HOLT McDOUGAL

Geometry

Edward B. Burger
David J. Chard
Paul A. Kennedy
Steven J. Leinwand
Freddie L. Renfro
Tom W. Roby
Dale G. Seymour
Bert K. Waits

HOLT McDOUGAL

HOUGHTON MIFFLIN HARCOURT

COMMON CORE EDITION

Printed in the U.S.A.

ISBN 978-0-547-64709-8

12 13 14 15 0868 22 21 20 19 18 17 16

4500602497 D E F G

Cover photo: © Micha Pawlitzki/Corbis

AUTHORS

Edward B. Burger, Ph.D., is Professor of Mathematics at Williams College and is the author of numerous articles, books, and videos. He has won several of the most prestigious writing and teaching awards offered by the Mathematical Association of America. Dr. Burger has made numerous television and radio appearances and has given countless mathematical presentations around the world.

David J. Chard, Ph.D., is the Leon Simmons Dean of the School of Education and Human Development at Southern Methodist University. He is a past president of the Divison of Research at the Council for Exceptional Children, a member of the International Academy for Research on Learning Disabilities, and has been the Principal Investigator on numerous research projects for the U.S. Department of Education.

Paul A. Kennedy, Ph.D., is a professor and Distinguished University Teaching Scholar in the Department of Mathematics at Colorado State University. Dr. Kennedy is a leader in mathematics education. His research focuses on developing algebraic thinking by using multiple representations and technology. He is the author of numerous publications.

Steven J. Leinwand is a Principal Research Analyst at the American Institutes for Research in Washington, D.C. He was previously, for 22 years, the Mathematics Supervisor with the Connecticut Department of Education.

Freddie L. Renfro, MA, has 35 years of experience in Texas education as a classroom teacher and director/coordinator of Mathematics PreK-12 for school districts in the Houston area. She has served as a reviewer and TXTEAM trainer for Texas Math Institutes and has presented at numerous math workshops.

Tom W. Roby, Ph.D., is Associate Professor of Mathematics and Director of the Quantitative Learning Center at the University of Connecticut. He founded and directed the Bay Area-based ACCLAIM professional development program. He also chaired the advisory board of the California Mathematics Project and reviewed content for the California Standards Tests.

Dale G. Seymour is a retired mathematics teacher, author, speaker and publisher. Dale founded Creative Publications in 1968, and went on to found two other mathematics publishing companies. Creating mathematical sculptures is one of his many hobbies.

Bert K. Waits, Ph.D., is a Professor Emeritus of Mathematics at The Ohio State University and cofounder of T³ (Teachers Teaching with Technology), a national professional development program. Dr. Waits is also a former board member of the NCTM and an author of the original NCTM Standards.

Contributing Authors

Linda Antinone
Fort Worth, TX
Ms. Antinone teaches mathematics at R. L. Paschal High School in Fort Worth, Texas. She has received the Presidential Award for Excellence in Teaching Mathematics and the National Radio Shack Teacher award. She has coauthored several books for Texas Instruments on the use of technology in mathematics.

Carmen Whitman
Pflugerville, TX
Ms. Whitman travels nationally helping districts improve mathematics education. She has been a program coordinator on the mathematics team at the Charles A. Dana Center, and has served as a secondary math specialist for the Austin Independent School District.

Reviewers

Robert Brouhle
Mathematics Department Chair, retired
Marina High School
Huntington Beach, CA

Carey Carter
Mathematics Teacher
Everman Joe C. Bean High School
Everman, TX

Greg Davis
Department Chair, retired
Lodi High School
Lodi, WI

Roger Fuller
Mathematics Department Chair
Grand Prairie High School
Grand Prairie, TX

Anthony Gugliotta
Supervisor of Math & Science
Rumson-Fair Haven Regional HS
Rumson, NJ

Marieta W. Harris
Mathematics Specialist
Memphis, TN

Debbie Hecky
Geometry Teacher
Scott High School
Covington, KY

Cynthia Hodges
Department Chair
Shoemaker High School
Killeen, TX

Kathleen Kelly
Mathematics Department Chair, retired
Lawrence High School
Fairfield, ME

Mike Kingery
Mathematics Teacher
Mayfield High School
Las Cruces, NM

Joy Lindsay
Mathematics Instructor
Bonita High School
LaVerne, CA

Kim Loggins
Geometry Teacher
Los Alamitos High School
Los Alamitos, CA

Elaine Pappas
Mathematics Department Chair
Cedar Shoals High School
Athens, GA

Terri Salas
Mathematics Consultant
Corpus Christi, TX

Jane Schneider
Mathematics Department Chair
Parkway West High School
Ballwin, MO

Jamae Sellari
Mathematics Instructor
Forest Hill High School
Jackson, MS

Caren Sorrells
Mathematics Coordinator
Birdville ISD
Haltom City, TX

E. Robin Staudenmeier
Middle/High School Math Coordinator
Olympia Community USD 16
Stanford, IL

Maureen "Marnie" Stockman
Geometry Specialist and Consultant
Cordova, MD

Anna Valdez
Geometry Teacher
Nikki Rowe High School
McAllen, TX

Lauralea Wright
Mathematics Teacher
Mauldin High School
Mauldin, SC

Denise Young
Mathematics Teacher
Blue Valley West High School
Overland Park, KS

Contributing Writer

Karen Droga Campe
Instructor
Yale University
New Haven, CT

Field Test Participants

Jill Morris
Navasota High School
Navasota, TX

Ruth Stutzman
Jefferson Forest High School
Forest, VA

Carey Carter
Alvarado High School
Alvarado, TX

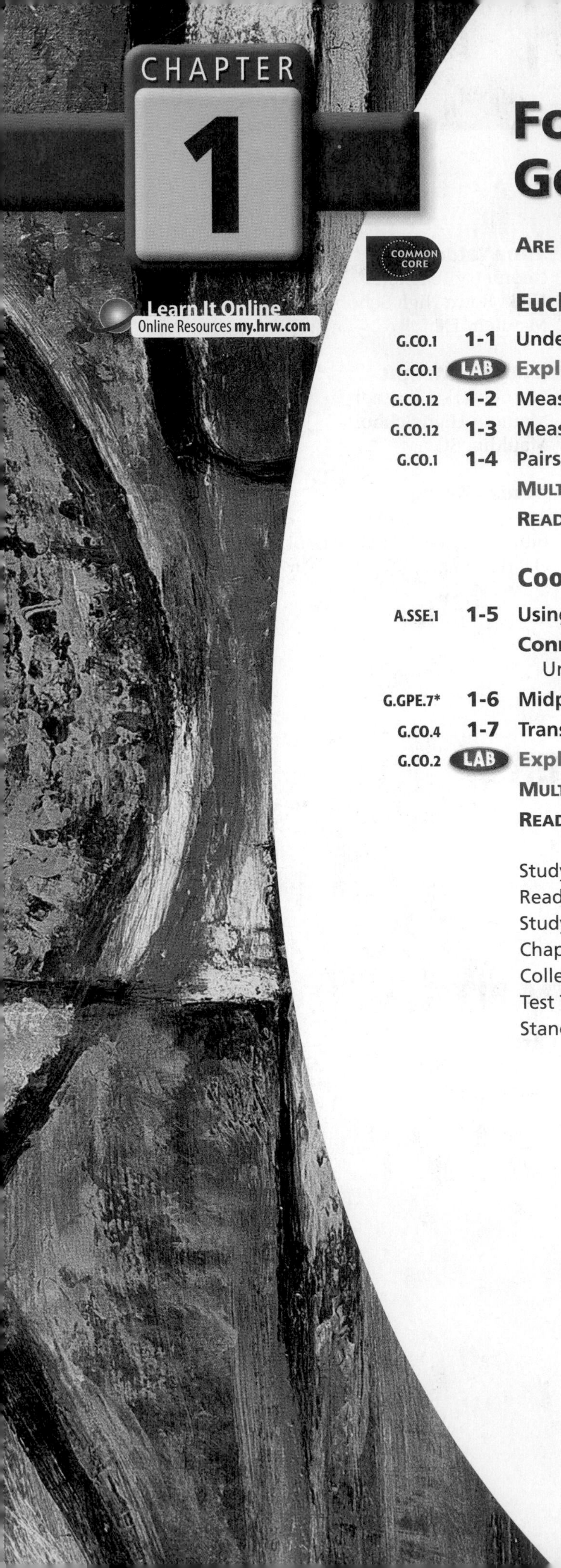

CHAPTER 1

Foundations for Geometry

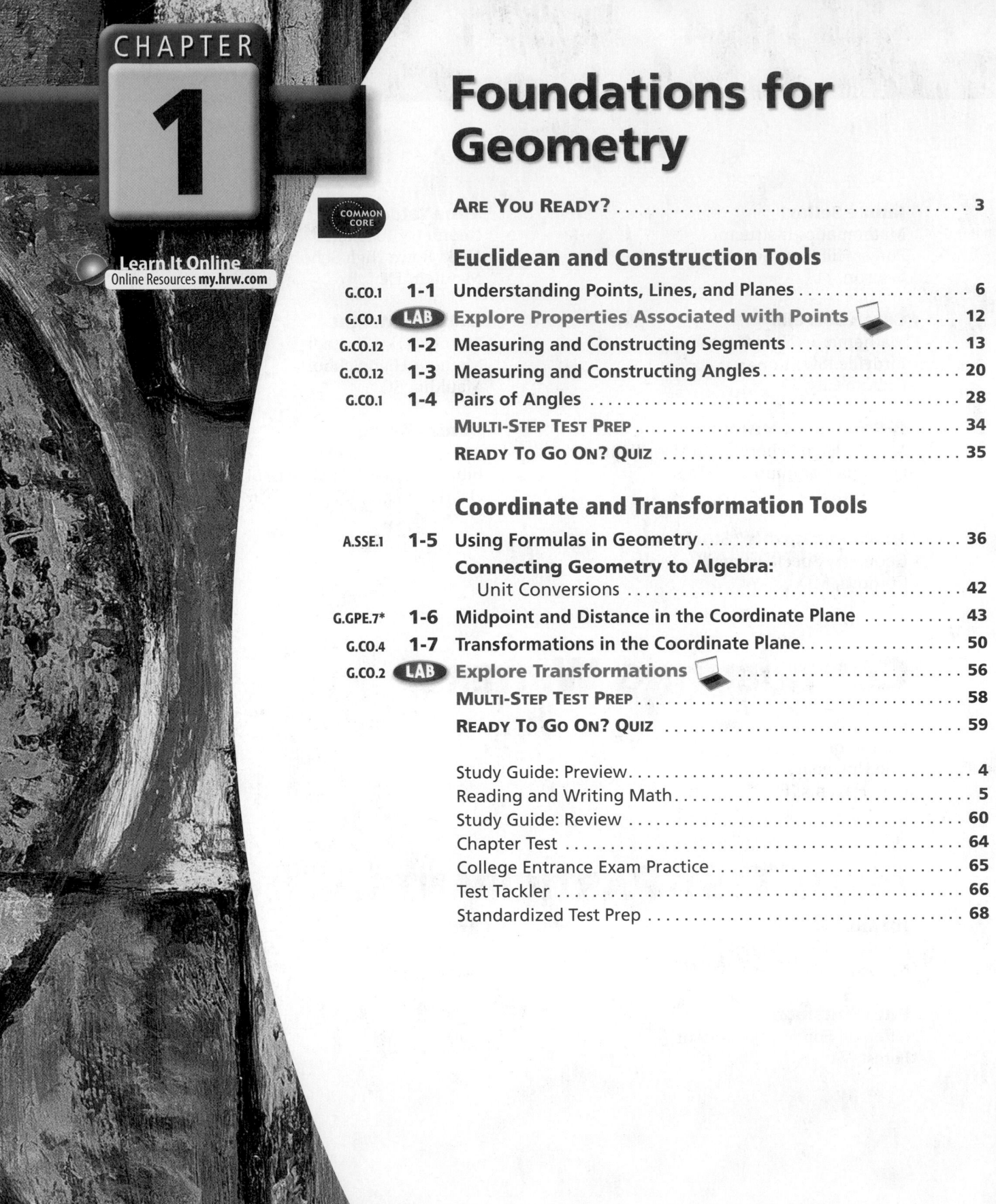

COMMON CORE

Painted design/Photolibrary.com

Geometric Reasoning

COMMON CORE

Kelly-Mooney Photography/CORBIS

CHAPTER

3

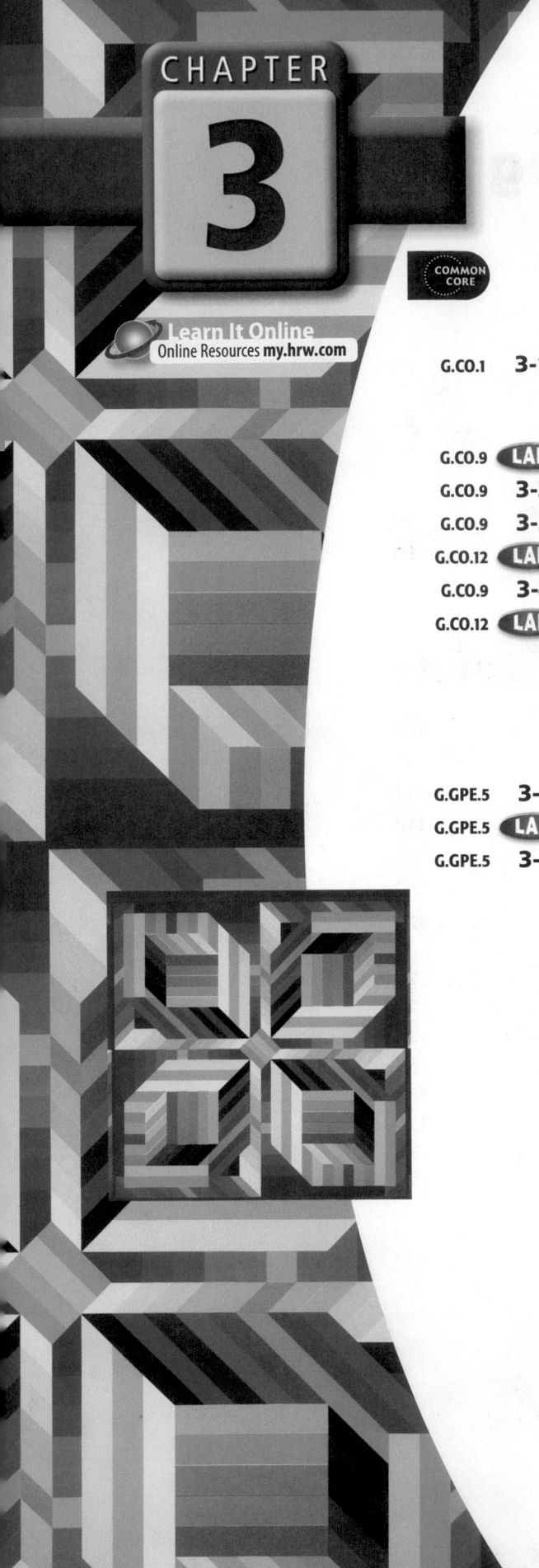

Parallel and Perpendicular Lines

COMMON CORE

Learn It Online
Online Resources my.hrw.com

CHAPTER 4

Triangle Congruence

Learn It Online
Online Resources my.hrw.com

COMMON CORE

Alamy Images

CHAPTER 5

Properties and Attributes of Triangles

COMMON CORE

Learn It Online
Online Resources my.hrw.com

Robert Shantz/Alamy

Polygons and Quadrilaterals

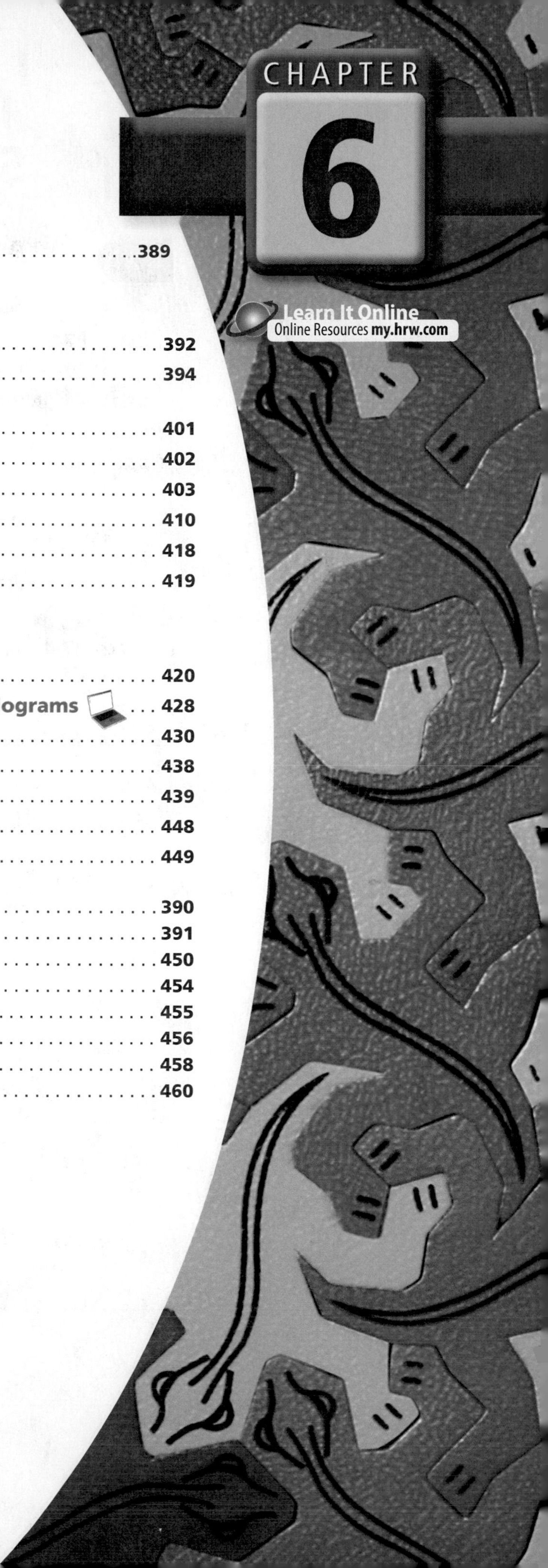

COMMON CORE

CHAPTER 7

Similarity

COMMON CORE

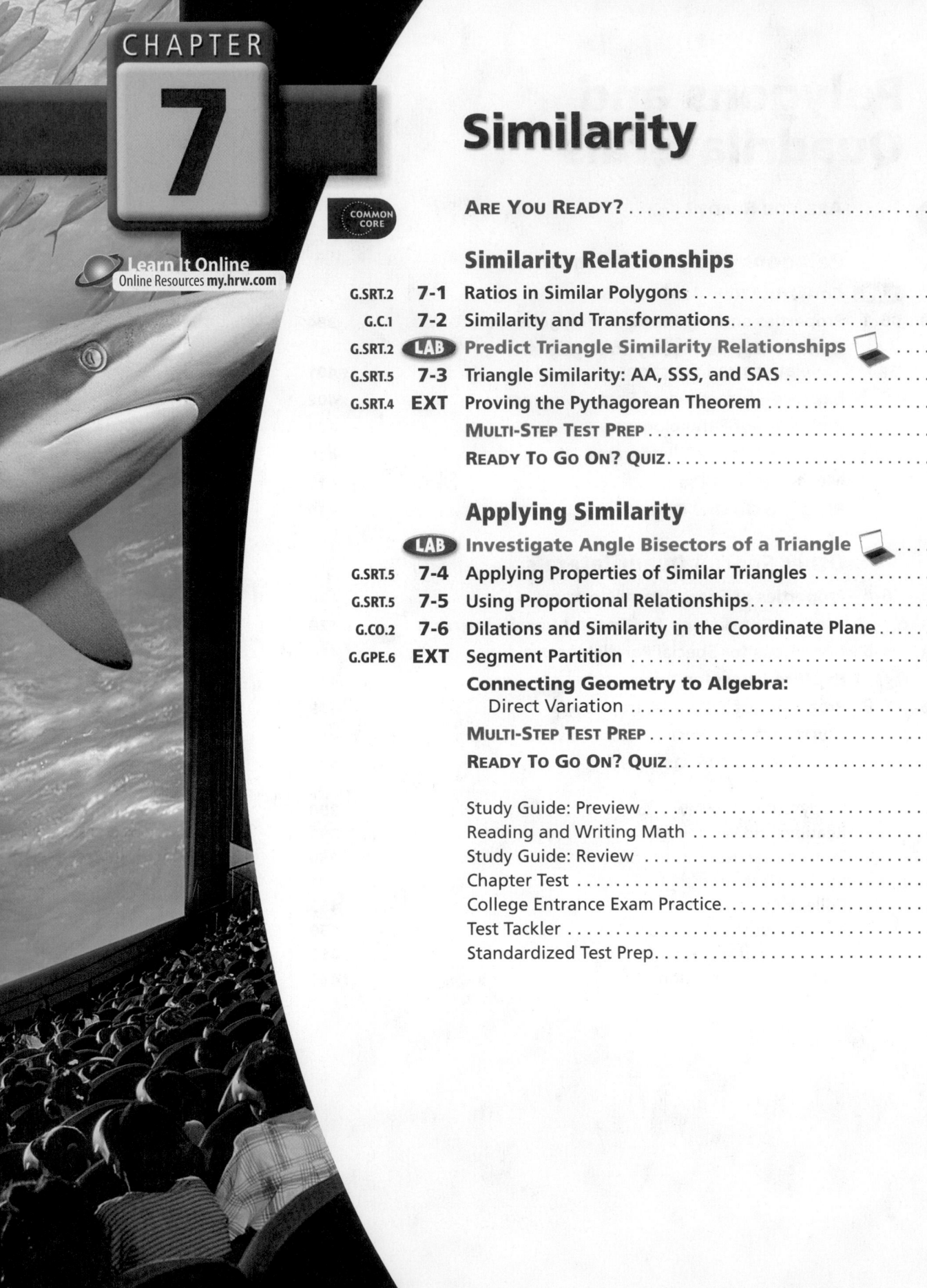

CHAPTER 8

Right Triangles and Trigonometry

COMMON CORE

Learn It Online
Online Resources my.hrw.com

CHAPTER 9

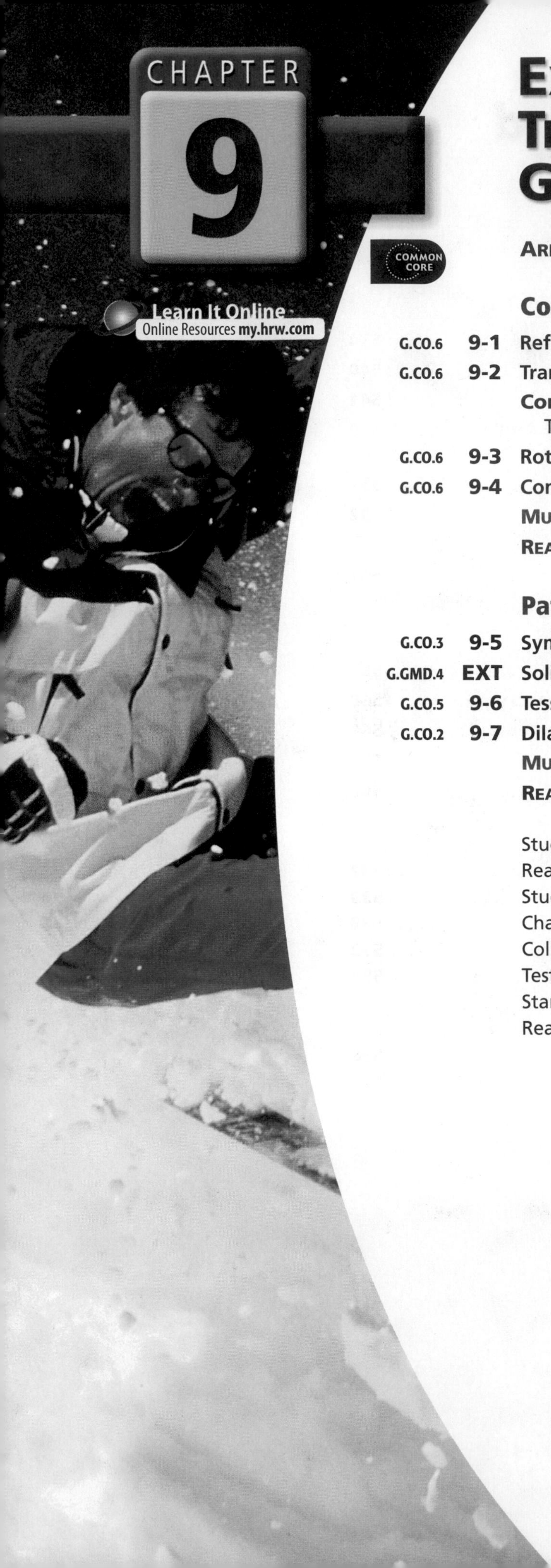

Learn It Online
Online Resources my.hrw.com

Extending Transformational Geometry

COMMON CORE

CHAPTER 10

Extending Perimeter, Circumference, and Area

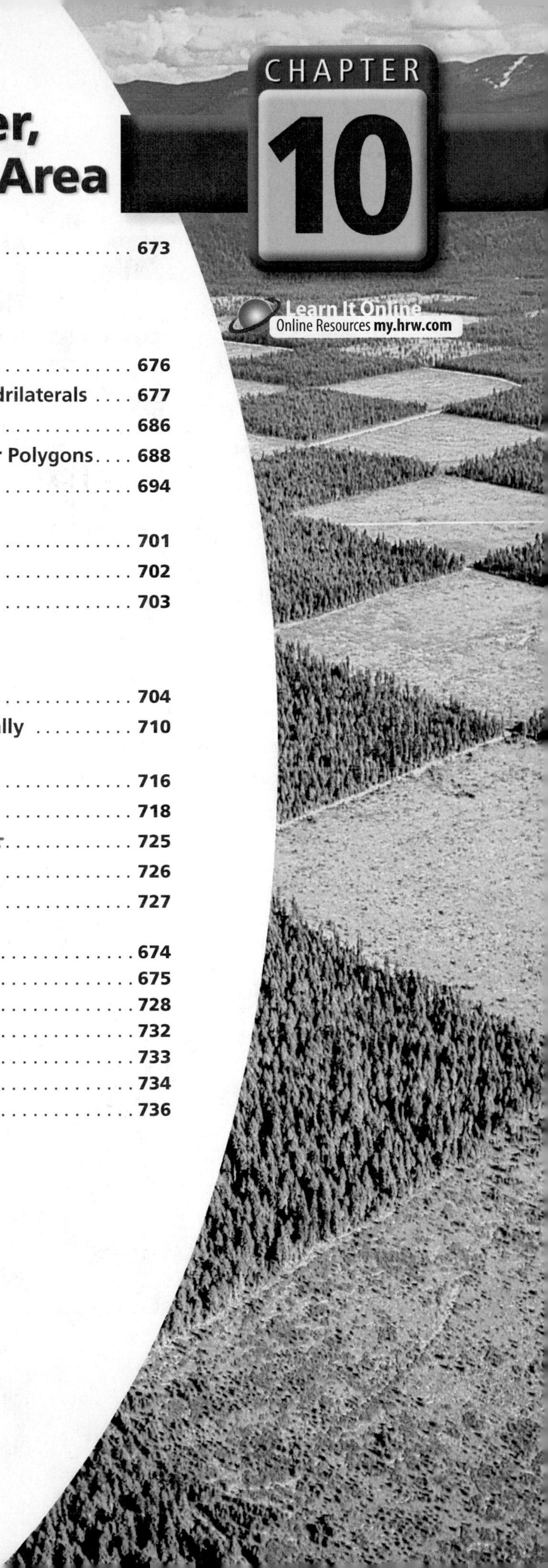

COMMON CORE

Jim Wark

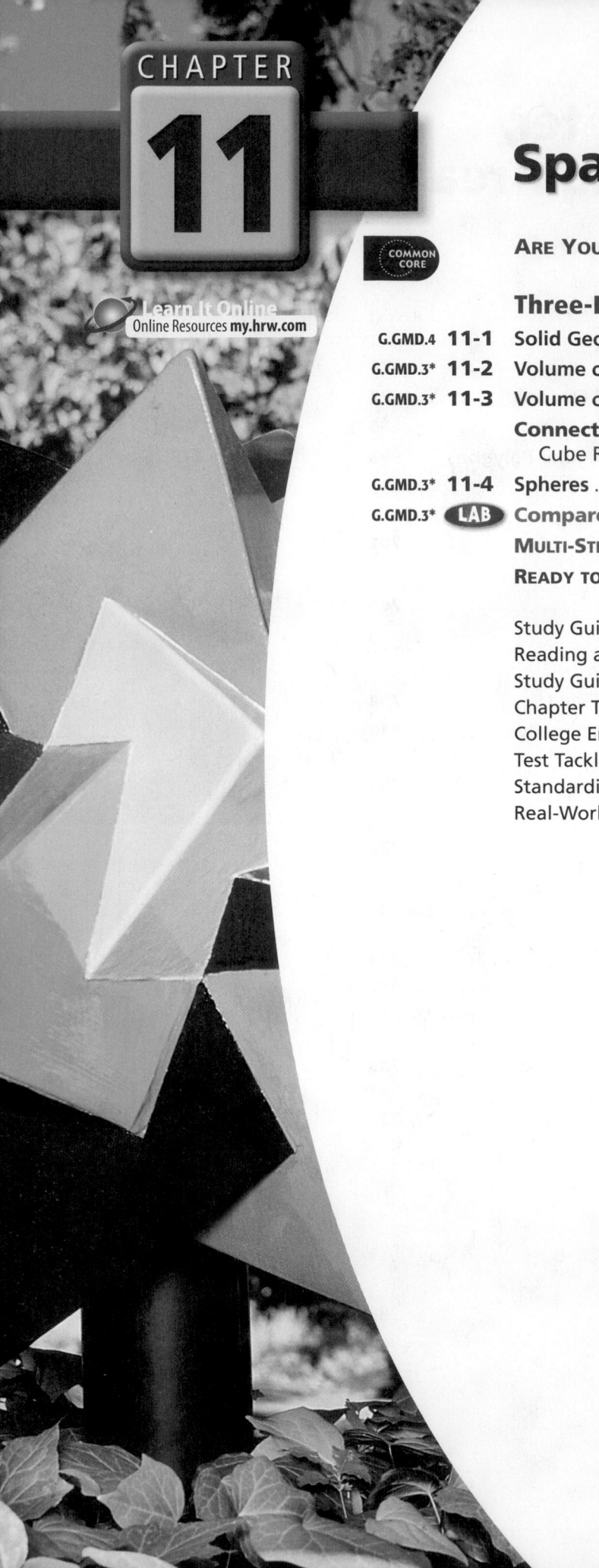

Spatial Reasoning

Erik Pawassar/Getty Images Photo Assignments/HMH Photo/Sculpture by Dale Seymour

CHAPTER 12

Circles

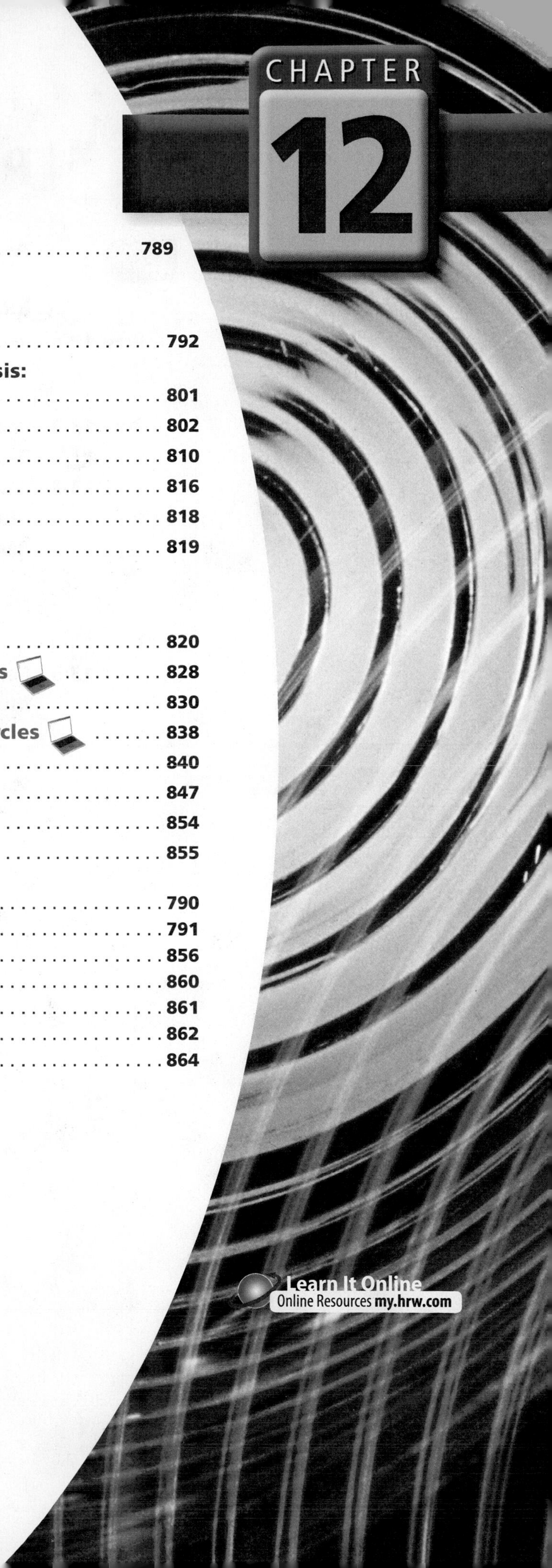

George B. Diebold/CORBIS

CHAPTER

13

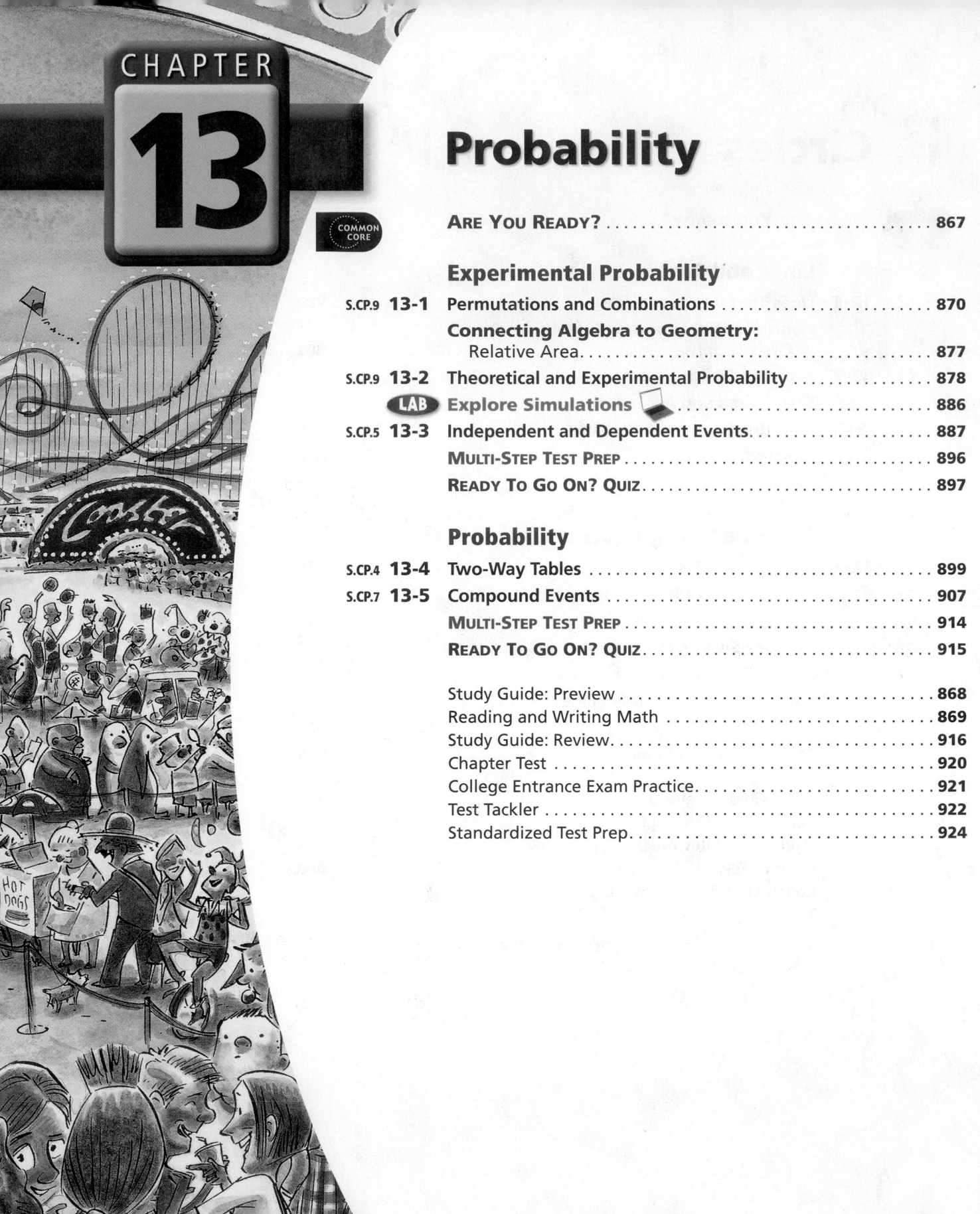

Probability

COMMON CORE

COMMON CORE

Standards for Mathematical Content
Correlation for Holt McDougal Algebra 1, Geometry, and Algebra 2

Standards	Descriptor	Algebra 1	Geometry	Algebra 2
Standards for Mathematical Content				
(+ = advanced; * = also a Modeling Standard)				
Number and Quantity				
CC.9-12.N.RN.1	Explain how the definition of the meaning of rational exponents follows from extending the properties of integer exponents to those values, allowing for a notation for radicals in terms of rational exponents.	SE: 392–393, 398–402		SE: 358–360, 395
CC.9-12.N.RN.2	Rewrite expressions involving radicals and rational exponents using the properties of exponents.	SE: 400–402	SE: 358	SE: 358–365, 392, 394, 398
CC.9-12.N.RN.3	Explain why the sum or product of two rational numbers is rational; that the sum of a rational number and an irrational number is irrational; and that the product of a nonzero rational number and an irrational number is irrational.	SE: 431–432		
CC.9-12.N.Q.1	Use units as a way to understand problems and to guide the solution of multi-step problems; choose and interpret units consistently in formulas; choose and interpret the scale and the origin in graphs and data displays.*	SE: 10, 26–30, 43–45, 53, 56–58, 59, 61, 62–68, 70–74, 83, 85–86, 88, 93, 108, 110, 115, 118, 122–124, 144, 159, 176, 184–185, 189–191, 194, 202, 208–209, 212, 213, 223, 265, 271–273, 279–281, 284, 488, 534, 536–537, 539–542, 549–550, 553, 556–558, 564–566, 572, 577–578, 598, 603, 628, 639–641	SE: 105, 108, 140, 186, 193–195, 197, 200, 211, 273, 445, 461, 528, 586, 593, 657, 671, 684–685, 695, 697–698, 703, 708, 713, 715, 727, 750, 753–756, 777, 786, 800, 865	SE: 12, 39, 90, 122, 229, 265, 293–294, 325, 340, 345–348, 363–364, 373, 381, 383, 437, 506, 650, 713, 732

SE = Student Edition

Standards	Descriptor	Algebra 1	Geometry	Algebra 2
Standards for Mathematical Content				
(+ = advanced; * = also a Modeling Standard)				
Number and Quantity				
CC.9-12.N.Q.2	Define appropriate quantities for the purpose of descriptive modeling.*	SE: 62–68, 75–81, 686–694, 695–701		
CC.9-12.N.Q.3	Choose a level of accuracy appropriate to limitations on measurement when reporting quantities.*	SE: 75–81		
CC.9-12.N.CN.1	Know there is a complex number i such that $i^2 = -1$, and every complex number has the form $a + bi$ with a and b real.			SE: 94–95, 138
CC.9-12.N.CN.2	Use the relation $i^2 = -1$ and the commutative, associative, and distributive properties to add, subtract, and multiply complex numbers.			SE: 128–131, 139, 141, 477
CC.9-12.N.CN.3	(+) Find the conjugate of a complex number; use conjugates to find moduli and quotients of complex numbers.			SE: 96–99, 126–133, 138, 145, 226
CC.9-12.N.CN.4	(+) Represent complex numbers on the complex plane in rectangular and polar form (including real and imaginary numbers), and explain why the rectangular and polar forms of a given complex number represent the same number.			*Opportunities to address this standard can be found on the following pages:* SE: 126–128, 139
CC.9-12.N.CN.5	(+) Represent addition, subtraction, multiplication, and conjugation of complex numbers geometrically on the complex plane; use properties of this representation for computation.			*Opportunities to address this standard can be found on the following pages:* SE: 126–133

SE = Student Edition

Standards	Descriptor	Algebra 1	Geometry	Algebra 2
Standards for Mathematical Content				
(+ = advanced; * = also a Modeling Standard)				
Number and Quantity				
CC.9-12.N.CN.6	(+) Calculate the distance between numbers in the complex plane as the modulus of the difference, and the midpoint of a segment as the average of the numbers at its endpoints.	*This standard is outside the scope of the Holt McDougal AGA series.*		
CC.9-12.N.CN.7	Solve quadratic equations with real coefficients that have complex solutions.			SE: 96–99, 101–107, 109, 138, 140, 190–195, 221
CC.9-12.N.CN.8	(+) Extend polynomial identities to the complex numbers.			SE: 189–195, 221
CC.9-12.N.CN.9	(+) Know the Fundamental Theorem of Algebra; show that it is true for quadratic polynomials.			SE: 189–195, 221, 222
CC.9-12.N.VM.1	(+) Recognize vector quantities as having both magnitude and direction. Represent vector quantities by directed line segments, and use appropriate symbols for vectors and their magnitudes (e.g., ***v***, |***v***|, ||***v***||, *v*).		SE: 577–585	
CC.9-12.N.VM.2	(+) Find the components of a vector by subtracting the coordinates of an initial point from the coordinates of a terminal point.		SE: 577	
CC.9-12.N.VM.3	(+) Solve problems involving velocity and other quantities that can be represented by vectors.		SE: 577–585, 586, 587, 591, 592, 593, 595	

SE = Student Edition

Standards	Descriptor	Algebra 1	Geometry	Algebra 2
Standards for Mathematical Content				
(+ = advanced; * = also a Modeling Standard)				
Number and Quantity				
CC.9-12.N.VM.4	(+) Add and subtract vectors. a. Add vectors end-to-end, component-wise, and by the parallelogram rule. Understand that the magnitude of a sum of two vectors is typically not the sum of the magnitudes. b. Given two vectors in magnitude and direction form, determine the magnitude and direction of their sum. c. Understand vector subtraction $v - w$ as $v + (-w)$, where $-w$ is the additive inverse of w, with the same magnitude as w and pointing in the opposite direction. Represent vector subtraction graphically by connecting the tips in the appropriate order, and perform vector subtraction component-wise.		SE: 577–585, 586, 587, 591, 596, 785	
CC.9-12.N.VM.5	(+) Multiply a vector by a scalar. a. Represent scalar multiplication graphically by scaling vectors and possibly reversing their direction; perform scalar multiplication component-wise, e.g., as $c(v_x, v_y) = (cv_x, cv_y)$. b. Compute the magnitude of a scalar multiple cv using $\|\|cv\|\| = \|c\|v$. Compute the direction of cv knowing that when $\|c\|v \neq 0$, the direction of cv is either along v (for $c > 0$) or against v (for $c < 0$).		SE: 577–585	
CC.9-12.N.VM.6	(+) Use matrices to represent and manipulate data, e.g., to represent payoffs or incidence relationships in a network.	*This standard is outside the scope of the Holt McDougal AGA series.*		

SE = Student Edition

Standards	Descriptor	Algebra 1	Geometry	Algebra 2
Standards for Mathematical Content				
(+ = advanced; * = also a Modeling Standard)				
Number and Quantity				
CC.9-12.N.VM.7	(+) Multiply matrices by scalars to produce new matrices, e.g., as when all of the payoffs in a game are doubled.	*This standard is outside the scope of the Holt McDougal AGA series.*		
CC.9-12.N.VM.8	(+) Add, subtract, and multiply matrices of appropriate dimensions.			SE: 144
CC.9-12.N.VM.9	(+) Understand that, unlike multiplication of numbers, matrix multiplication for square matrices is not a commutative operation, but still satisfies the associative and distributive properties.	*This standard is outside the scope of the Holt McDougal AGA series.*		
CC.9-12.N.VM.10	(+) Understand that the zero and identity matrices play a role in matrix addition and multiplication similar to the role of 0 and 1 in the real numbers. The determinant of a square matrix is nonzero if and only if the matrix has a multiplicative inverse.	*This standard is outside the scope of the Holt McDougal AGA series.*		
CC.9-12.N.VM.11	(+) Multiply a vector (regarded as a matrix with one column) by a matrix of suitable dimensions to produce another vector. Work with matrices as transformations of vectors.	*This standard is outside the scope of the Holt McDougal AGA series.*		
CC.9-12.N.VM.12	(+) Work with 2 × 2 matrices as a transformations of the plane, and interpret the absolute value of the determinant in terms of area.	*This standard is outside the scope of the Holt McDougal AGA series.*		

SE = Student Edition

Standards	Descriptor	Algebra 1	Geometry	Algebra 2
Standards for Mathematical Content				
(+ = advanced; * = also a Modeling Standard)				
Algebra				
CC.9-12.A.SSE.1	Interpret expressions that represent a quantity in terms of its context.* a. Interpret parts of an expression, such as terms, factors, and coefficients. b. Interpret complicated expressions by viewing one or more of their parts as a single entity.	SE: 10–11, 512, 514	SE: 36–41, 312–318, 689, 751, 757, 759	SE: 75, 234–240
CC.9-12.A.SSE.2	Use the structure of an expression to identify ways to rewrite it.	SE: 462, 463–469, 470–471, 472–479, 480–486, 487, 488, 489, 490–496, 498–503, 504, 505, 507–509, 510, 511, 514–515, 739	SE: 13–19	SE: 75, 141, 174–179, 219
CC.9-12.A.SSE.3	Choose and produce an equivalent form of an expression to reveal and explain properties of the quantity represented by the expression. a. Factor a quadratic expression to reveal the zeros of the function it defines. b. Complete the square in a quadratic expression to reveal the maximum or minimum value of the function it defines. c. Use the properties of exponents to transform expressions for exponential functions.	SE: a. & b.) 470–471, 472–479, 480–486, 487, 488, 489, 490–496, 499–503, 504, 505, 508–509, 510, 511, 514, 739 a.) 562–563, 636–641		SE: a. & b.) 75, 76, 77–84, 86–93, 137, 307 c.) 239
CC.9-12.A.SSE.4	Derive the formula for the sum of a finite geometric series (when the common ratio is not 1), and use the formula to solve problems.			SE: 658, 660–661, 678, 680

SE = Student Edition

Standards	Descriptor	Algebra 1	Geometry	Algebra 2
Standards for Mathematical Content				
(+ = advanced; * = also a Modeling Standard)				
Algebra				
CC.9-12.A.APR.1	Understand that polynomials form a system analogous to the integers, namely, they are closed under the operations of addition, subtraction, and multiplication; add, subtract, and multiply polynomials.	SE: 414–419, 422–429, 433–439		SE: 150–156, 158–164, 181, 218, 219, 222, 223, 224, 227, 307, 309, 335–338, 399, 403, 751
CC.9-12.A.APR.2	Know and apply the Remainder Theorem: For a polynomial $p(x)$ and a number a, the remainder on division by $x - a$ is $p(a)$, so $p(a) = 0$ if and only if $(x - a)$ is a factor of $p(x)$.			SE: 166–172, 174–179, 189–195, 220, 222
CC.9-12.A.APR.3	Identify zeros of polynomials when suitable factorizations are available, and use the zeros to construct a rough graph of the function defined by the polynomial.	SE: 562–567, 600–601		SE: 176–179, 181, 182–188, 219, 220, 223, 880
CC.9-12.A.APR.4	Prove polynomial identities and use them to describe numerical relationships.	SE: 433–439, 490–496, 497		SE: 158–161, 174–179
CC.9-12.A.APR.5	(+) Know and apply the Binomial Theorem for the expansion of $(x + y)^n$ in powers of x and y for a positive integer n, where x and y are any numbers, with coefficients determined for example by Pascal's Triangle. (The Binomial Theorem can be proved by mathematical induction or by a combinatorial argument.)			SE: 157, 158–164, 531, 532, 587, 590, 684
CC.9-12.A.APR.6	Rewrite simple rational expressions in different forms; write $a(x)/b(x)$ in the form $q(x) + r(x)/b(x)$, where $a(x)$, $b(x)$, $q(x)$, and $r(x)$ are polynomials with the degree of $r(x)$ less than the degree of $b(x)$, using inspection, long division, or, for the more complicated examples, a computer algebra system.		SE: 682, 685	SE: 166–172, 219, 222, 224, 537

SE = Student Edition

Standards	Descriptor	Algebra 1	Geometry	Algebra 2
Standards for Mathematical Content				
(+ = advanced; * = also a Modeling Standard)				
Algebra				
CC.9-12.A.APR.7	(+) Understand that rational expressions form a system analogous to the rational numbers, closed under addition, subtraction, multiplication, and division by a nonzero rational expression; add, subtract, multiply, and divide rational expressions.			SE: 321–326, 327–334, 335–338, 357, 391, 394, 395, 881
CC.9-12.A.CED.1	Create equations and inequalities in one variable and use them to solve problems. Include equations arising from linear and quadratic functions, and simple rational and exponential functions.*	SE: 19–22, 26–29, 34–38, 42–46, 54–59, 100–105, 107–111, 114–117, 118, 119, 122–125, 127–132, 144–147, 148, 149, 150–153, 154, 156–157, 158–159, 562–567, 568–573, 575–581, 582–589, 624–630		SE: 42, 46, 77–84, 85–92, 94–99, 100–107, 110–117, 144, 182–188, 189–195, 266–272, 348–355, 376–383, 474, 785–797
CC.9-12.A.CED.2	Create equations in two or more variables to represent relationships between quantities; graph equations on coordinate axes with labels and scales.*	SE: 179–185, 186–192, 230–236, 237–242, 244–251, 254–259, 260–265, 268–274, 275–282, 293–299, 301–307, 329–334, 336–342, 343–349, 352–357, 538–543, 545–551, 554–559, 582–589, 635–642, 649–655	SE: 182–187, 190–197, 201, 205, 206, 517	SE: 15–21, 24–30, 32–39, 44, 46, 59–66, 67–74, 118–125, 150–156, 197–203, 204–209, 210–215, 226, 234–240, 242–248, 249–255, 275–280, 281–288, 289–295, 313–320, 340–347, 367–375, 422–429, 432–439, 442–448, 450–456, 458–465, 536, 749, 754–761, 767

SE = Student Edition

Standards	Descriptor	Algebra 1	Geometry	Algebra 2
Standards for Mathematical Content				
(+ = advanced; * = also a Modeling Standard)				
Algebra				
CC.9-12.A.CED.3	Represent constraints by equations or inequalities, and by systems of equations and/or inequalities, and interpret solutions as viable or nonviable options in a modeling context.*	SE: 179–185, 230–236, 237–242, 260–265, 268–274, 275–282, 301–307, 331–334, 339–342, 346–349, 350–351, 354–356, 358, 359, 369–371, 374, 375, 376–378, 380, 381, 384–385, 451, 538–543, 554–559, 562–567, 568–573, 575–581, 582–589, 613, 635–642, 649–655		SE: 15–21, 24–30, 32–39, 59–66, 67–74, 110–117, 118–125, 150–156, 197–203, 204–209, 210–215, 234–240, 242–248, 249–255, 275–280, 281–288, 289–295, 313–320, 340–347, 367–375, 422–429, 432–439, 442–448, 450–456, 458–465, 749, 754–761, 762–767
CC.9-12.A.CED.4	Rearrange formulas to highlight a quantity of interest, using the same reasoning as in solving equations.*	SE: 49–53, 59, 68, 85, 88, 161	SE: 41, 673, 674, 676, 685	SE: 449
CC.9-12.A.REI.1	Explain each step in solving a simple equation as following from the equality of numbers asserted at the previous step, starting from the assumption that the original equation has a solution. Construct a viable argument to justify a solution method.	SE: 17–22, 24–30, 32–38, 40–46, 54–59, 61, 84–85	SE: 104–109, 127, 132, 134	SE: 77–84, 85–92, 100–107, 182–188, 266–272, 348–355, 376–383
CC.9-12.A.REI.2	Solve simple rational and radical equations in one variable, and give examples showing how extraneous solutions may arise.	SE: 669, 673, 674	SE: 466–471, 482–489, 493, 495–501, 520	SE: 348–355, 357, 376–383, 388, 389, 392, 393, 394, 395, 398, 399, 476, 809

SE = Student Edition

Standards	Descriptor	Algebra 1	Geometry	Algebra 2
Standards for Mathematical Content				
(+ = advanced; * = also a Modeling Standard)				
Algebra				
CC.9-12.A.REI.3	Solve linear equations and inequalities in one variable, including equations with coefficients represented by letters.	SE: 16, 17–22, 24–30, 31, 32–38, 39, 40–46, 53, 59, 60, 61, 68, 84–85, 88, 89, 92–93, 97, 106–111, 112–117, 118, 119, 120–125, 126–132, 140, 147, 148, 149, 151–152, 154, 155, 158–159, 161, 169, 185, 192, 203, 211, 222, 223, 236, 274, 299, 325, 334, 397, 403, 419, 450, 469, 519, 612, 623, 630, 679, 701, 721, 760		SE: 43, 46, 47, 48
CC.9-12.A.REI.4	Solve quadratic equations in one variable. a. Use the method of completing the square to transform any quadratic equation in x into an equation of the form $(x - p)^2 = q$ that has the same solutions. Derive the quadratic formula from this form. b. Solve quadratic equations by inspection (e.g., for $x^2 = 49$), taking square roots, completing the square, the quadratic formula and factoring, as appropriate to the initial form of the equation. Recognize when the quadratic formula gives complex solutions and write them as $a \pm bi$ for real numbers a and b.	SE: 554–559, 560–561, 562–567, 568–573, 576–581, 582–583, 585–589, 598, 599, 606–607, 608, 609, 613, 655	SE: 27, 45, 47–48, 55, 59, 63, 243, 245, 289, 338, 361–367, 377, 381, 382, 400, 427, 442, 444–446, 508, 798, 842, 844–846	SE: 77–84, 85–92, 96–99, 100–107, 108, 109, 137, 140, 143, 145, 307, 309, 684, 749
CC.9-12.A.REI.5	Prove that, given a system of two equations in two variables, replacing one equation by the sum of that equation and a multiple of the other produces a system with the same solutions.	SE: 343–349		

SE = Student Edition

Standards	Descriptor	Algebra 1	Geometry	Algebra 2
Standards for Mathematical Content				
(+ = advanced; * = also a Modeling Standard)				
Algebra				
CC.9-12.A.REI.6	Solve systems of linear equations exactly and approximately (e.g., with graphs), focusing on pairs of linear equations in two variables.	SE: 329–334, 336–342, 343–349, 350–351, 352–357, 358, 359, 376–378, 380, 381, 383, 384	SE: 152–153, 158–160, 161, 176, 194, 195, 328, 329–330	SE: 684
CC.9-12.A.REI.7	Solve a simple system consisting of a linear equation and a quadratic equation in two variables algebraically and graphically.	SE: 590–597	SE: 853	SE: 809, 862–869, 871, 872, 876, 877
CC.9-12.A.REI.8	(+) Represent a system of linear equations as a single matrix equation in a vector variable.	*This standard is outside the scope of the Holt McDougal AGA series.*		
CC.9-12.A.REI.9	(+) Find the inverse of a matrix if it exists and use it to solve systems of linear equations (using technology for matrices of dimension 3 × 3 or greater).	*This standard is outside the scope of the Holt McDougal AGA series.*		
CC.9-12.A.REI.10	Understand that the graph of an equation in two variables is the set of all its solutions plotted in the coordinate plane, often forming a curve (which could be a line).	SE: 186–192, 193, 216		SE: 43, 46
CC.9-12.A.REI.11	Explain why the *x*-coordinates of the points where the graphs of the equations $y = f(x)$ and $y = g(x)$ intersect are the solutions of the equation $f(x) = g(x)$; find the solutions approximately, e.g., using technology to graph the functions, make tables of values, or find successive approximations. Include cases where $f(x)$ and/or $g(x)$ are linear, polynomial, rational, absolute value, exponential, and logarithmic functions.*	SE: 47–48, 554–559, 560–561, 628, 629		SE: 79–80, 182–186, 191–192, 268–269, 351–352, 384–387

SE = Student Edition

Standards	Descriptor	Algebra 1	Geometry	Algebra 2
Standards for Mathematical Content				
(+ = advanced; * = also a Modeling Standard)				
Algebra				
CC.9-12.A.REI.12	Graph the solutions to a linear inequality in two variables as a half-plane (excluding the boundary in the case of a strict inequality), and graph the solution set to a system of linear inequalities in two variables as the intersection of the corresponding half-planes.	SE: 360–366, 368–372, 373, 374, 375, 379, 380, 381, 486		SE: 44, 46, 47, 50, 307, 880
CC.9-12.F.IF.1	Understand that a function from one set (called the domain) to another set (called the range) assigns to each element of the domain exactly one element of the range. If *f* is a function and *x* is an element of its domain, then $f(x)$ denotes the output of *f* corresponding to the input *x*. The graph of *f* is the graph of the equation $y = f(x)$.	SE: 170–176, 177, 179–186, 187–192, 193, 195, 215, 219, 222		
CC.9-12.F.IF.2	Use function notation, evaluate functions for inputs in their domains, and interpret statements that use function notation in terms of a context.	SE: 180–185, 192, 195, 216, 218, 219, 223, 322, 397, 629		SE: 50
CC.9-12.F.IF.3	Recognize that sequences are functions, sometimes defined recursively, whose domain is a subset of the integers.	SE: 206–211, 618–623		SE: 626–632
CC.9-12.F.IF.4	For a function that models a relationship between two quantities, interpret key features of graphs and tables in terms of the quantities, and sketch graphs showing key features given a verbal description of the relationship. Key features include: intercepts; intervals where the function is increasing, decreasing, positive, or negative; relative maximums and minimums; symmetries; end behavior; and periodicity.*	SE: 165, 167–168, 195, 214, 230, 234–235, 237–238, 240–242, 266, 267, 271–273, 309, 310–313, 315, 318, 531–532, 535–537, 541–543, 545–551, 552, 553, 554–559, 600–601, 603, 604–605, 608, 613, 630, 641, 644–647, 649–655, 565–659		SE: 7–14, 24–30, 43, 59–66, 67–74, 77–84, 109, 137, 140, 153–156, 183–188, 197–203, 204–209, 218, 220, 221, 222, 223, 236–240, 251–255, 275–280, 281–288, 313–320, 340–347, 367–375, 399, 406–413, 422–429, 432–439, 457, 476, 754–761, 762–767

SE = Student Edition

Standards	Descriptor	Algebra 1	Geometry	Algebra 2
Standards for Mathematical Content				
(+ = advanced; * = also a Modeling Standard)				
Functions				
CC.9-12.F.IF.5	Relate the domain of a function to its graph and, where applicable, to the quantitative relationship it describes.*	SE: 170–176, 182–184, 186–192, 194, 195, 218, 223, 233–235, 241, 260–265, 310–311, 313, 314, 323, 486, 525–529, 542–543, 545–551, 553, 600–601, 603, 669, 672, 674, 675	SE: 401, 685	SE: 14, 19–21, 65, 70, 72–73, 134, 172, 196, 226, 240, 241, 242, 245, 247, 253, 263, 280, 285–286, 288, 299, 302, 341, 345, 367–368, 371–372, 375, 388, 389, 392–393, 394, 413, 428–429, 439, 441, 453–454, 467, 470, 472, 685, 713, 719, 749, 754–761, 767, 851
CC.9-12.F.IF.6	Calculate and interpret the average rate of change of a function (presented symbolically or as a table) over a specified interval. Estimate the rate of change from a graph.*	SE: 244–245, 248–251, 254–259, 267, 268–274, 308, 315, 318, 323, 469, 656–659, 660–667, 739		SE: 44, 210–215, 408–413, 414–421, 468

SE = Student Edition

Standards	Descriptor	Algebra 1	Geometry	Algebra 2
Standards for Mathematical Content				
(+ = advanced; * = also a Modeling Standard)				
Functions				
CC.9-12.F.IF.7	Graph functions expressed symbolically and show key features of the graph, by hand in simple cases and using technology for more complicated cases.* a. Graph linear and quadratic functions and show intercepts, maxima, and minima. b. Graph square root, cube root, and piecewise-defined functions, including step functions and absolute value functions. c. Graph polynomial functions, identifying zeros when suitable factorizations are available, and showing end behavior. d. (+) Graph rational functions, identifying zeros and asymptotes when suitable factorizations are available, and showing end behavior. e. Graph exponential and logarithmic functions, showing intercepts and end behavior, and trigonometric functions, showing period, midline, and amplitude.	SE: a.) 186–192, 193, 195, 216, 218, 219, 220, 230–236, 237–242, 260–265, 266, 267, 268–274, 275–282, 283, 301–307, 309, 314–317, 318, 320, 321, 522–529, 531–537, 538–543, 553, 554–559, 605, 608, 609, 649–655 b.) 310–313 c.) 544, 545–551, 600–603 e.) 624–630		SE: a.) 24–30, 43, 46, 59–66, 67–74, 76, 77–84, 109, 137, 140, 144, 226, 476 b.) 45, 46, 367–375, 388, 389, 393, 394, 398, 422–429, 430–431, 441, 469, 685 c.) 153–156, 182–188, 196, 197–203, 204–209, 218, 220, 221 d.) 339, 340–347, 357, 392, 395, 399 e.) 234–240, 251–255, 275–280, 297, 298, 302, 754–755, 762–767, 768, 769, 800, 801, 804, 807
CC.9–12.F.IF.8	Write a function defined by an expression in different but equivalent forms to reveal and explain different properties of the function. a. Use the process of factoring and completing the square in a quadratic function to show zeros, extreme values, and symmetry of the graph, and interpret these in terms of a context. b. Use the properties of exponents to interpret expressions for exponential functions.	SE: 530, 533–534, 536–537, 541, 543, 553, 605, 608, 624–630		SE: a.) 67–74, 77–84, 85–92, 109, 881 b.) 234–240, 265, 302, 684

SE = Student Edition

Standards	Descriptor	Algebra 1	Geometry	Algebra 2
Standards for Mathematical Content				
(+ = advanced; * = also a Modeling Standard)				
Functions				
CC.9-12.F.IF.9	Compare properties of two functions each represented in a different way (algebraically, graphically, numerically in tables, or by verbal descriptions).	SE: 230–236, 310–313, 531–537, 538–543, 600–601, 624–630, 660–667		SE: 414–421
CC.9-12.F.BF.1	Write a function that describes a relationship between two quantities.* a. Determine an explicit expression, a recursive process, or steps for calculation from a context. b. Combine standard function types using arithmetic operations. c. (+) Compose functions.	SE: 179–185, 230–236, 268–274, 275–282, 545–551, 568–573, 635–642, 644–647, 649–655		SE: 32–39, 118–125, 159–163, 169–171, 180, 181, 206–209, 210–215, 219, 221, 222, 278, 289–295, 425–429, 434–438, 442–448, 450–456, 458–465, 470, 472, 475, 476, 881
CC.9-12.F.BF.2	Write arithmetic and geometric sequences both recursively and with an explicit formula, use them to model situations, and translate between the two forms.*	SE: 206–210, 622–623, 644–647		SE: 626–632, 647–650, 653, 654–663, 676, 677, 678, 680, 681, 684, 685, 749
CC.9-12.F.BF.3	Identify the effect on the graph of replacing $f(x)$ by $f(x) + k$, $k f(x)$, $f(kx)$, and $f(x + k)$ for specific values of k (both positive and negative); find the value of k given the graphs. Experiment with cases and illustrate an explanation of the effects on the graph using technology. Include recognizing even and odd functions from their graphs and algebraic expressions for them.	SE: 300, 301–307, 309, 310–313, 317, 318, 544, 545–551, 553, 559, 606, 608, 732, 747	SE: 101, 374, 618, 638, 640, 748	SE: 7–14, 15–21, 22, 23, 24–30, 44, 46, 51, 59–66, 109, 136, 204–209, 221, 222, 223, 225, 227, 281–288, 301, 302, 306, 368–375, 388, 389, 432–439, 469, 472, 473, 684, 748, 756–761, 762–767

SE = Student Edition

Standards	Descriptor	Algebra 1	Geometry	Algebra 2
Standards for Mathematical Content				
(+ = advanced; * = also a Modeling Standard)				
Functions				
CC.9-12.F.BF.4	Find inverse functions. a. Solve an equation of the form $f(x) = c$ for a simple function f that has an inverse and write an expression for the inverse. b. (+) Verify by composition that one function is the inverse of another. c. (+) Read values of an inverse function from a graph or a table, given that the function has an inverse. d. (+) Produce an invertible function from a non-invertible function by restricting the domain.		SE: 551, 558	SE: a.–c.) 241, 242–248, 251–255, 265, 299, 302, 303, 306, 450–456, 470, 472, 473, 684, 881 c.) 367
CC.9-12.F.BF.5	(+) Understand the inverse relationship between exponents and logarithms and use this relationship to solve problems involving logarithms and exponents.			SE: 249–255, 256–263, 264, 265, 266–272, 275–280, 297, 300, 302, 303, 306, 399, 881
CC.9-12.F.LE.1	Distinguish between situations that can be modeled with linear functions and with exponential functions.* a. Prove that linear functions grow by equal differences over equal intervals, and that exponential functions grow by equal factors over equal intervals. b. Recognize situations in which one quantity changes at a constant rate per unit interval relative to another. c. Recognize situations in which a quantity grows or decays by a constant percent rate per unit interval relative to another.	SE: 625–628, 649–655		SE: a.) 210–215, 406–413, 458–465 b.) 406–413, 441, 458–465, 471, 472 c.) 234–240, 458–465, 471, 472

SE = Student Edition

Standards	Descriptor	Algebra 1	Geometry	Algebra 2
Standards for Mathematical Content				
(+ = advanced; * = also a Modeling Standard)				
Functions				
CC.9-12.F.LE.2	Construct linear and exponential functions, including arithmetic and geometric sequences, given a graph, a description of a relationship, or two input-output pairs (include reading these from a table).*	SE: 206–211, 213, 216–217, 218, 219, 220, 230–236, 237–242, 260–265, 268–274, 275–282, 309, 314–317, 318, 320, 321, 618–623, 633, 635–642, 644–647, 649–655		SE: 44, 46, 234–240, 305, 398, 406–413, 441, 458–465, 468, 471, 472, 537, 643–651, 654–753, 880
CC.9-12.F.LE.3	Observe using graphs and tables that a quantity increasing exponentially eventually exceeds a quantity increasing linearly, quadratically, or (more generally) as a polynomial function.*	SE: 630, 660–667		SE: 234–240, 458–465
CC.9-12.F.LE.4	For exponential models, express as *a* logarithm the solution to $ab^{ct} = d$ where *a*, *c*, and *d* are numbers and the base *b* is 2, 10, or *e*; evaluate the logarithm using technology.*			SE: 249–255, 268–272, 274, 275–280
CC.9-12.F.LE.5	Interpret the parameters in a linear or exponential function in terms of a context.*	SE: 268–274, 635–642		SE: 234–240, 299
CC.9-12.F.TF.1	Understand radian measure of an angle as the length of the arc on the unit circle subtended by the angle.			SE: 707–713
CC.9-12.F.TF.2	Explain how the unit circle in the coordinate plane enables the extension of trigonometric functions to all real numbers, interpreted as radian measures of angles traversed counterclockwise around the unit circle.			SE: 700–702, 706–709

SE = Student Edition

Standards	Descriptor	Algebra 1	Geometry	Algebra 2
Standards for Mathematical Content				
(+ = advanced; * = also a Modeling Standard)				
Functions				
CC.9-12.F.TF.3	(+) Use special triangles to determine geometrically the values of sine, cosine, tangent for $\pi/3$, $\pi/4$ and $\pi/6$, and use the unit circle to express the values of sine, cosines, and tangent for x, $\pi + x$, and $2\pi - x$ in terms of their values for x, where x is any real number.			SE: 693–699, 706–713, 721, 741, 744, 745
CC.9-12.F.TF.4	(+) Use the unit circle to explain symmetry (odd and even) and periodicity of trigonometric functions.			*Opportunities to address this standard can be found on the following pages:* SE: 707–713, 754–761
CC.9-12.F.TF.5	Choose trigonometric functions to model periodic phenomena with specified amplitude, frequency, and midline.*			SE: 756–760, 762–767
CC.9-12.F.TF.6	(+) Understand that restricting a trigonometric function to a domain on which it is always increasing or always decreasing allows its inverse to be constructed.			SE: 714–719
CC.9-12.F.TF.7	(+) Use inverse functions to solve trigonometric equations that arise in modeling contexts; evaluate the solutions using technology, and interpret them in terms of the context.*		SE: 551, 552–559	SE: 716–719, 721, 742, 744, 745, 748, 791–797
CC.9-12.F.TF.8	Prove the Pythagorean identity $sin^2(\theta) + cos^2(\theta) = 1$ and use it to calculate trigonometric ratios.			SE: 772–777, 801, 804, 807
CC.9-12.F.TF.9	(+) Prove the addition and subtraction formulas for sine, cosine, and tangent and use them to solve problems.			SE: 778–783, 799, 802, 804, 805, 808

SE = Student Edition

Standards	Descriptor	Algebra 1	Geometry	Algebra 2
Standards for Mathematical Content				
(+ = advanced; * = also a Modeling Standard)				
Geometry				
CC.9-12.G.CO.1	Know precise definitions of angle, circle, perpendicular line, parallel line, and line segment, based on the undefined notions of point, line, distance along a line, and distance around a circular arc.		SE: 6–11, 20–27, 35, 64, 68, 69, 146–151, 688–693	SE: 700–705, 707–713
CC.9-12.G.CO.2	Represent transformations in the plane using, e.g., transparencies and geometry software; describe transformations as functions that take points in the plane as inputs and give other points as outputs. Compare transformations that preserve distance and angle to those that do not (e.g., translation versus horizontal stretch).		SE: 50–55, 56–57, 509–514, 523, 529, 596, 604–610, 611–617, 619–625, 626–631, 633, 650–657, 660–663, 664, 668, 669, 785	
CC.9-12.G.CO.3	Given a rectangle, parallelogram, trapezoid, or regular polygon, describe the rotations and reflections that carry it onto itself.		SE: 604–610, 611–617, 619–625, 626–631, 633, 634–640, 660–663, 664, 665	
CC.9-12.G.CO.4	Develop definitions of rotations, reflections, and translations in terms of angles, circles, perpendicular lines, parallel lines, and line segments.		SE: 50–55, 604–610, 611–617, 619–625, 633, 660, 661, 664	
CC.9-12.G.CO.5	Given a geometric figure and a rotation, reflection, or translation, draw the transformed figure using, e.g., graph paper, tracing paper, or geometry software. Specify a sequence of transformations that will carry a given figure onto another.		SE: 50–55, 56–57, 59, 63, 64, 604–610, 611–617, 619–625, 626–631, 633, 660–663, 664, 665, 668, 669, 785	

SE = Student Edition

Standards	Descriptor	Algebra 1	Geometry	Algebra 2
Standards for Mathematical Content				
(+ = advanced; * = also a Modeling Standard)				
Geometry				
CC.9-12.G.CO.6	Use geometric descriptions of rigid motions to transform figures and to predict the effect of a given rigid motion on a given figure; given two figures, use the definition of congruence in terms of rigid motions to decide if they are congruent.		SE: 220–223, 258–267, 274–277, 293, 298, 300, 604–610, 611–617, 619–625	
CC.9-12.G.CO.7	Use the definition of congruence in terms of rigid motions to show that two triangles are congruent if and only if corresponding pairs of sides and corresponding pairs of angles are congruent.	SE: 69–74	SE: 220–223, 268–273, 274–277, 293, 294–295, 298, 300	
CC.9-12.G.CO.8	Explain how the criteria for triangle congruence (ASA, SAS, and SSS) follow from the definition of congruence in terms of rigid motions.		SE: 248–249, 250–257, 260–267, 293, 297, 300, 302, 304, 387	
CC.9-12.G.CO.9	Prove geometric theorems about lines and angles. Theorems include: vertical angles are congruent; when a transversal crosses parallel lines, alternate interior angles are congruent and corresponding angles are congruent; points on a perpendicular bisector of a line segment are exactly those equidistant from the segment's endpoints.		SE: 118–125, 155–159, 162, 169, 181, 203–204, 206, 312–318	

SE = Student Edition

Standards	Descriptor	Algebra 1	Geometry	Algebra 2
Standards for Mathematical Content				
(+ = advanced; * = also a Modeling Standard)				
Geometry				
CC.9-12.G.CO.10	Prove theorems about triangles. Theorems include: measures of interior angles of a triangle sum to 180°; base angles of isosceles triangles are congruent; the segment joining midpoints of two sides of a triangle is parallel to the third side and half the length; the medians of a triangle meet at a point.		SE: 231–238, 247, 285–291, 293, 296, 299, 300, 326–331, 334–339, 341, 379, 380	
CC.9-12.G.CO.11	Prove theorems about parallelograms. Theorems include: opposite sides are congruent, the diagonals of a parallelogram bisect each other, and conversely, rectangles are parallelograms with congruent diagonals.	SE: 294, 297, 299	SE: 403–404, 419, 420–427, 451, 454	
CC.9-12.G.CO.12	Make formal geometric constructions with a variety of tools and methods (compass and straightedge, string, reflective devices, paper folding, dynamic geometry software, etc.). Copying a segment; copying an angle; bisecting a segment; bisecting an angle; constructing perpendicular lines, including the perpendicular bisector of a line segment; and constructing a line parallel to a given line through a point not on the line.		SE: 14, 16, 17-18, 22–27, 35, 61, 170–171, 172, 177, 179	
CC.9-12.G.CO.13	Construct an equilateral triangle, a square, and a regular hexagon inscribed in a circle.		SE: 392–393, 826	

SE = Student Edition

Standards	Descriptor	Algebra 1	Geometry	Algebra 2
Standards for Mathematical Content				
(+ = advanced; * = also a Modeling Standard)				
Geometry				
CC.9-12.G.SRT.1	Verify experimentally the properties of dilations given by a center and a scale factor: a. A dilation takes a line not passing through the center of the dilation to a parallel line, and leaves a line passing through the center unchanged. b. The dilation of a line segment is longer or shorter in the ratio given by the scale factor.		SE: 472–479, 509–514, 650–657, 659, 663, 664	
CC.9-12.G.SRT.2	Given two figures, use the definition of similarity in terms of similarity transformations to decide if they are similar; explain using similarity transformations the meaning of similarity for triangles as the equality of all corresponding angles and the proportionality of all corresponding pairs of sides.		SE: 466–471, 472–479, 480–481, 482–489, 493, 495–501, 519, 521, 524, 525, 526, 527, 531, 597	
CC.9-12.G.SRT.3	Use the properties of similarity transformations to establish the AA criterion for two triangles to be similar.		SE: 482–489, 521, 524	
CC.9-12.G.SRT.4	Prove theorems about triangles. Theorems include: a line parallel to one side of a triangle divides the other two proportionally, and conversely; the Pythagorean Theorem proved using triangle similarity.	SE: 69–70, 72–74, 83, 86, 88, 89, 185, 236, 323	SE: 312–318, 341, 359, 360–367, 377, 378, 490–491, 495, 501, 522, 696	
CC.9-12.G.SRT.5	Use congruence and similarity criteria for triangles to solve problems and prove relationships in geometric figures.		SE: 250–257, 258–267, 268–273, 293, 297–298, 300, 302, 304, 482–489, 493, 495–501, 519, 521, 524	

SE = Student Edition

Standards	Descriptor	Algebra 1	Geometry	Algebra 2
Standards for Mathematical Content				
(+ = advanced; * = also a Modeling Standard)				
Geometry				
CC.9-12.G.SRT.6	Understand that by similarity, side ratios in right triangles are properties of the angles in the triangle, leading to definitions of trigonometric ratios for acute angles.		SE: 534–539, 540, 541–548, 561, 588, 589, 592	SE: 693
CC.9-12.G.SRT.7	Explain and use the relationship between the sine and cosine of complementary angles.		SE: 549–550	
CC.9-12.G.SRT.8	Use trigonometric ratios and the Pythagorean Theorem to solve right triangles in applied problems.		SE: 360–371, 377, 381, 382, 383, 385, 552–559, 560, 561, 562–567, 568, 587, 589, 590, 592, 594, 596, 865	SE: 689, 693–699, 721, 740, 744, 745, 749, 809
CC.9-12.G.SRT.9	(+) Derive the formula $A = \frac{1}{2} ab \sin(C)$ for the area of a triangle by drawing an auxiliary line from a vertex perpendicular to the opposite side.		SE: 701	SE: 722
CC.9-12.G.SRT.10	(+) Prove the Laws of Sines and Cosines and use them to solve problems.		SE: 569–576, 587, 590, 592, 593	SE: 722–729, 730–737, 739, 742–743, 744, 745, 748
CC.9-12.G.SRT.11	(+) Understand and apply the Law of Sines and the Law of Cosines to find unknown measurements in right and non-right triangles (e.g., surveying problems, resultant forces).		SE: 569–576, 587, 590, 592, 593	SE: 725–729, 733–737, 739, 742–743, 744
CC.9-12.G.C.1	Prove that all circles are similar.		SE: 472–479	

SE = Student Edition

Standards	Descriptor	Algebra 1	Geometry	Algebra 2
Standards for Mathematical Content				
(+ = advanced; * = also a Modeling Standard)				
Geometry				
CC.9-12.G.C.2	Identify and describe relationships among inscribed angles, radii, and chords. Include the relationship between central, inscribed, and circumscribed angles; inscribed angles on a diameter are right angles; the radius of a circle is perpendicular to the tangent where the radius intersects the circle.		SE: 820–827, 830–837, 840–846, 855, 856, 860, 863, 864	
CC.9-12.G.C.3	Construct the inscribed and circumscribed circles of a triangle, and prove properties of angles for a quadrilateral inscribed in a circle.		SE: 319, 325, 823–827, 855, 858, 865	
CC.9-12.G.C.4	(+) Construct a tangent line from a point outside a given circle to the circle.		SE: 827	
CC.9-12.G.C.5	Derive using similarity the fact that the length of the arc intercepted by an angle is proportional to the radius, and define the radian measure of the angle as the constant of proportionality; derive the formula for the area of a sector.		SE: 810–815, 816–817	SE: 707–713
CC.9-12.G.GPE.1	Derive the equation of a circle of given center and radius using the Pythagorean Theorem; complete the square to find the center and radius of a circle given by an equation.		SE: 847–853, 859, 860	SE: 823–828, 858–860, 870, 871
CC.9-12.G.GPE.2	Derive the equation of a parabola given a focus and directrix.			SE: 845–851, 853, 871, 874, 876, 880

SE = Student Edition

Standards	Descriptor	Algebra 1	Geometry	Algebra 2
Standards for Mathematical Content				
(+ = advanced; * = also a Modeling Standard)				
Geometry				
CC.9–12.G.GPE.3	(+) Derive the equations of ellipses and hyperbolas given foci and directrices.			SE: 748, 830–836, 837, 838–844, 852, 853, 871, 873–874, 876, 881
CC.9-12.G.GPE.4	Use coordinates to prove simple geometric theorems algebraically.		SE: 279–284	SE: 820, 821
CC.9-12.G.GPE.5	Prove the slope criteria for parallel and perpendicular lines and use them to solve geometric problems (e.g., find the equation of line parallel or perpendicular to a given line that passes through a given point).	SE: 293–299, 307, 309, 317, 318, 323, 384, 450, 573, 761	SE: 190–197, 216–219, 412–417, 419, 426–427, 452, 454, 669	
CC.9-12.G.GPE.6	Find the point on a directed line segment between two given points that partitions the segment in a given ratio.	SE: 267, 316	SE: 515–516, 704–709	
CC.9-12.G.GPE.7	Use coordinates to compute perimeters of polygons and areas of triangles and rectangles, e.g., using the distance formula.*		SE: 704–705, 706–709, 727, 730, 732, 737	
CC.9-12.G.GMD.1	Give an informal argument for the formulas for the circumference of a circle, area of a circle, volume of a cylinder, pyramid, and cone. Use dissection arguments, Cavalieri's principle, and informal limit arguments.		SE: 688–693, 749–751, 757	
CC.9-12.G.GMD.2	(+) Give an informal argument using Cavalieri's principle for the formulas for the volume of a sphere and other solid figures.		SE: 749–756, 757–763, 765–772	

SE = Student Edition

Standards	Descriptor	Algebra 1	Geometry	Algebra 2
Standards for Mathematical Content				
(+ = advanced; * = also a Modeling Standard)				
Geometry				
CC.9-12.G.GMD.3	Use volume formulas for cylinders, pyramids, cones, and spheres to solve problems.*	SE: 402–403, 429, 430, 503, 573, 631	SE: 668, 749–756, 757–764, 766–773, 777, 779, 781, 784, 785, 864	SE: 172, 191–192, 325, 366, 816, 829
CC.9-12.G.GMD.4	Identify the shapes of two-dimensional cross-sections of three-dimensional objects, and identify three-dimensional objects generated by rotations of two-dimensional objects.		SE: 742–748, 778	
CC.9-12.G.MG.1	Use geometric shapes, their measures, and their properties to describe objects (e.g., modeling a tree trunk or a human torso as a cylinder).*	SE: 365, 410, 417, 428, 441, 477, 479, 485, 495, 577–578, 580	SE: 226–228, 235–237, 243–244, 253, 256, 266, 290, 291, 300, 316–317, 322–323, 336–337, 440, 444–446, 448, 449, 453, 544–547, 560, 750, 753–755, 758, 761–763, 797–799, 808, 813–814, 841, 843–845	
CC.9-12.G.MG.2	Apply concepts of density based on area and volume in modeling situations (e.g., persons per square mile, BTUs per cubic foot).*	SE: 68	SE: 750, 753, 755, 777	
CC.9-12.G.MG.3	Apply geometric methods to solve design problems (e.g., designing an object or structure to satisfy physical constraints or minimize cost; working with typographic grid systems based on ratios).*		SE: 105, 264, 268, 283, 323, 325, 329–330, 348, 372, 415, 445, 460–461, 471, 512–513, 605, 627, 695, 724, 748	

SE = Student Edition

Standards	Descriptor	Algebra 1	Geometry	Algebra 2
Standards for Mathematical Content				
(+ = advanced; * = also a Modeling Standard)				
Statistics and Probability				
CC.9-12.S.ID.1	Represent data with plots on the real number line (dot plots, histograms, and box plots).*	SE: 686–694, 695–701, 704–709, 710–713, 752, 753, 756		SE: 531, 532, 543–544, 547–548, 749
CC.9-12.S.ID.2	Use statistics appropriate to the shape of the data distribution to compare center (median, mean) and spread (interquartile range, standard deviation) of two or more different data sets.*	SE: 702–709		SE: 548, 576
CC.9-12.S.ID.3	Interpret differences in shape, center, and spread in the context of the data sets, accounting for possible effects of extreme data points (outliers).*	SE: 702–709, 710–713		SE: 527, 543–548
CC.9-12.S.ID.4	Use the mean and standard deviation of a data set to fit it to a normal distribution and to estimate population percentages. Recognize that there are data sets for which such a procedure is not appropriate. Use calculators, spreadsheets, and tables to estimate areas under the normal curve.*			SE: 594–595, 596–603
CC.9-12.S.ID.5	Summarize categorical data for two categories in two-way frequency tables. Interpret relative frequencies in the context of the data (including joint, marginal, and conditional relative frequencies). Recognize possible associations and trends in the data.*			SE: 501, 503–506, 509, 511–518, 530, 536

SE = Student Edition

Standards	Descriptor	Algebra 1	Geometry	Algebra 2
Standards for Mathematical Content				
(+ = advanced; * = also a Modeling Standard)				
Statistics and Probability				
CC.9-12.S.ID.6	Represent data on two quantitative variables on a scatter plot, and describe how the variables are related.* a. Fit a function to the data; use functions fitted to data to solve problems in the context of the data. Use given functions or choose a function suggested by the context. Emphasize linear and exponential models. b. Informally assess the fit of a function by plotting and analyzing residuals. c. Fit a linear function for a scatter plot that suggests a linear association.	SE: 196–198, 200–203, 204, 205, 211, 212, 213, 217, 218, 284, 285–292, 551, 649–655		SE: 32–39, 45, 46, 120–125, 135, 140, 210–215, 289–295, 296, 297, 301, 307, 458–465
CC.9-12.S.ID.7	Interpret the slope (rate of change) and the intercept (constant term) of a linear model in the context of the data.*	SE: 284, 285–292	SE: 183, 186, 193, 194, 195	SE: 32–39, 45
CC.9-12.S.ID.8	Compute (using technology) and interpret the correlation coefficient of a linear fit.*	SE: 285–292		SE: 32–39, 45, 46, 306
CC.9-12.S.ID.9	Distinguish between correlation and causation.*	SE: 285–292		
CC.9-12.S.IC.1	Understand statistics as a process for making inferences about population parameters based on a random sample from that population.*	SE: 716–721		SE: 551–558
CC.9-12.S.IC.2	Decide if a specified model is consistent with results from a given data-generating process, e.g., using simulation.*			SE: 505

SE = Student Edition

Standards	Descriptor	Algebra 1	Geometry	Algebra 2
Standards for Mathematical Content				
(+ = advanced; * = also a Modeling Standard)				
Statistics and Probability				
CC.9-12.S.IC.3	Recognize the purposes of and differences among sample surveys, experiments, and observational studies; explain how randomization relates to each.*	SE: 722–723		SE: 559–566
CC.9-12.S.IC.4	Use data from a sample survey to estimate a population mean or proportion; develop a margin of error through the use of simulation models for random sampling.*			SE: 579–586
CC.9-12.S.IC.5	Use data from a randomized experiment to compare two treatments; use simulations to decide if differences between parameters are significant.*			SE: 567–574
CC.9-12.S.IC.6	Evaluate reports based on data.*	SE: 716–721, 725, 754, 756		SE: 579–586
CC.9-12.S.CP.1	Describe events as subsets of a sample space (the set of outcomes) using characteristics (or categories) of the outcomes, or as unions, intersections, or complements of other events ("or," "and," "not").*	SE: 727–732, 734–739, 740–747		SE: 490–497, 509, 519–525, 530, 533, 534
CC.9-12.S.CP.2	Understand that two events *A* and *B* are independent if the probability of *A* and *B* occurring together is the product of their probabilities, and use this characterization to determine if they are independent.*	SE: 741–746, 755, 756	SE: 238	SE: 499–506, 509, 530, 532, 533

SE = Student Edition

Standards	Descriptor	Algebra 1	Geometry	Algebra 2
Standards for Mathematical Content				
(+ = advanced; * = also a Modeling Standard)				
Statistics and Probability				
CC.9-12.S.CP.3	Understand the conditional probability of *A* given *B* as *P*(*A* and *B*)/*P*(*B*), and interpret independence of *A* and *B* as saying that the conditional probability of *A* given *B* is the same as the probability of *A*, and the conditional probability of *B* given *A* is the same as the probability of *B*.*	SE: 740–747	SE: 351, 583	SE: 499–506, 530, 685
CC.9-12.S.CP.4	Construct and interpret two-way frequency tables of data when two categories are associated with each object being classified. Use the two-way table as a sample space to decide if events are independent and to approximate conditional probabilities.*			SE: 493–500, 511–518
CC.9-12.S.CP.5	Recognize and explain the concepts of conditional probability and independence in everyday language and everyday situations.*	SE: 740–741, 744–746		SE: 511–518
CC.9-12.S.CP.6	Find the conditional probability of *A* given *B* as the fraction of *B*'s outcomes that also belong to *A*, and interpret the answer in terms of the model.*	SE: 740–747		SE: 499–506, 530
CC.9-12.S.CP.7	Apply the Addition Rule, $P(A \text{ or } B) = P(A) + P(B) - P(A \text{ and } B)$, and interpret the answer in terms of the model.*	SE: 748–749		SE: 509, 519–525, 530, 535

SE = Student Edition

Standards	Descriptor	Algebra 1	Geometry	Algebra 2
Standards for Mathematical Content				
(+ = advanced; * = also a Modeling Standard)				
Statistics and Probability				
CC.9-12.S.CP.8	(+) Apply the general Multiplication Rule in a uniform probability model, $P(A \text{ and } B) = P(A)P(B\|A) = P(B)P(A\|B)$, and interpret the answer in terms of the model.*	SE: 740–747		SE: 499–506, 509, 530, 533
CC.9-12.S.CP.9	(+) Use permutations and combinations to compute probabilities of compound events and solve problems.*			SE: 482–488, 490–497, 509, 519–525, 528, 532, 534, 536, 809
CC.9-12.S.MD.1	(+) Define a random variable for a quantity of interest by assigning a numerical value to each event in a sample space; graph the corresponding probability distribution using the same graphical displays as for data distributions.*			SE: 592, 594
CC.9-12.S.MD.2	(+) Calculate the expected value of a random variable; interpret it as the mean of the probability distribution.*			SE: 527, 531, 532, 533, 545, 547
CC.9-12.S.MD.3	(+) Develop a probability distribution for a random variable defined for a sample space in which theoretical probabilities can be calculated; find the expected value. *			SE: 550

SE = Student Edition

Standards	Descriptor	Algebra 1	Geometry	Algebra 2
Standards for Mathematical Content				
(+ = advanced; * = also a Modeling Standard)				
Statistics and Probability				
CC.9-12.S.MD.4	(+) Develop a probability distribution for a random variable defined for a sample space in which probabilities are assigned empirically; find the expected value.*			SE: 527, 531, 532, 588–593
CC.9-12.S.MD.5	(+) Weigh the possible outcomes of a decision by assigning probabilities to payoff values and finding expected values.* a. Find the expected payoff for a game of chance. b. Evaluate and compare strategies on the basis of expected values.			SE: 509, 522–526
CC.9-12.S.MD.6	(+) Use probabilities to make fair decisions (e.g., drawing by lots, using a random number generator).*			SE: 551–558
CC.9-12.S.MD.7	(+) Analyze decisions and strategies using probability concepts (e.g., product testing, medical testing, pulling a hockey goalie at the end of a game).*	SE: 729, 731, 746, 748–749, 750, 754, 756		SE: 495–496, 504, 524, 526, 604–609

SE = Student Edition

MATHEMATICAL PRACTICES

Mastering the Standards
for Mathematical Practice

The topics described in the Standards for Mathematical Content will vary from year to year. However, the *way* in which you learn, study, and think about mathematics will not. The Standards for Mathematical Practice describe skills that you will use in all of your math courses. These pages show some features of your book that will help you gain these skills and use them to master this year's topics.

Getty Images/PhotoDisc

① Make sense of problems and persevere in solving them.

Mathematically proficient students start by explaining to themselves the meaning of a problem... They analyze givens, constraints, relationships, and goals. They make conjectures about the form... of the solution and plan a solution pathway...

In your book

Focus on Problem Solving describes a four-step plan for problem solving. The plan is introduced at the beginning of your book, and practice appears throughout.

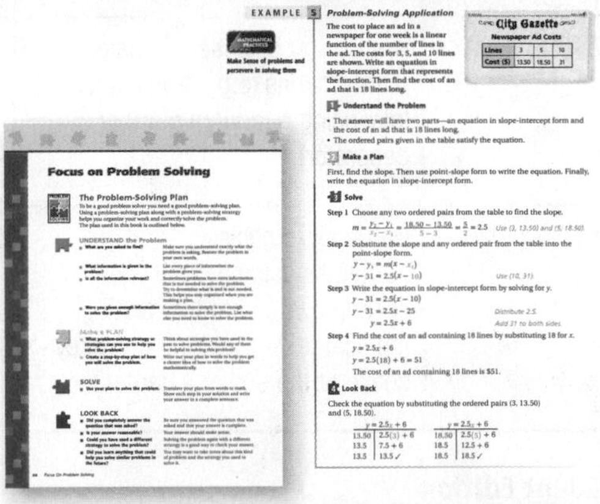

② Reason abstractly and quantitatively.
③ Construct viable arguments and critique the reasoning of others.

Mathematically proficient students... justify their conclusions, [and]... distinguish correct... reasoning from that which is flawed.

In your book

Think and Discuss asks you to evaluate statements, explain relationships, apply mathematical principles, and justify your reasoning.

MATHEMATICAL PRACTICES

THINK AND DISCUSS

1. Explain how multiplying the second equation in a system by −1 and eliminating by adding is the same as elimination by subtraction. Give an example of a system for which this applies.
2. Explain why it does not matter which variable you solve for first when solving a system by elimination.
3. **GET ORG**... an examp... given met...

MATHEMATICAL PRACTICES

THINK AND DISCUSS

1. Give a situation in which order matters and one in which order does not matter.
2. Give the value of $_nC_n$, where n is any integer. Explain your answer.
3. Tell what $_3C_4$ would mean in the real world and why it is not possible.
4. **GET ORGANIZED** Copy and complete the graphic organizer.

	Fundamental Counting Principle	Permutation	Combination
Formula			
Examples			

4 Model with mathematics.

Mathematically proficient students can apply... mathematics... to... problems... in everyday life, society, and the workplace...

In your book

Multi-Step Test Prep and **Real-World Connections** apply mathematics to other disciplines and in real-world scenarios.

5 Use appropriate tools strategically.

Mathematically proficient students consider the available tools when solving a... problem... [and] are... able to use technological tools to explore and deepen their understanding...

In your book

Algebra Labs and **Technology Labs** use concrete and technological tools to explore mathematical concepts.

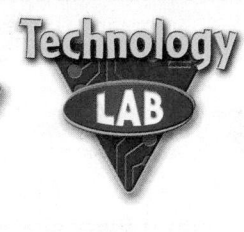

6 Attend to precision.

Mathematically proficient students... communicate precisely... with others and in their own reasoning... [They] give carefully formulated explanations...

In your book

Reading and Writing Math and **Write About It** help you learn and use the language of math to communicate mathematics precisely.

7 Look for and make use of structure.
8 Look for and express regularity in repeated reasoning.

Mathematically proficient students... look both for general methods and for shortcuts...

In your book

Lesson examples group similar types of problems together, and the solutions are carefully stepped out. This allows you to make generalizations about—and notice variations in—the underlying structures.

EXAMPLE 3 Finding Products in the Form $(a + b)(a - b)$

Multiply.

A $(x + 6)(x - 6)$

$(a + b)(a - b) = a^2 - b^2$ — *Use the rule for $(a + b)(a - b)$.*

$(x + 6)(x - 6) = x^2 - 6^2$ — *Identify a and b: $a = x$ and $b = 6$.*

$= x^2 - 36$ — *Simplify.*

B $(x^2 + 2y)(x^2 - 2y)$

$(a + b)(a - b) = a^2 - b^2$ — *Use the rule for $(a + b)(a - b)$.*

$(x^2 + 2y)(x^2 - 2y) = (x^2)^2 - (2y)^2$ — *Identify a and b: $a = x^2$ and $b = 2y$.*

$= x^4 - 4y^2$ — *Simplify.*

C $(7 + n)(7 - n)$

$(a + b)(a - b) = a^2 - b^2$ — *Use the rule for $(a + b)(a - b)$.*

$(7 + n)(7 - n) = 7^2 - n^2$ — *Identify a and b: $a = 7$ and $b = n$.*

$= 49 - n^2$ — *Simplify.*

WEEK 1

DAY 1

Which statement about a number line is true?

(A) Values increase toward the right.

(B) Values increase toward the left.

(C) Whole numbers are toward the right and decimal numbers are toward the left.

(D) Negative numbers are toward the right and positive numbers are toward the left.

DAY 2

If $a = b$ and $b = c$, which statement must be true?

(F) $a > c$

(G) $-a - c = 0$

(H) $a + c = 0$

(J) $a = c$

DAY 3

If the width of each square in the grid is 1 centimeter, what is the diameter of the circle?

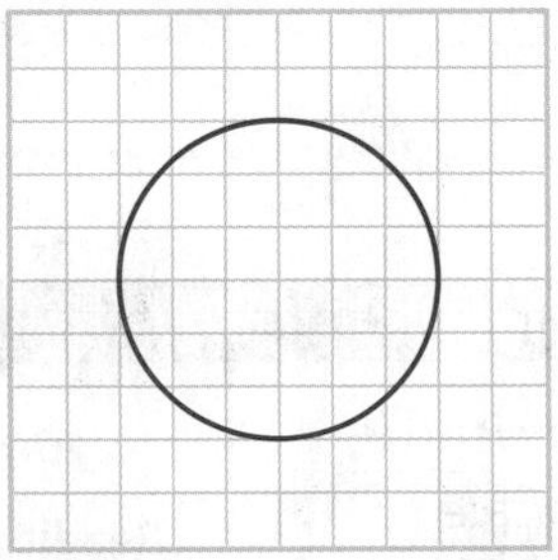

(A) 1 centimeter

(B) 3 centimeters

(C) 6 centimeters

(D) 12 centimeters

DAY 4

Which shape is NOT included in the figure?

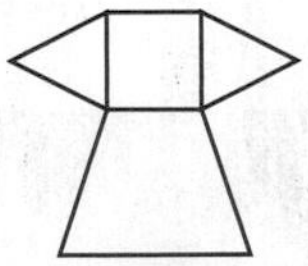

(F) Circle

(G) Square

(H) Triangle

(J) Trapezoid

DAY 5

Which statement best describes these two figures?

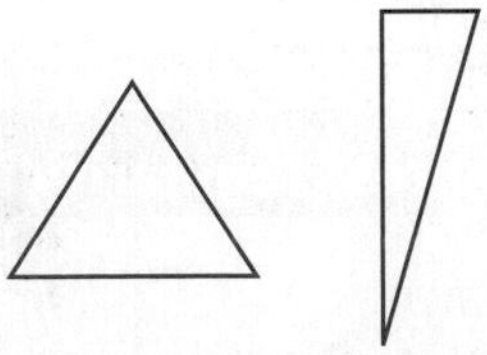

(A) They cover the same area.

(B) They are the same size.

(C) They have the same number of sides.

(D) The distance around each figure is the same.

Countdown to Mastery

WEEK 2

DAY 1

What is the length of $\overline{FD}$?

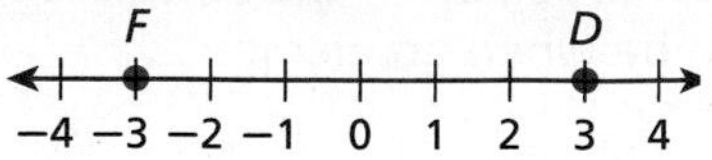

Ⓐ 0

Ⓑ 3

Ⓒ 6

Ⓓ 9

DAY 2

$\angle ABC$ is an obtuse angle. Which of these could be the measure of $\angle ABC$?

Ⓕ 0°

Ⓖ 53°

Ⓗ 90°

Ⓙ 108°

DAY 3

Which point is described by the coordinates $(-2, 3)$?

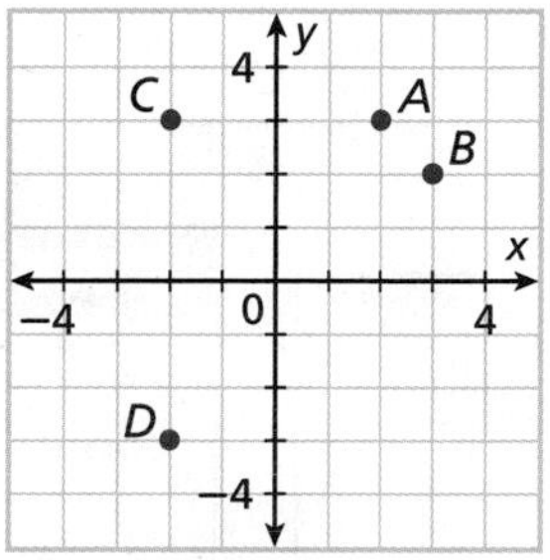

Ⓐ *A*

Ⓑ *B*

Ⓒ *C*

Ⓓ *D*

DAY 4

An architect is sketching a blueprint of a patio for a new home. On the blueprint, *C* is the midpoint of $\overline{AD}$, which represents one side of the patio. Point *B* is the midpoint of $\overline{AC}$. If $BC = 8$ feet, what is the length of $\overline{AD}$?

Ⓕ 8 feet

Ⓖ 16 feet

Ⓗ 24 feet

Ⓙ 32 feet

DAY 5

$\overrightarrow{OB}$ bisects $\angle AOC$, and $m\angle AOC = 60°$. What is $m\angle BOE$?

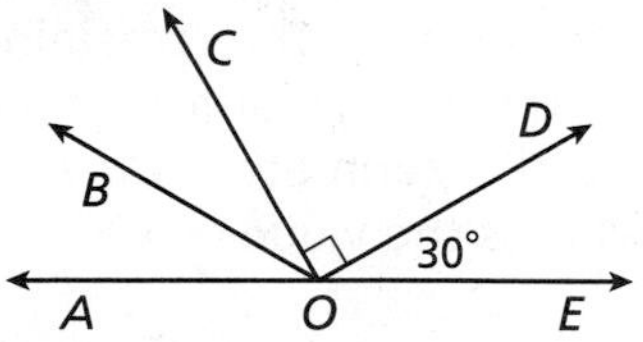

Ⓐ 30°

Ⓑ 60°

Ⓒ 120°

Ⓓ 150°

Countdown to Mastery

WEEK 3

DAY 1

The figure below shows the first three elements in a pattern. The area of the white region in the first element is 8 cm^2, and the area of the white region in the second element is 16 cm^2. What will the area of the white region be when an element contains six circles?

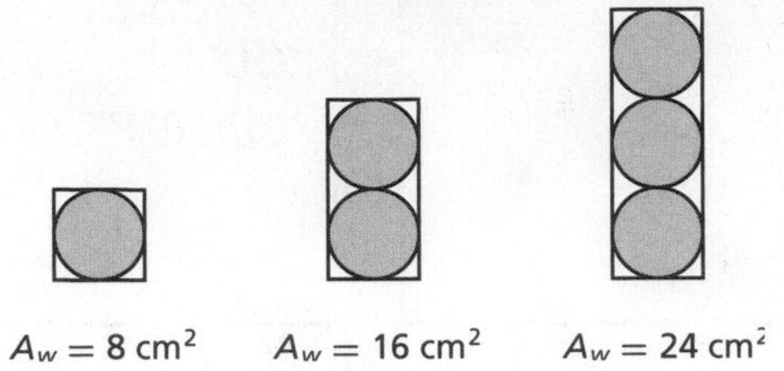

Ⓐ 36 square centimeters

Ⓑ 48 square centimeters

Ⓒ 144 square centimeters

Ⓓ 168 square centimeters

DAY 2

Which of these is a unit that can describe the perimeter of a figure?

Ⓕ Meters

Ⓖ Square centimeters

Ⓗ Cubic inches

Ⓙ Seconds

DAY 3

Point X is the midpoint of $\overline{HI}$. What is the coordinate of the point X?

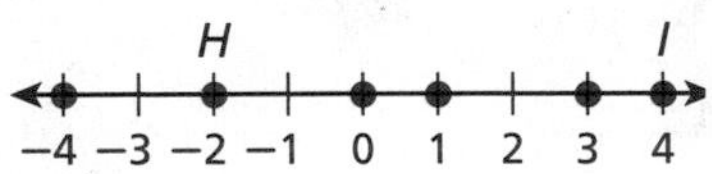

Ⓐ −4

Ⓑ 0

Ⓒ 1

Ⓓ 3

DAY 4

A hexagon has two congruent sides that are each 10 cm long. The remaining sides are congruent to each other, with length $(x - 3)$ cm. The perimeter of the polygon is 44 cm. What is the value of x?

Ⓕ 4.5

Ⓖ 6

Ⓗ 6.75

Ⓙ 9

DAY 5

A line segment is drawn between the points $(5, 8)$ and $(-1, 6)$. What are the coordinates of the midpoint of the segment?

Ⓐ $(3, 1)$

Ⓑ $(4, 14)$

Ⓒ $(2, 7)$

Ⓓ $\left(-\frac{1}{2}, 3\right)$

Countdown to Mastery

WEEK 4

DAY 1

Which equation below represents the second step of the solution process?

Step 1: $6x - 12 = 3(5 - x)$

Step 2: ?

Step 3: $9x - 12 = 15$

Step 4: $9x = 27$

Step 5: $x = 3$

(A) $6x - 12 = 15 - x$

(B) $6x - 12 = 15 - 3x$

(C) $6x - 12 = 5 - 3x$

(D) $6x = 3(5 - x) - 12$

DAY 2

Which conjecture best describes a rule for the pattern below?

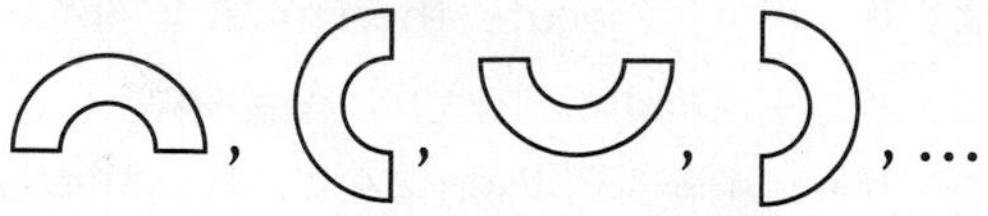

(F) Rotate counterclockwise 90°

(G) Rotate clockwise 90°

(H) Rotate counterclockwise 180°

(J) Rotate clockwise 180°

DAY 3

Given: A triangle is a right triangle.

Conclusion: Two of the sides are congruent.

This conclusion—

(A) is true because right triangles have exactly one angle that measures 90°.

(B) is true because all right triangles have two congruent angles.

(C) is false because, for example, the sides of a 30°-60°-90° right triangle have different lengths.

(D) is false because a right triangle cannot have two congruent angles.

DAY 4

Which of the following best describes the value of $4n + 1$ when n is an integer?

(F) The value is always negative.

(G) The value is always positive.

(H) The value is always even.

(J) The value is always odd.

DAY 5

$\overrightarrow{MN}$ bisects $\angle LMO$. Which statement must be true?

(A) $m\angle LMN = m\angle OMN$

(B) $m\angle LMO = m\angle OMN$

(C) $m\angle LMN = m\angle OML$

(D) $m\angle LMO = m\angle ONM$

DAY 1

Which statement is the converse of the conditional statement "If m∠A = 48°, then ∠A is acute?"

(A) If ∠A is not acute, then m∠A ≠ 48°.

(B) If ∠A is acute, then m∠A = 48°.

(C) If m∠A ≠ 48°, then ∠A is not acute.

(D) If ∠A is not acute, then it must be obtuse.

DAY 2

Which of the following statements is true, based on the figure?

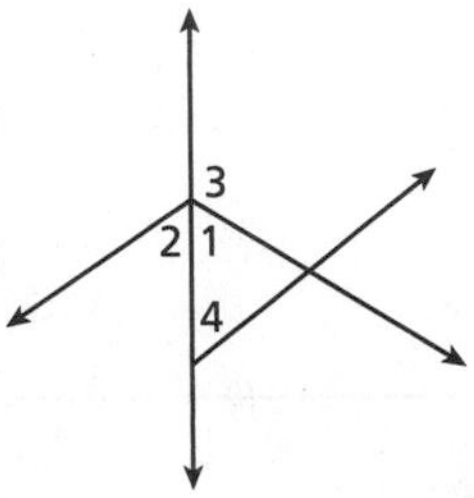

(F) ∠2 and ∠4 are not adjacent but form a linear pair.

(G) ∠2 and ∠4 are adjacent angles that form a linear pair.

(H) ∠1 and ∠3 are adjacent angles and form a linear pair.

(J) ∠1 and ∠3 are not adjacent angles but form a linear pair.

DAY 3

Let *a* represent "Three points are not collinear," and let *b* represent "The three points lie in exactly one plane." Which symbolic sentence represents the statement "If three points lie in exactly one plane, then the three points are not collinear"?

(A) $a \rightarrow b$

(B) $b \rightarrow a$

(C) $\sim a \rightarrow \sim b$

(D) $\sim b \rightarrow \sim a$

DAY 4

The figure below shows a pattern of right triangles and their areas, *A*. Based on the pattern, what will be the area of a right triangle with a height of 64 units?

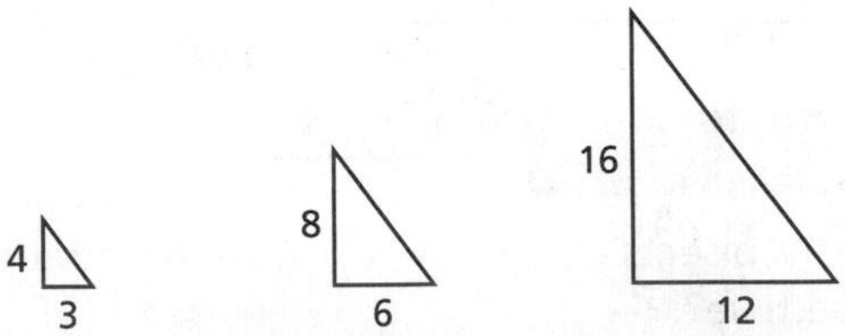

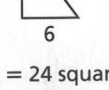

A = 6 square units   *A* = 24 square units   *A* = 96 square units

(F) 4 square units

(G) 100 square units

(H) 364 square units

(J) 1536 square units

DAY 5

How many pairs of vertical angles are in the diagram?

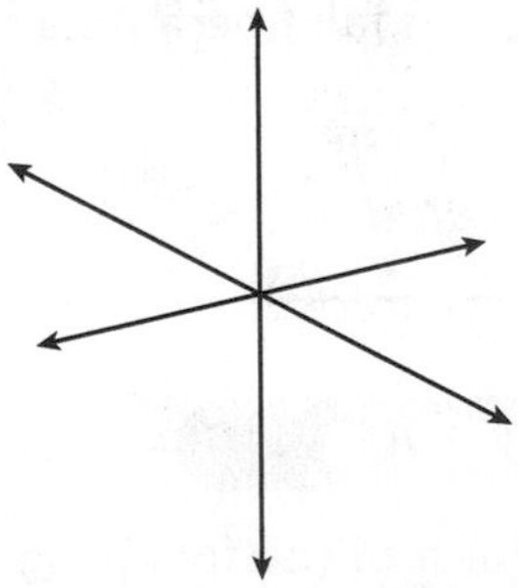

(A) 2

(B) 3

(C) 6

(D) 12

Countdown to Mastery

WEEK 6

DAY 1

A transversal crosses two parallel lines. If two angles are on opposite sides of the transversal and inside the two parallel lines, then they are alternate interior angles. If two angles are alternate interior angles, then they are congruent. $\angle 1$ and $\angle 2$ are alternate interior angles.

Which conclusion can be drawn from the given information?

Ⓐ $\angle 1$ and $\angle 2$ are parallel.

Ⓑ $\angle 1$ and $\angle 2$ are suppplementary

Ⓒ $\angle 1$ and $\angle 2$ are complementary.

Ⓓ $\angle 1$ and $\angle 2$ are congruent.

DAY 2

Two angles are labeled in the figure below. Which of the following statements best describes this angle pair?

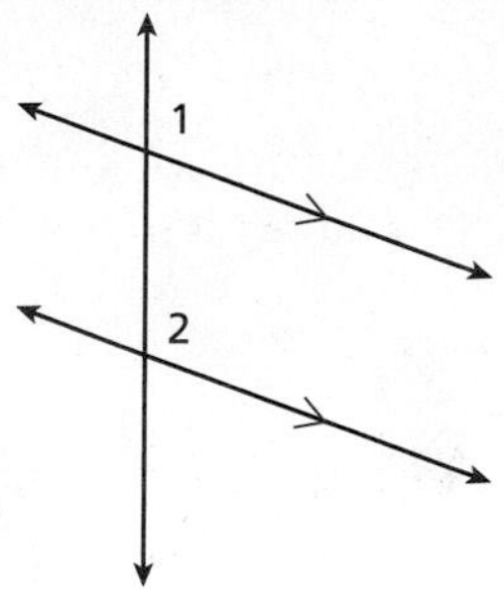

Ⓕ They are complementary angles.

Ⓖ They are congruent angles.

Ⓗ They are supplementary angles.

Ⓙ They are parallel angles.

DAY 3

If line a is parallel to line b, and $m\angle 8 = 62°$, what is $m\angle 1$?

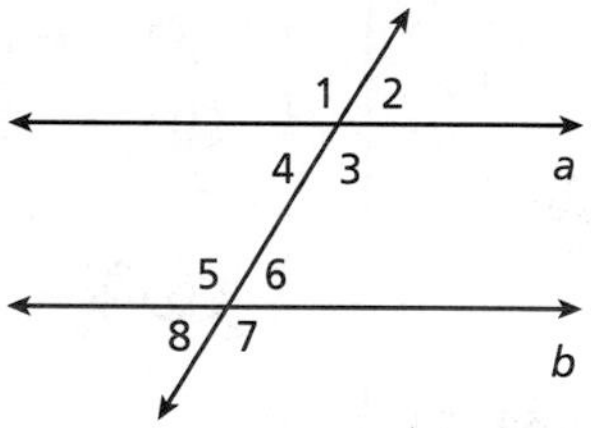

Ⓐ 28°

Ⓑ 62°

Ⓒ 118°

Ⓓ 180°

DAY 4

In $\triangle JKL$, $\angle J \approx \angle K$ and $\angle K \approx \angle L$. Which property of congruence of angles proves that $\angle J \approx \angle L$?

Ⓕ Reflexive

Ⓖ Symmetry

Ⓗ Transitive

Ⓙ None of the above

DAY 5

B is in the interior of $\angle AOC$. Which of the following statements must be true?

Ⓐ $m\angle AOB + m\angle BOC = m\angle AOC$

Ⓑ $m\angle AOB = m\angle BOC$

Ⓒ $m\angle AOB + m\angle AOC = m\angle BOC$

Ⓓ $m\angle BOC + m\angle AOC = m\angle AOB$

Countdown to Mastery

WEEK 7

DAY 1

Four rays are drawn from the origin through each of the following points: $S(-2, 5)$, $T(0, 4)$, $U(-1, -3)$, and $V(2, 6)$. Which point is on the ray that forms an acute angle with the ray in the figure?

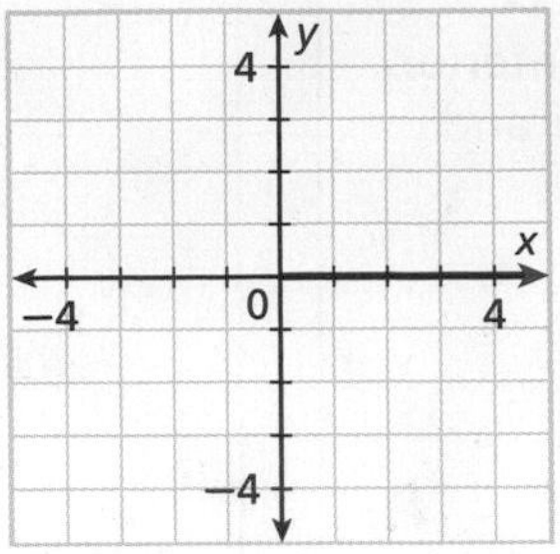

Ⓐ S

Ⓑ T

Ⓒ U

Ⓓ V

DAY 2

What must be true if two nonvertical lines are perpendicular?

Ⓕ Their slopes add to 0.

Ⓖ The product of their slopes is −1.

Ⓗ Their slopes are equal.

Ⓙ Their y-intercepts are equal.

DAY 3

Which line is parallel to $y = 2x + 3$?

Ⓐ $y = 2x - 8$

Ⓑ $y = 3x + 2$

Ⓒ $2y = -4x + 6$

Ⓓ $y = -2x + 3$

DAY 4

In $\triangle ABC$, $AC = 4x - 10$, $BC = 2x + 4$, and $\overline{DE}$ is a midsegment of $\triangle ABC$. If $DE = 8$, what is the value of x?

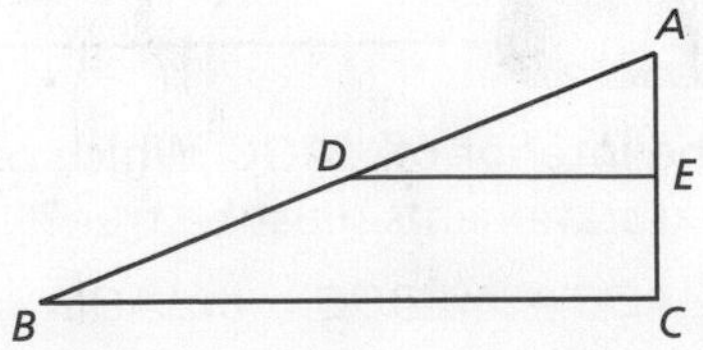

Ⓕ 2

Ⓖ 4.5

Ⓗ 6

Ⓙ 6.5

DAY 5

Two parallel lines are cut by a transversal. The measures of two corresponding angles are $(x + 20)°$ and $(3x - 10)°$. What is the value of x?

Ⓐ 7

Ⓑ 15

Ⓒ 35

Ⓓ 42

Countdown to Mastery — WEEK 8

DAY 1

What is the slope of the given line segment?

Ⓐ -2

Ⓑ $-\frac{1}{2}$

Ⓒ 1

Ⓓ 2

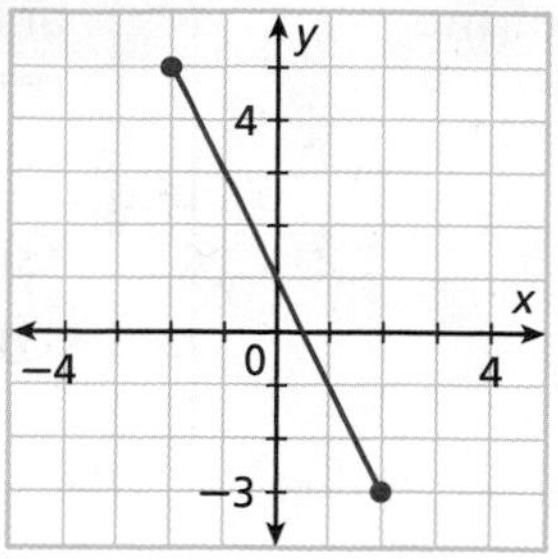

DAY 2

Which two lines are perpendicular?

Ⓕ $y = -5x + 2$ and $2y - 10x = 4$

Ⓖ $y = \frac{1}{4}x + 1$ and $y = 4x + 2$

Ⓗ $y = 3x + 1$ and $y - 4x = 6$

Ⓙ $y = \frac{1}{2}x + 2$ and $y + 2x = -4$

DAY 3

Which of the following is the best classification for the given triangle?

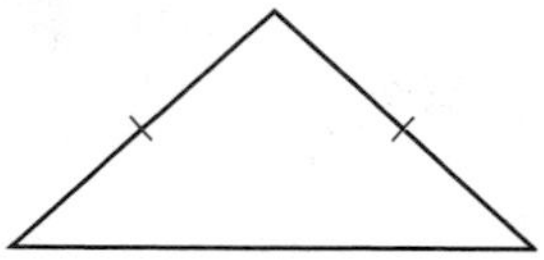

Ⓐ Equilateral

Ⓑ Isosceles

Ⓒ Scalene

Ⓓ Right

DAY 4

$\triangle SQT$ is an equilateral triangle. $\overline{QR}$ bisects $\angle SQT$. What are the measures of the angles of $\triangle SQR$?

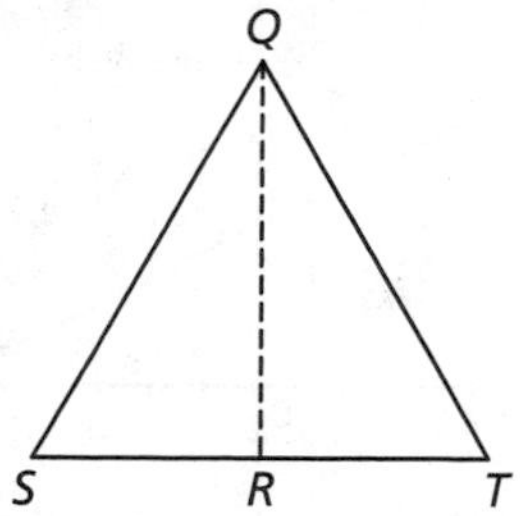

Ⓕ 30°-30°-30°

Ⓖ 30°-60°-90°

Ⓗ 30°-60°-60°

Ⓙ 60°-60°-60°

DAY 5

In $\triangle ABC$, $m\angle A = 62°$, $m\angle B = (3x + 3)°$, and $m\angle C = (4x + 10)°$. Find the value of x.

Ⓐ 7

Ⓑ 11

Ⓒ 13

Ⓓ 15

DAY 1

$\overleftrightarrow{AB}$ is perpendicular to $\overleftrightarrow{XY}$. If $A(3, 5)$, $B(9, 3)$, and $X(-2, -5)$, which of the following is a point on $\overleftrightarrow{XY}$?

(A) (6, 8)
(B) (1, 4)
(C) (3, 1)
(D) (2, 5)

DAY 2

$\angle ABC$ is formed by $\overrightarrow{BA}$ and $\overrightarrow{BC}$. If $A(-4, 1)$ and $B(-4, 6)$, what coordinates for C will result in an obtuse angle?

(F) (−1, 2)
(G) (−2, 9)
(H) (0, 5)
(J) (2, 6)

DAY 3

$\overleftrightarrow{AB} \parallel \overleftrightarrow{CD}$ and $\overleftrightarrow{AC} \parallel \overleftrightarrow{BD}$. Which of the following is true?

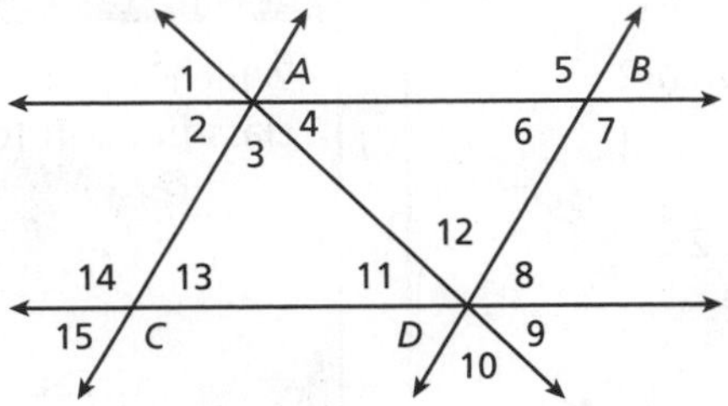

(A) $\angle 1$ is congruent to $\angle 5$.
(B) $\angle 2$ is supplementary to $\angle 14$.
(C) $\angle 8$ is congruent to $\angle 11$.
(D) $\angle 6$ is supplementary to $\angle 13$.

DAY 4

What is the length of the given segment to the nearest unit?

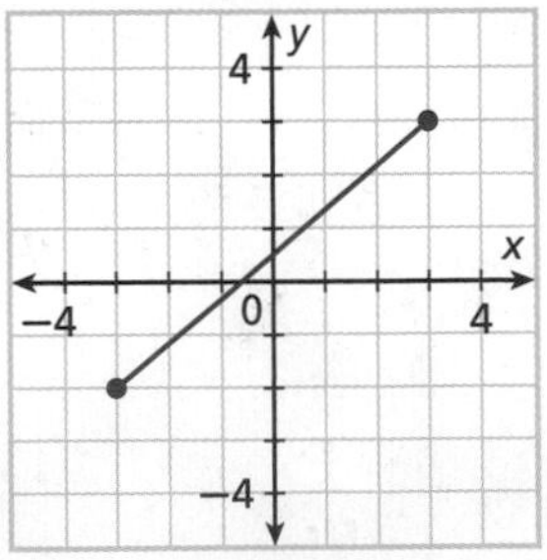

(F) 1
(G) 5
(H) 8
(J) 10

DAY 5

Which equation best represents the line in the graph?

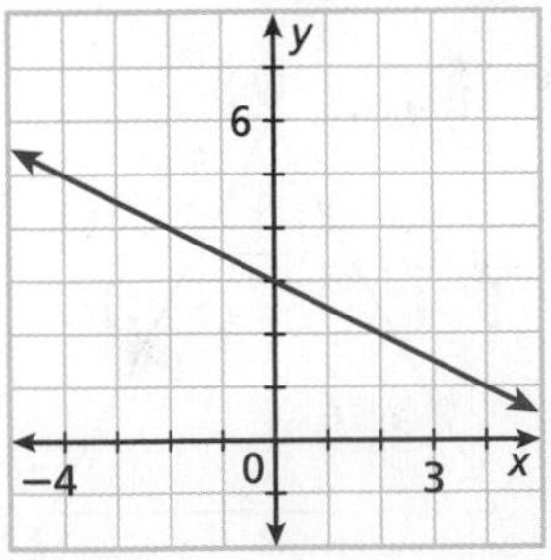

(A) $y = \frac{1}{2}x + 3$
(B) $y = 3x + 1$
(C) $y = -2x - 3$
(D) $y = -\frac{1}{2}x + 3$

DAY 1

Which set of angle measures can be used to conclude that lines x and y are parallel?

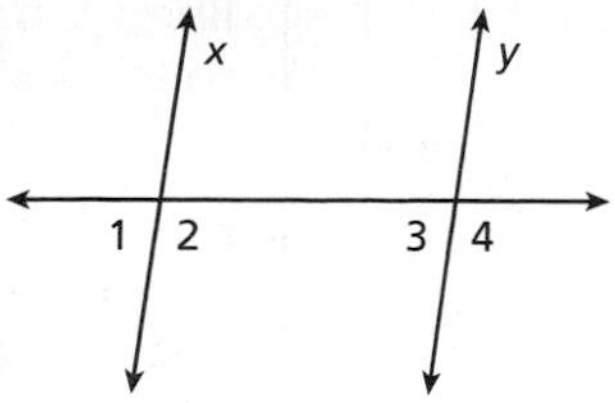

Ⓐ $m\angle 1 = 87°$ and $m\angle 3 = 93°$

Ⓑ $m\angle 1 = 82°$ and $m\angle 4 = 98°$

Ⓒ $m\angle 1 = 80°$ and $m\angle 2 = 100°$

Ⓓ $m\angle 3 = 88°$ and $m\angle 4 = 92°$

DAY 2

Which postulate or theorem can be used to prove that these triangles are congruent?

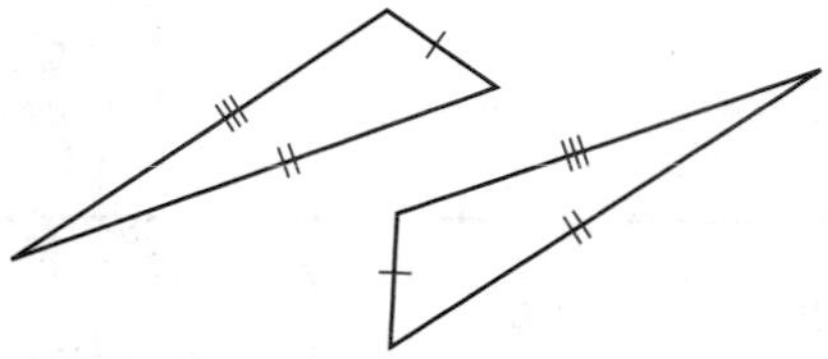

Ⓕ SAS

Ⓖ ASA

Ⓗ AAS

Ⓙ SSS

DAY 3

Which of the following conjectures is false?

Ⓐ The product of an even number and an odd number is even.

Ⓑ The difference of two negative numbers is a positive number.

Ⓒ If x is negative, then $-x$ is positive.

Ⓓ If x is even, then $x + 1$ is odd.

DAY 4

How many line segments can be determined by four points, no three of which are collinear?

Ⓕ 4

Ⓖ 6

Ⓗ 8

Ⓙ 10

DAY 5

The centroid of a triangle divides each median of the triangle into two segments. What of the following is the ratio of the length of the longer segment to the length of the shorter segment?

Ⓐ 1:1

Ⓑ 1:3

Ⓒ 2:3

Ⓓ 2:1

Countdown to Mastery — WEEK 11

DAY 1

What conclusion can you draw from the figure?

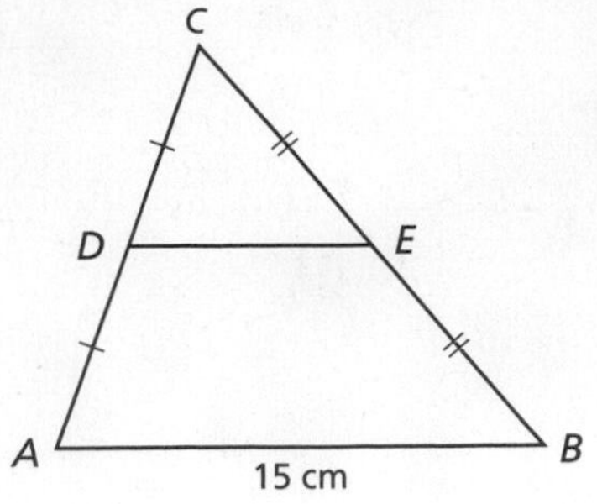

Ⓐ $\triangle ABC$ is isosceles.

Ⓑ The perimeter of $\triangle ABC$ is 45 centimeters.

Ⓒ $DE = 10$ centimeters

Ⓓ $DE = \frac{1}{2}AB$

DAY 2

Jan drew the figure below and claims that line ℓ is parallel to line m. Which of the following proves her statement true?

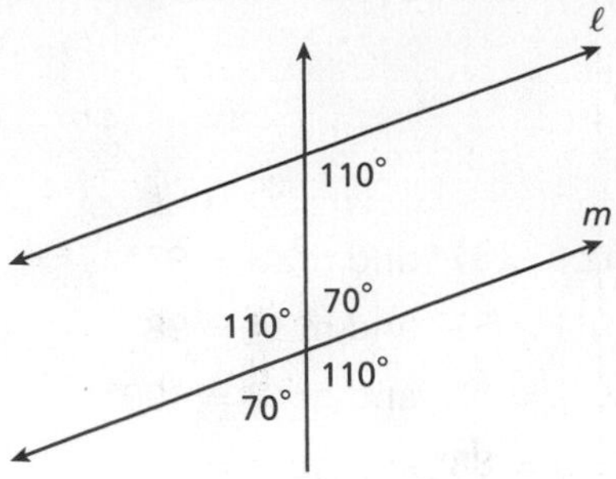

Ⓕ Angles on opposite sides of the transversal are equal.

Ⓖ Corresponding angles on the same side of the transversal are congruent.

Ⓗ More than two angles in the diagram have the same value.

Ⓙ Two straight lines pass through the same transversal.

DAY 3

Which of the following can you use to prove that two angles are complementary?

Ⓐ The sum of their measures is 90°.

Ⓑ The sum of their measures is 180°.

Ⓒ The angles have the same measure.

Ⓓ The measure of one angle is twice the other measure.

DAY 4

If $X(5, 5)$ and $Y(0, 0)$, what are the coordinates of Z so that $m\angle XYZ = 90°$?

Ⓕ (5, −5)

Ⓖ (−5, −5)

Ⓗ (5, 0)

Ⓙ (0, 5)

DAY 5

$\overrightarrow{OZ}$ is a bisector of $\angle XOY$. Which of the following statements is NOT true?

Ⓐ $2m\angle ZOY = m\angle XOY$

Ⓑ $2m\angle XOZ = m\angle XOY$

Ⓒ $m\angle ZOY = m\angle XOY$

Ⓓ $m\angle XOZ = \frac{1}{2}m\angle XOY$

Countdown to Mastery

WEEK 12

DAY 1

Which of the following correctly completes the congruence statement?

$\overline{AB} \cong$ ___?___

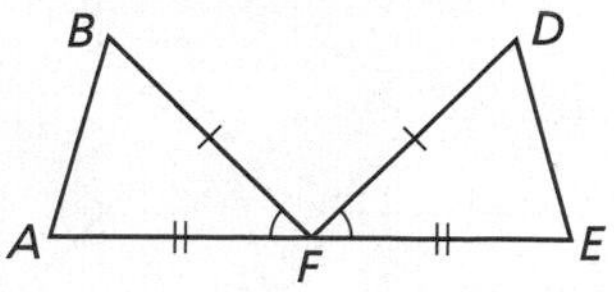

Ⓐ $\overline{FD}$

Ⓑ $\overline{AF}$

Ⓒ $\overline{EF}$

Ⓓ $\overline{ED}$

DAY 2

Based on the figure, which inequality is correct?

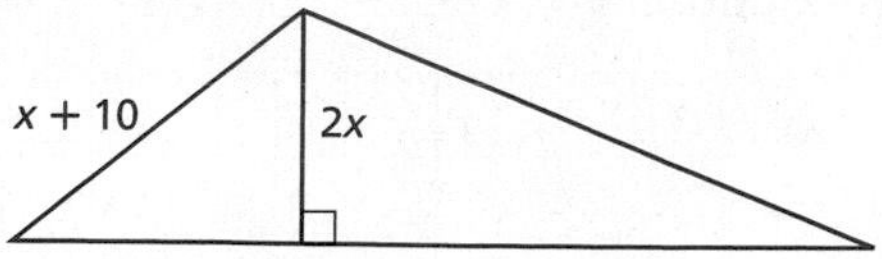

Ⓕ $2x > x + 10$

Ⓖ $2x < 10$

Ⓗ $x < 10$

Ⓙ $x > 8$

DAY 3

Roberta is attaching wooden trim around a stained glass window. The window is made up of eight congruent isosceles triangles.

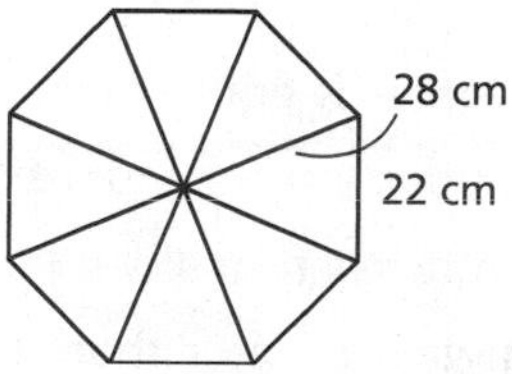

What length of trim does Roberta need in order to surround the entire window?

Ⓐ 22 centimeters

Ⓑ 78 centimeters

Ⓒ 176 centimeters

Ⓓ 624 centimeters

DAY 4

How many different segments can be created from eight collinear points?

Ⓕ 8

Ⓖ 13

Ⓗ 28

Ⓙ 36

DAY 5

Which of these conditional statements is true?

Ⓐ If two angles are vertical angles, then they are congruent.

Ⓑ If two angles are congruent, then they are right angles.

Ⓒ If four points are given, then they lie in exactly one plane.

Ⓓ If one angle of a triangle measures 60°, then the triangle is a right triangle.

DAY 1

What is an equation of a line that passes through P and is perpendicular to the line with equation $y = x + 2$?

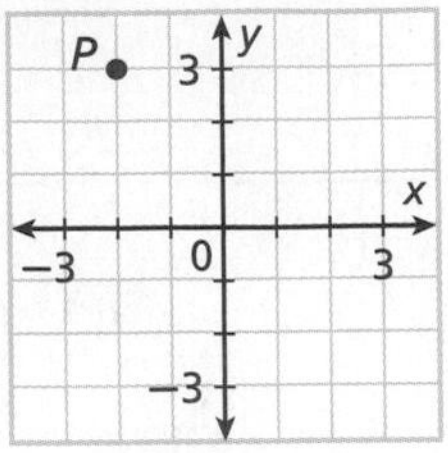

Ⓐ $y = x + 1$

Ⓑ $y = -x + 1$

Ⓒ $y = x + 5$

Ⓓ $y = -x + 5$

DAY 2

Which postulate or theorem can be used to verify the congruence of these two triangles?

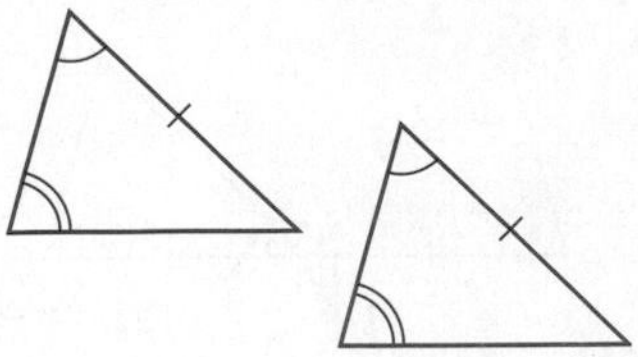

Ⓕ SSS

Ⓖ HL

Ⓗ AAS

Ⓙ SAS

DAY 3

Which conjecture is true?

Ⓐ If a figure is a rectangle, its perimeter is equal to its area.

Ⓑ If a figure is a triangle, all three sides are congruent.

Ⓒ If a figure is a quadrilateral, then it has four sides.

Ⓓ If a figure is a circle, its area is always greater than its circumference.

DAY 4

The layout of a swimming pool is plotted on the coordinate grid below. If each unit on the grid represents 2 meters, what is the length of the pool?

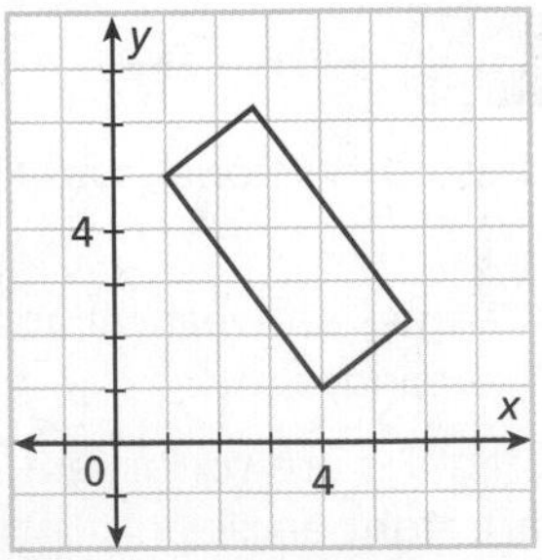

Ⓕ 5 meters

Ⓖ 8 meters

Ⓗ 10 meters

Ⓙ 25 meters

DAY 5

$\triangle LMN$ is shown on the grid. What is the slope of $\overline{MN}$?

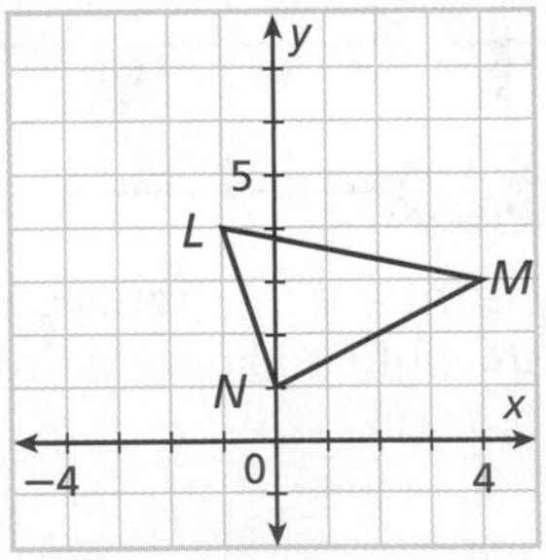

Ⓐ $-\frac{1}{2}$

Ⓑ -4

Ⓒ $\frac{1}{2}$

Ⓓ 2

DAY 1

A ceramic tile is in the shape of a 30°-60°-90° triangle. The side across from the 30° angle is 6.25 centimeters long. How long is the hypotenuse of the tile?

Ⓐ 3.125 centimeters

Ⓑ $6.25\sqrt{3}$ centimeters

Ⓒ 12.5 centimeters

Ⓓ 15 centimeters

DAY 2

What is the slope of this line?

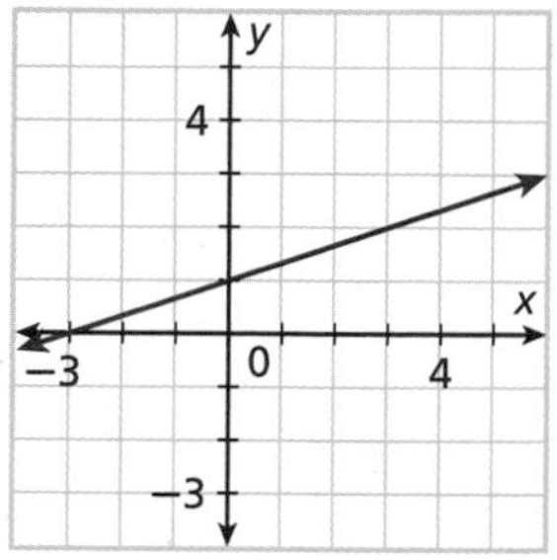

Ⓕ 1

Ⓖ $\frac{1}{3}$

Ⓗ 3

Ⓙ $-\frac{1}{3}$

DAY 3

Which equation should Aretha use to find the distance *c* between two points across a river?

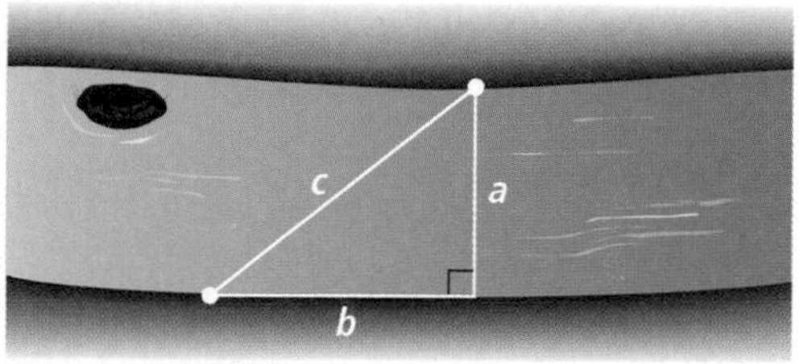

Ⓐ $c = a^2 + b^2$

Ⓑ $c = a + b$

Ⓒ $c^2 = \sqrt{a + b}$

Ⓓ $c = \sqrt{a^2 + b^2}$

DAY 4

The sums of the angle measures of three polygons are given. Based on the pattern, what will be the sum of the measures of a hexagon?

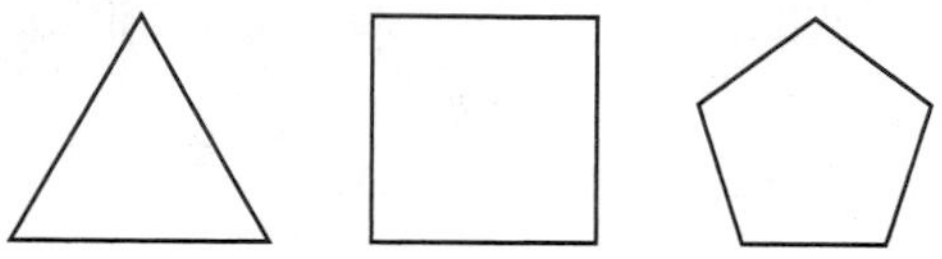

Ⓕ 240°

Ⓖ 420°

Ⓗ 600°

Ⓙ 720°

DAY 5

Which line in the graph is described by the equation $y = x + 2$?

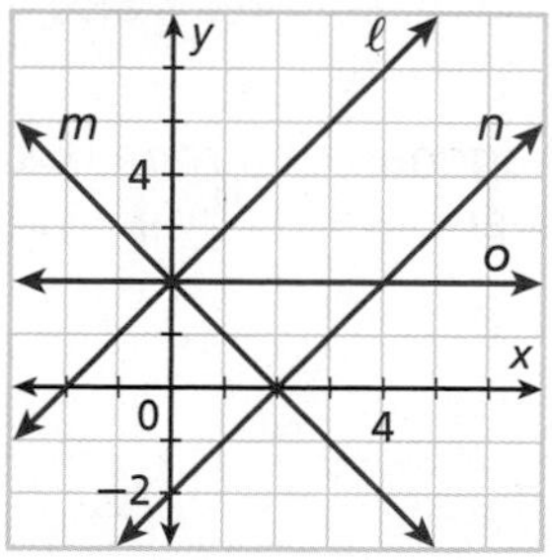

Ⓐ ℓ

Ⓑ m

Ⓒ n

Ⓓ o

Countdown to Mastery

WEEK 15

DAY 1

Three coordinates of ▱*ABCD* are *A*(4, 5), *C*(7, 3), and *D*(1, 3). Which coordinates could represent point *B*?

Ⓐ (1, 5)

Ⓑ (3, 7)

Ⓒ (5, 1)

Ⓓ (10, 5)

DAY 2

Which two lines are parallel?

Ⓕ $y = 6x + 8$ and $y + \frac{1}{6}x = 3$

Ⓖ $y = \frac{1}{3}x - 1$ and $y = 3x + 1$

Ⓗ $y - 2x = 2$ and $y = 2 - 2x$

Ⓙ $y = \frac{1}{4}x$ and $y - \frac{1}{4}x = 1$

DAY 3

What is the midpoint of $\overline{QR}$?

Ⓐ (1, −2)

Ⓑ (−2, 1)

Ⓒ (1, 2)

Ⓓ (−1, −2)

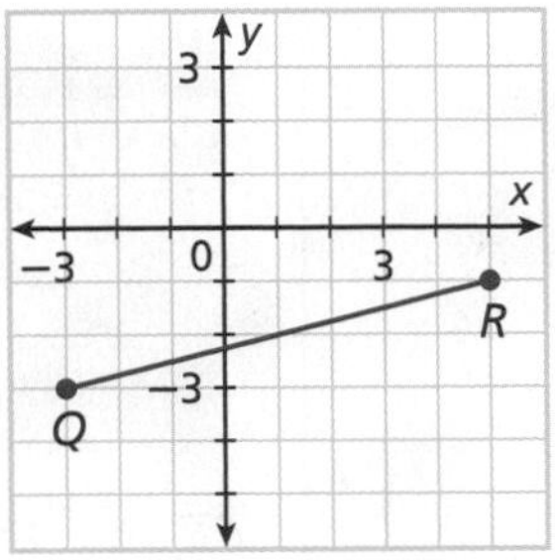

DAY 4

Which of these statements is true?

Ⓕ All quadrilaterals are parallelograms.

Ⓖ Every rectangle is a parallelogram.

Ⓗ Every parallelogram is also a rectangle.

Ⓙ The diagonals of a rhombus are congruent.

DAY 5

Which expression describes the total number of diagonals in a polygon with *n* sides?

No. of sides	3	4	5	6	7
No. of diagonals	0	2	5	9	14

Ⓐ $\frac{n(n-3)}{2}$

Ⓑ $2n$

Ⓒ $\frac{3n}{2}$

Ⓓ $\frac{2n+6}{3}$

DAY 1

The coordinates of the vertices of $\triangle ABC$ are (1, 1), (6, 1) and (1, 8). Which of the following could be the coordinates of the vertices of a triangle congruent to $\triangle ABC$?

Ⓐ (−8, −2), (−3, −2), (−3, −9)
Ⓑ (4, 1), (6, 2), (8, 10)
Ⓒ (−2, 5), (−2, −9), (−8, 3)
Ⓓ (0, 0), (−1, 8), (5, 2)

DAY 2

Natalia is using indirect measurement to find the distance across a pond. Which Pythagorean triple is represented by the triangle?

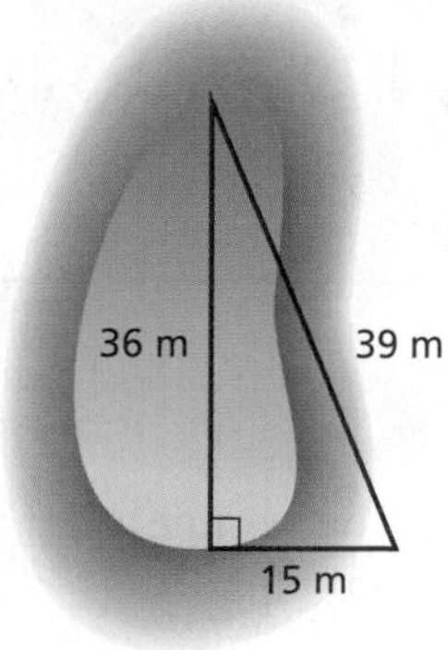

Ⓕ 3-4-5
Ⓖ 5-12-13
Ⓗ 8-15-17
Ⓙ 7-24-25

DAY 3

Which of the following sets of measurements could represent the side lengths of a right triangle?

Ⓐ 3, 5, 9
Ⓑ 4.5, 12, 8.5
Ⓒ 6, 7, 10
Ⓓ 2.5, 6, 6.5

DAY 4

What is the perimeter of the composite figure?

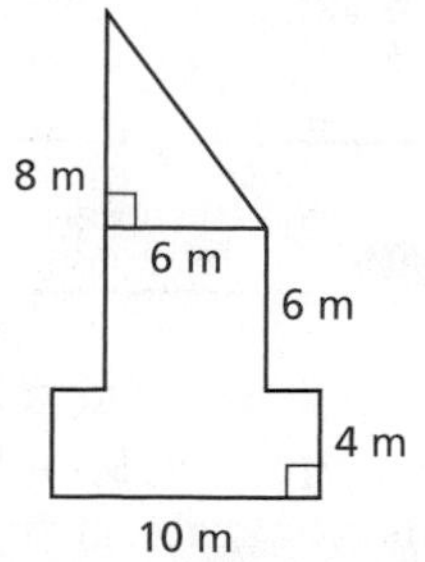

Ⓕ 52 meters
Ⓖ 58 meters
Ⓗ 100 meters
Ⓙ 124 meters

DAY 5

What is the measure of $\angle 3$ in the regular hexagon?

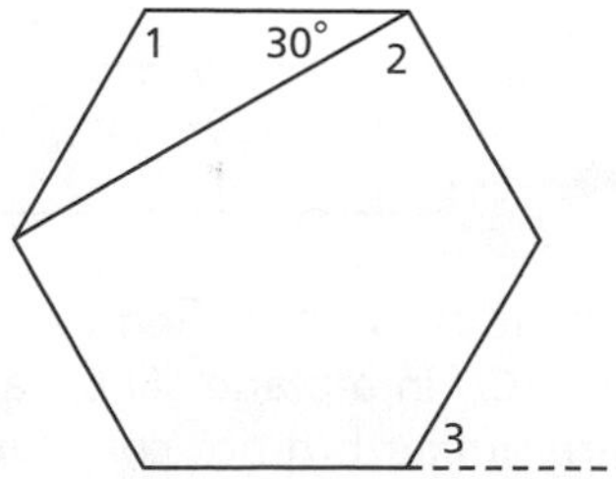

Ⓐ 30°
Ⓑ 60°
Ⓒ 90°
Ⓓ 120°

DAY 1

Which two lines are perpendicular?

(A) $y = x + 6$ and $y = x - 6$

(B) $y + \frac{2}{3}x = 1$ and $y = \frac{3}{2}x - 4$

(C) $y = \frac{1}{2}x - 2$ and $y = -\frac{1}{2}x + 3$

(D) $y - 2x = 5$ and $y = 2x + 2$

DAY 2

What is the perimeter of the composite figure to the nearest centimeter?

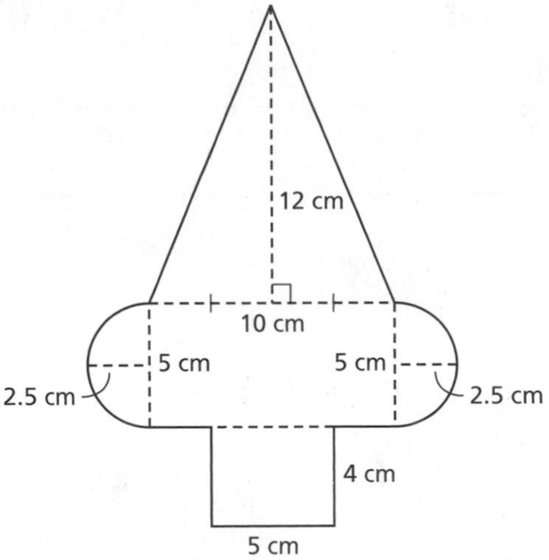

(F) 44 centimeters

(G) 52 centimeters

(H) 60 centimeters

(J) 83 centimeters

DAY 3

What is the measure of ∠1 in the triangle below?

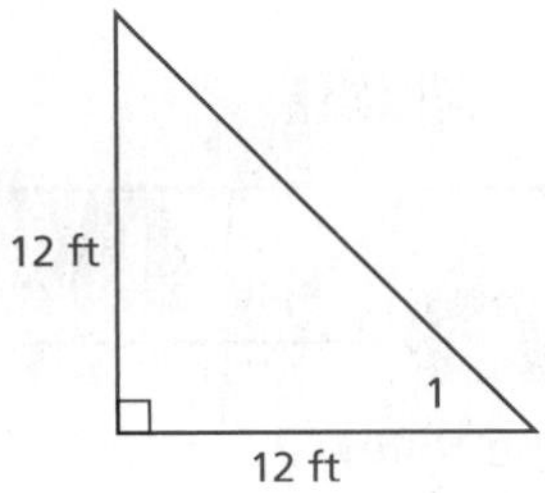

(A) 30°

(B) 45°

(C) 60°

(D) 90°

DAY 4

A transformation *M* is applied to a rectangle *ABCD* in a plane. *ABCD* and *A′B′C′D′* are similar but not congruent. Which of the following could describe *M*?

(F) Translation

(G) Rotation

(H) Dilation

(J) Reflection

DAY 5

The vertices of polygon *ABCD* are *A*(1, 5), *B*(8, 5), *C*(8, 3), and *D*(1, 3). Which of the following statements about this polygon is true?

(A) It is a square.

(B) Its width is 2 units.

(C) Its perimeter is 6 units.

(D) Its area is 9 square units.

DAY 1

Based on the pattern of similar triangles below, what is the value of x?

Ⓐ 2

Ⓑ 4

Ⓒ $4\sqrt{3}$

Ⓓ 8

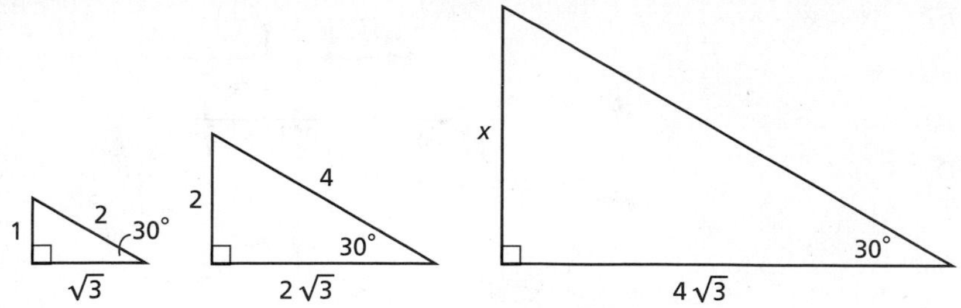

DAY 2

Which ratio is equivalent to $\sin B$?

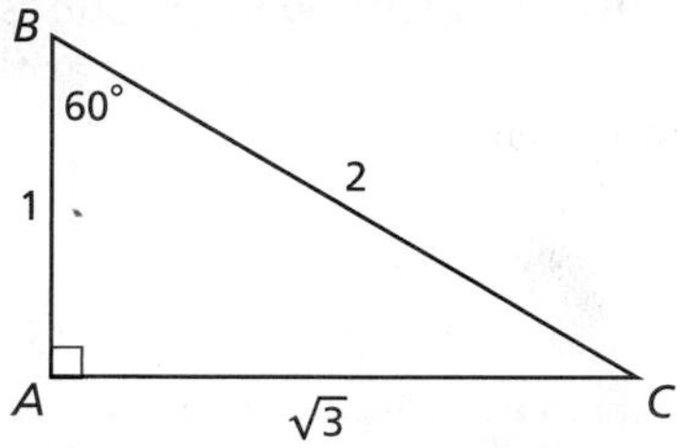

Ⓕ $\frac{2\sqrt{3}}{3}$

Ⓖ $\sqrt{3}$

Ⓗ $\frac{\sqrt{3}}{2}$

Ⓙ $\frac{1}{2}$

DAY 3

What is the value of x to the nearest tenth of a millimeter?

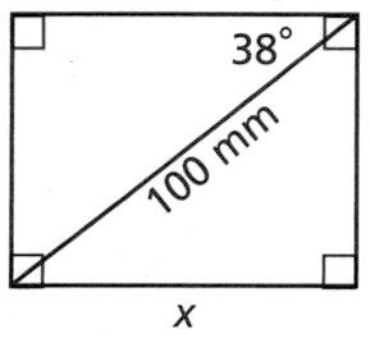

Ⓐ 52.0 millimeters

Ⓑ 61.6 millimeters

Ⓒ 78.8 millimeters

Ⓓ 140.4 millimeters

DAY 4

What is the value of x in the regular pentagon below?

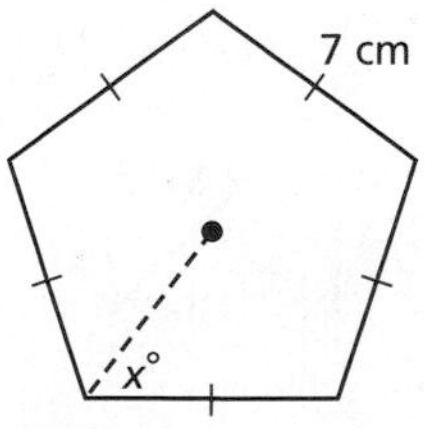

Ⓕ 54°

Ⓖ 90°

Ⓗ 108°

Ⓙ 180°

DAY 5

Which conjecture about polygons is NOT true?

Ⓐ The area of a parallelogram is the product of its base and height.

Ⓑ A rhombus has four right angles.

Ⓒ A square has four congruent sides.

Ⓓ A trapezoid has exactly one pair of parallel sides.

DAY 1

Which two line segments are congruent?

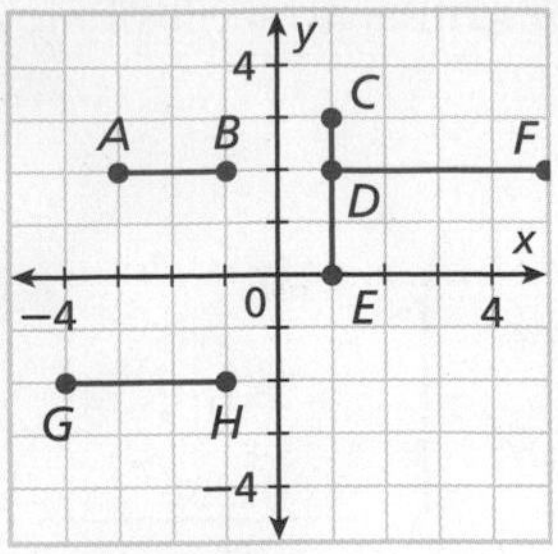

Ⓐ $\overline{AB}$ and $\overline{DF}$

Ⓑ $\overline{CE}$ and $\overline{GH}$

Ⓒ $\overline{GH}$ and $\overline{AB}$

Ⓓ $\overline{CD}$ and $\overline{DE}$

DAY 2

Which two angles satisfy the equation $\sin(3x + 2) = \cos(x + 8)$?

Ⓕ 11°, 79°

Ⓖ 20°, 70°

Ⓗ 44°, 46°

Ⓙ 62°, 28°

DAY 3

At a certain time of the day, a 24-foot tree casts an 18-foot shadow. How long is the shadow cast by a 4-foot mailbox at the same time of day?

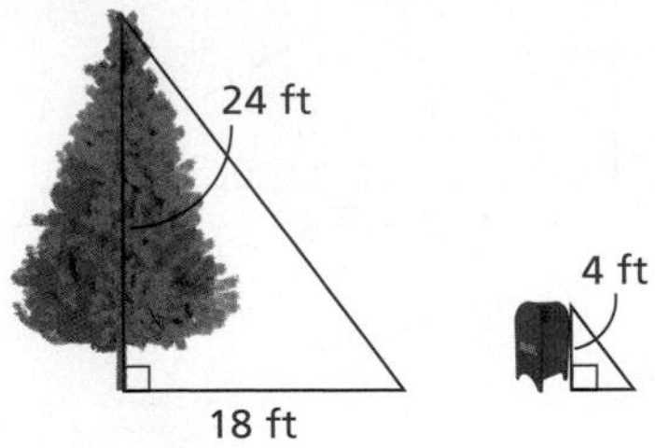

Ⓐ 1.3 feet

Ⓑ 3 feet

Ⓒ 4.5 feet

Ⓓ 5 feet

DAY 4

A school playground is a 25 m by 40 m rectangle. The school increases the width to 40 m and increases the length so that the original rectangle and the new one are similar. By how much does the perimeter of the playground increase?

Ⓕ 30 m

Ⓖ 60 m

Ⓗ 200 m

Ⓙ 225 m

DAY 5

What is x?

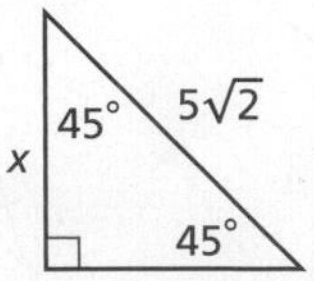

Ⓐ 2

Ⓑ 5

Ⓒ 10

Ⓓ 30

Countdown to Mastery WEEK 20

DAY 1

The figure shows the measure of each interior angle for several regular polygons.

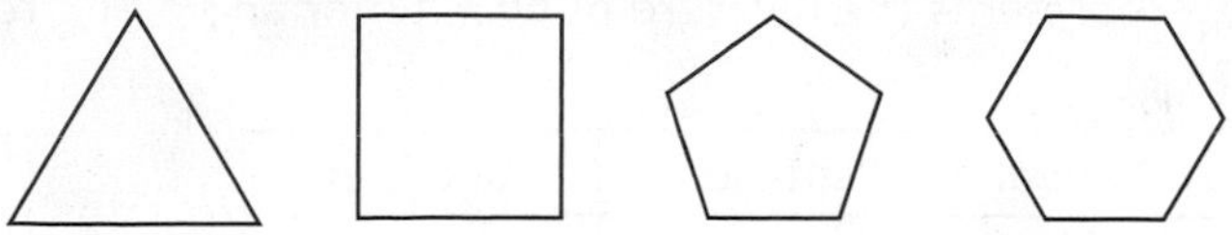

Which algebraic expression best represents the measure of an interior angle of a regular polygon with *n* sides?

Ⓐ $\frac{(n-2)180}{n}$

Ⓑ $\frac{360n}{n+2}$

Ⓒ $(n-2)180$

Ⓓ $\frac{180n}{2}$

DAY 2

The transformation $(x, y) \rightarrow (x + 3, y - 2)$ is applied to the hexagon. What are the coordinates of the image of point *P*?

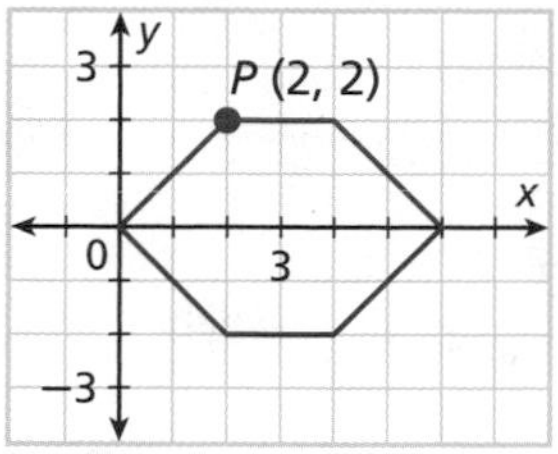

Ⓕ (−1, 5)

Ⓖ (5, 0)

Ⓗ (−1, −1)

Ⓙ (5, 4)

DAY 3

The two triangles in the figure are similar. What is the length of $\overline{MN}$?

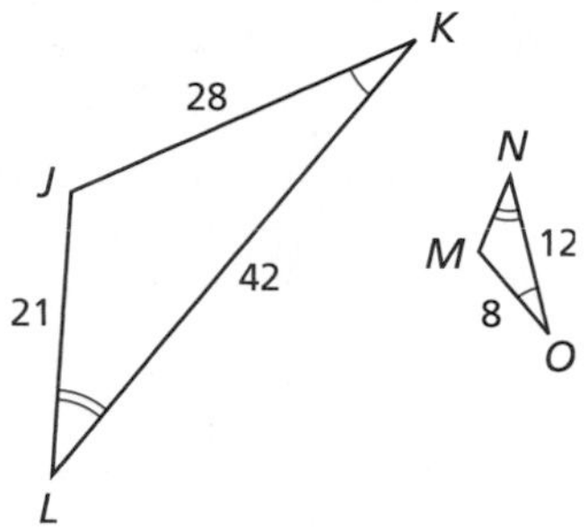

Ⓐ 3.5

Ⓑ 6

Ⓒ 7

Ⓓ 17.5

DAY 4

Two regular pentagons have perimeters of 30 and 75 respectively. What scale factor relates the smaller figure to the larger one?

Ⓕ 1:2.5

Ⓖ 1:6

Ⓗ 1:15

Ⓙ 1:21

DAY 5

Alissa is painting a diagonal line across a square tile. What is the length of the line?

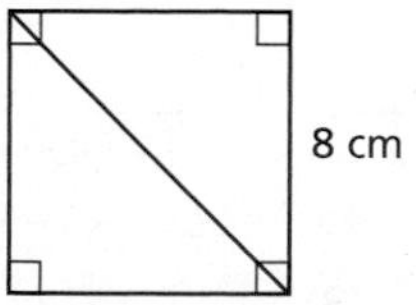

Ⓐ $2\sqrt{8}$ centimeters

Ⓑ 6 centimeters

Ⓒ 8 centimeters

Ⓓ $8\sqrt{2}$ centimeters

DAY 1

The table lists the measure of an exterior angle for the given regular polygon. Which expression best represents the measure of an exterior angle of a regular polygon with *n* sides?

Figure	Quadrilateral	Pentagon	Decagon
Exterior angle	90°	72°	36°

Ⓐ $\frac{360}{n-2}$

Ⓑ $\frac{360+n}{2+n}$

Ⓒ $360n$

Ⓓ $\frac{360}{n}$

DAY 2

Carrie is building a skateboard ramp with the dimensions below. What is the approximate measure of *x*?

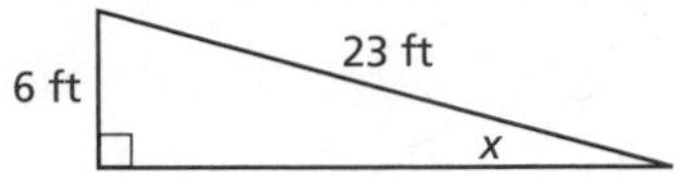

Ⓕ 4°

Ⓖ 8°

Ⓗ 12°

Ⓙ 15°

DAY 3

What is the value of *z*?

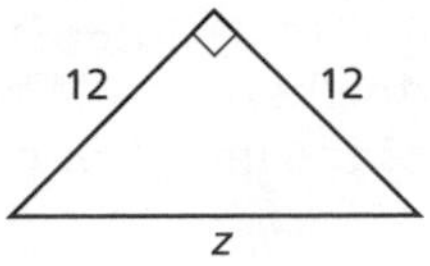

Ⓐ 12

Ⓑ $12\sqrt{2}$

Ⓒ $12\sqrt{3}$

Ⓓ 17

DAY 4

Which equation best describes the line containing the hypotenuse of this triangle?

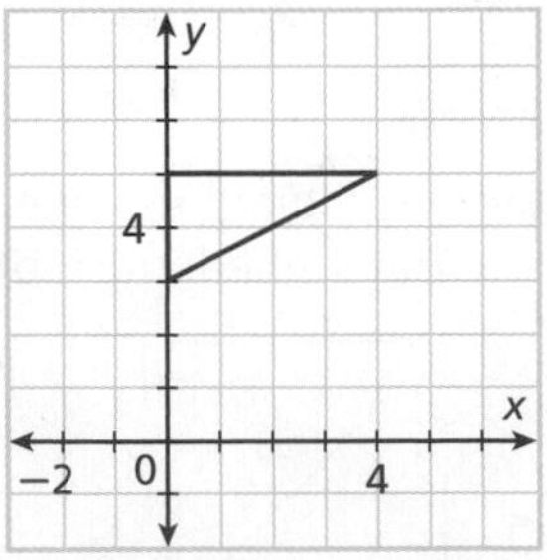

Ⓕ $y = \frac{1}{2}x + 3$

Ⓖ $y = 5$

Ⓗ $y = x + 3$

Ⓙ $y = -\frac{1}{2}x - 3$

DAY 5

The center of circle *C* is the midpoint of $\overline{AB}$. What are the coordinates of the midpoint?

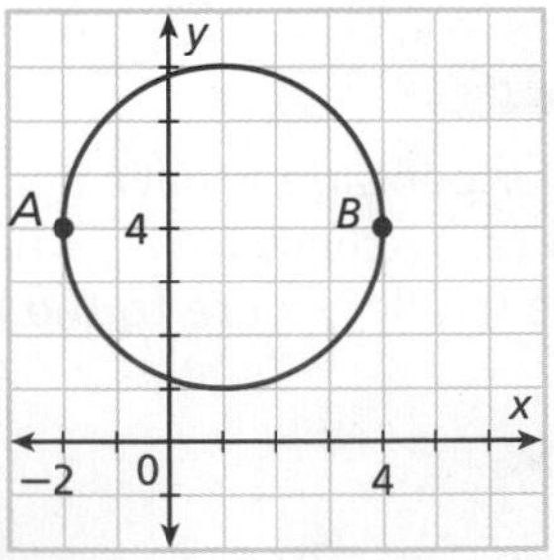

Ⓐ (0, 4)

Ⓑ (1, 4)

Ⓒ (2, 4)

Ⓓ (3, 3)

DAY 1

If this pattern is continued, how many shaded triangles will there be in the fourth element of the pattern?

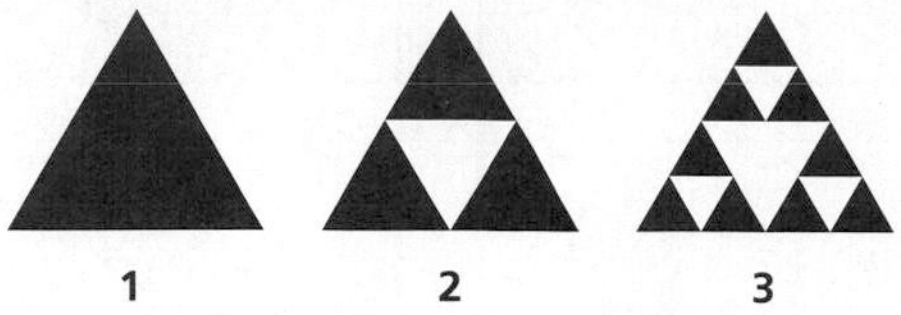

Ⓐ 9
Ⓑ 13
Ⓒ 27
Ⓓ 40

DAY 2

What is the slope of the line?

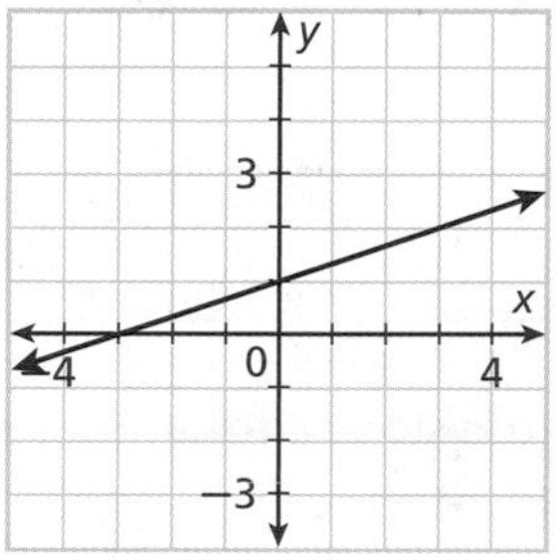

Ⓕ $-\frac{1}{2}$
Ⓖ $\frac{1}{3}$
Ⓗ $\frac{1}{2}$
Ⓙ 3

DAY 3

A delivery truck travels 13.5 mi east and then 18 mi north. How far is the truck from its starting point?

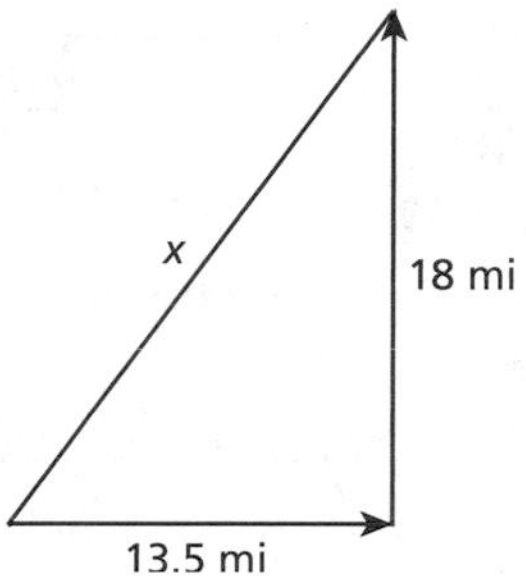

Ⓐ 4.5 miles
Ⓑ 20.25 miles
Ⓒ 22.5 miles
Ⓓ 31.5 miles

DAY 4

What are the side lengths of the triangle?

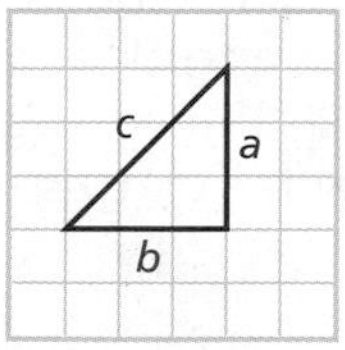

Ⓕ 3, 4, and 5
Ⓖ 2, 3, and 5
Ⓗ 3, 3, and 3
Ⓙ 3, 3, and $3\sqrt{2}$

DAY 5

An 18-foot ladder reaches the top of a building when placed at an angle of 45° with the horizontal. What is the approximate height of the building?

Ⓐ 9.0 feet
Ⓑ 12.7 feet
Ⓒ 14.4 feet
Ⓓ 30.9 feet

DAY 1

$\triangle RST$ is a 30°-60°-90° triangle. What is the y-coordinate of R if $a = -5$ and $c = -2$?

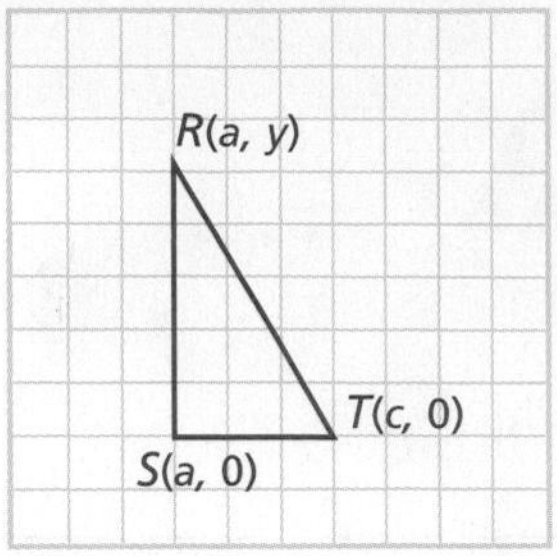

Ⓐ 3
Ⓑ $3\sqrt{2}$
Ⓒ $3\sqrt{3}$
Ⓓ 6

DAY 2

What is x if y is 12.8 and z is 16 in the right triangle below?

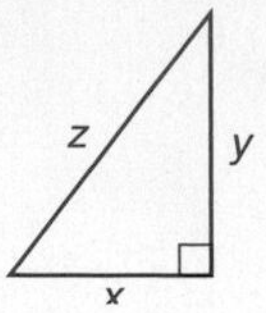

Ⓕ 3.2
Ⓖ 4.0
Ⓗ 9.6
Ⓙ 12.8

DAY 3

How does the slope of the hypotenuse of $\triangle ABC$ compare with the slope of the hypotenuse of $\triangle DBC$?

Ⓐ They have the same value.
Ⓑ They have opposite signs.
Ⓒ They have the same sign.
Ⓓ They are reciprocals.

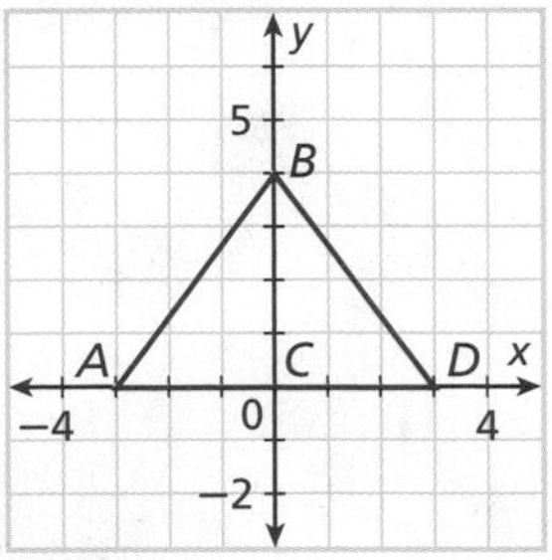

DAY 4

How many sides does a regular polygon have if each interior angle measures 120°?

Ⓕ 3
Ⓖ 4
Ⓗ 6
Ⓙ 8

DAY 5

An electrician is standing at the top of a tower. He sees a truck at an angle of depression of 3°. If the tower is 300 feet tall, about how far away is the truck?

Ⓐ 16 feet
Ⓑ 300 feet
Ⓒ 1052 feet
Ⓓ 5724 feet

DAY 1

Quadrilaterals *ABCD* and *WXYZ* are similar. What is *XY*?

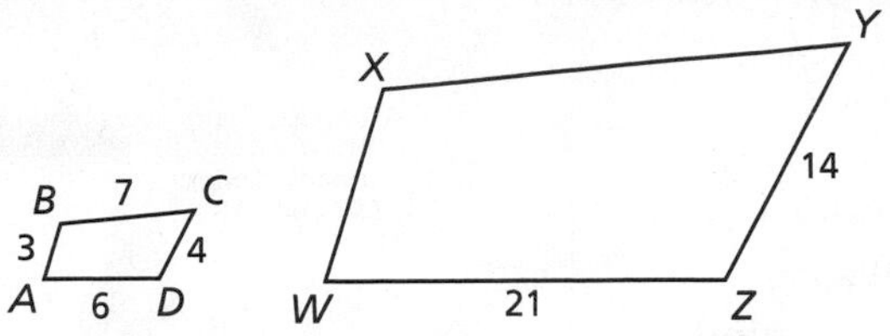

Ⓐ 3.5
Ⓑ 21
Ⓒ 24.5
Ⓓ 35

DAY 2

What is the second term in a proportion in which the first, third, and fourth terms are 3, 9, and 12, respectively?

Ⓕ 3
Ⓖ 4
Ⓗ 6
Ⓙ 8

DAY 3

The endpoints of a segment are *Q*(−2, 6) and *R*(5, −4). What is the length of the segment to the nearest tenth?

Ⓐ 3.6 units
Ⓑ 4.1 units
Ⓒ 8.5 units
Ⓓ 12.2 units

DAY 4

Which Pythagorean triple would be most helpful in finding the value of *a*?

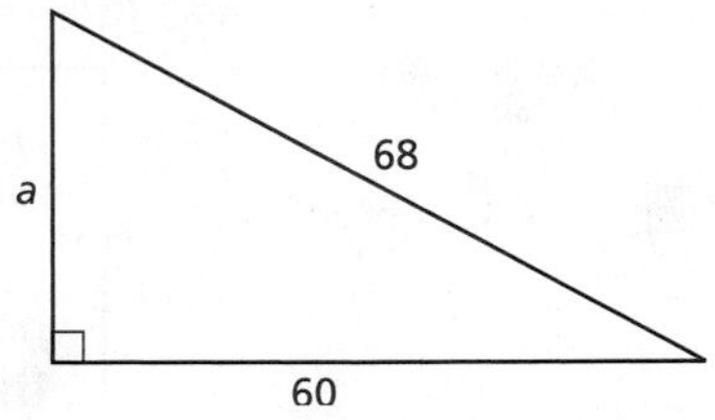

Ⓕ 3-4-5
Ⓖ 5-12-14
Ⓗ 8-15-17
Ⓙ 7-24-25

DAY 5

What is the perimeter of the square?

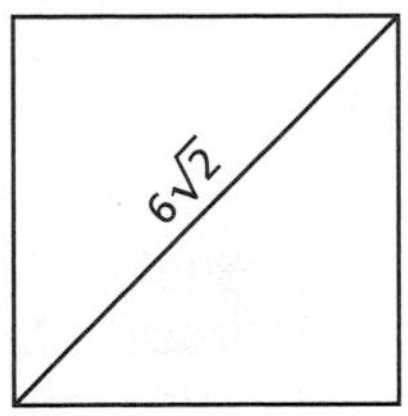

Ⓐ 6
Ⓑ 12
Ⓒ 24
Ⓓ 36

How to Study Geometry

This book has many features designed to help you learn and study effectively. Becoming familiar with these features will prepare you for greater success on your exams.

Learn

The **vocabulary** is listed at the beginning of every lesson.

Look for the **Know-It-Note** icons to identify important information.

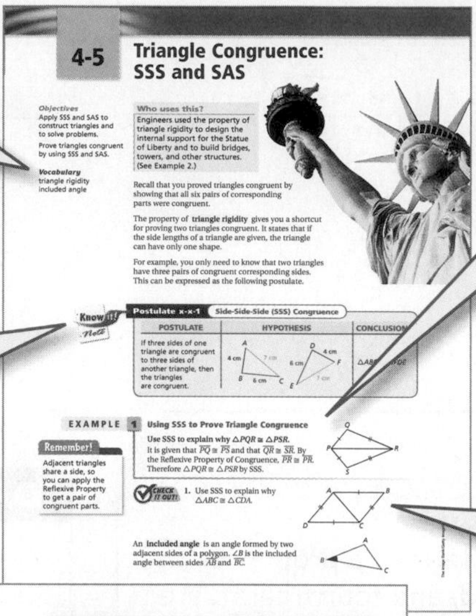

4-5 Triangle Congruence: SSS and SAS

Objectives
Apply SSS and SAS to construct triangles and to solve problems.
Prove triangles congruent by using SSS and SAS.

Vocabulary
triangle rigidity
included angle

Who uses this?
Engineers used the property of triangle rigidity to design the internal support for the Statue of Liberty and to build bridges, towers, and other structures. (See Example 2.)

Recall that you proved triangles congruent by showing that all six pairs of corresponding parts were congruent.

The property of **triangle rigidity** gives you a shortcut for proving two triangles congruent. It states that if the side lengths of a triangle are given, the triangle can have only one shape.

For example, you only need to know that two triangles have three pairs of congruent corresponding sides. This can be expressed as the following postulate.

Know It! Note — Postulate x-x-1 Side-Side-Side (SSS) Congruence

POSTULATE	HYPOTHESIS	CONCLUSION
If three sides of one triangle are congruent to three sides of another triangle, then the triangles are congruent.		$\triangle AB$…

EXAMPLE 1 **Using SSS to Prove Triangle Congruence**
Use SSS to explain why $\triangle PQR \cong \triangle PSR$.
It is given that $\overline{PQ} \cong \overline{PS}$ and that $\overline{QR} \cong \overline{SR}$. By the Reflexive Property of Congruence, $\overline{PR} \cong \overline{PR}$. Therefore $\triangle PQR \cong \triangle PSR$ by SSS.

Remember! Adjacent triangles share a side, so you can apply the Reflexive Property to get a pair of congruent parts.

CHECK IT OUT! 1. Use SSS to explain why $\triangle ABC \cong \triangle CDA$.

An **included angle** is an angle formed by two adjacent sides of a polygon. $\angle B$ is the included angle between sides $\overline{AB}$ and $\overline{BC}$.

Study the **examples** to apply new concepts and skills. Examples include stepped out solutions.

Test your understanding of examples by trying the **Check It Out** problems. Check your work in the Selected Answers.

Practice

Use a **graphic organizer** to summarize each lesson.

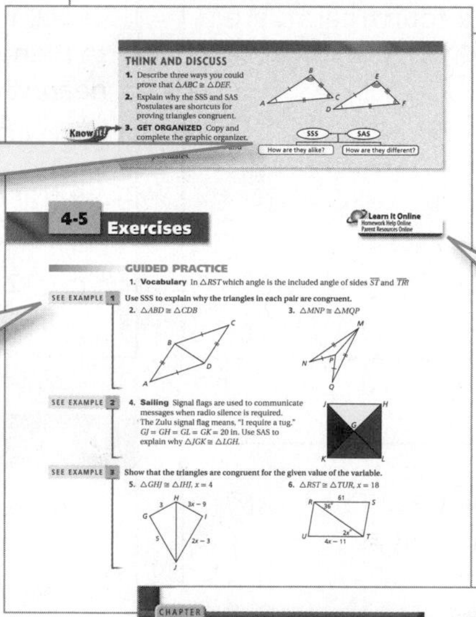

THINK AND DISCUSS
1. Describe three ways you could prove that $\triangle ABC \cong \triangle DEF$.
2. Explain why the SSS and SAS Postulates are shortcuts for proving triangles congruent.
3. **GET ORGANIZED** Copy and complete the graphic organizer.

SSS — SAS — How are they alike? — How are they different?

4-5 Exercises

Learn It Online
Homework Help Online
Parent Resources Online

GUIDED PRACTICE
1. **Vocabulary** In $\triangle RST$ which angle is the included angle of sides $\overline{ST}$ and $\overline{TR}$?

SEE EXAMPLE 1 Use SSS to explain why the triangles in each pair are congruent.
2. $\triangle ABD \cong \triangle CDB$
3. $\triangle MNP \cong \triangle MQP$

SEE EXAMPLE 2 4. **Sailing** Signal flags are used to communicate messages when radio silence is required. The Zulu signal flag means, "I require a tug." $GJ = GH = GL = GK = 20$ in. Use SAS to explain why $\triangle JGK \cong \triangle LGH$.

SEE EXAMPLE 3 Show that the triangles are congruent for the given value of the variable.
5. $\triangle GHJ \cong \triangle IHJ$, $x = 4$
6. $\triangle RST \cong \triangle TUR$, $x = 18$

Refer to the examples from the lesson to solve the **Guided Practice** exercises.

If you get stuck, use the internet for **Homework Help Online**.

Review

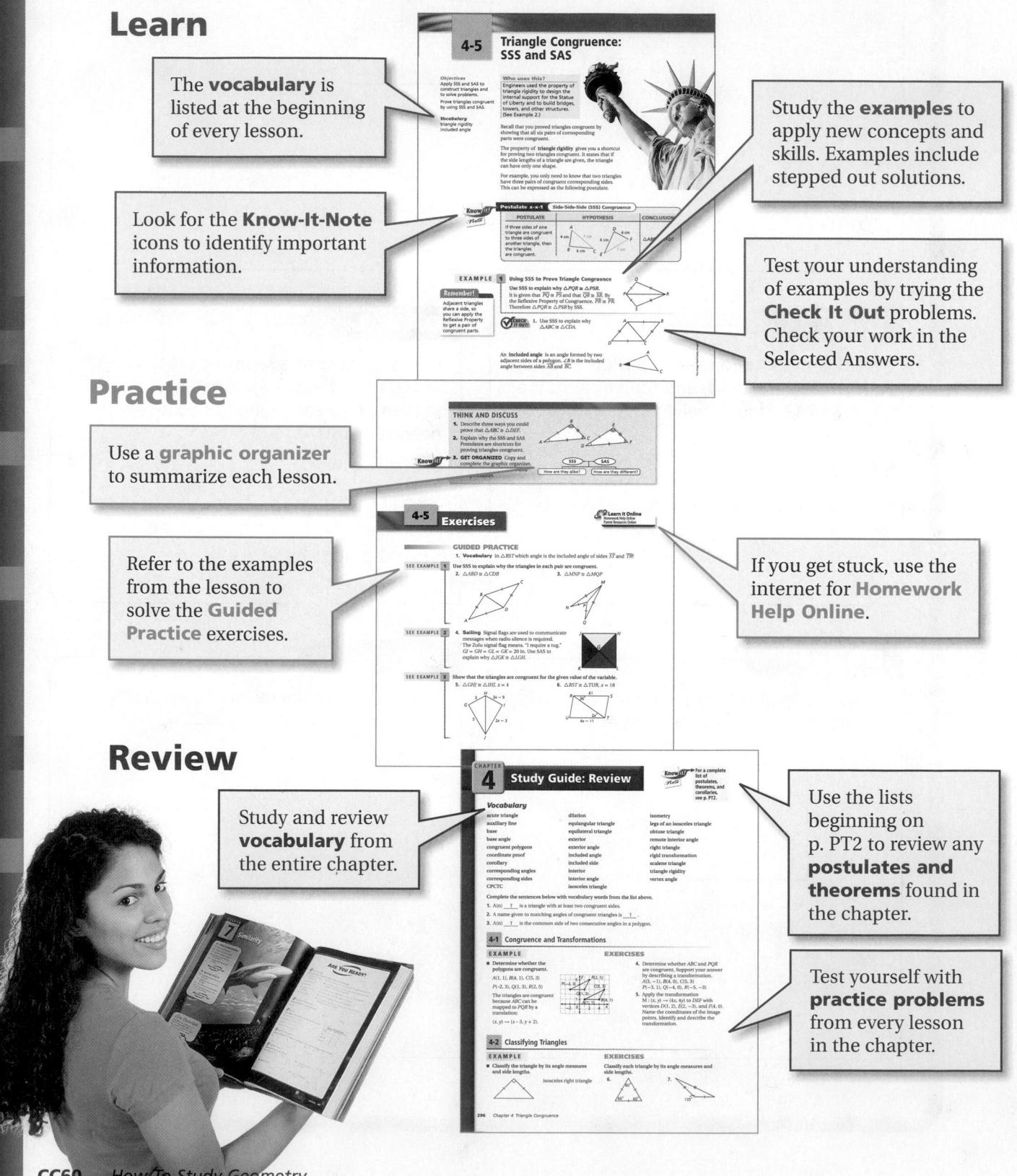

Study and review **vocabulary** from the entire chapter.

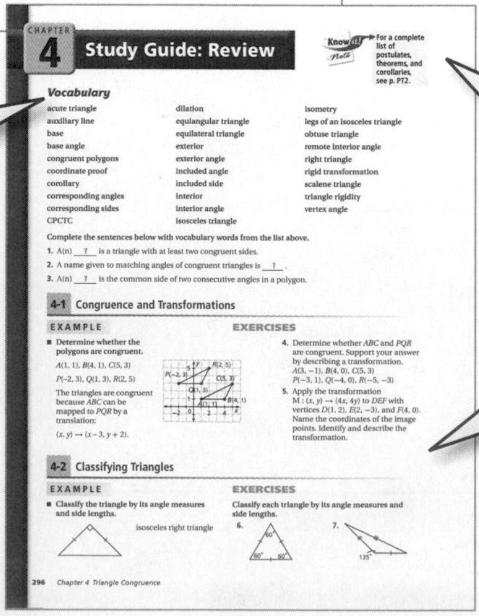

Chapter 4 Study Guide: Review

Know It! Note — For a complete list of postulates, theorems, and corollaries, see p. PT2.

Vocabulary

acute triangle	dilation	isometry
auxiliary line	equiangular triangle	legs of an isosceles triangle
base	equilateral triangle	obtuse triangle
base angle	exterior	remote interior angle
congruent polygons	exterior angle	right triangle
coordinate proof	included angle	rigid transformation
corollary	included side	scalene triangle
corresponding angles	interior	triangle rigidity
corresponding sides	interior angle	vertex angle
CPCTC	isosceles triangle	

Complete the sentences below with vocabulary words from the list above.
1. A(n) __?__ is a triangle with at least two congruent sides.
2. A name given to matching angles of congruent triangles is __?__.
3. A(n) __?__ is the common side of two consecutive angles in a polygon.

4-1 Congruence and Transformations

EXAMPLE
- Determine whether the polygons are congruent.
$A(1, 1), B(4, 1), C(5, 3)$
$P(-2, 3), Q(1, 3), R(2, 5)$
The triangles are congruent because ABC can be mapped to PQR by a translation:
$(x, y) \rightarrow (x - 3, y + 2)$.

EXERCISES
4. Determine whether ABC and PQR are congruent. Support your answer by describing a transformation.
$A(3, -1), B(4, 0), C(5, 3)$
$P(-3, 1), Q(-4, 0), R(-5, -3)$
5. Apply the transformation $M: (x, y) \rightarrow (4x, 4y)$ to DEF with vertices $D(1, 2)$, $E(2, -3)$, and $F(4, 0)$. Name the coordinates of the image points. Identify and describe the transformation.

4-2 Classifying Triangles

EXAMPLE
- Classify the triangle by its angle measures and side lengths.
isosceles right triangle

EXERCISES
Classify each triangle by its angle measures and side lengths.
6.
7.

296 Chapter 4 Triangle Congruence

Use the lists beginning on p. PT2 to review any **postulates and theorems** found in the chapter.

Test yourself with **practice problems** from every lesson in the chapter.

Focus on Problem Solving

The Problem Solving Plan

Mathematical problems are a part of daily life. You need to use a good problem-solving plan to be a good problem solver. The plan used in this textbook is outlined below.

UNDERSTAND the Problem

First make sure you understand the problem you are asked to solve.

■ **What are you asked to find?**	Restate the question in your own words.
■ **What information is given?**	Identify the key facts given in the problem.
■ **What information do you need?**	Determine what information you need to solve the problem.
■ **Do you have all the information needed?**	Determine if you need more information.
■ **Do you have too much information?**	Determine if there is unnecessary information and eliminate it from your list of important facts.

Make a PLAN

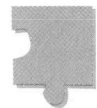

Plan how to use the information you are given.

■ **Have you solved similar problems?**	Think about similar problems you have solved successfully.
■ **What problem solving strategy or strategies could you use to solve this problem?**	Choose an appropriate problem solving strategy and decide how you will use it.

SOLVE

Use your plan to solve the problem. Show the steps in the solution, and write a final statement that gives the solution to the problem.

LOOK BACK

Check your answer against the original problem.

■ **Have you answered the question?**	Make sure you have answered the original question.
■ **Is the answer reasonable?**	The answer must make sense in relation to the question.
■ **Are your calculations correct?**	Check to make sure your calculations are accurate.
■ **Can you use another strategy or solve the problem in another way?**	Using another strategy is a good way to check your answer.
■ **Did you learn anyting that could help you solve similar problems in the future?**	Try to remember the types of problems you have solved and the strategies you applied.

ARE YOU READY?

Pre-Course Test

Measure with Customary and Metric Units

Measure each segment to the nearest eighth of an inch and to the nearest half of a centimeter.

1. ____________________

2. ____________________________

Measure Angles

Use a protractor to measure each angle.

3. 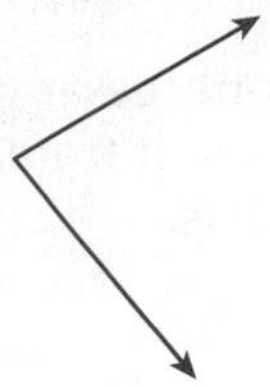

4. 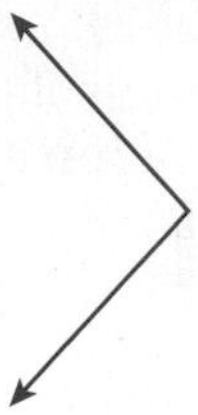

Ordered Pairs

Graph each point.

5. $A(1, 3)$

6. $B(-4, 5)$

7. $C(-3, -1)$

8. $D(2, -4)$

Connect Words and Algebra

9. Write an expression that represents the sum of a number x and 11.

10. Angelica has 15 comic books, and each month she buys 3 more comic books. Write an equation representing the number of comic books c she has at the end of any month m.

Evaluate Expressions

Evaluate each expression for the given value of the variable.

11. $3p + 6$ for $p = 4$

12. $6 - 4q$ for $q = 8$

Combine Like Terms

Simplify each expression by combining like terms.

13. $8b - 11b$

14. $12m^2 + 6m^2$

Solve One-Step Equations

Solve.

15. $8g = 56$

16. $h - 6 = -9$

Solve Multi-Step Equations

Solve.

17. $8p + 6 = 30$

18. $\frac{d}{4} - 6 = -9$

Solve and Graph Inequalities

Solve and graph each inequality.

19. $3g > 18$

20. $-4k > 8$

Simplify Fractions

Write each fraction in simplest form.

21. $\frac{14}{22}$

22. $\frac{20}{36}$

Solve Proportions

Solve each proportion.

23. $\frac{3}{4} = \frac{h}{36}$

24. $\frac{2}{9} = \frac{k}{6}$

Name and Classify Angles

Name and classify each angle.

25. 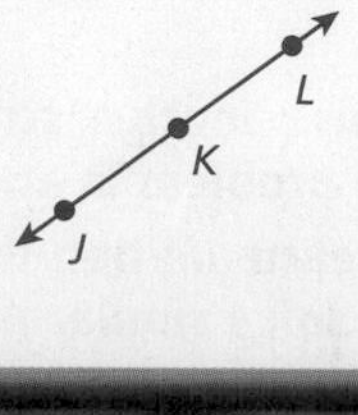

26. 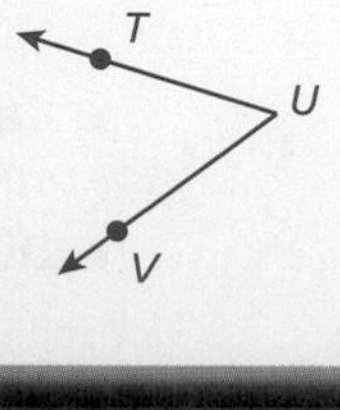

Angle Relationships

Give an example of each angle pair.

27. vertical angles

28. complementary angles

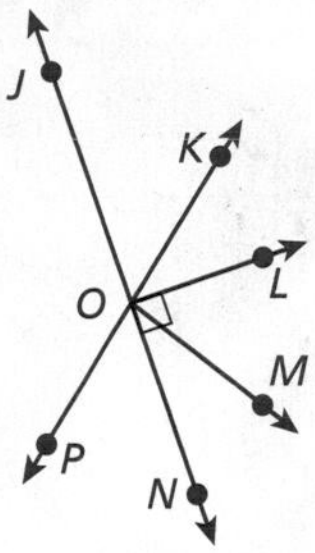

Parallel Lines and Transversals

Find the measure of each angle.

29. $\angle 1$

30. $\angle 2$

31. $\angle 4$

32. $\angle 6$

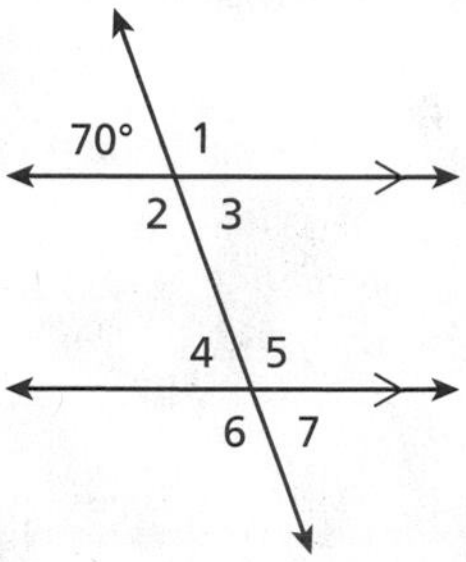

Classify Triangles

Tell whether each triangle is acute, right, or obtuse.

33.

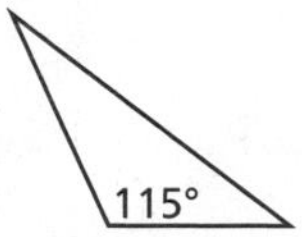

34.

Evaluate Powers

Find the value of each expression.

35. 9^2

36. 12^3

Simplify Radical Expressions

Simplify each expression.

37. $\sqrt{49} \cdot \sqrt{100}$

38. $\sqrt{2} \cdot \sqrt{32}$

Rounding and Estimation

Round each decimal to the indicated place value.

39. 7.449; tenth

40. 9.028; hundredth

Pythagorean Theorem

Find x in each right triangle. If the length is not a whole number, give the answer in simplest radical form.

41.

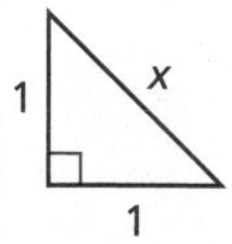

42.

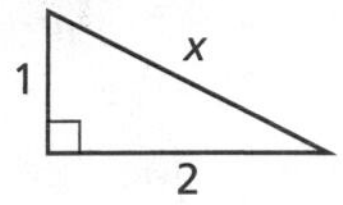

43.

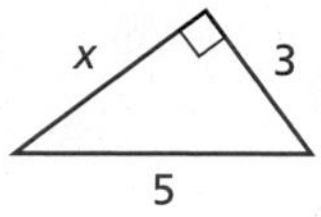

44.

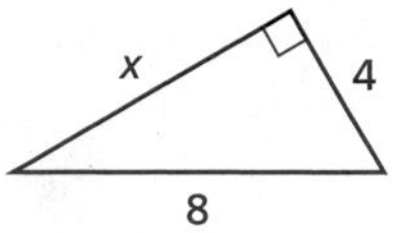

Find Perimeter

Find the perimeter of each figure.

45. equilateral triangle with side length 4 in.

46. rectangle with length 10 cm and width 5 cm

Area of Polygons

Find the area of each figure.

47. square with side length 6 cm

48. rectangle with length 4.5 in. and width 2 in.

Volume

Find the volume of each solid.

49. cube with side length 5 cm

50. rectangular prism with height 7 in., width 4 in., and length 3 in.

CHAPTER 1

Foundations for Geometry

COMMON CORE

Chapter

- Use the correct terminology for basic geometric figures.
- Apply basic formulas in and out of the coordinate plane.

Picture This!

Many geometric concepts and shapes may be used in creating works of art. Unique designs can be made using only points, lines, planes, or circles.

Learn It Online
Chapter Project Online

AP Photo/Tim Ockenden/library.com

ARE YOU READY?

Vocabulary

Match each term on the left with a definition on the right.

1. coordinate
2. metric system of measurement
3. expression
4. order of operations

A. a mathematical phrase that contains operations, numbers, and/or variables
B. the measurement system often used in the United States
C. one of the numbers of an ordered pair that locates a point on a coordinate graph
D. a list of rules for evaluating expressions
E. a decimal system of weights and measures that is used universally in science and commonly throughout the world

Measure with Customary and Metric Units

For each object tell which is the better measurement.

5. length of an unsharpened pencil
$7\frac{1}{2}$ in. or $9\frac{3}{4}$ in.
6. the diameter of a quarter
1 m or $2\frac{1}{2}$ cm
7. length of a soccer field
100 yd or 40 yd
8. height of a classroom
5 ft or 10 ft
9. height of a student's desk
30 in. or 4 ft
10. length of a dollar bill
15.6 cm or 35.5 cm

Combine Like Terms

Simplify each expression.

11. $-y + 3y - 6y + 12y$
12. $63 + 2x - 7 - 4x$
13. $-5 - 9 - 7x + 6x$
14. $24 - 3y + y + 7$

Evaluate Expressions

Evaluate each expression for the given value of the variable.

15. $x + 3x + 7x$ for $x = -5$
16. $5p + 10$ for $p = 78$
17. $2a - 8a$ for $a = 12$
18. $3n - 3$ for $n = 16$

Ordered Pairs

Write the ordered pair for each point.

19. *A*
20. *B*
21. *C*
22. *D*
23. *E*
24. *F*

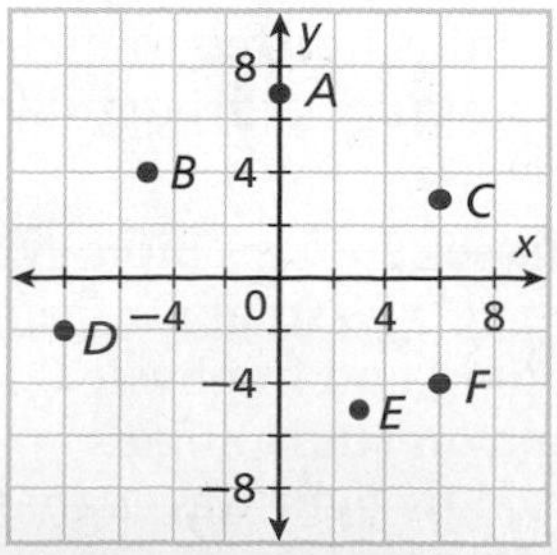

CHAPTER 1

Study Guide: Preview

Where You've Been

Previously, you

- used the order of operations.
- used variables and expressions to represent situations.
- located points in the coordinate plane.
- solved equations.

In This Chapter

You will study

- applying basic facts about points, lines, planes, segments, and angles.
- measuring and constructing segments and angles.
- using formulas to find distance and the coordinates of a midpoint.
- identifying reflections, rotations, and translations.

Where You're Going

You can use the skills learned in this chapter

- to find distances between cities.
- to determine how much material is needed to make a rectangular or triangular object.
- in classes such as Biology, when you learn about gene mapping and in physics, when you study angles formed by light waves that bounce off objects.

Key Vocabulary/Vocabulario

angle	ángulo
area	área
coordinate plane	plano cartesiano
line	línea
perimeter	perímetro
plane	plano
point	punto
transformation	transformación
undefined term	término indefinido

Vocabulary Connections

To become familiar with some of the vocabulary terms in the chapter, consider the following. You may refer to the chapter, the glossary, or a dictionary if you like.

1. A *definition* is a statement that gives the meaning of a word or phrase. What do you think the phrase **undefined term** means?
2. *Coordinates* are numbers used to describe a location. A *plane* is a flat surface. How can you use these meanings to understand the term **coordinate plane** ?
3. A **point** is often represented by a dot. What real-world items could represent points?
4. *Trans-* is a prefix that means "across," as in movement. A *form* is a shape. How can you use these meanings to understand the term **transformation** ?

Reading and Writing Math

Reading Strategy: Use Your Book for Success

Understanding how your textbook is organized will help you locate and use helpful information.

As you read through an example problem, pay attention to the notes in the **margin.** These notes highlight key information about the concept and will help you to avoid common mistakes.

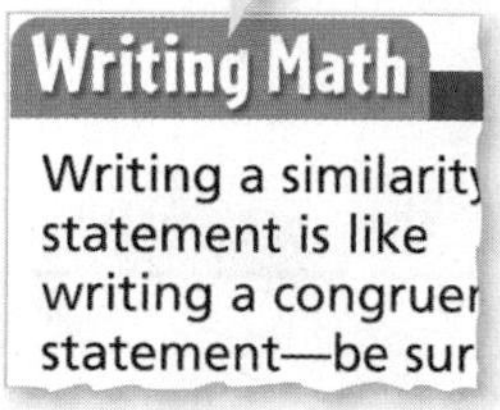
Writing Math

Writing a similarity statement is like writing a congruent statement—be sur

Helpful Hint

When writing an indirect proof, loo for a contradiction one of the followi

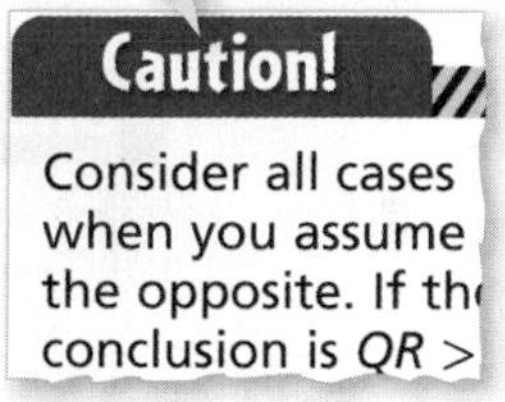
Caution!

Consider all cases when you assume the opposite. If th conclusion is *QR* >

The **Glossary** is found in the back of your textbook. Use it when you need a definition of an unfamiliar word or phrase.

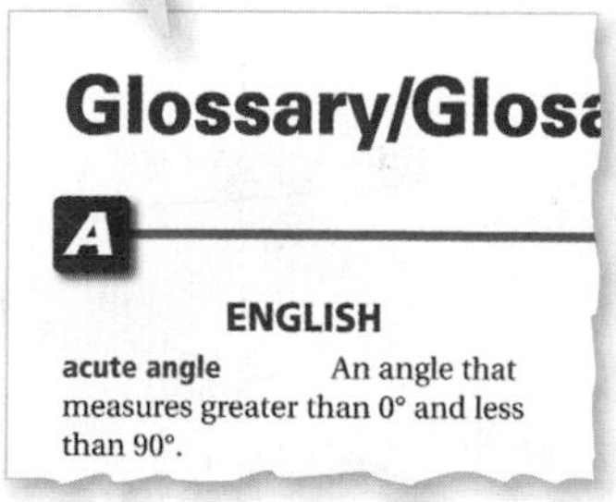
Glossary/Glosa

A

ENGLISH

acute angle An angle that measures greater than 0° and less than 90°.

The **Index** is located at the end of your textbook. If you need to locate the page where a particular concept is explained, use the **Index** to find the corresponding page number.

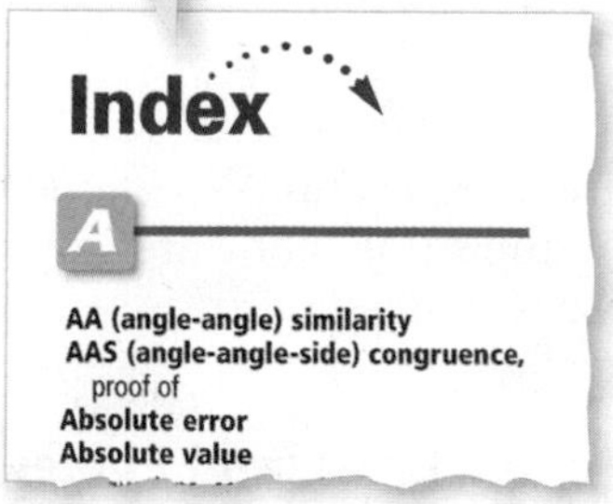
Index

A

AA (angle-angle) similarity
AAS (angle-angle-side) congruence,
proof of
Absolute error
Absolute value

The **Problem-Solving Handbook** is found in the back of your textbook. These pages review strategies that can help you solve real-world problems.

Problem-Sol

Draw a Diagra

When a problem involves obj drawing a diagram can mak

Try This

Use your textbook for the following problems.

1. Use the index to find the page where *right angle* is defined.
2. What formula does the Know-It Note on the first page of the lesson *Midpoint and Distance in the Coordinate Plane* refer to?
3. Use the glossary to find the definition of *congruent segments.*

COMMON CORE

1-1 Understanding Points, Lines, and Planes

CC.9-12.G.CO.1 Know precise definitions…based on the undefined notions of point, line…

Objectives
Identify, name, and draw points, lines, segments, rays, and planes.

Apply basic facts about points, lines, and planes.

Vocabulary
undefined term
point
line
plane
collinear
coplanar
segment
endpoint
ray
opposite rays
postulate

Who uses this?
Architects use representations of points, lines, and planes to create models of buildings. Interwoven segments were used to model the beams of Beijing's National Stadium for the 2008 Olympics.

The most basic figures in geometry are **undefined terms**, which cannot be defined by using other figures. The undefined terms *point, line,* and *plane* are the building blocks of geometry.

Know it! Note

Undefined Terms

TERM	NAME	DIAGRAM
A **point** names a location and has no size. It is represented by a dot.	A capital letter point ***P***	
A **line** is a straight path that has no thickness and extends forever.	A lowercase letter or two points on the line line ℓ, $\overleftrightarrow{XY}$ or $\overleftrightarrow{YX}$	
A **plane** is a flat surface that has no thickness and extends forever.	A script capital letter or three points not on a line plane $\mathcal{R}$ or plane ***ABC***	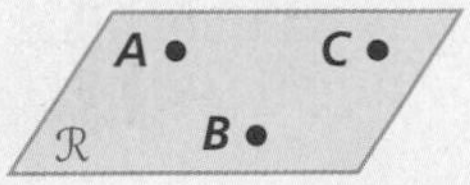

Points that lie on the same line are **collinear**. *K, L,* and *M* are collinear. *K, L,* and *N* are *noncollinear.* Points that lie in the same plane are **coplanar**. Otherwise they are *noncoplanar.*

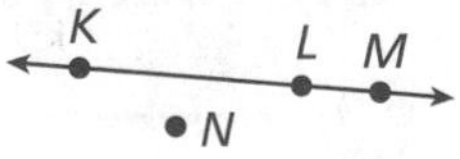

EXAMPLE 1 **Naming Points, Lines, and Planes**

Helpful Hint
A plane may be named by any three noncollinear points on that plane. Plane *ABC* may also be named *BCA, CAB, CBA, ACB,* or *BAC.*

Refer to the design in the roof of Beijing's National Stadium.

A **Name four coplanar points.**
K, L, M, and *N* all lie in plane $\mathcal{R}$.

B **Name three lines.**
$\overleftrightarrow{AB}$, $\overleftrightarrow{BC}$, and $\overleftrightarrow{CA}$.

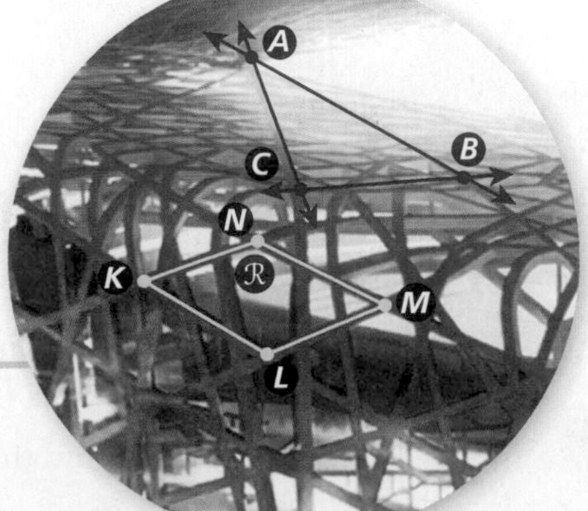

CHECK IT OUT! **1.** Use the diagram to name two planes.

Segments and Rays

DEFINITION	NAME	DIAGRAM
A **segment**, or line segment, is the part of a line consisting of two points and all points between them.	The two endpoints $\overline{AB}$ or $\overline{BA}$	
An **endpoint** is a point at one end of a segment or the starting point of a *ray*.	A capital letter *C* and *D*	
A **ray** is a part of a line that starts at an endpoint and extends forever in one direction.	Its endpoint and any other point on the ray $\overrightarrow{RS}$	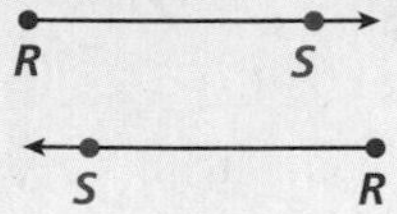
Opposite rays are two rays that have a common endpoint and form a line.	The common endpoint and any other point on each ray $\overrightarrow{EF}$ and $\overrightarrow{EG}$	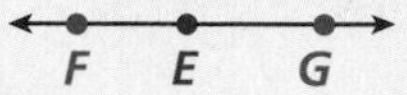

EXAMPLE 2 Drawing Segments and Rays

Draw and label each of the following.

A a segment with endpoints *U* and *V*

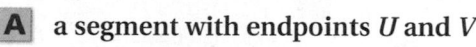

B opposite rays with a common endpoint *Q*

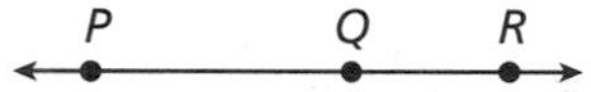

CHECK IT OUT! **2.** Draw and label a ray with endpoint *M* that contains *N*.

A **postulate**, or *axiom*, is a statement that is accepted as true without proof. Postulates about points, lines, and planes help describe geometric properties.

Postulates Points, Lines, and Planes

1-1-1 Through any two points there is exactly one line.

1-1-2 Through any three noncollinear points there is exactly one plane containing them.

1-1-3 If two points lie in a plane, then the line containing those points lies in the plane.

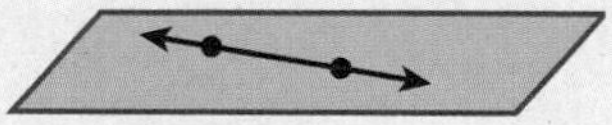

EXAMPLE 3 Identifying Points and Lines in a Plane

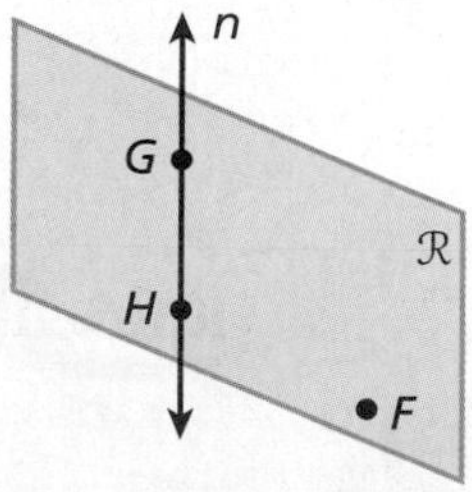

Name a line that passes through two points.

There is exactly one line *n* passing through *G* and *H*.

CHECK IT OUT! **3.** Name a plane that contains three noncollinear points.

Recall that a system of equations is a set of two or more equations containing two or more of the same variables. The coordinates of the solution of the system satisfy all equations in the system. These coordinates also locate the point where all the graphs of the equations in the system *intersect.*

An *intersection* is the set of all points that two or more figures have in common. The next two postulates describe intersections involving lines and planes.

Know it! Note

Postulates **Intersection of Lines and Planes**

1-1-4 If two lines intersect, then they intersect in exactly one point.

1-1-5 If two planes intersect, then they intersect in exactly one line.

Use a dashed line to show the hidden parts of any figure that you are drawing. A dashed line will indicate the part of the figure that is not seen.

EXAMPLE 4 Representing Intersections

Sketch a figure that shows each of the following.

A **A line intersects a plane, but does not lie in the plane.**

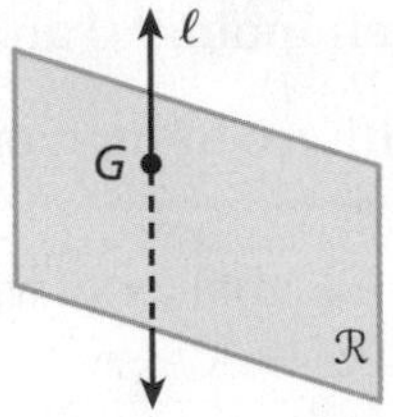

B **Two planes intersect in one line.**

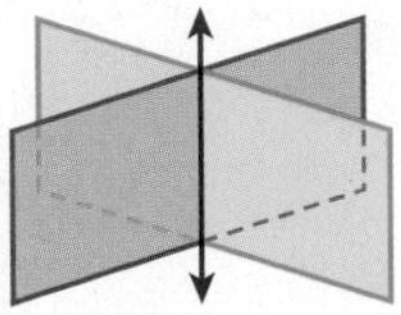

CHECK IT OUT! **4.** Sketch a figure that shows two lines intersect in one point in a plane, but only one of the lines lies in the plane.

MATHEMATICAL PRACTICES

THINK AND DISCUSS

1. Explain why any two points are collinear.

2. Which postulate explains the fact that two straight roads cannot cross each other more than once?

3. Explain why points and lines may be coplanar even when the plane containing them is not drawn.

4. Name all the possible lines, segments, and rays for the points *A* and *B*. Then give the maximum number of planes that can be determined by these points.

Know it! Note

5. **GET ORGANIZED** Copy and complete the graphic organizer below. In each box, name, describe, and illustrate one of the undefined terms.

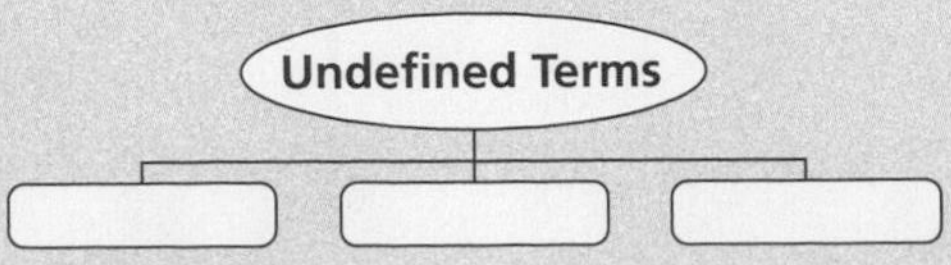

1-1 Exercises

Learn It Online
Homework Help Online
Parent Resources Online

GUIDED PRACTICE

Vocabulary **Apply the vocabulary from this lesson to answer each question.**

1. Give an example from your classroom of three *collinear* points.
2. Make use of the fact that *endpoint* is a compound of *end* and *point* and name the *endpoint* of $\overrightarrow{ST}$.

SEE EXAMPLE 1

Use the figure to name each of the following.

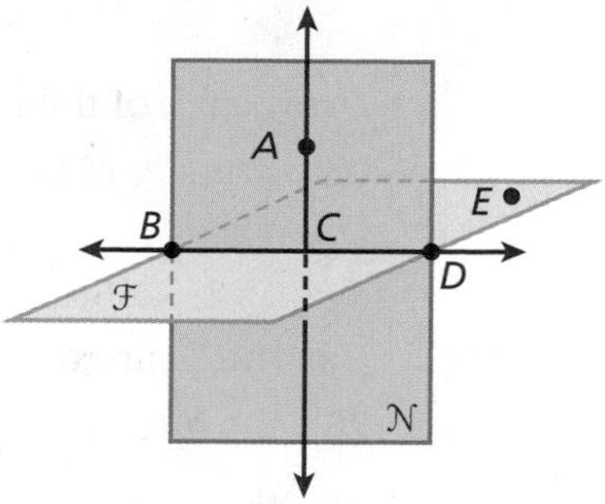

3. five points
4. two lines
5. two planes
6. point on $\overleftrightarrow{BD}$

SEE EXAMPLE 2

Draw and label each of the following.

7. a segment with endpoints M and N
8. a ray with endpoint F that passes through G

SEE EXAMPLE 3

Use the figure to name each of the following.

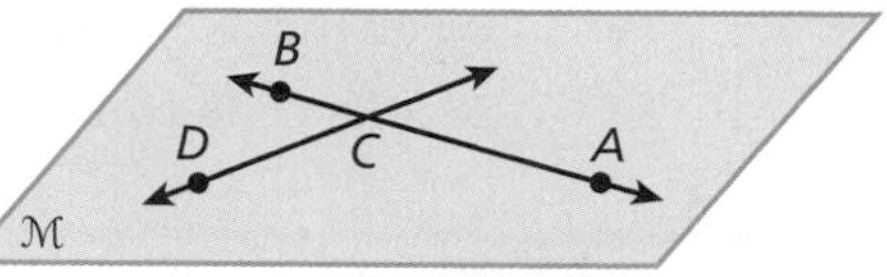

9. a line that contains A and C
10. a plane that contains A, D, and C

SEE EXAMPLE 4

Sketch a figure that shows each of the following.

11. three coplanar lines that intersect in a common point
12. two lines that do not intersect

PRACTICE AND PROBLEM SOLVING

Independent Practice

For Exercises	See Example
13–15	1
16–17	2
18–19	3
20–21	4

Extra Practice

See Extra Practice for more Skills Practice and Applications Practice exercises.

Use the figure to name each of the following.

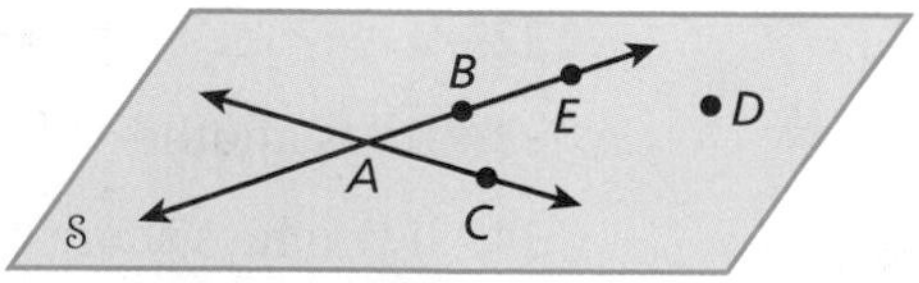

13. three collinear points
14. four coplanar points
15. a plane containing E

Draw and label each of the following.

16. a line containing X and Y
17. a pair of opposite rays that both contain R

Use the figure to name each of the following.

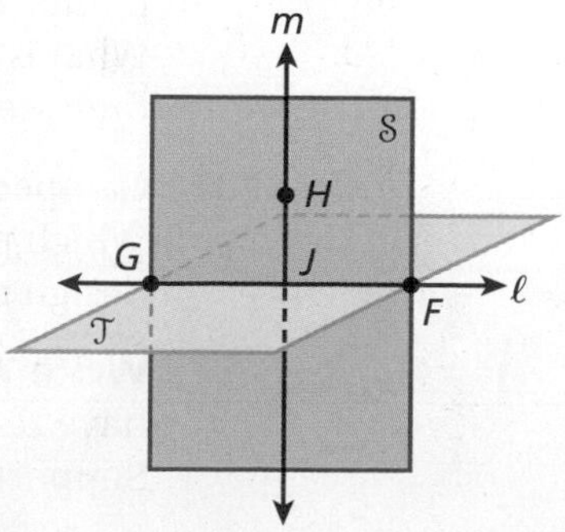

18. two points and a line that lie in plane $\mathcal{T}$
19. two planes that contain ℓ

Sketch a figure that shows each of the following.

20. a line that intersects two nonintersecting planes
21. three coplanar lines that intersect in three different points

MULTI-STEP TEST PREP

22. Name an object at the archaeological site shown that is represented by each of the following.
    a. a point
    b. a segment
    c. a plane

Draw each of the following.

23. plane $\mathcal{H}$ containing two lines that intersect at M
24. $\overleftrightarrow{ST}$ intersecting plane $\mathcal{M}$ at R

Use the figure to name each of the following.

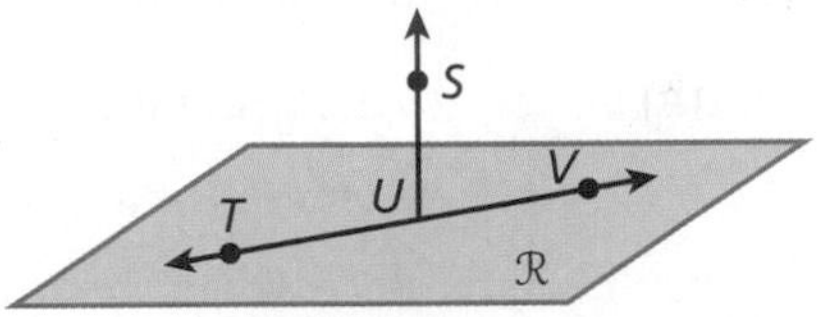

25. the intersection of $\overleftrightarrow{TV}$ and $\overrightarrow{US}$
26. the intersection of $\overrightarrow{US}$ and plane $\mathcal{R}$
27. the intersection of $\overline{TU}$ and $\overline{UV}$

Write the postulate that justifies each statement.

28. The line connecting two dots on a sheet of paper lies on the same sheet of paper as the dots.
29. If two ants are walking in straight lines but in different directions, their paths cannot cross more than once.
30. **Critical Thinking** Is it possible to draw three points that are noncoplanar? Explain.

Tell whether each statement is sometimes, always, or never true. Support your answer with a sketch.

31. If two planes intersect, they intersect in a straight line.
32. If two lines intersect, they intersect at two different points.
33. $\overleftrightarrow{AB}$ is another name for $\overleftrightarrow{BA}$.
34. If two rays share a common endpoint, then they form a line.
35. **Art** Pointillism is a technique in which tiny dots of complementary colors are combined to form a picture. Which postulate ensures that a line connecting two of these points also lies in the plane containing the points?
36. **Probability** Three of the labeled points are chosen at random. What is the probability that they are collinear?

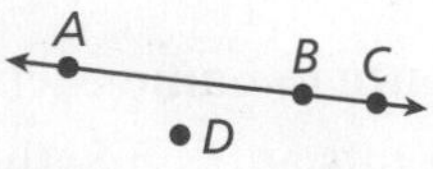

37. Campers often use a cooking stove with three legs. Which postulate explains why they might prefer this design to a stove that has four legs?
38. **Write About It** Explain why three coplanar lines may have zero, one, two, or three points of intersection. Support your answer with a sketch.

TEST PREP

39. Which of the following is a set of noncollinear points?

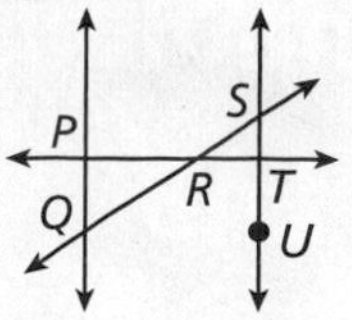

Ⓐ *P, R, T* Ⓒ *P, Q, R*

Ⓑ *Q, R, S* Ⓓ *S, T, U*

40. What is the greatest number of intersection points four coplanar lines can have?

Ⓕ 6 Ⓗ 2

Ⓖ 4 Ⓙ 0

41. Two flat walls meet in the corner of a classroom. Which postulate best describes this situation?

Ⓐ Through any three noncollinear points there is exactly one plane.

Ⓑ If two points lie in a plane, then the line containing them lies in the plane.

Ⓒ If two lines intersect, then they intersect in exactly one point.

Ⓓ If two planes intersect, then they intersect in exactly one line.

42. Gridded Response What is the greatest number of planes determined by four noncollinear points?

CHALLENGE AND EXTEND

Use the table for Exercises 43–45.

Figure			
Number of Points	2	3	4
Maximum Number of Segments	1	3	

43. What is the maximum number of segments determined by 4 points?

44. Multi-Step Extend the table. What is the maximum number of segments determined by 10 points?

45. Write a formula for the maximum number of segments determined by *n* points.

46. Critical Thinking Explain how rescue teams could use two of the postulates from this lesson to locate a distress signal.

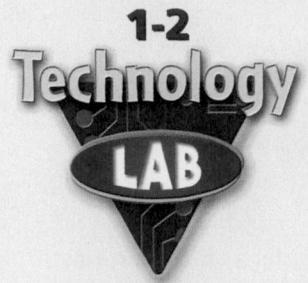

1-2

Technology LAB

Explore Properties Associated with Points

Use with Measuring and Constructing Segments

The two endpoints of a segment determine its length. Other points on the segment are *between* the endpoints. Only one of these points is the *midpoint* of the segment. In this lab, you will use geometry software to measure lengths of segments and explore properties of points on segments.

MATHEMATICAL PRACTICES **Use appropriate tools strategically.**

CC.9-12.G.CO.1 Know precise definitions… based on the undefined notions of point, line…

Learn It Online
Lab Resources Online

Activity

1. Construct a segment and label its endpoints A and C.

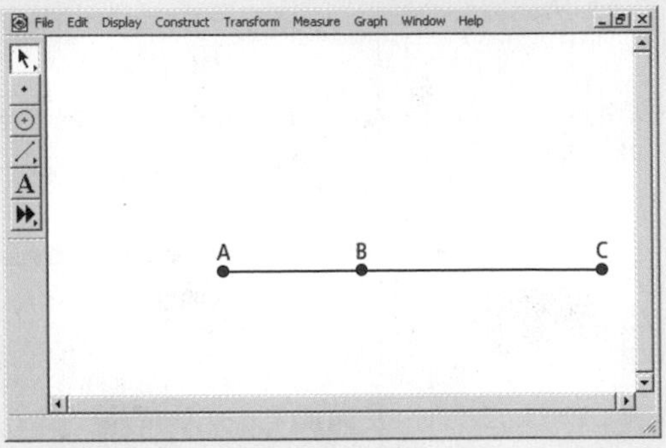

2. Create point B on $\overline{AC}$.

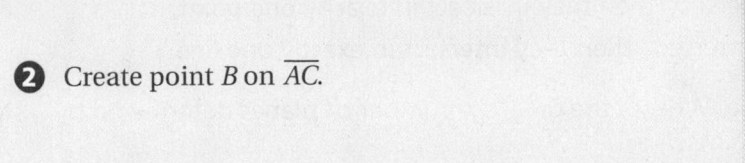

3. Measure the distances from A to B and from B to C. Use the Calculate tool to calculate the sum of AB and BC.

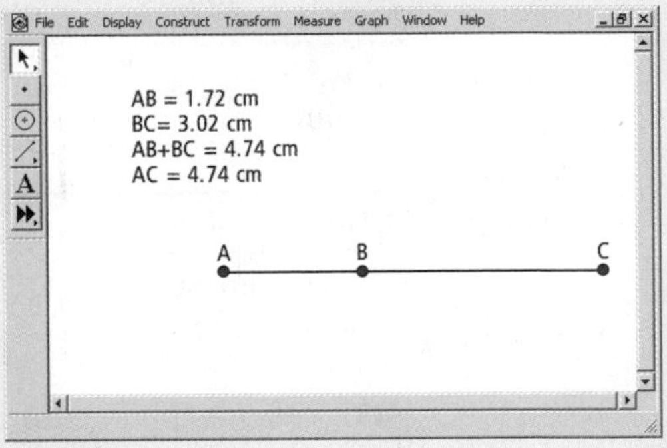

4. Measure the length of $\overline{AC}$. What do you notice about this length compared with the measurements found in Step 3?

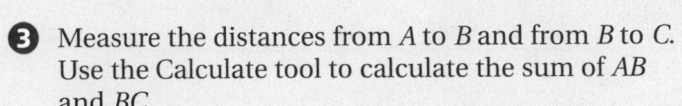

5. Drag point B along $\overline{AC}$. Drag one of the endpoints of $\overline{AC}$. What relationships do you think are true about the three measurements?

6. Construct the midpoint of $\overline{AC}$ and label it M.

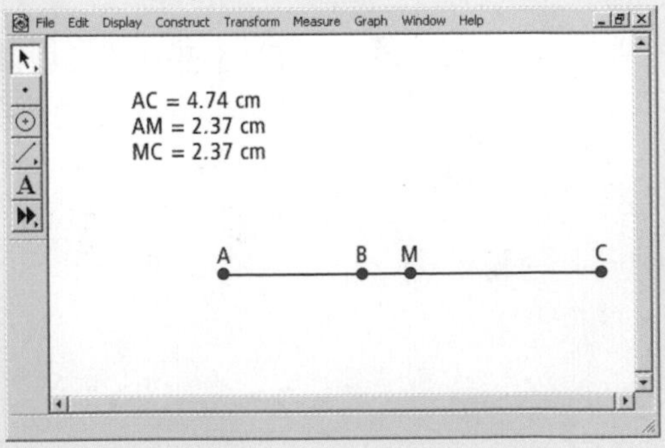

7. Measure $\overline{AM}$ and $\overline{MC}$. What relationships do you think are true about the lengths of $\overline{AC}$, $\overline{AM}$, and $\overline{MC}$? Use the Calculate tool to confirm your findings.

8. How many midpoints of $\overline{AC}$ exist?

Try This

1. Repeat the activity with a new segment. Drag each of the points in your figure (the endpoints, the point on the segment, and the midpoint). Write down any relationships you observe about the measurements.
2. Create a point D not on $\overline{AC}$. Measure $\overline{AD}$, $\overline{DC}$, and $\overline{AC}$. Does $AD + DC = AC$? What do you think has to be true about D for the relationship to always be true?

COMMON CORE

1-2 Measuring and Constructing Segments

CC.9-12.G.CO.12 Make formal geometric constructions with a variety of tools and methods…

Objectives

Use length and midpoint of a segment.

Construct midpoints and congruent segments.

Vocabulary

coordinate
distance
length
congruent segments
construction
between
midpoint
bisect
segment bisector

Why learn this?

You can measure a segment to calculate the distance between two locations. Maps of a race are used to show the distance between stations on the course. (See Example 4.)

A ruler can be used to measure the distance between two points. A point corresponds to one and only one number on the ruler. This number is called a **coordinate** . The following postulate summarizes this concept.

Know it! Note

Postulate 1-2-1 **Ruler Postulate**

The points on a line can be put into a one-to-one correspondence with the real numbers.

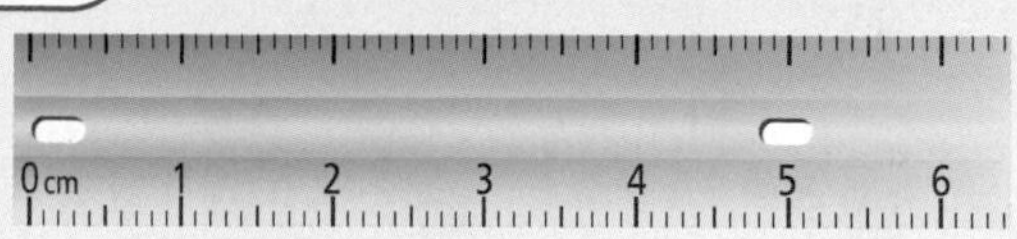

The **distance** between any two points is the absolute value of the difference of the coordinates. If the coordinates of points A and B are a and b, then the distance between A and B is $|a-b|$ or $|b-a|$. The distance between A and B is also called the **length** of $\overline{AB}$, or AB.

$AB = |a-b| = |b-a|$

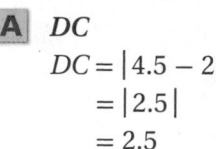

EXAMPLE 1 **Finding the Length of a Segment**

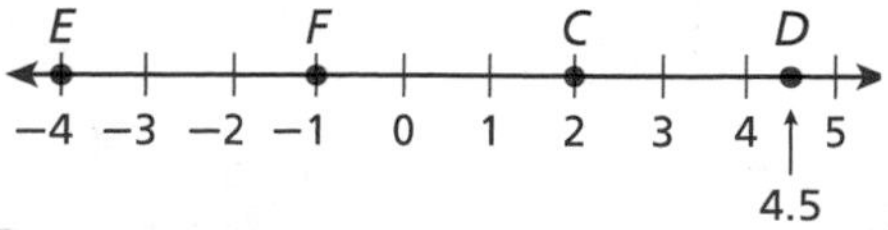

Find each length.

A DC

$DC = |4.5-2|$
$= |2.5|$
$= 2.5$

B EF

$EF = |-4-(-1)|$
$= |-4+1|$
$= |-3|$
$= 3$

CHECK IT OUT! **Find each length.**

1a. XY

1b. XZ

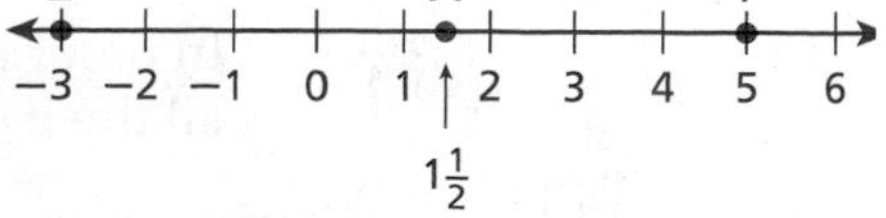

Caution!

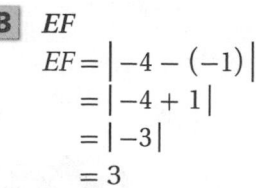

PQ represents a number, while $\overline{PQ}$ represents a geometric figure. Be sure to use equality for numbers ($PQ = RS$) and congruence for figures ($\overline{PQ} \cong \overline{RS}$).

Congruent segments are segments that have the same length. In the diagram, $PQ = RS$, so you can write $\overline{PQ} \cong \overline{RS}$. This is read as "segment PQ is congruent to segment RS." ***Tick marks*** are used in a figure to show congruent segments.

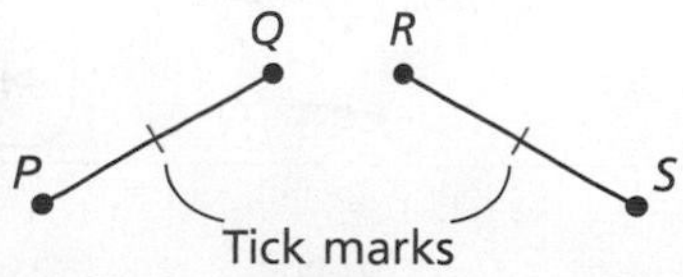

You can make a sketch or measure and draw a segment. These may not be exact. A **construction** is a way of creating a figure that is more precise. One way to make a geometric construction is to use a compass and straightedge.

Construction Congruent Segment

Construct a segment congruent to $\overline{AB}$.

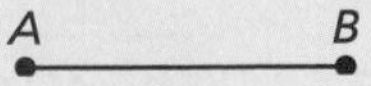

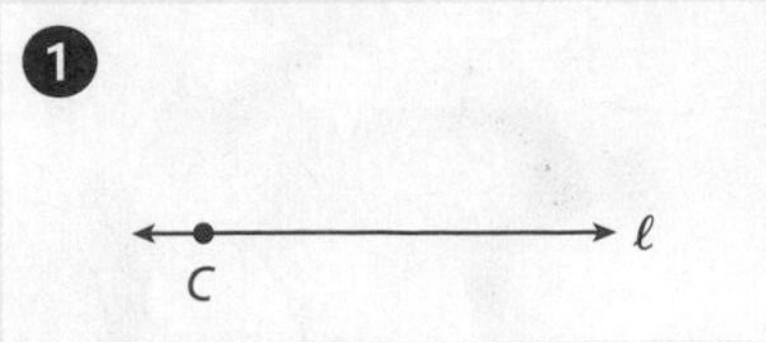

Draw ℓ. Choose a point on ℓ and label it C.

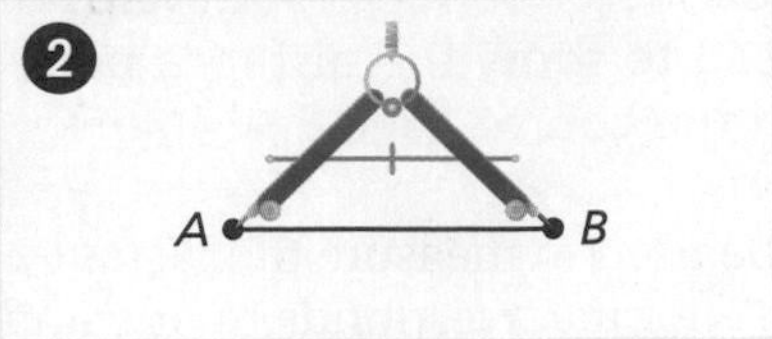

Open the compass to distance AB.

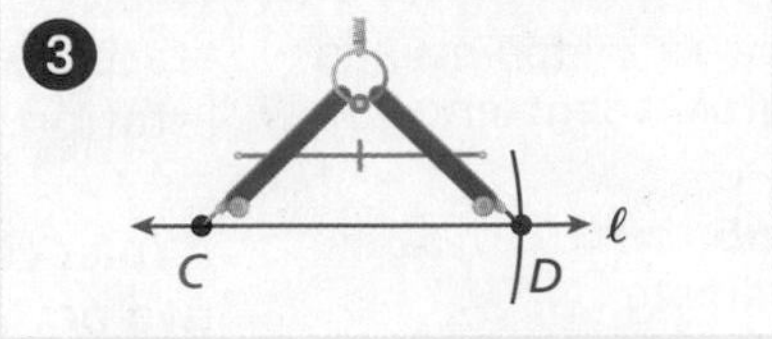

Place the point of the compass at C and make an arc through ℓ. Find the point where the arc and ℓ intersect and label it D.

$\overline{CD} \cong \overline{AB}$

EXAMPLE 2 Copying a Segment

Sketch, draw, and construct a segment congruent to $\overline{MN}$.

Step 1 Estimate and sketch.
Estimate the length of $\overline{MN}$ and sketch $\overline{PQ}$ approximately the same length.

Step 2 Measure and draw.
Use a ruler to measure $\overline{MN}$. MN appears to be 3.1 cm. Use a ruler and draw $\overline{XY}$ to have length 3.1 cm.

Step 3 Construct and compare.
Use a compass and straightedge to construct $\overline{ST}$ congruent to $\overline{MN}$.

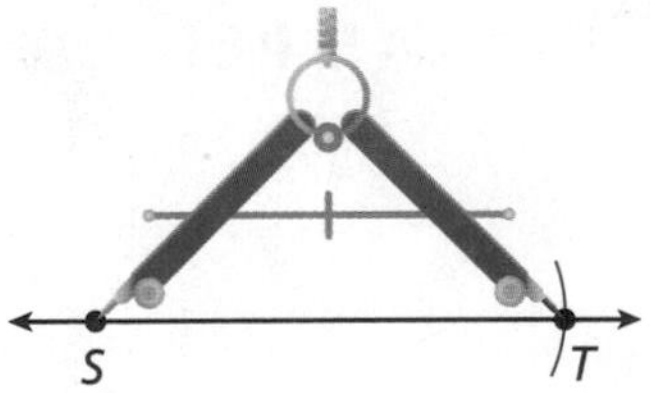

A ruler shows that $\overline{PQ}$ and $\overline{XY}$ are approximately the same length as $\overline{MN}$, but $\overline{ST}$ is precisely the same length.

CHECK IT OUT! 2. Sketch, draw, and construct a segment congruent to $\overline{JK}$.

In order for you to say that a point B is **between** two points A and C, all three of the points must lie on the same line, and $AB + BC = AC$.

Know it! Note

Postulate 1-2-2 Segment Addition Postulate

If B is between A and C, then $AB + BC = AC$.

EXAMPLE 3 Using the Segment Addition Postulate

Algebra

A **B is between A and C, $AC = 14$, and $BC = 11.4$. Find AB.**

$AC = AB + BC$	*Seg. Add. Post.*
$14 = AB + 11.4$	*Substitute 14 for AC and 11.4 for BC.*
$-11.4 \qquad -11.4$	*Subtract 11.4 from both sides.*
$2.6 = AB$	*Simplify.*

B **S is between R and T. Find RT.**

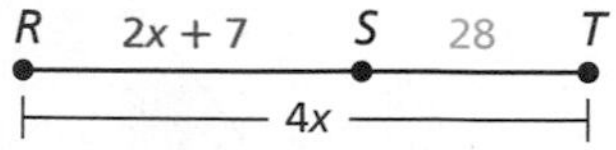

$RT = RS + ST$	*Seg. Add. Post.*
$4x = (2x + 7) + 28$	*Substitute the given values.*
$4x = 2x + 35$	*Simplify.*
$-2x \qquad -2x$	*Subtract 2x from both sides.*
$2x = 35$	*Simplify.*
$\frac{2x}{2} = \frac{35}{2}$	*Divide both sides by 2.*
$x = \frac{35}{2}$, or 17.5	*Simplify.*
$RT = 4x$	
$= 4(17.5) = 70$	*Substitute 17.5 for x.*

CHECK IT OUT!

3a. Y is between X and Z, $XZ = 3$, and $XY = 1\frac{1}{3}$. Find YZ.

3b. E is between D and F. Find DF.

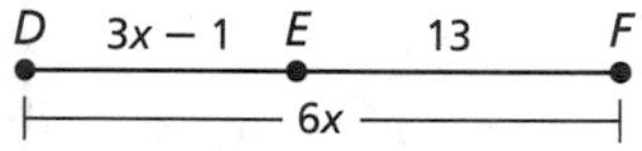

The **midpoint** M of $\overline{AB}$ is the point that **bisects**, or divides, the segment into two congruent segments. If M is the midpoint of $\overline{AB}$, then $AM = MB$. So if $AB = 6$, then $AM = 3$ and $MB = 3$.

EXAMPLE 4 *Recreation Application*

Algebra

The map shows the route for a race. You are 365 m from drink station R and 2 km from drink station S. The first-aid station is located at the midpoint of the two drink stations. How far are you from the first-aid station?

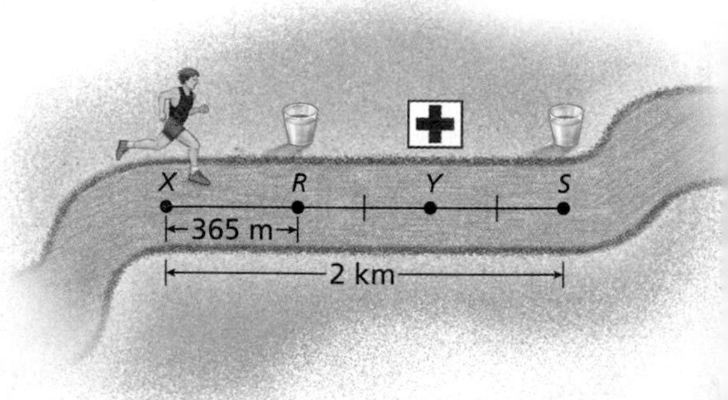

Let your current location be X and the location of the first-aid station be Y.

$XR + RS = XS$	*Seg. Add. Post.*
$365 + RS = 2000$	*Substitute 365 for XR and 2000 for XS.*
$-365 \qquad -365$	*Subtract 365 from both sides.*
$RS = 1635$	*Simplify.*
$RY = 817.5$	*Y is the mdpt. of $\overline{RS}$, so $RY = \frac{1}{2}RS$.*
$XY = XR + RY$	
$= \mathbf{365} + \mathbf{817.5} = 1182.5$ m	*Substitute 365 for XR and 817.5 for RY.*

You are 1182.5 m from the first-aid station.

CHECK IT OUT!

4. What is the distance to a drink station located at the midpoint between your current location and the first-aid station?

A **segment bisector** is any ray, segment, or line that intersects a segment at its midpoint. It divides the segment into two equal parts at its midpoint.

Construction Segment Bisector

1

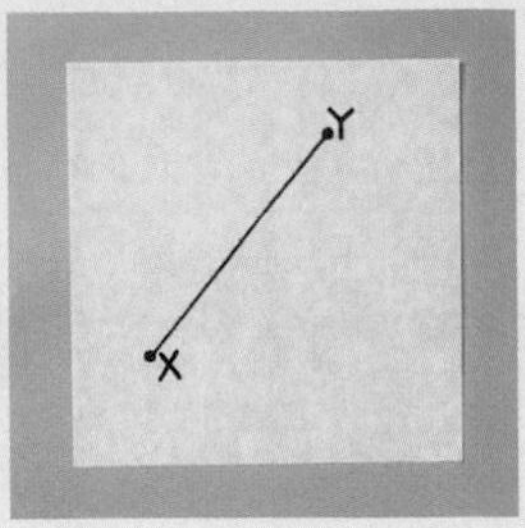

Draw $\overline{XY}$ on a sheet of paper.

2

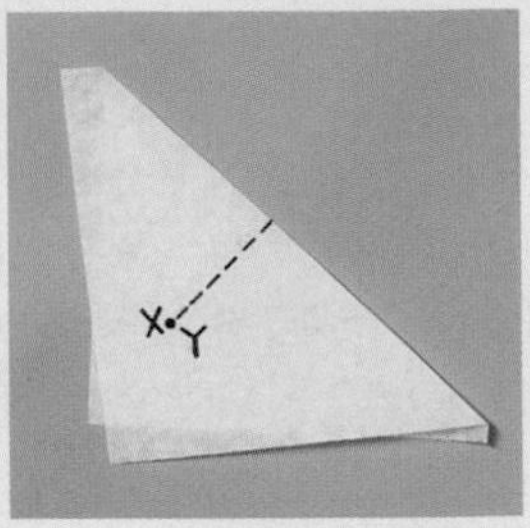

Fold the paper so that Y is on top of X.

3

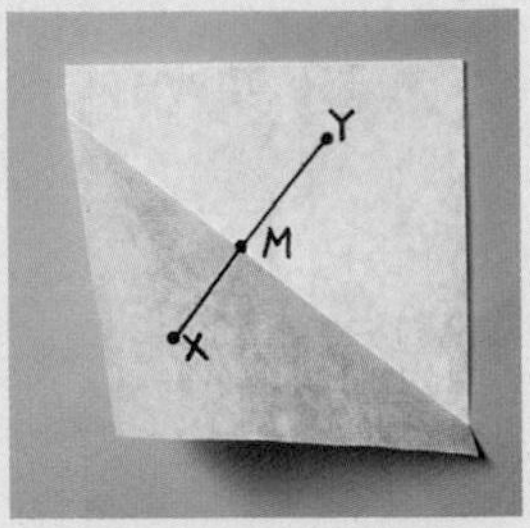

Unfold the paper. The line represented by the crease bisects $\overline{XY}$. Label the midpoint M.

$XM = MY$

EXAMPLE 5 Using Midpoints to Find Lengths

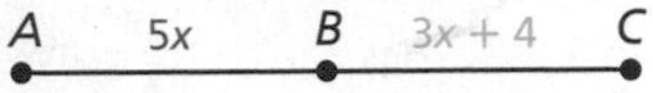

Algebra

B is the midpoint of $\overline{AC}$, $AB = 5x$, and $BC = 3x + 4$. Find AB, BC, and AC.

Step 1 Solve for x.

$AB = BC$	*B is the mdpt. of $\overline{AC}$.*
$5x = 3x + 4$	*Substitute 5x for AB and 3x + 4 for BC.*
$-3x \quad -3x$	*Subtract 3x from both sides.*
$2x = 4$	*Simplify.*
$\frac{2x}{2} = \frac{4}{2}$	*Divide both sides by 2.*
$x = 2$	*Simplify.*

Step 2 Find AB, BC, and AC.

$AB = 5x$ $\quad$ $BC = 3x + 4$ $\quad$ $AC = AB + BC$

$= 5(2) = 10$ $\quad$ $= 3(2) + 4 = 10$ $\quad$ $= 10 + 10 = 20$

CHECK IT OUT!

5. S is the midpoint of $\overline{RT}$, $RS = -2x$, and $ST = -3x - 2$. Find RS, ST, and RT.

MATHEMATICAL PRACTICES

THINK AND DISCUSS

1. Suppose R is the midpoint of $\overline{ST}$. Explain how SR and ST are related.

Know it! Note

2. GET ORGANIZED Copy and complete the graphic organizer. Make a sketch and write an equation to describe each relationship.

	B is between A and C.	B is the midpoint of $\overline{AC}$.
Sketch		
Equation		

1-2 Exercises

Learn It Online
Homework Help Online
Parent Resources Online

GUIDED PRACTICE

Vocabulary **Apply the vocabulary from this lesson to answer each question.**

1. Line ℓ bisects $\overline{XY}$ at M and divides $\overline{XY}$ into two equal parts. Name a pair of congruent segments.

2. __?__ is the amount of space between two points on a line. It is always expressed as a nonnegative number. (*distance* or *midpoint*)

SEE EXAMPLE 1

Find each length.

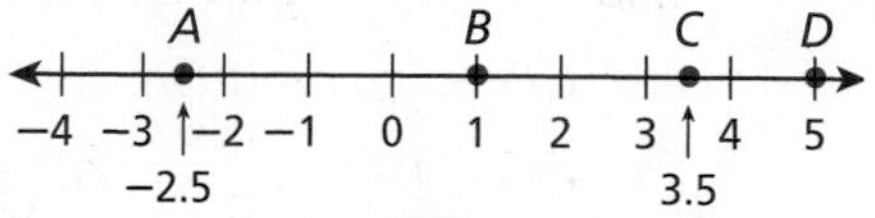

3. AB
4. BC

SEE EXAMPLE 2

5. Sketch, draw, and construct a segment congruent to $\overline{RS}$.

SEE EXAMPLE 3

6. B is between A and C, $AC = 15.8$, and $AB = 9.9$. Find BC.

7. Find MP.

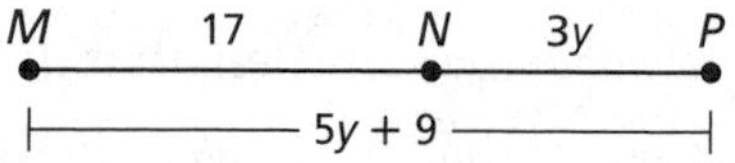

SEE EXAMPLE 4

8. **Travel** If a picnic area is located at the midpoint between Sacramento and Oakland, find the distance to the picnic area from the road sign.

SEE EXAMPLE 5

9. **Multi-Step** K is the midpoint of $\overline{JL}$, $JL = 4x - 2$, and $JK = 7$. Find x, KL, and JL.

10. E bisects $\overline{DF}$, $DE = 2y$, and $EF = 8y - 3$. Find DE, EF, and DF.

PRACTICE AND PROBLEM SOLVING

Independent Practice

For Exercises	See Example
11–12	1
13	2
14–15	3
16	4
17–18	5

Extra Practice

See Extra Practice for more Skills Practice and Applications Practice exercises.

Find each length.

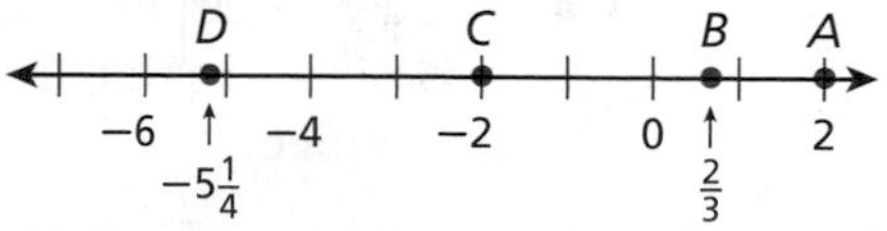

11. DB
12. CD

13. Sketch, draw, and construct a segment twice the length of $\overline{AB}$.

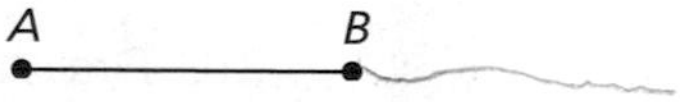

14. D is between C and E, $CE = 17.1$, and $DE = 8$. Find CD.

15. Find MN.

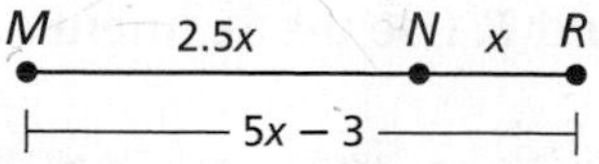

16. **Sports** During a football game, a quarterback standing at the 9-yard line passes the ball to a receiver at the 24-yard line. The receiver then runs with the ball halfway to the 50-yard line. How many total yards (passing plus running) did the team gain on the play?

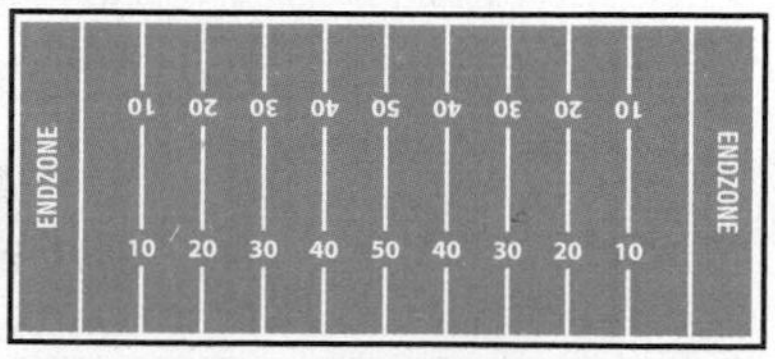

17. **Multi-Step** E is the midpoint of $\overline{DF}$, $DE = 2x + 4$, and $EF = 3x - 1$. Find DE, EF, and DF.

18. Q bisects $\overline{PR}$, $PQ = 3y$, and $PR = 42$. Find y and QR.

MULTI-STEP TEST PREP

19. Prep. Archaeologists at Valley Forge were eager to find what remained of the winter camp that soldiers led by George Washington called home for several months. The diagram represents one of the restored log cabins.

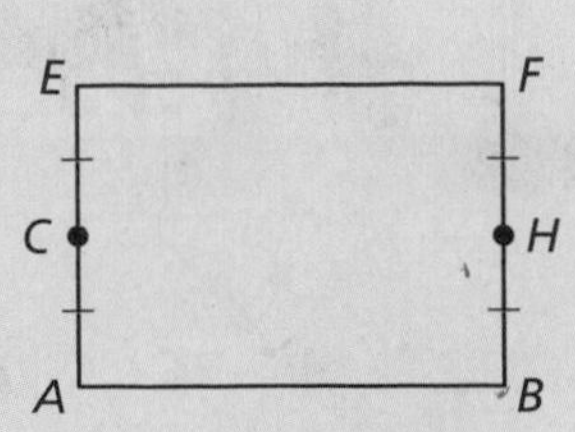

a. How is C related to $\overline{AE}$?

b. If $AC = 7$ ft, $EF = 2(AC) + 2$, and $AB = 2(EF) - 16$, what are AB and EF?

Use the diagram for Exercises 20–23.

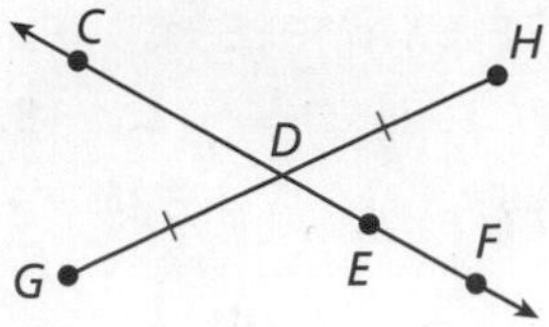

20. $GD = 4\frac{2}{3}$. Find GH.

21. $\overline{CD} \cong \overline{DF}$, E bisects $\overline{DF}$, and $CD = 14.2$. Find EF.

22. $GH = 4x - 1$, and $DH = 8$. Find x.

23. $\overline{GH}$ bisects $\overline{CF}$, $CF = 2y - 2$, and $CD = 3y - 11$. Find CD.

Tell whether each statement is sometimes, always, or never true. Support each of your answers with a sketch.

24. Two segments that have the same length must be congruent.

25. If M is between A and B, then M bisects $\overline{AB}$.

26. If Y is between X and Z, then X, Y, and Z are collinear.

27. **///ERROR ANALYSIS///** Below are two statements about the midpoint of $\overline{AB}$. Which is incorrect? Explain the error.

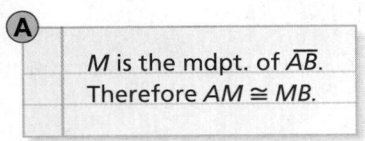

A

M is the mdpt. of $\overline{AB}$.
Therefore $AM \cong MB$.

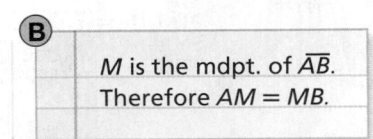

B

M is the mdpt. of $\overline{AB}$.
Therefore $AM = MB$.

28. Carpentry A carpenter has a wooden dowel that is 72 cm long. She wants to cut it into two pieces so that one piece is 5 times as long as the other. What are the lengths of the two pieces?

29. The coordinate of M is 2.5, and $MN = 4$. What are the possible coordinates for N?

30. Draw three collinear points where E is between D and F. Then write an equation using these points and the Segment Addition Postulate.

Suppose S is between R and T. Use the Segment Addition Postulate to solve for each variable.

31. $RS = 7y - 4$
$ST = y + 5$
$RT = 28$

32. $RS = 3x + 1$
$ST = \frac{1}{2}x + 3$
$RT = 18$

33. $RS = 2z + 6$
$ST = 4z - 3$
$RT = 5z + 12$

34. Write About It In the diagram, B is not between A and C. Explain.

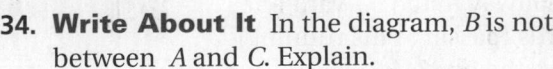

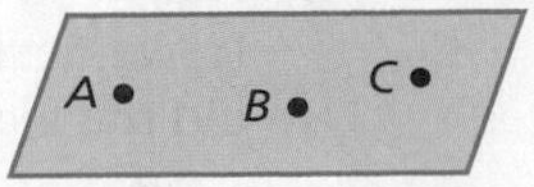

35. Construction Use a compass and straightedge to construct a segment whose length is $AB + CD$.

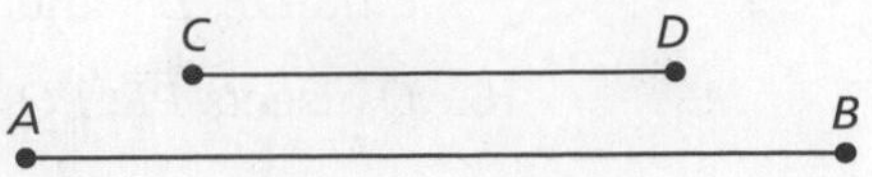

TEST PREP

36. Q is between P and R. S is between Q and R, and R is between Q and T. $PT = 34$, $QR = 8$, and $PQ = SQ = SR$. What is the length of $\overline{RT}$?

Ⓐ 9 Ⓑ 10 Ⓒ 18 Ⓓ 22

37. C is the midpoint of $\overline{AD}$. B is the midpoint of $\overline{AC}$. $BC = 12$. What is the length of $\overline{AD}$?

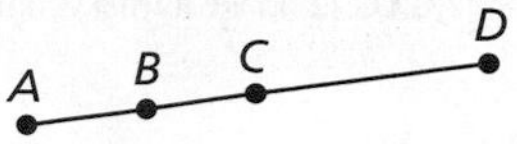

Ⓕ 12 Ⓖ 24 Ⓗ 36 Ⓙ 48

38. Which expression correctly states that $\overline{XY}$ is congruent to $\overline{VW}$?

Ⓐ $XY \cong VW$ Ⓑ $\overline{XY} \cong \overline{VW}$ Ⓒ $\overline{XY} = \overline{VW}$ Ⓓ $XY = VW$

39. A, B, C, D, and E are collinear points. $AE = 34$, $BD = 16$, and $AB = BC = CD$. What is the length of $\overline{CE}$?

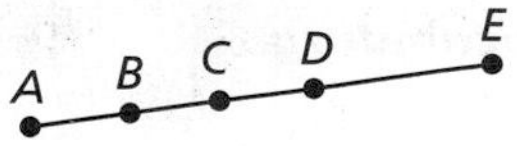

Ⓕ 10 Ⓖ 16 Ⓗ 18 Ⓙ 24

CHALLENGE AND EXTEND

40. HJ is twice JK. J is between H and K. If $HJ = 4x$ and $HK = 78$, find JK.

41. A, D, N, and X are collinear points. D is between N and A. $NA + AX = NX$. Draw a diagram that represents this information.

LINK

Sports

Joanna Hayes, of the United States, clears a hurdle on her way to winning the gold medal in the women's 100 m hurdles during the 2004 Olympic Games.

Sports **Use the following information for Exercises 42 and 43.**

The table shows regulation distances between hurdles in women's and men's races. In both the women's and men's events, the race consists of a straight track with 10 equally spaced hurdles.

Event	Distance of Race	Distance from Start to First Hurdle	Distance Between Hurdles	Distance from Last Hurdle to Finish
Women's	100 m	13.00 m	8.50 m	
Men's	110 m	13.72 m	9.14 m	

42. Find the distance from the last hurdle to the finish line for the women's race.

43. Find the distance from the last hurdle to the finish line for the men's race.

44. **Critical Thinking** Given that J, K, and L are collinear and that K is between J and L, is it possible that $JK = JL$? If so, draw an example. If not, explain.

COMMON CORE

1-3 Measuring and Constructing Angles

CC.9-12.G.CO.12 Make formal geometric constructions with a variety of tools and methods… *Also* **CC.9-12.G.CO.1**

Objectives

Name and classify angles.

Measure and construct angles and angle bisectors.

Vocabulary

angle
vertex
interior of an angle
exterior of an angle
measure
degree
acute angle
right angle
obtuse angle
straight angle
congruent angles
angle bisector

Who uses this?

Surveyors use angles to help them measure and map the earth's surface. (See Exercise 27.)

A transit is a tool for measuring angles. It consists of a telescope that swivels horizontally and vertically. Using a transit, a surveyor can measure the *angle* formed by his or her location and two distant points.

An **angle** is a figure formed by two rays, or sides, with a common endpoint called the **vertex** (plural: *vertices*). You can name an angle several ways: by its vertex, by a point on each ray and the vertex, or by a number.

The set of all points between the sides of the angle is the **interior of an angle**. The **exterior of an angle** is the set of all points outside the angle.

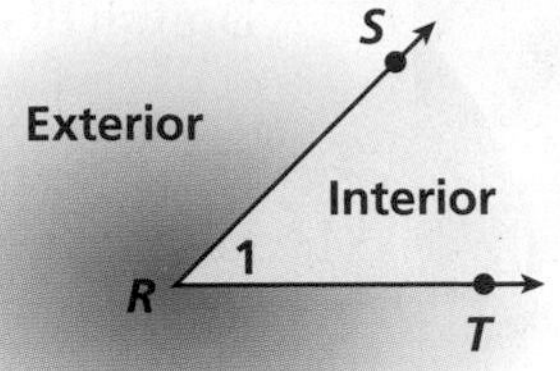

Angle Name

$\angle R$, $\angle SRT$, $\angle TRS$, or $\angle 1$

You cannot name an angle just by its vertex if the point is the vertex of more than one angle. In this case, you must use all three points to name the angle, and the middle point is always the vertex.

EXAMPLE 1 Naming Angles

A surveyor recorded the angles formed by a transit (point *T*) and three distant points, *Q*, *R*, and *S*. Name three of the angles.

$\angle QTR$, $\angle QTS$, and $\angle RTS$

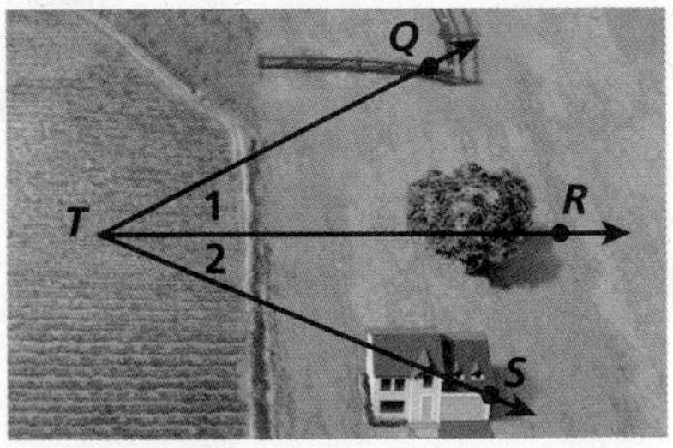

CHECK IT OUT!

1. Write the different ways you can name the angles in the diagram.

The **measure** of an angle is usually given in degrees. Since there are 360° in a circle, one **degree** is $\frac{1}{360}$ of a circle. When you use a protractor to measure angles, you are applying the following postulate.

Know it! Note

Postulate 1-3-1 Protractor Postulate

Given $\overleftrightarrow{AB}$ and a point O on $\overleftrightarrow{AB}$, all rays that can be drawn from O can be put into a one-to-one correspondence with the real numbers from 0 to 180.

Student to Student

Using a Protractor

José Muñoz
Lincoln High School

Most protractors have two sets of numbers around the edge. When I measure an angle and need to know which number to use, I first ask myself whether the angle is acute, right, or obtuse. For example, ∠RST looks like it is obtuse, so I know its measure must be 110°, not 70°.

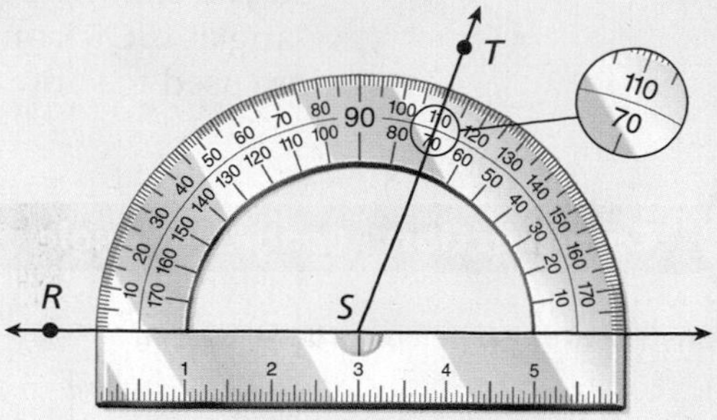

You can use the Protractor Postulate to help you classify angles by their measure. The measure of an angle is the absolute value of the difference of the real numbers that the rays correspond with on a protractor. If $\overrightarrow{OC}$ corresponds with c and $\overrightarrow{OD}$ corresponds with d, $m\angle DOC = |d - c|$ or $|c - d|$.

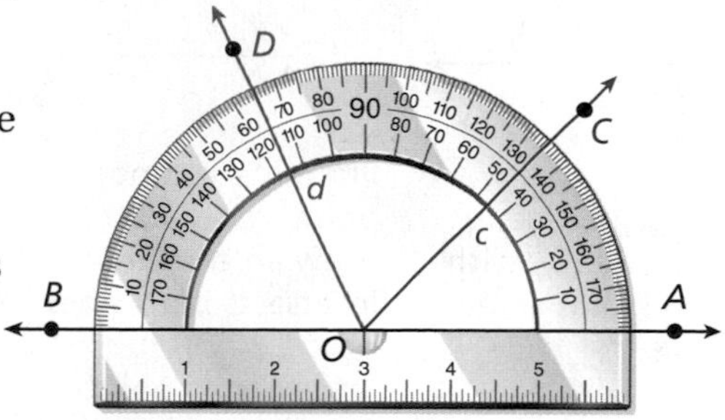

Know it! Note

Types of Angles

Acute Angle	Right Angle	Obtuse Angle	Straight Angle
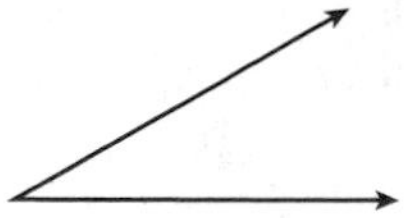	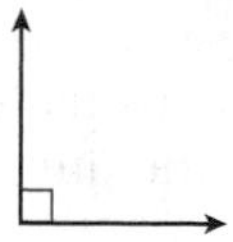	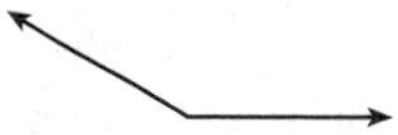	
Measures greater than 0° and less than 90°	Measures 90°	Measures greater than 90° and less than 180°	Formed by two opposite rays and meaures 180°

EXAMPLE 2 Measuring and Classifying Angles

Find the measure of each angle. Then classify each as acute, right, or obtuse.

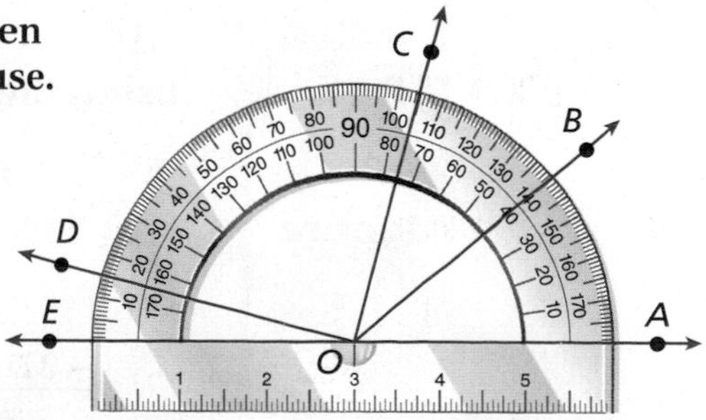

A $\angle AOD$

$m\angle AOD = 165°$

$\angle AOD$ is obtuse.

B $\angle COD$

$m\angle COD = |165 - 75| = 90°$

$\angle COD$ is a right angle.

CHECK IT OUT! **Use the diagram to find the measure of each angle. Then classify each as acute, right, or obtuse.**

2a. $\angle BOA$ **2b.** $\angle DOB$ **2c.** $\angle EOC$

Congruent angles are angles that have the same measure. In the diagram, $m\angle ABC = m\angle DEF$, so you can write $\angle ABC \cong \angle DEF$. This is read as "angle *ABC* is congruent to angle *DEF*." ***Arc marks*** are used to show that the two angles are congruent.

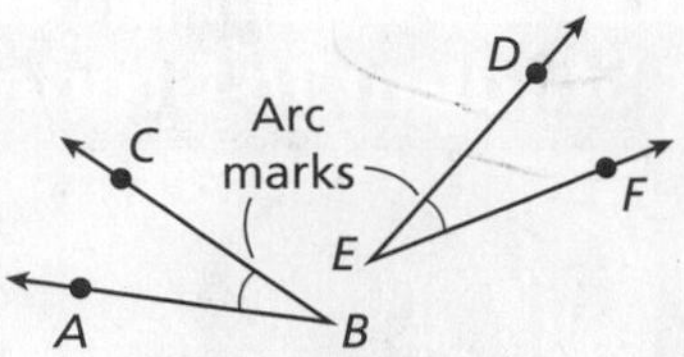

Construction Congruent Angle

Construct an angle congruent to ∠A.

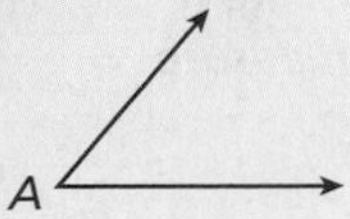

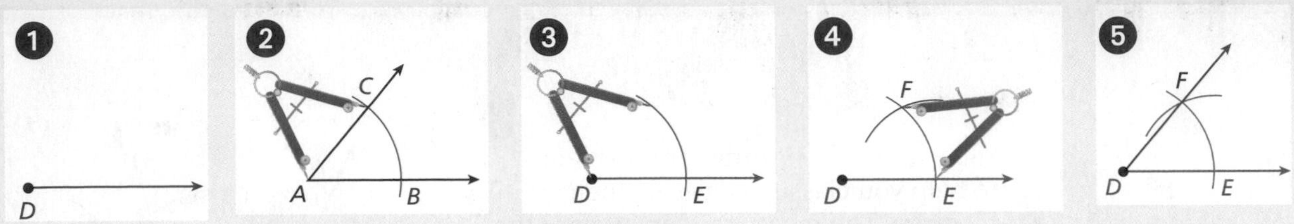

1. Use a straightedge to draw a ray with endpoint ***D***.
2. Place the compass point at *A* and draw an arc that intersects both sides of ∠*A*. Label the intersection points ***B*** and ***C***.
3. Using the same compass setting, place the compass point at ***D*** and draw an arc that intersects the ray. Label the intersection ***E***.
4. Place the compass point at *B* and open it to the distance *BC*. Place the point of the compass at ***E*** and draw an arc. Label its intersection with the first arc ***F***.
5. Use a straightedge to draw $\overrightarrow{DF}$.

   $\angle D \cong \angle A$

The Angle Addition Postulate is very similar to the Segment Addition Postulate that you learned in the previous lesson.

Know it! Note

Postulate 1-3-2 Angle Addition Postulate

If *S* is in the interior of ∠*PQR*, then $m\angle PQS + m\angle SQR = m\angle PQR$.

(∠ Add. Post.)

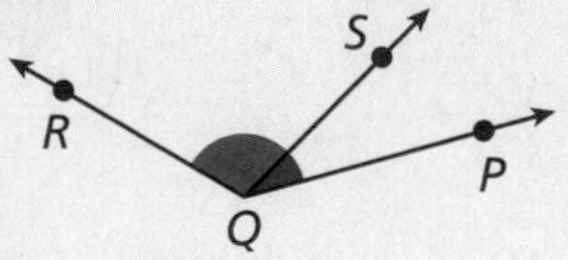

EXAMPLE 3 Using the Angle Addition Postulate

Algebra

$m\angle ABD = 37°$ and $m\angle ABC = 84°$. Find $m\angle DBC$.

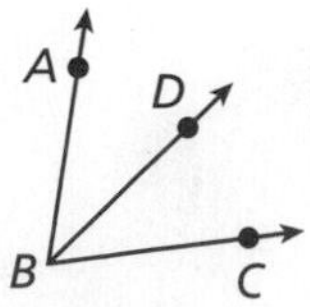

$m\angle ABC = m\angle ABD + m\angle DBC$	*∠ Add. Post.*
$84° = 37° + m\angle DBC$	*Substitute the given values.*
$\underline{-37\quad -37}$	*Subtract 37 from both sides.*
$47° = m\angle DBC$	*Simplify.*

CHECK IT OUT!

3. $m\angle XWZ = 121°$ and $m\angle XWY = 59°$. Find $m\angle YWZ$.

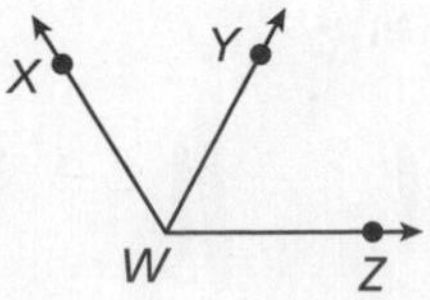

An **angle bisector** is a ray that divides an angle into two congruent angles. $\overrightarrow{JK}$ bisects $\angle LJM$; thus $\angle LJK \cong \angle KJM$.

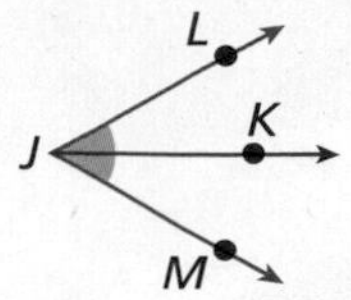

Construction Angle Bisector

Construct the bisector of ∠A.

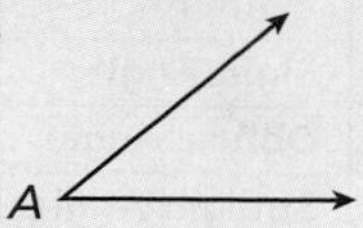

1

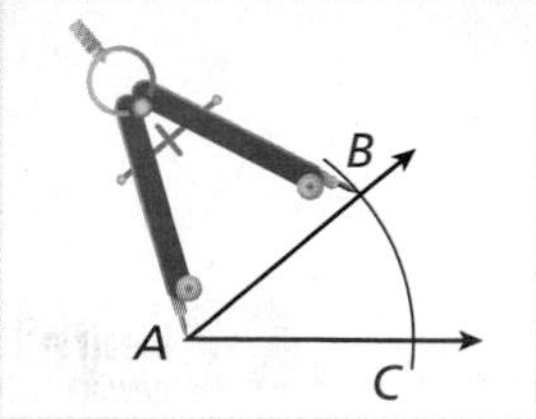

Place the point of the compass at *A* and draw an arc. Label its points of intersection with ∠*A* as *B* and *C*.

2

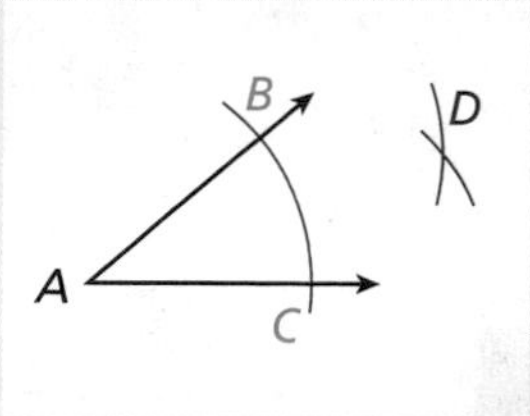

Without changing the compass setting, draw intersecting arcs from *B* and *C*. Label the intersection of the arcs as *D*.

3

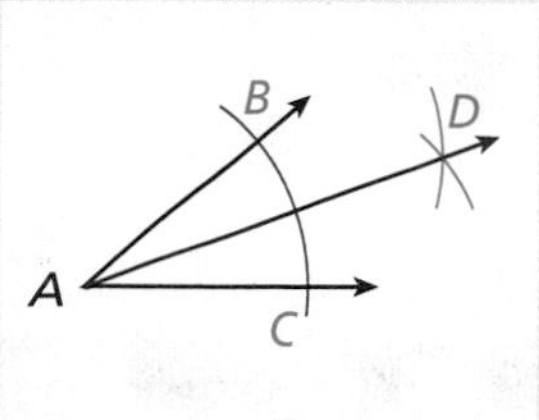

Use a straightedge to draw $\overrightarrow{AD}$.

$\overrightarrow{AD}$ bisects ∠*A*.

EXAMPLE 4 Finding the Measure of an Angle

Algebra

$\overrightarrow{BD}$ bisects $\angle ABC$, $m\angle ABD = (6x + 3)°$, and $m\angle DBC = (8x - 7)°$. Find $m\angle ABD$.

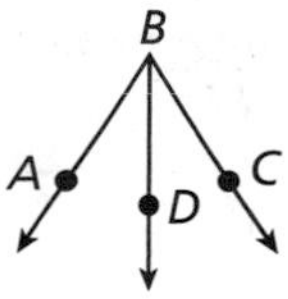

Step 1 Find *x*.

$m\angle ABD = m\angle DBC$	*Def. of ∠ bisector*
$(6x + 3)° = (8x - 7)°$	*Substitute the given values.*
$\underline{\quad +7 \quad} \quad \underline{\quad +7 \quad}$	*Add 7 to both sides.*
$6x + 10 = 8x$	*Simplify.*
$\underline{-6x \quad} \quad \underline{-6x \quad}$	*Subtract 6x from both sides.*
$10 = 2x$	*Simplify.*
$\frac{10}{2} = \frac{2x}{2}$	*Divide both sides by 2.*
$5 = x$	*Simplify.*

Step 2 Find $m\angle ABD$.

$m\angle ABD = 6x + 3$	
$= 6(5) + 3$	*Substitute 5 for x.*
$= 33°$	*Simplify.*

CHECK IT OUT!

Find the measure of each angle.

4a. $\overrightarrow{QS}$ bisects $\angle PQR$, $m\angle PQS = (5y - 1)°$, and $m\angle PQR = (8y + 12)°$. Find $m\angle PQS$.

4b. $\overrightarrow{JK}$ bisects $\angle LJM$, $m\angle LJK = (-10x + 3)°$, and $m\angle KJM = (-x + 21)°$. Find $m\angle LJM$.

MATHEMATICAL PRACTICES

THINK AND DISCUSS

1. Explain why any two right angles are congruent.

2. $\overrightarrow{BD}$ bisects $\angle ABC$. How are $m\angle ABC$, $m\angle ABD$, and $m\angle DBC$ related?

Know it! Note

3. GET ORGANIZED Copy and complete the graphic organizer. In the cells sketch, measure, and name an example of each angle type.

	Diagram	Measure	Name
Acute Angle			
Right Angle			
Obtuse Angle			
Straight Angle			

1-3 Exercises

Learn It Online
Homework Help Online
Parent Resources Online

GUIDED PRACTICE

Vocabulary **Apply the vocabulary from this lesson to answer each question.**

1. $\angle A$ is an acute angle. $\angle O$ is an obtuse angle. $\angle R$ is a right angle. Put $\angle A$, $\angle O$, and $\angle R$ in order from least to greatest by measure.

2. Which point is the vertex of $\angle BCD$? Which rays form the sides of $\angle BCD$?

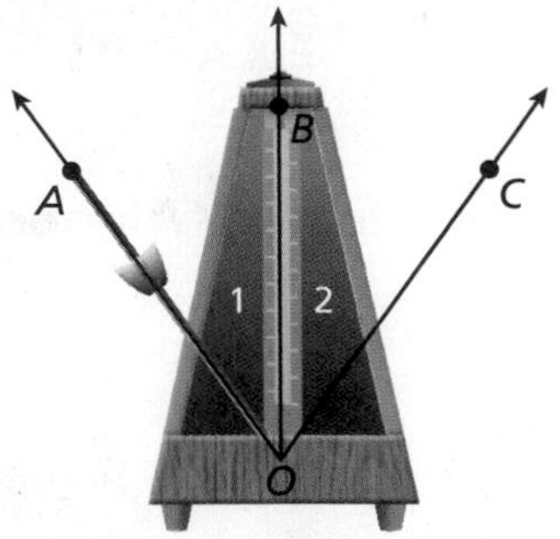

SEE EXAMPLE 1

3. **Music** Musicians use a metronome to keep time as they play. The metronome's needle swings back and forth in a fixed amount of time. Name all of the angles in the diagram.

SEE EXAMPLE 2

Use the protractor to find the measure of each angle. Then classify each as acute, right, or obtuse.

4. $\angle VXW$

5. $\angle TXW$

6. $\angle RXU$

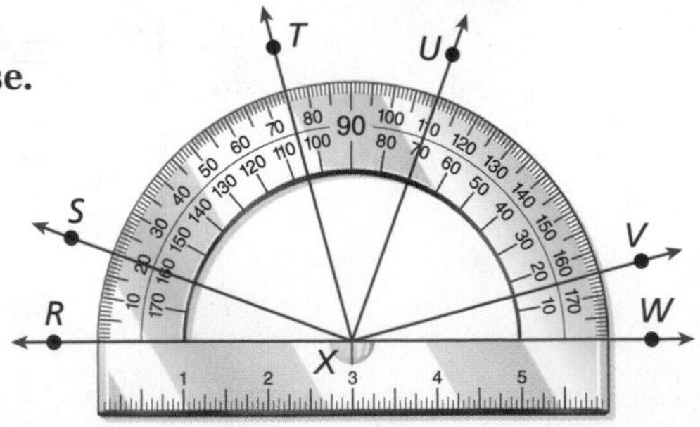

SEE EXAMPLE 3

L is in the interior of $\angle JKM$. Find each of the following.

7. $m\angle JKM$ if $m\angle JKL = 42°$ and $m\angle LKM = 28°$

8. $m\angle LKM$ if $m\angle JKL = 56.4°$ and $m\angle JKM = 82.5°$

SEE EXAMPLE 4

Multi-Step $\overrightarrow{BD}$ **bisects** $\angle ABC$. **Find each of the following.**

9. $m\angle ABD$ if $m\angle ABD = (6x + 4)°$ and $m\angle DBC = (8x - 4)°$

10. $m\angle ABC$ if $m\angle ABD = (5y - 3)°$ and $m\angle DBC = (3y + 15)°$

PRACTICE AND PROBLEM SOLVING

Independent Practice

For Exercises	See Example
11	1
12–14	2
15–16	3
17–18	4

Extra Practice

See Extra Practice for more Skills Practice and Applications Practice exercises.

11. Physics Pendulum clocks have been used since 1656 to keep time. The pendulum swings back and forth once or twice per second. Name all of the angles in the diagram.

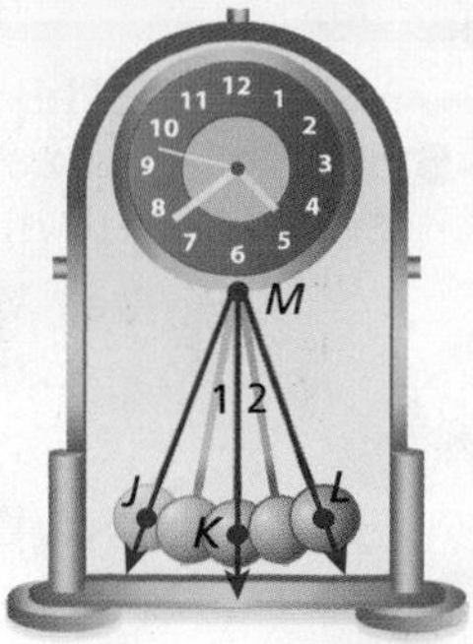

Use the protractor to find the measure of each angle. Then classify each as acute, right, or obtuse.

12. $\angle CGE$ **13.** $\angle BGD$ **14.** $\angle AGB$

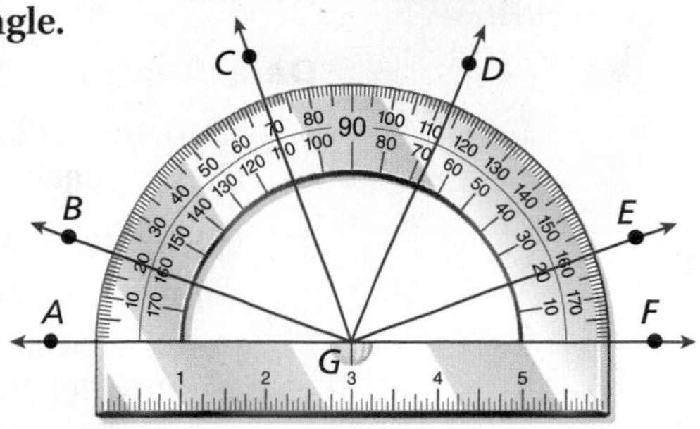

***T* is in the interior of $\angle RSU$. Find each of the following.**

15. $m\angle RSU$ if $m\angle RST = 38°$ and $m\angle TSU = 28.6°$

16. $m\angle RST$ if $m\angle TSU = 46.7°$ and $m\angle RSU = 83.5°$

Multi-Step $\overrightarrow{SP}$ **bisects $\angle RST$. Find each of the following.**

17. $m\angle RST$ if $m\angle RSP = (3x - 2)°$ and $m\angle PST = (9x - 26)°$

18. $m\angle RSP$ if $m\angle RST = \frac{5}{2}y°$ and $m\angle PST = (y + 5)°$

Estimation **Use the following information for Exercises 19–22.**

Assume the corner of a sheet of paper is a right angle. Use the corner to estimate the measure and classify each angle in the diagram.

19. $\angle BOA$ **20.** $\angle COA$

21. $\angle EOD$ **22.** $\angle EOB$

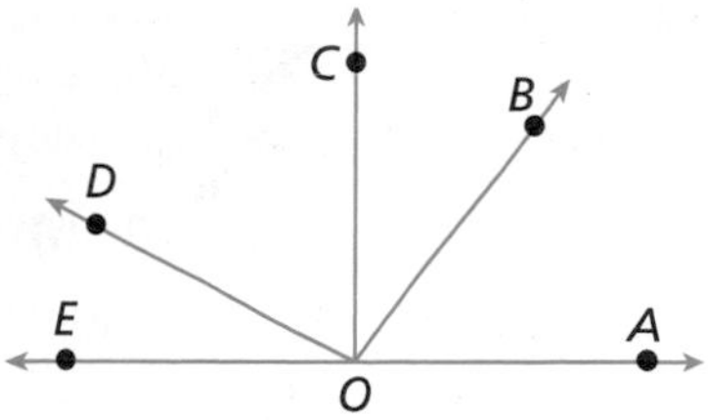

Use a protractor to draw an angle with each of the following measures.

23. 33° **24.** 142° **25.** 90° **26.** 168°

27. Surveying A surveyor at point *S* discovers that the angle between peaks *A* and *B* is 3 times as large as the angle between peaks *B* and *C*. The surveyor knows that $\angle ASC$ is a right angle. Find $m\angle ASB$ and $m\angle BSC$.

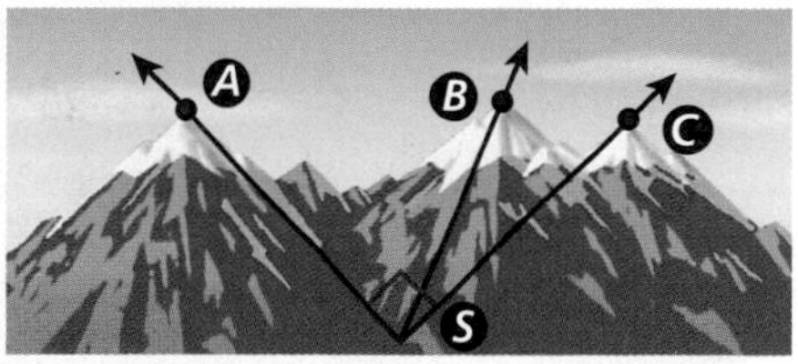

28. Math History As far back as the 5th century B.C., mathematicians have been fascinated by the problem of trisecting an angle. It is possible to construct an angle with $\frac{1}{4}$ the measure of a given angle. Explain how to do this.

Find the value of *x*.

29. $m\angle AOC = 7x - 2$, $m\angle DOC = 2x + 8$, $m\angle EOD = 27$

30. $m\angle AOB = 4x - 2$, $m\angle BOC = 5x + 10$, $m\angle COD = 3x - 8$

31. $m\angle AOB = 6x + 5$, $m\angle BOC = 4x - 2$, $m\angle AOC = 8x + 21$

32. Multi-Step *Q* is in the interior of right $\angle PRS$. If $m\angle PRQ$ is 4 times as large as $m\angle QRS$, what is $m\angle PRQ$?

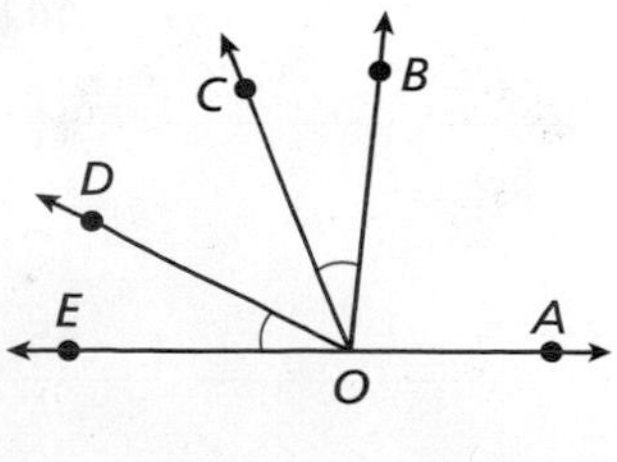

MULTI-STEP TEST PREP

33. This problem will prepare you for the Multi-Step Test Prep. An archaeologist standing at O looks for clues on where to dig for artifacts.

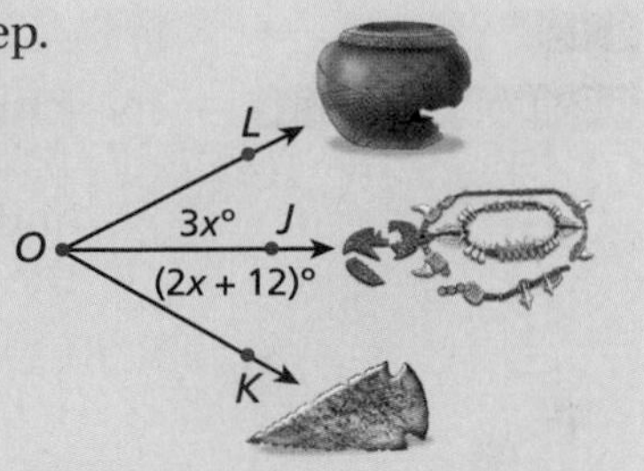

a. What value of x will make the angle between the pottery and the arrowhead measure 57°?

b. What value of x makes $\angle LOJ \cong \angle JOK$?

c. What values of x make $\angle LOK$ an acute angle?

Data Analysis Use the circle graph for Exercises 34–36.

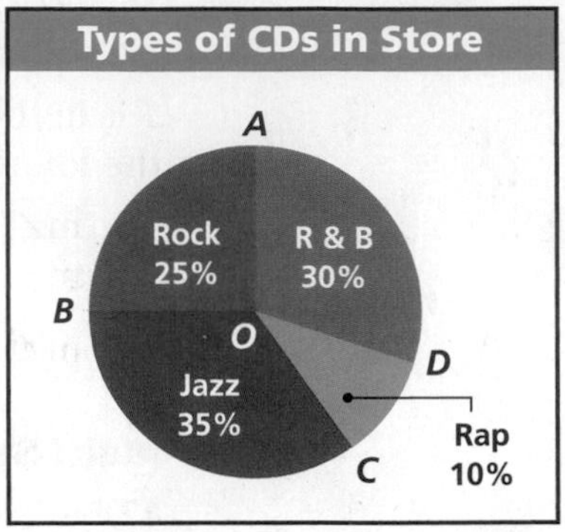

34. Find $m\angle AOB$, $m\angle BOC$, $m\angle COD$, and $m\angle DOA$. Classify each angle as acute, right, or obtuse.

35. What if...? Next year, the music store will use some of the shelves currently holding jazz music to double the space for rap. What will $m\angle COD$ and $m\angle BOC$ be next year?

36. Suppose a fifth type of music, salsa, is added. If the space is divided equally among the five types, what will be the angle measure for each type of music in the circle graph?

37. Critical Thinking Can an obtuse angle be congruent to an acute angle? Why or why not?

38. The measure of an obtuse angle is $(5x + 45)°$. What is the largest value for x?

39. Write About It $\overrightarrow{FH}$ bisects $\angle EFG$. Use the Angle Addition Postulate to explain why $m\angle EFH = \frac{1}{2}m\angle EFG$.

40. Multi-Step Use a protractor to draw a 70° angle. Then use a compass and straightedge to bisect the angle. What do you think will be the measure of each angle formed? Use a protractor to support your answer.

TEST PREP

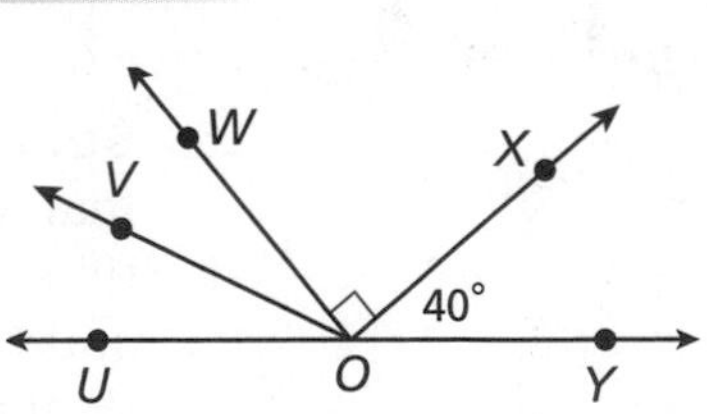

41. $m\angle UOW = 50°$, and $\overrightarrow{OV}$ bisects $\angle UOW$. What is $m\angle VOY$?

Ⓐ 25° Ⓒ 130°

Ⓑ 65° Ⓓ 155°

42. What is $m\angle UOX$?

Ⓕ 50° Ⓖ 115° Ⓗ 140° Ⓙ 165°

43. $\overrightarrow{BD}$ bisects $\angle ABC$, $m\angle ABC = (4x + 5)°$, and $m\angle ABD = (3x - 1)°$. What is the value of x?

Ⓐ 2.2 Ⓑ 3 Ⓒ 3.5 Ⓓ 7

44. If an angle is bisected and then 30° is added to the measure of the bisected angle, the result is the measure of a right angle. What is the measure of the original angle?

Ⓕ 30° Ⓖ 60° Ⓗ 75° Ⓙ 120°

45. Short Response If an obtuse angle is bisected, are the resulting angles acute or obtuse? Explain.

CHALLENGE AND EXTEND

46. Find the measure of the angle formed by the hands of a clock when it is 7:00.

47. $\overrightarrow{QS}$ bisects $\angle PQR$, $m\angle PQR = (x^2)°$, and $m\angle PQS = (2x + 6)°$. Find all the possible measures for $\angle PQR$.

48. For more precise measurements, a degree can be divided into 60 minutes, and each minute can be divided into 60 seconds. An angle measure of 42 degrees, 30 minutes, and 10 seconds is written as 42°30′10″. Subtract this angle measure from the measure 81°24′15″.

49. If 1 degree equals 60 minutes and 1 minute equals 60 seconds, how many seconds are in 2.25 degrees?

50. $\angle ABC \cong \angle DBC$. $m\angle ABC = \left(\frac{3x}{2} + 4\right)°$ and $m\angle DBC = \left(2x - 27\frac{1}{4}\right)°$. Is $\angle ABD$ a straight angle? Explain.

Using Technology Segment and Angle Bisectors

1. Construct the bisector of $\overline{MN}$.

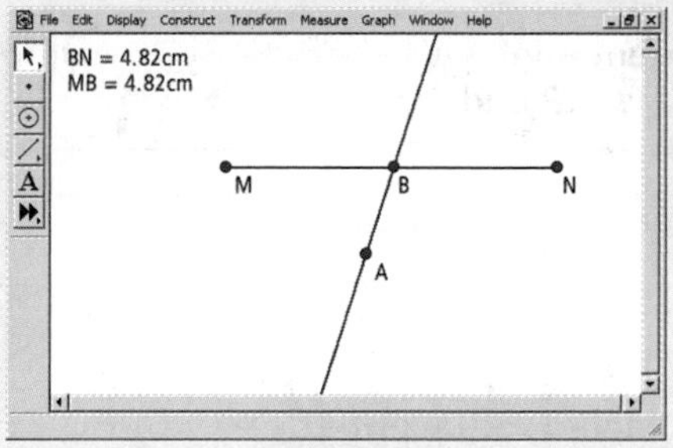

a. Draw $\overline{MN}$ and construct the midpoint B.

b. Construct a point A not on the segment.

c. Construct bisector $\overleftrightarrow{AB}$ and measure $\overline{MB}$ and $\overline{NB}$.

d. Drag M and N and observe MB and NB.

2. Construct the bisector of $\angle BAC$.

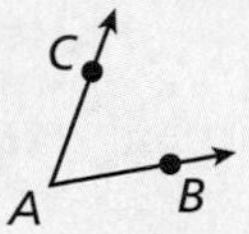

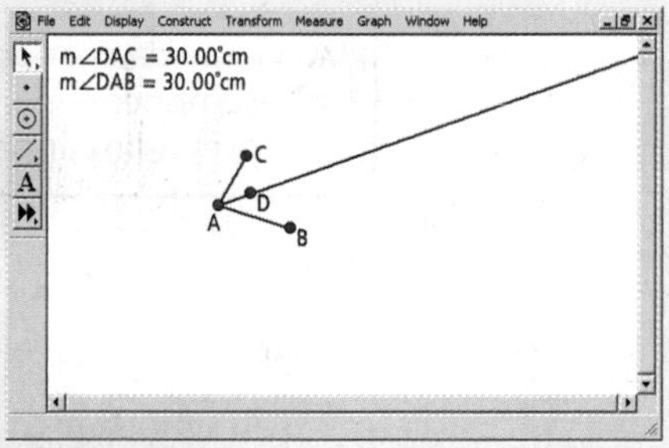

a. Draw $\angle BAC$.

b. Construct the angle bisector $\overrightarrow{AD}$ and measure $\angle DAC$ and $\angle DAB$.

c. Drag the angle and observe $m\angle DAB$ and $m\angle DAC$.

COMMON CORE

1-4 Pairs of Angles

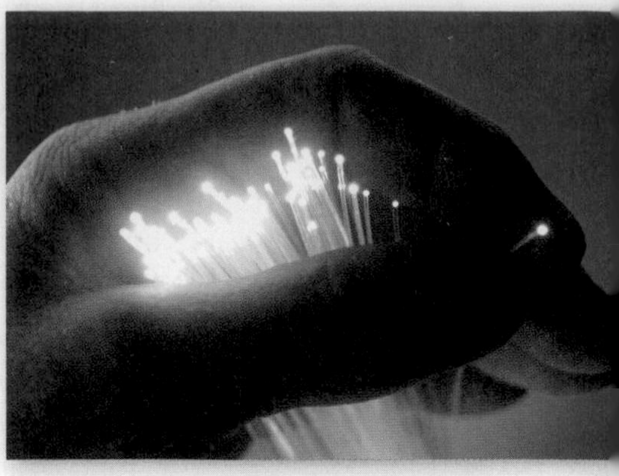

CC.9-12.G.CO.1 Know precise definitions…based on the undefined notions of point, line,…

Objectives
Identify adjacent, vertical, complementary, and supplementary angles.

Find measures of pairs of angles.

Vocabulary
adjacent angles
linear pair
complementary angles
supplementary angles
vertical angles

Who uses this?
Scientists use properties of angle pairs to design fiber-optic cables. (See Example 4.)

A fiber-optic cable is a strand of glass as thin as a human hair. Data can be transmitted over long distances by bouncing light off the inner walls of the cable.

Many pairs of angles have special relationships. Some relationships are because of the measurements of the angles in the pair. Other relationships are because of the positions of the angles in the pair.

Know it! Note

Pairs of Angles

Adjacent angles are two angles in the same plane with a common vertex and a common side, but no common interior points. ∠1 and ∠2 are adjacent angles.

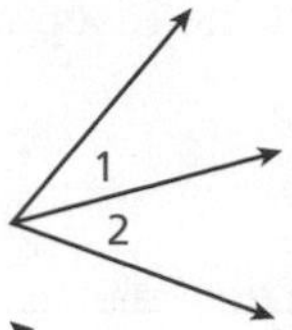

A **linear pair** of angles is a pair of adjacent angles whose noncommon sides are opposite rays. ∠3 and ∠4 form a linear pair.

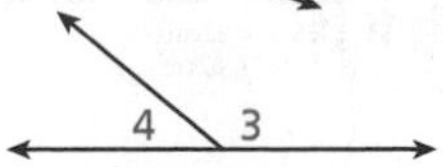

EXAMPLE 1 Identifying Angle Pairs

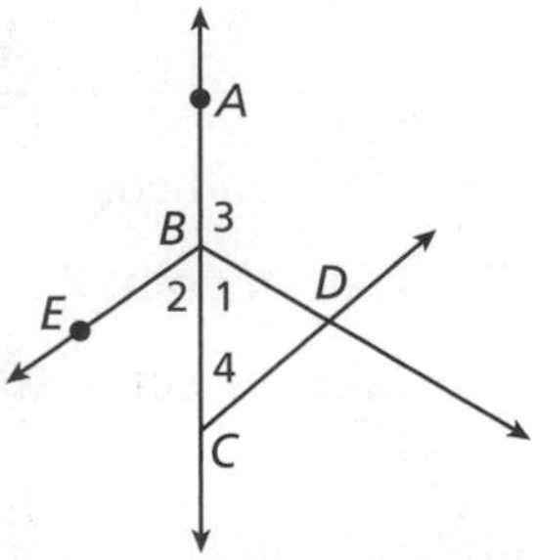

Tell whether the angles are only adjacent, adjacent and form a linear pair, or not adjacent.

A **∠1 and ∠2**

∠1 and ∠2 have a common vertex, *B*, a common side, $\overrightarrow{BC}$, and no common interior points. Therefore ∠1 and ∠2 are only adjacent angles.

B **∠2 and ∠4**

∠2 and ∠4 share $\overline{BC}$ but do not have a common vertex, so ∠2 and ∠4 are not adjacent angles.

C **∠1 and ∠3**

∠1 and ∠3 are adjacent angles. Their noncommon sides, $\overrightarrow{BC}$ and $\overrightarrow{BA}$, are opposite rays, so ∠1 and ∠3 also form a linear pair.

CHECK IT OUT!

Tell whether the angles are only adjacent, adjacent and form a linear pair, or not adjacent.

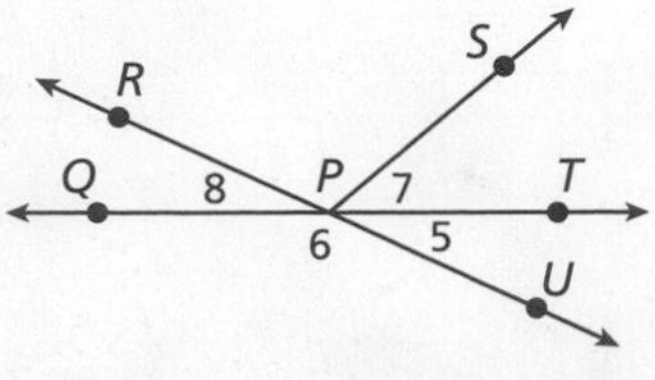

1a. ∠5 and ∠6

1b. ∠7 and ∠*SPU*

1c. ∠7 and ∠8

Know it! Note — Complementary and Supplementary Angles

Complementary angles are two angles whose measures have a sum of 90°.
$\angle A$ and $\angle B$ are complementary.

Supplementary angles are two angles whose measures have a sum of 180°.
$\angle A$ and $\angle C$ are supplementary.

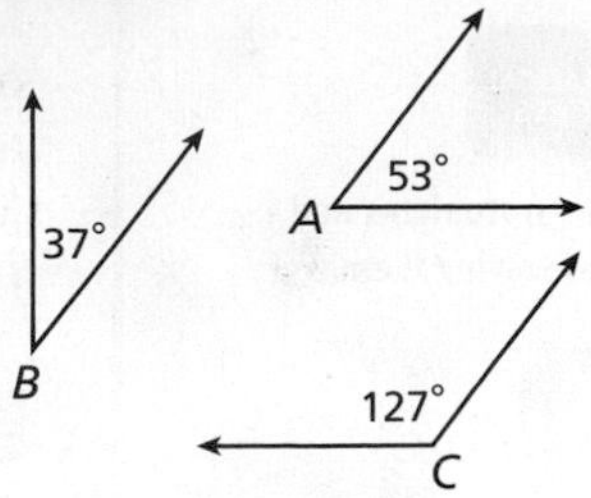

You can find the complement of an angle that measures $x°$ by subtracting its measure from 90°, or $(90 - x)°$. You can find the supplement of an angle that measures $x°$ by subtracting its measure from 180°, or $(180 - x)°$.

EXAMPLE 2 Finding the Measures of Complements and Supplements

Find the measure of each of the following.

A complement of $\angle M$

$(90 - x)°$

$90° - 26.8° = 63.2°$

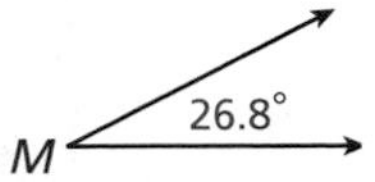

B supplement of $\angle N$

$(180 - x)°$

$180° - (2y + 20)° = 180° - 2y - 20$

$= (160 - 2y)°$

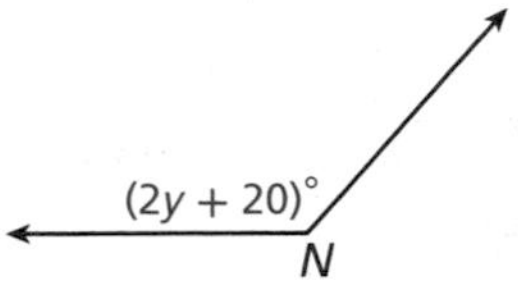

CHECK IT OUT! **Find the measure of each of the following.**

2a. complement of $\angle E$

2b. supplement of $\angle F$

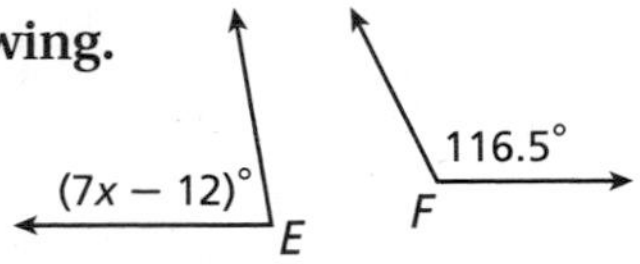

EXAMPLE 3 Using Complements and Supplements to Solve Problems

Algebra

An angle measures 3 degrees less than twice the measure of its complement. Find the measure of its complement.

Step 1 Let $m\angle A = x°$. Then $\angle B$, its complement, measures $(90 - x)°$.

Step 2 Write and solve an equation.

$m\angle A = 2m\angle B - 3$

$x = 2(90 - x) - 3$	*Substitute x for m∠A and 90 − x for m∠B.*
$x = 180 - 2x - 3$	*Distrib. Prop.*
$x = 177 - 2x$	*Combine like terms.*
$+2x \quad\quad +2x$	*Add 2x to both sides.*
$3x = 177$	*Simplify.*
$\frac{3x}{3} = \frac{177}{3}$	*Divide both sides by 3.*
$x = 59$	*Simplify.*

The measure of the complement, $\angle B$, is $(90 - 59)° = 31°$.

CHECK IT OUT! **3.** An angle's measure is 12° more than $\frac{1}{2}$ the measure of its supplement. Find the measure of the angle.

EXAMPLE 4 Problem-Solving Application

MATHEMATICAL PRACTICES

Make sense of problems and persevere in solving them.

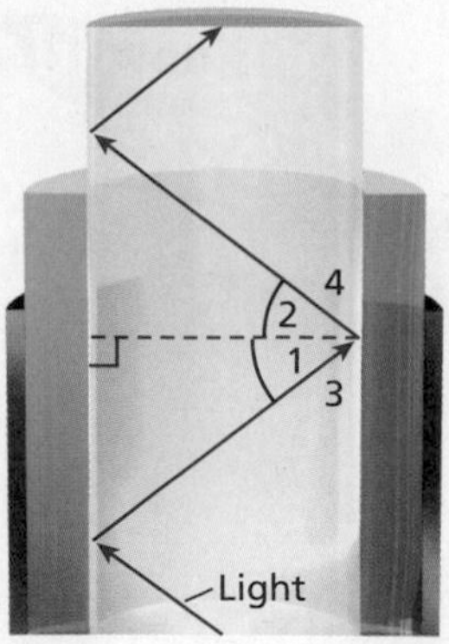

Light passing through a fiber optic cable reflects off the walls in such a way that ∠1 ≅ ∠2. ∠1 and ∠3 are complementary, and ∠2 and ∠4 are complementary.
If m∠1 = 38°, find m∠2, m∠3, and m∠4.

1 Understand the Problem

The **answers** are the measures of ∠2, ∠3, and ∠4.

List the important information:

- ∠1 ≅ ∠2
- ∠1 and ∠3 are complementary, and ∠2 and ∠4 are complementary.
- m∠1 = 38°

2 Make a Plan

If ∠1 ≅ ∠2, then m∠1 = m∠2.
If ∠3 and ∠1 are complementary, then m∠3 = (90 − 38)°.
If ∠4 and ∠2 are complementary, then m∠4 = (90 − 38)°.

3 Solve

By the Transitive Property of Equality, if m∠1 = 38° and m∠1 = m∠2, then m∠2 = 38°. Since ∠3 and ∠1 are complementary, m∠3 = 52°. Similarly, since ∠2 and ∠4 are complementary, m∠4 = 52°.

4 Look Back

The answer makes sense because 38° + 52° = 90°, so ∠1 and ∠3 are complementary, and ∠2 and ∠4 are complementary. Thus m∠2 = 38°, m∠3 = 52°, and m∠4 = 52°.

CHECK IT OUT! **4. What if...?** Suppose m∠3 = 27.6°. Find m∠1, m∠2, and m∠4.

Another angle pair relationship exists between two angles whose sides form two pairs of opposite rays. **Vertical angles** are two nonadjacent angles formed by two intersecting lines. ∠1 and ∠3 are vertical angles, as are ∠2 and ∠4.

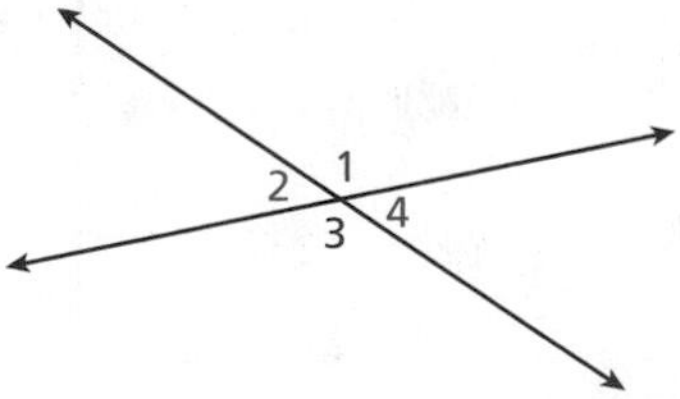

EXAMPLE 5 Identifying Vertical Angles

Name one pair of vertical angles.
Do they appear to have the same measure?
Check by measuring with a protractor.

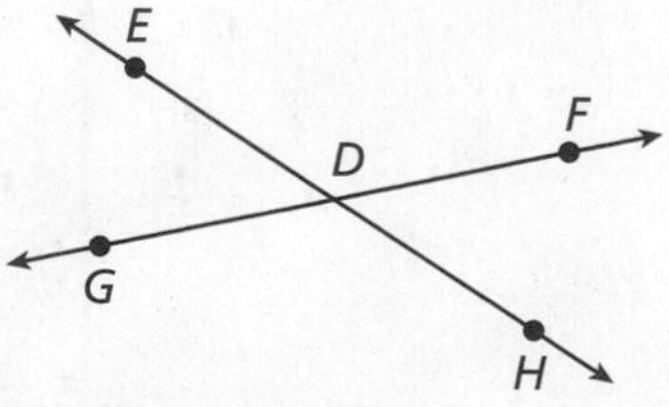

∠EDF and *∠GDH* are vertical angles and appear to have the same measure.

Check m∠*EDF* ≈ m∠*GDH* ≈ *135°.*

CHECK IT OUT! **5.** Name another pair of vertical angles. Do they appear to have the same measure? Check by measuring with a protractor.

THINK AND DISCUSS

1. Explain why any two right angles are supplementary.
2. Is it possible for a pair of vertical angles to also be adjacent? Explain.
3. **GET ORGANIZED** Copy and complete the graphic organizer below. In each box, draw a diagram and write a definition of the given angle pair.

Know it! Note

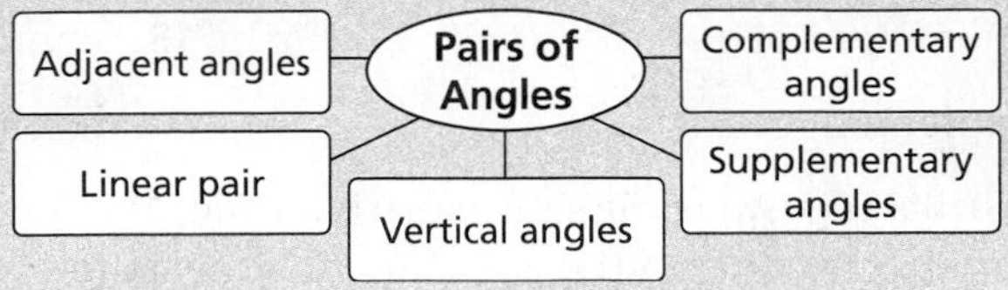

1-4 Exercises

GUIDED PRACTICE

Vocabulary **Apply the vocabulary from this lesson to answer each question.**

1. An angle measures $x°$. What is the measure of its *complement*? What is the measure of its *supplement*?
2. $\angle ABC$ and $\angle CBD$ are *adjacent angles*. Which side do the angles have in common?

SEE EXAMPLE 1

Tell whether the angles are only adjacent, adjacent and form a linear pair, or not adjacent.

3. $\angle 1$ and $\angle 2$
4. $\angle 1$ and $\angle 3$
5. $\angle 2$ and $\angle 4$
6. $\angle 2$ and $\angle 3$

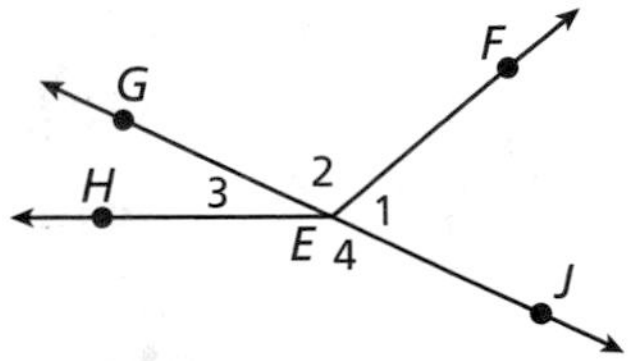

SEE EXAMPLE 2

Find the measure of each of the following.

7. supplement of $\angle A$
8. complement of $\angle A$
9. supplement of $\angle B$
10. complement of $\angle B$

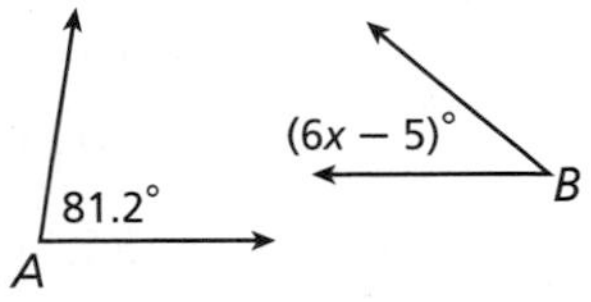

SEE EXAMPLE 3

11. **Multi-Step** An angle's measure is 6 degrees more than 3 times the measure of its complement. Find the measure of the angle.

SEE EXAMPLE 4

12. **Landscaping** A sprinkler swings back and forth between A and B in such a way that $\angle 1 \cong \angle 2$. $\angle 1$ and $\angle 3$ are complementary, and $\angle 2$ and $\angle 4$ are complementary. If $m\angle 1 = 47.5°$, find $m\angle 2$, $m\angle 3$, and $m\angle 4$.

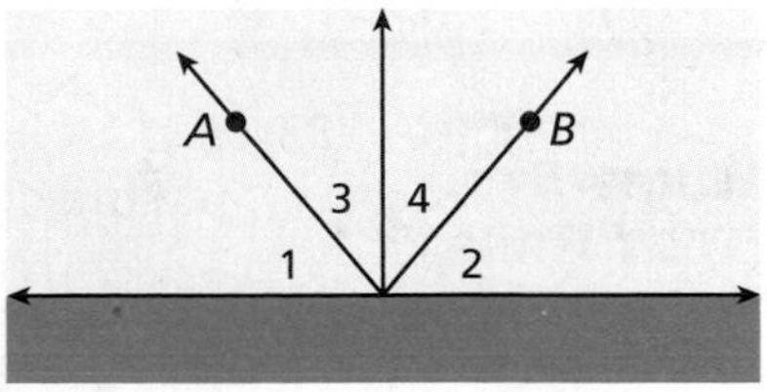

SEE EXAMPLE 5

13. Name each pair of vertical angles.

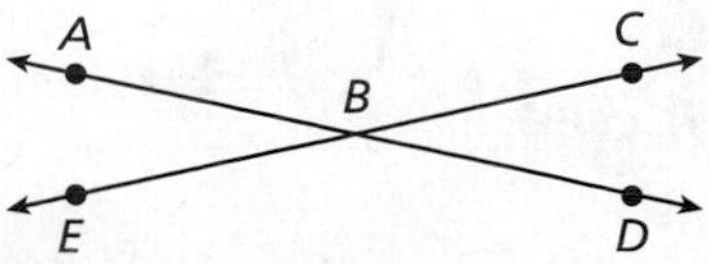

PRACTICE AND PROBLEM SOLVING

Independent Practice

For Exercises	See Example
14–17	1
18–21	2
22	3
23	4
24	5

Extra Practice

See Extra Practice for more Skills Practice and Applications Practice exercises.

Tell whether the angles are only adjacent, adjacent and form a linear pair, or not adjacent.

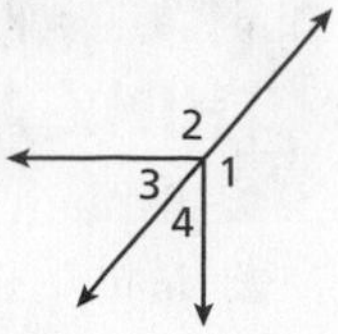

14. $\angle 1$ and $\angle 4$
15. $\angle 2$ and $\angle 3$
16. $\angle 3$ and $\angle 4$
17. $\angle 3$ and $\angle 1$

Given $m\angle A = 56.4°$ and $m\angle B = (2x - 4)°$, find the measure of each of the following.

18. supplement of $\angle A$
19. complement of $\angle A$
20. supplement of $\angle B$
21. complement of $\angle B$
22. **Multi-Step** An angle's measure is 3 times the measure of its complement. Find the measure of the angle and the measure of its complement.
23. **Art** In the stained glass pattern, $\angle 1 \cong \angle 2$. $\angle 1$ and $\angle 3$ are complementary, and $\angle 2$ and $\angle 4$ are complementary. If $m\angle 1 = 22.3°$, find $m\angle 2$, $m\angle 3$, and $m\angle 4$.

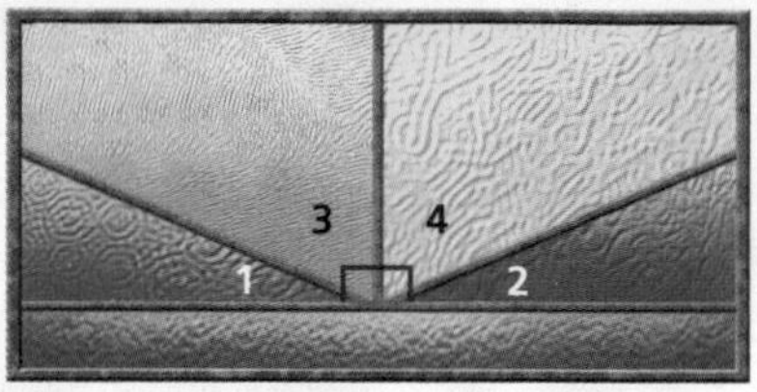

24. Name the pairs of vertical angles.

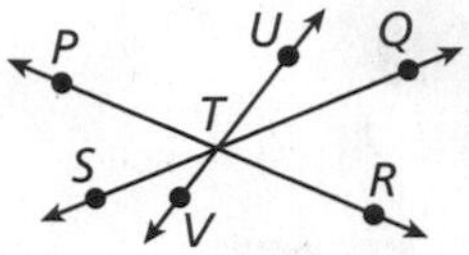

25. **Probability** The angle measures 30°, 60°, 120°, and 150° are written on slips of paper. You choose two slips of paper at random. What is the probability that the angle measures are supplementary?

Multi-Step **$\angle ABD$ and $\angle BDE$ are supplementary. Find the measures of both angles.**

26. $m\angle ABD = 5x°$, $m\angle BDE = (17x - 18)°$
27. $m\angle ABD = (3x + 12)°$, $m\angle BDE = (7x - 32)°$
28. $m\angle ABD = (12x - 12)°$, $m\angle BDE = (3x + 48)°$

Multi-Step **$\angle ABD$ and $\angle BDC$ are complementary. Find the measures of both angles.**

29. $m\angle ABD = (5y + 1)°$, $m\angle BDC = (3y - 7)°$
30. $m\angle ABD = (4y + 5)°$, $m\angle BDC = (4y + 8)°$
31. $m\angle ABD = (y - 30)°$, $m\angle BDC = 2y°$
32. **Critical Thinking** Explain why an angle that is supplementary to an acute angle must be an obtuse angle.

MULTI-STEP TEST PREP

33. H is in the interior of $\angle JAK$. $m\angle JAH = (3x - 8)°$, and $m\angle KAH = (x + 2)°$. Draw a picture of each relationship. Then find the measure of each angle.
    a. $\angle JAH$ and $\angle KAH$ are complementary angles.
    b. $\angle JAH$ and $\angle KAH$ form a linear pair.
    c. $\angle JAH$ and $\angle KAH$ are congruent angles.

Determine whether each statement is true or false. If false, explain why.

34. If an angle is acute, then its complement must be greater than its supplement.

35. A pair of vertical angles may also form a linear pair.

36. If two angles are supplementary and congruent, the measure of each angle is 90°.

37. If a ray divides an angle into two complementary angles, then the original angle is a right angle.

38. Write About It Describe a situation in which two angles are both congruent and complementary. Explain.

TEST PREP

39. What is the value of x in the diagram?

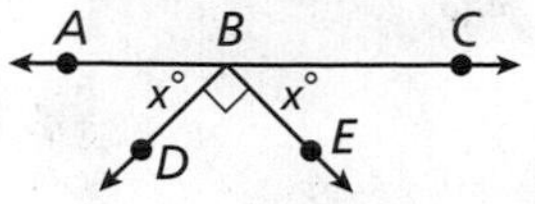

Ⓐ 15 Ⓑ 30 Ⓒ 45 Ⓓ 90

40. The ratio of the measures of two complementary angles is 1:2. What is the measure of the larger angle? (*Hint:* Let x and $2x$ represent the angle measures.)

Ⓕ 30° Ⓖ 45° Ⓗ 60° Ⓙ 120°

41. $m\angle A = 3y$, and $m\angle B = 2m\angle A$. Which value of y makes $\angle A$ supplementary to $\angle B$?

Ⓐ 10 Ⓑ 18 Ⓒ 20 Ⓓ 36

42. The measures of two supplementary angles are in the ratio 7:5. Which value is the measure of the smaller angle? (*Hint:* Let $7x$ and $5x$ represent the angle measures.)

Ⓕ 37.5 Ⓖ 52.5 Ⓗ 75 Ⓙ 105

CHALLENGE AND EXTEND

43. How many pairs of vertical angles are in the diagram?

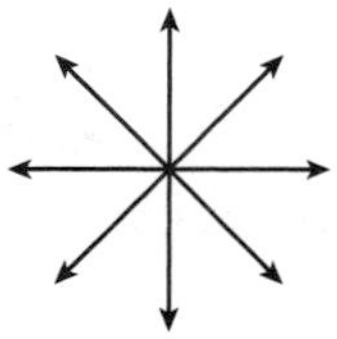

44. The supplement of an angle is 4 more than twice its complement. Find the measure of the angle.

45. An angle's measure is twice the measure of its complement. The larger angle is how many degrees greater than the smaller angle?

46. The supplement of an angle is 36° less than twice the supplement of the complement of the angle. Find the measure of the supplement.

MULTI-STEP TEST PREP

MATHEMATICAL PRACTICES **Reason abstractly and quantitatively.**

Euclidean and Construction Tools

Can You Dig It? A group of college and high school students participated in an archaeological dig. The team discovered four fossils. To organize their search, Sierra used a protractor and ruler to make a diagram of where different members of the group found fossils. She drew the locations based on the location of the campsite. The campsite is located at *X* on $\overleftrightarrow{XB}$. The four fossils were found at *R, T, W,* and *M.*

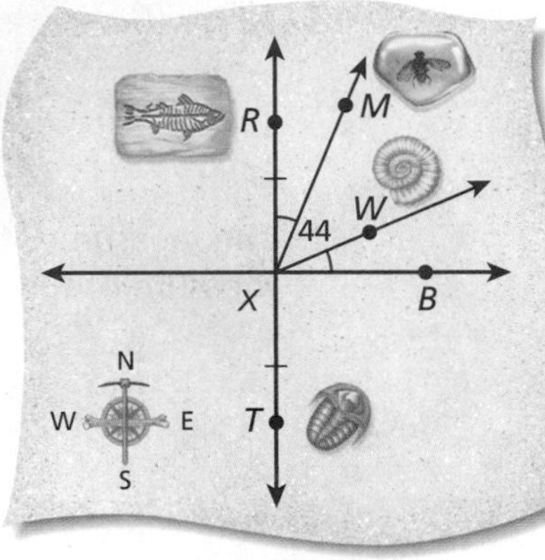

1. Are the locations of the campsite at *X* and the fossils at *R* and *T* collinear or noncollinear?
2. How is *X* related to $\overline{RT}$? If $RX = 10x - 6$ and $XT = 3x + 8$, what is the distance between the locations of the fossils at *R* and *T*?
3. $\angle RXB$ and $\angle BXT$ are right angles. Find the measure of each angle formed by the locations of the fossils and the campsite. Then classify each angle by its measure.
4. Identify the special angle pairs shown in the diagram of the archaeological dig.

READY TO GO ON?

Quiz for Lessons 1-1 Through 1-4

1-1 Understanding Points, Lines, and Planes

Draw and label each of the following.

1. a segment with endpoints *X* and *Y*
2. a ray with endpoint *M* that passes through *P*
3. three coplanar lines intersecting at a point
4. two points and a line that lie in a plane

Use the figure to name each of the following.

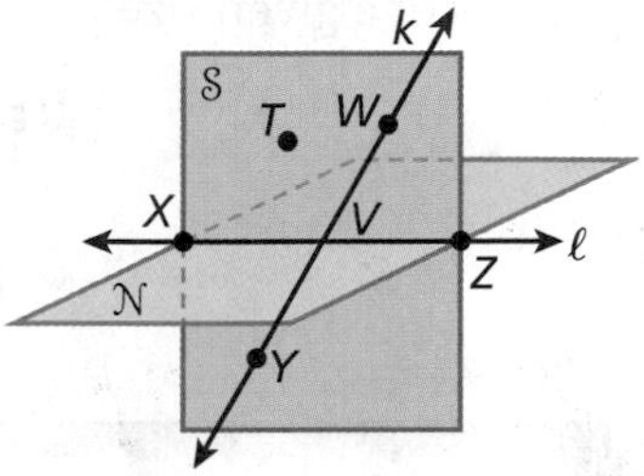

5. three coplanar points
6. two lines
7. a plane containing *T*, *V*, and *X*
8. a line containing *V* and *Z*

1-2 Measuring and Constructing Segments

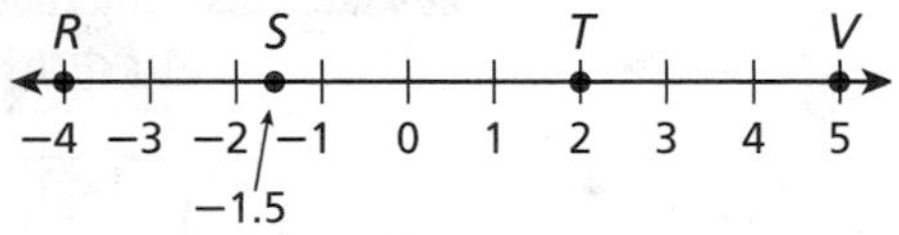

Find the length of each segment.

9. $\overline{SV}$ 10. $\overline{TR}$ 11. $\overline{ST}$

12. The diagram represents a straight highway with three towns, Henri, Joaquin, and Kenard. Find the distance from Henri *H* to Joaquin *J*.

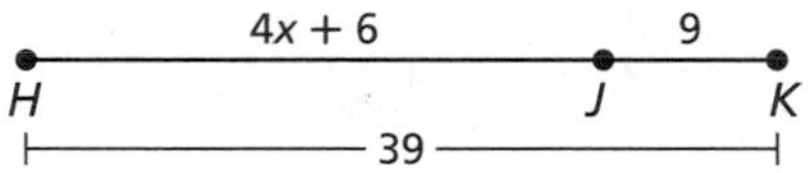

13. Sketch, draw, and construct a segment congruent to $\overline{CD}$.

14. *Q* is the midpoint of $\overline{PR}$, $PQ = 2z$, and $PR = 8z - 12$. Find *z*, *PQ*, and *PR*.

1-3 Measuring and Constructing Angles

15. Name all the angles in the diagram.

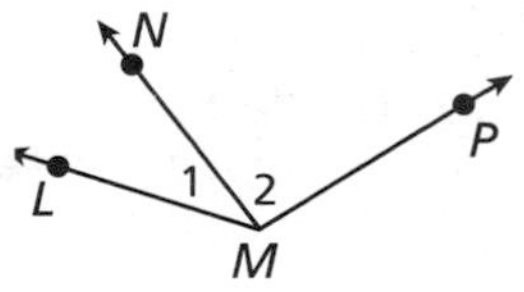

Classify each angle by its measure.

16. $m\angle PVQ = 21°$ 17. $m\angle RVT = 96°$ 18. $m\angle PVS = 143°$
19. $\overrightarrow{RS}$ bisects $\angle QRT$, $m\angle QRS = (3x + 8)°$, and $m\angle SRT = (9x - 4)°$. Find $m\angle SRT$.
20. Use a protractor and straightedge to draw a 130° angle. Then bisect the angle.

1-4 Pairs of Angles

Tell whether the angles are only adjacent, adjacent and form a linear pair, or not adjacent.

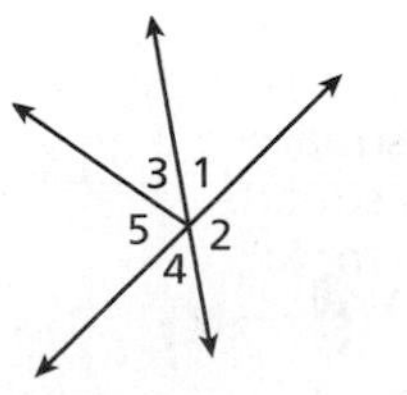

21. $\angle 1$ and $\angle 2$ 22. $\angle 4$ and $\angle 5$ 23. $\angle 3$ and $\angle 4$

If $m\angle T = (5x - 10)°$, find the measure of each of the following.

24. supplement of $\angle T$ 25. complement of $\angle T$

COMMON CORE

1-5 Using Formulas in Geometry

CC.9-12.A.SSE.1 Interpret expressions that represent a quantity in terms of its context.* *Also* **CC.9-12.A.CED.4***

Objective
Apply formulas for perimeter, area, and circumference.

Vocabulary
perimeter
area
base
height
diameter
radius
circumference
pi

Why learn this?
Puzzles use geometric-shaped pieces. Formulas help determine the amount of materials needed. (See Exercise 6.)

The **perimeter** P of a plane figure is the sum of the side lengths of the figure. The **area** A of a plane figure is the number of nonoverlapping square units of a given size that exactly cover the figure.

area = 2 units × 5 units

= 10 square units

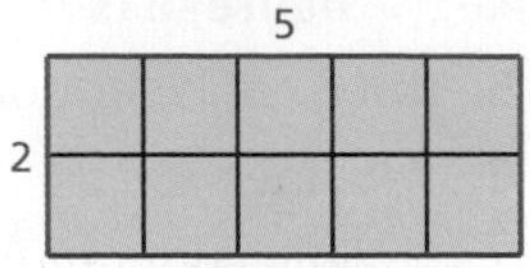

Know it! Note

Perimeter and Area

RECTANGLE	SQUARE	TRIANGLE
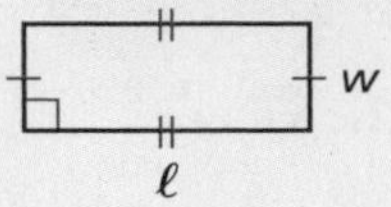	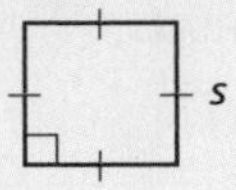	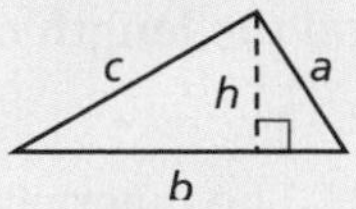
$P = 2\ell + 2w$ or $2(\ell + w)$ $A = \ell w$	$P = 4s$ $A = s^2$	$P = a + b + c$ $A = \frac{1}{2}bh$ or $\frac{bh}{2}$

The **base** b can be any side of a triangle. The **height** h is a segment from a vertex that forms a right angle with a line containing the base. The height may be a side of the triangle or in the interior or the exterior of the triangle.

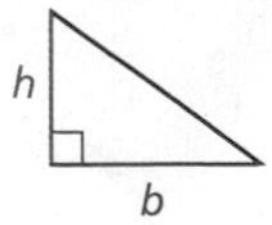

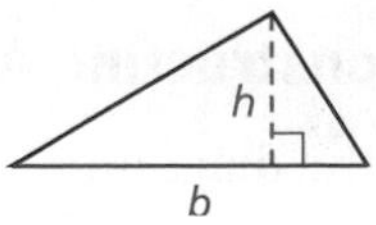

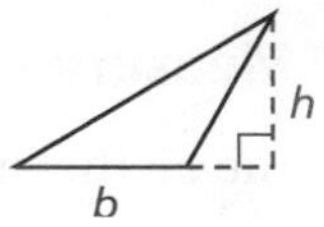

EXAMPLE 1 Finding Perimeter and Area

Find the perimeter and area of each figure.

A rectangle in which $\ell = 17$ cm and $w = 5$ cm

$P = 2\ell + 2w$
$= 2(17) + 2(5)$
$= 34 + 10 = 44$ cm

$A = \ell w$
$= (17)(5) = 85 \text{ cm}^2$

B triangle in which $a = 8$, $b = (x + 1)$, $c = 4x$, and $h = 6$

$P = a + b + c$
$= 8 + (x + 1) + 4x$
$= 5x + 9$

$A = \frac{1}{2}bh$
$= \frac{1}{2}(x + 1)(6) = 3x + 3$

Remember!
Perimeter is expressed in linear units, such as inches (in.) or meters (m). Area is expressed in square units, such as square centimeters (cm^2).

CHECK IT OUT! **1.** Find the perimeter and area of a square with $s = 3.5$ in.

EXAMPLE 2 Crafts Application

The Texas Treasures quilt block includes 24 purple triangles. The base and height of each triangle are about 3 in. Find the approximate amount of fabric used to make the 24 triangles.

The area of one triangle is

$$A = \frac{1}{2}bh = \frac{1}{2}(3)(3) = 4\frac{1}{2} \text{ in}^2.$$

The total area of the 24 triangles is

$$24\left(4\frac{1}{2}\right) = 108 \text{ in}^2.$$

CHECK IT OUT! 2. Find the amount of fabric used to make the four rectangles. Each rectangle has a length of $6\frac{1}{2}$ in. and a width of $2\frac{1}{2}$ in.

In a circle a **diameter** is a segment that passes through the center of the circle and whose endpoints are on the circle. A **radius** of a circle is a segment whose endpoints are the center of the circle and a point on the circle. The **circumference** of a circle is the distance around the circle.

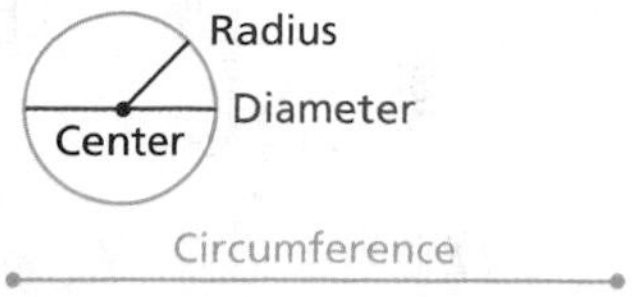

Know it! Note

Circumference and Area of a Circle

The circumference C of a circle is given by the formula $C = \pi d$ or $C = 2\pi r$.

The area A of a circle is given by the formula $A = \pi r^2$.

The ratio of a circle's circumference to its diameter is the same for all circles. This ratio is represented by the Greek letter **π (pi)**. The value of π is irrational. Pi is often approximated as 3.14 or $\frac{22}{7}$.

EXAMPLE 3 Finding the Circumference and Area of a Circle

Find the circumference and area of the circle.

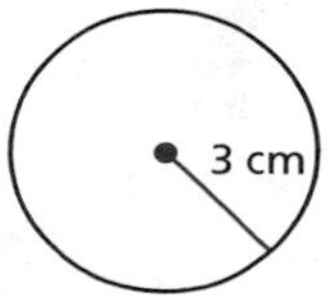

$$\begin{aligned} C &= 2\pi r \\ &= 2\pi(3) = 6\pi \\ &\approx 18.8 \text{ cm} \end{aligned}$$

$$\begin{aligned} A &= \pi r^2 \\ &= \pi(3)^2 = 9\pi \\ &\approx 28.3 \text{ cm}^2 \end{aligned}$$

CHECK IT OUT! 3. Find the circumference and area of a circle with radius 14 m.

MATHEMATICAL PRACTICES

THINK AND DISCUSS

1. Describe three different figures whose areas are each 16 in^2.

Know it! Note

2. **GET ORGANIZED** Copy and complete the graphic organizer. In each shape, write the formula for its area and perimeter.

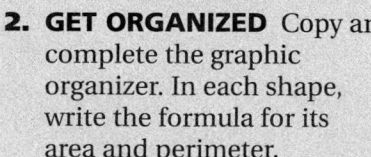

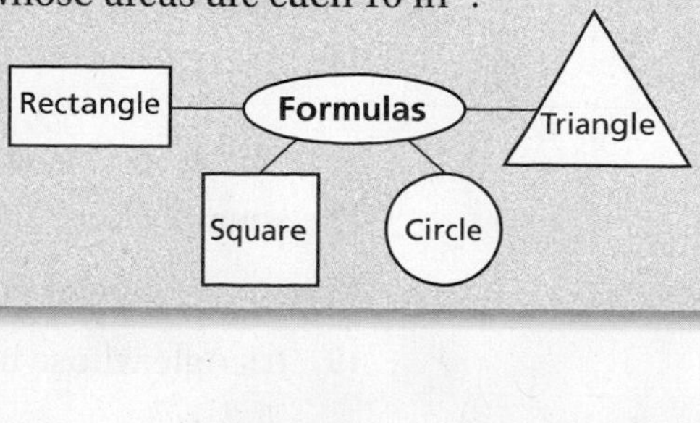

1-5 Exercises

Learn It Online
Homework Help Online
Parent Resources Online

GUIDED PRACTICE

Vocabulary **Apply the vocabulary from this lesson to answer each question.**

1. Explain how the concepts of *perimeter* and *circumference* are related.
2. For a rectangle, length and width are sometimes used in place of __?__. (*base and height* or *radius and diameter*)

SEE EXAMPLE 1

Find the perimeter and area of each figure.

3. 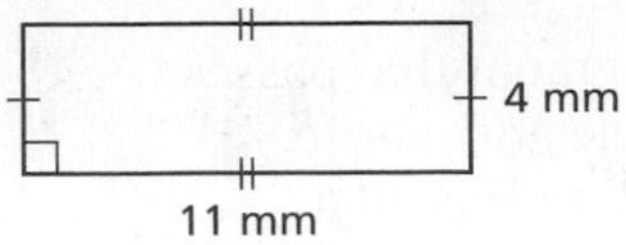

4. 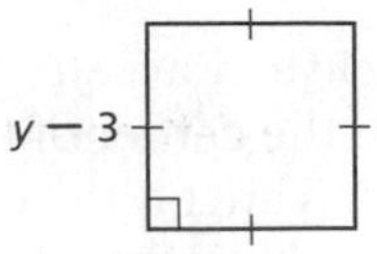

5. 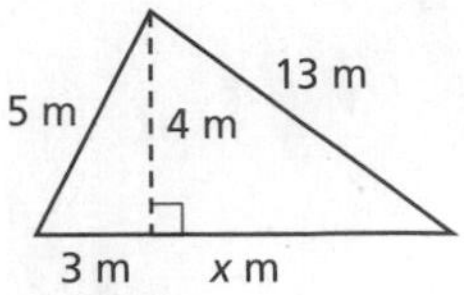

SEE EXAMPLE 2

6. **Manufacturing** A puzzle contains a triangular piece with a base of 3 in. and a height of 4 in. A manufacturer wants to make 80 puzzles. Find the amount of wood used if each puzzle contains 20 triangular pieces.

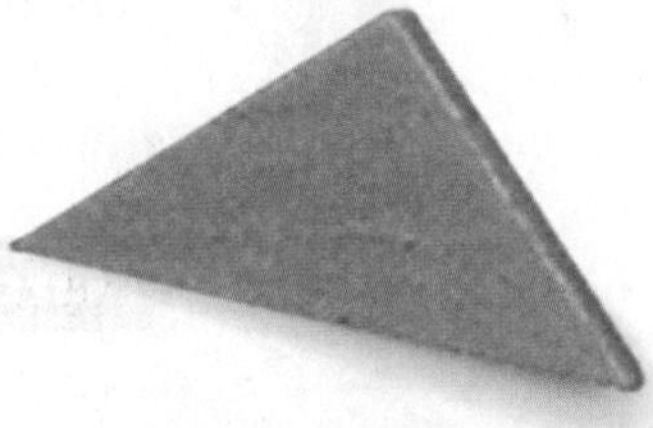

SEE EXAMPLE 3

Find the circumference and area of each circle. Use the π key on your calculator. Round to the nearest tenth.

7. 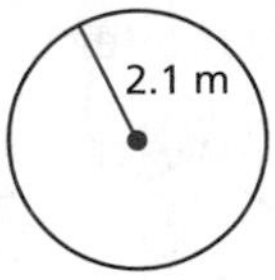

8. 

9. 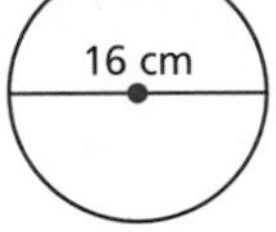

PRACTICE AND PROBLEM SOLVING

Independent Practice

For Exercises	See Example
10–12	1
13	2
14–16	3

Extra Practice

See Extra Practice for more Skills Practice and Applications Practice exercises.

Find the perimeter and area of each figure.

10. 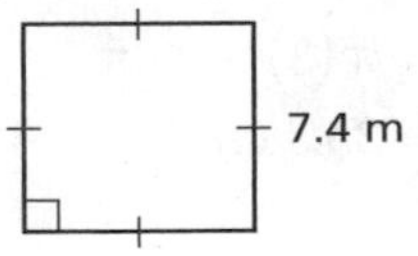

11. 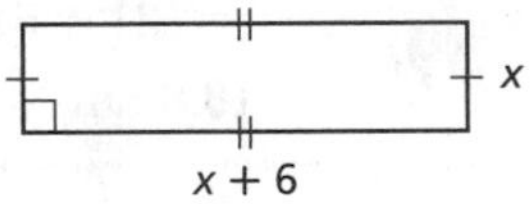

12. 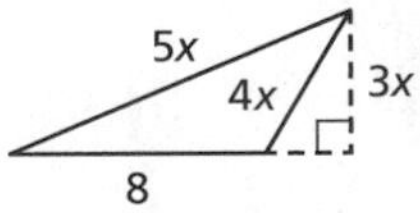

13. **Crafts** The quilt pattern includes 32 small triangles. Each has a base of 3 in. and a height of 1.5 in. Find the amount of fabric used to make the 32 triangles.

Find the circumference and area of each circle with the given radius or diameter. Use the π key on your calculator. Round to the nearest tenth.

14. $r = 12$ m
15. $d = 12.5$ ft
16. $d = \frac{1}{2}$ mi

Find the area of each of the following.

17. square whose sides are 9.1 yd in length
18. square whose sides are $(x + 1)$ in length
19. triangle whose base is $5\frac{1}{2}$ in. and whose height is $2\frac{1}{4}$ in.

Given the area of each of the following figures, find each unknown measure.

20. The area of a triangle is 6.75 m^2. If the base of the triangle is 3 m, what is the height of the triangle?

21. A rectangle has an area of 347.13 cm^2. If the length is 20.3 cm, what is the width of the rectangle?

22. The area of a circle is 64π. Find the radius of the circle.

23. **/// ERROR ANALYSIS ///** Below are two statements about the area of the circle. Which is incorrect? Explain the error.

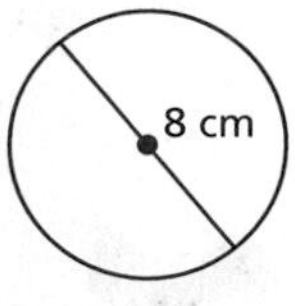

A

$A = \pi r^2$
$= \pi(8)^2$
$= 64\pi \text{ cm}^2$

B

$A = \pi r^2$
$= \pi(4)^2$
$= 16\pi \text{ cm}^2$

Find the area of each circle. Leave answers in terms of π.

24. circle with a diameter of 28 m

25. circle with a radius of $3y$

26. **Geography** The radius r of the earth at the equator is approximately 3964 mi. Find the distance around the earth at the equator. Use the π key on your calculator and round to the nearest mile.

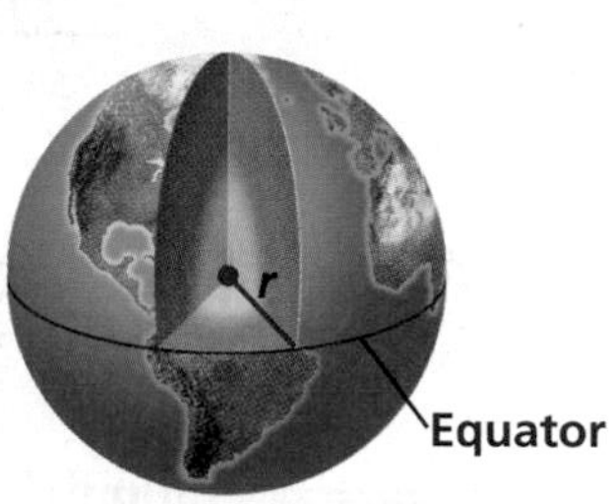

27. **Critical Thinking** Explain how the formulas for the perimeter and area of a square may be derived from the corresponding formulas for a rectangle.

28. Find the perimeter and area of a rectangle whose length is $(x + 1)$ and whose width is $(x - 3)$. Express your answer in terms of x.

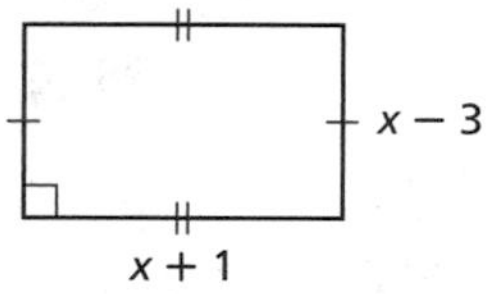

29. **Multi-Step** If the height h of a triangle is 3 inches less than the length of the base b, and the area A of the triangle is 19 times the length of the base, find b and h.

MULTI-STEP TEST PREP

30. A landscaper is to install edging around a garden. The edging costs $1.39 for each 24-inch-long strip. The landscaper estimates it will take 4 hours to install the edging.

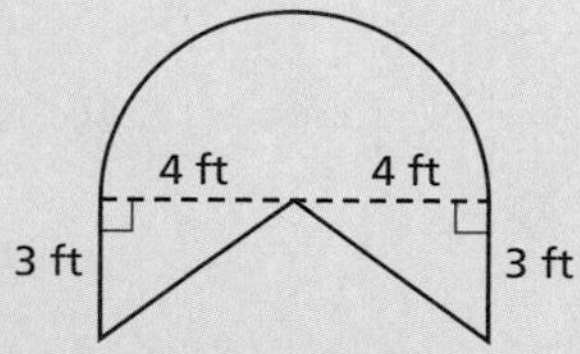

a. If the total cost is $120.30, what is the cost of the material purchased?

b. What is the charge for labor?

c. What is the area of the semicircle to the nearest tenth?

d. What is the area of each triangle?

e. What is the total area of the garden to the nearest foot?

31. **Algebra** The large rectangle has length $a + b$ and width $c + d$. Therefore, its area is $(a + b)(c + d)$.

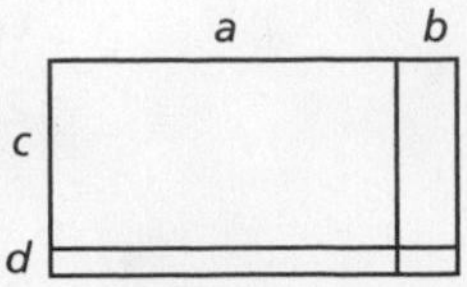

a. Find the area of each of the four small rectangles in the figure. Then find the sum of these areas. Explain why this sum must be equal to the product $(a + b)(c + d)$.

b. Suppose $b = d = 1$. Write the area of the large rectangle as a product of its length and width. Then find the sum of the areas of the four small rectangles. Explain why this sum must be equal to the product $(a + 1)(c + 1)$.

c. Suppose $b = d = 1$ and $a = c$. Write the area of the large rectangle as a product of its length and width. Then find the sum of the areas of the four small rectangles. Explain why this sum must be equal to the product $(a + 1)^2$.

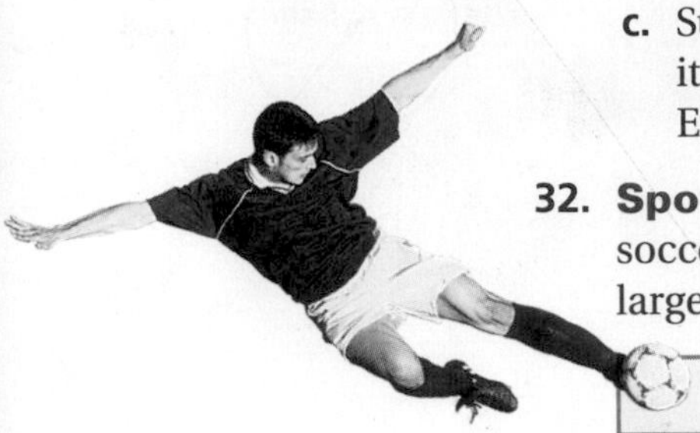

32. **Sports** The table shows the minimum and maximum dimensions for rectangular soccer fields used in international matches. Find the difference in area of the largest possible field and the smallest possible field.

	Minimum	Maximum
Length	100 m	110 m
Width	64 m	75 m

Find the value of each missing measure of a triangle.

33. $b = 2$ ft; $h =$ ▬ ft; $A = 28$ ft^2

34. $b =$ ▬ ft; $h = 22.6$ yd; $A = 282.5$ yd^2

Find the area of each rectangle with the given base and height.

35. 9.8 ft; 2.7 ft

36. 4 mi 960 ft; 440 ft

37. 3 yd 12 ft; 11 ft

Find the perimeter of each rectangle with the given base and height.

38. 21.4 in.; 7.8 in.

39. 4 ft 6 in.; 6 in.

40. 2 yd 8 ft; 6 ft

Find the diameter of the circle with the given measurement. Leave answers in terms of π.

41. $C = 14$

42. $A = 100\pi$

43. $C = 50\pi$

44. A skate park consists of a two adjacent rectangular regions as shown. Find the perimeter and area of the park.

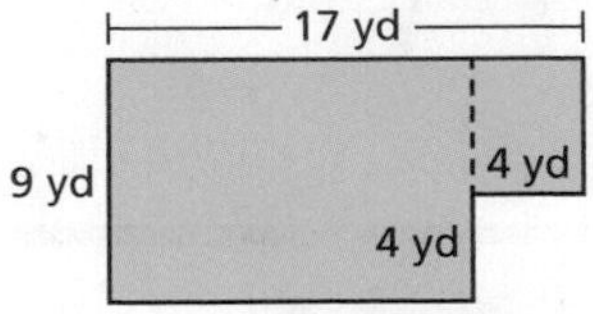

45. **Critical Thinking** Explain how you would measure a triangular piece of paper if you wanted to find its area.

46. **Write About It** A student wrote in her journal, "To find the perimeter of a rectangle, add the length and width together and then double this value." Does her method work? Explain.

TEST PREP

47. Manda made a circular tabletop that has an area of 452 in^2. Which is closest to the radius of the tabletop?

Ⓐ 9 in. Ⓑ 12 in. Ⓒ 24 in. Ⓓ 72 in.

48. A piece of wire 48 m long is bent into the shape of a rectangle whose length is twice its width. Find the length of the rectangle.

Ⓕ 8 m Ⓖ 16 m Ⓗ 24 m Ⓙ 32 m

49. Which equation best represents the area A of the triangle?

Ⓐ $A = 2x^2 + 4x$

Ⓑ $A = 4x(x + 2)$

Ⓒ $A = 2x^2 + 2$

Ⓓ $A = 4x^2 + 8$

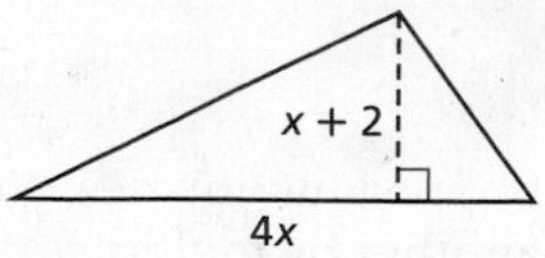

50. Ryan has a 30 ft piece of string. He wants to use the string to lay out the boundary of a new flower bed in his garden. Which of these shapes would use all the string?

Ⓕ A circle with a radius of about 37.2 in.

Ⓖ A rectangle with a length of 6 ft and a width of 5 ft

Ⓗ A triangle with each side 9 ft long

Ⓙ A square with each side 90 in. long

CHALLENGE AND EXTEND

51. A circle with a 6 in. diameter is stamped out of a rectangular piece of metal as shown. Find the area of the remaining piece of metal. Use the π key on your calculator and round to the nearest tenth.

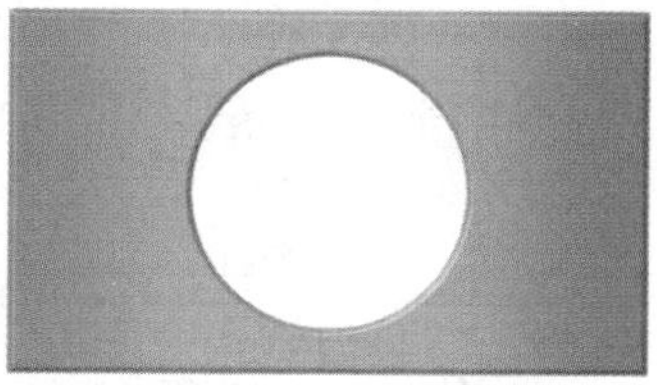

52. **a.** Solve $P = 2\ell + 2w$ for w.

b. Use your result from part **a** to find the width of a rectangle that has a perimeter of 9 ft and a length of 3 ft.

53. Find all possible areas of a rectangle whose sides are natural numbers and whose perimeter is 12.

LINK

Math History

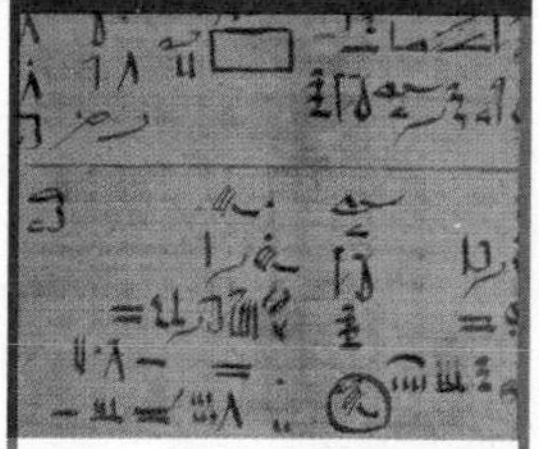

The Ahmes Papyrus is an ancient Egyptian source of information about mathematics. A page of the Ahmes Papyrus is about 1 foot wide and 18 feet long.

Source: scholars.nus.edu.sg

54. **Estimation** The Ahmes Papyrus dates from approximately 1650 B.C.E. Lacking a precise value for π, the author assumed that the area of a circle with a diameter of 9 units had the same area as a square with a side length of 8 units. By what percent did the author overestimate or underestimate the actual area of the circle?

55. **Multi-Step** The width of a painting is $\frac{4}{5}$ the measure of the length of the painting. If the area is 320 in^2, what are the length and width of the painting?

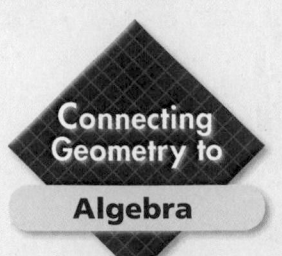

Connecting Geometry to **Algebra**

Unit Conversions

In previous courses, you learned to convert a measurement from one unit to another by multiplying it by a *conversion factor.* A conversion factor is a ratio of two equal quantities in different units of measurement.

Example

Find the perimeter, in centimeters, of the rectangle. (*Hint:* 1 in. = 2.54 cm.)

Find the perimeter in inches first.

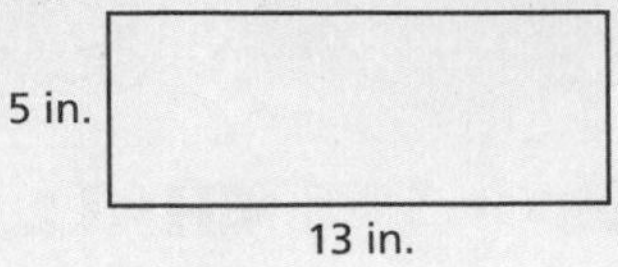

$p = 2\ell + 2w$

$p = 2(13) + 2(5)$ — *Substitute 13 for ℓ and 5 for w.*

$s = 26 + 10 = 36$ — *Simplify.*

The perimeter of the rectangle is 36 in. Multiply by a conversion factor to change the unit to centimeters.

$36 \text{ in} \times \dfrac{2.54 \text{ cm}}{1 \text{ in.}}$ — *Write the conversion factor*

$= 36 \cancel{\text{in}} \times \dfrac{2.54 \text{ cm}}{1 \cancel{\text{in}}.}$ — *Cancel out the like units and simplify.*

$= 36 \times 2.54 \text{ cm} = 91.44 \text{ cm}$

The perimeter of the rectangle is 91.44 cm.

Try This

Find the perimeter of each rectangle in the units given. Round to the nearest tenth.

1. feet

(*Hint:* 1 ft = 0.3048 m)

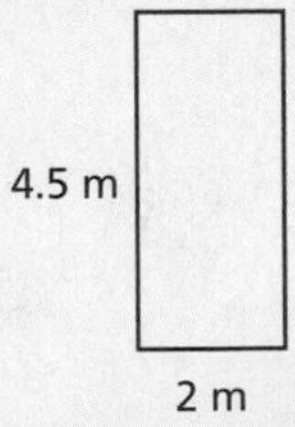

2. kilometers

(*Hint:* 1 mi ≈ 1.609 km)

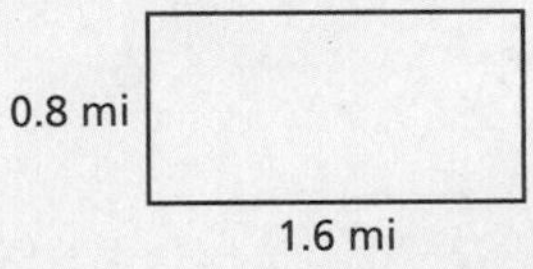

3. millimeters

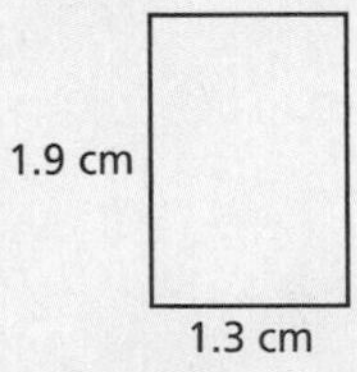

4. The radius of a circle is 3.5 in. Find the circumference of the circle in centimeters. Use 3.14 for π, and round your answer to the nearest tenth.

5. The side length of a square is 7 in.

a. What is the area of the square in square inches?

b. How could you change the conversion factor from the example to convert square inches to square centimeters?

c. Find the area of the square in square centimeters. Round to the nearest tenth.

COMMON CORE

1-6 Midpoint and Distance in the Coordinate Plane

CC.9-12.G.GPE.7 Use coordinates to compute perimeters…, e.g., using the distance formula.*

Objectives

Develop and apply the formula for midpoint.

Use the Distance Formula and the Pythagorean Theorem to find the distance between two points.

Vocabulary

coordinate plane
leg
hypotenuse

Why learn this?

You can use a coordinate plane to help you calculate distances. (See Example 5.)

Major League baseball fields are laid out according to strict guidelines. Once you know the dimensions of a field, you can use a coordinate plane to find the distance between two of the bases.

A **coordinate plane** is a plane that is divided into four regions by a horizontal line (x-axis) and a vertical line (y-axis). The location, or coordinates, of a point are given by an ordered pair (x, y).

You can find the midpoint of a segment by using the coordinates of its endpoints. Calculate the average of the x-coordinates and the average of the y-coordinates of the endpoints.

Know it! Note — **Midpoint Formula**

The midpoint M of $\overline{AB}$ with endpoints $A(x_1, y_1)$ and $B(x_2, y_2)$ is found by

$$M\left(\frac{x_1 + x_2}{2}, \frac{y_1 + y_2}{2}\right).$$

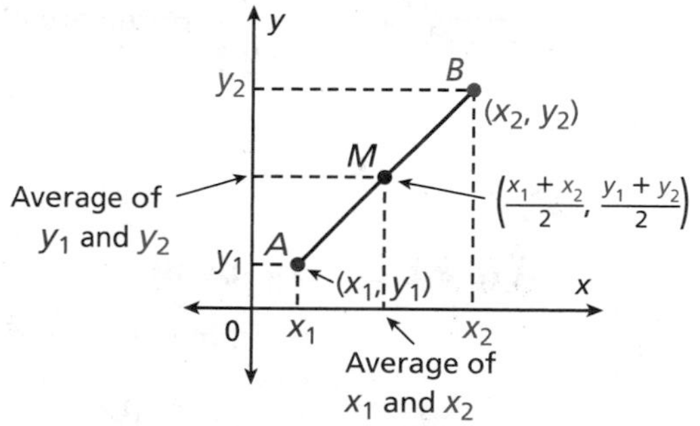

EXAMPLE 1 Finding the Coordinates of a Midpoint

Find the coordinates of the midpoint of $\overline{CD}$ with endpoints $C(-2, -1)$ and $D(4, 2)$.

$$M\left(\frac{x_1 + x_2}{2}, \frac{y_1 + y_2}{2}\right)$$

$$\frac{-2 + 4}{2}, \frac{-1 + 2}{2} = \left(\frac{2}{2}, \frac{1}{2}\right)$$

$$= \left(1, \frac{1}{2}\right)$$

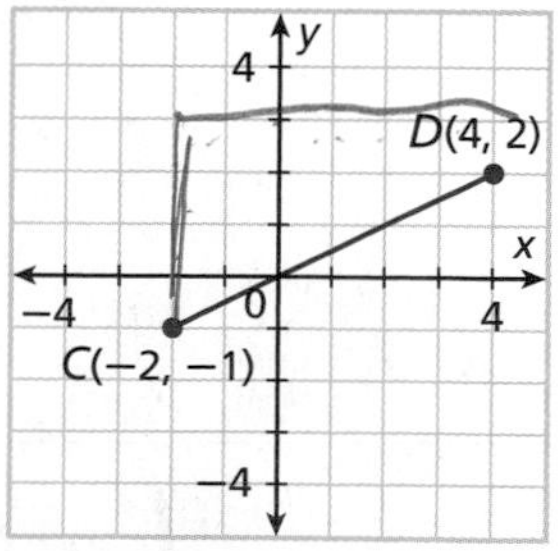

Helpful Hint

To make it easier to picture the problem, plot the segment's endpoints on a coordinate plane.

CHECK IT OUT! 1. Find the coordinates of the midpoint of $\overline{EF}$ with endpoints $E(-2, 3)$ and $F(5, -3)$.

EXAMPLE 2 Finding the Coordinates of an Endpoint

x^2y Algebra

M is the midpoint of $\overline{AB}$. A has coordinates $(2, 2)$, and M has coordinates $(4, -3)$. Find the coordinates of B.

Step 1 Let the coordinates of B equal (x, y).

Step 2 Use the Midpoint Formula: $(4, -3) = \left(\frac{2 + x}{2}, \frac{2 + y}{2}\right)$.

Step 3 Find the x-coordinate. Find the y-coordinate.

x-coordinate		y-coordinate
$4 = \frac{2 + x}{2}$	*Set the coordinates equal.*	$-3 = \frac{2 + y}{2}$
$2(4) = 2\left(\frac{2 + x}{2}\right)$	*Multiply both sides by 2.*	$2(-3) = 2\left(\frac{2 + y}{2}\right)$
$8 = 2 + x$	*Simplify.*	$-6 = 2 + y$
$-2 \quad -2$	*Subtract 2 from both sides.*	$-2 \quad -2$
$6 = x$	*Simplify.*	$-8 = y$

The coordinates of B are $(6, -8)$.

CHECK IT OUT! **2.** S is the midpoint of $\overline{RT}$. R has coordinates $(-6, -1)$, and S has coordinates $(-1, 1)$. Find the coordinates of T.

The Ruler Postulate can be used to find the distance between two points on a number line. The Distance Formula is used to calculate the distance between two points in a coordinate plane.

Know it! Note

Distance Formula

In a coordinate plane, the distance d between two points (x_1, y_1) and (x_2, y_2) is

$$d = \sqrt{(x_2 - x_1)^2 + (y_2 - y_1)^2}.$$

EXAMPLE 3 Using the Distance Formula

Find AB and CD. Then determine if $\overline{AB} \cong \overline{CD}$.

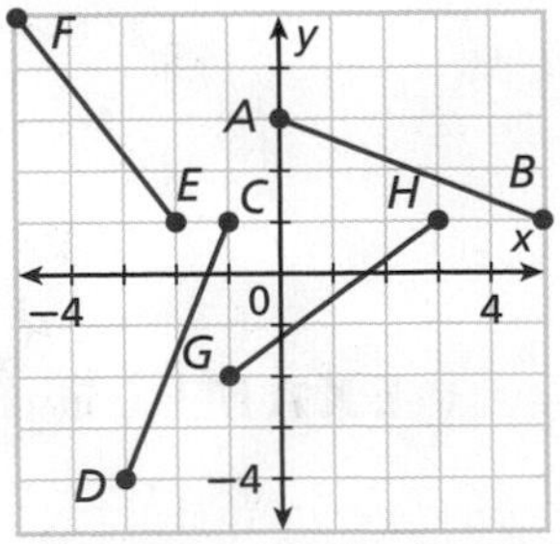

Step 1 Find the coordinates of each point.
$A(0, 3)$, $B(5, 1)$, $C(-1, 1)$, and $D(-3, -4)$

Step 2 Use the Distance Formula.

$$d = \sqrt{(x_2 - x_1)^2 + (y_2 - y_1)^2}$$

$$AB = \sqrt{(5 - 0)^2 + (1 - 3)^2} = \sqrt{5^2 + (-2)^2} = \sqrt{25 + 4} = \sqrt{29}$$

$$CD = \sqrt{[-3 - (-1)]^2 + (-4 - 1)^2} = \sqrt{(-2)^2 + (-5)^2} = \sqrt{4 + 25} = \sqrt{29}$$

Since $AB = CD$, $\overline{AB} \cong \overline{CD}$.

CHECK IT OUT! **3.** Find EF and GH. Then determine if $\overline{EF} \cong \overline{GH}$.

You can also use the Pythagorean Theorem to find the distance between two points in a coordinate plane. You will learn more about the Pythagorean Theorem later in this course.

In a right triangle, the two sides that form the right angle are the **legs** . The side across from the right angle that stretches from one leg to the other is the **hypotenuse** . In the diagram, ***a*** and ***b*** are the lengths of the shorter sides, or legs, of the right triangle. The longest side is called the hypotenuse and has length *c*.

Know it! Note

Theorem 1-6-1 **Pythagorean Theorem**

In a right triangle, the sum of the squares of the lengths of the *legs* is equal to the square of the length of the *hypotenuse*.

$$a^2 + b^2 = c^2$$

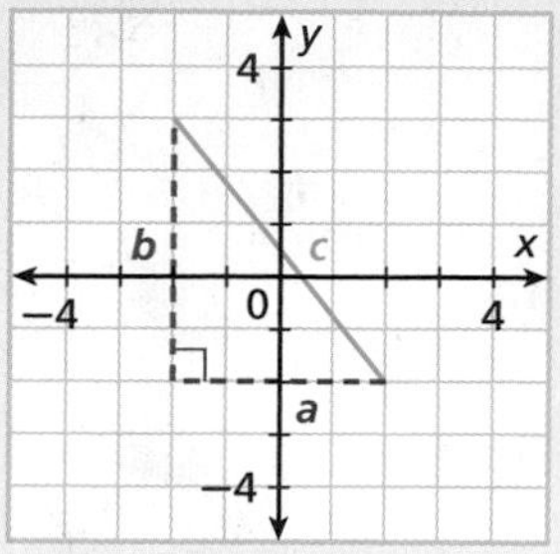

EXAMPLE 4 Finding Distances in the Coordinate Plane

Use the Distance Formula and the Pythagorean Theorem to find the distance, to the nearest tenth, from *A* to *B*.

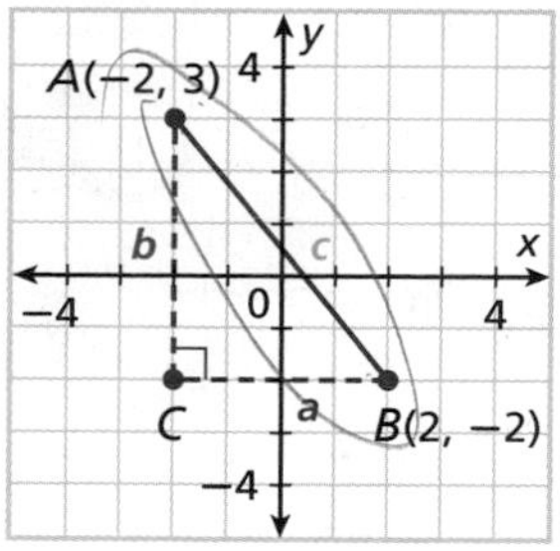

Method 1

Use the Distance Formula. Substitute the values for the coordinates of *A* and *B* into the Distance Formula.

$$\begin{aligned} AB &= \sqrt{(x_2 - x_1)^2 + (y_2 - y_1)^2} \\ &= \sqrt{[2 - (-2)]^2 + (-2 - 3)^2} \\ &= \sqrt{4^2 + (-5)^2} \\ &= \sqrt{16 + 25} \\ &= \sqrt{41} \\ &\approx 6.4 \end{aligned}$$

Method 2

Use the Pythagorean Theorem. Count the units for sides ***a*** and ***b***.

$a = 4$ and $b = 5$.

$$\begin{aligned} c^2 &= a^2 + b^2 \\ &= 4^2 + 5^2 \\ &= 16 + 25 \\ &= 41 \\ c &= \sqrt{41} \\ c &\approx 6.4 \end{aligned}$$

CHECK IT OUT! **Use the Distance Formula and the Pythagorean Theorem to find the distance, to the nearest tenth, from *R* to *S*.**

4a. $R(3, 2)$ and $S(-3, -1)$

4b. $R(-4, 5)$ and $S(2, -1)$

EXAMPLE 5 Sports Application

The four bases on a baseball field form a square with 90 ft sides. When a player throws the ball from home plate to second base, what is the distance of the throw, to the nearest tenth?

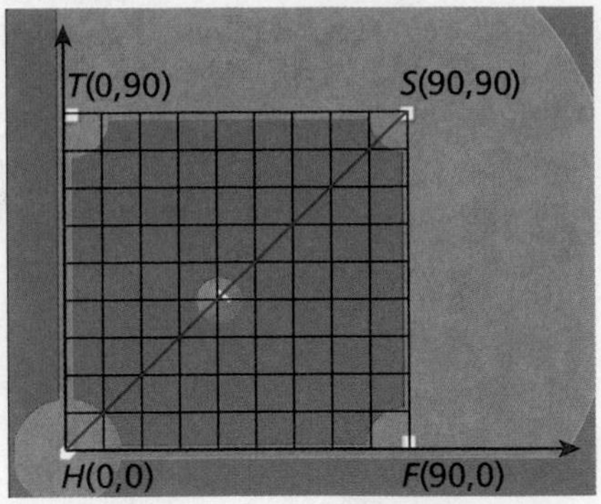

Set up the field on a coordinate plane so that home plate H is at the origin, first base F has coordinates $(90, 0)$, second base S has coordinates $(90, 90)$, and third base T has coordinates $(0, 90)$.

The distance HS from home plate to second base is the length of the hypotenuse of a right triangle.

$$HS = \sqrt{(x_2 - x_1)^2 + (y_2 - y_1)^2}$$
$$= \sqrt{(90 - 0)^2 + (90 - 0)^2}$$
$$= \sqrt{90^2 + 90^2}$$
$$= \sqrt{8100 + 8100}$$
$$= \sqrt{16{,}200}$$
$$\approx 127.3 \text{ ft}$$

CHECK IT OUT! 5. The center of the pitching mound has coordinates $(42.8, 42.8)$. When a pitcher throws the ball from the center of the mound to home plate, what is the distance of the throw, to the nearest tenth?

MATHEMATICAL PRACTICES

THINK AND DISCUSS

1. Can you exchange the coordinates (x_1, y_1) and (x_2, y_2) in the Midpoint Formula and still find the correct midpoint? Explain.
2. A right triangle has sides lengths of r, s, and t. Given that $s^2 + t^2 = r^2$, which variables represent the lengths of the legs and which variable represents the length of the hypotenuse?
3. Do you always get the same result using the Distance Formula to find distance as you do when using the Pythagorean Theorem? Explain your answer.
4. Why do you think that most cities are laid out in a rectangular grid instead of a triangular or circular grid?

Know it! Note

5. **GET ORGANIZED** Copy and complete the graphic organizer below. In each box, write a formula. Then make a sketch that will illustrate the formula.

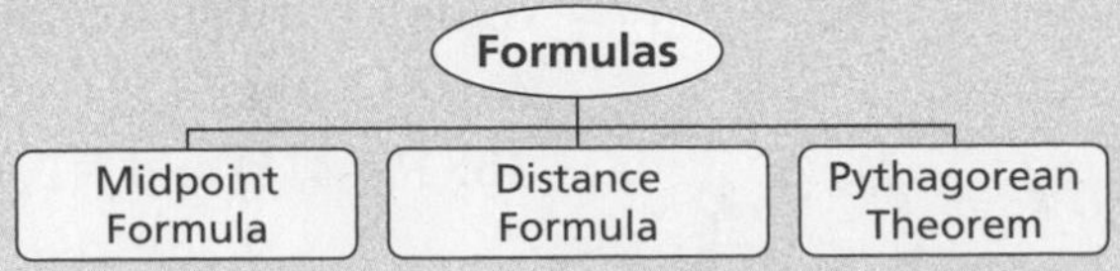

1-6 Exercises

Learn It Online
Homework Help Online
Parent Resources Online

GUIDED PRACTICE

1. **Vocabulary** The ___?___ is the side of a right triangle that is directly across from the right angle. (*hypotenuse* or *leg*)

SEE EXAMPLE 1

Find the coordinates of the midpoint of each segment.

2. $\overline{AB}$ with endpoints $A(4, -6)$ and $B(-4, 2)$
3. $\overline{CD}$ with endpoints $C(0, -8)$ and $D(3, 0)$

SEE EXAMPLE 2

4. M is the midpoint of $\overline{LN}$. L has coordinates $(-3, -1)$, and M has coordinates $(0, 1)$. Find the coordinates of N.
5. B is the midpoint of $\overline{AC}$. A has coordinates $(-3, 4)$, and B has coordinates $\left(-1\frac{1}{2}, 1\right)$. Find the coordinates of C.

SEE EXAMPLE 3

Multi-Step Find the length of the given segments and determine if they are congruent.

6. $\overline{JK}$ and $\overline{FG}$
7. $\overline{JK}$ and $\overline{RS}$

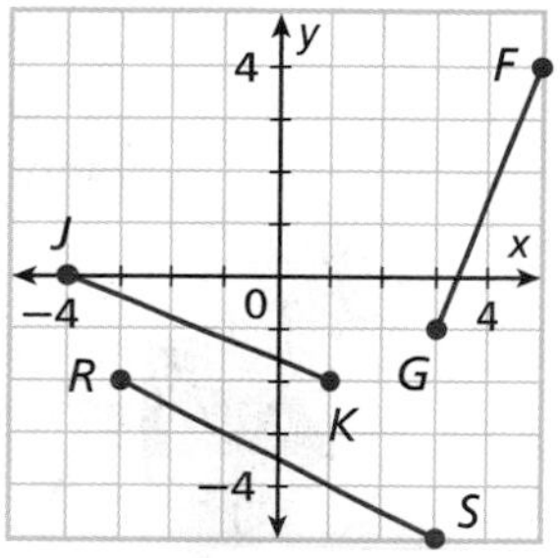

SEE EXAMPLE 4

Use the Distance Formula and the Pythagorean Theorem to find the distance, to the nearest tenth, between each pair of points.

8. $A(1, -2)$ and $B(-4, -4)$
9. $X(-2, 7)$ and $Y(-2, -8)$
10. $V(2, -1)$ and $W(-4, 8)$

SEE EXAMPLE 5

11. **Architecture** The plan for a rectangular living room shows electrical wiring will be run in a straight line from the entrance E to a light L at the opposite corner of the room. What is the length of the wire to the nearest tenth?

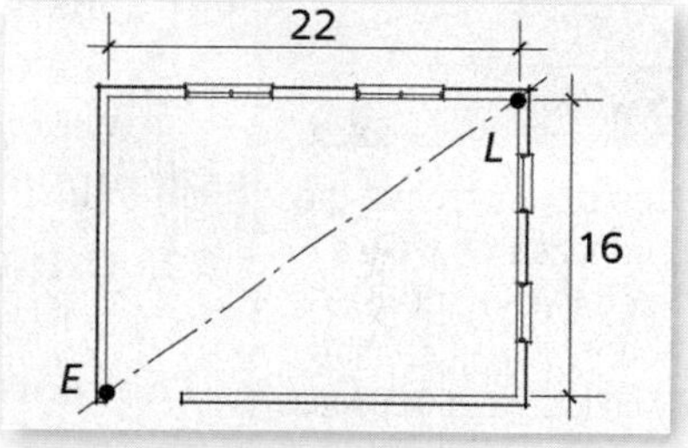

PRACTICE AND PROBLEM SOLVING

Independent Practice

For Exercises	See Example
12–13	1
14–15	2
16–17	3
18–20	4
21	5

Extra Practice

See Extra Practice for more Skills Practice and Applications Practice exercises.

Find the coordinates of the midpoint of each segment.

12. $\overline{XY}$ with endpoints $X(-3, -7)$ and $Y(-1, 1)$
13. $\overline{MN}$ with endpoints $M(12, -7)$ and $N(-5, -2)$
14. M is the midpoint of $\overline{QR}$. Q has coordinates $(-3, 5)$, and M has coordinates $(7, -9)$. Find the coordinates of R.
15. D is the midpoint of $\overline{CE}$. E has coordinates $(-3, -2)$, and D has coordinates $\left(2\frac{1}{2}, 1\right)$. Find the coordinates of C.

Multi-Step Find the length of the given segments and determine if they are congruent.

16. $\overline{DE}$ and $\overline{FG}$
17. $\overline{DE}$ and $\overline{RS}$

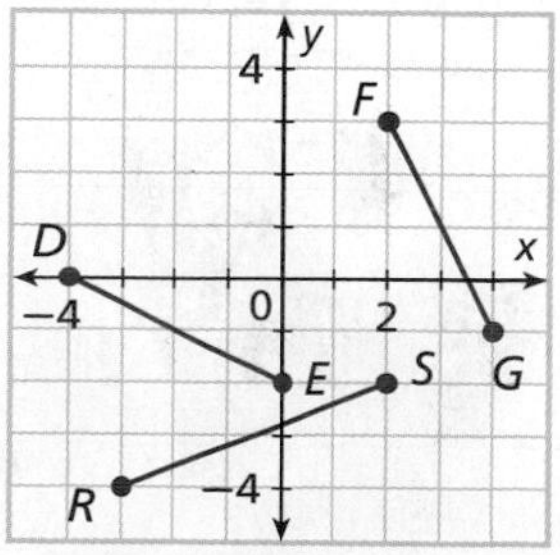

Use the Distance Formula and the Pythagorean Theorem to find the distance, to the nearest tenth, between each pair of points.

18. $U(0, 1)$ and $V(-3, -9)$ 19. $M(10, -1)$ and $N(2, -5)$ 20. $P(-10, 1)$ and $Q(5, 5)$

21. **Consumer Application** Televisions and computer screens are usually advertised based on the length of their diagonals. If the height of a computer screen is 11 in. and the width is 14 in., what is the length of the diagonal? Round to the nearest inch.

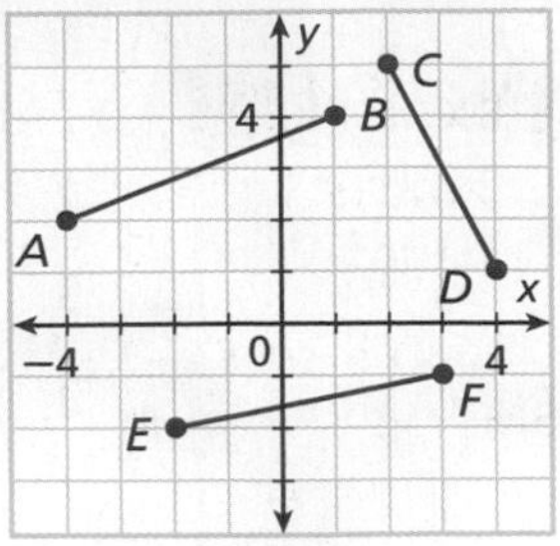

22. **Multi-Step** Use the Distance Formula to order $\overline{AB}$, $\overline{CD}$, and $\overline{EF}$ from shortest to longest.

23. Use the Pythagorean Theorem to find the distance from A to E. Round to the nearest hundredth.

24. X has coordinates $(a, 3a)$, and Y has coordinates $(-5a, 0)$. Find the coordinates of the midpoint of $\overline{XY}$.

25. Describe a shortcut for finding the midpoint of a segment when one of its endpoints has coordinates (a, b) and the other endpoint is the origin.

On the map, each square of the grid represents 1 square mile. Find each distance to the nearest tenth of a mile.

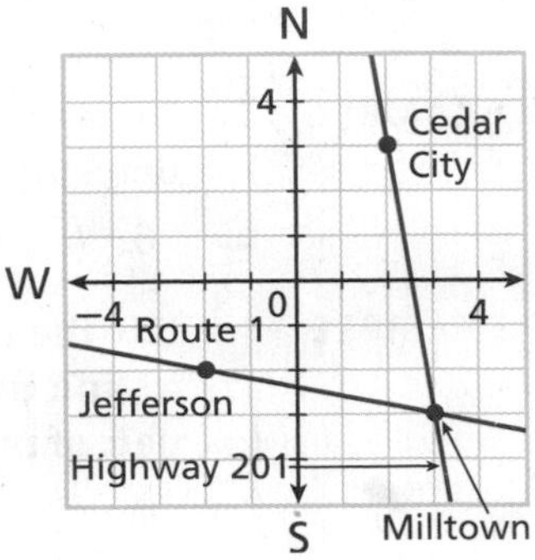

26. Find the distance along Highway 201 from Cedar City to Milltown.

27. A car breaks down on Route 1, at the midpoint between Jefferson and Milltown. A tow truck is sent out from Jefferson. How far does the truck travel to reach the car?

LINK

History

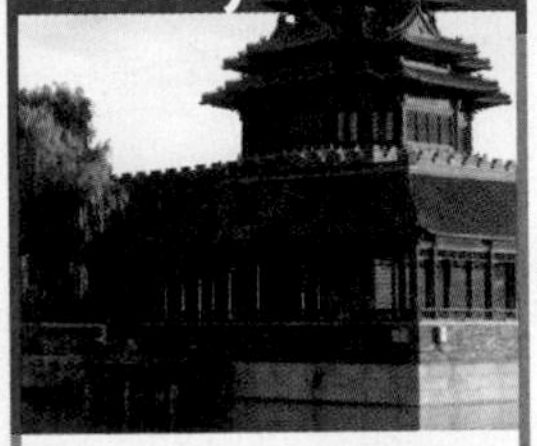

The construction of the Forbidden City lasted for 14 years. It began in 1406 with an estimated workforce of 200,000 men.

Source: www.wikipedia.com

28. **History** The Forbidden City in Beijing, China, is the world's largest palace complex. Surrounded by a wall and a moat, the rectangular complex is 960 m long and 750 m wide. Find the distance, to the nearest meter, from one corner of the complex to the opposite corner.

29. **Critical Thinking** Give an example of a line segment with midpoint $(0, 0)$.

The coordinates of the vertices of $\triangle ABC$ are $A(1, 4)$, $B(-2, -1)$, and $C(-3, -2)$.

30. Find the perimeter of $\triangle ABC$ to the nearest tenth.

31. The height h to side $\overline{BC}$ is $\sqrt{2}$, and b is the length of $\overline{BC}$. What is the area of $\triangle ABC$?

32. **Write About It** Explain why the Distance Formula is not needed to find the distance between two points that lie on a horizontal or a vertical line.

MULTI-STEP TEST PREP

33. Tania uses a coordinate plane to map out plans for landscaping a rectangular patio area. On the plan, one square represents 2 feet. She plans to plant a tree at the midpoint of $\overline{AC}$. How far from each corner of the patio does she plant the tree? Round to the nearest tenth.

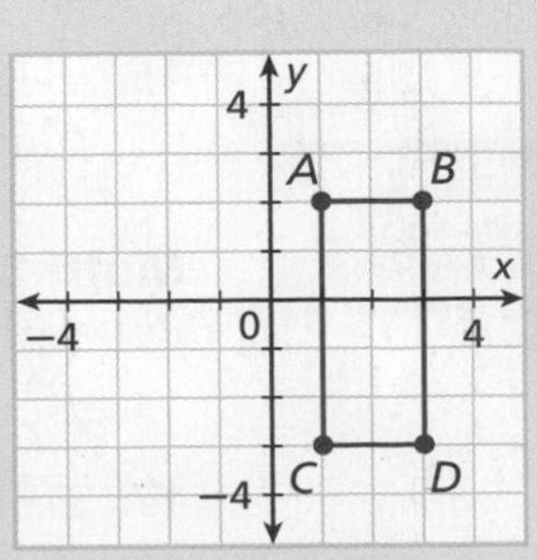

TEST PREP

34. Which segment has a length closest to 4 units?

Ⓐ $\overline{EF}$ Ⓒ $\overline{JK}$

Ⓑ $\overline{GH}$ Ⓓ $\overline{LM}$

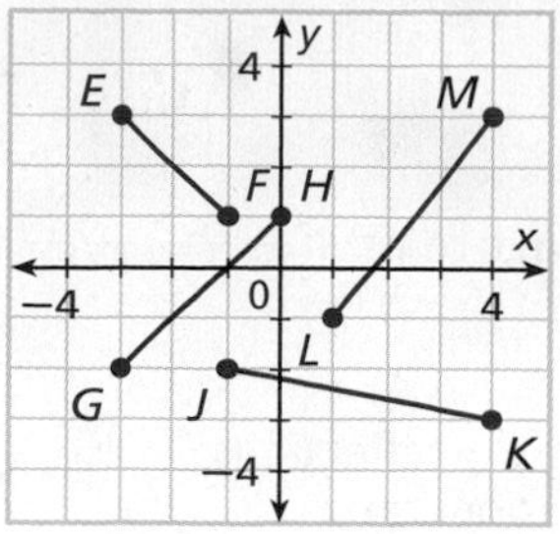

35. Find the distance, to the nearest tenth, between the midpoints of $\overline{LM}$ and $\overline{JK}$.

Ⓕ 1.8 Ⓗ 4.0

Ⓖ 3.6 Ⓙ 5.3

36. What are the coordinates of the midpoint of a line segment that connects the points $(7, -3)$ and $(-5, 6)$?

Ⓐ $\left(6, -4\frac{1}{2}\right)$ Ⓒ $\left(2, \frac{1}{2}\right)$

Ⓑ $(2, 3)$ Ⓓ $\left(1, 1\frac{1}{2}\right)$

37. A coordinate plane is placed over the map of a town. A library is located at $(-5, 1)$, and a museum is located at $(3, 5)$. What is the distance, to the nearest tenth, from the library to the museum?

Ⓕ 4.5 Ⓖ 5.7 Ⓗ 6.3 Ⓙ 8.9

CHALLENGE AND EXTEND

38. Use the diagram to find the following.

a. P is the midpoint of $\overline{AB}$, and R is the midpoint of $\overline{BC}$. Find the coordinates of Q.

b. Find the area of rectangle $PBRQ$.

c. Find DB. Round to the nearest tenth.

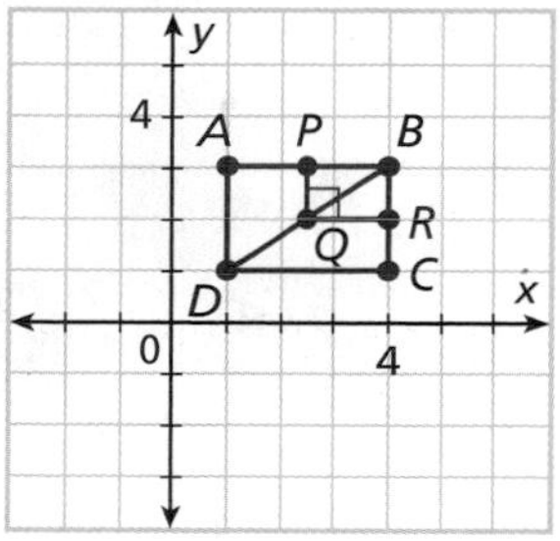

39. The coordinates of X are $(a - 5, -2a)$. The coordinates of Y are $(a + 1, 2a)$. If the distance between X and Y is 10, find the value of a.

40. Find two points on the y-axis that are a distance of 5 units from $(4, 2)$.

41. Given $\angle ACB$ is a right angle of $\triangle ABC$, $AC = x$, and $BC = y$, find AB in terms of x and y.

D: $\sqrt{(x_2 - x_1)^2 + (y_2 - y_1)}$

COMMON CORE

1-7 Transformations in the Coordinate Plane

CC.9-12.G.CO.4 Develop definitions of rotations, reflections, and translations... *Also* **CC.9-12.G.CO.2, CC.9-12.G.CO.5**

Objectives

Identify reflections, rotations, and translations.

Graph transformations in the coordinate plane.

Vocabulary

transformation
preimage
image
reflection
rotation
translation

Who uses this?

Artists use transformations to create decorative patterns. (See Example 4.)

The Alhambra, a 13th-century palace in Granada, Spain, is famous for the geometric patterns that cover its walls and floors. To create a variety of designs, the builders based the patterns on several different *transformations.*

A **transformation** is a change in the position, size, or shape of a figure. The original figure is called the **preimage** . The resulting figure is called the **image** . A transformation *maps* the preimage to the image. Arrow notation (→) is used to describe a transformation, and primes (′) are used to label the image.

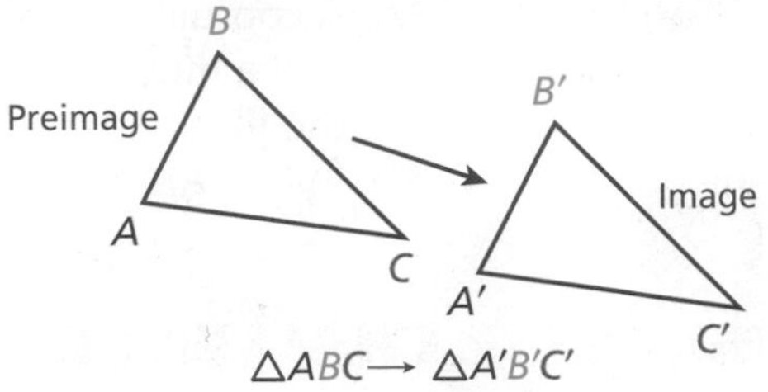

$\triangle ABC \rightarrow \triangle A'B'C'$

Know it! Note

Transformations

REFLECTION	ROTATION	TRANSLATION
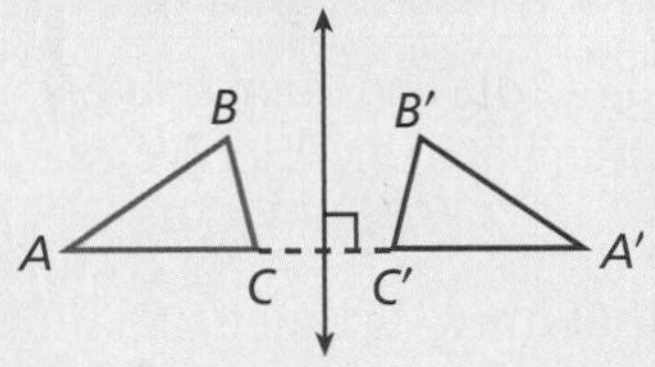	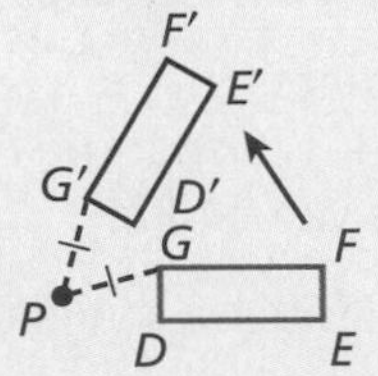	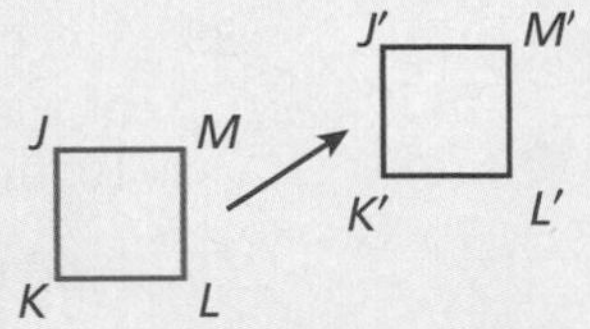
A **reflection** (or *flip*) is a transformation across a line, called the line of reflection. Each point and its image are the same distance from the line of reflection.	A **rotation** (or *turn*) is a transformation about a point *P*, called the center of rotation. Each point and its image are the same distance from *P*.	A **translation** (or *slide*) is a transformation in which all the points of a figure move the same distance in the same direction.

EXAMPLE 1 **Identifying Transformations**

Identify the transformation. Then use arrow notation to describe the transformation.

A

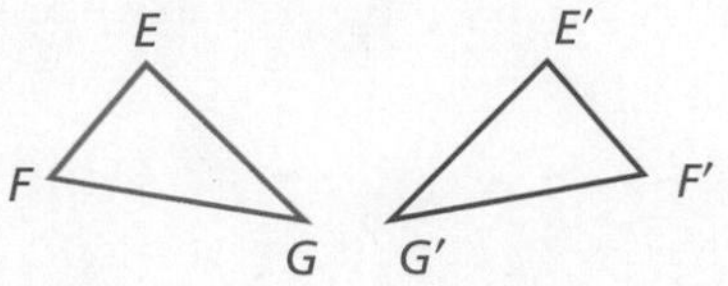

The transformation cannot be a translation because each point and its image are not in the same position.

The transformation is a reflection. $\triangle EFG \rightarrow \triangle E'F'G'$

Identify the transformation. Then use arrow notation to describe the transformation.

B

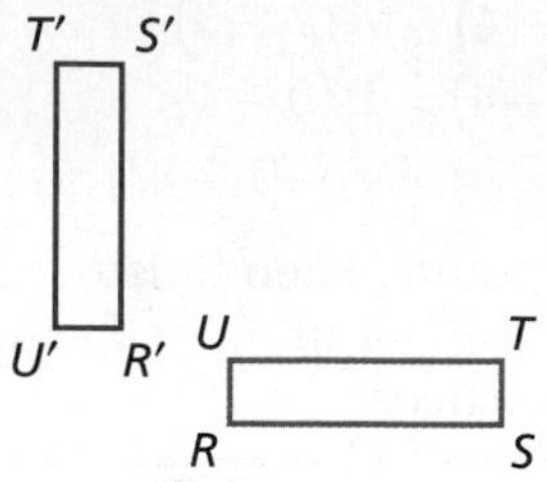

The transformation cannot be a reflection because each point and its image are not the same distance from a line of reflection.

The transformation is a 90° rotation. $RSTU \rightarrow R'S'T'U'$

CHECK IT OUT! **Identify each transformation. Then use arrow notation to describe the transformation.**

1a.

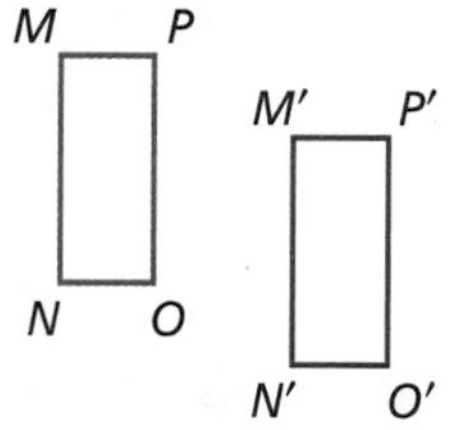

1b.

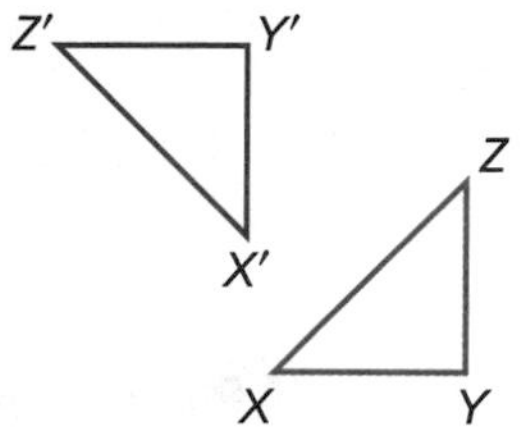

EXAMPLE 2 Drawing and Identifying Transformations

A figure has vertices at $A(-1, 4)$, $B(-1, 1)$, and $C(3, 1)$. After a transformation, the image of the figure has vertices at $A'(-1, -4)$, $B'(-1, -1)$, and $C'(3, -1)$. Draw the preimage and image. Then identify the transformation.

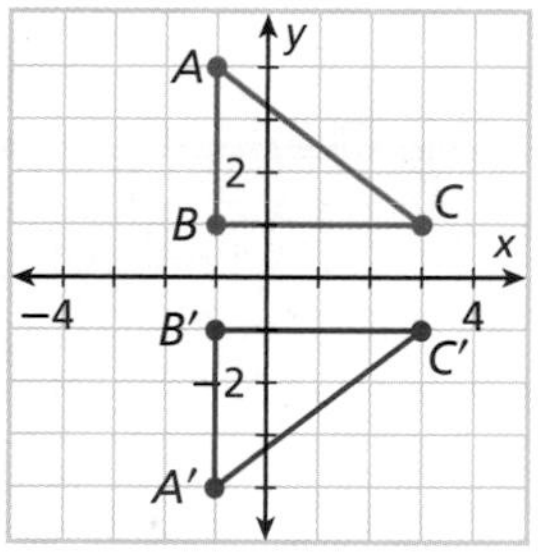

Plot the points. Then use a straightedge to connect the vertices.

The transformation is a reflection across the x-axis because each point and its image are the same distance from the x-axis.

CHECK IT OUT! **2.** A figure has vertices at $E(2, 0)$, $F(2, -1)$, $G(5, -1)$, and $H(5, 0)$. After a transformation, the image of the figure has vertices at $E'(0, 2)$, $F'(1, 2)$, $G'(1, 5)$, and $H'(0, 5)$. Draw the preimage and image. Then identify the transformation.

To find coordinates for the image of a figure in a translation, add a to the x-coordinates of the preimage and add b to the y-coordinates of the preimage. Translations can also be described by a rule such as $(x, y) \rightarrow (x + a, y + b)$.

EXAMPLE 3 Translations in the Coordinate Plane

Find the coordinates for the image of $\triangle ABC$ after the translation $(x, y) \rightarrow (x + 3, y - 4)$. Draw the image.

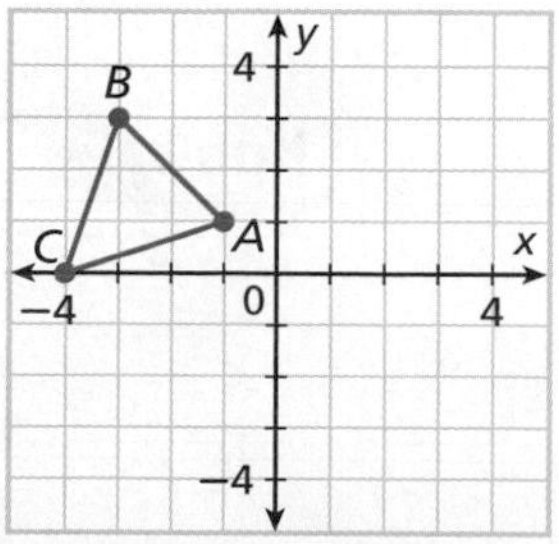

Step 1 Find the coordinates of $\triangle ABC$.

The vertices of $\triangle ABC$ are $A(-1, 1)$, $B(-3, 3)$, and $C(-4, 0)$.

Step 2 Apply the rule to find the vertices of the image.

$A'(-1 + 3, 1 - 4) = A'(2, -3)$
$B'(-3 + 3, 3 - 4) = B'(0, -1)$
$C'(-4 + 3, 0 - 4) = C'(-1, -4)$

Step 3 Plot the points. Then finish drawing the image by using a straightedge to connect the vertices.

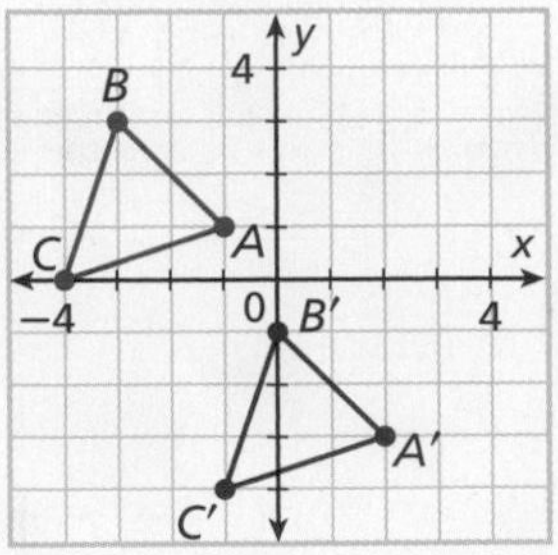

CHECK IT OUT!

3. Find the coordinates for the image of *JKLM* after the translation $(x, y) \rightarrow (x - 2, y + 4)$. Draw the image.

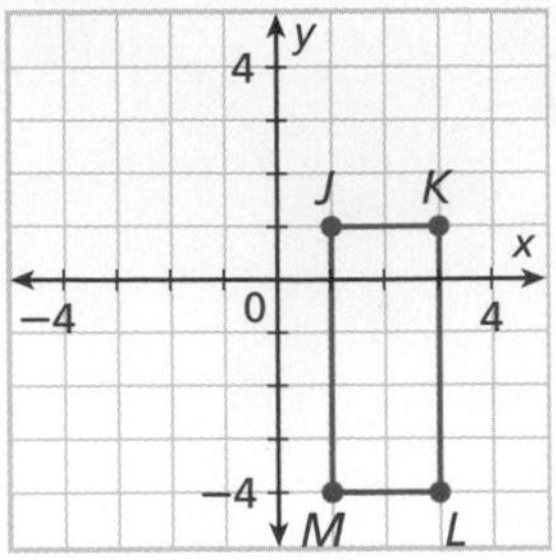

EXAMPLE 4 Art History Application

The pattern shown is similar to a pattern on a wall of the Alhambra. Write a rule for the translation of square 1 to square 2.

Step 1 Choose 2 points

Choose a point A on the preimage and a corresponding point A' on the image. A has coordinates $(3, 1)$, and A' has coordinates $(1, 3)$.

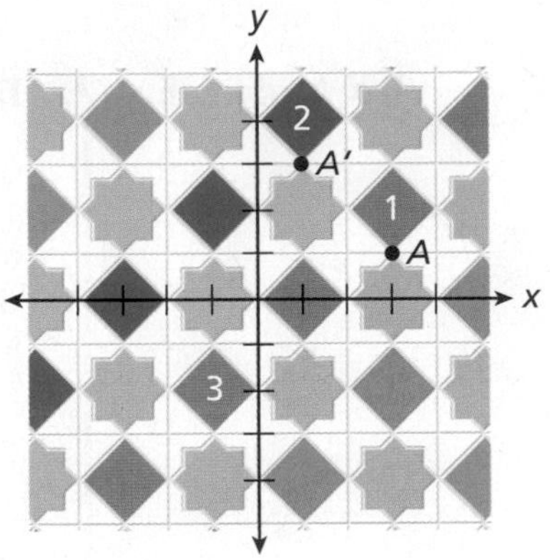

Step 2 Translate

To translate A to A', 2 units are subtracted from the x-coordinate and 2 units are added to the y-coordinate. Therefore, the translation rule is $(x, y) \rightarrow (x - 2, y + 2)$.

CHECK IT OUT!

4. Use the diagram to write a rule for the translation of square 1 to square 3.

MATHEMATICAL PRACTICES

THINK AND DISCUSS

1. Explain how to recognize a reflection when given a figure and its image.

Know it! Note

2. GET ORGANIZED Copy and complete the graphic organizer. In each box, sketch an example of each transformation.

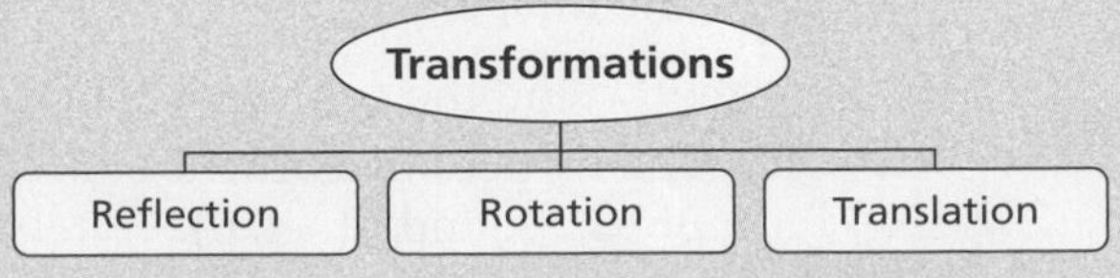

1-7 Exercises

Learn It Online
Homework Help Online
Parent Resources Online

GUIDED PRACTICE

Vocabulary **Apply the vocabulary from this lesson to answer each question.**

1. Given the transformation $\triangle XYZ \rightarrow \triangle X'Y'Z'$, name the preimage and image of the transformation.
2. The types of transformations of geometric figures in the coordinate plane can be described as a slide, a flip, or a turn. What are the other names used to identify these transformations?

SEE EXAMPLE 1

Identify each transformation. Then use arrow notation to describe the transformation.

3.
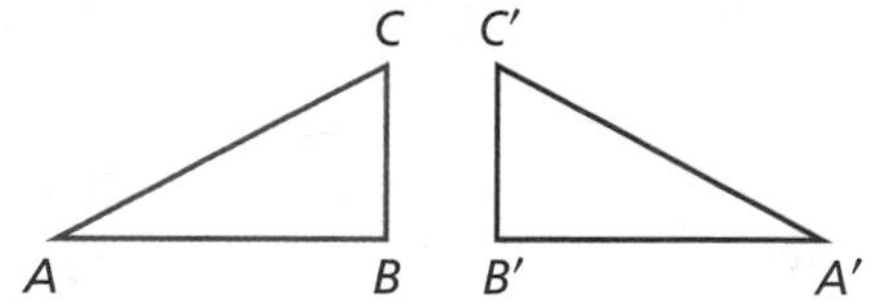

4.
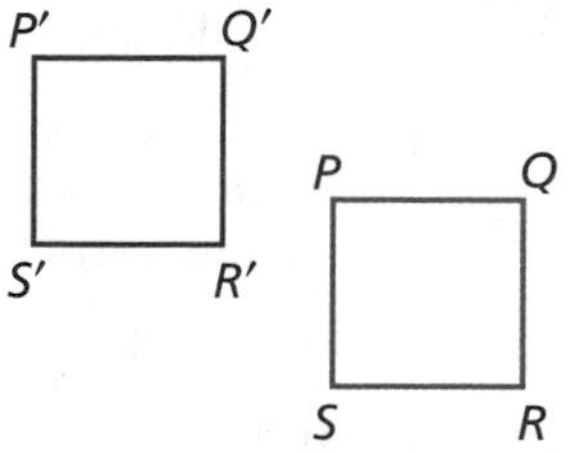

SEE EXAMPLE 2

5. A figure has vertices at $A(-3, 2)$, $B(-1, -1)$, and $C(-4, -2)$. After a transformation, the image of the figure has vertices at $A'(3, 2)$, $B'(1, -1)$, and $C'(4, -2)$. Draw the preimage and image. Then identify the transformation.

SEE EXAMPLE 3

6. **Multi-Step** The coordinates of the vertices of $\triangle DEF$ are $D(2, 3)$, $E(1, 1)$, and $F(4, 0)$. Find the coordinates for the image of $\triangle DEF$ after the translation $(x, y) \rightarrow (x - 3, y - 2)$. Draw the preimage and image.

SEE EXAMPLE 4

7. **Animation** In an animated film, a simple scene can be created by translating a figure against a still background. Write a rule for the translation that maps the rocket from position 1 to position 2.

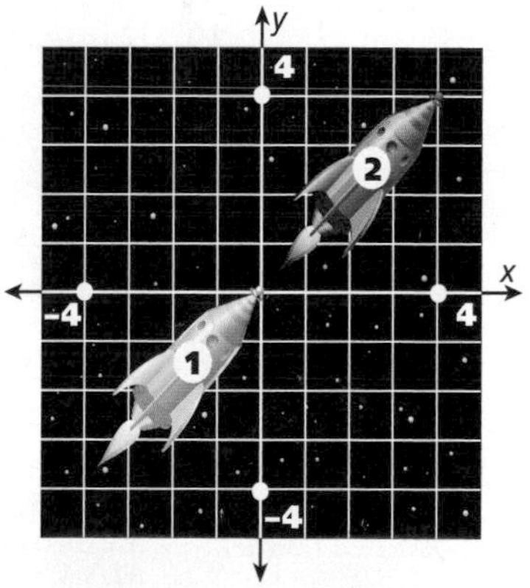

PRACTICE AND PROBLEM SOLVING

Independent Practice

For Exercises	See Example
8–9	1
10	2
11	3
12	4

Extra Practice

See Extra Practice for more Skills Practice and Applications Practice exercises.

Identify each transformation. Then use arrow notation to describe the transformation.

8.
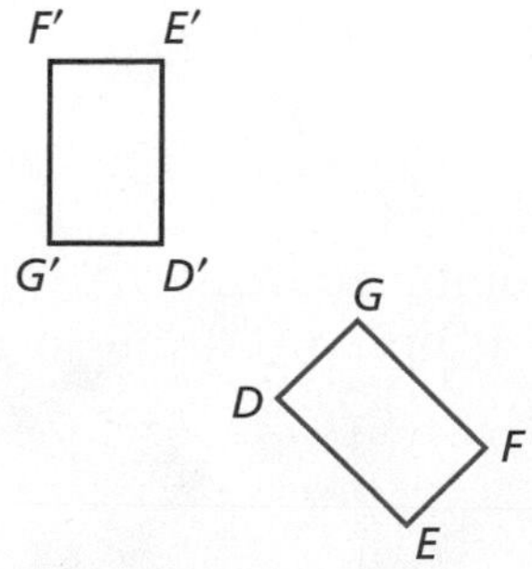

9.
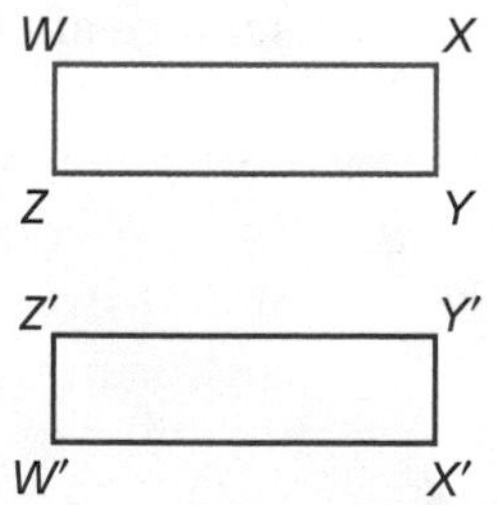

10. A figure has vertices at $J(-2, 3)$, $K(0, 3)$, $L(0, 1)$, and $M(-2, 1)$. After a transformation, the image of the figure has vertices at $J'(2, 1)$, $K'(4, 1)$, $L'(4, -1)$, and $M'(2, -1)$. Draw the preimage and image. Then identify the transformation.

11. **Multi-Step** The coordinates of the vertices of rectangle $ABCD$ are $A(-4, 1)$, $B(1, 1)$, $C(1, -2)$, and $D(-4, -2)$. Find the coordinates for the image of rectangle $ABCD$ after the translation $(x, y) \rightarrow (x + 3, y - 2)$. Draw the preimage and the image.

12. **Travel** Write a rule for the translation that maps the descent of the hot air balloon.

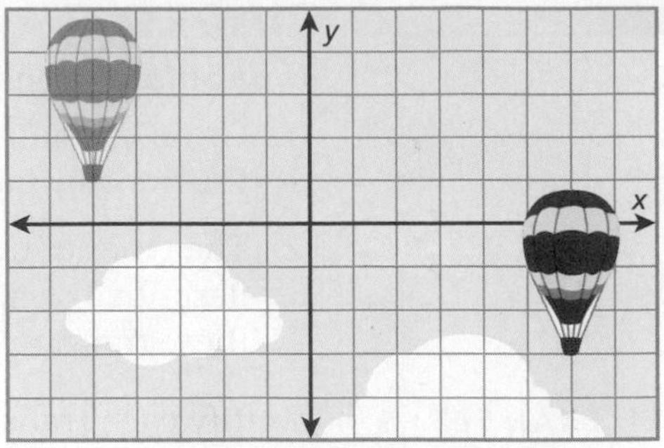

Which transformation is suggested by each of the following?

13. mountain range and its image on a lake

14. straight line path of a band marching down a street

15. wings of a butterfly

Given points $F(3, 5)$, $G(-1, 4)$, and $H(5, 0)$, draw $\triangle FGH$ and its reflection across each of the following lines.

16. the x-axis

17. the y-axis

18. Find the vertices of one of the triangles on the graph. Then use arrow notation to write a rule for translating the other three triangles.

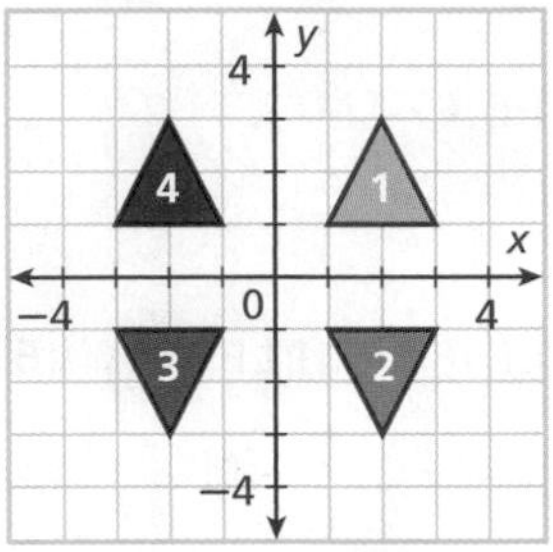

A transformation maps A onto B and C onto D.

19. Name the image of A.

20. Name the preimage of B.

21. Name the image of C.

22. Name the preimage of D.

23. Find the coordinates for the image of $\triangle RST$ with vertices $R(1, -4)$, $S(-1, -1)$, and $T(-5, 1)$ after the translation $(x, y) \rightarrow (x - 2, y - 8)$.

24. **Critical Thinking** Consider the translations $(x, y) \rightarrow (x + 5, y + 3)$ and $(x, y) \rightarrow (x + 10, y + 5)$. Compare the two translations.

Graph each figure and its image after the given translation.

25. $\overline{MN}$ with endpoints $M(2, 8)$ and $N(-3, 4)$ after the translation $(x, y) \rightarrow (x + 2, y - 5)$

26. $\overline{KL}$ with endpoints $K(-1, 1)$ and $L(3, -4)$ after the translation $(x, y) \rightarrow (x - 4, y + 3)$

27. **Write About It** Given a triangle in the coordinate plane, explain how to draw its image after the translation $(x, y) \rightarrow (x + 1, y + 1)$.

MULTI-STEP TEST PREP

28. Greg wants to rearrange the triangular pattern of colored stones on his patio. What combination of transformations could he use to transform $\triangle CAE$ to the image on the coordinate plane?

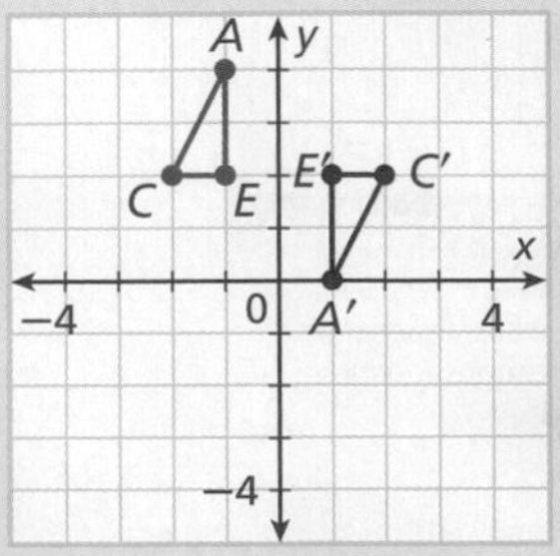

(tl), Ocean/Corbis; (bl), Sam Dudgeon/HMH

TEST PREP

29. Which type of transformation maps $\triangle XYZ$ to $\triangle X'Y'Z'$?

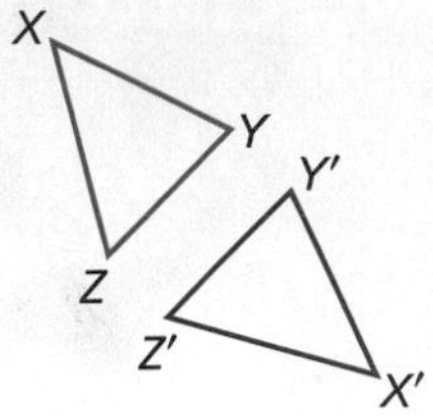

Ⓐ Reflection   Ⓒ Translation
Ⓑ Rotation   Ⓓ Not here

30. $\triangle DEF$ has vertices at $D(-4, 2)$, $E(-3, -3)$, and $F(1, 4)$. Which of these points is a vertex of the image of $\triangle DEF$ after the translation $(x, y) \rightarrow (x - 2, y + 1)$?

Ⓕ $(-2, 1)$ Ⓗ $(-5, -2)$
Ⓖ $(3, 3)$ Ⓙ $(-6, -1)$

31. Consider the translation $(1, 4) \rightarrow (-2, 3)$. What number was added to the x-coordinate?

Ⓐ -3 Ⓑ -1 Ⓒ 1   Ⓓ 7

32. Consider the translation $(-5, -7) \rightarrow (-2, -1)$. What number was added to the y-coordinate?

Ⓕ -3 Ⓖ 3   Ⓗ 6   Ⓙ 8

CHALLENGE AND EXTEND

33. $\triangle RST$ with vertices $R(-2, -2)$, $S(-3, 1)$, and $T(1, 1)$ is translated by $(x, y) \rightarrow (x - 1, y + 3)$. Then the image, $\triangle R'S'T'$, is translated by $(x, y) \rightarrow (x + 4, y - 1)$, resulting in $\triangle R''S''T''$.
    a. Find the coordinates for the vertices of $\triangle R''S''T''$.
    b. Write a rule for a single translation that maps $\triangle RST$ to $\triangle R''S''T''$.

34. Find the angle through which the minute hand of a clock rotates over a period of 12 minutes.

35. A triangle has vertices $A(1, 0)$, $B(5, 0)$, and $C(2, 3)$. The triangle is rotated 90° counterclockwise about the origin. Draw and label the image of the triangle.

Determine the coordinates for the reflection image of any point $A(x, y)$ across the given line.

36. x-axis   37. y-axis

1-7
Technology LAB

Use with Transformations in the Coordinate Plane

Explore Transformations

A transformation is a movement of a figure from its original position (preimage) to a new position (image). In this lab, you will use geometry software to perform transformations and explore their properties.

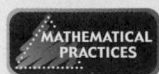

MATHEMATICAL PRACTICES **Use appropriate tools strategically.**

CC.9-12.G.CO.2 Represent transformations in the plane using…geometry software… *Also* **CC.9-12.G.CO.5**

Learn It Online
Lab Resources Online

Activity 1

1. Construct a triangle using the segment tool. Use the text tool to label the vertices *A, B,* and *C.*

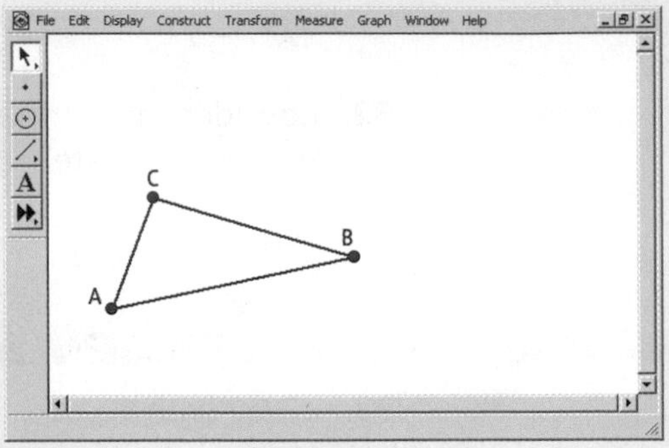

2. Select points *A* and *B* in that order. Choose Mark Vector from the Transform menu.

3. Select $\triangle ABC$ by clicking on all three segments of the triangle.

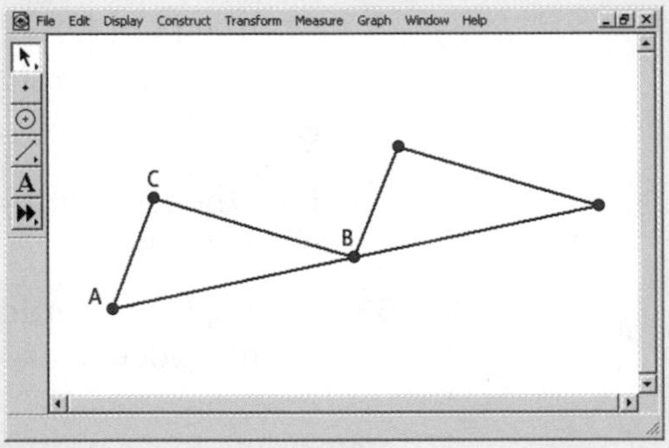

4. Choose Translate from the Transform menu, using *Marked* as the translation vector. What do you notice about the relationship between your preimage and its image?

5. What happens when you drag a vertex or a side of $\triangle ABC$?

Try This

For Problems 1 and 2 choose New Sketch from the File menu.

1. Construct a triangle and a segment outside the triangle. Mark this segment as a translation vector as you did in Step 2 of Activity 1. Use Step 4 of Activity 1 to translate the triangle. What happens when you drag an endpoint of the new segment?

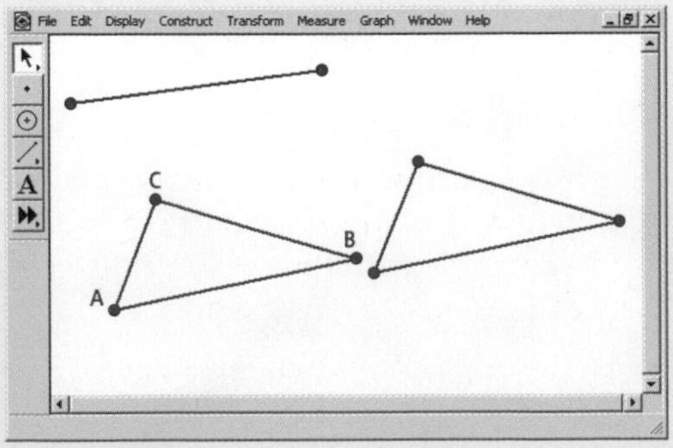

2. Instead of translating by a marked vector, use *Rectangular* as the translation vector and translate by a horizontal distance of 1 cm and a vertical distance of 2 cm. Compare this method with the marked vector method. What happens when you drag a side or vertex of the triangle?
3. Select the angles and sides of the preimage and image triangles. Use the tools in the Measure menu to measure length, angle measure, perimeter, and area. What do you think is true about these two figures?

Activity 2

1. Construct a triangle. Label the vertices *G, H,* and *I.*

2. Select point *H* and choose Mark Center from the Transform menu.

3. Select ∠*GHI* by selecting points *G, H,* and *I* in that order. Choose Mark Angle from the Transform menu.

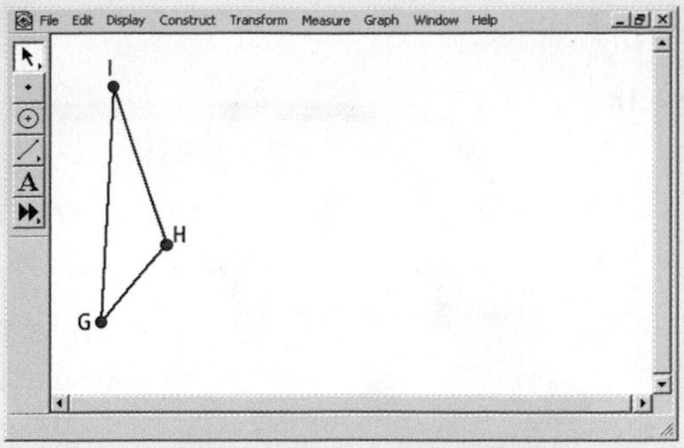

4. Select the entire triangle △*GHI* by dragging a selection box around the figure.

5. Choose Rotate from the Transform menu, using *Marked Angle* as the angle of rotation.

6. What happens when you drag a vertex or a side of △*GHI*?

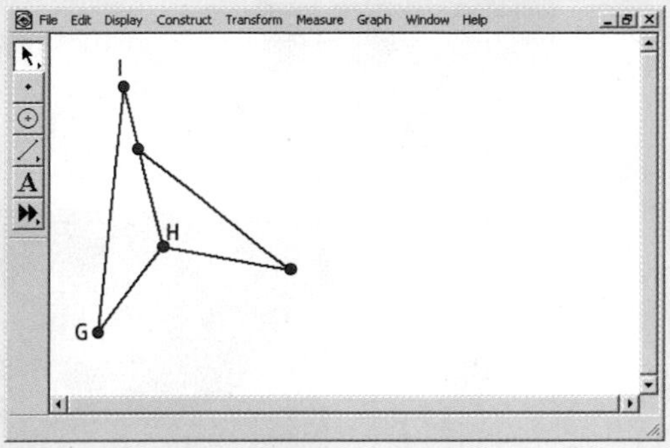

Try This

For Problems 4–6 choose New Sketch from the File menu.

4. Instead of selecting an angle of the triangle as the rotation angle, draw a new angle outside of the triangle. Mark this angle. Mark ∠*GHI* as Center and rotate the triangle. What happens when you drag one of the points that form the rotation angle?

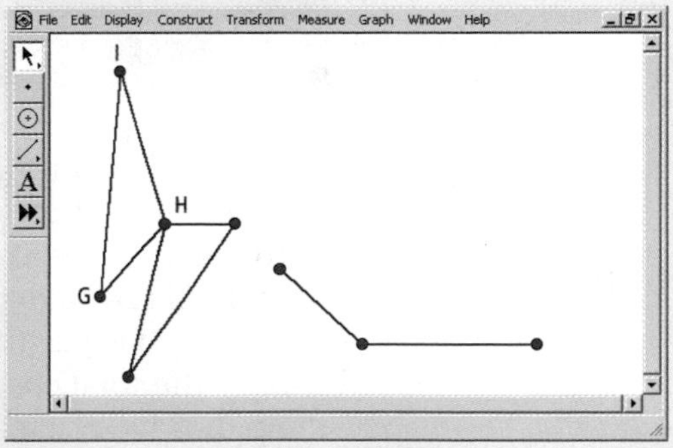

5. Construct △*QRS,* a new rotation angle, and a point *P* not on the triangle. Mark *P* as the center and mark the angle. Rotate the triangle. What happens when you drag *P* outside, inside, or on the preimage triangle?

6. Instead of rotating by a marked angle, use *Fixed Angle* as the rotation method and rotate by a fixed angle measure of 30°. Compare this method with the marked angle method.

7. Using the fixed angle method of rotation, can you find an angle measure that will result in an image figure that exactly covers the preimage figure?

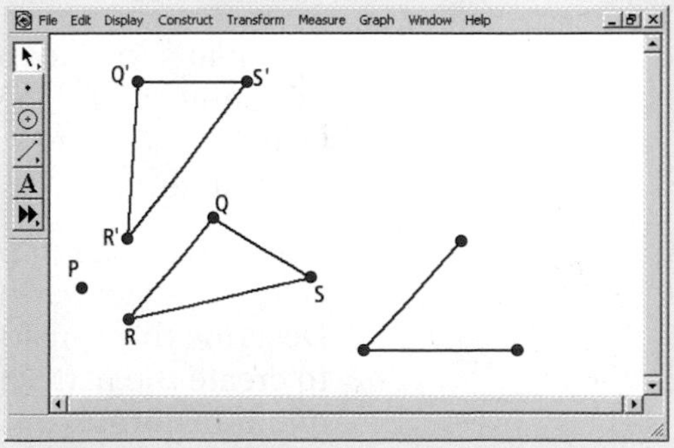

CHAPTER 1

MULTI-STEP TEST PREP

SECTION 1B

MATHEMATICAL PRACTICES **Reason abstractly and quantitatively.**

Coordinate and Transformation Tools

Pave the Way Julia wants to use L-shaped paving stones to pave a patio. Two stones will cover a 12 in. by 18 in. rectangle.

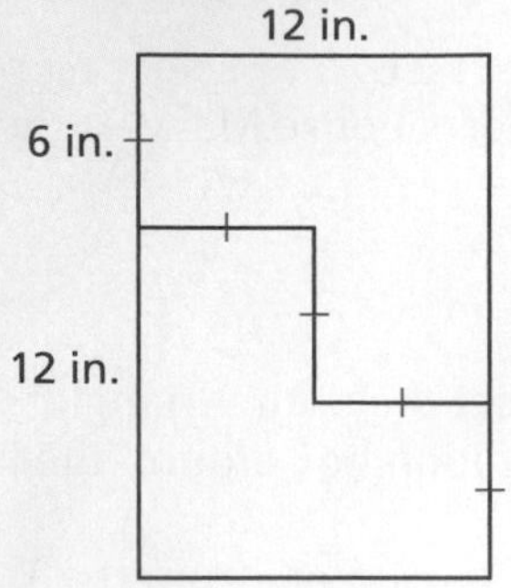

1. She drew diagram *ABCDEF* to represent the patio. Find the area and perimeter of the patio. How many paving stones would Julia need to purchase to pave the patio? If each stone costs $2.25, what is the total cost of the stones for the patio? Describe how you calculated your answer.

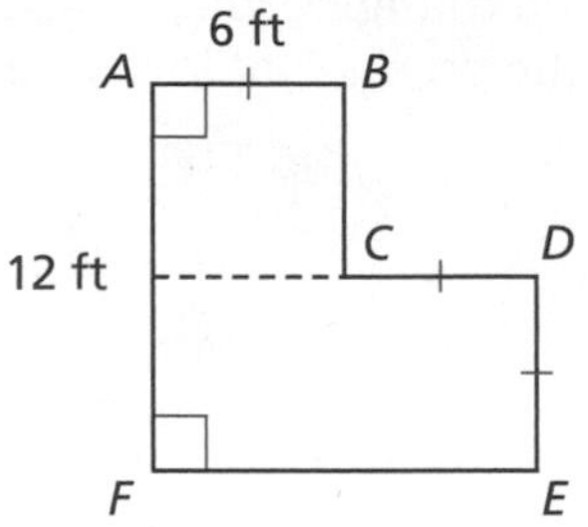

2. Julia plans to place a fountain at the midpoint of $\overline{AF}$. How far is the fountain from *B*, *C*, *E*, and *F*? Round to the nearest tenth.

3. Julia used a pair of paving stones to create another pattern for the patio. Describe the transformation she used to create the pattern. If she uses just one transformation, how many other patterns can she create using two stones? Draw all the possible combinations. Describe the transformation used to create each pattern.

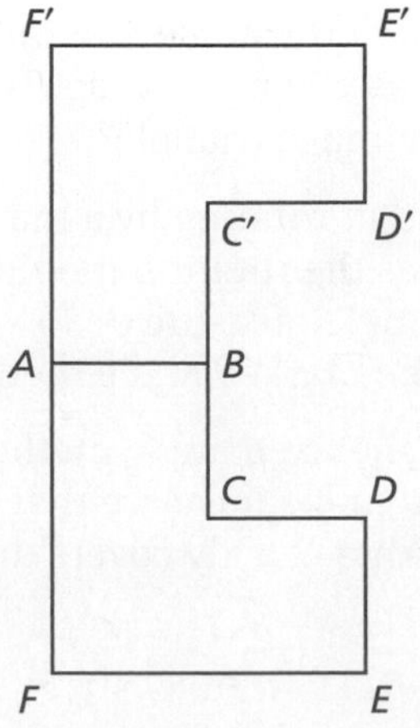

READY TO GO ON?

CHAPTER 1

SECTION 1B

Quiz for Lessons 1-5 Through 1-7

1-5 Using Formulas in Geometry

Find the perimeter and area of each figure.

1.

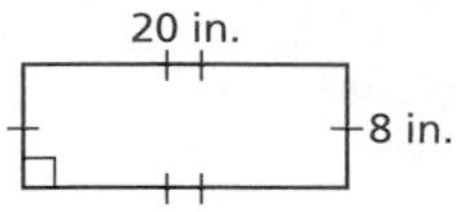

2.

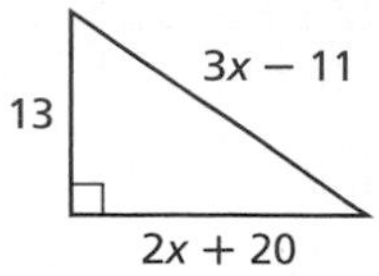

3.

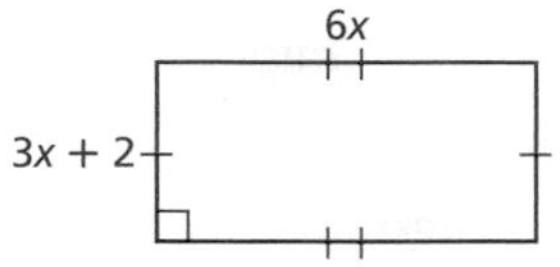

4.

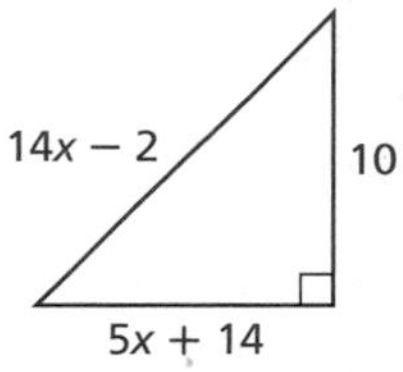

5. Find the circumference and area of a circle with a radius of 6 m. Use the π key on your calculator and round to the nearest tenth.

1-6 Midpoint and Distance in the Coordinate Plane

6. Find the coordinates for the midpoint of $\overline{XY}$ with endpoints $X(-4, 6)$ and $Y(3, 8)$.
7. J is the midpoint of $\overline{HK}$, H has coordinates $(6, -2)$, and J has coordinates $(9, 3)$. Find the coordinates of K.
8. Using the Distance Formula, find QR and ST to the nearest tenth. Then determine if $\overline{QR} \cong \overline{ST}$.
9. Using the Distance Formula and the Pythagorean Theorem, find the distance, to the nearest tenth, from $F(4, 3)$ to $G(-3, -2)$.

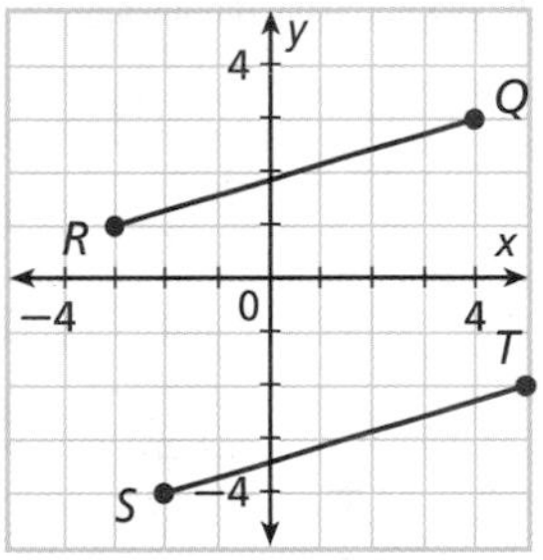

1-7 Transformations in the Coordinate Plane

Identify the transformation. Then use arrow notation to describe the transformation.

10.

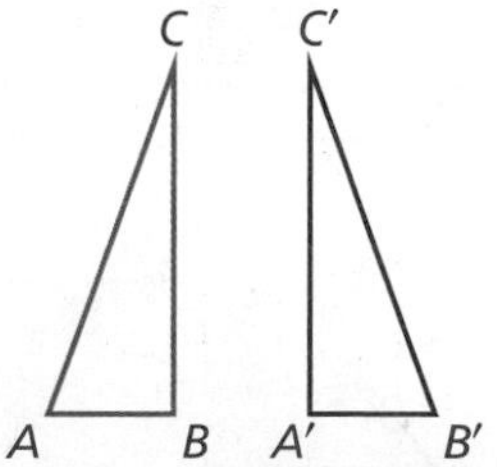

11.

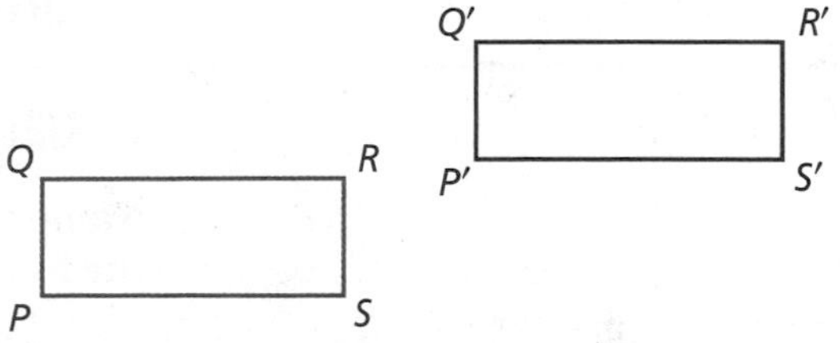

12. A graphic designer used the translation $(x, y) \rightarrow (x - 3, y + 2)$ to transform square $HJKL$. Find the coordinates and graph the image of square $HJKL$.
13. A figure has vertices at $X(1, 1)$, $Y(3, 1)$, and $Z(3, 4)$. After a transformation, the image of the figure has vertices at $X'(-1, -1)$, $Y'(-3, -1)$, and $Z'(-3, -4)$. Graph the preimage and image. Then identify the transformation.

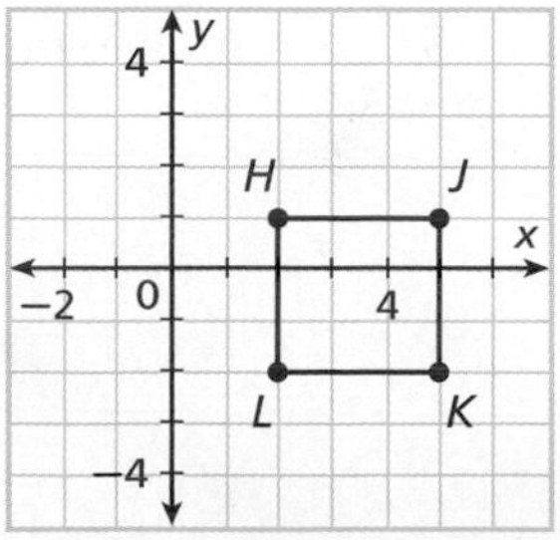

CHAPTER 1

Study Guide: Review

Know it! Note

For a complete list of postulates, theorems, and corollaries, see p. PT2.

Vocabulary

acute angle
adjacent angles
angle
angle bisector
area
base
between
bisect
circumference
collinear
complementary angles
congruent angles
congruent segments
construction
coordinate
coordinate plane
coplanar
degree
diameter
distance
endpoint
exterior of an angle
height
hypotenuse
image
interior of an angle
leg
length
line
linear pair
measure
midpoint
obtuse angle
opposite rays
perimeter
pi
plane
point
postulate
preimage
radius
ray
reflection
right angle
rotation
segment
segment bisector
straight angle
supplementary angles
transformation
translation
undefined term
vertex
vertical angles

Complete the sentences below with vocabulary words from the list above.

1. A(n) ___?___ divides an angle into two congruent angles.
2. ___?___ are two angles whose measures have a sum of 90°.
3. The length of the longest side of a right triangle is called the ___?___ .

1-1 Understanding Points, Lines, and Planes

EXAMPLES

■ **Name the common endpoint of $\overrightarrow{SR}$ and $\overrightarrow{ST}$.**

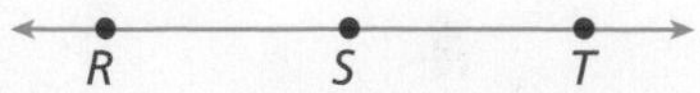

$\overrightarrow{SR}$ and $\overrightarrow{ST}$ are opposite rays with common endpoint *S*.

EXERCISES

Name each of the following.

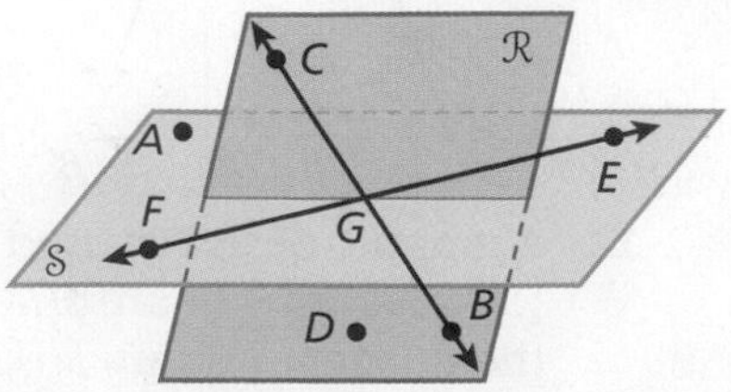

4. four coplanar points
5. line containing *B* and *C*
6. plane that contains *A*, *G*, and *E*

- **Draw and label three coplanar lines intersecting in one point.**

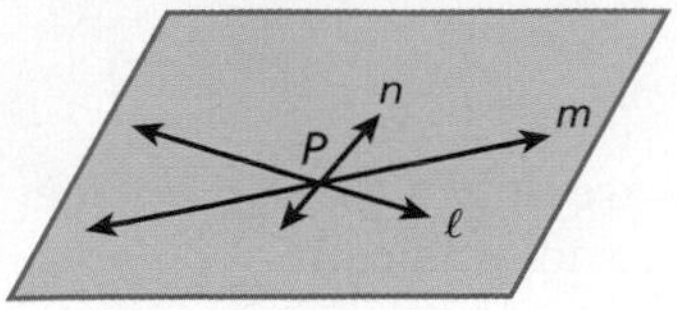

Draw and label each of the following.

7. line containing P and Q
8. pair of opposite rays both containing C
9. $\overleftrightarrow{CD}$ intersecting plane $\mathcal{P}$ at B

1-2 Measuring and Constructing Segments

EXAMPLES

- **Find the length of $\overline{XY}$.**

$XY = |-2 - 1|$
$= |-3| = 3$

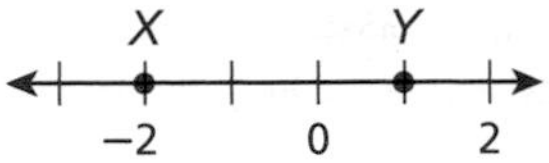

- **S is between R and T. Find RT.**

$RT = RS + ST$
$3x + 2 = 5x - 6 + 2x$
$3x + 2 = 7x - 6$
$x = 2$
$RT = 3(2) + 2 = 8$

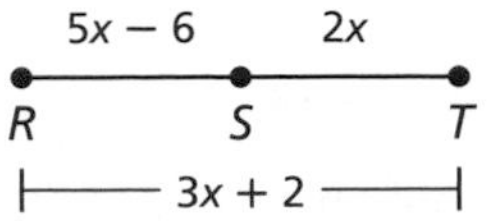

EXERCISES

Find each length.

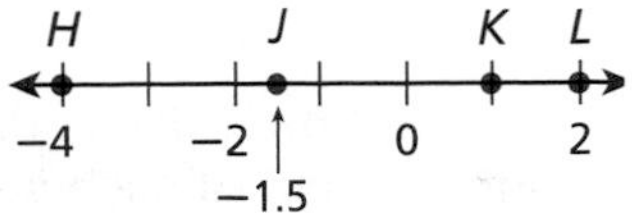

10. JL
11. HK
12. Y is between X and Z, $XY = 13.8$, and $XZ = 21.4$. Find YZ.
13. Q is between P and R. Find PR.

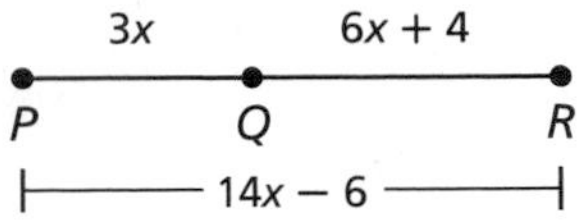

14. U is the midpoint of $\overline{TV}$, $TU = 3x + 4$, and $UV = 5x - 2$. Find TU, UV, and TV.
15. E is the midpoint of $\overline{DF}$, $DE = 9x$, and $EF = 4x + 10$. Find DE, EF, and DF.

1-3 Measuring and Constructing Angles

EXAMPLES

- **Classify each angle as acute, right, or obtuse.**

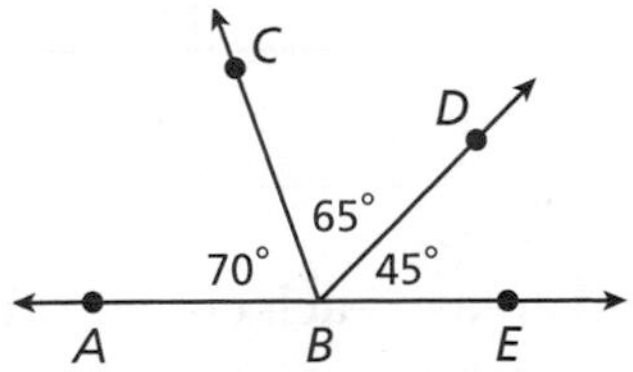

$\angle ABC$ acute;
$\angle CBD$ acute;
$\angle ABD$ obtuse;
$\angle DBE$ acute;
$\angle CBE$ obtuse

- **$\overline{KM}$ bisects $\angle JKL$, $m\angle JKM = (3x + 4)°$, and $m\angle MKL = (6x - 5)°$. Find $m\angle JKL$.**

$3x + 4 = 6x - 5$	*Def. of ∠ bisector*
$3x + 9 = 6x$	*Add 5 to both sides.*
$9 = 3x$	*Subtract 3x from both sides.*
$x = 3$	*Divide both sides by 3.*

$m\angle JKL = 3x + 4 + 6x - 5$
$= 9x - 1$
$= 9(3) - 1 = 26°$

EXERCISES

16. Classify each angle as acute, right, or obtuse.

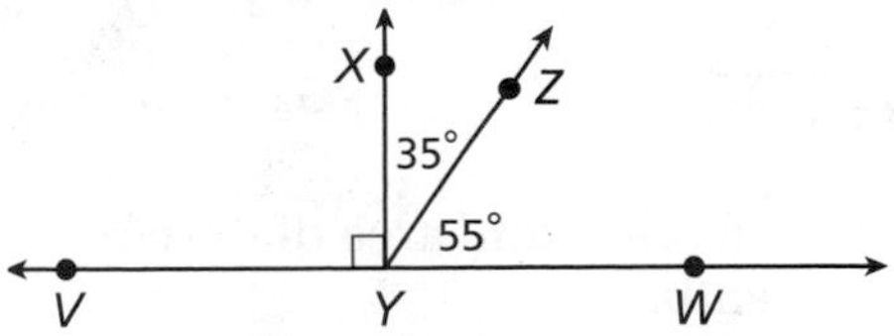

17. $m\angle HJL = 116°$. Find $m\angle HJK$.
18. $\overrightarrow{NP}$ bisects $\angle MNQ$, $m\angle MNP = (6x - 12)°$, and $m\angle PNQ = (4x + 8)°$. Find $m\angle MNQ$.

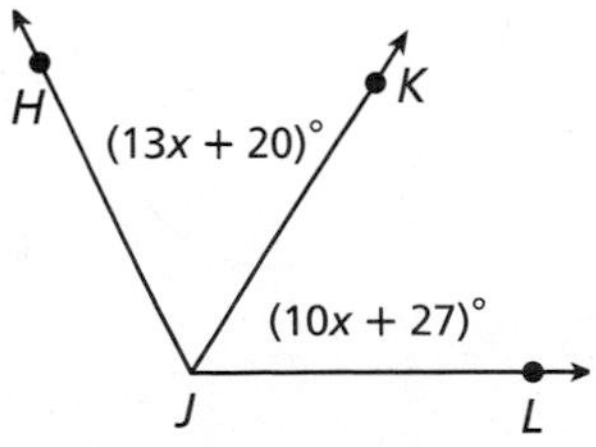

1-4 Pairs of Angles

EXAMPLES

■ **Tell whether the angles are only adjacent, adjacent and form a linear pair, or not adjacent.**

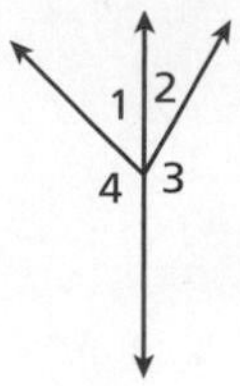

$\angle 1$ and $\angle 2$ are only adjacent.

$\angle 2$ and $\angle 4$ are not adjacent.

$\angle 2$ and $\angle 3$ are adjacent and form a linear pair.

$\angle 1$ and $\angle 4$ are adjacent and form a linear pair.

■ **Find the measure of the complement and supplement of each angle.**

$90 - 67.3 = 22.7°$

$180 - 67.3 = 112.7°$

$90 - (3x - 8) = (98 - 3x)°$

$180 - (3x - 8) = (188 - 3x)°$

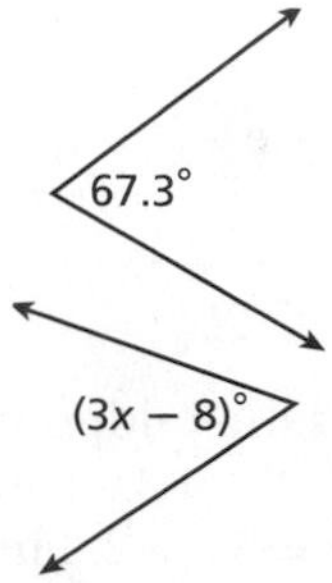

EXERCISES

Tell whether the angles are only adjacent, adjacent and form a linear pair, or not adjacent.

19. $\angle 1$ and $\angle 2$

20. $\angle 3$ and $\angle 4$

21. $\angle 2$ and $\angle 5$

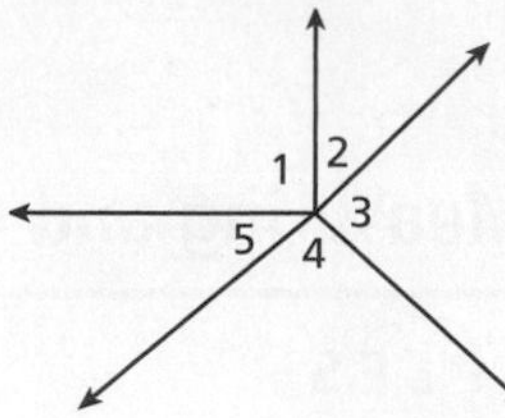

Find the measure of the complement and supplement of each angle.

22.

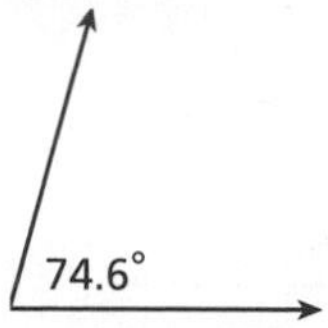

23.

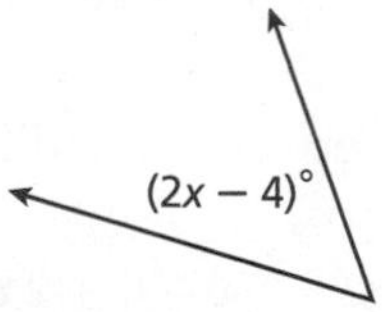

24. An angle measures 5 degrees more than 4 times its complement. Find the measure of the angle.

1-5 Using Formulas in Geometry

EXAMPLES

■ **Find the perimeter and area of the triangle.**

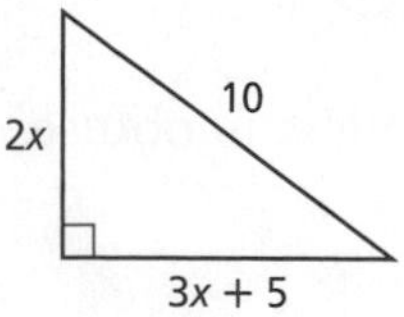

$P = 2x + 3x + 5 + 10$
$= 5x + 15$
$A = \frac{1}{2}(3x + 5)(2x)$
$= 3x^2 + 5x$

■ **Find the circumference and area of the circle to the nearest tenth.**

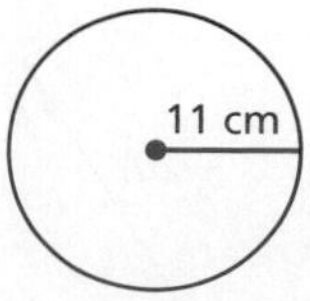

$C = 2\pi r$
$= 2\pi(11)$
$= 22\pi$
≈ 69.1 cm
$A = \pi r^2$
$= \pi(11)^2$
$= 121\pi$
$\approx 380.1 \text{ cm}^2$

EXERCISES

Find the perimeter and area of each figure.

25.

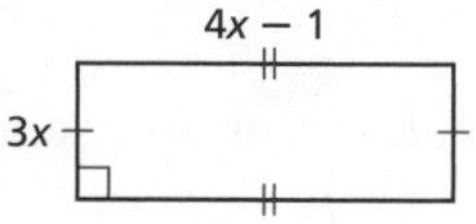

26.

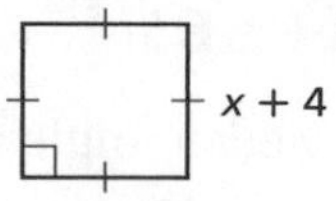

27.

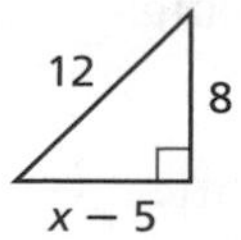

28.

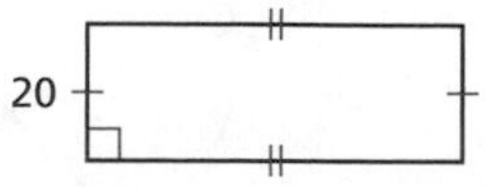

Find the circumference and area of each circle to the nearest tenth.

29.

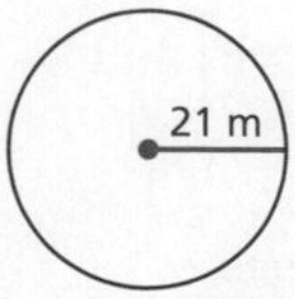

30.

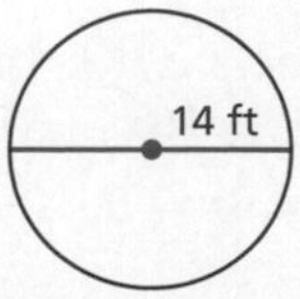

31. The area of a triangle is 102 m^2. The base of the triangle is 17 m. What is the height of the triangle?

1-6 Midpoint and Distance in the Coordinate Plane

EXAMPLES

■ **X is the midpoint of $\overline{CD}$. C has coordinates $(-4, 1)$, and X has coordinates $(3, -2)$. Find the coordinates of D.**

$$(3, -2) = \left(\frac{-4 + x}{2}, \frac{1 + y}{2}\right)$$

$$3 = \frac{-4 + x}{2} \qquad -2 = \frac{1 + y}{2}$$

$$6 = -4 + x \qquad -4 = 1 + y$$

$$10 = x \qquad -5 = y$$

The coordinates of D are $(10, -5)$.

■ **Use the Distance Formula and the Pythagorean Theorem to find the distance, to the nearest tenth, from $(1, 6)$ to $(4, 2)$.**

$$d = \sqrt{(4 - 1)^2 + (2 - 6)^2} \qquad c^2 = a^2 + b^2$$

$$= \sqrt{3^2 + (-4)^2} \qquad = 3^2 + 4^2$$

$$= \sqrt{9 + 16} \qquad = 9 + 16 = 25$$

$$= \sqrt{25} \qquad c = \sqrt{25}$$

$$= 5.0 \qquad = 5.0$$

EXERCISES

Y is the midpoint of $\overline{AB}$. Find the missing coordinates of each point.

32. $A(3, 2)$; $B(-1, 4)$; $Y(■, ■)$

33. $A(5, 0)$; $B(■, ■)$; $Y(-2, 3)$

34. $A(■, ■)$; $B(-4, 4)$; $Y(-2, 3)$

Use the Distance Formula and the Pythagorean Theorem to find the distance, to the nearest tenth, between each pair of points.

35. $X(-2, 4)$ and $Y(6, 1)$

36. $H(0, 3)$ and $K(-2, -4)$

37. $L(-4, 2)$ and $M(3, -2)$

1-7 Transformations in the Coordinate Plane

EXAMPLES

■ **Identify the transformation. Then use arrow notation to describe the transformation.**

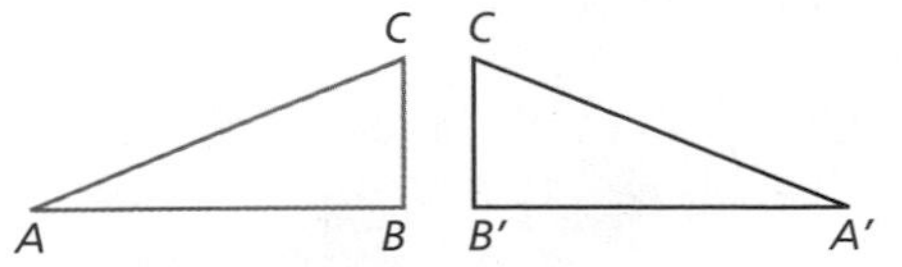

The transformation is a reflection.
$\triangle ABC \rightarrow \triangle A'B'C'$

■ **The coordinates of the vertices of rectangle $HJKL$ are $H(2, -1)$, $J(5, -1)$, $K(5, -3)$, and $L(2, -3)$. Find the coordinates of the image of rectangle $HJKL$ after the translation $(x, y) \rightarrow (x - 4, y + 1)$.**

$H' = (2 - 4, -1 + 1) = H'(-2, 0)$
$J' = (5 - 4, -1 + 1) = J'(1, 0)$
$K' = (5 - 4, -3 + 1) = K'(1, -2)$
$L' = (2 - 4, -3 + 1) = L'(-2, -2)$

EXERCISES

Identify each transformation. Then use arrow notation to describe the transformation.

38.

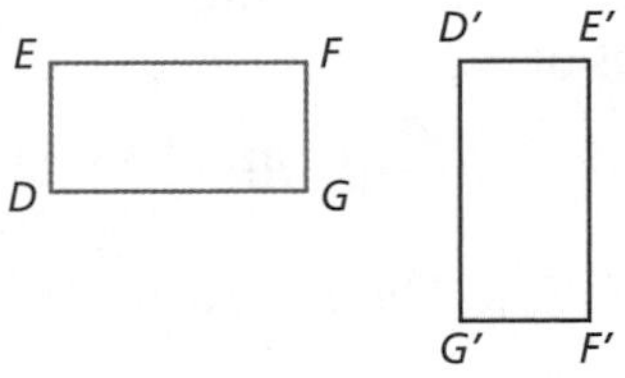

39.

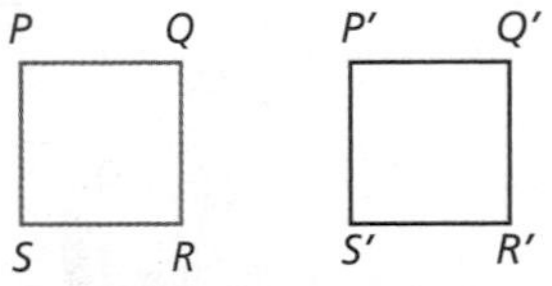

40. The coordinates for the vertices of $\triangle XYZ$ are $X(-5, -4)$, $Y(-3, -1)$, and $Z(-2, -2)$. Find the coordinates for the image of $\triangle XYZ$ after the translation $(x, y) \rightarrow (x + 4, y + 5)$.

CHAPTER 1

CHAPTER TEST

1. Draw and label plane $\mathcal{N}$ containing two lines that intersect at B.

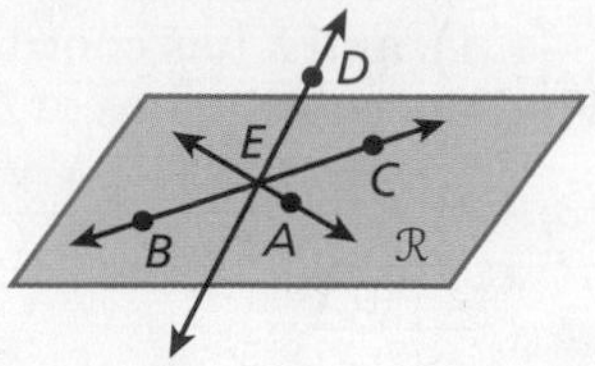

Use the figure to name each of the following.

2. four noncoplanar points
3. line containing B and E
4. The coordinate of A is -3, and the coordinate of B is 0.5. Find AB.
5. E, F, and G represent mile markers along a straight highway. Find EF.

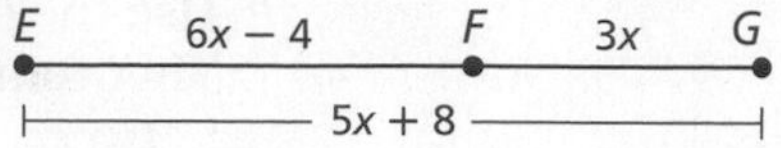

6. J is the midpoint of $\overline{HK}$. Find HJ, JK, and HK.

Classify each angle by its measure.

7. $m\angle LMP = 70°$
8. $m\angle QMN = 90°$
9. $m\angle PMN = 125°$
10. $\overrightarrow{TV}$ bisects $\angle RTS$. If the $m\angle RTV = (16x - 6)°$ and $m\angle VTS = (13x + 9)°$, what is the $m\angle RTV$?
11. An angle's measure is 5 degrees less than 3 times the measure of its supplement. Find the measure of the angle and its supplement.

Tell whether the angles are only adjacent, adjacent and form a linear pair, or not adjacent.

12. $\angle 2$ and $\angle 3$
13. $\angle 4$ and $\angle 5$
14. $\angle 1$ and $\angle 4$

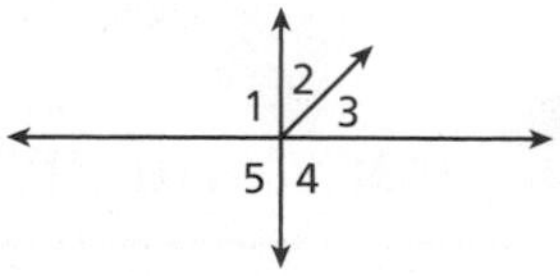

15. Find the perimeter and area of a rectangle with $b = 8$ ft and $h = 4$ ft.

Find the circumference and area of each circle to the nearest tenth.

16. $r = 15$ m
17. $d = 25$ ft
18. $d = 2.8$ cm
19. Find the midpoint of the segment with endpoints $(-4, 6)$ and $(3, 2)$.
20. M is the midpoint of $\overline{LN}$. M has coordinates $(-5, 1)$, and L has coordinates $(2, 4)$. Find the coordinates of N.
21. Given $A(-5, 1)$, $B(-1, 3)$, $C(1, 4)$, and $D(4, 1)$, is $\overline{AB} \cong \overline{CD}$? Explain.

Identify each transformation. Then use arrow notation to describe the transformation.

22.

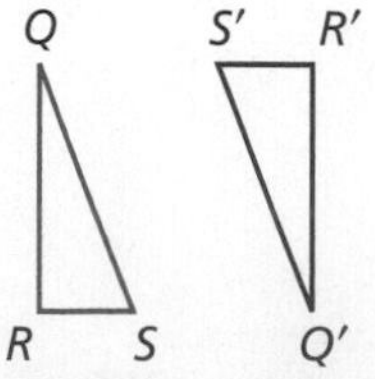

23.

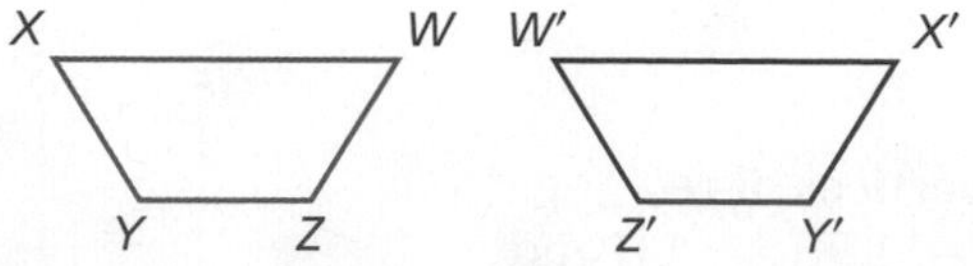

24. A designer used the translation $(x, y) \rightarrow (x + 3, y - 3)$ to transform a triangular-shaped pin ABC. Find the coordinates and draw the image of $\triangle ABC$.

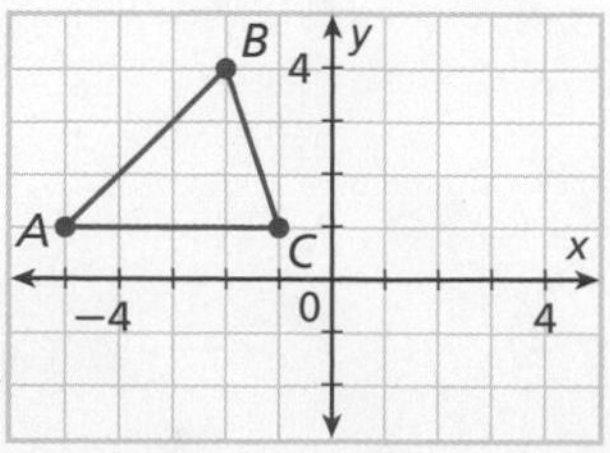

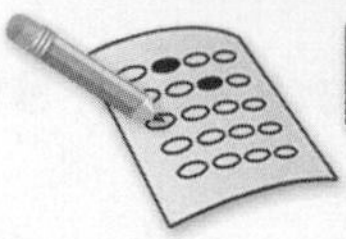

College Entrance Exam Practice

CHAPTER 1

FOCUS ON SAT

The SAT* has three sections: Mathematics, Critical Reading, and Writing. Your SAT scores show how you compare with other students. It can be used by colleges to determine admission and to award merit-based financial aid.

HOT TIP! **On SAT multiple-choice questions, you receive one point for each correct answer, but you lose a fraction of a point for each incorrect response. Guess only when you can eliminate at least one of the answer choices.**

You may want to time yourself as you take this practice test. It should take you about 6 minutes to complete.

1. Points D, E, F, and G are on a line, in that order. If $DE = 2$, $FG = 5$, and $DF = 6$, what is the value of $EG(DG)$?

(A) 13

(B) 18

(C) 19

(D) 42

(E) 99

2. $\overrightarrow{QS}$ bisects $\angle PQR$, $m\angle PQR = (4x + 2)°$, and $m\angle SQR = (3x - 6)°$. What is the value of x?

(A) 1

(B) 4

(C) 7

(D) 10

(E) 19

3. A rectangular garden is enclosed by a brick border. The total length of bricks used to enclose the garden is 42 meters. If the length of the garden is twice the width, what is the area of the garden?

(A) 7 meters

(B) 14 meters

(C) 42 meters

(D) 42 square meters

(E) 98 square meters

4. What is the area of the square?

(A) 16

(B) 25

(C) 32

(D) 36

(E) 41

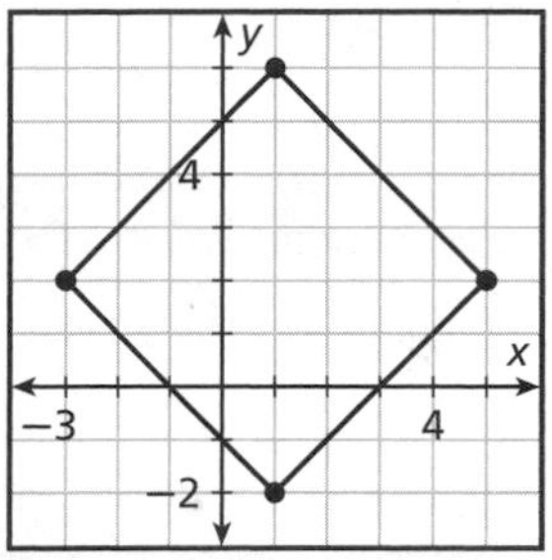

5. If $\angle BFD$ and $\angle AFC$ are right angles and $m\angle CFD = 72°$, what is the value of x?

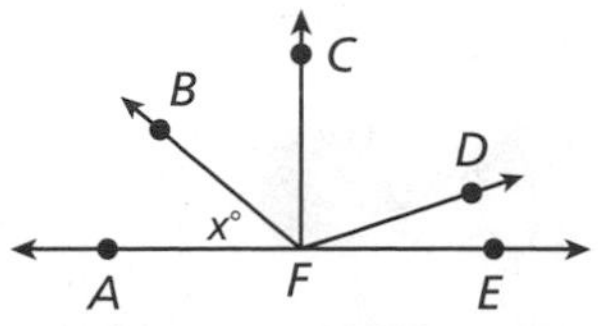

Note: Figure not drawn to scale.

(A) 18

(B) 36

(C) 72

(D) 90

(E) 108

*SAT is a registered trademark of the College Board, which was not involved in the production of, and does not endorse, this product.

CHAPTER 1

TEST TACKLER

Standardized Test Strategies

Multiple Choice: Work Backward

When you do not know how to solve a multiple-choice test item, use the answer choices and work the question backward. Plug in the answer choices to see which choice makes the question true.

EXAMPLE 1

T is the midpoint of $\overline{RC}$, $RT = 12x - 8$, and $TC = 28$. What is the value of x?

Ⓐ -4 Ⓒ 3

Ⓑ 2 Ⓓ 28

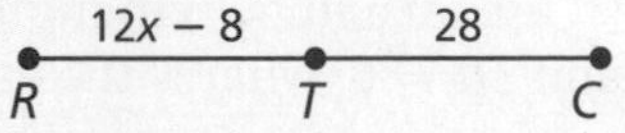

Since T is the midpoint of $\overline{RC}$, then $RT = RC$, or $12x - 8 = 28$.
Find what value of x makes the left side of the equation equal 28.

Try choice A: If $x = -4$, then $12x - 8 = 12(-4) - 8 = -56$.
This choice is not correct because length is always a positive number.

Try choice B: If $x = 2$, then $12x - 8 = 12(2) - 8 = 16$.
Since $16 \neq 28$, choice B is not the answer.

Try choice C: If $x = 3$, then $12x - 8 = 12(3) - 8 = 28$.

Since $28 = 28$, the correct answer is C, 3.

EXAMPLE 2

Joel used 6400 feet of fencing to make a rectangular horse pen. The width of the pen is 4 times as long as the length. What is the length of the horse pen?

Ⓕ 25 feet Ⓗ 640 feet

Ⓖ 480 feet Ⓙ 1600 feet

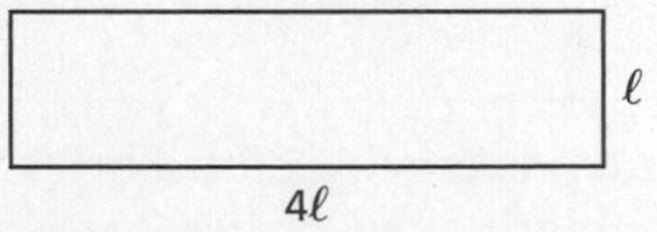

Use the formula $P = 2\ell + 2w$. $P = 6400$ and $w = 4\ell$. You can work backward to determine which answer choice is the most reasonable.

Try choice J: Use mental math. If $\ell = 1600$, then $4\ell = 6400$. This choice is not reasonable because the perimeter of the pen would then be far greater than 6400 feet.

Try choice F: Use mental math. If $\ell = 25$, then $4\ell = 100$. This choice is incorrect because the perimeter of the pen is 6400 ft, which is far greater than $2(25) + 2(100)$.

Try choice H: If $\ell = 640$, then $4\ell = 2560$. When you substitute these values into the perimeter formula, it makes a true statement.

The correct answer is H, 640 ft.

Read each test item and answer the questions that follow.

Item A

The measure of an angle is 3 times as great as that of its complement. Which value is the measure of the smaller angle?

Ⓐ 22.5° Ⓒ 63.5°

Ⓑ 27.5° Ⓓ 67.5°

1. Are there any definitions that you can use to solve this problem? If so, what are they?
2. Describe how to work backward to find the correct answer.

Item B

In a town's annual relay marathon race, the second runner of each team starts at mile marker 4 and runs to the halfway point of the 26-mile marathon. At that point the second runner passes the relay baton to the third runner of the team. How many total miles does the second runner of each team run?

Ⓕ 4 miles Ⓗ 9 miles

Ⓖ 6.5 miles Ⓙ 13 miles

3. Which answer choice should you plug in first? Why?
4. Describe, by working backward, how you know that choices F and G are not correct.

Item C

Consider the translation $(-2, 8) \rightarrow (8, -4)$. What number was added to the x-coordinate?

Ⓐ −12 Ⓒ 4

Ⓑ −6 Ⓓ 10

5. Which answer choice should you plug in first? Why?
6. Explain how to work the test question backward to determine the correct answer.

HOT TIP! When you work a test question backward start with choice C. The choices are usually listed in order from least to greatest. If choice C is incorrect because it is too low, you do not need to plug in the smaller numbers.

Item D

$\triangle QRS$ has vertices at $Q(3, 5)$, $R(3, 9)$, and $S(7, 5)$. Which of these points is a vertex of the image of $\triangle QRS$ after the translation $(x, y) \rightarrow (x - 7, y - 6)$?

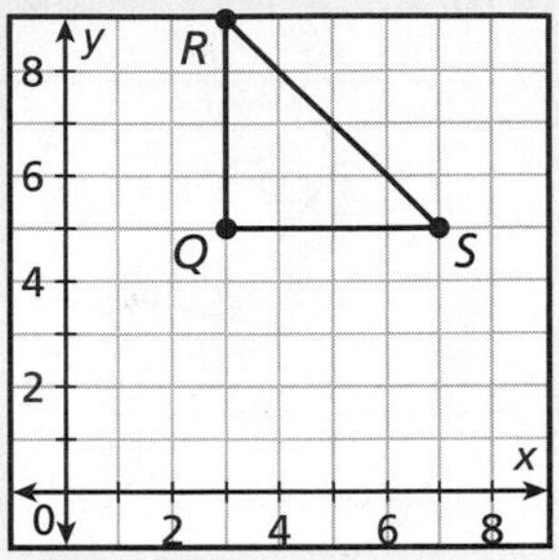

Ⓕ $(-4, 3)$ Ⓗ $(4, 1)$

Ⓖ $(0, 0)$ Ⓙ $(4, -3)$

7. Explain how to use mental math to find an answer that is NOT reasonable.
8. Describe, by working backward, how you can determine the correct answer.

Item E

$\overrightarrow{TS}$ bisects $\angle PTR$. If $m\angle PTS = (9x + 2)°$ and $m\angle STR = (x + 18)°$, what is the value of x?

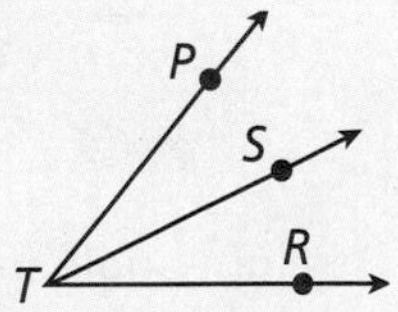

Ⓐ −10 Ⓒ 2

Ⓑ 0 Ⓓ 20

9. Explain how to use mental math to find an answer that is NOT reasonable.
10. Describe how to use the answer choices to work backward to find which answer is reasonable.

CHAPTER 1

STANDARDIZED TEST PREP

Learn It Online
State Test Practice

CUMULATIVE ASSESSMENT

Multiple Choice

Use the diagram for Items 1–3.

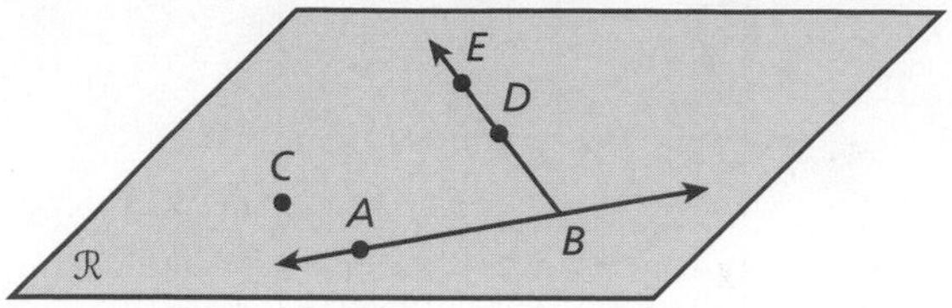

1. Which points are collinear?

Ⓐ A, B, and C Ⓒ A, B, and E

Ⓑ B, C, and D Ⓓ B, D, and E

2. What is another name for plane R?

Ⓕ Plane $\mathcal{C}$ Ⓗ Plane ACE

Ⓖ Plane AB Ⓙ Plane BDE

3. Use your protractor to find the approximate measure of $\angle ABD$.

Ⓐ 123° Ⓒ 77°

Ⓑ 117° Ⓓ 63°

4. S is between R and T. The distance between R and T is 4 times the distance between S and T. If $RS = 18$, what is RT?

Ⓕ 24 Ⓗ 14.4

Ⓖ 22.5 Ⓙ 6

5. A ray bisects a straight angle into two congruent angles. Which term describes each of the congruent angles that are formed?

Ⓐ Acute Ⓒ Right

Ⓑ Obtuse Ⓓ Straight

6. Which expression states that $\overline{AB}$ is congruent to $\overline{CD}$?

Ⓕ $AB \cong CD$ Ⓗ $\overline{AB} = \overline{CD}$

Ⓖ $AB = CD$ Ⓙ $\overline{AB} \cong \overline{CD}$

7. The measure of an angle is 35°. What is the measure of its complement?

Ⓐ 35° Ⓒ 55°

Ⓑ 45° Ⓓ 145°

Use the diagram for Items 8–10.

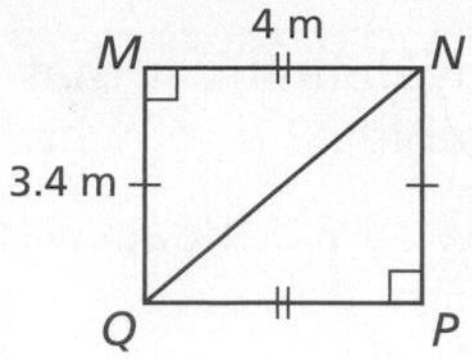

8. Which of these angles is adjacent to $\angle MQN$?

Ⓕ $\angle QMN$ Ⓗ $\angle QNP$

Ⓖ $\angle NPQ$ Ⓙ $\angle PQN$

9. What is the area of $\triangle NQP$?

Ⓐ 3.7 square meters Ⓒ 7.4 square meters

Ⓑ 6.8 square meters Ⓓ 13.6 square meters

10. Which of the following pairs of angles are complementary?

Ⓕ $\angle MNQ$ and $\angle QNP$

Ⓖ $\angle NQP$ and $\angle QPN$

Ⓗ $\angle MNP$ and $\angle QNP$

Ⓙ $\angle QMN$ and $\angle NPQ$

11. K is the midpoint of $\overline{JL}$. J has coordinates $(2, -1)$, and K has coordinates $(-4, 3)$. What are the coordinates of L?

Ⓐ $(3, -2)$ Ⓒ $(-1, 1)$

Ⓑ $(1, -1)$ Ⓓ $(-10, 7)$

12. A circle with a diameter of 10 inches has a circumference equal to the perimeter of a square. To the nearest tenth, what is the length of each side of the square?

Ⓕ 2.5 inches Ⓗ 5.6 inches

Ⓖ 3.9 inches Ⓙ 7.9 inches

13. The map coordinates of a campground are $(1, 4)$, and the coordinates of a fishing pier are $(4, 7)$. Each unit on the map represents 1 kilometer. If Alejandro walks in a straight line from the campground to the pier, how many kilometers, to the nearest tenth, will he walk?

Ⓐ 3.5 kilometers Ⓒ 6.0 kilometers

Ⓑ 4.2 kilometers Ⓓ 12.1 kilometers

HOT TIP! For many types of geometry problems, it may be helpful to draw a diagram and label it with the information given in the problem. This method is a good way of organizing the information and helping you decide how to solve the problem.

14. m∠*R* is 57°. What is the measure of its supplement?

(F) 33° (H) 123°

(G) 43° (J) 133°

15. What rule would you use to translate a triangle 4 units to the right?

(A) $(x, y) \rightarrow (x + 4, y)$

(B) $(x, y) \rightarrow (x - 4, y)$

(C) $(x, y) \rightarrow (x, y + 4)$

(D) $(x, y) \rightarrow (x, y - 4)$

16. If $\overrightarrow{WZ}$ bisects ∠*XWY*, which of the following statements is true?

(F) m∠*XWZ* > m∠*YWZ*

(G) m∠*XWZ* < m∠*YWZ*

(H) m∠*XWZ* = m∠*YWZ*

(J) m∠*XWZ* ≅ m∠*YWZ*

17. The *x*- and *y*-axes separate the coordinate plane into four regions, called quadrants. If (c, d) is a point that is not on the axes, such that $c < 0$ and $d < 0$, which quadrant would contain point (c, d)?

(A) I (C) III

(B) II (D) IV

Gridded Response

18. The measure of ∠1 is 4 times the measure of its supplement. What is the measure, in degrees, of ∠1?

19. The exits for Market St. and Finch St. are 3.5 miles apart on a straight highway. The exit for King St. is at the midpoint between these two exits. How many miles apart are the King St. and Finch St. exits?

20. *R* has coordinates $(-4, 9)$. *S* has coordinates $(4, -6)$. What is *RS*?

21. If ∠*A* is a supplement of ∠*B* and is a right angle, then what is m∠*B* in degrees?

22. ∠*C* and ∠*D* are complementary. m∠*C* is 4 times m∠*D*. What is m∠*C*?

Short Response

23. △*ABC* has vertices $A(-2, 0)$, $B(0, 0)$, and $C(0, 3)$. The image of △*ABC* has vertices $A'(1, -4)$, $B'(3, -4)$, and $C'(3, -1)$.

a. Draw △*ABC* and its image △*A′B′C′* on a coordinate plane.

b. Write a rule for the transformation of △*ABC* using arrow notation.

24. You are given the measure of ∠4. You also know the following angles are supplementary: ∠1 and ∠2, ∠2 and ∠3, and ∠1 and ∠4.

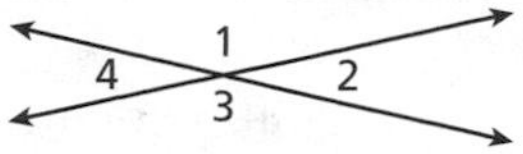

Explain how you can determine the measures of ∠1, ∠2, and ∠3.

25. Marian is making a circular tablecloth from a rectangular piece of fabric that measures 6 yards by 4 yards. What is the area of the largest circular piece that can be cut from the fabric? Leave your answer in terms of π. Show your work or explain in words how you found your answer.

Extended Response

26. Demara is creating a design using a computer illustration program. She begins by drawing the rectangle shown on the coordinate grid.

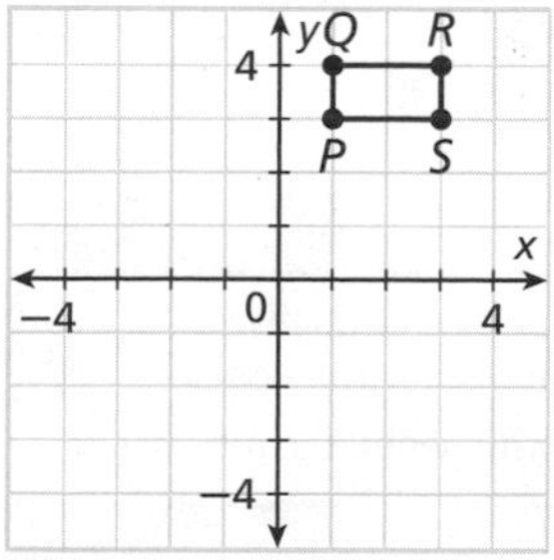

a. Demara translates rectangle *PQRS* using the rule $(x, y) \rightarrow (x - 4, y - 6)$. On a copy of the coordinate grid, draw this translation and label each vertex.

b. Describe one way that Demara could have moved rectangle *PQRS* to the same position in part **a** using a reflection and then a translation.

c. On the same coordinate grid, Demara reflects rectangle *PQRS* across the *x*-axis. She draws a figure with vertices at $(1, -3)$, $(3, -3)$, $(3, -5)$, and $(1, -5)$. Did Demara reflect rectangle *PQRS* correctly? Explain your answer.

CHAPTER 2

Geometric Reasoning

COMMON CORE

Chapter

- Use inductive and deductive reasoning to make arguments
- Plan and write geometric proofs

Winning Strategies

Mathematical reasoning is not just for geometry. It also gives you an edge when you play chess and other strategy games.

Learn It Online
Chapter Project Online

ARE YOU READY?

Vocabulary

Match each term on the left with a definition on the right.

1. angle
2. line
3. midpoint
4. plane
5. segment

A. a straight path that has no thickness and extends forever
B. a figure formed by two rays with a common endpoint
C. a flat surface that has no thickness and extends forever
D. a part of a line between two points
E. names a location and has no size
F. a point that divides a segment into two congruent segments

Angle Relationships

Select the best description for each labeled angle pair.

6.

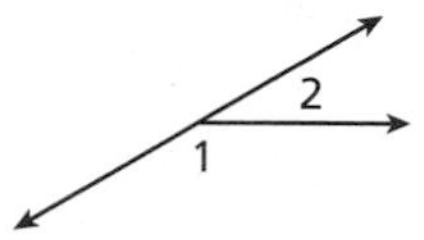

linear pair or vertical angles

7.

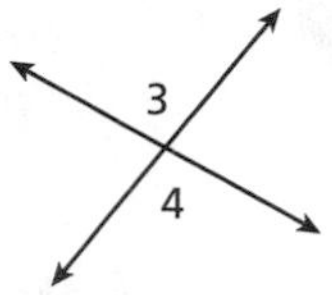

adjacent angles or vertical angles

8.

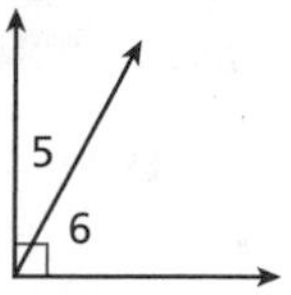

supplementary angles or complementary angles

Classify Real Numbers

Tell if each number is a natural number, a whole number, an integer, or a rational number. Give all the names that apply.

9. 6
10. –0.8
11. –3
12. 5.2
13. $\frac{3}{8}$
14. 0

Points, Lines, and Planes

Name each of the following.

15. a point
16. a line
17. a ray
18. a segment
19. a plane

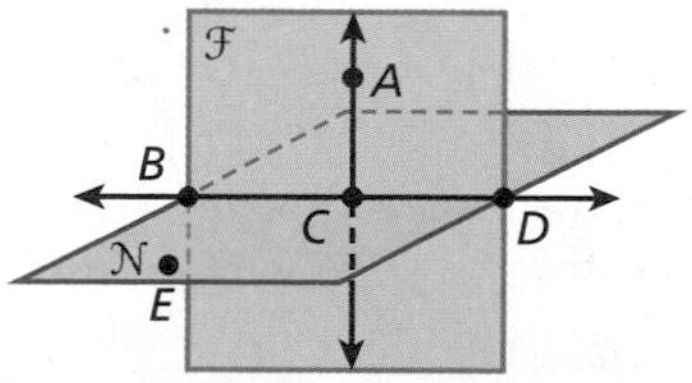

Solve One-Step Equations

Solve.

20. $8 + x = 5$
21. $6y = -12$
22. $9 = 6s$
23. $p - 7 = 9$
24. $\frac{z}{5} = 5$
25. $8.4 = -1.2r$

CHAPTER 2

Study Guide: Preview

Where You've Been

Previously, you

- studied relationships among points, lines, and planes.
- identified congruent segments and angles.
- examined angle relationships.
- used geometric formulas for perimeter and area.

In This Chapter

You will study

- inductive and deductive reasoning.
- using conditional statements and biconditional statements.
- justifying solutions to algebraic equations.
- writing two-column, flowchart, and paragraph proofs.

Where You're Going

You can use the skills learned in this chapter

- when you write proofs in geometry, algebra, and advanced math courses.
- when you use logical reasoning to draw conclusions in science and social studies courses.
- when you assess the validity of arguments in politics and advertising.

Key Vocabulary/Vocabulario

conjecture	conjetura
counterexample	contraejemplo
deductive reasoning	razonamiento deductivo
inductive reasoning	razonamiento inductivo
polygon	polígono
proof	demostración
quadrilateral	cuadrilátero
theorem	teorema
triangle	triángulo

Vocabulary Connections

To become familiar with some of the vocabulary terms in the chapter, consider the following. You may refer to the chapter, the glossary, or a dictionary if you like.

1. The word **counterexample** is made up of two words: *counter* and *example.* In this case, *counter* is related to the Spanish word *contra,* meaning "against." What is a counterexample to the statement "All numbers are positive"?
2. The root of the word **inductive** is *ducere,* which means "to lead." When you are inducted into a club, you are "led into" membership. When you use inductive reasoning in math, you start with specific examples. What do you think inductive reasoning leads you to?
3. The word **deductive** comes from *de,* which means "down from," and *ducere,* the same root as *inductive.* What do you think the phrase "lead down from" would mean when applied to reasoning in math?
4. In Greek, the word *poly* means "many," and the word *gon* means "angle." How can you use these meanings to understand the term **polygon**?

Reading and Writing Math

Reading Strategy: Read and Interpret a Diagram

A diagram is an informational tool. To correctly read a diagram, you must know what you can and cannot assume based on what you see in it.

What You CAN Assume	What You CANNOT Assume
✔ Collinear points	✘ Measures of segments
✔ Betweenness of points	✘ Measures of angles
✔ Coplanar points	✘ Congruent segments
✔ Straight angles and lines	✘ Congruent angles
✔ Adjacent angles	✘ Right angles
✔ Linear pairs of angles	
✔ Vertical angles	

If a diagram includes labeled information, such as an angle measure or a right angle mark, treat this information as given.

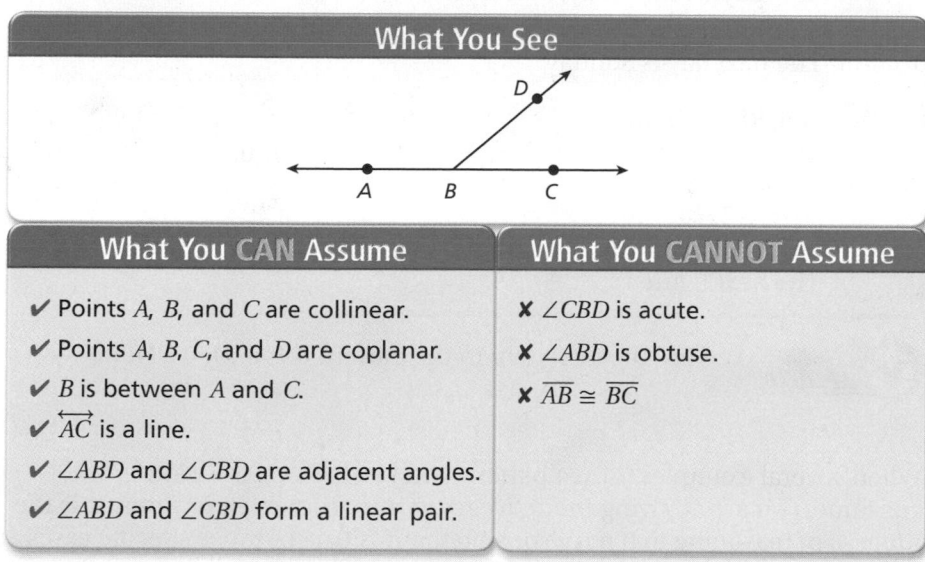

What You See

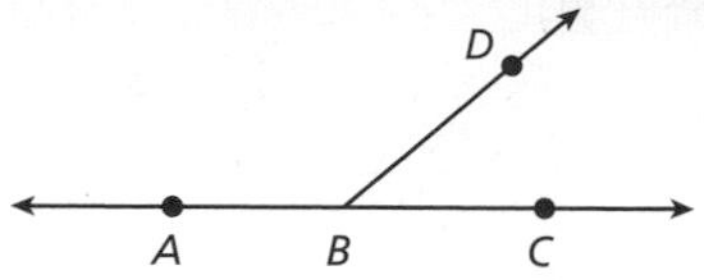

What You CAN Assume	What You CANNOT Assume
✔ Points *A*, *B*, and *C* are collinear.	✘ $\angle CBD$ is acute.
✔ Points *A*, *B*, *C*, and *D* are coplanar.	✘ $\angle ABD$ is obtuse.
✔ *B* is between *A* and *C*.	✘ $\overline{AB} \cong \overline{BC}$
✔ $\overleftrightarrow{AC}$ is a line.	
✔ $\angle ABD$ and $\angle CBD$ are adjacent angles.	
✔ $\angle ABD$ and $\angle CBD$ form a linear pair.	

Try This

List what you can and cannot assume from each diagram.

1.
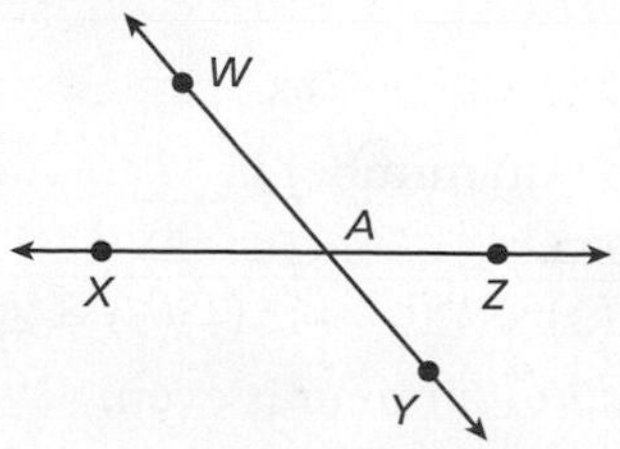

2.
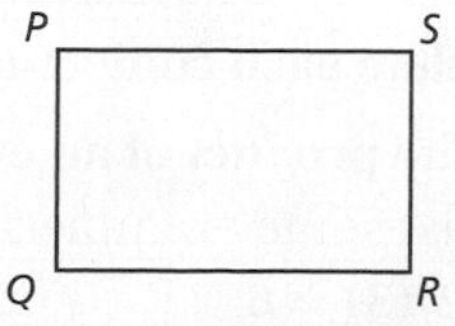

COMMON CORE

2-1 Using Inductive Reasoning to Make Conjectures

Prep for CC.9-12.G.CO.9 Prove theorems about lines and angles. *Also* **Prep for CC.9-12.G.CO.10, Prep for CC.9-12.G.CO.11, Prep for CC.9-12.G.SRT.4**

Objectives

Use inductive reasoning to identify patterns and make conjectures.

Find counterexamples to disprove conjectures.

Vocabulary

inductive reasoning
conjecture
counterexample

Who uses this?

Biologists use inductive reasoning to develop theories about migration patterns.

Biologists studying the migration patterns of California gray whales developed two theories about the whales' route across Monterey Bay. The whales either swam directly across the bay or followed the shoreline.

EXAMPLE 1 Identifying a Pattern

Find the next item in each pattern.

A **Monday, Wednesday, Friday, ...**

Alternating days of the week make up the pattern.
The next day is Sunday.

B **3, 6, 9, 12, 15, ...**

Multiples of 3 make up the pattern. The next multiple is 18.

C ←, ↖, ↑, ...

In this pattern, the figure rotates 45° clockwise each time.
The next figure is ↗.

CHECK IT OUT! **1.** Find the next item in the pattern 0.4, 0.04, 0.004, ...

When several examples form a pattern and you assume the pattern will continue, you are applying *inductive reasoning*. **Inductive reasoning** is the process of reasoning that a rule or statement is true because specific cases are true. You may use inductive reasoning to draw a conclusion from a pattern. A statement you believe to be true based on inductive reasoning is called a **conjecture**.

EXAMPLE 2 Making a Conjecture

Complete each conjecture.

A **The product of an even number and an odd number is ___?___.**

List some examples and look for a pattern.

$(2)(3) = 6$ $(2)(5) = 10$ $(4)(3) = 12$ $(4)(5) = 20$

The product of an even number and an odd number is even.

Complete each conjecture.

B **The number of segments formed by n collinear points is $\underline{\ ?\ }$.**

Draw a segment. Mark points on the segment, and count the number of individual segments formed. Be sure to include overlapping segments.

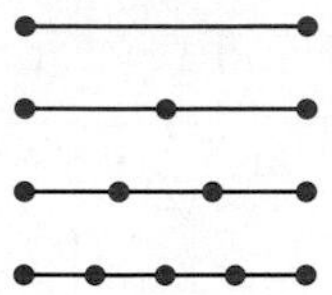

Points	Segments
2	1
3	$2 + 1 = 3$
4	$3 + 2 + 1 = 6$
5	$4 + 3 + 2 + 1 = 10$

The number of segments formed by n collinear points is the sum of the whole numbers less than n.

CHECK IT OUT! **2.** Complete the conjecture: The product of two odd numbers is $\underline{\ ?\ }$.

EXAMPLE 3 *Biology Application*

To learn about the migration behavior of California gray whales, biologists observed whales along two routes. For seven days they counted the numbers of whales seen along each route. Make a conjecture based on the data.

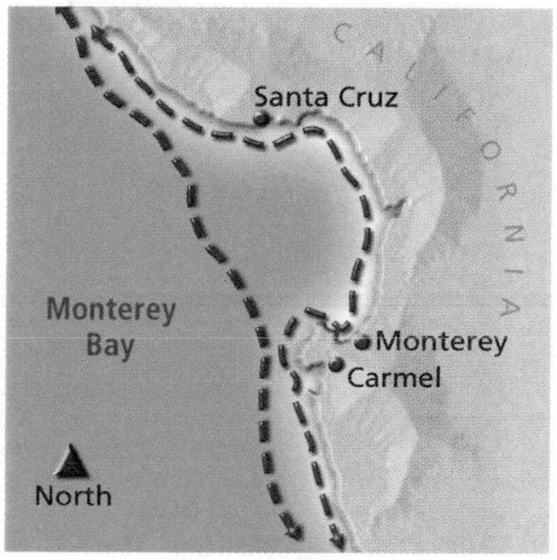

Numbers of Whales Each Day							
Direct Route	1	3	0	2	1	1	0
Shore Route	7	9	5	8	8	6	7

More whales were seen along the shore route each day. The data supports the conjecture that most California gray whales migrate along the shoreline.

CHECK IT OUT! **3.** Make a conjecture about the lengths of male and female whales based on the data.

Average Whale Lengths						
Length of Female (ft)	49	51	50	48	51	47
Length of Male (ft)	47	45	44	46	48	48

To show that a conjecture is always true, you must prove it. To show that a conjecture is false, you have to find only one example in which the conjecture is not true. This case is called a **counterexample**. A counterexample can be a drawing, a statement, or a number.

Know it! Note

Inductive Reasoning
1. Look for a pattern
2. Make a conjecture.
3. Prove the conjecture or find a counterexample.

EXAMPLE 4 Finding a Counterexample

Show that each conjecture is false by finding a counterexample.

A **For all positive numbers n, $\frac{1}{n} \le n$.**

Pick positive values for n and substitute them into the equation to see if the conjecture holds.

Let $n = 1$. Since $\frac{1}{n} = 1$ and $1 \le 1$, the conjecture holds.

Let $n = 2$. Since $\frac{1}{n} = \frac{1}{2}$ and $\frac{1}{2} \le 2$, the conjecture holds.

Let $n = \frac{1}{2}$. Since $\frac{1}{n} = \frac{1}{\frac{1}{2}} = 2$ and $2 \not\le \frac{1}{2}$, the conjecture is false.

$n = \frac{1}{2}$ is a counterexample.

B **For any three points in a plane, there are three different lines that contain two of the points.**

Draw three collinear points.

If the three points are collinear, the conjecture is false.

C **The temperature in Abilene, Texas, never exceeds 100°F during the spring months (March, April, and May).**

Monthly High Temperatures (°F) in Abilene, Texas

Jan	Feb	Mar	Apr	May	Jun	Jul	Aug	Sep	Oct	Nov	Dec
88	89	97	99	107	109	110	107	106	103	92	89

The temperature in May was 107°F, so the conjecture is false.

CHECK IT OUT! **Show that each conjecture is false by finding a counterexample.**

4a. For any real number x, $x^2 \ge x$.

4b. Supplementary angles are adjacent.

4c. The radius of every planet in the solar system is less than 50,000 km.

Planets' Diameters (km)

Mercury	Venus	Earth	Mars	Jupiter	Saturn	Uranus	Neptune
4880	12,100	12,800	6790	143,000	121,000	51,100	49,500

MATHEMATICAL PRACTICES

THINK AND DISCUSS

1. Can you prove a conjecture by giving one example in which the conjecture is true? Explain your reasoning.

Know it! Note

2. **GET ORGANIZED** Copy and complete the graphic organizer. In each box, describe the steps of the inductive reasoning process.

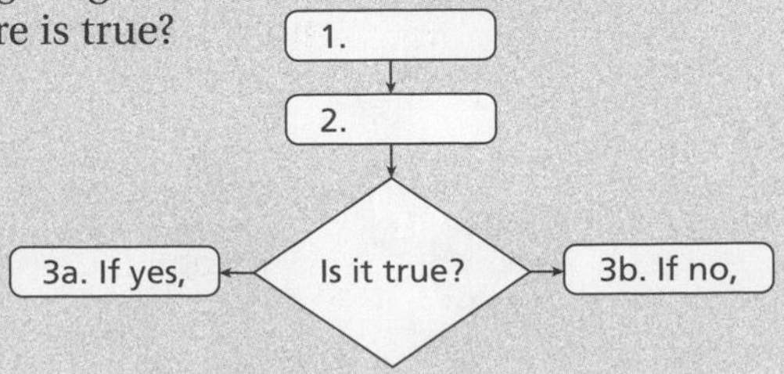

2-1 Exercises

Learn It Online
Homework Help Online
Parent Resources Online

GUIDED PRACTICE

1. **Vocabulary** Explain why a *conjecture* may be true or false.

SEE EXAMPLE 1

Find the next item in each pattern.

2. March, May, July, ...
3. $\frac{1}{3}, \frac{2}{4}, \frac{3}{5}, \ldots$
4. 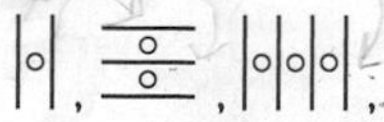

SEE EXAMPLE 2

Complete each conjecture.

5. The product of two even numbers is ___?___.
6. A rule in terms of n for the sum of the first n odd positive integers is ___?___.

SEE EXAMPLE 3

7. **Biology** A laboratory culture contains 150 bacteria. After twenty minutes, the culture contains 300 bacteria. After one hour, the culture contains 1200 bacteria. Make a conjecture about the rate at which the bacteria increases.

SEE EXAMPLE 4

Show that each conjecture is false by finding a counterexample.

8. Kennedy is the youngest U.S. president to be inaugurated.
9. Three points on a plane always form a triangle.
10. For any real number x, if $x^2 \geq 1$, then $x \geq 1$.

President	Age at Inauguration
Washington	57
T. Roosevelt	42
Truman	60
Kennedy	43
Clinton	46

PRACTICE AND PROBLEM SOLVING

Independent Practice

For Exercises	See Example
11–13	1
14–15	2
16	3
17–19	4

Extra Practice

See Extra Practice for more Skills Practice and Applications Practice exercises.

Find the next item in each pattern.

11. 8 A.M., 11 A.M., 2 P.M., ...
12. 75, 64, 53, ...
13. △, □, ⬠, ...

Complete each conjecture.

14. A rule in terms of n for the sum of the first n even positive integers is ___?___.
15. The number of nonoverlapping segments formed by n collinear points is ___?___.
16. **Industrial Arts** About 5% of the students at Lincoln High School usually participate in the robotics competition. There are 526 students in the school this year. Make a conjecture about the number of students who will participate in the robotics competition this year.

Show that each conjecture is false by finding a counterexample.

17. If $1 - y > 0$, then $0 < y < 1$.
18. For any real number x, $x^3 \geq x^2$.
19. Every pair of supplementary angles includes one obtuse angle.

Make a conjecture about each pattern. Write the next two items.

20. 2, 4, 16, ...
21. $\frac{1}{2}, \frac{1}{4}, \frac{1}{8}, \ldots$
22. –3, 6, –9, 12, ...
23. Draw a square of dots. Make a conjecture about the number of dots needed to increase the size of the square from $n \times n$ to $(n + 1) \times (n + 1)$.

Determine if each conjecture is true. If not, write or draw a counterexample.

24. Points X, Y, and Z are coplanar.

25. If n is an integer, then $-n$ is positive.

26. In a triangle with one right angle, two of the sides are congruent.

27. If $\overrightarrow{BD}$ bisects $\angle ABC$, then $m\angle ABD = m\angle CBD$.

28. Estimation The Westside High School band is selling coupon books to raise money for a trip. The table shows the amount of money raised for the first four days of the sale. If the pattern continues, estimate the amount of money raised during the sixth day.

Day	Money Raised ($)
1	146.25
2	195.75
3	246.25
4	295.50

LINK

Math History

Goldbach first stated his conjecture in a letter to Leonhard Euler in 1742. Euler, a Swiss mathematician who published over 800 papers, replied, "I consider [the conjecture] a theorem which is quite true, although I cannot demonstrate it."

29. Write each fraction in the pattern $\frac{1}{11}, \frac{2}{11}, \frac{3}{11}, \ldots$ as a repeating decimal. Then write a description of the fraction pattern and the resulting decimal pattern.

30. Math History Remember that a prime number is a whole number greater than 1 that has exactly two factors, itself and 1. Goldbach's conjecture states that every even number greater than 2 can be written as the sum of two primes. For example, $4 = 2 + 2$. Write the next five even numbers as the sum of two primes.

31. The pattern 1, 1, 2, 3, 5, 8, 13, 21, … is known as the *Fibonacci sequence*. Find the next three terms in the sequence and write a conjecture for the pattern.

32. Look at a monthly calendar and pick any three squares in a row—across, down, or diagonal. Make a conjecture about the number in the middle.

12	13	14
19	20	21
26	27	28

33. Make a conjecture about the value of $2n - 1$ when n is an integer.

34. Critical Thinking The turnaround date for migrating gray whales occurs when the number of northbound whales exceeds the number of southbound whales. Make a conjecture about the turnaround date, based on the table below. What factors might affect the validity of your conjecture in the future?

Migration Direction of Gray Whales

	Feb. 16	Feb. 17	Feb. 18	Feb. 19	Feb. 20	Feb. 21	Feb. 22
Southbound	0	2	3	0	1	1	0
Northbound	0	0	2	5	3	2	1

35. Write About It Explain why a true conjecture about even numbers does not necessarily hold for all numbers. Give an example to support your answer.

MULTI-STEP TEST PREP

36. a. For how many hours did the Mock Turtle do lessons on the third day?

b. On what day did the Mock Turtle do 1 hour of lessons?

"And how many hours a day did you do lessons?" said Alice, in a hurry to change the subject.

"Ten hours the first day," said the Mock Turtle: "nine the next, and so on."

TEST PREP

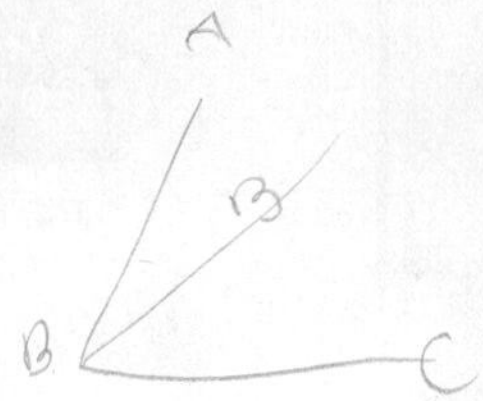

37. Which of the following conjectures is false?

Ⓐ If x is odd, then $x + 1$ is even.

Ⓑ The sum of two odd numbers is even.

Ⓒ The difference of two even numbers is positive.

Ⓓ If x is positive, then $-x$ is negative.

38. A student conjectures that if x is a prime number, then $x + 1$ is not prime. Which of the following is a counterexample?

Ⓕ $x = 11$ Ⓖ $x = 6$ Ⓗ $x = 3$ Ⓙ $x = 2$

39. The class of 2004 holds a reunion each year. In 2005, 87.5% of the 120 graduates attended. In 2006, 90 students went, and in 2007, 75 students went. About how many students do you predict will go to the reunion in 2010?

Ⓐ 12 Ⓑ 15 Ⓒ 24 Ⓓ 30

CHALLENGE AND EXTEND

40. Multi-Step Make a table of values for the rule $x^2 + x + 11$ when x is an integer from 1 to 8. Make a conjecture about the type of number generated by the rule. Continue your table. What value of x generates a counterexample?

41. Political Science Presidential elections are held every four years. U.S. senators are elected to 6-year terms, but only $\frac{1}{3}$ of the Senate is up for election every two years. If $\frac{1}{3}$ of the Senate is elected during a presidential election year, how many years must pass before these same senate seats are up for election during another presidential election year?

42. Physical Fitness Rob is training for the President's Challenge physical fitness program. During his first week of training, Rob does 15 sit-ups each day. He will add 20 sit-ups to his daily routine each week. His goal is to reach 150 sit-ups per day.

a. Make a table of the number of sit-ups Rob does each week from week 1 through week 10.

b. During which week will Rob reach his goal?

c. Write a conjecture for the number of sit-ups Rob does during week n.

43. Construction Draw $\overline{AB}$. Then construct point C so that it is not on $\overline{AB}$ and is the same distance from A and B. Construct $\overline{AC}$ and $\overline{BC}$. Compare $m\angle CAB$ and $m\angle CBA$ and compare AC and CB. Make a conjecture.

Connecting Geometry to Number Theory

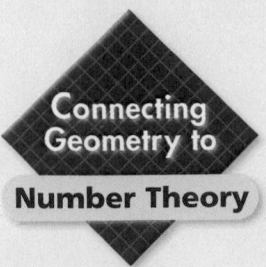

Venn Diagrams

Recall that in a Venn diagram, ovals are used to represent each set. The ovals can overlap if the sets share common elements.

The real number system contains an infinite number of subsets. The following chart shows some of them. Other examples of subsets are even numbers, multiples of 3, and numbers less than 6.

Set	Description	Examples
Natural numbers	The counting numbers	1, 2, 3, 4, 5, ...
Whole numbers	The set of natural numbers and 0	0, 1, 2, 3, 4, ...
Integers	The set of whole numbers and their opposites	..., −2, −1, 0, 1, 2, ...
Rational numbers	The set of numbers that can be written as a ratio of integers	$-\frac{3}{4}$, 5, −2, 0.5, 0
Irrational numbers	The set of numbers that cannot be written as a ratio of integers	$\pi, \sqrt{10}, 8 + \sqrt{2}$

Example

Draw a Venn diagram to show the relationship between the set of even numbers and the set of natural numbers.

The set of even numbers includes all numbers that are divisible by 2. This includes natural numbers such as 2, 4, and 6. But even numbers such as –4 and –10 are not natural numbers.

So the set of even numbers includes some, but not all, elements in the set of natural numbers. Similarly, the set of natural numbers includes some, but not all, even numbers.

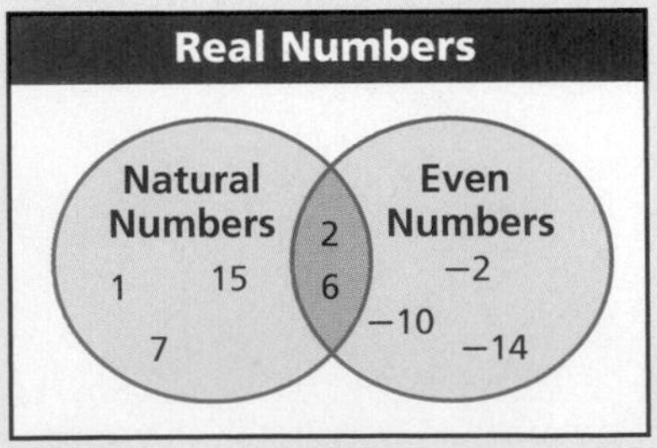

Draw a rectangle to represent all real numbers.

Draw overlapping ovals to represent the sets of even and natural numbers. You may write individual elements in each region.

Try This

Draw a Venn diagram to show the relationship between the given sets.

1. natural numbers, whole numbers
2. odd numbers, whole numbers
3. irrational numbers, integers

COMMON CORE

2-2 Conditional Statements

Prep for CC.9-12.G.CO.9 Prove theorems about lines and angles. *Also* **Prep for CC.9-12.G.CO.10, Prep for CC.9-12.G.CO.11, Prep for CC.9-12.G.SRT.4**

Objectives

Identify, write, and analyze the truth value of conditional statements.

Write the inverse, converse, and contrapositive of a conditional statement.

Vocabulary

conditional statement
hypothesis
conclusion
truth value
negation
converse
inverse
contrapositive
logically equivalent statements

Why learn this?

To identify a species of butterfly, you must know what characteristics one butterfly species has that another does not.

It is thought that the viceroy butterfly mimics the bad-tasting monarch butterfly to avoid being eaten by birds. By comparing the appearance of the two butterfly species, you can make the following conjecture:

If a butterfly has a curved black line on its hind wing, then it is a viceroy.

Know it! Note

Conditional Statements

DEFINITION	SYMBOLS	VENN DIAGRAM
A **conditional statement** is a statement that can be written in the form "if p, then q."		
The **hypothesis** is the part p of a conditional statement following the word *if*.	$p \to q$	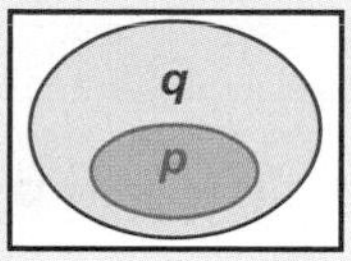
The **conclusion** is the part q of a conditional statement following the word *then*.		

By phrasing a conjecture as an if-then statement, you can quickly identify its hypothesis and conclusion.

Writing Math

"If p, then q" can also be written as "if p, q," "q, if p," "p implies q," and "p only if q."

EXAMPLE 1 Identifying the Parts of a Conditional Statement

Identify the hypothesis and conclusion of each conditional.

A **If a butterfly has a curved black line on its hind wing, then it is a viceroy.**

Hypothesis: A butterfly has a curved black line on its hind wing.

Conclusion: The butterfly is a Viceroy.

B **A number is an integer if it is a natural number.**

Hypothesis: A number is a natural number.

Conclusion: The number is an integer.

CHECK IT OUT! **1.** Identify the hypothesis and conclusion of the statement "A number is divisible by 3 if it is divisible by 6."

Many sentences without the words *if* and *then* can be written as conditionals. To do so, identify the sentence's hypothesis and conclusion by figuring out which part of the statement depends on the other.

EXAMPLE 2 Writing a Conditional Statement

Write a conditional statement from each of the following.

A **The midpoint *M* of a segment bisects the segment.**

The midpoint *M* of a segment **bisects the segment.** *Identify the hypothesis and conclusion.*

Conditional: If *M* is the midpoint of a segment, then *M* bisects the segment.

B

The inner oval represents the **hypothesis**, and the **outer** oval represents the **conclusion.**

Conditional: If an animal is a tarantula, then it is a spider.

CHECK IT OUT! **2.** Write a conditional statement from the sentence "Two angles that are complementary are acute."

A conditional statement has a **truth value** of either true (T) or false (F). It is false only when the hypothesis is true and the conclusion is false. Consider the conditional "If I get paid, I will take you to the movie." If I don't get paid, I haven't broken my promise. So the statement is still true.

To show that a conditional statement is false, you need to find only one counterexample where the hypothesis is true and the conclusion is false.

EXAMPLE 3 Analyzing the Truth Value of a Conditional Statement

Determine if each conditional is true. If false, give a counterexample.

A **If today is Sunday, then tomorrow is Monday.**

When the hypothesis is true, the conclusion is also true because Monday follows Sunday. So the conditional is true.

B **If an angle is obtuse, then it has a measure of 100°.**

You can draw an obtuse angle whose measure is not 100°. In this case, the hypothesis is true, but the conclusion is false. Since you can find a counterexample, the conditional is false.

C **If an odd number is divisible by 2, then 8 is a perfect square.**

An odd number is never divisible by 2, so the hypothesis is false. The number 8 is not a perfect square, so the conclusion is false. However, the conditional is true because the hypothesis is false.

Remember!

If the hypothesis is false, the conditional statement is true, regardless of the truth value of the conclusion.

CHECK IT OUT! **3.** Determine if the conditional "If a number is odd, then it is divisible by 3" is true. If false, give a counterexample.

The **negation** of statement *p* is "not *p*," written as $\sim p$. The negation of the statement "*M* is the midpoint of $\overline{AB}$" is "*M* is *not* the midpoint of $\overline{AB}$." The negation of a true statement is false, and the negation of a false statement is true. Negations are used to write related conditional statements.

Know it! Note

Related Conditionals

DEFINITION	SYMBOLS
A conditional is a statement that can be written in the form "If p, then q."	$p \rightarrow q$
The **converse** is the statement formed by exchanging the hypothesis and conclusion.	$q \rightarrow p$
The **inverse** is the statement formed by negating the hypothesis and the conclusion.	$\sim p \rightarrow \sim q$
The **contrapositive** is the statement formed by both exchanging and negating the hypothesis and conclusion.	$\sim q \rightarrow \sim p$

EXAMPLE 4 *Biology Application*

Moth

Butterfly

Write the converse, inverse, and contrapositive of the conditional statement. Use the photos to find the truth value of each.

If an insect is a butterfly, then it has four wings.

If **an insect is a butterfly**, then **it has four wings**.

Converse: If **an insect has four wings**, then **it is a butterfly**.

A moth also is an insect with four wings. So the converse is false.

Inverse: If **an insect is not a butterfly**, then **it does not have four wings**.

A moth is not a butterfly, but it has four wings. So the inverse is false.

Contrapositive: If **an insect does not have four wings**, then **it is not a butterfly**.

Butterflies must have four wings. So the contrapositive is true.

CHECK IT OUT! 4. Write the converse, inverse, and contrapositive of the conditional statement "If an animal is a cat, then it has four paws." Find the truth value of each.

Helpful Hint

The logical equivalence of a conditional and its contrapositive is known as the Law of Contrapositive.

In the example above, the conditional statement and its contrapositive are both true, and the converse and inverse are both false. Related conditional statements that have the same truth value are called **logically equivalent statements**. A conditional and its contrapositive are logically equivalent, and so are the converse and inverse.

Statement	Example	Truth Value
Conditional	If $m\angle A = 95°$, then $\angle A$ is obtuse.	T
Converse	If $\angle A$ is obtuse, then $m\angle A = 95°$.	F
Inverse	If $m\angle A \neq 95°$, then $\angle A$ is not obtuse.	F
Contrapositive	If $\angle A$ is not obtuse, then $m\angle A \neq 95°$.	T

However, the converse of a true conditional is not necessarily false. All four related conditionals can be true, or all four can be false, depending on the statement.

MATHEMATICAL PRACTICES

THINK AND DISCUSS

1. If a conditional statement is false, what are the truth values of its hypothesis and conclusion?

2. What is the truth value of a conditional whose hypothesis is false?

3. Can a conditional statement and its converse be logically equivalent? Support your answer with an example.

Know it! Note

4. GET ORGANIZED Copy and complete the graphic organizer. In each box, write the definition and give an example.

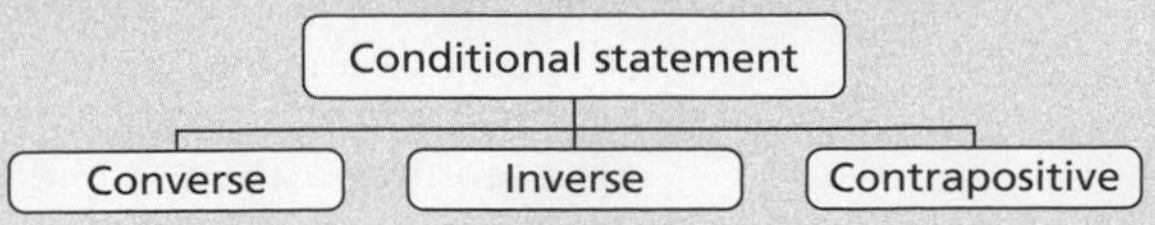

2-2 Exercises

Learn It Online
Homework Help Online
Parent Resources Online

GUIDED PRACTICE

Vocabulary **Apply the vocabulary from this lesson to answer each question.**

1. The ___?___ of a *conditional statement* is formed by exchanging the hypothesis and conclusion. (*converse, inverse,* or *contrapositive*)

2. A *conditional* and its *contrapositive* are ___?___ because they have the same truth value. (*logically equivalent* or *converses*)

SEE EXAMPLE 1

Identify the hypothesis and conclusion of each conditional.

3. If a person is at least 16 years old, then the person can drive a car.

4. A figure is a parallelogram if it is a rectangle.

5. The statement $a - b < a$ implies that b is a positive number.

SEE EXAMPLE 2

Write a conditional statement from each of the following.

6. Eighteen-year-olds are eligible to vote.

7. $\left(\frac{a}{b}\right)^2 < \frac{a}{b}$ when $0 < a < b$.

8.

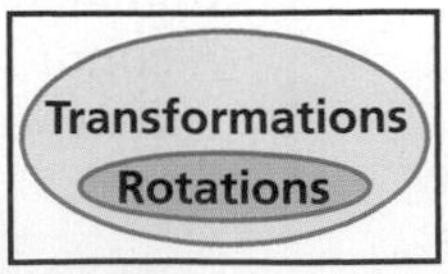

SEE EXAMPLE 3

Determine if each conditional is true. If false, give a counterexample.

9. If three points form the vertices of a triangle, then they lie in the same plane.

10. If $x > y$, then $|x| > |y|$.

11. If the season is spring, then the month is March.

SEE EXAMPLE 4

12. Travel Write the converse, inverse, and contrapositive of the following conditional statement. Find the truth value of each.

If Brielle drives at exactly 30 mi/h, then she travels 10 mi in 20 min.

PRACTICE AND PROBLEM SOLVING

Independent Practice

For Exercises	See Example
13–15	1
16–18	2
19–21	3
22–23	4

Extra Practice

See Extra Practice for more Skills Practice and Applications Practice exercises.

Identify the hypothesis and conclusion of each conditional.

13. If an animal is a tabby, then it is a cat.
14. Four angles are formed if two lines intersect.
15. If 8 ounces of cereal cost \$2.99, then 16 ounces of cereal cost \$5.98.

Write a conditional statement from each sentence.

16. You should monitor the heart rate of a patient who is ill.
17. After three strikes, the batter is out.
18. Congruent segments have equal measures.

Determine if each conditional is true. If false, give a counterexample.

19. If you subtract -2 from -6, then the result is -4.
20. If two planes intersect, then they intersect in exactly one point.
21. If a cat is a bird, then today is Friday.

Write the converse, inverse, and contrapositive of each conditional statement. Find the truth value of each.

22. **Probability** If the probability of an event is 0.1, then the event is unlikely to occur.
23. **Meteorology** If freezing rain is falling, then the air temperature is 32°F or less. (*Hint:* The freezing point of water is 32°F.)

Find the truth value of each statement.

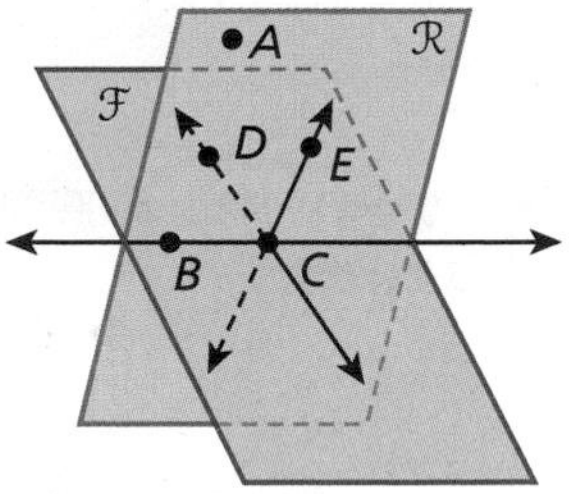

24. E lies in plane $\mathcal{R}$.
25. $\overleftrightarrow{CD}$ lies in plane $\mathcal{F}$.
26. C, E, and D are coplanar.
27. Plane $\mathcal{F}$ contains $\overrightarrow{ED}$.
28. B and E are collinear.
29. $\overleftrightarrow{BC}$ contains $\mathcal{F}$ and $\mathcal{R}$.

Draw a Venn diagram.

30. All integers are rational numbers.
31. All natural numbers are real.
32. All rectangles are quadrilaterals.
33. Plane is an undefined term.

Write a conditional statement from each Venn diagram.

34.
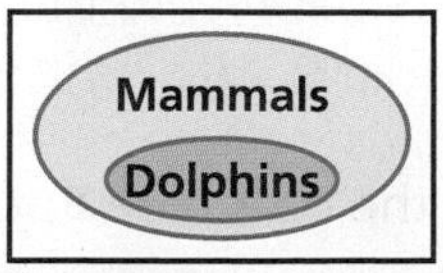

35.
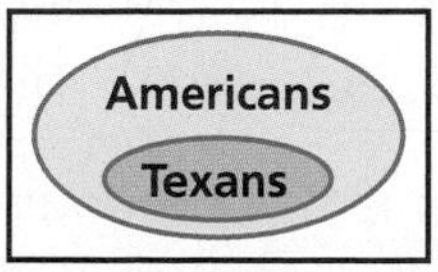

36.
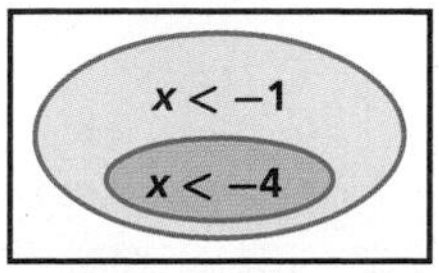

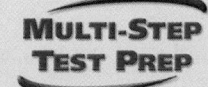

MULTI-STEP TEST PREP

37. a. Identify the hypothesis and conclusion in the Duchess's statement.
    b. Rewrite the Duchess's claim as a conditional statement.

"Tut, tut, child!" said the Duchess. "Everything's got a moral, if only you can find it." And she squeezed herself up closer to Alice's side as she spoke.

Find a counterexample to show that the converse of each conditional is false.

38. If $x = -5$, then $x^2 = 25$.

39. If two angles are vertical angles, then they are congruent.

40. If two angles are adjacent, then they share a vertex.

41. If you use sunscreen, then you will not get sunburned.

LINK

Geology

Diamond is four times as hard as the next mineral on Mohs' scale, corundum (ruby and sapphire).

Geology Mohs' scale is used to identify minerals. A mineral with a higher number is harder than a mineral with a lower number.

Use the table and the statements below for Exercises 42–47. Write each conditional and find its truth value.

Mohs' Scale	
Hardness	**Mineral**
1	Talc
2	Gypsum
3	Calcite
4	Fluorite
5	Apatite
6	Orthoclase
7	Quartz
8	Topaz
9	Corundum
10	Diamond

p: calcite q: not apatite

r: a hardness of 3 s: a hardness less than 5

42. $p \rightarrow r$ **43.** $s \rightarrow q$ **44.** $q \rightarrow s$

45. $q \rightarrow p$ **46.** $r \rightarrow q$ **47.** $p \rightarrow s$

48. Critical Thinking Consider the conditional "If two angles are congruent, then they have the same measure." Write the converse, inverse, and contrapositive and find the truth value of each. Use the related conditionals to draw a Venn diagram that represents the relationship between congruent angles and their measures.

49. Write About It When is a conditional statement false? Explain why a true conditional statement can have a hypothesis that is false.

TEST PREP

50. What is the inverse of "If it is Saturday, then it is the weekend"?

Ⓐ If it is the weekend, then it is Saturday.

Ⓑ If it is not Saturday, then it is the weekend.

Ⓒ If it is not Saturday, then it is not the weekend.

Ⓓ If it is not the weekend, then it is not Saturday.

51. Let *a* represent "Two lines are parallel to the same line," and let *b* represent "The two lines are parallel." Which symbolic statement represents the conditional "If two lines are NOT parallel, then they are parallel to the same line"?

Ⓕ $a \rightarrow b$ Ⓖ $b \rightarrow a$ Ⓗ $\sim b \rightarrow a$ Ⓙ $b \rightarrow \sim a$

52. Which statement is a counterexample for the conditional statement "If $f(x) = \sqrt{25 - x^2}$, then $f(x)$ is positive"?

Ⓐ $x = 0$ Ⓑ $x = 3$ Ⓒ $x = 4$ Ⓓ $x = 5$

53. Which statement has the same truth value as its converse?

Ⓕ If a triangle has a right angle, its side lengths are 3 centimeters, 4 centimeters, and 5 centimeters.

Ⓖ If an angle measures 104°, then the angle is obtuse.

Ⓗ If a number is an integer, then it is a natural number.

Ⓙ If an angle measures 90°, then it is an acute angle.

CHALLENGE AND EXTEND

For each Venn diagram, write two statements beginning with *Some, All,* or *No*.

54.

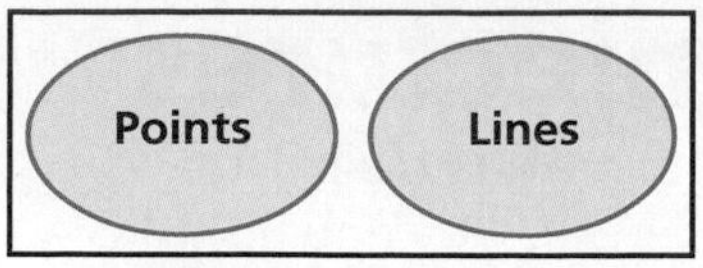

55.

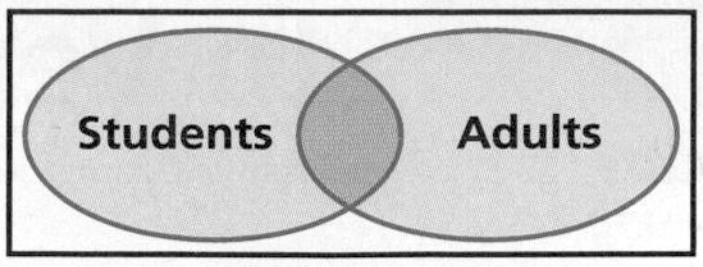

56. Given: If a figure is a square, then it is a rectangle. Figure A is not a rectangle. Conclusion: Figure A is not a square.

a. Draw a Venn diagram to represent the given conditional statement. Use the Venn diagram to explain why the conclusion is valid.

b. Write the contrapositive of the given conditional. How can you use the contrapositive to justify the conclusion?

57. Multi-Step How many true conditionals can you write using the statements below?

p: n is an integer. q: n is a whole number. r: n is a natural number.

Career Path

Learn It Online
Career Resources Online

Stephanie Poulin
Desktop Publisher
Daily Reporter

Q: What high school math classes did you take?
A: I took three years of math: Pre-Algebra, Algebra, and Geometry.

Q: What training do you need to be a desktop publisher?
A: Most of my training was done on the job. The computer science and typing classes I took in high school have been helpful.

Q: How do you use math?
A: Part of my job is to make sure all the text, charts, and photographs are formatted to fit the layout of each page. I have to manipulate things by comparing ratios, calculating areas, and using estimation.

Q: What future plans do you have?
A: My goal is to start my own business as a freelance graphic artist.

COMMON CORE

2-3 Using Deductive Reasoning to Verify Conjectures

Prep for CC.9-12.G.CO.9 Prove theorems about lines and angles. *Also* **Prep for CC.9-12.G.CO.10, Prep for CC.9-12.G.CO.11, Prep for CC.9-12.G.SRT.4**

Objective
Apply the Law of Detachment and the Law of Syllogism in logical reasoning.

Vocabulary
deductive reasoning

Why learn this?
You can use inductive and deductive reasoning to decide whether a common myth is accurate.

You have learned that one counterexample is enough to disprove a conjecture. But to prove that a conjecture is true, you must use *deductive reasoning*. **Deductive reasoning** is the process of using logic to draw conclusions from given facts, definitions, and properties.

EXAMPLE 1 *Media Application*

Urban legends and modern myths spread quickly through the media. Many Web sites and television shows are dedicated to confirming or disproving such myths. Is each conclusion a result of inductive or deductive reasoning?

A **There is a myth that toilets and sinks drain in opposite directions in the Southern and Northern Hemispheres. However, if you were to observe sinks draining in the two hemispheres, you would see that this myth is false.**

Since the conclusion is based on a pattern of observation, it is a result of inductive reasoning.

B **There is a myth that you should not touch a baby bird that has fallen from its nest because the mother bird will disown the baby if she detects human scent. However, biologists have shown that birds cannot detect human scent. Therefore, the myth cannot be true.**

The conclusion is based on logical reasoning from scientific research. It is a result of deductive reasoning.

CHECK IT OUT!

1. There is a myth that an eelskin wallet will demagnetize credit cards because the skin of the electric eels used to make the wallet holds an electric charge. However, eelskin products are not made from electric eels. Therefore, the myth cannot be true. Is this conclusion a result of inductive or deductive reasoning?

In deductive reasoning, if the given facts are true and you apply the correct logic, then the conclusion must be true. The Law of Detachment is one valid form of deductive reasoning.

Know it! Note

Law of Detachment

If $p \rightarrow q$ is a true statement and p is true, then q is true.

EXAMPLE 2 Verifying Conjectures by Using the Law of Detachment

Determine if each conjecture is valid by the Law of Detachment.

A **Given: If two segments are congruent, then they have the same length. $\overline{AB} \cong \overline{XY}$.**

Conjecture: $AB = XY$

Identify the hypothesis and conclusion in the given conditional.

If two segments are congruent, then they have the same length.

The given statement $\overline{AB} \cong \overline{XY}$ matches the hypothesis of a true conditional. By the Law of Detachment $AB = XY$. The conjecture is valid.

B **Given: If you are tardy 3 times, you must go to detention. Shea is in detention.**

Conjecture: Shea was tardy at least 3 times.

Identify the hypothesis and conclusion in the given conditional.

If you are tardy 3 times, you must go to detention.

The given statement "**Shea is in detention**" matches the conclusion of a true conditional. But this does not mean the hypothesis is true. Shea could be in detention for another reason. The conjecture is not valid.

CHECK IT OUT!

2. Determine if the conjecture is valid by the Law of Detachment.
Given: If a student passes his classes, the student is eligible to play sports. Ramon passed his classes.
Conjecture: Ramon is eligible to play sports.

Another valid form of deductive reasoning is the Law of Syllogism. It allows you to draw conclusions from two conditional statements when the conclusion of one is the hypothesis of the other.

Know it! Note

Law of Syllogism

If $p \rightarrow q$ and $q \rightarrow r$ are true statements, then $p \rightarrow r$ is a true statement.

EXAMPLE 3 Verifying Conjectures by Using the Law of Syllogism

Determine if each conjecture is valid by the Law of Syllogism.

A **Given: If $m\angle A < 90°$, then $\angle A$ is acute. If $\angle A$ is acute, then it is not a right angle.**

Conjecture: If $m\angle A < 90°$, then it is not a right angle.

Let p, q, and r represent the following.

p: The measure of an angle is less than 90°.

q: The angle is acute.

r: The angle is not a right angle.

You are given that $p \rightarrow q$ and $q \rightarrow r$. Since q is the conclusion of the first conditional and the hypothesis of the second conditional, you can conclude that $p \rightarrow r$. The conjecture is valid by the Law of Syllogism.

Caution!

It is possible to arrive at a true conclusion by applying invalid logical reasoning, as in Example 3B.

Determine if each conjecture is valid by the Law of Syllogism.

B **Given: If a number is divisible by 4, then it is divisible by 2.**
If a number is even, then it is divisible by 2.

Conjecture: If a number is divisible by 4, then it is even.

Let x, y, and z represent the following.

x: A number is divisible by 4.

y: A number is divisible by 2.

z: A number is even.

You are given that $x \rightarrow y$ and $z \rightarrow y$. The Law of Syllogism cannot be used to draw a conclusion since y is the conclusion of both conditionals. Even though the conjecture $x \rightarrow z$ is true, the logic used to draw the conclusion is not valid.

CHECK IT OUT!

3. Determine if the conjecture is valid by the Law of Syllogism.
Given: If an animal is a mammal, then it has hair.
If an animal is a dog, then it is a mammal.
Conjecture: If an animal is a dog, then it has hair.

EXAMPLE 4 Applying the Laws of Deductive Reasoning

Draw a conclusion from the given information.

A **Given: If a team wins 10 games, then they play in the finals. If a team plays in the finals, then they travel to Boston. The Ravens won 10 games.**

Conclusion: The Ravens will travel to Boston.

B **Given: If two angles form a linear pair, then they are adjacent. If two angles are adjacent, then they share a side. ∠1 and ∠2 form a linear pair.**

Conclusion: ∠1 and ∠2 share a side.

CHECK IT OUT!

4. Draw a conclusion from the given information.
Given: If a polygon is a triangle, then it has three sides.
If a polygon has three sides, then it is not a quadrilateral. Polygon P is a triangle.

MATHEMATICAL PRACTICES

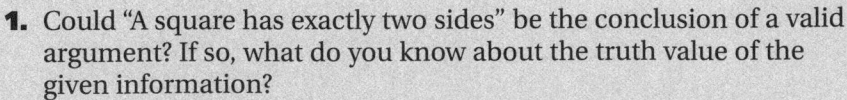

THINK AND DISCUSS

1. Could "A square has exactly two sides" be the conclusion of a valid argument? If so, what do you know about the truth value of the given information?
2. Explain why writing conditional statements as symbols might help you evaluate the validity of an argument.
3. **GET ORGANIZED** Copy and complete the graphic organizer. Write each law in your own words and give an example of each.

Know it! Note

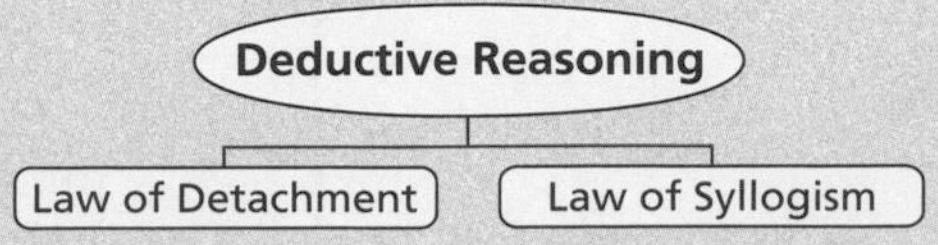

2-3 Exercises

Learn It Online
Homework Help Online
Parent Resources Online

GUIDED PRACTICE

1. **Vocabulary** Explain how *deductive reasoning* differs from inductive reasoning.

SEE EXAMPLE 1

Does each conclusion use inductive or deductive reasoning?

2. At Bell High School, students must take Biology before they take Chemistry. Sam is in Chemistry, so Marcia concludes that he has taken Biology.
3. A detective learns that his main suspect was out of town the day of the crime. He concludes that the suspect is innocent.

SEE EXAMPLE 2

Determine if each conjecture is valid by the Law of Detachment.

4. Given: If you want to go on a field trip, you must have a signed permission slip. Zola has a signed permission slip.
   Conjecture: Zola wants to go on a field trip.
5. Given: If the side lengths of a rectangle are 3 ft and 4 ft, then its area is 12 ft^2. A rectangle has side lengths of 3 ft and 4 ft.
   Conjecture: The area of the rectangle is 12 ft^2.

SEE EXAMPLE 3

Determine if each conjecture is valid by the Law of Syllogism.

6. Given: If you fly from Texas to California, you travel from the central to the Pacific time zone. If you travel from the central to the Pacific time zone, then you gain two hours.
   Conjecture: If you fly from Texas to California, you gain two hours.
7. Given: If a figure is a **square**, then the figure is a **rectangle**. If a figure is a **square**, then it is a **parallelogram.**
   Conjecture: If a figure is a **parallelogram**, then it is a **rectangle**.

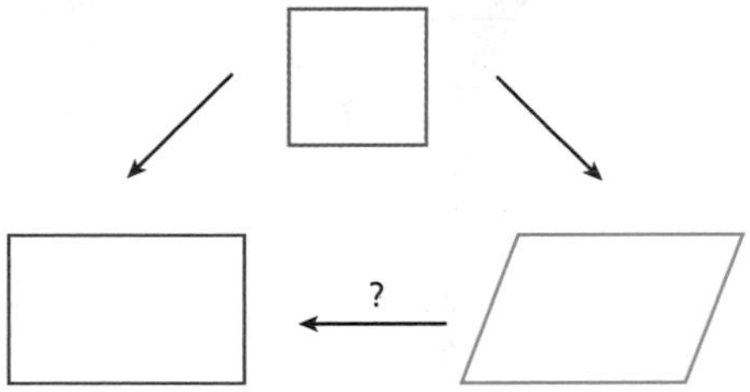

SEE EXAMPLE 4

8. Draw a conclusion from the given information.
   Given: If you leave your car lights on overnight, then your car battery will drain. If your battery is drained, your car might not start. Alex left his car lights on last night.

PRACTICE AND PROBLEM SOLVING

Independent Practice	
For Exercises	See Example
9–10	1
11	2
12	3
13	4

Extra Practice
See Extra Practice for more Skills Practice and Applications Practice exercises.

Does each conclusion use inductive or deductive reasoning?

9. The sum of the angle measures of a triangle is 180°. Two angles of a triangle measure 40° and 60°, so Kandy concludes that the third angle measures 80°.
10. All of the students in Henry's Geometry class are juniors. Alexander takes Geometry, but has another teacher. Henry concludes that Alexander is also a junior.
11. Determine if the conjecture is valid by the Law of Detachment.
    Given: If one integer is odd and another integer is even, their product is even. The product of two integers is 24.
    Conjecture: One of the two integers is odd.

12. **Science** Determine if the conjecture is valid by the Law of Syllogism.
Given: If an element is an alkali metal, then it reacts with water. If an element is in the first column of the periodic table, then it is an alkali metal.
Conjecture: If an element is in the first column of the periodic table, then it reacts with water.

13. Draw a conclusion from the given information.
Given: If Dakota watches the news, she is informed about current events.
If Dakota knows about current events, she gets better grades in Social Studies.
Dakota watches the news.

14. **Technology** Joseph downloads a file in 18 minutes with a dial-up modem. How long would it take to download the file with a Cheetah-Net cable modem?

CHEETAH-NET CABLE
75 Times As Fast As Dial-Up

LINK

Recreation

When the Gemini roller coaster opened in Cedar Point in 1978, it was the fastest roller coaster in the world. It no longer holds this title, but it is still a popular attraction.

Recreation Use the true statements below for Exercises 15–18. Determine whether each conclusion is valid.

I. The Gemini is at Cedar Point amusement park in Sandusky, OH.
II. Carter and Mary go to Cedar Point.
III. The Gemini roller coaster reaches speeds of 60 mi/h.
IV. When Carter goes to an amusement park, he rides all the roller coasters.

15. Carter went to Sandusky, OH.

16. Mary rode the Gemini.

17. Carter rode a roller coaster that travels 60 mi/h.

18. Mary rode a roller coaster that travels 60 mi/h.

19. **Critical Thinking** Is the argument below a valid application of the Law of Syllogism? Is the conclusion true? Explain your answers.
If $3 - x < 5$, then $x < -2$. If $x < -2$, then $-5x > 10$. Thus, if $3 - x < 5$, then $-5x > 10$.

20. **ERROR ANALYSIS** Below are two conclusions. Which is incorrect? Explain the error.
If two angles are complementary, their measures add to 90°. If an angle measures 90°, then it is a right angle. $\angle A$ and $\angle B$ are complementary.

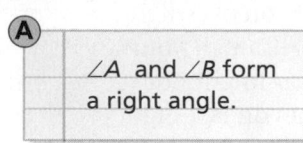

A $\angle A$ and $\angle B$ form a right angle.

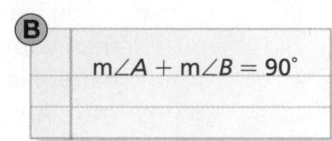

B $m\angle A + m\angle B = 90°$

21. **Write About It** Write one example of a real-life logical argument that uses the Law of Detachment and one that uses the Law of Syllogism. Explain why the conclusions are valid.

MULTI-STEP TEST PREP

22. When Alice meets the Pigeon in Wonderland, the Pigeon thinks she is a serpent. The Pigeon reasons that serpents eat eggs, and Alice confirms that she has eaten eggs.
a. Write "Serpents eat eggs" as a conditional statement.
b. Is the Pigeon's conclusion that Alice is a serpent valid? Explain your reasoning.

(cl) Dennis MacDonald / Alamy; (bl) Victoria Smith/HMH; (br) The Granger Collection, New York

TEST PREP

23. The Supershots scored over 75 points in each of ten straight games. The newspaper predicts that they will score more than 75 points tonight. Which form of reasoning is this conclusion based on?

Ⓐ Deductive reasoning, because the conclusion is based on logic

Ⓑ Deductive reasoning, because the conclusion is based on a pattern

Ⓒ Inductive reasoning, because the conclusion is based on logic

Ⓓ Inductive reasoning, because the conclusion is based on a pattern

24. $\overrightarrow{HF}$ bisects $\angle EHG$. Which conclusion is NOT valid?

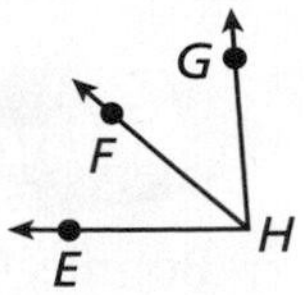

Ⓕ *E*, *F*, and *G* are coplanar.

Ⓖ $\angle EHF \cong \angle FHG$

Ⓗ $\overline{EF} \cong \overline{FG}$

Ⓙ $m\angle EHF = m\angle FHG$

25. Gridded Response If Whitney plays a low G on her piano, the frequency of the note is 24.50 hertz. The frequency of a note doubles with each octave. What is the frequency in hertz of a G note that is 3 octaves above low G?

CHALLENGE AND EXTEND

26. Political Science To be eligible to hold the office of the president of the United States, a person must be at least 35 years old, be a natural-born U.S. citizen, and have been a U.S. resident for at least 14 years. Given this information, what conclusion, if any, can be drawn from the statements below? Explain your reasoning.

Andre is not eligible to be the president of the United States.
Andre has lived in the United States for 16 years.

27. Multi-Step Consider the two conditional statements below.
If you live in San Diego, then you live in California.
If you live in California, then you live in the United States.

a. Draw a conclusion from the given conditional statements.

b. Write the contrapositive of each conditional statement.

c. Draw a conclusion from the two contrapositives.

d. How does the conclusion in part **a** relate to the conclusion in part **c**?

28. If Cassie goes to the skate park, Hanna and Amy will go. If Hanna or Amy goes to the skate park, then Marc will go. If Marc goes to the skate park, then Dallas will go. If only two of the five people went to the skate park, who were they?

2-3
Geometry LAB

Solve Logic Puzzles

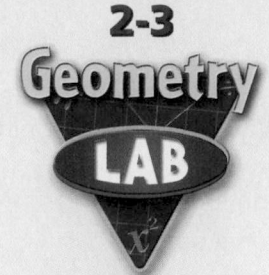

You have used deductive reasoning to analyze the truth values of conditional statements. Now you will learn some methods for diagramming conditional statements to help you solve logic puzzles.

Use with Conditional Statements

Activity 1

Bonnie, Cally, Daphne, and Fiona own a bird, cat, dog, and fish. No girl has a type of pet that begins with the same letter as her name. Bonnie is allergic to animal fur. Daphne feeds Fiona's bird when Fiona is away. Make a table to determine who owns which animal.

1 Since no girl has a type of pet that starts with the same letter as her name, place an X in each box along the diagonal of the table.

	Bird	Cat	Dog	Fish
Bonnie	×			
Cally		×		
Daphne			×	
Fiona				×

2 Bonnie cannot have a cat or dog because of her allergy. So she must own the fish, and no other girl can have the fish.

	Bird	Cat	Dog	Fish
Bonnie	×	×	×	✓
Cally		×		×
Daphne			×	×
Fiona				×

3 Fiona owns the bird, so place a check in Fiona's row, in the bird column. Place an X in the remaining boxes in the same column and row.

	Bird	Cat	Dog	Fish
Bonnie	×	×	×	✓
Cally	×	×		×
Daphne	×		×	×
Fiona	✓	×	×	×

4 Therefore, Daphne owns the cat, and Cally owns the dog.

	Bird	Cat	Dog	Fish
Bonnie	×	×	×	✓
Cally	×	×	✓	×
Daphne	×	✓	×	×
Fiona	✓	×	×	×

Try This

1. After figuring out that Fiona owns the bird in Step 3, why can you place an X in every other box in that row and column?

2. Ally, Emily, Misha, and Tracy go to a dance with Danny, Frank, Jude, and Kian. Ally and Frank are siblings. Jude and Kian are roommates. Misha does not know Kian. Emily goes with Kian's roommate. Tracy goes with Ally's brother. Who went to the dance with whom?

	Danny	Frank	Jude	Kian
Ally				
Emily				
Misha				
Tracy				

Activity 2

A farmer has a goat, a wolf, and a cabbage. He wants to transport all three from one side of a river to the other. He has a boat, but it has only enough room for the farmer and one thing. The wolf will eat the goat if they are left alone together, and the goat will eat the cabbage if they are left alone. How can the farmer get everything to the other side of the river?

You can use a *network* to solve this kind of puzzle. A **network** is a diagram of *vertices* and *edges*, also known as a graph. An **edge** is a curve or a segment that joins two *vertices* of the graph. A **vertex** is a point on the graph.

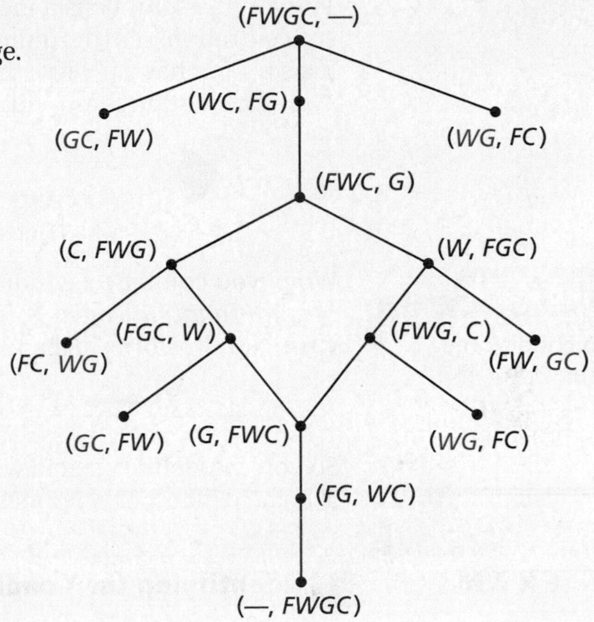

1. Let *F* represent the farmer, *W* represent the wolf, *G* represent the goat, and *C* represent the cabbage. Use an ordered pair to represent what is on each side of the river. The first ordered pair is (*FWGC*, —), and the desired result is (—, *FWGC*).
2. Draw a vertex and label it with the first ordered pair. Then draw an edge and vertex for each possible trip the farmer could make across the river. If at any point a path results in an unworkable combination of things, no more edges can be drawn from that vertex.
3. From each workable vertex, continue to draw edges and vertices that represent the next trip across the river. When you get to a vertex for (—, *FWGC*), the network is complete.
4. Use the network to write out the solution in words.

Try This

3. What combinations are unworkable? Why?
4. How many solutions are there to the farmer's transport problem? How many steps does each solution take?
5. What is the advantage of drawing a complete solution network rather than working out one solution with a diagram?
6. Madeline has two measuring cups—a 1-cup measuring cup and a $\frac{3}{4}$-cup measuring cup. Neither cup has any markings on it. How can Madeline get exactly $\frac{1}{2}$ cup of flour in the larger measuring cup? Complete the network below to solve the problem.

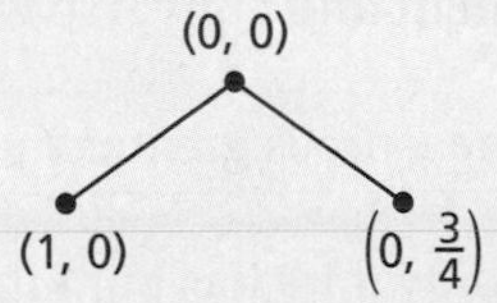

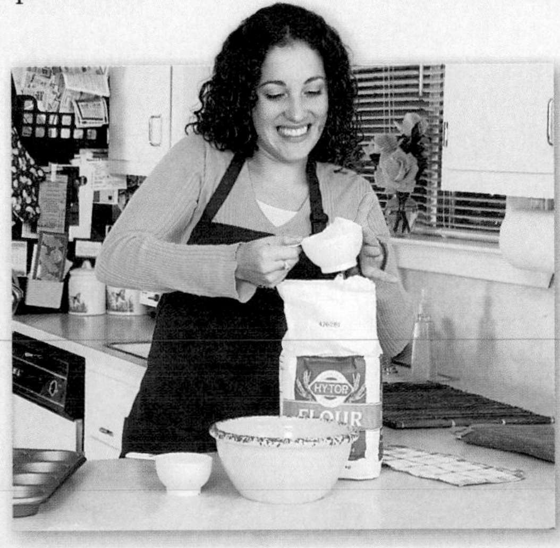

2-4 Biconditional Statements and Definitions

Prep for CC.9-12.G.CO.9 Prove theorems about lines and angles. *Also* **Prep for CC.9-12.G.CO.10, Prep for CC.9-12.G.CO.11, Prep for CC.9-12.G.SRT.4**

Objective
Write and analyze biconditional statements.

Vocabulary
biconditional statement
definition
polygon
triangle
quadrilateral

Who uses this?
A gardener can plan the color of the hydrangeas she plants by checking the pH of the soil.

The pH of a solution is a measure of the concentration of hydronium ions in the solution. If a solution has a pH less than 7, it is an acid. Also, if a solution is an acid, it has a pH less than 7.

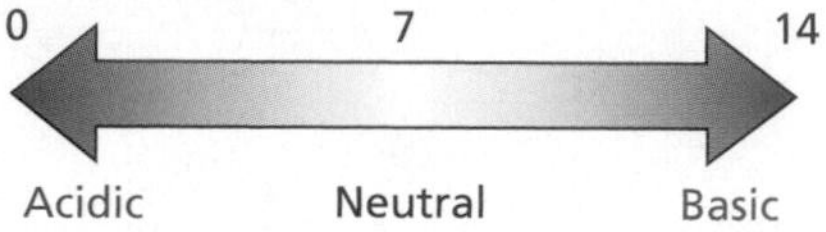

Writing Math
The biconditional "*p* if and only if *q*" can also be written as "*p* iff *q*" or $p \leftrightarrow q$.

When you combine a conditional statement and its converse, you create a *biconditional statement.* A **biconditional statement** is a statement that can be written in the form "*p* if and only if *q*." This means "if *p*, then *q*" and "if *q*, then *p*."

$$p \leftrightarrow q \text{ means } p \rightarrow q \text{ and } q \rightarrow p$$

So you can define an acid with the following biconditional statement: A solution is an acid if and only if it has a pH less than 7.

EXAMPLE 1 Identifying the Conditionals within a Biconditional Statement

Write the conditional statement and converse within each biconditional.

A **Two angles are congruent if and only if their measures are equal.**

Let *p* and *q* represent the following.

p: **Two angles are congruent.**
q: **Two angle measures are equal.**

The two parts of the biconditional $p \leftrightarrow q$ are $p \rightarrow q$ and $q \rightarrow p$.

Conditional: If **two angles are congruent**, then **their measures are equal.**

Converse: If **two angle measures are equal**, then **the angles are congruent.**

B **A solution is a base $\leftrightarrow$ it has a pH greater than 7.**

Let *x* and *y* represent the following.

x: **A solution is a base.**
y: **A solution has a pH greater than 7.**

The two parts of the biconditional $x \leftrightarrow y$ are $x \rightarrow y$ and $y \rightarrow x$.

Conditional: If **a solution is a base**, then **it has a pH greater than 7.**

Converse: If **a solution has a pH greater than 7**, then **it is a base.**

CHECK IT OUT! **Write the conditional statement and converse within each biconditional.**

1a. An angle is acute iff its measure is greater than 0° and less than 90°.

1b. Cho is a member if and only if he has paid the $5 dues.

EXAMPLE 2 Writing a Biconditional Statement

For each conditional, write the converse and a biconditional statement.

A **If $2x + 5 = 11$, then $x = 3$.**

Converse: If $x = 3$, then $2x + 5 = 11$.
Biconditional: $2x + 5 = 11$ if and only if $x = 3$.

B **If a point is a midpoint, then it divides the segment into two congruent segments.**

Converse: If a point divides a segment into two congruent segments, then the point is a midpoint.
Biconditional: A point is a midpoint if and only if it divides the segment into two congruent segments.

CHECK IT OUT! **For each conditional, write the converse and a biconditional statement.**

2a. If the date is July 4th, then it is Independence Day.

2b. If points lie on the same line, then they are collinear.

For a biconditional statement to be true, both the conditional statement and its converse must be true. If either the conditional or the converse is false, then the biconditional statement is false.

EXAMPLE 3 Analyzing the Truth Value of a Biconditional Statement

Determine if each biconditional is true. If false, give a counterexample.

A **A square has a side length of 5 if and only if it has an area of 25.**

Conditional: If a square has a side length of 5, then it has an area of 25. *The conditional is true.*

Converse: If a square has an area of 25, then it has a side length of 5. *The converse is true.*

Since the conditional and its converse are true, the biconditional is true.

B **The number n is a positive integer $\leftrightarrow$ $2n$ is a natural number.**

Conditional: If n is a positive integer, then $2n$ is a natural number. *The conditional is true.*

Converse: If $2n$ is a natural number, then n is a positive integer. *The converse is false.*

If $2n = 1$, then $n = \frac{1}{2}$, which is not an integer. Because the converse is false, the biconditional is false.

CHECK IT OUT! **Determine if each biconditional is true. If false, give a counterexample.**

3a. An angle is a right angle iff its measure is 90°.

3b. $y = -5 \leftrightarrow y^2 = 25$

In geometry, biconditional statements are used to write *definitions.* A **definition** is a statement that describes a mathematical object and can be written as a true biconditional. Most definitions in the glossary are not written as biconditional statements, but they can be. The "if and only if" is implied.

In the glossary, a **polygon** is defined as a closed plane figure formed by three or more line segments. Each segment intersects exactly two other segments only at their endpoints, and no two segments with a common endpoint are collinear.

A **triangle** is defined as a three-sided polygon, and a **quadrilateral** is a four-sided polygon.

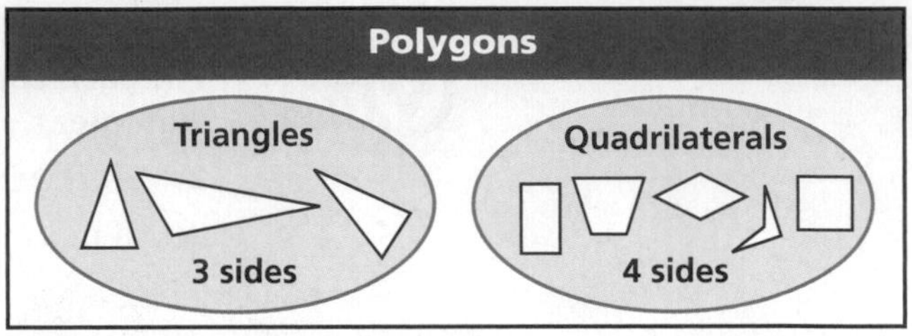

A good, precise definition can be used forward and backward. For example, if a figure is a quadrilateral, then it is a four-sided polygon. If a figure is a four-sided polygon, then it is a quadrilateral. To make sure a definition is precise, it helps to write it as a biconditional statement.

EXAMPLE 4 Writing Definitions as Biconditional Statements

Helpful Hint

Think of definitions as being reversible. Postulates, however, are not necessarily true when reversed.

Write each definition as a biconditional.

A **A triangle is a three-sided polygon.**

A figure is a triangle if and only if it is a three-sided polygon.

B **A segment bisector is a ray, segment, or line that divides a segment into two congruent segments.**

A ray, segment, or line is a segment bisector if and only if it divides a segment into two congruent segments.

CHECK IT OUT! **Write each definition as a biconditional.**

4a. A quadrilateral is a four-sided polygon.

4b. The measure of a straight angle is 180°.

MATHEMATICAL PRACTICES

THINK AND DISCUSS

1. How do you determine if a biconditional statement is true or false?

2. Compare a triangle and a quadrilateral.

Know it! Note

3. **GET ORGANIZED** Copy and complete the graphic organizer. Use the definition of a polygon to write a conditional, converse, and biconditional in the appropriate boxes.

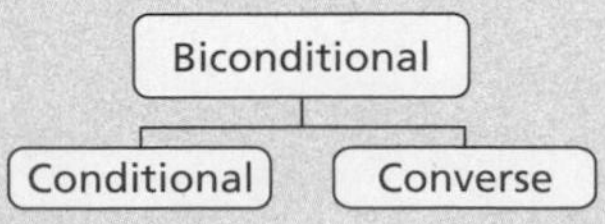

2-4 Exercises

Learn It Online
Homework Help Online
Parent Resources Online

GUIDED PRACTICE

1. **Vocabulary** How is a *biconditional statement* different from a conditional statement?

SEE EXAMPLE 1

Write the conditional statement and converse within each biconditional.

2. Perry can paint the entire living room if and only if he has enough paint.
3. Your medicine will be ready by 5 P.M. if and only if you drop your prescription off by 8 A.M.

SEE EXAMPLE 2

For each conditional, write the converse and a biconditional statement.

4. If a student is a sophomore, then the student is in the tenth grade.
5. If two segments have the same length, then they are congruent.

SEE EXAMPLE 3

Multi-Step Determine if each biconditional is true. If false, give a counterexample.

6. $xy = 0 \leftrightarrow x = 0$ or $y = 0$.
7. A figure is a quadrilateral if and only if it is a polygon.

SEE EXAMPLE 4

Write each definition as a biconditional.

8. Parallel lines are two coplanar lines that never intersect.
9. A hummingbird is a tiny, brightly colored bird with narrow wings, a slender bill, and a long tongue.

PRACTICE AND PROBLEM SOLVING

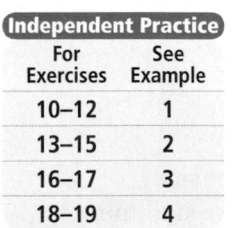

Independent Practice

For Exercises	See Example
10–12	1
13–15	2
16–17	3
18–19	4

Extra Practice
See Extra Practice for more Skills Practice and Applications Practice exercises.

Write the conditional statement and converse within each biconditional.

10. Three points are coplanar if and only if they lie in the same plane.
11. A parallelogram is a rectangle if and only if it has four right angles.
12. A lunar eclipse occurs if and only if Earth is between the Sun and the Moon.

For each conditional, write the converse and a biconditional statement.

13. If today is Saturday or Sunday, then it is the weekend.
14. If Greg has the fastest time, then he wins the race.
15. If a triangle contains a right angle, then it is a right triangle.

Multi-Step Determine if each biconditional is true. If false, give a counterexample.

16. Felipe is a swimmer if and only if he is an athlete.
17. The number $2n$ is even if and only if n is an integer.

Write each definition as a biconditional.

18. A circle is the set of all points in a plane that are a fixed distance from a given point.
19. A catcher is a baseball player who is positioned behind home plate and who catches throws from the pitcher.

Algebra **Determine if a true biconditional can be written from each conditional statement. If not, give a counterexample.**

20. If $a = b$, then $|a| = |b|$.

21. If $3x - 2 = 13$, then $\frac{4}{5}x + 8 = 12$.

22. If $y^2 = 64$, then $3y = 24$.

23. If $x > 0$, then $x^2 > 0$.

Use the diagrams to write a definition for each figure.

24.

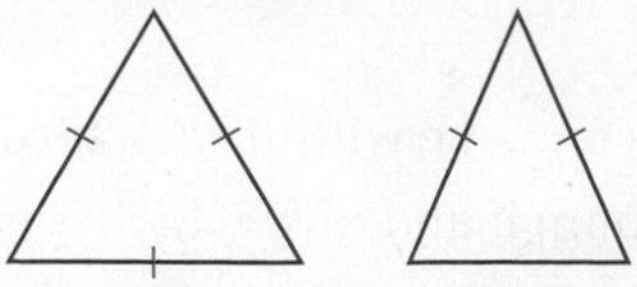

Equilateral triangle — Not an equilateral triangle

25.

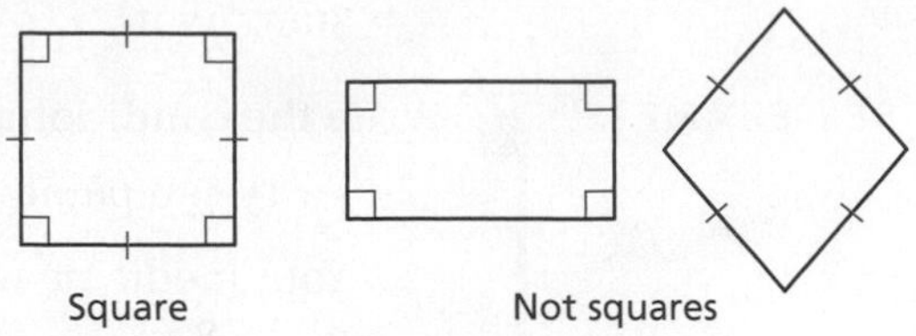

Square — Not squares

LINK

Biology

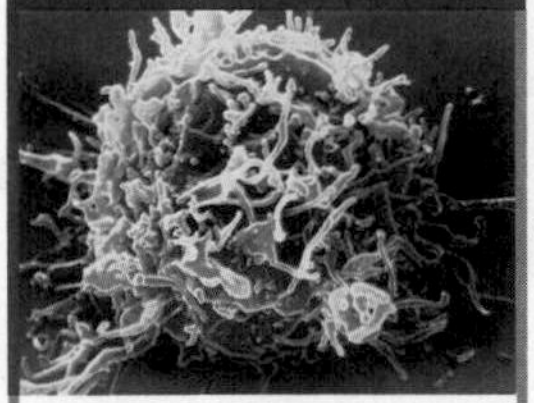

White blood cells live less than a few weeks. A drop of blood can contain anywhere from 7000 to 25,000 white blood cells.

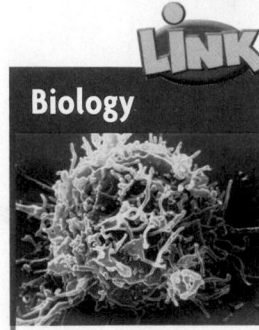

26. **Biology** White blood cells are cells that defend the body against invading organisms by engulfing them or by releasing chemicals called *antibodies*. Write the definition of a white blood cell as a biconditional statement.

Explain why the given statement is not a definition.

27. An automobile is a vehicle that moves along the ground.

28. A calculator is a machine that performs computations with numbers.

29. An angle is a geometric object formed by two rays.

Chemistry **Use the table for Exercises 30–32. Determine if a true biconditional statement can be written from each conditional.**

pH	Examples
0	Battery Acid
4	Acid rain, tomato juice
6	Saliva
8	Sea water
13	Bleach, oven cleaner
14	Drain cleaner

30. If a solution has a pH of 4, then it is tomato juice.

31. If a solution is bleach, then its pH is 13.

32. If a solution has a pH greater than 7, then it is not battery acid.

Complete each statement to form a true biconditional.

33. The circumference of a circle is 10π if and only if its radius is __?__.

34. Four points in a plane form a __?__ if and only if no three of them are collinear.

35. **Critical Thinking** Write the definition of a biconditional statement as a biconditional statement. Use the conditional and converse within the statement to explain why your biconditional is true.

36. **Write About It** Use the definition of an angle bisector to explain what is meant by the statement "A good definition is reversible."

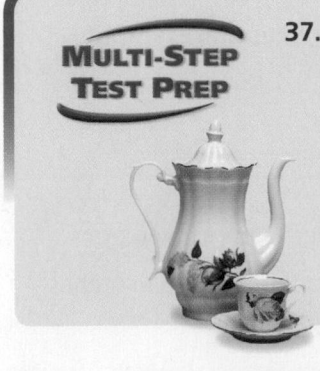

MULTI-STEP TEST PREP

37. a. Write "I say what I mean" and "I mean what I say" as conditionals.

b. Explain why the biconditional statement implied by Alice is false.

"Then you should say what you mean," the March Hare went on.

"I do," Alice hastily replied; "at least—at least I mean what I say—that's the same thing, you know."

TEST PREP

38. Which is a counterexample for the biconditional "An angle measures 80° if and only if the angle is acute"?

Ⓐ m∠S = 60°   Ⓑ m∠S = 115°   Ⓒ m∠S = 90°   Ⓓ m∠S = 360°

39. Which biconditional is equivalent to the spelling phrase "*I* before *E* except after *C*"?

Ⓕ The letter *I* comes before *E* if and only if *I* follows *C*.
Ⓖ The letter *E* comes before *I* if and only if *E* follows *C*.
Ⓗ The letter *E* comes before *I* if and only if *E* comes before *C*.
Ⓙ The letter *I* comes before *E* if and only if *I* comes before *C*.

40. Which conditional statement can be used to write a true biconditional?

Ⓐ If a number is divisible by 4, then it is even.
Ⓑ If a ratio compares two quantities measured in different units, the ratio is a rate.
Ⓒ If two angles are supplementary, then they are adjacent.
Ⓓ If an angle is right, then it is not acute.

41. **Short Response** Write the two conditional statements that make up the biconditional "You will get a traffic ticket if and only if you are speeding." Is the biconditional true or false? Explain your answer.

CHALLENGE AND EXTEND

42. **Critical Thinking** Describe what the Venn diagram of a true biconditional statement looks like. How does this support the idea that a definition can be written as a true biconditional?

43. Consider the conditional "If an angle measures 105°, then the angle is obtuse."
   a. Write the inverse of the conditional statement.
   b. Write the converse of the inverse.
   c. How is the converse of the inverse related to the original conditional?
   d. What is the truth value of the biconditional statement formed by the inverse of the original conditional and the converse of the inverse? Explain.

44. Suppose *A*, *B*, *C*, and *D* are coplanar, and *A*, *B*, and *C* are not collinear. What is the truth value of the biconditional formed from the true conditional "If $m\angle ABD + m\angle DBC = m\angle ABC$, then *D* is in the interior of $\angle ABC$"? Explain.

45. Find a counterexample for "n is divisible by 4 if and only if n^2 is even."

CHAPTER 2

MULTI-STEP TEST PREP

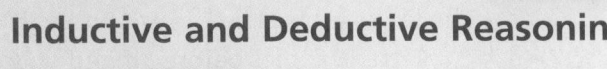

SECTION 2A

MATHEMATICAL PRACTICES **Construct viable arguments and critique the reasoning of others.**

Inductive and Deductive Reasoning

Rhyme or Reason

Alice's Adventures in Wonderland originated as a story told by Charles Lutwidge Dodgson (Lewis Carroll) to three young traveling companions. The story is famous for its wordplay and logical absurdities.

1. When Alice first meets the Cheshire Cat, she asks what sort of people live in Wonderland. The Cat explains that everyone in Wonderland is mad. What conjecture might the Cat make since Alice, too, is in Wonderland?

2. **"I don't much care where—" said Alice.**

   "Then it doesn't matter which way you go," said the Cat.

   "—so long as I get *somewhere*," Alice added as an explanation.

   "Oh, you're sure to do that," said the Cat, "if you only walk long enough."

Write the conditional statement implied by the Cat's response to Alice.

3. **"Well, then," the Cat went on, "you see a dog growls when it's angry, and wags its tail when it's pleased. Now I growl when I'm pleased, and wag my tail when I'm angry. Therefore I'm mad."**

Is the Cat's conclusion valid by the Law of Detachment or the Law of Syllogism? Explain your reasoning.

4. **"You might just as well say," added the Dormouse, who seemed to be talking in his sleep, "that 'I breathe when I sleep' is the same thing as 'I sleep when I breathe'!"**

Write a biconditional statement from the Dormouse's example. Explain why the biconditional statement is false.

READY TO GO ON?

Quiz for Lessons 2-1 Through 2-4

2-1 Using Inductive Reasoning to Make Conjectures

Find the next item in each pattern.

1. 1, 10, 18, 25, …
2. July, May, March, …
3. $\frac{1}{8}, -\frac{1}{4}, \frac{1}{2}, \ldots$
4. |, ┼, ╫, …
5. A biologist recorded the following data about the weight of male lions in a wildlife park in Africa. Use the table to make a conjecture about the average weight of a male lion.

ID Number	Weight (lb)
A1902SM	387.2
A1904SM	420.5
A1920SM	440.6
A1956SM	398.7
A1974SM	415.0

6. Complete the conjecture "The sum of two negative numbers is __?__."
7. Show that the conjecture "If an even number is divided by 2, then the result is an even number" is false by finding a counterexample.

2-2 Conditional Statements

8. Identify the hypothesis and conclusion of the conditional statement "An angle is obtuse if its measure is 107°."

Write a conditional statement from each of the following.

9. A whole number is an integer.
10. 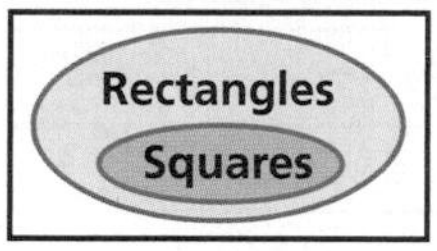

11. The diagonals of a square are congruent.

Determine if each conditional is true. If false, give a counterexample.

12. If an angle is acute, then it has a measure of 30°.
13. If $9x - 11 = 2x + 3$, then $x = 2$.
14. Write the converse, inverse, and contrapositive of the statement "If a number is even, then it is divisible by 4." Find the truth value of each.

2-3 Using Deductive Reasoning to Verify Conjectures

15. Determine if the following conjecture is valid by the Law of Detachment.
    Given: If Sue finishes her science project, she can go to the movie. Sue goes to the movie.
    Conjecture: Sue finished her science project.
16. Use the Law of Syllogism to draw a conclusion from the given information.
    Given: If one angle of a triangle is 90°, then the triangle is a right triangle. If a triangle is a right triangle, then its acute angle measures are complementary.

2-4 Biconditional Statements and Definitions

17. For the conditional "If two angles are supplementary, the sum of their measures is 180°," write the converse and a biconditional statement.
18. Determine if the biconditional "$\sqrt{x} = 4$ if and only if $x = 16$" is true. If false, give a counterexample.

COMMON CORE

2-5 Algebraic Proof

Prep for CC.9-12.G.CO.9 Prove theorems about lines and angles. *Also* **Prep for CC.9-12.G.CO.10, Prep for CC.9-12.G.CO.11, Prep for CC.9-12.G.SRT.4**

Objectives

Review properties of equality and use them to write algebraic proofs.

Identify properties of equality and congruence.

Vocabulary

proof

Who uses this?

Game designers and animators solve equations to simulate motion. (See Example 2.)

A **proof** is an argument that uses logic, definitions, properties, and previously proven statements to show that a conclusion is true.

If you've ever solved an equation in Algebra, then you've already done a proof! An algebraic proof uses algebraic properties such as the properties of equality and the Distributive Property.

Remember!

The Distributive Property states that $a(b + c) = ab + ac$.

Know it! Note

Properties of Equality

Addition Property of Equality	If $a = b$, then $a + c = b + c$.
Subtraction Property of Equality	If $a = b$, then $a - c = b - c$.
Multiplication Property of Equality	If $a = b$, then $ac = bc$.
Division Property of Equality	If $a = b$ and $c \neq 0$, then $\frac{a}{c} = \frac{b}{c}$.
Reflexive Property of Equality	$a = a$
Symmetric Property of Equality	If $a = b$, then $b = a$.
Transitive Property of Equality	If $a = b$ and $b = c$, then $a = c$.
Substitution Property of Equality	If $a = b$, then b can be substituted for a in any expression.

As you have learned, if you start with a true statement and each logical step is valid, then your conclusion is valid.

An important part of writing a proof is giving justifications to show that every step is valid. For each justification, you can use a definition, postulate, property, or a piece of information that is given.

EXAMPLE 1 Solving an Equation in Algebra

Solve the equation $-5 = 3n + 1$. Write a justification for each step.

$-5 = 3n + 1$	Given equation
$\underline{-1} \quad \underline{\quad -1}$	Subtraction Property of Equality
$-6 = 3n$	Simplify.
$\frac{-6}{3} = \frac{3n}{3}$	Division Property of Equality
$-2 = n$	Simplify.
$n = -2$	Symmetric Property of Equality

CHECK IT OUT! **1.** Solve the equation $\frac{1}{2}t = -7$. Write a justification for each step.

EXAMPLE 2 *Problem-Solving Application*

MATHEMATICAL PRACTICES

Make sense of problems and persevere in solving them.

To simulate the motion of an object in a computer game, the designer uses the formula $sr = 3.6p$ to find the number of pixels the object must travel during each second of animation. In the formula, s is the desired speed of the object in kilometers per hour, r is the scale of pixels per meter, and p is the number of pixels traveled per second.

The graphics in a game are based on a scale of 6 pixels per meter. The designer wants to simulate a vehicle moving at 75 km/h. How many pixels must the vehicle travel each second? Solve the equation for p and justify each step.

1 Understand the Problem

The **answer** will be the number of pixels traveled per second.

List the important information:

- $sr = 3.6p$
- p: pixels traveled per second
- $s = 75$ km/h
- $r = 6$ pixels per meter

2 Make a Plan

Substitute the given information into the formula and solve.

3 Solve

$sr = 3.6p$	Given equation
$(75)(6) = 3.6p$	Substitution Property of Equality
$450 = 3.6p$	Simplify.
$\frac{450}{3.6} = \frac{3.6p}{3.6}$	Division Property of Equality
$125 = p$	Simplify.
$p = 125$ pixels	Symmetric Property of Equality

4 Look Back

Check your answer by substituting it back into the original formula.

$$sr = 3.6p$$
$$(75)(6) = 3.6(125)$$
$$450 = 450 \checkmark$$

Helpful Hint

AB represents the length of $\overline{AB}$, so you can think of AB as a variable representing a number.

CHECK IT OUT! 2. What is the temperature in degrees Celsius C when it is 86°F? Solve the equation $C = \frac{5}{9}(F - 32)$ for C and justify each step.

Like algebra, geometry also uses numbers, variables, and operations. For example, segment lengths and angle measures are numbers. So you can use these same properties of equality to write algebraic proofs in geometry.

EXAMPLE 3 Solving an Equation in Geometry

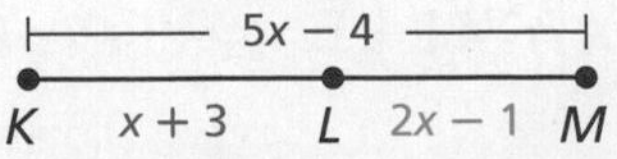

Write a justification for each step.

$KM = KL + LM$	Segment Addition Postulate
$5x - 4 = (x + 3) + (2x - 1)$	Substitution Property of Equality
$5x - 4 = 3x + 2$	Simplify.
$2x - 4 = 2$	Subtraction Property of Equality
$2x = 6$	Addition Property of Equality
$x = 3$	Division Property of Equality

CHECK IT OUT!

3. Write a justification for each step.

$m\angle ABC = m\angle ABD + m\angle DBC$

$8x° = (3x + 5)° + (6x - 16)°$

$8x = 9x - 11$

$-x = -11$

$x = 11$

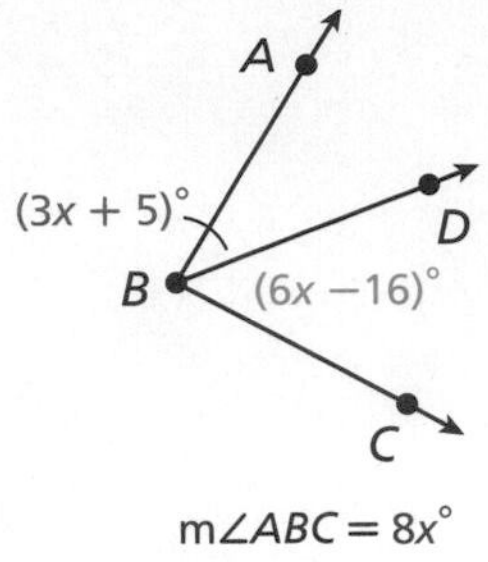

You have learned that segments with equal lengths are congruent and angles with equal measures are congruent. So the Reflexive, Symmetric, and Transitive Properties of Equality have corresponding properties of congruence.

Know it! Note

Properties of Congruence

SYMBOLS	EXAMPLE
Reflexive Property of Congruence figure *A* ≅ figure *A* (Reflex. Prop. of ≅)	$\overline{EF} \cong \overline{EF}$
Symmetric Property of Congruence If figure *A* ≅ figure *B*, then figure *B* ≅ figure *A*. (Sym. Prop. of ≅)	If $\angle 1 \cong \angle 2$, then $\angle 2 \cong \angle 1$.
Transitive Property of Congruence If figure *A* ≅ figure *B* and figure *B* ≅ figure *C*, then figure *A* ≅ figure *C*. (Trans. Prop. of ≅)	If $\overline{PQ} \cong \overline{RS}$ and $\overline{RS} \cong \overline{TU}$, then $\overline{PQ} \cong \overline{TU}$.

EXAMPLE 4 Identifying Properties of Equality and Congruence

Remember!

Numbers are equal (=) and figures are congruent (≅).

Identify the property that justifies each statement.

A	$m\angle 1 = m\angle 1$	Reflex. Prop. of =
B	$\overline{XY} \cong \overline{VW}$, so $\overline{VW} \cong \overline{XY}$.	Sym. Prop. of ≅
C	$\angle ABC \cong \angle ABC$	Reflex. Prop. of ≅
D	$\angle 1 \cong \angle 2$, and $\angle 2 \cong \angle 3$. So $\angle 1 \cong \angle 3$.	Trans. Prop. of ≅

CHECK IT OUT!

Identify the property that justifies each statement.

4a. $DE = GH$, so $GH = DE$.

4b. $94° = 94°$

4c. $0 = a$, and $a = x$. So $0 = x$.

4d. $\angle A \cong \angle Y$, so $\angle Y \cong \angle A$.

THINK AND DISCUSS

MATHEMATICAL PRACTICES

1. Tell what property you would use to solve the equation $\frac{k}{6} = 3.5$.
2. Explain when to use a congruence symbol instead of an equal sign.
3. **GET ORGANIZED** Copy and complete the graphic organizer. In each box, write an example of the property, using the correct symbol.

Know it! Note

Property	Equality	Congruence
Reflexive		
Symmetric		
Transitive		

2-5 Exercises

Learn It Online
Homework Help Online
Parent Resources Online

GUIDED PRACTICE

1. **Vocabulary** Write the definition of *proof* in your own words.

SEE EXAMPLE 1

Multi-Step Solve each equation. Write a justification for each step.

2. $y + 1 = 5$
3. $t - 3.2 = -8.3$
4. $2p - 30 = -4p + 6$
5. $\frac{x + 3}{-2} = 8$
6. $\frac{1}{2}n = \frac{3}{4}$
7. $0 = 2(r - 3) + 4$

SEE EXAMPLE 2

8. **Nutrition** Amy's favorite breakfast cereal has 102 Calories per serving. The equation $C = 9f + 90$ relates the grams of fat f in one serving to the Calories C in one serving. How many grams of fat are in one serving of the cereal? Solve the equation for f and justify each step.

9. **Movie Rentals** The equation $C = \$5.75 + \$0.89m$ relates the number of movie rentals m to the monthly cost C of a movie club membership. How many movies did Elias rent this month if his membership cost \$11.98? Solve the equation for m and justify each step.

SEE EXAMPLE 3

Write a justification for each step.

10.

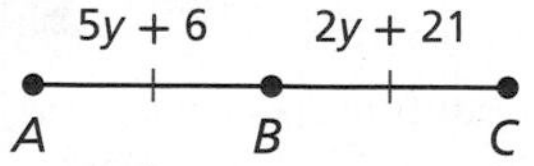

$AB = BC$

$5y + 6 = 2y + 21$

$3y + 6 = 21$

$3y = 15$

$y = 5$

11.

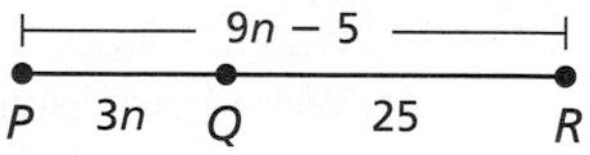

$PQ + QR = PR$

$3n + 25 = 9n - 5$

$25 = 6n - 5$

$30 = 6n$

$5 = n$

SEE EXAMPLE 4

Identify the property that justifies each statement.

12. $\overline{AB} \cong \overline{AB}$
13. $m\angle 1 = m\angle 2$, and $m\angle 2 = m\angle 4$. So $m\angle 1 = m\angle 4$.
14. $x = y$, so $y = x$.
15. $\overline{ST} \cong \overline{YZ}$, and $\overline{YZ} \cong \overline{PR}$. So $\overline{ST} \cong \overline{PR}$.

PRACTICE AND PROBLEM SOLVING

Independent Practice

For Exercises	See Example
16–21	1
22	2
23–24	3
25–28	4

Extra Practice

See Extra Practice for more Skills Practice and Applications Practice exercises.

Multi-Step Solve each equation. Write a justification for each step.

16. $5x - 3 = 4(x + 2)$ **17.** $1.6 = 3.2n$ **18.** $\frac{z}{3} - 2 = -10$

19. $-(h + 3) = 72$ **20.** $9y + 17 = -19$ **21.** $\frac{1}{2}(p - 16) = 13$

22. Ecology The equation $T = 0.03c + 0.05b$ relates the numbers of cans c and bottles b collected in a recycling rally to the total dollars T raised. How many cans were collected if $147 was raised and 150 bottles were collected? Solve the equation for c and justify each step.

Write a justification for each step.

23. $m\angle XYZ = m\angle 2 + m\angle 3$

$4n - 6 = 58 + (2n - 12)$

$4n - 6 = 2n + 46$

$2n - 6 = 46$

$2n = 52$

$n = 26$

24. $m\angle WYV = m\angle 1 + m\angle 2$

$5n = 3(n - 2) + 58$

$5n = 3n - 6 + 58$

$5n = 3n + 52$

$2n = 52$

$n = 26$

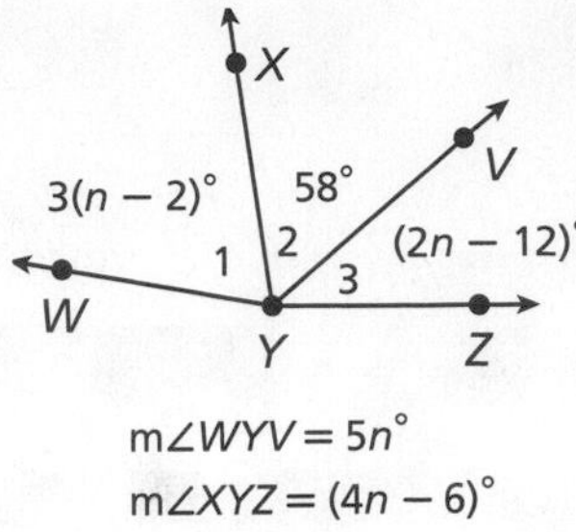

Identify the property that justifies each statement.

25. $\overline{KL} \cong \overline{PR}$, so $\overline{PR} \cong \overline{KL}$. **26.** $412 = 412$

27. If $a = b$ and $b = 0$, then $a = 0$. **28.** figure $A \cong$ figure A

29. Estimation Round the numbers in the equation $2(3.1x - 0.87) = 94.36$ to the nearest whole number and estimate the solution. Then solve the equation, justifying each step. Compare your estimate to the exact solution.

Use the indicated property to complete each statement.

30. Reflexive Property of Equality: $3x - 1 =$ __?__

31. Transitive Property of Congruence: If $\angle A \cong \angle X$ and $\angle X \cong \angle T$, then __?__.

32. Symmetric Property of Congruence: If $\overline{BC} \cong \overline{NP}$, then __?__.

33. Recreation The north campground is midway between the Northpoint Overlook and the waterfall. Use the midpoint formula to find the values of x and y, and justify each step.

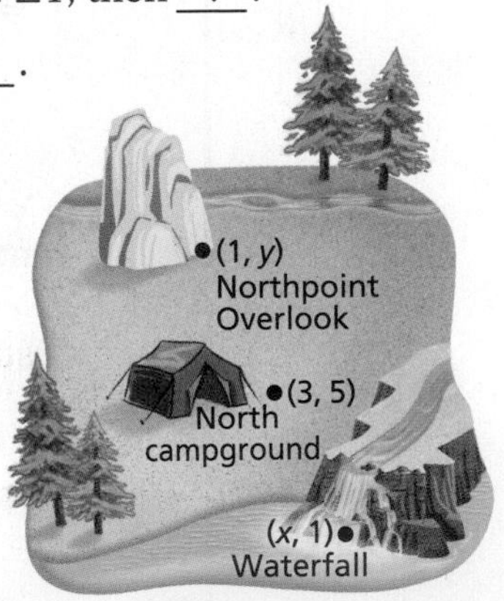

34. Business A computer repair technician charges $35 for each job plus $21 per hour of labor and 110% of the cost of parts. The total charge for a 3-hour job was $169.50. What was the cost of parts for this job? Write and solve an equation and justify each step in the solution.

35. Finance Morgan spent a total of $1,733.65 on her car last year. She spent $92.50 on registration, $79.96 on maintenance, and $983 on insurance. She spent the remaining money on gas. She drove a total of 10,820 miles.

a. How much on average did the gas cost per mile? Write and solve an equation and justify each step in the solution.

b. What if...? Suppose Morgan's car averages 32 miles per gallon of gas. How much on average did Morgan pay for a gallon of gas?

36. Critical Thinking Use the definition of segment congruence and the properties of equality to show that all three properties of congruence are true for segments.

MULTI-STEP TEST PREP

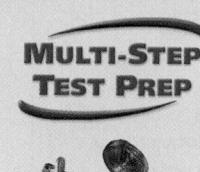

37. Recall from Algebra 1 that the Multiplication and Division Properties of Inequality tell you to reverse the inequality sign when multiplying or dividing by a negative number.

a. Solve the inequality $x + 15 \leq 63$ and write a justification for each step.

b. Solve the inequality $-2x > 36$ and write a justification for each step.

38. Write About It Compare the conclusion of a deductive proof and a conjecture based on inductive reasoning.

TEST PREP

39. Which could NOT be used to justify the statement $\overline{AB} \cong \overline{CD}$?

Ⓐ Definition of congruence
Ⓑ Reflexive Property of Congruence
Ⓒ Symmetric Property of Congruence
Ⓓ Transitive Property of Congruence

40. A club membership costs \$35 plus \$3 each time t the member uses the pool. Which equation represents the total cost C of the membership?

Ⓕ $35 = C + 3t$ Ⓖ $C + 35 = 3t$ Ⓗ $C = 35 + 3t$ Ⓙ $C = 35t + 3$

41. Which statement is true by the Reflexive Property of Equality?

Ⓐ $x = 35$ Ⓑ $\overline{CD} = \overline{CD}$ Ⓒ $\overline{RT} \cong \overline{TR}$ Ⓓ $CD = CD$

42. Gridded Response In the triangle, $m\angle 1 + m\angle 2 + m\angle 3 = 180°$. If $m\angle 3 = 2m\angle 1$ and $m\angle 1 = m\angle 2$, find $m\angle 3$ in degrees.

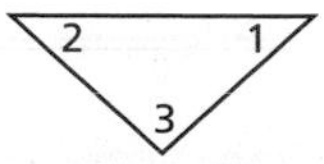

CHALLENGE AND EXTEND

43. In the gate, $PA = QB$, $QB = RA$, and $PA = 18$ in. Find PR, and justify each step.

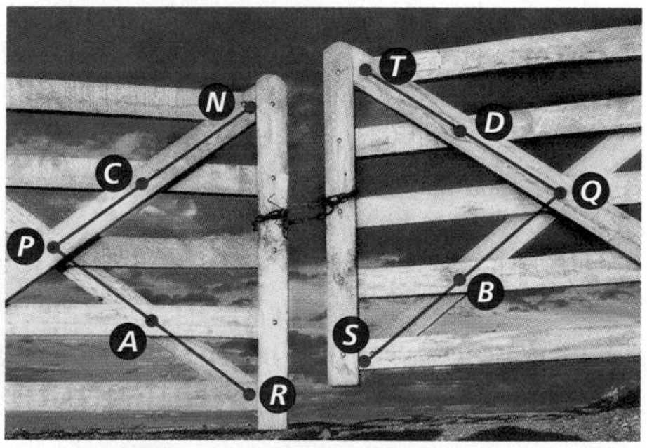

44. Critical Thinking Explain why there is no Addition Property of Congruence.

45. Algebra Justify each step in the solution of the inequality $7 - 3x > 19$.

COMMON CORE

2-6 Geometric Proof

CC.9-12.G.CO.9 Prove geometric theorems about lines and angles.

Objectives

Write two-column proofs.

Prove geometric theorems by using deductive reasoning.

Vocabulary

theorem
two-column proof

Who uses this?

To persuade your parents to increase your allowance, your argument must be presented logically and precisely.

When writing a geometric proof, you use deductive reasoning to create a chain of logical steps that move from the hypothesis to the conclusion of the conjecture you are proving. By proving that the conclusion is true, you have proven that the original conjecture is true.

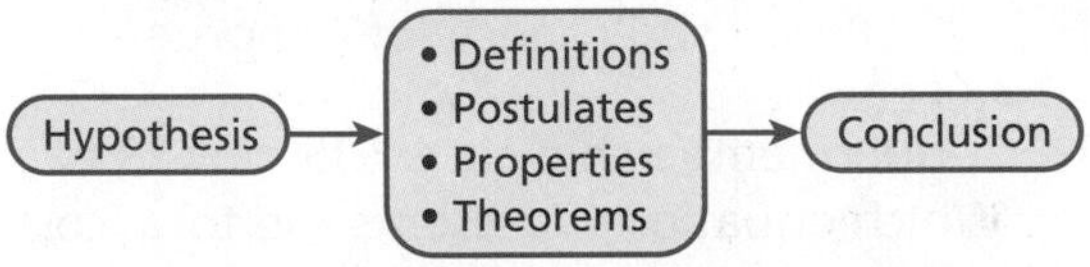

When writing a proof, it is important to justify each logical step with a reason. You can use symbols and abbreviations, but they must be clear enough so that anyone who reads your proof will understand them.

EXAMPLE 1 Writing Justifications

Helpful Hint

When a justification is based on more than the previous step, you can note this after the reason, as in Example 1 Step 5.

Write a justification for each step, given that $\angle A$ and $\angle B$ are complementary and $\angle A \cong \angle C$.

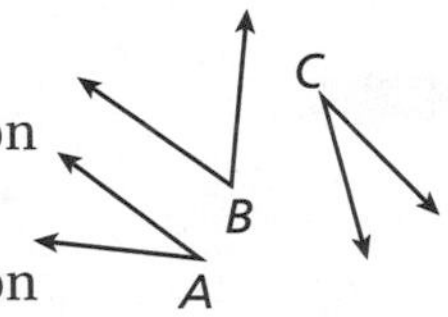

1. $\angle A$ and $\angle B$ are complementary. — Given information
2. $m\angle A + m\angle B = 90°$ — Def. of comp. ∠s
3. $\angle A \cong \angle C$ — Given information
4. $m\angle A = m\angle C$ — Def. of ≅ ∠s
5. $m\angle C + m\angle B = 90°$ — Subst. Prop. of = *Steps 2, 4*
6. $\angle C$ and $\angle B$ are complementary. — Def. of comp. ∠s

CHECK IT OUT!

1. Write a justification for each step, given that B is the midpoint of $\overline{AC}$ and $\overline{AB} \cong \overline{EF}$.

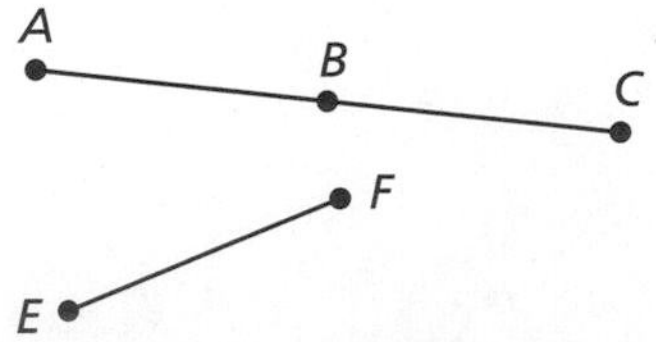

1. B is the midpoint of $\overline{AC}$.
2. $\overline{AB} \cong \overline{BC}$
3. $\overline{AB} \cong \overline{EF}$
4. $\overline{BC} \cong \overline{EF}$

A **theorem** is any statement that you can prove. Once you have proven a theorem, you can use it as a reason in later proofs.

Know it! Note

Theorem

	THEOREM	HYPOTHESIS	CONCLUSION
2-6-1	**Linear Pair Theorem** If two angles form a linear pair, then they are supplementary.	$\angle A$ and $\angle B$ form a linear pair.	$\angle A$ and $\angle B$ are supplementary.

Know it! Note

Theorem

THEOREM	HYPOTHESIS	CONCLUSION
2-6-2 Congruent Supplements Theorem If two angles are supplementary to the same angle (or to two congruent angles), then the two angles are congruent.	$\angle 1$ and $\angle 2$ are supplementary. $\angle 2$ and $\angle 3$ are supplementary.	$\angle 1 \cong \angle 3$

A geometric proof begins with *Given* and *Prove* statements, which restate the hypothesis and conclusion of the conjecture. In a **two-column proof**, you list the steps of the proof in the left column. You write the matching reason for each step in the right column.

EXAMPLE 2 Completing a Two-Column Proof

Fill in the blanks to complete a two-column proof of the Linear Pair Theorem.
Given: $\angle 1$ and $\angle 2$ form a linear pair.
Prove: $\angle 1$ and $\angle 2$ are supplementary.
Proof:

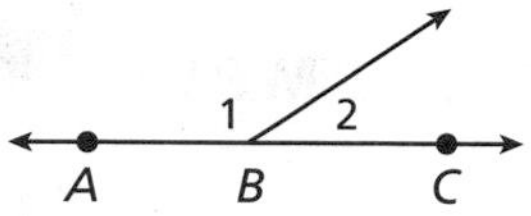

Statements	Reasons
1. $\angle 1$ and $\angle 2$ form a linear pair.	1. Given
2. $\overrightarrow{BA}$ and $\overrightarrow{BC}$ form a line.	2. Def. of lin. pair
3. $m\angle ABC = 180°$	3. Def. of straight $\angle$
4. a. ____?____	4. $\angle$ Add. Post.
5. b. ____?____	5. Subst. *Steps 3, 4*
6. $\angle 1$ and $\angle 2$ are supplementary.	6. c. ____?____

Writing Math

Since there is no other substitution property, the Substitution Property of Equality is often written as "Substitution" or "Subst."

Use the existing statements and reasons in the proof to fill in the blanks.

a. $m\angle 1 + m\angle 2 = m\angle ABC$ — *The $\angle$ Add. Post. is given as the reason.*

b. $m\angle 1 + m\angle 2 = 180°$ — *Substitute 180° for $m\angle ABC$.*

c. Def. of supp. $\angle$s — *The measures of supp. $\angle$s add to 180° by def.*

CHECK IT OUT!

2. Fill in the blanks to complete a two-column proof of one case of the Congruent Supplements Theorem.

Given: $\angle 1$ and $\angle 2$ are supplementary, and $\angle 2$ and $\angle 3$ are supplementary.

Prove: $\angle 1 \cong \angle 3$

Proof:

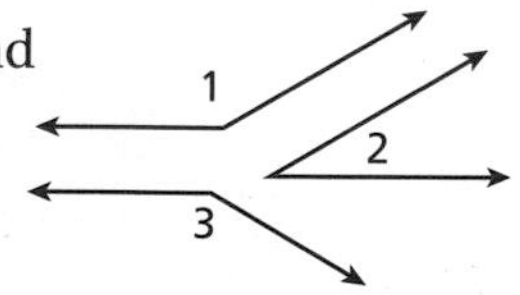

Statements	Reasons
1. a. ____?____	1. Given
2. $m\angle 1 + m\angle 2 = 180°$ $m\angle 2 + m\angle 3 = 180°$	2. Def. of supp. $\angle$s
3. b. ____?____	3. Subst.
4. $m\angle 2 = m\angle 2$	4. Reflex. Prop. of =
5. $m\angle 1 = m\angle 3$	5. c. ____?____
6. d. ____?____	6. Def. of $\cong$ $\angle$s

Before you start writing a proof, you should plan out your logic. Sometimes you will be given a plan for a more challenging proof. This plan will detail the major steps of the proof for you.

Know it! Note

Theorems

THEOREM	HYPOTHESIS	CONCLUSION
2-6-3 Right Angle Congruence Theorem All right angles are congruent.	$\angle A$ and $\angle B$ are right angles.	$\angle A \cong \angle B$
2-6-4 Congruent Complements Theorem If two angles are complementary to the same angle (or to two congruent angles), then the two angles are congruent.	$\angle 1$ and $\angle 2$ are complementary. $\angle 2$ and $\angle 3$ are complementary.	$\angle 1 \cong \angle 3$

EXAMPLE 3 Writing a Two-Column Proof from a Plan

Use the given plan to write a two-column proof of the Right Angle Congruence Theorem.

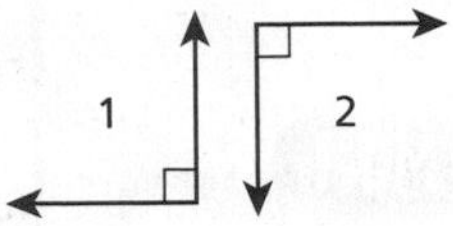

Given: $\angle 1$ and $\angle 2$ are right angles.
Prove: $\angle 1 \cong \angle 2$

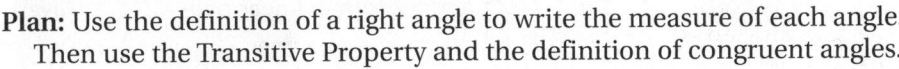

Plan: Use the definition of a right angle to write the measure of each angle. Then use the Transitive Property and the definition of congruent angles.

Proof:

Statements	Reasons
1. $\angle 1$ and $\angle 2$ are right angles.	1. Given
2. $m\angle 1 = 90°$, $m\angle 2 = 90°$	2. Def. of rt. $\angle$
3. $m\angle 1 = m\angle 2$	3. Trans. Prop. of =
4. $\angle 1 \cong \angle 2$	4. Def. of $\cong$ $\angle$s

Helpful Hint

If a diagram for a proof is not provided, draw your own and mark the given information on it. But do not mark the information in the Prove statement on it.

CHECK IT OUT!

3. Use the given plan to write a two-column proof of one case of the Congruent Complements Theorem.

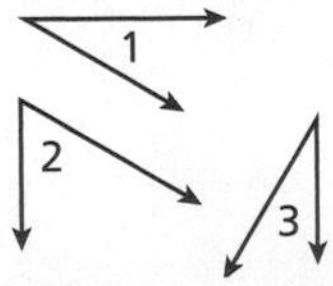

Given: $\angle 1$ and $\angle 2$ are complementary, and $\angle 2$ and $\angle 3$ are complementary.

Prove: $\angle 1 \cong \angle 3$

Plan: The measures of complementary angles add to 90° by definition. Use substitution to show that the sums of both pairs are equal. Use the Subtraction Property and the definition of congruent angles to conclude that $\angle 1 \cong \angle 3$.

Know it! Note

The Proof Process
1. Write the conjecture to be proven.
2. Draw a diagram to represent the hypothesis of the conjecture.
3. State the given information and mark it on the diagram.
4. State the conclusion of the conjecture in terms of the diagram.
5. Plan your argument and prove the conjecture.

MATHEMATICAL PRACTICES

THINK AND DISCUSS

1. Which step in a proof should match the Prove statement?
2. Why is it important to include every logical step in a proof?
3. List four things you can use to justify a step in a proof.

Know it! Note

4. **GET ORGANIZED** Copy and complete the graphic organizer. In each box, describe the steps of the proof process.

1. → 2. → 3. → 4. → 5.

2-6 Exercises

Learn It Online
Homework Help Online
Parent Resources Online

GUIDED PRACTICE

Vocabulary Apply the vocabulary from this lesson to answer each question.

1. In a *two-column proof,* you list the ___?___ in the left column and the ___?___ in the right column. (*statements* or *reasons*)

2. A ___?___ is a statement you can prove. (*postulate* or *theorem*)

SEE EXAMPLE 1

3. Write a justification for each step, given that $m\angle A = 60°$ and $m\angle B = 2m\angle A$.

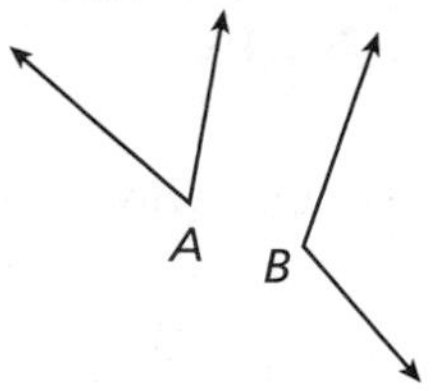

1. $m\angle A = 60°$, $m\angle B = 2m\angle A$
2. $m\angle B = 2(60°)$
3. $m\angle B = 120°$
4. $m\angle A + m\angle B = 60° + 120°$
5. $m\angle A + m\angle B = 180°$
6. $\angle A$ and $\angle B$ are supplementary.

SEE EXAMPLE 2

4. Fill in the blanks to complete the two-column proof.

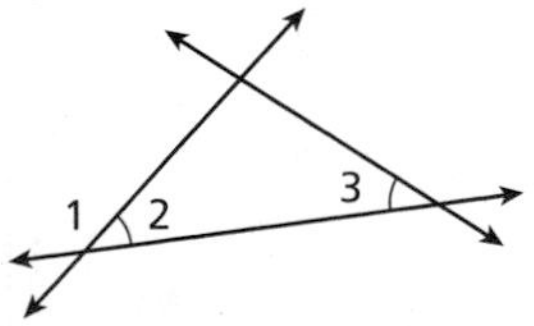

Given: $\angle 2 \cong \angle 3$
Prove: $\angle 1$ and $\angle 3$ are supplementary.
Proof:

Statements	Reasons
1. $\angle 2 \cong \angle 3$	**1.** Given
2. $m\angle 2 = m\angle 3$	**2. a.** ___?___
3. b. ___?___	**3.** Lin. Pair Thm.
4. $m\angle 1 + m\angle 2 = 180°$	**4.** Def. of supp. ∡
5. $m\angle 1 + m\angle 3 = 180°$	**5. c.** ___?___ *Steps 2, 4*
6. d. ___?___	**6.** Def. of supp. ∡

SEE EXAMPLE 3

5. Use the given plan to write a two-column proof.

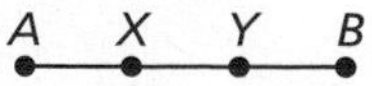

Given: X is the midpoint of $\overline{AY}$, and Y is the midpoint of $\overline{XB}$.
Prove: $\overline{AX} \cong \overline{YB}$
Plan: By the definition of midpoint, $\overline{AX} \cong \overline{XY}$, and $\overline{XY} \cong \overline{YB}$. Use the Transitive Property to conclude that $\overline{AX} \cong \overline{YB}$.

PRACTICE AND PROBLEM SOLVING

Independent Practice

For Exercises	See Example
6	1
7–8	2
9–10	3

Extra Practice

See Extra Practice for more Skills Practice and Applications Practice exercises.

6. Write a justification for each step, given that $\overrightarrow{BX}$ bisects $\angle ABC$ and $m\angle XBC = 45°$.

1. $\overrightarrow{BX}$ bisects $\angle ABC$.
2. $\angle ABX \cong \angle XBC$
3. $m\angle ABX = m\angle XBC$
4. $m\angle XBC = 45°$
5. $m\angle ABX = 45°$
6. $m\angle ABX + m\angle XBC = m\angle ABC$
7. $45° + 45° = m\angle ABC$
8. $90° = m\angle ABC$
9. $\angle ABC$ is a right angle.

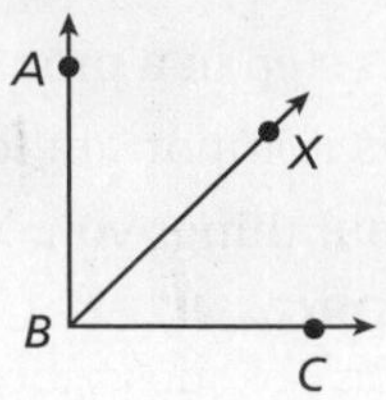

Fill in the blanks to complete each two-column proof.

7. Given: $\angle 1$ and $\angle 2$ are supplementary, and $\angle 3$ and $\angle 4$ are supplementary. $\angle 2 \cong \angle 3$

Prove: $\angle 1 \cong \angle 4$

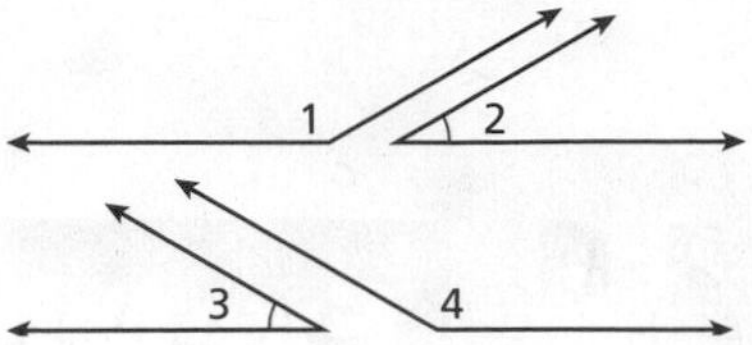

Proof:

Statements	Reasons
1. $\angle 1$ and $\angle 2$ are supplementary. $\angle 3$ and $\angle 4$ are supplementary.	**1.** Given
2. a. ___?___	**2.** Def. of supp. $\angle$s
3. $m\angle 1 + m\angle 2 = m\angle 3 + m\angle 4$	**3. b.** ___?___
4. $\angle 2 \cong \angle 3$	**4.** Given
5. $m\angle 2 = m\angle 3$	**5.** Def. of $\cong$ $\angle$s
6. c. ___?___	**6.** Subtr. Prop. of = *Steps 3, 5*
7. $\angle 1 \cong \angle 4$	**7. d.** ___?___

8. Given: $\angle BAC$ is a right angle. $\angle 2 \cong \angle 3$

Prove: $\angle 1$ and $\angle 3$ are complementary.

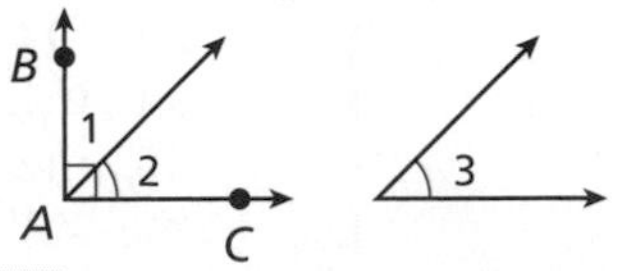

Proof:

Statements	Reasons
1. $\angle BAC$ is a right angle.	**1.** Given
2. $m\angle BAC = 90°$	**2. a.** ___?___
3. b. ___?___	**3.** $\angle$ Add. Post.
4. $m\angle 1 + m\angle 2 = 90°$	**4.** Subst. *Steps 2, 3*
5. $\angle 2 \cong \angle 3$	**5.** Given
6. c. ___?___	**6.** Def. of $\cong$ $\angle$s
7. $m\angle 1 + m\angle 3 = 90°$	**7. d.** ___?___ *Steps 4, 6*
8. e. ___?___	**8.** Def. of comp. $\angle$s

Use the given plan to write a two-column proof.

9. Given: $\overline{BE} \cong \overline{CE}$, $\overline{DE} \cong \overline{AE}$

Prove: $\overline{AB} \cong \overline{CD}$

Plan: Use the definition of congruent segments to write the given information in terms of lengths. Then use the Segment Addition Postulate to show that $AB = CD$ and thus $\overline{AB} \cong \overline{CD}$.

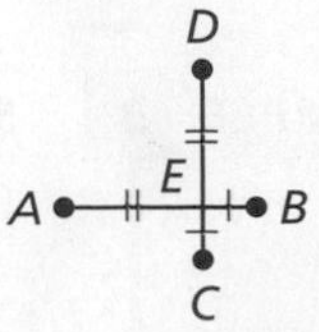

Use the given plan to write a two-column proof.

10. Given: ∠1 and ∠3 are complementary, and ∠2 and ∠4 are complementary. ∠3 ≅ ∠4

Prove: ∠1 ≅ ∠2

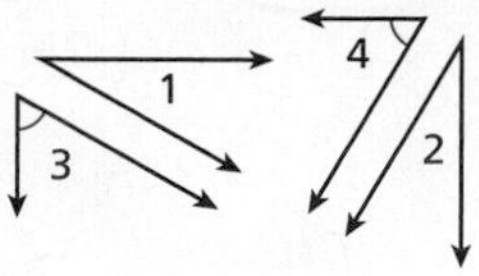

Plan: Since ∠1 and ∠3 are complementary and ∠2 and ∠4 are complementary, both pairs of angle measures add to 90°. Use substitution to show that the sums of both pairs are equal. Since ∠3 ≅ ∠4, their measures are equal. Use the Subtraction Property of Equality and the definition of congruent angles to conclude that ∠1 ≅ ∠2.

LINK Engineering

The Oresund Bridge, at 7845 meters long, is the world's longest single bridge. It carries both rail and car traffic between Denmark and Sweden.

Find each angle measure.

11. m∠1

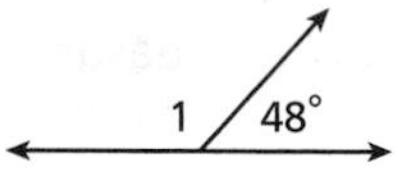

12. m∠2

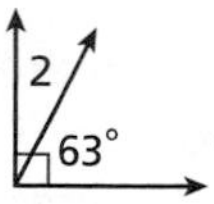

13. m∠3

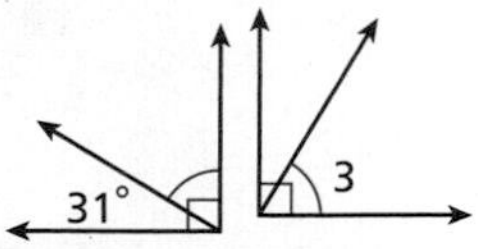

14. Engineering The Oresund Bridge, which connects the countries of Denmark and Sweden, was completed in 1999. If ∠1 ≅ ∠2, which theorem can you use to conclude that ∠3 ≅ ∠4?

15. Critical Thinking Explain why there are two cases to consider when proving the Congruent Supplements Theorem and the Congruent Complements Theorem.

Tell whether each statement is sometimes, always, or never true.

16. An angle and its complement are congruent.

17. A pair of right angles forms a linear pair.

18. An angle and its complement form a right angle.

19. A linear pair of angles is complementary.

Algebra **Find the value of each variable.**

20.

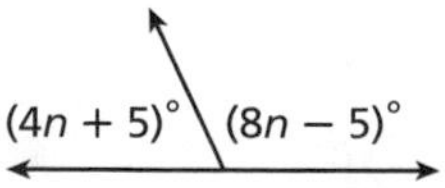

21.

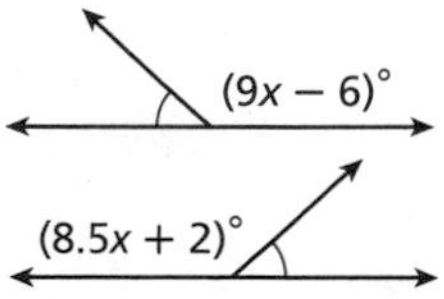

22.

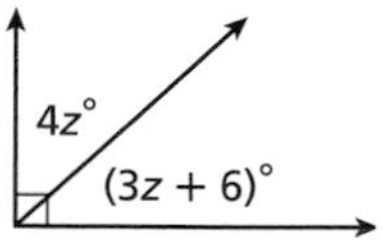

23. Write About It How are a theorem and a postulate alike? How are they different?

MULTI-STEP TEST PREP

24. Sometimes you may be asked to write a proof without a specific statement of the Given and Prove information being provided for you. For each of the following situations, use the triangle to write a Given and Prove statement.

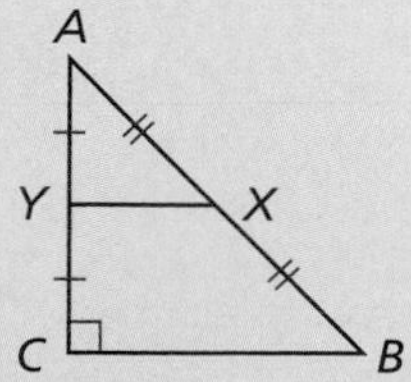

a. The segment connecting the midpoints of two sides of a triangle is half as long as the third side.

b. The acute angles of a right triangle are complementary.

c. In a right triangle, the sum of the squares of the legs is equal to the square of the hypotenuse.

TEST PREP

25. Which theorem justifies the conclusion that $\angle 1 \cong \angle 4$?

Ⓐ Linear Pair Theorem
Ⓑ Congruent Supplements Theorem
Ⓒ Congruent Complements Theorem
Ⓓ Right Angle Congruence Theorem

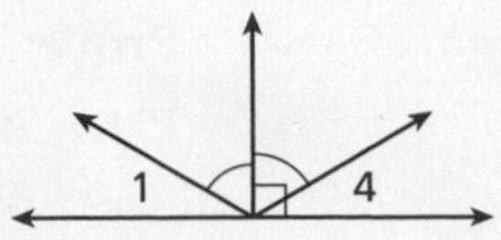

26. What can be concluded from the statement $m\angle 1 + m\angle 2 = 180°$?

Ⓕ $\angle 1$ and $\angle 2$ are congruent.
Ⓖ $\angle 1$ and $\angle 2$ are supplementary.
Ⓗ $\angle 1$ and $\angle 2$ are complementary.
Ⓙ $\angle 1$ and $\angle 2$ form a linear pair.

27. Given: Two angles are complementary. The measure of one angle is 10° less than the measure of the other angle. Conclusion: The measures of the angles are 85° and 95°. Which statement is true?

Ⓐ The conclusion is correct because 85° is 10° less than 95°.
Ⓑ The conclusion is verified by the first statement given.
Ⓒ The conclusion is invalid because the angles are not congruent.
Ⓓ The conclusion is contradicted by the first statement given.

CHALLENGE AND EXTEND

28. Write a two-column proof.
Given: $m\angle LAN = 30°$, $m\angle 1 = 15°$
Prove: $\overrightarrow{AM}$ bisects $\angle LAN$.

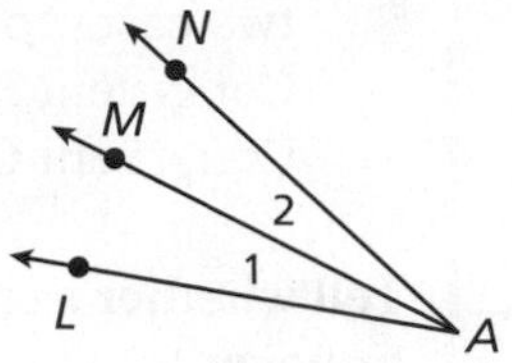

Multi-Step Find the value of the variable and the measure of each angle.

29.

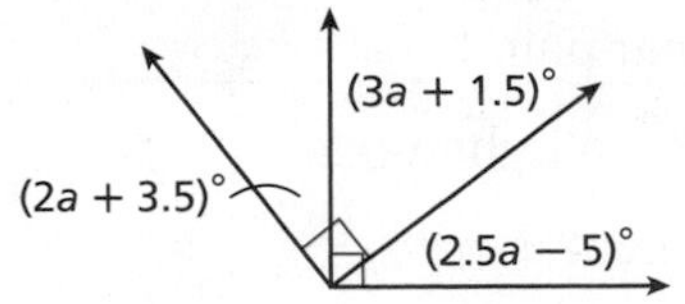

30.

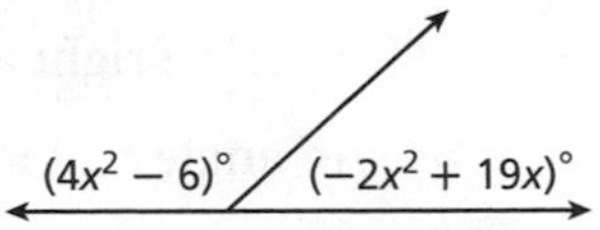

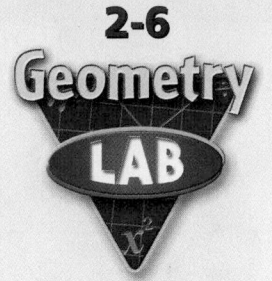

2-6
Geometry LAB

Use with Geometric Proof

Design Plans for Proofs

Sometimes the most challenging part of writing a proof is planning the logical steps that will take you from the Given statement to the Prove statement. Like working a jigsaw puzzle, you can start with any piece. Write down everything you know from the Given statement. If you don't see the connection right away, start with the Prove statement and work backward. Then connect the pieces into a logical order.

Activity

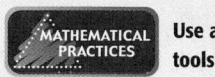

MATHEMATICAL PRACTICES **Use appropriate tools strategically**

CC.9-12.G.CO.9 Prove geometric theorems about lines and angles.

Prove the Common Angles Theorem.
Given: $\angle AXB \cong \angle CXD$
Prove: $\angle AXC \cong \angle BXD$

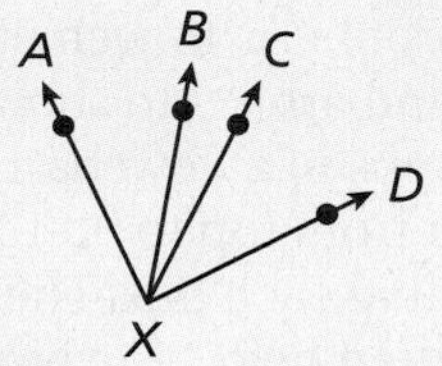

1 Start by considering the difference in the Given and Prove statements. How does $\angle AXB$ compare to $\angle AXC$? How does $\angle CXD$ compare to $\angle BXD$?

In both cases, ∠BXC is combined with the first angle to get the second angle.

2 The situation involves combining adjacent angle measures, so list any definitions, properties, postulates, and theorems that might be helpful.

Definition of congruent angles, Angle Addition Postulate, properties of equality, and Reflexive, Symmetric, and Transitive Properties of Congruence

3 Start with what you are given and what you are trying to prove and then work toward the middle.

$\angle AXB \cong \angle CXD$	*The first reason will be "Given."*
$m\angle AXB = m\angle CXD$	Def. of ≅ ∠s
???	???
$m\angle AXC = m\angle BXD$	???
$\angle AXC \cong \angle BXD$	*The last statement will be the Prove statement.*

4 Based on Step 1, $\angle BXC$ is the missing piece in the middle of the logical flow. So write down what you know about $\angle BXC$.

$\angle BXC \cong \angle BXC$	Reflex. Prop. of ≅
$m\angle BXC = m\angle BXC$	Reflex. Prop. of =

5 Now you can see that the Angle Addition Postulate needs to be used to complete the proof.

$m\angle AXB + m\angle BXC = m\angle AXC$	∠ Add. Post.
$m\angle BXC + m\angle CXD = m\angle BXD$	∠ Add. Post.

6 Use the pieces to write a complete two-column proof of the Common Angles Theorem.

Try This

1. Describe how a plan for a proof differs from the actual proof.

2. Write a plan and a two-column proof.
Given: $\overrightarrow{BD}$ bisects $\angle ABC$.
Prove: $2m\angle 1 = m\angle ABC$

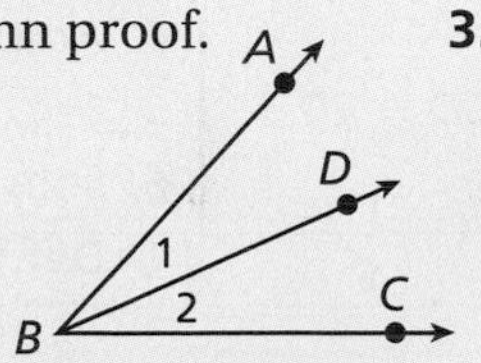

3. Write a plan and a two-column proof.
Given: $\angle LXN$ is a right angle.
Prove: $\angle 1$ and $\angle 2$ are complementary.

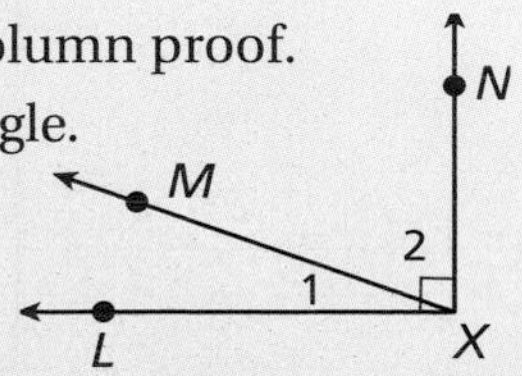

COMMON CORE

2-7 Flowchart and Paragraph Proofs

CC.9-12.G.CO.9 Prove theorems about lines and angles. *Also* **CC.9-12.G.CO.10**

Objectives

Write flowchart and paragraph proofs.

Prove geometric theorems by using deductive reasoning.

Vocabulary

flowchart proof
paragraph proof

Why learn this?

Flowcharts make it easy to see how the steps of a process are linked together.

A second style of proof is a **flowchart proof**, which uses boxes and arrows to show the structure of the proof. The steps in a flowchart proof move from left to right or from top to bottom, shown by the arrows connecting each box. The justification for each step is written below the box.

Know it! Note

Theorem 2-7-1 **Common Segments Theorem**

THEOREM	HYPOTHESIS	CONCLUSION
Given collinear points A, B, C, and D arranged as shown, if $\overline{AB} \cong \overline{CD}$, then $\overline{AC} \cong \overline{BD}$. 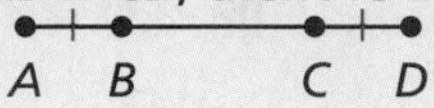	$\overline{AB} \cong \overline{CD}$	$\overline{AC} \cong \overline{BD}$

EXAMPLE 1 **Reading a Flowchart Proof**

Use the given flowchart proof to write a two-column proof of the Common Segments Theorem.

Given: $\overline{AB} \cong \overline{CD}$

Prove: $\overline{AC} \cong \overline{BD}$

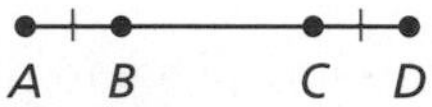

Flowchart proof:

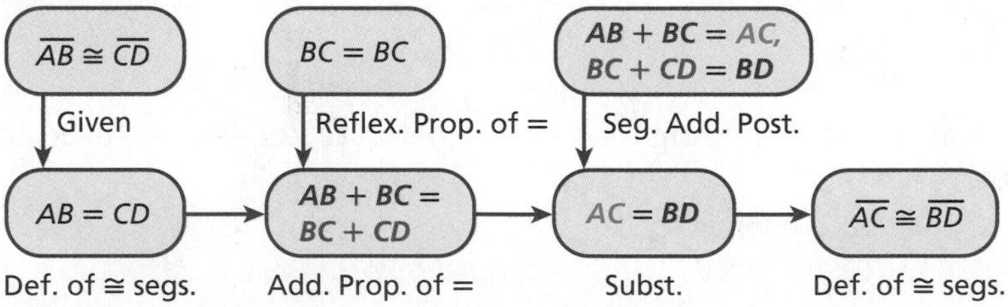

Two-column proof:

Statements	Reasons
1. $\overline{AB} \cong \overline{CD}$	1. Given
2. $AB = CD$	2. Def. of ≅ segs.
3. $BC = BC$	3. Reflex. Prop. of =
4. $AB + BC = BC + CD$	4. Add. Prop. of =
5. $AB + BC = AC$, $BC + CD = BD$	5. Seg. Add. Post.
6. $AC = BD$	6. Subst.
7. $\overline{AC} \cong \overline{BD}$	7. Def. of ≅ segs.

CHECK IT OUT!

1. Use the given flowchart proof to write a two-column proof.

Given: $RS = UV$, $ST = TU$

Prove: $\overline{RT} \cong \overline{TV}$

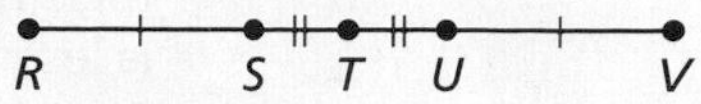

Flowchart proof:

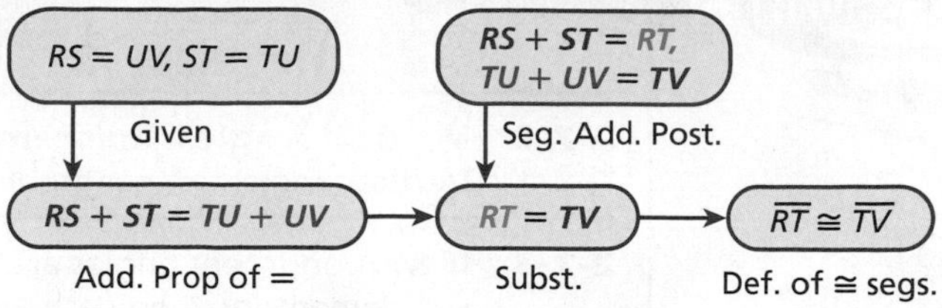

EXAMPLE 2 Writing a Flowchart Proof

Use the given two-column proof to write a flowchart proof of the Converse of the Common Segments Theorem.

Given: $\overline{AC} \cong \overline{BD}$

Prove: $\overline{AB} \cong \overline{CD}$

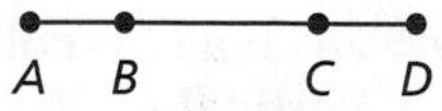

Two-column proof:

Statements	Reasons
1. $\overline{AC} \cong \overline{BD}$	1. Given
2. $AC = BD$	2. Def. of ≅ segs.
3. $AB + BC = AC$, $BC + CD = BD$	3. Seg. Add. Post.
4. $AB + BC = BC + CD$	4. Subst. *Steps 2, 3*
5. $BC = BC$	5. Reflex. Prop. of =
6. $AB = CD$	6. Subtr. Prop. of =
7. $\overline{AB} \cong \overline{CD}$	7. Def. of ≅ segs.

Helpful Hint

Like the converse of a conditional statement, the converse of a theorem is found by switching the hypothesis and conclusion.

Flowchart proof:

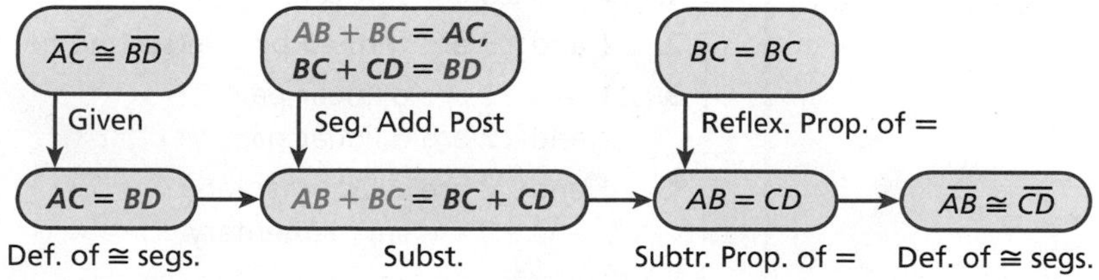

CHECK IT OUT!

2. Use the given two-column proof to write a flowchart proof.

Given: $\angle 2 \cong \angle 4$

Prove: $m\angle 1 = m\angle 3$

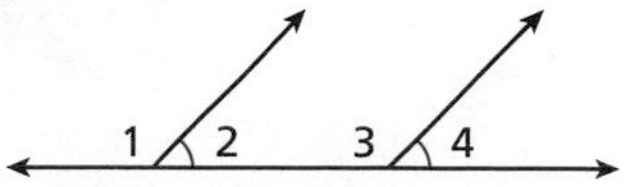

Two-column proof:

Statements	Reasons
1. $\angle 2 \cong \angle 4$	1. Given
2. $\angle 1$ and $\angle 2$ are supplementary. $\angle 3$ and $\angle 4$ are supplementary.	2. Lin. Pair Thm.
3. $\angle 1 \cong \angle 3$	3. ≅ Supps. Thm.
4. $m\angle 1 = m\angle 3$	4. Def. of ≅ $\angle$s

A **paragraph proof** is a style of proof that presents the steps of the proof and their matching reasons as sentences in a paragraph. Although this style of proof is less formal than a two-column proof, you still must include every step.

Know it! Note

Theorems

	THEOREM	HYPOTHESIS	CONCLUSION
2-7-2	**Vertical Angles Theorem** Vertical angles are congruent.	$\angle A$ and $\angle B$ are vertical angles.	$\angle A \cong \angle B$
2-7-3	If two congruent angles are supplementary, then each angle is a right angle. ($\cong$ ∠s supp. → rt. ∠s)	$\angle 1 \cong \angle 2$ $\angle 1$ and $\angle 2$ are supplementary.	$\angle 1$ and $\angle 2$ are right angles.

EXAMPLE 3

Reading a Paragraph Proof

Use the given paragraph proof to write a two-column proof of the Vertical Angles Theorem.

Given: $\angle 1$ and $\angle 3$ are vertical angles.
Prove: $\angle 1 \cong \angle 3$

Paragraph proof: $\angle 1$ and $\angle 3$ are vertical angles, so they are formed by intersecting lines. Therefore $\angle 1$ and $\angle 2$ are a linear pair, and $\angle 2$ and $\angle 3$ are a linear pair. By the Linear Pair Theorem, $\angle 1$ and $\angle 2$ are supplementary, and $\angle 2$ and $\angle 3$ are supplementary. So by the Congruent Supplements Theorem, $\angle 1 \cong \angle 3$.

Two-column proof:

Statements	Reasons
1. $\angle 1$ and $\angle 3$ are vertical angles.	**1.** Given
2. $\angle 1$ and $\angle 3$ are formed by intersecting lines.	**2.** Def. of vert. ∠s
3. $\angle 1$ and $\angle 2$ are a linear pair. $\angle 2$ and $\angle 3$ are a linear pair.	**3.** Def. of lin. pair
4. $\angle 1$ and $\angle 2$ are supplementary. $\angle 2$ and $\angle 3$ are supplementary.	**4.** Lin. Pair Thm.
5. $\angle 1 \cong \angle 3$	**5.** $\cong$ Supps. Thm.

CHECK IT OUT!

3. Use the given paragraph proof to write a two-column proof.

Given: $\angle WXY$ is a right angle. $\angle 1 \cong \angle 3$
Prove: $\angle 1$ and $\angle 2$ are complementary.

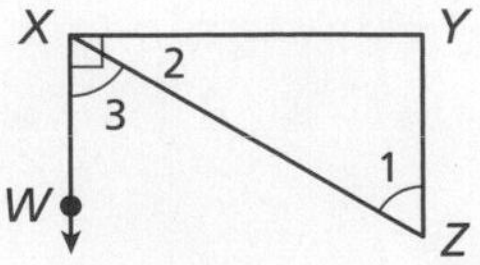

Paragraph proof: Since $\angle WXY$ is a right angle, $m\angle WXY = 90°$ by the definition of a right angle. By the Angle Addition Postulate, $m\angle WXY = m\angle 2 + m\angle 3$. By substitution, $m\angle 2 + m\angle 3 = 90°$. Since $\angle 1 \cong \angle 3$, $m\angle 1 = m\angle 3$ by the definition of congruent angles. Using substitution, $m\angle 2 + m\angle 1 = 90°$. Thus by the definition of complementary angles, $\angle 1$ and $\angle 2$ are complementary.

Student to Student

Writing a Proof

Claire Jeffords
Riverbend High School

When I have to write a proof and I don't see how to start, I look at what I'm supposed to be proving and see if it makes sense. If it does, I ask myself why. Sometimes this helps me to see what the reasons in the proof might be. If all else fails, I just start writing down everything I know based on the diagram and the given statement. By brainstorming like this, I can usually figure out the steps of the proof. You can even write each thing on a separate piece of paper and arrange the pieces of paper like a flowchart.

EXAMPLE 4 Writing a Paragraph Proof

Use the given two-column proof to write a paragraph proof of Theorem 2-7-3.

Given: ∠1 and ∠2 are supplementary. ∠1 ≅ ∠2
Prove: ∠1 and ∠2 are right angles.

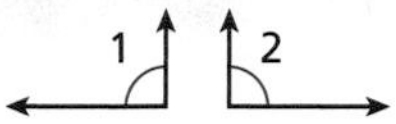

Two-column proof:

Statements	Reasons
1. ∠1 and ∠2 are supplementary. ∠1 ≅ ∠2	1. Given
2. m∠1 + m∠2 = 180°	2. Def. of supp. ∠s
3. m∠1 = m∠2	3. Def. of ≅ ∠s *Step 1*
4. m∠1 + m∠1 = 180°	4. Subst. *Steps 2, 3*
5. 2m∠1 = 180°	5. Simplification
6. m∠1 = 90°	6. Div. Prop. of =
7. m∠2 = 90°	7. Trans. Prop. of = *Steps 3, 6*
8. ∠1 and ∠2 are right angles.	8. Def. of rt. ∠

Paragraph proof: ∠1 and ∠2 are supplementary, so m∠1 + m∠2 = 180° by the definition of supplementary angles. They are also congruent, so their measures are equal by the definition of congruent angles. By substitution, m∠1 + m∠1 = 180°, so m∠1 = 90° by the Division Property of Equality. Because m∠1 = m∠2, m∠2 = 90° by the Transitive Property of Equality. So both are right angles by the definition of a right angle.

CHECK IT OUT!

4. Use the given two-column proof to write a paragraph proof.

Given: ∠1 ≅ ∠4
Prove: ∠2 ≅ ∠3

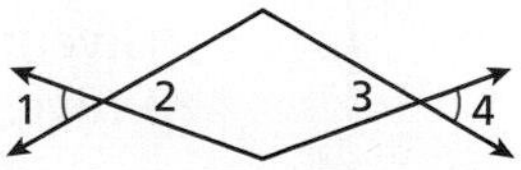

Two-column proof:

Statements	Reasons
1. ∠1 ≅ ∠4	1. Given
2. ∠1 ≅ ∠2, ∠3 ≅ ∠4	2. Vert. ∠s Thm.
3. ∠2 ≅ ∠4	3. Trans. Prop. of ≅ *Steps 1, 2*
4. ∠2 ≅ ∠3	4. Trans. Prop. of ≅ *Steps 2, 3*

MATHEMATICAL PRACTICES

THINK AND DISCUSS

1. Explain why there might be more than one correct way to write a proof.
2. Describe the steps you take when writing a proof.

Know it! Note

3. **GET ORGANIZED** Copy and complete the graphic organizer. In each box, describe the proof style in your own words.

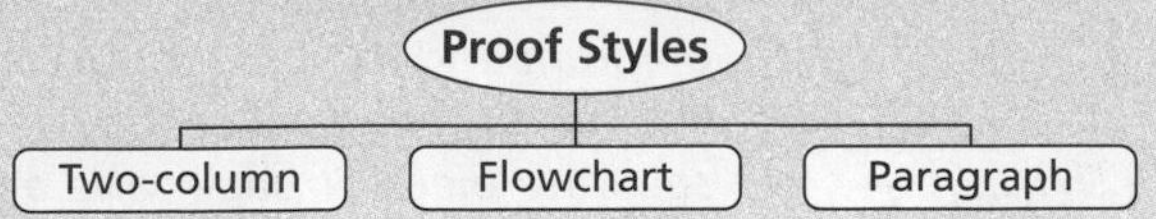

2-7 Exercises

Learn It Online
Homework Help Online
Parent Resources Online

GUIDED PRACTICE

Vocabulary **Apply the vocabulary from this lesson to answer each question.**

1. In a ___?___ proof, the logical order is represented by arrows that connect each step. (*flowchart* or *paragraph*)

2. The steps and reasons of a ___?___ proof are written out in sentences. (*flowchart* or *paragraph*)

SEE EXAMPLE 1

3. Use the given flowchart proof to write a two-column proof.

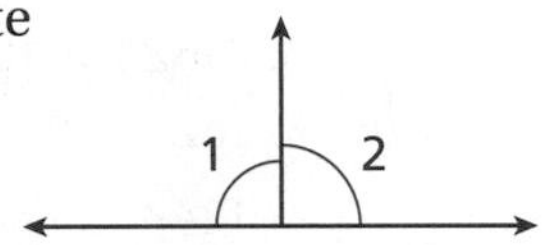

Given: $\angle 1 \cong \angle 2$
Prove: $\angle 1$ and $\angle 2$ are right angles.
Flowchart proof:

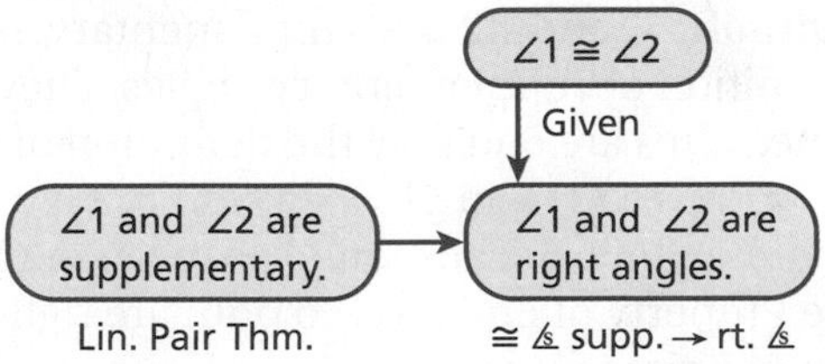

SEE EXAMPLE 2

4. Use the given two-column proof to write a flowchart proof.

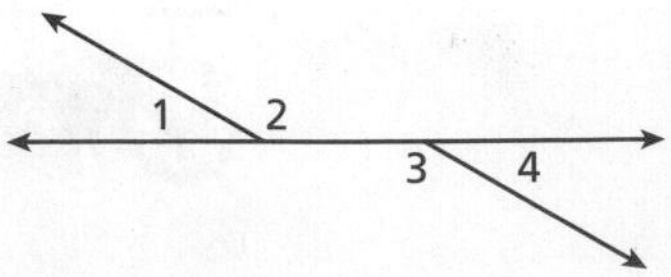

Given: $\angle 2$ and $\angle 4$ are supplementary.
Prove: $m\angle 2 = m\angle 3$
Two-column proof:

Statements	Reasons
1. $\angle 2$ and $\angle 4$ are supplementary.	1. Given
2. $\angle 3$ and $\angle 4$ are supplementary.	2. Lin. Pair Thm.
3. $\angle 2 \cong \angle 3$	3. $\cong$ Supps. Thm. *Steps 1, 2*
4. $m\angle 2 = m\angle 3$	4. Def. of $\cong$ ∠s

SEE EXAMPLE 3

5. Use the given paragraph proof to write a two-column proof.

Given: $\angle 2 \cong \angle 4$

Prove: $\angle 1 \cong \angle 3$

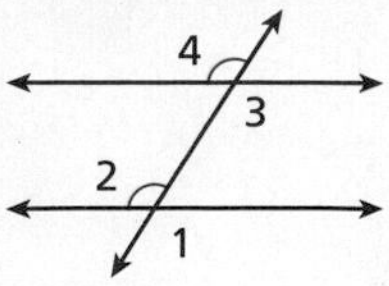

Paragraph proof:

By the Vertical Angles Theorem, $\angle 1 \cong \angle 2$, and $\angle 3 \cong \angle 4$. It is given that $\angle 2 \cong \angle 4$. By the Transitive Property of Congruence, $\angle 1 \cong \angle 4$, and thus $\angle 1 \cong \angle 3$.

SEE EXAMPLE 4

6. Use the given two-column proof to write a paragraph proof.

Given: $\overrightarrow{BD}$ bisects $\angle ABC$.

Prove: $\overrightarrow{BG}$ bisects $\angle FBH$.

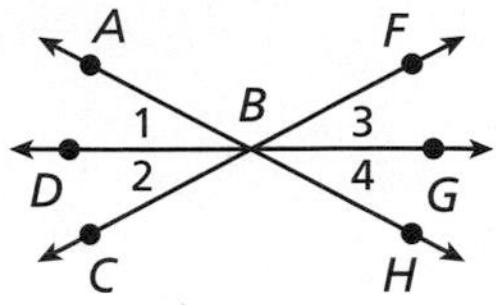

Two-column proof:

Statements	Reasons
1. $\overrightarrow{BD}$ bisects $\angle ABC$.	1. Given
2. $\angle 1 \cong \angle 2$	2. Def. of $\angle$ bisector
3. $\angle 1 \cong \angle 4$, $\angle 2 \cong \angle 3$	3. Vert. $\angle$s Thm.
4. $\angle 4 \cong \angle 2$	4. Trans. Prop. of $\cong$ *Steps 2, 3*
5. $\angle 4 \cong \angle 3$	5. Trans. Prop. of $\cong$ *Steps 3, 4*
6. $\overrightarrow{BG}$ bisects $\angle FBH$.	6. Def. of $\angle$ bisector

PRACTICE AND PROBLEM SOLVING

Independent Practice

For Exercises	See Example
7	1
8	2
9	3
10	4

Extra Practice

See Extra Practice for more Skills Practice and Applications Practice exercises.

7. Use the given flowchart proof to write a two-column proof.

Given: B is the midpoint of $\overline{AC}$.

$AD = EC$

Prove: $DB = BE$

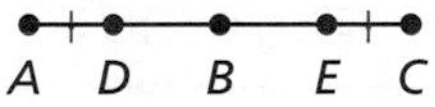

Flowchart proof:

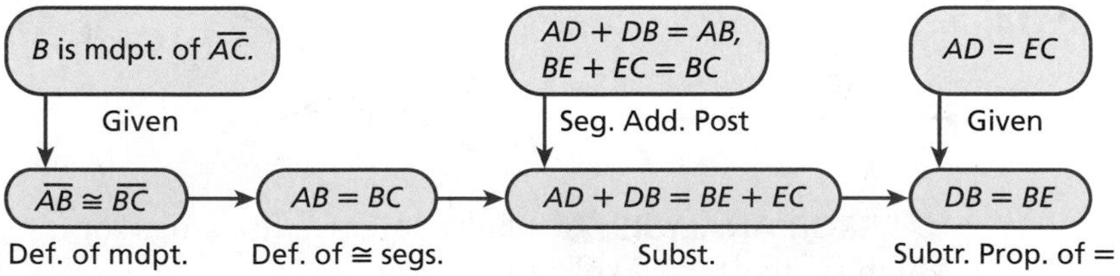

8. Use the given two-column proof to write a flowchart proof.

Given: $\angle 3$ is a right angle.

Prove: $\angle 4$ is a right angle.

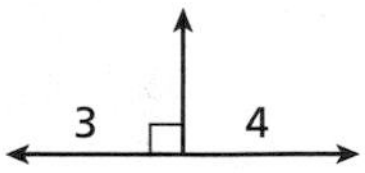

Two-column proof:

Statements	Reasons
1. $\angle 3$ is a right angle.	1. Given
2. $m\angle 3 = 90°$	2. Def. of rt. $\angle$
3. $\angle 3$ and $\angle 4$ are supplementary.	3. Lin. Pair Thm.
4. $m\angle 3 + m\angle 4 = 180°$	4. Def. of supp. $\angle$s
5. $90° + m\angle 4 = 180°$	5. Subst. *Steps 2, 4*
6. $m\angle 4 = 90°$	6. Subtr. Prop. of =
7. $\angle 4$ is a right angle.	7. Def. of rt. $\angle$

9. Use the given paragraph proof to write a two-column proof.

Given: $\angle 1 \cong \angle 4$

Prove: $\angle 2$ and $\angle 3$ are supplementary.

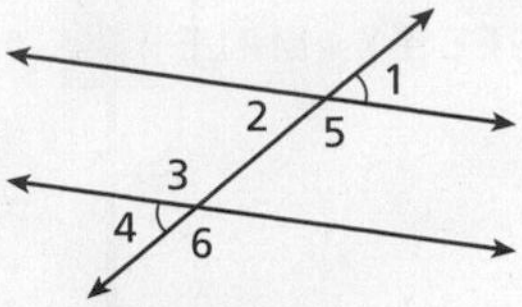

Paragraph proof:

$\angle 4$ and $\angle 3$ form a linear pair, so they are supplementary by the Linear Pair Theorem. Therefore, $m\angle 4 + m\angle 3 = 180°$. Also, $\angle 1$ and $\angle 2$ are vertical angles, so $\angle 1 \cong \angle 2$ by the Vertical Angles Theorem. It is given that $\angle 1 \cong \angle 4$. So by the Transitive Property of Congruence, $\angle 4 \cong \angle 2$, and by the definition of congruent angles, $m\angle 4 = m\angle 2$. By substitution, $m\angle 2 + m\angle 3 = 180°$, so $\angle 2$ and $\angle 3$ are supplementary by the definition of supplementary angles.

10. Use the given two-column proof to write a paragraph proof.

Given: $\angle 1$ and $\angle 2$ are complementary.

Prove: $\angle 2$ and $\angle 3$ are complementary.

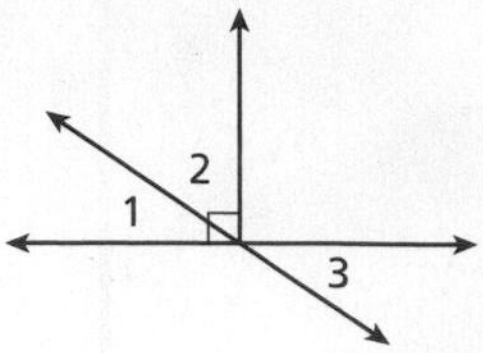

Two-column proof:

Statements	Reasons
1. $\angle 1$ and $\angle 2$ are complementary.	1. Given
2. $m\angle 1 + m\angle 2 = 90°$	2. Def. of comp. ∠s
3. $\angle 1 \cong \angle 3$	3. Vert. ∠s Thm.
4. $m\angle 1 = m\angle 3$	4. Def. of ≅ ∠s
5. $m\angle 3 + m\angle 2 = 90°$	5. Subst. *Steps 2, 4*
6. $\angle 2$ and $\angle 3$ are complementary.	6. Def. of comp. ∠s

Find each measure and name the theorem that justifies your answer.

11. AB

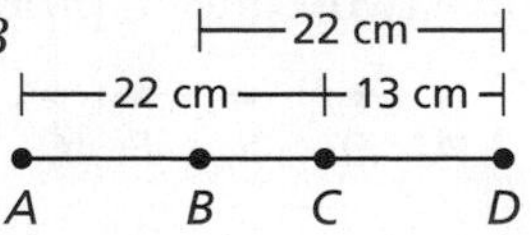

12. $m\angle 2$

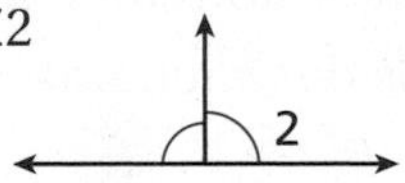

13. $m\angle 3$

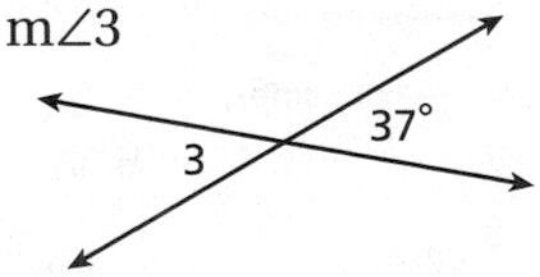

Algebra Find the value of each variable.

14.

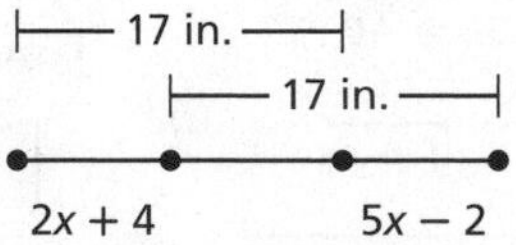

15.

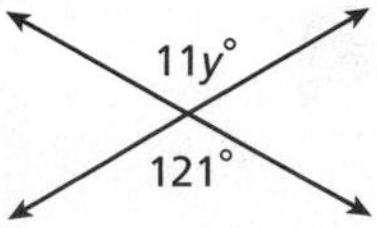

16.

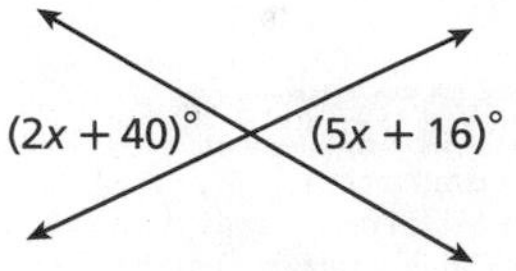

17. **ERROR ANALYSIS** Below are two drawings for the given proof. Which is incorrect? Explain the error.

Given: $\overline{AB} \cong \overline{BC}$

Prove: $\angle A \cong \angle C$

A

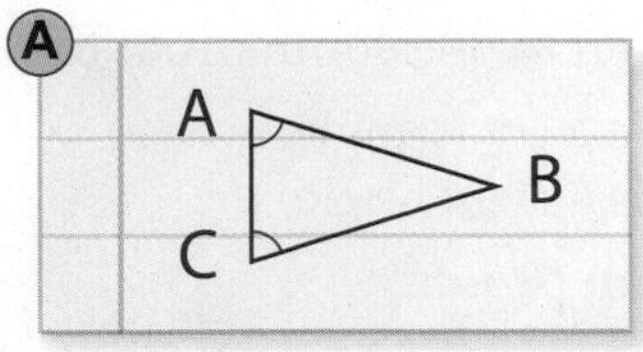

B

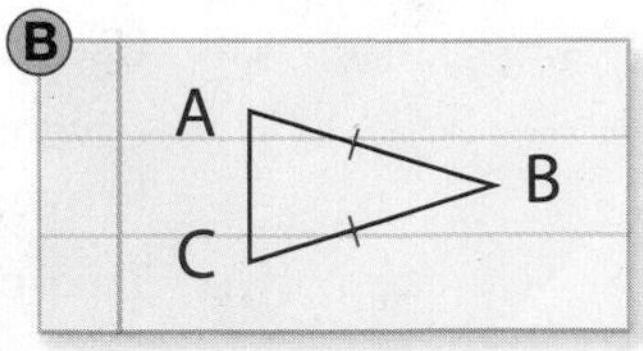

MULTI-STEP TEST PREP

18. Rearrange the pieces to create a flowchart proof.

$m\angle 1 + m\angle 2 = 180°$	$m\angle 1 = 117°$	$\angle 1$ and $\angle 2$ are supplementary.	$m\angle 2 = 63°$	$m\angle 1 + 63° = 180°$
Def. of supp. ∠s	Subtr. Prop. of =	Lin. Pair Thm.	Given	Subst.

19. Critical Thinking Two lines intersect, and one of the angles formed is a right angle. Explain why all four angles are congruent.

20. Write About It Which style of proof do you find easiest to write? to read?

TEST PREP

21. Which pair of angles in the diagram must be congruent?

Ⓐ ∠1 and ∠5 Ⓒ ∠5 and ∠8

Ⓑ ∠3 and ∠4 Ⓓ None of the above

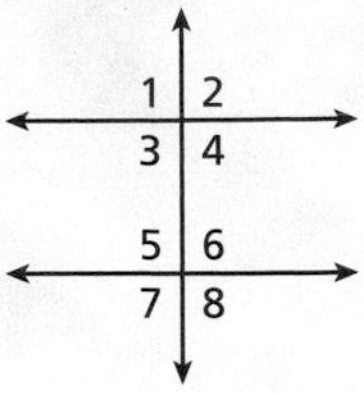

22. What is the measure of ∠2?

Ⓕ 38° Ⓗ 128°

Ⓖ 52° Ⓙ 142°

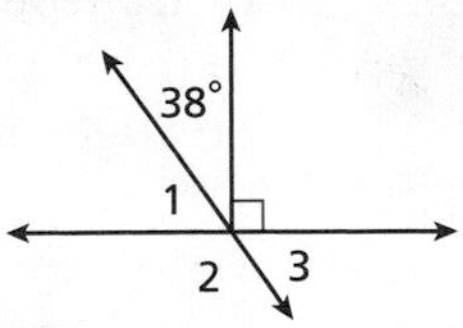

23. Which statement is NOT true if ∠2 and ∠6 are supplementary?

Ⓐ m∠2 + m∠6 = 180°

Ⓑ ∠2 and ∠3 are supplementary.

Ⓒ ∠1 and ∠6 are supplementary.

Ⓓ m∠1 + m∠4 = 180°

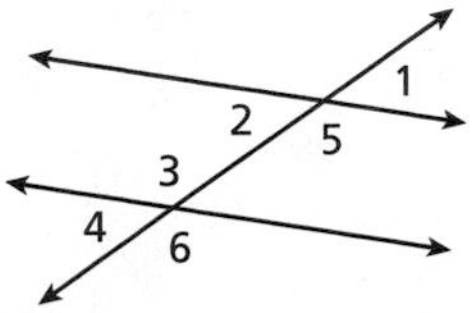

CHALLENGE AND EXTEND

24. Textiles Use the woven pattern to write a flowchart proof.

Given: ∠1 ≅ ∠3

Prove: m∠4 + m∠5 = m∠6

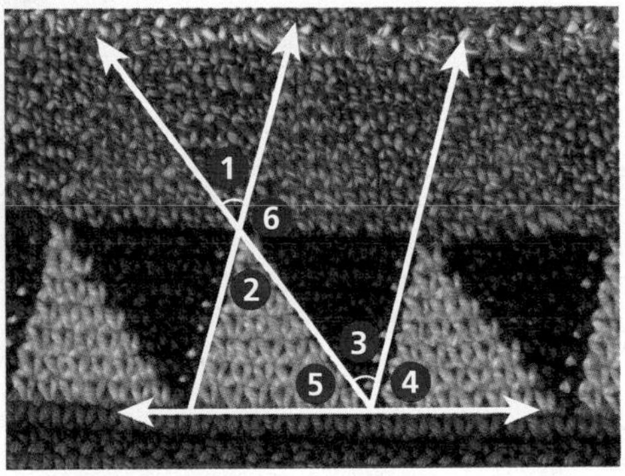

25. Write a two-column proof.

Given: ∠*AOC* ≅ ∠*BOD*

Prove: ∠*AOB* ≅ ∠*COD*

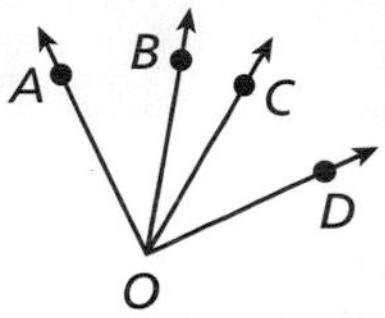

26. Write a paragraph proof.

Given: ∠2 and ∠5 are right angles.

m∠1 + m∠2 + m∠3 = m∠4 + m∠5 + m∠6

Prove: ∠1 ≅ ∠4

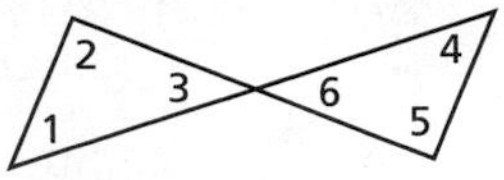

27. Multi-Step Find the value of each variable and the measures of all four angles.

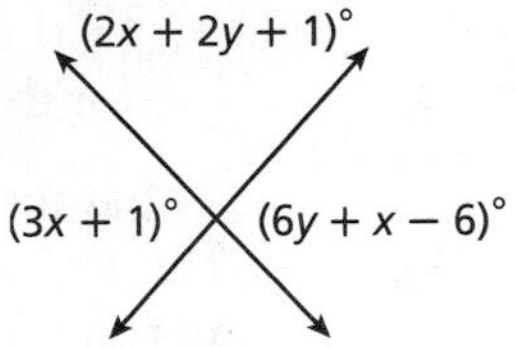

CHAPTER 2

MULTI-STEP TEST PREP

SECTION 2B

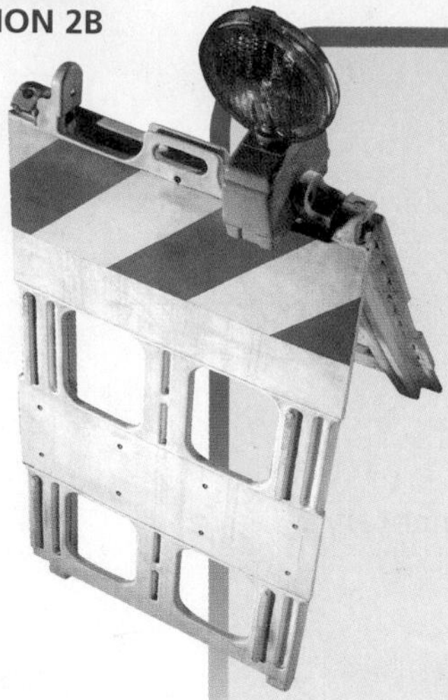

MATHEMATICAL PRACTICES **Construct viable arguments and critique the reasoning of others.**

Mathematical Proof

Intersection Inspection According to the U.S. Department of Transportation, it is ideal for two intersecting streets to form four 90° angles. If this is not possible, roadways should meet at an angle of 75° or greater for maximum safety and visibility.

1. Write a compound inequality to represent the range of measures an angle in an intersection should have.
2. Suppose that an angle in an intersection meets the guidelines specified by the U.S. Department of Transportation. Find the range of measures for the adjacent angle in the intersection.

The intersection of West Elm Street and Lamar Boulevard has a history of car accidents. The Southland neighborhood association is circulating a petition to have the city reconstruct the intersection. A surveyor measured the intersection, and one of the angles measures 145°.

3. Given that $m\angle 2 = 145°$, write a two-column proof to show that $m\angle 1$ and $m\angle 3$ are less than 75°.
4. Write a paragraph proof to justify the argument that the intersection of West Elm Street and Lamar Boulevard should be reconstructed.

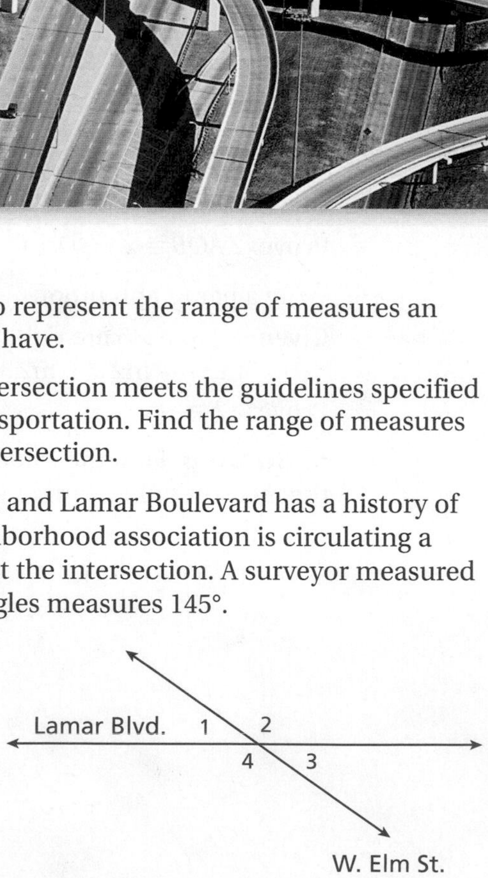

READY TO GO ON?

Quiz for Lessons 2-5 Through 2-7

2-5 Algebraic Proof

Solve each equation. Write a justification for each step.

1. $m - 8 = 13$
2. $4y - 1 = 27$
3. $-\frac{x}{3} = 2$

Identify the property that justifies each statement.

4. $m\angle XYZ = m\angle PQR$, so $m\angle PQR = m\angle XYZ$.
5. $\overline{AB} \cong \overline{AB}$
6. $\angle 4 \cong \angle A$, and $\angle A \cong \angle 1$. So $\angle 4 \cong \angle 1$.
7. $k = 7$, and $m = 7$. So $k = m$.

2-6 Geometric Proof

8. Fill in the blanks to complete the two-column proof.
   Given: $m\angle 1 + m\angle 3 = 180°$
   Prove: $\angle 1 \cong \angle 4$
   Proof:

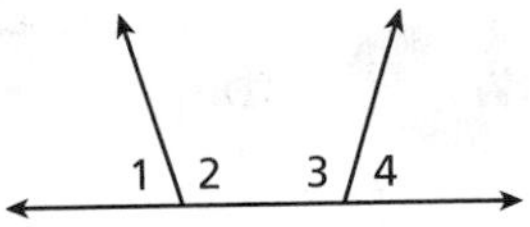

Statements	Reasons
1. $m\angle 1 + m\angle 3 = 180°$	1. a. ___?___
2. b. ___?___	2. Def. of supp. ∡
3. $\angle 3$ and $\angle 4$ are supplementary.	3. Lin. Pair Thm.
4. $\angle 3 \cong \angle 3$	4. c. ___?___
5. d. ___?___	5. ≅ Supps. Thm.

9. Use the given plan to write a two-column proof of the Symmetric Property of Congruence.
   Given: $\overline{AB} \cong \overline{EF}$
   Prove: $\overline{EF} \cong \overline{AB}$
   Plan: Use the definition of congruent segments to write $\overline{AB} \cong \overline{EF}$ as a statement of equality. Then use the Symmetric Property of Equality to show that $EF = AB$. So $\overline{EF} \cong \overline{AB}$ by the definition of congruent segments.

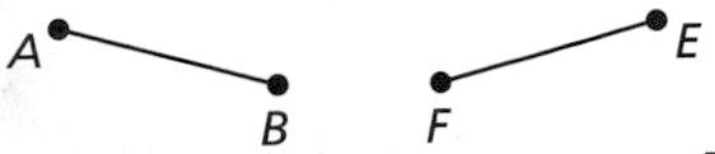

2-7 Flowchart and Paragraph Proofs

Use the given two-column proof to write the following.

Given: $\angle 1 \cong \angle 3$
Prove: $\angle 2 \cong \angle 4$
Proof:

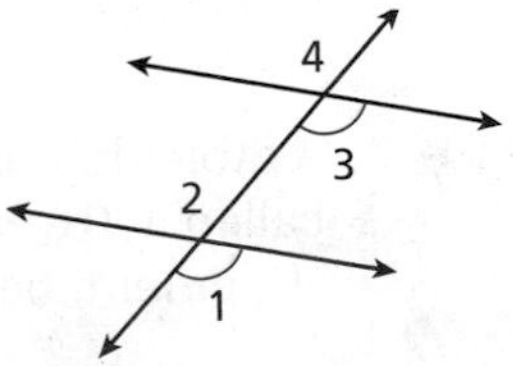

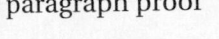

Statements	Reasons
1. $\angle 1 \cong \angle 3$	1. Given
2. $\angle 1 \cong \angle 2$, $\angle 3 \cong \angle 4$	2. Vert. ∡ Thm.
3. $\angle 2 \cong \angle 3$	3. Trans. Prop. of ≅
4. $\angle 2 \cong \angle 4$	4. Trans. Prop. of ≅

10. a flowchart proof
11. a paragraph proof

EXTENSION

Introduction to Symbolic Logic

Objectives
Analyze the truth value of conjunctions and disjunctions.

Construct truth tables to determine the truth value of logical statements.

Vocabulary
compound statement
conjunction
disjunction
truth table

Symbolic logic is used by computer programmers, mathematicians, and philosophers to analyze the truth value of statements, independent of their actual meaning.

A **compound statement** is created by combining two or more statements. Suppose p and q each represent a statement. Two compound statements can be formed by combining p and q: a *conjunction* and a *disjunction.*

Know it! Note

Compound Statements

TERM	WORDS	SYMBOLS	EXAMPLE
Conjunction	A compound statement that uses the word *and*	p AND q $p \wedge q$	Pat is a band member AND Pat plays tennis.
Disjunction	A compound statement that uses the word *or*	p OR q $p \vee q$	Pat is a band member OR Pat plays tennis.

A conjunction is true only when all of its parts are true. A disjunction is true if any one of its parts is true.

EXAMPLE 1 Analyzing Truth Values of Conjunctions and Disjunctions

Use p, q, and r to find the truth value of each compound statement.

p: Washington, D.C., is the capital of the United States.
q: The day after Monday is Tuesday.
r: California is the largest state in the United States.

A $q \vee r$
Since q is true,
the disjunction is true.

B $r \wedge p$
Since r is false,
the conjunction is false.

CHECK IT OUT! **Use the information given above to find the truth value of each compound statement.**

1a. $r \vee p$

1b. $p \wedge q$

A table that lists all possible combinations of truth values for a statement is called a **truth table**. A truth table shows you the truth value of a compound statement, based on the possible truth values of its parts.

Caution!
Make sure you include all possible combinations of truth values for each piece of the compound statement.

p	q	$p \rightarrow q$	$p \wedge q$	$p \vee q$
T	T	T	T	T
T	F	F	F	T
F	T	T	F	T
F	F	T	F	F

EXAMPLE 2 Constructing Truth Tables for Compound Statements

Construct a truth table for the compound statement $\sim u \wedge (v \vee w)$.

Since u, v, and w can each be either true or false, the truth table will have $(2)(2)(2) = 8$ rows.

u	v	w	$\sim u$	$v \vee w$	$\sim u \wedge (v \vee w)$
T	T	T	F	T	F
T	T	F	F	T	F
T	F	T	F	T	F
T	F	F	F	F	F
F	T	T	T	T	T
F	T	F	T	T	T
F	F	T	T	T	T
F	F	F	T	F	F

Remember!

The negation (~) of a statement has the opposite truth value.

CHECK IT OUT!

2. Construct a truth table for the compound statement $\sim u \wedge \sim v$.

EXTENSION Exercises

Use p, q, and r to find the truth value of each compound statement.

p: The day after Friday is Sunday.

q: $\frac{1}{2} = 0.5$

r: If $-4x - 2 = 10$, then $x = 3$.

1. $r \wedge q$

2. $r \vee p$

3. $p \vee r$

4. $q \wedge \sim q$

5. $\sim q \vee q$

6. $q \vee r$

Construct a truth table for each compound statement.

7. $s \wedge \sim t$

8. $\sim u \vee t$

9. $\sim u \vee (s \wedge t)$

Use a truth table to show that the two statements are logically equivalent.

10. $p \rightarrow q$; $\sim q \rightarrow \sim p$

11. $q \rightarrow p$; $\sim p \rightarrow \sim q$

12. A biconditional statement can be written as $(p \rightarrow q) \wedge (q \rightarrow p)$. Construct a truth table for this compound statement.

13. DeMorgan's Laws state that $\sim(p \wedge q) = \sim p \vee \sim q$ and that $\sim(p \vee q) = \sim p \wedge \sim q$.

a. Use truth tables to show that both statements are true.

b. If you think of disjunction and conjunction as inverse operations, DeMorgan's Laws are similar to which algebraic property?

14. The Law of Disjunctive Inference states that if $p \vee q$ is true and p is false, then q must be true.

a. Construct a truth table for $p \vee q$.

b. Use the truth table to explain why the Law of Disjunctive Inference is true.

CHAPTER 2

Study Guide: Review

Know it! Note: For a complete list of postulates, theorems, and corollaries, see p. PT2.

Vocabulary

biconditional statement
conclusion
conditional statement
conjecture
contrapositive
converse
counterexample
deductive reasoning
definition
flowchart proof
hypothesis
inductive reasoning
inverse
logically equivalent statements
negation
paragraph proof
polygon
proof
quadrilateral
theorem
triangle
truth value
two-column proof

Complete the sentences below with vocabulary words from the list above.

1. A statement you can prove and then use as a reason in later proofs is a(n) __?__.
2. __?__ is the process of using logic to draw conclusions from given facts, definitions, and properties.
3. A(n) __?__ is a case in which a conjecture is not true.
4. A statement you believe to be true based on inductive reasoning is called a(n) __?__.

2-1 Using Inductive Reasoning to Make Conjectures

EXAMPLES

■ **Find the next item in the pattern below.**

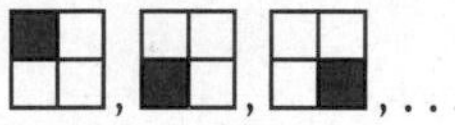

The red square moves in the counterclockwise direction. The next figure is 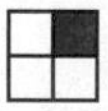.

■ **Complete the conjecture "The sum of two odd numbers is __?__."**

List some examples and look for a pattern.

$1 + 1 = 2 \quad 3 + 5 = 8 \quad 7 + 11 = 18$

The sum of two odd numbers is even.

■ **Show that the conjecture "For all non-zero integers, $-x < x$" is false by finding a counterexample.**

Pick positive and negative values for x and substitute to see if the conjecture holds.

Let $n = 3$. Since $-3 < 3$, the conjecture holds.

Let $n = -5$. Since $-(-5)$ is 5 and $5 \not< -5$, the conjecture is false.

$n = -5$ is a counterexample.

EXERCISES

Make a conjecture about each pattern. Write the next two items.

5. 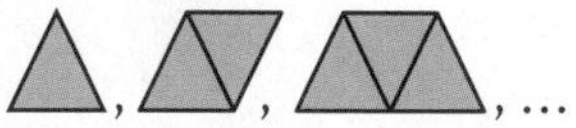

6. $\frac{1}{6}, \frac{1}{3}, \frac{1}{2}, \frac{2}{3}, \ldots$

7. 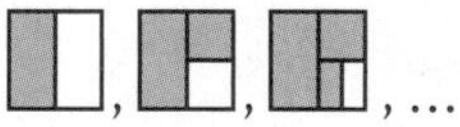

Complete each conjecture.

8. The sum of an even number and an odd number is __?__.
9. The square of a natural number is __?__.

Determine if each conjecture is true. If not, write or draw a counterexample.

10. All whole numbers are natural numbers.
11. If C is the midpoint of $\overline{AB}$, then $\overline{AC} \cong \overline{BC}$.
12. If $2x + 3 = 15$, then $x = 6$.
13. There are 28 days in February.
14. Draw a triangle. Construct the bisectors of each angle of the triangle. Make a conjecture about where the three angle bisectors intersect.

2-2 Conditional Statements

EXAMPLES

- **Write a conditional statement from the sentence "A rectangle has congruent diagonals."**

  If a figure is a rectangle, then it has congruent diagonals.

- **Write the inverse, converse, and contrapositive of the conditional statement "If m∠1 = 35°, then ∠1 is acute." Find the truth value of each.**

  Converse: If ∠1 is acute, then m∠1 = 35°. Not all acute angles measure 35°, so this is false.

  Inverse: If m∠1 ≠ 35°, then ∠1 is not acute. You can draw an acute angle that does not measure 35°, so this is false.

  Contrapositive: If ∠1 is not acute, then m∠1 ≠ 35°. An angle that measures 35° must be acute. So this statement is true.

EXERCISES

Write a conditional statement from each Venn diagram.

15.

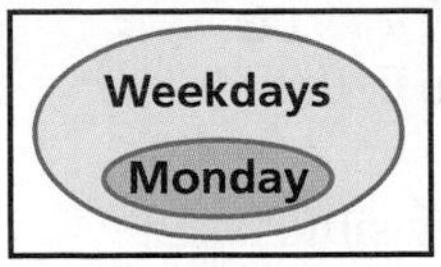

16.

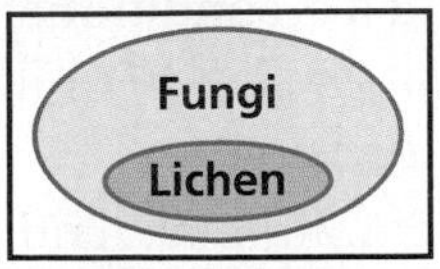

Determine if each conditional is true. If false, give a counterexample.

17. If two angles are adjacent, then they have a common ray.

18. If you multiply two irrational numbers, the product is irrational.

Write the converse, inverse, and contrapositive of each conditional statement. Find the truth value of each.

19. If ∠*X* is a right angle, then m∠*X* = 90°.

20. If x is a whole number, then $x = 2$.

2-3 Using Deductive Reasoning to Verify Conjectures

EXAMPLES

- **Determine if the conjecture is valid by the Law of Detachment or the Law of Syllogism.**

  Given: If $5c = 8y$, then $2w = -15$. If $5c = 8y$, then $x = 17$.

  Conjecture: If $2w = -15$, then $x = 17$.

  Let p be $5c = 8y$, q be $2w = -15$, and r be $x = 17$.

  Using symbols, the given information is written as $p \rightarrow q$ and $p \rightarrow r$. Neither the Law of Detachment nor the Law of Syllogism can be applied. The conjecture is not valid.

- **Draw a conclusion from the given information.**

  Given: If two points are distinct, then there is one line through them. *A* and *B* are distinct points.

  Let p be the hypothesis: two points are distinct.

  Let q be the conclusion: there is one line through the points.

  The statement "*A* and *B* are distinct points" matches the hypothesis, so you can conclude that there is one line through *A* and *B*.

EXERCISES

Use the true statements below to determine whether each conclusion is true or false.

Sue is a member of the swim team. When the team practices, Sue swims. The team begins practice when the pool opens. The pool opens at 8 A.M. on weekdays and at 12 noon on Saturday.

21. The swim team practices on weekdays only.

22. Sue swims on Saturdays.

23. Swim team practice starts at the same time every day.

Use the following information for Exercises 24–26.

The expression $2.15 + 0.07x$ gives the cost of a long-distance phone call, where x is the number of minutes after the first minute.

If possible, draw a conclusion from the given information. If not possible, explain why.

24. The cost of Sara's long-distance call is $2.57.

25. Paulo makes a long-distance call that lasts ten minutes.

26. Asa's long-distance phone bill for the month is $19.05.

2-4 Biconditional Statements and Definitions

EXAMPLES

■ **For the conditional "If a number is divisible by 10, then it ends in 0", write the converse and a biconditional statement.**

Converse: If a number ends in 0, then it is divisible by 10.

Biconditional: A number is divisible by 10 if and only if it ends in 0.

■ **Determine if the biconditional "The sides of a triangle measure 3, 7, and 15 if and only if the perimeter is 25" is true. If false, give a counterexample.**

Conditional: If the sides of a triangle measure 3, 7, and 15, then the perimeter is 25. True.

Converse: If the perimeter of a triangle is 25, then its sides measure 3, 7, and 15. False; a triangle with side lengths of 6, 10, and 9 also has a perimeter of 25.

Therefore the biconditional is false.

EXERCISES

Determine if a true biconditional can be written from each conditional statement. If not, give a counterexample.

27. If $3 - \frac{2x}{5} = 2$, then $x = \frac{5}{2}$.

28. If $x < 0$, then the value of x^4 is positive.

29. If a segment has endpoints at $(1, 5)$ and $(-3, 1)$, then its midpoint is $(-1, 3)$.

30. If the measure of one angle of a triangle is 90°, then the triangle is a right triangle.

Complete each statement to form a true biconditional.

31. Two angles are __?__ if and only if the sum of their measures is 90°.

32. $x^3 > 0$ if and only if x is __?__.

33. Trey can travel 100 miles in less than 2 hours if and only if his average speed is __?__.

34. The area of a square is equal to s^2 if and only if the perimeter of the square is __?__.

2-5 Algebraic Proof

EXAMPLES

■ **Solve the equation $5x - 3 = -18$. Write a justification for each step.**

$5x - 3 = -18$	Given
$\underline{+3 \quad +3}$	Add. Prop. of =
$5x = -15$	Simplify.
$\frac{5x}{5} = \frac{-15}{5}$	Div. Prop. of =
$x = -3$	Simplify.

■ **Write a justification for each step.**

$RS = ST$	Given
$5x - 18 = 4x$	Subst. Prop. of =
$x - 18 = 0$	Subtr. Prop. of =
$x = 18$	Add. Prop. of =

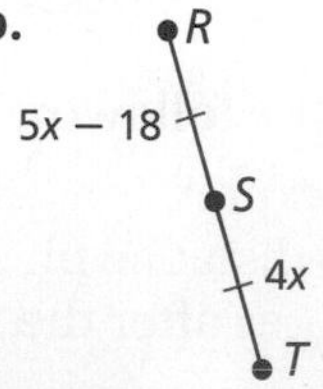

Identify the property that justifies each statement.

■ $\angle X \cong \angle 2$, so $\angle 2 \cong \angle X$.

Symmetric Property of Congruence

■ If $m\angle 2 = 180°$ and $m\angle 3 = 180°$, then $m\angle 2 = m\angle 3$.

Transitive Property of Equality

EXERCISES

Solve each equation. Write a justification for each step.

35. $\frac{m}{-5} + 3 = -4.5$

36. $-47 = 3x - 59$

Identify the property that justifies each statement.

37. $a + b = a + b$

38. If $\angle RST \cong \angle ABC$, then $\angle ABC \cong \angle RST$.

39. $2x = 9$, and $y = 9$. So $2x = y$.

Use the indicated property to complete each statement.

40. Reflex. Prop. of ≅: figure $ABCD \cong$ __?__

41. Sym. Prop. of =: If $m\angle 2 = m\angle 5$, then __?__.

42. Trans. Prop. of ≅: If $\overline{AB} \cong \overline{CD}$ and $\overline{AB} \cong \overline{EF}$, then __?__.

43. Kim borrowed money at an annual simple interest rate of 6% to buy a car. How much did she borrow if she paid $4200 in interest over the life of the 4-year loan? Solve the equation $I = Prt$ for P and justify each step.

2-6 Geometric Proof

EXAMPLES

- **Write a justification for each step, given that $m\angle 2 = 2m\angle 1$.**

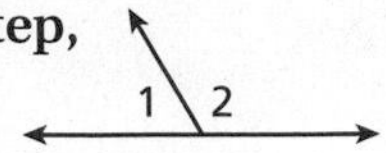

1. $\angle 1$ and $\angle 2$ supp.	Lin. Pair Thm.
2. $m\angle 1 + m\angle 2 = 180°$	Def. of supp. $\angle$s
3. $m\angle 2 = 2m\angle 1$	Given
4. $m\angle 1 + 2m\angle 1 = 180°$	Subst. *Steps 2, 3*
5. $3m\angle 1 = 180°$	Simplify
6. $m\angle 1 = 60°$	Div. Prop. of =

- **Use the given plan to write a two-column proof.**

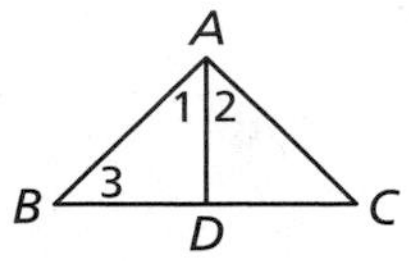

Given: $\overline{AD}$ bisects $\angle BAC$.
$\angle 1 \cong \angle 3$

Prove: $\angle 2 \cong \angle 3$

Plan: Use the definition of angle bisector to show that $\angle 1 \cong \angle 2$. Use the Transitive Property to conclude that $\angle 2 \cong \angle 3$.

Two-column proof:

Statements	Reasons
1. $\overline{AD}$ bisects $\angle BAC$.	**1.** Given
2. $\angle 1 \cong \angle 2$	**2.** Def. of $\angle$ bisector
3. $\angle 1 \cong \angle 3$	**3.** Given
4. $\angle 2 \cong \angle 3$	**4.** Trans. Prop. of $\cong$

EXERCISES

44. Write a justification for each step, given that $\angle 1$ and $\angle 2$ are complementary, and $\angle 1 \cong \angle 3$.

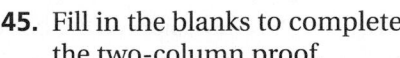

1. $\angle 1$ and $\angle 2$ comp.
2. $m\angle 1 + m\angle 2 = 90°$
3. $\angle 1 \cong \angle 3$
4. $m\angle 1 = m\angle 3$
5. $m\angle 3 + m\angle 2 = 90°$
6. $\angle 3$ and $\angle 2$ comp.

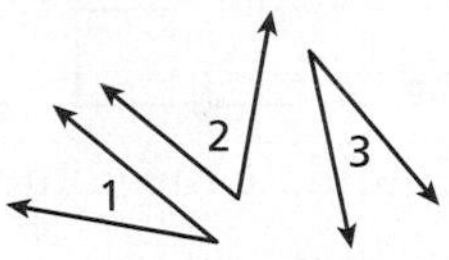

45. Fill in the blanks to complete the two-column proof.

Given: $\overline{TU} \cong \overline{UV}$

Prove: $SU + TU = SV$

Two-column proof:

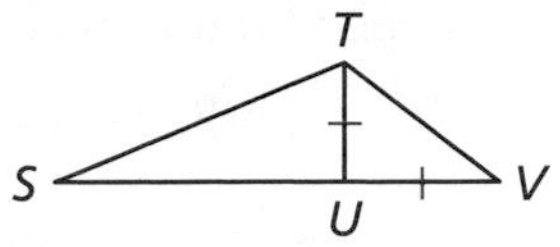

Statements	Reasons
1. $\overline{TU} \cong \overline{UV}$	**1. a.** ?
2. b. ?	**2.** Def. of $\cong$ segs.
3. c. ?	**3.** Seg. Add. Post.
4. $SU + TU = SV$	**4. d.** ?

Find the value of each variable.

46.

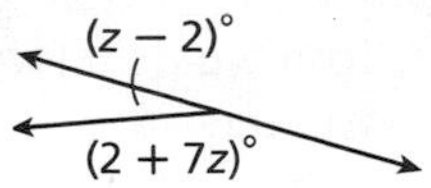

47.

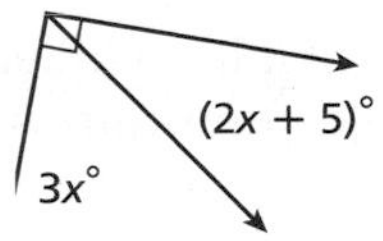

2-7 Flowchart and Paragraph Proofs

EXAMPLES

Use the two-column proof in the example for lesson *Geometric Proof* above to write each of the following.

- a flowchart proof

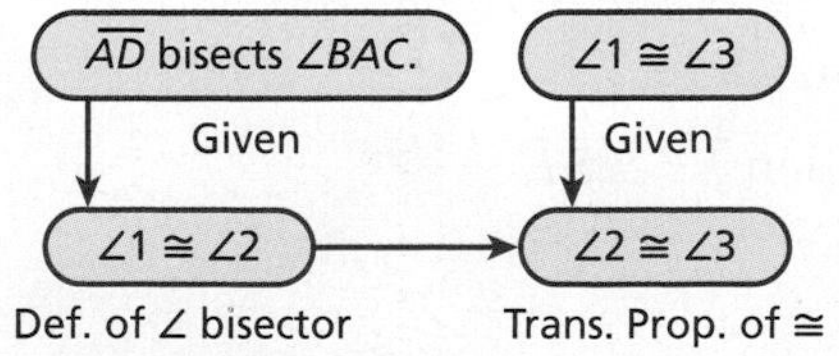

- a paragraph proof

Since $\overline{AD}$ bisects $\angle BAC$, $\angle 1 \cong \angle 2$ by the definition of angle bisector. It is given that $\angle 1 \cong \angle 3$. Therefore, $\angle 2 \cong \angle 3$ by the Transitive Property of Congruence.

EXERCISES

Use the given plan to write each of the following.

Given: $\angle ADE$ and $\angle DAE$ are complementary.
$\angle ADE$ and $\angle BAC$ are complementary.

Prove: $\angle DAC \cong \angle BAE$

Plan: Use the Congruent Complements Theorem to show that $\angle DAE \cong \angle BAC$. Since $\angle CAE \cong \angle CAE$, $\angle DAC \cong \angle BAE$ by the Common Angles Theorem.

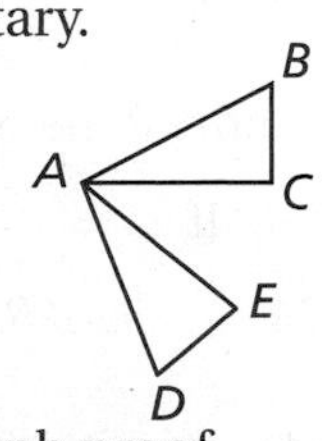

48. a flowchart proof

49. a paragraph proof

Find the value of each variable and name the theorem that justifies your answer.

50.

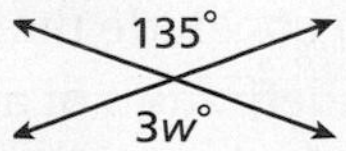

51.

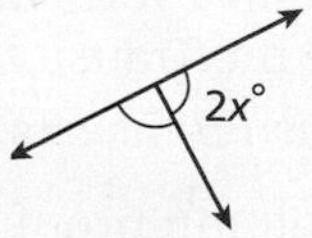

CHAPTER 2

CHAPTER TEST

Find the next item in each pattern.

1. 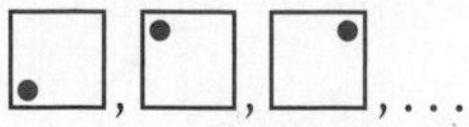

2. 405, 135, 45, 15, …

3. Complete the conjecture "The sum of two even numbers is __?__ ."

4. Show that the conjecture "All complementary angles are adjacent" is false by finding a counterexample.

5. Identify the hypothesis and conclusion of the conditional statement "The show is cancelled if it rains."

6. Write a conditional statement from the sentence "Parallel lines do not intersect."

Determine if each conditional is true. If false, give a counterexample.

7. If two lines intersect, then they form four right angles.

8. If a number is divisible by 10, then it is divisible by 5.

Use the conditional "If you live in the United States, then you live in Kentucky" for Items 9–11. Write the indicated type of statement and determine its truth value.

9. converse

10. inverse

11. contrapositive

12. Determine if the following conjecture is valid by the Law of Detachment.
Given: If it is colder than 50°F, Tom wears a sweater. It is 46°F today.
Conjecture: Tom is wearing a sweater.

13. Use the Law of Syllogism to draw a conclusion from the given information.
Given: If a figure is a square, then it is a quadrilateral. If a figure is a quadrilateral, then it is a polygon. Figure *ABCD* is a square.

14. Write the conditional statement and converse within the biconditional "Chad will work on Saturday if and only if he gets paid overtime."

15. Determine if the biconditional "B is the midpoint of $\overline{AC}$ iff $AB = BC$" is true. If false, give a counterexample.

Solve each equation. Write a justification for each step.

16. $8 - 5s = 1$

17. $0.4t + 3 = 1.6$

18. $38 = -3w + 2$

Identify the property that justifies each statement.

19. If $2x = y$ and $y = 7$, then $2x = 7$.

20. $m\angle DEF = m\angle DEF$

21. $\angle X \cong \angle P$, and $\angle P \cong \angle D$. So $\angle X \cong \angle D$.

22. If $\overline{ST} \cong \overline{XY}$, then $\overline{XY} \cong \overline{ST}$.

Use the given plan to write a proof in each format.

Given: $\angle AFB \cong \angle EFD$
Prove: $\overrightarrow{FB}$ bisects $\angle AFC$.
Plan: Since vertical angles are congruent, $\angle EFD \cong \angle BFC$.
Use the Transitive Property to conclude that $\angle AFB \cong \angle BFC$.
Thus $\overrightarrow{FB}$ bisects $\angle AFC$ by the definition of angle bisector.

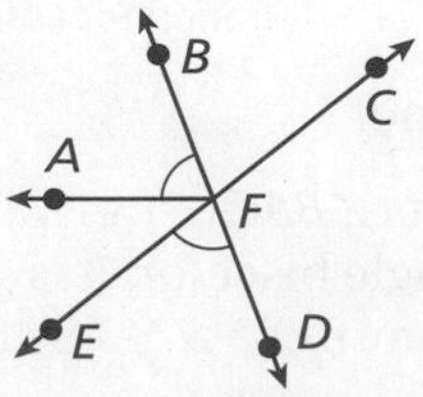

23. two-column proof

24. paragraph proof

25. flowchart proof

COLLEGE ENTRANCE EXAM PRACTICE

FOCUS ON SAT MATHEMATICS SUBJECT TESTS

Some colleges require that you take the SAT Subject Tests. There are two math subject tests—Level 1 and Level 2. Take the Mathematics Subject Test Level 1 when you have completed three years of college-prep mathematics courses.

HOT TIP! **On SAT Mathematics Subject Test questions, you receive one point for each correct answer, but you lose a fraction of a point for each incorrect response. Guess only when you can eliminate at least one of the answer choices.**

You may want to time yourself as you take this practice test. It should take you about 6 minutes to complete.

---

1. In the figure below, m∠1 = m∠2. What is the value of *y*?

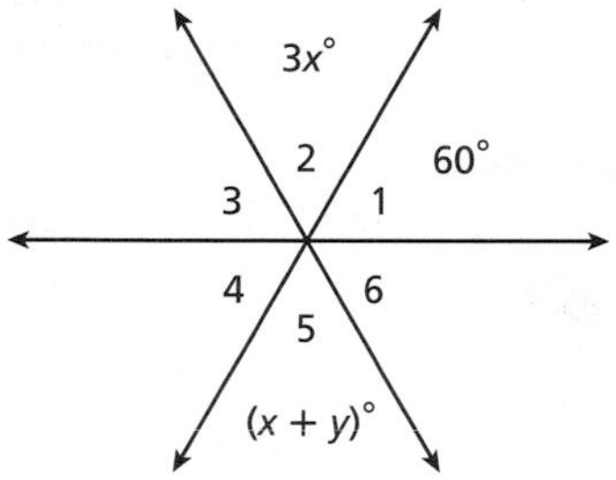

Note: Figure not drawn to scale.

(A) 10 **(B)** 30

(C) 40 **(D)** 50

(E) 60

---

2. The statement "I will cancel my appointment if and only if I have a conflict" is true. Which of the following can be concluded?

I. If I have a conflict, then I will cancel my appointment.

II. If I do not cancel my appointment, then I do not have a conflict.

III. If I cancel my appointment, then I have a conflict.

(A) I only **(B)** II only

(C) III only **(D)** I and III

(E) I, II, and III

---

3. What is the contrapositive of the statement "If it is raining, then the football team will win"?

(A) If it is not raining, then the football team will not win.

(B) If it is raining, then the football team will not win.

(C) If the football team wins, then it is raining.

(D) If the football team does not win, then it is not raining.

(E) If it is not raining, then the football team will win.

---

4. Given the points $D(1, 5)$ and $E(-2, 3)$, which conclusion is NOT valid?

(A) The midpoint of $\overline{DE}$ is $\left(-\frac{1}{2}, 4\right)$.

(B) *D* and *E* are collinear.

(C) The distance between *D* and *E* is $\sqrt{5}$.

(D) $\overline{DE} \cong \overline{ED}$

(E) *D* and *E* are distinct points.

---

5. For all integers *x*, what conclusion can be drawn about the value of the expression $\frac{x^2}{2}$?

(A) The value is negative.

(B) The value is not negative.

(C) The value is even.

(D) The value is odd.

(E) The value is not a whole number.

CHAPTER 2

TEST TACKLER

Standardized Test Strategies

Gridded Response: Record Your Answer

When responding to a gridded-response test item, you must fill out the grid on your answer sheet correctly, or the item will be marked as incorrect.

EXAMPLE 1

Gridded Response: Solve the equation $25 - 2(3x - 4) = 13$.

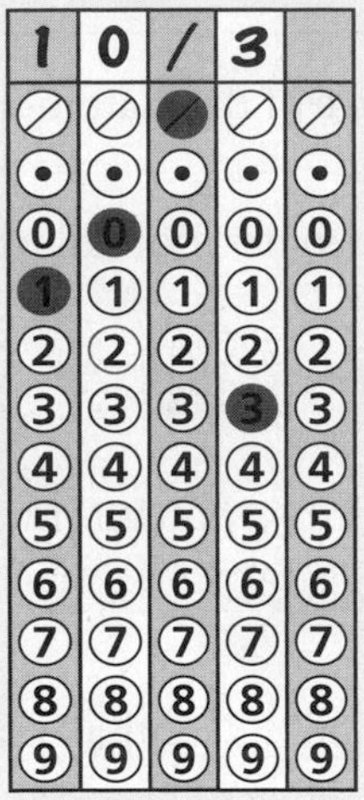

The value of x is $\frac{20}{6}$, $\frac{10}{3}$, $3\frac{1}{3}$, or $3.\overline{3}$.

- Mixed numbers and repeating decimals cannot be gridded, so you must grid the answer as $\frac{20}{6}$ or $\frac{10}{3}$.
- Using a pencil, write your answer in the answer boxes at the top of the grid.
- Put only one digit or symbol in each box. On some grids, the fraction bar and decimal point have a designated column.
- Do not leave a blank box in the middle of an answer.
- For each digit or symbol, shade the bubble that is in the same column as the digit or symbol in the answer box.

EXAMPLE 2

Gridded Response: The perimeter of a rectangle is 90 in. The width of the rectangle is 18 in. Find the length of the rectangle in feet.

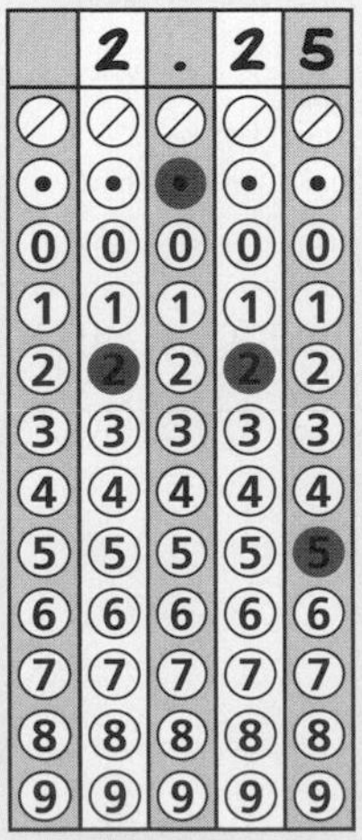

The length of the rectangle is 27 inches, but the problem asks for the measurement in feet.

27 inches = 2.25 or $\frac{9}{4}$ feet

- Using a pencil, write your answer in the answer boxes at the top of the grid.
- Put only one digit or symbol in each box. On some grids, the fraction bar and the decimal point have a designated column.
- Do not leave a blank box in the middle of an answer.
- For each digit or symbol, shade the bubble that is in the same column as the digit or symbol in the answer box.

HOT TIP! You cannot grid a negative number in a gridded-response item because the grid does not include the negative sign (–). So if you get a negative answer to a test item, rework the problem. You probably made a math error.

Read each statement and answer the questions that follow.

Sample A

The correct answer to a test item is $\frac{1}{6}$. A student gridded this answer as shown.

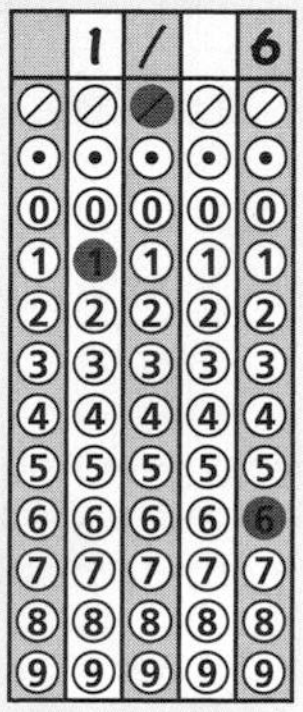

1. What error did the student make when filling out the grid?
2. Another student got an answer of $-\frac{1}{6}$. Explain why the student knew this answer was wrong.

Sample B

The perimeter of a triangle is $2\frac{3}{4}$ feet. A student gridded this answer as shown.

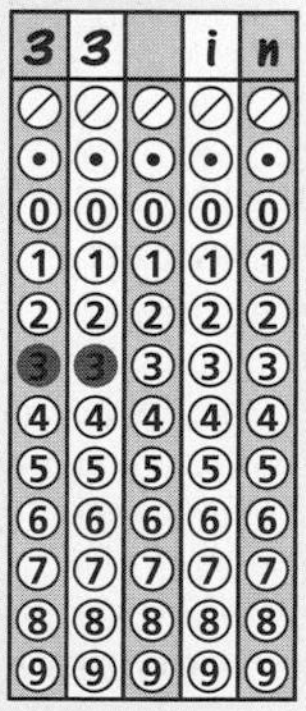

3. What error did the student make when filling out the grid?
4. Explain two ways to correctly grid the answer.

Sample C

The length of a segment is $7\frac{2}{5}$ units. A student gridded this answer as shown.

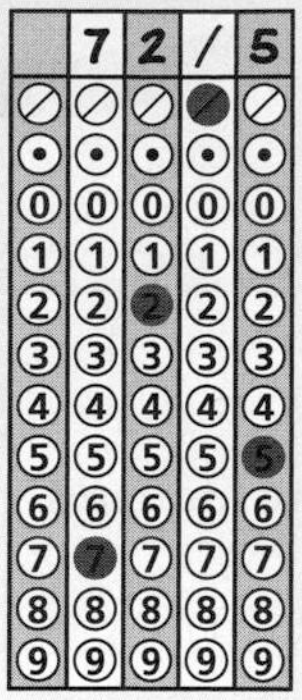

5. What answer does the grid show?
6. Explain why you cannot grid a mixed number.
7. Write the answer $7\frac{2}{5}$ in two forms that could be entered in the grid correctly.

Sample D

The measure of an angle is 48.9°. A student gridded this answer as shown.

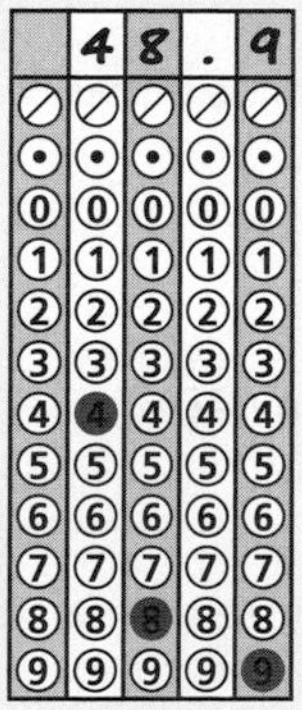

8. What error did the student make when filling out the grid?
9. Explain how to correctly grid the answer.
10. Another student plans to grid this answer as an improper fraction. Can this fraction be gridded? Explain.

STANDARDIZED TEST PREP

Learn It Online
State Test Practice

CUMULATIVE ASSESSMENT

Multiple Choice

Use the figure below for Items 1 and 2. In the figure, $\overrightarrow{DB}$ bisects ∠ADC.

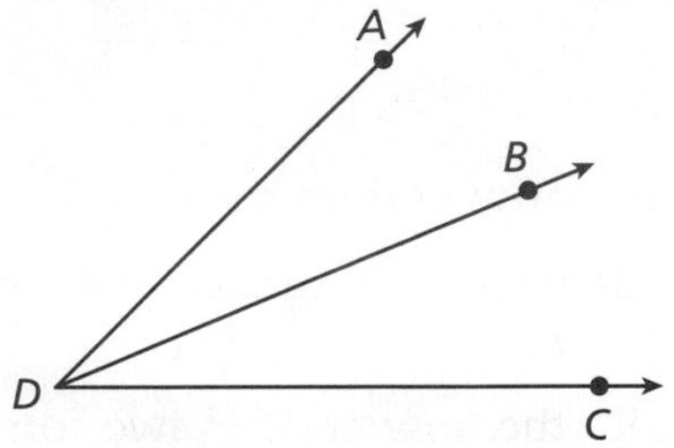

1. Which best describes the intersection of ∠ADB and ∠BDC?
   - (A) Exactly one ray
   - (B) Exactly one point
   - (C) Exactly one angle
   - (D) Exactly one segment

2. Which expression is equal to the measure of ∠ADC?
   - (F) 2(m∠ADB)
   - (G) 90° − m∠BDC
   - (H) 180° − 2(m∠ADC)
   - (J) m∠BDC − m∠ADB

3. What is the inverse of the statement, "If a polygon has 8 sides, then it is an octagon"?
   - (A) If a polygon is an octagon, then it has 8 sides.
   - (B) If a polygon is not an octagon, then it does not have 8 sides.
   - (C) If an octagon has 8 sides, then it is a polygon.
   - (D) If a polygon does not have 8 sides, then it is not an octagon.

4. Lily conjectures that if a number is divisible by 15, then it is also divisible by 9. Which of the following is a counterexample?
   - (F) 45
   - (G) 50
   - (H) 60
   - (J) 72

5. A diagonal of a polygon connects nonconsecutive vertices. The table shows the number of diagonals in a polygon with *n* sides.

Number of Sides	Number of Diagonals
4	2
5	5
6	9
7	14

   If the pattern continues, how many diagonals does a polygon with 8 sides have?
   - (A) 17
   - (B) 19
   - (C) 20
   - (D) 21

6. Which type of transformation maps figure *LMNP* onto figure *L′M′N′P′*?

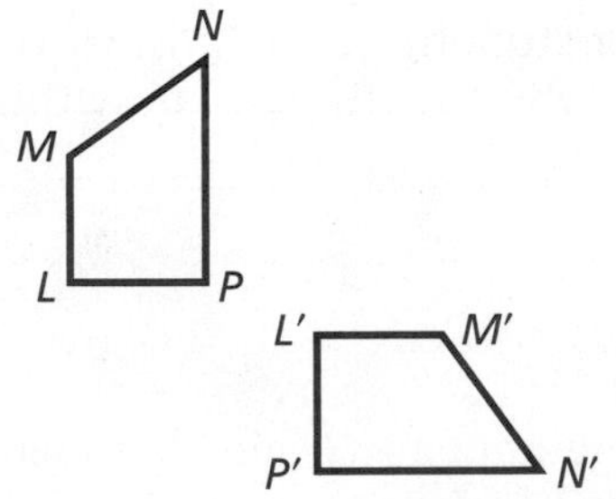

   - (F) Reflection
   - (G) Rotation
   - (H) Translation
   - (J) None of these

7. Miyoko went jogging on July 25, July 28, July 31, and August 3. If this pattern continues, when will Miyoko go jogging next?
   - (A) August 5
   - (B) August 6
   - (C) August 7
   - (D) August 8

8. Congruent segments have equal measures. A segment bisector divides a segment into two congruent segments. $\overleftrightarrow{XY}$ intersects $\overline{DE}$ at *X* and bisects $\overline{DE}$. Which conjecture is valid?
   - (F) m∠YXD = m∠YXE
   - (G) *Y* is between *D* and *E*.
   - (H) *DX* = *XE*
   - (J) *DE* = *YE*

9. Which statement is true by the Symmetric Property of Congruence?

(A) $\overline{ST} \cong \overline{ST}$

(B) $15 + MN = MN + 15$

(C) If $\angle P \cong \angle Q$, then $\angle Q \cong \angle P$.

(D) If $\angle D \cong \angle E$ and $\angle E \cong \angle F$, then $\angle D \cong \angle F$.

HOT TIP! **To find a counterexample for a biconditional statement, write the conditional statement and converse it contains. Then try to find a counterexample for one of these statements.**

10. Which is a counterexample for the following biconditional statement?

A pair of angles is supplementary if and only if the angles form a linear pair.

(F) The measures of supplementary angles add to 180°.

(G) A linear pair of angles is supplementary.

(H) Complementary angles do not form a linear pair.

(J) Two supplementary angles are not adjacent.

11. K is between J and L. The distance between J and K is 3.5 times the distance between K and L. If $JK = 14$, what is JL?

(A) 10.5 (C) 24.5

(B) 18 (D) 49

12. What is the length of the segment connecting the points $(-7, -5)$ and $(5, -2)$?

(F) $\sqrt{13}$ (H) $3\sqrt{17}$

(G) $\sqrt{53}$ (J) $\sqrt{193}$

Gridded Response

13. A segment has an endpoint at $(5, -2)$. The midpoint of the segment is $(2, 2)$. What is the length of the segment?

14. $\angle P$ measures 30° more than the measure of its supplement. What is the measure of $\angle P$ in degrees?

15. The perimeter of a square field is 1.6 kilometers. What is the area of the field in square kilometers?

Short Response

16. Solve the equation $2(AB) + 16 = 24$ to find the length of segment AB. Write a justification for each step.

17. Use the given two-column proof to write a flowchart proof.

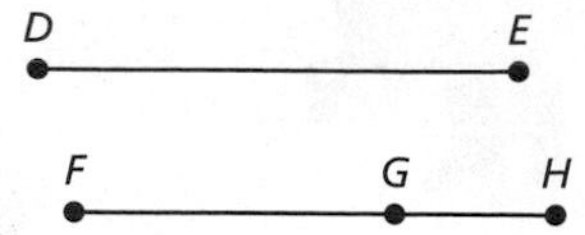

Given: $\overline{DE} \cong \overline{FH}$
Prove: $DE = FG + GH$

Two-column proof:

Statements	Reasons
1. $\overline{DE} \cong \overline{FH}$	1. Given
2. $DE = FH$	2. Def. of $\cong$ segs.
3. $FG + GH = FH$	3. Seg. Add. Post.
4. $DE = FG + GH$	4. Subst.

18. Consider the following conditional statement.

If two angles are complementary, then the angles are acute.

a. Determine if the conditional is true or false. If false, give a counterexample.

b. Write the converse of the conditional statement.

c. Determine whether the converse is true or false. If false, give a counterexample.

Extended Response

19. The figure below shows the intersection of two lines.

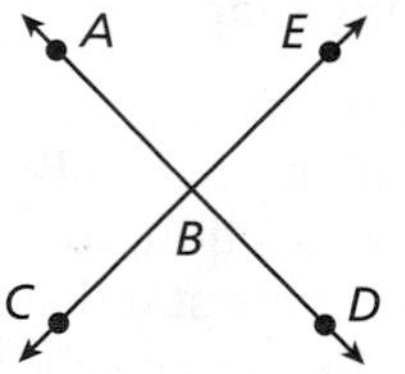

a. Name the linear pairs of angles in the figure. What conclusion can you make about each pair? Explain your reasoning.

b. Name the pairs of vertical angles in the figure. What conclusion can you make about each pair? Explain your reasoning.

c. Suppose $m\angle EBD = 90°$. What are the measures of the other angles in the figure? Write a two-column proof to support your answer.

Real-World CONNECTIONS

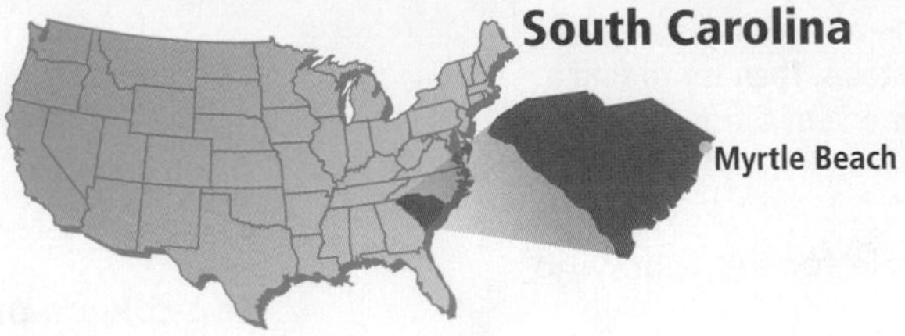

The Myrtle Beach Marathon

Every year in early February, runners take to the streets of Myrtle Beach to participate in a 26-mile marathon. It's an ideal time and place for long-distance running, with temperatures that average 60°F and a flat course that features breathtaking ocean views.

Choose one or more strategies to solve each problem.

1. During the marathon, a runner maintains a steady pace and completes the first 2.6 miles in 20 minutes. After 1 hour 20 minutes, she has completed 10.4 miles. Make a conjecture about the runner's average speed in miles per hour. How long do you expect it to take her to complete the marathon?
2. Along the course, medical stations are available every 2 miles. Portable toilets are available every 3 miles and at the end of the course. At how many points are there both a medical station and portable toilets?

For 3, use the map.

3. The course includes a straight section along Ocean Blvd. Along this section, runners pass a viewing stand and the race headquarters. The distance from the beginning of the straight section at 29th Ave. N. to the headquarters is 3.25 times the distance from 29th Ave. N. to the viewing stand. What is the distance from the viewing stand to the headquarters?

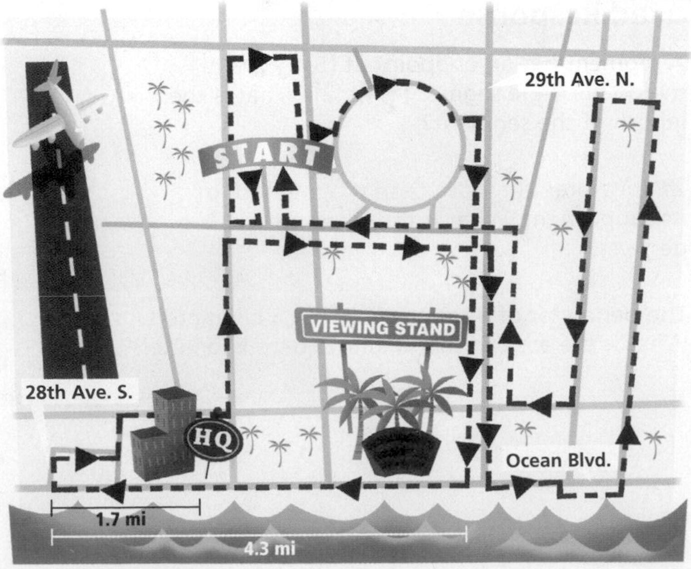

South Carolina's Waterfalls

The northwest corner of South Carolina is crisscrossed by hiking trails that lead to dozens of waterfalls, ranging from shallow cascades to the spectacular, 420-foot Raven Cliff Falls.

Choose one or more strategies to solve each problem.

1. A hiker made a round-trip hike of at least 3 miles and saw a waterfall that is less than 100 feet tall. Which waterfalls might the hiker have visited?

2. A travel brochure includes the following statements about South Carolina's waterfalls. Determine if each statement is true or false. If false, explain why.

a. If your round-trip hike is greater than 4 miles, you will be rewarded with an incredible view of a waterfall that is more than 400 feet tall.

b. If you haven't been to Lower Whitewater Falls, then you haven't seen a waterfall at least 200 feet tall.

c. If you don't want to hike 3 or more miles but want to see a 70-foot waterfall, then you should visit King Creek Falls.

3. Lower Brasstown Falls is a 120-foot waterfall consisting of three separate falls. The upper falls are 15 feet taller than the middle falls. The middle falls and lower falls are the same height. What is the height of each falls?

South Carolina Waterfalls

Waterfall	Height (ft)	Trail Length, One Way (mi)
Falls Creek Falls	100	1.5
King Creek Falls	70	0.7
Lower Whitewater Falls	200	2.0
Mill Creek Falls	25	2.5
Raven Cliff Falls	420	2.2
Yellow Branch Falls	50	1.5

Real-World Connections

CHAPTER

3 Parallel and Perpendicular Lines

COMMON CORE

Chapter Focus

- Use and prove properties of parallel lines and the angles formed by parallel lines and transversals.
- Represent lines in the coordinate plane.

Seeing is Disbelieving!

Many optical illusions are based on parallel and perpendicular lines. You can use these types of lines to create your own optical illusions.

Learn It Online
Chapter Project Online

ARE YOU READY?

Vocabulary

Match each term on the left with a definition on the right.

1. acute angle
2. congruent angles
3. obtuse angle
4. collinear
5. congruent segments

A. segments that have the same length
B. an angle that measures greater than 90° and less than 180°
C. points that lie in the same plane
D. angles that have the same measure
E. points that lie on the same line
F. an angle that measures greater than 0° and less than 90°

Conditional Statements

Identify the hypothesis and conclusion of each conditional.

6. If E is on $\overleftrightarrow{AC}$, then E lies in plane P.
7. If A is not in plane Q, then A is not on $\overleftrightarrow{BD}$.
8. If plane P and plane Q intersect, then they intersect in a line.

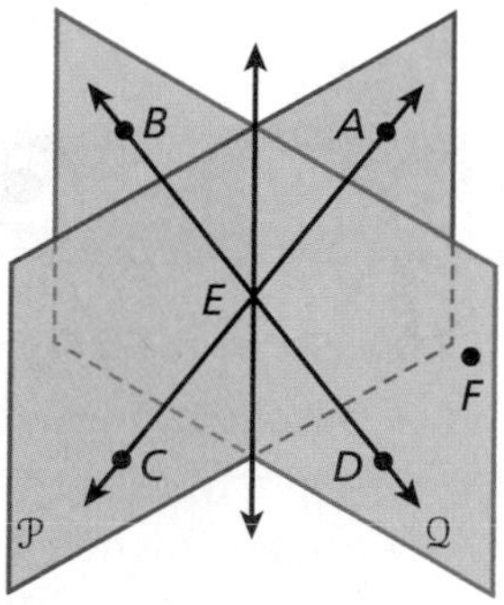

Name and Classify Angles

Name and classify each angle.

9. 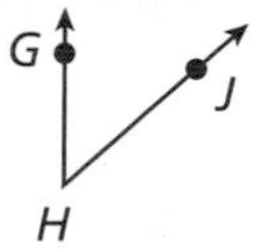

10. 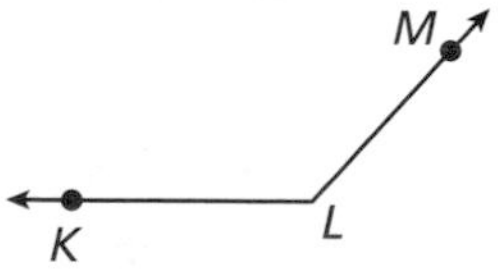

11. 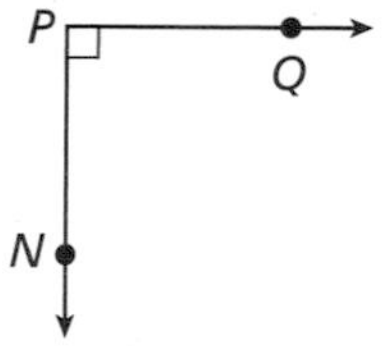

12. 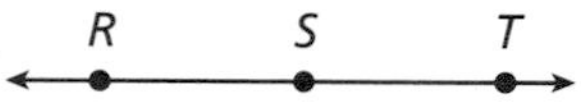

Angle Relationships

Give an example of each angle pair.

13. vertical angles
14. adjacent angles
15. complementary angles
16. supplementary angles

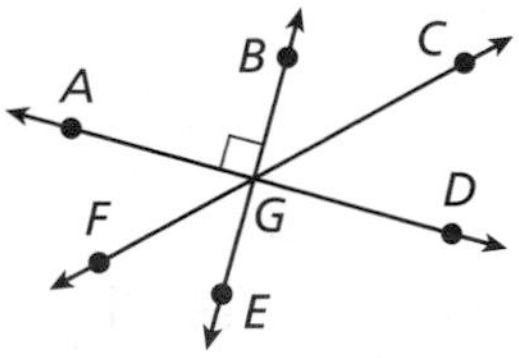

Evaluate Expressions

Evaluate each expression for the given value of the variable.

17. $4x + 9$ for $x = 31$
18. $6x - 16$ for $x = 43$
19. $97 - 3x$ for $x = 20$
20. $5x + 3x + 12$ for $x = 17$

Solve Multi-Step Equations

Solve each equation for x.

21. $4x + 8 = 24$
22. $2 = 2x - 8$
23. $4x + 3x + 6 = 90$
24. $21x + 13 + 14x - 8 = 180$

CHAPTER 3

Study Guide: Preview

Where You've Been

Previously, you

- identified and named points, lines, and planes.
- named and classified angles.
- found measures of angle pairs.
- developed and applied the formula for midpoint.

In This Chapter

You will study

- parallel and perpendicular lines.
- angles formed by parallel lines and a transversal.
- lines in a coordinate plane.

Where You're Going

You can use the skills learned in this chapter

- in Calculus, to find slopes of lines tangent to curves.
- in other classes, such as Physics and Economics, to analyze rates of change.
- in fields such as architecture and construction, to ensure that opposite walls of a building are parallel and adjacent walls are perpendicular.

Key Vocabulary/Vocabulario

alternate exterior angles	ángulos alternos externos
alternate interior angles	ángulos alternos internos
corresponding angles	ángulos correspondientes
parallel lines	líneas paralelas
perpendicular bisector	mediatriz
perpendicular lines	líneas perpendiculares
same-side interior angles	ángulos internos del mismo lado
slope	pendiente
transversal	transversal

Vocabulary Connections

To become familiar with some of the vocabulary terms in the chapter, answer the following questions. You may refer to the chapter, the glossary, or a dictionary if you like.

1. The root *trans-* means "across." What do you think a **transversal** of two lines does?
2. The *slope* of a mountain trail describes the steepness of the climb. What might the **slope** of a line describe?
3. What does the word *corresponding* mean? What do you think the term **corresponding angles** means?
4. What does the word *interior* mean? What might the phrase "interior of a pair of lines" describe? The word *alternate* means "to change from one to another." If two lines are crossed by a third line, where do you think a pair of **alternate interior angles** might be?

Reading and Writing Math

Study Strategy: Take Effective Notes

Taking effective notes is an important study strategy. The Cornell system of note taking is a good way to organize and review main ideas. In the Cornell system, the paper is divided into three main sections. The note-taking column is where you take notes during lecture. The cue column is where you write questions and key phrases as you review your notes. The summary area is where you write a brief summary of the lecture.

Step 1: Notes
Draw a vertical line about 2.5 inches from the left side of your paper. During class, write your notes about the main points of the lecture in the right column.

Step 2: Cues
After class, write down key phrases or questions in the left column.

Step 3: Summary
Use your cues to restate the main points in your own words.

9/4 page 1

What can you use to justify steps in a proof?	Geometric proof: Start with hypothesis, and then use defs., posts., and thms. to reach conclusion. Justify each step.
What kind of angles form a linear pair?	Linear Pair Theorem If 2 ∠s form a lin. pair, then they are supp.
What is true about two supplements of the same angle?	Congruent Supplements Theorem If 2 ∠s are supp. to the same ∠ (or to 2 ≅ ∠s), then the 2 ∠s are ≅.

Summary: A proof uses definitions, postulates, and theorems to show that a conclusion is true. The Linear Pair Theorem says that two angles that form a linear pair are supplementary. The Congruent Supplements Theorem says that two supplements to the same angle are congruent.

Try This

1. Research and write a paragraph describing the Cornell system of note taking. Describe how you can benefit from using this type of system.
2. In your next class, use the Cornell system of note taking. Compare these notes to your notes from a previous lecture.

COMMON CORE

3-1 Lines and Angles

CC.9-12.G.CO.1 Know precise definitions…based on the undefined notions of point, line…

Objectives

Identify parallel, perpendicular, and skew lines.

Identify the angles formed by two lines and a transversal.

Vocabulary

parallel lines
perpendicular lines
skew lines
parallel planes
transversal
corresponding angles
alternate interior angles
alternate exterior angles
same-side interior angles

Who uses this?

Card architects use playing cards to build structures that contain parallel and perpendicular planes.

In 1992, Bryan Berg broke the Guinness World Record for card structures by building a tower 14 feet 6 inches tall. Since then, he has built structures more than 25 feet tall.

Know it! Note

Parallel, Perpendicular, and Skew Lines

Parallel lines (||) are coplanar and do not intersect. In the figure, $\overleftrightarrow{AB} \parallel \overleftrightarrow{EF}$, and $\overleftrightarrow{EG} \parallel \overleftrightarrow{FH}$.

Perpendicular lines (⊥) intersect at 90° angles. In the figure, $\overleftrightarrow{AB} \perp \overleftrightarrow{AE}$, and $\overleftrightarrow{EG} \perp \overleftrightarrow{GH}$.

Skew lines are not coplanar. Skew lines are not parallel and do not intersect. In the figure, $\overleftrightarrow{AB}$ and $\overleftrightarrow{EG}$ are skew.

Parallel planes are planes that do not intersect. In the figure, plane ABE || plane CDG.

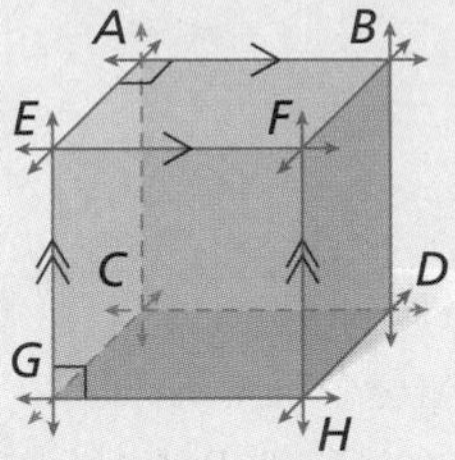

Arrows are used to show that $\overleftrightarrow{AB} \parallel \overleftrightarrow{EF}$ and $\overleftrightarrow{EG} \parallel \overleftrightarrow{FH}$.

EXAMPLE 1 **Identifying Types of Lines and Planes**

Identify each of the following.

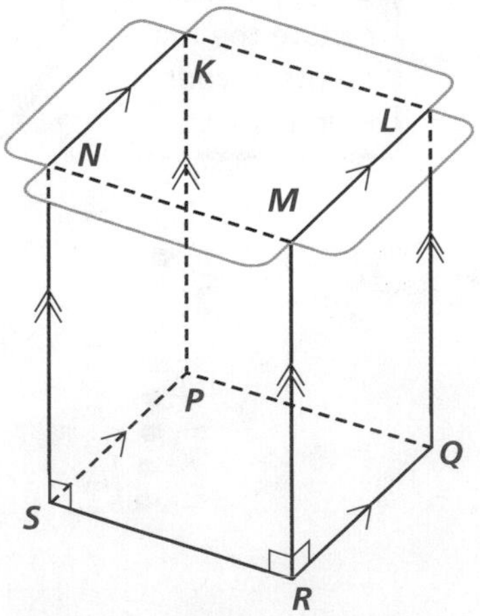

A **a pair of parallel segments**

$\overline{KN} \parallel \overline{PS}$

B **a pair of skew segments**

$\overline{LM}$ and $\overline{RS}$ are skew.

C **a pair of perpendicular segments**

$\overline{MR} \perp \overline{RS}$

D **a pair of parallel planes**

plane KPS || plane LQR

Helpful Hint

Segments or rays are parallel, perpendicular, or skew if the lines that contain them are parallel, perpendicular, or skew.

CHECK IT OUT!

Identify each of the following.

1a. a pair of parallel segments

1b. a pair of skew segments

1c. a pair of perpendicular segments

1d. a pair of parallel planes

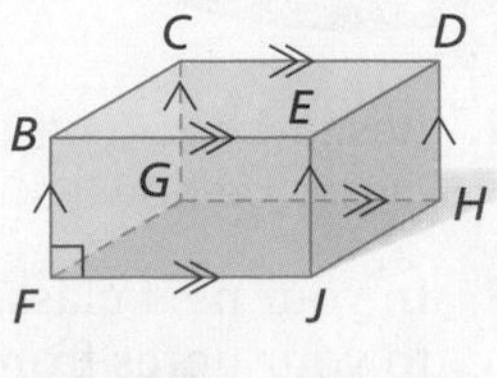

Know it! Note

Angle Pairs Formed by a Transversal

TERM	EXAMPLE
A **transversal** is a line that intersects two coplanar lines at two different points. The transversal *t* and the other two lines *r* and *s* form eight angles.	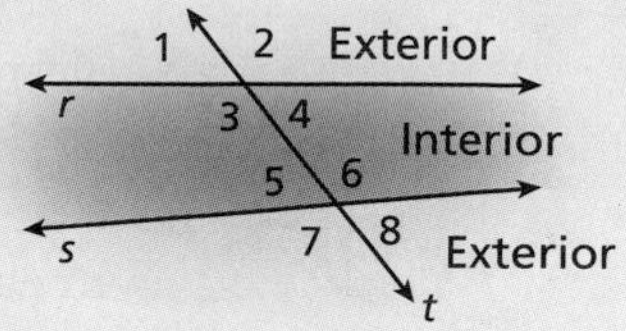
Corresponding angles lie on the same side of the transversal *t*, on the same sides of lines *r* and *s*.	∠1 and ∠5
Alternate interior angles are nonadjacent angles that lie on opposite sides of the transversal *t*, between lines *r* and *s*.	∠3 and ∠6
Alternate exterior angles lie on opposite sides of the transversal *t*, outside lines *r* and *s*.	∠1 and ∠8
Same-side interior angles or *consecutive interior angles* lie on the same side of the transversal *t*, between lines *r* and *s*.	∠3 and ∠5

EXAMPLE 2 Classifying Pairs of Angles

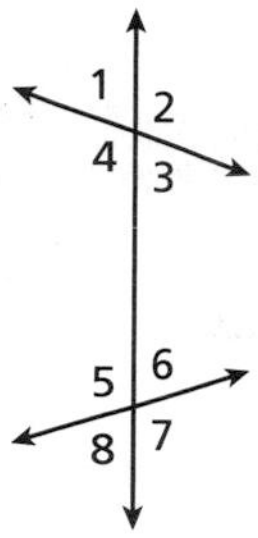

Give an example of each angle pair.

A corresponding angles
∠4 and ∠8

B alternate interior angles
∠4 and ∠6

C alternate exterior angles
∠2 and ∠8

D same-side interior angles
∠4 and ∠5

CHECK IT OUT! **Give an example of each angle pair.**

2a. corresponding angles
2b. alternate interior angles
2c. alternate exterior angles
2d. same-side interior angles

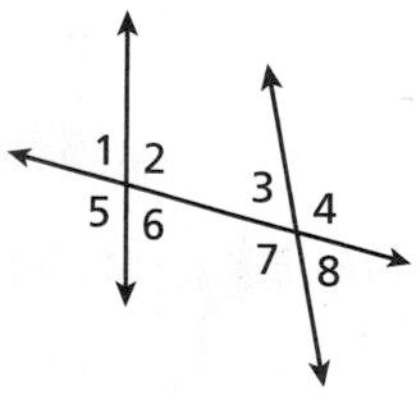

EXAMPLE 3 Identifying Angle Pairs and Transversals

Helpful Hint

To determine which line is the transversal for a given angle pair, locate the line that connects the vertices.

Identify the transversal and classify each angle pair.

A ∠1 and ∠5
transversal: *n*; alternate interior angles

B ∠3 and ∠6
transversal: *m*; corresponding angles

C ∠1 and ∠4
transversal: ℓ; alternate exterior angles

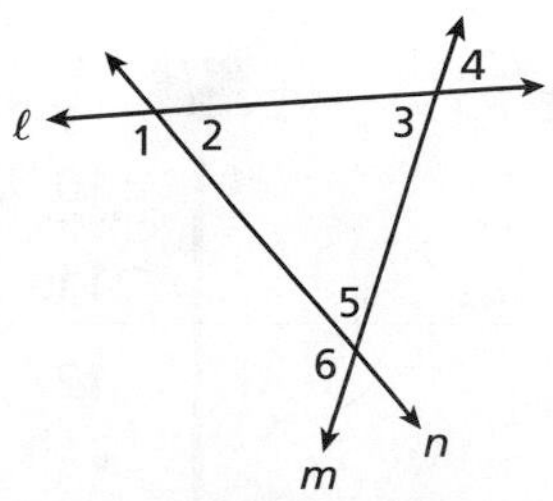

CHECK IT OUT! **3.** Identify the transversal and classify the angle pair ∠2 and ∠5 in the diagram above.

MATHEMATICAL PRACTICES

THINK AND DISCUSS

1. Compare perpendicular and intersecting lines.
2. Describe the positions of two alternate exterior angles formed by lines *m* and *n* with transversal *p*.

Know it! Note

3. **GET ORGANIZED** Copy the diagram and graphic organizer. In each box, list all the angle pairs of each type in the diagram.

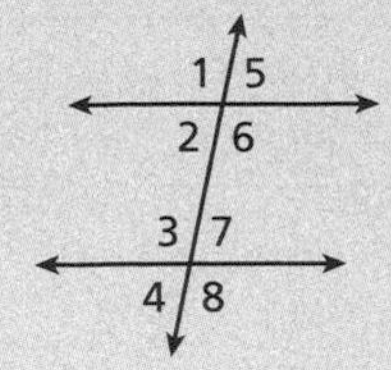

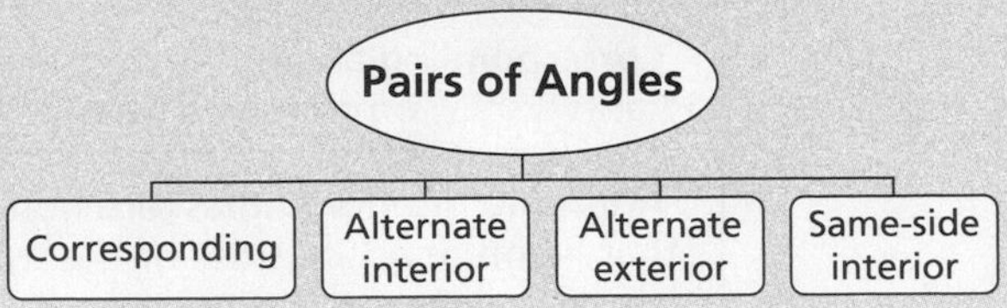

3-1 Exercises

Learn It Online
Homework Help Online
Parent Resources Online

GUIDED PRACTICE

1. **Vocabulary** __?__ are located on opposite sides of a transversal, between the two lines that intersect the transversal. (*corresponding angles, alternate interior angles, alternate exterior angles,* or *same-side interior angles*)

SEE EXAMPLE 1

Identify each of the following.

2. one pair of perpendicular segments
3. one pair of skew segments
4. one pair of parallel segments
5. one pair of parallel planes

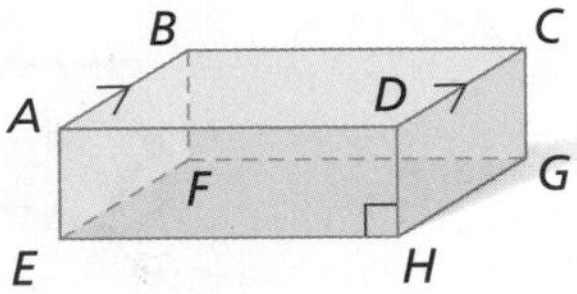

SEE EXAMPLE 2

Give an example of each angle pair.

6. alternate interior angles
7. alternate exterior angles
8. corresponding angles
9. same-side interior angles

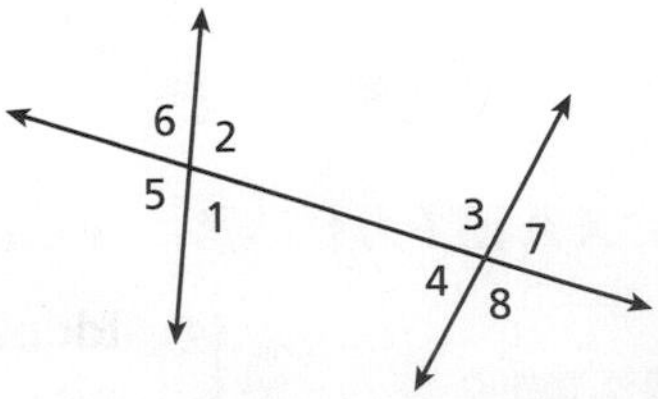

SEE EXAMPLE 3

Identify the transversal and classify each angle pair.

10. ∠1 and ∠2
11. ∠2 and ∠3
12. ∠2 and ∠4
13. ∠4 and ∠5

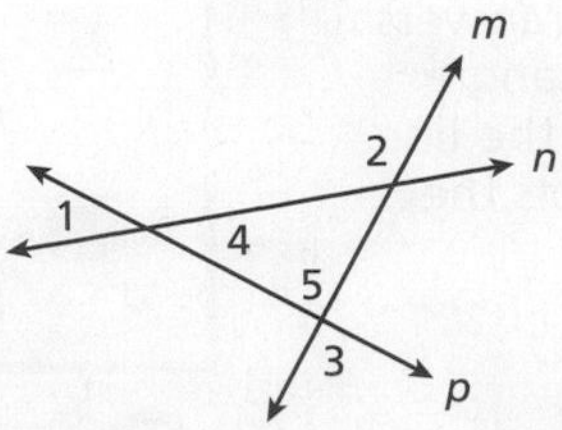

For Exercises	See Example
14–17	1
18–21	2
22–25	3

Independent Practice

Extra Practice

See Extra Practice for more Skills Practice and Applications Practice exercises.

PRACTICE AND PROBLEM SOLVING

Identify each of the following.

14. one pair of parallel segments

15. one pair of skew segments

16. one pair of perpendicular segments

17. one pair of parallel planes

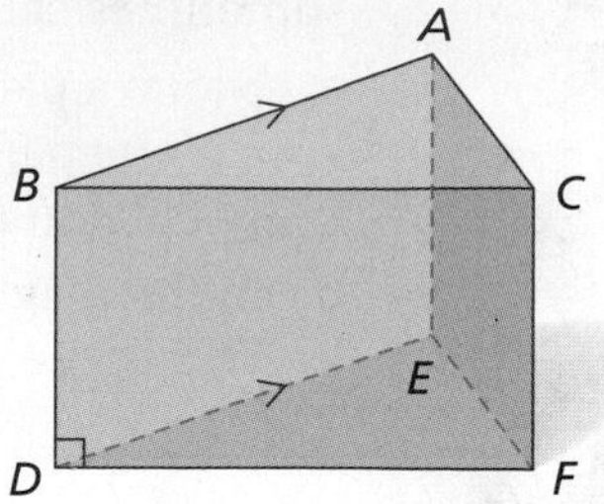

Give an example of each angle pair.

18. same-side interior angles

19. alternate exterior angles

20. corresponding angles

21. alternate interior angles

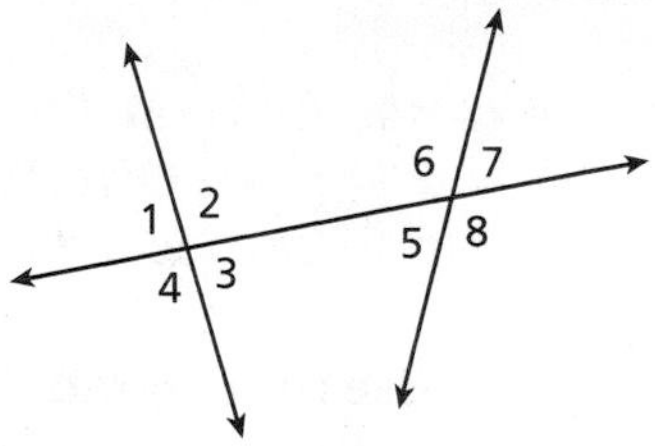

Identify the transversal and classify each angle pair.

22. ∠2 and ∠3

23. ∠4 and ∠5

24. ∠2 and ∠4

25. ∠1 and ∠2

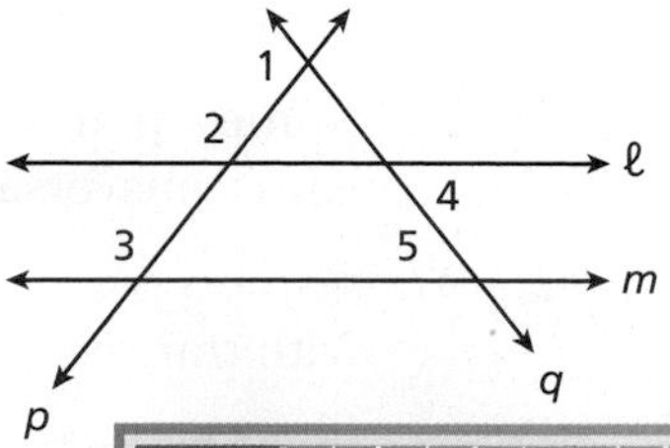

26. Sports A football player runs across the 30-yard line at an angle. He continues in a straight line and crosses the goal line at the same angle. Describe two parallel lines and a transversal in the diagram.

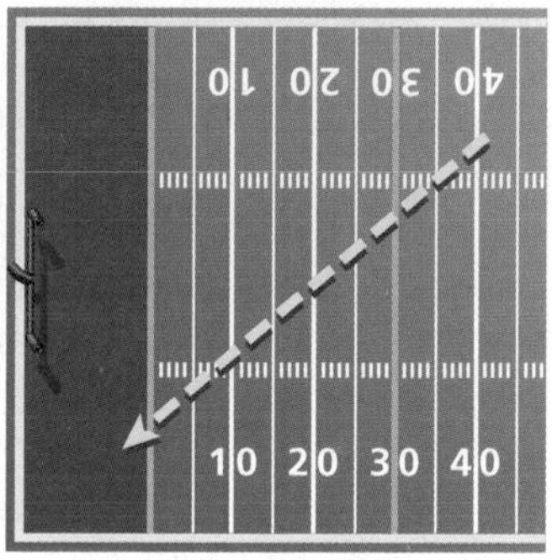

Name the type of angle pair shown in each letter.

27. F

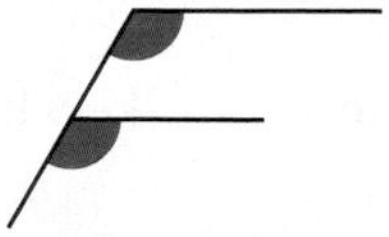

28. Z

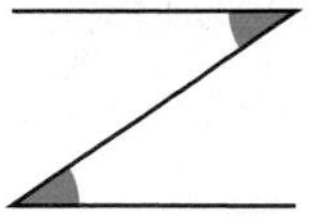

29. C

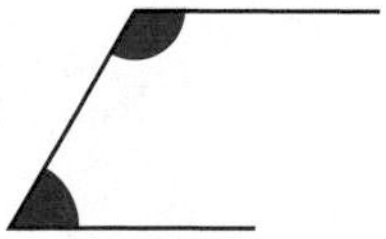

LINK

Entertainment

In an Ames room, two people of the same height that are standing in different parts of the room appear to be different sizes.

Entertainment **Use the following information for Exercises 30–32.**

In an Ames room, the floor is tilted and the back wall is closer to the front wall on one side.

30. Name a pair of parallel segments in the diagram.

31. Name a pair of skew segments in the diagram.

32. Name a pair of perpendicular segments in the diagram.

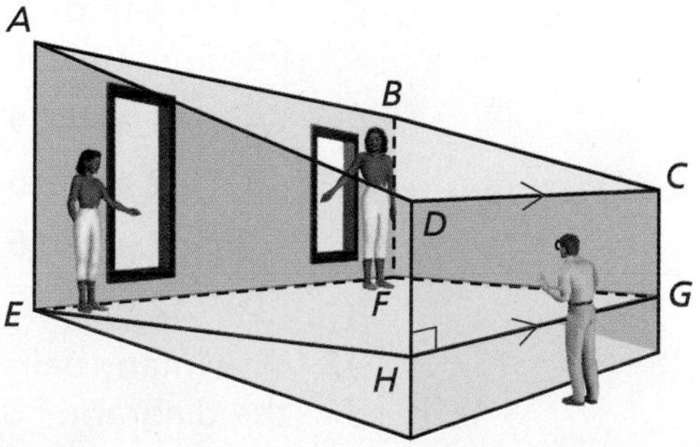

Multi-Step Test Prep

33. Buildings that are tilted like the one shown are sometimes called mystery spots.

a. Name a plane parallel to plane *KLP*, a plane parallel to plane *KNP*, and a plane parallel to *KLM*.

b. In the diagram, $\overline{QR}$ is a transversal to $\overline{PQ}$ and $\overline{RS}$. What type of angle pair is $\angle PQR$ and $\angle QRS$?

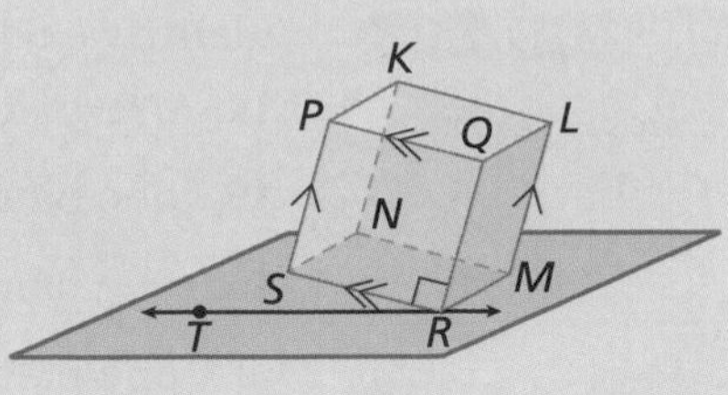

34. Critical Thinking Line ℓ is contained in plane P and line m is contained in plane Q. If P and Q are parallel, what are the possible classifications of ℓ and m? Include diagrams to support your answer.

Use the diagram for Exercises 35–40.

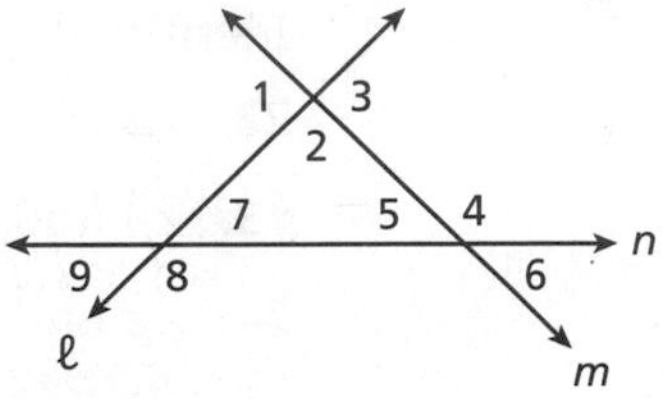

35. Name a pair of alternate interior angles with transversal n.

36. Name a pair of same-side interior angles with transversal ℓ.

37. Name a pair of corresponding angles with transversal m.

38. Identify the transversal and classify the angle pair for $\angle 3$ and $\angle 7$.

39. Identify the transversal and classify the angle pair for $\angle 5$ and $\angle 8$.

40. Identify the transversal and classify the angle pair for $\angle 1$ and $\angle 6$.

41. Aviation Describe the type of lines formed by two planes when flight 1449 is flying from San Francisco to Atlanta at 32,000 feet and flight 2390 is flying from Dallas to Chicago at 28,000 feet.

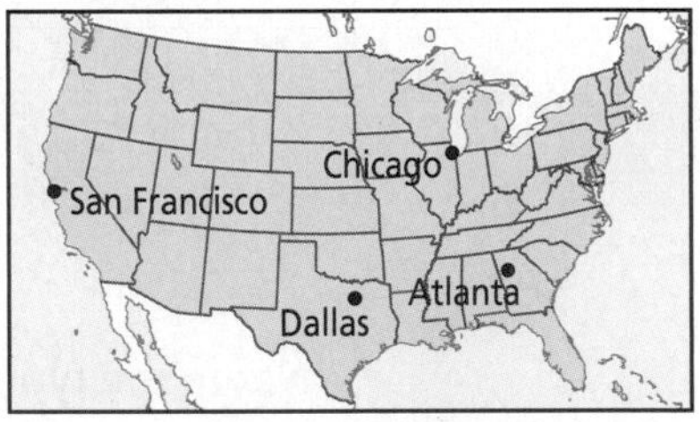

42. Multi-Step Draw line p, then draw two lines m and n that are both perpendicular to p. Make a conjecture about the relationship between lines m and n.

43. Write About It Discuss a real-world example of skew lines. Include a sketch.

Test Prep

44. Which pair of angles in the diagram are alternate interior angles?

Ⓐ $\angle 1$ and $\angle 5$

Ⓑ $\angle 2$ and $\angle 6$

Ⓒ $\angle 7$ and $\angle 5$

Ⓓ $\angle 2$ and $\angle 3$

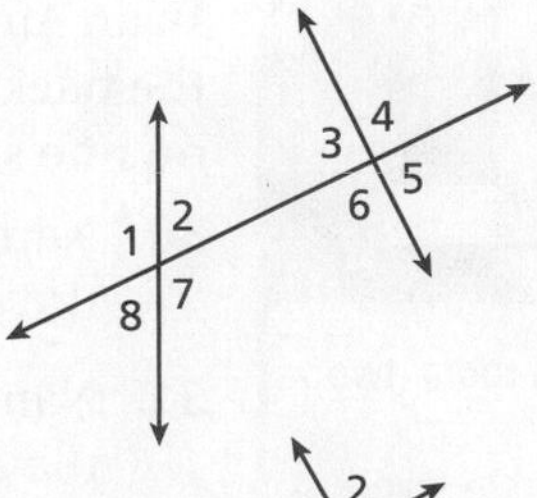

45. How many pairs of corresponding angles are in the diagram?

Ⓕ 2　　Ⓗ 8

Ⓖ 4　　Ⓙ 16

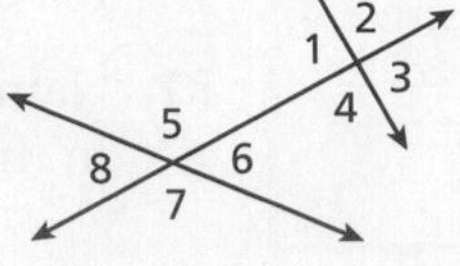

Rick Davis/Darkhouse and Fun Enthusiast

46. Which type of lines are NOT represented in the diagram?

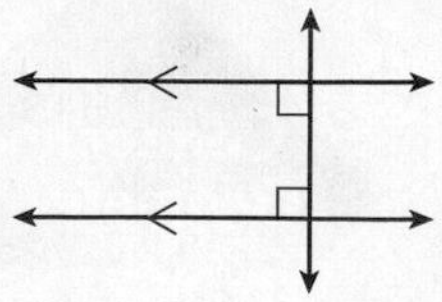

Ⓐ Parallel lines　　Ⓒ Skew lines

Ⓑ Intersecting lines　　Ⓓ Perpendicular lines

47. For two lines and a transversal, ∠1 and ∠8 are alternate exterior angles, and ∠1 and ∠5 are corresponding angles. Classify the angle pair ∠5 and ∠8.

Ⓕ Vertical angles

Ⓖ Alternate interior angles

Ⓗ Adjacent angles

Ⓙ Same-side interior angles

48. Which angles in the diagram are NOT corresponding angles?

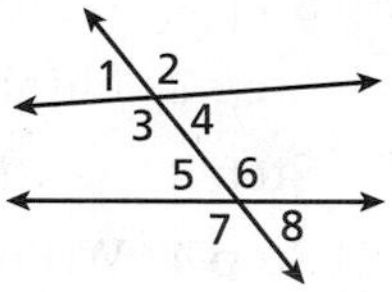

Ⓐ ∠1 and ∠5　　Ⓒ ∠4 and ∠8

Ⓑ ∠2 and ∠6　　Ⓓ ∠2 and ∠7

CHALLENGE AND EXTEND

Name all the angle pairs of each type in the diagram. Identify the transversal for each pair.

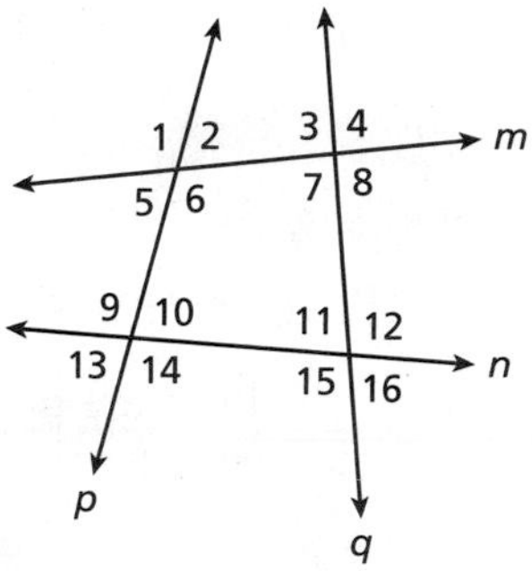

49. corresponding　　**50.** alternate interior

51. alternate exterior　　**52.** same-side interior

53. Multi-Step Draw two lines and a transversal such that ∠1 and ∠3 are corresponding angles, ∠1 and ∠2 are alternate interior angles, and ∠3 and ∠4 are alternate exterior angles. What type of angle pair is ∠2 and ∠4?

54. If the figure shown is folded to form a cube, which faces of the cube will be parallel?

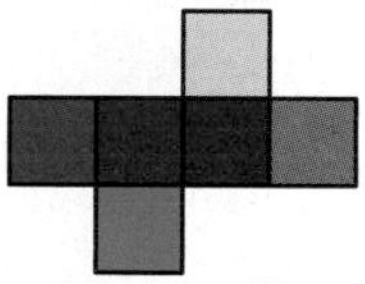

Connecting Geometry to

Algebra

Systems of Equations

Sometimes angle measures are given as algebraic expressions. When you know the relationship between two angles, you can write and solve a system of equations to find angle measures.

Solving Systems of Equations by Using Elimination	
Step 1	Write the system so that like terms are under one another.
Step 2	Eliminate one of the variables.
Step 3	Substitute that value into one of the original equations and solve.
Step 4	Write the answers as an ordered pair, (x, y).
Step 5	Check your solution.

Example 1

Solve for x and y.

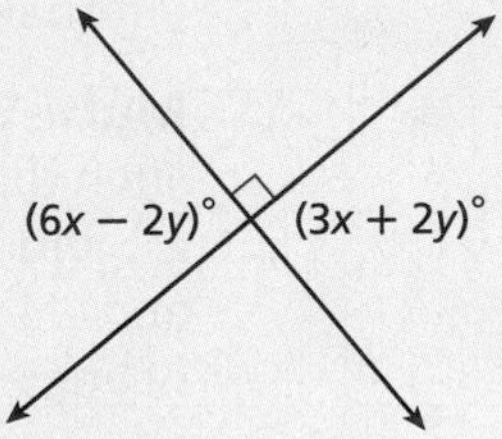

Since the lines are perpendicular, all of the angles are right angles. To write two equations, you can set each expression equal to 90°.

$$(3x + 2y)^\circ = 90^\circ,\ (6x - 2y)^\circ = 90^\circ$$

Step 1 $3x + 2y = 90$; $6x - 2y = 90$ — *Write the system so that like terms are under one another.*

Step 2 $9x + 0 = 180$ — *Add like terms on each side of the equations. The y-term has been eliminated.*

$x = 20$ — *Divide both sides by 9 to solve for x.*

Step 3 $3x + 2y = 90$ — *Write one of the original equations.*

$3(20) + 2y = 90$ — *Substitute 20 for x.*

$60 + 2y = 90$ — *Simplify.*

$2y = 30$ — *Subtract 60 from both sides.*

$y = 15$ — *Divide by 2 on both sides.*

Step 4 $(20, 15)$ — *Write the solution as an ordered pair.*

Step 5 Check the solution by substituting 20 for x and 15 for y in the original equations.

$3x + 2y$	$= 90$
$3(20) + 2(15)$	90
$60 + 30$	90
90	90 ✓

$6x - 2y$	$= 90$
$6(20) - 2(15)$	90
$120 - 30$	90
90	90 ✓

In some cases, before you can do Step 1 you will need to multiply one or both of the equations by a number so that you can eliminate a variable.

Example 2

Solve for x and y.

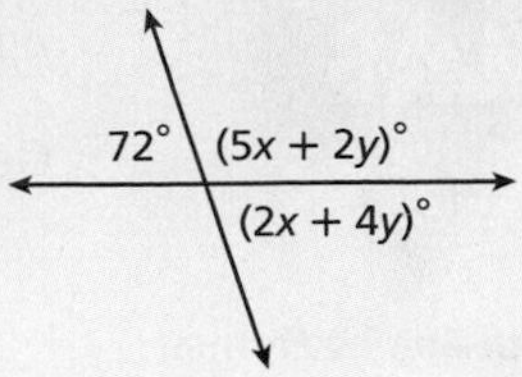

$(2x + 4y)^\circ = 72^\circ$ *Vertical Angles Theorem*

$(5x + 2y)^\circ = 108^\circ$ *Linear Pair Theorem*

The equations cannot be added or subtracted to eliminate a variable. Multiply the second equation by −2 to get opposite y-coefficients.

$5x + 2y = 108 \rightarrow -2(5x + 2y) = -2(108) \rightarrow -10x - 4y = -216$

Step 1 $\begin{array}{r} 2x + 4y = 72 \\ -10x - 4y = -216 \\ \hline \end{array}$ *Write the system so that like terms are under one another.*

Step 2 $-8x = -144$ *Add like terms on both sides of the equations. The y-term has been eliminated.*

$x = 18$ *Divide both sides by −8 to solve for x.*

Step 3 $2x + 4y = 72$ *Write one of the original equations.*

$2(18) + 4y = 72$ *Substitute 18 for x.*

$36 + 4y = 72$ *Simplify.*

$4y = 36$ *Subtract 36 from both sides.*

$y = 9$ *Divide by 4 on both sides.*

Step 4 $(18, 9)$ *Write the solution as an ordered pair.*

Step 5 Check the solution by substituting 18 for x and 9 for y in the original equations.

$2x + 4y$	$= 72$
$3(18) + 4(9)$	72
$36 + 36$	72
72	72 ✓

$5x + 2y$	$= 108$
$5(18) + 2(9)$	108
$90 + 18$	108
108	108 ✓

Try This

Solve for x and y.

1.

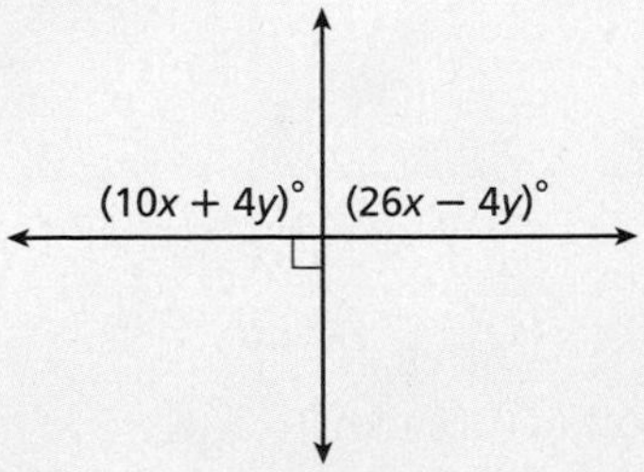

2.

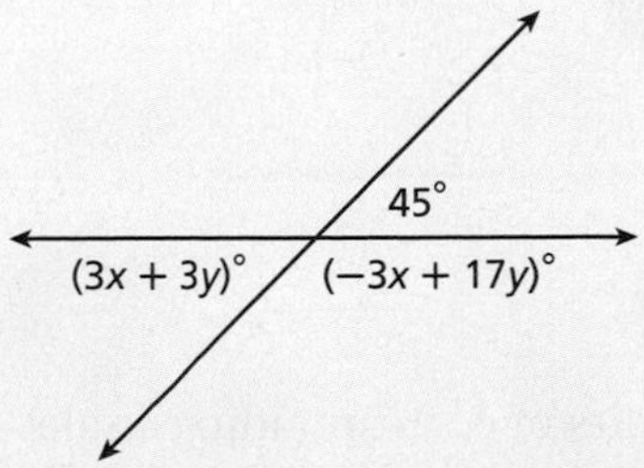

3.

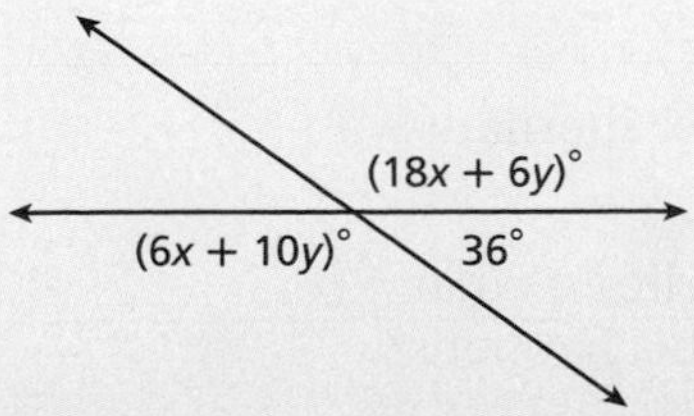

4.

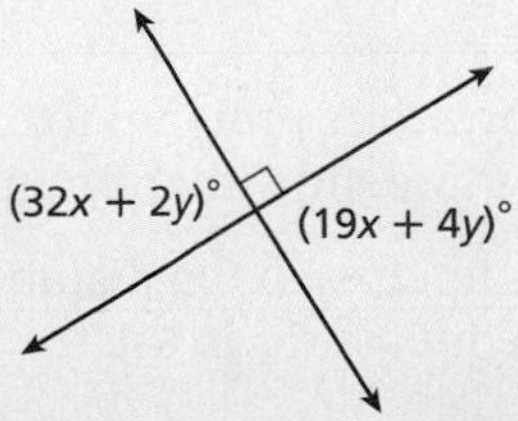

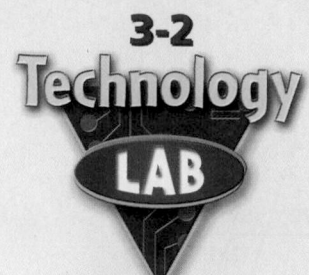

3-2 Technology LAB

Explore Parallel Lines and Transversals

Geometry software can help you explore angles that are formed when a transversal intersects a pair of parallel lines.

Use with Angles Formed by Parallel Lines and Transversals

MATHEMATICAL PRACTICES **Use appropriate tools strategically.**

CC.9-12.G.CO.9 Prove geometric theorems about lines and angles.

Learn It Online
Lab Resources Online

Activity

1. Construct a line and label two points on the line *A* and *B*.

2. Create point *C* not on $\overleftrightarrow{AB}$. Construct a line parallel to $\overleftrightarrow{AB}$ through point *C*. Create another point on this line and label it *D*.

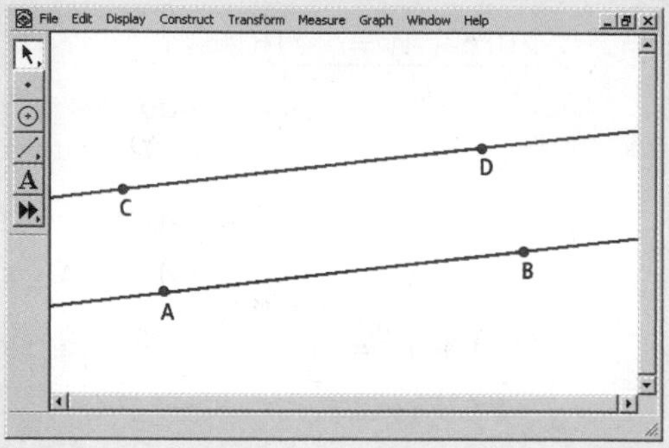

3. Create two points outside the two parallel lines and label them *E* and *F*. Construct transversal $\overleftrightarrow{EF}$. Label the points of intersection *G* and *H*.

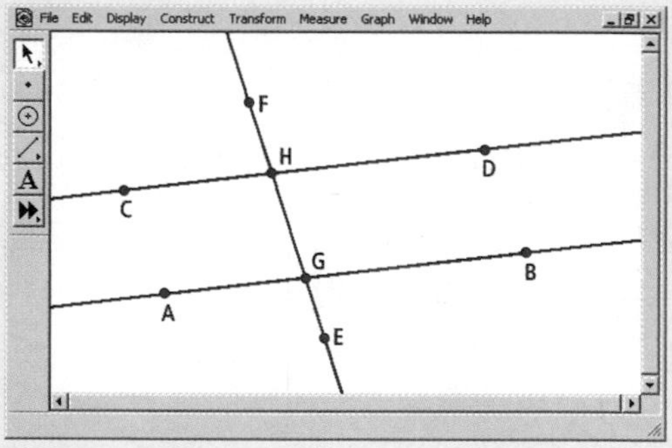

4. Measure the angles formed by the parallel lines and the transversal. Write the angle measures in a chart like the one below. Drag point *E* or *F* and chart with the new angle measures. What relationships do you notice about the angle measures? What conjectures can you make?

Angle	∠*AGE*	∠*BGE*	∠*AGH*	∠*BGH*	∠*CHG*	∠*DHG*	∠*CHF*	∠*DHF*
Measure								
Measure								

Try This

1. Identify the pairs of corresponding angles in the diagram. What conjecture can you make about their angle measures? Drag a point in the figure to confirm your conjecture.
2. Repeat steps in the previous problem for alternate interior angles, alternate exterior angles, and same-side interior angles.
3. Try dragging point *C* to change the distance between the parallel lines. What happens to the angle measures in the figure? Why do you think this happens?

COMMON CORE

3-2 Angles Formed by Parallel Lines and Transversals

CC.9-12.G.CO.9 Prove geometric theorems about lines and angles.

Objective
Prove and use theorems about the angles formed by parallel lines and a transversal.

Who uses this?
Piano makers use parallel strings for the higher notes. The longer strings used to produce the lower notes can be viewed as transversals. (See Example 3.)

When parallel lines are cut by a transversal, the angle pairs formed are either congruent or supplementary.

Know it! Note

Postulate 3-2-1 Corresponding Angles Postulate

POSTULATE	HYPOTHESIS	CONCLUSION
If two parallel lines are cut by a transversal, then the pairs of corresponding angles are congruent.	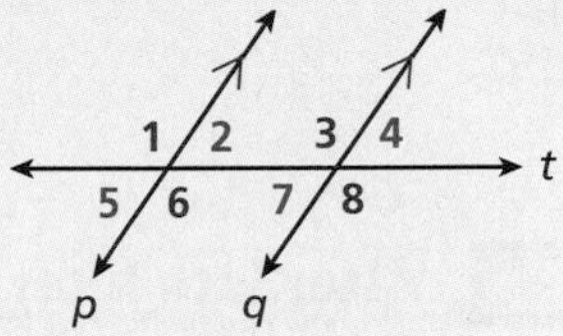	$\angle 1 \cong \angle 3$ $\angle 2 \cong \angle 4$ $\angle 5 \cong \angle 7$ $\angle 6 \cong \angle 8$

EXAMPLE 1 **Using the Corresponding Angles Postulate**

Find each angle measure.

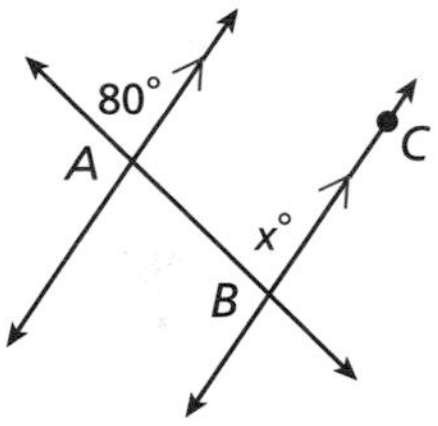

A m∠*ABC*

$x = 80$ *Corr. ∠s Post.*

$m\angle ABC = 80°$

x^2y **Algebra**

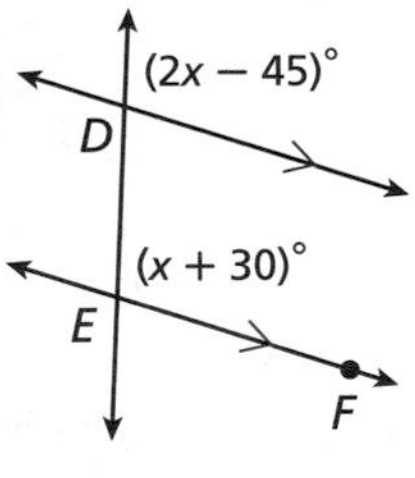

B m∠*DEF*

$(2x - 45)° = (x + 30)°$ *Corr. ∠s Post.*

$x - 45 = 30$ *Subtract x from both sides.*

$x = 75$ *Add 45 to both sides.*

$m\angle DEF = x + 30$

$= 75 + 30$ *Substitute 75 for x.*

$= 105°$

CHECK IT OUT!

1. Find m∠*QRS*.

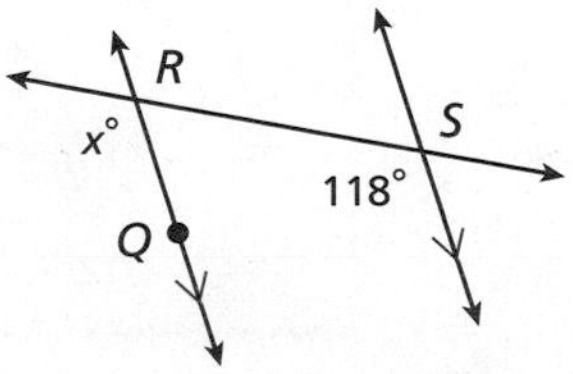

Remember that postulates are statements that are accepted without proof. Since the Corresponding Angles Postulate is given as a postulate, it can be used to prove the next three theorems.

Alamy Photos

Know it! Note

Theorems — Parallel Lines and Angle Pairs

	THEOREM	HYPOTHESIS	CONCLUSION
3-2-2	**Alternate Interior Angles Theorem** If two parallel lines are cut by a transversal, then the pairs of alternate interior angles are congruent.	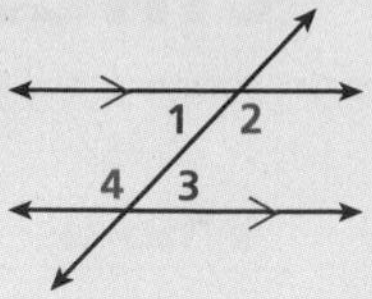	$\angle 1 \cong \angle 3$ $\angle 2 \cong \angle 4$
3-2-3	**Alternate Exterior Angles Theorem** If two parallel lines are cut by a transversal, then the two pairs of alternate exterior angles are congruent.	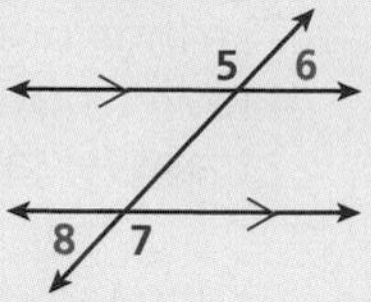	$\angle 5 \cong \angle 7$ $\angle 6 \cong \angle 8$
3-2-4	**Same-Side Interior Angles Theorem** If two parallel lines are cut by a transversal, then the two pairs of same-side interior angles are supplementary.	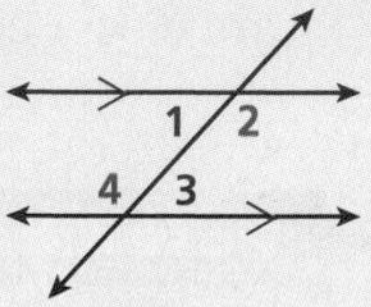	$m\angle 1 + m\angle 4 = 180°$ $m\angle 2 + m\angle 3 = 180°$

Helpful Hint

If a transversal is perpendicular to two parallel lines, all eight angles are congruent.

You will prove Theorems 3-2-3 and 3-2-4 in Exercises 25 and 26.

PROOF

Alternate Interior Angles Theorem

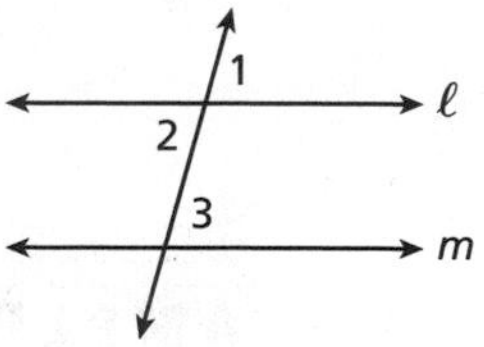

Given: $\ell \parallel m$
Prove: $\angle 2 \cong \angle 3$
Proof:

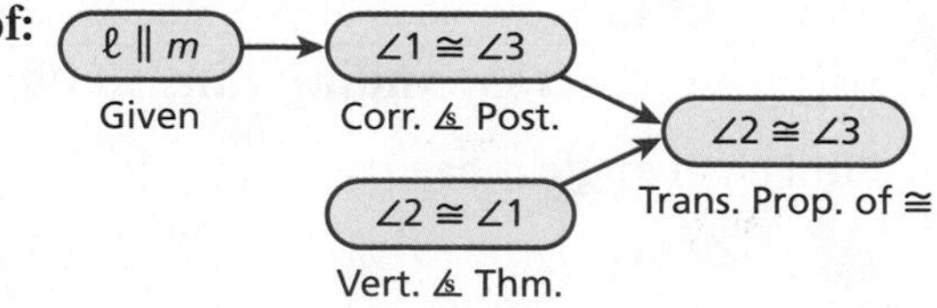

EXAMPLE 2 Finding Angle Measures

Find each angle measure.

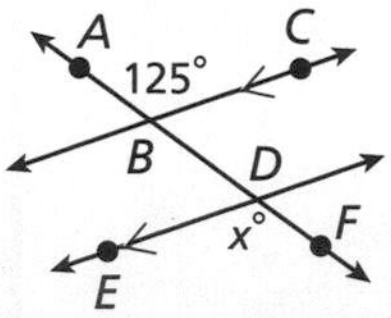

A $m\angle EDF$

$x = 125$

$m\angle EDF = 125°$ *Alt. Ext. ∠s Thm.*

Algebra

B $m\angle TUS$

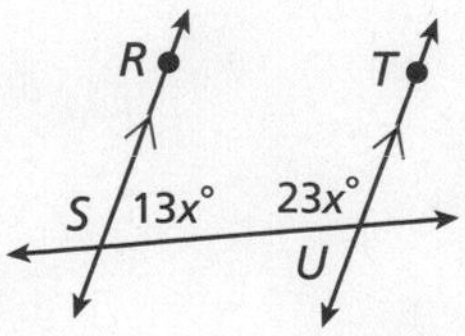

$13x° + 23x° = 180°$ *Same-Side Int. ∠s Thm.*

$36x = 180$ *Combine like terms.*

$x = 5$ *Divide both sides by 36.*

$m\angle TUS = 23(5) = 115°$ *Substitute 5 for x.*

CHECK IT OUT! 2. Find $m\angle ABD$.

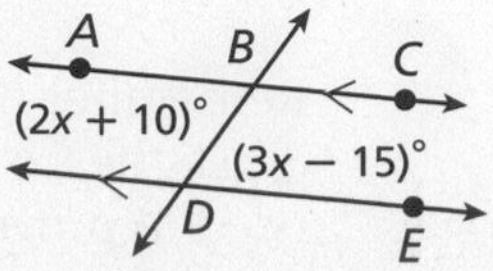

Student to Student

Parallel Lines and Transversals

Nancy Martin
East Branch
High School

When I solve problems with parallel lines and transversals, I remind myself that every pair of angles is either congruent or supplementary.

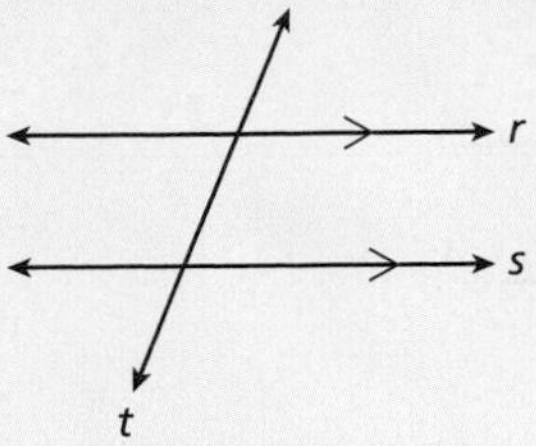

If r || s, all the acute angles are congruent and all the obtuse angles are congruent. The acute angles are supplementary to the obtuse angles.

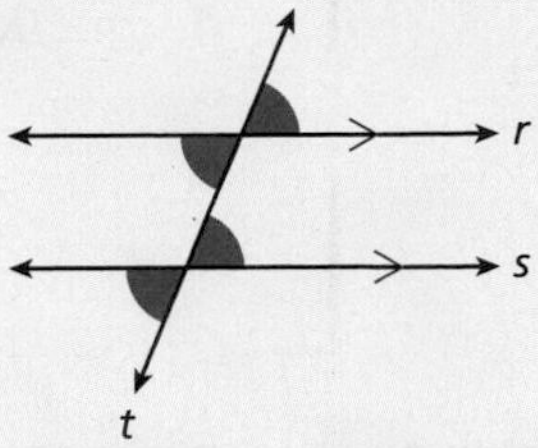

EXAMPLE 3 Music Application

Algebra

The treble strings of a grand piano are parallel. Viewed from above, the bass strings form transversals to the treble strings. Find x and y in the diagram.

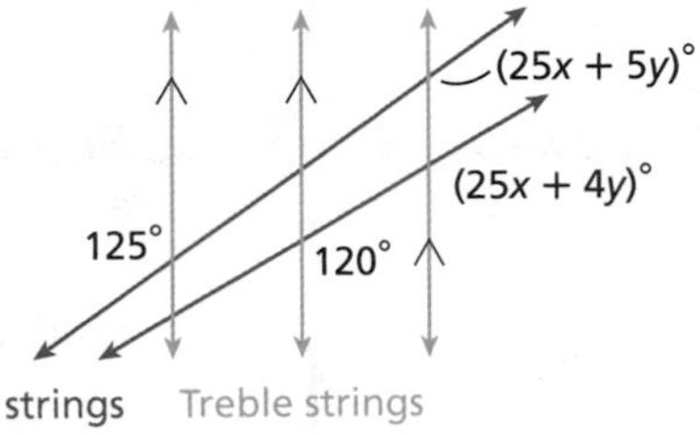

By the Alternate Exterior Angles Theorem, $(25x + 5y)^\circ = 125^\circ$.

By the Corresponding Angles Postulate, $(25x + 4y)^\circ = 120^\circ$.

$$25x + 5y = 125$$

$$-(25x + 4y = 120)$$ *Subtract the second equation from the first equation.*

$$y = 5$$

$$25x + 5(5) = 125$$ *Substitute 5 for y in 25x + 5y = 125. Simplify and solve for x.*

$$x = 4, y = 5$$

CHECK IT OUT! 3. Find the measures of the acute angles in the diagram.

MATHEMATICAL PRACTICES

THINK AND DISCUSS

1. Explain why a transversal that is perpendicular to two parallel lines forms eight congruent angles.

Know it! Note

2. GET ORGANIZED Copy the diagram and graphic organizer. Complete the graphic organizer by explaining why each of the three theorems is true.

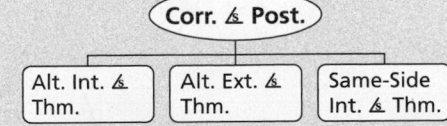

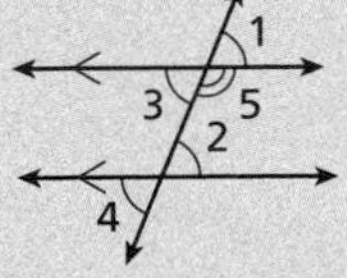

Corr. ∠s Post.

Alt. Int. ∠s Thm.	Alt. Ext. ∠s Thm.	Same-Side Int. ∠s Thm.

3-2 Exercises

Learn It Online
Homework Help Online
Parent Resources Online

GUIDED PRACTICE

SEE EXAMPLE 1

Find each angle measure.

1. $m\angle JKL$

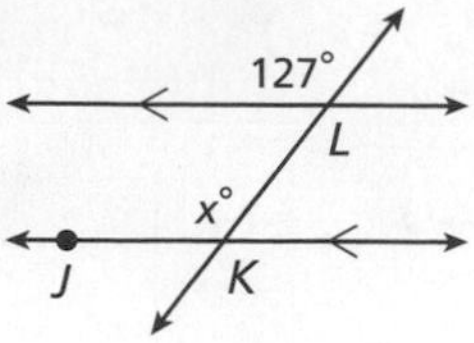

2. $m\angle BEF$

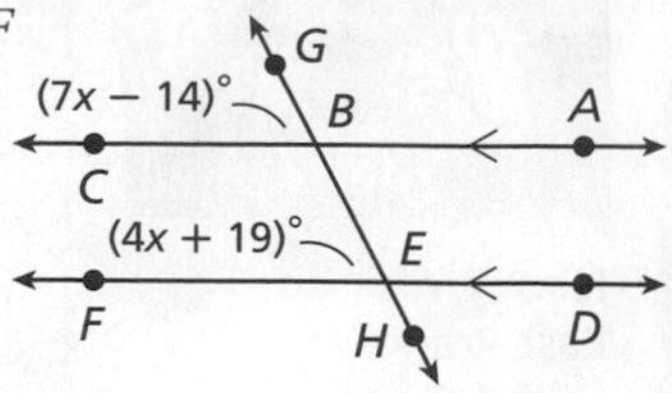

SEE EXAMPLE 2

3. $m\angle 1$

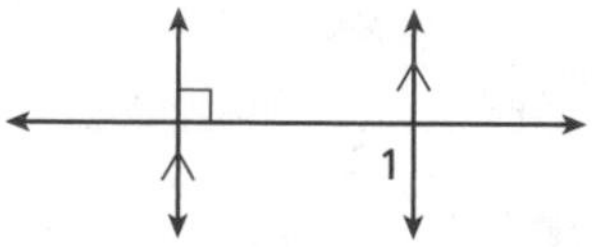

4. $m\angle CBY$

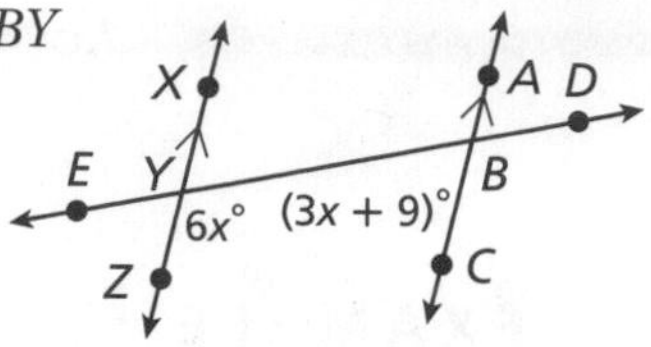

SEE EXAMPLE 3

5. Safety The railing of a wheelchair ramp is parallel to the ramp. Find x and y in the diagram.

PRACTICE AND PROBLEM SOLVING

Independent Practice	
For Exercises	See Example
6–7	1
8–11	2
12	3

Extra Practice
See Extra Practice for more Skills Practice and Applications Practice exercises.

Find each angle measure.

6. $m\angle KLM$

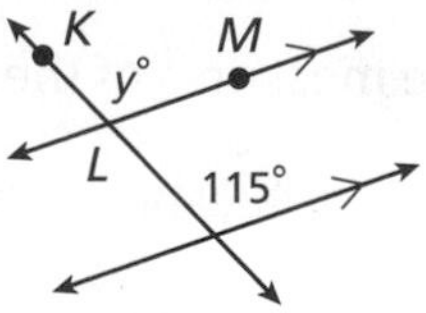

7. $m\angle VYX$

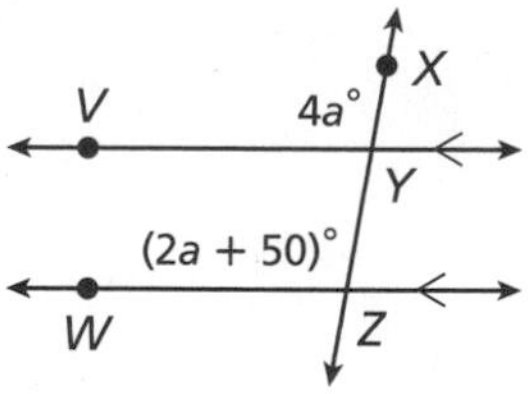

8. $m\angle ABC$

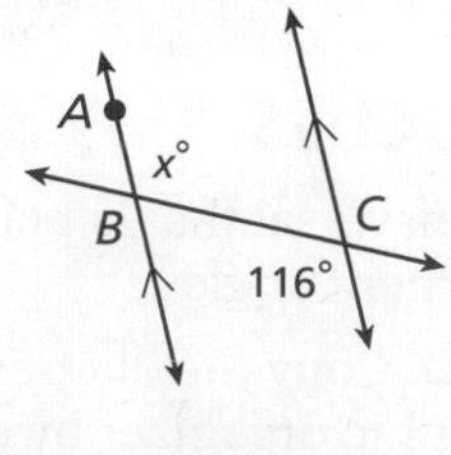

9. $m\angle EFG$

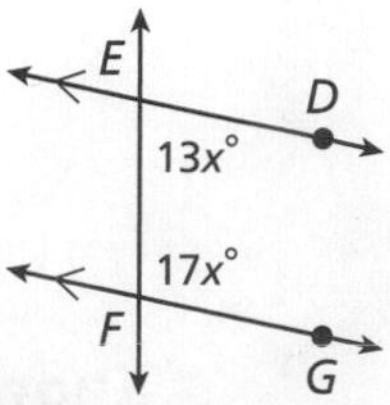

10. $m\angle PQR$

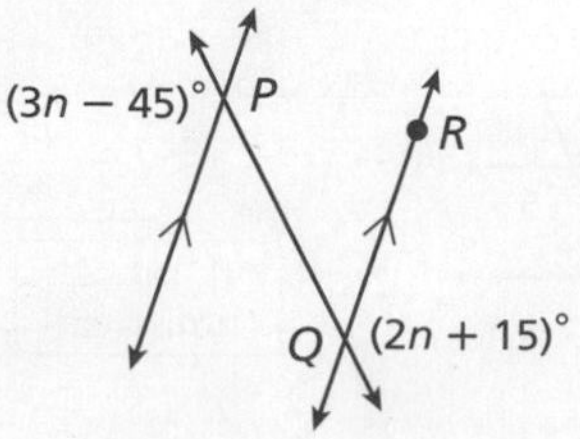

11. $m\angle STU$

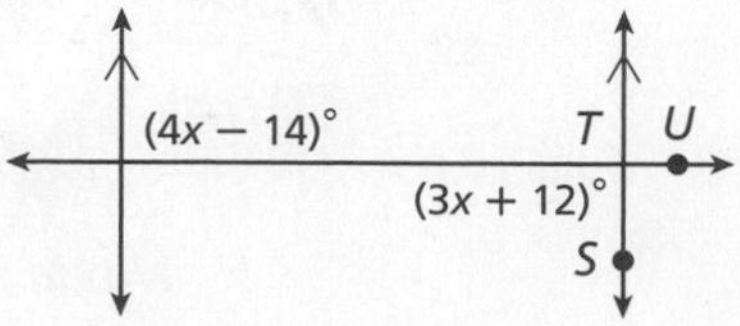

12. **Parking** In the parking lot shown, the lines that mark the width of each space are parallel.
$m\angle 1 = (2x - 3y)^\circ$
$m\angle 2 = (x + 3y)^\circ$
Find x and y.

Find each angle measure. Justify each answer with a postulate or theorem.

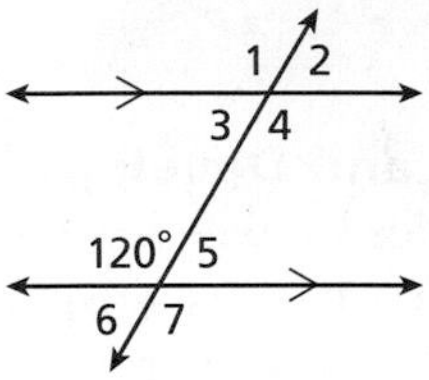

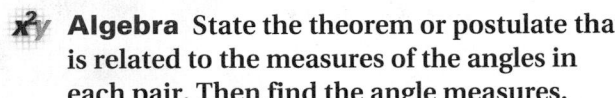

13. $m\angle 1$
14. $m\angle 2$
15. $m\angle 3$
16. $m\angle 4$
17. $m\angle 5$
18. $m\angle 6$
19. $m\angle 7$

Algebra State the theorem or postulate that is related to the measures of the angles in each pair. Then find the angle measures.

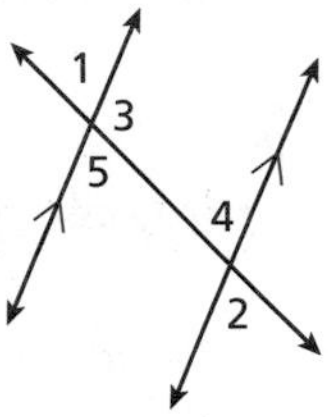

20. $m\angle 1 = (7x + 15)^\circ$, $m\angle 2 = (10x - 9)^\circ$
21. $m\angle 3 = (23x + 11)^\circ$, $m\angle 4 = (14x + 21)^\circ$
22. $m\angle 4 = (37x - 15)^\circ$, $m\angle 5 = (44x - 29)^\circ$
23. $m\angle 1 = (6x + 24)^\circ$, $m\angle 4 = (17x - 9)^\circ$

LINK

Architecture

The Luxor hotel is 600 feet wide, 600 feet long, and 350 feet high. The atrium in the hotel measures 29 million cubic feet.

24. **Architecture** The Luxor Hotel in Las Vegas, Nevada, is a 30-story pyramid. The hotel uses an elevator called an inclinator to take people up the side of the pyramid. The inclinator travels at a 39° angle. Which theorem or postulate best illustrates the angles formed by the path of the inclinator and each parallel floor? (*Hint:* Draw a picture.)

25. **Complete the two-column proof of the Alternate Exterior Angles Theorem.**
Given: $\ell \parallel m$
Prove: $\angle 1 \cong \angle 2$
Proof:

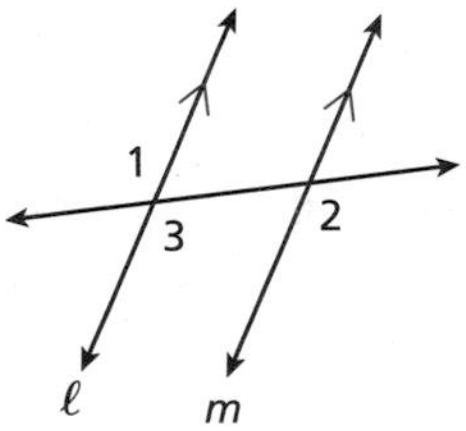

Statements	Reasons
1. $\ell \parallel m$	1. Given
2. a. ___?___	2. Vert. ∠s Thm.
3. $\angle 3 \cong \angle 2$	3. b. ___?___
4. c. ___?___	4. d. ___?___

26. **Write a paragraph proof of the Same-Side Interior Angles Theorem.**
Given: $r \parallel s$
Prove: $m\angle 1 + m\angle 2 = 180°$

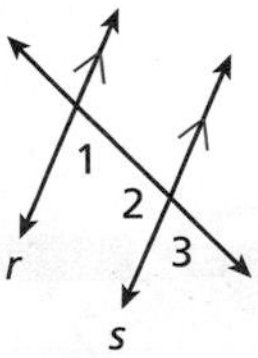

Draw the given situation or tell why it is impossible.

27. Two parallel lines are intersected by a transversal so that the corresponding angles are supplementary.

28. Two parallel lines are intersected by a transversal so that the same-side interior angles are complementary.

MULTI-STEP TEST PREP

29. In the diagram, which represents the side view of a mystery spot, $m\angle SRT = 25°$. $\overleftrightarrow{RT}$ is a transversal to $\overleftrightarrow{PS}$ and $\overleftrightarrow{QR}$.

a. What type of angle pair is $\angle QRT$ and $\angle STR$?

b. Find $m\angle STR$. Use a theorem or postulate to justify your answer.

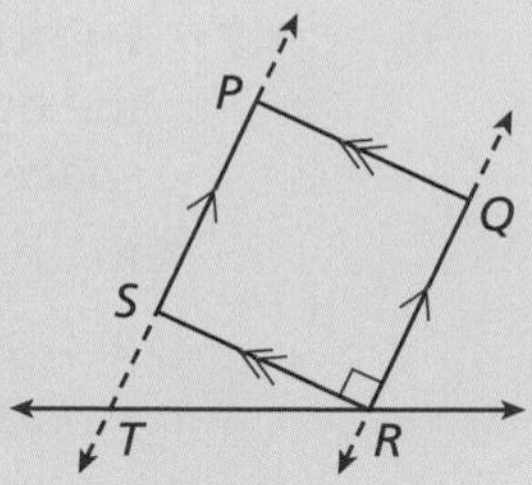

30. Land Development A piece of property lies between two parallel streets as shown. $m\angle 1 = (2x + 6)°$, and $m\angle 2 = (3x + 9)°$. What is the relationship between the angles? What are their measures?

31. ERROR ANALYSIS In the figure, $m\angle ABC = (15x + 5)°$, and $m\angle BCD = (10x + 25)°$. Which value of $m\angle BCD$ is incorrect? Explain.

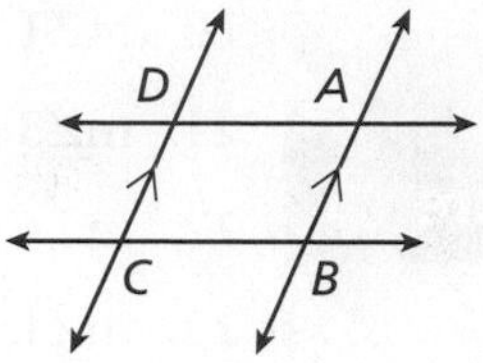

(A)

$$\begin{aligned} 15x + 5 &= 10x + 25 \\ -10x \quad &\quad -10x \\ 5x + 5 &= 25 \\ -5 \quad &\quad -5 \\ 5x &= 20 \\ x &= 4 \end{aligned}$$

$m\angle BCD = 10(4) + 25 = 65°$

(B)

$$\begin{aligned} (15x + 5) + (10x + 25) &= 180 \\ 25x + 30 &= 180 \\ -30 \quad &\quad -30 \\ 25x &= 150 \\ x &= 6 \end{aligned}$$

$m\angle BCD = 10(6) + 25 = 85°$

32. Critical Thinking In the diagram, $\ell \parallel m$. Explain why $\frac{x}{y} = 1$.

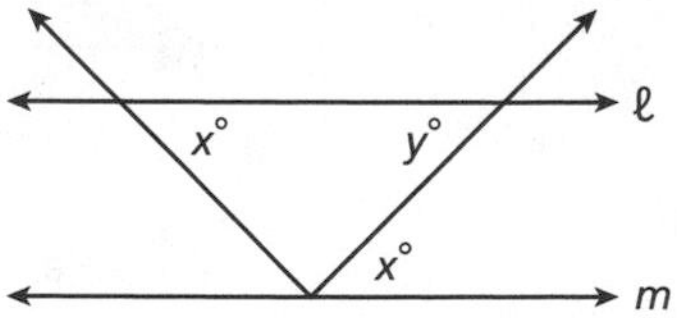

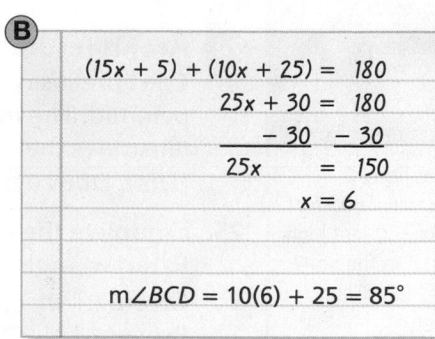

33. Write About It Suppose that lines ℓ and m are intersected by transversal p. One of the angles formed by ℓ and p is congruent to every angle formed by m and p. Draw a diagram showing lines ℓ, m, and p, mark any congruent angles that are formed, and explain what you know is true.

TEST PREP

34. $m\angle RST = (x + 50)°$, and $m\angle STU = (3x + 20)°$. Find $m\angle RVT$.

Ⓐ 15° Ⓒ 65°

Ⓑ 27.5° Ⓓ 77.5°

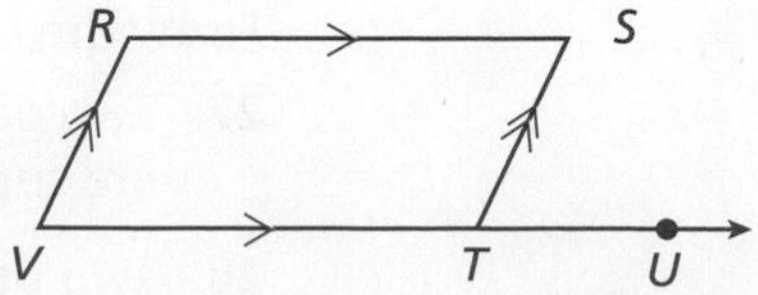

35. For two parallel lines and a transversal, m∠1 = 83°. For which pair of angle measures is the sum the least?

Ⓕ ∠1 and a corresponding angle

Ⓖ ∠1 and a same-side interior angle

Ⓗ ∠1 and its supplement

Ⓙ ∠1 and its complement

36. Short Response Given $a \parallel b$ with transversal t, explain why ∠1 and ∠3 are supplementary.

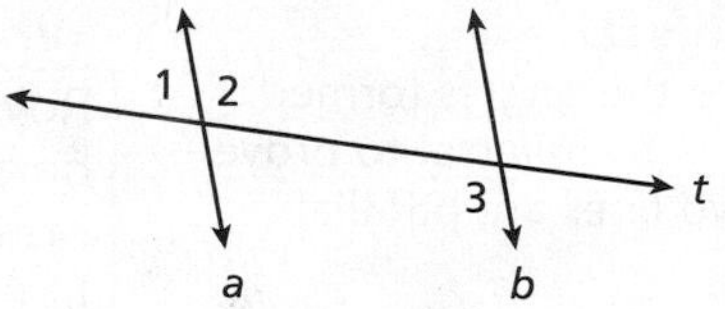

CHALLENGE AND EXTEND

Multi-Step Find m∠1 in each diagram. (*Hint:* Draw a line parallel to the given parallel lines.)

37.

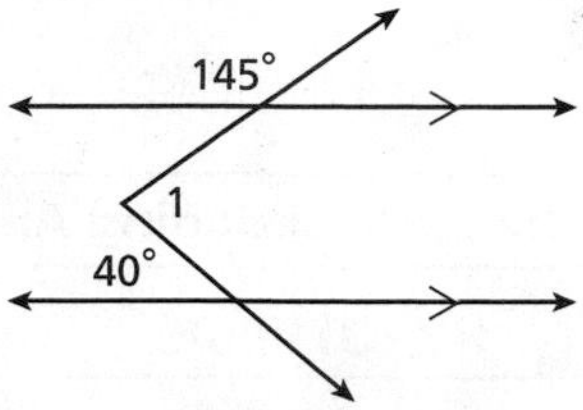

38.

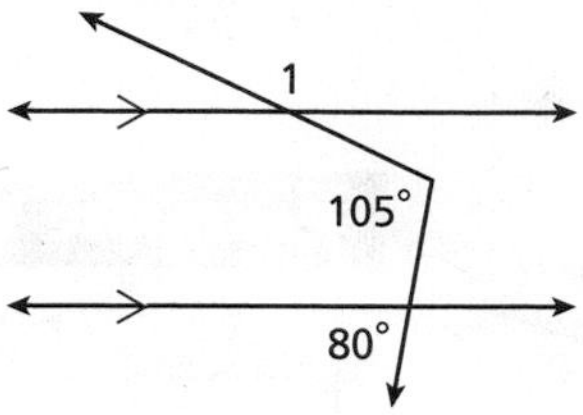

39. Find x and y in the diagram. Justify your answer.

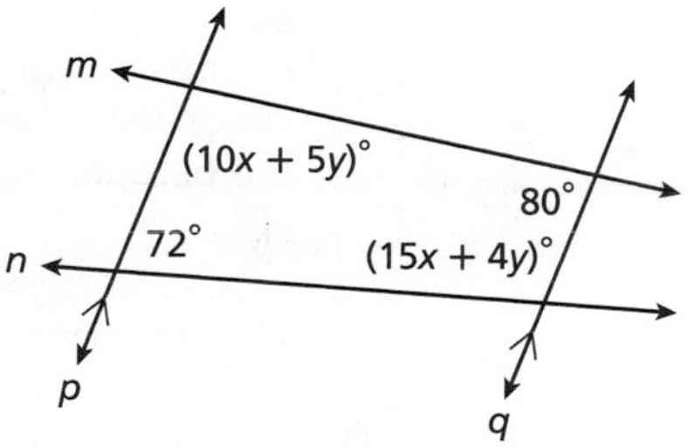

40. Two lines are parallel. The measures of two corresponding angles are $a°$ and $2b°$, and the measures of two same-side interior angles are $a°$ and $b°$. Find the value of a.

COMMON CORE

3-3 Proving Lines Parallel

CC.9-12.G.CO.9 Prove geometric theorems about lines and angles. *Also* **CC.9-12.G.CO.12**

Objective
Use the angles formed by a transversal to prove two lines are parallel.

Who uses this?
Rowers have to keep the oars on each side parallel in order to travel in a straight line. (See Example 4.)

Recall that the converse of a theorem is found by exchanging the hypothesis and conclusion. The converse of a theorem is not automatically true. If it is true, it must be stated as a postulate or proved as a separate theorem.

Know it! Note

Postulate 3-3-1 Converse of the Corresponding Angles Postulate

POSTULATE	HYPOTHESIS	CONCLUSION
If two coplanar lines are cut by a transversal so that a pair of corresponding angles are congruent, then the two lines are parallel.	$\angle 1 \cong \angle 2$ 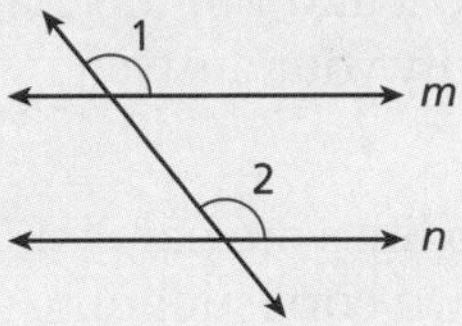	$m \parallel n$

EXAMPLE 1 Using the Converse of the Corresponding Angles Postulate

Use the Converse of the Corresponding Angles Postulate and the given information to show that $\ell \parallel m$.

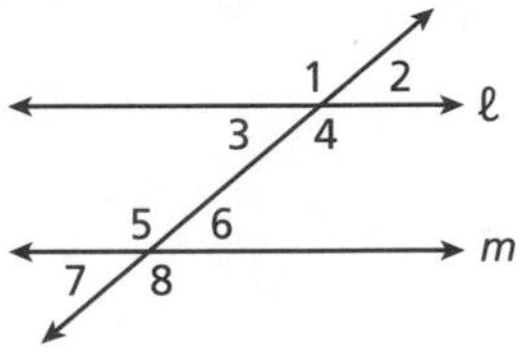

A $\angle 1 \cong \angle 5$

$\angle 1 \cong \angle 5$ — *∠1 and ∠5 are corresponding angles.*

$\ell \parallel m$ — *Conv. of Corr. ∠s Post.*

Algebra

B $m\angle 4 = (2x + 10)°$, $m\angle 8 = (3x - 55)°$, $x = 65$

$m\angle 4 = 2(65) + 10 = 140$ — *Substitute 65 for x.*

$m\angle 8 = 3(65) - 55 = 140$ — *Substitute 65 for x.*

$m\angle 4 = m\angle 8$ — *Trans. Prop. of Equality*

$\angle 4 \cong \angle 8$ — *Def. of ≅ ∠s*

$\ell \parallel m$ — *Conv. of Corr. ∠s Post.*

CHECK IT OUT!

Use the Converse of the Corresponding Angles Postulate and the given information to show that $\ell \parallel m$.

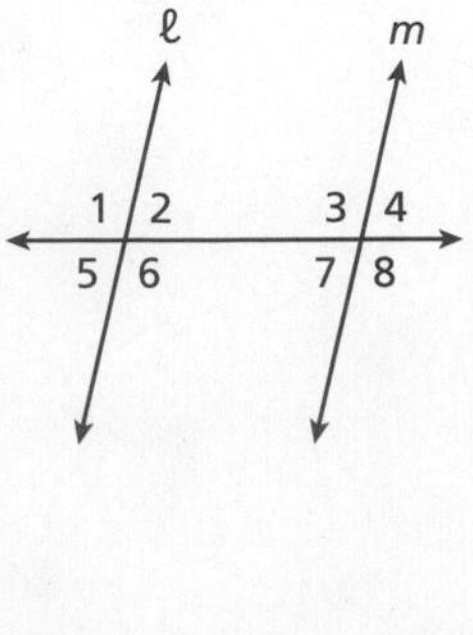

1a. $m\angle 1 = m\angle 3$

1b. $m\angle 7 = (4x + 25)°$, $m\angle 5 = (5x + 12)°$, $x = 13$

Ken Hawkins/Mira.com

Postulate 3-3-2 Parallel Postulate

Through a point P not on line ℓ, there is exactly one line parallel to ℓ.

The Converse of the Corresponding Angles Postulate is used to construct parallel lines. The Parallel Postulate guarantees that for any line ℓ, you can always construct a parallel line through a point that is not on ℓ.

Construction Parallel Lines

1. Draw a line ℓ and a point P that is not on ℓ.

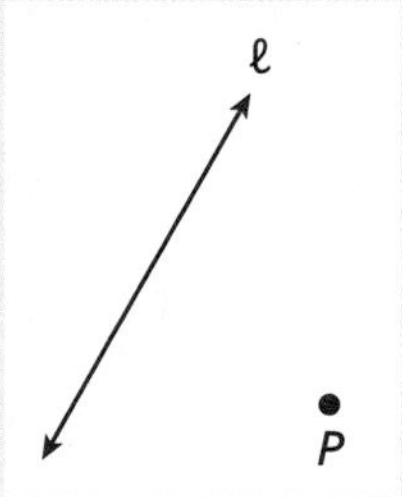

2. Draw a line m through P that intersects ℓ. Label the angle 1.

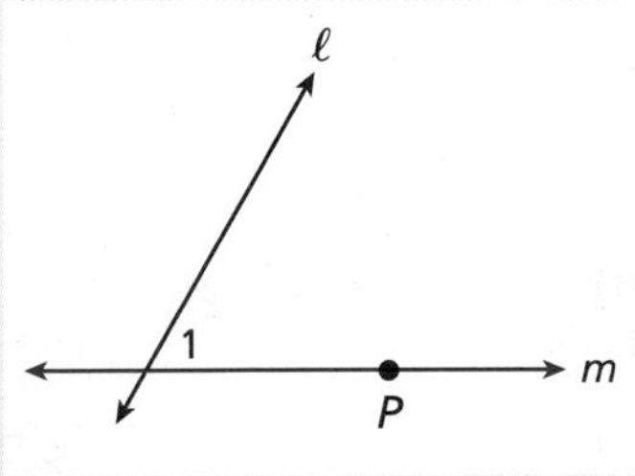

3. Construct an angle congruent to $\angle 1$ at P. By the converse of the Corresponding Angles Postulate, $\ell \parallel n$.

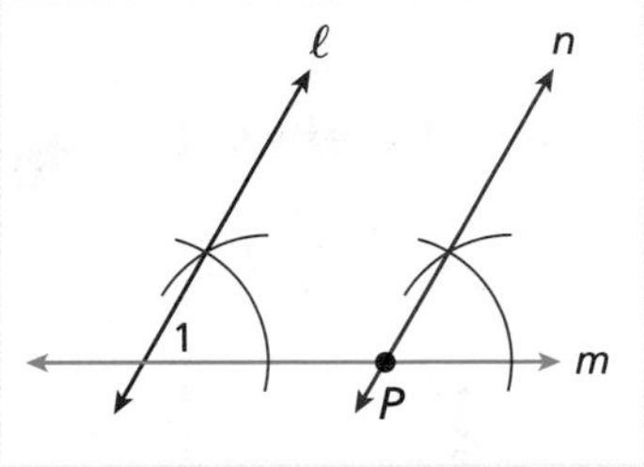

Theorems Proving Lines Parallel

THEOREM	HYPOTHESIS	CONCLUSION
3-3-3 **Converse of the Alternate Interior Angles Theorem** If two coplanar lines are cut by a transversal so that a pair of alternate interior angles are congruent, then the two lines are parallel.	$\angle 1 \cong \angle 2$ 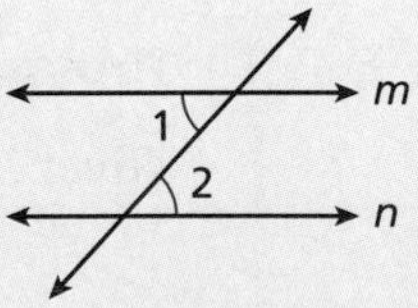	$m \parallel n$
3-3-4 **Converse of the Alternate Exterior Angles Theorem** If two coplanar lines are cut by a transversal so that a pair of alternate exterior angles are congruent, then the two lines are parallel.	$\angle 3 \cong \angle 4$ 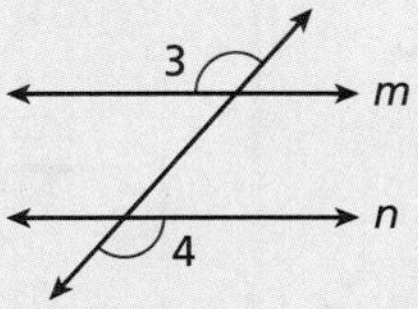	$m \parallel n$
3-3-5 **Converse of the Same-Side Interior Angles Theorem** If two coplanar lines are cut by a transversal so that a pair of same-side interior angles are supplementary, then the two lines are parallel.	$m\angle 5 + m\angle 6 = 180°$ 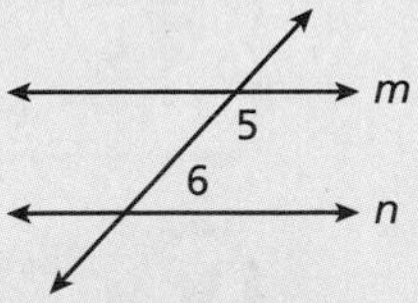	$m \parallel n$

You will prove Theorems 3-3-3 and 3-3-5 in Exercises 38–39.

PROOF **Converse of the Alternate Exterior Angles Theorem**

Given: $\angle 1 \cong \angle 2$
Prove: $\ell \parallel m$
Proof: It is given that $\angle 1 \cong \angle 2$. Vertical angles are congruent, so $\angle 1 \cong \angle 3$. By the Transitive Property of Congruence, $\angle 2 \cong \angle 3$. So $\ell \parallel m$ by the Converse of the Corresponding Angles Postulate.

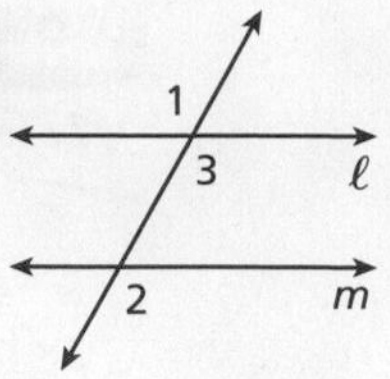

EXAMPLE 2 Determining Whether Lines are Parallel

Use the given information and the theorems you have learned to show that $r \parallel s$.

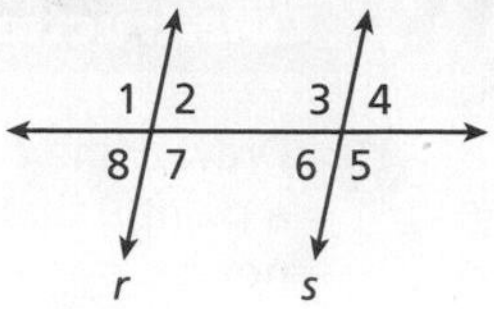

A $\angle 2 \cong \angle 6$

$\angle 2 \cong \angle 6$ — *$\angle 2$ and $\angle 6$ are alternate interior angles.*

$r \parallel s$ — *Conv. of Alt. Int. $\angle$s Thm.*

x^2y **Algebra**

B $m\angle 6 = (6x + 18)°$, $m\angle 7 = (9x + 12)°$, $x = 10$

$m\angle 6 = 6x + 18$

$= 6(10) + 18 = 78°$ — *Substitute 10 for x.*

$m\angle 7 = 9x + 12$

$= 9(10) + 12 = 102°$ — *Substitute 10 for x.*

$m\angle 6 + m\angle 7 = 78° + 102°$

$= 180°$ — *$\angle 6$ and $\angle 7$ are same-side interior angles.*

$r \parallel s$ — *Conv. of Same-Side Int. $\angle$s Thm.*

CHECK IT OUT! **Refer to the diagram above. Use the given information and the theorems you have learned to show that $r \parallel s$.**

2a. $m\angle 4 = m\angle 8$ **2b.** $m\angle 3 = 2x°$, $m\angle 7 = (x + 50)°$, $x = 50$

EXAMPLE 3 Proving Lines Parallel

Given: $\ell \parallel m$, $\angle 1 \cong \angle 3$
Prove: $r \parallel p$

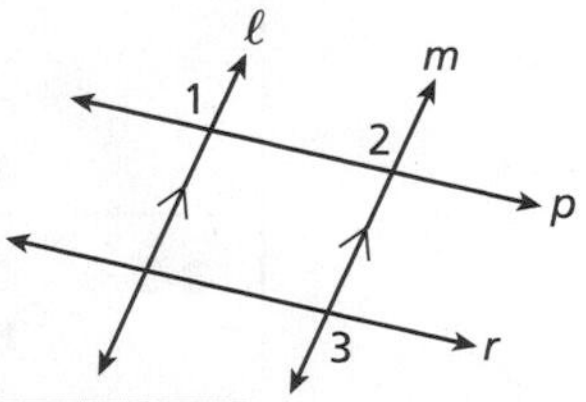

Proof:

Statements	Reasons
1. $\ell \parallel m$	**1.** Given
2. $\angle 1 \cong \angle 2$	**2.** Corr. $\angle$s Post.
3. $\angle 1 \cong \angle 3$	**3.** Given
4. $\angle 2 \cong \angle 3$	**4.** Trans. Prop. of $\cong$
5. $r \parallel p$	**5.** Conv. of Alt. Ext. $\angle$s Thm.

CHECK IT OUT! **3. Given:** $\angle 1 \cong \angle 4$, $\angle 3$ and $\angle 4$ are supplementary.
Prove: $\ell \parallel m$

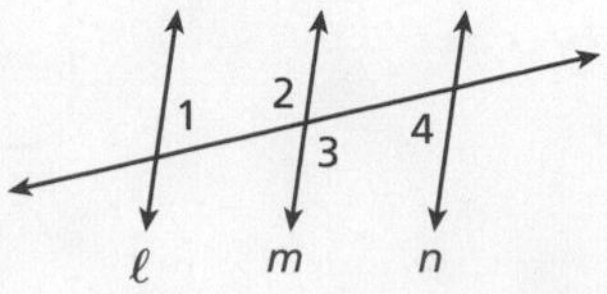

EXAMPLE 4 *Sports Application*

During a race, all members of a rowing team should keep the oars parallel on each side. If m∠1 = $(3x + 13)°$, m∠2 = $(5x - 5)°$, and $x = 9$, show that the oars are parallel.

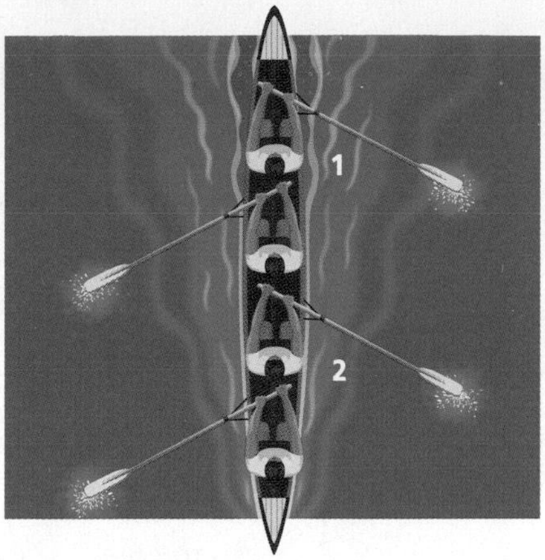

A line through the center of the boat forms a transversal to the two oars on each side of the boat.

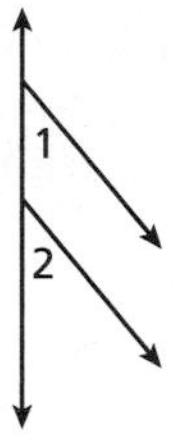

∠1 and ∠2 are corresponding angles.
If ∠1 ≅ ∠2, then the oars are parallel.

Substitute 9 for x in each expression:

m∠1 = $3x + 13$
$= 3(9) + 13 = 40°$ *Substitute 9 for x in each expression.*
m∠2 = $5x - 5$
$= 5(9) - 5 = 40°$ *m∠1 = m∠2, so ∠1 ≅ ∠2.*

The corresponding angles are congruent, so the oars are parallel by the Converse of the Corresponding Angles Postulate.

CHECK IT OUT!

4. **What if...?** Suppose the corresponding angles on the opposite side of the boat measure $(4y - 2)°$ and $(3y + 6)°$, where $y = 8$. Show that the oars are parallel.

THINK AND DISCUSS

MATHEMATICAL PRACTICES

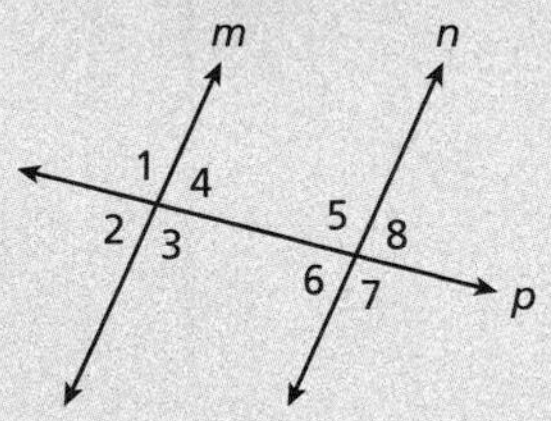

1. Explain three ways of proving that two lines are parallel.

2. If you know m∠1, how could you use the measures of ∠5, ∠6, ∠7, or ∠8 to prove $m \parallel n$?

Know it! Note

3. **GET ORGANIZED** Copy and complete the graphic organizer. Use it to compare the Corresponding Angles Postulate with the Converse of the Corresponding Angles Postulate.

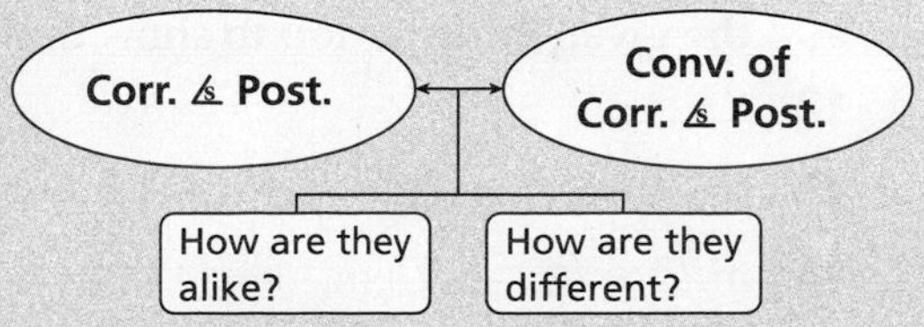

3-3 Exercises

Learn It Online
Homework Help Online
Parent Resources Online

GUIDED PRACTICE

SEE EXAMPLE 1

Use the Converse of the Corresponding Angles Postulate and the given information to show that $p \parallel q$.

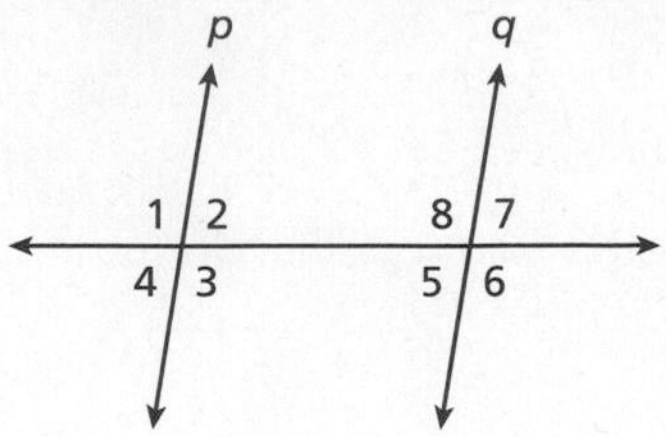

1. $\angle 4 \cong \angle 5$
2. $m\angle 1 = (4x + 16)^\circ$, $m\angle 8 = (5x - 12)^\circ$, $x = 28$
3. $m\angle 4 = (6x - 19)^\circ$, $m\angle 5 = (3x + 14)^\circ$, $x = 11$

SEE EXAMPLE 2

Use the theorems and given information to show that $r \parallel s$.

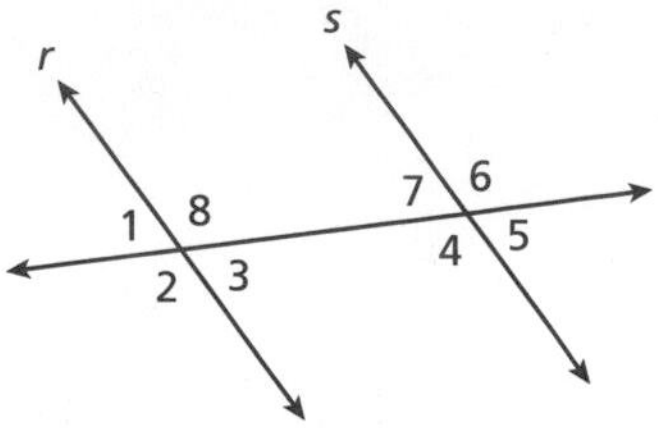

4. $\angle 1 \cong \angle 5$
5. $m\angle 3 + m\angle 4 = 180^\circ$
6. $\angle 3 \cong \angle 7$
7. $m\angle 4 = (13x - 4)^\circ$, $m\angle 8 = (9x + 16)^\circ$, $x = 5$
8. $m\angle 8 = (17x + 37)^\circ$, $m\angle 7 = (9x - 13)^\circ$, $x = 6$
9. $m\angle 2 = (25x + 7)^\circ$, $m\angle 6 = (24x + 12)^\circ$, $x = 5$

SEE EXAMPLE 3

10. Complete the following two-column proof.

Given: $\angle 1 \cong \angle 2$, $\angle 3 \cong \angle 1$
Prove: $\overline{XY} \parallel \overline{WV}$

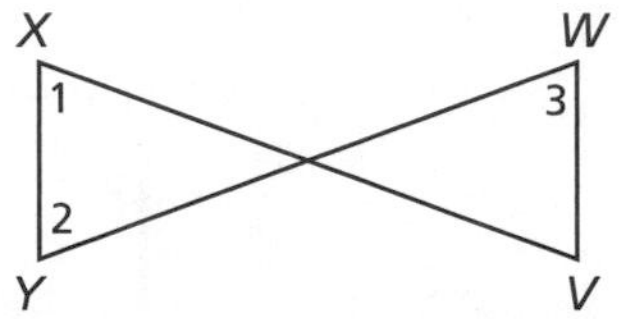

Proof:

Statements	Reasons
1. $\angle 1 \cong \angle 2$, $\angle 3 \cong \angle 1$	**1.** Given
2. $\angle 2 \cong \angle 3$	**2. a.** ___?___
3. b. ___?___	**3. c.** ___?___

SEE EXAMPLE 4

11. **Architecture** In the fire escape, $m\angle 1 = (17x + 9)^\circ$, $m\angle 2 = (14x + 18)^\circ$, and $x = 3$. Show that the two landings are parallel.

PRACTICE AND PROBLEM SOLVING

Use the Converse of the Corresponding Angles Postulate and the given information to show that $\ell \parallel m$.

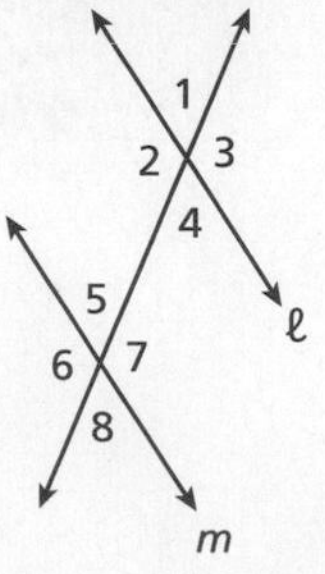

12. $\angle 3 \cong \angle 7$
13. $m\angle 4 = 54^\circ$, $m\angle 8 = (7x + 5)^\circ$, $x = 7$
14. $m\angle 2 = (8x + 4)^\circ$, $m\angle 6 = (11x - 41)^\circ$, $x = 15$
15. $m\angle 1 = (3x + 19)^\circ$, $m\angle 5 = (4x + 7)^\circ$, $x = 12$

Independent Practice

For Exercises	See Example
12–15	1
16–21	2
22	3
23	4

Extra Practice

See Extra Practice for more Skills Practice and Applications Practice exercises.

Use the theorems and given information to show that $n \parallel p$.

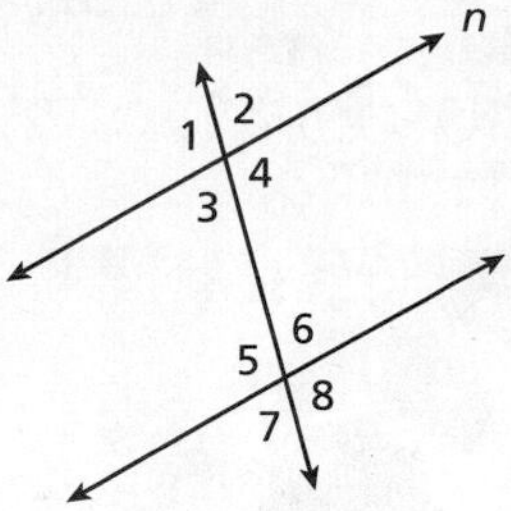

16. $\angle 3 \cong \angle 6$

17. $\angle 2 \cong \angle 7$

18. $m\angle 4 + m\angle 6 = 180°$

19. $m\angle 1 = (8x - 7)°$, $m\angle 8 = (6x + 21)°$, $x = 14$

20. $m\angle 4 = (4x + 3)°$, $m\angle 5 = (5x - 22)°$, $x = 25$

21. $m\angle 3 = (2x + 15)°$, $m\angle 5 = (3x + 15)°$, $x = 30$

22. Complete the following two-column proof.

Given: $\overline{AB} \parallel \overline{CD}$, $\angle 1 \cong \angle 2$, $\angle 3 \cong \angle 4$
Prove: $\overline{BC} \parallel \overline{DE}$

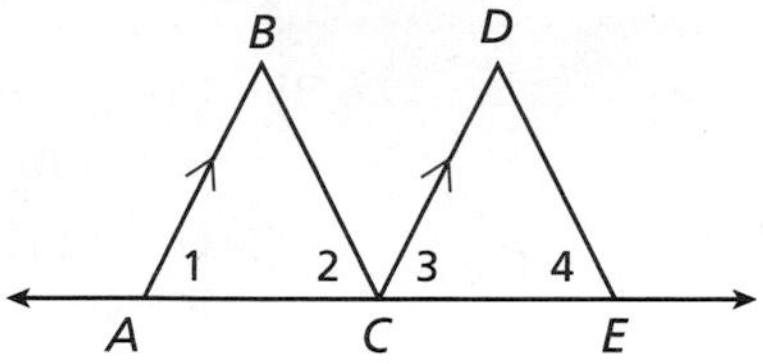

Proof:

Statements	Reasons
1. $\overline{AB} \parallel \overline{CD}$	1. Given
2. $\angle 1 \cong \angle 3$	2. a. ___?___
3. $\angle 1 \cong \angle 2$, $\angle 3 \cong \angle 4$	3. b. ___?___
4. $\angle 2 \cong \angle 4$	4. c. ___?___
5. d. ___?___	5. e. ___?___

23. Art Edmund Dulac used perspective when drawing the floor titles in an illustration for *The Wind's Tale* by Hans Christian Andersen. Show that $\overline{DJ} \parallel \overline{EK}$ if $m\angle 1 = (3x + 2)°$, $m\angle 2 = (5x - 10)°$, and $x = 6$.

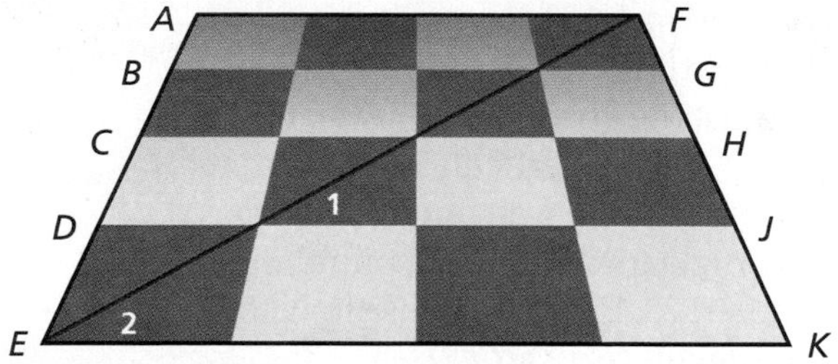

Name the postulate or theorem that proves that $\ell \parallel m$.

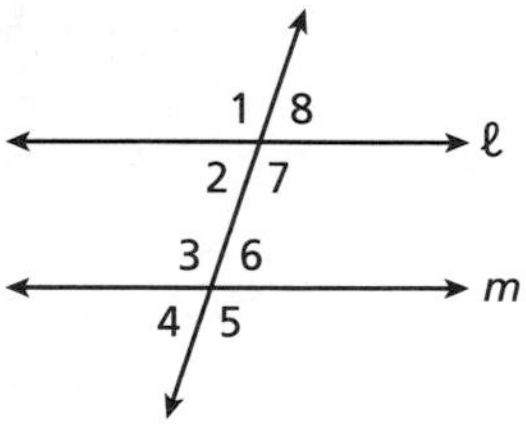

24. $\angle 8 \cong \angle 6$

25. $\angle 8 \cong \angle 4$

26. $\angle 2 \cong \angle 6$

27. $\angle 7 \cong \angle 5$

28. $\angle 3 \cong \angle 7$

29. $m\angle 2 + m\angle 3 = 180°$

For the given information, tell which pair of lines must be parallel. Name the postulate or theorem that supports your answer.

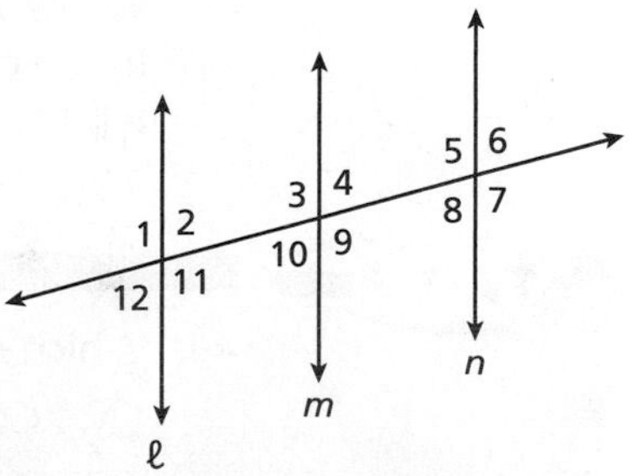

30. $m\angle 2 = m\angle 10$

31. $m\angle 8 + m\angle 9 = 180°$

32. $\angle 1 \cong \angle 7$

33. $m\angle 10 = m\angle 6$

34. $\angle 11 \cong \angle 5$

35. $m\angle 2 + m\angle 5 = 180°$

36. Multi-Step Two lines are intersected by a transversal so that $\angle 1$ and $\angle 2$ are corresponding angles, $\angle 1$ and $\angle 3$ are alternate exterior angles, and $\angle 3$ and $\angle 4$ are corresponding angles. If $\angle 2 \cong \angle 4$, what theorem or postulate can be used to prove the lines parallel?

MULTI-STEP TEST PREP

37. In the diagram, which represents the side view of a mystery spot, m∠*SRT* = 25°, and m∠*SUR* = 65°.

a. Name a same-side interior angle of ∠*SUR* for lines $\overleftrightarrow{SU}$ and $\overleftrightarrow{RT}$ with transversal $\overline{RU}$. What is its measure? Explain your reasoning.

b. Prove that $\overleftrightarrow{SU}$ and $\overleftrightarrow{RT}$ are parallel.

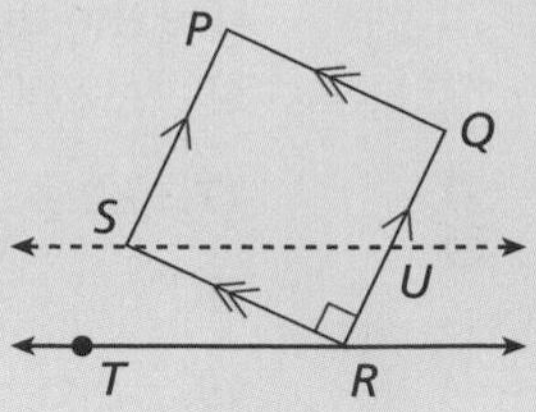

38. Complete the flowchart proof of the Converse of the Alternate Interior Angles Theorem.

Given: ∠2 ≅ ∠3

Prove: ℓ ∥ *m*

Proof:

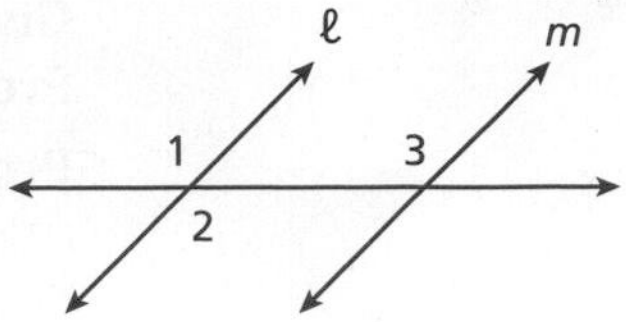

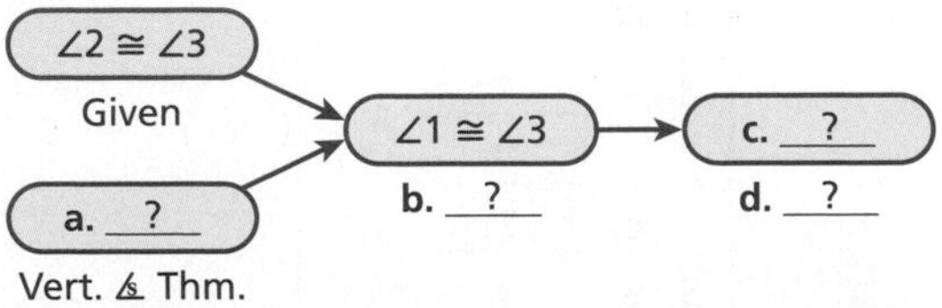

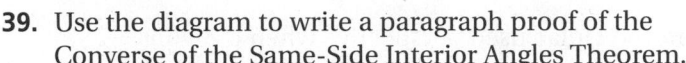

39. Use the diagram to write a paragraph proof of the Converse of the Same-Side Interior Angles Theorem.

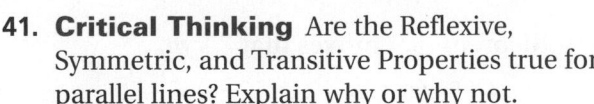

Given: ∠1 and ∠2 are supplementary.

Prove: ℓ ∥ *m*

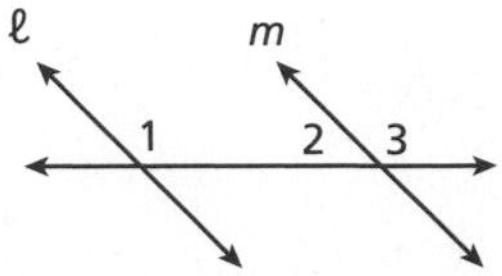

40. Carpentry A *plumb bob* is a weight hung at the end of a string, called a *plumb line*. The weight pulls the string down so that the plumb line is perfectly vertical. Suppose that the angle formed by the wall and the roof is 123° and the angle formed by the plumb line and the roof is 123°. How does this show that the wall is perfectly vertical?

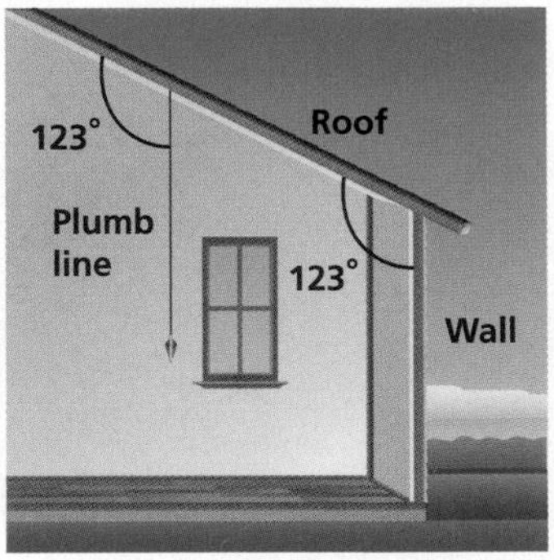

41. Critical Thinking Are the Reflexive, Symmetric, and Transitive Properties true for parallel lines? Explain why or why not.

Reflexive: ℓ ∥ ℓ

Symmetric: If ℓ ∥ *m*, then *m* ∥ ℓ.

Transitive: If ℓ ∥ *m* and *m* ∥ *n*, then ℓ ∥ *n*.

42. Write About It Does the information given in the diagram allow you to conclude that *a* ∥ *b*? Explain.

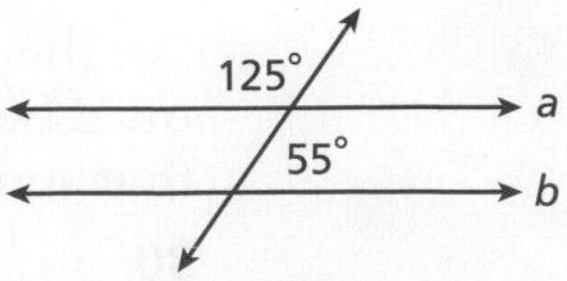

TEST PREP

43. Which postulate or theorem can be used to prove ℓ ∥ *m*?

Ⓐ Converse of the Corresponding Angles Postulate

Ⓑ Converse of the Alternate Interior Angles Theorem

Ⓒ Converse of the Alternate Exterior Angles Theorem

Ⓓ Converse of the Same-Side Interior Angles Theorem

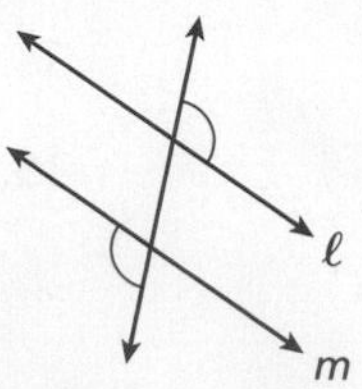

Rick Davis/Darkhouse and Fun Enthusiast

44. Two coplanar lines are cut by a transversal. Which condition does NOT guarantee that the two lines are parallel?

Ⓐ A pair of alternate interior angles are congruent.

Ⓑ A pair of same-side interior angles are supplementary.

Ⓒ A pair of corresponding angles are congruent.

Ⓓ A pair of alternate exterior angles are complementary.

45. Gridded Response Find the value of x so that $\ell \parallel m$.

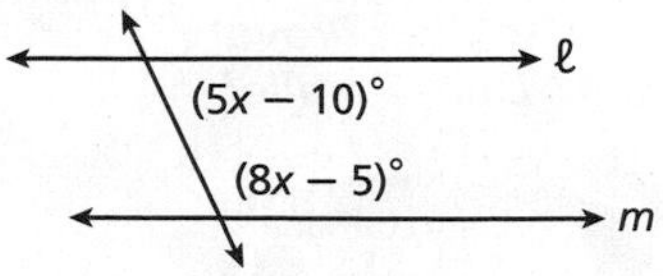

CHALLENGE AND EXTEND

Determine which lines, if any, can be proven parallel using the given information. Justify your answers.

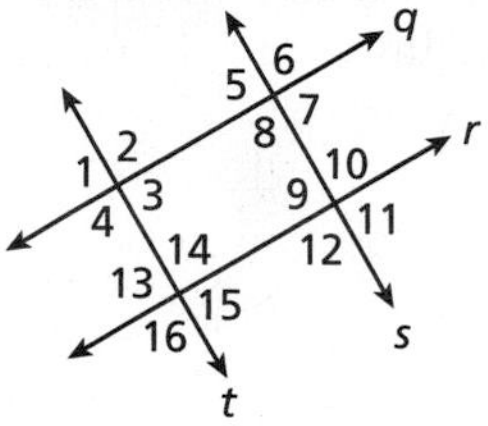

46. $\angle 1 \cong \angle 15$

47. $\angle 8 \cong \angle 14$

48. $\angle 3 \cong \angle 7$

49. $\angle 8 \cong \angle 10$

50. $\angle 6 \cong \angle 8$

51. $\angle 13 \cong \angle 11$

52. $m\angle 12 + m\angle 15 = 180°$

53. $m\angle 5 + m\angle 8 = 180°$

54. Write a paragraph proof that $\overline{AE} \parallel \overline{BD}$.

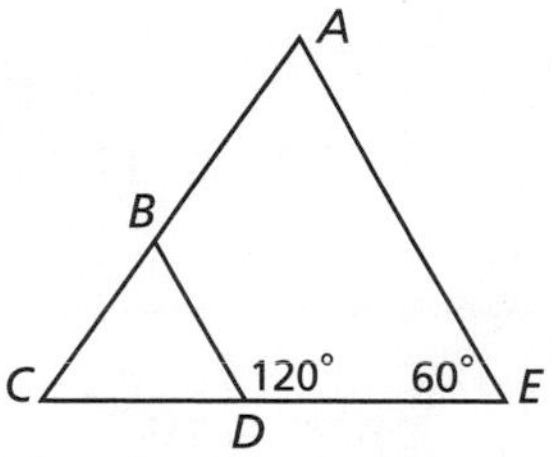

Use the diagram for Exercises 55 and 56.

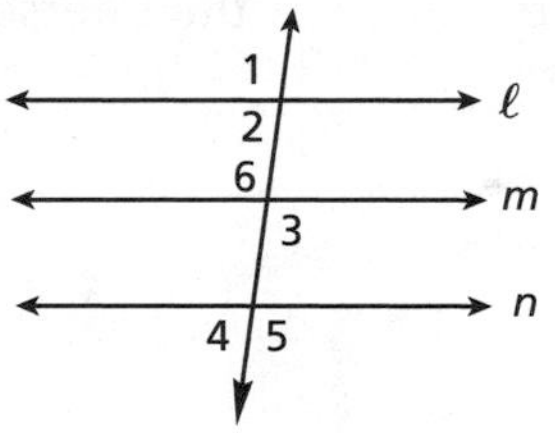

55. Given: $m\angle 2 + m\angle 3 = 180°$
Prove: $\ell \parallel m$

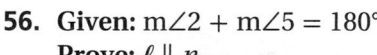

56. Given: $m\angle 2 + m\angle 5 = 180°$
Prove: $\ell \parallel n$

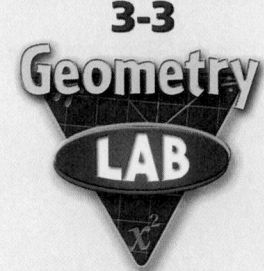

3-3 Geometry LAB

Construct Parallel Lines

Use with Proving Lines Parallel

You have learned one method of constructing parallel lines using a compass and straightedge. Another method, called the rhombus method, uses a property of a figure called a *rhombus*. The rhombus method is shown below.

MATHEMATICAL PRACTICES **Use appropriate tools strategically.**

CC.9-12.G.CO.12 Make formal geometric constructions with a variety of tools and methods…

Activity 1

1. Draw a line ℓ and a point P not on the line.

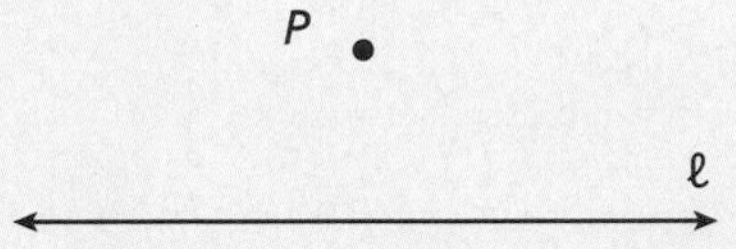

2. Choose a point Q on the line. Place your compass point at Q and draw an arc through P that intersects ℓ. Label the intersection R.

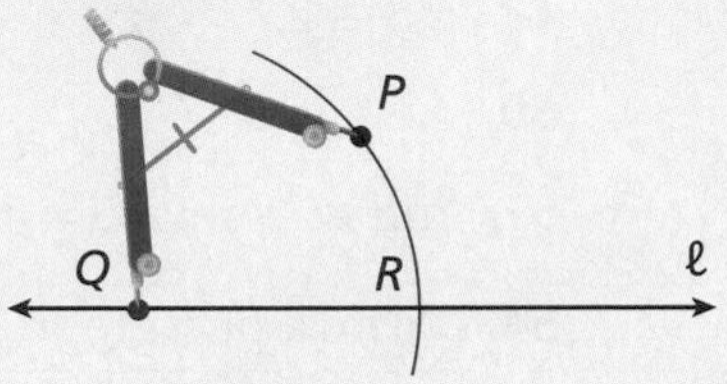

3. Using the same compass setting as the first arc, draw two more arcs: one from P, the other from R. Label the intersection of the two arcs S.

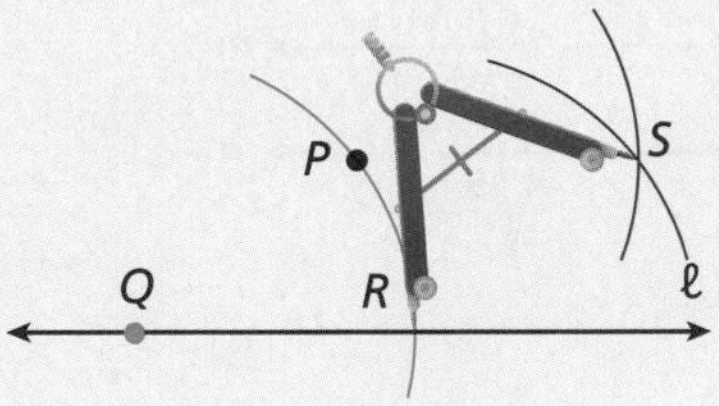

4. Draw $\overleftrightarrow{PS} \parallel \ell$.

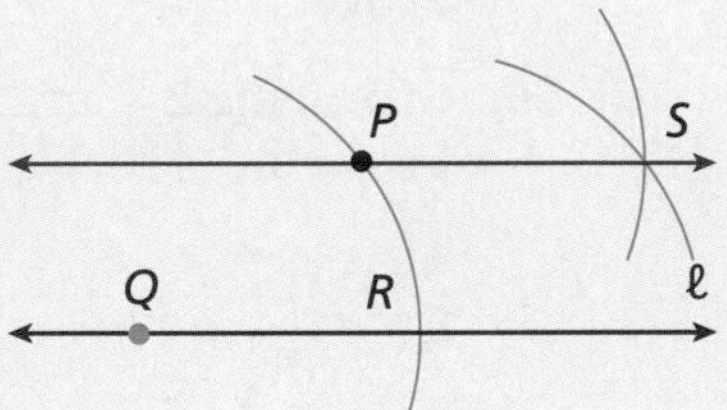

Try This

1. Repeat Activity 1 using a different point not on the line. Are your results the same?
2. Using the lines you constructed in Problem 1, draw transversal $\overleftrightarrow{PQ}$. Verify that the lines are parallel by using a protractor to measure alternate interior angles.
3. What postulate ensures that this construction is always possible?
4. A *rhombus* is a quadrilateral with four congruent sides. Explain why this method is called the rhombus method.

Activity 2

1. Draw a line ℓ and point P on a piece of patty paper.

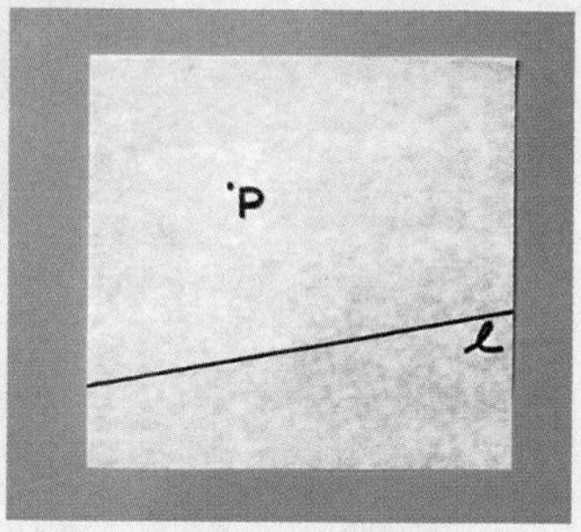

2. Fold the paper through P so that both sides of line ℓ match up

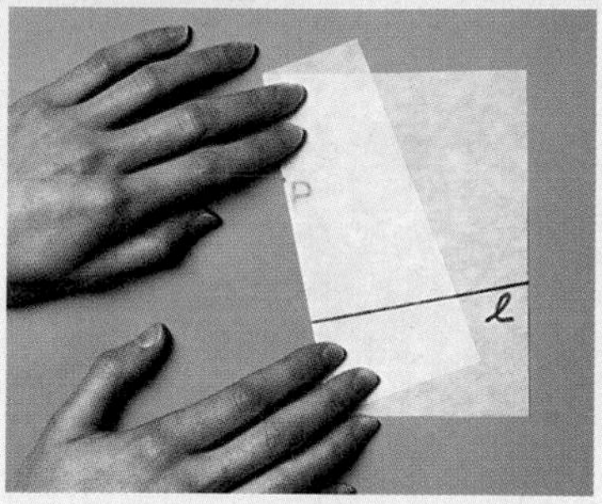

3. Crease the paper to form line m. P should be on line m.

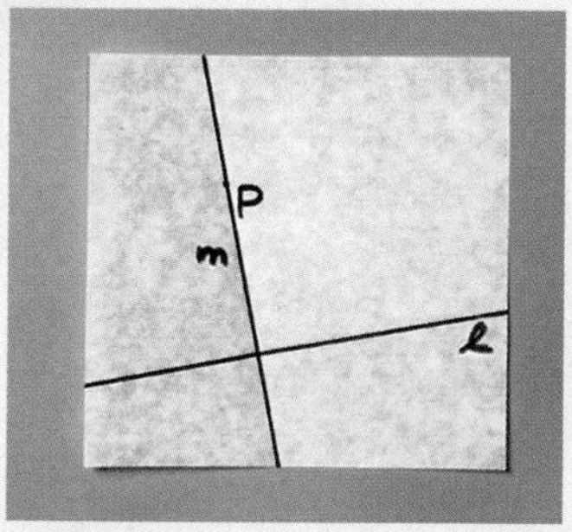

4. Fold the paper again through P so that both sides of line m match up.

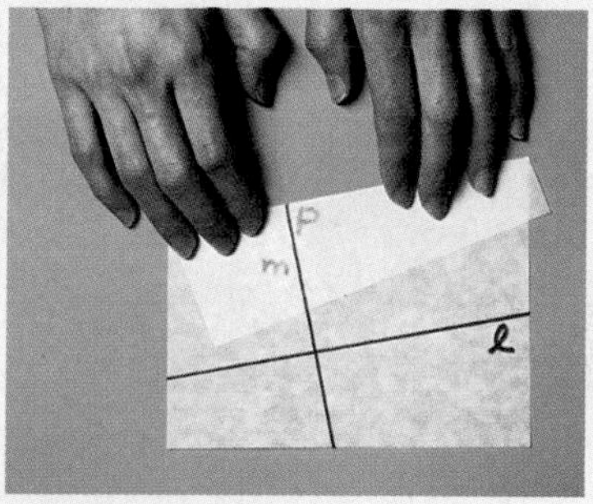

5. Crease the paper to form line n. Line n is parallel to line ℓ through P.

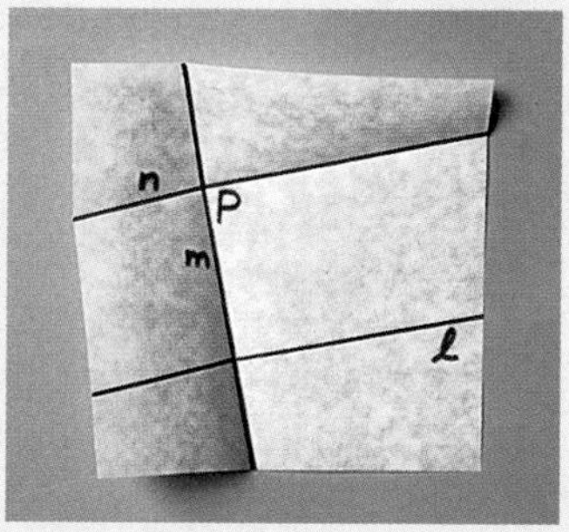

Try This

5. Repeat Activity 2 using a point in a different place not on the line. Are your results the same?
6. Use a protractor to measure corresponding angles. How can you tell that the lines are parallel?
7. Draw a triangle and construct a line parallel to one side through the vertex that is not on that side.
8. Line m is perpendicular to both ℓ and n. Use this statement to complete the following conjecture: If two lines in a plane are perpendicular to the same line, then ____?____ .

COMMON CORE

3-4 Perpendicular Lines

CC.9-12.G.CO.9 Prove geometric theorems about lines and angles. *Also* **CC.9-12.G.CO.12**

Objective
Prove and apply theorems about perpendicular lines.

Vocabulary
perpendicular bisector
distance from a point to a line

Why learn this?
Rip currents are strong currents that flow away from the shoreline and are perpendicular to it. A swimmer who gets caught in a rip current can get swept far out to sea. (See Example 3.)

The **perpendicular bisector** of a segment is a line perpendicular to a segment at the segment's midpoint. A construction of a perpendicular bisector is shown below.

Construction Perpendicular Bisector of a Segment

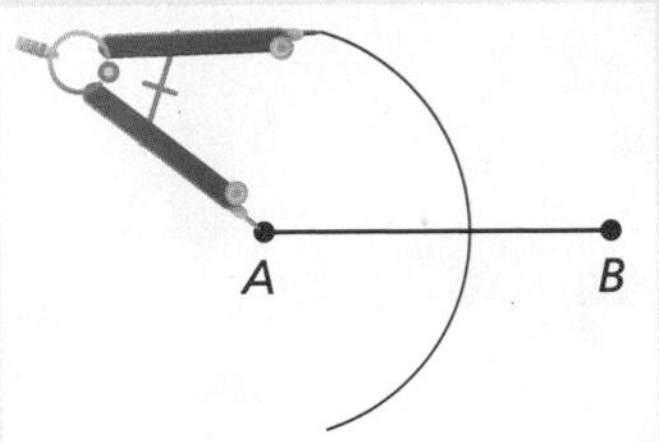

1. Draw $\overline{AB}$. Open the compass wider than half of AB and draw an arc centered at A.

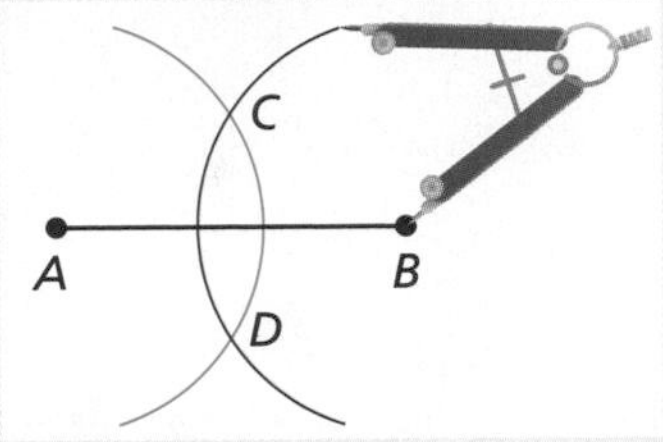

2. Using the same compass setting, draw an arc centered at B that intersects the first arc at C and D.

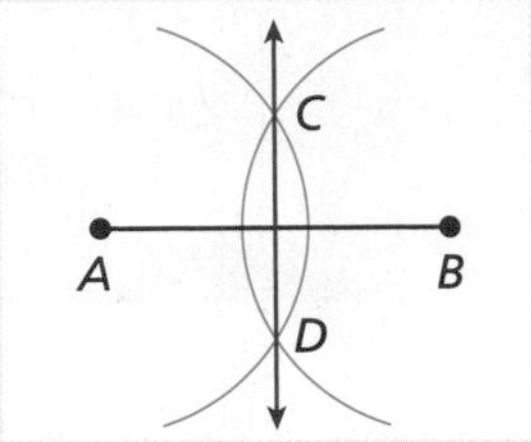

3. Draw $\overleftrightarrow{CD}$. $\overleftrightarrow{CD}$ is the perpendicular bisector of $\overline{AB}$.

The shortest segment from a point to a line is perpendicular to the line. This fact is used to define the **distance from a point to a line** as the length of the perpendicular segment from the point to the line.

EXAMPLE 1 Distance From a Point to a Line

A **Name the shortest segment from P to $\overleftrightarrow{AC}$.**
The shortest distance from a point to a line is the length of the perpendicular segment, so $\overline{PB}$ is the shortest segment from P to $\overleftrightarrow{AC}$.

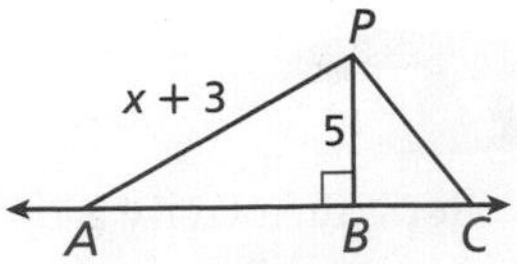

x^2y **Algebra**

B **Write and solve an inequality for x.**

$PA > PB$	*$\overline{PB}$ is the shortest segment.*
$x + 3 > 5$	*Substitute $x + 3$ for PA and 5 for PB.*
$-3 \quad -3$	*Subtract 3 from both sides of the inequality.*
$x > 2$	

CHECK IT OUT!

1a. Name the shortest segment from A to $\overleftrightarrow{BC}$.
1b. Write and solve an inequality for x.

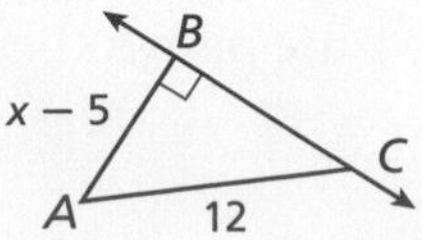

Know it! Note

Theorems

	THEOREM	HYPOTHESIS	CONCLUSION
3-4-1	If two intersecting lines form a linear pair of congruent angles, then the lines are perpendicular. (2 intersecting lines form lin. pair of $\cong$ ∠s $\rightarrow$ lines $\perp$.)	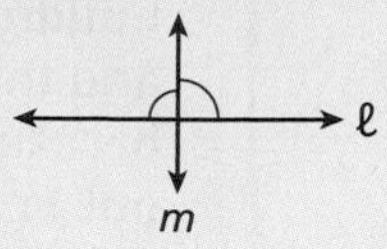	$\ell \perp m$
3-4-2	**Perpendicular Transversal Theorem** In a plane, if a transversal is perpendicular to one of two parallel lines, then it is perpendicular to the other line.	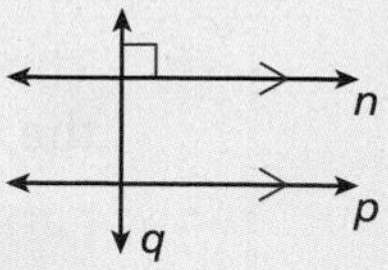	$q \perp p$
3-4-3	If two coplanar lines are perpendicular to the same line, then the two lines are parallel to each other. (2 lines $\perp$ to same line $\rightarrow$ 2 lines $\parallel$.)	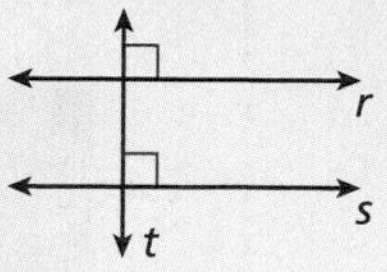	$r \parallel s$

You will prove Theorems 3-4-1 and 3-4-3 in Exercises 37 and 38.

PROOF

Perpendicular Transversal Theorem

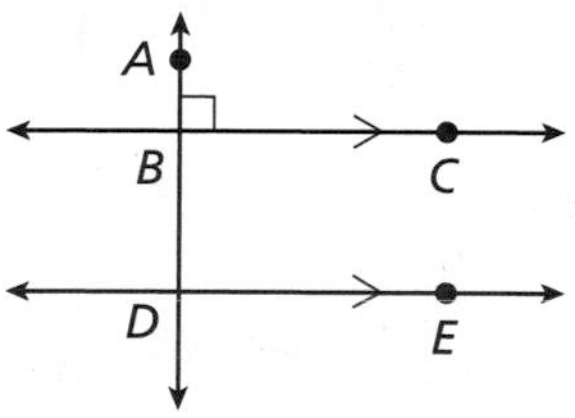

Given: $\overleftrightarrow{BC} \parallel \overleftrightarrow{DE}$, $\overleftrightarrow{AB} \perp \overleftrightarrow{BC}$

Prove: $\overleftrightarrow{AB} \perp \overleftrightarrow{DE}$

Proof:

It is given that $\overleftrightarrow{BC} \parallel \overleftrightarrow{DE}$, so $\angle ABC \cong \angle BDE$ by the Corresponding Angles Postulate. It is also given that $\overleftrightarrow{AB} \perp \overleftrightarrow{BC}$, so $m\angle ABC = 90°$. By the definition of congruent angles, $m\angle ABC = m\angle BDE$, so $m\angle BDE = 90°$ by the Transitive Property of Equality. By the definition of perpendicular lines, $\overleftrightarrow{AB} \perp \overleftrightarrow{DE}$.

EXAMPLE 2

Proving Properties of Lines

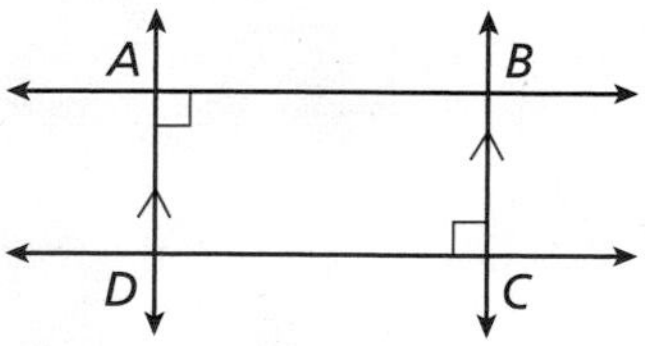

Write a two-column proof.

Given: $\overleftrightarrow{AD} \parallel \overleftrightarrow{BC}$, $\overleftrightarrow{AD} \perp \overleftrightarrow{AB}$, $\overleftrightarrow{BC} \perp \overleftrightarrow{DC}$

Prove: $\overleftrightarrow{AB} \parallel \overleftrightarrow{DC}$

Proof:

Statements	Reasons
1. $\overleftrightarrow{AD} \parallel \overleftrightarrow{BC}$, $\overleftrightarrow{BC} \perp \overleftrightarrow{DC}$	1. Given
2. $\overleftrightarrow{AD} \perp \overleftrightarrow{DC}$	2. $\perp$ Transv. Thm.
3. $\overleftrightarrow{AD} \perp \overleftrightarrow{AB}$	3. Given
4. $\overleftrightarrow{AB} \parallel \overleftrightarrow{DC}$	4. 2 lines $\perp$ to same line $\rightarrow$ 2 lines $\parallel$.

CHECK IT OUT!

2. Write a two-column proof.
Given: $\angle EHF \cong \angle HFG$, $\overleftrightarrow{FG} \perp \overleftrightarrow{GH}$
Prove: $\overleftrightarrow{EH} \perp \overleftrightarrow{GH}$

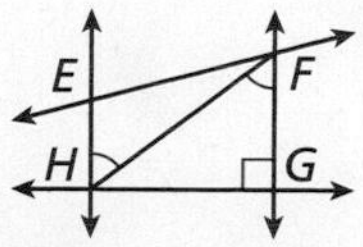

EXAMPLE 3 *Oceanography Application*

Rip currents may be caused by a sandbar parallel to the shoreline. Waves cause a buildup of water between the sandbar and the shoreline. When this water breaks through the sandbar, it flows out in a direction perpendicular to the sandbar. Why must the rip current be perpendicular to the shoreline?

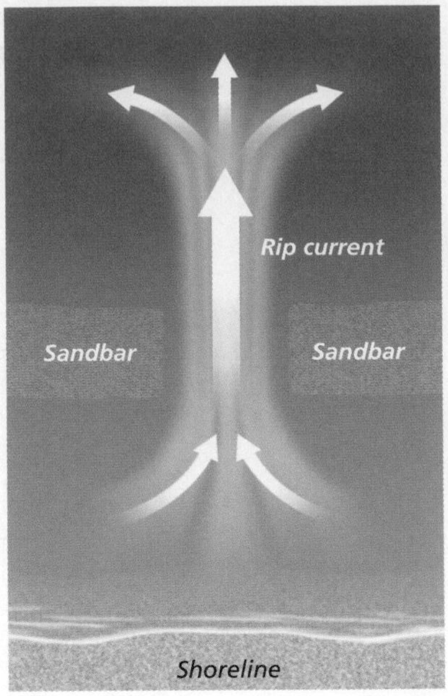

The rip current forms a transversal to the shoreline and the sandbar.

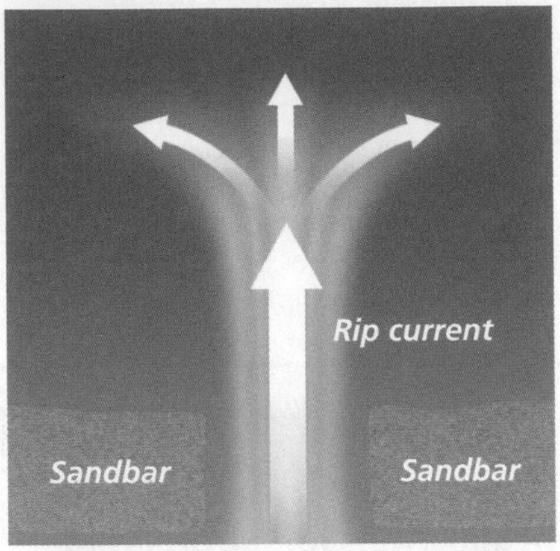

The shoreline and the sandbar are parallel, and the rip current is perpendicular to the sandbar. So by the Perpendicular Transversal Theorem, the rip current is perpendicular to the shoreline.

CHECK IT OUT! **3.** A swimmer who gets caught in a rip current should swim in a direction perpendicular to the current. Why should the path of the swimmer be parallel to the shoreline?

MATHEMATICAL PRACTICES

THINK AND DISCUSS

1. Describe what happens if two intersecting lines form a linear pair of congruent angles.

2. Explain why a transversal that is perpendicular to two parallel lines forms eight congruent angles.

Know it! Note

3. GET ORGANIZED Copy and complete the graphic organizer. Use the diagram and the theorems from this lesson to complete the table.

Diagram	If you are given . . .	Then you can conclude . . .
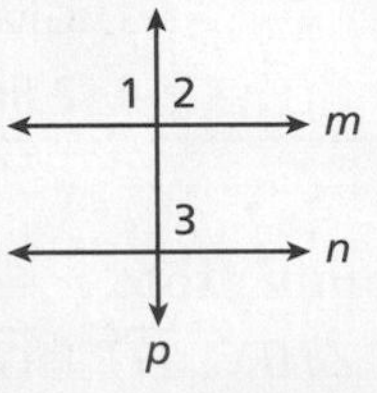	$m\angle 1 = m\angle 2$	
	$m\angle 2 = 90°$ $m\angle 3 = 90°$	
	$m\angle 2 = 90°$ $m \parallel n$	

3-4 Exercises

Learn It Online
Homework Help Online
Parent Resources Online

GUIDED PRACTICE

1. **Vocabulary** $\overleftrightarrow{CD}$ is the *perpendicular bisector* of $\overline{AB}$. $\overleftrightarrow{CD}$ intersects $\overline{AB}$ at C. What can you say about $\overline{AB}$ and $\overleftrightarrow{CD}$? What can you say about $\overline{AC}$ and $\overline{BC}$?

SEE EXAMPLE 1

2. Name the shortest segment from point E to $\overleftrightarrow{AD}$.
3. Write and solve an inequality for x.

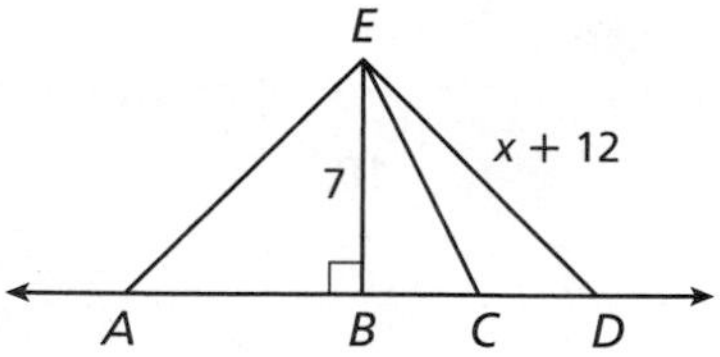

SEE EXAMPLE 2

4. Complete the two-column proof.
Given: $\angle ABC \cong \angle CBE$, $\overleftrightarrow{DE} \perp \overleftrightarrow{AF}$
Prove: $\overleftrightarrow{CB} \parallel \overleftrightarrow{DE}$
Proof:

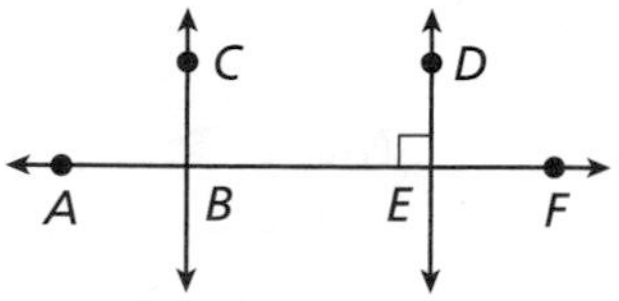

Statements	Reasons
1. $\angle ABC \cong \angle CBE$	1. Given
2. $\overleftrightarrow{CB} \perp \overleftrightarrow{AF}$	2. a. ___?___
3. b. ___?___	3. Given
4. $\overleftrightarrow{CB} \parallel \overleftrightarrow{DE}$	4. c. ___?___

SEE EXAMPLE 3

5. **Sports** The center line in a tennis court is perpendicular to both service lines. Explain why the service lines must be parallel to each other.

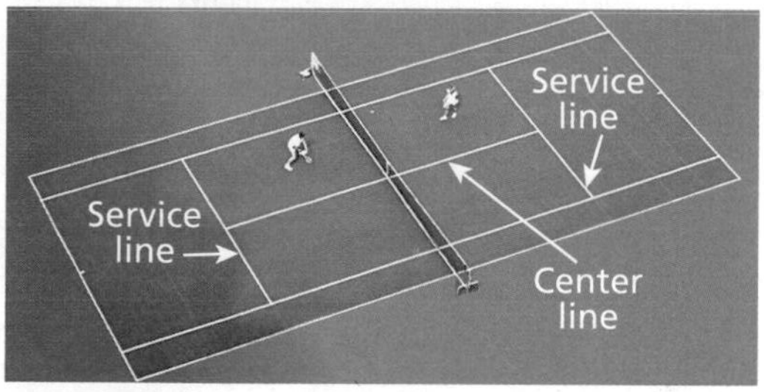

PRACTICE AND PROBLEM SOLVING

Independent Practice

For Exercises	See Example
6–7	1
8	2
9	3

Extra Practice

See Extra Practice for more Skills Practice and Applications Practice exercises.

6. Name the shortest segment from point W to $\overline{XZ}$.
7. Write and solve an inequality for x.

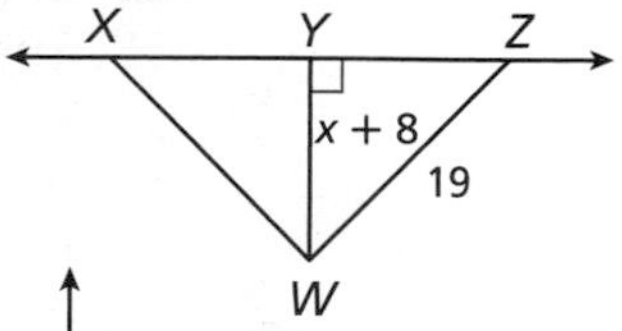

8. Complete the two-column proof below.
Given: $\overleftrightarrow{AB} \perp \overleftrightarrow{BC}$, $m\angle 1 + m\angle 2 = 180°$
Prove: $\overleftrightarrow{BC} \perp \overleftrightarrow{CD}$
Proof:

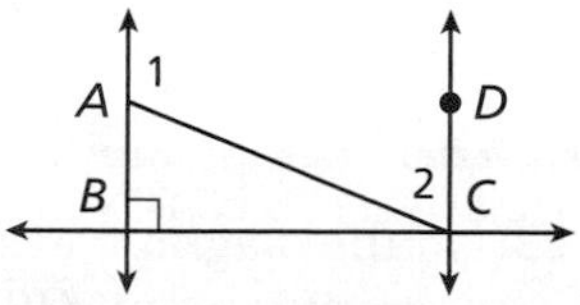

Statements	Reasons
1. $\overleftrightarrow{AB} \perp \overleftrightarrow{BC}$	1. Given
2. $m\angle 1 + m\angle 2 = 180°$	2. a. ___?___
3. $\angle 1$ and $\angle 2$ are supplementary.	3. Def. of supplementary
4. b. ___?___	4. Converse of the Same-Side Interior Angles Theorem
5. $\overleftrightarrow{BC} \perp \overleftrightarrow{CD}$	5. c. ___?___

9. **Music** The *frets* on a guitar are all perpendicular to one of the strings. Explain why the frets must be parallel to each other.

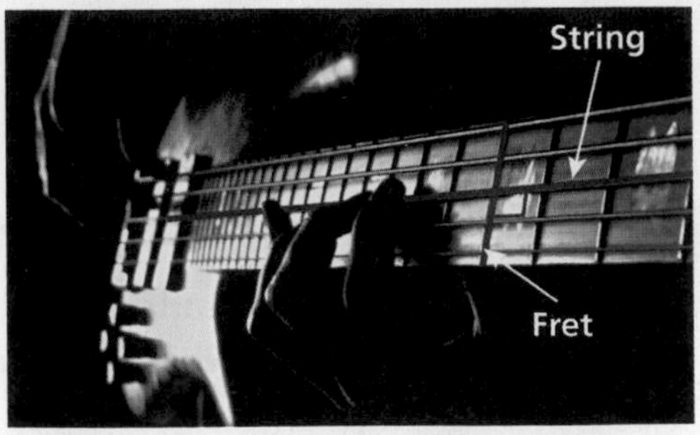

For each diagram, write and solve an inequality for x.

10.

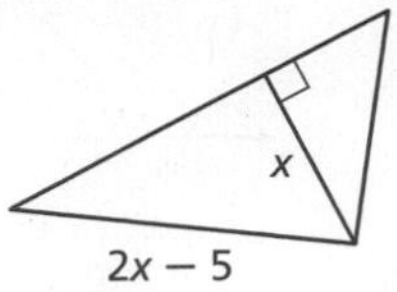

11.

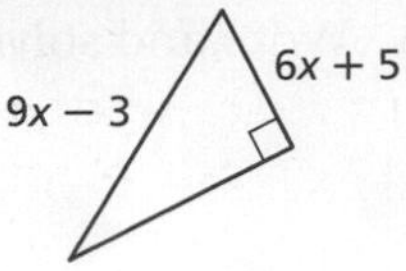

Multi-Step Solve to find x and y in each diagram.

12.

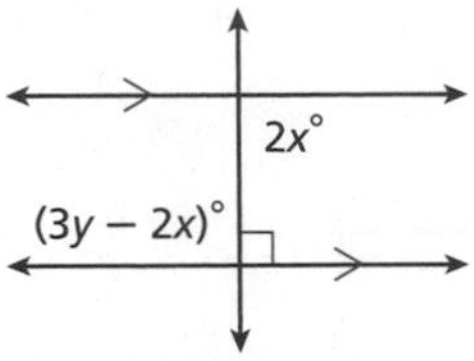

13.

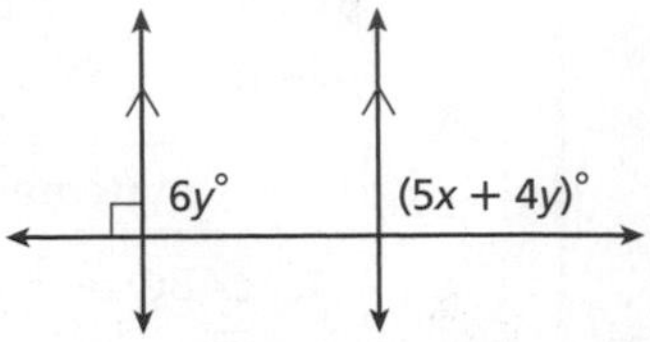

14.

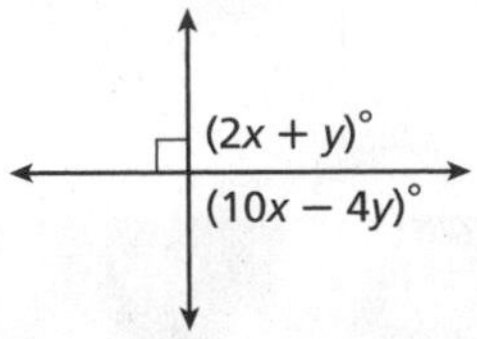

15.

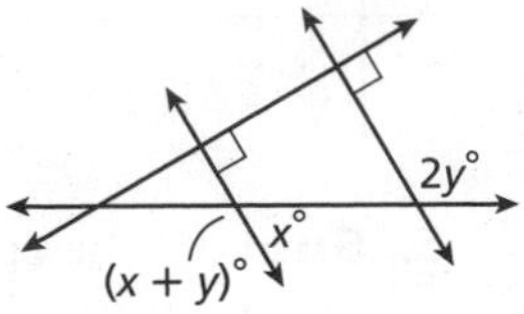

Determine if there is enough information given in the diagram to prove each statement.

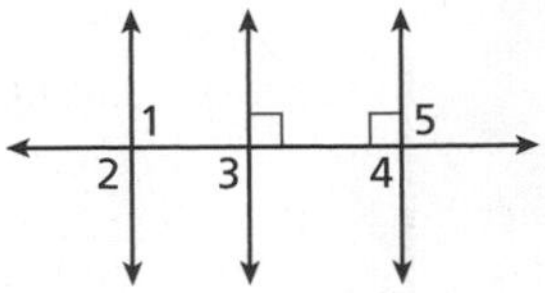

16. $\angle 1 \cong \angle 2$ 17. $\angle 1 \cong \angle 3$

18. $\angle 2 \cong \angle 3$ 19. $\angle 2 \cong \angle 4$

20. $\angle 3 \cong \angle 4$ 21. $\angle 3 \cong \angle 5$

22. **Critical Thinking** Are the Reflexive, Symmetric, and Transitive Properties true for perpendicular lines? Explain why or why not.
Reflexive: $\ell \perp \ell$
Symmetric: If $\ell \perp m$, then $m \perp \ell$.
Transitive: If $\ell \perp m$ and $m \perp n$, then $\ell \perp n$.

MULTI-STEP TEST PREP

23. In the diagram, which represents the side view of a mystery spot, $\overline{QR} \perp \overline{PQ}$, $\overline{PQ} \parallel \overline{RS}$, and $\overline{PS} \parallel \overline{QR}$.
   a. Prove $\overline{QR} \perp \overline{RS}$ and $\overline{PS} \perp \overline{RS}$.
   b. Prove $\overline{PQ} \perp \overline{PS}$.

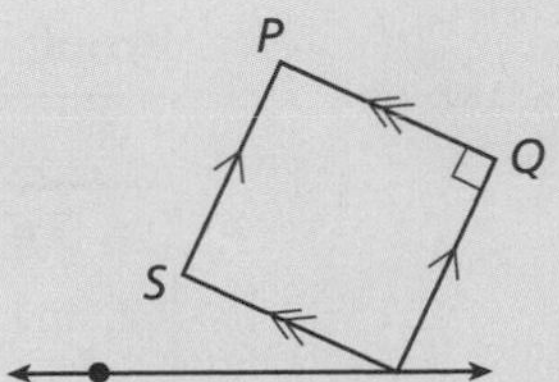

24. **Geography** Felton Avenue, Arlee Avenue, and Viehl Avenue are all parallel. Broadway Street is perpendicular to Felton Avenue. Use the satellite photo and the given information to determine the values of x and y.

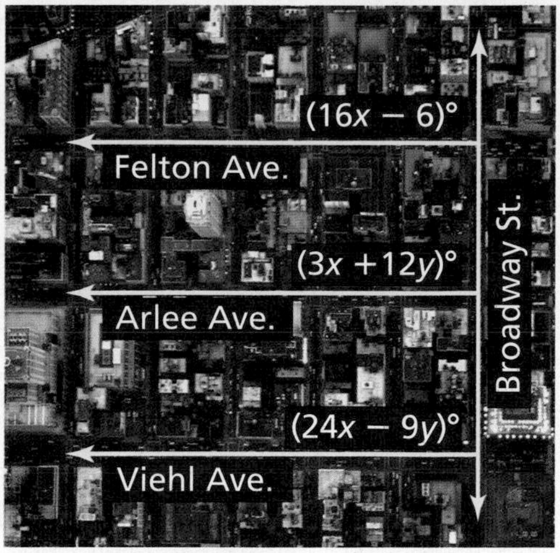

25. **Estimation** Copy the diagram onto a grid with 1 cm by 1 cm squares. Estimate the distance from point P to line ℓ.

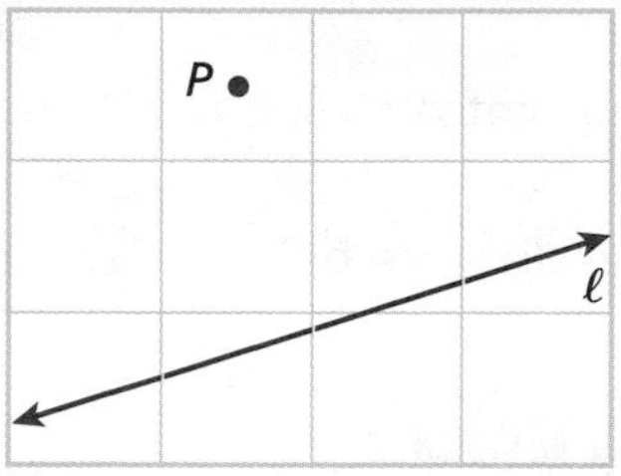

26. **Critical Thinking** Draw a figure to show that Theorem 3-4-3 is not true if the lines are not in the same plane.

27. Draw a figure in which $\overline{AB}$ is a perpendicular bisector of $\overline{XY}$ but $\overline{XY}$ is not a perpendicular bisector of $\overline{AB}$.

28. **Write About It** A ladder is formed by rungs that are perpendicular to the sides of the ladder. Explain why the rungs of the ladder are parallel.

Construction Construct a segment congruent to each given segment and then construct its perpendicular bisector.

29.

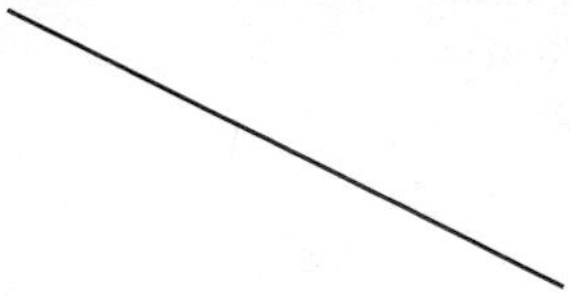

30.

TEST PREP

31. Which inequality is correct for the given diagram?

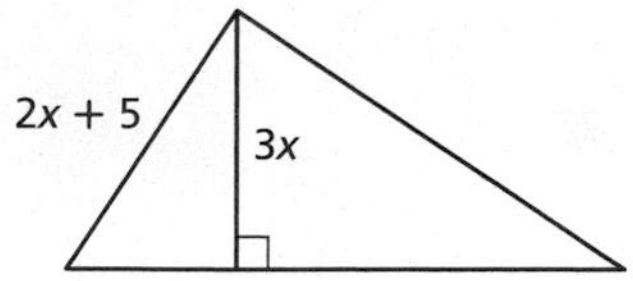

Ⓐ $2x + 5 < 3x$
Ⓒ $2x + 5 > 3x$
Ⓑ $x > 1$
Ⓓ $x > 5$

32. In the diagram, $\ell \perp m$. Find x and y.

Ⓕ $x = 5, y = 7$
Ⓖ $x = 7, y = 5$
Ⓗ $x = 90, y = 90$
Ⓙ $x = 10, y = 5$

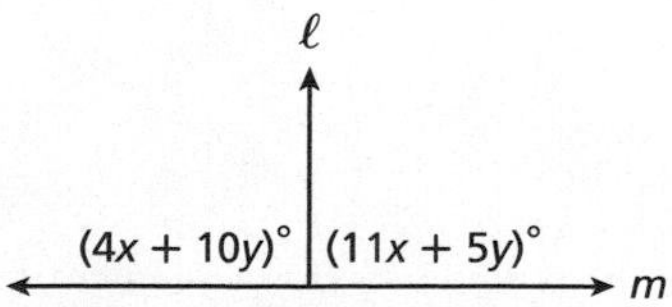

33. If $\ell \perp m$, which statement is NOT correct?

Ⓐ $m\angle 2 = 90°$
Ⓑ $m\angle 1 + m\angle 2 = 180°$
Ⓒ $\angle 1 \cong \angle 2$
Ⓓ $\angle 1 \perp \angle 2$

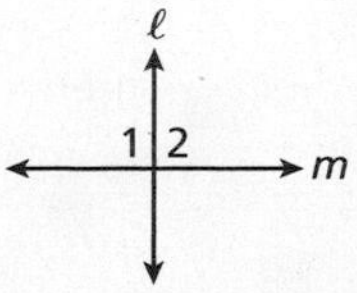

34. In a plane, both lines *m* and *n* are perpendicular to both lines *p* and *q*. Which conclusion CANNOT be made?

Ⓐ $p \parallel q$

Ⓑ $m \parallel n$

Ⓒ $p \perp q$

Ⓓ All angles formed by lines *m*, *n*, *p*, and *q* are congruent.

35. Extended Response Lines *m* and *n* are parallel. Line *p* intersects line *m* at *A* and line *n* at *B*, and is perpendicular to line *m*.

a. What is the relationship between line *n* and line *p*? Draw a diagram to support your answer.

b. What is the distance from point *A* to line *n*? What is the distance from point *B* to line *m*? Explain.

c. How would you define the distance between two parallel lines in a plane?

CHALLENGE AND EXTEND

36. Multi-Step Find m∠1 in the diagram. (*Hint:* Draw a line parallel to the given parallel lines.)

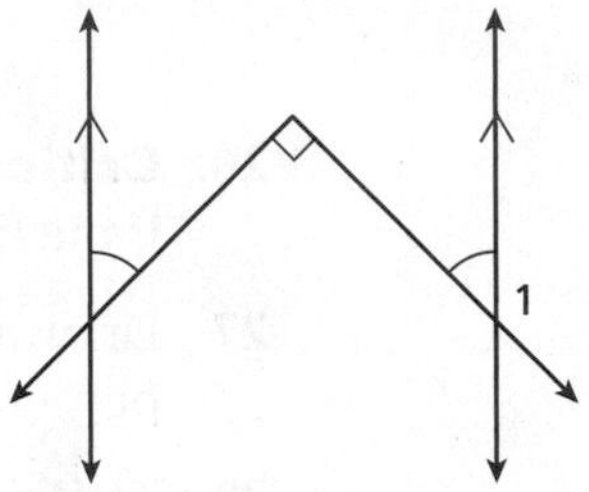

37. Prove Theorem 3-4-1: If two intersecting lines form a linear pair of congruent angles, then the two lines are perpendicular.

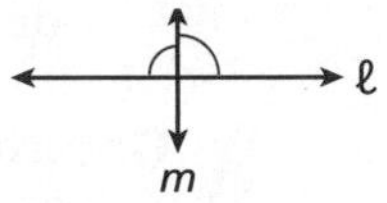

38. Prove Theorem 3-4-3: If two coplanar lines are perpendicular to the same line, then the two lines are parallel to each other.

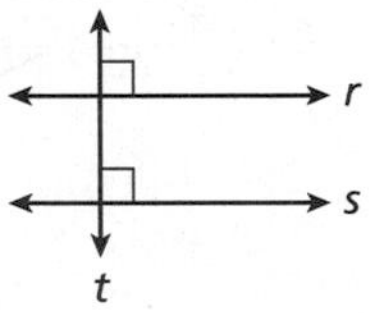

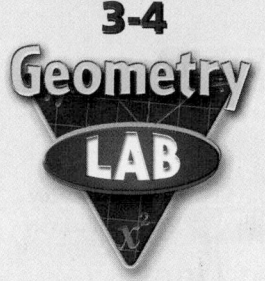

3-4 Geometry LAB

Construct Perpendicular Lines

Use with Perpendicular Lines

You have learned to construct the perpendicular bisector of a segment. This is the basis of the construction of a line perpendicular to a given line through a given point. The steps in the construction are the same whether the point is on or off the line.

MATHEMATICAL PRACTICES **Use appropriate tools strategically.**

CC.9-12.G.CO.12 Make formal geometric constructions with a variety of tools and methods…

Activity

Copy the given line ℓ and point P.

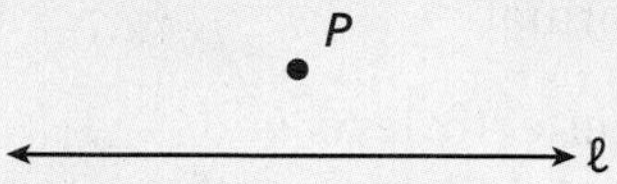

1. Place the compass point on P and draw an arc that intersects ℓ at two points. Label the points A and B.

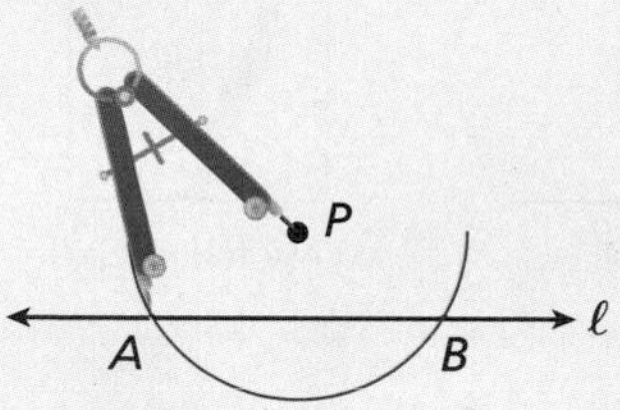

2. Construct the perpendicular bisector of $\overline{AB}$.

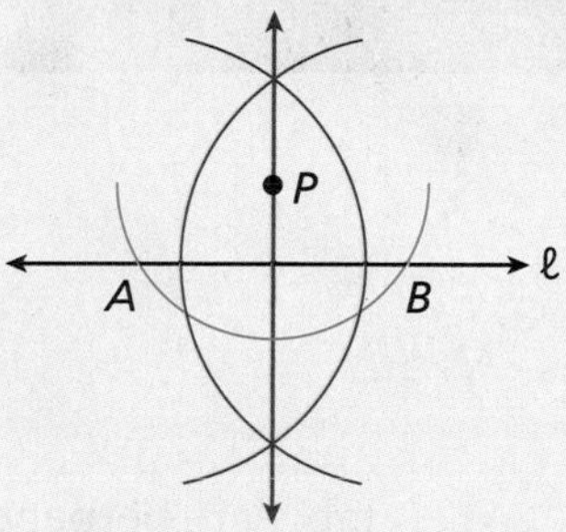

Try This

Copy each diagram and construct a line perpendicular to line ℓ through point P. Use a protractor to verify that the lines are perpendicular.

1.

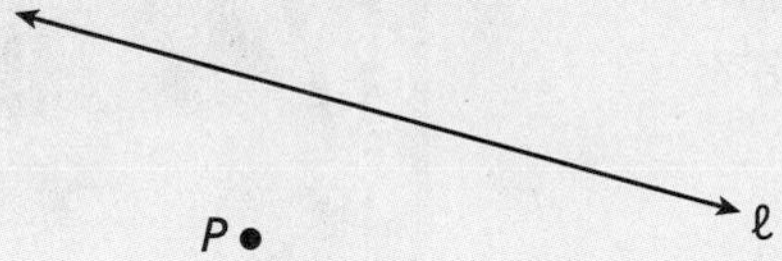

2.

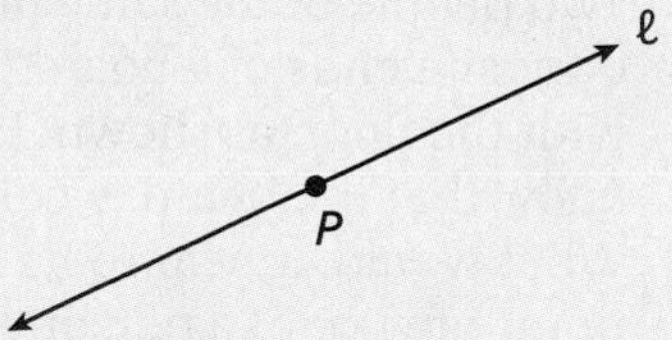

3. Follow the steps below to construct two parallel lines. Explain why ℓ ∥ n.

Step 1 Given a line ℓ, draw a point P not on ℓ.

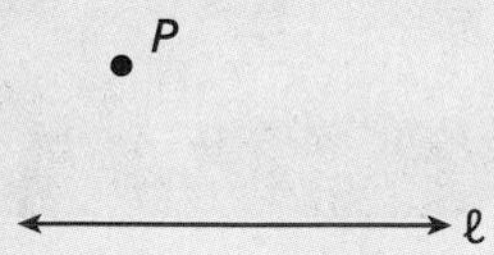

Step 2 Construct line m perpendicular to ℓ through P.

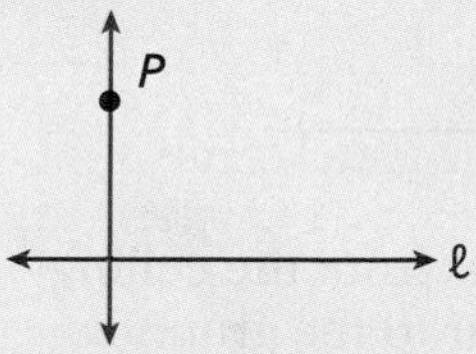

Step 3 Construct line n perpendicular to m through P.

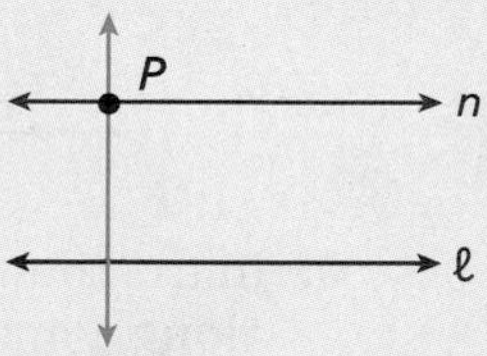

CHAPTER 3

MULTI-STEP TEST PREP

SECTION 3A

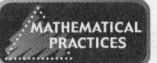

MATHEMATICAL PRACTICES **Reason abstractly and quantitatively.**

Parallel and Perpendicular Lines and Transversals

On the Spot Inside a mystery spot building, objects can appear to roll uphill, and people can look as if they are standing at impossible angles. This is because there is no view of the outside, so the room appears to be normal.

Suppose that the ground is perfectly level and the floor of the building forms a 25° angle with the ground. The floor and ceiling are parallel, and the walls are perpendicular to the floor.

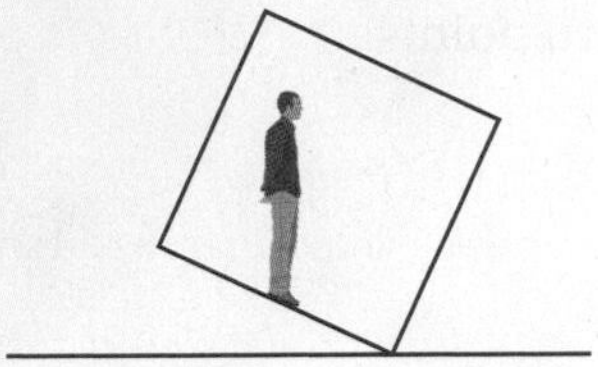

View from outside

View from inside

1. A table is placed in the room. The legs of the table are perpendicular to the floor, and the top is perpendicular to the legs. Draw a diagram and describe the relationship of the tabletop to the floor, walls, and ceiling of the room.
2. Find the angle of the table top relative to the ground. Suppose a ball is placed on the table. Describe what would happen and how it would appear to a person in the room.
3. Two people of the same height are standing on opposite ends of a board that makes a 25° angle with the floor, as shown. Explain how you know that the board is parallel to the ground. What would appear to be happening from the point of view of a person inside the room?

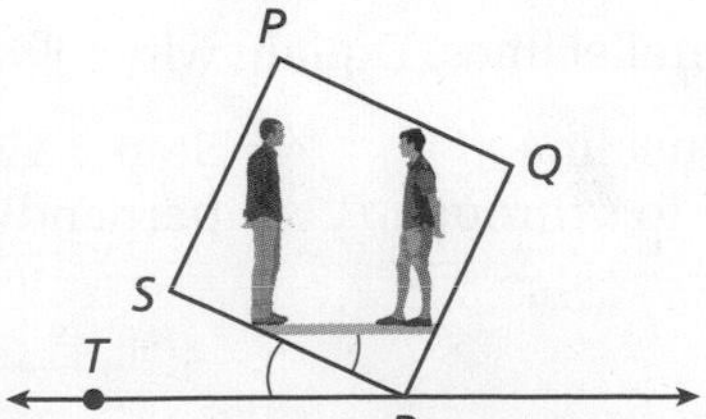

4. In the room, a lamp hangs from the ceiling along a line perpendicular to the ground. Find the angle the line makes with the walls. Describe how it would appear to a person standing in the room.

READY TO GO ON?

Quiz for Lessons 3-1 Through 3-4

3-1 Lines and Angles

Identify each of the following.

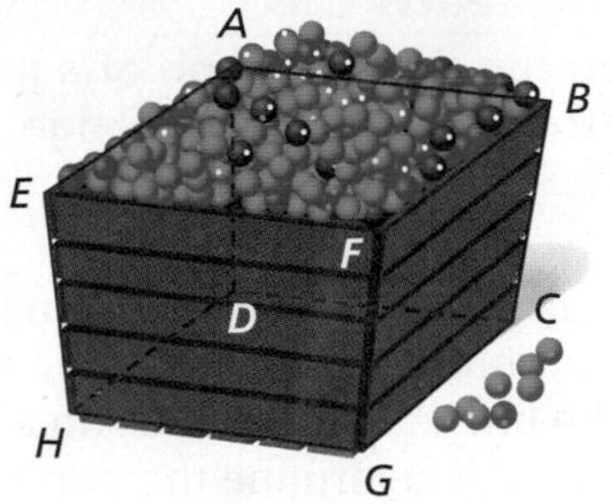

1. a pair of perpendicular segments
2. a pair of skew segments
3. a pair of parallel segments
4. a pair of parallel planes

Give an example of each angle pair.

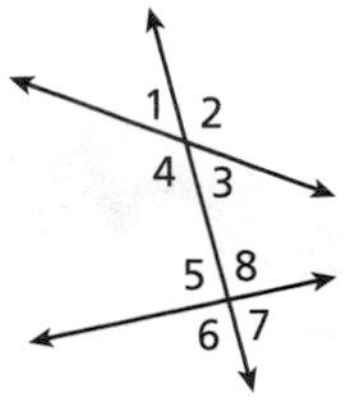

5. alternate interior angles
6. alternate exterior angles
7. corresponding angles
8. same-side interior angles

3-2 Angles Formed by Parallel Lines and Transversals

Find each angle measure.

9.

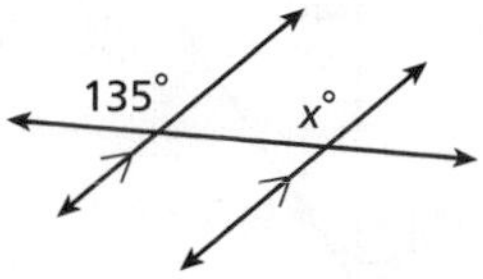

10.

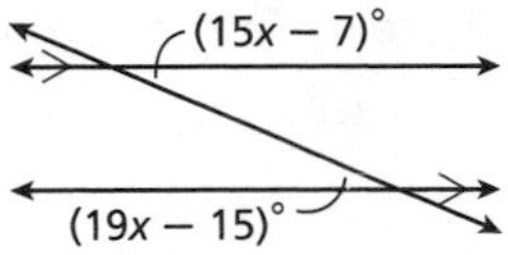

11.

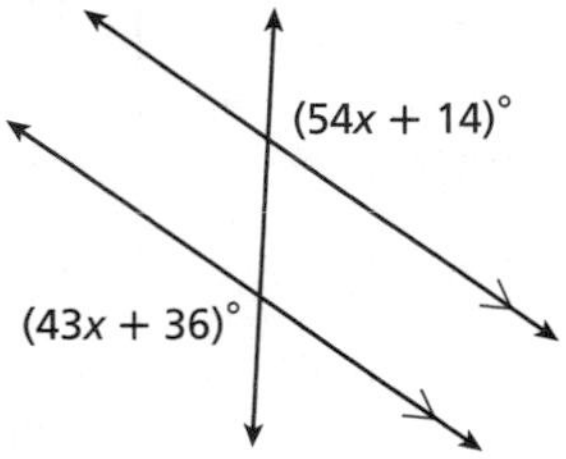

3-3 Proving Lines Parallel

Use the given information and the theorems and postulates you have learned to show that $a \parallel b$.

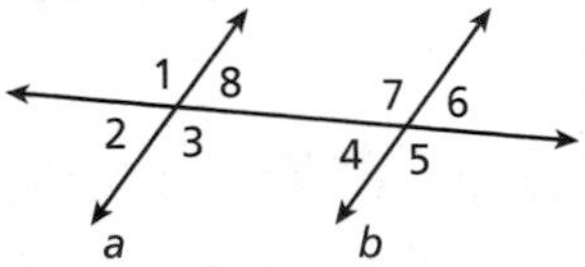

12. $m\angle 8 = (13x + 20)^\circ$, $m\angle 6 = (7x + 38)^\circ$, $x = 3$
13. $\angle 1 \cong \angle 5$
14. $m\angle 8 + m\angle 7 = 180^\circ$
15. $m\angle 8 = m\angle 4$
16. The tower shown is supported by guy wires such that $m\angle 1 = (3x + 12)^\circ$, $m\angle 2 = (4x - 2)^\circ$, and $x = 14$. Show that the guy wires are parallel.

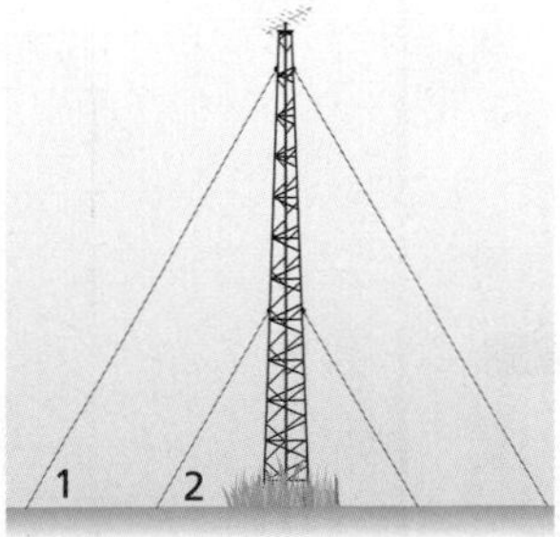

3-4 Perpendicular Lines

17. Write a two-column proof.
Given: $\angle 1 \cong \angle 2$, $\ell \perp n$
Prove: $\ell \perp p$

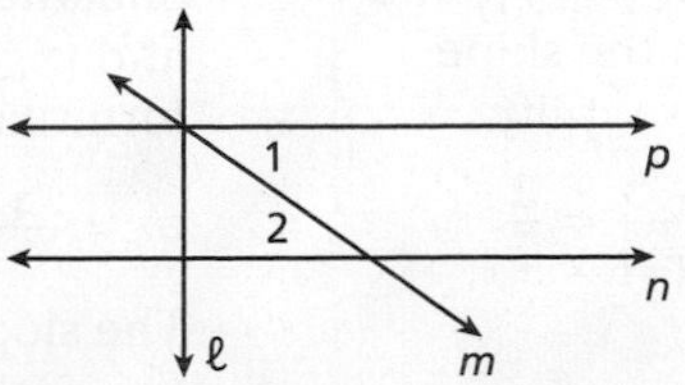

COMMON CORE

3-5 Slopes of Lines

CC.9-12.G.GPE.5 Prove the slope criteria for parallel and perpendicular lines and use them to solve… problems…

Objectives

Find the slope of a line.

Use slopes to identify parallel and perpendicular lines.

Vocabulary

rise

run

slope

Why learn this?

You can use the graph of a line to describe your rate of change, or speed, when traveling. (See Example 2.)

The *slope* of a line in a coordinate plane is a number that describes the steepness of the line. Any two points on a line can be used to determine the slope.

Know it! Note

Slope of a Line

DEFINITION	EXAMPLE
The **rise** is the difference in the *y*-values of two points on a line.	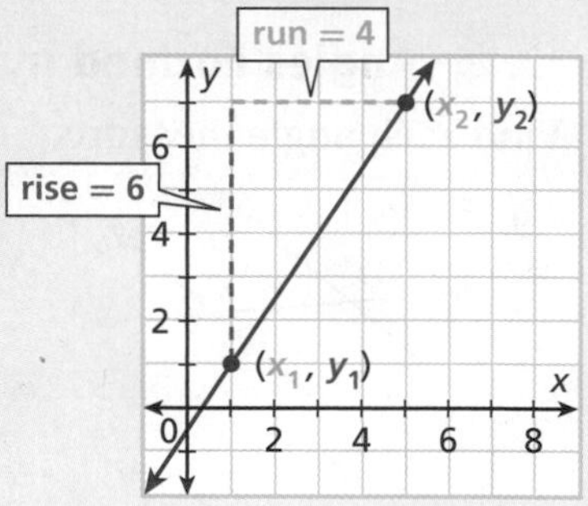
The **run** is the difference in the *x*-values of two points on a line.	
The **slope** of a line is the ratio of rise to run. If (x_1, y_1) and (x_2, y_2) are any two points on a line, the slope of the line is $m = \frac{y_2 - y_1}{x_2 - x_1}$.	slope $= \frac{6}{4} = \frac{3}{2}$

EXAMPLE 1 Finding the Slope of a Line

Algebra

Use the slope formula to determine the slope of each line.

A $\overleftrightarrow{AB}$

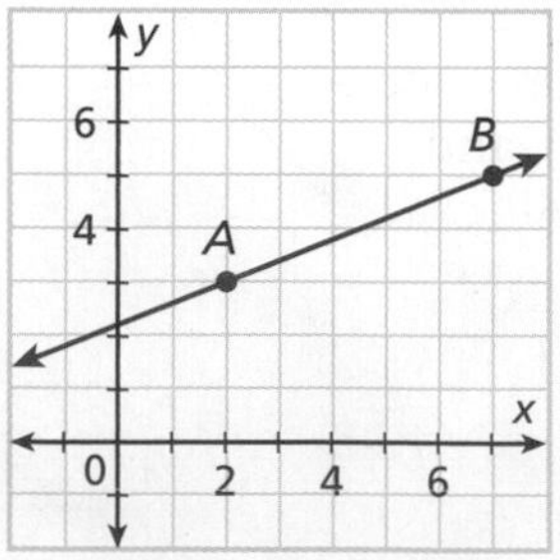

Substitute $(2, 3)$ for (x_1, y_1) and $(7, 5)$ for (x_2, y_2) in the slope formula and then simplify.

$$m = \frac{y_2 - y_1}{x_2 - x_1} = \frac{5 - 3}{7 - 2} = \frac{2}{5}$$

B $\overleftrightarrow{CD}$

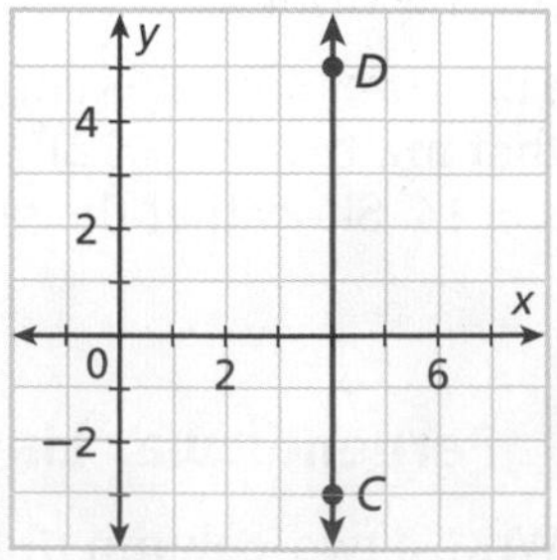

Substitute $(4, -3)$ for (x_1, y_1) and $(4, 5)$ for (x_2, y_2) in the slope formula and then simplify.

$$m = \frac{y_2 - y_1}{x_2 - x_1} = \frac{5 - (-3)}{4 - 4} = \frac{8}{0}$$

The slope is undefined.

Remember!

A fraction with zero in the denominator is undefined because it is impossible to divide by zero.

Use the slope formula to determine the slope of each line.

C $\overleftrightarrow{EF}$

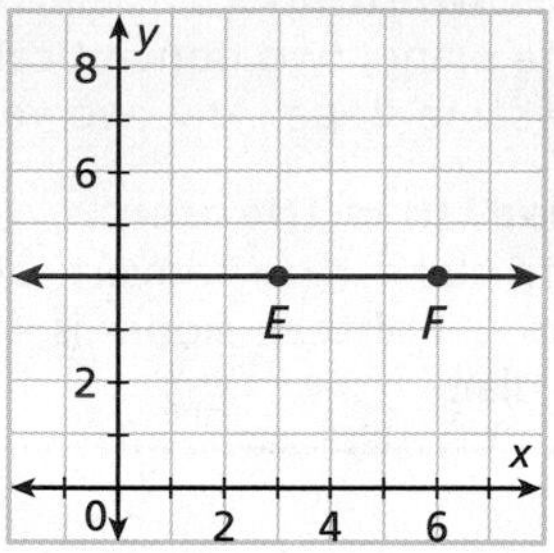

Substitute (3, 4) for (x_1, y_1) and (6, 4) for (x_2, y_2) in the slope formula and then simplify.

$$m = \frac{y_2 - y_1}{x_2 - x_1} = \frac{4 - 4}{6 - 3} = \frac{0}{3} = 0$$

D $\overleftrightarrow{GH}$

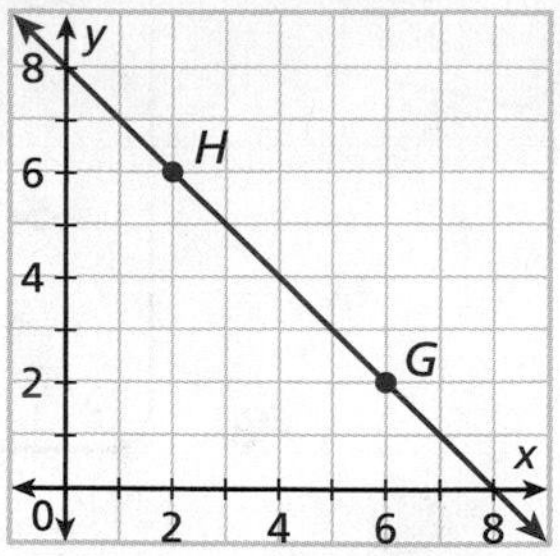

Substitute (6, 2) for (x_1, y_1) and (2, 6) for (x_2, y_2) in the slope formula and then simplify.

$$m = \frac{y_2 - y_1}{x_2 - x_1} = \frac{6 - 2}{2 - 6} = \frac{4}{-4} = -1$$

CHECK IT OUT! **1.** Use the slope formula to determine the slope of $\overleftrightarrow{JK}$ through $J(3, 1)$ and $K(2, -1)$.

Summary: Slope of a Line

Positive Slope	Negative Slope	Zero Slope	Undefined Slope
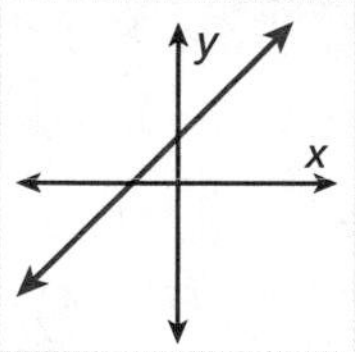	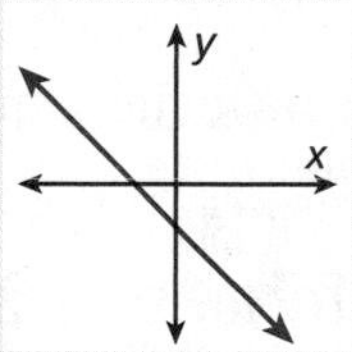	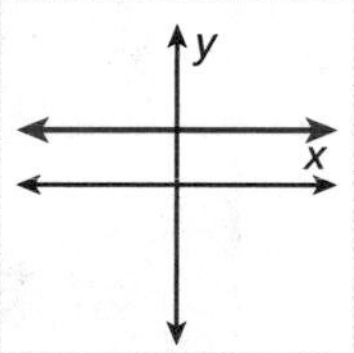	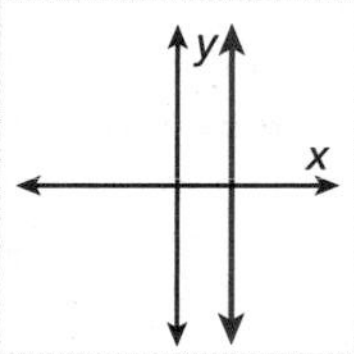

One interpretation of slope is a *rate of change.* If y represents miles traveled and x represents time in hours, the slope gives the rate of change in miles per hour.

EXAMPLE 2 *Transportation Application*

Tony is driving from Dallas, Texas, to Atlanta, Georgia. At 3:00 P.M., he is 180 miles from Dallas. At 5:30 P.M., he is 330 miles from Dallas. Graph the line that represents Tony's distance from Dallas at a given time. Find and interpret the slope of the line.

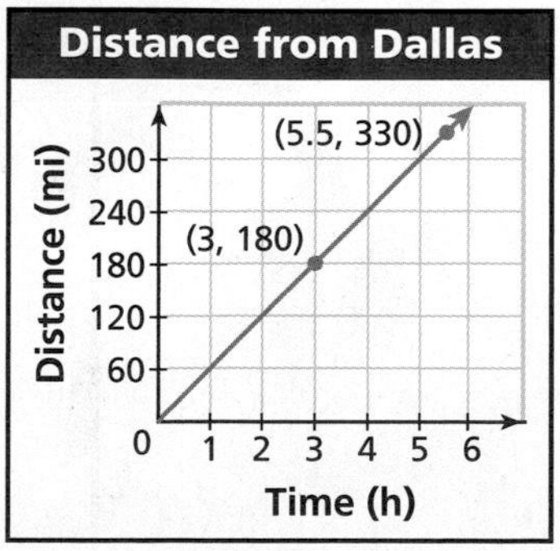

Use the points (3, 180) and (5.5, 330) to graph the line and find the slope.

$$m = \frac{330 - 180}{5.5 - 3} = \frac{150}{2.5} = 60$$

The slope is 60, which means he is traveling at an average speed of 60 miles per hour.

CHECK IT OUT! **2. What if...?** Use the graph above to estimate how far Tony will have traveled by 6:30 P.M. if his average speed stays the same.

Know it! Note

Slopes of Parallel and Perpendicular Lines

3-5-1 Parallel Lines Theorem
In a coordinate plane, two nonvertical lines are parallel if and only if they have the same slope. Any two vertical lines are parallel.

3-5-2 Perpendicular Lines Theorem
In a coordinate plane, two nonvertical lines are perpendicular if and only if the product of their slopes is −1. Vertical and horizontal lines are perpendicular.

If a line has a slope of $\frac{a}{b}$, then the slope of a perpendicular line is $-\frac{b}{a}$. The ratios $\frac{a}{b}$ and $-\frac{b}{a}$ are called *opposite reciprocals.*

EXAMPLE 3 Determining Whether Lines Are Parallel, Perpendicular, or Neither

Algebra

Graph each pair of lines. Use slopes to determine whether the lines are parallel, perpendicular, or neither.

A $\overleftrightarrow{AB}$ **and** $\overleftrightarrow{CD}$ **for** $A(2, 1)$, $B(1, 5)$, $C(4, 2)$, **and** $D(5, -2)$

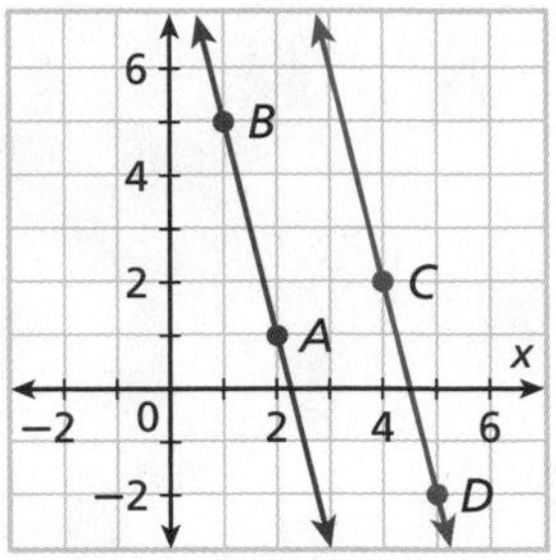

slope of $\overleftrightarrow{AB} = \frac{5-1}{1-2} = \frac{4}{-1} = -4$

slope of $\overleftrightarrow{CD} = \frac{-2-2}{5-4} = \frac{-4}{1} = -4$

The lines have the same slope, so they are parallel.

B $\overleftrightarrow{ST}$ **and** $\overleftrightarrow{UV}$ **for** $S(-2, 2)$, $T(5, -1)$, $U(3, 4)$, **and** $V(-1, -4)$

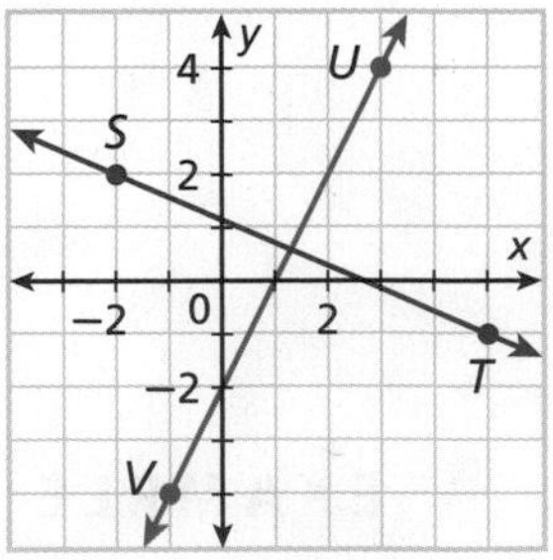

slope of $\overleftrightarrow{ST} = \frac{-1-2}{5-(-2)} = \frac{-3}{7} = -\frac{3}{7}$

slope of $\overleftrightarrow{UV} = \frac{-4-4}{-1-3} = \frac{-8}{-4} = 2$

The slopes are not the same, so the lines are not parallel. The product of the slopes is not −1, so the lines are not perpendicular.

Caution!

Four given points do not always determine two lines. Graph the lines to make sure the points are not collinear.

C $\overleftrightarrow{FG}$ **and** $\overleftrightarrow{HJ}$ **for** $F(1, 1)$, $G(2, 2)$, $H(2, 1)$, **and** $J(1, 2)$

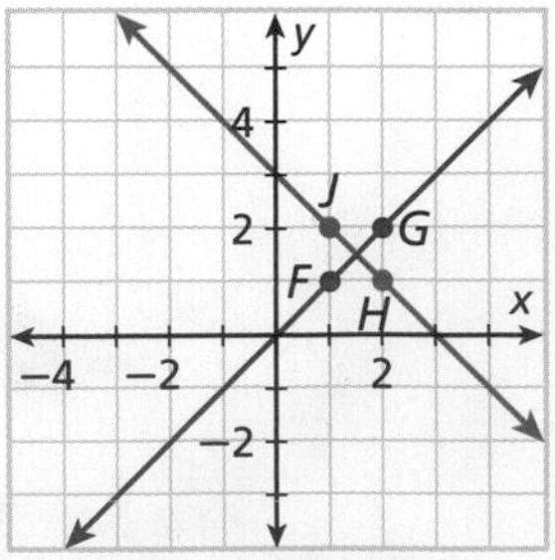

slope of $\overleftrightarrow{FG} = \frac{2-1}{2-1} = \frac{1}{1} = 1$

slope of $\overleftrightarrow{HJ} = \frac{2-1}{1-2} = \frac{1}{-1} = -1$

The product of the slopes is $1(-1) = -1$, so the lines are perpendicular.

CHECK IT OUT! **Graph each pair of lines. Use slopes to determine whether the lines are parallel, perpendicular, or neither.**

3a. $\overleftrightarrow{WX}$ and $\overleftrightarrow{YZ}$ for $W(3, 1)$, $X(3, -2)$, $Y(-2, 3)$, and $Z(4, 3)$

3b. $\overleftrightarrow{KL}$ and $\overleftrightarrow{MN}$ for $K(-4, 4)$, $L(-2, -3)$, $M(3, 1)$, and $N(-5, -1)$

3c. $\overleftrightarrow{BC}$ and $\overleftrightarrow{DE}$ for $B(1, 1)$, $C(3, 5)$, $D(-2, -6)$, and $E(3, 4)$

THINK AND DISCUSS

MATHEMATICAL PRACTICES

1. Explain how to find the slope of a line when given two points.
2. Compare the slopes of horizontal and vertical lines.
3. **GET ORGANIZED** Copy and complete the graphic organizer.

Know it! Note

Pairs of Lines		
Type	**Slopes**	**Example**
Parallel		
Perpendicular		

3-5 Exercises

Learn It Online
Homework Help Online
Parent Resources Online

GUIDED PRACTICE

1. **Vocabulary** The *slope* of a line is the ratio of its ___?___ to its ___?___. (*rise* or *run*)

SEE EXAMPLE 1

Use the slope formula to determine the slope of each line.

2. $\overleftrightarrow{MN}$

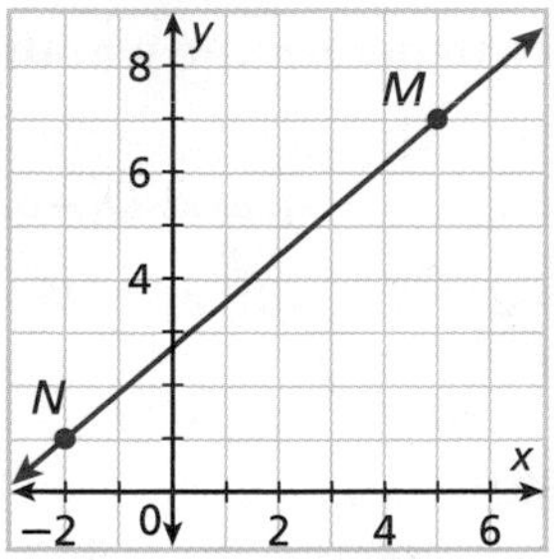

3. $\overleftrightarrow{CD}$

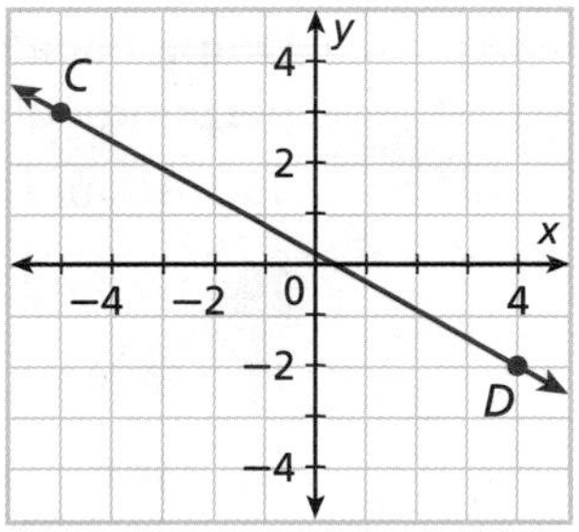

4. $\overleftrightarrow{AB}$

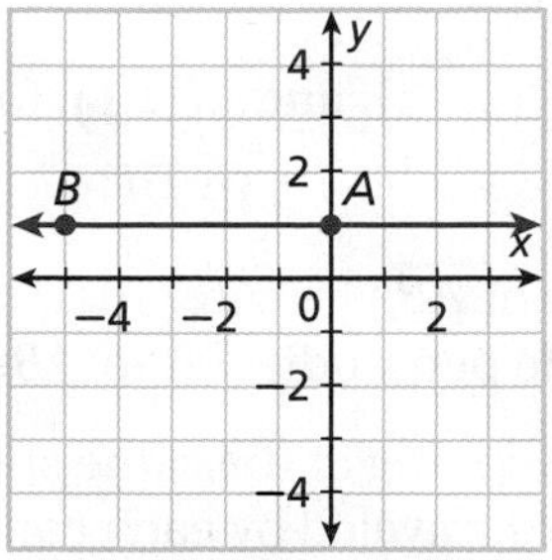

5. $\overleftrightarrow{ST}$

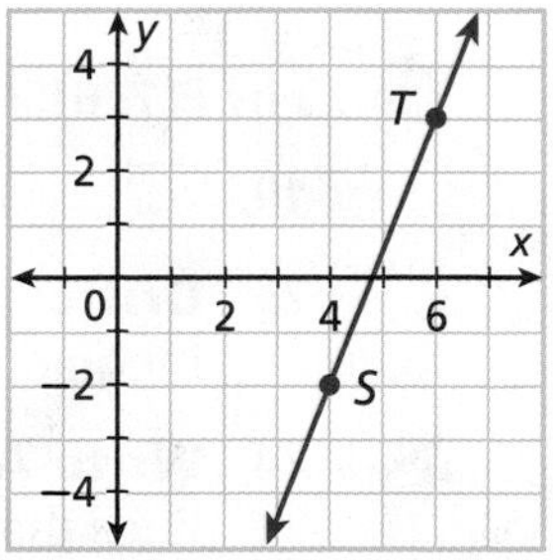

SEE EXAMPLE 2

6. **Biology** A migrating bird flying at a constant speed travels 80 miles by 8:00 A.M. and 200 miles by 11:00 A.M. Graph the line that represents the bird's distance traveled. Find and interpret the slope of the line.

SEE EXAMPLE 3

Graph each pair of lines. Use slopes to determine whether the lines are parallel, perpendicular, or neither.

7. $\overleftrightarrow{HJ}$ and $\overleftrightarrow{KM}$ for $H(3, 2)$, $J(4, 1)$, $K(-2, -4)$, and $M(-1, -5)$
8. $\overleftrightarrow{LM}$ and $\overleftrightarrow{NP}$ for $L(-2, 2)$, $M(2, 5)$, $N(0, 2)$, and $P(3, -2)$
9. $\overleftrightarrow{QR}$ and $\overleftrightarrow{ST}$ for $Q(6, 1)$, $R(-2, 4)$, $S(5, 3)$, and $T(-3, -1)$

PRACTICE AND PROBLEM SOLVING

Independent Practice

For Exercises	See Example
10–13	1
14	2
15–17	3

Extra Practice

See Extra Practice for more Skills Practice and Applications Practice exercises.

Use the slope formula to determine the slope of each line.

10. $\overleftrightarrow{AB}$

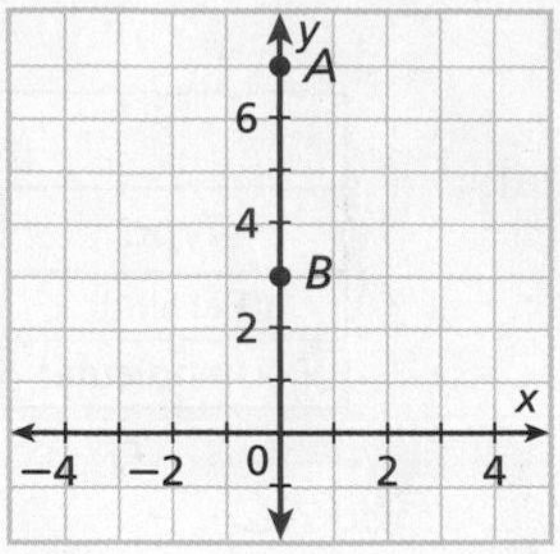

11. $\overleftrightarrow{CD}$

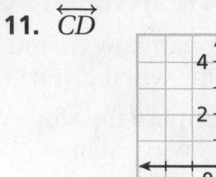

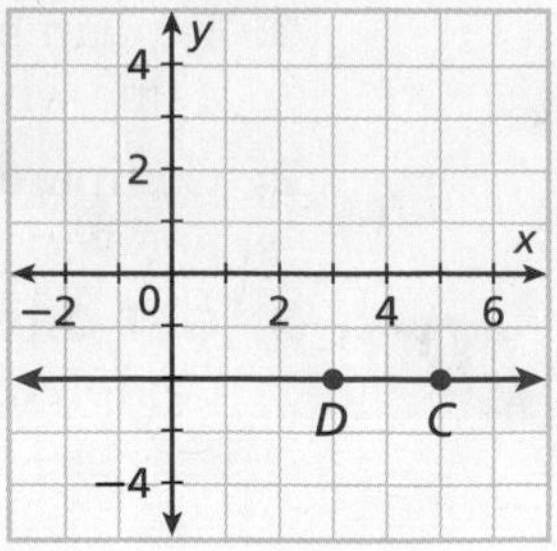

12. $\overleftrightarrow{EF}$

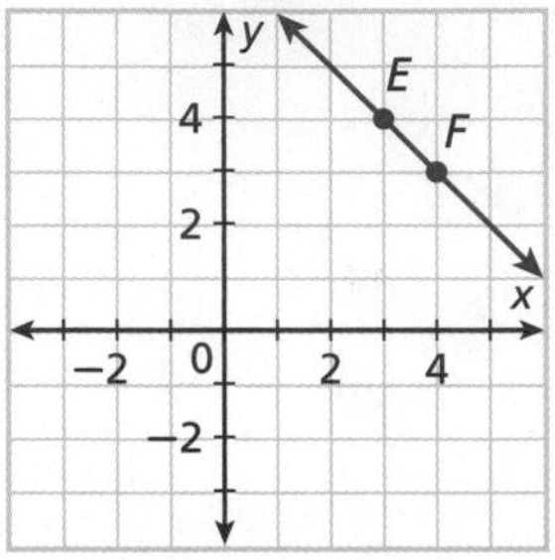

13. $\overleftrightarrow{GH}$

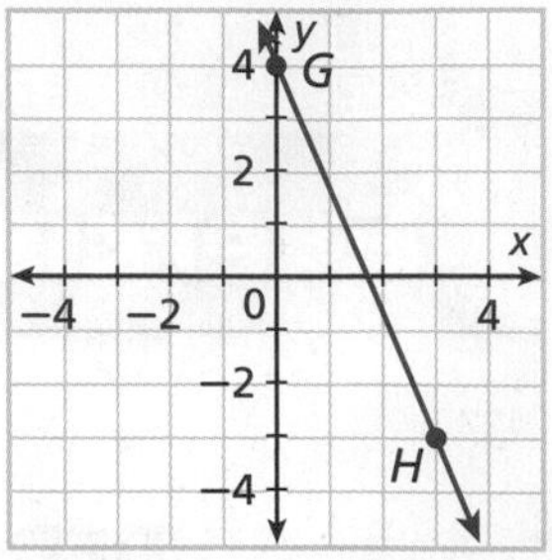

14. Aviation A pilot traveling at a constant speed flies 100 miles by 2:30 P.M. and 475 miles by 5:00 P.M. Graph the line that represents the pilot's distance flown. Find and interpret the slope of the line.

Graph each pair of lines. Use slopes to determine whether the lines are parallel, perpendicular, or neither.

15. $\overleftrightarrow{AB}$ and $\overleftrightarrow{CD}$ for $A(2, -1)$, $B(7, 2)$, $C(2, -3)$, and $D(-3, -6)$

16. $\overleftrightarrow{XY}$ and $\overleftrightarrow{ZW}$ for $X(-2, 5)$, $Y(6, -2)$, $Z(-3, 6)$, and $W(4, 0)$

17. $\overleftrightarrow{JK}$ and $\overleftrightarrow{JL}$ for $J(-4, -2)$, $K(4, -2)$, and $L(-4, 6)$

18. Geography A point on a river has an elevation of about 1150 meters above sea level. The length of the river from that point to where it enters the sea is about 2400 km. Find and interpret the slope of the river.

For $F(7, 6)$, $G(-3, 5)$, $H(-2, -3)$, $J(4, -2)$, and $K(6, 1)$, find each slope.

19. $\overleftrightarrow{FG}$ **20.** $\overleftrightarrow{GJ}$ **21.** $\overleftrightarrow{HK}$ **22.** $\overleftrightarrow{GK}$

23. Critical Thinking The slope of $\overleftrightarrow{AB}$ is greater than 0 and less than 1. Write an inequality for the slope of a line perpendicular to $\overleftrightarrow{AB}$.

24. Write About It Two cars are driving at the same speed. What is true about the lines that represent the distance traveled by each car at a given time?

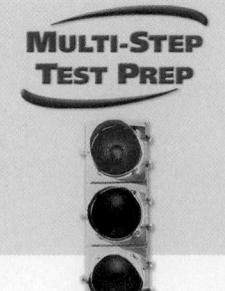

MULTI-STEP TEST PREP

25. A traffic engineer calculates the speed of vehicles as they pass a traffic light. While the light is green, a taxi passes at a constant speed. After 2 s the taxi is 132 ft past the light. After 5 s it is 330 ft past the light.

a. Find the speed of the taxi in feet per second.

b. Use the fact that 22 ft/s = 15 mi/h to find the taxi's speed in miles per hour.

Test Prep

26. $\overleftrightarrow{AB} \perp \overleftrightarrow{CD}$ for $A(1, 3)$, $B(4, -2)$, $C(6, 1)$, and $D(x, y)$. Which are possible values of x and y?

    (A) $x = 1, y = -2$
    (B) $x = 3, y = 6$
    (C) $x = 3, y = -4$
    (D) $x = -2, y = -4$

27. Classify $\overleftrightarrow{MN}$ and $\overleftrightarrow{PQ}$ for $M(-3, 1)$, $N(1, 3)$, $P(8, 4)$, and $Q(2, 1)$.

    (F) Parallel
    (G) Perpendicular
    (H) Vertical
    (J) Skew

28. In the formula $d = rt$, d represents distance, and r represents the rate of change, or slope. Which ray on the graph represents a slope of 45 miles per hour?

    (A) A
    (B) B
    (C) C
    (D) D

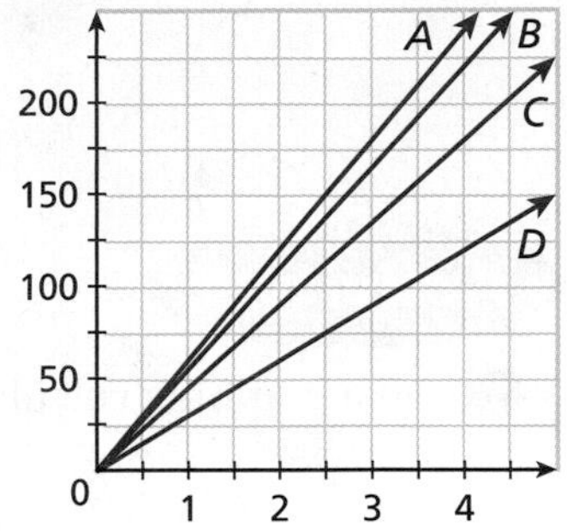

CHALLENGE AND EXTEND

Use the given information to classify $\overleftrightarrow{JK}$ for $J(a, b)$ and $K(c, d)$.

29. $a = c$

30. $b = d$

31. The vertices of square $ABCD$ are $A(0, -2)$, $B(6, 4)$, $C(0, 10)$, $D(-6, 4)$.
    a. Show that the opposite sides are parallel.
    b. Show that the consecutive sides are perpendicular.
    c. Show that all sides are congruent.

32. $\overleftrightarrow{ST} \parallel \overleftrightarrow{VW}$ for $S(-3, 5)$, $T(1, -1)$, $V(x, -3)$, and $W(1, y)$. Find a set of possible values for x and y.

33. $\overleftrightarrow{MN} \perp \overleftrightarrow{PQ}$ for $M(2, 1)$, $N(-3, 0)$, $P(x, 4)$, and $Q(3, y)$. Find a set of possible values for x and y.

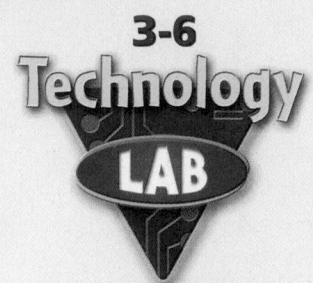

3-6 Technology LAB

Use with Lines in the Coordinate Plane

Explore Parallel and Perpendicular Lines

A graphing calculator can help you explore graphs of parallel and perpendicular lines. To graph a line on a calculator, you can enter the equation of the line in *slope-intercept form*. The slope-intercept form of the equation of a line is $y = mx + b$, where m is the slope and b is the y-intercept. For example, the line $y = 2x + 3$ has a slope of 2 and crosses the y-axis at (0, 3).

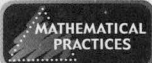

MATHEMATICAL PRACTICES **Use appropriate tools strategically.**

Learn It Online Lab Resources Online

CC.9-12.G.GPE.5 Prove the slope criteria for parallel and perpendicular lines and use them to solve ...problems...

Activity 1

1. On a graphing calculator, graph the lines $y = 3x - 4$, $y = -3x - 4$, and $y = 3x + 1$. Which lines appear to be parallel? What do you notice about the slopes of the parallel lines?

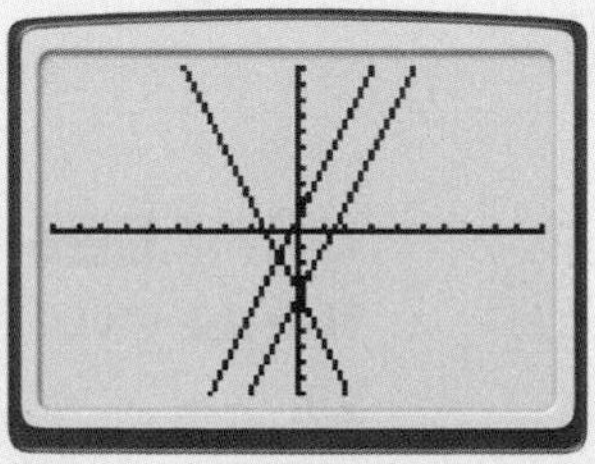

2. Graph $y = 2x$. Experiment with other equations to find a line that appears parallel to $y = 2x$. If necessary, graph $y = 2x$ on graph paper and construct a parallel line. What is the slope of this new line?

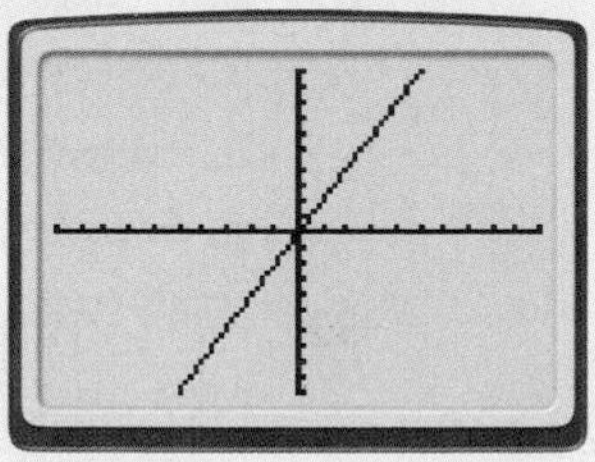

3. Graph $y = -\frac{1}{2}x + 3$. Try to graph a line that appears parallel to $y = -\frac{1}{2}x + 3$. What is the slope of this new line?

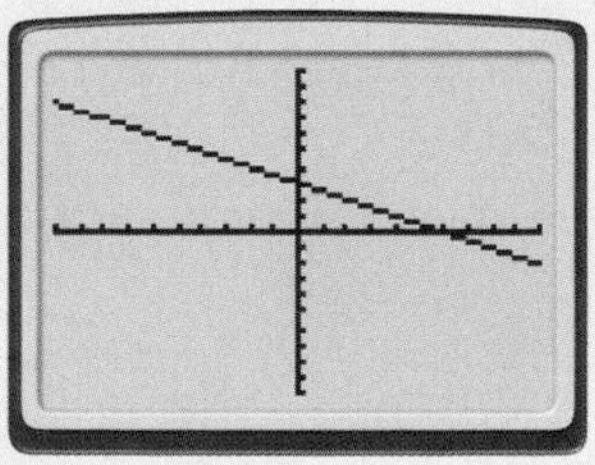

Try This

1. Create two new equations of lines that you think will be parallel. Graph these to confirm your conjecture.
2. Graph two lines that you think are parallel. Change the window settings on the calculator. Do the lines still appear parallel? Describe your results.
3. Try changing the y-intercepts of one of the parallel lines. Does this change whether the lines appear to be parallel?

On a graphing calculator, perpendicular lines may not appear to be perpendicular on the screen. This is because the unit distances on the x-axis and y-axis can have different lengths. To make sure that the lines appear perpendicular on the screen, use a *square window*, which shows the x-axis and y-axis as having equal unit distances.

One way to get a square window is to use the **Zoom** feature. On the **Zoom** menu, the **ZDecimal** and **ZSquare** commands change the window to a square window. The **ZStandard** command does not produce a square window.

Activity 2

1 Graph the lines $y = x$ and $y = -x$ in a square window. Do the lines appear to be perpendicular?

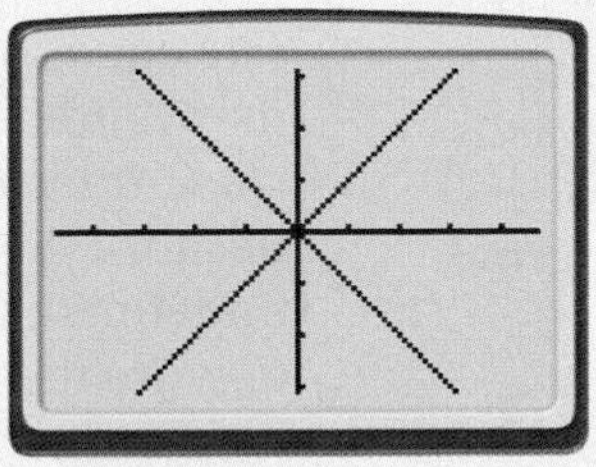

2 Graph $y = 3x - 2$ in a square window. Experiment with other equations to find a line that appears perpendicular to $y = 3x - 2$. If necessary, graph $y = 3x - 2$ on graph paper and construct a perpendicular line. What is the slope of this new line?

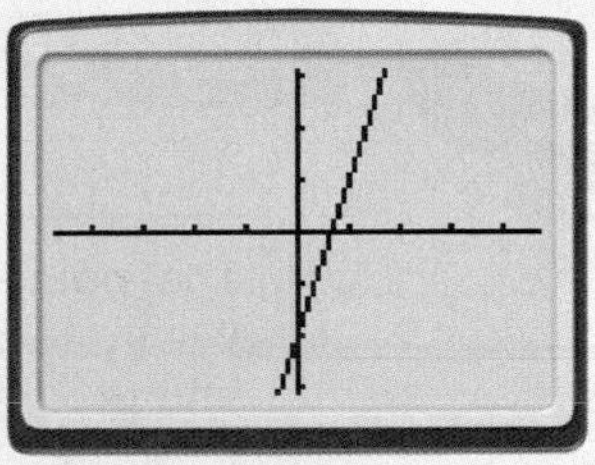

3 Graph $y = \frac{2}{3}x$ in a square window. Try to graph a line that appears perpendicular to $y = \frac{2}{3}x$. What is the slope of this new line?

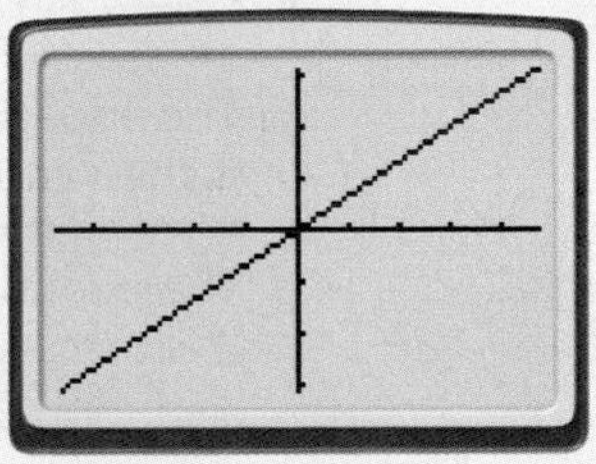

Try This

4. Create two new equations of lines that you think will be perpendicular. Graph these in a square window to confirm your conjecture.
5. Graph two lines that you think are perpendicular. Change the window settings on the calculator. Do the lines still appear perpendicular? Describe your results.
6. Try changing the y-intercepts of one of the perpendicular lines. Does this change whether the lines appear to be perpendicular?

COMMON CORE

3-6 Lines in the Coordinate Plane

CC.9-12.G.GPE.5 Prove the slope criteria for parallel and perpendicular lines and use them to solve… problems…

Objectives
Graph lines and write their equations in slope-intercept and point-slope form.

Classify lines as parallel, intersecting, or coinciding.

Vocabulary
point-slope form
slope-intercept form

Why learn this?
The cost of some health club plans includes a one-time enrollment fee and a monthly fee. You can use the equations of lines to determine which plan is best for you. (See Example 4.)

CLOSE TO HOME
JOHN McPHERSON

"A one-year membership is $10,000, but to encourage you to work out, we give you back $25 every time you use the facility."

The equation of a line can be written in many different forms. The *point-slope* and *slope-intercept* forms of a line are equivalent. Because the slope of a vertical line is undefined, these forms cannot be used to write the equation of a vertical line.

Know it! Note

Forms of the Equation of a Line

FORM	EXAMPLE
The **point-slope form** of a line is $y - y_1 = m(x - x_1)$, where m is the slope and (x_1, y_1) is a given point on the line.	$y - 3 = 2(x - 4)$ $m = 2$, $(x_1, y_1) = (4, 3)$
The **slope-intercept form** of a line is $y = mx + b$, where m is the slope and b is the y-intercept.	$y = 3x + 6$ $m = 3$, $b = 6$
The equation of a vertical line is $x = a$, where a is the x-intercept.	$x = 5$
The equation of a horizontal line is $y = b$, where b is the y-intercept.	$y = 2$

You will use a proof to derive the slope-intercept form of a line in Exercise 54.

PROOF

Point-Slope Form of a Line

Given: The slope of a line through points (x_1, y_1) and (x_2, y_2) is $m = \frac{y_2 - y_1}{x_2 - x_1}$.
Prove: The equation of the line through (x_1, y_1) with slope m is $y - y_1 = m(x - x_1)$.
Proof:
Let (x, y) be any point on the line.

$m = \frac{y_2 - y_1}{x_2 - x_1}$	*Slope formula*
$m = \frac{y - y_1}{x - x_1}$	*Substitute (x, y) for (x_2, y_2).*
$(x - x_1)m = (x - x_1)\frac{y - y_1}{x - x_1}$	*Multiply both sides by $(x - x_1)$.*
$m(x - x_1) = (y - y_1)$	*Simplify.*
$y - y_1 = m(x - x_1)$	*Sym. Prop. of =*

EXAMPLE 1 **Writing Equations of Lines**

Algebra

Write the equation of each line in the given form.

A the line with slope 3 through (2, 1) in point-slope form

$y - y_1 = m(x - x_1)$ *Point-slope form*

$y - 1 = 3(x - 2)$ *Substitute 3 for m, 2 for x_1, and 1 for y_1.*

B the line through (0, 4) and (−1, 2) in slope-intercept form

$m = \frac{2-4}{-1-0} = \frac{-2}{-1} = 2$ *Find the slope.*

$y = mx + b$ *Slope-intercept form*

$4 = 2(0) + b$ *Substitute 2 for m, 0 for x, and 4 for y to find b.*

$4 = b$ *Simplify.*

$y = 2x + 4$ *Write in slope-intercept form using m = 2 and b = 4.*

Remember!

A line with y-intercept b contains the point (0, b).
A line with x-intercept a contains the point (a, 0).

C the line with x-intercept 2 and y-intercept 3 in point-slope form

$m = \frac{3-0}{0-2} = -\frac{3}{2}$ *Use the points (2, 0) and (0, 3) to find the slope.*

$y - y_1 = m(x - x_1)$ *Point-slope form*

$y - 0 = -\frac{3}{2}(x - 2)$ *Substitute $-\frac{3}{2}$ for m, 2 for x_1, and 0 for y_1.*

$y = -\frac{3}{2}(x - 2)$ *Simplify.*

CHECK IT OUT! Write the equation of each line in the given form.

1a. the line with slope 0 through (4, 6) in slope-intercept form

1b. the line through (−3, 2) and (1, 2) in point-slope form

EXAMPLE 2 **Graphing Lines**

Algebra

Graph each line.

A $y = \frac{3}{2}x + 3$

The equation is given in slope-intercept form, with a slope of $\frac{3}{2}$ and a y-intercept of 3.

Plot the point (0, 3) and then rise 3 and run 2 to find another point.

Draw the line containing the two points.

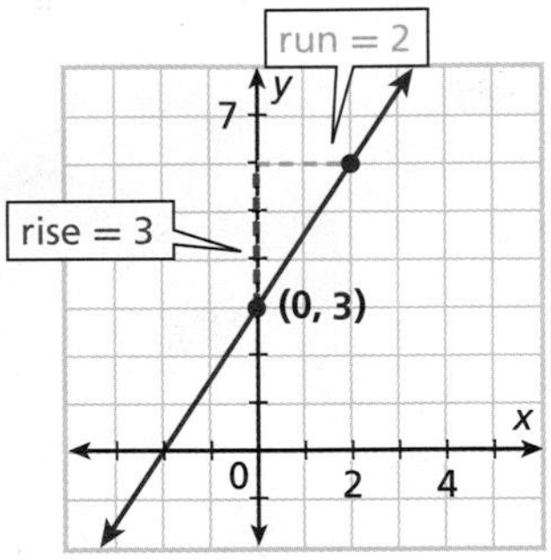

B $y + 3 = -2(x - 1)$

The equation is given in point-slope form, with a slope of $-2 = \frac{-2}{1}$ through the point (1, −3).

Plot the point (1, −3) and then rise −2 and run 1 to find another point.

Draw the line containing the two points.

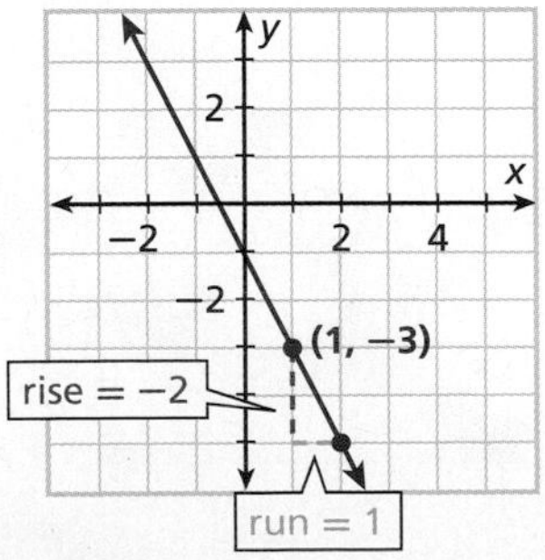

Graph the line.

C $x = 3$

The equation is given in the form for a vertical line with an x-intercept of 3. The equation tells you that the x-coordinate of every point on the line is 3. Draw the vertical line through $(3, 0)$.

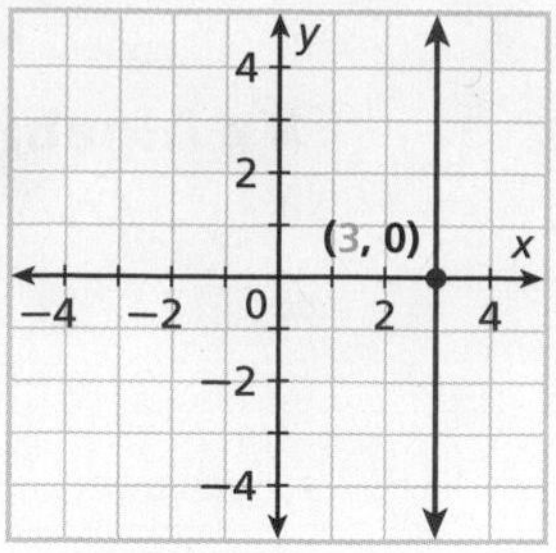

CHECK IT OUT! **Graph each line.**

2a. $y = 2x - 3$ **2b.** $y - 1 = -\frac{2}{3}(x + 2)$ **2c.** $y = -4$

A system of two linear equations in two variables represents two lines. The lines can be parallel, intersecting, or coinciding. Lines that coincide are the same line, but the equations may be written in different forms.

Know it! Note — **Pairs of Lines**

Parallel Lines	Intersecting Lines	Coinciding Lines
$y = 5x + 8$ $y = 5x - 4$	$y = 2x - 5$ $y = 4x + 3$	$y = 2x - 4$ $y = 2x - 4$
Same slope different y-intercept	Different slopes	Same slope same y-intercept

EXAMPLE 3 Classifying Pairs of Lines

Determine whether the lines are parallel, intersect, or coincide.

A $y = 2x + 3, y = 2x - 1$

Both lines have a slope of 2, and the y-intercepts are different. So the lines are parallel.

B $y = 3x - 5, 6x - 2y = 10$

Solve the second equation for y to find the slope-intercept form.

$6x - 2y = 10$

$-2y = -6x + 10$

$y = 3x - 5$

Both lines have a slope of 3 and a y-intercept of −5, so they coincide.

C $3x + 2y = 7, 3y = 4x + 7$

Solve both equations for y to find the slope-intercept form.

$3x + 2y = 7$

$2y = -3x + 7$

$y = -\frac{3}{2}x + \frac{7}{2}$ *The slope is* $-\frac{3}{2}$.

$3y = 4x + 7$

$y = \frac{4}{3}x + \frac{7}{3}$ *The slope is* $\frac{4}{3}$.

The lines have different slopes, so they intersect.

CHECK IT OUT! **3.** Determine whether the lines $3x + 5y = 2$ and $3x + 6 = -5y$ are parallel, intersect, or coincide.

EXAMPLE 4 Problem-Solving Application

MATHEMATICAL PRACTICES

Make sense of problems and persevere in solving them.

Audrey is trying to decide between two health club plans. After how many months would both plans' total costs be the same?

	Plan A	Plan B
Enrollment Fee	\$140	\$60
Monthly Fee	\$35	\$55

1 Understand the Problem

The **answer** is the number of months after which the costs of the two plans would be the same. Plan A costs \$140 for enrollment and \$35 per month. Plan B costs \$60 for enrollment and \$55 per month.

2 Make a Plan

Write an equation for each plan, and then graph the equations. The solution is the intersection of the two lines. Find the intersection by solving the system of equations.

3 Solve

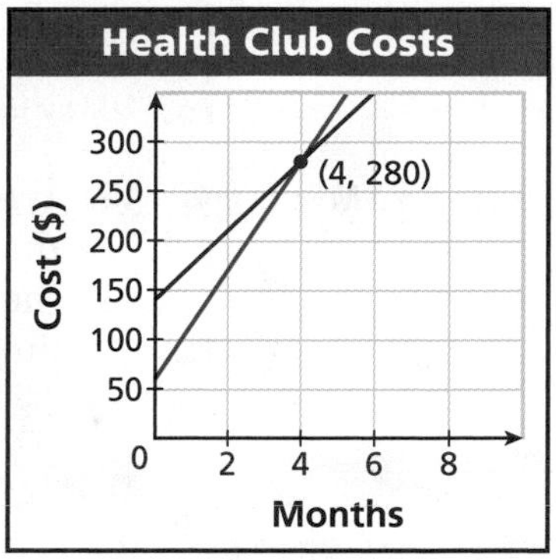

Plan A: $y = 35x + 140$

Plan B: $y = 55x + 60$

$0 = -20x + 80$ *Subtract the second equation from the first.*

$x = 4$ *Solve for x.*

$y = 35(4) + 140 = 280$ *Substitute 4 for x in the first equation.*

The lines cross at $(4, 280)$.
Both plans cost \$280 after 4 months.

4 Look Back

Check your answer for each plan in the original problem. For 4 months, plan A costs \$140 plus \$35(4) = \$140 + \$140 = \$280. Plan B costs \$60 + \$55(4) = \$60 + \$220 = \$280, so the plans cost the same.

CHECK IT OUT! **Use the information above to answer the following.**

4. **What if...?** Suppose the rate for Plan B was also \$35 per month. What would be true about the lines that represent the cost of each plan?

MATHEMATICAL PRACTICES

THINK AND DISCUSS

1. Explain how to use the slopes and y-intercepts to determine if two lines are parallel.
2. Describe the relationship between the slopes of perpendicular lines.
3. **GET ORGANIZED** Copy and complete the graphic organizer.

Know it! Note

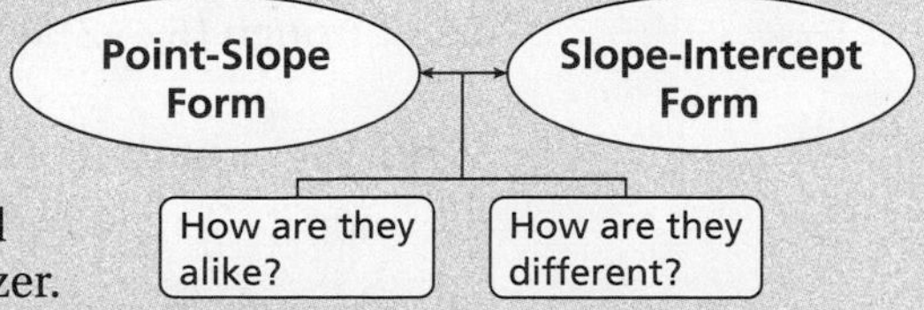

3-6 Exercises

Learn It Online
Homework Help Online
Parent Resources Online

GUIDED PRACTICE

1. **Vocabulary** How can you recognize the *slope-intercept form* of an equation?

SEE EXAMPLE 1

Write the equation of each line in the given form.

2. the line through $(4, 7)$ and $(-2, 1)$ in slope-intercept form
3. the line through $(-4, 2)$ with slope $\frac{3}{4}$ in point-slope form.
4. the line with x-intercept 4 and y-intercept -2 in slope-intercept form

SEE EXAMPLE 2

Graph each line.

5. $y = -3x + 4$
6. $y + 4 = \frac{2}{3}(x - 6)$
7. $x = 5$

SEE EXAMPLE 3

Determine whether the lines are parallel, intersect, or coincide.

8. $y = -3x + 4,\ y = -3x + 1$
9. $6x - 12y = -24,\ 3y = 2x + 18$
10. $y = \frac{1}{3}x + \frac{2}{3},\ 3y = x + 2$
11. $4x + 2y = 10,\ y = -2x + 15$

SEE EXAMPLE 4

12. **Transportation** A speeding ticket in Conroe costs \$115 for the first 10 mi/h over the speed limit and \$1 for each additional mi/h. In Lakeville, a ticket costs \$50 for the first 10 mi/h over the speed limit and \$10 for each additional mi/h. If the speed limit is 55 mi/h, at what speed will the tickets cost approximately the same?

PRACTICE AND PROBLEM SOLVING

Homework Help

For Exercises	See Example
13–15	1
16–18	2
19–22	3
23	4

Extra Practice

See Extra Practice for more Skills Practice and Applications Practice exercises.

Write the equation of each line in the given form.

13. the line through $(0, -2)$ and $(4, 6)$ in point-slope form
14. the line through $(5, 2)$ and $(-2, 2)$ in slope-intercept form
15. the line through $(6, -4)$ with slope $\frac{2}{3}$ in point-slope form

Graph each line.

16. $y - 7 = x + 4$
17. $y = \frac{1}{2}x - 2$
18. $y = 2$

Determine whether the lines are parallel, intersect, or coincide.

19. $y = x - 7,\ y = -x + 3$
20. $y = \frac{5}{2}x + 4,\ 2y = 5x - 4$
21. $x + 2y = 6,\ y = -\frac{1}{2}x + 3$
22. $7x + 2y = 10,\ 3y = 4x - 5$
23. **Business** Chris is comparing two sales positions that he has been offered. The first pays a weekly salary of \$375 plus a 20% commission. The second pays a weekly salary of \$325 plus a 25% commission. How much must he make in sales per week for the two jobs to pay the same?

Write the equation of each line in slope-intercept form. Then graph the line.

24. through $(-6, 2)$ and $(3, 6)$
25. horizontal line through $(2, 3)$
26. through $(5, -2)$ with slope $\frac{2}{3}$
27. x-intercept 4, y-intercept -3

Write the equation of each line in point-slope form. Then graph the line.

28. slope $-\frac{1}{2}$, y-intercept 2
29. slope $\frac{3}{4}$, x-intercept -2
30. through $(5, -1)$ with slope -1
31. through $(4, 6)$ and $(-2, -5)$

32. **ERROR ANALYSIS** Write the equation of the line with slope −2 through the point (−4, 3) in slope-intercept form. Which equation is incorrect? Explain.

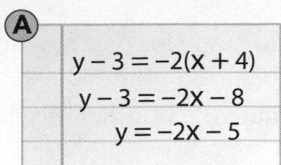

A

$y - 3 = -2(x + 4)$
$y - 3 = -2x - 8$
$y = -2x - 5$

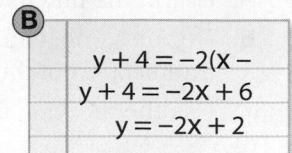

B

$y + 4 = -2(x -$
$y + 4 = -2x + 6$
$y = -2x + 2$

Determine whether the lines are perpendicular.

33. $y = 3x - 5,\ y = -3x + 1$

34. $y = -x + 1,\ y = x + 2$

35. $y = -\frac{2}{3}x + 5,\ y = \frac{3}{2}x - 8,$

36. $y = -2x + 4,\ y = -\frac{1}{2}x - 2$

Multi-Step Given the equation of the line and point *P* not on the line, find the equation of a line parallel to the given line and a line perpendicular to the given line through the given point.

37. $y = 3x + 7,\ P(2, 3)$

38. $y = -2x - 5,\ P(-1, 4)$

39. $4x + 3y = 8,\ P(4, -2)$

40. $2x - 5y = 7,\ P(-2, 4)$

LINK

Food

In 2004, the world's largest pizza was baked in Italy. The diameter of the pizza was 5.19 m (about 17 ft) and it weighed 124 kg (about 273 lb).

Multi-Step Use slope to determine if each triangle is a right triangle. If so, which angle is the right angle?

41. $A(-5, 3),\ B(0, -2),\ C(5, 3)$

42. $D(1, 0),\ E(2, 7),\ F(5, 1)$

43. $G(3, 4),\ H(-3, 4),\ J(1, -2)$

44. $K(-2, 4),\ L(2, 1),\ M(1, 8)$

45. **Food** A restaurant charges \$8 for a large cheese pizza plus \$1.50 per topping. Another restaurant charges \$11 for a large cheese pizza plus \$0.75 per topping. How many toppings does a pizza have that costs the same at both restaurants?

46. **Estimation** Estimate the solution of the system of equations represented by the lines in the graph.

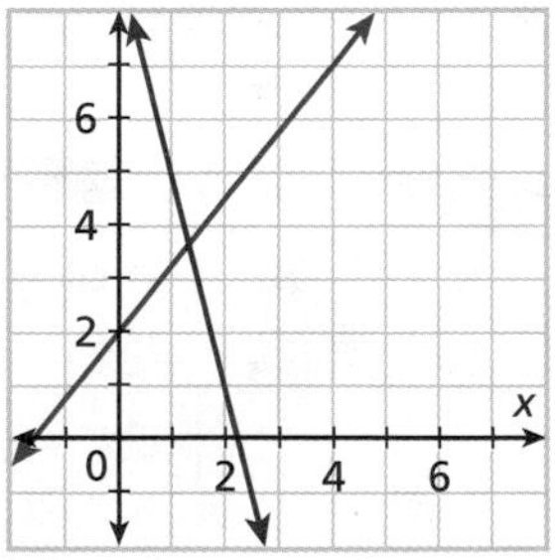

Write the equation of the perpendicular bisector of the segment with the given endpoints.

47. (2, 5) and (4, 9)

48. (1, 1) and (3, 1)

49. (1, 3) and (−1, 4)

50. (−3, 2) and (−3, −10)

51. Line ℓ has equation $y = -\frac{1}{2}x + 4$, and point P has coordinates (3, 5).
   a. Find the equation of line m that passes through P and is perpendicular to ℓ.
   b. Find the coordinates of the intersection of ℓ and m.
   c. What is the distance from P to ℓ?

52. Line p has equation $y = x + 3$, and line q has equation $y = x - 1$.
   a. Find the equation of a line r that is perpendicular to p and q.
   b. Find the coordinates of the intersection of p and r and the coordinates of the intersection of q and r.
   c. Find the distance between lines p and q.

MULTI-STEP TEST PREP

53. For a car moving at 60 mi/h, the equation $d = 88t$ gives the distance in feet d that the car travels in t seconds.

a. Graph the line $d = 88t$.

b. On the same graph you made for part **a**, graph the line $d = 300$. What does the intersection of the two lines represent?

c. Use the graph to estimate the number of seconds it takes the car to travel 300 ft.

54. Prove the slope-intercept form of a line, given the point-slope form.
Given: The equation of the line through (x_1, y_1) with slope m is $y - y_1 = m(x - x_1)$.
Prove: The equation of the line through $(0, b)$ with slope m is $y = mx + b$.
Plan: Substitute $(0, b)$ for (x_1, y_1) in the equation $y - y_1 = m(x - x_1)$ and simplify.

55. Data Collection Use a graphing calculator and a motion detector to do the following: Walk in front of the motion detector at a constant speed, and write the equation of the resulting graph.

56. Critical Thinking A line contains the points $(-4, 6)$ and $(2, 2)$. Write a convincing argument that the line crosses the x-axis at $(5, 0)$. Include a graph to verify your argument.

57. Write About It Determine whether the lines are parallel. Use slope to explain your answer.

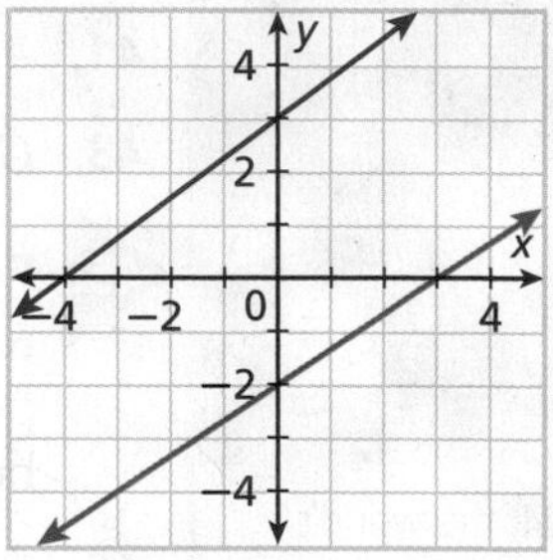

TEST PREP

58. Which graph best represents a solution to this system of equations?

$$\begin{cases} -3x + y = 7 \\ 2x + y = -3 \end{cases}$$

Ⓐ

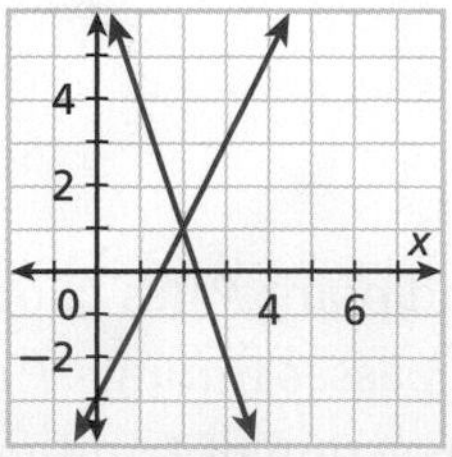

Ⓒ

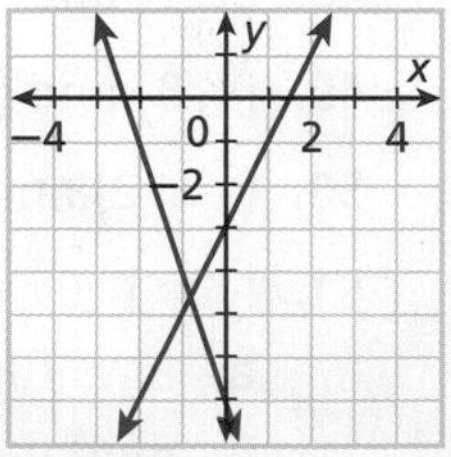

Ⓑ

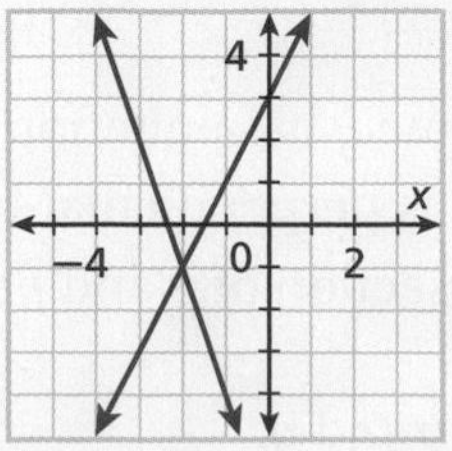

Ⓓ

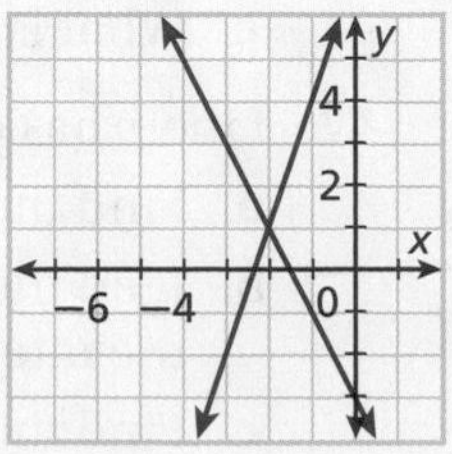

59. Which line is parallel to the line with the equation $y = -2x + 5$?

Ⓕ $\overleftrightarrow{AB}$ through $A(2, 3)$ and $B(1, 1)$
Ⓗ $4x + 2y = 10$
Ⓖ $y = -\frac{1}{2}x - 3$
Ⓙ $x + \frac{1}{2}y = 1$

60. Which equation best describes the graph shown?

Ⓐ $y = -\frac{3}{2}x + 3$
Ⓒ $y = -\frac{2}{3}x + 2$
Ⓑ $y = 3x - \frac{2}{3}$
Ⓓ $y = -\frac{2}{3}x + 3$

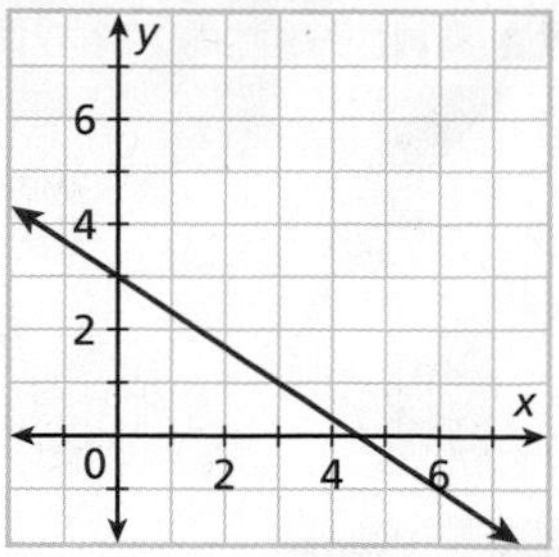

61. Which line includes the points $(-4, 2)$ and $(6, -3)$?

Ⓕ $y = 2x - 4$
Ⓗ $y = -\frac{1}{2}x - 4$
Ⓖ $y = 2x$
Ⓙ $y = -\frac{1}{2}x$

CHALLENGE AND EXTEND

62. A right triangle is formed by the x-axis, the y-axis, and the line $y = -2x + 5$. Find the length of the hypotenuse.

63. If the length of the hypotenuse of a right triangle is 17 units and the legs lie along the x-axis and y-axis, find a possible equation that describes the line that contains the hypotenuse.

$x^2 + y^2 = \sqrt{17}^2$

64. Find the equations of three lines that form a triangle with a hypotenuse of 13 units.

65. Multi-Step Are the points $(-2, -4)$, $(5, -2)$ and $(2, -3)$ collinear? Explain the method you used to determine your answer.

66. For the line $y = x + 1$ and the point $P(3, 2)$, let d represent the distance from P to a point (x, y) on the line.

a. Write an expression for d^2 in terms of x and y. Substitute the expression $x + 1$ for y and simplify.

b. How could you use this expression to find the shortest distance from P to the line? Compare your result to the distance along a perpendicular line.

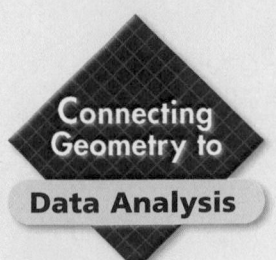

Connecting Geometry to **Data Analysis**

Scatter Plots and Lines of Best Fit

Recall that a line has an infinite number of points on it. You can compute the slope of a line if you can identify two distinct points on the line.

Example 1

The table shows several possible measures of an angle and its supplement. Graph the points in the table. Then draw the line that best represents the data and write the equation of the line.

x	$y = 180 - x$
30	150
60	120
90	90
120	60
150	30

Step 1
Use the table to write ordered pairs $(x, 180 - x)$ and then plot the points.

$(30, 150), (60, 120), (90, 90), (120, 60), (150, 30)$

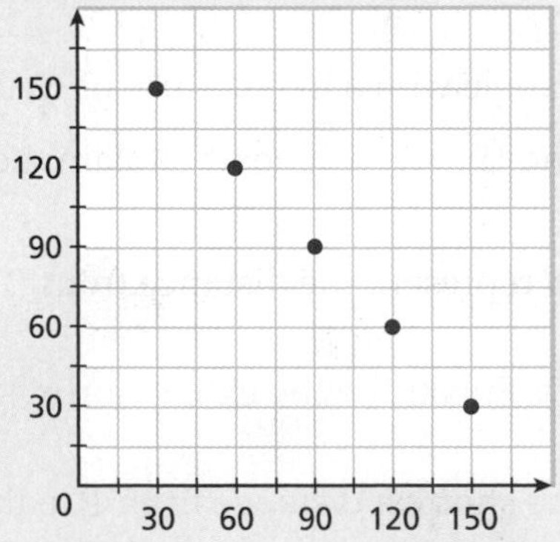

Step 2
Draw a line that passes through all the points.

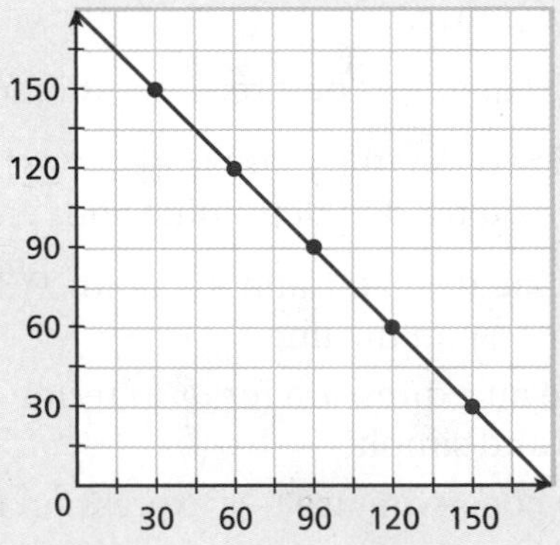

Step 3 Choose two points from the line, such as (30, 150) and (120, 60). Use them to find the slope.

$$m = \frac{y_2 - y_1}{x_2 - x_1}$$ *Slope formula*

$$= \frac{60 - 150}{120 - 30}$$ *Substitute (30, 150) for (x_1, y_1) and (120, 60) for (x_2, y_2).*

$$= \frac{-90}{90} = -1$$ *Simplify.*

Step 4 Use the point-slope form to find the equation of the line and then simplify.

$$y - y_1 = m(x - x_1)$$ *Point-slope form*

$$y - 150 = -1(x - 30)$$ *Substitute (30, 150) for (x_1, y_1) and −1 for m.*

$$y = -x + 180$$ *Simplify.*

If you can draw a line through all the points in a set of data, the relationship is linear. If the points are close to a line, you can approximate the relationship with a *line of best fit.*

Example 2

A physical therapist evaluates a client's progress by measuring the angle of motion of an injured joint. The table shows the angle of motion of a client's wrist over six weeks. Estimate the equation of the line of best fit.

Week	Angle Measure
1	30
2	36
3	46
4	48
5	54
6	62

Step 1
Use the table to write ordered pairs and then plot the points.

$(1, 30), (2, 36), (3, 46), (4, 48), (5, 54), (6, 62)$

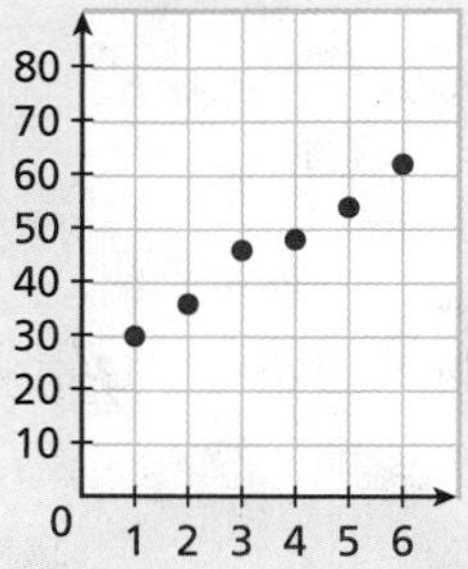

Step 2
Use a ruler to estimate a line of best fit. Try to get the edge of the ruler closest to all the points on the line.

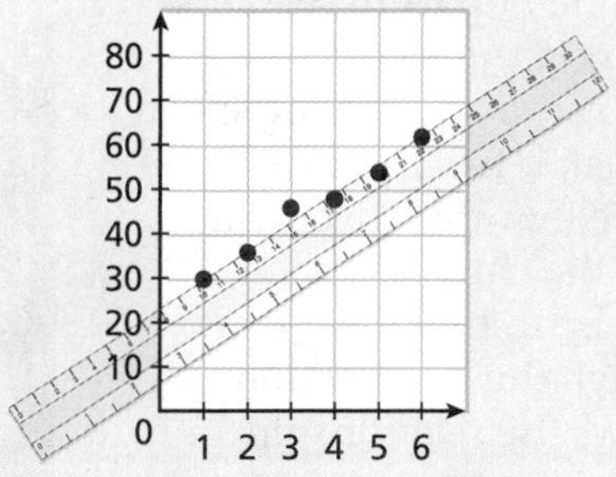

Step 3 A line passing through $(2, 36)$ and $(6, 62)$ seems to be closest to all the points. Draw this line. Use the points $(2, 36)$ and $(6, 62)$ to find the slope of the line.

$$m = \frac{y_2 - y_1}{x_2 - x_1} = \frac{62 - 36}{6 - 2} = 6.5$$ *Substitute $(2, 36)$ for (x_1, y_1) and $(6, 62)$ for (x_2, y_2).*

Step 4 Use the point-slope form to find the equation of the line and then simplify.

$$y - y_1 = m(x - x_1)$$ *Point-slope form*

$$y - 36 = 6.5(x - 2)$$ *Substitute $(2, 36)$ for (x_1, y_1) and 6.5 for m.*

$$y = 6.5x + 23$$ *Simplify.*

Try This

Estimate the equation of the line of best fit for each relationship.

1.

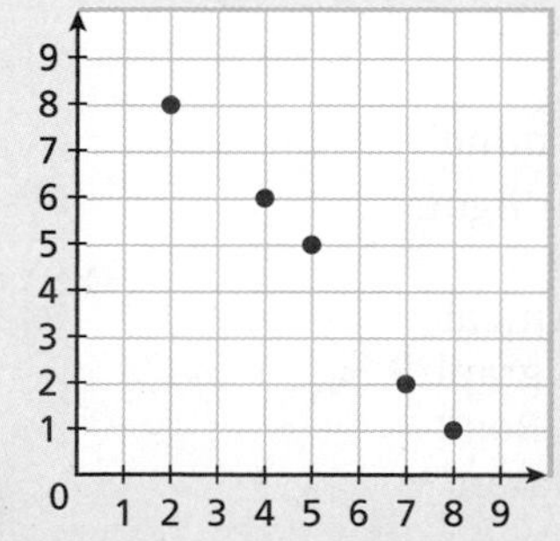

2. the relationship between an angle and its complement

3. **Data Collection** Use a graphing calculator and a motion detector to do the following: Set the equipment so that the graph shows distance on the y-axis and time on the x-axis. Walk in front of the motion dector while varying your speed slightly and use the resulting graph.

CHAPTER 3

MULTI-STEP TEST PREP

SECTION 3B

MATHEMATICAL PRACTICES **Model with mathematics.**

Coordinate Geometry

Red Light, Green Light When a driver approaches an intersection and sees a yellow traffic light, she must decide if she can make it through the intersection before the light turns red. Traffic engineers use graphs and equations to study this situation.

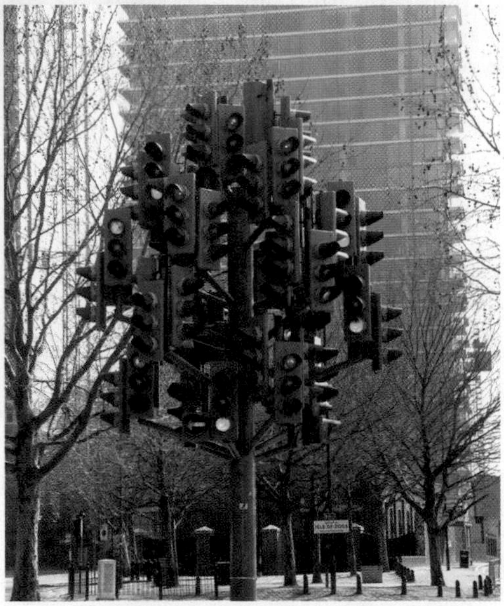

1. Traffic engineers can set the duration of the yellow lights on Lincoln Road for any length of time *t* up to 10 seconds. For each value of *t*, there is a critical distance *d*. If a car moving at the speed limit is more than *d* feet from the light when it turns yellow, the driver will have to stop. If the car is less than *d* feet from the light, the driver can continue through the intersection. The graph shows the relationship between *t* and *d*. Find the speed limit on Lincoln Road in miles per hour. (*Hint:* 22 ft/s = 15 mi/h)

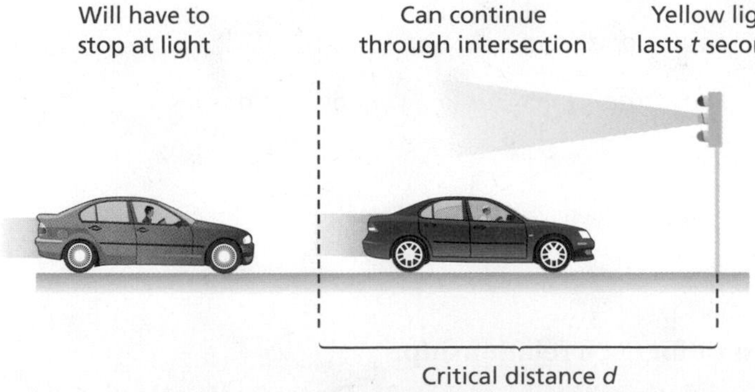

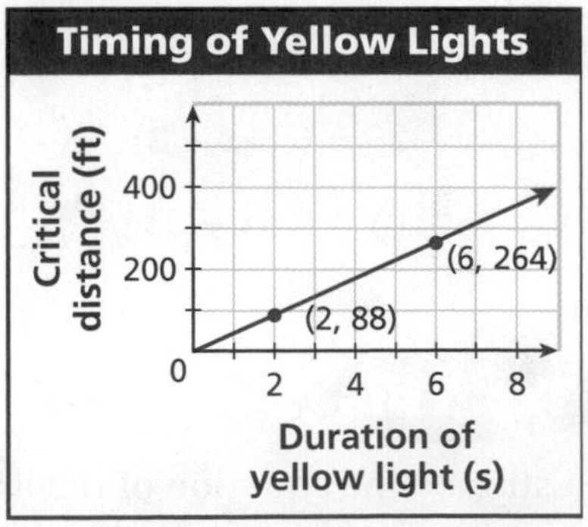

2. Traffic engineers use the equation $d = \frac{22}{15}st$ to determine the critical distance for various durations of a yellow light. In the equation, *s* is the speed limit. The speed limit on Porter Street is 45 mi/h. Write the equation of the critical distance for a yellow light on Porter Street and then graph the line. Does this line intersect the line for Lincoln Road? If so, where? Is the line for Porter Street steeper or flatter than the line for Lincoln Road? Explain how you know.

READY TO GO ON?

Quiz for Lesson 3-5 and 3-6

3-5 Slopes of Lines

Use the slope formula to determine the slope of each line.

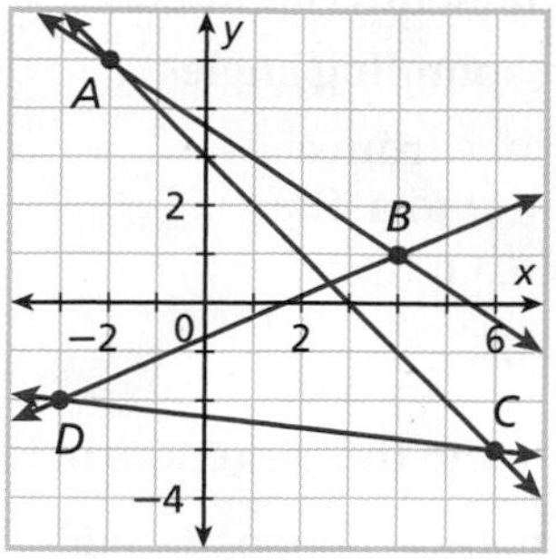

1. $\overleftrightarrow{AC}$ 2. $\overleftrightarrow{CD}$ 3. $\overleftrightarrow{AB}$ 4. $\overleftrightarrow{BD}$

Find the slope of the line through the given points.

5. $M(2, 3)$ and $N(0, 7)$
6. $F(-1, 4)$ and $G(5, -1)$
7. $P(4, 0)$ and $Q(1, -3)$
8. $K(4, 2)$ and $L(-3, 2)$
9. Sonia is walking 2.5 miles home from school. She leaves at 4:00 P.M., and gets home at 4:45 P.M. Graph the line that represents Sonia's distance from school at a given time. Find and interpret the slope of the line.

Graph each pair of lines and use their slopes to determine if they are parallel, perpendicular, or neither.

10. $\overleftrightarrow{EF}$ and $\overleftrightarrow{GH}$ for $E(-2, 3)$, $F(6, 1)$, $G(6, 4)$, and $H(2, 5)$
11. $\overleftrightarrow{JK}$ and $\overleftrightarrow{LM}$ for $J(4, 3)$, $K(5, -1)$, $L(-2, 4)$, and $M(3, -5)$
12. $\overleftrightarrow{NP}$ and $\overleftrightarrow{QR}$ for $N(5, -3)$, $P(0, 4)$, $Q(-3, -2)$, and $R(4, 3)$
13. $\overleftrightarrow{ST}$ and $\overleftrightarrow{VW}$ for $S(0, 3)$, $T(0, 7)$, $V(2, 3)$, and $W(5, 3)$

3-6 Lines in the Coordinate Plane

Write the equation of each line in the given form.

14. the line through $(3, 8)$ and $(-3, 4)$ in slope-intercept form
15. the line through $(-5, 4)$ with slope $\frac{2}{3}$ in point-slope form
16. the line with y-intercept 2 through the point $(4, 1)$ in slope-intercept form

Graph each line.

17. $y = -2x + 5$
18. $y + 3 = \frac{1}{4}(x - 4)$
19. $x = 3$

Write the equation of each line.

20.

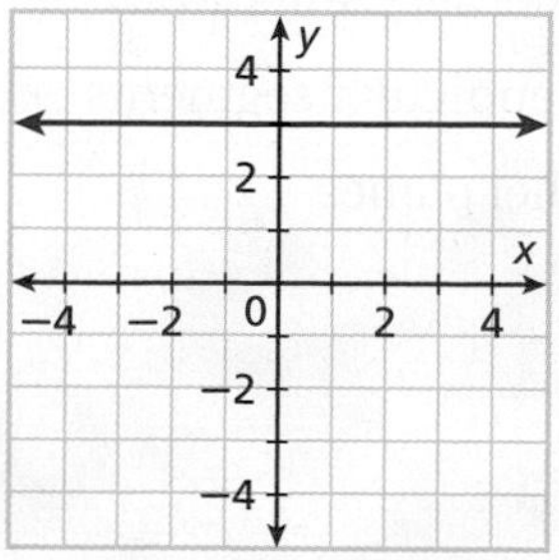

21.

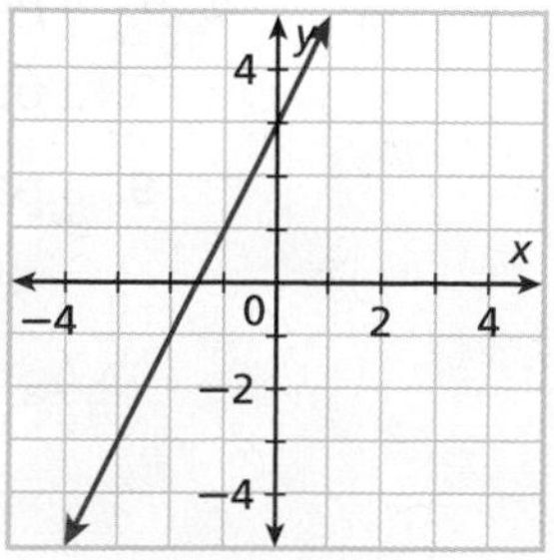

22.

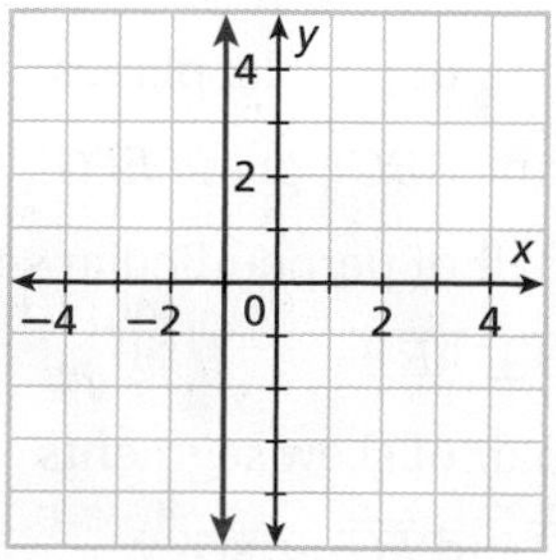

Determine whether the lines are parallel, intersect, or coincide.

23. $y = -2x + 5$
 $y = -2x - 5$
24. $3x + 2y = 8$
 $y = -\frac{3}{2}x + 4$
25. $y = 4x - 5$
 $3x + 4y = 7$

CHAPTER 3 Study Guide: Review

Know it! Note For a complete list of postulates, theorems, and corollaries, see p. PT2.

Vocabulary

alternate exterior angles
alternate interior angles
corresponding angles
distance from a point to a line
parallel lines
parallel planes
perpendicular bisector
perpendicular lines
point-slope form
rise
run
same-side interior angles
skew lines
slope
slope-intercept form
transversal

Complete the sentences below with vocabulary words from the list above.

1. Angles on opposite sides of a transversal and between the lines it intersects are __?__ .
2. Lines that are in different planes are __?__ .
3. A(n) __?__ is a line that intersects two coplanar lines at two points.
4. The __?__ is used to write the equation of a line with a given slope that passes through a given point.
5. The slope of a line is the ratio of the __?__ to the __?__ .

3-1 Lines and Angles

EXAMPLES

Identify each of the following.

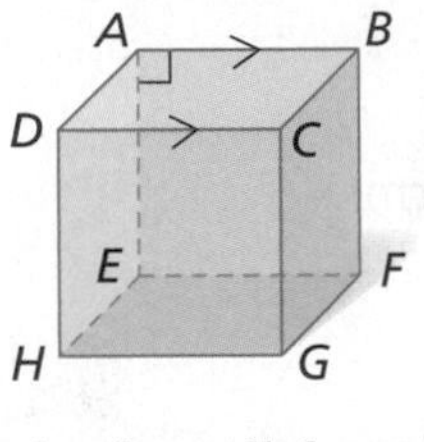

- a pair of parallel segments
  $\overline{AB} \parallel \overline{CD}$
- a pair of parallel planes
  plane *ABC* || plane *EFG*
- a pair of perpendicular segments
  $\overline{AB} \perp \overline{AE}$
- a pair of skew segments
  $\overline{AB}$ and $\overline{FG}$ are skew.

EXERCISES

Identify each of the following.

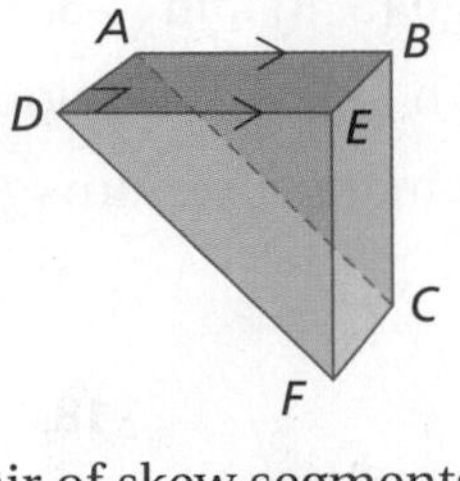

6. a pair of skew segments
7. a pair of parallel segments
8. a pair of perpendicular segments
9. a pair of parallel planes

Identify the transversal and classify each angle pair.

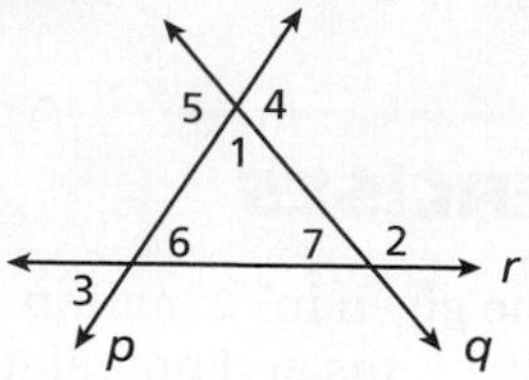

- $\angle 4$ and $\angle 6$

  p, corresponding angles
- $\angle 1$ and $\angle 2$

  q, alternate interior angles
- $\angle 3$ and $\angle 4$

  p, alternate exterior angles
- $\angle 6$ and $\angle 7$

  r, same-side interior angles

Identify the transversal and classify each angle pair.

10. $\angle 5$ and $\angle 2$

11. $\angle 6$ and $\angle 3$

12. $\angle 2$ and $\angle 4$

13. $\angle 1$ and $\angle 2$

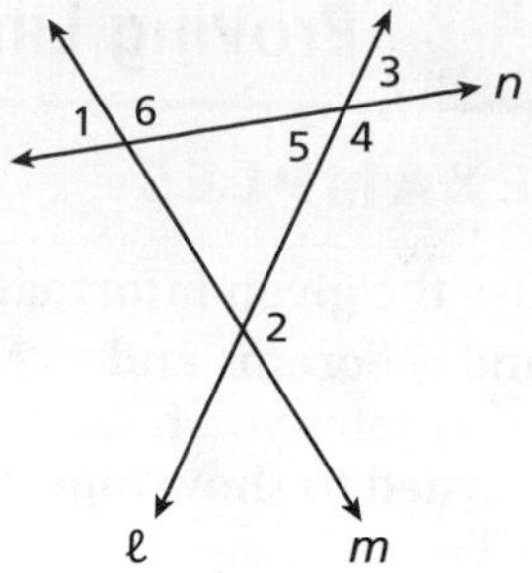

3-2 Angles Formed by Parallel Lines and Transversals

EXAMPLES

Find each angle measure.

- m$\angle TUV$

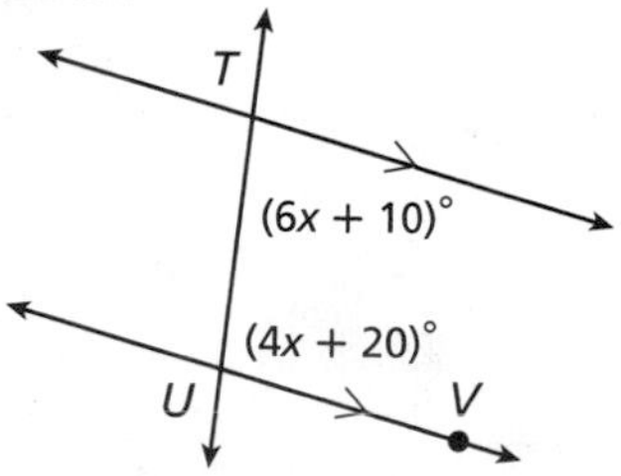

By the Same-Side Interior Angles Theorem, $(6x + 10) + (4x + 20) = 180$.

$x = 15$ *Solve for x.*

Substitute the value for x into the expression for m$\angle TUV$.
m$\angle TUV = 4(15) + 20 = 80°$

- m$\angle ABC$

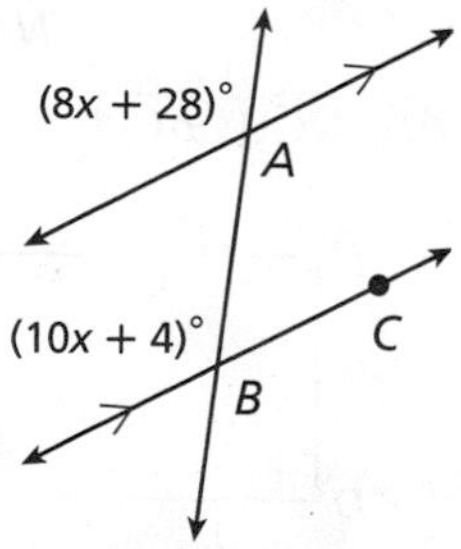

By the Corresponding Angles Postulate, $8x + 28 = 10x + 4$.

$x = 12$ *Solve for x.*

Substitute the value for x into the expression for one of the obtuse angles.
$10(12) + 4 = 124°$

$\angle ABC$ is supplementary to the 124° angle, so m$\angle ABC = 180 - 124 = 56°$.

EXERCISES

Find each angle measure.

14. m$\angle WYZ$

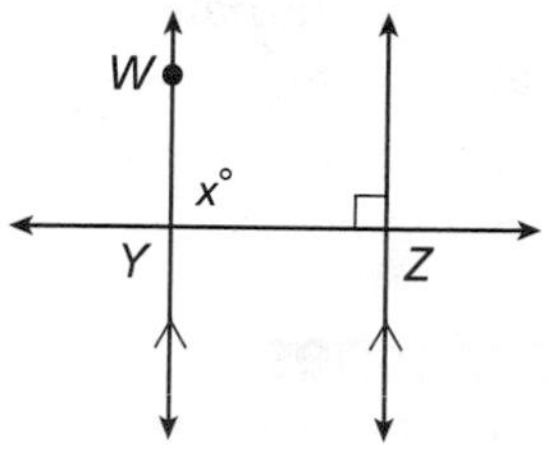

15. m$\angle KLM$

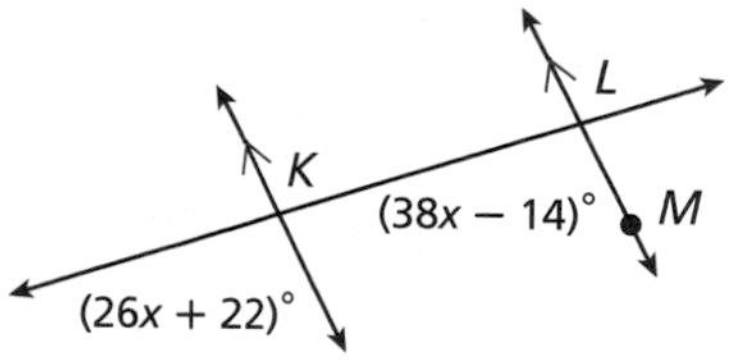

16. m$\angle DEF$

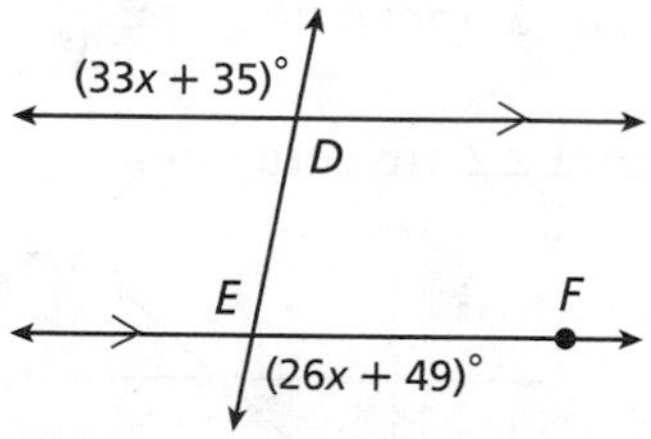

17. m$\angle QRS$

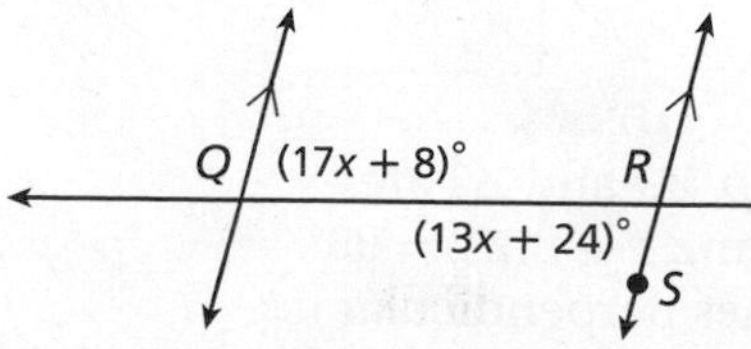

3-3 Proving Lines Parallel

EXAMPLES

Use the given information and theorems and postulates you have learned to show that $p \parallel q$.

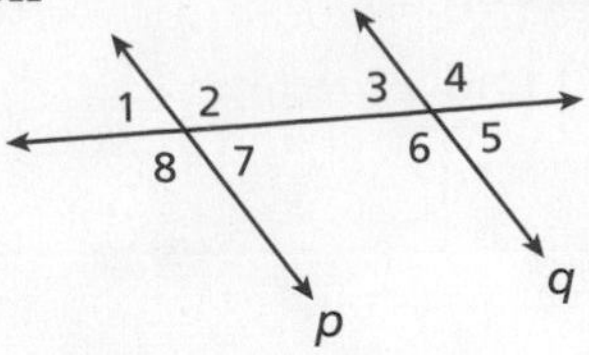

- $m\angle 2 + m\angle 3 = 180°$

  $\angle 2$ and $\angle 3$ are supplementary, so $p \parallel q$ by the Converse of the Same-Side Interior Angles Theorem.

- $\angle 8 \cong \angle 6$

  $\angle 8 \cong \angle 6$, so $p \parallel q$ by the Converse of the Corresponding Angles Postulate.

- $m\angle 1 = (7x - 3)°$, $m\angle 5 = 5x + 15$, $x = 9$

  $m\angle 1 = 60°$, and $m\angle 5 = 60°$. So $\angle 1 \cong \angle 5$. $p \parallel q$ by the Converse of the Alternate Exterior Angles Theorem.

EXERCISES

Use the given information and theorems and postulates you have learned to show that $c \parallel d$.

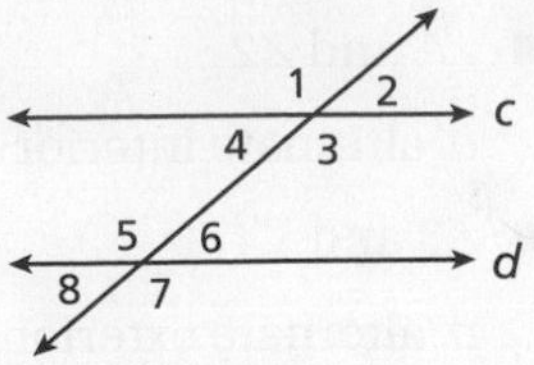

18. $m\angle 4 = 58°$, $m\angle 6 = 58°$

19. $m\angle 1 = (23x + 38)°$, $m\angle 5 = (17x + 56)°$, $x = 3$

20. $m\angle 6 = (12x + 6)°$, $m\angle 3 = (21x + 9)°$, $x = 5$

21. $m\angle 1 = 99°$, $m\angle 7 = (13x + 8)°$, $x = 7$

3-4 Perpendicular Lines

EXAMPLES

- **Name the shortest segment from point X to $\overline{WY}$.**

  $\overline{XZ}$

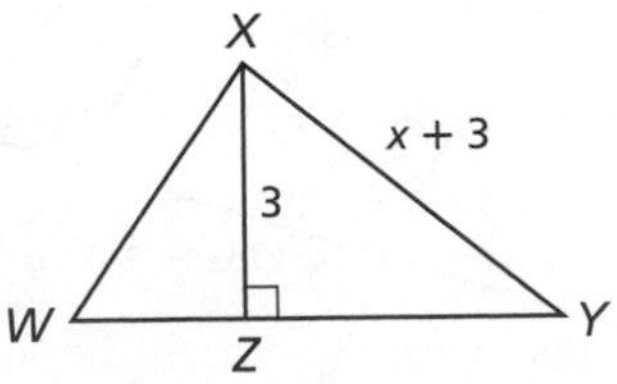

- **Write and solve an inequality for x.**

  $x + 3 > 3$

  $x > 0$ *Subtract 3 from both sides.*

- **Given: $m \perp p$, $\angle 1$ and $\angle 2$ are complementary.**
  Prove: $p \parallel q$

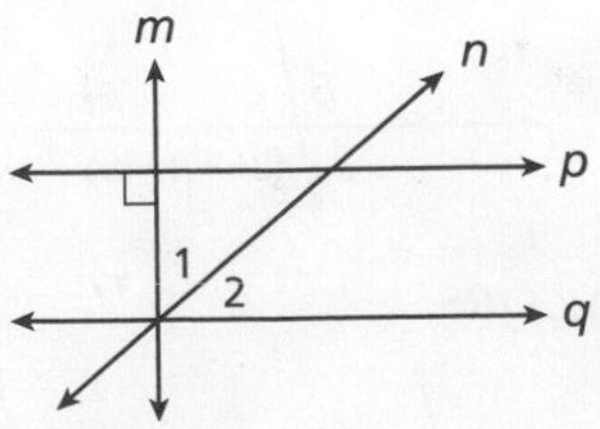

Proof:
It is given that $m \perp p$. $\angle 1$ and $\angle 2$ are complementary, so $m\angle 1 + m\angle 2 = 90°$. Thus $m \perp q$. Two lines perpendicular to the same line are parallel, so $p \parallel q$.

EXERCISES

22. Name the shortest segment from point K to $\overline{LN}$.

23. Write and solve an inequality for x.

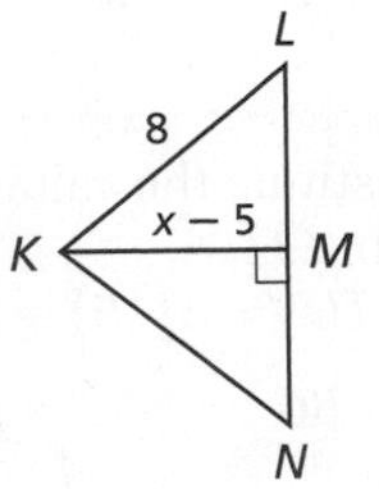

24. Given: $\overline{AD} \parallel \overline{BC}$, $\overline{AD} \perp \overline{AB}$, $\overline{DC} \perp \overline{BC}$

Prove: $\overline{AB} \parallel \overline{CD}$

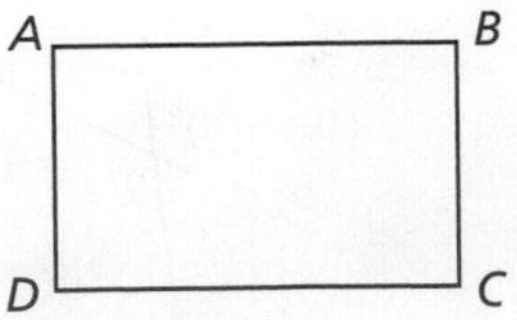

3-5 Slopes of Lines

EXAMPLES

- **Use the slope formula to determine the slope of the line.**

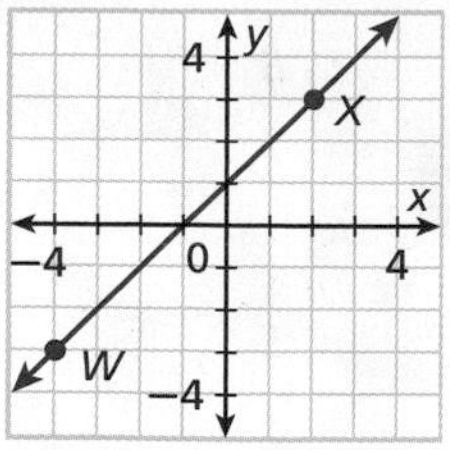

slope of $\overleftrightarrow{WX} = \frac{y_2 - y_1}{x_2 - x_1} = \frac{3-(-3)}{2-(-4)} = \frac{6}{6} = 1$

- **Use slopes to determine whether $\overleftrightarrow{AB}$ and $\overleftrightarrow{CD}$ are parallel, perpendicular, or neither for $A(-1, 5)$, $B(-3, 4)$, $C(3, -1)$, and $D(4, -3)$.**

slope of $\overleftrightarrow{AB} = \frac{4-5}{-3-(-1)} = \frac{1}{2}$

slope of $\overleftrightarrow{CD} = \frac{-3-(-1)}{4-3} = \frac{-2}{1} = -2$

The slopes are opposite reciprocals, so the lines are perpendicular.

EXERCISES

Use the slope formula to determine the slope of each line.

25.

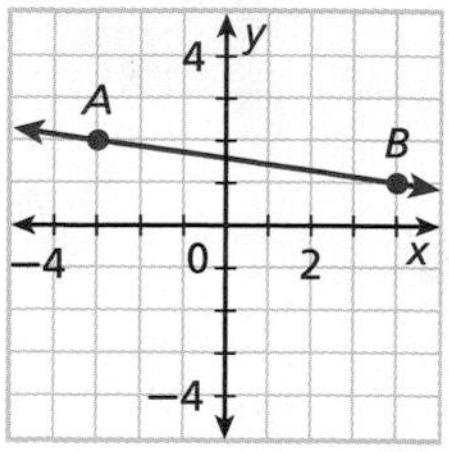

26.

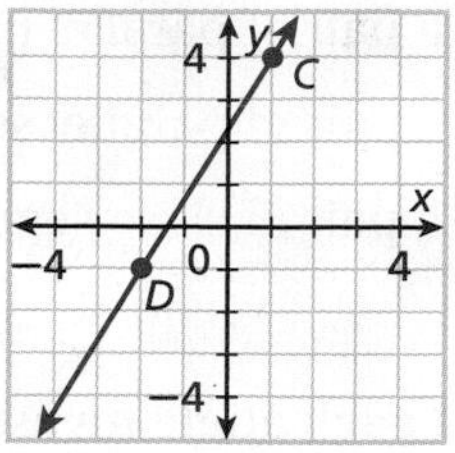

Use slopes to determine if the lines are parallel, perpendicular, or neither.

27. $\overleftrightarrow{EF}$ and $\overleftrightarrow{GH}$ for $E(8, 2)$, $F(-3, 4)$, $G(6, 1)$, and $H(-4, 3)$

28. $\overleftrightarrow{JK}$ and $\overleftrightarrow{LM}$ for $J(4, 3)$, $K(-4, -2)$, $L(5, 6)$, and $M(-3, 1)$

29. $\overleftrightarrow{ST}$ and $\overleftrightarrow{UV}$ for $S(-4, 5)$, $T(2, 3)$, $U(3, 1)$, and $V(4, 4)$

3-6 Lines in the Coordinate Plane

EXAMPLES

- **Write the equation of the line through $(5, -2)$ with slope $\frac{3}{5}$ in slope-intercept form.**

$y - (-2) = \frac{3}{5}(x - 5)$ *Point-slope form*

$y + 2 = \frac{3}{5}x - 3$ *Simplify.*

$y = \frac{3}{5}x - 5$ *Solve for y.*

- **Determine whether the lines $y = 4x + 6$ and $8x - 2y = 4$ are parallel, intersect, or coincide.**

Solve the second equation for y to find the slope-intercept form.

$8x - 2y = 4$

$y = 4x - 2$

Both the lines have a slope of 4 and have different y-intercepts, so they are parallel.

EXERCISES

Write the equation of each line in the given form.

30. the line through $(6, 1)$ and $(-3, 5)$ in slope-intercept form

31. the line through $(-3, -4)$ with slope $\frac{2}{3}$ in slope-intercept form

32. the line with x-intercept 1 and y-intercept −2 in point-slope form

Determine whether the lines are parallel, intersect, or coincide.

33. $-3x + 2y = 5$, $6x - 4y = 8$

34. $y = 4x - 3$, $5x + 2y = 1$

35. $y = 2x + 1$, $2x - y = -1$

CHAPTER 3

CHAPTER TEST

Identify each of the following.

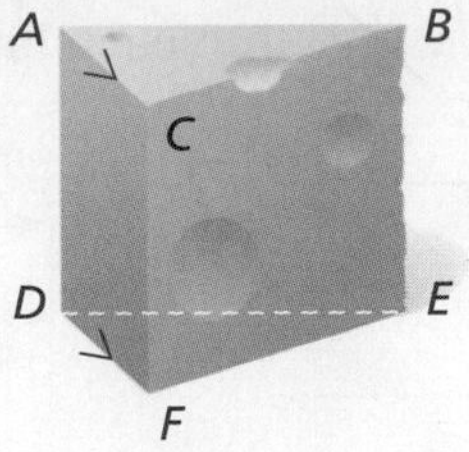

1. a pair of parallel planes
2. a pair of parallel segments
3. a pair of skew segments

Find each angle measure.

4. 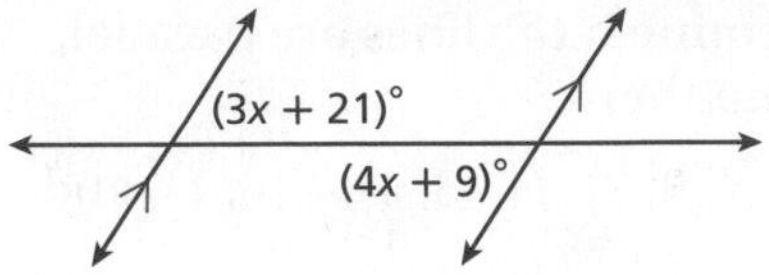

5. 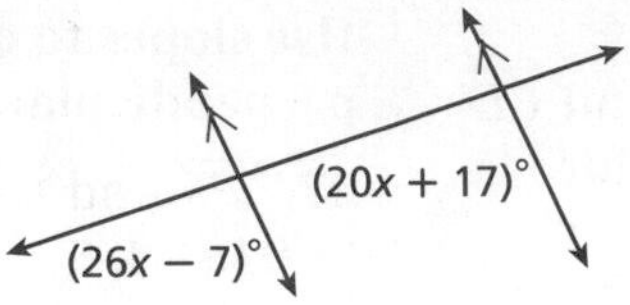

6. 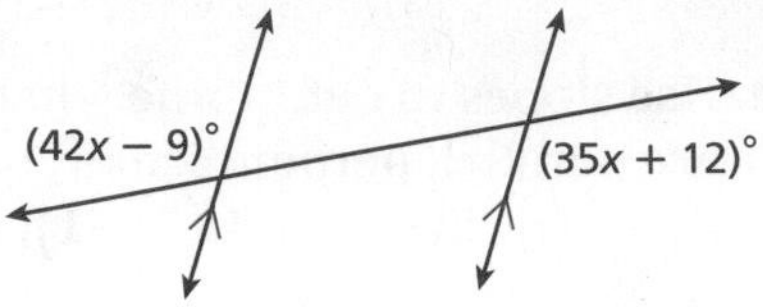

Use the given information and the theorems and postulates you have learned to show $f \parallel g$.

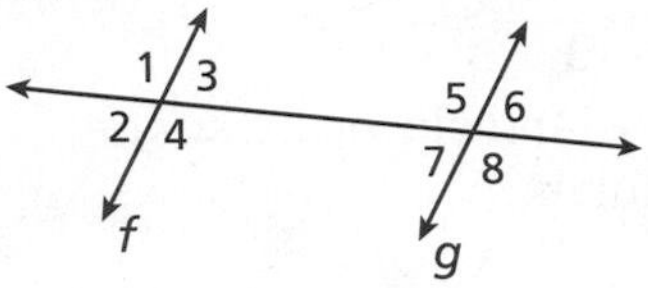

7. $m\angle 4 = (16x + 20)°$, $m\angle 5 = (12x + 32)°$, $x = 3$
8. $m\angle 3 = (18x + 6)°$, $m\angle 5 = (21x + 18)°$, $x = 4$

Write a two-column proof.

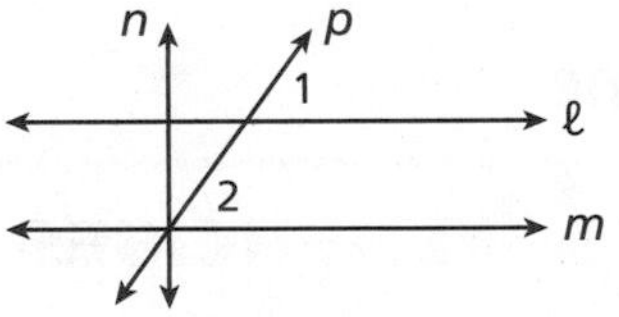

9. Given: $\angle 1 \cong \angle 2$, $n \perp \ell$

   Prove: $n \perp m$

Use the slope formula to determine the slope of each line.

10. 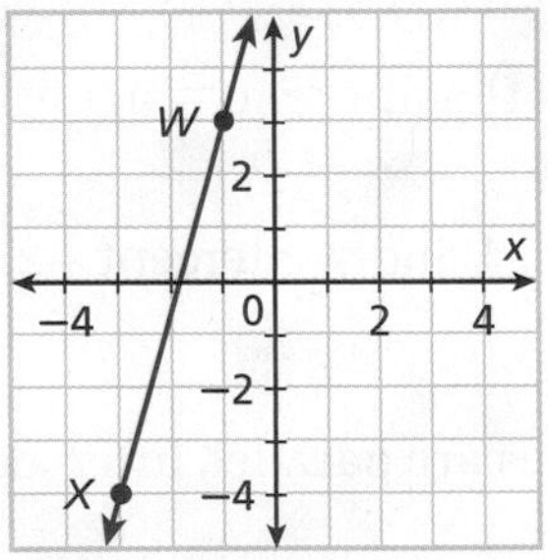

11. 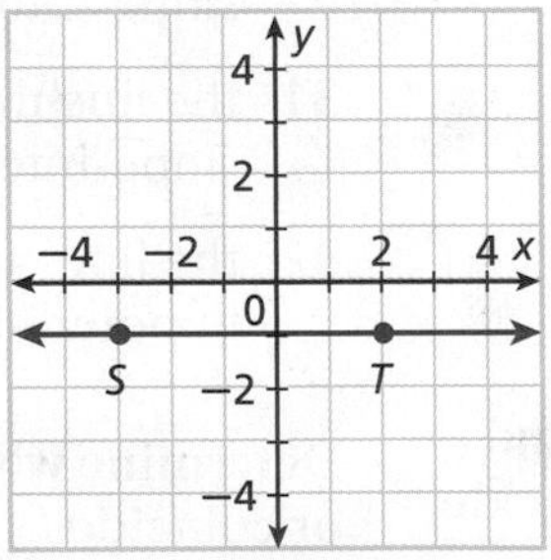

12. 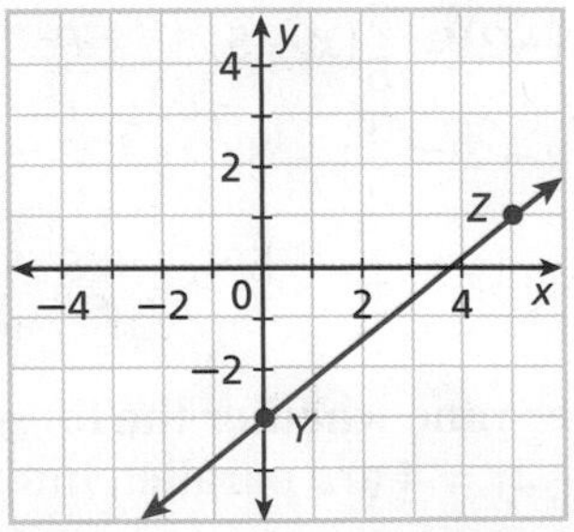

13. Greg is on a 32-mile bicycle trail from Elroy, Wisconsin, to Sparta, Wisconsin. He leaves Elroy at 9:30 A.M. and arrives in Sparta at 2:00 P.M. Graph the line that represents Greg's distance from Elroy at a given time. Find and interpret the slope of the line.
14. Graph $\overleftrightarrow{QR}$ and $\overleftrightarrow{ST}$ for $Q(3, 3)$, $R(6, -5)$, $S(-4, 6)$, and $T(-1, -2)$. Use slopes to determine whether the lines are parallel, perpendicular, or neither.
15. Write the equation of the line through $(-2, -5)$ with slope $-\frac{3}{4}$ in point-slope form.
16. Determine whether the lines $6x + y = 3$ and $2x + 3y = 1$ are parallel, intersect, or coincide.

COLLEGE ENTRANCE EXAM PRACTICE

FOCUS ON ACT

When you take the ACT Mathematics Test, you receive a separate subscore for each of the following areas:
- Pre-Algebra/Elementary Algebra,
- Intermediate Algebra/Coordinate Geometry, and
- Plane Geometry/Trigonometry.

HOT TIP! **Find out what percent of questions are from each area and concentrate on content that represents the greatest percent of questions.**

You may want to time yourself as you take this practice test. It should take you about 5 minutes to complete.

---

1. Which of the following is an equation of the line that passes through the point $(2, -3)$ and is parallel to the line $4x - 5y = 1$?

(A) $-4x + 5y = -23$

(B) $-5x - 4y = 2$

(C) $-2x - 5y = 11$

(D) $-4x - 5y = 7$

(E) $-5x + 4y = -22$

---

2. In the figure below, line t crosses parallel lines ℓ and m. Which of the following statements are true?

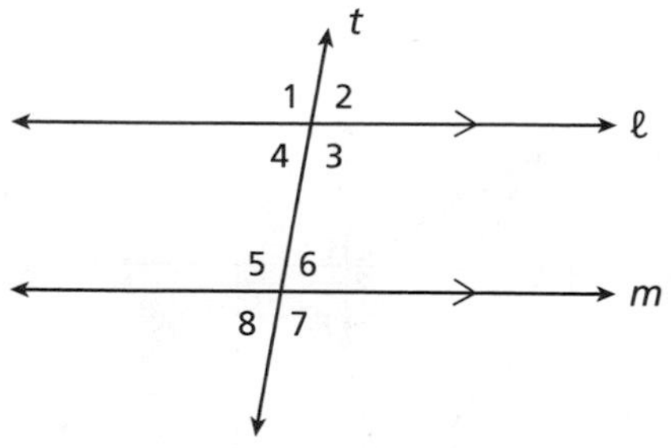

I. $\angle 1$ and $\angle 6$ are alternate interior angles.

II. $\angle 2 \cong \angle 4$

III. $\angle 2 \cong \angle 8$

(F) I only

(G) II only

(H) III only

(J) I and II only

(K) II and III only

---

3. In the standard (x, y) coordinate plane, the line that passes through $(1, -7)$ and $(-8, 5)$ is perpendicular to the line that passes through $(3, 6)$ and $(-1, b)$. What is the value of b?

(A) 2

(B) 3

(C) 7

(D) 9

(E) 10

---

4. Lines m and n are cut by a transversal so that $\angle 2$ and $\angle 5$ are corresponding angles. If $m\angle 2 = (x + 18)°$ and $m\angle 5 = (2x - 28)°$, which value of x makes lines m and n parallel?

(F) $3\frac{1}{3}$

(G) $33\frac{1}{3}$

(H) 46

(J) $63\frac{1}{3}$

(K) 72

---

5. What is the distance between point $G(4, 2)$ and the line through the points $E(1, -2)$ and $F(7, -2)$?

(A) 3

(B) 4

(C) 5

(D) 6

(E) 7

CHAPTER 3

TEST TACKLER

Standardized Test Strategies

Short Response: Write Short Responses

Short response test items are designed to test mathematical understanding. In your response, you have to show your work and possibly describe your reasoning to show that you understand the concept. Scores are based on a 2-point scoring rubric.

Some short response questions require you to draw and label a diagram. Make sure you draw the figure as described in the problem statement and provide all markings and labeling as needed.

EXAMPLE 1

Short Response Draw and label $\angle ABC$ and $\angle CBD$, a pair of adjacent, supplementary angles. Then draw a line perpendicular to line AD though point B and name two right angles.

Scoring Rubric

2 points: The student shows an understanding of adjacent and supplementary angles and perpendicular lines. The diagram is correct, and all labels and markings are included. The student correctly names two right angles.

1 point: The student correctly sketches the diagram, but labels it incorrectly, does not name two right angles, or incorrectly names two right angles. OR the student makes minor flaws in the diagram but correctly names two right angles.

0 points: The diagram is completely incorrect, or the student gives no response.

Here are examples of how different responses were scored using the scoring rubric shown.

2-point response:

$\angle ABG$ and $\angle GBD$ are right angles.

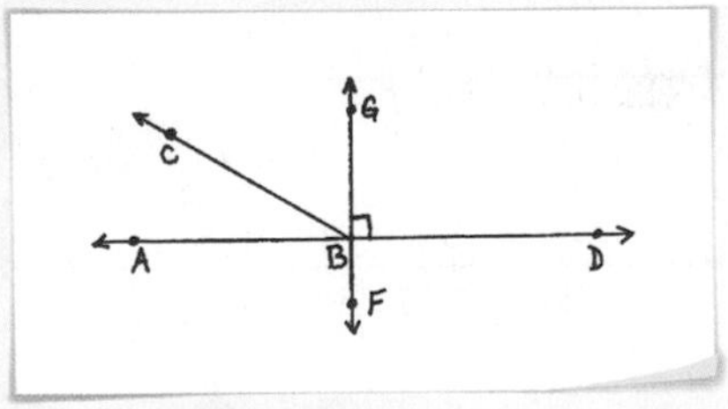

Notice that the diagram is correct and all labels and markings are included. Student correctly identified two right angles.

1-point response:

$\angle GCD$ is a right angle.

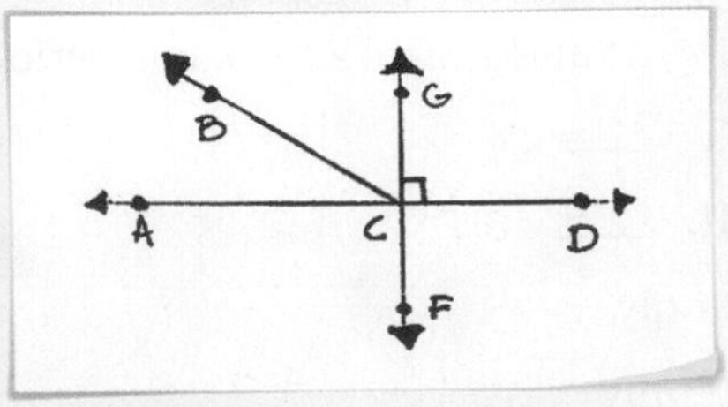

Notice that the diagram is almost correct, but points B and C are mislabeled. Also, the student only identified one right angle, not two.

0-point response:

Notice that the student did not complete the required diagram, and it appears to be completely incorrect.

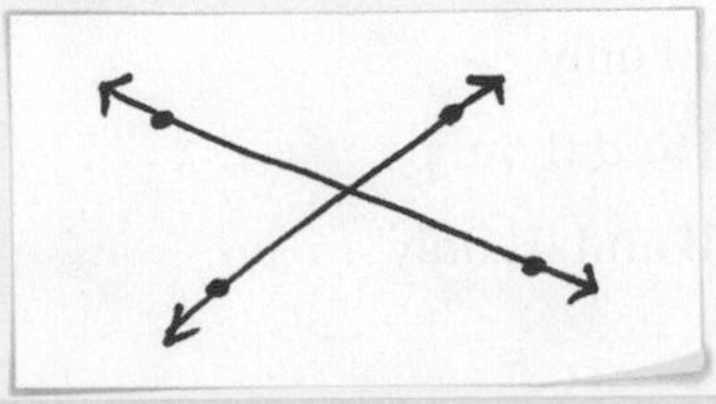

Read each test item, and use the scoring rubric to answer each question.

Scoring Rubric

2 points: The student's response is correct and complete. The answer contains complete explanations and/or adequate work when required.

1 point: The student's response demonstrates only partial understanding. The response may include the correct process with an incorrect answer, or a correct answer without the required work.

0 points: The student's response demonstrates no understanding of the mathematical concepts. The response may include a correct response using an obviously incorrect procedure.

Item A

Short Response Find $m\angle JKM$. Identify any postulates used to determine the answer.

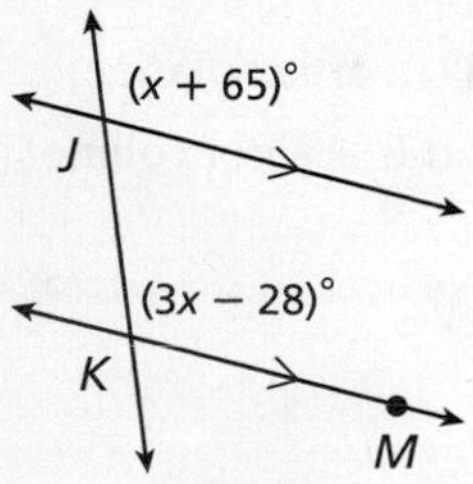

1. What should be included in a student's response in order to receive 2 points?

2. A student wrote this response:

The angles look like they have the same measure, so:

$(x+65)° = (3x-28)°$

$-2x = -93$

$x = 46.5$

$(3x-28) = 3(46.5)-28 = 111.5$

$m\angle JKM = 111.5°$

What score should this response receive? What needs to be added to the response, if anything, in order to receive 2 points?

HOT TIP! To receive full credit, make sure your explanations or descriptions are complete sentences.

Item B

Short Response Write a paragraph proof.

Given: $\overleftrightarrow{YT} \parallel \overleftrightarrow{ZW}$; $\overleftrightarrow{XZ} \perp \overleftrightarrow{ZW}$

Prove: $\overleftrightarrow{XY} \perp \overleftrightarrow{YT}$

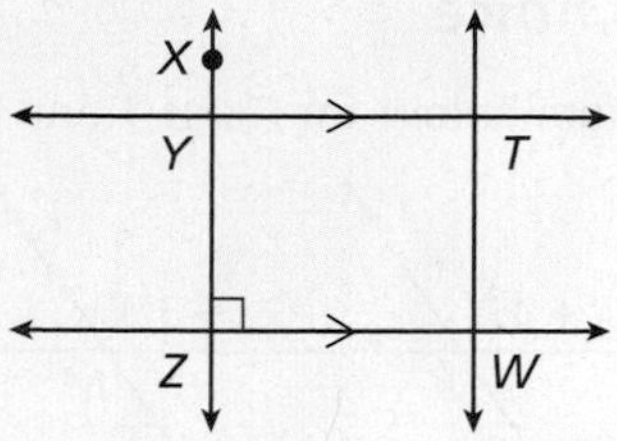

So far, Issac has these thoughts written down on his paper.

I know $\overleftrightarrow{YT} \parallel \overleftrightarrow{ZW}$, and it looks like $\overleftrightarrow{YZ} \parallel \overleftrightarrow{TW}$. $\angle YZW$ and $\angle XYT$ are corr. ∠s, so they must be ≅.

I also know $\overleftrightarrow{XZ} \perp \overleftrightarrow{ZW}$, so the ∠s formed by these lines are rt. ∠s. It also looks like $\overleftrightarrow{TW} \perp \overleftrightarrow{ZW}$, which means more rt. ∠s.

I think I need to show $\angle YZW \cong \angle XYT$ so that I can say they both measure 90°. Then by def. of ⊥ lines, $\overleftrightarrow{XY} \perp \overleftrightarrow{YT}$.

3. What information is NOT necessary for Isaac to include in his proof?

4. Rewrite Issac's paragraph so that it would receive 2 points.

CHAPTER 3

STANDARDIZED TEST PREP

Learn It Online
State Test Practice

CUMULATIVE ASSESSMENT

Multiple Choice

Use the diagram below for Items 1 and 2.

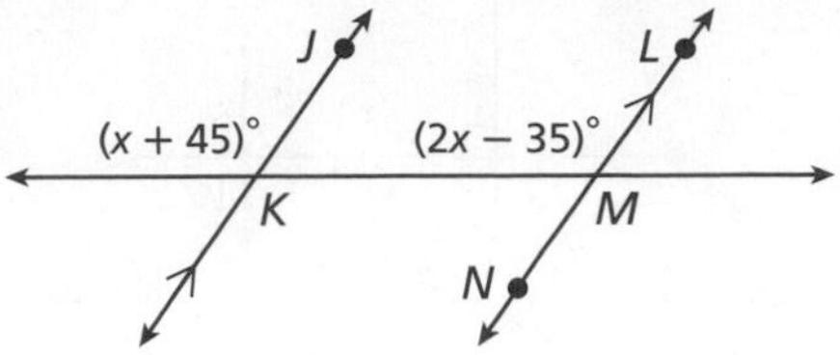

1. What type of angle pair are $\angle JKM$ and $\angle KMN$?

(A) Corresponding angles

(B) Alternate exterior angles

(C) Same-side interior angles

(D) Alternate interior angles

2. What is $m\angle KML$?

(F) 57° (H) 102°

(G) 80° (J) 125°

3. What is a possible value of x in the diagram?

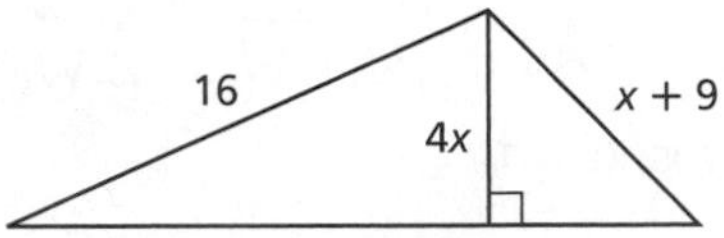

(A) 2 (C) 4

(B) 3 (D) 5

4. A graphic artist used a computer illustration program to draw a line connecting points with coordinates $(3, -1)$ and $(4, 6)$. She needs to draw a second line parallel to the first line. What slope should the second line have?

(F) $\frac{1}{7}$ (H) 5

(G) $\frac{1}{5}$ (J) 7

5. Which term describes a pair of vertical angles that are also supplementary?

(A) Acute (C) Right

(B) Obtuse (D) Straight

6. What is the equation of the line that passes through the points $(-1, 8)$ and $(4, -2)$?

(F) $y = -2x + 6$ (H) $y = \frac{1}{2}x - 4$

(G) $y = -\frac{1}{2}x$ (J) $y = 2x + 10$

7. Given the points $R(-5, 3)$, $S(-5, 4)$, $T(-3, 4)$, and $U(-3, 1)$, which line is perpendicular to $\overleftrightarrow{TU}$?

(A) $\overleftrightarrow{RS}$ (C) $\overleftrightarrow{ST}$

(B) $\overleftrightarrow{RT}$ (D) $\overleftrightarrow{SU}$

8. Which of following is true if $\overleftrightarrow{XY}$ and $\overleftrightarrow{UV}$ are skew?

(F) $\overleftrightarrow{XY}$ and $\overleftrightarrow{UV}$ are coplanar.

(G) X, Y, and U are noncollinear.

(H) $\overleftrightarrow{XY} \parallel \overleftrightarrow{UV}$

(J) $\overleftrightarrow{XY} \perp \overleftrightarrow{UV}$

HOT TIP! **Make sure that you answer the question that is asked. Some problems require more than one step. You must perform *all* of the steps to get the correct answer.**

9. Point C is the midpoint of $\overline{AB}$ for $A(1, -2)$ and $B(7, 2)$. What is the length of $\overline{AC}$? Round to the nearest tenth.

(A) 3.0 (C) 5.0

(B) 3.6 (D) 7.2

Use the diagram below for Items 10 and 11.

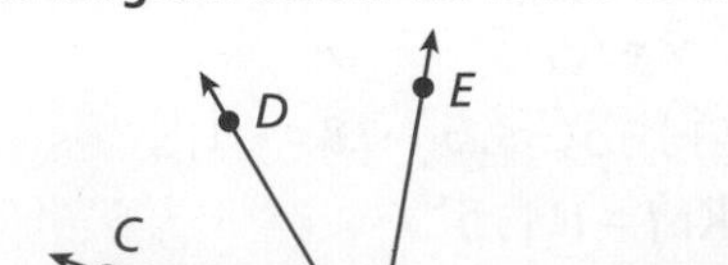

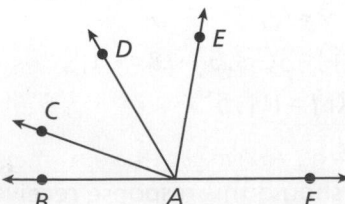

10. $\overrightarrow{AD}$ bisects $\angle CAE$, and $\overrightarrow{AE}$ bisects $\angle CAF$. If $m\angle DAF = 120°$, what is $m\angle DAE$?

(F) 40° (G) 60° (H) 80° (J) 100°

11. What is the intersection of $\overrightarrow{AF}$ and $\overrightarrow{AD}$?

(A) A (B) F (C) $\overline{FD}$ (D) $\angle DAF$

12. Which statement is true by the Transitive Property of Equality?

Ⓕ If $x + 3 = y$, then $y = x + 3$.

Ⓖ If $k = 6$, then $2k = 12$.

Ⓗ If $a = b$ and $b = 8$, then $a = 8$.

Ⓙ If $m = n$, then $m + 7 = n + 7$.

13. Which condition guarantees that $r \parallel s$?

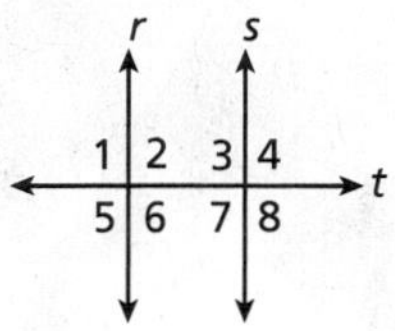

Ⓐ $\angle 1 \cong \angle 2$

Ⓑ $\angle 2 \cong \angle 7$

Ⓒ $\angle 2 \cong \angle 3$

Ⓓ $\angle 1 \cong \angle 4$

14. What is the converse of the following statement?

If $x = 2$, then $x + 3 = 5$.

Ⓕ If $x \neq 2$, then $x + 3 = 5$.

Ⓖ If $x = 2$, then $x + 3 \neq 5$.

Ⓗ If $x + 3 \neq 5$, then $x \neq 2$.

Ⓙ If $x + 3 = 5$, then $x = 2$.

Gridded Response

15. Two lines a and b are cut by a transversal so that $\angle 1$ and $\angle 2$ are same-side interior angles. If $m\angle 1 = (2x + 30)^\circ$ and $m\angle 2 = (4x - 75)^\circ$, what value of x proves that $a \parallel b$?

16. What is the slope of the line that passes through (3, 7) and (−5, 1)?

17. $\angle 1$ and $\angle 2$ form a linear pair. $m\angle 1 = (4x + 18)^\circ$ and $m\angle 2 = (3x - 6)^\circ$. What is the value of x?

18. Points A, B, and C are collinear, and B is between A and C. $AB = 16$ and $AC = 27$. What is the distance BC?

19. Ms. Nelson wants to put a chain-link fence around 3 sides of a square-shaped lawn. Chain-link fencing is sold in sections that are each 6 feet wide. If Ms. Nelson's lawn has an area of 3600 square feet, how many sections of fencing will she need?

20. What is the next number in this pattern?

67, 76, 83, 88,...

Short Response

21. Given $\ell \parallel m$ with transversal t, explain why $\angle 1$ and $\angle 8$ are supplementary.

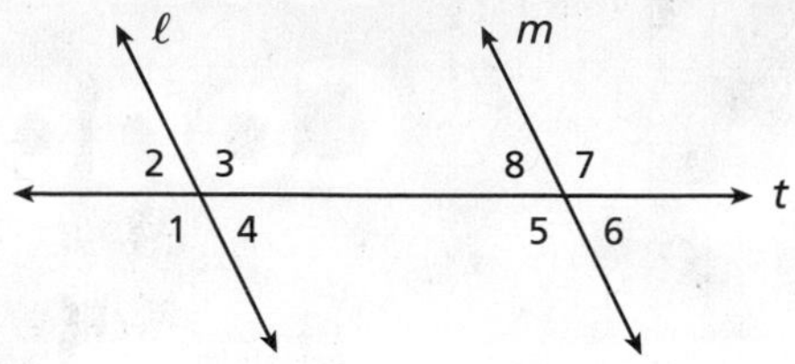

22. Read the following conditional statement.

If two angles are vertical angles, then they are congruent.

a. Write the converse of this conditional statement.

b. Give a counterexample to show that the converse is false.

23. Assume that the following statements are true when the bases are loaded in a baseball game.

If a batter hits the ball over the fence, then the batter hits a home run.
A batter hits a home run if and only if the result is four runs scored.

a. If a batter hits the ball over the fence when the bases are loaded, can you conclude that four runs were scored? Explain your answer.

b. If a batter hits a home run when the bases are loaded, can you conclude that the batter hit the ball over the fence? Explain your answer.

Extended Response

24. A car passes through a tollbooth at 8:00 A.M. and begins traveling east at an average speed of 45 miles per hour. A second car passes through the same tollbooth an hour later and begins traveling east at an average speed of 60 miles per hour.

a. Write an equation for each car that relates the number of hours x since 8:00 A.M. to the distance in miles y the car has traveled. Explain what the slope of each equation represents.

b. Graph the system of equations on the coordinate plane.

c. If neither car stops, at what time will the second car catch up to the first car? Explain how you determined your answer.

CHAPTER

4 Triangle Congruence

COMMON CORE

Chapter

- Prove and use the Triangle Sum Theorem
- Understand congruence and prove and apply congruence relationships for triangles

Flexible Creations

When you turn a kaleidoscope, the shapes flip to form a variety of designs. You can create flexagons that also flip to form patterns.

Learn It Online
Chapter Project Online

ARE YOU READY?

Vocabulary

Match each term on the left with a definition on the right.

1. acute angle
2. congruent segments
3. obtuse angle
4. postulate
5. triangle

A. a statement that is accepted as true without proof
B. an angle that measures greater than 90° and less than 180°
C. a statement that you can prove
D. segments that have the same length
E. a three-sided polygon
F. an angle that measures greater than 0° and less than 90°

Measure Angles

Use a protractor to measure each angle.

6.

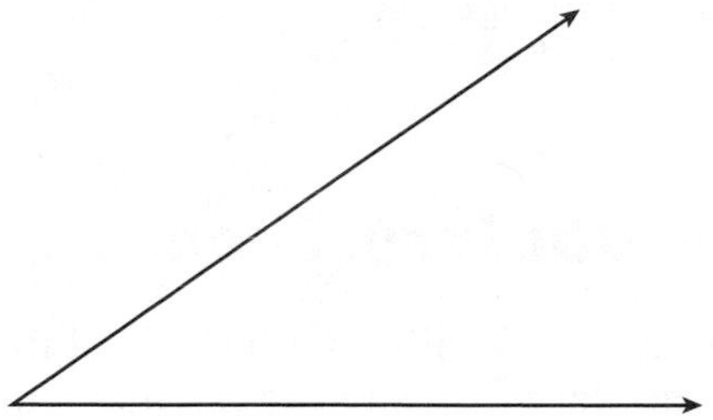

7.

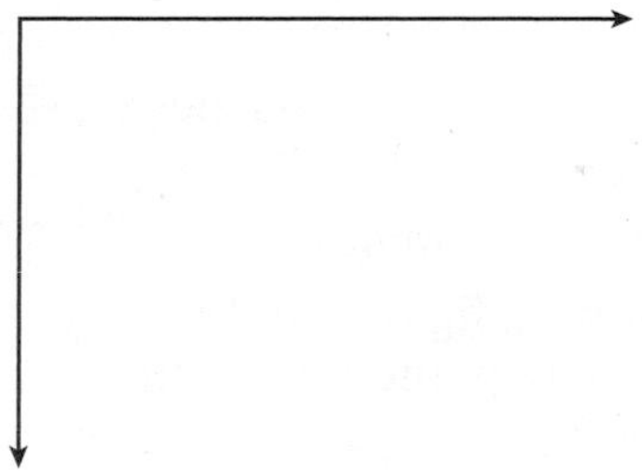

Use a protractor to draw an angle with each of the following measures.

8. 20°
9. 63°
10. 105°
11. 158°

Solve Equations with Fractions

Solve.

12. $\frac{9}{2}x + 7 = 25$
13. $3x - \frac{2}{3} = \frac{4}{3}$
14. $x - \frac{1}{5} = \frac{12}{5}$
15. $2y = 5y - \frac{21}{2}$

Connect Words and Algebra

Write an equation for each statement.

16. Tanya's age t is three times Martin's age m.
17. Twice the length of a segment x is 9 ft.
18. The sum of 53° and twice an angle measure y is 90°.
19. The price of a radio r is $25 less than the price of a CD player p.
20. Half the amount of liquid j in a jar is 5 oz more than the amount of liquid b in a bowl.

CHAPTER 4

Study Guide: Preview

Where You've Been

Previously, you

- measured and classified angles.
- wrote definitions for triangles and other polygons.
- used deductive reasoning.
- planned and wrote proofs.

In This Chapter

You will study

- classifying triangles.
- proving triangles congruent.
- using corresponding parts of congruent triangles in proofs.
- positioning figures in the coordinate plane for use in proofs.
- proving theorems about isosceles and equilateral triangles.

Where You're Going

You can use the skills learned in this chapter

- in Algebra 2 and Precalculus.
- in other classes, such as in Physics when you solve for various measures of a triangle and in Geography when you identify a location using coordinates.
- outside of school to make greeting cards or to design jewelry or whenever you create sets of objects that have the same size and shape.

Key Vocabulary/Vocabulario

acute triangle	triángulo acutángulo
congruent polygons	polígonos congruentes
corollary	corolario
equilateral triangle	triángulo equilátero
exterior angle	ángulo externo
interior angle	ángulo interno
isosceles triangle	triángulo isósceles
obtuse triangle	triángulo obtusángulo
right triangle	triángulo rectángulo
scalene triangle	triángulo escaleno

Vocabulary Connections

To become familiar with some of the vocabulary terms in the chapter, consider the following. You may refer to the chapter, the glossary, or a dictionary if you like.

1. The Latin word *acutus* means "pointed" or "sharp." Draw a triangle that looks pointed or sharp. Do you think this is an **acute triangle** ?
2. Consider the everyday meaning of the word *exterior*. Where do you think an **exterior angle** of a triangle is located?
3. You already know the definition of an obtuse angle. Use this meaning to make a conjecture about an **obtuse triangle** .
4. *Scalene* comes from a Greek word that means "uneven." If the sides of a **scalene triangle** are uneven, draw an example of such a triangle.

Reading and Writing Math

Reading Strategy: Read Geometry Symbols

In Geometry we often use symbols to communicate information. When studying each lesson, read both the symbols and the words slowly and carefully. Reading aloud can sometimes help you translate symbols into words.

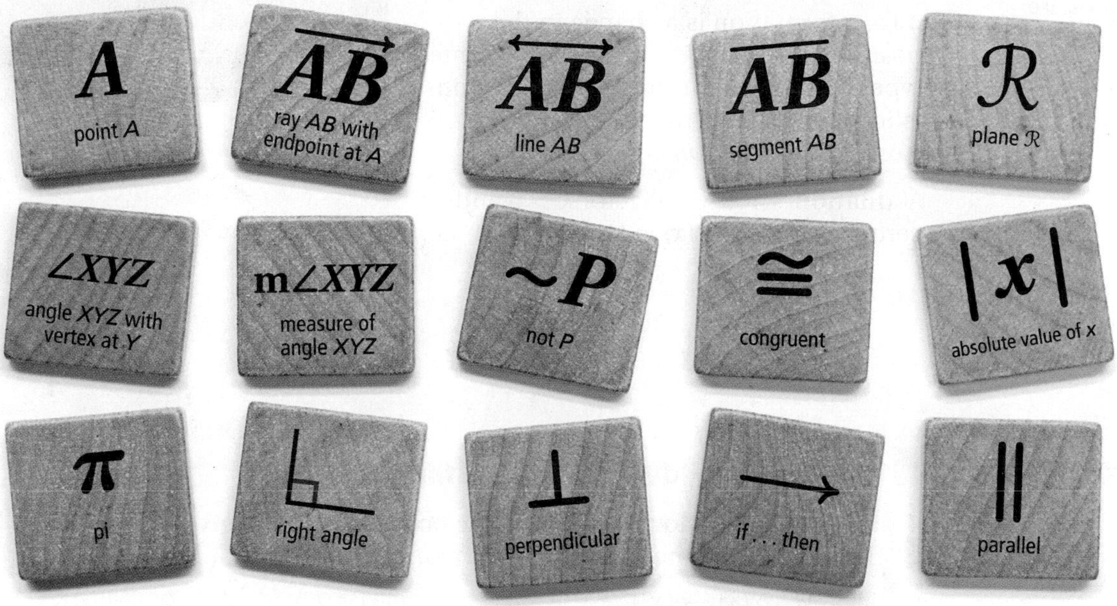

Throughout this course, you will use these symbols and combinations of these symbols to represent various geometric statements.

Symbol Combinations	Translated into Words
$\overleftrightarrow{ST} \parallel \overleftrightarrow{UV}$	Line *ST* is parallel to line *UV*.
$\overline{BC} \perp \overline{GH}$	Segment *BC* is perpendicular to segment *GH*.
$p \rightarrow q$	If *p*, then *q*.
$m\angle QRS = 45°$	The measure of angle *QRS* is 45 degrees.
$\angle CDE \cong \angle LMN$	Angle *CDE* is congruent to angle *LMN*.

Try This

Rewrite each statement using symbols.

1. the absolute value of 2 times pi
2. The measure of angle 2 is 125 degrees.
3. Segment *XY* is perpendicular to line *BC*.
4. If not *p*, then not *q*.

Translate the symbols into words.

5. $m\angle FGH = m\angle VWX$
6. $\overleftrightarrow{ZA} \parallel \overleftrightarrow{TU}$
7. $\sim p \rightarrow q$
8. $\overrightarrow{ST}$ bisects $\angle TSU$.

COMMON CORE

4-1 Congruence and Transformations

CC.9-12.G.CO.6 ...Given two figures, use...rigid motions to decide if they are congruent. *Also* **CC.9-12.G.CO.7**

Objectives

Draw, identify, and describe transformations in the coordinate plane.

Use properties of rigid motions to determine whether figures are congruent and to prove figures congruent.

Vocabulary

dilation
isometry
rigid transformation

Why learn this?

Transformations can be used to create frieze patterns in art and architecture, such as in this cast iron gate.

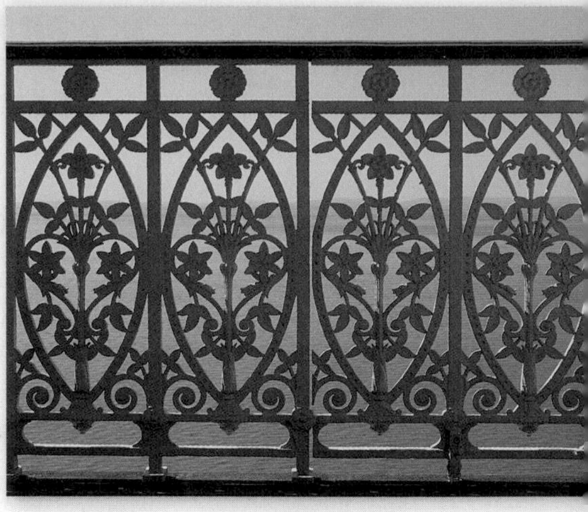

A transformation is a change in the position, shape, or size of a figure. Some types of transformations are translations (slides), reflections (flips), rotations (turns), and *dilations.*

A **dilation** with scale factor $k > 0$ and center (0, 0) maps (x, y) to (kx, ky).

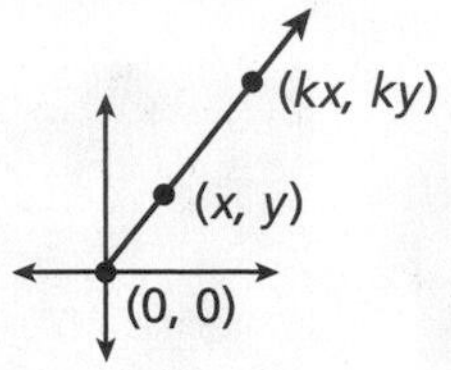

EXAMPLE 1 Drawing and Identifying Transformations

Apply the transformation M to the polygon with the given vertices. Identify and describe the transformation.

A $M: (x, y) \rightarrow (x + 2, y - 5)$
$P(1, 2)$, $Q(4, 4)$, $R(4, 2)$

This is a translation 2 units right and 5 units down.

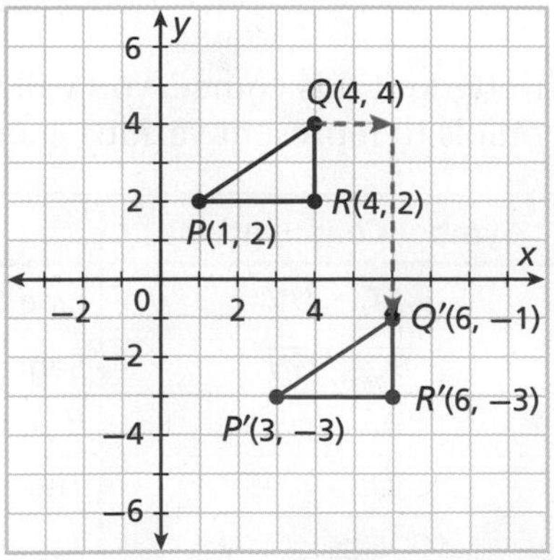

Remember!

In a transformation, the original figure is the preimage. The resulting figure is the image.

B $M: (x, y) \rightarrow (-x, y)$
$A(1, 1)$, $B(3, 2)$, $C(3, 5)$

This is a reflection across the *y*-axis.

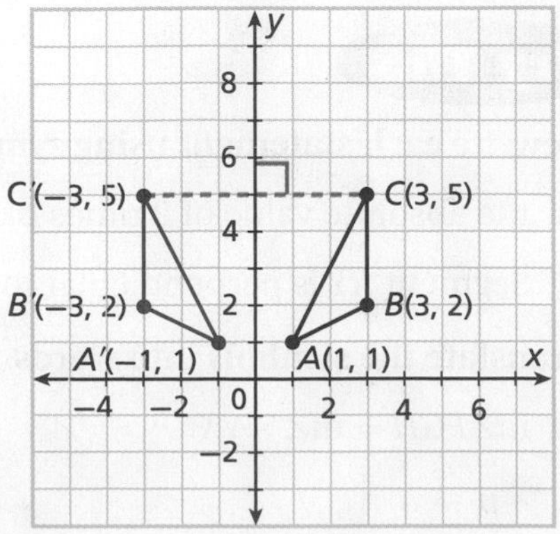

C $M: (x, y) \rightarrow (-y, x)$
$R(1, 2)$, $E(1, 4)$, $C(5, 4)$, $T(5, 2)$

This is a 90° rotation counterclockwise with center of rotation (0, 0).

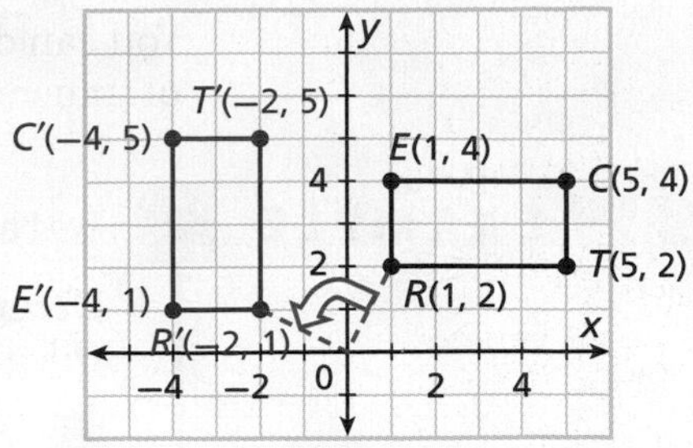

D $M: (x, y) \rightarrow (2x, 2y)$
$K(-1, 2)$, $L(2, 2)$, $N(1, 3)$

This is a dilation with scale factor 2 and center (0, 0).

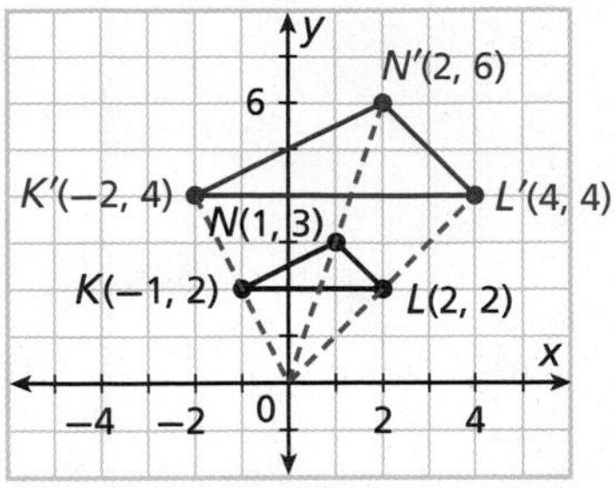

CHECK IT OUT!

1. Apply the transformation $M: (x, y) \rightarrow (3x, 3y)$ to the polygon with vertices $D(1, 3)$, $E(1, -2)$, and $F(3, 0)$. Name the coordinates of the image points. Identify and describe the transformation.

Representing Transformations in the Coordinate Plane

TRANSFORMATION	COORDINATE MAPPING AND DESCRIPTION
Translation	$(x, y) \rightarrow (x + a, y + b)$ Translation *a* units horizontally and *b* units vertically
Reflection	$(x, y) \rightarrow (-x, y)$ Reflection across *y*-axis $(x, y) \rightarrow (x, -y)$ Reflection across *x*-axis
Rotation	$(x, y) \rightarrow (y, -x)$ Rotation about (0, 0), 90° clockwise $(x, y) \rightarrow (-y, x)$ Rotation about (0, 0), 90° counterclockwise $(x, y) \rightarrow (-x, -y)$ Rotation about (0, 0), 180°
Dilation	$(x, y) \rightarrow (kx, ky)$, $k > 0$ Dilation with scale factor *k* and center (0, 0)

An **isometry** is a transformation that preserves length, angle measure, and area. Because of these properties, an isometry produces an image that is congruent to the preimage. A **rigid transformation** is another name for an isometry.

Transformations and Congruence

Translations, reflections, and rotations produce images that are congruent to their preimages.

Dilations with scale factor $k \neq 1$ produce images that are not congruent to their preimages.

You can determine whether some figures are congruent by determining what type of transformation(s) can be applied to one figure to produce the other figure.

EXAMPLE 2 Determining Whether Figures are Congruent

Determine whether the polygons with the given vertices are congruent.

A $A(1, 1)$, $B(4, 1)$, $C(4, 3)$
$P(-4, 2)$, $Q(-1, 2)$, $R(-1, 4)$

The triangles are congruent because $\triangle ABC$ can be mapped to $\triangle PQR$ by a translation:

$(x, y) \rightarrow (x - 5, y + 1)$.

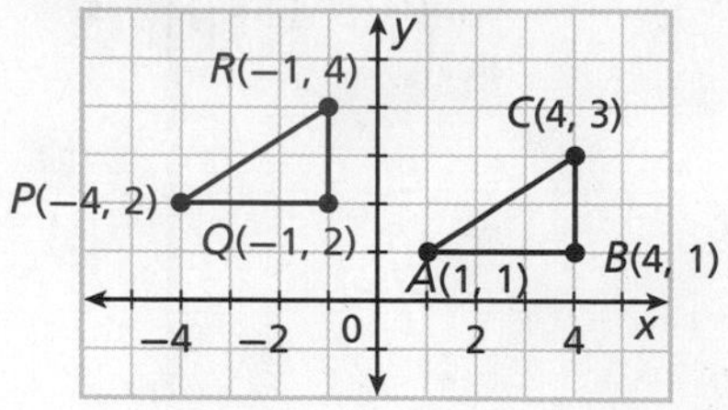

B $A(2, 2)$, $B(-4, 4)$, $C(2, 4)$
$P(3, 3)$, $Q(-6, 6)$, $R(3, 6)$

The triangles are not congruent because $\triangle ABC$ can be mapped to $\triangle PQR$ by a dilation with scale factor $k \neq 1$:

$(x, y) \rightarrow (1.5x, 1.5y)$.

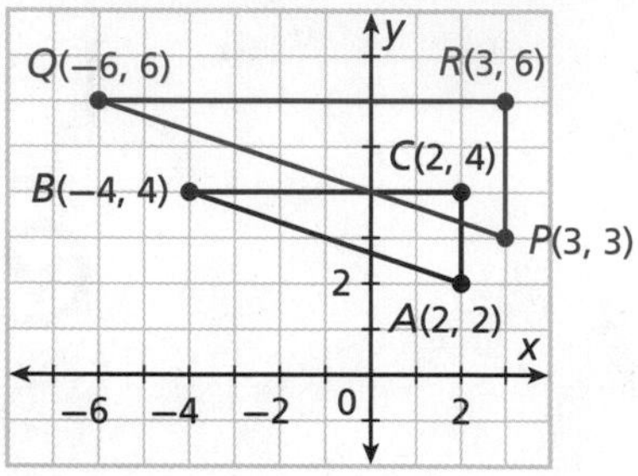

CHECK IT OUT! 2. Determine whether the polygons with the given vertices are congruent. Support your answer by describing a transformation: $A(2, -1)$, $B(3, 0)$, $C(2, 3)$ and $P(1, 2)$, $Q(0, 3)$, $R(-3, 2)$.

You can prove two figures are congruent by showing there are one or more translations, reflections, or rotations that map one figure to the other.

EXAMPLE 3 Applying Transformations

Prove that the polygons with the given vertices are congruent.

$A(3, 1)$, $B(2, -1)$, $C(7, -1)$
$P(-3, -2)$, $Q(-5, -1)$, $R(-5, -6)$

Graph the triangles. There is no apparent single transformation that maps $\triangle ABC$ to $\triangle PQR$. Look for a combination of congruence transformations that map $\triangle ABC$ to $\triangle PQR$.

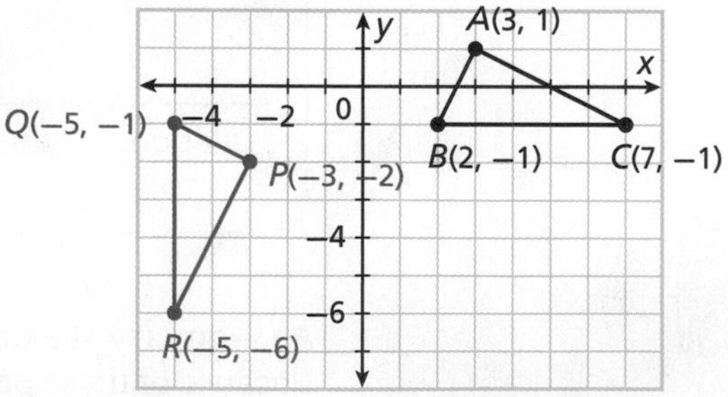

The triangles are congruent because $\triangle ABC$ can be mapped to $\triangle A'B'C'$ by a translation:

$(x, y) \rightarrow (x - 1, y - 4)$; and $\triangle A'B'C'$ can then be mapped to $\triangle PQR$ by a rotation:

$(x, y) \rightarrow (y, -x)$.

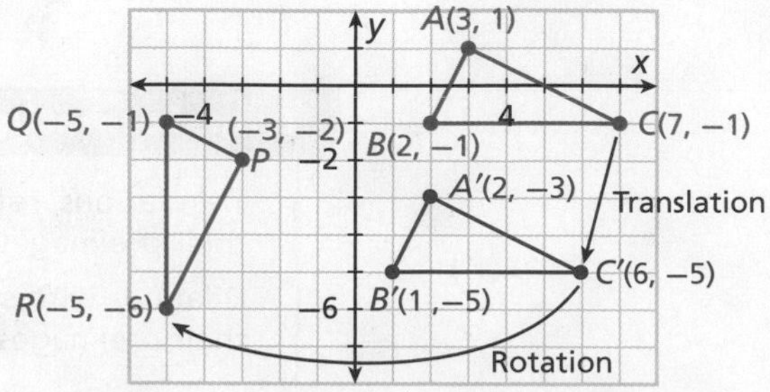

CHECK IT OUT! **3.** Prove that the polygons with the given vertices are congruent: $A(-4, -2)$, $B(-2, 1)$, $C(-2, -2)$ and $P(1, 0)$, $Q(3, -3)$, $R(3, 0)$.

EXAMPLE 4 ***Architecture Application***

Helpful Hint

Translations, reflections, and rotations can be called congruence transformations.

What transformation is used to create the frieze pattern in this cast iron gate? Are sections of the gate congruent? Explain your answer.

Repeated horizontal translations create the frieze pattern. A translation of any section either to the left or to the right by a distance equal to the width of the section produces an image that is congruent to the preimage.

CHECK IT OUT! **4.** Sketch a frieze pattern that can be produced by using reflections.

MATHEMATICAL PRACTICES

THINK AND DISCUSS

1. Think of the transformation mapping $(x, y) \rightarrow (x + 5, y - 2)$ as a function with input (x, y). What is the output of the function? If the transformation is applied to a polygon, describe the size, shape, and position of the image compared to the preimage.

2. What type of transformation preserves angle but does not preserve distance?

3. Describe a dilation with center (0, 0) that would produce an image such that every image point is closer to (0, 0) than its corresponding preimage point.

4. GET ORGANIZED Copy and complete the graphic organizer, including coordinate transformation rules.

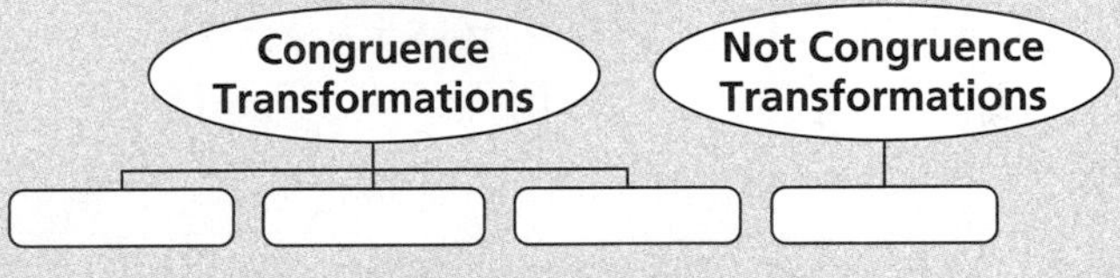

4-1 Exercises

GUIDED PRACTICE

Vocabulary **Apply the vocabulary from this lesson to answer each question.**

1. Dilations with scale factor $k \neq 1$ produce images that ___?___ *(are, are not)* congruent to their preimages.

2. An ___?___ (isometry, image) is a transformation that preserves length, angle, and area; it is also called a ___?___ (translation, rigid transformation).

SEE EXAMPLE 1

Apply the transformation M to the polygon with the given vertices. Name the coordinates of the image points. Identify and describe the transformation.

3. $M: (x, y) \rightarrow (x, -y)$
$A(2, 1), B(5, 4), C(5, 1)$

4. $M: (x, y) \rightarrow (3x, 3y)$
$P(-2, 1), Q(-1, 2), R(0, 1)$

5. $M: (x, y) \rightarrow (y, -x)$
$L(3, 1), M(3, 4), N(5, 4), O(5, 1)$

6. $M: (x, y) \rightarrow (x - 3, y + 2)$
$D(4, -1), E(7, 3), F(7, -1)$

SEE EXAMPLE 2

Determine whether the polygons with the given vertices are congruent. Support your answer by describing a transformation.

7. $A(-4, 4), B(-4, 6), C(2, 6), D(2, 4)$ and $W(-2, 2), X(-2, 3), Y(1, 3), Z(1, 2)$

8. $A(-2, -2), B(-4, -1), C(-1, -1)$ and $T(2, 2), U(4, 1), V(1, 1)$

SEE EXAMPLE 3

Prove that the polygons with the given vertices are congruent.

9. $J(-5, 2), K(-2, 5), L(-2, 2)$ and $M(5, 0), N(2, 3), O(2, 0)$

10. $D(-1, -5), E(-4, -4), F(-1, -2)$ and $X(3, 4), Y(6, 3), Z(3, 1)$

SEE EXAMPLE 4

11. Victorian Crafts What transformation is used to create the frieze pattern in the wallpaper shown? Are there any congruent sections of the wallpaper? Explain your answer.

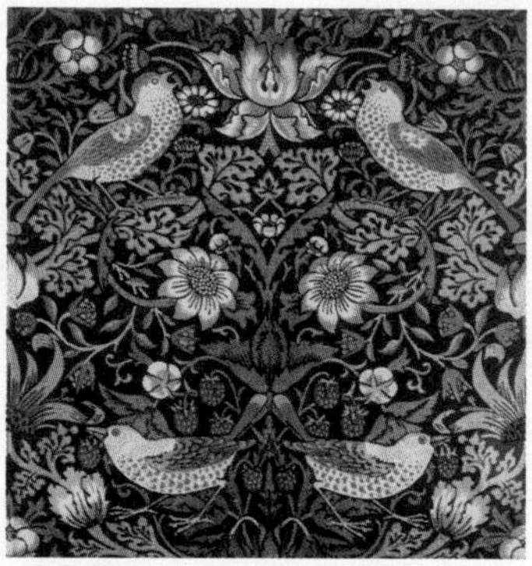

12. Sketch a frieze pattern that can be produced by using reflections and/or translations.

PRACTICE AND PROBLEM SOLVING

Independent Practice	
For Exercises	See Example
13–18	1
19–21	2
22–24	3
25	4

Apply the transformation M to the polygon with the given vertices. Name the coordinates of the image points. Identify and describe the transformation.

13. $M: (x, y) \rightarrow (x + 5, y - 4)$
$G(4, -1), H(7, 3), I(7, -1)$

14. $M: (x, y) \rightarrow (-x, y)$
$P(3, 2), Q(6, 2), R(3, 5)$

15. $M: (x, y) \rightarrow (1.5x, 1.5y)$
$L(-1, 4), M(-4, 4), N(-4, 3)$

16. $M: (x, y) \rightarrow (-y, x)$
$A(-7, 6), B(-7, 4), C(-4, 6), D(-4, 4)$

17. $M: (x, y) \rightarrow (x - 1, y + 1)$
$N(1, -2), O(0, 4), P(2, 4)$

18. $M: (x, y) \rightarrow (-x, -y)$
$W(5, 2), X(2, 2), Y(5, 5)$

Determine whether the polygons with the given vertices are congruent. Support your answer by describing a transformation.

19. $J(-4, 4), K(-4, 6), L(2, 6), M(2, 4)$ and $A(4, 4), B(6, 4), C(6, -2), D(4, -2)$

20. $P(-2, -2), Q(-4, -1), R(-1, -1)$ and $X(2, 2), Y(4, 1), Z(1, 1)$

21. $E(-1, -1), F(2, 2), G(-3, 3)$ and $U(-1, 2), V(2, 5), W(-3, 6)$

Prove that the polygons with the given vertices are congruent.

22. $D(-5, -1), E(-2, 1), F(2, -1)$ and $X(-1, 1), Y(2, -1), Z(6, 1)$

23. $A(2, -1), B(4, -2), C(6, 0)$ and $D(-3, -2), E(-4, -4), F(-2, -6)$

24. $P(-7, 3), Q(-8, 7), R(-4, 7)$ and $G(4, -3), H(5, -7), I(1, -7)$

25. Quilting Jennifer is designing a quilt. She made this diagram to follow when making her quilt.

a. What transformation or combination of transformations is used to create the pattern in this quilt design?

b. Are sections of the quilt congruent? Explain your answer.

c. What if . . . ? How might the design look different if she had used 180° rotations instead?

Apply the transformation M to the polygon with the given vertices. Name the coordinates of the image points. Identify and describe the transformation.

26. $M: (x, y) \rightarrow (x - 3, y + 2)$

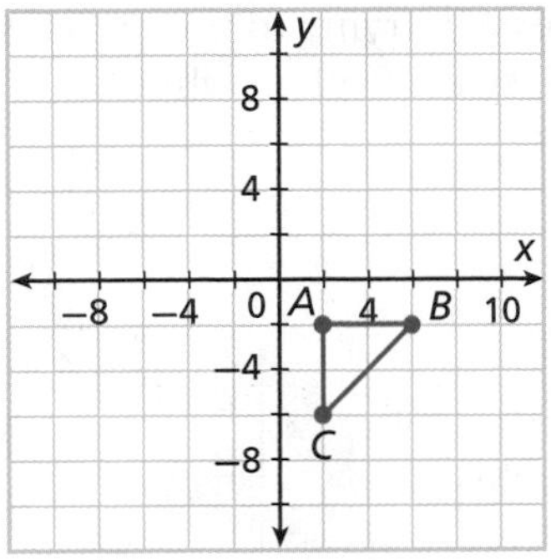

27. $M: (x, y) \rightarrow (y, -x)$

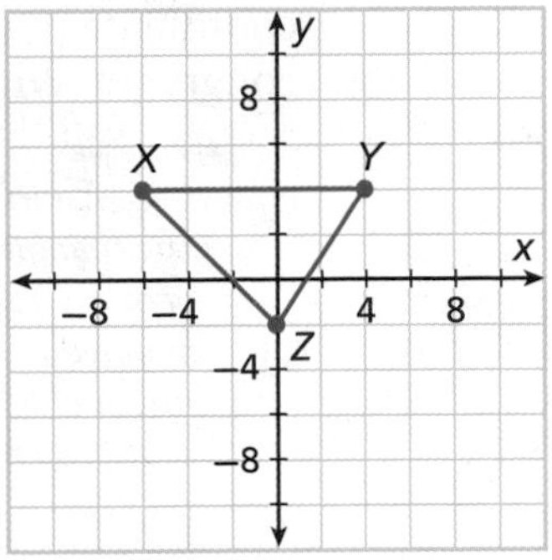

28. Logo Design Eli made this logo design for a company letterhead. What transformation(s) did he use to make the design? Are there any congruent shapes in the design?

Apply the transformations M to the polygon with the given vertices. Name the coordinates of the image points. Identify and describe the transformations.

29. $M: (x, y) \rightarrow (x, -y) \rightarrow (x + 3, y)$

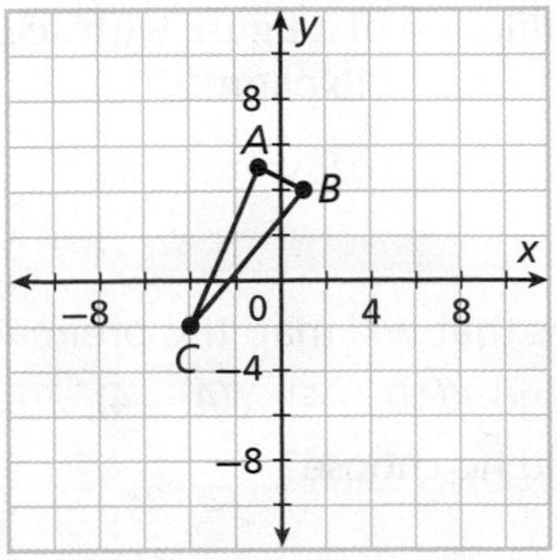

30. $M: (x, y) \rightarrow (3x, 3y) \rightarrow (-y, x)$

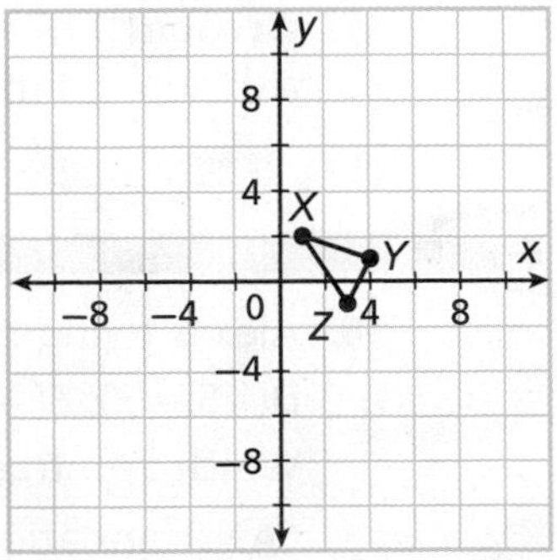

31. Tessellations Frank developed a tessellating shape to use in a repeating design. Describe the series of transformations he used to create this square design of his tessellated shape.

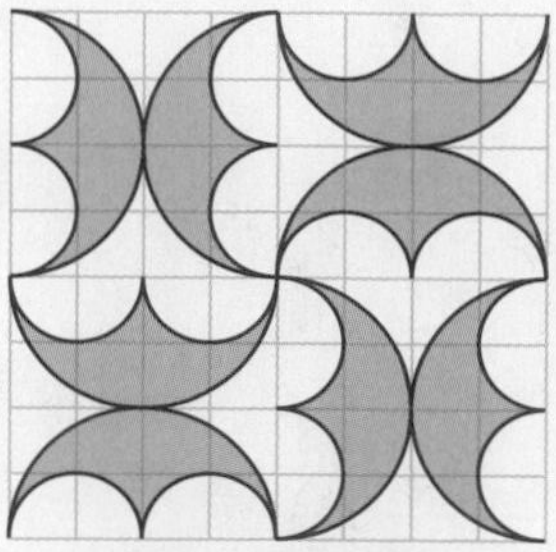

32. Signal Flags Seth is going to recreate this signal flag out of fabric. He has light blue and dark blue fabric. What transformations will he perform on the light blue triangles to position them correctly, if he starts in the upper left corner?

33. ERROR ANALYSIS Erin and Dave are looking at the triangles on the coordinate plane shown. They are each trying to prove that the triangles are congruent. Who has the correct answer? Explain why.

Erin's Answer
The triangles are congruent because $\triangle ABC$ can be mapped to $\triangle DEF$ by a rotation: $(x, y) \rightarrow (-y, x)$. Then $\triangle DEF$ can be mapped to $\triangle XYZ$ by a translation: $(x, y) \rightarrow (x + 2, y + 3)$.

Dave's Answer
The triangles are congruent because $\triangle ABC$ can be mapped to $\triangle DEF$ by a reflection: $(x, y) \rightarrow (x, -y)$. Then $\triangle DEF$ can be mapped to $\triangle XYZ$ by a translation: $(x, y) \rightarrow (x + 2, y + 3)$.

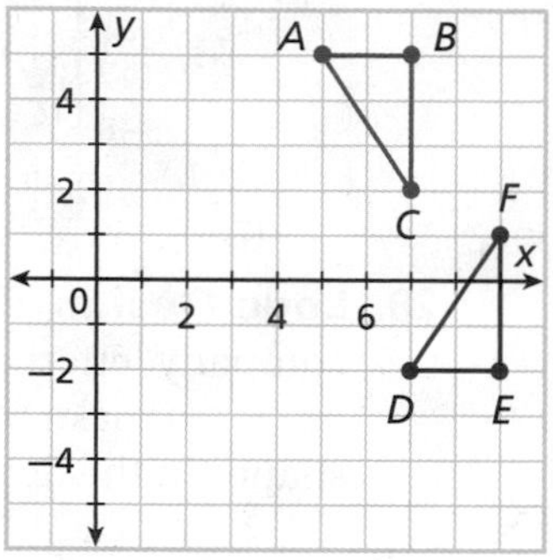

34. Write About It Describe the differences in reflecting a polygon and rotating a polygon in terms of the coordinate mapping directions.

35. Critical Thinking How does a dilation of a figure with scale factor 0.5 compare to a dilation of the figure with scale factor 2? Explain.

TEST PREP

36. Alex is trying two transformations that will map the preimage to the image. $D(-5, -2)$, $E(-2, -2)$, $F(-4, -5)$ and $X(10, -4)$, $Y(4, -4)$, $Z(8, -10)$
Which two transformations should he choose?

Ⓐ translation and reflection
Ⓑ dilation and reflection
Ⓒ reflection and rotation
Ⓓ rotation and dilation

37. Bill applied the transformation M to the polygon. What are the coordinates of the image points for the polygon?

$M: (x, y) \rightarrow (x, -y)$

Ⓐ $A'(1, 1), B'(6, 4), C'(8, -2)$

Ⓑ $A'(-1, 1), B'(-6, 4), C'(-8, -2)$

Ⓒ $A'(-1, -1), B'(-6, -4), C'(-8, 2)$

Ⓓ $A'(1, -1), B'(6, -4), C'(8, 2)$

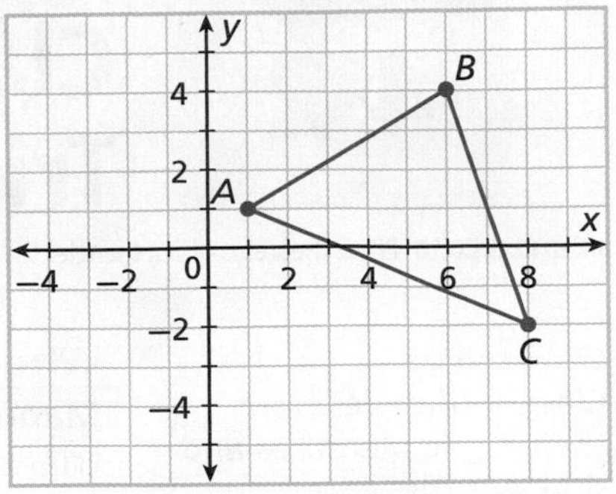

CHALLENGE AND EXTEND

38. **Architecture** Steve was visiting the ruins at Mitla, an archeological site in Mexico. He saw this frieze design.

a. Does the frieze have congruent shapes? What transformation or combination of tranformations are used to create the pattern in this frieze design?

b. **What if ... ?** How might the design have looked if the designers had rotated the S-shapes 90 degrees clockwise and then translated an entire row to make the next row? Sketch your answer.

COMMON CORE

4-2 Classifying Triangles

CC.9-12.G.CO.10 Prove theorems about triangles.

Objectives

Classify triangles by their angle measures and side lengths.

Use triangle classification to find angle measures and side lengths.

Vocabulary

acute triangle
equiangular triangle
right triangle
obtuse triangle
equilateral triangle
isosceles triangle
scalene triangle

Who uses this?

Manufacturers use properties of triangles to calculate the amount of material needed to make triangular objects. (See Example 4.)

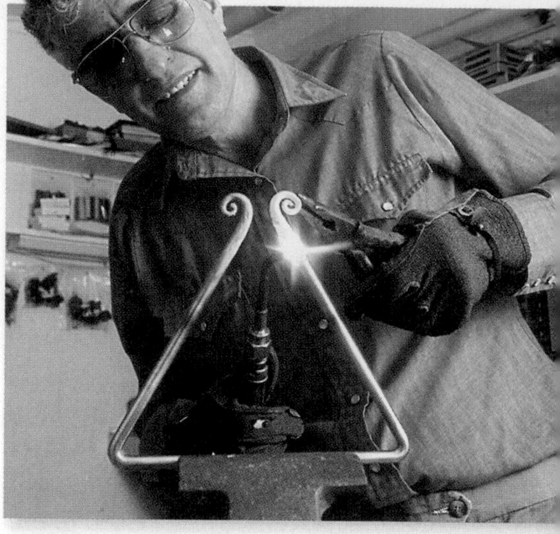

A triangle is a steel percussion instrument in the shape of an *equilateral triangle.* Different-sized triangles produce different musical notes when struck with a metal rod.

Recall that a *triangle* ($\triangle$) is a polygon with three sides. Triangles can be classified in two ways: by their angle measures or by their side lengths.

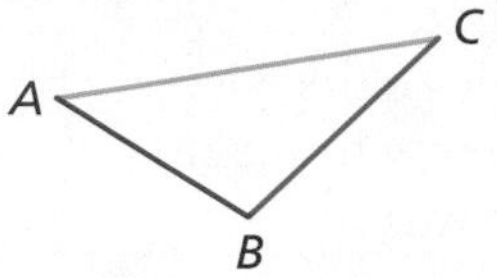

$\overline{AB}$, $\overline{BC}$, and $\overline{AC}$ are the *sides* of $\triangle ABC$. *A, B,* and *C* are the triangle's *vertices.*

Know it! Note

Triangle Classification **By Angle Measures**

Acute Triangle	Equiangular Triangle	Right Triangle	Obtuse Triangle
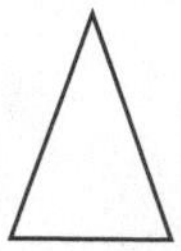	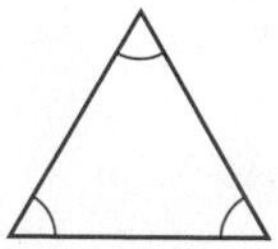	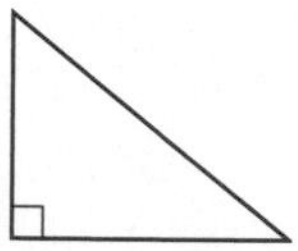	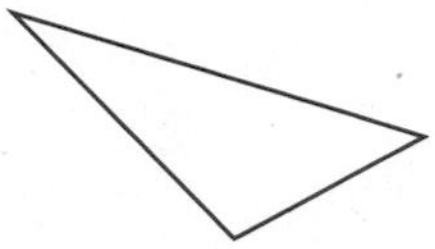
Three acute angles	Three congruent acute angles	One right angle	One obtuse angle

EXAMPLE 1 **Classifying Triangles by Angle Measures**

Classify each triangle by its angle measures.

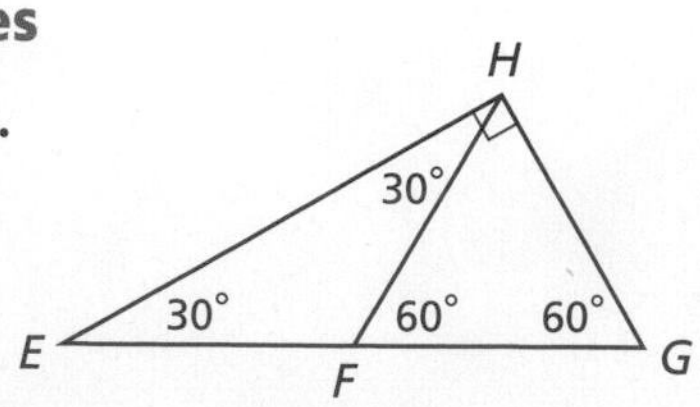

A $\triangle EHG$

$\angle EHG$ is a right angle. So $\triangle EHG$ is a right triangle.

B $\triangle EFH$

$\angle EFH$ and $\angle HFG$ form a linear pair, so they are supplementary. Therefore $m\angle EFH + m\angle HFG = 180°$. By substitution, $m\angle EFH + \mathbf{60°} = 180°$. So $m\angle EFH = 120°$. $\triangle EFH$ is an obtuse triangle by definition.

CHECK IT OUT! **1.** Use the diagram to classify $\triangle FHG$ by its angle measures.

Know it! Note

Triangle Classification | **By Side Lengths**

Equilateral Triangle	Isosceles Triangle	Scalene Triangle
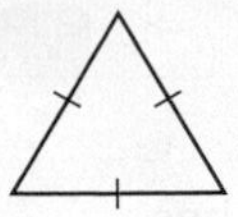	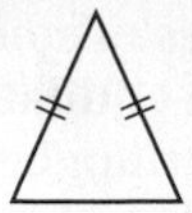	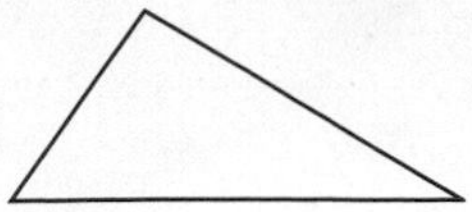
Three congruent sides	At least two congruent sides	No congruent sides

EXAMPLE 2 Classifying Triangles by Side Lengths

Remember!
When you look at a figure, you cannot assume segments are congruent based on their appearance. They must be marked as congruent.

Classify each triangle by its side lengths.

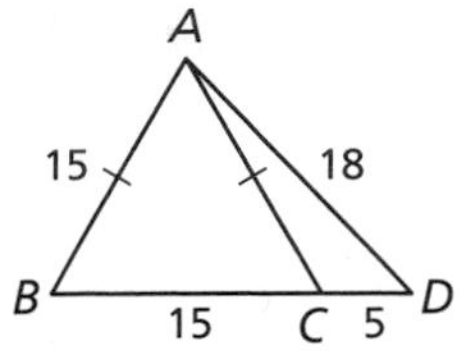

A $\triangle ABC$
From the figure, $\overline{AB} \cong \overline{AC}$. So $AC = 15$, and $\triangle ABC$ is equilateral.

B $\triangle ABD$
By the Segment Addition Postulate,
$BD = BC + CD = 15 + 5 = 20.$
Since no sides are congruent, $\triangle ABD$ is scalene.

CHECK IT OUT! 2. Use the diagram to classify $\triangle ACD$ by its side lengths.

EXAMPLE 3 Using Triangle Classification

Algebra

Find the side lengths of the triangle.

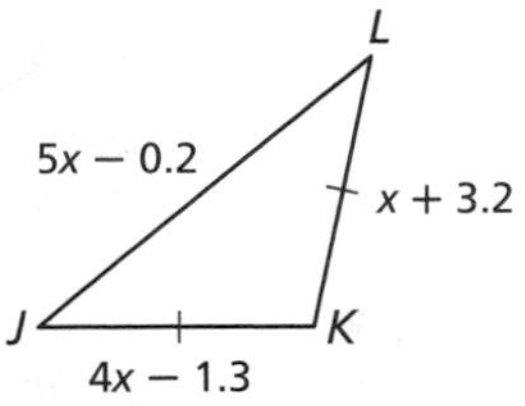

Step 1 Find the value of x.

$\overline{JK} \cong \overline{KL}$	*Given*
$JK = KL$	*Def. of ≅ segs.*
$(4x - 1.3) = (x + 3.2)$	*Substitute (4x − 13) for JK and (x + 3.2) for KL.*
$3x = 4.5$	*Add 1.3 and subtract x from both sides.*
$x = 1.5$	*Divide both sides by 3.*

Step 2 Substitute 1.5 into the expressions to find the side lengths.

$JK = 4x - 1.3$
$= 4(1.5) - 1.3 = 4.7$
$KL = x + 3.2$
$= (1.5) + 3.2 = 4.7$
$JL = 5x - 0.2$
$= 5(1.5) - 0.2 = 7.3$

CHECK IT OUT! 3. Find the side lengths of equilateral $\triangle FGH$.

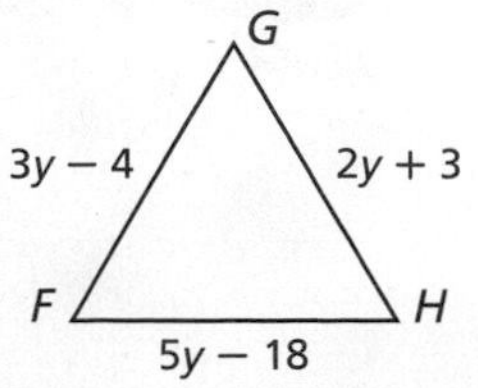

EXAMPLE 4 *Music Application*

A manufacturer produces musical triangles by bending pieces of steel into the shape of an equilateral triangle. The triangles are available in side lengths of 4 inches, 7 inches, and 10 inches. How many 4-inch triangles can the manufacturer produce from a 100 inch piece of steel?

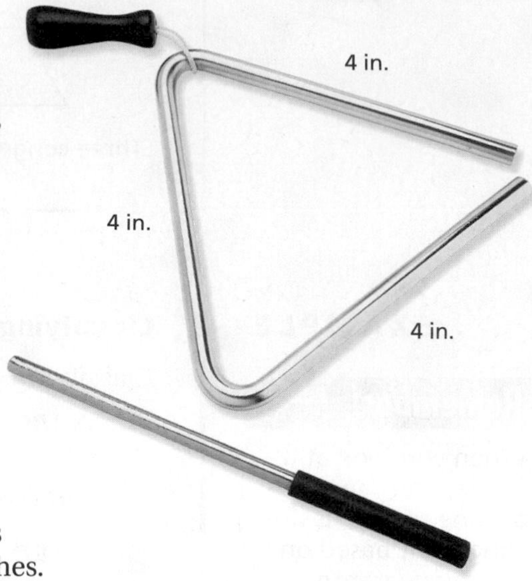

The amount of steel needed to make one triangle is equal to the perimeter P of the equilateral triangle.

$P = 3(4)$
$= 12$ in.

To find the number of triangles that can be made from 100 inches. of steel, divide 100 by the amount of steel needed for one triangle.

$100 \div 12 = 8\frac{1}{3}$ triangles

There is not enough steel to complete a ninth triangle. So the manufacturer can make 8 triangles from a 100 in. piece of steel.

CHECK IT OUT! **Each measure is the side length of an equilateral triangle. Determine how many triangles can be formed from a 100 in. piece of steel.**

4a. 7 in. **4b.** 10 in.

MATHEMATICAL PRACTICES

THINK AND DISCUSS

1. For $\triangle DEF$, name the three pairs of consecutive sides and the vertex formed by each.
2. Sketch an example of an obtuse isosceles triangle, or explain why it is not possible to do so.
3. Is every acute triangle equiangular? Explain and support your answer with a sketch.
4. Use the Pythagorean Theorem to explain why you cannot draw an equilateral right triangle.

Know it! Note

5. **GET ORGANIZED** Copy and complete the graphic organizer. In each box, describe each type of triangle.

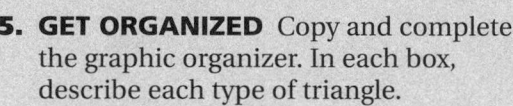

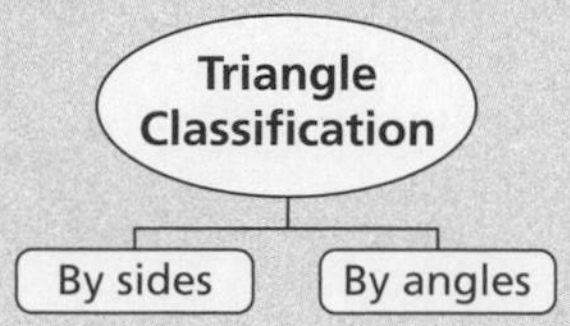

4-2 Exercises

Learn It Online
Homework Help Online
Parent Resources Online

GUIDED PRACTICE

Vocabulary **Apply the vocabulary from this lesson to answer each question.**

1. In $\triangle JKL$, JK, KL, and JL are *equal*. How does this help you classify $\triangle JKL$ by its side lengths?
2. $\triangle XYZ$ is an *obtuse* triangle. What can you say about the types of angles in $\triangle XYZ$?

SEE EXAMPLE 1

Classify each triangle by its angle measures.

3. $\triangle DBC$ 4. $\triangle ABD$ 5. $\triangle ADC$

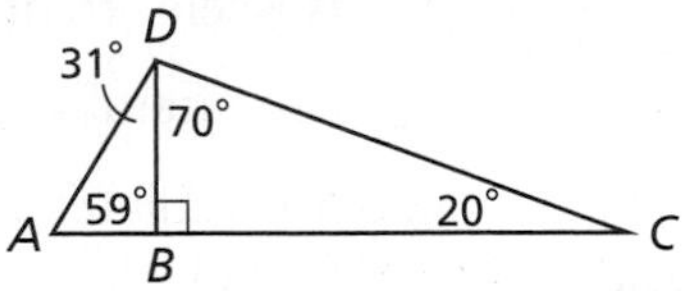

SEE EXAMPLE 2

Classify each triangle by its side lengths.

6. $\triangle EGH$ 7. $\triangle EFH$ 8. $\triangle HFG$

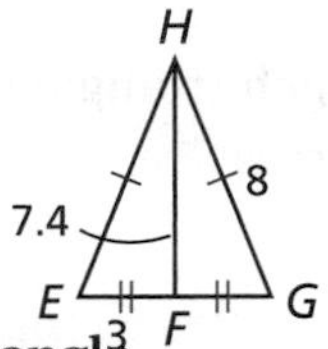

SEE EXAMPLE 3

Multi-Step **Find the side lengths of each triangle.**

9.

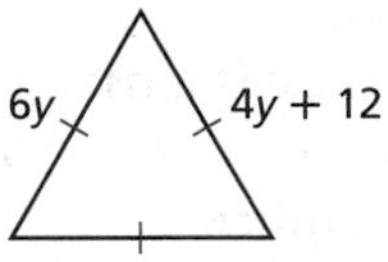

10.

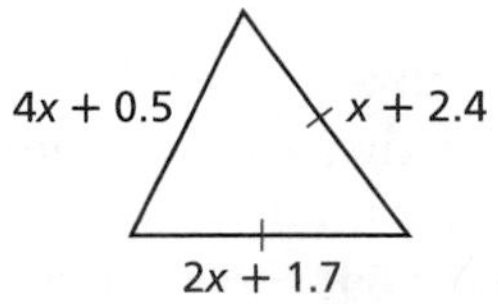

SEE EXAMPLE 4

11. **Crafts** A jeweler creates triangular earrings by bending pieces of silver wire. Each earring is an isosceles triangle with the dimensions shown. How many earrings can be made from a piece of wire that is 50 cm long?

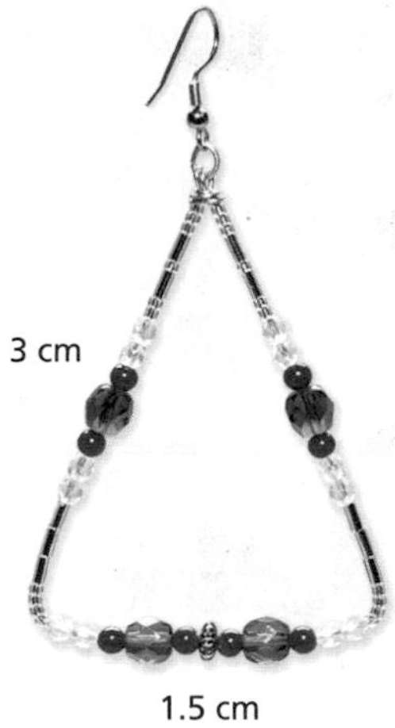

PRACTICE AND PROBLEM SOLVING

Independent Practice

For Exercises	See Example
12–14	1
15–17	2
18–20	3
21–22	4

Extra Practice
See Extra Practice for more Skills Practice and Applications Practice exercises.

Classify each triangle by its angle measures.

12. $\triangle BEA$
13. $\triangle DBC$
14. $\triangle ABC$

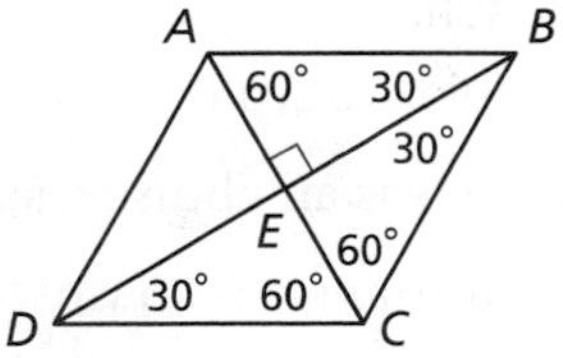

Classify each triangle by its side lengths.

15. $\triangle PST$ 16. $\triangle RSP$ 17. $\triangle RPT$

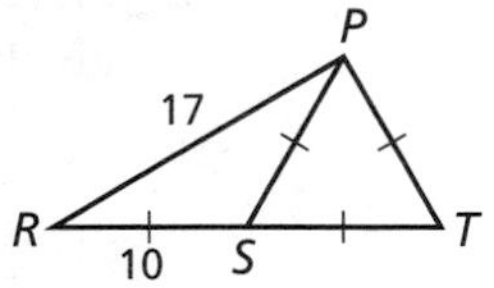

Multi-Step **Find the side lengths of each triangle.**

18.

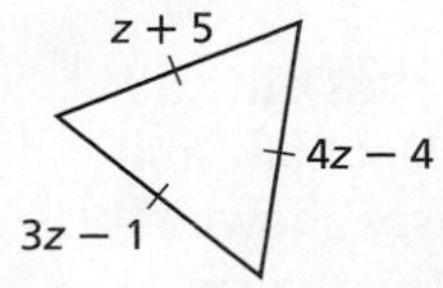

19.

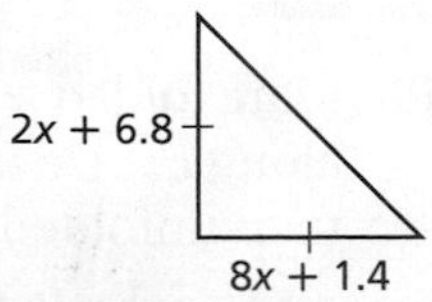

20. Draw a triangle large enough to measure. Label the vertices X, Y, and Z.
    a. Name the three sides and three angles of the triangle.
    b. Use a ruler and protractor to classify the triangle by its side lengths and angle measures.

Carpentry **Use the following information for Exercises 21 and 22.** A manufacturer makes trusses, or triangular supports, for the roofs of houses. Each truss is the shape of an isosceles triangle in which $\overline{PQ} \cong \overline{PR}$. The length of the base $\overline{QR}$ is $\frac{4}{3}$ the length of each of the congruent sides.

21. The perimeter of each truss is 60 ft. Find each side length.

22. How many trusses can the manufacturer make from 150 feet of lumber?

Draw an example of each type of triangle or explain why it is not possible.

23. isosceles right **24.** equiangular obtuse **25.** scalene right

26. equilateral acute **27.** scalene equiangular **28.** isosceles acute

29. An equilateral triangle has a perimeter of 105 in. What is the length of each side of the triangle?

Classify each triangle by its angles and sides.

30. $\triangle ABC$ **31.** $\triangle ACD$

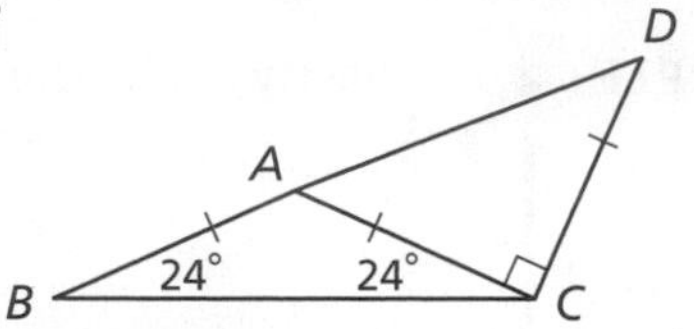

32. An isosceles triangle has a perimeter of 34 cm. The congruent sides measure $(4x - 1)$ cm. The length of the third side is x cm. What is the value of x?

33. **Architecture** The base of the Flatiron Building is a triangle bordered by three streets: Broadway, Fifth Avenue, and East Twenty-second Street. The Fifth Avenue side is 1 ft shorter than twice the East Twenty-second Street side. The East Twenty-second Street side is 8 ft shorter than half the Broadway side. The Broadway side is 190 ft.

a. Find the two unknown side lengths.

b. Classify the triangle by its side lengths.

LINK

Architecture

Daniel Burnham designed and built the 22-story Flatiron Building in New York City in 1902.

Source: www.greatbuildings.com

34. **Critical Thinking** Is every isosceles triangle equilateral? Is every equilateral triangle isosceles? Explain.

Tell whether each statement is sometimes, always, or never true. Support your answer with a sketch.

35. An acute triangle is a scalene triangle.

36. A scalene triangle is an obtuse triangle.

37. An equiangular triangle is an isosceles triangle.

38. **Write About It** Write a formula for the side length s of an equilateral triangle, given the perimeter P. Explain how you derived the formula.

39. **Construction** Use the method for constructing congruent segments to construct an equilateral triangle.

MULTI-STEP TEST PREP

40. Marc folded a rectangular sheet of paper, $ABCD$, in half along $\overline{EF}$. He folded the resulting square diagonally and then unfolded the paper to create the creases shown.

a. Use the Pythagorean Theorem to find DE and CE.

b. What is the $m\angle DEC$?

c. Classify $\triangle DEC$ by its side lengths and by its angle measures.

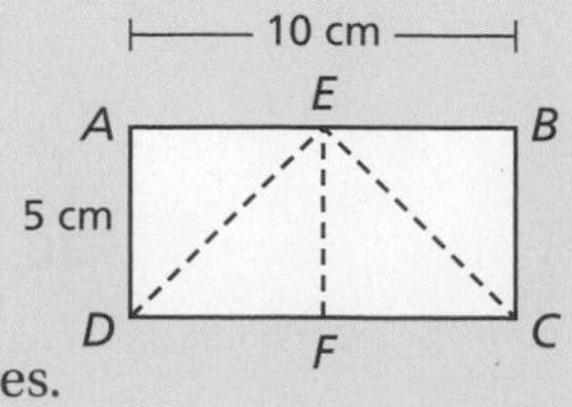

TEST PREP

41. What is the side length of an equilateral triangle with a perimeter of $36\frac{2}{3}$ inches?

Ⓐ $36\frac{2}{3}$ inches
Ⓒ $12\frac{1}{3}$ inches
Ⓑ $18\frac{1}{3}$ inches
Ⓓ $12\frac{2}{9}$ inches

42. The vertices of $\triangle RST$ are $R(3, 2)$, $S(-2, 3)$, and $T(-2, 1)$. Which of these best describes $\triangle RST$?

Ⓕ Isosceles Ⓖ Scalene Ⓗ Equilateral Ⓙ Right

43. Which of the following is NOT a correct classification of $\triangle LMN$?

Ⓐ Acute
Ⓒ Isosceles
Ⓑ Equiangular
Ⓓ Right

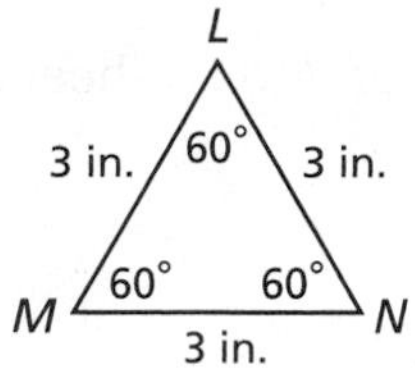

44. Gridded Response $\triangle ABC$ is isosceles, and $\overline{AB} \cong \overline{AC}$. $AB = \left(\frac{1}{2}x + \frac{1}{4}\right)$, and $BC = \left(\frac{5}{2} - x\right)$. What is the perimeter of $\triangle ABC$?

CHALLENGE AND EXTEND

45. A triangle has vertices with coordinates $(0, 0)$, $(a, 0)$, and $(0, a)$, where $a \neq 0$. Classify the triangle in two different ways. Explain your answer.

46. Write a two-column proof.
Given: $\triangle ABC$ is equiangular.
$EF \parallel AC$
Prove: $\triangle EFB$ is equiangular.

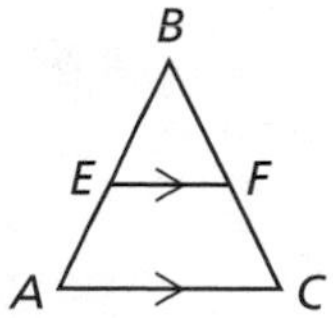

47. Two sides of an equilateral triangle measure $(y + 10)$ units and $(y^2 - 2)$ units. If the perimeter of the triangle is 21 units, what is the value of y?

48. Multi-Step The average length of the sides of $\triangle PQR$ is 24. How much longer then the average is the longest side?

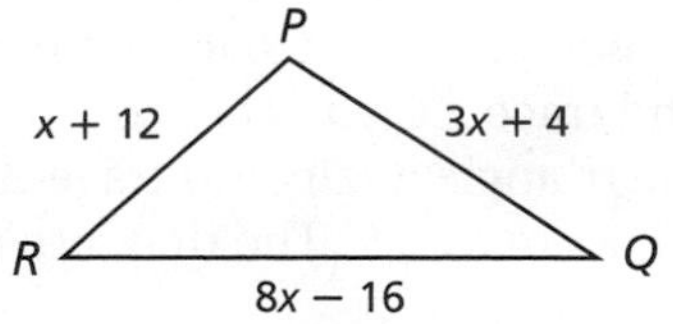

4-3 Geometry LAB

Develop the Triangle Sum Theorem

In this lab, you will use patty paper to discover a relationship between the measures of the interior angles of a triangle.

Use with *Angle Relationships in Triangles*

MATHEMATICAL PRACTICES **Look for and express regularity in repeated reasoning.**

CC.9-12.G.CO.10 Prove theorems about triangles.

Activity

1. Draw and label $\triangle ABC$ on a sheet of notebook paper.

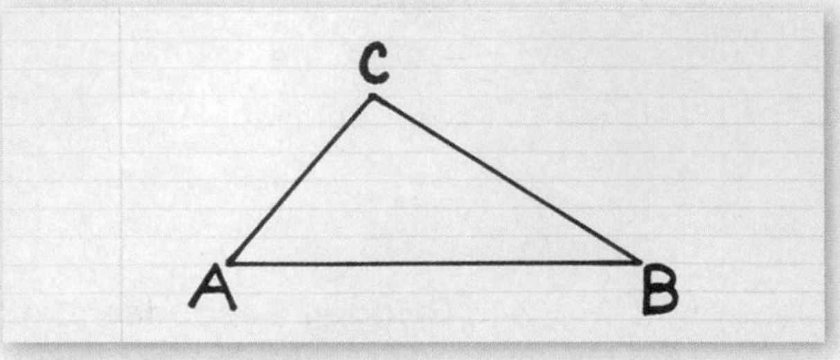

2. On patty paper draw a line ℓ and label a point P on the line.

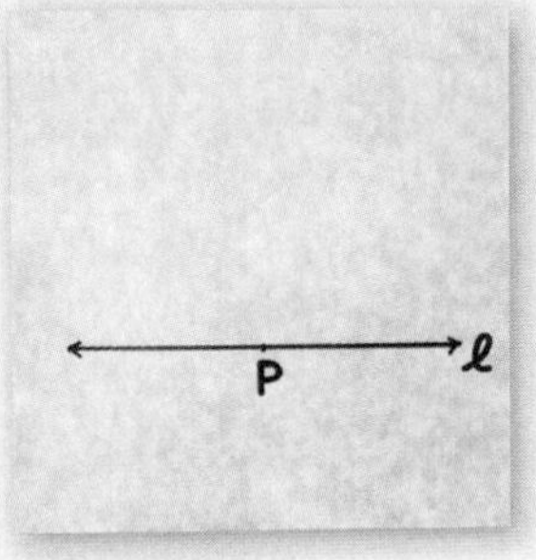

3. Place the patty paper on top of the triangle you drew. Align the papers so that $\overline{AB}$ is on line ℓ and P and B coincide. Trace $\angle B$. Rotate the triangle and trace $\angle C$ adjacent to $\angle B$. Rotate the triangle again and trace $\angle A$ adjacent to $\angle C$. The diagram shows your final step.

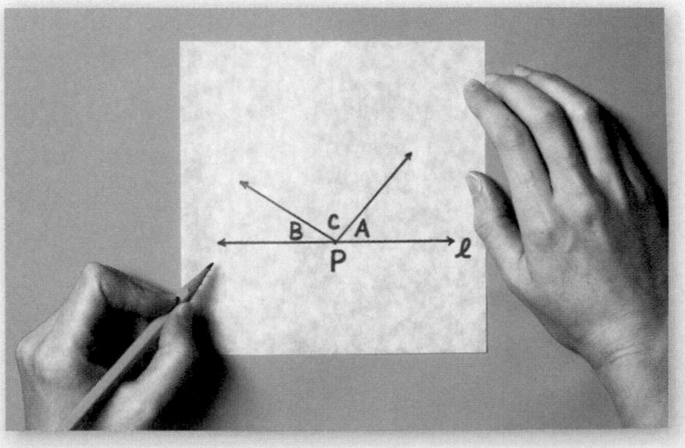

Try This

1. What do you notice about the three angles of the triangle that you traced?
2. Repeat the activity two more times using two different triangles. Do you get the same results each time?
3. Write an equation describing the relationship among the measures of the angles of $\triangle ABC$.
4. Use inductive reasoning to write a conjecture about the sum of the measures of the angles of a triangle.

COMMON CORE

4-3 Angle Relationships in Triangles

CC.9-12.G.CO.10 Prove theorems about triangles.

Objectives
Find the measures of interior and exterior angles of triangles.

Apply theorems about the interior and exterior angles of triangles.

Vocabulary
auxiliary line
corollary
interior
exterior
interior angle
exterior angle
remote interior angle

Who uses this?
Surveyors use triangles to make measurements and create boundaries. (See Example 1.)

Triangulation is a method used in surveying. Land is divided into adjacent triangles. By measuring the sides and angles of one triangle and applying properties of triangles, surveyors can gather information about adjacent triangles.

This engraving shows the county surveyor and commissioners laying out the town of Baltimore in 1730.

Know it! Note

Theorem 4-3-1 **Triangle Sum Theorem**

The sum of the angle measures of a triangle is 180°.

$m\angle A + m\angle B + m\angle C = 180°$

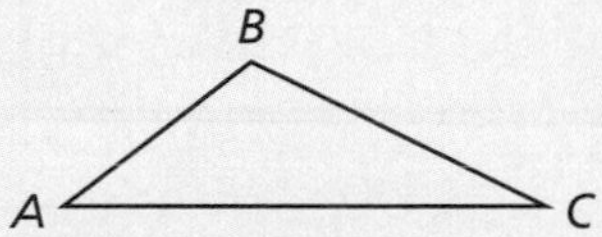

The proof of the Triangle Sum Theorem uses an *auxiliary line*. An **auxiliary line** is a line that is added to a figure to aid in a proof.

PROOF **Triangle Sum Theorem**

Given: $\triangle ABC$
Prove: $m\angle 1 + m\angle 2 + m\angle 3 = 180°$

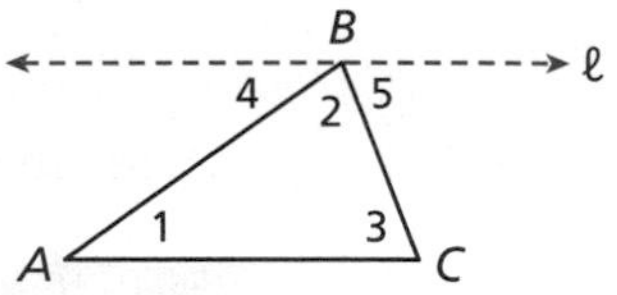

Proof:

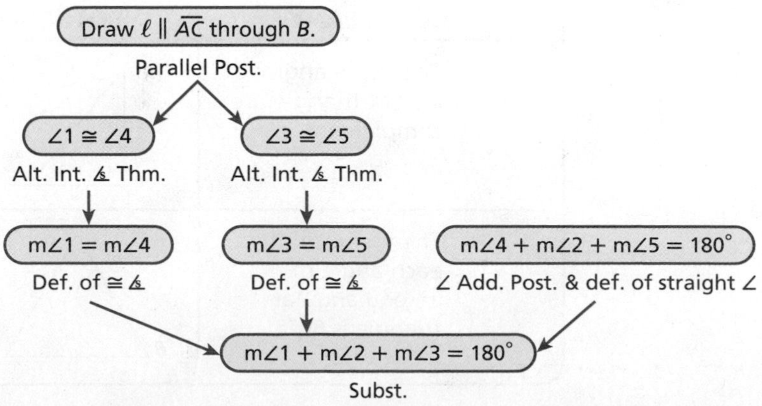

EXAMPLE 1 *Surveying Application*

The map of France commonly used in the 1600s was significantly revised as a result of a triangulation land survey. The diagram shows part of the survey map. Use the diagram to find the indicated angle measures.

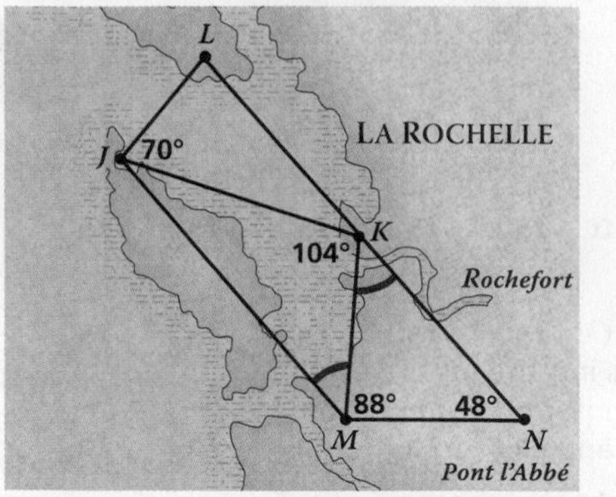

Algebra

A $m\angle NKM$

$m\angle KMN + m\angle MNK + m\angle NKM = 180°$	*△ Sum Thm.*
$\mathbf{88} + \mathbf{48} + m\angle NKM = 180$	*Substitute 88 for m∠KMN and 48 for m∠MNK.*
$136 + m\angle NKM = 180$	*Simplify.*
$m\angle NKM = 44°$	*Subtract 136 from both sides.*

B $m\angle JLK$

Step 1 Find $m\angle JKL$.

$m\angle NKM + m\angle MKJ + m\angle JKL = 180°$	*Lin. Pair Thm. & ∠ Add. Post.*
$\mathbf{44} + \mathbf{104} + m\angle JKL = 180$	*Substitute 44 for m∠NKM and 104 for m∠MKJ.*
$148 + m\angle JKL = 180$	*Simplify.*
$m\angle JKL = 32°$	*Subtract 148 from both sides.*

Step 2 Use substitution and then solve for $m\angle JLK$.

$m\angle JLK + m\angle JKL + m\angle KJL = 180°$	*△ Sum Thm.*
$m\angle JLK + \mathbf{32} + \mathbf{70} = 180$	*Substitute 32 for m∠JKL and 70 for m∠KJL.*
$m\angle JLK + 102 = 180$	*Simplify.*
$m\angle JLK = 78°$	*Subtract 102 from both sides.*

CHECK IT OUT! **1.** Use the diagram to find $m\angle MJK$.

A **corollary** is a theorem whose proof follows directly from another theorem. Here are two corollaries to the Triangle Sum Theorem.

Know it! Note — **Corollaries**

COROLLARY		HYPOTHESIS	CONCLUSION
4-3-2	The acute angles of a right triangle are complementary.	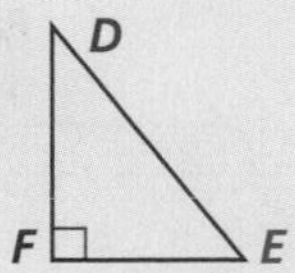	$\angle D$ and $\angle E$ are complementary. $m\angle D + m\angle E = 90°$
4-3-3	The measure of each angle of an equiangular triangle is 60°.	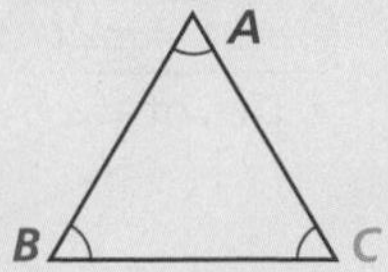	$m\angle A = m\angle B = m\angle C = 60°$

You will prove Corollaries 4-3-2 and 4-3-3 in Exercises 24 and 25.

EXAMPLE 2 Finding Angle Measures in Right Triangles

Algebra

One of the acute angles in a right triangle measures 22.9°. What is the measure of the other acute angle?

Let the acute angles be $\angle M$ and $\angle N$, with $m\angle M = 22.9°$.

$m\angle M + m\angle N = 90$	*Acute ∠s of rt. △ are comp.*
$22.9 + m\angle N = 90$	*Substitute 22.9 for m∠M.*
$m\angle N = 67.1°$	*Subtract 22.9 from both sides.*

CHECK IT OUT! **The measure of one of the acute angles in a right triangle is given. What is the measure of the other acute angle?**

2a. $63.7°$ **2b.** $x°$ **2c.** $48\frac{2}{5}°$

The **interior** is the set of all points inside the figure. The **exterior** is the set of all points outside the figure. An **interior angle** is formed by two sides of a triangle. An **exterior angle** is formed by one side of the triangle and the extension of an adjacent side. Each exterior angle has two *remote interior angles.* A **remote interior angle** is an interior angle that is not adjacent to the exterior angle.

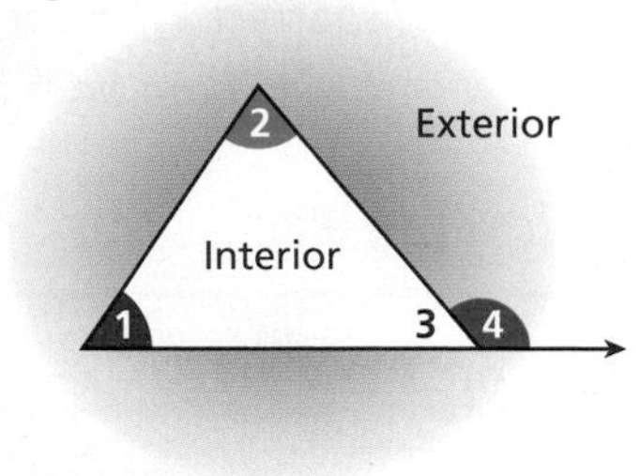

$\angle 4$ is an exterior angle. Its remote interior angles are $\angle 1$ and $\angle 2$.

Know it! Note

Theorem 4-3-4 Exterior Angle Theorem

The measure of an exterior angle of a triangle is equal to the sum of the measures of its remote interior angles.

$m\angle 4 = m\angle 1 + m\angle 2$

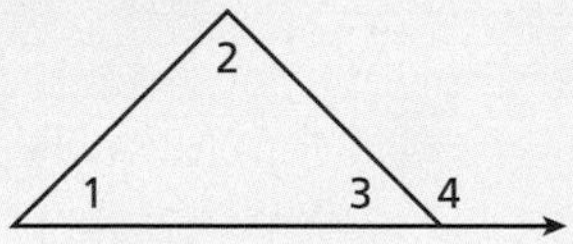

You will prove Theorem 4-3-4 in Exercise 28.

EXAMPLE 3 Applying the Exterior Angle Theorem

Algebra

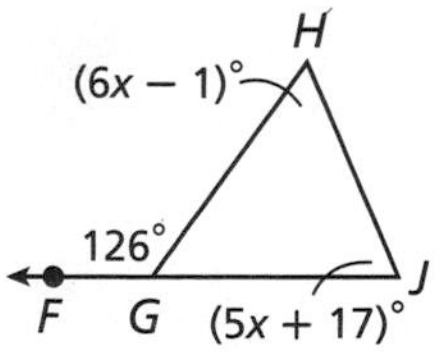

Find $m\angle J$.

$m\angle J + m\angle H = m\angle FGH$	*Ext. ∠ Thm.*
$5x + 17 + 6x - 1 = 126$	*Substitute 5x + 17 for m∠J, 6x − 1 for m∠H, and 126 for m∠FGH.*
$11x + 16 = 126$	*Simplify.*
$11x = 110$	*Subtract 16 from both sides.*
$x = 10$	*Divide both sides by 11.*

$m\angle J = 5x + 17 = 5(10) + 17 = 67°$

CHECK IT OUT! **3.** Find $m\angle ACD$.

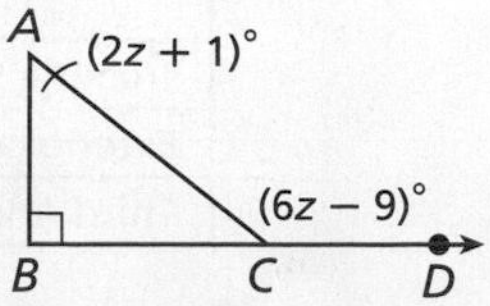

Know it! Note

Theorem 4-3-5 Third Angles Theorem

THEOREM	HYPOTHESIS	CONCLUSION
If two angles of one triangle are congruent to two angles of another triangle, then the third pair of angles are congruent.	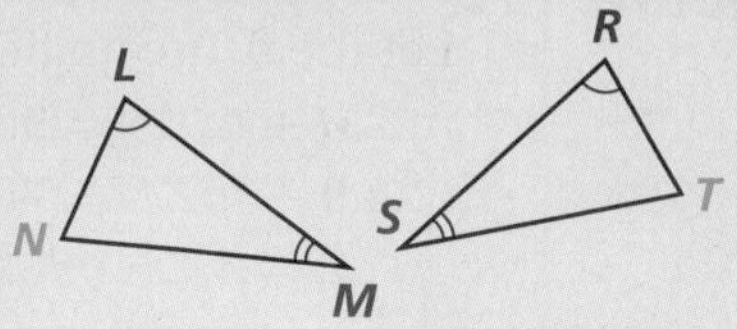	$\angle N \cong \angle T$

You will prove Theorem 4-3-5 in Exercise 27.

EXAMPLE 4 Applying the Third Angles Theorem

Algebra

Find $m\angle C$ and $m\angle F$.

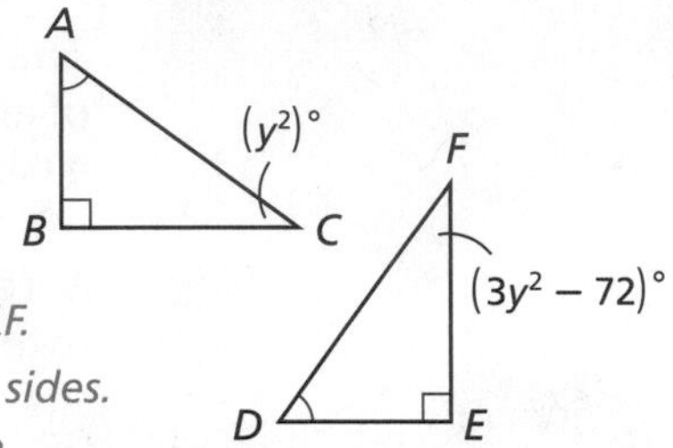

$\angle C \cong \angle F$	*Third $\triangle$s Thm.*
$m\angle C = m\angle F$	*Def. of $\cong$ $\triangle$s.*
$y^2 = 3y^2 - 72$	*Substitute y^2 for $m\angle C$ and $3y^2 - 72$ for $m\angle F$.*
$-2y^2 = -72$	*Subtract $3y^2$ from both sides.*
$y^2 = 36$	*Divide both sides by -2.*

So $m\angle C = 36°$.

Since $m\angle F = m\angle C$, $m\angle F = 36°$.

Helpful Hint

You can use substitution to verify that $m\angle F = 36°$.
$m\angle F = (3 \cdot 36 - 72) = 36°$.

CHECK IT OUT!

4. Find $m\angle P$ and $m\angle T$.

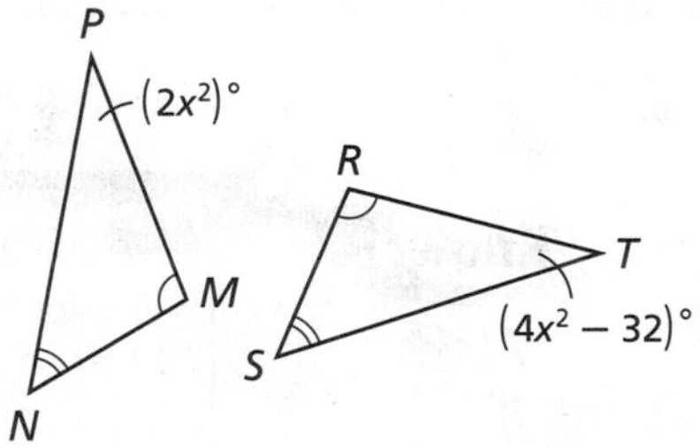

MATHEMATICAL PRACTICES

THINK AND DISCUSS

1. Use the Triangle Sum Theorem to explain why the supplement of one of the angles of a triangle equals in measure the sum of the other two angles of the triangle. Support your answer with a sketch.

2. Sketch a triangle and draw all of its exterior angles. How many exterior angles are there at each vertex of the triangle? How many total exterior angles does the triangle have?

Know it! Note

3. GET ORGANIZED Copy and complete the graphic organizer. In each box, write each theorem in words and then draw a diagram to represent it.

Theorem	Words	Diagram
Triangle Sum Theorem		
Exterior Angle Theorem		
Third Angles Theorem		

4-3 Exercises

Learn It Online
Homework Help Online
Parent Resources Online

GUIDED PRACTICE

Vocabulary **Apply the vocabulary from this lesson to answer each question.**

1. To remember the meaning of *remote interior angle,* think of a television remote control. What is another way to remember the term *remote*?
2. An *exterior angle* is drawn at vertex E of $\triangle DEF$. What are its *remote interior angles*?
3. What do you call segments, rays, or lines that are added to a given diagram?

SEE EXAMPLE 1

Astronomy **Use the following information for Exercises 4 and 5.**

An *asterism* is a group of stars that is easier to recognize than a constellation. One popular asterism is the Summer Triangle, which is composed of the stars Deneb, Altair, and Vega.

4. What is the value of y?
5. What is the measure of each angle in the Summer Triangle?

SEE EXAMPLE 2

The measure of one of the acute angles in a right triangle is given. What is the measure of the other acute angle?

6. $20.8°$
7. $y°$
8. $24\frac{2}{3}°$

SEE EXAMPLE 3

Find each angle measure.

9. $m\angle M$

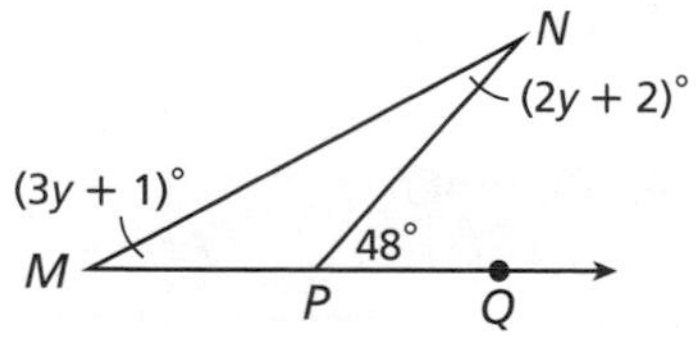

10. $m\angle L$

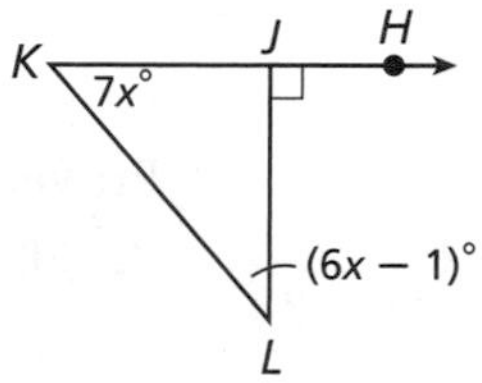

11. In $\triangle ABC$, $m\angle A = 65°$, and the measure of an exterior angle at C is $117°$. Find $m\angle B$ and the $m\angle BCA$.

SEE EXAMPLE 4

12. $m\angle C$ and $m\angle F$

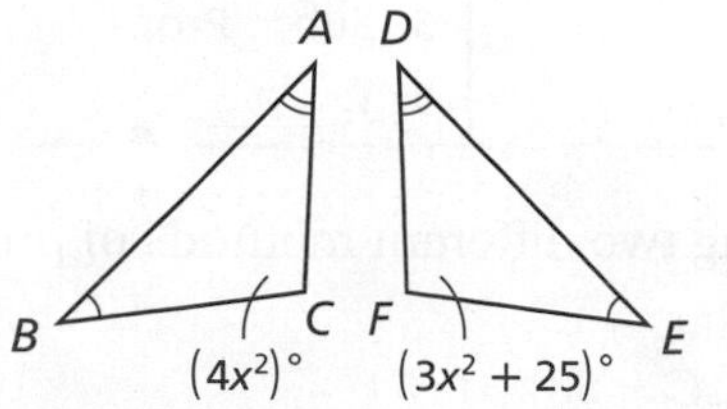

13. $m\angle S$ and $m\angle U$

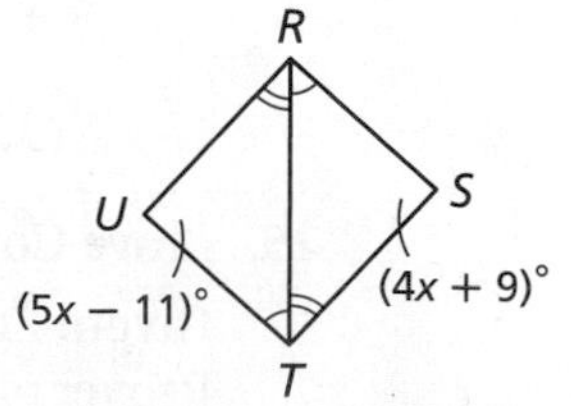

14. For $\triangle ABC$ and $\triangle XYZ$, $m\angle A = m\angle X$ and $m\angle B = m\angle Y$. Find the measures of $\angle C$ and $\angle Z$ if $m\angle C = 4x + 7$ and $m\angle Z = 3(x + 5)$.

PRACTICE AND PROBLEM SOLVING

Independent Practice

For Exercises	See Example
15	1
16–18	2
19–20	3
21–22	4

Extra Practice

See Extra Practice for more Skills Practice and Applications Practice exercises.

15. **Navigation** A sailor on ship A measures the angle between ship B and the pier and finds that it is 39°. A sailor on ship B measures the angle between ship A and the pier and finds that it is 57°. What is the measure of the angle between ships A and B?

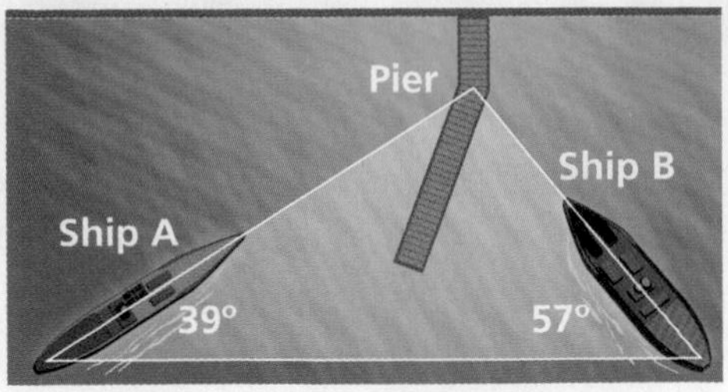

The measure of one of the acute angles in a right triangle is given. What is the measure of the other acute angle?

16. $76\frac{1}{4}°$

17. $2x°$

18. 56.8°

Find each angle measure.

19. $m\angle XYZ$

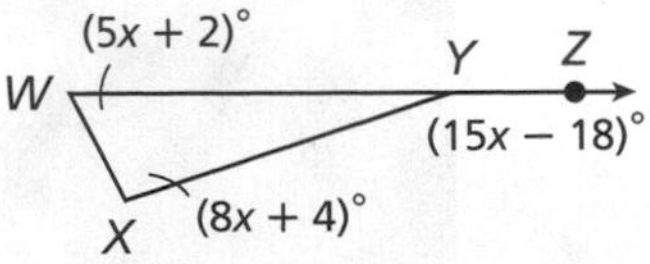

20. $m\angle C$

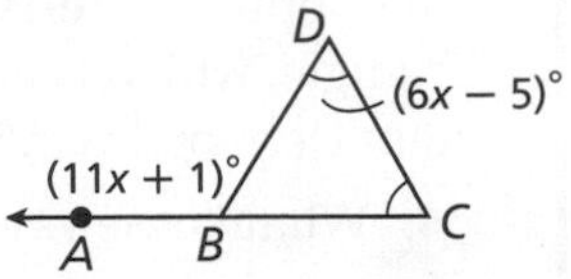

21. $m\angle N$ and $m\angle P$

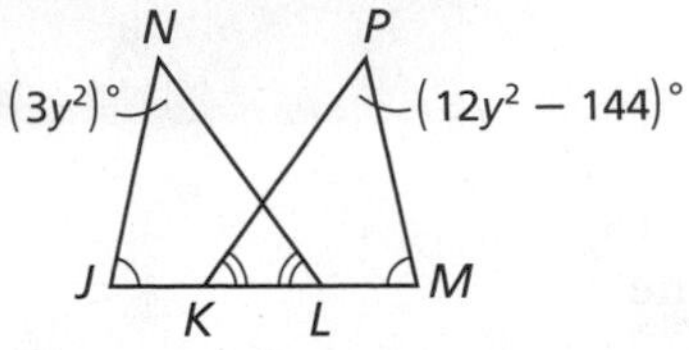

22. $m\angle Q$ and $m\angle S$

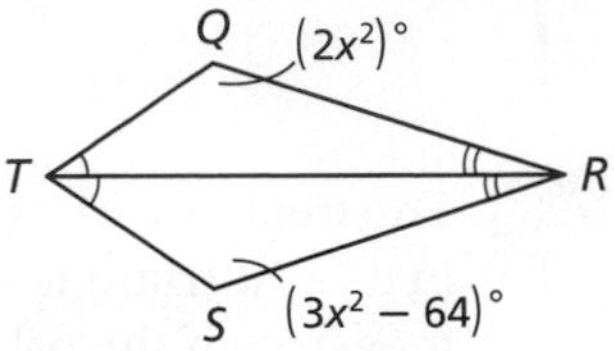

23. **Multi-Step** The measures of the angles of a triangle are in the ratio 1 : 4 : 7. What are the measures of the angles? (*Hint:* Let x, $4x$, and $7x$ represent the angle measures.)

24. Complete the proof of Corollary 4-3-2.

Given: $\triangle DEF$ with right $\angle F$

Prove: $\angle D$ and $\angle E$ are complementary.

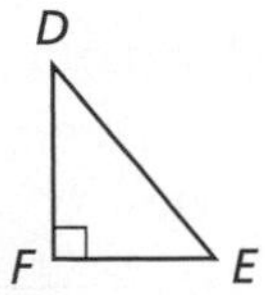

Proof:

Statements	Reasons
1. $\triangle DEF$ with rt. $\angle F$	1. a. ___?___
2. b. ___?___	2. Def. of rt. $\angle$
3. $m\angle D + m\angle E + m\angle F = 180°$	3. c. ___?___
4. $m\angle D + m\angle E + 90° = 180°$	4. d. ___?___
5. e. ___?___	5. Subtr. Prop.
6. $\angle D$ and $\angle E$ are comp.	6. f. ___?___

25. Prove Corollary 4-3-3 using two different methods of proof.

Given: $\triangle ABC$ is equiangular.

Prove: $m\angle A = m\angle B = m\angle C = 60°$

26. **Multi-Step** The measure of one acute angle in a right triangle is $1\frac{1}{4}$ times the measure of the other acute angle. What is the measure of the larger acute angle?

27. Write a two-column proof of the Third Angles Theorem.

28. Prove the Exterior Angle Theorem.

Given: $\triangle ABC$ with exterior angle $\angle ACD$
Prove: $m\angle ACD = m\angle A + m\angle B$
(*Hint:* $\angle BCA$ and $\angle DCA$ form a linear pair.)

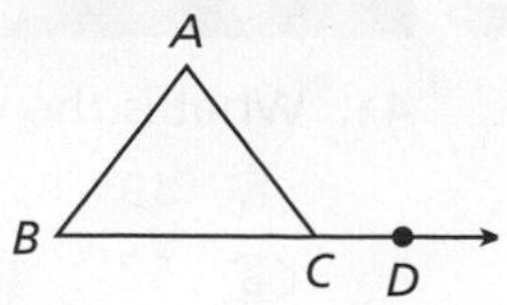

Find each angle measure.

29. $\angle UXW$
30. $\angle UWY$
31. $\angle WZX$
32. $\angle XYZ$

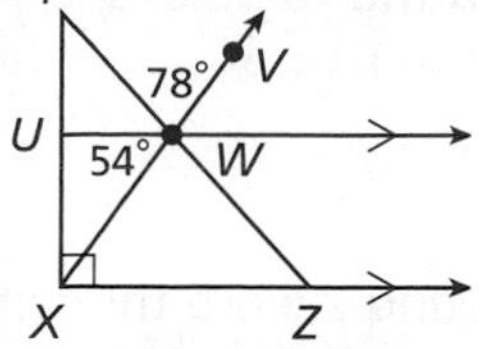

33. **Critical Thinking** What is the measure of any exterior angle of an equiangular triangle? What is the sum of the exterior angle measures?

34. Find $m\angle SRQ$, given that $\angle P \cong \angle U$, $\angle Q \cong \angle T$, and $m\angle RST = 37.5°$.

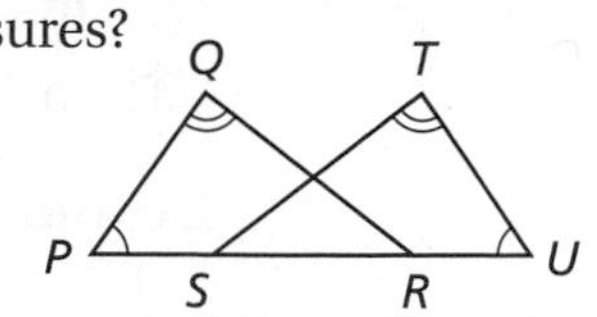

35. **Multi-Step** In a right triangle, one acute angle measure is 4 times the other acute angle measure. What is the measure of the smaller angle?

36. **Aviation** To study the forces of lift and drag, the Wright brothers built a glider, attached two ropes to it, and flew it like a kite. They modeled the two wind forces as the legs of a right triangle.

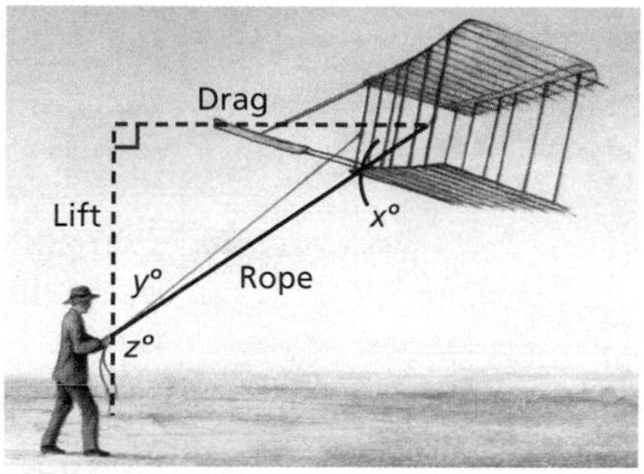

a. What part of a right triangle is formed by each rope?
b. Use the Triangle Sum Theorem to write an equation relating the angle measures in the right triangle.
c. Simplify the equation from part **b**. What is the relationship between x and y?
d. Use the Exterior Angle Theorem to write an expression for z in terms of x.
e. If $x = 37°$, use your results from parts **c** and **d** to find y and z.

37. **Estimation** Draw a triangle and two exterior angles at each vertex. Estimate the measure of each angle. How are the exterior angles at each vertex related? Explain.

38. **Given:** $\overline{AB} \perp \overline{BD}$, $\overline{BD} \perp \overline{DC}$, $\angle A \cong \angle C$
Prove: $\overline{AD} \parallel \overline{CB}$

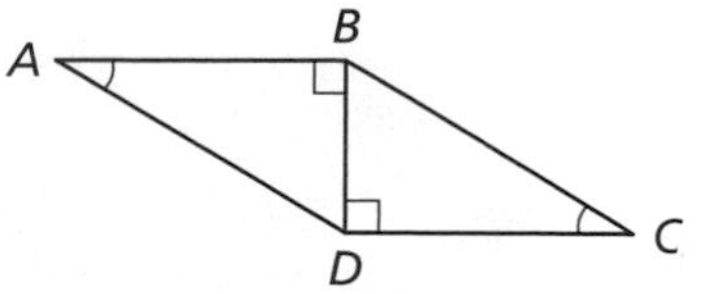

39. **Write About It** A triangle has angle measures of 115°, 40°, and 25°. Explain how to find the measures of the triangle's exterior angles. Support your answer with a sketch.

MULTI-STEP TEST PREP

40. One of the steps in making an origami crane involves folding a square sheet of paper into the shape shown.

a. $\angle DCE$ is a right angle. $\overline{FC}$ bisects $\angle DCE$, and $\overline{BC}$ bisects $\angle FCE$. Find $m\angle FCB$.
b. Use the Triangle Sum Theorem to find $m\angle CBE$.

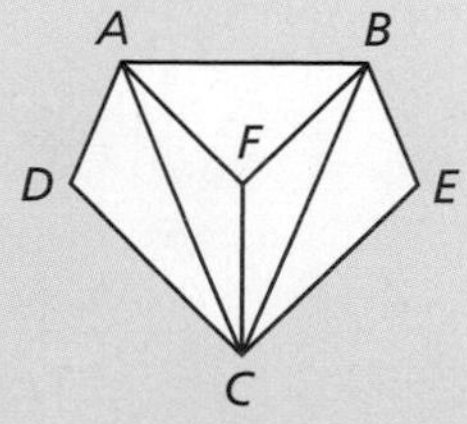

TEST PREP

41. What is the value of x?

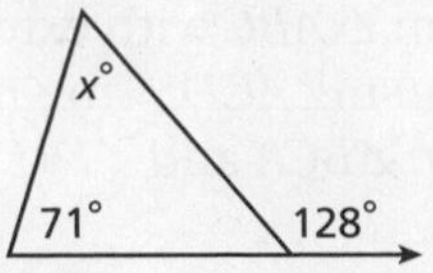

Ⓐ 19
Ⓑ 52
Ⓒ 57
Ⓓ 71

42. Find the value of s.

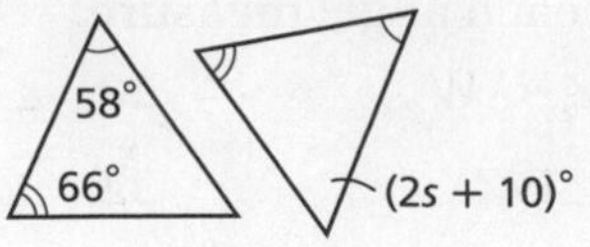

Ⓕ 23
Ⓖ 28
Ⓗ 34
Ⓙ 56

43. $\angle A$ and $\angle B$ are the remote interior angles of $\angle BCD$ in $\triangle ABC$. Which of these equations must be true?

Ⓐ $m\angle A - 180° = m\angle B$
Ⓑ $m\angle A = 90° - m\angle B$
Ⓒ $m\angle BCD = m\angle BCA - m\angle A$
Ⓓ $m\angle B = m\angle BCD - m\angle A$

44. **Extended Response** The measures of the angles in a triangle are in the ratio 2:3:4. Describe how to use algebra to find the measures of these angles. Then find the measure of each angle and classify the triangle.

CHALLENGE AND EXTEND

45. An exterior angle of a triangle measures 117°. Its remote interior angles measure $(2y^2 + 7)°$ and $(61 - y^2)°$. Find the value of y.

46. Two parallel lines are intersected by a transversal. What type of triangle is formed by the intersection of the angle bisectors of two same-side interior angles? Explain. (*Hint:* Use geometry software or construct a diagram of the angle bisectors of two same-side interior angles.)

47. **Critical Thinking** Explain why an exterior angle of a triangle cannot be congruent to a remote interior angle.

48. **Probability** The measure of each angle in a triangle is a multiple of 30°. What is the probability that the triangle has at least two congruent angles?

49. In $\triangle ABC$, $m\angle B$ is 5° less than $1\frac{1}{2}$ times $m\angle A$. $m\angle C$ is 5° less than $2\frac{1}{2}$ times $m\angle A$. What is $m\angle A$ in degrees?

COMMON CORE

4-4 Congruent Triangles

CC.9-12.G.SRT.5 Use congruence…criteria for triangles to solve problems and prove relationships…

Objectives

Use properties of congruent triangles.

Prove triangles congruent by using the definition of congruence.

Vocabulary

corresponding angles
corresponding sides
congruent polygons

Who uses this?

Machinists used triangles to construct a model of the International Space Station's support structure.

Geometric figures are congruent if they are the same size and shape. **Corresponding angles** and **corresponding sides** are in the same position in polygons with an equal number of sides. Two polygons are **congruent polygons** if and only if their corresponding angles and sides are congruent. Thus triangles that are the same size and shape are congruent.

Know it! Note

Properties of Congruent Polygons

DIAGRAM	CORRESPONDING ANGLES	CORRESPONDING SIDES
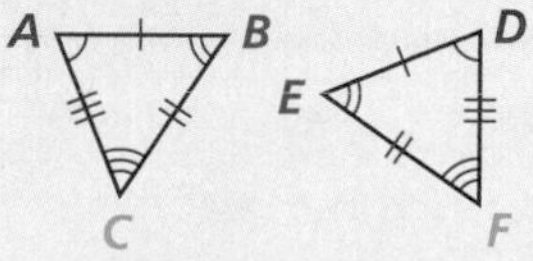 $\triangle ABC \cong \triangle DEF$	$\angle A \cong \angle D$ $\angle B \cong \angle E$ $\angle C \cong \angle F$	$\overline{AB} \cong \overline{DE}$ $\overline{BC} \cong \overline{EF}$ $\overline{AC} \cong \overline{DF}$
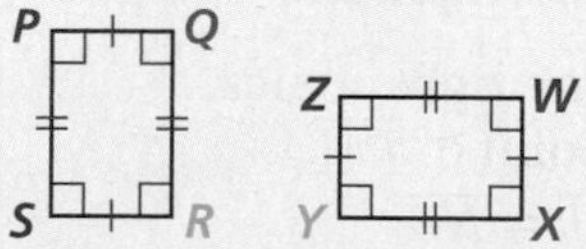 polygon $PQRS \cong$ polygon $WXYZ$	$\angle P \cong \angle W$ $\angle Q \cong \angle X$ $\angle R \cong \angle Y$ $\angle S \cong \angle Z$	$\overline{PQ} \cong \overline{WX}$ $\overline{QR} \cong \overline{XY}$ $\overline{RS} \cong \overline{YZ}$ $\overline{PS} \cong \overline{WZ}$

Helpful Hint

Two vertices that are the endpoints of a side are called consecutive vertices. For example, *P* and *Q* are consecutive vertices.

To name a polygon, write the vertices in consecutive order. For example, you can name polygon *PQRS* as *QRSP* or *SRQP*, but **not** as *PRQS*. In a congruence statement, the order of the vertices indicates the corresponding parts.

EXAMPLE 1 **Naming Congruent Corresponding Parts**

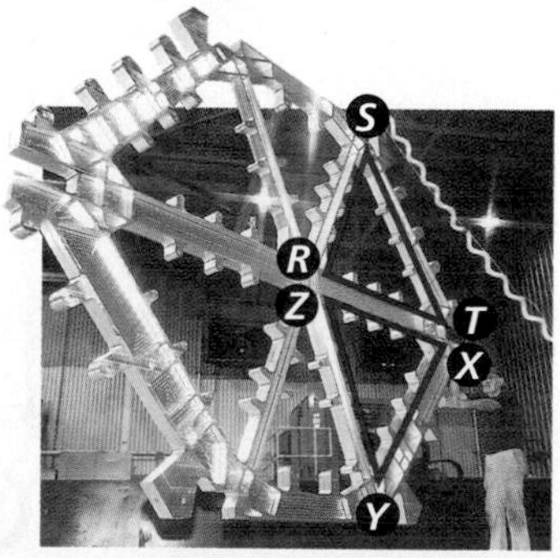

$\triangle RST$ and $\triangle XYZ$ represent the triangles of the space station's support structure. If $\triangle RST \cong \triangle XYZ$, identify all pairs of congruent corresponding parts.

Angles: $\angle R \cong \angle X$, $\angle S \cong \angle Y$, $\angle T \cong \angle Z$

Sides: $\overline{RS} \cong \overline{XY}$, $\overline{ST} \cong \overline{YZ}$, $\overline{RT} \cong \overline{XZ}$

CHECK IT OUT!

1. If polygon $LMNP \cong$ polygon $EFGH$, identify all pairs of corresponding congruent parts.

EXAMPLE 2 Using Corresponding Parts of Congruent Triangles

Algebra

Given: $\triangle EFH \cong \triangle GFH$

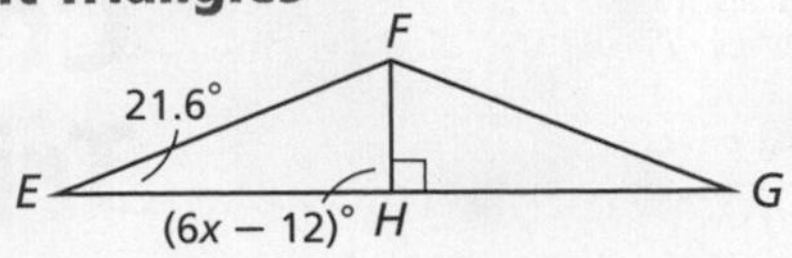

A Find the value of x.

$\angle FHE$ and $\angle FHG$ are rt. ∠s.	*Def. of ⊥ lines*
$\angle FHE \cong \angle FHG$	*Rt. ∠ ≅ Thm.*
$m\angle FHE = m\angle FHG$	*Def. of ≅ ∠s*
$(6x - 12)° = 90°$	*Substitute values for m∠FHE and m∠FHG.*
$6x = 102$	*Add 12 to both sides.*
$x = 17$	*Divide both sides by 6.*

Helpful Hint

When you write a statement such as $\triangle ABC \cong \triangle DEF$, you are also stating which parts are congruent.

B Find $m\angle GFH$.

$m\angle EFH + m\angle FHE + m\angle E = 180°$	*△ Sum Thm.*
$m\angle EFH + 90 + 21.6 = 180$	*Substitute values for m∠FHE and m∠E.*
$m\angle EFH + 111.6 = 180$	*Simplify.*
$m\angle EFH = 68.4$	*Subtract 111.6 from both sides.*
$\angle GFH \cong \angle EFH$	*Corr. ∠s of ≅ △s are ≅.*
$m\angle GFH = m\angle EFH$	*Def. of ≅ ∠s*
$m\angle GFH = 68.4°$	*Trans. Prop. of =*

CHECK IT OUT! Given: $\triangle ABC \cong \triangle DEF$

2a. Find the value of x.

2b. Find $m\angle F$.

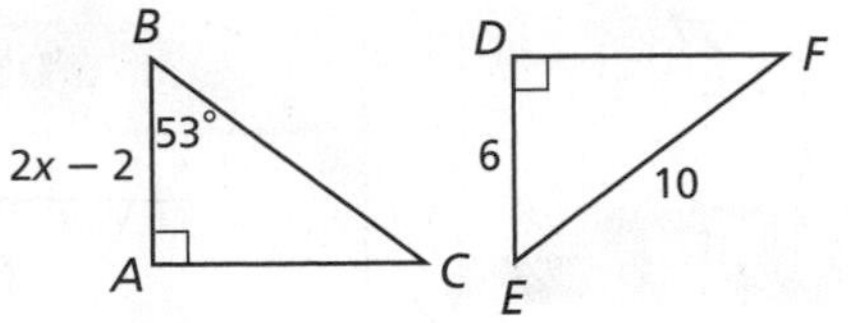

EXAMPLE 3 Proving Triangles Congruent

Given: $\angle P$ and $\angle M$ are right angles.
R is the midpoint of $\overline{PM}$.
$\overline{PQ} \cong \overline{MN}$, $\overline{QR} \cong \overline{NR}$

Prove: $\triangle PQR \cong \triangle MNR$

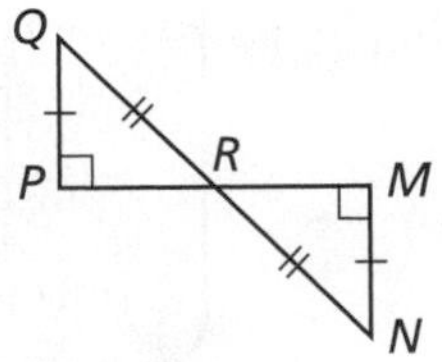

Proof:

Statements	Reasons
1. $\angle P$ and $\angle M$ are rt. ∠s	1. Given
2. $\angle P \cong \angle M$	2. Rt. ∠ ≅ Thm.
3. $\angle PRQ \cong \angle MRN$	3. Vert. ∠s Thm.
4. $\angle Q \cong \angle N$	4. Third ∠s Thm.
5. R is the mdpt. of $\overline{PM}$.	5. Given
6. $\overline{PR} \cong \overline{MR}$	6. Def. of mdpt.
7. $\overline{PQ} \cong \overline{MN}$; $\overline{QR} \cong \overline{NR}$	7. Given
8. $\triangle PQR \cong \triangle MNR$	8. Def. of ≅ △s

CHECK IT OUT! **3.** Given: $\overline{AD}$ bisects $\overline{BE}$.
$\overline{BE}$ bisects $\overline{AD}$.
$\overline{AB} \cong \overline{DE}$, $\angle A \cong \angle D$

Prove: $\triangle ABC \cong \triangle DEC$

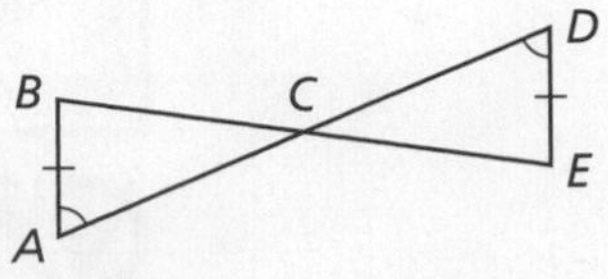

Student to Student

Overlapping Triangles

Cecelia Medina
Lamar High School

"With overlapping triangles, it helps me to redraw the triangles separately. That way I can mark what I know about one triangle without getting confused by the other one."

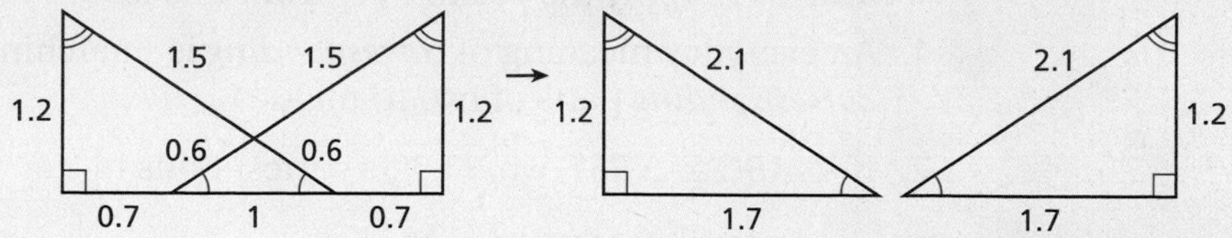

EXAMPLE 4 ***Engineering Application***

The bars that give structural support to a roller coaster form triangles. Since the angle measures and the lengths of the corresponding sides are the same, the triangles are congruent.

Given: $\overline{JK} \perp \overline{KL}$, $\overline{ML} \perp \overline{KL}$, $\angle KLJ \cong \angle LKM$, $\overline{JK} \cong \overline{ML}$, $\overline{JL} \cong \overline{MK}$

Prove: $\triangle JKL \cong \triangle MLK$

Proof:

Statements	Reasons
1. $\overline{JK} \perp \overline{KL}$, $\overline{ML} \perp \overline{KL}$	**1.** Given
2. $\angle JKL$ and $\angle MLK$ are rt. $\angle$s.	**2.** Def. of $\perp$ lines
3. $\angle JKL \cong \angle MLK$	**3.** Rt. $\angle \cong$ Thm.
4. $\angle KLJ \cong \angle LKM$	**4.** Given
5. $\angle KJL \cong \angle LMK$	**5.** Third $\angle$s Thm.
6. $\overline{JK} \cong \overline{ML}$, $\overline{JL} \cong \overline{MK}$	**6.** Given
7. $\overline{KL} \cong \overline{LK}$	**7.** Reflex. Prop. of $\cong$
8. $\triangle JKL \cong \triangle MLK$	**8.** Def. of $\cong$ $\triangle$s

CHECK IT OUT! **4.** Use the diagram to prove the following.
Given: $\overline{MK}$ bisects $\overline{JL}$. $\overline{JL}$ bisects $\overline{MK}$. $\overline{JK} \cong \overline{ML}$, $\overline{JK} \parallel \overline{ML}$
Prove: $\triangle JKN \cong \triangle LMN$

THINK AND DISCUSS

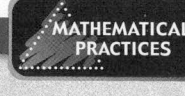

MATHEMATICAL PRACTICES

1. A roof truss is a triangular structure that supports a roof. How can you be sure that two roof trusses are the same size and shape?

Know it! Note

2. GET ORGANIZED Copy and complete the graphic organizer. In each box, name the congruent corresponding parts.

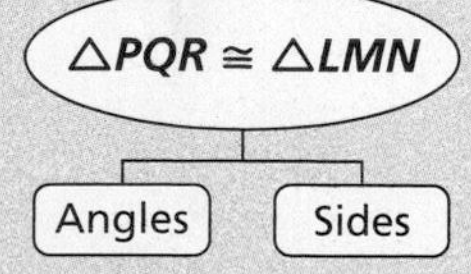

4-4 Exercises

Learn It Online
Homework Help Online
Parent Resources Online

GUIDED PRACTICE

Vocabulary **Apply the vocabulary from this lesson to answer each question.**

1. An everyday meaning of *corresponding* is "matching." How can this help you find the *corresponding* parts of two triangles?

2. If $\triangle ABC \cong \triangle RST$, what angle corresponds to $\angle S$?

SEE EXAMPLE 1

Given: $\triangle RST \cong \triangle LMN$. Identify the congruent corresponding parts.

3. $\overline{RS} \cong$ ___?___
4. $\overline{LN} \cong$ ___?___
5. $\angle S \cong$ ___?___
6. $\overline{TS} \cong$ ___?___
7. $\angle L \cong$ ___?___
8. $\angle N \cong$ ___?___

SEE EXAMPLE 2

Given: $\triangle FGH \cong \triangle JKL$. Find each value.

9. KL
10. x

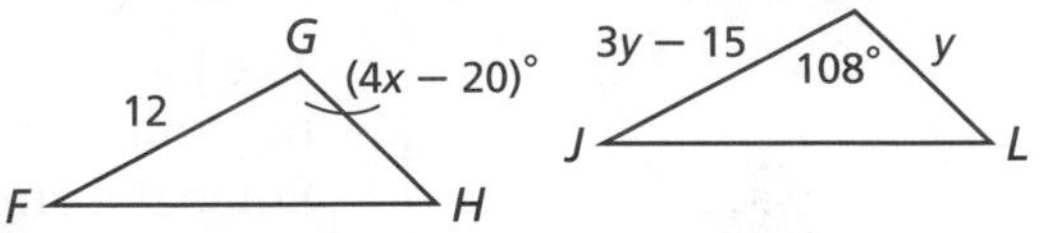

SEE EXAMPLE 3

11. **Given:** E is the midpoint of $\overline{AC}$ and $\overline{BD}$.
$\overline{AB} \cong \overline{CD}$, $\overline{AB} \parallel \overline{CD}$

Prove: $\triangle ABE \cong \triangle CDE$

Proof:

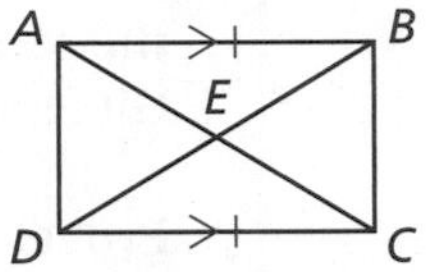

Statements	Reasons
1. $\overline{AB} \parallel \overline{CD}$	1. a. ___?___
2. $\angle ABE \cong \angle CDE$, $\angle BAE \cong \angle DCE$	2. b. ___?___
3. $\overline{AB} \cong \overline{CD}$	3. c. ___?___
4. E is the mdpt. of $\overline{AC}$ and $\overline{BD}$.	4. d. ___?___
5. e. ___?___	5. Def. of mdpt.
6. $\angle AEB \cong \angle CED$	6. f. ___?___
7. $\triangle ABE \cong \triangle CDE$	7. g. ___?___

SEE EXAMPLE 4

12. **Engineering** The geodesic dome shown is a 14-story building that models Earth. Use the given information to prove that the triangles that make up the sphere are congruent.

Given: $\overline{SU} \cong \overline{ST} \cong \overline{SR}$, $\overline{TU} \cong \overline{TR}$,
$\angle UST \cong \angle RST$,
and $\angle U \cong \angle R$

Prove: $\triangle RTS \cong \triangle UTS$

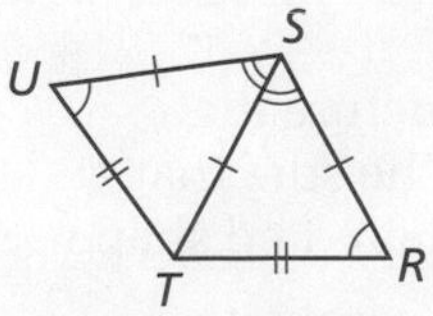

PRACTICE AND PROBLEM SOLVING

Independent Practice

For Exercises	See Example
13–16	1
17–18	2
19	3
20	4

Extra Practice

See Extra Practice for more Skills Practice and Applications Practice exercises.

Given: Polygon $CDEF \cong$ polygon $KLMN$. Identify the congruent corresponding parts.

13. $\overline{DE} \cong$ ___?___

14. $\overline{KN} \cong$ ___?___

15. $\angle F \cong$ ___?___

16. $\angle L \cong$ ___?___

Given: $\triangle ABD \cong \triangle CBD$. Find each value.

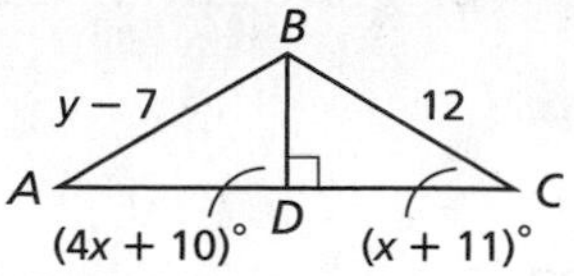

17. $m\angle C$

18. y

19. Given: $\overline{MP}$ bisects $\angle NMR$. P is the midpoint of $\overline{NR}$. $\overline{MN} \cong \overline{MR}$, $\angle N \cong \angle R$

Prove: $\triangle MNP \cong \triangle MRP$

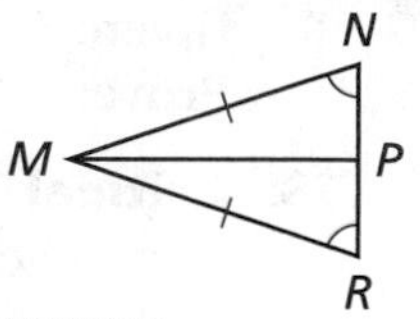

Proof:

Statements	Reasons
1. $\angle N \cong \angle R$	1. a. ___?___
2. $\overline{MP}$ bisects $\angle NMR$.	2. b. ___?___
3. c. ___?___	3. Def. of ∠ bisector
4. d. ___?___	4. Third ⊿ Thm.
5. P is the mdpt. of $\overline{NR}$.	5. e. ___?___
6. f. ___?___	6. Def. of mdpt.
7. $\overline{MN} \cong \overline{MR}$	7. g. ___?___
8. $\overline{MP} \cong \overline{MP}$	8. h. ___?___
9. $\triangle MNP \cong \triangle MRP$	9. Def. of ≅ ⊿

20. Hobbies In a garden, triangular flower beds are separated by straight rows of grass as shown.

Given: $\angle ADC$ and $\angle BCD$ are right angles.
$\overline{AC} \cong \overline{BD}$, $\overline{AD} \cong \overline{BC}$
$\angle DAC \cong \angle CBD$

Prove: $\triangle ADC \cong \triangle BCD$

21. For two triangles, the following corresponding parts are given:
$\overline{GS} \cong \overline{KP}$, $\overline{GR} \cong \overline{KH}$, $\overline{SR} \cong \overline{PH}$,
$\angle S \cong \angle P$, $\angle G \cong \angle K$, and $\angle R \cong \angle H$.
Write three different congruence statements.

22. The two polygons in the diagram are congruent. Complete the following congruence statement for the polygons.
polygon R ___?___ $\cong$ polygon V ___?___

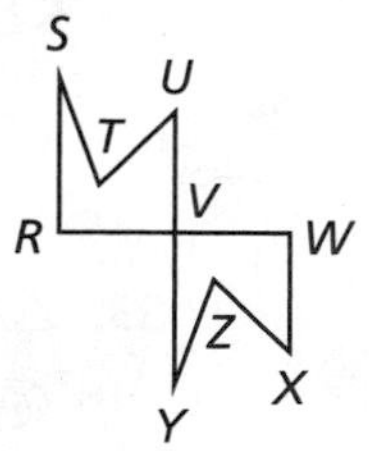

Write and solve an equation for each of the following.

23. $\triangle ABC \cong \triangle DEF$. $AB = 2x - 10$, and $DE = x + 20$. Find the value of x and AB.

24. $\triangle JKL \cong \triangle MNP$. $m\angle L = (x^2 + 10)^\circ$, and $m\angle P = (2x^2 + 1)^\circ$. What is $m\angle L$?

25. Polygon $ABCD \cong$ polygon $PQRS$. $BC = 6x + 5$, and $QR = 5x + 7$. Find the value of x and BC.

Multi-Step Test Prep

26. Many origami models begin with a square piece of paper, *JKLM*, that is folded along both diagonals to make the creases shown. $\overline{JL}$ and $\overline{MK}$ are perpendicular bisectors of each other, and $\angle NML \cong \angle NKL$.
    a. Explain how you know that $\overline{KL}$ and $\overline{ML}$ are congruent.
    b. Prove $\triangle NML \cong \triangle NKL$.

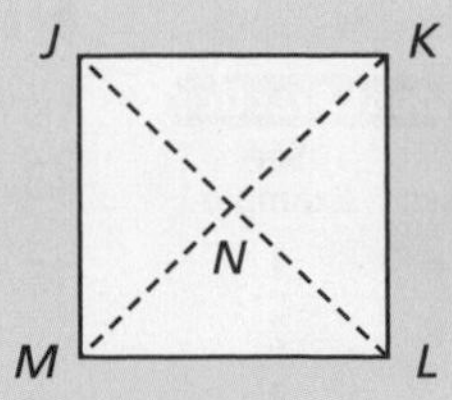

27. Draw a diagram and then write a proof.
    Given: $\overline{BD} \perp \overline{AC}$. *D* is the midpoint of $\overline{AC}$. $\overline{AB} \cong \overline{CB}$, and $\overline{BD}$ bisects $\angle ABC$.
    Prove: $\triangle ABD \cong \triangle CBD$

28. **Critical Thinking** Draw two triangles that are not congruent but have an area of 4 cm^2 each.

29. **///ERROR ANALYSIS///** Given $\triangle MPQ \cong \triangle EDF$. Two solutions for finding $m\angle E$ are shown. Which is incorrect? Explain the error.

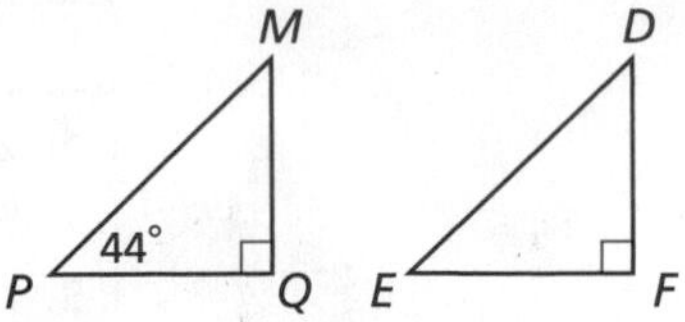

A

Since corr. parts of ≅ $\triangle$s are ≅, $\angle E \cong \angle P$. So $m\angle E = m\angle P = 44°$.

B

Since the acute $\angle$s of a rt. $\triangle$ are comp., $m\angle M = 46°$. $\angle E \cong \angle M$, so $m\angle E = 46°$.

30. **Write About It** Given the diagram of the triangles, is there enough information to prove that $\triangle HKL$ is congruent to $\triangle YWX$? Explain.

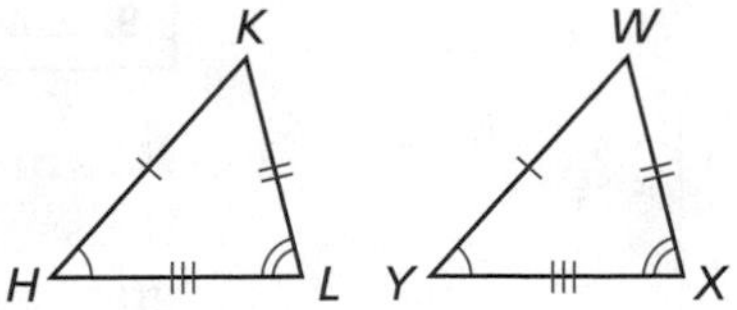

Test Prep

31. Which congruence statement correctly indicates that the two given triangles are congruent?
    Ⓐ $\triangle ABC \cong \triangle EFD$ Ⓒ $\triangle ABC \cong \triangle DEF$
    Ⓑ $\triangle ABC \cong \triangle FDE$ Ⓓ $\triangle ABC \cong \triangle FED$

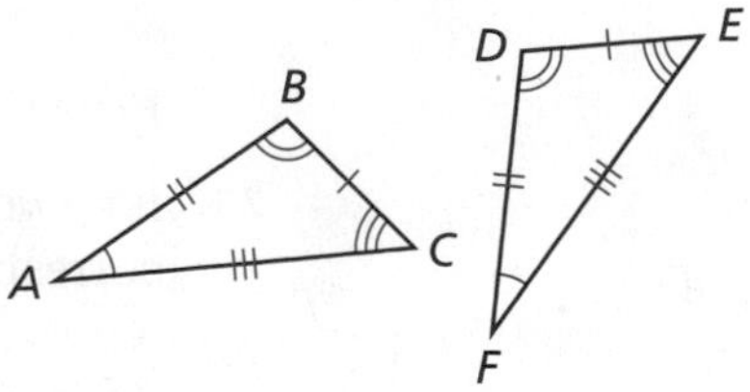

32. $\triangle MNP \cong \triangle RST$. What are the values of *x* and *y*?
    Ⓕ $x = 26, y = 21\frac{1}{3}$ Ⓗ $x = 25, y = 20\frac{2}{3}$
    Ⓖ $x = 27, y = 20$ Ⓙ $x = 30\frac{1}{3}, y = 16\frac{2}{3}$

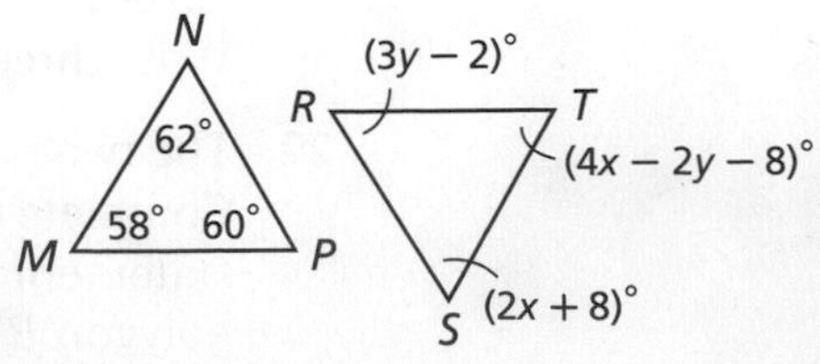

33. $\triangle ABC \cong \triangle XYZ$. $m\angle A = 47.1°$, and $m\angle C = 13.8°$. Find $m\angle Y$.
    Ⓐ 13.8 Ⓒ 76.2
    Ⓑ 42.9 Ⓓ 119.1

34. $\triangle MNR \cong \triangle SPQ$, $NL = 18$, $SP = 33$, $SR = 10$, $RQ = 24$, and $QP = 30$. What is the perimeter of $\triangle MNR$?
    Ⓕ 79 Ⓗ 87
    Ⓖ 85 Ⓙ 97

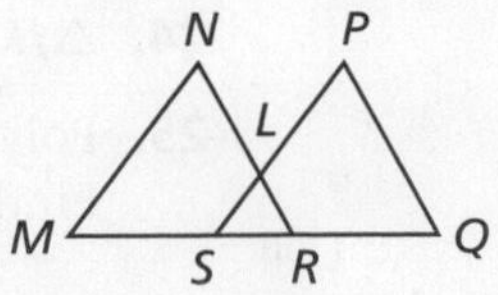

CHALLENGE AND EXTEND

35. Multi-Step Given that the perimeter of $TUVW$ is 149 units, find the value of x. Is $\triangle TUV \cong \triangle TWV$? Explain.

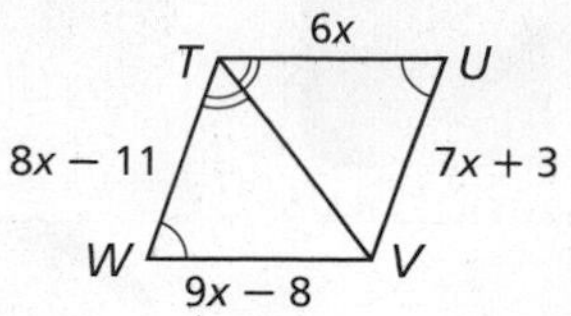

36. Multi-Step Polygon $ABCD \cong$ polygon $EFGH$. $\angle A$ is a right angle. $m\angle E = (y^2 - 10)°$, and $m\angle H = (2y^2 - 132)°$. Find $m\angle D$.

37. Given: $\overline{RS} \cong \overline{RT}$, $\angle S \cong \angle T$
Prove: $\triangle RST \cong \triangle RTS$

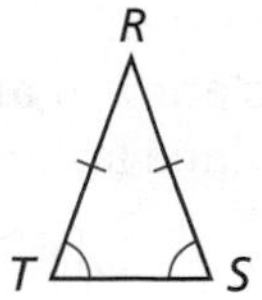

Career Path

Learn It Online
Career Resources Online

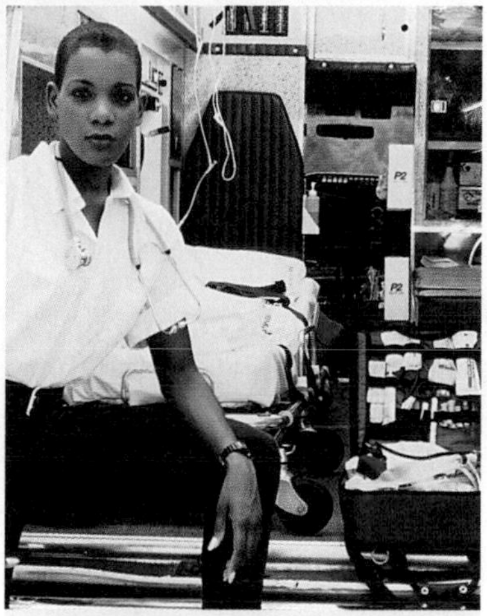

Jordan Carter
Emergency Medical
Services Program

Q: What math classes did you take in high school?
A: Algebra 1 and 2, Geometry, Precalculus

Q: What kind of degree or certification will you receive?
A: I will receive an associate's degree in applied science. Then I will take an exam to be certified as an EMT or paramedic.

Q: How do you use math in your hands-on training?
A: I calculate dosages based on body weight and age. I also calculate drug doses in milligrams per kilogram per hour or set up an IV drip to deliver medications at the correct rate.

Q: What are your future career plans?
A: When I am certified, I can work for a private ambulance service or with a fire department. I could also work in a hospital, transporting critically ill patients by ambulance or helicopter.

CHAPTER 4

MULTI-STEP TEST PREP

SECTION 4A

MATHEMATICAL PRACTICES **Construct viable arguments and critique the reasoning of others.**

Triangles and Congruence

Origami Origami is the Japanese art of paper folding. The Japanese word *origami* literally means "fold paper." This ancient art form relies on properties of geometry to produce fascinating and beautiful shapes.

Each of the figures shows a step in making an origami swan from a square piece of paper. The final figure shows the creases of an origami swan that has been unfolded.

Step 1

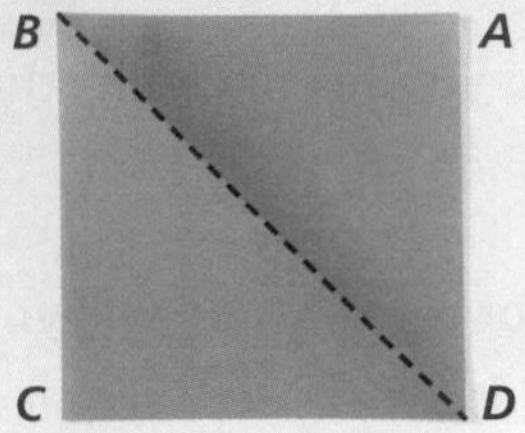

Fold the paper in half diagonally and crease it. Turn it over.

Step 2

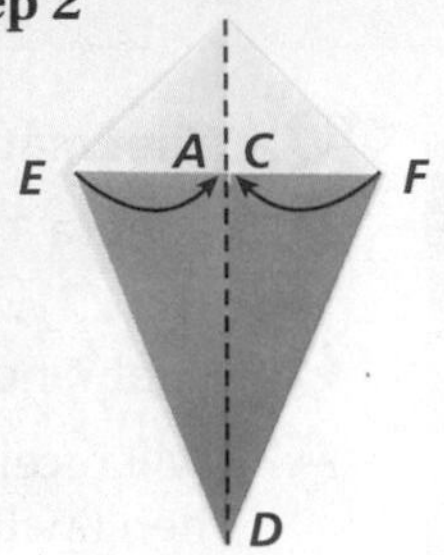

Fold corners *A* and *C* to the center line and crease. Turn it over.

Step 3

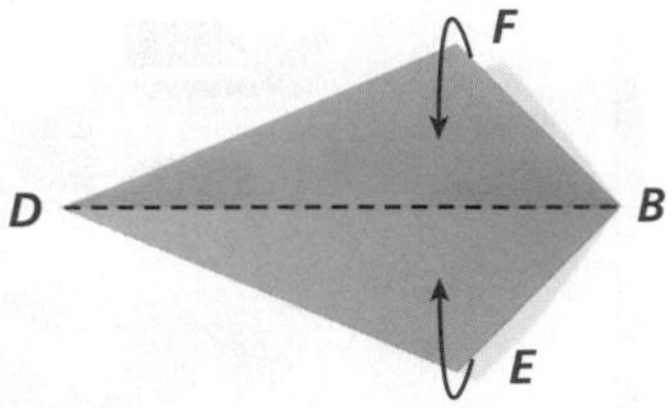

Fold in half along the center crease so that $\overline{DE}$ and $\overline{DF}$ are together.

Step 4

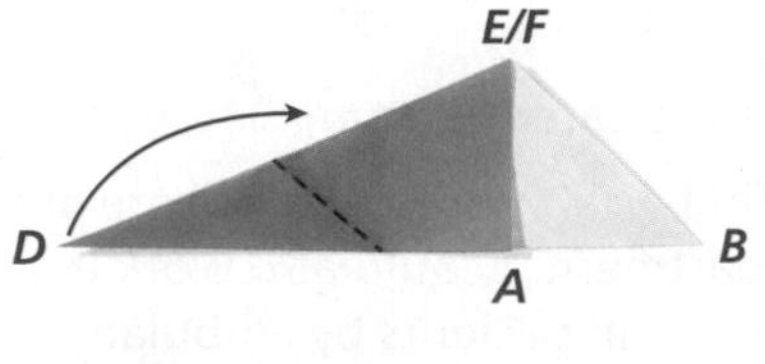

Fold the narrow point upward at a 90° angle and crease. Push in the fold so that the neck is inside the body.

Step 5

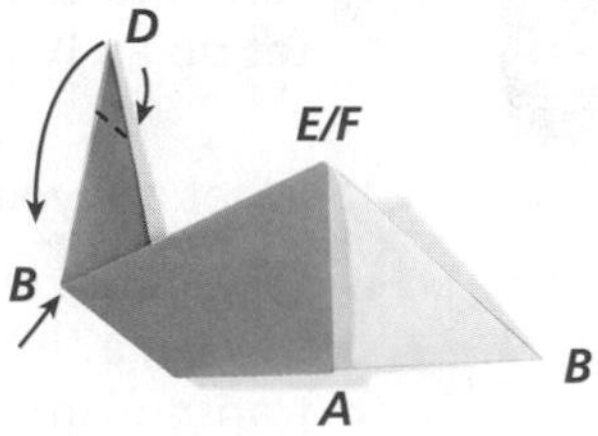

Fold the tip downward and crease. Push in the fold so that the head is inside the neck.

Step 6

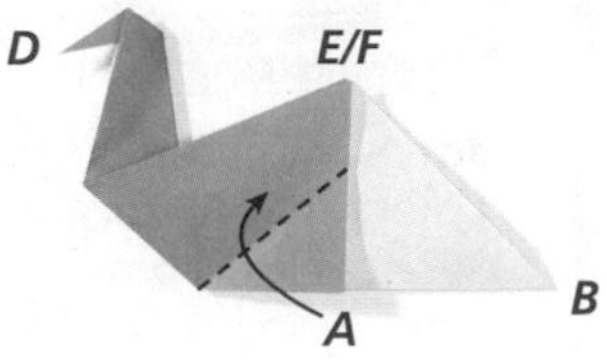

Fold up the flap to form the wing.

1. Use the fact that *ABCD* is a square to classify $\triangle ABD$ by its side lengths and by its angle measures.
2. $\overline{DB}$ bisects $\angle ABC$ and $\angle ADC$. $\overline{DE}$ bisects $\angle ADB$. Find the measures of the angles in $\triangle EDB$. Explain how you found the measures.
3. Given that $\overline{DB}$ bisects $\angle ABC$ and $\angle EDF$, $\overline{BE} \cong \overline{BF}$, and $\overline{DE} \cong \overline{DF}$, prove that $\triangle EDB \cong \triangle FDB$.

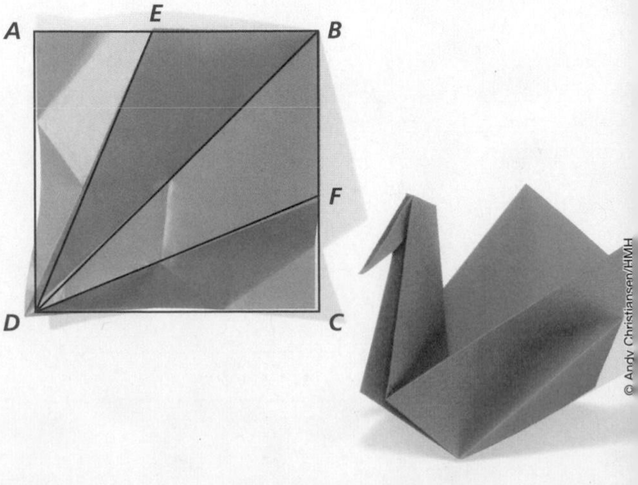

READY TO GO ON?

Quiz for Lessons 4-1 Through 4-4

4-1 Congruence and Transformations

Apply the transformation M to the polygon with vertices $A(5, 2)$, $B(-3, 4)$, and $C(-1, -6)$. Identify and describe the transformation.

1. $M: (x, y) \rightarrow (x - 2, y + 3)$
2. $M: (x, y) \rightarrow (x, -y)$
3. $M: (x, y) \rightarrow (-y, x)$
4. $M: (x, y) \rightarrow (3x, 3y)$

4-2 Classifying Triangles

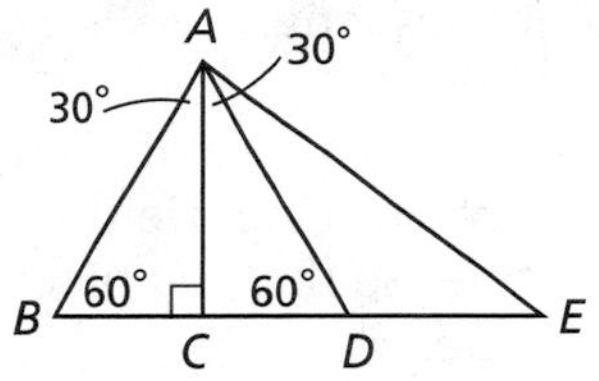

Classify each triangle by its angle measures.

5. $\triangle ACD$ 6. $\triangle ABD$ 7. $\triangle ADE$

Classify each triangle by its side lengths.

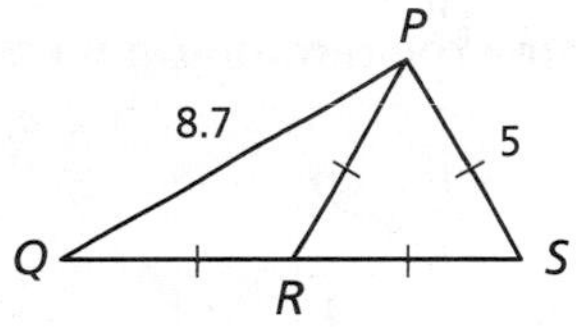

8. $\triangle PQR$ 9. $\triangle PRS$ 10. $\triangle PQS$

4-3 Angle Relationships in Triangles

Find each angle measure.

11. $m\angle M$

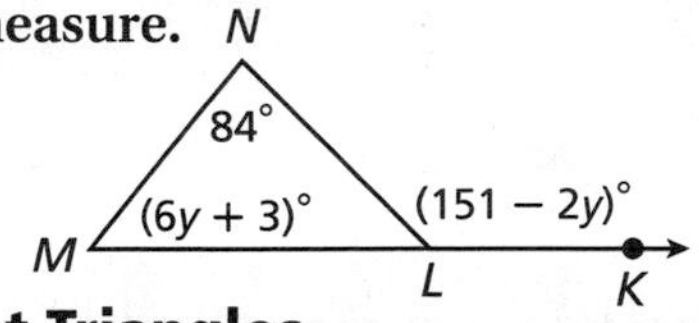

12. $m\angle ABC$

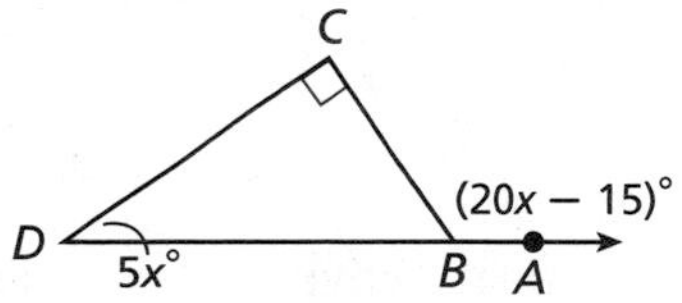

4-4 Congruent Triangles

Given: $\triangle JKL \cong \triangle DEF$. Identify the congruent corresponding parts.

13. $\overline{KL} \cong$ ___?___ 14. $\overline{DF} \cong$ ___?___ 15. $\angle K \cong$ ___?___ 16. $\angle F \cong$ ___?___

17. **Given:** $\overleftrightarrow{AB} \parallel \overleftrightarrow{CD}$, $\overline{AB} \cong \overline{CD}$, $\overline{AC} \cong \overline{BD}$, $\overline{AC} \perp \overline{CD}$, $\overline{DB} \perp \overline{AB}$

Prove: $\triangle ACD \cong \triangle DBA$

Proof:

Statements	Reasons
1. $\overleftrightarrow{AB} \parallel \overleftrightarrow{CD}$	1. a. ___?___
2. $\angle BAD \cong \angle CDA$	2. b. ___?___
3. $\overline{AC} \perp \overline{CD}$, $\overline{DB} \perp \overline{AB}$	3. c. ___?___
4. $\angle ACD$ and $\angle DBA$ are rt. ∠s	4. d. ___?___
5. e. ___?___	5. Rt. ∠ ≅ Thm.
6. f. ___?___	6. Third ∠s Thm.
7. $\overline{AB} \cong \overline{CD}$, $\overline{AC} \cong \overline{BD}$	7. g. ___?___
8. h. ___?___	8. Reflex Prop. of ≅
9. $\triangle ACD \cong \triangle DBA$	9. i. ___?___

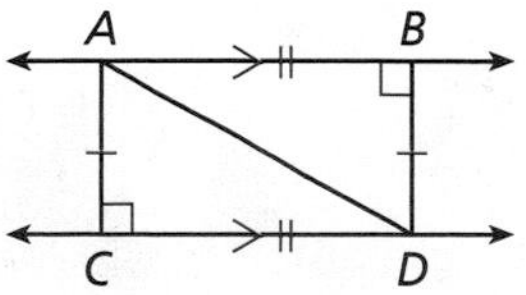

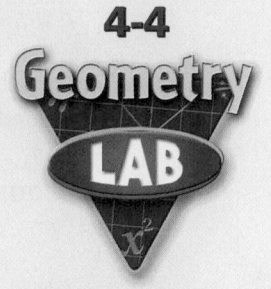

4-4 Geometry LAB

Explore SSS and SAS Triangle Congruence

Use with *Triangle Congruence: SSS and SAS*

You have used the definition of congruent triangles to prove triangles congruent. To use the definition, you need to prove that all three pairs of corresponding sides and all three pairs of corresponding angles are congruent.

In this lab, you will discover some shortcuts for proving triangles congruent.

MATHEMATICAL PRACTICES **Use appropriate tools strategically.** **CC.9-12.G.CO.8** Explain how the criteria for triangle congruence…follow from the definition of congruence…

Activity 1

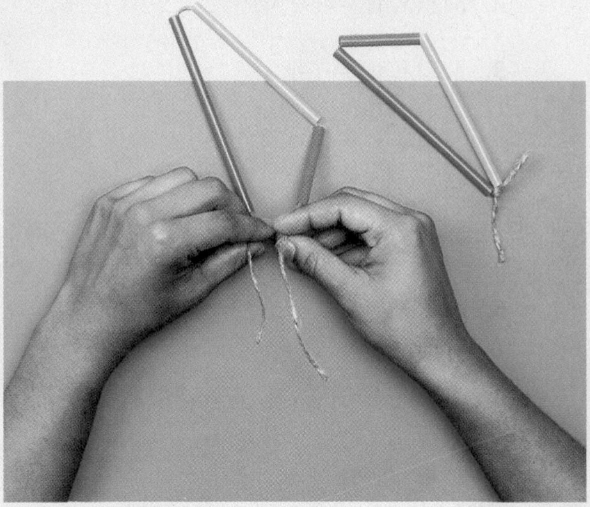

1. Measure and cut six pieces from the straws: two that are 2 inches long, two that are 4 inches long, and two that are 5 inches long.
2. Cut two pieces of string that are each about 20 inches long.
3. Thread one piece of each size of straw onto a piece of string. Tie the ends of the string together so that the pieces of straw form a triangle.
4. Using the remaining pieces, try to make another triangle with the same side lengths that is *not* congruent to the first triangle.

Try This

1. Repeat Activity 1 using side lengths of your choice. Are your results the same?
2. Do you think it is possible to make two triangles that have the same side lengths but that are not congruent? Why or why not?
3. How does your answer to Problem 2 provide a shortcut for proving triangles congruent?
4. Complete the following conjecture based on your results. Two triangles are congruent if ____?____.

Activity 2

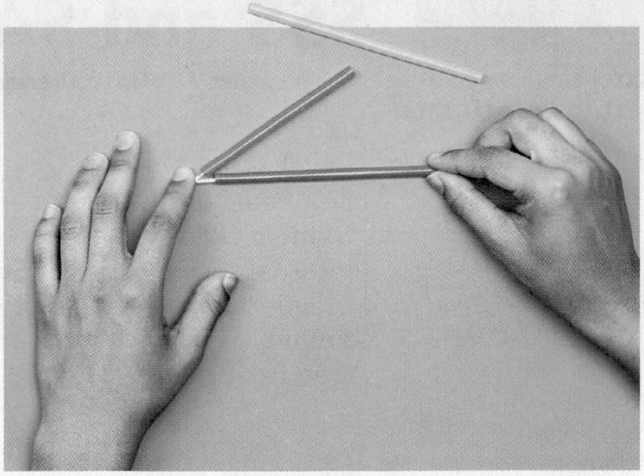

1. Measure and cut two pieces from the straws: one that is 4 inches long and one that is 5 inches long.

2. Use a protractor to help you bend a paper clip to form a 30° angle.

3. Place the pieces of straw on the sides of the 30° angle. The straws will form two sides of your triangle.

4. Without changing the angle formed by the paper clip, use a piece of straw to make a third side for your triangle, cutting it to fit as necessary. Use additional paper clips or string to hold the straws together in a triangle.

Try This

5. Repeat Activity 2 using side lengths and an angle measure of your choice. Are your results the same?
6. Suppose you know two side lengths of a triangle and the measure of the angle between these sides. Can the length of the third side be any measure? Explain.
7. How does your answer to Problem 6 provide a shortcut for proving triangles congruent?
8. Use the two given sides and the given angle from Activity 2 to form a triangle that is not congruent to the triangle you formed. (*Hint:* One of the given sides does not have to be adjacent to the given angle.)
9. Complete the following conjecture based on your results. Two triangles are congruent if ______?______ .

COMMON CORE

4-5 Triangle Congruence: SSS and SAS

CC.9-12.G.CO.8 Explain how the criteria for triangle congruence...follow from the definition of congruence...
Also **CC.9-12.G.CO.7, CC.9-12.G.SRT.5**

Objectives
Apply SSS and SAS to construct triangles and to solve problems.

Prove triangles congruent by using SSS and SAS.

Vocabulary
triangle rigidity
included angle

Who uses this?
Engineers used the property of triangle rigidity to design the internal support for the Statue of Liberty and to build bridges, towers, and other structures. (See Example 2.)

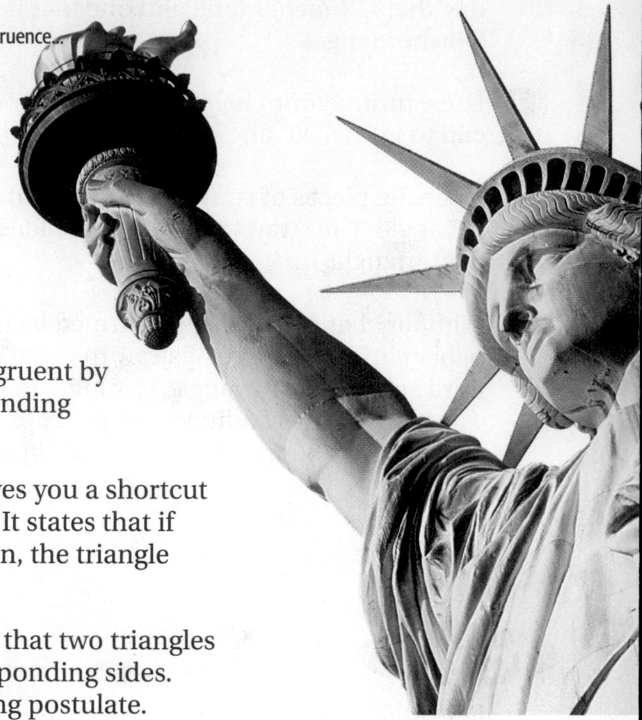

Recall that you proved triangles congruent by showing that all six pairs of corresponding parts were congruent.

The property of **triangle rigidity** gives you a shortcut for proving two triangles congruent. It states that if the side lengths of a triangle are given, the triangle can have only one shape.

For example, you only need to know that two triangles have three pairs of congruent corresponding sides. This can be expressed as the following postulate.

Know it! Note

Postulate 4-5-1 Side-Side-Side (SSS) Congruence

POSTULATE	HYPOTHESIS	CONCLUSION
If three sides of one triangle are congruent to three sides of another triangle, then the triangles are congruent.	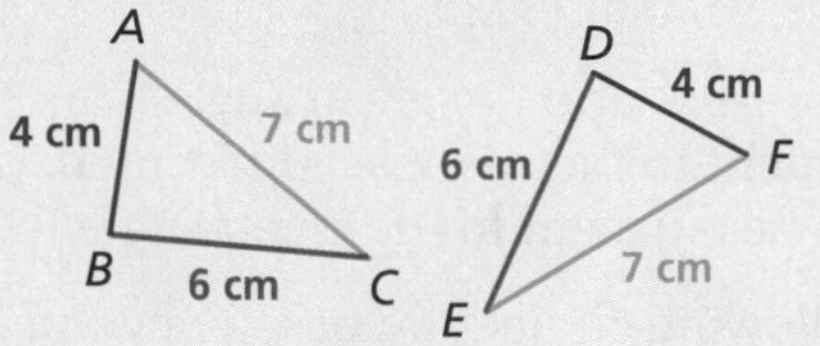	$\triangle ABC \cong \triangle FDE$

EXAMPLE 1 **Using SSS to Prove Triangle Congruence**

Use SSS to explain why $\triangle PQR \cong \triangle PSR$.
It is given that $\overline{PQ} \cong \overline{PS}$ and that $\overline{QR} \cong \overline{SR}$. By the Reflexive Property of Congruence, $\overline{PR} \cong \overline{PR}$. Therefore $\triangle PQR \cong \triangle PSR$ by SSS.

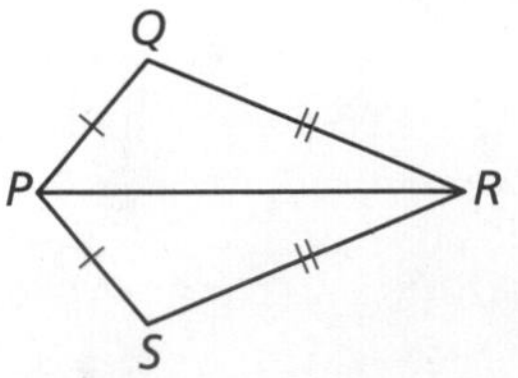

Remember!
Adjacent triangles share a side, so you can apply the Reflexive Property to get a pair of congruent parts.

CHECK IT OUT!
1. Use SSS to explain why $\triangle ABC \cong \triangle CDA$.

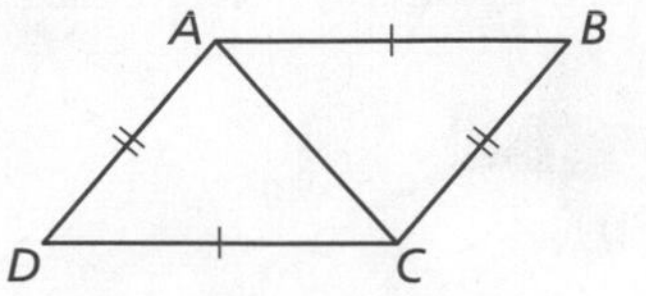

An **included angle** is an angle formed by two adjacent sides of a polygon. $\angle B$ is the included angle between sides $\overline{AB}$ and $\overline{BC}$.

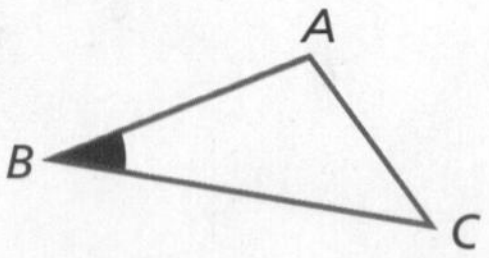

It can also be shown that only two pairs of congruent corresponding sides are needed to prove the congruence of two triangles if the included angles are also congruent.

Know it! Note

Postulate 4-5-2 Side-Angle-Side (SAS) Congruence

POSTULATE	HYPOTHESIS	CONCLUSION
If two sides and the included angle of one triangle are congruent to two sides and the included angle of another triangle, then the triangles are congruent.	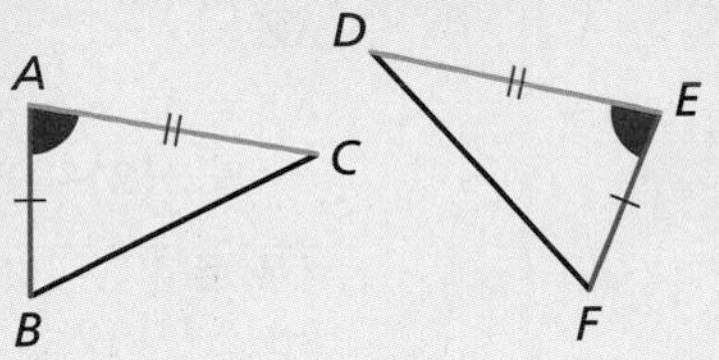	$\triangle ABC \cong \triangle EFD$

EXAMPLE 2 *Engineering Application*

Caution!

The letters SAS are written in that order because the congruent angles must be between pairs of congruent corresponding sides.

The figure shows part of the support structure of the Statue of Liberty. Use SAS to explain why $\triangle KPN \cong \triangle LPM$.

It is given that $\overline{KP} \cong \overline{LP}$ and that $\overline{NP} \cong \overline{MP}$. By the Vertical Angles Theorem, $\angle KPN \cong \angle LPM$. Therefore $\triangle KPN \cong \triangle LPM$ by SAS.

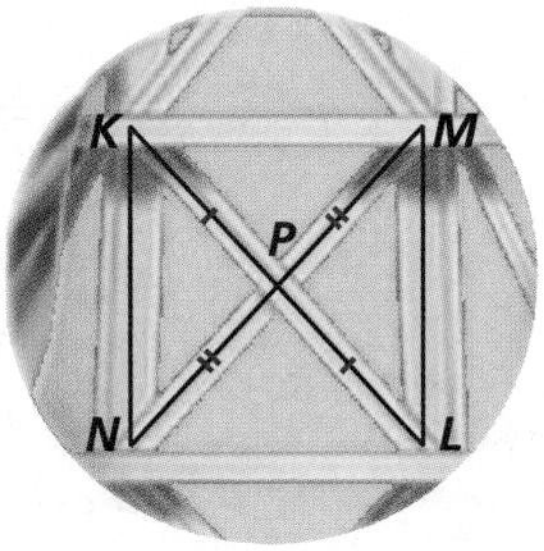

CHECK IT OUT!

2. Use SAS to explain why $\triangle ABC \cong \triangle DBC$.

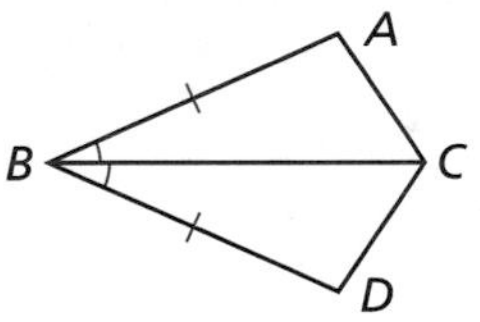

The SAS Postulate guarantees that if you are given the lengths of two sides and the measure of the included angle, you can construct one and only one triangle.

Construction Congruent Triangles Using SAS

Use a straightedge to draw two segments and one angle, or copy the given segments and angle.

1

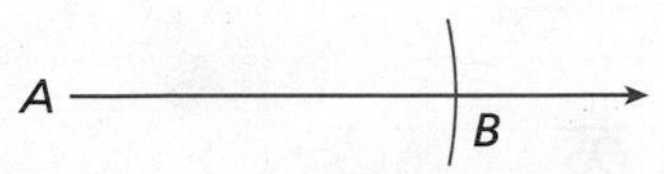

Construct $\overline{AB}$ congruent to one of the segments.

2

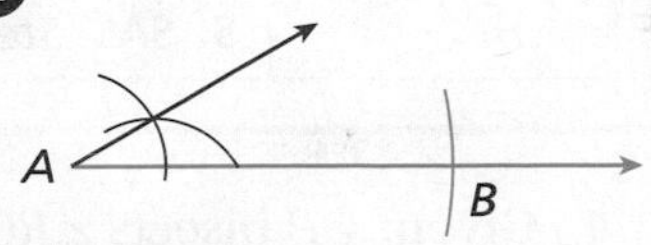

Construct $\angle A$ congruent to the given angle.

3

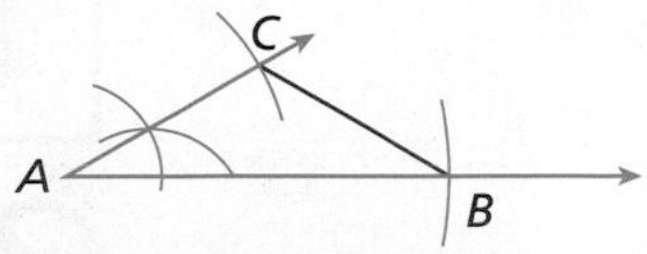

Construct $\overline{AC}$ congruent to the other segment. Draw $\overline{CB}$ to complete $\triangle ABC$.

EXAMPLE 3 Verifying Triangle Congruence

x^2 Algebra

Show that the triangles are congruent for the given value of the variable.

A $\triangle UVW \cong \triangle YXZ, x = 3$

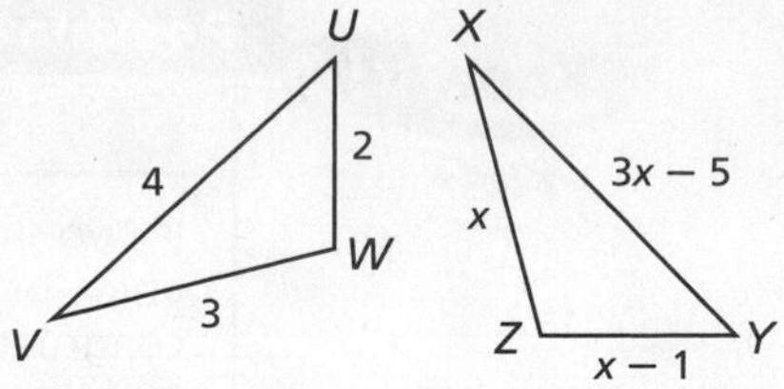

$ZY = x - 1$
$= 3 - 1 = 2$
$XZ = x = 3$
$XY = 3x - 5$
$= 3(3) - 5 = 4$

$\overline{UV} \cong \overline{YX}$. $\overline{VW} \cong \overline{XZ}$, and $\overline{UW} \cong \overline{YZ}$.
So $\triangle UVW \cong \triangle YXZ$ by SSS.

B $\triangle DEF \cong \triangle JGH, y = 7$

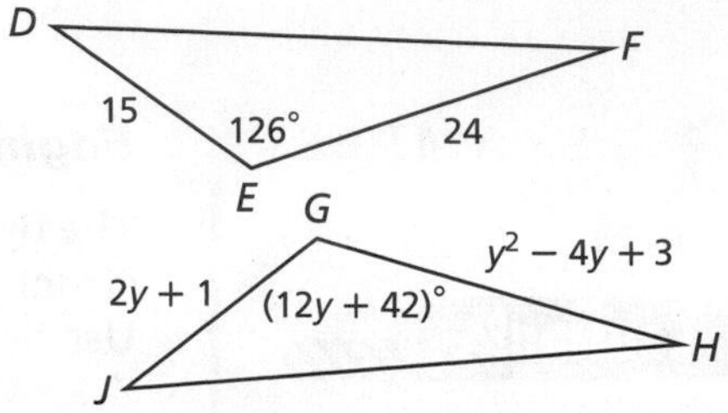

$JG = 2y + 1$
$= 2(7) + 1$
$= 15$
$GH = y^2 - 4y + 3$
$= (7)^2 - 4(7) + 3$
$= 24$
$m\angle G = 12y + 42$
$= 12(7) + 42$
$= 126°$

$\overline{DE} \cong \overline{JG}$. $\overline{EF} \cong \overline{GH}$, and $\angle E \cong \angle G$.
So $\triangle DEF \cong \triangle JGH$ by SAS.

CHECK IT OUT!

3. Show that $\triangle ADB \cong \triangle CDB$ when $t = 4$.

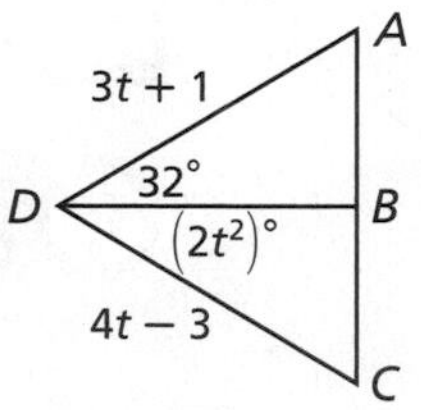

EXAMPLE 4 Proving Triangles Congruent

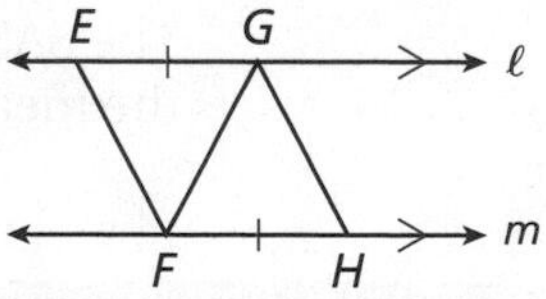

Given: $\ell \parallel m$, $\overline{EG} \cong \overline{HF}$
Prove: $\triangle EGF \cong \triangle HFG$
Proof:

Statements	Reasons
1. $\overline{EG} \cong \overline{HF}$	1. Given
2. $\ell \parallel m$	2. Given
3. $\angle EGF \cong \angle HFG$	3. Alt. Int. ∠s Thm.
4. $\overline{FG} \cong \overline{GF}$	4. Reflex Prop. of ≅
5. $\triangle EGF \cong \triangle HFG$	5. SAS *Steps 1, 3, 4*

CHECK IT OUT!

4. **Given:** $\overrightarrow{QP}$ bisects $\angle RQS$. $\overline{QR} \cong \overline{QS}$
Prove: $\triangle RQP \cong \triangle SQP$

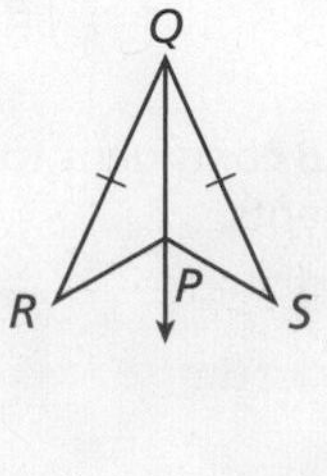

MATHEMATICAL PRACTICES

THINK AND DISCUSS

1. Describe three ways you could prove that $\triangle ABC \cong \triangle DEF$.

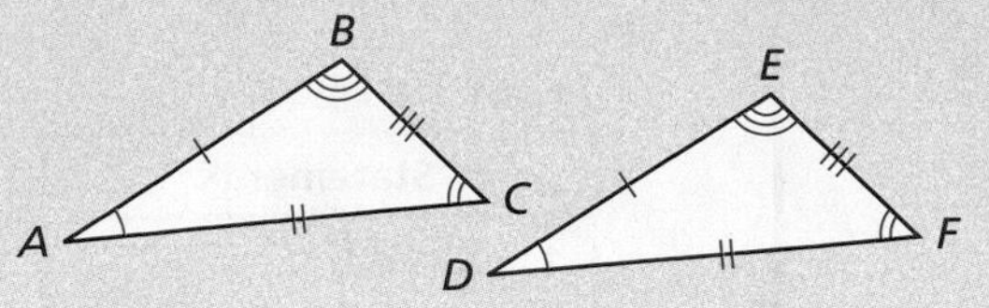

2. Explain why the SSS and SAS Postulates are shortcuts for proving triangles congruent.

Know it! Note

3. **GET ORGANIZED** Copy and complete the graphic organizer. Use it to compare the SSS and SAS postulates.

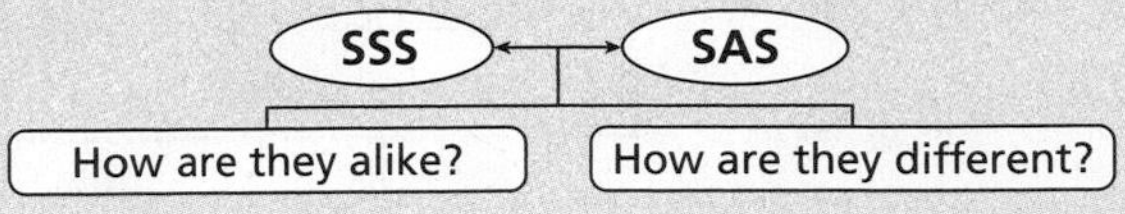

4-5 Exercises

Learn It Online
Homework Help Online
Parent Resources Online

GUIDED PRACTICE

1. **Vocabulary** In $\triangle RST$ which angle is the included angle of sides $\overline{ST}$ and $\overline{TR}$?

SEE EXAMPLE 1

Use SSS to explain why the triangles in each pair are congruent.

2. $\triangle ABD \cong \triangle CDB$

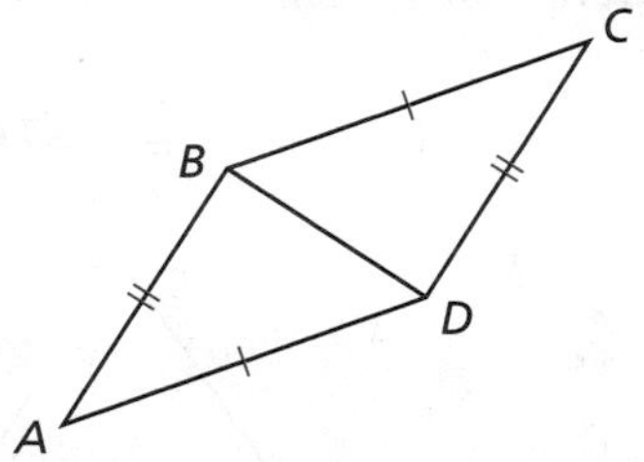

3. $\triangle MNP \cong \triangle MQP$

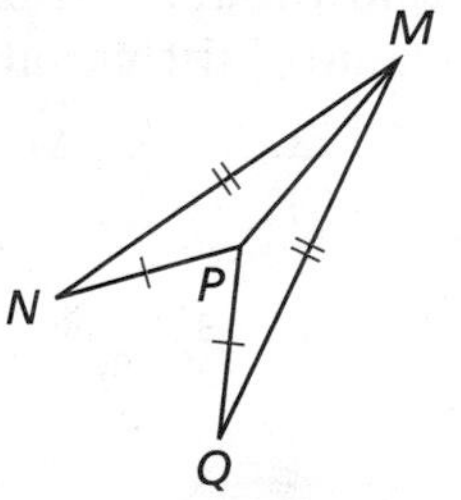

SEE EXAMPLE 2

4. **Sailing** Signal flags are used to communicate messages when radio silence is required. The Zulu signal flag means, "I require a tug." $GJ = GH = GL = GK = 20$ in. Use SAS to explain why $\triangle JGK \cong \triangle LGH$.

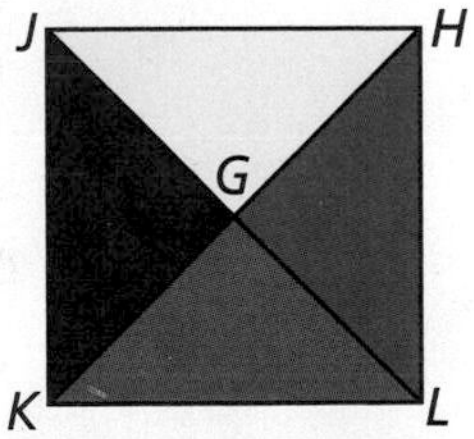

SEE EXAMPLE 3

Show that the triangles are congruent for the given value of the variable.

5. $\triangle GHJ \cong \triangle IHJ$, $x = 4$

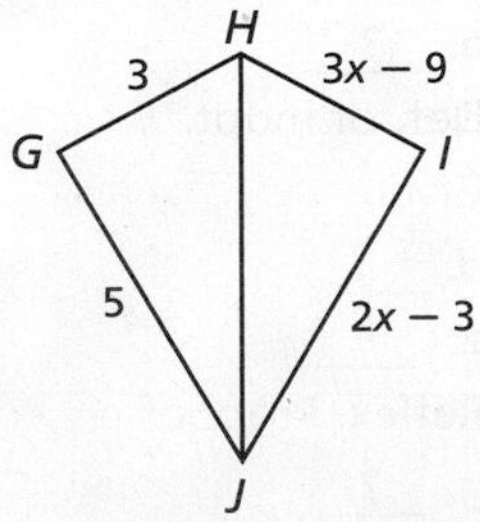

6. $\triangle RST \cong \triangle TUR$, $x = 18$

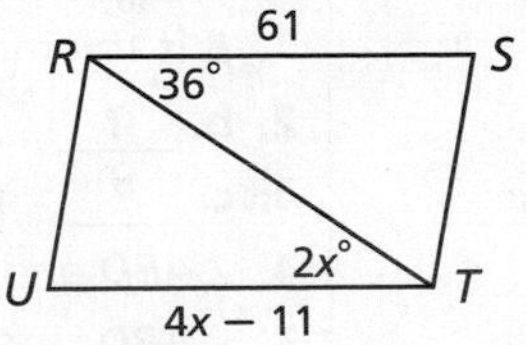

SEE EXAMPLE 4

7. **Given:** $\overline{JK} \cong \overline{ML}$, $\angle JKL \cong \angle MLK$
Prove: $\triangle JKL \cong \triangle MLK$

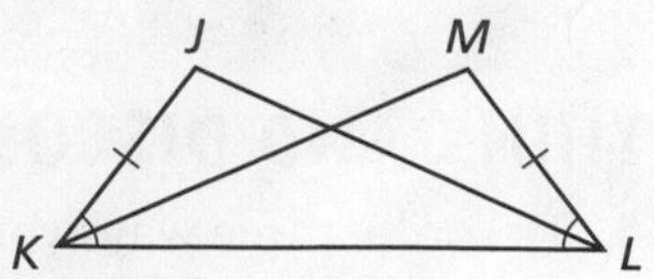

Proof:

Statements	Reasons
1. $\overline{JK} \cong \overline{ML}$	1. a. ___?___
2. b. ___?___	2. Given
3. $\overline{KL} \cong \overline{LK}$	3. c. ___?___
4. $\triangle JKL \cong \triangle MLK$	4. d. ___?___

PRACTICE AND PROBLEM SOLVING

Independent Practice

For Exercises	See Example
8–9	1
10	2
11–12	3
13	4

Extra Practice

See Extra Practice for more Skills Practice and Applications Practice exercises.

Use SSS to explain why the triangles in each pair are congruent.

8. $\triangle BCD \cong \triangle EDC$

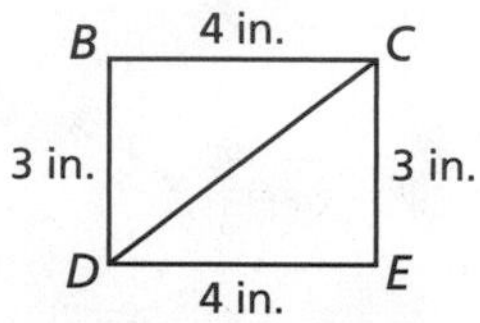

9. $\triangle GJK \cong \triangle GJL$

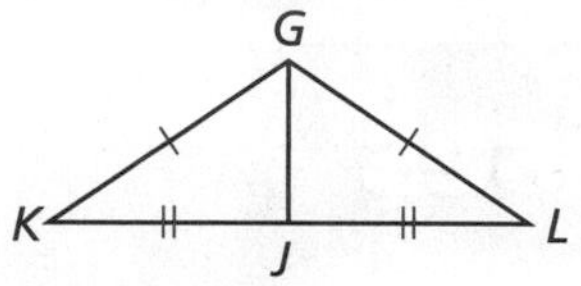

10. **Theater** The lights shining on a stage appear to form two congruent right triangles. Given $\overline{EC} \cong \overline{DB}$, use SAS to explain why $\triangle ECB \cong \triangle DBC$.

Show that the triangles are congruent for the given value of the variable.

11. $\triangle MNP \cong \triangle QNP$, $y = 3$

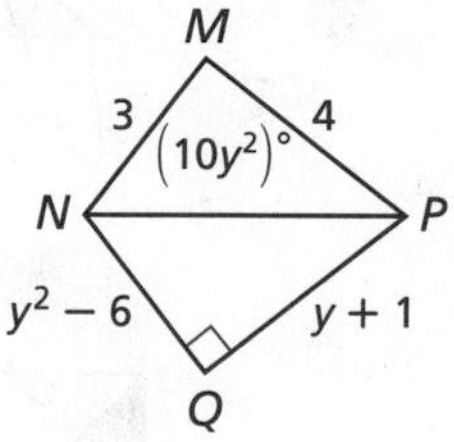

12. $\triangle XYZ \cong \triangle STU$, $t = 5$

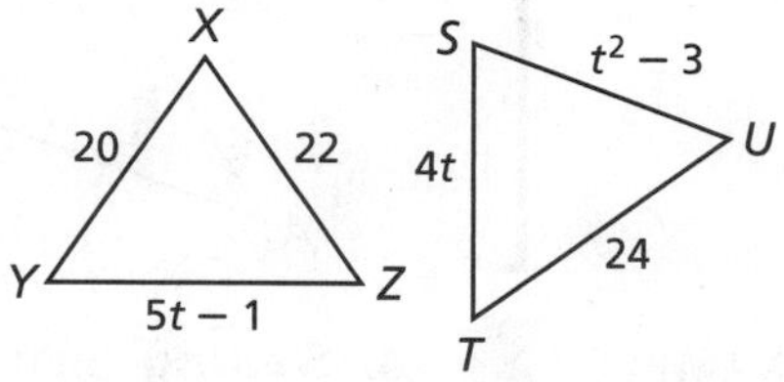

13. **Given:** B is the midpoint of $\overline{DC}$. $\overline{AB} \perp \overline{DC}$
Prove: $\triangle ABD \cong \triangle ABC$

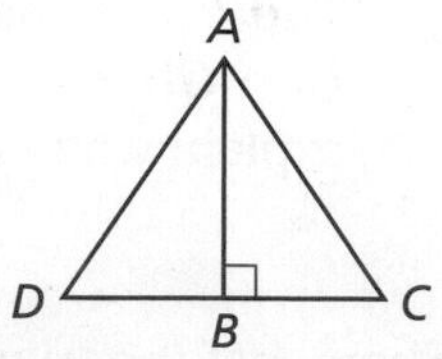

Proof:

Statements	Reasons
1. B is the mdpt. of $\overline{DC}$.	1. a. ___?___
2. b. ___?___	2. Def. of mdpt.
3. c. ___?___	3. Given
4. $\angle ABD$ and $\angle ABC$ are rt. $\angle$s.	4. d. ___?___
5. $\angle ABD \cong \angle ABC$	5. e. ___?___
6. f. ___?___	6. Reflex. Prop. of $\cong$
7. $\triangle ABD \cong \triangle ABC$	7. g. ___?___

Which postulate, if any, can be used to prove the triangles congruent?

14.

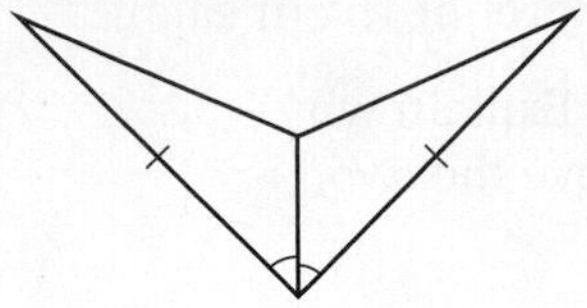

15.

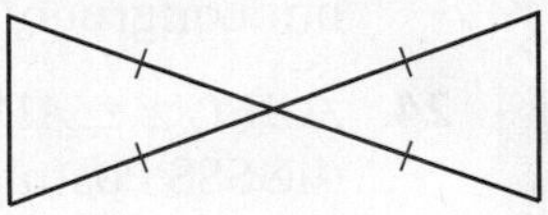

16.

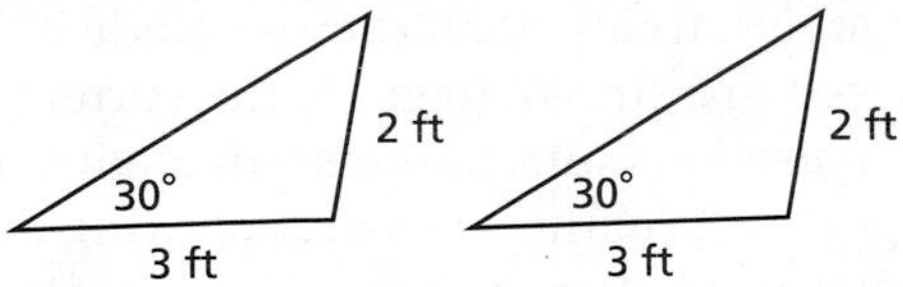

17.

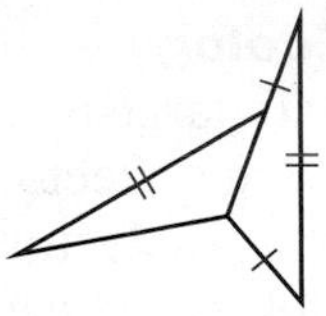

18. Explain what additional information, if any, you would need to prove $\triangle ABC \cong \triangle DEC$ by each postulate.

a. SSS **b.** SAS

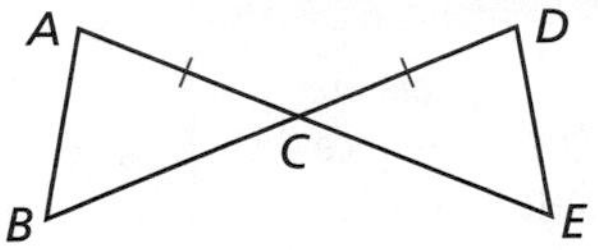

Multi-Step **Graph each triangle. Then use the Distance Formula and the SSS Postulate to determine whether the triangles are congruent.**

19. $\triangle QRS$ and $\triangle TUV$
$Q(-2, 0)$, $R(1, -2)$, $S(-3, -2)$
$T(5, 1)$, $U(3, -2)$, $V(3, 2)$

20. $\triangle ABC$ and $\triangle DEF$
$A(2, 3)$, $B(3, -1)$, $C(7, 2)$
$D(-3, 1)$, $E(1, 2)$, $F(-3, 5)$

21. Given: $\angle ZVY \cong \angle WYV$, $\angle ZVW \cong \angle WYZ$, $\overline{VW} \cong \overline{YZ}$

Prove: $\triangle ZVY \cong \triangle WYV$

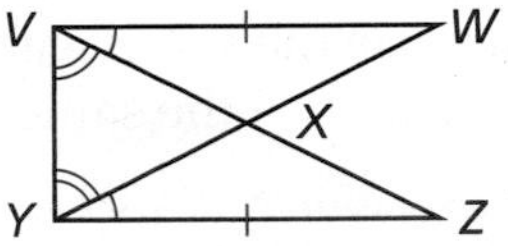

Proof:

Statements	Reasons
1. $\angle ZVY \cong \angle WYV$, $\angle ZVW \cong WYZ$	1. a. ___?___
2. $m\angle ZVY = m\angle WYV$, $m\angle ZVW = m\angle WYZ$	2. b. ___?___
3. $m\angle ZVY + m\angle ZVW = m\angle WYV + m\angle WYZ$	3. Add. Prop. of =
4. c. ___?___	4. ∠ Add. Post.
5. $\angle WVY \cong \angle ZYV$	5. d. ___?___
6. $\overline{VW} \cong \overline{YZ}$	6. e. ___?___
7. f. ___?___	7. Reflex. Prop. of ≅
8. $\triangle ZVY \cong \triangle WYV$	8. g. ___?___

MULTI-STEP TEST PREP

22. The diagram shows two triangular trusses that were built for the roof of a doghouse.

a. You can use a protractor to check that $\angle A$ and $\angle D$ are right angles. Explain how you could make just two additional measurements on each truss to ensure that the trusses are congruent.

b. You verify that the trusses are congruent and find that $AB = AC = 2.5$ ft. Find the length of $\overline{EF}$ to the nearest tenth. Explain.

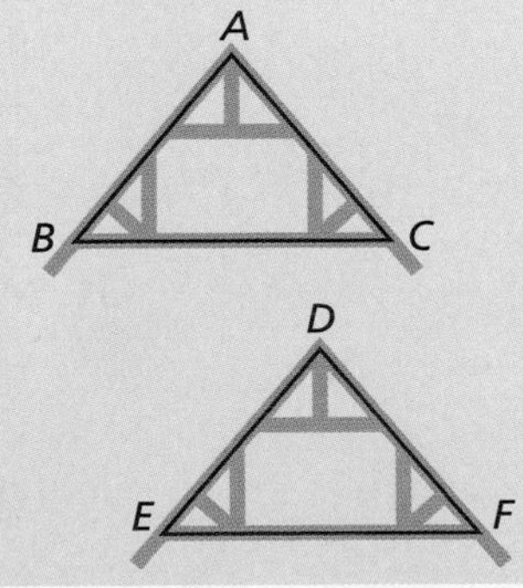

23. **Critical Thinking** Draw two isosceles triangles that are not congruent but that have a perimeter of 15 cm each.

24. $\triangle ABC \cong \triangle ADC$ for what value of x? Explain why the SSS Postulate can be used to prove the two triangles congruent.

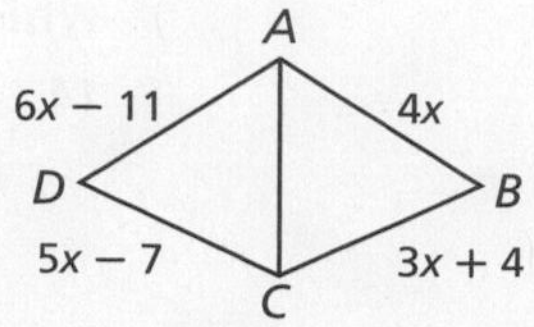

LINK Ecology

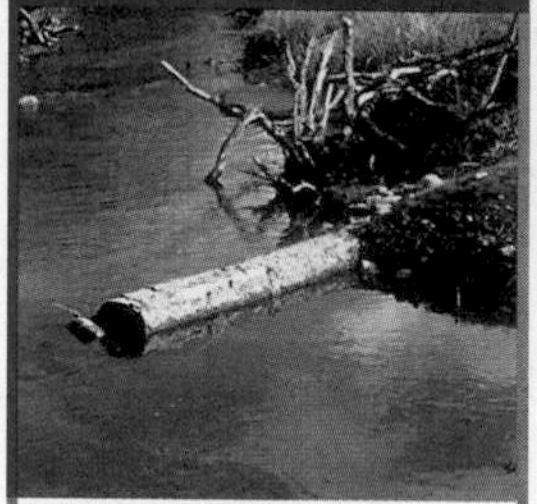

Wing deflectors are designed to reduce the width-to-depth ratio of a stream. Reducing the width increases the velocity of the stream.

25. **Ecology** A *wing deflector* is a triangular structure made of logs that is filled with large rocks and placed in a stream to guide the current or prevent erosion. Wing deflectors are often used in pairs. Suppose an engineer wants to build two wing deflectors. The logs that form the sides of each wing deflector are perpendicular. How can the engineer make sure that the two wing deflectors are congruent?

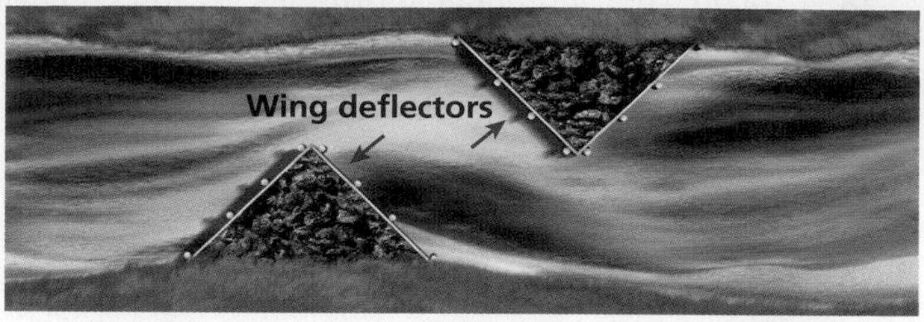

26. **Write About It** If you use the same two sides and included angle to repeat the construction of a triangle, are your two constructed triangles congruent? Explain.

27. **Construction** Use three segments (SSS) to construct a scalene triangle. Suppose you then use the same segments in a different order to construct a second triangle. Will the result be the same? Explain.

TEST PREP

28. Which of the three triangles below can be proven congruent by SSS or SAS?

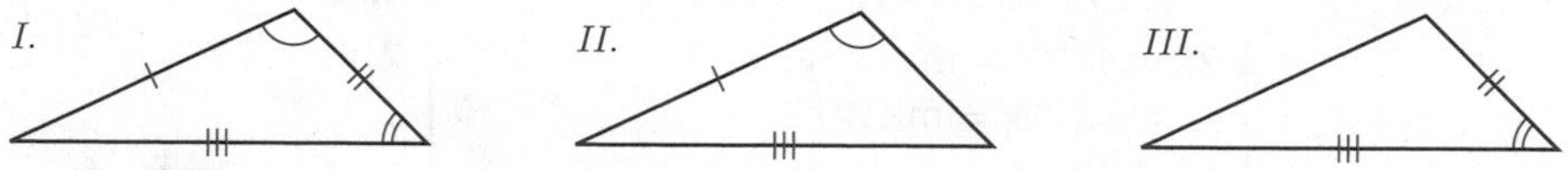

Ⓐ I and II Ⓑ II and III Ⓒ I and III Ⓓ I, II, and III

29. What is the perimeter of polygon $ABCD$?

Ⓕ 29.9 cm Ⓗ 49.8 cm

Ⓖ 39.8 cm Ⓙ 59.8 cm

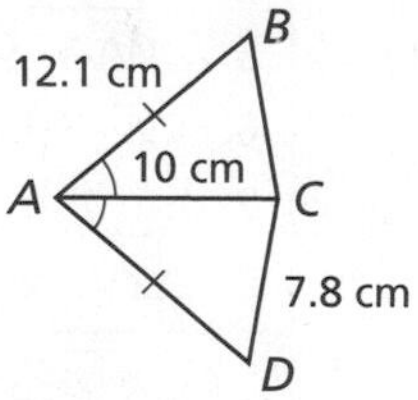

30. Jacob wants to prove that $\triangle FGH \cong \triangle JKL$ using SAS. He knows that $\overline{FG} \cong \overline{JK}$ and $\overline{FH} \cong \overline{JL}$. What additional piece of information does he need?

Ⓐ $\angle F \cong \angle J$ Ⓒ $\angle H \cong \angle L$

Ⓑ $\angle G \cong \angle K$ Ⓓ $\angle F \cong \angle G$

31. What must the value of x be in order to prove that $\triangle EFG \cong \triangle EHG$ by SSS?

Ⓕ 1.5 Ⓗ 4.67

Ⓖ 4.25 Ⓙ 5.5

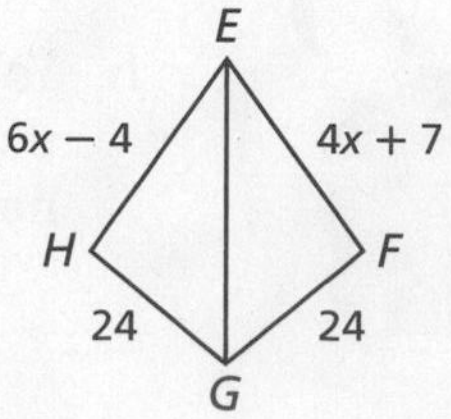

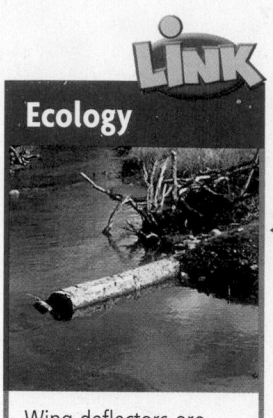

CHALLENGE AND EXTEND

32. Given: $\angle ADC$ and $\angle BCD$ are supplementary. $\overline{AD} \cong \overline{CB}$

Prove: $\triangle ADB \cong \triangle CBD$

(*Hint:* Draw an auxiliary line.)

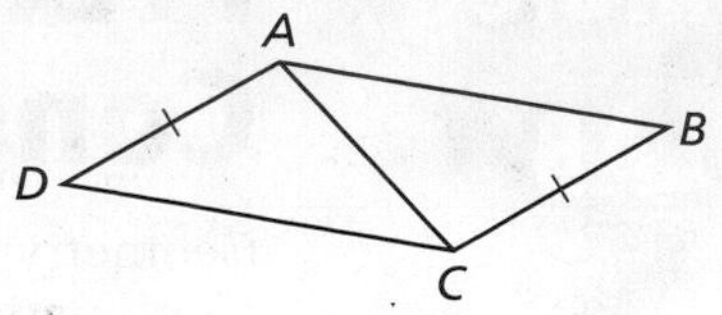

33. Given: $\angle QPS \cong \angle TPR$, $\overline{PQ} \cong \overline{PT}$, $\overline{PR} \cong \overline{PS}$

Prove: $\triangle PQR \cong \triangle PTS$

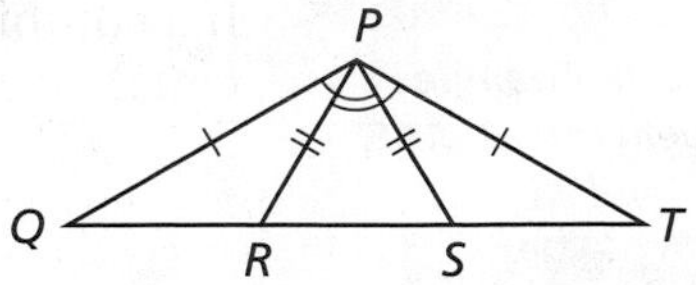

Algebra **Use the following information for Exercises 34 and 35.** Find the value of x. Then use SSS or SAS to write a paragraph proof showing that two of the triangles are congruent.

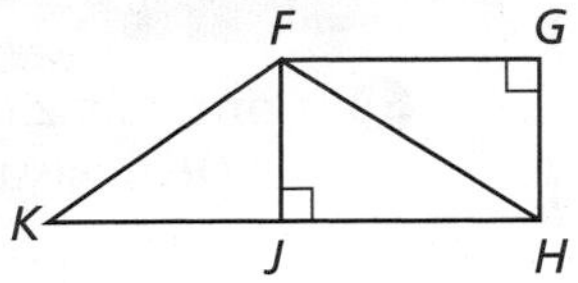

34. $m\angle FKJ = 2x°$
$m\angle KFJ = (3x + 10)°$
$KJ = 4x + 8$
$HJ = 6(x - 4)$

35. $\overline{FJ}$ bisects $\angle KFH$.
$m\angle KFJ = (2x + 6)°$
$m\angle HFJ = (3x - 21)°$
$FK = 8x - 45$
$FH = 6x + 9$

Using Technology

Use geometry software to complete the following.

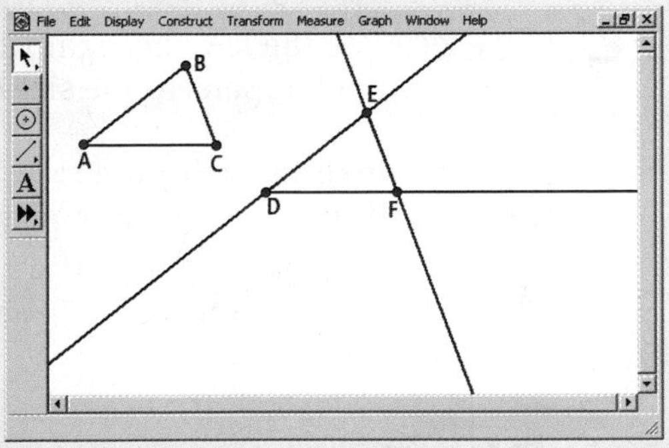

1. Draw a triangle and label the vertices A, B, and C. Draw a point and label it D. Mark a vector from A to B and translate D by the marked vector. Label the image E. Draw $\overleftrightarrow{DE}$. Mark $\angle BAC$ and rotate $\overleftrightarrow{DE}$ about D by the marked angle. Mark $\angle ABC$ and rotate $\overleftrightarrow{DE}$ about E by the marked angle. Label the intersection F.
2. Drag A, B, and C to different locations. What do you notice about the two triangles?
3. Write a conjecture about $\triangle ABC$ and $\triangle DEF$.
4. Test your conjecture by measuring the sides and angles of $\triangle ABC$ and $\triangle DEF$.

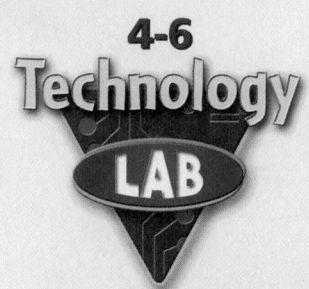

4-6 Technology LAB

Predict Other Triangle Congruence Relationships

Use with *Triangle Congruence: ASA, AAS, and HL*

Geometry software can help you investigate whether certain combinations of triangle parts will make only one triangle. If a combination makes only one triangle, then this arrangement can be used to prove two triangles congruent.

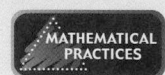

MATHEMATICAL PRACTICES **Use appropriate tools strategically.**

CC.9-12.G.SRT.5 Use congruence…criteria for triangles to solve problems and prove relationships...

Activity 1

1. Construct $\angle CAB$ measuring 45° and $\angle EDF$ measuring 110°.

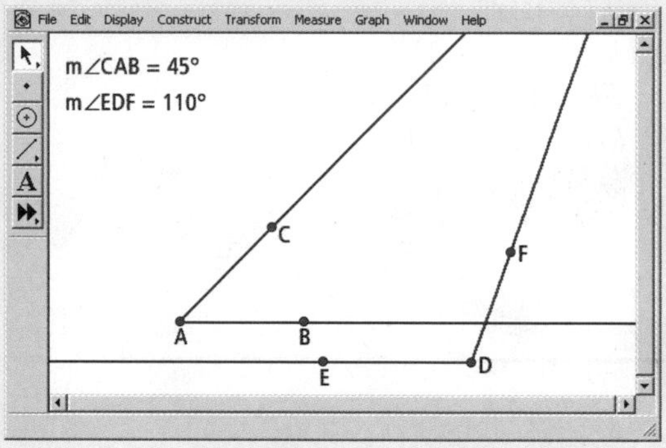

2. Move $\angle EDF$ so that $\overrightarrow{DE}$ overlays $\overrightarrow{BA}$. Where $\overrightarrow{DF}$ and $\overrightarrow{AC}$ intersect, label the point G. Measure $\angle DGA$.

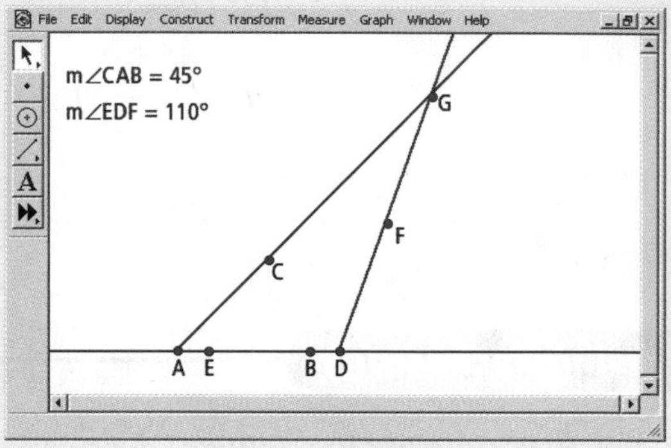

3. Move $\angle CAB$ to the left and right without changing the measures of the angles. Observe what happens to the size of $\angle DGA$.

4. Measure the distance from A to D. Try to change the shape of the triangle without changing AD and the measures of $\angle A$ and $\angle D$.

Try This

1. Repeat Activity 1 using angle measures of your choice. Are your results the same? Explain.
2. Do the results change if one of the given angles measures 90°?
3. What theorem proves that the measure of $\angle DGA$ in Step 2 will always be the same?
4. In Step 3 of the activity, the angle measures in $\triangle ADG$ stayed the same as the size of the triangle changed. Does Angle-Angle-Angle, like Side-Side-Side, make only one triangle? Explain.
5. Repeat Step 4 of the activity but measure the length of $\overline{AG}$ instead of $\overline{AD}$. Are your results the same? Does this lead to a new congruence postulate or theorem?
6. If you are given two angles of a triangle, what additional piece of information is needed so that only one triangle is made? Make a conjecture based on your findings in Step 5.

Activity 2

1. Construct $\overline{YZ}$ with a length of 6.5 cm.

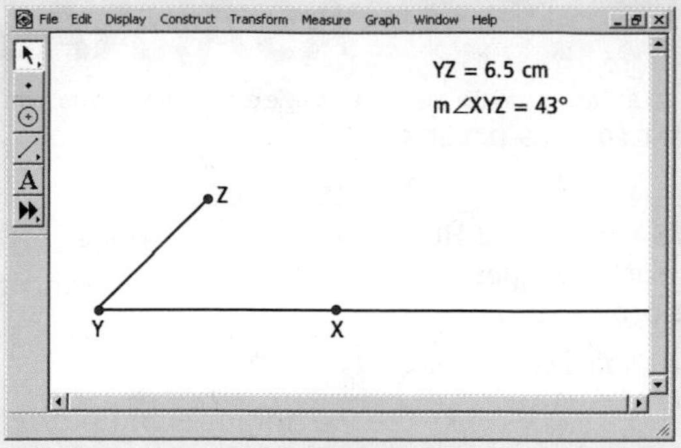

2. Using $\overline{YZ}$ as a side, construct $\angle XYZ$ measuring 43°.

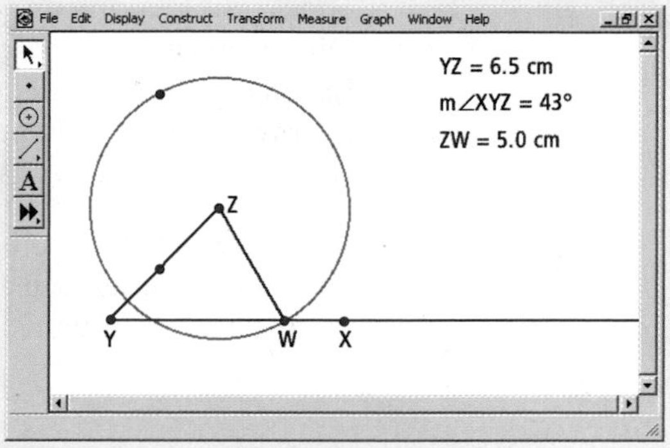

3. Draw a circle at Z with a radius of 5 cm. Construct $\overline{ZW}$, a radius of circle Z.

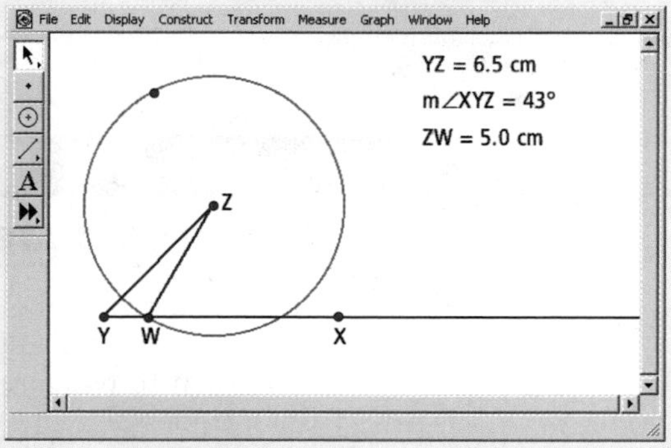

4. Move W around circle Z. Observe the possible shapes of $\triangle YZW$.

Try This

7. In Step 4 of the activity, how many different triangles were possible? Does Side-Side-Angle make only one triangle?
8. Repeat Activity 2 using an angle measure of 90° in Step 2 and a circle with a radius of 7 cm in Step 3. How many different triangles are possible in Step 4?
9. Repeat the activity again using a measure of 90° in Step 2 and a circle with a radius of 8.25 cm in Step 3. Classify the resulting triangle by its angle measures.
10. Based on your results, complete the following conjecture. In a Side-Side-Angle combination, if the corresponding nonincluded angles are ___?___ , then only one triangle is possible.

COMMON CORE

4-6 Triangle Congruence: ASA, AAS, and HL

CC.9-12.G.CO.8 Explain how the criteria for triangle congruence...follow from the definition of congruence...
Also **CC.9-12.G.CO.7, CC.9-12.G.SRT.5**

Objectives

Apply ASA, AAS, and HL to construct triangles and to solve problems.

Prove triangles congruent by using ASA, AAS, and HL.

Vocabulary

included side

Why use this?

Bearings are used to convey direction, helping people find their way to specific locations.

Participants in an *orienteering* race use a map and a compass to find their way to checkpoints along an unfamiliar course. Directions are given by *bearings*, which are based on compass headings. For example, to travel along the bearing S 43° E, you face south and then turn 43° to the east.

An **included side** is the common side of two consecutive angles in a polygon. The following postulate uses the idea of an *included side.*

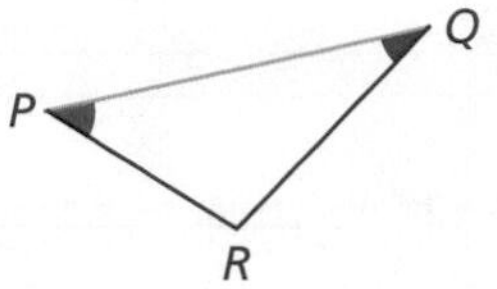

$\overline{PQ}$ is the included side of $\angle P$ and $\angle Q$.

Know it! Note

Postulate 4-6-1 Angle-Side-Angle (ASA) Congruence

POSTULATE	HYPOTHESIS	CONCLUSION
If two angles and the included side of one triangle are congruent to two angles and the included side of another triangle, then the triangles are congruent.	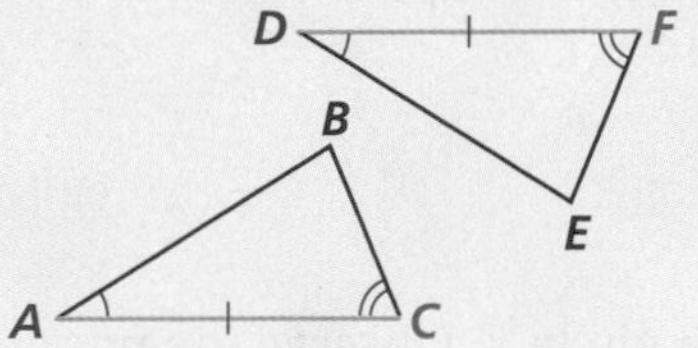	$\triangle ABC \cong \triangle DEF$

EXAMPLE 1 *Problem-Solving Application*

MATHEMATICAL PRACTICES

Make sense of problems and persevere in solving them.

Organizers of an orienteering race are planning a course with checkpoints *A*, *B*, and *C*. Does the table give enough information to determine the location of the checkpoints?

	Bearing	Distance
A to *B*	N 55° E	7.6 km
B to *C*	N 26° W	▆
C to *A*	S 20° W	▆

1 Understand the Problem

The **answer** is whether the information in the table can be used to find the position of checkpoints *A*, *B*, and *C*. List the **important information:** The bearing from *A* to *B* is N 55° E. From *B* to *C* is N 26° W, and from *C* to *A* is S 20° W. The distance from *A* to *B* is 7.6 km.

2 Make a Plan

Draw the course using vertical lines to show north-south directions. Then use these parallel lines and the alternate interior angles to help find angle measures of $\triangle ABC$.

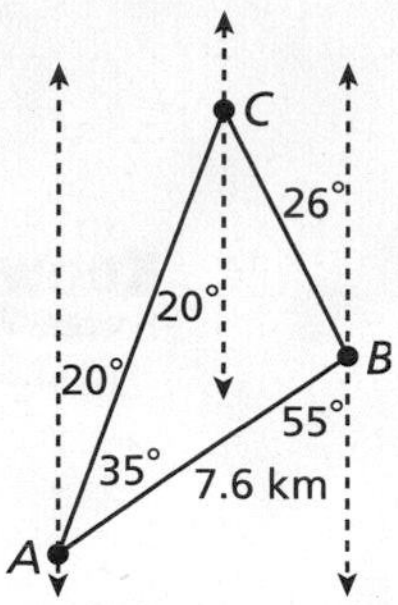

3 Solve

$m\angle CAB = 55° - 20° = 35°$

$m\angle CBA = 180° - (26° + 55°) = 99°$

You know the measures of $\angle CAB$ and $\angle CBA$ and the length of the included side $\overline{AB}$. Therefore by ASA, a unique triangle ABC is determined.

4 Look Back

One and only one triangle can be made using the information in the table, so the table does give enough information to determine the location of all the checkpoints.

CHECK IT OUT! 1. **What if...?** If 7.6 km is the distance from B to C, is there enough information to determine the location of all the checkpoints? Explain.

EXAMPLE 2 Applying ASA Congruence

Determine if you can use ASA to prove $\triangle UVX \cong \triangle WVX$. Explain.

$\angle UXV \cong \angle WXV$ as given. Since $\angle WVX$ is a right angle that forms a linear pair with $\angle UVX$, $\angle WVX \cong \angle UVX$. Also $\overline{VX} \cong \overline{VX}$ by the Reflexive Property. Therefore $\triangle UVX \cong \triangle WVX$ by ASA.

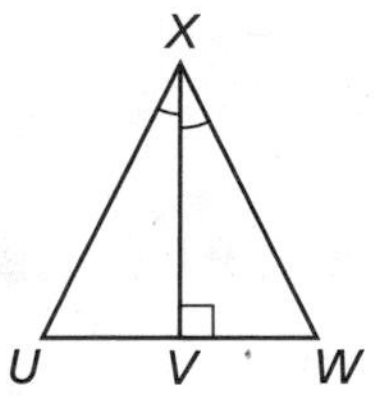

CHECK IT OUT! 2. Determine if you can use ASA to prove $\triangle NKL \cong \triangle LMN$. Explain.

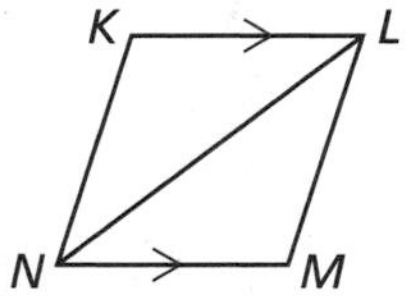

Construction Congruent Triangles Using ASA

Use a straightedge to draw a segment and two angles, or copy the given segment and angles.

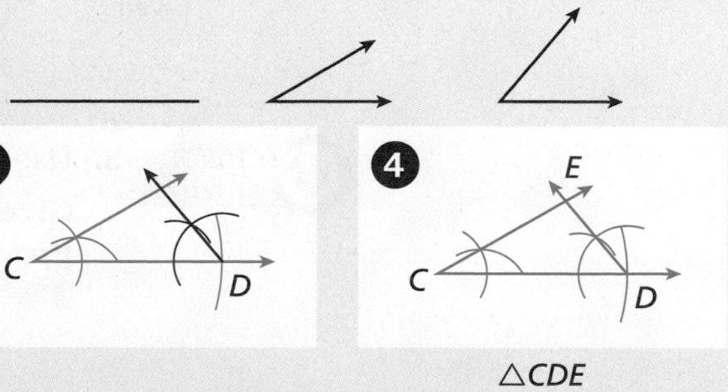

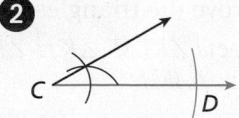

1. Construct $\overline{CD}$ congruent to the given segment.
2. Construct $\angle C$ congruent to one of the angles.
3. Construct $\angle D$ congruent to the other angle.
4. Label the intersection of the rays as E.

You can use the Third Angles Theorem to prove another congruence relationship based on ASA. This theorem is Angle-Angle-Side (AAS).

Know it! Note

Theorem 4-6-2 Angle-Angle-Side (AAS) Congruence

THEOREM	HYPOTHESIS	CONCLUSION
If two angles and a nonincluded side of one triangle are congruent to the corresponding angles and nonincluded side of another triangle, then the triangles are congruent.	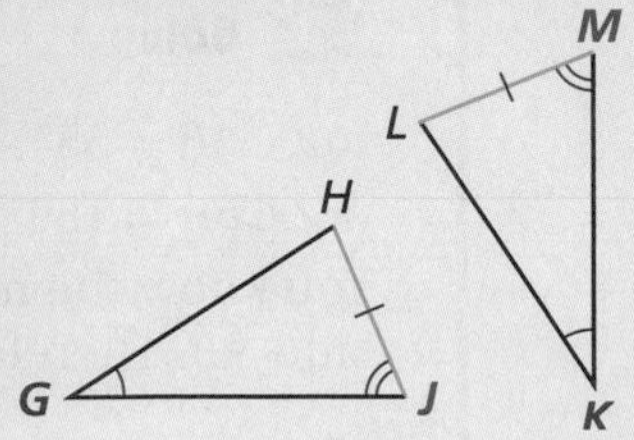	$\triangle GHJ \cong \triangle KLM$

PROOF

Angle-Angle-Side Congruence

Given: $\angle G \cong \angle K$, $\angle J \cong \angle M$, $\overline{HJ} \cong \overline{LM}$
Prove: $\triangle GHJ \cong \triangle KLM$
Proof:

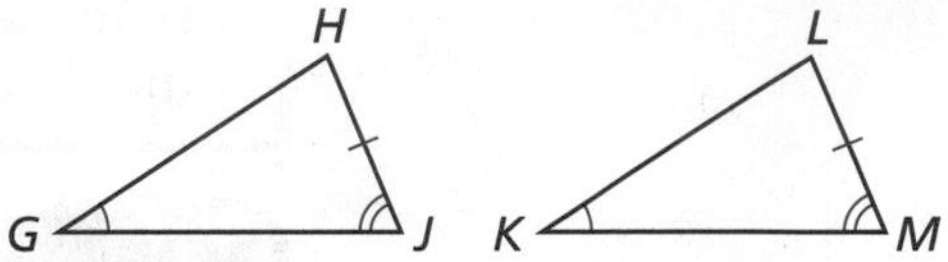

Statements	Reasons
1. $\angle G \cong \angle K$, $\angle J \cong \angle M$	1. Given
2. $\angle H \cong \angle L$	2. Third ∠s Thm.
3. $\overline{HJ} \cong \overline{LM}$	3. Given
4. $\triangle GHJ \cong \triangle KLM$	4. ASA *Steps 1, 3, and 2*

EXAMPLE 3 Using AAS to Prove Triangles Congruent

Use AAS to prove the triangles congruent.
Given: $\overline{AB} \parallel \overline{ED}$, $\overline{BC} \cong \overline{DC}$
Prove: $\triangle ABC \cong \triangle EDC$
Proof:

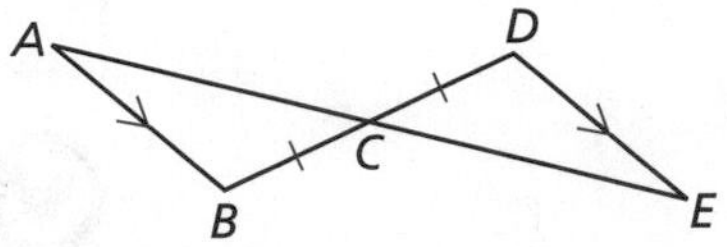

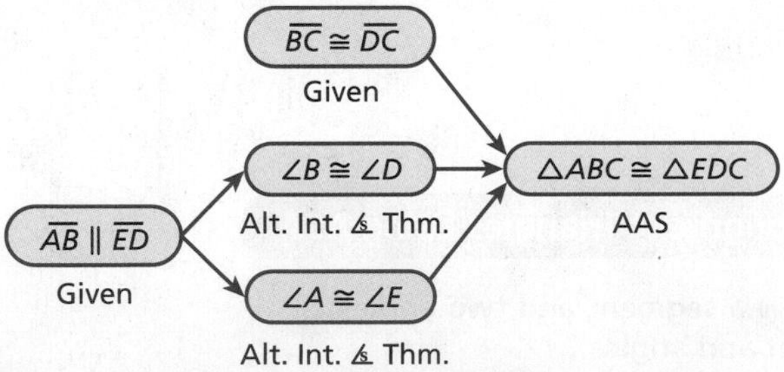

CHECK IT OUT!

3. Use AAS to prove the triangles congruent.
Given: $\overline{JL}$ bisects $\angle KLM$. $\angle K \cong \angle M$
Prove: $\triangle JKL \cong \triangle JML$

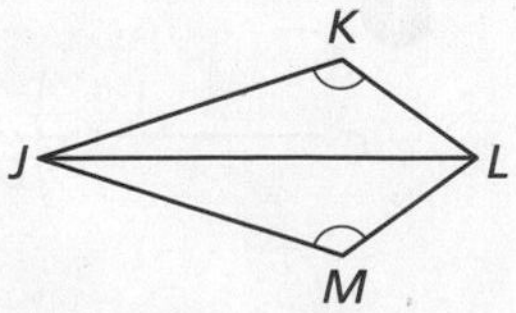

There are four theorems for right triangles that are not used for acute or obtuse triangles. They are Leg-Leg (LL), Hypotenuse-Angle (HA), Leg-Angle (LA), and Hypotenuse-Leg (HL). You will prove LL, HA, and LA in Exercises 21, 23, and 33.

Know it! Note

Theorem 4-6-3 Hypotenuse-Leg (HL) Congruence

THEOREM	HYPOTHESIS	CONCLUSION
If the hypotenuse and a leg of a right triangle are congruent to the hypotenuse and a leg of another right triangle, then the triangles are congruent.	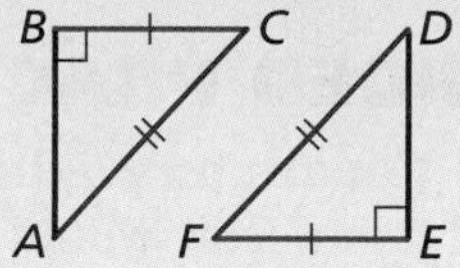	$\triangle ABC \cong \triangle DEF$

You will prove the Hypotenuse-Leg Theorem in lesson Isosceles and Equilateral Triangles

EXAMPLE 4 Applying HL Congruence

Determine if you can use the HL Congruence Theorem to prove the triangles congruent. If not, tell what else you need to know.

A $\triangle VWX$ **and** $\triangle YXW$

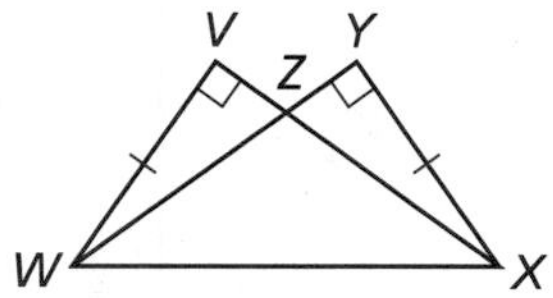

According to the diagram, $\triangle VWX$ and $\triangle YXW$ are right triangles that share hypotenuse $\overline{WX}$. $\overline{WX} \cong \overline{XW}$ by the Reflexive Property. It is given that $\overline{WV} \cong \overline{XY}$, therefore $\triangle VWX \cong \triangle YXW$ by HL.

B $\triangle VWZ$ **and** $\triangle YXZ$

This conclusion cannot be proved by HL. According to the diagram, $\triangle VWZ$ and $\triangle YXZ$ are right triangles, and $\overline{WV} \cong \overline{XY}$. You do not know that hypotenuse $\overline{WZ}$ is congruent to hypotenuse $\overline{XZ}$.

CHECK IT OUT!

4. Determine if you can use the HL Congruence Theorem to prove $\triangle ABC \cong \triangle DCB$. If not, tell what else you need to know.

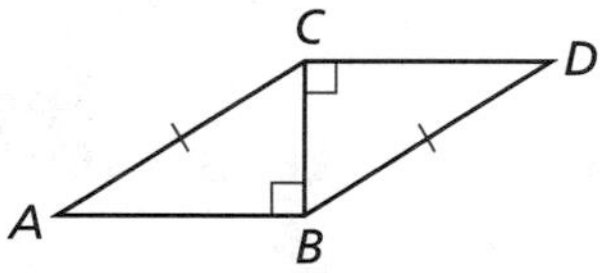

MATHEMATICAL PRACTICES

THINK AND DISCUSS

1. Could you use AAS to prove that these two triangles are congruent? Explain.

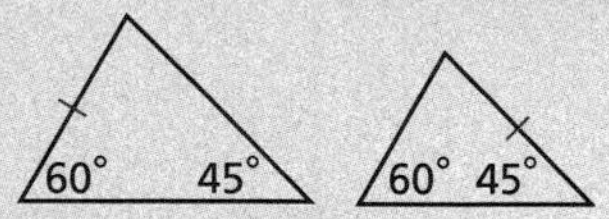

2. The arrangement of the letters in ASA matches the arrangement of what parts of congruent triangles? Include a sketch to support your answer.

Know it! Note

3. **GET ORGANIZED** Copy and complete the graphic organizer. In each column, write a description of the method and then sketch two triangles, marking the appropriate congruent parts.

Proving Triangles Congruent						
	Def. of $\triangle \cong$	SSS	SAS	ASA	AAS	HL
Words						
Pictures						

4-6 Exercises

Learn It Online
Homework Help Online
Parent Resources Online

GUIDED PRACTICE

1. **Vocabulary** A triangle contains ∠*ABC* and ∠*ACB* with $\overline{BC}$ "closed in" between them. How would this help you remember the definition of *included side*?

SEE EXAMPLE 1

Surveying **Use the table for Exercises 2 and 3.** A landscape designer surveyed the boundaries of a triangular park. She made the following table for the dimensions of the land.

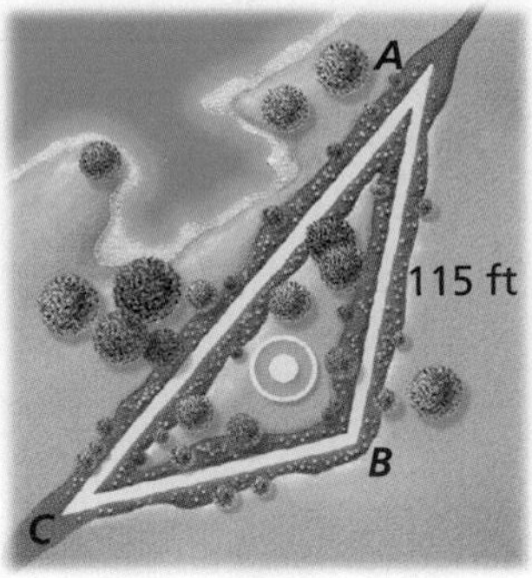

	A to *B*	*B* to *C*	*C* to *A*
Bearing	E	S 25° E	N 62° W
Distance	115 ft	?	?

2. Draw the plot of land described by the table. Label the measures of the angles in the triangle.

3. Does the table have enough information to determine the locations of points *A*, *B*, and *C*? Explain.

SEE EXAMPLE 2

Determine if you can use ASA to prove the triangles congruent. Explain.

4. △*VRS* and △*VTS*, given that $\overline{VS}$ bisects ∠*RST* and ∠*RVT*

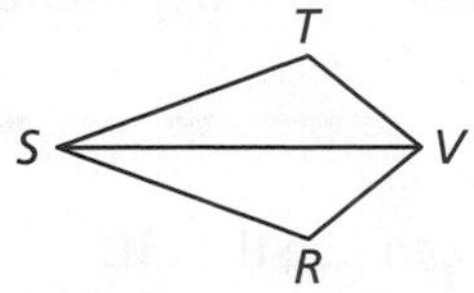

5. △*DEH* and △*FGH*

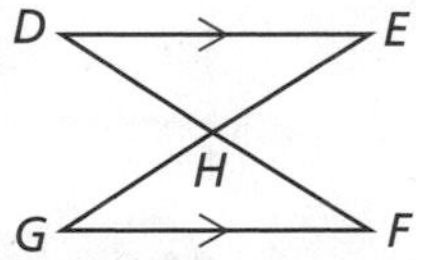

SEE EXAMPLE 3

6. Use AAS to prove the triangles congruent.

Given: ∠*R* and ∠*P* are right angles.
$\overline{QR} \parallel \overline{SP}$

Prove: △*QPS* ≅ △*SRQ*

Proof:

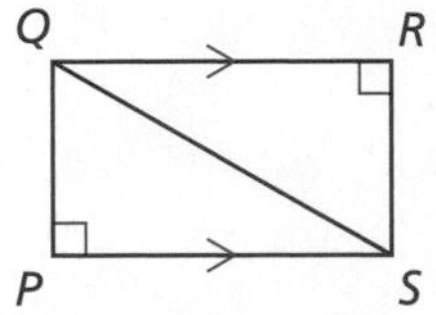

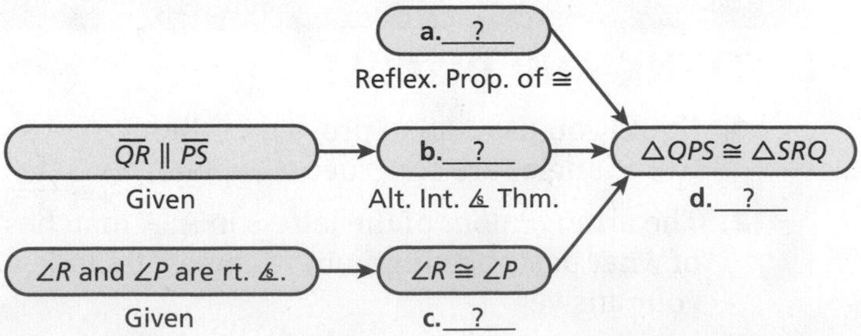

SEE EXAMPLE 4

Determine if you can use the HL Congruence Theorem to prove the triangles congruent. If not, tell what else you need to know.

7. △*ABC* and △*CDA*

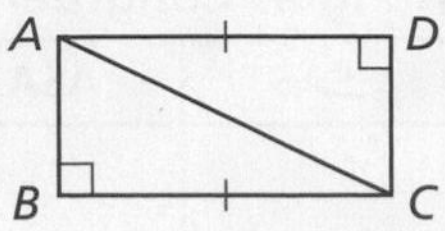

8. △*XYV* and △*ZYV*

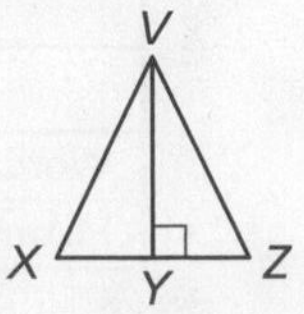

PRACTICE AND PROBLEM SOLVING

Independent Practice

For Exercises	See Example
9–10	1
11–12	2
13	3
14–15	4

Extra Practice

See Extra Practice for more Skills Practice and Applications Practice exercises.

LINK

Math History

Euclid wrote the mathematical text *The Elements* around 2300 years ago. It may be the second most reprinted book in history.

Surveying Use the table for Exercises 9 and 10.
From two different observation towers a fire is sighted. The locations of the towers are given in the following table.

	X to *Y*	*X* to *F*	*Y* to *F*
Bearing	E	N 53° E	N 16° W
Distance	6 km	?	?

9. Draw the diagram formed by observation tower *X*, observation tower *Y*, and the fire *F*. Label the measures of the angles.

10. Is there enough information given in the table to pinpoint the location of the fire? Explain.

Determine if you can use ASA to prove the triangles congruent. Explain.

11. $\triangle MKJ$ and $\triangle MKL$

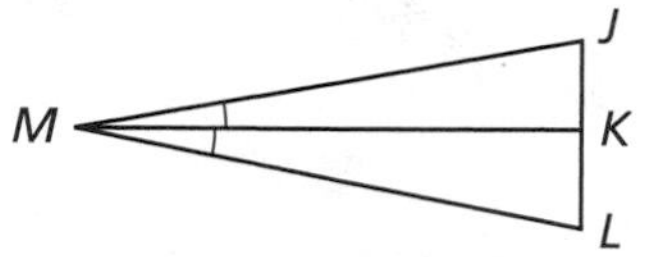

12. $\triangle RST$ and $\triangle TUR$

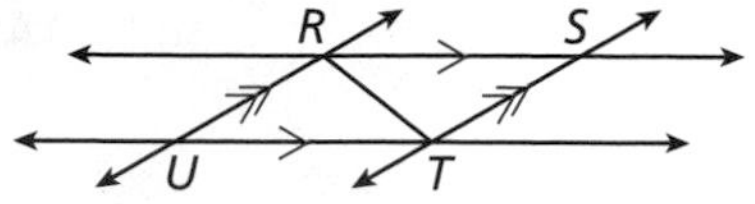

13. **Given:** $\overline{AB} \cong \overline{DE}$, $\angle C \cong \angle F$
Prove: $\triangle ABC \cong \triangle DEF$

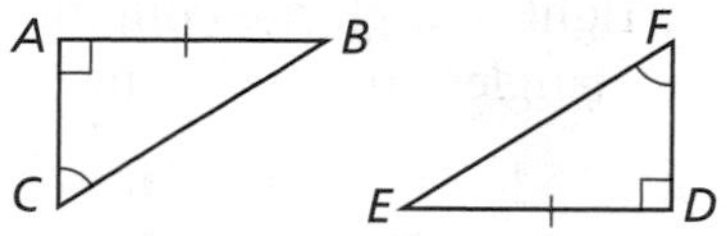

Proof:

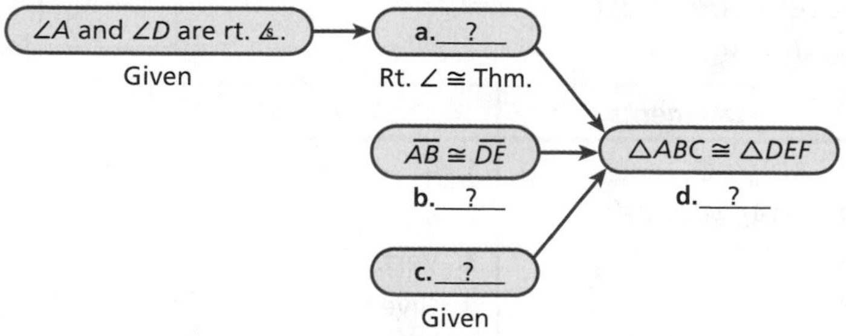

Determine if you can use the HL Congruence Theorem to prove the triangles congruent. If not, tell what else you need to know.

14. $\triangle GHJ$ and $\triangle JKG$

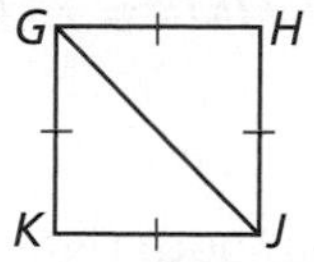

15. $\triangle ABE$ and $\triangle DCE$, given that E is the midpoint of $\overline{AD}$ and $\overline{BC}$

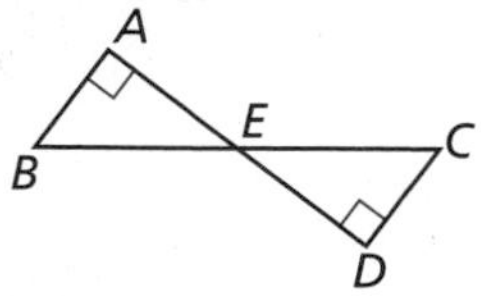

Multi-Step For each pair of triangles write a triangle congruence statement. Identify the transformation that moves one triangle to the position of the other triangle.

16.

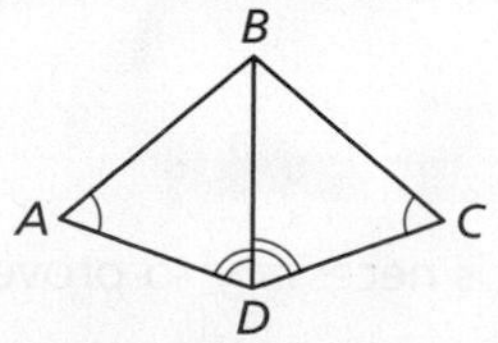

17.

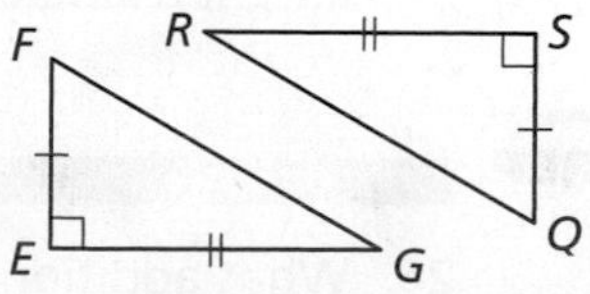

18. **Critical Thinking** Side-Side-Angle (SSA) cannot be used to prove two triangles congruent. Draw a diagram that shows why this is true.

MULTI-STEP TEST PREP

19. A carpenter built a truss to support the roof of a doghouse.

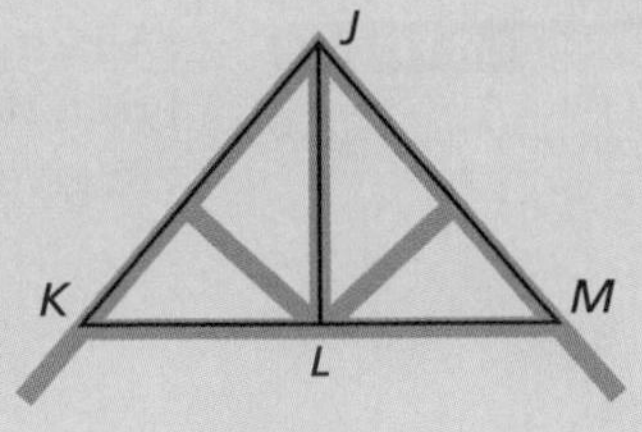

a. The carpenter knows that $\overline{KJ} \cong \overline{MJ}$. Can the carpenter conclude that $\triangle KJL \cong \triangle MJL$? Why or why not?

b. Suppose the carpenter also knows that $\angle JLK$ is a right angle. Which theorem can be used to show that $\triangle KJL \cong \triangle MJL$?

20. **///ERROR ANALYSIS///** Two proofs that $\triangle EFH \cong \triangle GHF$ are given. Which is incorrect? Explain the error.

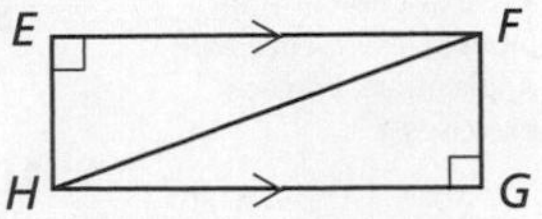

A

It is given that $\overline{EF} \parallel \overline{GH}$. By the Alt. Int. ∠s Thm., $\angle EFH \cong \angle GHF$. $\angle E \cong \angle G$ by the Rt. $\angle \cong$ Thm. By the Reflex. Prop. of $\cong$, $\overline{HF} \cong \overline{HF}$. So by AAS, $\triangle EFH \cong \triangle GHF$.

B

$\overline{HF}$ is the hyp. of both rt. △s. $\overline{HF} \cong \overline{HF}$ by the Reflex. Prop. of $\cong$. Since the opp. sides of a rect. are $\cong$, $\overline{EF} \cong \overline{GH}$. So by HL, $\triangle EFH \cong \triangle FHG$.

21. Write a paragraph proof of the Leg-Leg (LL) Congruence Theorem. If the legs of one right triangle are congruent to the corresponding legs of another right triangle, the triangles are congruent.

22. Use AAS to prove the triangles congruent.
Given: $\overline{AD} \parallel \overline{BC}$, $\overline{AD} \cong \overline{CB}$
Prove: $\triangle AED \cong \triangle CEB$

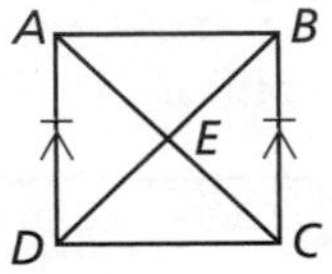

Proof:

Statements	Reasons
1. $\overline{AD} \parallel \overline{BC}$	1. a. ___?___
2. $\angle DAE \cong \angle BCE$	2. b. ___?___
3. c. ___?___	3. Vert. ∠s Thm.
4. d. ___?___	3. Given
5. e. ___?___	4. f. ___?___

23. Prove the Hypotenuse-Angle (HA) Theorem.
Given: $\overline{KM} \perp \overline{JL}$, $\overline{JM} \cong \overline{LM}$, $\angle JMK \cong \angle LMK$
Prove: $\triangle JKM \cong \triangle LKM$

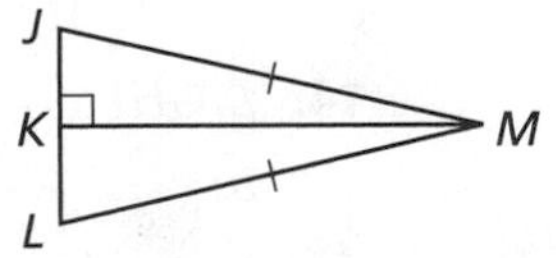

24. **Write About It** The legs of both right $\triangle DEF$ and right $\triangle RST$ are 3 cm and 4 cm. They each have a hypotenuse 5 cm in length. Describe two different ways you could prove that $\triangle DEF \cong \triangle RST$.

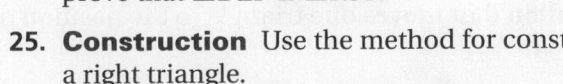

25. **Construction** Use the method for constructing perpendicular lines to construct a right triangle.

TEST PREP

26. What additional congruence statement is necessary to prove $\triangle XWY \cong \triangle XVZ$ by ASA?

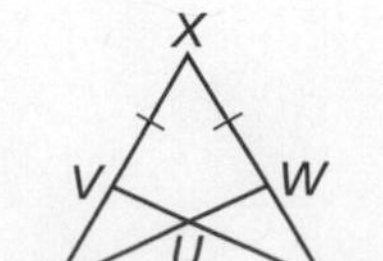

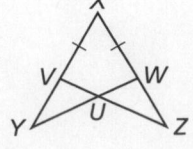

Ⓐ $\angle XVZ \cong \angle XWY$

Ⓑ $\angle VUY \cong \angle WUZ$

Ⓒ $\overline{VZ} \cong \overline{WY}$

Ⓓ $\overline{XZ} \cong \overline{XY}$

27. Which postulate or theorem justifies the congruence statement $\triangle STU \cong \triangle VUT$?

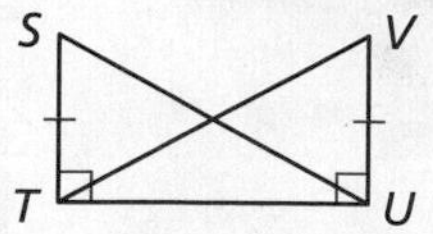

Ⓕ ASA　　Ⓗ HL
Ⓖ SSS　　Ⓙ SAS

28. Which of the following congruence statements is true?

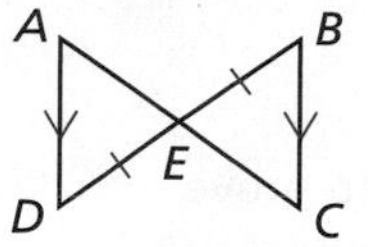

Ⓐ $\angle A \cong \angle B$　　Ⓒ $\triangle AED \cong \triangle CEB$
Ⓑ $\overline{CE} \cong \overline{DE}$　　Ⓓ $\triangle AED \cong \triangle BEC$

29. In $\triangle RST$, $RT = 6y - 2$. In $\triangle UVW$, $UW = 2y + 7$. $\angle R \cong \angle U$, and $\angle S \cong \angle V$. What must be the value of y in order to prove that $\triangle RST \cong \triangle UVW$?

Ⓕ 1.25　　Ⓖ 2.25　　Ⓗ 9.0　　Ⓙ 11.5

30. **Extended Response** Draw a triangle. Construct a second triangle that has the same angle measures but is not congruent. Compare the lengths of each pair of corresponding sides. Consider the relationship between the lengths of the sides and the measures of the angles. Explain why Angle-Angle-Angle (AAA) is not a congruence principle.

CHALLENGE AND EXTEND

31. **Sports** This bicycle frame includes $\triangle VSU$ and $\triangle VTU$, which lie in intersecting planes. From the given angle measures, can you conclude that $\triangle VSU \cong \triangle VTU$? Explain.

$m\angle VUS = (7y - 2)^\circ$　　$m\angle VUT = \left(5\frac{1}{2}x - \frac{1}{2}\right)^\circ$

$m\angle USV = 5\frac{2}{3}y^\circ$　　$m\angle UTV = (4x + 8)^\circ$

$m\angle SVU = (3y - 6)^\circ$　　$m\angle TVU = 2x^\circ$

32. **Given:** $\triangle ABC$ is equilateral. C is the midpoint of $\overline{DE}$. $\angle DAC$ and $\angle EBC$ are congruent and supplementary.
Prove: $\triangle DAC \cong \triangle EBC$

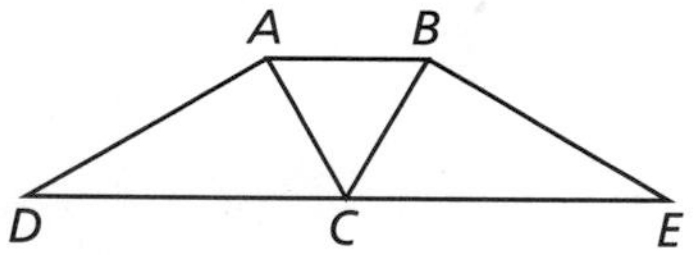

33. Write a two-column proof of the Leg-Angle (LA) Congruence Theorem. If a leg and an acute angle of one right triangle are congruent to the corresponding parts of another right triangle, the triangles are congruent. (*Hint:* There are two cases to consider.)

34. If two triangles are congruent by ASA, what theorem could you use to prove that the triangles are also congruent by AAS? Explain.

COMMON CORE

4-7 Triangle Congruence: CPCTC

CC.9-12.G.SRT.5 Use congruence…criteria for triangles to solve problems and prove relationships… *Also* **CC.9-12.G.MG.3***

Objective
Use CPCTC to prove parts of triangles are congruent.

Vocabulary
CPCTC

Why learn this?
You can use congruent triangles to estimate distances.

CPCTC is an abbreviation for the phrase "Corresponding Parts of Congruent Triangles are Congruent." It can be used as a justification in a proof after you have proven two triangles congruent.

Remember!
SSS, SAS, ASA, AAS, and HL use corresponding parts to prove triangles congruent. CPCTC uses congruent triangles to prove corresponding parts congruent.

EXAMPLE 1 *Engineering Application*

To design a bridge across a canyon, you need to find the distance from *A* to *B*. Locate points *C*, *D*, and *E* as shown in the figure. If *DE* = 600 ft, what is *AB*?

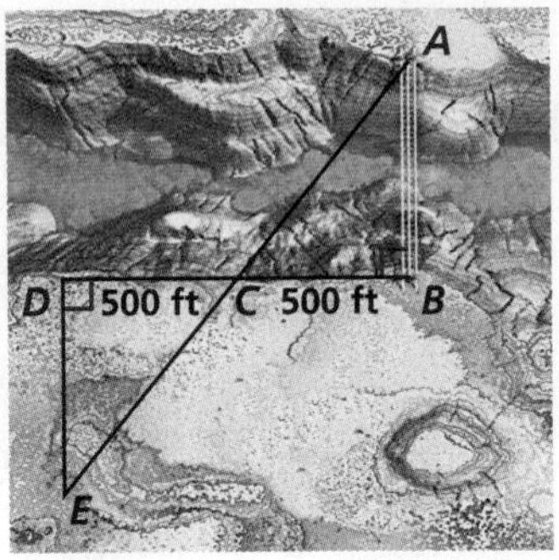

$\angle D \cong \angle B$, because they are both right angles.
$\overline{DC} \cong \overline{CB}$, because $DC = CB = 500$ ft.
$\angle DCE \cong \angle BCA$, because vertical angles are congruent. Therefore $\triangle DCE \cong \triangle BCA$ by ASA or LA. By CPCTC, $\overline{ED} \cong \overline{AB}$, so $AB = ED = 600$ ft.

CHECK IT OUT!

1. A landscape architect sets up the triangles shown in the figure to find the distance *JK* across a pond. What is *JK*?

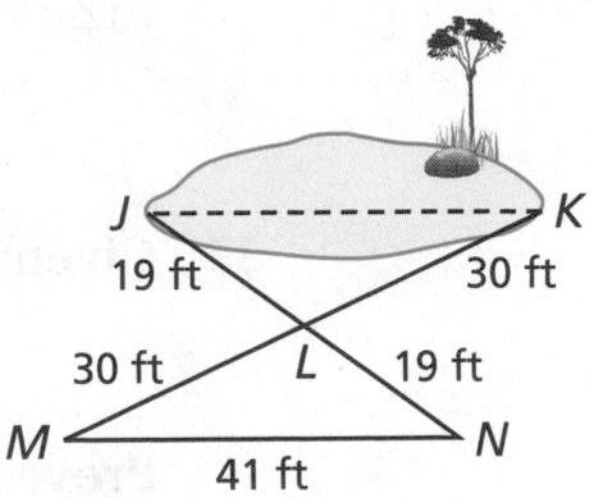

EXAMPLE 2 **Proving Corresponding Parts Congruent**

Given: $\overline{AB} \cong \overline{DC}$, $\angle ABC \cong \angle DCB$
Prove: $\angle A \cong \angle D$

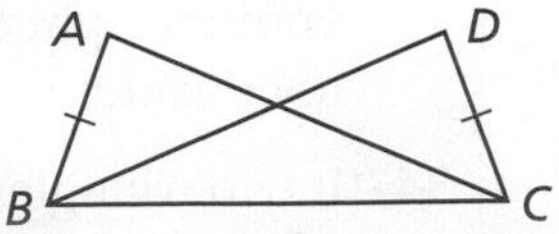

Proof:

- $\overline{AB} \cong \overline{DC}$ (Given)
- $\angle ABC \cong \angle DCB$ (Given)
- $\overline{BC} \cong \overline{CB}$ (Reflex. Prop. of ≅)
- → $\triangle ABC \cong \triangle DCB$ (SAS)
- → $\angle A \cong \angle D$ (CPCTC)

CHECK IT OUT!

2. Given: $\overline{PR}$ bisects $\angle QPS$ and $\angle QRS$.
Prove: $\overline{PQ} \cong \overline{PS}$

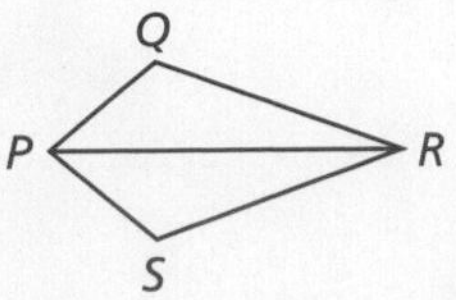

EXAMPLE 3 Using CPCTC in a Proof

Helpful Hint

Work backward when planning a proof. To show that $\overline{ED} \parallel \overline{GF}$, look for a pair of angles that are congruent. Then look for triangles that contain these angles.

Given: $\overline{EG} \parallel \overline{DF}$, $\overline{EG} \cong \overline{DF}$
Prove: $\overline{ED} \parallel \overline{GF}$
Proof:

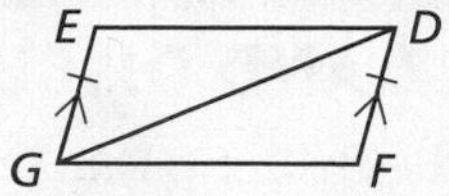

Statements	Reasons
1. $\overline{EG} \cong \overline{DF}$	1. Given
2. $\overline{EG} \parallel \overline{DF}$	2. Given
3. $\angle EGD \cong \angle FDG$	3. Alt. Int. ∠s Thm.
4. $\overline{GD} \cong \overline{DG}$	4. Reflex. Prop. of ≅
5. $\triangle EGD \cong \triangle FDG$	5. SAS *Steps 1, 3, and 4*
6. $\angle EDG \cong \angle FGD$	6. CPCTC
7. $\overline{ED} \parallel \overline{GF}$	7. Converse of Alt. Int. ∠s Thm.

CHECK IT OUT! 3. **Given:** J is the midpoint of $\overline{KM}$ and $\overline{NL}$.
Prove: $\overline{KL} \parallel \overline{MN}$

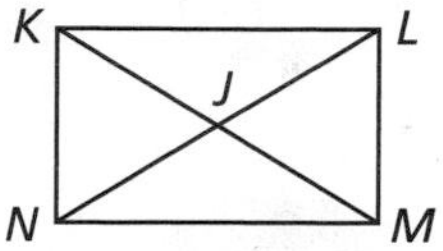

You can also use CPCTC when triangles are on a coordinate plane. You use the Distance Formula to find the lengths of the sides of each triangle. Then, after showing that the triangles are congruent, you can make conclusions about their corresponding parts.

EXAMPLE 4 Using CPCTC in the Coordinate Plane

Algebra

Given: $A(2, 3)$, $B(5, -1)$, $C(1, 0)$, $D(-4, -1)$, $E(0, 2)$, $F(-1, -2)$
Prove: $\angle ABC \cong \angle DEF$

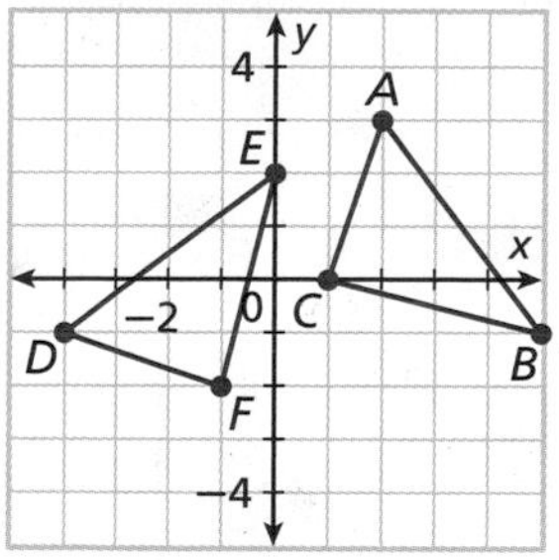

Step 1 Plot the points on a coordinate plane.
Step 2 Use the Distance Formula to find the lengths of the sides of each triangle.

$$D = \sqrt{(x_2 - x_1)^2 + (y_2 - y_1)^2}$$

$$AB = \sqrt{(5-2)^2 + (-1-3)^2} = \sqrt{9+16} = \sqrt{25} = 5$$

$$DE = \sqrt{(0-(-4))^2 + (2-(-1))^2} = \sqrt{16+9} = \sqrt{25} = 5$$

$$BC = \sqrt{(1-5)^2 + (0-(-1))^2} = \sqrt{16+1} = \sqrt{17}$$

$$EF = \sqrt{(-1-0)^2 + (-2-2)^2} = \sqrt{1+16} = \sqrt{17}$$

$$AC = \sqrt{(1-2)^2 + (0-3)^2} = \sqrt{1+9} = \sqrt{10}$$

$$DF = \sqrt{(-1-(-4))^2 + (-2-(-1))^2} = \sqrt{9+1} = \sqrt{10}$$

So $\overline{AB} \cong \overline{DE}$, $\overline{BC} \cong \overline{EF}$, and $\overline{AC} \cong \overline{DF}$. Therefore $\triangle ABC \cong \triangle DEF$ by SSS, and $\angle ABC \cong \angle DEF$ by CPCTC.

CHECK IT OUT! 4. **Given:** $J(-1, -2)$, $K(2, -1)$, $L(-2, 0)$, $R(2, 3)$, $S(5, 2)$, $T(1, 1)$
Prove: $\angle JKL \cong \angle RST$

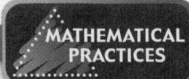

MATHEMATICAL PRACTICES

THINK AND DISCUSS

1. In the figure, $\overline{UV} \cong \overline{XY}$, $\overline{VW} \cong \overline{YZ}$, and $\angle V \cong \angle Y$. Explain why $\triangle UVW \cong \triangle XYZ$. By CPCTC, which additional parts are congruent?

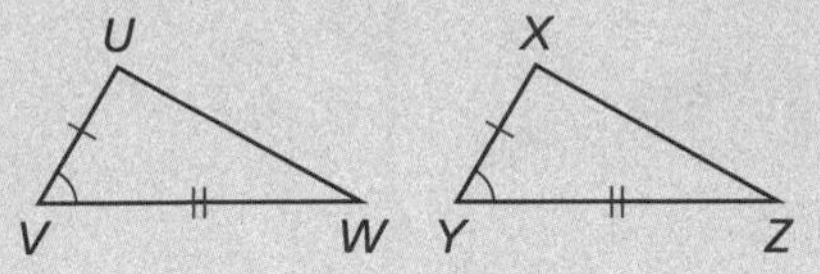

Know it! Note

2. **GET ORGANIZED** Copy and complete the graphic organizer. Write all conclusions you can make using CPCTC.

4-7 Exercises

Learn It Online
Homework Help Online
Parent Resources Online

GUIDED PRACTICE

1. **Vocabulary** You use CPCTC after proving triangles are congruent. Which parts of congruent triangles are referred to as corresponding parts?

SEE EXAMPLE 1

2. **Archaeology** An archaeologist wants to find the height AB of a rock formation. She places a marker at C and steps off the distance from C to B. Then she walks the same distance from C and places a marker at D. If $DE = 6.3$ m, what is AB?

SEE EXAMPLE 2

3. **Given:** X is the midpoint of $\overline{ST}$. $\overline{RX} \perp \overline{ST}$
Prove: $\overline{RS} \cong \overline{RT}$

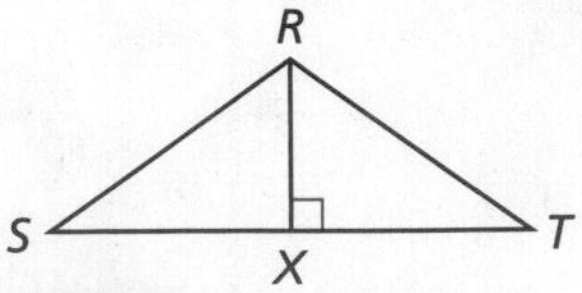

Proof:

- $\overline{RX} \perp \overline{ST}$ (Given) → $\angle RXS$ and $\angle RXT$ are rt. ∠s. (**a.** ?) → $\angle RXS \cong \angle RXT$ (**b.** ?)
- $\overline{RX} \cong \overline{RX}$ (**c.** ?)
- X is the mdpt. of $\overline{ST}$. (Given) → $\overline{SX} \cong \overline{TX}$ (**d.** ?)
- **e.** ? (SAS) → $\overline{RS} \cong \overline{RT}$ (**f.** ?)

SEE EXAMPLE 3

4. **Given:** $\overline{AC} \cong \overline{AD}$, $\overline{CB} \cong \overline{DB}$
Prove: $\overline{AB}$ bisects $\angle CAD$.

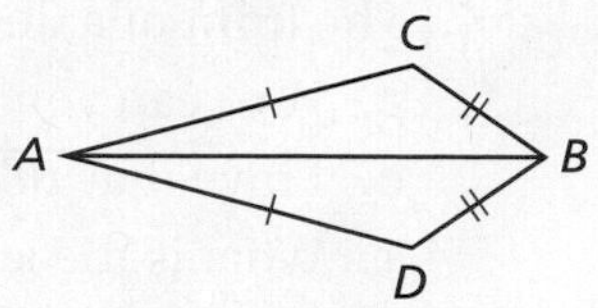

Proof:

Statements	Reasons
1. $\overline{AC} \cong \overline{AD}$, $\overline{CB} \cong \overline{DB}$	1. a. ___?___
2. b. ___?___	2. Reflex. Prop. of $\cong$
3. $\triangle ACB \cong \triangle ADB$	3. c. ___?___
4. $\angle CAB \cong \angle DAB$	4. d. ___?___
5. $\overline{AB}$ bisects $\angle CAD$	5. e. ___?___

SEE EXAMPLE 4

Multi-Step Use the given set of points to prove each congruence statement.

5. $E(-3, 3)$, $F(-1, 3)$, $G(-2, 0)$, $J(0, -1)$, $K(2, -1)$, $L(1, 2)$; $\angle EFG \cong \angle JKL$
6. $A(2, 3)$, $B(4, 1)$, $C(1, -1)$, $R(-1, 0)$, $S(-3, -2)$, $T(0, -4)$; $\angle ACB \cong \angle RTS$

PRACTICE AND PROBLEM SOLVING

Independent Practice

For Exercises	See Example
7	1
8–9	2
10–11	3
12–13	4

Extra Practice

See Extra Practice for more Skills Practice and Applications Practice exercises.

7. **Surveying** To find the distance AB across a river, a surveyor first locates point C. He measures the distance from C to B. Then he locates point D the same distance east of C. If $DE = 420$ ft, what is AB?

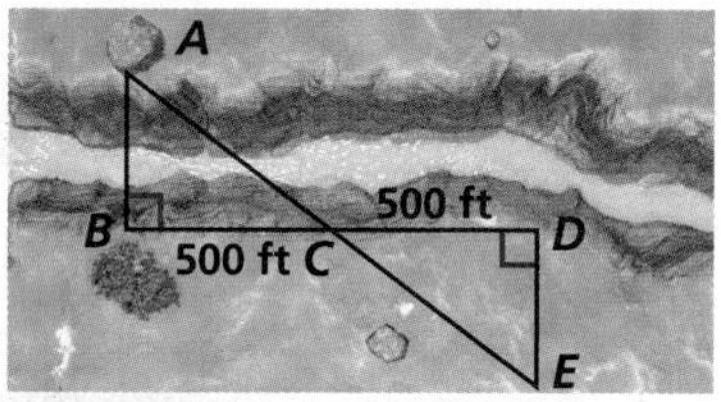

8. **Given:** M is the midpoint of $\overline{PQ}$ and $\overline{RS}$.
Prove: $\overline{QR} \cong \overline{PS}$

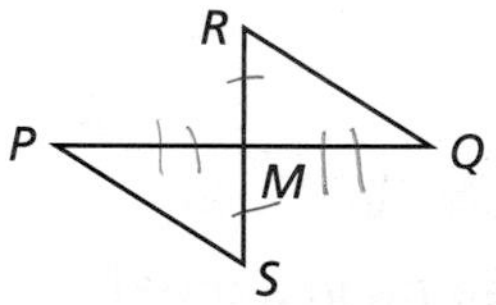

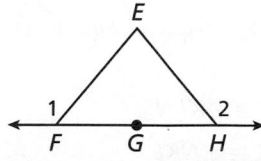

9. **Given:** $\overline{WX} \cong \overline{XY} \cong \overline{YZ} \cong \overline{ZW}$
Prove: $\angle W \cong \angle Y$

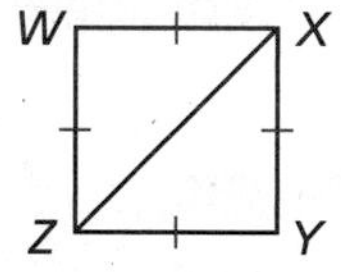

10. **Given:** G is the midpoint of $\overline{FH}$.
$\overline{EF} \cong \overline{EH}$
Prove: $\angle 1 \cong \angle 2$

11. **Given:** $\overline{LM}$ bisects $\angle JLK$. $\overline{JL} \cong \overline{KL}$
Prove: M is the midpoint of $\overline{JK}$.

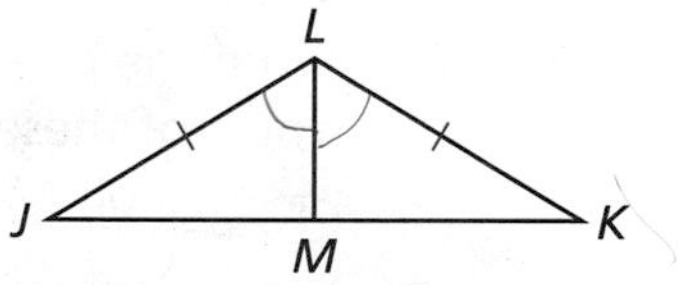

Multi-Step Use the given set of points to prove each congruence statement.

12. $R(0, 0)$, $S(2, 4)$, $T(-1, 3)$, $U(-1, 0)$, $V(-3, -4)$, $W(-4, -1)$; $\angle RST \cong \angle UVW$
13. $A(-1, 1)$, $B(2, 3)$, $C(2, -2)$, $D(2, -3)$, $E(-1, -5)$, $F(-1, 0)$; $\angle BAC \cong \angle EDF$
14. **Given:** $\triangle QRS$ is adjacent to $\triangle QTS$. $\overline{QS}$ bisects $\angle RQT$. $\angle R \cong \angle T$
Prove: $\overline{QS}$ bisects $\overline{RT}$.
15. **Given:** $\triangle ABE$ and $\triangle CDE$ with E the midpoint of $\overline{AC}$ and $\overline{BD}$
Prove: $\overline{AB} \parallel \overline{CD}$

MULTI-STEP TEST PREP

16. The front of a doghouse has the dimensions shown.
    a. How can you prove that $\triangle ADB \cong \triangle ADC$?
    b. Prove that $\overline{BD} \cong \overline{CD}$.
    c. What is the length of $\overline{BD}$ and $\overline{BC}$ to the nearest tenth?

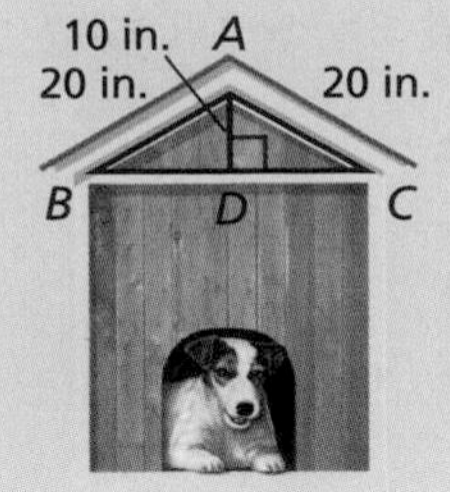

Multi-Step Find the value of *x*.

17.

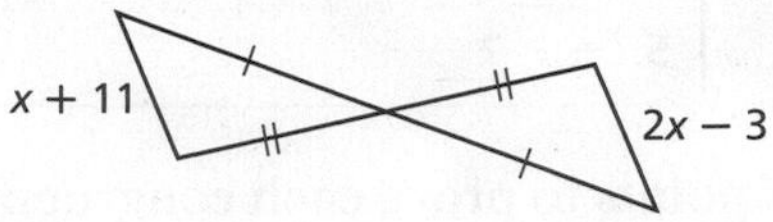

18.

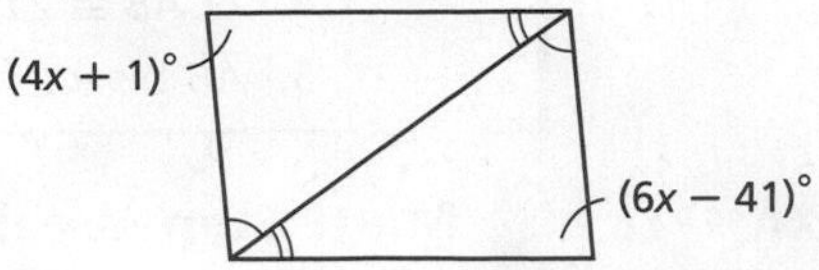

Use the diagram for Exercises 19–21.

19. **Given:** $PS = RQ$, $m\angle 1 = m\angle 4$
    Prove: $m\angle 3 = m\angle 2$

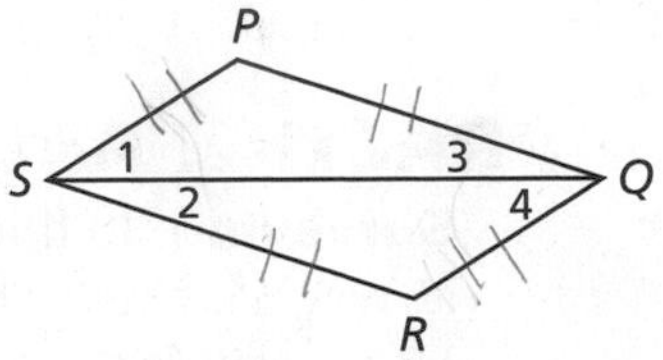

20. **Given:** $m\angle 1 = m\angle 2$, $m\angle 3 = m\angle 4$
    Prove: $PS = RS$

21. **Given:** $PS = RQ$, $PQ = RS$
    Prove: $\overline{PQ} \parallel \overline{RS}$

22. **Critical Thinking** Does the diagram contain enough information to allow you to conclude that $\overline{JK} \parallel \overline{ML}$? Explain.

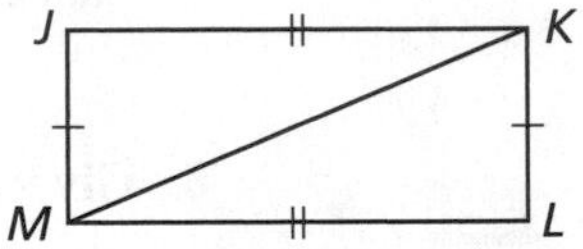

23. **Write About It** Draw a diagram and explain how a surveyor can set up triangles to find the distance across a lake. Label each part of your diagram. List which sides or angles must be congruent.

TEST PREP

24. Which of these will NOT be used as a reason in a proof of $\overline{AC} \cong \overline{AD}$?

    Ⓐ SAS　　Ⓒ ASA
    Ⓑ CPCTC　　Ⓓ Reflexive Property

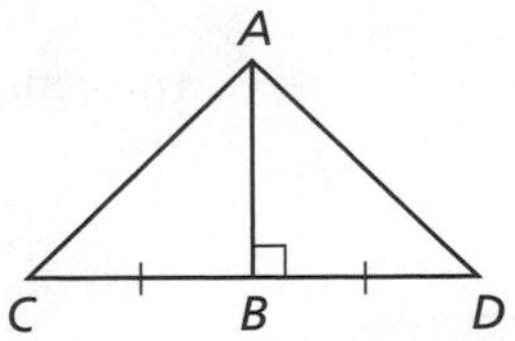

25. Given the points $K(1, 2)$, $L(0, -4)$, $M(-2, -3)$, and $N(-1, 3)$, which of these is true?

    Ⓕ $\angle KNL \cong \angle MNL$　　Ⓗ $\angle MLN \cong \angle KLN$
    Ⓖ $\angle LNK \cong \angle NLM$　　Ⓙ $\angle MNK \cong \angle NKL$

26. What is the value of *y*?

    Ⓐ 10　　Ⓒ 35
    Ⓑ 20　　Ⓓ 85

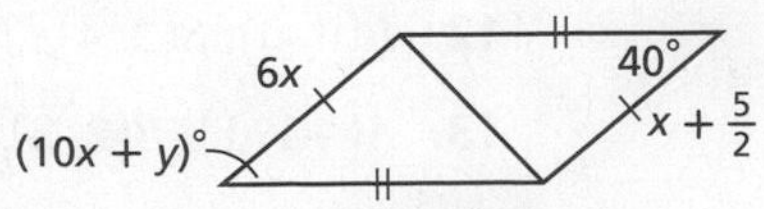

27. Which of these are NOT used to prove angles congruent?

    Ⓕ congruent triangles　　Ⓗ parallel lines
    Ⓖ noncorresponding parts　　Ⓙ perpendicular lines

28. Which set of coordinates represents the vertices of a triangle congruent to $\triangle RST$? (*Hint:* Find the lengths of the sides of $\triangle RST$.)

Ⓐ (3, 4), (3, 0), (0, 0)

Ⓑ (3, 3), (0, 4), (0, 0)

Ⓒ (3, 1), (3, 3), (4, 6)

Ⓓ (3, 0), (4, 4), (0, 6)

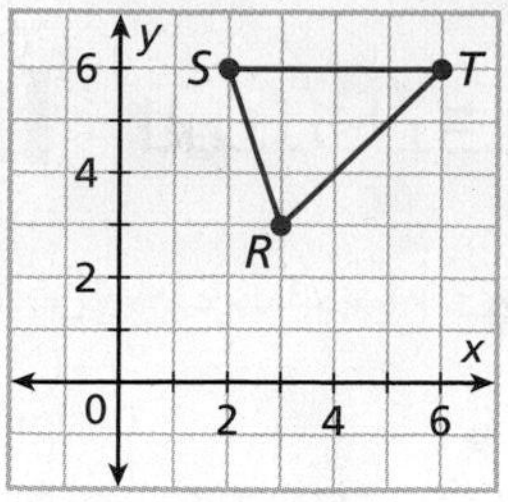

CHALLENGE AND EXTEND

29. All of the edges of a cube are congruent. All of the angles on each face of a cube are right angles. Use CPCTC to explain why any two diagonals on the faces of a cube (for example, $\overline{AC}$ and $\overline{AF}$) must be congruent.

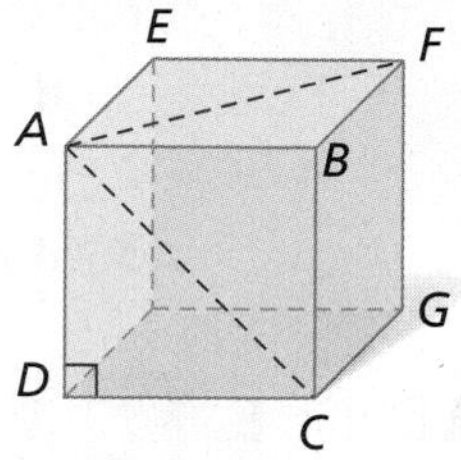

30. **Given:** $\overline{JK} \cong \overline{ML}$, $\overline{JM} \cong \overline{KL}$
Prove: $\angle J \cong \angle L$
(*Hint:* Draw an auxiliary line.)

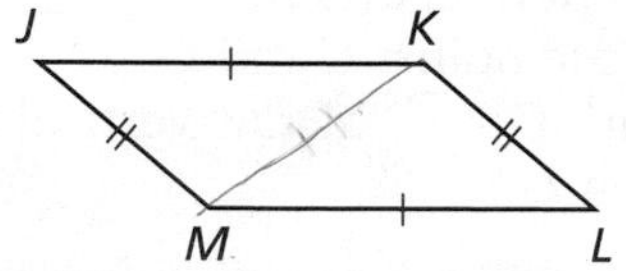

31. **Given:** R is the midpoint of $\overline{AB}$.
S is the midpoint of $\overline{DC}$.
$\overline{RS} \perp \overline{AB}$, $\angle ASD \cong \angle BSC$
Prove: $\triangle ASD \cong \triangle BSC$

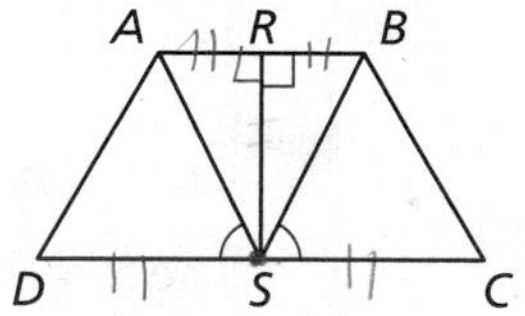

32. $\triangle ABC$ is in plane $\mathcal{M}$. $\triangle CDE$ is in plane $\mathcal{P}$. Both planes have C in common and $\angle A \cong \angle E$. What is the height AB to the nearest foot?

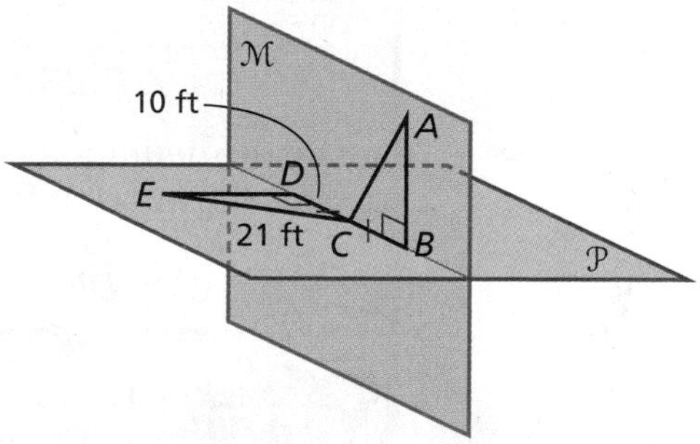

COMMON CORE

EXTENSION Lines and Slopes

CC.9-12.G.GPE.5 Prove the slope criteria for parallel and perpendicular lines and use them to solve…problems…

Objective
Prove the slope criteria for parallel and perpendicular lines.

Slopes can be used to determine if two lines in a coordinate plane are parallel or perpendicular. In this lesson, you will prove the Parallel Lines Theorem and the Perpendicular Lines Theorem. Suppose that L_1 and L_2 are two lines in the coordinate plane with slopes m_1 and m_2. The proof of the Parallel Lines Theorem can be broken into three parts:

1. If $L_1 \parallel L_2$ and L_1 and L_2 are not vertical, then $m_1 = m_2$.
2. If $m_1 = m_2$, then $L_1 \parallel L_2$.
3. If L_1 and L_2 are vertical, then $L_1 \parallel L_2$.

EXAMPLE 1 Proving the Parallel Lines Theorem

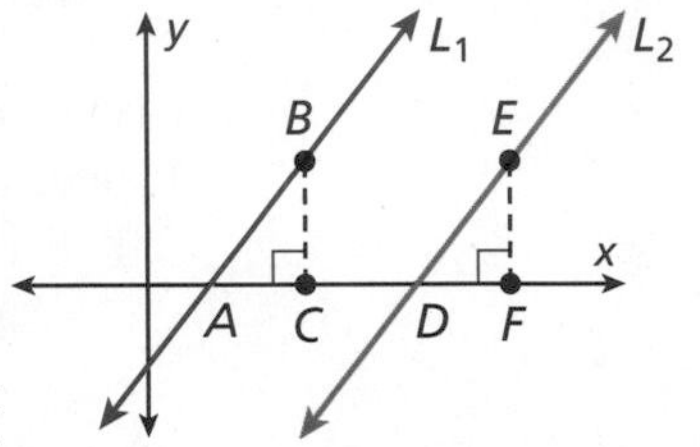

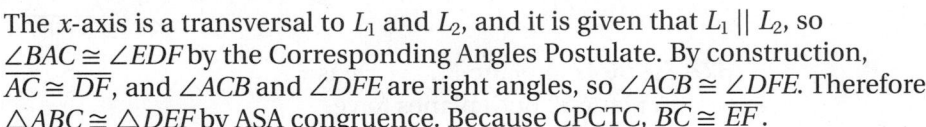

Given: $L_1 \parallel L_2$, L_1 and L_2 are not vertical
Prove: $m_1 = m_2$
Proof:

Assume that L_1 and L_2 are not horizontal. Locate point A at the x-intercept of L_1 and point D at the x-intercept of L_2. Locate points C and F on the x-axis as shown so that $\overline{AC} \cong \overline{DF}$. Draw vertical segments $\overline{BC}$ and $\overline{EF}$ such that B is on L_1 and E is on L_2.

The x-axis is a transversal to L_1 and L_2, and it is given that $L_1 \parallel L_2$, so $\angle BAC \cong \angle EDF$ by the Corresponding Angles Postulate. By construction, $\overline{AC} \cong \overline{DF}$, and $\angle ACB$ and $\angle DFE$ are right angles, so $\angle ACB \cong \angle DFE$. Therefore, $\triangle ABC \cong \triangle DEF$ by ASA congruence. Because CPCTC, $\overline{BC} \cong \overline{EF}$.

By the definition of congruent segments, $AC = DF$ and $BC = EF$. By the Substitution Property of Equality and the definition of slope, $m_1 = \frac{BC}{AC} = \frac{EF}{DF} = m_2$.

CHECK IT OUT!

1. Complete the two-column proof, using the figure in Example 1.
Given: $m_1 = m_2$
Prove: $L_1 \parallel L_2$
Proof:

Statements	Reasons
1. $m_1 = m_2$	1. ?
2. $\frac{BC}{AC} = \frac{EF}{DF}$	2. ?
3. $AC = DF$	3. By construction
4. $\frac{BC}{AC} = \frac{EF}{AC}$	4. ?
5. $BC = EF$	5. ?
6. $\angle ACB \cong \angle DFE$	6. By construction, all right angles are $\cong$
7. $\triangle ABC \cong \triangle DEF$	7. ?
8. $\angle BAC \cong \angle EDF$	8. ?
9. $L_1 \parallel L_2$	9. ?

The proof of the Perpendicular Lines Theorem can be broken into three parts:

1. If $L_1 \perp L_2$ and L_1 and L_2 are not vertical, then $m_1 m_2 = -1$.
2. If $m_1 m_2 = -1$, then $L_1 \perp L_2$.
3. If L_1 is horizontal and L_2 is vertical, then $L_1 \perp L_2$.

The third statement will be used in the proof of the second statement. Proof of the third statement is left as an exercise.

EXAMPLE 2 Proving the Perpendicular Lines

Given: $L_1 \perp L_2$, L_1 and L_2 are not vertical
Prove: $m_1 m_2 = -1$
Proof:

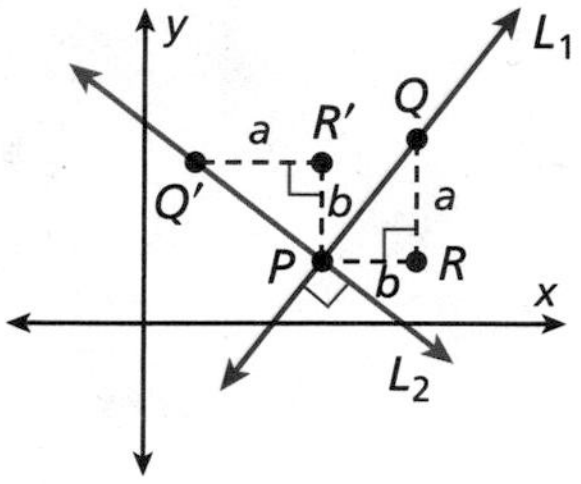

Suppose that $m_1 = \frac{a}{b}$ and that L_1 and L_2 intersect at point P. Draw a right triangle $\triangle PQR$ with side $\overline{PQ}$ on L_1, where $\overline{PR}$ is a horizontal side of length b representing the run, and $\overline{QR}$ is a vertical side of length a representing the rise.

Rotate $\triangle PQR$ by 90° counterclockwise around point P to form the image $\triangle PQ'R'$. Because $L_1 \perp L_2$, the image Q' will lie on point L_2. $\overline{PR'}$ is a 90° rotation of $\overline{PR}$, so it is vertical with length b, and $\overline{QR'}$ is a 90° rotation of $\overline{QR}$ so it is horizontal, with length a.

The slope of L_2 is $m_2 = \frac{-b}{a}$, so $m_1 m_2 = \frac{a}{b}\left(\frac{-b}{a}\right) = -1$.

CHECK IT OUT!

2. Complete the paragraph proof below.
Given: $m1 \cdot m2 = -1$
Prove: $L1 \perp L2$
Proof:

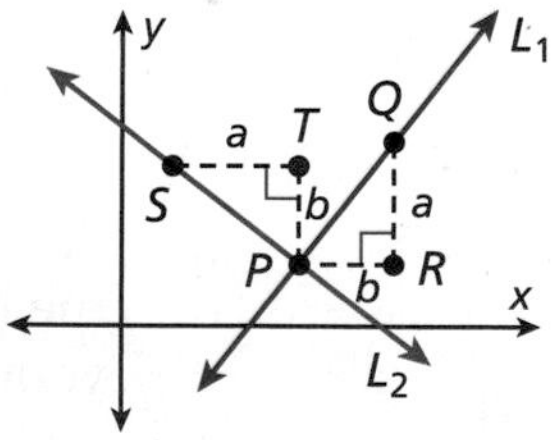

Let $m_1 = \frac{a}{b}$. Then $m_2 = -\frac{b}{a}$.
Draw PQR with sides of length a and b and a right angle at R to represent the rise and run of L_1, and $\triangle PST$ with sides of length b and a to represent the rise and run of L_2.

$\triangle PQR \cong \triangle PST$ by **a.**__?__, so $\angle QPR \cong \angle SPT$ because **b.**__?__.

$m\angle QPR = m\angle SPT$ by **c.**__?__.

By construction, $\overline{PT} \perp \overline{PR}$, so $m\angle RPT = 90°$ by the definition of perpendicular lines.

$m\angle QPT + m\angle QPR = 90°$ by **e.**__?__.

Then $m\angle QPT + m\angle SPT = 90°$ by **f.**__?__, so $m\angle SPQ = 90°$ by **g.**__?__.

$L_1 \perp L_2$ by **h.**__?__.

EXTENSION Exercises

Determine whether the lines shown are parallel, perpendicular, or neither.

1.

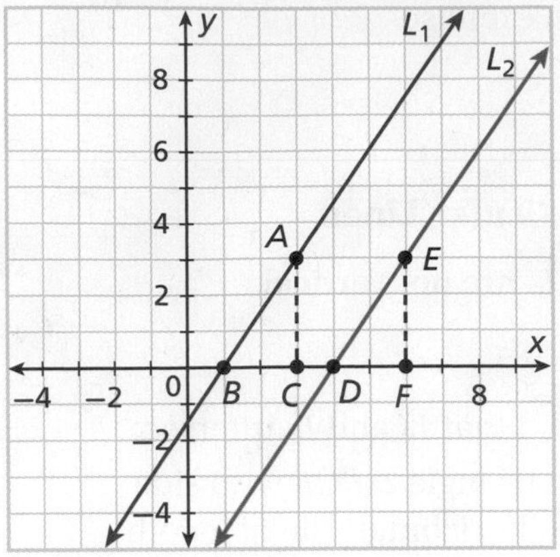

2.

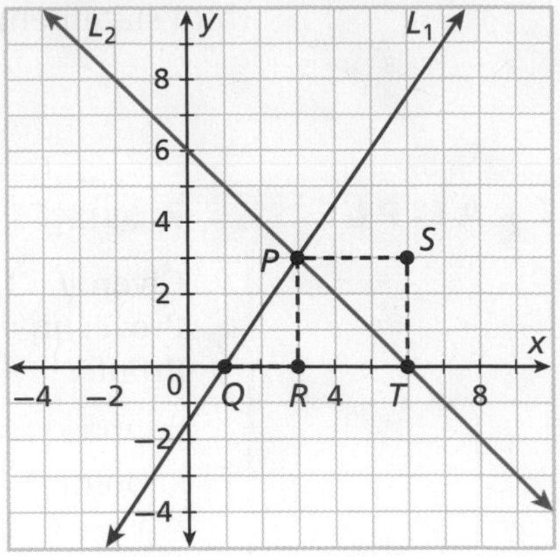

3.

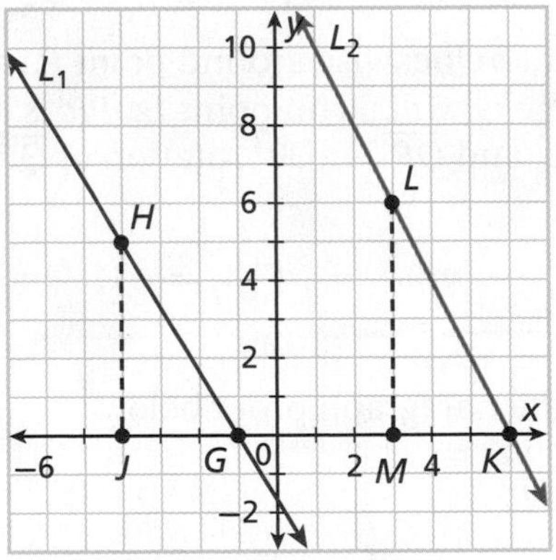

4.

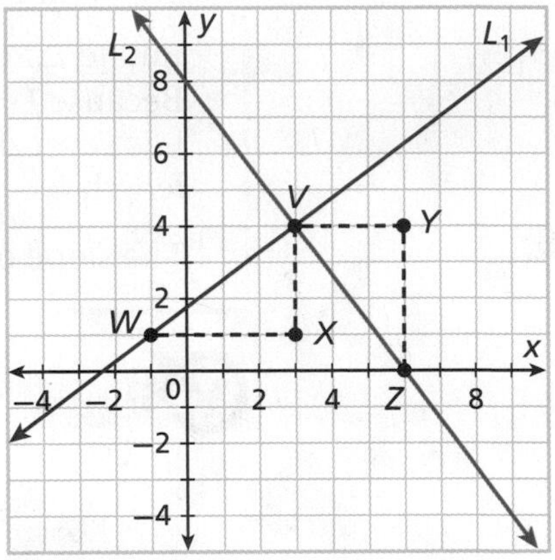

5. The coordinate plane shows two lines. Determine whether or not the lines are perpendicular. Explain your answer.

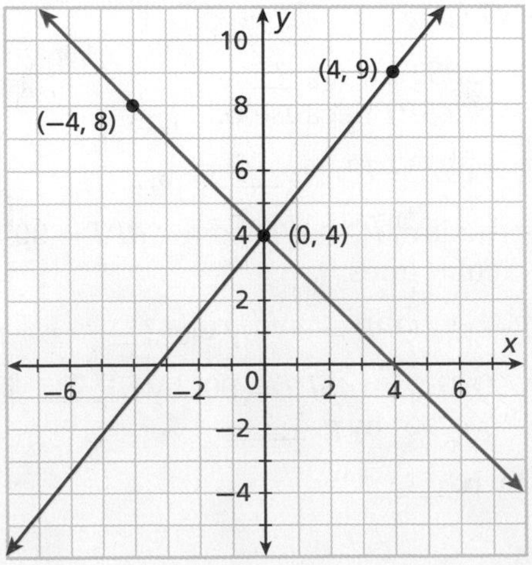

6. The coordinate plane shows two lines. Determine whether or not the lines are parallel. Explain your answer.

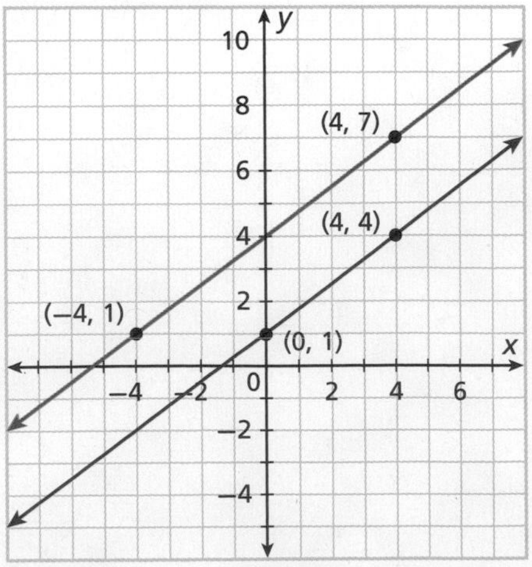

7. Find the equation of the line parallel to the line shown that passes through the point (4, 8).

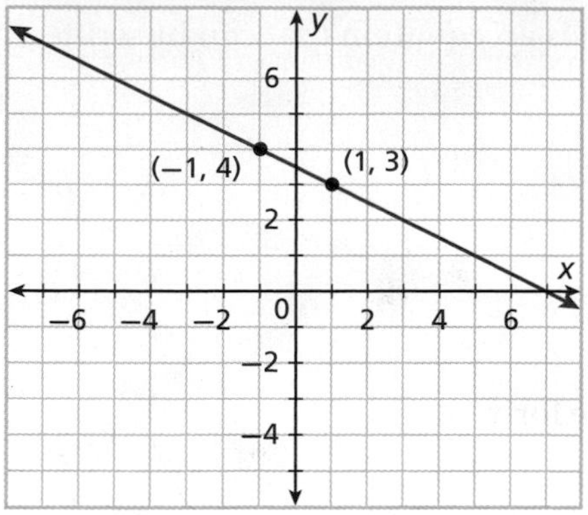

8. Find the equation of the line perpendicular to the line shown that passes through the point (–3, 1).

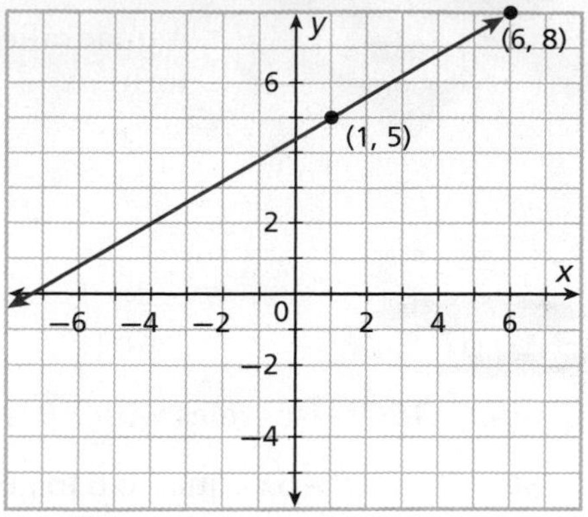

Challenge **Prove the remaining parts of the Parallel Lines Theorem and Perpendicular Lines Theorem below. You may use the reasons below in your proofs.**

- **Definition of coordinate plane: The coordinate plane is divided into four regions by two perpendicular lines, called the *x*-axis and the *y*-axis.**
- **Definition of horizontal line: A horizontal line is parallel to the *x*-axis.**
- **Definition of vertical line: A vertical line is parallel to the *y*-axis.**

9. **Given:** L_1 and L_2 with $m_1 = m_2 = 0$
Prove: $L_1 \parallel L_2$

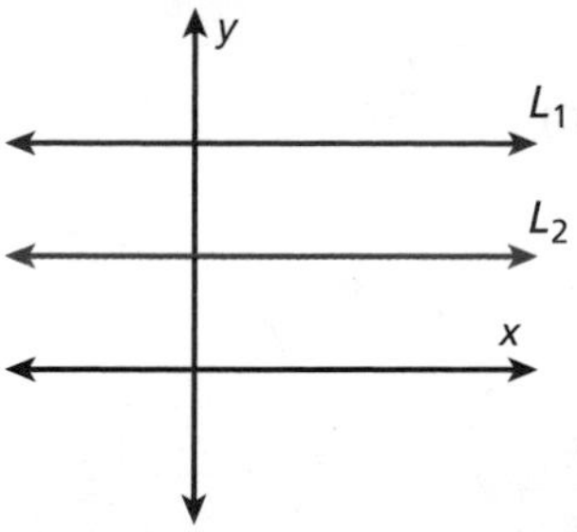

10. **Given:** L_1 and L_2 are vertical.
Prove: $L_1 \parallel L_2$

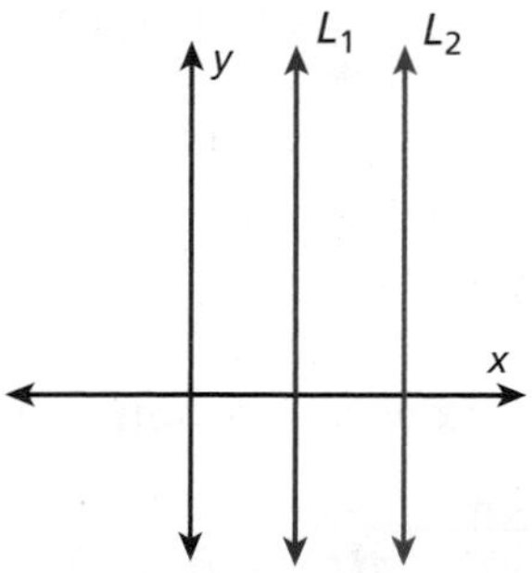

11. **Given:** L_1 is horizontal and L_2 is vertical
Prove: $L_1 \perp L_2$

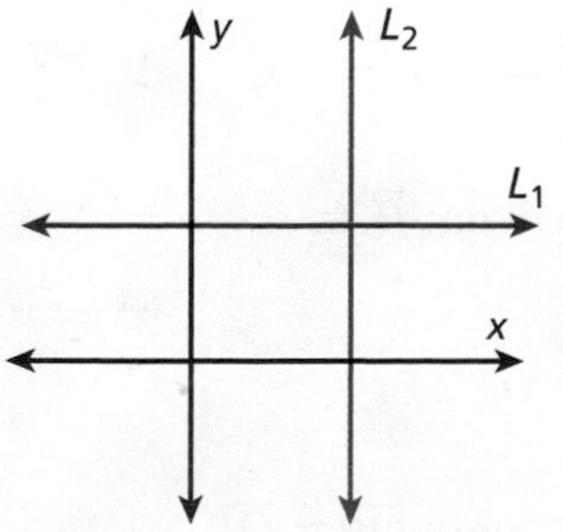

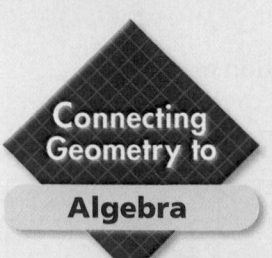

Connecting Geometry to

Algebra

Quadratic Equations

A quadratic equation is an equation that can be written in the form $ax^2 + bx + c = 0$.

Example

Given: $\triangle ABC$ is isosceles with $\overline{AB} \cong \overline{AC}$. Solve for x.

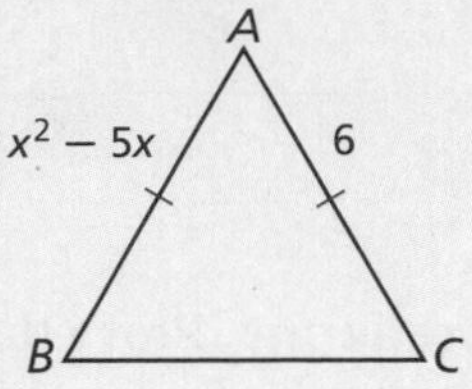

Step 1 Set $x^2 - 5x$ equal to 6 to get $x^2 - 5x = 6$.

Step 2 Rewrite the quadratic equation by subtracting 6 from each side to get $x^2 - 5x - 6 = 0$.

Step 3 Solve for x.

Method 1: Factoring		Method 2: Quadratic Formula	
$x^2 - 5x - 6 = 0$		$x = \dfrac{-b \pm \sqrt{b^2 - 4ac}}{2a}$	
$(x - 6)(x + 1) = 0$	*Factor.*	$x = \dfrac{-(-5) \pm \sqrt{(-5)^2 - 4(1)(-6)}}{2(1)}$	*Substitute 1 for a, −5 for b, and −6 for c.*
$x - 6 = 0$ or $x + 1 = 0$	*Set each factor equal to 0.*	$x = \dfrac{5 \pm \sqrt{49}}{2}$	*Simplify.*
$x = 6$ or $x = -1$	*Solve.*	$x = \dfrac{5 \pm 7}{2}$	*Find the square root.*
		$x = \dfrac{12}{2}$ or $x = \dfrac{-2}{2}$	*Simplify.*
		$x = 6$ or $x = -1$	

Step 4 Check each solution in the original equation.

$x^2 - 5x$	$= 6$
$(6)^2 - 5(6)$	6
$36 - 30$	6
6	6 ✓

$x^2 - 5x$	$= 6$
$(-1)^2 - 5(-1)$	6
$1 + 5$	6
6	6 ✓

Try This

Solve for x in each isosceles triangle.

1. **Given: $\overline{FE} \cong \overline{FG}$**

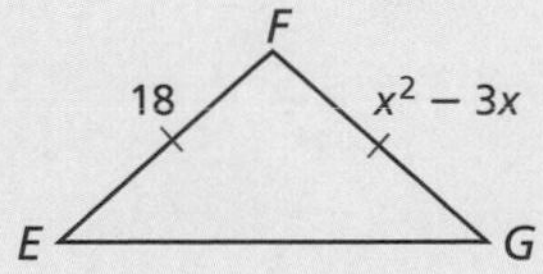

2. **Given: $\overline{JK} \cong \overline{JL}$**

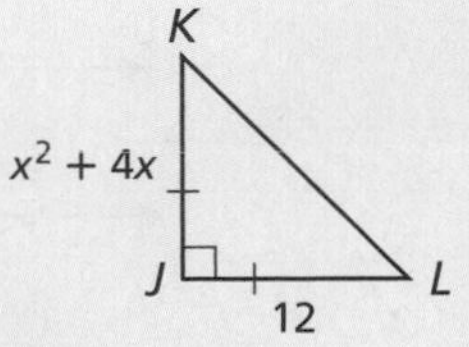

3. **Given: $\overline{YX} \cong \overline{YZ}$**

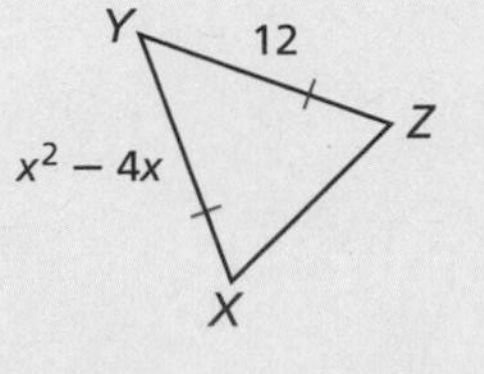

4. **Given: $\overline{QP} \cong \overline{QR}$**

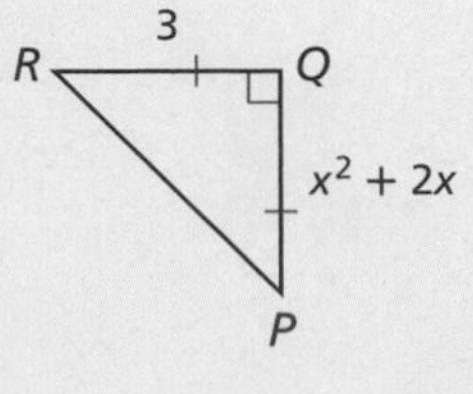

COMMON CORE

4-8 Introduction to Coordinate Proof

CC.9-12.G.GPE.4 Use coordinates to prove simple...theorems... *Also* **CC.9-12.G.GPE.7*, CC.9-12.G.MG.3***

Objectives

Position figures in the coordinate plane for use in coordinate proofs.

Prove geometric concepts by using coordinate proof.

Vocabulary

coordinate proof

Who uses this?

The Bushmen in South Africa use the Global Positioning System to transmit data about endangered animals to conservationists. (See Exercise 24.)

You have used coordinate geometry to find the midpoint of a line segment and to find the distance between two points. Coordinate geometry can also be used to prove conjectures.

A **coordinate proof** is a style of proof that uses coordinate geometry and algebra. The first step of a coordinate proof is to position the given figure in the plane. You can use any position, but some strategies can make the steps of the proof simpler.

Know it! Note

Strategies for Positioning Figures in the Coordinate Plane

- Use the origin as a vertex, keeping the figure in Quadrant I.
- Center the figure at the origin.
- Center a side of the figure at the origin.
- Use one or both axes as sides of the figure.

EXAMPLE 1 Positioning a Figure in the Coordinate Plane

Position a rectangle with a length of 8 units and a width of 3 units in the coordinate plane.

Method 1 You can center the longer side of the rectangle at the origin.

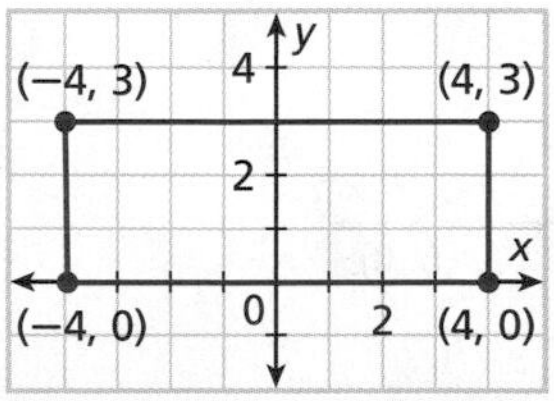

Method 2 You can use the origin as a vertex of the rectangle.

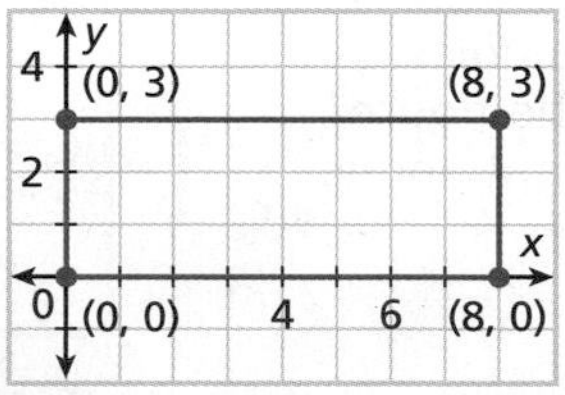

Depending on what you are using the figure to prove, one solution may be better than the other. For example, if you need to find the midpoint of the longer side, use the first solution.

CHECK IT OUT!

1. Position a right triangle with leg lengths of 2 and 4 units in the coordinate plane. (*Hint:* Use the origin as the vertex of the right angle.)

Once the figure is placed in the coordinate plane, you can use slope, the coordinates of the vertices, the Distance Formula, or the Midpoint Formula to prove statements about the figure.

EXAMPLE 2 Writing a Proof Using Coordinate Geometry

Write a coordinate proof.

Given: Right $\triangle ABC$ has vertices $A(0, 6)$, $B(0, 0)$, and $C(4, 0)$. D is the midpoint of $\overline{AC}$.

Prove: The area of $\triangle DBC$ is one half the area of $\triangle ABC$.

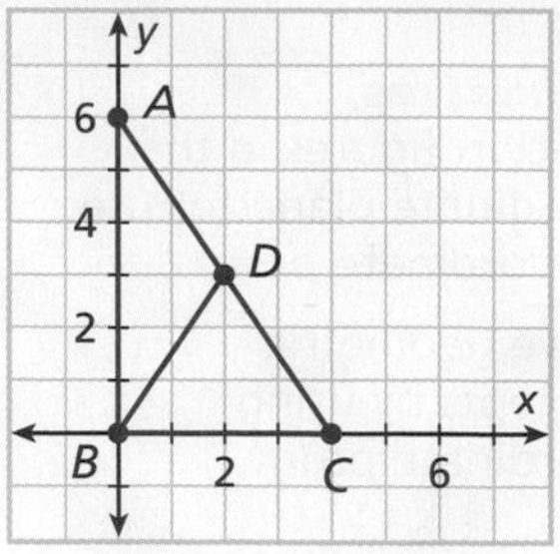

Proof: $\triangle ABC$ is a right triangle with height AB and base BC.

area of $\triangle ABC = \frac{1}{2}bh$

$= \frac{1}{2}(4)(6) = 12$ square units

By the Midpoint Formula, the coordinates of $D = \left(\frac{0+4}{2}, \frac{6+0}{2}\right) = (2, 3)$. The y-coordinate of D is the height of $\triangle DBC$, and the base is 4 units.

area of $\triangle DBC = \frac{1}{2}bh$

$= \frac{1}{2}(4)(3) = 6$ square units

Since $6 = \frac{1}{2}(12)$, the area of $\triangle DBC$ is one half the area of $\triangle ABC$.

CHECK IT OUT! **2.** Use the information in Example 2 to write a coordinate proof showing that the area of $\triangle ADB$ is one half the area of $\triangle ABC$.

A coordinate proof can also be used to prove that a certain relationship is always true. You can prove that a statement is true for all right triangles without knowing the side lengths. To do this, assign variables as the coordinates of the vertices.

EXAMPLE 3 Assigning Coordinates to Vertices

Position each figure in the coordinate plane and give the coordinates of each vertex.

Caution!

Do not use both axes when positioning a figure unless you know the figure has a right angle.

A **a right triangle with leg lengths a and b**

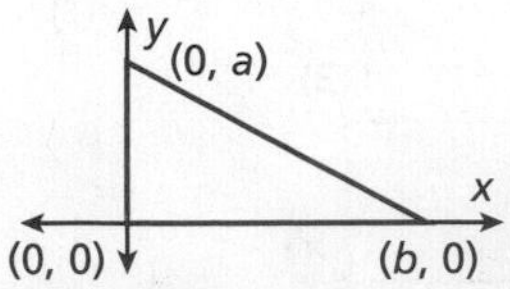

B **a rectangle with length c and width d**

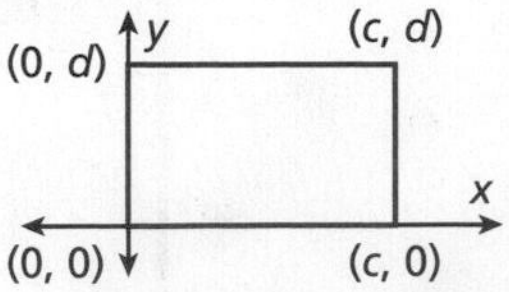

CHECK IT OUT! **3.** Position a square with side length $4p$ in the coordinate plane and give the coordinates of each vertex.

If a coordinate proof requires calculations with fractions, choose coordinates that make the calculations simpler. For example, use multiples of 2 when you are to find coordinates of a midpoint. Once you have assigned the coordinates of the vertices, the procedure for the proof is the same, except that your calculations will involve variables.

EXAMPLE 4 Writing a Coordinate Proof

Given: $\angle B$ is a right angle in $\triangle ABC$. D is the midpoint of $\overline{AC}$.
Prove: The area of $\triangle DBC$ is one half the area of $\triangle ABC$.

Step 1 Assign coordinates to each vertex.
The coordinates of A are $(0, 2j)$,
the coordinates of B are $(0, 0)$,
and the coordinates of C are $(2n, 0)$.

Since you will use the Midpoint Formula to find the coordinates of D, use multiples of 2 for the leg lengths.

Step 2 Position the figure in the coordinate plane.

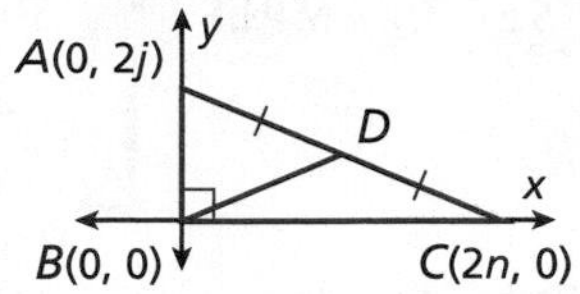

Step 3 Write a coordinate proof.

Proof: $\triangle ABC$ is a right triangle with height $2j$ and base $2n$.

$$\text{area of } \triangle ABC = \frac{1}{2}bh$$
$$= \frac{1}{2}(2n)(2j)$$
$$= 2nj \text{ square units}$$

By the Midpoint Formula, the coordinates of $D = \left(\frac{0+2n}{2}, \frac{2j+0}{2}\right) = (n, j)$.

The height of $\triangle DBC$ is j units, and the base is $2n$ units.

$$\text{area of } \triangle DBC = \frac{1}{2}bh$$
$$= \frac{1}{2}(2n)(j)$$
$$= nj \text{ square units}$$

Since $nj = \frac{1}{2}(2nj)$, the area of $\triangle DBC$ is one half the area of $\triangle ABC$.

Remember!
Because the x- and y-axes intersect at right angles, they can be used to form the sides of a right triangle.

CHECK IT OUT!
4. Use the information in Example 4 to write a coordinate proof showing that the area of $\triangle ADB$ is one half the area of $\triangle ABC$.

THINK AND DISCUSS

MATHEMATICAL PRACTICES

1. When writing a coordinate proof why are variables used instead of numbers as coordinates for the vertices of a figure?

2. How does the way you position a figure in the coordinate plane affect your calculations in a coordinate proof?

3. Explain why it might be useful to assign $2p$ as a coordinate instead of just p.

Know it! Note

4. GET ORGANIZED Copy and complete the graphic organizer. In each row, draw an example of each strategy that might be used when positioning a figure for a coordinate proof.

Positioning Strategy	Example
Use origin as a vertex.	
Center figure at origin.	
Center side of figure at origin.	
Use axes as sides of figure.	

4-8 Exercises

Learn It Online
Homework Help Online
Parent Resources Online

GUIDED PRACTICE

1. **Vocabulary** What is the relationship between *coordinate geometry*, *coordinate plane*, and *coordinate proof*?

SEE EXAMPLE 1

Position each figure in the coordinate plane.

2. a rectangle with a length of 4 units and width of 1 unit
3. a right triangle with leg lengths of 1 unit and 3 units

SEE EXAMPLE 2

Write a proof using coordinate geometry.

4. **Given:** Right $\triangle PQR$ has coordinates $P(0, 6)$, $Q(8, 0)$, and $R(0, 0)$. A is the midpoint of $\overline{PR}$. B is the midpoint of $\overline{QR}$.
   Prove: $AB = \frac{1}{2}PQ$

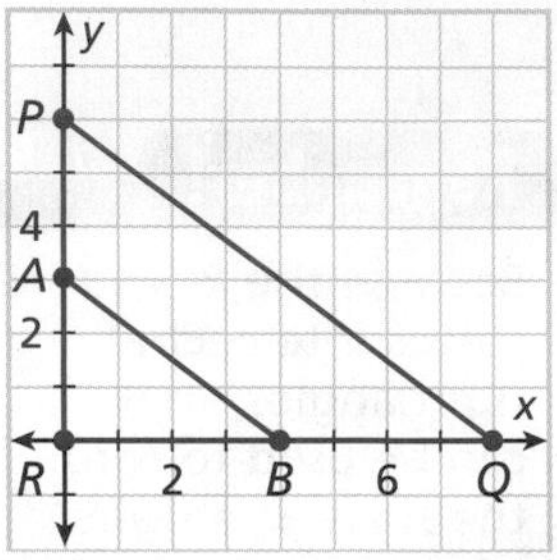

SEE EXAMPLE 3

Position each figure in the coordinate plane and give the coordinates of each vertex.

5. a right triangle with leg lengths m and n
6. a rectangle with length a and width b

SEE EXAMPLE 4

Multi-Step **Assign coordinates to each vertex and write a coordinate proof.**

7. **Given:** $\angle R$ is a right angle in $\triangle PQR$. A is the midpoint of $\overline{PR}$. B is the midpoint of $\overline{QR}$.
   Prove: $AB = \frac{1}{2}PQ$

PRACTICE AND PROBLEM SOLVING

Independent Practice

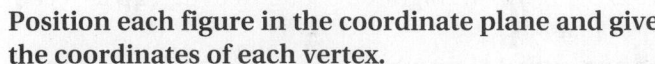

For Exercises	See Example
8–9	1
10	2
11–12	3
13	4

Extra Practice

See Extra Practice for more Skills Practice and Applications Practice exercises.

Position each figure in the coordinate plane.

8. a square with side lengths of 2 units
9. a right triangle with leg lengths of 1 unit and 5 units

Write a proof using coordinate geometry.

10. **Given:** Rectangle $ABCD$ has coordinates $A(0, 0)$, $B(0, 10)$, $C(6, 10)$, and $D(6, 0)$. E is the midpoint of $\overline{AB}$, and F is the midpoint of $\overline{CD}$.
    Prove: $EF = BC$

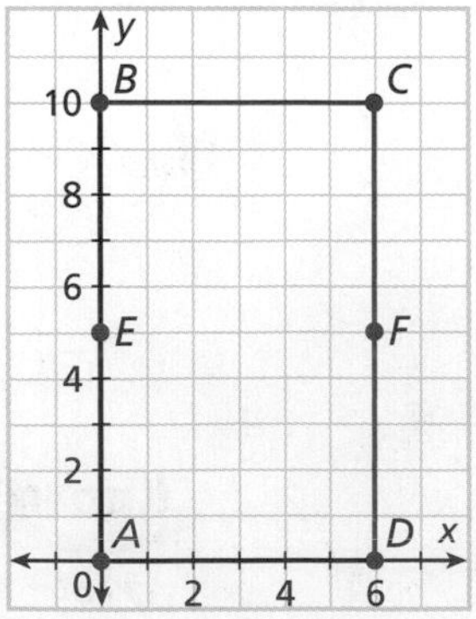

Position each figure in the coordinate plane and give the coordinates of each vertex.

11. a square with side length $2m$
12. a rectangle with dimensions x and $3x$

Multi-Step **Assign coordinates to each vertex and write a coordinate proof.**

13. **Given:** E is the midpoint of $\overline{AB}$ in rectangle $ABCD$. F is the midpoint of $\overline{CD}$.
    Prove: $EF = AD$
14. **Critical Thinking** Use variables to write the general form of the endpoints of a segment whose midpoint is $(0, 0)$.

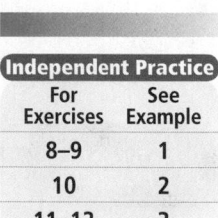

15. **Recreation** A hiking trail begins at $E(0, 0)$. Bryan hikes from the start of the trail to a waterfall at $W(3, 3)$ and then makes a 90° turn to a campsite at $C(6, 0)$.
   a. Draw Bryan's route in the coordinate plane.
   b. If one grid unit represents 1 mile, what is the total distance Bryan hiked? Round to the nearest tenth.

Find the perimeter and area of each figure.

16. a right triangle with leg lengths of a and $2a$ units

17. a rectangle with dimensions s and t units

Find the missing coordinates for each figure.

18.

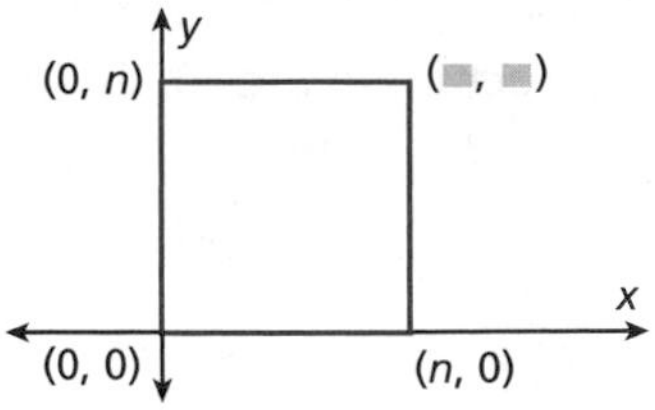

19.

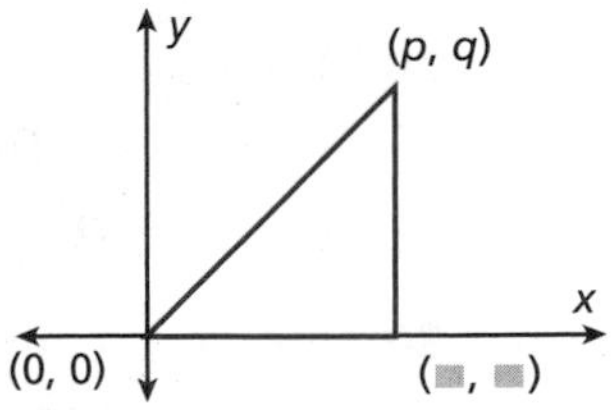

LINK
Conservation

The origin of the springbok's name may come from its habit of *pronking*, or bouncing. When pronking, a springbok can leap up to 13 feet in the air. Springboks can run up to 53 miles per hour.

20. **Conservation** The Bushmen have sighted animals at the following coordinates: $(-25, 31.5)$, $(-23.2, 31.4)$, and $(-24, 31.1)$. Prove that the distance between two of these locations is approximately twice the distance between two other.

21. **Navigation** Two ships depart from a port at $P(20, 10)$. The first ship travels to a location at $A(-30, 50)$, and the second ship travels to a location at $B(70, -30)$. Each unit represents one nautical mile. Find the distance to the nearest nautical mile between the two ships. Verify that the port is at the midpoint between the two.

Write a coordinate proof.

22. **Given:** Rectangle $PQRS$ has coordinates $P(0, 2)$, $Q(3, 2)$, $R(3, 0)$, and $S(0, 0)$. $\overline{PR}$ and $\overline{QS}$ intersect at $T(1.5, 1)$.
    Prove: The area of $\triangle RST$ is $\frac{1}{4}$ of the area of the rectangle.

23. **Given:** $A(x_1, y_1)$, $B(x_2, y_2)$, with midpoint $M\left(\frac{x_1 + x_2}{2}, \frac{y_1 + y_2}{2}\right)$
    Prove: $AM = \frac{1}{2}AB$

24. Plot the points on a coordinate plane and connect them to form $\triangle KLM$ and $\triangle MPK$. Write a coordinate proof.
    Given: $K(-2, 1)$, $L(-2, 3)$, $M(1, 3)$, $P(1, 1)$
    Prove: $\triangle KLM \cong \triangle MPK$

25. **Write About It** When you place two sides of a figure on the coordinate axes, what are you assuming about the figure?

MULTI-STEP TEST PREP

26. Paul designed a doghouse to fit against the side of his house. His plan consisted of a right triangle on top of a rectangle.
   a. Find BD and CE.
   b. Before building the doghouse, Paul sketched his plan on a coordinate plane. He placed A at the origin and $\overline{AB}$ on the x-axis. Find the coordinates of B, C, D, and E, assuming that each unit of the coordinate plane represents one inch.

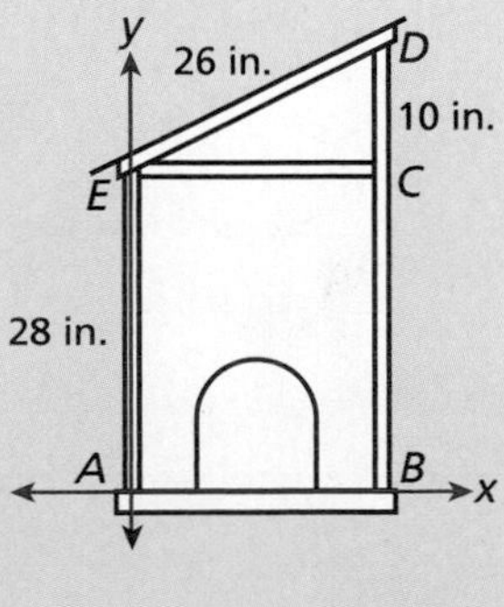

TEST PREP

27. The coordinates of the vertices of a right triangle are $(0, 0)$, $(4, 0)$, and $(0, 2)$. Which is a true statement?

Ⓐ The vertex of the right angle is at $(4, 2)$.
Ⓑ The midpoints of the two legs are at $(2, 0)$ and $(0, 1)$.
Ⓒ The hypotenuse of the triangle is $\sqrt{6}$ units.
Ⓓ The shortest side of the triangle is positioned on the *x*-axis.

28. A rectangle has dimensions of $2g$ and $2f$ units. If one vertex is at the origin, which coordinates could NOT represent another vertex?

Ⓕ $(2f, g)$ Ⓖ $(2f, 0)$ Ⓗ $(2g, 2f)$ Ⓙ $(-2f, 2g)$

29. The coordinates of the vertices of a rectangle are $(0, 0)$, $(a, 0)$, (a, b), and $(0, b)$. What is the perimeter of the rectangle?

Ⓐ $a + b$ Ⓑ ab Ⓒ $\frac{1}{2}ab$ Ⓓ $2a + 2b$

30. A coordinate grid is placed over a map. City A is located at $(-1, 2)$ and city C is located at $(3, 5)$. If city C is at the midpoint between city A and city B, what are the coordinates of city B?

Ⓕ $(1, 3.5)$ Ⓖ $(-5, -1)$ Ⓗ $(7, 8)$ Ⓙ $(2, 7)$

CHALLENGE AND EXTEND

Find the missing coordinates for each figure.

31.

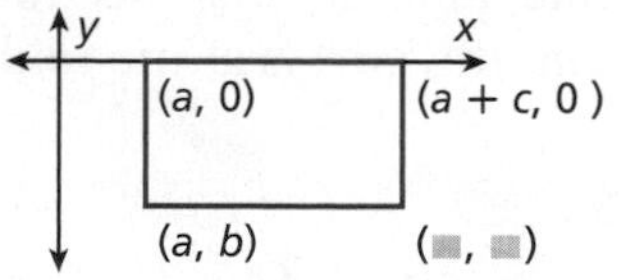

32.

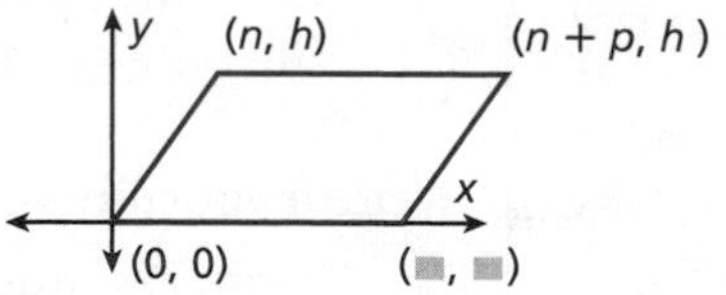

33. The vertices of a right triangle are at $(-2s, 2s)$, $(0, 2s)$, and $(0, 0)$. What coordinates could be used so that a coordinate proof would be easier to complete?

34. Rectangle $ABCD$ has dimensions of $2f$ and $2g$ units. The equation of the line containing $\overline{BD}$ is $y = \frac{g}{f}x$, and the equation of the line containing $\overline{AC}$ is $y = -\frac{g}{f}x + 2g$. Use algebra to show that the coordinates of E are (f, g).

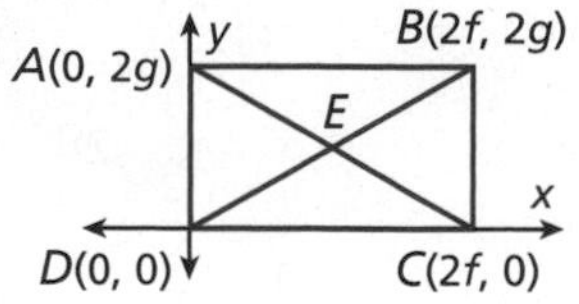

COMMON CORE

4-9 Isosceles and Equilateral Triangles

CC.9-12.G.CO.10 Prove theorems about triangles.

Objectives

Prove theorems about isosceles and equilateral triangles.

Apply properties of isosceles and equilateral triangles.

Vocabulary

legs of an isosceles triangle
vertex angle
base
base angles

Who uses this?

Astronomers use geometric methods. (See Example 1.)

Recall that an isosceles triangle has at least two congruent sides. The congruent sides are called the **legs**. The **vertex angle** is the angle formed by the legs. The side opposite the vertex angle is called the **base**, and the **base angles** are the two angles that have the base as a side.

∠3 is the vertex angle.
∠1 and ∠2 are the base angles.

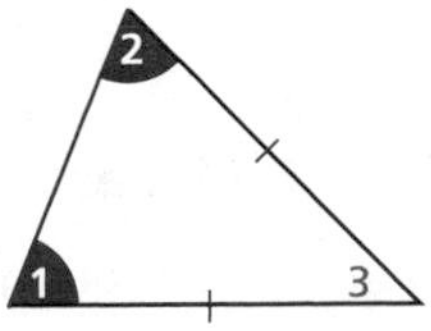

Know it! Note

Theorems Isosceles Triangle

THEOREM	HYPOTHESIS	CONCLUSION
4-9-1 **Isosceles Triangle Theorem** If two sides of a triangle are congruent, then the angles opposite the sides are congruent.	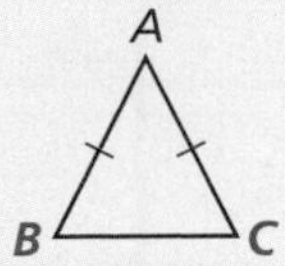	$\angle B \cong \angle C$
4-9-2 **Converse of Isosceles Triangle Theorem** If two angles of a triangle are congruent, then the sides opposite those angles are congruent.	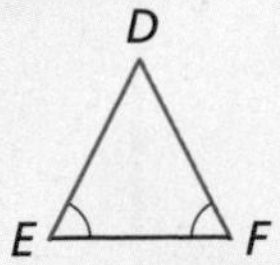	$\overline{DE} \cong \overline{DF}$

Theorem 4-9-1 is proven below. You will prove Theorem 4-9-2 in Exercise 35.

PROOF **Isosceles Triangle Theorem**

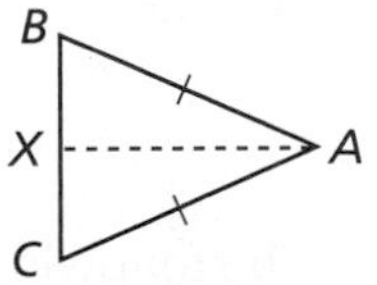

Given: $\overline{AB} \cong \overline{AC}$
Prove: $\angle B \cong \angle C$
Proof:

Statements	Reasons
1. Draw X, the mdpt. of $\overline{BC}$.	**1.** Every seg. has a unique mdpt.
2. Draw the auxiliary line $\overline{AX}$.	**2.** Through two pts. there is exactly one line.
3. $\overline{BX} \cong \overline{CX}$	**3.** Def. of mdpt.
4. $\overline{AB} \cong \overline{AC}$	**4.** Given
5. $\overline{AX} \cong \overline{AX}$	**5.** Reflex. Prop. of ≅
6. $\triangle ABX \cong \triangle ACX$	**6.** SSS *Steps 3, 4, 5*
7. $\angle B \cong \angle C$	**7.** CPCTC

Reading Math

The Isosceles Triangle Theorem is sometimes stated as "Base angles of an isosceles triangle are congruent."

EXAMPLE 1 Astronomy Application

The distance from Earth to nearby stars can be measured using the parallax method, which requires observing the positions of a star 6 months apart. If the distance *LM* to a star in July is 4.0×10^{13} km, explain why the distance *LK* to the star in January is the same. (Assume the distance from Earth to the Sun does not change.)

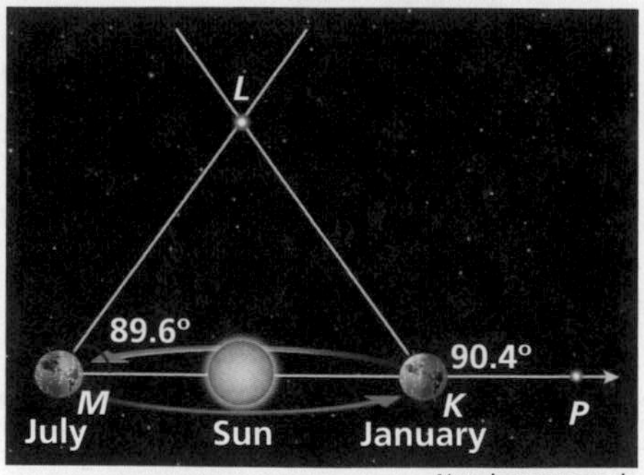

Not drawn to scale

$m\angle LKM = 180 - 90.4$, so $m\angle LKM = 89.6°$. Since $\angle LKM \cong \angle M$, $\triangle LMK$ is isosceles by the Converse of the Isosceles Triangle Theorem. Thus $LK = LM = 4.0 \times 10^{13}$ km.

CHECK IT OUT! 1. If the distance from Earth to a star in September is 4.2×10^{13} km, what is the distance from Earth to the star in March? Explain.

EXAMPLE 2 Finding the Measure of an Angle

Algebra

Find each angle measure.

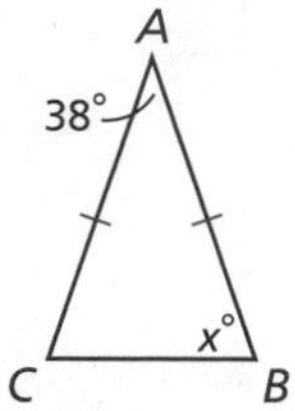

A $m\angle C$

$m\angle C = m\angle B = x°$ — *Isosc. △ Thm.*

$m\angle C + m\angle B + m\angle A = 180$ — *△ Sum Thm.*

$x + x + 38 = 180$ — *Substitute the given values.*

$2x = 142$ — *Simplify and subtract 38 from both sides.*

$x = 71$ — *Divide both sides by 2.*

Thus $m\angle C = 71°$.

B $m\angle S$

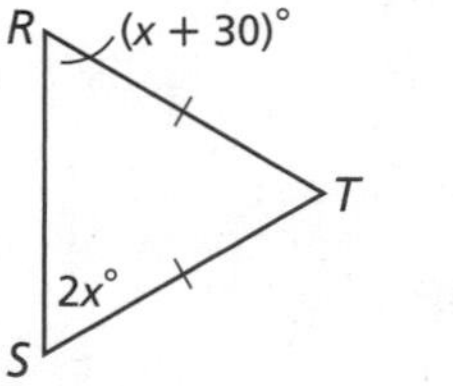

$m\angle S = m\angle R$ — *Isosc. △ Thm.*

$2x° = (x + 30)°$ — *Substitute the given values.*

$x = 30$ — *Subtract x from both sides.*

Thus $m\angle S = 2x° = 2(30) = 60°$.

CHECK IT OUT! **Find each angle measure.**

2a. $m\angle H$ **2b.** $m\angle N$

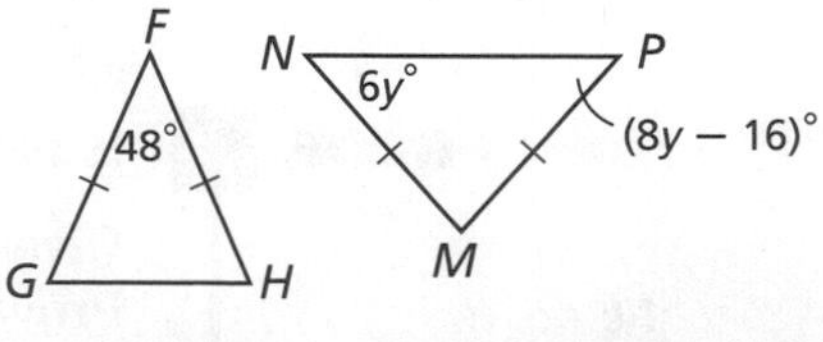

The following corollary and its converse show the connection between equilateral triangles and equiangular triangles.

Know it! Note

Corollary 4-9-3 Equilateral Triangle

COROLLARY	HYPOTHESIS	CONCLUSION
If a triangle is equilateral, then it is equiangular. (equilateral △ → equiangular △)	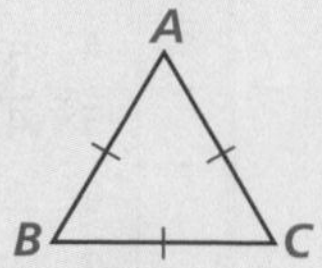	$\angle A \cong \angle B \cong \angle C$

You will prove Corollary 4-9-3 in Exercise 36.

Know it! Note

Corollary 4-9-4 Equiangular Triangle

COROLLARY	HYPOTHESIS	CONCLUSION
If a triangle is equiangular, then it is equilateral. (equiangular $\triangle \rightarrow$ equilateral $\triangle$)	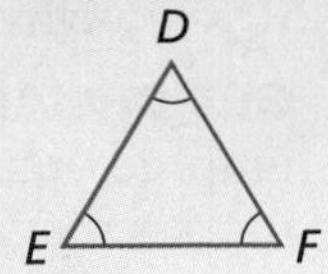	$\overline{DE} \cong \overline{DF} \cong \overline{EF}$

You will prove Corollary 4-9-4 in Exercise 37.

EXAMPLE 3 Using Properties of Equilateral Triangles

Algebra

Find each value.

A x

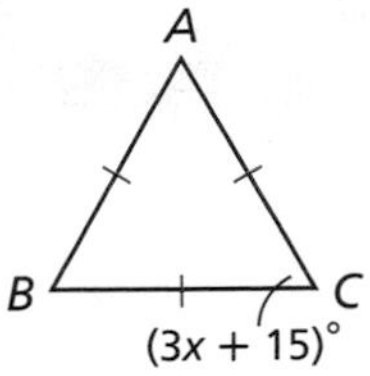

$\triangle ABC$ is equiangular.	*Equilateral $\triangle \rightarrow$ equiangular $\triangle$*
$(3x + 15)^\circ = 60^\circ$	*The measure of each $\angle$ of an equiangular $\triangle$ is 60°.*
$3x = 45$	*Subtract 15 from both sides.*
$x = 15$	*Divide both sides by 3.*

B t

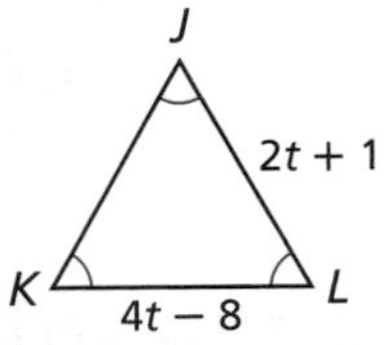

$\triangle JKL$ is equilateral.	*Equiangular $\triangle \rightarrow$ equilateral $\triangle$*
$4t - 8 = 2t + 1$	*Def. of equilateral $\triangle$*
$2t = 9$	*Subtract 2t and add 8 to both sides.*
$t = 4.5$	*Divide both sides by 2.*

CHECK IT OUT! **3.** Use the diagram to find JL.

EXAMPLE 4 Using Coordinate Proof

Remember!

A coordinate proof may be easier if you place one side of the triangle along the x-axis and locate a vertex at the origin or on the y-axis.

Prove that the triangle whose vertices are the midpoints of the sides of an isosceles triangle is also isosceles.

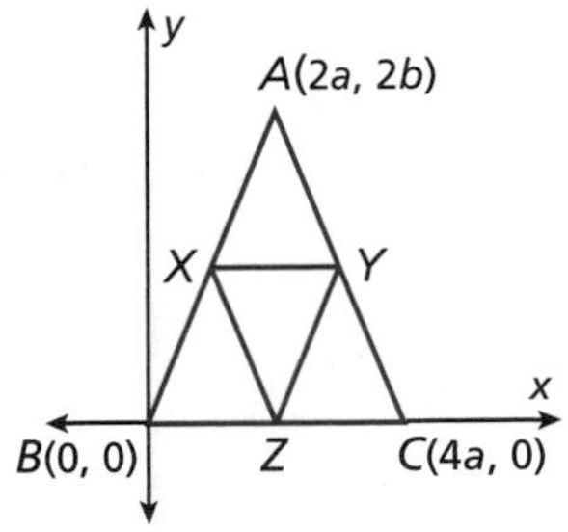

Given: $\triangle ABC$ is isosceles. X is the mdpt. of $\overline{AB}$. Y is the mdpt. of $\overline{AC}$. Z is the mdpt. of $\overline{BC}$.
Prove: $\triangle XYZ$ is isosceles.

Proof:
Draw a diagram and place the coordinates of $\triangle ABC$ and $\triangle XYZ$ as shown. By the Midpoint Formula, the coordinates of X are $\left(\frac{2a+0}{2}, \frac{2b+0}{2}\right) = (a, b)$, the coordinates of Y are $\left(\frac{2a+4a}{2}, \frac{2b+0}{2}\right) = (3a, b)$, and the coordinates of Z are $\left(\frac{4a+0}{2}, \frac{0+0}{2}\right) = (2a, 0)$.
By the Distance Formula, $XZ = \sqrt{(2a-a)^2 + (0-b)^2} = \sqrt{a^2 + b^2}$, and $YZ = \sqrt{(2a-3a)^2 + (0-b)^2} = \sqrt{a^2+b^2}$.
Since $XZ = YZ$, $\overline{XZ} \cong \overline{YZ}$ by definition. So $\triangle XYZ$ is isosceles.

CHECK IT OUT! **4. What if...?** The coordinates of $\triangle ABC$ are $A(0, 2b)$, $B(-2a, 0)$, and $C(2a, 0)$. Prove $\triangle XYZ$ is isosceles.

MATHEMATICAL PRACTICES

THINK AND DISCUSS

Know it! Note

1. Explain why each of the angles in an equilateral triangle measures 60°.
2. **GET ORGANIZED** Copy and complete the graphic organizer. In each box, draw and mark a diagram for each type of triangle.

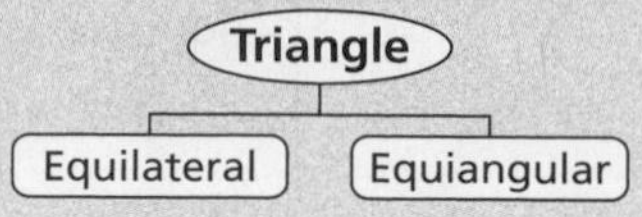

4-9 Exercises

Learn It Online
Homework Help Online
Parent Resources Online

GUIDED PRACTICE

1. **Vocabulary** Draw isosceles $\triangle JKL$ with $\angle K$ as the vertex angle. Name the legs, base, and base angles of the triangle.

SEE EXAMPLE 1

2. **Surveying** To find the distance QR across a river, a surveyor locates three points Q, R, and S. $QS = 41$ m, and $m\angle S = 35°$. The measure of exterior $\angle PQS = 70°$. Draw a diagram and explain how you can find QR.

SEE EXAMPLE 2

Find each angle measure.

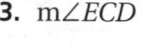

3. $m\angle ECD$

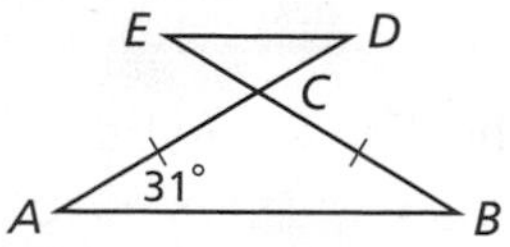

4. $m\angle K$

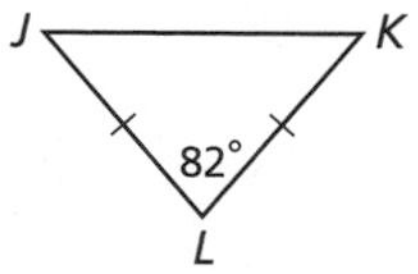

5. $m\angle X$

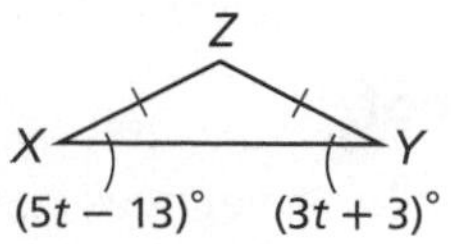

6. $m\angle A$

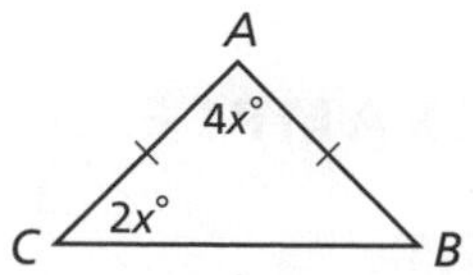

SEE EXAMPLE 3

Find each value.

7. y

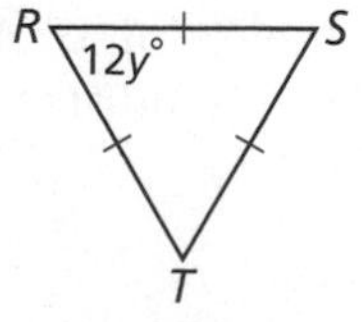

8. x

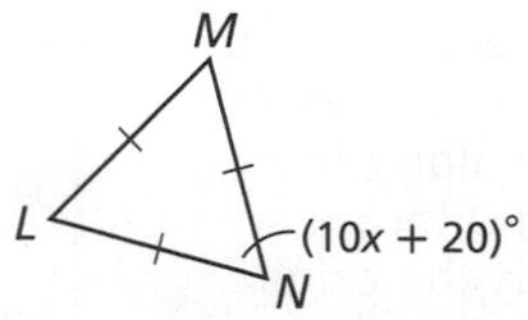

9. BC

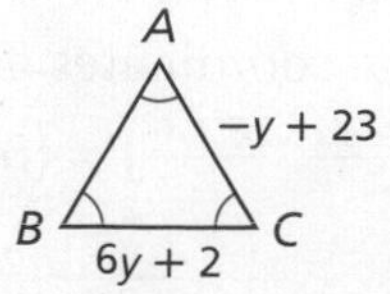

10. JK

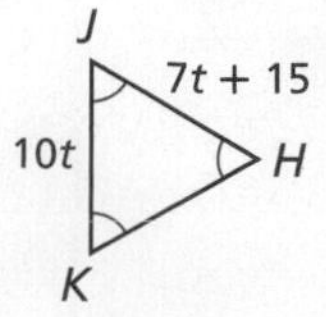

SEE EXAMPLE 4

11. **Given:** $\triangle ABC$ is right isosceles. X is the midpoint of $\overline{AC}$. $\overline{AB} \cong \overline{BC}$

    Prove: $\triangle AXB$ is isosceles.

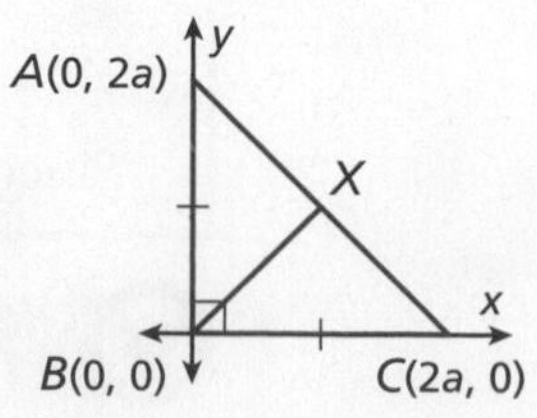

PRACTICE AND PROBLEM SOLVING

Independent Practice

For Exercises	See Example
12	1
13–16	2
17–20	3
21	4

Extra Practice

See Extra Practice for more Skills Practice and Applications Practice exercises.

12. Aviation A plane is flying parallel to the ground along $\overrightarrow{AC}$. When the plane is at A, an air-traffic controller in tower T measures the angle to the plane as 40°. After the plane has traveled 2.4 mi to B, the angle to the plane is 80°. How can you find BT?

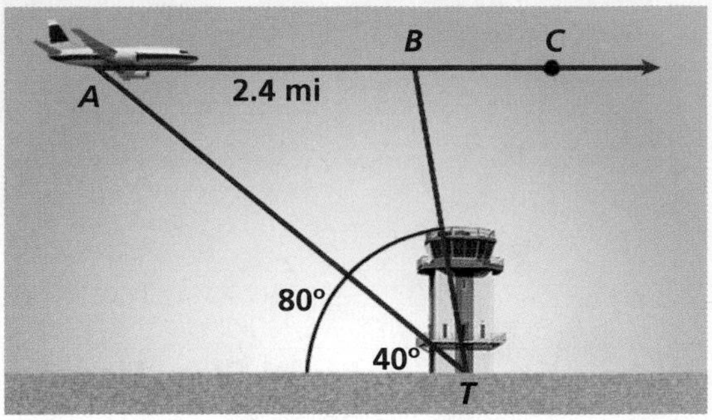

Find each angle measure.

13. $m\angle E$

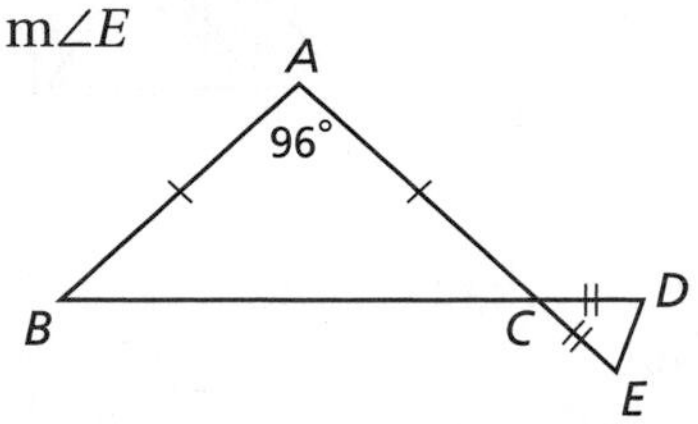

14. $m\angle TRU$

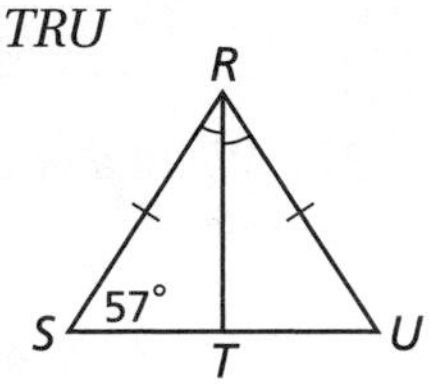

15. $m\angle F$

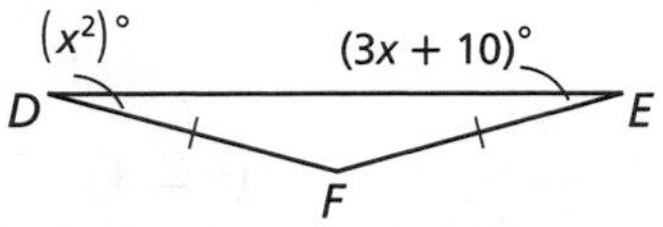

16. $m\angle A$

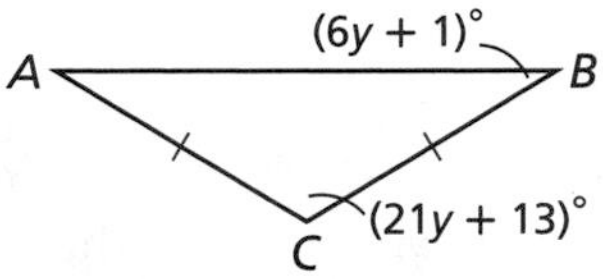

Find each value.

17. z

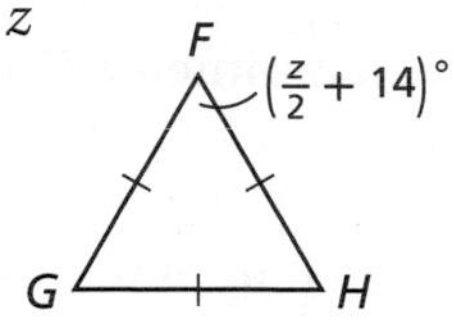

18. y

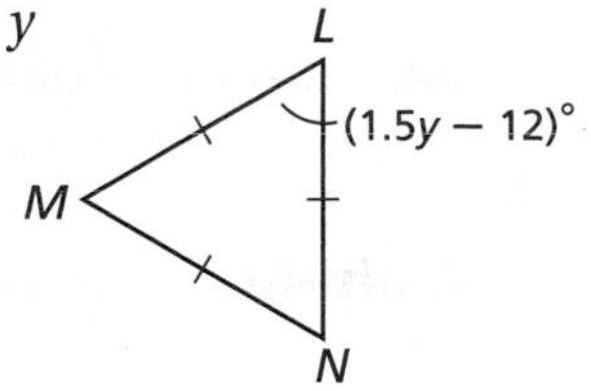

19. BC

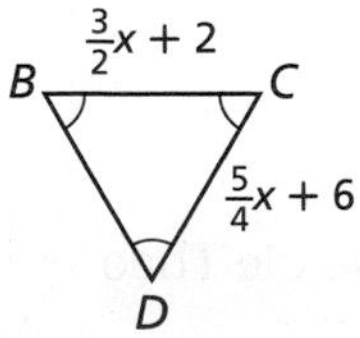

20. XZ

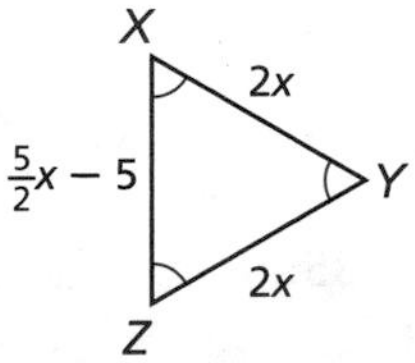

21. Given: $\triangle ABC$ is isosceles. P is the midpoint of $\overline{AB}$. Q is the midpoint of $\overline{AC}$. $\overline{AB} \cong \overline{AC}$
Prove: $\overline{PC} \cong \overline{QB}$

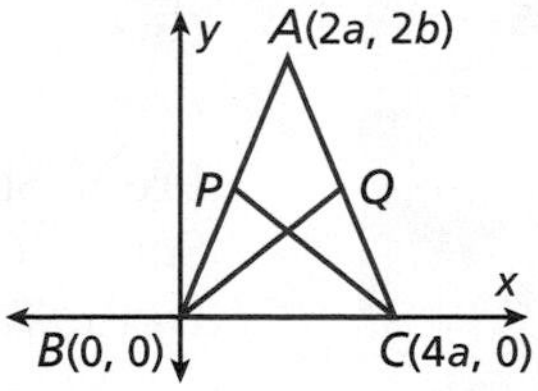

Tell whether each statement is sometimes, always, or never true. Support your answer with a sketch.

22. An equilateral triangle is an isosceles triangle.

23. The vertex angle of an isosceles triangle is congruent to the base angles.

24. An isosceles triangle is a right triangle.

25. An equilateral triangle and an obtuse triangle are congruent.

26. Critical Thinking Can a base angle of an isosceles triangle be an obtuse angle? Why or why not?

MULTI-STEP TEST PREP

27. The diagram shows the inside view of the support structure of the back of a doghouse. $\overline{PQ} \cong \overline{PR}$, $\overline{PS} \cong \overline{PT}$, $m\angle PST = 71°$, and $m\angle QPS = m\angle RPT = 18°$.

a. Find $m\angle SPT$.

b. Find $m\angle PQR$ and $m\angle PRQ$.

Multi-Step Find the measure of each numbered angle.

28.

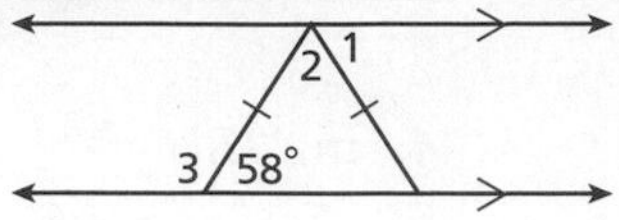

29.

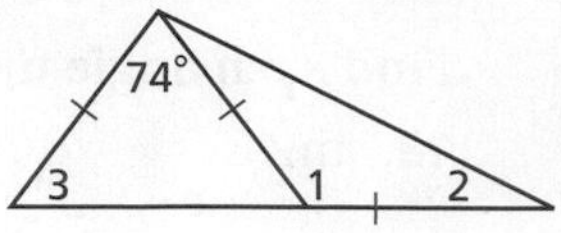

30. Write a coordinate proof.

Given: $\angle B$ is a right angle in isosceles right $\triangle ABC$. X is the midpoint of $\overline{AC}$. $\overline{BA} \cong \overline{BC}$

Prove: $\triangle AXB \cong \triangle CXB$

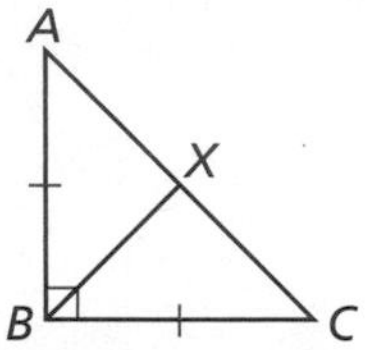

31. Estimation Draw the figure formed by $(-2, 1)$, $(5, 5)$, and $(-1, -7)$. Estimate the measure of each angle and make a conjecture about the classification of the figure. Then use a protractor to measure each angle. Was your conjecture correct? Why or why not?

32. How many different isosceles triangles have a perimeter of 18 and sides whose lengths are natural numbers? Explain.

Multi-Step Find the value of the variable in each diagram.

33.

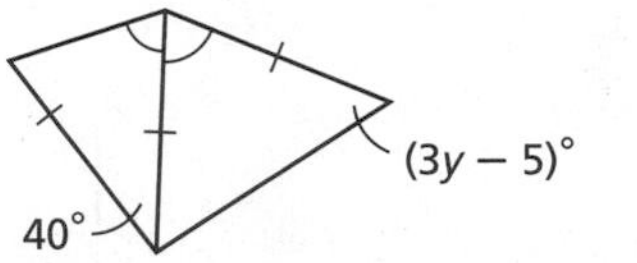

34.

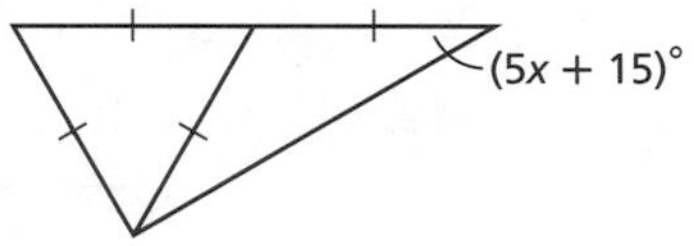

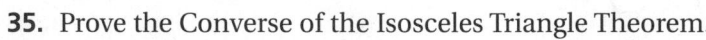

35. Prove the Converse of the Isosceles Triangle Theorem.

36. Complete the proof of Corollary 4-9-3.

Given: $\overline{AB} \cong \overline{AC} \cong \overline{BC}$

Prove: $\angle A \cong \angle B \cong \angle C$

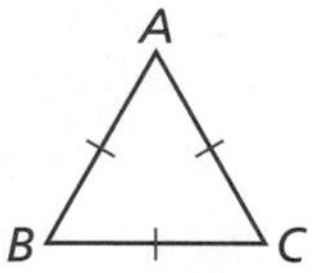

Proof: Since $\overline{AB} \cong \overline{AC}$, **a.** ___?___ by the Isosceles Triangle Theorem. Since $\overline{AC} \cong \overline{BC}$, $\angle A \cong \angle B$ by **b.** ___?___ . Therefore $\angle A \cong \angle C$ by **c.** ___?___ . By the Transitive Property of $\cong$, $\angle A \cong \angle B \cong \angle C$.

37. Prove Corollary 4-9-4.

LINK

Navigation

The taffrail log is dragged from the stern of a vessel to measure the speed or distance traveled during a voyage. The log consists of a rotator, recording device, and governor.

38. Navigation The captain of a ship traveling along $\overrightarrow{AB}$ sights an island C at an angle of 45°. The captain measures the distance the ship covers until it reaches B, where the angle to the island is 90°. Explain how to find the distance BC to the island.

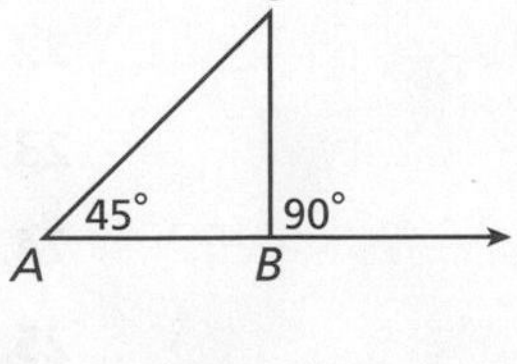

39. Given: $\triangle ABC \cong \triangle CBA$

Prove: $\triangle ABC$ is isosceles.

40. Write About It Write the Isosceles Triangle Theorem and its converse as a biconditional.

41. Rewrite the paragraph proof of the Hypotenuse-Leg (HL) Congruence Theorem as a two-column proof.

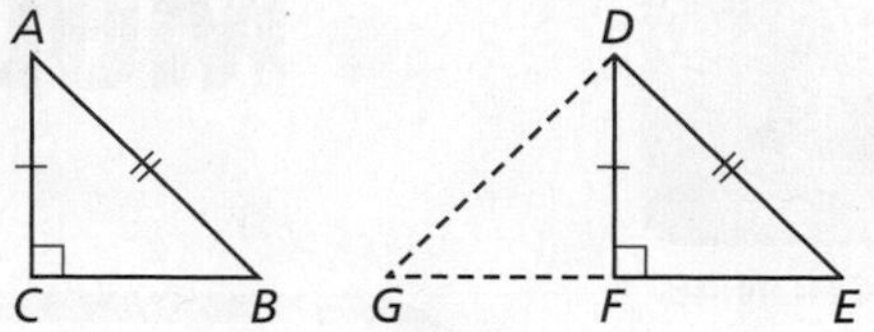

Given: $\triangle ABC$ and $\triangle DEF$ are right triangles.
$\angle C$ and $\angle F$ are right angles.
$\overline{AC} \cong \overline{DF}$, and $\overline{AB} \cong \overline{DE}$.

Prove: $\triangle ABC \cong \triangle DEF$

Proof: On $\triangle DEF$ draw $\overrightarrow{EF}$. Mark G so that $FG = CB$. Thus $\overline{FG} \cong \overline{CB}$. From the diagram, $\overline{AC} \cong \overline{DF}$ and $\angle C$ and $\angle F$ are right angles. $\overline{DF} \perp \overline{EG}$ by definition of perpendicular lines. Thus $\angle DFG$ is a right angle, and $\angle DFG \cong \angle C$. $\triangle ABC \cong \triangle DGF$ by SAS. $\overline{DG} \cong \overline{AB}$ by CPCTC. $\overline{AB} \cong \overline{DE}$ as given. $\overline{DG} \cong \overline{DE}$ by the Transitive Property. By the Isosceles Triangle Theorem $\angle G \cong \angle E$. $\angle DFG \cong \angle DFE$ since right angles are congruent. So $\triangle DGF \cong \triangle DEF$ by AAS. Therefore $\triangle ABC \cong \triangle DEF$ by the Transitive Property.

TEST PREP

42. Lorena is designing a window so that $\angle R$, $\angle S$, $\angle T$, and $\angle U$ are right angles, $\overline{VU} \cong \overline{VT}$, and $m\angle UVT = 20°$. What is $m\angle RUV$?

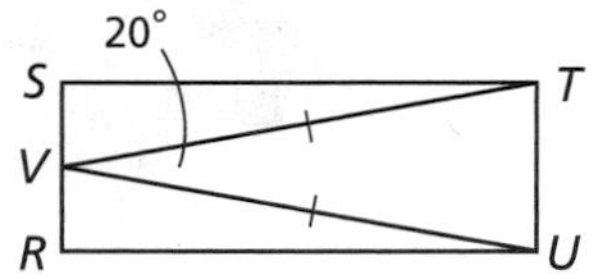

Ⓐ 10°
Ⓑ 70°
Ⓒ 20°
Ⓓ 80°

43. Which of these values of y makes $\triangle ABC$ isosceles?

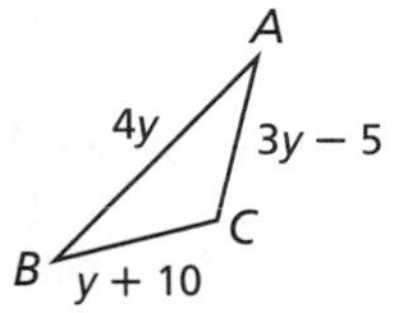

Ⓕ $1\frac{1}{4}$
Ⓖ $2\frac{1}{2}$
Ⓗ $7\frac{1}{2}$
Ⓙ $15\frac{1}{2}$

44. Gridded Response The vertex angle of an isosceles triangle measures $(6t - 9)°$, and one of the base angles measures $(4t)°$. Find t.

CHALLENGE AND EXTEND

45. In the figure, $\overline{JK} \cong \overline{JL}$, and $\overline{KM} \cong \overline{KL}$. Let $m\angle J = x°$. Prove $m\angle MKL$ must also be $x°$.

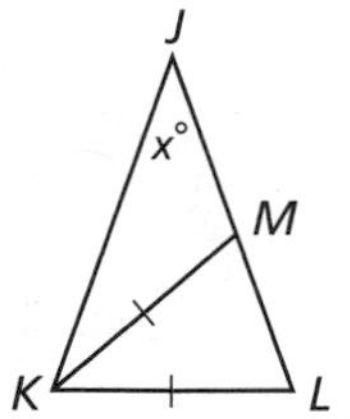

46. An equilateral $\triangle ABC$ is placed on a coordinate plane. Each side length measures $2a$. B is at the origin, and C is at $(2a, 0)$. Find the coordinates of A.

47. An isosceles triangle has coordinates $A(0, 0)$ and $B(a, b)$. What are all possible coordinates of the third vertex?

CHAPTER 4

MULTI-STEP TEST PREP

SECTION 4B

MATHEMATICAL PRACTICES **Reason abstractly and quantitatively.**

Proving Triangles Congruent

Gone to the Dogs You are planning to build a doghouse for your dog. The pitched roof of the doghouse will be supported by four trusses. Each truss will be an isosceles triangle with the dimensions shown. To determine the materials you need to purchase and how you will construct the trusses, you must first plan carefully.

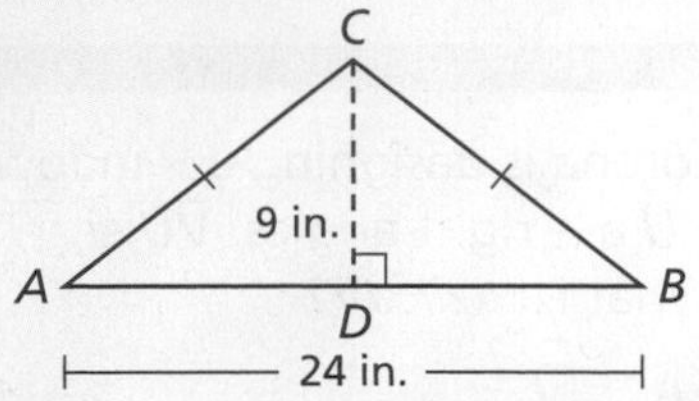

1. You want to be sure that all four trusses are exactly the same size and shape. Explain how you could measure three lengths on each truss to ensure this. Which postulate or theorem are you using?
2. Prove that the two triangular halves of the truss are congruent.
3. What can you say about $\overline{AD}$ and $\overline{DB}$? Why is this true? Use this to help you find the lengths of $\overline{AD}$, $\overline{DB}$, $\overline{AC}$, and $\overline{BC}$.
4. You want to make careful plans on a coordinate plane before you begin your construction of the trusses. Each unit of the coordinate plane represents 1 inch. How could you assign coordinates to vertices *A*, *B*, and *C*?
5. $m\angle ACB = 106°$. What is the measure of each of the acute angles in the truss? Explain how you found your answer.
6. You can buy the wood for the trusses at the building supply store for \$0.80 a foot. The store sells the wood in 6-foot lengths only. How much will you have to spend to get enough wood for the 4 trusses of the doghouse?

READY TO GO ON?

CHAPTER 4

SECTION 4B

Quiz for Lessons 4-5 Through 4-9

4-5 Triangle Congruence: SSS and SAS

1. The figure shows one tower and the cables of a suspension bridge. Given that $\overline{AC} \cong \overline{BC}$, use SAS to explain why $\triangle ACD \cong \triangle BCD$.

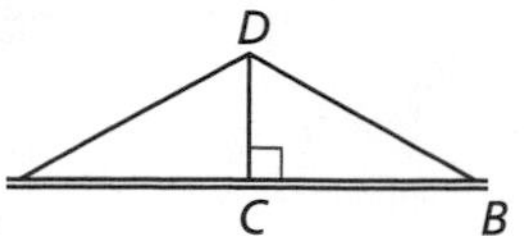

2. **Given:** $\overline{JK}$ bisects $\angle MJN$. $\overline{MJ} \cong \overline{NJ}$
   Prove: $\triangle MJK \cong \triangle NJK$

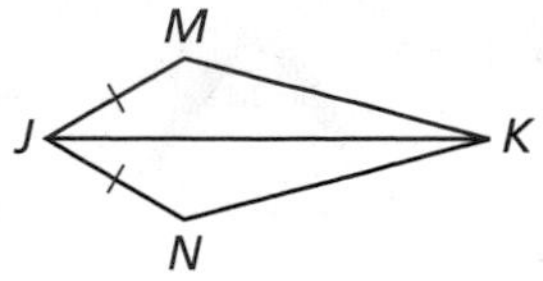

4-6 Triangle Congruence: ASA, AAS, and HL

Determine if you can use the HL Congruence Theorem to prove the triangles congruent. If not, tell what else you need to know.

3. $\triangle RSU$ and $\triangle TUS$

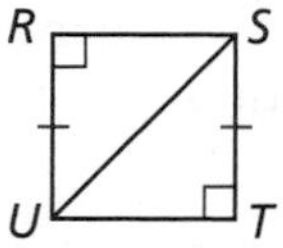

4. $\triangle ABC$ and $\triangle DCB$

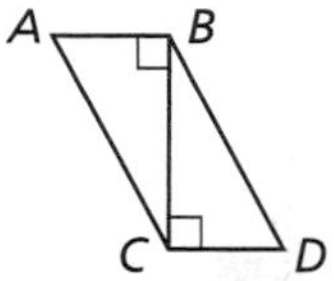

Observers in two lighthouses *K* and *L* spot a ship *S*.

5. Draw a diagram of the triangle formed by the lighthouses and the ship. Label each measure.
6. Is there enough data in the table to pinpoint the location of the ship? Why?

	K to *L*	*K* to *S*	*L* to *S*
Bearing	E	N 58° E	N 77° W
Distance	12 km	?	?

4-7 Triangle Congruence: CPCTC

7. **Given:** $\overline{CD} \parallel \overline{BE}$, $\overline{DE} \parallel \overline{CB}$
   Prove: $\angle D \cong \angle B$

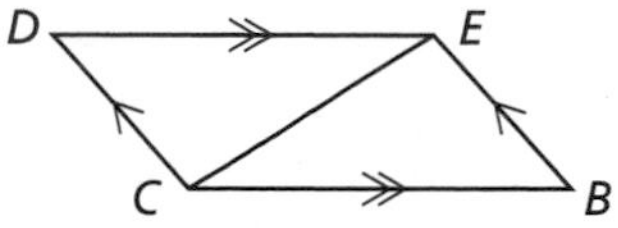

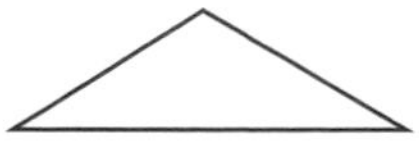

4-8 Introduction to Coordinate Proof

8. Position a square with side lengths of 9 units in the coordinate plane
9. Assign coordinates to each vertex and write a coordinate proof.
   Given: *ABCD* is a rectangle with *M* as the midpoint of $\overline{AB}$. *N* is the midpoint of $\overline{AD}$.
   Prove: The area of $\triangle AMN$ is $\frac{1}{8}$ the area of rectangle *ABCD*.

4-9 Isosceles and Equilateral Triangles

Find each value.

10. m$\angle C$

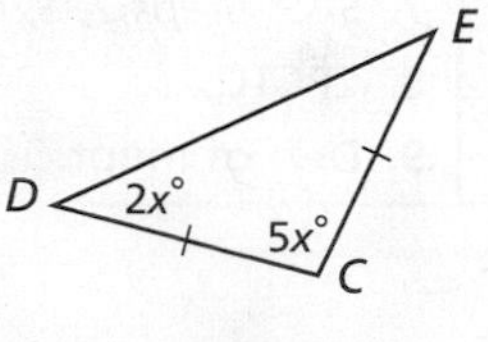

11. *ST*

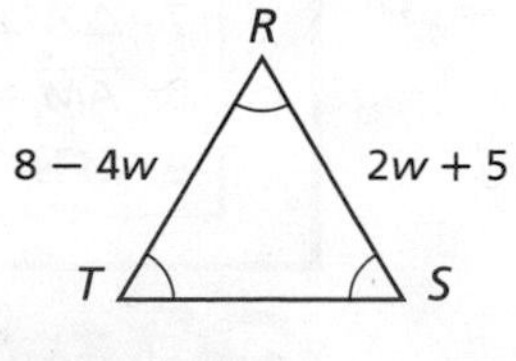

12. **Given:** Isosceles $\triangle JKL$ has coordinates $J(0, 0)$, $K(2a, 2b)$, and $L(4a, 0)$. *M* is the midpoint of $\overline{JK}$, and *N* is the midpoint of $\overline{KL}$.
    Prove: $\triangle KMN$ is isosceles.

COMMON CORE

EXTENSION Proving Constructions Valid

CC.9-12.G.CO.12 Make formal geometric constructions with a variety of tools and methods…

Objective
Use congruent triangles to prove constructions valid.

When performing a compass and straight edge construction, the compass setting remains the same width until you change it. This fact allows you to construct a segment congruent to a given segment. You can assume that two distances constructed with the same compass setting are congruent.

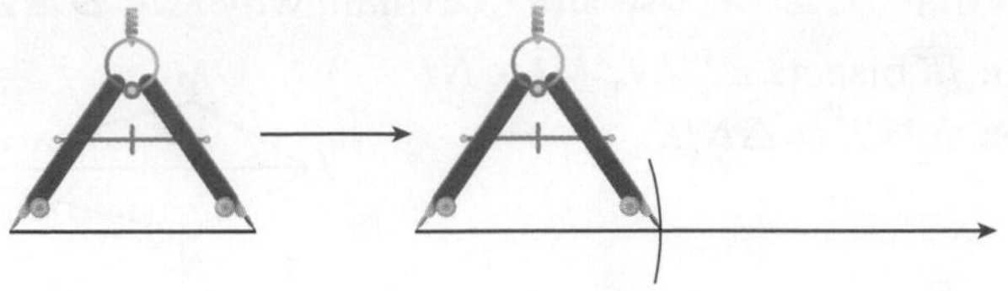

The steps in the construction of a figure can be justified by combining the assumptions of compass and straightedge constructions and the postulates and theorems that are used for proving triangles congruent.

You have learned that there exists exactly one midpoint on any line segment. The proof below justifies the construction of a midpoint.

EXAMPLE 1 Proving the Construction of a Midpoint

Given: diagram showing the steps in the construction
Prove: M is the midpoint of $\overline{AB}$.

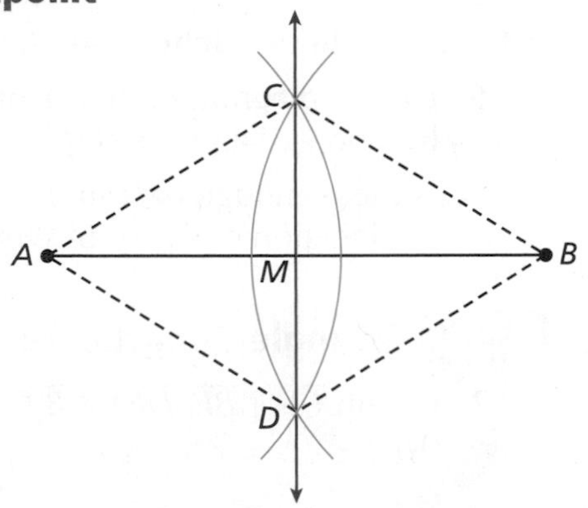

Remember!
To construct a midpoint, see the construction of a perpendicular bisector in *Perpendicular Lines*.

Proof:

Statements	Reasons
1. Draw $\overline{AC}$, $\overline{BC}$, $\overline{AD}$, and $\overline{BD}$.	1. Through any two pts. there is exactly one line.
2. $\overline{AC} \cong \overline{BC} \cong \overline{AD} \cong \overline{BD}$	2. Same compass setting used
3. $\overline{CD} \cong \overline{CD}$	3. Reflex. Prop. of $\cong$
4. $\triangle ACD \cong \triangle BCD$	4. SSS *Steps 2, 3*
5. $\angle ACD \cong \angle BCD$	5. CPCTC
6. $\overline{CM} \cong \overline{CM}$	6. Reflex. Prop. of $\cong$
7. $\triangle ACM \cong \triangle BCM$	7. SAS *Steps 2, 5, 6*
8. $\overline{AM} \cong \overline{BM}$	8. CPCTC
9. M is the midpt. of $\overline{AB}$.	9. Def. of mdpt.

CHECK IT OUT! **1. Given:** above diagram
Prove: $\overleftrightarrow{CD}$ is the perpendicular bisector of $\overline{AB}$.

EXAMPLE 2 Proving the Construction of an Angle

Given: diagram showing the steps in the construction

Prove: $\angle A \cong \angle D$

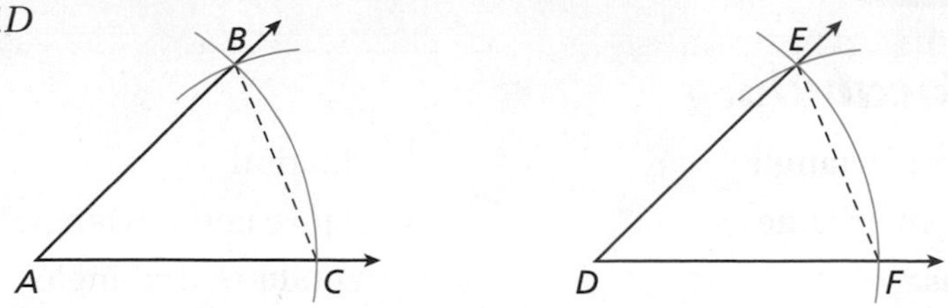

Proof: Since there is a straight line through any two points, you can draw $\overline{BC}$ and $\overline{EF}$. The same compass setting was used to construct $\overline{AC}$, $\overline{AB}$, $\overline{DF}$, and $\overline{DE}$, so $\overline{AC} \cong \overline{AB} \cong \overline{DF} \cong \overline{DE}$. The same compass setting was used to construct $\overline{BC}$ and $\overline{EF}$, so $\overline{BC} \cong \overline{EF}$. Therefore $\triangle BAC \cong \triangle EDF$ by SSS, and $\angle A \cong \angle D$ by CPCTC.

Remember!

To review the construction of an angle congruent to another angle, see *Measuring and Constructing Angles*.

CHECK IT OUT!

2. Prove the construction for bisecting an angle.

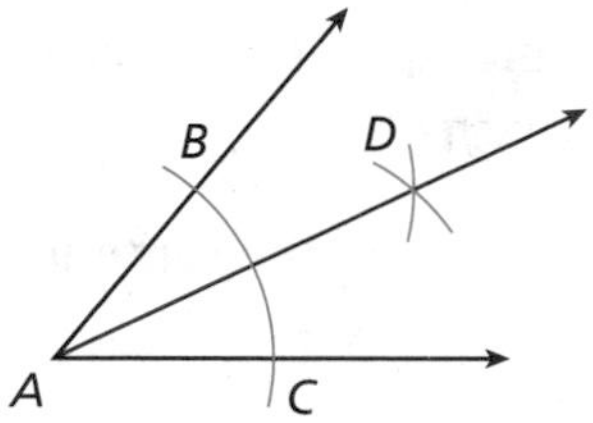

EXTENSION Exercises

Use each diagram to prove the construction valid.

1. parallel lines

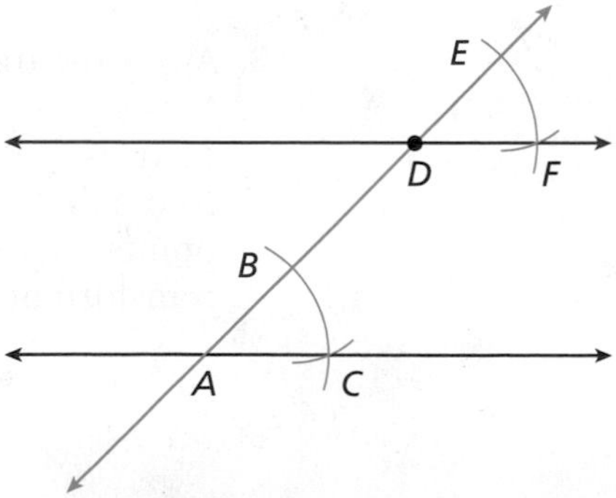

2. a perpendicular through a point not on the line

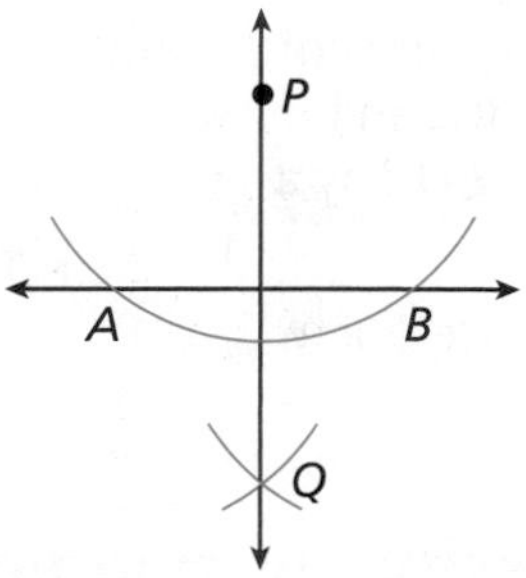

3. constructing a triangle using SAS

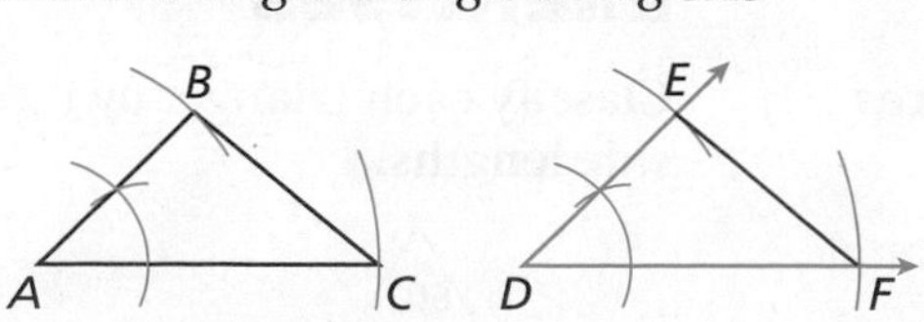

4. constructing a triangle using ASA

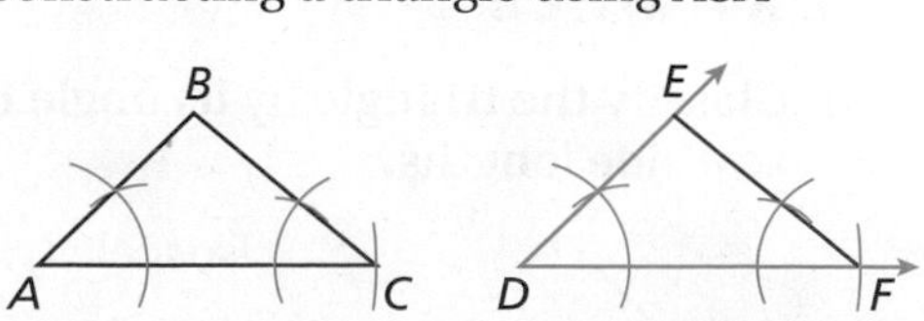

CHAPTER 4

Study Guide: Review

Know it! Note

For a complete list of postulates, theorems, and corollaries, see p. PT2.

Vocabulary

acute triangle
auxiliary line
base
base angle
congruent polygons
coordinate proof
corollary
corresponding angles
corresponding sides
CPCTC
dilation
equiangular triangle
equilateral triangle
exterior
exterior angle
included angle
included side
interior
interior angle
isosceles triangle
isometry
legs of an isosceles triangle
obtuse triangle
remote interior angle
right triangle
rigid transformation
scalene triangle
triangle rigidity
vertex angle

Complete the sentences below with vocabulary words from the list above.

1. A(n) __?__ is a triangle with at least two congruent sides.

2. A name given to matching angles of congruent triangles is __?__ .

3. A(n) __?__ is the common side of two consecutive angles in a polygon.

4-1 Congruence and Transformations

EXAMPLE

- **Determine whether the polygons are congruent.**

$A(1, 1)$, $B(4, 1)$, $C(5, 3)$

$P(-2, 3)$, $Q(1, 3)$, $R(2, 5)$

The triangles are congruent because ABC can be mapped to PQR by a translation:

$(x, y) \rightarrow (x - 3, y + 2)$.

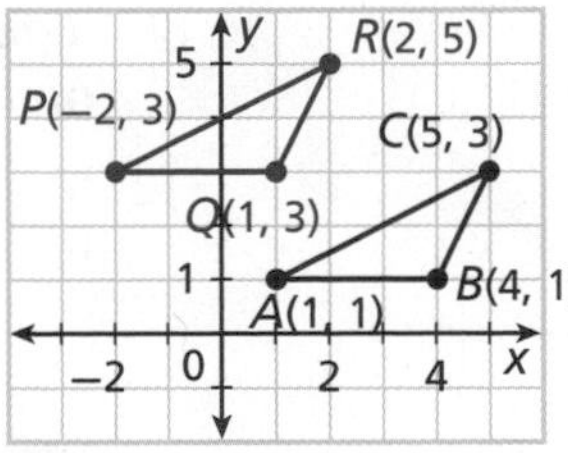

EXERCISES

4. Determine whether ABC and PQR are congruent. Support your answer by describing a transformation.
$A(3, -1)$, $B(4, 0)$, $C(5, 3)$
$P(-3, 1)$, $Q(-4, 0)$, $R(-5, -3)$

5. Apply the transformation $M : (x, y) \rightarrow (4x, 4y)$ to DEF with vertices $D(1, 2)$, $E(2, -3)$, and $F(4, 0)$. Name the coordinates of the image points. Identify and describe the transformation.

4-2 Classifying Triangles

EXAMPLE

- **Classify the triangle by its angle measures and side lengths.**

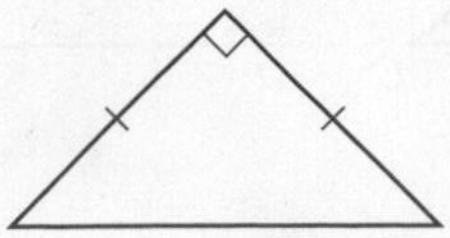

isosceles right triangle

EXERCISES

Classify each triangle by its angle measures and side lengths.

6.

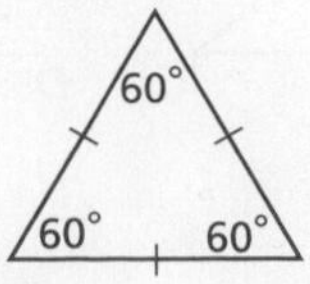

7.

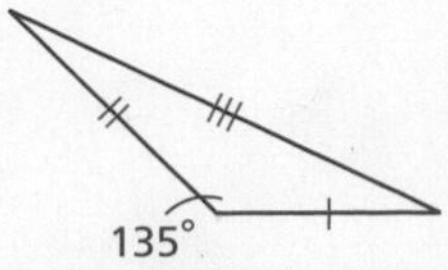

4-3 Angle Relationships in Triangles

EXAMPLE

■ **Find m∠S.**

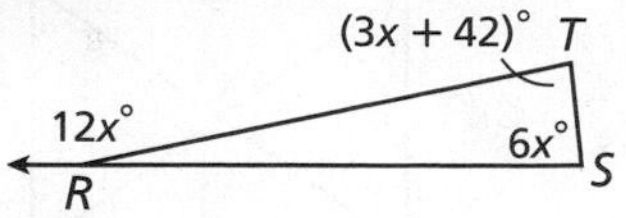

$12x = 3x + 42 + 6x$

$12x = 9x + 42$

$3x = 42$

$x = 14$

$m\angle S = 6(14) = 84°$

EXERCISES

Find m∠N.

8.

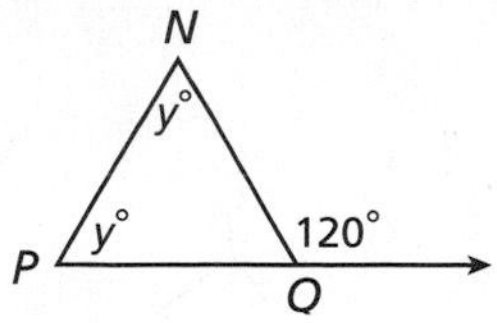

9. In $\triangle LMN$, $m\angle L = 8x°$, $m\angle M = (2x + 1)°$, and $m\angle N = (6x - 1)°$.

4-4 Congruent Triangles

EXAMPLE

■ **Given: $\triangle DEF \cong \triangle JKL$. Identify all pairs of congruent corresponding parts. Then find the value of x.**

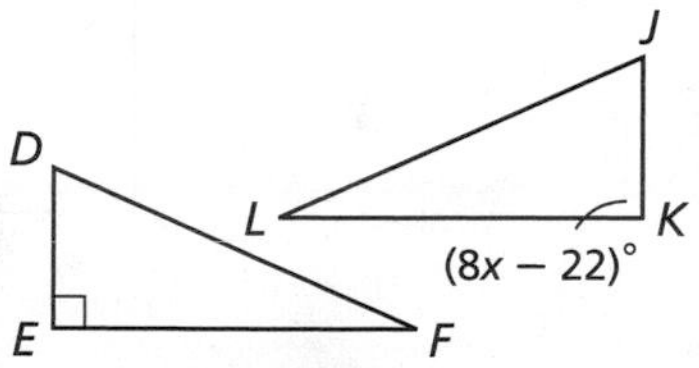

The congruent pairs follow: $\angle D \cong \angle J$, $\angle E \cong \angle K$, $\angle F \cong \angle L$, $\overline{DE} \cong \overline{JK}$, $\overline{EF} \cong \overline{KL}$, and $\overline{DF} \cong \overline{JL}$.

Since $m\angle E = m\angle K$, $90 = 8x - 22$. After 22 is added to both sides, $112 = 8x$. So $x = 14$.

EXERCISES

Given: $\triangle PQR \cong \triangle XYZ$. Identify the congruent corresponding parts.

10. $\overline{PR} \cong$ __?__ **11.** $\angle Y \cong$ __?__

Given: $\triangle ABC \cong \triangle CDA$
Find each value.

12. x

13. CD

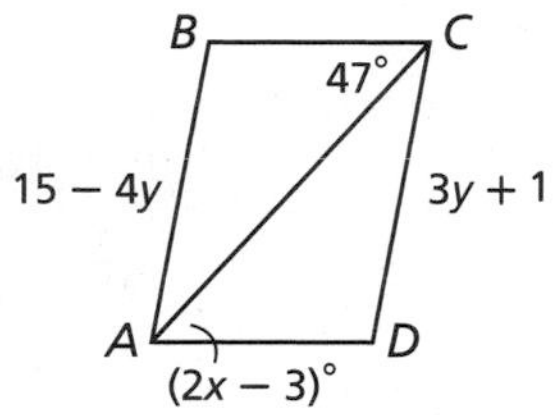

4-5 Triangle Congruence: SSS and SAS

EXAMPLES

■ **Given: $\overline{RS} \cong \overline{UT}$, and $\overline{VS} \cong \overline{VT}$. V is the midpoint of $\overline{RU}$.**

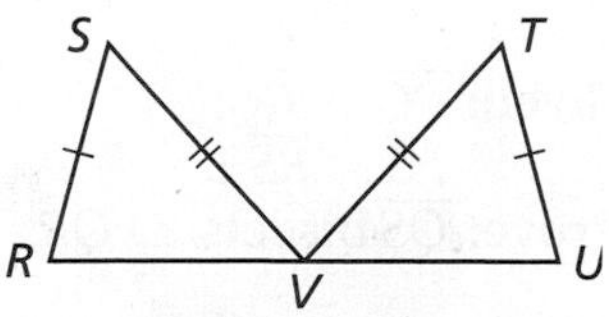

Prove: $\triangle RSV \cong \triangle UTV$

Proof:

Statements	Reasons
1. $\overline{RS} \cong \overline{UT}$	1. Given
2. $\overline{VS} \cong \overline{VT}$	2. Given
3. *V is the mdpt. of* $\overline{RU}$.	3. Given
4. $\overline{RV} \cong \overline{UV}$	4. Def. of mdpt.
5. $\triangle RSV \cong \triangle UTV$	5. SSS *Steps 1, 2, 4*

EXERCISES

14. Given: $\overline{AB} \cong \overline{DE}$, $\overline{DB} \cong \overline{AE}$
Prove: $\triangle ADB \cong \triangle DAE$

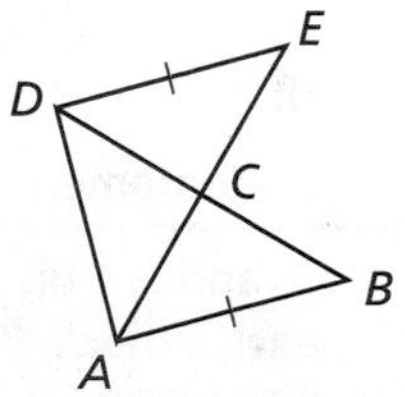

15. Given: $\overline{GJ}$ bisects $\overline{FH}$, and $\overline{FH}$ bisects $\overline{GJ}$.
Prove: $\triangle FGK \cong \triangle HJK$

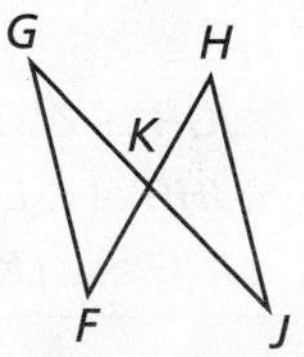

4-6 Triangle Congruence: ASA, AAS, and HL

EXAMPLES

- **Given:** B is the midpoint of $\overline{AE}$.
  $\angle A \cong \angle E$,
  $\angle ABC \cong \angle EBD$
  Prove: $\triangle ABC \cong \triangle EBD$

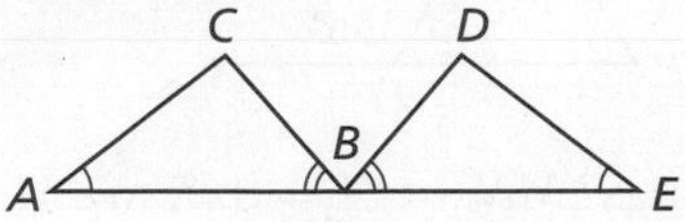

Proof:

Statements	Reasons
1. $\angle A \cong \angle E$	1. Given
2. $\angle ABC \cong \angle EBD$	2. Given
3. B is the mdpt. of $\overline{AE}$.	3. Given
4. $\overline{AB} \cong \overline{EB}$	4. Def. of mdpt.
5. $\triangle ABC \cong \triangle EBD$	5. ASA *Steps 1, 4, 2*

EXERCISES

16. Given: C is the midpoint of $\overline{AG}$.
$\overline{HA} \parallel \overline{GB}$
Prove: $\triangle HAC \cong \triangle BGC$

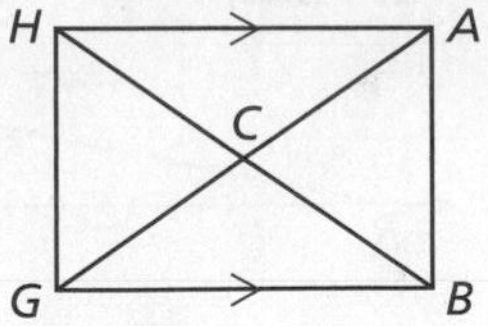

17. Given: $\overline{WX} \perp \overline{XZ}$,
$\overline{YZ} \perp \overline{ZX}$,
$\overline{WZ} \cong \overline{YX}$
Prove: $\triangle WZX \cong \triangle YXZ$

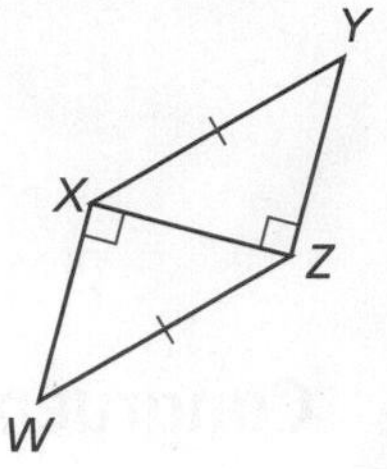

18. Given: $\angle S$ and $\angle V$ are right angles.
$RT = UW$.
$m\angle T = m\angle W$
Prove: $\triangle RST \cong \triangle UVW$

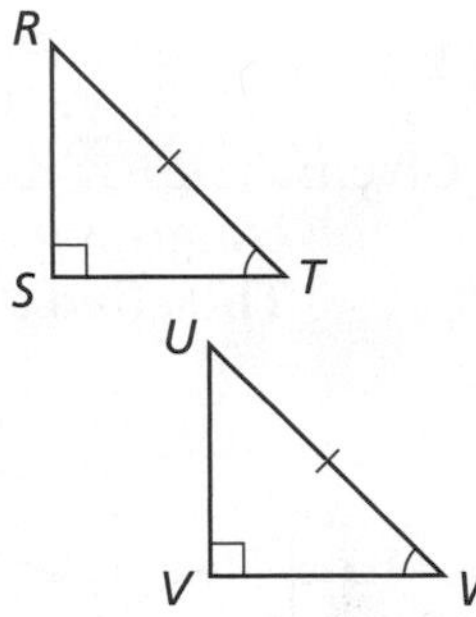

4-7 Triangle Congruence: CPCTC

EXAMPLES

- **Given:** $\overline{JL}$ and $\overline{HK}$ bisect each other.
  Prove: $\angle JHG \cong \angle LKG$

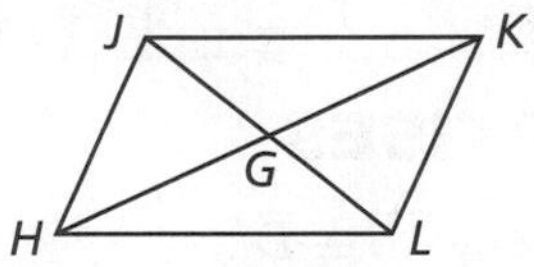

Proof:

Statements	Reasons
1. $\overline{JL}$ and $\overline{HK}$ bisect each other.	1. Given
2. $\overline{JG} \cong \overline{LG}$, and $\overline{HG} \cong \overline{KG}$.	2. Def. of bisect
3. $\angle JGH \cong \angle LGK$	3. Vert. ∠s Thm.
4. $\triangle JHG \cong \triangle LKG$	4. SAS *Steps 2, 3*
5. $\angle JHG \cong \angle LKG$	5. CPCTC

EXERCISES

19. Given: M is the midpoint of $\overline{BD}$.
$\overline{BC} \cong \overline{DC}$
Prove: $\angle 1 \cong \angle 2$

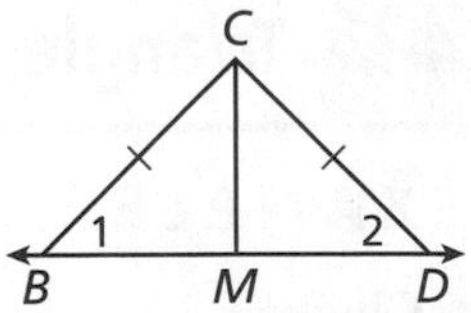

20. Given: $\overline{PQ} \cong \overline{RQ}$,
$\overline{PS} \cong \overline{RS}$
Prove: $\overline{QS}$ bisects $\angle PQR$.

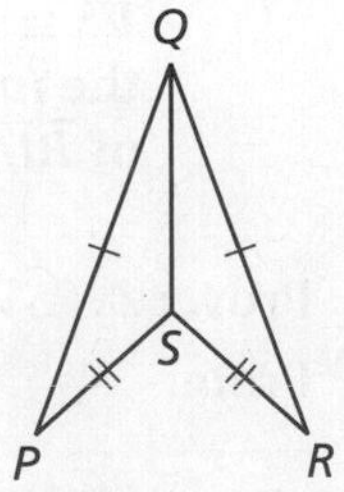

21. Given: H is the midpoint of $\overline{GJ}$.
L is the midpoint of $\overline{MK}$.
$\overline{GM} \cong \overline{KJ}$, $\overline{GJ} \cong \overline{KM}$,
$\angle G \cong \angle K$
Prove: $\angle GMH \cong \angle KJL$

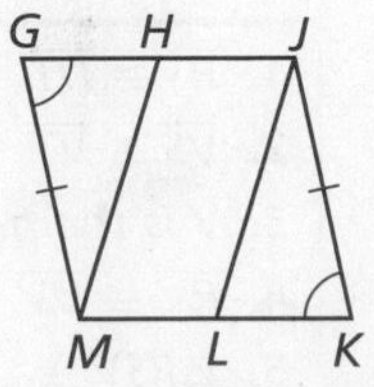

4-8 Introduction to Coordinate Proof

EXAMPLES

■ **Given: $\angle B$ is a right angle in isosceles right $\triangle ABC$. E is the midpoint of $\overline{AB}$. D is the midpoint of $\overline{CB}$. $\overline{AB} \cong \overline{CB}$**

Prove: $\overline{CE} \cong \overline{AD}$

Proof: Use the coordinates $A(0, 2a)$, $B(0, 0)$, and $C(2a, 0)$. Draw $\overline{AD}$ and $\overline{CE}$.

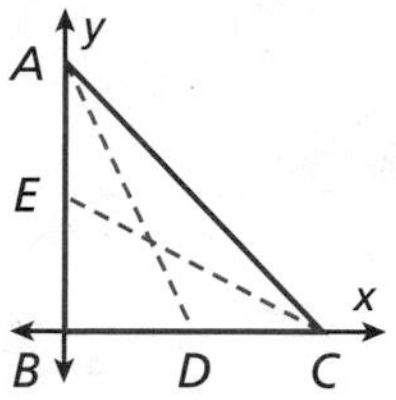

By the Midpoint Formula,

$$E = \left(\frac{0+0}{2}, \frac{2a+0}{2}\right) = (0, a) \text{ and}$$

$$D = \left(\frac{0+2a}{2}, \frac{0+0}{2}\right) = (a, 0)$$

By the Distance Formula,

$$CE = \sqrt{(2a-0)^2 + (0-a)^2}$$
$$= \sqrt{4a^2 + a^2} = a\sqrt{5}$$
$$AD = \sqrt{(a-0)^2 + (0-2a)^2}$$
$$= \sqrt{a^2 + 4a^2} = a\sqrt{5}$$

Thus $\overline{CE} \cong \overline{AD}$ by the definition of congruence.

EXERCISES

Position each figure in the coordinate plane and give the coordinates of each vertex.

22. a right triangle with leg lengths r and s

23. a rectangle with length $2p$ and width p

24. a square with side length $8m$

For exercises 25 and 26 assign coordinates to each vertex and write a coordinate proof.

25. Given: In rectangle $ABCD$, E is the midpoint of $\overline{AB}$, F is the midpoint of $\overline{BC}$, G is the midpoint of $\overline{CD}$, and H is the midpoint of $\overline{AD}$.

Prove: $\overline{EF} \cong \overline{GH}$

26. Given: $\triangle PQR$ has a right $\angle Q$. M is the midpoint of $\overline{PR}$.

Prove: $MP = MQ = MR$

27. Show that a triangle with vertices at $(3, 5)$, $(3, 2)$, and $(2, 5)$ is a right triangle.

4-9 Isosceles and Equilateral Triangles

EXAMPLE

■ **Find the value of x.**

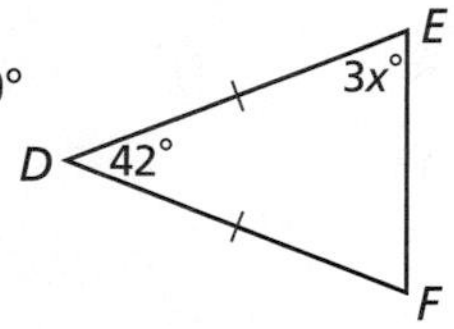

$m\angle D + m\angle E + m\angle F = 180°$ by the Triangle Sum Theorem. $m\angle E = m\angle F$ by the Isosceles Triangle Theorem.

$m\angle D + 2m\angle E = 180°$	*Substitution*
$42 + 2(3x) = 180$	*Substitute the given values.*
$6x = 138$	*Simplify.*
$x = 23$	*Divide both sides by 6.*

EXERCISES

Find each value.

28. x

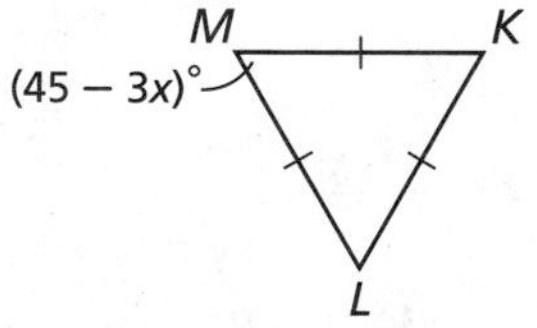

29. RS

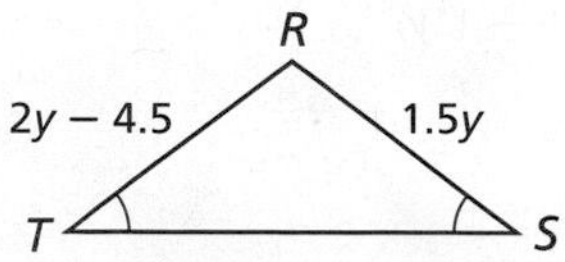

30. Given: $\triangle ACD$ is isosceles with $\angle D$ as the vertex angle. B is the midpoint of $\overline{AC}$. $AB = x + 5$, $BC = 2x - 3$, and $CD = 2x + 6$. Find the perimeter of $\triangle ACD$.

CHAPTER 4

CHAPTER TEST

1. Classify $\triangle ACD$ by its angle measures.

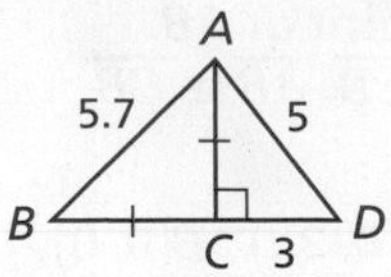

Classify each triangle by its side lengths.

2. $\triangle ACD$ 3. $\triangle ABC$ 4. $\triangle ABD$

5. While surveying the triangular plot of land shown, a surveyor finds that $m\angle S = 43°$. The measure of $\angle RTP$ is twice that of $\angle RTS$. What is $m\angle R$?

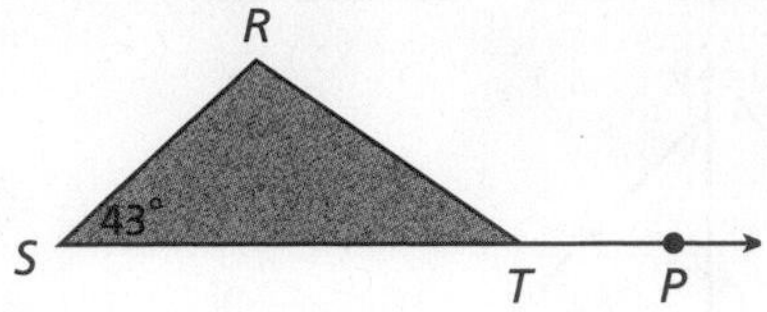

Given: $\triangle XYZ \cong \triangle JKL$
Identify the congruent corresponding parts.

6. $\overline{JL} \cong$ __?__ 7. $\angle Y \cong$ __?__ 8. $\angle L \cong$ __?__ 9. $\overline{YZ} \cong$ __?__

10. **Given:** T is the midpoint of $\overline{PR}$ and $\overline{SQ}$.
Prove: $\triangle PTS \cong \triangle RTQ$

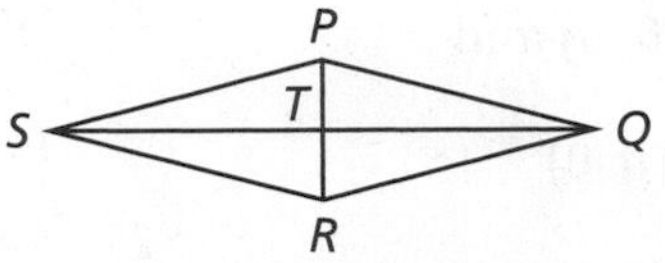

11. The figure represents a walkway with triangular supports. Given that $\overline{GJ}$ bisects $\angle HGK$ and $\angle H \cong \angle K$, use AAS to prove $\triangle HGJ \cong \triangle KGJ$

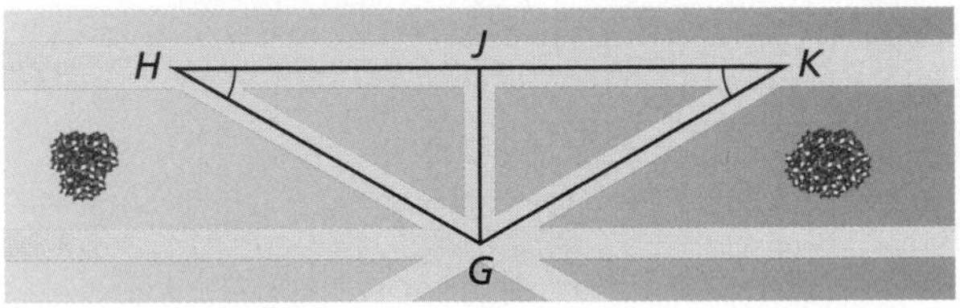

12. **Given:** $\overline{AB} \cong \overline{DC}$, $\overline{AB} \perp \overline{AC}$, $\overline{DC} \perp \overline{DB}$
Prove: $\triangle ABC \cong \triangle DCB$

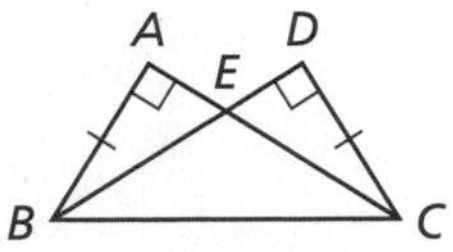

13. **Given:** $\overline{PQ} \parallel \overline{SR}$, $\angle S \cong \angle Q$
Prove: $\overline{PS} \parallel \overline{QR}$

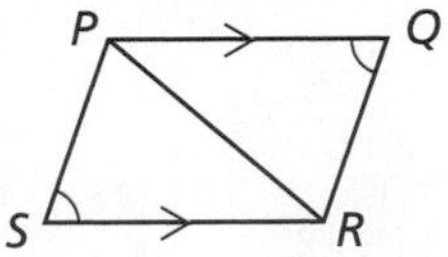

14. Position a right triangle with legs 3 m and 4 m long in the coordinate plane. Give the coordinates of each vertex.

15. Assign coordinates to each vertex and write a coordinate proof.
Given: Square $ABCD$
Prove: $\overline{AC} \cong \overline{BD}$

Find each value.

16. y

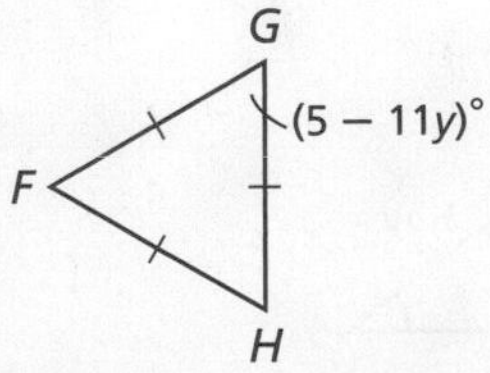

17. $m\angle S$

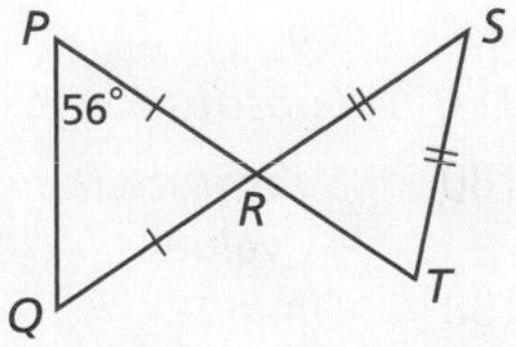

18. **Given:** Isosceles $\triangle ABC$ has coordinates $A(2a, 0)$, $B(0, 2b)$, and $C(-2a, 0)$. D is the midpoint of $\overline{AC}$, and E is the midpoint of $\overline{AB}$.
Prove: $\triangle AED$ is isosceles.

COLLEGE ENTRANCE EXAM PRACTICE

FOCUS ON ACT

The ACT Mathematics Test is one of four tests in the ACT. You are given 60 minutes to answer 60 multiple-choice questions. The questions cover material typically taught through the end of eleventh grade. You will need to know basic formulas but nothing too difficult.

HOT TIP! **There is no penalty for guessing on the ACT. If you are unsure of the correct answer, eliminate as many answer choices as possible and make your best guess. Make sure you have entered an answer for every question before time runs out.**

You may want to time yourself as you take this practice test. It should take you about 5 minutes to complete.

---

1. For the figure below, which of the following must be true?

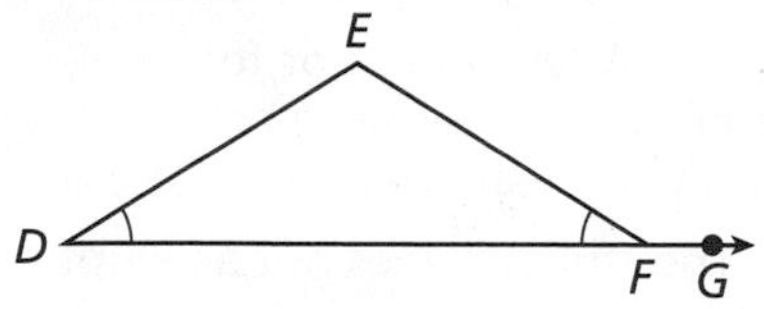

I. m$\angle EFG >$ m$\angle DEF$

II. m$\angle EDF =$ m$\angle EFD$

III. m$\angle DEF +$ m$\angle EDF >$ m$\angle EFG$

(A) I only

(B) II only

(C) I and II only

(D) II and III only

(E) I, II, and III

---

2. In the figure below, $\triangle ABD \cong \triangle CDB$, m$\angle A = (2x + 14)^\circ$, m$\angle C = (3x - 15)^\circ$, and m$\angle DBA = 49°$. What is the measure of $\angle BDA$?

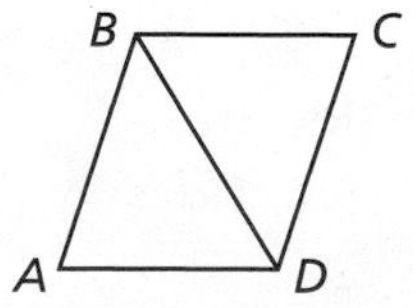

(F) 29°

(G) 49°

(H) 59°

(J) 72°

(K) 101°

---

3. Which of the following best describes a triangle with vertices having coordinates $(-1, 0)$, $(0, 3)$, and $(1, -4)$?

(A) Equilateral

(B) Isosceles

(C) Right

(D) Scalene

(E) Equiangular

---

4. In the figure below, what is the value of y?

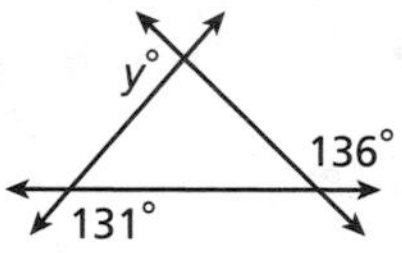

(F) 49

(G) 87

(H) 93

(J) 131

(K) 136

---

5. In $\triangle RST$, $RS = 2x + 10$, $ST = 3x - 2$, and $RT = \frac{1}{2}x + 28$. If $\triangle RST$ is equiangular, what is the value of x?

(A) 2

(B) $5\frac{1}{3}$

(C) 6

(D) 12

(E) 34

CHAPTER 4

TEST TACKLER

Standardized Test Strategies

Extended Response: Write Extended Responses

Extended-response questions are designed to assess your ability to apply and explain what you have learned. These test items are graded using a 4-point scoring rubric.

Scoring Rubric

4 points: The student shows an understanding of properties relating to parallel lines, triangle congruence, and the differences between ASA, SSS, and SAS.

3 points: The student correctly chooses which theorem to use but does not completely defend the choice or leaves out crucial understanding of parallel lines.

2 points: The student chooses the correct theorem but only defends part of it.

1 point: The student does not follow directions or does not provide any explanation for the answer.

0 points: The student does not attempt to answer.

EXAMPLE 1

Extended Response Given $p \parallel q$, state which theorem, AAS, ASA, SSS, or SAS, you would use to prove that $\triangle ABC \cong \triangle DCB$. Explain your reasoning.

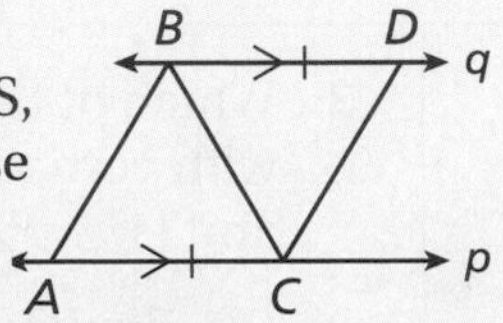

4-point response:

The correct theorem to use is SAS. According to the figure, $\overline{AC} \cong \overline{DB}$. By the Reflexive Property, $\overline{BC} \cong \overline{BC}$. So it just needs to be shown that $\angle BCA \cong \angle CBD$. Since $p \parallel q$ and they are cut by transversal $\overline{BC}$, $\angle BCA \cong \angle CBD$ by the Alternate Interior Angles Theorem. So by SAS, $\triangle ABC \cong \triangle DCB$. SSS cannot be used to prove that $\triangle ABC \cong \triangle DCB$ because it cannot be proven that $\overline{AB} \cong \overline{DC}$. ASA cannot be used because it cannot be proven that $\angle BAC \cong \angle CDB$. AAS cannot be used because it cannot be proven that $\angle ABC \cong \angle DCB$.

The student gave a complete, correct response to the question and provided an explanation as to why the other theorems could not be used.

3-point response:

The theorem to use is SAS because, according to the figure, two sides and their included angle in each triangle can be shown to be congruent. Side 1: $\overline{AC} \cong \overline{DB}$ according to the figure. Side 2: $\overline{BC} \cong \overline{BC}$ because of the Reflexive Property. $\angle BCA \cong \angle CBD$ because of the Alternate Interior Angles Theorem.

The reasoning is correct, but the student did not explain why other theorems could not be used.

2-point response:

You can use SAS because the picture shows that the triangles share one side. There are congruence marks on $\overline{AC}$ and $\overline{BD}$, so these sides are congruent.

The answer is correct, but the student did not explain why the included angles are congruent.

1-point response:

You can use SAS.

The student did not provide any reasoning.

HOT TIP! To receive full credit, make sure all parts of the problem are answered. Be sure to provide a complete explanation for your reasoning.

Read each test item and answer the questions that follow.

Scoring Rubric:

4 points: The student demonstrates a thorough understanding of the concept, correctly answers the question, and provides a complete explanation.

3 points: The student correctly answers the question but does not show all work or does not provide an explanation.

2 points: The student makes minor errors resulting in an incorrect solution but shows and explains an understanding of the concept.

1 point: The student gives a response showing no work or explanation.

0 points: The student gives no response.

Item A

What theorem(s) can you use, other than the HL Theorem, to prove that $\triangle MNP \cong \triangle XYZ$? Explain your reasoning.

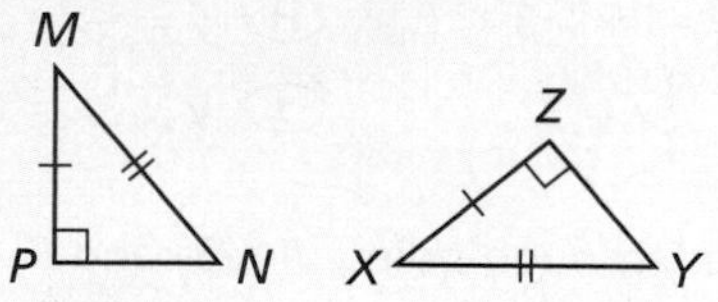

1. What should a full-credit response to this test item include?

2. A student wrote this response:

   You can use the Pythagorean Theorem.

   What score should this response receive? Why?

3. Write a list of the ways to prove triangles congruent. Is the Pythagorean Theorem on your list?

4. Add to the response so that it receives a score of 4-points.

Item B

Can an equilateral triangle be an obtuse triangle? Explain your answer. Include a sketch to support your reasoning.

5. What should a full-credit response to this test item include?

6. A student wrote this response:

   No, an equilateral triangle cannot be an obtuse triangle because an equilateral triangle has three congruent sides and three congruent acute angles. An acute angle has a measure less than 90°. By definition, an obtuse triangle has one obtuse angle, which is an angle with a measure greater than 90°.

   Why will this response not receive a score of 4 points?

7. Correct the response so that it receives full credit.

Item C

An isosceles right triangle has two sides, each with length $y + 4$.

Describe how you would find the length of the hypotenuse. Provide a sketch in your explanation.

8. A student began trying to find the length of the hypotenuse by writing the following:

$$(y+4)^2 + (y+4)^2 = (\text{hypotenuse})^2$$
$$(y^2+8y+16)+(y^2+8y+16) = (\text{hypotenuse})^2$$
$$2y^2 + 16y + 32 = (\text{hypotenuse})^2$$
$$\sqrt{2y^2 + 16y + 32} = \text{hypotenuse}$$

   Is the student on his way to receiving a 4-point response? Explain.

9. Describe a different method the student could use for this response.

CHAPTER 4

STANDARDIZED TEST PREP

Learn It Online
State Test Practice

CUMULATIVE ASSESSMENT

Multiple Choice

Use the diagram for Items 1 and 2.

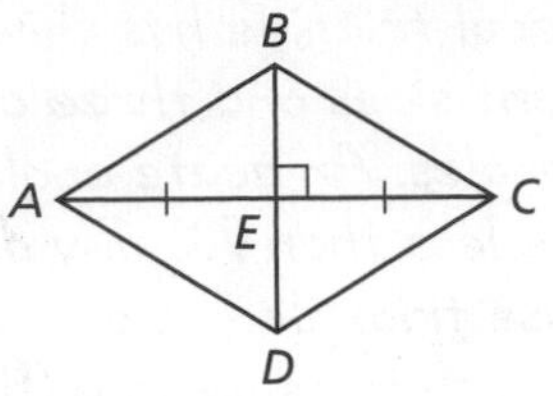

1. Which of these congruence statements can be proved from the information given in the figure?
   - (A) $\triangle AEB \cong \triangle CED$
   - (B) $\triangle BAC \cong \triangle DAC$
   - (C) $\triangle ABD \cong \triangle BCA$
   - (D) $\triangle DEC \cong \triangle DEA$

2. What other information is needed to prove that $\triangle CEB \cong \triangle AED$ by the HL Congruence Theorem?
   - (F) $\overline{AD} \cong \overline{AB}$
   - (G) $\overline{BE} \cong \overline{AE}$
   - (H) $\overline{CB} \cong \overline{AD}$
   - (J) $\overline{DE} \cong \overline{CE}$

3. Which biconditional statement is true?
   - (A) Tomorrow is Monday if and only if today is not Saturday.
   - (B) Next month is January if and only if this month is December.
   - (C) Today is a weekend day if and only if yesterday was Friday.
   - (D) This month had 31 days if and only if last month had 30 days.

4. What must be true if $\overleftrightarrow{PQ}$ intersects $\overleftrightarrow{ST}$ at more than one point?
   - (F) *P*, *Q*, *S*, and *T* are collinear.
   - (G) *P*, *Q*, *S*, and *T* are noncoplanar.
   - (H) $\overrightarrow{PQ}$ and $\overrightarrow{ST}$ are opposite rays.
   - (J) $\overleftrightarrow{PQ}$ and $\overleftrightarrow{ST}$ are perpendicular.

5. $\triangle ABC \cong \triangle DEF$, $EF = x^2 - 7$, and $BC = 4x - 2$. Find the values of *x*.
   - (A) −1 and 5
   - (B) −1 and 6
   - (C) 1 and 5
   - (D) 2 and 3

6. Which conditional statement has the same truth value as its inverse?
   - (F) If $n < 0$, then $n^2 > 0$.
   - (G) If a triangle has three congruent sides, then it is an isosceles triangle.
   - (H) If an angle measures less than 90°, then it is an acute angle.
   - (J) If *n* is a negative integer, then $n < 0$.

7. On a map, an island has coordinates (3, 5), and a reef has coordinates (6, 8). If each map unit represents 1 mile, what is the distance between the island and the reef to the nearest tenth of a mile?
   - (A) 4.2 miles
   - (B) 6.0 miles
   - (C) 9.0 miles
   - (D) 15.8 miles

8. A line has an *x*-intercept of −8 and a *y*-intercept of 3. What is the equation of the line?
   - (F) $y = -8x + 3$
   - (G) $y = \frac{3}{8}x + 3$
   - (H) $y = \frac{8}{3}x - 8$
   - (J) $y = 3x - 8$

9. $\overleftrightarrow{JK}$ passes through points $J(1, 3)$ and $K(-3, 11)$. Which of these lines is perpendicular to $\overleftrightarrow{JK}$?
   - (A) $y = -\frac{1}{2}x + \frac{1}{3}$
   - (B) $y = \frac{1}{2}x + 6$
   - (C) $y = -2x - \frac{1}{5}$
   - (D) $y = 2x - 4$

10. If $PQ = 2(RS) + 4$ and $RS = TU + 1$, which equation is true by the Substitution Property of Equality?
    - (F) $PQ = TU + 5$
    - (G) $PQ = TU + 6$
    - (H) $PQ = 2(TU) + 5$
    - (J) $PQ = 2(TU) + 6$

11. Which of the following is NOT valid for proving that triangles are congruent?
    - (A) AAA
    - (B) ASA
    - (C) SAS
    - (D) HL

Use this diagram for Items 12 and 13.

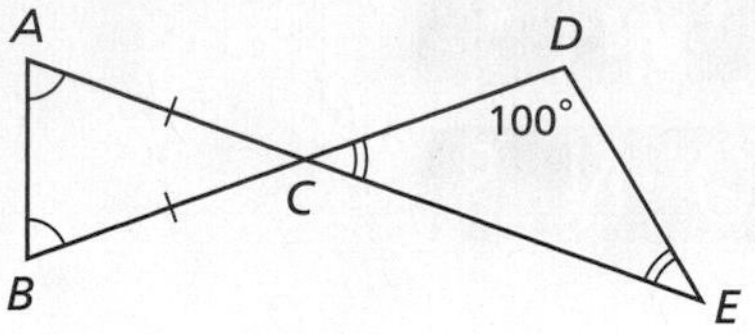

12. What is the measure of $\angle ACD$?

Ⓕ 40°
Ⓖ 80°
Ⓗ 100°
Ⓙ 140°

13. What type of triangle is $\triangle ABC$?

Ⓐ Isosceles acute
Ⓑ Equilateral acute
Ⓒ Isosceles obtuse
Ⓓ Scalene acute

HOT TIP! **Take some time to learn the directions for filling in a grid. Check and recheck to make sure you are filling in the grid properly. You will only get credit if the ovals below the boxes are filled in correctly. To check your answer, solve the problem using a different method from the one you originally used. If you made a mistake the first time, you are unlikely to make the same mistake when you solve a different way.**

Gridded Response

14. $\triangle CDE \cong \triangle JKL$. $m\angle E = (3x + 4)°$, and $m\angle L = (6x - 5)°$. What is the value of x?

15. Lucy, Eduardo, Carmen, and Frank live on the same street. Eduardo's house is halfway between Lucy's house and Frank's house. Lucy's house is halfway between Carmen's house and Frank's house. If the distance between Eduardo's house and Lucy's house is 150 ft, what is the distance in feet between Carmen's house and Eduardo's house?

16. $\triangle JKL \cong \triangle XYZ$, and $JK = 10 - 2n$. $XY = 2$, and $YZ = n^2$. Find KL.

17. An angle is its own supplement. What is its measure?

18. The area of a circle is 154 square inches. What is its circumference to the nearest inch?

19. The measure of $\angle P$ is $3\frac{1}{2}$ times the measure of $\angle Q$. If $\angle P$ and $\angle Q$ are complementary, what is $m\angle P$ in degrees?

Short Response

20. Given $\ell \parallel m$ with transversal n, explain why $\angle 2$ and $\angle 3$ are complementary.

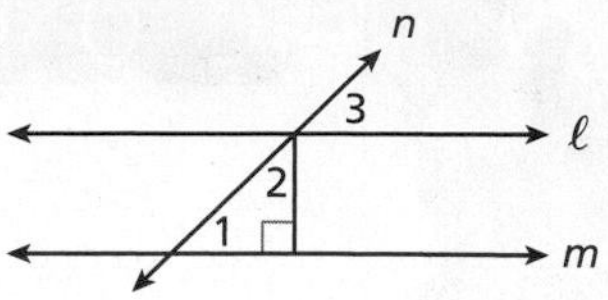

21. $\angle G$ and $\angle H$ are supplementary angles. $m\angle G = (2x + 12)°$, and $m\angle H = x°$.

a. Write an equation that can be used to determine the value of x. Solve the equation and justify each step.

b. Explain why $\angle H$ has a complement but $\angle G$ does not.

22. A manager conjectures that for every 1000 parts a factory produces, 60 are defective.

a. If the factory produces 1500 parts in one day, how many of them can be expected to be defective based on the manager's conjecture? Explain how you found your answer.

b. Use the data in the table below to show that the manager's conjecture is false.

Day	1	2	3	4	5
Parts	1000	2000	500	1500	2500
Defective Parts	60	150	30	90	150

23. $\overline{BD}$ is the perpendicular bisector of $\overline{AC}$.

a. What are the conclusions you can make from this statement?

b. Suppose $\overline{BD}$ intersects $\overline{AC}$ at D. Explain why $\overline{BD}$ is the shortest path from B to $\overline{AC}$.

Extended Response

24. $\triangle ABC$ and $\triangle DEF$ are isosceles triangles. $\overline{BC} \cong \overline{EF}$, and $\overline{AC} \cong \overline{DF}$. $m\angle C = 42.5°$, and $m\angle E = 95°$.

a. What is $m\angle D$? Explain how you determined your answer.

b. Show that $\triangle ABC$ and $\triangle DEF$ are congruent.

c. Given that $EF = 2x + 7$ and $AB = 3x + 2$, find the value for x. Explain how you determined your answer.

Real-World CONNECTIONS

The Queen's Cup

The annual Queen's Cup race is one of the most exciting sailing events of the year. Traditionally held at the end of June, the race attracts hundreds of yachts that compete to cross Lake Michigan—at night—in the fastest time possible.

Choose one or more strategies to solve each problem.

1. The race starts in Milwaukee, Wisconsin, and ends in Grand Haven, Michigan. The boats don't sail from the start to the finish in a straight line. They follow a zigzag course to take advantage of the wind. Suppose one of the boats leaves Milwaukee at a bearing of N 50° E and follows the course shown. At what bearing does the boat approach Grand Haven?

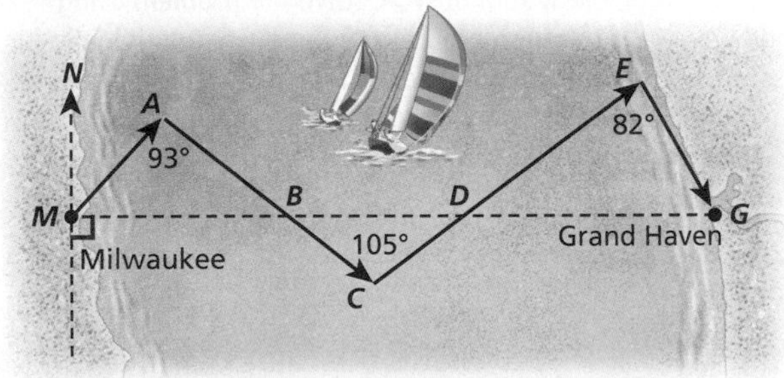

2. The Queen's Cup race is 78.75 miles long. In 2004, the winning sailboat completed the first 29.4 miles in about 3 hours and the first 49 miles in about 5 hours. Suppose it had continued at this rate. What would the winning time have been?

3. During the race one of the boats leaves Milwaukee *M*, sails to *X*, and then sails to *Y*. The team discovers a problem with the boat so it has to return directly to Milwaukee. Does the table contain enough information to determine the course to return to *M*? Explain.

	Bearing	Distance (mi)
M to *X*	N 42° E	3.1
X to *Y*	S 59° E	2.4
Y to *M*	■	■

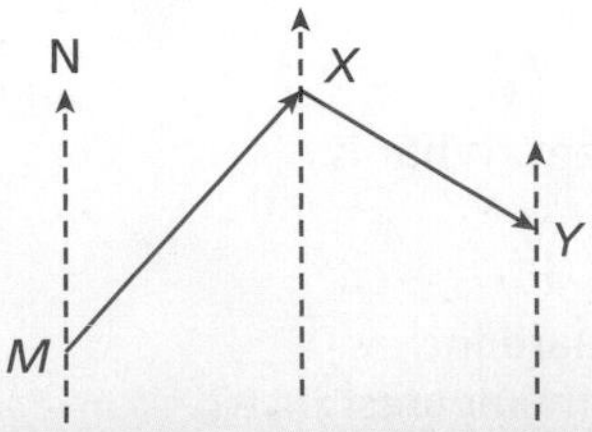

The Air Zoo

Located in Kalamazoo, Michigan, the Air Zoo offers visitors a thrilling, interactive voyage through the history of flight. It features full-motion flight simulators, a "4-D" theater, and more than 80 rare aircraft. The Air Zoo is also home to *The Century of Flight*, the world's largest indoor mural.

Choose one or more strategies to solve each problem.

1. *The Century of Flight* mural measures 28,800 square feet—approximately the size of three football fields! The table gives data on the rate at which the mural was painted. How many months did it take to complete the mural?

Painting *The Century of Flight*

Months of Work	Amount Completed (ft^2)
2	5,236
5	13,091
7	18,327

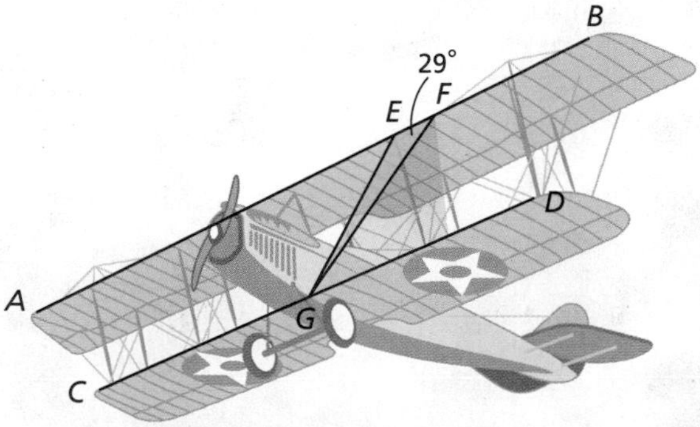

2. Visitors to the Air Zoo can see a replica of a Curtiss JN-4 "Jenny," the plane that flew the first official U.S. airmail route in 1918. The plane has two parallel wings $\overline{AB}$ and $\overline{CD}$ that are connected by bracing wires. The wires are arranged so that $m\angle EFG = 29°$ and $\overline{GF}$ bisects $\angle EGD$. What is $m\angle AEG$?

3. The Air Zoo's flight simulators let visitors practice takeoffs and landings. To determine the position of a plane during takeoff, an airport uses two cameras mounted 1000 ft apart. What is the distance d that the plane has moved along the runway since it passed camera 1?

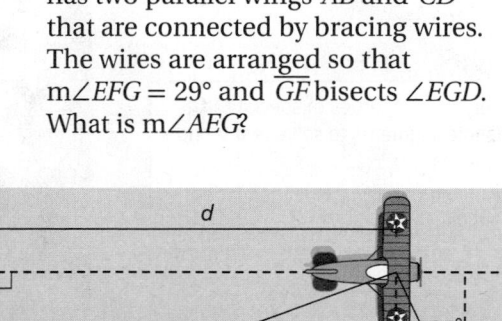

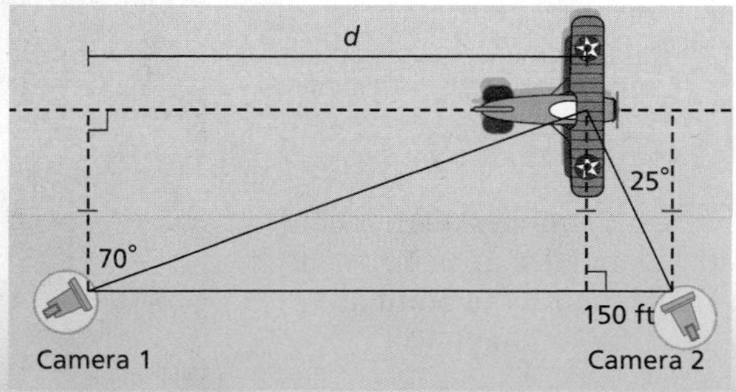

Real-World Connections

CHAPTER

5 Properties and Attributes of Triangles

COMMON CORE

Chapter

- Apply the properties of special triangle segments to solve real-world problems.
- Justify and apply inequality relationships in triangles.

Balancing Act

Sculptures and mobiles often include carefully balanced shapes. You can use medians to find the point at which a triangular shape will balance.

Learn It Online
Chapter Project Online

ARE YOU READY?

Vocabulary

Match each term on the left with a definition on the right.

1. angle bisector
2. conclusion
3. hypotenuse
4. leg of a right triangle
5. perpendicular bisector of a segment

A. the side opposite the right angle in a right triangle
B. a line that is perpendicular to a segment at its midpoint
C. the phrase following the word *then* in a conditional statement
D. one of the two sides that form the right angle in a right triangle
E. a line or ray that divides an angle into two congruent angles
F. the phrase following the word *if* in a conditional statement

Classify Triangles

Tell whether each triangle is acute, right, or obtuse.

6.
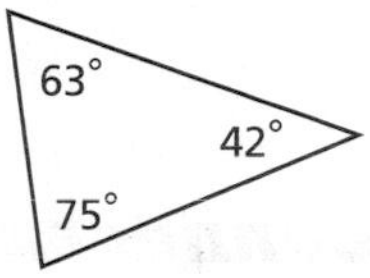

7.
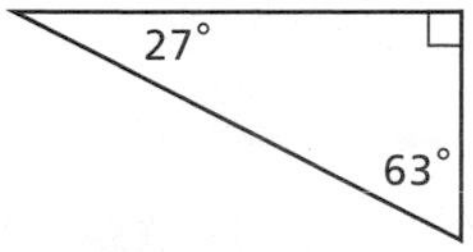

8.
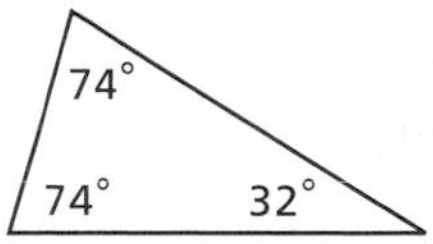

9.
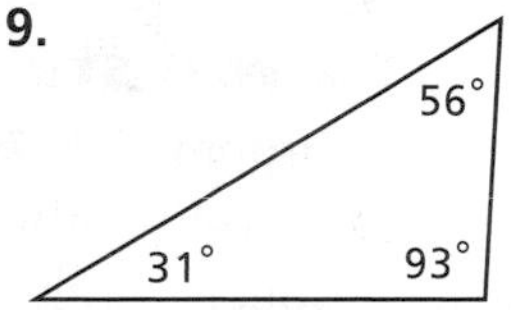

Squares and Square Roots

Simplify each expression.

10. 8^2
11. $(-12)^2$
12. $\sqrt{49}$
13. $-\sqrt{36}$

Simplify Radical Expressions

Simplify each expression.

14. $\sqrt{9+16}$
15. $\sqrt{100-36}$
16. $\sqrt{\frac{81}{25}}$
17. $\sqrt{2^2}$

Solve and Graph Inequalities

Solve each inequality. Graph the solutions on a number line.

18. $d+5<1$
19. $-4 \le w-7$
20. $-3s \ge 6$
21. $-2 > \frac{m}{10}$

Logical Reasoning

Draw a conclusion from each set of true statements.

22. If two lines intersect, then they are not parallel.
Lines ℓ and m intersect at P.
23. If M is the midpoint of $\overline{AB}$, then $AM = MB$.
If $AM = MB$, then $AM = \frac{1}{2}AB$ and $MB = \frac{1}{2}AB$.

CHAPTER 5

Study Guide: Preview

Where You've Been

Previously, you

- studied points, lines, rays, segments, and angles.
- learned properties of triangles.
- identified congruent triangles.
- used the Pythagorean Theorem to find distances.
- used deductive reasoning to write proofs.

In This Chapter

You will study

- properties of perpendicular bisectors and angle bisectors.
- special points, segments, and lines related to triangles.
- inequalities in one triangle and in two triangles.
- Pythagorean inequalities and special right triangles.
- how to write an indirect proof.

Where You're Going

You can use the skills learned in this chapter

- to study trigonometry in geometry, algebra, and advanced math courses.
- to study motion and forces in physics courses.
- to estimate travel distances and to assess the validity of indirect arguments outside of school.

Key Vocabulary/Vocabulario

altitude of a triangle	altura de un triángulo
centroid of a triangle	centroide de un triángulo
circumcenter of a triangle	circuncentro de un triángulo
concurrent	concurrente
equidistant	equidistante
incenter of a triangle	incentro de un triángulo
median of a triangle	mediana de un triángulo
midsegment of a triangle	segmento medio de un triángulo
orthocenter of a triangle	orthocentro de un triángulo

Vocabulary Connections

To become familiar with some of the vocabulary terms in the chapter, consider the following. You may refer to the chapter, the glossary, or a dictionary if you like.

1. In Latin, *co* means "together with," and *currere* means "to run." How can you use these meanings to understand what **concurrent** lines are?
2. The endpoints of a **midsegment of a triangle** are on two sides of the triangle. Where on the sides do you think the endpoints are located?
3. The strip of concrete or grass in the middle of some roadways is called the *median*. What do you think the term **median of a triangle** means?
4. The word **equidistant** begins with *equi-*, which means "equal." List three other words that begin with *equi-*. What is the meaning of each word?
5. Think of the everyday meaning of *altitude*. What do you think the **altitude of a triangle** is?

Reading and Writing Math

Reading Strategy: Learn Math Vocabulary

Mathematics has a vocabulary all its own. To learn and remember new vocabulary words, use the following study strategies.

- Try to figure out the meaning of a new word based on its context.
- Use a dictionary to look up the root word or prefix.
- Relate the new word to familiar everyday words.

Once you know what a word means, write its definition in your own words.

Term	Study Notes	Definition
Polygon	*The prefix poly means "many" or "several."*	*A closed plane figure formed by three or more line segments*
Bisect	*The prefix bi means "two."*	*Cuts or divides something into two equal parts*
Slope	*Think of a ski slope.*	*The measure of the steepness of a line*
Intersection	*The root word intersect means "to overlap." Think of the intersection of two roads.*	*The set of points that two or more lines have in common*

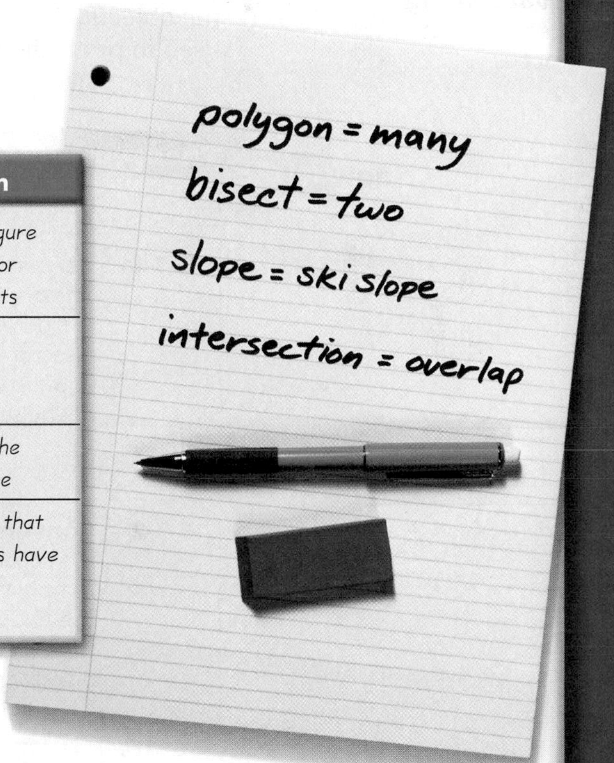

Try This

Complete the table below.

	Term	Study Notes	Definition
1.	Trinomial		
2.	Equiangular triangle		
3.	Perimeter		
4.	Deductive reasoning		

Use the given prefix and its meanings to write a definition for each vocabulary word.

5. *circum* (about, around); circumference

6. *co* (with, together); coplanar

7. *trans* (across, beyond, through); translation

COMMON CORE

5-1 Perpendicular and Angle Bisectors

CC.9-12.G.CO.9 Prove geometric theorems about lines and angles. *Also* **CC.9-12.G.SRT.4**

Objectives
Prove and apply theorems about perpendicular bisectors.

Prove and apply theorems about angle bisectors.

Vocabulary
equidistant
locus

Who uses this?
The suspension and steering lines of a parachute keep the sky diver centered under the parachute. (See Example 3.)

When a point is the same distance from two or more objects, the point is said to be **equidistant** from the objects. Triangle congruence theorems can be used to prove theorems about equidistant points.

Know it! *Note*

Theorems **Distance and Perpendicular Bisectors**

THEOREM		HYPOTHESIS	CONCLUSION
5-1-1	**Perpendicular Bisector Theorem** If a point is on the perpendicular bisector of a segment, then it is equidistant from the endpoints of the segment.	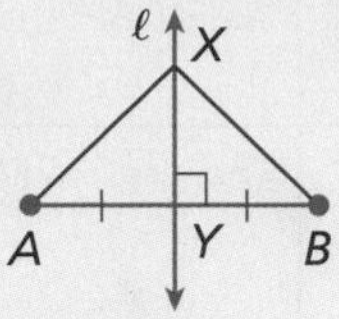 $\overline{XY} \perp \overline{AB}$ $\overline{YA} \cong \overline{YB}$	$XA = XB$
5-1-2	**Converse of the Perpendicular Bisector Theorem** If a point is equidistant from the endpoints of a segment, then it is on the perpendicular bisector of the segment.	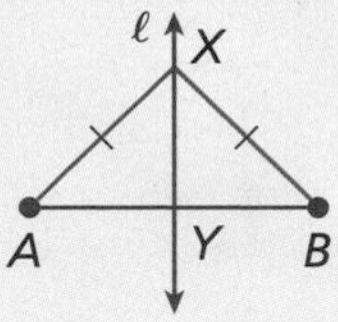 $XA = XB$	$\overline{XY} \perp \overline{AB}$ $\overline{YA} \cong \overline{YB}$

You will prove Theorem 5-1-2 in Exercise 30.

PROOF

Perpendicular Bisector Theorem

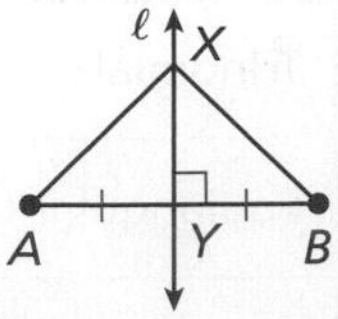

Given: ℓ is the perpendicular bisector of $\overline{AB}$.
Prove: $XA = XB$

Proof:

Since ℓ is the perpendicular bisector of $\overline{AB}$, $\ell \perp \overline{AB}$ and Y is the midpoint of $\overline{AB}$. By the definition of perpendicular, $\angle AYX$ and $\angle BYX$ are right angles and $\angle AYX \cong \angle BYX$. By the definition of midpoint, $\overline{AY} \cong \overline{BY}$. By the Reflexive Property of Congruence, $\overline{XY} \cong \overline{XY}$. So $\triangle AYX \cong \triangle BYX$ by SAS, and $\overline{XA} \cong \overline{XB}$ by CPCTC. Therefore $XA = XB$ by the definition of congruent segments.

Reading Math

The word *locus* comes from the Latin word for location. The plural of *locus* is *loci*, which is pronounced LOW-sigh.

A **locus** is a set of points that satisfies a given condition. The perpendicular bisector of a segment can be defined as the locus of points in a plane that are equidistant from the endpoints of the segment.

EXAMPLE 1 Applying the Perpendicular Bisector Theorem and Its Converse

Find each measure.

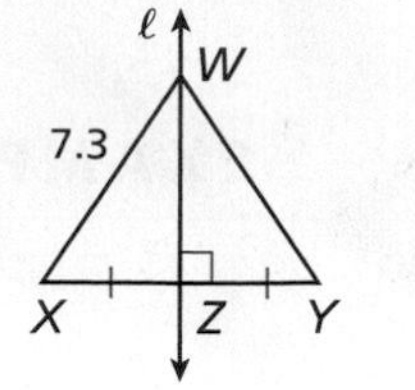

A *YW*

$YW = XW$	*⊥ Bisector Thm.*
$YW = 7.3$	*Substitute 7.3 for XW.*

B *BC*

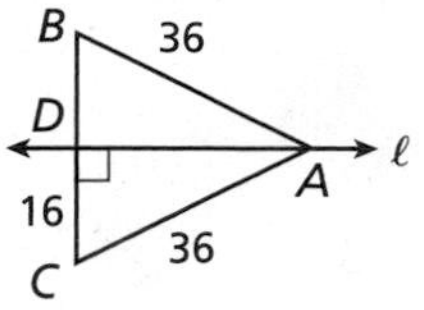

Since $AB = AC$ and $\ell \perp \overline{BC}$, ℓ is the perpendicular bisector of $\overline{BC}$ by the Converse of the Perpendicular Bisector Theorem.

$BC = 2CD$	*Def. of seg. bisector*
$BC = 2(16) = 32$	*Substitute 16 for CD.*

Algebra

C *PR*

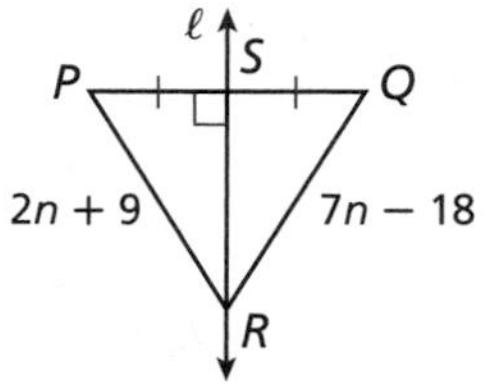

$PR = RQ$	*⊥ Bisector Thm.*
$2n + 9 = 7n - 18$	*Substitute the given values.*
$9 = 5n - 18$	*Subtract 2n from both sides.*
$27 = 5n$	*Add 18 to both sides.*
$5.4 = n$	*Divide both sides by 5.*

So $PR = 2(5.4) + 9 = 19.8$.

CHECK IT OUT! **Find each measure.**

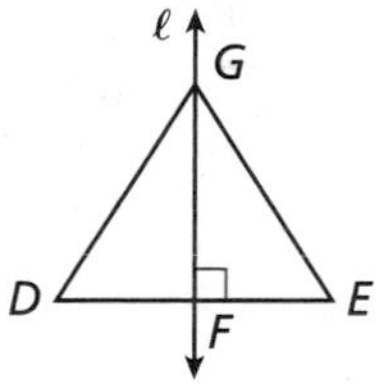

1a. Given that line ℓ is the perpendicular bisector of $\overline{DE}$ and $EG = 14.6$, find DG.

1b. Given that $DE = 20.8$, $DG = 36.4$, and $EG = 36.4$, find EF.

Remember that the distance between a point and a line is the length of the perpendicular segment from the point to the line.

Know it! Note

Theorems Distance and Angle Bisectors

THEOREM		HYPOTHESIS	CONCLUSION
5-1-3	**Angle Bisector Theorem** If a point is on the bisector of an angle, then it is equidistant from the sides of the angle.	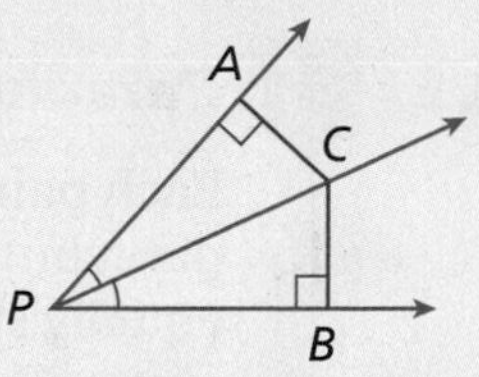 $\angle APC \cong \angle BPC$	$AC = BC$
5-1-4	**Converse of the Angle Bisector Theorem** If a point in the interior of an angle is equidistant from the sides of the angle, then it is on the bisector of the angle.	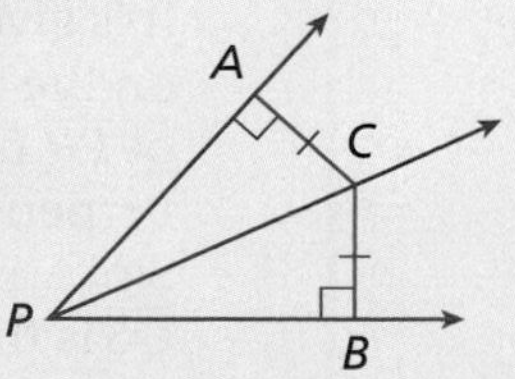 $AC = BC$	$\angle APC \cong \angle BPC$

You will prove these theorems in Exercises 31 and 40.

Based on these theorems, an angle bisector can be defined as the locus of all points in the interior of the angle that are equidistant from the sides of the angle.

EXAMPLE 2 Applying the Angle Bisector Theorems

Find each measure.

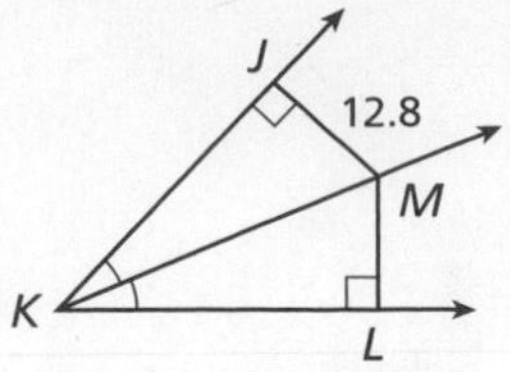

A *LM*

$LM = JM$	*∠ Bisector Thm.*
$LM = 12.8$	*Substitute 12.8 for JM.*

B **m∠*ABD*, given that m∠*ABC* = 112°**

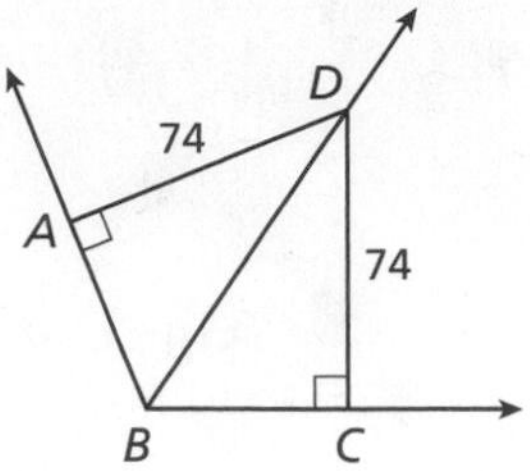

Since $AD = DC$, $\overline{AD} \perp \overline{BA}$, and $\overline{DC} \perp \overline{BC}$, $\overrightarrow{BD}$ bisects ∠*ABC* by the Converse of the Angle Bisector Theorem.

$m\angle ABD = \frac{1}{2} m\angle ABC$	*Def. of ∠ bisector*
$m\angle ABD = \frac{1}{2}(112°) = 56°$	*Substitute 112° for m∠ABC.*

Algebra

C m∠*TSU*

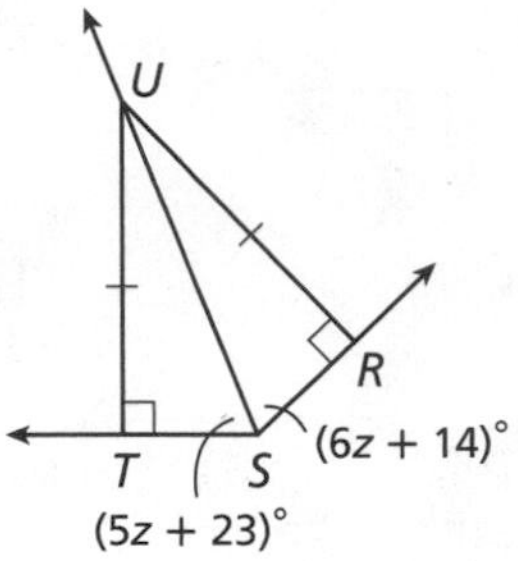

Since $RU = UT$, $\overline{RU} \perp \overline{SR}$, and $\overline{UT} \perp \overline{ST}$, $\overrightarrow{SU}$ bisects ∠*RST* by the Converse of the Angle Bisector Theorem.

$m\angle RSU = m\angle TSU$	*Def. of ∠ bisector*
$6z + 14 = 5z + 23$	*Substitute the given values.*
$z + 14 = 23$	*Subtract 5z from both sides.*
$z = 9$	*Subtract 14 from both sides.*

So $m\angle TSU = [5(9) + 23]° = 68°$.

CHECK IT OUT! **Find each measure.**

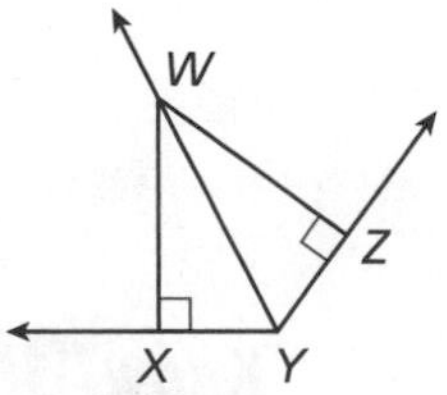

2a. Given that $\overrightarrow{YW}$ bisects ∠*XYZ* and $WZ = 3.05$, find *WX*.

2b. Given that m∠*WYZ* = 63°, $XW = 5.7$, and $ZW = 5.7$, find m∠*XYZ*.

EXAMPLE 3 *Parachute Application*

Each pair of suspension lines on a parachute are the same length and are equally spaced from the center of the chute. How do these lines keep the sky diver centered under the parachute?

It is given that $\overline{PQ} \cong \overline{RQ}$. So *Q* is on the perpendicular bisector of $\overline{PR}$ by the Converse of the Perpendicular Bisector Theorem. Since *S* is the midpoint of $\overline{PR}$, $\overline{QS}$ is the perpendicular bisector of $\overline{PR}$. Therefore the sky diver remains centered under the chute.

CHECK IT OUT! **3.** S is equidistant from each pair of suspension lines. What can you conclude about $\overrightarrow{QS}$?

EXAMPLE 4 Writing Equations of Bisectors in the Coordinate Plane

Algebra

Write an equation in point-slope form for the perpendicular bisector of the segment with endpoints $A(-1, 6)$ and $B(3, 4)$.

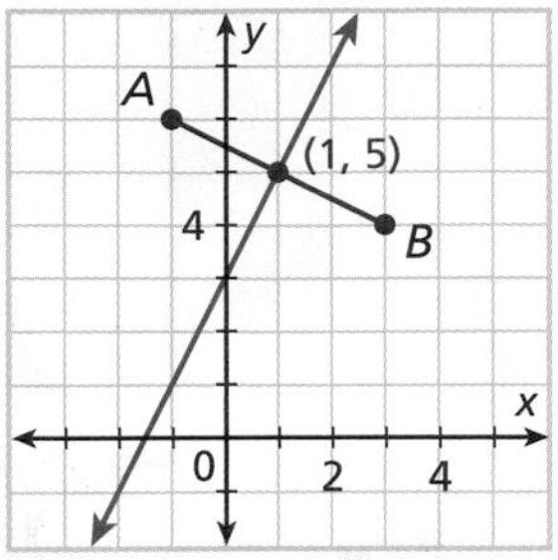

Step 1 Graph $\overline{AB}$.

The perpendicular bisector of $\overline{AB}$ is perpendicular to $\overline{AB}$ at its midpoint.

Step 2 Find the midpoint of $\overline{AB}$.

$\left(\frac{x_1 + x_2}{2}, \frac{y_1 + y_2}{2}\right)$ *Midpoint formula*

mdpt. of $\overline{AB} = \left(\frac{-1 + 3}{2}, \frac{6 + 4}{2}\right) = (1, 5)$

Step 3 Find the slope of the perpendicular bisector.

slope $= \frac{y_2 - y_1}{x_2 - x_1}$ *Slope formula*

slope of $\overline{AB} = \frac{4 - 6}{3 - (-1)} = \frac{-2}{4} = -\frac{1}{2}$

Since the slopes of perpendicular lines are opposite reciprocals, the slope of the perpendicular bisector is 2.

Step 4 Use point-slope form to write an equation.

The perpendicular bisector of $\overline{AB}$ has slope 2 and passes through $(1, 5)$.

$y - y_1 = m(x - x_1)$ *Point-slope form*

$y - 5 = 2(x - 1)$ *Substitute 5 for y_1, 2 for m, and 1 for x_1.*

CHECK IT OUT! **4.** Write an equation in point-slope form for the perpendicular bisector of the segment with endpoints $P(5, 2)$ and $Q(1, -4)$.

MATHEMATICAL PRACTICES

THINK AND DISCUSS

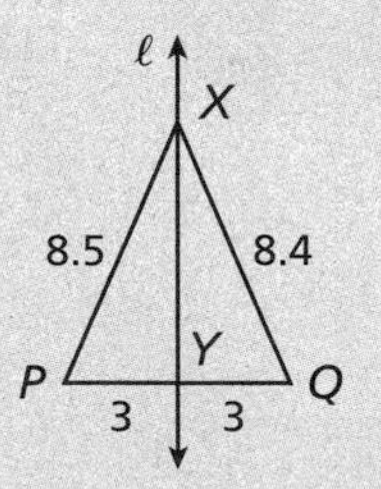

1. Is line ℓ a bisector of $\overline{PQ}$? Is it a perpendicular bisector of $\overline{PQ}$? Explain.

2. Suppose that M is in the interior of $\angle JKL$ and $MJ = ML$. Can you conclude that $\overrightarrow{KM}$ is the bisector of $\angle JKL$? Explain.

Know it! Note

3. **GET ORGANIZED** Copy and complete the graphic organizer. In each box, write the theorem or its converse in your own words.

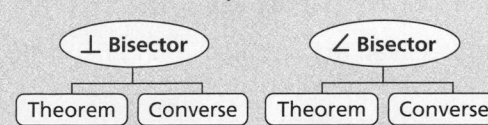

⊥ Bisector: Theorem | Converse

∠ Bisector: Theorem | Converse

5-1 Exercises

Learn It Online
Homework Help Online
Parent Resources Online

GUIDED PRACTICE

1. **Vocabulary** A ___?___ is the *locus* of all points in a plane that are *equidistant* from the endpoints of a segment. (*perpendicular bisector* or *angle bisector*)

SEE EXAMPLE 1

Use the diagram for Exercises 2–4.

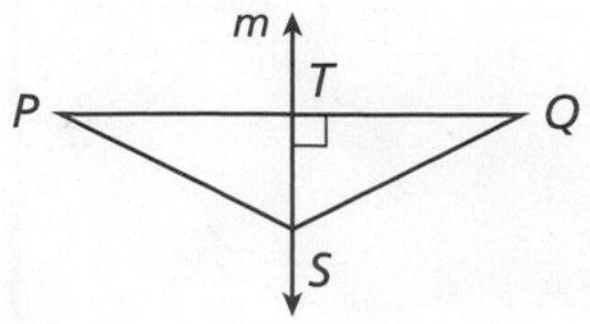

2. Given that $PS = 53.4$, $QT = 47.7$, and $QS = 53.4$, find PQ.
3. Given that m is the perpendicular bisector of $\overline{PQ}$ and $SQ = 25.9$, find SP.
4. Given that m is the perpendicular bisector of $\overline{PQ}$, $PS = 4a$, and $QS = 2a + 26$, find QS.

SEE EXAMPLE 2

Use the diagram for Exercises 5–7.

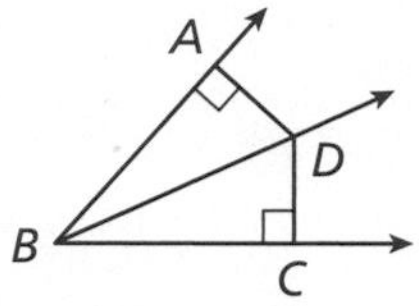

5. Given that $\overrightarrow{BD}$ bisects $\angle ABC$ and $CD = 21.9$, find AD.
6. Given that $AD = 61$, $CD = 61$, and $m\angle ABC = 48°$, find $m\angle CBD$.
7. Given that $DA = DC$, $m\angle DBC = (10y + 3)°$, and $m\angle DBA = (8y + 10)°$, find $m\angle DBC$.

SEE EXAMPLE 3

8. **Carpentry** For a king post truss to be constructed correctly, P must lie on the bisector of $\angle JLN$. How can braces $\overline{PK}$ and $\overline{PM}$ be used to ensure that P is in the proper location?

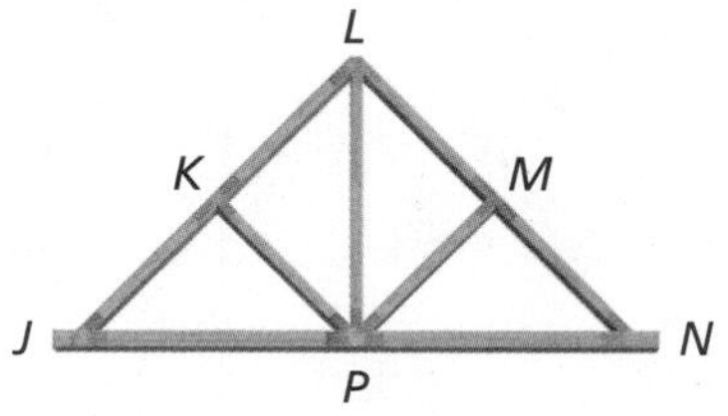

SEE EXAMPLE 4

Write an equation in point-slope form for the perpendicular bisector of the segment with the given endpoints.

9. $M(-5, 4)$, $N(1, -2)$
10. $U(2, -6)$, $V(4, 0)$
11. $J(-7, 5)$, $K(1, -1)$

PRACTICE AND PROBLEM SOLVING

Independent Practice

For Exercises	See Example
12–14	1
15–17	2
18	3
19–21	4

Extra Practice

See Extra Practice for more Skills Practice and Applications Practice exercises.

Use the diagram for Exercises 12–14.

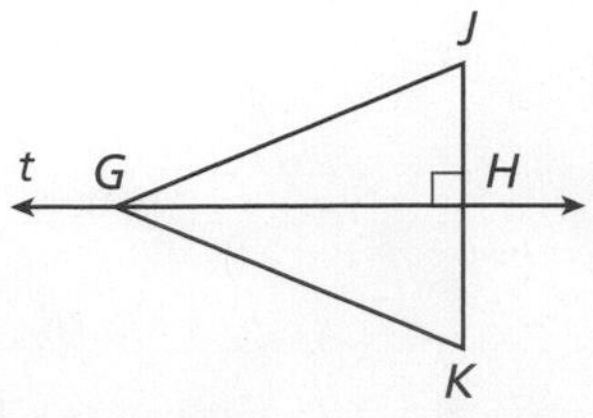

12. Given that line t is the perpendicular bisector of $\overline{JK}$ and $GK = 8.25$, find GJ.
13. Given that line t is the perpendicular bisector of $\overline{JK}$, $JG = x + 12$, and $KG = 3x - 17$, find KG.
14. Given that $GJ = 70.2$, $JH = 26.5$, and $GK = 70.2$, find JK.

Use the diagram for Exercises 15–17.

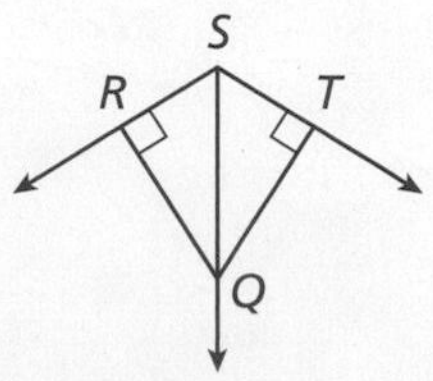

15. Given that $m\angle RSQ = m\angle TSQ$ and $TQ = 1.3$, find RQ.
16. Given that $m\angle RSQ = 58°$, $RQ = 49$, and $TQ = 49$, find $m\angle RST$.
17. Given that $RQ = TQ$, $m\angle QSR = (9a + 48)°$, and $m\angle QST = (6a + 50)°$, find $m\angle QST$.

18. **City Planning** The planners for a new section of the city want every location on Main Street to be equidistant from Elm Street and Grove Street. How can the planners ensure that this is the case?

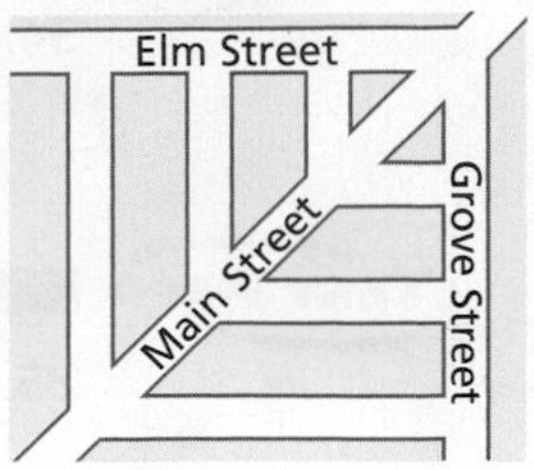

Write an equation in point-slope form for the perpendicular bisector of the segment with the given endpoints.

19. $E(-4, -7)$, $F(0, 1)$ 20. $X(-7, 5)$, $Y(-1, -1)$ 21. $M(-3, -1)$, $N(7, -5)$

22. $\overline{PQ}$ is the perpendicular bisector of $\overline{ST}$. Find the values of m and n.

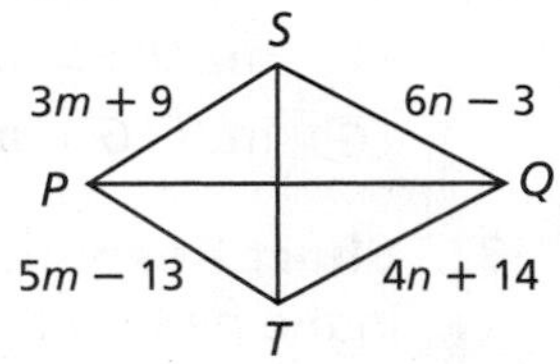

One of the first recorded shuffleboard games was played in England in 1532. In this game, Henry VIII supposedly lost £9 to Lord William.

Shuffleboard **Use the diagram of a shuffleboard and the following information to find each length in Exercises 23–28.**

$\overline{KZ}$ is the perpendicular bisector of $\overline{GN}$, $\overline{HM}$, and $\overline{JL}$.

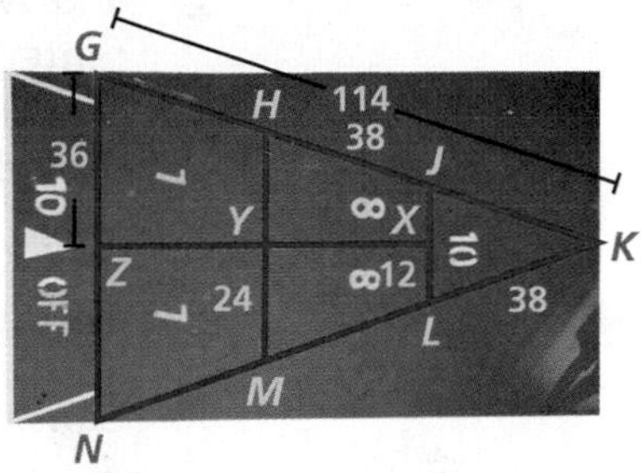

23. JK 24. GN 25. ML

26. HY 27. JL 28. NM

29. **Multi-Step** The endpoints of $\overline{AB}$ are $A(-2, 1)$ and $B(4, -3)$. Find the coordinates of a point C other than the midpoint of $\overline{AB}$ that is on the perpendicular bisector of $\overline{AB}$. How do you know it is on the perpendicular bisector?

30. Write a paragraph proof of the Converse of the Perpendicular Bisector Theorem.

Given: $AX = BX$

Prove: X is on the perpendicular bisector of $\overline{AB}$.

Plan: Draw ℓ perpendicular to $\overline{AB}$ through X. Show that $\triangle AYX \cong \triangle BYX$ and thus $\overline{AY} \cong \overline{BY}$. By definition, ℓ is the perpendicular bisector of $\overline{AB}$.

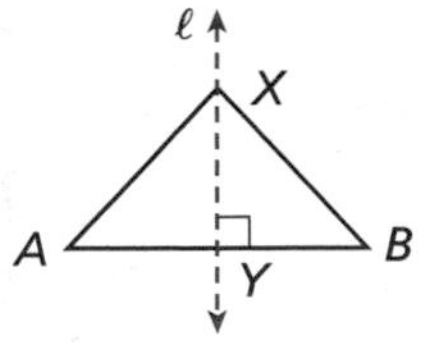

31. Write a two-column proof of the Angle Bisector Theorem.

Given: $\overrightarrow{PS}$ bisects $\angle QPR$. $\overline{SQ} \perp \overrightarrow{PQ}$, $\overline{SR} \perp \overrightarrow{PR}$

Prove: $SQ = SR$

Plan: Use the definitions of angle bisector and perpendicular to identify two pairs of congruent angles. Show that $\triangle PQS \cong \triangle PRS$ and thus $\overline{SQ} \cong \overline{SR}$.

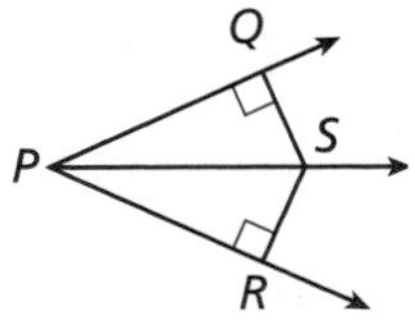

32. **Critical Thinking** In the Converse of the Angle Bisector Theorem, why is it important to say that the point must be in the interior of the angle?

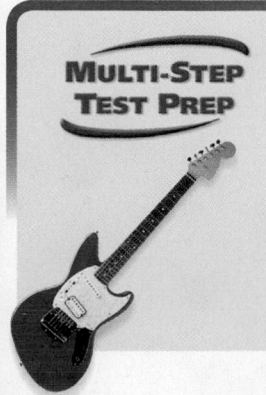

MULTI-STEP TEST PREP

33. A music company has stores in Abby $(-3, -2)$ and Cardenas $(3, 6)$. Each unit in the coordinate plane represents 1 mile.

   a. The company president wants to build a warehouse that is equidistant from the two stores. Write an equation that describes the possible locations.

   b. A straight road connects Abby and Cardenas. The warehouse will be located exactly 4 miles from the road. How many locations are possible?

   c. To the nearest tenth of a mile, how far will the warehouse be from each store?

34. **Write About It** How is the construction of the perpendicular bisector of a segment related to the Converse of the Perpendicular Bisector Theorem?

TEST PREP

35. If $\overleftrightarrow{JK}$ is perpendicular to $\overline{XY}$ at its midpoint M, which statement is true?

   (A) $JX = KY$ (B) $JX = KX$ (C) $JM = KM$ (D) $JX = JY$

36. What information is needed to conclude that $\overrightarrow{EF}$ is the bisector of $\angle DEG$?

   (F) $m\angle DEF = m\angle DEG$
   (G) $m\angle FEG = m\angle DEF$
   (H) $m\angle GED = m\angle GEF$
   (J) $m\angle DEF = m\angle EFG$

37. **Short Response** The city wants to build a visitor center in the park so that it is equidistant from Park Street and Washington Avenue. They also want the visitor center to be equidistant from the museum and the library. Find the point V where the visitor center should be built. Explain your answer.

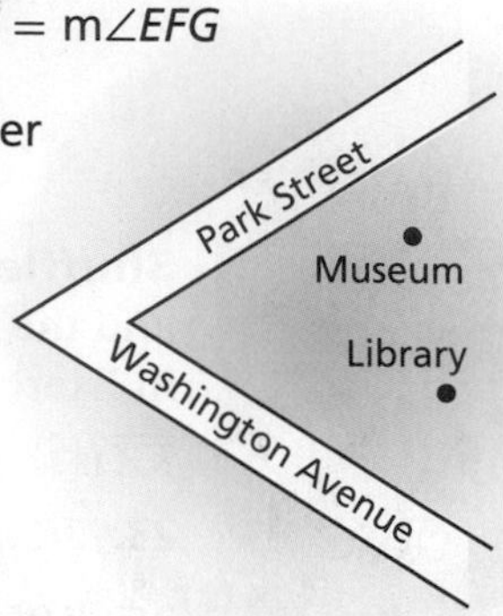

CHALLENGE AND EXTEND

38. Consider the points $P(2, 0)$, $A(-4, 2)$, $B(0, -6)$, and $C(6, -3)$.
   a. Show that P is on the bisector of $\angle ABC$.
   b. Write an equation of the line that contains the bisector of $\angle ABC$.

39. Find the locus of points that are equidistant from the x-axis and y-axis.

40. Write a two-column proof of the Converse of the Angle Bisector Theorem.

   Given: $\overline{VX} \perp \overrightarrow{YX}$, $\overline{VZ} \perp \overrightarrow{YZ}$, $VX = VZ$
   Prove: $\overrightarrow{YV}$ bisects $\angle XYZ$.

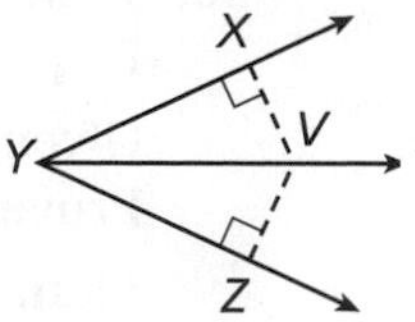

41. Write a paragraph proof.

   Given: $\overline{KN}$ is the perpendicular bisector of $\overline{JL}$.
   $\overline{LN}$ is the perpendicular bisector of $\overline{KM}$.
   $\overline{JR} \cong \overline{MT}$
   Prove: $\angle JKM \cong \angle MLJ$

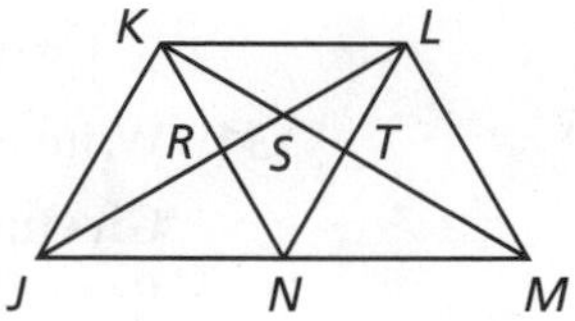

COMMON CORE

5-2 Bisectors of Triangles

CC.9-12.G.C.3 Construct… inscribed and circumscribed circles of a triangle… *Also* **CC.9-12.G.CO.12, CC.9-12.G.MG.2***

Objectives

Prove and apply properties of perpendicular bisectors of a triangle.

Prove and apply properties of angle bisectors of a triangle.

Vocabulary

concurrent
point of concurrency
circumcenter of a triangle
circumscribed
incenter of a triangle
inscribed

Who uses this?

An event planner can use perpendicular bisectors of triangles to find the best location for a fireworks display. (See Example 4.)

Since a triangle has three sides, it has three perpendicular bisectors. When you construct the perpendicular bisectors, you find that they have an interesting property.

Construction Circumcenter of a Triangle

1 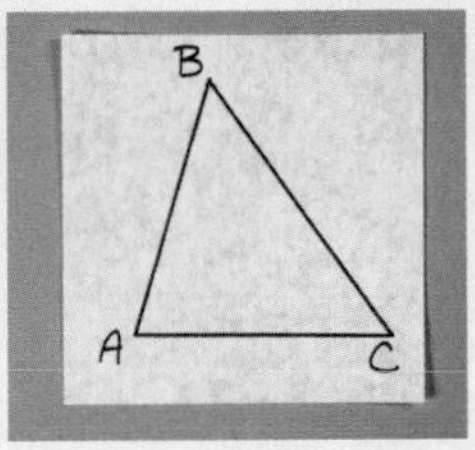

Draw a large scalene acute triangle *ABC* on a piece of patty paper.

2 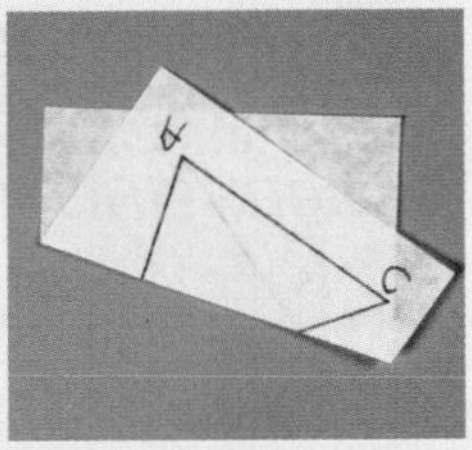

Fold the perpendicular bisector of each side.

3 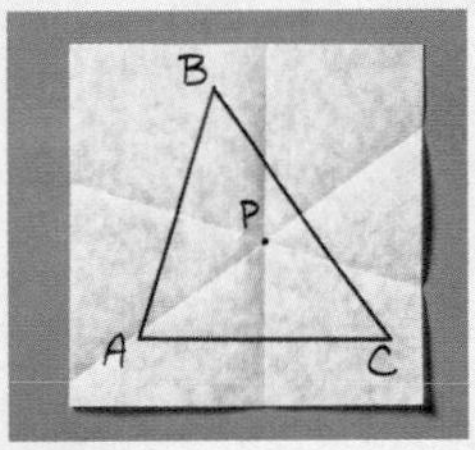

Label the point where the three perpendicular bisectors intersect as *P*.

Helpful Hint

The perpendicular bisector of a side of a triangle does not always pass through the opposite vertex.

When three or more lines intersect at one point, the lines are said to be **concurrent**. The **point of concurrency** is the point where they intersect. In the construction, you saw that the three perpendicular bisectors of a triangle are concurrent. This point of concurrency is the **circumcenter of the triangle**.

Know it! Note

Theorem 5-2-1 Circumcenter Theorem

The circumcenter of a triangle is equidistant from the vertices of the triangle.

$PA = PB = PC$

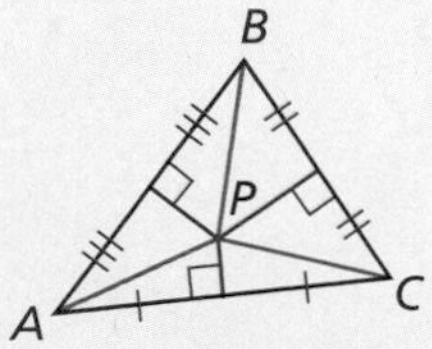

The circumcenter can be inside the triangle, outside the triangle, or on the triangle.

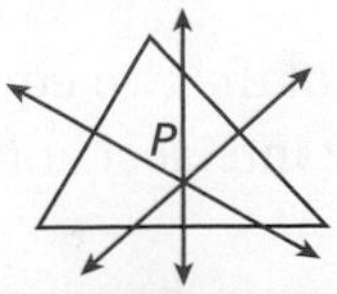

Acute triangle

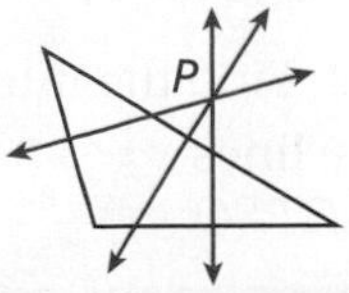

Obtuse triangle

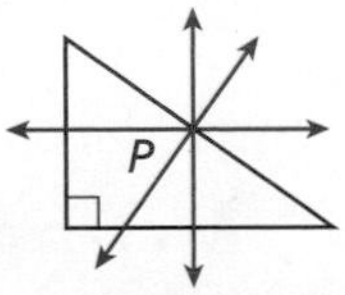

Right triangle

(tr), Firefly Productions/CORBIS; (cl)(c)(cr), Sam Dudgeon/HMH Photo;

The circumcenter of $\triangle ABC$ is the center of its *circumscribed* circle. A circle that contains all the vertices of a polygon is **circumscribed** about the polygon.

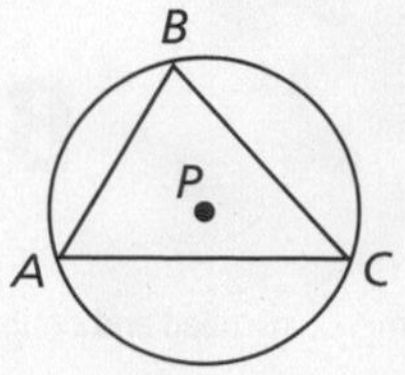

PROOF

Circumcenter Theorem

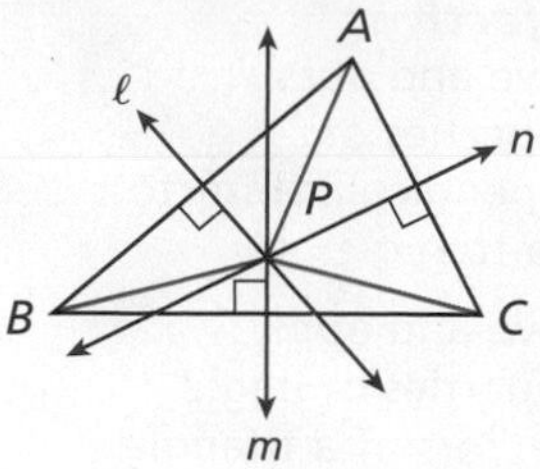

Given: Lines ℓ, m, and n are the perpendicular bisectors of $\overline{AB}$, $\overline{BC}$, and $\overline{AC}$, respectively.

Prove: $PA = PB = PC$

Proof:

P is the circumcenter of $\triangle ABC$. Since P lies on the perpendicular bisector of $\overline{AB}$, $PA = PB$ by the Perpendicular Bisector Theorem. Similarly, P also lies on the perpendicular bisector of $\overline{BC}$, so $PB = PC$. Therefore $PA = PB = PC$ by the Transitive Property of Equality.

EXAMPLE 1 Using Properties of Perpendicular Bisectors

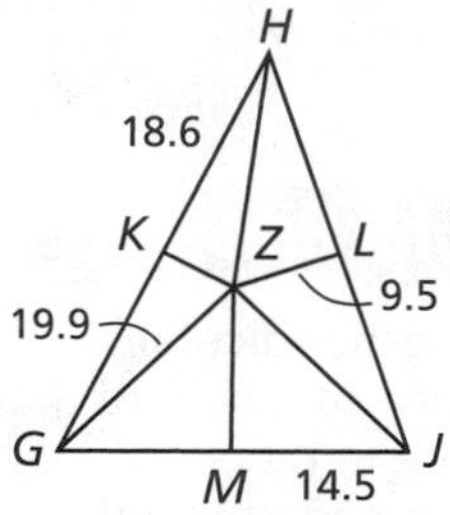

$\overline{KZ}$, $\overline{LZ}$, and $\overline{MZ}$ are the perpendicular bisectors of $\triangle GHJ$. Find HZ.

Z is the circumcenter of $\triangle GHJ$. By the Circumcenter Theorem, Z is equidistant from the vertices of $\triangle GHJ$.

$HZ = GZ$	*Circumcenter Thm.*
$HZ = 19.9$	*Substitute 19.9 for GZ.*

CHECK IT OUT! **Use the diagram above. Find each length.**

1a. GM **1b.** GK **1c.** JZ

EXAMPLE 2 Finding the Circumcenter of a Triangle

Algebra

Find the circumcenter of $\triangle RSO$ with vertices $R(-6, 0)$, $S(0, 4)$, and $O(0, 0)$.

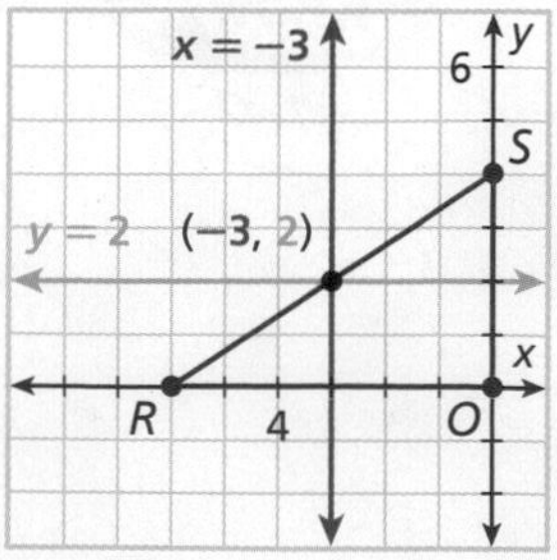

Step 1 Graph the triangle.

Step 2 Find equations for two perpendicular bisectors.

Since two sides of the triangle lie along the axes, use the graph to find the perpendicular bisectors of these two sides. The perpendicular bisector of $\overline{RO}$ is $x = -3$, and the perpendicular bisector of $\overline{OS}$ is $y = 2$.

Step 3 Find the intersection of the two equations.

The lines $x = -3$ and $y = 2$ intersect at $(-3, 2)$, the circumcenter of $\triangle RSO$.

CHECK IT OUT! 2. Find the circumcenter of $\triangle GOH$ with vertices $G(0, -9)$, $O(0, 0)$, and $H(8, 0)$.

A triangle has three angles, so it has three angle bisectors. The angle bisectors of a triangle are also concurrent. This point of concurrency is the **incenter of the triangle**.

Know it! Note

Theorem 5-2-2 Incenter Theorem

The incenter of a triangle is equidistant from the sides of the triangle.

$PX = PY = PZ$

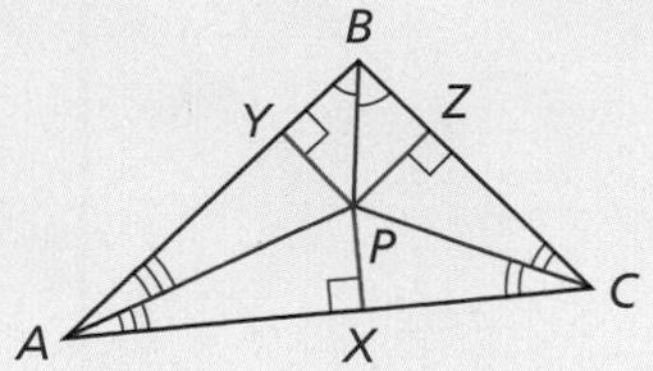

You will prove Theorem 5-2-2 in Exercise 35.

Remember!

The distance between a point and a line is the length of the perpendicular segment from the point to the line.

Unlike the circumcenter, the incenter is always inside the triangle.

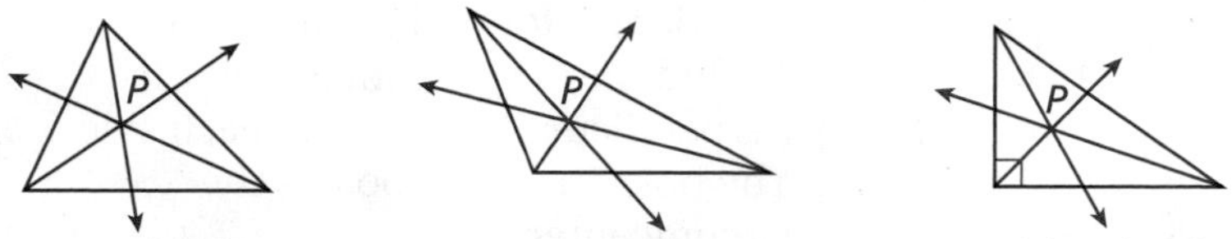

Acute triangle   Obtuse triangle   Right triangle

The incenter is the center of the triangle's *inscribed circle.* A circle **inscribed** in a polygon intersects each line that contains a side of the polygon at exactly one point.

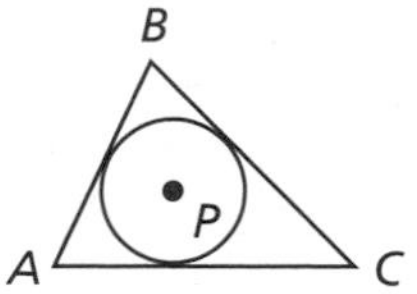

EXAMPLE 3 Using Properties of Angle Bisectors

$\overline{JV}$ and $\overline{KV}$ are angle bisectors of $\triangle JKL$. Find each measure.

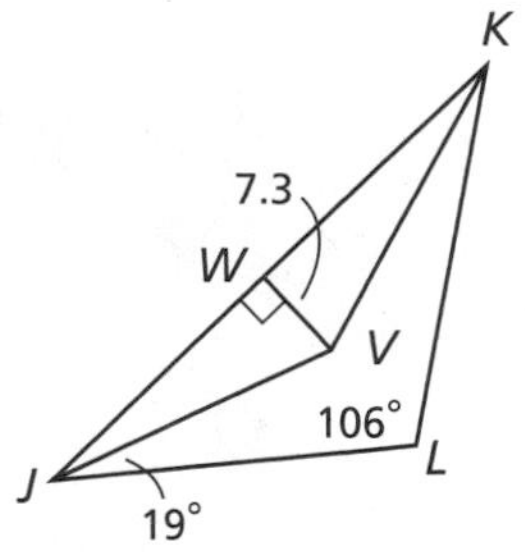

A **the distance from V to $\overline{KL}$**

V is the incenter of $\triangle JKL$. By the Incenter Theorem, V is equidistant from the sides of $\triangle JKL$.

The distance from V to $\overline{JK}$ is 7.3.

So the distance from V to $\overline{KL}$ is also 7.3.

B **$m\angle VKL$**

$m\angle KJL = 2m\angle VJL$	*$\overline{JV}$ is the bisector of $\angle KJL$.*
$m\angle KJL = 2(19°) = 38°$	*Substitute 19° for $m\angle VJL$.*
$m\angle KJL + m\angle JLK + m\angle JKL = 180°$	*$\triangle$ Sum Thm.*
$38 + 106 + m\angle JKL = 180$	*Substitute the given values.*
$m\angle JKL = 36°$	*Subtract 144° from both sides.*
$m\angle VKL = \frac{1}{2}m\angle JKL$	*$\overline{KV}$ is the bisector of $\angle JKL$.*
$m\angle VKL = \frac{1}{2}(36°) = 18°$	*Substitute 36° for $m\angle JKL$.*

CHECK IT OUT! $\overline{QX}$ and $\overline{RX}$ are angle bisectors of $\triangle PQR$. Find each measure.

3a. the distance from X to $\overline{PQ}$

3b. $m\angle PQX$

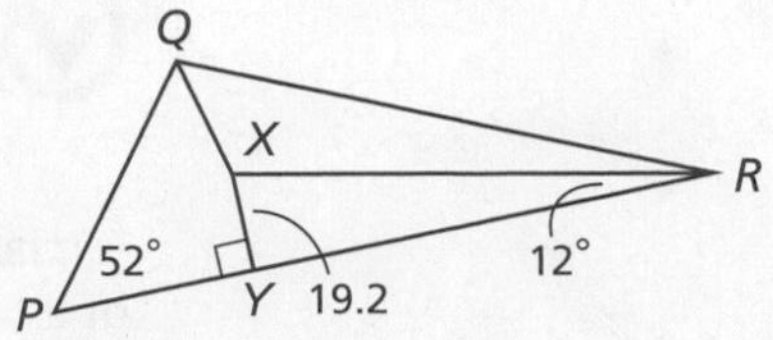

EXAMPLE 4 Community Application

For the next Fourth of July, the towns of Ashton, Bradford, and Clearview will launch a fireworks display from a boat in the lake. Draw a sketch to show where the boat should be positioned so that it is the same distance from all three towns. Justify your sketch.

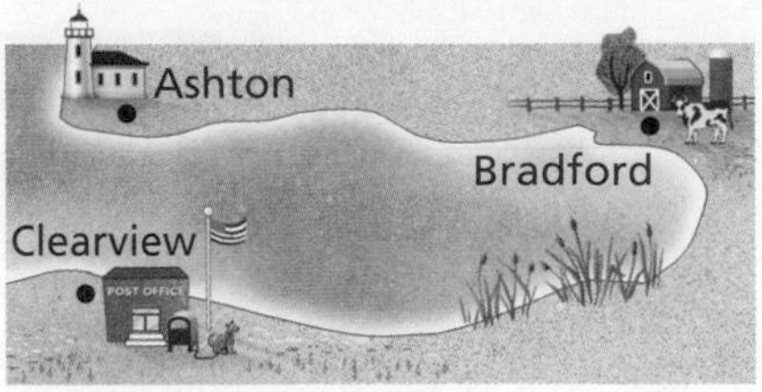

Let the three towns be vertices of a triangle. By the Circumcenter Theorem, the circumcenter of the triangle is equidistant from the vertices.

Trace the outline of the lake. Draw the triangle formed by the towns. To find the circumcenter, find the perpendicular bisectors of each side. The position of the boat is the circumcenter, *F*.

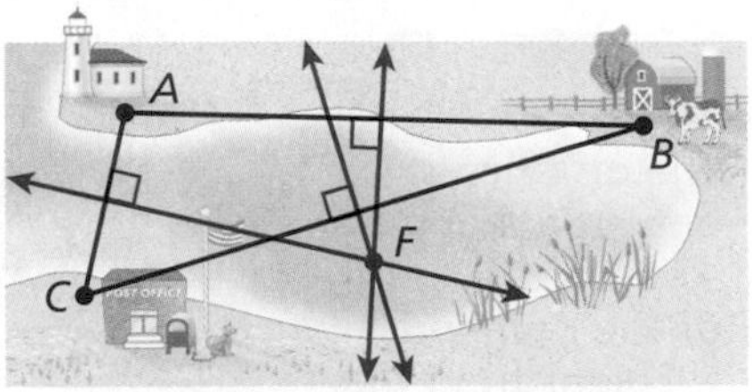

CHECK IT OUT! **4.** A city plans to build a firefighters' monument in the park between three streets. Draw a sketch to show where the city should place the monument so that it is the same distance from all three streets. Justify your sketch.

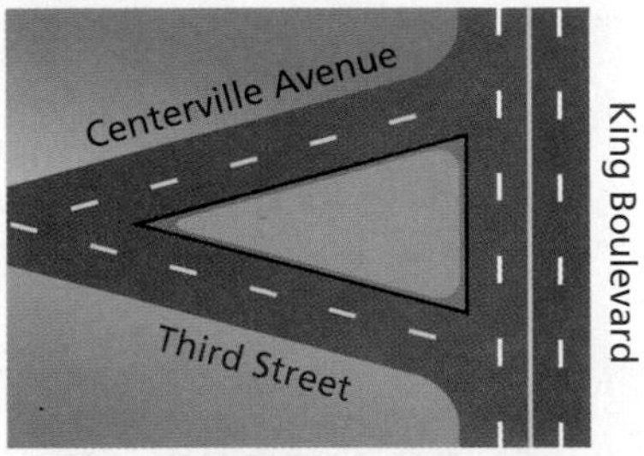

MATHEMATICAL PRACTICES

THINK AND DISCUSS

1. Sketch three lines that are concurrent.

2. *P* and *Q* are the circumcenter and incenter of $\triangle RST$, but not necessarily in that order. Which point is the circumcenter? Which point is the incenter? Explain how you can tell without constructing any of the bisectors.

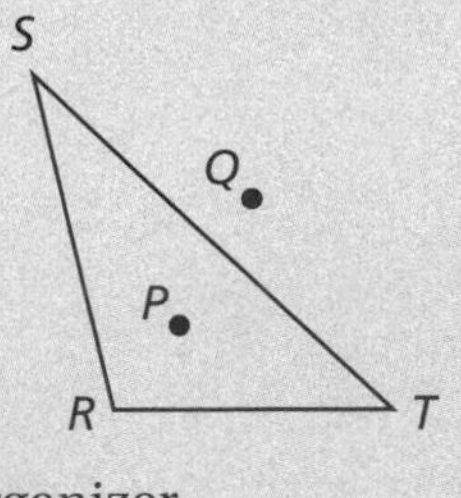

Know it! Note

3. GET ORGANIZED Copy and complete the graphic organizer. Fill in the blanks to make each statement true.

	Circumcenter	Incenter
Definition	The point of concurrency of the __?__	The point of concurrency of the __?__
Distance	Equidistant from the __?__	Equidistant from the __?__
Location (Inside, Outside, or On)	Can be __?__ the triangle	__?__ the triangle

5-2 Exercises

Learn It Online
Homework Help Online
Parent Resources Online

GUIDED PRACTICE

Vocabulary **Apply the vocabulary from this lesson to answer each question.**

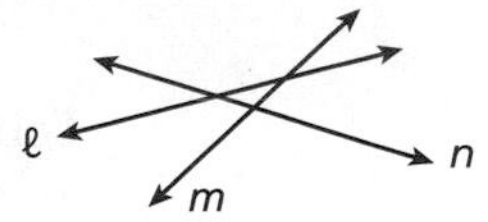

1. Explain why lines ℓ, m, and n are NOT *concurrent.*
2. A circle that contains all the vertices of a polygon is ___?___ the polygon. (*circumscribed about* or *inscribed in*)

SEE EXAMPLE 1

$\overline{SN}$, $\overline{TN}$, and $\overline{VN}$ are the perpendicular bisectors of $\triangle PQR$. Find each length.

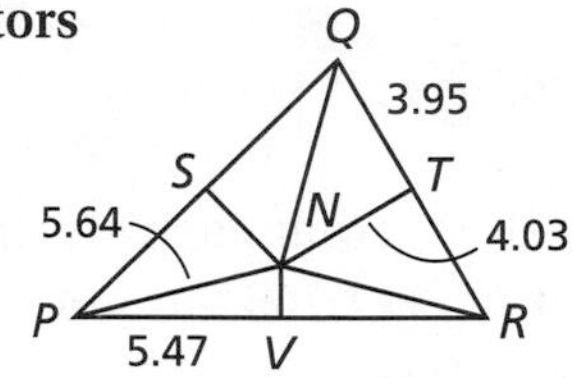

3. NR
4. RV
5. TR
6. QN

SEE EXAMPLE 2

Multi-Step **Find the circumcenter of a triangle with the given vertices.**

7. $O(0, 0)$, $K(0, 12)$, $L(4, 0)$
8. $A(-7, 0)$, $O(0, 0)$, $B(0, -10)$

SEE EXAMPLE 3

$\overline{CF}$ and $\overline{EF}$ are angle bisectors of $\triangle CDE$. Find each measure.

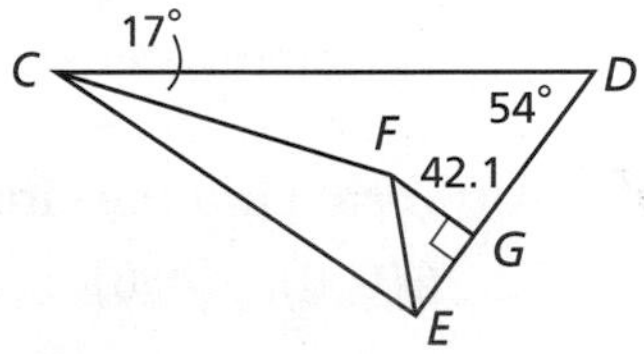

9. the distance from F to $\overline{CD}$
10. $m\angle FED$

SEE EXAMPLE 4

11. **Design** The designer of the Newtown High School pennant wants the circle around the bear emblem to be as large as possible. Draw a sketch to show where the center of the circle should be located. Justify your sketch.

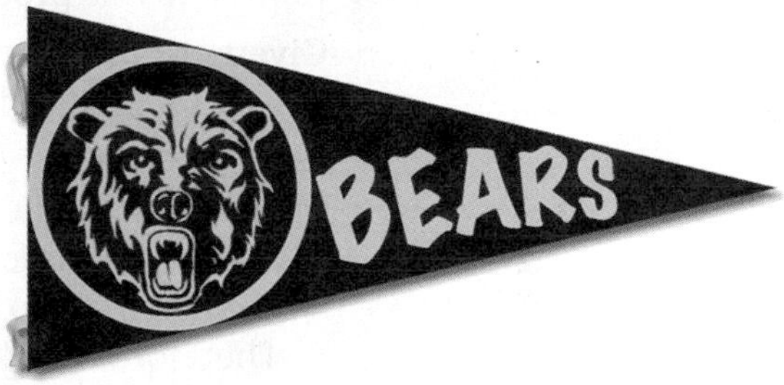

PRACTICE AND PROBLEM SOLVING

Independent Practice

For Exercises	See Example
12–15	1
16–17	2
18–19	3
20	4

Extra Practice

See Extra Practice for more Skills Practice and Applications Practice exercises.

$\overline{DY}$, $\overline{EY}$, and $\overline{FY}$ are the perpendicular bisectors of $\triangle ABC$. Find each length.

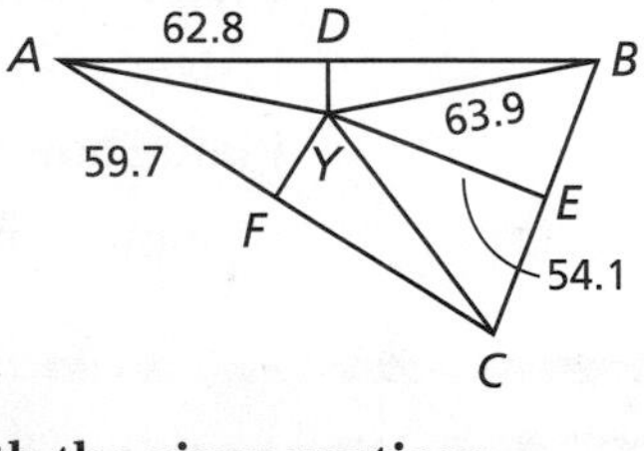

12. CF
13. YC
14. DB
15. AY

Multi-Step **Find the circumcenter of a triangle with the given vertices.**

16. $M(-5, 0)$, $N(0, 14)$, $O(0, 0)$
17. $O(0, 0)$, $V(0, 19)$, $W(-3, 0)$

$\overline{TJ}$ and $\overline{SJ}$ are angle bisectors of $\triangle RST$. Find each measure.

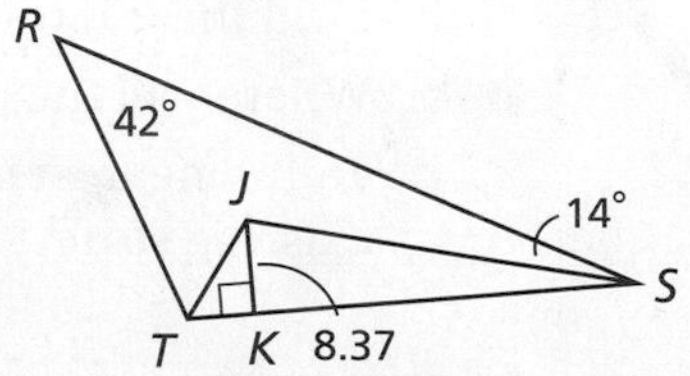

18. the distance from J to $\overline{RS}$
19. $m\angle RTJ$

20. **Business** A company repairs photocopiers in Harbury, Gaspar, and Knowlton. Draw a sketch to show where the company should locate its office so that it is the same distance from each city. Justify your sketch.

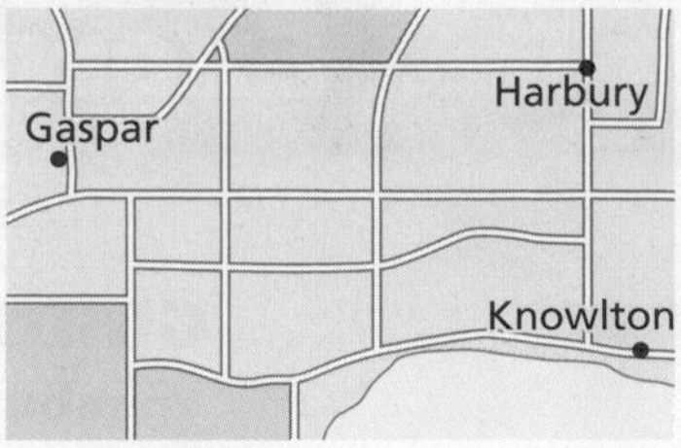

21. **Critical Thinking** If M is the incenter of $\triangle JKL$, explain why $\angle JML$ cannot be a right angle.

Tell whether each segment lies on a perpendicular bisector, an angle bisector, or neither. Justify your answer.

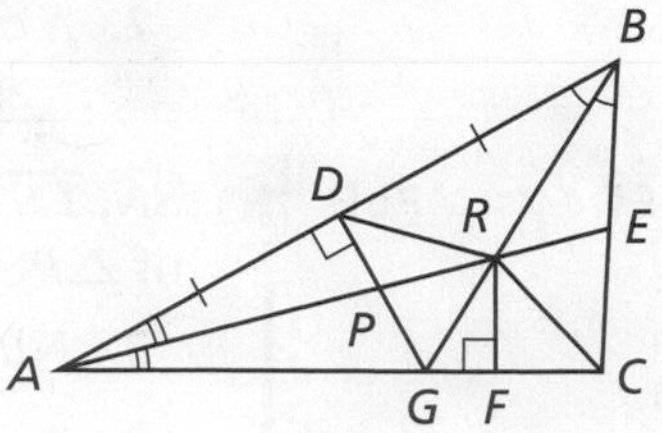

22. $\overline{AE}$
23. $\overline{DG}$
24. $\overline{BG}$
25. $\overline{CR}$
26. $\overline{FR}$
27. $\overline{DR}$

Tell whether each statement is sometimes, always, or never true. Support your answer with a sketch.

28. The angle bisectors of a triangle intersect at a point outside the triangle.
29. An angle bisector of a triangle bisects the opposite side.
30. A perpendicular bisector of a triangle passes through the opposite vertex.
31. The incenter of a right triangle is on the triangle.
32. The circumcenter of a scalene triangle is inside the triangle.

Algebra Find the circumcenter of the triangle with the given vertices.

33. $O(0, 0)$, $A(4, 8)$, $B(8, 0)$
34. $O(0, 0)$, $Y(0, 12)$, $Z(6, 6)$

35. Complete this proof of the Incenter Theorem by filling in the blanks.

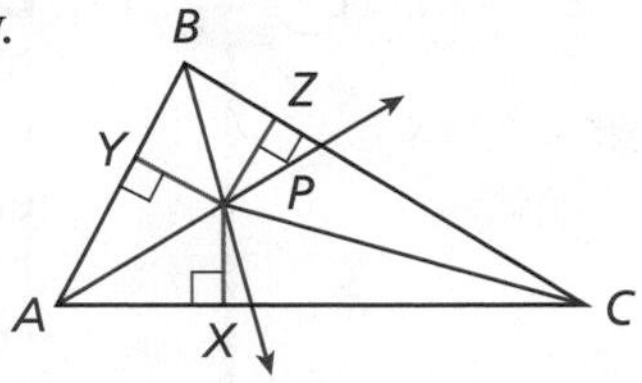

Given: $\overrightarrow{AP}$, $\overrightarrow{BP}$, and $\overrightarrow{CP}$ bisect $\angle A$, $\angle B$, and $\angle C$, respectively. $\overline{PX} \perp \overline{AC}$, $\overline{PY} \perp \overline{AB}$, $\overline{PZ} \perp \overline{BC}$

Prove: $PX = PY = PZ$

Proof: Let P be the incenter of $\triangle ABC$. Since P lies on the bisector of $\angle A$, $PX = PY$ by **a.** ___?___ . Similarly, P also lies on **b.** ___?___ , so $PY = PZ$. Therefore **c.** ___?___ by the Transitive Property of Equality.

36. Prove that the bisector of the vertex angle of an isosceles triangle is the perpendicular bisector of the base.

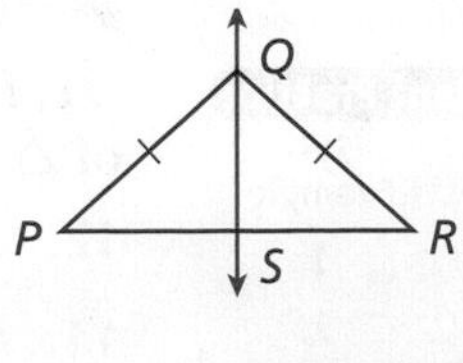

Given: $\overleftrightarrow{QS}$ bisects $\angle PQR$. $\overline{PQ} \cong \overline{RQ}$

Prove: $\overleftrightarrow{QS}$ is the perpendicular bisector of $\overline{PR}$.

Plan: Show that $\triangle PQS \cong \triangle RQS$. Then use CPCTC to show that S is the midpoint of $\overline{PR}$ and that $\overleftrightarrow{QS} \perp \overline{PR}$.

MULTI-STEP TEST PREP

37. A music company has stores at $A(0, 0)$, $B(8, 0)$, and $C(4, 3)$, where each unit of the coordinate plane represents one mile.
    a. A new store will be built so that it is equidistant from the three existing stores. Find the coordinates of the new store's location.
    b. Where will the new store be located in relation to $\triangle ABC$?
    c. To the nearest tenth of a mile, how far will the new store be from each of the existing stores?

38. **Write About It** How are the inscribed circle and the circumscribed circle of a triangle alike? How are they different?

39. **Construction** Draw a large scalene acute triangle.
   a. Construct the angle bisectors to find the incenter. Inscribe a circle in the triangle.
   b. Construct the perpendicular bisectors to find the circumcenter. Circumscribe a circle around the triangle.

TEST PREP

40. P is the incenter of $\triangle ABC$. Which must be true?

   Ⓐ $PA = PB$ Ⓒ $YA = YB$
   Ⓑ $PX = PY$ Ⓓ $AX = BZ$

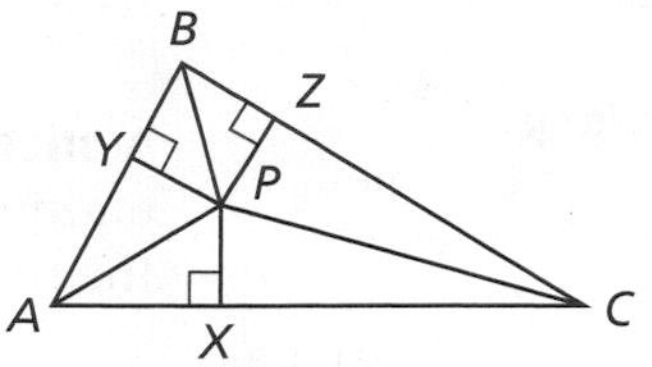

41. Lines r, s, and t are concurrent. The equation of line r is $x = 5$, and the equation of line s is $y = -2$. Which could be the equation of line t?

   Ⓕ $y = x - 7$ Ⓗ $y = x + 3$
   Ⓖ $y = x - 3$ Ⓙ $y = x + 7$

42. **Gridded Response** Lines a, b, and c are the perpendicular bisectors of $\triangle KLM$. Find LN.

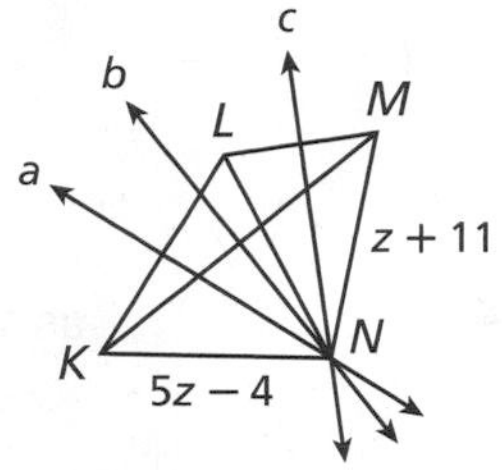

CHALLENGE AND EXTEND

43. Use the right triangle with the given coordinates.
   a. Prove that the midpoint of the hypotenuse of a right triangle is equidistant from all three vertices.
   b. Make a conjecture about the circumcenter of a right triangle.

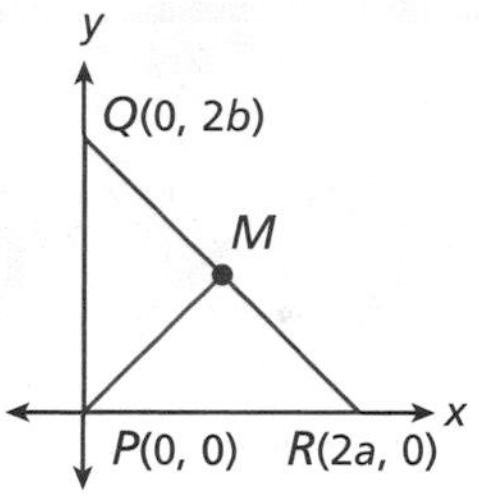

Design LINK

The trefoil shape, as seen in this stained glass window, has been used in design for centuries.

44. **Design** A *trefoil* is created by constructing three overlapping circles. In the figure, an equilateral triangle is inscribed inside a trefoil, and $\overline{AB}$ is a perpendicular bisector of the triangle. If the distance from one vertex to the circumcenter is 28 cm, what is the distance AB across the trefoil?

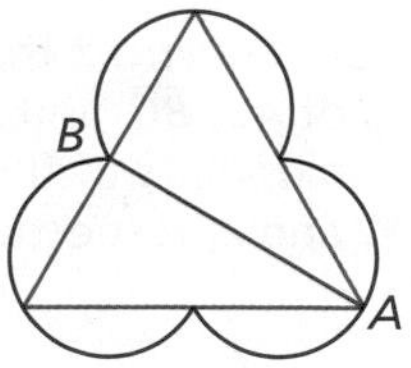

COMMON CORE

5-3 Medians and Altitudes of Triangles

CC.9-12.G.CO.10 Prove theorems about triangles. *Also* **CC.9-12.G.CO.12, CC.9-12.G.MG.3***

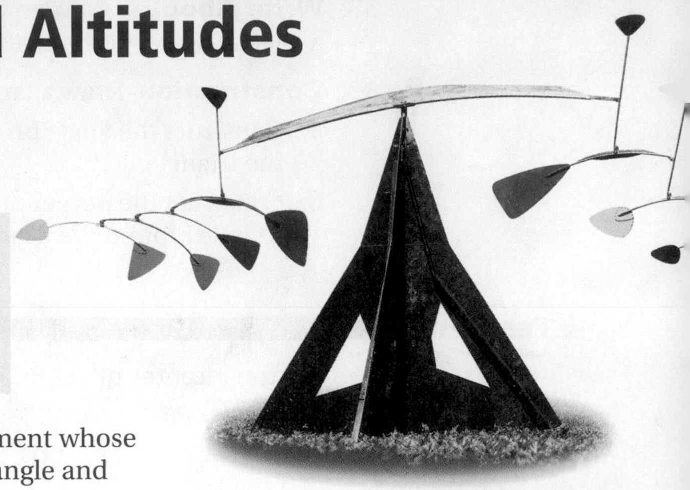

Objectives

Apply properties of medians of a triangle.

Apply properties of altitudes of a triangle.

Vocabulary

median of a triangle
centroid of a triangle
altitude of a triangle
orthocenter of a triangle

Who uses this?

Sculptors who create mobiles of moving objects can use centers of gravity to balance the objects. (See Example 2.)

A **median of a triangle** is a segment whose endpoints are a vertex of the triangle and the midpoint of the opposite side.

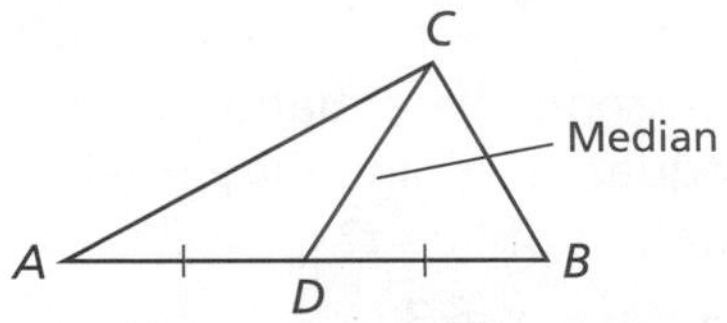

Every triangle has three medians, and the medians are concurrent, as shown in the construction below.

Construction Centroid of a Triangle

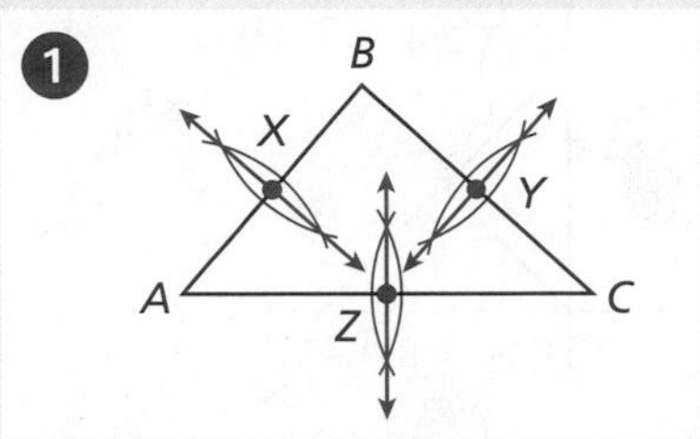

Draw $\triangle ABC$. Construct the midpoints of $\overline{AB}$, $\overline{BC}$, and $\overline{AC}$. Label the midpoints of the sides X, Y, and Z, respectively.

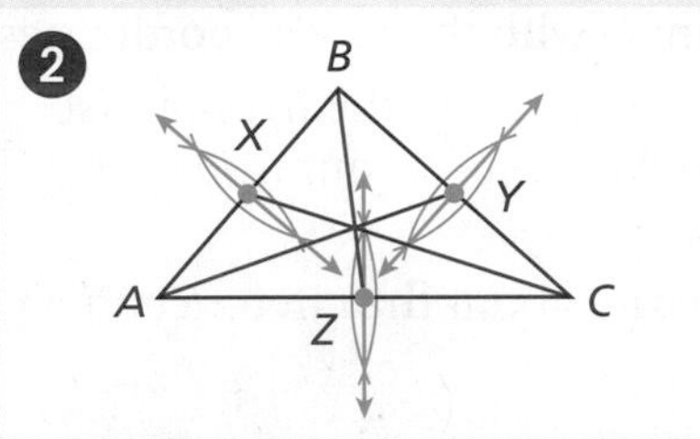

Draw $\overline{AY}$, $\overline{BZ}$, and $\overline{CX}$. These are the three medians of $\triangle ABC$.

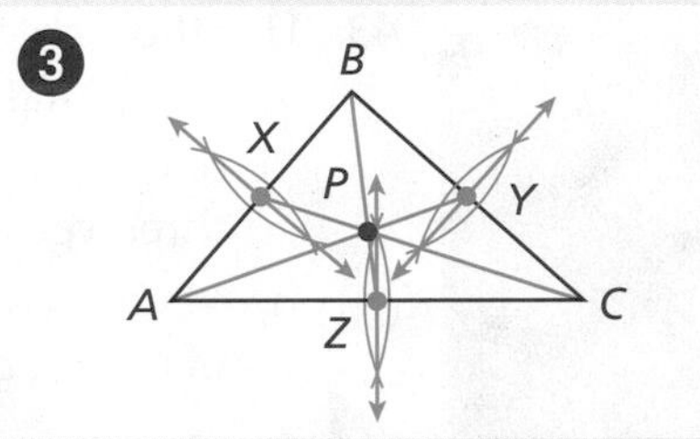

Label the point where $\overline{AY}$, $\overline{BZ}$, and $\overline{CX}$ intersect as P.

The point of concurrency of the medians of a triangle is the **centroid of the triangle**. The centroid is always inside the triangle. The centroid is also called the *center of gravity* because it is the point where a triangular region will balance.

Know it! Note

Theorem 5-3-1 **Centroid Theorem**

The centroid of a triangle is located $\frac{2}{3}$ of the distance from each vertex to the midpoint of the opposite side.

$AP = \frac{2}{3}AY \qquad BP = \frac{2}{3}BZ \qquad CP = \frac{2}{3}CX$

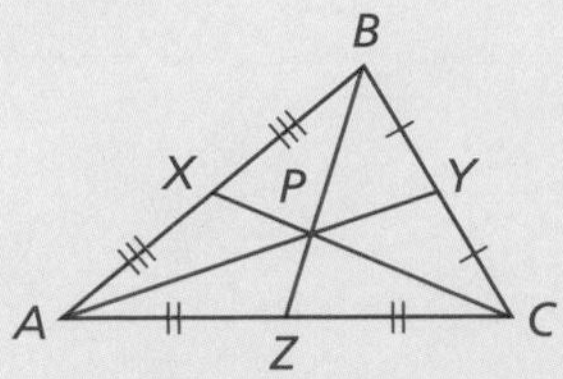

EXAMPLE 1 Using the Centroid to Find Segment Lengths

In $\triangle ABC$, $AF = 9$, and $GE = 2.4$. Find each length.

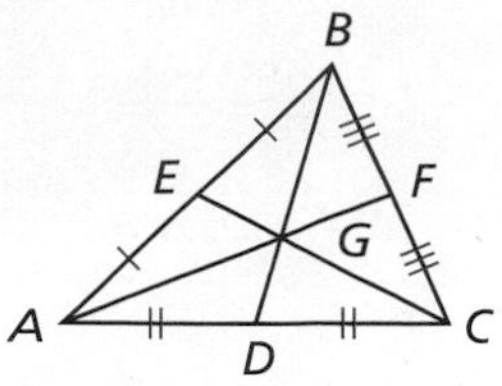

A AG

$AG = \frac{2}{3}AF$	*Centroid Thm.*
$AG = \frac{2}{3}(9)$	*Substitute 9 for AF.*
$AG = 6$	*Simplify.*

B CE

$CG = \frac{2}{3}CE$	*Centroid Thm.*
$CG + GE = CE$	*Seg. Add. Post.*
$\frac{2}{3}CE + GE = CE$	*Substitute $\frac{2}{3}CE$ for CG.*
$GE = \frac{1}{3}CE$	*Subtract $\frac{2}{3}CE$ from both sides.*
$2.4 = \frac{1}{3}CE$	*Substitute 2.4 for GE.*
$7.2 = CE$	*Multiply both sides by 3.*

CHECK IT OUT! **In $\triangle JKL$, $ZW = 7$, and $LX = 8.1$. Find each length.**

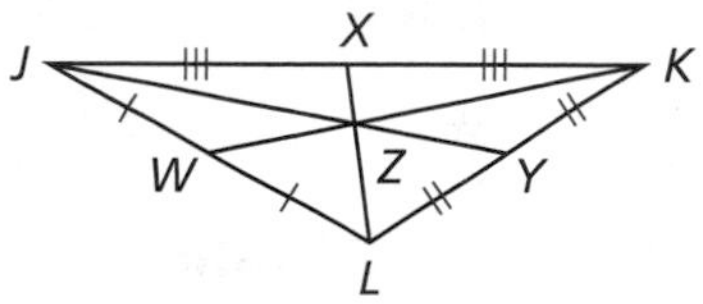

1a. KW

1b. LZ

EXAMPLE 2 *Problem-Solving Application*

MATHEMATICAL PRACTICES

Make sense of problems and persevere in solving them.

The diagram shows the plan for a triangular piece of a mobile. Where should the sculptor attach the support so that the triangle is balanced?

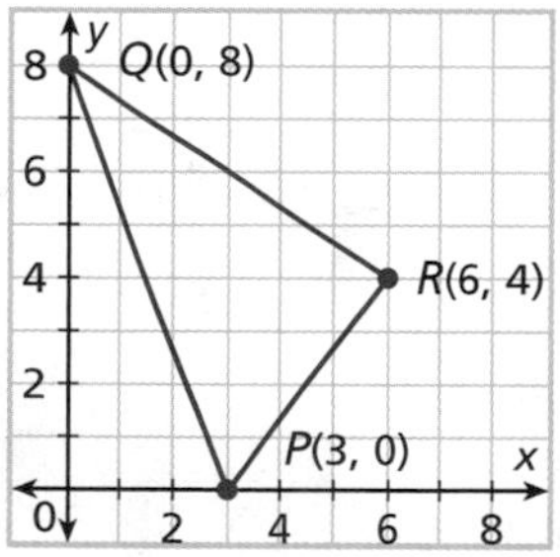

1 Understand the Problem

The **answer** will be the coordinates of the centroid of $\triangle PQR$. The **important information** is the location of the vertices, $P(3, 0)$, $Q(0, 8)$, and $R(6, 4)$.

2 Make a Plan

The centroid of the triangle is the point of intersection of the three medians. So write the equations for two medians and find their point of intersection.

3 Solve

Let M be the midpoint of $\overline{QR}$ and N be the midpoint of $\overline{QP}$.

$$M = \left(\frac{0+6}{2}, \frac{8+4}{2}\right) = (3, 6) \qquad N = \left(\frac{0+3}{2}, \frac{8+0}{2}\right) = (1.5, 4)$$

$\overline{PM}$ is vertical. Its equation is $x = 3$. $\overline{RN}$ is horizontal. Its equation is $y = 4$. The coordinates of the centroid are $S(3, 4)$.

4 Look Back

Let L be the midpoint of $\overline{PR}$. The equation for $\overline{QL}$ is $y = -\frac{4}{3}x + 8$, which intersects $x = 3$ at $S(3, 4)$.

CHECK IT OUT! **2.** Find the average of the x-coordinates and the average of the y-coordinates of the vertices of $\triangle PQR$. Make a conjecture about the centroid of a triangle.

Helpful Hint

The height of a triangle is the length of an altitude.

An **altitude of a triangle** is a perpendicular segment from a vertex to the line containing the opposite side. Every triangle has three altitudes. An altitude can be inside, outside, or on the triangle.

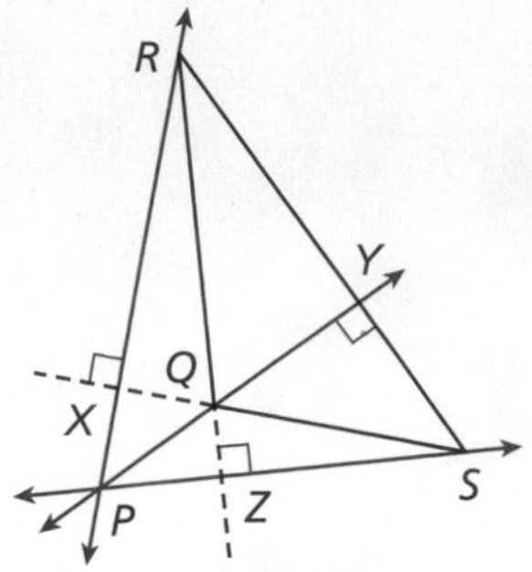

In $\triangle QRS$, altitude $\overline{QY}$ is inside the triangle, but $\overline{RX}$ and $\overline{SZ}$ are not. Notice that the lines containing the altitudes are concurrent at P. This point of concurrency is the **orthocenter of the triangle**.

EXAMPLE 3 Finding the Orthocenter

Algebra

Find the orthocenter of $\triangle JKL$ with vertices $J(-4, 2)$, $K(-2, 6)$, and $L(2, 2)$.

Step 1 Graph the triangle.

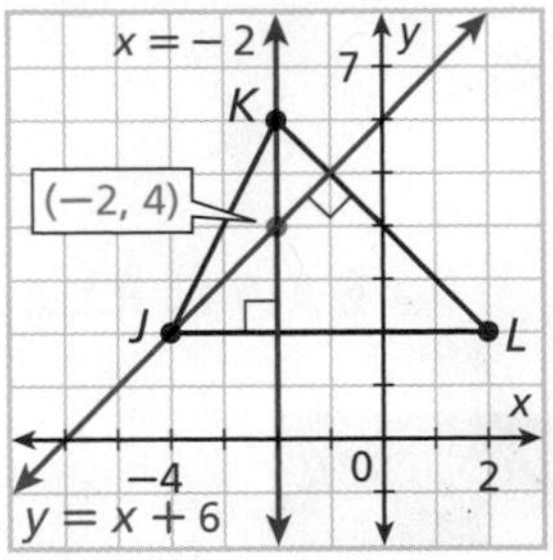

Step 2 Find an equation of the line containing the altitude from K to $\overline{JL}$.

Since $\overleftrightarrow{JL}$ is horizontal, the altitude is vertical. The line containing it must pass through $K(-2, 6)$, so the equation of the line is $x = -2$.

Step 3 Find an equation of the line containing the altitude from J to $\overline{KL}$.

$$\text{slope of } \overleftrightarrow{KL} = \frac{2 - 6}{2 - (-2)} = -1$$

The slope of a line perpendicular to $\overleftrightarrow{KL}$ is 1. This line must pass through $J(-4, 2)$.

$y - y_1 = m(x - x_1)$	*Point-slope form*
$y - 2 = 1[x - (-4)]$	*Substitute 2 for y_1, 1 for m, and −4 for x_1.*
$y - 2 = x + 4$	*Distribute 1.*
$y = x + 6$	*Add 2 to both sides.*

Step 4 Solve the system to find the coordinates of the orthocenter.

$$\begin{cases} x = -2 \\ y = x + 6 \end{cases}$$

$y = -2 + 6 = 4$ *Substitute −2 for x.*

The coordinates of the orthocenter are $(-2, 4)$.

CHECK IT OUT! **3.** Show that the altitude to $\overline{JK}$ passes through the orthocenter of $\triangle JKL$.

MATHEMATICAL PRACTICES

THINK AND DISCUSS

1. Draw a triangle in which a median and an altitude are the same segment. What type of triangle is it?
2. Draw a triangle in which an altitude is also a side of the triangle. What type of triangle is it?
3. The centroid of a triangle divides each median into two segments. What is the ratio of the two lengths of each median?

Know it! Note

4. **GET ORGANIZED** Copy and complete the graphic organizer. Fill in the blanks to make each statement true.

	Centroid	Orthocenter
Definition	The point of concurrency of the ___?___	The point of concurrency of the ___?___
Location (Inside, Outside, or On)	___?___ the triangle	Can be ___?___ the triangle

5-3 Exercises

Learn It Online
Homework Help Online
Parent Resources Online

GUIDED PRACTICE

Vocabulary **Apply the vocabulary from this lesson to answer each question.**

1. The ___?___ of a triangle is located $\frac{2}{3}$ of the distance from each vertex to the midpoint of the opposite side. (*centroid* or *orthocenter*)

2. The ___?___ of a triangle is perpendicular to the line containing a side. (*altitude* or *median*)

SEE EXAMPLE 1

$VX = 204$, and $RW = 104$. Find each length.

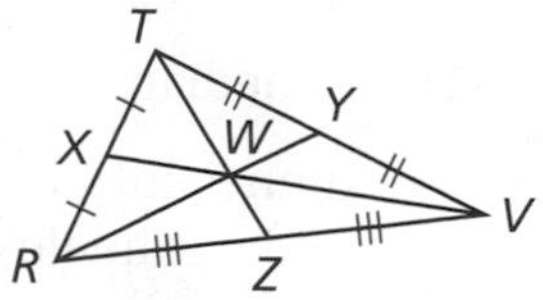

3. VW
4. WX
5. RY
6. WY

SEE EXAMPLE 2

7. **Design** The diagram shows a plan for a piece of a mobile. A chain will hang from the centroid of the triangle. At what coordinates should the artist attach the chain?

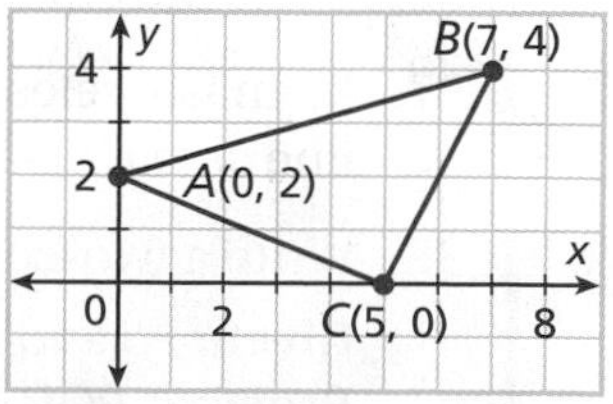

SEE EXAMPLE 3

Multi-Step **Find the orthocenter of a triangle with the given vertices.**

8. $K(2, -2)$, $L(4, 6)$, $M(8, -2)$
9. $U(-4, -9)$, $V(-4, 6)$, $W(5, -3)$
10. $P(-5, 8)$, $Q(4, 5)$, $R(-2, 5)$
11. $C(-1, -3)$, $D(-1, 2)$, $E(9, 2)$

PRACTICE AND PROBLEM SOLVING

Independent Practice

For Exercises	See Example
12–15	1
16	2
17–20	3

Extra Practice

See Extra Practice for more Skills Practice and Applications Practice exercises.

$PA = 2.9$, and $HC = 10.8$. Find each length.

12. PC **13.** HP

14. JA **15.** JP

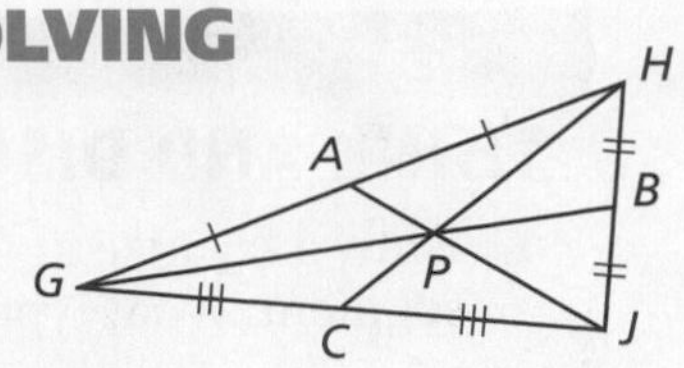

16. Design In the plan for a table, the triangular top has coordinates $(0, 10)$, $(4, 0)$, and $(8, 14)$. The tabletop will rest on a single support placed beneath it. Where should the support be attached so that the table is balanced?

Multi-Step Find the orthocenter of a triangle with the given vertices.

17. $X(-2, -2)$, $Y(6, 10)$, $Z(6, -6)$ **18.** $G(-2, 5)$, $H(6, 5)$, $J(4, -1)$

19. $R(-8, 9)$, $S(-2, 9)$, $T(-2, 1)$ **20.** $A(4, -3)$, $B(8, 5)$, $C(8, -8)$

Find each measure.

21. GL **22.** PL

23. HL **24.** GJ

25. perimeter of $\triangle GHJ$ **26.** area of $\triangle GHJ$

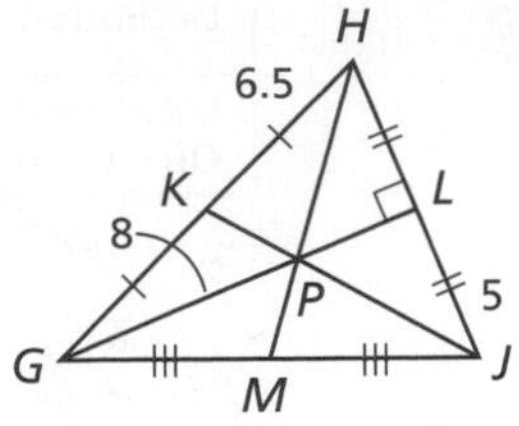

Algebra Find the centroid of a triangle with the given vertices.

27. $A(0, -4)$, $B(14, 6)$, $C(16, -8)$ **28.** $X(8, -1)$, $Y(2, 7)$, $Z(5, -3)$

Find each length.

29. PZ **30.** PX

31. QZ **32.** YZ

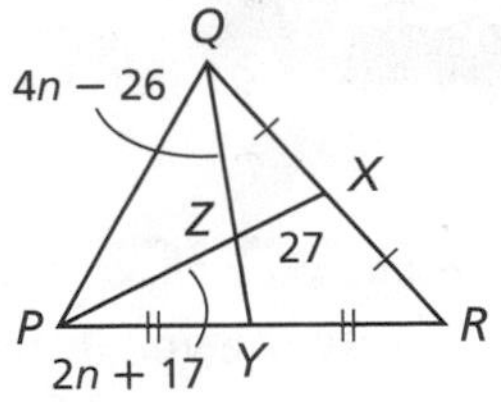

LINK

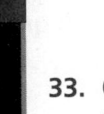

Math History

In 1678, Giovanni Ceva published his famous theorem that states the conditions necessary for three *Cevians* (segments from a vertex of a triangle to the opposite side) to be concurrent. The medians and altitudes of a triangle meet these conditions.

33. Critical Thinking Draw an isosceles triangle and its line of symmetry. What are four other names for this segment?

Tell whether each statement is sometimes, always, or never true. Support your answer with a sketch.

34. A median of a triangle bisects one of the angles.

35. If one altitude of a triangle is in the triangle's exterior, then a second altitude is also in the triangle's exterior.

36. The centroid of a triangle lies in its exterior.

37. In an isosceles triangle, the altitude and median from the vertex angle are the same line as the bisector of the vertex angle.

38. Write a two-column proof.

Given: $\overline{PS}$ and $\overline{RT}$ are medians of $\triangle PQR$. $\overline{PS} \cong \overline{RT}$

Prove: $\triangle PQR$ is an isosceles triangle.

Plan: Show that $\triangle PTR \cong \triangle RSP$ and use CPCTC to conclude that $\angle QPR \cong \angle QRP$.

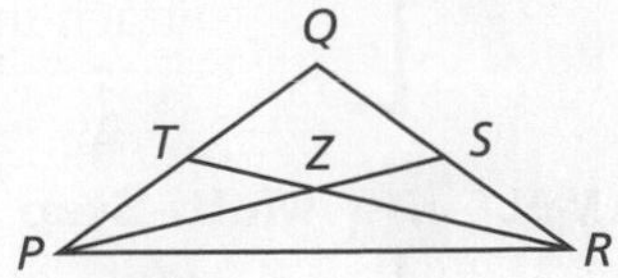

39. Write About It Draw a large triangle on a sheet of paper and cut it out. Find the centroid by paper folding. Try to balance the shape on the tip of your pencil at a point other than the centroid. Now try to balance the shape at its centroid. Explain why the centroid is also called the center of gravity.

MULTI-STEP TEST PREP

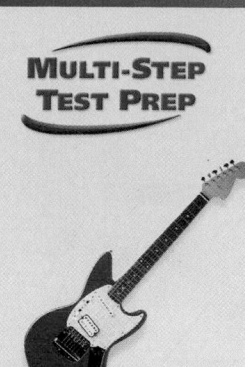

40. The towns of Davis, El Monte, and Fairview have the coordinates shown in the table, where each unit of the coordinate plane represents one mile. A music company has stores in each city and a distribution warehouse at the centroid of $\triangle DEF$.

City	Location
Davis	$D(0, 0)$
El Monte	$E(0, 8)$
Fairview	$F(8, 0)$

   a. What are the coordinates of the warehouse?
   b. Find the distance from the warehouse to the Davis store. Round your answer to the nearest tenth of a mile.
   c. A straight road connects El Monte and Fairview. What is the distance from the warehouse to the road?

TEST PREP

41. $\overline{QT}$, $\overline{RV}$, and $\overline{SW}$ are medians of $\triangle QRS$. Which statement is NOT necessarily true?

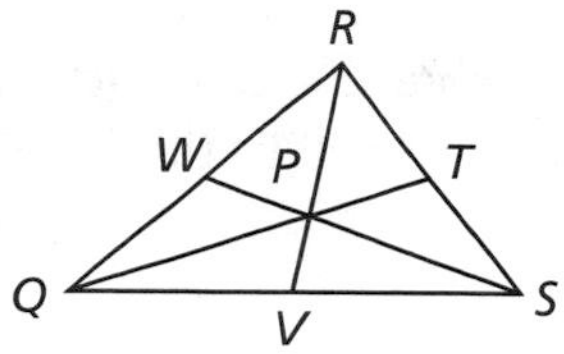

   Ⓐ $QP = \frac{2}{3}QT$ Ⓒ $RT = ST$
   Ⓑ $RP = 2PV$ Ⓓ $QT = SW$

42. Suppose that the orthocenter of a triangle lies outside the triangle. Which points of concurrency are inside the triangle?
   I. incenter   **II.** circumcenter   **III.** centroid
   Ⓕ I and II only   Ⓗ II and III only
   Ⓖ I and III only   Ⓙ I, II, and III

43. In the diagram, which of the following correctly describes $\overline{LN}$?

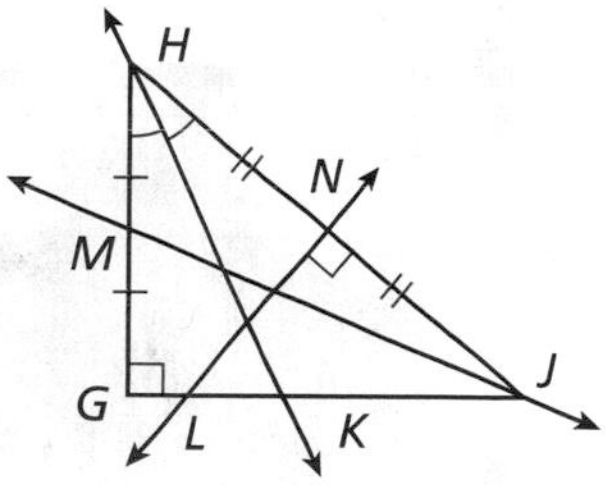

   Ⓐ Altitude   Ⓒ Median
   Ⓑ Angle bisector   Ⓓ Perpendicular bisector

CHALLENGE AND EXTEND

44. Draw an equilateral triangle.
   a. Explain why the perpendicular bisector of any side contains the vertex opposite that side.
   b. Explain why the perpendicular bisector through any vertex also contains the median, the altitude, and the angle bisector through that vertex.
   c. Explain why the incenter, circumcenter, centroid, and orthocenter are the same point.

45. Use coordinates to show that the lines containing the altitudes of a triangle are concurrent.

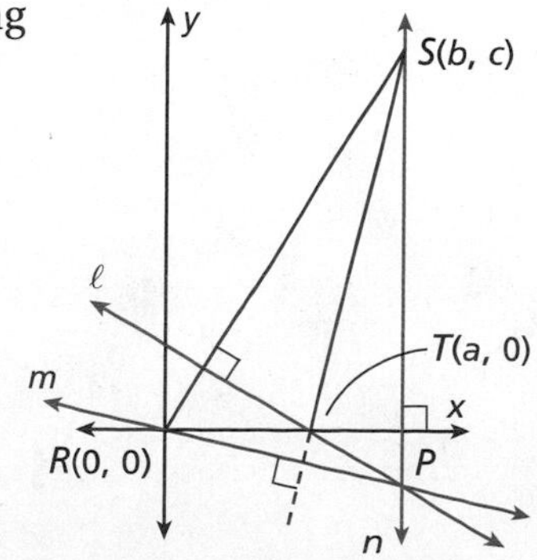

   a. Find the slopes of $\overline{RS}$, $\overline{ST}$, and $\overline{RT}$.
   b. Find the slopes of lines ℓ, m, and n.
   c. Write equations for lines ℓ, m, and n.
   d. Solve a system of equations to find the point P where lines ℓ and m intersect.
   e. Show that line n contains P.
   f. What conclusion can you draw?

Construction Orthocenter of a Triangle

1

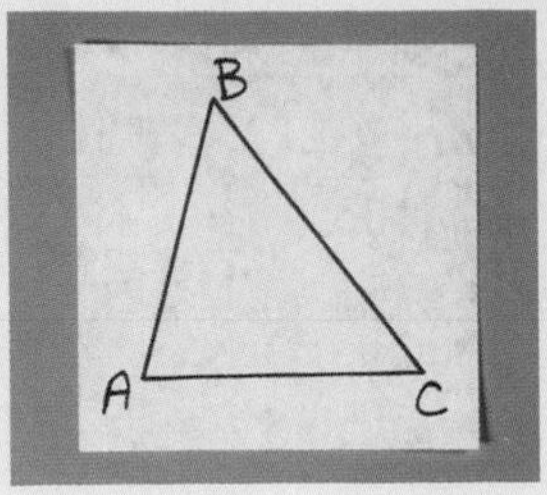

Draw a large scalene acute triangle *ABC* on a piece of patty paper.

2

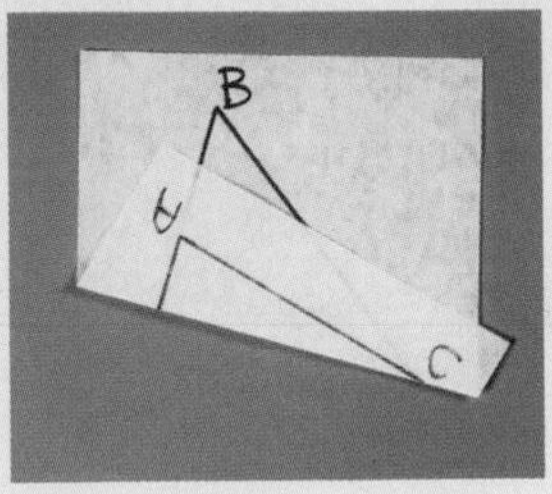

Find the altitude of each side by folding the side so that it overlaps itself and so that the fold intersects the opposite vertex.

3

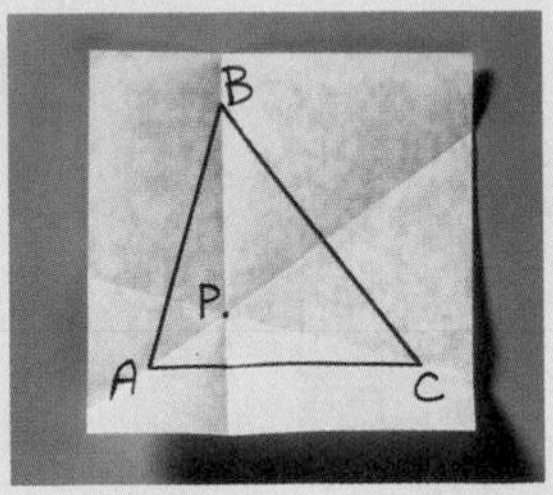

Mark the point where the three lines containing the altitudes intersect and label it *P*. *P* is the orthocenter of $\triangle ABC$.

---

1. Repeat the construction for a scalene obtuse triangle and a scalene right triangle.
2. Make a conjecture about the location of the orthocenter in an acute, an obtuse, and a right triangle.

Career Path

Learn It Online
Career Resources Online

Alex Peralta
Electrician

Q: What high school math classes did you take?

A: Algebra 1, Geometry, and Statistics.

Q: What type of training did you receive?

A: In high school, I took classes in electricity, electronics, and drafting. I began an apprenticeship program last year to prepare for the exam to get my license.

Q: How do you use math?

A: Determining the locations of outlets and circuits on blueprints requires good spatial sense. I also use ratios and proportions, calculate distances, work with formulas, and estimate job costs.

5-3 Technology LAB

Special Points in Triangles

In this lab you will use geometry software to explore properties of the four points of concurrency you have studied.

Learn It Online
Lab Resources Online

Use with Medians and Altitudes of Triangles

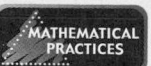

MATHEMATICAL PRACTICES **Use appropriate tools strategically.**

CC.9-12.G.CO.10 Prove theorems about triangles.

Activity

1. Construct a triangle.
2. Construct the perpendicular bisector of each side of the triangle. Construct the point of intersection of these three lines. This is the circumcenter of the triangle. Label it *U* and hide the perpendicular bisectors.

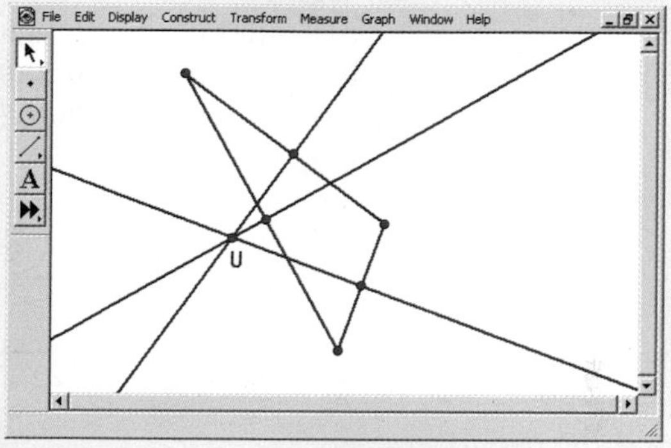

3. In the same triangle, construct the bisector of each angle. Construct the point of intersection of these three lines. This is the incenter of the triangle. Label it *I* and hide the angle bisectors.
4. In the same triangle, construct the midpoint of each side. Then construct the three medians. Construct the point of intersection of these three lines. Label the centroid *C* and hide the medians.

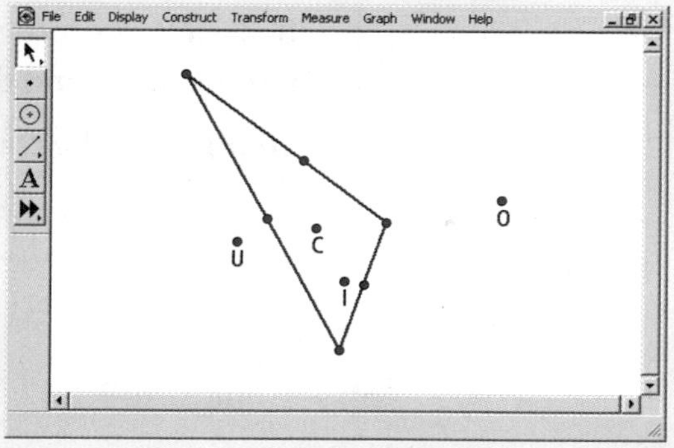

5. In the same triangle, construct the altitude to each side. Construct the point of intersection of these three lines. Label the orthocenter *O* and hide the altitudes.
6. Move a vertex of the triangle and observe the positions of the four points of concurrency. In 1765, Swiss mathematician Leonhard Euler showed that three of these points are always collinear. The line containing them is called the *Euler line.*

Try This

1. Which three points of concurrency lie on the Euler line?
2. **Make a Conjecture** Which point on the Euler line is always between the other two? Measure the distances between the points. Make a conjecture about the relationship of the distances between these three points.
3. **Make a Conjecture** Move a vertex of the triangle until all four points of concurrency are collinear. In what type of triangle are all four points of concurrency on the Euler line?
4. **Make a Conjecture** Find a triangle in which all four points of concurrency coincide. What type of triangle has this special property?

COMMON CORE

5-4 The Triangle Midsegment Theorem

CC.9-12.G.CO.10 Prove theorems about triangles.

Objective
Prove and use properties of triangle midsegments.

Vocabulary
midsegment of a triangle

Why learn this?
You can use triangle midsegments to make indirect measurements of distances, such as the distance across a volcano. (See Example 3.)

A **midsegment of a triangle** is a segment that joins the midpoints of two sides of the triangle. Every triangle has three midsegments, which form the *midsegment triangle*.

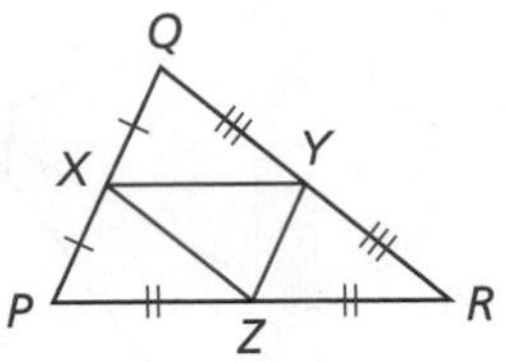

Midsegments: $\overline{XY}, \overline{YZ}, \overline{ZX}$
Midsegment triangle: $\triangle XYZ$

EXAMPLE 1 Examining Midsegments in the Coordinate Plane

In $\triangle GHJ$, show that midsegment $\overline{KL}$ is parallel to $\overline{GJ}$ and that $KL = \frac{1}{2}GJ$.

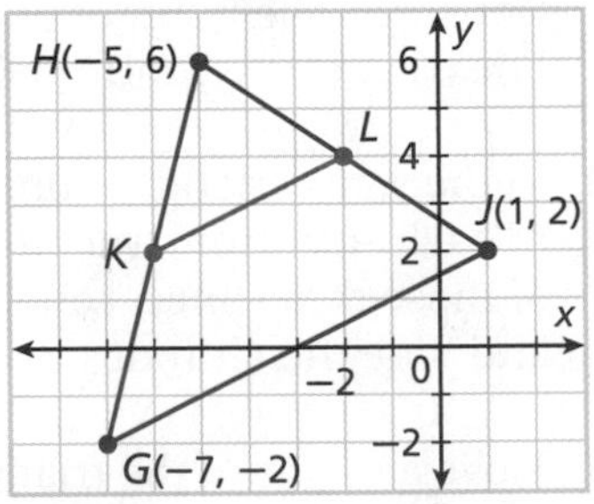

Step 1 Find the coordinates of K and L.

$$\text{mdpt. of } \overline{GH} = \left(\frac{-7 + (-5)}{2}, \frac{-2 + 6}{2}\right)$$
$$= (-6, 2)$$

$$\text{mdpt. of } \overline{HJ} = \left(\frac{-5 + 1}{2}, \frac{6 + 2}{2}\right) = (-2, 4)$$

Step 2 Compare the slopes of $\overline{KL}$ and $\overline{GJ}$.

$$\text{slope of } \overline{KL} = \frac{4 - 2}{-2 - (-6)} = \frac{1}{2} \qquad \text{slope of } \overline{GJ} = \frac{2 - (-2)}{1 - (-7)} = \frac{1}{2}$$

Since the slopes are the same, $\overline{KL} \parallel \overline{GJ}$.

Step 3 Compare the lengths of $\overline{KL}$ and $\overline{GJ}$.

$$KL = \sqrt{\left[-2 - (-6)\right]^2 + (4 - 2)^2} = 2\sqrt{5}$$
$$GJ = \sqrt{\left[1 - (-7)\right]^2 + \left[2 - (-2)\right]^2} = 4\sqrt{5}$$

Since $2\sqrt{5} = \frac{1}{2}(4\sqrt{5})$, $KL = \frac{1}{2}GJ$.

CHECK IT OUT! 1. The vertices of $\triangle RST$ are $R(-7, 0)$, $S(-3, 6)$, and $T(9, 2)$. M is the midpoint of $\overline{RT}$, and N is the midpoint of $\overline{ST}$. Show that $\overline{MN} \parallel \overline{RS}$ and $MN = \frac{1}{2}RS$.

The relationship shown in Example 1 is true for the three midsegments of every triangle.

Know it! Note

Theorem 5-4-1 **Triangle Midsegment Theorem**

A midsegment of a triangle is parallel to a side of the triangle, and its length is half the length of that side.

$\overline{DE} \parallel \overline{AC},\ DE = \frac{1}{2}AC$

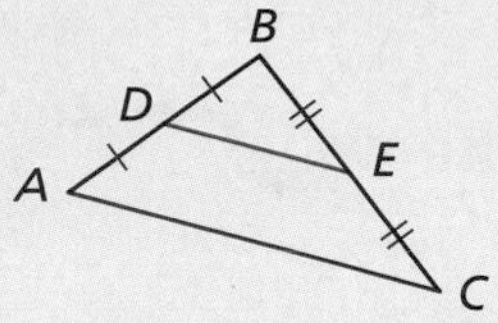

You will prove Theorem 5-4-1 in Exercise 38.

EXAMPLE 2 Using the Triangle Midsegment Theorem

Find each measure.

A UW

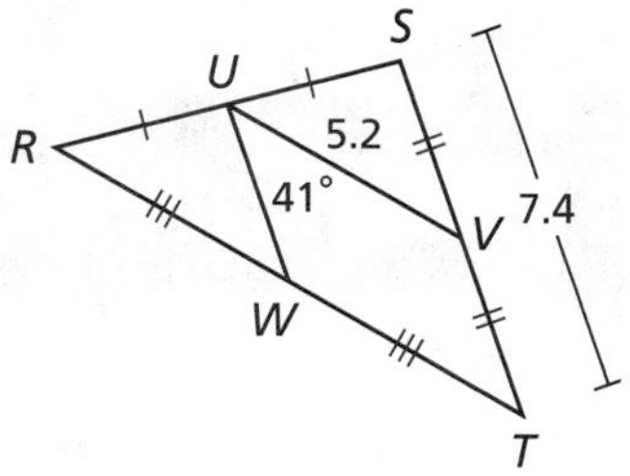

$UW = \frac{1}{2}ST$	*△ Midsegment Thm.*
$UW = \frac{1}{2}(7.4)$	*Substitute 7.4 for ST.*
$UW = 3.7$	*Simplify.*

B $m\angle SVU$

$\overline{UW} \parallel \overline{ST}$	*△ Midsegment Thm.*
$m\angle SVU = m\angle VUW$	*Alt. Int. ∠s Thm.*
$m\angle SVU = 41°$	*Substitute 41° for m∠VUW.*

CHECK IT OUT! **Find each measure.**

2a. JL **2b.** PM **2c.** $m\angle MLK$

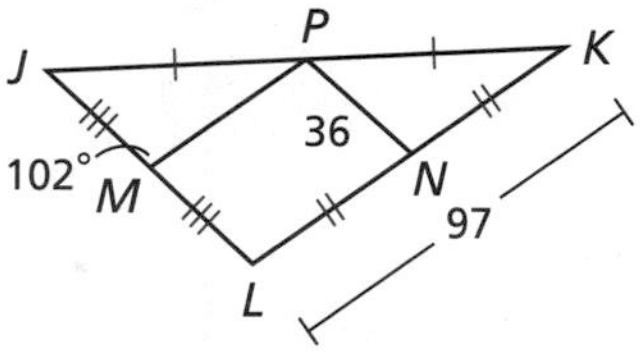

EXAMPLE 3 *Indirect Measurement Application*

Anna wants to find the distance across the base of Capulin Volcano, an extinct volcano in New Mexico. She measures a triangle at one side of the volcano as shown in the diagram. What is AE?

$BD = \frac{1}{2}AE$	*△ Midsegment Thm.*
$775 = \frac{1}{2}AE$	*Substitute 775 for BD.*
$1550 = AE$	*Multiply both sides by 2.*

The distance AE across the base of the volcano is about 1550 meters.

CHECK IT OUT! **3. What if...?** Suppose Anna's result in Example 3 is correct. To check it, she measures a second triangle. How many meters will she measure between H and F?

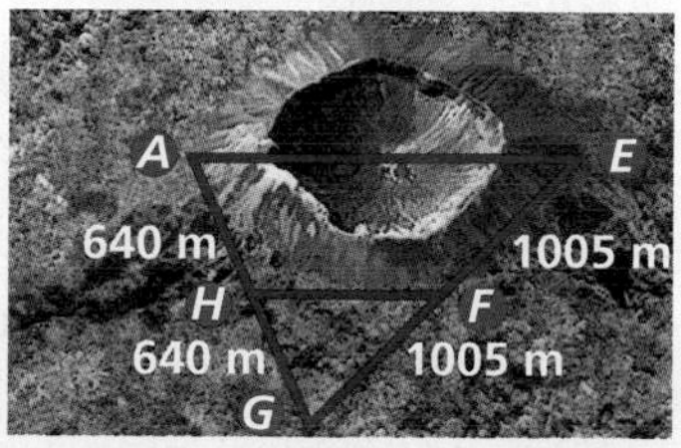

THINK AND DISCUSS

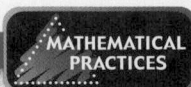

MATHEMATICAL PRACTICES

1. Explain why $\overline{XY}$ is NOT a midsegment of the triangle.

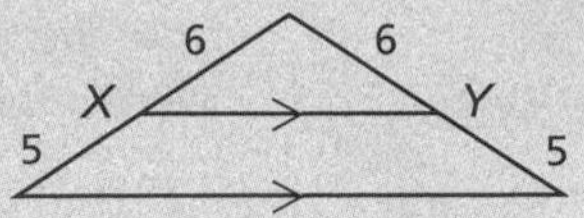

Know it! Note

2. **GET ORGANIZED** Copy and complete the graphic organizer. Write the definition of a triangle midsegment and list its properties. Then draw an example and a nonexample.

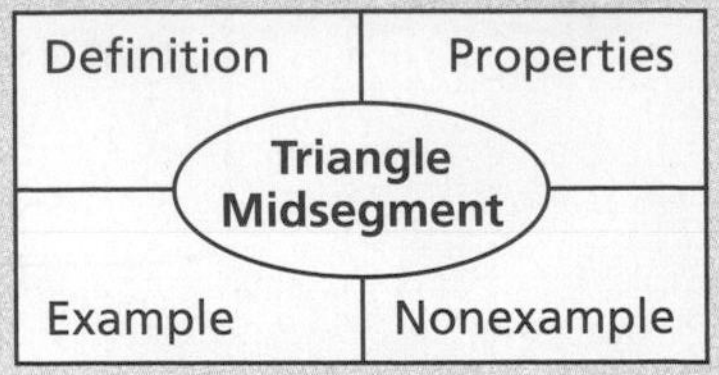

5-4 Exercises

Learn It Online
Homework Help Online
Parent Resources Online

GUIDED PRACTICE

1. **Vocabulary** The *midsegment of a triangle* joins the ___?___ of two sides of the triangle. (*endpoints* or *midpoints*)

SEE EXAMPLE 1

2. The vertices of $\triangle PQR$ are $P(-4, -1)$, $Q(2, 9)$, and $R(6, 3)$. S is the midpoint of $\overline{PQ}$, and T is the midpoint of $\overline{QR}$. Show that $\overline{ST} \parallel \overline{PR}$ and $ST = \frac{1}{2}PR$.

SEE EXAMPLE 2

Find each measure.

3. NM
4. XZ
5. NZ
6. $m\angle LMN$
7. $m\angle YXZ$
8. $m\angle XLM$

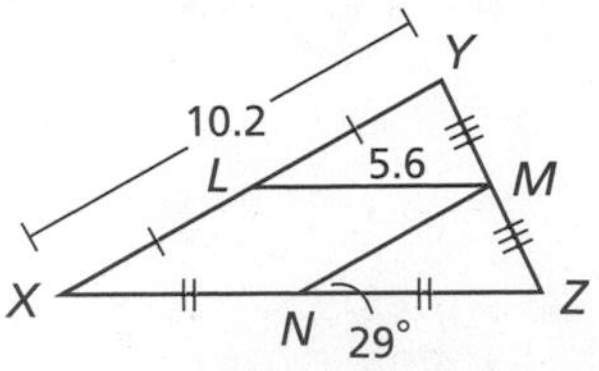

SEE EXAMPLE 3

9. **Architecture** In this A-frame house, the width of the first floor $\overline{XZ}$ is 30 feet. The second floor $\overline{CD}$ is slightly above and parallel to the midsegment of $\triangle XYZ$. Is the width of the second floor more or less than 5 yards? Explain.

PRACTICE AND PROBLEM SOLVING

Independent Practice	
For Exercises	See Example
10	1
11–16	2
17	3

Extra Practice
See Extra Practice for more Skills Practice and Applications Practice exercises.

10. The vertices of $\triangle ABC$ are $A(-6, 11)$, $B(6, -3)$, and $C(-2, -5)$. D is the midpoint of $\overline{AC}$, and E is the midpoint of $\overline{AB}$. Show that $\overline{DE} \parallel \overline{CB}$ and $DE = \frac{1}{2}CB$.

Find each measure.

11. GJ
12. RQ
13. RJ
14. $m\angle PQR$
15. $m\angle HGJ$
16. $m\angle GPQ$

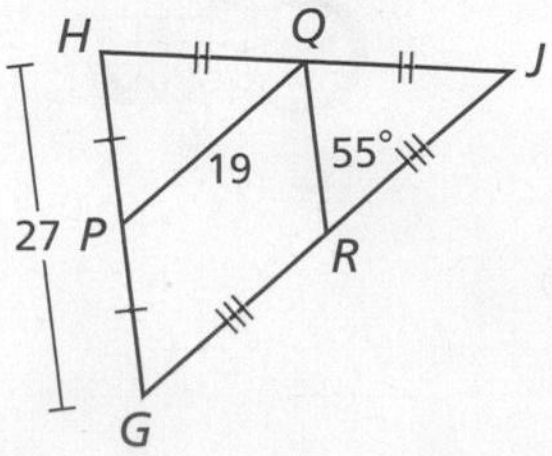

17. **Carpentry** In each support for the garden swing, the crossbar $\overline{DE}$ is attached at the midpoints of legs $\overline{BA}$ and $\overline{BC}$. The distance AC is $4\frac{1}{2}$ feet. The carpenter has a timber that is 30 inches long. Is this timber long enough to be used as one of the crossbars? Explain.

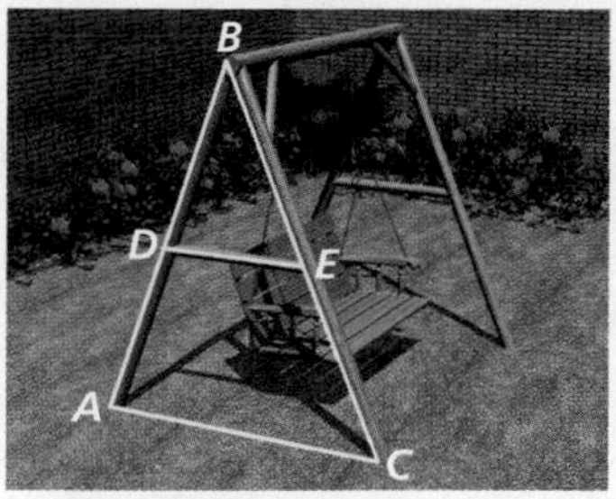

$\triangle KLM$ is the midsegment triangle of $\triangle GHJ$.

18. What is the perimeter of $\triangle GHJ$?

19. What is the perimeter of $\triangle KLM$?

20. What is the relationship between the perimeter of $\triangle GHJ$ and the perimeter of $\triangle KLM$?

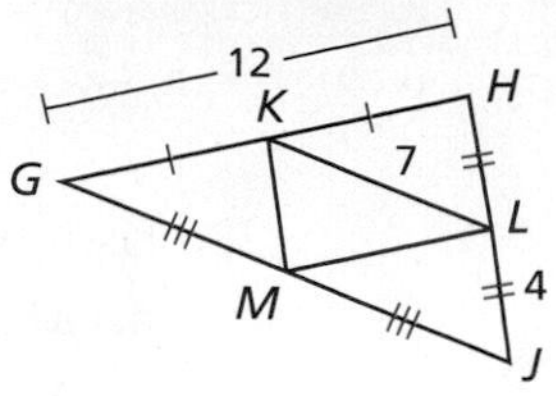

Algebra Find the value of n in each triangle.

21.

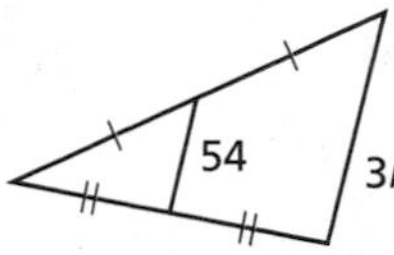

22.

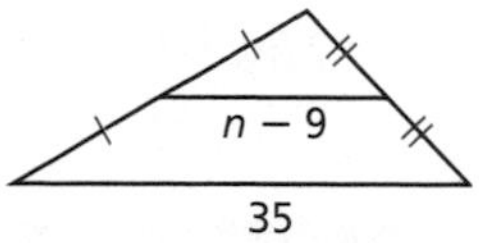

23.

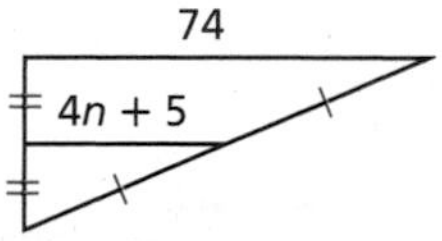

24.

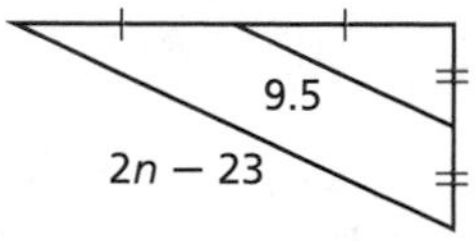

25.

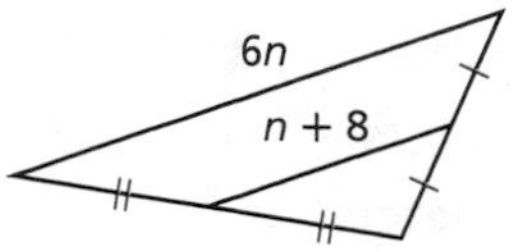

26.

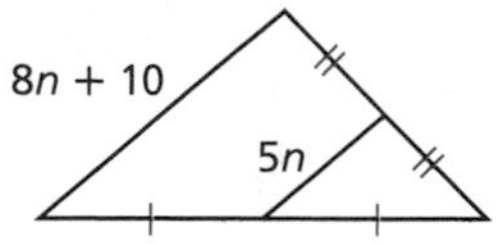

27. **ERROR ANALYSIS** Below are two solutions for finding BC. Which is incorrect? Explain the error.

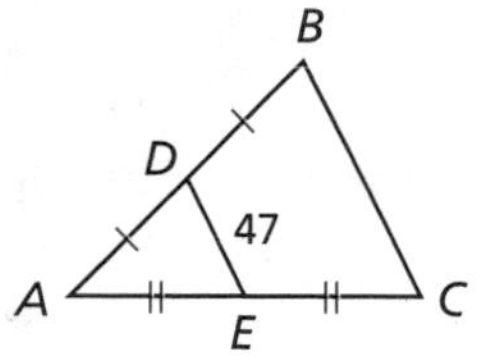

A

$DE = 0.5BC$
$47 = 0.5BC$
$94 = BC$

B

$BC = 0.5DE$
$BC = 0.5(47)$
$BC = 23.5$

28. **Critical Thinking** Draw scalene $\triangle DEF$. Label X as the midpoint of $\overline{DE}$, Y as the midpoint of $\overline{EF}$, and Z as the midpoint of $\overline{DF}$. Connect the three midpoints. List all of the congruent angles in your drawing.

29. **Estimation** The diagram shows the sketch for a new street. Parallel parking spaces will be painted on both sides of the street. Each parallel parking space is 23 feet long. About how many parking spaces can the city accommodate on both sides of the new street? Explain your answer.

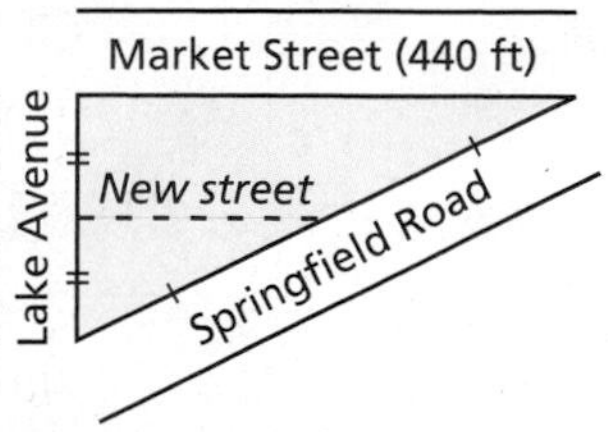

$\overline{CG}$, $\overline{EH}$, and $\overline{FJ}$ are midsegments of $\triangle ABD$, $\triangle GCD$, and $\triangle GHE$, respectively. Find each measure.

30. CG 31. EH 32. FJ

33. $m\angle DCG$ 34. $m\angle GHE$ 35. $m\angle FJH$

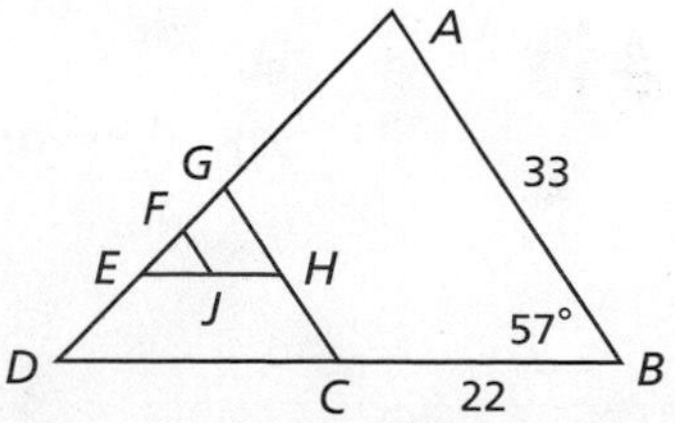

36. **Write About It** An isosceles triangle has two congruent sides. Does it also have two congruent midsegments? Explain.

MULTI-STEP TEST PREP

37. The figure shows the roads connecting towns A, B, and C. A music company has a store in each town and a distribution warehouse W at the midpoint of road $\overline{XY}$.
   a. What is the distance from the warehouse to point X?
   b. A truck starts at the warehouse, delivers instruments to the stores in towns A, B, and C (in this order) and then returns to the warehouse. What is the total length of the trip, assuming the driver takes the shortest possible route?

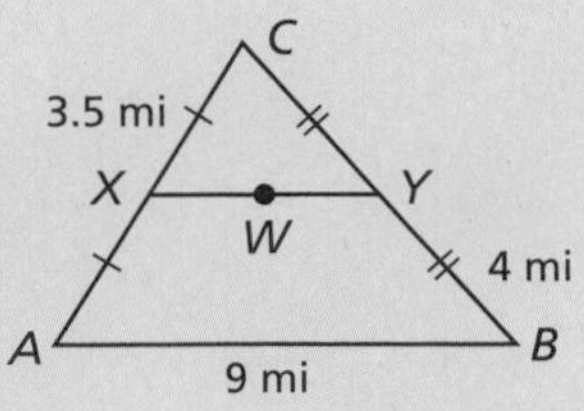

38. Use coordinates to prove the Triangle Midsegment Theorem.
   a. M is the midpoint of $\overline{PQ}$. What are its coordinates?
   b. N is the midpoint of $\overline{QR}$. What are its coordinates?
   c. Find the slopes of $\overline{PR}$ and $\overline{MN}$. What can you conclude?
   d. Find PR and MN. What can you conclude?

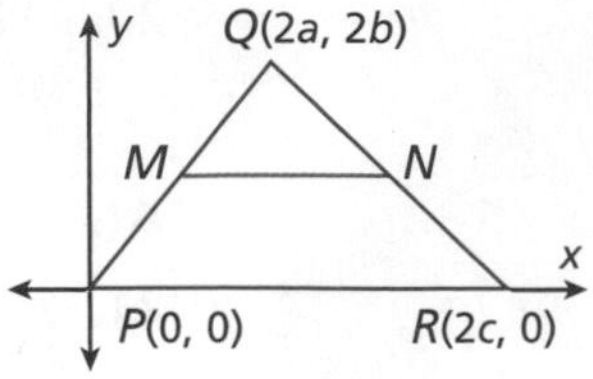

TEST PREP

39. $\overline{PQ}$ is a midsegment of $\triangle RST$. What is the length of $\overline{RT}$?
   (A) 9 meters
   (B) 21 meters
   (C) 45 meters
   (D) 63 meters

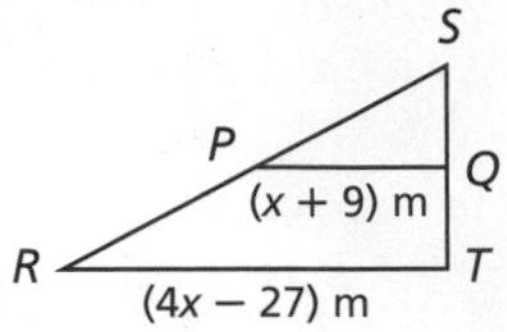

40. In $\triangle UVW$, M is the midpoint of $\overline{VU}$, and N is the midpoint of $\overline{VW}$. Which statement is true?
   (F) $VM = VN$
   (G) $MN = UV$
   (H) $VU = 2VM$
   (J) $VW = \frac{1}{2}VN$

41. $\triangle XYZ$ is the midsegment triangle of $\triangle JKL$, $XY = 8$, $YK = 14$, and $m\angle YKZ = 67°$. Which of the following measures CANNOT be determined?
   (A) KL
   (B) JY
   (C) $m\angle XZL$
   (D) $m\angle KZY$

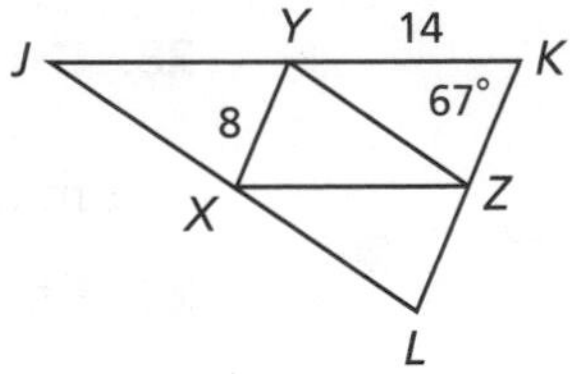

CHALLENGE AND EXTEND

42. **Multi-Step** The midpoints of the sides of a triangle are $A(-6, 3)$, $B(2, 1)$, and $C(0, -3)$. Find the coordinates of the vertices of the triangle.

43. **Critical Thinking** Classify the midsegment triangle of an equilateral triangle by its side lengths and angle measures.

Algebra Find the value of n in each triangle.

44.

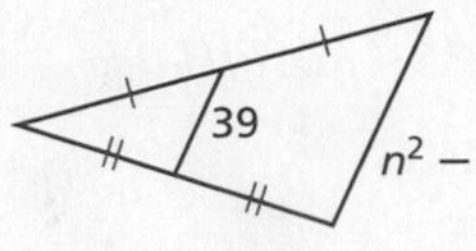

45.

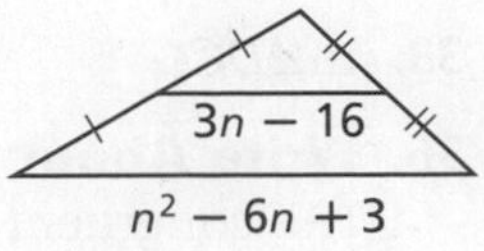

46. $\triangle XYZ$ is the midsegment triangle of $\triangle PQR$. Write a congruence statement involving all four of the smaller triangles. What is the relationship between the area of $\triangle XYZ$ and $\triangle PQR$?

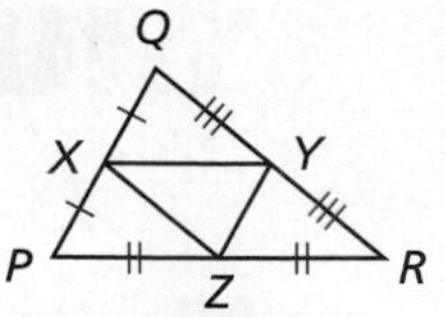

47. $\overline{AB}$ is a midsegment of $\triangle XYZ$. $\overline{CD}$ is a midsegment of $\triangle ABZ$. $\overline{EF}$ is a midsegment of $\triangle CDZ$, and $\overline{GH}$ is a midsegment of $\triangle EFZ$.

a. Copy and complete the table.

Number of Midsegment	1	2	3	4
Length of Midsegment	■	■	■	■

b. If this pattern continues, what will be the length of midsegment 8?

c. Write an algebraic expression to represent the length of midsegment n. (*Hint*: Think of the midsegment lengths as powers of 2.)

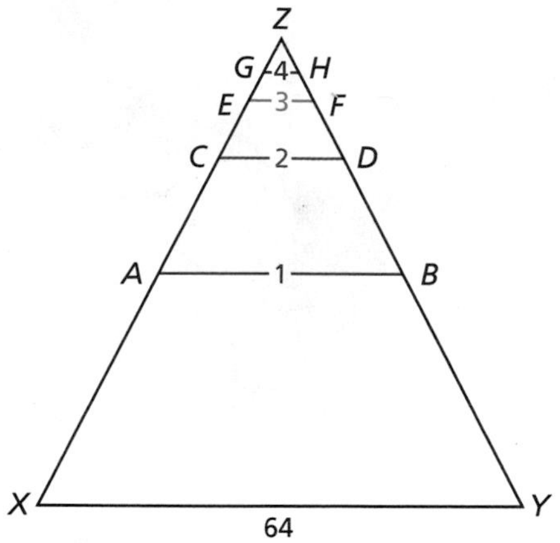

Construction Midsegment of a Triangle

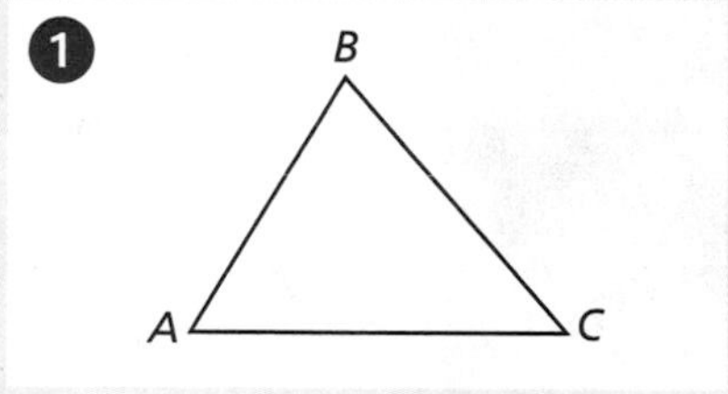

Draw a large triangle. Label the vertices *A*, *B*, and *C*.

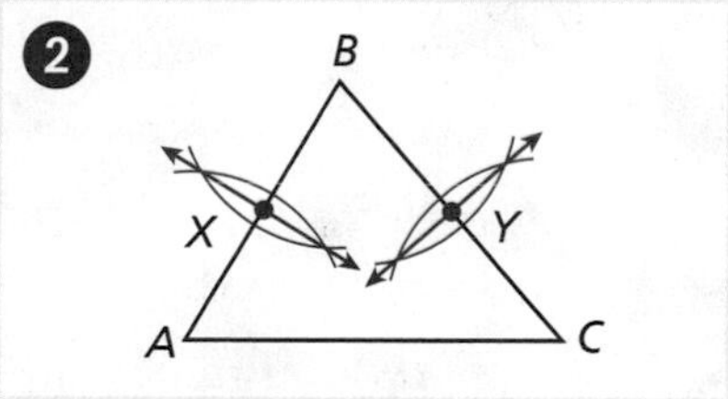

Construct the midpoints of $\overline{AB}$ and $\overline{BC}$. Label the midpoints *X* and *Y*, respectively.

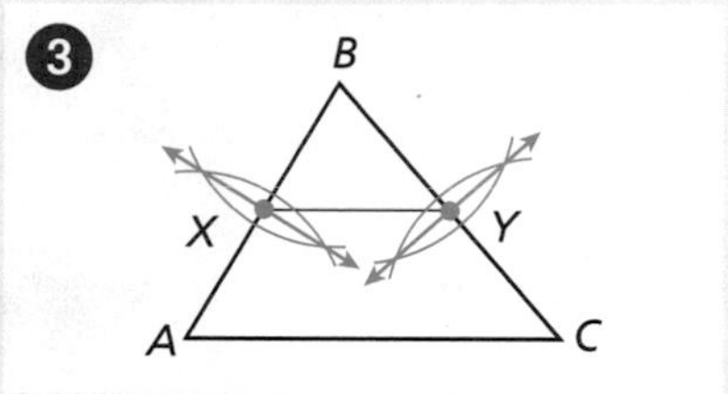

Draw the midsegment $\overline{XY}$.

1. Using a ruler, measure $\overline{XY}$ and $\overline{AC}$. How are the two lengths related?

2. How can you use a protractor to verify that $\overline{XY}$ is parallel to $\overline{AC}$?

CHAPTER 5

MULTI-STEP TEST PREP

SECTION 5A

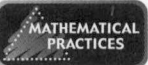

MATHEMATICAL PRACTICES **Model with mathematics.**

Segments in Triangles

Location Contemplation

A chain of music stores has locations in Ashville, Benton, and Carson. The directors of the company are using a coordinate plane to decide on the location for a new distribution warehouse. Each unit on the plane represents one mile.

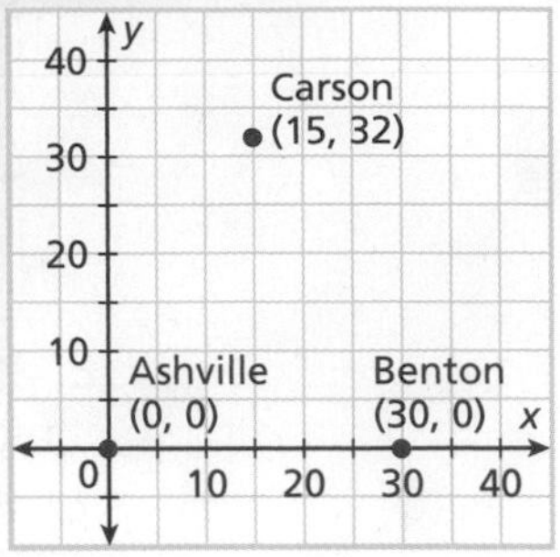

1. A plot of land is available at the centroid of the triangle formed by the three cities. What are the coordinates for this location?
2. If the directors build the warehouse at the centroid, about how far will it be from each of the cities?
3. Another plot of land is available at the orthocenter of the triangle. What are the coordinates for this location?
4. About how far would the warehouse be from each city if it were built at the orthocenter?
5. A third option is to build the warehouse at the circumcenter of the triangle. What are the coordinates for this location?
6. About how far would the warehouse be from each city if it were built at the circumcenter?
7. The directors decide that the warehouse should be equidistant from each city. Which location should they choose?

READY TO GO ON?

Quiz for Lessons 5-1 Through 5-4

5-1 Perpendicular and Angle Bisectors

Find each measure.

1. *PQ*

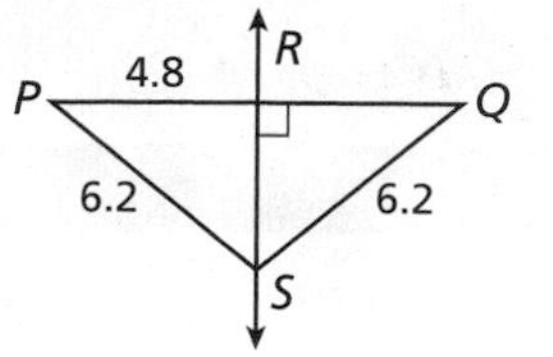

2. *JM*

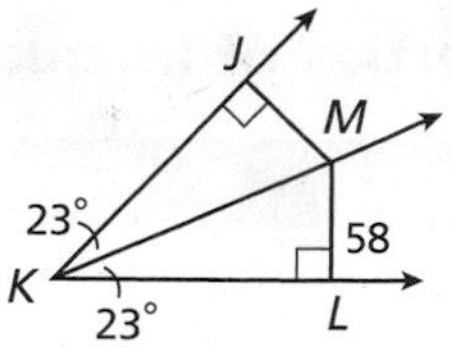

3. *AC*

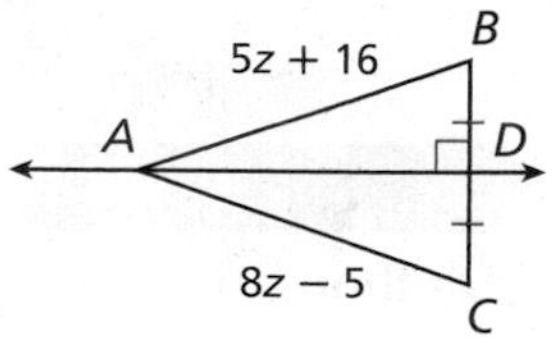

4. Write an equation in point-slope form for the perpendicular bisector of the segment with endpoints $M(-1, -3)$ and $N(7, 1)$.

5-2 Bisectors of Triangles

5. $\overline{PX}$, $\overline{PY}$, and $\overline{PZ}$ are the perpendicular bisectors of $\triangle RST$. Find *PS* and *XT*.

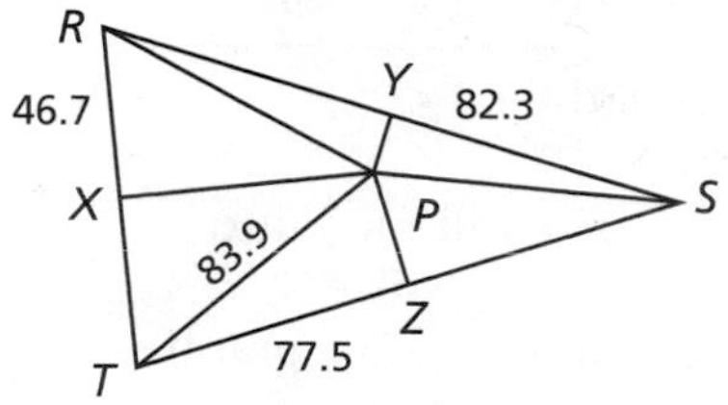

6. $\overline{JK}$ and $\overline{HK}$ are angle bisectors of $\triangle GHJ$. Find $m\angle GJK$ and the distance from *K* to $\overline{HJ}$.

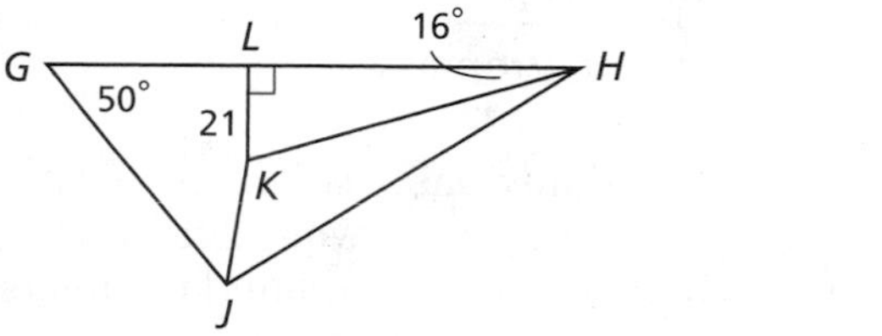

7. Find the circumcenter of $\triangle TVO$ with vertices $T(9, 0)$, $V(0, -4)$, and $O(0, 0)$.

5-3 Medians and Altitudes of Triangles

8. In $\triangle DEF$, $BD = 87$, and $WE = 38$. Find *BW*, *CW*, and *CE*.
9. Paula cuts a triangle with vertices at coordinates $(0, 4)$, $(8, 0)$, and $(10, 8)$ from grid paper. At what coordinates should she place the tip of a pencil to balance the triangle?
10. Find the orthocenter of $\triangle PSV$ with vertices $P(2, 4)$, $S(8, 4)$, and $V(4, 0)$.

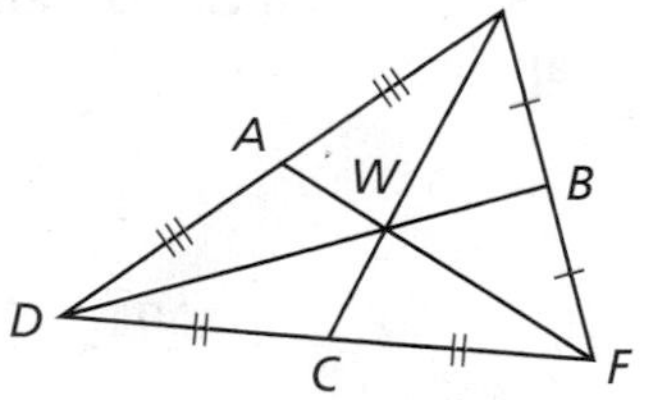

5-4 The Triangle Midsegment Theorem

11. Find *ZV*, *PM*, and $m\angle RZV$ in $\triangle JMP$.

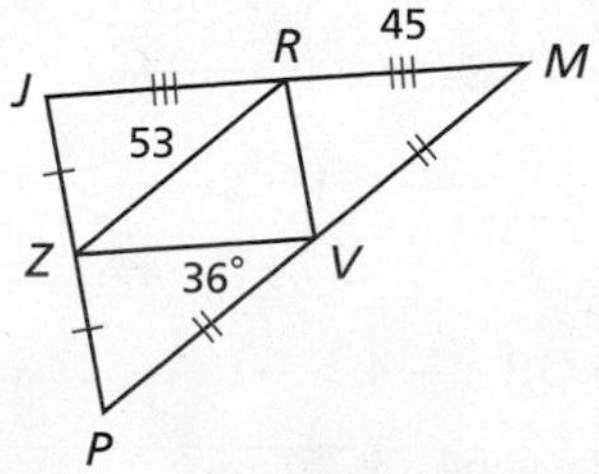

12. What is the distance *XZ* across the pond?

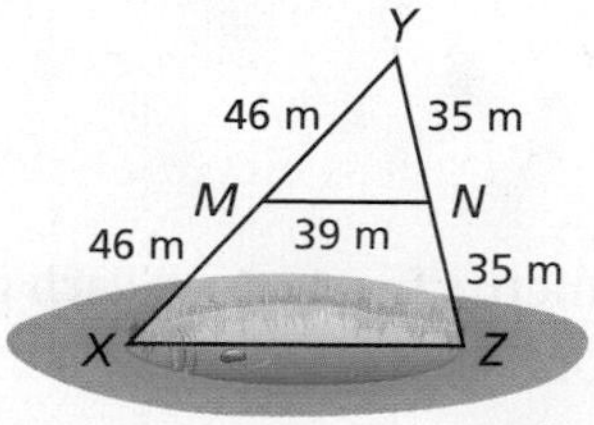

Connecting Geometry to Algebra

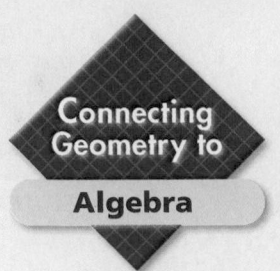

Solving Compound Inequalities

To solve an inequality, you use the Properties of Inequality and inverse operations to undo the operations in the inequality one at a time.

Properties of Inequality

PROPERTY	ALGEBRA
Addition Property	If $a < b$, then $a + c < b + c$.
Subtraction Property	If $a < b$, then $a - c < b - c$.
Multiplication Property	If $a < b$ and $c > 0$, then $ac < bc$. If $a < b$ and $c < 0$, then $ac > bc$.
Division Property	If $a < b$ and $c > 0$, then $\frac{a}{c} < \frac{b}{c}$. If $a < b$ and $c < 0$, then $\frac{a}{c} > \frac{b}{c}$.
Transitive Property	If $a < b$ and $b < c$, then $a < c$.
Comparison Property	If $a + b = c$ and $b > 0$, then $a < c$.

A compound inequality is formed when two simple inequalities are combined into one statement with the word *and* or *or*. To solve a compound inequality, solve each simple inequality and find the intersection or union of the solutions. The graph of a compound inequality may represent a line, a ray, two rays, or a segment.

Example

Solve the compound inequality $5 < 20 - 3a \leq 11$. What geometric figure does the graph represent?

$5 < 20 - 3a$	AND	$20 - 3a \leq 11$	*Rewrite the compound inequality as two simple inequalities.*
$-15 < -3a$	AND	$-3a \leq -9$	*Subtract 20 from both sides.*
$5 > a$	AND	$a \geq 3$	*Divide both sides by −3 and reverse the inequality symbols.*
	$3 \leq a < 5$		*Combine the two solutions into a single statement.*

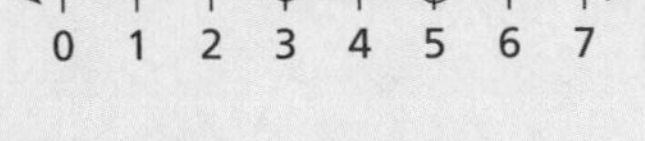

The graph represents a segment.

Try This

Solve. What geometric figure does each graph represent?

1. $-4 + x > 1$ OR $-8 + 2x < -6$
2. $2x - 3 \geq -5$ OR $x - 4 > -1$
3. $-6 < 7 - x \leq 12$
4. $22 < -2 - 2x \leq 54$
5. $3x \geq 0$ OR $x + 5 < 7$
6. $2x - 3 \leq 5$ OR $-2x + 3 \leq -9$

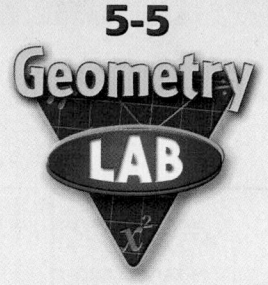

5-5

Geometry LAB

Explore Triangle Inequalities

Many of the triangle relationships you have learned so far involve a statement of equality. For example, the circumcenter of a triangle is equidistant from the vertices of the triangle, and the incenter is equidistant from the sides of the triangle. Now you will investigate some triangle relationships that involve inequalities.

Use with Indirect Proof and Inequalities in One Triangle

Activity 1

MATHEMATICAL PRACTICES **Use appropriate tools strategically.**

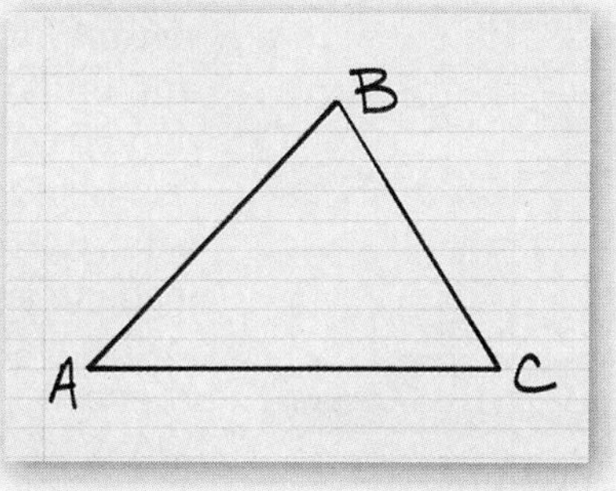

1. Draw a large scalene triangle. Label the vertices *A*, *B*, and *C*.

2. Measure the sides and the angles. Copy the table below and record the measures in the first row.

	BC	*AC*	*AB*	m∠*A*	m∠*B*	m∠*C*
Triangle 1						
Triangle 2						
Triangle 3						
Triangle 4						

Try This

1. In the table, draw a circle around the longest side length, and draw a circle around the greatest angle measure of △*ABC*. Draw a square around the shortest side length, and draw a square around the least angle measure.
2. **Make a Conjecture** Where is the longest side in relation to the largest angle? Where is the shortest side in relation to the smallest angle?
3. Draw three more scalene triangles and record the measures in the table. Does your conjecture hold?

Activity 2

1. Cut three sets of chenille stems to the following lengths.
   3 inches, 4 inches, 6 inches
   3 inches, 4 inches, 7 inches
   3 inches, 4 inches, 8 inches

2. Try to make a triangle with each set of chenille stems.

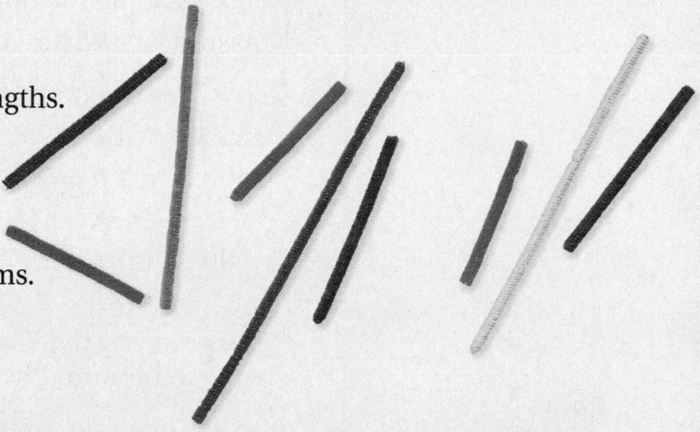

Try This

4. Which sets of chenille stems make a triangle?
5. **Make a Conjecture** For each set of chenille stems, compare the sum of any two lengths with the third length. What is the relationship?
6. Select a different set of three lengths and test your conjecture. Does your conjecture hold?

COMMON CORE

5-5 Indirect Proof and Inequalities in One Triangle

CC.9-12.G.CO.10 Prove theorems about triangles.

Objectives
Write indirect proofs.

Apply inequalities in one triangle.

Vocabulary
indirect proof

Why learn this?

You can use a triangle inequality to find a reasonable range of values for an unknown distance. (See Example 5.)

Getting in shape for the Summer Olympics.

So far you have written proofs using *direct reasoning*. You began with a true hypothesis and built a logical argument to show that a conclusion was true. In an **indirect proof**, you begin by assuming that the conclusion is false. Then you show that this assumption leads to a contradiction. This type of proof is also called a *proof by contradiction*.

Helpful Hint

When writing an indirect proof, look for a contradiction of one of the following: the given information, a definition, a postulate, or a theorem.

Writing an Indirect Proof
1. Identify the conjecture to be proven.
2. Assume the opposite (the negation) of the conclusion is true.
3. Use direct reasoning to show that the assumption leads to a contradiction.
4. Conclude that since the assumption is false, the original conjecture must be true.

EXAMPLE 1 Writing an Indirect Proof

Write an indirect proof that a right triangle cannot have an obtuse angle.

Step 1 Identify the conjecture to be proven.

Given: $\triangle JKL$ is a right triangle.
Prove: $\triangle JKL$ does not have an obtuse angle.

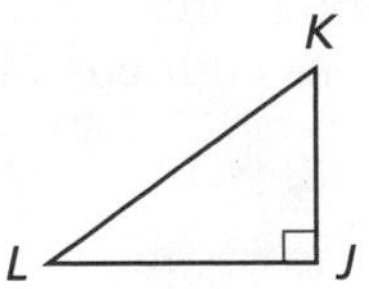

Step 2 Assume the opposite of the conclusion.

Assume $\triangle JKL$ has an obtuse angle. Let $\angle K$ be obtuse.

Step 3 Use direct reasoning to lead to a contradiction.

$m\angle K + m\angle L = 90°$	*The acute ∠s of a rt. △ are comp.*
$m\angle K = 90° - m\angle L$	*Subtr. Prop. of =*
$m\angle K > 90°$	*Def. of obtuse ∠*
$90° - m\angle L > 90°$	*Substitute 90° − m∠L for m∠K.*
$m\angle L < 0°$	*Subtract 90° from both sides and solve for m∠L.*

However, by the Protractor Postulate, a triangle cannot have an angle with a measure less than 0°.

Step 4 Conclude that the original conjecture is true.

The assumption that $\triangle JKL$ has an obtuse angle is false.

Therefore $\triangle JKL$ does not have an obtuse angle.

CHECK IT OUT! **1.** Write an indirect proof that a triangle cannot have two right angles.

The positions of the longest and shortest sides of a triangle are related to the positions of the largest and smallest angles.

Know it! Note

Theorems Angle-Side Relationships in Triangles

THEOREM	HYPOTHESIS	CONCLUSION
5-5-1 If two sides of a triangle are not congruent, then the larger angle is opposite the longer side. (In △, larger ∠ is opp. longer side.)	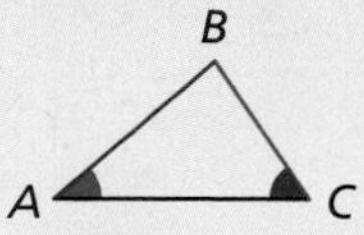 $AB > BC$	$m\angle C > m\angle A$
5-5-2 If two angles of a triangle are not congruent, then the longer side is opposite the larger angle. (In △, longer side is opp. larger ∠.)	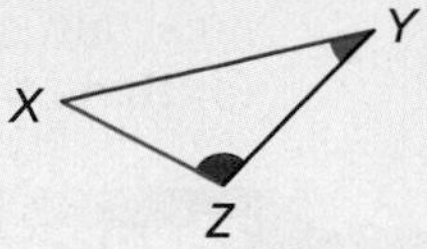 $m\angle Z > m\angle Y$	$XY > XZ$

You will prove Theorem 5-5-1 in Exercise 67.

PROOF

Theorem 5-5-2

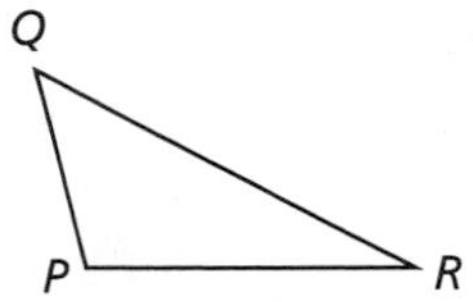

Given: $m\angle P > m\angle R$
Prove: $QR > QP$

Indirect Proof:
Assume $QR \ngtr QP$. This means that either $QR < QP$ or $QR = QP$.

Case 1 If $QR < QP$, then $m\angle P < m\angle R$ because the larger angle is opposite the longer side. This contradicts the given information. So $QR \nless QP$.

Case 2 If $QR = QP$, then $m\angle P = m\angle R$ by the Isosceles Triangle Theorem. This also contradicts the given information, so $QR \neq QP$.

The assumption $QR \ngtr QP$ is false. Therefore $QR > QP$.

Caution!

Consider all cases when you assume the opposite. If the conclusion is $QR > QP$, the negation includes $QR < QP$ and $QR = QP$.

EXAMPLE 2 Ordering Triangle Side Lengths and Angle Measures

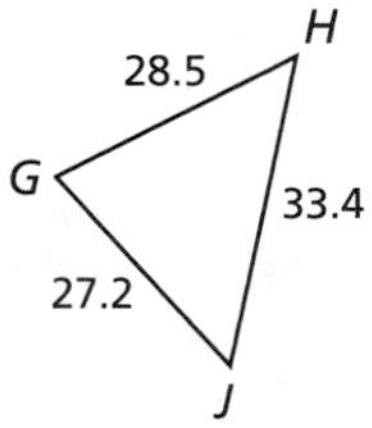

A **Write the angles in order from smallest to largest.**

The shortest side is $\overline{GJ}$, so the smallest angle is $\angle H$.
The longest side is $\overline{HJ}$, so the largest angle is $\angle G$.
The angles from smallest to largest are $\angle H$, $\angle J$, and $\angle G$.

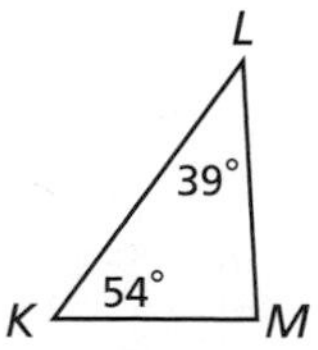

B **Write the sides in order from shortest to longest.**

$m\angle M = 180° - (39° + 54°) = 87°$ *△ Sum Thm.*
The smallest angle is $\angle L$, so the shortest side is $\overline{KM}$.
The largest angle is $\angle M$, so the longest side is $\overline{KL}$.
The sides from shortest to longest are $\overline{KM}$, $\overline{LM}$, and $\overline{KL}$.

CHECK IT OUT!

2a. Write the angles in order from smallest to largest.

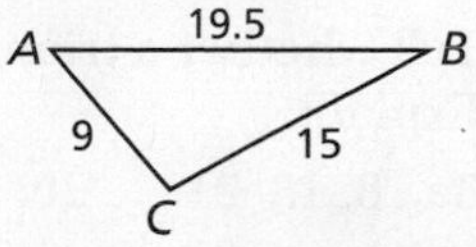

2b. Write the sides in order from shortest to longest.

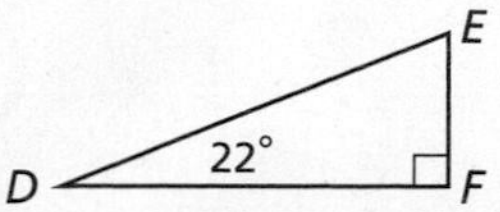

A triangle is formed by three segments, but not every set of three segments can form a triangle.

Segments with lengths of 7, 4, and 4 can form a triangle.

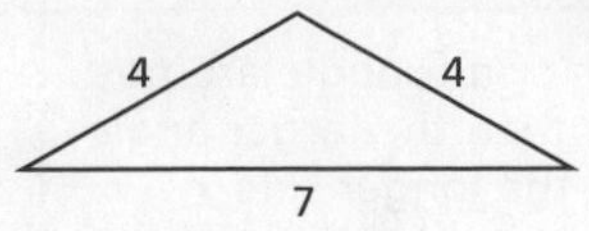

Segments with lengths of 7, 3, and 3 cannot form a triangle.

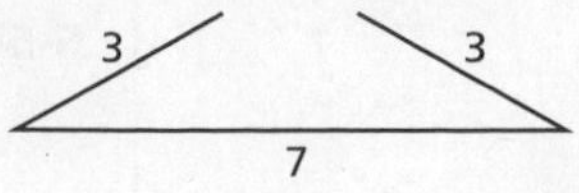

A certain relationship must exist among the lengths of three segments in order for them to form a triangle.

Know it! Note

Theorem 5-5-3 **Triangle Inequality Theorem**

The sum of any two side lengths of a triangle is greater than the third side length.

$AB + BC > AC$
$BC + AC > AB$
$AC + AB > BC$

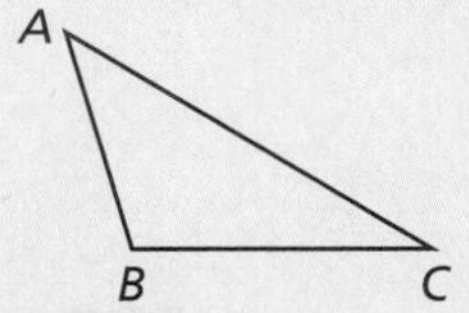

You will prove Theorem 5-5-3 in Exercise 68.

EXAMPLE 3 Applying the Triangle Inequality Theorem

Tell whether a triangle can have sides with the given lengths. Explain.

A **3, 5, 7**

$3 + 5 \overset{?}{>} 7$ $\quad$ $3 + 7 \overset{?}{>} 5$ $\quad$ $5 + 7 \overset{?}{>} 3$

$8 > 7$ ✓ $\quad$ $10 > 5$ ✓ $\quad$ $12 > 3$ ✓

Yes—the sum of each pair of lengths is greater than the third length.

Helpful Hint

To show that three lengths cannot be the side lengths of a triangle, you only need to show that one of the three triangle inequalities is false.

B **4, 6.5, 11**

$4 + 6.5 \overset{?}{>} 11$

$10.5 \not> 11$

No—by the Triangle Inequality Theorem, a triangle cannot have these side lengths.

C $n + 5, n^2, 2n$**, when** $n = 3$

Step 1 Evaluate each expression when $n = 3$.

$n + 5$	n^2	$2n$
$3 + 5$	3^2	$2(3)$
8	9	6

Step 2 Compare the lengths.

$8 + 9 \overset{?}{>} 6$ $\quad$ $8 + 6 \overset{?}{>} 9$ $\quad$ $9 + 6 \overset{?}{>} 8$

$17 > 6$ ✓ $\quad$ $14 > 9$ ✓ $\quad$ $15 > 8$ ✓

Yes—the sum of each pair of lengths is greater than the third length.

CHECK IT OUT! **Tell whether a triangle can have sides with the given lengths. Explain.**

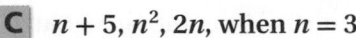

3a. 8, 13, 21 $\quad$ **3b.** 6.2, 7, 9 $\quad$ **3c.** $t - 2, 4t, t^2 + 1$, when $t = 4$

EXAMPLE 4 Finding Side Lengths

The lengths of two sides of a triangle are 6 centimeters and 11 centimeters. Find the range of possible lengths for the third side.

Let s represent the length of the third side. Then apply the Triangle Inequality Theorem.

$s + 6 > 11$	$s + 11 > 6$	$6 + 11 > s$
$s > 5$	$s > -5$	$17 > s$

Combine the inequalities. So $5 < s < 17$. The length of the third side is greater than 5 centimeters and less than 17 centimeters.

CHECK IT OUT! **4.** The lengths of two sides of a triangle are 22 inches and 17 inches. Find the range of possible lengths for the third side.

EXAMPLE 5 *Travel Application*

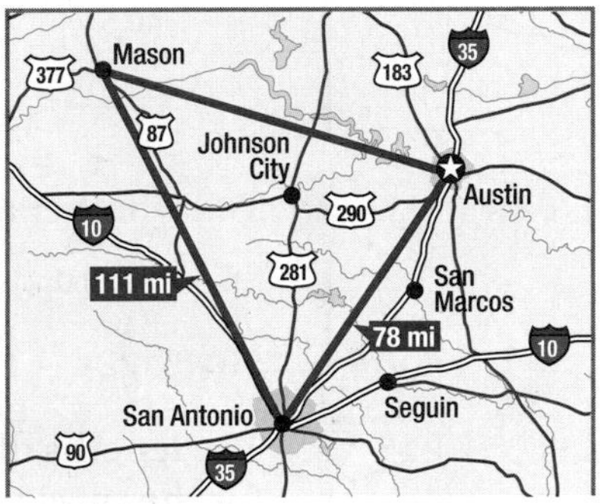

The map shows the approximate distances from San Antonio to Mason and from San Antonio to Austin. What is the range of distances from Mason to Austin?

Let d be the distance from Mason to Austin.

$d + 111 > 78$	$d + 78 > 111$	$111 + 78 > d$	*△ Inequal. Thm.*
$d > -33$	$d > 33$	$189 > d$	*Subtr. Prop. of Inequal.*
	$33 < d < 189$		*Combine the inequalities.*

The distance from Mason to Austin is greater than 33 miles and less than 189 miles.

CHECK IT OUT! **5.** The distance from San Marcos to Johnson City is 50 miles, and the distance from Seguin to San Marcos is 22 miles. What is the range of distances from Seguin to Johnson City?

MATHEMATICAL PRACTICES

THINK AND DISCUSS

1. To write an indirect proof that an angle is obtuse, a student assumes that the angle is acute. Is this the correct assumption? Explain.

2. Give an example of three measures that can be the lengths of the sides of a triangle. Give an example of three lengths that cannot be the sides of a triangle.

Know it! Note

3. GET ORGANIZED Copy and complete the graphic organizer. In each box, explain what you know about $\triangle ABC$ as a result of the theorem.

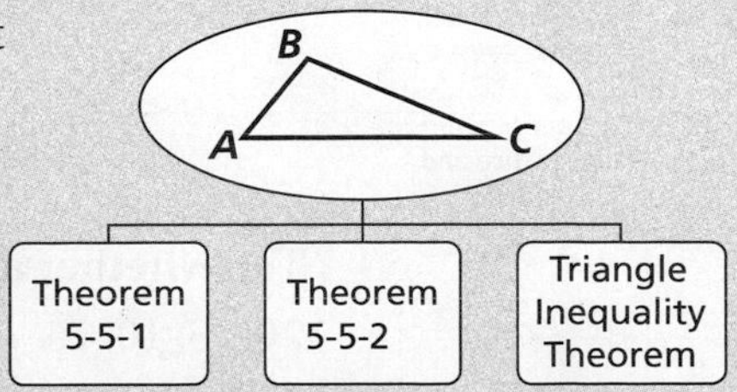

5-5 Exercises

Learn It Online
Homework Help Online
Parent Resources Online

GUIDED PRACTICE

1. **Vocabulary** Describe the process of an *indirect proof* in your own words.

SEE EXAMPLE 1

Write an indirect proof of each statement.

2. A scalene triangle cannot have two congruent angles.
3. An isosceles triangle cannot have a base angle that is a right angle.

SEE EXAMPLE 2

4. Write the angles in order from smallest to largest.

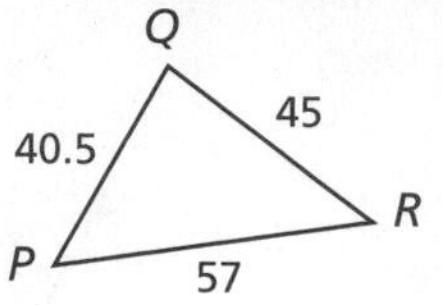

5. Write the sides in order from shortest to longest.

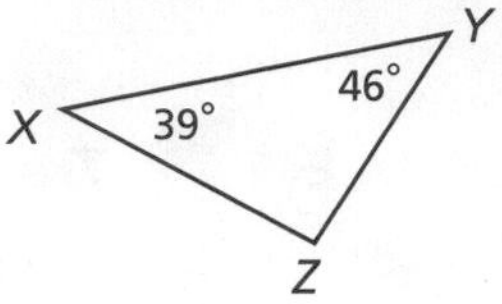

SEE EXAMPLE 3

Tell whether a triangle can have sides with the given lengths. Explain.

6. 4, 7, 10
7. 2, 9, 12
8. $3\frac{1}{2}, 3\frac{1}{2}, 6$
9. 3, 1.1, 1.7
10. $3x, 2x - 1, x^2$, when $x = 5$
11. $7c + 6, 10c - 7, 3c^2$, when $c = 2$

SEE EXAMPLE 4

The lengths of two sides of a triangle are given. Find the range of possible lengths for the third side.

12. 8 mm, 12 mm
13. 16 ft, 16 ft
14. 11.4 cm, 12 cm

SEE EXAMPLE 5

15. **Design** The refrigerator, stove, and sink in a kitchen are at the vertices of a path called the work triangle.
    a. If the angle at the sink is the largest, which side of the work triangle will be the longest?
    b. The designer wants the longest side of this triangle to be 9 feet long. Can the lengths of the other sides be 5 feet and 4 feet? Explain.

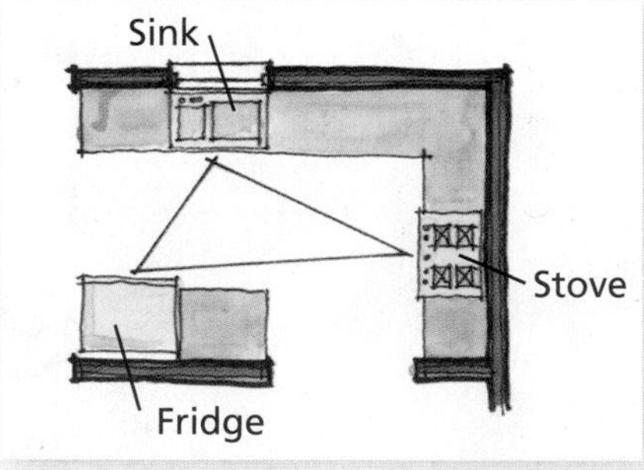

PRACTICE AND PROBLEM SOLVING

Independent Practice

For Exercises	See Example
16–17	1
18–19	2
20–25	3
26–31	4
32	5

Extra Practice
See Extra Practice for more Skills Practice and Applications Practice exercises.

Write an indirect proof of each statement.

16. A scalene triangle cannot have two congruent midsegments.
17. Two supplementary angles cannot both be obtuse angles.
18. Write the angles in order from smallest to largest.

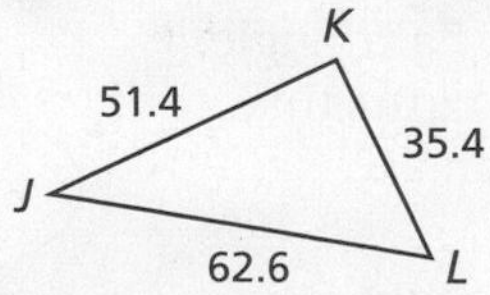

19. Write the sides in order from shortest to longest.

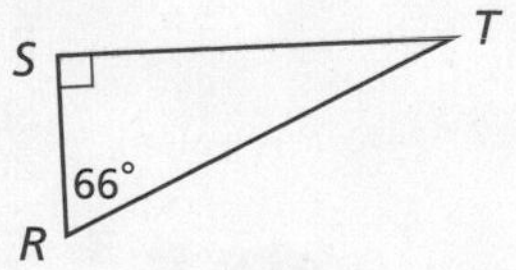

Tell whether a triangle can have sides with the given lengths. Explain.

20. 6, 10, 15
21. 14, 18, 32
22. 11.9, 5.8, 5.8
23. 103, 41.9, 62.5
24. $z + 8, 3z + 5, 4z - 11$, when $z = 6$
25. $m + 11, 8m, m^2 + 1$, when $m = 3$

LINK Bicycles

On June 26, 2004, Terry Goertzen of Winnipeg, Canada, attained the new Guinness world record for the tallest bicycle with his 5.5-meter-tall bike.

The lengths of two sides of a triangle are given. Find the range of possible lengths for the third side.

26. 4 yd, 19 yd

27. 28 km, 23 km

28. 9.2 cm, 3.8 cm

29. 3.07 m, 1.89 m

30. $2\frac{1}{8}$ in., $3\frac{5}{8}$ in.

31. $3\frac{5}{6}$ ft, $6\frac{1}{2}$ ft

32. Bicycles The five steel tubes of this mountain bike frame form two triangles. List the five tubes in order from shortest to longest. Explain your answer.

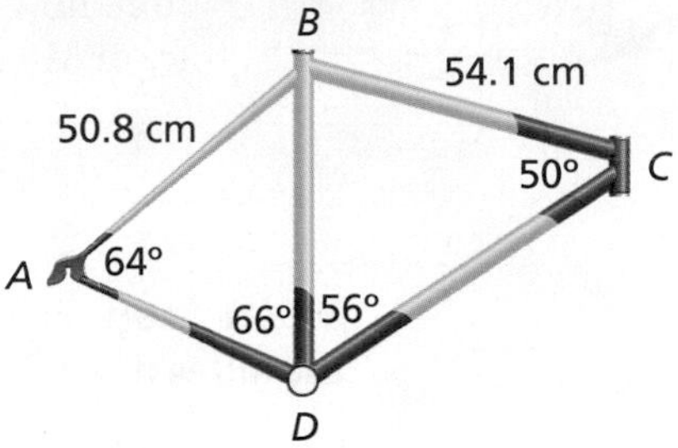

33. Critical Thinking The length of the base of an isosceles triangle is 15. What is the range of possible lengths for each leg? Explain.

List the sides of each triangle in order from shortest to longest.

34.

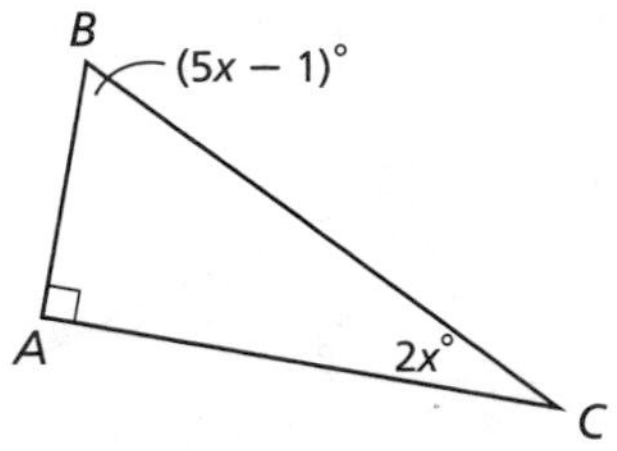

35.

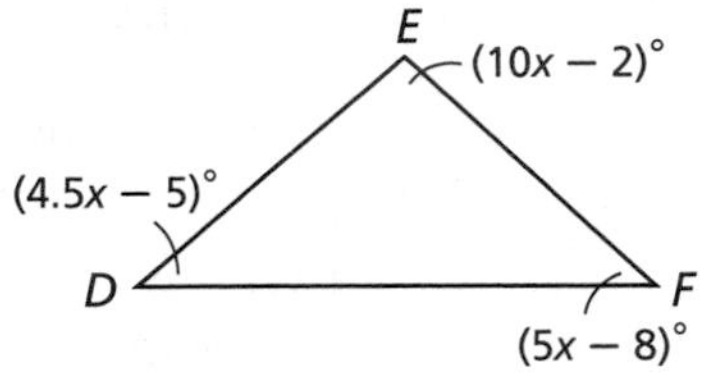

In each set of statements, name the two that contradict each other.

36. $\triangle PQR$ is a right triangle.
$\triangle PQR$ is a scalene triangle.
$\triangle PQR$ is an acute triangle.

37. $\angle Y$ is supplementary to $\angle Z$.
$m\angle Y < 90°$
$\angle Y$ is an obtuse angle.

38. $\triangle JKL$ is isosceles with base $\overline{JL}$.
In $\triangle JKL$, $m\angle K > m\angle J$
In $\triangle JKL$, $JK > LK$

39. $\overline{AB} \perp \overline{BC}$
$\overline{AB} \cong \overline{CD}$
$\overline{AB} \parallel \overline{BC}$

40. Figure A is a polygon.
Figure A is a triangle.
Figure A is a quadrilateral.

41. x is even.
x is a multiple of 4.
x is prime.

Compare. Write <, >, or =.

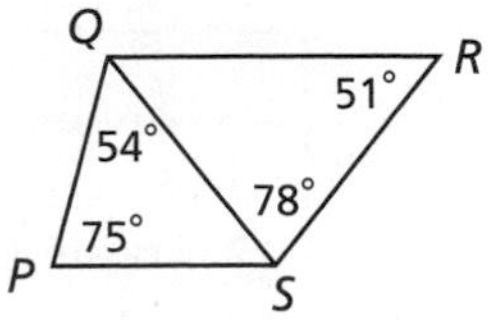

42. QS ▩ PS

43. PQ ▩ QS

44. QS ▩ QR

45. QS ▩ RS

46. PQ ▩ RS

47. RS ▩ PS

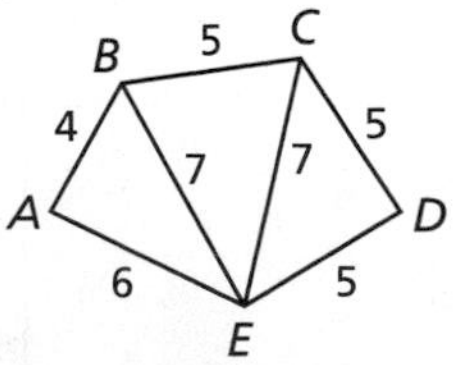

48. $m\angle ABE$ ▩ $m\angle BEA$

49. $m\angle CBE$ ▩ $m\angle CEB$

50. $m\angle DCE$ ▩ $m\angle DEC$

51. $m\angle DCE$ ▩ $m\angle CDE$

52. $m\angle ABE$ ▩ $m\angle EAB$

53. $m\angle EBC$ ▩ $m\angle ECB$

List the angles of $\triangle JKL$ in order from smallest to largest.

54. $J(-3, -2)$, $K(3, 6)$, $L(8, -2)$

55. $J(-5, -10)$, $K(-5, 2)$, $L(7, -5)$

56. $J(-4, 1)$, $K(-3, 8)$, $L(3, 4)$

57. $J(-10, -4)$, $K(0, 3)$, $L(2, -8)$

58. Critical Thinking An attorney argues that her client did not commit a burglary because a witness saw her client in a different city at the time of the burglary. Explain how this situation is an example of indirect reasoning.

MULTI-STEP TEST PREP

59. The figure shows an airline's routes between four cities.

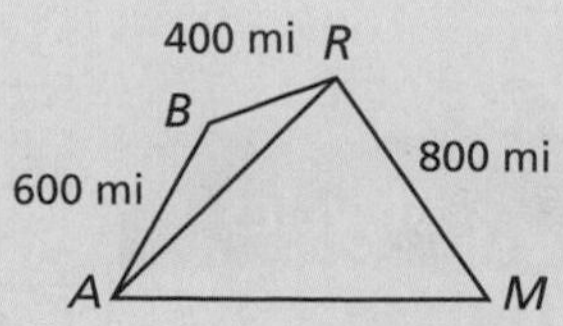

a. The airline's planes fly at an average speed of 500 mi/h. What is the range of time it might take to fly from Auburn (A) to Raymond (R)?

b. The airline offers one frequent-flier mile for every mile flown. Is it possible to earn 1800 miles by flying from Millford (M) to Auburn (A)? Explain.

Multi-Step **Each set of expressions represents the lengths of the sides of a triangle. Find the range of possible values of n.**

60. $n, 6, 8$ **61.** $2n, 5, 7$ **62.** $n + 1, 3, 6$

63. $n + 1, n + 2, n + 3$ **64.** $n + 2, n + 3, 3n - 2$ **65.** $n, n + 2, 2n + 1$

66. Given that P is in the interior of $\triangle XYZ$, prove that $XY + XP + PZ > YZ$.

67. Complete the proof of Theorem 5-5-1 by filling in the blanks.

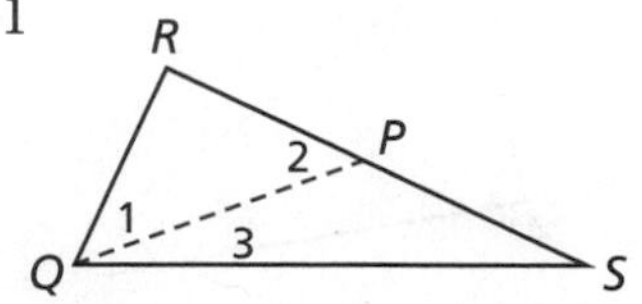

Given: $RS > RQ$

Prove: $m\angle RQS > m\angle S$

Proof:

Locate P on $\overline{RS}$ so that $RP = RQ$. So $\overline{RP} \cong \overline{RQ}$ by **a.** ___?___ . Then $\angle 1 \cong \angle 2$ by **b.** ___?___ , and $m\angle 1 = m\angle 2$ by **c.** ___?___ . By the Angle Addition Postulate, $m\angle RQS =$ **d.** ___?___ . So $m\angle RQS > m\angle 1$ by the Comparison Property of Inequality. Then $m\angle RQS > m\angle 2$ by **e.** ___?___ . By the Exterior Angle Theorem, $m\angle 2 = m\angle 3 +$ **f.** ___?___ . So $m\angle 2 > m\angle S$ by the Comparison Property of Inequality. Therefore $m\angle RQS > m\angle S$ by **g.** ___?___ .

68. Complete the proof of the Triangle Inequality Theorem.

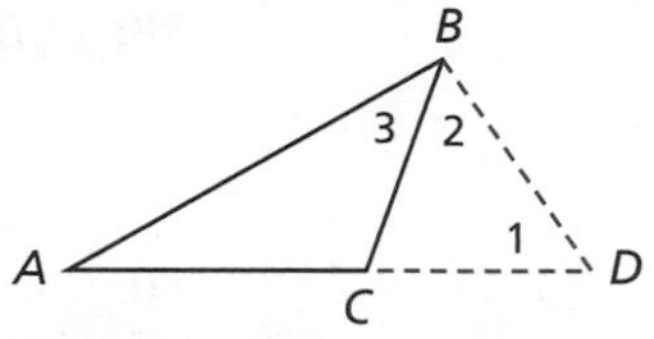

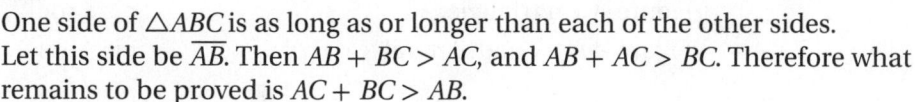

Given: $\triangle ABC$

Prove: $AB + BC > AC, AB + AC > BC, AC + BC > AB$

Proof:

One side of $\triangle ABC$ is as long as or longer than each of the other sides. Let this side be $\overline{AB}$. Then $AB + BC > AC$, and $AB + AC > BC$. Therefore what remains to be proved is $AC + BC > AB$.

Statements	Reasons
1. **a.** ___?___	1. Given
2. Locate D on $\overrightarrow{AC}$ so that $BC = DC$.	2. Ruler Post.
3. $AC + DC =$ **b.** ___?___	3. Seg. Add. Post.
4. $\angle 1 \cong \angle 2$	4. **c.** ___?___
5. $m\angle 1 = m\angle 2$	5. **d.** ___?___
6. $m\angle ABD = m\angle 2 +$ **e.** ___?___	6. $\angle$ Add. Post.
7. $m\angle ABD > m\angle 2$	7. Comparison Prop. of Inequal.
8. $m\angle ABD > m\angle 1$	8. **f.** ___?___
9. $AD > AB$	9. **g.** ___?___
10. $AC + DC > AB$	10. **h.** ___?___
11. **i.** ___?___	11. Subst.

69. **Write About It** Explain why the hypotenuse is always the longest side of a right triangle. Explain why the diagonal of a square is longer than each side.

TEST PREP

70. The lengths of two sides of a triangle are 3 feet and 5 feet. Which could be the length of the third side?

Ⓐ 3 feet Ⓑ 8 feet Ⓒ 15 feet Ⓓ 16 feet

71. Which statement about $\triangle GHJ$ is false?

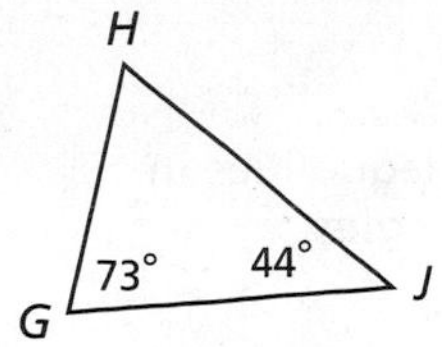

Ⓕ $GH < GJ$ Ⓗ $GH + HJ < GJ$

Ⓖ $m\angle H > m\angle J$ Ⓙ $\triangle GHJ$ is a scalene triangle.

72. In $\triangle RST$, $m\angle S = 92°$. Which is the longest side of $\triangle RST$?

Ⓐ $\overline{RS}$ Ⓒ $\overline{RT}$

Ⓑ $\overline{ST}$ Ⓓ Cannot be determined

CHALLENGE AND EXTEND

73. **Probability** A bag contains five sticks. The lengths of the sticks are 1 inch, 3 inches, 5 inches, 7 inches, and 9 inches. Suppose you pick three sticks from the bag at random. What is the probability you can form a triangle with the three sticks?

74. Complete this indirect argument that $\sqrt{2}$ is irrational. Assume that **a.** __?__ . Then $\sqrt{2} = \frac{p}{q}$, where p and q are positive integers that have no common factors. Thus $2 =$ **b.** __?__ , and $p^2 =$ **c.** __?__ . This implies that p^2 is even, and thus p is even. Since p^2 is the square of an even number, p^2 is divisible by 4 because **d.** __?__ . But then q^2 must be even because **e.** __?__ , and so q is even. Then p and q have a common factor of 2, which contradicts the assumption that p and q have no common factors.

75. Prove that the perpendicular segment from a point to a line is the shortest segment from the point to the line.

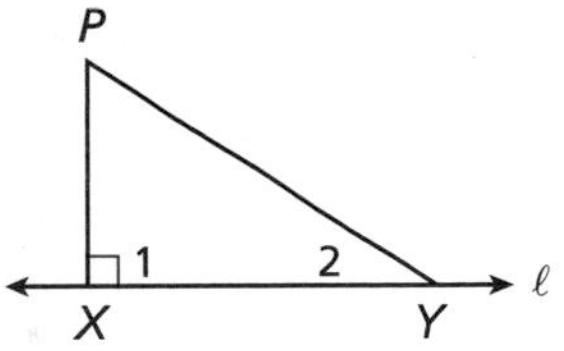

Given: $\overline{PX} \perp \ell$. Y is any point on ℓ other than X.
Prove: $PY > PX$
Plan: Show that $\angle 2$ and $\angle P$ are complementary. Use the Comparison Property of Inequality to show that $90° > m\angle 2$. Then show that $m\angle 1 > m\angle 2$ and thus $PY > PX$.

5-6 Inequalities in Two Triangles

CC.9-12.G.CO.10 Prove theorems about triangles.

Objective
Apply inequalities in two triangles.

Who uses this?
Designers of this circular swing ride can use the angle of the swings to determine how high the chairs will be at full speed. (See Example 2.)

In this lesson, you will apply inequality relationships between two triangles.

Know it! Note

Theorems Inequalities in Two Triangles

THEOREM	HYPOTHESIS	CONCLUSION
5-6-1 **Hinge Theorem** If two sides of one triangle are congruent to two sides of another triangle and the included angles are not congruent, then the longer third side is across from the larger included angle.	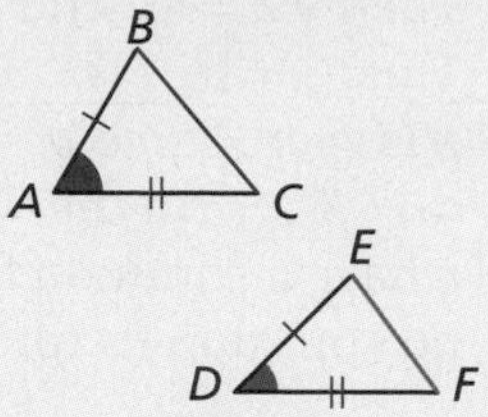 $m\angle A > m\angle D$	$BC > EF$
5-6-2 **Converse of the Hinge Theorem** If two sides of one triangle are congruent to two sides of another triangle and the third sides are not congruent, then the larger included angle is across from the longer third side.	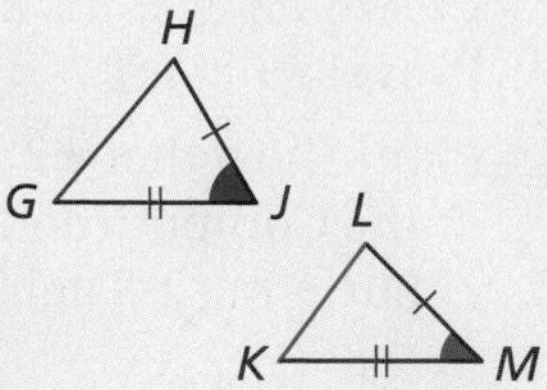 $GH > KL$	$m\angle J > m\angle M$

You will prove Theorem 5-6-1 in Exercise 35.

PROOF

Converse of the Hinge Theorem

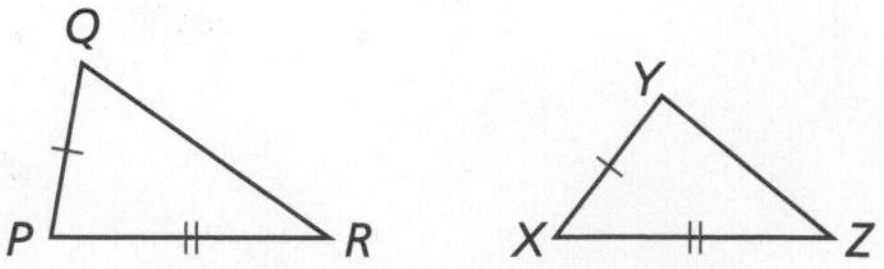

Given: $\overline{PQ} \cong \overline{XY}$, $\overline{PR} \cong \overline{XZ}$, $QR > YZ$
Prove: $m\angle P > m\angle X$

Indirect Proof:
Assume $m\angle P \not> m\angle X$. So either $m\angle P < m\angle X$, or $m\angle P = m\angle X$.

Case 1 If $m\angle P < m\angle X$, then $QR < YZ$ by the Hinge Theorem. This contradicts the given information that $QR > YZ$. So $m\angle P \not< m\angle X$.

Case 2 If $m\angle P = m\angle X$, then $\angle P \cong \angle X$. So $\triangle PQR \cong \triangle XYZ$ by SAS. Then $\overline{QR} \cong \overline{YZ}$ by CPCTC, and $QR = YZ$. This also contradicts the given information. So $m\angle P \neq m\angle X$.

The assumption $m\angle P \not> m\angle X$ is false. Therefore $m\angle P > m\angle X$.

EXAMPLE 1 Using the Hinge Theorem and Its Converse

A **Compare m∠*PQS* and m∠*RQS*.**

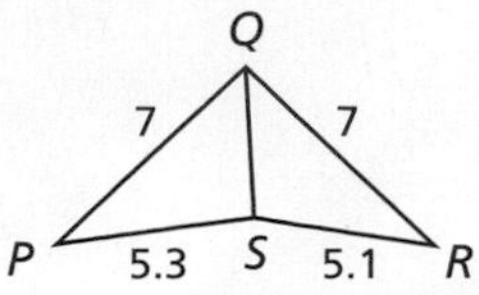

Compare the side lengths in △*PQS* and △*RQS*.

$PQ = RQ \qquad QS = QS \qquad PS > RS$

By the Converse of the Hinge Theorem, m∠*PQS* > m∠*RQS*.

B **Compare *KL* and *MN*.**

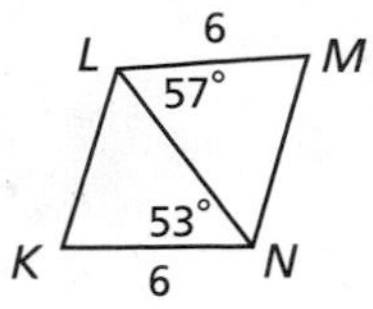

Compare the sides and angles in △*KLN* and △*MNL*.

$KN = ML \qquad LN = LN \qquad m\angle LNK < m\angle NLM$

By the Hinge Theorem, *KL* < *MN*.

x^2y Algebra

C **Find the range of values for *z*.**

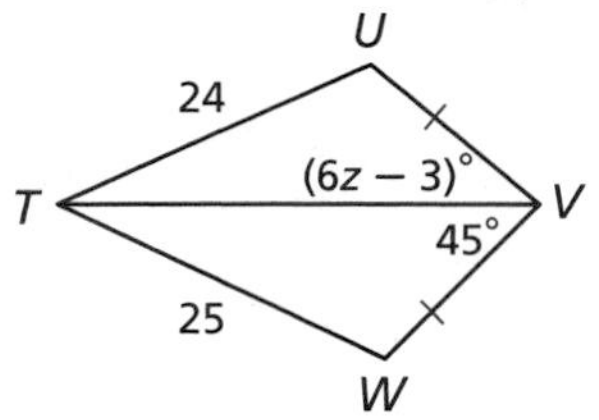

Step 1 Compare the side lengths in △*TUV* and △*TWV*.

$TV = TV \qquad VU = VW \qquad TU < TW$

By the Converse of the Hinge Theorem, m∠*UVT* < m∠*WVT*.

$6z - 3 < 45$ *Substitute the given values.*

$z < 8$ *Add 3 to both sides and divide both sides by 6.*

Step 2 Since ∠*UVT* is in a triangle, m∠*UVT* > 0°.

$6z - 3 > 0$ *Substitute the given value.*

$z > 0.5$ *Add 3 to both sides and divide both sides by 6.*

Step 3 Combine the inequalities.

The range of values for *z* is $0.5 < z < 8$.

CHECK IT OUT! **Compare the given measures.**

1a. m∠*EGH* and m∠*EGF*

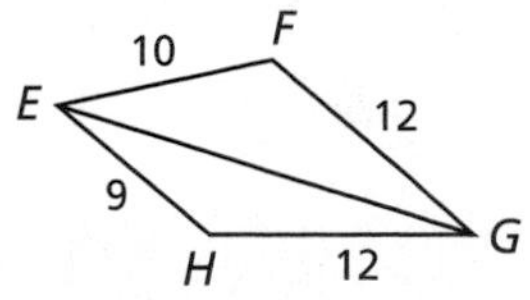

1b. *BC* and *AB*

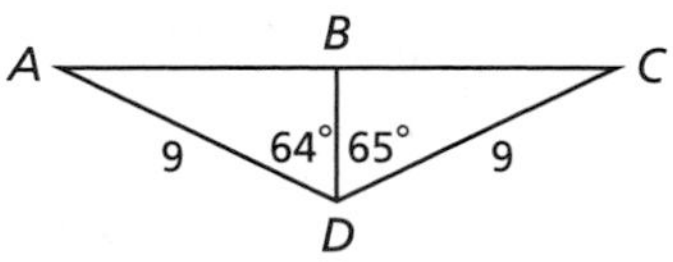

EXAMPLE 2 *Entertainment Application*

The angle of the swings in a circular swing ride changes with the speed of the ride. The diagram shows the position of one swing at two different speeds. Which rider is farther from the base of the swing tower? Explain.

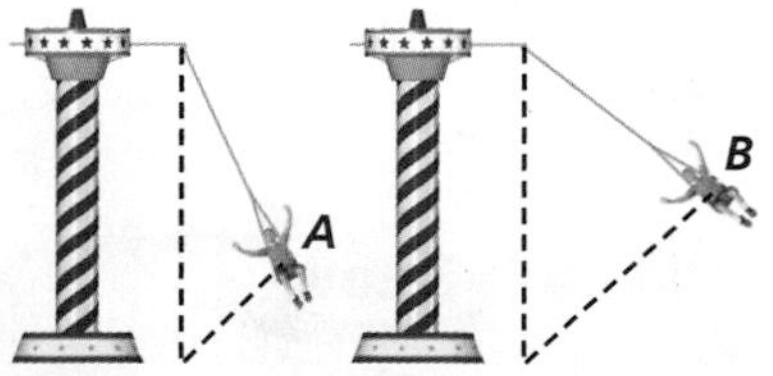

The height of the tower and the length of the cable holding the chair are the same in both triangles.

The angle formed by the swing in position *A* is smaller than the angle formed by the swing in position *B*. So rider *B* is farther from the base of the tower than rider *A* by the Hinge Theorem.

CHECK IT OUT!

2. When the swing ride is at full speed, the chairs are farthest from the base of the swing tower. What can you conclude about the angles of the swings at full speed versus low speed? Explain.

EXAMPLE 3 Proving Triangle Relationships

Write a two-column proof.
Given: $\overline{KL} \cong \overline{NL}$
Prove: $KM > NM$

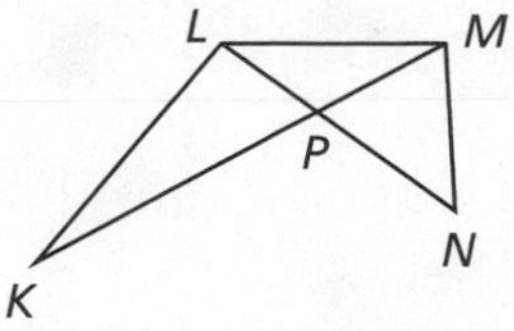

Proof:

Statements	Reasons
1. $\overline{KL} \cong \overline{NL}$	1. Given
2. $\overline{LM} \cong \overline{LM}$	2. Reflex. Prop. of $\cong$
3. $m\angle KLM = m\angle NLM + m\angle KLN$	3. $\angle$ Add. Post.
4. $m\angle KLM > m\angle NLM$	4. Comparison Prop. of Inequal.
5. $KM > NM$	5. Hinge Thm.

CHECK IT OUT!

Write a two-column proof.

3a. Given: C is the midpoint of $\overline{BD}$.
$m\angle 1 = m\angle 2$
$m\angle 3 > m\angle 4$
Prove: $AB > ED$

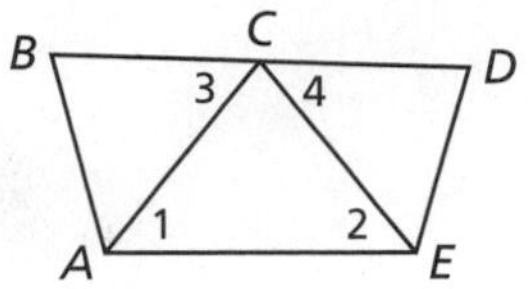

3b. Given: $\angle SRT \cong \angle STR$
$TU > RU$
Prove: $m\angle TSU > m\angle RSU$

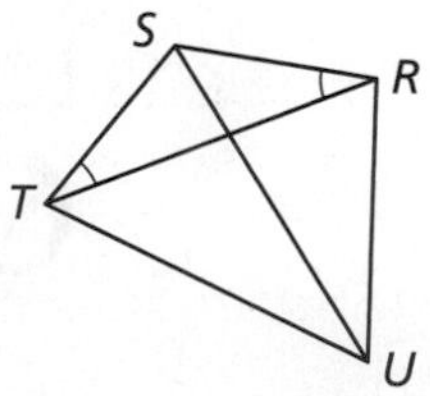

MATHEMATICAL PRACTICES

THINK AND DISCUSS

1. Describe a real-world object that shows the Hinge Theorem or its converse.
2. Can you make a conclusion about the triangles shown at right by applying the Hinge Theorem? Explain.

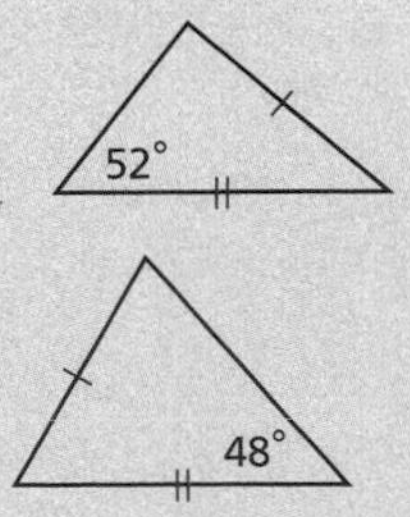

Know it! Note

3. **GET ORGANIZED** Copy and complete the graphic organizer. In each box, use the given triangles to write a statement for the theorem.

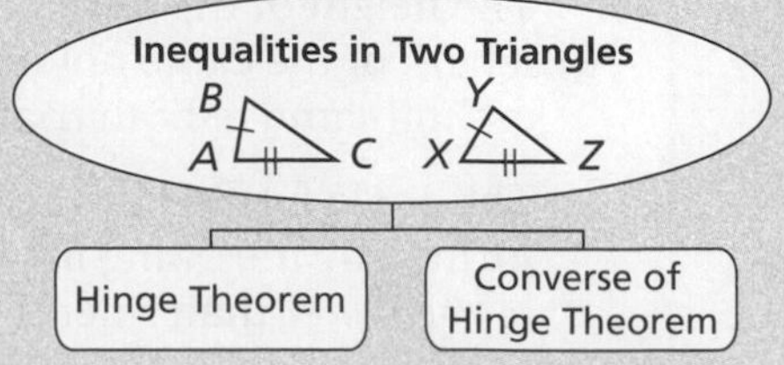

5-6 Exercises

Learn It Online
Homework Help Online
Parent Resources Online

GUIDED PRACTICE

SEE EXAMPLE 1

Compare the given measures.

1. *AC* and *XZ*

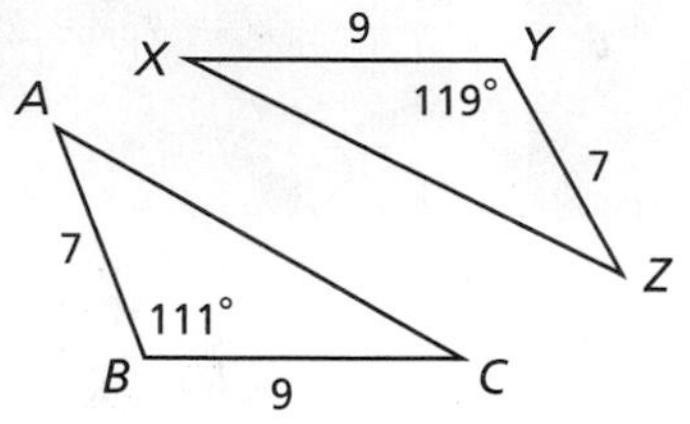

2. m∠*SRT* and m∠*QRT*

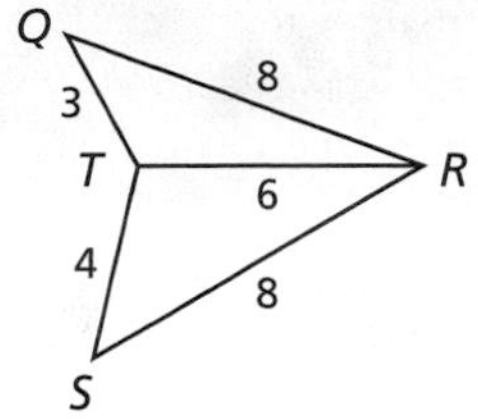

3. *KL* and *KN*

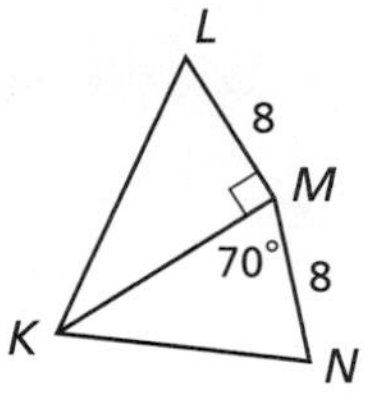

Find the range of values for *x*.

4.

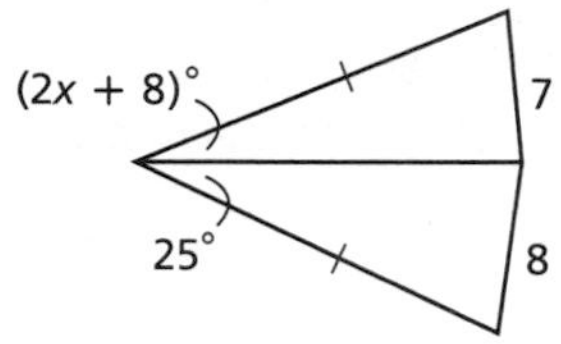

5.

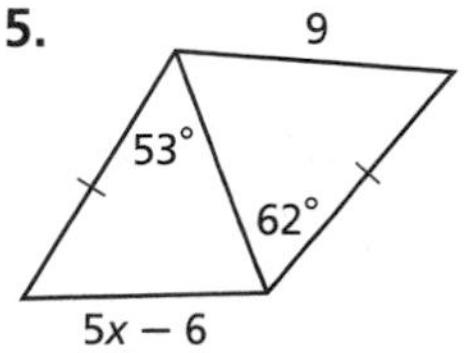

6.

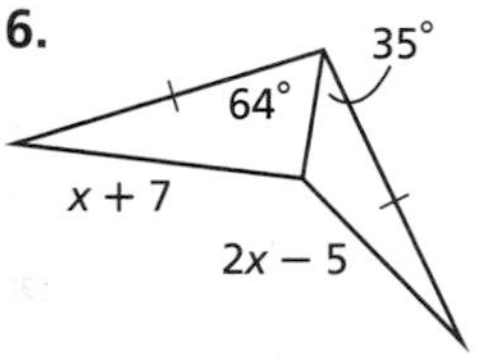

SEE EXAMPLE 2

7. Health A therapist can take measurements to gauge the flexibility of a patient's elbow joint. In which position is the angle measure at the elbow joint greater? Explain.

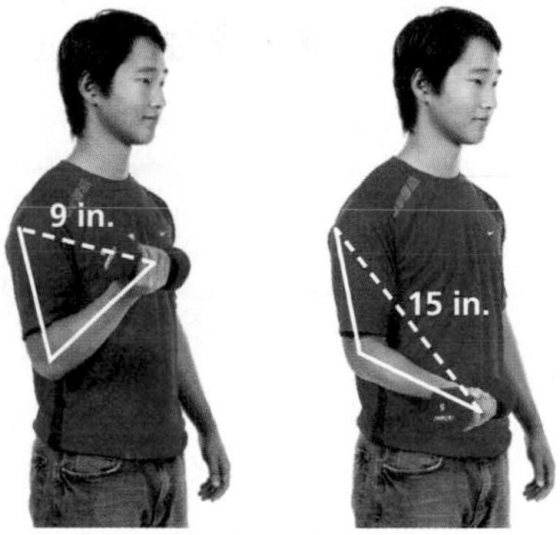

SEE EXAMPLE 3

8. Write a two-column proof.

Given: $\overline{FH}$ is a median of △*DFG*.
m∠*DHF* > m∠*GHF*

Prove: *DF* > *GF*

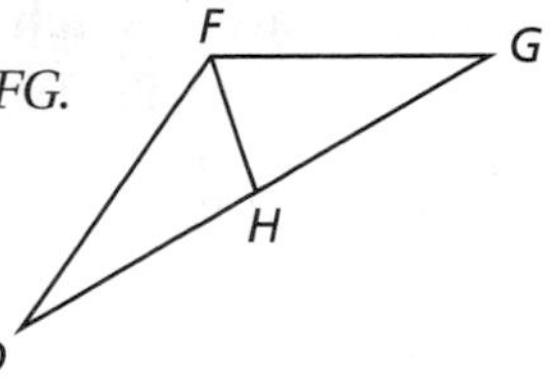

PRACTICE AND PROBLEM SOLVING

Independent Practice

For Exercises	See Example
9–14	1
15	2
16	3

Extra Practice

See Extra Practice for more Skills Practice and Applications Practice exercises.

Compare the given measures.

9. m∠*DCA* and m∠*BCA*

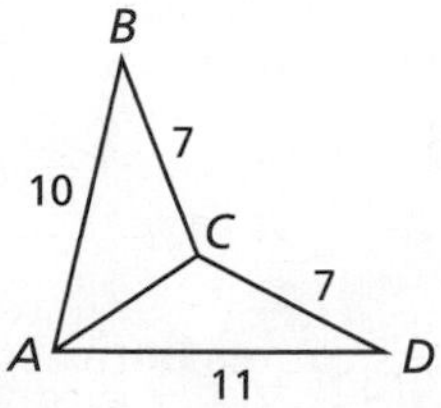

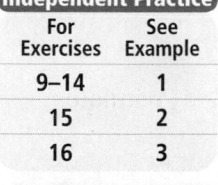

10. m∠*GHJ* and m∠*KLM*

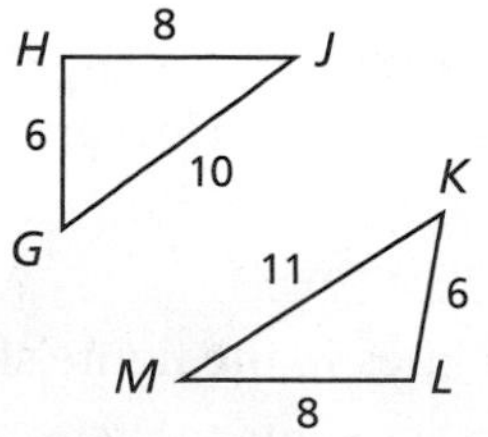

11. *TU* and *SV*

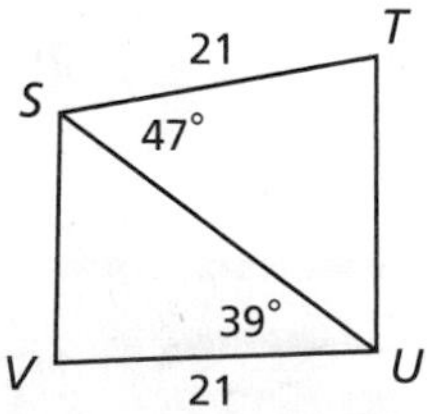

Find the range of values for *z*.

12.

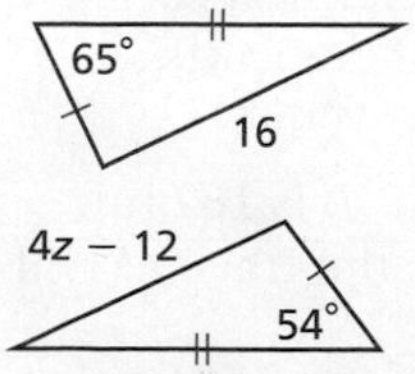

13.

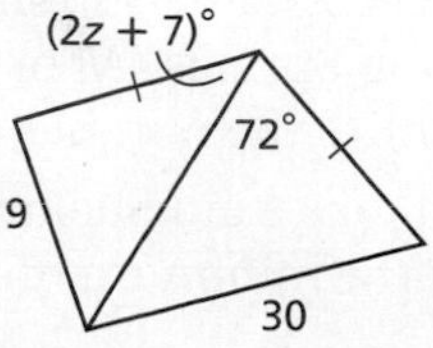

14.

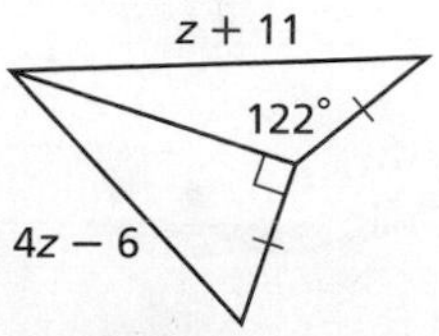

15. **Industry** The operator of a backhoe changes the distance between the cab and the bucket by changing the angle formed by the arms. In which position is the distance from the cab to the bucket greater? Explain.

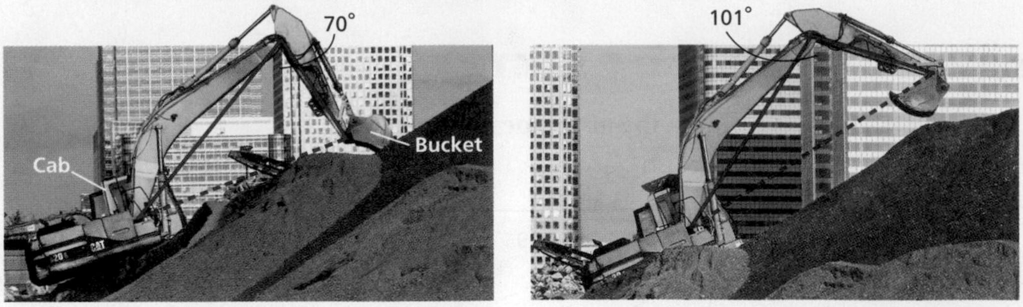

16. Write a two-column proof.
Given: $\overline{JK} \cong \overline{NM}$, $\overline{KP} \cong \overline{MQ}$, $JQ > NP$
Prove: $m\angle K > m\angle M$

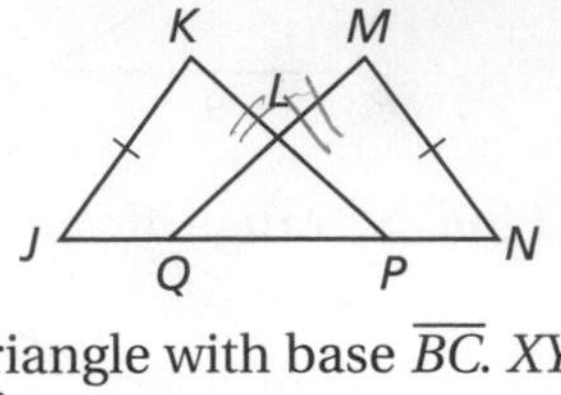

17. **Critical Thinking** ABC is an isosceles triangle with base $\overline{BC}$. XYZ is an isosceles triangle with base $\overline{YZ}$. Given that $\overline{AB} \cong \overline{XY}$ and $m\angle A = m\angle X$, compare BC and YZ.

Compare. Write <, >, or =.

18. $m\angle QRP$ ■ $m\angle SRP$
19. $m\angle QPR$ ■ $m\angle QRP$
20. $m\angle PRS$ ■ $m\angle RSP$
21. $m\angle RSP$ ■ $m\angle RPS$
22. $m\angle QPR$ ■ $m\angle RPS$
23. $m\angle PSR$ ■ $m\angle PQR$

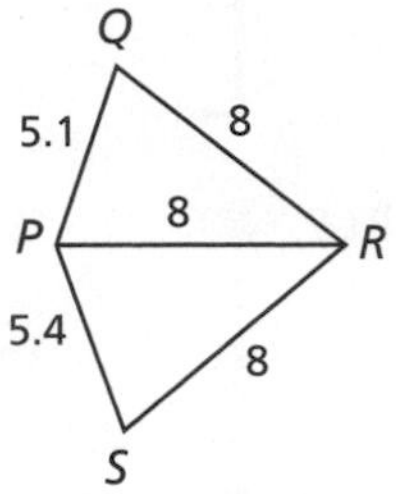

Make a conclusion based on the Hinge Theorem or its converse. (*Hint*: Draw a sketch.)

24. In $\triangle ABC$ and $\triangle DEF$, $\overline{AB} \cong \overline{DE}$, $\overline{BC} \cong \overline{EF}$, $m\angle B = 59°$, and $m\angle E = 47°$.
25. $\triangle RST$ is isosceles with base $\overline{RT}$. The endpoints of $\overline{SV}$ are vertex S and a point V on $\overline{RT}$. $RV = 4$, and $TV = 5$.
26. In $\triangle GHJ$ and $\triangle KLM$, $\overline{GH} \cong \overline{KL}$, and $\overline{GJ} \cong \overline{KM}$. $\angle G$ is a right angle, and $\angle K$ is an acute angle.
27. In $\triangle XYZ$, $\overline{XM}$ is the median to $\overline{YZ}$, and $YX > ZX$.
28. **Write About It** The picture shows a door hinge in two different positions. Use the picture to explain why Theorem 5-6-1 is called the Hinge Theorem.

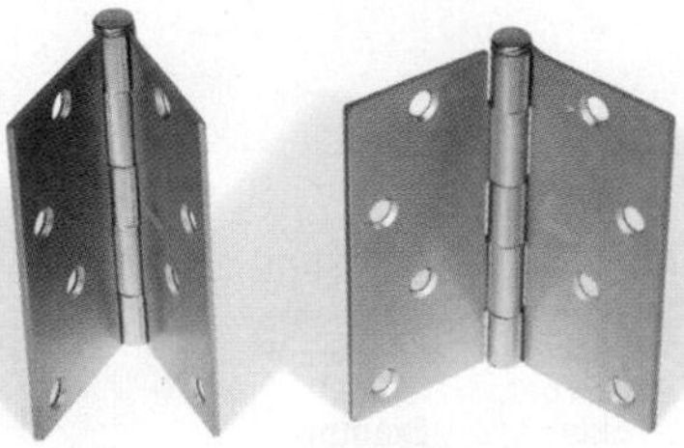

29. **Write About It** Compare the Hinge Theorem to the SAS Congruence Postulate. How are they alike? How are they different?

MULTI-STEP TEST PREP

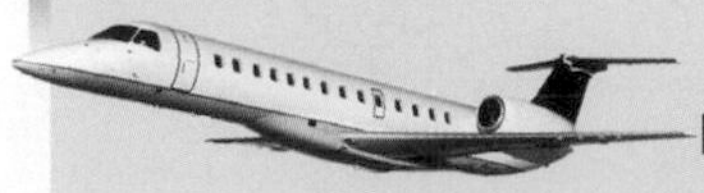

30. The solid lines in the figure show an airline's routes between four cities.
    a. A traveler wants to fly from Jackson (J) to Shelby (S), but there is no direct flight between these cities. Given that $m\angle NSJ < m\angle HSJ$, should the traveler first fly to Newton Springs (N) or to Hollis (H) if he wants to minimize the number of miles flown? Why?
    b. The distance from Shelby (S) to Jackson (J) is 182 mi. What is the minimum number of miles the traveler will have to fly?

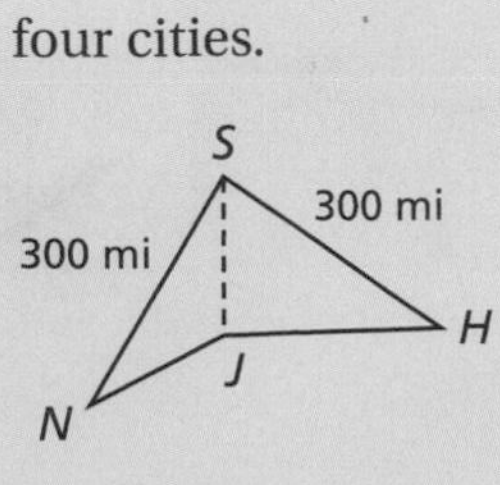

TEST PREP

31. $\overline{ML}$ is a median of $\triangle JKL$. Which inequality best describes the range of values for x?

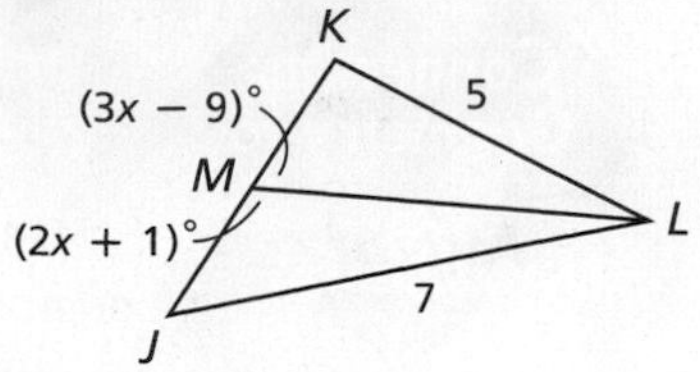

Ⓐ $x > 2$　　Ⓒ $3 < x < 4\frac{2}{3}$

Ⓑ $x > 10$　　Ⓓ $3 < x < 10$

32. $\overline{DC}$ is a median of $\triangle ABC$. Which of the following statements is true?

Ⓕ $BC < AC$　　Ⓖ $BC > AC$　　Ⓗ $AD = DB$　　Ⓙ $DC = AB$

33. **Short Response** Two groups start hiking from the same camp. Group A hikes 6.5 miles due west and then hikes 4 miles in the direction N 35° W. Group B hikes 6.5 miles due east and then hikes 4 miles in the direction N 45° E. At this point, which group is closer to the camp? Explain.

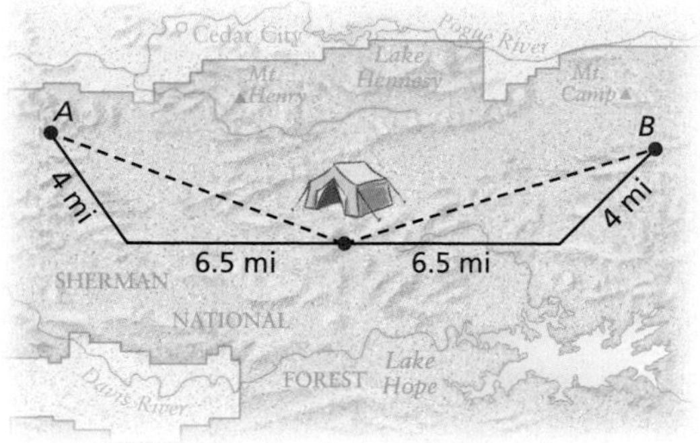

CHALLENGE AND EXTEND

34. **Multi-Step** In $\triangle XYZ$, $XZ = 5x + 15$, $XY = 8x - 6$, and $m\angle XVZ > m\angle XVY$. Find the range of values for x.

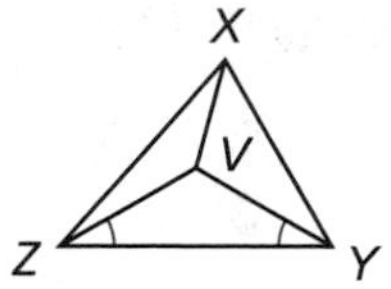

35. Use these steps to write a paragraph proof of the Hinge Theorem.

Given: $\overline{AB} \cong \overline{DE}$, $\overline{BC} \cong \overline{EF}$, $m\angle ABC > m\angle DEF$
Prove: $AC > DF$

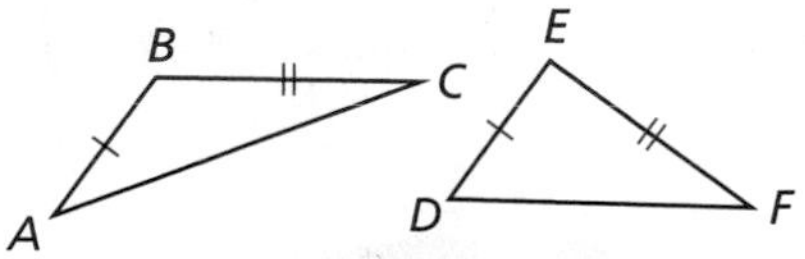

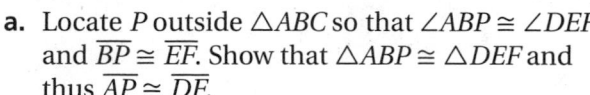

a. Locate P outside $\triangle ABC$ so that $\angle ABP \cong \angle DEF$ and $\overline{BP} \cong \overline{EF}$. Show that $\triangle ABP \cong \triangle DEF$ and thus $\overline{AP} \cong \overline{DF}$.

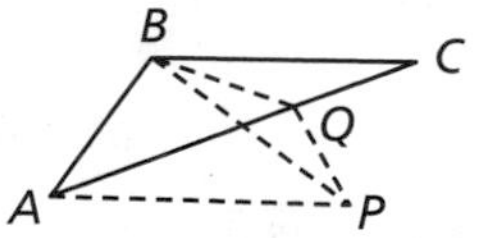

b. Locate Q on $\overline{AC}$ so that $\overline{BQ}$ bisects $\angle PBC$. Draw $\overline{QP}$. Show that $\triangle BQP \cong \triangle BQC$ and thus $\overline{QP} \cong \overline{QC}$.

c. Justify the statements $AQ + QP > AP$, $AQ + QC = AC$, $AQ + QC > AP$, $AC > AP$, and $AC > DF$.

Connecting Geometry to Algebra

Simplest Radical Form

When a problem involves square roots, you may be asked to give the answer in simplest radical form. Recall that the radicand is the expression under the radical sign.

Simplest Form of a Square-Root Expression

An expression containing square roots is in simplest form when

- the radicand has no perfect square factors other than 1.
- the radicand has no fractions.
- there are no square roots in any denominator.

To simplify a radical expression, remember that the square root of a product is equal to the product of the square roots. Also, the square root of a quotient is equal to the quotient of the square roots.

$$\sqrt{ab} = \sqrt{a} \cdot \sqrt{b}, \text{ when } a \geq 0 \text{ and } b \geq 0$$

$$\sqrt{\frac{a}{b}} = \frac{\sqrt{a}}{\sqrt{b}}, \text{ when } a \geq 0 \text{ and } b > 0$$

Examples

Write each expression in simplest radical form.

A $\sqrt{216}$

$\sqrt{216}$	*216 has a perfect-square factor of 36, so the expression is not in simplest radical form.*
$\sqrt{(36)(6)}$	*Factor the radicand.*
$\sqrt{36} \cdot \sqrt{6}$	*Product Property of Square Roots*
$6\sqrt{6}$	*Simplify.*

B $\frac{6}{\sqrt{2}}$

$\frac{6}{\sqrt{2}}$	*There is a square root in the denominator, so the expression is not in simplest radical form.*
$\frac{6}{\sqrt{2}}\left(\frac{\sqrt{2}}{\sqrt{2}}\right)$	*Multiply by a form of 1 to eliminate the square root in the denominator.*
$\frac{6\sqrt{2}}{2}$	*Simplify.*
$3\sqrt{2}$	*Divide.*

Try This

Write each expression in simplest radical form.

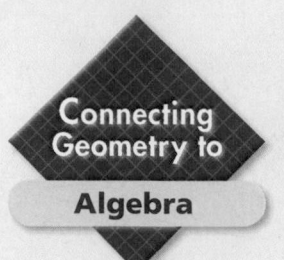

1. $\sqrt{720}$ **2.** $\sqrt{\frac{3}{16}}$ **3.** $\frac{10}{\sqrt{2}}$ **4.** $\sqrt{\frac{1}{3}}$ **5.** $\sqrt{45}$

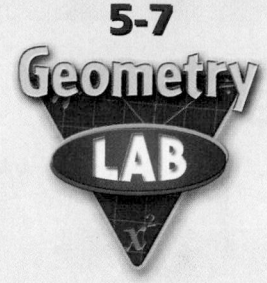

5-7 Geometry LAB

Hands-on Proof of the Pythagorean Theorem

In this activity, you will build figures and compare their areas to justify the Pythagorean Theorem.

Use with The Pythagorean Theorem

MATHEMATICAL PRACTICES **Construct viable arguments and critique the reasoning of others.**

CC.9-12.G.SRT.4 Prove theorems about triangles.

Activity

1. Draw a large scalene right triangle on graph paper. Draw three copies of the triangle. On each triangle, label the shorter leg a, the longer leg b, and the hypotenuse c.

2. Draw a square with a side length of $b - a$. Label each side of the square.

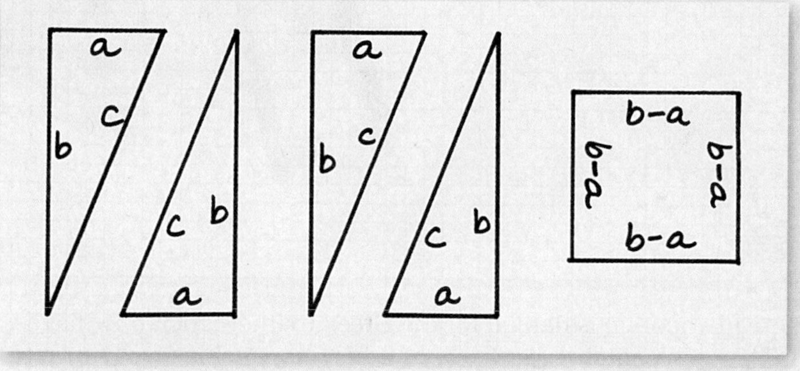

3. Cut out the five figures. Arrange them to make the composite figure shown at right.

4. You can think of this composite figure as being made of the two squares outlined in red. What are the side length and area of the small red square? of the large red square?

5. Use your results from Step 4 to write an algebraic expression for the area of the composite figure.

6. Now rearrange the five figures to make a single square with side length c. Write an algebraic expression for the area of this square.

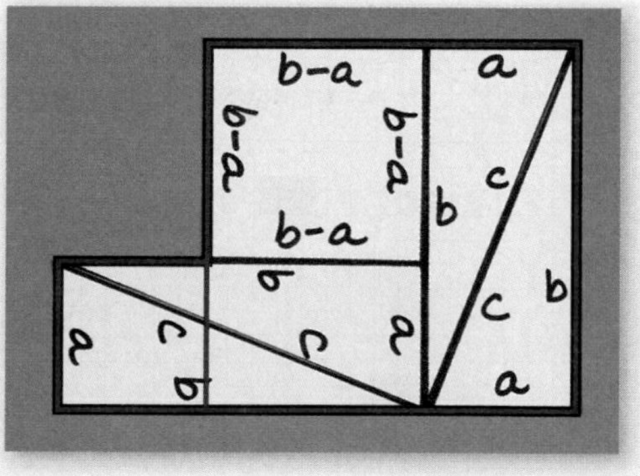

Try This

1. Since the composite figure and the square with side length c are made of the same five shapes, their areas are equal. Write and simplify an equation to represent this relationship. What conclusion can you make?
2. Draw a scalene right triangle with different side lengths. Repeat the activity. Do you reach the same conclusion?

COMMON CORE

5-7 The Pythagorean Theorem

CC.9-12.G.SRT.8 Use...the Pythagorean Theorem to solve right triangles...* *Also* CC.9-12.G.SRT.4

Objectives
Use the Pythagorean Theorem and its converse to solve problems.

Use Pythagorean inequalities to classify triangles.

Vocabulary
Pythagorean triple

Why learn this?
You can use the Pythagorean Theorem to determine whether a ladder is in a safe position. (See Example 2.)

The Pythagorean Theorem is probably the most famous mathematical relationship. The theorem states that in a right triangle, the sum of the squares of the lengths of the legs equals the square of the length of the hypotenuse.

$$a^2 + b^2 = c^2$$

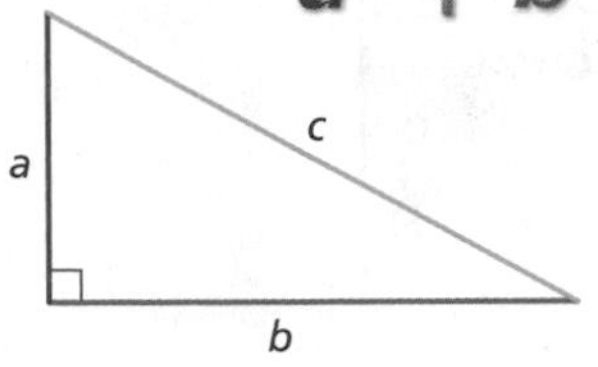

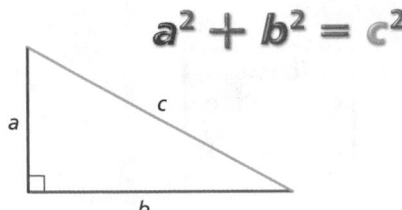

The Pythagorean Theorem is named for the Greek mathematician Pythagoras, who lived in the sixth century B.C.E. However, this relationship was known to earlier people, such as the Babylonians, Egyptians, and Chinese.

There are many different proofs of the Pythagorean Theorem. The one below uses area and algebra.

PROOF

Pythagorean Theorem

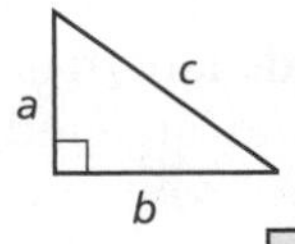

Given: A right triangle with leg lengths a and b and hypotenuse of length c

Prove: $a^2 + b^2 = c^2$

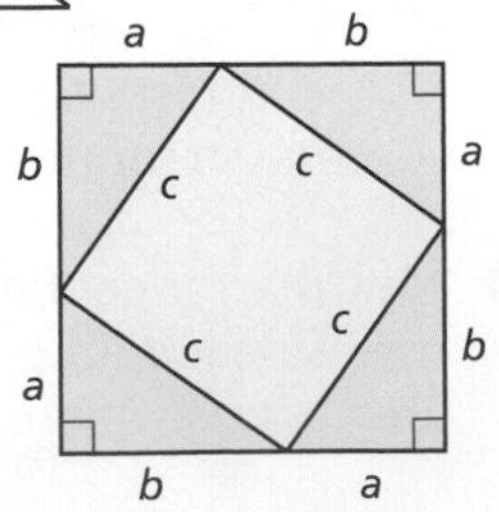

Proof: Arrange four copies of the triangle as shown. The sides of the triangles form two squares.

The area of the outer square is $(a + b)^2$. The area of the inner square is c^2. The area of each blue triangle is $\frac{1}{2}ab$.

area of outer square = area of 4 blue triangles + area of inner square

$$(a + b)^2 = 4\left(\frac{1}{2}ab\right) + c^2 \qquad \textit{Substitute the areas.}$$

$$a^2 + 2ab + b^2 = 2ab + c^2 \qquad \textit{Simplify.}$$

$$a^2 + b^2 = c^2 \qquad \textit{Subtract 2ab from both sides.}$$

Remember!
The area A of a square with side length s is given by the formula $A = s^2$.
The area A of a triangle with base b and height h is given by the formula $A = \frac{1}{2}bh$.

The Pythagorean Theorem gives you a way to find unknown side lengths when you know a triangle is a right triangle.

EXAMPLE 1 Using the Pythagorean Theorem

Find the value of x. Give your answer in simplest radical form.

A

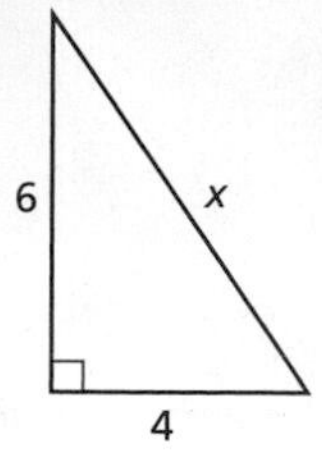

$a^2 + b^2 = c^2$ *Pythagorean Theorem*

$6^2 + 4^2 = x^2$ *Substitute 6 for a, 4 for b, and x for c.*

$52 = x^2$ *Simplify.*

$\sqrt{52} = x$ *Find the positive square root.*

$x = \sqrt{(4)(13)} = 2\sqrt{13}$ *Simplify the radical.*

B

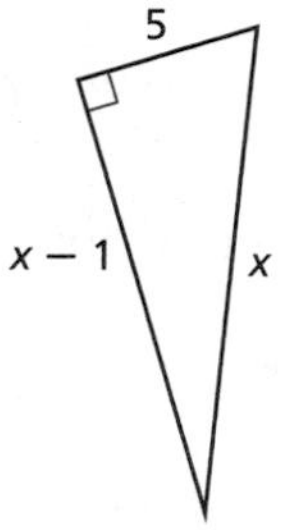

$a^2 + b^2 = c^2$ *Pythagorean Theorem*

$5^2 + (x - 1)^2 = x^2$ *Substitute 5 for a, x − 1 for b, and x for c.*

$25 + x^2 - 2x + 1 = x^2$ *Multiply.*

$-2x + 26 = 0$ *Combine like terms.*

$26 = 2x$ *Add 2x to both sides.*

$x = 13$ *Divide both sides by 2.*

CHECK IT OUT! **Find the value of x. Give your answer in simplest radical form.**

1a.

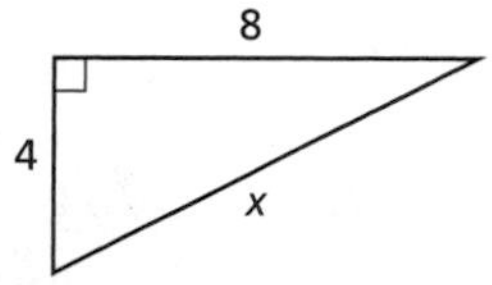

1b.

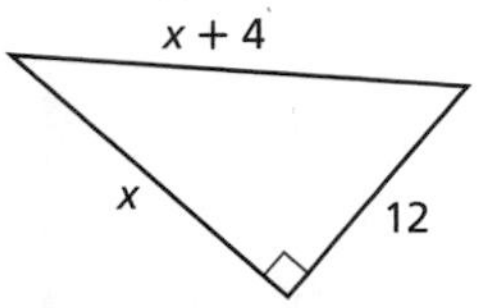

EXAMPLE 2 *Safety Application*

To prevent a ladder from shifting, safety experts recommend that the ratio of $a:b$ be 4:1. How far from the base of the wall should you place the foot of a 10-foot ladder? Round to the nearest inch.

Let x be the distance in feet from the foot of the ladder to the base of the wall. Then $4x$ is the distance in feet from the top of the ladder to the base of the wall.

$a^2 + b^2 = c^2$ *Pythagorean Theorem*

$(4x)^2 + x^2 = 10^2$ *Substitute.*

$17x^2 = 100$ *Multiply and combine like terms.*

$x^2 = \frac{100}{17}$ *Divide both sides by 17.*

$x = \sqrt{\frac{100}{17}} \approx 2$ ft 5 in. *Find the positive square root and round it.*

CHECK IT OUT! 2. **What if...?** According to the recommended ratio, how high will a 30-foot ladder reach when placed against a wall? Round to the nearest inch.

A set of three nonzero whole numbers a, b, and c such that $a^2 + b^2 = c^2$ is called a **Pythagorean triple**.

Common Pythagorean Triples			
3, 4, 5	5, 12, 13,	8, 15, 17	7, 24, 25

EXAMPLE 3 Identifying Pythagorean Triples

Find the missing side length. Tell if the side lengths form a Pythagorean triple. Explain.

A

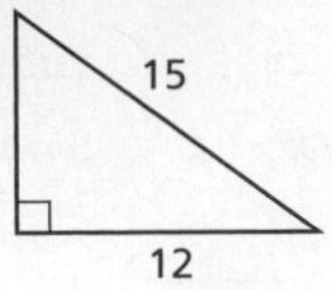

$a^2 + b^2 = c^2$	*Pythagorean Theorem*
$12^2 + b^2 = 15^2$	*Substitute 12 for a and 15 for c.*
$b^2 = 81$	*Multiply and subtract 144 from both sides.*
$b = 9$	*Find the positive square root.*

The side lengths are nonzero whole numbers that satisfy the equation $a^2 + b^2 = c^2$, so they form a Pythagorean triple.

B

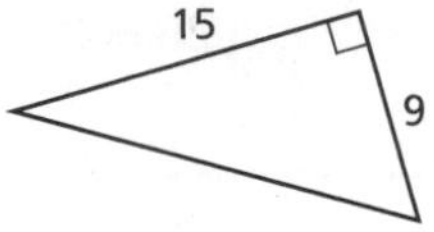

$a^2 + b^2 = c^2$	*Pythagorean Theorem*
$9^2 + 15^2 = c^2$	*Substitute 9 for a and 15 for b.*
$306 = c^2$	*Multiply and add.*
$c = \sqrt{306} = 3\sqrt{34}$	*Find the positive square root and simplify.*

The side lengths do not form a Pythagorean triple because $3\sqrt{34}$ is not a whole number.

CHECK IT OUT! **Find the missing side length. Tell if the side lengths form a Pythagorean triple. Explain.**

3a.

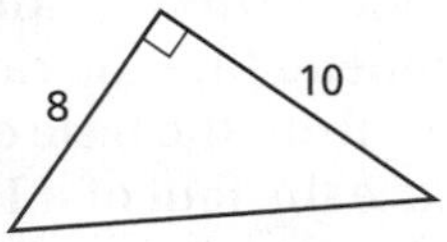

3b.

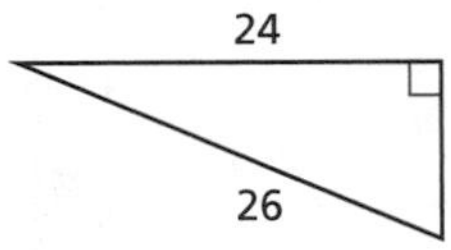

3c.

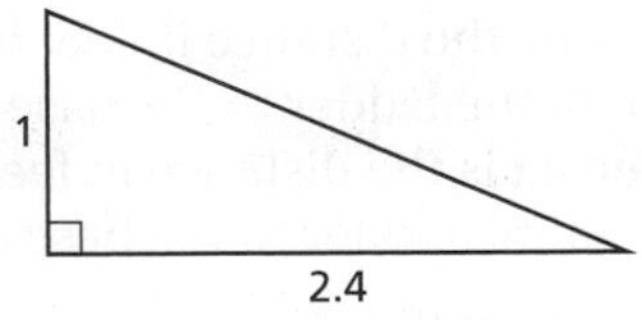

3d.

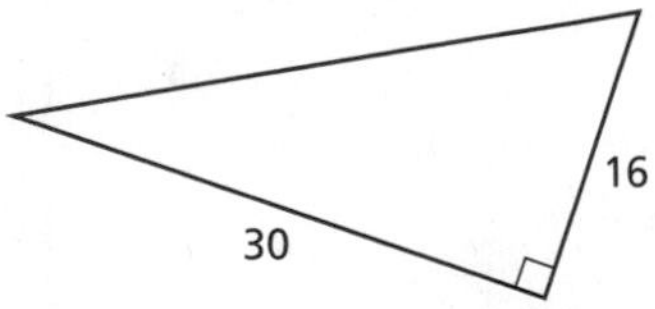

The converse of the Pythagorean Theorem gives you a way to tell if a triangle is a right triangle when you know the side lengths.

Know it! Note

Theorems 5-7-1 Converse of the Pythagorean Theorem

THEOREM	HYPOTHESIS	CONCLUSION
If the sum of the squares of the lengths of two sides of a triangle is equal to the square of the length of the third side, then the triangle is a right triangle.	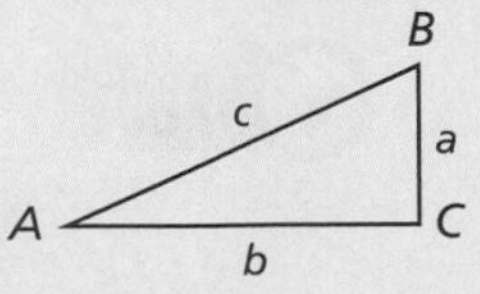 $a^2 + b^2 = c^2$	$\triangle ABC$ is a right triangle.

You will prove Theorem 5-7-1 in Exercise 45.

You can also use side lengths to classify a triangle as acute or obtuse.

Know it! Note

Theorems 5-7-2 Pythagorean Inequalities Theorem

In $\triangle ABC$, c is the length of the longest side.

If $c^2 > a^2 + b^2$, then $\triangle ABC$ is an **obtuse** triangle.

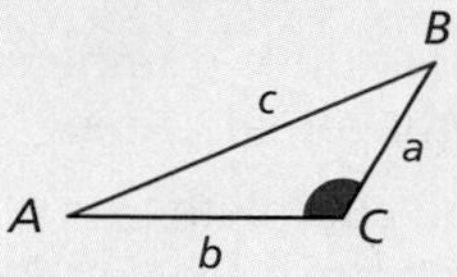

If $c^2 < a^2 + b^2$, then $\triangle ABC$ is an **acute** triangle.

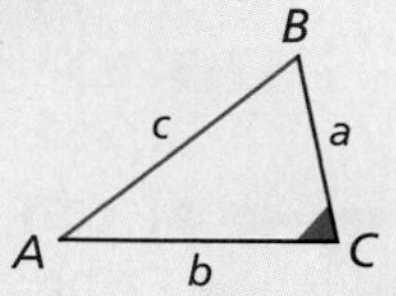

To understand why the Pythagorean inequalities are true, consider $\triangle ABC$.

If $c^2 = a^2 + b^2$, then $\triangle ABC$ is a right triangle by the Converse of the Pythagorean Theorem. So $m\angle C = 90°$.

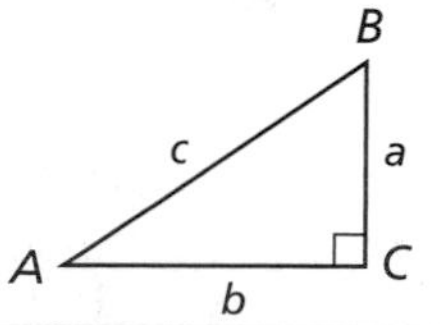

If $c^2 > a^2 + b^2$, then c has increased. By the Converse of the Hinge Theorem, $m\angle C$ has also increased. So $m\angle C > 90°$.

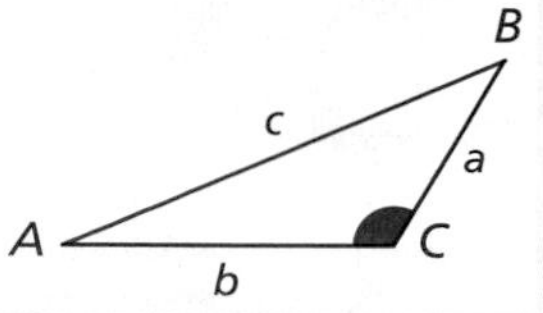

If $c^2 < a^2 + b^2$, then c has decreased. By the Converse of the Hinge Theorem, $m\angle C$ has also decreased. So $m\angle C < 90°$.

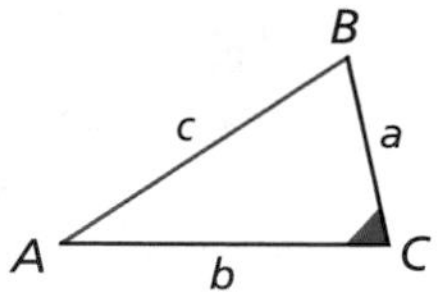

EXAMPLE 4 Classifying Triangles

Tell if the measures can be the side lengths of a triangle. If so, classify the triangle as acute, obtuse, or right.

A **8, 11, 13**

Step 1 Determine if the measures form a triangle.

By the Triangle Inequality Theorem, 8, 11, and 13 can be the side lengths of a triangle.

Step 2 Classify the triangle.

$c^2 \stackrel{?}{=} a^2 + b^2$	*Compare c^2 to $a^2 + b^2$.*
$13^2 \stackrel{?}{=} 8^2 + 11^2$	*Substitute the longest side length for c.*
$169 \stackrel{?}{=} 64 + 121$	*Multiply.*
$169 < 185$	*Add and compare.*

Since $c^2 < a^2 + b^2$, the triangle is **acute**.

B **5.8, 9.3, 15.6**

Step 1 Determine if the measures form a triangle.

Since $5.8 + 9.3 = 15.1$ and $15.1 \not> 15.6$, these cannot be the side lengths of a triangle.

Remember!

By the Triangle Inequality Theorem, the sum of any two side lengths of a triangle is greater than the third side length.

CHECK IT OUT! **Tell if the measures can be the side lengths of a triangle. If so, classify the triangle as acute, obtuse, or right.**

4a. 7, 12, 16 **4b.** 11, 18, 34 **4c.** 3.8, 4.1, 5.2

MATHEMATICAL PRACTICES

THINK AND DISCUSS

1. How do you know which numbers to substitute for *c*, *a*, and *b* when using the Pythagorean Inequalities?
2. Explain how the figure at right demonstrates the Pythagorean Theorem.

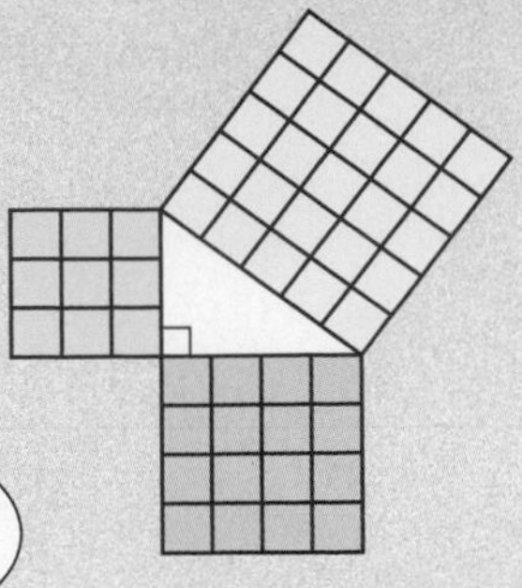

3. List the conditions that a set of three numbers must satisfy in order to form a Pythagorean triple.

Know it! Note

4. **GET ORGANIZED** Copy and complete the graphic organizer. In each box, summarize the Pythagorean relationship.

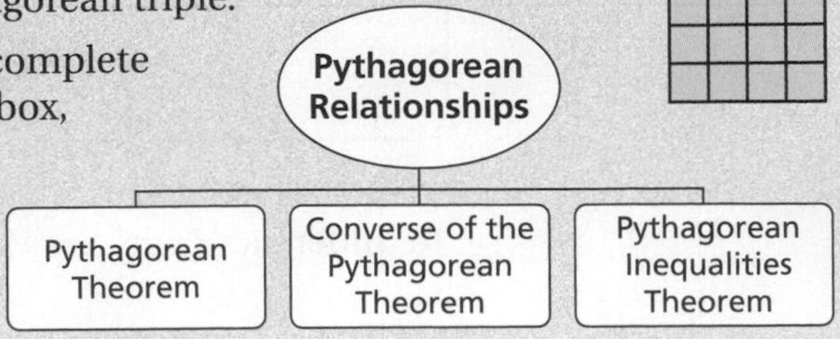

5-7 Exercises

Learn It Online
Homework Help Online
Parent Resources Online

GUIDED PRACTICE

1. **Vocabulary** Do the numbers 2.7, 3.6, and 4.5 form a *Pythagorean triple*? Explain why or why not.

SEE EXAMPLE 1

Find the value of x. Give your answer in simplest radical form.

2. 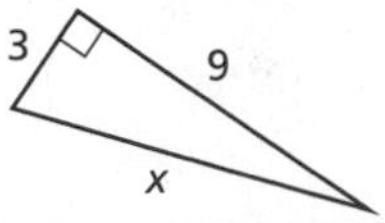

3. 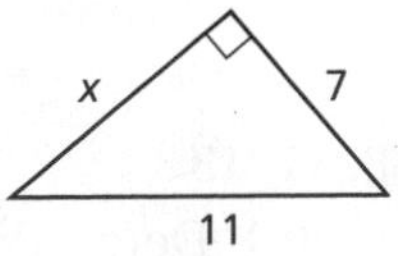

4. 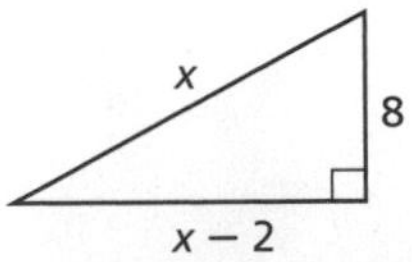

SEE EXAMPLE 2

5. **Computers** The size of a computer monitor is usually given by the length of its diagonal. A monitor's aspect ratio is the ratio of its width to its height. This monitor has a diagonal length of 19 inches and an aspect ratio of 5 : 4. What are the width and height of the monitor? Round to the nearest tenth of an inch.

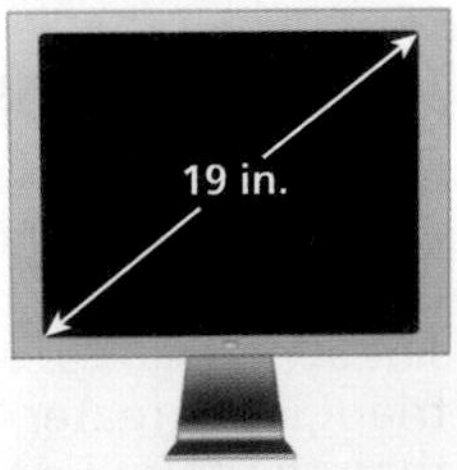

SEE EXAMPLE 3

Find the missing side length. Tell if the side lengths form a Pythagorean triple. Explain.

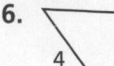

6. 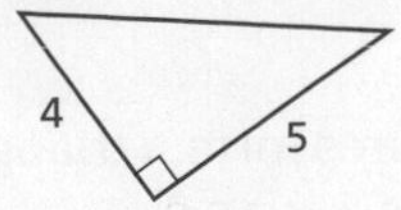

7. 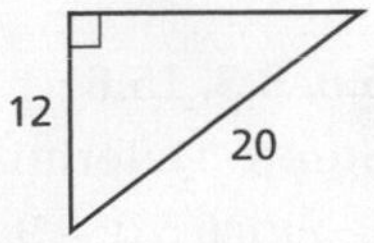

8. 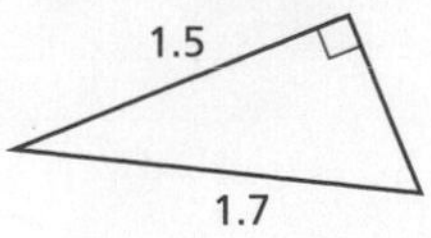

SEE EXAMPLE 4

Multi-Step Tell if the measures can be the side lengths of a triangle. If so, classify the triangle as acute, obtuse, or right.

9. 7, 10, 12
10. 9, 11, 15
11. 9, 40, 41
12. $1\frac{1}{2}, 1\frac{3}{4}, 3\frac{1}{4}$
13. 5.9, 6, 8.4
14. $11, 13, 7\sqrt{6}$

PRACTICE AND PROBLEM SOLVING

Independent Practice	
For Exercises	See Example
15–17	1
18	2
19–21	3
22–27	4

Extra Practice

See Extra Practice for more Skills Practice and Applications Practice exercises.

Find the value of x. Give your answer in simplest radical form.

15. 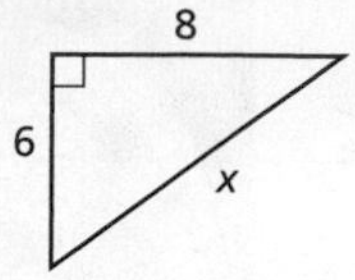

16. 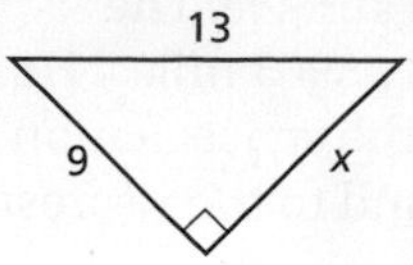

17. 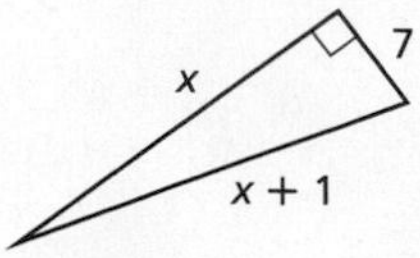

18. **Safety** The safety rules for a playground state that the height of the slide and the distance from the base of the ladder to the front of the slide must be in a ratio of 3:5. If a slide is about 8 feet long, what are the height of the slide and the distance from the base of the ladder to the front of the slide? Round to the nearest inch.

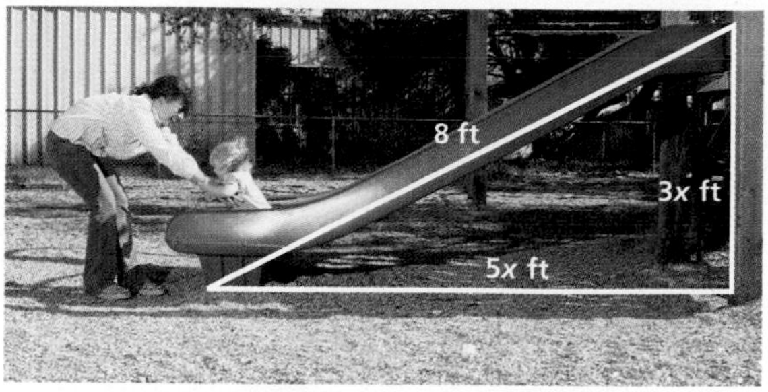

Find the missing side length. Tell if the side lengths form a Pythagorean triple. Explain.

19. 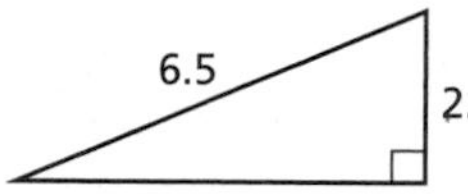

20. 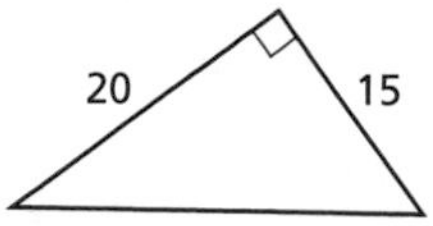

21. 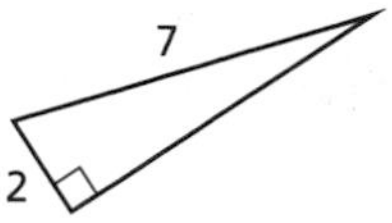

Multi-Step **Tell if the measures can be the side lengths of a triangle. If so, classify the triangle as acute, obtuse, or right.**

22. 10, 12, 15
23. 8, 13, 23
24. 9, 14, 17
25. $1\frac{1}{2}, 2, 2\frac{1}{2}$
26. 0.7, 1.1, 1.7
27. $7, 12, 6\sqrt{5}$

LINK

Surveying

Ancient Egyptian surveyors were referred to as *rope-stretchers.* The standard surveying rope was 100 royal cubits. A cubit is 52.4 cm long.

28. **Surveying** It is believed that surveyors in ancient Egypt laid out right angles using a rope divided into twelve sections by eleven equally spaced knots. How could the surveyors use this rope to make a right angle?

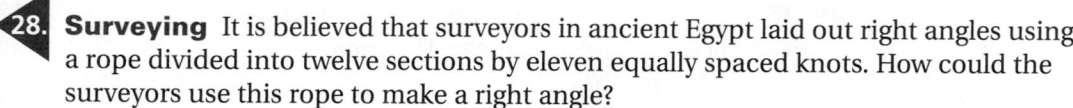

29. **ERROR ANALYSIS** Below are two solutions for finding x. Which is incorrect? Explain the error.

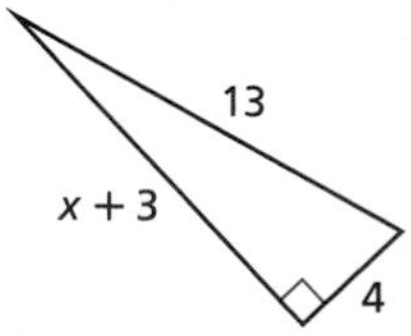

A

$a^2 + 4^2 = 13^2$
$a^2 = 169 - 16 = 153$
$a \approx 12.4$
$x + 3 \approx 12.4$
$x \approx 9.4$

B

$(x + 3)^2 + 4^2 = 13^2$
$x^2 + 9 + 16 = 169$
$x^2 = 144$
$x = 12$

Find the value of x. Give your answer in simplest radical form.

30. 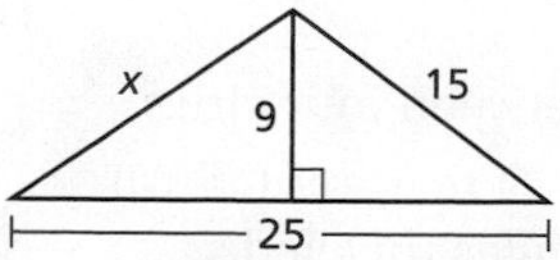

31. 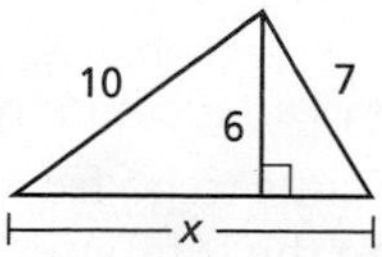

32. 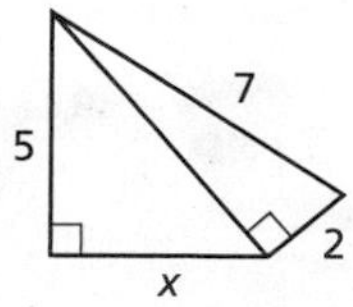

33. 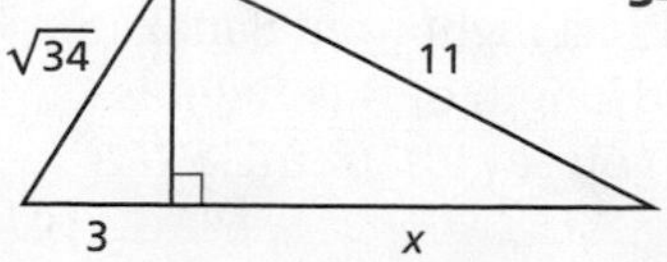

34. 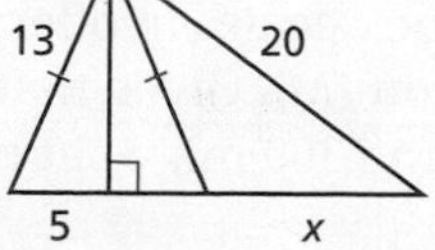

35. 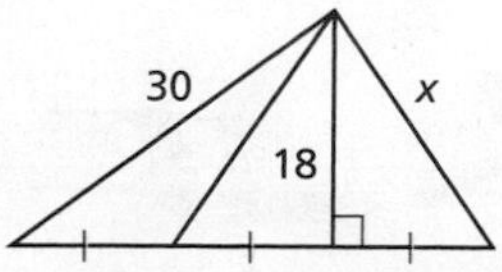

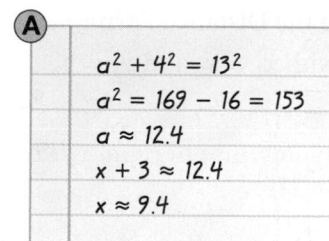

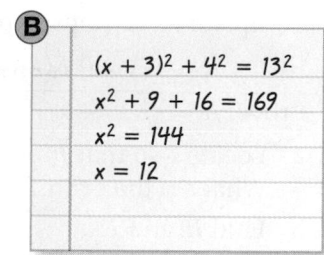

36. **Space Exploration** The International Space Station orbits at an altitude of about 250 miles above Earth's surface. The radius of Earth is approximately 3963 miles. How far can an astronaut in the space station see to the horizon? Round to the nearest mile.

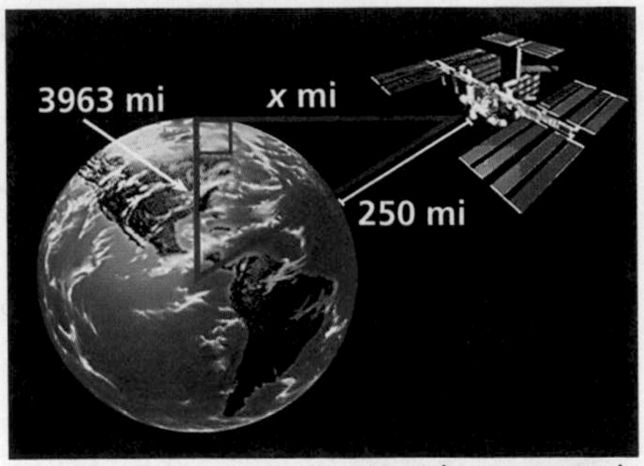

Not drawn to scale

37. **Critical Thinking** In the proof of the Pythagorean Theorem on the first page of this lesson, how do you know the outer figure is a square? How do you know the inner figure is a square?

Multi-Step **Find the perimeter and the area of each figure. Give your answer in simplest radical form.**

38. 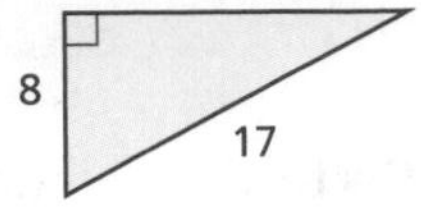

39. 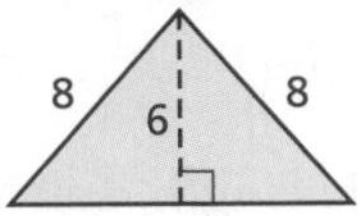

40. 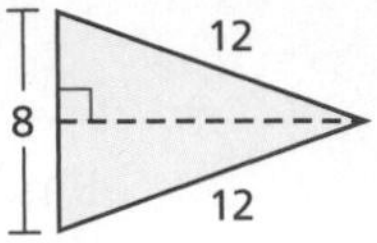

41. 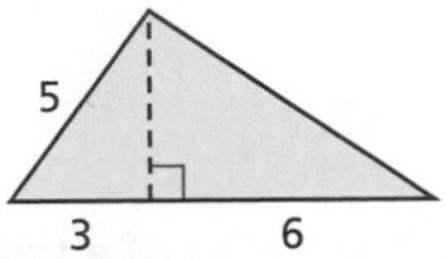

42. 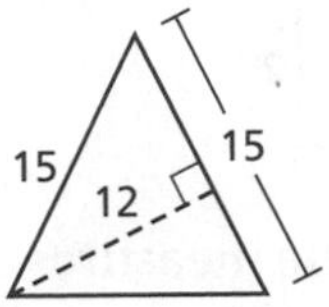

43. 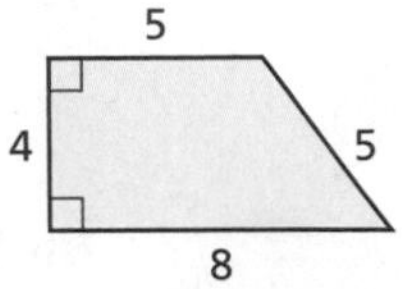

44. **Write About It** When you apply both the Pythagorean Theorem and its converse, you use the equation $a^2 + b^2 = c^2$. Explain in your own words how the two theorems are different.

45. Use this plan to write a paragraph proof of the Converse of the Pythagorean Theorem.

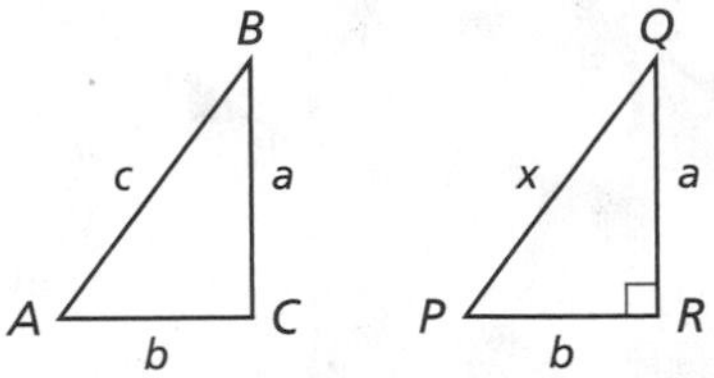

Given: $\triangle ABC$ with $a^2 + b^2 = c^2$
Prove: $\triangle ABC$ is a right triangle.
Plan: Draw $\triangle PQR$ with $\angle R$ as the right angle, leg lengths of a and b, and a hypotenuse of length x. By the Pythagorean Theorem, $a^2 + b^2 = x^2$. Use substitution to compare x and c. Show that $\triangle ABC \cong \triangle PQR$ and thus $\angle C$ is a right angle.

46. Complete these steps to prove the Distance Formula.

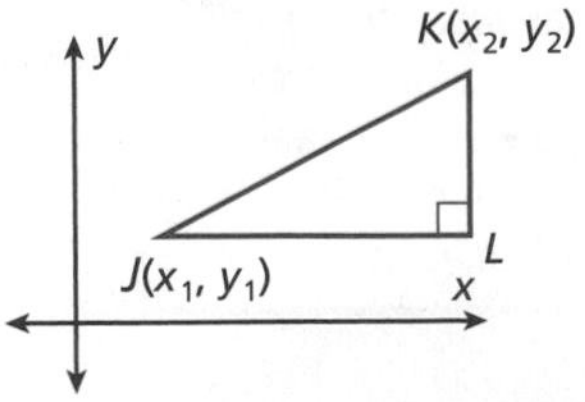

Given: $J(x_1, y_1)$ and $K(x_2, y_2)$ with $x_1 \neq x_2$ and $y_1 \neq y_2$
Prove: $JK = \sqrt{(x_2 - x_1)^2 + (y_2 - y_1)^2}$

a. Locate L so that $\overline{JK}$ is the hypotenuse of right $\triangle JKL$. What are the coordinates of L?
b. Find JL and LK.
c. By the Pythagorean Theorem, $JK^2 = JL^2 + LK^2$. Find JK.

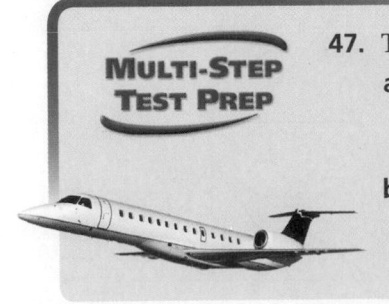

MULTI-STEP TEST PREP

47. The figure shows an airline's routes between four cities.

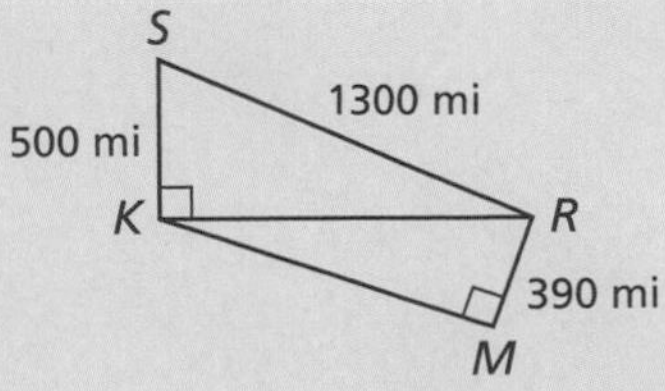

a. A traveler wants to go from Sanak (S) to Manitou (M). To minimize the total number of miles traveled, should she first fly to King City (K) or to Rice Lake (R)?
b. The airline decides to offer a direct flight from Sanak (S) to Manitou (M). Given that the length of this flight is more than 1360 mi, what can you say about m$\angle SRM$?

TEST PREP

48. **Gridded Response** $\overline{KX}$, $\overline{LX}$, and $\overline{MX}$ are the perpendicular bisectors of $\triangle GHJ$. Find GJ to the nearest tenth of a unit.

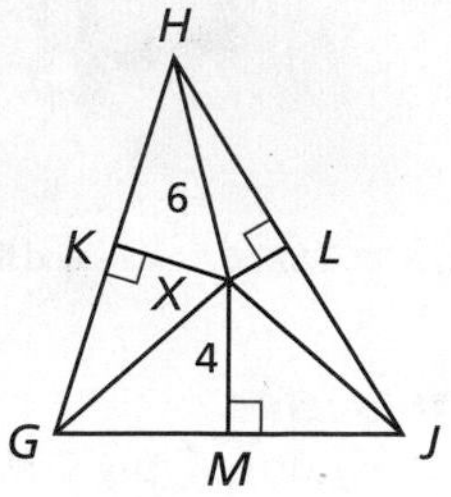

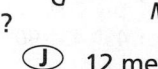

49. Which number forms a Pythagorean triple with 24 and 25?

Ⓐ 1 Ⓑ 7 Ⓒ 26 Ⓓ 49

50. The lengths of two sides of an obtuse triangle are 7 meters and 9 meters. Which could NOT be the length of the third side?

Ⓕ 4 meters Ⓖ 5 meters Ⓗ 11 meters Ⓙ 12 meters

51. **Extended Response** The figure shows the first six triangles in a pattern of triangles.

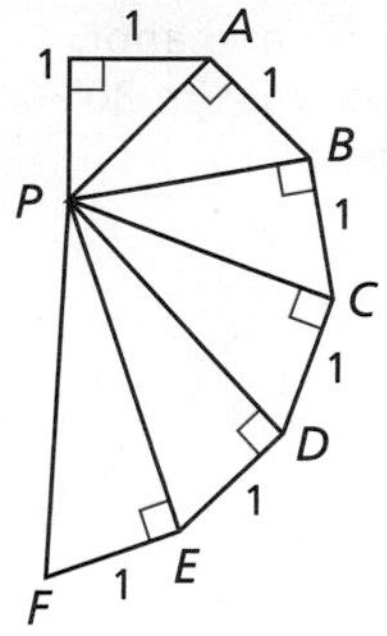

a. Find PA, PB, PC, PD, PE, and PF in simplest radical form.

b. If the pattern continues, what would be the length of the hypotenuse of the ninth triangle? Explain your answer.

c. Write a rule for finding the length of the hypotenuse of the nth triangle in the pattern. Explain your answer.

CHALLENGE AND EXTEND

52. **Algebra** Find all values of k so that $(-1, 2)$, $(-10, 5)$, and $(-4, k)$ are the vertices of a right triangle.

53. **Critical Thinking** Use a diagram of a right triangle to explain why $a + b > \sqrt{a^2 + b^2}$ for any positive numbers a and b.

54. In a right triangle, the leg lengths are a and b, and the length of the altitude to the hypotenuse is h. Write an expression for h in terms of a and b. (*Hint*: Think of the area of the triangle.)

55. **Critical Thinking** Suppose the numbers a, b, and c form a Pythagorean triple. Is each of the following also a Pythagorean triple? Explain.

a. $a + 1, b + 1, c + 1$

b. $2a, 2b, 2c$

c. a^2, b^2, c^2

d. $\sqrt{a}, \sqrt{b}, \sqrt{c}$

COMMON CORE

5-8 Applying Special Right Triangles

CC.9-12.G.SRT.6 Understand that ... side ratios in right triangles are properties of the angles in the triangle...

Objectives

Justify and apply properties of 45°-45°-90° triangles.

Justify and apply properties of 30°-60°-90° triangles.

Who uses this?

You can use properties of special right triangles to calculate the correct size of a bandana for your dog. (See Example 2.)

A diagonal of a square divides it into two congruent isosceles right triangles. Since the base angles of an isosceles triangle are congruent, the measure of each acute angle is 45°. So another name for an isosceles right triangle is a 45°-45°-90° triangle.

A 45°-45°-90° triangle is one type of *special right triangle*. You can use the Pythagorean Theorem to find a relationship among the side lengths of a 45°-45°-90° triangle.

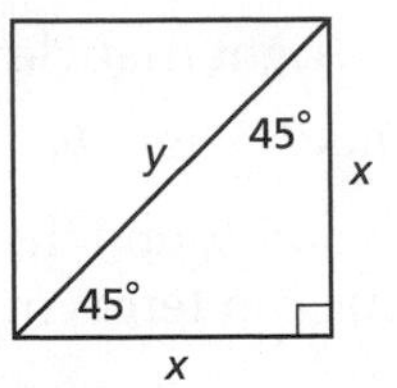

$a^2 + b^2 = c^2$	*Pythagorean Theorem*
$x^2 + x^2 = y^2$	*Substitute the given values.*
$2x^2 = y^2$	*Simplify.*
$\sqrt{2x^2} = \sqrt{y^2}$	*Find the square root of both sides.*
$x\sqrt{2} = y$	*Simplify.*

Know it! Note

Theorem 5-8-1 **45°-45°-90° Triangle Theorem**

In a 45°-45°-90° triangle, both legs are congruent, and the length of the hypotenuse is the length of a leg times $\sqrt{2}$.

$AC = BC = \ell$ $\quad$ $AB = \ell\sqrt{2}$

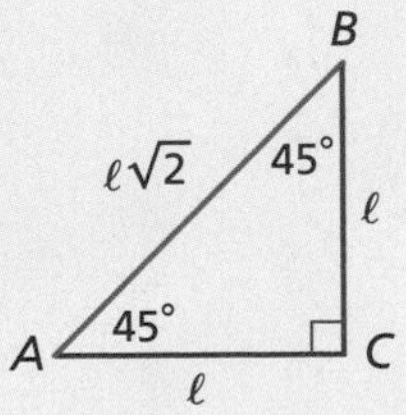

EXAMPLE 1 **Finding Side Lengths in a 45°-45°-90° Triangle**

Find the value of x. Give your answer in simplest radical form.

A

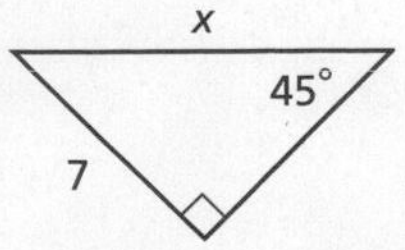

By the Triangle Sum Theorem, the measure of the third angle of the triangle is 45°. So it is a 45°-45°-90° triangle with a leg length of 7.

$x = 7\sqrt{2}$ $\quad$ *Hypotenuse = leg$\sqrt{2}$*

Find the value of x. Give your answer in simplest radical form.

B

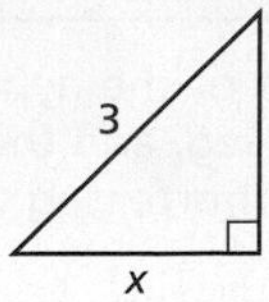

The triangle is an isosceles right triangle, which is a 45°-45°-90° triangle. The length of the hypotenuse is 3.

$3 = x\sqrt{2}$ — *Hypotenuse = leg$\sqrt{2}$*

$\frac{3}{\sqrt{2}} = x$ — *Divide both sides by $\sqrt{2}$.*

$\frac{3\sqrt{2}}{2} = x$ — *Rationalize the denominator.*

CHECK IT OUT! **Find the value of x. Give your answer in simplest radical form.**

1a.

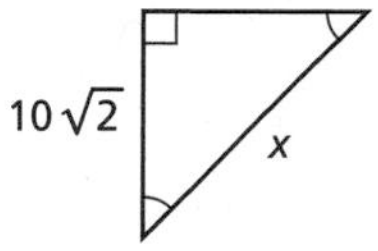

1b.

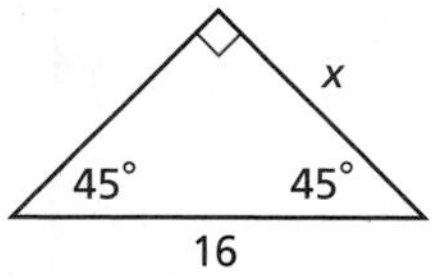

EXAMPLE 2 *Craft Application*

Tessa wants to make a bandana for her dog by folding a square of cloth into a 45°-45°-90° triangle. Her dog's neck has a circumference of about 32 cm. The folded bandana needs to be an extra 16 cm long so Tessa can tie it around her dog's neck. What should the side length of the square be? Round to the nearest centimeter.

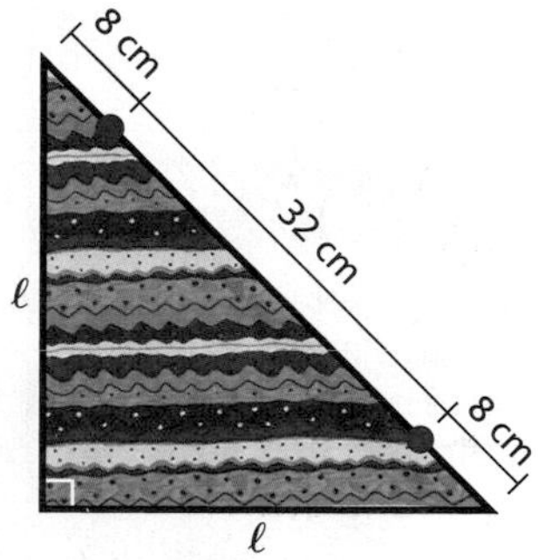

Tessa needs a 45°-45°-90° triangle with a hypotenuse of 48 cm.

$48 = \ell\sqrt{2}$ — *Hypotenuse = leg$\sqrt{2}$*

$\ell = \frac{48}{\sqrt{2}} \approx 34$ cm — *Divide by $\sqrt{2}$ and round.*

CHECK IT OUT! **2. What if...?** Tessa's other dog is wearing a square bandana with a side length of 42 cm. What would you expect the circumference of the other dog's neck to be? Round to the nearest centimeter.

A 30°-60°-90° triangle is another special right triangle. You can use an equilateral triangle to find a relationship between its side lengths.

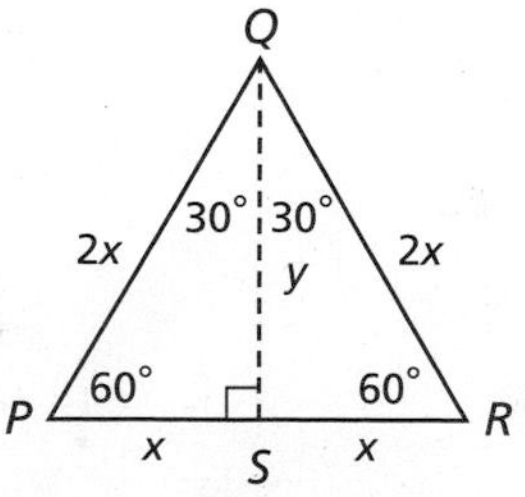

Draw an altitude in $\triangle PQR$. Since $\triangle PQS \cong \triangle RQS$, $\overline{PS} \cong \overline{RS}$. Label the side lengths in terms of x, and use the Pythagorean Theorem to find y.

$a^2 + b^2 = c^2$ — *Pythagorean Theorem*

$x^2 + y^2 = (2x)^2$ — *Substitute x for a, y for b, and 2x for c.*

$y^2 = 3x^2$ — *Multiply and combine like terms.*

$\sqrt{y^2} = \sqrt{3x^2}$ — *Find the square root of both sides.*

$y = x\sqrt{3}$ — *Simplify.*

Know it! Note

Theorem 5-8-2 — 30°-60°-90° Triangle Theorem

In a 30°-60°-90° triangle, the length of the hypotenuse is is 2 times the length of the shorter leg, and the length of the longer leg is the length of the shorter leg times $\sqrt{3}$.

$AC = s$ $\quad AB = 2s$ $\quad BC = s\sqrt{3}$

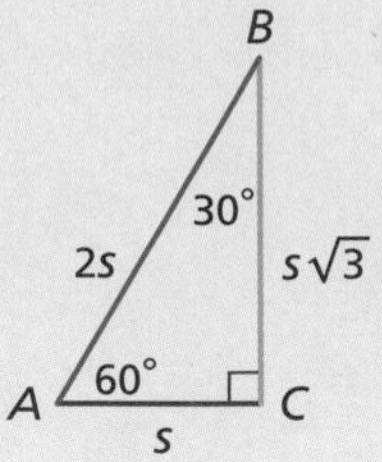

EXAMPLE 3 Finding Side Lengths in a 30°-60°-90° Triangle

Find the values of x and y. Give your answers in simplest radical form.

A

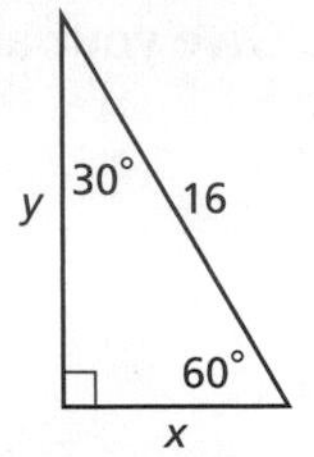

$16 = 2x$	*Hypotenuse = 2(shorter leg)*
$8 = x$	*Divide both sides by 2.*
$y = x\sqrt{3}$	*Longer leg = (shorter leg)$\sqrt{3}$*
$y = 8\sqrt{3}$	*Substitute 8 for x.*

> **Remember!**
> If two angles of a triangle are not congruent, the shorter side lies opposite the smaller angle.

B

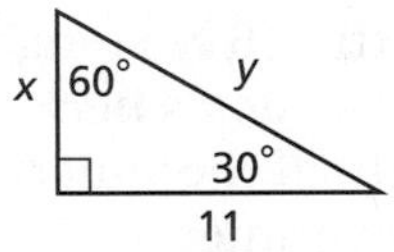

$11 = x\sqrt{3}$	*Longer leg = (shorter leg)$\sqrt{3}$*
$\dfrac{11}{\sqrt{3}} = x$	*Divide both sides by $\sqrt{3}$.*
$\dfrac{11\sqrt{3}}{3} = x$	*Rationalize the denominator.*
$y = 2x$	*Hypotenuse = 2(shorter leg)*
$y = 2\left(\dfrac{11\sqrt{3}}{3}\right)$	*Substitute $\frac{11\sqrt{3}}{3}$ for x.*
$y = \dfrac{22\sqrt{3}}{3}$	*Simplify.*

CHECK IT OUT! **Find the values of x and y. Give your answers in simplest radical form.**

3a.

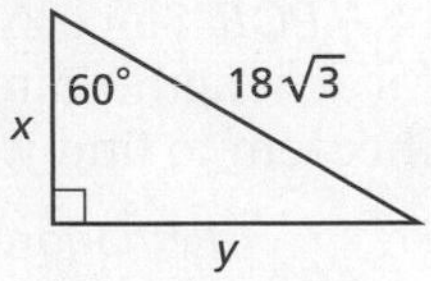

3b.

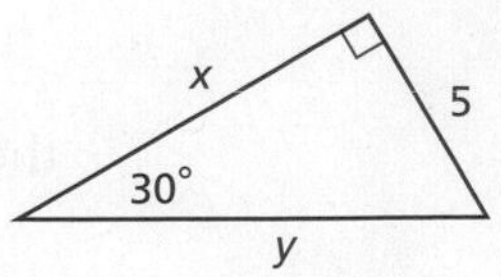

3c.

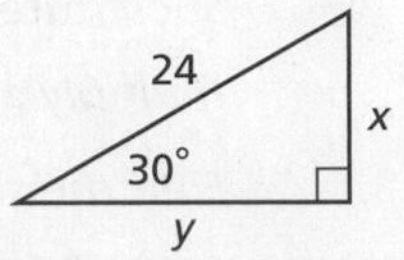

3d.

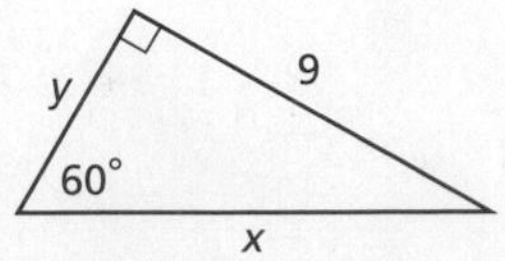

Student to Student

30°-60°-90° Triangles

Marcus Maiello
Johnson High School

To remember the side relationships in a 30°-60°-90° triangle, I draw a simple "1-2-$\sqrt{3}$" triangle like this.

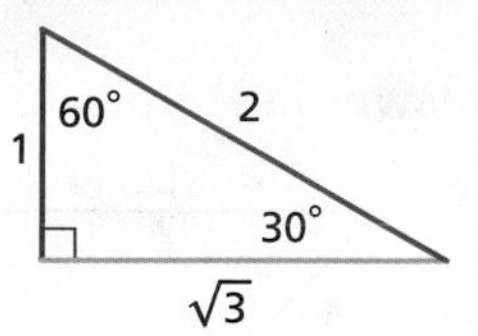

$2 = 2(1)$, so
***hypotenuse** = 2(**shorter leg**).*

$\sqrt{3} = \sqrt{3}(1)$, so
*longer leg = $\sqrt{3}$(**shorter leg**).*

EXAMPLE 4 **Using the 30°-60°-90° Triangle Theorem**

The frame of the clock shown is an equilateral triangle. The length of one side of the frame is 20 cm. Will the clock fit on a shelf that is 18 cm below the shelf above it?

Step 1 Divide the equilateral triangle into two 30°-60°-90° triangles.

The height of the frame is the length of the longer leg.

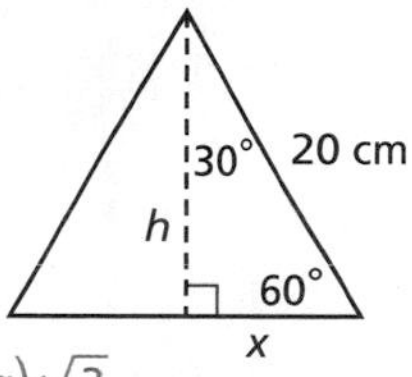

Step 2 Find the length x of the shorter leg.

$20 = 2x$ *Hypotenuse = 2(shorter leg)*

$10 = x$ *Divide both sides by 2.*

Step 3 Find the length h of the longer leg.

$h = 10\sqrt{3} \approx 17.3$ cm *Longer leg = (shorter leg)$\sqrt{3}$*

The frame is approximately 17.3 centimeters tall. So the clock will fit on the shelf.

CHECK IT OUT! **4. What if...?** A manufacturer wants to make a larger clock with a height of 30 centimeters. What is the length of each side of the frame? Round to the nearest tenth.

MATHEMATICAL PRACTICES

THINK AND DISCUSS

1. Explain why an isosceles right triangle is a 45°-45°-90° triangle.

2. Describe how finding x in triangle I is different from finding x in triangle II.

I.

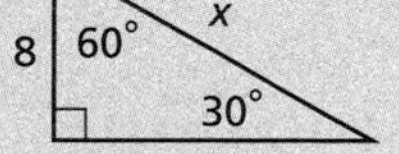

II.

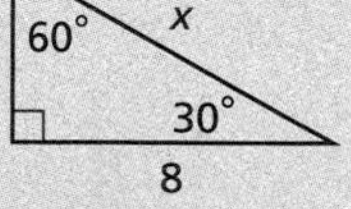

Know it! Note

3. GET ORGANIZED Copy and complete the graphic organizer. In each box, sketch the special right triangle and label its side lengths in terms of s.

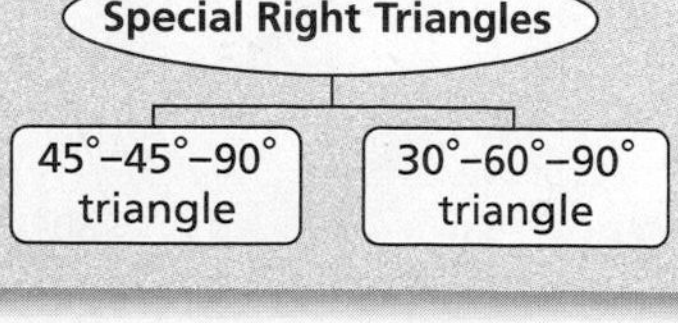

5-8 Exercises

GUIDED PRACTICE

SEE EXAMPLE 1 Find the value of x. Give your answer in simplest radical form.

1. 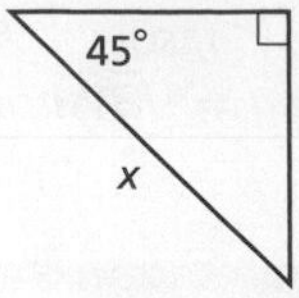

2. 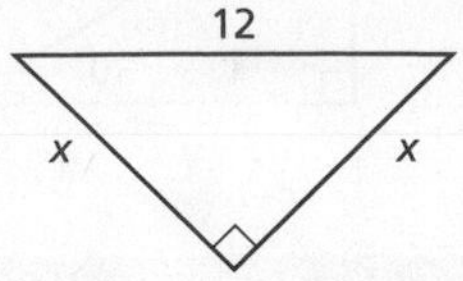

3. 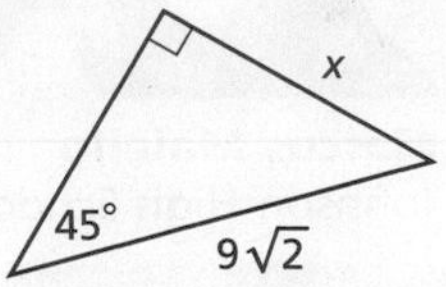

SEE EXAMPLE 2

4. **Transportation** The two arms of the railroad sign are perpendicular bisectors of each other. In Pennsylvania, the lengths marked in red must be 19.5 inches. What is the distance labeled d? Round to the nearest tenth of an inch.

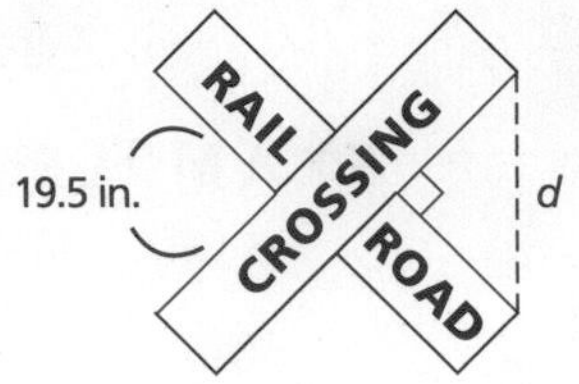

SEE EXAMPLE 3 Find the values of x and y. Give your answers in simplest radical form.

5. 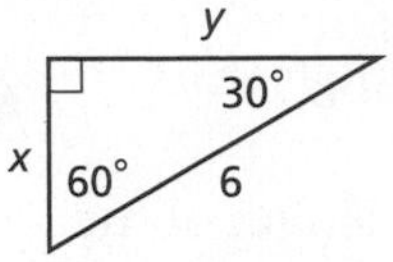

6. 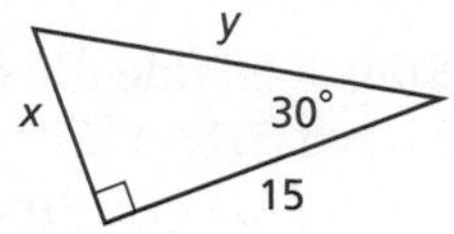

7. 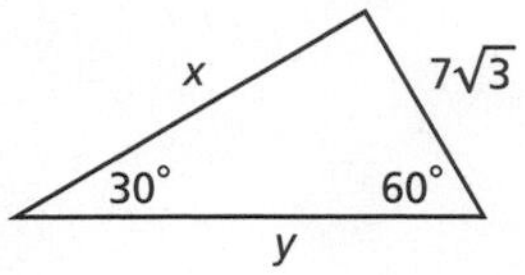

SEE EXAMPLE 4

8. **Entertainment** Regulation billiard balls are $2\frac{1}{4}$ inches in diameter. The rack used to group 15 billiard balls is in the shape of an equilateral triangle. What is the approximate height of the triangle formed by the rack? Round to the nearest quarter of an inch.

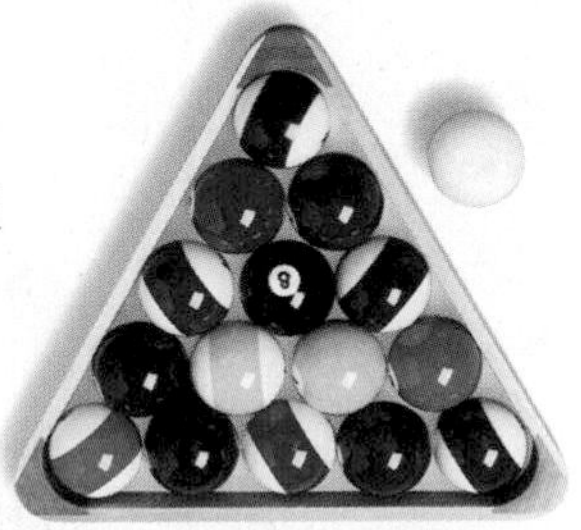

PRACTICE AND PROBLEM SOLVING

Independent Practice

For Exercises	See Example
9–11	1
12	2
13–15	3
16	4

Extra Practice

See Extra Practice for more Skills Practice and Applications Practice exercises.

Find the value of x. Give your answer in simplest radical form.

9. 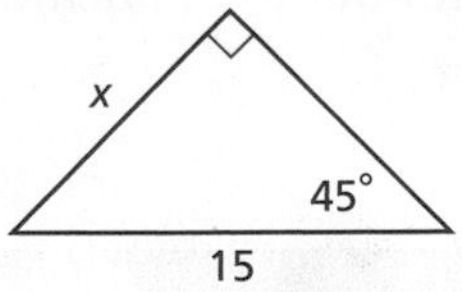

10. 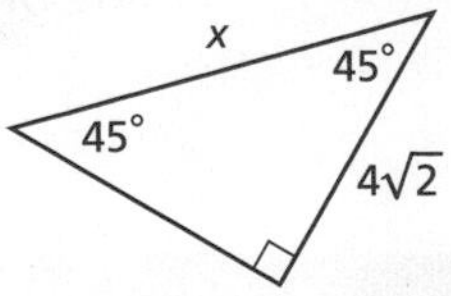

11. 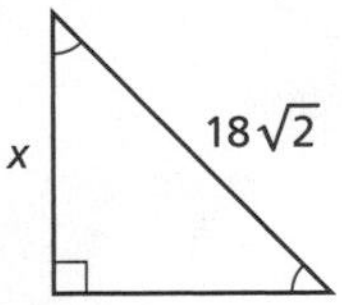

12. **Design** This tabletop is an isosceles right triangle. The length of the front edge of the table is 48 inches. What is the length w of each side edge? Round to the nearest tenth of an inch.

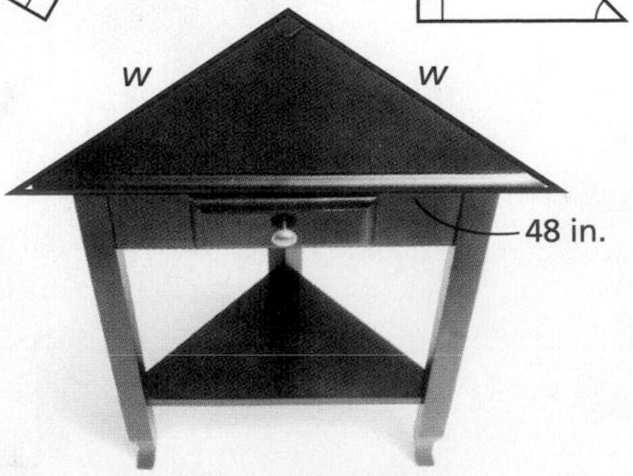

Find the value of x and y. Give your answers in simplest radical form.

13. 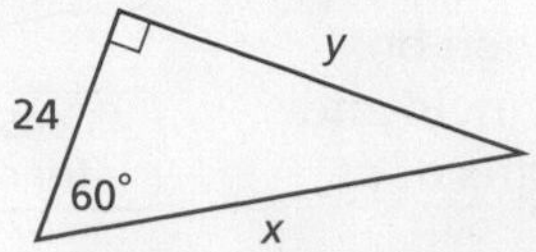

14. 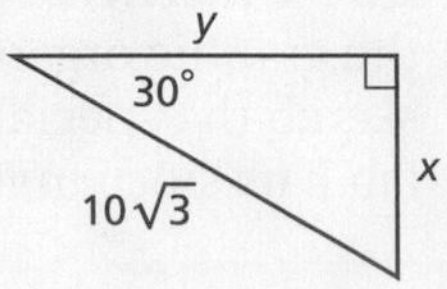

15. 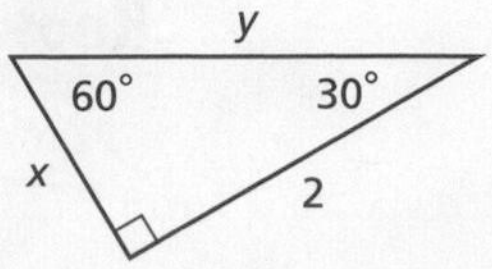

16. **Pets** A dog walk is used in dog agility competitions. In this dog walk, each ramp makes an angle of 30° with the ground.

  a. How long is one ramp?

  b. How long is the entire dog walk, including both ramps?

Multi-Step Find the perimeter and area of each figure. Give your answers in simplest radical form.

17. a 45°-45°-90° triangle with hypotenuse length 12 inches

18. a 30°-60°-90° triangle with hypotenuse length 28 centimeters

19. a square with diagonal length 18 meters

20. an equilateral triangle with side length 4 feet

21. an equilateral triangle with height 30 yards

22. **Estimation** The triangle loom is made from wood strips shaped into a 45°-45°-90° triangle. Pegs are placed every $\frac{1}{2}$ inch along the hypotenuse and every $\frac{1}{4}$ inch along each leg. Suppose you make a loom with an 18-inch hypotenuse. Approximately how many pegs will you need?

23. **Critical Thinking** The angle measures of a triangle are in the ratio 1:2:3. Are the side lengths also in the ratio 1:2:3? Explain your answer.

Find the coordinates of point *P* under the given conditions. Give your answers in simplest radical form.

24. $\triangle PQR$ is a 45°-45°-90° triangle with vertices $Q(4, 6)$ and $R(-6, -4)$, and $m\angle P = 90°$. P is in Quadrant II.

25. $\triangle PST$ is a 45°-45°-90° triangle with vertices $S(4, -3)$ and $T(-2, 3)$, and $m\angle S = 90°$. P is in Quadrant I.

26. $\triangle PWX$ is a 30°-60°-90° triangle with vertices $W(-1, -4)$ and $X(4, -4)$, and $m\angle W = 90°$. P is in Quadrant II.

27. $\triangle PYZ$ is a 30°-60°-90° triangle with vertices $Y(-7, 10)$ and $Z(5, 10)$, and $m\angle Z = 90°$. P is in Quadrant IV.

28. **Write About It** Why do you think 30°-60°-90° triangles and 45°-45°-90° triangles are called *special right triangles*?

MULTI-STEP TEST PREP

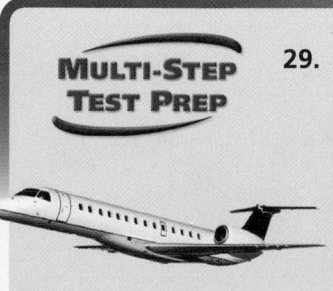

29. The figure shows an airline's routes among four cities. The airline offers one frequent-flier mile for each mile flown (rounded to the nearest mile). How many frequent-flier miles do you earn for each flight?

  a. Nelson (N) to Belton (B)

  b. Idria (I) to Nelson (N)

  c. Belton (B) to Idria (I)

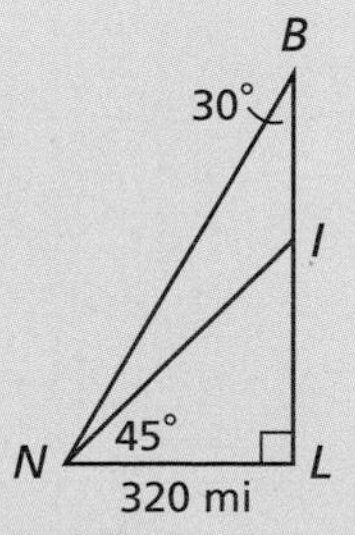

TEST PREP

30. Which is a true statement?

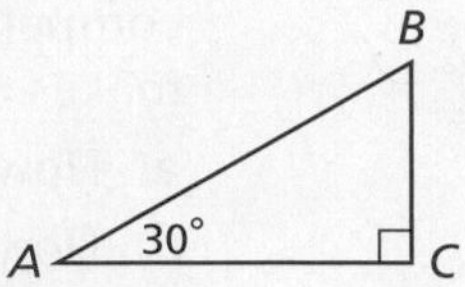

Ⓐ $AB = BC\sqrt{2}$ Ⓒ $AC = BC\sqrt{3}$

Ⓑ $AB = BC\sqrt{3}$ Ⓓ $AC = AB\sqrt{2}$

31. An 18-foot pole is broken during a storm. The top of the pole touches the ground 12 feet from the base of the pole. How tall is the part of the pole left standing?

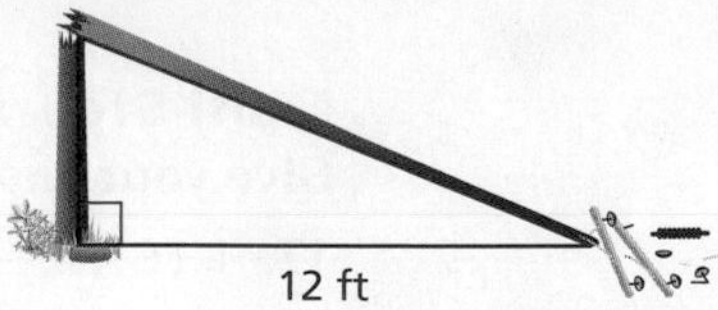

Ⓕ 5 feet Ⓗ 13 feet

Ⓖ 6 feet Ⓙ 22 feet

32. The length of the hypotenuse of an isosceles right triangle is 24 inches. What is the length of one leg of the triangle, rounded to the nearest tenth of an inch?

Ⓐ 13.9 inches Ⓒ 33.9 inches

Ⓑ 17.0 inches Ⓓ 41.6 inches

33. **Gridded Response** Find the area of the rectangle to the nearest tenth of a square inch.

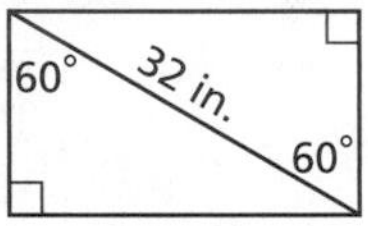

CHALLENGE AND EXTEND

Multi-Step Find the value of x in each figure.

34.

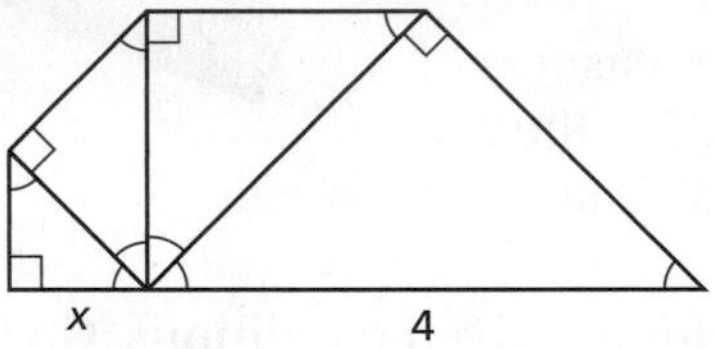

35.

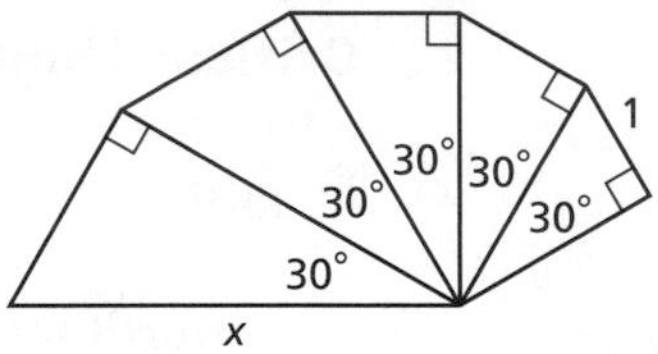

36. Each edge of the cube has length e.

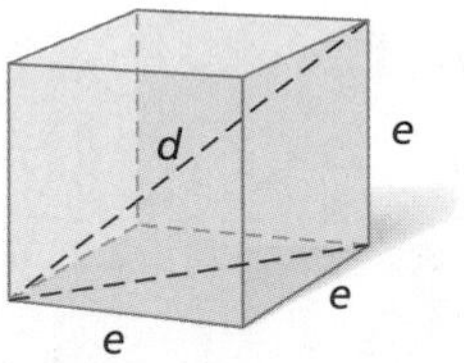

a. Find the diagonal length d when $e = 1$, $e = 2$, and $e = 3$. Give the answers in simplest radical form.

b. Write a formula for d for any positive value of e.

37. Write a paragraph proof to show that the altitude to the hypotenuse of a 30°-60°-90° triangle divides the hypotenuse into two segments, one of which is 3 times as long as the other.

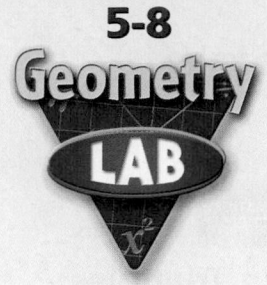

5-8

Geometry LAB

Graph Irrational Numbers

Numbers such as $\sqrt{2}$ and $\sqrt{3}$ are irrational. That is, they cannot be written as the ratio of two integers. In decimal form, they are infinite nonrepeating decimals. You can round the decimal form to estimate the location of these numbers on a number line, or you can use right triangles to construct their locations exactly.

Use with Applying Special Right Triangles

MATHEMATICAL PRACTICES **Use appropriate tools strategically.**

Activity

1 Draw a line. Mark two points near the left side of the line and label them 0 and 1. The distance from 0 to 1 is 1 unit.

2 Set your compass to 1 unit and mark increments at 2, 3, 4, and 5 units to construct a number line.

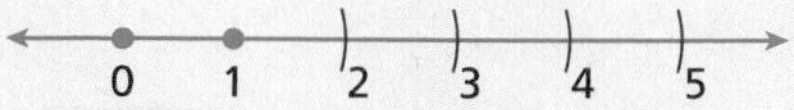

3 Construct a perpendicular to the line through 1.

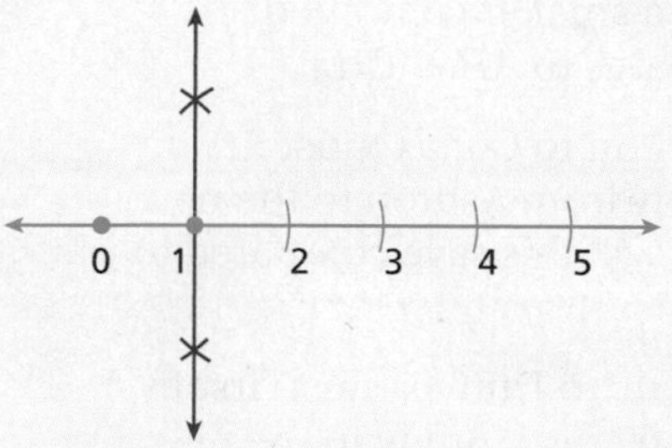

4 Using your compass, mark 1 unit up from the number line and then draw a right triangle. The legs both have length 1, so by the Pythagorean Theorem, the hypotenuse has a length of $\sqrt{2}$.

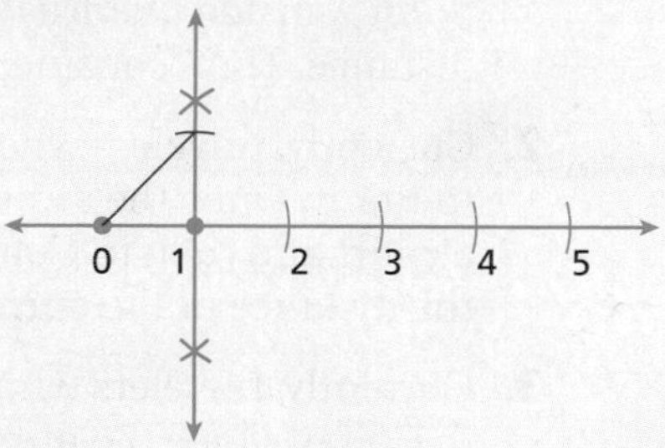

5 Set your compass to the length of the hypotenuse. Draw an arc centered at 0 that intersects the number line at $\sqrt{2}$.

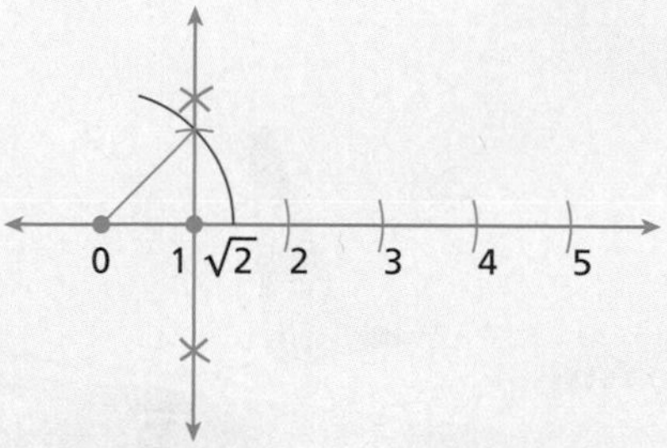

6 Repeat Steps 3 through 5, starting at $\sqrt{2}$, to construct a segment of length $\sqrt{3}$.

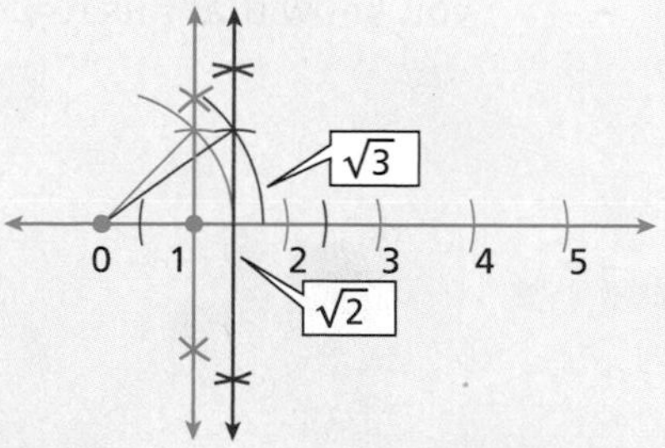

Try This

1. Sketch the two right triangles from Step 6. Label the side lengths and use the Pythagorean Theorem to show why the construction is correct.
2. Construct $\sqrt{4}$ and verify that it is equal to 2.
3. Construct $\sqrt{5}$ through $\sqrt{9}$ and verify that $\sqrt{9}$ is equal to 3.
4. Set your compass to the length of the segment from 0 to $\sqrt{2}$. Mark off another segment of length $\sqrt{2}$ to show that $\sqrt{8}$ is equal to $2\sqrt{2}$.

CHAPTER 5

MULTI-STEP TEST PREP

SECTION 5B

MATHEMATICAL PRACTICES **Model with mathematics.**

Relationships in Triangles

Fly Away! A commuter airline serves the four cities of Ashton, Brady, Colfax, and Dumas, located at points *A*, *B*, *C*, and *D*, respectively. The solid lines in the figure show the airline's existing routes. The airline is building an airport at *H*, which will serve as a hub. This will add four new routes to their schedule: $\overline{AH}$, $\overline{BH}$, $\overline{CH}$, and $\overline{DH}$.

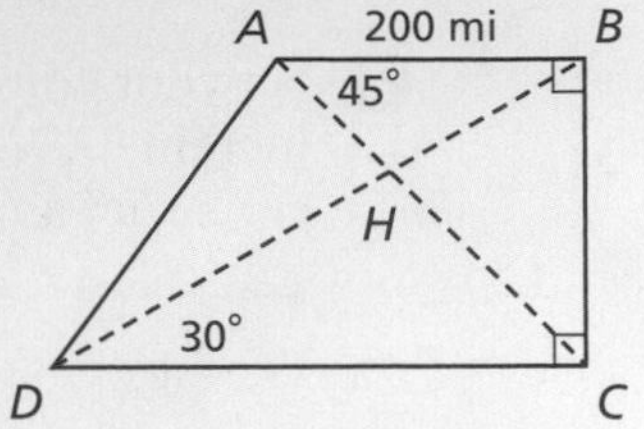

1. The airline wants to locate the airport so that the combined distance to the cities $(AH + BH + CH + DH)$ is as small as possible. Give an indirect argument to explain why the airline should locate the airport at the intersection of the diagonals $\overline{AC}$ and $\overline{BD}$. (*Hint*: Assume that a different point *X* inside quadrilateral *ABCD* results in a smaller combined distance. Then consider how $AX + CX$ compares to $AH + CH$.)

2. Currently, travelers who want to go from Ashton to Colfax must first fly to Brady. Once the airport is built, they will fly from Ashton to the new airport and then to Colfax. How many miles will this save compared to the distance of the current trip?

3. Currently, travelers who want to go from Brady to Dumas must first fly to Colfax. Once the airport is built, they will fly from Brady to the new airport and then to Dumas. How many miles will this save?

4. Once the airport is built, the airline plans to serve a meal only on its longest flight. On which route should they serve the meal? How do you know that this route is the longest?

READY TO GO ON?

Quiz for Lessons 5-5 Through 5-8

5-5 Indirect Proof and Inequalities in One Triangle

1. Write an indirect proof that the supplement of an acute angle cannot be an acute angle.

2. Write the angles of $\triangle KLM$ in order from smallest to largest.

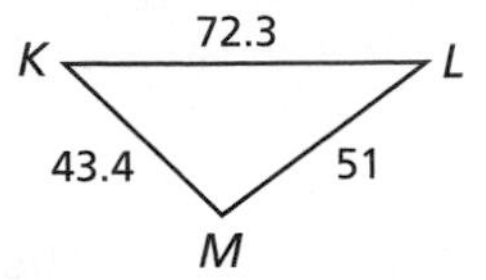

3. Write the sides of $\triangle DEF$ in order from shortest to longest.

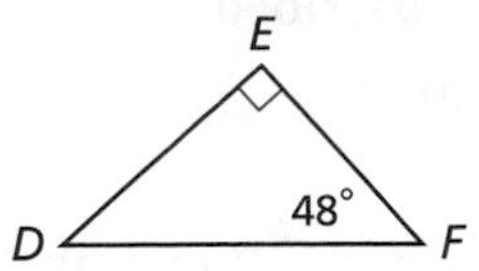

Tell whether a triangle can have sides with the given lengths. Explain.

4. 8.3, 10.5, 18.8

5. $4s$, $s + 10$, s^2, when $s = 4$

6. The distance from Kara's school to the theater is 9 km. The distance from her school to the zoo is 16 km. If the three locations form a triangle, what is the range of distances from the theater to the zoo?

5-6 Inequalities in Two Triangles

7. Compare PR and SV.

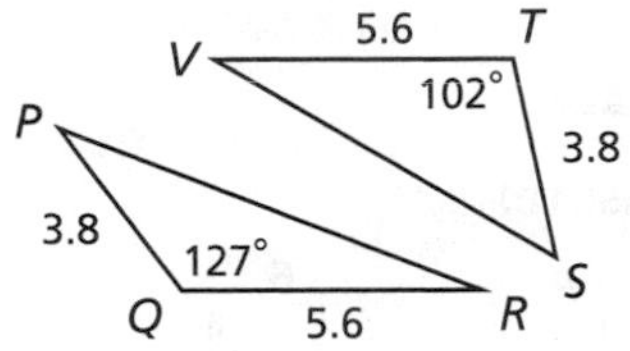

8. Compare $m\angle KJL$ and $m\angle MJL$.

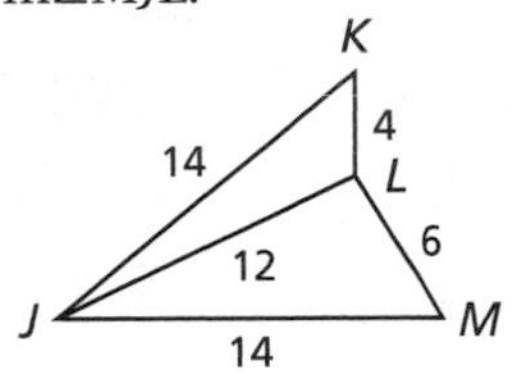

9. Find the range of values for x.

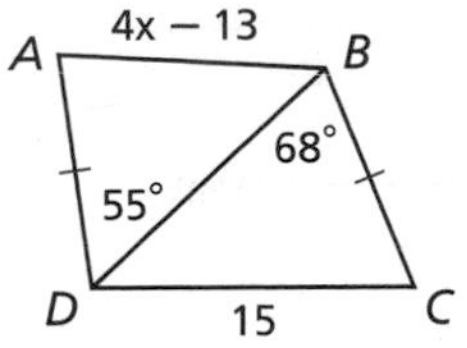

5-7 The Pythagorean Theorem

10. Find the value of x. Give the answer in simplest radical form.

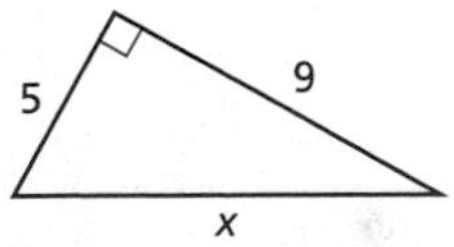

11. Find the missing side length. Tell if the side lengths form a Pythagorean triple. Explain.

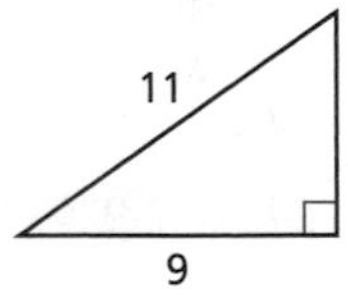

12. Tell if the measures 10, 12, and 16 can be the side lengths of a triangle. If so, classify the triangle as acute, obtuse, or right.

13. A landscaper wants to place a stone walkway from one corner of the rectangular lawn to the opposite corner. What will be the length of the walkway? Round to the nearest inch.

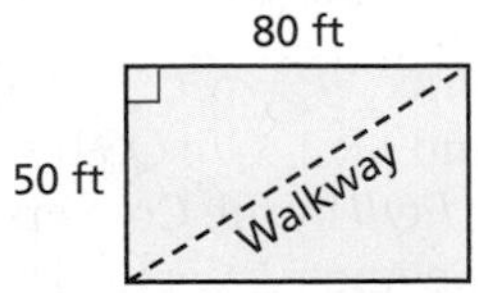

5-8 Applying Special Right Triangles

14. A yield sign is an equilateral triangle with a side length of 36 inches. What is the height h of the sign? Round to the nearest inch.

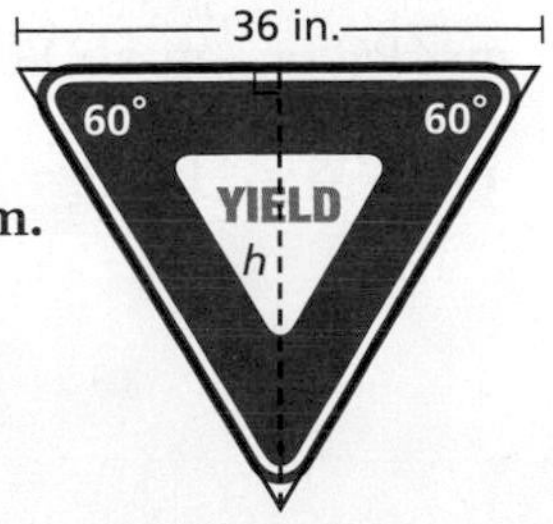

Find the values of the variables. Give your answers in simplest radical form.

15.

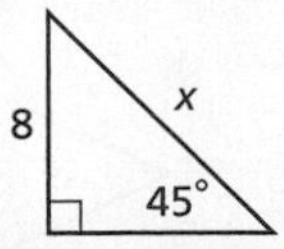

16.

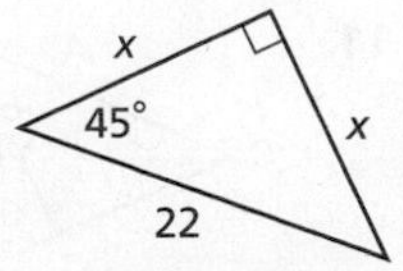

17.

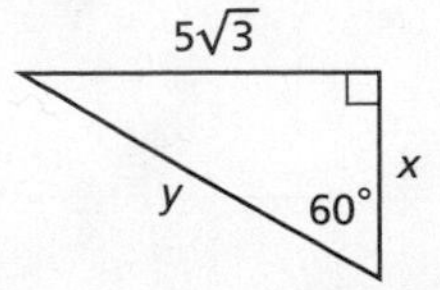

CHAPTER 5

Study Guide: Review

Know it! Note

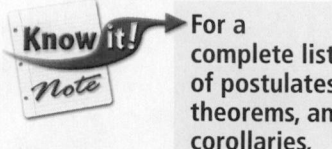

For a complete list of postulates, theorems, and corollaries, see p. PT2.

Vocabulary

altitude of a triangle	equidistant	median of a triangle
centroid of a triangle	incenter of a triangle	midsegment of a triangle
circumcenter of a triangle	indirect proof	orthocenter of a triangle
circumscribed	inscribed	point of concurrency
concurrent	locus	Pythagorean triple

Complete the sentences below with vocabulary words from the list above.

1. A point that is the same distance from two or more objects is __?__ from the objects.

2. A __?__ is a segment that joins the midpoints of two sides of the triangle.

3. The point of concurrency of the angle bisectors of a triangle is the __?__ .

4. A __?__ is a set of points that satisfies a given condition.

5-1 Perpendicular and Angle Bisectors

EXAMPLES

Find each measure.

■ *JL*

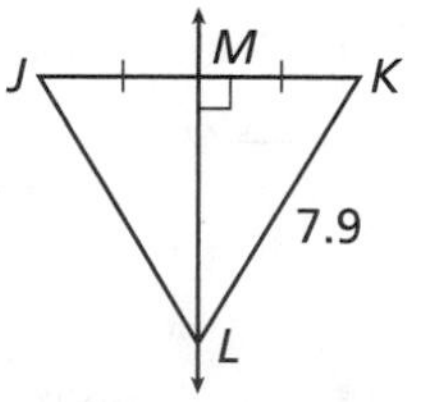

Because $\overline{JM} \cong \overline{MK}$ and $\overline{ML} \perp \overline{JK}$, $\overline{ML}$ is the perpendicular bisector of $\overline{JK}$.

$JL = KL$ *⊥ Bisector Thm.*

$JL = 7.9$ *Substitute 7.9 for KL.*

■ m∠*PQS*, given that m∠*PQR* = 68°

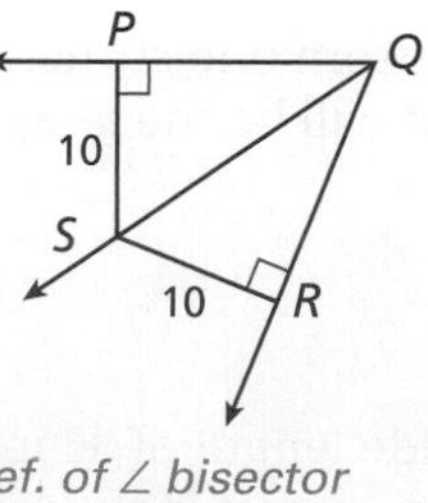

Since $SP = SR$, $\overline{SP} \perp \overline{QP}$, and $\overline{SR} \perp \overline{QR}$, $\overrightarrow{QS}$ bisects ∠*PQR* by the Converse of the Angle Bisector Theorem.

$m\angle PQS = \frac{1}{2} m\angle PQR$ *Def. of ∠ bisector*

$m\angle PQS = \frac{1}{2}(68°) = 34°$ *Substitute 68° for m∠PQR.*

EXERCISES

Find each measure.

5. *BD*

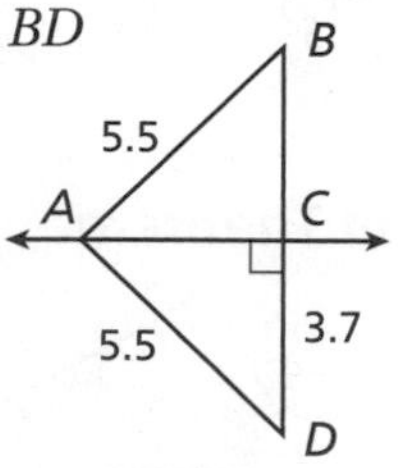

6. *YZ*

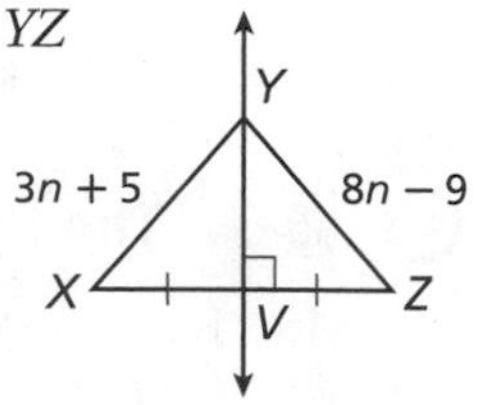

7. *HT*

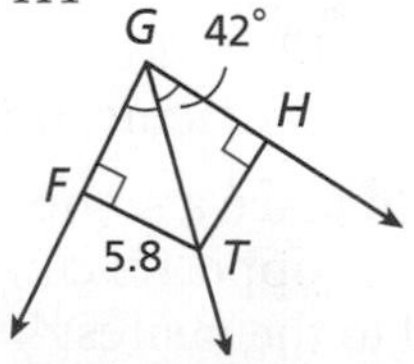

8. m∠*MNP*

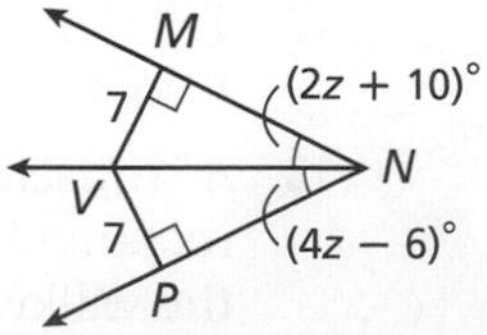

Write an equation in point-slope form for the perpendicular bisector of the segment with the given endpoints.

9. $A(-4, 5)$, $B(6, -5)$

10. $X(3, 2)$, $Y(5, 10)$

Tell whether the given information allows you to conclude that *P* is on the bisector of ∠*ABC*.

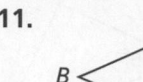

11.

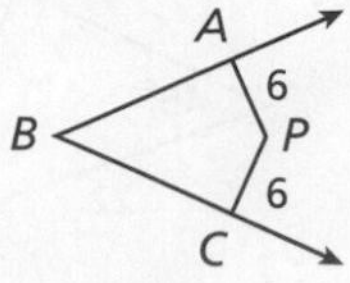

12.

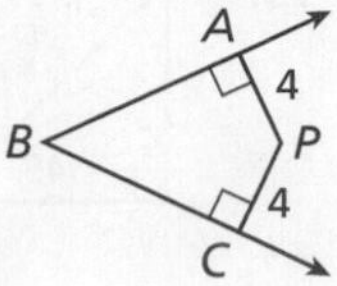

5-2 Bisectors of Triangles

EXAMPLES

- **$\overline{DG}$, $\overline{EG}$, and $\overline{FG}$ are the perpendicular bisectors of $\triangle ABC$. Find AG.**

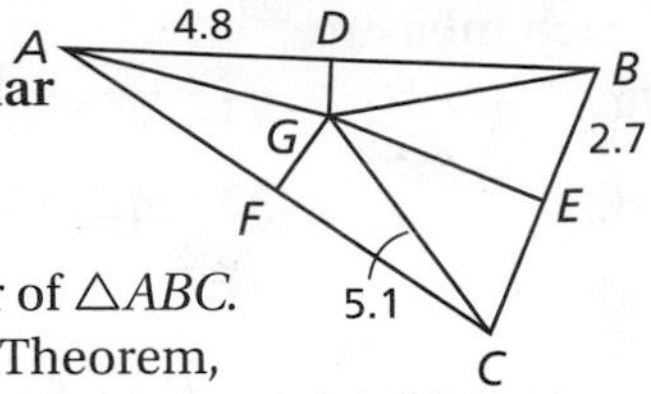

G is the circumcenter of $\triangle ABC$. By the Circumcenter Theorem, G is equidistant from the vertices of $\triangle ABC$.

$AG = CG$ *Circumcenter Thm.*

$AG = 5.1$ *Substitute 5.1 for CG.*

- **$\overline{QS}$ and $\overline{RS}$ are angle bisectors of $\triangle PQR$. Find the distance from S to $\overline{PR}$.**

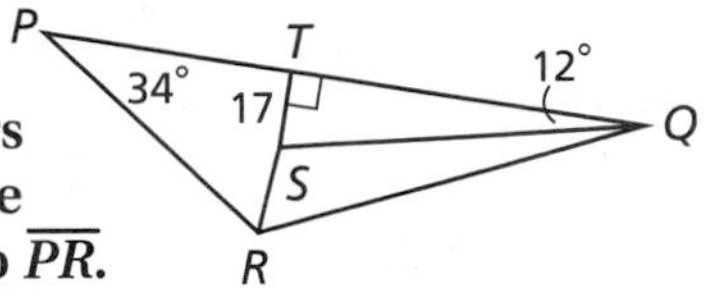

S is the incenter of $\triangle PQR$. By the Incenter Theorem, S is equidistant from the sides of $\triangle PQR$. The distance from S to $\overline{PQ}$ is 17, so the distance from S to $\overline{PR}$ is also 17.

EXERCISES

$\overline{PX}$, $\overline{PY}$, and $\overline{PZ}$ are the perpendicular bisectors of $\triangle GHJ$. Find each length.

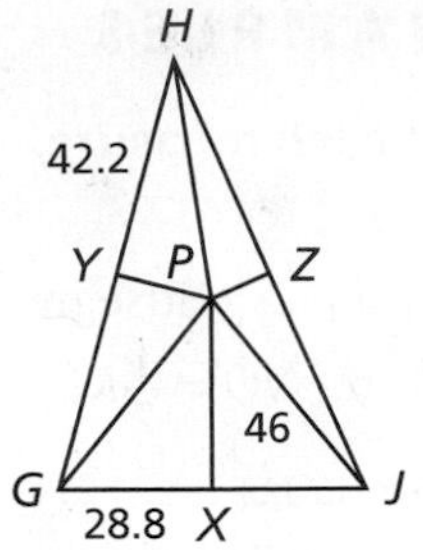

13. GY **14.** GP

15. GJ **16.** PH

$\overline{UA}$ and $\overline{VA}$ are angle bisectors of $\triangle UVW$. Find each measure.

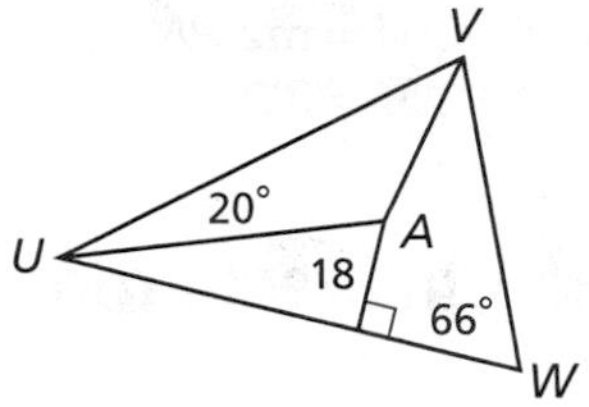

17. the distance from A to $\overline{UV}$

18. $m\angle WVA$

Find the circumcenter of a triangle with the given vertices.

19. $M(0, 6)$, $N(8, 0)$, $O(0, 0)$

20. $O(0, 0)$, $R(0, -7)$, $S(-12, 0)$

5-3 Medians and Altitudes of Triangles

EXAMPLES

- **In $\triangle JKL$, $JP = 42$. Find JQ.**

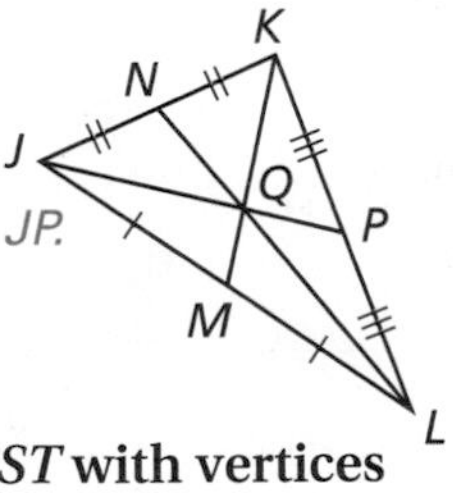

$JQ = \frac{2}{3}JP$ *Centroid Thm.*

$JQ = \frac{2}{3}(42)$ *Substitute 42 for JP.*

$JQ = 28$ *Multiply.*

- **Find the orthocenter of $\triangle RST$ with vertices $R(-5, 3)$, $S(-2, 5)$, and $T(-2, 0)$.**

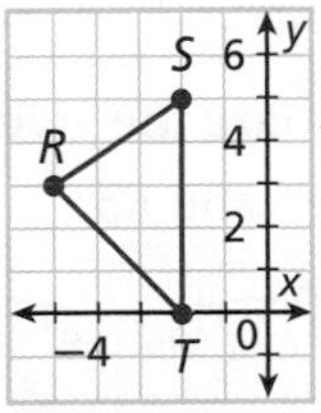

Since $\overline{ST}$ is vertical, the equation of the line containing the altitude from R to $\overline{ST}$ is $y = 3$.

slope of $\overline{RT} = \dfrac{3 - 0}{-5 - (-2)} = -1$

The slope of the altitude to $\overline{RT}$ is 1. This line must pass through $S(-2, 5)$.

$y - y_1 = m(x - x_1)$ *Point-slope form*

$y - 5 = 1(x + 2)$ *Substitution*

Solve the system $\begin{cases} y = 3 \\ y = x + 7 \end{cases}$ to find that the coordinates of the orthocenter are $(-4, 3)$.

EXERCISES

In $\triangle DEF$, $DB = 24.6$, and $EZ = 11.6$. Find each length.

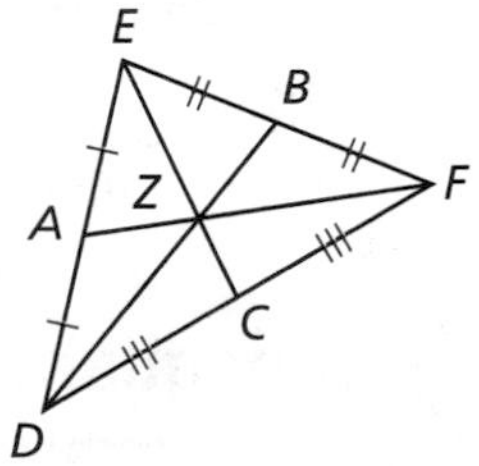

21. DZ **22.** ZB

23. ZC **24.** EC

Find the orthocenter of a triangle with the given vertices.

25. $J(-6, 7)$, $K(-6, 0)$, $L(-11, 0)$

26. $A(1, 2)$, $B(6, 2)$, $C(1, -8)$

27. $R(2, 3)$, $S(7, 8)$, $T(8, 3)$

28. $X(-3, 2)$, $Y(5, 2)$, $Z(3, -4)$

29. The coordinates of a triangular piece of a mobile are $(0, 4)$, $(3, 8)$, and $(6, 0)$. The piece will hang from a chain so that it is balanced. At what coordinates should the chain be attached?

5-4 The Triangle Midsegment Theorem

EXAMPLES

Find each measure.

- *NQ*

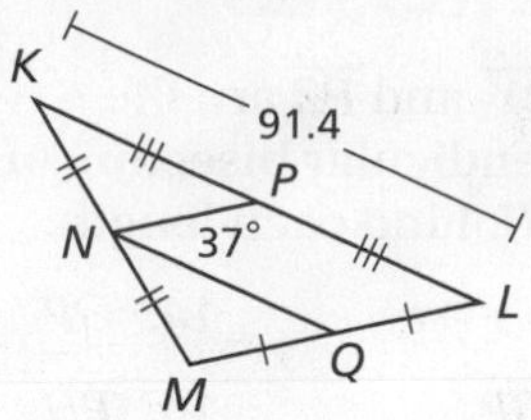

By the △ Midsegment Thm., $NQ = \frac{1}{2}KL = 45.7$.

- m∠*NQM*

$\overline{NP} \parallel \overline{ML}$	*△ Midsegment Thm.*
m∠*NQM* = m∠*PNQ*	*Alt. Int. ∠s Thm.*
m∠*NQM* = 37°	*Substitution*

EXERCISES

Find each measure.

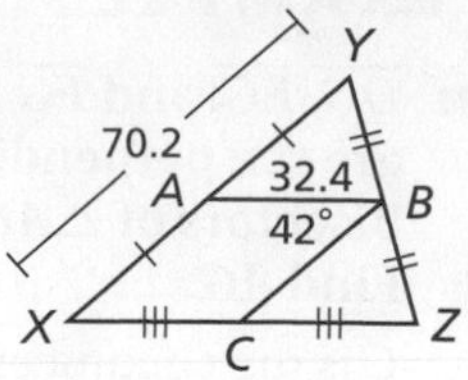

30. *BC* **31.** *XZ*

32. *XC* **33.** m∠*BCZ*

34. m∠*BAX* **35.** m∠*YXZ*

36. The vertices of △*GHJ* are *G*(−4, −7), *H*(2, 5), and *J*(10, −3). *V* is the midpoint of $\overline{GH}$, and *W* is the midpoint of $\overline{HJ}$. Show that $\overline{VW} \parallel \overline{GJ}$ and $VW = \frac{1}{2}GJ$.

5-5 Indirect Proof and Inequalities in One Triangle

EXAMPLES

- **Write the angles of △*RST* in order from smallest to largest.**

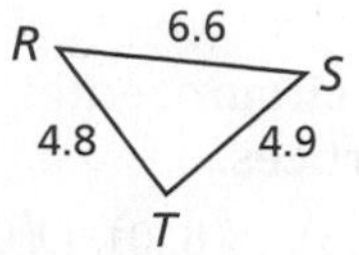

The smallest angle is opposite the shortest side. In order, the angles are ∠*S*, ∠*R*, and ∠*T*.

- **The lengths of two sides of a triangle are 15 inches and 12 inches. Find the range of possible lengths for the third side.**

Let *s* be the length of the third side.

$s + 15 > 12$	$s + 12 > 15$	$15 + 12 > s$
$s > -3$	$s > 3$	$27 > s$

By the Triangle Inequality Theorem, 3 in. < *s* < 27 in.

EXERCISES

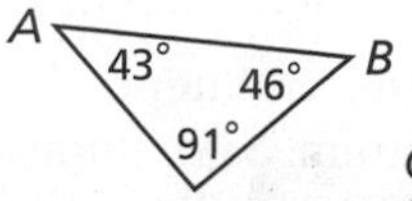

37. Write the sides of △*ABC* in order from shortest to longest.

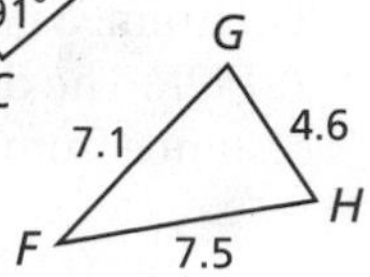

38. Write the angles of △*FGH* in order from smallest to largest.

39. The lengths of two sides of a triangle are 13.5 centimeters and 4.5 centimeters. Find the range of possible lengths for the third side.

Tell whether a triangle can have sides with the given lengths. Explain.

40. 6.2, 8.1, 14.2 **41.** *z*, *z*, 3*z*, when *z* = 5

42. Write an indirect proof that a triangle cannot have two obtuse angles.

5-6 Inequalities in Two Triangles

EXAMPLES

Compare the given measures.

- *KL* and *ST*

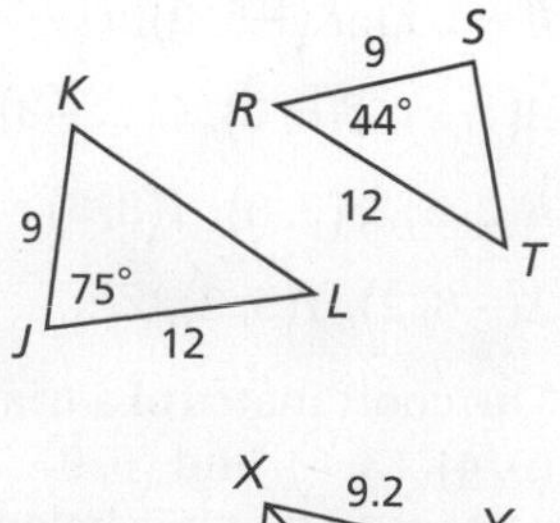

KJ = *RS*, *JL* = *RT*, and m∠*J* > m∠*R*. By the Hinge Theorem, *KL* > *ST*.

- m∠*ZXY* and m∠*XZW*

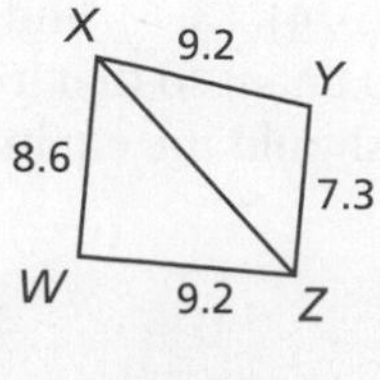

XY = *WZ*, *XZ* = *XZ*, and *YZ* < *XW*. By the Converse of the Hinge Theorem, m∠*ZXY* < m∠*XZW*.

EXERCISES

Compare the given measures.

43. *PS* and *RS*

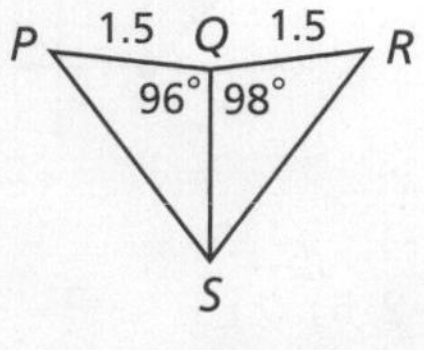

44. m∠*BCA* and m∠*DCA*

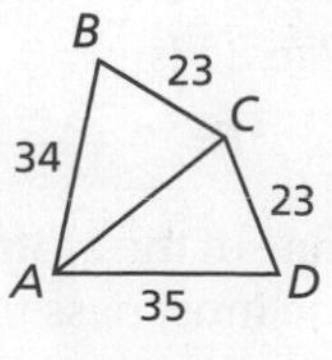

Find the range of values for *n*.

45.

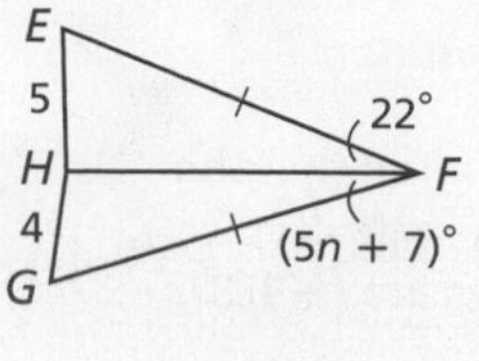

46.

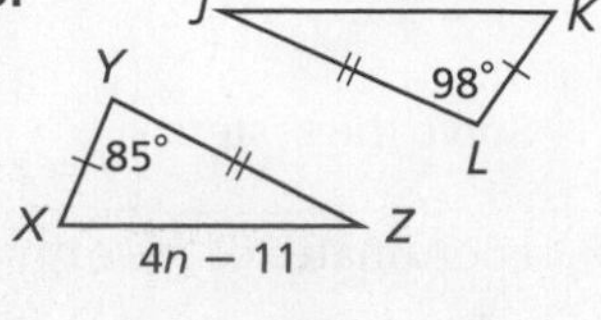

5-7 The Pythagorean Theorem

EXAMPLES

- **Find the value of x. Give your answer in simplest radical form.**

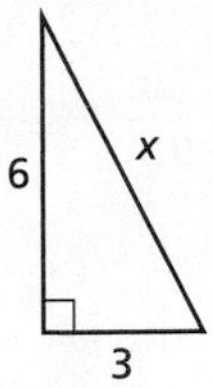

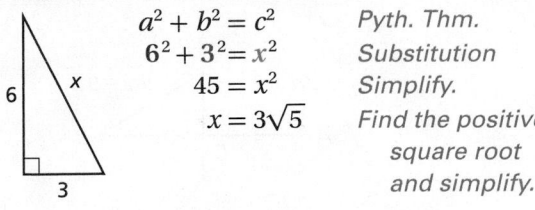

$a^2 + b^2 = c^2$	*Pyth. Thm.*
$6^2 + 3^2 = x^2$	*Substitution*
$45 = x^2$	*Simplify.*
$x = 3\sqrt{5}$	*Find the positive square root and simplify.*

- **Find the missing side length. Tell if the sides form a Pythagorean triple. Explain.**

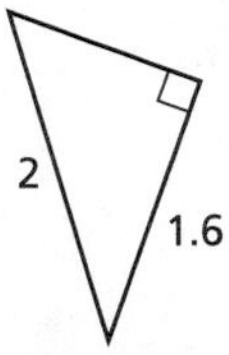

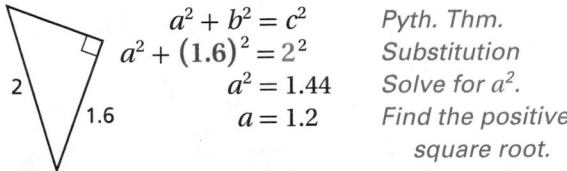

$a^2 + b^2 = c^2$	*Pyth. Thm.*
$a^2 + (1.6)^2 = 2^2$	*Substitution*
$a^2 = 1.44$	*Solve for a^2.*
$a = 1.2$	*Find the positive square root.*

The side lengths do not form a Pythagorean triple because 1.2 and 1.6 are not whole numbers.

EXERCISES

Find the value of x. Give your answer in simplest radical form.

47.

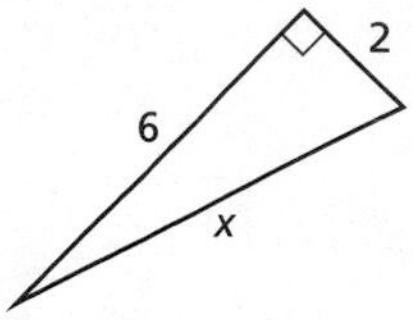

48.

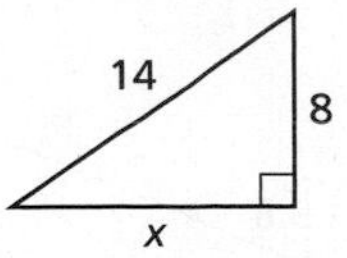

Find the missing side length. Tell if the sides form a Pythagorean triple. Explain.

49.

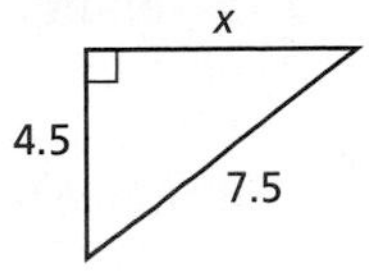

50.

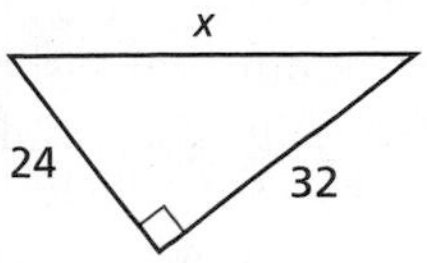

Tell if the measures can be the side lengths of a triangle. If so, classify the triangle as acute, obtuse, or right.

51. 9, 12, 16

52. 11, 14, 27

53. 1.5, 3.6, 3.9

54. 2, 3.7, 4.1

5-8 Applying Special Right Triangles

EXAMPLES

Find the values of the variables. Give your answers in simplest radical form.

- 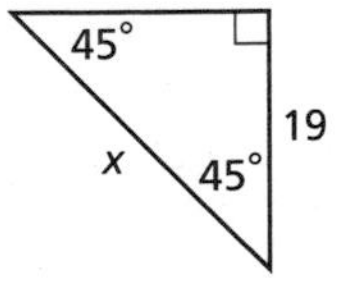

This is a 45°-45°-90° triangle.

$x = 19\sqrt{2}$ *Hyp. = leg$\sqrt{2}$*

- 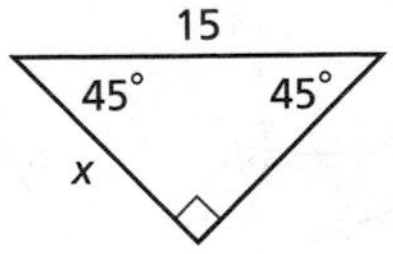

This is a 45°-45°-90° triangle.

$15 = x\sqrt{2}$ *Hyp. = leg$\sqrt{2}$*

$\frac{15}{\sqrt{2}} = x$ *Divide both sides by $\sqrt{2}$.*

$\frac{15\sqrt{2}}{2} = x$ *Rationalize the denominator.*

- 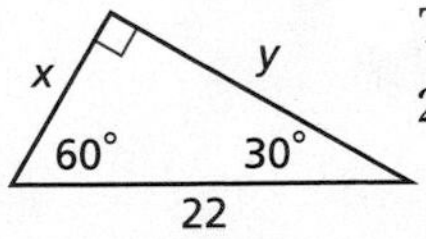

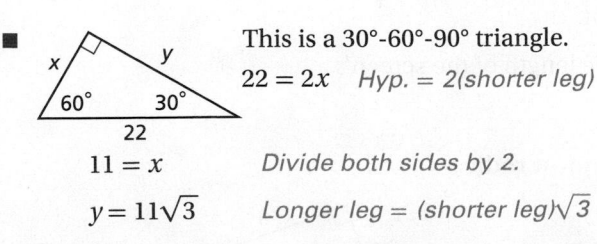

This is a 30°-60°-90° triangle.

$22 = 2x$ *Hyp. = 2(shorter leg)*

$11 = x$ *Divide both sides by 2.*

$y = 11\sqrt{3}$ *Longer leg = (shorter leg)$\sqrt{3}$*

EXERCISES

Find the values of the variables. Give your answers in simplest radical form.

55.

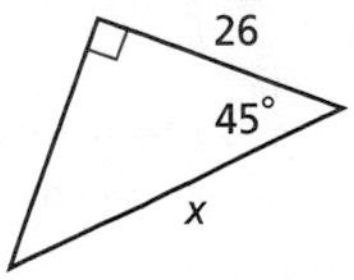

56.

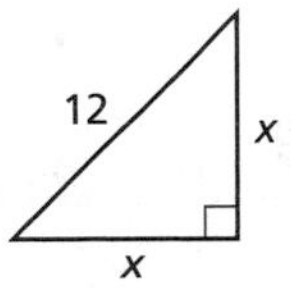

57.

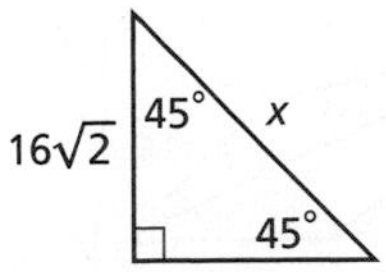

58.

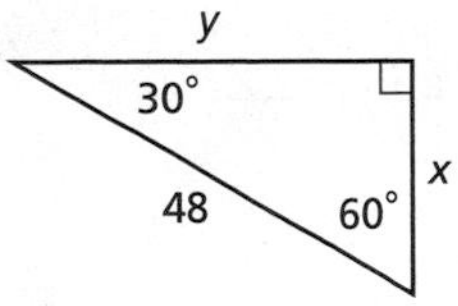

59.

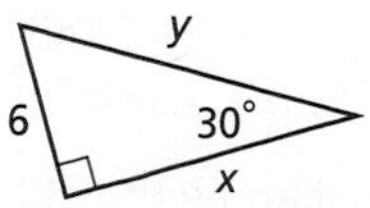

60.

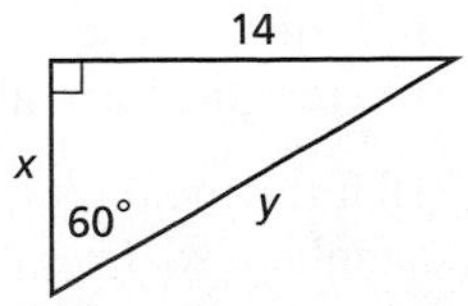

Find the value of each variable. Round to the nearest inch.

61.

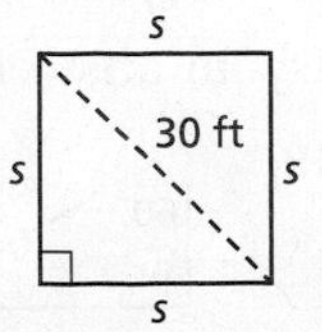

62.

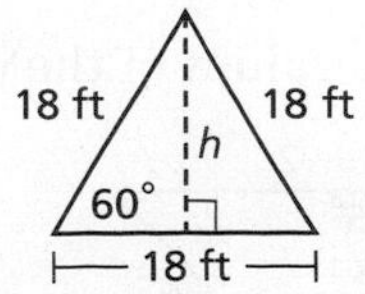

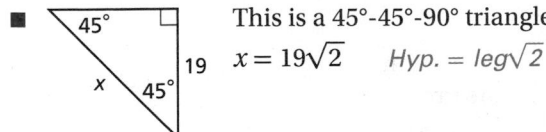

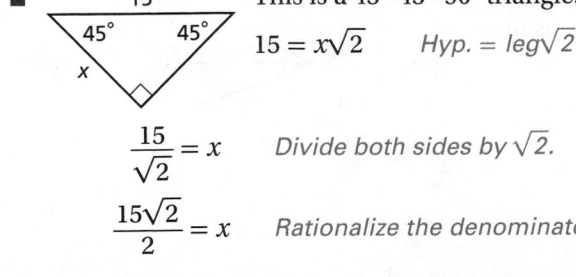

CHAPTER TEST

Find each measure.

1. KL

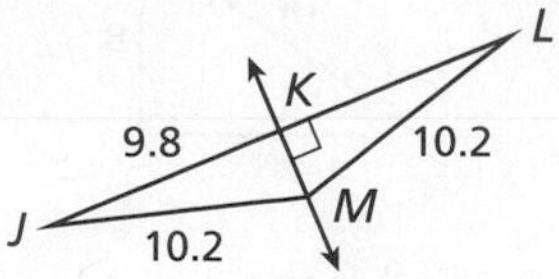

2. m∠WXY

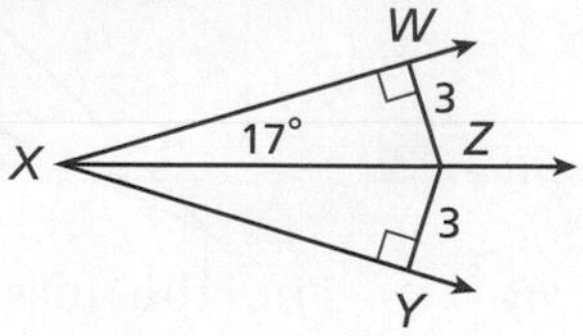

3. BC

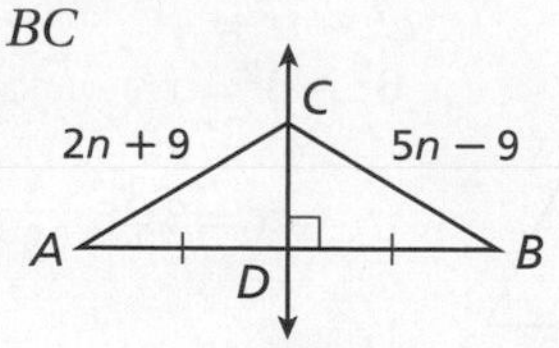

4. $\overline{MQ}$, $\overline{NQ}$, and $\overline{PQ}$ are the perpendicular bisectors of $\triangle RST$. Find RS and RQ.

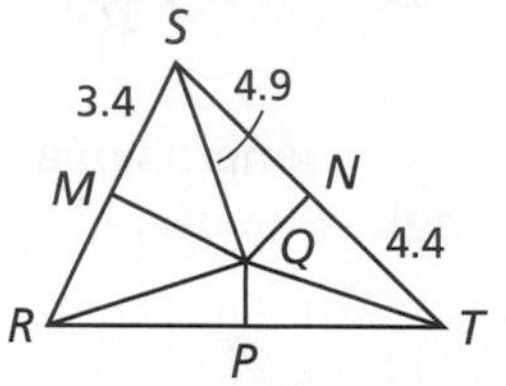

5. $\overline{EG}$ and $\overline{FG}$ are angle bisectors of $\triangle DEF$. Find m∠GEF and the distance from G to $\overline{DF}$.

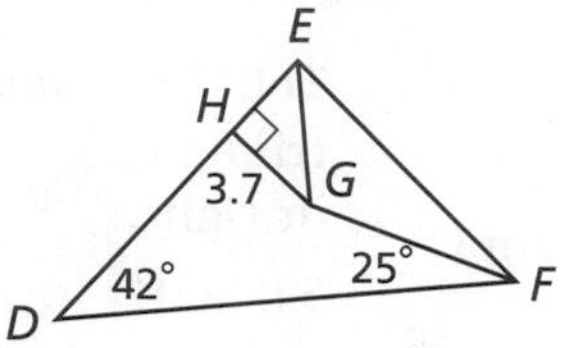

6. In $\triangle XYZ$, $XC = 261$, and $ZW = 118$. Find XW, BW, and BZ.

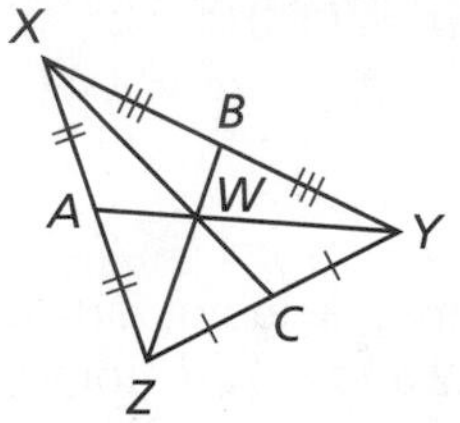

7. Find the orthocenter of $\triangle JKL$ with vertices $J(-5, 2)$, $K(-5, 10)$, and $L(1, 4)$.

8. In $\triangle GHJ$ at right, find PR, GJ, and m∠GRP.

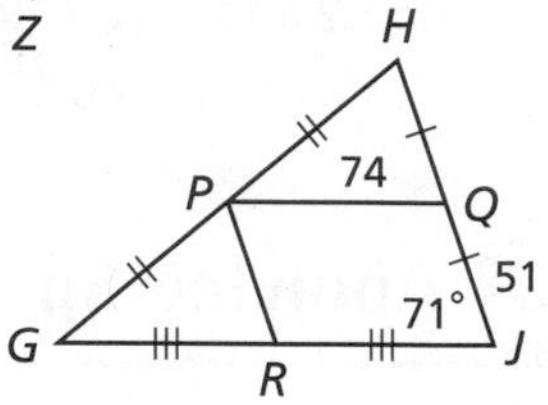

9. Write an indirect proof that two obtuse angles cannot form a linear pair.

10. Write the angles of $\triangle BEH$ in order from smallest to largest.

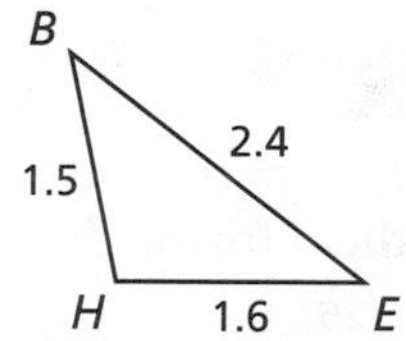

11. Write the sides of $\triangle RTY$ in order from shortest to longest.

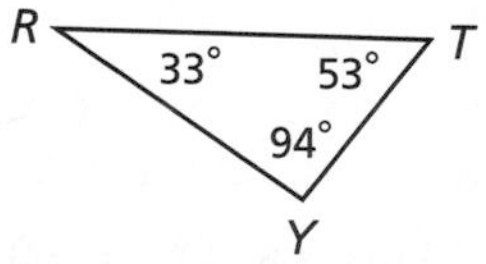

12. The distance from Arville to Branton is 114 miles. The distance from Branton to Camford is 247 miles. If the three towns form a triangle, what is the range of distances from Arville to Camford?

13. Compare m∠SPV and m∠ZPV.

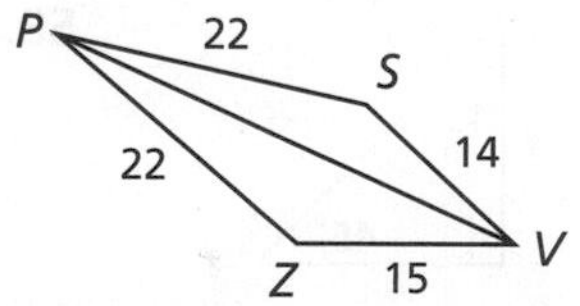

14. Find the range of values for x.

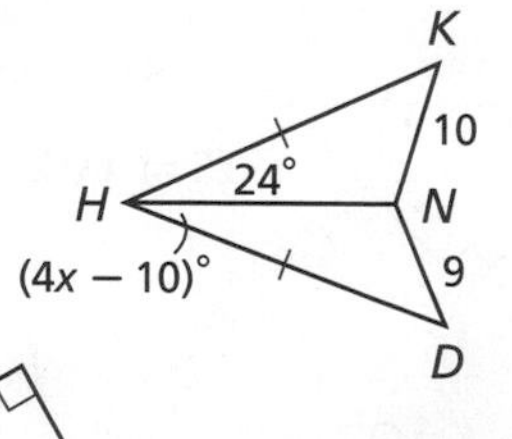

15. Find the missing side length in the triangle. Tell if the side lengths form a Pythagorean triple. Explain.

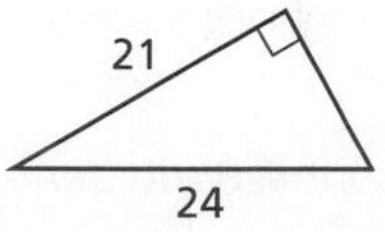

16. Tell if the measures 18, 20, and 27 can be the side lengths of a triangle. If so, classify the triangle as acute, obtuse, or right.

17. An IMAX screen is 62 feet tall and 82 feet wide. What is the length of the screen's diagonal? Round to the nearest inch.

Find the values of the variables. Give your answers in simplest radical form.

18.

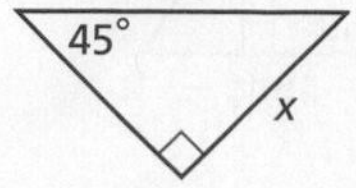

19.

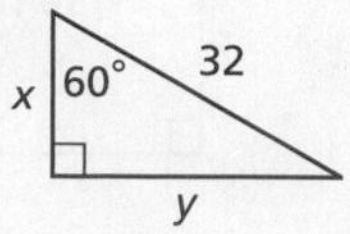

20.

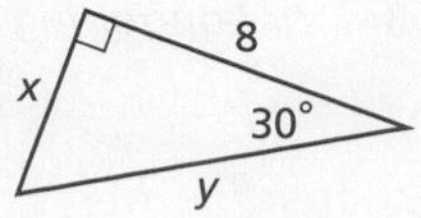

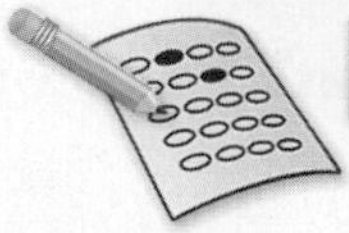

College Entrance Exam Practice

FOCUS ON SAT MATHEMATICS SUBJECT TESTS

Some questions on the SAT Mathematics Subject Tests require the use of a calculator. You can take the test without one, but it is not recommended. The calculator you use must meet certain criteria. For example, calculators that make noise or have typewriter-like keypads are not allowed.

HOT TIP! If you have both a scientific and a graphing calculator, bring the graphing calculator to the test. Make sure you spend time getting used to a new calculator before the day of the test.

You may want to time yourself as you take this practice test. It should take you about 6 minutes to complete.

1. In $\triangle ABC$, $m\angle C = 2m\angle A$, and $CB = 3$ units. What is AB to the nearest hundredth unit?

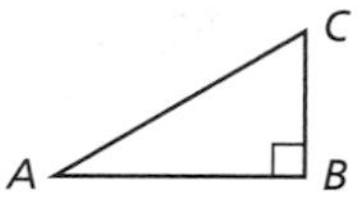

(A) 1.73 units

(B) 4.24 units

(C) 5.20 units

(D) 8.49 units

(E) 10.39 units

2. What is the perimeter of $\triangle ABC$ if D is the midpoint of $\overline{AB}$, E is the midpoint of $\overline{BC}$, and F is the midpoint of $\overline{AC}$?

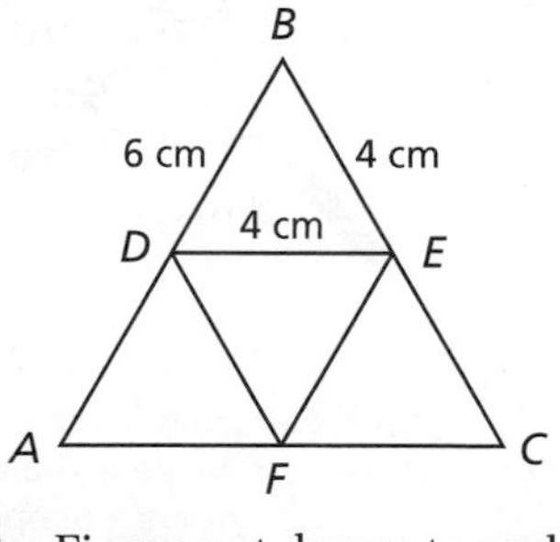

Note: Figure not drawn to scale.

(A) 8 centimeters

(B) 14 centimeters

(C) 20 centimeters

(D) 28 centimeters

(E) 35 centimeters

3. The side lengths of a right triangle are 2, 5, and c, where $c > 5$. What is the value of c?

(A) $\sqrt{21}$

(B) $\sqrt{29}$

(C) 7

(D) 9

(E) $\sqrt{145}$

4. In the triangle below, which of the following CANNOT be the length of the unknown side?

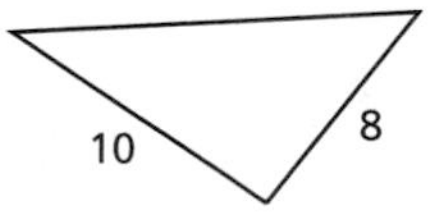

(A) 2.2

(B) 6

(C) 12.8

(D) 17.2

(E) 18.1

5. Which of the following points is on the perpendicular bisector of the segment with endpoints $(3, 4)$ and $(9, 4)$?

(A) $(4, 2)$

(B) $(4, 5)$

(C) $(5, 4)$

(D) $(6, -1)$

(E) $(7, 4)$

CHAPTER 5

TEST TACKLER

Standardized Test Strategies

Any Question Type: Check with a Different Method

It is important to check all of your answers on a test. An effective way to do this is to use a different method to answer the question a second time. If you get the same answer with two different methods, then your answer is probably correct.

EXAMPLE 1

Short Response **What are the coordinates of the centroid of $\triangle ABC$ with $A(-2, 4)$, $B(4, 6)$, and $C(1, -1)$? Show your work.**

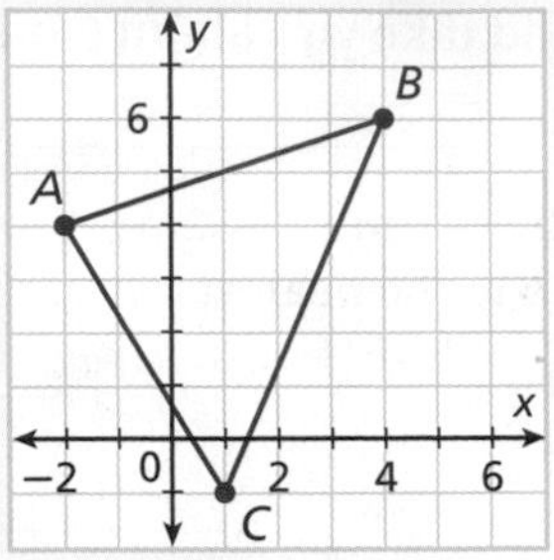

Method 1: The centroid of a triangle is the point of concurrency of the medians. Write the equations of two medians and find their point of intersection.

Let D be the midpoint of $\overline{AB}$ and let E be the midpoint of $\overline{BC}$.

$$D = \left(\frac{-2+4}{2}, \frac{4+6}{2}\right) = (1, 5) \qquad E = \left(\frac{4+1}{2}, \frac{6+(-1)}{2}\right) = (2.5, 2.5)$$

The median from C to D contains $C(1, -1)$ and $D(1, 5)$. It is vertical, so its equation is $x = 1$.

The median from A to E contains $A(-2, 4)$ and $E(2.5, 2.5)$.

slope of $\overline{AE} = \frac{4-2.5}{-2-2.5} = \frac{1.5}{-4.5} = -\frac{1}{3}$

$y - y_1 = m(x - x_1)$	*Point-slope form*
$y - 4 = -\frac{1}{3}(x + 2)$	*Substitute 4 for y_1, $-\frac{1}{3}$ for m, and −2 for x_1.*

Solve the system $\begin{cases} x = 1 \\ y - 4 = -\frac{1}{3}(x + 2) \end{cases}$ *to find the point of intersection.*

$y - 4 = -\frac{1}{3}(1 + 2)$	*Substitute 1 for x.*
$y = 3$	*Simplify.*

The coordinates of the centroid are $(1, 3)$.

Method 2: To check this answer, use a different method. By the Centroid Theorem, the centroid of a triangle is $\frac{2}{3}$ of the distance from each vertex to the midpoint of the opposite side. $\overline{CD}$ is vertical with a length of 6 units. $\frac{2}{3}(6) = 4$, and the coordinates of the point that is 4 units up from C is $(1, 3)$.

This method confirms the first answer.

Problem Solving Strategies

- Draw a Diagram
- Make a Model
- Guess and Test
- Work Backward
- Find a Pattern
- Make a Table
- Solve a Simpler Problem
- Use Logical Reasoning
- Use a Venn Diagram
- Make an Organized List

If you can't think of a different method to use to check your answer, circle the question and come back to it later.

Read each test item and answer the questions that follow.

Item A

Multiple Choice Given that ℓ is the perpendicular bisector of $\overline{AB}$, $AC = 3n + 1$, and $BC = 6n - 11$, what is the value of n?

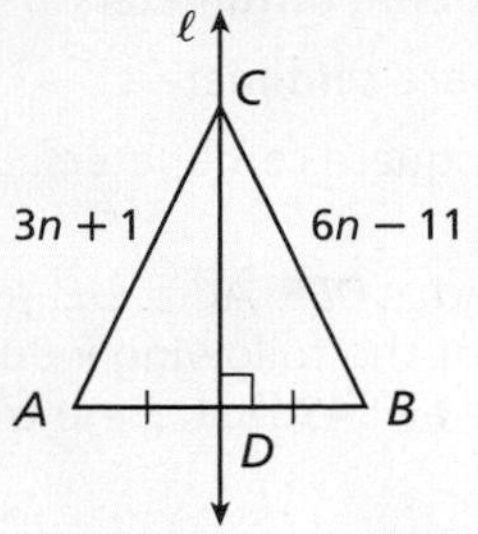

Ⓐ -4　Ⓒ $\frac{4}{3}$

Ⓑ $\frac{3}{4}$　Ⓓ 4

1. How can you use the given answer choices to solve this problem?
2. Describe how to solve this problem differently.

Item B

Multiple Choice Which number forms a Pythagorean triple with 15 and 17?

Ⓕ 5　Ⓗ 8

Ⓖ 7　Ⓙ 10

3. How can you use the given answer choices to find the answer?
4. Describe a different method you can use to check your answer.

Item C

Gridded Response Find the area of the square in square centimeters.

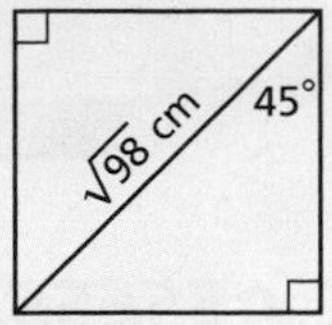

5. How can you use special right triangles to answer this question?
6. Explain how you can check your answer by using the Pythagorean Theorem.

Item D

Short Response Do the ordered pairs $A(-8, 4)$, $B(0, -2)$, and $C(8, 4)$ form a right triangle? Explain your answer.

7. Explain how to use slope to determine if $\triangle ABC$ is a right triangle.
8. How can you use the Converse of the Pythagorean Theorem to check your answer?

Item E

Short Response Find the orthocenter of $\triangle RST$. Show your work.

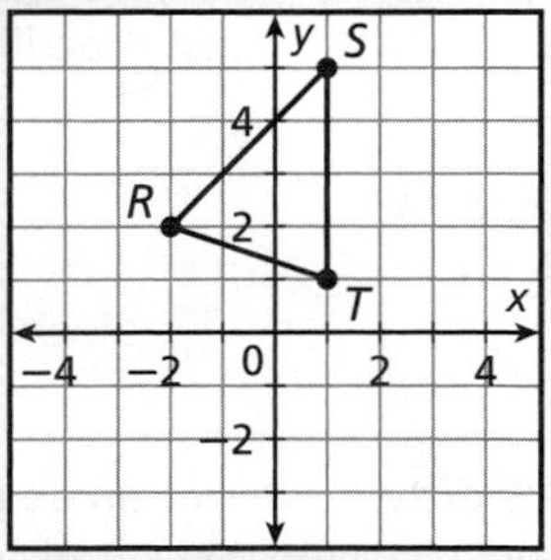

9. Describe how you would solve this problem.
10. How can you use the third altitude of the triangle to confirm that your answer is correct?

CHAPTER 5

STANDARDIZED TEST PREP

Learn It Online
State Test Practice

CUMULATIVE ASSESSMENT

Multiple Choice

1. $\overline{GJ}$ is a midsegment of $\triangle DEF$, and $\overline{HK}$ is a midsegment of $\triangle GFJ$. What is the length of $\overline{HK}$?

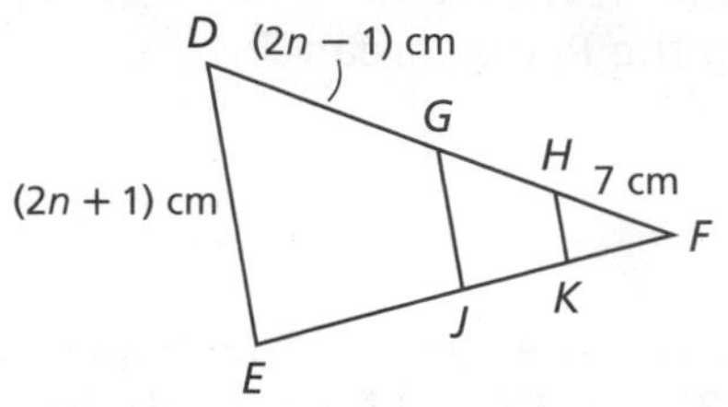

Ⓐ 2.25 centimeters

Ⓑ 4 centimeters

Ⓒ 7.5 centimeters

Ⓓ 9 centimeters

2. In $\triangle RST$, $SR < ST$, and $RT > ST$. If $m\angle R = (2x + 10)°$ and $m\angle T = (3x - 25)°$, which is a possible value of x?

Ⓕ 25 Ⓗ 35

Ⓖ 30 Ⓙ 40

3. The vertex angle of an isosceles triangle measures $(7a - 2)°$, and one of the base angles measures $(4a + 1)°$. Which term best describes this triangle?

Ⓐ Acute

Ⓑ Equiangular

Ⓒ Right

Ⓓ Obtuse

4. The lengths of two sides of an acute triangle are 8 inches and 10 inches. Which of the following could be the length of the third side?

Ⓕ 5 inches Ⓗ 12 inches

Ⓖ 6 inches Ⓙ 13 inches

5. For the coordinates $M(-1, 0)$, $N(-2, 2)$, $P(10, y)$, and $Q(4, 6)$, $\overline{MN} \parallel \overline{PQ}$. What is the value of y?

Ⓐ −18 Ⓒ 6

Ⓑ −6 Ⓓ 18

6. What is the area of an equilateral triangle that has a perimeter of 18 centimeters?

Ⓕ 9 square centimeters

Ⓖ $9\sqrt{3}$ square centimeters

Ⓗ 18 square centimeters

Ⓙ $18\sqrt{3}$ square centimeters

7. In $\triangle ABC$ and $\triangle DEF$, $\overline{AC} \cong \overline{DE}$, and $\angle A \cong \angle E$. Which of the following would allow you to conclude by SAS that these triangles are congruent?

Ⓐ $\overline{AB} \cong \overline{DF}$

Ⓑ $\overline{AC} \cong \overline{EF}$

Ⓒ $\overline{BA} \cong \overline{FE}$

Ⓓ $\overline{CB} \cong \overline{DF}$

8. For the segment below, $AB = \frac{1}{2}AC$, and $CD = 2BC$. Which expression is equal to the length of $\overline{AD}$?

Ⓕ $2AB + BC$

Ⓖ $2AC + AB$

Ⓗ $3AB$

Ⓙ $4BC$

9. In $\triangle DEF$, $m\angle D = 2(m\angle E + m\angle F)$. Which term best describes $\triangle DEF$?

Ⓐ Acute

Ⓑ Equiangular

Ⓒ Right

Ⓓ Obtuse

10. Which point of concurrency is always located inside the triangle?

Ⓕ The centroid of an obtuse triangle

Ⓖ The circumcenter of an obtuse triangle

Ⓗ The circumcenter of a right triangle

Ⓙ The orthocenter of a right triangle

HOT TIP! If a diagram is not provided, draw your own. Use the given information to label the diagram.

11. The length of one leg of a right triangle is 3 times the length of the other, and the length of the hypotenuse is 10. What is the length of the longest leg?

(A) 3 (C) $\sqrt{10}$

(B) $3\sqrt{10}$ (D) $12\sqrt{5}$

12. Which statement is true by the Transitive Property of Congruence?

(F) If $\angle A \cong \angle T$, then $\angle T \cong \angle A$.

(G) If $m\angle L = m\angle S$, then $\angle L \cong \angle S$.

(H) $5QR + 10 = 5(QR + 2)$

(J) If $\overline{BD} \cong \overline{DE}$ and $\overline{DE} \cong \overline{EF}$, then $\overline{BD} \cong \overline{EF}$.

Gridded Response

13. P is the incenter of $\triangle JKL$. The distance from P to $\overline{KL}$ is $2y - 9$. What is the distance from P to $\overline{JK}$?

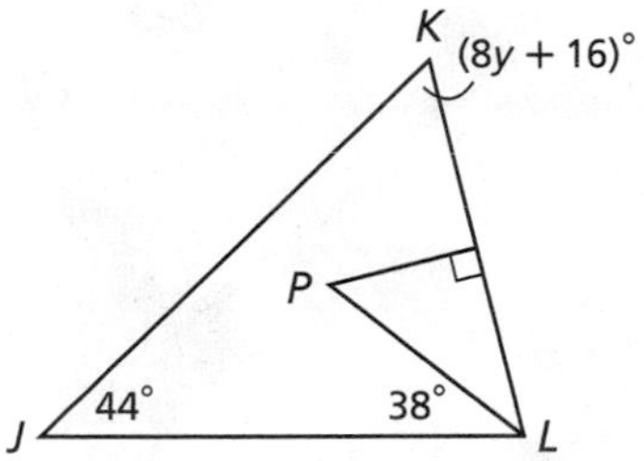

14. In a plane, $r \parallel s$, and $s \perp t$. How many right angles are formed by the lines r, s, and t?

15. What is the measure, in degrees, of $\angle H$?

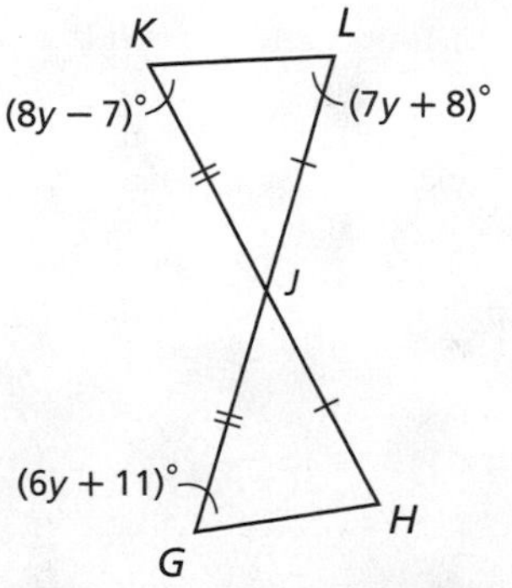

16. The point T is in the interior of $\angle XYZ$. If $m\angle XYZ = (25x + 10)°$, $m\angle XYT = 90°$, and $m\angle TYZ = (9x)°$, what is the value of x?

Short Response

17. In $\triangle RST$, S is on the perpendicular bisector of $\overline{RT}$, $m\angle S = (4n + 16)°$, and $m\angle R = (3n - 18)°$. Find $m\angle R$. Show your work and explain how you determined your answer.

18. Given that $\overline{BD} \parallel \overline{AC}$ and $\overline{AB} \cong \overline{BD}$, explain why $AC < DC$.

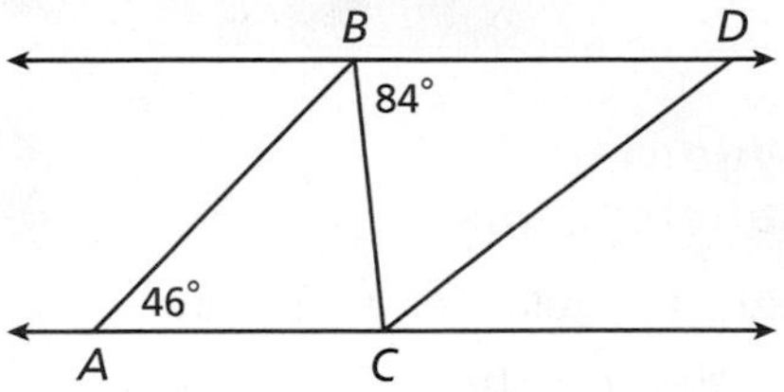

19. Write an indirect proof that an acute triangle cannot contain a pair of complementary angles.

Given: $\triangle XYZ$ is an acute triangle.

Prove: $\triangle XYZ$ does not contain a pair of complementary angles.

20. Find the coordinates of the orthocenter of $\triangle JKL$. Show your work and explain how you found your answer.

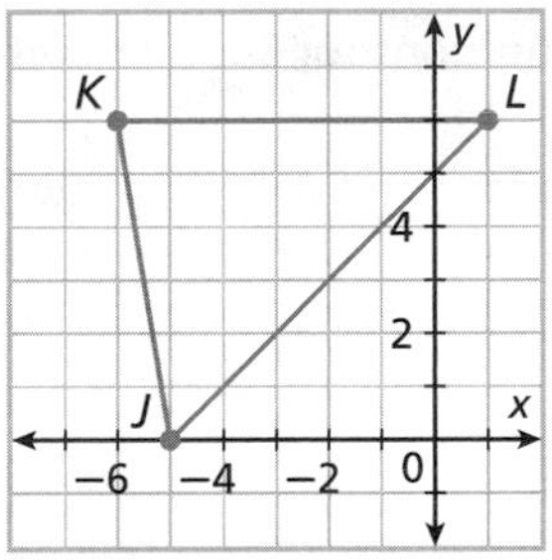

Extended Response

21. Consider the statement "If a triangle is equiangular, then it is acute."

a. Write the converse, inverse, and contrapositive of this conditional statement.

b. Write a biconditional statement from the conditional statement.

c. Determine the truth value of the biconditional statement. If it is false, give a counterexample.

d. Determine the truth value of each statement below. Give an example or counterexample to justify your reasoning.

"For any conditional, if the inverse and contrapositive are true, then the biconditional is true."

"For any conditional, if the inverse and converse are true, then the biconditional is true."

CHAPTER 6

Polygons and Quadrilaterals

COMMON CORE

Chapter

- Apply the properties of regular polygons to solve real-world problems.
- Justify and apply the properties of special parallelograms.

Divide and Conquer

Some of the trickiest puzzles are based on simple polygonal shapes. You can use polygons to solve and create a variety of puzzles.

Learn It Online
Chapter Project Online

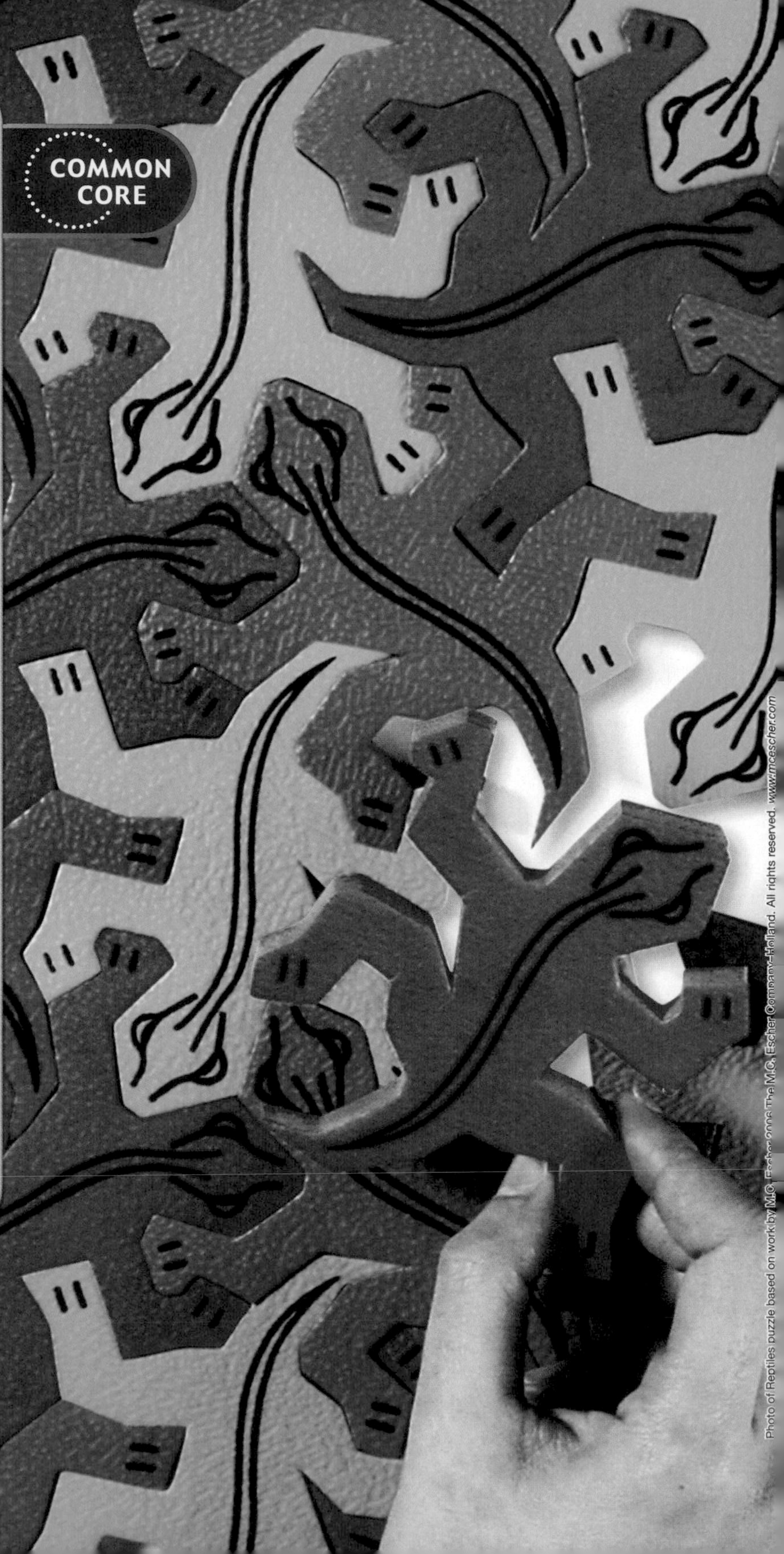

ARE YOU READY?

Vocabulary

Match each term on the left with a definition on the right.

1. exterior angle
2. parallel lines
3. perpendicular lines
4. polygon
5. quadrilateral

A. lines that intersect to form right angles

B. lines in the same plane that do not intersect

C. two angles of a polygon that share a side

D. a closed plane figure formed by three or more segments that intersect only at their endpoints

E. a four-sided polygon

F. an angle formed by one side of a polygon and the extension of a consecutive side

Triangle Sum Theorem

Find the value of x.

6. 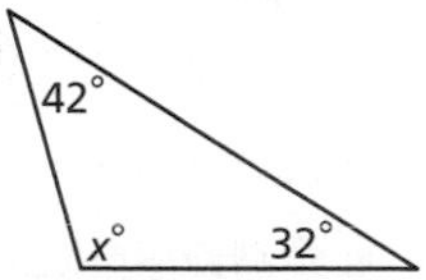

7. 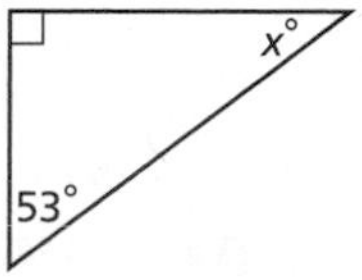

8. 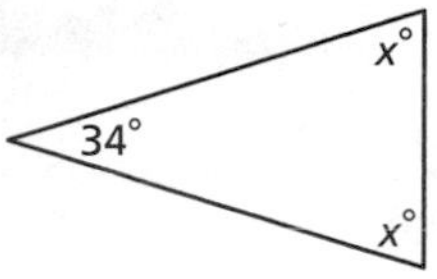

9. 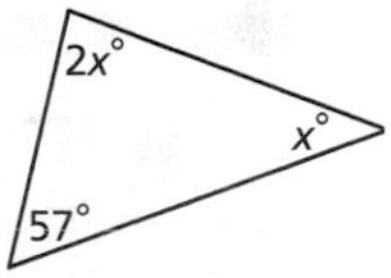

Parallel Lines and Transversals

Find the measure of each numbered angle.

10. 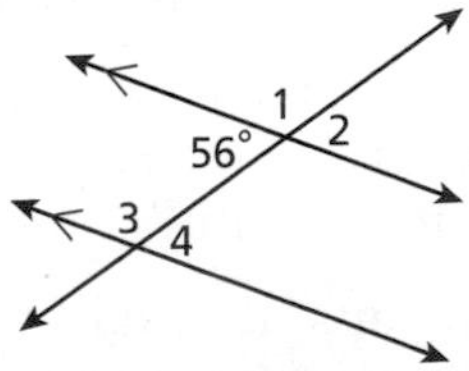

11. 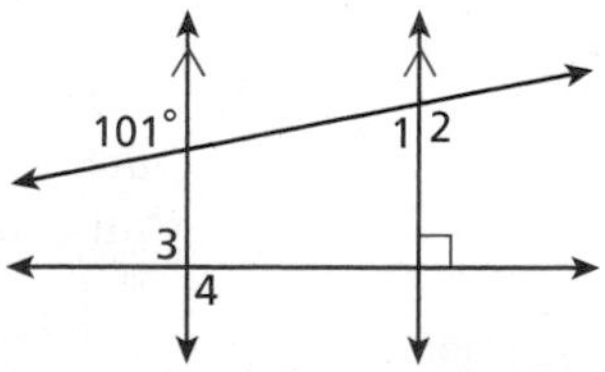

12. 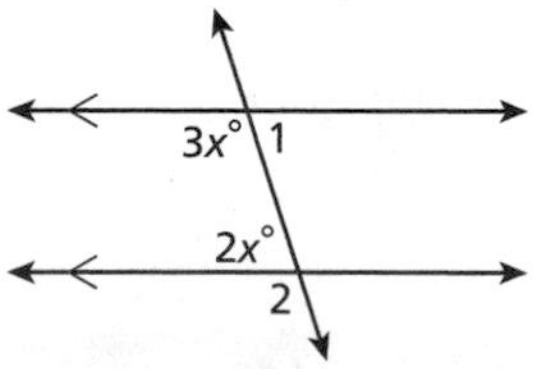

Special Right Triangles

Find the value of x. Give the answer in simplest radical form.

13. 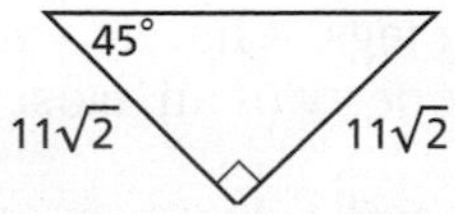

14. 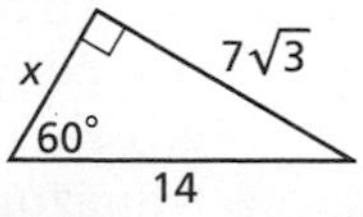

15. 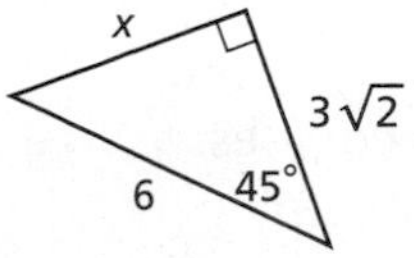

16. 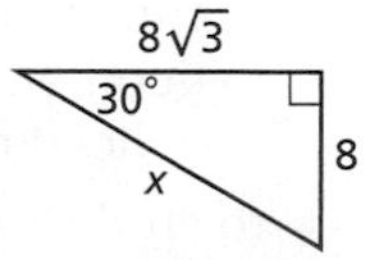

Conditional Statements

Tell whether the given statement is true or false. Write the converse. Tell whether the converse is true or false.

17. If two angles form a linear pair, then they are supplementary.

18. If two angles are congruent, then they are right angles.

19. If a triangle is a scalene triangle, then it is an acute triangle.

CHAPTER 6

Study Guide: Preview

Where You've Been

Previously, you

- learned properties of triangles.
- studied properties of parallel and perpendicular lines.
- classified triangles based on their side lengths and angle measures.
- wrote proofs involving congruent triangles.

In This Chapter

You will study

- properties of polygons.
- properties of special quadrilaterals.
- how to show that a polygon is a special quadrilateral.
- how to write proofs involving special quadrilaterals.

Where You're Going

You can use the skills learned in this chapter

- to find areas and volumes in geometry, algebra, and advanced math courses.
- to study motion and mechanics in physics courses.
- to use devices such as cameras and binoculars and to work on hobbies and craft projects outside of school.

Key Vocabulary/Vocabulario

concave	cóncavo
diagonal	diagonal
isosceles trapezoid	trapecio isósceles
kite	cometa
parallelogram	paralelogramo
rectangle	rectángulo
regular polygon	polígono regular
rhombus	rombo
square	cuadrado
trapezoid	trapecio

Vocabulary Connections

To become familiar with some of the vocabulary terms in the chapter, consider the following. You may refer to the chapter, the glossary, or a dictionary if you like.

1. The word **concave** is made up of two parts: *con* and *cave*. Sketch a polygon that looks like it caves in.
2. In Greek, *dia* means "through" or "across," and *gonia* means "angle" or "corner." How can you use these meanings to understand the term **diagonal** ?
3. If a triangle is *isosceles*, then it has two congruent legs. What do you think is a special property of an **isosceles trapezoid** ?
4. A **parallelogram** has four sides. What do you think is a special property of the sides of a parallelogram?
5. One of the meanings of the word *regular* is "orderly." What do you think the term **regular polygon** means?

Reading and Writing Math

Writing Strategy: Write a Convincing Argument

Throughout this book, the icon identifies exercises that require you to write an explanation or argument to support an idea. Your response to a Write About It exercise shows that you have a solid understanding of the mathematical concept.

To be effective, a written argument should contain

- a clear statement of your mathematical claim.
- evidence or reasoning that supports your claim.

Example

36. Write About It An isosceles triangle has two congruent sides. Does it also have two congruent midsegments? Explain.

Step 1 **Make a statement of your mathematical claim.**

Draw a sketch to investigate the properties of the midsegments of an isosceles triangle. You will find that the midsegments parallel to the legs of the isosceles triangle are congruent.

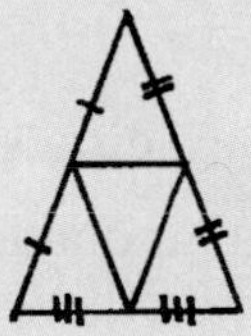

Claim: The midsegments parallel to the legs of an isosceles triangle are congruent.

Step 2 **Give evidence to support your claim.**

Identify any properties or theorems that support your claim. In this case, the Triangle Midsegment Theorem states that the length of a midsegment of a triangle is $\frac{1}{2}$ the length of the parallel side.

To clarify your argument, label your diagram and use it in your response.

Step 3 **Write a complete response.**

Yes, the two midsegments parallel to the legs of an isosceles triangle are congruent. Suppose $\triangle ABC$ is isosceles with $\overline{AB} \cong \overline{AC}$. $\overline{XZ}$ and $\overline{YZ}$ are midsegments of $\triangle ABC$. By the Triangle Midsegment Theorem, $XZ = \frac{1}{2}AC$ and $YZ = \frac{1}{2}AB$. Since $\overline{AB} \cong \overline{AC}$, $AB = AC$. So $\frac{1}{2}AB = \frac{1}{2}AC$ by the Multiplication Property of Equality. By substitution, $XZ = YZ$, so $\overline{XZ} \cong \overline{YZ}$.

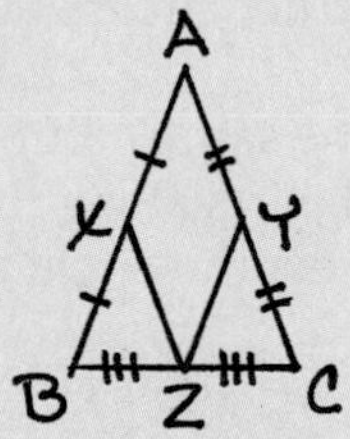

Try This

Write a convincing argument.

1. Compare the circumcenter and the incenter of a triangle.
2. If you know the side lengths of a triangle, how do you determine which angle is the largest?

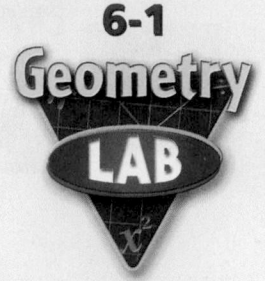

6-1 Geometry LAB

Construct Regular Polygons

Use with *Properties and Attributes of Polygons*

An equilateral triangle is a triangle with three congruent sides. You also learned that an equilateral triangle is equiangular, meaning that all its angles are congruent.

In this lab, you will construct polygons that are both equilateral and equiangular by inscribing them in circles.

MATHEMATICAL PRACTICES **Use appropriate tools strategically.**

CC.9-12.G.CO.13 Construct an equilateral triangle, a square, and a regular hexagon inscribed in a circle.

Activity 1

1. Construct circle *P*. Draw a diameter $\overline{AC}$.
2. Construct the perpendicular bisector of $\overline{AC}$. Label the intersections of the bisector and the circle as *B* and *D*.
3. Draw $\overline{AB}$, $\overline{BC}$, $\overline{CD}$, and $\overline{DA}$. The polygon *ABCD* is a *regular quadrilateral.* This means it is a four-sided polygon that has four congruent sides and four congruent angles.

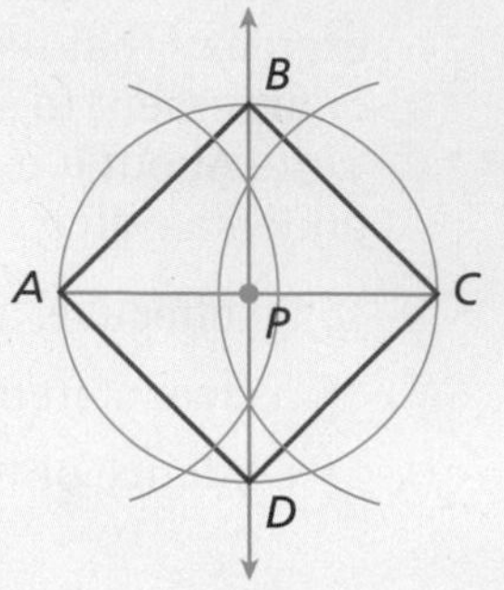

Try This

1. Describe a different method for constructing a regular quadrilateral.
2. The regular quadrilateral in Activity 1 is inscribed in the circle. What is the relationship between the circle and the regular quadrilateral?
3. A *regular octagon* is an eight-sided polygon that has eight congruent sides and eight congruent angles. Use angle bisectors to construct a regular octagon from a regular quadrilateral.

Activity 2

1. Construct circle *P*. Draw a point *A* on the circle.
2. Use the same compass setting. Starting at *A*, draw arcs to mark off equal parts along the circle. Label the other points where the arcs intersect the circle as *B, C, D, E,* and *F.*
3. Draw $\overline{AB}$, $\overline{BC}$, $\overline{CD}$, $\overline{DE}$, $\overline{EF}$, and $\overline{FA}$. The polygon *ABCDEF* is a *regular hexagon.* This means it is a six-sided polygon that has six congruent sides and six congruent angles.

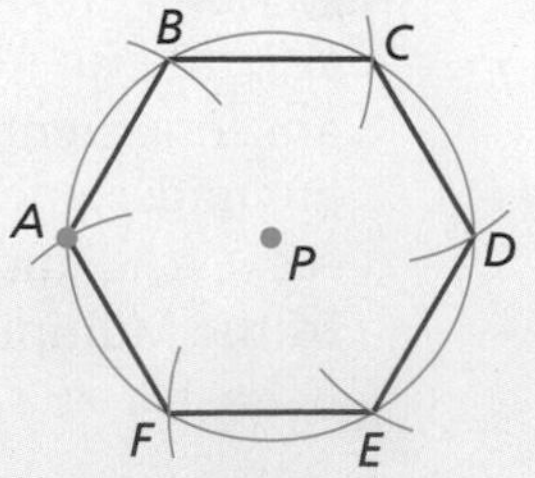

Try This

4. Justify the conclusion that *ABCDEF* is a regular hexagon. (*Hint:* Draw diameters $\overline{AD}$, $\overline{BE}$, and $\overline{CF}$. What types of triangles are formed?)
5. A *regular dodecagon* is a 12-sided polygon that has 12 congruent sides and 12 congruent angles. Use the construction of a regular hexagon to construct a regular dodecagon. Explain your method.

Activity 3

1 Construct circle P. Draw a diameter $\overline{AB}$.

2 Construct the perpendicular bisector of $\overline{AB}$. Label one point where the bisector intersects the circle as point E.

3 Construct the midpoint of radius $\overline{PB}$. Label it as point C.

4 Set your compass to the length CE. Place the compass point at C and draw an arc that intersects $\overline{AB}$. Label the point of intersection D.

5 Set the compass to the length ED. Starting at E, draw arcs to mark off equal parts along the circle. Label the other points where the arcs intersect the circle as F, G, H, and J.

6 Draw $\overline{EF}$, $\overline{FG}$, $\overline{GH}$, $\overline{HJ}$, and $\overline{JE}$. The polygon $EFGHJ$ is a *regular pentagon.* This means it is a five-sided polygon that has five congruent sides and five congruent angles.

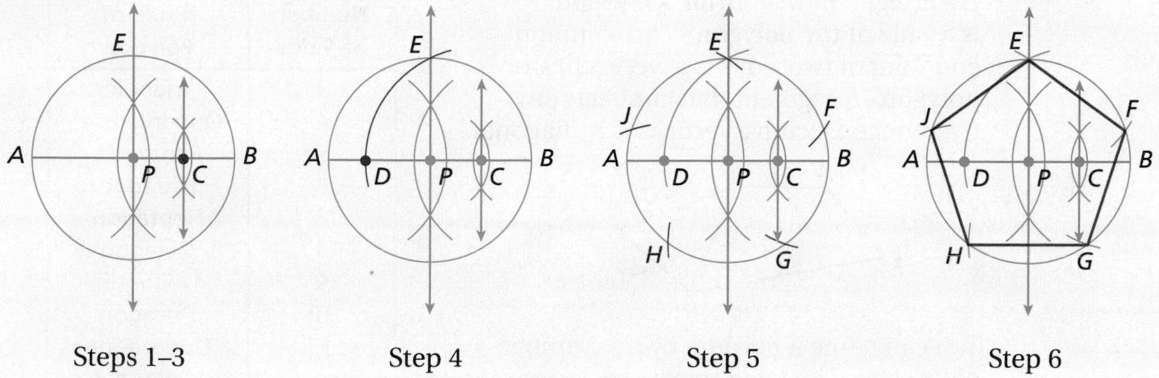

Try This

6. A *regular decagon* is a ten-sided polygon that has ten congruent sides and ten congruent angles. Use the construction of a regular pentagon to construct a regular decagon. Explain your method.

7. Measure each angle of the regular polygons in Activities 1–3 and complete the following table.

REGULAR POLYGONS				
Number of Sides	3	4	5	6
Measure of Each Angle	60°			
Sum of Angle Measures	180°			

8. Make a Conjecture What is a general rule for finding the sum of the angle measures in a regular polygon with n sides?

9. Make a Conjecture What is a general rule for finding the measure of each angle in a regular polygon with n sides?

COMMON CORE

6-1 Properties and Attributes of Polygons

CC.9-12.G.CO.11 Prove theorems about parallelograms.

Objectives

Classify polygons based on their sides and angles.

Find and use the measures of interior and exterior angles of polygons.

Vocabulary

side of a polygon
vertex of a polygon
diagonal
regular polygon
concave
convex

Why learn this?

The opening that lets light into a camera lens is created by an aperture, a set of blades whose edges may form a polygon. (See Example 5.)

You have learned the definition of a polygon. Now you will learn about the parts of a polygon and about ways to classify polygons.

Each segment that forms a polygon is a **side of the polygon**. The common endpoint of two sides is a **vertex of the polygon**. A segment that connects any two nonconsecutive vertices is a **diagonal**.

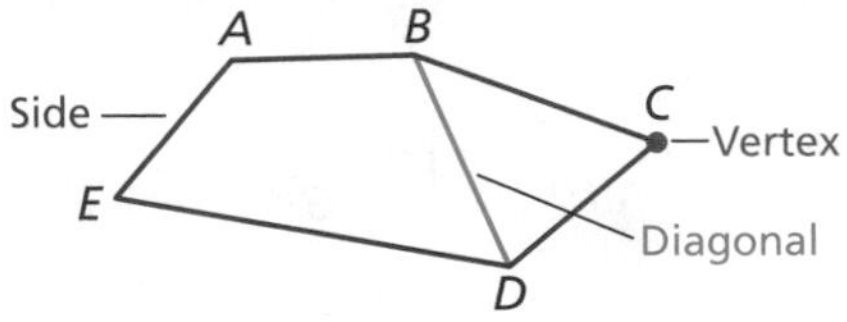

You can name a polygon by the number of its sides. The table shows the names of some common polygons. Polygon *ABCDE* is a pentagon.

Number of Sides	Name of Polygon
3	Triangle
4	Quadrilateral
5	Pentagon
6	Hexagon
7	Heptagon
8	Octagon
9	Nonagon
10	Decagon
12	Dodecagon
n	*n*-gon

Remember!

A polygon is a closed plane figure formed by three or more segments that intersect only at their endpoints.

EXAMPLE 1 Identifying Polygons

Tell whether each figure is a polygon. If it is a polygon, name it by the number of its sides.

A

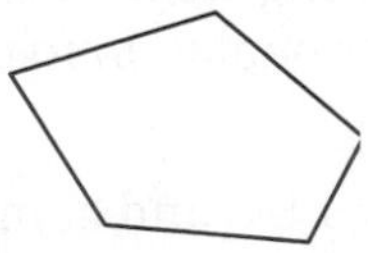

polygon, pentagon

B

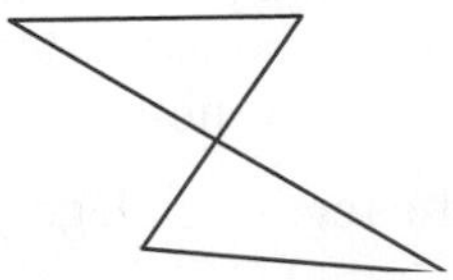

not a polygon

C

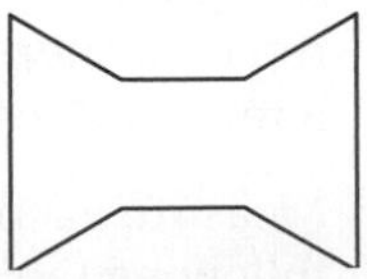

polygon, octagon

CHECK IT OUT! **Tell whether each figure is a polygon. If it is a polygon, name it by the number of its sides.**

1a.

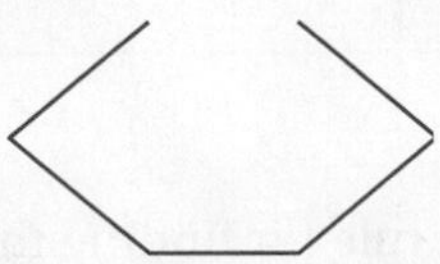

1b.

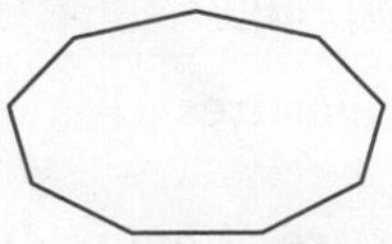

1c.

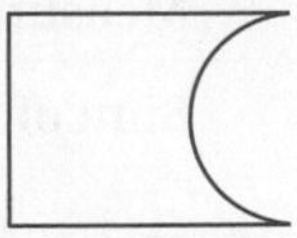

All the sides are congruent in an equilateral polygon. All the angles are congruent in an equiangular polygon. A **regular polygon** is one that is both equilateral and equiangular. If a polygon is not regular, it is called irregular.

A polygon is **concave** if any part of a diagonal contains points in the exterior of the polygon. If no diagonal contains points in the exterior, then the polygon is **convex**. A regular polygon is always convex.

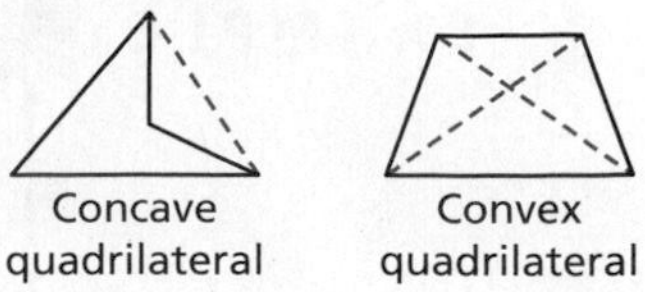

EXAMPLE 2 Classifying Polygons

Tell whether each polygon is regular or irregular. Tell whether it is concave or convex.

A

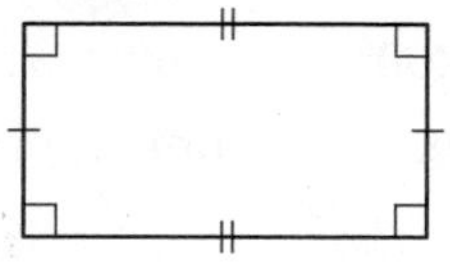

irregular, convex

B

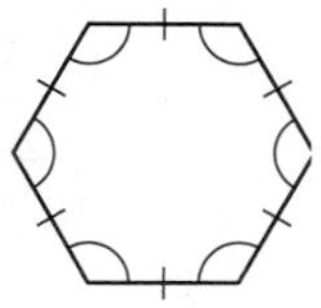

regular, convex

C

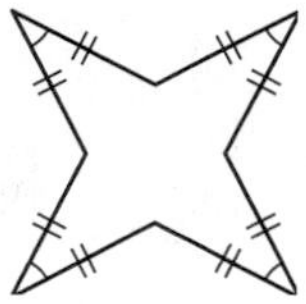

irregular, concave

CHECK IT OUT! **Tell whether each polygon is regular or irregular. Tell whether it is concave or convex.**

2a.

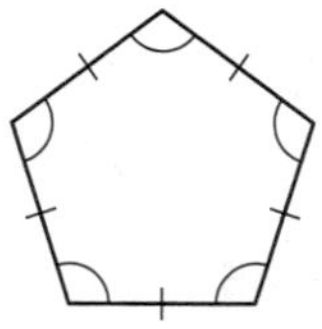

2b.

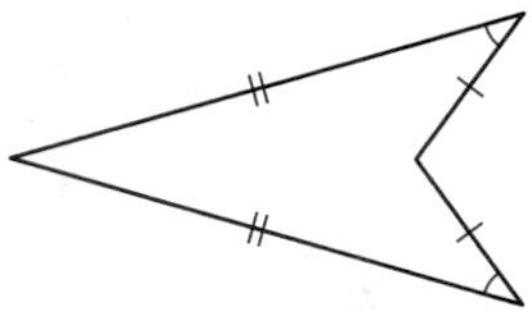

Remember!

By the Triangle Sum Theorem, the sum of the interior angle measures of a triangle is 180°.

To find the sum of the interior angle measures of a convex polygon, draw all possible diagonals from one vertex of the polygon. This creates a set of triangles. The sum of the angle measures of all the triangles equals the sum of the angle measures of the polygon.

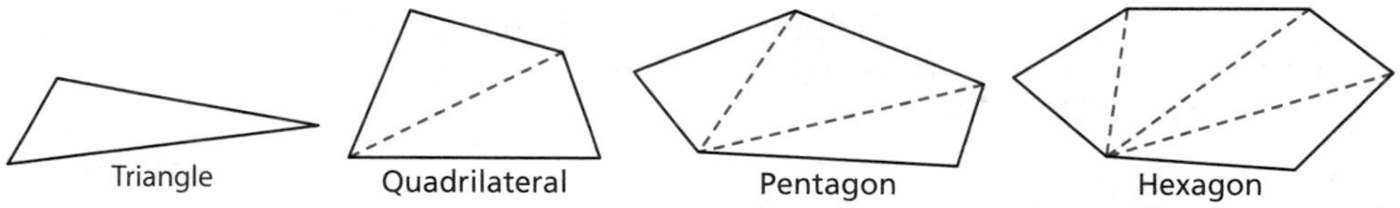

Polygon	Number of Sides	Number of Triangles	Sum of Interior Angle Measures
Triangle	3	1	$(1)180° = 180°$
Quadrilateral	4	2	$(2)180° = 360°$
Pentagon	5	3	$(3)180° = 540°$
Hexagon	6	4	$(4)180° = 720°$
n-gon	n	$n - 2$	$(n - 2)180°$

In each convex polygon, the number of triangles formed is two less than the number of sides n. So the sum of the angle measures of all these triangles is $(n - 2)180°$.

Know it! Note

Theorem 6-1-1 **Polygon Angle Sum Theorem**

The sum of the interior angle measures of a convex polygon with n sides is $(n - 2)180°$.

EXAMPLE 3 Finding Interior Angle Measures and Sums in Polygons

A **Find the sum of the interior angle measures of a convex octagon.**

$(n - 2)180°$ — *Polygon ∠ Sum Thm.*

$(8 - 2)180°$ — *An octagon has 8 sides, so substitute 8 for n.*

$1080°$ — *Simplify.*

B **Find the measure of each interior angle of a regular nonagon.**

Step 1 Find the sum of the interior angle measures.

$(n - 2)180°$ — *Polygon ∠ Sum Thm.*

$(9 - 2)180° = 1260°$ — *Substitute 9 for n and simplify.*

Step 2 Find the measure of one interior angle.

$\frac{1260°}{9} = 140°$ — *The int. ∠s are ≅, so divide by 9.*

Algebra

C **Find the measure of each interior angle of quadrilateral *PQRS*.**

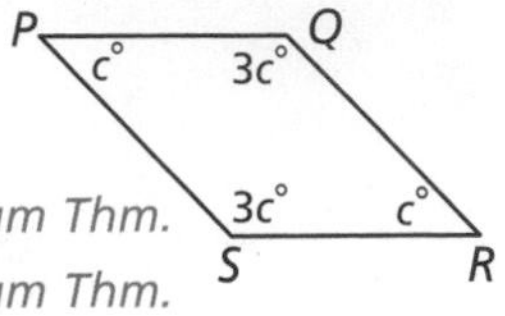

$(4 - 2)180° = 360°$ — *Polygon ∠ Sum Thm.*

$m\angle P + m\angle Q + m\angle R + m\angle S = 360°$ — *Polygon ∠ Sum Thm.*

$c + 3c + c + 3c = 360$ — *Substitute.*

$8c = 360$ — *Combine like terms.*

$c = 45$ — *Divide both sides by 8.*

$m\angle P = m\angle R = 45°$

$m\angle Q = m\angle S = 3(45°) = 135°$

CHECK IT OUT!

3a. Find the sum of the interior angle measures of a convex 15-gon.

3b. Find the measure of each interior angle of a regular decagon.

In the polygons below, an exterior angle has been measured at each vertex. Notice that in each case, the sum of the exterior angle measures is 360°.

Remember!

An exterior angle is formed by one side of a polygon and the extension of a consecutive side.

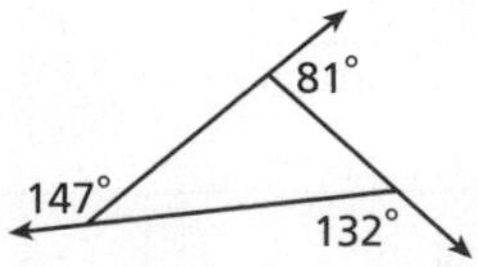

$147° + 81° + 132° = 360°$

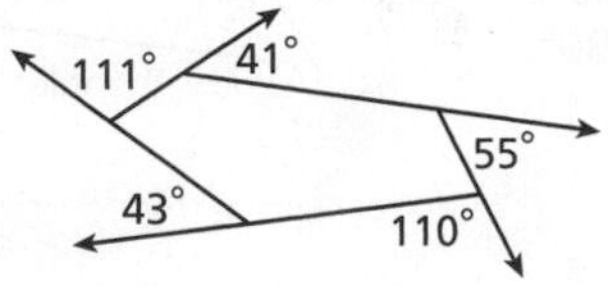

$43° + 111° + 41° + 55° + 110° = 360°$

Know it! Note

Theorem 6-1-2 Polygon Exterior Angle Sum Theorem

The sum of the exterior angle measures, one angle at each vertex, of a convex polygon is 360°.

EXAMPLE 4 Finding Exterior Angle Measures in Polygons

A **Find the measure of each exterior angle of a regular hexagon.**

A hexagon has 6 sides and 6 vertices.

sum of ext. ∠s = 360° — *Polygon Ext. ∠ Sum Thm.*

measure of one ext. $\angle = \frac{360°}{6} = 60°$ — *A regular hexagon has 6 ≅ ext. ∠s, so divide the sum by 6.*

The measure of each exterior angle of a regular hexagon is 60°.

Algebra

B **Find the value of a in polygon $RSTUV$.**

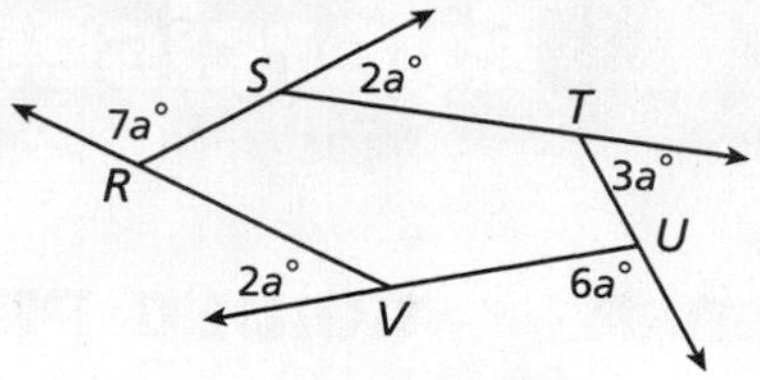

$7a° + 2a° + 3a° + 6a° + 2a° = 360°$ *Polygon Ext. ∠ Sum Thm.*

$20a = 360$ *Combine like terms.*

$a = 18$ *Divide both sides by 20.*

CHECK IT OUT!

4a. Find the measure of each exterior angle of a regular dodecagon.

4b. Find the value of r in polygon $JKLM$.

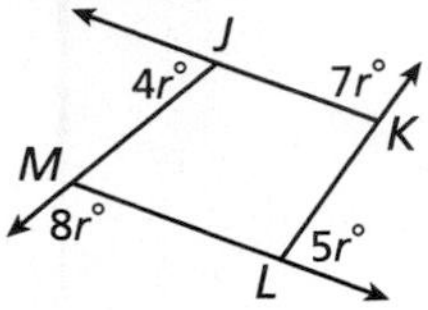

EXAMPLE 5 *Photography Application*

The aperture of the camera is formed by ten blades. The blades overlap to form a regular decagon. What is the measure of ∠CBD?

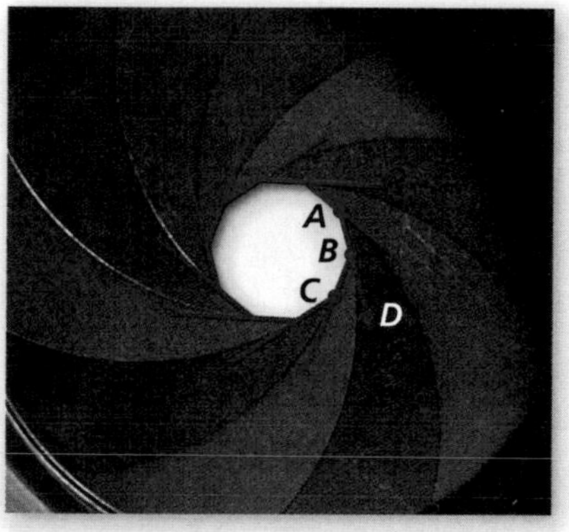

∠CBD is an exterior angle of a regular decagon. By the Polygon Exterior Angle Sum Theorem, the sum of the exterior angle measures is 360°.

$m\angle CBD = \frac{360°}{10} = 36°$ *A regular decagon has 10 ≅ ext. ∠s, so divide the sum by 10.*

CHECK IT OUT!

5. What if...? Suppose the shutter were formed by 8 blades. What would the measure of each exterior angle be?

MATHEMATICAL PRACTICES

THINK AND DISCUSS

1. Draw a concave pentagon and a convex pentagon. Explain the difference between the two figures.
2. Explain why you cannot use the expression $\frac{360°}{n}$ to find the measure of an exterior angle of an irregular n-gon.
3. Know it! Note **GET ORGANIZED** Copy and complete the graphic organizer. In each cell, write the formula for finding the indicated value for a regular convex polygon with n sides.

	Interior Angles	Exterior Angles
Sum of Angle Measures		
One Angle Measure		

6-1 Exercises

Learn It Online
Homework Help Online
Parent Resources Online

GUIDED PRACTICE

1. **Vocabulary** Explain why an equilateral polygon is not necessarily a *regular* polygon.

SEE EXAMPLE 1

Tell whether each outlined shape is a polygon. If it is a polygon, name it by the number of its sides.

2. 

3. 

4. 

5. 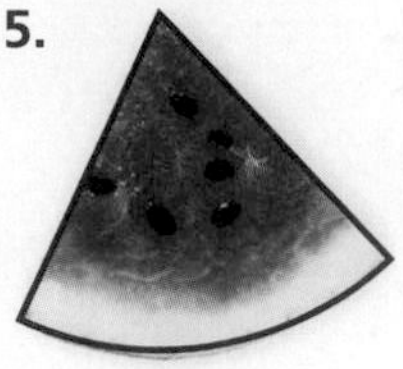

SEE EXAMPLE 2

Tell whether each polygon is regular or irregular. Tell whether it is concave or convex.

6. 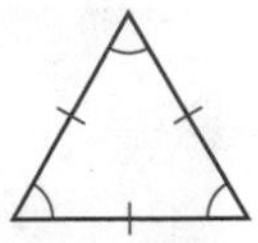

7. 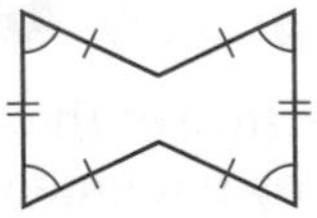

8. 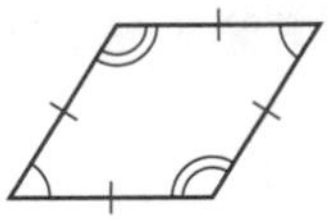

SEE EXAMPLE 3

9. Find the measure of each interior angle of pentagon *ABCDE*.

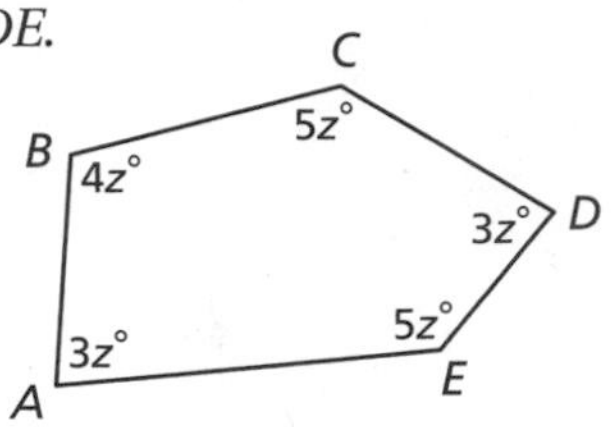

10. Find the measure of each interior angle of a regular dodecagon.

11. Find the sum of the interior angle measures of a convex 20-gon.

SEE EXAMPLE 4

12. Find the value of y in polygon *JKLM*.

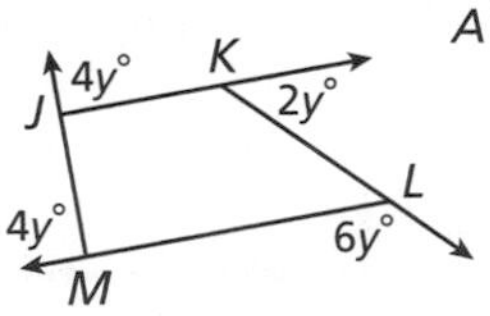

13. Find the measure of each exterior angle of a regular pentagon.

SEE EXAMPLE 5

Safety **Use the photograph of the traffic sign for Exercises 14 and 15.**

14. Name the polygon by the number of its sides.

15. In the polygon, $\angle P$, $\angle R$, and $\angle T$ are right angles, and $\angle Q \cong \angle S$. What are $m\angle Q$ and $m\angle S$?

PRACTICE AND PROBLEM SOLVING

Independent Practice	
For Exercises	See Example
16–18	1
19–21	2
22–24	3
25–26	4
27–28	5

Extra Practice

See Extra Practice for more Skills Practice and Applications Practice exercises.

Tell whether each figure is a polygon. If it is a polygon, name it by the number of its sides.

16. 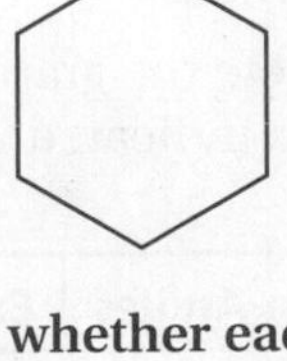

17. 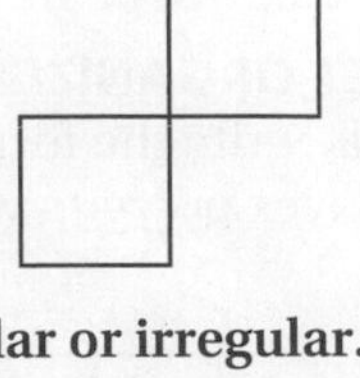

18. 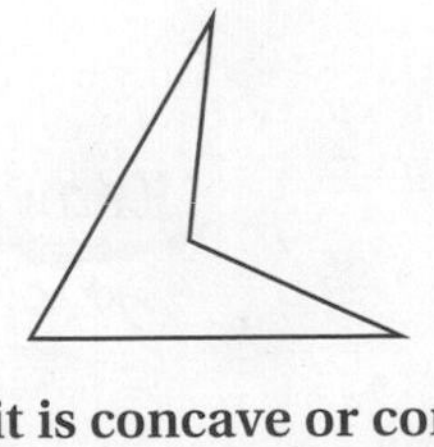

Tell whether each polygon is regular or irregular. Tell whether it is concave or convex.

19. 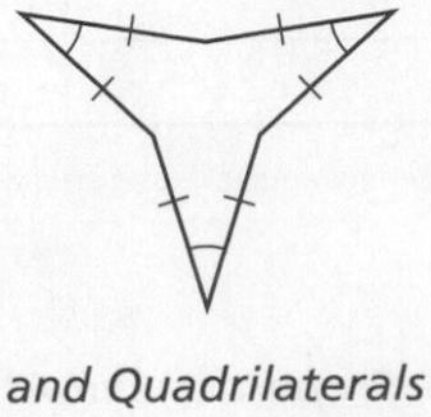

20. 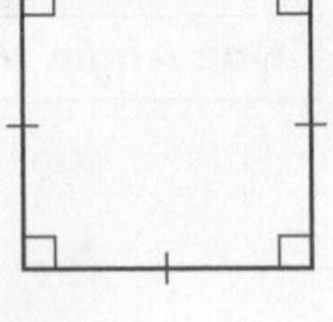

21. 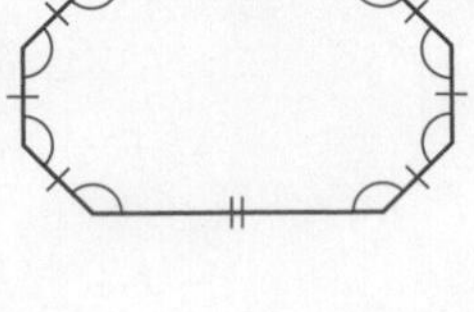

22. Find the measure of each interior angle of quadrilateral *RSTV*.

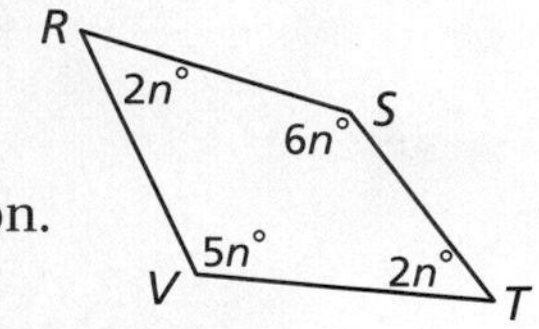

23. Find the measure of each interior angle of a regular 18-gon.

24. Find the sum of the interior angle measures of a convex heptagon.

25. Find the measure of each exterior angle of a regular nonagon.

26. A pentagon has exterior angle measures of $5a°$, $4a°$, $10a°$, $3a°$, and $8a°$. Find the value of *a*.

Crafts The folds on the lid of the gift box form a regular hexagon. Find each measure.

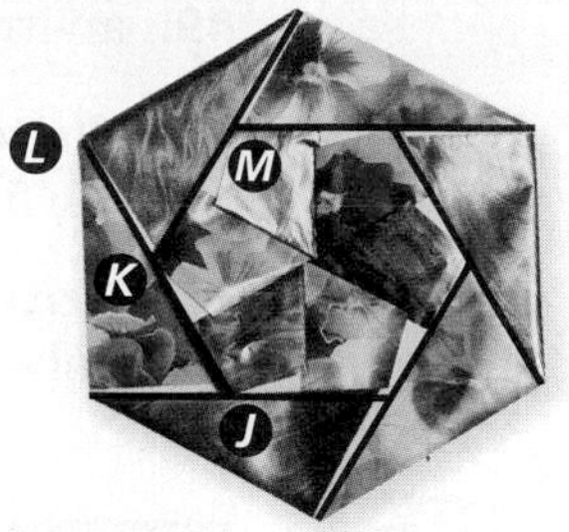

27. m∠*JKM*

28. m∠*MKL*

Algebra Find the value of *x* in each figure.

29.

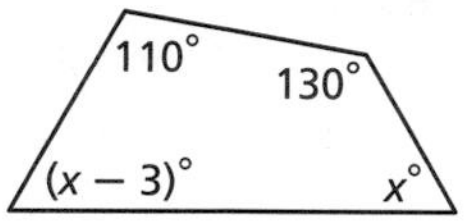

30.

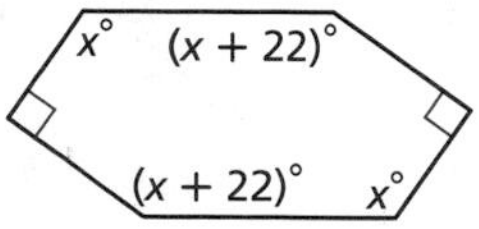

31.

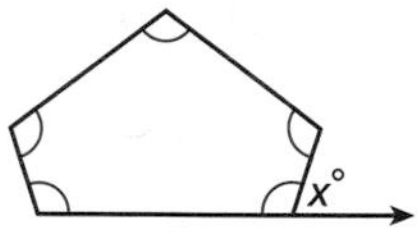

Find the number of sides a regular polygon must have to meet each condition.

32. Each interior angle measure equals each exterior angle measure.

33. Each interior angle measure is four times the measure of each exterior angle.

34. Each exterior angle measure is one eighth the measure of each interior angle.

Name the convex polygon whose interior angle measures have each given sum.

35. 540° 36. 900° 37. 1800° 38. 2520°

Multi-Step An exterior angle measure of a regular polygon is given. Find the number of its sides and the measure of each interior angle.

39. 120° 40. 72° 41. 36° 42. 24°

43. **ERROR ANALYSIS** Which conclusion is incorrect? Explain the error.

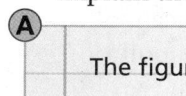

A: The figure is a polygon.

B: The figure is not a polygon.

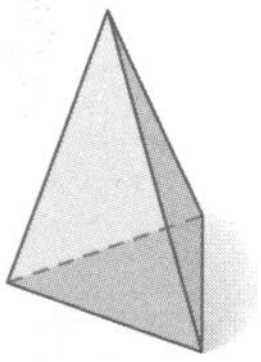

44. **Estimation** Graph the polygon formed by the points $A(-2, -6)$, $B(-4, -1)$, $C(-1, 2)$, $D(4, 0)$, and $E(3, -5)$. Estimate the measure of each interior angle. Make a conjecture about whether the polygon is equiangular. Now measure each interior angle with a protractor. Was your conjecture correct?

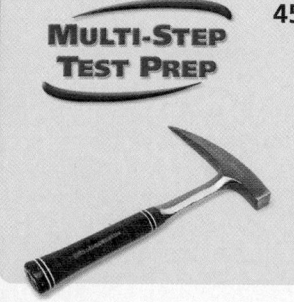

MULTI-STEP TEST PREP

45. In this quartz crystal, $m\angle A = 95°$, $m\angle B = 125°$, $m\angle E = m\angle D = 130°$, and $\angle C \cong \angle F \cong \angle G$.

a. Name polygon *ABCDEFG* by the number of sides.

b. What is the sum of the interior angle measures of *ABCDEFG*?

c. Find m∠*F*.

46. The perimeter of a regular polygon is 45 inches. The length of one side is 7.5 inches. Name the polygon by the number of its sides.

Draw an example of each figure.

47. a regular quadrilateral

48. an irregular concave heptagon

49. an irregular convex pentagon

50. an equilateral polygon that is not equiangular

51. Write About It Use the terms from the lesson to describe the figure as specifically as possible.

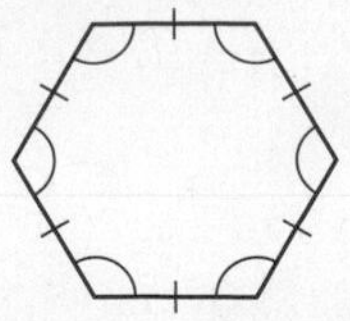

52. Critical Thinking What geometric figure does a regular polygon begin to resemble as the number of sides increases?

TEST PREP

53. Which terms describe the figure shown?

I. quadrilateral   II. concave   III. regular

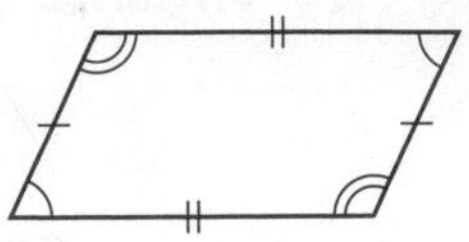

Ⓐ I only

Ⓑ II only

Ⓒ I and II

Ⓓ I and III

54. Which statement is NOT true about a regular 16-gon?

Ⓕ It is a convex polygon.

Ⓖ It has 16 congruent sides.

Ⓗ The sum of the interior angle measures is 2880°.

Ⓙ The sum of the exterior angles, one at each vertex, is 360°.

55. In polygon *ABCD*, $m\angle A = 49°$, $m\angle B = 107°$, and $m\angle C = 2m\angle D$. What is $m\angle C$?

Ⓐ 24°   Ⓑ 68°   Ⓒ 102°   Ⓓ 136°

CHALLENGE AND EXTEND

56. The interior angle measures of a convex pentagon are consecutive multiples of 4. Find the measure of each interior angle.

57. Polygon *PQRST* is a regular pentagon. Find the values of *x*, *y*, and *z*.

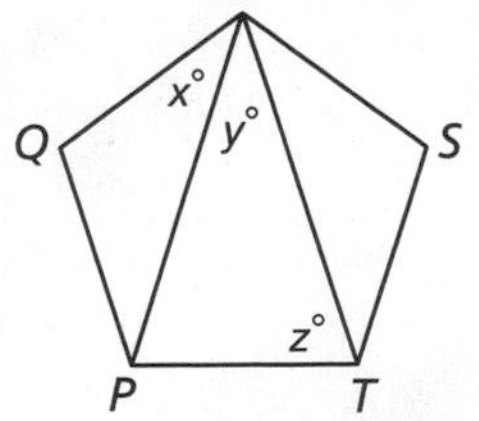

58. Multi-Step Polygon *ABCDEFGHJK* is a regular decagon. Sides $\overline{AB}$ and $\overline{DE}$ are extended so that they meet at point *L* in the exterior of the polygon. Find $m\angle BLD$.

59. Critical Thinking Does the Polygon Angle Sum Theorem work for concave polygons? Draw a sketch to support your answer.

Connecting Geometry to **Algebra**

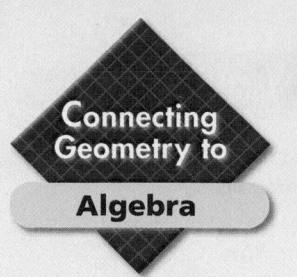

Relations and Functions

Many numeric relationships in geometry can be represented by algebraic relations. These relations may or may not be functions, depending on their domain and range.

A *relation* is a set of ordered pairs. All the first coordinates in the set of ordered pairs are the *domain* of the relation. All the second coordinates are the *range* of the relation.

A *function* is a type of relation that pairs each element in the domain with exactly one element in the range.

Example

Give the domain and range of the relation $y = \dfrac{6}{x-6}$. Tell whether the relation is a function.

Step 1 Make a table of values for the relation.

x	-6	0	5	6	7	12
y	-0.5	-1	-6	Undefined	6	1

Step 2 Plot the points and connect them with smooth curves.

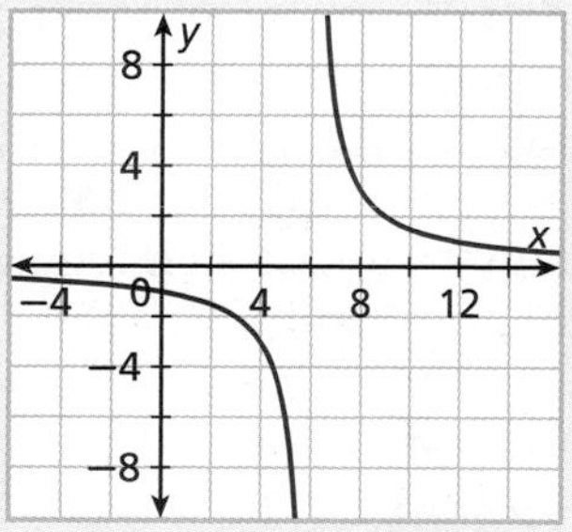

Step 3 Identify the domain and range.
Since y is undefined at $x = 6$, the domain of the relation is the set of all real numbers except 6. Since there is no x-value such that $y = 0$, the range of the relation is the set of all real numbers except 0.

Step 4 Determine whether the relation is a function.
From the graph, you can see that only one y-value exists for each x-value, so the relation is a function.

Try This

Give the domain and range of each relation. Tell whether the relation is a function.

1. $y = (x - 2)180$
2. $y = 360$
3. $y = \dfrac{(x-2)180}{x}$
4. $y = \dfrac{360}{x}$
5. $x = 3y - 10$
6. $x^2 + y^2 = 9$
7. $x = -2$
8. $y = x^2 + 4$
9. $-x + 8y = 5$

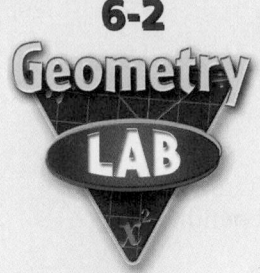

6-2 Geometry LAB

Use with Properties of Parallelograms

Explore Properties of Parallelograms

MATHEMATICAL PRACTICES Use appropriate tools strategically.

CC.9-12.G.CO.11 Prove theorems about parallelograms.

In this lab you will investigate the relationships among the angles and sides of a special type of quadrilateral called a *parallelogram*. You will need to apply the Transitive Property of Congruence. That is, if figure $A \cong$ figure B and figure $B \cong$ figure C, then figure $A \cong$ figure C.

Activity

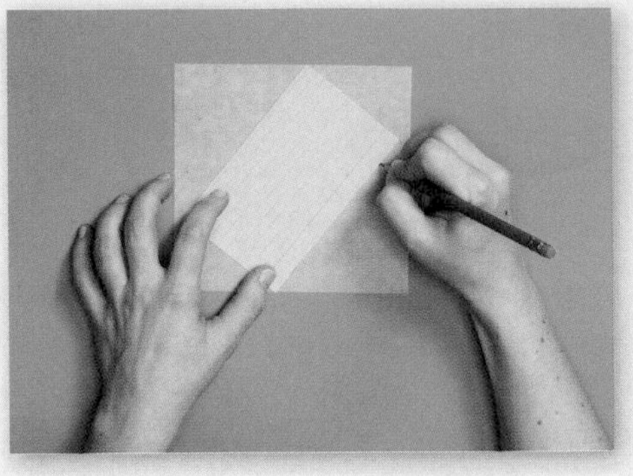

1. Use opposite sides of an index card to draw a set of parallel lines on a piece of patty paper. Then use opposite sides of a ruler to draw a second set of parallel lines that intersects the first. Label the points of intersection *A, B, C,* and *D,* in that order. Quadrilateral *ABCD* has two pairs of parallel sides. It is a *parallelogram.*

2. Place a second piece of patty paper over the first and trace *ABCD*. Label the points that correspond to *A, B, C,* and *D* as *Q, R, S,* and *T,* in that order. The parallelograms *ABCD* and *QRST* are congruent. Name all the pairs of congruent corresponding sides and angles.

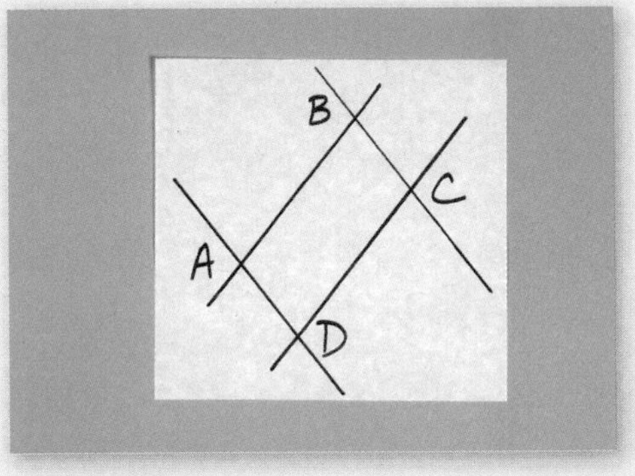

3. Lay *ABCD* over *QRST* so that $\overline{AB}$ overlays $\overline{ST}$. What do you notice about their lengths? What does this tell you about $\overline{AB}$ and $\overline{CD}$? Now move *ABCD* so that $\overline{DA}$ overlays $\overline{RS}$. What do you notice about their lengths? What does this tell you about $\overline{DA}$ and $\overline{BC}$?

4. Lay *ABCD* over *QRST* so that $\angle A$ overlays $\angle S$. What do you notice about their measures? What does this tell you about $\angle A$ and $\angle C$? Now move *ABCD* so that $\angle B$ overlays $\angle T$. What do you notice about their measures? What does this tell you about $\angle B$ and $\angle D$?

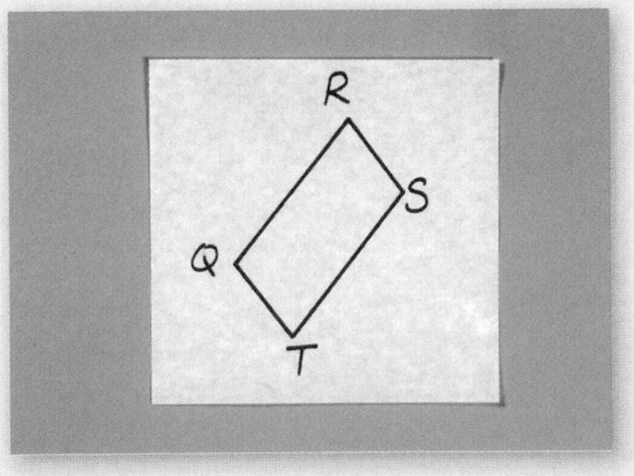

5. Arrange the pieces of patty paper so that $\overline{RS}$ overlays $\overline{AD}$. What do you notice about $\overline{QR}$ and $\overline{AB}$? What does this tell you about $\angle A$ and $\angle R$? What can you conclude about $\angle A$ and $\angle B$?

6. Draw diagonals $\overline{AC}$ and $\overline{BD}$. Fold *ABCD* so that *A* matches *C*, making a crease. Unfold the paper and fold it again so that *B* matches *D*, making another crease. What do you notice about the creases? What can you conclude about the diagonals?

Try This

1. Repeat the above steps with a different parallelogram. Do you get the same results?
2. **Make a Conjecture** How do you think the sides of a parallelogram are related to each other? the angles? the diagonals? Write your conjectures as conditional statements.

COMMON CORE

6-2 Properties of Parallelograms

CC.9-12.G.CO.11 Prove theorems about parallelograms.

Objectives
Prove and apply properties of parallelograms.
Use properties of parallelograms to solve problems.

Vocabulary
parallelogram

Who uses this?
Race car designers can use a parallelogram-shaped linkage to keep the wheels of the car vertical on uneven surfaces. (See Example 1.)

Any polygon with four sides is a quadrilateral. However, some quadrilaterals have special properties. These *special quadrilaterals* are given their own names.

Helpful Hint

Opposite sides of a quadrilateral do not share a vertex. Opposite angles do not share a side.

A quadrilateral with two pairs of parallel sides is a **parallelogram**. To write the name of a parallelogram, you use the symbol ▱.

Parallelogram *ABCD*
▱*ABCD*

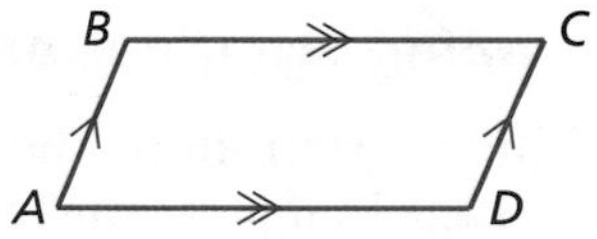

$\overline{AB} \parallel \overline{CD}$, $\overline{BC} \parallel \overline{DA}$

Know it! Note

Theorem 6-2-1 Properties of Parallelograms

THEOREM	HYPOTHESIS	CONCLUSION
If a quadrilateral is a parallelogram, then its opposite sides are congruent. (▱ → opp. sides ≅)	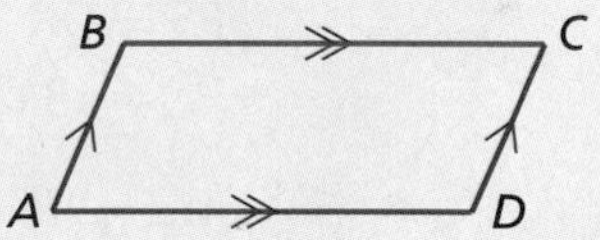	$\overline{AB} \cong \overline{CD}$ $\overline{BC} \cong \overline{DA}$

PROOF

Theorem 6-2-1

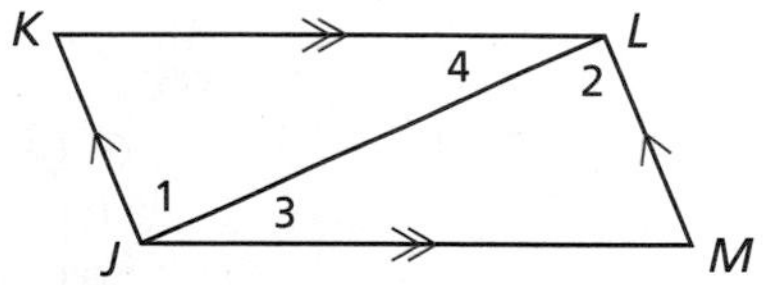

Given: *JKLM* is a parallelogram.
Prove: $\overline{JK} \cong \overline{LM}$, $\overline{KL} \cong \overline{MJ}$

Proof:

Statements	Reasons
1. *JKLM* is a parallelogram.	1. Given
2. $\overline{JK} \parallel \overline{LM}$, $\overline{KL} \parallel \overline{MJ}$	2. Def. of ▱
3. $\angle 1 \cong \angle 2$, $\angle 3 \cong \angle 4$	3. Alt. Int. ∠s Thm.
4. $\overline{JL} \cong \overline{JL}$	4. Reflex. Prop. of ≅
5. $\triangle JKL \cong \triangle LMJ$	5. ASA *Steps 3, 4*
6. $\overline{JK} \cong \overline{LM}$, $\overline{KL} \cong \overline{MJ}$	6. CPCTC

Know it! Note

Theorems Properties of Parallelograms

THEOREM		HYPOTHESIS	CONCLUSION
6-2-2	If a quadrilateral is a parallelogram, then its opposite angles are congruent. (▱ → opp. ∠s ≅)	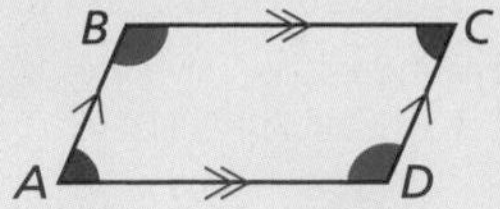	$\angle A \cong \angle C$ $\angle B \cong \angle D$
6-2-3	If a quadrilateral is a parallelogram, then its consecutive angles are supplementary. (▱ → cons. ∠s supp.)	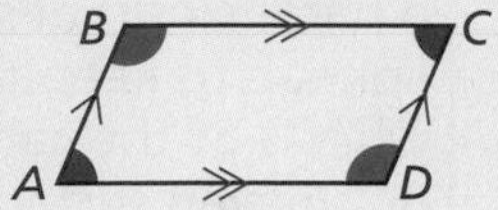	$m\angle A + m\angle B = 180°$ $m\angle B + m\angle C = 180°$ $m\angle C + m\angle D = 180°$ $m\angle D + m\angle A = 180°$
6-2-4	If a quadrilateral is a parallelogram, then its diagonals bisect each other. (▱ → diags. bisect each other)	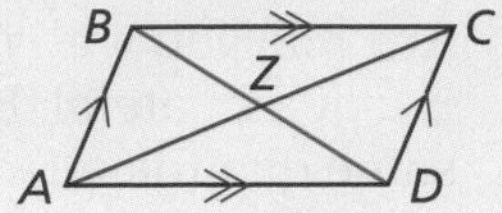	$\overline{AZ} \cong \overline{CZ}$ $\overline{BZ} \cong \overline{DZ}$

You will prove Theorems 6-2-3 and 6-2-4 in Exercises 45 and 44.

EXAMPLE 1 *Racing Application*

The diagram shows the parallelogram-shaped linkage that joins the frame of a race car to one wheel of the car. In ▱*PQRS*, *QR* = 48 cm, *RT* = 30 cm, and m∠*QPS* = 73°. Find each measure.

A *PS*

$\overline{PS} \cong \overline{QR}$ — *▱ → opp. sides ≅*

$PS = QR$ — *Def. of ≅ segs.*

$PS = 48$ cm — *Substitute 48 for QR.*

B m∠*PQR*

$m\angle PQR + m\angle QPS = 180°$ — *▱ → cons. ∠s supp.*

$m\angle PQR + 73 = 180$ — *Substitute 73 for m∠QPS.*

$m\angle PQR = 107°$ — *Subtract 73 from both sides.*

C *PT*

$\overline{PT} \cong \overline{RT}$ — *▱ → diags. bisect each other*

$PT = RT$ — *Def. of ≅ segs.*

$PT = 30$ cm — *Substitute 30 for RT.*

CHECK IT OUT! **In ▱*KLMN*, *LM* = 28 in., *LN* = 26 in., and m∠*LKN* = 74°. Find each measure.**

1a. *KN*

1b. m∠*NML*

1c. *LO*

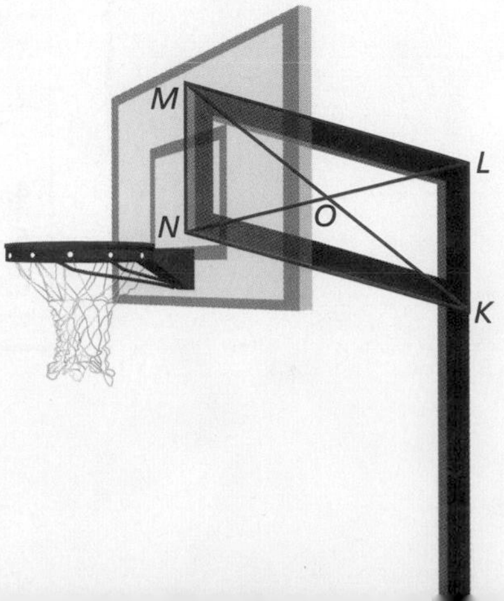

EXAMPLE 2 Using Properties of Parallelograms to Find Measures

Algebra

$ABCD$ is a parallelogram. Find each measure.

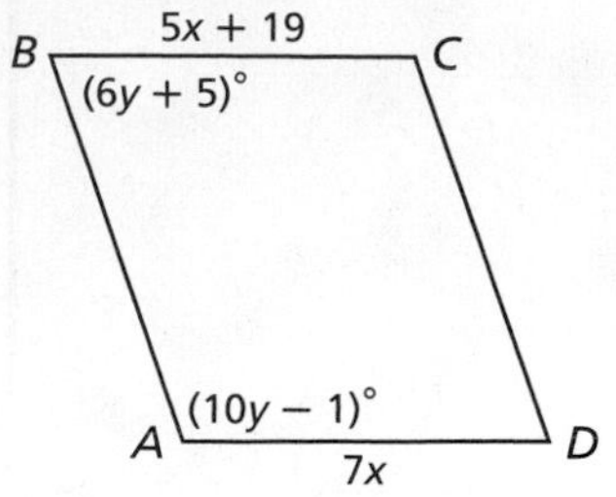

A AD

$\overline{AD} \cong \overline{BC}$	*▱ → opp. sides ≅*
$AD = BC$	*Def. of ≅ segs.*
$7x = 5x + 19$	*Substitute the given values.*
$2x = 19$	*Subtract 5x from both sides.*
$x = 9.5$	*Divide both sides by 2.*

$AD = 7x = 7(9.5) = 66.5$

B $m\angle B$

$m\angle A + m\angle B = 180°$	*▱ → cons. ∡ supp.*
$(10y - 1) + (6y + 5) = 180$	*Substitute the given values.*
$16y + 4 = 180$	*Combine like terms.*
$16y = 176$	*Subtract 4 from both sides.*
$y = 11$	*Divide both sides by 16.*

$m\angle B = (6y + 5)° = [6(11) + 5]° = 71°$

CHECK IT OUT! **$EFGH$ is a parallelogram. Find each measure.**

2a. JG

2b. FH

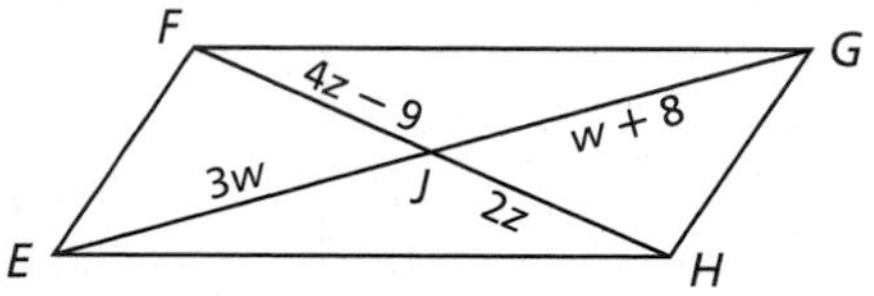

EXAMPLE 3 Parallelograms in the Coordinate Plane

Three vertices of ▱$ABCD$ are $A(1, -2)$, $B(-2, 3)$, and $D(5, -1)$. Find the coordinates of vertex C.

Since $ABCD$ is a parallelogram, both pairs of opposite sides must be parallel.

> **Remember!**
> When you are drawing a figure in the coordinate plane, the name $ABCD$ gives the order of the vertices.

Step 1 Graph the given points.

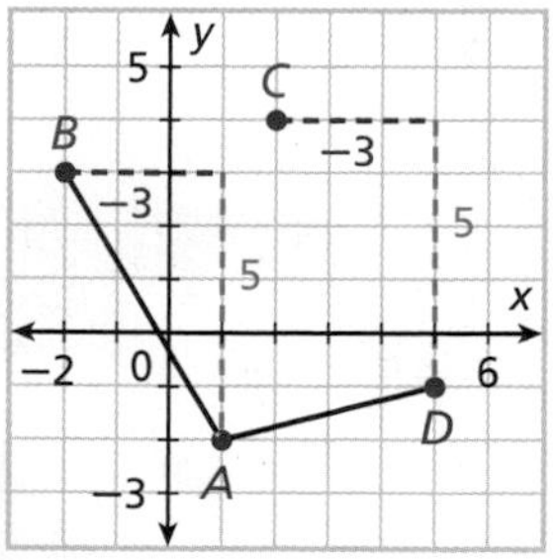

Step 2 Find the slope of $\overline{AB}$ by counting the units from A to B.
The rise from −2 to 3 is 5.
The run from 1 to −2 is −3.

Step 3 Start at D and count the same number of units.
A rise of 5 from −1 is 4.
A run of −3 from 5 is 2. Label $(2, 4)$ as vertex C.

Step 4 Use the slope formula to verify that $\overline{BC} \parallel \overline{AD}$.

$$\text{slope of } \overline{BC} = \frac{4 - 3}{2 - (-2)} = \frac{1}{4}$$

$$\text{slope of } \overline{AD} = \frac{-1 - (-2)}{5 - 1} = \frac{1}{4}$$

The coordinates of vertex C are $(2, 4)$.

CHECK IT OUT! **3.** Three vertices of ▱$PQRS$ are $P(-3, -2)$, $Q(-1, 4)$, and $S(5, 0)$. Find the coordinates of vertex R.

EXAMPLE 4 Using Properties of Parallelograms in a Proof

Write a two-column proof.

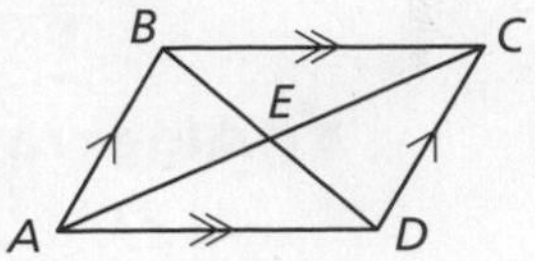

A Theorem 6-2-2

Given: *ABCD* is a parallelogram.

Prove: $\angle BAD \cong \angle DCB$, $\angle ABC \cong \angle CDA$

Proof:

Statements	Reasons
1. *ABCD* is a parallelogram.	1. Given
2. $\overline{AB} \cong \overline{CD}$, $\overline{DA} \cong \overline{BC}$	2. ▱ → opp. sides ≅
3. $\overline{BD} \cong \overline{BD}$	3. Reflex. Prop. of ≅
4. $\triangle BAD \cong \triangle DCB$	4. SSS *Steps 2, 3*
5. $\angle BAD \cong \angle DCB$	5. CPCTC
6. $\overline{AC} \cong \overline{AC}$	6. Reflex. Prop. of ≅
7. $\triangle ABC \cong \triangle CDA$	7. SSS *Steps 2, 6*
8. $\angle ABC \cong \angle CDA$	8. CPCTC

B **Given:** *GHJN* and *JKLM* are parallelograms. *H* and *M* are collinear. *N* and *K* are collinear.

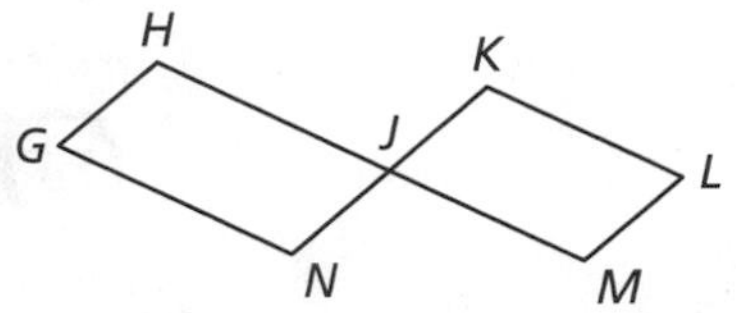

Prove: $\angle G \cong \angle L$

Proof:

Statements	Reasons
1. *GHJN* and *JKLM* are parallelograms.	1. Given
2. $\angle HJN \cong \angle G$, $\angle MJK \cong \angle L$	2. ▱ → opp. ∠s ≅
3. $\angle HJN \cong \angle MJK$	3. Vert. ∠s Thm.
4. $\angle G \cong \angle L$	4. Trans. Prop. of ≅

CHECK IT OUT!

4. Use the figure in Example 4B to write a two-column proof.
Given: *GHJN* and *JKLM* are parallelograms. *H* and *M* are collinear. *N* and *K* are collinear.
Prove: $\angle N \cong \angle K$

MATHEMATICAL PRACTICES

THINK AND DISCUSS

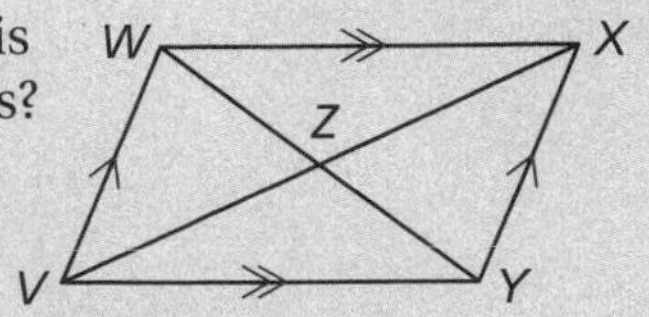

1. The measure of one angle of a parallelogram is 71°. What are the measures of the other angles?
2. In ▱*VWXY*, $VW = 21$, and $WY = 36$. Find as many other measures as you can. Justify your answers.

Know it! Note

3. **GET ORGANIZED** Copy and complete the graphic organizer. In each cell, draw a figure with markings that represents the given property.

Properties of Parallelograms				
Opp. sides ∥	Opp. sides ≅	Opp. ∠s ≅	Cons. ∠s supp.	Diags. bisect each other.

6-2 Exercises

Learn It Online
Homework Help Online
Parent Resources Online

GUIDED PRACTICE

Vocabulary **Apply the vocabulary from this lesson to answer each question.**

1. Explain why the figure at right is NOT a *parallelogram*.
2. Draw ▱*PQRS*. Name the opposite sides and opposite angles.

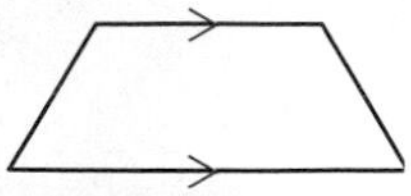

SEE EXAMPLE 1

Safety **The handrail is made from congruent parallelograms. In ▱*ABCD*, *AB* = 17.5, *DE* = 18, and m∠*BCD* = 110°. Find each measure.**

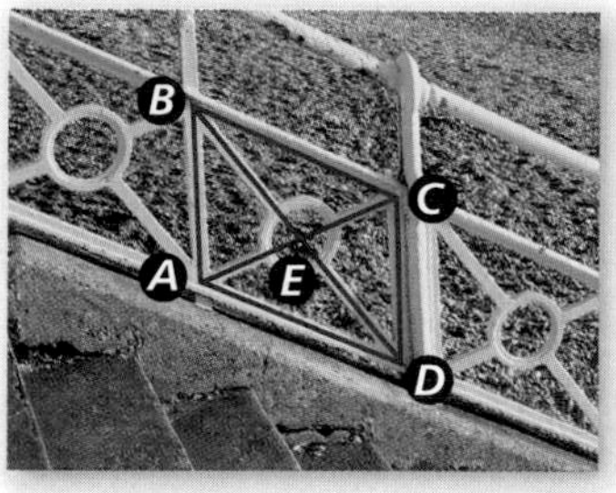

3. *BD*
4. *CD*
5. *BE*
6. m∠*ABC*
7. m∠*ADC*
8. m∠*DAB*

SEE EXAMPLE 2

JKLM **is a parallelogram. Find each measure.**

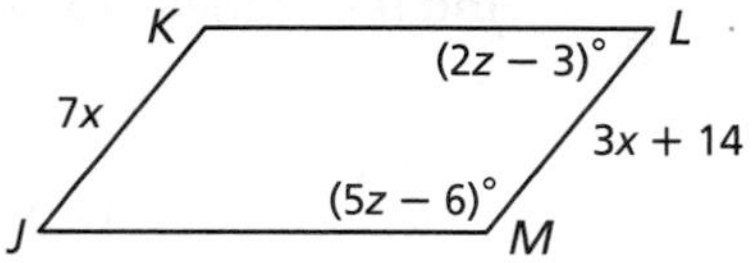

9. *JK*
10. *LM*
11. m∠*L*
12. m∠*M*

SEE EXAMPLE 3

13. **Multi-Step** Three vertices of ▱*DFGH* are *D*(−9, 4), *F*(−1, 5), and *G*(2, 0). Find the coordinates of vertex *H*.

SEE EXAMPLE 4

14. Write a two-column proof.
Given: *PSTV* is a parallelogram. $\overline{PQ} \cong \overline{RQ}$
Prove: ∠*STV* ≅ ∠*R*

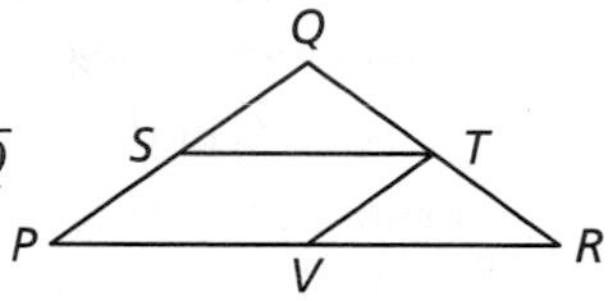

PRACTICE AND PROBLEM SOLVING

Independent Practice	
For Exercises	See Example
15–20	1
21–24	2
25	3
26	4

Extra Practice
See Extra Practice for more Skills Practice and Applications Practice exercises.

Shipping **Cranes can be used to load cargo onto ships. In ▱*JKLM*, *JL* = 165.8, *JK* = 110, and m∠*JML* = 50°. Find the measure of each part of the crane.**

15. *JN*
16. *LM*
17. *LN*
18. m∠*JKL*
19. m∠*KLM*
20. m∠*MJK*

WXYZ **is a parallelogram. Find each measure.**

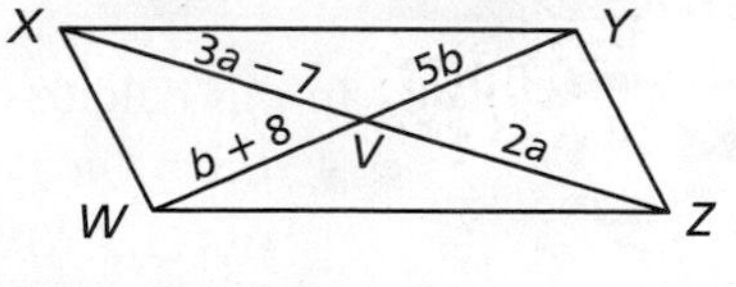

21. *WV*
22. *YW*
23. *XZ*
24. *ZV*

25. **Multi-Step** Three vertices of ▱*PRTV* are *P*(−4, −4), *R*(−10, 0), and *V*(5, −1). Find the coordinates of vertex *T*.

26. Write a two-column proof.
Given: *ABCD* and *AFGH* are parallelograms.
Prove: ∠*C* ≅ ∠*G*

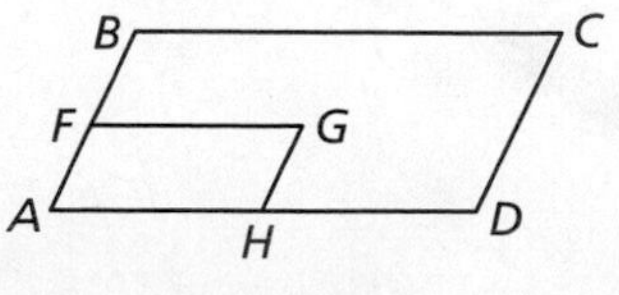

Algebra The perimeter of $\square PQRS$ is 84. Find the length of each side of $\square PQRS$ under the given conditions.

27. $PQ = QR$ **28.** $QR = 3(RS)$ **29.** $RS = SP - 7$ **30.** $SP = RS^2$

31. Cars To repair a large truck, a mechanic might use a *parallelogram lift*. In the lift, $\overline{FG} \cong \overline{GH} \cong \overline{LK} \cong \overline{KJ}$, and $\overline{FL} \cong \overline{GK} \cong \overline{HJ}$.

a. Which angles are congruent to $\angle 1$? Justify your answer.

b. What is the relationship between $\angle 1$ and each of the remaining labeled angles? Justify your answer.

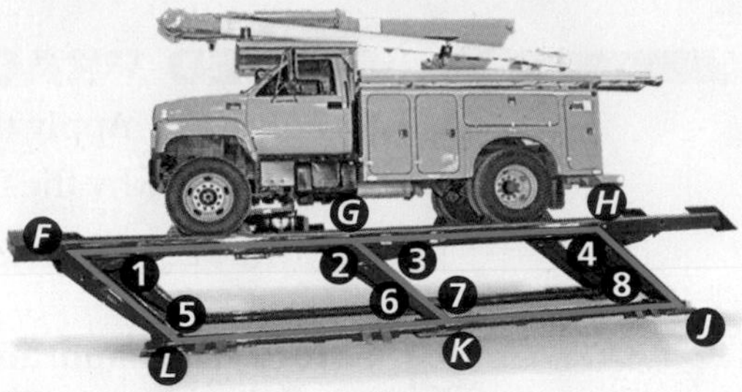

Complete each statement about $\square KMPR$. Justify your answer.

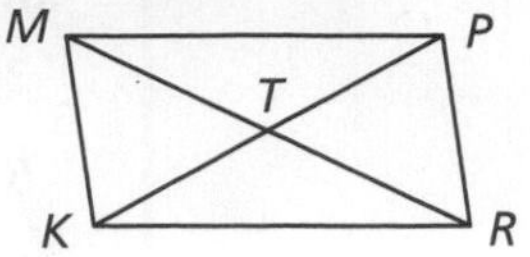

32. $\angle MPR \cong$ ___?___ **33.** $\angle PRK \cong$ ___?___ **34.** $\overline{MT} \cong$ ___?___

35. $\overline{PR} \cong$ ___?___ **36.** $\overline{MP} \parallel$ ___?___ **37.** $\overline{MK} \parallel$ ___?___

38. $\angle MPK \cong$ ___?___ **39.** $\angle MTK \cong$ ___?___ **40.** $m\angle MKR + m\angle PRK =$ ___?___

Find the values of x, y, and z in each parallelogram.

41.

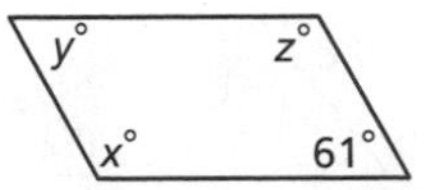

42.

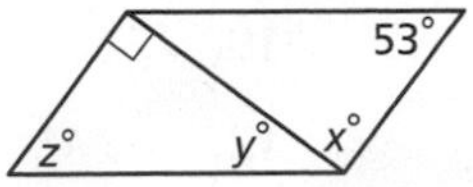

43.

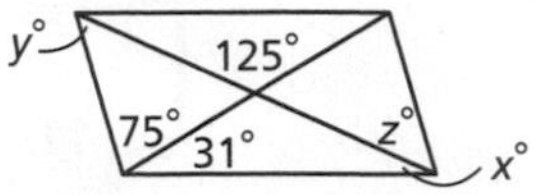

44. Complete the paragraph proof of Theorem 6-2-4 by filling in the blanks.

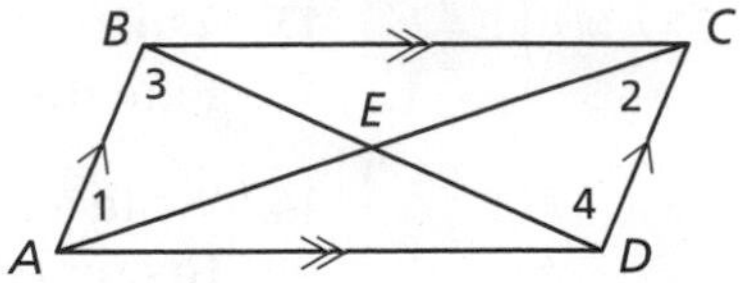

Given: $ABCD$ is a parallelogram.
Prove: $\overline{AC}$ and $\overline{BD}$ bisect each other at E.

Proof: It is given that $ABCD$ is a parallelogram. By the definition of a parallelogram, $\overline{AB} \parallel$ **a.** ___?___ . By the Alternate Interior Angles Theorem, $\angle 1 \cong$ **b.** ___?___ , and $\angle 3 \cong$ **c.** ___?___ . $\overline{AB} \cong \overline{CD}$ because **d.** ___?___ . This means that $\triangle ABE \cong \triangle CDE$ by **e.** ___?___ . So by **f.** ___?___ , $\overline{AE} \cong \overline{CE}$, and $\overline{BE} \cong \overline{DE}$. Therefore $\overline{AC}$ and $\overline{BD}$ bisect each other at E by the definition of **g.** ___?___ .

45. Write a two-column proof of Theorem 6-2-3: If a quadrilateral is a parallelogram, then its consecutive angles are supplementary.

Algebra Find the values of x and y in each parallelogram.

46.

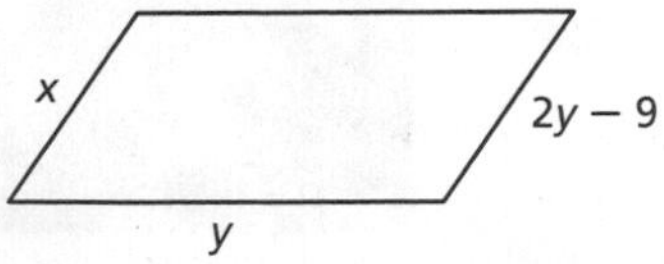

47.

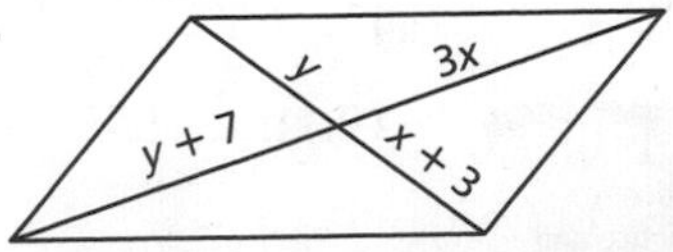

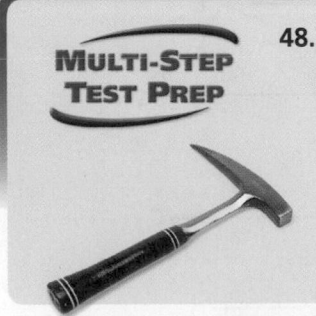

MULTI-STEP TEST PREP

48. In this calcite crystal, the face $ABCD$ is a parallelogram.

a. In $\square ABCD$, $m\angle B = (6x + 12)°$, and $m\angle D = (9x - 33)°$. Find $m\angle B$.

b. Find $m\angle A$ and $m\angle C$. Which theorem or theorems did you use to find these angle measures?

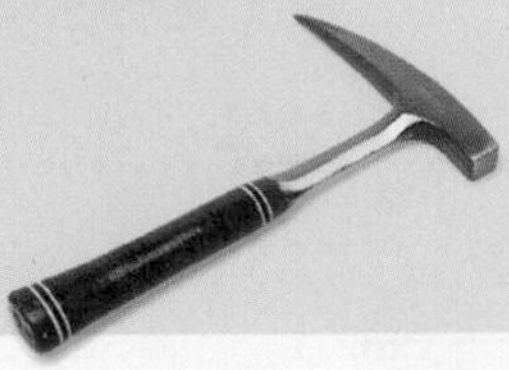

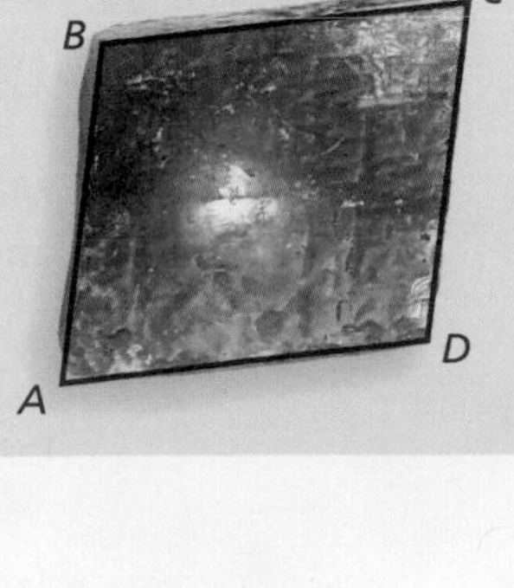

49. **Critical Thinking** Draw any parallelogram. Draw a second parallelogram whose corresponding sides are congruent to the sides of the first parallelogram but whose corresponding angles are not congruent to the angles of the first.

   a. Is there an SSSS congruence postulate for parallelograms? Explain.

   b. Remember the meaning of triangle rigidity. Is a parallelogram rigid? Explain.

50. **Write About It** Explain why every parallelogram is a quadrilateral but every quadrilateral is not necessarily a parallelogram.

TEST PREP

51. What is the value of x in ▱$PQRS$?

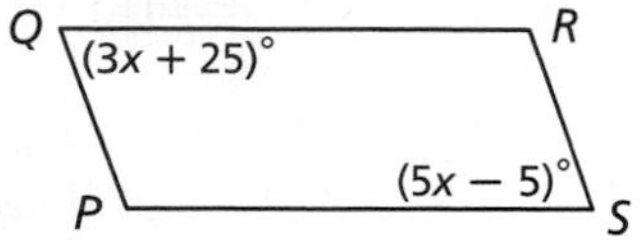

   Ⓐ 15 Ⓒ 30

   Ⓑ 20 Ⓓ 70

52. The diagonals of ▱$JKLM$ intersect at Z. Which statement is true?

   Ⓕ $JL = KM$ Ⓖ $JL = \frac{1}{2}KM$ Ⓗ $JL = \frac{1}{2}JZ$ Ⓙ $JL = 2JZ$

53. **Gridded Response** In ▱$ABCD$, $BC = 8.2$, and $CD = 5$. What is the perimeter of ▱$ABCD$?

CHALLENGE AND EXTEND

The coordinates of three vertices of a parallelogram are given. Give the coordinates for all possible locations of the fourth vertex.

54. $(0, 5), (4, 0), (8, 5)$

55. $(-2, 1), (3, -1), (-1, -4)$

56. The feathers on an arrow form two congruent parallelograms that share a common side. Each parallelogram is the reflection of the other across the line they share. Show that $y = 2x$.

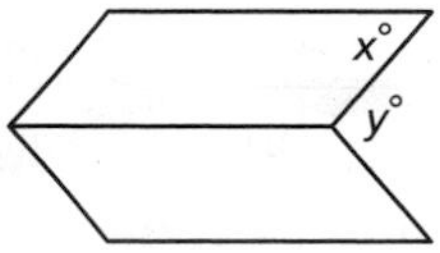

57. Prove that the bisectors of two consecutive angles of a parallelogram are perpendicular.

COMMON CORE

6-3 Conditions for Parallelograms

CC.9-12.G.CO.11 Prove theorems about parallelograms. *Also* **CC.9-12.G.GPE.5, C.9-12.G.MG.3***

Objective
Prove that a given quadrilateral is a parallelogram.

Who uses this?
A bird watcher can use a *parallelogram mount* to adjust the height of a pair of binoculars without changing the viewing angle. (See Example 4.)

You have learned to identify the properties of a parallelogram. Now you will be given the properties of a quadrilateral and will have to tell if the quadrilateral is a parallelogram. To do this, you can use the definition of a parallelogram or the conditions below.

Know it! Note

Remember!
In the converse of a theorem, the hypothesis and conclusion are exchanged.

Theorems **Conditions for Parallelograms**

THEOREM	EXAMPLE
6-3-1 If one pair of opposite sides of a quadrilateral are parallel and congruent, then the quadrilateral is a parallelogram. (quad. with pair of opp. sides $\parallel$ and $\cong \rightarrow \square$)	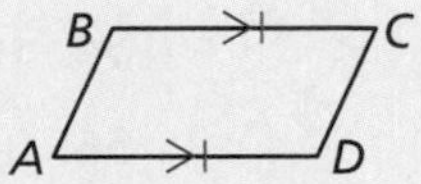
6-3-2 If both pairs of opposite sides of a quadrilateral are congruent, then the quadrilateral is a parallelogram. (quad. with opp. sides $\cong \rightarrow \square$)	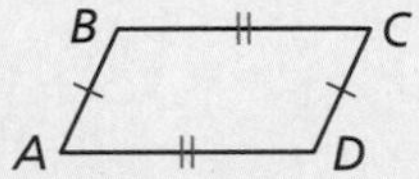
6-3-3 If both pairs of opposite angles of a quadrilateral are congruent, then the quadrilateral is a parallelogram. (quad. with opp. $\angle s \cong \rightarrow \square$)	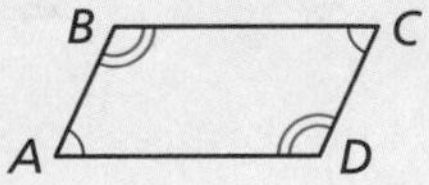

You will prove Theorems 6-3-2 and 6-3-3 in Exercises 26 and 29.

PROOF **Theorem 6-3-1**

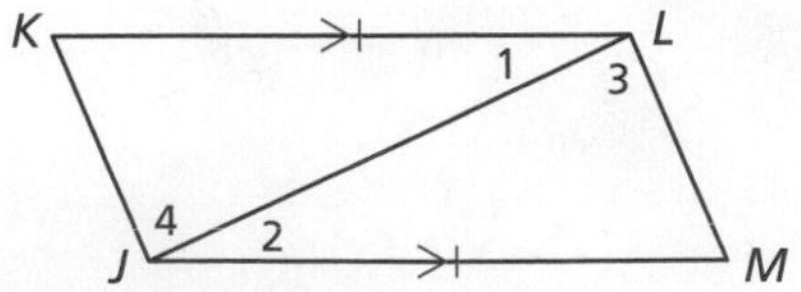

Given: $\overline{KL} \parallel \overline{MJ}$, $\overline{KL} \cong \overline{MJ}$
Prove: *JKLM* is a parallelogram.

Proof:
It is given that $\overline{KL} \cong \overline{MJ}$. Since $\overline{KL} \parallel \overline{MJ}$, $\angle 1 \cong \angle 2$ by the Alternate Interior Angles Theorem. By the Reflexive Property of Congruence, $\overline{JL} \cong \overline{JL}$. So $\triangle JKL \cong \triangle LMJ$ by SAS. By CPCTC, $\angle 3 \cong \angle 4$, and $\overline{JK} \parallel \overline{LM}$ by the Converse of the Alternate Interior Angles Theorem. Since the opposite sides of *JKLM* are parallel, *JKLM* is a parallelogram by definition.

The two theorems below can also be used to show that a given quadrilateral is a parallelogram.

Know it! Note

Theorems **Conditions for Parallelograms**

	THEOREM	EXAMPLE
6-3-4	If an angle of a quadrilateral is supplementary to both of its consecutive angles, then the quadrilateral is a parallelogram. (quad. with ∠ supp. to cons. ∠s → ▱)	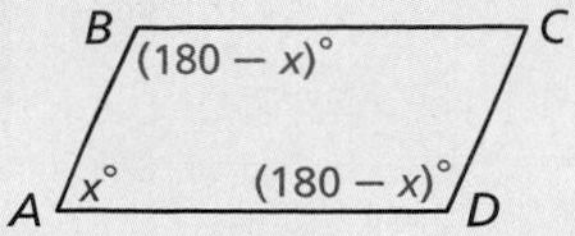
6-3-5	If the diagonals of a quadrilateral bisect each other, then the quadrilateral is a parallelogram. (quad. with diags. bisecting each other → ▱)	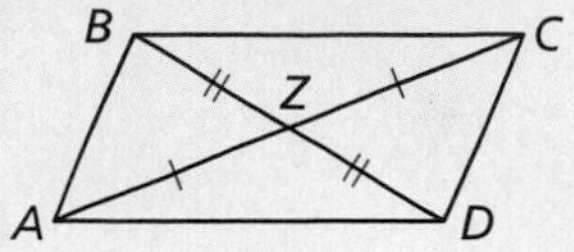

You will prove Theorems 6-3-4 and 6-3-5 in Exercises 27 and 30.

EXAMPLE 1 Verifying Figures are Parallelograms

Algebra

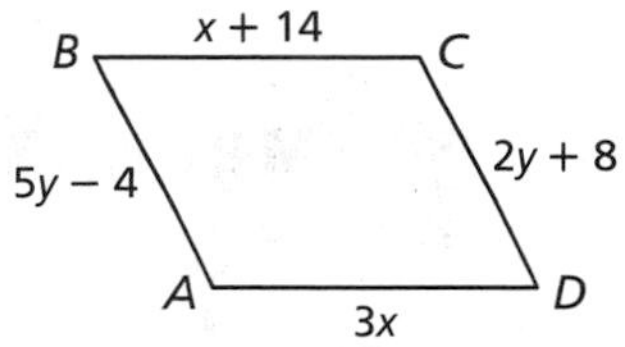

A **Show that $ABCD$ is a parallelogram for $x = 7$ and $y = 4$.**

Step 1 Find BC and DA.

$BC = x + 14$	*Given*	$DA = 3x$
$BC = 7 + 14 = 21$	*Substitute and simplify.*	$DA = 3x = 3(7) = 21$

Step 2 Find AB and CD.

$AB = 5y - 4$	*Given*	$CD = 2y + 8$
$AB = 5(4) - 4 = 16$	*Substitute and simplify.*	$CD = 2(4) + 8 = 16$

Since $BC = DA$ and $AB = CD$, $ABCD$ is a parallelogram by Theorem 6-3-2.

B **Show that $EFGH$ is a parallelogram for $z = 11$ and $w = 4.5$.**

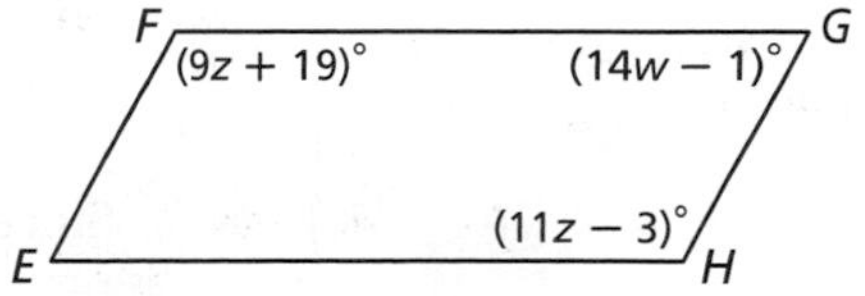

$m\angle F = (9z + 19)^\circ$	*Given*
$m\angle F = [9(11) + 19]^\circ = 118^\circ$	*Substitute 11 for z and simplify.*
$m\angle H = (11z - 3)^\circ$	*Given*
$m\angle H = [11(11) - 3]^\circ = 118^\circ$	*Substitute 11 for z and simplify.*
$m\angle G = (14w - 1)^\circ$	*Given*
$m\angle G = [14(4.5) - 1]^\circ = 62^\circ$	*Substitute 4.5 for w and simplify.*

Since $118^\circ + 62^\circ = 180^\circ$, $\angle G$ is supplementary to both $\angle F$ and $\angle H$. $EFGH$ is a parallelogram by Theorem 6-3-4.

CHECK IT OUT!

1. Show that $PQRS$ is a parallelogram for $a = 2.4$ and $b = 9$.

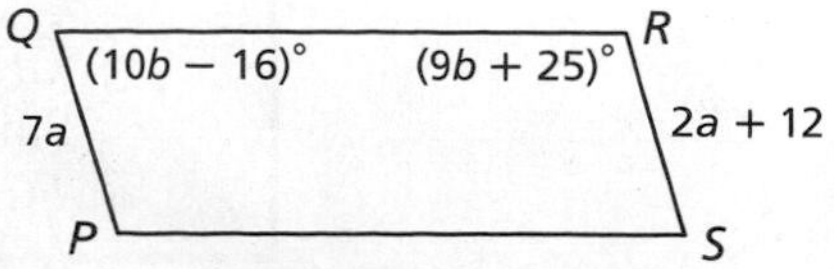

EXAMPLE 2 Applying Conditions for Parallelograms

Determine if each quadrilateral must be a parallelogram. Justify your answer.

A

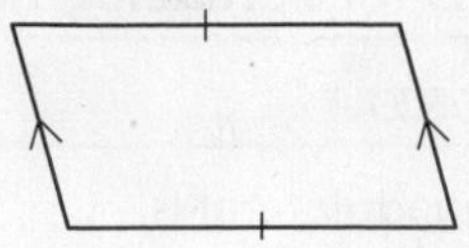

No. One pair of opposite sides are parallel. A different pair of opposite sides are congruent. The conditions for a parallelogram are not met.

B

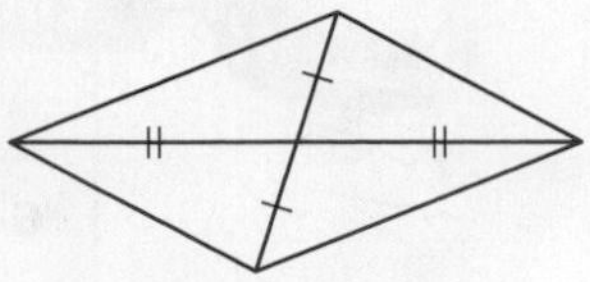

Yes. The diagonals bisect each other. By Theorem 6-3-5, the quadrilateral is a parallelogram.

CHECK IT OUT! **Determine if each quadrilateral must be a parallelogram. Justify your answer.**

2a.

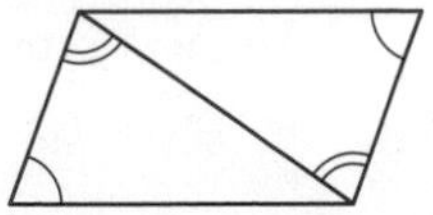

2b.

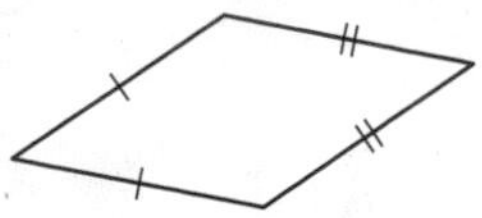

EXAMPLE 3 Proving Parallelograms in the Coordinate Plane

Show that quadrilateral *ABCD* is a parallelogram by using the given definition or theorem.

A $A(-3, 2)$, $B(-2, 7)$, $C(2, 4)$, $D(1, -1)$; **definition of parallelogram**

Find the slopes of both pairs of opposite sides.

$$\text{slope of } \overline{AB} = \frac{7-2}{-2-(-3)} = \frac{5}{1} = 5$$

$$\text{slope of } \overline{CD} = \frac{-1-4}{1-2} = \frac{-5}{-1} = 5$$

$$\text{slope of } \overline{BC} = \frac{4-7}{2-(-2)} = \frac{-3}{4} = -\frac{3}{4}$$

$$\text{slope of } \overline{DA} = \frac{2-(-1)}{-3-1} = \frac{3}{-4} = -\frac{3}{4}$$

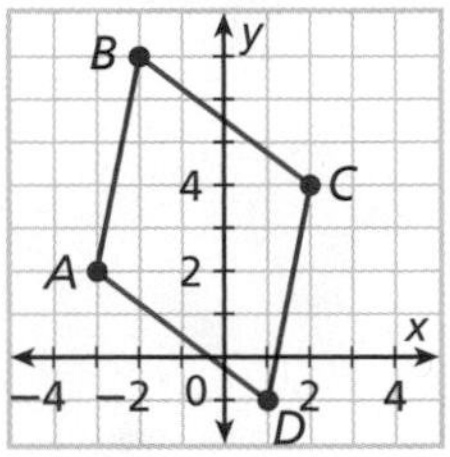

Since both pairs of opposite sides are parallel, *ABCD* is a parallelogram by definition.

B $F(-4, -2)$, $G(-2, 2)$, $H(4, 3)$, $J(2, -1)$; **Theorem 6-3-1**

Find the slopes and lengths of one pair of opposite sides.

$$\text{slope of } \overline{GH} = \frac{3-2}{4-(-2)} = \frac{1}{6}$$

$$\text{slope of } \overline{JF} = \frac{-2-(-1)}{-4-2} = \frac{-1}{-6} = \frac{1}{6}$$

$$GH = \sqrt{[4-(-2)]^2 + (3-2)^2} = \sqrt{37}$$

$$JF = \sqrt{(-4-2)^2 + [-2-(-1)]^2} = \sqrt{37}$$

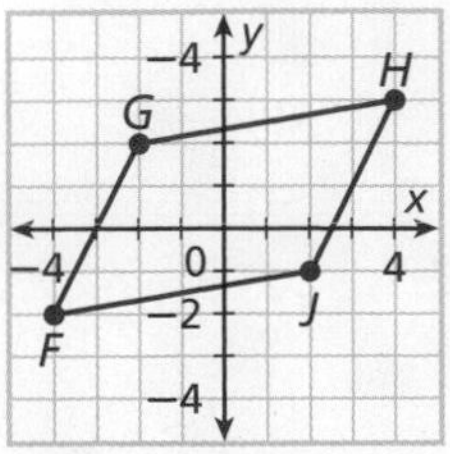

$\overline{GH}$ and $\overline{JF}$ have the same slope, so $\overline{GH} \parallel \overline{JF}$. Since $GH = JF$, $\overline{GH} \cong \overline{JF}$. So by Theorem 6-3-1, *FGHJ* is a parallelogram.

Helpful Hint

To say that a quadrilateral is a parallelogram *by definition*, you must show that both pairs of opposite sides are parallel.

CHECK IT OUT! **3.** Use the definition of a parallelogram to show that the quadrilateral with vertices $K(-3, 0)$, $L(-5, 7)$, $M(3, 5)$, and $N(5, -2)$ is a parallelogram.

You have learned several ways to determine whether a quadrilateral is a parallelogram. You can use the given information about a figure to decide which condition is best to apply.

Helpful Hint

To show that a quadrilateral is a parallelogram, you only have to show that it satisfies one of these sets of conditions.

Conditions for Parallelograms
Both pairs of opposite sides are parallel. (definition)
One pair of opposite sides are parallel and congruent. (Theorem 6-3-1)
Both pairs of opposite sides are congruent. (Theorem 6-3-2)
Both pairs of opposite angles are congruent. (Theorem 6-3-3)
One angle is supplementary to both of its consecutive angles. (Theorem 6-3-4)
The diagonals bisect each other. (Theorem 6-3-5)

EXAMPLE 4 *Bird-Watching Application*

In the parallelogram mount, there are bolts at *P*, *Q*, *R*, and *S* such that *PQ* = *RS* and *QR* = *SP*. The frame *PQRS* moves when you raise or lower the binoculars. Why is *PQRS* always a parallelogram?

When you move the binoculars, the angle measures change, but *PQ*, *QR*, *RS*, and *SP* stay the same. So it is always true that *PQ* = *RS* and *QR* = *SP*. Since both pairs of opposite sides of the quadrilateral are congruent, *PQRS* is always a parallelogram.

CHECK IT OUT! **4.** The frame is attached to the tripod at points *A* and *B* such that *AB* = *RS* and *BR* = *SA*. So *ABRS* is also a parallelogram. How does this ensure that the angle of the binoculars stays the same?

MATHEMATICAL PRACTICES

THINK AND DISCUSS

1. What do all the theorems in this lesson have in common?

2. How are the theorems in this lesson different from the theorems in the lesson *Properties of Parallelograms*?

Know it! Note

3. GET ORGANIZED Copy and complete the graphic organizer. In each box, write one of the six conditions for a parallelogram. Then sketch a parallelogram and label it to show how it meets the condition.

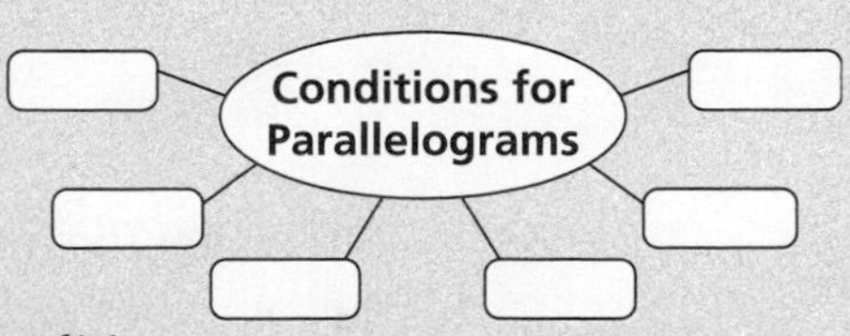

6-3 Exercises

Learn It Online
Homework Help Online
Parent Resources Online

GUIDED PRACTICE

SEE EXAMPLE 1

1. Show that *EFGH* is a parallelogram for $s = 5$ and $t = 6$.

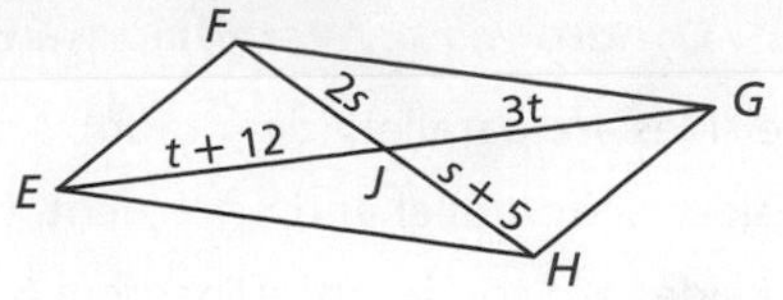

2. Show that *KLPQ* is a parallelogram for $m = 14$ and $n = 12.5$.

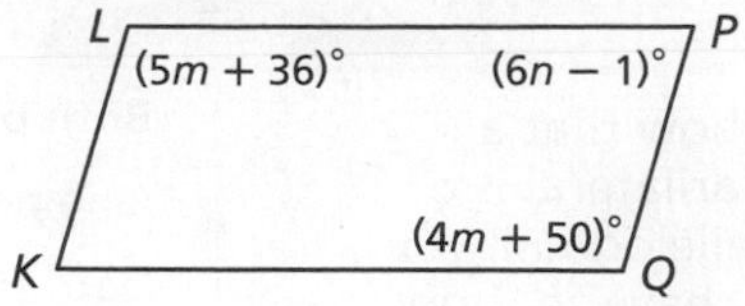

SEE EXAMPLE 2

Determine if each quadrilateral must be a parallelogram. Justify your answer.

3. 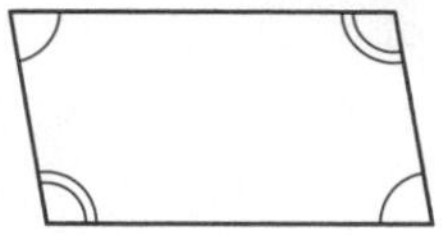

4. 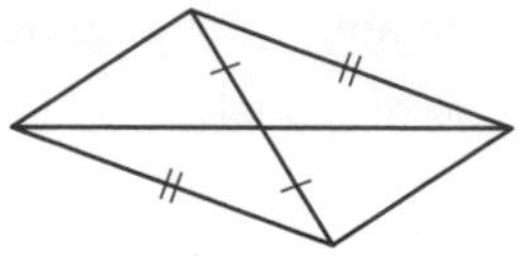

5. 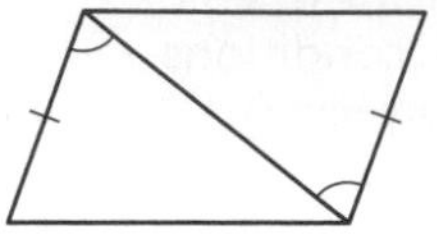

SEE EXAMPLE 3

Show that the quadrilateral with the given vertices is a parallelogram.

6. $W(-5, -2)$, $X(-3, 3)$, $Y(3, 5)$, $Z(1, 0)$
7. $R(-1, -5)$, $S(-2, -1)$, $T(4, -1)$, $U(5, -5)$

SEE EXAMPLE 4

8. **Navigation** A parallel rule can be used to plot a course on a navigation chart. The tool is made of two rulers connected at hinges to two congruent crossbars $\overline{AD}$ and $\overline{BC}$. You place the edge of one ruler on your desired course and then move the second ruler over the compass rose on the chart to read the bearing for your course. If $\overline{AD} \parallel \overline{BC}$, why is $\overline{AB}$ always parallel to $\overline{CD}$?

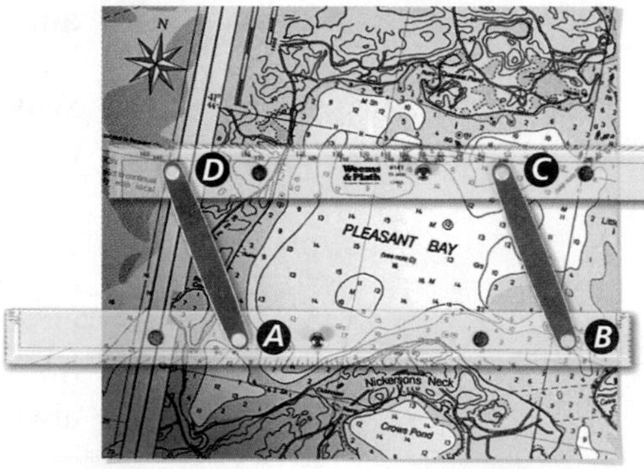

PRACTICE AND PROBLEM SOLVING

Independent Practice

For Exercises	See Example
9–10	1
11–13	2
14–15	3
16	4

Extra Practice
See Extra Practice for more Skills Practice and Applications Practice exercises.

9. Show that *BCGH* is a parallelogram for $x = 3.2$ and $y = 7$.

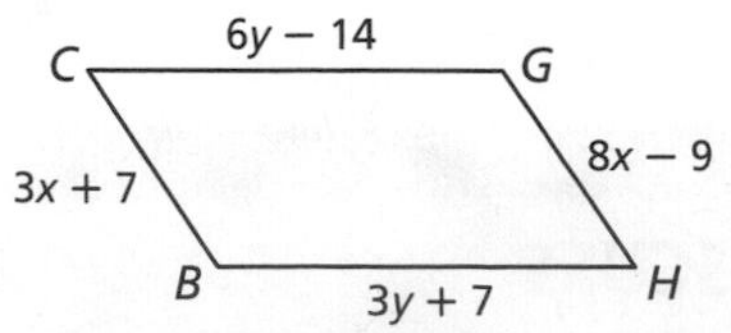

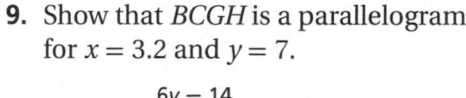

10. Show that *TUVW* is a parallelogram for $a = 19.5$ and $b = 22$.

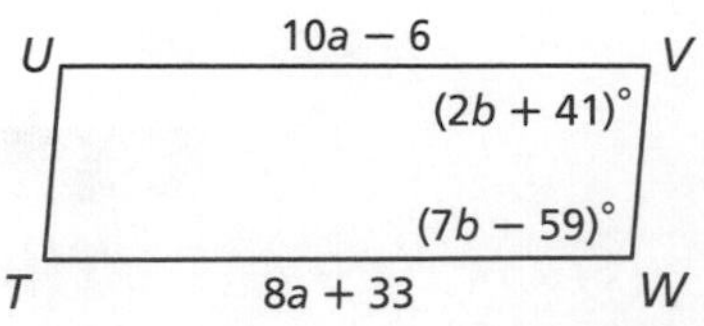

Determine if each quadrilateral must be a parallelogram. Justify your answer.

11. 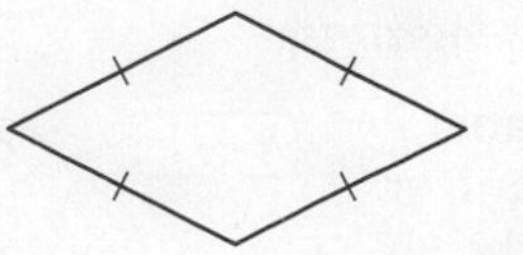

12. 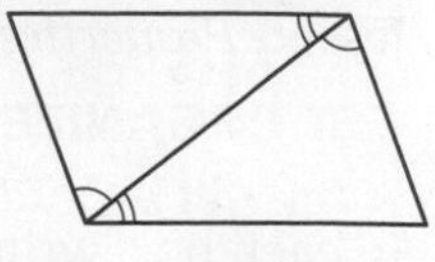

13. 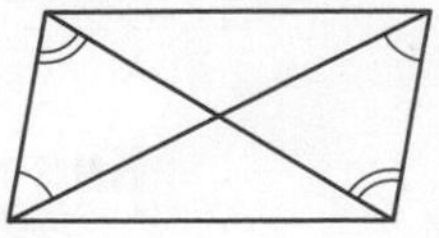

Show that the quadrilateral with the given vertices is a parallelogram.

14. $J(-1, 0)$, $K(-3, 7)$, $L(2, 6)$, $M(4, -1)$
15. $P(-8, -4)$, $Q(-5, 1)$, $R(1, -5)$, $S(-2, -10)$

16. **Design** The toolbox has cantilever trays that pull away from the box so that you can reach the items beneath them. Two congruent brackets connect each tray to the box. Given that $AD = BC$, how do the brackets $\overline{AB}$ and $\overline{CD}$ keep the tray horizontal?

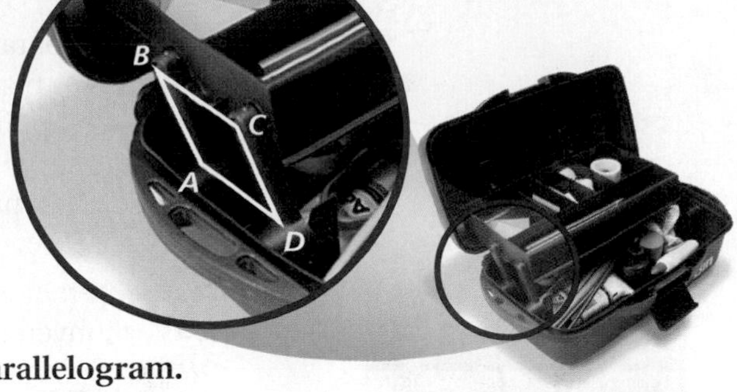

Determine if each quadrilateral must be a parallelogram. Justify your answer.

17.

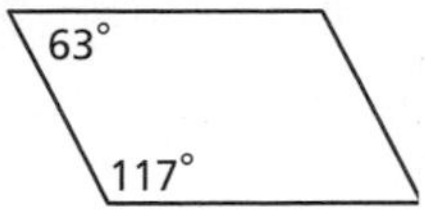

18.

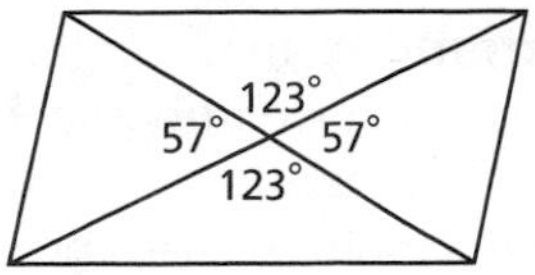

19.

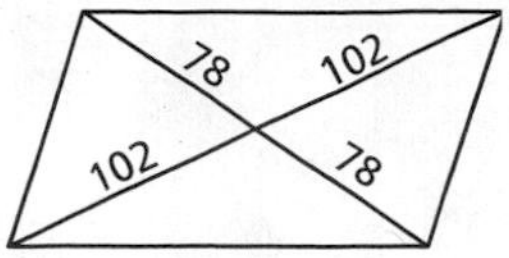

Algebra Find the values of a and b that would make the quadrilateral a parallelogram.

20.

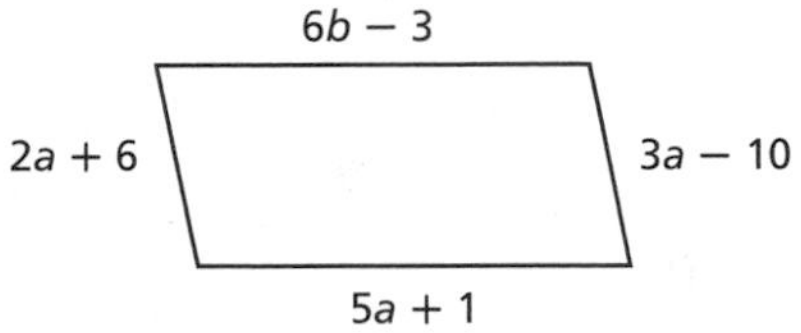

21.

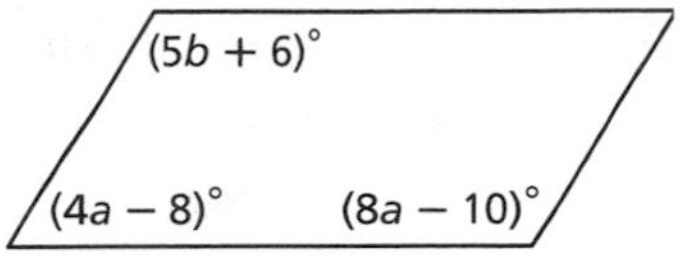

22.

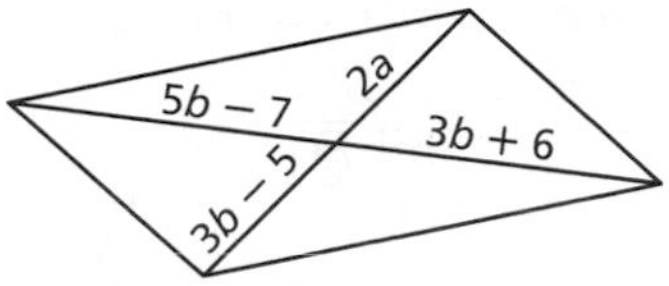

23.

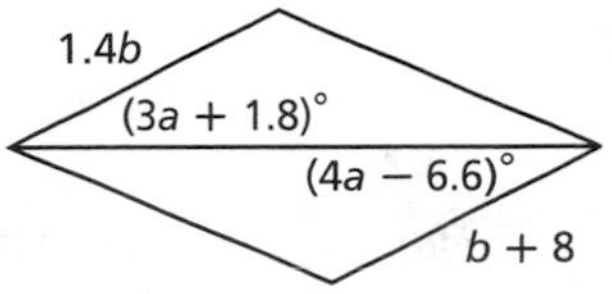

24. **Critical Thinking** Draw a quadrilateral that has congruent diagonals but is not a parallelogram. What can you conclude about using congruent diagonals as a condition for a parallelogram?

25. **Social Studies** The angles at the corners of the flag of the Republic of the Congo are right angles. The red and green triangles are congruent isosceles right triangles. Why is the shape of the yellow stripe a parallelogram?

26. Complete the two-column proof of Theorem 6-3-2 by filling in the blanks.

Given: $\overline{AB} \cong \overline{CD}$, $\overline{BC} \cong \overline{DA}$

Prove: $ABCD$ is a parallelogram.

Proof:

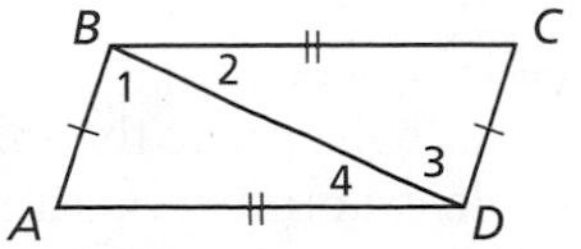

Statements	Reasons
1. $\overline{AB} \cong \overline{CD}$, $\overline{BC} \cong \overline{DA}$	1. Given
2. $\overline{BD} \cong \overline{BD}$	2. a. ____?____
3. $\triangle DAB \cong$ b. ____?____	3. c. ____?____
4. $\angle 1 \cong$ d. ____?____, $\angle 4 \cong$ e. ____?____	4. CPCTC
5. $\overline{AB} \parallel \overline{CD}$, $\overline{BC} \parallel \overline{DA}$	5. f. ____?____
6. $ABCD$ is a parallelogram.	6. g. ____?____

27. Complete the paragraph proof of Theorem 6-3-4 by filling in the blanks.
Given: $\angle P$ is supplementary to $\angle Q$.
$\angle P$ is supplementary to $\angle S$.
Prove: *PQRS* is a parallelogram.

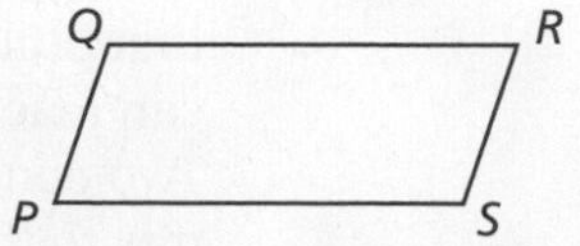

Proof:
It is given that $\angle P$ is supplementary to **a.** ___?___ and **b.** ___?___ . By the Converse of the Same-Side Interior Angles Theorem, $\overline{QR} \parallel$ **c.** ___?___ and $\overline{PQ} \parallel$ **d.** ___?___ . So *PQRS* is a parallelogram by the definition of **e.** ___?___ .

LINK
Measurement

Ancient balance scales had one beam that moved on a single hinge. The stress on the hinge often made the scale imprecise.

28. **Measurement** In the eighteenth century, Gilles Personne de Roberval designed a scale with two beams and two hinges. In $\square ABCD$, *E* is the midpoint of $\overline{AB}$, and *F* is the midpoint of $\overline{CD}$. Write a paragraph proof that *AEFD* and *EBCF* are parallelograms.

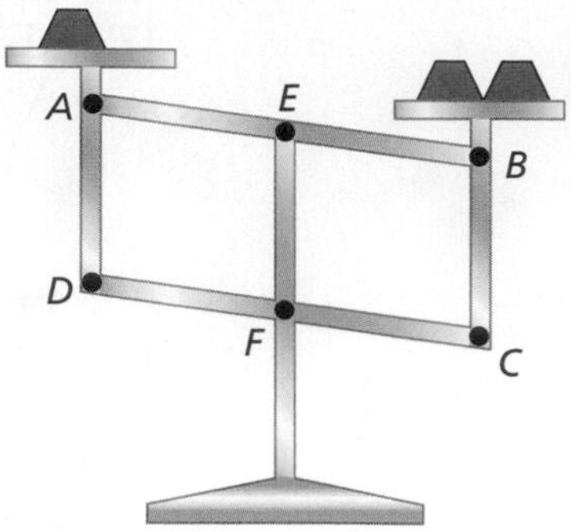

Prove each theorem.

29. Theorem 6-3-3
Given: $\angle E \cong \angle G$, $\angle F \cong \angle H$
Prove: *EFGH* is a parallelogram.

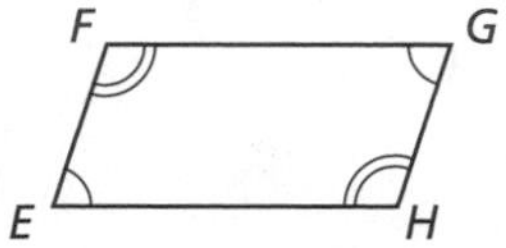

Plan: Show that the sum of the interior angles of *EFGH* is 360°. Then apply properties of equality to show that $m\angle E + m\angle F = 180°$ and $m\angle E + m\angle H = 180°$. Then you can conclude that $\overline{EF} \parallel \overline{GH}$ and $\overline{FG} \parallel \overline{HE}$.

30. Theorem 6-3-5
Given: $\overline{JL}$ and $\overline{KM}$ bisect each other.
Prove: *JKLM* is a parallelogram.

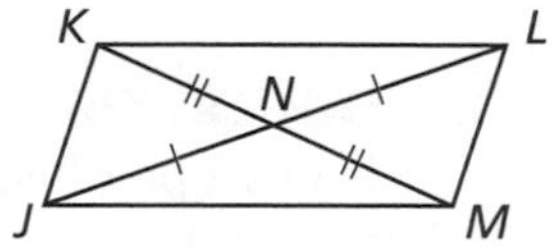

Plan: Show that $\triangle JNK \cong \triangle LNM$ and $\triangle KNL \cong \triangle MNJ$. Then use the fact that the corresponding angles are congruent to show $\overline{JK} \parallel \overline{LM}$ and $\overline{KL} \parallel \overline{MJ}$.

31. Prove that the figure formed by two midsegments of a triangle and their corresponding bases is a parallelogram.

32. **Write About It** Use the theorems about properties of parallelograms to write three biconditional statements about parallelograms.

33. **Construction** Explain how you can construct a parallelogram based on the conditions of Theorem 6-3-1. Use your method to construct a parallelogram.

MULTI-STEP TEST PREP

34. A geologist made the following observations while examining this amethyst crystal. Tell whether each set of observations allows the geologist to conclude that *PQRS* is a parallelogram. If so, explain why.
a. $\overline{PQ} \cong \overline{SR}$, and $\overline{PS} \parallel \overline{QR}$.
b. $\angle S$ and $\angle R$ are supplementary, and $\overline{PS} \cong \overline{QR}$.
c. $\angle S \cong \angle Q$, and $\overline{PQ} \parallel \overline{SR}$.

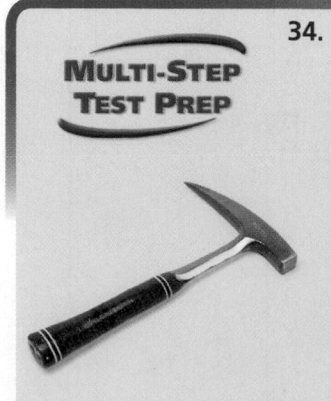

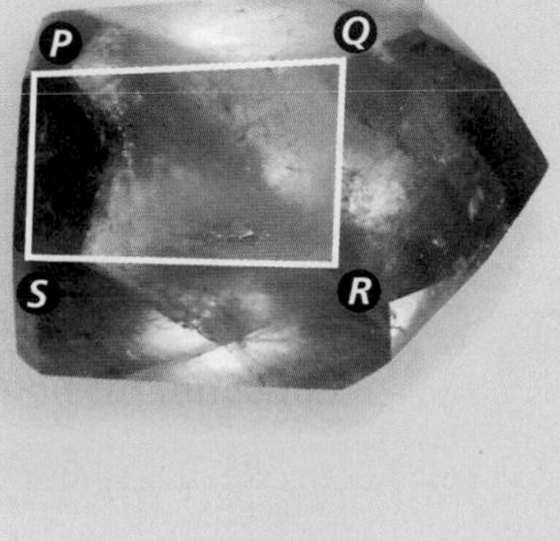

TEST PREP

35. What additional information would allow you to conclude that *WXYZ* is a parallelogram?

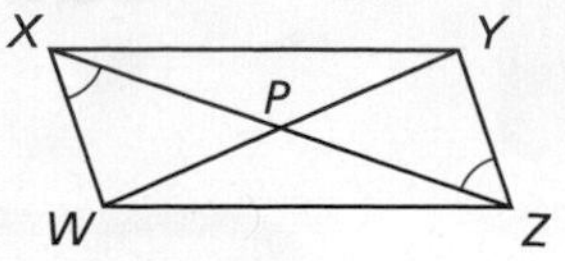

Ⓐ $\overline{XY} \cong \overline{ZW}$ Ⓒ $\overline{WY} \cong \overline{WZ}$

Ⓑ $\overline{WX} \cong \overline{YZ}$ Ⓓ $\angle XWY \cong \angle ZYW$

36. Which could be the coordinates of the fourth vertex of ▱*ABCD* with $A(-1, -1)$, $B(1, 3)$, and $C(6, 1)$?

Ⓕ $D(8, 5)$ Ⓖ $D(4, -3)$ Ⓗ $D(13, 3)$ Ⓙ $D(3, 7)$

37. Short Response The vertices of quadrilateral *RSTV* are $R(-5, 0)$, $S(-1, 3)$, $T(5, 1)$, and $V(2, -2)$. Is *RSTV* a parallelogram? Justify your answer.

CHALLENGE AND EXTEND

38. Write About It As the upper platform of the movable staircase is raised and lowered, the height of each step changes. How does the upper platform remain parallel to the ground?

39. Multi-Step The diagonals of a parallelogram intersect at $(-2, 1.5)$. Two vertices are located at $(-7, 2)$ and $(2, 6.5)$. Find the coordinates of the other two vertices.

40. Given: *D* is the midpoint of $\overline{AC}$, and *E* is the midpoint of $\overline{BC}$.

Prove: $\overline{DE} \parallel \overline{AB}$, $DE = \frac{1}{2}AB$

(*Hint:* Extend $\overline{DE}$ to form $\overline{DF}$ so that $\overline{EF} \cong \overline{DE}$. Then show that *DFBA* is a parallelogram.)

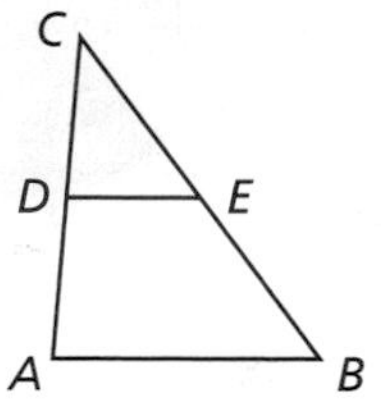

CHAPTER 6

MULTI-STEP TEST PREP

SECTION 6A

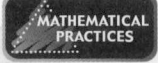

MATHEMATICAL PRACTICES **Reason abstractly and quantitatively.**

Polygons and Parallelograms

Crystal Clear A crystal is a mineral formation that has polygonal faces. Geologists classify crystals based on the types of polygons that the faces form.

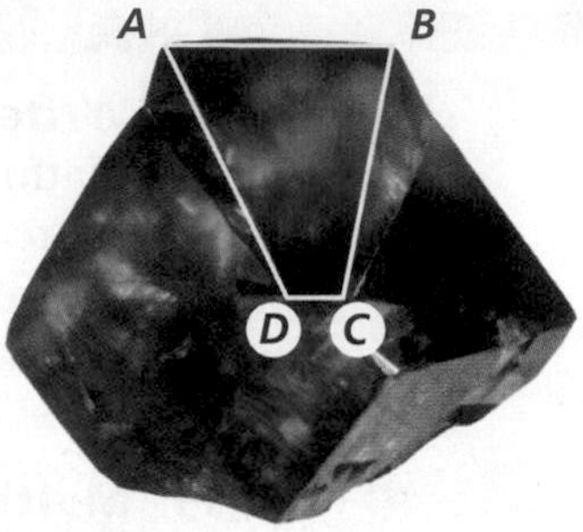

1. What type of polygon is *ABCD* in the fluorite crystal? Given that $\overline{AB} \parallel \overline{DC}$, $m\angle B = 82°$, $m\angle D = 116°$, find $m\angle A$.

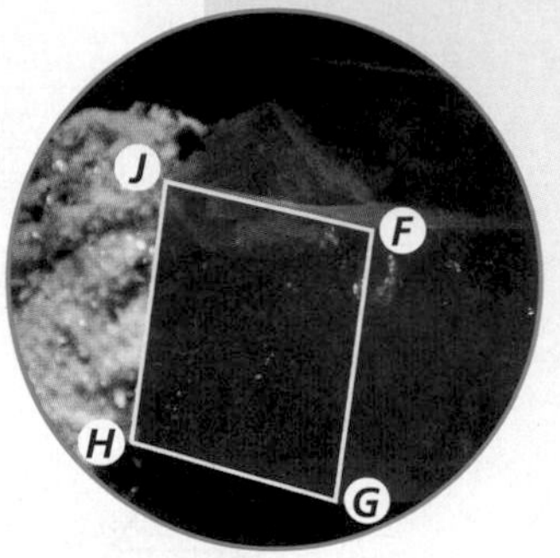

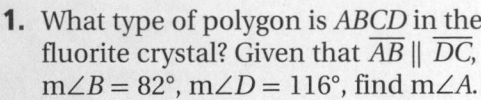

2. The red crystals are called rhodochrosite. The face *FGHJ* is a parallelogram. Given that $m\angle F = (9x - 13)°$ and $m\angle J = (7x + 1)°$, find $m\angle G$. Explain how you found this angle measure.

3. While studying the amazonite crystal, a geologist found that $\overline{MN} \cong \overline{QP}$ and $\angle NQP \cong \angle QNM$. Can the geologist conclude that *MNPQ* is a parallelogram? Why or why not? Justify your answer.

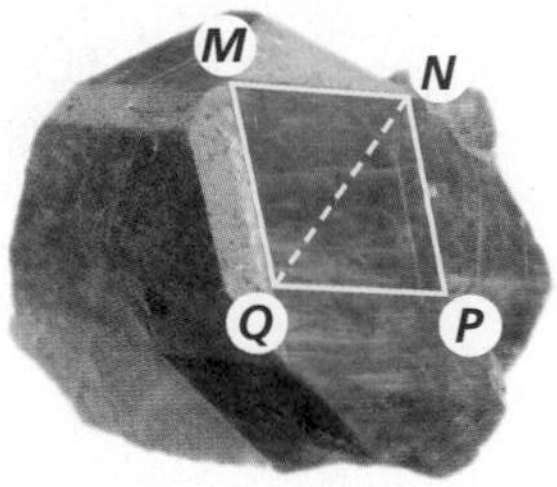

READY TO GO ON?

Quiz for Lessons 6-1 Through 6-3

6-1 Properties and Attributes of Polygons

Tell whether each figure is a polygon. If it is a polygon, name it by the number of its sides.

1. 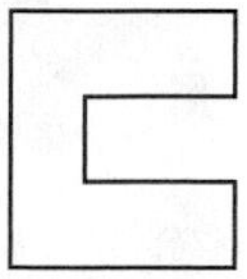

2. 

3. 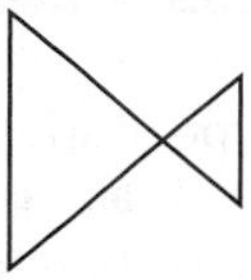

4. 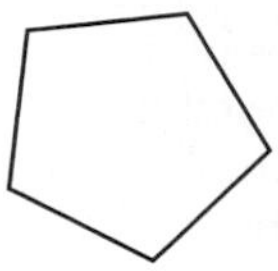

5. Find the sum of the interior angle measures of a convex 16-gon.

6. The surface of a trampoline is in the shape of a regular hexagon. Find the measure of each interior angle of the trampoline.

7. A park in the shape of quadrilateral *PQRS* is bordered by four sidewalks. Find the measure of each exterior angle of the park.

8. Find the measure of each exterior angle of a regular decagon.

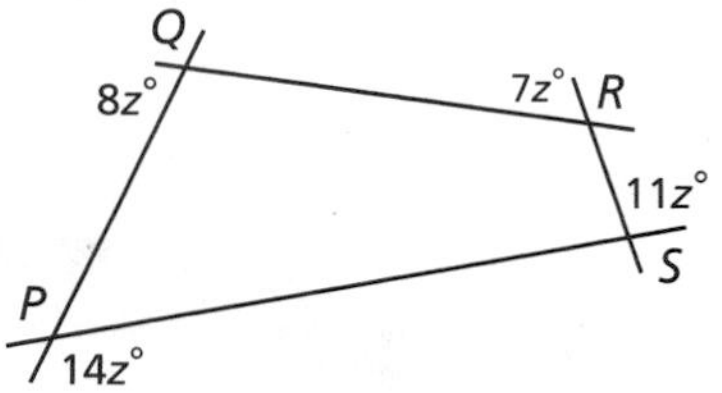

6-2 Properties of Parallelograms

A pantograph is used to copy drawings. Its legs form a parallelogram. In ▱*JKLM*, $LM = 17$ cm, $KN = 13.5$ cm, and $m\angle KJM = 102°$. Find each measure.

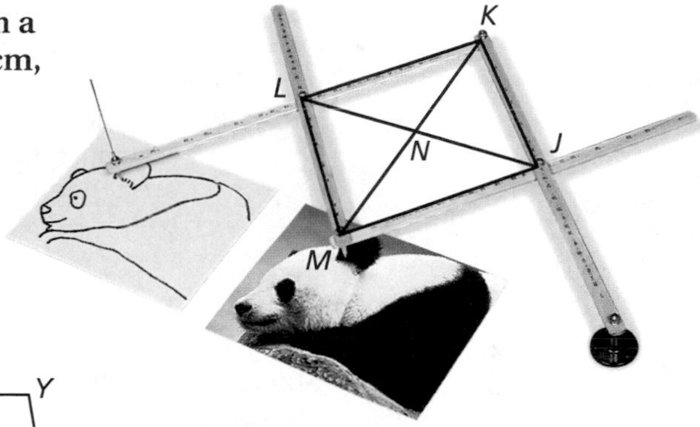

9. *KM* **10.** *KJ* **11.** *MN*

12. $m\angle JKL$ **13.** $m\angle JML$ **14.** $m\angle KLM$

15. Three vertices of ▱*ABCD* are $A(-3, 1)$, $B(5, 7)$, and $C(6, 2)$. Find the coordinates of vertex *D*.

***WXYZ* is a parallelogram. Find each measure.**

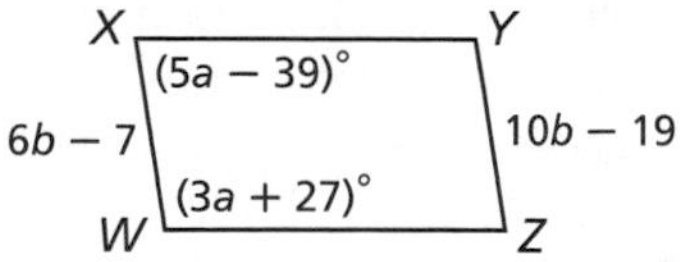

16. *WX* **17.** *YZ*

18. $m\angle X$ **19.** $m\angle W$

6-3 Conditions for Parallelograms

20. Show that *RSTV* is a parallelogram for $x = 6$ and $y = 4.5$.

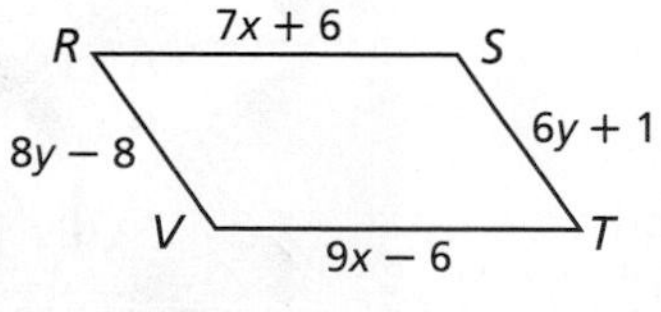

21. Show that *GHJK* is a parallelogram for $m = 12$ and $n = 9.5$.

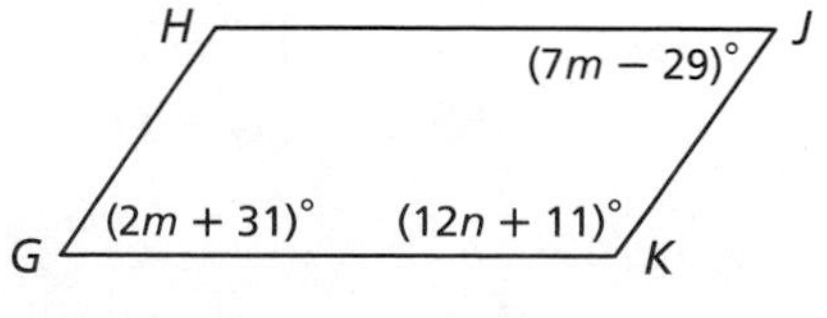

Determine if each quadrilateral must be a parallelogram. Justify your answer.

22. 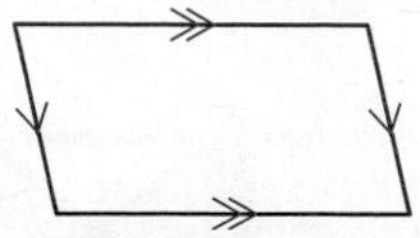

23. 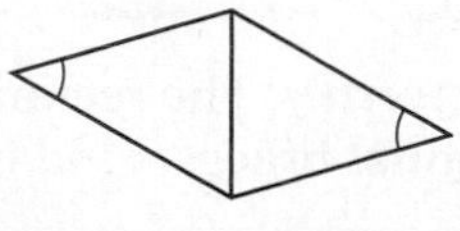

24. 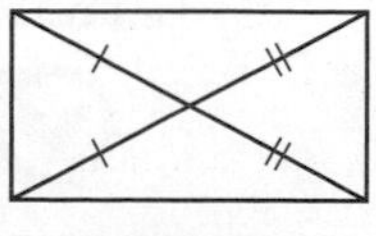

25. Show that a quadrilateral with vertices $C(-9, 4)$, $D(-4, 8)$, $E(2, 6)$, and $F(-3, 2)$ is a parallelogram.

COMMON CORE

6-4 Properties of Special Parallelograms

CC.9-12.G.CO.11 Prove theorems about parallelograms.

Objectives

Prove and apply properties of rectangles, rhombuses, and squares.

Use properties of rectangles, rhombuses, and squares to solve problems.

Vocabulary

rectangle
rhombus
square

Who uses this?

Artists who work with stained glass can use properties of rectangles to cut materials to the correct sizes.

A second type of special quadrilateral is a *rectangle*. A **rectangle** is a quadrilateral with four right angles.

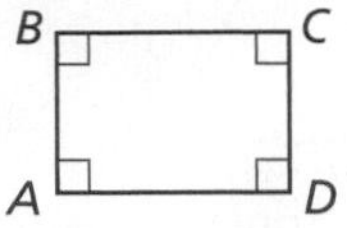

Rectangle *ABCD*

Know it! Note

Theorems Properties of Rectangles

	THEOREM	HYPOTHESIS	CONCLUSION
6-4-1	If a quadrilateral is a rectangle, then it is a parallelogram. (rect. → ▱)	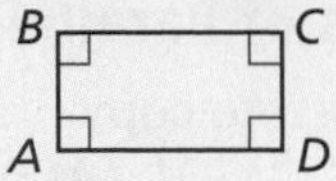	*ABCD* is a parallelogram.
6-4-2	If a parallelogram is a rectangle, then its diagonals are congruent. (rect. → diags. ≅)	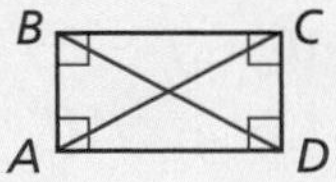	$\overline{AC} \cong \overline{BD}$

You will prove Theorems 6-4-1 and 6-4-2 in Exercises 38 and 35.

Since a rectangle is a parallelogram by Theorem 6-4-1, a rectangle "inherits" all the properties of parallelograms.

EXAMPLE 1 ***Craft Application***

An artist connects stained glass pieces with lead strips. In this rectangular window, the strips are cut so that $FG = 24$ in. and $FH = 34$ in. Find JG.

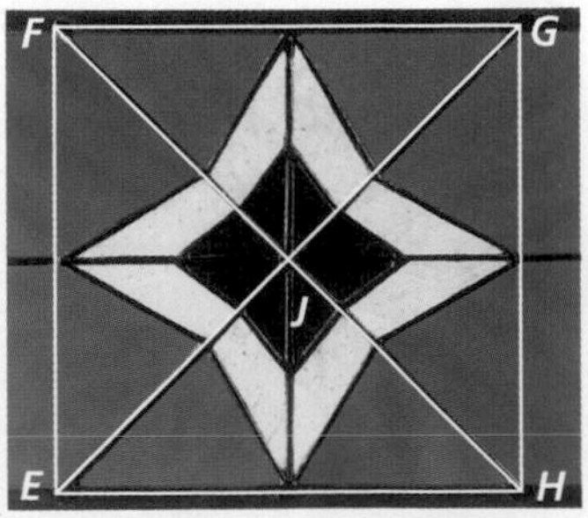

$\overline{EG} \cong \overline{FH}$	*Rect. → diags. ≅*
$EG = FH = 34$	*Def. of ≅ segs.*
$JG = \frac{1}{2}EG$	*▱ → diags. bisect each other*
$JG = \frac{1}{2}(34) = 17$ in.	*Substitute and simplify.*

CHECK IT OUT! **Carpentry** **The rectangular gate has diagonal braces. Find each length.**

1a. *HJ* **1b.** *HK*

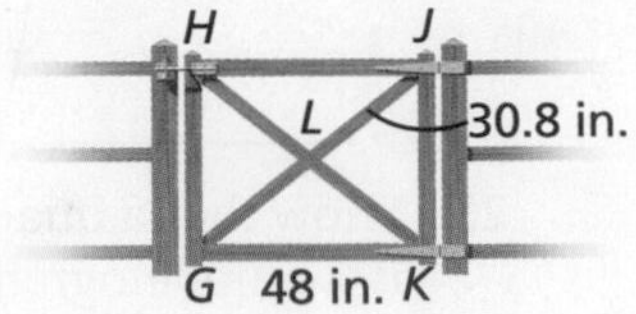

A *rhombus* is another special quadrilateral. A **rhombus** is a quadrilateral with four congruent sides.

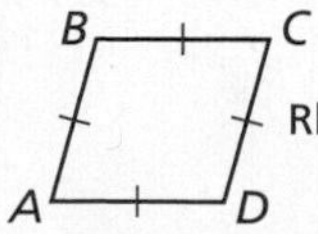

Rhombus *ABCD*

Know it! Note

Theorems **Properties of Rhombuses**

THEOREM		HYPOTHESIS	CONCLUSION
6-4-3	If a quadrilateral is a rhombus, then it is a parallelogram. (rhombus → ▱)	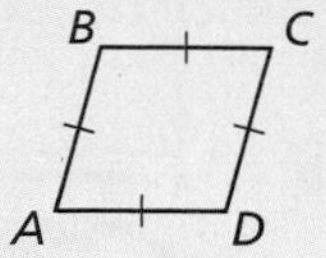	*ABCD* is a parallelogram.
6-4-4	If a parallelogram is a rhombus, then its diagonals are perpendicular. (rhombus → diags. ⊥)	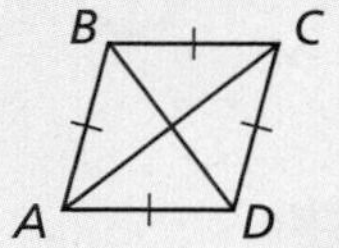	$\overline{AC} \perp \overline{BD}$
6-4-5	If a parallelogram is a rhombus, then each diagonal bisects a pair of opposite angles. (rhombus → each diag. bisects opp. ∠s)	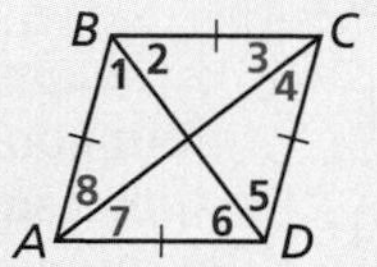	$\angle 1 \cong \angle 2$ $\angle 3 \cong \angle 4$ $\angle 5 \cong \angle 6$ $\angle 7 \cong \angle 8$

You will prove Theorems 6-4-3 and 6-4-4 in Exercises 34 and 37.

PROOF **Theorem 6-4-5**

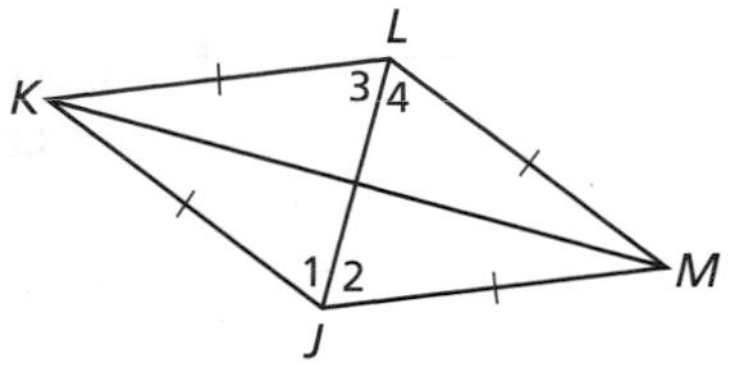

Given: *JKLM* is a rhombus.
Prove: $\overline{JL}$ bisects $\angle KJM$ and $\angle KLM$.
$\overline{KM}$ bisects $\angle JKL$ and $\angle JML$.

Proof:
Since *JKLM* is a rhombus, $\overline{JK} \cong \overline{JM}$, and $\overline{KL} \cong \overline{ML}$ by the definition of a rhombus. By the Reflexive Property of Congruence, $\overline{JL} \cong \overline{JL}$. Thus $\triangle JKL \cong \triangle JML$ by SSS. Then $\angle 1 \cong \angle 2$, and $\angle 3 \cong \angle 4$ by CPCTC. So $\overline{JL}$ bisects $\angle KJM$ and $\angle KLM$ by the definition of an angle bisector. By similar reasoning, $\overline{KM}$ bisects $\angle JKL$ and $\angle JML$.

Like a rectangle, a rhombus is a parallelogram. So you can apply the properties of parallelograms to rhombuses.

EXAMPLE 2 Using Properties of Rhombuses to Find Measures

Algebra

RSTV is a rhombus. Find each measure.

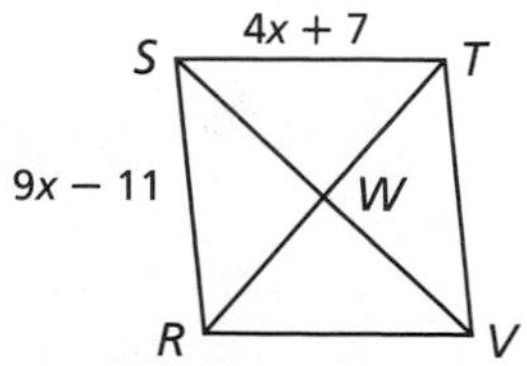

A *VT*

$ST = SR$	*Def. of rhombus*
$4x + 7 = 9x - 11$	*Substitute the given values.*
$18 = 5x$	*Subtract 4x from both sides and add 11 to both sides.*
$3.6 = x$	*Divide both sides by 5.*
$VT = ST$	*Def. of rhombus*
$VT = 4x + 7$	*Substitute 4x + 7 for ST.*
$VT = 4(3.6) + 7 = 21.4$	*Substitute 3.6 for x and simplify.*

***RSTV* is a rhombus. Find each measure.**

B $m\angle WSR$

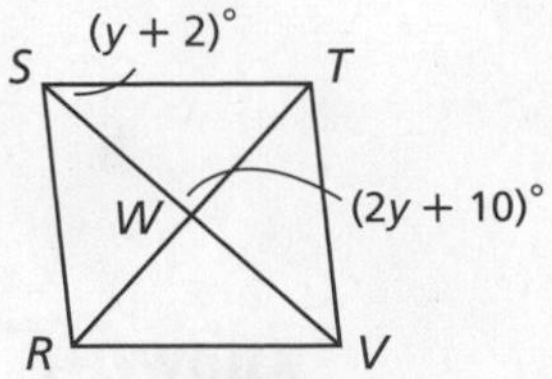

$m\angle SWT = 90°$	*Rhombus → diags. ⊥*
$2y + 10 = 90$	*Substitute 2y + 10 for m∠SWT.*
$y = 40$	*Subtract 10 from both sides and divide both sides by 2.*
$m\angle WSR = m\angle TSW$	*Rhombus → each diag. bisects opp. ∠s*
$m\angle WSR = (y + 2)°$	*Substitute y + 2 for m∠TSW.*
$m\angle WSR = (40 + 2)° = 42°$	*Substitute 40 for y and simplify.*

CHECK IT OUT! ***CDFG* is a rhombus. Find each measure.**

2a. CD

2b. $m\angle GCH$ if $m\angle GCD = (b + 3)°$ and $m\angle CDF = (6b - 40)°$

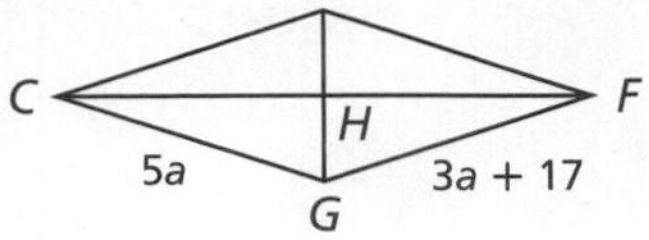

Helpful Hint

Rectangles, rhombuses, and squares are sometimes referred to as *special parallelograms*.

A **square** is a quadrilateral with four right angles and four congruent sides. In the exercises, you will show that a square is a parallelogram, a rectangle, and a rhombus. So a square has the properties of all three.

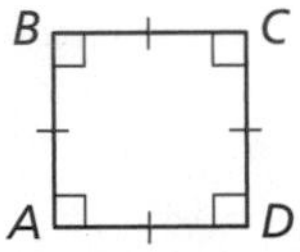

Square *ABCD*

EXAMPLE 3 Verifying Properties of Squares

Show that the diagonals of square *ABCD* are congruent perpendicular bisectors of each other.

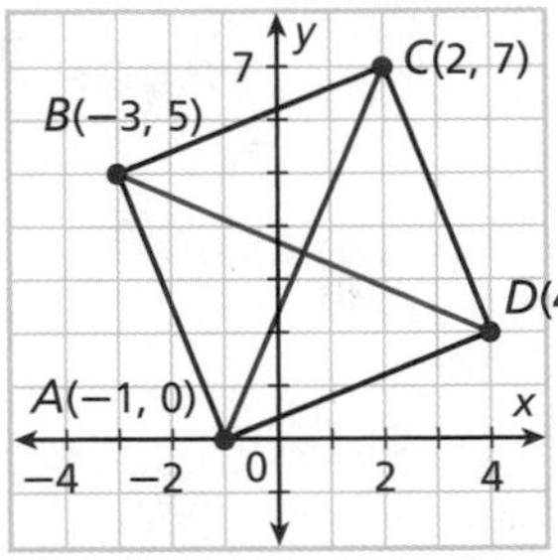

Step 1 Show that $\overline{AC}$ and $\overline{BD}$ are congruent.

$$AC = \sqrt{[2-(-1)]^2 + (7-0)^2} = \sqrt{58}$$

$$BD = \sqrt{[4-(-3)]^2 + (2-5)^2} = \sqrt{58}$$

Since $AC = BD$, $\overline{AC} \cong \overline{BD}$.

Step 2 Show that $\overline{AC}$ and $\overline{BD}$ are perpendicular.

$$\text{slope of } \overline{AC} = \frac{7-0}{2-(-1)} = \frac{7}{3}$$

$$\text{slope of } \overline{BD} = \frac{2-5}{4-(-3)} = \frac{-3}{7} = -\frac{3}{7}$$

Since $\left(\frac{7}{3}\right)\left(-\frac{3}{7}\right) = -1$, $\overline{AC} \perp \overline{BD}$.

Step 3 Show that $\overline{AC}$ and $\overline{BD}$ bisect each other.

$$\text{mdpt. of } \overline{AC}: \left(\frac{-1+2}{2}, \frac{0+7}{2}\right) = \left(\frac{1}{2}, \frac{7}{2}\right)$$

$$\text{mdpt. of } \overline{BD}: \left(\frac{-3+4}{2}, \frac{5+2}{2}\right) = \left(\frac{1}{2}, \frac{7}{2}\right)$$

Since $\overline{AC}$ and $\overline{BD}$ have the same midpoint, they bisect each other.

The diagonals are congruent perpendicular bisectors of each other.

CHECK IT OUT! **3.** The vertices of square *STVW* are $S(-5, -4)$, $T(0, 2)$, $V(6, -3)$, and $W(1, -9)$. Show that the diagonals of square *STVW* are congruent perpendicular bisectors of each other.

Student to Student

Special Parallelograms

Taylor Gallinghouse
Central High School

*To remember the properties of rectangles, rhombuses, and squares, I start with a **square**, which has all the properties of the others.*

*To get a **rectangle** that is not a square, I stretch the square in one direction. Its diagonals are still congruent, but they are no longer perpendicular.*

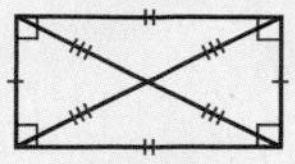

*To get a **rhombus** that is not a square, I go back to the square and slide the top in one direction. Its diagonals are still perpendicular and bisect the opposite angles, but they aren't congruent.*

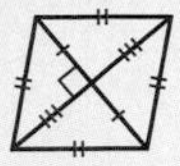

EXAMPLE 4 **Using Properties of Special Parallelograms in Proofs**

Given: *EFGH* **is a rectangle.** *J* **is the midpoint of** $\overline{EH}$.
Prove: $\triangle FJG$ **is isosceles.**

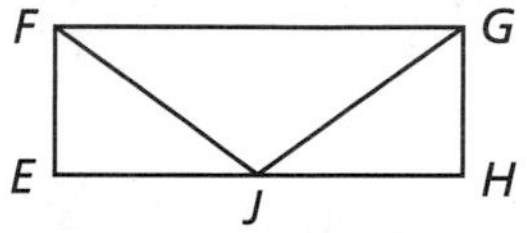

Proof:

Statements	Reasons
1. *EFGH* is a rectangle. *J* is the midpoint of $\overline{EH}$.	1. Given
2. $\angle E$ and $\angle H$ are right angles.	2. Def. of rect.
3. $\angle E \cong \angle H$	3. Rt. $\angle \cong$ Thm.
4. *EFGH* is a parallelogram.	4. Rect. → ▱
5. $\overline{EF} \cong \overline{HG}$	5. ▱ → opp. sides ≅
6. $\overline{EJ} \cong \overline{HJ}$	6. Def. of mdpt.
7. $\triangle FJE \cong \triangle GJH$	7. SAS *Steps 3, 5, 6*
8. $\overline{FJ} \cong \overline{GJ}$	8. CPCTC
9. $\triangle FJG$ is isosceles.	9. Def. of isosc. △

CHECK IT OUT!

4. Given: *PQTS* is a rhombus with diagonal $\overline{PR}$.
Prove: $\overline{RQ} \cong \overline{RS}$

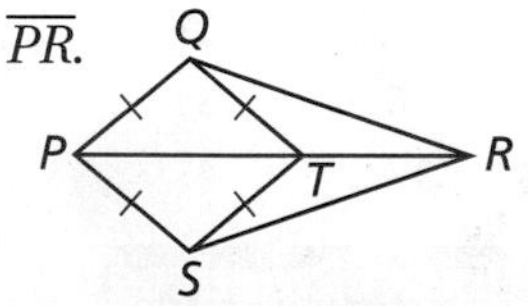

MATHEMATICAL PRACTICES

THINK AND DISCUSS

1. Which theorem means "The diagonals of a rectangle are congruent"? Why do you think the theorem is written as a conditional?

2. What properties of a rhombus are the same as the properties of all parallelograms? What special properties does a rhombus have?

Know it! Note

3. GET ORGANIZED Copy and complete the graphic organizer. Write the missing terms in the three unlabeled sections. Then write a definition of each term.

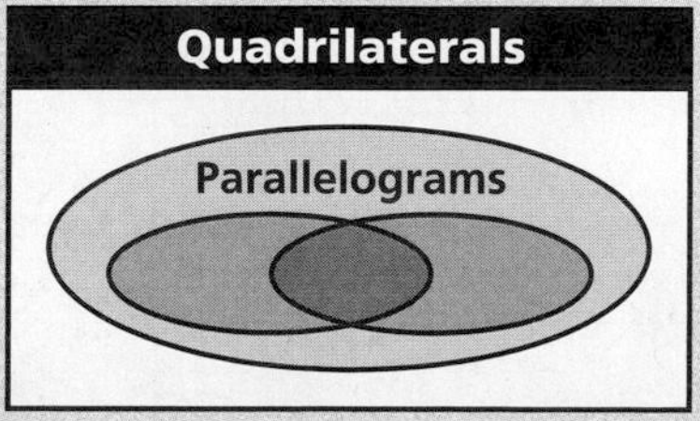

6-4 Exercises

Learn It Online
Homework Help Online
Parent Resources Online

GUIDED PRACTICE

1. **Vocabulary** What is another name for an *equilateral quadrilateral*? an *equiangular quadrilateral*? a *regular quadrilateral*?

SEE EXAMPLE 1

Engineering The braces of the bridge support lie along the diagonals of rectangle *PQRS*. $RS = 160$ ft, and $QS = 380$ ft. Find each length.

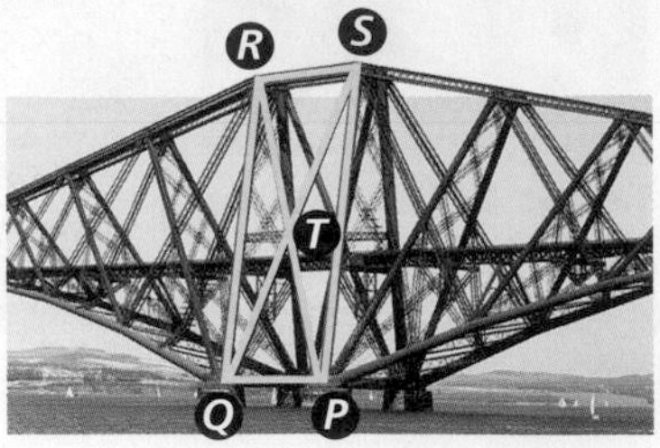

2. TQ
3. PQ
4. ST
5. PR

SEE EXAMPLE 2

ABCD **is a rhombus. Find each measure.**

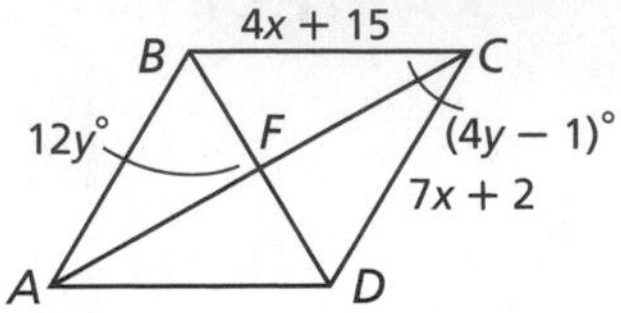

6. AB
7. $m\angle ABC$

SEE EXAMPLE 3

8. **Multi-Step** The vertices of square *JKLM* are $J(-3, -5)$, $K(-4, 1)$, $L(2, 2)$, and $M(3, -4)$. Show that the diagonals of square *JKLM* are congruent perpendicular bisectors of each other.

SEE EXAMPLE 4

9. **Given:** *RECT* is a rectangle. $\overline{RX} \cong \overline{TY}$
Prove: $\triangle REY \cong \triangle TCX$

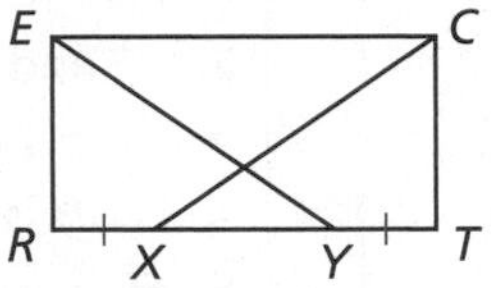

PRACTICE AND PROBLEM SOLVING

Independent Practice

For Exercises	See Example
10–13	1
14–15	2
16	3
17	4

Extra Practice
See Extra Practice for more Skills Practice and Applications Practice exercises.

Carpentry A carpenter measures the diagonals of a piece of wood. In rectangle *JKLM*, $JM = 25$ in., and $JP = 14\frac{1}{2}$ in. Find each length.

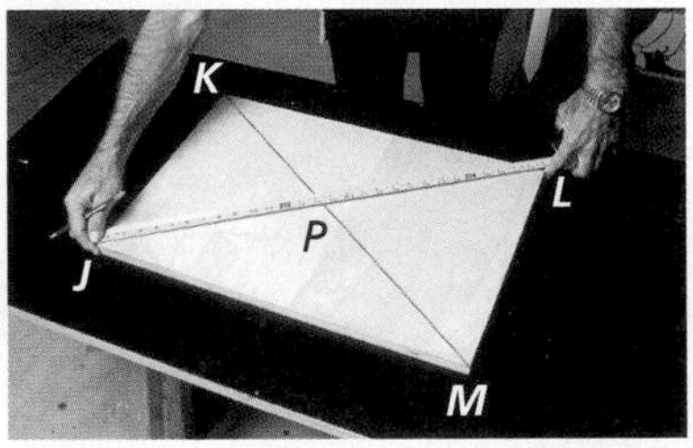

10. JL
11. KL
12. KM
13. MP

VWXY **is a rhombus. Find each measure.**

14. VW
15. $m\angle VWX$ and $m\angle WYX$ if $m\angle WVY = (4b + 10)^\circ$ and $m\angle XZW = (10b - 5)^\circ$

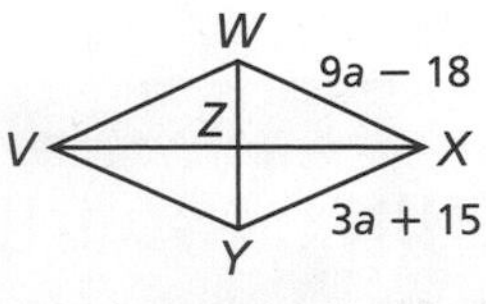

16. **Multi-Step** The vertices of square *PQRS* are $P(-4, 0)$, $Q(4, 3)$, $R(7, -5)$, and $S(-1, -8)$. Show that the diagonals of square *PQRS* are congruent perpendicular bisectors of each other.

17. **Given:** *RHMB* is a rhombus with diagonal $\overline{HB}$.
Prove: $\angle HMX \cong \angle HRX$

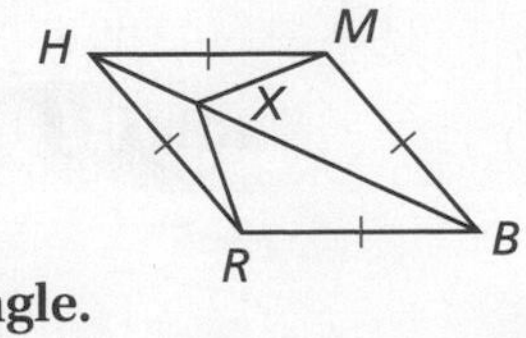

Find the measures of the numbered angles in each rectangle.

18.

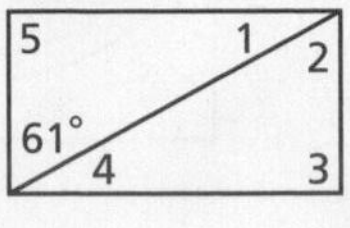

19.

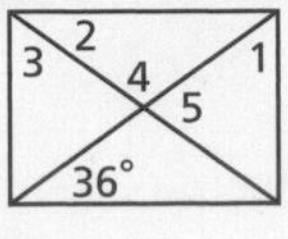

20.

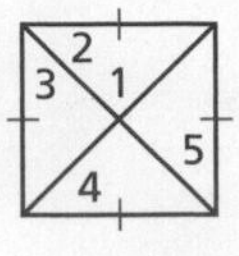

Find the measures of the numbered angles in each rhombus.

21.

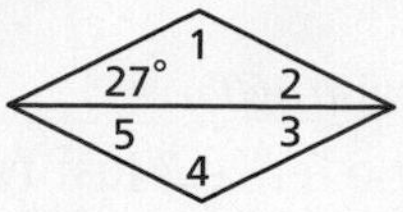

22.

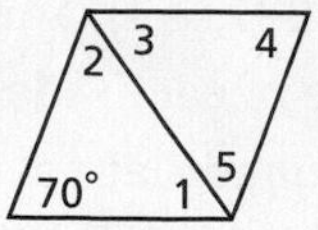

23.

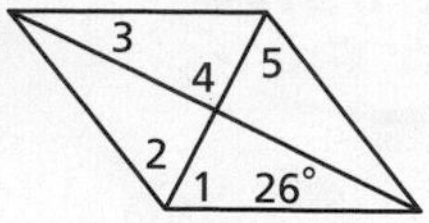

Tell whether each statement is sometimes, always, or never true. (*Hint:* Refer to your graphic organizer for this lesson.)

24. A rectangle is a parallelogram.

25. A rhombus is a square.

26. A parallelogram is a rhombus.

27. A rhombus is a rectangle.

28. A square is a rhombus.

29. A rectangle is a quadrilateral.

30. A square is a rectangle.

31. A rectangle is a square.

32. Critical Thinking A triangle is equilateral if and only if the triangle is equiangular. Can you make a similar statement about a quadrilateral? Explain your answer.

33. History There are five shapes of clay tiles in this tile mosaic from the ruins of Pompeii.

a. Make a sketch of each shape of tile and tell whether the shape is a polygon.

b. Name each polygon by its number of sides. Does each shape appear to be regular or irregular?

c. Do any of the shapes appear to be special parallelograms? If so, identify them by name.

d. Find the measure of each interior angle of the center polygon.

34. ///ERROR ANALYSIS/// Find and correct the error in this proof of Theorem 6-4-3.

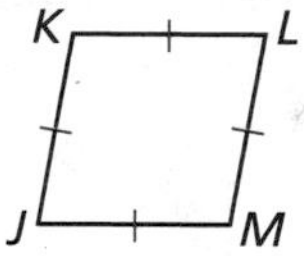

Given: *JKLM* is a rhombus.
Prove: *JKLM* is a parallelogram.

Proof:

It is given that *JKLM* is a rhombus. So by the definition of a rhombus, $\overline{JK} \cong \overline{LM}$, and $\overline{KL} \cong \overline{MJ}$. If a quadrilateral is a parallelogram, then its opposite sides are congruent. So *JKLM* is a parallelogram.

35. Complete the two-column proof of Theorem 6-4-2 by filling in the blanks.

Given: *EFGH* is a rectangle.
Prove: $\overline{FH} \cong \overline{GE}$

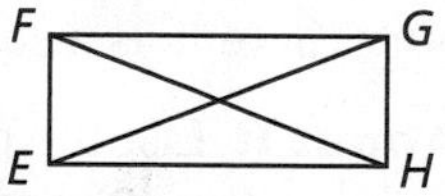

Proof:

Statements	Reasons
1. *EFGH* is a rectangle.	1. Given
2. *EFGH* is a parallelogram.	2. a. ___?___
3. $\overline{EF} \cong$ b. ___?___	3. ▱ → opp. sides ≅
4. $\overline{EH} \cong \overline{EH}$	4. c. ___?___
5. ∠*FEH* and ∠*GHE* are right angles.	5. d. ___?___
6. ∠*FEH* ≅ e. ___?___	6. Rt. ∠ ≅ Thm.
7. △*FEH* ≅ △*GHE*	7. f. ___?___
8. $\overline{FH} \cong \overline{GE}$	8. g. ___?___

MULTI-STEP TEST PREP

36. The organizers of a fair plan to fence off a plot of land given by the coordinates $A(2, 4)$, $B(4, 2)$, $C(-1, -3)$, and $D(-3, -1)$.

a. Find the slope of each side of quadrilateral *ABCD*.

b. What type of quadrilateral is formed by the fences? Justify your answer.

c. The organizers plan to build a straight path connecting *A* and *C* and another path connecting *B* and *D*. Explain why these two paths will have the same length.

37. Use this plan to write a proof of Theorem 6-4-4.

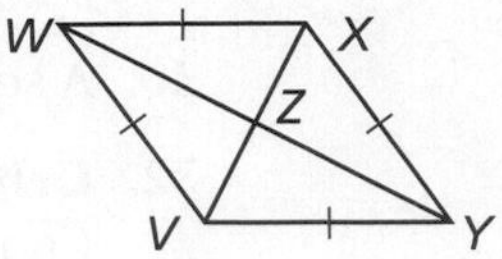

Given: *VWXY* is a rhombus.

Prove: $\overline{VX} \perp \overline{WY}$

Plan: Use the definition of a rhombus and the properties of parallelograms to show that $\triangle WZX \cong \triangle YZX$. Then use CPCTC to show that $\angle WZX$ and $\angle YZX$ are right angles.

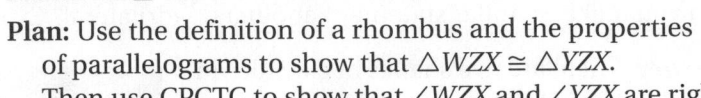

38. Write a paragraph proof of Theorem 6-4-1.

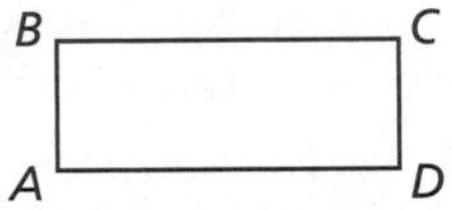

Given: *ABCD* is a rectangle.

Prove: *ABCD* is a parallelogram.

39. Write a two-column proof.

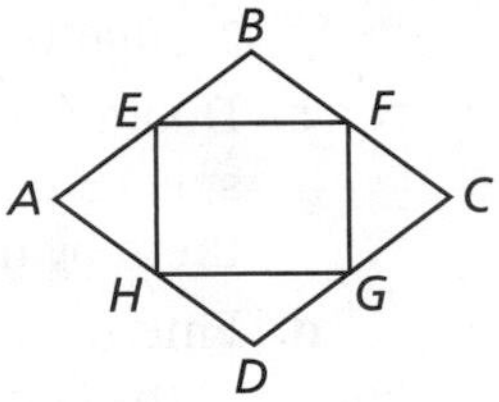

Given: *ABCD* is a rhombus. *E*, *F*, *G*, and *H* are the midpoints of the sides.

Prove: *EFGH* is a parallelogram.

Multi-Step Find the perimeter and area of each figure. Round to the nearest hundredth, if necessary.

40.

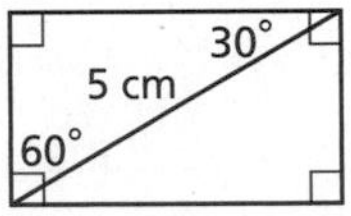

41.

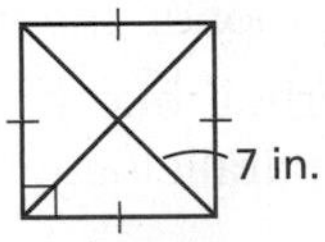

42.

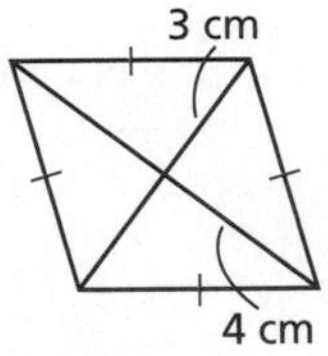

43. Write About It Explain why each of these conditional statements is true.

a. If a quadrilateral is a square, then it is a parallelogram.

b. If a quadrilateral is a square, then it is a rectangle.

c. If a quadrilateral is a square, then it is a rhombus.

44. Write About It List the properties that a square "inherits" because it is (1) a parallelogram, (2) a rectangle, and (3) a rhombus.

TEST PREP

45. Which expression represents the measure of $\angle J$ in rhombus *JKLM*?

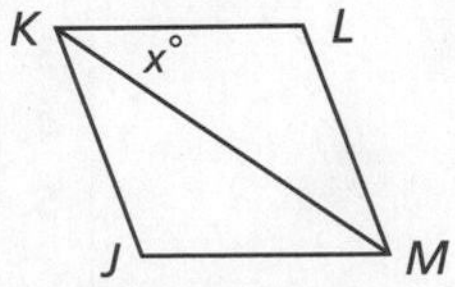

Ⓐ $x°$　　Ⓒ $(180 - x)°$

Ⓑ $2x°$　　Ⓓ $(180 - 2x)°$

46. Short Response The diagonals of rectangle *QRST* intersect at point *P*. If $QR = 1.8$ cm, $QP = 1.5$ cm, and $QT = 2.4$ cm, find the perimeter of $\triangle RST$. Explain how you found your answer.

47. Which statement is NOT true of a rectangle?

Ⓕ Both pairs of opposite sides are congruent and parallel.

Ⓖ Both pairs of opposite angles are congruent and supplementary.

Ⓗ All pairs of consecutive sides are congruent and perpendicular.

Ⓙ All pairs of consecutive angles are congruent and supplementary.

CHALLENGE AND EXTEND

48. **Algebra** Find the value of x in the rhombus.

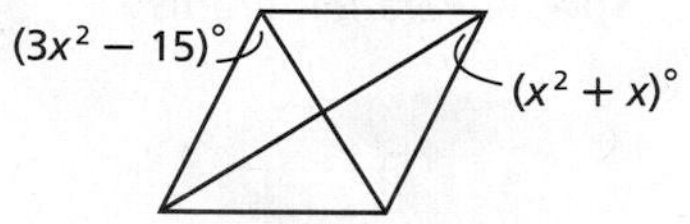

49. Prove that the segment joining the midpoints of two consecutive sides of a rhombus is perpendicular to one diagonal and parallel to the other.

50. Extend the definition of a triangle midsegment to write a definition for the midsegment of a rectangle. Prove that a midsegment of a rectangle divides the rectangle into two congruent rectangles.

51. The figure is formed by joining eleven congruent squares. How many rectangles are in the figure?

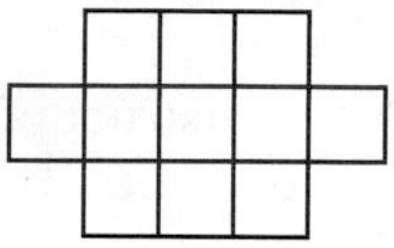

Construction Rhombus

1

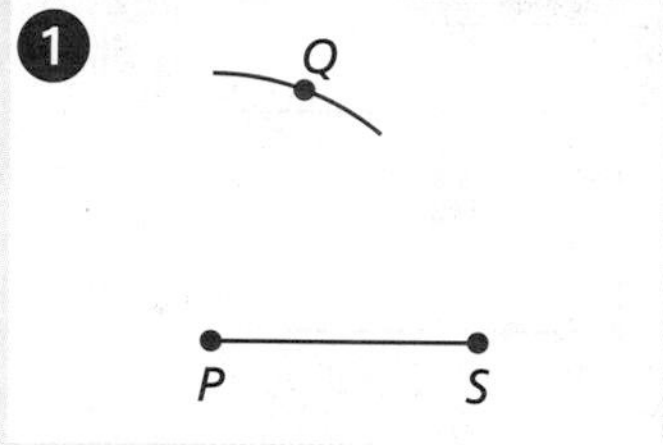

Draw $\overline{PS}$. Set the compass to the length of $\overline{PS}$. Place the compass point at P and draw an arc above $\overline{PS}$. Label a point **Q** on the arc.

2

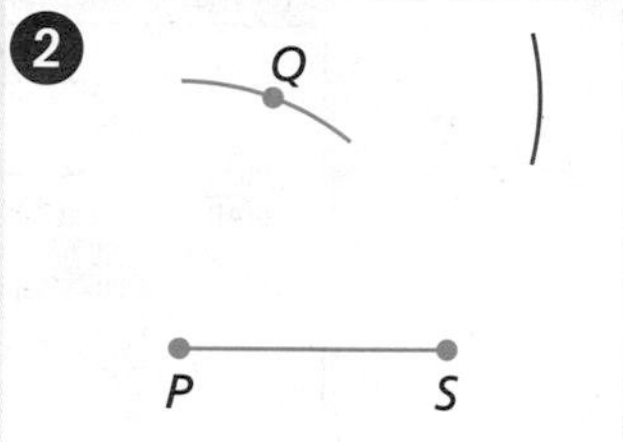

Place the compass point at Q and draw an arc to the right of Q.

3

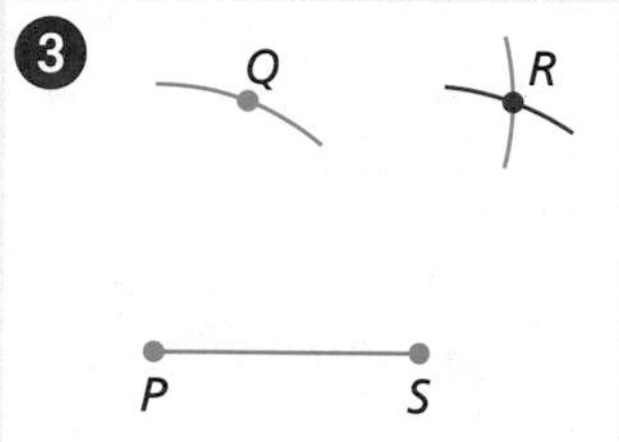

Place the compass point at S and draw an arc that intersects the arc drawn from Q. Label the point of intersection **R**.

4

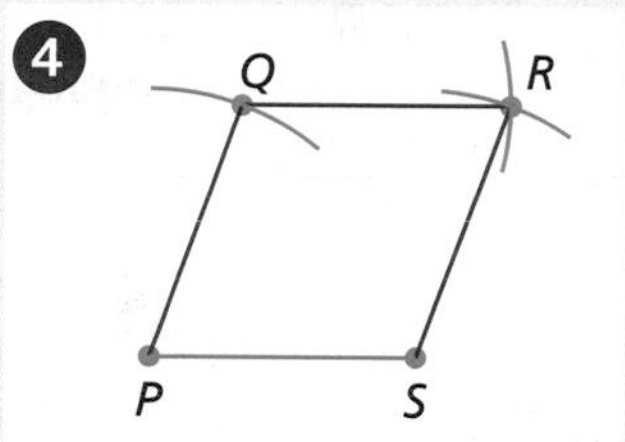

Draw $\overline{PQ}$, $\overline{QR}$, and $\overline{RS}$.

6-5 Technology LAB

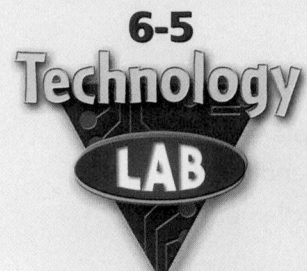

Predict Conditions for Special Parallelograms

In this lab, you will use geometry software to predict the conditions that are sufficient to prove that a parallelogram is a rectangle, rhombus, or square.

Use with *Conditions for Special Parallelograms*

MATHEMATICAL PRACTICES **Use appropriate tools strategically.**

Learn It Online
Lab Resources Online

Activity 1

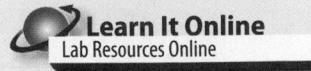

CC.9-12.G.CO.11 Prove theorems about parallelograms.

1. Construct $\overline{AB}$ and $\overline{AD}$ with a common endpoint A. Construct a line through D parallel to $\overline{AB}$. Construct a line through B parallel to $\overline{AD}$.

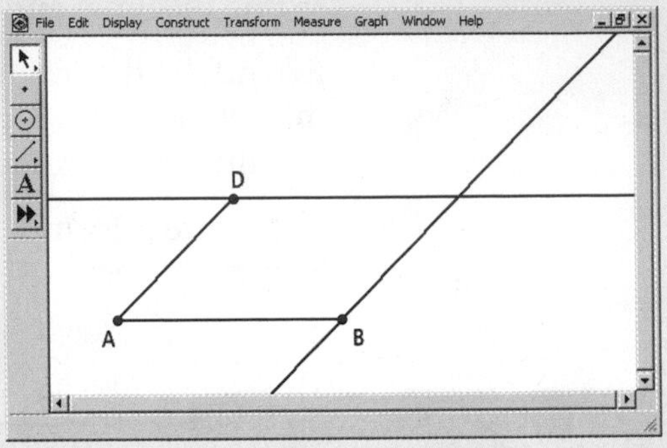

2. Construct point C at the intersection of the two lines. Hide the lines and construct $\overline{BC}$ and $\overline{CD}$ to complete the parallelogram.

3. Measure the four sides and angles of the parallelogram.

4. Move A so that $m\angle ABC = 90°$. What type of special parallelogram results?

5. Move A so that $m\angle ABC \neq 90°$.

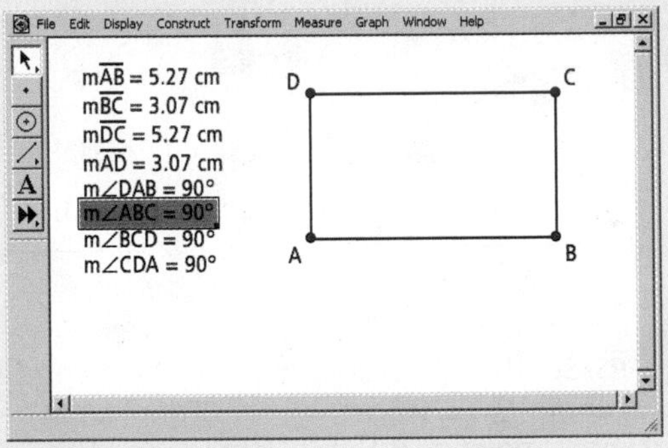

6. Construct $\overline{AC}$ and $\overline{BD}$ and measure their lengths. Move A so that $AC = BD$. What type of special parallelogram results?

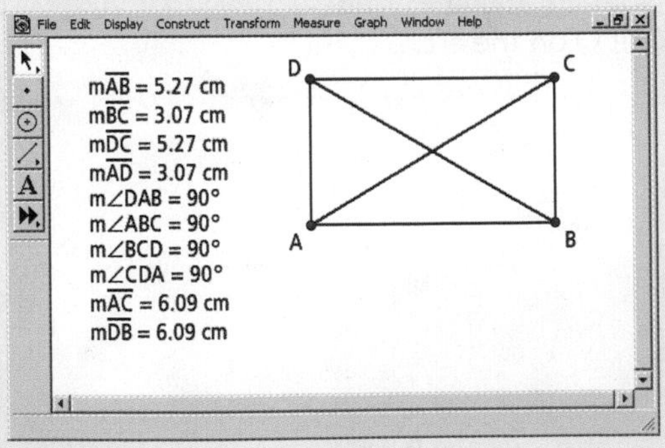

Try This

1. How does the method of constructing $ABCD$ in Steps 1 and 2 guarantee that the quadrilateral is a parallelogram?

2. **Make a Conjecture** What are two conditions for a rectangle? Write your conjectures as conditional statements.

Activity 2

1. Use the parallelogram you constructed in Activity 1. Move A so that $AB = BC$. What type of special parallelogram results?

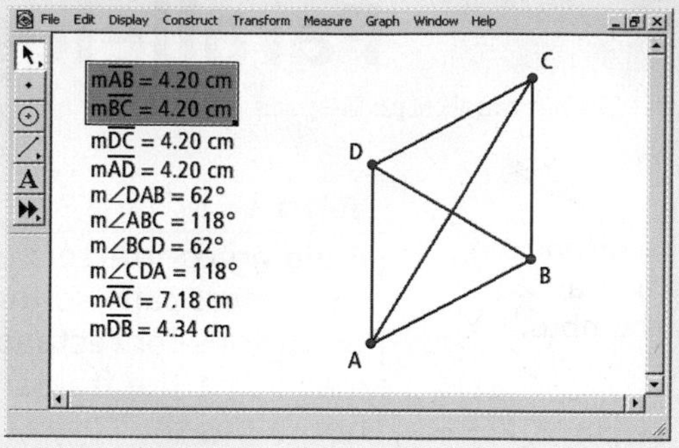

2. Move A so that $AB \neq BC$.

3. Label the intersection of the diagonals as E. Measure $\angle AEB$.

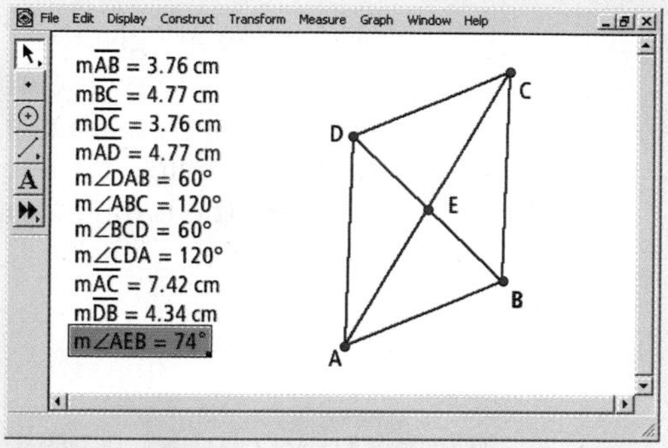

4. Move A so that $m\angle AEB = 90°$. What type of special parallelogram results?

5. Move A so that $m\angle AEB \neq 90°$.

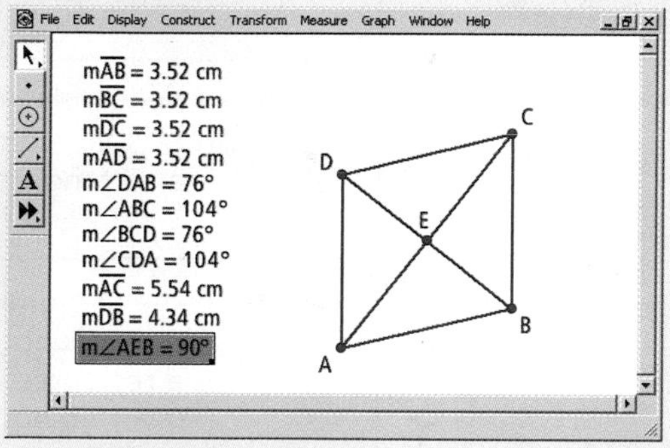

6. Measure $\angle ABD$ and $\angle CBD$. Move A so that $m\angle ABD = m\angle CBD$. What type of special parallelogram results?

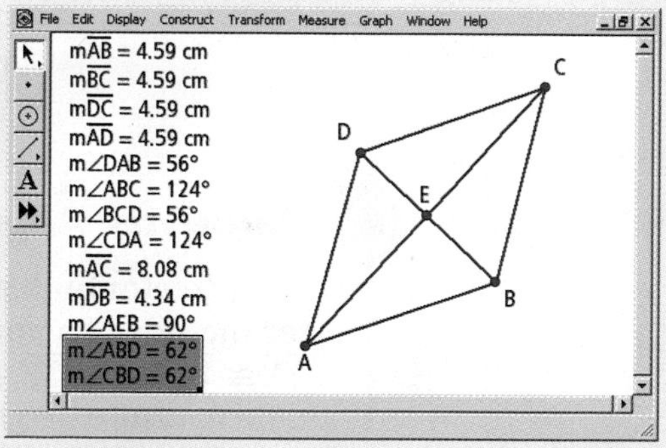

Try This

3. **Make a Conjecture** What are three conditions for a rhombus? Write your conjectures as conditional statements.

4. **Make a Conjecture** A square is both a rectangle and a rhombus. What conditions do you think must hold for a parallelogram to be a square?

COMMON CORE

6-5 Conditions for Special Parallelograms

CC.9-12.G.CO.11 Prove theorems about parallelograms.

Objective
Prove that a given quadrilateral is a rectangle, rhombus, or square.

Who uses this?
Building contractors and carpenters can use the conditions for rectangles to make sure the frame for a house has the correct shape.

When you are given a parallelogram with certain properties, you can use the theorems below to determine whether the parallelogram is a rectangle.

Know it! Note

Theorems Conditions for Rectangles

	THEOREM	EXAMPLE
6-5-1	If one angle of a parallelogram is a right angle, then the parallelogram is a rectangle. (▱ with one rt. ∠ → rect.)	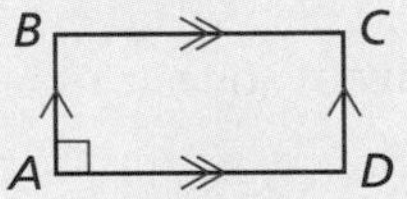
6-5-2	If the diagonals of a parallelogram are congruent, then the parallelogram is a rectangle. (▱ with diags. ≅ → rect.)	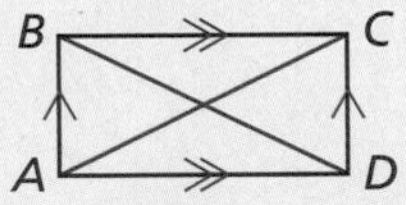 $\overline{AC} \cong \overline{BD}$

You will prove Theorems 6-5-1 and 6-5-2 in Exercises 31 and 28.

EXAMPLE 1 *Carpentry Application*

A contractor built a wood frame for the side of a house so that $\overline{XY} \cong \overline{WZ}$ and $\overline{XW} \cong \overline{YZ}$. Using a tape measure, the contractor found that $XZ = WY$. Why must the frame be a rectangle?

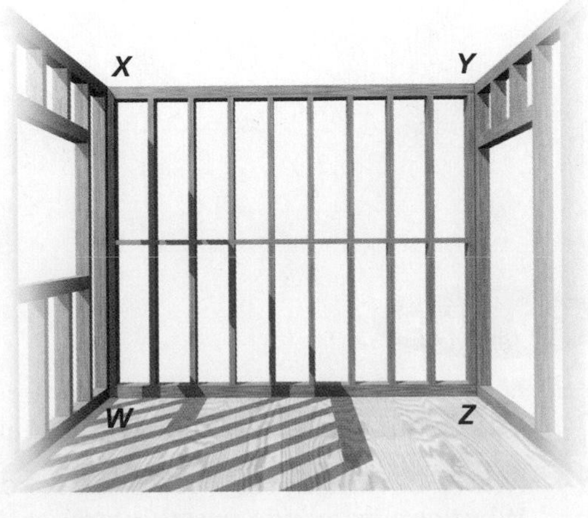

Both pairs of opposite sides of $WXYZ$ are congruent, so $WXYZ$ is a parallelogram. Since $XZ = WY$, the diagonals of ▱$WXYZ$ are congruent. Therefore the frame is a rectangle by Theorem 6-5-2.

CHECK IT OUT! **1.** A carpenter's square can be used to test that an angle is a right angle. How could the contractor use a carpenter's square to check that the frame is a rectangle?

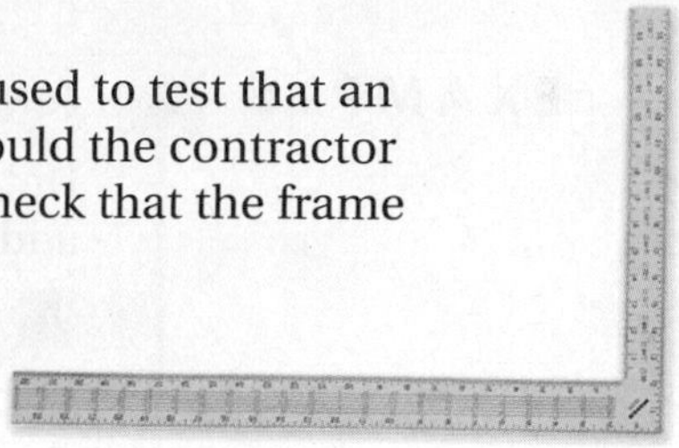

Below are some conditions you can use to determine whether a parallelogram is a rhombus.

Know it! Note

Theorems **Conditions for Rhombuses**

	THEOREM	EXAMPLE
6-5-3	If one pair of consecutive sides of a parallelogram are congruent, then the parallelogram is a rhombus. (▱ with one pair cons. sides ≅ → rhombus)	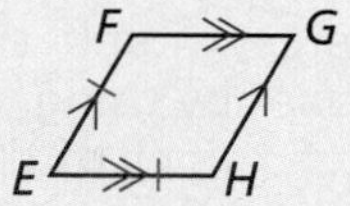
6-5-4	If the diagonals of a parallelogram are perpendicular, then the parallelogram is a rhombus. (▱ with diags. ⊥ → rhombus)	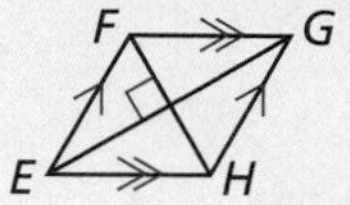
6-5-5	If one diagonal of a parallelogram bisects a pair of opposite angles, then the parallelogram is a rhombus. (▱ with diag. bisecting opp. ∠s → rhombus)	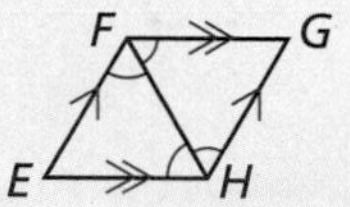

You will prove Theorems 6-5-3 and 6-5-4 in Exercises 32 and 30.

Caution!

In order to apply Theorems 6-5-1 through 6-5-5, the quadrilateral must be a parallelogram.

PROOF

Theorem 6-5-5

Given: *JKLM* is a parallelogram.
$\overline{JL}$ bisects ∠*KJM* and ∠*KLM*.
Prove: *JKLM* is a rhombus.
Proof:

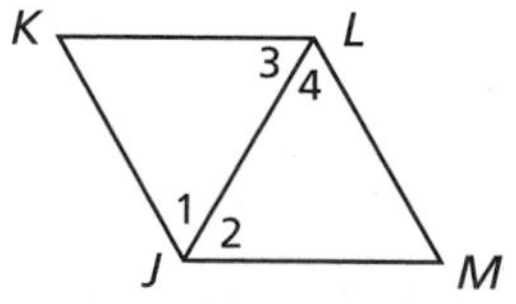

Statements	Reasons
1. *JKLM* is a parallelogram. $\overline{JL}$ bisects ∠*KJM* and ∠*KLM*.	**1.** Given
2. ∠1 ≅ ∠2, ∠3 ≅ ∠4	**2.** Def. of ∠ bisector
3. $\overline{JL} \cong \overline{JL}$	**3.** Reflex. Prop. of ≅
4. △*JKL* ≅ △*JML*	**4.** ASA *Steps 2, 3*
5. $\overline{JK} \cong \overline{JM}$	**5.** CPCTC
6. *JKLM* is a rhombus.	**6.** ▱ with one pair cons. sides ≅ → rhombus

To prove that a given quadrilateral is a square, it is sufficient to show that the figure is both a rectangle and a rhombus. You will explain why this is true in Exercise 43.

EXAMPLE 2 Applying Conditions for Special Parallelograms

Determine if the conclusion is valid. If not, tell what additional information is needed to make it valid.

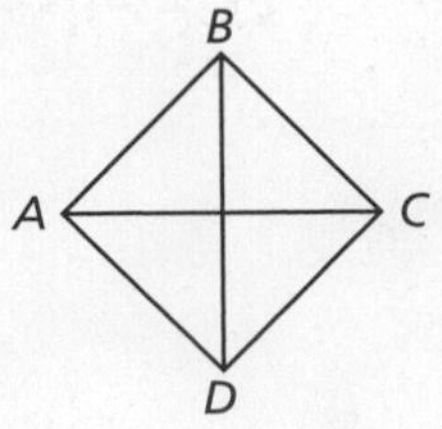

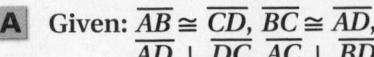

A **Given:** $\overline{AB} \cong \overline{CD}$, $\overline{BC} \cong \overline{AD}$, $\overline{AD} \perp \overline{DC}$, $\overline{AC} \perp \overline{BD}$

Conclusion: *ABCD* **is a square.**

Step 1 Determine if *ABCD* is a parallelogram.

$\overline{AB} \cong \overline{CD}$, $\overline{BC} \cong \overline{AD}$	*Given*
ABCD is a parallelogram.	*Quad. with opp. sides ≅ → ▱*

Step 2 Determine if *ABCD* is a rectangle.

$\overline{AD} \perp \overline{DC}$, so $\angle ADC$ is a right angle.	*Def. of ⊥*
ABCD is a rectangle.	*▱ with one rt. ∠ → rect.*

Step 3 Determine if *ABCD* is a rhombus.

$\overline{AC} \perp \overline{BD}$	*Given*
ABCD is a rhombus.	*▱ with diags. ⊥ → rhombus*

Step 4 Determine if *ABCD* is a square.

Since *ABCD* is a rectangle and a rhombus, it has four right angles and four congruent sides. So *ABCD* is a square by definition. The conclusion is valid.

B **Given:** $\overline{AB} \cong \overline{BC}$

Conclusion: *ABCD* **is a rhombus.**

The conclusion is not valid. By Theorem 6-5-3, if one pair of consecutive sides of a parallelogram are congruent, then the parallelogram is a rhombus. To apply this theorem, you must first know that *ABCD* is a parallelogram.

Remember!

You can also prove that a given quadrilateral is a rectangle, rhombus, or square by using the definitions of the special quadrilaterals.

CHECK IT OUT!

2. Determine if the conclusion is valid. If not, tell what additional information is needed to make it valid.
Given: $\angle ABC$ is a right angle.
Conclusion: *ABCD* is a rectangle.

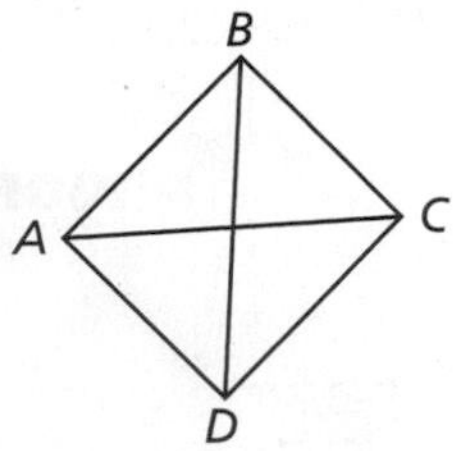

EXAMPLE 3 Identifying Special Parallelograms in the Coordinate Plane

Use the diagonals to determine whether a parallelogram with the given vertices is a rectangle, rhombus, or square. Give all the names that apply.

A $A(0, 2)$, $B(3, 6)$, $C(8, 6)$, $D(5, 2)$

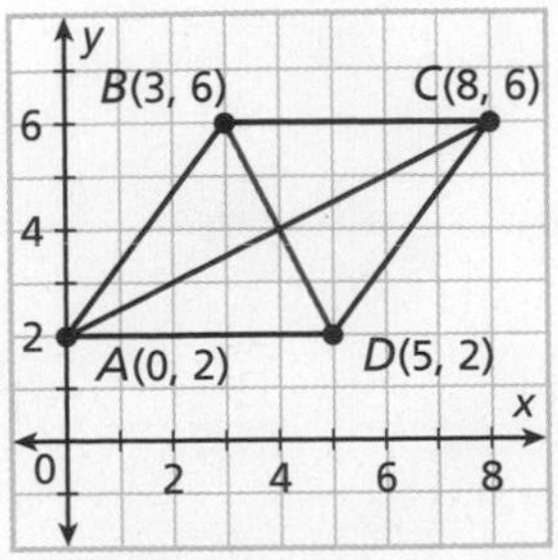

Step 1 Graph ▱*ABCD*.

Step 2 Determine if *ABCD* is a rectangle.

$$AC = \sqrt{(8-0)^2 + (6-2)^2} = \sqrt{80} = 4\sqrt{5}$$

$$BD = \sqrt{(5-3)^2 + (2-6)^2} = \sqrt{20} = 2\sqrt{5}$$

Since $4\sqrt{5} \neq 2\sqrt{5}$, *ABCD* is not a rectangle. Thus *ABCD* is not a square.

Step 3 Determine if *ABCD* is a rhombus.

slope of $\overline{AC} = \frac{6-2}{8-0} = \frac{1}{2}$ slope of $\overline{BD} = \frac{2-6}{5-3} = -2$

Since $\left(\frac{1}{2}\right)(-2) = -1$, $\overline{AC} \perp \overline{BD}$. *ABCD* is a rhombus.

B $E(-4, -1), F(-3, 2), G(3, 0), H(2, -3)$

Step 1 Graph ▱*EFGH*.

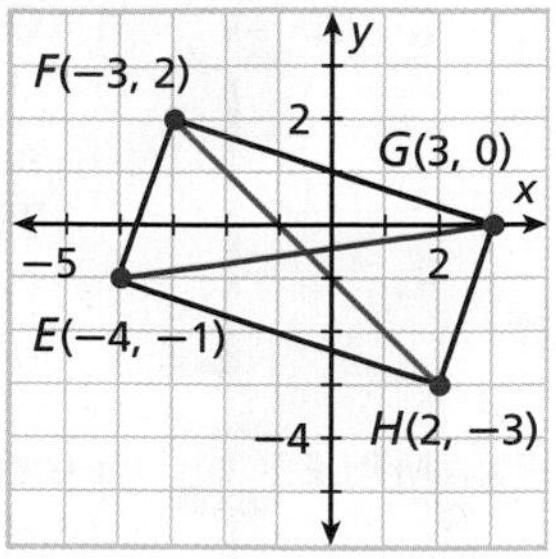

Step 2 Determine if *EFGH* is a rectangle.

$EG = \sqrt{[3-(-4)]^2 + [0-(-1)]^2}$
$= \sqrt{50} = 5\sqrt{2}$

$FH = \sqrt{[2-(-3)]^2 + (-3-2)^2}$
$= \sqrt{50} = 5\sqrt{2}$

Since $5\sqrt{2} = 5\sqrt{2}$, the diagonals are congruent. *EFGH* is a rectangle.

Step 3 Determine if *EFGH* is a rhombus.

slope of $\overline{EG} = \frac{0-(-1)}{3-(-4)} = \frac{1}{7}$

slope of $\overline{FH} = \frac{-3-2}{2-(-3)} = \frac{-5}{5} = -1$

Since $\left(\frac{1}{7}\right)(-1) \neq -1$, $\overline{EG} \not\perp \overline{FH}$.

So *EFGH* is a not a rhombus and cannot be a square.

CHECK IT OUT! **Use the diagonals to determine whether a parallelogram with the given vertices is a rectangle, rhombus, or square. Give all the names that apply.**

3a. $K(-5, -1), L(-2, 4), M(3, 1), N(0, -4)$

3b. $P(-4, 6), Q(2, 5), R(3, -1), S(-3, 0)$

MATHEMATICAL PRACTICES

THINK AND DISCUSS

1. What special parallelogram is formed when the diagonals of a parallelogram are congruent? when the diagonals are perpendicular? when the diagonals are both congruent and perpendicular?
2. Draw a figure that shows why this statement is not necessarily true: If one angle of a quadrilateral is a right angle, then the quadrilateral is a rectangle.
3. A rectangle can also be defined as a parallelogram with a right angle. Explain why this definition is accurate.

Know it! Note

4. **GET ORGANIZED** Copy and complete the graphic organizer. In each box, write at least three conditions for the given parallelogram.

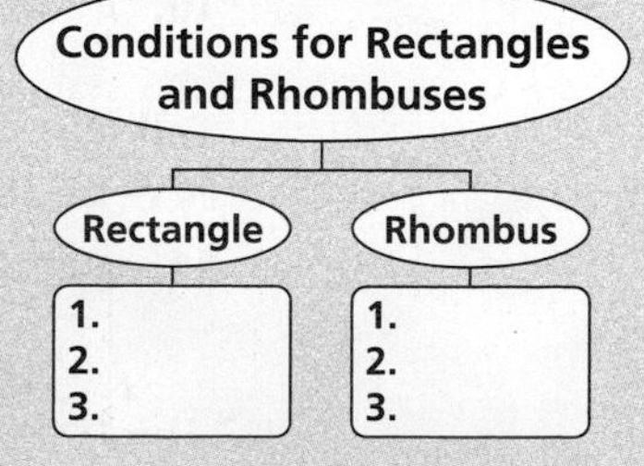

6-5 Exercises

Learn It Online
Homework Help Online
Parent Resources Online

GUIDED PRACTICE

SEE EXAMPLE 1

1. **Gardening** A city garden club is planting a square garden. They drive pegs into the ground at each corner and tie strings between each pair. The pegs are spaced so that $\overline{WX} \cong \overline{XY} \cong \overline{YZ} \cong \overline{ZW}$. How can the garden club use the diagonal strings to verify that the garden is a square?

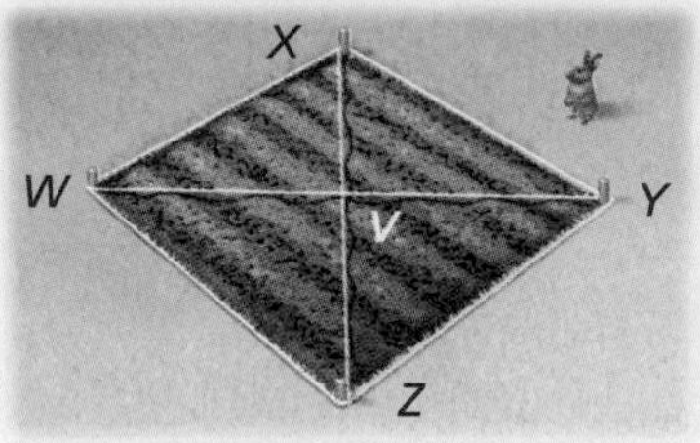

SEE EXAMPLE 2

Determine if the conclusion is valid. If not, tell what additional information is needed to make it valid.

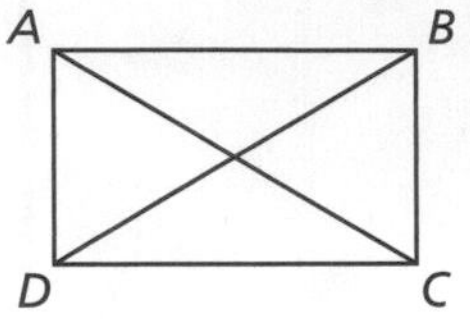

2. Given: $\overline{AC} \cong \overline{BD}$
   Conclusion: *ABCD* is a rectangle.
3. Given: $\overline{AB} \parallel \overline{CD}$, $\overline{AB} \cong \overline{CD}$, $\overline{AB} \perp \overline{BC}$
   Conclusion: *ABCD* is a rectangle.

SEE EXAMPLE 3

Multi-Step Use the diagonals to determine whether a parallelogram with the given vertices is a rectangle, rhombus, or square. Give all the names that apply.

4. $P(-5, 2)$, $Q(4, 5)$, $R(6, -1)$, $S(-3, -4)$
5. $W(-6, 0)$, $X(1, 4)$, $Y(2, -4)$, $Z(-5, -8)$

PRACTICE AND PROBLEM SOLVING

Independent Practice

For Exercises	See Example
6	1
7–8	2
9–10	3

Extra Practice
See Extra Practice for more Skills Practice and Applications Practice exercises.

6. **Crafts** A framer uses a clamp to hold together the pieces of a picture frame. The pieces are cut so that $\overline{PQ} \cong \overline{RS}$ and $\overline{QR} \cong \overline{SP}$. The clamp is adjusted so that *PZ, QZ, RZ,* and *SZ* are all equal. Why must the frame be a rectangle?

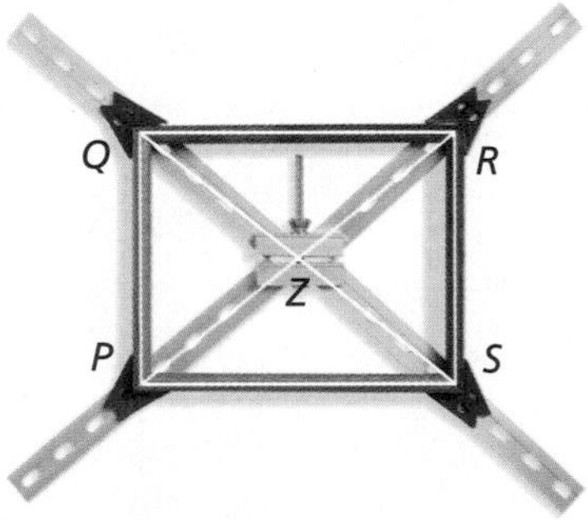

Determine if the conclusion is valid. If not, tell what additional information is needed to make it valid.

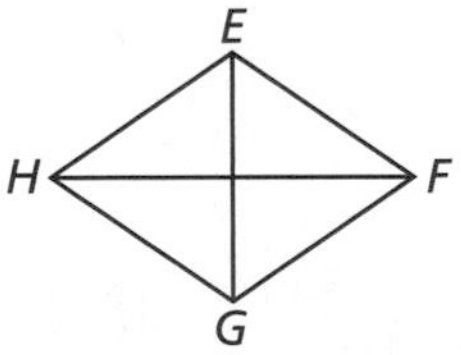

7. Given: $\overline{EG}$ and $\overline{FH}$ bisect each other. $\overline{EG} \perp \overline{FH}$
   Conclusion: *EFGH* is a rhombus.
8. Given: $\overline{FH}$ bisects $\angle EFG$ and $\angle EHG$.
   Conclusion: *EFGH* is a rhombus.

Multi-Step Use the diagonals to determine whether a parallelogram with the given vertices is a rectangle, rhombus, or square. Give all the names that apply.

9. $A(-10, 4)$, $B(-2, 10)$, $C(4, 2)$, $D(-4, -4)$
10. $J(-9, -7)$, $K(-4, -2)$, $L(3, -3)$, $M(-2, -8)$

Tell whether each quadrilateral is a parallelogram, rectangle, rhombus, or square. Give all the names that apply.

11. 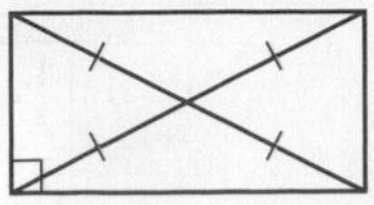

12. 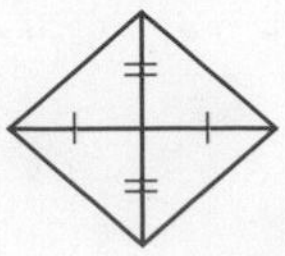

13. 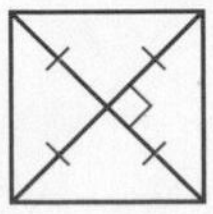

Tell whether each quadrilateral is a parallelogram, rectangle, rhombus, or square. Give all the names that apply.

14.

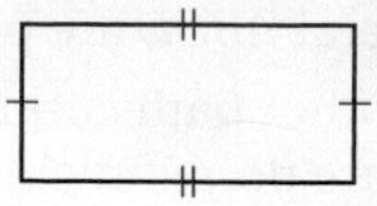

15.

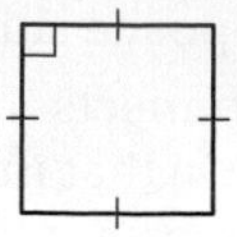

16.

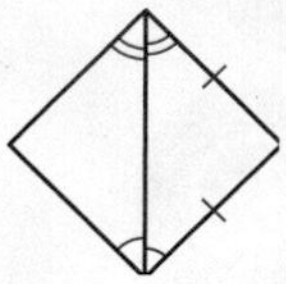

17. ///ERROR ANALYSIS/// In ▱*ABCD*, $\overline{AC} \cong \overline{BD}$. Which conclusion is incorrect? Explain the error.

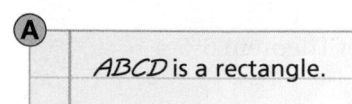

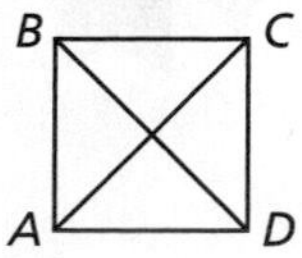

A *ABCD* is a rectangle.

B *ABCD* is a square.

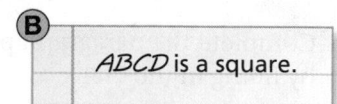

Give one characteristic of the diagonals of each figure that would make the conclusion valid.

18. Conclusion: *JKLM* is a rhombus.

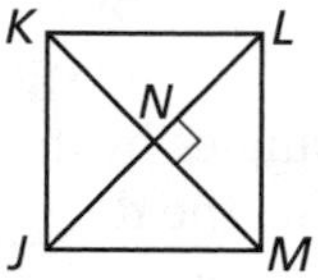

19. Conclusion: *PQRS* is a square.

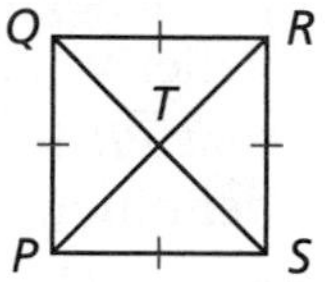

The coordinates of three vertices of ▱*ABCD* are given. Find the coordinates of *D* so that the given type of figure is formed.

20. $A(4, -2)$, $B(-5, -2)$, $C(4, 4)$; rectangle

21. $A(-5, 5)$, $B(0, 0)$, $C(7, 1)$; rhombus

22. $A(0, 2)$, $B(4, -2)$, $C(0, -6)$; square

23. $A(2, 1)$, $B(-1, 5)$, $C(-5, 2)$; square

Find the value of *x* that makes each parallelogram the given type.

24. rectangle

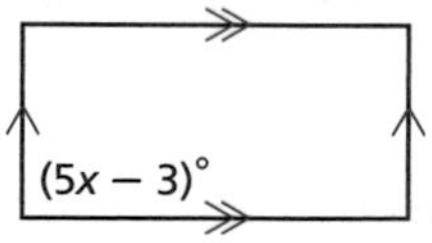

25. rhombus

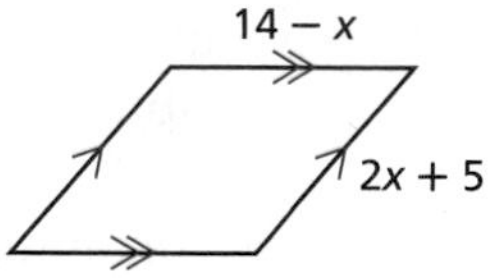

26. square

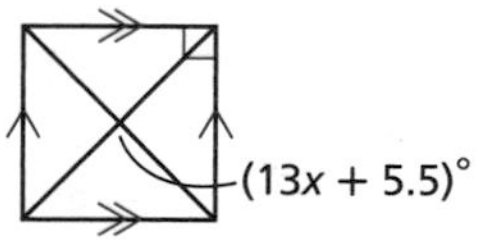

27. Critical Thinking The diagonals of a quadrilateral are perpendicular bisectors of each other. What is the best name for this quadrilateral? Explain your answer.

28. Complete the two-column proof of Theorem 6-5-2 by filling in the blanks.

Given: *EFGH* is a parallelogram.
$\overline{EG} \cong \overline{HF}$

Prove: *EFGH* is a rectangle.

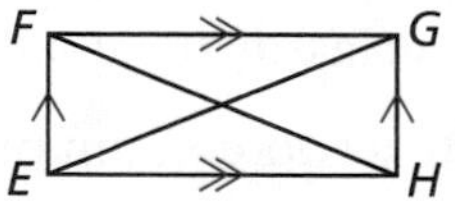

Proof:

Statements	Reasons
1. *EFGH* is a parallelogram. $\overline{EG} \cong \overline{HF}$	1. Given
2. $\overline{EF} \cong \overline{HG}$	2. a. ___?___
3. b. ___?___	3. Reflex. Prop. of ≅
4. △*EFH* ≅ △*HGE*	4. c. ___?___
5. ∠*FEH* ≅ d. ___?___	5. e. ___?___
6. ∠*FEH* and ∠*GHE* are supplementary.	6. f. ___?___
7. g. ___?___	7. ≅ ∡ supp. → rt. ∡
8. *EFGH* is a rectangle.	8. h. ___?___

MULTI-STEP TEST PREP

29. A state fair takes place on a plot of land given by the coordinates $A(-2, 3)$, $B(1, 2)$, $C(2, -1)$, and $D(-1, 0)$.

a. Show that the opposite sides of quadrilateral *ABCD* are parallel.

b. A straight path connects *A* and *C*, and another path connects *B* and *D*. Use slopes to prove that these two paths are perpendicular.

c. What can you conclude about *ABCD*? Explain your answer.

30. Complete the paragraph proof of Theorem 6-5-4 by filling in the blanks.

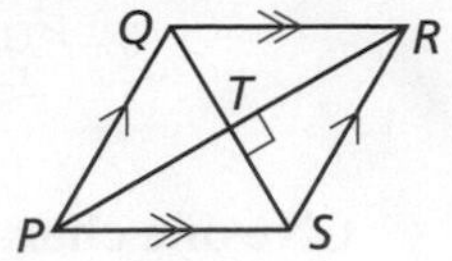

Given: *PQRS* is a parallelogram. $\overline{PR} \perp \overline{QS}$

Prove: *PQRS* is a rhombus.

Proof:

It is given that *PQRS* is a parallelogram. The diagonals of a parallelogram bisect each other, so $\overline{PT} \cong$ **a.** ___?___ . By the Reflexive Property of Congruence, $\overline{QT} \cong$ **b.** ___?___ . It is given that $\overline{PR} \perp \overline{QS}$, so $\angle QTP$ and $\angle QTR$ are right angles by the definition of **c.** ___?___ . Then $\angle QTP \cong \angle QTR$ by the **d.** ___?___ . So $\triangle QTP \cong \triangle QTR$ by **e.** ___?___ , and $\overline{QP} \cong$ **f.** ___?___ , by CPCTC. By Theorem 6-5-3, if one pair of consecutive sides of a parallelogram are congruent, then the parallelogram is a **g.** ___?___ . Therefore *PQRS* is rhombus.

31. Write a two-column proof of Theorem 6-5-1.

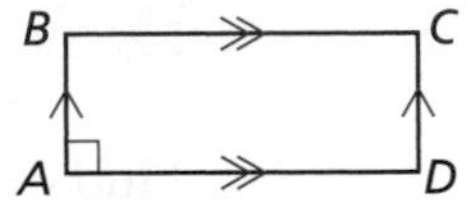

Given: *ABCD* is a parallelogram. $\angle A$ is a right angle.

Prove: *ABCD* is a rectangle.

32. Write a paragraph proof of Theorem 6-5-3.

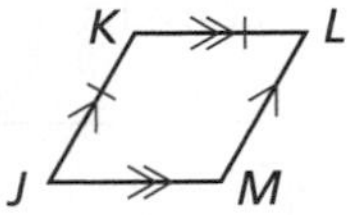

Given: *JKLM* is a parallelogram. $\overline{JK} \cong \overline{KL}$

Prove: *JKLM* is a rhombus.

33. Algebra Four lines are represented by the equations below.

ℓ: $y = -x + 1$ $\quad$ m: $y = -x + 7$ $\quad$ n: $y = 2x + 1$ $\quad$ p: $y = 2x + 7$

a. Graph the four lines in the coordinate plane.

b. Classify the quadrilateral formed by the lines.

c. What if...? Suppose the slopes of lines n and p change to 1. Reclassify the quadrilateral.

34. Write a two-column proof.

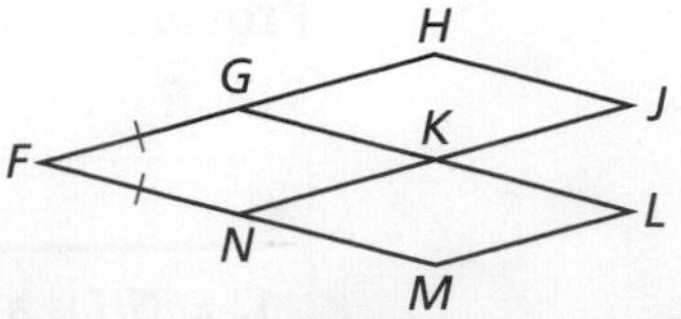

Given: *FHJN* and *GLMF* are parallelograms.
$\overline{FG} \cong \overline{FN}$

Prove: *FGKN* is a rhombus.

35. Write About It Write a biconditional statement based on the theorems about the diagonals of rectangles. Write a biconditional statement based on the theorems about the diagonals of rhombuses. Can you write a biconditional statement based on the theorems about opposite angles in parallelograms? Explain your answer.

Construction Use the diagonals to construct each figure. Then use the theorems from this lesson to explain why your method works.

36. rectangle $\qquad$ **37.** rhombus $\qquad$ **38.** square

TEST PREP

39. In ▱$PQRS$, $\overline{PR}$ and $\overline{QS}$ intersect at T. What additional information is needed to conclude that $PQRS$ is a rectangle?

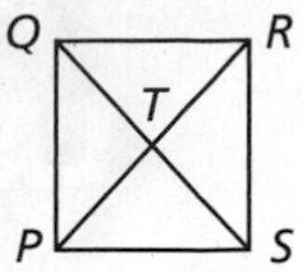

Ⓐ $\overline{PT} \cong \overline{QT}$ Ⓒ $\overline{PT} \perp \overline{QT}$
Ⓑ $\overline{PT} \cong \overline{RT}$ Ⓓ $\overline{PT}$ bisects $\angle QPS$.

40. Which of the following is the best name for figure $WXYZ$ with vertices $W(-3, 1)$, $X(1, 5)$, $Y(8, -2)$, and $Z(4, -6)$?

Ⓕ Parallelogram Ⓖ Rectangle Ⓗ Rhombus Ⓙ Square

41. **Extended Response**

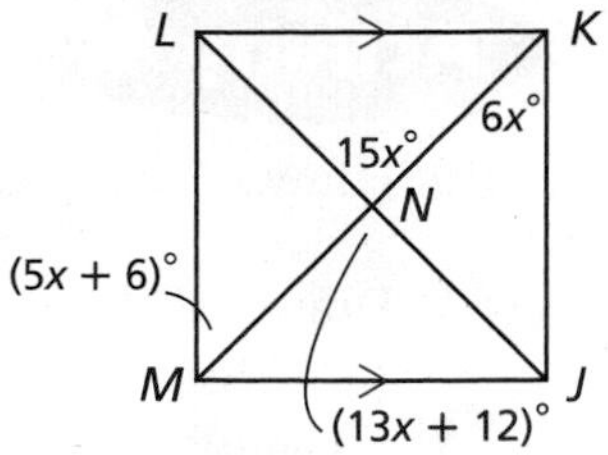

a. Write and solve an equation to find the value of x.
b. Is $JKLM$ a parallelogram? Explain.
c. Is $JKLM$ a rectangle? Explain.
d. Is $JKLM$ a rhombus? Explain.

CHALLENGE AND EXTEND

42. **Given:** $\overline{AC} \cong \overline{DF}$, $\overline{AB} \cong \overline{DE}$, $\overline{AB} \perp \overline{BC}$, $\overline{DE} \perp \overline{EF}$, $\overline{BE} \perp \overline{EF}$, $\overline{BC} \parallel \overline{EF}$
Prove: $EBCF$ is a rectangle.

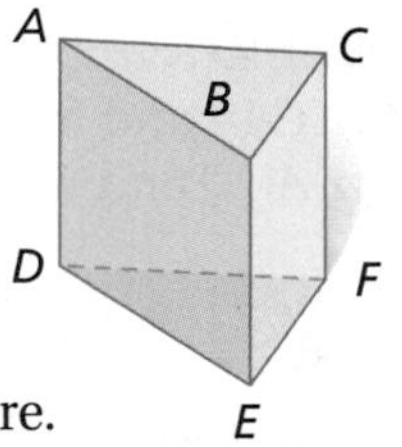

43. **Critical Thinking** Consider the following statement: If a quadrilateral is a rectangle and a rhombus, then it is a square.
a. Explain why the statement is true.
b. If a quadrilateral is a rectangle, is it necessary to show that all four sides are congruent in order to conclude that it is a square? Explain.
c. If a quadrilateral is a rhombus, is it necessary to show that all four angles are right angles in order to conclude that it is a square? Explain.

44. **Cars** As you turn the crank of a car jack, the platform that supports the car rises. Use the diagonals of the parallelogram to explain whether the jack forms a rectangle, rhombus, or square.

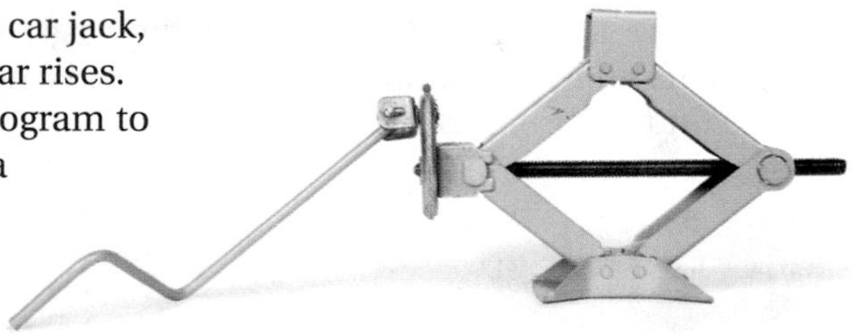

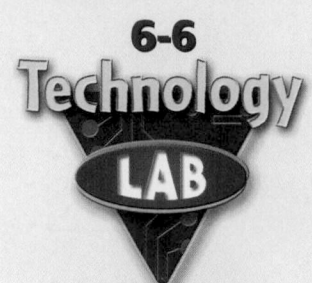

6-6 Technology LAB

Explore Isosceles Trapezoids

In this lab you will investigate the properties and conditions of an *isosceles trapezoid.* A *trapezoid* is a quadrilateral with one pair of parallel sides, called *bases.* The sides that are not parallel are called *legs.* In an isosceles trapezoid, the legs are congruent.

Use with Properties of Kites and Trapezoids

Learn It Online
Lab Resources Online

MATHEMATICAL PRACTICES **Use appropriate tools strategically.**

Activity 1

1. Draw $\overline{AB}$ and a point C not on $\overline{AB}$. Construct a parallel line ℓ through C.
2. Draw point D on line ℓ. Construct $\overline{AC}$ and $\overline{BD}$.
3. Measure AC, BD, $\angle CAB$, $\angle ABD$, $\angle ACD$, and $\angle CDB$.
4. Move D until $AC = BD$. What do you notice about $m\angle CAB$ and $m\angle ABD$? What do you notice about $m\angle ACD$ and $m\angle CDB$?
5. Move D so that $AC \neq BD$. Now move D so that $m\angle CAB = m\angle ABD$. What do you notice about AC and BD?

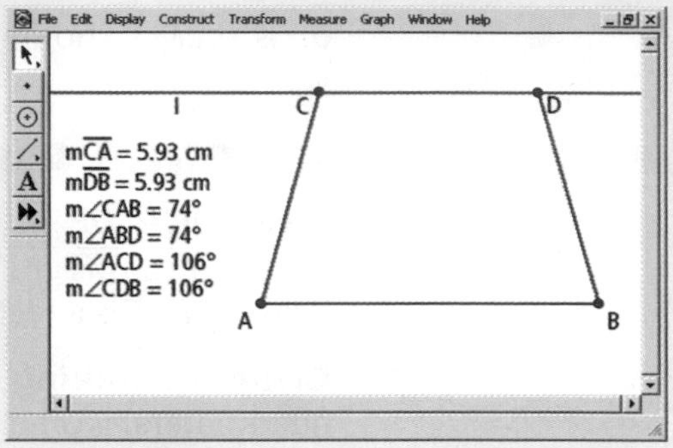

Try This

1. **Make a Conjecture** What is true about the base angles of an isosceles trapezoid? Write your conjecture as a conditional statement.
2. **Make a Conjecture** How can the base angles of a trapezoid be used to determine if the trapezoid is isosceles? Write your conjecture as a conditional statement.

Activity 2

1. Construct $\overline{AD}$ and $\overline{CB}$.
2. Measure AD and CB.
3. Move D until $AC = BD$. What do you notice about AD and CB?
4. Move D so that $AC \neq BD$. Now move D so that $AD = BC$. What do you notice about AC and BD?

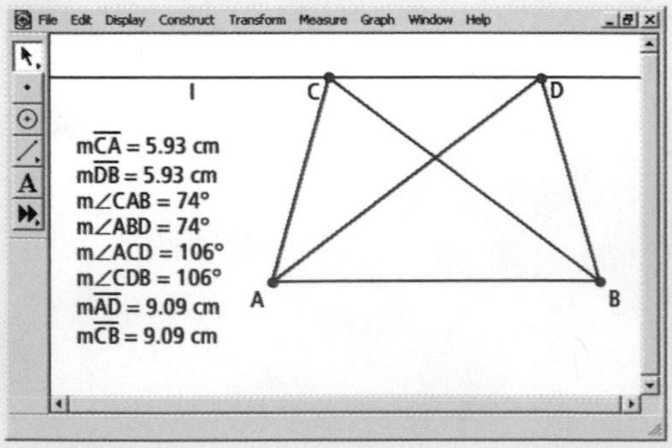

Try This

3. **Make a Conjecture** What is true about the diagonals of an isosceles trapezoid? Write your conjecture as a conditional statement.
4. **Make a Conjecture** How can the diagonals of a trapezoid be used to determine if the trapezoid is isosceles? Write your conjecture as a conditional statement.

COMMON CORE

6-6 Properties of Kites and Trapezoids

CC.9-12.G.SRT.5 Use congruence…criteria for triangles to solve problems and prove relationships…

Objectives

Use properties of kites to solve problems.

Use properties of trapezoids to solve problems.

Vocabulary

kite
trapezoid
base of a trapezoid
leg of a trapezoid
base angle of a trapezoid
isosceles trapezoid
midsegment of a trapezoid

Why learn this?

The design of a simple kite flown at the beach shares the properties of the geometric figure called a *kite*.

A **kite** is a quadrilateral with exactly two pairs of congruent consecutive sides.

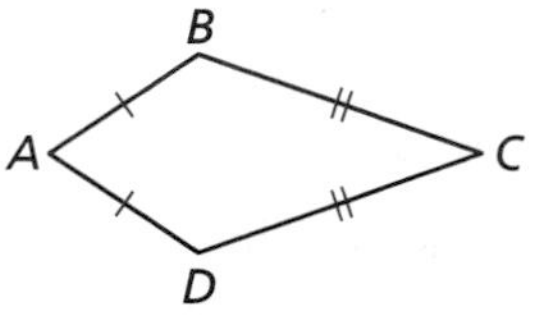

Kite *ABCD*

Know it! Note

Theorems Properties of Kites

	THEOREM	HYPOTHESIS	CONCLUSION
6-6-1	If a quadrilateral is a kite, then its diagonals are perpendicular. (kite → diags. ⊥)	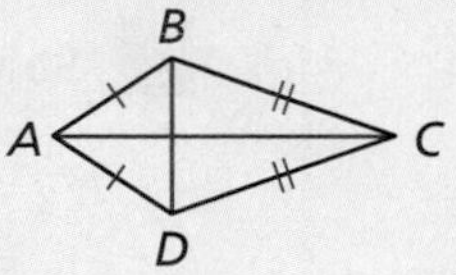	$\overline{AC} \perp \overline{BD}$
6-6-2	If a quadrilateral is a kite, then exactly one pair of opposite angles are congruent. (kite → one pair opp. ∠s ≅)	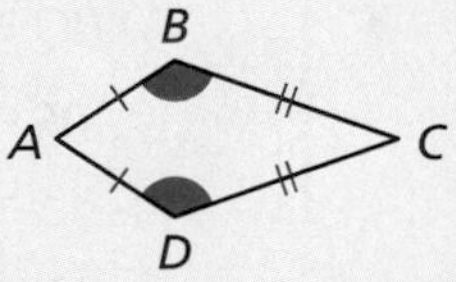	$\angle B \cong \angle D$ $\angle A \ncong \angle C$

You will prove Theorem 6-6-1 in Exercise 39.

PROOF

Theorem 6-6-2

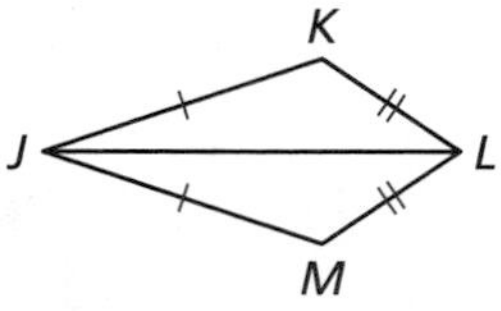

Given: *JKLM* is a kite with $\overline{JK} \cong \overline{JM}$ and $\overline{KL} \cong \overline{ML}$.
Prove: $\angle K \cong \angle M$, $\angle KJM \ncong \angle KLM$

Proof:

Step 1 Prove $\angle K \cong \angle M$.

It is given that $\overline{JK} \cong \overline{JM}$ and $\overline{KL} \cong \overline{ML}$. By the Reflexive Property of Congruence, $\overline{JL} \cong \overline{JL}$. This means that $\triangle JKL \cong \triangle JML$ by SSS. So $\angle K \cong \angle M$ by CPCTC.

Step 2 Prove $\angle KJM \ncong \angle KLM$.

If $\angle KJM \cong \angle KLM$, then both pairs of opposite angles of *JKLM* are congruent. This would mean that *JKLM* is a parallelogram. But this contradicts the given fact that *JKLM* is a kite. Therefore $\angle KJM \ncong \angle KLM$.

EXAMPLE 1 Problem-Solving Application

MATHEMATICAL PRACTICES

Make sense of problems and persevere in solving them.

Alicia is using a pattern to make a kite. She has made the frame of the kite by placing wooden sticks along the diagonals. She also has cut four triangular pieces of fabric and has attached them to the frame. To finish the kite, Alicia must cover the outer edges with a cloth binding. There are 2 yards of binding in one package. What is the total amount of binding needed to cover the edges of the kite? How many packages of binding must Alicia buy?

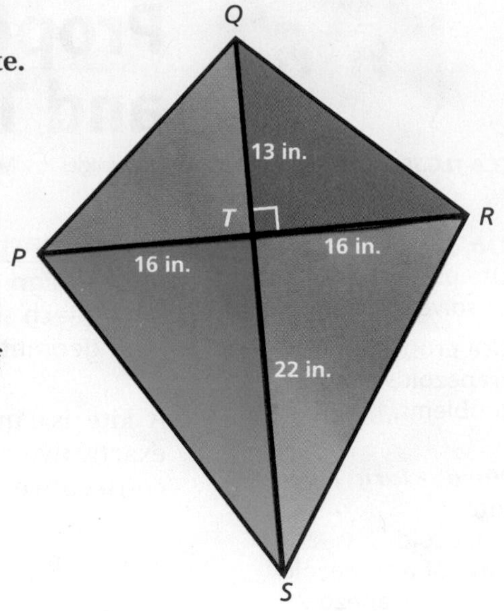

1 Understand the Problem

The **answer** has two parts.

- the total length of binding Alicia needs
- the number of packages of binding Alicia must buy

2 Make a Plan

The diagonals of a kite are perpendicular, so the four triangles are right triangles. Use the Pythagorean Theorem and the properties of kites to find the unknown side lengths. Add these lengths to find the perimeter of the kite.

3 Solve

$PQ = \sqrt{16^2 + 13^2}$ *Pyth. Thm.*

$= \sqrt{425} = 5\sqrt{17}$ in.

$RQ = PQ = 5\sqrt{17}$ in. $\overline{PQ} \cong \overline{RQ}$

$PS = \sqrt{16^2 + 22^2}$ *Pyth. Thm.*

$= \sqrt{740} = 2\sqrt{185}$ in.

$RS = PS = 2\sqrt{185}$ in. $\overline{RS} \cong \overline{PS}$

perimeter of $PQRS = 5\sqrt{17} + 5\sqrt{17} + 2\sqrt{185} + 2\sqrt{185} \approx 95.6$ in.

Alicia needs approximately 95.6 inches of binding.

One package of binding contains 2 yards, or 72 inches.

$\frac{95.6}{72} \approx 1.3$ packages of binding

In order to have enough, Alicia must buy 2 packages of binding.

4 Look Back

To estimate the perimeter, change the side lengths into decimals and round. $5\sqrt{17} \approx 21$, and $2\sqrt{185} \approx 27$. The perimeter of the kite is approximately $2(21) + 2(27) = 96$. So 95.6 is a reasonable answer.

CHECK IT OUT!

1. What if...? Daryl is going to make a kite by doubling all the measures in the kite above. What is the total amount of binding needed to cover the edges of his kite? How many packages of binding must Daryl buy?

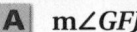

EXAMPLE 2 Using Properties of Kites

In kite *EFGH*, m∠*FEJ* = 25°, and m∠*FGJ* = 57°. Find each measure.

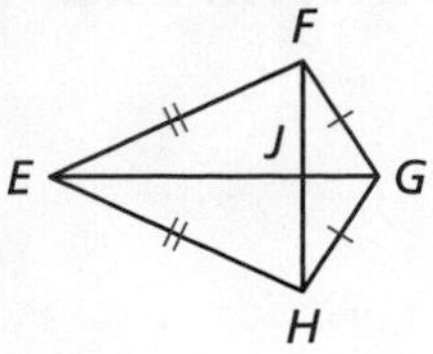

A m∠*GFJ*

m∠*FJG* = 90°	*Kite → diags. ⊥*
m∠*GFJ* + m∠*FGJ* = 90	*Acute ∠s of rt. △ are comp.*
m∠*GFJ* + 57 = 90	*Substitute 57 for m∠FGJ.*
m∠*GFJ* = 33°	*Subtract 57 from both sides.*

B m∠*JFE*

△*FJE* is also a right triangle, so m∠*JFE* + m∠*FEJ* = 90°. By substituting 25° for m∠*FEJ*, you find that m∠*JFE* = 65°.

C m∠*GHE*

∠*GHE* ≅ ∠*GFE*	*Kite → one pair opp. ∠s ≅*
m∠*GHE* = m∠*GFE*	*Def. of ≅ ∠s*
m∠*GFE* = m∠*GFJ* + m∠*JFE*	*∠ Add. Post.*
m∠*GHE* = 33° + 65° = 98°	*Substitute.*

CHECK IT OUT! **In kite *PQRS*, m∠*PQR* = 78°, and m∠*TRS* = 59°. Find each measure.**

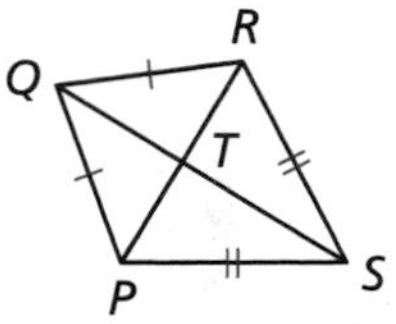

2a. m∠*QRT* **2b.** m∠*QPS* **2c.** m∠*PSR*

A **trapezoid** is a quadrilateral with exactly one pair of parallel sides. Each of the parallel sides is called a **base**. The nonparallel sides are called **legs**. **Base angles** of a trapezoid are two consecutive angles whose common side is a base.

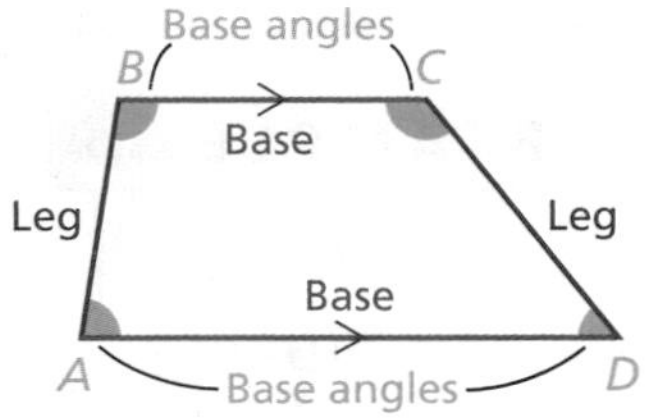

If the legs of a trapezoid are congruent, the trapezoid is an **isosceles trapezoid**. The following theorems state the properties of an isosceles trapezoid.

Know it! Note

Theorems Isosceles Trapezoids

	THEOREM	DIAGRAM	EXAMPLE
6-6-3	If a quadrilateral is an isosceles trapezoid, then each pair of base angles are congruent. (isosc. trap. → base ∠s ≅)	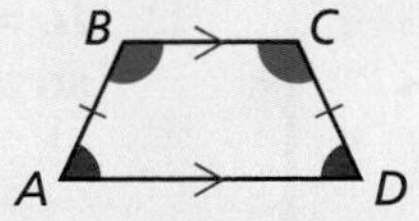	∠*A* ≅ ∠*D* ∠*B* ≅ ∠*C*
6-6-4	If a trapezoid has one pair of congruent base angles, then the trapezoid is isosceles. (trap. with pair base ∠s ≅ → isosc. trap.)	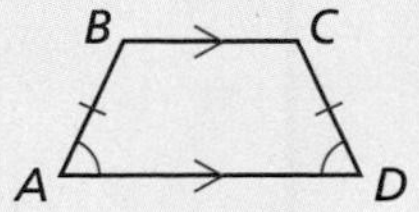	*ABCD* is isosceles.
6-6-5	A trapezoid is isosceles if and only if its diagonals are congruent. (isosc. trap. ↔ diags. ≅)	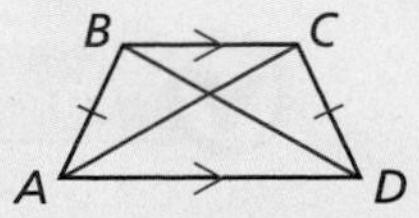	$\overline{AC} \cong \overline{DB}$ ↔ *ABCD* is isosceles.

Remember!

Theorem 6-6-5 is a biconditional statement. So it is true both "forward" and "backward."

EXAMPLE 3 Using Properties of Isosceles Trapezoids

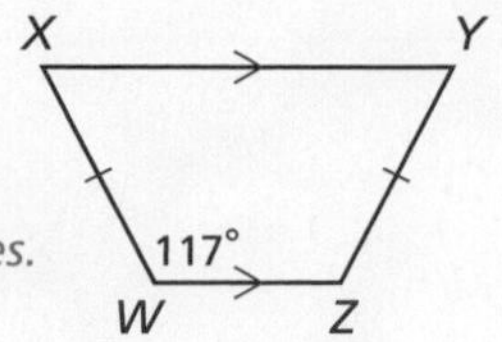

A **Find m∠Y.**

m∠W + m∠X = 180°	*Same-Side Int. ∠s Thm.*
117 + m∠X = 180	*Substitute 117 for m∠W.*
m∠X = 63°	*Subtract 117 from both sides.*
∠Y ≅ ∠X	*Isosc. trap. → base ∠s ≅*
m∠Y = m∠X	*Def. of ≅ ∠s*
m∠Y = 63°	*Substitute 63 for m∠X.*

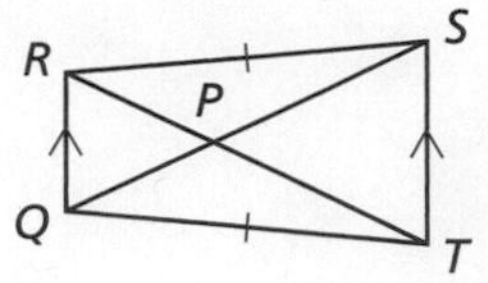

B **$RT = 24.1$, and $QP = 9.6$. Find PS.**

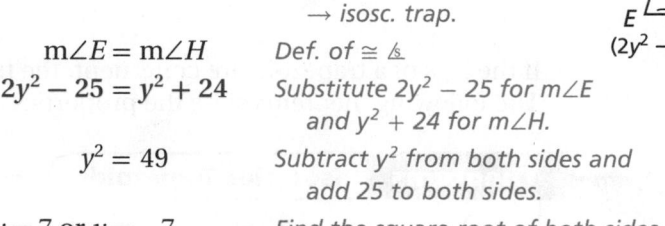

$\overline{QS} \cong \overline{RT}$	*Isosc. trap. → diags. ≅*
$QS = RT$	*Def. of ≅ segs.*
$QS = 24.1$	*Substitute 24.1 for RT.*
$QP + PS = QS$	*Seg. Add. Post.*
$9.6 + PS = 24.1$	*Substitute 9.6 for QP and 24.1 for QS.*
$PS = 14.5$	*Subtract 9.6 from both sides.*

CHECK IT OUT!

3a. Find m∠F.

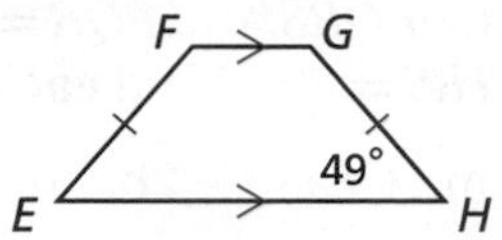

3b. $JN = 10.6$, and $NL = 14.8$. Find KM.

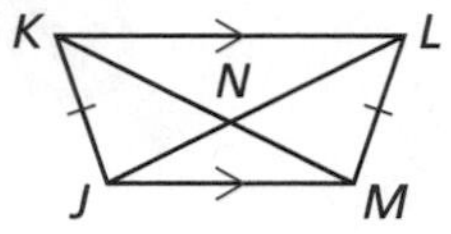

EXAMPLE 4 Applying Conditions for Isosceles Trapezoids

Algebra

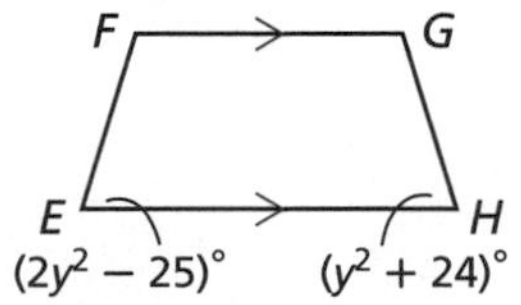

A **Find the value of y so that $EFGH$ is isosceles.**

∠E ≅ ∠H	*Trap. with pair base ∠s ≅ → isosc. trap.*
m∠E = m∠H	*Def. of ≅ ∠s*
$2y^2 - 25 = y^2 + 24$	*Substitute $2y^2 - 25$ for m∠E and $y^2 + 24$ for m∠H.*
$y^2 = 49$	*Subtract y^2 from both sides and add 25 to both sides.*
$y = 7$ or $y = -7$	*Find the square root of both sides.*

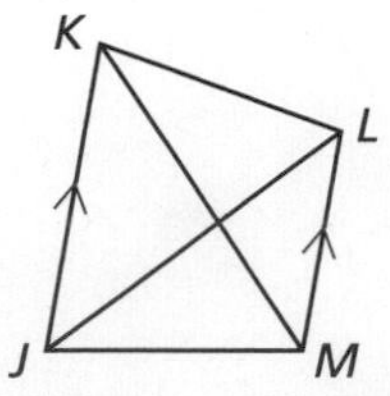

B **$JL = 5z + 3$, and $KM = 9z - 12$. Find the value of z so that $JKLM$ is isosceles.**

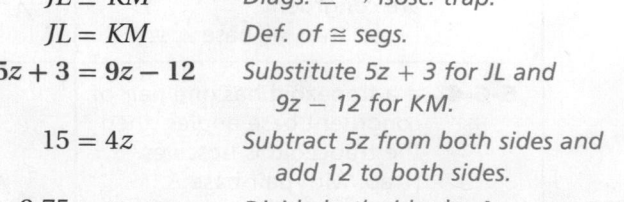

$\overline{JL} \cong \overline{KM}$	*Diags. ≅ → isosc. trap.*
$JL = KM$	*Def. of ≅ segs.*
$5z + 3 = 9z - 12$	*Substitute $5z + 3$ for JL and $9z - 12$ for KM.*
$15 = 4z$	*Subtract 5z from both sides and add 12 to both sides.*
$3.75 = z$	*Divide both sides by 4.*

CHECK IT OUT!

4. Find the value of x so that $PQST$ is isosceles.

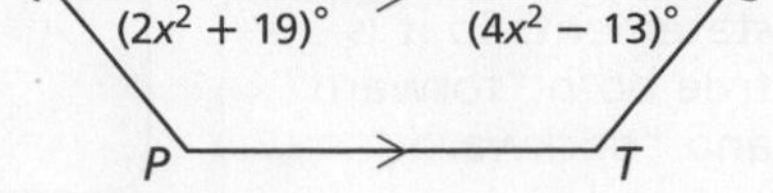

The **midsegment of a trapezoid** is the segment whose endpoints are the midpoints of the legs. The Trapezoid Midsegment Theorem is similar to the Triangle Midsegment Theorem.

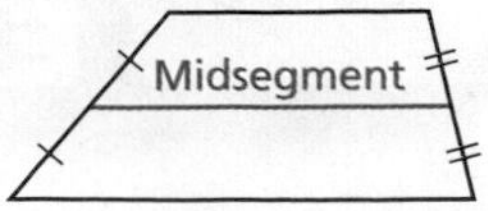

Know it! Note

Theorem 6-6-6 **Trapezoid Midsegment Theorem**

The midsegment of a trapezoid is parallel to each base, and its length is one half the sum of the lengths of the bases.

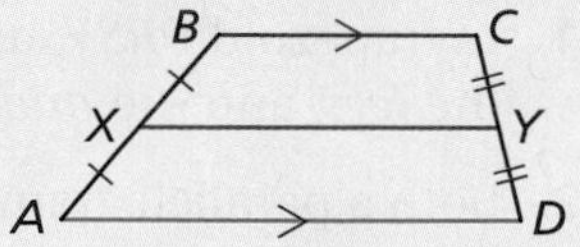

$\overline{XY} \parallel \overline{BC}$, $\overline{XY} \parallel \overline{AD}$

$XY = \frac{1}{2}(BC + AD)$

You will prove the Trapezoid Midsegment Theorem in Exercise 46.

EXAMPLE 5 Finding Lengths Using Midsegments

Find *ST*.

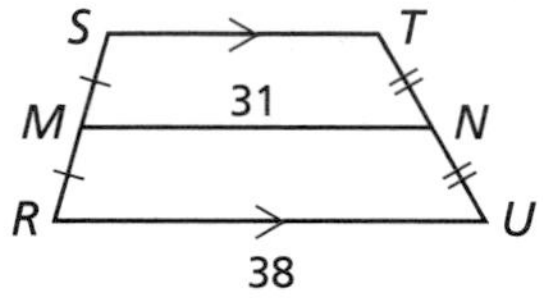

$MN = \frac{1}{2}(ST + RU)$	*Trap. Midsegment Thm.*
$31 = \frac{1}{2}(ST + 38)$	*Substitute the given values.*
$62 = ST + 38$	*Multiply both sides by 2.*
$24 = ST$	*Subtract 38 from both sides.*

CHECK IT OUT! **5.** Find *EH*.

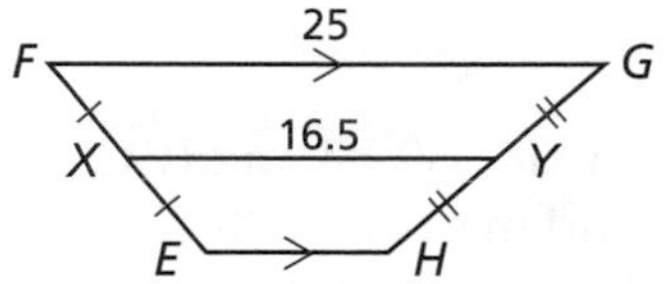

MATHEMATICAL PRACTICES

THINK AND DISCUSS

1. Is it possible for the legs of a trapezoid to be parallel? Explain.

2. How is the midsegment of a trapezoid similar to a midsegment of a triangle? How is it different?

Know it! Note

3. GET ORGANIZED Copy and complete the graphic organizer. Write the missing terms in the unlabeled sections. Then write a definition of each term.

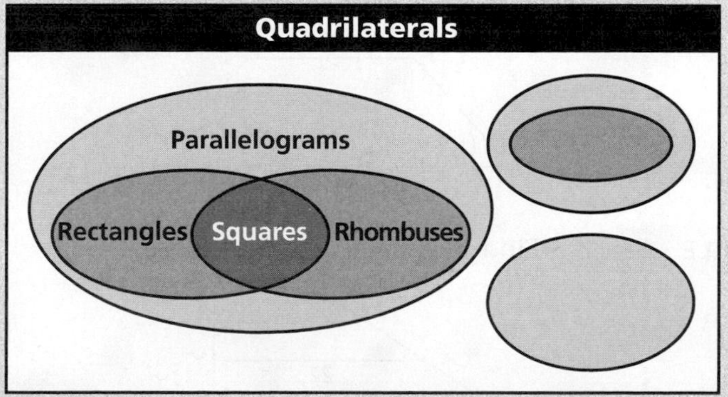

6-6 Exercises

Learn It Online
Homework Help Online
Parent Resources Online

GUIDED PRACTICE

Vocabulary **Apply the vocabulary from this lesson to answer each question.**

1. In trapezoid *PRSV*, name the *bases*, the *legs*, and the *midsegment*.

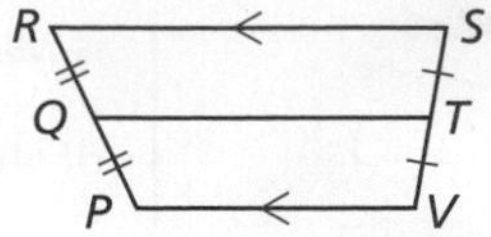

2. Both a parallelogram and a *kite* have two pairs of congruent sides. How are the congruent sides of a kite different from the congruent sides of a parallelogram?

SEE EXAMPLE 1

3. **Crafts** The edges of the kite-shaped glass in the sun catcher are sealed with lead strips. *JH*, *KH*, and *LH* are 2.75 inches, and *MH* is 5.5 inches. How much lead is needed to seal the edges of the sun catcher? If the craftsperson has two 3-foot lengths of lead, how many sun catchers can be sealed?

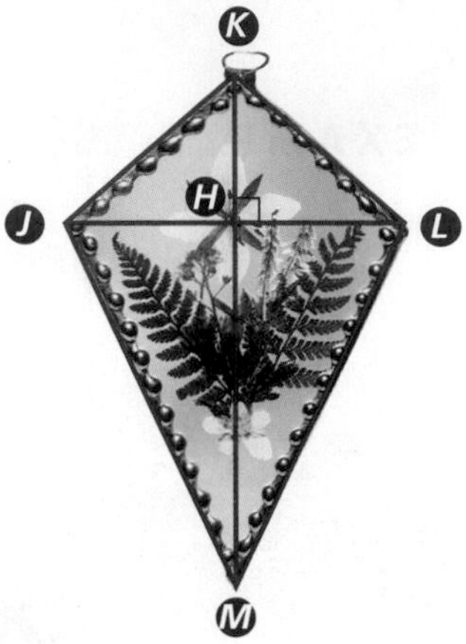

SEE EXAMPLE 2

In kite *WXYZ*, m∠*WXY* = 104°, and m∠*VYZ* = 49°. Find each measure.

4. m∠*VZY*
5. m∠*VXW*
6. m∠*XWZ*

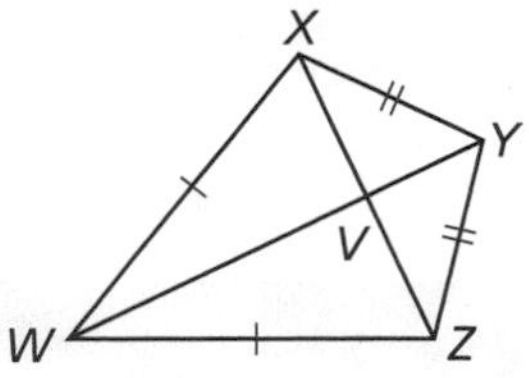

SEE EXAMPLE 3

7. Find m∠*A*.

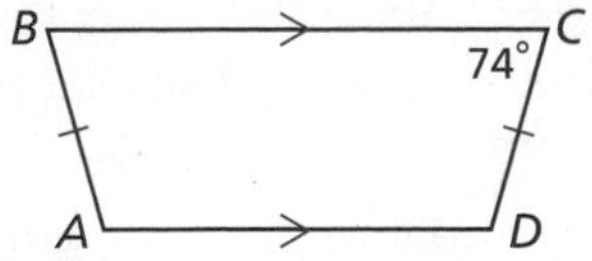

8. *RW* = 17.7, and *SV* = 23.3. Find *TW*.

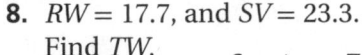

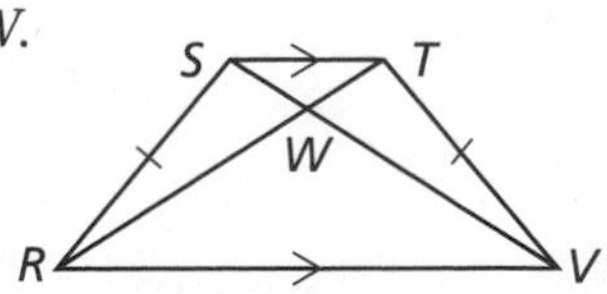

SEE EXAMPLE 4

9. Find the value of *z* so that *EFGH* is isosceles.

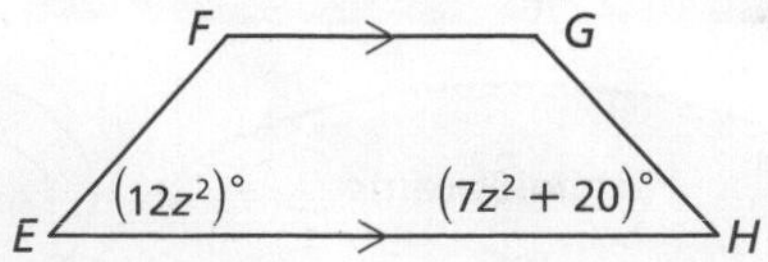

10. *MQ* = 7*y* − 6, and *LP* = 4*y* + 11. Find the value of *y* so that *LMPQ* is isosceles.

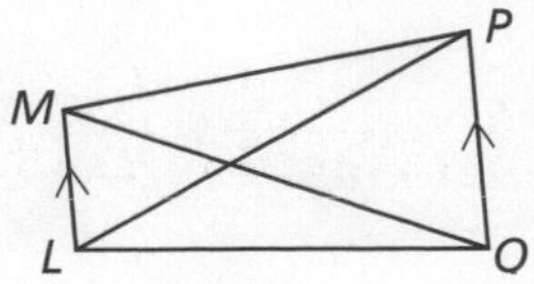

SEE EXAMPLE 5

11. Find *QR*.

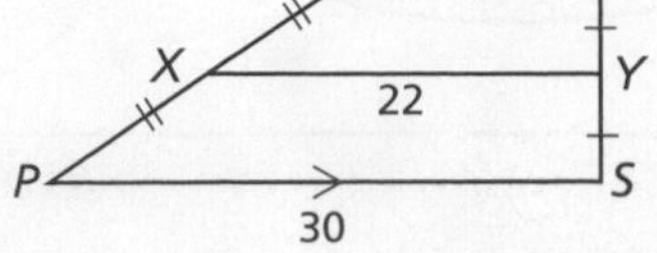

12. Find *AZ*.

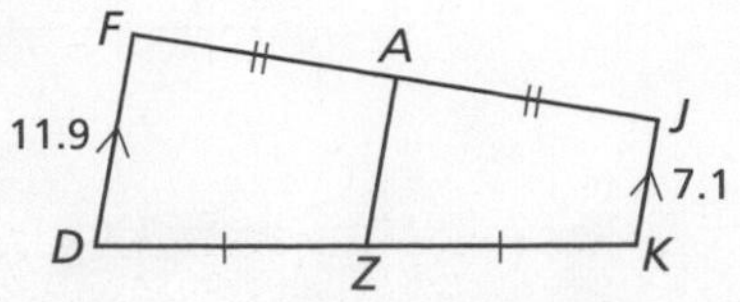

Independent Practice	
For Exercises	See Example
13	1
14–16	2
17–18	3
19–20	4
21–22	5

Extra Practice

See Extra Practice for more Skills Practice and Applications Practice exercises.

PRACTICE AND PROBLEM SOLVING

13. Design Each square section in the iron railing contains four small kites. The figure shows the dimensions of one kite. What length of iron is needed to outline one small kite? How much iron is needed to outline one complete section, including the square?

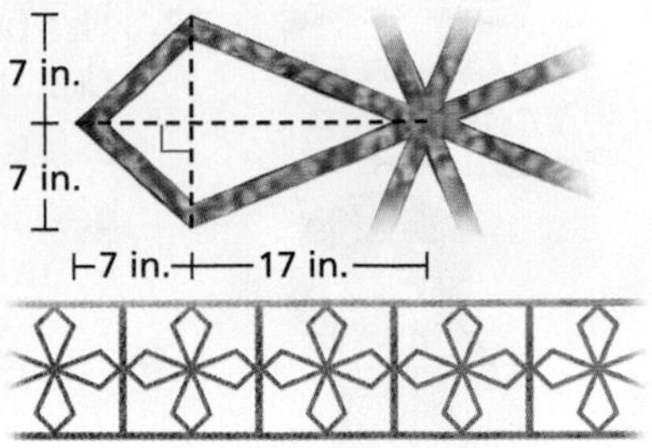

In kite $ABCD$, $m\angle DAX = 32°$, and $m\angle XDC = 64°$. Find each measure.

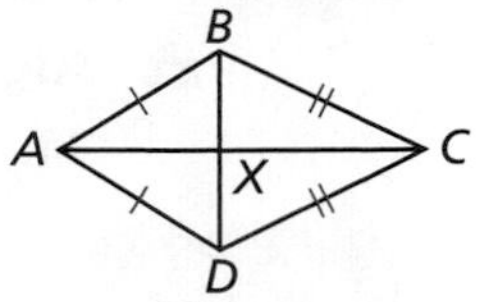

14. $m\angle XDA$

15. $m\angle ABC$

16. $m\angle BCD$

17. Find $m\angle Q$.

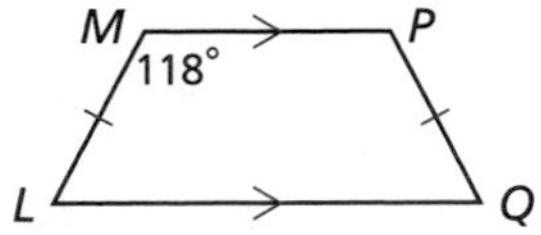

18. $SZ = 62.6$, and $KZ = 34$. Find RJ.

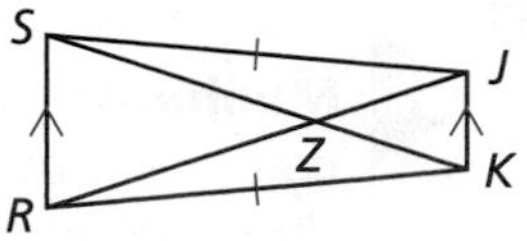

19. Algebra Find the value of a so that $XYZW$ is isosceles. Give your answer as a simplified radical.

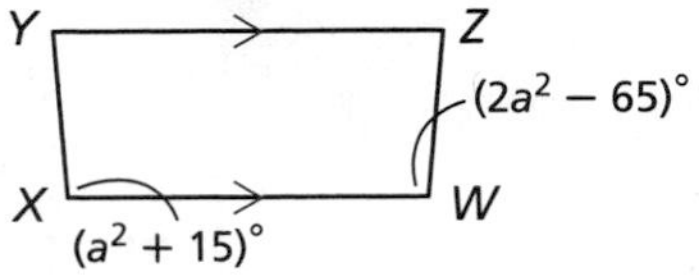

20. Algebra $GJ = 4x - 1$, and $FH = 9x - 15$. Find the value of x so that $FGHJ$ is isosceles.

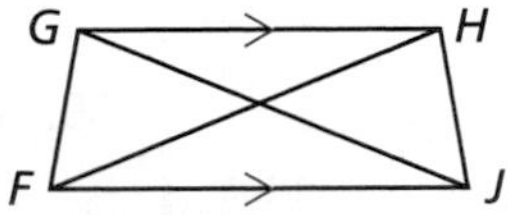

21. Find PQ.

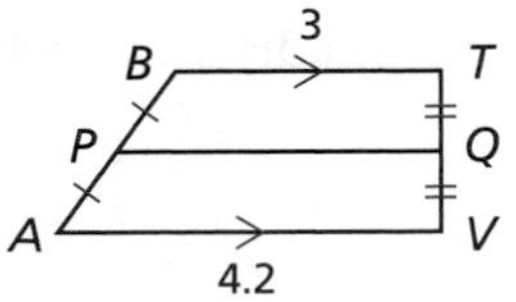

22. Find KR.

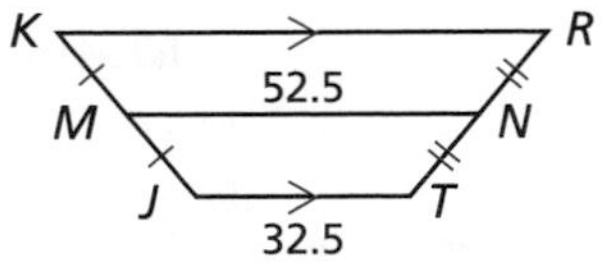

Tell whether each statement is sometimes, always, or never true.

23. The opposite angles of a trapezoid are supplementary.

24. The opposite angles of a kite are supplementary.

25. A pair of consecutive angles in a kite are supplementary.

26. Estimation Hal is building a trapezoid-shaped frame for a flower bed. The lumber costs \$1.29 per foot. Based on Hal's sketch, estimate the cost of the lumber. (*Hint:* Find the angle measures in the triangle formed by the dashed line.)

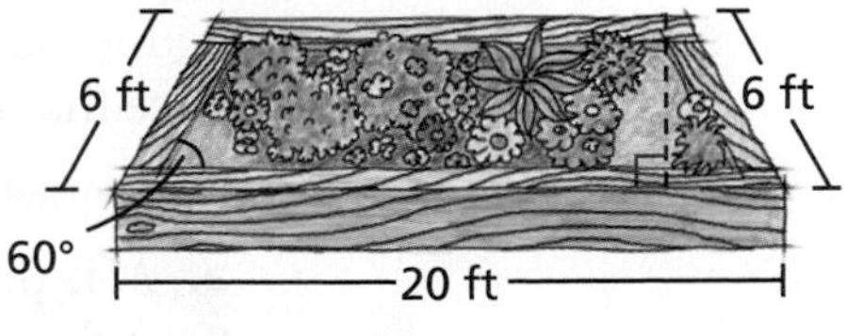

Find the measure of each numbered angle.

27.

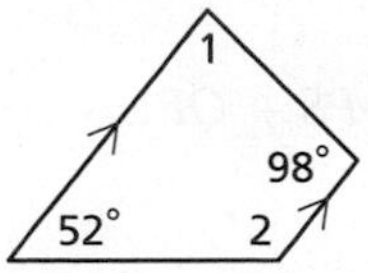

28.

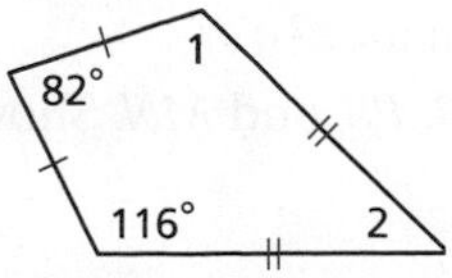

29.

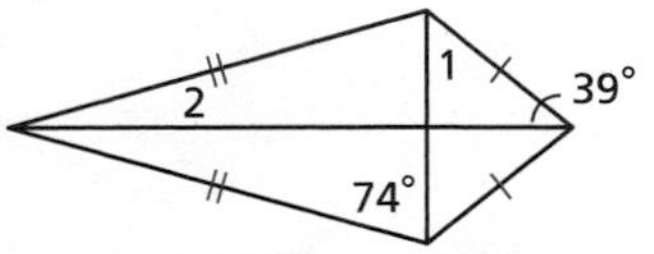

30.

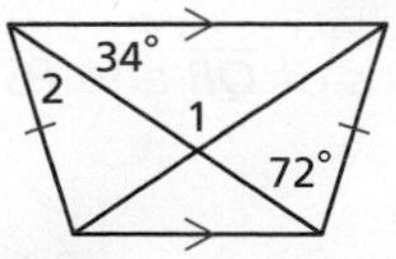

31.

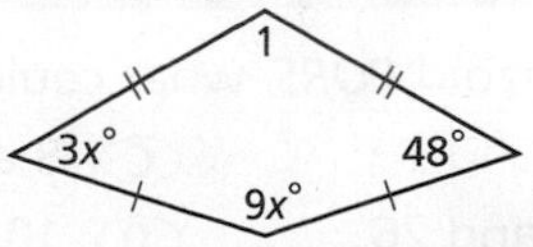

32.

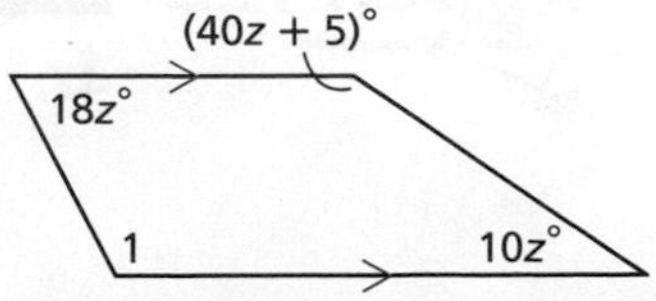

MULTI-STEP TEST PREP

33. The boundary of a fairground is a quadrilateral with vertices at $E(-1, 3)$, $F(3, 4)$, $G(2, 0)$, and $H(-3, -2)$.

a. Use the Distance Formula to show that *EFGH* is a kite.

b. The organizers need to know the angle measure at each vertex. Given that $m\angle H = 46°$ and $m\angle F = 62°$, find $m\angle E$ and $m\angle G$.

Algebra **Find the length of the midsegment of each trapezoid.**

34.

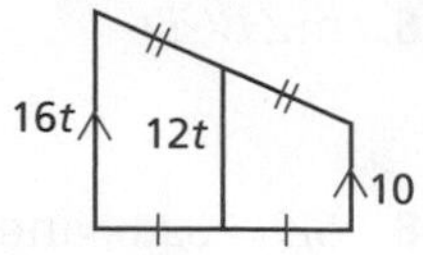

35.

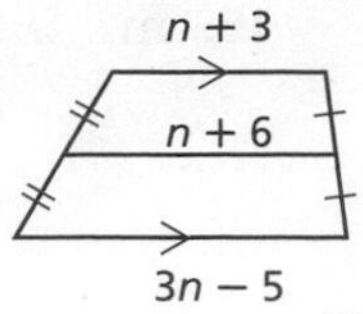

36.

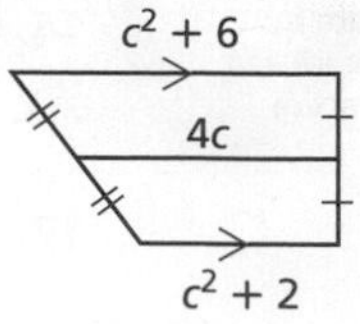

LINK

Mechanics

The Peaucellier cell, invented in 1864, converts circular motion into linear motion. This type of linkage was supposedly used in the fans that ventilated the Houses of Parliament in London prior to the invention of electric fans.

The Granger Collection, New York

37. **Mechanics** A *Peaucellier cell* is made of seven rods connected by joints at the labeled points. *AQBP* is a rhombus, and $\overline{OA} \cong \overline{OB}$. As *P* moves along a circular path, *Q* moves along a linear path. In the position shown, $m\angle AQB = 72°$, and $m\angle AOB = 28°$. What are $m\angle PAQ$, $m\angle OAQ$, and $m\angle OBP$?

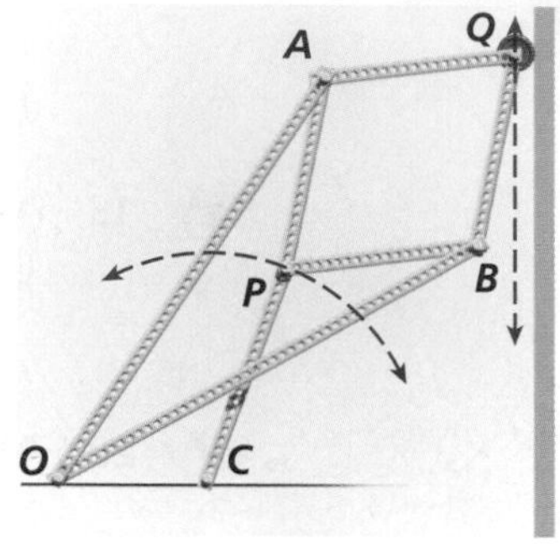

38. Prove that one diagonal of a kite bisects a pair of opposite angles and the other diagonal.

39. Prove Theorem 6-6-1: If a quadrilateral is a kite, then its diagonals are perpendicular.

Multi-Step **Give the best name for a quadrilateral with the given vertices.**

40. $(-4, -1)$, $(-4, 6)$, $(2, 6)$, $(2, -4)$

41. $(-5, 2)$, $(-5, 6)$, $(-1, 6)$, $(2, -1)$

42. $(-2, -2)$, $(1, 7)$, $(4, 4)$, $(1, -5)$

43. $(-4, -3)$, $(0, 3)$, $(4, 3)$, $(8, -3)$

44. **Carpentry** The window frame is a regular octagon. It is made from eight pieces of wood shaped like congruent isosceles trapezoids. What are $m\angle A$, $m\angle B$, $m\angle C$, and $m\angle D$?

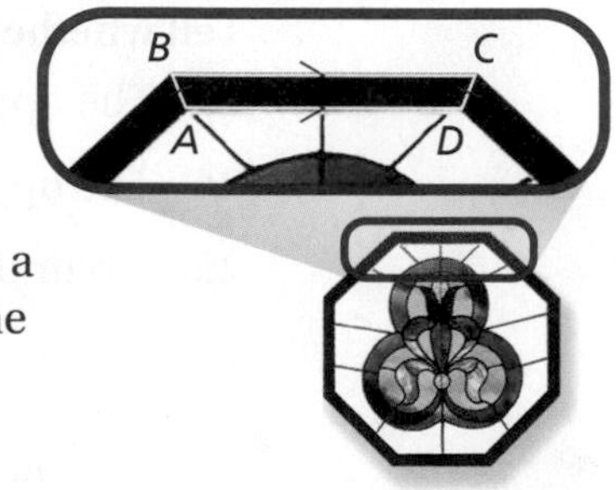

45. **Write About It** Compare an isosceles trapezoid to a trapezoid that is not isosceles. What properties do the figures have in common? What properties does one have that the other does not?

46. Use coordinates to verify the Trapezoid Midsegment Theorem.

a. *M* is the midpoint of $\overline{QP}$. What are its coordinates?

b. *N* is the midpoint of $\overline{RS}$. What are its coordinates?

c. Find the slopes of $\overline{QR}$, $\overline{PS}$, and $\overline{MN}$. What can you conclude?

d. Find *QR*, *PS*, and *MN*. Show that $MN = \frac{1}{2}(PS + QR)$.

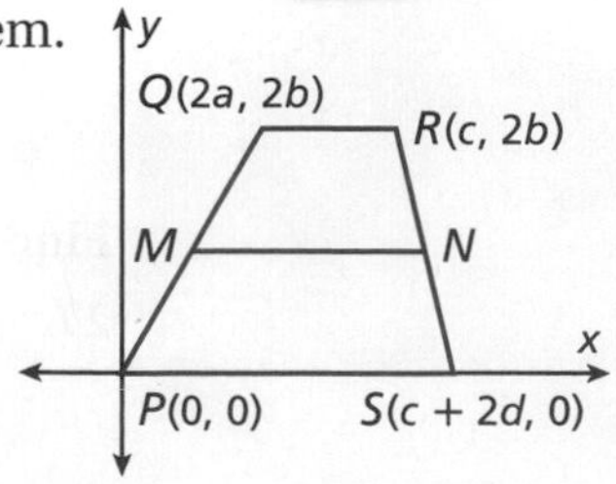

TEST PREP

47. In trapezoid *PQRS*, what could be the lengths of $\overline{QR}$ and $\overline{PS}$?

Ⓐ 6 and 10

Ⓑ 6 and 26

Ⓒ 8 and 32

Ⓓ 10 and 24

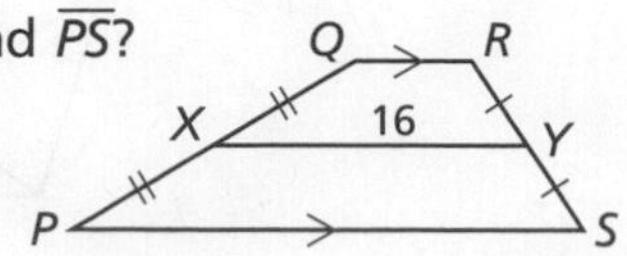

48. Which statement is never true for a kite?

(F) The diagonals are perpendicular.

(G) One pair of opposite angles are congruent.

(H) One pair of opposite sides are parallel.

(J) Two pairs of consecutive sides are congruent.

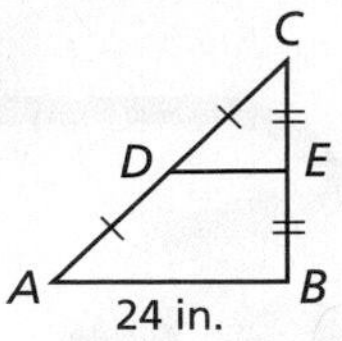

49. **Gridded Response** What is the length of the midsegment of trapezoid *ADEB* in inches?

CHALLENGE AND EXTEND

50. Write a two-column proof. (*Hint:* If there is a line and a point not on the line, then there is exactly one line through the point perpendicular to the given line. Use this fact to draw auxiliary lines $\overline{UX}$ and $\overline{VY}$ so that $\overline{UX} \perp \overline{WZ}$ and $\overline{VY} \perp \overline{WZ}$.)

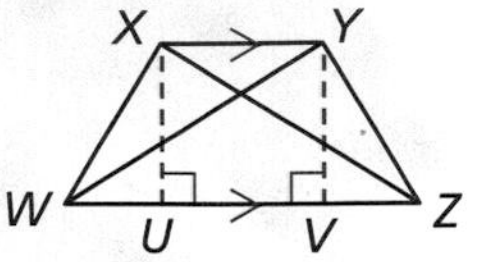

Given: *WXYZ* is a trapezoid with $\overline{XZ} \cong \overline{YW}$.
Prove: *WXYZ* is an isosceles trapezoid.

51. The perimeter of isosceles trapezoid *ABCD* is 27.4 inches. If $BC = 2(AB)$, find *AD*, *AB*, *BC*, and *CD*.

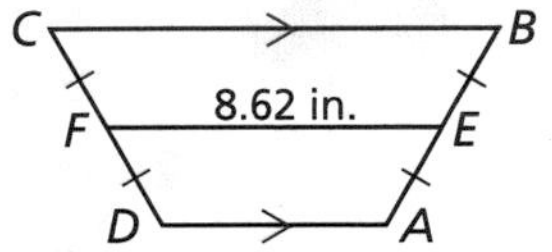

Construction Kite

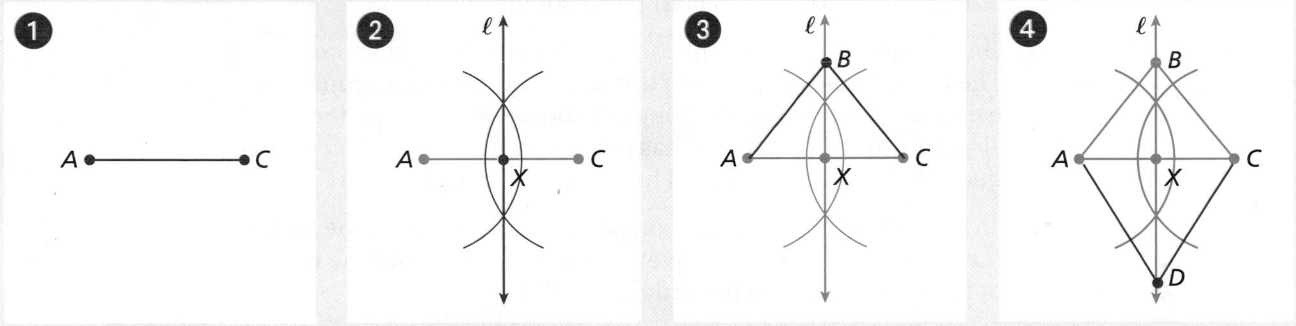

Draw a segment $\overline{AC}$.

Construct line ℓ as the perpendicular bisector of $\overline{AC}$. Label the intersection as *X*.

Draw a point *B* on ℓ above $\overline{AC}$. Draw $\overline{AB}$ and $\overline{CB}$.

Draw a point *D* on ℓ below $\overline{AC}$ so that $DX \neq BX$. Draw $\overline{AD}$ and $\overline{CD}$.

1. **Critical Thinking** How would you modify the construction above so that *ABCD* is a concave kite?

MULTI-STEP TEST PREP

MATHEMATICAL PRACTICES **Model with mathematics.**

Other Special Quadrilaterals

A Fair Arrangement The organizers of a county fair are using a coordinate plane to plan the layout of the fairground. The fence that surrounds the fairground will have vertices at $A(-1, 4)$, $B(7, 8)$, $C(3, 0)$, and $D(-5, -4)$.

1. The organizers consider creating two straight paths through the fairground: one from point A to point C and another from point B to point D. Use a theorem from this chapter to prove that these paths would be perpendicular.

2. The organizers instead decide to put an entry gate at the midpoint of each side of the fence, as shown. They plan to create straight paths that connect the gates. Show that the paths $\overline{PQ}$, $\overline{QR}$, $\overline{RS}$, and $\overline{SP}$ form a parallelogram.

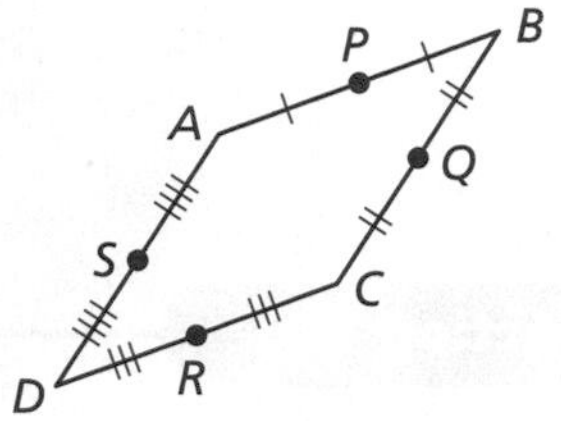

3. Use the paths $\overline{PR}$ and $\overline{SQ}$ to tell whether $\square PQRS$ is a rhombus, rectangle, or square.

4. One section of the fair will contain all the rides and games. The organizers will fence off this area within the fairground by using the existing fences along $\overline{AB}$ and $\overline{BC}$ and adding fences along $\overline{AE}$ and $\overline{CE}$, where E has coordinates $(-1, 0)$. What type of quadrilateral will be formed by these four fences?

5. To construct the fences, the organizers need to know the angle measures at each vertex. Given that $m\angle B = 37°$, find the measures of the other angles in quadrilateral $ABCE$.

(tl), Lew Robertson/Getty; (b), Design Pics Inc./Alamy

READY TO GO ON?

Quiz for Lessons 6-4 Through 6-6

6-4 Properties of Special Parallelograms

The flag of Jamaica is a rectangle with stripes along the diagonals. In rectangle *QRST*, $QS = 80.5$, and $RS = 36$. Find each length.

1. SP **2.** QT **3.** TR **4.** TP

***GHJK* is a rhombus. Find each measure.**

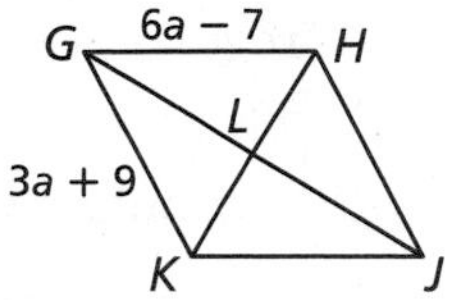

5. HJ

6. $m\angle HJG$ and $m\angle GHJ$ if $m\angle JLH = (4b - 6)^\circ$ and $m\angle JKH = (2b + 11)^\circ$

7. **Given:** $QSTV$ is a rhombus. $\overline{PT} \cong \overline{RT}$
Prove: $\overline{PQ} \cong \overline{RQ}$

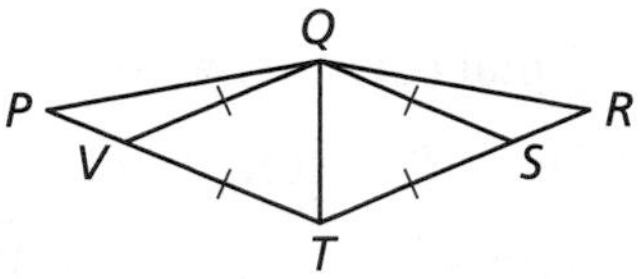

6-5 Conditions for Special Parallelograms

Determine if the conclusion is valid. If not, tell what additional information is needed to make it valid.

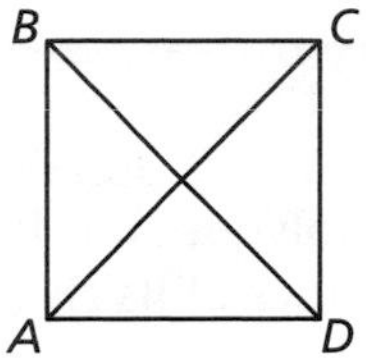

8. Given: $\overline{AC} \perp \overline{BD}$
Conclusion: $ABCD$ is a rhombus.

9. Given: $\overline{AB} \cong \overline{CD}$, $\overline{AC} \cong \overline{BD}$, $\overline{AB} \parallel \overline{CD}$
Conclusion: $ABCD$ is a rectangle.

Use the diagonals to determine whether a parallelogram with the given vertices is a rectangle, rhombus, or square. Give all the names that apply.

10. $W(-2, 2)$, $X(1, 5)$, $Y(7, -1)$, $Z(4, -4)$ **11.** $M(-4, 5)$, $N(1, 7)$, $P(3, 2)$, $Q(-2, 0)$

12. **Given:** $\overline{VX}$ and $\overline{ZX}$ are midsegments of $\triangle TWY$. $\overline{TW} \cong \overline{TY}$
Prove: $TVXZ$ is a rhombus.

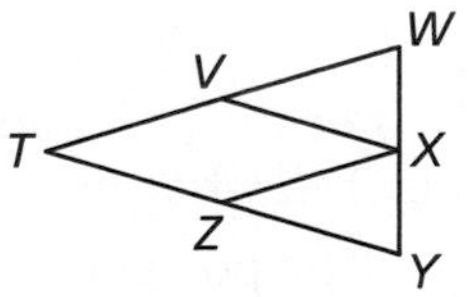

6-6 Properties of Kites and Trapezoids

In kite *EFGH*, $m\angle FHG = 68^\circ$, and $m\angle FEH = 62^\circ$. Find each measure.

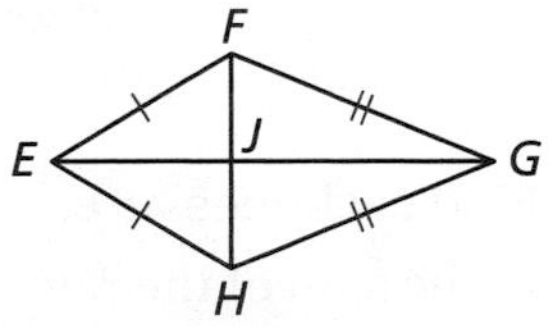

13. $m\angle FEJ$ **14.** $m\angle EHJ$

15. $m\angle FGJ$ **16.** $m\angle EHG$

17. Find $m\angle R$.

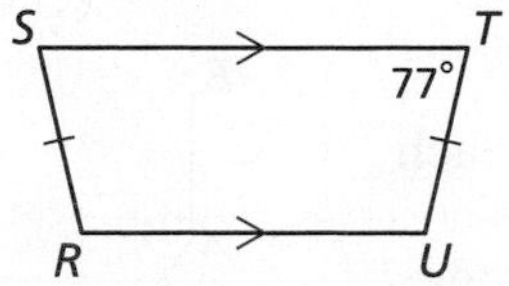

18. $YZ = 34.2$, and $VX = 53.4$. Find WZ.

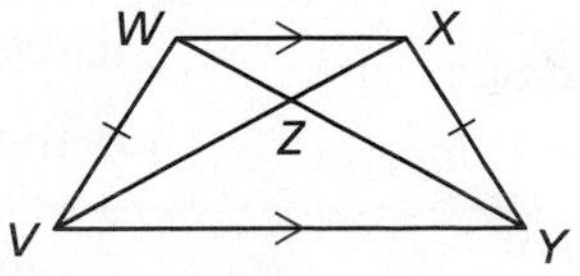

19. A dulcimer is a trapezoid-shaped stringed instrument. The bases are 43 in. and 23 in. long. If a string is attached at the midpoint of each leg of the trapezoid, how long is the string?

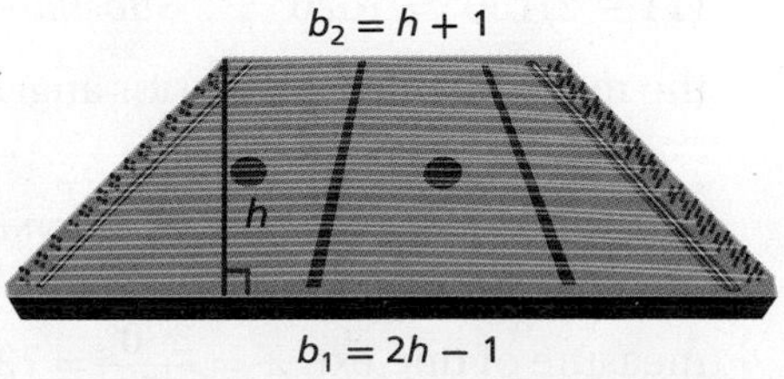

CHAPTER 6

Study Guide: Review

Know it! Note

For a complete list of postulates, theorems, and corollaries, see p. PT2.

Vocabulary

base of a trapezoid	kite	rhombus
base angle of a trapezoid	leg of a trapezoid	side of a polygon
concave	midsegment of a trapezoid	square
convex	parallelogram	trapezoid
diagonal	rectangle	vertex of a polygon
isosceles trapezoid	regular polygon	

Complete the sentences below with vocabulary words from the list above.

1. The common endpoint of two sides of a polygon is a(n) __?__ .

2. A polygon is __?__ if no diagonal contains points in the exterior.

3. A(n) __?__ is a quadrilateral with four congruent sides.

4. Each of the parallel sides of a trapezoid is called a(n) __?__ .

6-1 Properties and Attributes of Polygons

EXAMPLES

■ **Tell whether the figure is a polygon. If it is a polygon, name it by the number of its sides.**

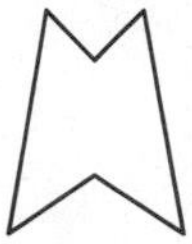

The figure is a closed plane figure made of segments that intersect only at their endpoints, so it is a polygon. It has six sides, so it is a hexagon.

■ **Tell whether the polygon is regular or irregular. Tell whether it is concave or convex.**

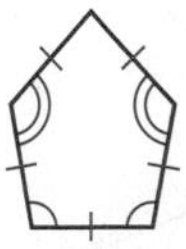

The polygon is equilateral, but it is not equiangular. So it is not regular. No diagonal contains points in the exterior, so it is convex.

Find each measure.

■ the sum of the interior angle measures of a convex 11-gon

$(n - 2)180°$ *Polygon ∠ Sum Thm.*

$(11 - 2)180° = 1620°$ *Substitute 11 for n.*

■ the measure of each exterior angle of a regular pentagon

sum of ext. ∠s = 360° *Polygon Ext. ∠ Sum Thm.*

measure of one ext. $\angle = \frac{360°}{5} = 72°$

EXERCISES

Tell whether each figure is a polygon. If it is a polygon, name it by the number of its sides.

5.

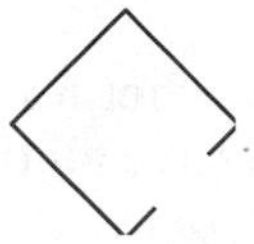

6.

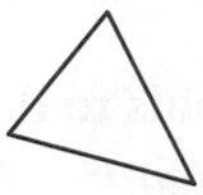

7.

Tell whether each polygon is regular or irregular. Tell whether it is concave or convex.

8.

9.

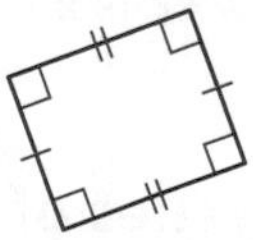

10.

Find each measure.

11. the sum of the interior angle measures of a convex dodecagon

12. the measure of each interior angle of a regular 20-gon

13. the measure of each exterior angle of a regular quadrilateral

14. the measure of each interior angle of hexagon *ABCDEF*

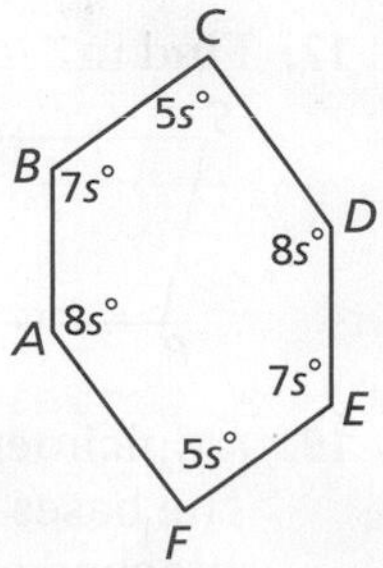

6-2 Properties of Parallelograms

EXAMPLES

■ **In ▱*PQRS*, m∠*RSP* = 99°, *PQ* = 19.8, and *RT* = 12.3. Find *PT*.**

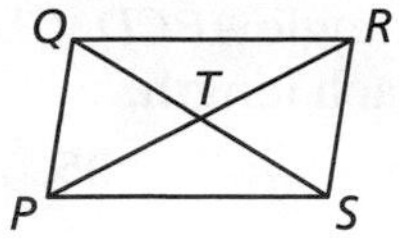

$\overline{PT} \cong \overline{RT}$	*▱ → diags. bisect each other*
$PT = RT$	*Def. of ≅ segs.*
$PT = 12.3$	*Substitute 12.3 for RT.*

***JKLM* is a parallelogram. Find each measure.**

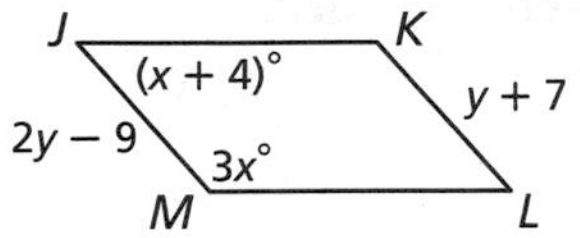

■ *LK*

$\overline{JM} \cong \overline{LK}$	*▱ → opp. sides ≅*
$JM = LK$	*Def. of ≅ segs.*
$2y - 9 = y + 7$	*Substitute the given values.*
$y = 16$	*Solve for y.*
$LK = 16 + 7 = 23$	

■ m∠*M*

$m\angle J + m\angle M = 180°$	*▱ → cons. ∠s supp.*
$(x + 4) + 3x = 180$	*Substitute the given values.*
$x = 44$	*Solve for x.*
$m\angle M = 3(44) = 132°$	

EXERCISES

In ▱*ABCD*, m∠*ABC* = 79°, *BC* = 62.4, and *BD* = 75. Find each measure.

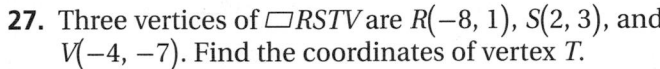

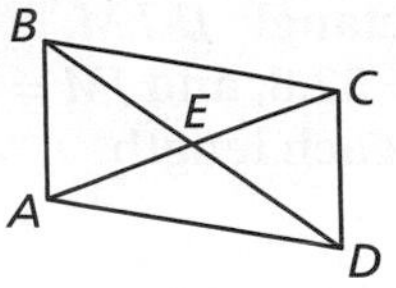

15. *BE* **16.** *AD*

17. *ED* **18.** m∠*CDA*

19. m∠*BCD* **20.** m∠*DAB*

***WXYZ* is a parallelogram. Find each measure.**

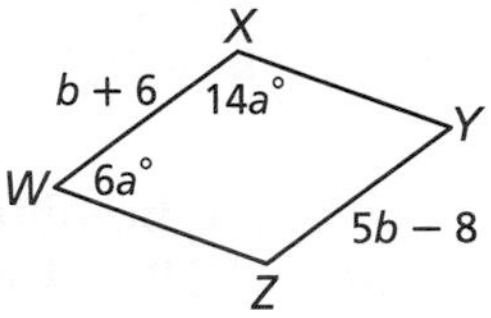

21. *WX* **22.** *YZ*

23. m∠*W* **24.** m∠*X*

25. m∠*Y* **26.** m∠*Z*

27. Three vertices of ▱*RSTV* are *R*(−8, 1), *S*(2, 3), and *V*(−4, −7). Find the coordinates of vertex *T*.

28. Write a two-column proof.
Given: *GHLM* is a parallelogram.
∠*L* ≅ ∠*JMG*
Prove: △*GJM* is isosceles.

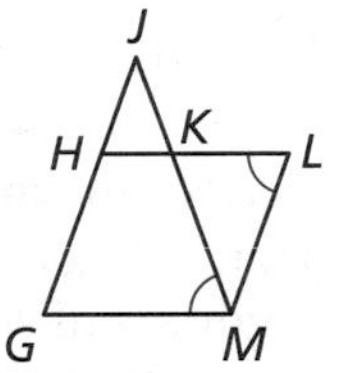

6-3 Conditions for Parallelograms

EXAMPLES

■ **Show that *MNPQ* is a parallelogram for *a* = 6 and *b* = 1.6.**

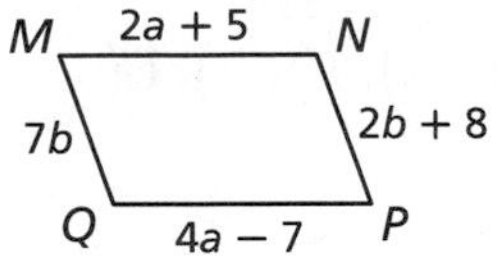

$MN = 2a + 5$	$QP = 4a - 7$
$MN = 2(6) + 5 = 17$	$QP = 4(6) - 7 = 17$
$MQ = 7b$	$NP = 2b + 8$
$MQ = 7(1.6) = 11.2$	$NP = 2(1.6) + 8 = 11.2$

Since its opposite sides are congruent, *MNPQ* is a parallelogram.

■ **Determine if the quadrilateral must be a parallelogram. Justify your answer.**

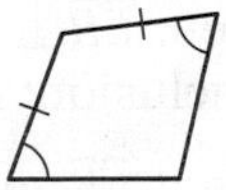

No. One pair of opposite angles are congruent, and one pair of consecutive sides are congruent. None of the conditions for a parallelogram are met.

EXERCISES

Show that the quadrilateral is a parallelogram for the given values of the variables.

29. $m = 13$, $n = 27$ **30.** $x = 25$, $y = 7$

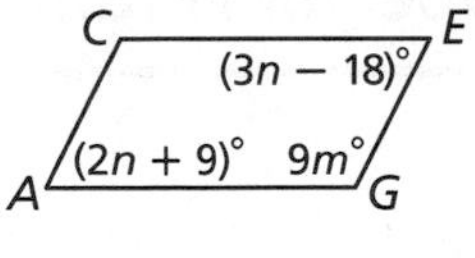

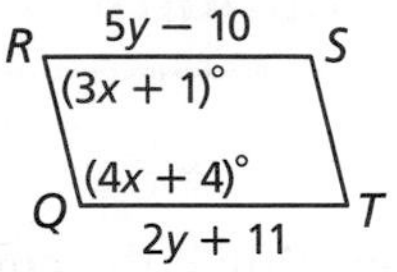

Determine if the quadrilateral must be a parallelogram. Justify your answer.

31.

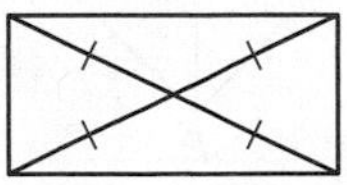

32.

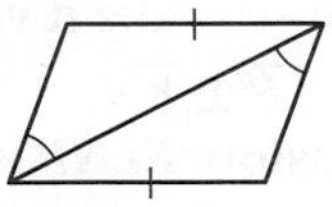

33. Show that the quadrilateral with vertices *B*(−4, 3), *D*(6, 5), *F*(7, −1), and *H*(−3, −3) is a parallelogram.

6-4 Properties of Special Parallelograms

EXAMPLES

In rectangle $JKLM$, $KM = 52.8$, and $JM = 45.6$. Find each length.

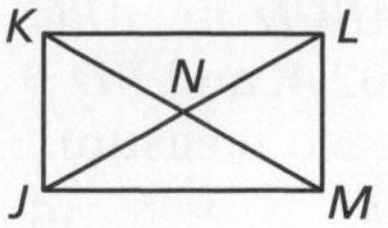

- KL

$JKLM$ is a ▱. *Rect. → ▱*

$KL = JM = 45.6$ *▱ → opp. sides ≅*

- NL

$JL = KM = 52.8$ *Rect. → diags. ≅*

$NL = \frac{1}{2}JL = 26.4$ *▱ → diags. bisect each other*

- **$PQRS$ is a rhombus. Find $m\angle QPR$, given that $m\angle QTR = (6y + 6)°$ and $m\angle SPR = 3y°$.**

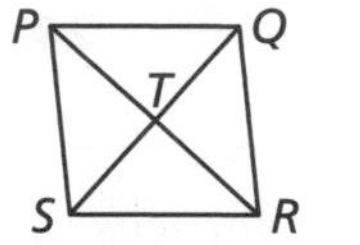

$m\angle QTR = 90°$ *Rhombus → diags. ⊥*

$6y + 6 = 90$ *Substitute the given value.*

$y = 14$ *Solve for y.*

$m\angle QPR = m\angle SPR$ *Rhombus → each diag. bisects opp. ∠s*

$m\angle QPR = 3(14)° = 42°$

- **The vertices of square $ABCD$ are $A(5, 0)$, $B(2, 4)$, $C(-2, 1)$, and $D(1, -3)$. Show that the diagonals of square $ABCD$ are congruent perpendicular bisectors of each other.**

$AC = BD = 5\sqrt{2}$ *Diags. are ≅.*

slope of $\overline{AC} = -\frac{1}{7}$ *Product of slopes is −1, so diags. are ⊥.*

slope of $\overline{BD} = 7$

mdpt. of $\overline{AC}$ = mdpt. of $\overline{BD} = \left(\frac{3}{2}, \frac{1}{2}\right)$ *Diags. bisect each other.*

EXERCISES

In rectangle $ABCD$, $CD = 18$, and $CE = 19.8$. Find each length.

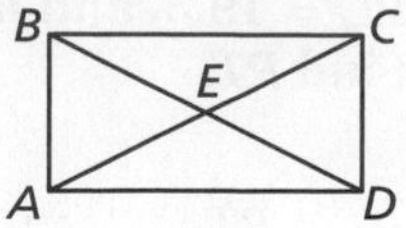

34. AB **35.** AC

36. BD **37.** BE

In rhombus $WXYZ$, $WX = 7a + 1$, $WZ = 9a - 6$, and $VZ = 3a$. Find each measure.

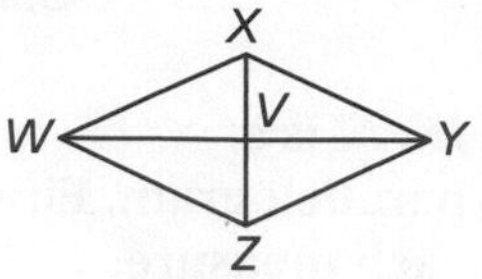

38. WZ **39.** XV

40. XY **41.** XZ

In rhombus $RSTV$, $m\angle TZV = (8n + 18)°$, and $m\angle SRV = (9n + 1)°$. Find each measure.

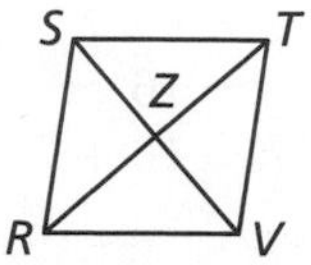

42. $m\angle TRS$ **43.** $m\angle RSV$

44. $m\angle STV$ **45.** $m\angle TVR$

Find the measures of the numbered angles in each figure.

46. rectangle $MNPQ$

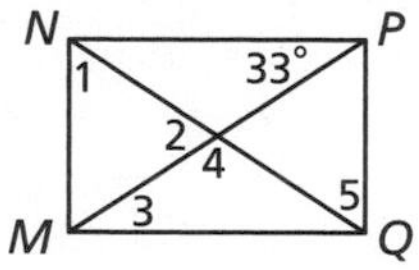

47. rhombus $CDGH$

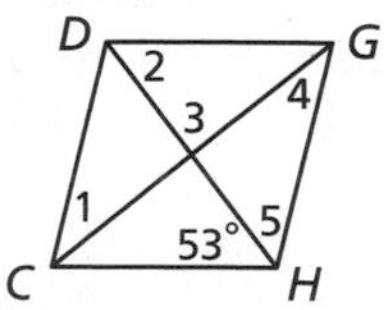

Show that the diagonals of the square with the given vertices are congruent perpendicular bisectors of each other.

48. $R(-5, 0)$, $S(-1, -2)$, $T(-3, -6)$, and $U(-7, -4)$

49. $E(2, 1)$, $F(5, 1)$, $G(5, -2)$, and $H(2, -2)$

6-5 Conditions for Special Parallelograms

EXAMPLES

- **Determine if the conclusion is valid. If not, tell what additional information is needed to make it valid.**

Given: $\overline{LP} \perp \overline{KN}$

Conclusion: $KLNP$ is a rhombus.

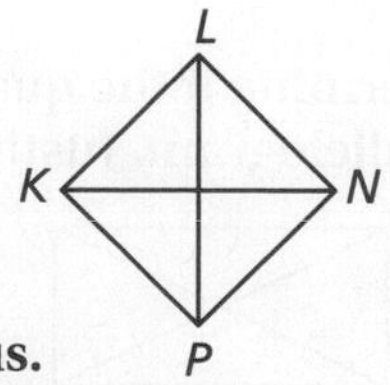

The conclusion is not valid. If the diagonals of a parallelogram are perpendicular, then the parallelogram is a rhombus. To apply this theorem, you must first know that $KLNP$ is a parallelogram.

EXERCISES

Determine if the conclusion is valid. If not, tell what additional information is needed to make it valid.

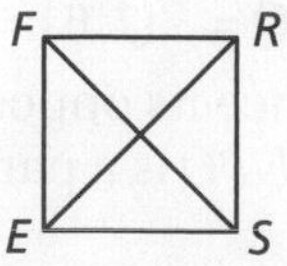

50. Given: $\overline{ER} \perp \overline{FS}$, $\overline{ER} \cong \overline{FS}$
Conclusion: $EFRS$ is a square.

51. Given: $\overline{ER}$ and $\overline{FS}$ bisect each other.
$\overline{ER} \cong \overline{FS}$
Conclusion: $EFRS$ is a rectangle.

52. Given: $\overline{EF} \parallel \overline{RS}$, $\overline{FR} \parallel \overline{ES}$, $\overline{EF} \cong \overline{ES}$
Conclusion: $EFRS$ is a rhombus.

- Use the diagonals to tell whether a parallelogram with vertices $P(-5, 3)$, $Q(0, 1)$, $R(2, -4)$, and $S(-3, -2)$ is a rectangle, rhombus, or square. Give all the names that apply.

$PR = \sqrt{98} = 7\sqrt{2}$ *Distance Formula*
$QS = \sqrt{18} = 3\sqrt{2}$ *Distance Formula*

Since $PR \neq QS$, $PQRS$ is not a rectangle and not a square.

slope of $\overline{PR} = \frac{7}{-7} = -1$ *Slope Formula*

slope of $\overline{QS} = \frac{3}{3} = 1$ *Slope Formula*

Since the product of the slopes is -1, the diagonals are perpendicular. $PQRS$ is a rhombus.

Use the diagonals to tell whether a parallelogram with the given vertices is a rectangle, rhombus, or square. Give all the names that apply.

53. $B(-3, 0)$, $F(-2, 7)$, $J(5, 8)$, $N(4, 1)$

54. $D(-4, -3)$, $H(5, 6)$, $L(8, 3)$, $P(-1, -6)$

55. $Q(-8, -2)$, $T(-6, 8)$, $W(4, 6)$, $Z(2, -4)$

6-6 Properties of Kites and Trapezoids

EXAMPLES

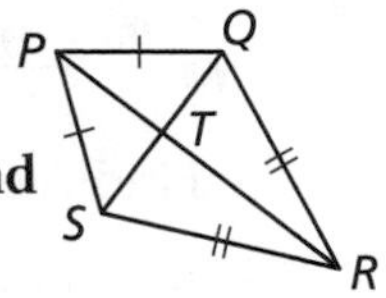

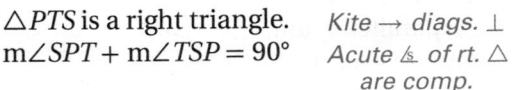

- **In kite $PQRS$, $m\angle SRT = 24°$, and $m\angle TSP = 53°$. Find $m\angle SPT$.**

$\triangle PTS$ is a right triangle. *Kite → diags. ⊥*
$m\angle SPT + m\angle TSP = 90°$ *Acute ∡ of rt. △ are comp.*

$m\angle SPT + 53 = 90$ *Substitute 53 for m∠TSP.*
$m\angle SPT = 37°$ *Subtract 53 from both sides.*

- **Find $m\angle D$.**

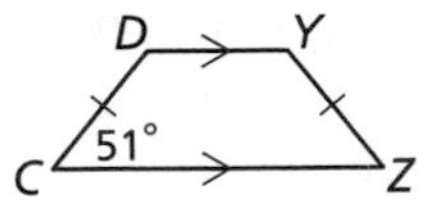

$m\angle C + m\angle D = 180°$ *Same-Side Int. ∡ Thm.*
$51 + m\angle D = 180$ *Substitute 51 for m∠C.*
$m\angle D = 129°$ *Subtract.*

- **In trapezoid $HJLN$, $JP = 32.5$, and $HL = 50$. Find PN.**

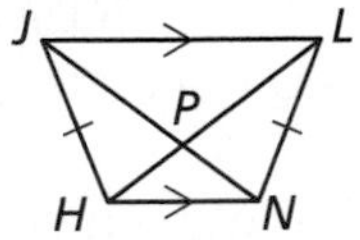

$\overline{JN} \cong \overline{HL}$ *Isosc. trap. → diags. ≅*
$JN = HL = 50$ *Def. of ≅ segs.*
$JP + PN = JN$ *Seg. Add. Post.*
$32.5 + PN = 50$ *Substitute.*
$PN = 17.5$ *Subtract 32.5 from both sides.*

- **Find WZ.**

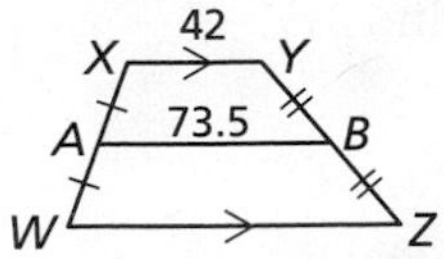

$AB = \frac{1}{2}(XY + WZ)$ *Trap. Midsegment Thm.*
$73.5 = \frac{1}{2}(42 + WZ)$ *Substitute.*
$147 = 42 + WZ$ *Multiply both sides by 2.*
$105 = WZ$ *Solve for WZ.*

EXERCISES

In kite $WXYZ$, $m\angle VXY = 58°$, and $m\angle ZWX = 50°$. Find each measure.

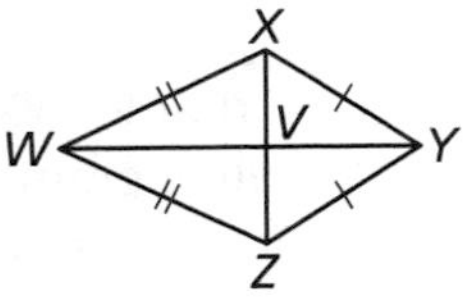

56. $m\angle XYZ$ **57.** $m\angle ZWV$

58. $m\angle VZW$ **59.** $m\angle WZY$

Find each measure.

60. $m\angle R$ and $m\angle S$

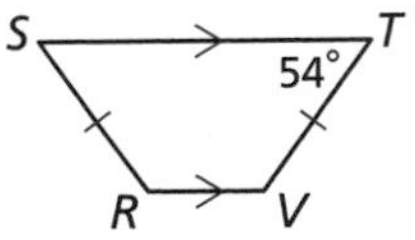

61. BZ if $ZH = 70$ and $EK = 121.6$

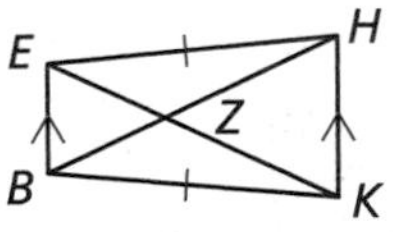

62. MN

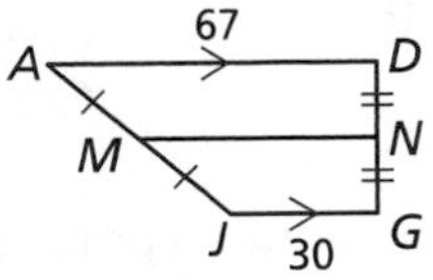

63. EQ

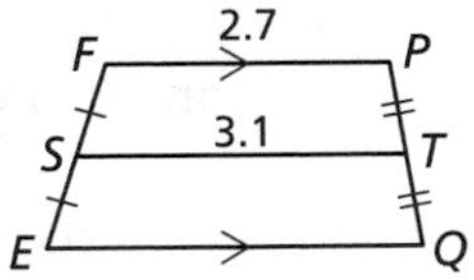

64. Find the value of n so that $PQXY$ is isosceles.

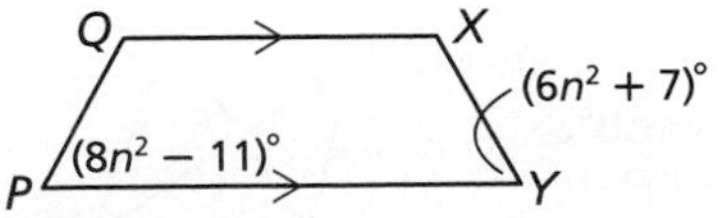

Give the best name for a quadrilateral whose vertices have the given coordinates.

65. $(-4, 5)$, $(-1, 8)$, $(5, 5)$, $(-1, 2)$

66. $(1, 4)$, $(5, 4)$, $(5, -4)$, $(1, -1)$

67. $(-6, -1)$, $(-4, 2)$, $(0, 2)$, $(2, -1)$

CHAPTER TEST

Tell whether each figure is a polygon. If it is a polygon, name it by the number of its sides.

1.

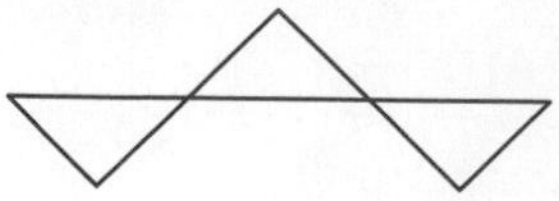

2.

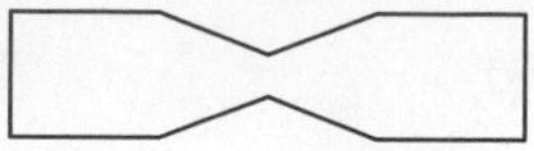

3. The base of a fountain is in the shape of a quadrilateral, as shown. Find the measure of each interior angle of the fountain.

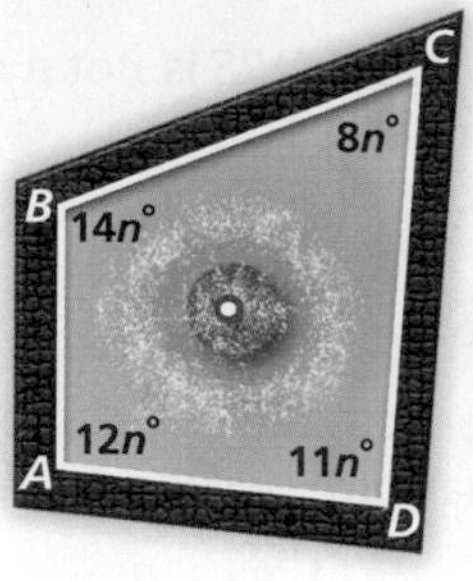

4. Find the sum of the interior angle measures of a convex nonagon.

5. Find the measure of each exterior angle of a regular 15-gon.

6. In ▱$EFGH$, $EH = 28$, $HZ = 9$, and $m\angle EHG = 145°$. Find FH and $m\angle FEH$.

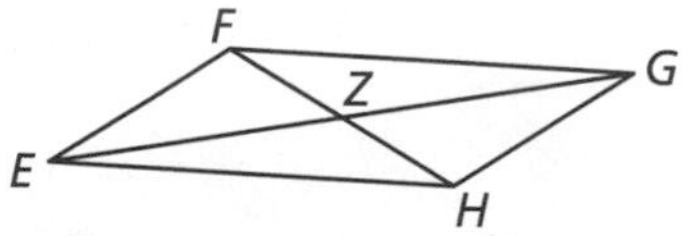

7. $JKLM$ is a parallelogram. Find KL and $m\angle L$.

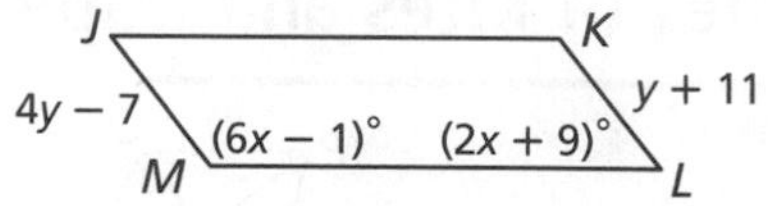

8. Three vertices of ▱$PQRS$ are $P(-2, -3)$, $R(7, 5)$, and $S(6, 1)$. Find the coordinates of Q.

9. Show that $WXYZ$ is a parallelogram for $a = 4$ and $b = 3$.

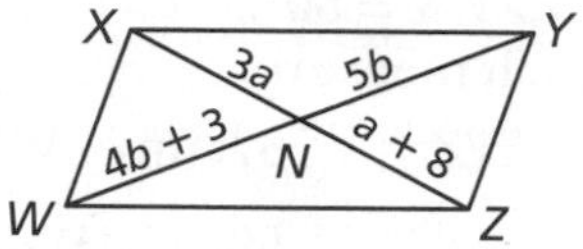

10. Determine if $CDGH$ must be a parallelogram. Justify your answer.

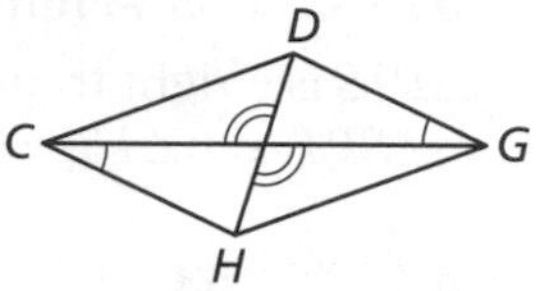

11. Show that a quadrilateral with vertices $K(-7, -3)$, $L(2, 0)$, $S(5, -4)$, and $T(-4, -7)$ is a parallelogram.

12. In rectangle $PLCM$, $LC = 19$, and $LM = 23$. Find PT and PM.

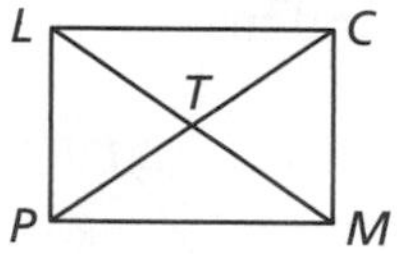

13. In rhombus $EHKN$, $m\angle NQK = (7z + 6)°$, and $m\angle ENQ = (5z + 1)°$. Find $m\angle HEQ$ and $m\angle EHK$.

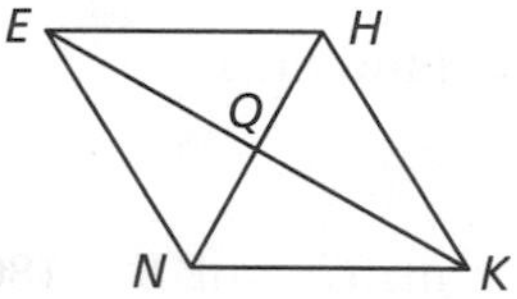

Determine if the conclusion is valid. If not, tell what additional information is needed to make it valid.

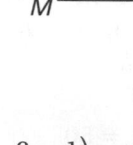

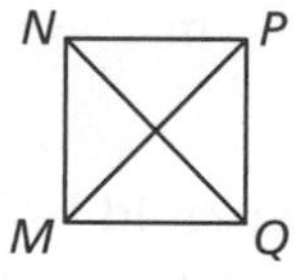

14. Given: $\overline{NP} \cong \overline{PQ} \cong \overline{QM} \cong \overline{MN}$
Conclusion: $MNPQ$ is a square.

15. Given: $\overline{NP} \cong \overline{MQ}$, $\overline{NM} \cong \overline{PQ}$, $\overline{NQ} \cong \overline{MP}$
Conclusion: $MNPQ$ is a rectangle.

Use the diagonals to determine whether a parallelogram with the given vertices is a rectangle, rhombus, or square. Give all the names that apply.

16. $A(-5, 7)$, $C(3, 6)$, $E(7, -1)$, $G(-1, 0)$

17. $P(4, 1)$, $Q(3, 4)$, $R(-3, 2)$, $S(-2, -1)$

18. $m\angle JFR = 43°$, and $m\angle JNB = 68°$. Find $m\angle FBN$.

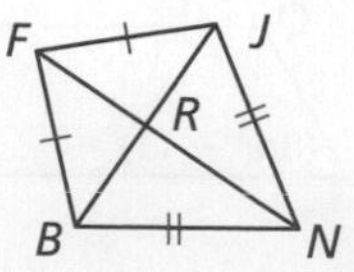

19. $PV = 61.1$, and $YS = 24.7$. Find MY.

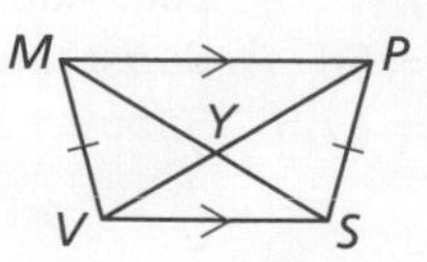

20. Find HR.

College Entrance Exam Practice

FOCUS ON SAT

The scores for each SAT section range from 200 to 800. Your score is calculated by subtracting a fraction for each incorrect multiple-choice answer from the total number of correct answers. No points are deducted for incorrect grid-in answers or items you left blank.

HOT TIP! If you have time, go back through each section of the test and check as many of your answers as possible. Try to use a different method of solving the problem than you used the first time.

You may want to time yourself as you take this practice test. It should take you about 6 minutes to complete.

---

1. Given the quadrilateral below, what value of x would allow you to conclude that the figure is a parallelogram?

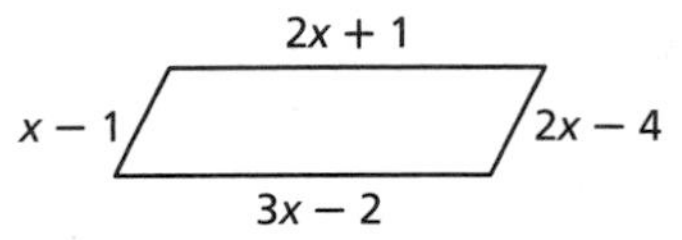

(A) −2

(B) 0

(C) 1

(D) 2

(E) 3

2. In the figure below, if $ABCD$ is a rectangle, what type of triangle must $\triangle ABE$ be?

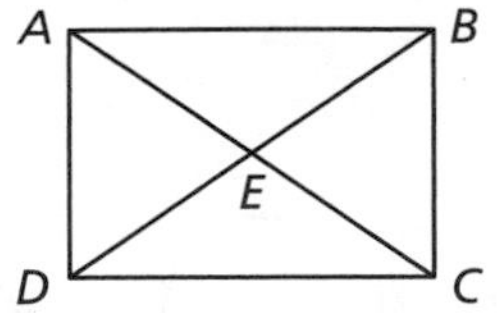

(A) Equilateral

(B) Right

(C) Equiangular

(D) Isosceles

(E) Scalene

3. Which of the following terms best describes the figure below?

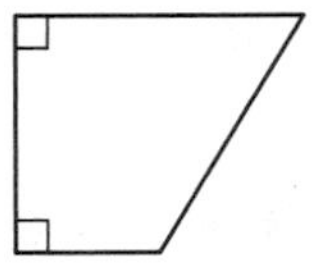

(A) Rhombus

(B) Trapezoid

(C) Quadrilateral

(D) Square

(E) Parallelogram

4. Three vertices of $\square MNPQ$ are $M(3, 1)$, $N(0, 6)$, and $P(4, 7)$. Which of the following could be the coordinates of vertex Q?

(A) $(7, 0)$

(B) $(-1, 1)$

(C) $(7, 2)$

(D) $(11, 3)$

(E) $(9, 4)$

5. If $ABCDE$ is a regular pentagon, what is the measure of $\angle C$?

(A) 45°

(B) 60°

(C) 90°

(D) 108°

(E) 120°

CHAPTER 6

TEST TACKLER

Standardized Test Strategies

Multiple Choice: Eliminate Answer Choices

For some multiple-choice test items, you can eliminate one or more of the answer choices without having to do many calculations. Use estimation or logic to help you decide which answer choices can be eliminated.

EXAMPLE 1

What is the value of *x* in the figure?

Ⓐ 3°   Ⓒ 83°

Ⓑ 63°   Ⓓ 153°

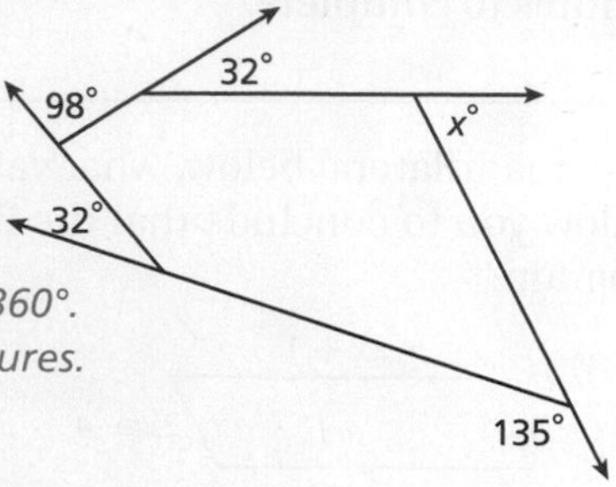

The sum of the exterior angle measures of a convex polygon is 360°. By rounding, you can estimate the sum of the given angle measures.

$100° + 30° + 140° + 30° = 300°$

If $x = 153°$, the sum of the angle measures would be far greater than 360°. So eliminate D.

If $x = 3°$, the sum would be far less than 360°. So eliminate A.

From your estimate, it seems likely that the correct choice is B, 63°. Confirm that this is correct by doing the actual calculation.

$98° + 32° + 63° + 135° + 32° = 360°$

The correct answer is B, 63°.

EXAMPLE 2

What is m∠*B* in the isosceles trapezoid?

Ⓕ 216°   Ⓗ 72°

Ⓖ 108°   Ⓙ 58°

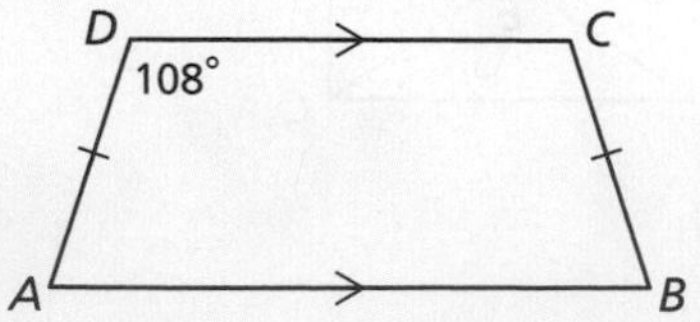

Base angles of an isosceles trapezoid are congruent. Since ∠D and ∠B are not a pair of base angles, their measures are not equal. Eliminate G, 108°.

∠D and ∠C are base angles, so $m\angle C = 108°$. ∠B and ∠C are same-side interior angles formed by parallel lines. So they are supplementary angles. Therefore the measure of angle B cannot be greater than 180°. You can eliminate F.

$m\angle B = 180° - 108° = 72°$

The correct answer is H, 72°.

HOT TIP! Try to eliminate unreasonable answer choices. Some choices may be too large or too small or may have incorrect units.

Read each test item and answer the questions that follow.

Item A

The diagonals of rectangle *MNPQ* intersect at *S*. If $MN = 4.1$ meters, $MS = 2.35$ meters, and $MQ = 2.3$ meters, what is the area of $\triangle MPQ$ to the nearest tenth?

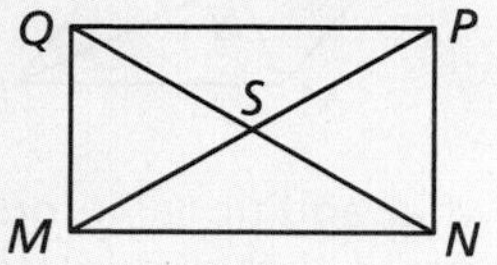

Ⓐ 4.7 square meters

Ⓑ 5.4 meters

Ⓒ 9.4 square meters

Ⓓ 12.8 meters

1. Are there any answer choices you can eliminate immediately? If so, which choices and why?
2. Describe how to use estimation to eliminate at least one more answer choice.

Item B

What is the sum of the interior angles of a convex hexagon?

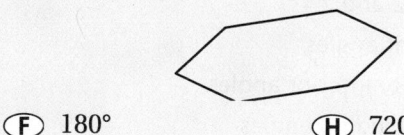

Ⓕ 180°   Ⓗ 720°

Ⓖ 500°   Ⓙ 1080°

3. Can any of the answer choices be eliminated immediately? If so, which choices and why?
4. How can you use the fact that 500 is not a multiple of 180 to eliminate choice G?
5. A student answered this problem with J. Explain the mistake the student made.

Item C

In isosceles trapezoid *ABCD*, $AC = 18.2$, and $DG = 6.3$. What is *GB*?

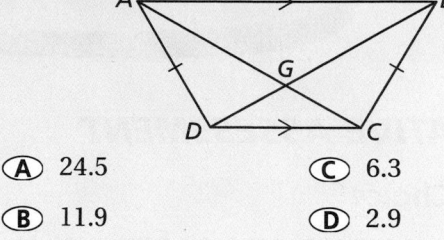

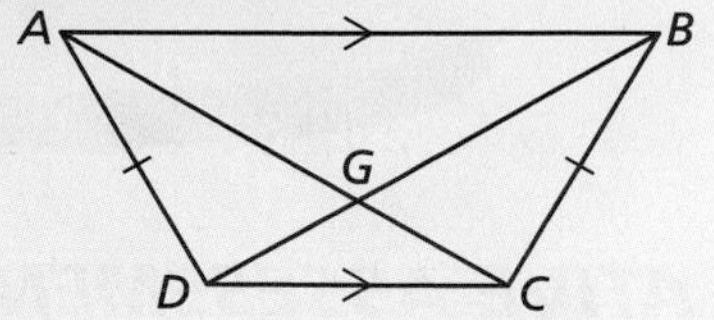

Ⓐ 24.5   Ⓒ 6.3

Ⓑ 11.9   Ⓓ 2.9

6. Will the measure of $\overline{GB}$ be more than, less than, or equal to the measure of $\overline{AC}$? What answer choices can you eliminate and why?
7. Explain how to use estimation to answer this problem.

Item D

In trapezoid *LMNP*, $XY = 25$ feet. What are two possible lengths for $\overline{LM}$ and $\overline{PN}$?

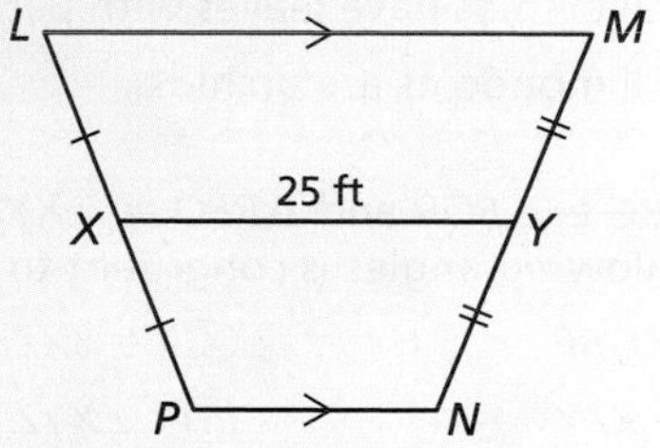

Ⓕ 18 feet and 32 feet

Ⓖ 49 feet and 2 feet

Ⓗ 10 feet and 15 feet

Ⓙ 7 inches and 43 inches

8. Which answer choice can you eliminate immediately? Why?
9. A student used logic to eliminate choice H. Do you agree with the student's decision? Explain.
10. A student used estimation and answered this problem with G. Explain the mistake the student made.

STANDARDIZED TEST PREP

Learn It Online
State Test Practice

CUMULATIVE ASSESSMENT

Multiple Choice

1. The exterior angles of a triangle have measures of $(x + 10)°$, $(2x + 20)°$, and $3x°$. What is the measure of the smallest interior angle of the triangle?

Ⓐ 15° Ⓒ 55°

Ⓑ 35° Ⓓ 65°

2. If a plant is a monocot, then its leaves have parallel veins. If a plant is an orchid, then it is a monocot. A Mexican vanilla plant is an orchid. Based on this information, which conclusion is NOT valid?

Ⓕ The leaves of a Mexican vanilla plant have parallel veins.

Ⓖ A Mexican vanilla plant is a monocot.

Ⓗ All orchids have leaves with parallel veins.

Ⓙ All monocots are orchids.

3. If $\triangle ABC \cong \triangle PQR$ and $\triangle RPQ \cong \triangle XYZ$, which of the following angles is congruent to $\angle CAB$?

Ⓐ $\angle QRP$ Ⓒ $\angle YXZ$

Ⓑ $\angle XZY$ Ⓓ $\angle XYZ$

4. Which line coincides with the line $2y + 3x = 4$?

Ⓕ $3y + 2x = 4$

Ⓖ $y = \frac{2}{3}x + 2$

Ⓗ a line through $(-1, 1)$ and $(2, 3)$

Ⓙ a line through $(0, 2)$ and $(4, -4)$

5. What is the value of x in polygon $ABCDEF$?

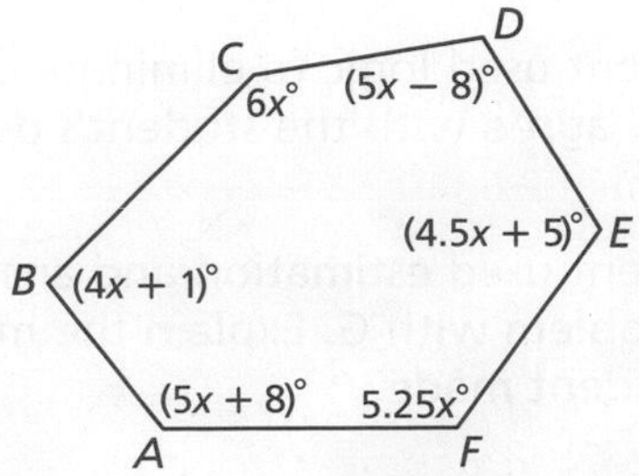

Ⓐ 12 Ⓒ 24

Ⓑ 18 Ⓓ 36

Use the figure below for Items 6 and 7.

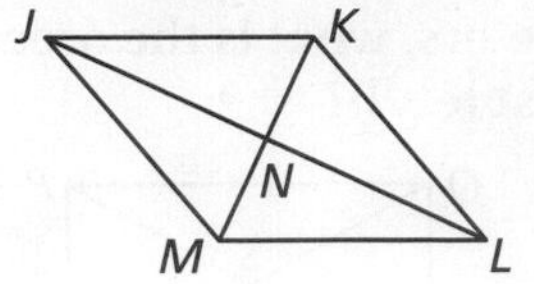

6. If $\overline{JK} \parallel \overline{ML}$, what additional information do you need to prove that quadrilateral $JKLM$ is a parallelogram?

Ⓕ $\overline{JM} \cong \overline{KL}$

Ⓖ $\overline{MN} \cong \overline{LN}$

Ⓗ $\angle MLK$ and $\angle LKJ$ are right angles.

Ⓙ $\angle JML$ and $\angle KLM$ are supplementary.

7. Given that $JKLM$ is a parallelogram and that $m\angle KLN = 25°$, $m\angle JMN = 65°$, and $m\angle JML = 130°$, which term best describes quadrilateral $JKLM$?

Ⓐ Rectangle

Ⓑ Rhombus

Ⓒ Square

Ⓓ Trapezoid

8. For two lines and a transversal, $\angle 1$ and $\angle 2$ are same-side interior angles, $\angle 2$ and $\angle 3$ are vertical angles, and $\angle 3$ and $\angle 4$ are alternate exterior angles. Which classification best describes the angle pair $\angle 2$ and $\angle 4$?

Ⓕ Adjacent angles

Ⓖ Alternate interior angles

Ⓗ Corresponding angles

Ⓙ Vertical angles

9. For $\triangle ABC$ and $\triangle DEF$, $\angle A \cong \angle F$, and $\overline{AC} \cong \overline{EF}$. Which of the following would allow you to conclude that these triangles are congruent by AAS?

Ⓐ $\angle ABC \cong \angle EDF$

Ⓑ $\angle ACB \cong \angle EDF$

Ⓒ $\angle BAC \cong \angle FDE$

Ⓓ $\angle CBA \cong \angle FED$

10. The vertices of ▱$ABCD$ are $A(1, 4)$, $B(4, y)$, $C(3, -2)$, and $D(0, -3)$. What is the value of y?

Ⓕ 3 Ⓗ 5

Ⓖ 4 Ⓙ 6

11. Quadrilateral $RSTU$ is a kite. What is the length of $\overline{RV}$?

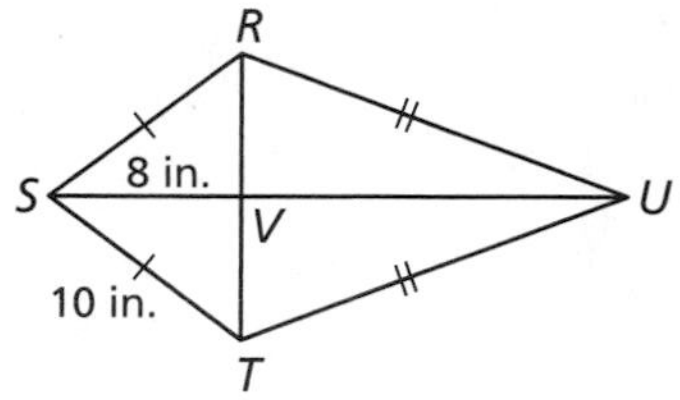

Ⓐ 4 inches Ⓒ 6 inches

Ⓑ 5 inches Ⓓ 13 inches

12. What is the measure of each interior angle in a regular dodecagon?

Ⓕ 30° Ⓗ 150°

Ⓖ 144° Ⓙ 162°

13. The coordinates of the vertices of quadrilateral $RSTU$ are $R(1, 3)$, $S(2, 7)$, $T(10, 5)$, and $U(9, 1)$. Which term best describes quadrilateral $RSTU$?

Ⓐ Parallelogram Ⓒ Rhombus

Ⓑ Rectangle Ⓓ Trapezoid

HOT TIP! **Mixed numbers cannot be entered into the grid for gridded-response questions. For example, if you get an answer of $7\frac{1}{4}$, you must grid either 7.25 or $\frac{29}{4}$.**

Gridded Response

14. If quadrilateral $MNPQ$ is a parallelogram, what is the value of x?

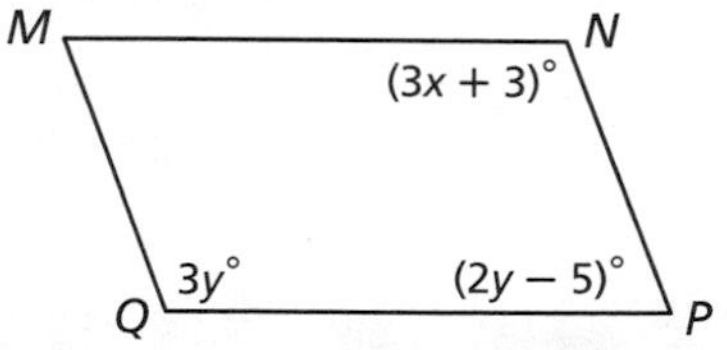

15. What is the greatest number of line segments determined by six coplanar points when no three are collinear?

16. Quadrilateral $RSTU$ is a rectangle with diagonals $\overline{RT}$ and $\overline{SU}$. If $RT = 4a + 2$ and $SU = 6a - 25$, what is the value of a?

Short Response

17. In $\triangle ABC$, $AE = 9x - 11.25$, and $AF = x + 4$.

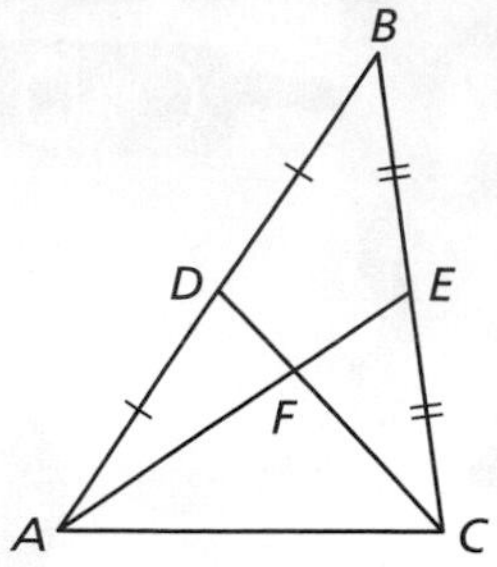

a. Find the value of x. Show your work and explain how you found your answer.

b. If $\overline{DF} \cong \overline{EF}$, show that $\triangle AFD \cong \triangle CFE$. State any theorems or postulates used.

18. Consider quadrilateral $ABCD$.

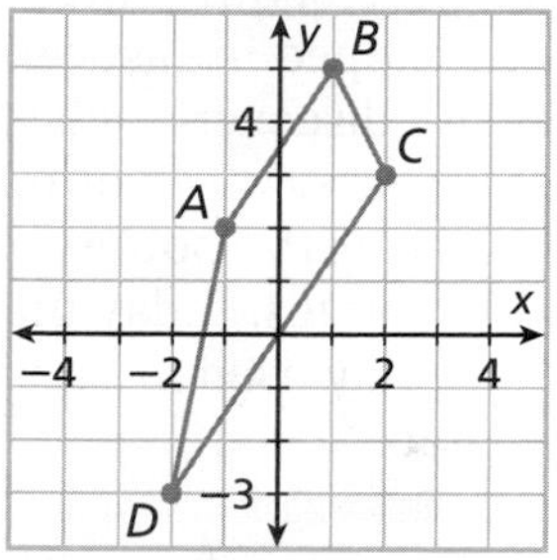

a. Show that $ABCD$ is a trapezoid. Justify your answer.

b. What are the coordinates for the endpoints of the midsegment of trapezoid $ABCD$?

19. Suppose that $\angle M$ is complementary to $\angle N$ and $\angle N$ is complementary to $\angle P$. Explain why the measurements of these three angles cannot be the angle measurements of a triangle.

Extended Response

20. Given $\triangle ABC$ and $\triangle XYZ$, suppose that $\overline{AB} \cong \overline{XY}$ and $\overline{BC} \cong \overline{YZ}$.

a. If $AB = 5$, $BC = 6$, $AC = 8$, and $m\angle B < m\angle Y$, explain why $\triangle XYZ$ is obtuse. Justify your reasoning and state any theorems or postulates used.

b. If $AB = 3$, $BC = 5$, $AC = 5$, and $m\angle B > m\angle Y$, find the length of $\overline{XZ}$ so that $\triangle XYZ$ is a right triangle. Justify your reasoning and state any theorems or postulates used.

c. If $AB = 8$ and $BC = 4$, find the range of possible values for the length of $\overline{AC}$. Justify your answer.

Real-World CONNECTIONS

Handmade Tiles

During the nineteenth century, an important industry developed in east central Ohio thanks to an "earthy" discovery—clay! The region's rich soil and easy access to river transportation helped establish Ohio as the pottery and ceramic capital of the United States. Today the majority of the earthenware clay used in handmade tiles is still mined in Ohio.

Choose one or more strategies to solve each problem.

1. In tile making, soft clay is pressed into long rectangular wooden trays. After the clay has dried, tiles are cut from the rectangular slab. A tile manufacturer wants to make parallelogram-shaped tiles with the dimensions shown. What is the maximum number of such tiles that can be cut from a 12 in. by 40 in. slab of clay?

2. An interior designer is buying tiles that are in the shape of isosceles trapezoids. Each tile has bases that are 1 in. and 3 in. long, and the tiles can be arranged as shown to form a rectangle. How many tiles should the designer buy in order to frame a 25 in. by 49 in. window?

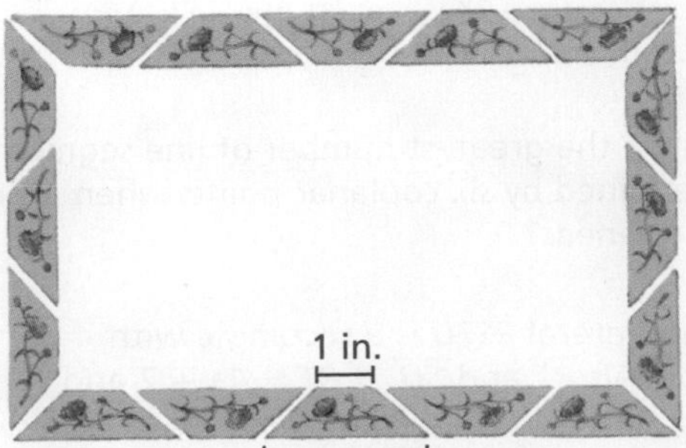

3. A tile manufacturer wants to make a tile in the shape of a rhombus where one diagonal is twice the length of the other diagonal. What should the lengths of the diagonals be in order to make a tile with sides 7 cm long? Round to the nearest hundredth.

The Millennium Force Roller Coaster

When it opened in May 2000, the Millennium Force roller coaster broke all previous records and became the tallest and fastest roller coaster in the world. One of 16 roller coasters at Cedar Point in Sandusky, Ohio, the Millennium Force takes riders on a wild journey that features 1.25 miles of track, a top speed of 93 miles per hour, and a breathtaking 310-foot drop!

Choose one or more strategies to solve each problem.

1. The first hill of the Millennium Force is 310 ft tall. The ascent to the top of the hill is at a 45° angle. What is the length of the ascent to the nearest tenth of a foot?
2. The Millennium Force was the first coaster in which an elevator lift system was used to pull the trains to the top of the first hill. The system pulls the trains at a speed of 20 ft/s. How long does it take a train to reach the top of the hill?

The figure shows the support structure for the first hill of the Millennium Force. For 3 and 4, use the figure.

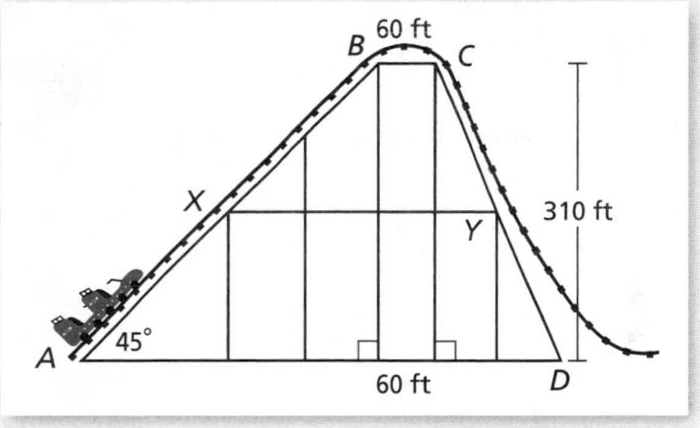

3. The length of the first descent $\overline{CD}$ is 314.8 ft. To the nearest foot, what is the total horizontal distance AD that the train covers as it goes over the first hill?
4. Engineers designed the support beam $\overline{XY}$ so that X is the midpoint of the ascent $\overline{AB}$ and Y is the midpoint of the descent $\overline{CD}$. What is the length of the beam to the nearest foot?

CHAPTER

7 Similarity

COMMON CORE

Chapter

- Justify conditions for triangle similarity.
- Apply similarity to solve real-world problems.

Close Encounters

IMAX films use a wide array of modern technology. The mathematics of similarity and perspective are key to making realistic movie images.

Learn It Online
Chapter Project Online

ARE YOU READY?

Vocabulary

Match each term on the left with a definition on the right.

1. side of a polygon
2. denominator
3. numerator
4. vertex of a polygon
5. vertical angles

A. two nonadjacent angles formed by two intersecting lines
B. the top number of a fraction, which tells how many parts of a whole are being considered
C. a point that corresponds to one and only one number
D. the intersection of two sides of a polygon
E. one of the segments that form a polygon
F. the bottom number of a fraction, which tells how many equal parts are in the whole

Simplify Fractions

Write each fraction in simplest form.

6. $\frac{16}{20}$
7. $\frac{14}{21}$
8. $\frac{33}{121}$
9. $\frac{56}{80}$

Ratios

Use the table to write each ratio in simplest form.

10. jazz CDs to country CDs
11. hip-hop CDs to jazz CDs
12. rock CDs to total CDs
13. total CDs to country CDs

Ryan's CD Collection	
Rock	36
Jazz	18
Hip-hop	34
Country	24

Identify Polygons

Determine whether each figure is a polygon. If so, name it by the number of sides.

14. 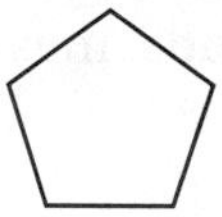

15. 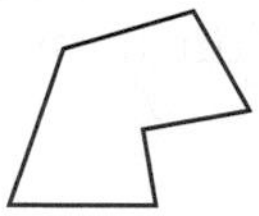

16. 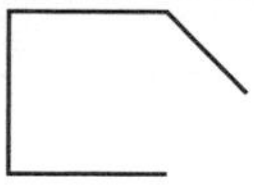

17. 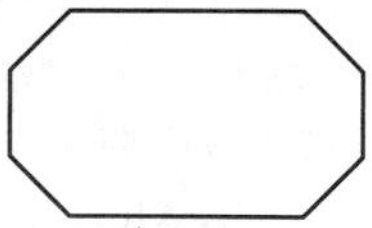

Find Perimeter

Find the perimeter of each figure.

18. rectangle *PQRS*

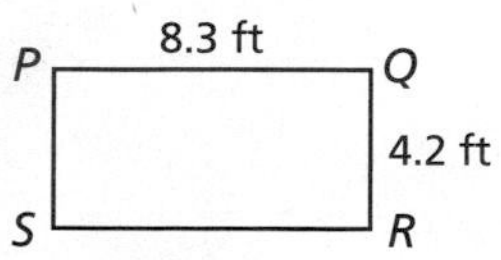

19. regular hexagon *ABCDEF*

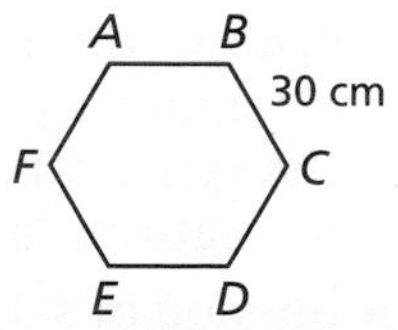

20. rhombus *JKLM*

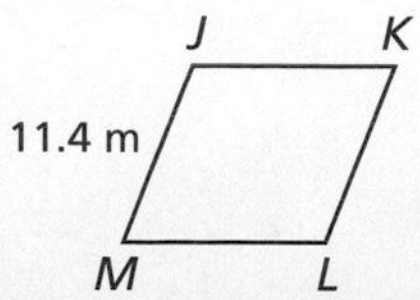

21. regular pentagon *UVWXY*

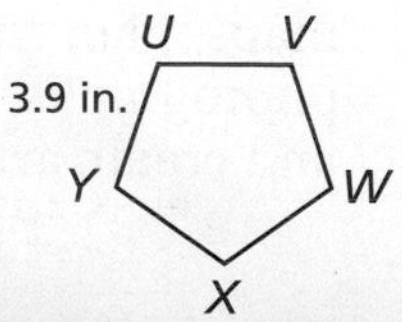

CHAPTER 7

Study Guide: Preview

Where You've Been

Previously, you

- classified polygons based on their sides and angles.
- used properties of polygons.
- wrote proofs about polygons.

In This Chapter

You will study

- verifying that polygons are similar using corresponding angles and sides.
- using properties of similar polygons.
- writing proofs about similar polygons.

Where You're Going

You can use the skills learned in this chapter

- in Algebra 2 and Precalculus.
- in other classes, such as in Physics when you study the symmetries of nature, in Geography when you look at the symmetry of many natural formations, and in Art.
- outside of school to read maps, plan trips, enlarge photographs, build models, and create art.

Key Vocabulary/Vocabulario

dilation	dilatación
scale	escala
scale drawing	dibujo a escala
scale factor	factor de escala
similar	semejante
similar polygons	polígonos semejantes
similarity ratio	razón de semejanza

Vocabulary Connections

To become familiar with some of the vocabulary terms in the chapter, consider the following. You may refer to the chapter, the glossary, or a dictionary if you like.

1. When an eye doctor dilates your eyes, the pupils become enlarged. What might it mean for one geometric figure to be a **dilation** of another figure?
2. A blueprint is a scale drawing of a building. What do you think is the definition of a **scale drawing**?
3. What does the word *similar* mean in everyday language? What do you think the term **similar polygons** means?

Reading Strategy: Read and Understand the Problem

Many of the concepts you are learning are used in real-world situations. Throughout the text, there are examples and exercises that are real-world word problems. Listed below are strategies for solving word problems.

Problem Solving Strategies

- Read slowly and carefully. Determine what information is given and what you are asked to find.
- If a diagram is provided, read the labels and make sure that you understand the information. If you do not, resketch and relabel the diagram so it makes sense to you. If a diagram is not provided, make a quick sketch and label it.
- Use the given information to set up and solve the problem.
- Decide whether your answer makes sense.

Look at how the Polygon Exterior Angle Theorem is used in photography.

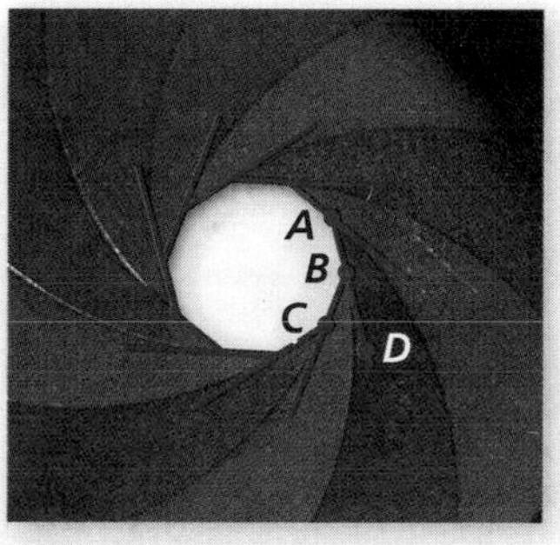

PROBLEM SOLVING

Photography Application

The aperture of the camera shown is formed by ten blades. The blades overlap to form a regular decagon. What is the measure of $\angle CBD$?

Step	Procedure	Result
Understand the Problem	• List the **important information**. • The **answer** will be the measure of $\angle CBD$.	$\angle CBD$ is one of the exterior angles of the regular decagon formed by the apeture.
Make a Plan	• A **diagram** is provided, and it is labeled accurately.	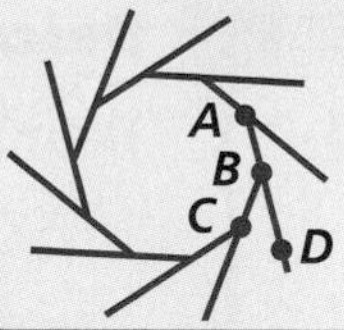
Solve	• You can use the **Polygon Exterior Angle Theorem**. Then divide to find the measure of **one** of the exterior angles.	$m\angle CBD = \frac{360°}{10} = 36°$
Look Back	• The **answer** is reasonable since a decagon has 10 angles.	$10(36°) = 360°$

Try This

Use the problem-solving strategies for the following problem.

1. A painter's scaffold is constructed so that the braces lie along the diagonals of rectangle $PQRS$. Given $RS = 28$ and $QS = 85$, find QT.

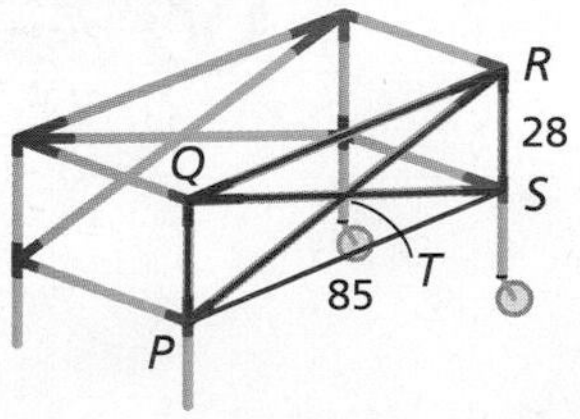

COMMON CORE

7-1 Ratios in Similar Polygons

CC.9-12.G.SRT.2 Given two figures,…decide if they are similar… *Also* **CC.9-12.G.MG.3***

Objectives

Identify similar polygons.

Apply properties of similar polygons to solve problems.

Vocabulary

similar

similar polygons

similarity ratio

Why learn this?

Similar polygons are used to build models of actual objects. (See Example 3.)

Figures that are **similar** (~) have the same shape but not necessarily the same size.

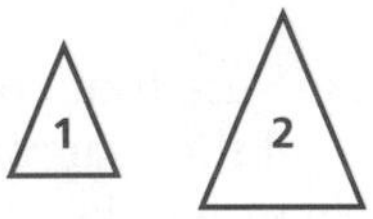

$\triangle 1$ is similar to $\triangle 2 (\triangle 1 \sim \triangle 2)$.

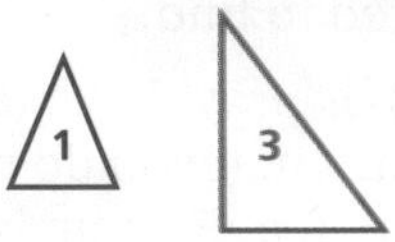

$\triangle 1$ is not similar to $\triangle 3 (\triangle 1 \nsim \triangle 3)$.

Know it! Note

Similar Polygons

DEFINITION	DIAGRAM	STATEMENTS
Two polygons are **similar polygons** if and only if their corresponding angles are congruent and their corresponding side lengths are proportional.	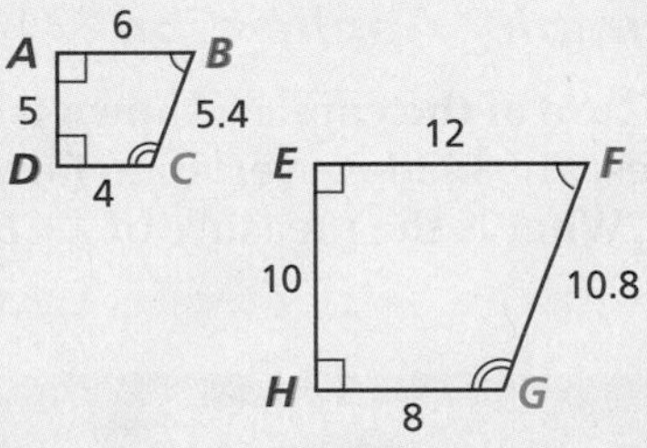 ABCD ~ EFGH	$\angle A \cong \angle E$ $\angle B \cong \angle F$ $\angle C \cong \angle G$ $\angle D \cong \angle H$ $\frac{AB}{EF} = \frac{BC}{FG} = \frac{CD}{GH} = \frac{DA}{HE} = \frac{1}{2}$

EXAMPLE 1 Describing Similar Polygons

Identify the pairs of congruent angles and corresponding sides.

$\angle Z \cong \angle R$ and $\angle Y \cong \angle Q$. By the Third Angles Theorem, $\angle X \cong \angle S$.

$\frac{XY}{SQ} = \frac{6}{9} = \frac{2}{3}, \frac{YZ}{QR} = \frac{12}{18} = \frac{2}{3},$

$\frac{XZ}{SR} = \frac{9}{13.5} = \frac{2}{3}$

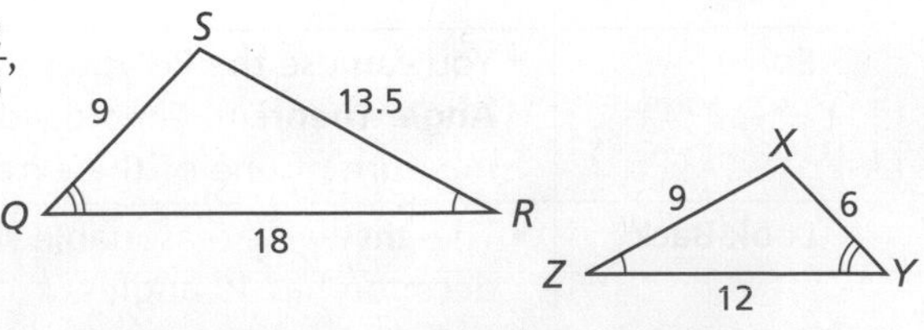

CHECK IT OUT!

1. Identify the pairs of congruent angles and corresponding sides.

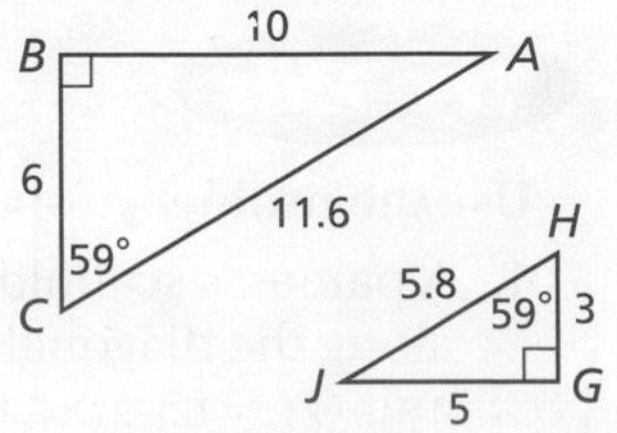

A **similarity ratio** is the ratio of the lengths of the corresponding sides of two similar polygons. The similarity ratio of $\triangle ABC$ to $\triangle DEF$ is $\frac{3}{6}$, or $\frac{1}{2}$. The similarity ratio of $\triangle DEF$ to $\triangle ABC$ is $\frac{6}{3}$, or 2.

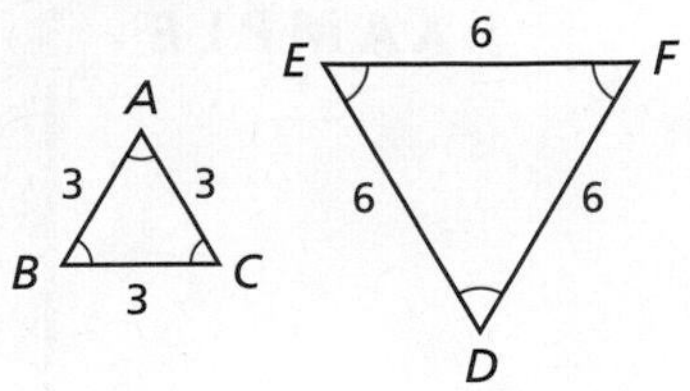

EXAMPLE 2 Identifying Similar Polygons

Determine whether the polygons are similar. If so, write the similarity ratio and a similarity statement.

A rectangles *PQRS* and *TUVW*

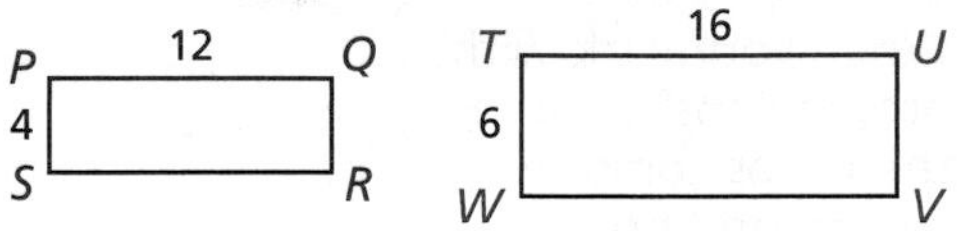

Step 1 Identify pairs of congruent angles.

$\angle P \cong \angle T$, $\angle Q \cong \angle U$,
$\angle R \cong \angle V$, and $\angle S \cong \angle W$ *All ∠s of a rect. are rt. ∠s and are ≅.*

Step 2 Compare corresponding sides.

$$\frac{PQ}{TU} = \frac{12}{16} = \frac{3}{4}, \quad \frac{PS}{TW} = \frac{4}{6} = \frac{2}{3}$$

Since corresponding sides are not proportional, the rectangles are not similar.

B $\triangle ABC$ and $\triangle DEF$

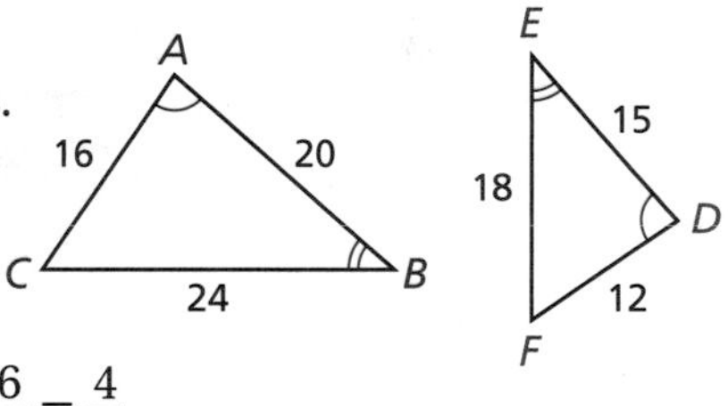

Step 1 Identify pairs of congruent angles.

$\angle A \cong \angle D$, $\angle B \cong \angle E$ *Given*
$\angle C \cong \angle F$ *Third ∠s Thm.*

Step 2 Compare corresponding sides.

$$\frac{AB}{DE} = \frac{20}{15} = \frac{4}{3}, \quad \frac{BC}{EF} = \frac{24}{18} = \frac{4}{3}, \quad \frac{AC}{DF} = \frac{16}{12} = \frac{4}{3}$$

Thus the similarity ratio is $\frac{4}{3}$, and $\triangle ABC \sim \triangle DEF$.

Writing Math

Writing a similarity statement is like writing a congruence statement—be sure to list corresponding vertices in the same order.

CHECK IT OUT! 2. Determine if $\triangle JLM \sim \triangle NPS$. If so, write the similarity ratio and a similarity statement.

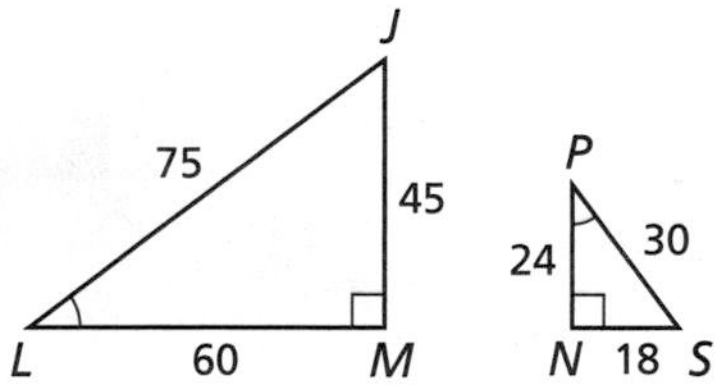

Student to Student

Proportions with Similar Figures

Anna Woods
Westwood High School

When I set up a proportion, I make sure each ratio compares the figures in the same order. To find x, I wrote $\frac{10}{4} = \frac{6}{x}$. This will work because the first ratio compares the lengths starting with rectangle ABCD. The second ratio compares the widths, also starting with rectangle ABCD.

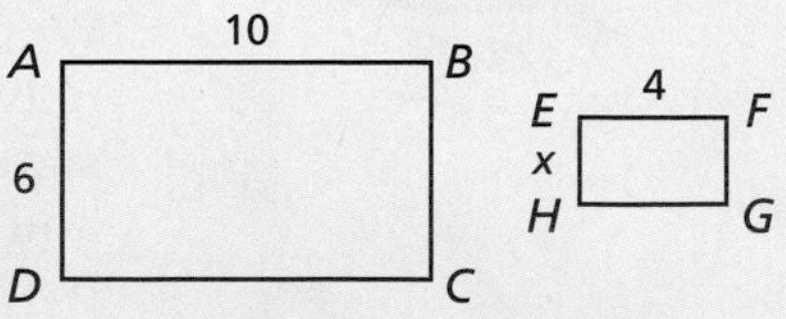

ABCD ~ EFGH

EXAMPLE 3 *Hobby Application*

A Railbox boxcar can be used to transport auto parts. If the length of the actual boxcar is 50 ft, find the width of the actual boxcar to the nearest tenth of a foot.

Let x be the width of the actual boxcar in feet. The rectangular model of a boxcar is similar to the rectangular boxcar, so the corresponding lengths are proportional.

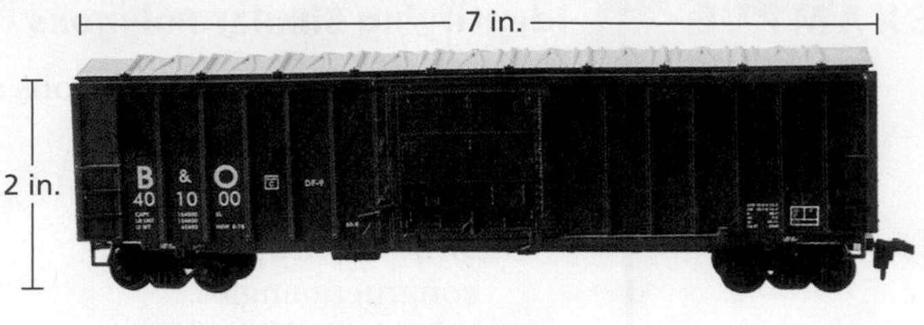

> **Helpful Hint**
>
> When you work with proportions, be sure the ratios compare corresponding measures.

$$\frac{\text{length of boxcar}}{\text{length of model}} = \frac{\text{width of boxcar}}{\text{width of model}}$$

$$\frac{50}{7} = \frac{x}{2}$$

$7x = (50)(2)$ *Cross Products Prop.*

$7x = 100$ *Simplify.*

$x \approx 14.3$ *Divide both sides by 7.*

The width of the model is approximately 14.3 ft.

CHECK IT OUT! **3.** A boxcar has the dimensions shown. A model of the boxcar is 1.25 in. wide. Find the length of the model to the nearest inch.

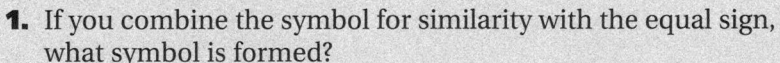

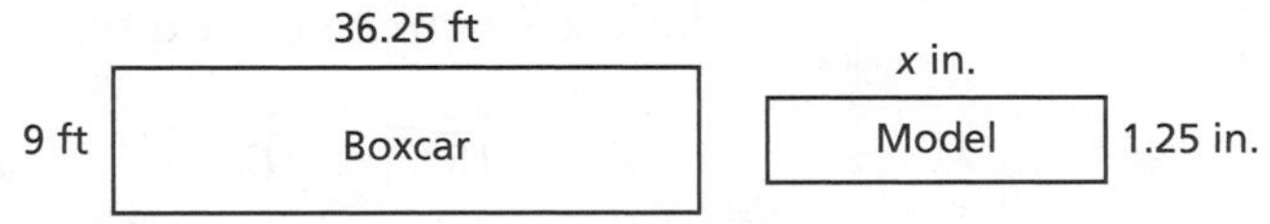

MATHEMATICAL PRACTICES

THINK AND DISCUSS

1. If you combine the symbol for similarity with the equal sign, what symbol is formed?
2. The similarity ratio of rectangle *ABCD* to rectangle *EFGH* is $\frac{1}{9}$. How do the side lengths of rectangle *ABCD* compare to the corresponding side lengths of rectangle *EFGH*?
3. What shape(s) are always similar?
4. **GET ORGANIZED** Copy and complete the graphic organizer. Write the definition of similar polygons, and a similarity statement. Then draw examples and nonexamples of similar polygons.

Know it! Note

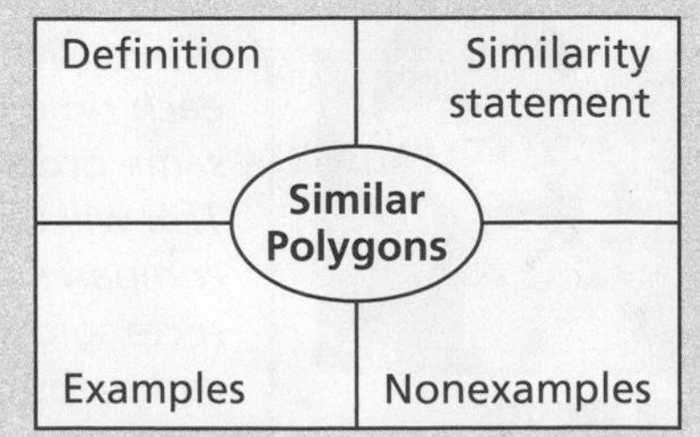

7-1 Exercises

Learn It Online
Homework Help Online
Parent Resources Online

GUIDED PRACTICE

1. **Vocabulary** Give an example of similar figures in your classroom.

SEE EXAMPLE 1

Identify the pairs of congruent angles and corresponding sides.

2.

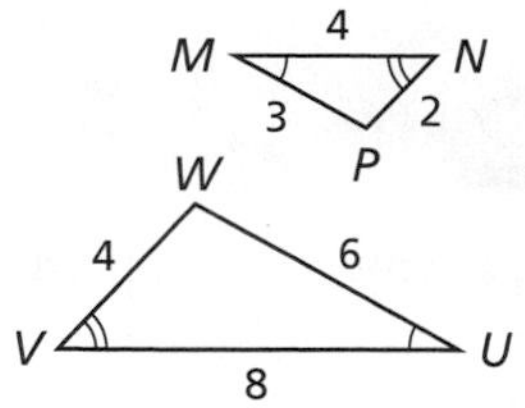

3.

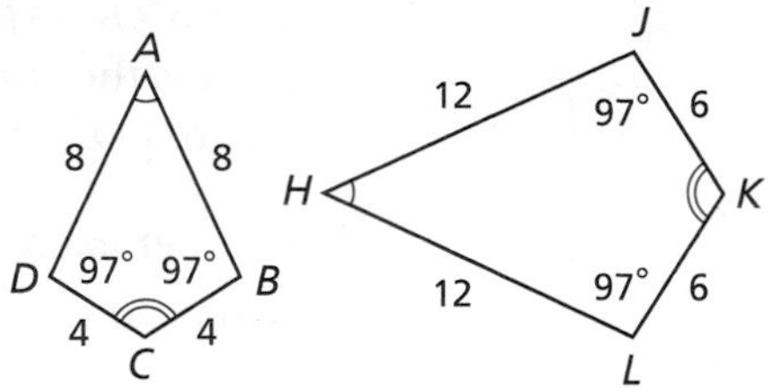

SEE EXAMPLE 2

Multi-Step Determine whether the polygons are similar. If so, write the similarity ratio and a similarity statement.

4. rectangles *ABCD* and *EFGH*

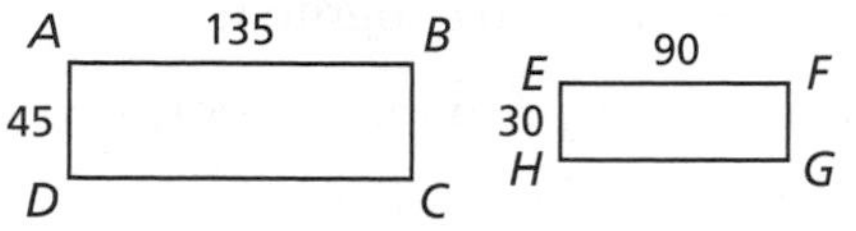

5. $\triangle RMP$ and $\triangle UWX$

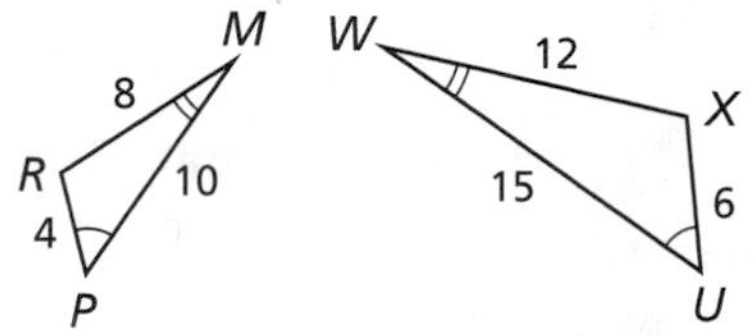

SEE EXAMPLE 3

6. **Art** The town of Goodland, Kansas, claims that it has one of the world's largest easels. It holds an enlargement of a van Gogh painting that is 24 ft wide. The original painting is 58 cm wide and 73 cm tall. If the reproduction is similar to the original, what is the height of the reproduction to the nearest foot?

PRACTICE AND PROBLEM SOLVING

Independent Practice

For Exercises	See Example
7–8	1
9–10	2
11	3

Extra Practice

See Extra Practice for more Skills Practice and Applications Practice exercises.

Identify the pairs of congruent angles and corresponding sides.

7.

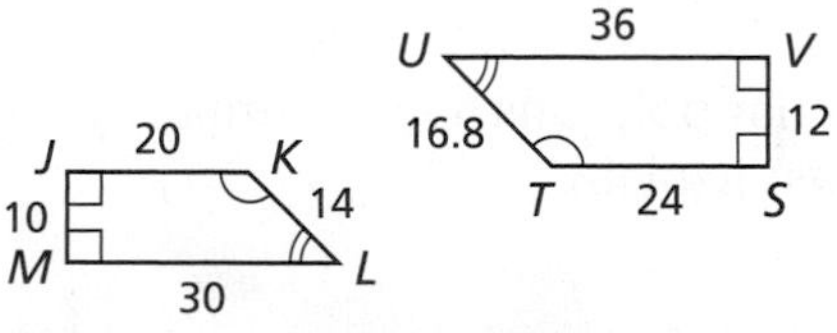

8.

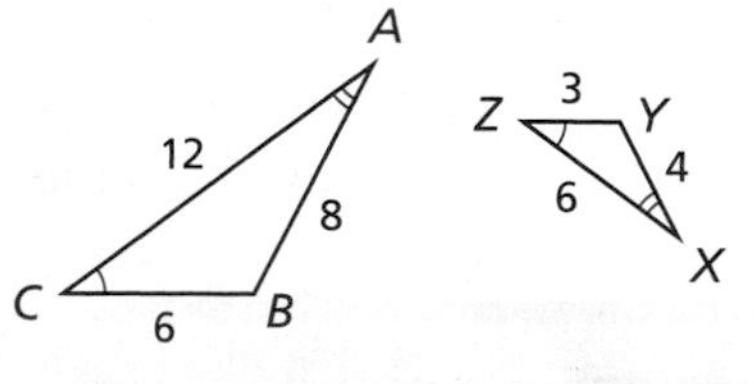

Multi-Step Determine whether the polygons are similar. If so, write the similarity ratio and a similarity statement.

9. $\triangle RSQ$ and $\triangle UXZ$

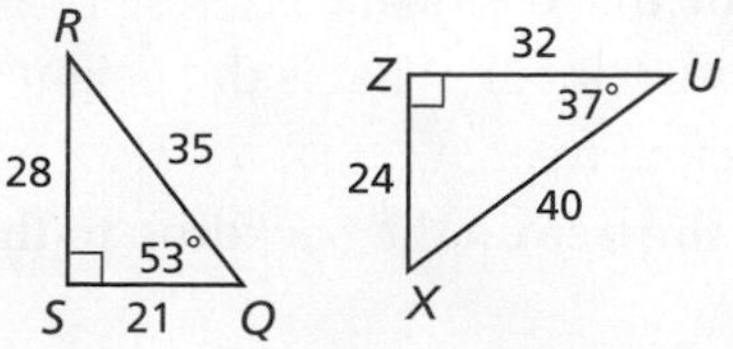

10. rectangles *ABCD* and *JKLM*

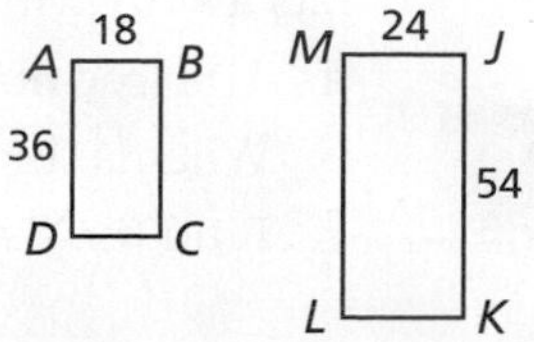

11. **Hobbies** The ratio of the model car's dimensions to the actual car's dimensions is $\frac{1}{56}$. The model has a length of 3 in. What is the length of the actual car?

12. Square *ABCD* has an area of 4 m^2. Square *PQRS* has an area of 36 m^2. What is the similarity ratio of square *ABCD* to square *PQRS*? What is the similarity ratio of square *PQRS* to square *ABCD*?

Tell whether each statement is sometimes, always, or never true.

13. Two right triangles are similar.

14. Two squares are similar.

15. A parallelogram and a trapezoid are similar.

16. If two polygons are congruent, they are also similar.

17. If two polygons are similar, they are also congruent.

18. **Critical Thinking** Explain why any two regular polygons having the same number of sides are similar.

LINK

Monument

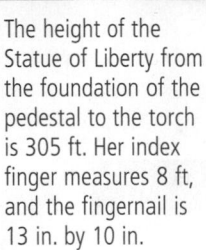

The height of the Statue of Liberty from the foundation of the pedestal to the torch is 305 ft. Her index finger measures 8 ft, and the fingernail is 13 in. by 10 in.

Source: libertystatepark.org

Find the value of *x*.

19. $ABCD \sim EFGH$

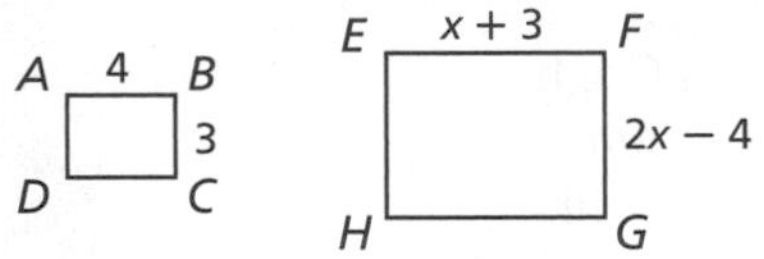

20. $\triangle MNP \sim \triangle XYZ$

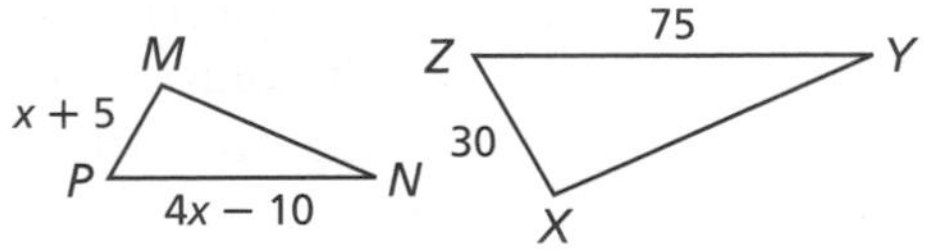

21. **Estimation** The Statue of Liberty's hand is 16.4 ft long. Assume that your own body is similar to that of the Statue of Liberty and estimate the length of the Statue of Liberty's nose. (*Hint:* Use a ruler to measure your own hand and nose. Then set up a proportion.)

22. Write the definition of similar polygons as two conditional statements.

23. $\square JKLM \sim \square NOPQ$. If $m\angle K = 75°$, name two 75° angles in $\square NOPQ$.

24. A dining room is 18 ft long and 14 ft wide. On a blueprint for the house, the dining room is 3.5 in. long. To the nearest tenth of an inch, what is the width of the dining room on the blueprint?

25. **Write About It** Two similar polygons have a similarity ratio of 1 : 1. What can you say about the two polygons? Explain.

MULTI-STEP TEST PREP

26. A stage set consists of a painted backdrop with some wooden flats in front of it. One of the flats shows a tree that has a similarity ratio of $\frac{1}{2}$ to an actual tree. To give an illusion of distance, the backdrop includes a small painted tree that has a similarity ratio of $\frac{1}{10}$ to the tree on the flat.
    a. The tree on the backdrop is 0.9 ft tall. What is the height of the tree on the flat?
    b. What is the height of the actual tree?
    c. Find the similarity ratio of the tree on the backdrop to the actual tree.

TEST PREP

27. Which value of y makes the two rectangles similar?

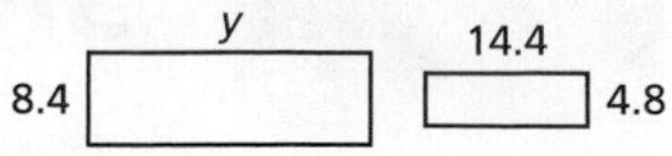

Ⓐ 3 Ⓒ 25.2

Ⓑ 8.2 Ⓓ 28.8

28. $\triangle CGL \sim \triangle MPS$. The similarity ratio of $\triangle CGL$ to $\triangle MPS$ is $\frac{5}{2}$. What is the length of $\overline{PS}$?

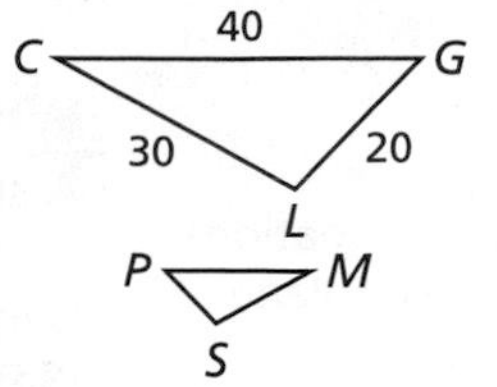

Ⓕ 8 Ⓗ 50

Ⓖ 12 Ⓙ 75

29. **Short Response** Explain why 1.5, 2.5, 3.5 and 6, 10, 12 cannot be corresponding sides of similar triangles.

CHALLENGE AND EXTEND

30. **Architecture** An architect is designing a building that is 200 ft long and 140 ft wide. She builds a model so that the similarity ratio of the model to the building is $\frac{1}{500}$. What is the length and width of the model in inches?

31. Write a paragraph proof.

Given: $\overline{QR} \parallel \overline{ST}$

Prove: $\triangle PQR \sim \triangle PST$

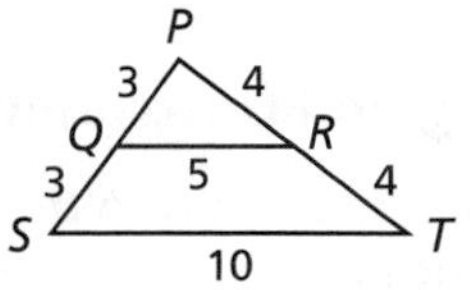

32. In the figure, D is the midpoint of $\overline{AC}$.

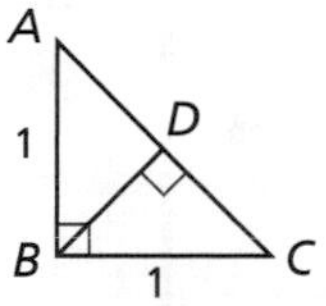

a. Find AC, DC, and DB.

b. Use your results from part **a** to help you explain why $\triangle ABC \sim \triangle CDB$.

33. A golden rectangle has the following property: If a square is cut from one end of the rectangle, the rectangle that remains is similar to the original rectangle.

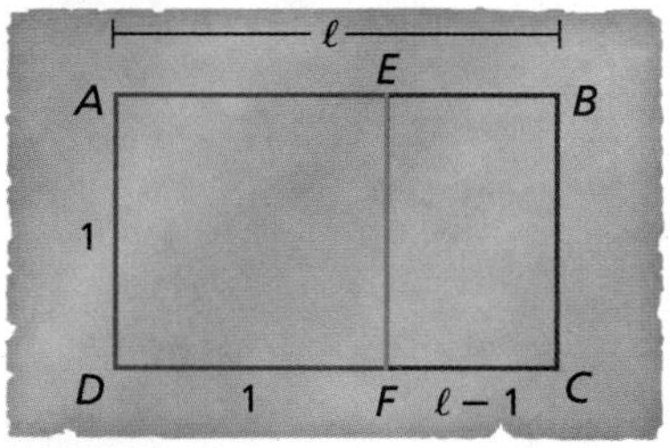

a. Rectangle $ABCD$ is a golden rectangle. Write a similarity statement for rectangle $ABCD$ and rectangle $BCFE$.

b. Write a proportion using the corresponding sides of these rectangles.

c. Solve the proportion for ℓ. (*Hint:* Use the Quadratic Formula.)

d. The value of ℓ is known as the golden ratio. Use a calculator to find ℓ to the nearest tenth.

COMMON CORE

7-2 Similarity and Transformations

CC.9-12.G.C.1 Prove that all circles are similar. *Also* **CC.9-12.G.SRT.1**

Objectives

Draw and describe similarity transformations in the coordinate plane.

Use properties of similarity transformations to determine whether polygons are similar and to prove circles are similar.

Vocabulary

similarity transformation

Who uses this?

A sign maker can use a similarity transformation to create a banner showing state flags. (See Example 4.)

A transformation that maps (x, y) to (kx, ky), where $k > 0$, is a dilation with center $(0, 0)$ and scale factor k. If $0 < k < 1$, the dilation is a *reduction.* If $k > 1$, the dilation is an *enlargement.*

EXAMPLE 1 Drawing and Describing Dilations

Apply the dilation D to the polygon with the given vertices. Describe the dilation.

A $D: (x, y) \to (2x, 2y)$

$A(2, 1)$, $B(2, 3)$, $C(5, 1)$

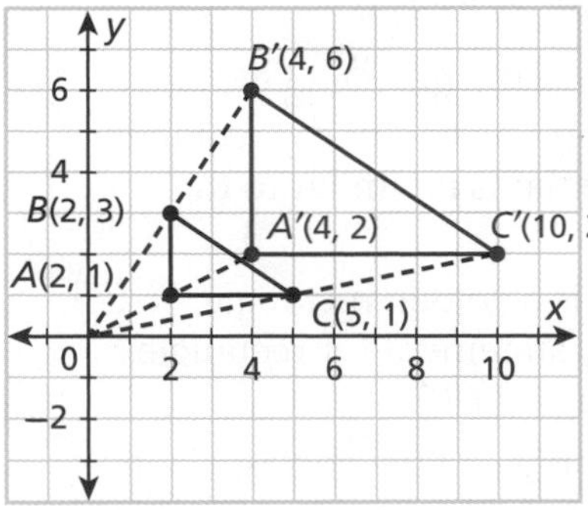

This is a dilation with center (0, 0) and scale factor 2.

B $D: (x, y) \to \left(\frac{2}{3}x, \frac{2}{3}y\right)$

$P(-6, 3)$, $Q(-3, 9)$, $R(3, 6)$

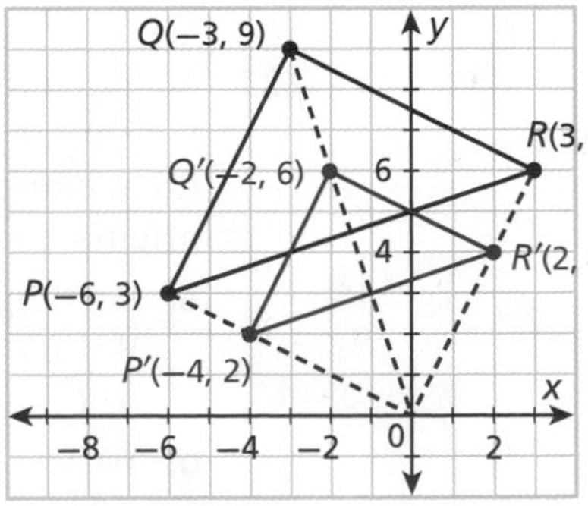

This is a dilation with center (0, 0) and scale factor $\frac{2}{3}$.

CHECK IT OUT! **1.** Apply the dilation $D: (x, y) \to \left(\frac{1}{4}x, \frac{1}{4}y\right)$ to the polygon with vertices $D(-8, 0)$, $E(-8, -4)$, and $F(-4, -8)$. Name the coordinates of the image points. Describe the dilation.

Remember!

Translations, reflections, and rotations are congruence transformations.

In a dilation, the image and the preimage are similar because they have the same shape. When the figures in a dilation are polygons, the image and preimage are similar polygons, so corresponding side lengths are proportional and corresponding angles are congruent. That is, dilations preserve angle measure.

A transformation that produces similar figures is a *similarity transformation.* A **similarity transformation** is a dilation or a composite of one or more dilations and one or more congruence transformations. Two figures are similar if and only if there is a similarity transformation that maps one figure to the other figure.

EXAMPLE 2 Determining Whether Polygons are Similar

Determine whether the polygons with the given vertices are similar.

> **Helpful Hint**
>
> Every dilation has an inverse, and the scale factors are reciprocals. In Example 2A, you can say *HJKL* is mapped to *ABCD* using the scale factor $\frac{3}{2}$.

A $A(-3, -3)$, $B(-3, 6)$, $C(6, 6)$, $D(6, -3)$
$H(-2, -2)$, $J(-2, 4)$, $K(4, 4)$, $L(4, -2)$

Yes; *ABCD* can be mapped to *HJKL* by a dilation: $(x, y) \rightarrow \left(\frac{2}{3}x, \frac{2}{3}y\right)$.

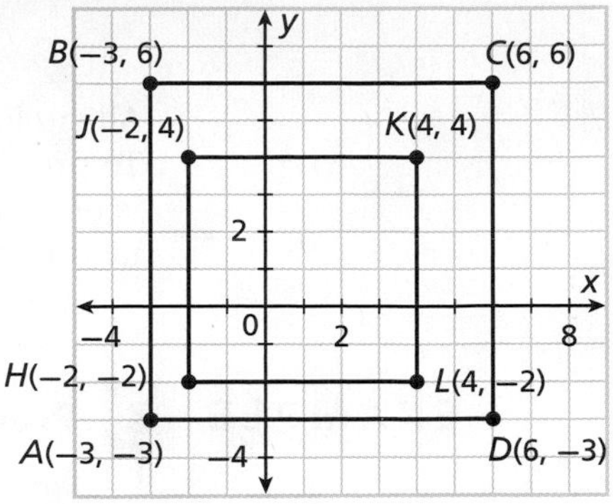

B $P(2, 2)$, $Q(2, 4)$, $R(6, 4)$, $S(6, 2)$
$W(5, 5)$, $X(5, 9)$, $Y(12, 9)$, $Z(12, 5)$

No;

The rule $(x, y) \rightarrow (2.5x, 2.5y)$ maps *P* to *W*, but not *Q* to *X*. No similarity transformation maps *PQRS* to *WXYZ*.

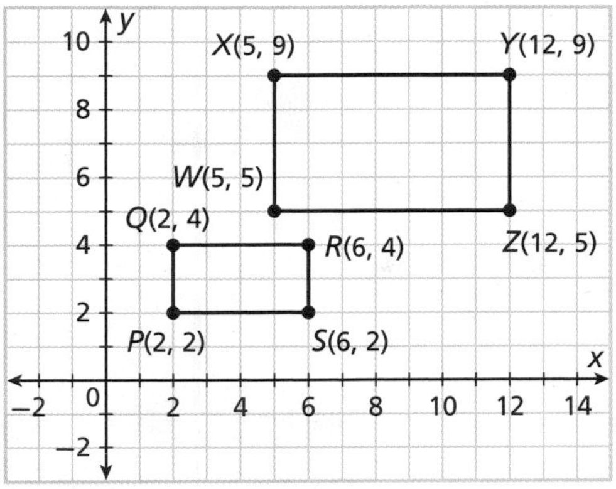

C $A(2, 1)$, $B(4, 2)$, $C(4, 1)$
$D(-9, 6)$, $E(-3, 6)$, $F(-3, 9)$

Yes; Translate $\triangle ABC$ to the left and up. Then enlarge the image to obtain $\triangle DEF$.

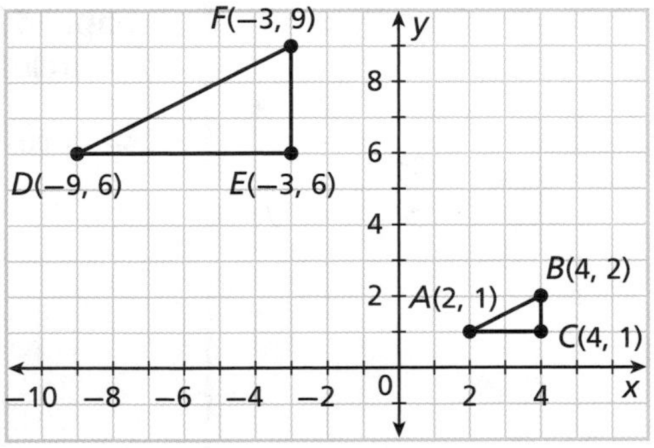

Yes; $\triangle ABC$ can be mapped to $\triangle A'B'C'$ by a translation: $(x, y) \rightarrow (x - 5, y + 1)$. Then $\triangle A'B'C'$ can be mapped to $\triangle DEF$ by a dilation: $(x, y) \rightarrow (3x, 3y)$.

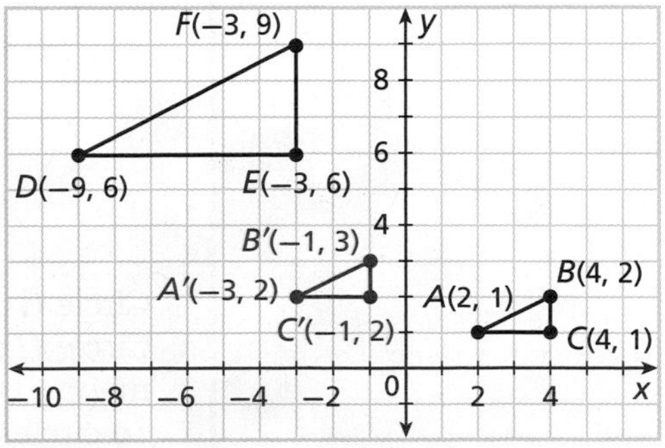

CHECK IT OUT! **2.** Determine whether the polygons with the given vertices are similar: $A(2, -1)$, $B(3, -1)$, $C(3, -4)$ and $P(3, 6)$, $Q(3, 9)$, $R(12, 9)$.

All circles are similar because they all have the same shape. To prove this, it is helpful to use a dilation whose center is not (0, 0). In general, a dilation with center C and scale factor k maps P to P' so that P' is on $\overline{CP}$ and $CP' = k \cdot CP$.

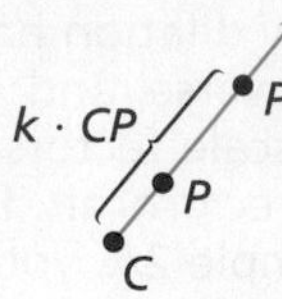

EXAMPLE 3 Proving Circles Similar

A **Prove that circle A with center (0, 0) and radius 1 is similar to circle B with center (5, 0) and radius 2.**

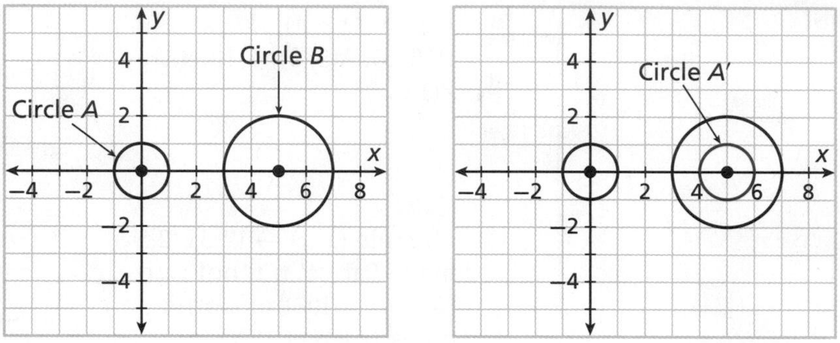

Circle A can be mapped to circle A' by a translation: $(x, y) \rightarrow (x + 5, y)$. Circle A' and circle B both have center (5, 0). Then circle A' can be mapped to circle B by a dilation with center (5, 0) and scale factor 2. So circles A and B are similar.

B **Prove that circle C with center (−2, 0) and radius 2 is similar to circle D with center (4, 1) and radius 3.**

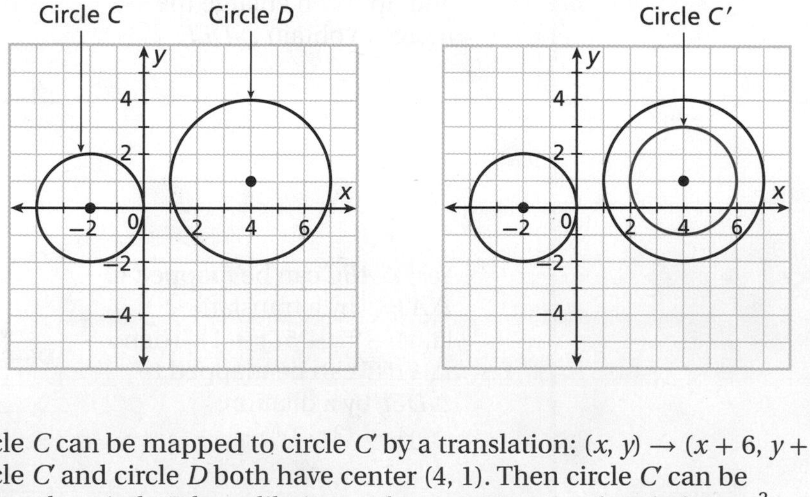

Circle C can be mapped to circle C' by a translation: $(x, y) \rightarrow (x + 6, y + 1)$. Circle C' and circle D both have center (4, 1). Then circle C' can be mapped to circle D by a dilation with center (4, 1) and scale factor $\frac{3}{2}$. So circles C and D are similar.

CHECK IT OUT! **3.** Prove that circle A with center (2, 1) and radius 4 is similar to circle B with center (−1, −1) and radius 2.

EXAMPLE 4 *Business Application*

Tia makes signs and banners. She is making a banner that shows five Texas flags. The middle flag is 3 times the size of each of the other flags. Tia will first draw the lower left flag and then the middle flag. How can she draw those flags?

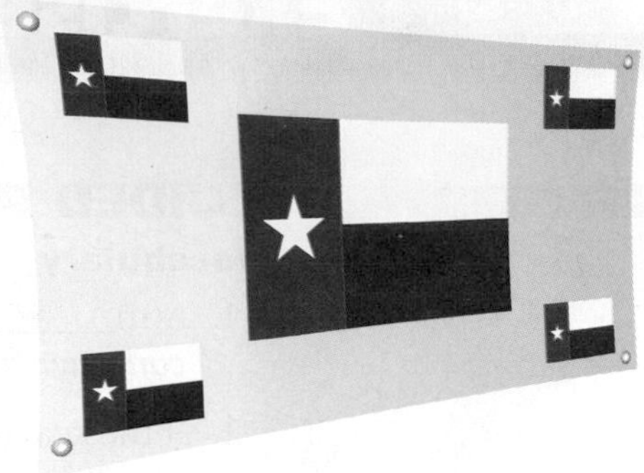

Place the lower left flag on a coordinate plane in a convenient position, such as that shown by rectangle *ABCD*.

Apply the dilation with center (0, 0) and scale factor 3: $(x, y) \rightarrow (3x, 3y)$.

The image, *A′B′C′D′*, represents the middle flag.

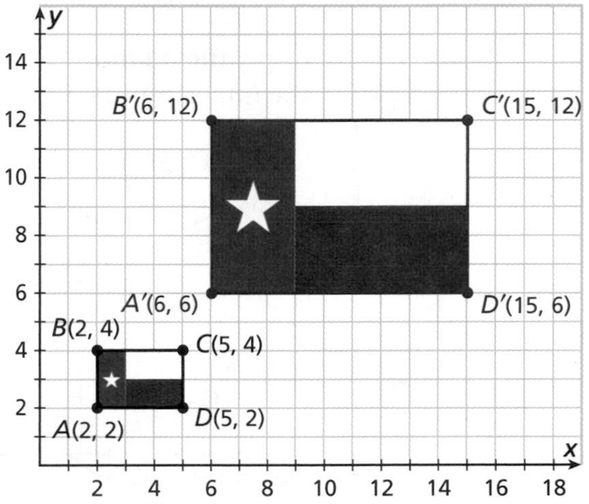

CHECK IT OUT! **4. What if...?** How could Tia draw the middle flag to make it 4 times the size of each of the other flags?

MATHEMATICAL PRACTICES

THINK AND DISCUSS

1. Consider this dilation applied to a polygon: $(x, y) \rightarrow (1.5x, 1.5y)$. Describe the corresponding side lengths, corresponding angle measures, and position of the image compared to the preimage.

2. Explain why the rules $(x, y) \rightarrow (y, -x)$ and then $(x, y) \rightarrow (2x, 2y)$ form a similarity transformation.

3. GET ORGANIZED Copy and complete the graphic organizer.

Determining if polygons are similar	
Proving circles are similar	

7-2 Exercises

GUIDED PRACTICE

Vocabulary **Apply the vocabulary from this lesson to answer each question.**

1. A(n) ___?___ transformation produces figures that are similar. (*similarity, congruence,* or *scale factor*)

2. If the scale factor k in a dilation is a value between 0 and 1, the dilation is a(n) ___?___. (*enlargement, reduction,* or *translation*)

SEE EXAMPLE 1

Apply the dilation D to the polygon with the given vertices. Name the coordinates of the image points. Identify and describe the transformation.

3. $D: (x, y) \rightarrow (4x, 4y)$

   $A(-1, -1)$, $B(2, 1)$, $C(-2, 1)$

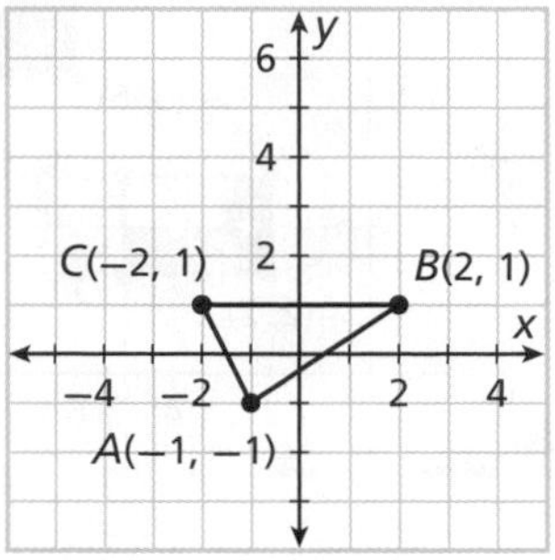

4. $D: (x, y) \rightarrow \left(\frac{1}{3}x, \frac{1}{3}y\right)$

   $A(3, 9)$, $B(-6, 3)$, $C(3, -3)$

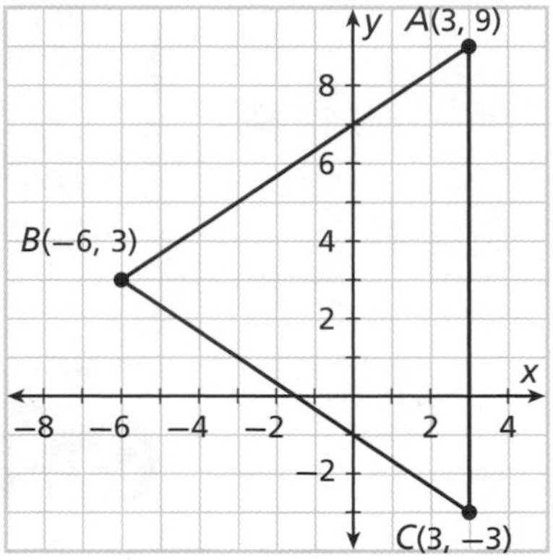

5. $D: (x, y) \rightarrow (2.5x, 2.5y)$

   $A(2, 3)$, $B(5, -2)$, $C(-4, -2)$

6. $D: (x, y) \rightarrow \left(\frac{3}{4}x, \frac{3}{4}y\right)$

   $A(4, 8)$, $B(-8, 4)$, $C(8, -4)$

SEE EXAMPLE 2

Determine whether the polygons with the given vertices are similar. Support your answer by describing a transformation.

7. $L(1, -4)$, $M(1, -9)$, $N(5, -2)$, $O(9, -5)$
   $P(2, 5)$, $Q(2, -5)$, $R(10, 9)$, $S(18, 3)$

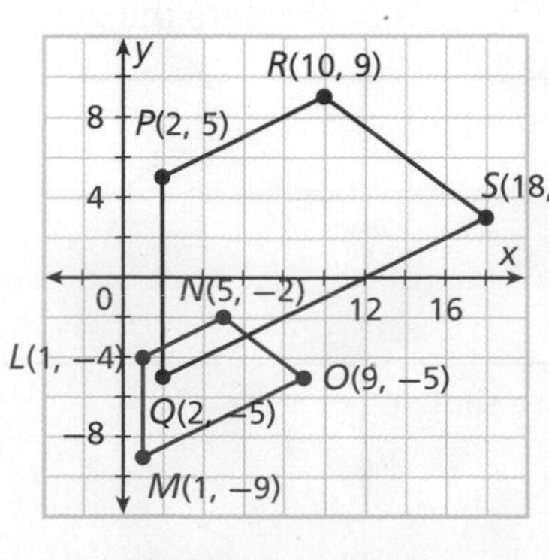

8. $W(-4, 2)$, $X(-4, 6)$, $Y(6, 2)$, $Z(6, 6)$
   $D(-2, 1)$, $E(-8, 12)$, $F(3, 10)$, $G(3, 3)$

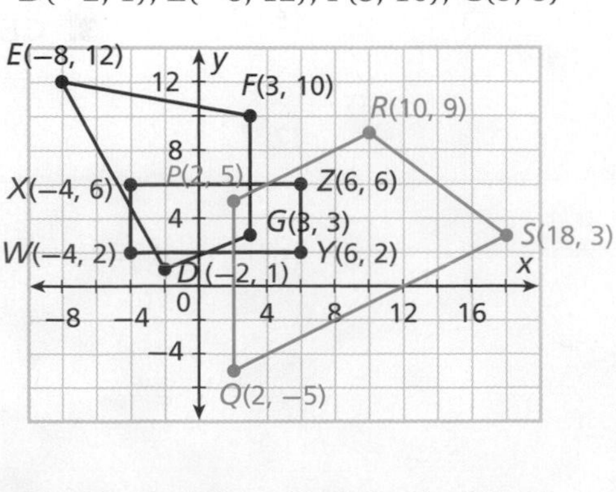

9. $A(3, 0)$, $B(3, 6)$, $C(9, 6)$
   $X(4, 0)$, $Y(4, -8)$, $Z(12, -8)$

10. $L(-10, 5)$, $M(-5, 0)$, $N(0, 0)$, $O(5, 5)$
    $D(4, 2)$, $E(2, 0)$, $F(0, 0)$, $G(-2, 2)$

SEE EXAMPLE 3

11. Prove that circle A with center (4, 0) and radius 5 is similar to circle B with center (−6, −3) and radius 3.

12. Prove that circle A with center (6, −9) and radius 4 is similar to circle B with center (3, −8) and radius 5.

SEE EXAMPLE 4

13. Hector is making an art project by cutting and gluing shapes to a wooden board. His design includes two similar triangles, with one 4 times the size of the other. He cuts and traces the small triangle first onto grid paper. Describe how he can use the tracing to make a pattern for the large fabric triangle.

PRACTICE AND PROBLEM SOLVING

Independent Practice

For Exercises	See Example
14–15	1
16–17	2
22	3
23	4

Apply the dilation D to the polygon with the given vertices. Name the coordinates of the image points. Identify and describe the transformation.

14. $D: (x, y) \rightarrow (0.5x, 0.5y)$

$A(1, -2)$, $B(1, -4)$, $C(5, -2)$ $D(5, -4)$

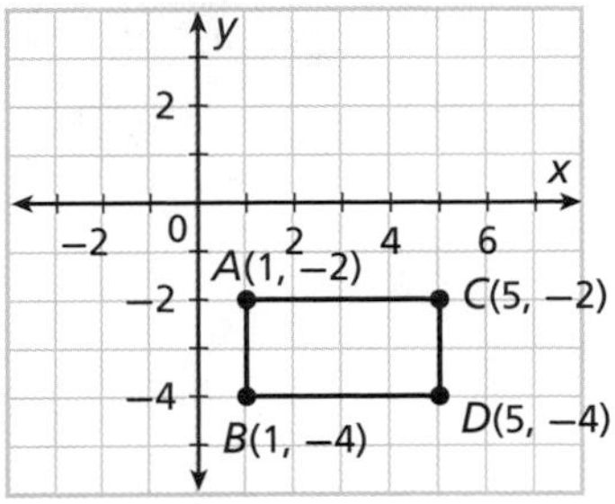

15. $D: (x, y) \rightarrow \left(\frac{3}{10}x, \frac{3}{10}y\right)$

$A(20, 10)$, $B(0, -20)$, $C(10, 30)$

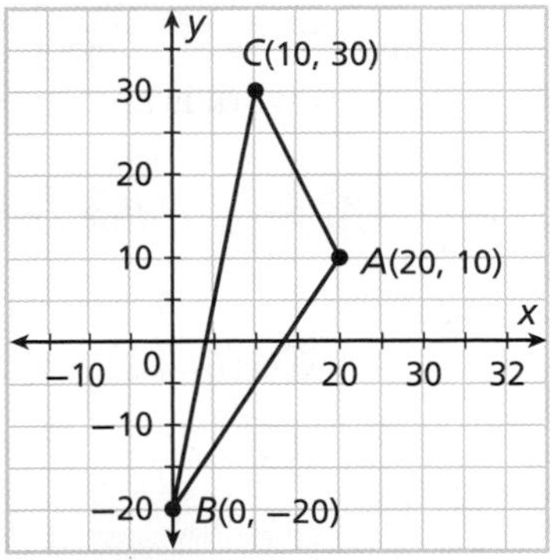

Determine whether the polygons with the given vertices are similar. Support your answer by describing a transformation.

16. $V(3, 2)$, $W(8, 2)$, $X(1, 5)$

$R(6, 4)$, $S(16, 4)$, $T(3, 15)$

17. $A(-2, -3)$, $B(-2, 0)$, $C(10, -3)$

$P(-4, 2)$, $Q(-4, 4)$, $R(4, 2)$

18. Write About It Triangle ABC is dilated by a scale factor of 5. The image is $A'B'C'$. Compare the angle measures and side lengths of the original triangle and its image after dilation.

Determine whether the polygons shown are similar. If they are similar, describe the transformation in two different ways, from the larger to the smaller figure, and from the smaller to the larger figure.

19.

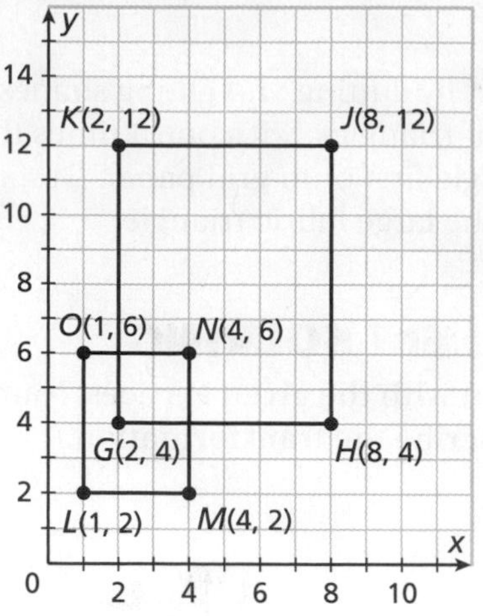

20.

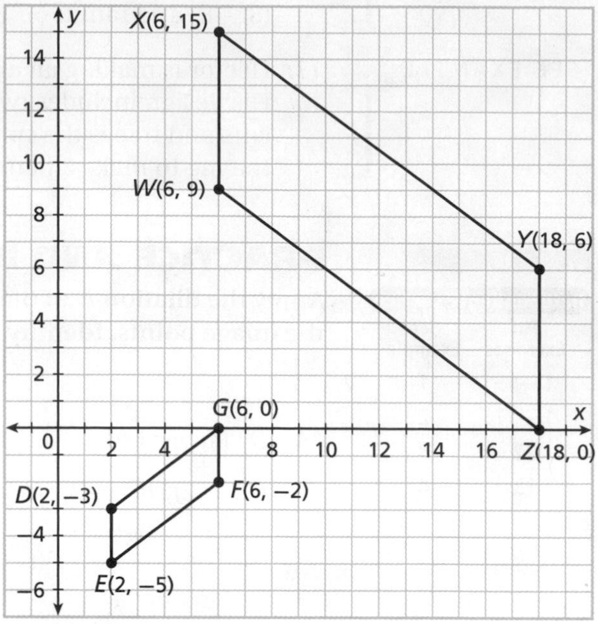

21. **ERROR ANALYSIS** Triangle *ABC* has vertices at $A(-12, -6)$, $B(-6, 12)$, and $C(6, 12)$. The images of *A* and *B* after the similarity transformation *D* are $A'(-8, -4)$ and $B'(-4, 8)$. Reggie and Hillary find different coordinates for C', the image of *C*. Their work is shown below. Who made an error? Describe the error.

Hillary's Work

$C': (6, 12) \rightarrow \left(\frac{2}{3} \cdot 6, \frac{2}{3} \cdot 12\right)$

$\rightarrow (4, 8)$

Reggie's Work

$C': (6, 12) \rightarrow \left(\frac{3}{2} \cdot 6, \frac{3}{2} \cdot 12\right)$

$\rightarrow (9, 18)$

22. A baby pool with radius 2 meters is being built near a larger pool with radius 4 meters at a recreation center. The plans for the construction are laid out on the coordinate system shown. Prove that the baby pool is similar to the larger pool.

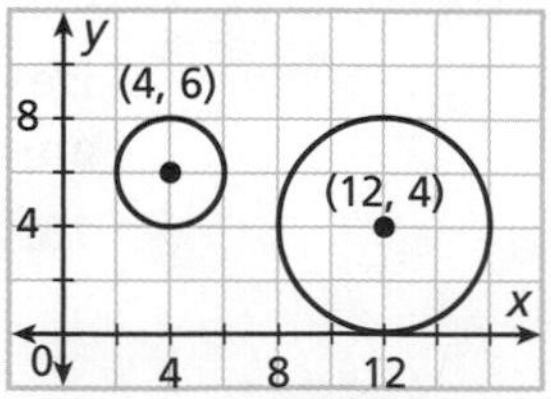

23. **Architecture** An architect is making a scale drawing of two buildings whose floor plans are to be similar rectangles. He has already drawn the smaller building. The larger building will be located to the upper right and will have dimensions 5 times those of the smaller building. How can he draw the larger building?

24. **Critical Thinking** To map a figure *A* to a similar figure *B*, first *A* is mapped to A' by a dilation: $(x, y) \rightarrow \left(\frac{5}{3}x, \frac{5}{3}y\right)$. Then A' is mapped to *B* by a translation $(x, y) \rightarrow (x - 2, y + 1)$. The vertices of A' are $W(-10, 0)$, $X(-5, 10)$, $Y(5, 10)$, and $Z(-5, 0)$. Find the vertices of *A* and *B*.

TEST PREP

25. Triangle *ABC* undergoes a transformation *T* to produce the image *EFG*. Given the vertices of the triangles below, which is a true statement about *T*?

$A(4, 8), B(0, 4), C(4, 0)$
$E(3, 6), F(0, 3), G(3, 0)$

Ⓐ *T* is a similarity transformation in which *ABC* is dilated by a scale factor of $\frac{3}{4}$.

Ⓑ *T* is a congruence transformation in which *ABC* is dilated by a scale factor of $\frac{3}{4}$.

Ⓒ *T* is a similarity transformation in which *ABC* is dilated by a scale factor of of $\frac{4}{3}$.

Ⓓ *T* is a congruence transformation in which *ABC* is dilated by a scale factor of $\frac{4}{3}$.

26. Figure *ABCD* with the vertices given below is translated 6 units left and 7 units down. It is then dilated to produce the similar figure *EFGH* with the vertices given below. By what scale is the figure dilated?

$A(10, 15), B(14, 7), C(6, 7), D(6, 11)$

$E(5, 10), F(10, 0), G(0, 0), H(0, 5)$

Ⓐ 0.5
Ⓑ 0.8
Ⓒ 1.25
Ⓓ 1.5

CHALLENGE AND EXTEND

27. The area of a square is 16 square units and its lower left vertex is positioned at (2, 0). After a similarity transformation, the image of the lower left vertex is positioned at (−8, 0). Name the other three vertices of the image and find its area.

28. The hypotenuse of a right triangle *ABC* in a coordinate plane is $\overline{AB}$, with *A* at (1, 2) and *B* at (3, 6). The image of the hypotenuse after a rotation of 180° and a dilation is $\overline{A'B'}$, with *A′* at (−3.5, −7) and *B′* at (−10.5, −21). Give two possible locations of *C′*, the image of *C*.

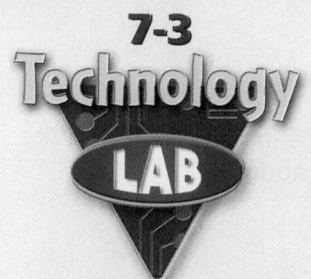

7-3
Technology LAB

Predict Triangle Similarity Relationships

Use with Triangle Similarity: AA, SSS, and SAS

You have found shortcuts for determining that two triangles are congruent. Now you will use geometry software to find ways to determine that triangles are similar.

MATHEMATICAL PRACTICES **Use appropriate tools strategically.**

Learn It Online
Lab Resources Online

Activity 1

CC.9-12.G.SRT.2 ...Explain...the meaning of similarity for triangles...

1. Construct $\triangle ABC$. Construct $\overline{DE}$ longer than any of the sides of $\triangle ABC$. Rotate $\overline{DE}$ around D by rotation $\angle BAC$. Rotate $\overline{DE}$ around E by rotation $\angle ABC$. Label the intersection point of the two rotated segments as F.

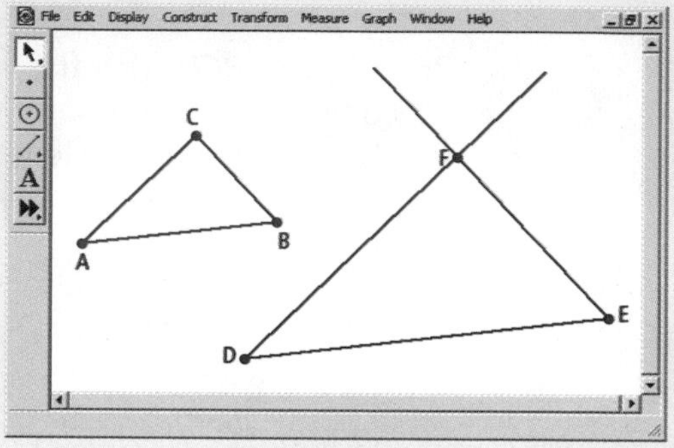

2. Measure angles to confirm that $\angle BAC \cong \angle EDF$ and $\angle ABC \cong \angle DEF$. Drag a vertex of $\triangle ABC$ or an endpoint of $\overline{DE}$ to show that the two triangles have two pairs of congruent angles.

3. Measure the side lengths of both triangles. Divide each side length of $\triangle ABC$ by the corresponding side length of $\triangle DEF$. Compare the resulting ratios. What do you notice?

Try This

1. What theorem guarantees that the third pair of angles in the triangles are also congruent?
2. Will the ratios of corresponding sides found in Step 3 always be equal? Drag a vertex of $\triangle ABC$ or an endpoint of $\overline{DE}$ to investigate this question. State a conjecture based on your results.

Activity 2

1. Construct a new $\triangle ABC$. Create P in the interior of the triangle. Create $\triangle DEF$ by enlarging $\triangle ABC$ around P by a multiple of 2 using the Dilation command. Drag P outside of $\triangle ABC$ to separate the triangles.

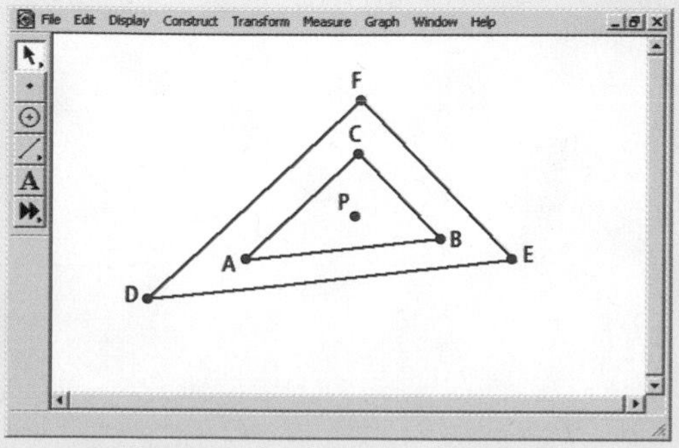

2 Measure the side lengths of $\triangle DEF$ to confirm that each side is twice as long as the corresponding side of $\triangle ABC$. Drag a vertex of $\triangle ABC$ to verify that this relationship is true.

3 Measure the angles of both triangles. What do you notice?

Try This

3. Did the construction of the triangles with three pairs of sides in the same ratio guarantee that the corresponding angles would be congruent? State a conjecture based on these results.

4. Compare your conjecture to the SSS Congruence Theorem. How are they similar and how are they different?

Activity 3

1 Construct a different $\triangle ABC$. Create P in the interior of the triangle. Expand $\overline{AB}$ and $\overline{AC}$ around P by a multiple of 2 using the Dilation command. Create an angle congruent to $\angle BAC$ with sides that are each twice as long as $\overline{AB}$ and $\overline{AC}$.

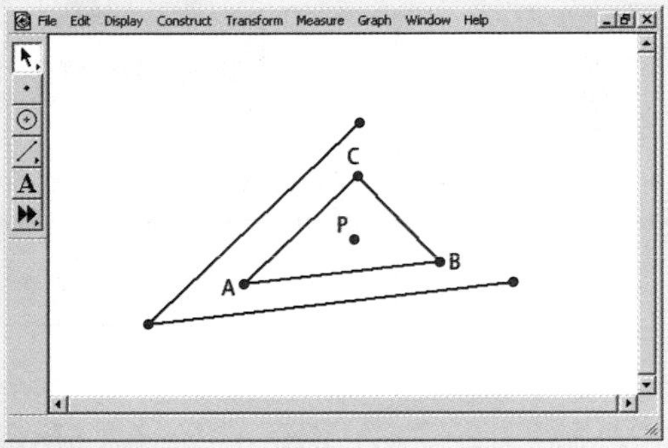

2 Use a segment to create the third side of a new triangle and label it $\triangle DEF$. Drag P outside of $\triangle ABC$ to separate the triangles.

3 Measure each side length and determine the relationship between corresponding sides of $\triangle ABC$ and $\triangle DEF$.

4 Measure the angles of both triangles. What do you notice?

Try This

5. Tell whether $\triangle ABC$ is similar to $\triangle DEF$. Explain your reasoning.

6. Write a conjecture based on the activity. What congruency theorem is related to your conjecture?

COMMON CORE

7-3 Triangle Similarity: AA, SSS, and SAS

CC.9-12.G.SRT.5 Use...similarity criteria for triangles to solve problems... *Also* **CC.9-12.G.SRT.3, CC.9-12.G.SRT.2**

Objectives

Prove certain triangles are similar by using AA, SSS, and SAS.

Use triangle similarity to solve problems.

Who uses this?

Engineers use similar triangles when designing buildings, such as the Pyramid Building in San Diego, California. (See Example 5.)

There are several ways to prove certain triangles are similar. The following postulate, as well as the SSS and SAS Similarity Theorems, will be used in proofs just as SSS, SAS, ASA, HL, and AAS were used to prove triangles congruent.

Know it! Note

Postulate 7-3-1 Angle-Angle (AA) Similarity

POSTULATE	HYPOTHESIS	CONCLUSION
If two angles of one triangle are congruent to two angles of another triangle, then the triangles are similar.	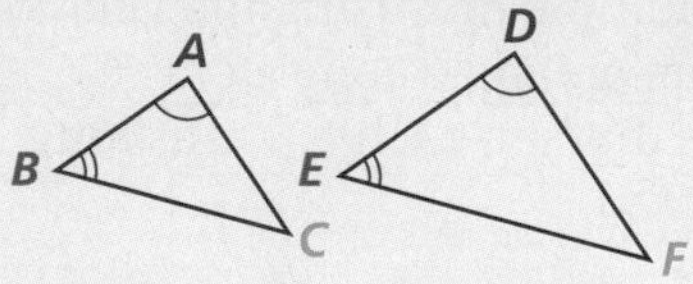	$\triangle ABC \sim \triangle DEF$

EXAMPLE 1 Using the AA Similarity Postulate

Explain why the triangles are similar and write a similarity statement.

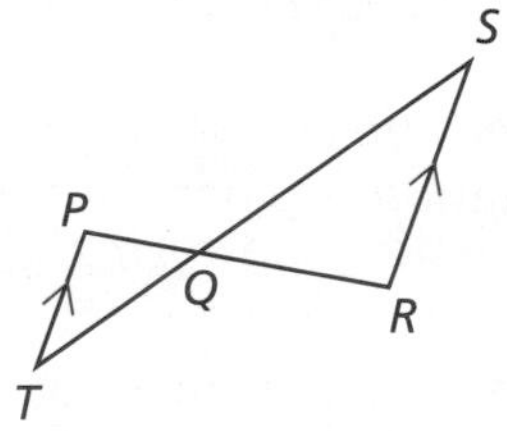

Since $\overline{PT} \parallel \overline{SR}$, $\angle P \cong \angle R$, and $\angle T \cong \angle S$ by the Alternate Interior Angles Theorem. Therefore $\triangle PQT \sim \triangle RQS$ by AA $\sim$.

CHECK IT OUT!

1. Explain why the triangles are similar and write a similarity statement.

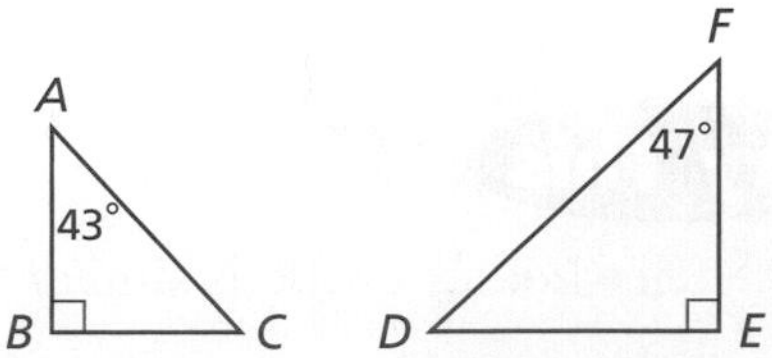

Know it! Note

Theorem 7-3-2 Side-Side-Side (SSS) Similarity

THEOREM	HYPOTHESIS	CONCLUSION
If the three sides of one triangle are proportional to the three corresponding sides of another triangle, then the triangles are similar.	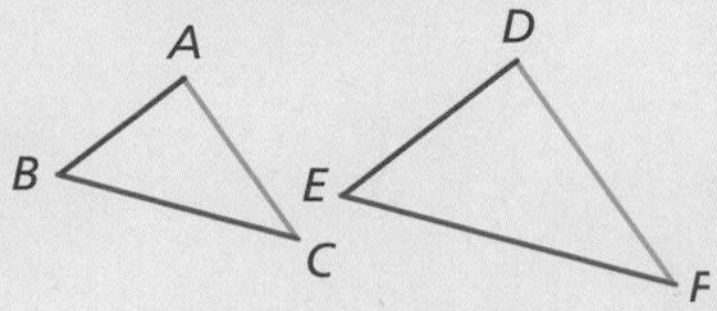	$\triangle ABC \sim \triangle DEF$

You will prove Theorem 7-3-2 in Exercise 38.

Know it! Note

Theorem 7-3-3 Side-Angle-Side (SAS) Similarity

THEOREM	HYPOTHESIS	CONCLUSION
If two sides of one triangle are proportional to two sides of another triangle and their included angles are congruent, then the triangles are similar.	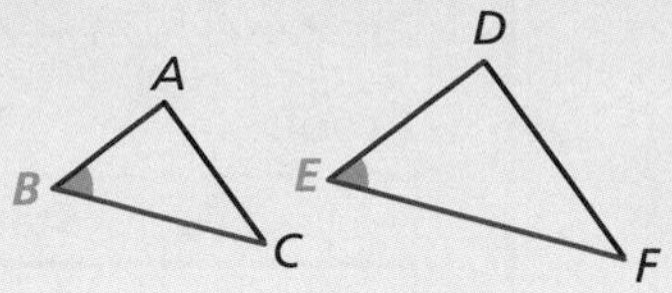 $\angle B \cong \angle E$	$\triangle ABC \sim \triangle DEF$

You will prove Theorem 7-3-3 in Exercise 39.

EXAMPLE 2 Verifying Triangle Similarity

Verify that the triangles are similar.

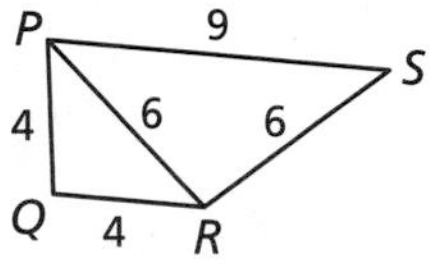

A $\triangle PQR$ **and** $\triangle PRS$

$\frac{PQ}{PR} = \frac{4}{6} = \frac{2}{3}, \frac{QR}{RS} = \frac{4}{6} = \frac{2}{3}, \frac{PR}{PS} = \frac{6}{9} = \frac{2}{3}$

Therefore $\triangle PQR \sim \triangle PRS$ by SSS ~.

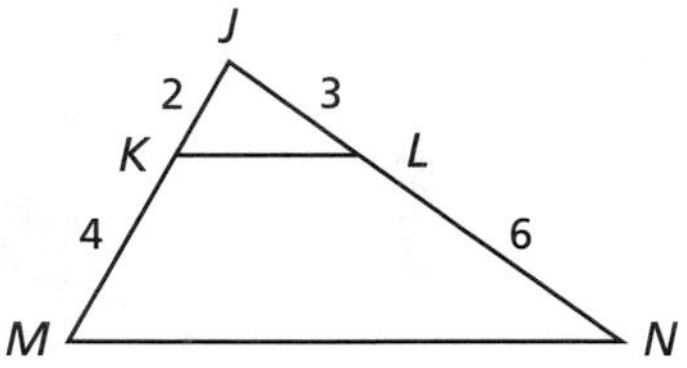

B $\triangle JKL$ **and** $\triangle JMN$

$\angle J \cong \angle J$ by the Reflexive Property of $\cong$.

$\frac{JK}{JM} = \frac{2}{6} = \frac{1}{3}, \frac{JL}{JN} = \frac{3}{9} = \frac{1}{3}$

Therefore $\triangle JKL \sim \triangle JMN$ by SAS ~.

CHECK IT OUT! **2.** Verify that $\triangle TXU \sim \triangle VXW$.

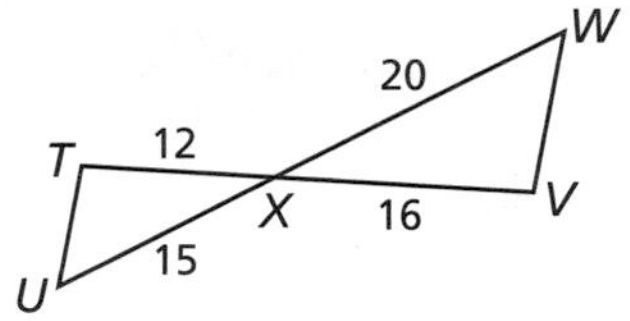

EXAMPLE 3 Finding Lengths in Similar Triangles

Explain why $\triangle ABC \sim \triangle DBE$ and then find BE.

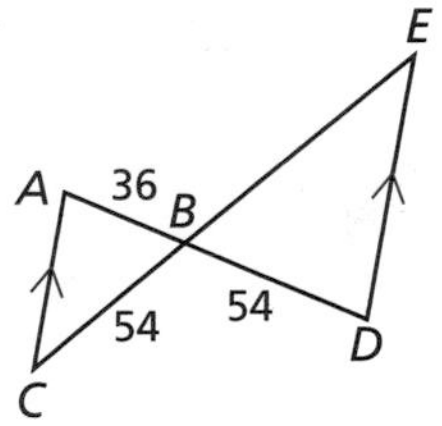

Step 1 Prove triangles are similar.

As shown $\overline{AC} \parallel \overline{ED}$, $\angle A \cong \angle D$, and $\angle C \cong \angle E$ by the Alternate Interior Angles Theorem. Therefore $\triangle ABC \sim \triangle DBE$ by AA ~.

Step 2 Find BE.

$\frac{AB}{DB} = \frac{BC}{BE}$	*Corr. sides are proportional.*
$\frac{36}{54} = \frac{54}{BE}$	*Substitute 36 for AB, 54 for DB, and 54 for BC.*
$36(BE) = 54^2$	*Cross Products Prop.*
$36(BE) = 2916$	*Simplify.*
$BE = 81$	*Divide both sides by 36.*

CHECK IT OUT! **3.** Explain why $\triangle RSV \sim \triangle RTU$ and then find RT.

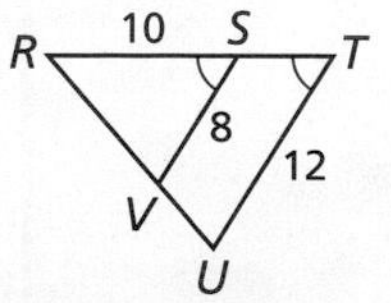

EXAMPLE 4 Writing Proofs with Similar Triangles

Given: A is the midpoint of $\overline{BC}$.
D is the midpoint of $\overline{BE}$.

Prove: $\triangle BDA \sim \triangle BEC$

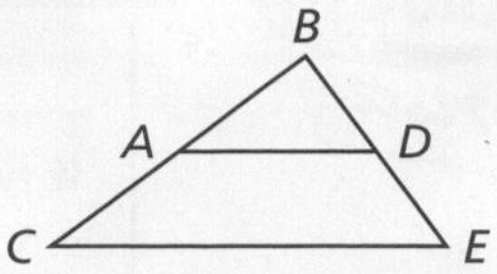

Proof:

Statements	Reasons
1. A is the mdpt. of $\overline{BC}$. D is the mdpt. of $\overline{BE}$.	1. Given
2. $\overline{BA} \cong \overline{AC}$, $\overline{BD} \cong \overline{DE}$	2. Def. of mdpt.
3. $BA = AC$, $BD = DE$	3. Def. of $\cong$ seg.
4. $BC = BA + AC$, $BE = BD + DE$	4. Seg. Add. Post.
5. $BC = BA + BA$, $BE = BD + BD$	5. Subst. Prop.
6. $BC = 2BA$, $BE = 2BD$	6. Simplify.
7. $\frac{BC}{BA} = 2$, $\frac{BE}{BD} = 2$	7. Div. Prop. of =
8. $\frac{BC}{BA} = \frac{BE}{BD}$	8. Trans. Prop. of =
9. $\angle B \cong \angle B$	9. Reflex. Prop. of $\cong$
10. $\triangle BDA \sim \triangle BEC$	10. SAS $\sim$ *Steps 8, 9*

CHECK IT OUT!

4. **Given:** M is the midpoint of $\overline{JK}$.
N is the midpoint of $\overline{KL}$,
and P is the midpoint of $\overline{JL}$.

Prove: $\triangle JKL \sim \triangle NPM$
(*Hint:* Use the Triangle Midsegment Theorem and SSS $\sim$.)

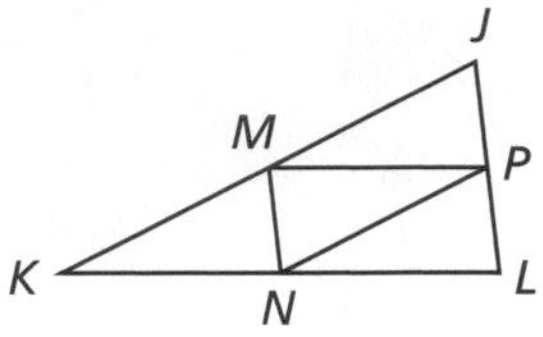

EXAMPLE 5 *Engineering Application*

The photo shows a gable roof. $\overline{AC} \parallel \overline{FG}$. Use similar triangles to prove $\triangle ABC \sim \triangle FBG$ and then find BF to the nearest tenth of a foot.

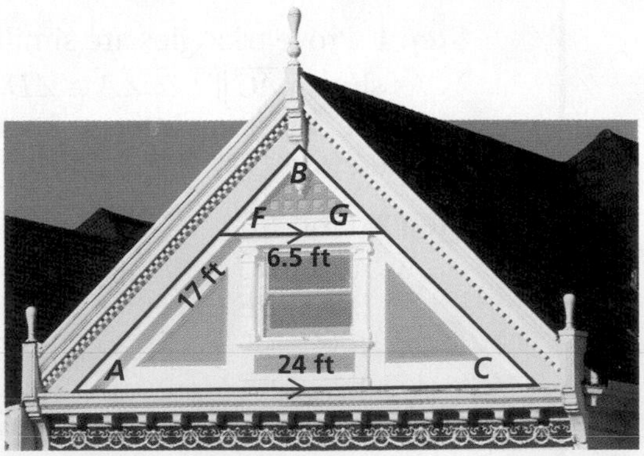

Step 1 Prove the triangles are similar.

$\overline{AC} \parallel \overline{FG}$ — *Given*

$\angle BFG \cong \angle BAC$ — *Corr. ∠s Thm.*

$\angle B \cong \angle B$ — *Reflex. Prop. of $\cong$*

Therefore $\triangle ABC \sim \triangle FBG$ by AA $\sim$.

Step 2 Find BF.

$\frac{BA}{AC} = \frac{BF}{FG}$	*Corr. sides are proportional.*
$\frac{x+17}{24} = \frac{x}{6.5}$	*Substitute the given values.*
$6.5(x+17) = 24x$	*Cross Products Prop.*
$6.5x + 110.5 = 24x$	*Distrib. Prop.*
$110.5 = 17.5x$	*Subtract 6.5x from both sides.*
$6.3 \approx x$ or BF	*Divide both sides by 17.5.*

CHECK IT OUT! **5. What if...?** If $AB = 4x$, $AC = 5x$, and $BF = 4$, find FG.

The Reflexive, Symmetric, and Transitive Properties of Equality have corresponding properties of congruence. These properties also hold true for similarity of triangles.

Know it! Note

Properties of Similarity

Reflexive Property of Similarity

$\triangle ABC \sim \triangle ABC$ (Reflex. Prop. of $\sim$)

Symmetric Property of Similarity

If $\triangle ABC \sim \triangle DEF$, then $\triangle DEF \sim \triangle ABC$. (Sym. Prop. of $\sim$)

Transitive Property of Similarity

If $\triangle ABC \sim \triangle DEF$ and $\triangle DEF \sim \triangle XYZ$, then $\triangle ABC \sim \triangle XYZ$. (Trans. Prop. of $\sim$)

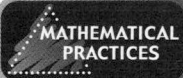

MATHEMATICAL PRACTICES

THINK AND DISCUSS

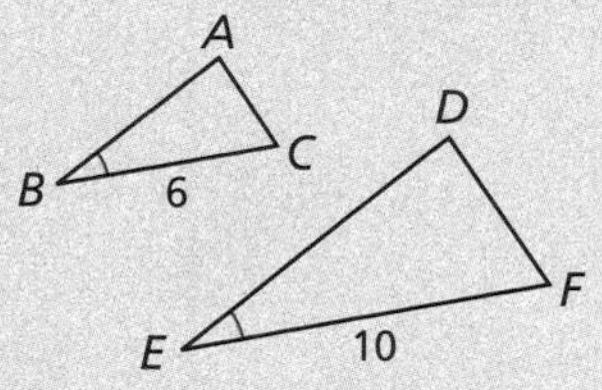

1. What additional information, if any, would you you need in order to show that $\triangle ABC \sim \triangle DEF$ by the AA Similarity Postulate?

2. What additional information, if any, would you need in order to show that $\triangle ABC \sim \triangle DEF$ by the SAS Similarity Theorem?

3. Do corresponding sides of similar triangles need to be proportional and congruent? Explain.

Know it! Note

4. GET ORGANIZED Copy and complete the graphic organizer. If possible, write a congruence or similarity theorem or postulate in each section of the table. Include a marked diagram for each.

	Congruence	Similarity
SSS		
SAS		
AA		

7-3 Exercises

Learn It Online
Homework Help Online
Parent Resources Online

GUIDED PRACTICE

SEE EXAMPLE 1

Explain why the triangles are similar and write a similarity statement.

1.

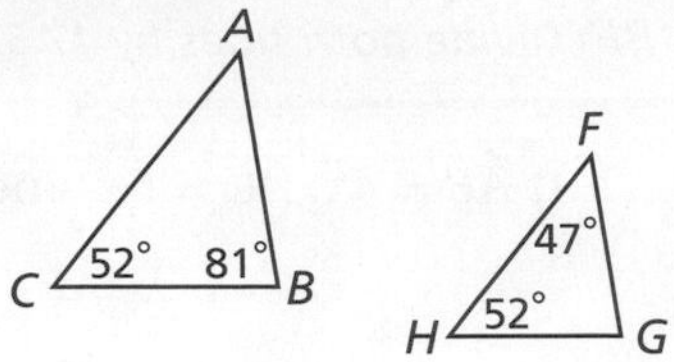

2.

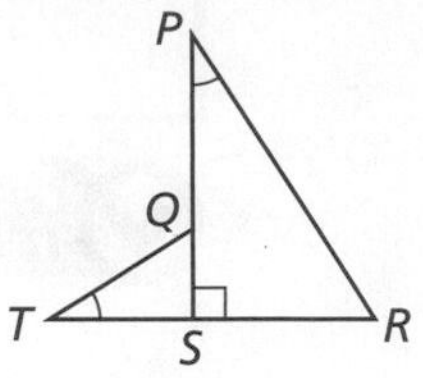

SEE EXAMPLE 2

Verify that the triangles are similar.

3. $\triangle DEF$ and $\triangle JKL$

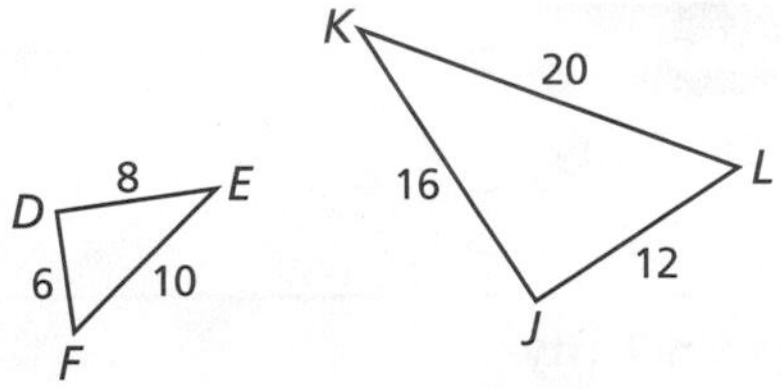

4. $\triangle MNP$ and $\triangle MRQ$

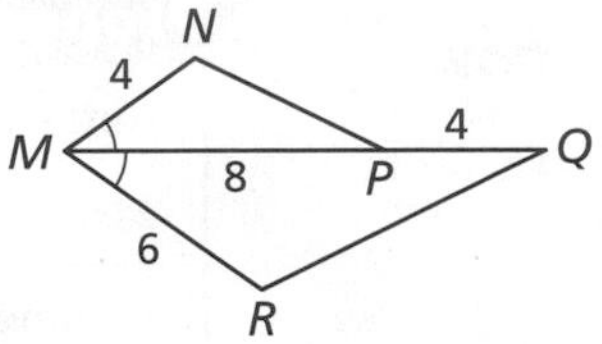

SEE EXAMPLE 3

Multi-Step **Explain why the triangles are similar and then find each length.**

5. AB

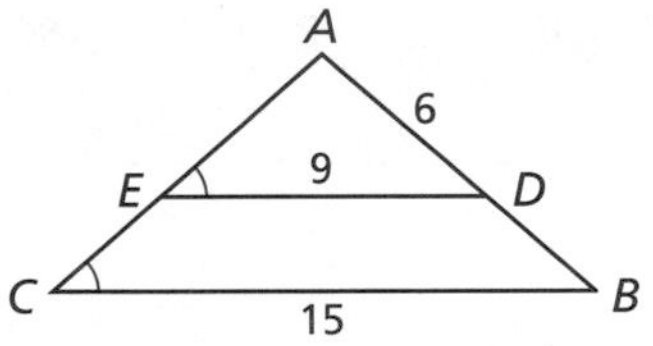

6. WY

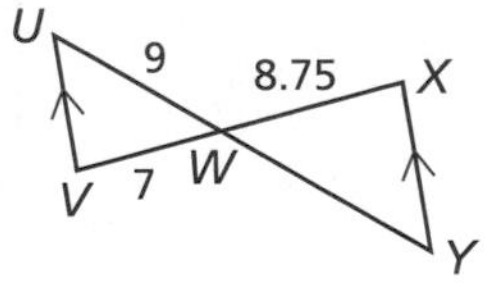

SEE EXAMPLE 4

7. Given: $\overleftrightarrow{MN} \parallel \overline{KL}$
Prove: $\triangle JMN \sim \triangle JKL$

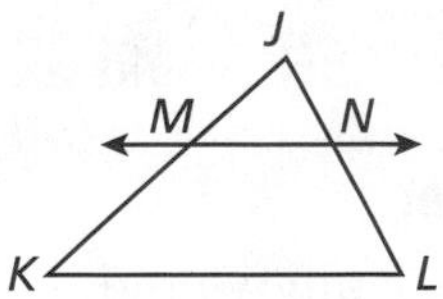

8. Given: $SQ = 2QP$, $TR = 2RP$
Prove: $\triangle PQR \sim \triangle PST$

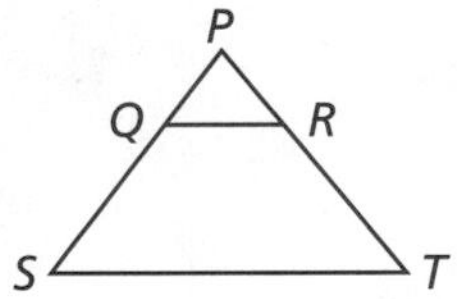

9. The coordinates of A, B, and C are $A(0, 0)$, $B(2, 6)$, and $C(8, -2)$. What theorem or postulate justifies the statement $\triangle ABC \sim \triangle ADE$, if the coordinates of D and E are twice the coordinates of B and C?

SEE EXAMPLE 5

10. Surveying In order to measure the distance AB across the meteorite crater, a surveyor at S locates points A, B, C, and D as shown. What is AB to the nearest meter? nearest kilometer?

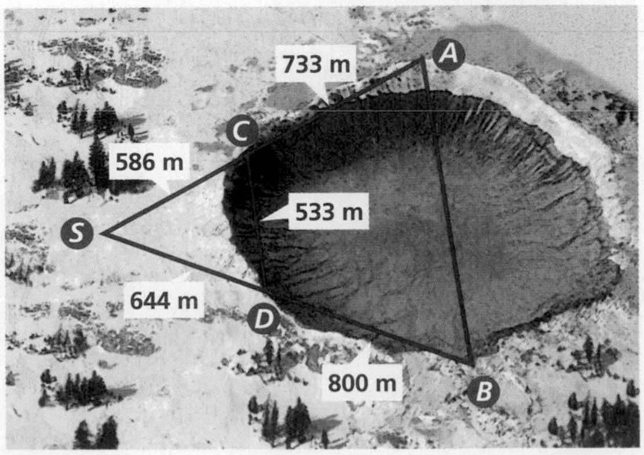

PRACTICE AND PROBLEM SOLVING

Independent Practice

For Exercises	See Example
11–12	1
13–14	2
15–16	3
17–18	4
19	5

Extra Practice

See Extra Practice for more Skills Practice and Applications Practice exercises.

Explain why the triangles are similar and write a similarity statement.

11.

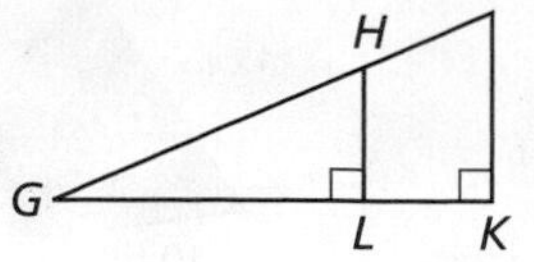

12.

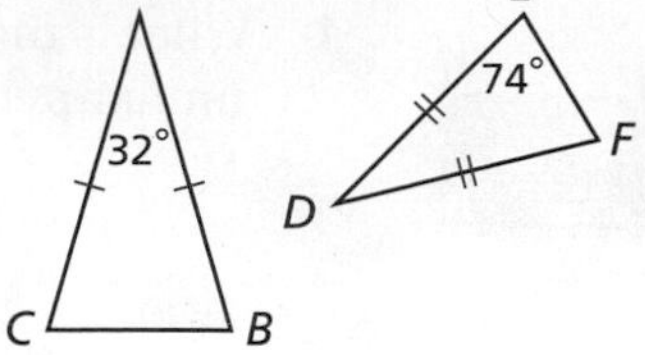

Verify that the given triangles are similar.

13. $\triangle KLM$ and $\triangle KNL$

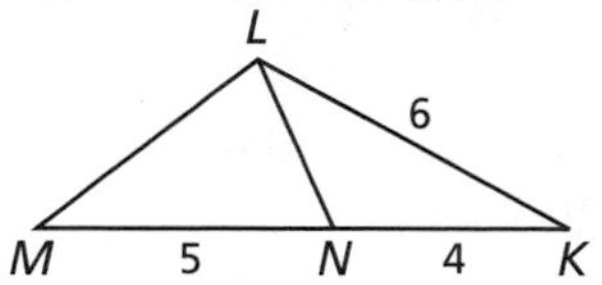

14. $\triangle UVW$ and $\triangle XYZ$

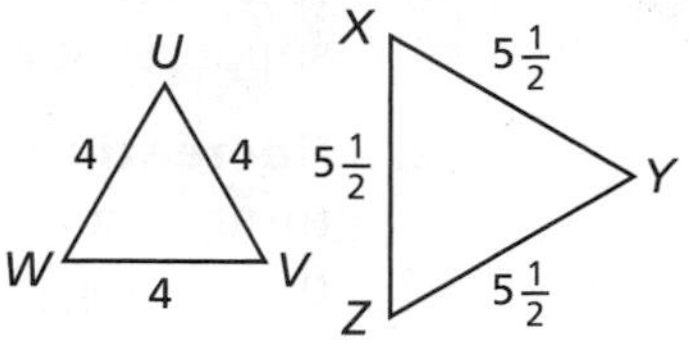

Multi-Step **Explain why the triangles are similar and then find each length.**

15. AB

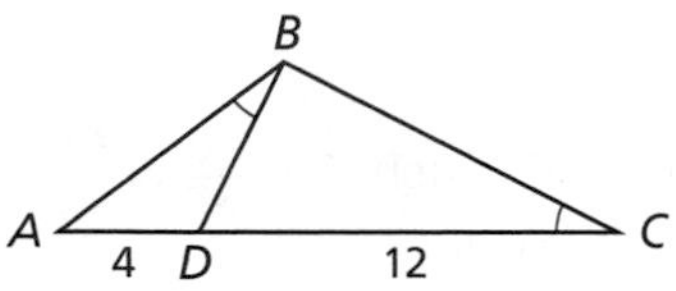

16. PS

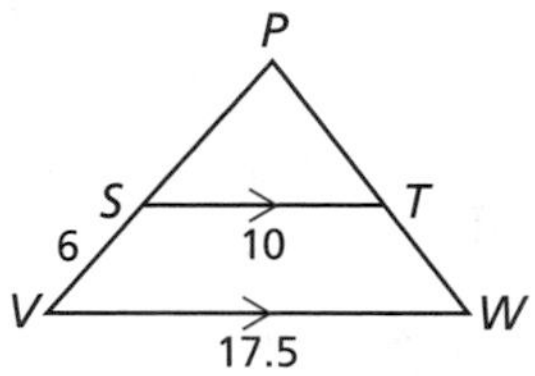

17. **Given:** $CD = 3AC$, $CE = 3BC$

Prove: $\triangle ABC \sim \triangle DEC$

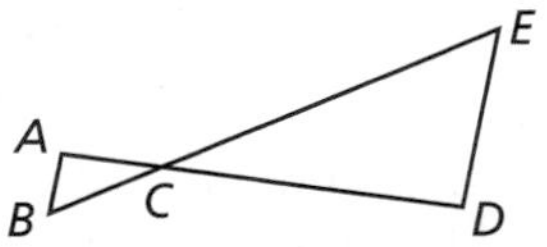

18. **Given:** $\frac{PR}{MR} = \frac{QR}{NR}$

Prove: $\angle 1 \cong \angle 2$

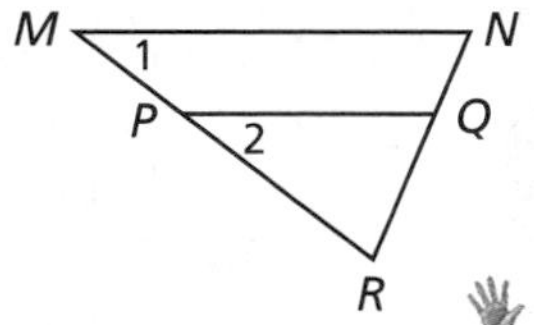

19. **Photography** The picture shows a person taking a pinhole photograph of himself. Light entering the opening reflects his image on the wall, forming similar triangles. What is the height of the image to the nearest tenth of a foot?

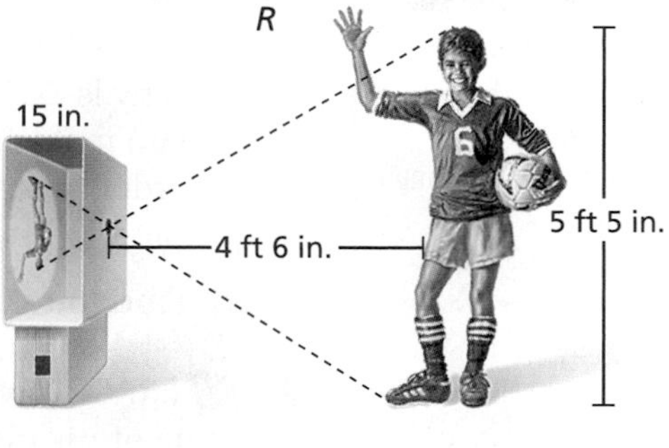

Draw $\triangle JKL$ and $\triangle MNP$. Determine if you can conclude that $\triangle JKL \sim \triangle MNP$ based on the given information. If so, which postulate or theorem justifies your response?

20. $\angle K \cong \angle N$, $\frac{JK}{MN} = \frac{KL}{NP}$

21. $\frac{JK}{MN} = \frac{KL}{NP} = \frac{JL}{MP}$

22. $\angle J \cong \angle M$, $\frac{JL}{MP} = \frac{KL}{NP}$

Find the value of x.

23.

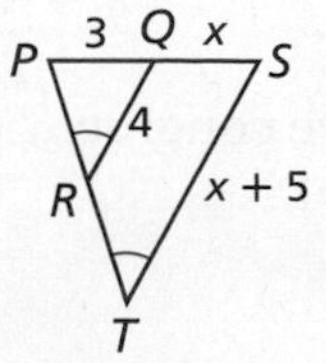

24.

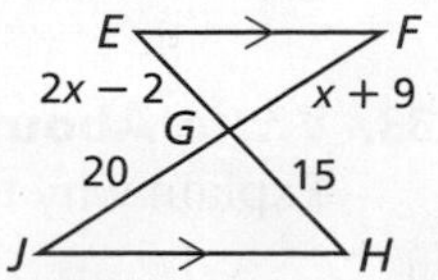

MULTI-STEP TEST PREP

25. The set for an animated film includes three small triangles that represent pyramids.

a. Which pyramids are similar? Why?

b. What is the similarity ratio of the similar pyramids?

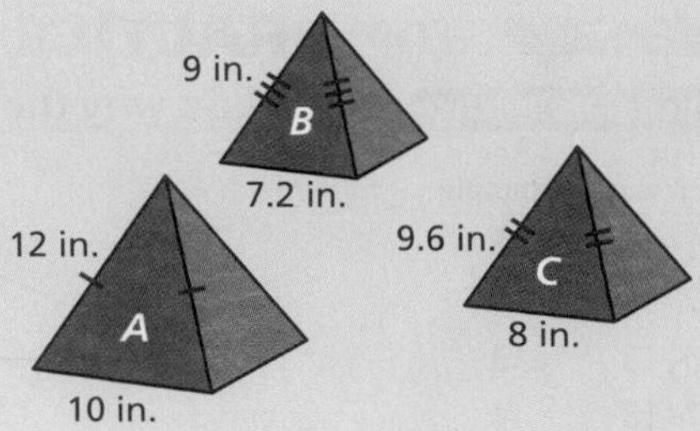

26. Critical Thinking $\triangle ABC$ is not similar to $\triangle DEF$, and $\triangle DEF$ is not similar to $\triangle XYZ$. Could $\triangle ABC$ be similar to $\triangle XYZ$? Why or why not? Make a sketch to support your answer.

27. Recreation To play shuffleboard, two teams take turns sliding disks on a court. The dimensions of the scoring area for a standard shuffleboard court are shown. What are JK and MN?

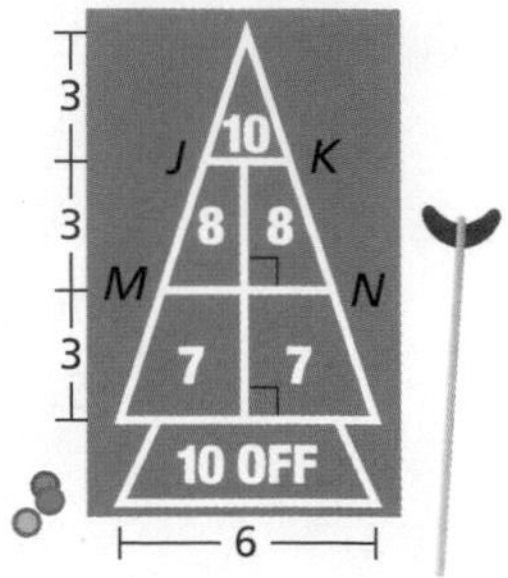

28. Prove the Transitive Property of Similarity.
Given: $\triangle ABC \sim \triangle DEF$, $\triangle DEF \sim \triangle XYZ$
Prove: $\triangle ABC \sim \triangle XYZ$

29. Draw and label $\triangle PQR$ and $\triangle STU$ such that $\frac{PQ}{ST} = \frac{QR}{TU}$ but $\triangle PQR$ is NOT similar to $\triangle STU$.

LINK

Meteorology

A tropical storm is classified as a hurricane if its winds reach a speed of at least 74 mi/h.

Source: http://www.nhc.noaa.gov

30. Given: $\triangle KNJ$ is isosceles with $\angle N$ as the vertex angle. $\angle H \cong \angle L$
Prove: $\triangle GHJ \sim \triangle MLK$

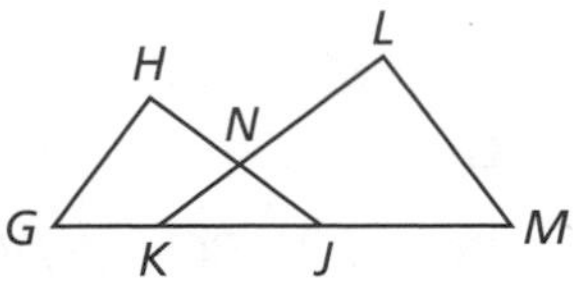

31. Meteorology Satellite photography makes it possible to measure the diameter of a hurricane. The figure shows that a camera's aperture YX is 35 mm and its focal length WZ is 50 mm. The satellite W holding the camera is 150 mi above the hurricane, centered at C.

a. Why is $\triangle XYZ \sim \triangle ABZ$? What assumption must you make about the position of the camera in order to make this conclusion?

b. What other triangles in the figure must be similar? Why?

c. Find the diameter AB of the hurricane.

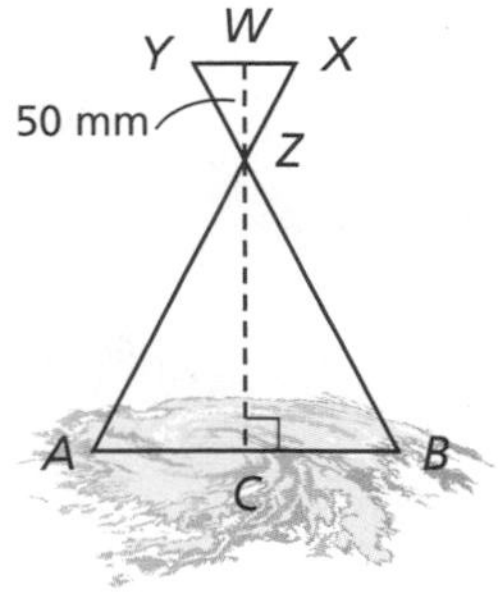

32. ERROR ANALYSIS Which solution for the value of y is incorrect? Explain the error.

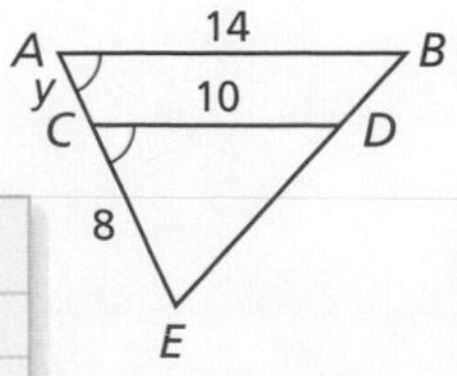

A

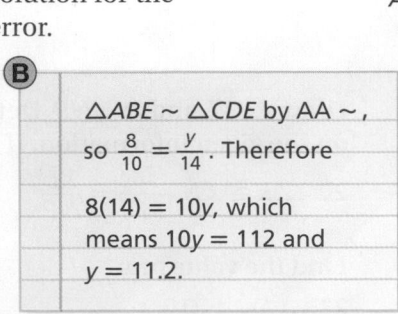

$\triangle ABE \sim \triangle CDE$ by AA $\sim$,
so $\frac{14}{8+y} = \frac{10}{8}$. Then
$10(8 + y) = 8(14)$, or
$80 + 10y = 112$. So
$10y = 32$ and $y = 3.2$.

B

$\triangle ABE \sim \triangle CDE$ by AA $\sim$,
so $\frac{8}{10} = \frac{y}{14}$. Therefore
$8(14) = 10y$, which
means $10y = 112$ and
$y = 11.2$.

33. Write About It Two isosceles triangles have congruent vertex angles. Explain why the two triangles must be similar.

TEST PREP

34. What is the length of $\overline{TU}$?

Ⓐ 36 Ⓒ 48

Ⓑ 40 Ⓓ 90

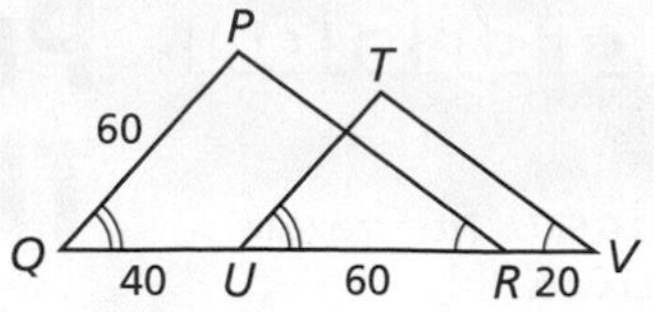

35. Which dimensions guarantee that $\triangle BCD \sim \triangle FGH$?

Ⓕ $FG = 11.6$, $GH = 8.4$

Ⓖ $FG = 12$, $GH = 14$

Ⓗ $FG = 11.4$, $GH = 11.4$

Ⓙ $FG = 10.5$, $GH = 14.5$

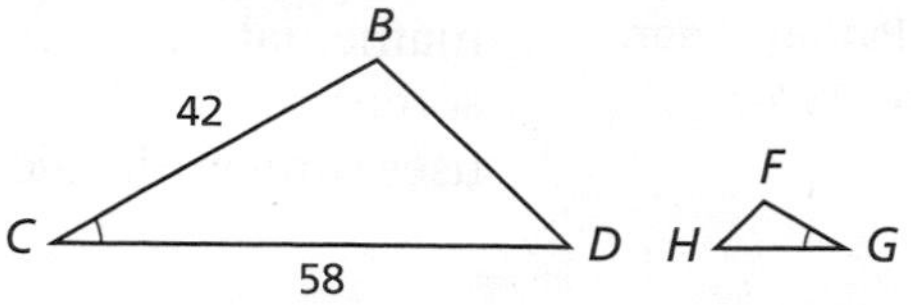

36. $\square ABCD \sim \square EFGH$. Which similarity postulate or theorem lets you conclude that $\triangle BCD \sim \triangle FGH$?

Ⓐ AA Ⓒ SAS

Ⓑ SSS Ⓓ None of these

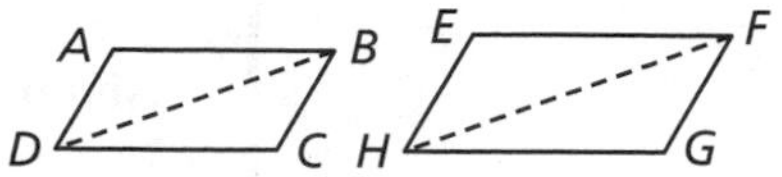

37. Gridded Response If 6, 8, and 12 and 15, 20, and x are the lengths of the corresponding sides of two similar triangles, what is the value of x?

CHALLENGE AND EXTEND

38. Prove the SSS Similarity Theorem.

Given: $\frac{AB}{DE} = \frac{BC}{EF} = \frac{AC}{DF}$

Prove: $\triangle ABC \sim \triangle DEF$

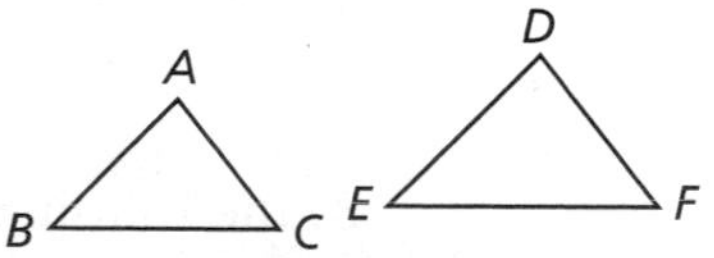

(*Hint:* Assume that $AB < DE$ and choose point X on $\overline{DE}$ so that $\overline{AB} \cong \overline{DX}$. Then choose point Y on $\overline{DF}$ so that $\overleftrightarrow{XY} \parallel \overline{EF}$. Show that $\triangle DXY \sim \triangle DEF$ and that $\triangle ABC \cong \triangle DXY$.)

39. Prove the SAS Similarity Theorem.

Given: $\angle B \cong \angle E$, $\frac{AB}{DE} = \frac{BC}{EF}$

Prove: $\triangle ABC \sim \triangle DEF$

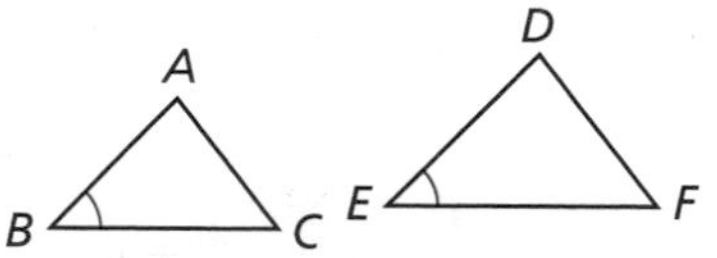

(*Hint:* Assume that $AB < DE$ and choose point X on $\overline{DE}$ so that $\overline{EX} \cong \overline{BA}$. Then choose point Y on $\overline{EF}$ so that $\angle EXY \cong \angle EDF$. Show that $\triangle XEY \sim \triangle DEF$ and that $\triangle ABC \cong \triangle XEF$.)

40. Given $\triangle ABC \sim \triangle XYZ$, $m\angle A = 50°$, $m\angle X = (2x + 5y)°$, $m\angle Z = (5x + y)°$, and that $m\angle B = (102 - x)°$, find $m\angle Z$.

COMMON CORE

EXTENSION

Proving the Pythagorean Theorem

CC.9-12.G.SRT.4 Prove theorems about triangles.

Objective
Prove the Pythagorean Theorem using similar triangles.

The Pythagorean Theorem is one of the most widely used and well-known mathematical theorems. The theorem has been proven in many different ways, some of which involve subdividing the triangle in some way. The following proof uses similar triangles.

EXAMPLE 1 Proving the Pythagorean Theorem Using Similar Triangles

Prove the Pythagorean Theorem using similar triangles.
Given: $\triangle ABC$ with right $\angle C$
Prove: $a^2 + b^2 = c^2$

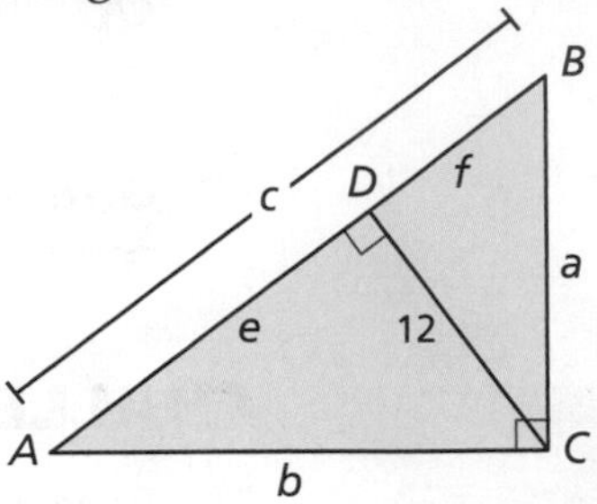

Proof: Draw an altitude from vertex C to side c as shown. By the Reflexive Property of Congruence, $\angle A \cong \angle A$ and $\angle B \cong \angle B$. All right angles are congruent, so $\angle ADC \cong \angle ACB$ and $\angle BDC \cong \angle ACB$. Therefore, $\triangle ACD \sim \triangle ABC$ and $\triangle CBD \sim \triangle ABC$ by the AA Similarity Postulate.

By the Transitive Property of Similarity, $\triangle ACD \sim \triangle CBD$.

Corresponding sides of similar triangles are proportional, so $\frac{c}{a} = \frac{a}{f}$ and $\frac{c}{b} = \frac{b}{e}$.

$\frac{c}{a} = \frac{a}{f}$	$\frac{c}{b} = \frac{b}{e}$	
$cf = a^2$	$ce = b^2$	*Cross-multiply.*
	$a^2 + ce = a^2 + b^2$	*Add a^2 to both sides.*
→	$cf + ce = a^2 + b^2$	$cf = a^2$
	$c(f + e) = a^2 + b^2$	*Factor.*
	$c^2 = a^2 + b^2$	$c = e + f$ *(Segment Addition)*

CHECK IT OUT!

1. In the figure, find c, e, and f.

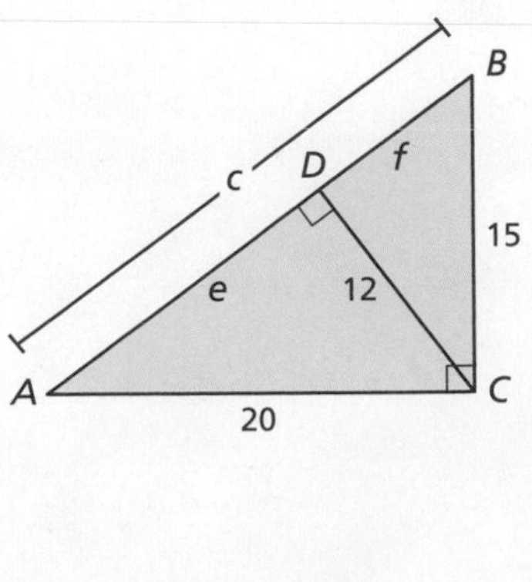

EXAMPLE 2 Applying the Pythagorean Theorem

Mike places a 20-foot ladder diagonally against the wall of the building. The bottom of the ladder is 3.5 feet from the building. The top of the ladder reaches how many feet above the ground?

Use the Pythagorean Theorem. The ladder is the hypotenuse of the triangle.

$$a^2 + b^2 = c^2$$
$$3.5^2 + b^2 = 20^2$$
$$12.25 + b^2 = 400$$
$$b^2 = 387.75$$
$$b \approx 19.7$$

The ladder reaches approximately 19.7 ft above the ground.

CHECK IT OUT! 2. Jackie drives 5 miles east and 3 miles north from home to school. What is the shortest distance from Jackie's home to school?

EXTENSION Exercises

Find the unknown values in each figure. Give your answers in simplest radical form.

1.

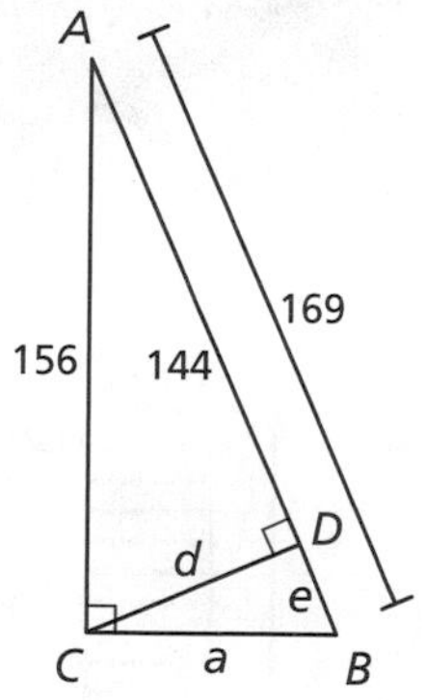

2.

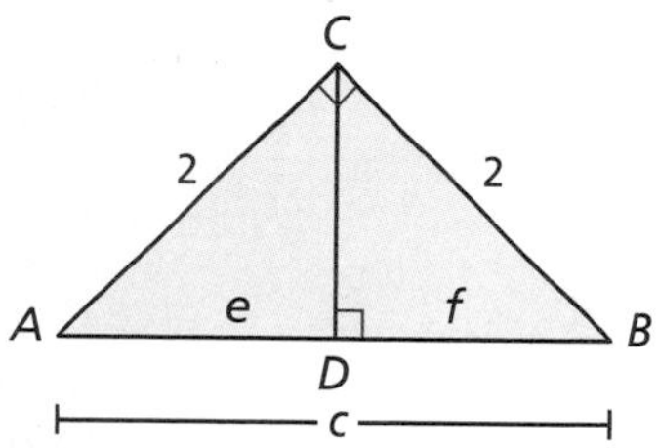

3. **Critical Thinking** Explain why any triple a, $2a$, $a\sqrt{3}$ are possible side lengths of a right triangle for any constant a.

4. The figure shows a loading dock with a ramp used to unload packages. What is the length of the ramp?

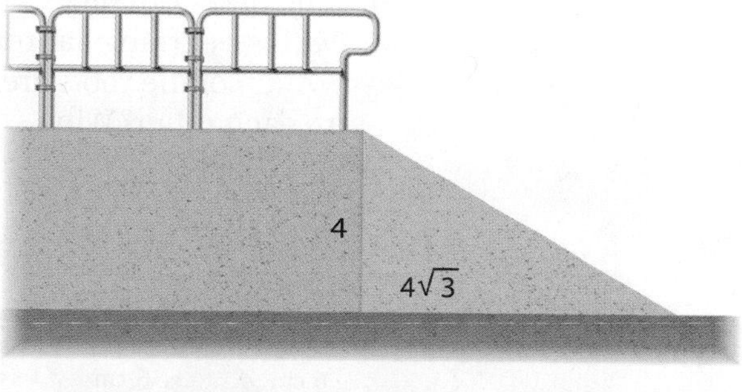

CHAPTER 7

SECTION 7A

MULTI-STEP TEST PREP

MATHEMATICAL PRACTICES **Model with mathematics.**

Similarity Relationships

Lights! Camera! Action! Lorenzo, Maria, Sam, and Tia are working on a video project for their history class. They decide to film a scene where the characters in the scene are on a train arriving at a town. Since Lorenzo collects model trains, they decide to use one of his trains and to build a set behind it. To create the set, they use a film technique called forced perspective. They want to use small objects to create an illusion of great distance in a very small space.

1. Lorenzo's model train is $\frac{1}{87}$ the size of the original train. He measures the engine of the model train and finds that it is $2\frac{1}{2}$ in. tall. What is the height of the real engine to the nearest foot?

2. The closest building to the train needs to be made using the same scale as the train. Maria and Sam estimate that the height of an actual station is 20 ft. How tall would they need to build their model of the train station to the nearest $\frac{1}{4}$ in.?

3. To give depth to their scene, they want to construct partial buildings behind the train station. Lorenzo decided to build a restaurant. If the height of the restaurant is actually 24 ft, how tall would they need to build their model of the restaurant to the nearest inch?

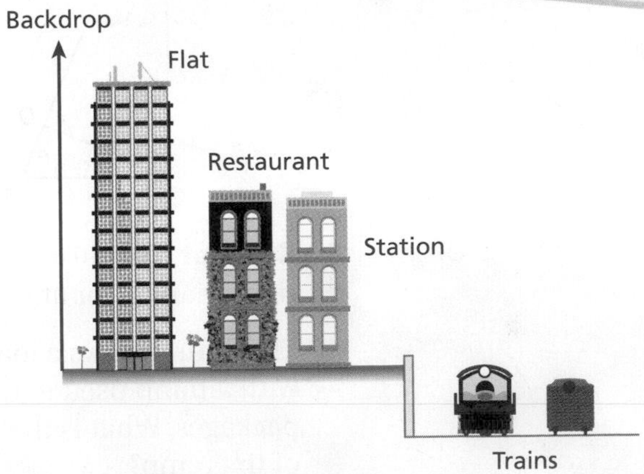

4. The other buildings on the set will have triangular roofs. Which of the roofs are similar to each other? Why?

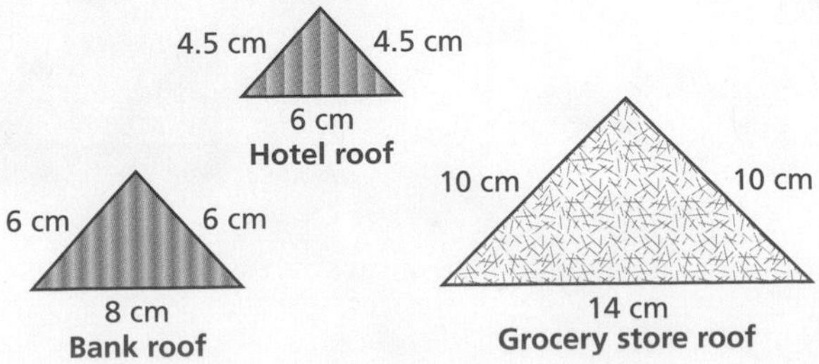

READY TO GO ON?

CHAPTER 7

SECTION 7A

Quiz for Lessons 7-1 Through 7-3

7-1 Ratios in Similar Polygons

Determine whether the two polygons are similar. If so, write the similarity ratio and a similarity statement.

1. rectangles *ABCD* and *WXYZ*

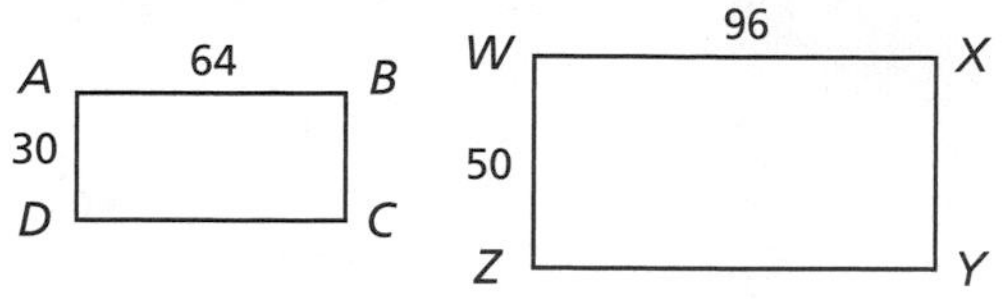

2. $\triangle JMR$ and $\triangle KNP$

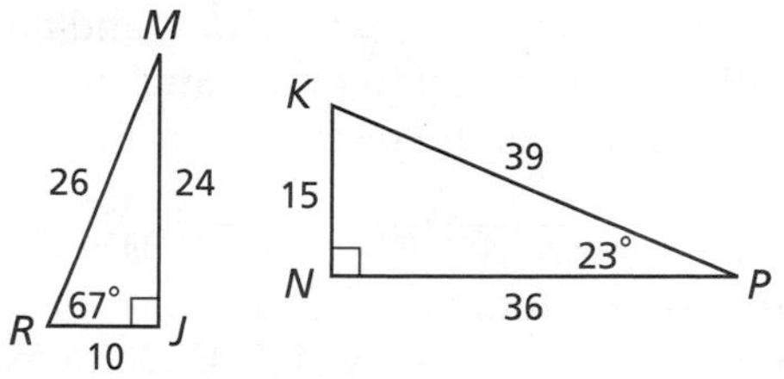

3. Leonardo da Vinci's famous portrait the *Mona Lisa* is 30 in. long and 21 in. wide. Janelle has a refrigerator magnet of the painting that is 3.5 cm wide. What is the length of the magnet?

7-2 Similarity and Transformations

Apply the dilation to the polygon with the given vertices. Name the coordinates of the points. Identify and describe the transformation.

4. $D: (x, y) \rightarrow (3x, 3y)$; $A(0, 0)$, $B(1, 2)$, $C(3, -2)$
5. $D: (x, y) \rightarrow (0.5x, 0.5y)$; $A(10, 6)$, $B(8, -4)$, $C(-2, 0)$

Determine whether the polygons with the given vertices are similar. Support your answer by describing a transformation.

6. $A(0, 0)$, $B(-2, 0)$, $C(-2, 1)$
   $X(10, 0)$, $Y(6, 0)$, $Z(6, 2)$

7. $A(0, 0)$, $B(1, 3)$, $C(-1, 4)$
   $X(0, 0)$, $Y(3, 9)$, $Z(-2, 8)$

7-3 Triangle Similarity: AA, SSS, and SAS

8. **Given:** $\square ABCD$
   Prove: $\triangle EDG \sim \triangle FBG$

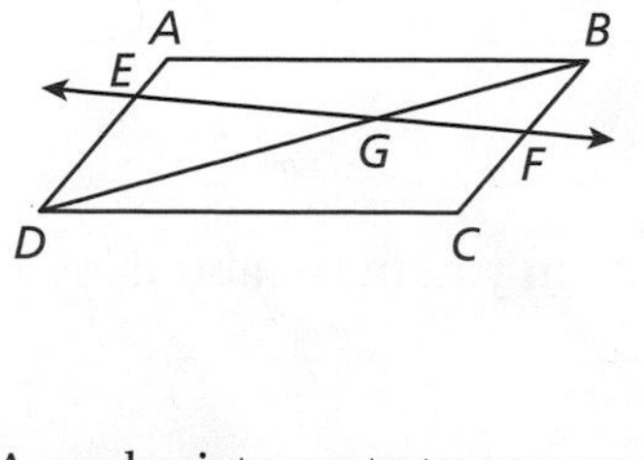

9. **Given:** $MQ = \frac{1}{3}MN$, $MR = \frac{1}{3}MP$
   Prove: $\triangle MQR \sim \triangle MNP$

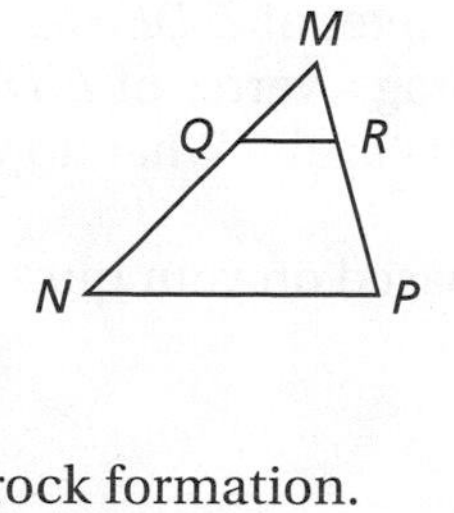

10. A geologist wants to measure the length *XY* of a rock formation. To do so, she locates points *U, V, X, Y,* and *Z* as shown. What is *XY*?

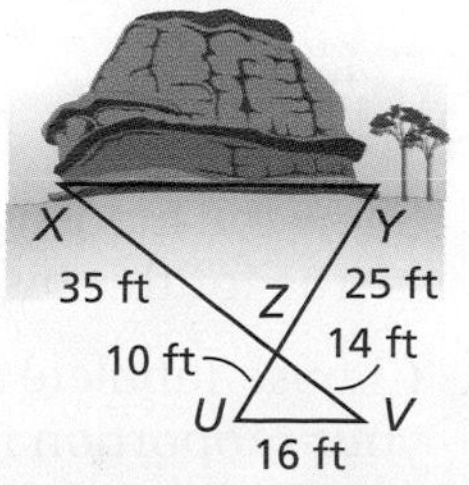

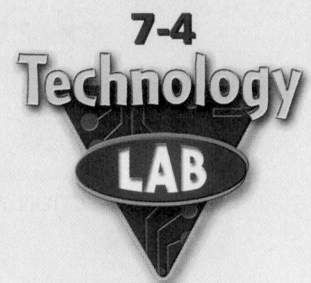

7-4 Technology LAB

Use with *Applying Properties of Similar Triangles*

Investigate Angle Bisectors of a Triangle

In a triangle, an angle bisector divides the opposite side into two segments. You will use geometry software to explore the relationships between these segments.

Learn It Online
Lab Resources Online

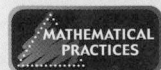

MATHEMATICAL PRACTICES **Use appropriate tools strategically.**

Activity 1

1. Construct $\triangle ABC$. Bisect $\angle BAC$ and create the point of intersection of the angle bisector and $\overline{BC}$. Label the intersection D.

2. Measure $\overline{AB}$, $\overline{AC}$, $\overline{BD}$, and $\overline{CD}$. Use these measurements to write ratios. What are the results? Drag a vertex of $\triangle ABC$ and examine the ratios again. What do you notice?

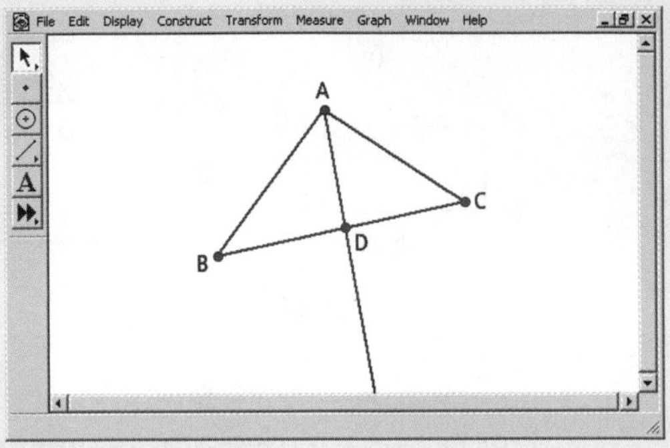

Try This

1. Choose Tabulate and create a table using the four lengths and the ratios from Step 2. Drag a vertex of $\triangle ABC$ and add the new measurements to the table. What conjecture can you make about the segments created by an angle bisector?
2. Write a proportion based on your conjecture.

Activity 2

1. Construct $\triangle DEF$. Create the *incenter* of the triangle and label it I. Hide the angle bisectors of $\angle E$ and $\angle F$. Find the point of intersection of $\overline{EF}$ and the bisector of $\angle D$. Label the intersection G.

2. Find DI, DG, and the perimeter of $\triangle DEF$.

3. Divide the length of $\overline{DI}$ by the length of DG. Add the lengths of $\overline{DE}$ and $\overline{DF}$. Then divide this sum by the perimeter of $\triangle DEF$. Compare the two quotients. Drag a vertex of $\triangle DEF$ and examine the quotients again. What do you notice?

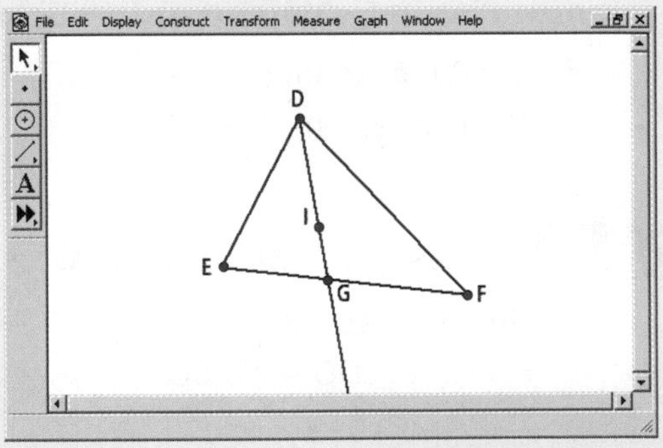

4. Write a proportion based on your quotients. What conjecture can you make about this relationship?

Try This

3. Show the hidden angle bisector of $\angle E$ or $\angle F$. Confirm that your conjecture is true for this bisector. Drag a vertex of $\triangle DEF$ and observe the results.
4. Choose Tabulate and create a table with the measurements you used in your proportion in Step 4.

COMMON CORE

7-4 Applying Properties of Similar Triangles

CC.9-12.G.SRT.5 Use...similarity criteria for triangles to solve problems... *Also* **CC.9-12.G.SRT.4, CC.9-12.G.SRT.2**

Objectives

Use properties of similar triangles to find segment lengths.

Apply proportionality and triangle angle bisector theorems.

Who uses this?

Artists use similarity and proportionality to give paintings an illusion of depth. (See Example 3.)

Artists use mathematical techniques to make two-dimensional paintings appear three-dimensional. The invention of *perspective* was based on the observation that far away objects look smaller and closer objects look larger.

Mathematical theorems like the Triangle Proportionality Theorem are important in making perspective drawings.

Know it! Note

Theorem 7-4-1 **Triangle Proportionality Theorem**

THEOREM	HYPOTHESIS	CONCLUSION
If a line parallel to a side of a triangle intersects the other two sides, then it divides those sides proportionally.	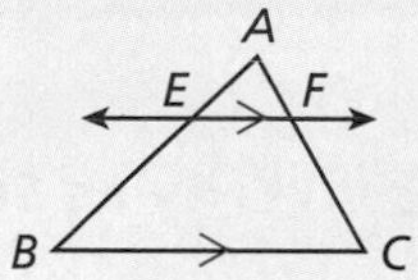 $\overline{EF} \parallel \overline{BC}$	$\frac{AE}{EB} = \frac{AF}{FC}$

You can use a compass-and-straightedge construction to verify this theorem. Although the construction is not a proof, it should help convince you that the theorem is true. After you have completed the construction, use a ruler to measure $\overline{AE}$, $\overline{EB}$, $\overline{AF}$, and $\overline{FC}$ to see that $\frac{AE}{EB} = \frac{AF}{FC}$.

Construction Triangle Proportionality Theorem

Construct a line parallel to a side of a triangle.

1

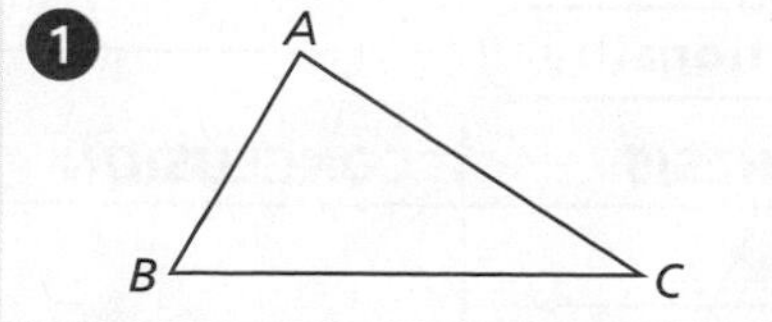

Use a straightedge to draw $\triangle ABC$.

2

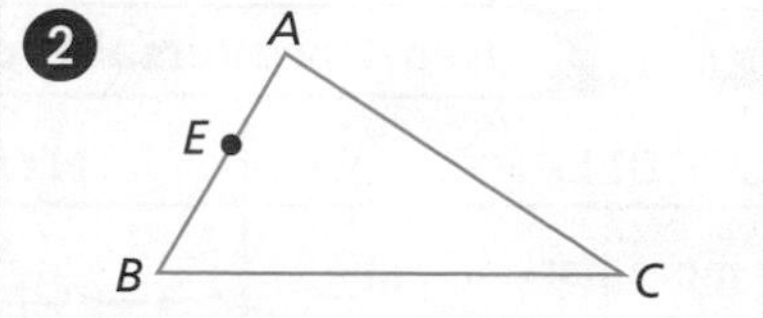

Label E on AB.

3

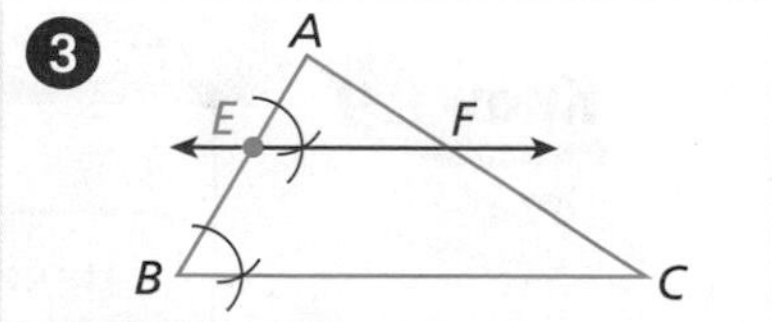

Construct $\angle E \cong \angle B$. Label the intersection of $\overleftrightarrow{EF}$ and $\overline{AC}$ as F. $\overleftrightarrow{EF} \parallel \overline{BC}$ by the Converse of the Corresponding Angles Postulate.

EXAMPLE 1 Finding the Length of a Segment

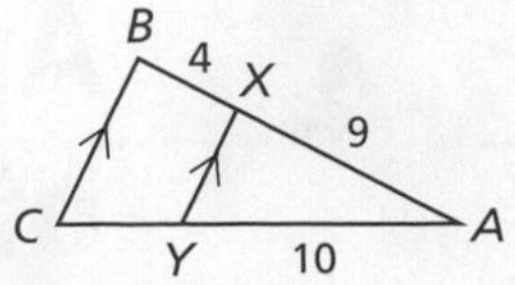

Find CY.

It is given that $\overline{XY} \parallel \overline{BC}$, so $\frac{AX}{XB} = \frac{AY}{YC}$ by the Triangle Proportionality Theorem.

$\frac{9}{4} = \frac{10}{CY}$ — *Substitute 9 for AX, 4 for XB, and 10 for AY.*

$9(CY) = 40$ — *Cross Products Prop.*

$CY = \frac{40}{9}$, or $4\frac{4}{9}$ — *Divide both sides by 9.*

CHECK IT OUT! **1.** Find PN.

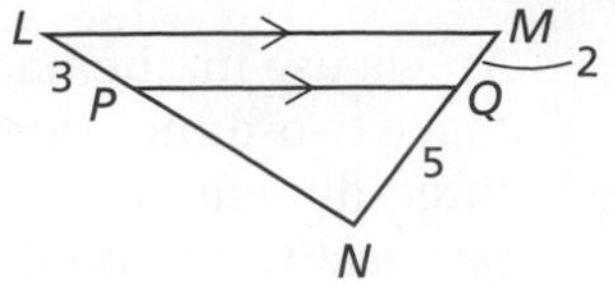

Know it! Note

Theorem 7-4-2 Converse of the Triangle Proportionality Theorem

THEOREM	HYPOTHESIS	CONCLUSION
If a line divides two sides of a triangle proportionally, then it is parallel to the third side.	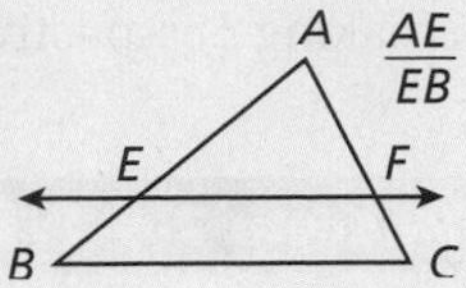 $\frac{AE}{EB} = \frac{AF}{FC}$	$\overleftrightarrow{EF} \parallel \overline{BC}$

You will prove Theorem 7-4-2 in Exercise 23.

EXAMPLE 2 Verifying Segments are Parallel

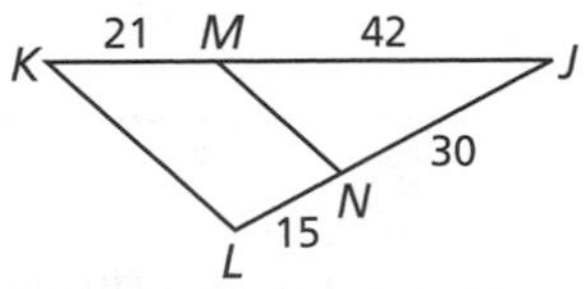

Verify that $\overline{MN} \parallel \overline{KL}$.

$\frac{JM}{MK} = \frac{42}{21} = 2$

$\frac{JN}{NL} = \frac{30}{15} = 2$

Since $\frac{JM}{MK} = \frac{JN}{NL}$, $\overline{MN} \parallel \overline{KL}$ by the Converse of the Triangle Proportionality Theorem.

CHECK IT OUT! **2.** $AC = 36$ cm, and $BC = 27$ cm. Verify that $\overline{DE} \parallel \overline{AB}$.

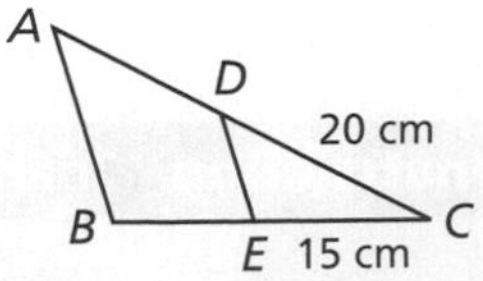

Know it! Note

Corollary 7-4-3 Two-Transversal Proportionality

COROLLARY	HYPOTHESIS	CONCLUSION
If three or more parallel lines intersect two transversals, then they divide the transversals proportionally.	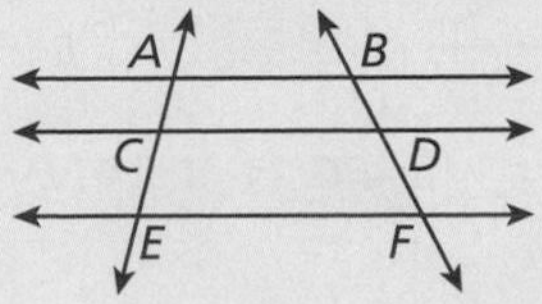	$\frac{AC}{CE} = \frac{BD}{DF}$

You will prove Corollary 7-4-3 in Exercise 24.

EXAMPLE 3 Art Application

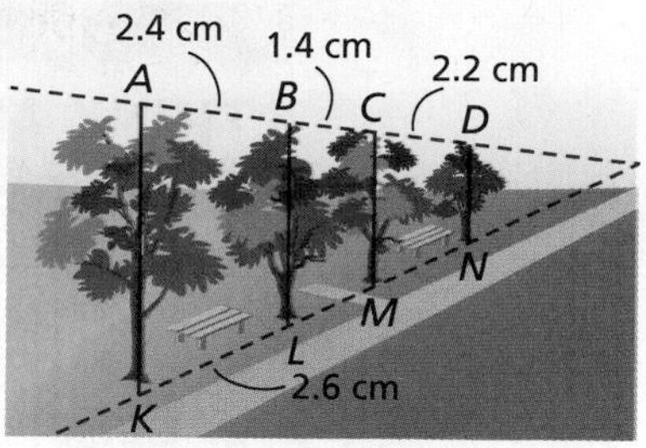

An artist used perspective to draw guidelines to help her sketch a row of parallel trees. She then checked the drawing by measuring the distances between the trees. What is *LN*?

$\overline{AK} \parallel \overline{BL} \parallel \overline{CM} \parallel \overline{DN}$ *Given*

$\frac{KL}{LN} = \frac{AB}{BD}$ *2-Transv. Proportionality Corollary*

$BD = BC + CD$ *Seg. Add. Post.*

$BD = 1.4 + 2.2 = 3.6 \text{ cm}$ *Substitute 1.4 for BC and 2.2 for CD.*

$\frac{2.6}{LN} = \frac{2.4}{3.6}$ *Substitute the given values.*

$2.4(LN) = 3.6(2.6)$ *Cross Products Prop.*

$LN = 3.9 \text{ cm}$ *Divide both sides by 2.4.*

CHECK IT OUT! **3.** Use the diagram to find *LM* and *MN* to the nearest tenth.

The previous theorems and corollary lead to the following conclusion.

Know it! Note

Theorem 7-4-4 Triangle Angle Bisector Theorem

THEOREM	HYPOTHESIS	CONCLUSION
An angle bisector of a triangle divides the opposite side into two segments whose lengths are proportional to the lengths of the other two sides. (△ ∠ Bisector Thm.)	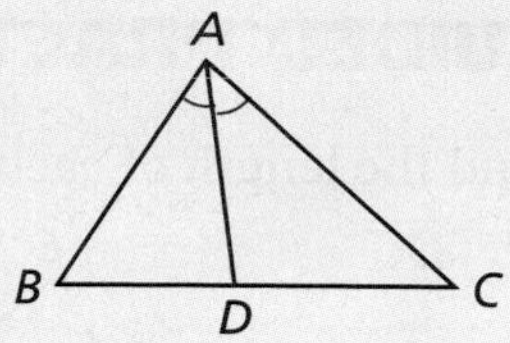	$\frac{BD}{DC} = \frac{AB}{AC}$

You will prove Theorem 7-4-4 in Exercise 38.

EXAMPLE 4 Using the Triangle Angle Bisector Theorem

Algebra

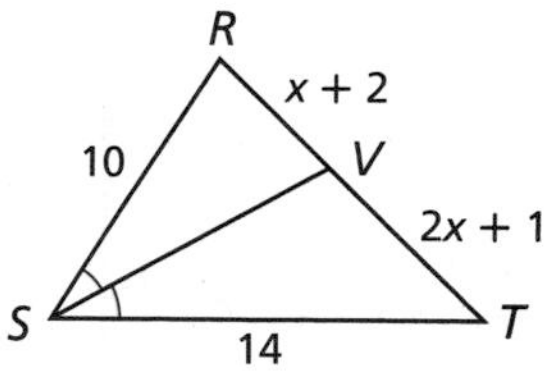

Find *RV* and *VT*.

$\frac{RV}{VT} = \frac{SR}{ST}$ by the △ ∠ Bisector Thm.

$\frac{x+2}{2x+1} = \frac{10}{14}$ *Substitute the given values.*

$14(x+2) = 10(2x+1)$ *Cross Products Prop.*

$14x + 28 = 20x + 10$ *Dist. Prop.*

$18 = 6x$ *Simplify.*

$x = 3$ *Divide both sides by 6.*

$RV = x + 2 = 3 + 2 = 5$ $\quad VT = 2x + 1 = 2(3) + 1 = 7$ *Substitute 3 for x.*

Helpful Hint

You can check your answer by substituting the values into the proportion.

$\frac{RV}{VT} = \frac{SR}{ST}$

$\frac{5}{7} = \frac{10}{14}$

$\frac{5}{7} = \frac{5}{7}$

CHECK IT OUT! **4.** Find *AC* and *DC*.

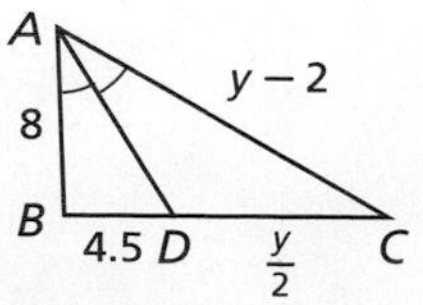

MATHEMATICAL PRACTICES

THINK AND DISCUSS

1. $\overline{XY} \parallel \overline{BC}$. Use what you know about similarity and proportionality to state as many different proportions as possible.

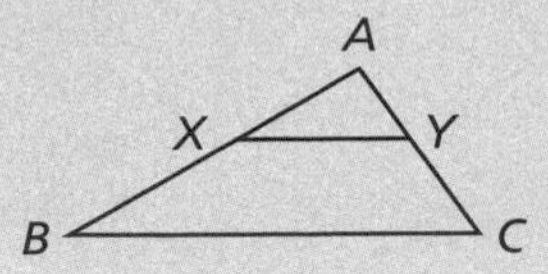

Know it! Note

2. **GET ORGANIZED** Copy and complete the graphic organizer. Draw a figure for each proportionality theorem or corollary and then measure it. Use your measurements to write an if-then statement about each figure.

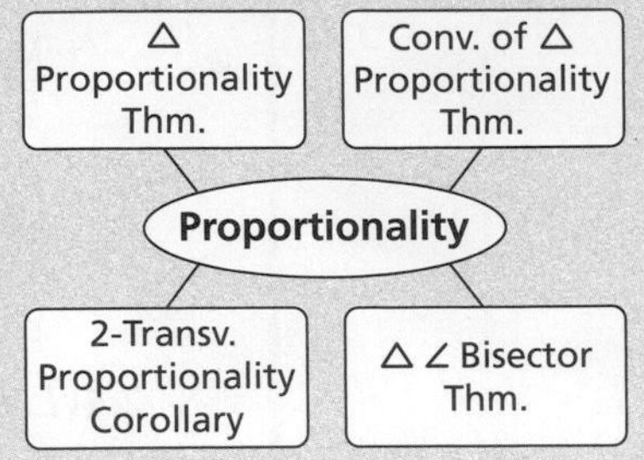

7-4 Exercises

Learn It Online
Homework Help Online
Parent Resources Online

GUIDED PRACTICE

SEE EXAMPLE 1

Find the length of each segment.

1. $\overline{DG}$

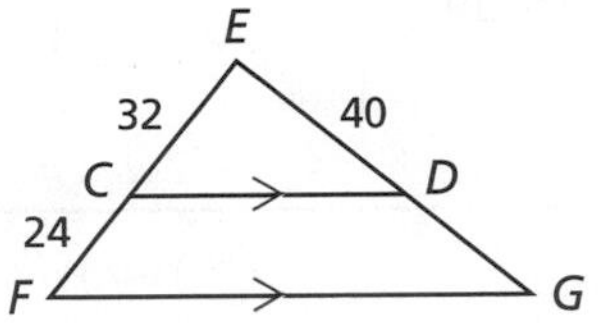

2. $\overline{RN}$

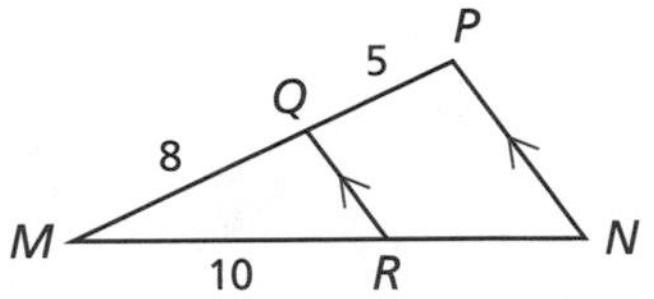

SEE EXAMPLE 2

Verify that the given segments are parallel.

3. $\overline{AB}$ and $\overline{CD}$

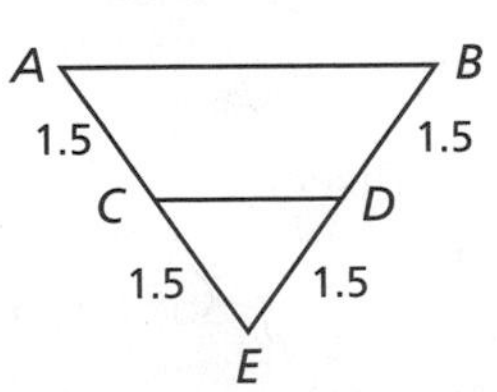

4. $\overline{TU}$ and $\overline{RS}$

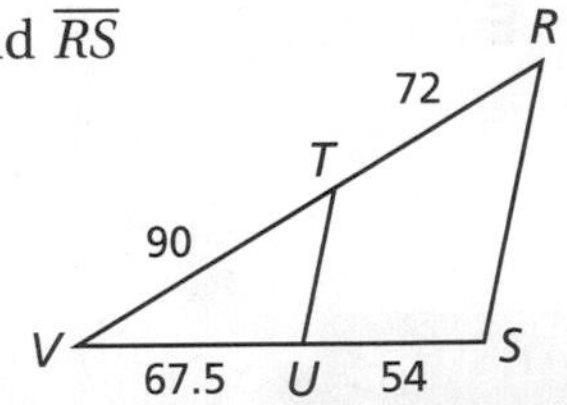

SEE EXAMPLE 3

5. **Travel** The map shows the area around Herald Square in Manhattan, New York, and the approximate length of several streets. If the numbered streets are parallel, what is the length of Broadway between 34th St. and 35th St. to the nearest foot?

SEE EXAMPLE 4 Find the length of each segment.

6. $\overline{QR}$ and $\overline{RS}$

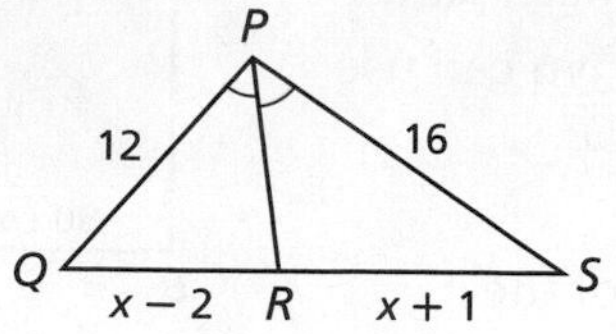

7. $\overline{CD}$ and $\overline{AD}$

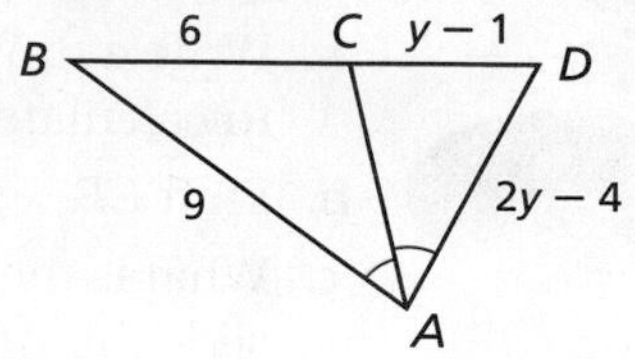

PRACTICE AND PROBLEM SOLVING

Independent Practice

For Exercises	See Example
8–9	1
10–11	2
12	3
13–14	4

Extra Practice

See Extra Practice for more Skills Practice and Applications Practice exercises.

Find the length of each segment.

8. $\overline{KL}$

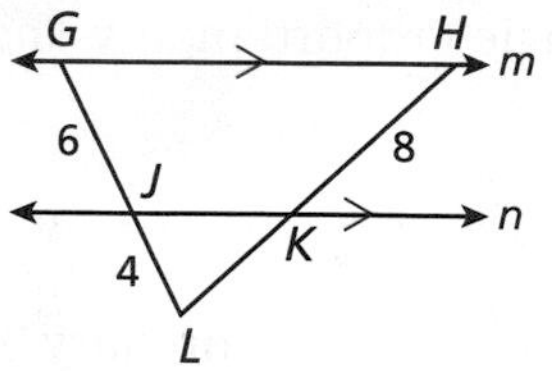

9. $\overline{XZ}$

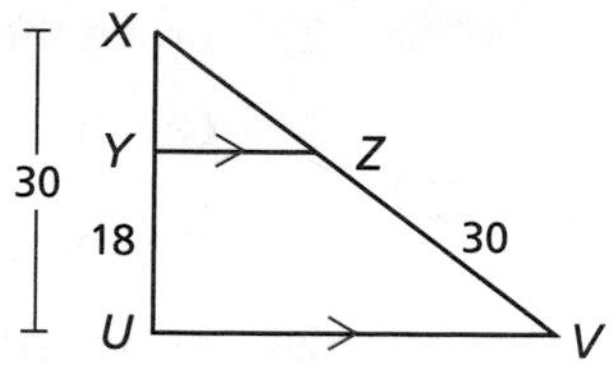

Verify that the given segments are parallel.

10. $\overline{AB}$ and $\overline{CD}$

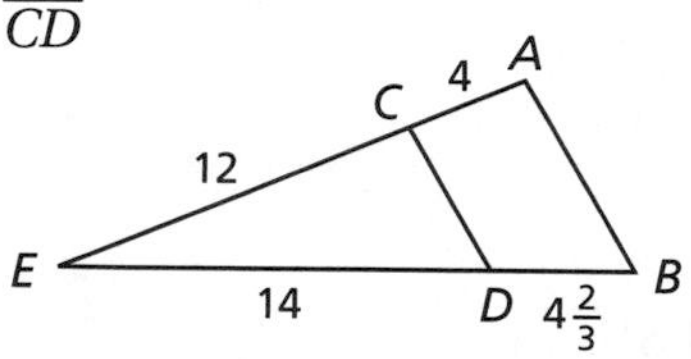

11. $\overline{MN}$ and $\overline{QR}$

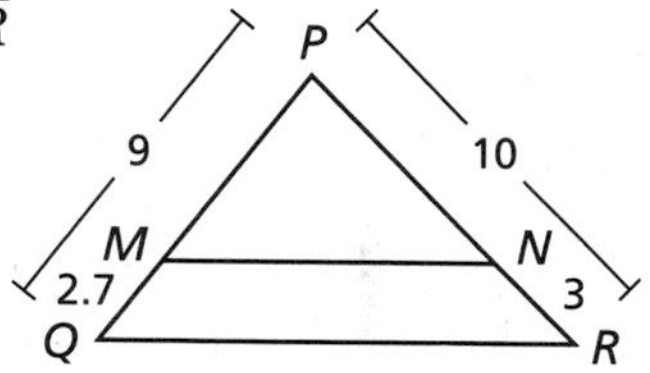

12. **Architecture** The wooden treehouse has horizontal siding that is parallel to the base. What are *LM* and *MN* to the nearest hundredth?

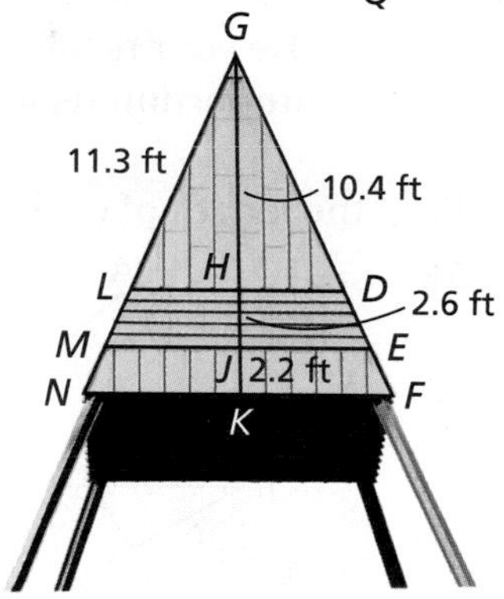

Find the length of each segment.

13. $\overline{BC}$ and $\overline{CD}$

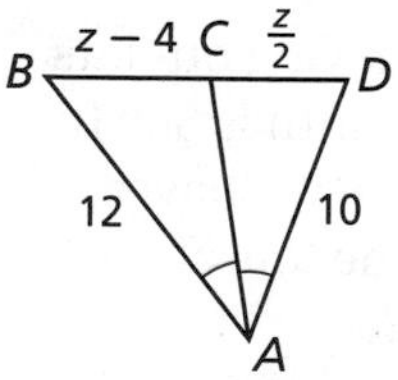

14. $\overline{ST}$ and $\overline{TU}$

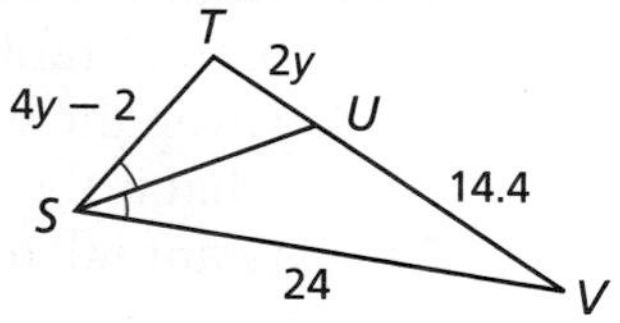

In the figure, $\overleftrightarrow{BC} \parallel \overleftrightarrow{DE} \parallel \overleftrightarrow{FG}$. Complete each proportion.

15. $\frac{AB}{BD} = \frac{AC}{\blacksquare}$

16. $\frac{\blacksquare}{DF} = \frac{AE}{EG}$

17. $\frac{DF}{\blacksquare} = \frac{EG}{CE}$

18. $\frac{AF}{AB} = \frac{\blacksquare}{AC}$

19. $\frac{BD}{CE} = \frac{\blacksquare}{EG}$

20. $\frac{AB}{AC} = \frac{BF}{\blacksquare}$

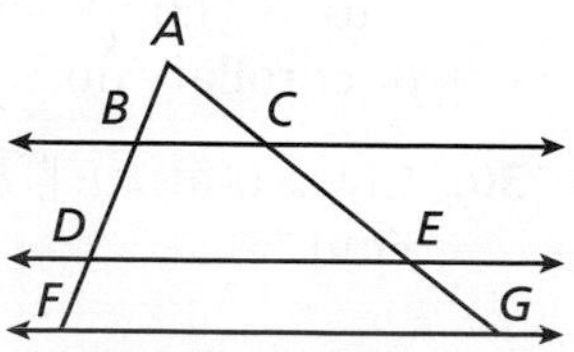

21. The bisector of an angle of a triangle divides the opposite side of the triangle into segments that are 12 in. and 16 in. long. Another side of the triangle is 20 in. long. What are two possible lengths for the third side?

MULTI-STEP TEST PREP

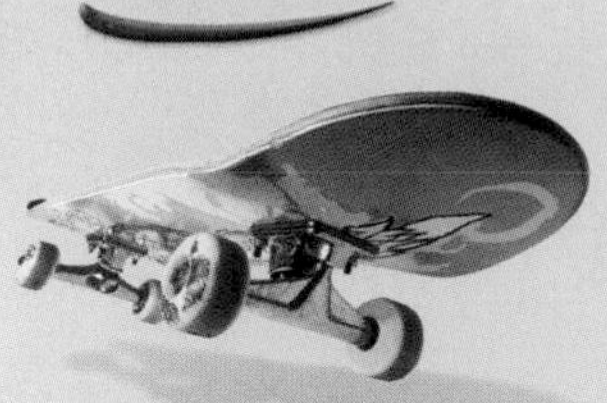

22. Jaclyn is building a slide rail, the narrow, slanted beam found in skateboard parks.

a. Write a proportion that Jaclyn can use to calculate the length of $\overline{CE}$.

b. Find CE.

c. What is the overall length of the slide rail AJ?

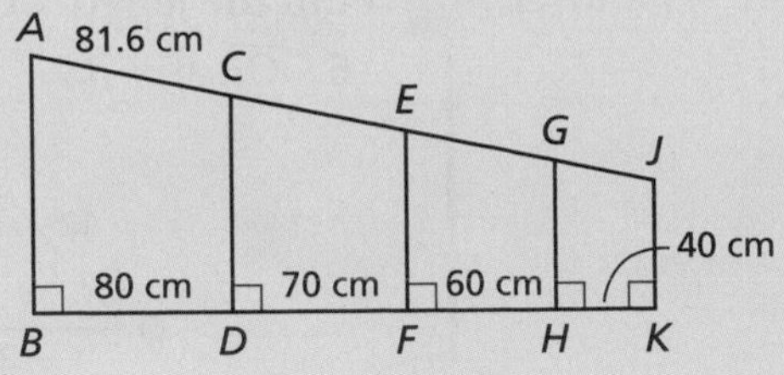

23. Prove the Converse of the Triangle Proportionality Theorem.

Given: $\frac{AE}{EB} = \frac{AF}{FC}$

Prove: $\overleftrightarrow{EF} \parallel \overline{BC}$

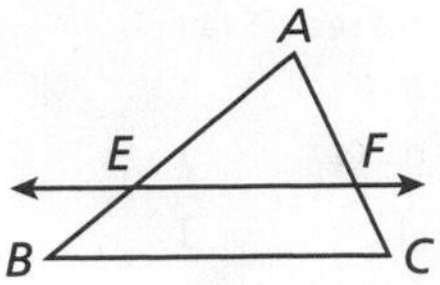

24. Prove the Two-Transversal Proportionality Corollary.

Given: $\overleftrightarrow{AB} \parallel \overleftrightarrow{CD}$, $\overleftrightarrow{CD} \parallel \overleftrightarrow{EF}$

Prove: $\frac{AC}{CE} = \frac{BD}{DF}$

(*Hint:* Draw $\overleftrightarrow{BE}$ through X.)

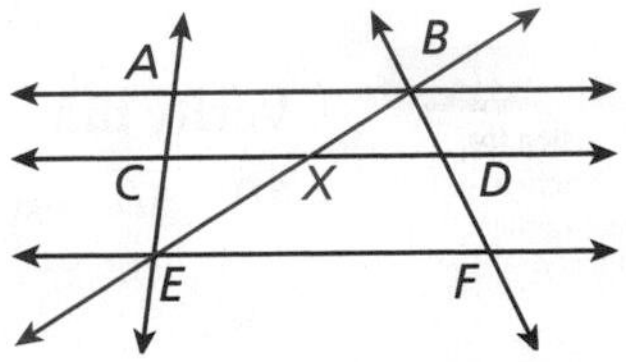

25. Given that $\overleftrightarrow{PQ} \parallel \overleftrightarrow{RS} \parallel \overleftrightarrow{TU}$

a. Find PR, RT, QS, and SU.

b. Use your results from part **b** to write a proportion relating the segment lengths.

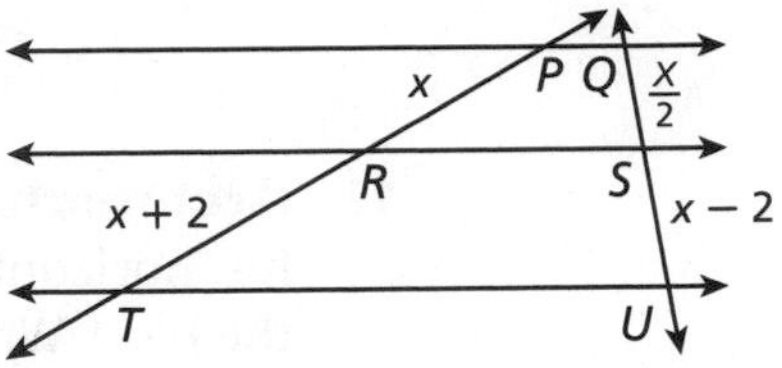

Find the length of each segment.

26. $\overline{EF}$

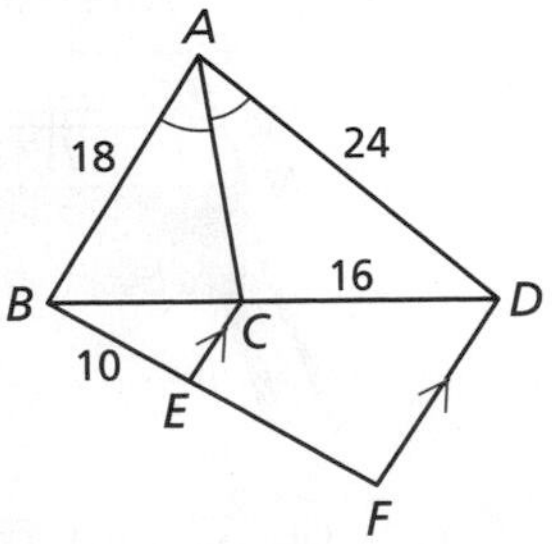

27. $\overline{ST}$

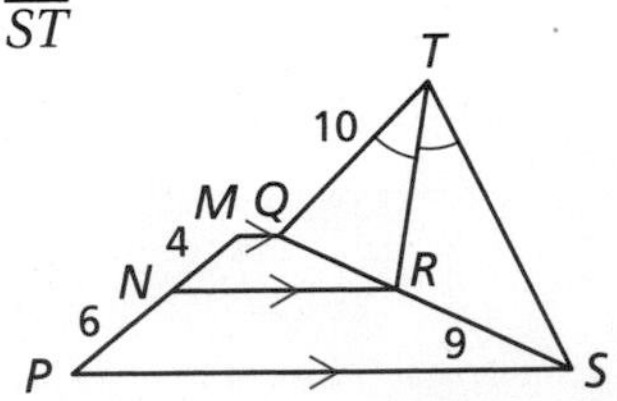

28. Real Estate A developer is laying out lots along Grant Rd. whose total width is 500 ft. Given the width of each lot along Chavez St., what is the width of each of the lots along Grant Rd. to the nearest foot?

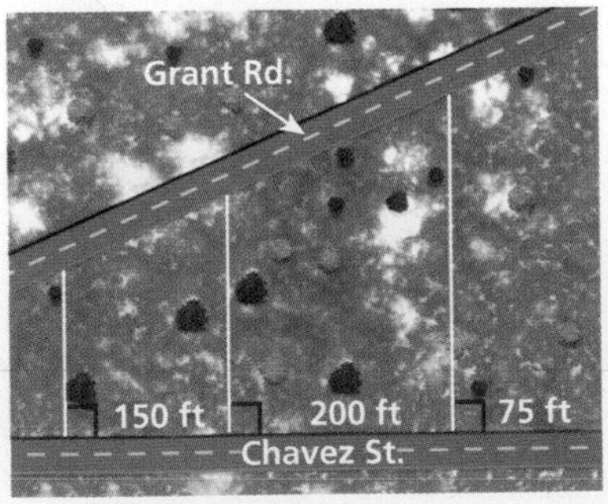

29. Critical Thinking Explain how to use a sheet of lined notebook paper to divide a segment into five congruent segments. Which theorem or corollary do you use?

30. Given that $\overline{DE} \parallel \overline{BC}$, $\overline{XY} \parallel \overline{AD}$
Find EC.

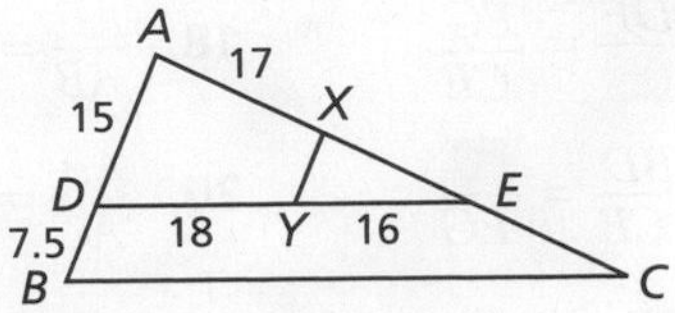

31. Write About It In $\triangle ABC$, $\overrightarrow{AD}$ bisects $\angle BAC$. Write a proportionality statement for the triangle. What theorem supports your conclusion?

TEST PREP

32. Which dimensions let you conclude that $\overline{UV} \parallel \overline{ST}$?

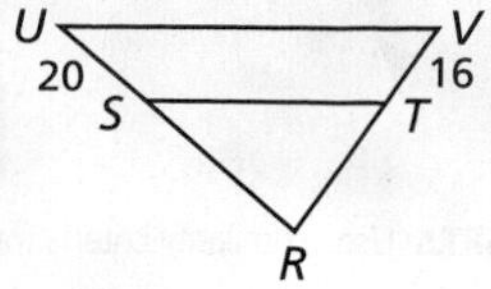

Ⓐ $SR = 12$, $TR = 9$
Ⓑ $SR = 16$, $TR = 20$
Ⓒ $SR = 35$, $TR = 28$
Ⓓ $SR = 50$, $TR = 48$

33. In $\triangle ABC$, the bisector of $\angle A$ divides $\overline{BC}$ into segments with lengths 16 and 20. $AC = 25$. Which of these could be the length of $\overline{AB}$?

Ⓕ 12.8 Ⓖ 16 Ⓗ 18.75 Ⓙ 20

34. On the map, 1st St. and 2nd St. are parallel. What is the distance from City Hall to 2nd St. along Cedar Rd.?

Ⓐ 1.8 mi
Ⓑ 3.2 mi
Ⓒ 4.2 mi
Ⓓ 5.6 mi

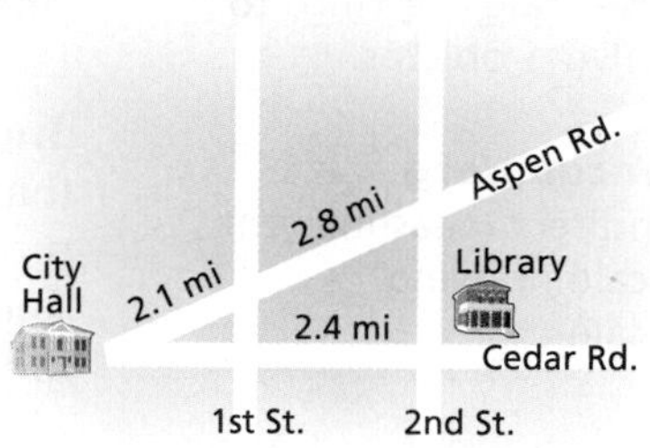

35. Extended Response Two segments are divided proportionally. The first segment is divided into lengths 20, 15, and x. The corresponding lengths in the second segment are 16, y, and 24. Find the value of x and y. Use these values and write six proportions.

CHALLENGE AND EXTEND

36. The perimeter of $\triangle ABC$ is 29 m. $\overline{AD}$ bisects $\angle A$. Find AB and AC.

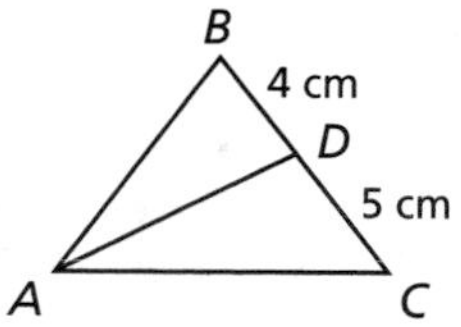

37. Prove that if two triangles are similar, then the ratio of their corresponding angle bisectors is the same as the ratio of their corresponding sides.

38. Prove the Triangle Angle Bisector Theorem.

Given: In $\triangle ABC$, $\overline{AD}$ bisects $\angle A$.

Prove: $\frac{BD}{DC} = \frac{AB}{AC}$

Plan: Draw $\overline{BX} \parallel \overline{AD}$ and extend $\overline{AC}$ to X. Use properties of parallel lines and the Converse of the Isosceles Triangle Theorem to show that $\overline{AX} \cong \overline{AB}$. Then apply the Triangle Proportionality Theorem.

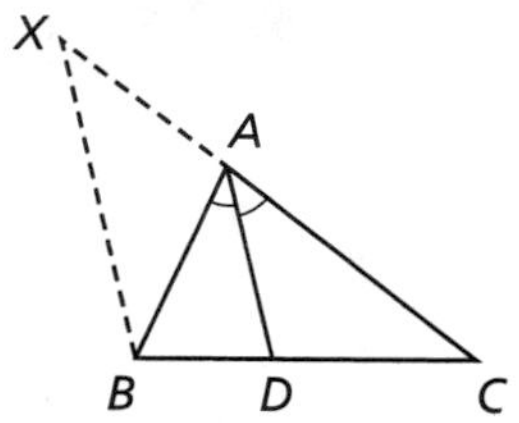

39. Construction Construct three parallel lines cut by a transversal. Construct a second transversal that forms line segments twice the length of the corresponding segments on the first transversal.

COMMON CORE

7-5 Using Proportional Relationships

CC.9-12.G.SRT.5 Use…similarity criteria for triangles to solve problems and prove relationships...

Objectives
Use ratios to make indirect measurements.

Use scale drawings to solve problems.

Vocabulary
indirect measurement
scale drawing
scale

Why learn this?
Proportional relationships help you find distances that cannot be measured directly.

Indirect measurement is any method that uses formulas, similar figures, and/or proportions to measure an object. The following example shows one indirect measurement technique.

EXAMPLE 1 *Measurement Application*

A student wanted to find the height of a statue of a pineapple in Nambour, Australia. She measured the pineapple's shadow and her own shadow. The student's height is 5 ft 4 in. What is the height of the pineapple?

Step 1 Convert the measurements to inches.

$AC = 5 \text{ ft } 4 \text{ in.} = (5 \cdot 12) \text{ in.} + 4 \text{ in.} = 64 \text{ in.}$

$BC = 2 \text{ ft} = (2 \cdot 12) \text{ in.} = 24 \text{ in.}$

$EF = 8 \text{ ft } 9 \text{ in.} = (8 \cdot 12) \text{ in.} + 9 \text{ in.} = 105 \text{ in.}$

Step 2 Find similar triangles.

Because the sun's rays are parallel, $\angle 1 \cong \angle 2$. Therefore $\triangle ABC \sim \triangle DEF$ by $AA \sim$.

Step 3 Find DF.

$\frac{AC}{DF} = \frac{BC}{EF}$ *Corr. sides are proportional.*

$\frac{64}{DF} = \frac{24}{105}$ *Substitute 64 for AC, 24 for BC, and 105 for EF.*

$24(DF) = 64 \cdot 105$ *Cross Products Prop.*

$DF = 280$ *Divide both sides by 24.*

The height of the pineapple is 280 in., or 23 ft 4 in.

Helpful Hint

Whenever dimensions are given in both feet and inches, you must convert them to either feet or inches before doing any calculations.

CHECK IT OUT! **1.** A student who is 5 ft 6 in. tall measured shadows to find the height LM of a flagpole. What is LM?

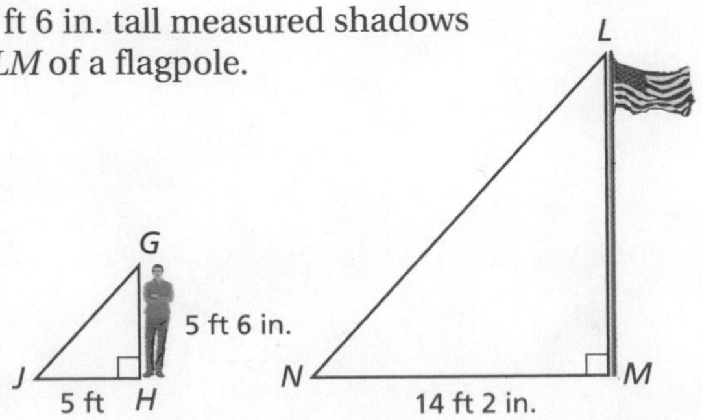

A **scale drawing** represents an object as smaller than or larger than its actual size. The drawing's **scale** is the ratio of any length in the drawing to the corresponding actual length. For example, on a map with a scale of 1 cm : 1500 m, one centimeter on the map represents 1500 m in actual distance.

EXAMPLE 2 Solving for a Dimension

The scale of this map of downtown Dallas is 1.5 cm : 300 m. Find the actual distance between Union Station and the Dallas Public Library.

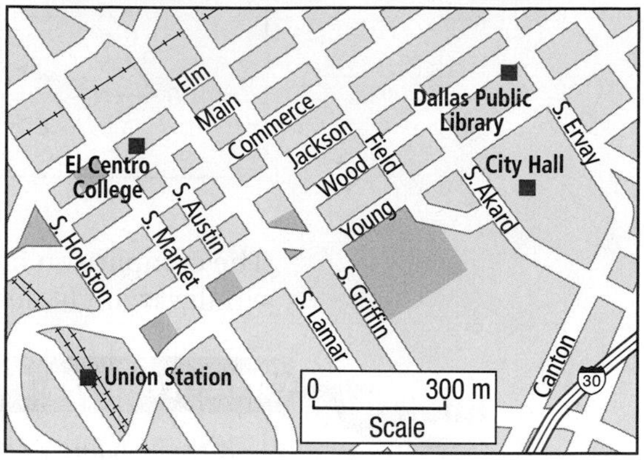

Use a ruler to measure the distance between Union Station and the Dallas Public Library. The distance is 6 cm.

> **Remember!**
> A proportion may compare measurements that have different units.

To find the actual distance x write a proportion comparing the map distance to the actual distance.

$$\frac{6}{x} = \frac{1.5}{300}$$

$1.5x = 6(300)$	*Cross Products Prop.*
$1.5x = 1800$	*Simplify.*
$x = 1200$	*Divide both sides by 1.5.*

The actual distance is 1200 m, or 1.2 km.

CHECK IT OUT! **2.** Find the actual distance between City Hall and El Centro College.

EXAMPLE 3 Making a Scale Drawing

The Lincoln Memorial in Washington, D.C., is approximately 57 m long and 36 m wide. Make a scale drawing of the base of the building using a scale of 1 cm : 15 m.

Step 1 Set up proportions to find the length ℓ and width w of the scale drawing.

$\frac{\ell}{57} = \frac{1}{15}$	$\frac{w}{36} = \frac{1}{15}$
$15\ell = 57$	$15w = 36$
$\ell = 3.8$ m	$w = 2.4$ cm

Step 2 Use a ruler to draw a rectangle with these dimensions.

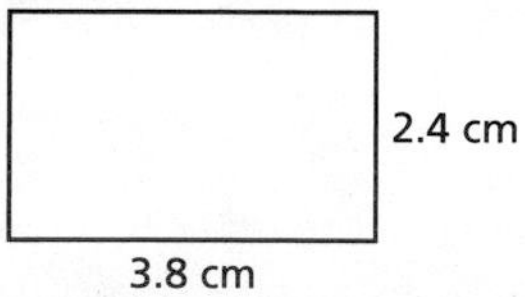

CHECK IT OUT! **3.** The rectangular central chamber of the Lincoln Memorial is 74 ft long and 60 ft wide. Make a scale drawing of the floor of the chamber using a scale of 1 in. : 20 ft.

Similar Triangles — Similarity, Perimeter, and Area Ratios

STATEMENT	RATIO
$\triangle ABC \sim \triangle DEF$ 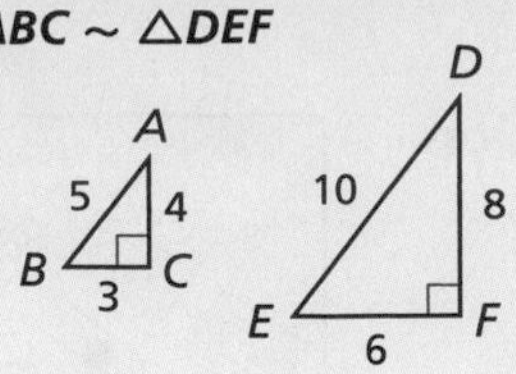	Similarity ratio: $\frac{AB}{DE} = \frac{AC}{DF} = \frac{BC}{EF} = \frac{1}{2}$ Perimeter ratio: $\frac{\text{perimeter } \triangle ABC}{\text{perimeter } \triangle DEF} = \frac{12}{24} = \frac{1}{2}$ Area ratio: $\frac{\text{area } \triangle ABC}{\text{area } \triangle DEF} = \frac{6}{24} = \frac{1}{4} = \left(\frac{1}{2}\right)^2$

The comparison of the similarity ratio and the ratio of perimeters and areas of similar triangles leads to the following theorem.

Theorem 7-5-1 — Proportional Perimeters and Areas Theorem

If the similarity ratio of two similar figures is $\frac{a}{b}$, then the ratio of their perimeters is $\frac{a}{b}$, and the ratio of their areas is $\frac{a^2}{b^2}$, or $\left(\frac{a}{b}\right)^2$.

You will prove Theorem 7-5-1 in Exercises 44 and 45.

EXAMPLE 4 Using Ratios to Find Perimeters and Areas

Given that $\triangle RST \sim \triangle UVW$, find the perimeter P and area A of $\triangle UVW$.

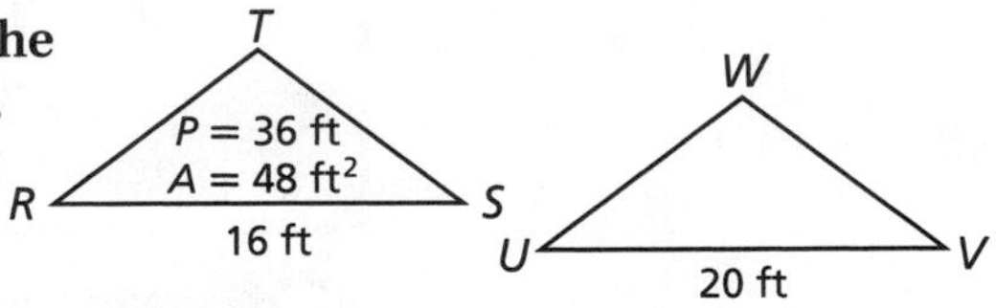

The similarity ratio of $\triangle RST$ to $\triangle UVW$ is $\frac{16}{20}$, or $\frac{4}{5}$.

By the Proportional Perimeters and Areas Theorem, the ratio of the triangles' perimeters is also $\frac{4}{5}$, and the ratio of the triangles' areas is $\left(\frac{4}{5}\right)^2$, or $\frac{16}{25}$.

Perimeter	Area
$\frac{36}{P} = \frac{4}{5}$	$\frac{48}{A} = \frac{16}{25}$
$4P = 5(36)$	$16A = 25 \cdot 48$
$P = 45$ ft	$A = 75 \text{ ft}^2$

The perimeter of $\triangle UVW$ is 45 ft, and the area is 75 ft^2.

CHECK IT OUT! 4. $\triangle ABC \sim \triangle DEF$, $BC = 4$ mm, and $EF = 12$ mm. If $P = 42$ mm and $A = 96 \text{ mm}^2$ for $\triangle DEF$, find the perimeter and area of $\triangle ABC$.

MATHEMATICAL PRACTICES

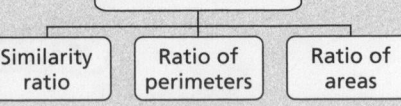

THINK AND DISCUSS

1. Explain how to find the actual distance between two cities 5.5 in. apart on a map that has a scale of 1 in. : 25 mi.
2. **GET ORGANIZED** Copy and complete the graphic organizer. Draw and measure two similar figures. Then write their ratios.

Similar Figures
- Similarity ratio
- Ratio of perimeters
- Ratio of areas

7-5 Exercises

Learn It Online
Homework Help Online
Parent Resources Online

GUIDED PRACTICE

1. **Vocabulary** Finding distances using similar triangles is called ___?___. (*indirect measurement* or *scale drawing*)

SEE EXAMPLE 1

2. **Measurement** To find the height of a dinosaur in a museum, Amir placed a mirror on the ground 40 ft from its base. Then he stepped back 4 ft so that he could see the top of the dinosaur in the mirror. Amir's eyes were approximately 5 ft 6 in. above the ground. What is the height of the dinosaur?

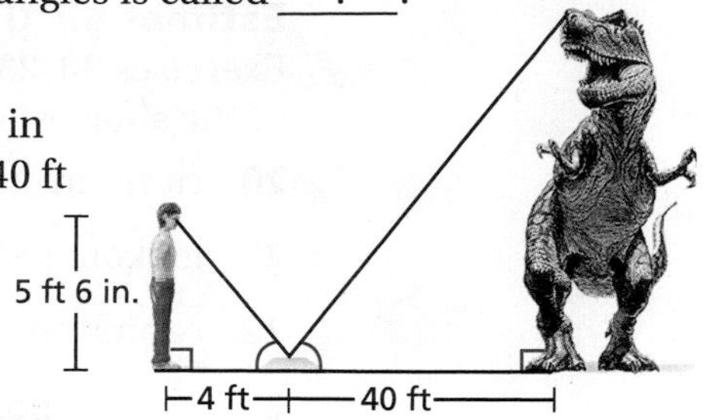

SEE EXAMPLE 2

The scale of this blueprint of an art gallery is 1 in.:48 ft. Find the actual lengths of the following walls.

3. $\overline{AB}$
4. $\overline{CD}$
5. $\overline{EF}$
6. $\overline{FG}$

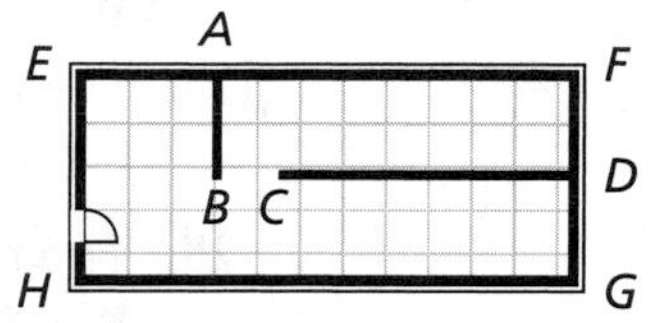

SEE EXAMPLE 3

Multi-Step A rectangular classroom is 10 m long and 4.6 m wide. Make a scale drawing of the classroom using the following scales.

7. 1 cm:1 m
8. 1 cm:2 m
9. 1 cm:2.3 m

SEE EXAMPLE 4

Given: rectangle *MNPQ* ~ rectangle *RSTU*

10. Find the perimeter of rectangle *RSTU*.
11. Find the area of rectangle *RSTU*.

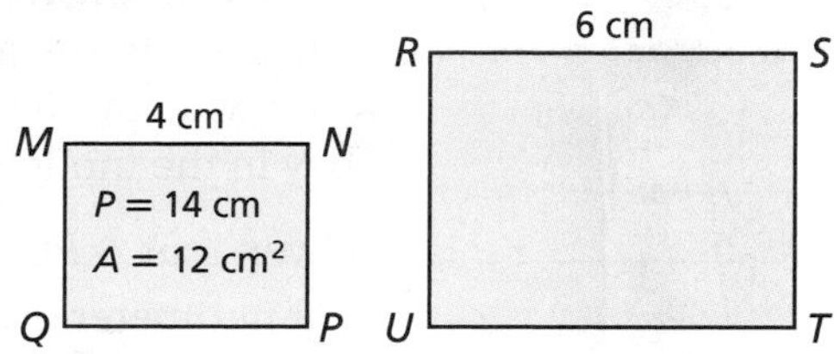

PRACTICE AND PROBLEM SOLVING

Independent Practice

For Exercises	See Example
12	1
13–14	2
15–17	3
18–19	4

Extra Practice

See Extra Practice for more Skills Practice and Applications Practice exercises.

12. **Measurement** Jenny is 5 ft 2 in. tall. To find the height of a light pole, she measured her shadow and the pole's shadow. What is the height of the pole?

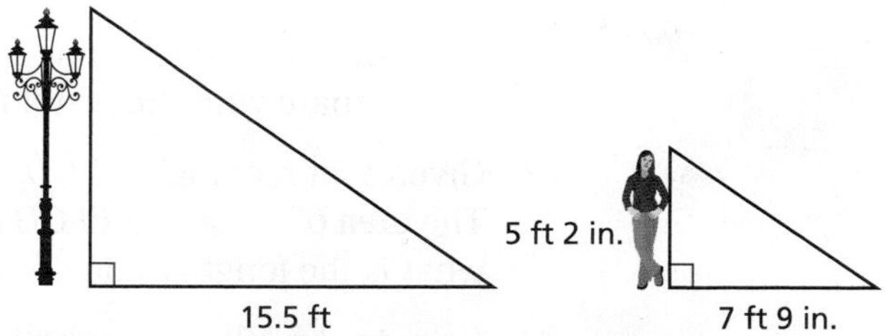

Space Exploration Use the following information for Exercises 13 and 14.

This is a map of the Mars Exploration Rover *Opportunity's* predicted landing site on Mars. The scale is 1 cm:9.4 km. What are the approximate measures of the actual length and width of the ellipse?

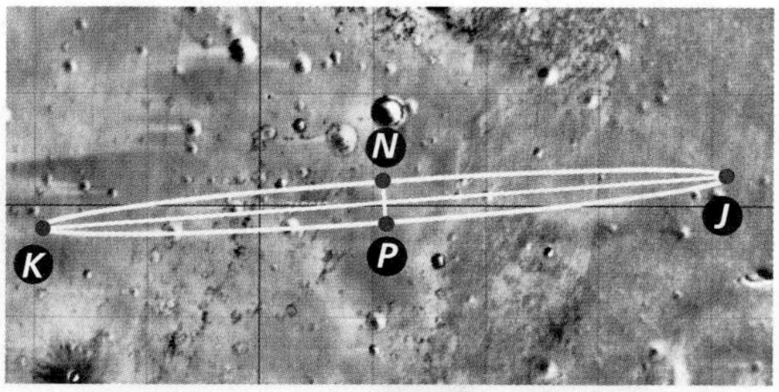

13. *KJ*
14. *NP*

Multi-Step A park at the end of a city block is a right triangle with legs 150 ft and 200 ft long. Make a scale drawing of the park using the following scales.

15. 1.5 in.:100 ft
16. 1 in.:300 ft
17. 1 in.:150 ft

Given that pentagon $ABCDE \sim$ pentagon $FGHJK$, find each of the following.

18. perimeter of pentagon $FGHJK$

19. area of pentagon $FGHJK$

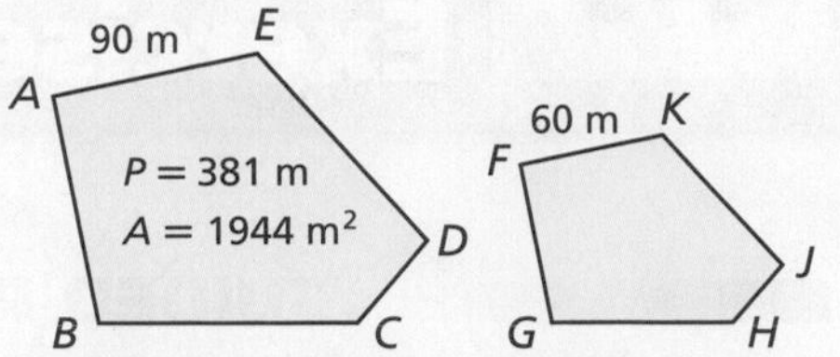

Estimation Use the scale on the map for Exercises 20–23. Give the approximate distance of the shortest route between each pair of sites.

20. campfire and the lake

21. lookout point and the campfire

22. cabins and the dining hall

23. lookout point and the lake

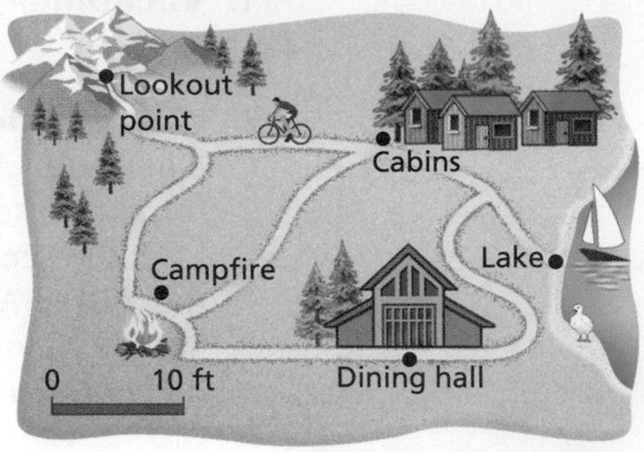

Given: $\triangle ABC \sim \triangle DEF$

24. The ratio of the perimeter of $\triangle ABC$ to the perimeter of $\triangle DEF$ is $\frac{8}{9}$. What is the similarity ratio of $\triangle ABC$ to $\triangle DEF$?

25. The ratio of the area of $\triangle ABC$ to the area of $\triangle DEF$ is $\frac{16}{25}$. What is the similarity ratio of $\triangle ABC$ to $\triangle DEF$?

26. The ratio of the area of $\triangle ABC$ to the area of $\triangle DEF$ is $\frac{4}{81}$. What is the ratio of the perimeter of $\triangle ABC$ to the perimeter of $\triangle DEF$?

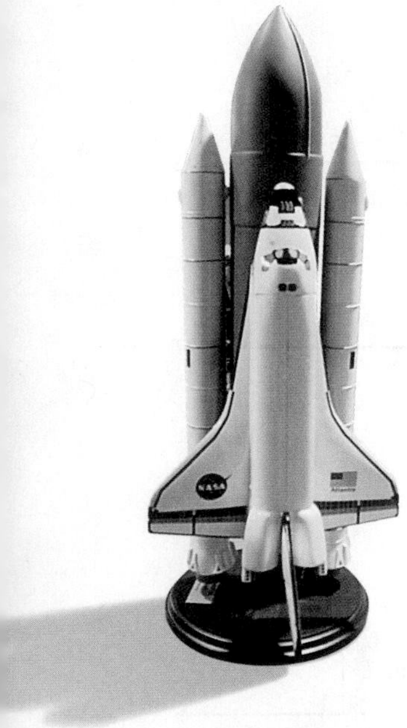

27. **Space Exploration** The scale of this model of the space shuttle is 1 ft : 50 ft. In the actual space shuttle, the main cargo bay measures 15 ft wide by 60 ft long. What are the dimensions of the cargo bay in the model?

28. Given that $\triangle PQR \sim \triangle WXY$, find each ratio.

a. $\dfrac{\text{perimeter of } \triangle PQR}{\text{perimeter of } \triangle WXY}$

b. $\dfrac{\text{area of } \triangle PQR}{\text{area of } \triangle WXY}$

c. How does the result in part **a** compare with the result in part **b**?

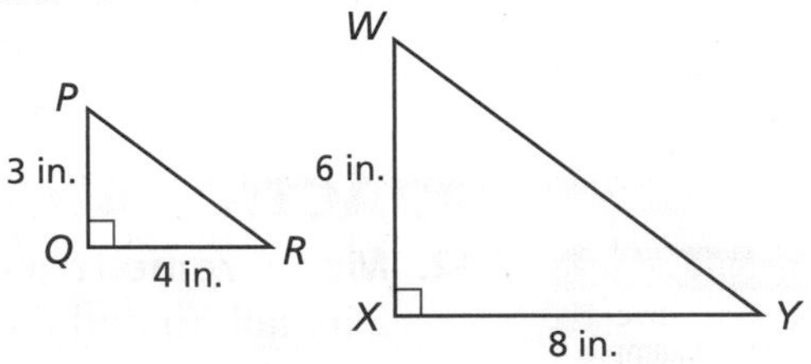

29. Given that rectangle $ABCD \sim EFGH$. The area of rectangle $ABCD$ is 135 in^2. The area of rectangle $EFGH$ is 240 in^2. If the width of rectangle $ABCD$ is 9 in., what is the length and width of rectangle $EFGH$?

30. **Sports** An NBA basketball court is 94 ft long and 50 ft wide. Make a scale drawing of a court using a scale of $\frac{1}{4}$ in. : 10 ft.

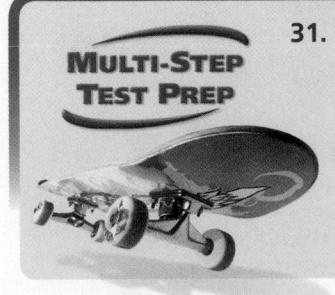

MULTI-STEP TEST PREP

31. A blueprint for a skateboard ramp has a scale of 1 in. : 2 ft. On the blueprint, the rectangular piece of wood that forms the ramp measures 2 in. by 3 in.

a. What is the similarity ratio of the blueprint to the actual ramp?

b. What is the ratio of the area of the ramp on the blueprint to its actual area?

c. Find the area of the actual ramp.

32. **Estimation** The photo shows a person who is 5 ft 1 in. tall standing by a statue in Jamestown, North Dakota. Estimate the actual height of the head of the statue by using a ruler to measure her height and the height of the head of the statue in the photo.

33. **Math History** In A.D. 1076, the mathematician Shen Kua was asked by the emperor of China to produce maps of all Chinese territories. Shen created 23 maps, each drawn with a scale of 1 cm:900,000 cm. How many centimeters long would a 1 km road be on such a map?

34. Points X, Y, and Z are the midpoints of $\overline{JK}$, $\overline{KL}$, and $\overline{LJ}$, respectively. What is the ratio of the area of $\triangle JKL$ to the area of $\triangle XYZ$?

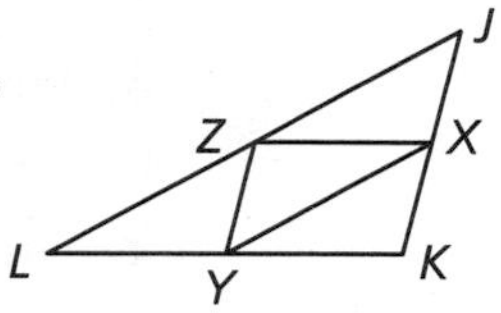

35. **Critical Thinking** Keisha is making two scale drawings of her school. In one drawing, she uses a scale of 1 cm:1 m. In the other drawing, she uses a scale of 1 cm:5 m. Which of these scales will produce a smaller drawing? Explain.

36. The ratio of the perimeter of square $ABCD$ to the perimeter of square $EFGH$ is $\frac{4}{9}$. Find the side lengths of each square.

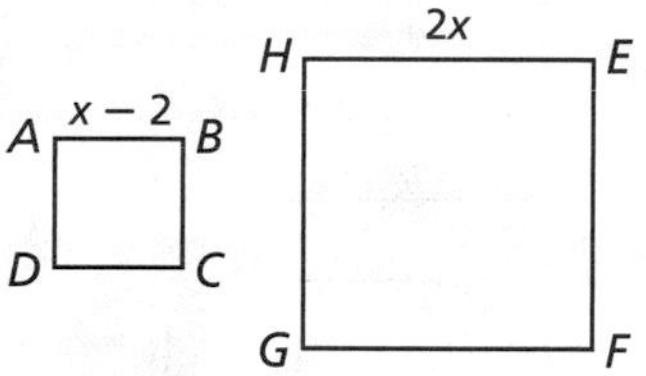

37. **Write About It** Explain what it would mean to make a scale drawing with a scale of 1:1.

38. **Write About It** One square has twice the area of another square. Explain why it is impossible for both squares to have side lengths that are whole numbers.

TEST PREP

39. $\triangle ABC \sim \triangle RST$, and the area of $\triangle ABC$ is 24 m^2. What is the area of $\triangle RST$?

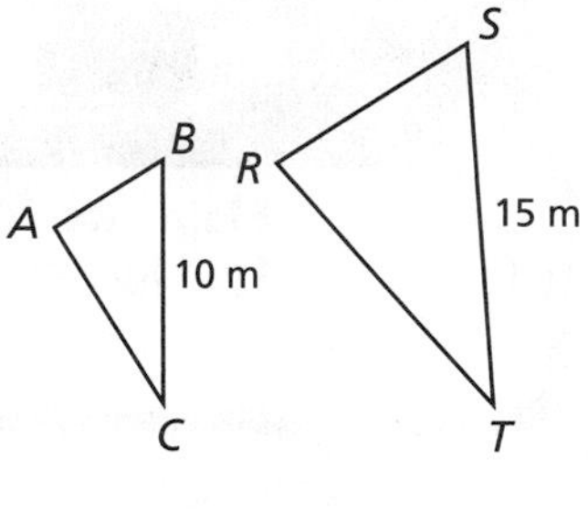

Ⓐ 16 m^2 Ⓒ 36 m^2
Ⓑ 29 m^2 Ⓓ 54 m^2

40. A blueprint for a museum uses a scale of $\frac{1}{4}$ in.:1 ft. One of the rooms on the blueprint is $3\frac{3}{4}$ in. long. How long is the actual room?

Ⓕ 4 ft Ⓖ 15 ft Ⓗ 45 ft Ⓙ 180 ft

41. The similarity ratio of two similar pentagons is $\frac{9}{4}$. What is the ratio of the perimeters of the pentagons?

Ⓐ $\frac{2}{3}$ Ⓑ $\frac{3}{2}$ Ⓒ $\frac{9}{4}$ Ⓓ $\frac{81}{16}$

42. Of two similar triangles, the second triangle has sides half the length of the first. Given that the area of the first triangle is 16 ft^2, find the area of the second.

Ⓕ 4 ft^2 Ⓖ 8 ft^2 Ⓗ 16 ft^2 Ⓙ 32 ft^2

CHALLENGE AND EXTEND

43. **Astronomy** The Falkland Islands has a scale model of the solar system nearly 6 km long. The model's scale is 1 km : 1 billion km.
    a. Earth is 150,000,000 km from the Sun. How many meters apart are Earth and the Sun in the model?
    b. The diameter of Earth is 12,800 km. What is the diameter, in centimeters, of Earth in the model?

44. **Given:** $\triangle ABC \sim \triangle DEF$
    Prove: $\dfrac{AB + BC + AC}{DE + EF + DF} = \dfrac{AB}{DE}$

45. **Given:** $\triangle PQR \sim \triangle WXY$
    Prove: $\dfrac{\text{Area } \triangle PQR}{\text{Area } \triangle WXY} = \dfrac{PR^2}{WY^2}$

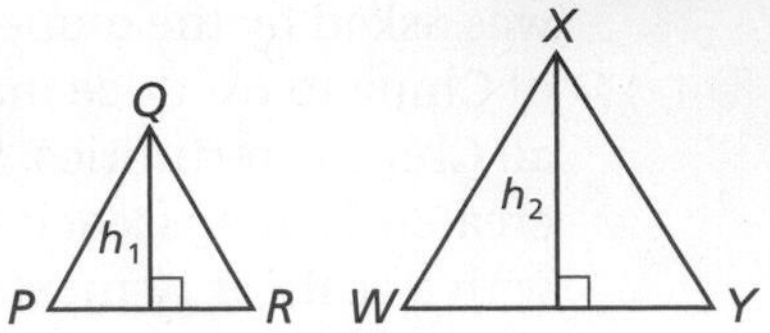

46. Quadrilateral *PQRS* has side lengths of 6 m, 7 m, 10 m, and 12 m. The similarity ratio of quadrilateral *PQRS* to quadrilateral *WXYZ* is 1 : 2.
    a. Find the lengths of the sides of quadrilateral *WXYZ*.
    b. Make a table of the lengths of the sides of both figures.
    c. Graph the data in the table.
    d. Determine an equation that relates the lengths of the sides of quadrilateral *PQRS* to the lengths of the sides of quadrilateral *WXYZ*.

Career Path

Learn It Online
Career Resources Online

Elaine Koch
Photogrammetrist

Q: What math classes did you take in high school?
A: Algebra, Geometry, and Probability and Statistics

Q: What math-related classes did you take in college?
A: Trigonometry, Precalculus, Drafting, and System Design

Q: How do photogrammetrists use math?
A: Photogrammetrists use aerial photographs to make detailed maps. To prepare maps, I use computers and perform a lot of scale measures to make sure the maps are accurate.

Q: What are your future plans?
A: My favorite part of making maps is designing scale drawings. Someday I'd like to apply these skills toward architectural work.

COMMON CORE

7-6 Dilations and Similarity in the Coordinate Plane

CC.9-12.G.CO.2 Represent transformations in the plane... *Also* **CC.9-12.G.SRT.1, CC.9-12.G.MG.3***

Objectives

Apply similarity properties in the coordinate plane.

Use coordinate proof to prove figures similar.

Vocabulary

dilation

scale factor

Who uses this?

Computer programmers use coordinates to enlarge or reduce images.

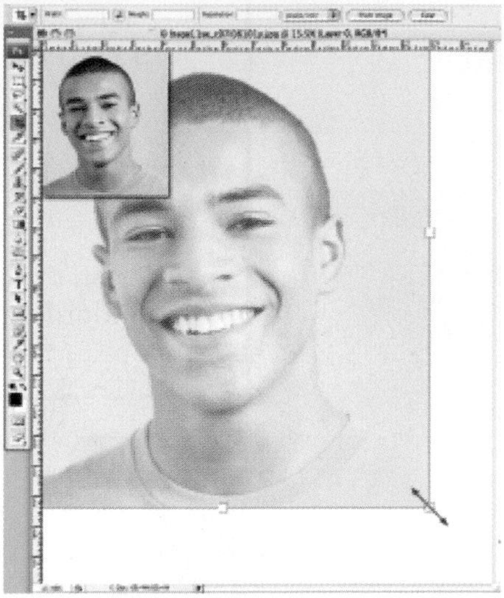

Many photographs on the Web are in JPEG format, which is short for Joint Photographic Experts Group. When you drag a corner of a JPEG image in order to enlarge it or reduce it, the underlying program uses coordinates and similarity to change the image's size.

A **dilation** is a transformation that changes the size of a figure but not its shape. The preimage and the image are always similar. A **scale factor** describes how much the figure is enlarged or reduced. For a dilation with scale factor k, you can find the image of a point by multiplying each coordinate by k: $(a, b) \rightarrow (ka, kb)$.

EXAMPLE 1 *Computer Graphics Application*

The figure shows the position of a JPEG photo. Draw the border of the photo after a dilation with scale factor $\frac{3}{2}$.

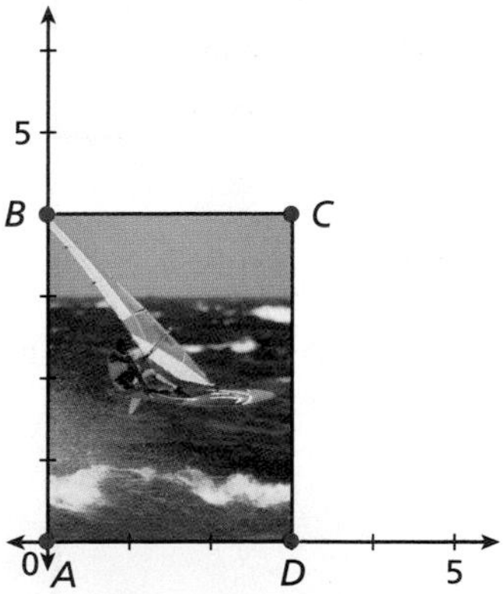

Step 1 Multiply the vertices of the photo $A(0, 0)$, $B(0, 4)$, $C(3, 4)$, and $D(3, 0)$ by $\frac{3}{2}$.

Rectangle *ABCD*	Rectangle *A′B′C′D′*
$A(0, 0) \rightarrow A'\left(0 \cdot \frac{3}{2}, 0 \cdot \frac{3}{2}\right)$	$\rightarrow A'(0, 0)$
$B(0, 4) \rightarrow B'\left(0 \cdot \frac{3}{2}, 4 \cdot \frac{3}{2}\right)$	$\rightarrow B'(0, 6)$
$C(3, 4) \rightarrow C'\left(3 \cdot \frac{3}{2}, 4 \cdot \frac{3}{2}\right)$	$\rightarrow C'(4.5, 6)$
$D(3, 0) \rightarrow D'\left(3 \cdot \frac{3}{2}, 0 \cdot \frac{3}{2}\right)$	$\rightarrow D'(4.5, 0)$

Step 2 Plot points $A'(0, 0)$, $B'(0, 6)$, $C'(4.5, 6)$, and $D'(4.5, 0)$. Draw the rectangle.

Helpful Hint

If the scale factor of a dilation is greater than 1 ($k > 1$), it is an *enlargement*. If the scale factor is less than 1 ($k < 1$), it is a *reduction*.

CHECK IT OUT!

1. What if...? Draw the border of the original photo after a dilation with scale factor $\frac{1}{2}$.

EXAMPLE 2 Finding Coordinates of Similar Triangles

Given that $\triangle AOB \sim \triangle COD$, find the coordinates of D and the scale factor.

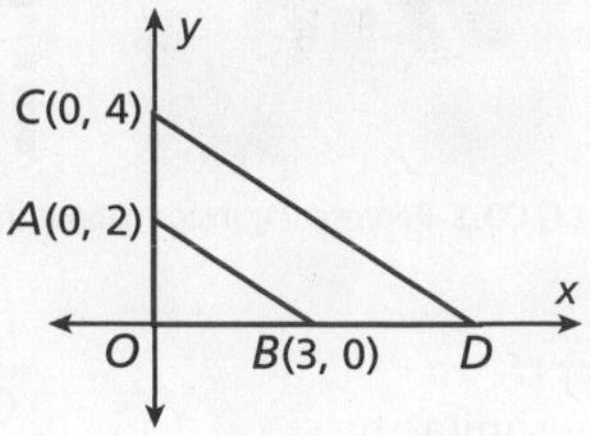

Since $\triangle AOB \sim \triangle COD$,

$$\frac{AO}{CO} = \frac{OB}{OD}$$

$$\frac{2}{4} = \frac{3}{OD}$$ *Substitute 2 for AO, 4 for CO, and 3 for OB.*

$$2OD = 12$$ *Cross Products Prop.*

$$OD = 6$$ *Divide both sides by 2.*

D lies on the x-axis, so its y-coordinate is 0. Since $OD = 6$, its x-coordinate must be 6. The coordinates of D are $(6, 0)$. $(3, 0) \rightarrow (3 \cdot 2, 0 \cdot 2) \rightarrow (6, 0)$, so the scale factor is 2.

CHECK IT OUT!

2. Given that $\triangle MON \sim \triangle POQ$ and coordinates $P(-15, 0)$, $M(-10, 0)$, and $Q(0, -30)$, find the coordinates of N and the scale factor.

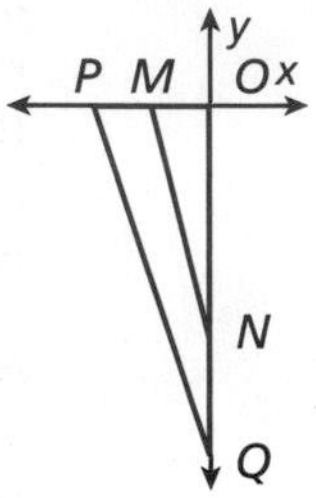

EXAMPLE 3 Proving Triangles Are Similar

Given: $A(1, 5)$, $B(-1, 3)$, $C(3, 4)$, $D(-3, 1)$, and $E(5, 3)$

Prove: $\triangle ABC \sim \triangle ADE$

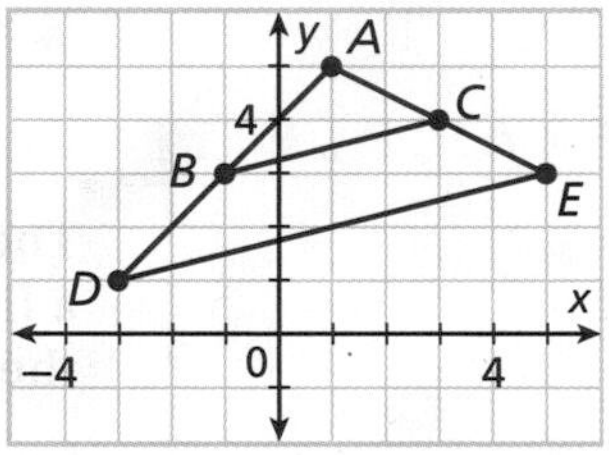

Step 1 Plot the points and draw the triangles.

Step 2 Use the Distance Formula to find the side lengths.

$$AB = \sqrt{(-1 - 1)^2 + (3 - 5)^2} = \sqrt{8} = 2\sqrt{2}$$

$$AC = \sqrt{(3 - 1)^2 + (4 - 5)^2} = \sqrt{5}$$

$$AD = \sqrt{(-3 - 1)^2 + (1 - 5)^2} = \sqrt{32} = 4\sqrt{2}$$

$$AE = \sqrt{(5 - 1)^2 + (3 - 5)^2} = \sqrt{20} = 2\sqrt{5}$$

Step 3 Find the similarity ratio.

$$\frac{AB}{AD} = \frac{2\sqrt{2}}{4\sqrt{2}} = \frac{2}{4} = \frac{1}{2}$$

$$\frac{AC}{AE} = \frac{\sqrt{5}}{2\sqrt{5}} = \frac{1}{2}$$

Since $\frac{AB}{AD} = \frac{AC}{AE}$ and $\angle A \cong \angle A$ by the Reflexive Property, $\triangle ABC \sim \triangle ADE$ by SAS $\sim$.

CHECK IT OUT!

3. Given: $R(-2, 0)$, $S(-3, 1)$, $T(0, 1)$, $U(-5, 3)$, and $V(4, 3)$
Prove: $\triangle RST \sim \triangle RUV$

EXAMPLE 4 Using the SSS Similarity Theorem

Graph the image of $\triangle ABC$ after a dilation with scale factor 2. Verify that $\triangle A'B'C' \sim \triangle ABC$.

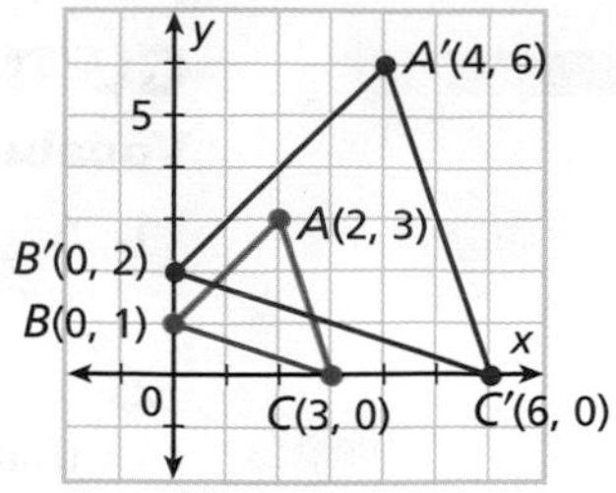

Step 1 Multiply each coordinate by 2 to find the coordinates of the vertices of $\triangle A'B'C'$.

$$A(2, 3) \rightarrow A'(2 \cdot 2, 3 \cdot 2) = A'(4, 6)$$
$$B(0, 1) \rightarrow B'(0 \cdot 2, 1 \cdot 2) = B'(0, 2)$$
$$C(3, 0) \rightarrow C'(3 \cdot 2, 0 \cdot 2) = C'(6, 0)$$

Step 2 Graph $\triangle A'B'C'$.

Step 3 Use the Distance Formula to find the side lengths.

$$AB = \sqrt{(2-0)^2 + (3-1)^2} = \sqrt{8} = 2\sqrt{2} \qquad A'B' = \sqrt{(4-0)^2 + (6-2)^2} = \sqrt{32} = 4\sqrt{2}$$

$$BC = \sqrt{(3-0)^2 + (0-1)^2} = \sqrt{10} \qquad B'C' = \sqrt{(6-0)^2 + (0-2)^2} = \sqrt{40} = 2\sqrt{10}$$

$$AC = \sqrt{(3-2)^2 + (0-3)^2} = \sqrt{10} \qquad A'C' = \sqrt{(6-4)^2 + (0-6)^2} = \sqrt{40} = 2\sqrt{10}$$

Step 4 Find the similarity ratio.

$$\frac{A'B'}{AB} = \frac{4\sqrt{2}}{2\sqrt{2}} = 2, \quad \frac{B'C'}{BC} = \frac{2\sqrt{10}}{\sqrt{10}} = 2, \quad \frac{A'C'}{AC} = \frac{2\sqrt{10}}{\sqrt{10}} = 2$$

Since $\frac{A'B'}{AB} = \frac{B'C'}{BC} = \frac{A'C'}{AC}$, $\triangle ABC \sim \triangle A'B'C'$ by SSS $\sim$.

CHECK IT OUT!

4. Graph the image of $\triangle MNP$ after a dilation with scale factor 3. Verify that $\triangle M'N'P' \sim \triangle MNP$.

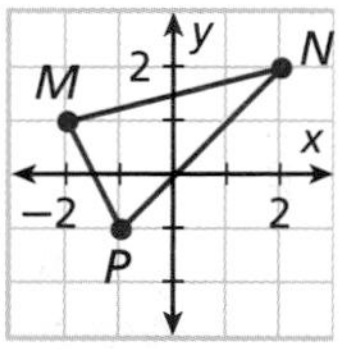

MATHEMATICAL PRACTICES

THINK AND DISCUSS

1. $\triangle JKL$ has coordinates $J(0, 0)$, $K(0, 2)$, and $L(3, 0)$. Its image after a dilation has coordinates $J'(0, 0)$, $K'(0, 8)$, and $L'(12, 0)$. Explain how to find the scale factor of the dilation.

Know it! Note

2. GET ORGANIZED Copy and complete the graphic organizer. Write the definition of a dilation, a property of dilations, and an example and nonexample of a dilation.

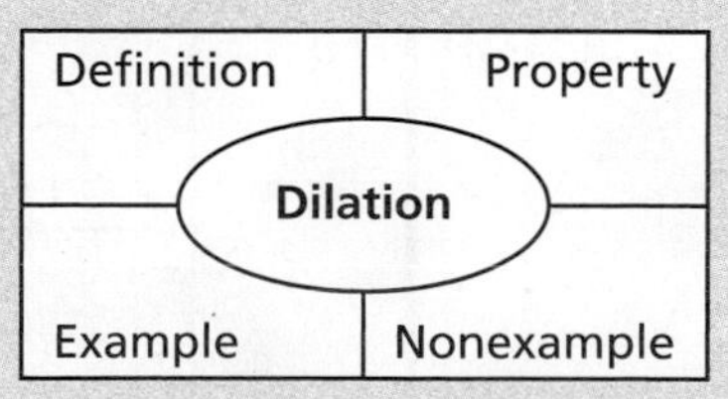

7-6 Exercises

GUIDED PRACTICE

Vocabulary **Apply the vocabulary from this lesson to answer each question.**

1. A __?__ is a transformation that proportionally reduces or enlarges a figure, such as the pupil of an eye. (*dilation* or *scale factor*)

2. A ratio that describes or determines the dimensional relationship of a figure to that which it represents, such as a map scale of 1 in.: 45 ft, is called a __?__. (*dilation* or *scale factor*)

SEE EXAMPLE 1

3. **Graphic Design** A designer created this logo for a real estate agent but needs to make the logo twice as large for use on a sign. Draw the logo after a dilation with scale factor 2.

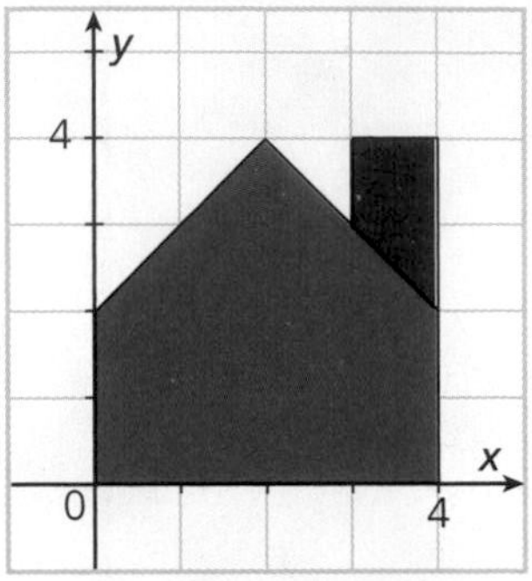

SEE EXAMPLE 2

4. Given that $\triangle AOB \sim \triangle COD$, find the coordinates of C and the scale factor.

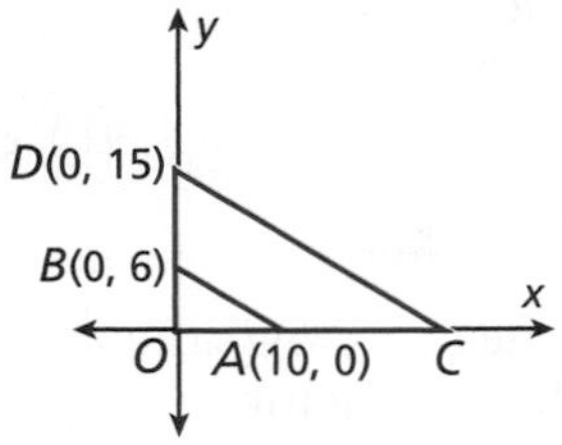

5. Given that $\triangle ROS \sim \triangle POQ$, find the coordinates of S and the scale factor.

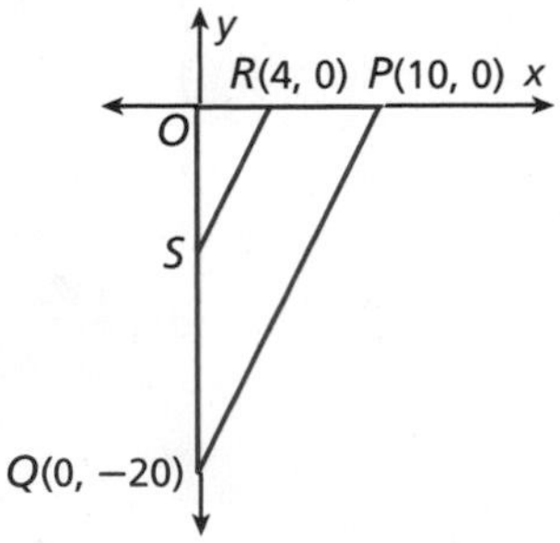

SEE EXAMPLE 3

6. **Given:** $A(0, 0)$, $B(-1, 1)$, $C(3, 2)$, $D(-2, 2)$, and $E(6, 4)$
   Prove: $\triangle ABC \sim \triangle ADE$

7. **Given:** $J(-1, 0)$, $K(-3, -4)$, $L(3, -2)$, $M(-4, -6)$, and $N(5, -3)$
   Prove: $\triangle JKL \sim \triangle JMN$

SEE EXAMPLE 4

Multi-Step **Graph the image of each triangle after a dilation with the given scale factor. Then verify that the image is similar to the given triangle.**

8. scale factor 2

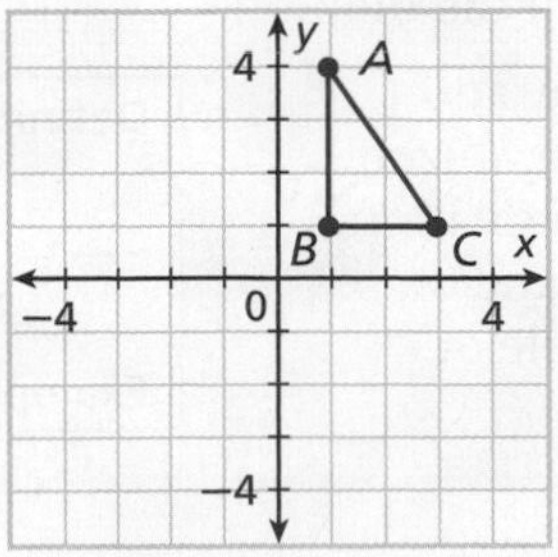

9. scale factor $\frac{3}{2}$

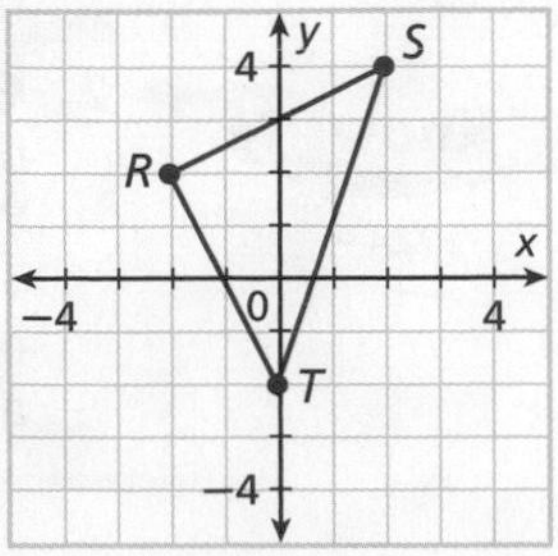

PRACTICE AND PROBLEM SOLVING

Independent Practice	
For Exercises	See Example
10	1
11–12	2
13–14	3
15–16	4

Extra Practice

See Extra Practice for more Skills Practice and Applications Practice exercises.

10. **Advertising** A promoter produced this design for a street festival. She now wants to make the design smaller to use on postcards. Sketch the design after a dilation with scale factor $\frac{1}{2}$.

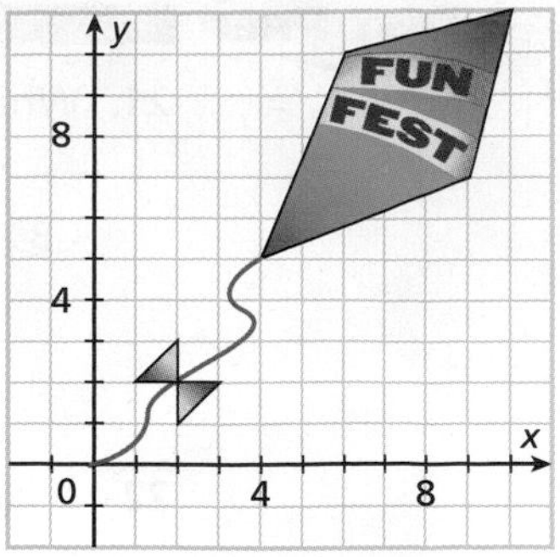

11. Given that $\triangle UOV \sim \triangle XOY$, find the coordinates of X and the scale factor.

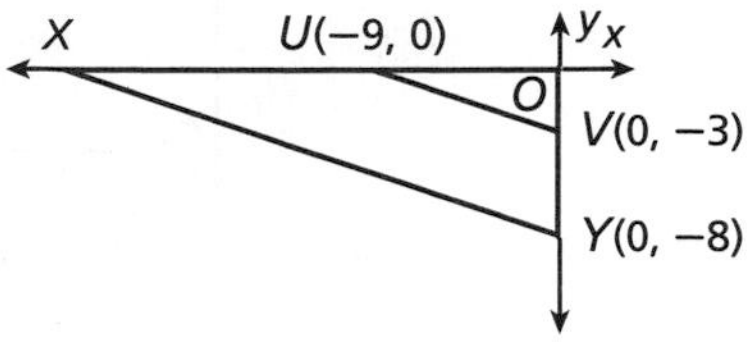

12. Given that $\triangle MON \sim \triangle KOL$, find the coordinates of K and the scale factor.

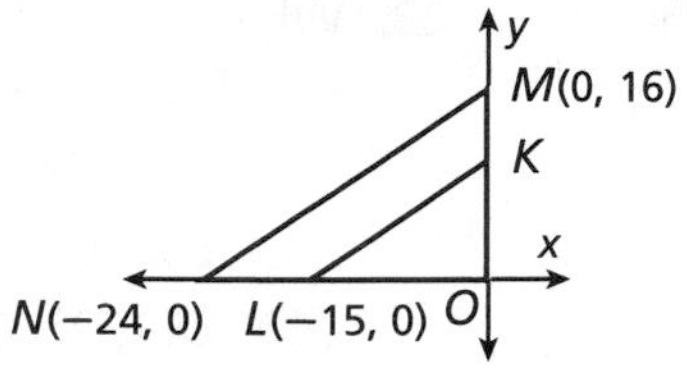

13. **Given:** $D(-1, 3)$, $E(-3, -1)$, $F(3, -1)$, $G(-4, -3)$, and $H(5, -3)$
Prove: $\triangle DEF \sim \triangle DGH$

14. **Given:** $M(0, 10)$, $N(5, 0)$, $P(15, 15)$, $Q(10, -10)$, and $R(30, 20)$
Prove: $\triangle MNP \sim \triangle MQR$

Multi-Step Graph the image of each triangle after a dilation with the given scale factor. Then verify that the image is similar to the given triangle.

15. $J(-2, 0)$ and $K(-1, -1)$, and $L(-3, -2)$ with scale factor 3

16. $M(0, 4)$, $N(4, 2)$, and $P(2, -2)$ with scale factor $\frac{1}{2}$

17. **Critical Thinking** Consider the transformation given by the mapping $(x, y) \rightarrow (2x, 4y)$. Is this transformation a dilation? Why or why not?

18. **/// ERROR ANALYSIS ///** Which solution to find the scale factor of the dilation that maps $\triangle RST$ to $\triangle UVW$ is incorrect? Explain the error.

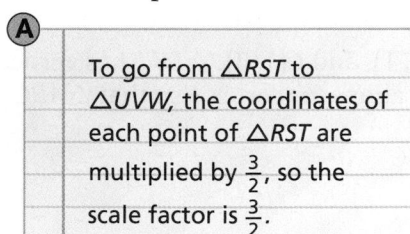

A

To go from $\triangle RST$ to $\triangle UVW$, the coordinates of each point of $\triangle RST$ are multiplied by $\frac{3}{2}$, so the scale factor is $\frac{3}{2}$.

B

The scale factor is the ratio of corresponding measures. Since $\frac{RT}{UW} = \frac{2}{3}$, the scale factor is $\frac{2}{3}$.

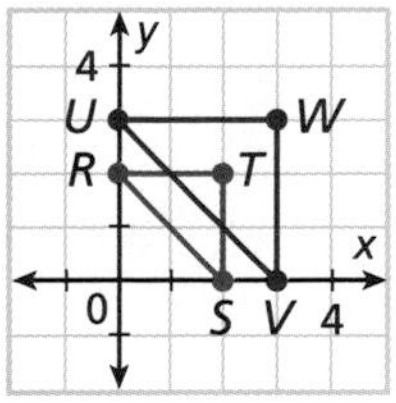

19. **Write About It** A dilation maps $\triangle ABC$ to $\triangle A'B'C'$. How is the scale factor of the dilation related to the similarity ratio of $\triangle ABC$ to $\triangle A'B'C'$? Explain.

MULTI-STEP TEST PREP

20. a. In order to build a skateboard ramp, Miles draws $\triangle JKL$ on a coordinate plane. One unit on the drawing represents 60 cm of actual distance. Explain how he should assign coordinates for the vertices of $\triangle JKL$.

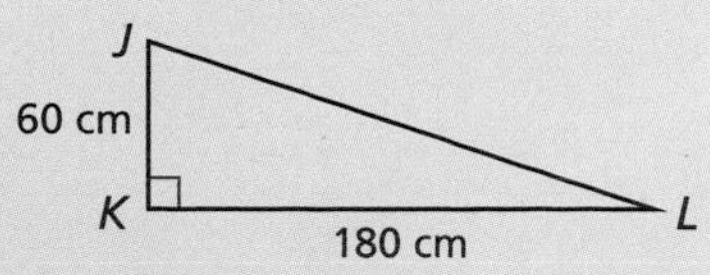

b. Graph the image of $\triangle JKL$ after a dilation with scale factor 3.

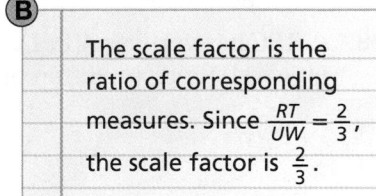

TEST PREP

21. Which coordinates for *C* make $\triangle COD$ similar to $\triangle AOB$?

Ⓐ (0, 2.4) Ⓒ (0, 3)
Ⓑ (0, 2.5) Ⓓ (0, 3.6)

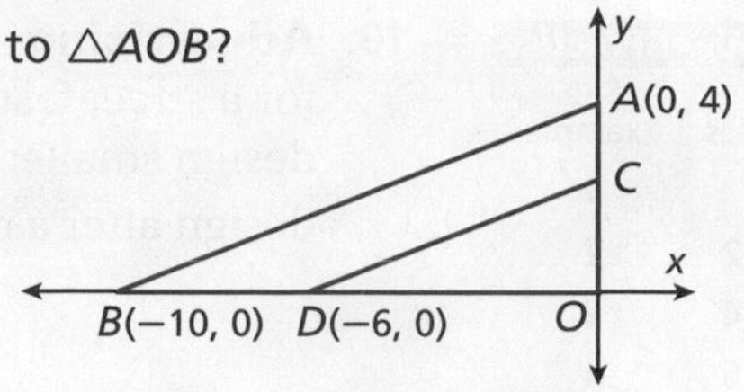

22. A dilation with scale factor 2 maps $\triangle RST$ to $\triangle R'S'T'$. The perimeter of $\triangle RST$ is 60. What is the perimeter of $\triangle R'S'T'$?

Ⓕ 30 Ⓖ 60 Ⓗ 120 Ⓙ 240

23. Which triangle with vertices *D*, *E*, and *F* is similar to $\triangle ABC$?

Ⓐ $D(1, 2)$, $E(3, 2)$, $F(2, 0)$
Ⓑ $D(-1, -2)$, $E(2, -2)$, $F(1, -5)$
Ⓒ $D(1, 2)$, $E(5, 2)$, $F(3, 0)$
Ⓓ $D(-2, -2)$, $E(0, 2)$, $F(-1, 0)$

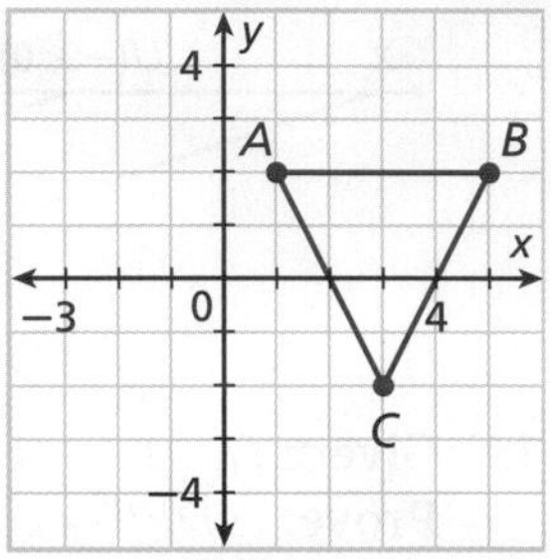

24. Gridded Resonse $\overline{AB}$ with endpoints $A(3, 2)$ and $B(7, 5)$ is dilated by a scale factor of 3. Find the length of $\overline{A'B'}$.

CHALLENGE AND EXTEND

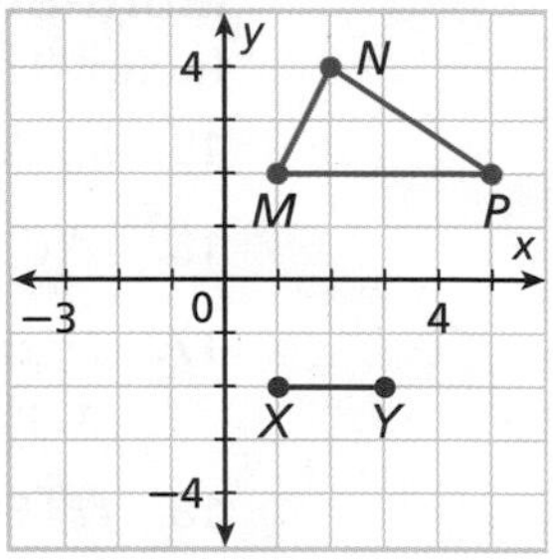

25. How many different triangles having $\overline{XY}$ as a side are similar to $\triangle MNP$?

26. $\triangle XYZ \sim \triangle MPN$. Find the coordinates of *Z*.

27. A rectangle has two of its sides on the *x*- and *y*-axes, a vertex at the origin, and a vertex on the line $y = 2x$. Prove that any two such rectangles are similar.

28. $\triangle ABC$ has vertices $A(0, 1)$, $B(3, 1)$, and $C(1, 3)$. $\triangle DEF$ has vertices $D(1, -1)$ and $E(7, -1)$. Find two different locations for vertex *F* so that $\triangle ABC \sim \triangle DEF$.

COMMON CORE

EXTENSION Segment Partition

CC.9-12.G.GPE.6 Find the point on a...segment...that partitions the segment in a given ratio.

Objectives
Divide a directed line segment into partitions.

A **directed line segment** is a segment between two points A and B with a specified direction, from A to B or from B to A. To partition a directed line segment is to divide it into two segments with a given ratio.

EXAMPLE 1 Finding the Coordinates of a Point in a Directed Line Segment

Vocabulary
directed line segment

Find the point P along the directed line segment from point $A(-8, -7)$ to point $B(8, 5)$ that divides the segment in the ratio 3 to 1.

First, find the rise and run of the directed line segment.

rise $= |-7 - 5| = 12$

run $= |8 - (-8)| = 16$

Point P is $\frac{3}{4}$ of the way between points A and B, so find $\frac{3}{4}$ of both the rise and the run:

$\frac{3}{4}$ of rise $= \frac{3}{4}(12) = 9$

$\frac{3}{4}$ of run $= \frac{3}{4}(16) = 12$

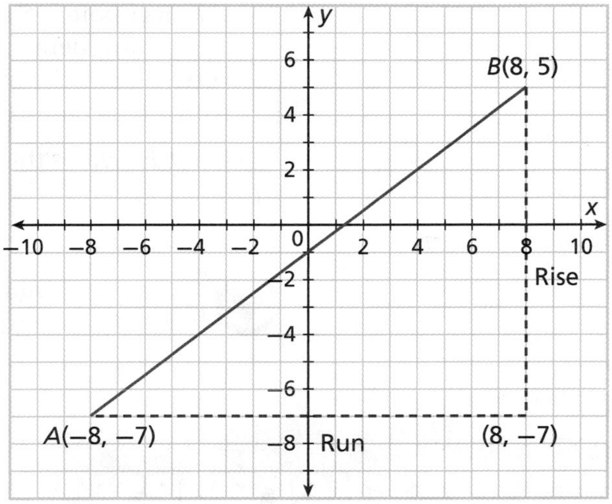

Point P is 9 units up and 12 units right from point A. Its coordinates are $(-8 + 12, -7 + 9)$, or $(4, 2)$.

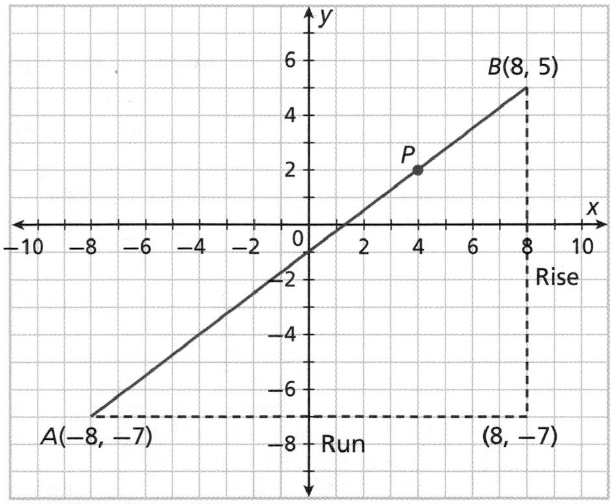

CHECK IT OUT!

1. Find the point Q along the directed line segment from point $R(-2, 4)$ to point $S(18, -6)$ that divides the segment in the ratio 3 to 7.

EXAMPLE 2 **Using Construction to Draw a Point in a Directed Line Segment**

Given the directed line segment from A to B, construct a point G that divides the segment in the ratio 1 to 1 from A to B.

Use a straightedge to draw the ray $\overrightarrow{AC}$. The exact measure of the angle is not important, but the construction is easiest for angles from about 30° to 60°.

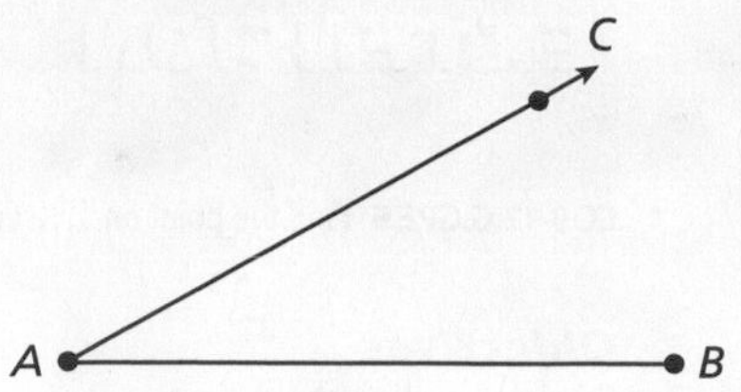

Place the compass point on A and draw an arc through $\overrightarrow{AC}$. Label the intersection D. Using the same compass setting, draw another arc centered on D, and label the intersection E.

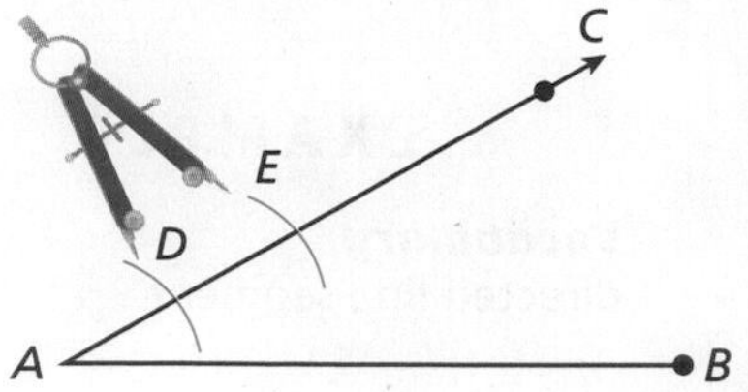

Connect points B and E. Construct an angle congruent to $\angle AEB$ with D as its vertex. Label the intersection of the angle with $\overrightarrow{AB}$ as point F.

Point F divides the segment in the ratio 1 to 2.

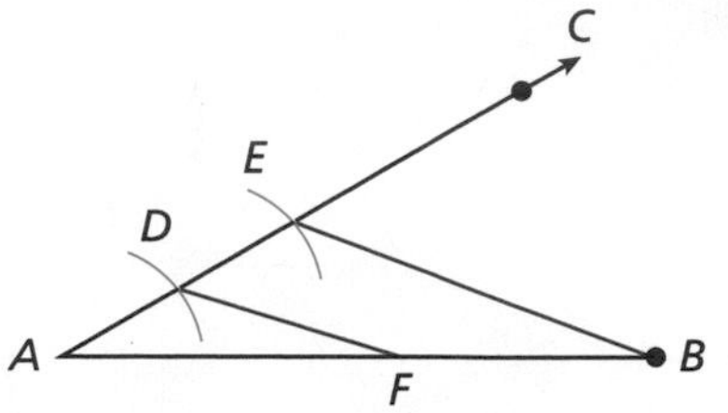

CHECK IT OUT! **2.** Draw a directed line segment from A to B, then construct point P that divides the segment in the ratio 2 to 3 from point B to point A.

EXTENSION Exercises

1. Find the point P along the directed line segment from point A to point B that divides the segment in the ratio 2 to 5.

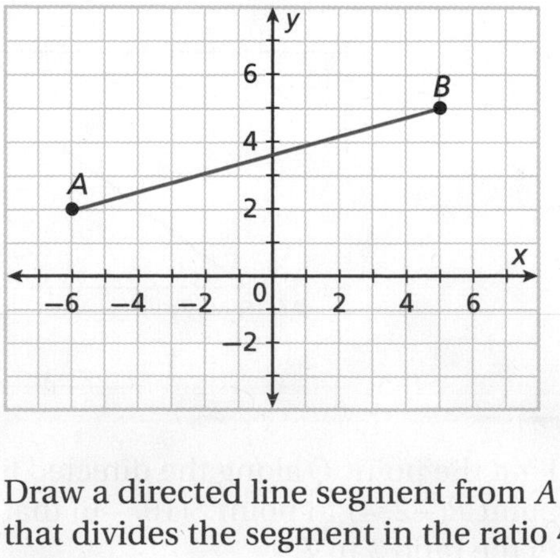

2. Find the point P along the directed line segment from point A to point B that divides the segment in the ratio 1 to 6.

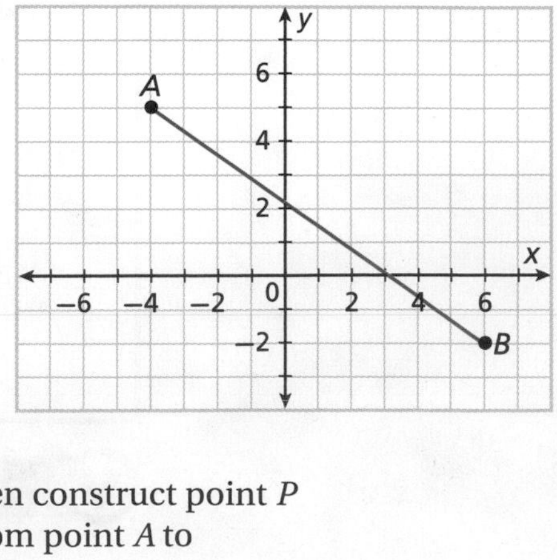

3. Draw a directed line segment from A to B, then construct point P that divides the segment in the ratio 4 to 1 from point A to point B.

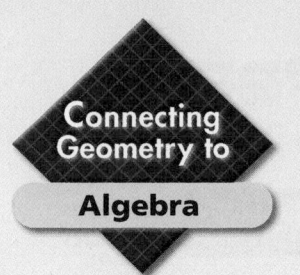

Connecting Geometry to Algebra

Direct Variation

For two similar figures, the measure of each point was multiplied by the same scale factor. Is the relationship between the scale factor and the perimeter of the figure a direct variation?

Recall from algebra that if y varies directly as x, then $y = kx$, or $\frac{y}{x} = k$, where k is the constant of variation.

Example

A rectangle has a length of 4 ft and a width of 2 ft. Find the relationship between the scale factors of similar rectangles and their corresponding perimeters. If the relationship is a direct variation, find the constant of variation.

Step 1 Make a table to record data.

Scale Factor x	Length $\ell = x(4)$	Width $w = x(2)$	Perimeter $P = 2\ell + 2w$
$\frac{1}{2}$	$\ell = \frac{1}{2}(4) = 2$	$w = \frac{1}{2}(2) = 1$	$2(2) + 2(1) = 6$
2	8	4	24
3	12	6	36
4	16	8	48
5	20	10	60

Step 2 Graph the points $\left(\frac{1}{2}, 6\right)$, $(2, 24)$, $(3, 36)$, $(4, 48)$, and $(5, 60)$.

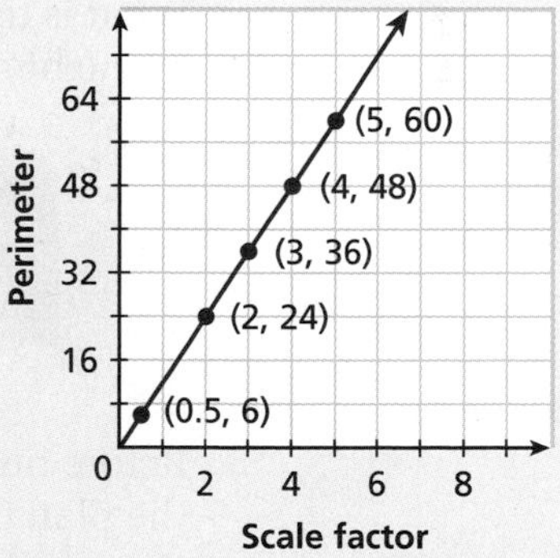

Since the points are collinear and the line that contains them includes the origin, the relationship is a direct variation.

Step 3 Find the equation of direct variation.

$y = kx$

$60 = k(5)$ *Substitute 60 for y and 5 for x.*

$12 = k$ *Divide both sides by 5.*

$y = 12x$ *Substitute 12 for k.*

Thus the constant of variation is 12.

Try This

Use the scale factors given in the above table. Find the relationship between the scale factors of similar figures and their corresponding perimeters. If the relationship is a direct variation, find the constant of variation.

1. regular hexagon with side length 6
2. triangle with side lengths 3, 6, and 7
3. square with side length 3

CHAPTER 7

MULTI-STEP TEST PREP

SECTION 7B

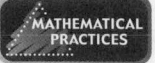

MATHEMATICAL PRACTICES **Model with mathematics.**

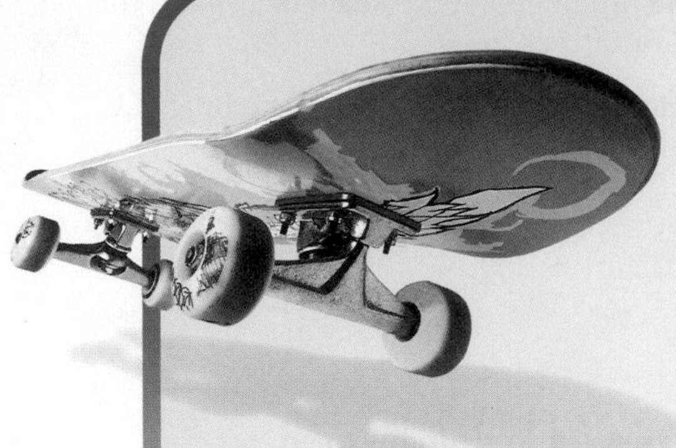

Applying Similarity

Ramp It Up Many companies sell plans for build-it-yourself skateboard ramps. The figures below show a ramp and the plan for the triangular support structure at the side of the ramp. In the plan, $\overline{AB}$, $\overline{EF}$, $\overline{GH}$, and $\overline{JK}$ are perpendicular to the base $\overline{BC}$.

1. The instructions call for extra pieces of wood to reinforce $\overline{AE}$, $\overline{EG}$, $\overline{GJ}$, and $\overline{JC}$. Given $AE = 42.2$ cm, find EG, GJ, and JC to the nearest tenth.

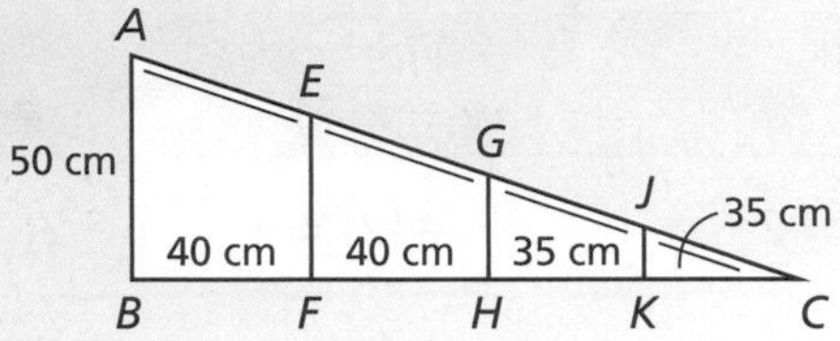

2. Once the support structure is built, it is covered with a triangular piece of plywood. Find the area of the piece of wood needed to cover $\triangle ABC$. A separate blueprint for the ramp uses a scale of 1 cm : 25 cm. What is the area of $\triangle ABC$ in the blueprint?

3. Before building the ramp, you transfer the plan to a coordinate plane. Draw $\triangle ABC$ on a coordinate plane so that 1 unit represents 25 cm and B is at the origin. Then draw the image of $\triangle ABC$ after a dilation with scale factor $\frac{3}{2}$.

READY TO GO ON?

Quiz for Lessons 7-4 Through 7-6

7-4 Applying Properties of Similar Triangles

Find the length of each segment.

1. $\overline{ST}$

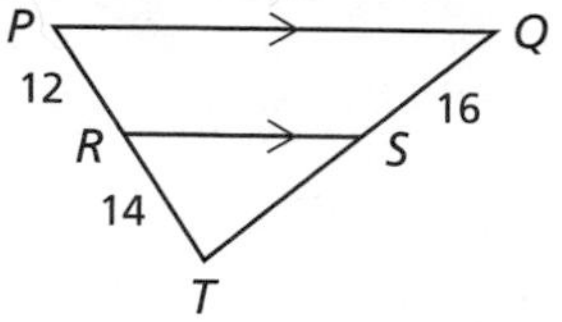

2. $\overline{AB}$ and $\overline{AC}$

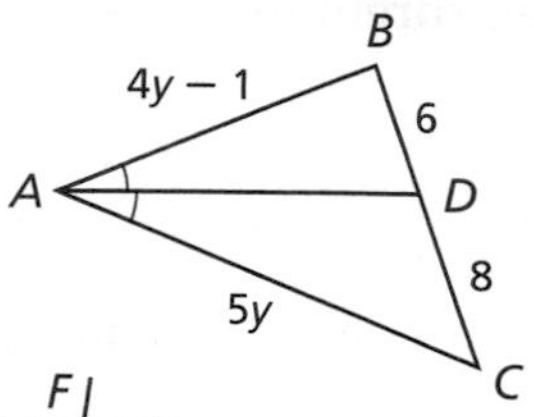

3. An artist drew a picture of railroad tracks such that the ties $\overline{EF}$, $\overline{GH}$, and $\overline{JK}$ are parallel. What is the length of $\overline{FH}$?

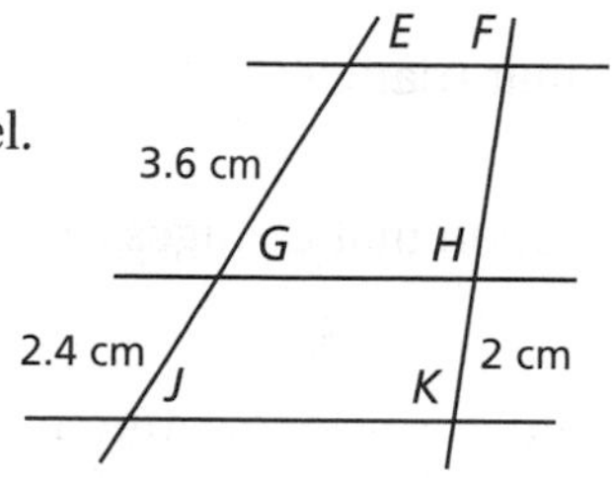

7-5 Using Proportional Relationships

The plan for a restaurant uses the scale of 1.5 in. : 60 ft. Find the actual length of the following walls.

4. $\overline{AB}$
5. $\overline{BC}$
6. $\overline{CD}$
7. $\overline{EF}$

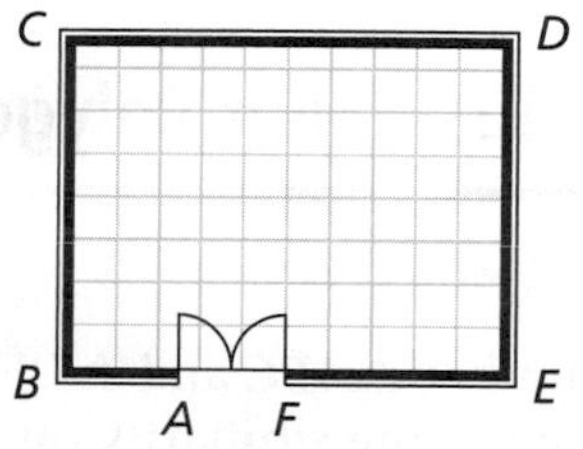

8. A student who is 5 ft 3 in. tall measured her shadow and the shadow cast by a water tower shaped like a golf ball. What is the height of the tower?

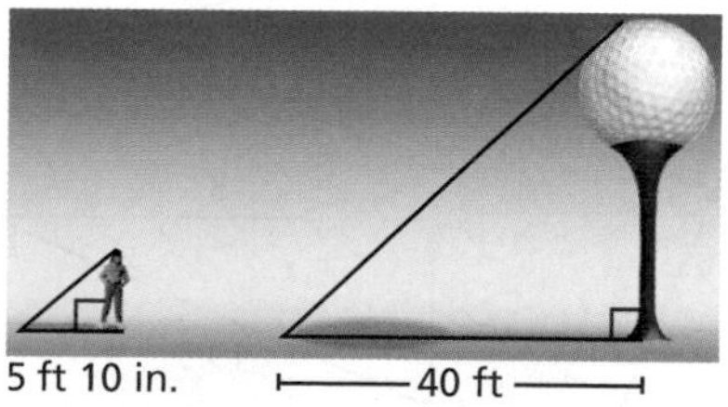

7-6 Dilations and Similarity in the Coordinate Plane

9. **Given:** $A(-1, 2)$, $B(-3, -2)$, $C(3, 0)$, $D(-2, 0)$, and $E(1, 1)$
   Prove: $\triangle ADE \sim \triangle ABC$
10. **Given:** $R(0, 0)$, $S(-2, -1)$, $T(0, -3)$, $U(4, 2)$, and $V(0, 6)$
    Prove: $\triangle RST \sim \triangle RUV$

Graph the image of each triangle after a dilation with the given scale factor. Then verify that the image is similar to the given triangle.

11. scale factor 3

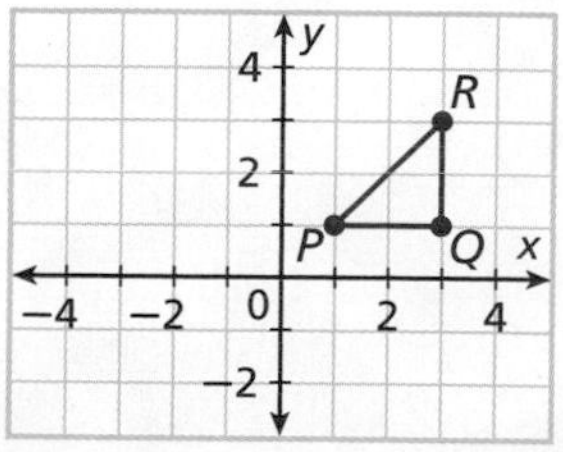

12. scale factor 1.5

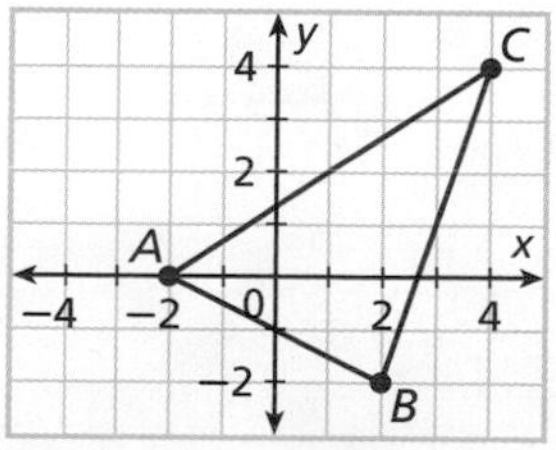

CHAPTER 7 Study Guide: Review

Know it! Note

For a complete list of postulates, theorems, and corollaries, see p. PT2.

Vocabulary

dilation	scale drawing	similar polygons
directed line segment	scale factor	similarity ratio
indirect measurement	similar	similarity transformation
scale		

Complete the sentences below with vocabulary words from the list above.

1. Using shadows and similar triangles to find the height of an object is an example of ___?___ .
2. A(n) ___?___ a transformation that changes the size of a figure but not its shape.
3. A ___?___ is the ratio of the lengths of the corresponding sides of two similar polygons.
4. The ___?___ of a dilation describes how much the figure is enlarged or reduced.

7-1 Ratios in Similar Polygons

EXAMPLE

■ **Determine whether △*ABC* and △*DEF* are similar. If so, write the similarity ratio and a similarity statement.**

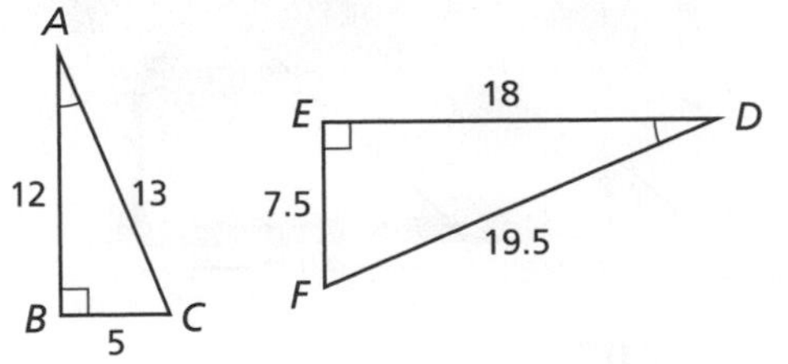

It is given that $\angle A \cong \angle D$ and $\angle B \cong \angle E$. $\angle C \cong \angle F$ by the Third Angles Theorem. $\frac{AB}{DE} = \frac{BC}{EF} = \frac{AC}{DF} = \frac{2}{3}$. Thus the similarity ratio is $\frac{2}{3}$, and $\triangle ABC \sim \triangle DEF$.

EXERCISES

Determine whether the polygons are similar. If so, write the similarity ratio and a similarity statement.

5. rectangles *JKLM* and *PQRS*

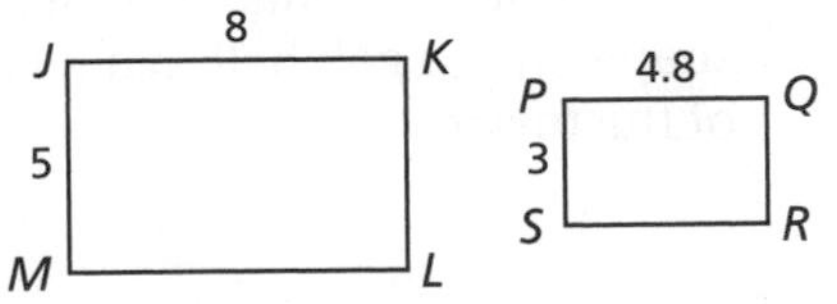

6. △*TUV* and △*WXY*

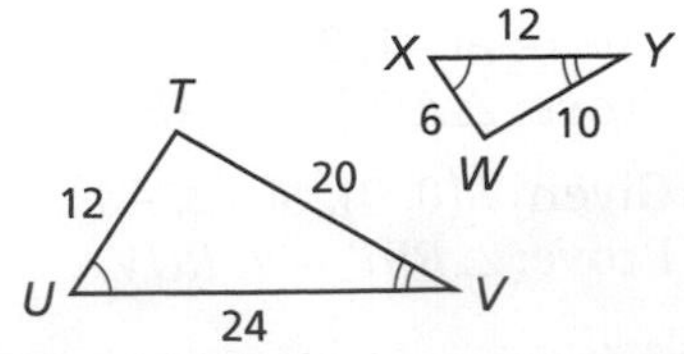

7-2 Similarity and Transformations

EXAMPLE

- Apply the dilation $D: (x, y) \rightarrow (1.5x, 1.5y)$ to the polygon with vertices $A(0, 0)$, $B(4, 6)$, and $C(8, -2)$. Name the coordinates of the image points. Describe the transformation.

$A'(0, 0)$
$B'(6, 9)$
$C'(12, -3)$

This is a dilation with center (0, 0) and scale factor 1.5.

EXERCISES

7. Apply the dilation $D: (x, y) \rightarrow (4x, 4y)$ to the polygon with vertices $A(1, 2)$, $B(3, -1)$, $C(-4, 0)$. Name the coordinates of the image points. Describe the transformation.

8. Determine whether the polygons with the given vertices are similar. Support your answer by describing a transformation.

$A(-3, 1)$, $B(-1, -1)$, $C(-3, -2)$

$X(5, 3)$, $Y(1, -1)$, $Z(5, -3)$

7-3 Triangle Similarity: AA, SSS, and SAS

EXAMPLE

- **Given:** $\overline{AB} \parallel \overline{CD}$, $AB = 2CD$, $AC = 2CE$
Prove: $\triangle ABC \sim \triangle CDE$

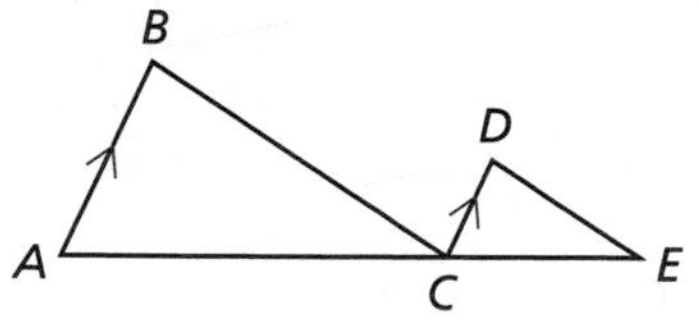

Proof:

Statements	Reasons
1. $\overline{AB} \parallel \overline{CD}$	1. Given
2. $\angle BAC \cong \angle DCE$	2. Corr. ∠s Post.
3. $AB = 2CD$, $AC = 2CE$	3. Given
4. $\frac{AB}{CD} = 2$, $\frac{AC}{CE} = 2$	4. Division Prop.
5. $\frac{AB}{CD} = \frac{AC}{CE}$	5. Trans. Prop. of =
6. $\triangle ABC \sim \triangle CDE$	6. SAS ~ *(Steps 2, 5)*

EXERCISES

9. Given: $JL = \frac{1}{3}JN$, $JK = \frac{1}{3}JM$
Prove: $\triangle JKL \sim \triangle JMN$

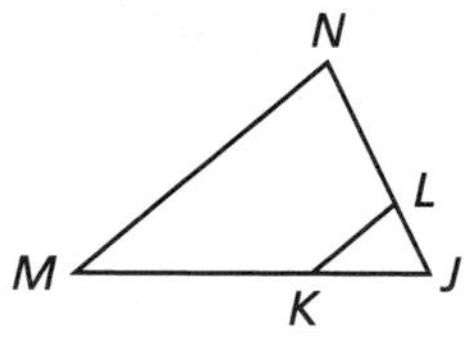

10. Given: $\overline{QR} \parallel \overline{ST}$
Prove: $\triangle PQR \sim \triangle PTS$

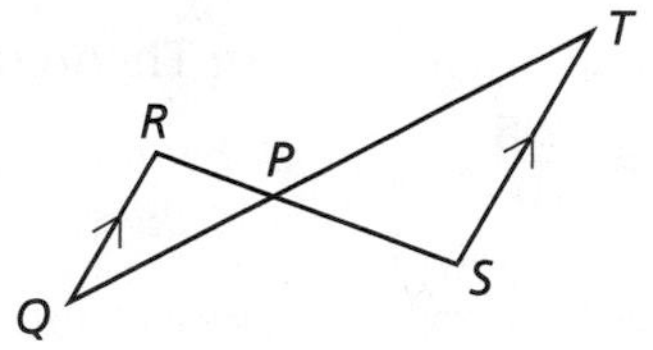

11. Given: $\overline{BD} \parallel \overline{CE}$
Prove: $AB(CE) = AC(BD)$

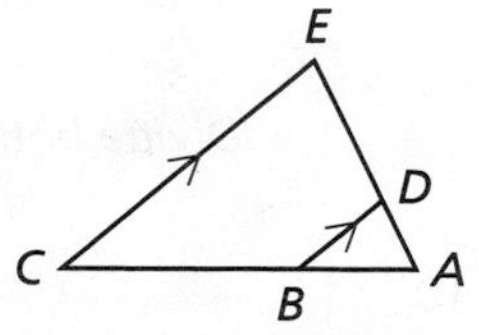

(*Hint:* After you have proved the triangles similar, look for a proportion using *AB*, *AC*, *CE*, and *BD*, the lengths of corresponding sides.)

7-4 Applying Properties of Similar Triangles

EXAMPLES

■ **Find *PQ*.**

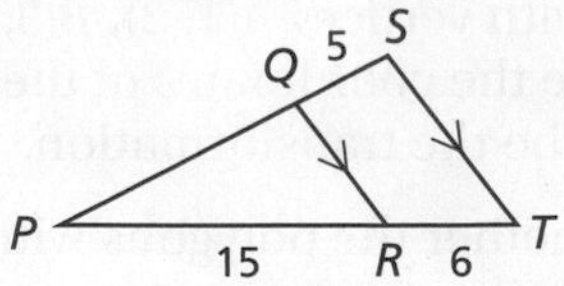

It is given that $\overline{QR} \parallel \overline{ST}$, so $\frac{PQ}{QS} = \frac{PR}{RT}$ by the Triangle Proportionality Theorem.

$\frac{PQ}{5} = \frac{15}{6}$ *Substitute 5 for QS, 15 for PR, and 6 for RT.*

$6(PQ) = 75$ *Cross Products Prop.*

$PQ = 12.5$ *Divide both sides by 6.*

■ **Verify that $\overline{AB} \parallel \overline{CD}$.**

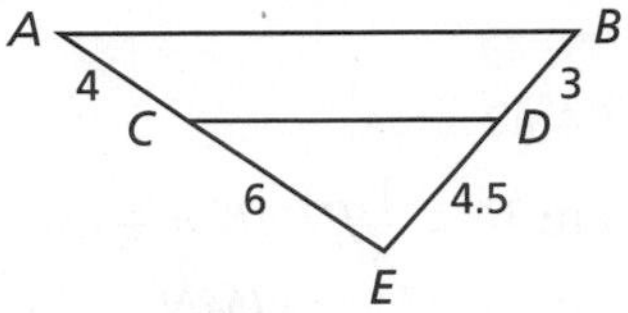

$\frac{EC}{CA} = \frac{6}{4} = 1.5$

$\frac{ED}{DB} = \frac{4.5}{3} = 1.5$

Since $\frac{EC}{CA} = \frac{ED}{DB}$, $\overline{AB} \parallel \overline{CD}$ by the Converse of the Triangle Proportionality Theorem.

■ **Find *JL* and *LK*.**

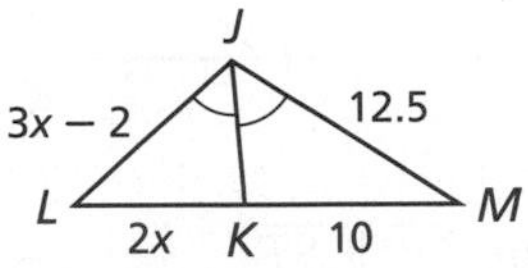

Since $\overline{JK}$ bisects $\angle LJM$, $\frac{JL}{LK} = \frac{JM}{MK}$ by the Triangle Angle Bisector Theorem.

$\frac{3x-2}{2x} = \frac{12.5}{10}$ *Substitute the given values.*

$10(3x - 2) = 12.5(2x)$ *Cross Products Prop.*

$30x - 20 = 25x$ *Simplify.*

$30x = 25x + 20$ *Add 20 to both sides.*

$5x = 20$ *Subtract 25x from both sides.*

$x = 4$ *Divide both sides by 5.*

$JL = 3x - 2$

$= 3(4) - 2 = 10$

$LK = 2x$

$= 2(4) = 8$

EXERCISES

Find each length.

12. *CE*

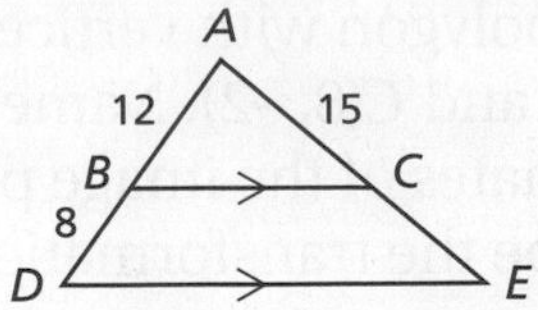

13. *ST*

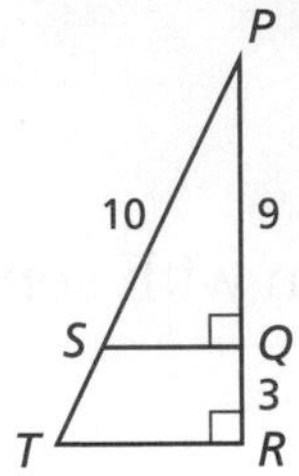

Verify that the given segments are parallel.

14. $\overline{KL}$ and $\overline{MN}$

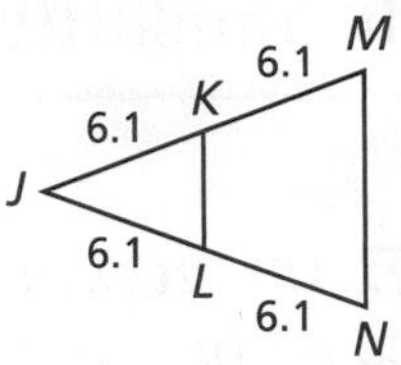

15. $\overline{AB}$ and $\overline{CD}$

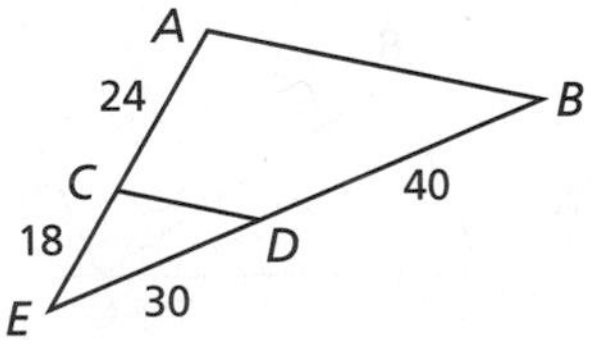

16. Find *SU* and *SV*.

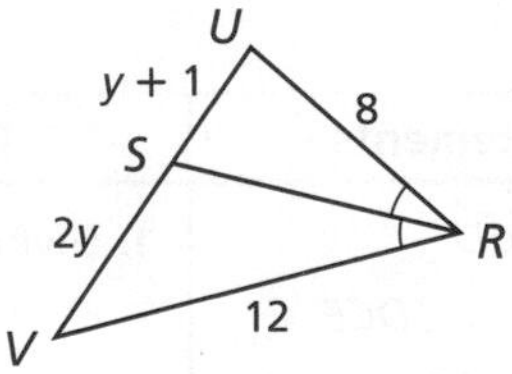

17. Find the length of the third side of $\triangle ABC$.

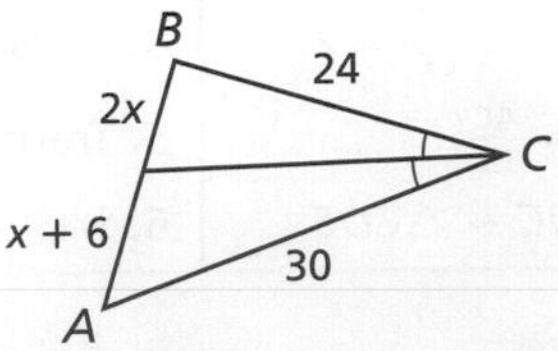

18. One side of a triangle is *x* inches longer than another side. The ray bisecting the angle formed by these sides divides the opposite side into 3-inch and 5-inch segments. Find the perimeter of the triangle in terms of *x*.

7-5 Using Proportional Relationships

EXAMPLE

■ **Use the dimensions in the diagram to find the height *h* of the tower.**

A student who is 5 ft 5 in. tall measured his shadow and a tower's shadow to find the height of the tower.

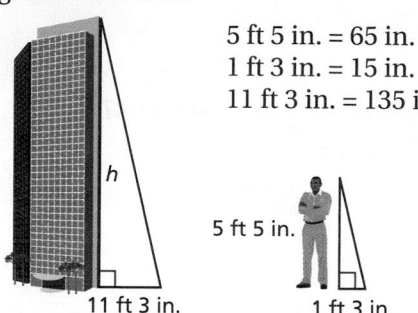

5 ft 5 in. = 65 in.
1 ft 3 in. = 15 in.
11 ft 3 in. = 135 in.

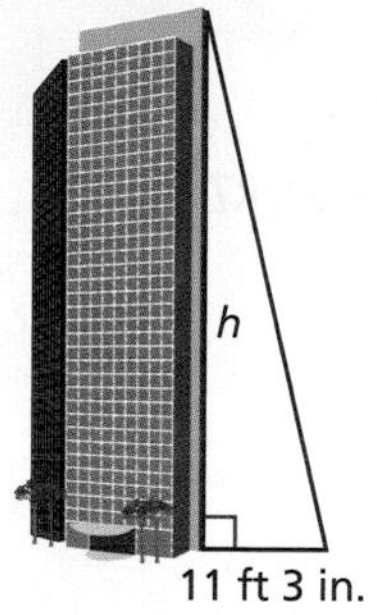

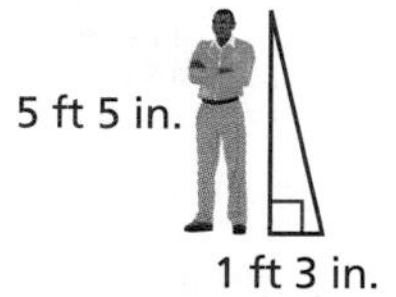

$\frac{h}{135} = \frac{65}{15}$ *Corr. sides are proportional.*

$15h = 65(135)$ *Cross Products Prop.*

$15h = 8775$ *Simplify.*

$h = 585$ in. *Divide both sides by 15.*

The height of the tower is 48 ft 9 in.

EXERCISES

19. To find the height of a flagpole, Casey measured her own shadow and the flagpole's shadow. Given that Casey's height is 5 ft 4 in., what is the height x of the flagpole?

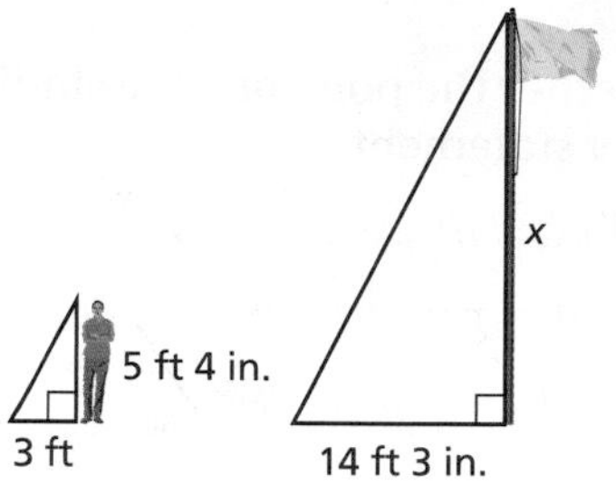

20. Jonathan is 3 ft from a lamppost that is 12 ft high. The lamppost and its shadow form the legs of a right triangle. Jonathan is 6 ft tall and is standing parallel to the lamppost. How long is Jonathan's shadow?

7-6 Dilations and Similarity in the Coordinate Plane

EXAMPLE

■ **Given:** $A(5, -4)$, $B(-1, -2)$, $C(3, 0)$, $D(-4, -1)$ and $E(2, 2)$

Prove: $\triangle ABC \sim \triangle ADE$

Proof: Plot the points and draw the triangles.

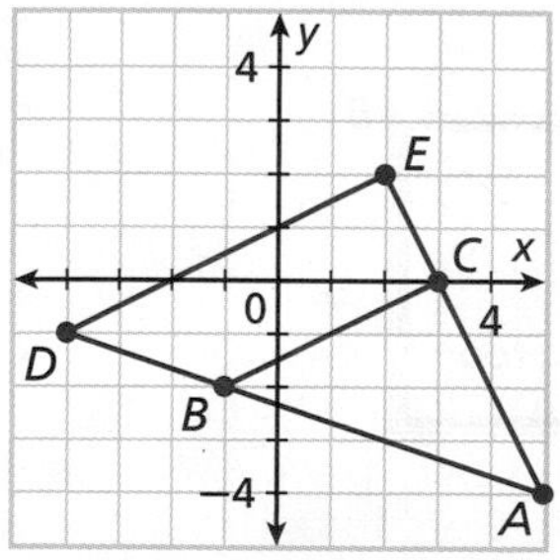

Use the Distance Formula to find the side lengths.

$AC = 2\sqrt{5}$, $AE = 3\sqrt{5}$

$AB = 2\sqrt{10}$, $AD = 3\sqrt{10}$

Therefore $\frac{AB}{AD} = \frac{AC}{AE} = \frac{2}{3}$.

Since corresponding sides are proportional and $\angle A \cong \angle A$ by the Reflexive Property, $\triangle ABC \sim \triangle ADE$ by SAS $\sim$.

EXERCISES

21. **Given:** $R(1, -3)$, $S(-1, -1)$, $T(2, 0)$, $U(-3, 1)$, and $V(3, 3)$

Prove: $\triangle RST \sim \triangle RUV$

22. **Given:** $J(4, 4)$, $K(2, 3)$, $L(4, 2)$, $M(-4, 0)$, and $N(4, -4)$

Prove: $\triangle JKL \sim \triangle JMN$

23. Given that $\triangle AOB \sim \triangle COD$, find the coordinates of B and the scale factor.

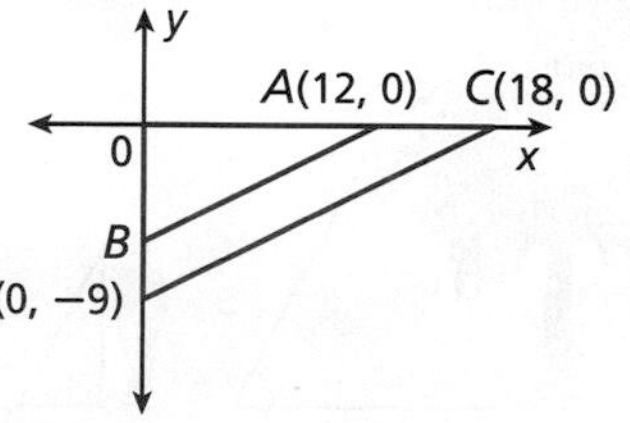

24. Graph the image of the triangle after a dilation with the given scale factor. Then verify that the image is similar to the given triangle. $K(0, 3)$, $L(0, 0)$, and $M(4, 0)$ with scale factor 3.

CHAPTER 7

CHAPTER TEST

Apply the dilation to the polygon with vertices at $A(0, 1)$, $B(-3, 2)$, $C(5, -4)$. Name the coordinates of the points. Identify and describe the transformation.

1. $D: (x, y) \rightarrow (4x, 4y)$

2. $D: (x, y) \rightarrow (0.2x, 0.2y)$

Determine whether the polygons are similar. If so, write the similarity ratio and a similarity statement.

3. $\triangle ABC$ and $\triangle MNP$

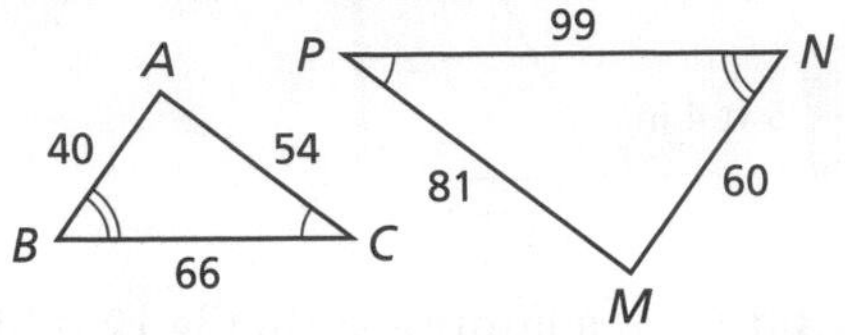

4. rectangle $DEFG$ and rectangle $HJKL$

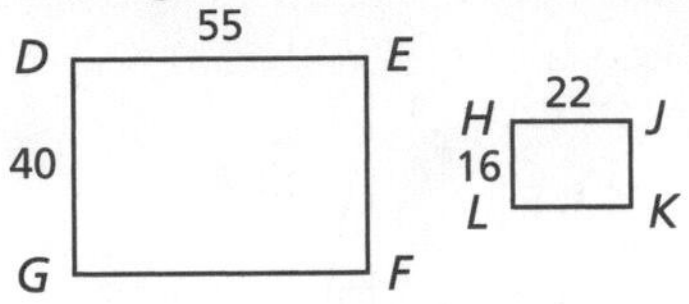

5. Given: ▱$RSTU$
Prove: $\triangle RWV \sim \triangle SWT$

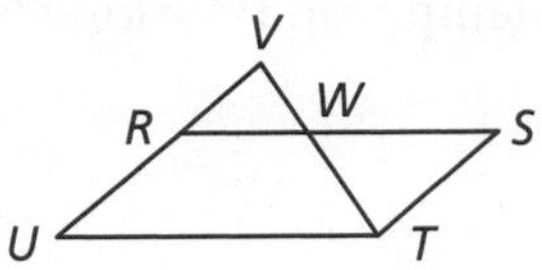

6. Derrick is building a skateboard ramp as shown. Given that $BD = DF = FG = 3$ ft, find CD and EF to the nearest tenth.

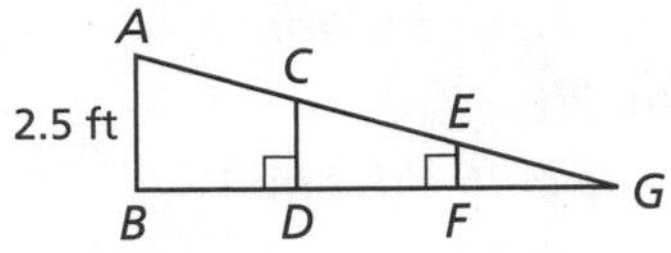

Find the length of each segment.

7. $\overline{PR}$

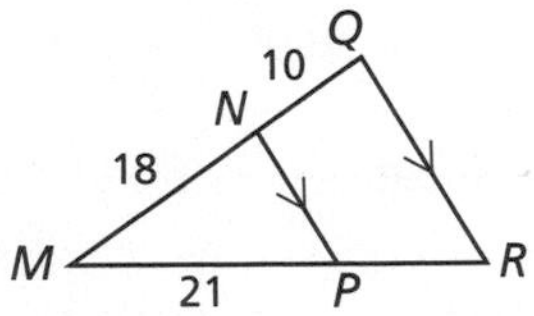

8. $\overline{YW}$ and $\overline{WZ}$

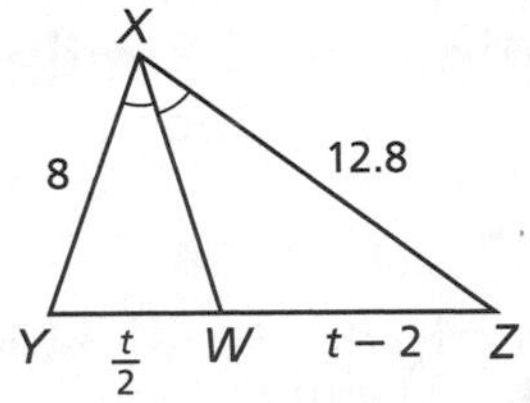

9. To find the height of a tree, a student measured the tree's shadow and her own shadow. If the student's height is 5 ft 8 in., what is the height of the tree?

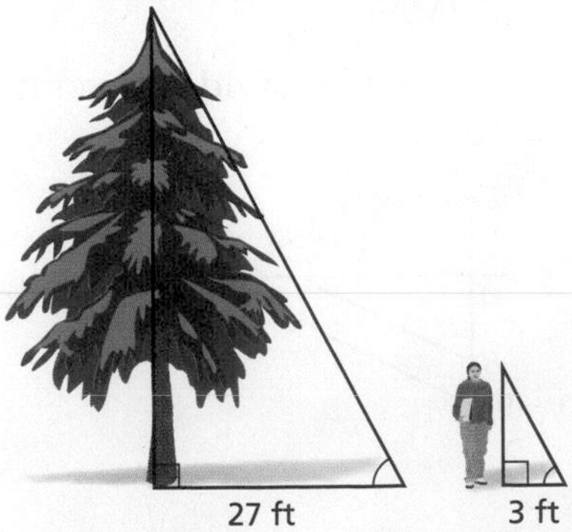

10. The plan for a living room uses the scale of 1.5 in.:30 ft. Use a ruler and find the length of the actual room's diagonal $\overline{AB}$.

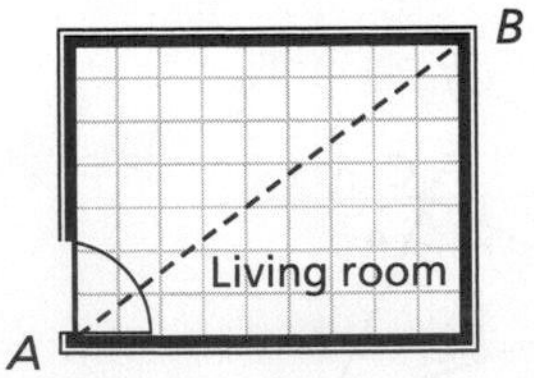

11. Given: $A(6, 5)$, $B(3, 4)$, $C(6, 3)$, $D(-3, 2)$, and $E(6, -1)$
Prove: $\triangle ABC \sim \triangle ADE$

12. A quilter designed this patch for a quilt but needs a larger version for a different project. Draw the quilt patch after a dilation with scale factor $\frac{3}{2}$.

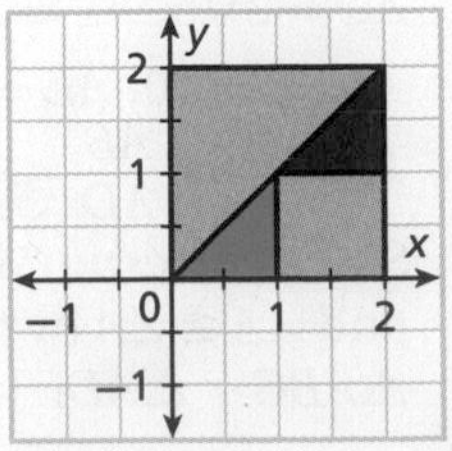

COLLEGE ENTRANCE EXAM PRACTICE

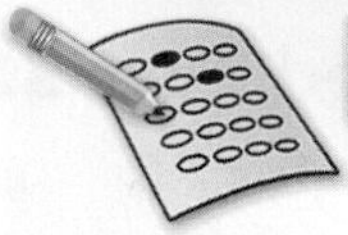

CHAPTER 7

FOCUS ON SAT

The SAT consists of seven test sections: three verbal, three math, and one more verbal or math section not used to compute your final score. The "extra" section is used to try out questions for future tests and to compare your score to previous tests.

HOT TIP! **Read each question carefully and make sure you answer the question being asked. Check that your answer makes sense in the context of the problem. If you have time, check your work.**

You may want to time yourself as you take this practice test. It should take you about 8 minutes to complete.

---

1. In the figure below, the coordinates of the vertices are $A(1, 5)$, $B(1, 1)$, $D(10, 1)$, and $E(10, -7)$. If the length of $\overline{CE}$ is 10, what are the coordinates of C?

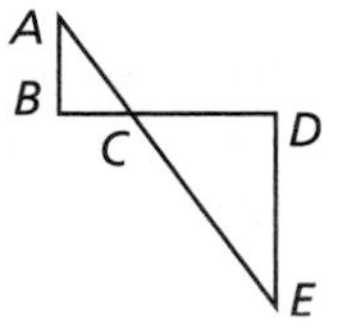

Note: Figure not drawn to scale.

(A) $(4, 1)$

(B) $(1, 4)$

(C) $(7, 1)$

(D) $(1, 7)$

(E) $(6, 1)$

---

2. In the figure below, triangles JKL and MKN are similar, and ℓ is parallel to segment JL. What is the length of $\overline{KM}$?

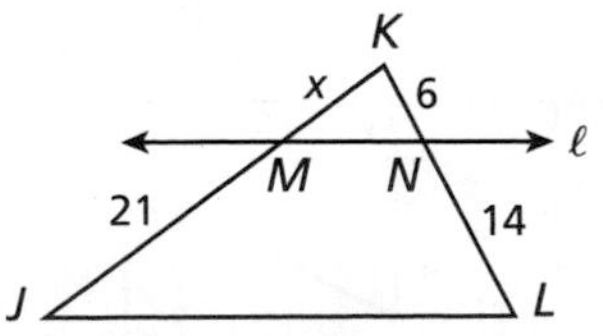

Note: Figure not drawn to scale.

(A) 4

(B) 8

(C) 9

(D) 13

(E) 18

---

3. Which set of vertices describe a triangle that is a dilation with scale factor 3 of ABC with vertices at $A(12, 6)$, $B(-18, 24)$, $C(0, 12)$?

(A) $X(4, 2)$, $Y(-3, 4)$, $Z(0, 4)$

(B) $X(9, 3)$, $Y(-21, 21)$, $Z(-3, 9)$

(C) $X(15, 9)$, $Y(-15, 27)$, $Z(3, 15)$

(D) $X(36, 18)$, $Y(-54, 72)$, $Z(0, 36)$

(E) $X(36, -18)$, $Y(54, 72)$, $Z(0, -24)$

---

4. A 35-foot flagpole casts a 9-foot shadow at the same time that a girl casts a 1.2-foot shadow. How tall is the girl?

(A) 3 feet 8 inches

(B) 4 feet 6 inches

(C) 4 feet 7 inches

(D) 4 feet 8 inches

(E) 5 feet 6 inches

---

5. What polygon is similar to every other polygon of the same name?

(A) Triangle

(B) Parallelogram

(C) Rectangle

(D) Square

(E) Trapezoid

CHAPTER 7

TEST TACKLER

Standardized Test Strategies

Any Question Type: Interpret A Diagram

When a diagram is included as part of a test question, do not make any assumptions about the diagram. Diagrams are not always drawn to scale and can be misleading if you are not careful.

EXAMPLE 1

Multiple Choice What is DE?

Ⓐ 3.6 Ⓒ 4.8

Ⓑ 4 Ⓓ 9

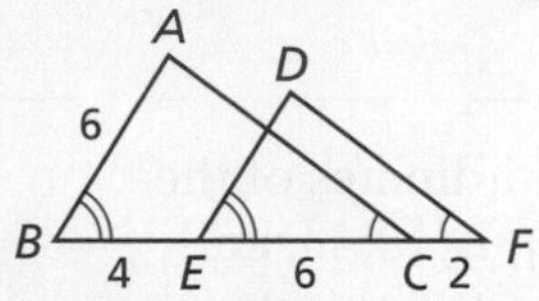

Make your own sketch of the diagram. Separate the two triangles so that you are able to find the side length measures.

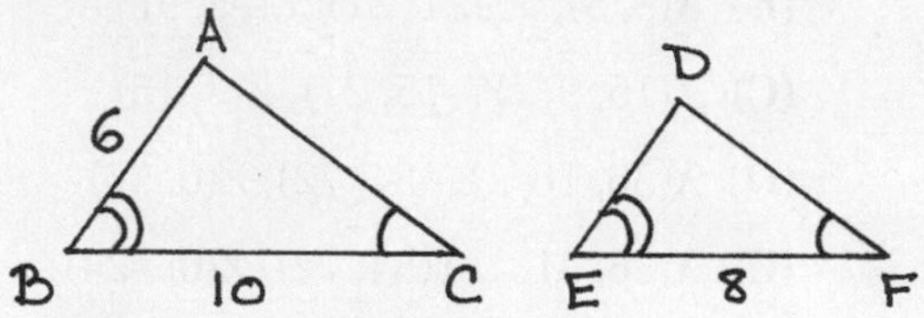

By redrawing the diagram, it is clear that the two triangles are similar. Set up a proportion to find DE.

$$\frac{AB}{BC} = \frac{DE}{EF}$$

$$\frac{6}{10} = \frac{DE}{8}$$

$$\frac{48}{10} = DE$$

$$DE = 4.8$$

The correct choice is C.

EXAMPLE 2

Gridded Response $\triangle X'Y'Z'$ is the image of $\triangle XYZ$ after a dilation with scale factor $\frac{1}{2}$. Find $X'Z'$.

Before you begin, look at the scale of both the x-axis and the y-axis. Do not assume that the scale is always 1.

At first glance, you might assume that XZ is 4. But by looking closely at the x-axis, notice that each increment represents 2 units. So XZ is actually 8.

When $\triangle XYZ$ is dilated by a factor of $\frac{1}{2}$, $X'Z'$ will be half of XZ.

$$X'Z' = \frac{1}{2}XZ = \frac{1}{2}(8) = 4$$

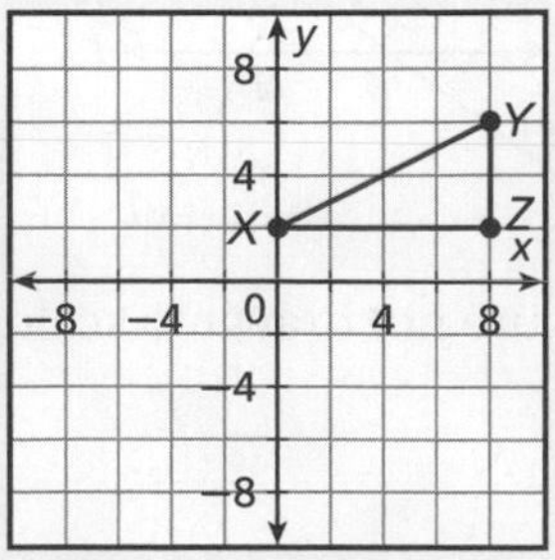

HOT TIP! If the diagram does not match the given information, draw one that is more accurate.

Read each test item and answer the questions that follow.

Item A

Multiple Choice What will the image of A be after a dilation with center at (0, 0) and scale factor 2 followed by a translation left by 5?

Ⓐ (25, 6)

Ⓑ (20, 6)

Ⓒ (1, 6)

Ⓓ (−4, 6)

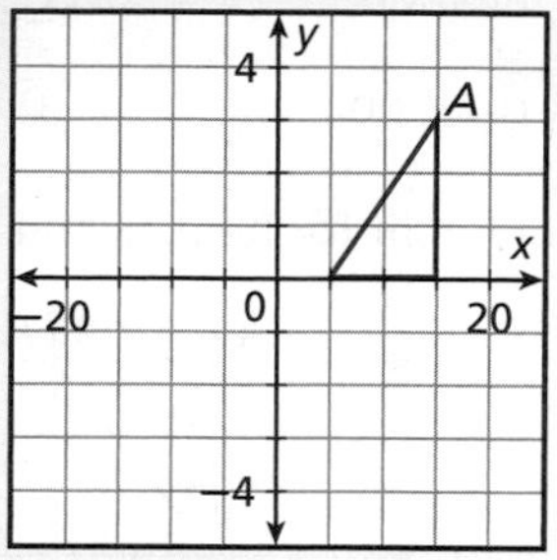

1. What is the scale of the y-axis? What is the y-coordinate of A after the dilation?
2. What is the scale of the x-axis? What is the x-coordinate of A after the dilation?
3. How does the translation left affect the coordinates of the image of A? What are the coordinates of A after the translation?
4. Anna selected Choice C as her answer. Is she correct? If not, what do you think she did wrong?

Item B

Gridded Response If $ABDC \sim MNPO$ and AC is 6, what is AB?

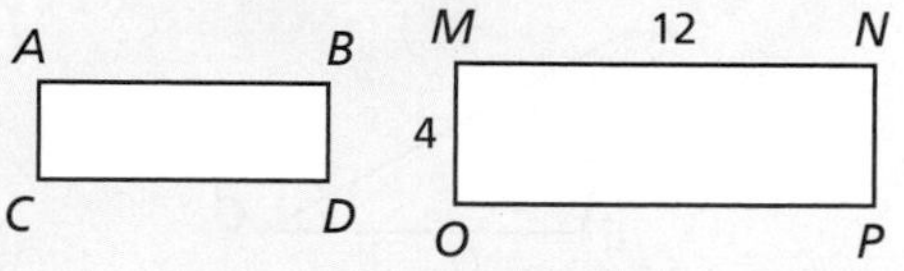

5. Examine the figures. Do you think $\overline{AB}$ is longer or shorter than $\overline{MN}$?
6. Do you think the drawings actually represent the given information? If not, explain why.
7. Create your own sketch of the figures to more accurately match the given information.

Item C

Short Response Find the measure of MN and PR.

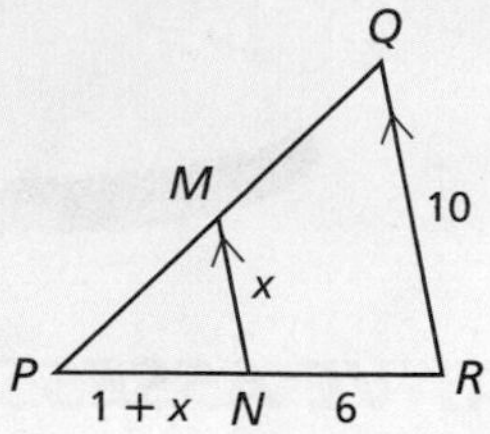

8. Describe how redrawing the figure can help you better understand the given information.
9. After reading this test question, a student redrew the figure as shown below. Explain if it is a correct interpretation of the original figure. If it is not, redraw and/or relabel it so that it is correct.

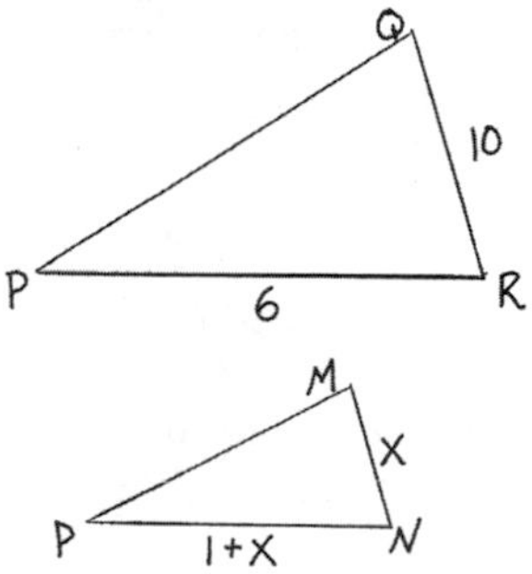

Item D

Multiple Choice Which is a similarity ratio for the triangles shown?

Ⓐ $\frac{20}{1}$

Ⓑ $\frac{10}{1}$

Ⓒ $\frac{2}{1}$

Ⓓ $\frac{15}{1}$

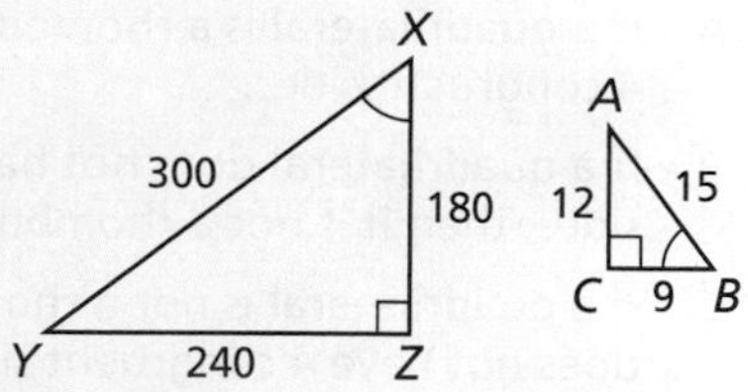

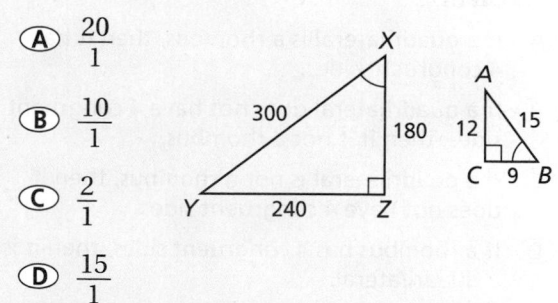

10. Chad determined that choice D was correct. Do you agree? If not, what do you think he did wrong?
11. Redraw the figures so that they are easier to understand. Write three statements that describe which vertices correspond to each other and three statements that describe which sides correspond to each other.

CHAPTER 7

STANDARDIZED TEST PREP

Learn It Online
State Test Practice

CUMULATIVE ASSESSMENT

Multiple Choice

1. Which similarity statement is true for rectangles *ABCD* and *MNPQ*, given that $AB = 3$, $AD = 4$, $MN = 6$, and $NP = 4.5$?

- (A) Rectangle $ABCD \sim$ rectangle $MNPQ$
- (B) Rectangle $ABCD \sim$ rectangle $PQMN$
- (C) Rectangle $ABCD \sim$ rectangle $MPNQ$
- (D) Rectangle $ABCD \sim$ rectangle $QMNP$

2. $\triangle ABC$ has perpendicular bisectors $\overline{XP}$, $\overline{YP}$, and $\overline{ZP}$. If $AP = 6$ and $ZP = 4.5$, what is the length of $\overline{BC}$ to the nearest tenth?

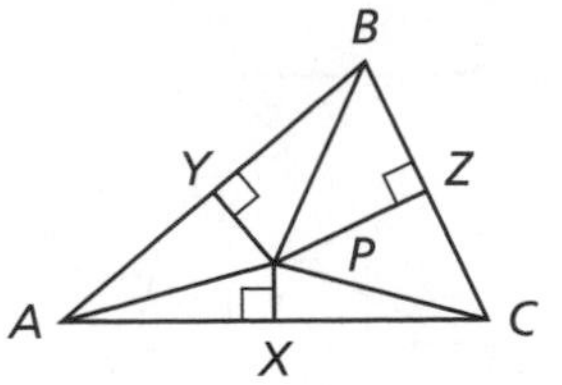

- (F) 4.0
- (G) 7.9
- (H) 9.0
- (J) 12.7

3. What is the converse of the statement "If a quadrilateral has 4 congruent sides, then it is a rhombus"?

- (A) If a quadrilateral is a rhombus, then it has 4 congruent sides.
- (B) If a quadrilateral does not have 4 congruent sides, then it is not a rhombus.
- (C) If a quadrilateral is not a rhombus, then it does not have 4 congruent sides.
- (D) If a rhombus has 4 congruent sides, then it is a quadrilateral.

4. A blueprint for a hotel uses a scale of 3 in.:100 ft. On the blueprint, the lobby has a width of 1.5 in. and a length of 2.25 in. If the carpeting for the lobby costs \$1.25 per square foot, how much will the carpeting for the entire lobby cost?

- (F) \$312.50
- (G) \$1406.25
- (H) \$3000.00
- (J) \$4687.50

5. Which of the following is NOT an isometry?

- (A) dilation
- (B) rotation
- (C) reflection
- (D) translation

Use the diagram for Items 6 and 7.

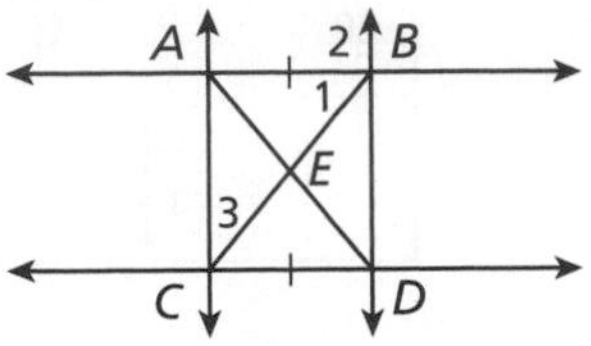

6. Given that $\overline{AB} \cong \overline{CD}$, which additional information would be sufficient to prove that *ABCD* is a parallelogram?

- (F) $\overline{AB} \parallel \overline{CD}$
- (G) $\overline{AC} \parallel \overline{BD}$
- (H) $\angle CAB \cong \angle CDB$
- (J) *E* is the midpoint of $\overline{AD}$.

7. If $\overleftrightarrow{AC}$ is parallel to $\overleftrightarrow{BD}$ and $m\angle 1 + m\angle 2 = 140°$, what is the measure of $\angle 3$?

- (A) 20°
- (B) 40°
- (C) 50°
- (D) 70°

8. If $\overline{AC}$ is twice as long as $\overline{AB}$, what is the length of $\overline{DC}$?

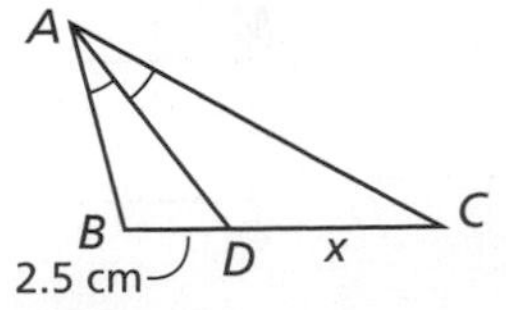

- (F) 2.5 centimeters
- (G) 3.75 centimeters
- (H) 5 centimeters
- (J) 15 centimeters

When writing proportions for similar figures, make sure that each ratio compares corresponding side lengths in each figure.

9. What type of triangle has angles that measure $(2x)°$, $(3x - 9)°$, and $(x + 27)°$?

(A) Isosceles acute triangle

(B) Isosceles right triangle

(C) Scalene acute triangle

(D) Scalene obtuse triangle

Use the diagram for Items 10 and 11.

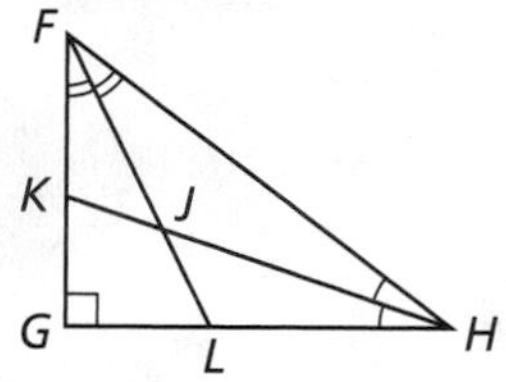

10. Which of these points is the orthocenter of $\triangle FGH$?

(F) F　　(H) H

(G) G　　(J) J

11. Which of the following could be the side lengths of $\triangle FGH$?

(A) $FG = 2$, $GH = 3$, and $FH = 4$

(B) $FG = 4$, $GH = 5$, and $FH = 6$

(C) $FG = 5$, $GH = 4$, and $FH = 3$

(D) $FG = 6$, $GH = 8$, and $FH = 10$

12. The measure of one of the exterior angles of a right triangle is 120°. What are the measures of the acute interior angles of the triangle?

(F) 30° and 60°　　(H) 40° and 80°

(G) 40° and 50°　　(J) 60° and 60°

Gridded Response

13. The ratio of a football field's length to its width is 9:4. If the length of the field is 360 ft, what is the width of the field in feet?

14. The sum of the measures of the interior angles of a convex polygon is 1260°. How many sides does the polygon have?

15. In kite *PQRS*, $\angle P$ and $\angle R$ are opposite angles. If $m\angle P = 25°$ and $m\angle R = 75°$, what is the measure of $\angle Q$ in degrees?

16. Heather is 1.6 m tall and casts a shadow of 3.5 m. At the same time, a barn casts a shadow of 17.5 m. Find the height of the barn in meters.

Short Response

17. $\triangle ABC$ has vertices $A(-2, 0)$, $B(2, 2)$, and $C(2, -2)$. $\triangle DEC$ has vertices $D(0, -1)$, $E(2, 0)$, and $C(2, -2)$. Prove that $\triangle ABC \sim \triangle DEC$.

18. $\angle TUV$ in the diagram below is an obtuse angle.

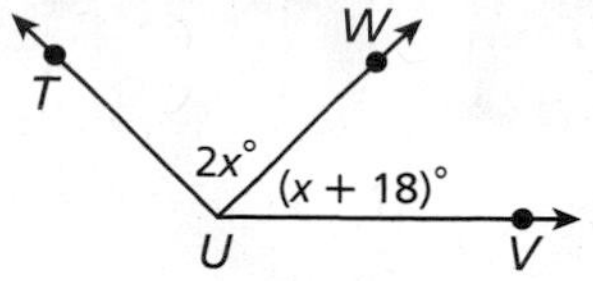

Write an inequality showing the range of possible measurements for $\angle TUW$. Show your work or explain your answer.

19. $\triangle ABC$ and $\triangle ABD$ share side $\overline{AB}$. Given that $\triangle ABC \sim \triangle ABD$, use AAS to explain why these two triangles must also be congruent.

20. Rectangle *ABCD* has a length of 2.6 cm and a width of 1.8 cm. Rectangle *WXYZ* has a length of 7.8 cm and a width of 5.4 cm. Determine whether rectangle *ABCD* is similar to rectangle *WXYZ*. Explain your reasoning.

21. If $\triangle ABC$ and $\triangle XYZ$ are similar triangles, there are six possible similarity statements.

a. What is the probability that $\triangle ABC \sim \triangle XYZ$ is correct?

b. If $\triangle ABC$ and $\triangle XYZ$ are isosceles, what is the probability that $\triangle ABC \sim \triangle XYZ$?

c. If $\triangle ABC$ and $\triangle XYZ$ are equilateral, what is the probability that $\triangle ABC \sim \triangle XYZ$? Explain.

Extended Response

22. a. Explain in words how you determine the possible values for *x* and *y* that would make the two triangles below similar.

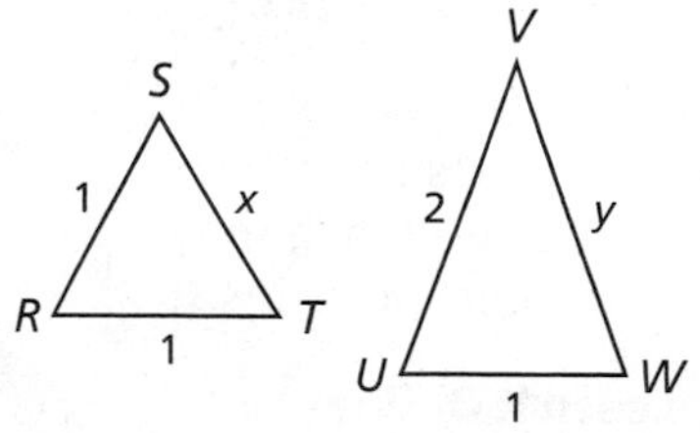

Note: Triangles not drawn to scale.

b. Pick values for x and y that satisfy the conditions you found in part a. Given those values, write a proof that the triangles are similar.

c. Explain why *x* cannot have a value of 1 if the two triangles in the diagram above are similar.

CHAPTER

8 Right Triangles and Trigonometry

COMMON CORE

Chapter

- Solve problems using the similarity relationships of right triangles.
- Apply trigonometric ratios to real-world situations.

Written in Stone

Plimpton 322, a 4000-year-old Babylonian tablet, lists columns of numbers based on Pythagorean triples and trigonometric ratios.

Learn It Online
Chapter Project Online

ARE YOU READY?

Vocabulary

Match each term on the left with a definition on the right.

1. altitude
2. proportion
3. ratio
4. right triangle

A. a comparison of two numbers by division

B. a segment from a vertex to the midpoint of the opposite side of a triangle

C. an equation stating that two ratios are equal

D. a perpendicular segment from the vertex of a triangle to a line containing the base

E. a triangle that contains a right angle

Identify Similar Figures

Determine if the two triangles are similar.

5. 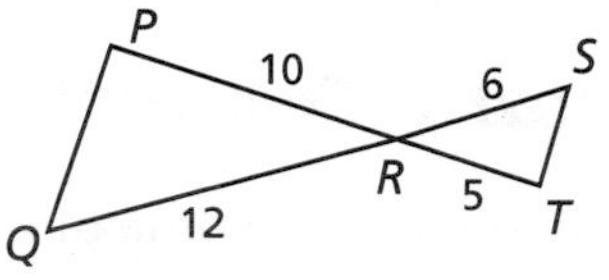

6. 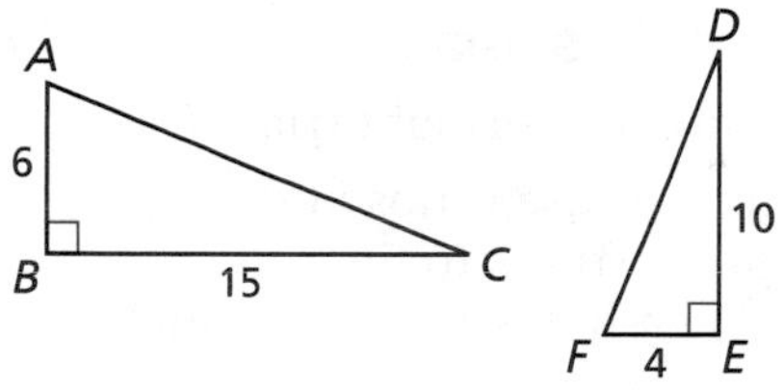

Special Right Triangles

Find the value of x. Give the answer in simplest radical form.

7. 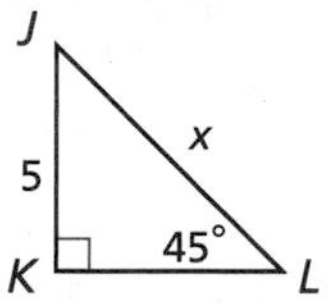

8. 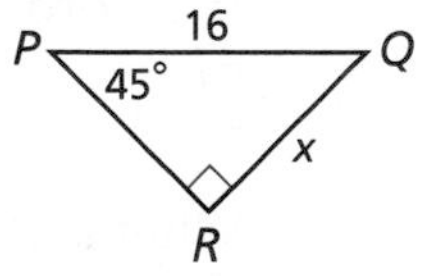

9. 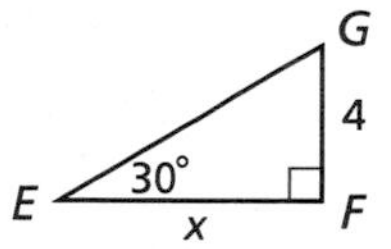

10. 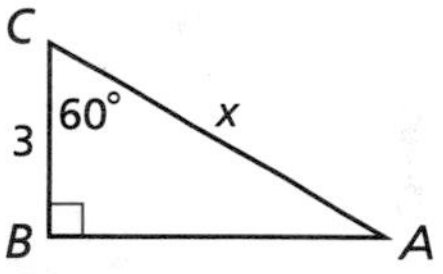

Solve Multi-Step Equations

Solve each equation.

11. $3(x - 1) = 12$
12. $-2(y + 5) = -1$
13. $6 = 8(x - 3)$
14. $2 = -1(z + 4)$

Solve Proportions

Solve each proportion.

15. $\frac{4}{y} = \frac{6}{18}$
16. $\frac{5}{8} = \frac{x}{32}$
17. $\frac{m}{9} = \frac{8}{12}$
18. $\frac{y}{4} = \frac{9}{y}$

Rounding and Estimation

Round each decimal to the indicated place value.

19. 13.118; hundredth
20. 37.91; tenth
21. 15.992; tenth
22. 173.05; whole number

CHAPTER 8

Study Guide: Preview

Where You've Been

Previously, you

- identified similar polygons and proved that triangles are similar.
- used ratios and proportions.
- solved real-world problems using similarity.

In This Chapter

You will study

- similarity of right triangles.
- how to use ratios and proportions to find missing side lengths in right triangles.
- how to use trigonometric ratios to solve real-world problems.

Where You're Going

You can use the skills learned in this chapter

- in your future math classes, especially Trigonometry.
- in other classes, such as Physics and Physical Education.
- outside of school to measure distances, to estimate heights, or to plan a course for hiking or kayaking.

Key Vocabulary/Vocabulario

angle of depression	ángulo de depresión
angle of elevation	ángulo de elevación
cosine	coseno
geometric mean	media geométrica
sine	seno
tangent	tangente
trigonometric ratio	razón trigonométrica
vector	vector

Vocabulary Connections

To become familiar with some of the vocabulary terms in the chapter, consider the following. You may refer to the chapter, the glossary, or a dictionary if you like.

1. The term **angle of elevation** includes the word *elevation.* What does *elevate* mean in everyday usage? What do you think an angle of elevation might be?
2. What is a *depression*? What do you think the term **angle of depression** means?
3. A **vector** is sometimes defined as "a directed line segment." How can you use this definition to understand this term?
4. The word *trigonometric* comes from the Greek word *trigonon,* which means "triangle," and the suffix *metric,* which means "measurement." Based on this, how do you think you might use a **trigonometric ratio** ?

CHAPTER 8

Reading and Writing Math

Reading Strategy: Read to Understand

As you read a lesson, read with a purpose. Lessons are about one or two specific objectives. These objectives are at the top of the first page of every lesson. Reading with the objectives in mind can help you understand the lesson.

Objective

Identify similar polygons.

→ Identify the **objectives** of the lesson.

Figures that are **similar** ($\sim$) have the same shape but not necessarily the same size.

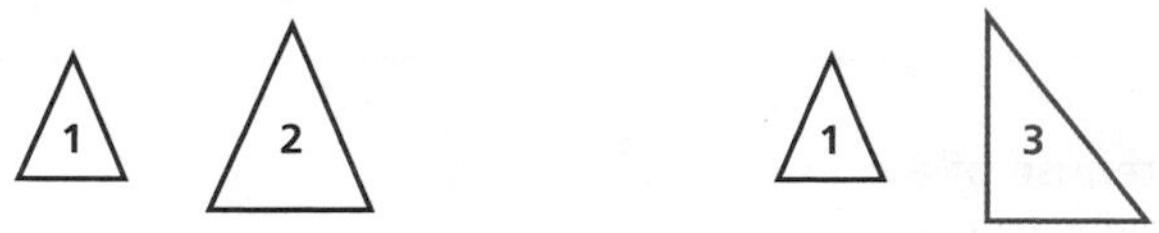

$\triangle 1$ is similar to $\triangle 2$ ($\triangle 1 \sim \triangle 2$).

$\triangle 1$ is not similar to $\triangle 3$ ($\triangle 1 \nsim \triangle 3$).

→ Read through the lesson to find where the objectives are explained.

Questions

- Can two polygons be both similar and congruent?
- In Example 1, the triangles are not oriented the same. How can you tell which angles are congruent and which sides are corresponding?

→ List any questions, problems, or trouble spots you may have.

New Vocabulary/Symbols

- Similarity is represented by the symbol $\sim$. Congruence is represented by the symbol $\cong$.
- Similar: same shape but not necessarily the same size

→ Write down any new vocabulary or symbols.

Try This

Use the first lesson of this chapter to complete each of the following.

1. What are the objectives of the lesson?
2. Identify any new vocabulary, formulas, and symbols.
3. Identify any examples that you need clarified.
4. Make a list of questions you need answered during class.

COMMON CORE

8-1 Similarity in Right Triangles

CC.9-12.G.SRT.6 Understand that…side ratios in right triangles are properties of the angles in the triangle…

Objectives

Use geometric mean to find segment lengths in right triangles.

Apply similarity relationships in right triangles to solve problems.

Vocabulary

geometric mean

Why learn this?

You can use similarity relationships in right triangles to find the height of Big Tex.

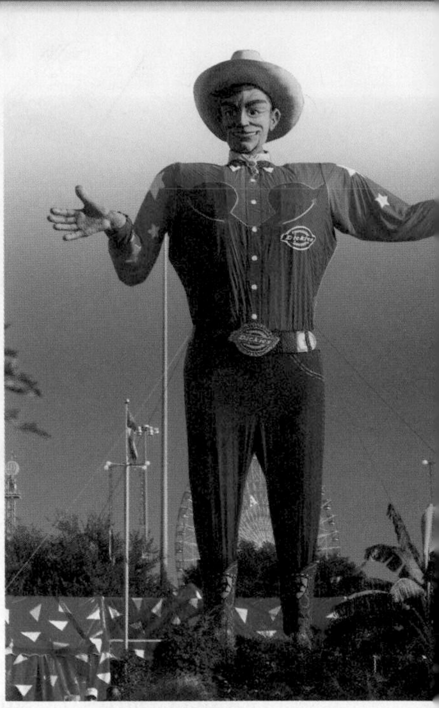

Big Tex debuted as the official symbol of the State Fair of Texas in 1952. This 6000-pound cowboy wears size 70 boots and a 75-gallon hat. In this lesson, you will learn how to use right triangle relationships to find Big Tex's height.

In a right triangle, an altitude drawn from the vertex of the right angle to the hypotenuse forms two right triangles.

Know it! Note

Theorem 8-1-1

The altitude to the hypotenuse of a right triangle forms two triangles that are similar to each other and to the original triangle.

$\triangle ABC \sim \triangle ACD \sim \triangle CBD$

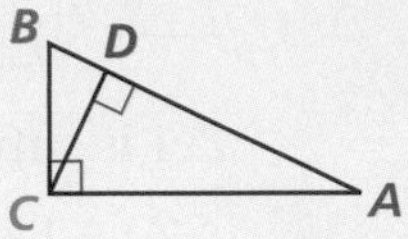

PROOF

Theorem 8-1-1

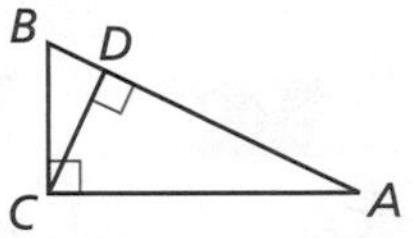

Given: $\triangle ABC$ is a right triangle with altitude $\overline{CD}$.
Prove: $\triangle ABC \sim \triangle ACD \sim \triangle CBD$

Proof: The right angles in $\triangle ABC$, $\triangle ACD$, and $\triangle CBD$ are all congruent. By the Reflexive Property of Congruence, $\angle A \cong \angle A$. Therefore $\triangle ABC \sim \triangle ACD$ by the AA Similarity Theorem. Similarly, $\angle B \cong \angle B$, so $\triangle ABC \sim \triangle CBD$. By the Transitive Property of Similarity, $\triangle ABC \sim \triangle ACD \sim \triangle CBD$.

EXAMPLE 1

Identifying Similar Right Triangles

Write a similarity statement comparing the three triangles.

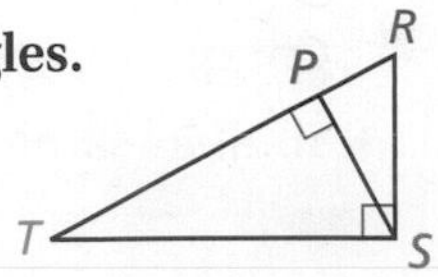

Sketch the three right triangles with the angles of the triangles in corresponding positions.

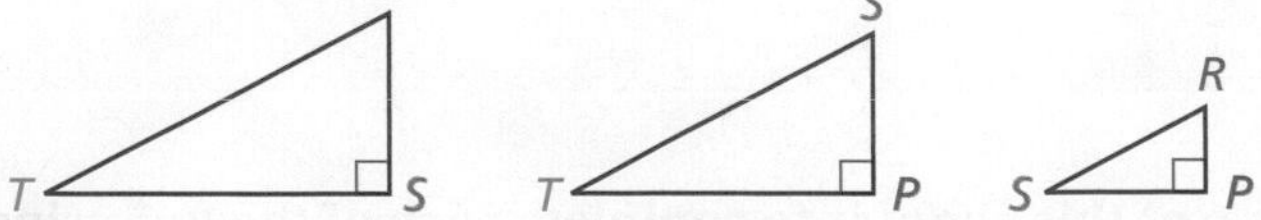

By Theorem 8-1-1, $\triangle RST \sim \triangle SPT \sim \triangle RPS$.

CHECK IT OUT!

1. Write a similarity statement comparing the three triangles.

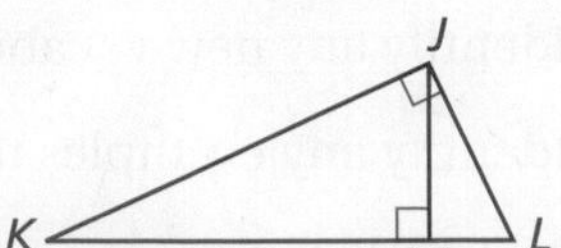

Consider the proportion $\frac{a}{x} = \frac{x}{b}$. In this case, the means of the proportion are the same number, and that number is the *geometric mean* of the extremes. The **geometric mean** of two positive numbers is the positive square root of their product. So the geometric mean of a and b is the positive number x such that $x = \sqrt{ab}$, or $x^2 = ab$.

EXAMPLE 2 Finding Geometric Means

Find the geometric mean of each pair of numbers. If necessary, give the answer in simplest radical form.

A 4 and 9

Let x be the geometric mean.

$x^2 = (4)(9) = 36$ *Def. of geometric mean*

$x = 6$ *Find the positive square root.*

B 6 and 15

Let x be the geometric mean.

$x^2 = (6)(15) = 90$ *Def. of geometric mean*

$x = \sqrt{90} = 3\sqrt{10}$ *Find the positive square root.*

CHECK IT OUT! **Find the geometric mean of each pair of numbers. If necessary, give the answer in simplest radical form.**

2a. 2 and 8   **2b.** 10 and 30   **2c.** 8 and 9

You can use Theorem 8-1-1 to write proportions comparing the side lengths of the triangles formed by the altitude to the hypotenuse of a right triangle. All the relationships in red involve geometric means.

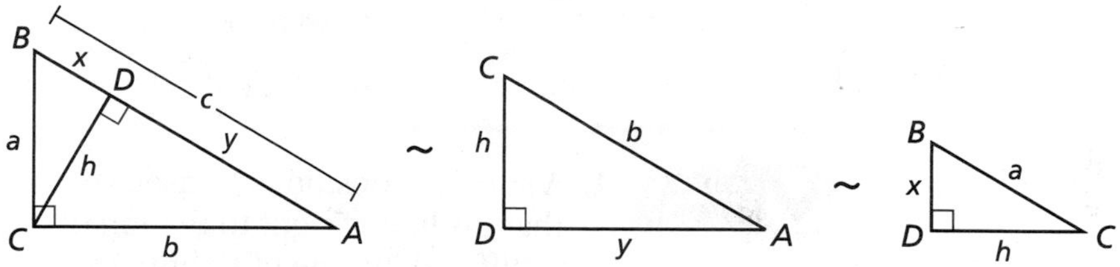

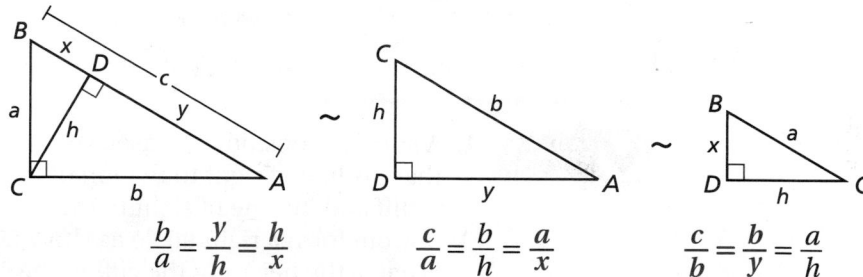

$\frac{b}{a} = \frac{y}{h} = \frac{h}{x}$ $\frac{c}{a} = \frac{b}{h} = \frac{a}{x}$ $\frac{c}{b} = \frac{b}{y} = \frac{a}{h}$

Know it! Note

Corollaries Geometric Means

COROLLARY	EXAMPLE	DIAGRAM
8-1-2 The length of the altitude to the hypotenuse of a right triangle is the geometric mean of the lengths of the two segments of the hypotenuse.	$h^2 = xy$	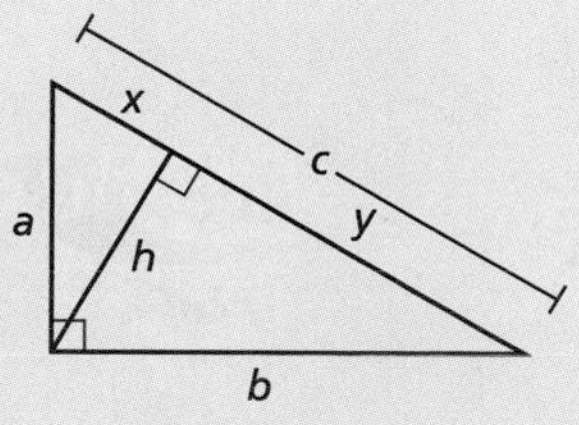
8-1-3 The length of a leg of a right triangle is the geometric mean of the lengths of the hypotenuse and the segment of the hypotenuse adjacent to that leg.	$a^2 = xc$ $b^2 = yc$	

EXAMPLE 3 Finding Side Lengths in Right Triangles

Helpful Hint

Once you've found the unknown side lengths, you can use the Pythagorean Theorem to check your answers.

Find *x*, *y*, and *z*.

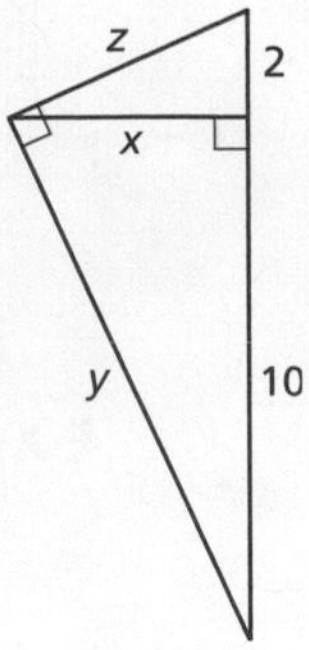

$x^2 = (2)(10) = 20$ — *x is the geometric mean of 2 and 10.*

$x = \sqrt{20} = 2\sqrt{5}$ — *Find the positive square root.*

$y^2 = (12)(10) = 120$ — *y is the geometric mean of 12 and 10.*

$y = \sqrt{120} = 2\sqrt{30}$ — *Find the positive square root.*

$z^2 = (12)(2) = 24$ — *z is the geometric mean of 12 and 2.*

$z = \sqrt{24} = 2\sqrt{6}$ — *Find the positive square root.*

CHECK IT OUT! **3.** Find *u*, *v*, and *w*.

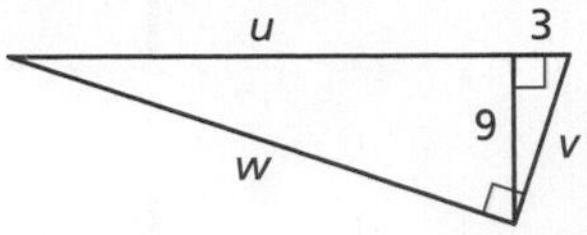

EXAMPLE 4 *Measurement Application*

To estimate the height of Big Tex at the State Fair of Texas, Michael steps away from the statue until his line of sight to the top of the statue and his line of sight to the bottom of the statue form a 90° angle. His eyes are 5 ft above the ground, and he is standing 15 ft 3 in. from Big Tex. How tall is Big Tex to the nearest foot?

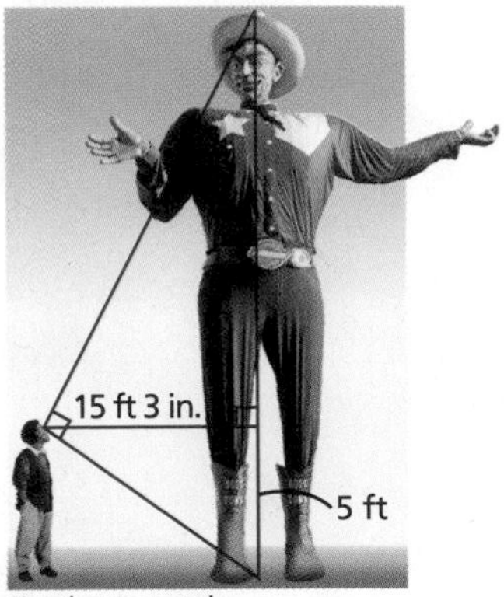

Not drawn to scale

Let x be the height of Big Tex above eye level.

15 ft 3 in. = 15.25 ft — *Convert 3 in. to 0.25 ft.*

$(15.25)^2 = 5x$ — *15.25 is the geometric mean of 5 and x.*

$x = 46.5125 \approx 47$ — *Solve for x and round.*

Big Tex is about 47 + 5, or 52 ft tall.

CHECK IT OUT! **4.** A surveyor positions himself so that his line of sight to the top of a cliff and his line of sight to the bottom form a right angle as shown. What is the height of the cliff to the nearest foot?

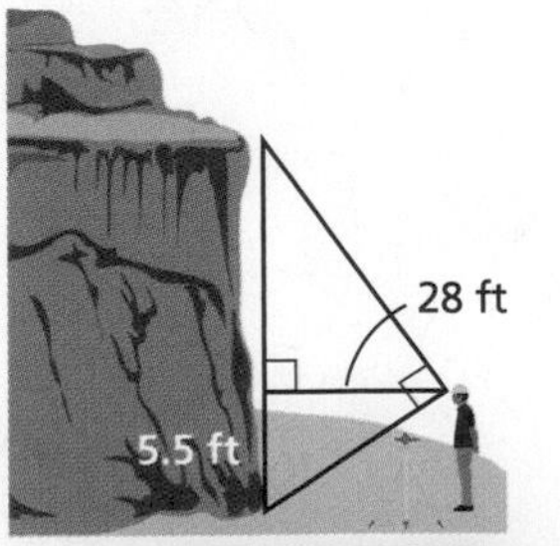

MATHEMATICAL PRACTICES

THINK AND DISCUSS

1. Explain how to find the geometric mean of 7 and 21.

Know it! Note

2. GET ORGANIZED Copy and complete the graphic organizer. Label the right triangle and draw the altitude to the hypotenuse. In each box, write a proportion in which the given segment is a geometric mean.

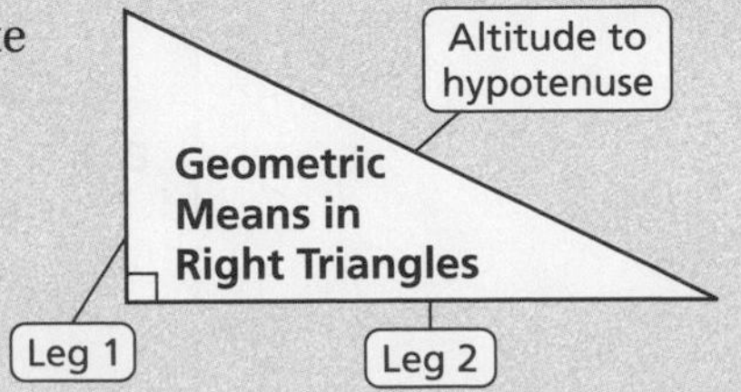

8-1 Exercises

Learn It Online
Homework Help Online
Parent Resources Online

GUIDED PRACTICE

1. **Vocabulary** In the proportion $\frac{2}{8} = \frac{8}{32}$, which number is the *geometric mean* of the other two numbers?

SEE EXAMPLE 1

Write a similarity statement comparing the three triangles in each diagram.

2. 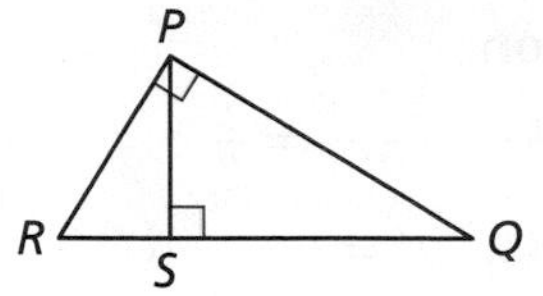

3. 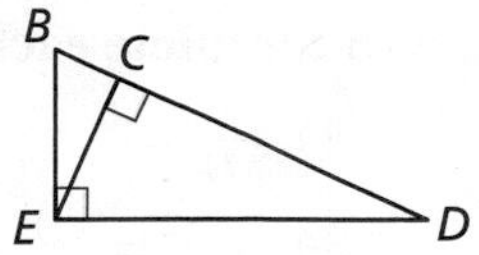

4. 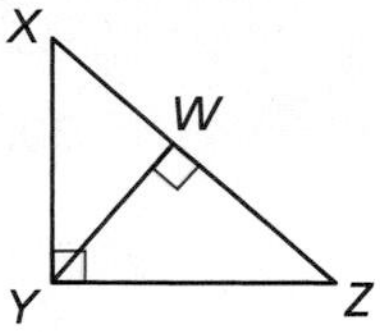

SEE EXAMPLE 2

Find the geometric mean of each pair of numbers. If necessary, give the answer in simplest radical form.

5. 2 and 50
6. 4 and 16
7. $\frac{1}{2}$ and 8
8. 9 and 12
9. 16 and 25
10. 7 and 11

SEE EXAMPLE 3

Find *x*, *y*, and *z*.

11. 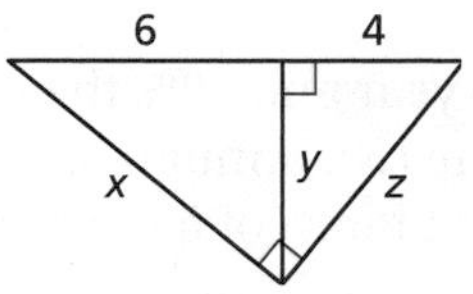

12. 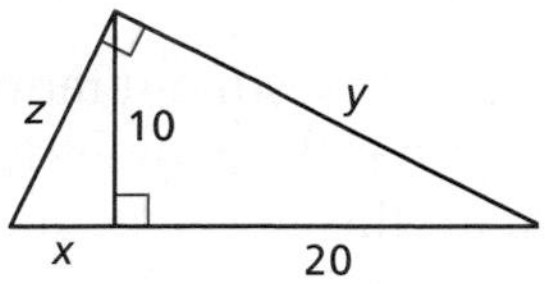

13. 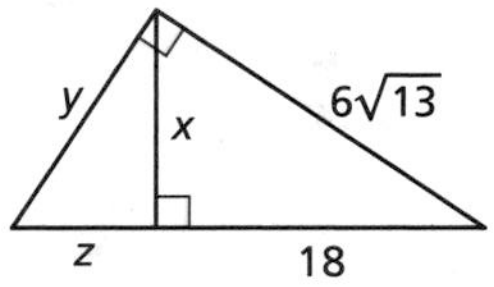

SEE EXAMPLE 4

14. **Measurement** To estimate the length of the USS *Constitution* in Boston harbor, a student locates points *T* and *U* as shown. What is *RS* to the nearest tenth?

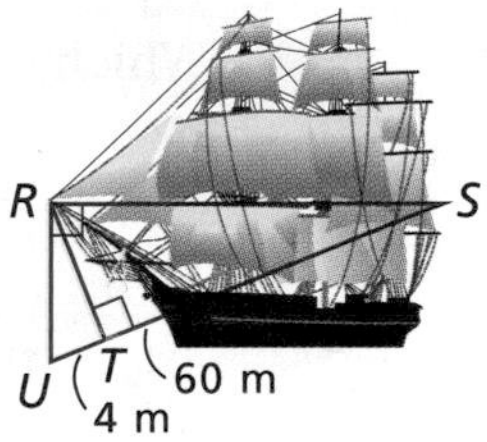

PRACTICE AND PROBLEM SOLVING

Independent Practice

For Exercises	See Example
15–17	1
18–23	2
24–26	3
27	4

Extra Practice

See Extra Practice for more Skills Practice and Applications Practice exercises.

Write a similarity statement comparing the three triangles in each diagram.

15. 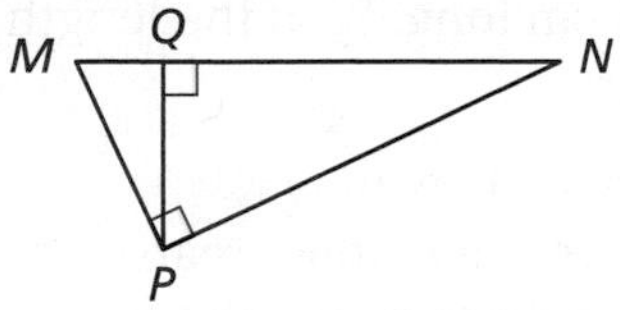

16. 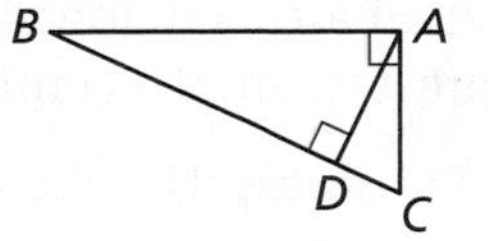

17. 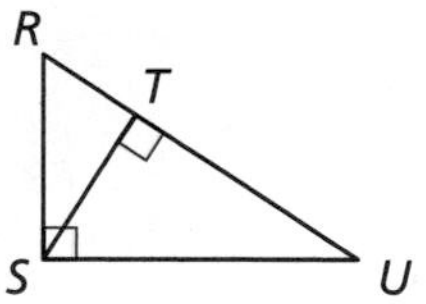

Find the geometric mean of each pair of numbers. If necessary, give the answer in simplest radical form.

18. 5 and 45
19. 3 and 15
20. 5 and 8
21. $\frac{1}{4}$ and 80
22. 1.5 and 12
23. $\frac{2}{3}$ and $\frac{27}{40}$

Find *x*, *y*, and *z*.

24. 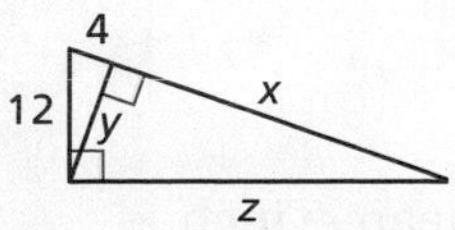

25. 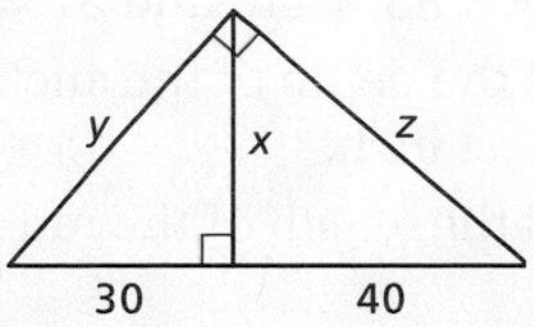

26. 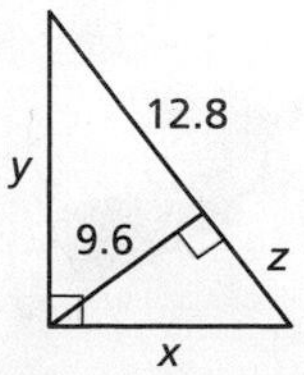

27. Measurement To estimate the height of the Taipei 101 tower, Andrew stands so that his lines of sight to the top and bottom of the tower form a 90° angle. What is the height of the tower to the nearest foot?

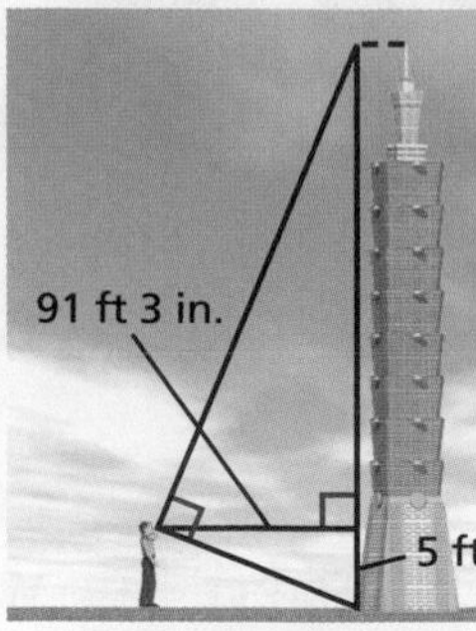

28. The geometric mean of two numbers is 8. One of the numbers is 2. Find the other number.

29. The geometric mean of two numbers is $2\sqrt{5}$. One of the numbers is 6. Find the other number.

Use the diagram to complete each equation.

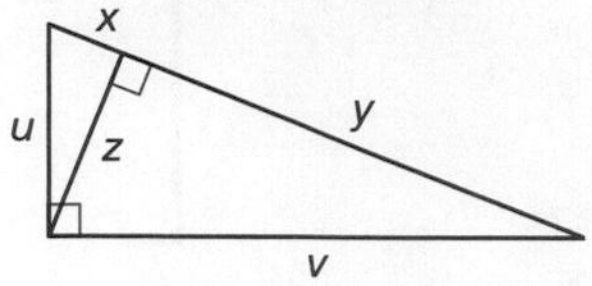

30. $\frac{x}{z} = \frac{z}{?}$ **31.** $\frac{?}{u} = \frac{u}{x}$ **32.** $\frac{x+y}{v} = \frac{v}{?}$

33. $\frac{y}{?} = \frac{z}{x}$ **34.** $(?)^2 = y(x+y)$ **35.** $u^2 = (x+y)(?)$

Give each answer in simplest radical form.

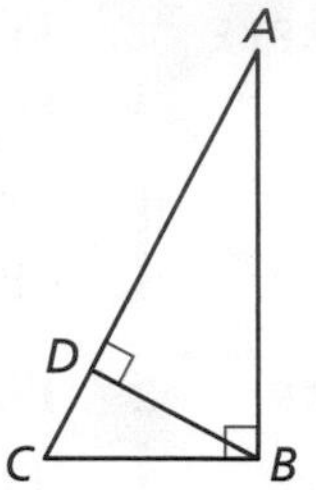

36. $AD = 12$, and $CD = 8$. Find BD.

37. $AC = 16$, and $CD = 5$. Find BC.

38. $AD = CD = \sqrt{2}$. Find BD.

39. $BC = \sqrt{5}$, and $AC = \sqrt{10}$. Find CD.

40. Finance An investment returns 3% one year and 10% the next year. The average rate of return is the geometric mean of the two annual rates. What is the average rate of return for this investment to the nearest tenth of a percent?

41. ERROR ANALYSIS Two students were asked to find EF. Which solution is incorrect? Explain the error.

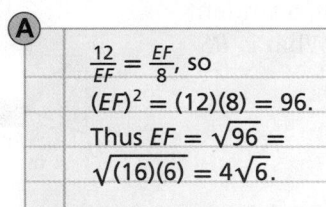

A

$\frac{12}{EF} = \frac{EF}{8}$, so
$(EF)^2 = (12)(8) = 96$.
Thus $EF = \sqrt{96} = \sqrt{(16)(6)} = 4\sqrt{6}$.

B

$\frac{8}{EF} = \frac{EF}{4}$, so
$(EF)^2 = (8)(4) = 32$.
Thus $EF = \sqrt{32} = \sqrt{(16)(2)} = 4\sqrt{2}$.

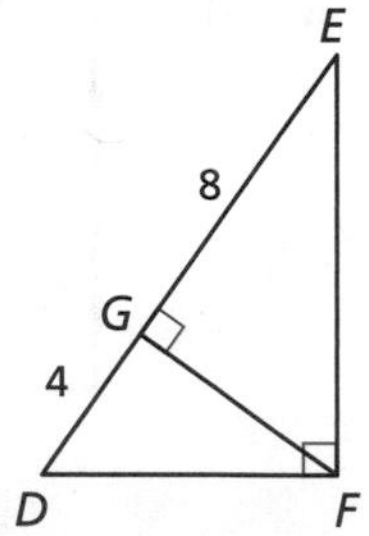

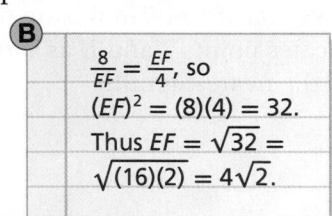

42. The altitude to the hypotenuse of a right triangle divides the hypotenuse into segments that are 2 cm long and 5 cm long. Find the length of the altitude to the nearest tenth of a centimeter.

43. Critical Thinking Use the figure to show how Corollary 8-1-3 can be used to derive the Pythagorean Theorem. (*Hint:* Use the corollary to write expressions for a^2 and b^2. Then add the expressions.)

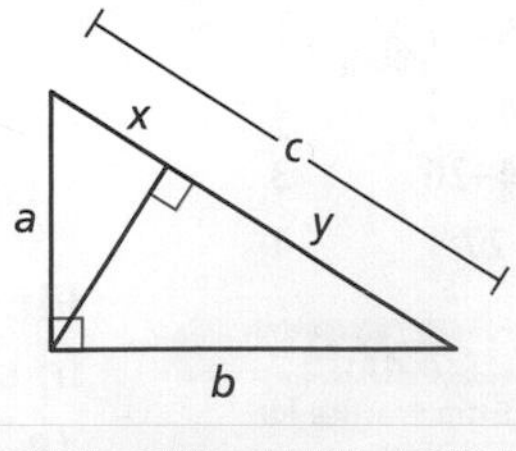

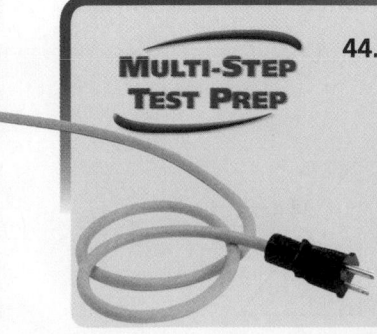

MULTI-STEP TEST PREP

44. Before installing a utility pole, a crew must first dig a hole and install the anchor for the guy wire that supports the pole. In the diagram, $\overline{SW} \perp \overline{RT}$, $\overline{RW} \perp \overline{WT}$, $RS = 4$ ft, and $ST = 3$ ft.

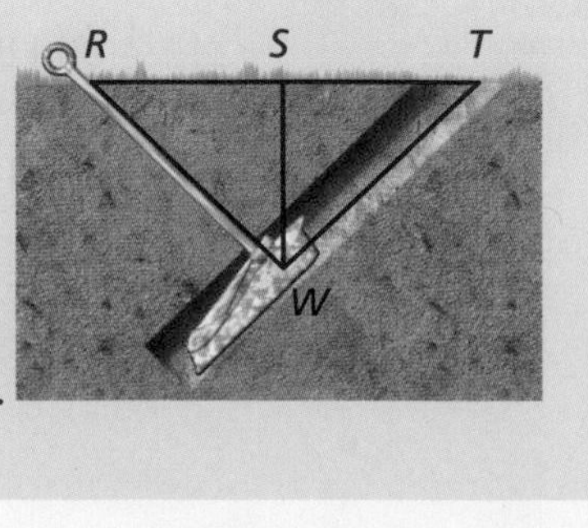

a. Find the depth of the anchor $\overline{SW}$ to the nearest inch.

b. Find the length of the rod $\overline{RW}$ to the nearest inch.

45. **Write About It** Suppose the rectangle and square have the same area. Explain why s must be the geometric mean of a and b.

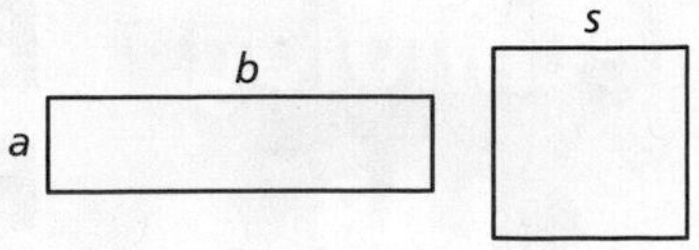

46. **Write About It** Explain why the geometric mean of two perfect squares must be a whole number.

TEST PREP

47. Lee is building a skateboard ramp based on the plan shown. Which is closest to the length of the ramp from point X to point Y?

(A) 4.9 feet (C) 8.5 feet

(B) 5.7 feet (D) 9.4 feet

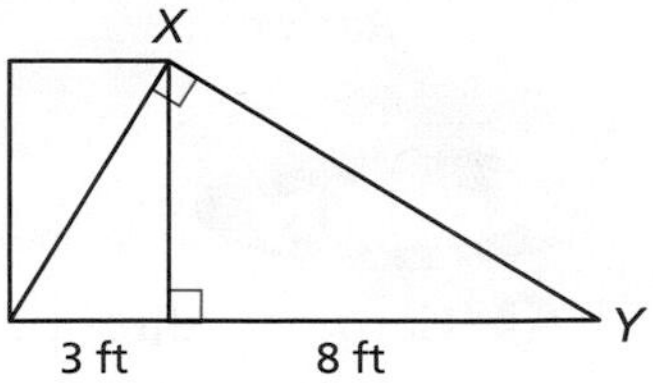

48. What is the area of $\triangle ABC$?

(F) 18 square meters (H) 39 square meters

(G) 36 square meters (J) 78 square meters

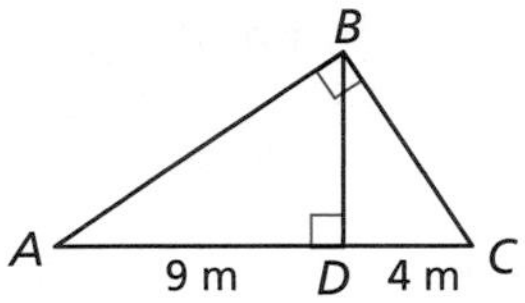

49. Which expression represents the length of $\overline{RS}$?

(A) $\sqrt{y+1}$ (C) y^2

(B) $\sqrt{y}$ (D) $y(y+1)$

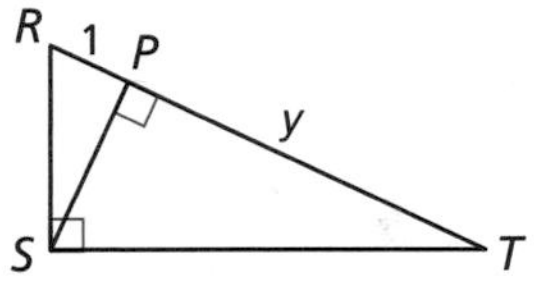

CHALLENGE AND EXTEND

50. **Algebra** An 8-inch-long altitude of a right triangle divides the hypotenuse into two segments. One segment is 4 times as long as the other. What are the lengths of the segments of the hypotenuse?

51. Use similarity in right triangles to find x, y, and z.

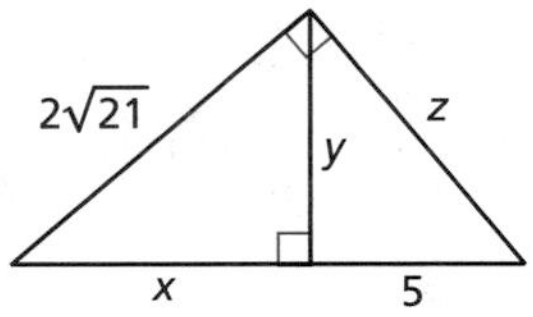

52. Prove the following. If the altitude to the hypotenuse of a right triangle bisects the hypotenuse, then the triangle is a 45°-45°-90° right triangle.

53. **Multi-Step** Find AC and AB to the nearest hundredth.

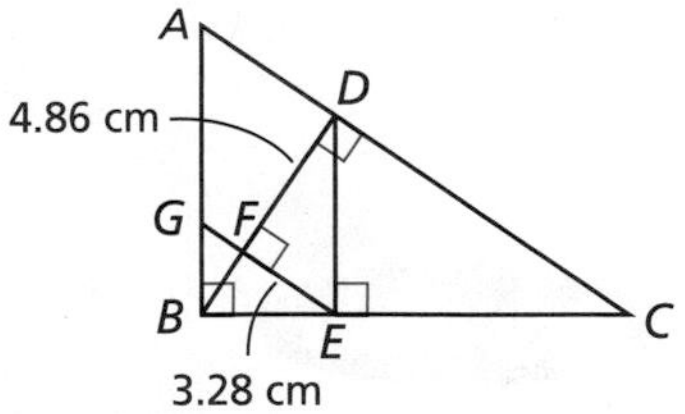

8-2 Technology LAB

Explore Trigonometric Ratios

Use with Trigonometric Ratios

In a right triangle, the ratio of two side lengths is known as a *trigonometric ratio.*

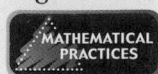

MATHEMATICAL PRACTICES **Use appropriate tools strategically.**

CC.9-12.G.SRT.6 Understand that… side ratios…are properties of the angles in the triangle, leading to definitions of trigonometric ratios…

Learn It Online
Lab Resources Online

Activity

1 Construct three points and label them A, B, and C. Construct rays $\overrightarrow{AB}$ and $\overrightarrow{AC}$ with common endpoint A. Move C so that $\angle A$ is an acute angle.

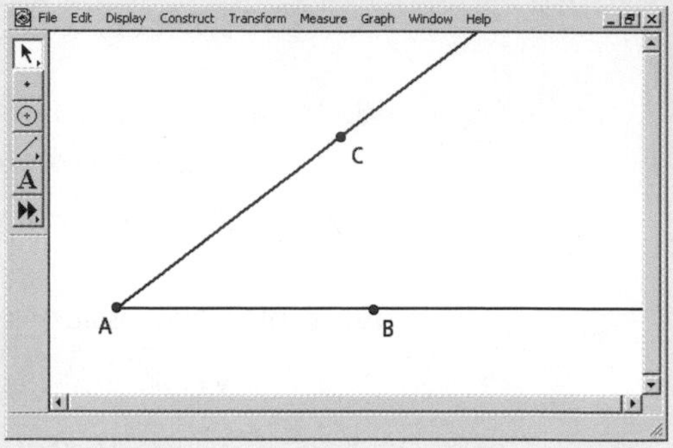

2 Construct point D on $\overrightarrow{AC}$. Construct a line through D perpendicular to $\overrightarrow{AB}$. Label the intersection of the perpendicular line and $\overrightarrow{AB}$ as E.

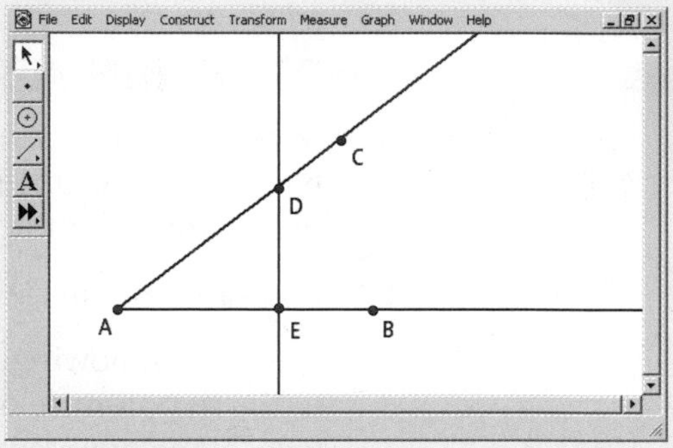

3 Measure $\angle A$. Measure DE, AE, and AD, the side lengths of $\triangle AED$.

4 Calculate the ratios $\frac{DE}{AD}$, $\frac{AE}{AD}$, and $\frac{DE}{AE}$.

Try This

1. Drag D along $\overrightarrow{AC}$. What happens to the measure of $\angle A$ as D moves? What postulate or theorem guarantees that the different triangles formed are similar to each other?
2. As you move D, what happens to the values of the three ratios you calculated? Use the properties of similar triangles to explain this result.
3. Move C. What happens to the measure of $\angle A$? With a new value for $m\angle A$, note the values of the three ratios. What happens to the ratios if you drag D?
4. Move C until $\frac{DE}{AD} = \frac{AE}{AD}$. What is the value of $\frac{DE}{AE}$? What is the measure of $\angle A$? Use the properties of special right triangles to justify this result.

COMMON CORE

8-2 Trigonometric Ratios

CC.9-12.G.SRT.6 Understand that…side ratios…are properties of the angles in the triangle, leading to definitions of trigonometric ratios…

Objectives

Find the sine, cosine, and tangent of an acute angle.

Use trigonometric ratios to find side lengths in right triangles and to solve real-world problems.

Vocabulary

trigonometric ratio
sine
cosine
tangent

Who uses this?

Contractors use trigonometric ratios to build ramps that meet legal requirements.

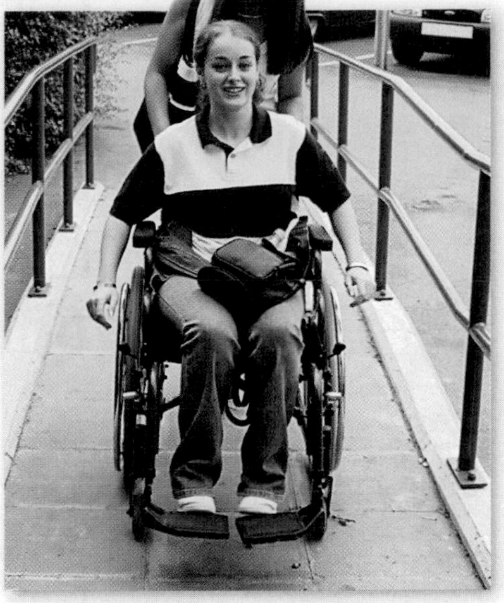

According to the Americans with Disabilities Act (ADA), the maximum slope allowed for a wheelchair ramp is $\frac{1}{12}$, which is an angle of about 4.8°. Properties of right triangles help builders construct ramps that meet this requirement.

By the AA Similarity Postulate, a right triangle with a given acute angle is similar to every other right triangle with that same acute angle measure. So $\triangle ABC \sim \triangle DEF \sim \triangle XYZ$, and $\frac{BC}{AC} = \frac{EF}{DF} = \frac{YZ}{XZ}$. These are *trigonometric ratios.* A **trigonometric ratio** is a ratio of two sides of a right triangle.

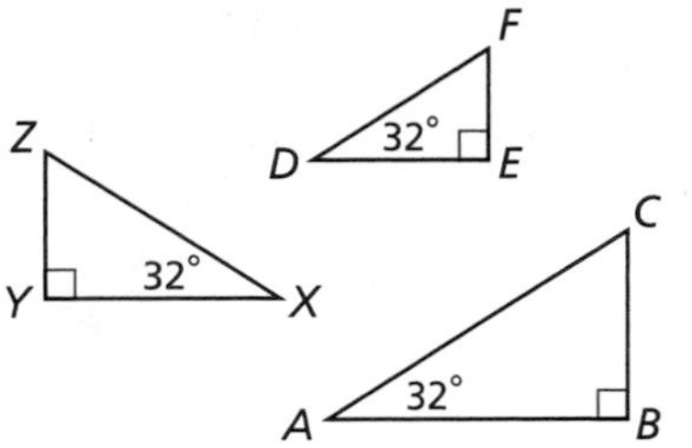

Know it! Note

Writing Math

In trigonometry, the letter of the vertex of the angle is often used to represent the measure of that angle. For example, the sine of ∠A is written as sin A.

Trigonometric Ratios

DEFINITION	SYMBOLS	DIAGRAM
The **sine** of an angle is the ratio of the length of the leg opposite the angle to the length of the hypotenuse.	$\sin A = \frac{\text{opposite leg}}{\text{hypotenuse}} = \frac{a}{c}$ $\sin B = \frac{\text{opposite leg}}{\text{hypotenuse}} = \frac{b}{c}$	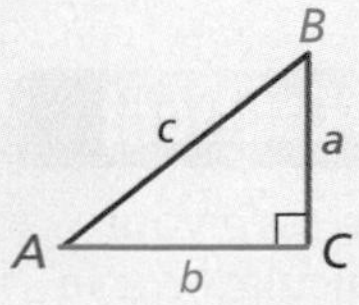
The **cosine** of an angle is the ratio of the length of the leg adjacent to the angle to the length of the hypotenuse.	$\cos A = \frac{\text{adjacent leg}}{\text{hypotenuse}} = \frac{b}{c}$ $\cos B = \frac{\text{adjacent leg}}{\text{hypotenuse}} = \frac{a}{c}$	
The **tangent** of an angle is the ratio of the length of the leg opposite the angle to the length of the leg adjacent to the angle.	$\tan A = \frac{\text{opposite leg}}{\text{adjacent leg}} = \frac{a}{b}$ $\tan B = \frac{\text{opposite leg}}{\text{adjacent leg}} = \frac{b}{a}$	

EXAMPLE 1 Finding Trigonometric Ratios

Write each trigonometric ratio as a fraction and as a decimal rounded to the nearest hundredth.

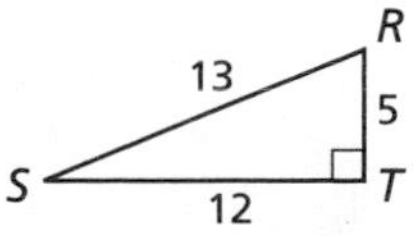

A $\sin R$

$\sin R = \frac{12}{13} \approx 0.92$ *The sine of an ∠ is* $\frac{\text{opp. leg}}{\text{hyp.}}$.

Write each trigonometric ratio as a fraction and as a decimal rounded to the nearest hundredth.

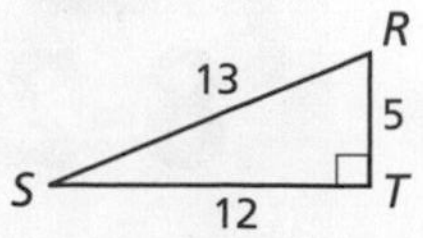

B $\cos R$

$\cos R = \frac{5}{13} \approx 0.38$ *The cosine of an ∠ is $\frac{\text{adj. leg}}{\text{hyp.}}$.*

C $\tan S$

$\tan S = \frac{5}{12} \approx 0.42$ *The tangent of an ∠ is $\frac{\text{opp. leg}}{\text{adj. leg}}$.*

CHECK IT OUT! Write each trigonometric ratio as a fraction and as a decimal rounded to the nearest hundredth.

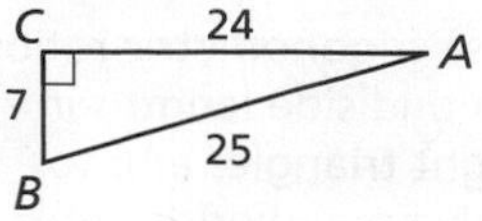

1a. $\cos A$ **1b.** $\tan B$ **1c.** $\sin B$

EXAMPLE 2 Finding Trigonometric Ratios in Special Right Triangles

Use a special right triangle to write sin 60° as a fraction.

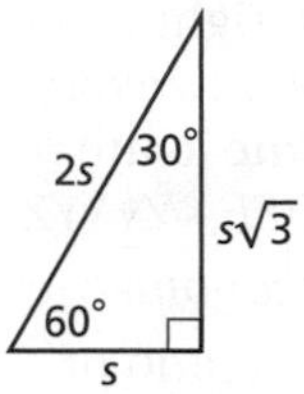

Draw and label a 30°-60°-90° △.

$\sin 60° = \frac{s\sqrt{3}}{2s} = \frac{\sqrt{3}}{2}$ *The sine of an ∠ is $\frac{\text{opp. leg}}{\text{hyp.}}$.*

CHECK IT OUT! **2.** Use a special right triangle to write tan 45° as a fraction.

EXAMPLE 3 Calculating Trigonometric Ratios

Use your calculator to find each trigonometric ratio. Round to the nearest hundredth.

Caution!

Be sure your calculator is in degree mode, not radian mode.

A cos 76°

$\cos 76° \approx 0.24$

B sin 8°

$\sin 8° \approx 0.14$

C tan 82°

$\tan 82° \approx 7.12$

CHECK IT OUT! Use your calculator to find each trigonometric ratio. Round to the nearest hundredth.

3a. tan 11° **3b.** sin 62° **3c.** cos 30°

The hypotenuse is always the longest side of a right triangle. So the denominator of a sine or cosine ratio is always greater than the numerator. Therefore the sine and cosine of an acute angle are always positive numbers less than 1. Since the tangent of an acute angle is the ratio of the lengths of the legs, it can have any value greater than 0.

EXAMPLE 4 Using Trigonometric Ratios to Find Lengths

Find each length. Round to the nearest hundredth.

A AB

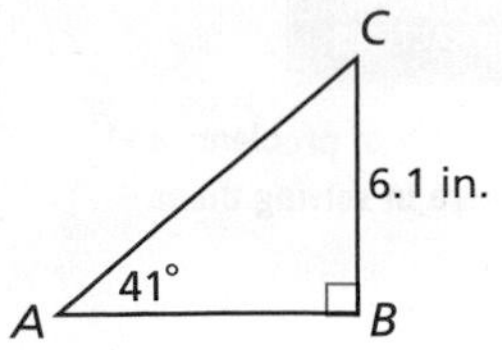

$\overline{AB}$ is adjacent to the given angle, $\angle A$. You are given BC, which is opposite $\angle A$. Since the adjacent and opposite legs are involved, use a tangent ratio.

$\tan A = \frac{\text{opp. leg}}{\text{adj. leg}} = \frac{BC}{AB}$ *Write a trigonometric ratio.*

$\tan 41° = \frac{6.1}{AB}$ *Substitute the given values.*

$AB = \frac{6.1}{\tan 41°}$ *Multiply both sides by AB and divide by tan 41°.*

$AB \approx 7.02$ in. *Simplify the expression.*

B MP

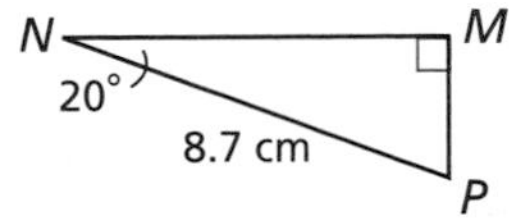

$\overline{MP}$ is opposite the given angle, $\angle N$. You are given NP, which is the hypotenuse. Since the opposite side and hypotenuse are involved, use a sine ratio.

$\sin N = \frac{\text{opp. leg}}{\text{hyp.}} = \frac{MP}{NP}$ *Write a trigonometric ratio.*

$\sin 20° = \frac{MP}{8.7}$ *Substitute the given values.*

$8.7(\sin 20°) = MP$ *Multiply both sides by 8.7.*

$MP \approx 2.98$ cm *Simplify the expression.*

Caution!

Do not round until the final step of your answer. Use the values of the trigonometric ratios provided by your calculator.

C YZ

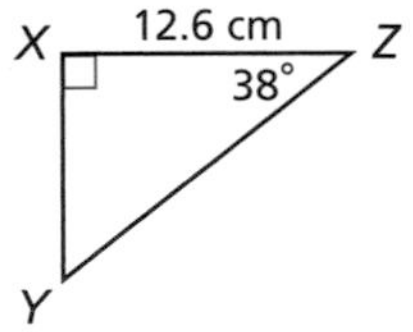

$\overline{YZ}$ is the hypotenuse. You are given XZ, which is adjacent to the given angle, $\angle Z$. Since the adjacent side and hypotenuse are involved, use a cosine ratio.

$\cos Z = \frac{\text{adj. leg}}{\text{hyp.}} = \frac{XZ}{YZ}$ *Write a trigonometric ratio.*

$\cos 38° = \frac{12.6}{YZ}$ *Substitute the given values.*

$YZ = \frac{12.6}{\cos 38°}$ *Multiply both sides by YZ and divide by cos 38°.*

$YZ \approx 15.99$ cm *Simplify the expression.*

CHECK IT OUT! **Find each length. Round to the nearest hundredth.**

4a. DF

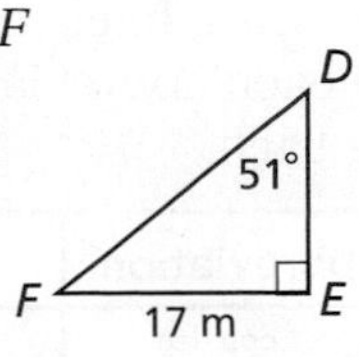

4b. ST

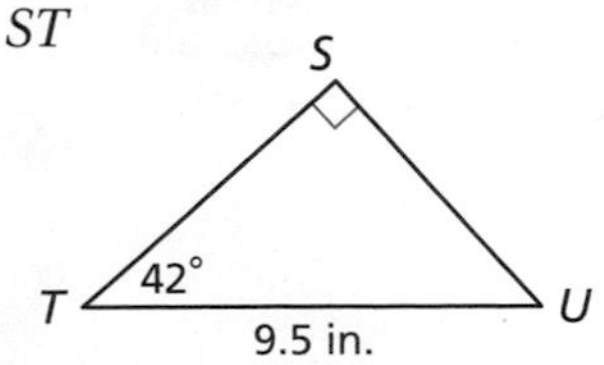

4c. BC

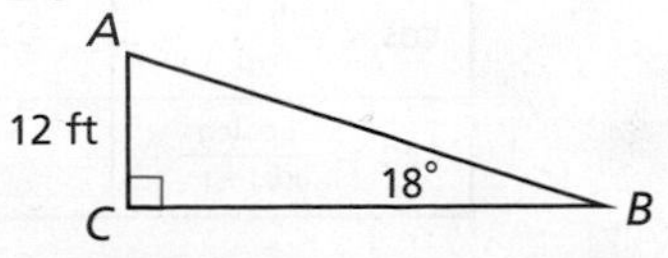

4d. JL

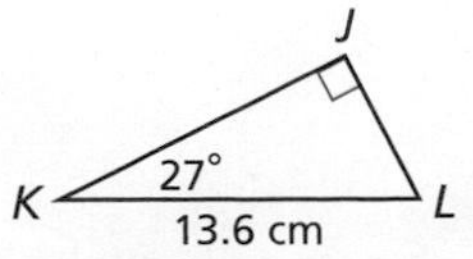

EXAMPLE 5 *Problem Solving Application*

MATHEMATICAL PRACTICES

Make sense of problems and persevere in solving them.

A contractor is building a wheelchair ramp for a doorway that is 1.2 ft above the ground. To meet ADA guidelines, the ramp will make an angle of 4.8° with the ground. To the nearest hundredth of a foot, what is the horizontal distance covered by the ramp?

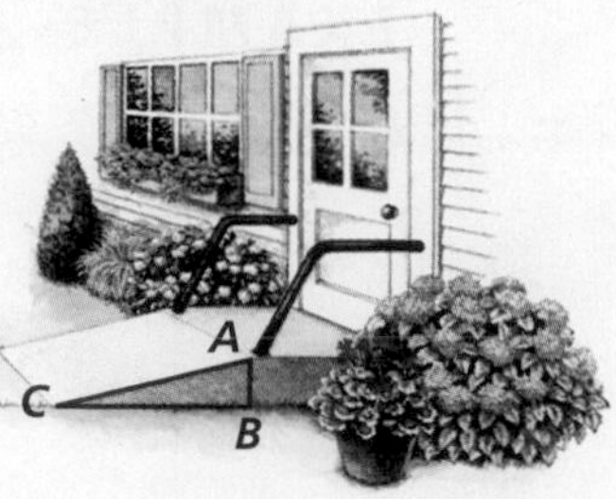

1 Understand the Problem

Make a sketch. The **answer** is *BC*.

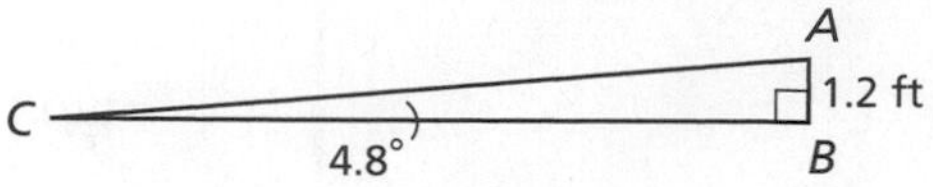

2 Make a Plan

$\overline{BC}$ is the leg adjacent to $\angle C$. You are given *AB*, which is the leg opposite $\angle C$. Since the opposite and adjacent legs are involved, write an equation using the tangent ratio.

3 Solve

$\tan C = \frac{AB}{BC}$	*Write a trigonometric ratio.*
$\tan 4.8° = \frac{1.2}{BC}$	*Substitute the given values.*
$BC = \frac{1.2}{\tan 4.8°}$	*Multiply both sides by BC and divide by tan 4.8°.*
$BC \approx 14.2904$ ft	*Simplify the expression.*

4 Look Back

The problem asks for *BC* rounded to the nearest hundredth, so round the length to 14.29. The ramp covers a horizontal distance of 14.29 ft.

CHECK IT OUT! **5.** Find *AC*, the length of the ramp in Example 5, to the nearest hundredth of a foot.

THINK AND DISCUSS

MATHEMATICAL PRACTICES

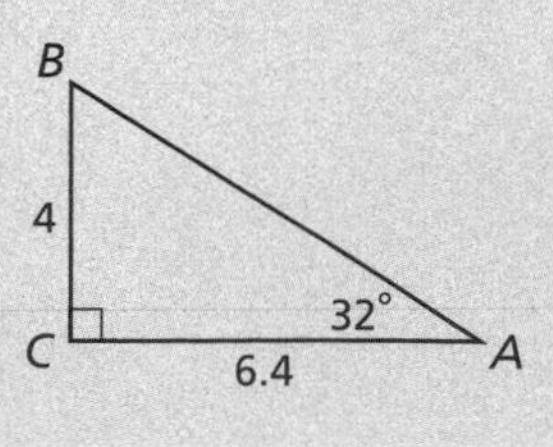

1. Tell how you could use a sine ratio to find *AB*.

2. Tell how you could use a cosine ratio to find *AB*.

Know it! Note

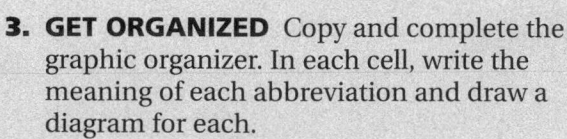

3. GET ORGANIZED Copy and complete the graphic organizer. In each cell, write the meaning of each abbreviation and draw a diagram for each.

Abbreviation	Words	Diagram
$\sin = \frac{\text{opp. leg}}{\text{hyp.}}$		
$\cos = \frac{\text{adj. leg}}{\text{hyp.}}$		
$\tan = \frac{\text{opp. leg}}{\text{adj. leg}}$		

8-2 Exercises

Learn It Online
Homework Help Online
Parent Resources Online

GUIDED PRACTICE

Vocabulary **Apply the vocabulary from this lesson to answer each question.**

1. In $\triangle JKL$, $\angle K$ is a right angle. Write the *sine* of $\angle J$ as a ratio of side lengths.
2. In $\triangle MNP$, $\angle M$ is a right angle. Write the *tangent* of $\angle N$ as a ratio of side lengths.

SEE EXAMPLE 1

Write each trigonometric ratio as a fraction and as a decimal rounded to the nearest hundredth.

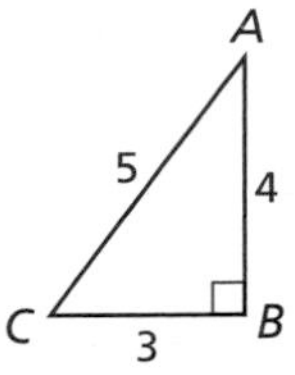

3. $\sin C$
4. $\tan A$
5. $\cos A$
6. $\cos C$
7. $\tan C$
8. $\sin A$

SEE EXAMPLE 2

Use a special right triangle to write each trigonometric ratio as a fraction.

9. $\cos 60°$
10. $\tan 30°$
11. $\sin 45°$

SEE EXAMPLE 3

Use your calculator to find each trigonometric ratio. Round to the nearest hundredth.

12. $\tan 67°$
13. $\sin 23°$
14. $\sin 49°$
15. $\cos 88°$
16. $\cos 12°$
17. $\tan 9°$

SEE EXAMPLE 4

Find each length. Round to the nearest hundredth.

18. *BC*

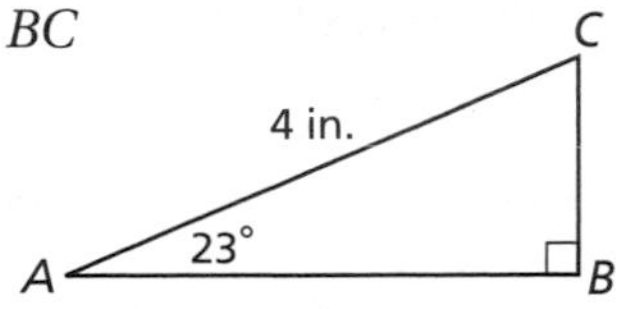

19. *QR*

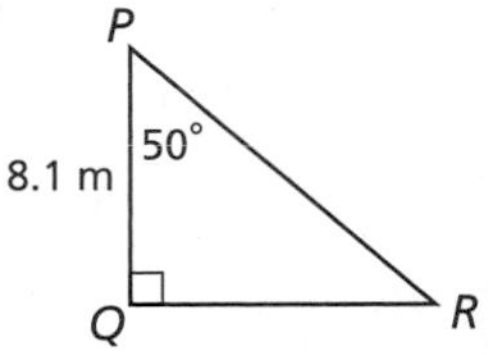

20. *KL*

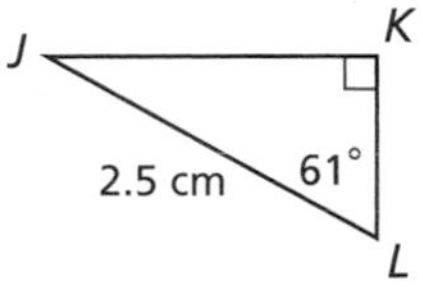

SEE EXAMPLE 5

21. **Architecture** A pediment has a pitch of 15°, as shown. If the width of the pediment, *WZ*, is 56 ft, what is *XY* to the nearest inch?

PRACTICE AND PROBLEM SOLVING

Independent Practice

For Exercises	See Example
22–27	1
28–30	2
31–36	3
37–42	4
43	5

Extra Practice

See Extra Practice for more Skills Practice and Applications Practice exercises.

Write each trigonometric ratio as a fraction and as a decimal rounded to the nearest hundredth.

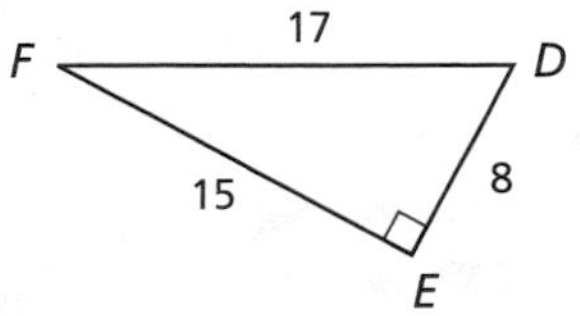

22. $\cos D$
23. $\tan D$
24. $\tan F$
25. $\cos F$
26. $\sin F$
27. $\sin D$

Use a special right triangle to write each trigonometric ratio as a fraction.

28. $\tan 60°$
29. $\sin 30°$
30. $\cos 45°$

Use your calculator to find each trigonometric ratio. Round to the nearest hundredth.

31. $\tan 51°$
32. $\sin 80°$
33. $\cos 77°$
34. $\tan 14°$
35. $\sin 55°$
36. $\cos 48°$

Find each length. Round to the nearest hundredth.

37. *PQ*

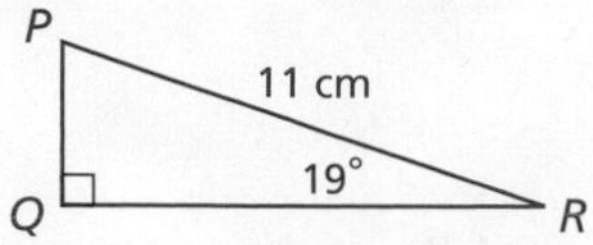

38. *AC*

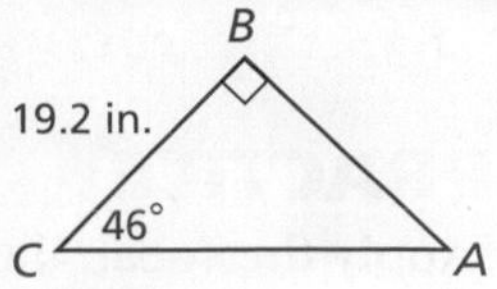

39. *GH*

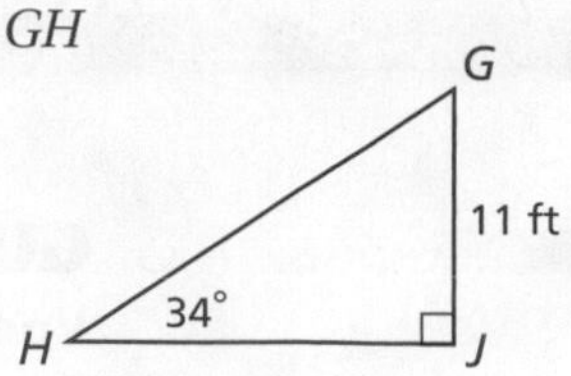

40. *XZ*

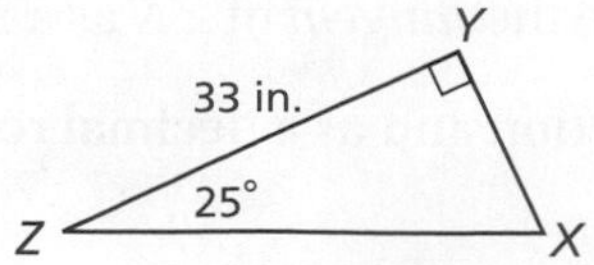

41. *KL*

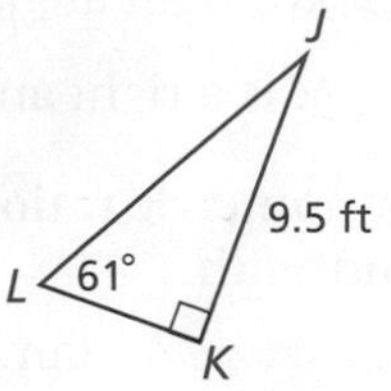

42. *EF*

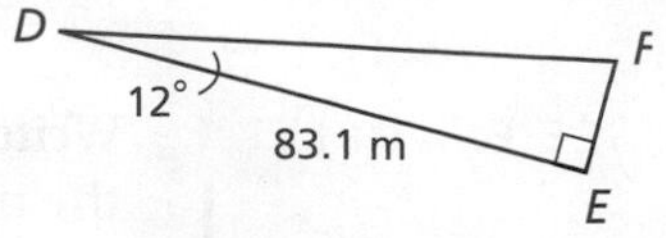

43. Sports A jump ramp for waterskiing makes an angle of 15° with the surface of the water. The ramp rises 1.58 m above the surface. What is the length of the ramp to the nearest hundredth of a meter?

Use special right triangles to complete each statement.

44. An angle that measures __?__ has a tangent of 1.

45. For a 45° angle, the __?__ and __?__ ratios are equal.

46. The sine of a __?__ angle is 0.5.

47. The cosine of a 30° angle is equal to the sine of a __?__ angle.

48. Safety According to the Occupational Safety and Health Administration (OSHA), a ladder that is placed against a wall should make a 75.5° angle with the ground for optimal safety. To the nearest tenth of a foot, what is the maximum height that a 10-ft ladder can safely reach?

Find the indicated length in each rectangle. Round to the nearest tenth.

49. *BC*

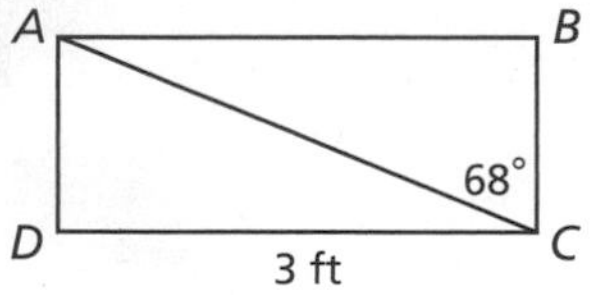

50. *SU*

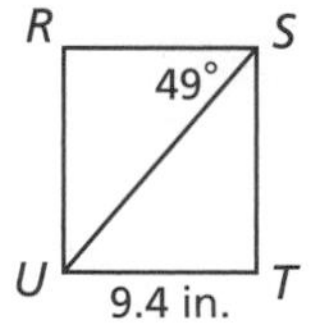

51. Critical Thinking For what angle measures is the tangent ratio less than 1? greater than 1? Explain.

MULTI-STEP TEST PREP

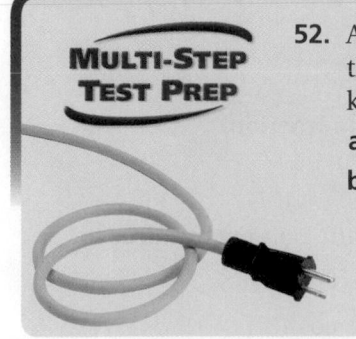

52. A utility worker is installing a 25-foot pole $\overline{AB}$ at the foot of a hill. Two guy wires, $\overline{AC}$ and $\overline{AD}$, will help keep the pole vertical.

a. To the nearest inch, how long should $\overline{AC}$ be?

b. $\overline{AD}$ is perpendicular to the hill, which makes an angle of 28° with a horizontal line. To the nearest inch, how long should this guy wire be?

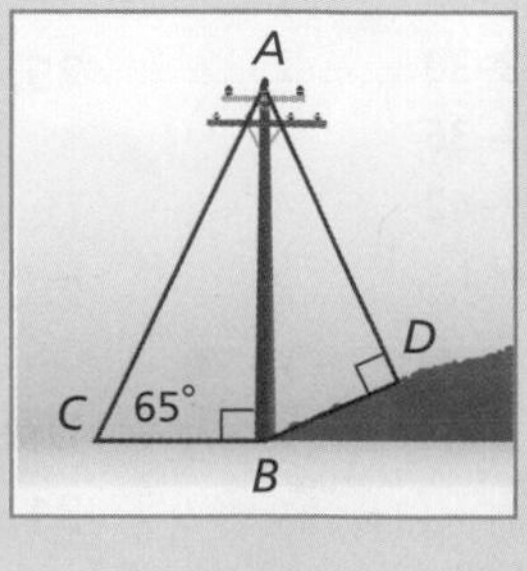

LINK

History

The Pyramid of Cheops consists of more than 2,000,000 blocks of stone with an average weight of 2.5 tons each.

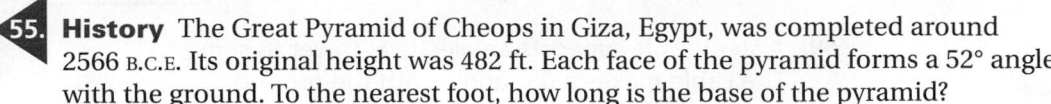

53. Find the sine of the smaller acute angle in a triangle with side lengths of 3, 4, and 5 inches.

54. Find the tangent of the greater acute angle in a triangle with side lengths of 7, 24, and 25 centimeters.

55. History The Great Pyramid of Cheops in Giza, Egypt, was completed around 2566 B.C.E. Its original height was 482 ft. Each face of the pyramid forms a 52° angle with the ground. To the nearest foot, how long is the base of the pyramid?

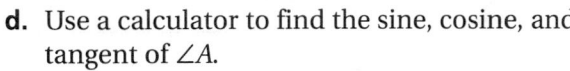

56. Measurement Follow these steps to calculate trigonometric ratios.

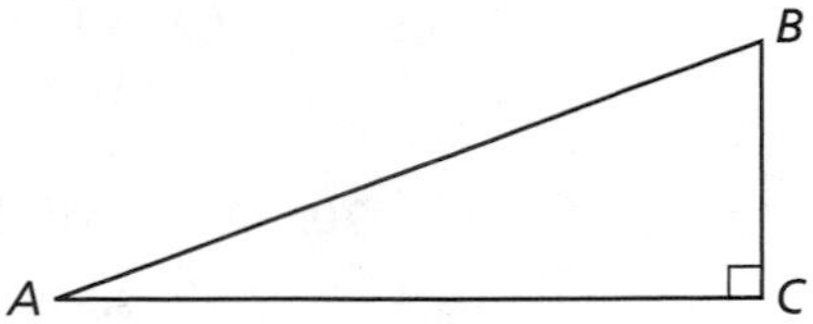

a. Use a centimeter ruler to find *AB*, *BC*, and *AC*.

b. Use your measurements from part **a** to find the sine, cosine, and tangent of $\angle A$.

c. Use a protractor to find $m\angle A$.

d. Use a calculator to find the sine, cosine, and tangent of $\angle A$.

e. How do the values in part **d** compare to the ones you found in part **b**?

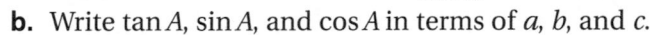

57. Algebra Recall from Algebra I that an *identity* is an equation that is true for all values of the variables.

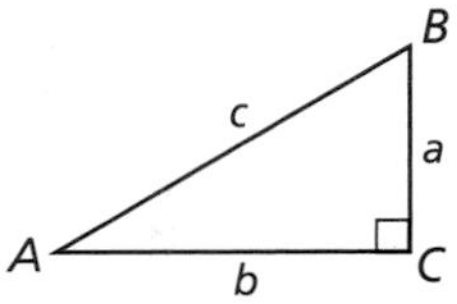

a. Show that the identity $\tan A = \dfrac{\sin A}{\cos A}$ is true when $m\angle A = 30°$.

b. Write $\tan A$, $\sin A$, and $\cos A$ in terms of *a*, *b*, and *c*.

c. Use your results from part **b** to prove the identity $\tan A = \dfrac{\sin A}{\cos A}$.

Verify that $(\sin A)^2 + (\cos A)^2 = 1$ for each angle measure.

58. $m\angle A = 45°$ **59.** $m\angle A = 30°$ **60.** $m\angle A = 60°$

61. Multi-Step The equation $(\sin A)^2 + (\cos A)^2 = 1$ is known as a Pythagorean Identity.

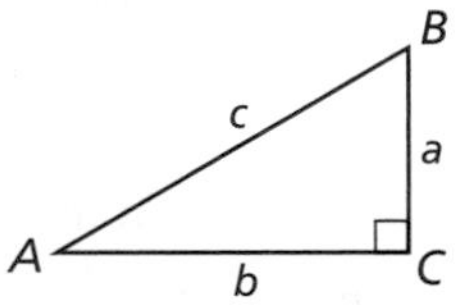

a. Write $\sin A$ and $\cos A$ in terms of *a*, *b*, and *c*.

b. Use your results from part **a** to prove the identity $(\sin A)^2 + (\cos A)^2 = 1$.

c. Write About It Why do you think this identity is called a Pythagorean identity?

Find the perimeter and area of each triangle. Round to the nearest hundredth.

62.

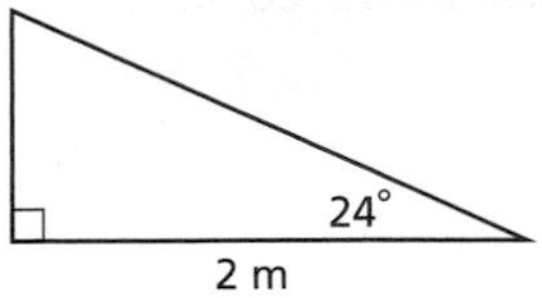

63.

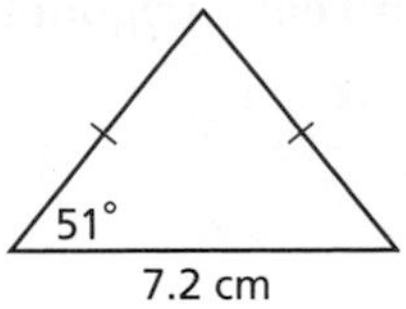

64.

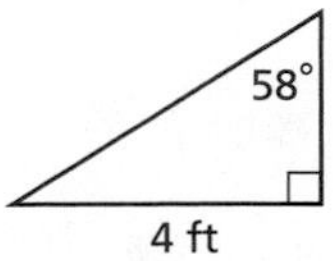

65.

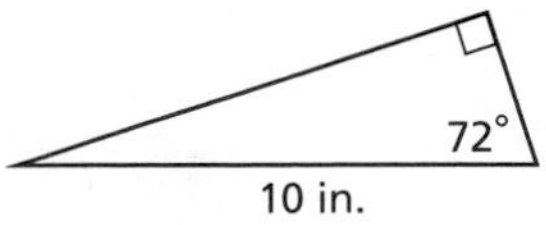

66. Critical Thinking Draw $\triangle ABC$ with $\angle C$ a right angle. Write $\sin A$ and $\cos B$ in terms of the side lengths of the triangle. What do you notice? How are $\angle A$ and $\angle B$ related? Make a conjecture based on your observations.

67. Write About It Explain how the tangent of an acute angle changes as the angle measure increases.

TEST PREP

68. Which expression can be used to find AB?

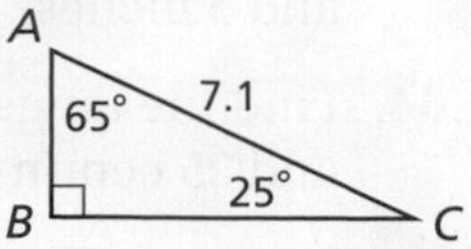

Ⓐ $7.1(\sin 25°)$ Ⓒ $7.1(\sin 65°)$

Ⓑ $7.1(\cos 25°)$ Ⓓ $7.1(\tan 65°)$

69. A steel cable supports an electrical tower as shown. The cable makes a 65° angle with the ground. The base of the cable is 17 ft from the tower. What is the height of the tower to the nearest foot?

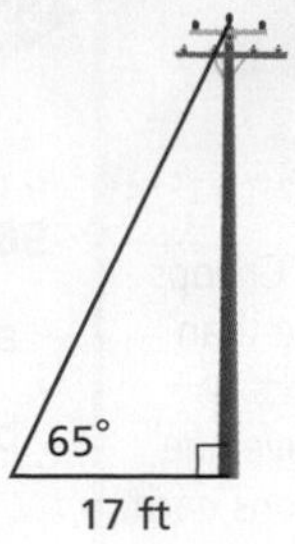

Ⓕ 8 feet Ⓗ 36 feet

Ⓖ 15 feet Ⓙ 40 feet

70. Which of the following has the same value as $\sin M$?

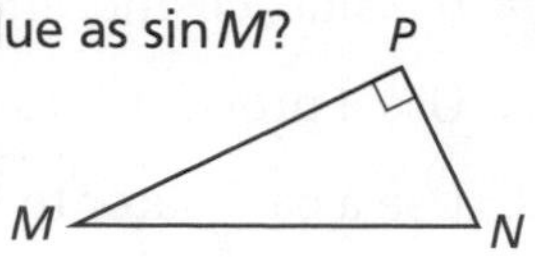

Ⓐ $\sin N$ Ⓒ $\cos N$

Ⓑ $\tan M$ Ⓓ $\cos M$

CHALLENGE AND EXTEND

Algebra **Find the value of x. Then find AB, BC, and AC. Round each to the nearest unit.**

71.

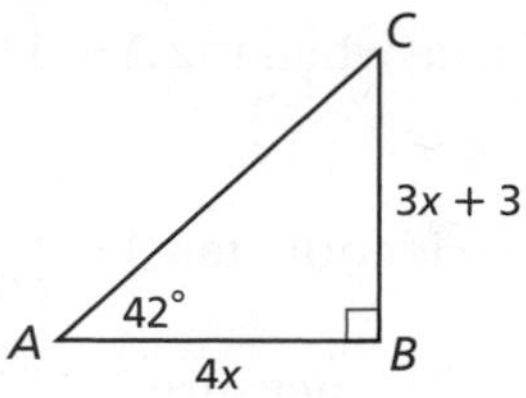

72.

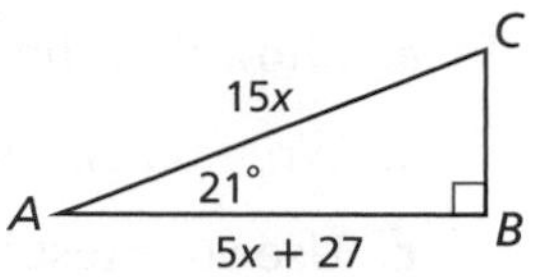

73. **Multi-Step** Prove the identity $(\tan A)^2 + 1 = \dfrac{1}{(\cos A)^2}$.

74. A regular pentagon with 1 in. sides is inscribed in a circle. Find the radius of the circle rounded to the nearest hundredth.

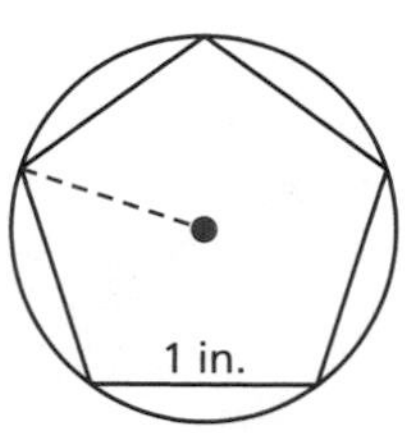

Each of the three trigonometric ratios has a reciprocal ratio, as defined below. These ratios are *cosecant* (csc), *secant* (sec), and *cotangent* (cot).

$\csc A = \dfrac{1}{\sin A}$ $\sec A = \dfrac{1}{\cos A}$ $\cot A = \dfrac{1}{\tan A}$

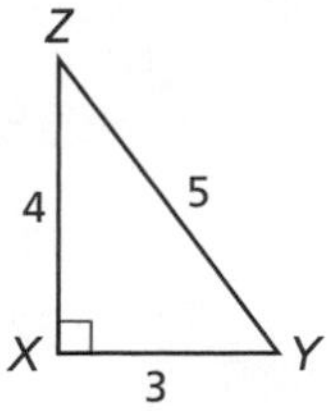

Find each trigonometric ratio to the nearest hundredth.

75. $\csc Y$ 76. $\sec Z$ 77. $\cot Y$

COMMON CORE

EXTENSION

Trigonometric Ratios and Complementary Angles

CC.9-12.G.SRT.7 Explain and use the relationship between the sine and cosine of complementary angles.

Objectives
Use the relationship between the sine and cosine of complementary angles.

Vocabulary
cofunction

The acute angles of a right triangle are complementary angles. If the measure of one of the two acute angles is given, the measure of the second acute angle can be found by subtracting the given measure from 90°.

EXAMPLE 1 Finding the Sine and Cosine of Acute Angles

Find the sine and cosine of the acute angles in the right triangle shown.

Start with the sine and cosine of $\angle A$.

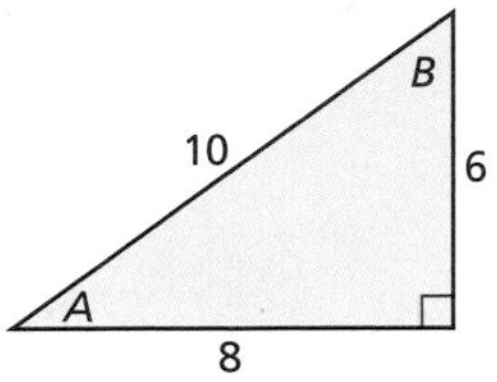

$$\sin A = \frac{\text{opposite}}{\text{hypotenuse}} = \frac{6}{10} = \frac{3}{5}$$

$$\cos A = \frac{\text{adjacent}}{\text{hypotenuse}} = \frac{8}{10} = \frac{4}{5}$$

Then, find the sine and cosine of $\angle B$.

$$\sin B = \frac{\text{opposite}}{\text{hypotenuse}} = \frac{8}{10} = \frac{4}{5}$$

$$\cos B = \frac{\text{adjacent}}{\text{hypotenuse}} = \frac{6}{10} = \frac{3}{5}$$

CHECK IT OUT!

1. Find the sine and cosine of the acute angles of a right triangle with sides 10, 24, 26. (Use A for the angle opposite the side with length 10 and B for the angle opposite the side with length 24.)

In Example 1, notice that $\sin A = \cos B$ and $\cos A = \sin B$. In general, the sine of an acute angle is equal to the cosine of the complement of that angle.

The trigonometric function of the complement of an angle is called a **cofunction.** The sine and cosines are cofunctions of each other.

EXAMPLE 2 Writing Sine in Cosine Terms and Cosine in Sine Terms

A **Write sin 42° in terms of the cosine.**

$$\sin 42° = \cos(90 - 42)°$$
$$= \cos 48°$$

B **Write cos 36° in terms of the sine.**

$$\cos 36° = \sin(90 - 36)°$$
$$= \sin 54°$$

CHECK IT OUT!

2a. Write sin 28° in terms of the cosine.

2b. Write cos 51° in terms of the sine.

EXAMPLE 3 Finding Unknown Angles

Find two angles that satisfy the equation.

$$\sin(2x - 4)° = \cos(3x + 9)°$$

If $\sin(2x - 4)° = \cos(3x + 9)°$, then $(2x - 4)°$ and $(3x + 9)°$ are the measures of complementary angles. The sum of the measures must be 90°.

$$(2x - 4) + (3x + 9) = 90$$
$$5x + 5 = 90$$
$$5x = 85$$
$$x = 17$$

Substitute the value of x into the original expression to find the angle measures.

$$2x - 4 = 2(17) - 4$$
$$= 30°$$

$$3x + 9 = 3(17) + 9$$
$$= 60°$$

The measurements of the two angles are 30° and 60°.

CHECK IT OUT! **Find the two angles that satisfy the equation**

3a. $\sin(3x + 2)° = \cos(x + 44)°$.

3b. $\sin(2x + 20)° = \cos(3x + 30)°$.

EXTENSION Exercises

Find the cosine and sine of the acute angles in the triangles shown.

1.

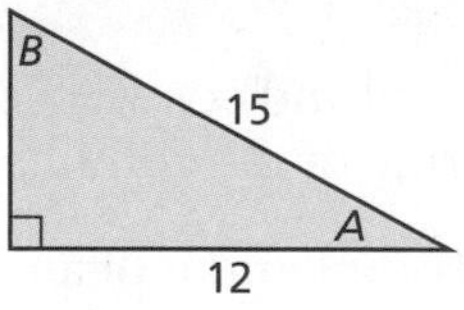

2.

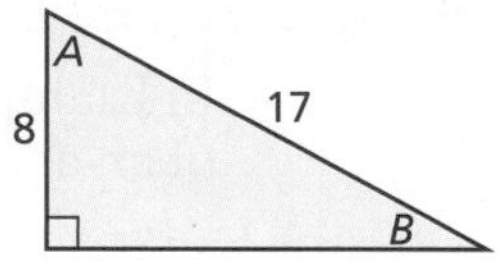

Write each trigonometric function in terms of its cofunction.

3. sin 64°

4. cos 84°

5. cos 38°

6. sin 24°

7. cos 72°

8. sin 45°

Find two angles that satisfy each equation.

9. $\sin(4x + 30)° = \cos(-2x + 54)°$

10. $\sin(-2x + 92)° = \cos(x + 8)°$

11. $\cos(5x + 49)° = \sin(3x + 57)°$

12. $\cos(-3x + 106)° = \sin(7x - 64)°$

13. $\sin(2x + 30)° = \cos(3x + 5)°$

14. $\sin(5x - 12)° = \cos(x + 54)°$

15. $\cos(3x - 10)° = \sin(3x - 20)°$

16. $\cos(7x - 68)° = \sin(-3x + 110)°$

Inverse Functions

In Algebra, you learned that a function is a relation in which each element of the domain is paired with exactly one element of the range. If you switch the domain and range of a one-to-one function, you create an *inverse function.*

The function $y = \sin^{-1} x$ is the inverse of the function $y = \sin x$.

If you know the value of a trigonometric ratio, you can use the inverse trigonometric function to find the angle measure. You can do this either with a calculator or by looking at the graph of the function.

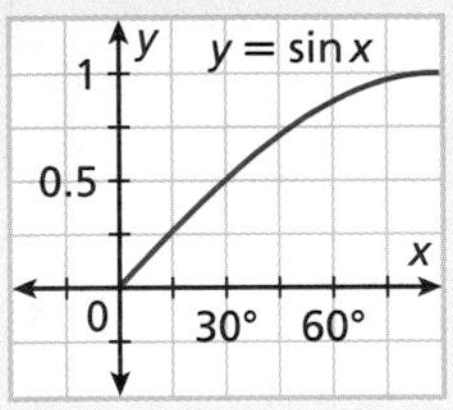

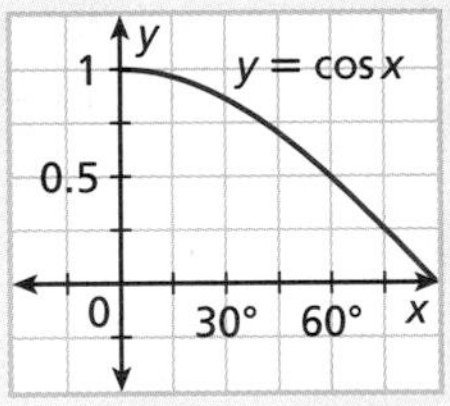

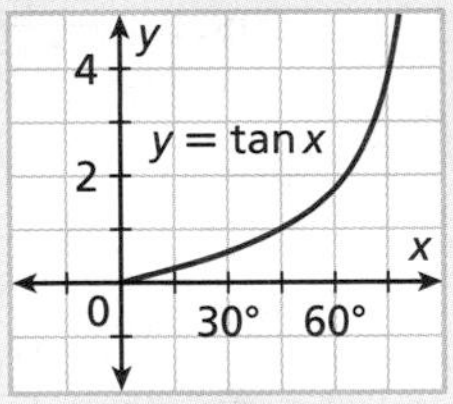

Example

Use the graphs above to find the value of x for $1 = \sin x$. Then write this expression using an inverse trigonometric function.

$1 = \sin x$ — *Look at the graph of $y = \sin x$. Find where the graph intersects the line $y = 1$ and read the corresponding x-coordinate.*

$x = 90°$

$90° = \sin^{-1}(1)$ — *Switch the x- and y-values.*

Try This

Use the graphs above to find the value of x for each of the following. Then write each expression using an inverse trigonometric function.

1. $0 = \sin x$

2. $\frac{1}{2} = \cos x$

3. $1 = \tan x$

4. $0 = \cos x$

5. $0 = \tan x$

6. $\frac{1}{2} = \sin x$

COMMON CORE

8-3 Solving Right Triangles

CC.9-12.G.SRT.8 Use trigonometric ratios and the Pythagorean Theorem to solve right triangles...*

Objective
Use trigonometric ratios to find angle measures in right triangles and to solve real-world problems.

Why learn this?
You can convert the percent grade of a road to an angle measure by solving a right triangle.

San Francisco, California, is famous for its steep streets. The steepness of a road is often expressed as a *percent grade.* Filbert Street, the steepest street in San Francisco, has a 31.5% grade. This means the road rises 31.5 ft over a horizontal distance of 100 ft, which is equivalent to a 17.5° angle. You can use trigonometric ratios to change a percent grade to an angle measure.

EXAMPLE 1 Identifying Angles from Trigonometric Ratios

Use the trigonometric ratio $\cos A = 0.6$ to determine which angle of the triangle is $\angle A$.

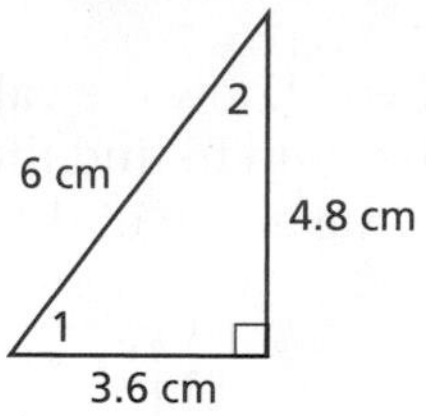

$\cos A = \dfrac{\text{adj. leg}}{\text{hyp.}}$ — *Cosine is the ratio of the adjacent leg to the hypotenuse.*

$\cos \angle 1 = \dfrac{3.6}{6} = 0.6$ — *The leg adjacent to ∠1 is 3.6. The hypotenuse is 6.*

$\cos \angle 2 = \dfrac{4.8}{6} = 0.8$ — *The leg adjacent to ∠2 is 4.8. The hypotenuse is 6.*

Since $\cos A = \cos \angle 1$, $\angle 1$ is $\angle A$.

CHECK IT OUT! **Use the given trigonometric ratio to determine which angle of the triangle is $\angle A$.**

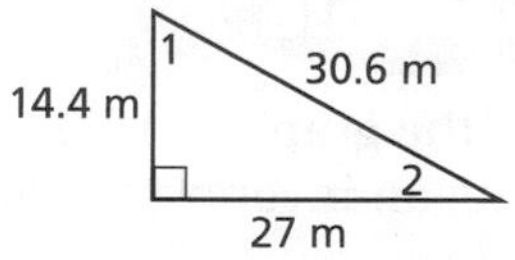

1a. $\sin A = \dfrac{8}{17}$ **1b.** $\tan A = 1.875$

You have learned that $\sin 30° = 0.5$. Conversely, if you know that the sine of an acute angle is 0.5, you can conclude that the angle measures 30°. This is written as $\sin^{-1}(0.5) = 30°$.

Reading Math
The expression $\sin^{-1} x$ is read "the inverse sine of x." It does *not* mean $\frac{1}{\sin x}$. You can think of $\sin^{-1} x$ as "the angle whose sine is x."

If you know the sine, cosine, or tangent of an acute angle measure, you can use the inverse trigonometric functions to find the measure of the angle.

Inverse Trigonometric Functions
If $\sin A = x$, then $\sin^{-1} x = m\angle A$.
If $\cos A = x$, then $\cos^{-1} x = m\angle A$.
If $\tan A = x$, then $\tan^{-1} x = m\angle A$.

EXAMPLE 2 Calculating Angle Measures from Trigonometric Ratios

> **Helpful Hint**
>
> When using your calculator to find the value of an inverse trigonometric expression, you may need to press the ARC, INV, or 2nd key.

Use your calculator to find each angle measure to the nearest degree.

A $\cos^{-1}(0.5)$

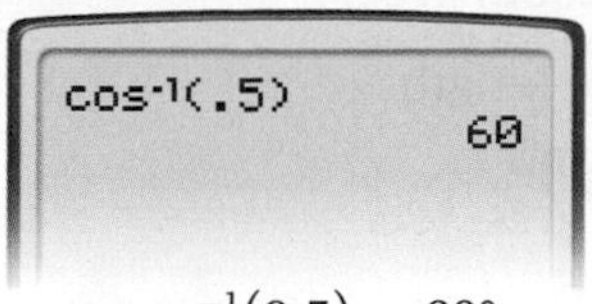

$\cos^{-1}(0.5) = 60°$

B $\sin^{-1}(0.45)$

$\sin^{-1}(0.45) \approx 27°$

C $\tan^{-1}(3.2)$

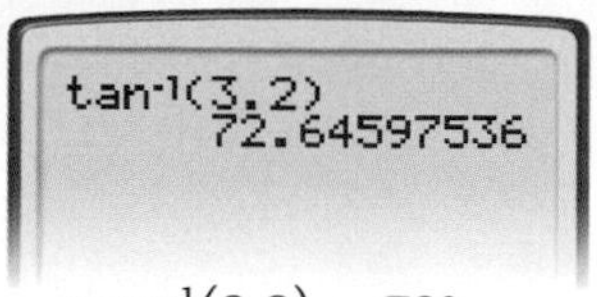

$\tan^{-1}(3.2) \approx 73°$

CHECK IT OUT! **Use your calculator to find each angle measure to the nearest degree.**

2a. $\tan^{-1}(0.75)$ **2b.** $\cos^{-1}(0.05)$ **2c.** $\sin^{-1}(0.67)$

Using given measures to find the unknown angle measures or side lengths of a triangle is known as *solving a triangle*. To solve a right triangle, you need to know two side lengths or one side length and an acute angle measure.

EXAMPLE 3 Solving Right Triangles

Find the unknown measures. Round lengths to the nearest hundredth and angle measures to the nearest degree.

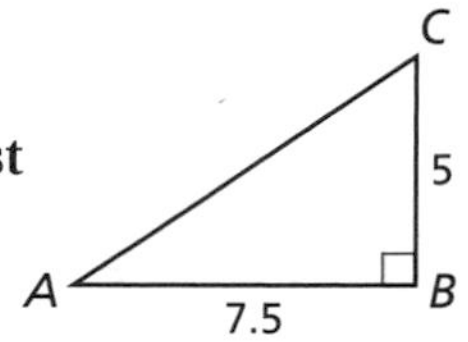

Method 1:

By the Pythagorean Theorem,

$AC^2 = AB^2 + BC^2.$

$= (7.5)^2 + 5^2 = 81.25$

So $AC = \sqrt{81.25} \approx 9.01$.

$m\angle A = \tan^{-1}\left(\frac{5}{7.5}\right) \approx 34°$

Since the acute angles of a right triangle are complementary, $m\angle C \approx 90° - 34° \approx 56°$.

Method 2:

$m\angle A = \tan^{-1}\left(\frac{5}{7.5}\right) \approx 34°$

Since the acute angles of a right triangle are complementary, $m\angle C \approx 90° - 34° \approx 56°$.

$\sin A = \frac{5}{AC}$, so $AC = \frac{5}{\sin A}$.

$$AC \approx \frac{5}{\sin\left[\tan^{-1}\left(\frac{5}{7.5}\right)\right]} \approx 9.01$$

CHECK IT OUT! **3.** Find the unknown measures. Round lengths to the nearest hundredth and angle measures to the nearest degree.

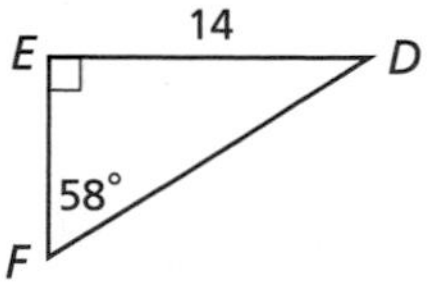

Student to Student

Solving Right Triangles

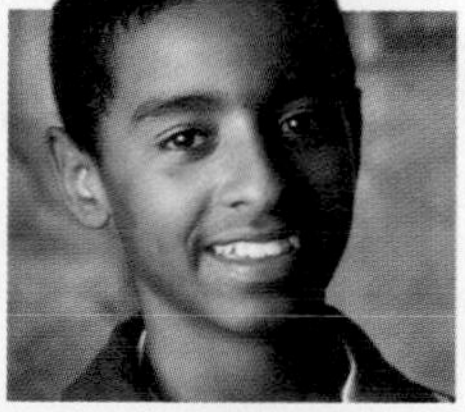

Kendell Waters
Marshall High School

Rounding can really make a difference! To find AC, I used the Pythagorean Theorem and got 15.62.

Then I did it a different way. I used $m\angle A = \tan^{-1}\left(\frac{10}{12}\right)$ *to find* $m\angle A = 39.8056°$*, which I rounded to 40°.* $\sin 40° = \frac{10}{AC}$, *so* $AC = \frac{10}{\sin 40°} \approx 15.56$.

The difference in the two answers reminded me not to round values until the last step.

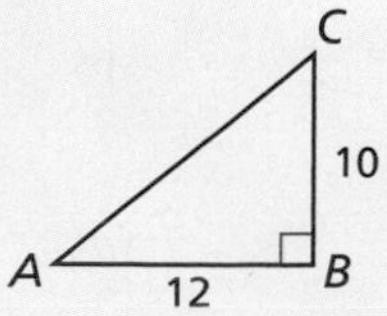

EXAMPLE 4 Solving a Right Triangle in the Coordinate Plane

The coordinates of the vertices of $\triangle JKL$ are $J(-1, 2)$, $K(-1, -3)$, and $L(3, -3)$. Find the side lengths to the nearest hundredth and the angle measures to the nearest degree.

Step 1 Find the side lengths.

Plot points *J*, *K*, and *L*.

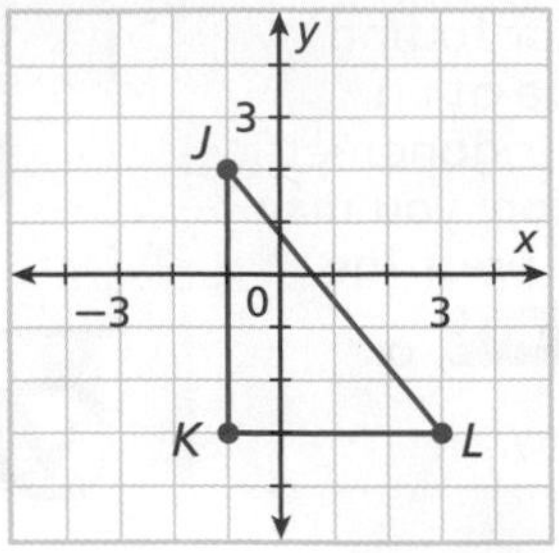

$JK = 5 \qquad KL = 4$

By the Distance Formula,

$$JL = \sqrt{[3-(-1)]^2 + (-3-2)^2}.$$
$$= \sqrt{4^2 + (-5)^2}$$
$$= \sqrt{16 + 25} = \sqrt{41} \approx 6.40$$

Step 2 Find the angle measures.

$m\angle K = 90°$ — *$\overline{JK}$ and $\overline{KL}$ are $\perp$.*

$m\angle J = \tan^{-1}\left(\frac{4}{5}\right) \approx 39°$ — *$\overline{KL}$ is opp. $\angle J$, and $\overline{JK}$ is adj. to $\angle J$.*

$m\angle L \approx 90° - 39° \approx 51°$ — *The acute $\angle$s of a rt. $\triangle$ are comp.*

CHECK IT OUT! 4. The coordinates of the vertices of $\triangle RST$ are $R(-3, 5)$, $S(4, 5)$, and $T(4, -2)$. Find the side lengths to the nearest hundredth and the angle measures to the nearest degree.

EXAMPLE 5 *Travel Application*

San Francisco's Lombard Street is known as one of "the crookedest streets in the world." The road's eight switchbacks were built in the 1920s to make the steep hill passable by cars. If the hill has a percent grade of 84%, what angle does the hill make with a horizontal line? Round to the nearest degree.

$84\% = \frac{84}{100}$ — *Change the percent grade to a fraction.*

An 84% grade means the hill rises 84 ft for every 100 ft of horizontal distance.

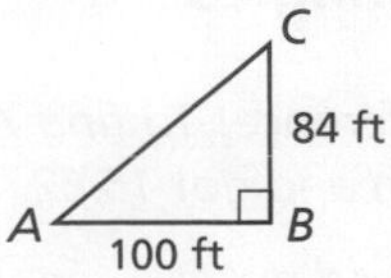

Draw a right triangle to represent the hill. $\angle A$ is the angle the hill makes with a horizontal line.

$m\angle A = \tan^{-1}\left(\frac{84}{100}\right) \approx 40°$

CHECK IT OUT! 5. Baldwin St. in Dunedin, New Zealand, is the steepest street in the world. It has a grade of 38%. To the nearest degree, what angle does Baldwin St. make with a horizontal line?

MATHEMATICAL PRACTICES

THINK AND DISCUSS

1. Describe the steps you would use to solve $\triangle RST$.

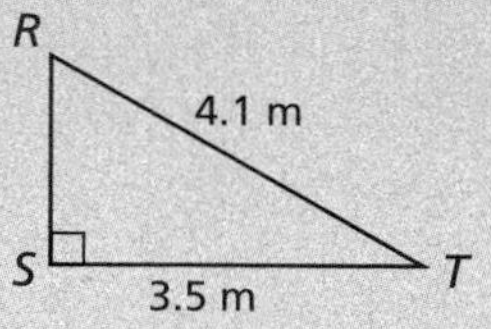

2. Given that $\cos Z = 0.35$, write an equivalent statement using an inverse trigonometric function.

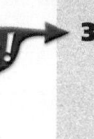

Know it! Note

3. **GET ORGANIZED** Copy and complete the graphic organizer. In each box, write a trigonometric ratio for $\angle A$. Then write an equivalent statement using an inverse trigonometric function.

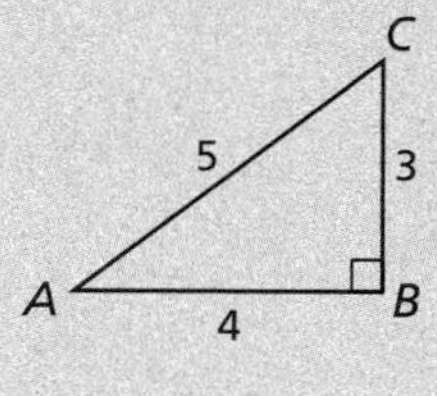

	Trigonometric Ratio	Inverse Trigonometric Function
Sine		
Cosine		
Tangent		

8-3 Exercises

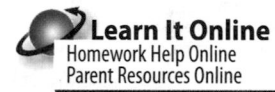

Learn It Online
Homework Help Online
Parent Resources Online

GUIDED PRACTICE

SEE EXAMPLE 1

Use the given trigonometric ratio to determine which angle of the triangle is $\angle A$.

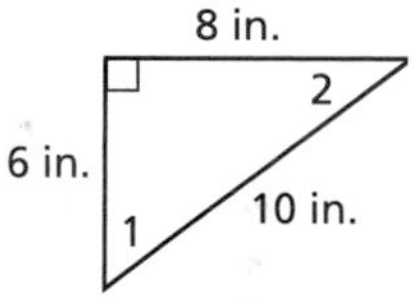

1. $\sin A = \frac{4}{5}$ 2. $\tan A = 1\frac{1}{3}$ 3. $\cos A = 0.6$
4. $\cos A = 0.8$ 5. $\tan A = 0.75$ 6. $\sin A = 0.6$

SEE EXAMPLE 2

Use your calculator to find each angle measure to the nearest degree.

7. $\tan^{-1}(2.1)$ 8. $\cos^{-1}\left(\frac{1}{3}\right)$ 9. $\cos^{-1}\left(\frac{5}{6}\right)$
10. $\sin^{-1}(0.5)$ 11. $\sin^{-1}(0.61)$ 12. $\tan^{-1}(0.09)$

SEE EXAMPLE 3

Multi-Step Find the unknown measures. Round lengths to the nearest hundredth and angle measures to the nearest degree.

13.
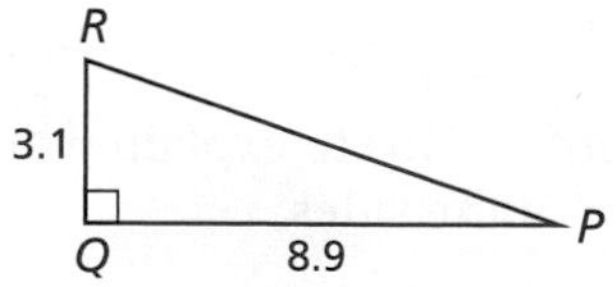

14.
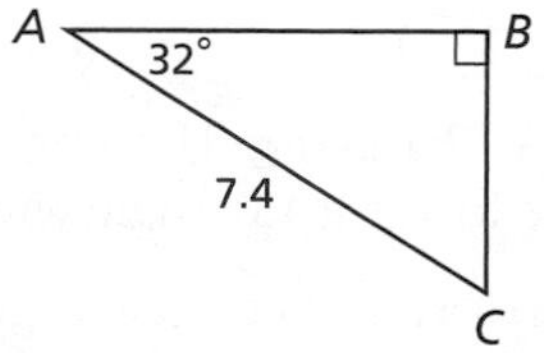

15.
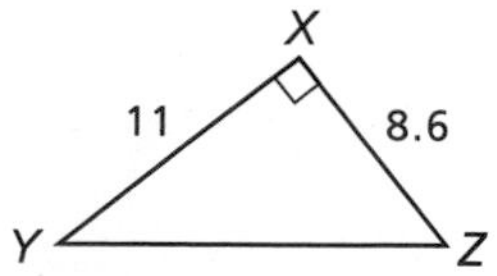

SEE EXAMPLE 4

Multi-Step For each triangle, find the side lengths to the nearest hundredth and the angle measures to the nearest degree.

16. $D(4, 1)$, $E(4, -2)$, $F(-2, -2)$ 17. $R(3, 3)$, $S(-2, 3)$, $T(-2, -3)$
18. $X(4, -6)$, $Y(-3, 1)$, $Z(-3, -6)$ 19. $A(-1, 1)$, $B(1, 1)$, $C(1, 5)$

SEE EXAMPLE 5

20. **Cycling** A hill in the Tour de France bike race has a grade of 8%. To the nearest degree, what is the angle that this hill makes with a horizontal line?

PRACTICE AND PROBLEM SOLVING

Independent Practice

For Exercises	See Example
21–26	1
27–32	2
33–35	3
36–37	4
38	5

Extra Practice

See Extra Practice for more Skills Practice and Applications Practice exercises.

Use the given trigonometric ratio to determine which angle of the triangle is $\angle A$.

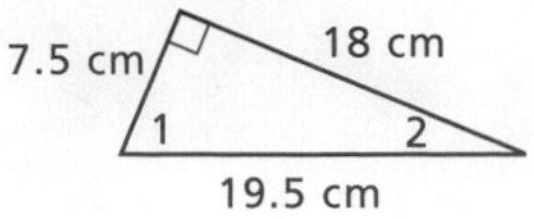

21. $\tan A = \frac{5}{12}$
22. $\tan A = 2.4$
23. $\sin A = \frac{12}{13}$
24. $\sin A = \frac{5}{13}$
25. $\cos A = \frac{12}{13}$
26. $\cos A = \frac{5}{13}$

Use your calculator to find each angle measure to the nearest degree.

27. $\sin^{-1}(0.31)$
28. $\tan^{-1}(1)$
29. $\cos^{-1}(0.8)$
30. $\cos^{-1}(0.72)$
31. $\tan^{-1}(1.55)$
32. $\sin^{-1}\left(\frac{9}{17}\right)$

Multi-Step **Find the unknown measures. Round lengths to the nearest hundredth and angle measures to the nearest degree.**

33.
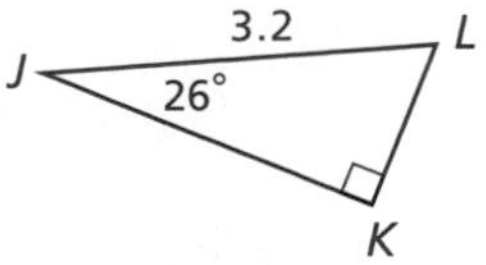

34.
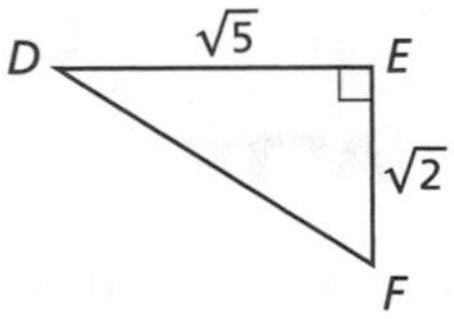

35.
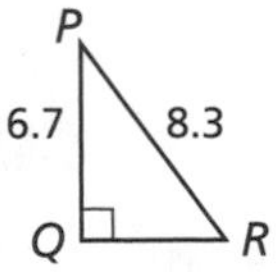

Multi-Step **For each triangle, find the side lengths to the nearest hundredth and the angle measures to the nearest degree.**

36. $A(2, 0), B(2, -5), C(1, -5)$
37. $M(3, 2), N(3, -2), P(-1, -2)$

38. **Building** For maximum accessibility, a wheelchair ramp should have a slope between $\frac{1}{16}$ and $\frac{1}{20}$. What is the range of angle measures that a ramp should make with a horizontal line? Round to the nearest degree.

Complete each statement. If necessary, round angle measures to the nearest degree. Round other values to the nearest hundredth.

39. tan ___?___ ≈ 3.5
40. sin ___?___ $\approx \frac{2}{3}$
41. ___?___ $42° \approx 0.74$
42. $\cos^{-1}$(___?___) $\approx 12°$
43. $\sin^{-1}$(___?___) $\approx 69°$
44. ___?___ $60° = \frac{1}{2}$

45. **Critical Thinking** Use trigonometric ratios to explain why the diagonal of a square forms a 45° angle with each of the sides.

46. **Estimation** You can use trigonometry to find angle measures when a protractor is not available.

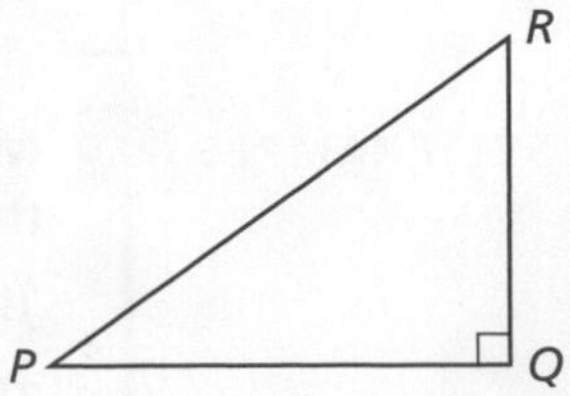

a. Estimate the measure of $\angle P$.
b. Use a centimeter ruler to find RQ and PQ.
c. Use your measurements from part **b** and an inverse trigonometric function to find $m\angle P$ to the nearest degree.
d. How does your result in part **c** compare to your estimate in part **a**?

MULTI-STEP TEST PREP

47. An electric company wants to install a vertical utility pole at the base of a hill that has an 8% grade.

a. To the nearest degree, what angle does the hill make with a horizontal line?

b. What is the measure of the angle between the pole and the hill? Round to the nearest degree.

c. A utility worker installs a 31-foot guy wire from the top of the pole to the hill. Given that the guy wire is perpendicular to the hill, find the height of the pole to the nearest inch.

LINK

Fitness

Running on a treadmill is slightly easier than running outdoors, since you don't have to overcome wind resistance. Set the treadmill to a 1% grade to match the intensity of an outdoor run.

The side lengths of a right triangle are given below. Find the measures of the acute angles in the triangle. Round to the nearest degree.

48. 3, 4, 5 **49.** 5, 12, 13 **50.** 8, 15, 17

51. What if...? A right triangle has leg lengths of 28 and 45 inches. Suppose the length of the longer leg doubles. What happens to the measure of the acute angle opposite that leg?

52. Fitness As part of off-season training, the Houston Texans football team must sprint up a ramp with a 28% grade. To the nearest degree, what angle does this ramp make with a horizontal line?

53. The coordinates of the vertices of a triangle are $A(-1, 0)$, $B(6, 1)$, and $C(0, 3)$.

a. Use the Distance Formula to find AB, BC, and AC.

b. Use the Converse of the Pythagorean Theorem to show that $\triangle ABC$ is a right triangle. Identify the right angle.

c. Find the measures of the acute angles of $\triangle ABC$. Round to the nearest degree.

Find the indicated measure in each rectangle. Round to the nearest degree.

54. $m\angle BDC$

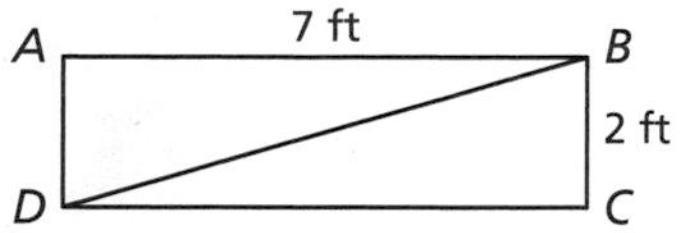

55. $m\angle STV$

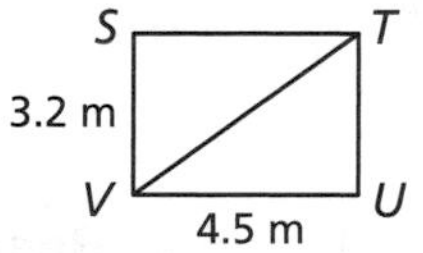

Find the indicated measure in each rhombus. Round to the nearest degree.

56. $m\angle DGF$

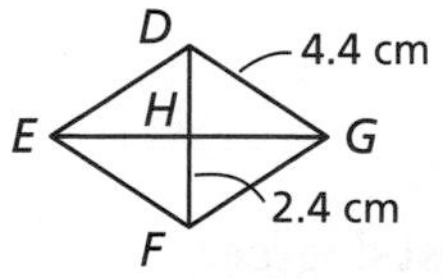

57. $m\angle LKN$

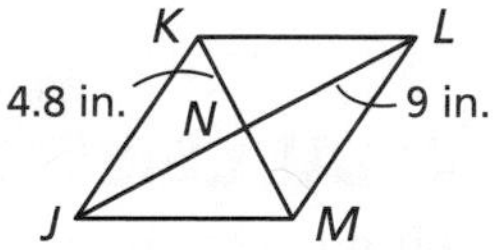

58. Critical Thinking Without using a calculator, compare the values of $\tan 60°$ and $\tan 70°$. Explain your reasoning.

The measure of an acute angle formed by a line with slope m and the x-axis can be found by using the expression $\tan^{-1}(m)$. Find the measure of the acute angle that each line makes with the x-axis. Round to the nearest degree.

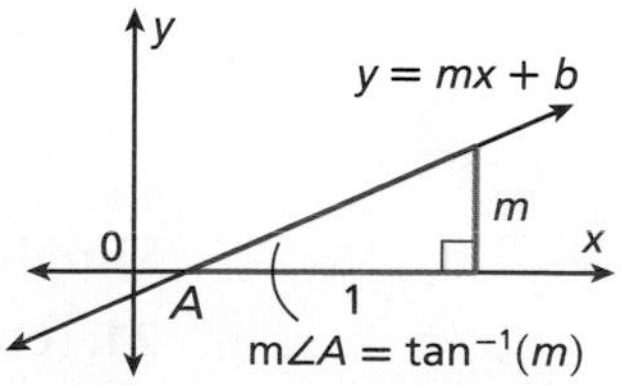

59. $y = 3x + 5$ **60.** $y = \frac{2}{3}x + 1$ **61.** $5y = 4x + 3$

62. **ERROR ANALYSIS** A student was asked to find m∠*C*. Explain the error in the student's solution.

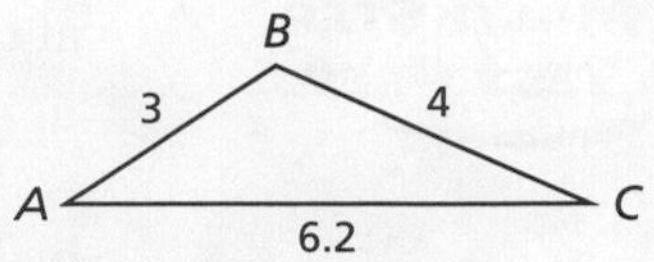

> Since $\tan C = \frac{3}{4}$, $m\angle C = \tan^{-1}\left(\frac{3}{4}\right)$, and $\tan^{-1}(0.75) \approx 37°$. So $m\angle C \approx 37°$.

63. **Write About It** A student claims that you must know the three side lengths of a right triangle before you can use trigonometric ratios to find the measures of the acute angles. Do you agree? Why or why not?

64. $\overline{DC}$ is an altitude of right △*ABC*. Use trigonometric ratios to find the missing lengths in the figure. Then use these lengths to verify the three relationships in the Geometric Mean Corollaries.

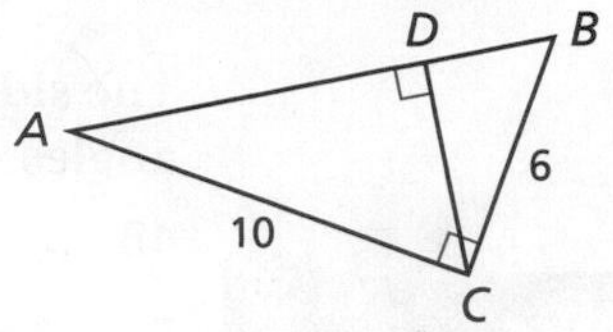

TEST PREP

65. Which expression can be used to find m∠*A*?

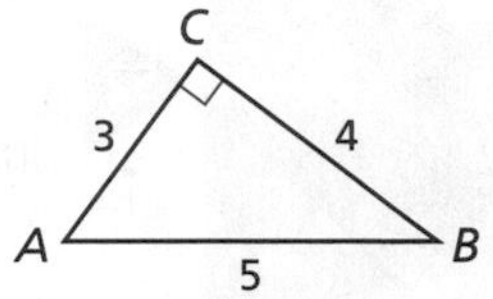

Ⓐ $\tan^{-1}(0.75)$ Ⓒ $\cos^{-1}(0.8)$

Ⓑ $\sin^{-1}\left(\frac{3}{5}\right)$ Ⓓ $\tan^{-1}\left(\frac{4}{3}\right)$

66. Which expression is NOT equivalent to cos 60°?

Ⓕ $\frac{1}{2}$ Ⓗ $\frac{\sin 60°}{\tan 60°}$

Ⓖ sin 30° Ⓙ $\cos^{-1}\left(\frac{1}{2}\right)$

67. To the nearest degree, what is the measure of the acute angle formed by Jefferson St. and Madison St.?

Ⓐ 27° Ⓒ 59°

Ⓑ 31° Ⓓ 63°

68. **Gridded Response** A highway exit ramp has a slope of $\frac{3}{20}$. To the nearest degree, find the angle that the ramp makes with a horizontal line.

CHALLENGE AND EXTEND

Find each angle measure. Round to the nearest degree.

69. m∠*J*

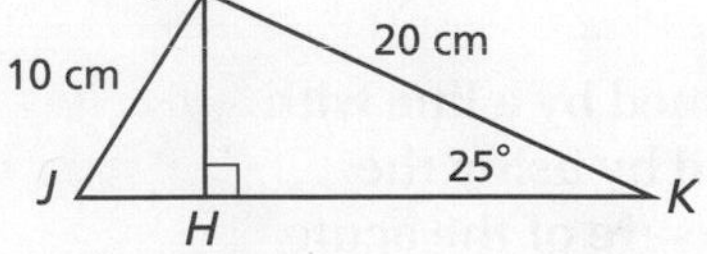

70. m∠*A*

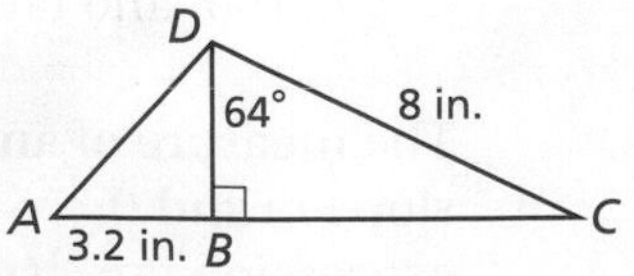

Simply each expression.

71. $\cos^{-1}(\cos 34°)$

72. $\tan[\tan^{-1}(1.5)]$

73. $\sin(\sin^{-1} x)$

74. A ramp has a 6% grade. The ramp is 40 ft long. Find the vertical distance that the ramp rises. Round your answer to the nearest hundredth.

75. Critical Thinking Explain why the expression $\sin^{-1}(1.5)$ does not make sense.

76. If you are given the lengths of two sides of $\triangle ABC$ and the measure of the included angle, you can use the formula $\frac{1}{2}bc \sin A$ to find the area of the triangle. Derive this formula. (*Hint:* Draw an altitude from B to $\overline{AC}$. Use trigonometric ratios to find the length of this altitude.)

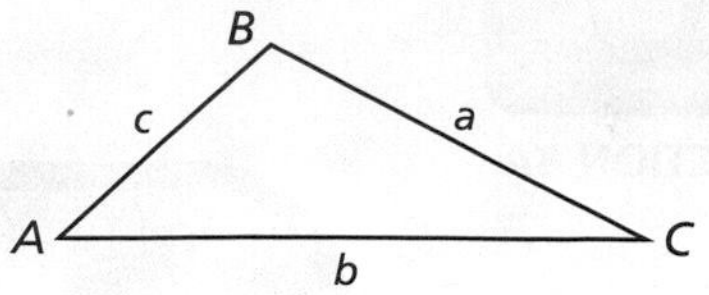

Using Technology

Use a spreadsheet to complete the following.

	A	B	C	D	E
1	**a**	**b**	**c**	**m(angle A)**	**m(angle B)**
2					

= SQRT(A2^2 + B2^2)

= DEGREES(ATAN(A2/B2))

= DEGREES(ATAN(B2/A2))

1. In cells A2 and B2, enter values for the leg lengths of a right triangle.
2. In cell C2, write a formula to calculate c, the length of the hypotenuse.
3. Write a formula to calculate the measure of $\angle A$ in cell D2. Be sure to use the Degrees function so that the answer is given in degrees. Format the value to include no decimal places.
4. Write a formula to calculate the measure of $\angle B$ in cell E2. Again, be sure to use the Degrees function and format the value to include no decimal places.
5. Use your spreadsheet to check your answers for Exercises 48–50.

CHAPTER 8

MULTI-STEP TEST PREP

SECTION 8A

MATHEMATICAL PRACTICES Reason abstractly and quantitatively.

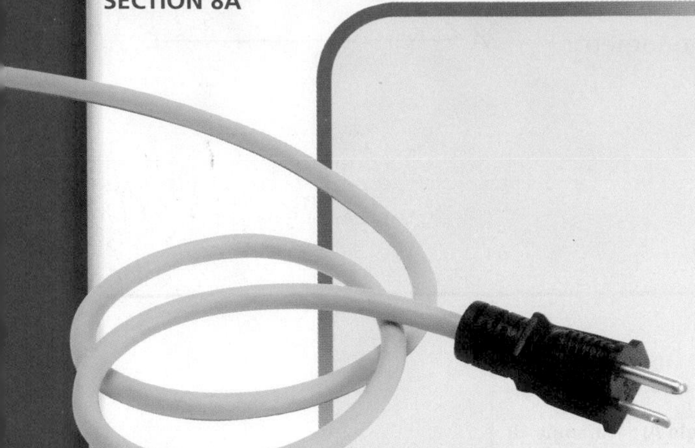

Trigonometric Ratios

It's Electrifying! Utility workers install and repair the utility poles and wires that carry electricity from generating stations to consumers. As shown in the figure, a crew of workers plans to install a vertical utility pole $\overline{AC}$ and a supporting guy wire $\overline{AB}$ that is perpendicular to the ground.

1. The utility pole is 30 ft tall. The crew finds that $DC = 6$ ft. What is the distance DB from the pole to the anchor point of the guy wire?
2. How long is the guy wire? Round to the nearest inch.
3. In the figure, $\angle ABD$ is called the *line angle.* In order to choose the correct weight of the cable for the guy wire, the crew needs to know the measure of the line angle. Find $m\angle ABD$ to the nearest degree.
4. To the nearest degree, what is the measure of the angle formed by the pole and the guy wire?
5. What is the percent grade of the hill on which the crew is working?

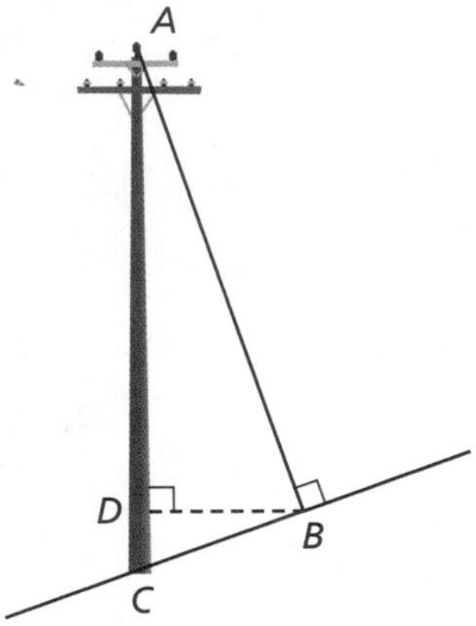

READY TO GO ON?

CHAPTER 8

SECTION 8A

Quiz for Lessons 8-1 Through 8-3

8-1 Similarity in Right Triangles

Find the geometric mean of each pair of numbers. If necessary, give the answer in simplest radical form.

1. 5 and 12 **2.** 2.75 and 44 **3.** $\frac{5}{2}$ and $\frac{15}{8}$

Find x, y, and z.

4.

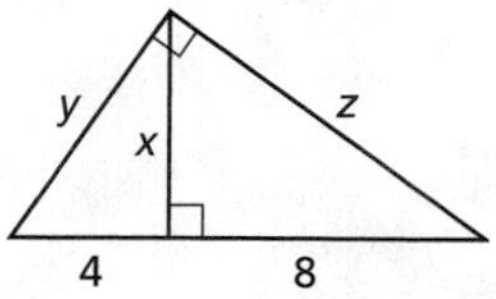

5.

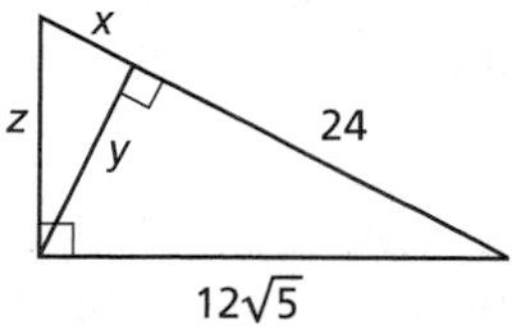

6.

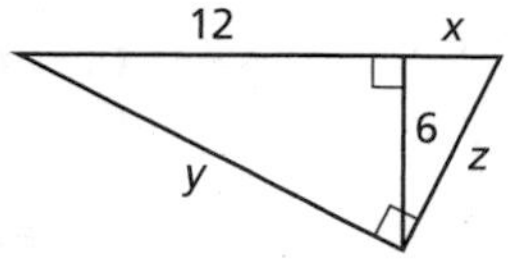

7. A land developer needs to know the distance across a pond on a piece of property. What is AB to the nearest tenth of a meter?

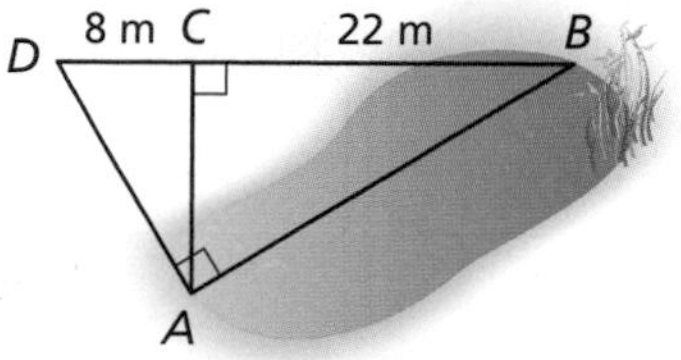

8-2 Trigonometric Ratios

Use a special right triangle to write each trigonometric ratio as a fraction.

8. $\tan 45°$ **9.** $\sin 30°$ **10.** $\cos 30°$

Use your calculator to find each trigonometric ratio. Round to the nearest hundredth.

11. $\sin 16°$ **12.** $\cos 79°$ **13.** $\tan 27°$

Find each length. Round to the nearest hundredth.

14. QR

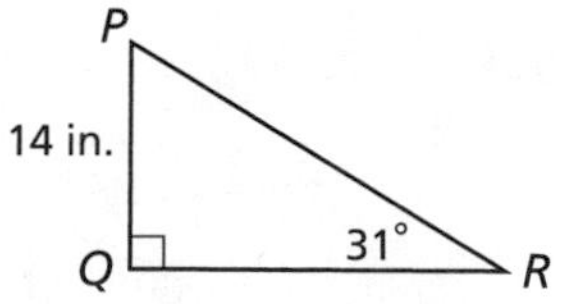

15. AB

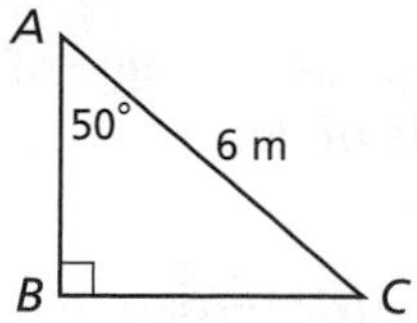

16. LM

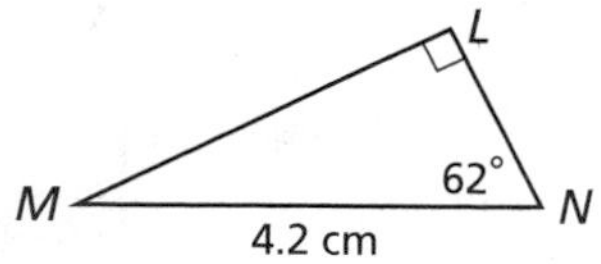

8-3 Solving Right Triangles

Find the unknown measures. Round lengths to the nearest hundredth and angle measures to the nearest degree.

17.

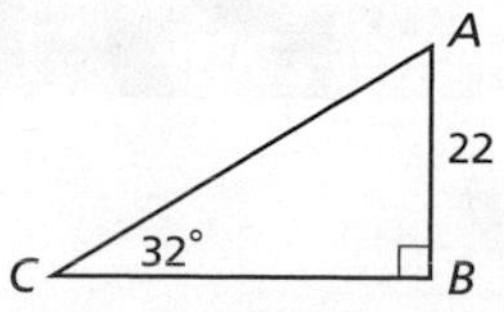

18.

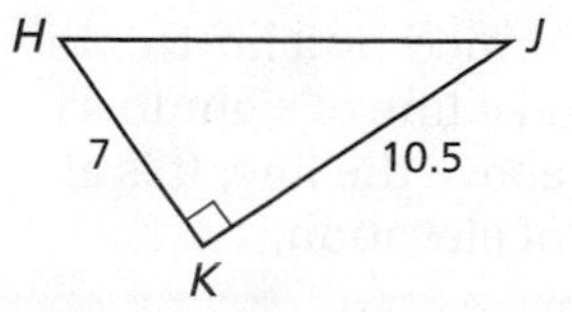

19.

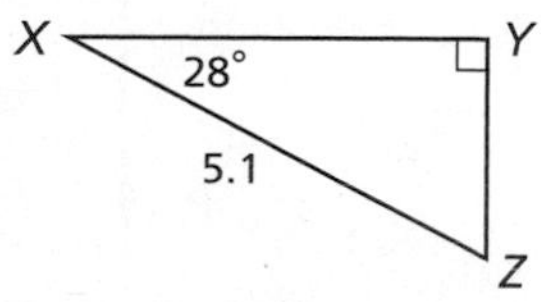

20. The wheelchair ramp at the entrance of the Mission Bay Library has a slope of $\frac{1}{18}$. What angle does the ramp make with the sidewalk? Round to the nearest degree.

COMMON CORE

8-4 Angles of Elevation and Depression

CC.9-12.G.SRT.8 Use trigonometric ratios and the Pythagorean Theorem to solve right triangles…*

Objective
Solve problems involving angles of elevation and angles of depression.

Vocabulary
angle of elevation
angle of depression

Who uses this?
Pilots and air traffic controllers use angles of depression to calculate distances.

An **angle of elevation** is the angle formed by a horizontal line and a line of sight to a point *above* the line. In the diagram, ∠1 is the angle of elevation from the tower T to the plane P.

An **angle of depression** is the angle formed by a horizontal line and a line of sight to a point *below* the line. ∠2 is the angle of depression from the plane to the tower.

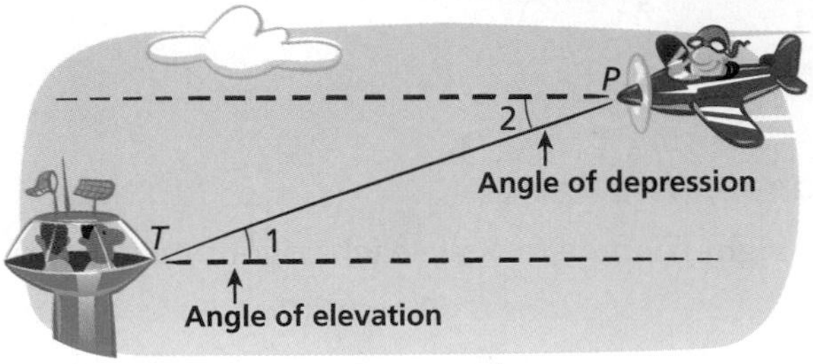

Since horizontal lines are parallel, ∠1 ≅ ∠2 by the Alternate Interior Angles Theorem. Therefore the angle of elevation from one point is congruent to the angle of depression from the other point.

EXAMPLE 1 Classifying Angles of Elevation and Depression

Classify each angle as an angle of elevation or angle of depression.

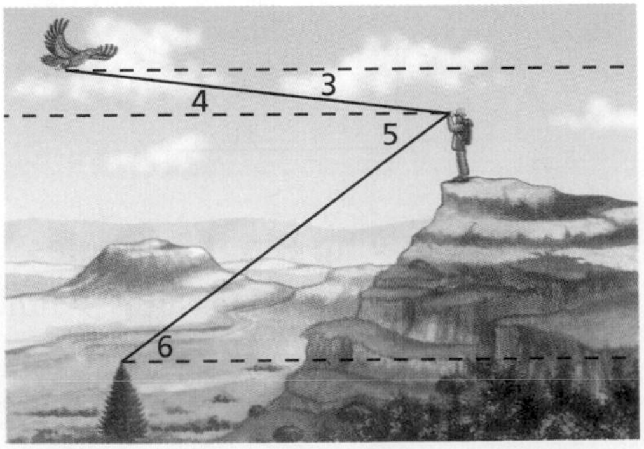

A ∠3

∠3 is formed by a horizontal line and a line of sight to a point below the line. It is an angle of depression.

B ∠4

∠4 is formed by a horizontal line and a line of sight to a point above the line. It is an angle of elevation.

CHECK IT OUT! **Use the diagram above to classify each angle as an angle of elevation or angle of depression.**

1a. ∠5 **1b.** ∠6

EXAMPLE 2 **Finding Distance by Using Angle of Elevation**

An air traffic controller at an airport sights a plane at an angle of elevation of 41°. The pilot reports that the plane's altitude is 4000 ft. What is the horizontal distance between the plane and the airport? Round to the nearest foot.

Draw a sketch to represent the given information. Let A represent the airport and let P represent the plane. Let x be the horizontal distance between the plane and the airport.

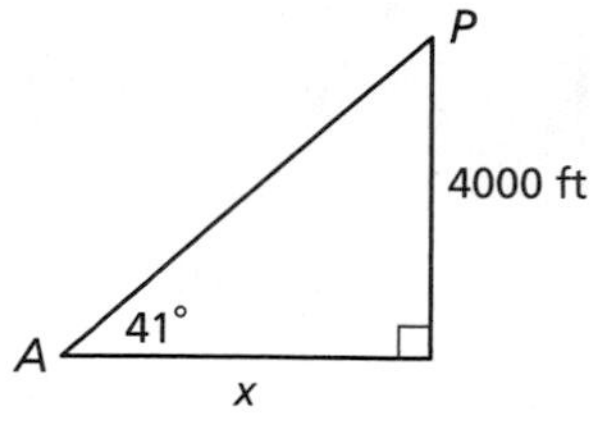

$\tan 41° = \frac{4000}{x}$ — *You are given the side opposite ∠A, and x is the side adjacent to ∠A. So write a tangent ratio.*

$x = \frac{4000}{\tan 41°}$ — *Multiply both sides by x and divide both sides by tan 41°.*

$x \approx 4601$ ft — *Simplify the expression.*

CHECK IT OUT! 2. **What if...?** Suppose the plane is at an altitude of 3500 ft and the angle of elevation from the airport to the plane is 29°. What is the horizontal distance between the plane and the airport? Round to the nearest foot.

EXAMPLE 3 **Finding Distance by Using Angle of Depression**

A forest ranger in a 90-foot observation tower sees a fire. The angle of depression to the fire is 7°. What is the horizontal distance between the tower and the fire? Round to the nearest foot.

Draw a sketch to represent the given information. Let T represent the top of the tower and let F represent the fire. Let x be the horizontal distance between the tower and the fire.

Caution!

The angle of depression may not be one of the angles in the triangle you are solving. It may be the complement of one of the angles in the triangle.

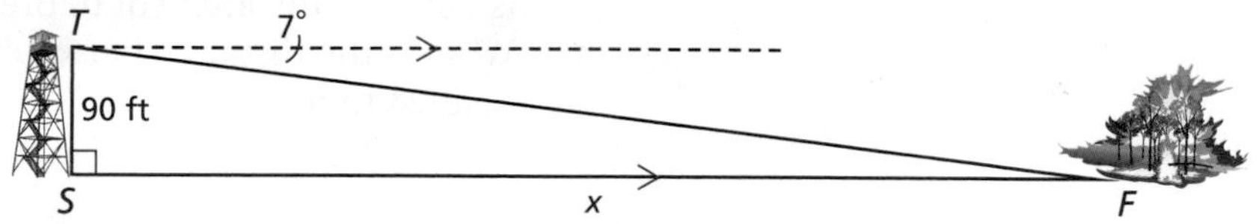

By the Alternate Interior Angles Theorem, $m\angle F = 7°$.

$\tan 7° = \frac{90}{x}$ — *Write a tangent ratio.*

$x = \frac{90}{\tan 7°}$ — *Multiply both sides by x and divide both sides by tan 7°.*

$x \approx 733$ ft — *Simplify the expression.*

CHECK IT OUT! 3. **What if...?** Suppose the ranger sees another fire and the angle of depression to the fire is 3°. What is the horizontal distance to this fire? Round to the nearest foot.

EXAMPLE 4 *Aviation Application*

A pilot flying at an altitude of 2.7 km sights two control towers directly in front of her. The angle of depression to the base of one tower is 37°. The angle of depression to the base of the other tower is 58°. What is the distance between the two towers? Round to the nearest tenth of a kilometer.

Step 1 Draw a sketch. Let P represent the plane and let A and B represent the two towers. Let x be the distance between the towers.

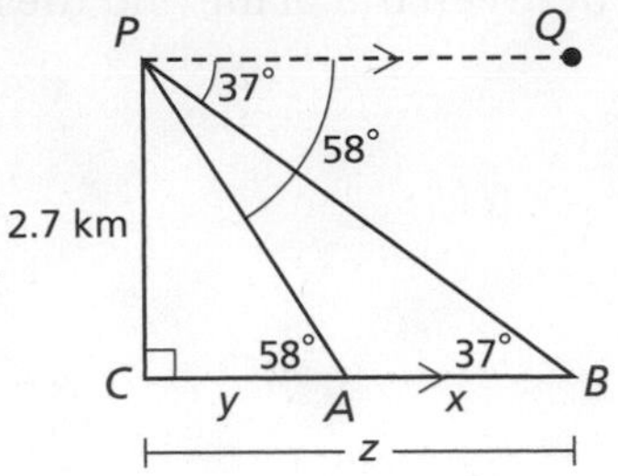

Helpful Hint

Always make a sketch to help you correctly place the given angle measure.

Step 2 Find y.

By the Alternate Interior Angles Theorem, $m\angle CAP = 58°$.

In $\triangle APC$, $\tan 58° = \frac{2.7}{y}$.

So $y = \frac{2.7}{\tan 58°} \approx 1.6871$ km.

Step 3 Find z.

By the Alternate Interior Angles Theorem, $m\angle CBP = 37°$.

In $\triangle BPC$, $\tan 37° = \frac{2.7}{z}$.

So $z = \frac{2.7}{\tan 37°} \approx 3.5830$ km.

Step 4 Find x.

$x = z - y$

$x \approx 3.5830 - 1.6871 \approx 1.9$ km

So the two towers are about 1.9 km apart.

CHECK IT OUT!

4. A pilot flying at an altitude of 12,000 ft sights two airports directly in front of him. The angle of depression to one airport is 78°, and the angle of depression to the second airport is 19°. What is the distance between the two airports? Round to the nearest foot.

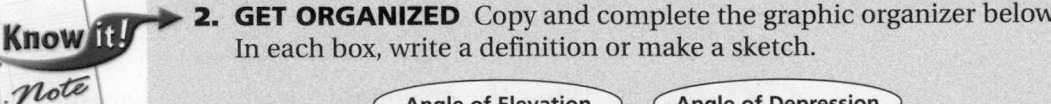

MATHEMATICAL PRACTICES

THINK AND DISCUSS

1. Explain what happens to the angle of elevation from your eye to the top of a skyscraper as you walk toward the skyscraper.

Know it! Note

2. GET ORGANIZED Copy and complete the graphic organizer below. In each box, write a definition or make a sketch.

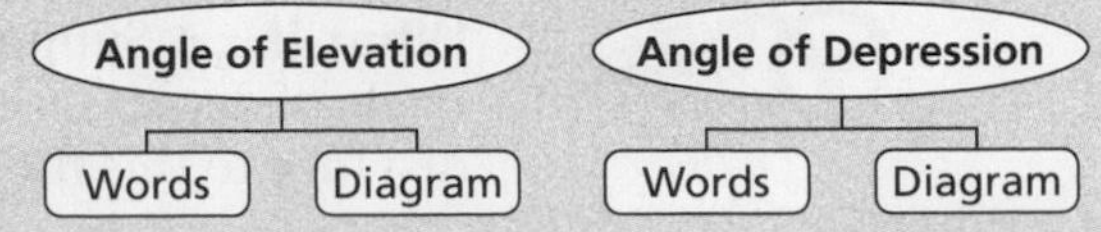

8-4 Exercises

Learn It Online
Homework Help Online
Parent Resources Online

GUIDED PRACTICE

Vocabulary **Apply the vocabulary from this lesson to answer each question.**

1. An angle of ___?___ is measured from a horizontal line to a point above that line. (*elevation* or *depression*)

2. An angle of ___?___ is measured from a horizontal line to a point below that line. (*elevation* or *depression*)

SEE EXAMPLE 1

Classify each angle as an angle of elevation or angle of depression.

3. ∠1
4. ∠2
5. ∠3
6. ∠4

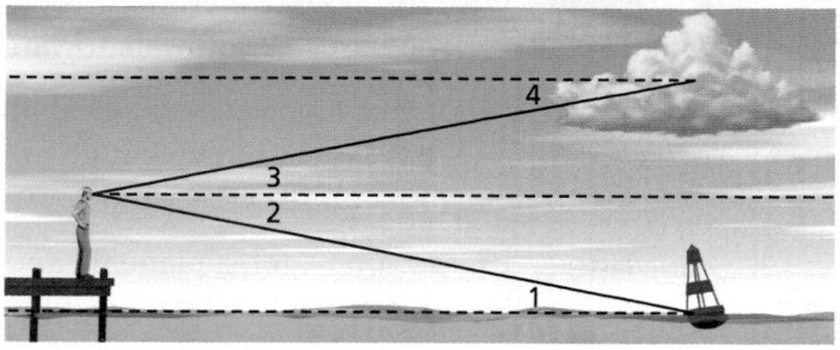

SEE EXAMPLE 2

7. **Measurement** When the angle of elevation to the sun is 37°, a flagpole casts a shadow that is 24.2 ft long. What is the height of the flagpole to the nearest foot?

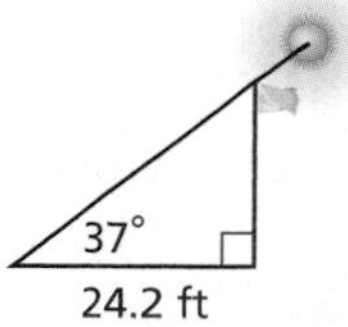

SEE EXAMPLE 3

8. **Aviation** The pilot of a traffic helicopter sights an accident at an angle of depression of 18°. The helicopter's altitude is 1560 ft. What is the horizontal distance from the helicopter to the accident? Round to the nearest foot.

SEE EXAMPLE 4

9. **Surveying** From the top of a canyon, the angle of depression to the far side of the river is 58°, and the angle of depression to the near side of the river is 74°. The depth of the canyon is 191 m. What is the width of the river at the bottom of the canyon? Round to the nearest tenth of a meter.

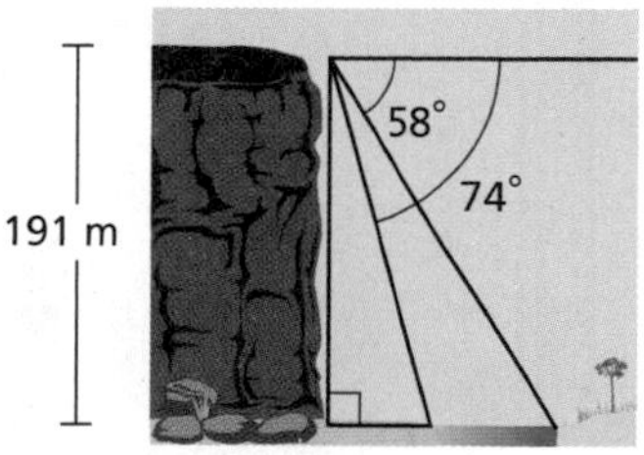

PRACTICE AND PROBLEM SOLVING

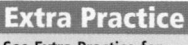

Independent Practice

For Exercises	See Example
10–13	1
14	2
15	3
16	4

Extra Practice

See Extra Practice for more Skills Practice and Applications Practice exercises.

Classify each angle as an angle of elevation or angle of depression.

10. ∠1
11. ∠2
12. ∠3
13. ∠4

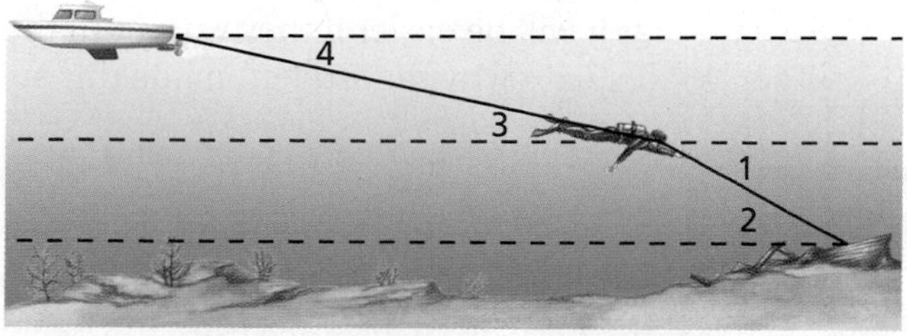

14. **Geology** To measure the height of a rock formation, a surveyor places her transit 100 m from its base and focuses the transit on the top of the formation. The angle of elevation is 67°. The transit is 1.5 m above the ground. What is the height of the rock formation? Round to the nearest meter.

LINK

Space Shuttle

During its launch, a space shuttle accelerates to more than 27,359 km/h in just over 8 minutes. So the shuttle travels 3219 km/h faster each minute.

15. **Forestry** A forest ranger in a 120 ft observation tower sees a fire. The angle of depression to the fire is 3.5°. What is the horizontal distance between the tower and the fire? Round to the nearest foot.

16. **Space Shuttle** Marion is observing the launch of a space shuttle from the command center. When she first sees the shuttle, the angle of elevation to it is 16°. Later, the angle of elevation is 74°. If the command center is 1 mi from the launch pad, how far did the shuttle travel while Marion was watching? Round to the nearest tenth of a mile.

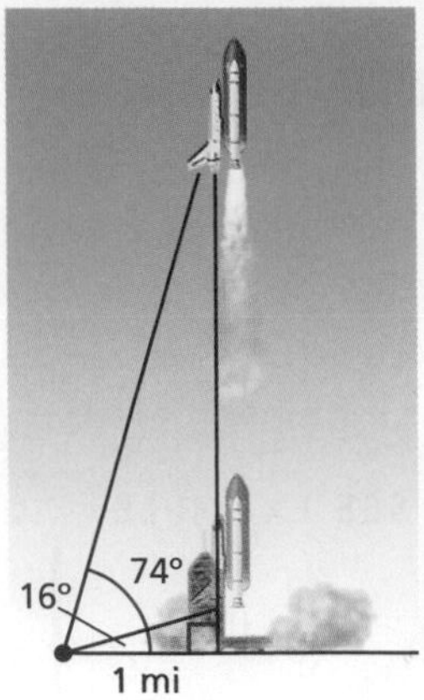

Tell whether each statement is true or false. If false, explain why.

17. The angle of elevation from your eye to the top of a tree increases as you walk toward the tree.

18. If you stand at street level, the angle of elevation to a building's tenth-story window is greater than the angle of elevation to one of its ninth-story windows.

19. As you watch a plane fly above you, the angle of elevation to the plane gets closer to 0° as the plane approaches the point directly overhead.

20. An angle of depression can never be more than 90°.

Use the diagram for Exercises 21 and 22.

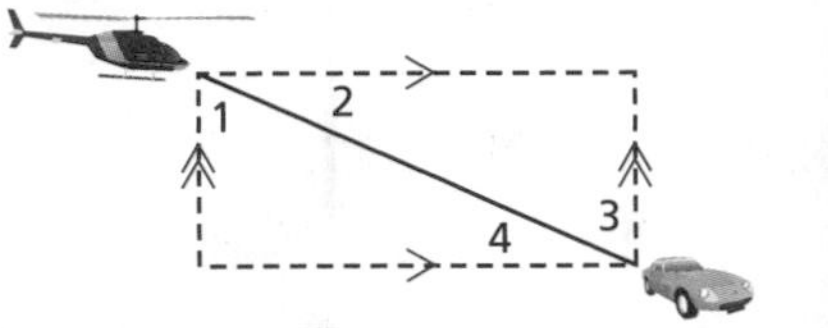

21. Which angles are not angles of elevation or angles of depression?

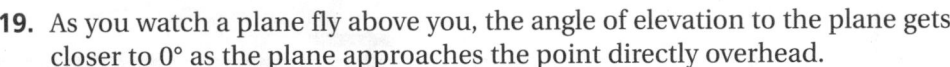

22. The angle of depression from the helicopter to the car is 30°. Find m∠1, m∠2, m∠3, and m∠4.

23. **Critical Thinking** Describe a situation in which the angle of depression to an object is decreasing.

24. An observer in a hot-air balloon sights a building that is 50 m from the balloon's launch point. The balloon has risen 165 m. What is the angle of depression from the balloon to the building? Round to the nearest degree.

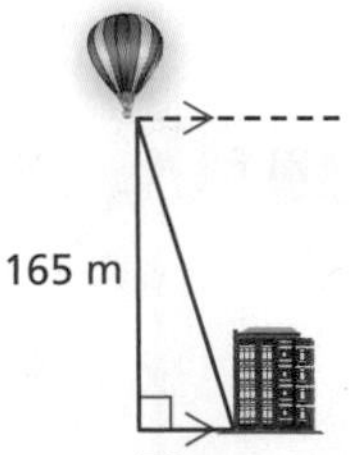

25. **Multi-Step** A surveyor finds that the angle of elevation to the top of a 1000 ft tower is 67°.
    a. To the nearest foot, how far is the surveyor from the base of the tower?
    b. How far back would the surveyor have to move so that the angle of elevation to the top of the tower is 55°? Round to the nearest foot.

26. **Write About It** Two students are using shadows to calculate the height of a pole. One says that it will be easier if they wait until the angle of elevation to the sun is exactly 45°. Explain why the student made this suggestion.

MULTI-STEP TEST PREP

27. The pilot of a rescue helicopter is flying over the ocean at an altitude of 1250 ft. The pilot sees a life raft at an angle of depression of 31°.
    a. What is the horizontal distance from the helicopter to the life raft, rounded to the nearest foot?
    b. The helicopter travels at 150 ft/s. To the nearest second, how long will it take until the helicopter is directly over the raft?

TEST PREP

28. Mai is flying a plane at an altitude of 1600 ft. She sights a stadium at an angle of depression of 35°. What is Mai's approximate horizontal distance from the stadium?

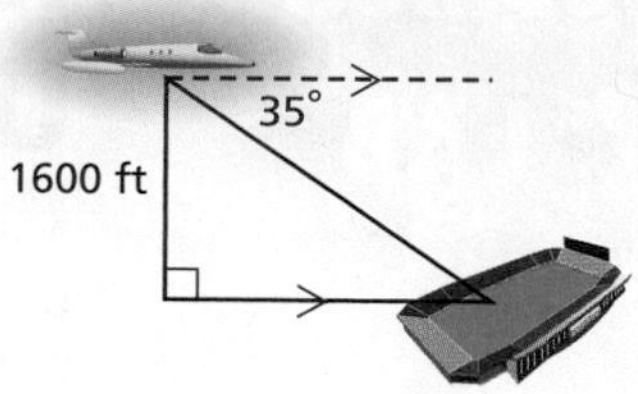

   (A) 676 feet (C) 1450 feet
   (B) 1120 feet (D) 2285 feet

29. Jeff finds that an office building casts a shadow that is 93 ft long when the angle of elevation to the sun is 60°. What is the height of the building?

   (F) 54 feet (G) 81 feet (H) 107 feet (J) 161 feet

30. **Short Response** Jim is rafting down a river that runs through a canyon. He sees a trail marker ahead at the top of the canyon and estimates the angle of elevation from the raft to the marker as 45°. Draw a sketch to represent the situation. Explain what happens to the angle of elevation as Jim moves closer to the marker.

CHALLENGE AND EXTEND

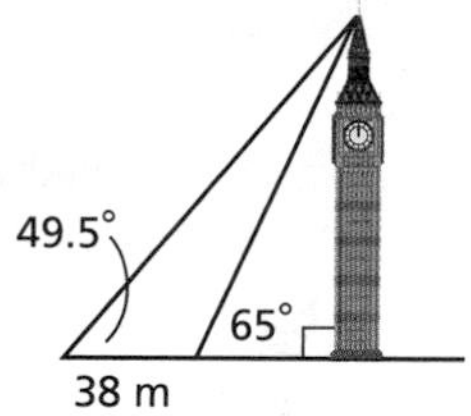

31. Susan and Jorge stand 38 m apart. From Susan's position, the angle of elevation to the top of Big Ben is 65°. From Jorge's position, the angle of elevation to the top of Big Ben is 49.5°. To the nearest meter, how tall is Big Ben?

32. A plane is flying at a constant altitude of 14,000 ft and a constant speed of 500 mi/h. The angle of depression from the plane to a lake is 6°. To the nearest minute, how much time will pass before the plane is directly over the lake?

33. A skyscraper stands between two school buildings. The two schools are 10 mi apart. From school *A*, the angle of elevation to the top of the skyscraper is 5°. From school *B*, the angle of elevation is 2°. What is the height of the skyscraper to the nearest foot?

34. Katie and Kim are attending a theater performance. Katie's seat is at floor level. She looks down at an angle of 18° to see the orchestra pit. Kim's seat is in the balcony directly above Katie. Kim looks down at an angle of 42° to see the pit. The horizontal distance from Katie's seat to the pit is 46 ft. What is the vertical distance between Katie's seat and Kim's seat? Round to the nearest inch.

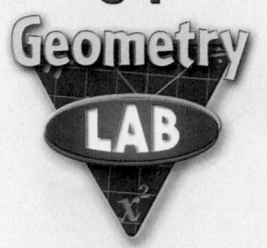

8-1 Geometry LAB

Use with Angles of Elevation and Depression

Indirect Measurement Using Trigonometry

A *clinometer* is a surveying tool that is used to measure angles of elevation and angles of depression. In this lab, you will make a simple clinometer and use it to find indirect measurements. Choose a tall object, such as a flagpole or tree, whose height you will measure.

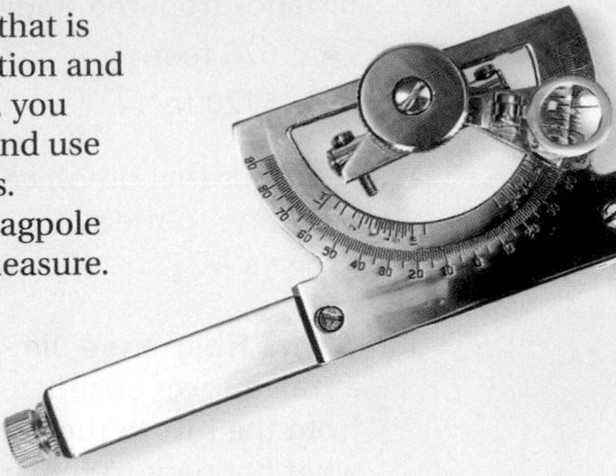

MATHEMATICAL PRACTICES **Use appropriate tools strategically.**

CC.9-12.G.SRT.8 Use trigonometric ratios and the Pythagorean Theorem to solve right triangles…*

Activity

1. Follow these instructions to make a clinometer.
   - **a.** Tie a washer or paper clip to the end of a 6-inch string.
   - **b.** Tape the string's other end to the midpoint of the straight edge of a protractor.
   - **c.** Tape a straw along the straight edge of the protractor.

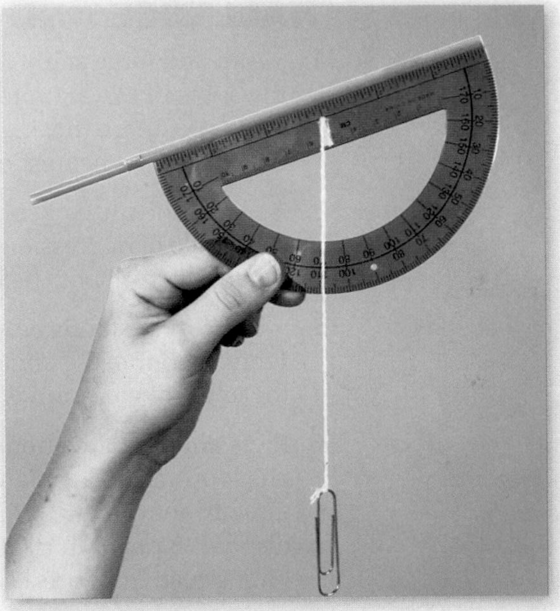

2. Stand back from the object you want to measure. Use a tape measure to measure and record the distance from your feet to the base of the object. Also measure the height of your eyes above the ground.
3. Hold the clinometer steady and look through the straw to sight the top of the object you are measuring. When the string stops moving, pinch it against the protractor and record the acute angle measure.

Try This

1. How is the angle reading from the clinometer related to the angle of elevation from your eye to the top of the object you are measuring?
2. Draw and label a diagram showing the object and the measurements you made. Then use trigonometric ratios to find the height of the object.
3. Repeat the activity, measuring the angle of elevation to the object from a different distance. How does your result compare to the previous one?
4. Describe possible measurement errors that can be made in the activity.
5. Explain why this method of indirect measurement is useful in real-world situations.

COMMON CORE

8-5 Law of Sines and Law of Cosines

CC.9-12.G.SRT.10 (+) Prove the Laws of Sines and Cosines and use them to solve problems. *Also* **CC.9-12.G.SRT.11 (+)**

Objective
Use the Law of Sines and the Law of Cosines to solve triangles.

Who uses this?
Engineers can use the Law of Sines and the Law of Cosines to solve construction problems.

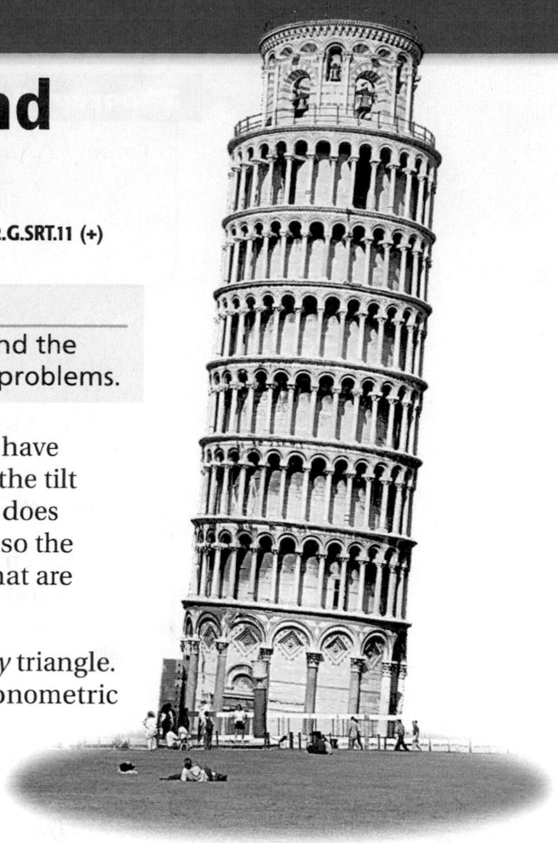

Since its completion in 1370, engineers have proposed many solutions for lessening the tilt of the Leaning Tower of Pisa. The tower does not form a right angle with the ground, so the engineers have to work with triangles that are not right triangles.

In this lesson, you will learn to solve *any* triangle. To do so, you will need to calculate trigonometric ratios for angle measures up to 180°. You can use a calculator to find these values.

EXAMPLE 1 Finding Trigonometric Ratios for Obtuse Angles

Use a calculator to find each trigonometric ratio. Round to the nearest hundredth.

A $\sin 135°$

$\sin 135° \approx 0.71$

B $\tan 98°$

$\tan 98° \approx -7.12$

C $\cos 108°$

$\cos 108° \approx -0.31$

CHECK IT OUT! **Use a calculator to find each trigonometric ratio. Round to the nearest hundredth.**

1a. $\tan 175°$ **1b.** $\cos 92°$ **1c.** $\sin 160°$

You can use the altitude of a triangle to find a relationship between the triangle's side lengths.

In $\triangle ABC$, let h represent the length of the altitude from C to $\overline{AB}$.

From the diagram, $\sin A = \frac{h}{b}$, and $\sin B = \frac{h}{a}$.

By solving for h, you find that $h = b\sin A$ and $h = a\sin B$. So $b\sin A = a\sin B$, and $\frac{\sin A}{a} = \frac{\sin B}{b}$.

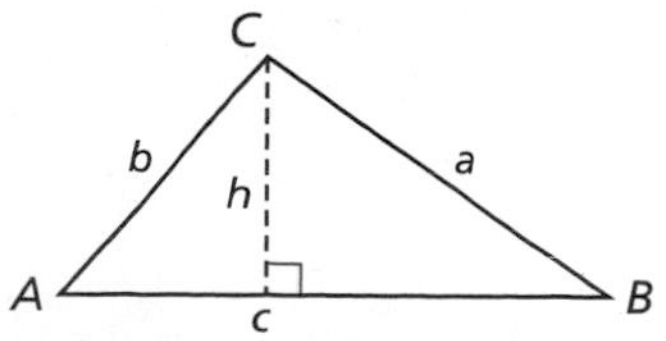

You can use another altitude to show that these ratios equal $\frac{\sin C}{c}$.

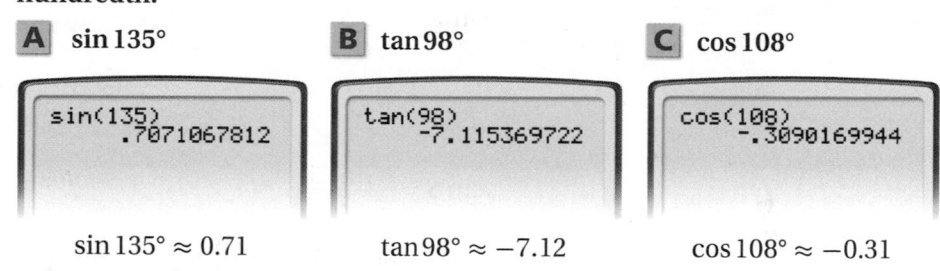

Know it! Note

Theorem 8-5-1 The Law of Sines

For any $\triangle ABC$ with side lengths *a*, *b*, and *c*,

$$\frac{\sin A}{a} = \frac{\sin B}{b} = \frac{\sin C}{c}.$$

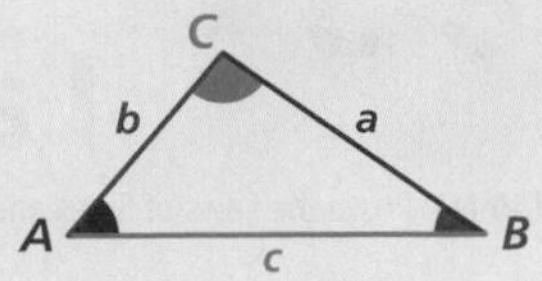

You can use the Law of Sines to solve a triangle if you are given

- two angle measures and any side length (ASA or AAS) or
- two side lengths and a non-included angle measure (SSA).

EXAMPLE 2 Using the Law of Sines

Find each measure. Round lengths to the nearest tenth and angle measures to the nearest degree.

A DF

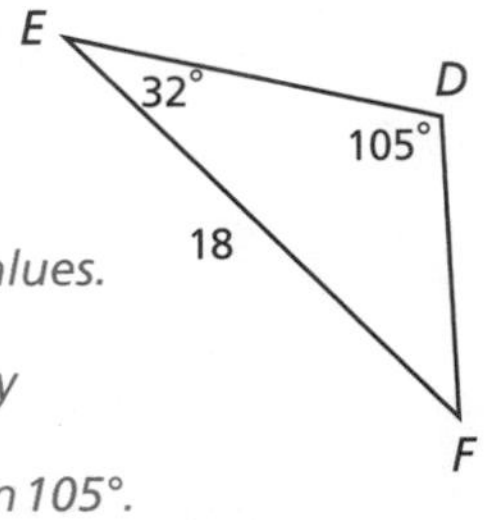

$\frac{\sin D}{EF} = \frac{\sin E}{DF}$ — *Law of Sines*

$\frac{\sin 105°}{18} = \frac{\sin 32°}{DF}$ — *Substitute the given values.*

$DF \sin 105° = 18 \sin 32°$ — *Cross Products Property*

$DF = \frac{18 \sin 32°}{\sin 105°} \approx 9.9$ — *Divide both sides by sin 105°.*

Remember!

In a proportion with three parts, you can use any of the two parts together.

B $m\angle S$

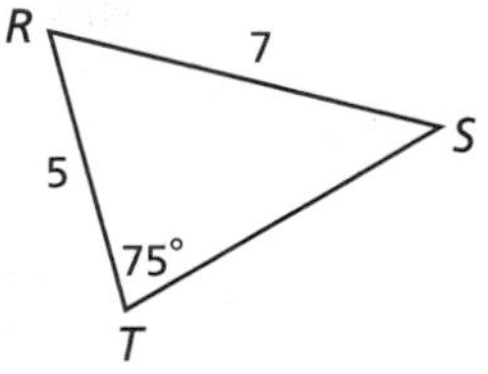

$\frac{\sin T}{RS} = \frac{\sin S}{RT}$ — *Law of Sines*

$\frac{\sin 75°}{7} = \frac{\sin S}{5}$ — *Substitute the given values.*

$\sin S = \frac{5 \sin 75°}{7}$ — *Multiply both sides by 5.*

$m\angle S \approx \sin^{-1}\left(\frac{5 \sin 75°}{7}\right) \approx 44°$ — *Use the inverse sine function to find m∠S.*

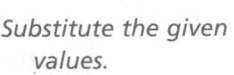

CHECK IT OUT! **Find each measure. Round lengths to the nearest tenth and angle measures to the nearest degree.**

2a. NP

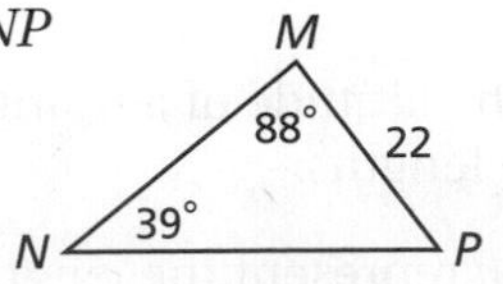

2b. $m\angle L$

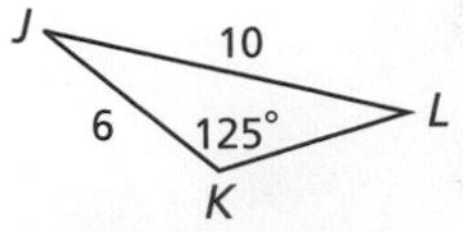

2c. $m\angle X$

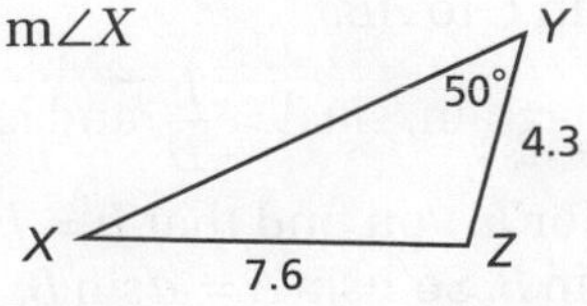

2d. AC

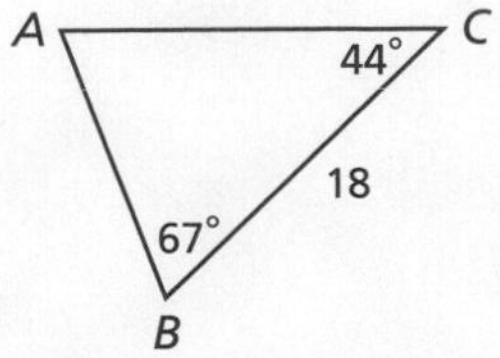

The Law of Sines cannot be used to solve every triangle. If you know two side lengths and the included angle measure or if you know all three side lengths, you cannot use the Law of Sines. Instead, you can apply the Law of Cosines.

Know it! Note

Theorem 8-5-2 The Law of Cosines

For any $\triangle ABC$ with side lengths a, b, and c:

$$a^2 = b^2 + c^2 - 2bc\cos A$$
$$b^2 = a^2 + c^2 - 2ac\cos B$$
$$c^2 = a^2 + b^2 - 2ab\cos C$$

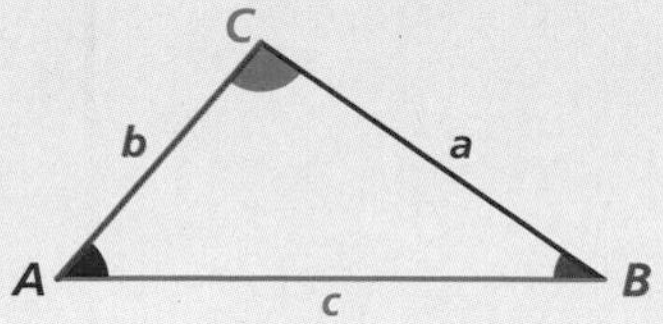

You will prove one case of the Law of Cosines in Exercise 57.

Helpful Hint

The angle referenced in the Law of Cosines is across the equal sign from its corresponding side.

You can use the Law of Cosines to solve a triangle if you are given
- two side lengths and the included angle measure (SAS) or
- three side lengths (SSS).

EXAMPLE 3 Using the Law of Cosines

Find each measure. Round lengths to the nearest tenth and angle measures to the nearest degree.

A BC

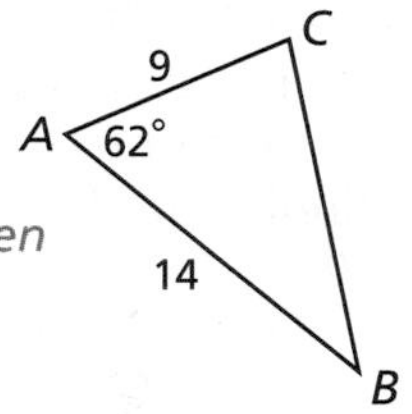

$BC^2 = AB^2 + AC^2 - 2(AB)(AC)\cos A$ *Law of Cosines*

$= 14^2 + 9^2 - 2(14)(9)\cos 62°$ *Substitute the given values.*

$BC^2 \approx 158.6932$ *Simplify.*

$BC \approx 12.6$ *Find the square root of both sides.*

B $m\angle R$

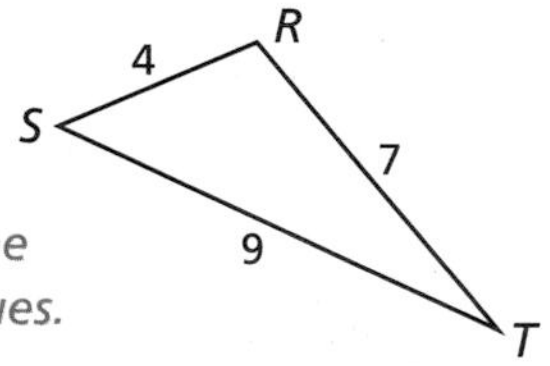

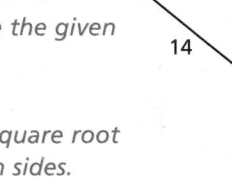

$ST^2 = RS^2 + RT^2 - 2(RS)(RT)\cos R$ *Law of Cosines*

$9^2 = 4^2 + 7^2 - 2(4)(7)\cos R$ *Substitute the given values.*

$81 = 65 - 56\cos R$ *Simplify.*

$16 = -56\cos R$ *Subtract 65 from both sides.*

$\cos R = -\frac{16}{56}$ *Solve for cos R.*

$m\angle R = \cos^{-1}\left(-\frac{16}{56}\right) \approx 107°$ *Use the inverse cosine function to find m∠R.*

CHECK IT OUT! **Find each measure. Round lengths to the nearest tenth and angle measures to the nearest degree.**

3a. DE

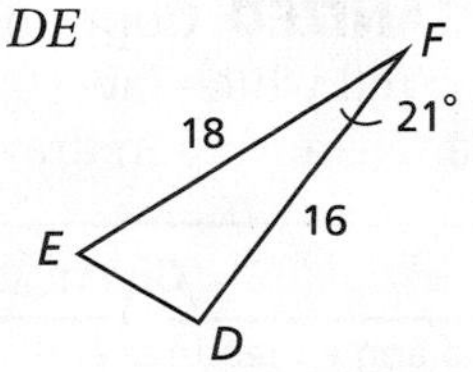

3b. $m\angle K$

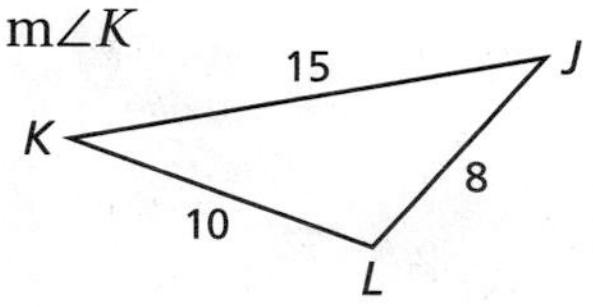

3c. YZ

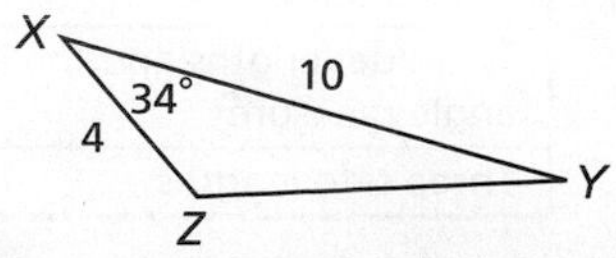

3d. $m\angle R$

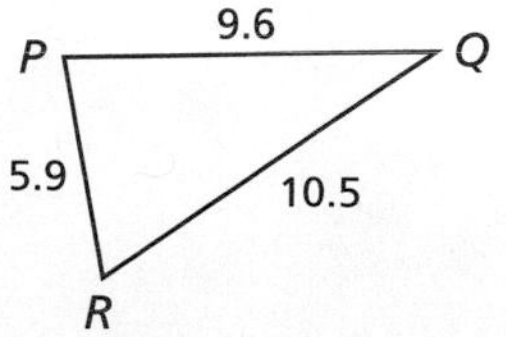

EXAMPLE 4 Engineering Application

The Leaning Tower of Pisa is 56 m tall. In 1999, the tower made a 100° angle with the ground. To stabilize the tower, an engineer considered attaching a cable from the top of the tower to a point that is 40 m from the base. How long would the cable be, and what angle would it make with the ground? Round the length to the nearest tenth and the angle measure to the nearest degree.

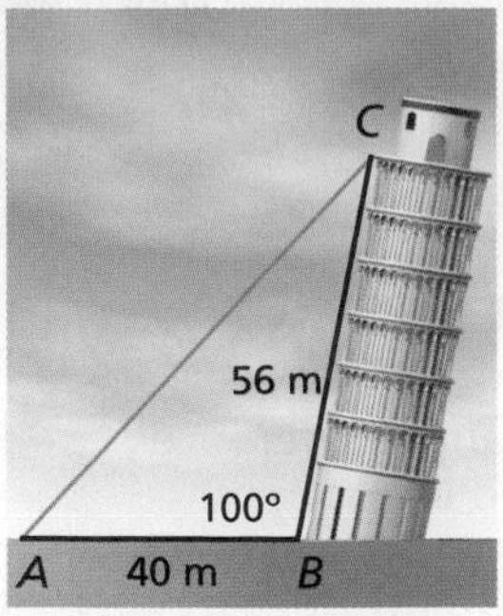

Step 1 Find the length of the cable.

$AC^2 = AB^2 + BC^2 - 2(AB)(BC)\cos B$ *Law of Cosines*

$= 40^2 + 56^2 - 2(40)(56)\cos 100°$ *Substitute the given values.*

$AC^2 \approx 5513.9438$ *Simplify.*

$AC \approx 74.3$ m *Find the square root of both sides.*

Step 2 Find the measure of the angle the cable would make with the ground.

$\frac{\sin A}{BC} = \frac{\sin B}{AC}$ *Law of Sines*

$\frac{\sin A}{56} \approx \frac{\sin 100°}{74.2559}$ *Substitute the calculated value for AC.*

$\sin A \approx \frac{56 \sin 100°}{74.2559}$ *Multiply both sides by 56.*

$m\angle A \approx \sin^{-1}\left(\frac{56 \sin 100°}{74.2559}\right) \approx 48°$ *Use the inverse sine function to find m∠A.*

Helpful Hint

Do not round your answer until the final step of the computation. If a problem has multiple steps, store the calculated answers to each part in your calculator.

CHECK IT OUT!

4. **What if...?** Another engineer suggested using a cable attached from the top of the tower to a point 31 m from the base. How long would this cable be, and what angle would it make with the ground? Round the length to the nearest tenth and the angle measure to the nearest degree.

MATHEMATICAL PRACTICES

THINK AND DISCUSS

1. Tell what additional information, if any, is needed to find BC using the Law of Sines.

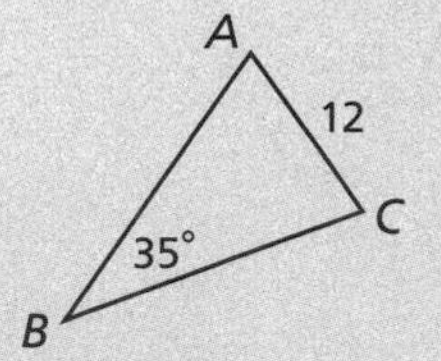

Know it! Note

2. **GET ORGANIZED** Copy and complete the graphic organizer. Tell which law you would use to solve each given triangle and then draw an example.

Given	Law	Example
Two angle measures and any side length		
Two side lengths and a nonincluded angle measure		
Two side lengths and the included angle measure		
Three side lengths		

8-5 Exercises

Learn It Online
Homework Help Online
Parent Resources Online

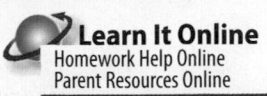

GUIDED PRACTICE

SEE EXAMPLE 1

Use a calculator to find each trigonometric ratio. Round to the nearest hundredth.

1. sin 100° **2.** cos 167° **3.** tan 92°

4. tan 141° **5.** cos 133° **6.** sin 150°

7. sin 147° **8.** tan 164° **9.** cos 156°

SEE EXAMPLE 2

Find each measure. Round lengths to the nearest tenth and angle measures to the nearest degree.

10. *RT*

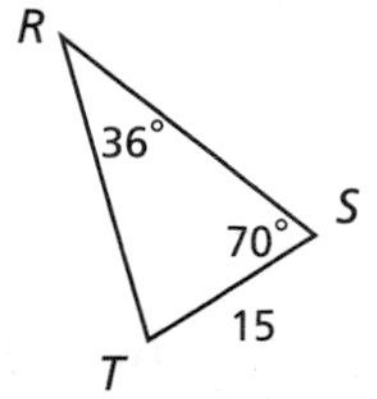

11. m∠*B*

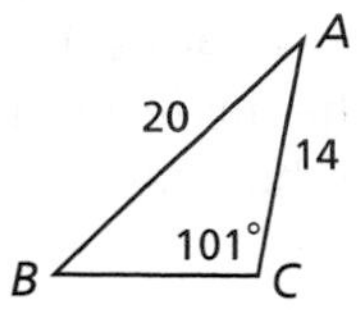

12. m∠*F*

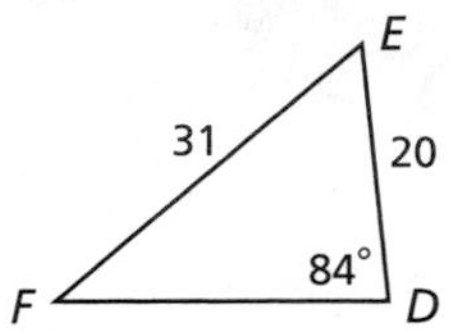

SEE EXAMPLE 3

13. m∠*Q*

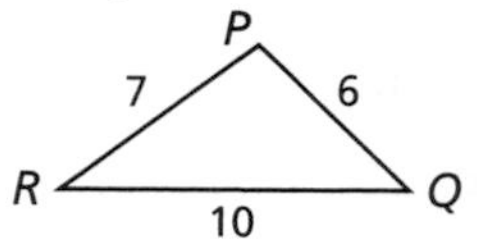

14. *MN*

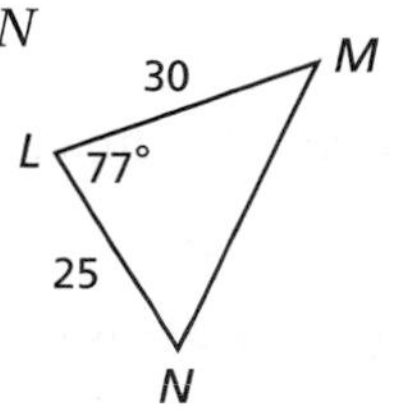

15. *AB*

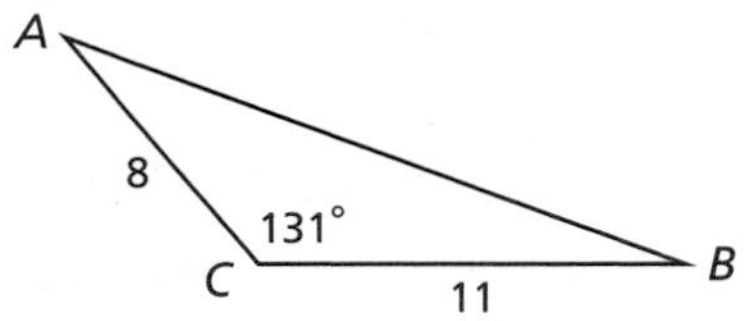

SEE EXAMPLE 4

16. Carpentry A carpenter makes a triangular frame by joining three pieces of wood that are 20 cm, 24 cm, and 30 cm long. What are the measures of the angles of the triangle? Round to the nearest degree.

PRACTICE AND PROBLEM SOLVING

Independent Practice

For Exercises	See Example
17–25	1
26–31	2
32–37	3
38	4

Extra Practice

See Extra Practice for more Skills Practice and Applications Practice exercises.

Use a calculator to find each trigonometric ratio. Round to the nearest hundredth.

17. cos 95° **18.** tan 178° **19.** tan 118°

20. sin 132° **21.** sin 98° **22.** cos 124°

23. tan 139° **24.** cos 145° **25.** sin 128°

Find each measure. Round lengths to the nearest tenth and angle measures to the nearest degree.

26. m∠*C*

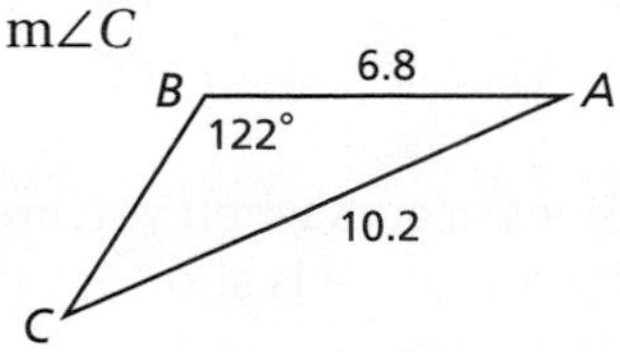

27. *PR*

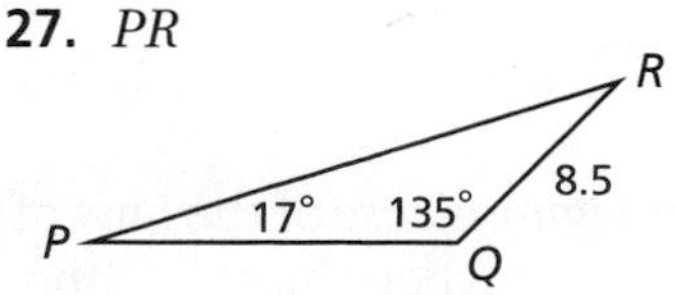

28. *JL*

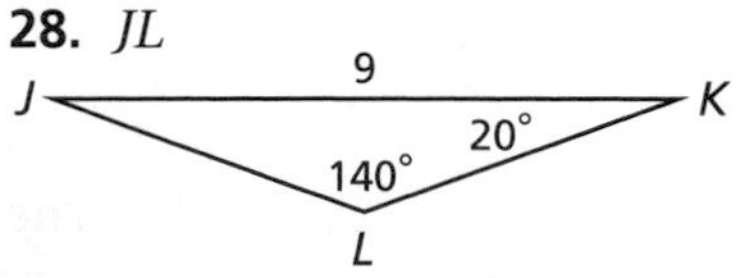

29. *EF*

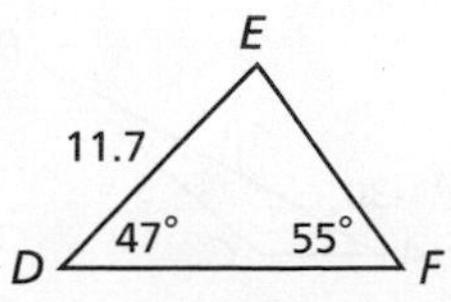

30. m∠*J*

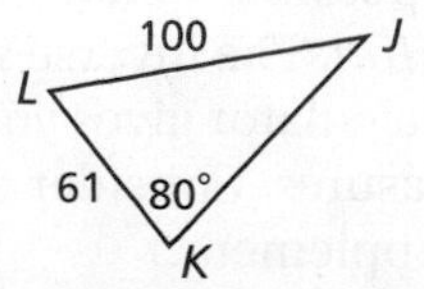

31. m∠*X*

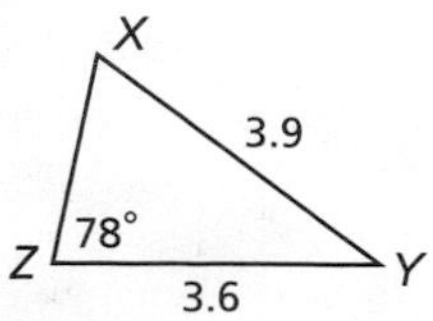

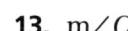

Find each measure. Round lengths to the nearest tenth and angle measures to the nearest degree.

32. AB

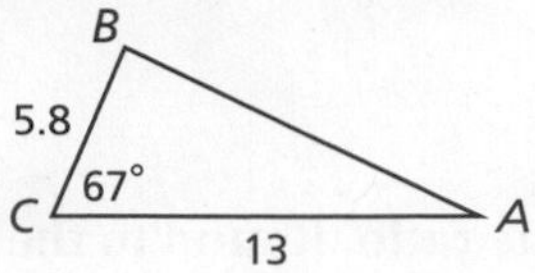

33. $m\angle Z$

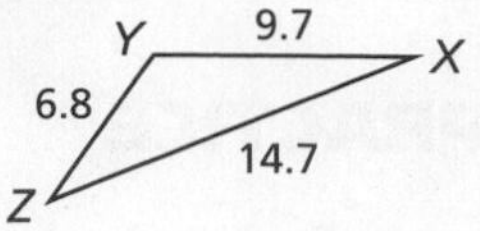

34. $m\angle R$

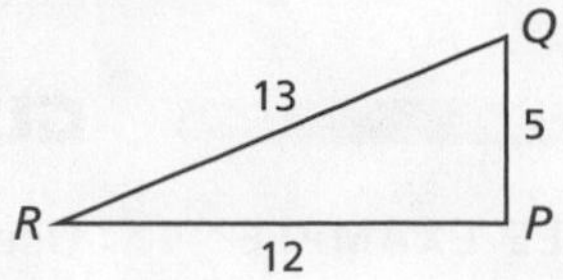

35. EF

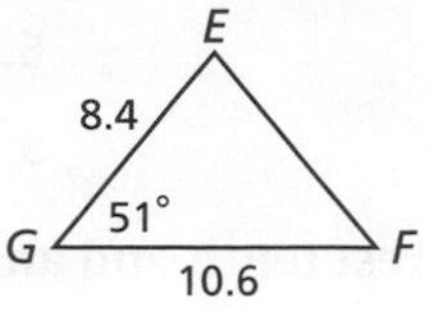

36. LM

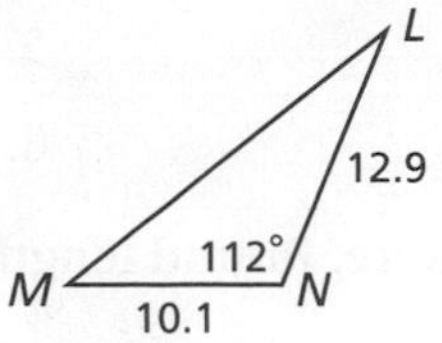

37. $m\angle G$

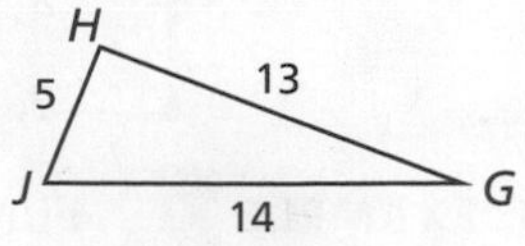

LINK

Surveying

Many modern surveys are done with GPS (Global Positioning System) technology. GPS uses orbiting satellites as reference points from which other locations are established.

38. Surveying To find the distance across a lake, a surveyor locates points A, B, and C as shown. What is AB to the nearest tenth of a meter, and what is $m\angle B$ to the nearest degree?

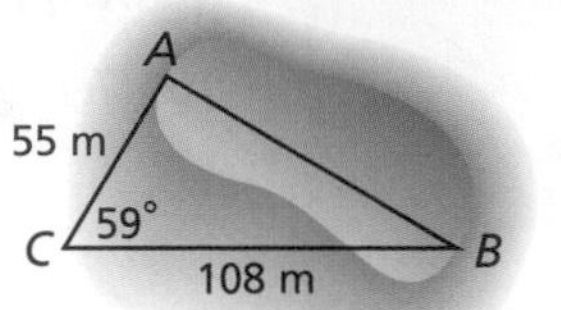

Use the figure for Exercises 39–42. Round lengths to the nearest tenth and angle measures to the nearest degree.

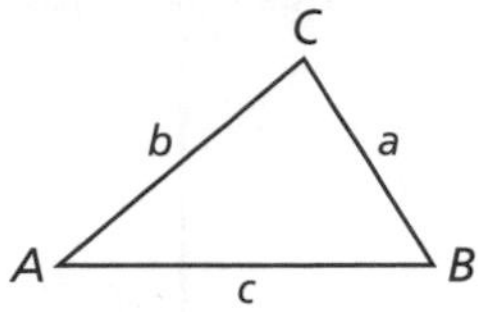

39. $m\angle A = 74°$, $m\angle B = 22°$, and $b = 3.2$ cm. Find a.

40. $m\angle C = 100°$, $a = 9.5$ in., and $b = 7.1$ in. Find c.

41. $a = 2.2$ m, $b = 3.1$ m, and $c = 4$ m. Find $m\angle B$.

42. $a = 10.3$ cm, $c = 8.4$ cm, and $m\angle A = 45°$. Find $m\angle C$.

43. Critical Thinking Suppose you are given the three angle measures of a triangle. Can you use the Law of Sines or the Law of Cosines to find the lengths of the sides? Why or why not?

44. What if...? What does the Law of Cosines simplify to when the given angle is a right angle?

45. Orienteering The map of a beginning orienteering course is shown at right. To the nearest degree, at what angle should a team turn in order to go from the first checkpoint to the second checkpoint?

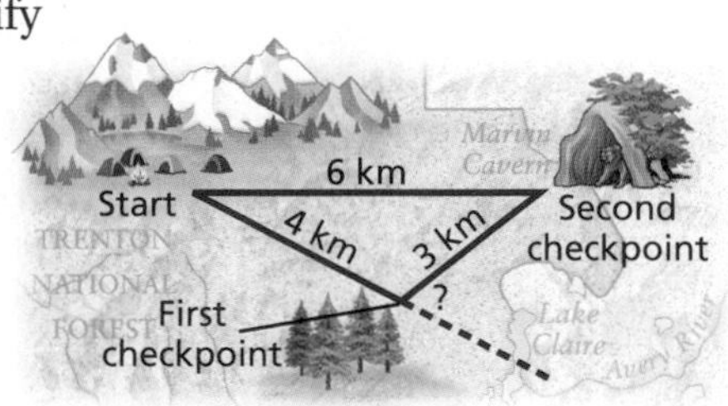

Multi-Step Find the perimeter of each triangle. Round to the nearest tenth.

46.

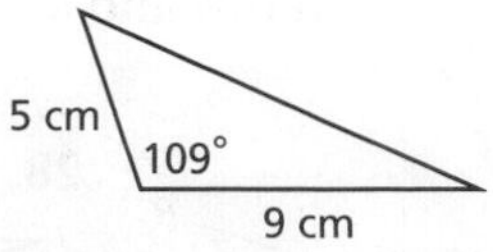

47.

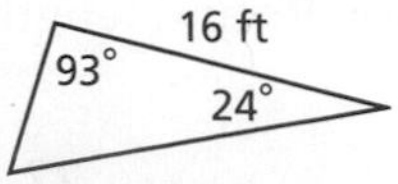

48.

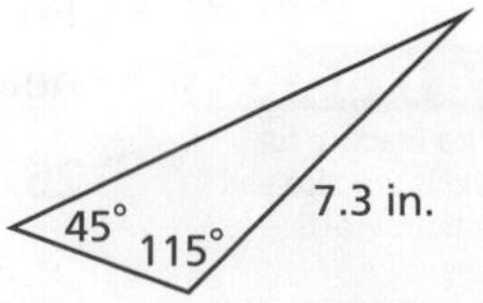

49. The *ambiguous case* of the Law of Sines occurs when you are given an acute angle measure and when the side opposite this angle is shorter than the other given side. In this case, there are two possible triangles.

Find two possible values for $m\angle C$ to the nearest degree. (*Hint:* The inverse sine function on your calculator gives you only acute angle measures. Consider this angle *and* its supplement.)

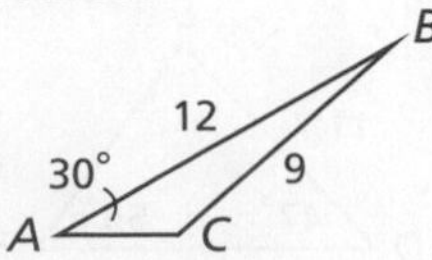

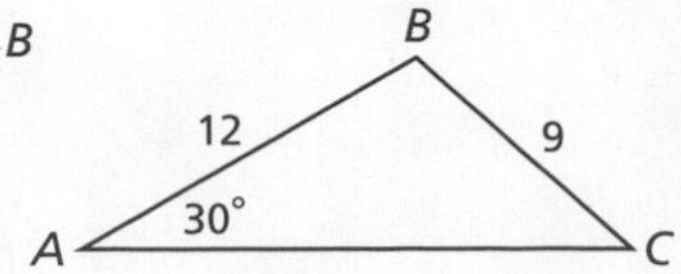

MULTI-STEP TEST PREP

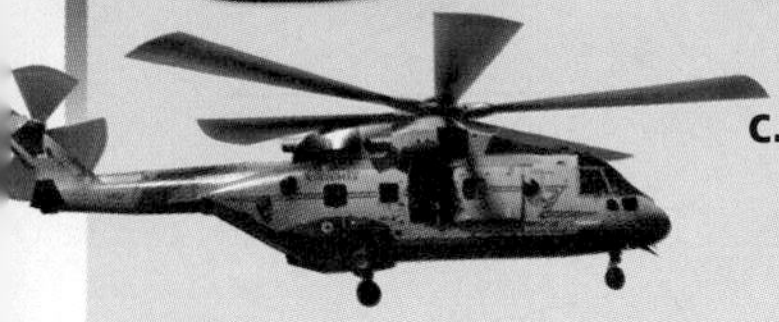

50. Rescue teams at two heliports, A and B, receive word of a fire at F.

a. What is $m\angle AFB$?

b. To the nearest mile, what are the distances from each heliport to the fire?

c. If a helicopter travels 150 mi/h, how much time is saved by sending a helicopter from A rather than B?

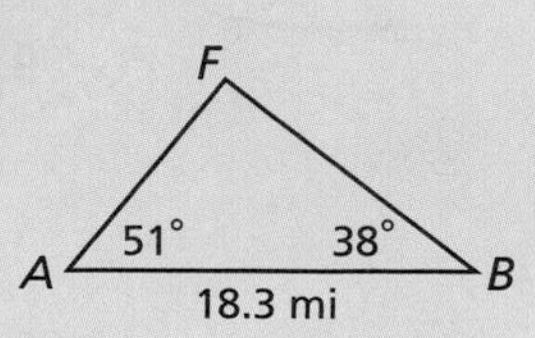

Identify whether you would use the Law of Sines or Law of Cosines as the first step when solving the given triangle.

51.

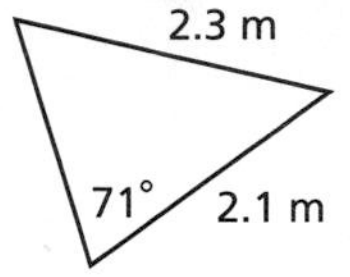

52.

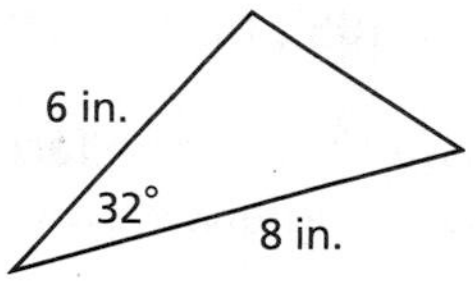

53.

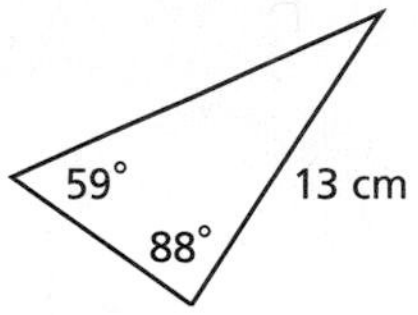

54. The coordinates of the vertices of $\triangle RST$ are $R(0, 3)$, $S(3, 1)$, and $T(-3, -1)$.

a. Find RS, ST, and RT.

b. Which angle of $\triangle RST$ is the largest? Why?

c. Find the measure of the largest angle in $\triangle RST$ to the nearest degree.

55. Art Jessika is creating a pattern for a piece of stained glass. Find BC, AB, and $m\angle ABC$. Round lengths to the nearest hundredth and angle measures to the nearest degree.

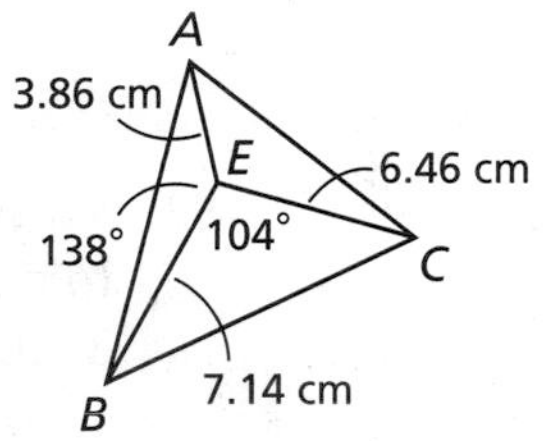

56. ERROR ANALYSIS Two students were asked to find x in $\triangle DEF$. Which solution is incorrect? Explain the error.

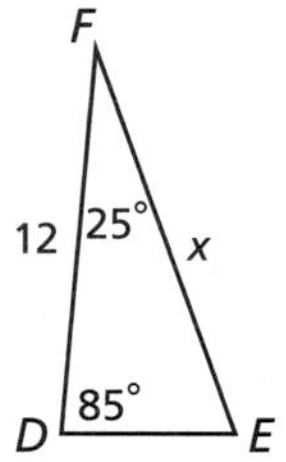

A

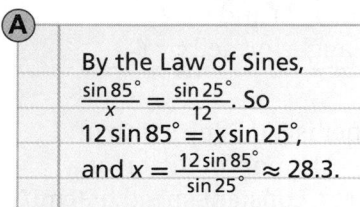

By the Law of Sines,
$\frac{\sin 85°}{x} = \frac{\sin 25°}{12}$. So
$12 \sin 85° = x \sin 25°$,
and $x = \frac{12 \sin 85°}{\sin 25°} \approx 28.3$.

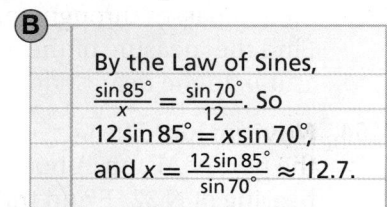

B

By the Law of Sines,
$\frac{\sin 85°}{x} = \frac{\sin 70°}{12}$. So
$12 \sin 85° = x \sin 70°$,
and $x = \frac{12 \sin 85°}{\sin 70°} \approx 12.7$.

57. Complete the proof of the Law of Cosines for the case when $\triangle ABC$ is an acute triangle.
Given: $\triangle ABC$ is acute with side lengths a, b, and c.
Prove: $a^2 = b^2 + c^2 - 2bc\cos A$

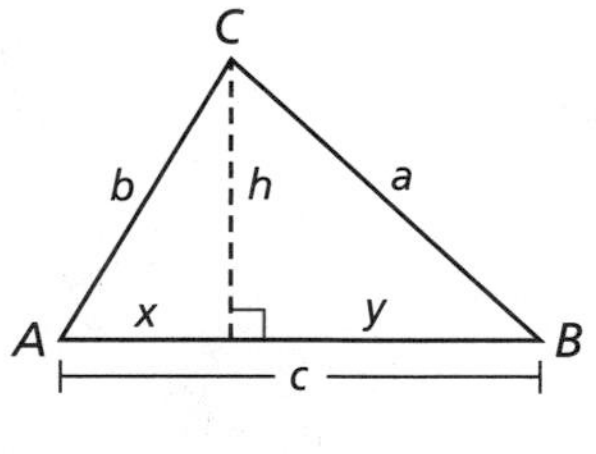

Proof: Draw the altitude from C to $\overline{AB}$. Let h be the length of this altitude. It divides $\overline{AB}$ into segments of lengths x and y. By the Pythagorean Theorem, $a^2 =$ **a.** ___?___ , and **b.** ___?___ $= h^2 + x^2$. Substitute $y = c - x$ into the first equation to get **c.** ___?___ . Rearrange the terms to get $a^2 = (h^2 + x^2) + c^2 - 2cx$. Substitute the expression for b^2 to get **d.** ___?___ . From the diagram, $\cos A = \frac{x}{b}$. So $x =$ **e.** ___?___ . Therefore $a^2 = b^2 + c^2 - 2bc\cos A$ by **f.** ___?___ .

58. Write About It Can you use the Law of Sines to solve $\triangle EFG$? Explain why or why not.

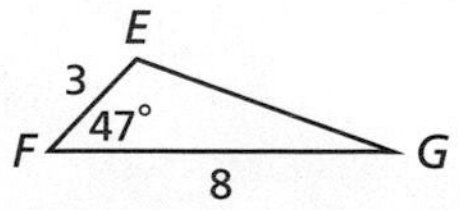

TEST PREP

59. Which of these is closest to the length of $\overline{AB}$?

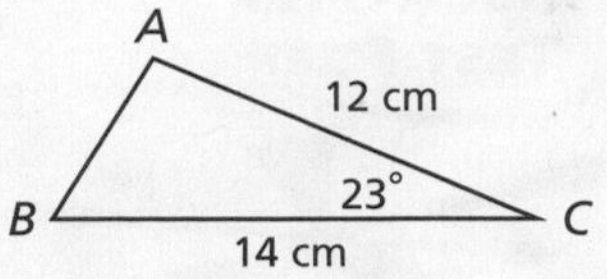

Ⓐ 5.5 centimeters Ⓒ 14.4 centimeters

Ⓑ 7.5 centimeters Ⓓ 22.2 centimeters

60. Which set of given information makes it possible to find x using the Law of Sines?

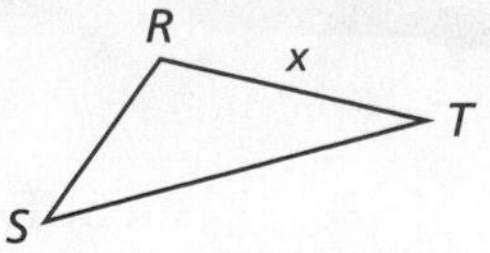

Ⓕ $m\angle T = 38°$, $RS = 8.1$, $ST = 15.3$

Ⓖ $RS = 4$, $m\angle S = 40°$, $ST = 9$

Ⓗ $m\angle R = 92°$, $m\angle S = 34°$, $ST = 7$

Ⓙ $m\angle R = 105°$, $m\angle S = 44°$, $m\angle T = 31°$

61. A surveyor finds that the face of a pyramid makes a 135° angle with the ground. From a point 100 m from the base of the pyramid, the angle of elevation to the top is 25°. How long is the face of the pyramid, $\overline{XY}$?

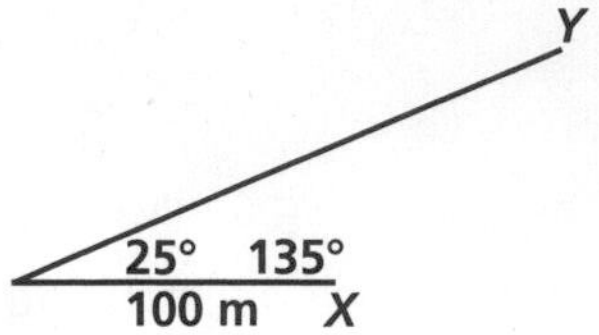

Ⓐ 48 meters Ⓒ 124 meters

Ⓑ 81 meters Ⓓ 207 meters

CHALLENGE AND EXTEND

62. **Multi-Step** Three circular disks are placed next to each other as shown. The disks have radii of 2 cm, 3 cm, and 4 cm. The centers of the disks form $\triangle ABC$. Find $m\angle ACB$ to the nearest degree.

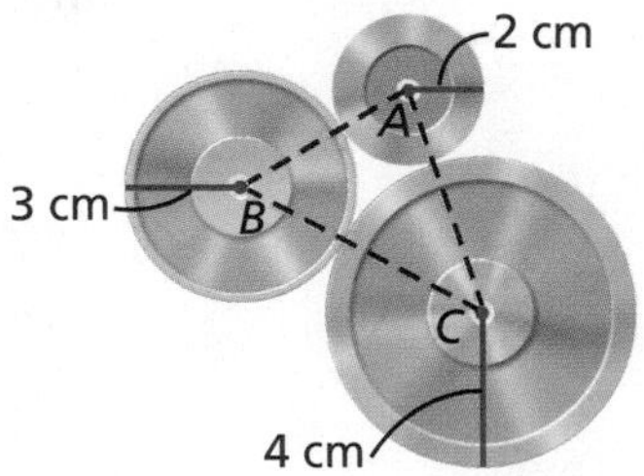

63. Line ℓ passes through points $(-1, 1)$ and $(1, 3)$. Line m passes through points $(-1, 1)$ and $(3, 2)$. Find the measure of the acute angle formed by ℓ and m to the nearest degree.

64. **Navigation** The port of Bonner is 5 mi due south of the port of Alston. A boat leaves the port of Alston at a bearing of N 32° E and travels at a constant speed of 6 mi/h. After 45 minutes, how far is the boat from the port of Bonner? Round to the nearest tenth of a mile.

COMMON CORE

8-6 Vectors

Objectives
Find the magnitude and direction of a vector.

Use vectors and vector addition to solve real-world problems.

Vocabulary
vector
component form
magnitude
direction
equal vectors
parallel vectors
resultant vector

Who uses this?
By using vectors, a kayaker can take water currents into account when planning a course. (See Example 5.)

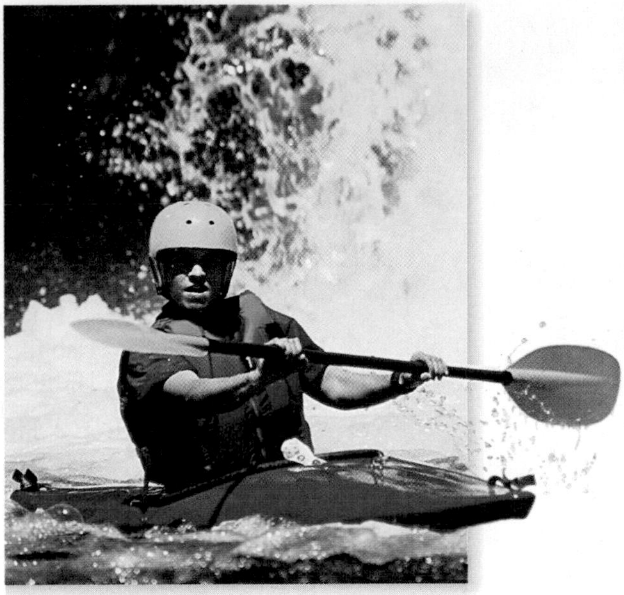

The speed and direction an object moves can be represented by a *vector*. A **vector** is a quantity that has both length and direction.

You can think of a vector as a directed line segment. The vector below may be named $\overrightarrow{AB}$ or $\vec{v}$.

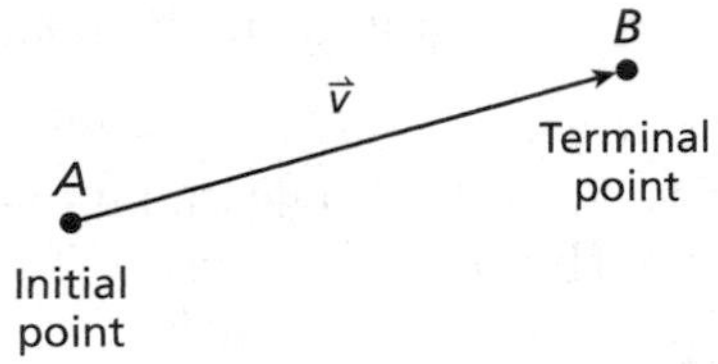

A vector can also be named using *component form*. The **component form** $\langle x, y\rangle$ of a vector lists the **horizontal** and vertical change from the initial point to the terminal point. The component form of $\overrightarrow{CD}$ is $\langle 2, 3\rangle$.

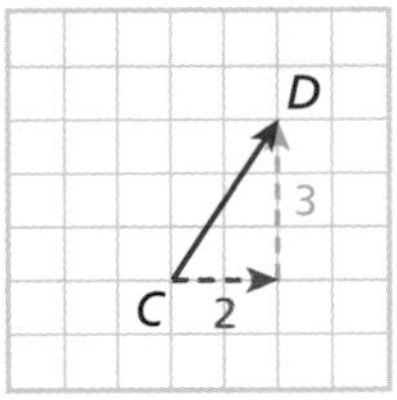

EXAMPLE 1 Writing Vectors in Component Form

Write each vector in component form.

A $\overrightarrow{EF}$

The horizontal change from E to F is 4 units.
The vertical change from E to F is -3 units.
So the component form of $\overrightarrow{EF}$ is $\langle 4, -3\rangle$.

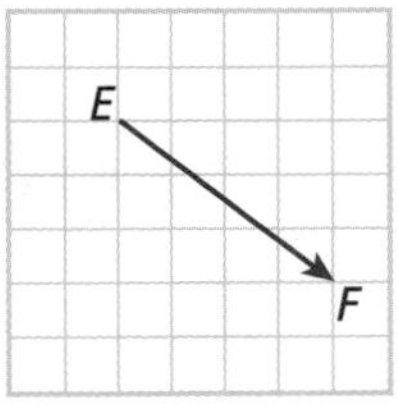

B $\overrightarrow{PQ}$ **with** $P(7, -5)$ **and** $Q(4, 3)$

$\overrightarrow{PQ} = \langle x_2 - x_1, y_2 - y_1\rangle$ *Subtract the coordinates of the initial point from the coordinates of the terminal point.*

$\overrightarrow{PQ} = \langle 4 - 7, 3 - (-5)\rangle$ *Substitute the coordinates of the given points.*

$\overrightarrow{PQ} = \langle -3, 8\rangle$ *Simplify.*

CHECK IT OUT! **Write each vector in component form.**

1a. $\vec{u}$

1b. the vector with initial point $L(-1, 1)$ and terminal point $M(6, 2)$

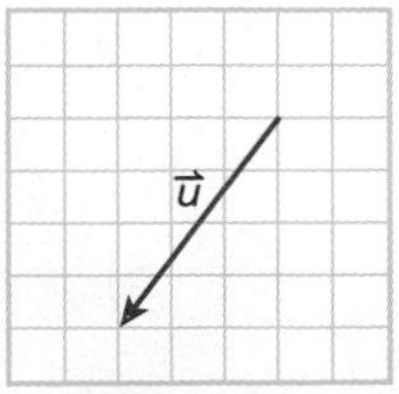

The **magnitude** of a vector is its length. The magnitude of a vector is written $|\overrightarrow{AB}|$ or $|\vec{v}|$.

When a vector is used to represent speed in a given direction, the magnitude of the vector equals the speed. For example, if a vector represents the course a kayaker paddles, the magnitude of the vector is the kayaker's speed.

EXAMPLE 2 Finding the Magnitude of a Vector

Draw the vector ⟨4, –2⟩ on a coordinate plane.
Find its magnitude to the nearest tenth.

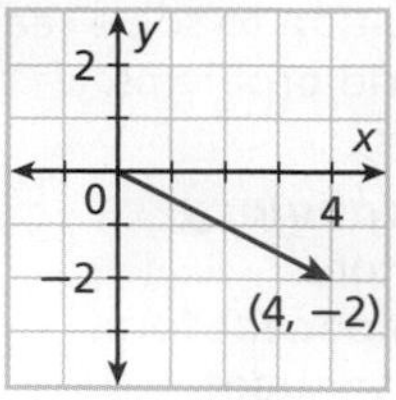

Step 1 Draw the vector on a coordinate plane.
Use the origin as the initial point. Then (4, –2) is the terminal point.

Step 2 Find the magnitude.
Use the Distance Formula.

$$|\langle 4, -2\rangle| = \sqrt{(4-0)^2 + (-2-0)^2} = \sqrt{20} \approx 4.5$$

CHECK IT OUT! **2.** Draw the vector ⟨–3, 1⟩ on a coordinate plane. Find its magnitude to the nearest tenth.

The **direction** of a vector is the angle that it makes with a horizontal line. This angle is measured counterclockwise from the positive *x*-axis. The direction of $\overrightarrow{AB}$ is 60°.

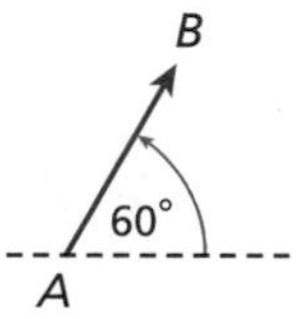

The direction of a vector can also be given as a bearing relative to the compass directions *north, south, east,* and *west.* $\overrightarrow{AB}$ has a bearing of N 30° E.

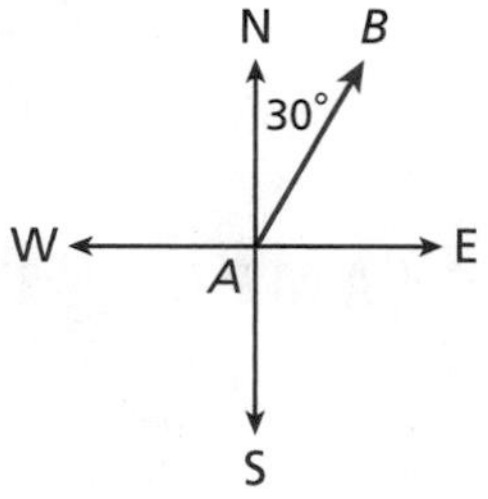

EXAMPLE 3 Finding the Direction of a Vector

A wind velocity is given by the vector ⟨2, 5⟩.
Draw the vector on a coordinate plane.
Find the direction of the vector to the nearest degree.

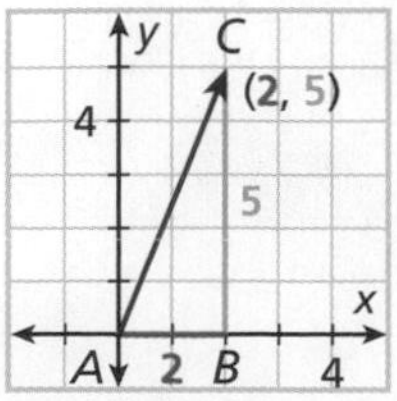

Step 1 Draw the vector on a coordinate plane.
Use the origin as the initial point.

Step 2 Find the direction.
Draw right triangle *ABC* as shown. ∠*A* is the angle formed by the vector and the *x*-axis, and $\tan A = \frac{5}{2}$. So $m\angle A = \tan^{-1}\left(\frac{5}{2}\right) \approx 68°$.

CHECK IT OUT! **3.** The force exerted by a tugboat is given by the vector ⟨7, 3⟩. Draw the vector on a coordinate plane. Find the direction of the vector to the nearest degree.

Caution!

Note that $\overrightarrow{AB} \neq \overrightarrow{BA}$ since these vectors do not have the same direction.

Two vectors are **equal vectors** if they have the same magnitude and the same direction. For example, $\vec{u} = \vec{v}$. Equal vectors do not have to have the same initial point and terminal point.

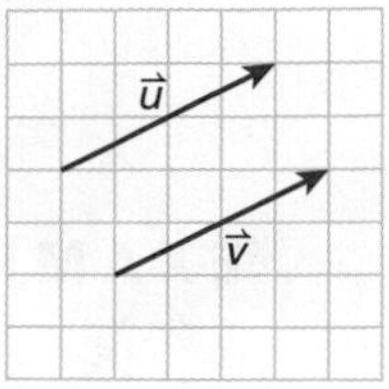

$|\vec{u}| = |\vec{v}| = 2\sqrt{5}$

Two vectors are **parallel vectors** if they have the same direction or if they have opposite directions. They may have different magnitudes. For example, $\vec{w} \parallel \vec{x}$. Equal vectors are always parallel vectors.

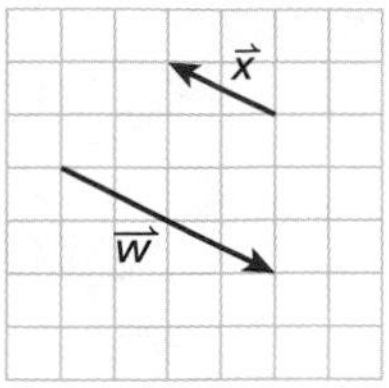

$|\vec{w}| = 2\sqrt{5}$
$|\vec{x}| = \sqrt{5}$

EXAMPLE 4 Identifying Equal and Parallel Vectors

Identify each of the following.

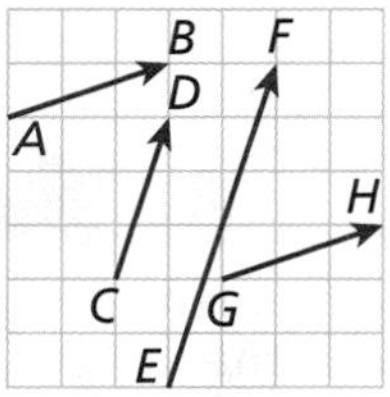

A equal vectors

$\overrightarrow{AB} = \overrightarrow{GH}$ *Identify vectors with the same magnitude and direction.*

B parallel vectors

$\overrightarrow{AB} \parallel \overrightarrow{GH}$ and $\overrightarrow{CD} \parallel \overrightarrow{EF}$ *Identify vectors with the same or opposite directions.*

CHECK IT OUT! **Identify each of the following.**

4a. equal vectors

4b. parallel vectors

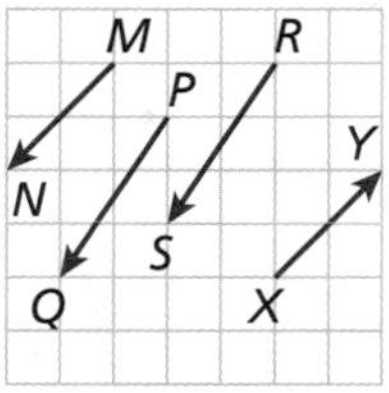

The **resultant vector** is the vector that represents the sum of two given vectors. To add two vectors geometrically, you can use the head-to-tail method or the parallelogram method.

Know it! Note

Vector Addition

METHOD	EXAMPLE
Head-to-Tail Method Place the initial point (tail) of the **second vector** on the terminal point (head) of the **first vector**. The **resultant** is the vector that joins the initial point of the **first vector** to the terminal point of the **second vector**.	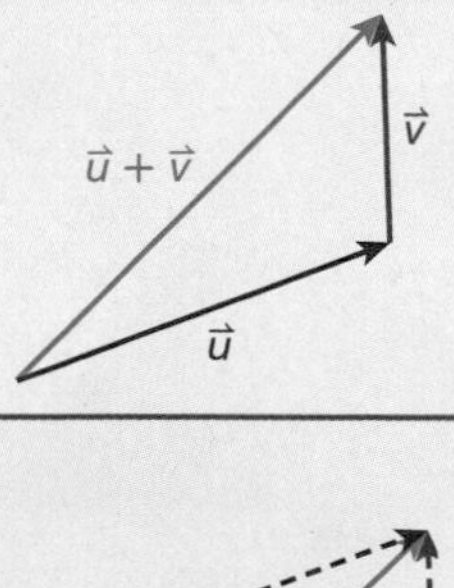
Parallelogram Method Use the same initial point for both of the given vectors. Create a parallelogram by adding a copy of each vector at the terminal point (head) of the other vector. The **resultant vector** is a diagonal of the parallelogram formed.	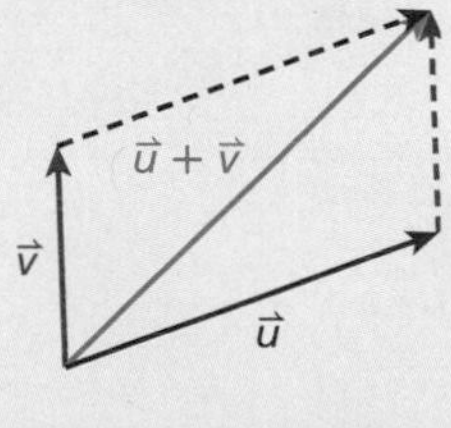

To add vectors numerically, add their components. If $\vec{u} = \langle x_1, y_1 \rangle$ and $\vec{v} = \langle x_2, y_2 \rangle$, then $\vec{u} + \vec{v} = \langle x_1 + x_2, y_1 + y_2 \rangle$.

EXAMPLE 5 *Sports Application*

A kayaker leaves shore at a bearing of N 55° E and paddles at a constant speed of 3 mi/h. There is a 1 mi/h current moving due east. What are the kayak's actual speed and direction? Round the speed to the nearest tenth and the direction to the nearest degree.

Step 1 Sketch vectors for the kayaker and the current.

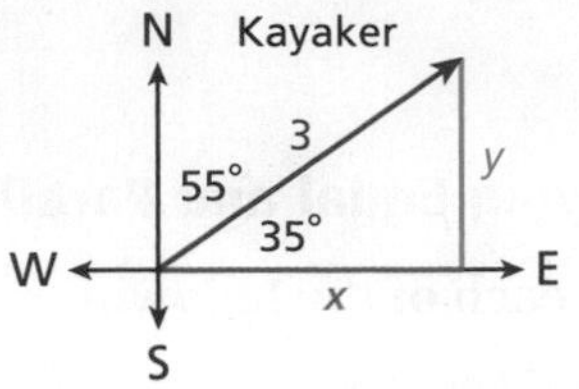

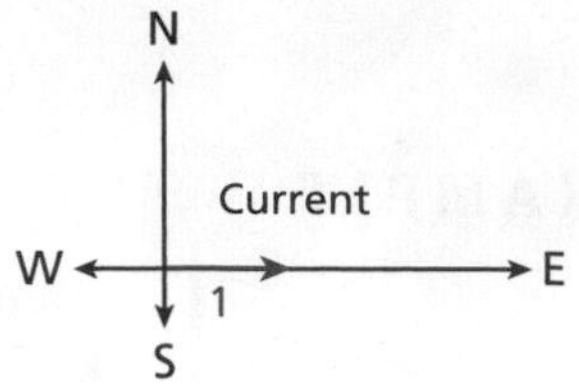

Step 2 Write the vector for the kayaker in component form.

The kayaker's vector has a magnitude of 3 mi/h and makes an angle of 35° with the x-axis.

$$\cos 35° = \frac{x}{3}, \text{ so } x = 3\cos 35° \approx 2.5.$$

$$\sin 35° = \frac{y}{3}, \text{ so } y = 3\sin 35° \approx 1.7.$$

The kayaker's vector is $\langle 2.5, 1.7 \rangle$.

Step 3 Write the vector for the current in component form.

Since the current moves 1 mi/h in the direction of the x-axis, it has a horizontal component of 1 and a vertical component of 0. So its vector is $\langle 1, 0 \rangle$.

Step 4 Find and sketch the resultant vector $\overrightarrow{AB}$.

Add the components of the kayaker's vector and the current's vector.

$$\langle 2.5, 1.7 \rangle + \langle 1, 0 \rangle = \langle 3.5, 1.7 \rangle$$

The resultant vector in component form is $\langle 3.5, 1.7 \rangle$.

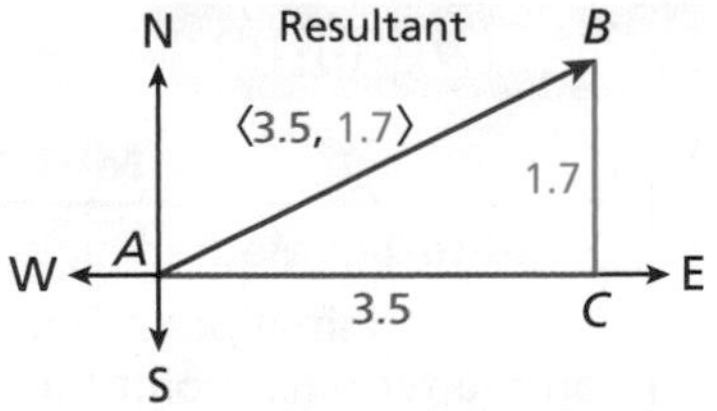

Step 5 Find the magnitude and direction of the resultant vector.

The magnitude of the resultant vector is the kayak's actual speed.

$$|\langle 3.5, 1.7 \rangle| = \sqrt{(3.5 - 0)^2 + (1.7 - 0)^2} \approx 3.9 \text{ mi/h}$$

The angle measure formed by the resultant vector gives the kayak's actual direction.

$$\tan A = \frac{1.7}{3.5}, \text{ so } A = \tan^{-1}\left(\frac{1.7}{3.5}\right) \approx 26°, \text{ or N } 64° \text{ E}.$$

Remember!

Component form gives the horizontal and vertical change from the initial point to the terminal point of the vector.

CHECK IT OUT! **5. What if...?** Suppose the kayaker in Example 5 instead paddles at 4 mi/h at a bearing of N 20° E. What are the kayak's actual speed and direction? Round the speed to the nearest tenth and the direction to the nearest degree.

THINK AND DISCUSS

MATHEMATICAL PRACTICES

1. Explain why the segment with endpoints $(0, 0)$ and $(1, 4)$ is not a vector.
2. Assume you are given a vector in component form. Other than the Distance Formula, what theorem can you use to find the vector's magnitude?
3. Describe how to add two vectors numerically.
4. **GET ORGANIZED** Copy and complete the graphic organizer.

Know it! Note

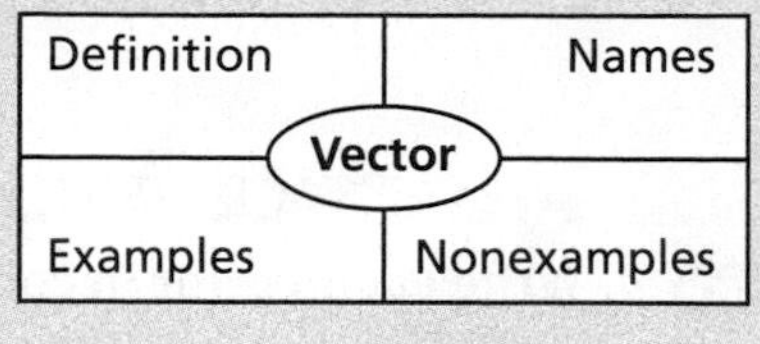

8-6 Exercises

Learn It Online
Homework Help Online
Parent Resources Online

GUIDED PRACTICE

Vocabulary **Apply the vocabulary from this lesson to answer each question.**

1. ___?___ vectors have the same magnitude and direction. (*equal, parallel,* or *resultant*)
2. ___?___ vectors have the same or opposite directions. (*equal, parallel,* or *resultant*)
3. The ___?___ of a vector indicates the vector's size. (*magnitude* or *direction*)

SEE EXAMPLE 1

Write each vector in component form.

4. $\overrightarrow{AC}$ with $A(1, 2)$ and $C(6, 5)$
5. the vector with initial point $M(-4, 5)$ and terminal point $N(4, -3)$
6. $\overrightarrow{PQ}$

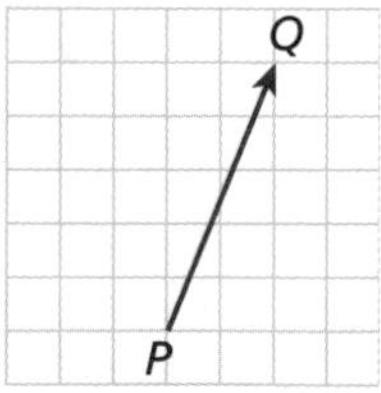

SEE EXAMPLE 2

Draw each vector on a coordinate plane. Find its magnitude to the nearest tenth.

7. $\langle 1, 4 \rangle$
8. $\langle -3, -2 \rangle$
9. $\langle 5, -3 \rangle$

SEE EXAMPLE 3

Draw each vector on a coordinate plane. Find the direction of the vector to the nearest degree.

10. A river's current is given by the vector $\langle 4, 6 \rangle$.
11. The velocity of a plane is given by the vector $\langle 5, 1 \rangle$.
12. The path of a hiker is given by the vector $\langle 6, 3 \rangle$.

SEE EXAMPLE 4

Identify each of the following.

13. equal vectors in diagram 1
14. parallel vectors in diagram 1
15. equal vectors in diagram 2
16. parallel vectors in diagram 2

Diagram 1

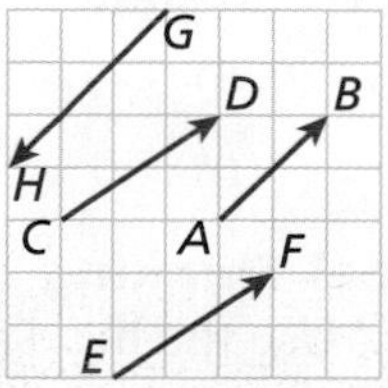

Diagram 2

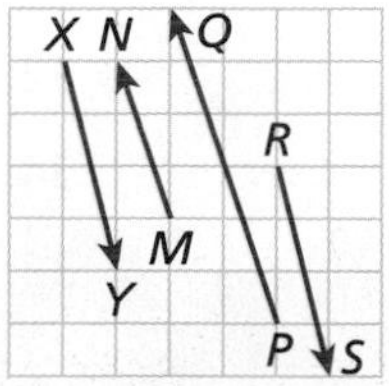

SEE EXAMPLE 5

17. **Recreation** To reach a campsite, a hiker first walks for 2 mi at a bearing of N 40° E. Then he walks 3 mi due east. What are the magnitude and direction of his hike from his starting point to the campsite? Round the distance to the nearest tenth of a mile and the direction to the nearest degree.

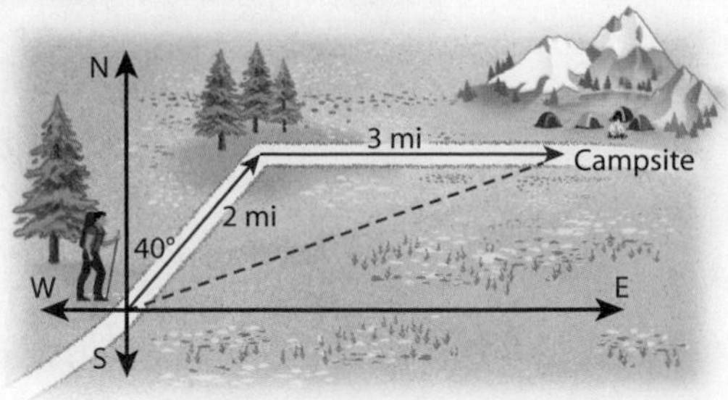

PRACTICE AND PROBLEM SOLVING

Independent Practice	
For Exercises	See Example
18–20	1
21–23	2
24–26	3
27–30	4
31	5

Extra Practice

See Extra Practice for more Skills Practice and Applications Practice exercises.

Write each vector in component form.

18. $\overrightarrow{JK}$ with $J(-6, -7)$ and $K(3, -5)$

19. $\overrightarrow{EF}$ with $E(1.5, -3)$ and $F(-2, 2.5)$

20. $\vec{w}$

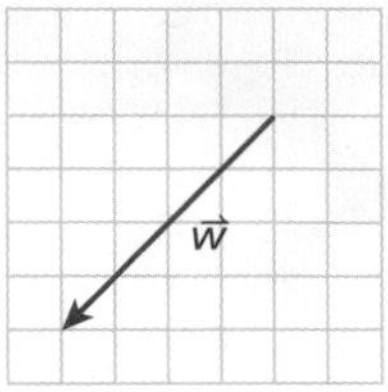

Draw each vector on a coordinate plane. Find its magnitude to the nearest tenth.

21. $\langle -2, 0 \rangle$

22. $\langle 1.5, 1.5 \rangle$

23. $\langle 2.5, -3.5 \rangle$

Draw each vector on a coordinate plane. Find the direction of the vector to the nearest degree.

24. A boat's velocity is given by the vector $\langle 4, 1.5 \rangle$.

25. The path of a submarine is given by the vector $\langle 3.5, 2.5 \rangle$.

26. The path of a projectile is given by the vector $\langle 2, 5 \rangle$.

Identify each of the following.

27. equal vectors in diagram 1

28. parallel vectors in diagram 1

29. equal vectors in diagram 2

30. parallel vectors in diagram 2

Diagram 1

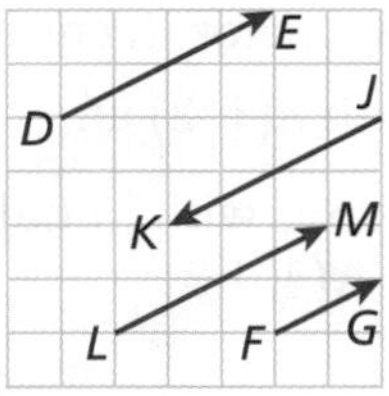

Diagram 2

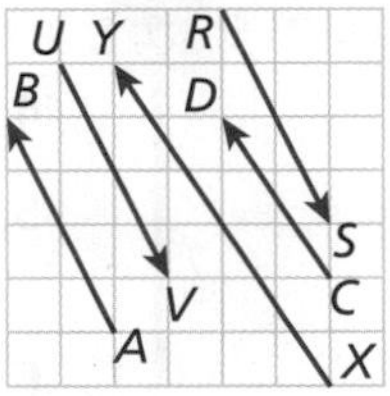

31. **Aviation** The pilot of a single-engine airplane flies at a constant speed of 200 km/h at a bearing of N 25° E. There is a 40 km/h crosswind blowing southeast (S 45° E). What are the plane's actual speed and direction? Round the speed to the nearest tenth and the direction to the nearest degree.

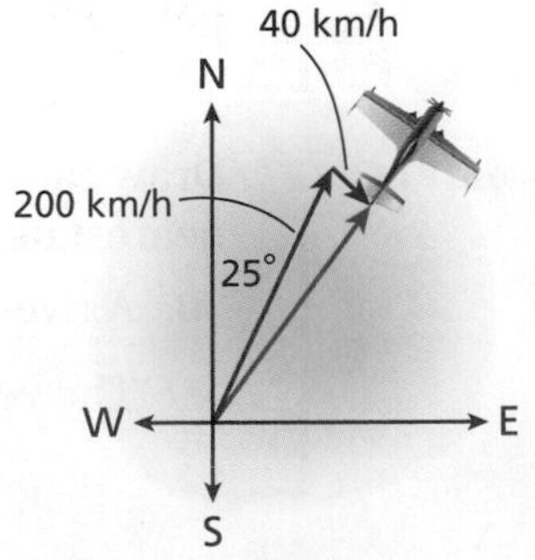

Find each vector sum.

32. $\langle 1, 2 \rangle + \langle 0, 6 \rangle$

33. $\langle -3, 4 \rangle + \langle 5, -2 \rangle$

34. $\langle 0, 1 \rangle + \langle 7, 0 \rangle$

35. $\langle 8, 3 \rangle + \langle -2, -1 \rangle$

36. **Critical Thinking** Is vector addition commutative? That is, is $\vec{u} + \vec{v}$ equal to $\vec{v} + \vec{u}$? Use the head-to-tail method of vector addition to explain why or why not.

MULTI-STEP TEST PREP

37. A helicopter at H must fly at 50 mi/h in the direction N 45° E to reach the site of a flood victim F. There is a 41 mi/h wind in the direction N 53° W. The pilot needs to the know the velocity vector $\overrightarrow{HX}$ he should use so that his resultant vector will be $\overrightarrow{HF}$.

    a. What is m∠F? (*Hint:* Consider a vertical line through F.)

    b. Use the Law of Cosines to find the magnitude of $\overrightarrow{HX}$ to the nearest tenth.

    c. Use the Law of Sines to find m∠FHX to the nearest degree.

    d. What is the direction of $\overrightarrow{HX}$?

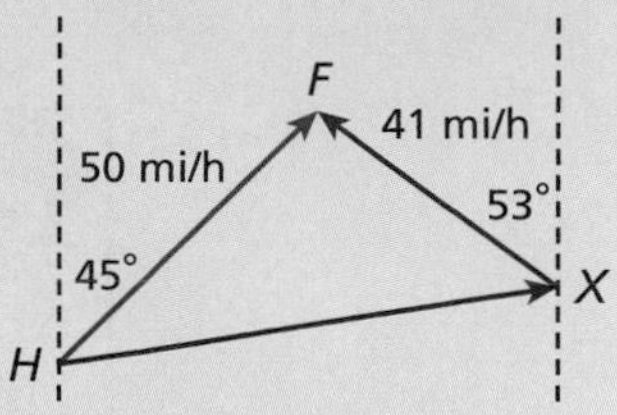

Write each vector in component form. Round values to the nearest tenth.

38. magnitude 15, direction 42°

39. magnitude 7.2, direction 9°

40. magnitude 12.1, direction N 57° E

41. magnitude 5.8, direction N 22° E

42. **Physics** A classroom has a window near the ceiling, and a long pole must be used to close it.

    a. Carla holds the pole at a 45° angle to the floor and applies 10 lb of force to the upper edge of the window. Find the vertical component of the vector representing the force on the window. Round to the nearest tenth.

    b. Taneka also applies 10 lb of force to close the window, but she holds the pole at a 75° angle to the floor. Find the vertical component of the force vector in this case. Round to the nearest tenth.

    c. Who will have an easier time closing the window, Carla or Taneka? (*Hint:* Who applies more vertical force?)

43. **Probability** The numbers 1, 2, 3, and 4 are written on slips of paper and placed in a hat. Two different slips of paper are chosen at random to be the x- and y-components of a vector.

    a. What is the probability that the vector will be equal to $\langle 1, 2\rangle$?

    b. What is the probability that the vector will be parallel to $\langle 1, 2\rangle$?

44. You can subtract one vector from another by subtracting the components of the second vector from the components of the first. If $\vec{a} = \langle x_1, y_1\rangle$ and $\vec{b} = \langle x_2, y_2\rangle$, then $\vec{a} - \vec{b} = \langle x_1 - x_2, y_1 - y_2\rangle$

    a. Find $\vec{a} - \vec{b}$ for $\vec{a} = \langle 4, -2\rangle$ and $\vec{b} = \langle 2, -1\rangle$.

    b. You can also think of subtracting a vector as adding its opposite. In symbols, $\vec{a} - \vec{b} = \vec{a} + (-\vec{b})$ and $-\vec{b} = \langle -x_2, -y_2\rangle$. Using the vectors given in part **a**, draw $\vec{a} + (-\vec{b})$ in the corrdinate plane using the head-to-tail method.

Multi-Step **Find the magnitude of each vector to the nearest tenth and the direction of each vector to the nearest degree.**

45. $\vec{u}$

46. $\vec{v}$

47. $\vec{w}$

48. $\vec{z}$

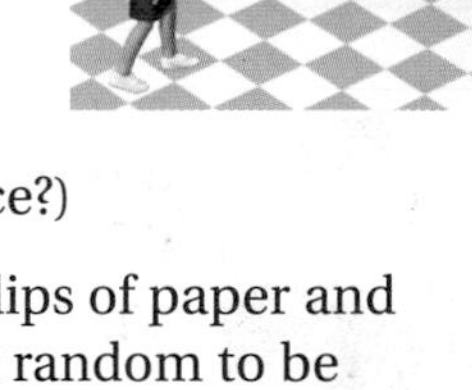

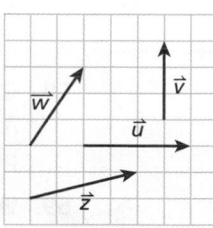

49. Football Write two vectors in component form to represent the pass pattern that Jason is told to run. Find the resultant vector and show that Jason's move is equivalent to the vector.

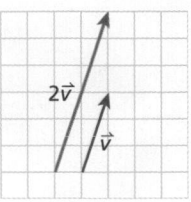

For each given vector, find another vector that has the same magnitude but a different direction. Then find a vector that has the same direction but a different magnitude.

50. $\langle -3, 6\rangle$ **51.** $\langle 12, 5\rangle$ **52.** $\langle 8, -11\rangle$

Multi-Step Find the sum of each pair of vectors. Then find the magnitude and direction of the resultant vector. Round the magnitude to the nearest tenth and the direction to the nearest degree.

53. $\vec{u} = \langle 1, 2\rangle$, $\vec{v} = \langle 2.5, -1\rangle$

54. $\vec{u} = \langle -2, 7\rangle$, $\vec{v} = \langle 4.8, -3.1\rangle$

55. $\vec{u} = \langle 6, 0\rangle$, $\vec{v} = \langle -2, 4\rangle$

56. $\vec{u} = \langle -1.2, 8\rangle$, $\vec{v} = \langle 5.2, -2.1\rangle$

LINK

Math History

August Ferdinand Möbius is best known for experimenting with the Möbius strip, a three-dimensional figure that has only one side and one edge.

57. Math History In 1827, the mathematician August Ferdinand Möbius published a book in which he introduced directed line segments (what we now call vectors). He showed how to perform *scalar multiplication* of vectors. For example, consider a hiker who walks along a path given by the vector $\vec{v}$. The path of another hiker who walks twice as far in the same direction is given by the vector $2\vec{v}$.

a. Write the component form of the vectors $\vec{v}$ and $2\vec{v}$.

b. Find the magnitude of $\vec{v}$ and $2\vec{v}$. How do they compare?

c. Find the direction of $\vec{v}$ and $2\vec{v}$. How do they compare?

d. Given the component form of a vector, explain how to find the components of the vector $k\vec{v}$, where k is a constant.

e. Use scalar multiplication with $k = -1$ to write the *negation of a vector* $\vec{v}$ in component form.

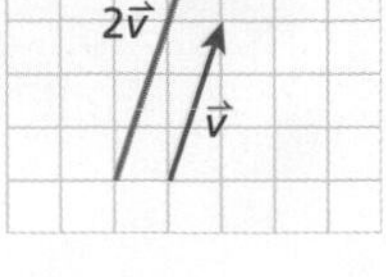

58. Critical Thinking A vector $\vec{u}$ points due west with a magnitude of u units. Another vector $\vec{v}$ points due east with a magnitude of v units. Describe three possible directions and magnitudes for the resultant vector.

59. Write About It Compare a line segment, a ray, and a vector.

TEST PREP

60. Which vector is parallel to $\langle 2, 1 \rangle$?

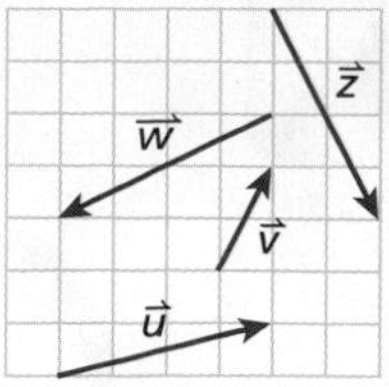

Ⓐ $\vec{u}$ Ⓒ $\vec{w}$

Ⓑ $\vec{v}$ Ⓓ $\vec{z}$

61. The vector $\langle 7, 9 \rangle$ represents the velocity of a helicopter. What is the direction of this vector to the nearest degree?

Ⓕ 38° Ⓖ 52° Ⓗ 128° Ⓙ 142°

62. A canoe sets out on a course given by the vector $\langle 5, 11 \rangle$. What is the length of the canoe's course to the nearest unit?

Ⓐ 6 Ⓑ 8 Ⓒ 12 Ⓓ 16

63. **Gridded Response** $\overrightarrow{AB}$ has an initial point of $(-3, 6)$ and a terminal point of $(-5, -2)$. Find the magnitude of $\overrightarrow{AB}$ to the nearest tenth.

CHALLENGE AND EXTEND

Recall that the angle of a vector's direction is measured counterclockwise from the positive *x*-axis. Find the direction of each vector to the nearest degree.

64. $\langle -2, 3 \rangle$ 65. $\langle -4, 0 \rangle$ 66. $\langle -5, -3 \rangle$

67. **Navigation** The captain of a ship is planning to sail in an area where there is a 4 mi/h current moving due east. What speed and bearing should the captain maintain so that the ship's actual course (taking the current into account) is 10 mi/h at a bearing of N 70° E? Round the speed to the nearest tenth and the direction to the nearest degree.

68. Aaron hikes from his home to a park by walking 3 km at a bearing of N 30° E, then 6 km due east, and then 4 km at a bearing of N 50° E. What are the magnitude and direction of the vector that represents the straight path from Aaron's home to the park? Round the magnitude to the nearest tenth and the direction to the nearest degree.

CHAPTER 8

MULTI-STEP TEST PREP

SECTION 8B

MATHEMATICAL PRACTICES **Reason abstractly and quantitatively.**

Applying Trigonometric Ratios

Help Is on the Way! Rescue helicopters were first used in the 1950s during the Korean War. The helicopters made it possible to airlift wounded soldiers to medical stations. Today, helicopters are used to rescue injured hikers, flood victims, and people who are stranded at sea.

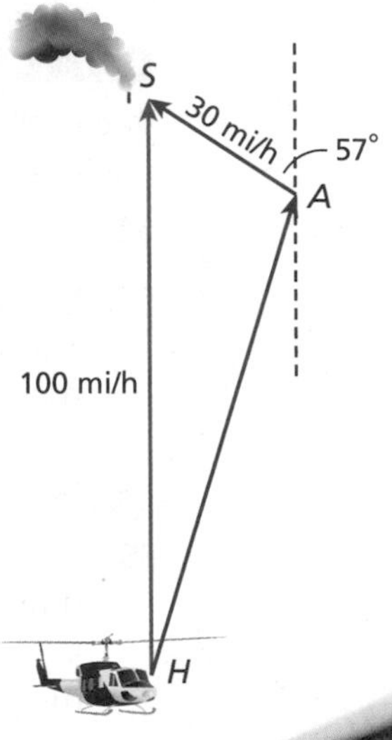

1. The pilot of a helicopter is searching for an injured hiker. While flying at an altitude of 1500 ft, the pilot sees smoke at an angle of depression of 14°. Assuming that the smoke is a distress signal from the hiker, what is the helicopter's horizontal distance to the hiker? Round to the nearest foot.
2. The pilot plans to fly due north at 100 mi/h from the helicopter's current position *H* to the location of the smoke *S*. However there is a 30 mi/h wind in the direction N 57° W. The pilot needs to know the velocity vector $\overrightarrow{HA}$ that he should use so that his resultant vector will be $\overrightarrow{HS}$. Find $m\angle S$ and then use the Law of Cosines to find the magnitude of $\overrightarrow{HA}$ to the nearest mile per hour.
3. Use the Law of Sines to find the direction of $\overrightarrow{HA}$ to the nearest degree.

(t) Pete Ryan/National Geographic/Getty (b) Stone/Getty Images

READY TO GO ON?

Quiz for Lessons 8-4 Through 8-6

8-4 Angles of Elevation and Depression

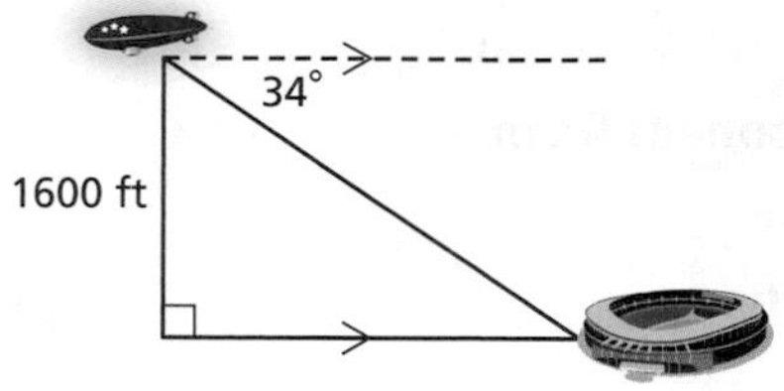

1. An observer in a blimp sights a football stadium at an angle of depression of 34°. The blimp's altitude is 1600 ft. What is the horizontal distance from the blimp to the stadium? Round to the nearest foot.

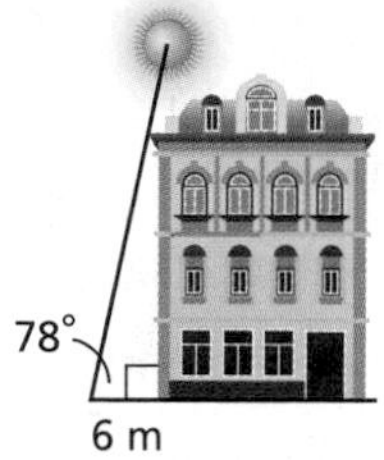

2. When the angle of elevation of the sun is 78°, a building casts a shadow that is 6 m long. What is the height of the building to the nearest tenth of a meter?

8-5 Law of Sines and Law of Cosines

Find each measure. Round lengths to the nearest tenth and angle measures to the nearest degree.

3. m∠A

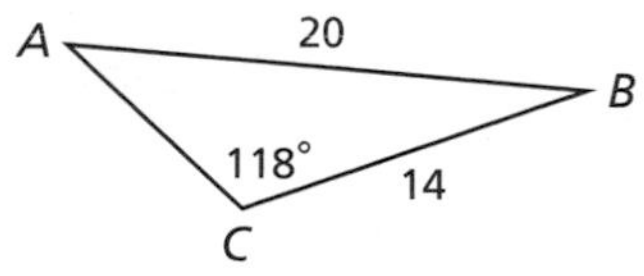

4. GH

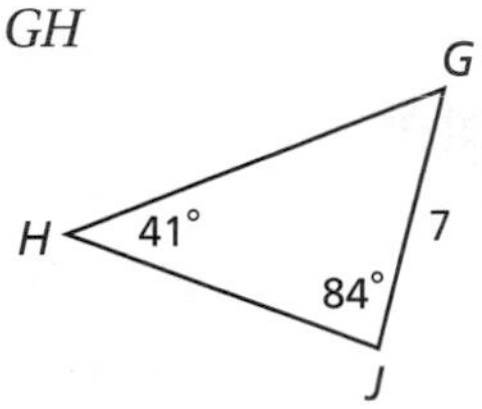

5. XZ

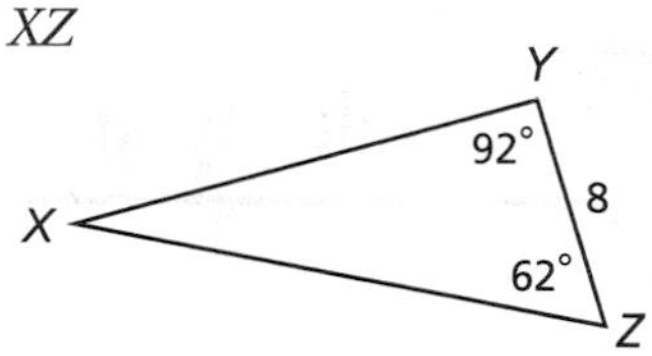

6. UV

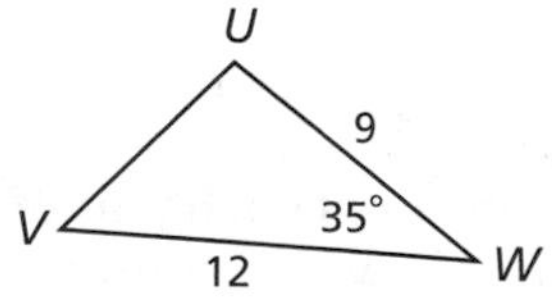

7. m∠F

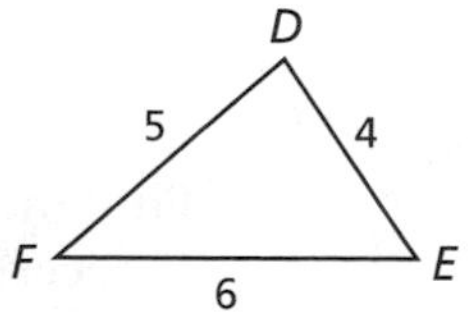

8. QS

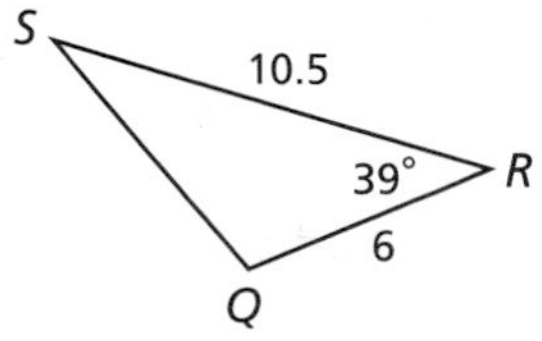

8-6 Vectors

Draw each vector on a coordinate plane. Find its magnitude to the nearest tenth.

9. $\langle 3, 1\rangle$
10. $\langle -2, -4\rangle$
11. $\langle 0, 5\rangle$

Draw each vector on a coordinate plane. Find the direction of the vector to the nearest degree.

12. A wind velocity is given by the vector $\langle 2, 1\rangle$.
13. The current of a river is given by the vector $\langle 5, 3\rangle$.
14. The force of a spring is given by the vector $\langle 4, 4\rangle$.

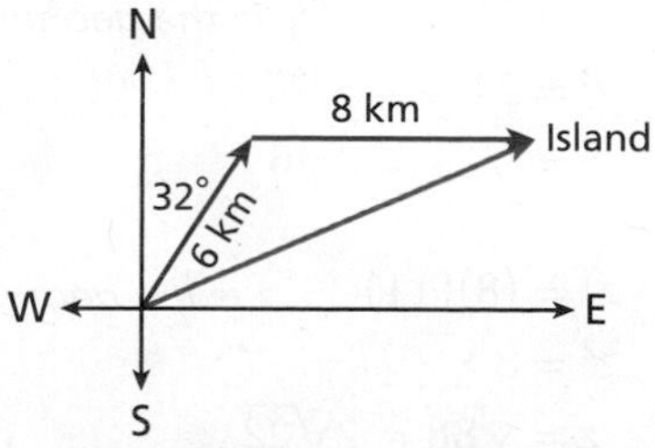

15. To reach an island, a ship leaves port and sails for 6 km at a bearing of N 32° E. It then sails due east for 8 km. What are the magnitude and direction of the voyage directly from the port to the island? Round the distance to the nearest tenth of a kilometer and the direction to the nearest degree.

CHAPTER 8

Study Guide: Review

Know it! Note — For a list of postulates, theorems, and corollaries, see page PT2.

Vocabulary

angle of depression
angle of elevation
component form
cosine
direction
equal vectors
geometric mean
magnitude
parallel vectors
resultant vector
sine
tangent
trigonometric ratio
vector

Complete the sentences below with vocabulary words from the list above.

1. The ___?___ of a vector gives the horizontal and vertical change from the initial point to the terminal point.
2. Two vectors with the same magnitude and direction are called ___?___.
3. If a and b are positive numbers, then $\sqrt{ab}$ is the ___?___ of a and b.
4. A(n) ___?___ is the angle formed by a horizontal line and a line of sight to a point above the horizontal line.
5. The sine, cosine, and tangent are all examples of a(n) ___?___.

8-1 Similarity in Right Triangles

EXAMPLES

■ **Find the geometric mean of 5 and 30.**

Let x be the geometric mean.

$x^2 = (5)(30) = 150$ *Def. of geometric mean*

$x = \sqrt{150} = 5\sqrt{6}$ *Find the positive square root.*

■ **Find x, y, and z.**

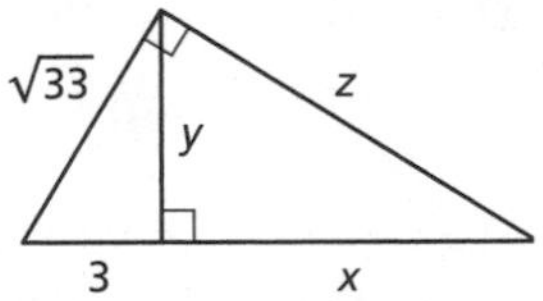

$\left(\sqrt{33}\right)^2 = 3(3 + x)$ *$\sqrt{33}$ is the geometric mean of 3 and 3 + x.*

$33 = 9 + 3x$

$24 = 3x$

$x = 8$

$y^2 = (3)(8)$ *y is the geometric mean of 3 and 8.*

$y^2 = 24$

$y = \sqrt{24} = 2\sqrt{6}$

$z^2 = (8)(11)$ *z is the geometric mean of 8 and 11.*

$z^2 = 88$

$z = \sqrt{88} = 2\sqrt{22}$

EXERCISES

6. Write a similarity statement comparing the three triangles.

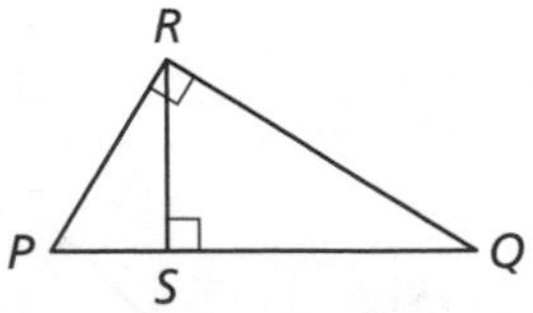

Find the geometric mean of each pair of numbers. If necessary, give the answer in simplest radical form.

7. $\frac{1}{4}$ and 100
8. 3 and 17

Find x, y, and z.

9.

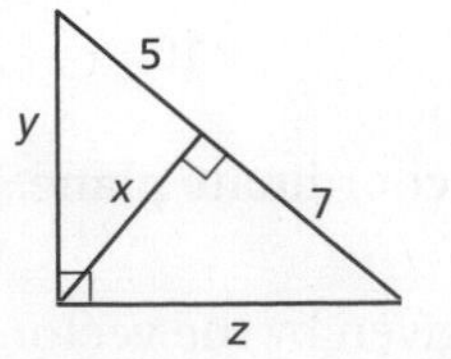

10.

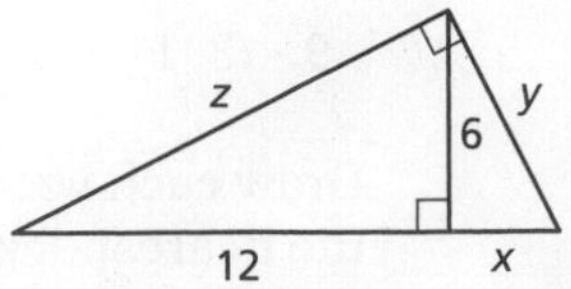

11.

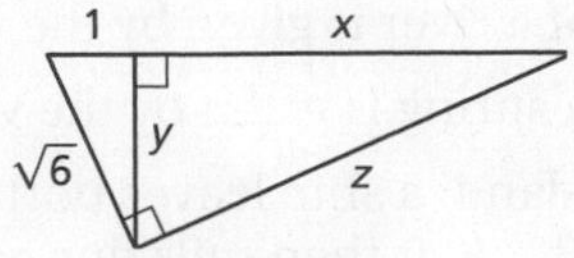

8-2 Trigonometric Ratios

EXAMPLES

Find each length. Round to the nearest hundredth.

■ EF

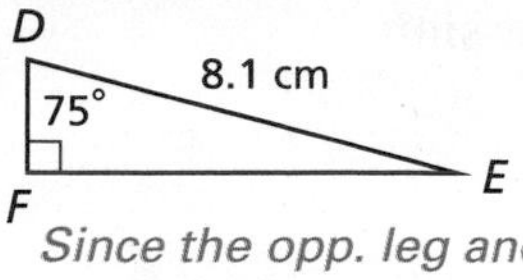

$$\sin 75° = \frac{EF}{8.1}$$

$$EF = 8.1(\sin 75°)$$

$$EF \approx 7.82 \text{ cm}$$

Since the opp. leg and hyp. are involved, use a sine ratio.

■ AB

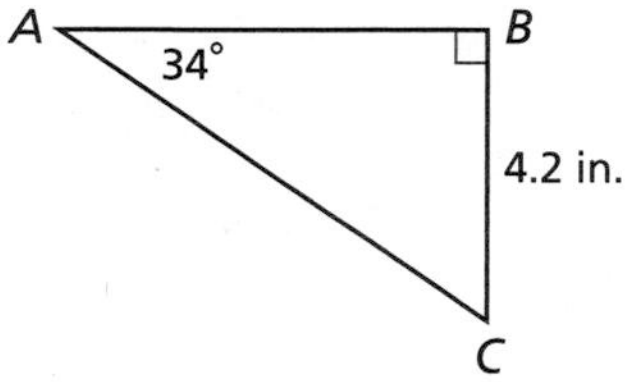

$$\tan 34° = \frac{4.2}{AB}$$

$$AB \tan 34° = 4.2$$

$$AB = \frac{4.2}{\tan 34°}$$

$$AB \approx 6.23 \text{ in.}$$

Since the opp. and adj. legs are involved, use a tangent ratio.

EXERCISES

Find each length. Round to the nearest hundredth.

12. UV

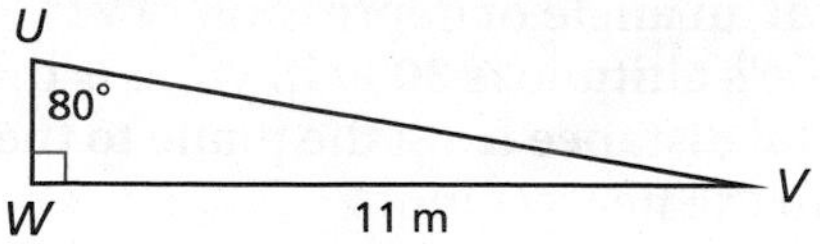

13. PR

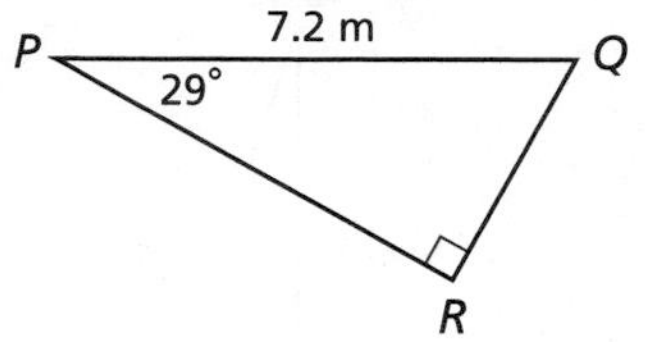

14. XY

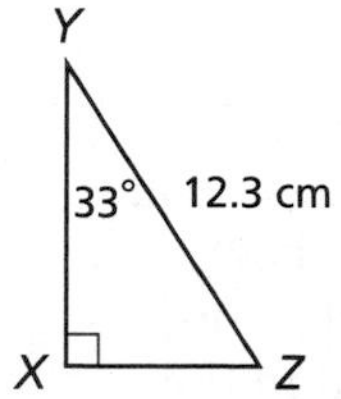

15. JL

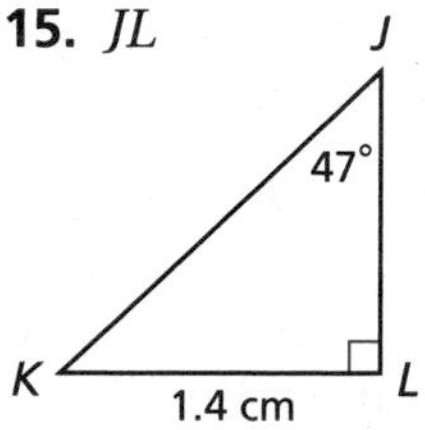

8-3 Solving Right Triangles

EXAMPLE

■ **Find the unknown measures in $\triangle LMN$. Round lengths to the nearest hundredth and angle measures to the nearest degree.**

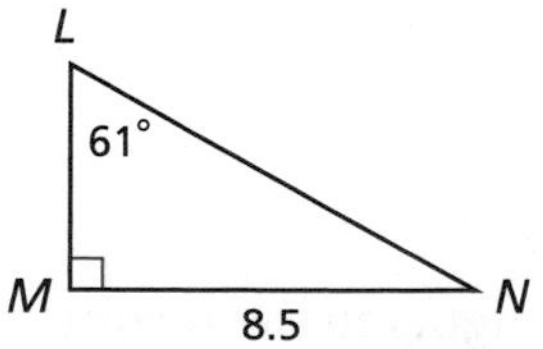

The acute angles of a right triangle are complementary. So $m\angle N = 90° - 61° = 29°$.

$\sin L = \frac{MN}{LN}$ — *Write a trig. ratio.*

$\sin 61° = \frac{8.5}{LN}$ — *Substitute the given values.*

$LN = \frac{8.5}{\sin 61°} \approx 9.72$ — *Solve for LN.*

$\tan L = \frac{MN}{LM}$ — *Write a trig. ratio.*

$\tan 61° = \frac{8.5}{LM}$ — *Substitute the given values.*

$LM = \frac{8.5}{\tan 61°} \approx 4.71$ — *Solve for LM.*

EXERCISES

Find the unknown measures. Round lengths to the nearest hundredth and angle measures to the nearest degree.

16.

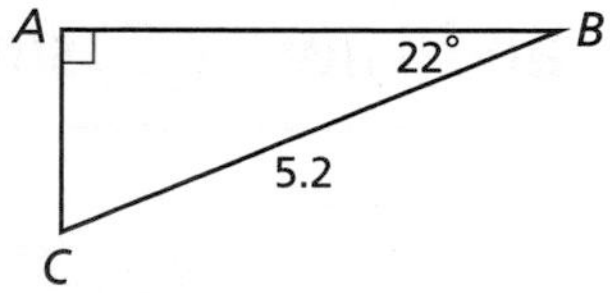

17.

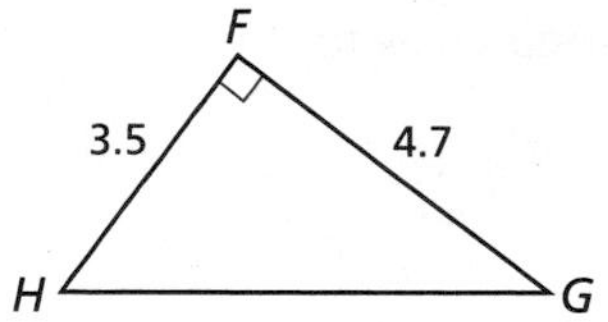

18.

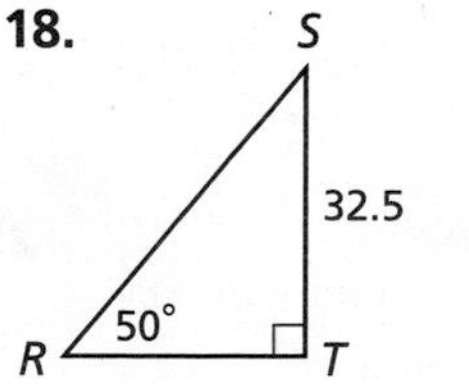

19.

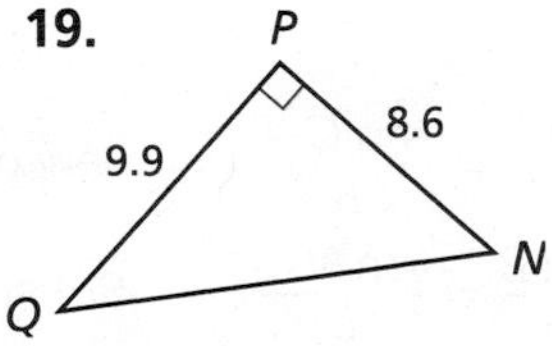

8-4 Angles of Elevation and Depression

EXAMPLES

■ **A pilot in a plane spots a forest fire on the ground at an angle of depression of 71°. The plane's altitude is 3000 ft. What is the horizontal distance from the plane to the fire? Round to the nearest foot.**

$\tan 71° = \frac{3000}{XF}$

$XF = \frac{3000}{\tan 71°}$

$XF \approx 1033$ ft

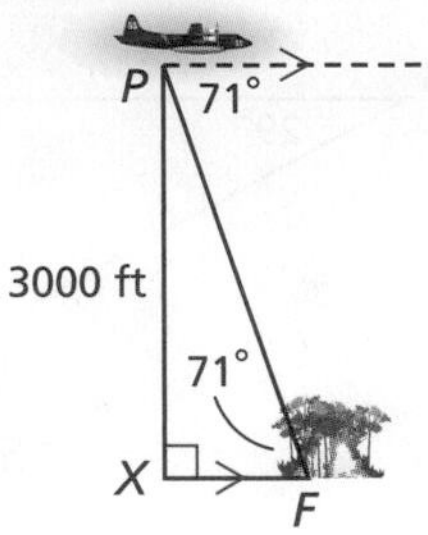

■ **A diver is swimming at a depth of 63 ft below sea level. He sees a buoy floating at sea level at an angle of elevation of 47°. How far must the diver swim so that he is directly beneath the buoy? Round to the nearest foot.**

$\tan 47° = \frac{63}{XD}$

$XD = \frac{63}{\tan 47°}$

$XD \approx 59$ ft

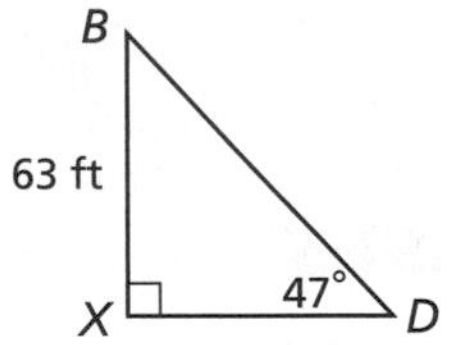

EXERCISES

Classify each angle as an angle of elevation or angle of depression.

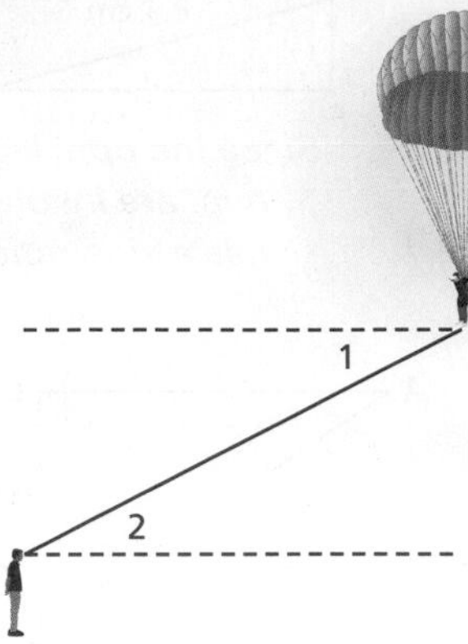

20. ∠1 **21.** ∠2

22. When the angle of elevation to the sun is 82°, a monument casts a shadow that is 5.1 ft long. What is the height of the monument to the nearest foot?

23. A ranger in a lookout tower spots a fire in the distance. The angle of depression to the fire is 4°, and the lookout tower is 32 m tall. What is the horizontal distance to the fire? Round to the nearest meter.

8-5 Law of Sines and Law of Cosines

EXAMPLES

Find each measure. Round lengths to the nearest tenth and angle measures to the nearest degree.

■ m∠*B*

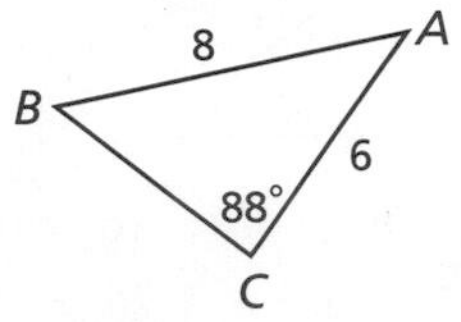

$\frac{\sin B}{AC} = \frac{\sin C}{AB}$ *Law of Sines*

$\frac{\sin B}{6} = \frac{\sin 88°}{8}$ *Substitute the given values.*

$\sin B = \frac{6 \sin 88°}{8}$ *Multiply both sides by 6.*

$m\angle B = \sin^{-1}\left(\frac{6 \sin 88°}{8}\right) \approx 49°$

EXERCISES

Find each measure. Round lengths to the nearest tenth and angle measures to the nearest degree.

24. m∠*Z*

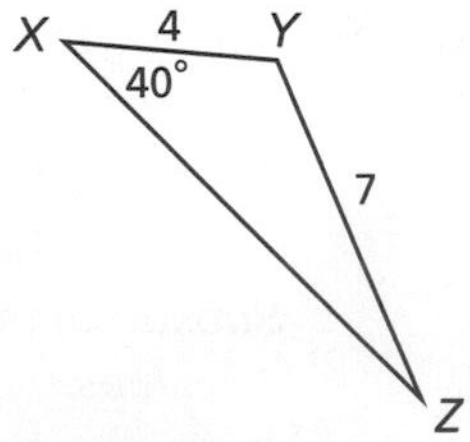

25. *MN*

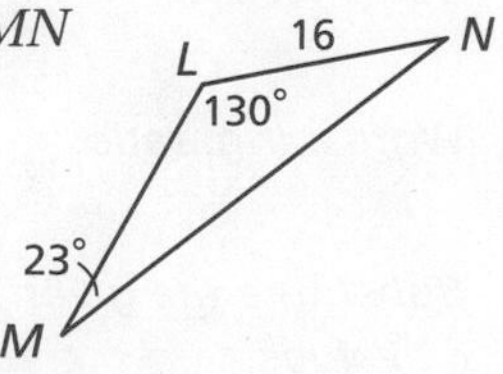

Find each measure. Round lengths to the nearest tenth and angle measures to the nearest degree.

■ *HJ*

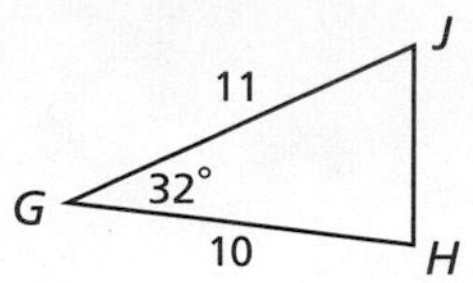

Use the Law of Cosines.

$HJ^2 = GH^2 + GJ^2 - 2(GH)(GJ)\cos G$

$= 10^2 + 11^2 - 2(10)(11)\cos 32°$

$HJ^2 \approx 34.4294$ *Simplify.*

$HJ \approx 5.9$ *Find the square root.*

Find each measure. Round lengths to the nearest tenth and angle measures to the nearest degree.

26. *EF*

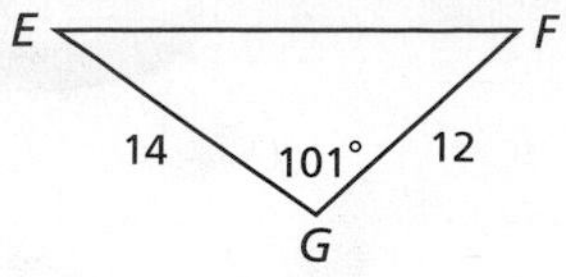

27. m∠*Q*

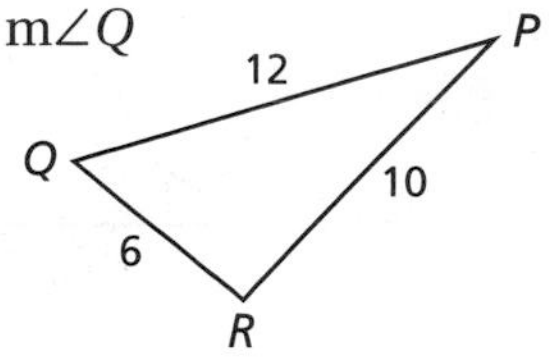

8-6 Vectors

EXAMPLES

■ **Draw the vector ⟨−1, 4⟩ on a coordinate plane. Find its magnitude to the nearest tenth.**

$|\langle -1, 4\rangle| = \sqrt{(-1)^2 + (4)^2}$

$= \sqrt{17} \approx 4.1$

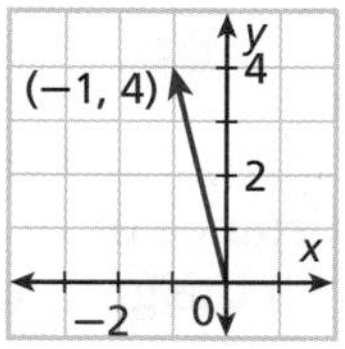

■ **The velocity of a jet is given by the vector ⟨4, 3⟩. Draw the vector on a coordinate plane. Find the direction of the vector to the nearest degree.**

In △*PQR*, $\tan P = \frac{3}{4}$, so

$m\angle P = \tan^{-1}\left(\frac{3}{4}\right) \approx 37°$.

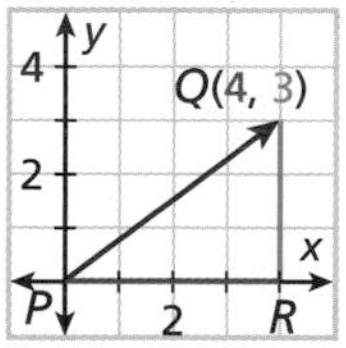

■ **Susan swims across a river at a bearing of N 75° E at a speed of 0.5 mi/h. The river's current moves due east at 1 mi/h. Find Susan's actual speed to the nearest tenth and her direction to the nearest degree.**

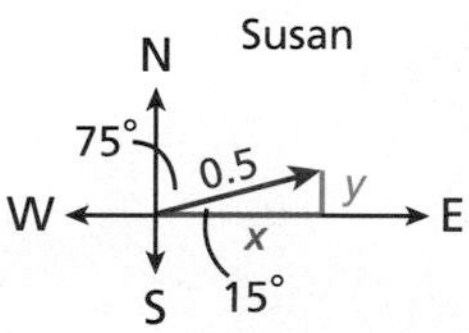

$\cos 15° = \frac{x}{0.5}$, so $x \approx 0.48$.

$\sin 15° = \frac{y}{0.5}$, so $y \approx 0.13$.

Susan's vector is ⟨**0.48**, **0.13**⟩. The current is ⟨**1**, **0**⟩. Susan's actual speed is the magnitude of the resultant vector, ⟨**1.48**, **0.13**⟩.

$|\langle 1.48, 0.13\rangle| = \sqrt{(1.48)^2 + (0.13)^2} \approx 1.5$ mi/h

Her direction is $\tan^{-1}\left(\frac{0.13}{1.48}\right) \approx 5°$, or N 85° E.

EXERCISES

Write each vector in component form.

28. $\overrightarrow{AB}$ with $A(5, 1)$ and $B(-2, 3)$

29. $\overrightarrow{MN}$ with $M(-2, 4)$ and $N(-1, -2)$

30. $\overrightarrow{RS}$

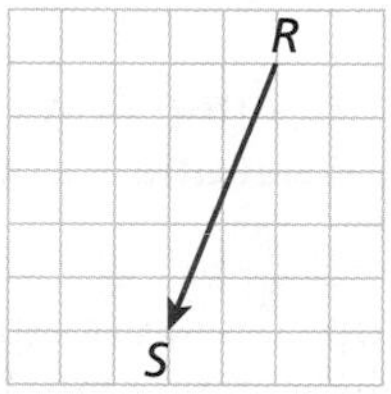

Draw each vector on a coordinate plane. Find its magnitude to the nearest tenth.

31. ⟨−5, −3⟩

32. ⟨−2, 0⟩

33. ⟨4, −4⟩

Draw each vector on a coordinate plane. Find the direction of the vector to the nearest degree.

34. The velocity of a helicopter is given by the vector ⟨4, 5⟩.

35. The force applied by a tugboat is given by the vector ⟨7, 2⟩.

36. A plane flies at a constant speed of 600 mi/h at a bearing of N 55° E. There is a 50 mi/h crosswind blowing due east. What are the plane's actual speed and direction? Round the speed to the nearest tenth and the direction to the nearest degree.

CHAPTER 8 CHAPTER TEST

Find *x*, *y*, and *z*.

1. 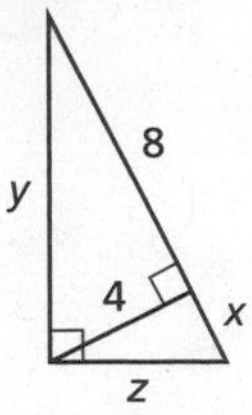

2. 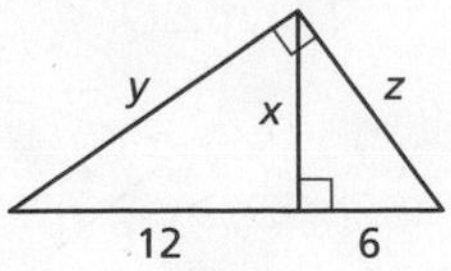

3. 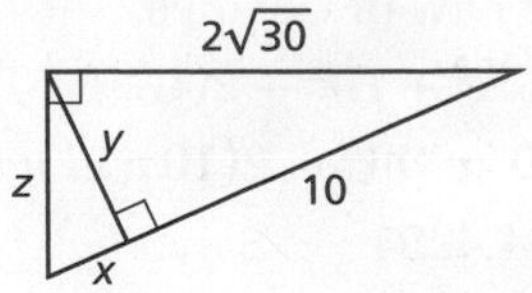

Use a special right triangle to write each trigonometric ratio as a fraction.

4. $\cos 60°$

5. $\sin 45°$

6. $\tan 60°$

Find each length. Round to the nearest hundredth.

7. *PR* 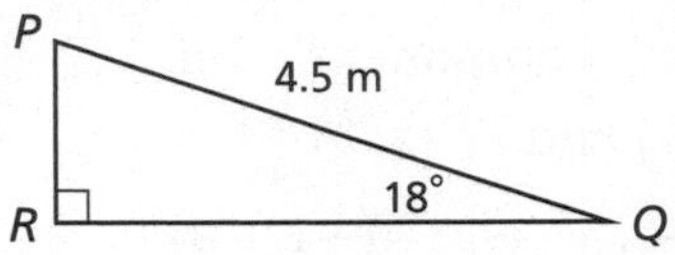

8. *AB* 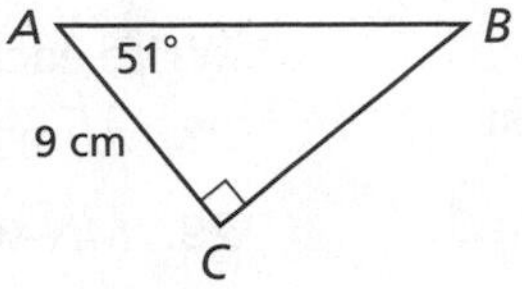

9. *FG* 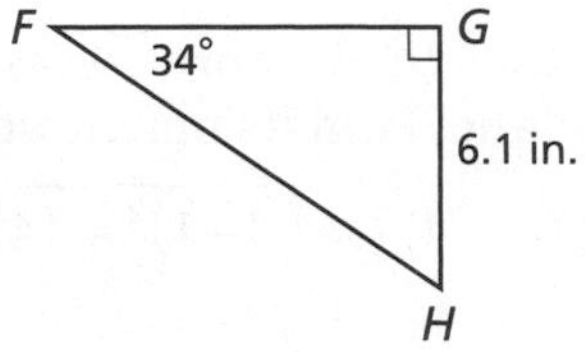

10. Nate built a skateboard ramp that covers a horizontal distance of 10 ft. The ramp rises a total of 3.5 ft. What angle does the ramp make with the ground? Round to the nearest degree.

11. An observer at the top of a skyscraper sights a tour bus at an angle of depression of 61°. The skyscraper is 910 ft tall. What is the horizontal distance from the base of the skyscraper to the tour bus? Round to the nearest foot.

Find each measure. Round lengths to the nearest tenth and angle measures to the nearest degree.

12. $m\angle B$ 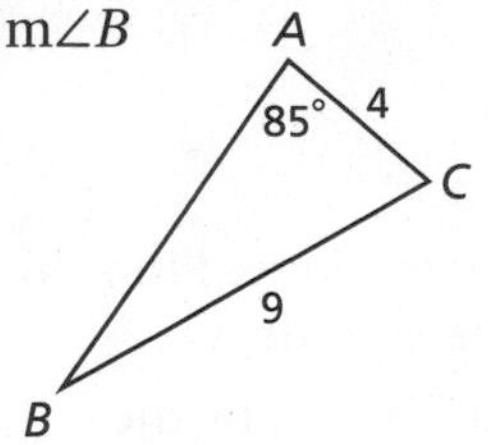

13. *RS* 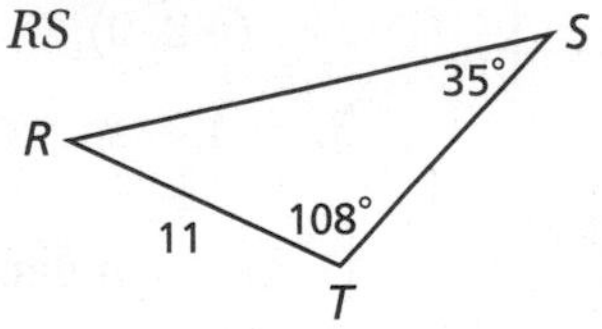

14. $m\angle M$ 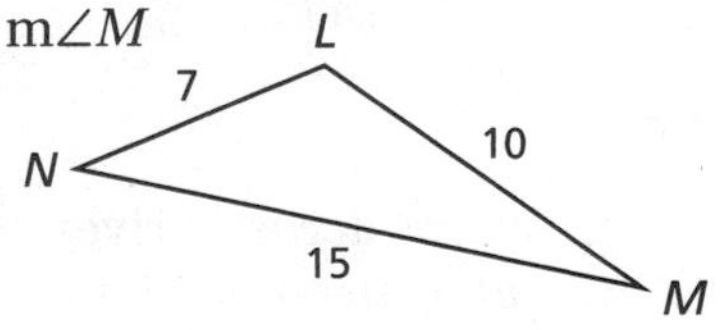

Draw each vector on a coordinate plane. Find its magnitude to the nearest tenth.

15. $\langle 1, 3\rangle$

16. $\langle -4, 1\rangle$

17. $\langle 2, -3\rangle$

Draw each vector on a coordinate plane. Find the direction of the vector to the nearest degree.

18. The velocity of a plane is given by the vector $\langle 3, 5\rangle$.

19. A wind velocity is given by the vector $\langle 4, 1\rangle$.

20. Kate is rowing across a river. She sets out at a bearing of N 40° E and paddles at a constant rate of 3.5 mi/h. There is a 2 mi/h current moving due east. What are Kate's actual speed and direction? Round the speed to the nearest tenth and the direction to the nearest degree.

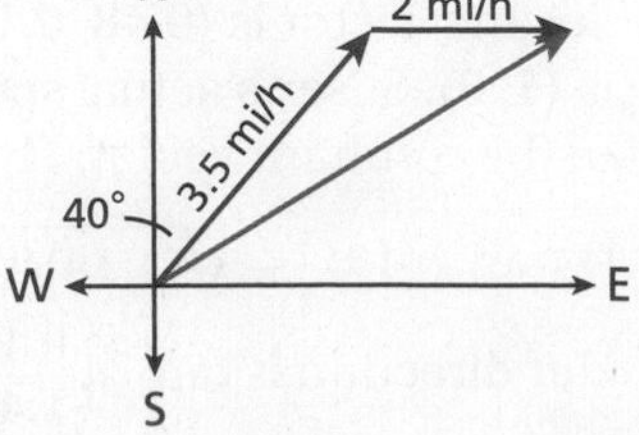

COLLEGE ENTRANCE EXAM PRACTICE

FOCUS ON SAT MATHEMATICS SUBJECT TESTS

The SAT Mathematics Subject Tests each consist of 50 multiple-choice questions. You are not expected to have studied every topic on the SAT Mathematics Subject Tests, so some questions may be unfamiliar.

HOT TIP! Though you can use a calculator on the SAT Mathematics Subject Tests, it may be faster to answer some questions without one. Remember to use test-taking strategies before you press buttons!

You may want to time yourself as you take this practice test. It should take you about 6 minutes to complete.

---

1. Let P be the acute angle formed by the line $-x + 4y = 12$ and the x-axis. What is the approximate measure of $\angle P$?

(A) 14°

(B) 18°

(C) 72°

(D) 76°

(E) 85°

---

2. In right triangle DEF, $DE = 15$, $EF = 36$, and $DF = 39$. What is the cosine of $\angle F$?

(A) $\frac{5}{12}$

(B) $\frac{12}{5}$

(C) $\frac{5}{13}$

(D) $\frac{12}{13}$

(E) $\frac{13}{12}$

---

3. A triangle has angle measures of 19°, 61°, and 100°. What is the approximate length of the side opposite the 100° angle if the side opposite the 61° angle is 8 centimeters long?

(A) 2.5 centimeters

(B) 3 centimeters

(C) 9 centimeters

(D) 12 centimeters

(E) 13 centimeters

---

4. A swimmer jumps into a river and starts swimming directly across it at a constant velocity of 2 meters per second. The speed of the current is 7 meters per second. Given the current, what is the actual speed of the swimmer to the nearest tenth?

(A) 0.3 meters per second

(B) 1.7 meters per second

(C) 5.0 meters per second

(D) 7.3 meters per second

(E) 9.0 meters per second

---

5. What is the approximate measure of the vertex angle of the isosceles triangle below?

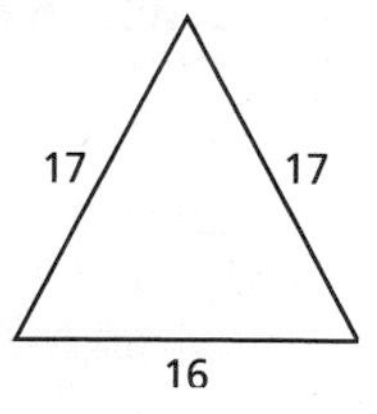

(A) 28.1°

(B) 56.1°

(C) 62.0°

(D) 112.2°

(E) 123.9°

CHAPTER 8

TEST TACKLER

Standardized Test Strategies

Any Question Type: Estimate

Once you find the answer to a test problem, take a few moments to check your answer by using estimation strategies. By doing so, you can verify that your final answer is reasonable.

EXAMPLE 1

Gridded Response **Find the geometric mean of 38 and 12 to the nearest hundredth.**

Let x be the geometric mean.

$x^2 = (38)(12) = 456$	*Def. of geometric mean*
$x \approx 21.35$	*Find the positive square root.*

Now use estimation to check that this answer is reasonable.

$x^2 \approx (40)(10) = 400$	*Round 38 to 40 and round 12 to 10.*
$x \approx 20$	*Find the positive square root.*

The estimate is close to the calculated answer, so 21.35 is a reasonable answer.

EXAMPLE 2

Multiple Choice **Which of the following is equal to sin X?**

Ⓐ 0.02 Ⓒ 0.91

Ⓑ 0.41 Ⓓ 2.44

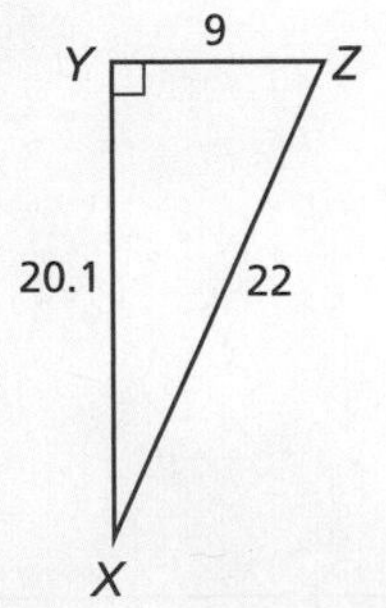

Use a trigonometric ratio to find the answer.

$\sin X = \frac{YZ}{XZ}$	*The sine of an ∠ is $\frac{\text{opp. leg}}{\text{hyp.}}$.*
$\sin X = \frac{9}{22} \approx 0.41$	*Substitute the given values and simplify.*

Now use estimation to check that this answer is reasonable.

$\sin X \approx \frac{10}{20} \approx 0.5$	*Round 9 to 10 and round 22 to 20.*

The estimate is close to the calculated answer, so B is a reasonable answer.

HOT TIP! An extra minute spent checking your answers can result in a better test score.

Read each test item and answer the questions that follow.

Item A

Gridded Response A cell phone tower casts a shadow that is 121 ft long when the angle of elevation to the sun is 48°. How tall is the cell phone tower? Round to the nearest foot.

1. A student estimated that the answer should be slightly greater than 121 by comparing tan 48° and tan 45°. Explain why this estimation strategy works.
2. Describe how to use the inverse tangent function to estimate whether an answer of 134 ft makes sense.

Item B

Short Response $\overrightarrow{BC}$ has an initial point of $(-1, 0)$ and a terminal point of $(4, 2)$.

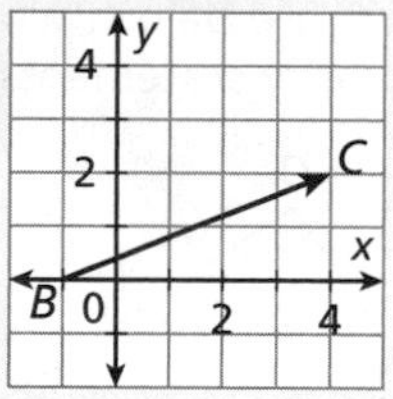

a. Write $\overrightarrow{BC}$ in component form.

b. Find the magnitude of $\overrightarrow{BC}$. Round to the nearest hundredth.

c. Find the direction of $\overrightarrow{BC}$. Round to the nearest degree.

3. A student correctly found the magnitude of $\overrightarrow{BC}$ as $\sqrt{29}$. The student then calculated the value of this radical as 6.39. Explain how to use perfect squares to estimate the value of $\sqrt{29}$. Is 6.39 a reasonable answer?
4. A student calculated the measure of the angle the vector forms with a horizontal line as 68°. Use estimation to explain why this answer is not reasonable.

Item C

Multiple Choice In $\triangle QRS$, what is the measure of $\overline{SQ}$ to the nearest tenth of a centimeter?

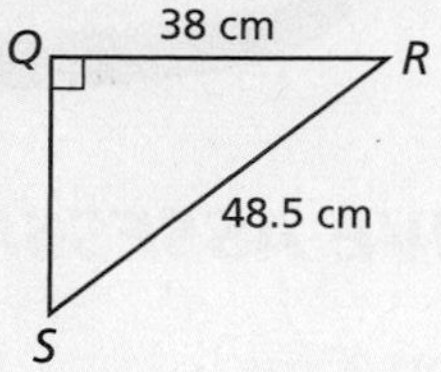

Ⓐ 9.3 centimeters

Ⓑ 10.5 centimeters

Ⓒ 30.1 centimeters

Ⓓ 61.7 centimeters

5. A student calculated the answer as 30.1 cm. The student then used the diagram to estimate that *SQ* is more than half of *RQ*. So the student decided that his answer was reasonable. Is this estimation method a good way to check your answer? Why or why not?
6. Describe how to use estimation and the Pythagorean Theorem to check your answer to this problem.

Item D

Multiple Choice The McCleods have a variable interest rate on their mortgage. The rate is 2.625% the first year and 4% the following year. The average interest rate is the geometric mean of these two rates. To the nearest hundredth of a percent, what is the average interest rate for their mortgage?

Ⓕ 1.38% Ⓗ 3.89%

Ⓖ 3.24% Ⓙ 10.50%

7. Describe how to use estimation to show that choices **F** and **J** are unreasonable.
8. To find the answer, a student uses the equation $x^2 = (2.625)(4)$. Which compatible numbers should the student use to quickly check the answer?

STANDARDIZED TEST PREP

Learn It Online
State Test Practice

CUMULATIVE ASSESSMENT

Multiple Choice

1. What is the length of $\overline{UX}$ to the nearest centimeter?

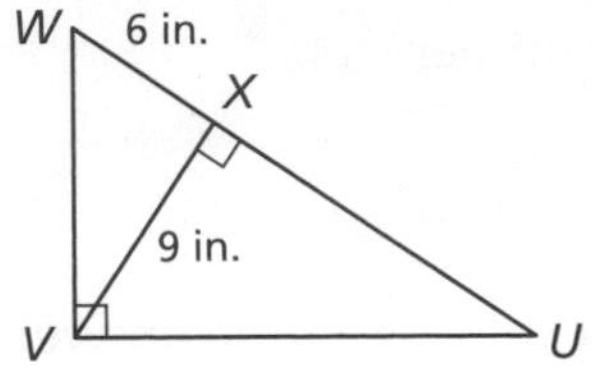

Ⓐ 3 centimeters
Ⓑ 7 centimeters
Ⓒ 9 centimeters
Ⓓ 13 centimeters

2. $\triangle ABC$ is a right triangle. $m\angle A = 20°$, $m\angle B = 90°$, $AC = 8$, and $AB = 3$. Which expression can be used to find BC?

Ⓕ $\dfrac{3}{\tan 70°}$ Ⓗ $8 \tan 20°$

Ⓖ $\dfrac{8}{\sin 20°}$ Ⓙ $3 \cos 70°$

3. A slide at a park is 25 ft long, and the top of the slide is 10 ft above the ground. What is the approximate measure of the angle the slide makes with the ground?

Ⓐ 21.8° Ⓒ 66.4°
Ⓑ 23.6° Ⓓ 68.2°

4. Which of the following vectors is equal to the vector with an initial point at $(2, -1)$ and a terminal point at $(-2, 4)$?

Ⓕ $\langle -4, -5 \rangle$ Ⓗ $\langle 5, -4 \rangle$
Ⓖ $\langle -4, 5 \rangle$ Ⓙ $\langle 5, 4 \rangle$

5. Which statement is true by the Addition Property of Equality?

Ⓐ If $3x + 6 = 9y$, then $x + 2 = 3y$.
Ⓑ If $t = 1$ and $s = t + 5$, then $s = 6$.
Ⓒ If $k + 1 = \ell + 2$, then $2k + 2 = 2\ell + 4$.
Ⓓ If $a + 2 = 3b$, then $a + 5 = 3b + 3$.

6. $\triangle ABC$ has vertices $A(-2, -2)$, $B(-3, 2)$, and $C(1, 3)$. Which translation produces an image with vertices at the coordinates $(-2, -2)$, $(2, -1)$, and $(-1, -6)$?

Ⓕ $(x, y) \rightarrow (x + 1, y - 4)$
Ⓖ $(x, y) \rightarrow (x + 2, y - 8)$
Ⓗ $(x, y) \rightarrow (x - 3, y - 5)$
Ⓙ $(x, y) \rightarrow (x - 4, y + 1)$

7. $\triangle ABC$ is a right triangle in which $m\angle A = 30°$ and $m\angle B = 60°$. Which of the following are possible lengths for the sides of this triangle?

Ⓐ $AB = \sqrt{3}$, $AC = \sqrt{2}$, and $BC = 1$
Ⓑ $AB = 4$, $AC = 2$, and $BC = 2\sqrt{3}$
Ⓒ $AB = 6\sqrt{3}$, $AC = 27$, and $BC = 3\sqrt{3}$
Ⓓ $AB = 8$, $AC = 4\sqrt{3}$, and $BC = 4$

8. Based on the figure below, which of the following similarity statements must be true?

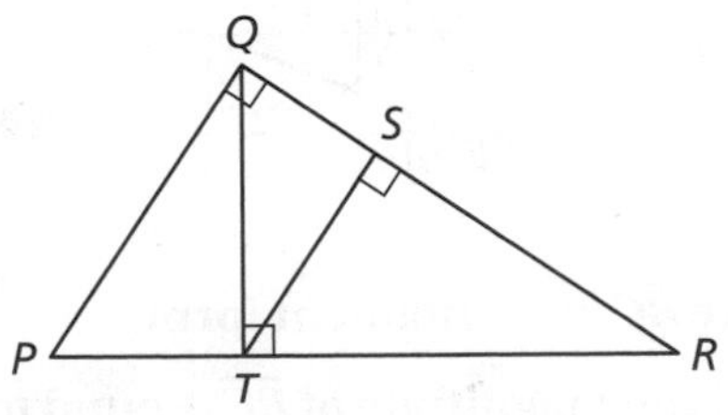

Ⓕ $\triangle PQR \sim \triangle TSR$
Ⓖ $\triangle PQR \sim \triangle RTQ$
Ⓗ $\triangle PQR \sim \triangle TSQ$
Ⓙ $\triangle PQR \sim \triangle TQP$

9. $ABCD$ is a rhombus with vertices $A(1, 1)$ and $C(3, 4)$. Which of the following lines is parallel to diagonal $\overline{BD}$?

Ⓐ $2x - 3y = 12$
Ⓑ $2x + 3y = 12$
Ⓒ $3x + 2y = 12$
Ⓓ $3x - 4y = 12$

10. Which of the following is NOT equivalent to sin 60°?

Ⓕ cos 30°

Ⓖ $\frac{\sqrt{3}}{2}$

Ⓗ (cos 60°)(tan 60°)

Ⓙ $\frac{\tan 30°}{\sin 30°}$

11. *ABCDE* is a convex pentagon. $\angle A \cong \angle B \cong \angle C$, $\angle D \cong \angle E$, and $m\angle A = 2m\angle D$. What is the measure of $\angle C$?

Ⓐ 67.5°

Ⓑ 135°

Ⓒ 154.2°

Ⓓ 225°

12. Which of the following sets of lengths can represent the side lengths of an obtuse triangle?

Ⓕ 4, 7.5, and 8.5

Ⓖ 7, 12, and 13

Ⓗ 9.5, 16.5, and 35

Ⓙ 36, 75, and 88

HOT TIP!

Be sure to correctly identify any pairs of parallel lines before using the Alternate Interior Angles Theorem or the Same-Side Interior Angles Theorem.

13. What is the value of *x*?

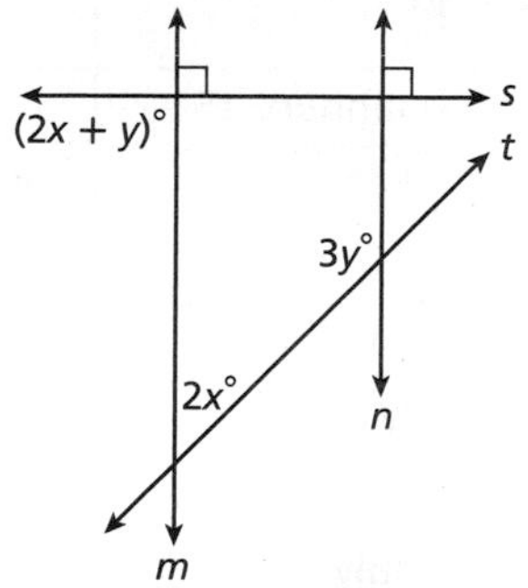

Ⓐ 22.5

Ⓑ 45

Ⓒ 90

Ⓓ 135

Gridded Response

14. Find the next item in the pattern below.

1, 3, 7, 13, 21, ...

15. In $\triangle XYZ$, $\angle X$ and $\angle Z$ are remote interior angles of exterior $\angle XYT$. If $m\angle X = (x + 15)°$, $m\angle Z = (50 - 3x)°$, and $m\angle XYT = (4x - 25)°$, what is the value of *x*?

16. In $\triangle ABC$ and $\triangle DEF$, $\angle A \cong \angle F$. If $EF = 4.5$, $DF = 3$, and $AC = 1.5$, what length for $\overline{AB}$ would let you conclude that $\triangle ABC \sim \triangle FED$?

Short Response

17. A building casts a shadow that is 85 ft long when the angle of elevation to the sun is 34°.

a. What is the height of the building? Round to the nearest inch and show your work.

b. What is the angle of elevation to the sun when the shadow is 42 ft 6 in. long? Round to the nearest tenth of a degree and show your work.

18. Use the figure to find each of the following. Round to the nearest tenth of a centimeter and show your work.

a. the length of $\overline{DC}$

b. the length of $\overline{AB}$

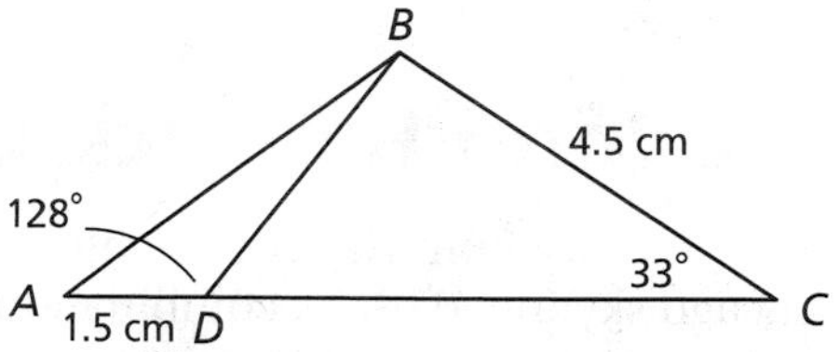

Extended Response

19. Tony and Paul are taking a vacation with their cousin, Greg. Tony and Paul live in the same house. Paul will go directly to the vacation spot, but Tony has to pick up Greg.

Tony travels 90 miles at a bearing of N 25° E to get to his cousin's house. He then travels due east for 50 miles to get to the vacation spot. Paul travels on one highway to get from his house to the vacation spot.

For each of the following, explain in words how you found your answer and round to the nearest tenth.

a. Write the vectors in component form for the route from Tony and Paul's house to their cousin's house and the route from their cousin's house to the vacation spot.

b. What are the direction and magnitude of Paul's direct route from his house to the vacation spot?

c. Tony and Paul leave the house at the same time and arrive at the vacation spot at the same time. If Tony traveled at an average speed of 50 mi/h, what was Paul's average speed?

The John Hancock Center

The 100-story John Hancock Center is one of the most distinctive features of the Chicago skyline. With its combination of stores, offices, and 49 floors of apartments, the John Hancock Center is the world's tallest multifunctional skyscraper.

Choose one or more strategies to solve each problem.

1. The building's observation deck is on the 94th floor, 1000 ft above street level. The deck is equipped with telescopes that offer close-up views of the surrounding city. Using one of the telescopes, a visitor spots a ship on Lake Michigan. The angle of depression to the ship is 10°. To the nearest foot, how far is the ship from the base of the building?

For 2–4, use the table.

2. At noon on May 15, the shadow of the John Hancock Center, including its antenna, is 818.2 ft long. Find the height of the building to the nearest foot.
3. How long is the shadow of the building at noon on October 15? Round to the nearest foot.
4. On which of the dates shown is the building's shadow the longest? What is the length of the shadow to the nearest foot?

Elevation of the Sun in Chicago, Illinois

Date	Angle of Elevation at Noon (°)
January 15	27
February 15	34
March 15	46
April 15	58
May 15	61
June 15	71
July 15	70
August 15	62
September 15	51
October 15	39
November 15	29
December 15	25

Ernest Hemingway's Birthplace

The Nobel Prize-winning author Ernest Hemingway (1899–1961) was born in Oak Park, Illinois. Visitors to Oak Park, a suburb of Chicago, can tour the home where Hemingway was born and spent much of his childhood. Thanks to a recent restoration, the house appears just as it did when Hemingway lived there.

Choose one or more strategies to solve each problem.

1. The blueprint shown below was used during the restoration of the first floor of Hemingway's house. As part of the restoration project, a narrow border of wallpaper was placed along the edge of the ceiling around the perimeter of the dining room. Approximately how many feet of wallpaper were needed?
2. During the restoration, the floor of the parlor and living room was covered with red carpet. Estimate the number of square feet of carpet that were used.
3. Hemingway's childhood bedroom is located on the second floor of the house. The bedroom has a perimeter of 40 ft, and its length is 4 ft more than its width. Assuming the blueprint for the second floor uses the same scale as the blueprint below, what are the dimensions of the bedroom on the blueprint for the second floor?

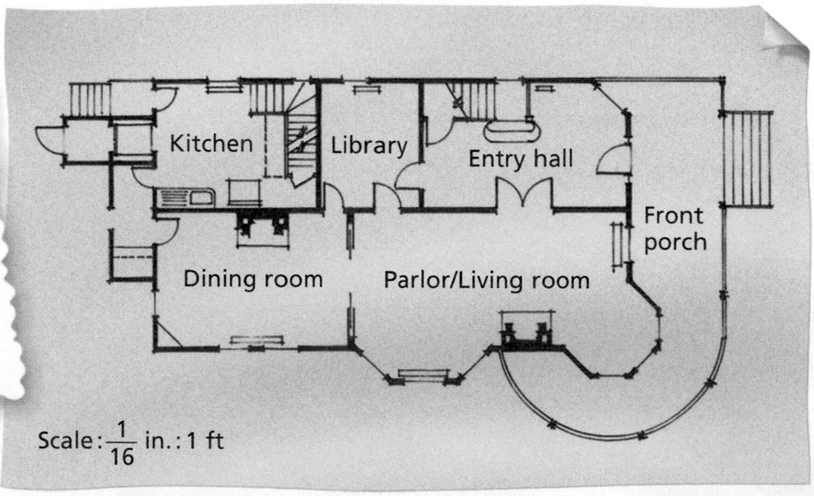

Real-World Connections

CHAPTER 9

Extending Transformational Geometry

COMMON CORE

Chapter

- Apply reflections, translations, and rotations to simple geometric figures in the coordinate plane.
- Understand how symmetry and transformations are related.

Let it Snow!

A blanket of snow is formed by trillions of symmetric crystals. You can use transformations and symmetry to explore snow crystals.

Learn It Online
Chapter Project Online

ARE YOU READY?

Vocabulary

Match each term on the left with a definition on the right.

1. image
2. preimage
3. transformation
4. vector

A. a mapping of a figure from its original position to a new position

B. a ray that divides an angle into two congruent angles

C. a shape that undergoes a transformation

D. a quantity that has both a size and a direction

E. the shape that results from a transformation of a figure

Ordered Pairs

Graph each ordered pair.

5. $(0, 4)$ **6.** $(-3, 2)$ **7.** $(4, 3)$

8. $(3, -1)$ **9.** $(-1, -3)$ **10.** $(-2, 0)$

Congruent Figures

Can you conclude that the given triangles are congruent? If so, explain why.

11. $\triangle PQS$ and $\triangle PRS$

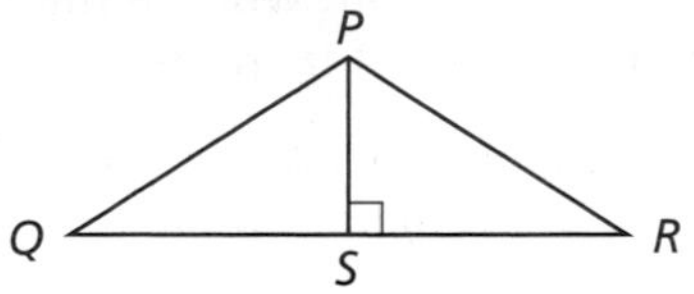

12. $\triangle DEG$ and $\triangle FGE$

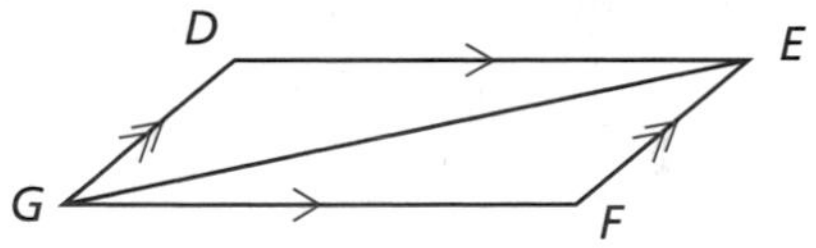

Identify Similar Figures

Can you conclude that the given figures are similar? If so, explain why.

13. $\triangle JKL$ and $\triangle JMN$

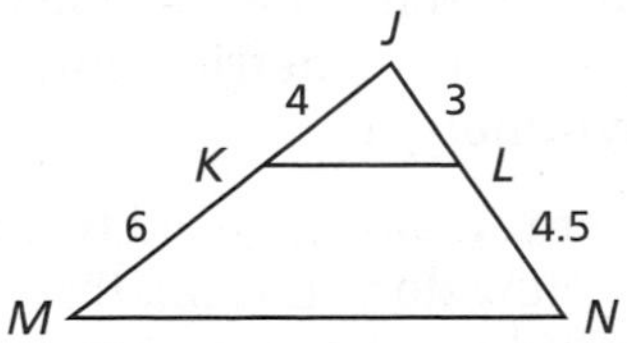

14. rectangle *PQRS* and rectangle *UVWX*

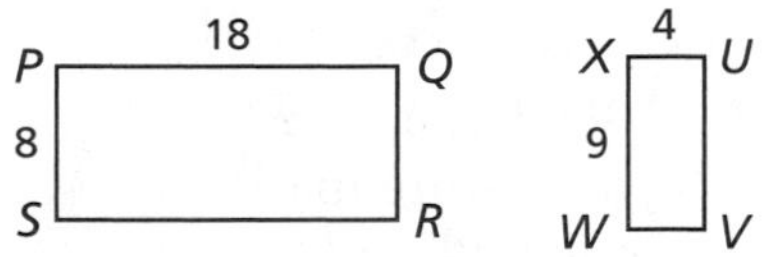

Angles in Polygons

15. Find the measure of each interior angle of a regular octagon.

16. Find the sum of the interior angle measures of a convex pentagon.

17. Find the measure of each exterior angle of a regular hexagon.

18. Find the value of *x* in hexagon *ABCDEF*.

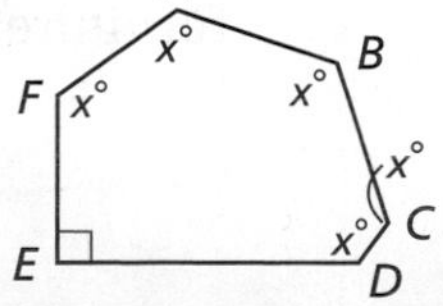

CHAPTER 9

Study Guide: Preview

Where You've Been

Previously, you

- graphed figures on a coordinate plane.
- studied congruent figures, similar figures, parallel lines, and perpendicular lines.
- used transformations to explore properties of figures.

In This Chapter

You will study

- rules for transformations in the coordinate plane.
- transformations that preserve congruence of figures.
- properties of figures such as symmetry.

Where You're Going

You can use the skills learned in this chapter

- in all your future math classes, including Algebra 2.
- in other classes, such as Art, Chemistry, Biology, and Physics.
- to find shortest paths, build furniture, and create artwork.

Key Vocabulary/Vocabulario

composition of transformations	composición de transformaciones
glide reflection	deslizamiento con inversión
isometry	isometría
symmetry	simetría
tessellation	teselado

Vocabulary Connections

To become familiar with some of the vocabulary terms in the chapter, consider the following. You may refer to the chapter, the glossary, or a dictionary if you like.

1. A *composition* is something that has been put together. How can you use this idea to understand what is meant by a **composition of transformations** ?
2. The prefix *iso-* means "equal." The suffix *-metry* means "measure." What do you think might be true about the preimage and image of a figure under a transformation that is an **isometry** ?
3. Give some examples of how the words *symmetry* and *symmetric* are used in everyday speech. What do you think it means for a geometric figure to have **symmetry** ?
4. *Tessera* are small tiles used to create a mosaic. How do you think this relates to the meaning of the word **tessellation** ?

Reading and Writing Math

Reading Strategy: Read to Solve Problems

A word problem may be overwhelming at first. Once you identify the important parts of the problem and translate the words into math language, you will find that the problem is similar to others you have solved.

Reading Tips:

- ✔ Read each phrase slowly. Write down what the words mean as you read them.
- ✔ Draw a diagram. Label the diagram so it makes sense to you.
- ✔ Read the problem again before finding your solution.
- ✔ Translate the words or phrases into math language.
- ✔ Highlight what is being asked.

Use the **Reading Tips** to help you understand this problem.

14. After a day hike, a group of hikers set up a camp 3 km east and 7 km north of the starting point. What is the distance from the camp to the starting point?

Identify Key Words

After a day hike, a group of hikers set up a camp *3 km east* and *7 km north* of the *starting point*.

What is the *distance* from the *camp* to the *starting point*?

Translate Words into Math

The *starting point* can be represented by the ordered pair *(0, 0)*.

The *camp* can be represented by the ordered pair *(3, 7)*.

Distance can be found using the *Distance Formula*.

Draw a Diagram

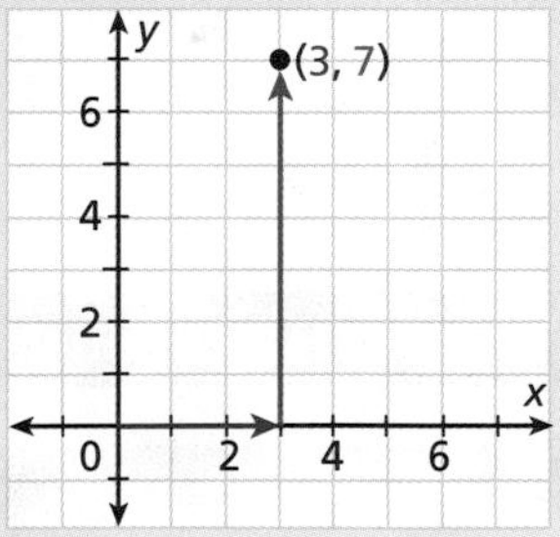

Use the Distance Formula to find the distance between the camp and the starting point.

$$d = \sqrt{(x_2 - x_1)^2 + (y_2 - y_1)^2}$$
$$= \sqrt{(3 - 0)^2 + (7 - 0)^2} \approx 7.6 \text{ km}$$

Try This

For the following problem, apply the following reading tips. Do not solve.

- Identify key words.
- Translate each phrase into math language.
- Draw a diagram to represent the problem.

1. The lengths of two sides of a triangle are 4 cm and 10 cm. Find the range of possible lengths of the third side.

COMMON CORE

9-1 Reflections

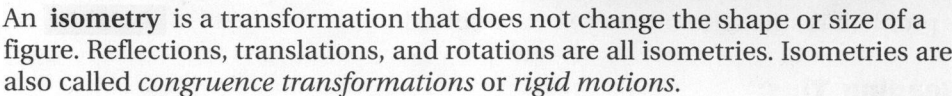

CC.9-12.G.CO.6 ...Transform figures and...predict the effect of a given rigid motion on a given figure...
Also **CC.9-12.G.CO.5, CC.9-12.G.CO.4, CC.9-12.G.CO.2**

Objective
Identify and draw reflections.

Vocabulary
isometry

Who uses this?
Trail designers use reflections to find shortest paths. (See Example 3.)

An **isometry** is a transformation that does not change the shape or size of a figure. Reflections, translations, and rotations are all isometries. Isometries are also called *congruence transformations* or *rigid motions.*

Recall that a reflection is a transformation that moves a figure (the preimage) by flipping it across a line. The reflected figure is called the image. A reflection is an isometry, so the image is always congruent to the preimage.

EXAMPLE 1 Identifying Reflections

Tell whether each transformation appears to be a reflection. Explain.

A

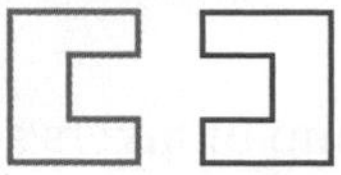

Yes; the image appears to be flipped across a line.

B

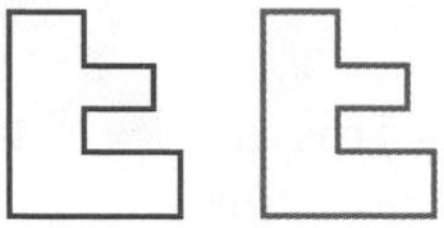

No; the figure does not appear to be flipped.

CHECK IT OUT! **Tell whether each transformation appears to be a reflection.**

1a.

1b.

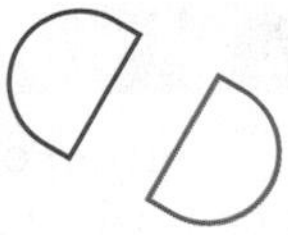

Construction Reflect a Figure Using Patty Paper

1

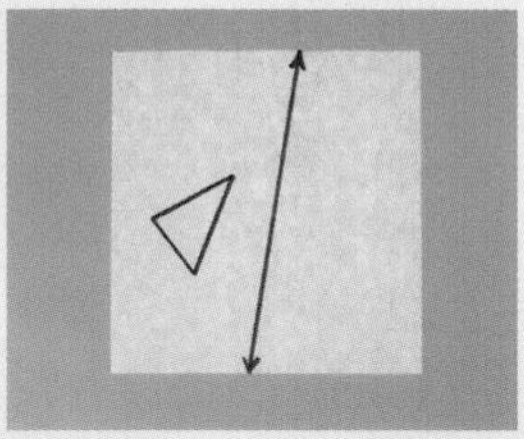

Draw a triangle and a line of reflection on a piece of patty paper.

2

Fold the patty paper back along the line of reflection.

3

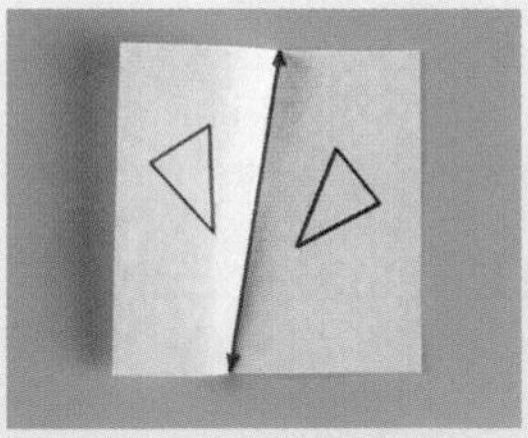

Trace the triangle. Then unfold the paper.

Draw a segment from each vertex of the preimage to the corresponding vertex of the image. Your construction should show that the line of reflection is the perpendicular bisector of every segment connecting a point and its image.

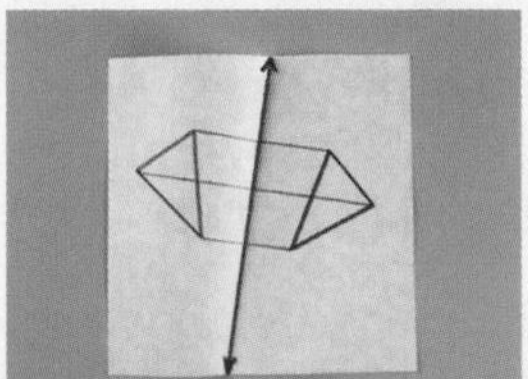

Know it! Note — Reflections

A reflection is a transformation across a line, called the line of reflection, so that the line of reflection is the perpendicular bisector of each segment joining each point and its image.

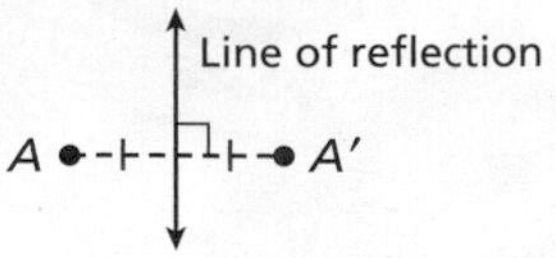

EXAMPLE 2 Drawing Reflections

Copy the quadrilateral and the line of reflection. Draw the reflection of the quadrilateral across the line.

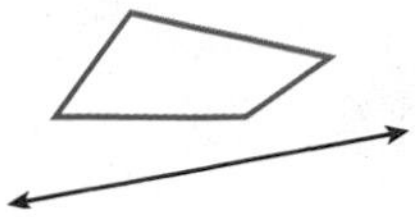

Step 1 Through each vertex draw a line perpendicular to the line of reflection.

Step 2 Measure the distance from each vertex to the line of reflection. Locate the image of each vertex on the opposite side of the line of reflection and the same distance from it.

Step 3 Connect the images of the vertices.

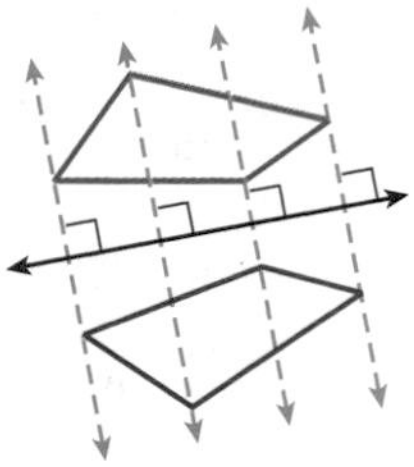

CHECK IT OUT! 2. Copy the quadrilateral and the line of reflection. Draw the reflection of the quadrilateral across the line.

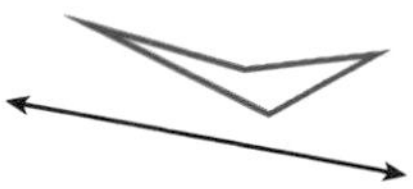

EXAMPLE 3 *Problem-Solving Application*

MATHEMATICAL PRACTICES

Make sense of problems and persevere in solving them.

A trail designer is planning two trails that connect campsites *A* and *B* to a point on the river. He wants the total length of the trails to be as short as possible. Where should the trail meet the river?

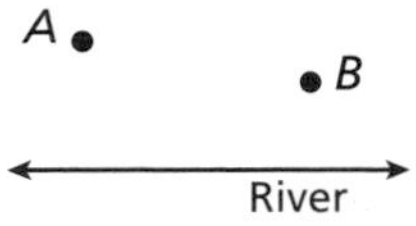

1 Understand the Problem

The problem asks you to locate point X on the river so that $AX + XB$ has the least value possible.

2 Make a Plan

Let B' be the reflection of point B across the river. For any point X on the river, $\overline{XB'} \cong \overline{XB}$, so $AX + XB = AX + XB'$. $AX + XB'$ is least when A, X, and B' are collinear.

3 Solve

Reflect B across the river to locate B'. Draw $\overline{AB'}$ and locate X at the intersection of $\overline{AB'}$ and the river.

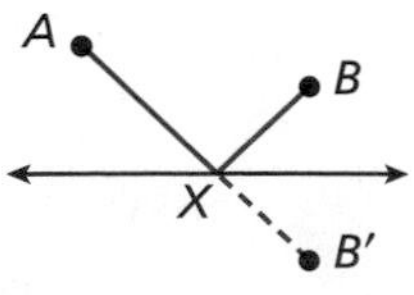

4 Look Back

To verify your answer, choose several possible locations for X and measure the total length of the trails for each location.

CHECK IT OUT! 3. **What if...?** If A and B were the same distance from the river, what would be true about $\overline{AX}$ and $\overline{BX}$?

Reflections in the Coordinate Plane

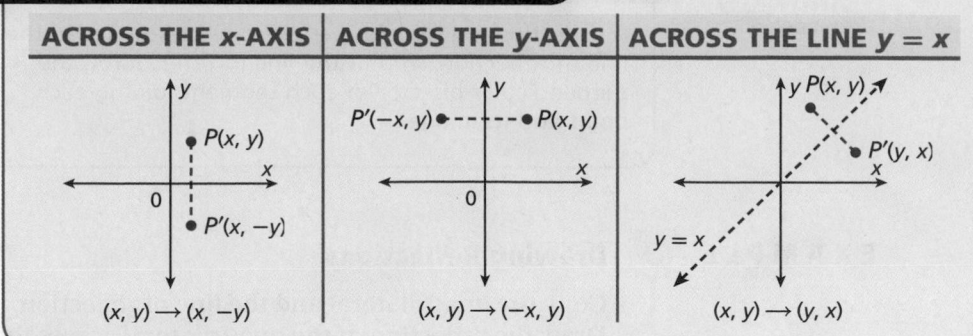

ACROSS THE x-AXIS	ACROSS THE y-AXIS	ACROSS THE LINE $y = x$
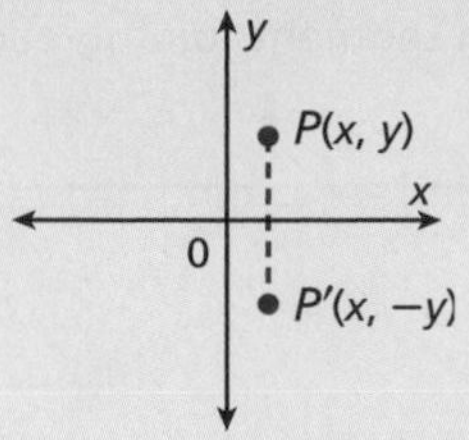	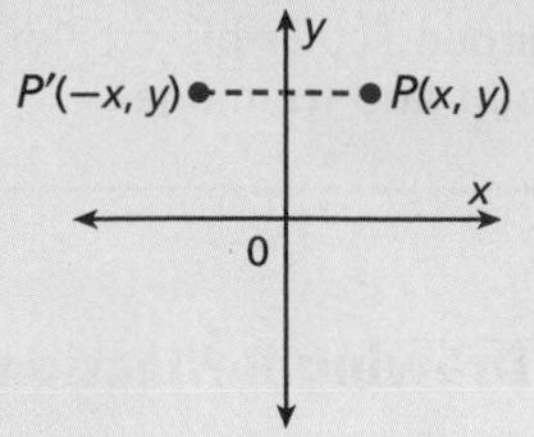	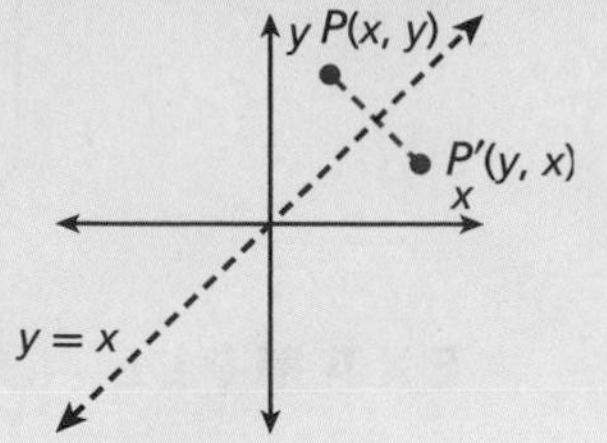
$(x, y) \rightarrow (x, -y)$	$(x, y) \rightarrow (-x, y)$	$(x, y) \rightarrow (y, x)$

EXAMPLE 4 **Drawing Reflections in the Coordinate Plane**

Reflect the figure with the given vertices across the given line.

A $M(1, 2), N(1, 4), P(3, 3)$; **$y$-axis**

The reflection of (x, y) is $(-x, y)$.

$M(1, 2) \rightarrow M'(-1, 2)$

$N(1, 4) \rightarrow N'(-1, 4)$

$P(3, 3) \rightarrow P'(-3, 3)$

Graph the preimage and image.

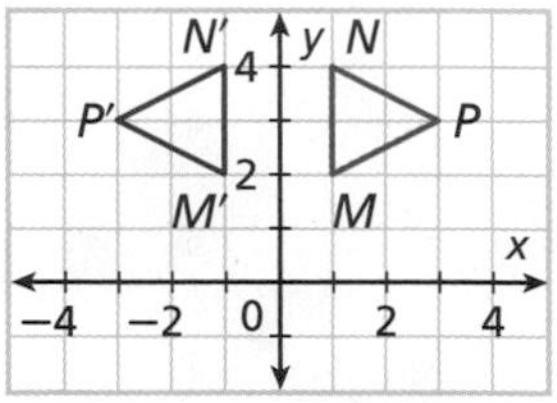

B $D(2, 0), E(2, 2), F(5, 2), G(5, 1); y = x$

The reflection of (x, y) is (y, x).

$D(2, 0) \rightarrow D'(0, 2)$

$E(2, 2) \rightarrow E'(2, 2)$

$F(5, 2) \rightarrow F'(2, 5)$

$G(5, 1) \rightarrow G'(1, 5)$

Graph the preimage and image.

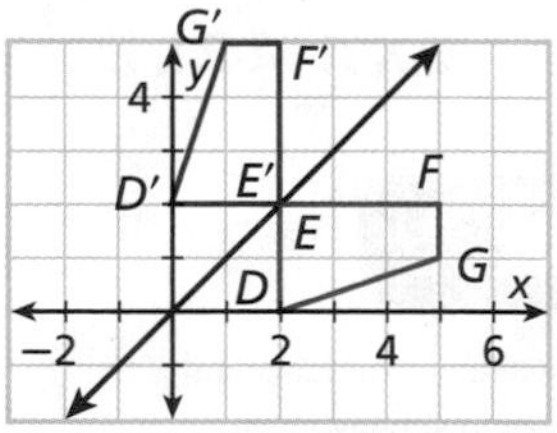

CHECK IT OUT! 4. Reflect the rectangle with vertices $S(3, 4)$, $T(3, 1)$, $U(-2, 1)$, and $V(-2, 4)$ across the x-axis.

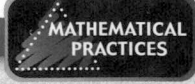

MATHEMATICAL PRACTICES

THINK AND DISCUSS

1. Acute scalene $\triangle ABC$ is reflected across $\overline{BC}$. Classify quadrilateral $ABA'C$. Explain your reasoning.
2. Point A' is a *reflection* of point A across line ℓ. What is the relationship of ℓ to $\overline{AA'}$?
3. **GET ORGANIZED** Copy and complete the graphic organizer.

Line of Reflection	Image of (a, b)	Example
x-axis		
y-axis		
$y = x$		

9-1 Exercises

Learn It Online
Homework Help Online
Parent Resources Online

GUIDED PRACTICE

1. **Vocabulary** If a transformation is an *isometry,* how would you describe the relationship between the preimage and the image?

SEE EXAMPLE 1

Tell whether each transformation appears to be a reflection.

2.

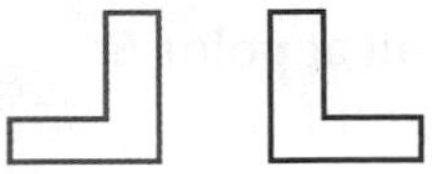

3.

4.

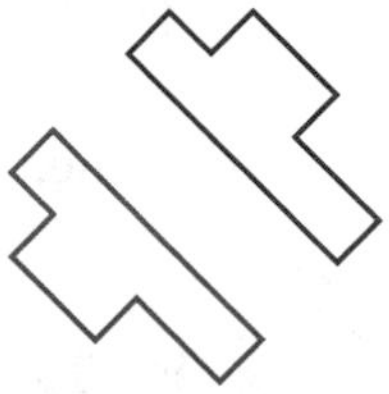

5.

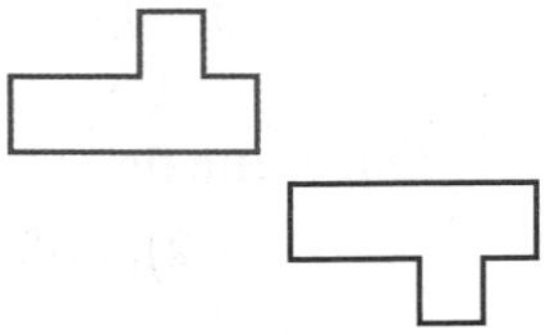

SEE EXAMPLE 2

Multi-Step **Copy each figure and the line of reflection. Draw the reflection of the figure across the line.**

6.

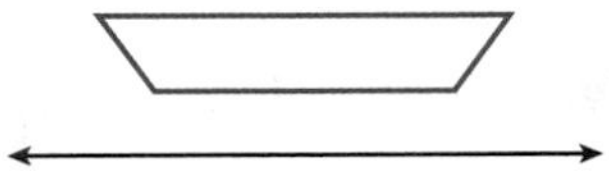

7.

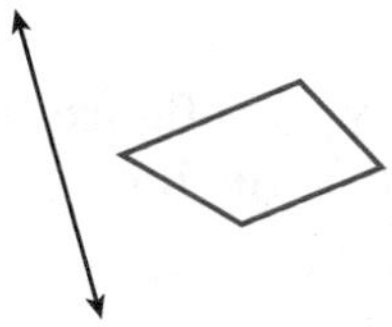

SEE EXAMPLE 3

8. **City Planning** The towns of San Pablo and Tanner are located on the same side of Highway 105. Two access roads are planned that connect the towns to a point P on the highway. Draw a diagram that shows where point P should be located in order to make the total length of the access roads as short as possible.

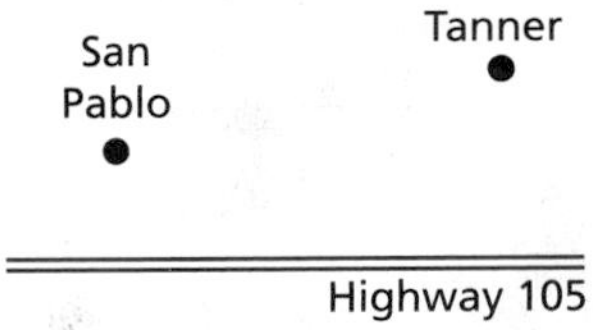

SEE EXAMPLE 4

Reflect the figure with the given vertices across the given line.

9. $A(-2, 1)$, $B(2, 3)$, $C(5, 2)$; x-axis
10. $R(0, -1)$, $S(2, 2)$, $T(3, 0)$; y-axis
11. $M(2, 1)$, $N(3, 1)$, $P(2, -1)$, $Q(1, -1)$; $y = x$
12. $A(-2, 2)$, $B(-1, 3)$, $C(1, 2)$, $D(-2, -2)$; $y = x$

PRACTICE AND PROBLEM SOLVING

Independent Practice

For Exercises	See Example
13–16	1
17–18	2
19	3
20–23	4

Extra Practice

See Extra Practice for more Skills Practice and Applications Practice exercises.

Tell whether each transformation appears to be a reflection.

13.

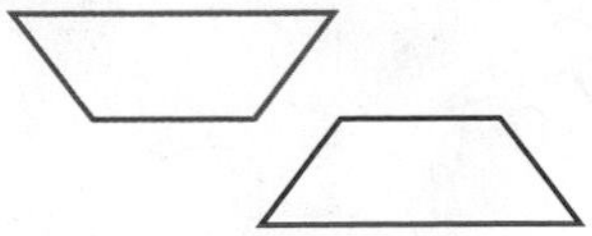

14.

15.

16.

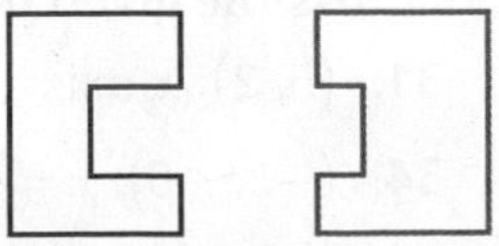

Multi-Step Copy each figure and the line of reflection. Draw the reflection of the figure across the line.

17.

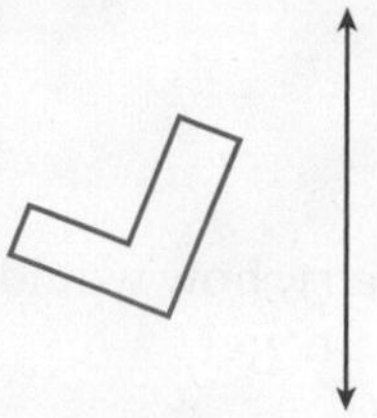

18.

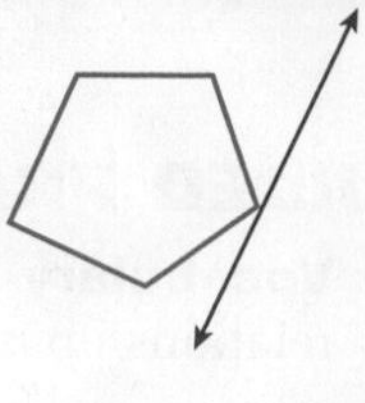

19. **Recreation** Cara is playing pool. She wants to hit the ball at point *A* without hitting the ball at point *B*. She has to bounce the cue ball, located at point *C*, off the side rail and into her ball. Draw a diagram that shows the exact point along the rail that Cara should aim for.

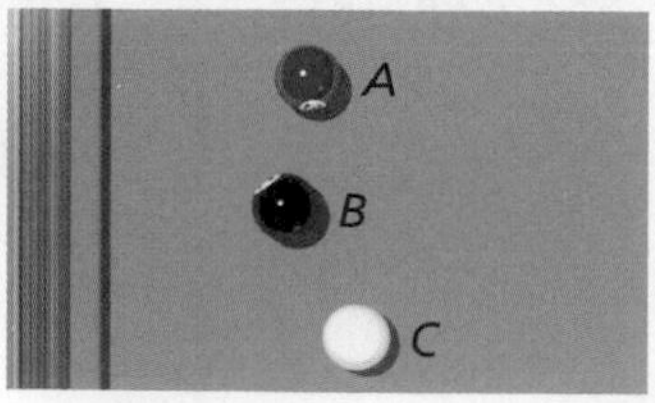

Reflect the figure with the given vertices across the given line.

20. $A(-3, 2)$, $B(0, 2)$, $C(-2, 0)$; y-axis

21. $M(-4, -1)$, $N(-1, -1)$, $P(-2, -2)$; $y = x$

22. $J(1, 2)$, $K(-2, -1)$, $L(3, -1)$; x-axis

23. $S(-1, 1)$, $T(1, 4)$, $U(3, 2)$, $V(1, -3)$; $y = x$

Copy each figure. Then complete the figure by drawing the reflection image across the line.

24.

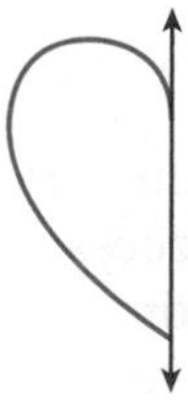

25.

26.

LINK

Chemistry

Louis Pasteur (1822–1895) is best known for the pasteurization process, which kills germs in milk. He discovered chemical chirality when he observed that two salt crystals were mirror images of each other.

27. **Chemistry** In chemistry, *chiral* molecules are mirror images of each other. Although they have similar structures, chiral molecules can have very different properties. For example, the compound R-(+)-limonene smells like oranges, while its mirror image, S-(−)-limonene, smells like lemons. Use the figure and the given line of reflection to draw S-(−)-limonene.

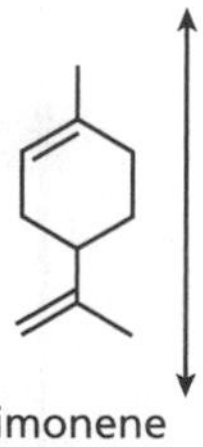

R-(+)-limonene

Each figure shows a preimage and image under a reflection. Copy the figure and draw the line of reflection.

28.

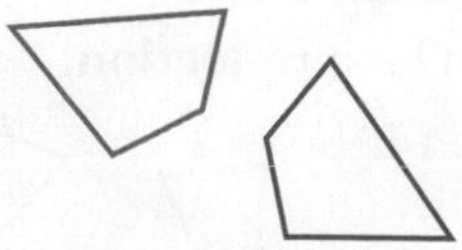

29.

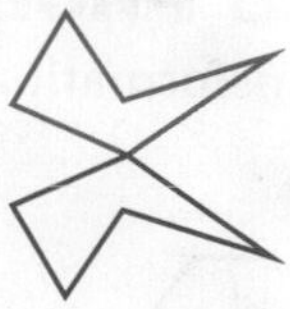

30.

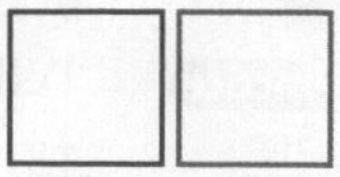

Use arrow notation to describe the mapping of each point when it is reflected across the given line.

31. $(5, 2)$; x-axis

32. $(-3, -7)$; y-axis

33. $(0, 12)$; x-axis

34. $(-3, -6)$; $y = x$

35. $(0, -5)$; $y = x$

36. $(4, 4)$; $y = x$

MULTI-STEP TEST PREP

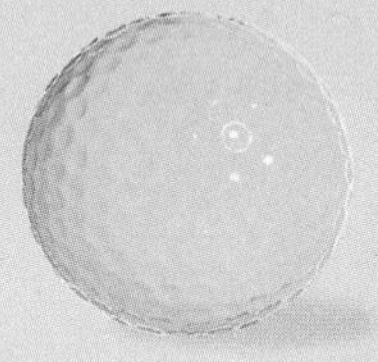

37. The figure shows one hole of a miniature golf course.

a. Is it possible to hit the ball in a straight line from the tee T to the hole H?

b. Find the coordinates of H', the reflection of H across $\overline{BC}$.

c. The point at which a player should aim in order to make a hole in one is the intersection of $\overline{TH'}$ and $\overline{BC}$. What are the coordinates of this point?

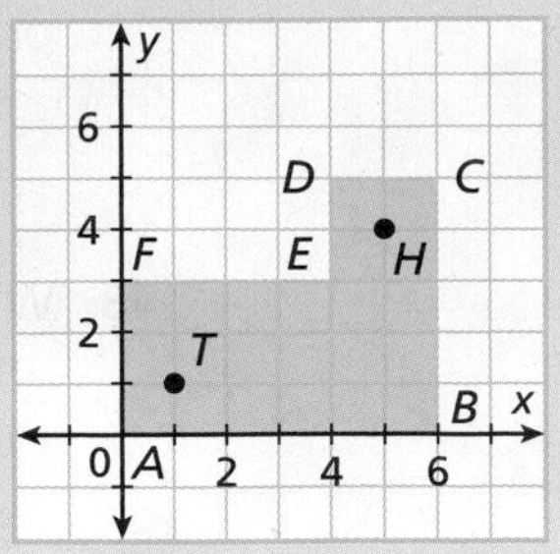

38. Critical Thinking Sketch the next figure in the sequence below.

39. Critical Thinking Under a reflection in the coordinate plane, the point (3, 5) is mapped to the point (5, 3). What is the line of reflection? Is this the only possible line of reflection? Explain.

Draw the reflection of the graph of each function across the given line.

40. x-axis

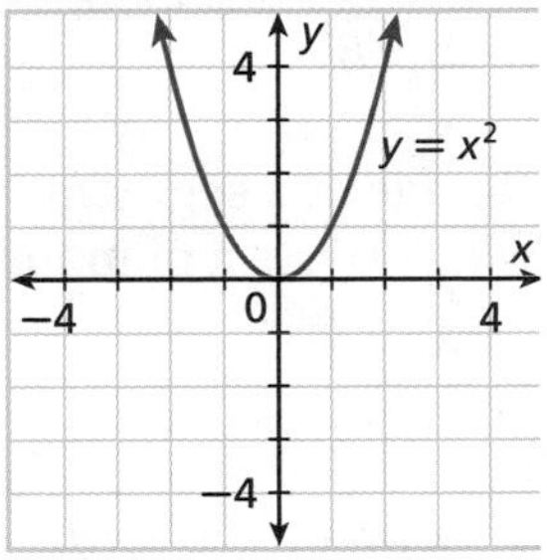

41. y-axis

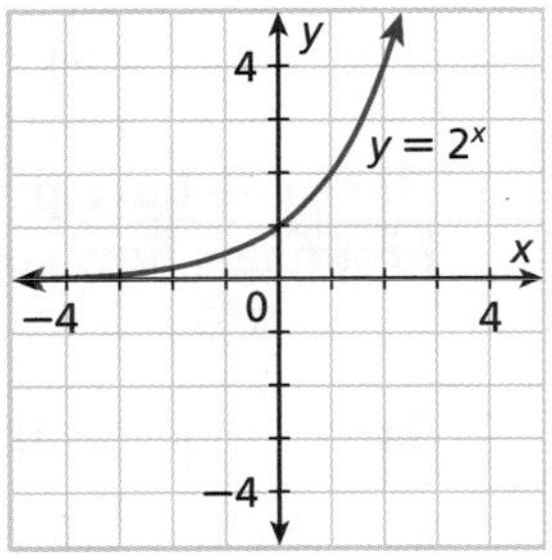

42. Write About It Imagine reflecting all the points in a plane across line ℓ. Which points remain fixed under this transformation? That is, for which points is the image the same as the preimage? Explain.

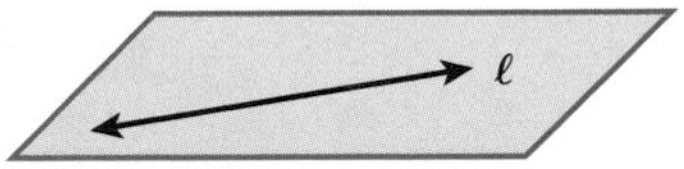

Construction **Use the construction of a line perpendicular to a given line through a given point and the construction of a segment congruent to a given segment to construct the reflection of each figure across a line.**

43. a point **44.** a segment **45.** a triangle

TEST PREP

46. Daryl is using a coordinate plane to plan a garden. He draws a flower bed with vertices (3, 1), (3, 4), (−2, 4), and (−2, 1). Then he creates a second flower bed by reflecting the first one across the x-axis. Which of these is a vertex of the second flower bed?

Ⓐ (−2, −4)
Ⓑ (−3, 1)
Ⓒ (2, 1)
Ⓓ (−3, −4)

47. In the reflection shown, the shaded figure is the preimage. Which of these represents the mapping?

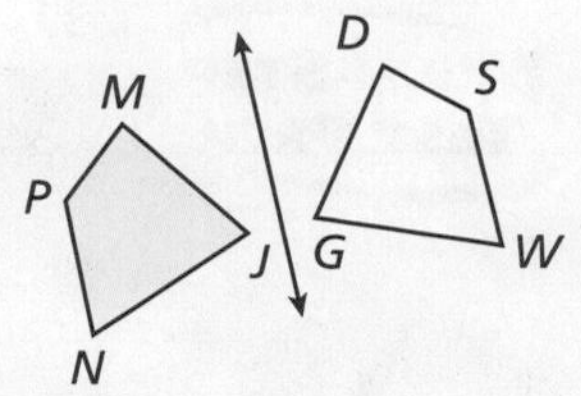

Ⓕ *MJNP* → *DSWG*
Ⓗ *JMPN* → *GWSD*
Ⓖ *DGWS* → *MJNP*
Ⓙ *PMJN* → *SDGW*

48. What is the image of the point (−3, 4) when it is reflected across the *y*-axis?

Ⓐ (4, −3)
Ⓒ (3, 4)
Ⓑ (−3, −4)
Ⓓ (−4, −3)

CHALLENGE AND EXTEND

Find the coordinates of the image when each point is reflected across the given line.

49. $(4, 2);\ y = 3$

50. $(-3, 2);\ x = 1$

51. $(3, 1);\ y = x + 2$

52. Prove that the reflection image of a segment is congruent to the preimage.
Given: $\overline{A'B'}$ is the reflection image of $\overline{AB}$ across line ℓ.
Prove: $\overline{AB} \cong \overline{A'B'}$
Plan: Draw auxiliary lines $\overline{AA'}$ and $\overline{BB'}$ as shown. First prove that $\triangle ACD \cong \triangle A'CD$. Then use CPCTC to conclude that $\angle CDA \cong \angle CDA'$. Therefore $\angle ADB \cong \angle A'DB'$, which makes it possible to prove that $\triangle ADB \cong \triangle A'DB'$. Finally use CPCTC to conclude that $\overline{AB} \cong \overline{A'B'}$.

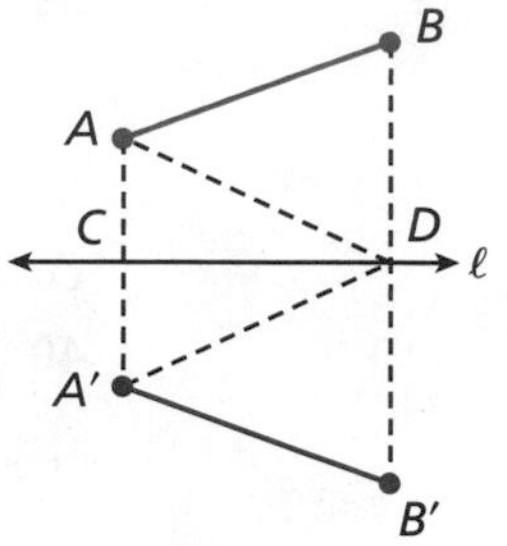

Once you have proved that the reflection image of a segment is congruent to the preimage, how could you prove the following? Write a plan for each proof.

53. If $\overline{A'B'}$ is the reflection of $\overline{AB}$, then $AB = A'B'$.

54. If $\angle A'B'C'$ is the reflection of $\angle ABC$, then $m\angle ABC = m\angle A'B'C'$.

55. The reflection $\triangle A'B'C'$ is congruent to the preimage $\triangle ABC$.

56. If point C is between points A and B, then the reflection C' is between A' and B'.

57. If points A, B, and C are collinear, then the reflections A', B', and C' are collinear.

COMMON CORE

9-2 Translations

CC.9-12.G.CO.6 ...Transform figures and...predict the effect of a given rigid motion on a given figure... *Also* **CC.9-12.G.CO.5, CC.9-12.G.CO.4, CC.9-12.G.CO.2**

Objective
Identify and draw translations.

Who uses this?
Marching band directors use translations to plan their bands' field shows. (See Example 4.)

A translation is a transformation where all the points of a figure are moved the same distance in the same direction. A translation is an isometry, so the image of a translated figure is congruent to the preimage.

EXAMPLE 1 Identifying Translations

Tell whether each transformation appears to be a translation. Explain.

A

No; not all of the points have moved the same distance.

B

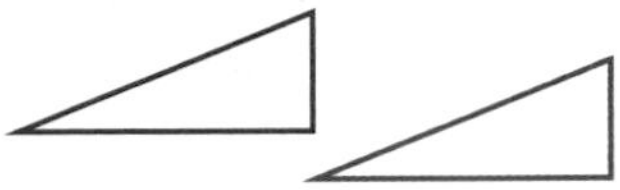

Yes; all of the points have moved the same distance in the same direction.

CHECK IT OUT! **Tell whether each transformation appears to be a translation.**

1a.

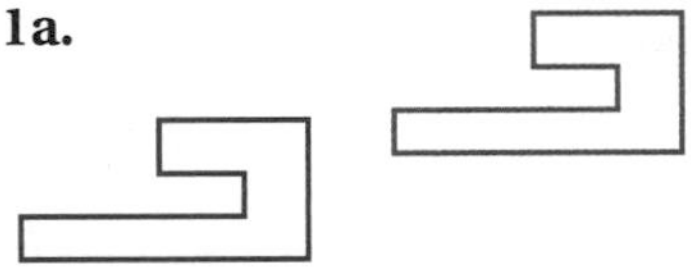

1b.

Construction Translate a Figure Using Patty Paper

1.

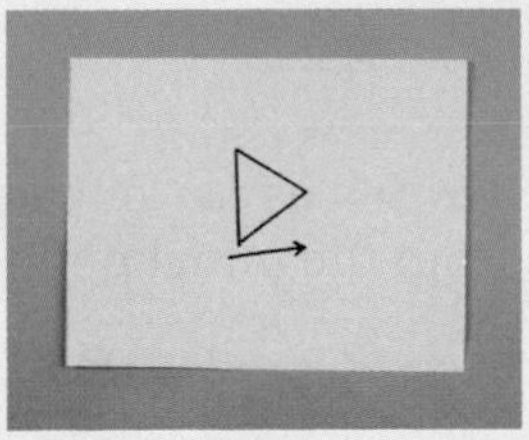

Draw a triangle and a translation vector on a sheet of paper.

2.

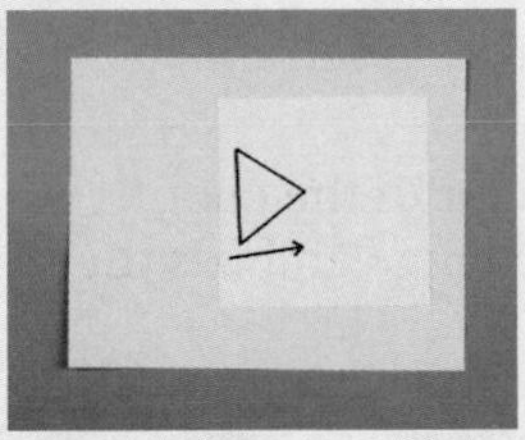

Place a sheet of patty paper on top of the diagram. Trace the triangle and vector.

3.

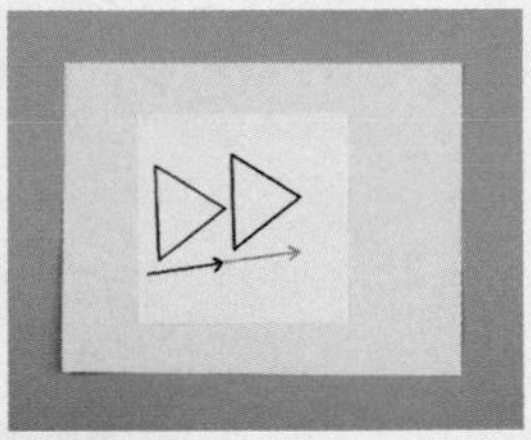

Slide the bottom paper in the direction of the vector until the head of the top vector aligns with the tail of the bottom vector. Trace the triangle.

Draw a segment from each vertex of the preimage to the corresponding vertex of the image. Your construction should show that every segment connecting a point and its image is the same length as the translation vector. These segments are also parallel to the translation vector.

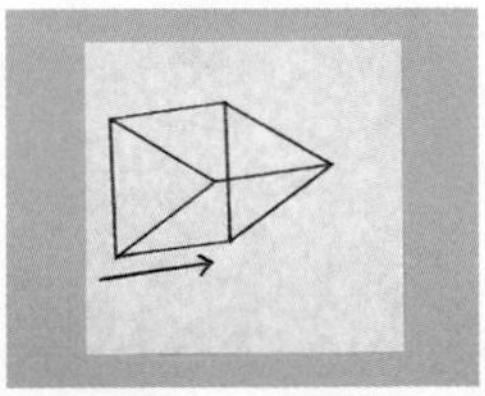

Know it! Note — Translations

A translation is a transformation along a vector such that each segment joining a point and its image has the same length as the vector and is parallel to the vector.

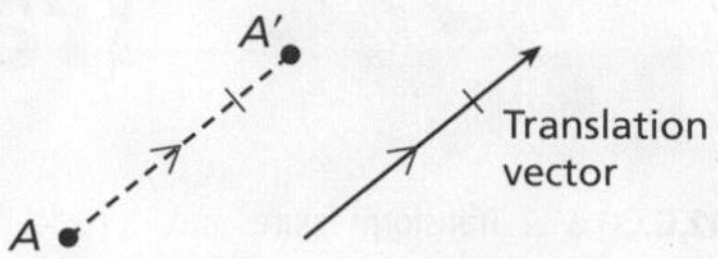

EXAMPLE 2 Drawing Translations

Copy the triangle and the translation vector. Draw the translation of the triangle along $\vec{v}$.

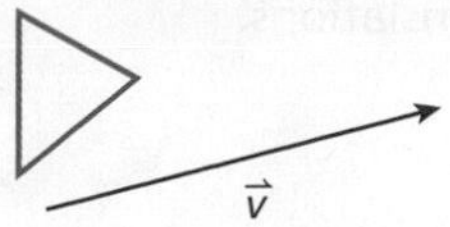

Step 1 Draw a line parallel to the vector through each vertex of the triangle.

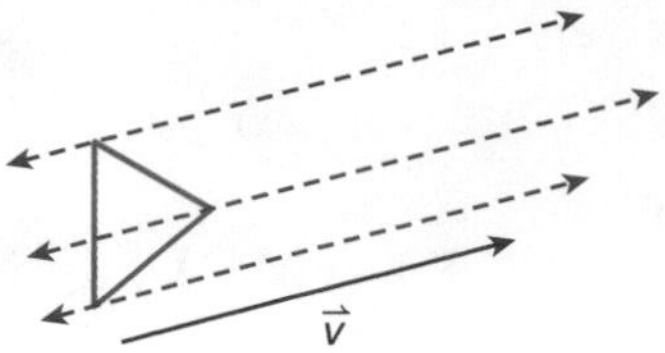

Step 2 Measure the length of the vector. Then, from each vertex mark off this distance in the same direction as the vector, on each of the parallel lines.

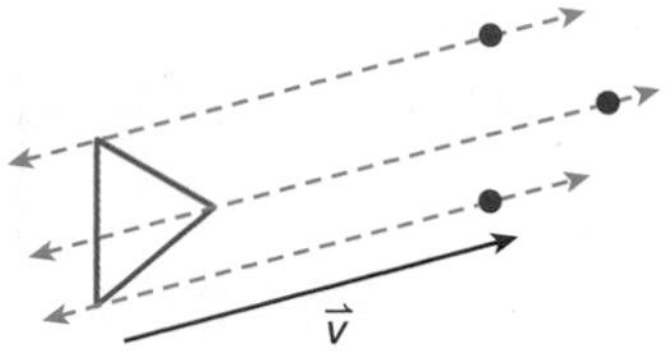

Step 3 Connect the images of the vertices.

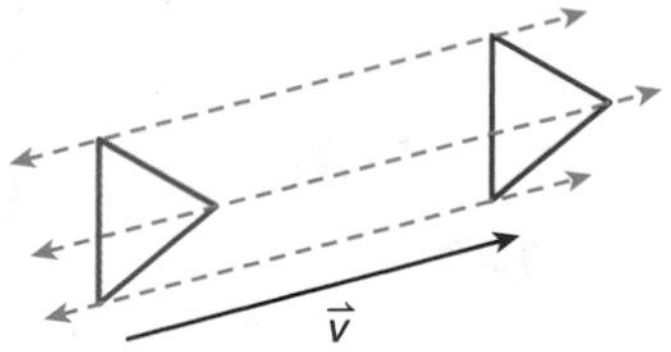

CHECK IT OUT!

2. Copy the quadrilateral and the translation vector. Draw the translation of the quadrilateral along $\vec{w}$.

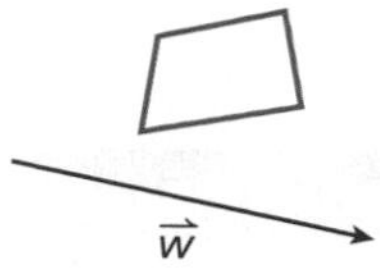

Recall that a vector in the coordinate plane can be written as $\langle a, b\rangle$, where a is the horizontal change and b is the vertical change from the initial point to the terminal point.

Know it! Note — Translations in the Coordinate Plane

HORIZONTAL TRANSLATION ALONG VECTOR $\langle a, 0\rangle$	VERTICAL TRANSLATION ALONG VECTOR $\langle 0, b\rangle$	GENERAL TRANSLATION ALONG VECTOR $\langle a, b\rangle$
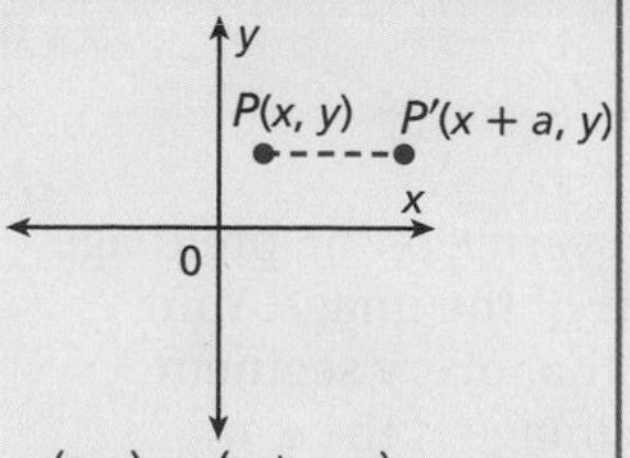	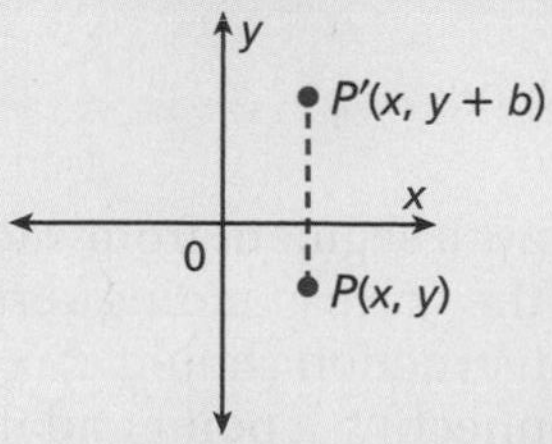	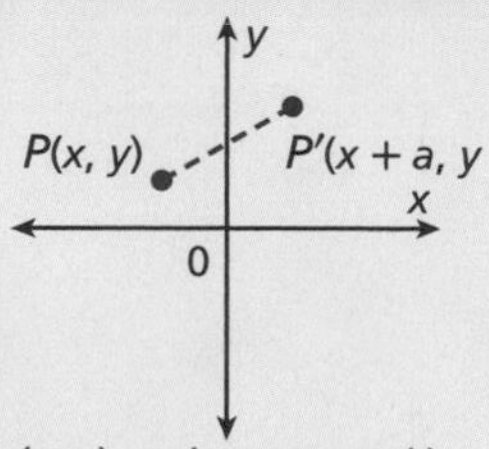
$(x, y) \rightarrow (x + a, y)$	$(x, y) \rightarrow (x, y + b)$	$(x, y) \rightarrow (x + a, y + b)$

EXAMPLE 3 Drawing Translations in the Coordinate Plane

Translate the triangle with vertices $A(-2, -4)$, $B(-1, -2)$, and $C(-3, 0)$ along the vector $\langle 2, 4 \rangle$.

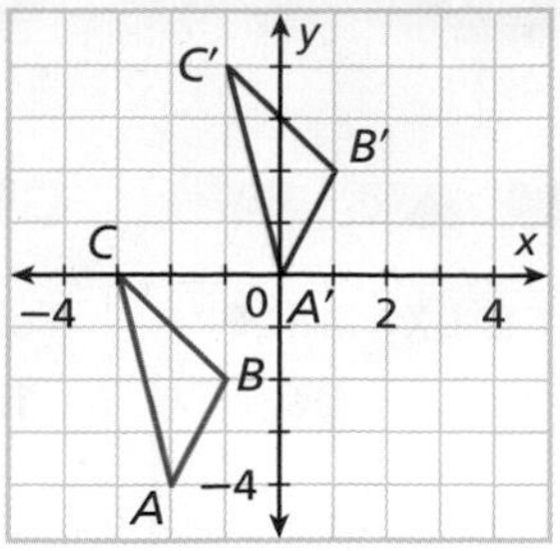

The image of (x, y) is $(x + 2, y + 4)$.

$A(-2, -4) \rightarrow A'(-2 + 2, -4 + 4) = A'(0, 0)$

$B(-1, -2) \rightarrow B'(-1 + 2, -2 + 4) = B'(1, 2)$

$C(-3, 0) \rightarrow C'(-3 + 2, 0 + 4) = C'(-1, 4)$

Graph the preimage and image.

CHECK IT OUT! **3.** Translate the quadrilateral with vertices $R(2, 5)$, $S(0, 2)$, $T(1, -1)$, and $U(3, 1)$ along the vector $\langle -3, -3 \rangle$.

EXAMPLE 4 *Entertainment Application*

In a marching drill, it takes 8 steps to march 5 yards. A drummer starts 8 steps to the left and 8 steps up from the center of the field. She marches 16 steps to the right to her second position. Then she marches 24 steps down the field to her final position. What is the drummer's final position? What single translation vector moves her from the starting position to her final position?

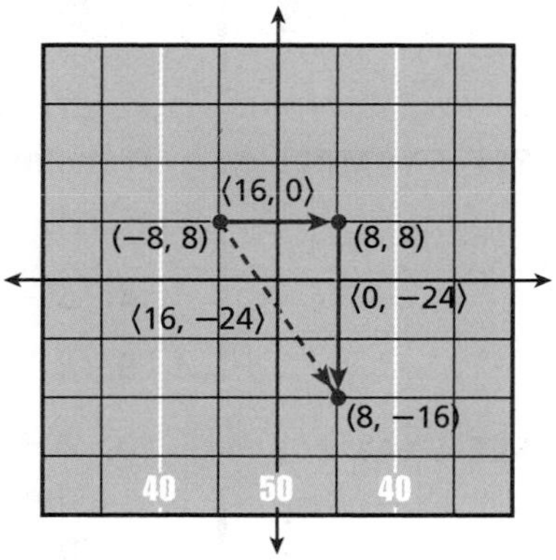

The drummer's starting coordinates are $(-8, 8)$.

Her second position is $(-8 + 16, 8) = (8, 8)$.

Her final position is $(8, 8 - 24) = (8, -16)$.

The vector that moves her directly from her starting position to her final position is $\langle 16, 0 \rangle + \langle 0, -24 \rangle = \langle 16, -24 \rangle$.

CHECK IT OUT! **4. What if...?** Suppose another drummer started at the center of the field and marched along the same vectors as above. What would this drummer's final position be?

MATHEMATICAL PRACTICES

THINK AND DISCUSS

1. Point A' is a *translation* of point A along $\vec{v}$. What is the relationship of $\vec{v}$ to $\overline{AA'}$?
2. $\overline{AB}$ is translated to form $\overline{A'B'}$. Classify quadrilateral $AA'B'B$. Explain your reasoning.
3. **GET ORGANIZED** Copy and complete the graphic organizer.

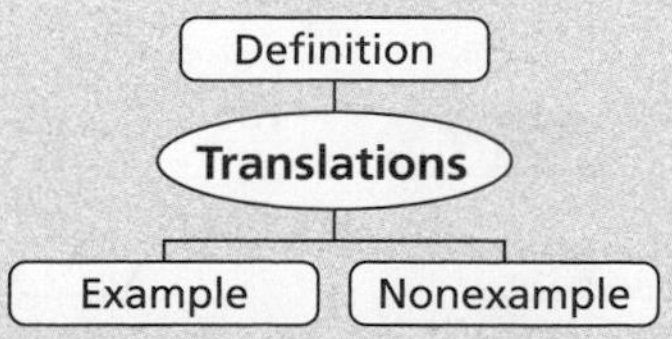

Know it! Note

9-2 Exercises

Learn It Online
Homework Help Online
Parent Resources Online

GUIDED PRACTICE

SEE EXAMPLE 1

Tell whether each transformation appears to be a translation.

1. 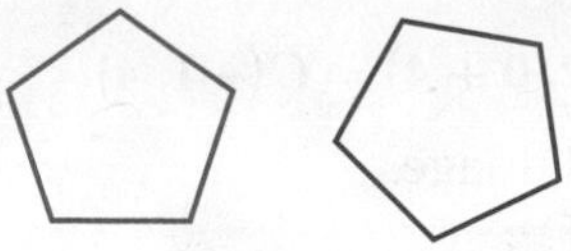

2. 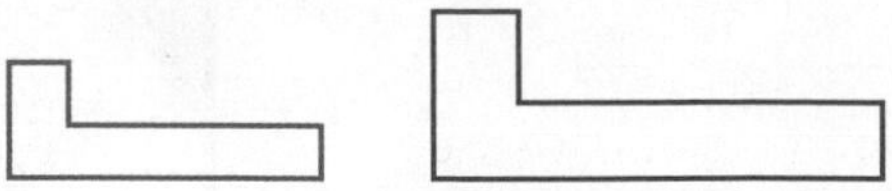

3. 

4. 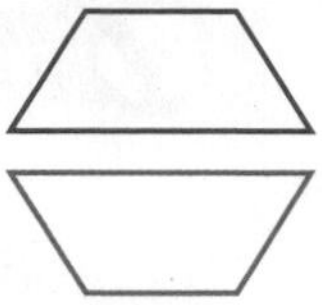

SEE EXAMPLE 2

Multi-Step **Copy each figure and the translation vector. Draw the translation of the figure along the given vector.**

5. 

6. 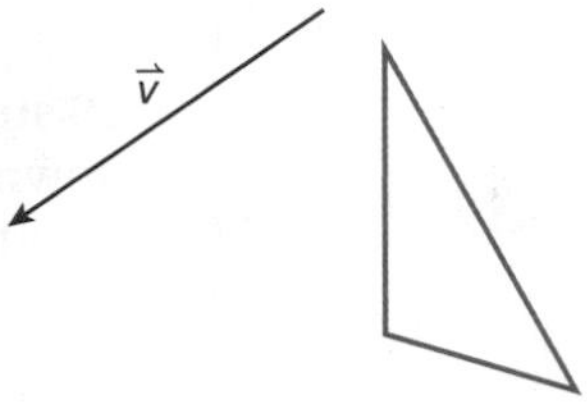

SEE EXAMPLE 3

Translate the figure with the given vertices along the given vector.

7. $A(-4, -4)$, $B(-2, -3)$, $C(-1, 3)$; $\langle 5, 0 \rangle$
8. $R(-3, 1)$, $S(-2, 3)$, $T(2, 3)$, $U(3, 1)$; $\langle 0, -4 \rangle$
9. $J(-2, 2)$, $K(-1, 2)$, $L(-1, -2)$, $M(-3, -1)$; $\langle 3, 2 \rangle$

SEE EXAMPLE 4

10. **Art** The Zulu people of southern Africa are known for their beadwork. To create a typical Zulu pattern, translate the polygon with vertices $(1, 5)$, $(2, 3)$, $(1, 1)$, and $(0, 3)$ along the vector $\langle 0, -4 \rangle$. Translate the image along the same vector. Repeat to generate a pattern. What are the vertices of the fourth polygon in the pattern?

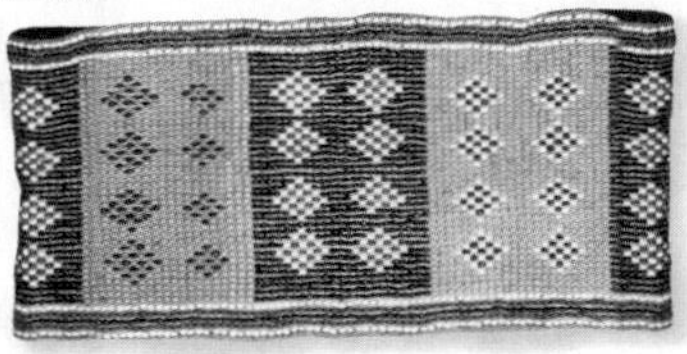

PRACTICE AND PROBLEM SOLVING

Independent Practice

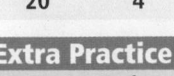

For Exercises	See Example
11–14	1
15–16	2
17–19	3
20	4

Extra Practice

See Extra Practice for more Skills Practice and Applications Practice exercises.

Tell whether each transformation appears to be a translation.

11. 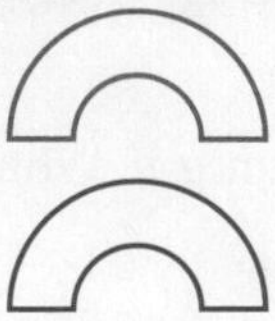

12. 

13. 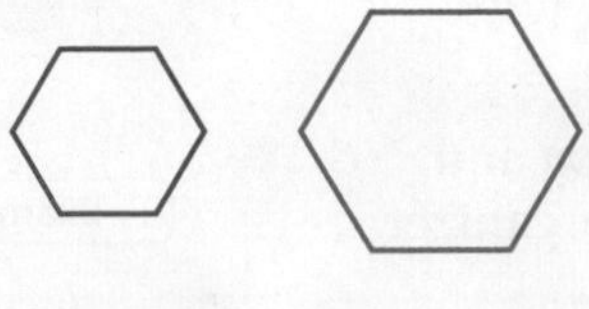

14. 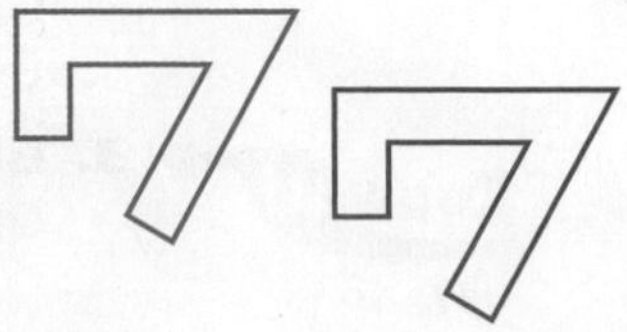

Multi-Step Copy each figure and the translation vector. Draw the translation of the figure along the given vector.

15.

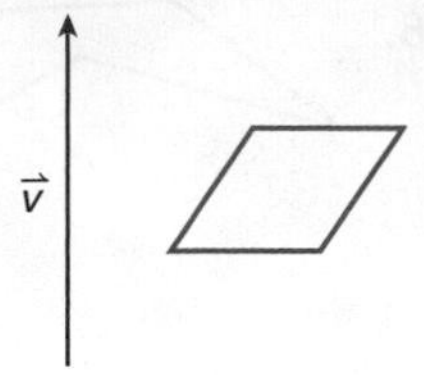

16.

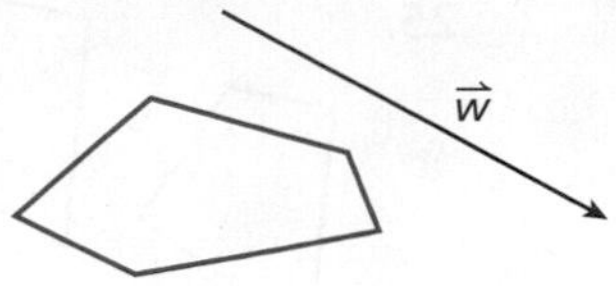

LINK

Animation

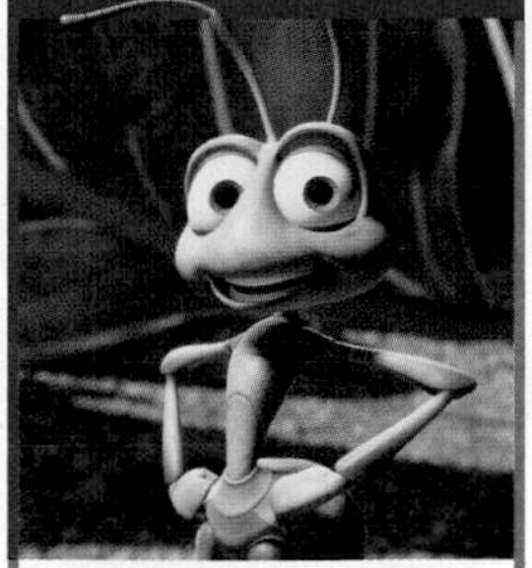

Each frame of a computer-animated feature represents $\frac{1}{24}$ of a second of film.

Source: www.pixar.com

Translate the figure with the given vertices along the given vector.

17. $P(-1, 2)$, $Q(1, -1)$, $R(3, 1)$, $S(2, 3)$; $\langle -3, 0 \rangle$

18. $A(1, 3)$, $B(-1, 2)$, $C(2, 1)$, $D(4, 2)$; $\langle -3, -3 \rangle$

19. $D(0, 15)$, $E(-10, 5)$, $F(10, -5)$; $\langle 5, -20 \rangle$

20. Animation An animator draws the ladybug shown and then translates it along the vector $\langle 1, 1 \rangle$, followed by a translation of the new image along the vector $\langle 2, 2 \rangle$, followed by a translation of the second image along the vector $\langle 3, 3 \rangle$.

a. Sketch the ladybug's final position.

b. What single vector moves the ladybug from its starting position to its final position?

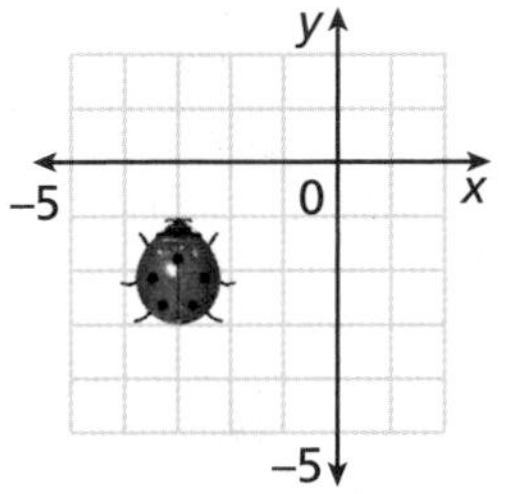

Draw the translation of the graph of each function along the given vector.

21. $\langle 3, 0 \rangle$

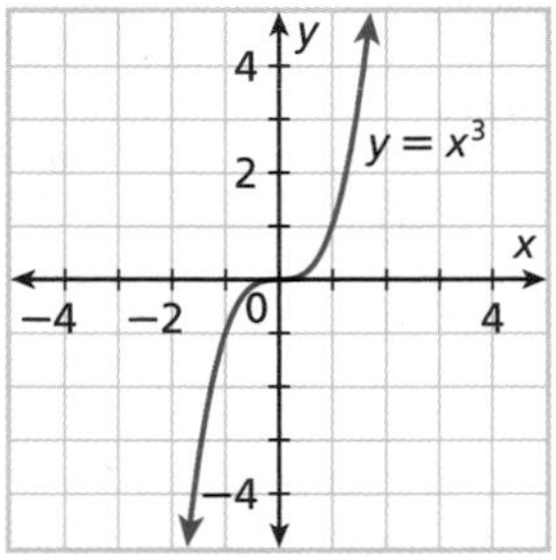

22. $\langle -1, -1 \rangle$

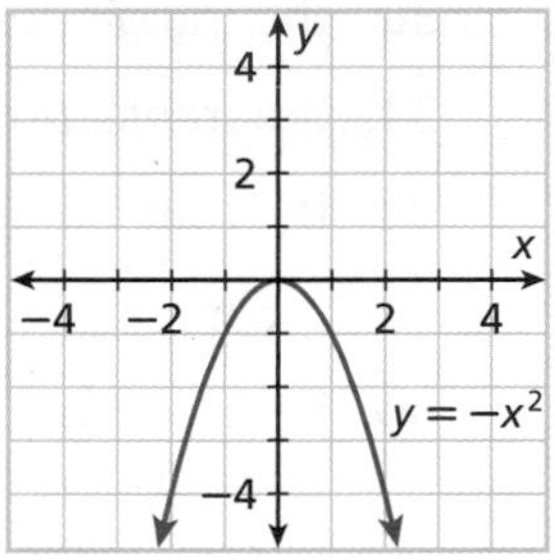

23. Probability The point $P(3, 2)$ is translated along one of the following four vectors chosen at random: $\langle -3, 0 \rangle$, $\langle -1, -4 \rangle$, $\langle 3, -2 \rangle$, and $\langle 2, 3 \rangle$. Find the probability of each of the following.

a. The image of P is in the fourth quadrant.

b. The image of P is on an axis.

c. The image of P is at the origin.

MULTI-STEP TEST PREP

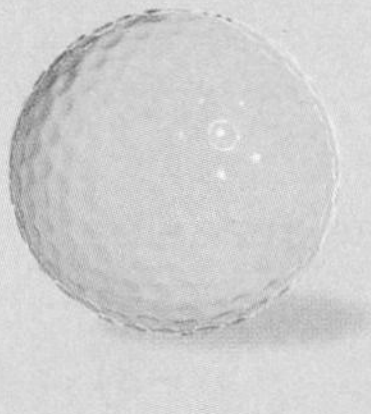

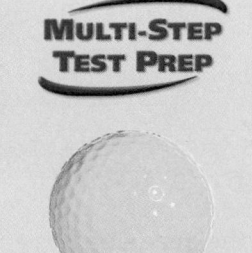

24. The figure shows one hole of a miniature golf course and the path of a ball from the tee T to the hole H.

a. What translation vector represents the path of the ball from T to $\overline{DC}$?

b. What translation vector represents the path of the ball from $\overline{DC}$ to H?

c. Show that the sum of these vectors is equal to the vector that represents the straight path from T to H.

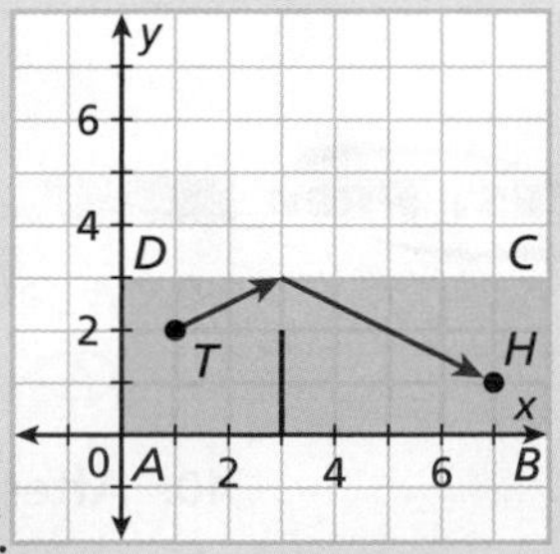

Each figure shows a preimage (blue) and its image (red) under a translation. Copy the figure and draw the vector along which the polygon is translated.

25.

26.

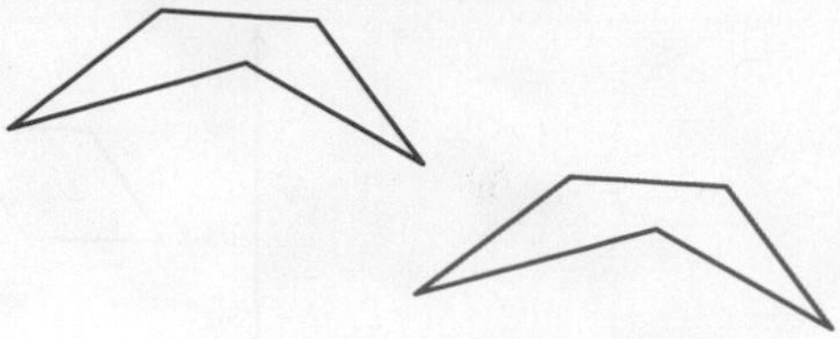

27. Critical Thinking The points of a plane are translated along the given vector $\overrightarrow{AB}$. Do any points remain fixed under this transformation? That is, are there any points for which the image coincides with the preimage? Explain.

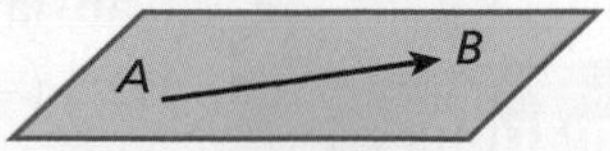

28. Carpentry Carpenters use a tool called *adjustable parallels* to set up level work areas and to draw parallel lines. Describe how a carpenter could use this tool to translate a given point along a given vector. What additional tools, if any, would be needed?

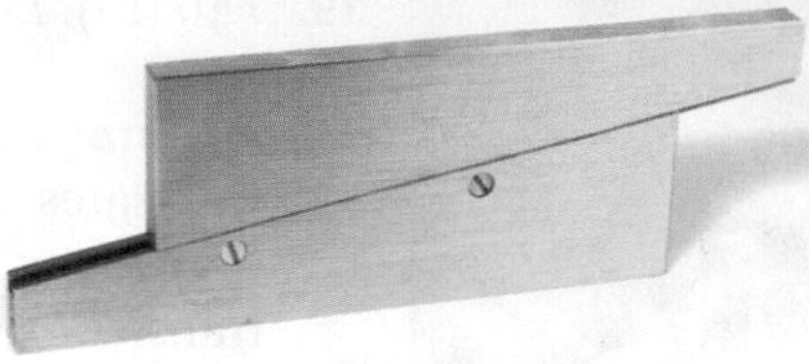

Find the vector associated with each translation. Then use arrow notation to describe the mapping of the preimage to the image.

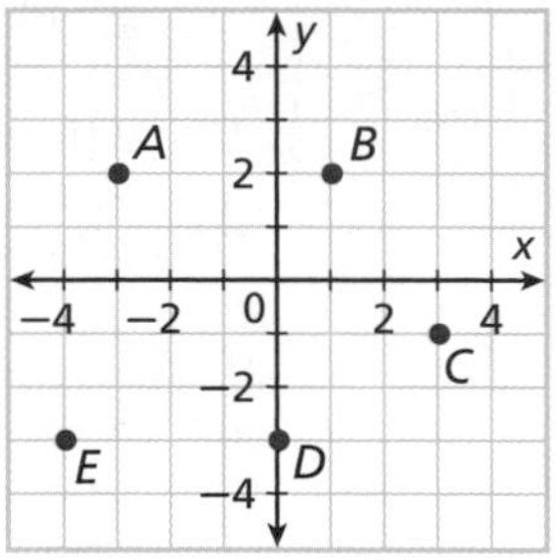

29. the translation that maps point A to point B

30. the translation that maps point B to point A

31. the translation that maps point C to point D

32. the translation that maps point E to point B

33. the translation that maps point C to the origin

34. Multi-Step The rectangle shown is translated two-thirds of the way along one of its diagonals. Find the area of the region where the rectangle and its image overlap.

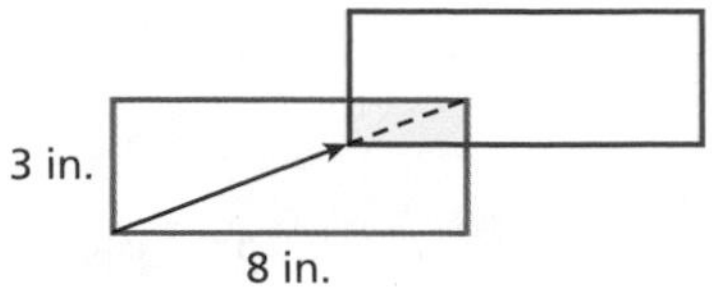

35. Write About It Point P is translated along the vector $\langle a, b\rangle$. Explain how to find the distance between point P and its image.

Construction **Use the construction of a line parallel to a given line through a given point and the construction of a segment congruent to a given segment to construct the translation of each figure along a vector.**

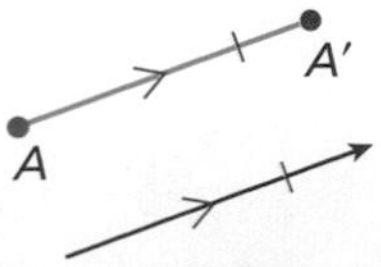

36. a point **37.** a segment **38.** a triangle

TEST PREP

39. What is the image of $P(1, 3)$ when it is translated along the vector $\langle -3, 5\rangle$?

Ⓐ $(-2, 8)$ Ⓑ $(0, 6)$ Ⓒ $(1, 3)$ Ⓓ $(0, 4)$

40. After a translation, the image of $A(-6, -2)$ is $B(-4, -4)$. What is the image of the point $(3, -1)$ after this translation?

Ⓕ $(-5, 1)$ Ⓖ $(5, -3)$ Ⓗ $(5, 1)$ Ⓙ $(-5, -3)$

41. Which vector translates point Q to point P?

Ⓐ $\langle -2, -4 \rangle$ Ⓒ $\langle -2, 4 \rangle$

Ⓑ $\langle 4, -2 \rangle$ Ⓓ $\langle 2, -4 \rangle$

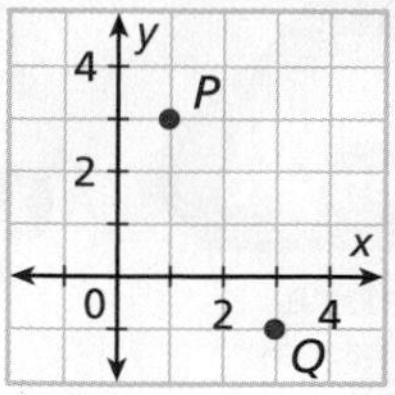

CHALLENGE AND EXTEND

42. The point $M(1, 2)$ is translated along a vector that is parallel to the line $y = 2x + 4$. The translation vector has magnitude $\sqrt{5}$. What are the possible images of point M?

43. A cube has edges of length 2 cm. Point P is translated along $\vec{u}$, $\vec{v}$, and $\vec{w}$ as shown.

a. Describe a single translation vector that maps point P to point Q.

b. Find the magnitude of this vector to the nearest hundredth.

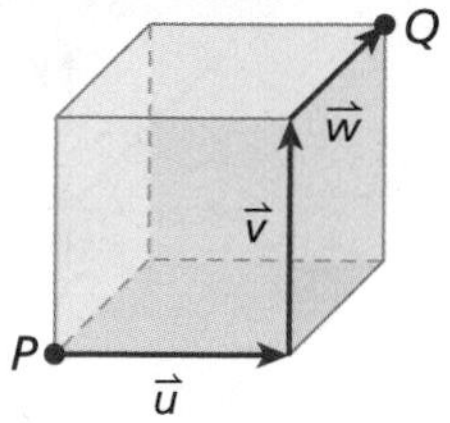

44. Prove that the translation image of a segment is congruent to the preimage.
Given: $\overline{A'B'}$ is the translation image of $\overline{AB}$.
Prove: $\overline{AB} \cong \overline{A'B'}$
(*Hint:* Draw auxiliary lines $\overline{AA'}$ and $\overline{BB'}$. What can you conclude about $\overline{AA'}$ and $\overline{BB'}$?)

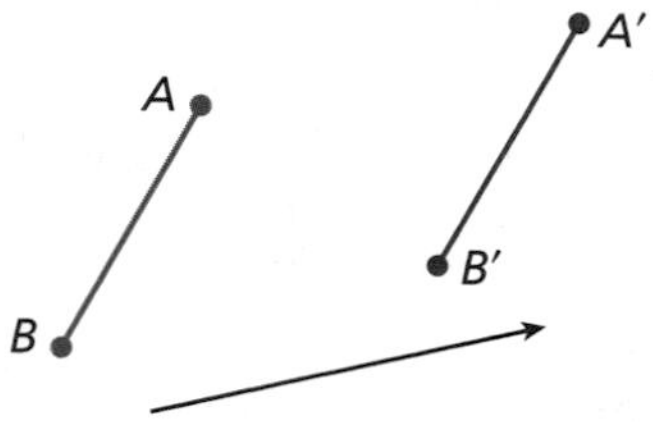

Once you have proved that the translation image of a segment is congruent to the preimage, how could you prove the following? Write a plan for each proof.

45. If $\overline{A'B'}$ is a translation of $\overline{AB}$, then $AB = A'B'$.

46. If $\angle A'B'C'$ is a translation of $\angle ABC$, then $m\angle ABC = m\angle A'B'C'$.

47. The translation $\triangle A'B'C'$ is congruent to the preimage $\triangle ABC$.

48. If point C is between points A and B, then the translation C' is between A' and B'.

49. If points A, B, and C are collinear, then the translations A', B', and C' are collinear.

Connecting Geometry to **Algebra**

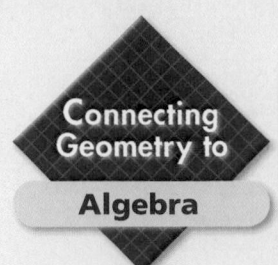

Transformations of Functions

Transformations can be used to graph complicated functions by using the graphs of simpler functions called *parent functions.* The following are examples of parent functions and their graphs.

$y = |x|$

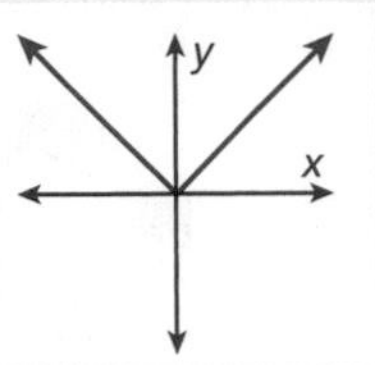

$y = \sqrt{x}$

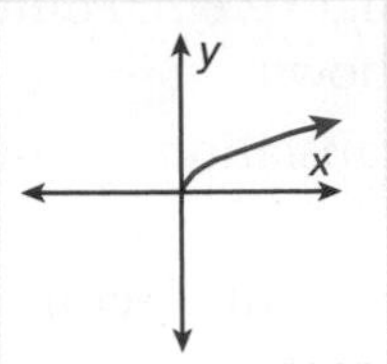

$y = x^2$

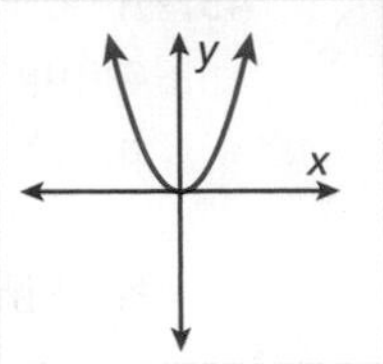

Transformation of Parent Function $y = f(x)$		
Reflection	**Vertical Translation**	**Horizontal Translation**
Across x-axis: $y = -f(x)$	$y = f(x) + k$	$y = f(x - h)$
Across y-axis: $y = f(-x)$	Up k units if $k > 0$	Right h units if $h > 0$
	Down k units if $k < 0$	Left h units if $h < 0$

Example

For the parent function $y = x^2$, write a function rule for the given transformation and graph the preimage and image.

A a reflection across the x-axis
function rule: $y = -x^2$
graph:

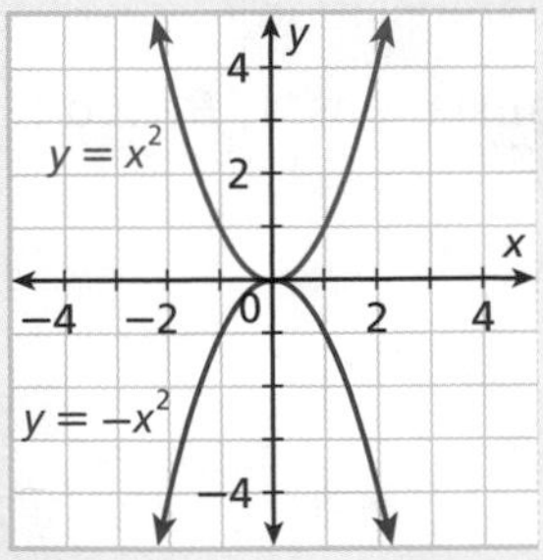

B a translation up 2 units and right 3 units
function rule: $y = (x - 3)^2 + 2$
graph:

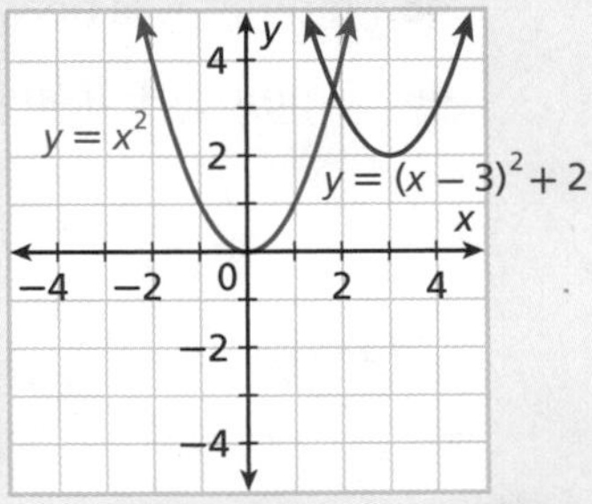

Try This

For each parent function, write a function rule for the given transformation and graph the preimage and image.

1. parent function: $y = x^2$
   transformation: a translation down 1 unit and right 4 units
2. parent function: $y = \sqrt{x}$
   transformation: a reflection across the x-axis
3. parent function: $y = |x|$
   transformation: a translation up 2 units and left 1 unit

COMMON CORE

9-3 Rotations

CC.9-12.G.CO.6 ...Transform figures and...predict the effect of a given rigid motion on a given figure...
Also CC.9-12.G.CO.5, CC.9-12.G.CO.4, CC.9-12.G.CO.2

Objective
Identify and draw rotations.

Who uses this?
Astronomers can use properties of rotations to analyze photos of star trails. (See Exercise 35.)

Remember that a rotation is a transformation that turns a figure around a fixed point, called the center of rotation. A rotation is an isometry, so the image of a rotated figure is congruent to the preimage.

EXAMPLE 1 Identifying Rotations

Tell whether each transformation appears to be a rotation. Explain.

A

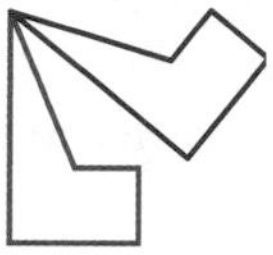

Yes; the figure appears to be turned around a point.

B

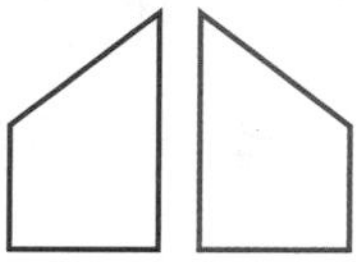

No; the figure appears to be flipped, not turned.

CHECK IT OUT! **Tell whether each transformation appears to be a rotation.**

1a.

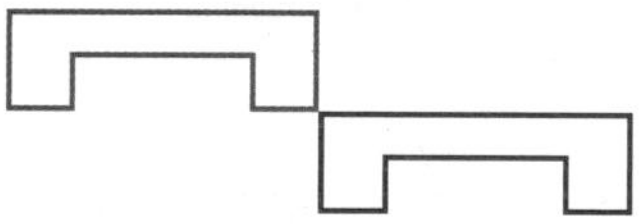

1b.

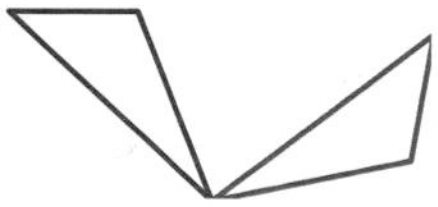

Construction Rotate a Figure Using Patty Paper

1

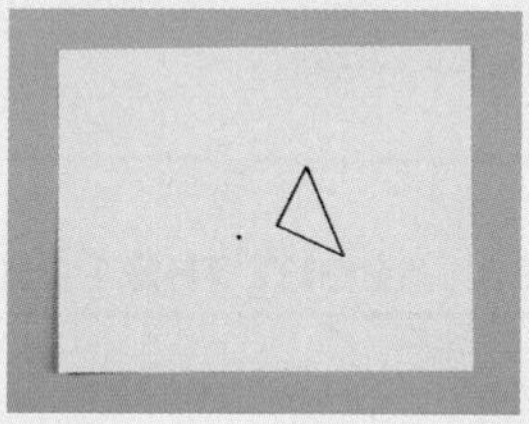

On a sheet of paper, draw a triangle and a point. The point will be the center of rotation.

2

Place a sheet of patty paper on top of the diagram. Trace the triangle and the point.

3

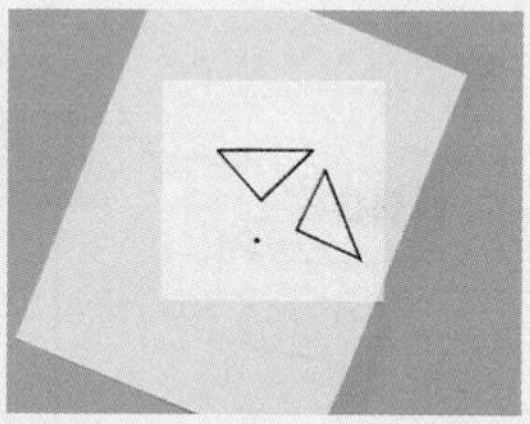

Hold your pencil down on the point and rotate the bottom paper counterclockwise. Trace the triangle.

Draw a segment from each vertex to the center of rotation. Your construction should show that a point's distance to the center of rotation is equal to its image's distance to the center of rotation. The angle formed by a point, the center of rotation, and the point's image is the angle by which the figure was rotated.

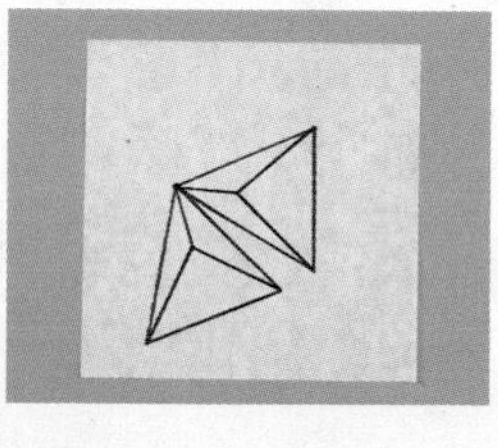

Know it! Note — Rotations

A rotation is a transformation about a point *P*, called the center of rotation, such that each point and its image are the same distance from *P*, and such that all angles with vertex *P* formed by a point and its image are congruent. In the figure, $\angle APA'$ is the angle of rotation.

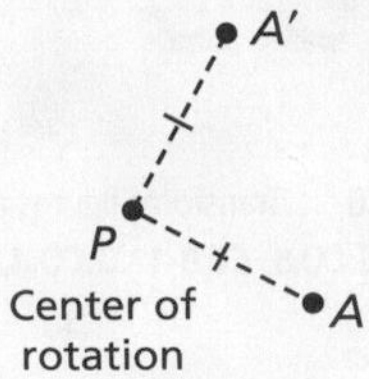

EXAMPLE 2 Drawing Rotations

Copy the figure and the angle of rotation. Draw the rotation of the triangle about point *P* by m∠*A*.

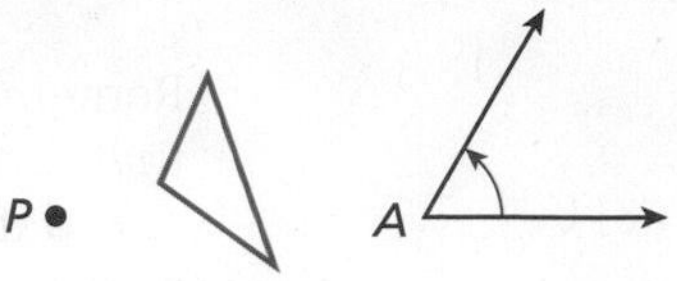

Step 1 Draw a segment from each vertex to point *P*.

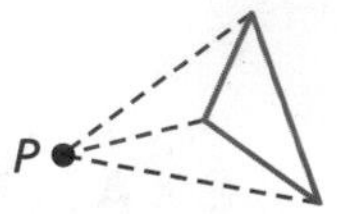

Step 2 Construct an angle congruent to ∠*A* onto each segment. Measure the distance from each vertex to point *P* and mark off this distance on the corresponding ray to locate the image of each vertex.

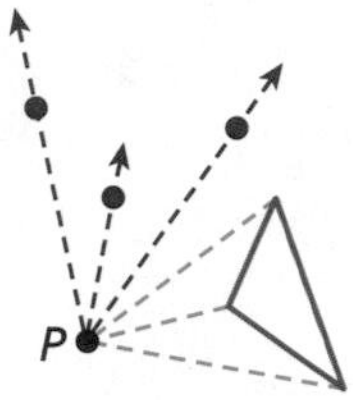

Step 3 Connect the images of the vertices.

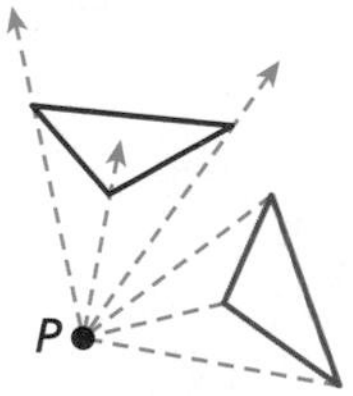

Helpful Hint

Unless otherwise stated, all rotations in this book are counterclockwise.

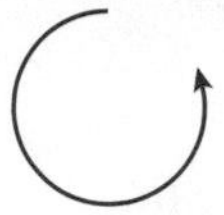

CHECK IT OUT!

2. Copy the figure and the angle of rotation. Draw the rotation of the segment about point *Q* by m∠*X*.

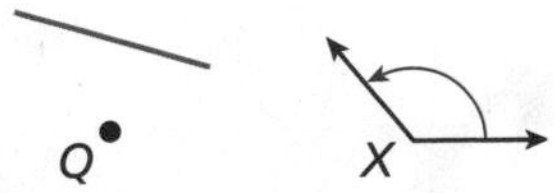

Know it! Note — Rotations in the Coordinate Plane

BY 90° ABOUT THE ORIGIN	BY 180° ABOUT THE ORIGIN
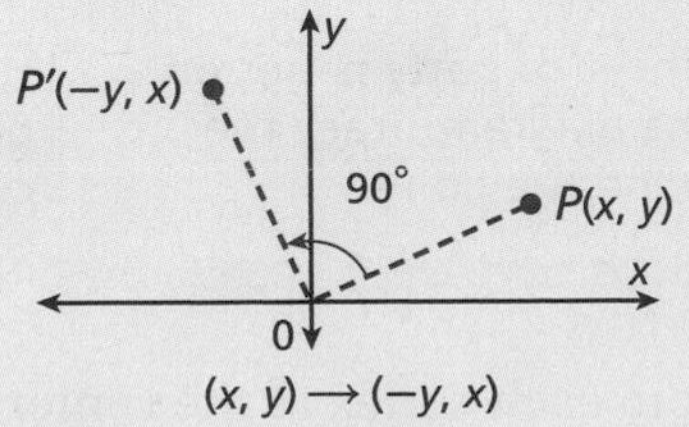	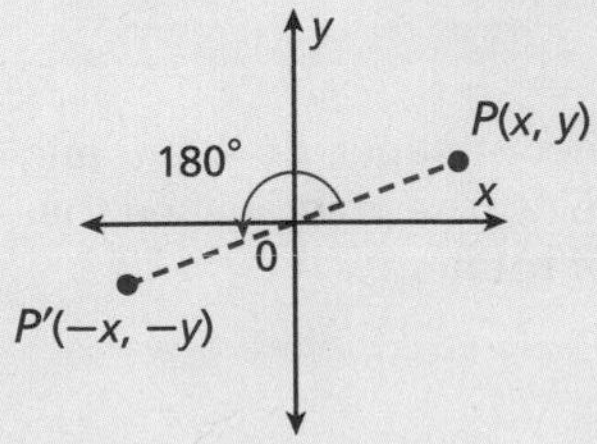
$(x, y) \rightarrow (-y, x)$	$(x, y) \rightarrow (-x, -y)$

If the angle of a rotation in the coordinate plane is not a multiple of 90°, you can use sine and cosine ratios to find the coordinates of the image.

EXAMPLE 3 Drawing Rotations in the Coordinate Plane

Rotate $\triangle ABC$ with vertices $A(2, -1)$, $B(4, 1)$, and $C(3, 3)$ by 90° about the origin.

The rotation of (x, y) is $(-y, x)$.

$A(2, -1) \rightarrow A'(1, 2)$

$B(4, 1) \rightarrow B'(-1, 4)$

$C(3, 3) \rightarrow C'(-3, 3)$

Graph the preimage and image.

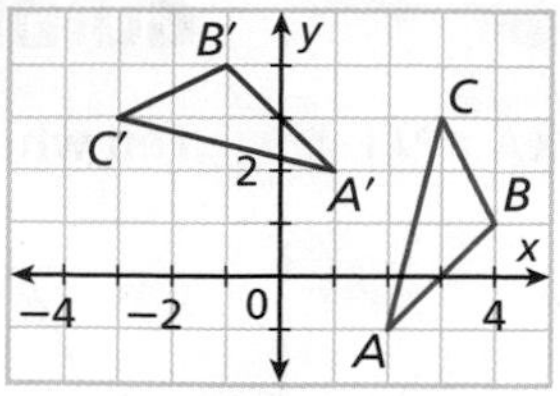

CHECK IT OUT! **3.** Rotate $\triangle ABC$ by 180° about the origin.

EXAMPLE 4 *Engineering Application*

The London Eye observation wheel has a radius of 67.5 m and takes 30 minutes to make a complete rotation. A car starts at position $(67.5, 0)$. What are the coordinates of the car's location after 5 minutes?

Step 1 Find the angle of rotation. Five minutes is $\frac{5}{30} = \frac{1}{6}$ of a complete rotation, or $\frac{1}{6}(360°) = 60°$.

Step 2 Draw a right triangle to represent the car's location (x, y) after a rotation of 60° about the origin.

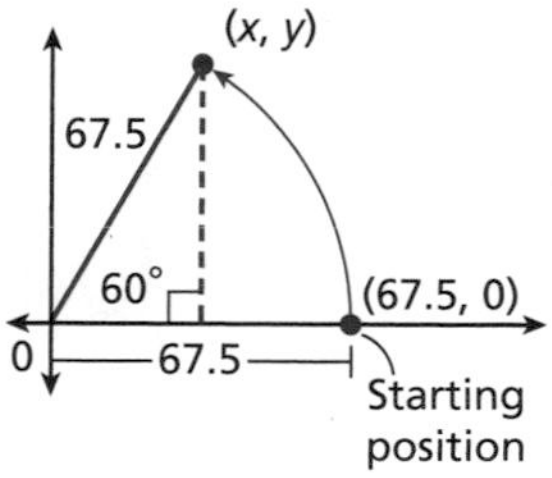

Step 3 Use the cosine ratio to find the x-coordinate.

$\cos 60° = \frac{x}{67.5}$ *$\cos = \frac{adj.}{hyp.}$*

$x = 67.5 \cos 60° \approx 33.8$ *Solve for x.*

Step 4 Use the sine ratio to find the y-coordinate.

$\sin 60° = \frac{y}{67.5}$ *$\sin = \frac{opp.}{hyp.}$*

$y = 67.5 \sin 60° \approx 58.5$ *Solve for y.*

The car's location after 5 minutes is approximately $(33.8, 58.5)$.

CHECK IT OUT! **4.** Find the coordinates of the observation car after 6 minutes. Round to the nearest tenth.

THINK AND DISCUSS

MATHEMATICAL PRACTICES

1. Describe the image of a rotation of a figure by an angle of 360°.

2. Point A' is a rotation of point A about point P. What is the relationship of $\overline{AP}$ to $\overline{A'P}$?

Know it! Note

3. GET ORGANIZED Copy and complete the graphic organizer.

	Reflection	Translation	Rotation
Definition			
Example			

9-3 Exercises

Learn It Online
Homework Help Online
Parent Resources Online

GUIDED PRACTICE

SEE EXAMPLE 1

Tell whether each transformation appears to be a rotation.

1.

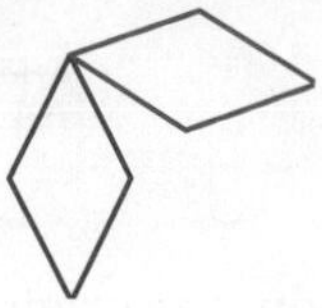

2.

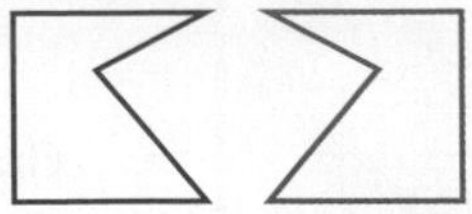

3.

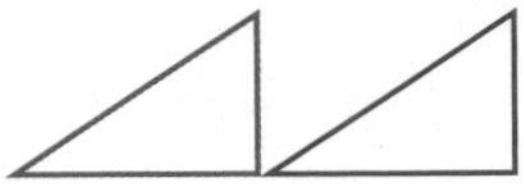

4.

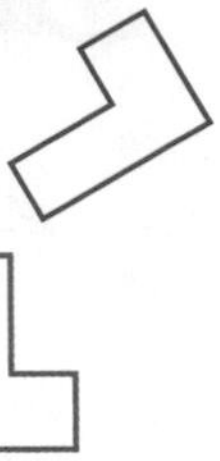

SEE EXAMPLE 2

Copy each figure and the angle of rotation. Draw the rotation of the figure about point *P* by m∠*A*.

5.

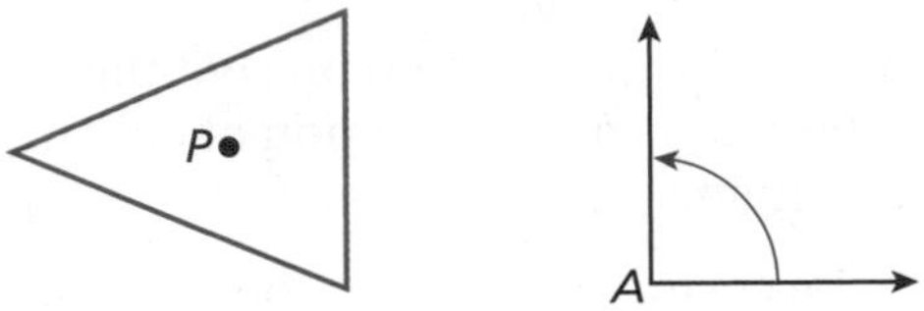

6.

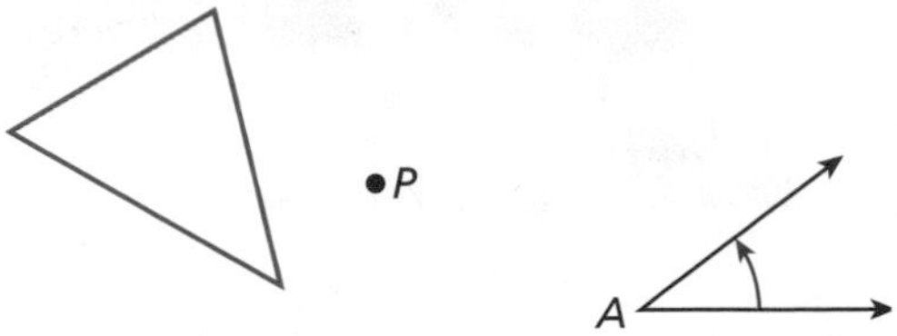

SEE EXAMPLE 3

Rotate the figure with the given vertices about the origin using the given angle of rotation.

7. $A(1, 0)$, $B(3, 2)$, $C(5, 0)$; 90°

8. $J(2, 1)$, $K(4, 3)$, $L(2, 4)$, $M(-1, 2)$; 90°

9. $D(2, 3)$, $E(-1, 2)$, $F(2, 1)$; 180°

10. $P(-1, -1)$, $Q(-4, -2)$, $R(0, -2)$; 180°

SEE EXAMPLE 4

11. Animation An artist uses a coordinate plane to plan the motion of an animated car. To simulate the car driving around a curve, the artist places the car at the point $(10, 0)$ and then rotates it about the origin by 30°. Give the car's final position, rounding the coordinates to the nearest tenth.

PRACTICE AND PROBLEM SOLVING

Independent Practice

For Exercises	See Example
12–15	1
16–17	2
18–21	3
22	4

Extra Practice

See Extra Practice for more Skills Practice and Applications Practice exercises.

Tell whether each transformation appears to be a rotation.

12.

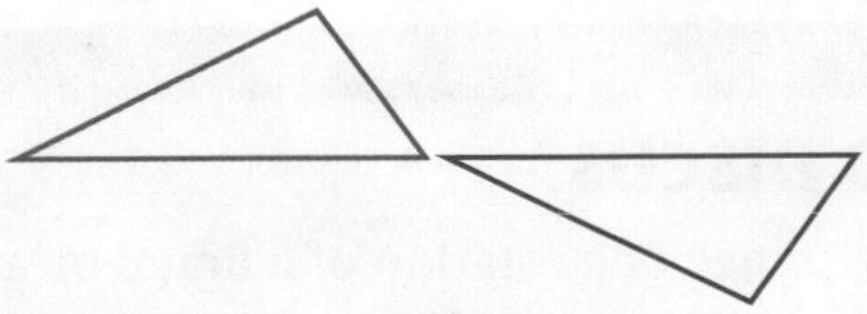

13.

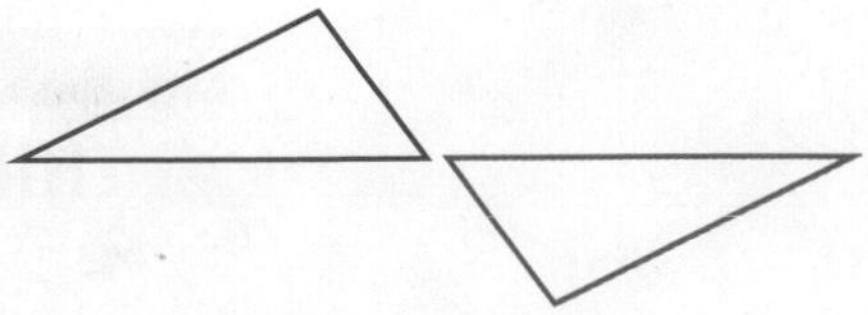

14.

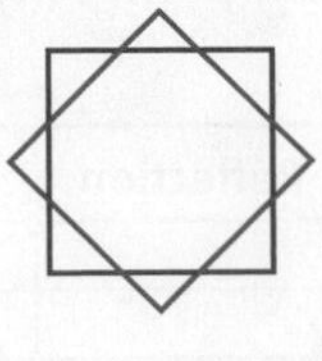

15.

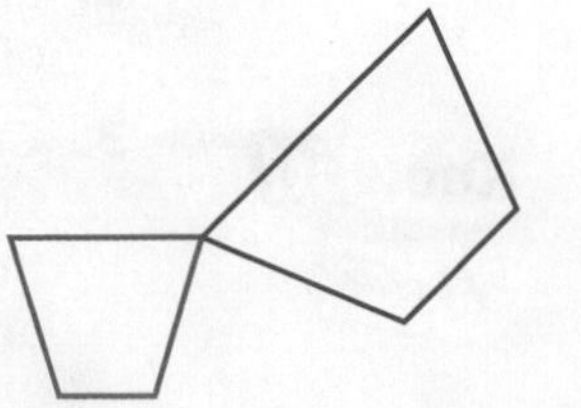

Copy each figure and the angle of rotation. Draw the rotation of the figure about point P by $m\angle A$.

16.

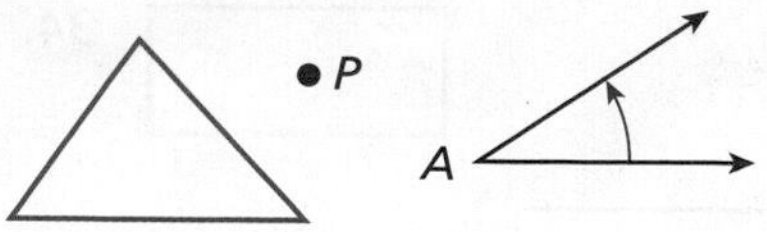

17.

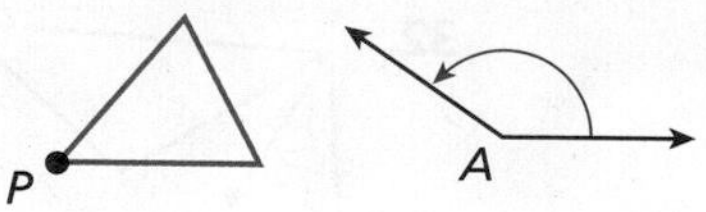

Rotate the figure with the given vertices about the origin using the given angle of rotation.

18. $E(-1, 2)$, $F(3, 1)$, $G(2, 3)$; 90°

19. $A(-1, 0)$, $B(-1, -3)$, $C(1, -3)$, $D(1, 0)$; 90°

20. $P(0, -2)$, $Q(2, 0)$, $R(3, -3)$; 180°

21. $L(2, 0)$, $M(-1, -2)$, $N(2, -2)$; 180°

22. **Architecture** The CN Tower in Toronto, Canada, features a revolving restaurant that takes 72 minutes to complete a full rotation. A table that is 50 feet from the center of the restaurant starts at position $(50, 0)$. What are the coordinates of the table after 6 minutes? Round coordinates to the nearest tenth.

Copy each figure. Then draw the rotation of the figure about the red point using the given angle measure.

23. 90°

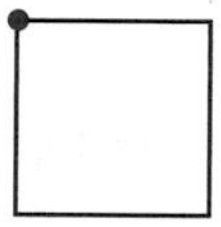

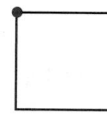

24. 180°

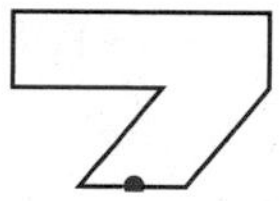

25. 180°

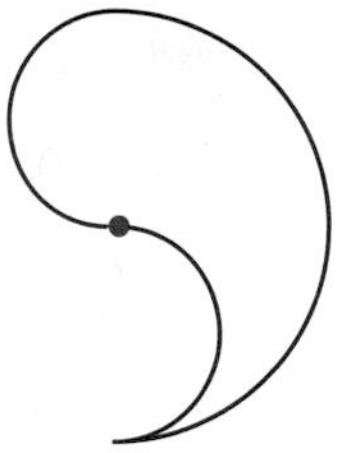

26. Point Q has coordinates $(2, 3)$. After a rotation about the origin, the image of point Q lies on the y-axis.
   a. Find the angle of rotation to the nearest degree.
   b. Find the coordinates of the image of point Q. Round to the nearest tenth.

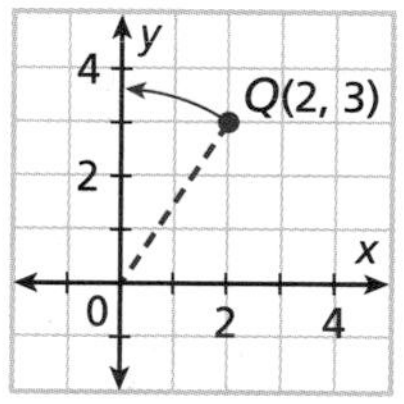

Rectangle $RSTU$ is the image of rectangle $LMNP$ under a 180° rotation about point A. Name each of the following.

27. the image of point N

28. the preimage of point S

29. the image of $\overline{MN}$

30. the preimage of $\overline{TU}$

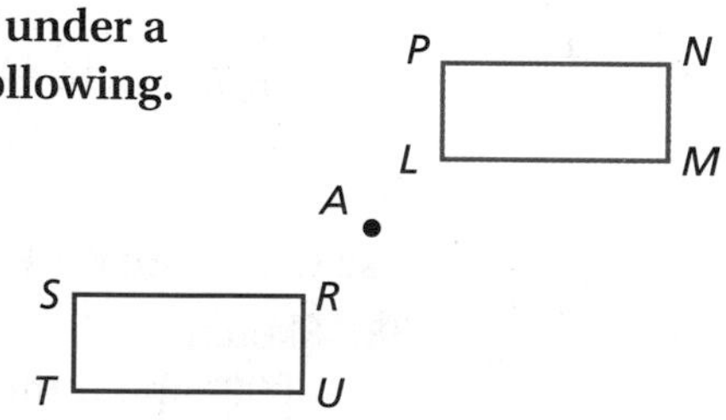

MULTI-STEP TEST PREP

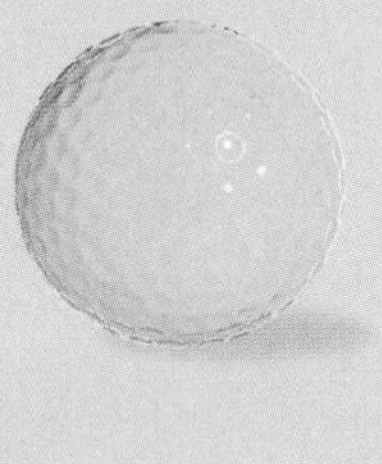

31. A miniature golf course includes a hole with a windmill. Players must hit the ball through the opening at the base of the windmill while the blades rotate.
   a. The blades take 20 seconds to make a complete rotation. Through what angle do the blades rotate in 4 seconds?
   b. Find the coordinates of point A after 4 seconds. (*Hint:* $(4, 3)$ is the center of rotation.)

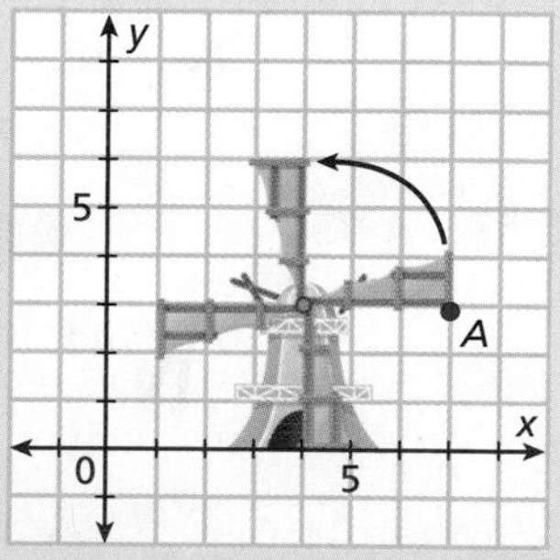

Each figure shows a preimage and its image under a rotation. Copy the figure and locate the center of rotation.

32.

33.

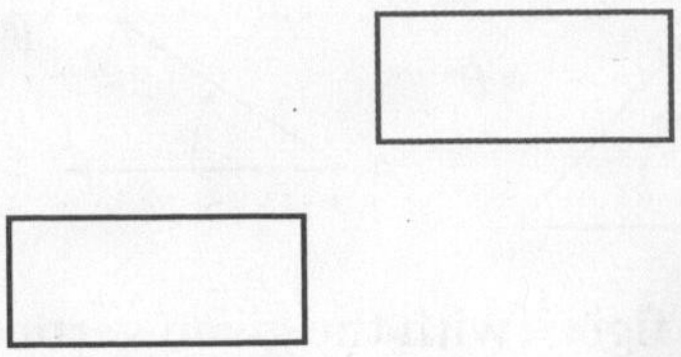

34.

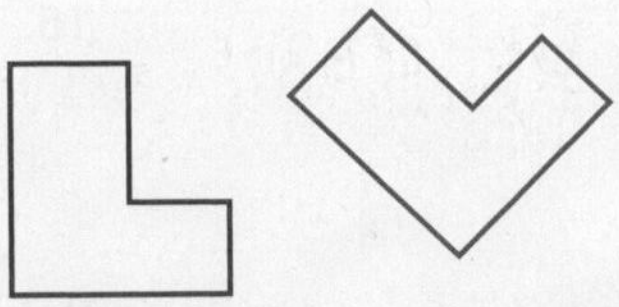

35. Astronomy The photograph was made by placing a camera on a tripod and keeping the camera's shutter open for a long time. Because of Earth's rotation, the stars appear to rotate around Polaris, also known as the North Star.

a. **Estimation** Estimate the angle of rotation of the stars in the photo.

b. **Estimation** Use your result from part **a** to estimate the length of time that the camera's shutter was open. (*Hint:* If the shutter was open for 24 hours, the stars would appear to make one complete rotation around Polaris.)

36. Estimation In the diagram, $\triangle ABC \rightarrow \triangle A'B'C'$ under a rotation about point P.

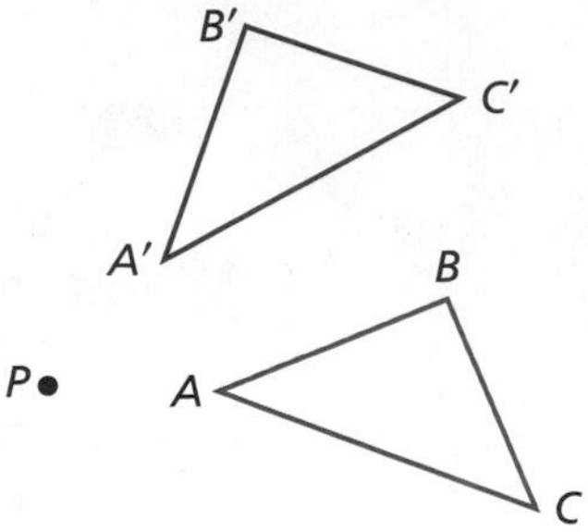

a. Estimate the angle of rotation.

b. Explain how you can draw two segments and can then use a protractor to measure the angle of rotation.

c. Copy the figure. Use the method from part **b** to find the angle of rotation. How does your result compare to your estimate?

37. Critical Thinking A student wrote the following in his math journal. "Under a rotation, every point moves around the center of rotation by the same angle measure. This means that every point moves the same distance." Do you agree? Explain.

Use the figure for Exercises 38–40.

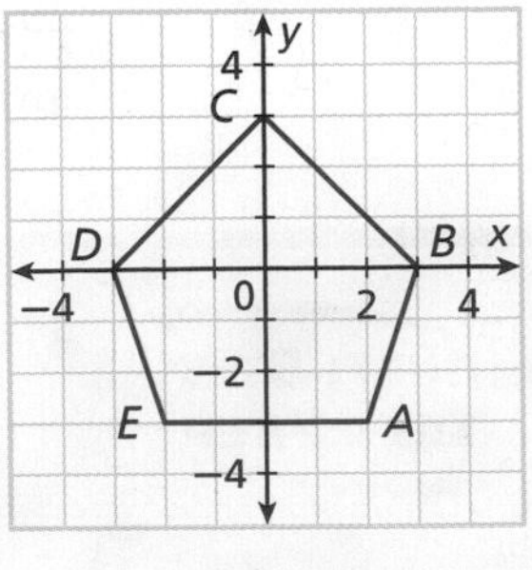

38. Sketch the image of pentagon *ABCDE* under a rotation of 90° about the origin. Give the vertices of the image.

39. Sketch the image of pentagon *ABCDE* under a rotation of 180° about the origin. Give the vertices of the image.

40. Write About It Is the image of *ABCDE* under a rotation of 180° about the origin the same as its image under a reflection across the *x*-axis? Explain your reasoning.

41. Construction Copy the figure. Use the construction of an angle congruent to a given angle to construct the image of point X under a rotation about point P by $m\angle A$.

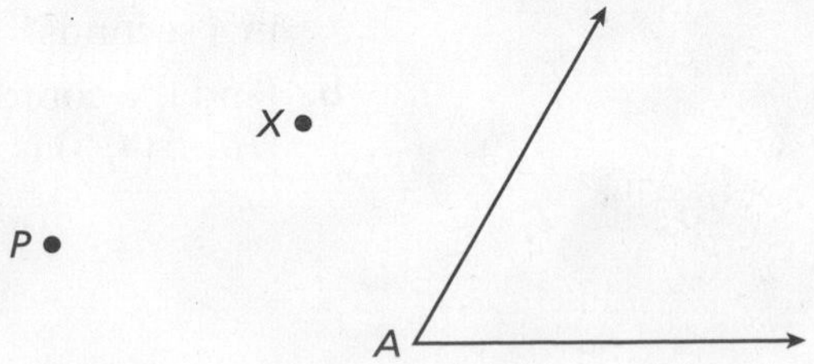

TEST PREP

42. What is the image of the point $(-2, 5)$ when it is rotated about the origin by 90°?
   Ⓐ $(-5, 2)$ Ⓑ $(5, -2)$ Ⓒ $(-5, -2)$ Ⓓ $(2, -5)$

43. The six cars of a Ferris wheel are located at the vertices of a regular hexagon. Which rotation about point *P* maps car *A* to car *C*?
   Ⓕ 60° Ⓖ 90° Ⓗ 120° Ⓙ 135°

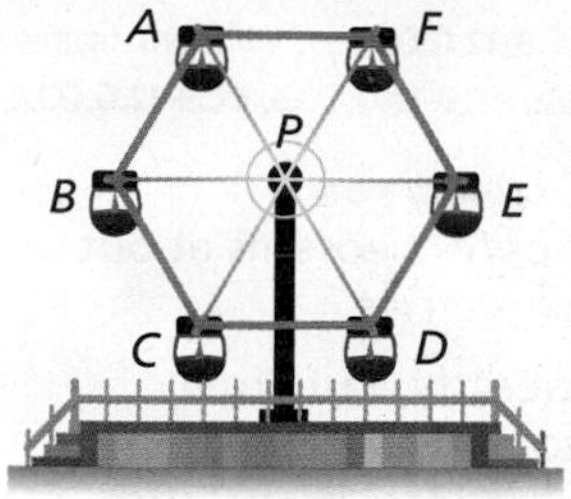

44. **Gridded Response** Under a rotation about the origin, the point $(-3, 4)$ is mapped to the point $(3, -4)$. What is the measure of the angle of rotation?

CHALLENGE AND EXTEND

45. **Engineering** Gears are used to change the speed and direction of rotating parts in pieces of machinery. In the diagram, suppose gear B makes one complete rotation in the counterclockwise direction. Give the angle of rotation and direction for the rotation of gear A. Explain how you got your answer.

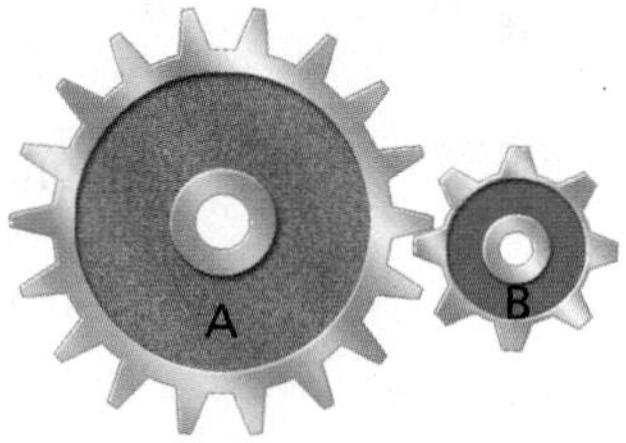

46. **Given:** $\overline{A'B'}$ is the rotation image of $\overline{AB}$ about point *P*.
   Prove: $\overline{AB} \cong \overline{A'B'}$
   (*Hint:* Draw auxiliary lines $\overline{AP}$, $\overline{BP}$, $\overline{A'P}$, and $\overline{B'P}$ and show that $\triangle APB \cong \triangle A'PB'$.)

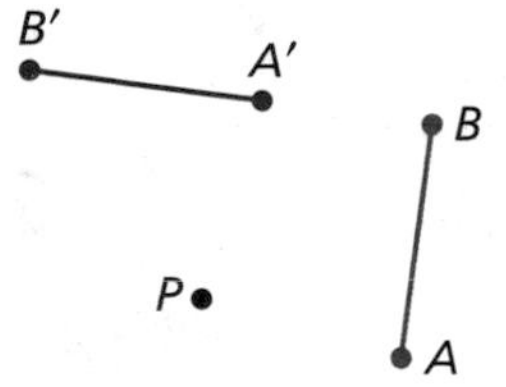

Once you have proved that the rotation image of a segment is congruent to the preimage, how could you prove the following? Write a plan for each proof.

47. If $\overline{A'B'}$ is a rotation of $\overline{AB}$, then $AB = A'B'$.

48. If $\angle A'B'C'$ is a rotation of $\angle ABC$, then $m\angle ABC = m\angle A'B'C'$.

49. The rotation $\triangle A'B'C'$ is congruent to the preimage $\triangle ABC$.

50. If point *C* is between points *A* and *B*, then the rotation *C′* is between *A′* and *B′*.

51. If points *A*, *B*, and *C* are collinear, then the rotations *A′*, *B′*, and *C′* are collinear.

COMMON CORE

9-4 Compositions of Transformations

CC.9-12.G.CO.6 ...Transform figures and...predict the effect of a given rigid motion on a given figure...
Also CC.9-12.G.CO.5, CC.9-12.G.CO.4, CC.9-12.G.CO.2

Objectives
Apply theorems about isometries.

Identify and draw compositions of transformations, such as glide reflections.

Vocabulary
composition of transformations
glide reflection

Why learn this?
Compositions of transformations can be used to describe chess moves. (See Exercise 11.)

A **composition of transformations** is one transformation followed by another. For example, a **glide reflection** is the composition of a translation and a reflection across a line parallel to the translation vector.

The glide reflection that maps $\triangle JKL$ to $\triangle J'K'L'$ is the composition of a translation along $\vec{v}$ followed by a reflection across line ℓ.

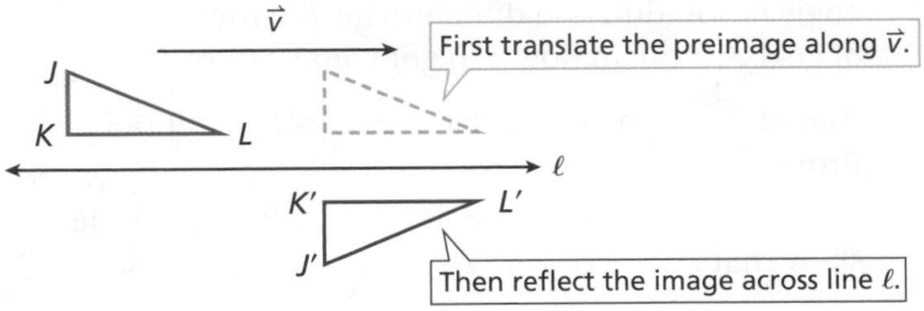

The image after each transformation is congruent to the previous image. By the Transitive Property of Congruence, the final image is congruent to the preimage. This leads to the following theorem.

Know it! Note

Theorem 9-4-1

A composition of two isometries is an isometry.

EXAMPLE 1 Drawing Compositions of Isometries

Draw the result of the composition of isometries.

A **Reflect $\triangle ABC$ across line ℓ and then translate it along $\vec{v}$.**

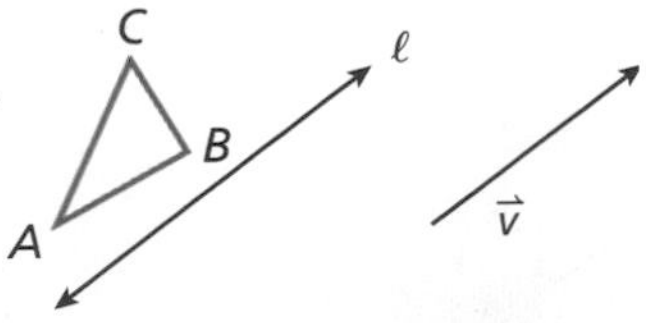

Step 1 Draw $\triangle A'B'C'$, the reflection image of $\triangle ABC$.

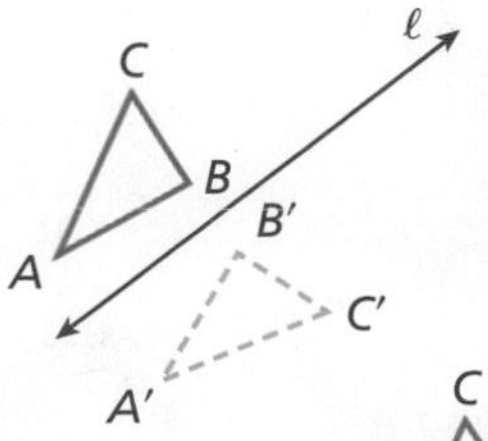

Step 2 Translate $\triangle A'B'C'$ along $\vec{v}$ to find the final image, $\triangle A''B''C''$.

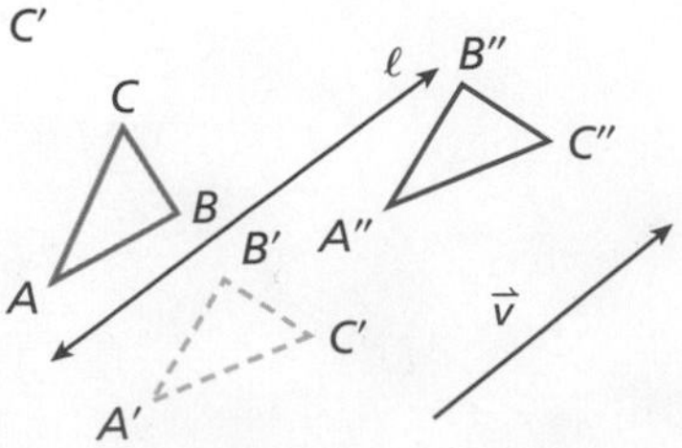

B $\triangle RST$ **has vertices** $R(1, 2)$, $S(1, 4)$, **and** $T(-3, 4)$. **Rotate** $\triangle RST$ **90° about the origin and then reflect it across the** y**-axis.**

Step 1 The rotation image of (x, y) is $(-y, x)$.
$R(1, 2) \rightarrow R'(-2, 1)$, $S(1, 4) \rightarrow S'(-4, 1)$, and $T(-3, 4) \rightarrow T'(-4, -3)$.

Step 2 The **reflection** image of (x, y) is $(-x, y)$.
$R'(-2, 1) \rightarrow R''(2, 1)$, $S'(-4, 1) \rightarrow S''(4, 1)$, and $T'(-4, -3) \rightarrow T''(4, -3)$.

Step 3 Graph the preimage and images.

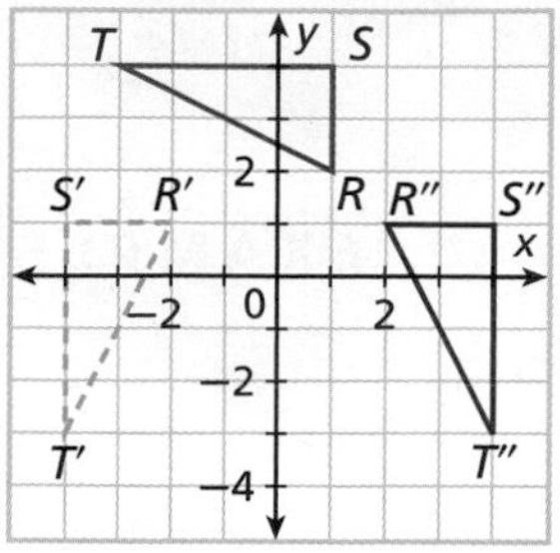

CHECK IT OUT! **1.** $\triangle JKL$ has vertices $J(1, -2)$, $K(4, -2)$, and $L(3, 0)$. Reflect $\triangle JKL$ across the x-axis and then rotate it 180° about the origin.

Know it! Note

Theorem 9-4-2

The composition of two reflections across two parallel lines is equivalent to a translation.

- The translation vector is perpendicular to the lines.
- The length of the translation vector is twice the distance between the lines.

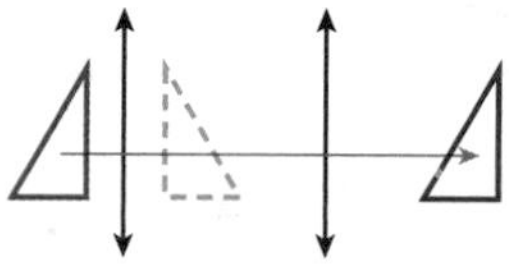

The composition of two reflections across two intersecting lines is equivalent to a rotation.

- The center of rotation is the intersection of the lines.
- The angle of rotation is twice the measure of the angle formed by the lines.

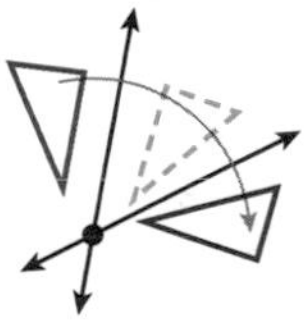

EXAMPLE 2 *Art Application*

Tabitha is creating a design for an art project. She reflects a figure across line ℓ and then reflects the image across line m. Describe a single transformation that moves the figure from its starting position to its final position.

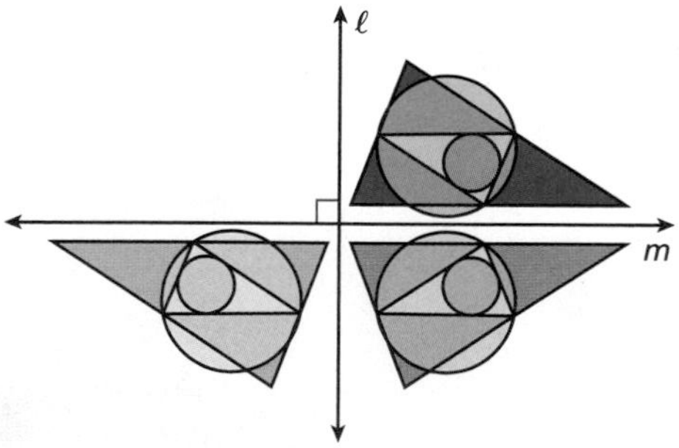

By Theorem 9-4-2, the composition of two reflections across intersecting lines is equivalent to a rotation about the point of intersection. Since the lines are perpendicular, they form a 90° angle. By Theorem 9-4-2, the angle of rotation is $2 \cdot 90° = 180°$.

CHECK IT OUT! **2. What if...?** Suppose Tabitha reflects the figure across line n and then the image across line p. Describe a single transformation that is equivalent to the two reflections.

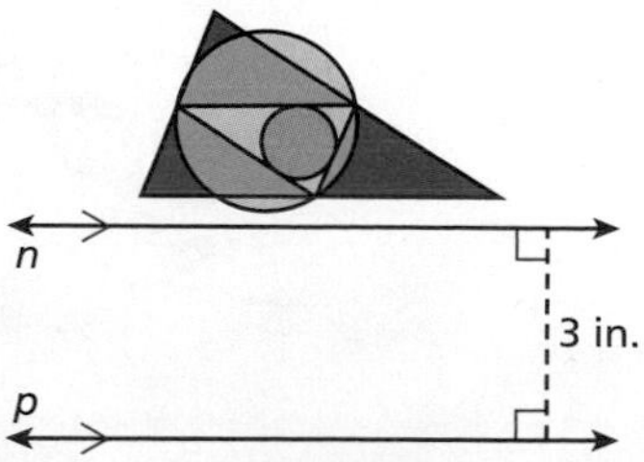

Know it! Note

Theorem 9-4-3

Any translation or rotation is equivalent to a composition of two reflections.

EXAMPLE 3 Describing Transformations in Terms of Reflections

Copy each figure and draw two lines of reflection that produce an equivalent transformation.

A translation: $\triangle ABC \rightarrow \triangle A'B'C'$

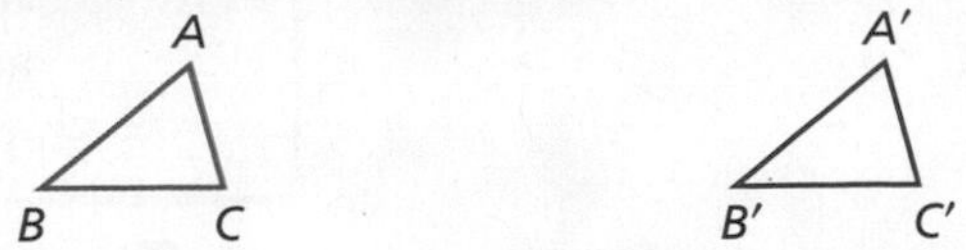

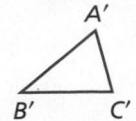

Step 1 Draw $\overline{AA'}$ and locate the midpoint M of $\overline{AA'}$.

Step 2 Draw the perpendicular bisectors of $\overline{AM}$ and $\overline{A'M}$.

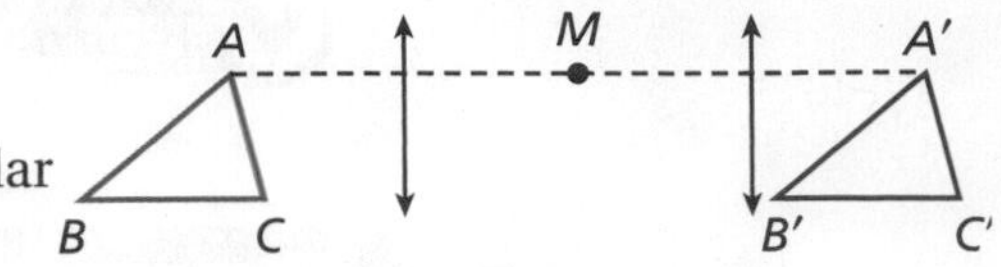

Remember!

To draw the perpendicular bisector of a segment, use a ruler to locate the midpoint, and then use a right angle to draw a perpendicular line.

B rotation with center P: $\triangle DEF \rightarrow \triangle D'E'F'$

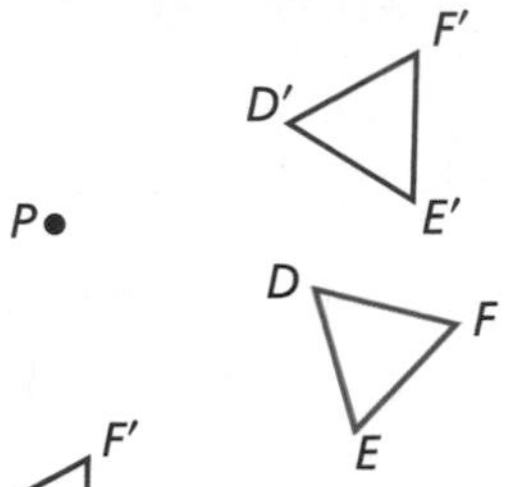

Step 1 Draw $\angle DPD'$. Draw the angle bisector $\overrightarrow{PX}$.

Step 2 Draw the bisectors of $\angle DPX$ and $\angle D'PX$.

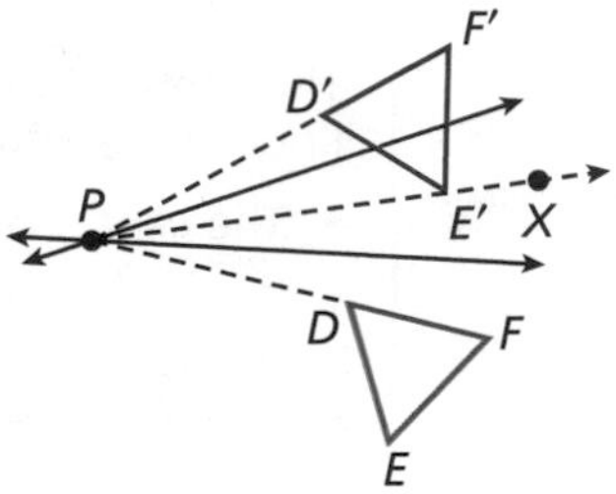

CHECK IT OUT!

3. Copy the figure showing the translation that maps $LMNP \rightarrow L'M'N'P'$. Draw the lines of reflection that produce an equivalent transformation.

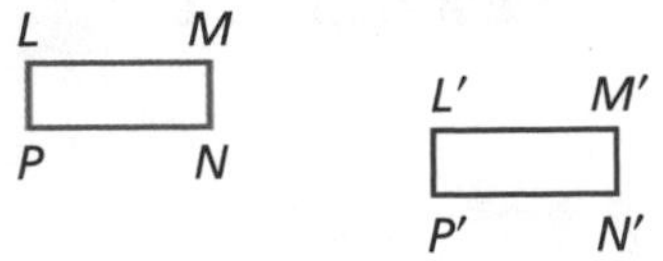

MATHEMATICAL PRACTICES

THINK AND DISCUSS

1. Which theorem explains why the image of a rectangle that is translated and then rotated is congruent to the preimage?
2. Point A' is a glide reflection of point A along $\vec{v}$ and across line ℓ. What is the relationship between $\vec{v}$ and ℓ? Explain the steps you would use to draw a glide reflection.
3. **GET ORGANIZED** Copy and complete the graphic organizer. In each box, describe an equivalent transformation and sketch an example.

Know it! Note

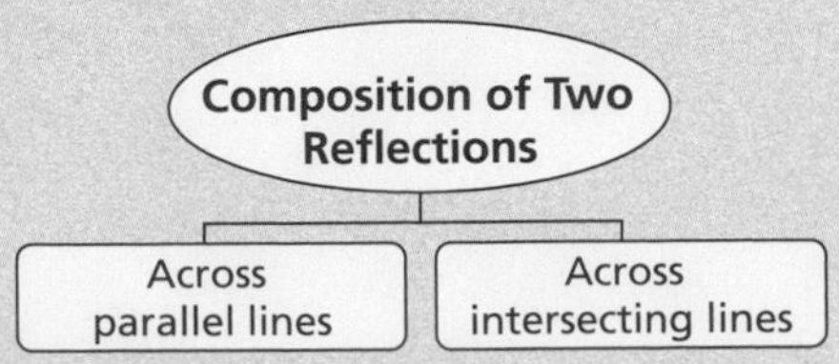

9-4 Exercises

Learn It Online
Homework Help Online
Parent Resources Online

GUIDED PRACTICE

1. **Vocabulary** Explain the steps you would use to draw a *glide reflection.*

SEE EXAMPLE 1

Draw the result of each composition of isometries.

2. Translate $\triangle DEF$ along $\vec{u}$ and then reflect it across line ℓ.

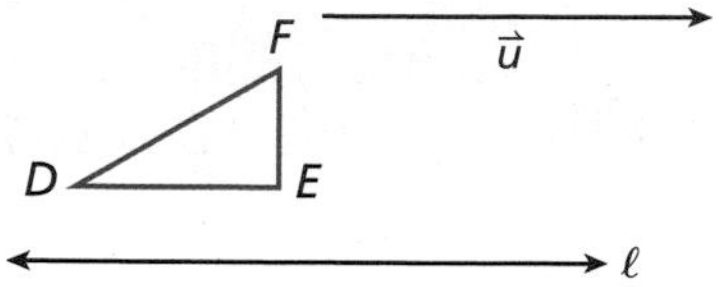

3. Reflect rectangle *PQRS* across line *m* and then translate it along $\vec{v}$.

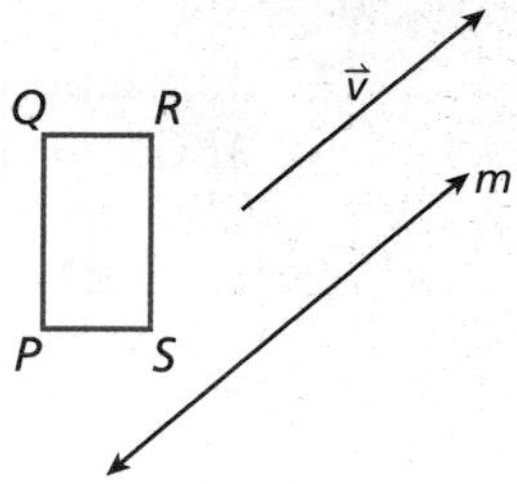

4. $\triangle ABC$ has vertices $A(1, -1)$, $B(4, -1)$, and $C(3, 2)$. Reflect $\triangle ABC$ across the *y*-axis and then translate it along the vector $\langle 0, -2 \rangle$.

SEE EXAMPLE 2

5. **Sports** To create the opening graphics for a televised football game, an animator reflects a picture of a football helmet across line ℓ. She then reflects its image across line *m*, which intersects line ℓ at a 50° angle. Describe a single transformation that moves the helmet from its starting position to its final position.

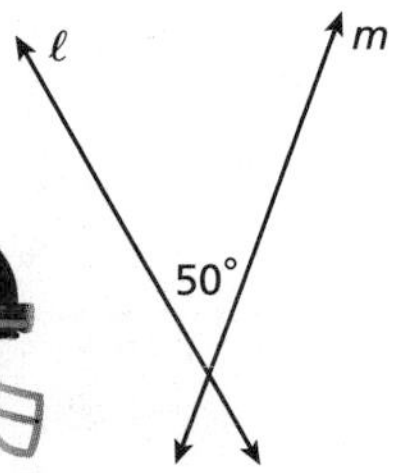

SEE EXAMPLE 3

Copy each figure and draw two lines of reflection that produce an equivalent transformation.

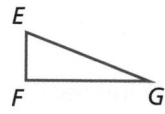

6. translation: $\triangle EFG \rightarrow \triangle E'F'G'$

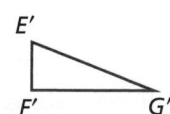

7. rotation with center *P*: $\triangle ABC \rightarrow \triangle A'B'C'$

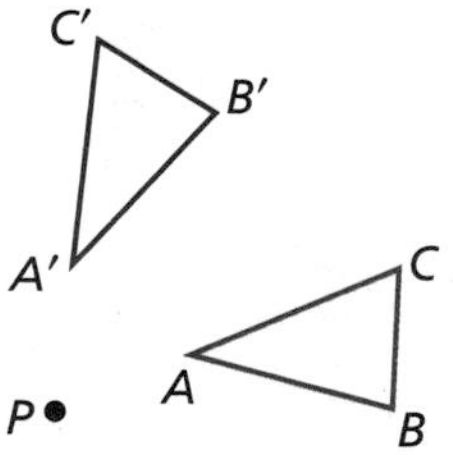

PRACTICE AND PROBLEM SOLVING

Independent Practice

For Exercises	See Example
8–10	1
11	2
12–13	3

Extra Practice

See Extra Practice for more Skills Practice and Applications Practice exercises.

Draw the result of each composition of isometries.

8. Translate $\triangle RST$ along $\vec{u}$ and then translate it along $\vec{v}$.

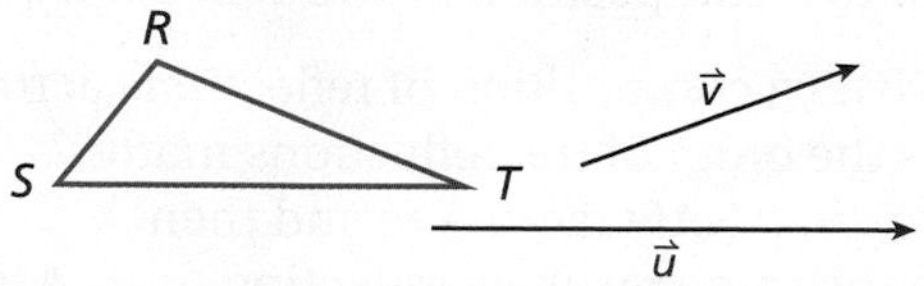

9. Rotate $\triangle ABC$ 90° about point *P* and then reflect it across line ℓ.

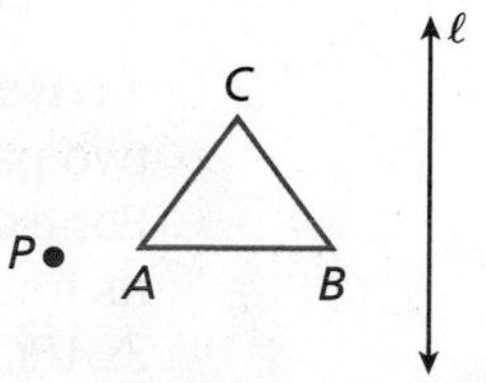

10. $\triangle GHJ$ has vertices $G(1, -1)$, $H(3, 1)$, and $J(3, -2)$. Reflect $\triangle GHJ$ across the line $y = x$ and then reflect it across the *x*-axis.

11. Games In chess, a knight moves in the shape of the letter L. The piece moves two spaces horizontally or vertically. Then it turns 90° in either direction and moves one more space.

a. Describe a knight's move as a composition of transformations.

b. Copy the chessboard with the knight. Label all the positions the knight can reach in one move.

c. Label all the positions the knight can reach in two moves.

Copy each figure and draw two lines of reflection that produce an equivalent transformation.

12. translation: $ABCD \to A'B'C'D'$

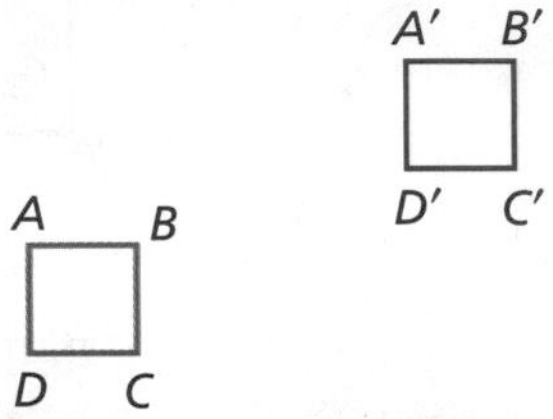

13. rotation with center Q: $\triangle JKL \to \triangle J'K'L'$

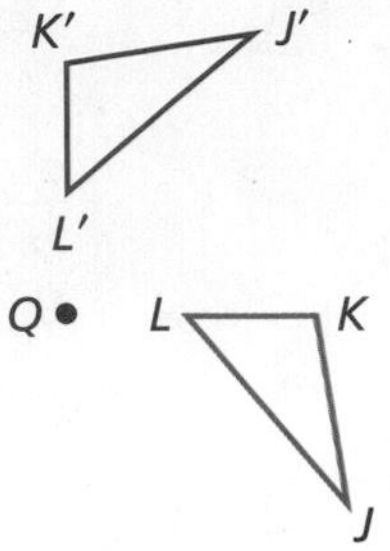

14. **///ERROR ANALYSIS///** The segment with endpoints $A(4, 2)$ and $B(2, 1)$ is reflected across the y-axis. The image is reflected across the x-axis. What transformation is equivalent to the composition of these two reflections? Which solution is incorrect? Explain the error.

A

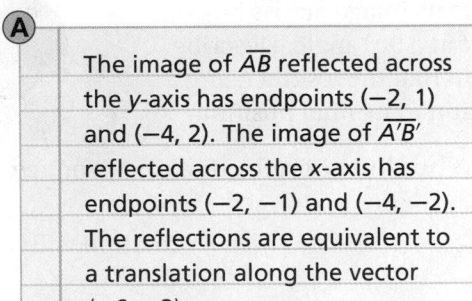

The image of $\overline{AB}$ reflected across the y-axis has endpoints $(-2, 1)$ and $(-4, 2)$. The image of $\overline{A'B'}$ reflected across the x-axis has endpoints $(-2, -1)$ and $(-4, -2)$. The reflections are equivalent to a translation along the vector $\langle -6, -3 \rangle$.

B

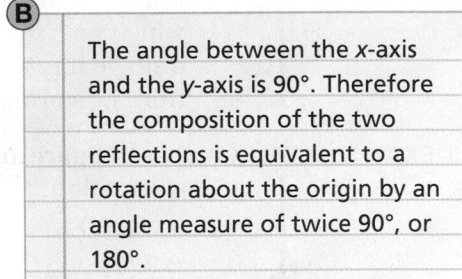

The angle between the x-axis and the y-axis is 90°. Therefore the composition of the two reflections is equivalent to a rotation about the origin by an angle measure of twice 90°, or 180°.

15. Equilateral $\triangle ABC$ is reflected across $\overline{AB}$. Then its image is translated along $\overrightarrow{BC}$. Copy $\triangle ABC$ and draw its final image.

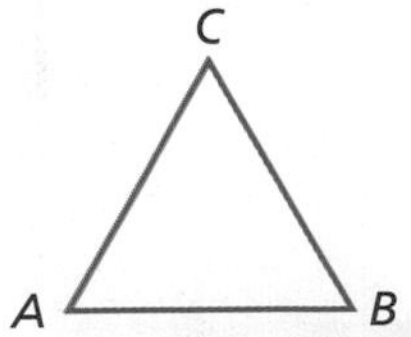

Tell whether each statement is sometimes, always, or never true.

16. The composition of two reflections is equivalent to a rotation.

17. An isometry changes the size of a figure.

18. The composition of two isometries is an isometry.

19. A rotation is equivalent to a composition of two reflections.

20. **Critical Thinking** Given a composition of reflections across two parallel lines, does the order of the reflections matter? For example, does reflecting $\triangle ABC$ across m and then its image across n give the same result as reflecting $\triangle ABC$ across n and then its image across m? Explain.

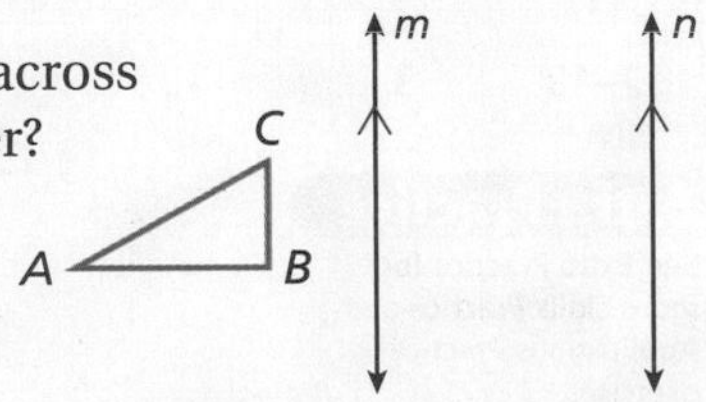

21. **Write About It** Under a glide reflection, $\triangle RST \to \triangle R'S'T'$. The vertices of $\triangle RST$ are $R(-3, -2)$, $S(-1, -2)$, and $T(-1, 0)$. The vertices of $\triangle R'S'T'$ are $R'(2, 2)$, $S'(4, 2)$, and $T'(4, 0)$. Describe the reflection and translation that make up the glide reflection.

MULTI-STEP TEST PREP

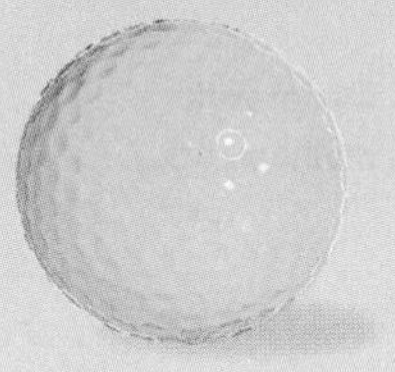

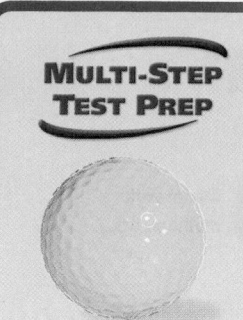

22. The figure shows one hole of a miniature golf course where T is the tee and H is the hole.

a. Yuriko makes a hole in one as shown by the red arrows. Write the ball's path as a composition of translations.

b. Find a different way to make a hole in one, and write the ball's path as a composition of translations.

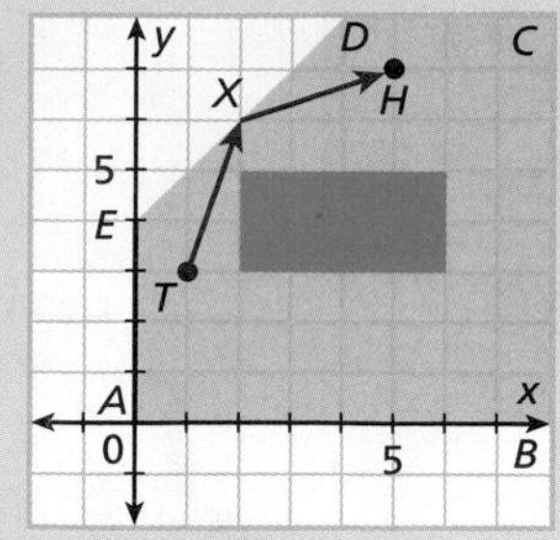

TEST PREP

23. $\triangle ABC$ is reflected across the y-axis. Then its image is rotated 90° about the origin. What are the coordinates of the final image of point A under this composition of transformations?

Ⓐ $(-1, -2)$ Ⓑ $(-2, 1)$ Ⓒ $(1, 2)$ Ⓓ $(-2, -1)$

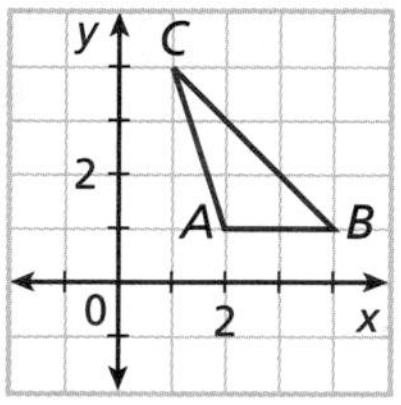

24. Which composition of transformations maps $\triangle ABC$ into the fourth quadrant?

Ⓕ Reflect across the x-axis and then reflect across the y-axis.

Ⓖ Rotate about the origin by 180° and then reflect across the y-axis.

Ⓗ Translate along the vector $\langle -5, 0 \rangle$ and then rotate about the origin by 90°.

Ⓙ Rotate about the origin by 90° and then translate along the vector $\langle 1, -2 \rangle$.

25. Which is equivalent to the composition of two translations?

Ⓐ Reflection Ⓑ Rotation Ⓒ Translation Ⓓ Glide reflection

CHALLENGE AND EXTEND

26. The point $A(3, 1)$ is rotated 90° about the point $P(-1, 2)$ and then reflected across the line $y = 5$. Find the coordinates of the image A'.

27. For any two congruent figures in a plane, one can be transformed to the other by a composition of no more than three reflections. Copy the figure. Show how to find a composition of three reflections that maps $\triangle MNP$ to $\triangle M'N'P'$.

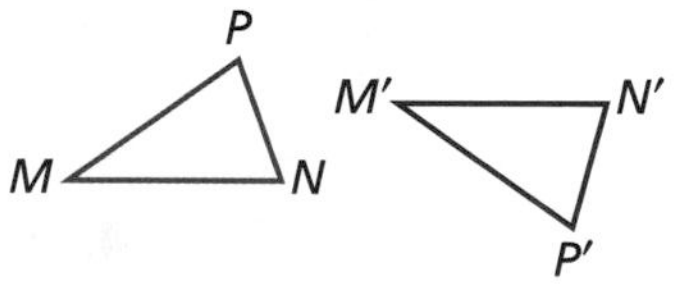

28. A figure in the coordinate plane is reflected across the line $y = x + 1$ and then across the line $y = x + 3$. Find a translation vector that is equivalent to the composition of the reflections. Write the vector in component form.

CHAPTER 9

MULTI-STEP TEST PREP

SECTION 9A

MATHEMATICAL PRACTICES **Model with mathematics.**

Congruence Transformations

A Hole in One The figure shows a plan for one hole of a miniature golf course. The tee is at point *T* and the hole is at point *H*. Each unit of the coordinate plane represents one meter.

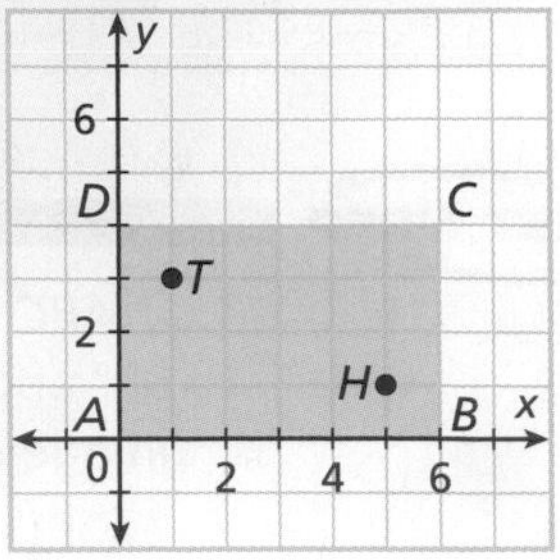

1. When a player hits the ball in a straight line from *T* to *H*, the path of the ball can be represented by a translation. What is the translation vector? How far does the ball travel? Round to the nearest tenth.

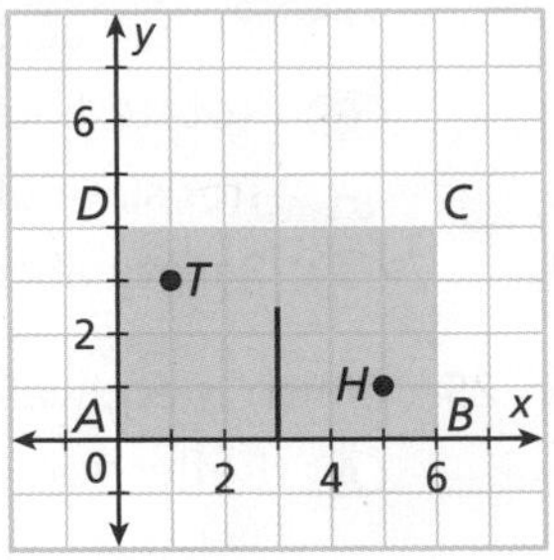

2. The designer of the golf course decides to make the hole more difficult by placing a barrier between the tee and the hole, as shown. To make a hole in one, a player must hit the ball so that it bounces off wall $\overline{DC}$. What point along the wall should a player aim for? Explain.

3. Write the path of the ball in Problem 2 as a composition of two translations. What is the total distance that the ball travels in this case? Round to the nearest tenth.

4. The designer decides to remove the barrier and put a revolving obstacle between the tee and the hole. The obstacle consists of a turntable with four equally spaced pillars, as shown. The designer wants the turntable to make one complete rotation in 16 seconds. What should be the coordinates of the pillar at (4, 2) after 2 seconds?

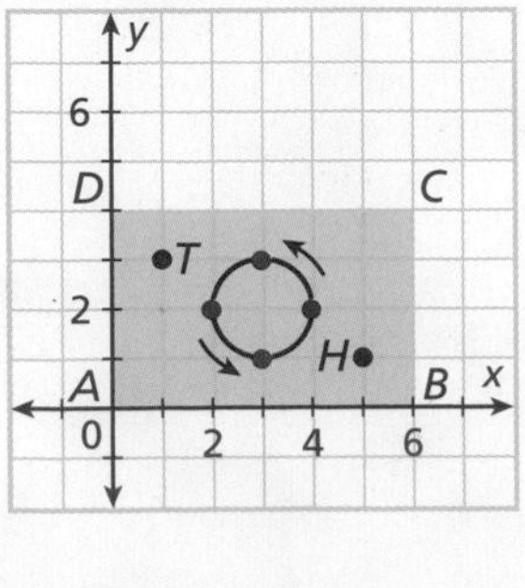

READY TO GO ON?

Quiz for Lessons 9-1 Through 9-4

9-1 Reflections

Tell whether each transformation appears to be a reflection.

1. 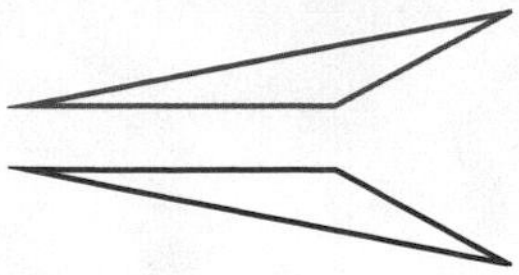

2. 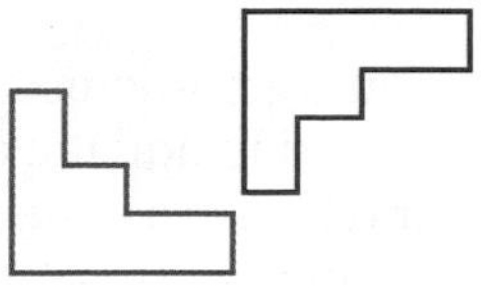

Copy each figure and the line of reflection. Draw the reflection of the figure across the line.

3. 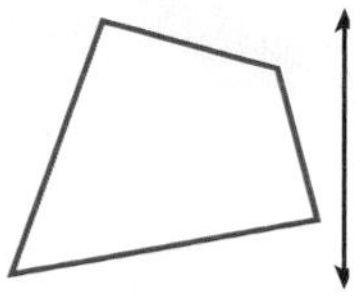

4. 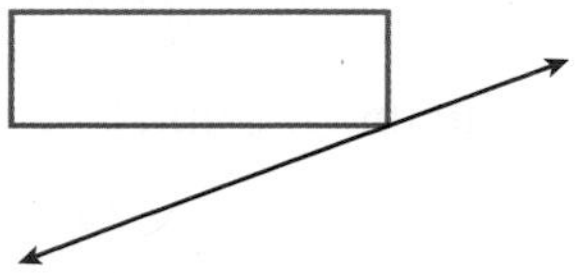

9-2 Translations

Tell whether each transformation appears to be a translation.

5. 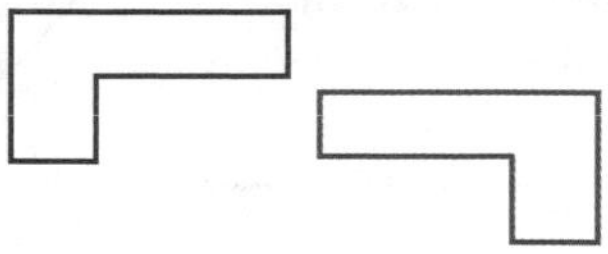

6. 

7. A landscape architect represents a flower bed by a polygon with vertices $(1, 0)$, $(4, 0)$, $(4, 2)$, and $(1, 2)$. She decides to move the flower bed to a new location by translating it along the vector $\langle -4, -3 \rangle$. Draw the flower bed in its final position.

9-3 Rotations

Tell whether each transformation appears to be a rotation.

8. 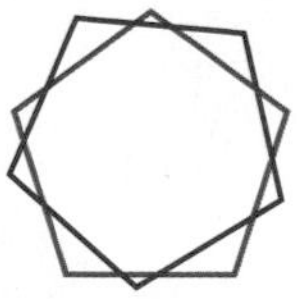

9. 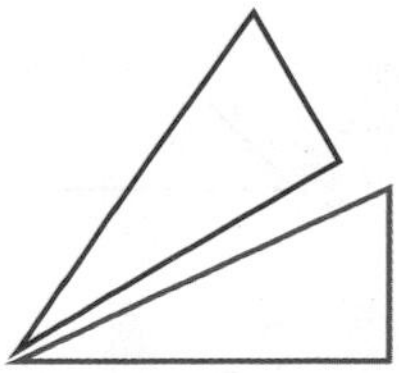

Rotate the figure with the given vertices about the origin using the given angle of rotation.

10. $A(1, 0)$, $B(4, 1)$, $C(3, 2)$; 180°

11. $R(-2, 0)$, $S(-2, 4)$, $T(-3, 4)$, $U(-3, 0)$; 90°

9-4 Compositions of Transformations

12. Draw the result of the following composition of transformations. Translate *GHJK* along $\vec{v}$ and then reflect it across line *m*.

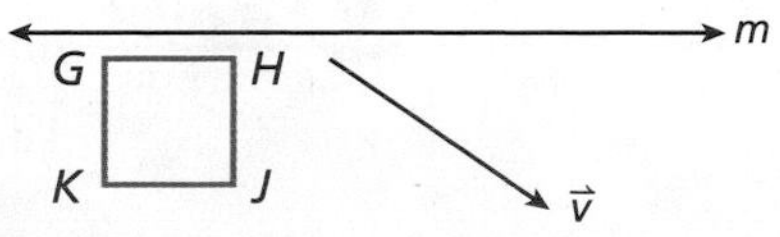

13. $\triangle ABC$ with vertices $A(1, 0)$, $B(1, 3)$, and $C(2, 3)$ is reflected across the *y*-axis, and then its image is reflected across the *x*-axis. Describe a single transformation that moves the triangle from its starting position to its final position.

COMMON CORE

9-5 Symmetry

CC.9-12.G.CO.3 Given a…polygon, describe the rotations and reflections that carry it onto itself.
Also **CC.9-12.G.CO.5, CC.9-12.G.CO.2**

Objective
Identify and describe symmetry in geometric figures.

Vocabulary
symmetry
line symmetry
line of symmetry
rotational symmetry

Who uses this?
Marine biologists use symmetry to classify diatoms.

Diatoms are microscopic algae that are found in aquatic environments. Scientists use a system that was developed in the 1970s to classify diatoms based on their *symmetry*.

A figure has **symmetry** if there is a transformation of the figure such that the image coincides with the preimage.

Know it! Note

Line Symmetry

A figure has **line symmetry** (or reflection symmetry) if it can be reflected across a line so that the image coincides with the preimage. The **line of symmetry** (also called the axis of symmetry) divides the figure into two congruent halves.

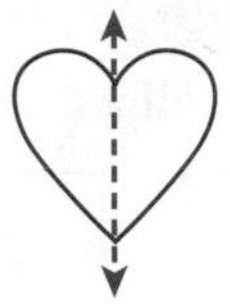

EXAMPLE 1 Identifying Line Symmetry

Tell whether each figure has line symmetry. If so, copy the shape and draw all lines of symmetry.

A 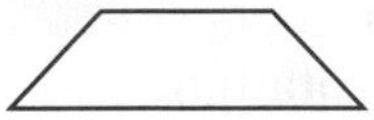 yes; one line of symmetry 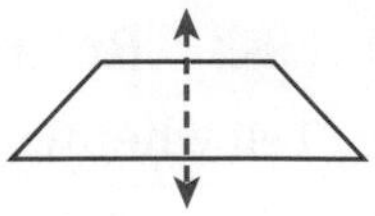

B 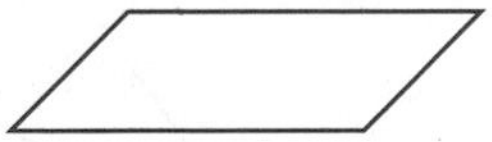 no line symmetry

C  yes; five lines of symmetry 

CHECK IT OUT! **Tell whether each figure has line symmetry. If so, copy the shape and draw all lines of symmetry.**

1a. 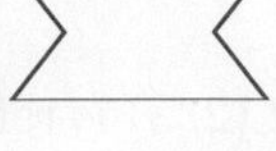 **1b.**  **1c.** 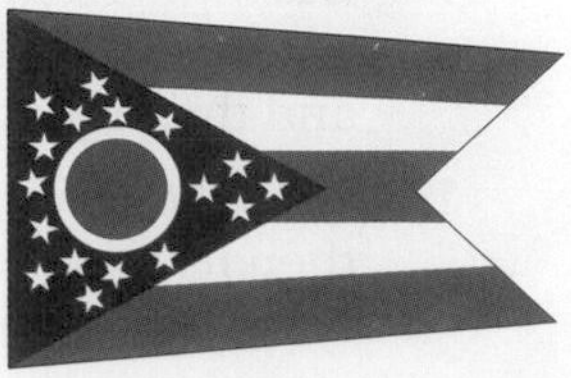

Rotational Symmetry

A figure has **rotational symmetry** (or *radial symmetry*) if it can be rotated about a point by an angle greater than 0° and less than 360° so that the image coincides with the preimage.

The *angle of rotational symmetry* is the smallest angle through which a figure can be rotated to coincide with itself. The number of times the figure coincides with itself as it rotates through 360° is called the *order* of the rotational symmetry.

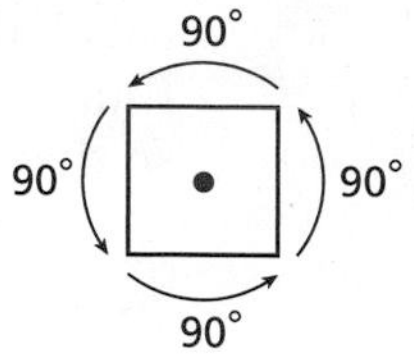

Angle of rotational symmetry: 90°
Order: 4

EXAMPLE 2 Identifying Rotational Symmetry

Tell whether each figure has rotational symmetry. If so, give the angle of rotational symmetry and the order of the symmetry.

A

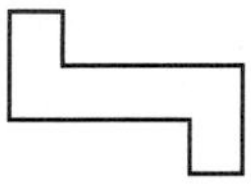

yes; 180°;
order: 2

B

no rotational symmetry

C

yes; 60°;
order: 6

CHECK IT OUT! **Tell whether each figure has rotational symmetry. If so, give the angle of rotational symmetry and the order of the symmetry.**

2a.

2b.

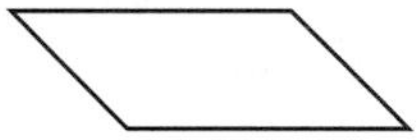

2c.

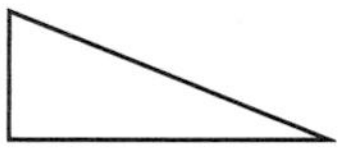

EXAMPLE 3 *Biology Application*

Describe the symmetry of each diatom. Copy the shape and draw any lines of symmetry. If there is rotational symmetry, give the angle and order.

A

line symmetry and rotational symmetry; angle of rotational symmetry: 180°; order: 2

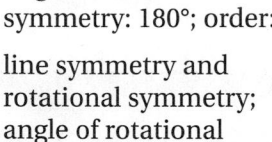

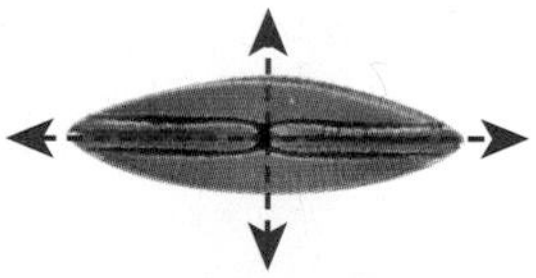

B

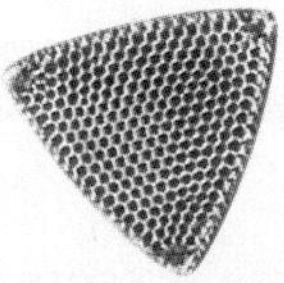

line symmetry and rotational symmetry; angle of rotational symmetry: 120°; order: 3

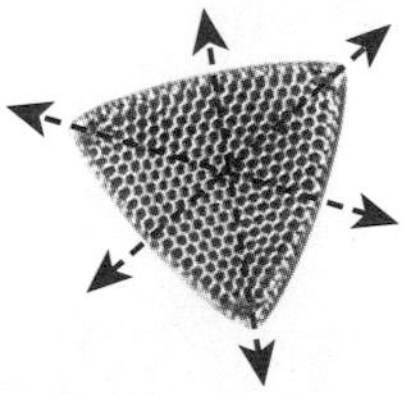

CHECK IT OUT! **Describe the symmetry of each diatom. Copy the shape and draw any lines of symmetry. If there is rotational symmetry, give the angle and order.**

3a.

3b.

A three-dimensional figure has *plane symmetry* if a plane can divide the figure into two congruent reflected halves.

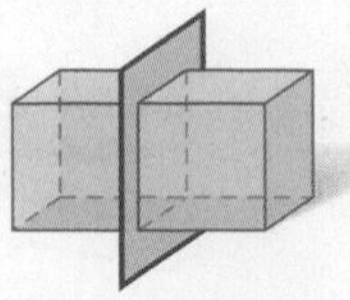

Plane symmetry

A three-dimensional figure has *symmetry about an axis* if there is a line about which the figure can be rotated (by an angle greater than 0° and less than 360°) so that the image coincides with the preimage.

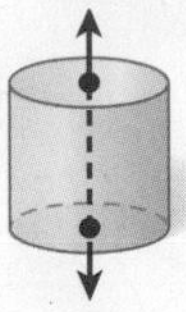

Symmetry about an axis

EXAMPLE 4 Identifying Symmetry in Three Dimensions

Tell whether each figure has plane symmetry, symmetry about an axis, or neither.

A **trapezoidal prism**

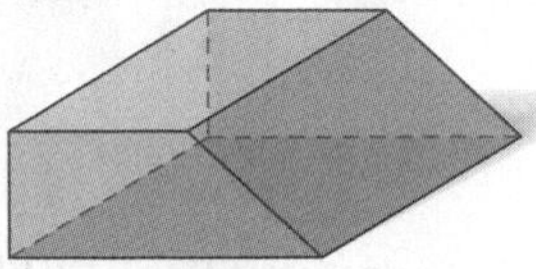

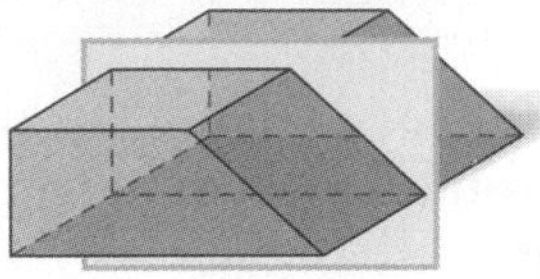

plane symmetry

B **equilateral triangular prism**

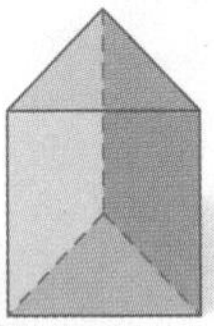

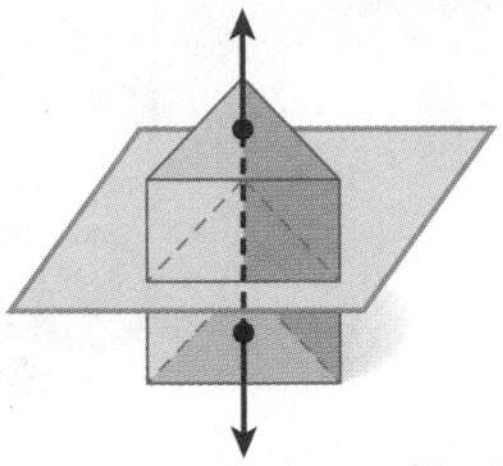

plane symmetry and symmetry about an axis

CHECK IT OUT! **Tell whether each figure has plane symmetry, symmetry about an axis, or no symmetry.**

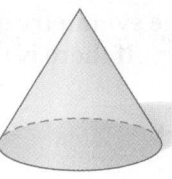

4a. cone

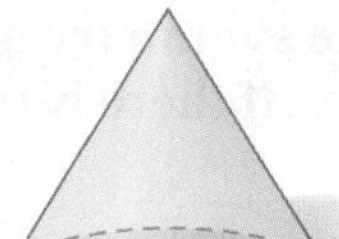

4b. pyramid

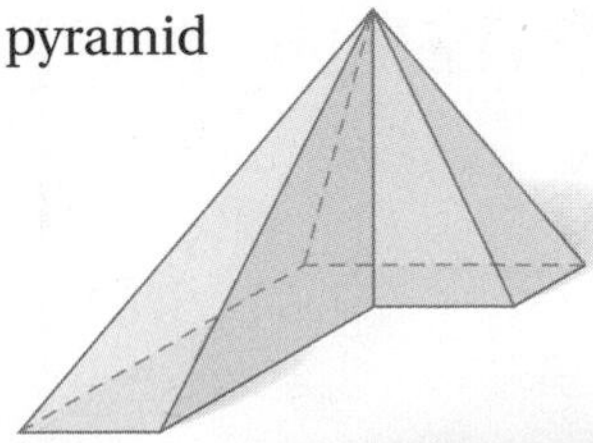

MATHEMATICAL PRACTICES

THINK AND DISCUSS

1. Explain how you could use scissors and paper to cut out a shape that has line symmetry.

2. Describe how you can find the angle of rotational symmetry for a regular polygon with *n* sides.

Know it! Note

3. **GET ORGANIZED** Copy and complete the graphic organizer. In each region, draw a figure with the given type of symmetry.

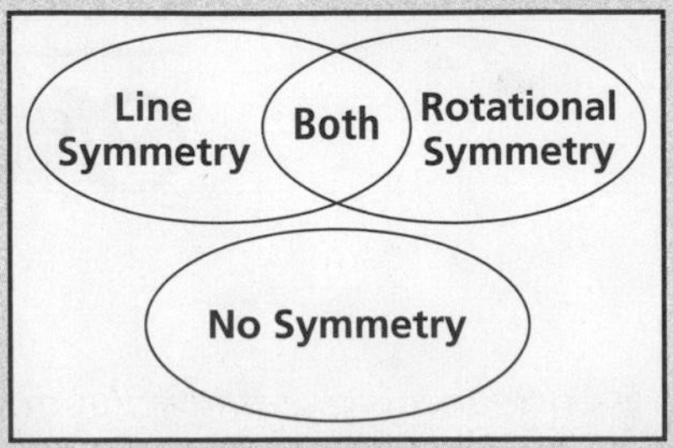

9-5 Exercises

Learn It Online
Homework Help Online
Parent Resources Online

GUIDED PRACTICE

Vocabulary **Apply the vocabulary from this lesson to answer each question.**

1. Describe the *line of symmetry* of an isosceles triangle.

2. The capital letter T has ___?___ . (*line symmetry* or *rotational symmetry*)

SEE EXAMPLE 1

Tell whether each figure has line symmetry. If so, copy the shape and draw all lines of symmetry.

3. 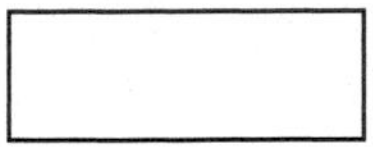

4. 

5. 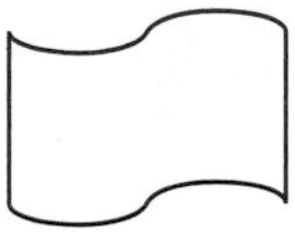

SEE EXAMPLE 2

Tell whether each figure has rotational symmetry. If so, give the angle of rotational symmetry and the order of the symmetry.

6. 

7. 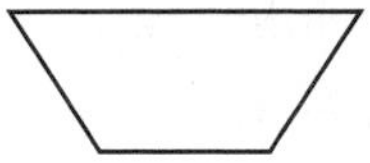

8. 

SEE EXAMPLE 3

9. **Architecture** The Pentagon in Alexandria, Virginia, is the world's largest office building. Copy the shape of the building and draw all lines of symmetry. Give the angle and order of rotational symmetry.

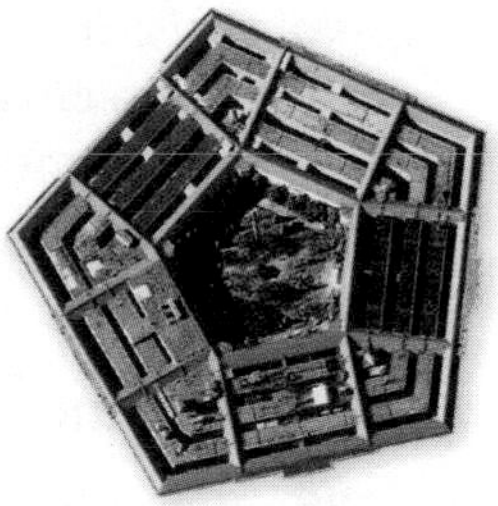

SEE EXAMPLE 4

Tell whether each figure has plane symmetry, symmetry about an axis, or neither.

10. prism 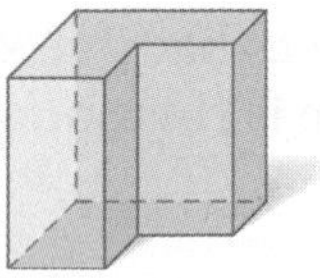

11. cylinder 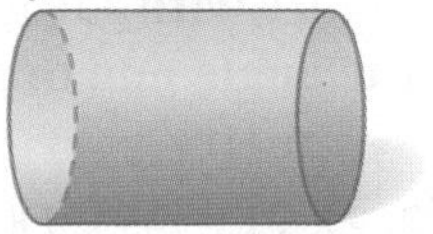

12. rectangular prism 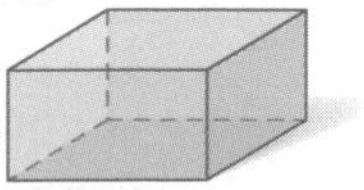

PRACTICE AND PROBLEM SOLVING

Independent Practice

For Exercises	See Example
13–15	1
16–18	2
19	3
20–22	4

Extra Practice
See Extra Practice for more Skills Practice and Applications Practice exercises.

Tell whether each figure has line symmetry. If so, copy the shape and draw all lines of symmetry.

13. 

14. 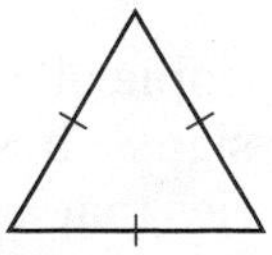

15. 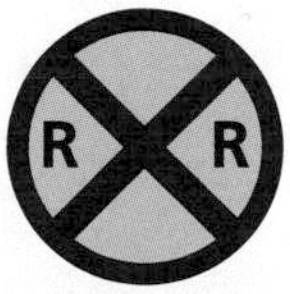

Tell whether each figure has rotational symmetry. If so, give the angle of rotational symmetry and the order of the symmetry.

16. 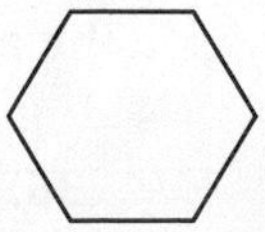

17. 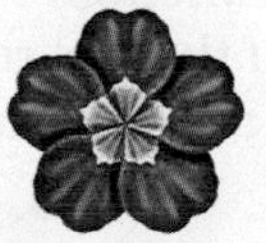

18. 

19. **Art** *Op art* is a style of art that uses optical effects to create an impression of movement in a painting or sculpture. The painting at right, *Vega-Tek*, by Victor Vasarely, is an example of op art. Sketch the shape in the painting and draw any lines of symmetry. If there is rotational symmetry, give the angle and order.

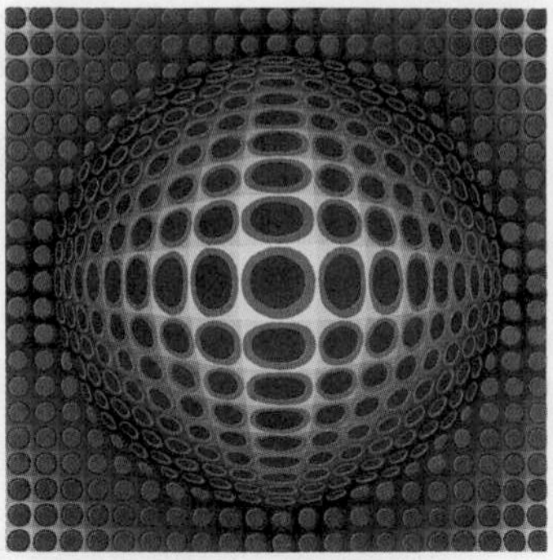

Tell whether each figure has plane symmetry, symmetry about an axis, or neither.

20. sphere

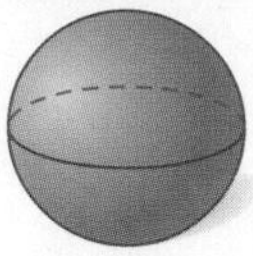

21. triangular pyramid

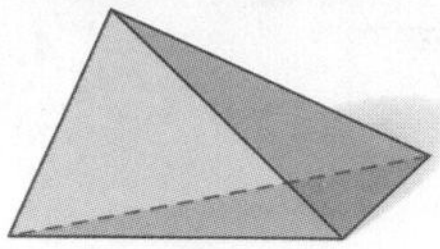

22. torus

Draw a triangle with the following number of lines of symmetry. Then classify the triangle.

23. exactly one line of symmetry
24. three lines of symmetry
25. no lines of symmetry

Data Analysis **The graph shown, called the** ***standard normal curve,*** **is used in statistical analysis. The area under the curve is 1 square unit. There is a vertical line of symmetry at $x = 0$. The areas of the shaded regions are indicated on the graph.**

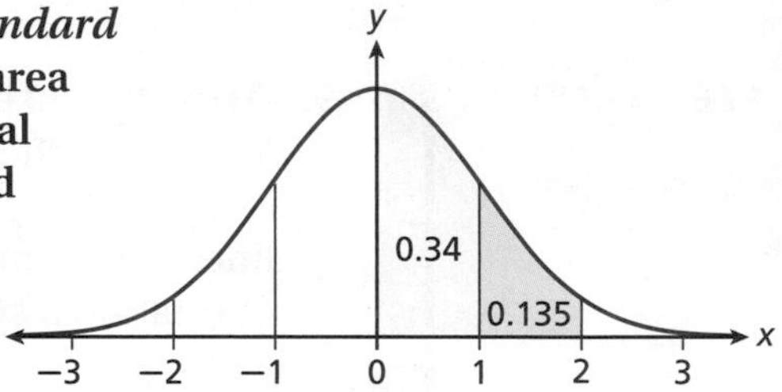

26. Find the area under the curve for $x > 0$.
27. Find the area under the curve for $x > 2$.
28. If a point under the curve is selected at random, what is the probability that the x-value of the point will be between -1 and 1?

Tell whether the figure with the given vertices has line symmetry and/or rotational symmetry. Give the angle and order if there is rotational symmetry. Draw the figure and any lines of symmetry.

29. $A(-2, 2)$, $B(2, 2)$, $C(1, -2)$, $D(-1, -2)$
30. $R(-3, 3)$, $S(3, 3)$, $T(3, -3)$, $U(-3, -3)$
31. $J(4, 4)$, $K(-2, 2)$, $L(2, -2)$
32. $A(3, 1)$, $B(0, 2)$, $C(-3, 1)$, $D(-3, -1)$, $E(0, -2)$, $F(3, -1)$

33. **Art** The Chokwe people of Angola are known for their traditional sand designs. These complex drawings are traced out to illustrate stories that are told at evening gatherings. Classify the symmetry of the Chokwe design shown.

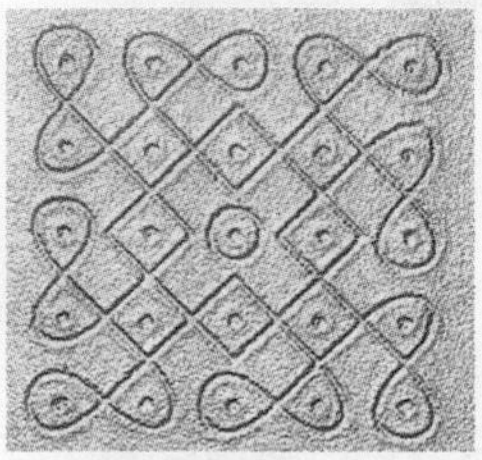

Algebra **Graph each function. Tell whether the graph has line symmetry and/or rotational symmetry. If there is rotational symmetry, give the angle and order. Write the equations of any lines of symmetry.**

34. $y = x^2$
35. $y = (x - 2)^2$
36. $y = x^3$

MULTI-STEP TEST PREP

37. This woodcut, entitled *Circle Limit III*, was made by Dutch artist M. C. Escher.

   a. Does the woodcut have line symmetry? If so, describe the lines of symmetry. If not, explain why not.
   b. Does the woodcut have rotational symmetry? If so, give the angle and order of the symmetry. If not, explain why not.
   c. Does your answer to part **b** change if color is not taken into account? Explain.

Classify the quadrilateral that meets the given conditions. First make a conjecture and then verify your conjecture by drawing a figure.

38. two lines of symmetry perpendicular to the sides and order-2 rotational symmetry

39. no line symmetry and order-2 rotational symmetry

40. two lines of symmetry through opposite vertices and order-2 rotational symmetry

41. four lines of symmetry and order-4 rotational symmetry

42. one line of symmetry through a pair of opposite vertices and no rotational symmetry

43. **Physics** High-speed photography makes it possible to analyze the physics behind a water splash. When a drop lands in a bowl of liquid, the splash forms a crown of evenly spaced points. What is the angle of rotational symmetry for a crown with 24 points?

44. **Critical Thinking** What can you conclude about a rectangle that has four lines of symmetry? Explain.

45. **Geography** The Isle of Man is an island in the Irish Sea. The island's symbol is a *triskelion* that consists of three running legs radiating from the center. Describe the symmetry of the triskelion.

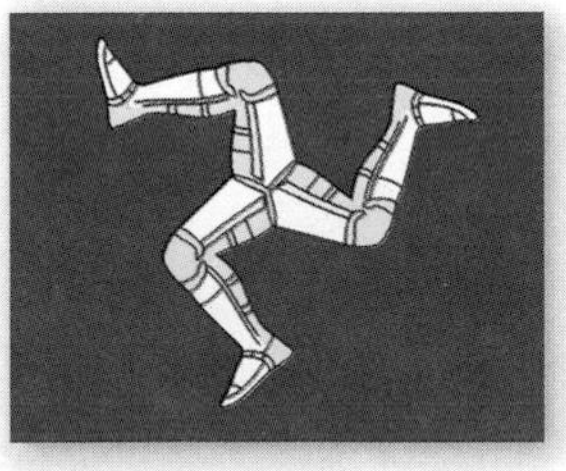

46. **Critical Thinking** Draw several examples of figures that have two perpendicular lines of symmetry. What other type of symmetry do these figures have? Make a conjecture based on your observation.

Each figure shows part of a shape with a center of rotation and a given rotational symmetry. Copy and complete each figure.

47. order 4

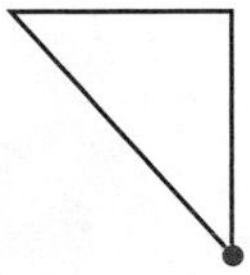

48. order 6

49. order 2

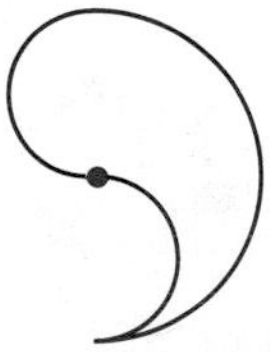

50. **Write About It** Explain the connection between the angle of rotational symmetry and the order of the rotational symmetry. That is, if you know one of these, explain how you can find the other.

TEST PREP

51. What is the order of rotational symmetry for the hexagon shown?

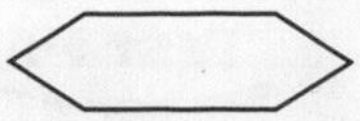

Ⓐ 2 Ⓑ 3 Ⓒ 4 Ⓓ 6

52. Which of these figures has exactly four lines of symmetry?

Ⓕ Regular octagon
Ⓖ Equilateral triangle
Ⓗ Isosceles triangle
Ⓙ Square

53. Consider the graphs of the following equations. Which graph has the *y*-axis as a line of symmetry?

Ⓐ $y = (x - 3)^2$ Ⓑ $y = x^3$ Ⓒ $y = x^2 - 3$ Ⓓ $y = |x + 3|$

54. Donnell designed a garden plot that has rotational symmetry, but not line symmetry. Which of these could be the shape of the plot?

Ⓕ 
Ⓖ 
Ⓗ 
Ⓙ 

CHALLENGE AND EXTEND

55. A regular polygon has an angle of rotational symmetry of 5°. How many sides does the polygon have?

56. How many lines of symmetry does a regular *n*-gon have if *n* is even? if *n* is odd? Explain your reasoning.

Find the equation of the line of symmetry for the graph of each function.

57. $y = (x + 4)^2$ **58.** $y = |x - 2|$ **59.** $y = 3x^2 + 5$

Give the number of axes of symmetry for each regular polyhedron. Describe all axes of symmetry.

60. cube

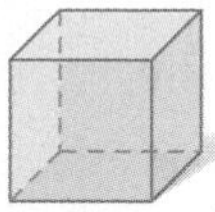

61. tetrahedron

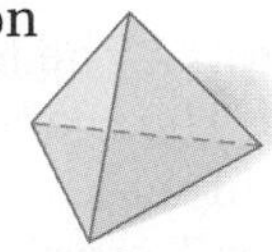

62. octahedron

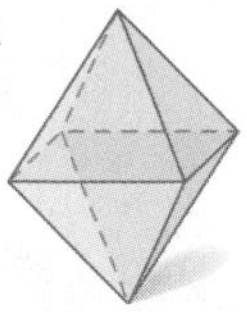

COMMON CORE

EXTENSION

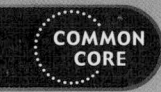

Solids of Revolution

CC.9-12.G.GMD.4 ...Identify three-dimensional objects generated by rotations of two-dimensional objects.

Objectives

Understand how solids can be produced by rotating a two-dimensional figure through space.

Vocabulary

solid of revolution

If you rotate a rectangle around one of its sides, the path it makes through space is a cylinder. A **solid of revolution** is a three-dimensional figure that is formed by rotating a two-dimensional shape around an axis.

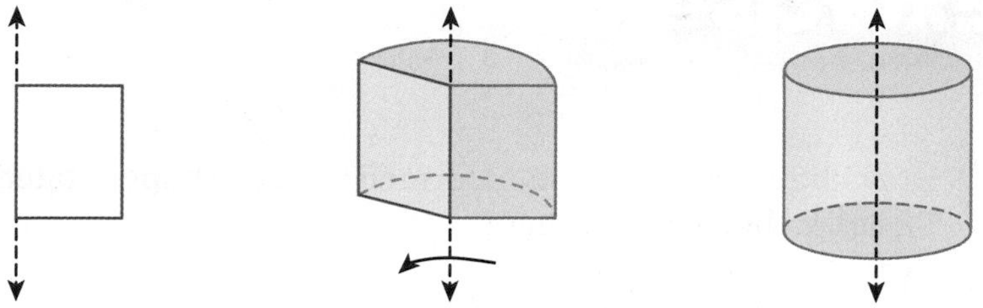

EXAMPLE 1 Sketching a Solid of Revolution

Draw the solid of revolution formed by the shape rotated around the axis given. Describe the resulting shape.

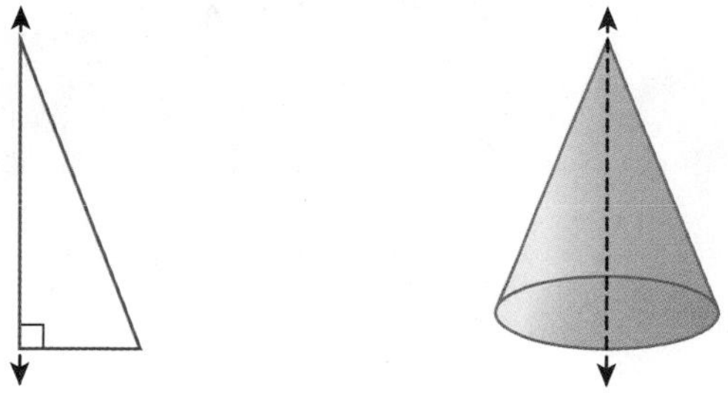

A right triangle rotated around an axis that passes through one of the legs forms a cone.

CHECK IT OUT!

1. Draw the solid of revolution formed by the given shape rotated around the axis given. Describe the resulting shape.

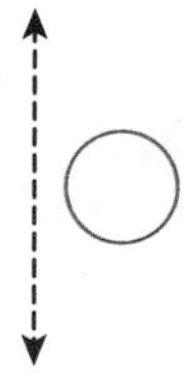

EXAMPLE 2 Recreation Application

A chess pawn is a solid of revolution. Draw a two-dimensional shape and an axis of rotation that could form the pawn.

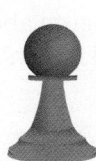

The two-dimensional shape should match the outline of one side of the pawn.

CHECK IT OUT!

2. Draw a two-dimensional shape and axis of rotation that could form the sports drink bottle.

EXTENSION Exercises

Draw the solid of revolution formed by each shape rotated around the axis given. Describe the resulting shape.

1.

2.

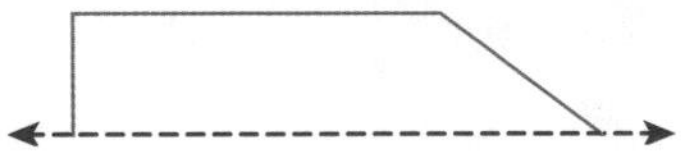

Draw a two-dimensional shape and axis of rotation that could form each figure.

3.

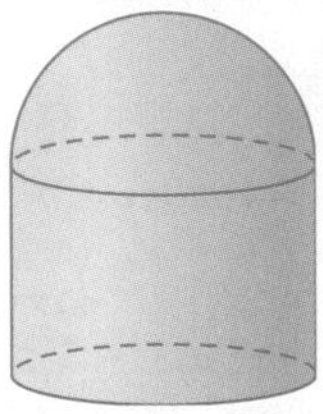

4.

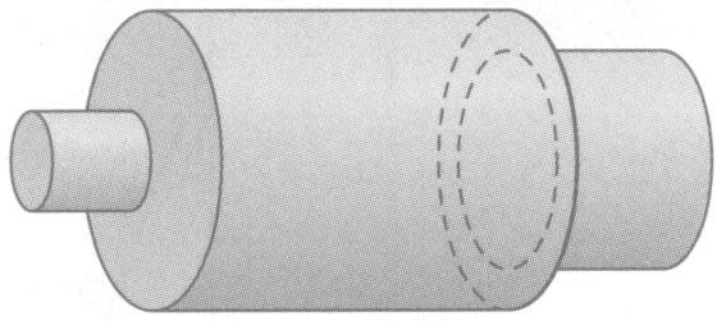

Draw the solid of revolution formed by each shape rotated around the *z*-axis. Then find the volume of the solid to the nearest tenth of a unit.

5.

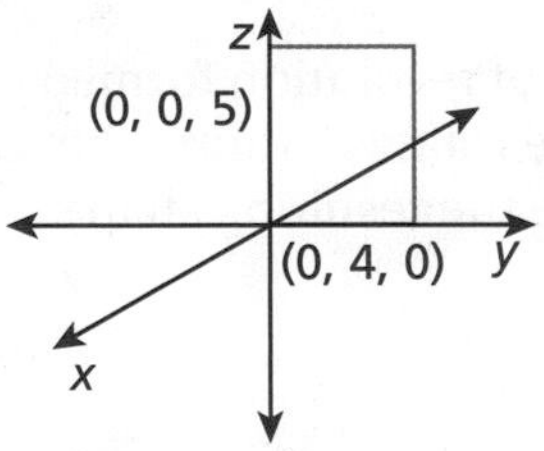

6.

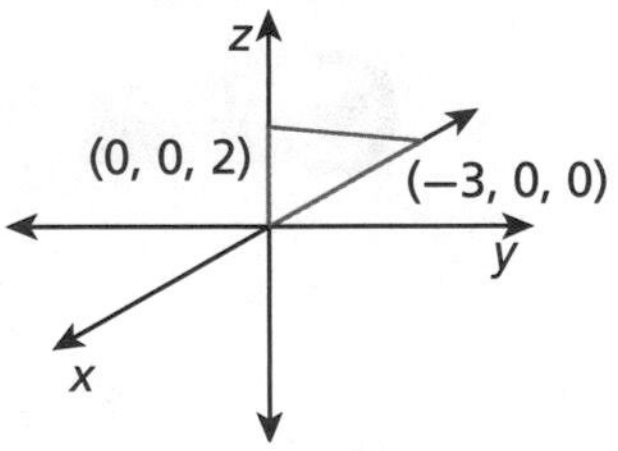

7. **Critical Thinking** If you find the cross section of a solid of revolution in a plane that's perpendicular to the axis of rotation, you will always get the same shape. What is it? Use drawings to support your answer.

8. **Write About It** Will rotation of the blue figure about either axis shown in the figure produce a sphere? Explain why or why not.

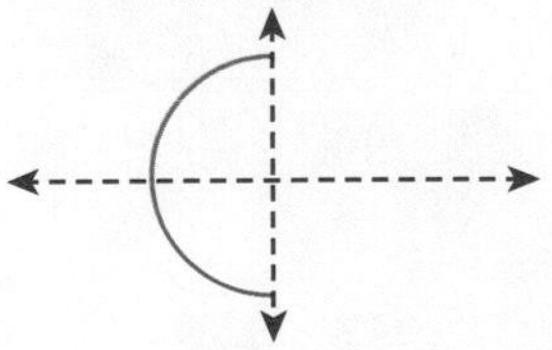

9. **Challenge** Is an oblique cylinder a solid of revolution? Explain your reasoning.

COMMON CORE

9-6 Tessellations

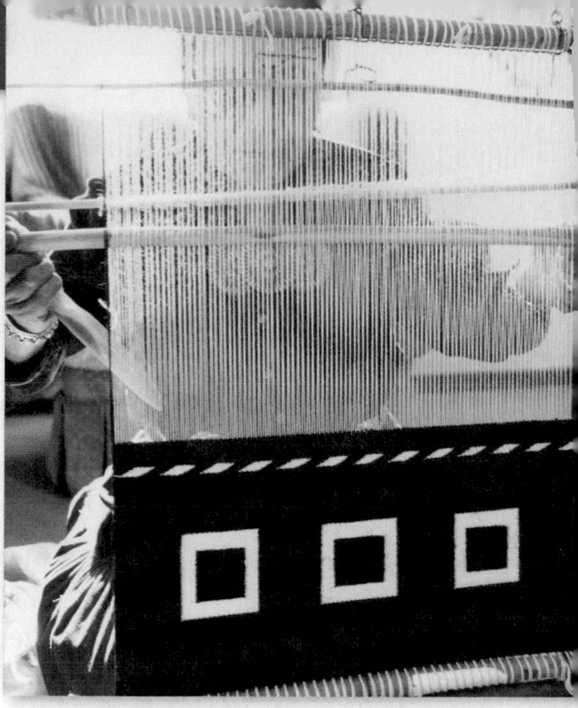

CC.9-12.G.CO.5 Given a geometric figure and a rotation, reflection, or translation, draw the transformed figure… *Also* **CC.9-12.G.CO.2**

Objectives

Use transformations to draw tessellations.

Identify regular and semiregular tessellations and figures that will tessellate.

Vocabulary

translation symmetry
frieze pattern
glide reflection symmetry
tessellation
regular tessellation
semiregular tessellation

Who uses this?

Repeating patterns play an important role in traditional Native American art.

A pattern has **translation symmetry** if it can be translated along a vector so that the image coincides with the preimage. A **frieze pattern** is a pattern that has translation symmetry along a line.

Both of the frieze patterns shown below have translation symmetry. The pattern on the right also has *glide reflection symmetry*. A pattern with **glide reflection symmetry** coincides with its image after a glide reflection.

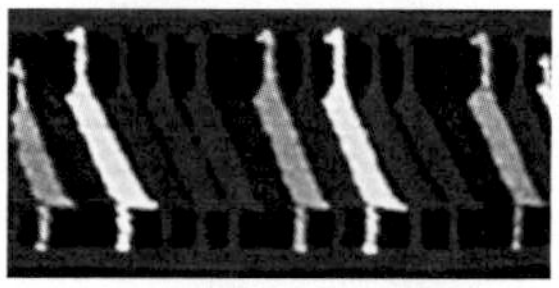

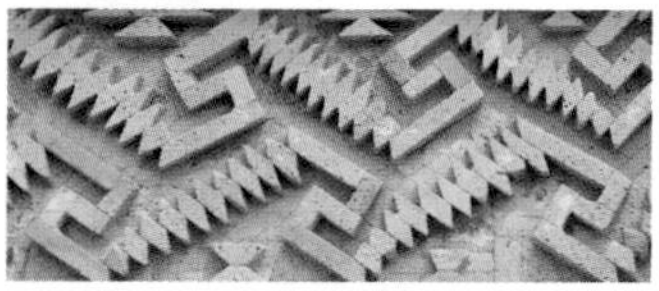

EXAMPLE 1 *Art Application*

Identify the symmetry in each frieze pattern.

A

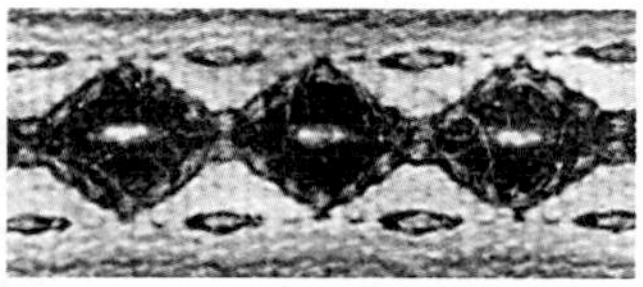

translation symmetry and glide reflection symmetry

B

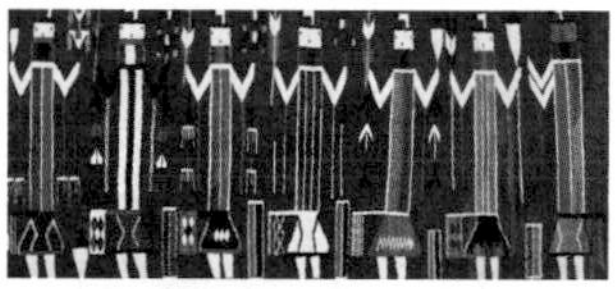

translation symmetry

Helpful Hint

When you are given a frieze pattern, you may assume that the pattern continues forever in both directions.

CHECK IT OUT! **Identify the symmetry in each frieze pattern.**

1a.

1b.

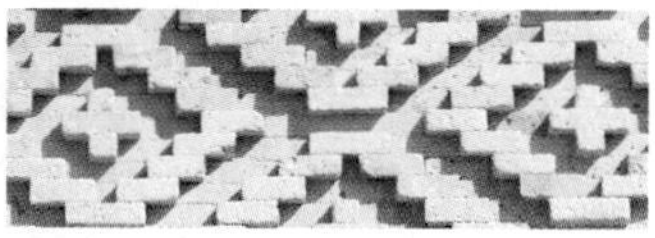

A **tessellation**, or *tiling*, is a repeating pattern that completely covers a plane with no gaps or overlaps. The measures of the angles that meet at each vertex must add up to 360°.

In the tessellation shown, each angle of the quadrilateral occurs once at each vertex. Because the angle measures of any quadrilateral add to 360°, any quadrilateral can be used to tessellate the plane. Four copies of the quadrilateral meet at each vertex.

The angle measures of any triangle add up to 180°. This means that any triangle can be used to tessellate a plane. Six copies of the triangle meet at each vertex, as shown.

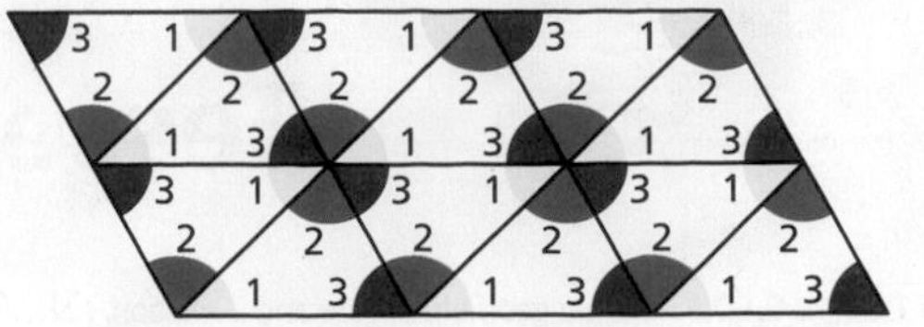

$$m\angle 1 + m\angle 2 + m\angle 3 = 180°$$
$$m\angle 1 + m\angle 2 + m\angle 3 + m\angle 1 + m\angle 2 + m\angle 3 = 360°$$

EXAMPLE 2 Using Transformations to Create Tessellations

Copy the given figure and use it to create a tessellation.

A

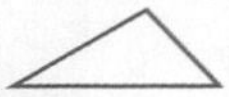

Step 1 Rotate the triangle 180° about the midpoint of one side.

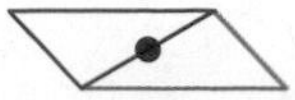

Step 2 Translate the resulting pair of triangles to make a row of triangles.

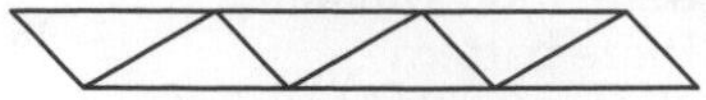

Step 3 Translate the row of triangles to make a tessellation.

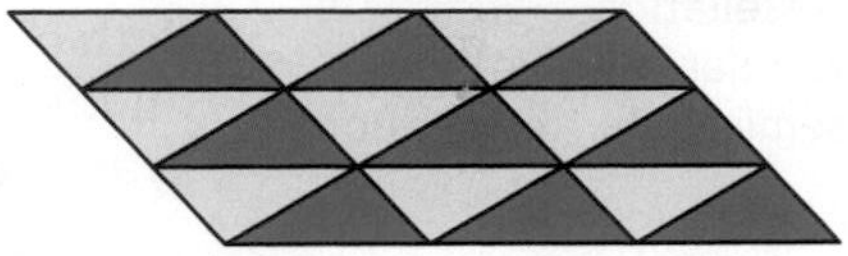

B

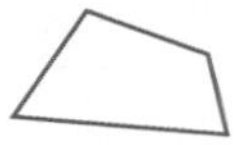

Step 1 Rotate the quadrilateral 180° about the midpoint of one side.

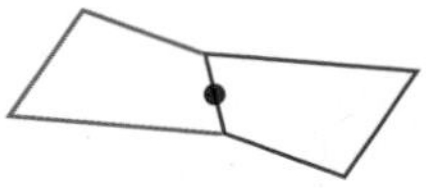

Step 2 Translate the resulting pair of quadrilaterals to make a row of quadrilaterals.

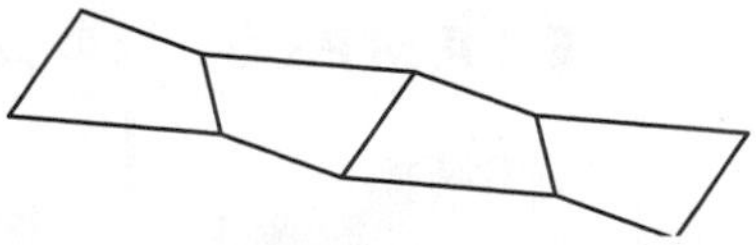

Step 3 Translate the row of quadrilaterals to make a tessellation.

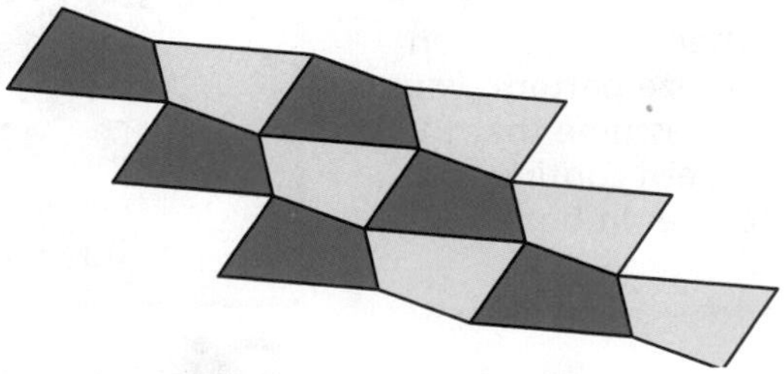

CHECK IT OUT!

2. Copy the given figure and use it to create a tessellation.

A **regular tessellation** is formed by congruent regular polygons. A **semiregular tessellation** is formed by two or more different regular polygons, with the same number of each polygon occurring in the same order at every vertex.

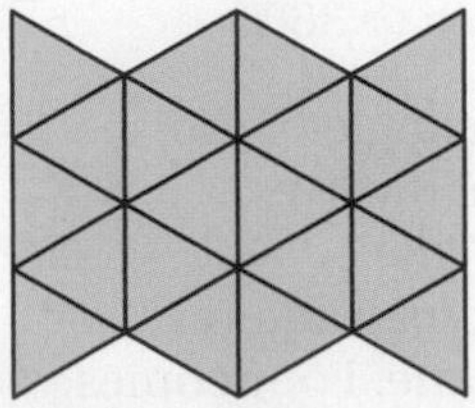

Regular tessellation

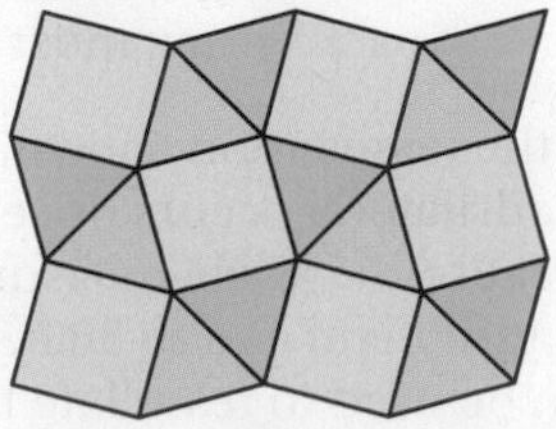

Semiregular tessellation

Every vertex has two squares and three triangles in this order: square, triangle, square, triangle, triangle.

Student to Student

Tessellations

Ryan Gray
Sunset High School

When I need to decide if given figures can be used to tessellate a plane, I look at angle measures. To form a regular tessellation, the angle measures of a regular polygon must be a divisor of 360°. To form a semiregular tessellation, the angle measures around a vertex must add up to 360°.

For example, regular octagons and equilateral triangles cannot be used to make a semiregular tessellation because no combination of 135° and 60° adds up to exactly 360°.

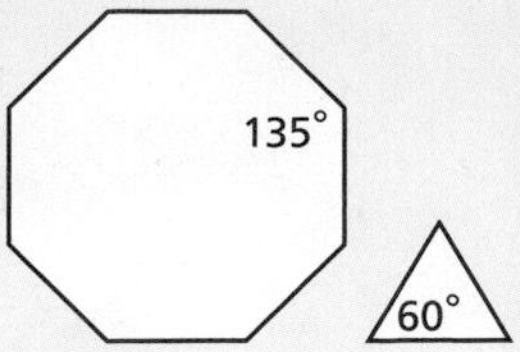

EXAMPLE 3 Classifying Tessellations

Classify each tessellation as regular, semiregular, or neither.

A

Two regular octagons and one square meet at each vertex. The tessellation is semiregular.

B

Only squares are used. The tessellation is regular.

C

Irregular hexagons are used in the tessellation. It is neither regular nor semiregular.

CHECK IT OUT! **Classify each tessellation as regular, semiregular, or neither.**

3a.

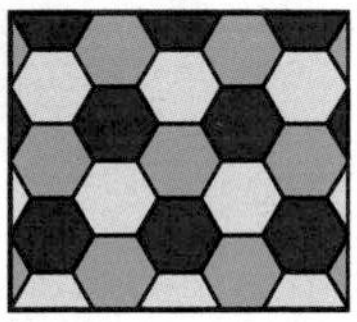

3b.

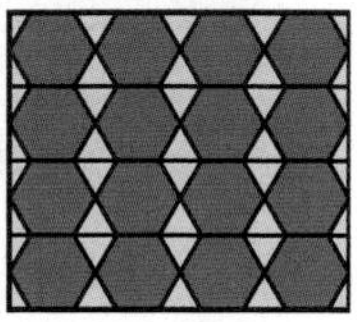

3c.

EXAMPLE 4 Determining Whether Polygons Will Tessellate

Determine whether the given regular polygon(s) can be used to form a tessellation. If so, draw the tessellation.

A

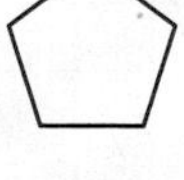

No; each angle of the pentagon measures 108°, and 108 is not a divisor of 360.

B

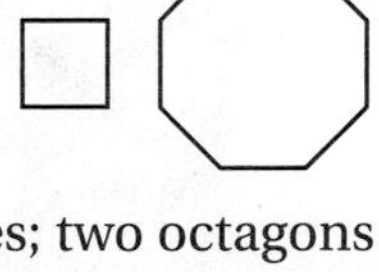

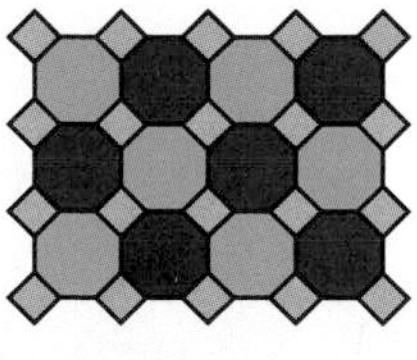

Yes; two octagons and one square meet at each vertex.
$135° + 135° + 90° = 360°$

CHECK IT OUT! **Determine whether the given regular polygon(s) can be used to form a tessellation. If so, draw the tessellation.**

4a.

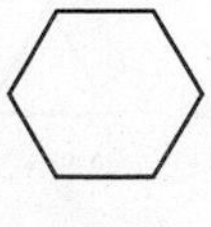

4b.

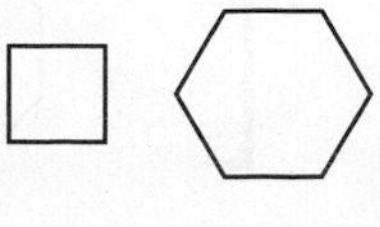

THINK AND DISCUSS

1. Explain how you can identify a frieze pattern that has glide reflection symmetry.
2. Is it possible to tessellate a plane using circles? Why or why not?
3. **GET ORGANIZED** Copy and complete the graphic organizer.

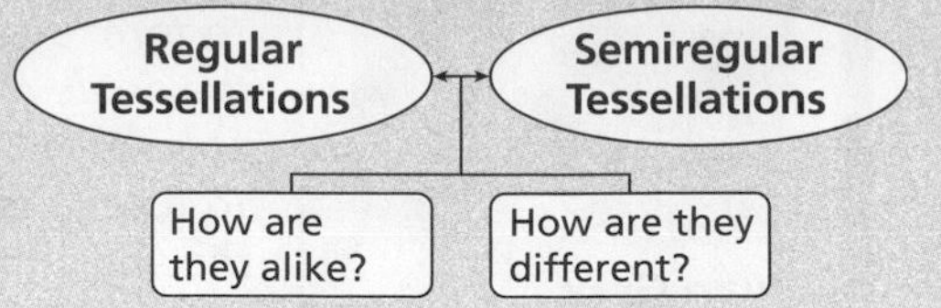

9-6 Exercises

Learn It Online
Homework Help Online
Parent Resources Online

GUIDED PRACTICE

Vocabulary Apply the vocabulary from this lesson to answer each question.

1. Sketch a pattern that has *glide reflection symmetry.*
2. Describe a real-world example of a *regular tessellation.*

SEE EXAMPLE 1

Transportation The tread of a tire is the part that makes contact with the ground. Various tread patterns help improve traction and increase durability. Identify the symmetry in each tread pattern.

3. 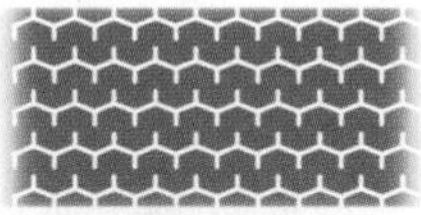
4. 
5. 

SEE EXAMPLE 2

Copy the given figure and use it to create a tessellation.

6. 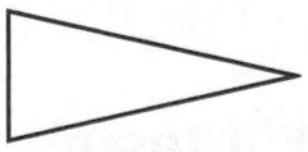
7. 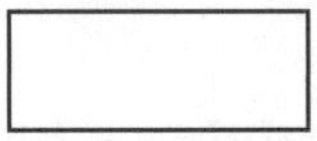
8. 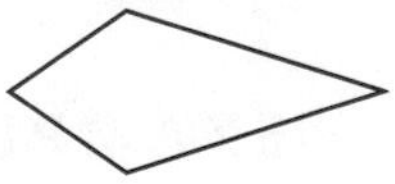

SEE EXAMPLE 3

Classify each tessellation as regular, semiregular, or neither.

9. 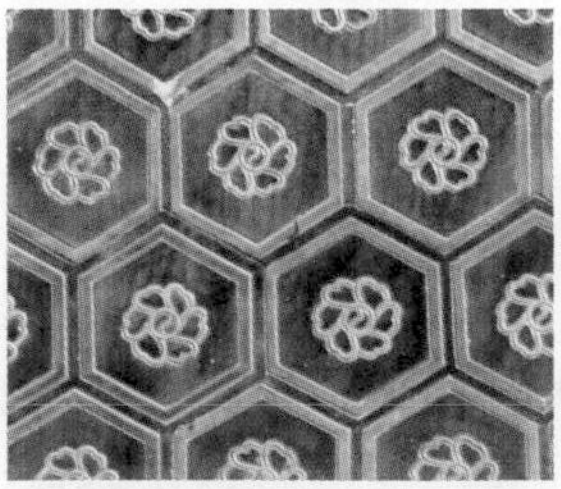
10. 
11. 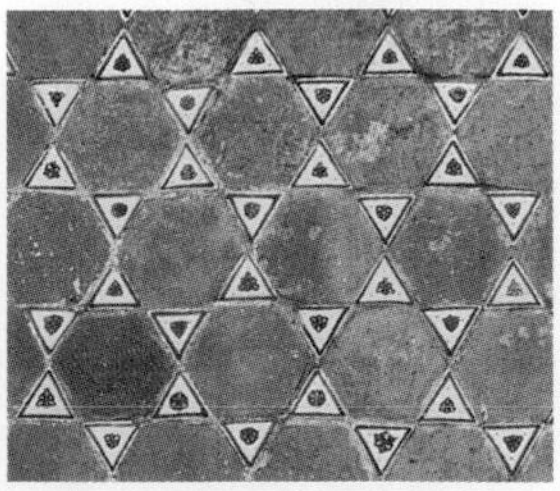

SEE EXAMPLE 4

Determine whether the given regular polygon(s) can be used to form a tessellation. If so, draw the tessellation.

12. 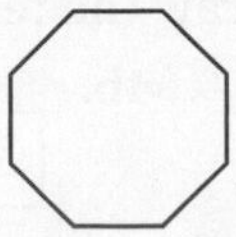
13. 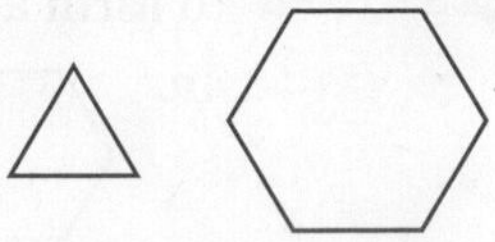
14. 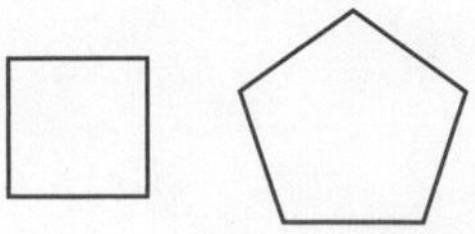

PRACTICE AND PROBLEM SOLVING

Independent Practice

For Exercises	See Example
15–17	1
18–20	2
21–23	3
24–26	4

Extra Practice

See Extra Practice for more Skills Practice and Applications Practice exercises.

Interior Decorating Identify the symmetry in each wallpaper border.

15. 

16. 

17. 

Copy the given figure and use it to create a tessellation.

18. 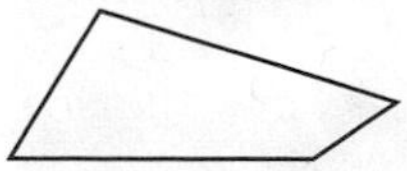

19. 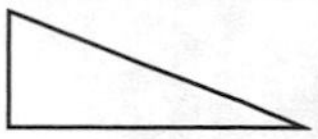

20. 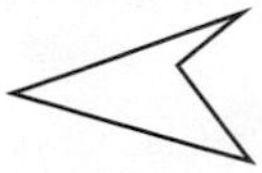

Classify each tessellation as regular, semiregular, or neither.

21. 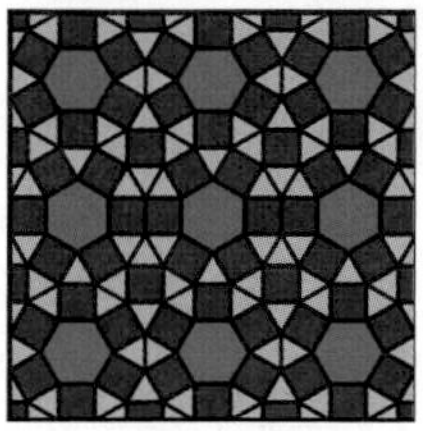

22. 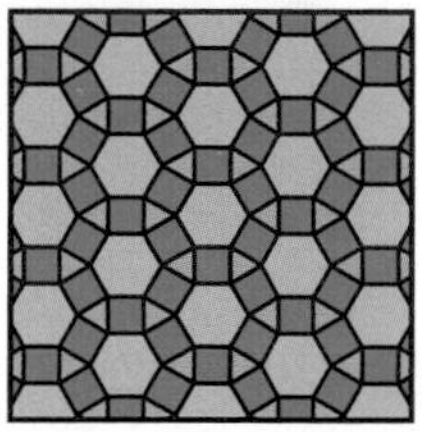

23. 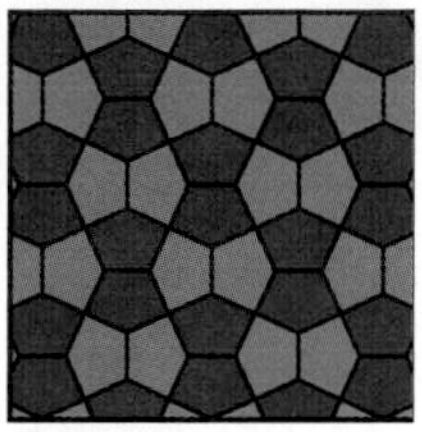

Determine whether the given regular polygon(s) can be used to form a tessellation. If so, draw the tessellation.

24. 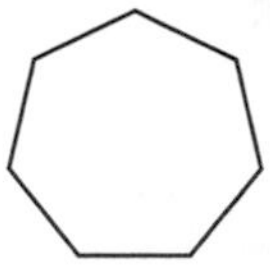

25. 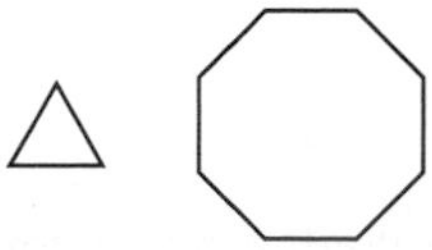

26. 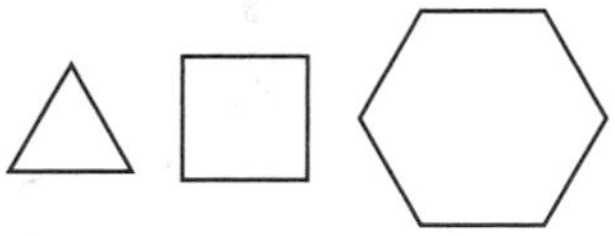

27. Physics A truck moving down a road creates whirling pockets of air called a *vortex train*. Use the figure to classify the symmetry of a vortex train.

Identify all of the types of symmetry (translation, glide reflection, and/or rotation) in each tessellation.

28. 

29. 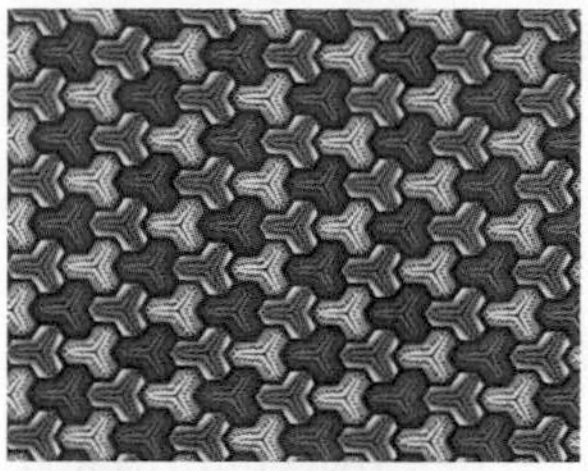

30. 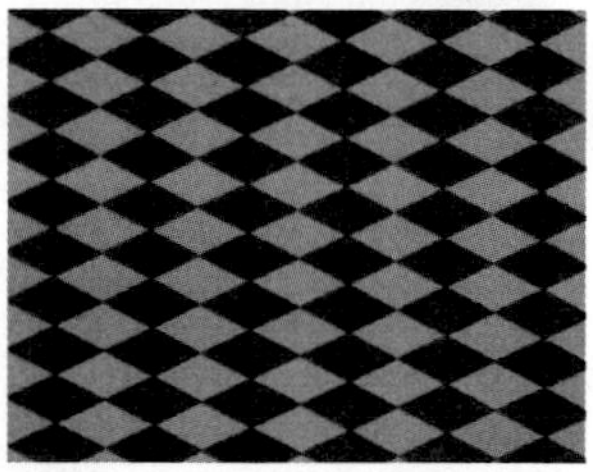

Tell whether each statement is sometimes, always, or never true.

31. A triangle can be used to tessellate a plane.

32. A frieze pattern has glide reflection symmetry.

33. The angles at a vertex of a tessellation add up to 360°.

34. It is possible to use a regular pentagon to make a regular tessellation.

35. A semiregular tessellation includes scalene triangles.

MULTI-STEP TEST PREP

36. Many of the patterns in M. C. Escher's works are based on simple tessellations. For example, the pattern at right is based on a tessellation of equilateral triangles. Identify the figure upon which each pattern is based.

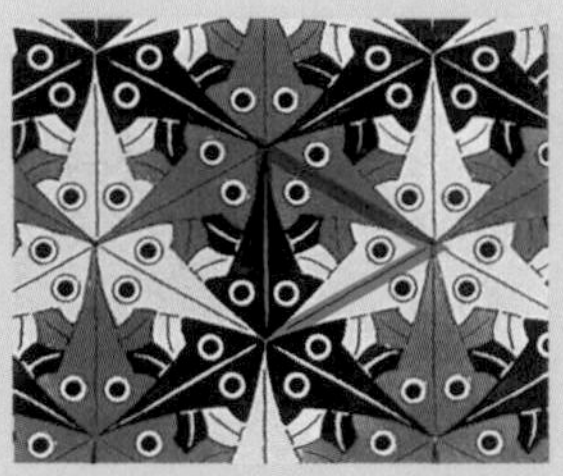

a.

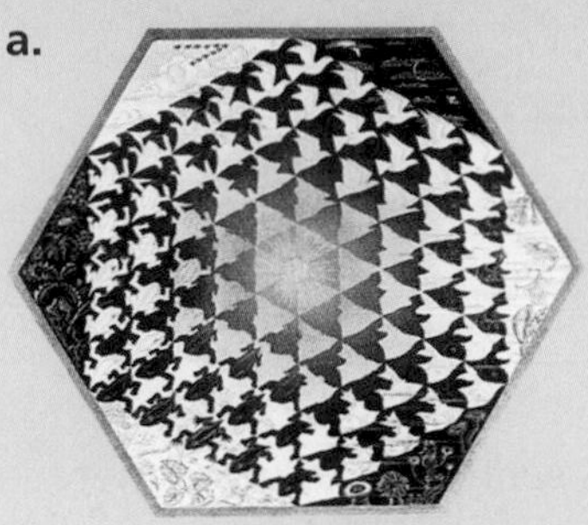

b.

Use the given figure to draw a frieze pattern with the given symmetry.

37. translation symmetry 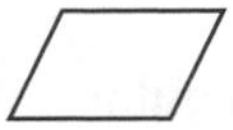

38. glide reflection symmetry 

39. translation symmetry 

40. glide reflection symmetry 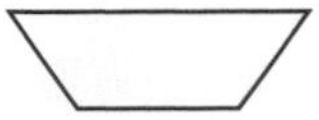

41. **Optics** A kaleidoscope is formed by three mirrors joined to form the lateral surface of a triangular prism. Copy the triangular faces and reflect it over each side. Repeat to form a tessellation. Describe the symmetry of the tessellation.

42. **Critical Thinking** The pattern on a soccer ball is a tessellation of a sphere using regular hexagons and regular pentagons. Can these two shapes be used to tessellate a plane? Explain your reasoning.

43. **Chemistry** A *polymer* is a substance made of repeating chemical units or molecules. The *repeat unit* is the smallest structure that can be repeated to create the chain. Draw the repeat unit for polypropylene, the polymer shown below.

$$- CH_2 - CH - CH_2 - CH - CH_2 - CH - CH_2 - CH -$$

(each CH bears a pendant CH_3 group)

$$CH_3 \quad CH_3 \quad CH_3 \quad CH_3$$

44. The *dual* of a tessellation is formed by connecting the centers of adjacent polygons with segments. Copy or trace the semiregular tessellation shown and draw its dual. What type of polygon makes up the dual tessellation?

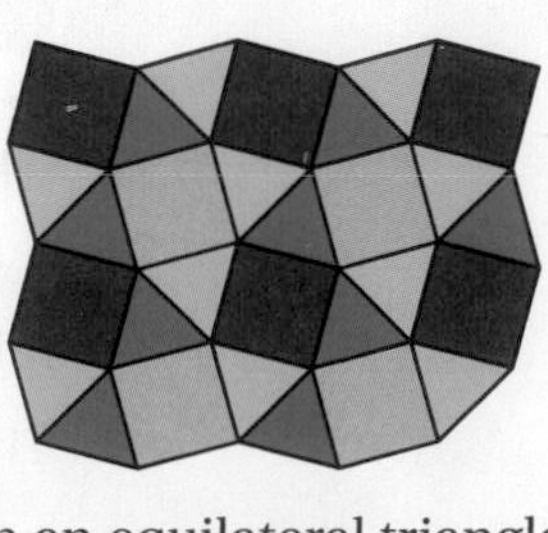

45. **Write About It** You can make a regular tessellation from an equilateral triangle, a square, or a regular hexagon. Explain why these are the only three regular tessellations that are possible.

TEST PREP

46. Which frieze pattern has glide reflection symmetry?

Ⓐ 

Ⓒ 

Ⓑ 

Ⓓ 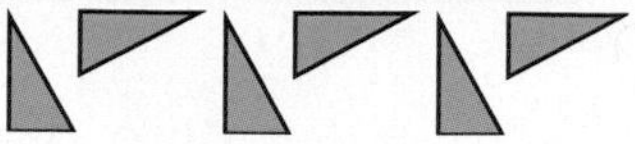

47. Which shape CANNOT be used to make a regular tessellation?

Ⓕ Equilateral triangle

Ⓗ Regular pentagon

Ⓖ Square

Ⓙ Regular hexagon

48. Which pair of regular polygons can be used to make a semiregular tessellation?

Ⓐ 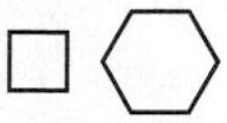

Ⓑ 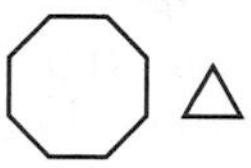

Ⓒ 

Ⓓ 

CHALLENGE AND EXTEND

49. Some shapes can be used to tessellate a plane in more than one way. Three tessellations that use the same rectangle are shown. Draw a parallelogram and draw at least three tessellations using that parallelogram.

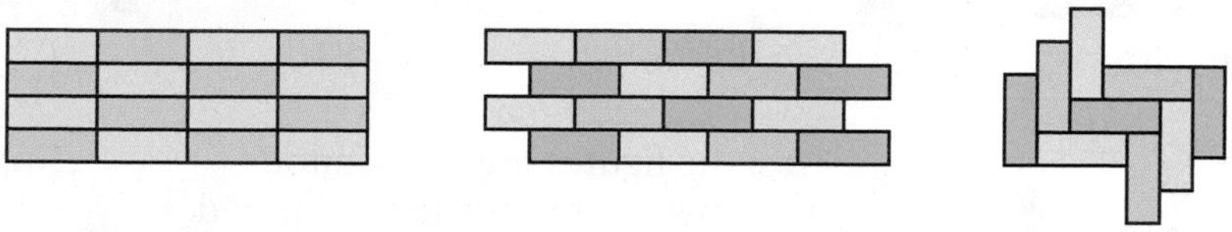

Determine whether each figure can be used to tessellate three-dimensional space.

50. 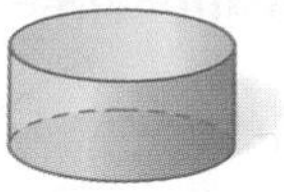

51. 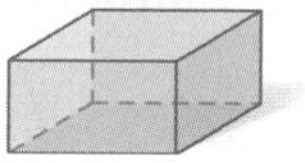

52. 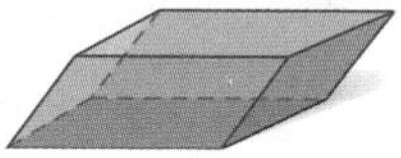

COMMON CORE

9-7 Dilations

CC.9-12.G.CO.2 Represent transformations in the plane… *Also* **CC.9-12.G.SRT.1**

Objective
Identify and draw dilations.

Vocabulary
center of dilation
enlargement
reduction

Who uses this?
Artists use dilations to turn sketches into large-scale paintings. (See Example 3.)

Recall that a dilation is a transformation that changes the size of a figure but not the shape. The image and the preimage of a figure under a dilation are similar.

EXAMPLE 1 Identifying Dilations

Helpful Hint
For a dilation with scale factor k, if $k > 0$, the figure is not turned or flipped. If $k < 0$, the figure is rotated by 180°.

Tell whether each transformation appears to be a dilation. Explain.

A

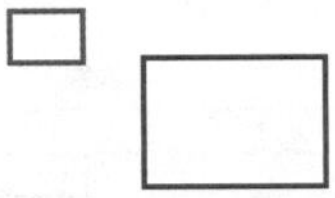

Yes; the figures are similar, and the image is not turned or flipped.

B

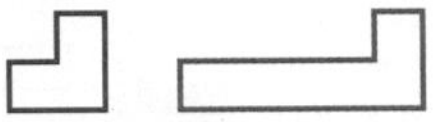

No; the figures are not similar.

CHECK IT OUT! **Tell whether each transformation appears to be a dilation.**

1a.

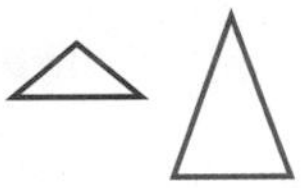

1b.

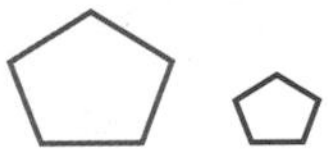

Construction Dilate a Figure by a Scale Factor of 2

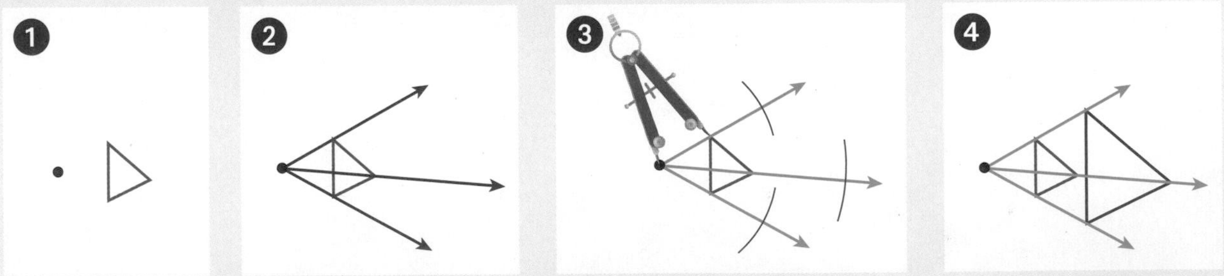

1. Draw a triangle and a point outside the triangle. The point is the *center of dilation.*
2. Use a straightedge to draw a line through the center of dilation and each vertex of the triangle.
3. Set the compass to the distance from the center of dilation to a vertex. Mark this distance along the line for each vertex as shown.
4. Connect the vertices of the image.

In the construction, the lines connecting points of the image with the corresponding points of the preimage all intersect at the center of dilation. Also, the distance from the center to each point of the image is twice the distance to the corresponding point of the preimage.

Know it! Note

Dilations

A dilation, or *similarity transformation*, is a transformation in which the lines connecting every point P with its image P' all intersect at a point C, called the **center of dilation**. $\frac{CP'}{CP}$ is the same for every point P.

The scale factor k of a dilation is the ratio of a linear measurement of the image to a corresponding measurement of the preimage. In the figure, $k = \frac{P'Q'}{PQ}$.

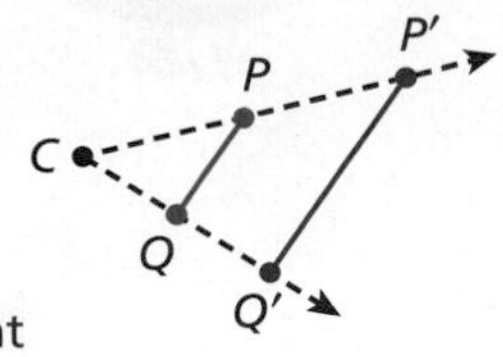

A dilation enlarges or reduces all dimensions proportionally. A dilation with a scale factor greater than 1 is an **enlargement**, or *expansion*. A dilation with a scale factor greater than 0 but less than 1 is a **reduction**, or *contraction*.

EXAMPLE 2 Drawing Dilations

Copy the triangle and the center of dilation P. Draw the image of $\triangle ABC$ under a dilation with a scale factor of $\frac{1}{2}$.

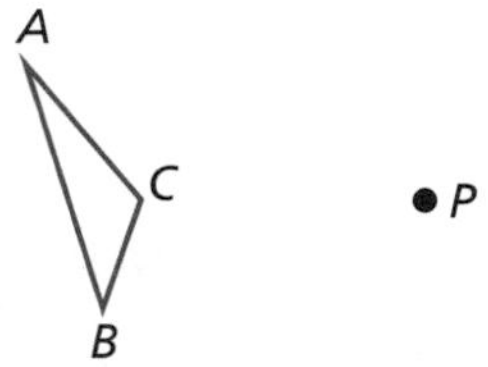

Step 1 Draw a line through P and each vertex.

Step 2 On each line, mark half the distance from P to the vertex.

Step 3 Connect the vertices of the image.

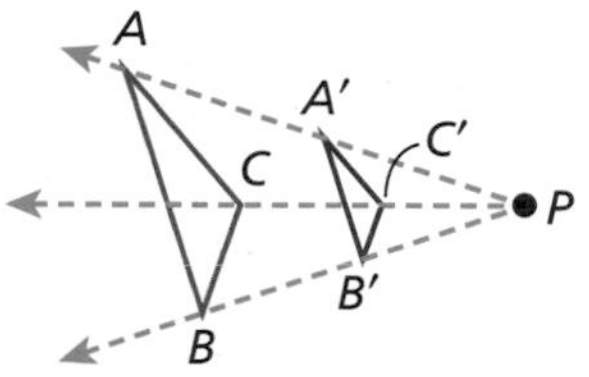

CHECK IT OUT!

2. Copy the figure and the center of dilation. Draw the dilation of $RSTU$ using center Q and a scale factor of 3.

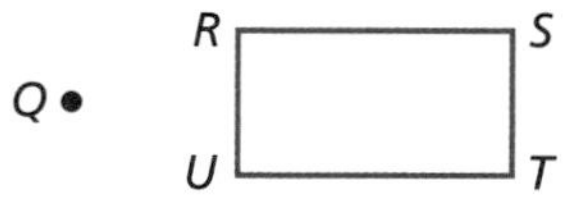

EXAMPLE 3 *Art Application*

An artist is creating a large painting from a photograph by dividing the photograph into squares and dilating each square by a scale factor of 4. If the photograph is 20 cm by 25 cm, what is the perimeter of the painting?

The scale factor of the dilation is 4, so a 1 cm by 1 cm square on the photograph represents a 4 cm by 4 cm square on the painting.

Find the dimensions of the painting.

$b = 4(25) = 100$ cm

$h = 4(20) = 80$ cm

Multiply each dimension by the scale factor, 4.

Find the perimeter of the painting.

$P = 2(100 + 80) = 360$ cm $P = 2(b + h)$

CHECK IT OUT!

3. **What if...?** In Example 3, suppose the photograph is a square with sides of length 10 in. Find the area of the painting.

Know it! Note

Dilations in the Coordinate Plane

If $P(x, y)$ is the preimage of a point under a dilation centered at the origin with scale factor k, then the image of the point is $P'(kx, ky)$.

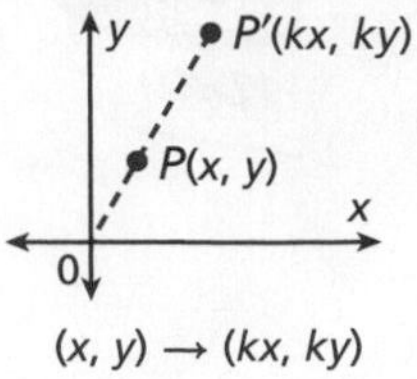

If the scale factor of a dilation is negative, the preimage is rotated by 180°. For $k > 0$, a dilation with a scale factor of $-k$ is equivalent to the composition of a dilation with a scale factor of k that is rotated 180° about the center of dilation.

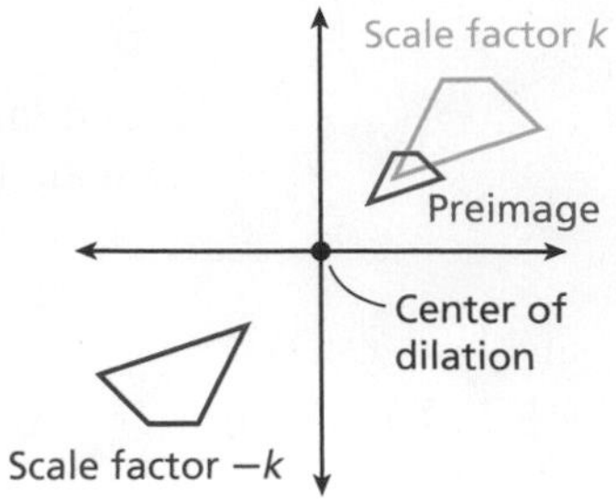

EXAMPLE 4 Drawing Dilations in the Coordinate Plane

Draw the image of a triangle with vertices $A(-1, 1)$, $B(-2, -1)$, and $C(-1, -2)$ under a dilation with a scale factor of -2 centered at the origin.

The dilation of (x, y) is $(-2x, -2y)$.

$A(-1, 1) \rightarrow A'(-2(-1), -2(1)) = A'(2, -2)$

$B(-2, -1) \rightarrow B'(-2(-2), -2(-1)) = B'(4, 2)$

$C(-1, -2) \rightarrow C'(-2(-1), -2(-2)) = C'(2, 4)$

Graph the preimage and image.

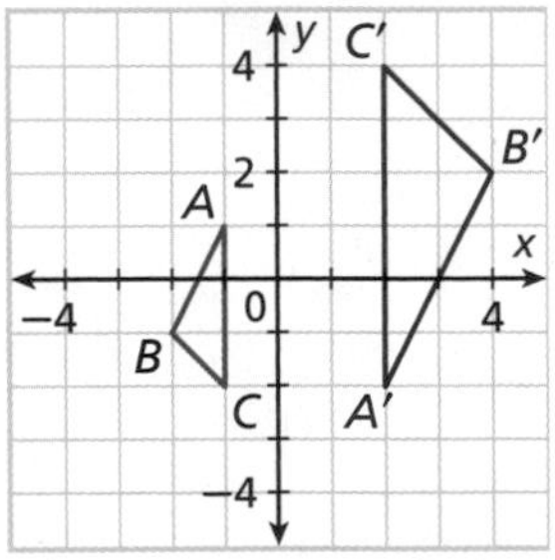

CHECK IT OUT! 4. Draw the image of a parallelogram with vertices $R(0, 0)$, $S(4, 0)$, $T(2, -2)$, and $U(-2, -2)$ under a dilation centered at the origin with a scale factor of $-\frac{1}{2}$.

MATHEMATICAL PRACTICES

THINK AND DISCUSS

1. Given a triangle and its image under a dilation, explain how you could use a ruler to find the scale factor of the dilation.
2. A figure is dilated by a scale factor of k, and then the image is rotated 180° about the center of dilation. What single transformation would produce the same image?
3. **GET ORGANIZED** Copy and complete the graphic organizer. In each box, describe the dilation with the given scale factor.

Know it! Note

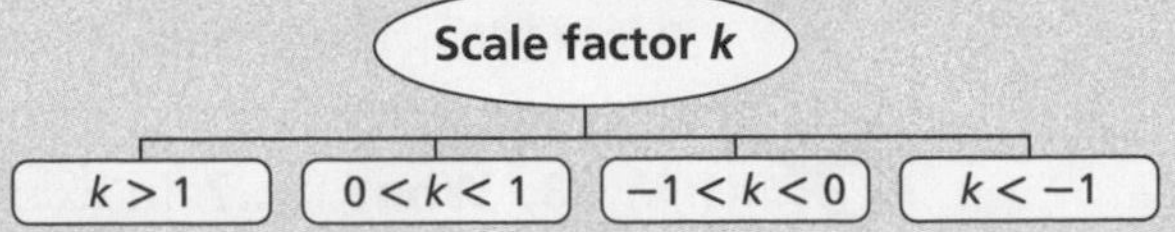

9-7 Exercises

GUIDED PRACTICE

1. **Vocabulary** What are the *center of dilation* and scale factor for the transformation $(x, y) \rightarrow (3x, 3y)$?

SEE EXAMPLE 1

Tell whether each transformation appears to be a dilation.

2.
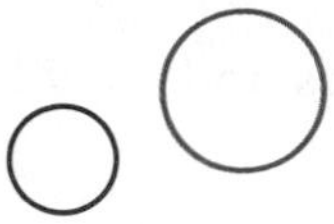

3.
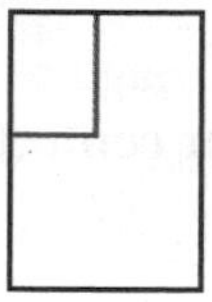

4.
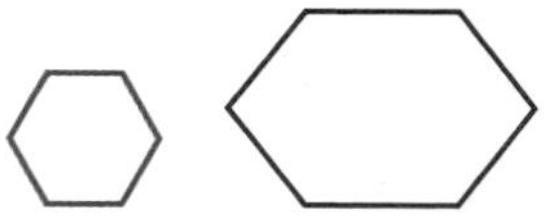

5.

SEE EXAMPLE 2

Copy each triangle and center of dilation *P*. Draw the image of the triangle under a dilation with the given scale factor.

6. Scale factor: 2
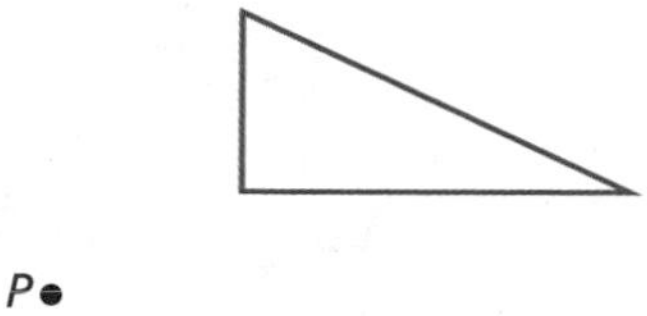

7. Scale factor: $\frac{1}{2}$

SEE EXAMPLE 3

8. **Architecture** A blueprint shows a reduction of a room using a scale factor of $\frac{1}{50}$. In the blueprint, the room's length is 8 in., and its width is 6 in. Find the perimeter of the room.

SEE EXAMPLE 4

Draw the image of the figure with the given vertices under a dilation with the given scale factor centered at the origin.

9. $A(1, 0)$, $B(2, 2)$, $C(4, 0)$; scale factor: 2
10. $J(-2, 2)$, $K(4, 2)$, $L(4, -2)$, $M(-2, -2)$; scale factor: $\frac{1}{2}$
11. $D(-3, 3)$, $E(3, 6)$, $F(3, 0)$; scale factor: $-\frac{1}{3}$
12. $P(-2, 0)$, $Q(-1, 0)$, $R(0, -1)$, $S(-3, -1)$; scale factor: -2

PRACTICE AND PROBLEM SOLVING

Independent Practice

For Exercises	See Example
13–16	1
17–18	2
19	3
20–23	4

Extra Practice

See Extra Practice for more Skills Practice and Applications Practice exercises.

Tell whether each transformation appears to be a dilation.

13.
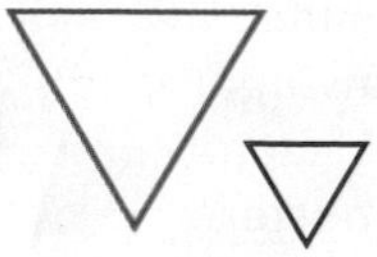

14.
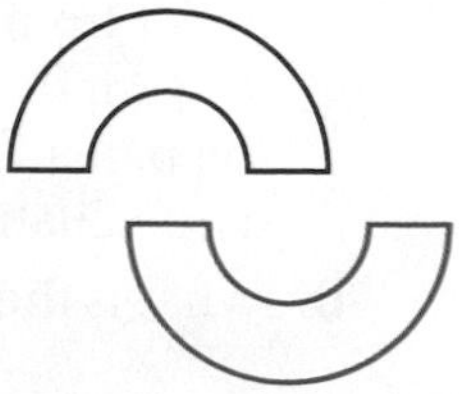

15.
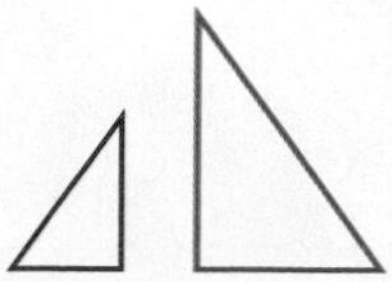

16.
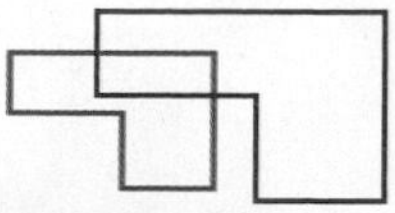

Copy each rectangle and the center of dilation *P*. Draw the image of the rectangle under a dilation with the given scale factor.

17. scale factor: 3

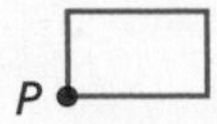

18. scale factor: $\frac{1}{2}$

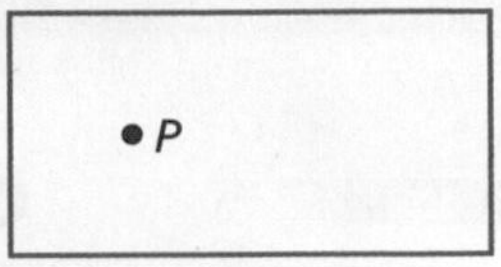

> **LINK**
> ### Art
> 
>
> Mosaic is an ancient art form that is over 4000 years old and is still popular today. Creators of early mosaics used pebbles and other objects, but mosaic titles, or *tesserae,* have been in use since at least 200 B.C.E.

19. **Art** Jeff is making a mosaic by gluing 1 cm square tiles onto a photograph. He starts with a 6 cm by 8 cm rectangular photo and enlarges it by a scale factor of 1.5. How many tiles will Jeff need in order to cover the enlarged photo?

Draw the image of the figure with the given vertices under a dilation with the given scale factor centered at the origin.

20. $M(0, 3)$, $N(6, 0)$, $P(0, -3)$; scale factor: $-\frac{1}{3}$

21. $A(-1, 3)$, $B(1, 1)$, $C(-4, 1)$; scale factor: -1

22. $R(1, 0)$, $S(2, 0)$, $T(2, -2)$, $U(-1, -2)$; scale factor: -2

23. $D(4, 0)$, $E(2, -4)$, $F(-2, -4)$, $G(-4, 0)$, $H(-2, 4)$, $J(2, 4)$; scale factor: $-\frac{1}{2}$

Each figure shows the preimage (blue) and image (red) under a dilation. Write a similarity statement based on the figure.

24.

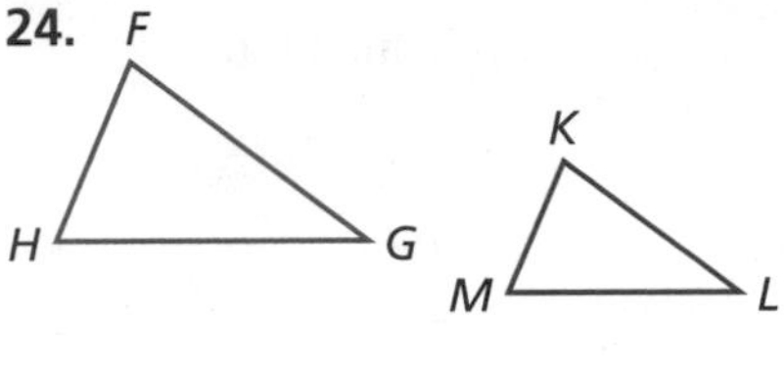

25.

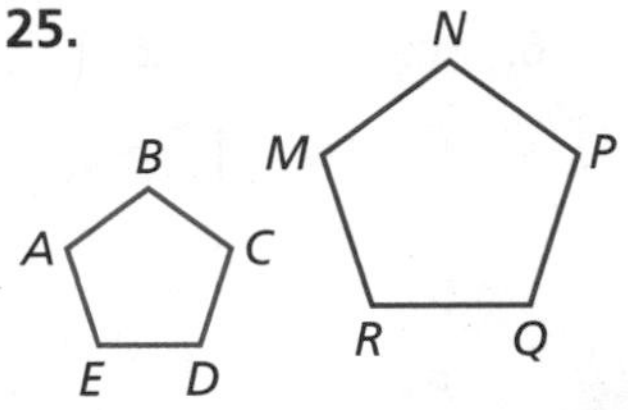

26. The rectangular prism shown is enlarged by a dilation with scale factor 4. Find the surface area and volume of the image.

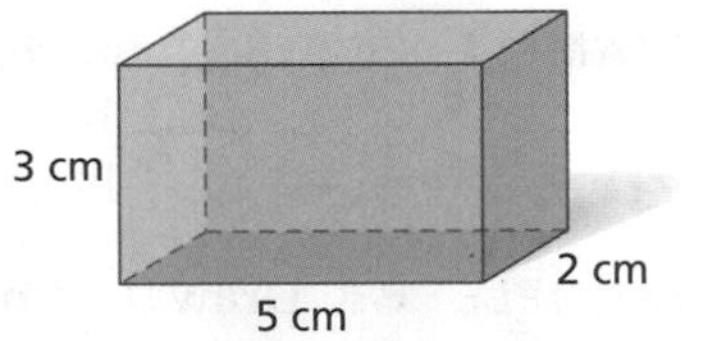

Copy each figure and locate the center of dilation.

27.

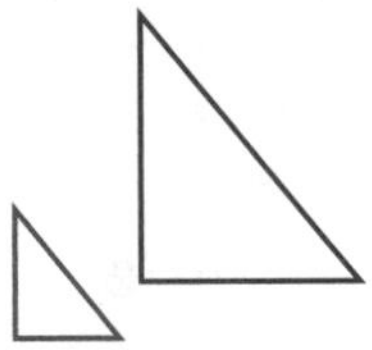

28.

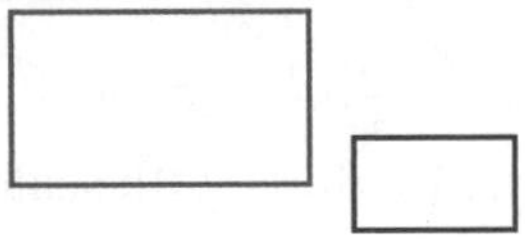

29.

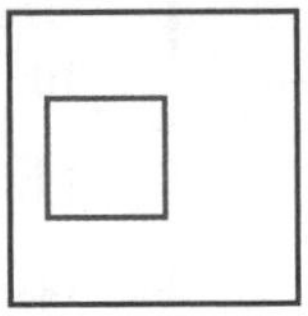

MULTI-STEP TEST PREP

30. a. In the original drawing, the rectangular piece of paper from which the hands emerge measures 27.6 cm by 19.9 cm. On a poster of the drawing, the paper is 82.8 cm long. What is the scale factor of the dilation that was used to make the poster?

b. What is the area of the paper on the poster?

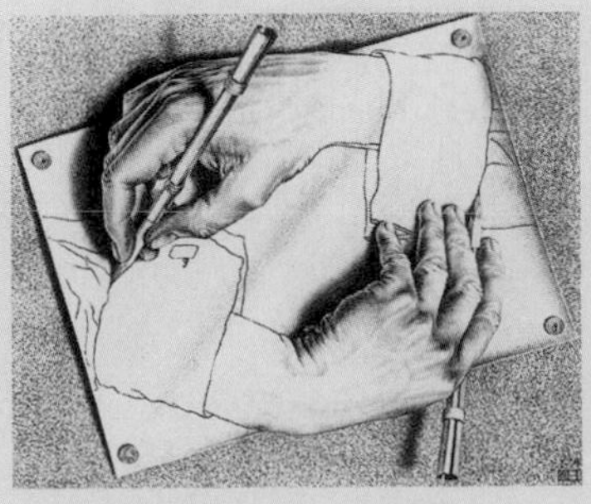

31. ERROR ANALYSIS Rectangle $A'B'C'D'$ is the image of rectangle $ABCD$ under a dilation. Which calculation of the area of rectangle $A'B'C'D'$ is incorrect? Explain the error.

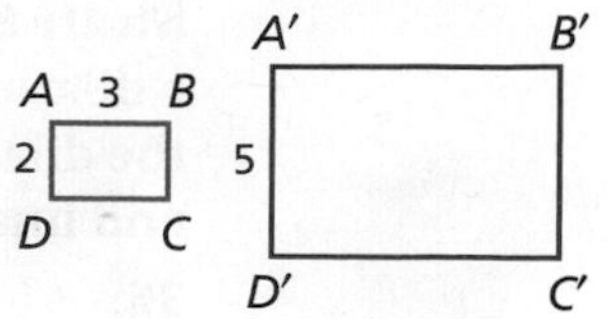

A

The scale factor of the dilation is $\frac{5}{2}$, or 2.5, so the length of $\overline{A'B'}$ must be $2.5 \times 3 = 7.5$. Then the area of rectangle $A'B'C'D'$ is $5 \times 7.5 = 37.5$.

B

The area of rectangle $ABCD$ is $2 \times 3 = 6$, and the scale factor of the dilation is $\frac{5}{2}$, or 2.5. Therefore the area of rectangle $A'B'C'D'$ is $2.5 \times 6 = 15$.

32. Optometry The pupil is the circular opening that allows light into the eye.

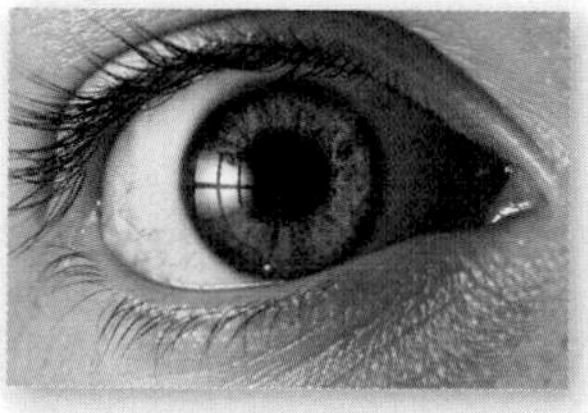

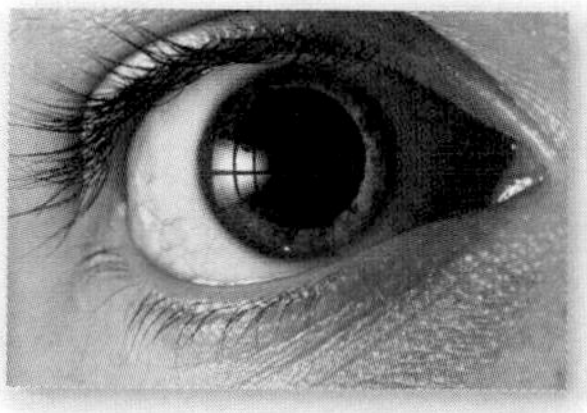

a. An optometrist dilates a patient's pupil from 6 mm to 8 mm. What is the scale factor for this dilation?

b. To the nearest tenth, find the area of the pupil before and after the dilation.

c. As a percentage, how much more light is admitted to the eye after the dilation?

33. Estimation In the diagram, $\triangle ABC \rightarrow \triangle A'B'C'$ under a dilation with center P.

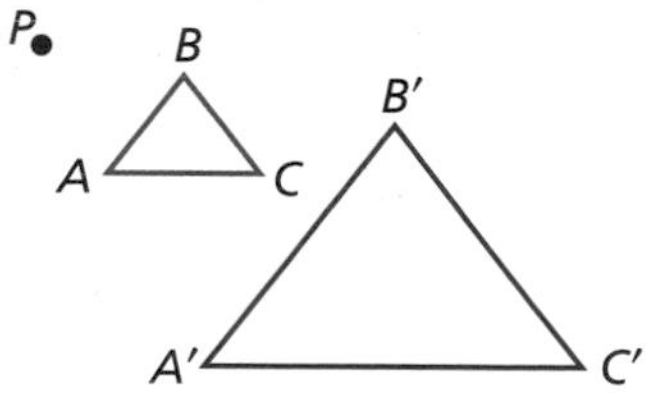

a. Estimate the scale factor of the dilation.

b. Explain how you can use a ruler to make measurements and to calculate the scale factor.

c. Use the method from part **b** to calculate the scale factor. How does your result compare to your estimate?

34. $\triangle ABC$ has vertices $A(-1, 1)$, $B(2, 1)$, and $C(2, 2)$.

a. Draw the image of $\triangle ABC$ under a dilation centered at the origin with scale factor 2 followed by a reflection across the x-axis.

b. Draw the image of $\triangle ABC$ under a reflection across the x-axis followed by a dilation centered at the origin with scale factor 2.

c. Compare the results of parts **a** and **b.** Does the order of the transformations matter?

35. Astronomy The image of the sun projected through the hole of a pinhole camera (the center of dilation) has a diameter of $\frac{1}{4}$ in. The diameter of the sun is 870,000 mi. What is the scale factor of the dilation?

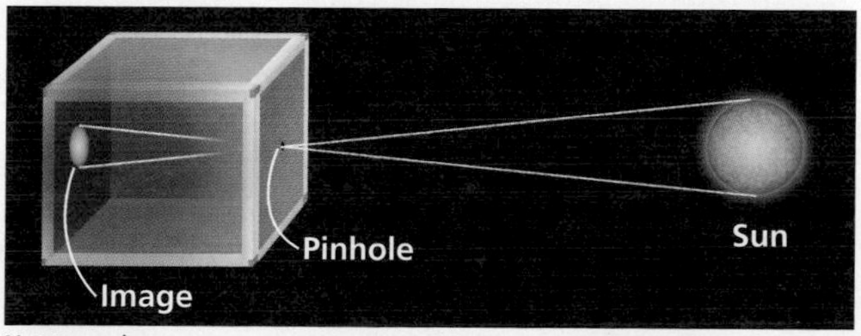

Not to scale

Multi-Step $\triangle ABC$ **with vertices** $A(-2, 2)$, $B(1, 3)$, **and** $C(1, -1)$ **is transformed by a dilation centered at the origin. For each given image point, find the scale factor of the dilation and the coordinates of the remaining image points. Graph the preimage and image on a coordinate plane.**

36. $A'(-4, 4)$ **37.** $C'(-2, 2)$ **38.** $B'(-1, -3)$

39. Critical Thinking For what values of the scale factor is the image of a dilation congruent to the preimage? Explain.

40. Write About It When is a dilation equivalent to a rotation by 180°? Why?

41. Write About It Is the composition of a dilation with scale factor m followed by a dilation with scale factor n equivalent to a single dilation with scale factor mn? Explain your reasoning.

Construction Copy each figure. Then use a compass and straightedge to construct the dilation of the figure with the given scale factor and point P **as the center of dilation.**

42. scale factor: $\frac{1}{2}$

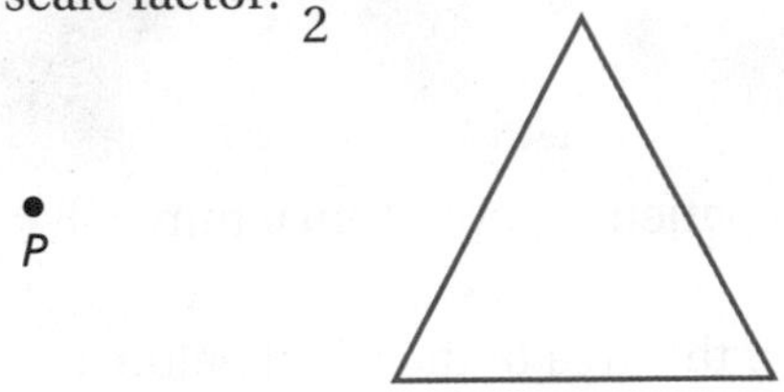

43. scale factor: 2

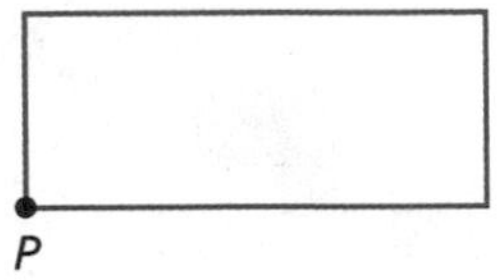

44. scale factor: -1

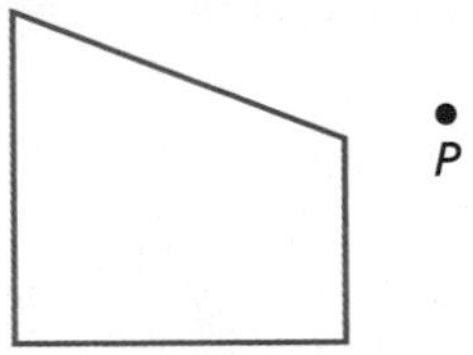

45. scale factor: -2

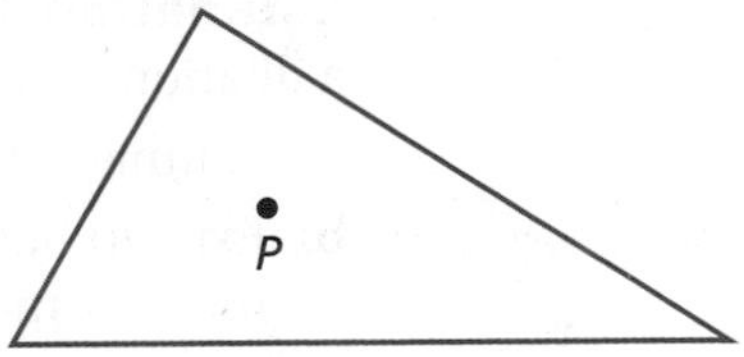

TEST PREP

46. Rectangle *ABCD* is transformed by a dilation centered at the origin. Which scale factor produces an image that has a vertex at $(0, -2)$?

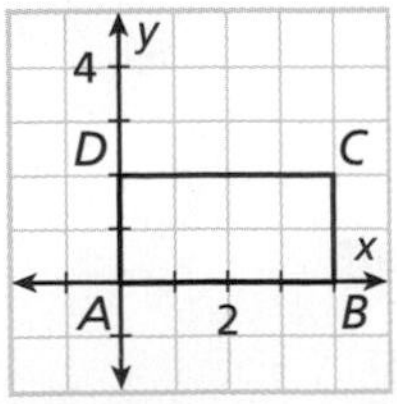

Ⓐ $-\frac{1}{2}$ Ⓒ -2

Ⓑ -1 Ⓓ -4

47. Rectangle *ABCD* is enlarged under a dilation centered at the origin with scale factor 2.5. What is the perimeter of the image?

Ⓕ 15 Ⓖ 24 Ⓗ 30 Ⓙ 50

48. Gridded Response What is the scale factor of a dilation centered at the origin that maps the point $(-2, 3)$ to the point $(-8.4, 12.6)$?

49. Short Response The rules for a photo contest state that entries must have an area no greater than 100 cm^2. Amber has a 6 cm by 8 cm digital photo, and she uses software to enlarge it by a scale factor of 1.5. Does the enlargement meet the requirements of the contest? Show the steps you used to decide your answer.

CHALLENGE AND EXTEND

50. Rectangle $ABCD$ has vertices $A(0, 2)$, $B(1, 2)$, $C(1, 0)$, and $D(0, 0)$.

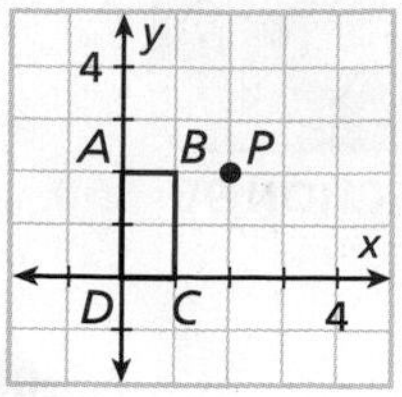

a. Draw the image of $ABCD$ under a dilation centered at point P with scale factor 2.

b. Describe the dilation in part **a** as a composition of a dilation centered at the origin followed by a translation.

c. Explain how a dilation with scale factor k and center of dilation (a, b) can be written as a composition of a dilation centered at the origin and a translation.

51. The equation of line ℓ is $y = -x + 2$. Find the equation of the image of line ℓ after a dilation centered at the origin with scale factor 3.

Using Technology

Use a graphing calculator to complete the following.

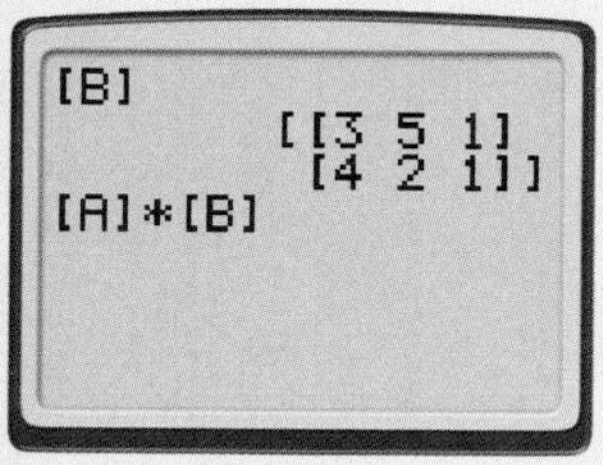

1. $\triangle ABC$ with vertices $A(3, 4)$, $B(5, 2)$, and $C(1, 1)$ can be represented by the point matrix $\begin{bmatrix} 3 & 5 & 1 \\ 4 & 2 & 1 \end{bmatrix}$. Enter these values into matrix **[B]** on your calculator.

2. The matrix $\begin{bmatrix} 2 & 0 \\ 0 & 2 \end{bmatrix}$ can be used to perform a dilation with scale factor 2. Enter these values into matrix **[A]** on your calculator and find **[A] * [B]**. Graph the triangle represented by the resulting point matrix.

3. Make a conjecture about the matrix that could be used to perform a dilation with scale factor $-\frac{1}{2}$. Enter the values into matrix **[A]** on your calculator.

4. Test your conjecture by finding **[A] * [B]** and graphing the triangle represented by the resulting point matrix.

CHAPTER 9

SECTION 9B

MULTI-STEP TEST PREP

MATHEMATICAL PRACTICES **Reason abstractly and quantitatively.**

Patterns

Tessellation Fascination A museum is planning an exhibition of works by the Dutch artist M. C. Escher (1898–1972). The exhibit will include the five drawings shown here.

1. Tell whether each drawing has parallel lines of symmetry, intersecting lines of symmetry, or no lines of symmetry.
2. Tell whether each drawing has rotational symmetry. If so, give the angle of rotational symmetry and the order of the symmetry.
3. Tell whether each drawing is a tessellation. If so, identify the basic figure upon which the tessellation is based.

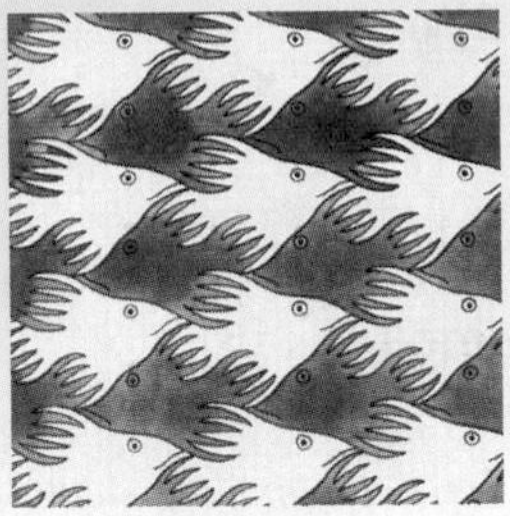

Drawing A

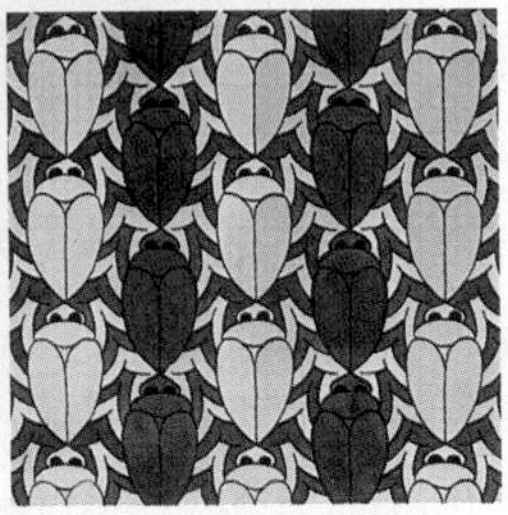

Drawing B

Drawing C

Drawing D

4. The entrance to the exhibit will include a large mural based on drawing E. In the original drawing, the cover of the book measures 13.2 cm by 11.1 cm. In the mural, the book cover will have an area of 21,098.88 cm^2. What is the scale factor of the dilation that will be used to make the mural?

Drawing E

READY TO GO ON?

CHAPTER 9

SECTION 9B

Quiz for Lessons 9-5 Through 9-7

9-5 Symmetry

Explain whether each figure has line symmetry. If so, copy the figure and draw all lines of symmetry.

1. 

2. 

3. 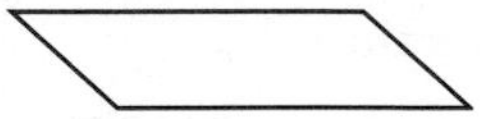

Explain whether each figure has rotational symmetry. If so, give the angle of rotational symmetry and the order of the symmetry.

4. 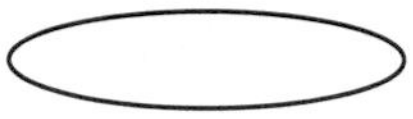

5. 

6. 

9-6 Tessellations

Copy the given figure and use it to create a tessellation.

7. 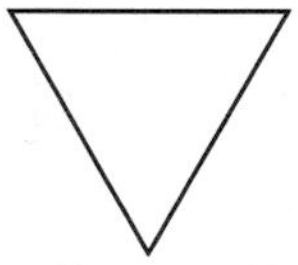

8. 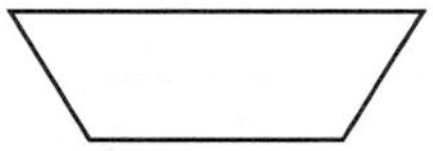

9. 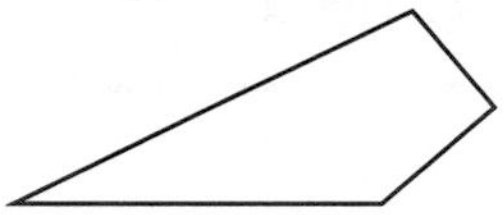

Classify each tessellation as regular, semiregular, or neither.

10. 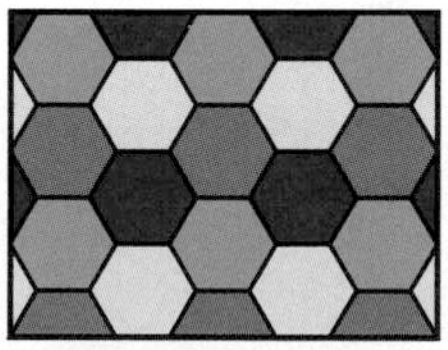

11. 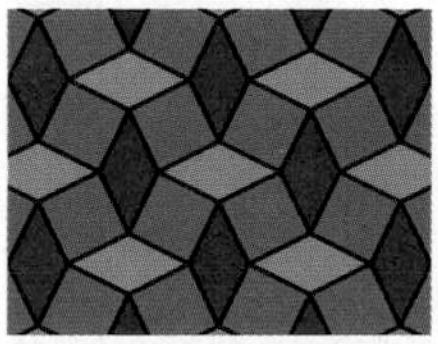

12. 

13. Determine whether it is possible to tessellate a plane with regular octagons. If so, draw the tessellation. If not, explain why.

9-7 Dilations

Tell whether each transformation appears to be a dilation.

14. 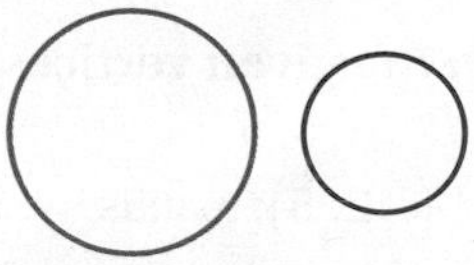

15. 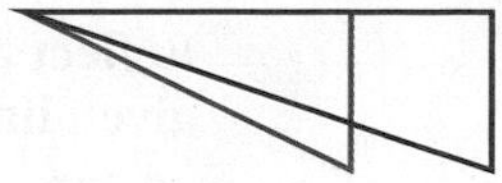

16. 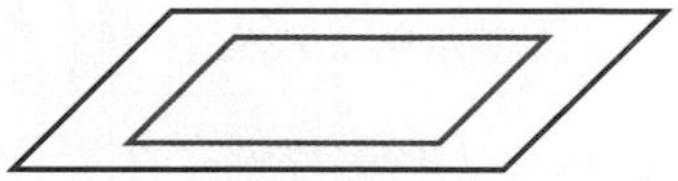

Draw the image of the figure with the given vertices under a dilation with the given scale factor centered at the origin.

17. $A(0, 2)$, $B(-1, 0)$, $C(0, -1)$, $D(1, 0)$; scale factor: 2

18. $P(-4, -2)$, $Q(0, -2)$, $R(0, 0)$, $S(-4, 0)$; scale factor: $-\frac{1}{2}$

CHAPTER
9 Study Guide: Review

Know it! Note

For a complete list of the postulates and theorems in this chapter, see p. PS12.

Vocabulary

center of dilation	line of symmetry
composition of transformations	reduction
enlargement	regular tessellation
frieze pattern	rotational symmetry
glide reflection	semiregular tessellation
glide reflection symmetry	symmetry
isometry	tessellation
line symmetry	translation symmetry

Complete the sentences below with vocabulary words from the list above.

1. A(n) __?__ is a pattern formed by congruent regular polygons.
2. A pattern that has translation symmetry along a line is called a(n) __?__ .
3. A transformation that does not change the size or shape of a figure is a(n) __?__ .
4. One transformation followed by another is called a(n) __?__ .

9-1 Reflections

EXAMPLE

- **Reflect the figure with the given vertices across the given line.**

$A(1, -2), B(4, -3), C(3, 0); y = x$

To reflect across the line $y = x$, interchange the x- and y-coordinates of each point. The images of the vertices are $A'(-2, 1)$, $B'(-3, 4)$, and $C'(0, 3)$.

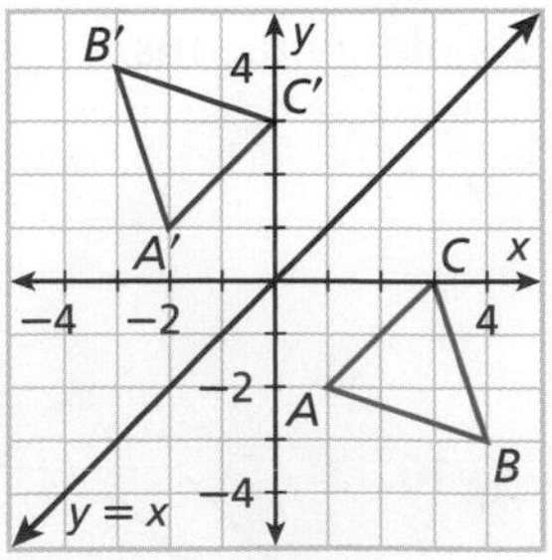

EXERCISES

Tell whether each transformation appears to be a reflection.

5. 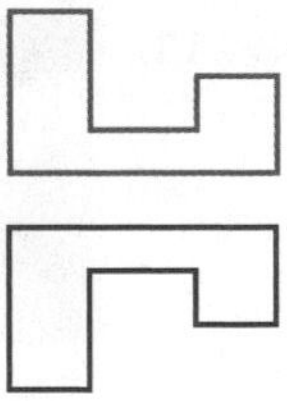

6. 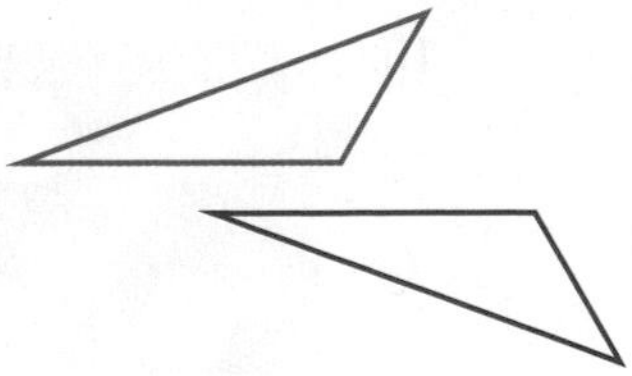

7. 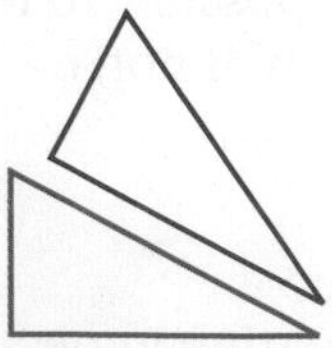

8. 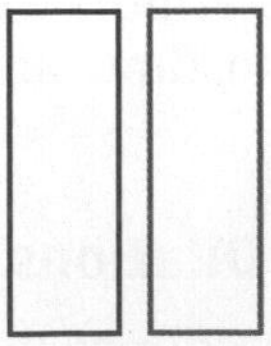

Reflect the figure with the given vertices across the given line.

9. $E(-3, 2), F(0, 2), G(-2, 5)$; x-axis
10. $J(2, -1), K(4, -2), L(4, -3), M(2, -3)$; y-axis
11. $P(2, -2), Q(4, -2), R(3, -4)$; $y = x$
12. $A(2, 2), B(-2, 2), C(-1, 4)$; $y = x$

9-2 Translations

EXAMPLE

■ **Translate the figure with the given vertices along the given vector.**

***D*(−4, 4), *E*(−4, 2), *F*(−1, 1), *G*(−2, 3); ⟨5, −5⟩**

To translate along ⟨5, −5⟩, add 5 to the *x*-coordinate of each point and add −5 to the *y*-coordinate of each point. The vertices of the image are *D′*(1, −1), *E′*(1, −3), *F′*(4, −4), and *G′*(3, −2).

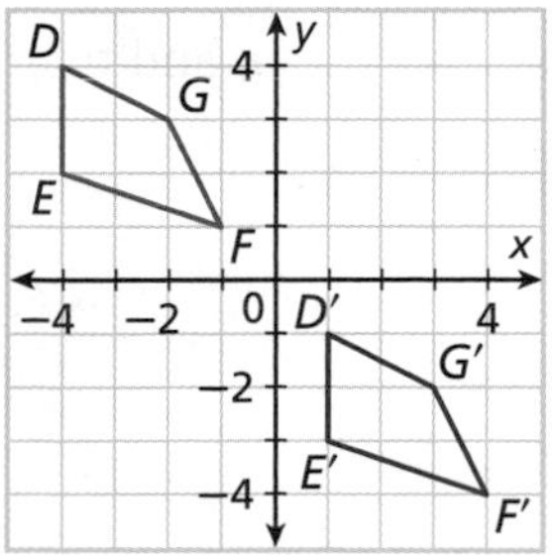

EXERCISES

Tell whether each transformation appears to be a translation.

13.

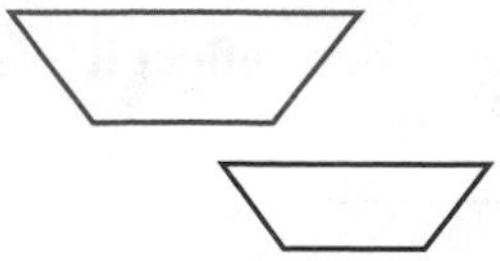

14.

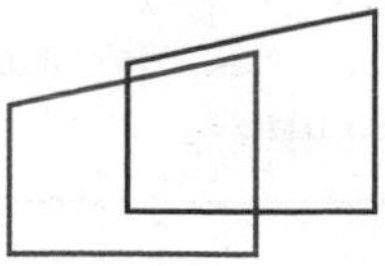

15.

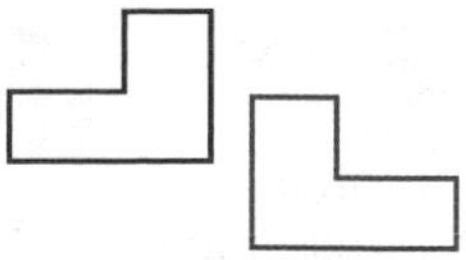

16.

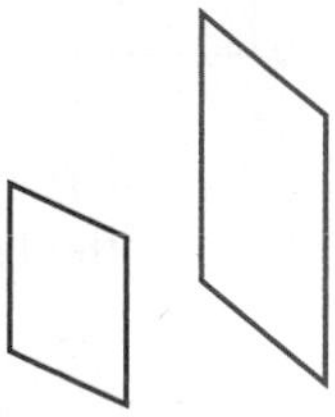

Translate the figure with the given vertices along the given vector.

17. *R*(1, −1), *S*(1, −3), *T*(4, −3), *U*(4, −1); ⟨−5, 2⟩

18. *A*(−4, −1), *B*(−3, 2), *C*(−1, −2); ⟨6, 0⟩

19. *M*(1, 4), *N*(4, 4), *P*(3, 1); ⟨−3, −3⟩

20. *D*(3, 1), *E*(2, −2), *F*(3, −4), *G*(4, −2); ⟨−6, 2⟩

9-3 Rotations

EXAMPLE

■ **Rotate the figure with the given vertices about the origin using the given angle of rotation.**

***A*(−2, 0), *B*(−1, 3), *C*(−4, 3); 180°**

To rotate by 180°, find the opposite of the *x*- and *y*-coordinate of each point. The vertices of the image are *A′*(2, 0), *B′*(1, −3), and *C′*(4, −3).

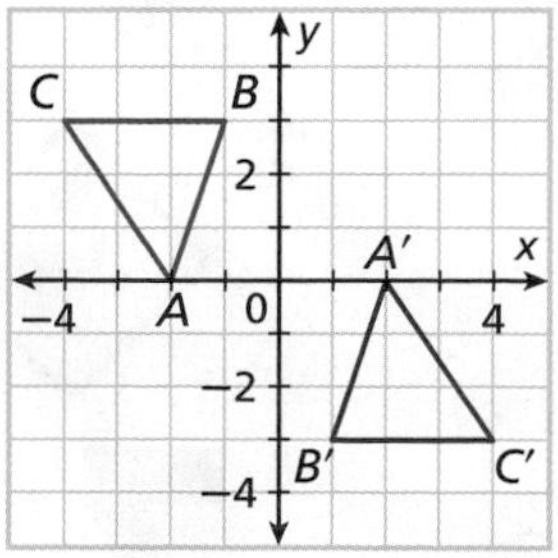

EXERCISES

Tell whether each transformation appears to be a rotation.

21.

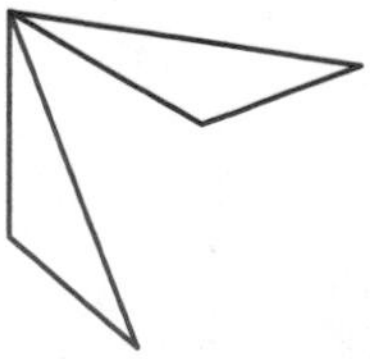

22.

23.

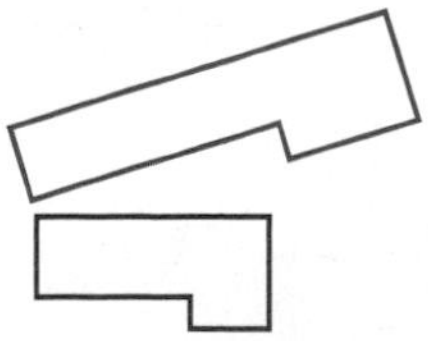

24.

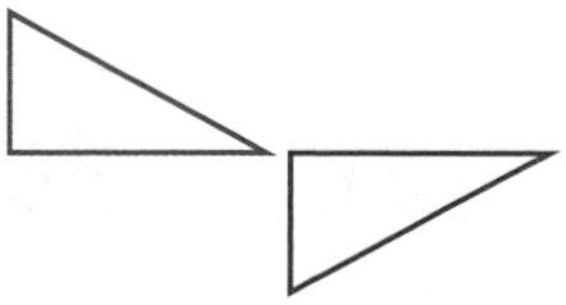

Rotate the figure with the given vertices about the origin using the given angle of rotation.

25. *A*(1, 3), *B*(4, 1), *C*(4, 4); 90°

26. *A*(1, 3), *B*(4, 1), *C*(4, 4); 180°

27. *M*(2, 2), *N*(5, 2), *P*(3, −2), *Q*(0, −2); 90°

28. *G*(−2, 1), *H*(−3, −2), *J*(−1, −4); 180°

9-4 Compositions of Transformations

EXAMPLE

■ **Draw the result of the composition of isometries.**

Translate $\triangle MNP$ along $\vec{v}$ and then reflect it across line ℓ.

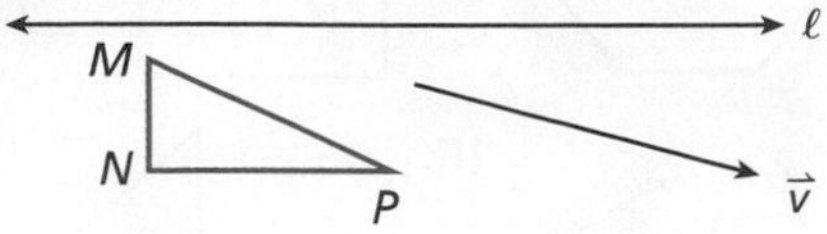

First draw $\triangle M'N'P'$, the translation image of $\triangle MNP$. Then reflect $\triangle M'N'P'$ across line ℓ to find the final image, $\triangle M''N''P''$.

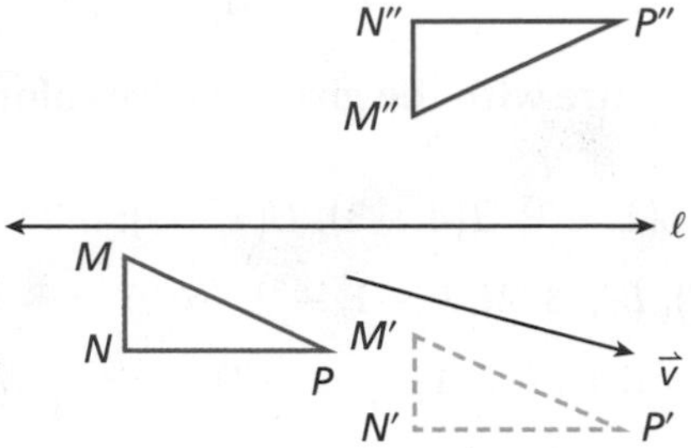

EXERCISES

Draw the result of the composition of isometries.

29. Translate $ABCD$ along $\vec{v}$ and then reflect it across line m.

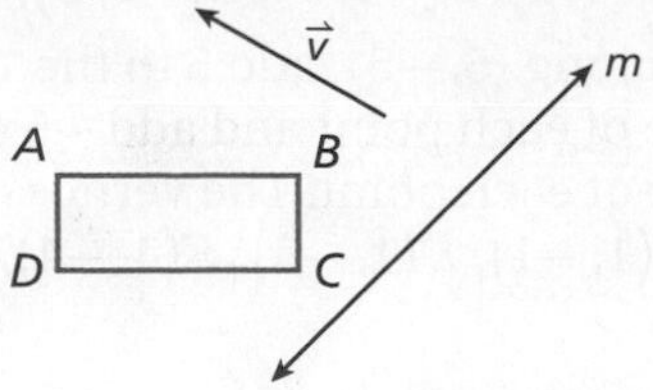

30. Reflect $\triangle JKL$ across line m and then rotate it 90° about point P.

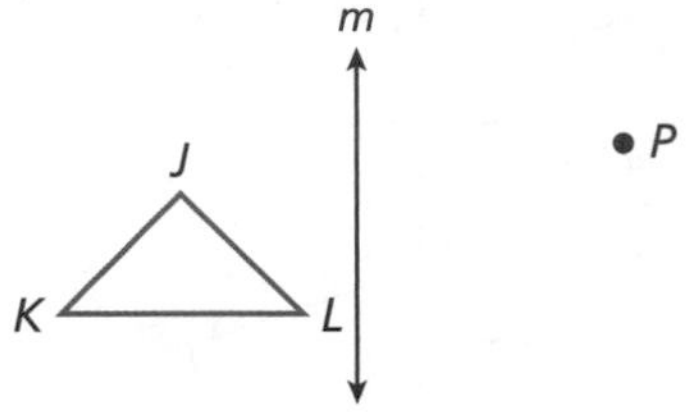

9-5 Symmetry

EXAMPLES

Tell whether each figure has rotational symmetry. If so, give the angle of rotational symmetry and the order of the symmetry.

■ 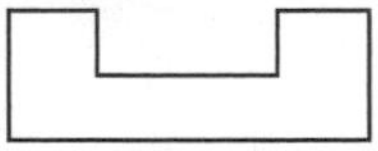

no rotational symmetry

■ 

The figure coincides with itself when it is rotated by 90°. Therefore the angle of rotational symmetry is 90°. The order of symmetry is 4.

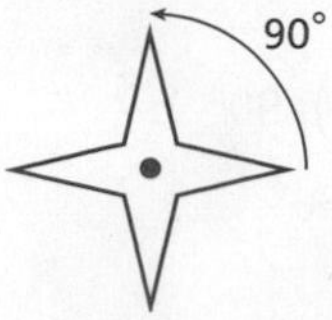

EXERCISES

Tell whether each figure has line symmetry. If so, copy the figure and draw all lines of symmetry.

31. 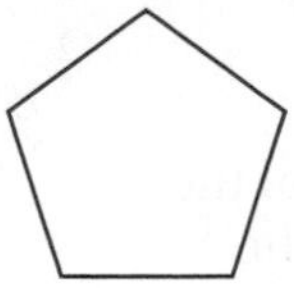

32. 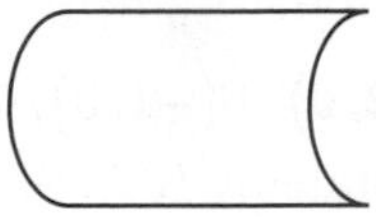

Tell whether each figure has rotational symmetry. If so, give the angle of rotational symmetry and the order of symmetry.

33. 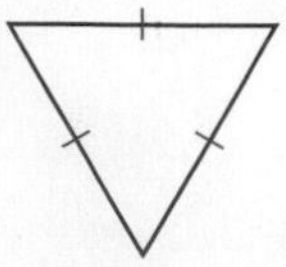

34. 

35. 

36. 

9-6 Tessellations

EXAMPLES

- **Copy the given figure and use it to create a tessellation. Rotate the quadrilateral 180° about the midpoint of one side.**

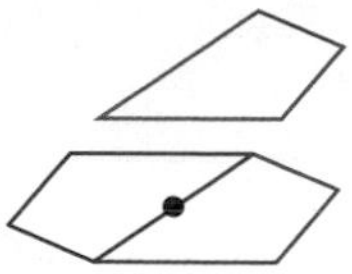

Translate the resulting pair of quadrilaterals to make a row.

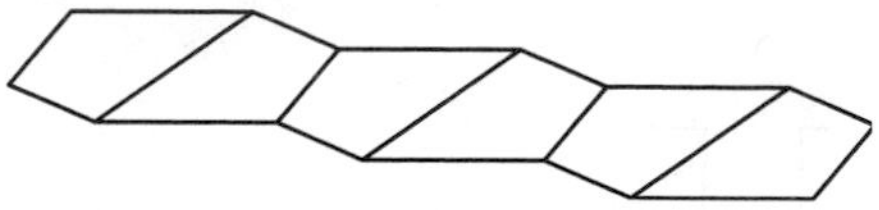

Translate the row to make a tessellation.

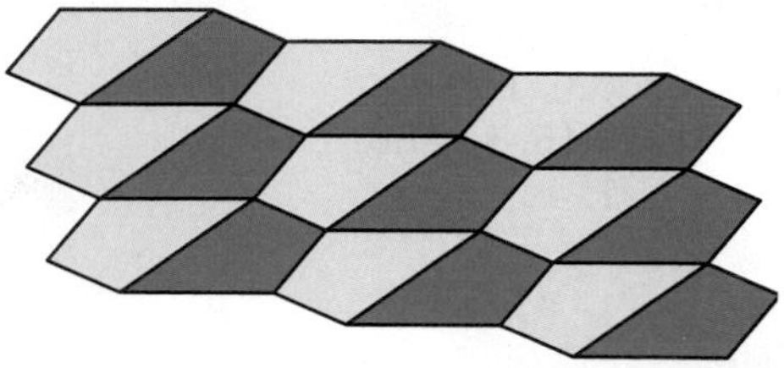

- **Classify the tessellation as regular, semiregular, or neither.**

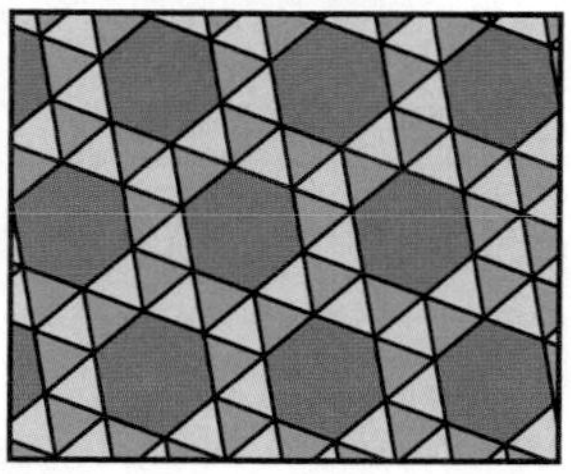

The tessellation is made of two different regular polygons, and each vertex has the same polygons in the same order. Therefore the tessellation is semiregular.

EXERCISES

Copy the given figure and use it to create a tessellation.

37.

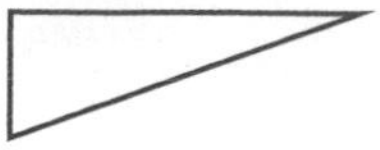

38.

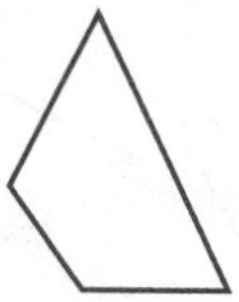

39.

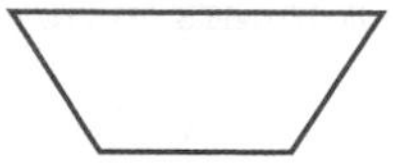

40.

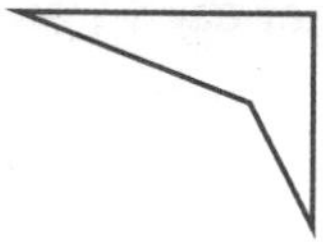

Classify each tessellation as regular, semiregular, or neither.

41.

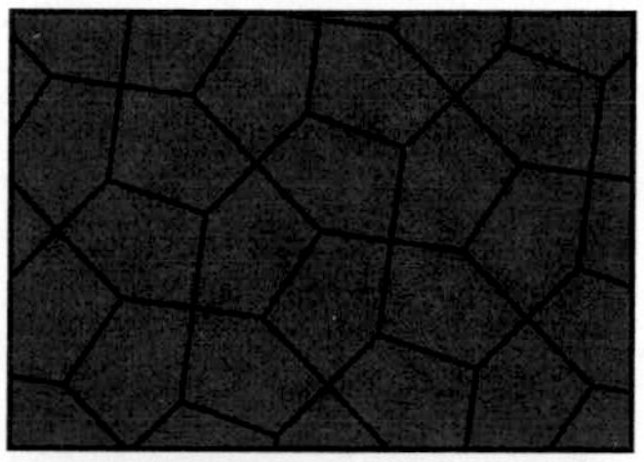

42.

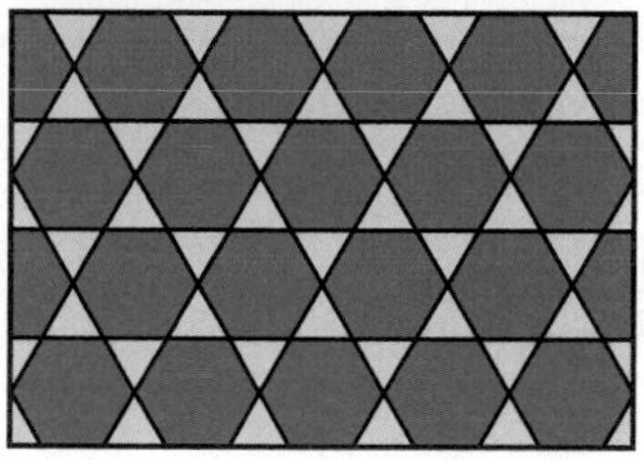

9-7 Dilations

EXAMPLE

- **Draw the image of the figure with the given vertices under a dilation centered at the origin using the given scale factor. $A(0, -2)$, $B(2, -2)$, $C(2, 0)$; scale factor: 2**

Multiply the x- and y-coordinates of each point by 2. The vertices of the image are $A'(0, -4)$, $B'(4, -4)$, and $C'(4, 0)$.

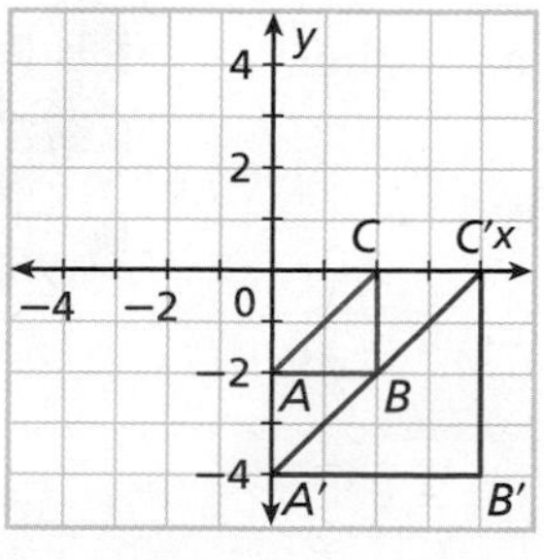

EXERCISES

Tell whether each transformation appears to be a dilation.

43.

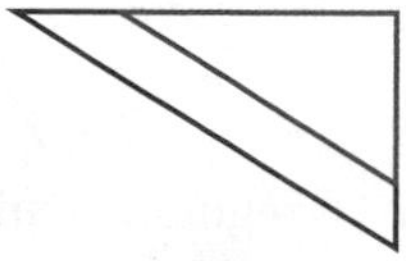

44.

Draw the image of the figure with the given vertices under a dilation centered at the origin using the given scale factor.

45. $R(0, 0)$, $S(4, 4)$, $T(4, -4)$; scale factor: $-\frac{1}{2}$

46. $D(0, 2)$, $E(-2, 2)$, $F(-2, 0)$; scale factor: -2

CHAPTER 9

CHAPTER TEST

Tell whether each transformation appears to be a reflection.

1. 

2. 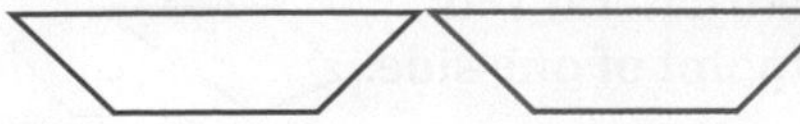

Tell whether each transformation appears to be a translation.

3. 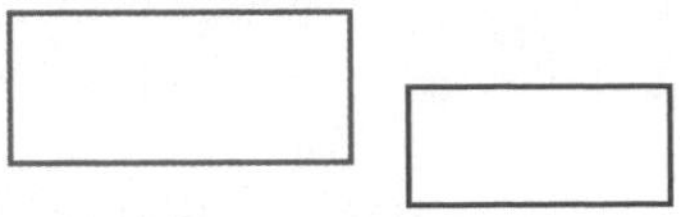

4. 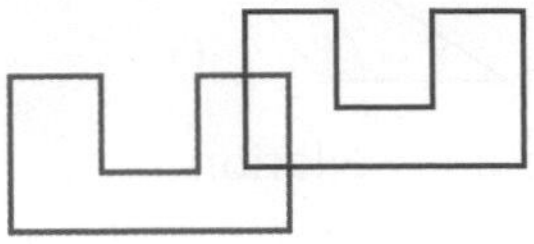

5. An interior designer is using a coordinate grid to place furniture in a room. The position of a sofa is represented by a rectangle with vertices $(1, 3)$, $(2, 2)$, $(5, 5)$, and $(4, 6)$. He decides to move the sofa by translating it along the vector $\langle -1, -1 \rangle$. Draw the sofa in its final position.

Tell whether each transformation appears to be a rotation.

6. 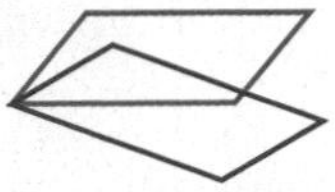

7. 

8. Rotate rectangle $DEFG$ with vertices $D(1, -1)$, $E(4, -1)$, $F(4, -3)$, and $G(1, -3)$ about the origin by 180°.

9. Rectangle $ABCD$ with vertices $A(3, -1)$, $B(3, -2)$, $C(1, -2)$, and $D(1, -1)$ is reflected across the y-axis, and then its image is reflected across the x-axis. Describe a single transformation that moves the rectangle from its starting position to its final position.

10. Tell whether the “no entry” sign has line symmetry. If so, copy the sign and draw all lines of symmetry.

11. Tell whether the “no entry” sign has rotational symmetry. If so, give the angle of rotational symmetry and the order of the symmetry.

Copy the given figure and use it to create a tessellation.

12. 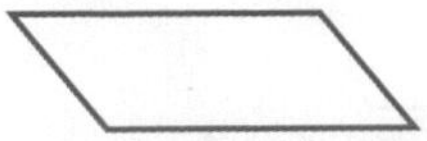

13. 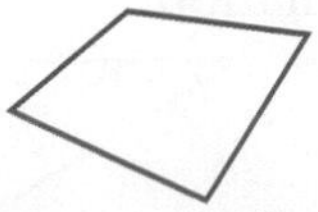

14. 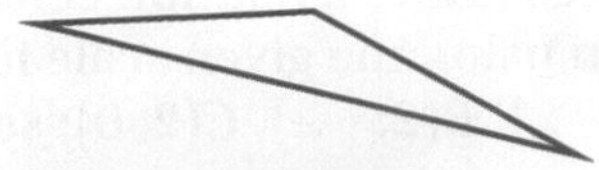

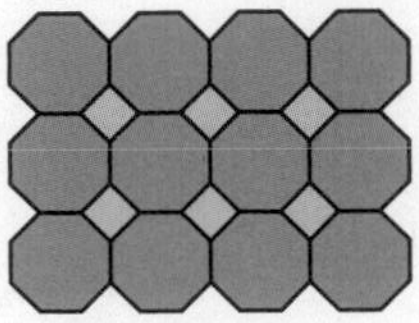

15. Classify the tessellation shown as regular, semiregular, or neither.

Tell whether each transformation appears to be a dilation.

16. 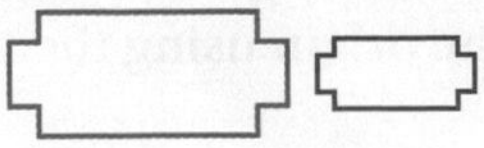

17. 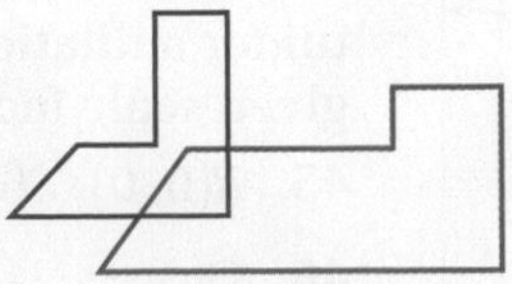

18. Draw the image of $\triangle ABC$ with vertices $A(2, -1)$, $B(1, -4)$, and $C(4, -4)$ under a dilation centered at the origin with scale factor $-\frac{1}{2}$.

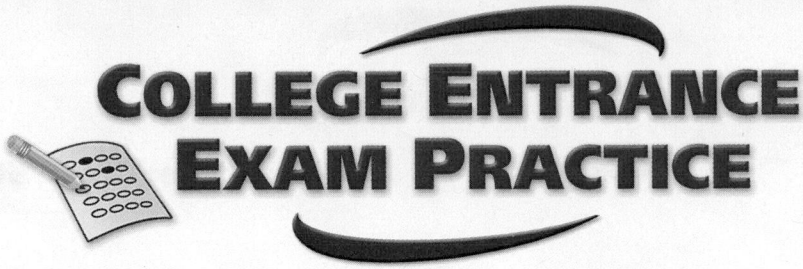

College Entrance Exam Practice

FOCUS ON ACT

No question on the ACT Mathematics Test requires the use of a calculator, but you may bring certain types of calculators to the test. Check www.actstudent.org for a descriptive list of calculators that are prohibited or allowed with slight modifications.

HOT TIP! If you are not sure how to solve a problem, looking through the answer choices may provide you with a clue to the solution method. It may take longer to work backward from the answers provided, so make sure you are monitoring your time.

You may want to time yourself as you take this practice test. It should take you about 5 minutes to complete.

---

1. Which of the following functions has a graph that is symmetric with respect to the *y*-axis?

(A) $f(x) = x^4 - 2$

(B) $f(x) = (x + 2)^4$

(C) $f(x) = 2x - 4$

(D) $f(x) = x^2 + 4x$

(E) $f(x) = (x - 4)^2$

---

2. What is the image of the point $(-4, 5)$ after the translation that maps the point $(1, -3)$ to the point $(-1, -7)$?

(F) $(4, 1)$

(G) $(-6, 1)$

(H) $(-8, 3)$

(J) $(-2, 9)$

(K) $(0, 7)$

---

3. When the point $(-2, -5)$ is reflected across the *x*-axis, what is the resulting image?

(A) $(-5, -2)$

(B) $(2, 5)$

(C) $(2, -5)$

(D) $(-2, 5)$

(E) $(5, 2)$

---

4. After a composition of transformations, the line segment from $A(1, 4)$ to $B(4, 2)$ maps to the line segment from $C(-1, -2)$ to $D(-4, -4)$. Which of the following describes the composition that is applied to $\overline{AB}$ to obtain $\overline{CD}$?

(F) Translate 5 units to the left and then reflect across the *y*-axis.

(G) Reflect across the *y*-axis and then reflect across the *x*-axis.

(H) Reflect across the *y*-axis and then translate 6 units down.

(J) Reflect across the *x*-axis and then reflect across the *y*-axis.

(K) Translate 6 units down and then reflect across the *x*-axis.

---

5. What is the image of the following figure after rotating it counterclockwise by 270°?

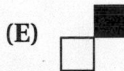

(A) 

(B) 

(C) 

(D) 

(E) 

CHAPTER 9

TEST TACKLER

Standardized Test Strategies

Any Question Type: Highlight Main Ideas

Before answering a test item, identify the important information given in the problem and make sure you clearly identify the question being asked. Outlining the question or breaking a problem into parts can help you to understand the main idea.

A common error in answering multi-step questions is to complete only the first step. In multiple-choice questions, partial answers are often used as the incorrect answer choices. If you start by outlining all steps needed to solve the problem, you are less likely to choose one of these incorrect answers.

EXAMPLE 1

Gridded Response

A blueprint shows a rectangular building's layout reduced using a scale factor of $\frac{1}{30}$. On the blueprint, the building's width is 15 in. and its length is 6 in. Find the area of the actual building in square feet.

What are you asked to find?

the area of the actual building in square feet

List the given information you need to solve the problem.

The scale factor is $\frac{1}{30}$.

On the blueprint, the width is 15 in. and the length is 6 in.

EXAMPLE 2

Short Response

An animator uses a coordinate plane to show the motion of a flying bird. The bird begins at the point $(12, 0)$ and is then rotated about the origin by 15° every 0.005 second. Give the bird's position after 0.015 second. Round the coordinates to the nearest tenth. Explain the steps you used to get your answer.

What are you asked to find?

the coordinates of the bird's position after 0.015 seconds, to the nearest tenth

What information are you given?

the initial position of the bird and the angle of rotation for every 0.005 second

HOT TIP! Sometimes important information is given in a diagram.

Read each test item and answer the questions that follow.

Item A

Multiple Choice **Jonas is using a coordinate plane to plan an archaeological dig. He outlines a rectangle with vertices at (5, 2), (5, 9), (10, 9), and (10, 2). Then he outlines a second rectangle by reflecting the first area across the x-axis and then across the y-axis. Which is a vertex of the second outlined rectangle?**

Ⓐ $(-5, 2)$ Ⓒ $(-2, -10)$

Ⓑ $(-5, -9)$ Ⓓ $(10, -9)$

1. Identify the sentence that gives the information regarding the coordinates of the initial rectangle.
2. What are you being asked to do?
3. How many transformations does Jonas perform before he sketches the second rectangle? Which sentence leads you to this answer?
4. A student incorrectly marked choice A as her response. What part of the test item did she fail to complete?

Item B

Short Response **A picture frame can hold a picture that is no greater than 320 in^2. Gabby has a digital photo with dimensions 3.5 in. by 5 in., and she uses software to enlarge it by a scale factor of 5. Does the enlargement fit the frame? Show the steps you used to decide your answer.**

5. Make a list stating the information given and what you are being asked to do.
6. Are there any intermediate steps you have to make to obtain a solution for the problem? If so, describe the steps.

Item C

Short Response **Rectangle $A'B'C'D'$ is the image of rectangle $ABCD$ under a dilation. Identify the scale factor and determine the area of rectangle $A'B'C'D'$.**

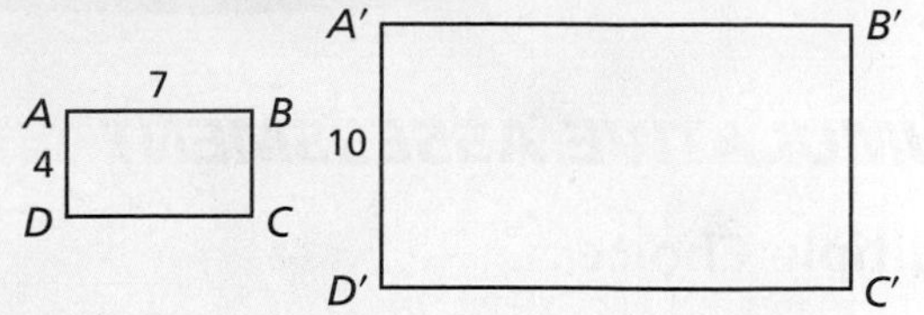

7. How many parts are there to this item? Make a list of what needs to be included in your response.
8. Where in the test item can you find the important information (data) needed to solve the problem? Make a list of this information.

Item D

Multiple Choice **$\triangle ABC$ is reflected across the x-axis. Then its image is rotated 180° about the origin. What are the coordinates of the image of point B after the reflection?**

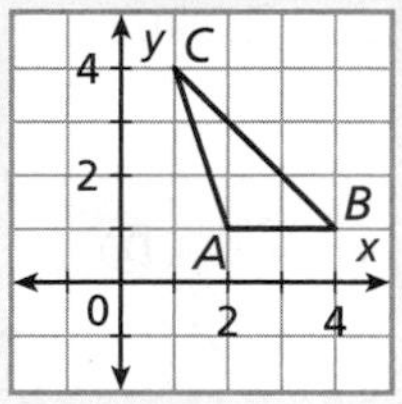

Ⓐ $(-4, -1)$ Ⓒ $(1, -4)$

Ⓑ $(-1, 4)$ Ⓓ $(4, -1)$

9. Identify the transformations described in the problem statement.
10. What are you being asked to do?
11. Identify any part of the problem statement that you will not use to answer the question.
12. There are only two pieces of information given in this test item that are important to answering this question. What are they?

CHAPTER 9

STANDARDIZED TEST PREP

Learn It Online
State Test Practice

CUMULATIVE ASSESSMENT

Multiple Choice

1. Parallelogram $ABCD$ has a diagonal $\overline{AC}$ with endpoints $A(1, 3)$ and $C(5, -3)$. If B has coordinates (x, y), which of the following represents the coordinates for D?

Ⓐ $(-3x, -y)$

Ⓑ $(-x, -y)$

Ⓒ $(-x + 6, -y)$

Ⓓ $(x - 3, y)$

2. Which of the following sets of lengths can represent the side lengths of an obtuse triangle?

Ⓕ 3, 5, and 10

Ⓖ 7, 12, and 13

Ⓗ 9, 15, and 22

Ⓙ 2, 3, and 5

3. The image of point A under a 90° rotation about the origin is $A'(10, -4)$. What are the coordinates of point A?

Ⓐ $(-10, -4)$

Ⓑ $(-10, 4)$

Ⓒ $(-4, -10)$

Ⓓ $(4, 10)$

4. What is the length of $\overline{UX}$ to the nearest inch?

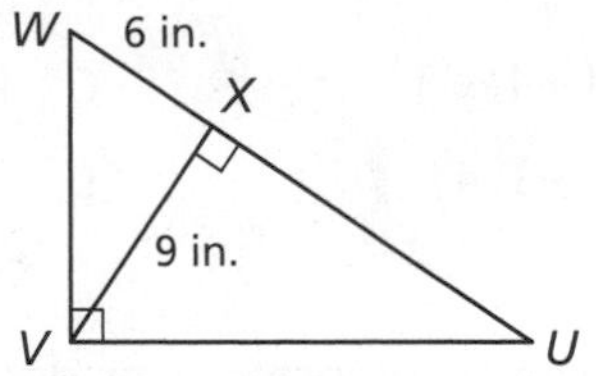

Ⓕ 4.5 inches

Ⓖ 10 inches

Ⓗ 12 inches

Ⓙ 18 inches

5. Marty conjectures that the sum of any two prime numbers is even. Which of the following is a counterexample that shows Marty's conjecture is false?

Ⓐ $2 + 2 = 4$

Ⓑ $2 + 7 = 9$

Ⓒ $2 + 9 = 11$

Ⓓ $3 + 5 = 8$

Use the graph for Items 6–8.

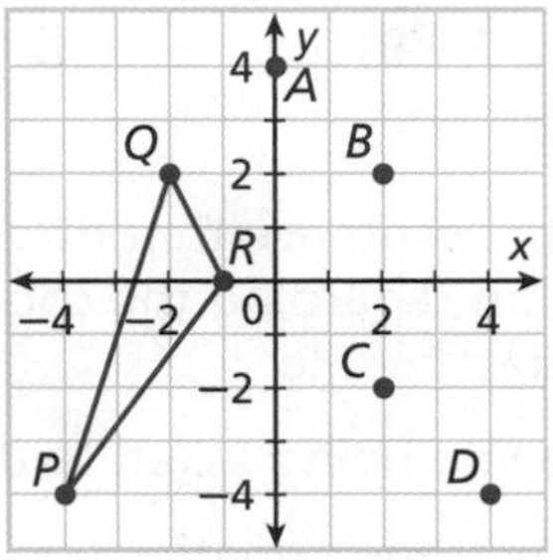

6. What are the coordinates of the image of point C under the same translation that maps point D to point B?

Ⓕ $(4, 4)$

Ⓖ $(0, 4)$

Ⓗ $(0, 8)$

Ⓙ $(4, -8)$

7. $\triangle PQR$ is the image of a triangle under a dilation centered at the origin with scale factor $-\frac{1}{2}$. Which point is a vertex of the preimage of $\triangle PQR$ under this dilation?

Ⓐ A

Ⓑ B

Ⓒ C

Ⓓ D

8. What is the measure of $\angle PRQ$? Round to the nearest degree.

Ⓕ 63°

Ⓖ 127°

Ⓗ 117°

Ⓙ 45°

9. Which mapping represents a rotation of 270° about the origin?

Ⓐ $(x, y) \rightarrow (-x, -y)$

Ⓑ $(x, y) \rightarrow (x, -y)$

Ⓒ $(x, y) \rightarrow (-y, -x)$

Ⓓ $(x, y) \rightarrow (y, -x)$

HOT TIP! When problems involve geometric figures in the coordinate plane, it may be useful to describe properties of the figures algebraically. For example, you can use slope to verify that sides of a figure are parallel or perpendicular, or you can use the Distance Formula to find side lengths of the figure.

10. $\triangle ABC$ is a right triangle. $m\angle A = 65°$, $m\angle B = 90°$, $AC = 7$, and $AB = 3$. Which expression can be used to find BC?

- (F) 3/tan 25°
- (G) 8/sin 65°
- (H) 7 tan 65°
- (J) 3 cos 25°

11. Which regular polygon can be used with an equilateral triangle to tessellate a plane?

- (A) Heptagon
- (B) Octagon
- (C) Nonagon
- (D) Dodecagon

12. Which line coincides with the line $3y - 2x = 6$?

- (F) a line through (4, 3) and (0, −3)
- (G) a line through (0, 2) and (1.5, 3)
- (H) $2y - 3x = 6$
- (J) $y = -\frac{1}{2}x + 6$

13. Given the points $B(-1, 2)$, $C(-7, y)$, $D(1, -3)$, and $E(-3, -2)$, what is the value of y if $\overline{BD} \parallel \overline{CE}$?

- (A) −12
- (B) −8
- (C) 3.5
- (D) 8

Gridded Response

14. $\triangle ABC$ is a right triangle such that $m\angle B = 90°$. If $AC = 12$ and $BC = 9$, what is the perimeter of $\triangle ABC$? Round to the nearest tenth.

15. A blueprint for an office space uses a scale of 3 inches: 20 feet. What is the area in square inches of the office space on the blueprint if the actual office space has area 1300 square feet?

16. How many lines of symmetry does a regular hexagon have?

17. What is the x-coordinate of the image of the point $A(12, -7)$ if A is reflected across the x-axis?

Short Response

18. $A(-4, -2)$, $B(-2, -3)$, and $C(-3, -5)$ are three of the vertices of rhombus $ABCD$. Show that $ABCD$ is a square. Justify your answer.

19. Rectangle $PQRS$ has a length of 1.3 feet and a width of 0.9 feet. Rectangle $TUVW$ has a length of 11.7 inches and a width of 8.1 inches. Determine whether rectangle $PQRS$ is similar to rectangle $TUVW$. Explain your reasoning.

20. Determine the value of x if $\triangle ABC \cong \triangle BDC$. Justify your answer.

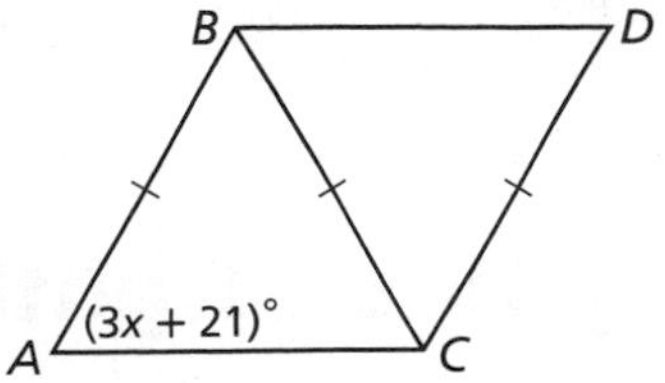

21. $\triangle ABC$ is reflected across line m.

a. What observations can be made about $\triangle ABC$ and its reflected image $\triangle A'B'C'$ regarding the following properties: collinearity, betweenness, angle measure, triangle congruence, and orientation?

b. Explain.

22. Given the coordinates of points A, B, and C, explain how you could demonstrate that the three points are collinear.

23. Proving that the diagonals of rectangle $KLMN$ are equal using a coordinate proof involves placement of the rectangle and selection of coordinates.

a. Is it possible to always position rectangle $KLMN$ so that one vertex coincides with the origin?

b. Why is it convenient to place rectangle $KLMN$ so that one vertex is at the origin?

Extended Response

24. $\overline{AB}$ has endpoints $A(0, 3)$ and $B(2, 5)$.

a. Draw $\overline{AB}$ and its image, $\overline{A'B'}$, under the translation $\langle 0, -8 \rangle$.

b. Find the equations of two lines such that the composition of the two reflections across the lines will also map $\overline{AB}$ to $\overline{A'B'}$. Show your work or explain in words how you found your answer.

c. Show that any glide reflection is equivalent to a composition of three reflections.

Real-World CONNECTIONS

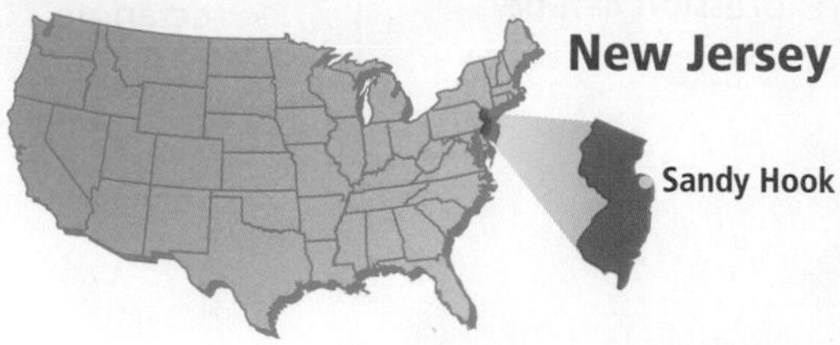

Sandy Hook Lighthouse

Sandy Hook Lighthouse in northern New Jersey has been guiding ships into New York Harbor for nearly 250 years. Built in 1764, the 85-foot tower is the oldest working lighthouse in the country.

Choose one or more strategies to solve each problem.

1. Suppose the side of the tower measures 86 feet in length along an edge. To the nearest degree, what angle does the edge of the side make with the ground?
2. The base of the lighthouse is a regular octagon. What is the sum of the measures of the angles of the octagon?
3. Most lighthouses use *Fresnel lenses,* named after their inventor, Augustine Fresnel. The chart shows the sizes, or *orders,* of the circular lenses. Find the scale factor from a fourth degree lens to a first degree lens.

Fresnel Lenses

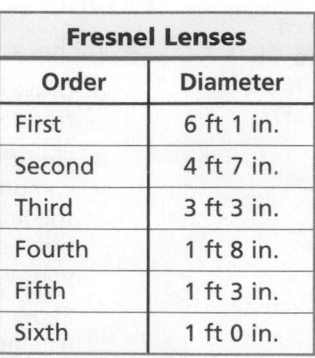

Order	Diameter
First	6 ft 1 in.
Second	4 ft 7 in.
Third	3 ft 3 in.
Fourth	1 ft 8 in.
Fifth	1 ft 3 in.
Sixth	1 ft 0 in.

Moveable Bridges

New Jersey is home to more than two dozen moveable bridges. A moveable bridge has a section that can be lifted, tilted, or swung out of the way so that tall boats can pass.

1. The Cape May Canal Bridge is a *swing bridge.* Part of the roadbed can pivot horizontally to let boats pass. What transformation describes the motion of the bridge? The pivoting section moves through an angle of 90°. How far does a point 10 ft from the pivot travel as the bridge opens?

A *lift bridge* contains a section that can be translated vertically. For 2–4, use the table.

Lift Bridges		
Name	**Vertical Clearance (Lowered Position)**	**Vertical Clearance (Raised Position)**
Burlington-Bristol Bridge	35 ft	138 ft
Delair Lift Bridge	49 ft	135 ft

2. It takes 2 min to completely lift the roadbed of the Burlington-Bristol Bridge. At what speed in feet per minute does the lifting mechanism translate the roadbed?

3. To the nearest second, how long does it take the Burlington-Bristol Bridge's lifting mechanism to translate the roadbed 10 ft?

4. Suppose the Delair Lift Bridge can be raised at the same speed as the Burlington-Bristol Bridge. To the nearest second, how long would it take to completely lift its roadbed?

5. The HX Drawbridge in Secaucus is a *bascule bridge.* Weights are used to raise part of its deck at an angle. The moveable section of the HX Drawbridge is 151 ft long. Find the height of the deck above the roadway after it has been rotated by an angle of 20°.

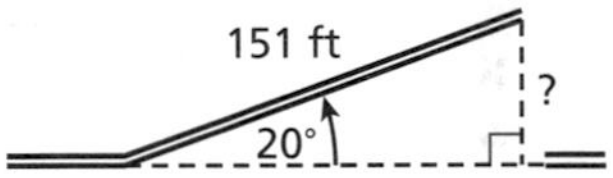

CHAPTER

10 Extending Perimeter, Circumference, and Area

COMMON CORE

Chapter Focus

- Develop and apply area formulas for circles, polygons, and composite figures.
- Use area to solve geometric probability problems.

It measures up!

How would you find the area of a field or the floor of an irregularly shaped building? You can use the ideas in this chapter to find out!

Learn It Online
Chapter Project Online

Air Photo/Jim Wark

ARE YOU READY?

Vocabulary

Match each term on the left with a definition on the right.

1. area
2. kite
3. perimeter
4. regular polygon

A. a polygon that is both equilateral and equiangular

B. a quadrilateral with exactly one pair of parallel sides

C. the number of nonoverlapping unit squares of a given size that exactly cover the interior of a figure

D. a quadrilateral with exactly two pairs of adjacent congruent sides

E. the distance around a closed plane figure

Convert Units

Use multiplication or division to change from one unit of measure to another.

5. 12 mi = ____ yd
6. 7.3 km = ____ m
7. 6 in. = ____ ft
8. 15 m = ____ mm

Length	
Metric	**Customary**
1 kilometer = 1000 meters 1 meter = 100 centimeters 1 centimeter = 10 millimeters	1 mile = 1760 yards 1 mile = 5280 feet 1 yard = 3 feet 1 foot = 12 inches

Pythagorean Theorem

Find x in each right triangle. Round to the nearest tenth, if necessary.

9.
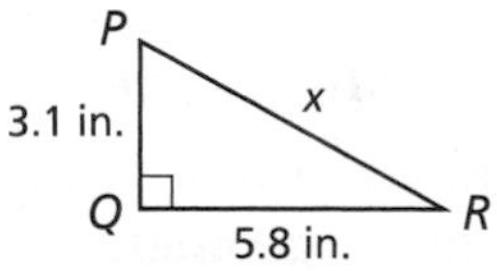

10.
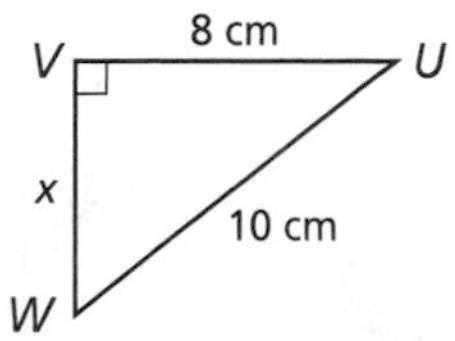

11.
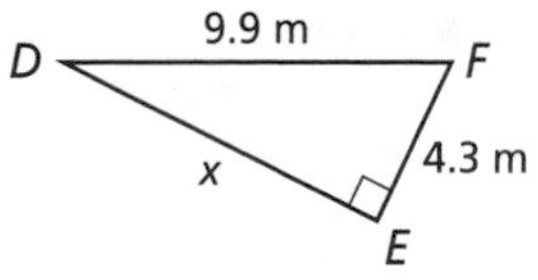

Measure with Customary and Metric Units

Measure each segment to the nearest eighth of an inch and to the nearest half of a centimeter.

12.

13.

14.
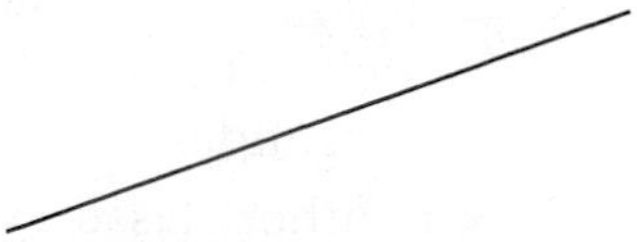

Solve for a Variable

Solve each equation for the indicated variable.

15. $A = \frac{1}{2}bh$ for b

16. $P = 2b + 2h$ for h

17. $A = \frac{1}{2}(b_1 + b_2)h$ for b_1

18. $A = \frac{1}{2}d_1d_2$ for d_1

CHAPTER 10

Study Guide: Preview

Where You've Been

Previously, you

- graphed ordered pairs.
- developed and used the Pythagorean Theorem.
- measured with customary and metric units.
- used formulas for area and perimeter.

In This Chapter

You will study

- areas and perimeters of figures whose vertices are given by ordered pairs.
- areas and perimeters of figures whose dimensions are found by using the Pythagorean Theorem.
- areas and perimeters of figures in customary and metric units.
- proofs of formulas for area and perimeter.

Where You're Going

You can use the skills learned in this chapter

- in your future math classes, such as Calculus, to find the area under a curve.
- in other classes, such as in Geography to find lengths of borders and areas of countries.
- outside of school to plan a garden, analyze data in the newspaper, and solve puzzles.

Key Vocabulary/Vocabulario

apothem	apotema
center of a circle	centro de un circulo
center of a regular polygon	centro de un poligono regular
central angle of a regular polygon	ángulo central de un poligono
circle	circulo
composite figure	figuras compuestas
geometric probability	probabilidad geométrica

Vocabulary Connections

To become familiar with some of the vocabulary terms in the chapter, consider the following. You may refer to the chapter, the glossary, or a dictionary if you like.

1. How can you use the everyday meaning of the word *center* to understand the term **center of a circle** ?
2. The word *composite* means "of separate parts." What do you think the term **composite figure** means?
3. What does the word *probability* mean? How do you think **geometric probability** differs from theoretical probability?
4. The word **apothem** begins with the root *apo-*, which means "away from." The apothem of a regular polygon is measured "away from" the center to the midpoint of a side. What do you think is true about the apothem and the side of the polygon?

Reading and Writing Math

Study Strategy: Memorize Formulas

Throughout a geometry course, you will learn many formulas, theorems, postulates, and corollaries. You may be required to memorize some of these. In order not to become overwhelmed by the amount of information, it helps to use flash cards.

In a right triangle, the two sides that form the right angle are the **legs**. The side across from the right angle that stretches from one leg to the other is the **hypotenuse**. In the diagram, *a* and *b* are the lengths of the shorter sides, or legs, of the right triangle. The longest side is called the hypotenuse and has length *c*.

Know it! Note

Theorem Pythagorean Theorem

In a right triangle, the sum of the squares of the lengths of the *legs* is equal to the square of the length of the *hypotenuse*.

$$a^2 + b^2 = c^2$$

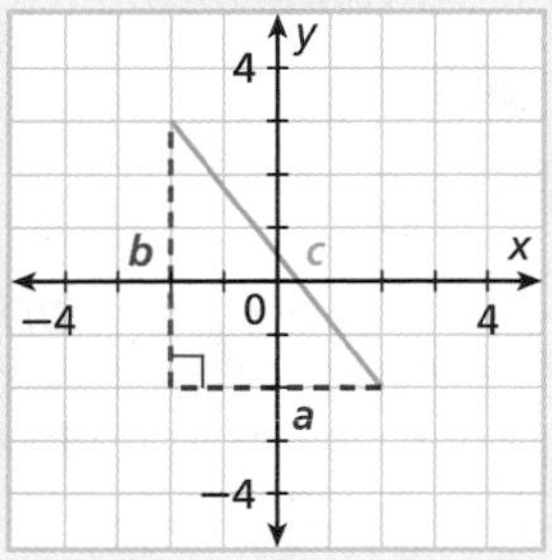

To create a flash card, write the name of the formula or theorem on the front of the card. Then clearly write the appropriate information on the back of the card. Be sure to include a labeled diagram.

Front

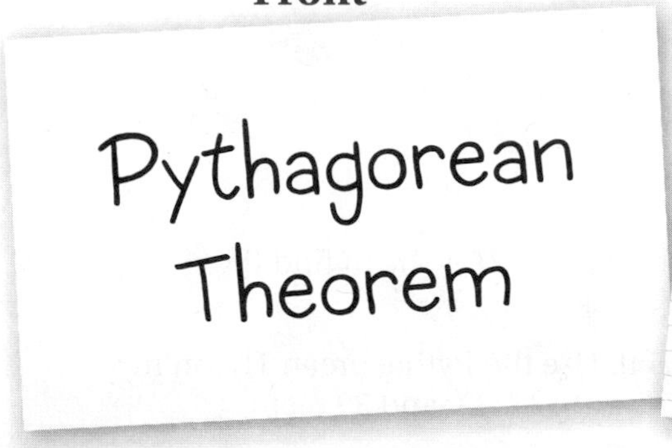

Back

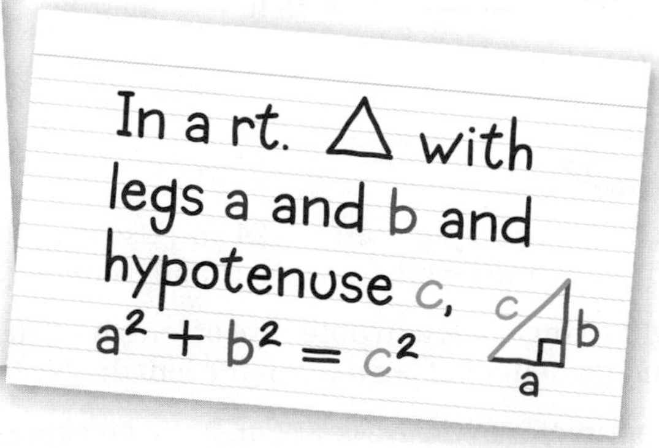

In a rt. △ with legs a and b and hypotenuse c,
a² + b² = c²
c
b
a

Try This

1. Choose a lesson from this book that you have already studied, and make flash cards of the formulas or theorems from the lesson.
2. Review your flash cards by looking at the front of each card and trying to recall the information on the back of the card.

Connecting Geometry to Algebra

Literal Equations

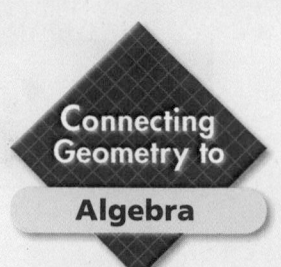

A *literal equation* contains two or more variables. Formulas you have used to find perimeter, circumference, area, and side relationships of right triangles are examples of literal equations.

If you want to evaluate a formula for several different values of a given variable, it is helpful to solve for the variable first.

Example

Danielle plans to use 50 feet of fencing to build a dog run. Use the formula $P = 2\ell + 2w$ to find the length ℓ when the width w is 4, 5, 6, and 10 feet.

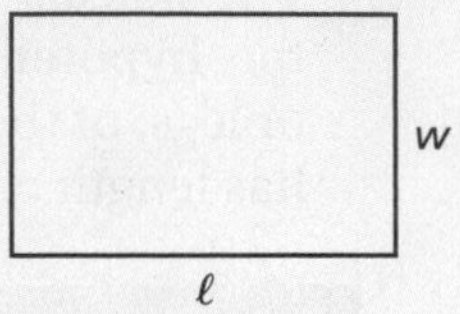

Solve the equation for ℓ.

First solve the formula for the variable.

$P = 2\ell + 2w$ — *Write the original equation.*

$P - 2w = 2\ell$ — *Subtract 2w from both sides.*

$\frac{P - 2w}{2} = \ell$ — *Divide both sides by 2.*

Use your result to find ℓ for each value of w.

$\ell = \frac{P - 2w}{2} = \frac{50 - 2(4)}{2} = 21 \text{ ft}$ — *Substitute 50 for P and 4 for w.*

$\ell = \frac{P - 2w}{2} = \frac{50 - 2(5)}{2} = 20 \text{ ft}$ — *Substitute 50 for P and 5 for w.*

$\ell = \frac{P - 2w}{2} = \frac{50 - 2(6)}{2} = 19 \text{ ft}$ — *Substitute 50 for P and 6 for w.*

$\ell = \frac{P - 2w}{2} = \frac{50 - 2(10)}{2} = 15 \text{ ft}$ — *Substitute 50 for P and 10 for w.*

Try This

1. A rectangle has a perimeter of 24 cm. Use the formula $P = 2\ell + 2w$ to find the width when the length is 2, 3, 4, 6, and 8 cm.
2. A right triangle has a hypotenuse of length $c = 65$ ft. Use the Pythagorean Theorem to find the length of leg a when the length of leg b is 16, 25, 33, and 39 feet.
3. The perimeter of $\triangle ABC$ is 112 in. Write an expression for a in terms of b and c, and use it to complete the following table.

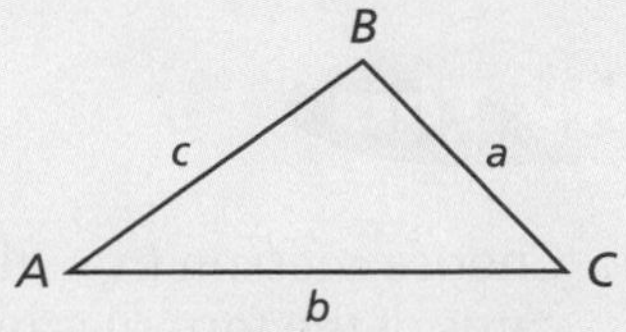

a	b	c
	48	35
	36	36
	14	50

10-1 Developing Formulas for Triangles and Quadrilaterals

CC.9-12.A.SSE.1 Interpret expressions that represent a quantity in terms of its context.* *Also* **CC.9-12.A.CED.4**

Objectives

Develop and apply the formulas for the areas of triangles and special quadrilaterals.

Solve problems involving perimeters and areas of triangles and special quadrilaterals.

Why learn this?

You can use formulas for area to help solve puzzles such as the tangram.

A tangram is an ancient Chinese puzzle made from a square. The pieces can be rearranged to form many different shapes. The area of a figure made with all the pieces is the sum of the areas of the pieces.

Know it! Note

Postulate 10-1-1 Area Addition Postulate

The area of a region is equal to the sum of the areas of its nonoverlapping parts.

Recall that a rectangle with base b and height h has an area of $A = bh$. You can use the Area Addition Postulate to see that a parallelogram has the same area as a rectangle with the same base and height.

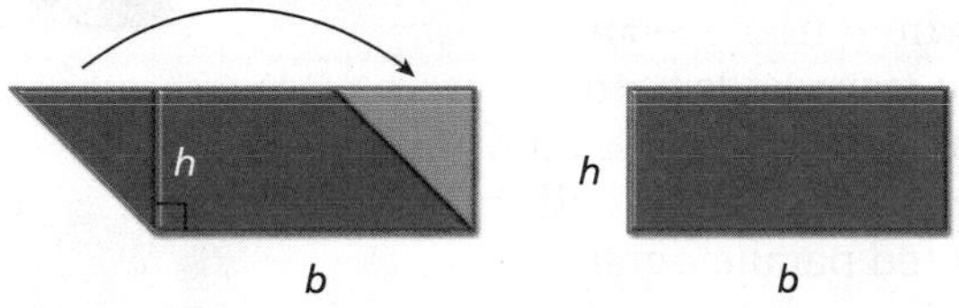

A triangle is cut off one side and translated to the other side.

Know it! Note

Area Parallelogram

The area of a parallelogram with base b and height h is $A = bh$.

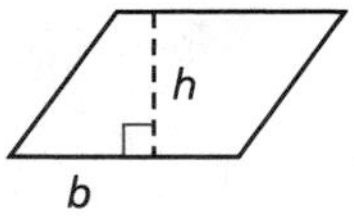

Remember that rectangles and squares are also parallelograms. The area of a square with side s is $A = s^2$, and the perimeter is $P = 4s$.

EXAMPLE 1 Finding Measurements of Parallelograms

Remember!

The height of a parallelogram is measured along a segment perpendicular to a line containing the base.

Find each measurement.

A the area of the parallelogram

Step 1 Use the Pythagorean Theorem to find the height h.

$3^2 + h^2 = 5^2$

$h = 4$

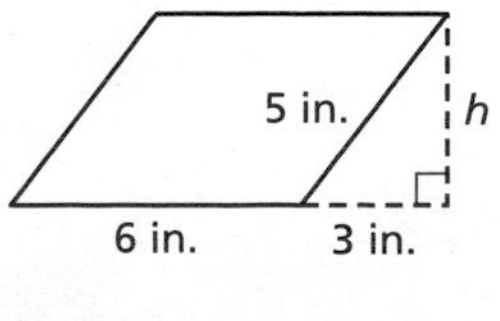

Step 2 Use h to find the area of the parallelogram.

$A = bh$ *Area of a parallelogram*

$A = 6(4)$ *Substitute 6 for b and 4 for h.*

$A = 24 \text{ in}^2$ *Simplify.*

Algebra

Find each measurement.

B **the height of a rectangle in which $b = 5$ cm and $A = (5x^2 - 5x)$ cm^2**

$A = bh$	*Area of a rectangle*
$5x^2 - 5x = 5h$	*Substitute $5x^2 - 5x$ for A and 5 for b.*
$5(x^2 - x) = 5h$	*Factor 5 out of the expression for A.*
$x^2 - x = h$	*Divide both sides by 5.*
$h = (x^2 - x)$ cm	*Sym. Prop. of =*

C **the perimeter of the rectangle, in which $A = 12x$ ft^2**

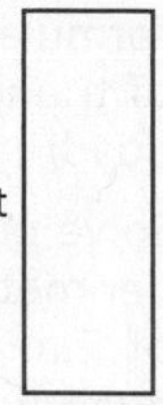

Step 1 Use the area and the height to find the base.

$A = bh$	*Area of a rectangle*
$12x = b(6)$	*Substitute 12x for A and 6 for h.*
$2x = b$	*Divide both sides by 6.*

Step 2 Use the base and the height to find the perimeter.

$P = 2b + 2h$	*Perimeter of a rectangle*
$P = 2(2x) + 2(6)$	*Substitute 2x for b and 6 for h.*
$P = (4x + 12)$ ft.	*Simplify.*

Remember!

The perimeter of a rectangle with base b and height h is $P = 2b + 2h$, or $P = 2(b + h)$.

CHECK IT OUT! 1. Find the base of a parallelogram in which $h = 56$ yd and $A = 28$ yd^2.

To understand the formula for the area of a triangle or trapezoid, notice that two congruent triangles or two congruent trapezoids fit together to form a parallelogram. Thus the area of a triangle or trapezoid is half the area of the related parallelogram.

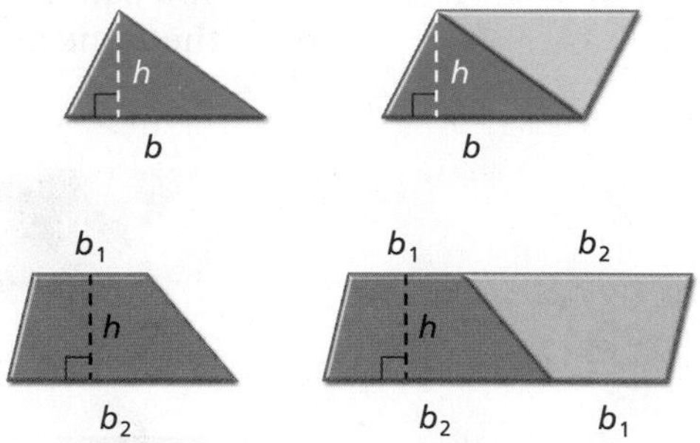

Know it! Note

Area **Triangles and Trapezoids**

The area of a triangle with base b and height h is $A = \frac{1}{2}bh$.

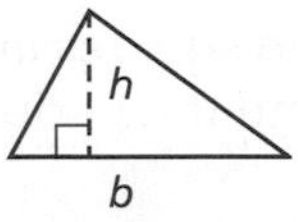

The area of a trapezoid with bases b_1 and b_2 and height h is $A = \frac{1}{2}(b_1 + b_2)h$, or

$$A = \frac{(b_1 + b_2)h}{2}.$$

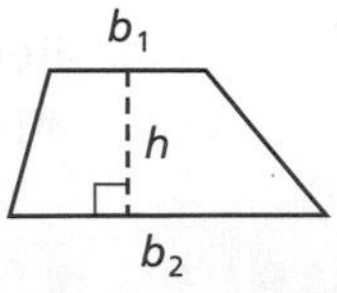

EXAMPLE 2 Finding Measurements of Triangles and Trapezoids

Find each measurement.

A **the area of a trapezoid in which $b_1 = 9$ cm, $b_2 = 12$ cm, and $h = 3$ cm**

$A = \frac{1}{2}(b_1 + b_2)h$	*Area of a trapezoid*
$A = \frac{1}{2}(9 + 12)3$	*Substitute 9 for b_1, 12 for b_2, and 3 for h.*
$A = 31.5$ cm^2	*Simplify.*

Find each measurement.

B **the base of the triangle, in which $A = x^2$ in^2**

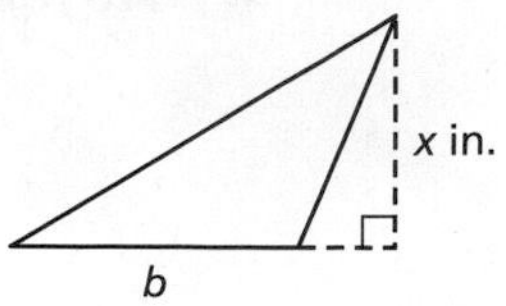

$A = \frac{1}{2}bh$ *Area of a triangle*

$x^2 = \frac{1}{2}bx$ *Substitute x^2 for A and x for h.*

$x = \frac{1}{2}b$ *Divide both sides by x.*

$2x = b$ *Multiply both sides by 2.*

$b = 2x$ in. *Sym. Prop. of =*

C **b_2 of the trapezoid, in which $A = 8$ ft^2**

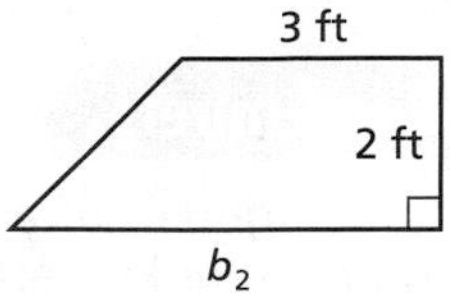

$A = \frac{1}{2}(b_1 + b_2)h$ *Area of a trapezoid*

$8 = \frac{1}{2}(3 + b_2)(2)$ *Substitute 8 for A, 3 for b_1, and 2 for h.*

$8 = 3 + b_2$ *Multiply $\frac{1}{2}$ by 2.*

$5 = b_2$ *Subtract 3 from both sides.*

$b_2 = 5$ ft *Sym. Prop. of =*

CHECK IT OUT! **2.** Find the area of the triangle.

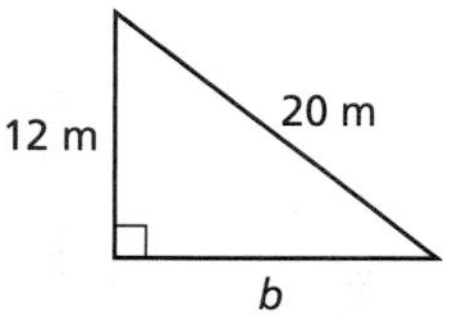

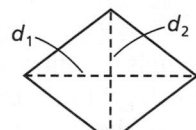

A kite or a rhombus with diagonals d_1 and d_2 can be divided into two congruent triangles with a base of d_1 and a height of $\frac{1}{2}d_2$.

area of each triangle: $A = \frac{1}{2}d_1\left(\frac{1}{2}d_2\right) = \frac{1}{4}d_1d_2$

total area: $A = 2\left(\frac{1}{4}d_1d_2\right) = \frac{1}{2}d_1d_2$

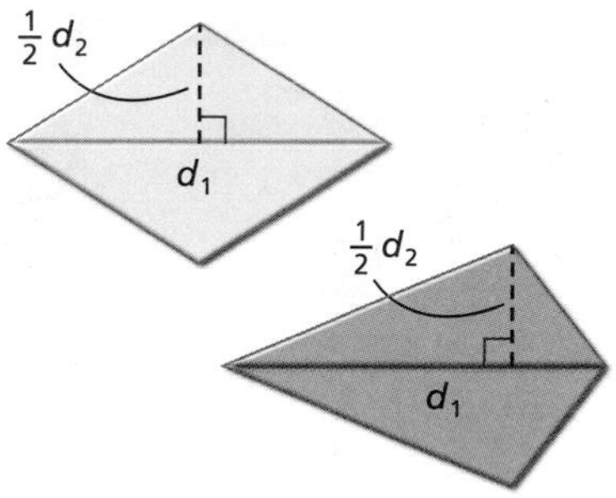

Know it! Note

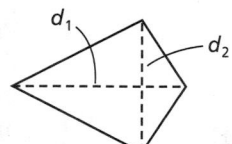

Area **Rhombuses and Kites**

The area of a rhombus or kite with diagonals d_1 and d_2 is $A = \frac{1}{2}d_1d_2$.

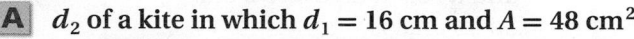

EXAMPLE 3 Finding Measurements of Rhombuses and Kites

Find each measurement.

A **d_2 of a kite in which $d_1 = 16$ cm and $A = 48$ cm^2**

$A = \frac{1}{2}d_1d_2$ *Area of a kite*

$48 = \frac{1}{2}(16)d_2$ *Substitute 48 for A and 16 for d_1.*

$6 = d_2$ *Solve for d_2.*

$d_2 = 6$ cm *Sym. Prop. of =*

x^2y **Algebra**

Find each measurement.

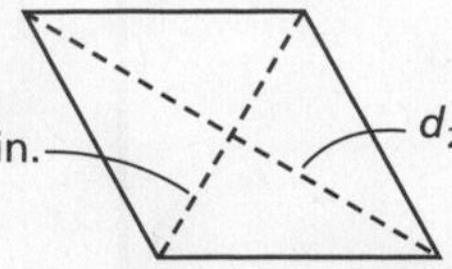

B **the area of the rhombus**

$A = \frac{1}{2}d_1d_2$

$A = \frac{1}{2}(6x + 4)(10x + 10)$ *Substitute $(6x + 4)$ for d_1 and $(10x + 10)$ for d_2.*

$A = \frac{1}{2}(60x^2 + 100x + 40)$ *Multiply the binomials (FOIL).*

$A = (30x^2 + 50x + 20)\ \text{in}^2$ *Distrib. Prop.*

Remember!

The diagonals of a rhombus or kite are perpendicular, and the diagonals of a rhombus bisect each other.

C **the area of the kite**

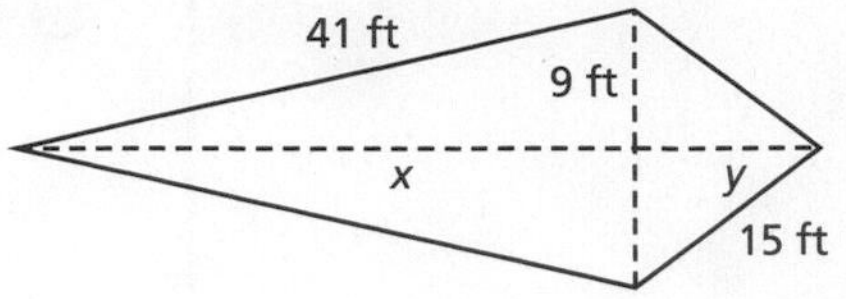

Step 1 The diagonals d_1 and d_2 form four right triangles. Use the Pythagorean Theorem to find x and y.

$9^2 + x^2 = 41^2$	$9^2 + y^2 = 15^2$
$x^2 = 1600$	$y^2 = 144$
$x = 40$	$y = 12$

Step 2 Use d_1 and d_2 to find the area. d_1 is equal to $x + y$, which is 52. Half of d_2 is equal to 9, so d_2 is equal to 18.

$A = \frac{1}{2}d_1d_2$ *Area of a kite*

$A = \frac{1}{2}(52)(18)$ *Substitute 52 for d_1 and 18 for d_2.*

$A = 468\ \text{ft}^2$ *Simplify.*

CHECK IT OUT! **3.** Find d_2 of a rhombus in which $d_1 = 3x$ m and $A = 12xy\ \text{m}^2$.

EXAMPLE 4 *Games Application*

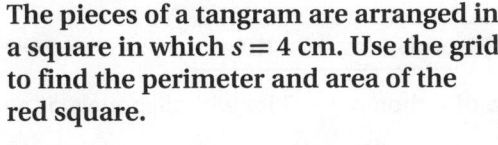

The pieces of a tangram are arranged in a square in which $s = 4$ cm. Use the grid to find the perimeter and area of the red square.

Perimeter:
Each side of the red square is the diagonal of a square of the grid. Each grid square has a side length of 1 cm, so the diagonal is $\sqrt{2}$ cm. The perimeter of the red square is $P = 4s = 4\sqrt{2}$ cm.

Area:

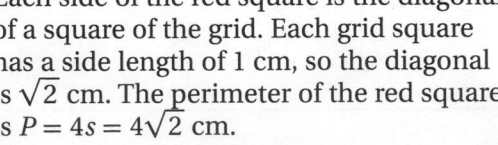

Method 1 The red square is also a rhombus. The diagonals d_1 and d_2 each measure 2 cm. So its area is

$A = \frac{1}{2}d_1d_2 = \frac{1}{2}(2)(2) = 2\ \text{cm}^2.$

Method 2 The side length of the red square is $\sqrt{2}$ cm, so the area is

$A = s^2 = (\sqrt{2})^2 = 2$ cm.

CHECK IT OUT! **4.** In the tangram above, find the perimeter and area of the large green triangle.

MATHEMATICAL PRACTICES

THINK AND DISCUSS

1. Explain why the area of a triangle is half the area of a parallelogram with the same base and height.
2. Compare the formula for the area of a trapezoid with the formula for the area of a rectangle.

Know it! Note

3. **GET ORGANIZED** Copy and complete the graphic organizer. Name all the shapes whose area is given by each area formula and sketch an example of each shape.

Area Formula	Shape(s)	Example(s)
$A = bh$		
$A = \frac{1}{2}bh$		
$A = \frac{1}{2}(b_1 + b_2)h$		
$A = \frac{1}{2}d_1d_2$		

10-1 Exercises

Learn It Online
Homework Help Online
Parent Resources Online

GUIDED PRACTICE

Find each measurement.

SEE EXAMPLE 1

1. the area of the parallelogram

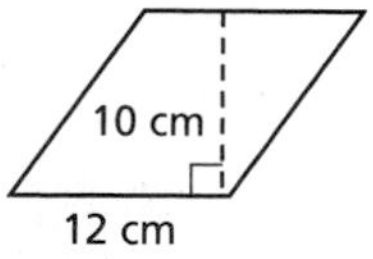

2. the height of the rectangle, in which $A = 10x^2$ ft^2

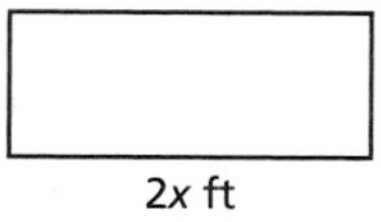

3. the perimeter of a square in which $A = 169$ cm^2

SEE EXAMPLE 2

4. the area of the trapezoid

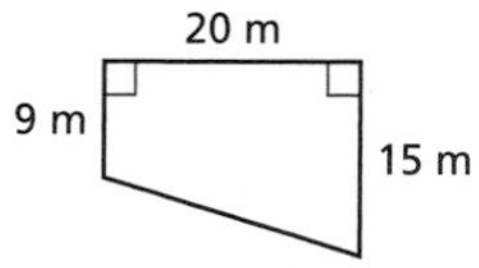

5. the base of the triangle, in which $A = 58.5$ in^2

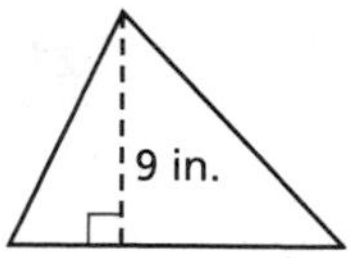

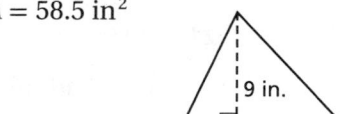

6. b_1 of a trapezoid in which $A = (48x + 68)$ in^2, $h = 8$ in., and $b_2 = (9x + 12)$ in.

SEE EXAMPLE 3

7. the area of the rhombus

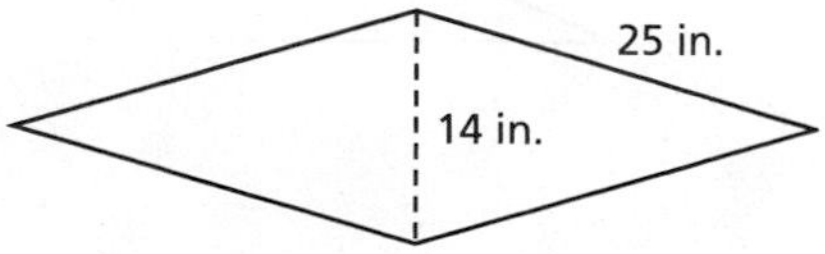

8. d_2 of the kite, in which $A = 187.5$ m^2

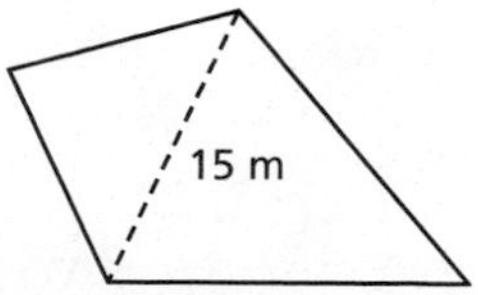

9. d_2 of a kite in which $A = 12x^2y^3$ cm^2, $d_1 = 3xy$ cm

SEE EXAMPLE 4

10. **Art** The stained-glass window shown is a rectangle with a base of 4 ft and a height of 3 ft. Use the grid to find the area of each piece.

PRACTICE AND PROBLEM SOLVING

Independent Practice

For Exercises	See Example
11–13	1
14–16	2
17–19	3
20–22	4

Extra Practice

See Extra Practice for more Skills Practice and Applications Practice exercises.

Find each measurement.

11. the height of the parallelogram, in which $A = 7.5\ \text{m}^2$

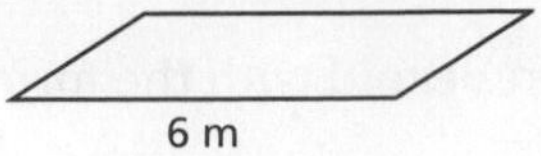

12. the perimeter of the rectangle

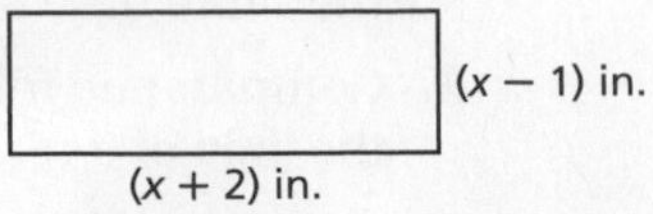

13. the area of a parallelogram in which $b = (3x + 5)$ ft and $h = (7x - 1)$ ft

14. the area of the triangle

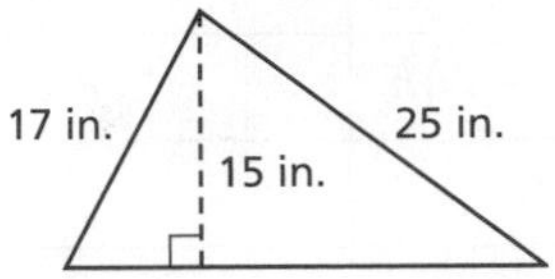

15. the height of the trapezoid, in which $A = 280\ \text{cm}^2$

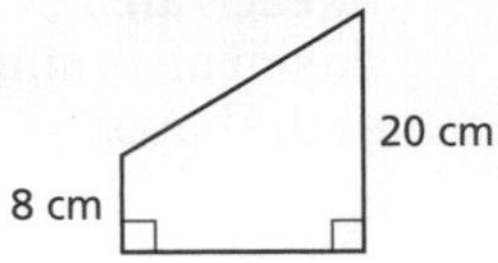

16. the area of a triangle in which $b = (x + 1)$ ft and $h = 8x$ ft

17. the area of the kite

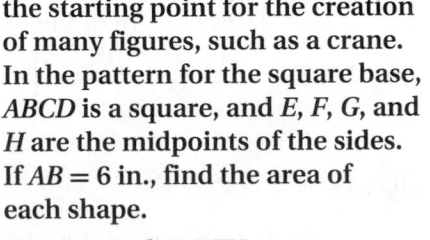

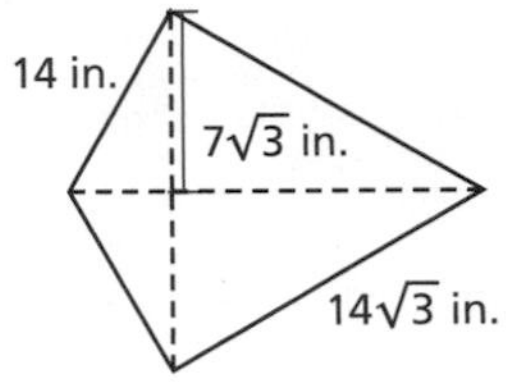

18. d_2 of the rhombus, in which $A = (3x^2 + 6x)\ \text{m}^2$

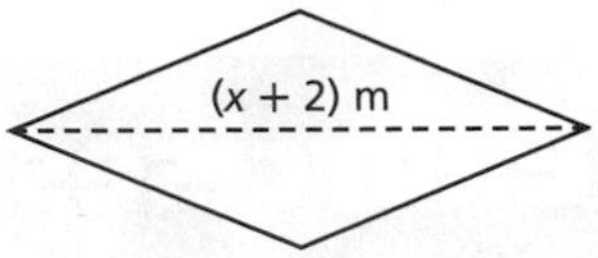

19. the area of a kite in which $d_1 = (6x + 5)$ ft and $d_2 = (4x + 8)$ ft

Crafts In origami, a *square base* is the starting point for the creation of many figures, such as a crane. In the pattern for the square base, *ABCD* is a square, and *E*, *F*, *G*, and *H* are the midpoints of the sides. If $AB = 6$ in., find the area of each shape.

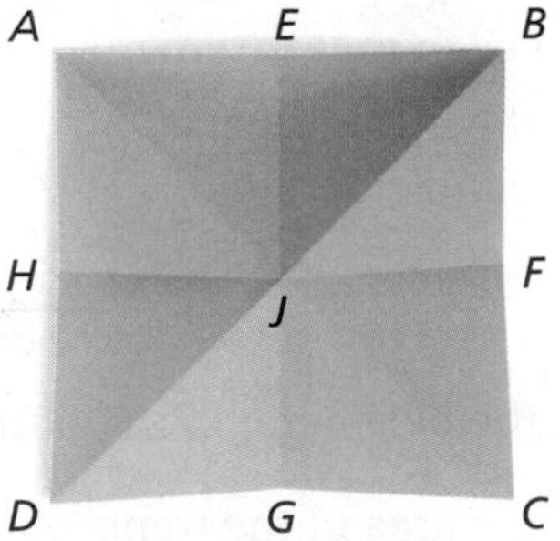

20. rectangle *ABFH*

21. $\triangle AEJ$

22. trapezoid *ABFJ*

Multi-Step Find the area of each figure. Round to the nearest tenth, if necessary.

23.

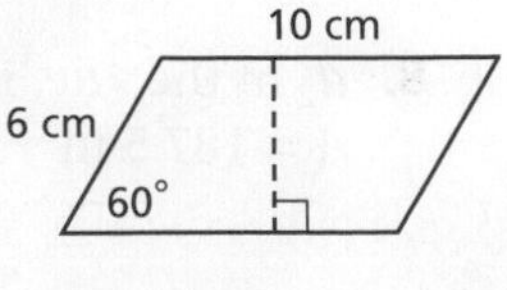

24.

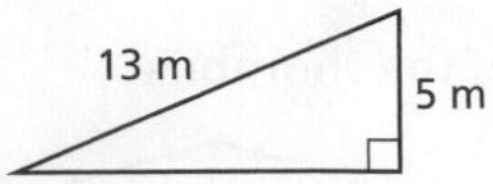

25.

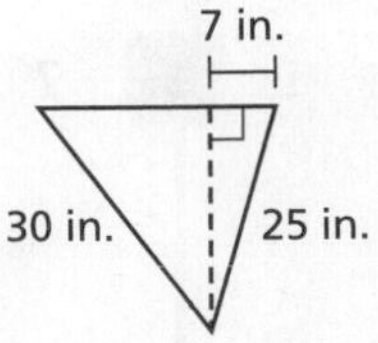

Write each area in terms of *x*.

26. equilateral triangle

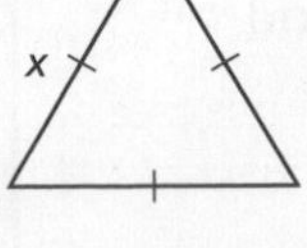

27. 30°-60°-90° triangle

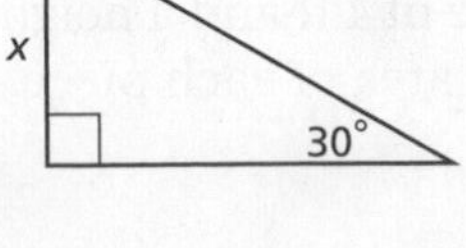

28. 45°-45°-90° triangle

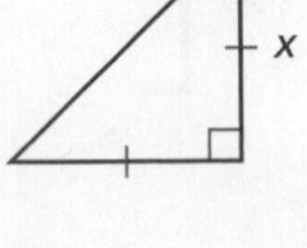

MULTI-STEP TEST PREP

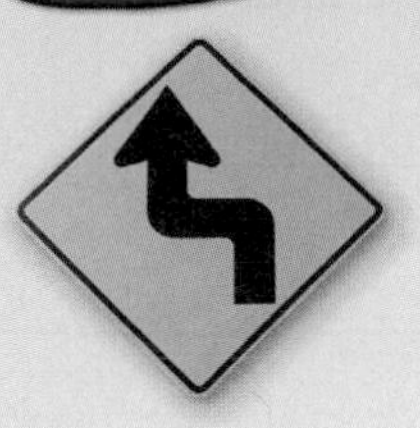

29. A sign manufacturer makes yield signs by cutting an equilateral triangle from a square piece of aluminum with the dimensions shown.

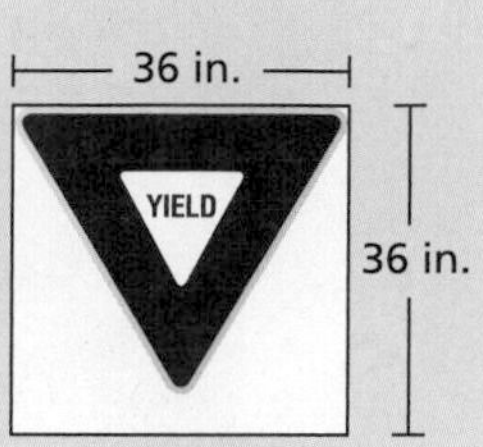

a. Find the height of the yield sign to the nearest tenth.

b. Find the area of the sign to the nearest tenth.

c. How much material is left after a sign is made?

Find the missing measurements for each rectangle.

	Base *b*	Height *h*	Area *A*	Perimeter *P*
30.	12	16		
31.	17		136	
32.		11		50
33.			216	66

34. The perimeter of a rectangle is 72 in. The base is 3 times the height. Find the area of the rectangle.

35. The area of a triangle is 50 cm^2. The base of the triangle is 4 times the height. Find the height of the triangle.

36. The perimeter of an isosceles trapezoid is 40 ft. The bases of the trapezoid are 11 ft and 19 ft. Find the area of the trapezoid.

Use the conversion table for Exercises 37–42.

37. $1\ yd^2 = \underline{\ \ ?\ \ }\ ft^2$

38. $1\ m^2 = \underline{\ \ ?\ \ }\ cm^2$

39. $1\ cm^2 = \underline{\ \ ?\ \ }\ mm^2$

40. $1\ mi^2 = \underline{\ \ ?\ \ }\ in^2$

Conversion Factors	
Metric	**Customary**
1 km = 1000 m	1 mi = 1760 yd
1 m = 100 cm	1 mi = 5280 ft
1 cm = 10 mm	1 yd = 3 ft
	1 ft = 12 in.

41. A triangle has a base of 3 yd and a height of 8 yd. Find the area in square feet.

42. A rhombus has diagonals 500 yd and 800 yd in length. Find the area in square miles.

LINK

History

President James Garfield was a classics professor and a major general in the Union Army. He was assassinated in 1881.

Source: www.whitehouse.gov

43. The following proof of the Pythagorean Theorem was discovered by President James Garfield in 1876 while he was a member of the House of Representatives.

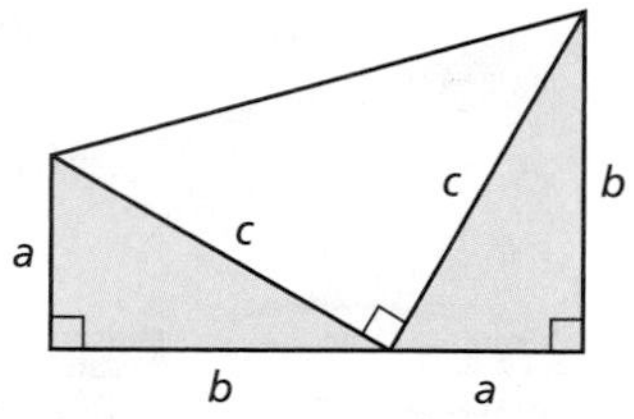

a. Write the area of the trapezoid in terms of a and b.

b. Write the areas of the three triangles in terms of a, b, and c.

c. Use the Area Addition Postulate to write an equation relating your results from parts **a** and **b**. Simplify the equation to prove the Pythagorean Theorem.

44. Use the diagram to prove the formula for the area of a rectangle, given the formula for the area of a square.

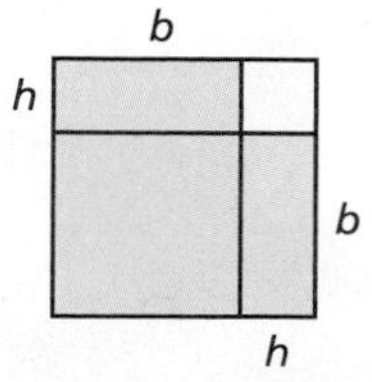

Given: Rectangle with base b and height h
Prove: The area of the rectangle is $A = bh$.
Plan: Use the formula for the area of a square to find the areas of the outer square and the two squares inside the figure. Write and solve an equation for the area of the rectangle.

Prove each area formula.

45. Given: Parallelogram with area $A = bh$
Prove: The area of the triangle is $A = \frac{1}{2}bh$.

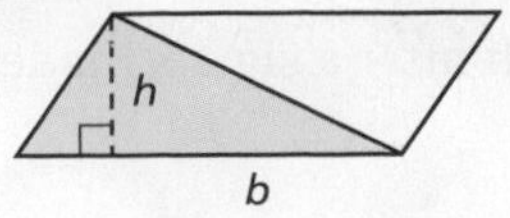

46. Given: Triangle with area $A = \frac{1}{2}bh$
Prove: The area of the trapezoid is $A = \frac{1}{2}(b_1 + b_2)h$.

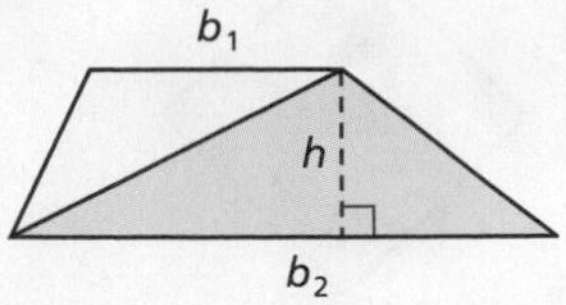

47. Measurement Choose an appropriate unit of measurement and measure the base and height of each parallelogram.

a. Find the area of each parallelogram. Give your answer with the correct precision.

b. Which has the greatest area?

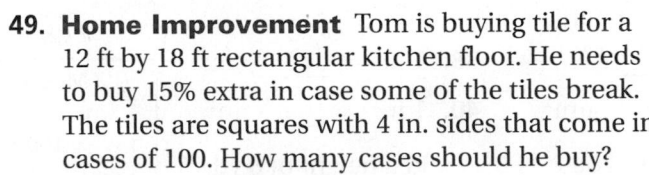

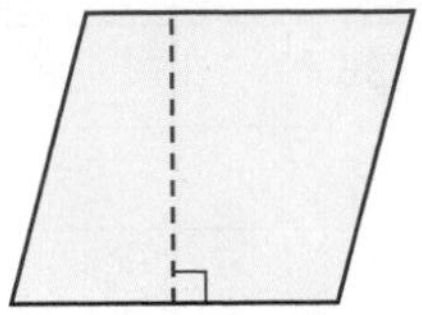
Figure A

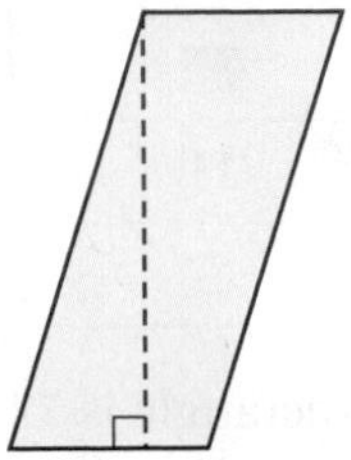
Figure B

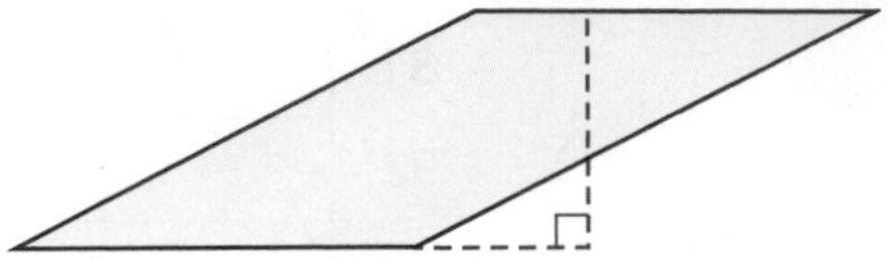
Figure C

48. Hobbies Tina is making a kite according to the plans at right. The fabric weighs about 40 grams per square meter. The diagonal braces, or *spars*, weigh about 20 grams per meter. Estimate the weight of the kite.

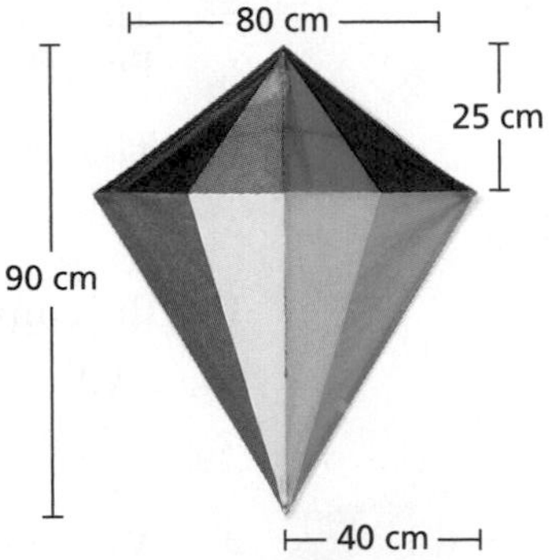

49. Home Improvement Tom is buying tile for a 12 ft by 18 ft rectangular kitchen floor. He needs to buy 15% extra in case some of the tiles break. The tiles are squares with 4 in. sides that come in cases of 100. How many cases should he buy?

50. Critical Thinking If the maximum error in the given measurements of the rectangle is 0.1 cm, what is the greatest possible error in the area? Explain.

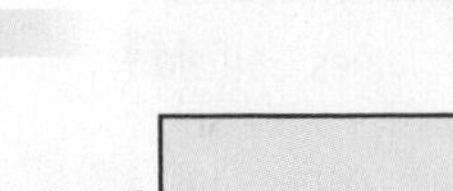

51. Write About It A square is also a parallelogram, a rectangle, and a rhombus. Prove that the area formula for each shape gives the same result as the formula for the area of a square.

TEST PREP

52. Which expression best represents the area of the rectangle?

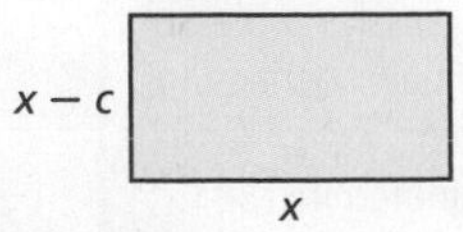

Ⓐ $2x + 2(x - c)$
Ⓑ $x(x - c)$
Ⓒ $x^2 + (x - c)^2$
Ⓓ $2x(x - c)$

53. The length of a rectangle is 3 times the width. The perimeter is 48 inches. Which system of equations can be used to find the dimensions of the rectangle?

Ⓕ $\ell = w + 3$
$2(\ell + w) = 48$

Ⓖ $\ell = 3w$
$2\ell + 6w = 48$

Ⓗ $\ell = 3w$
$2(\ell + w) = 48$

Ⓙ $\ell = w + 3$
$2\ell + 6w = 48$

54. A 16- by 18-foot rectangular section of a wall will be covered by square tiles that measure 2 feet on each side. If the tiles are not cut, how many of them will be needed to cover the section of the wall?

Ⓐ 288 Ⓑ 144 Ⓒ 72 Ⓓ 17

55. The area of trapezoid $HJKM$ is 90 square centimeters. Which is closest to the length of $\overline{JK}$?

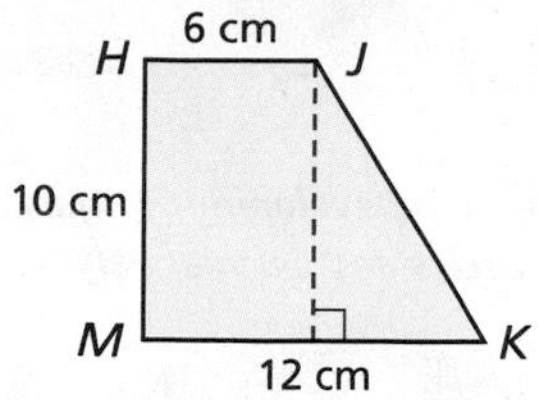

Ⓕ 10 centimeters Ⓗ 11.7 centimeters

Ⓖ 10.5 centimeters Ⓙ 16 centimeters

56. **Gridded Response** A driveway is shaped like a parallelogram with a base of 28 feet and a height of 17 feet. Covering the driveway with crushed stone will cost $2.75 per square foot. How much will it cost to cover the driveway with crushed stone?

CHALLENGE AND EXTEND

Multi-Step Find h in each parallelogram.

57.

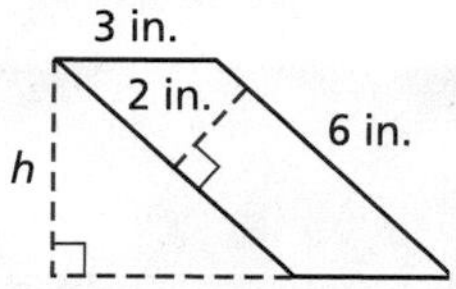

58.

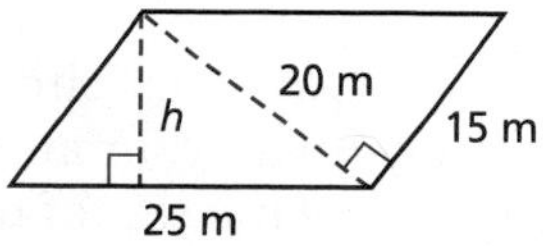

59. **Algebra** A rectangle has a perimeter of $(26x + 16)$ cm and an area of $(42x^2 + 51x + 15)$ cm^2. Find the dimensions of the rectangle in terms of x.

60. Prove that the area of any quadrilateral with perpendicular diagonals is $\frac{1}{2}d_1d_2$.

61. **Gardening** A gardener has 24 feet of fencing to enclose a rectangular garden.

a. Let x and y represent the side lengths of the rectangle. Solve the perimeter formula $2x + 2y = 24$ for y, and substitute the expression into the area formula $A = xy$.

b. Graph the resulting function on a coordinate plane. What are the domain and range of the function?

c. What are the dimensions of the rectangle that will enclose the greatest area?

d. **Write About It** How would you find the dimensions of the rectangle with the least perimeter that would enclose a rectangular area of 100 square feet?

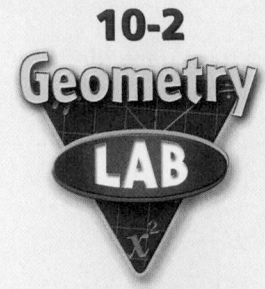

10-2
Geometry LAB

Develop π

The ratio of the circumference of a circle to its diameter is defined as π. All circles are similar, so this ratio is the same for all circles:

$$\pi = \frac{\text{circumference}}{\text{diameter}}.$$

Use with Developing Formulas for Circles and Regular Polygons

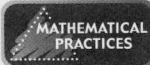

MATHEMATICAL PRACTICES **Use appropriate tools strategically.**

CC.9-12.G.GMD.1 Give an informal argument for the formulas for the circumference of a circle, area of a circle…

Activity 1

1. Use your compass to draw a large circle on a piece of cardboard and then cut it out.

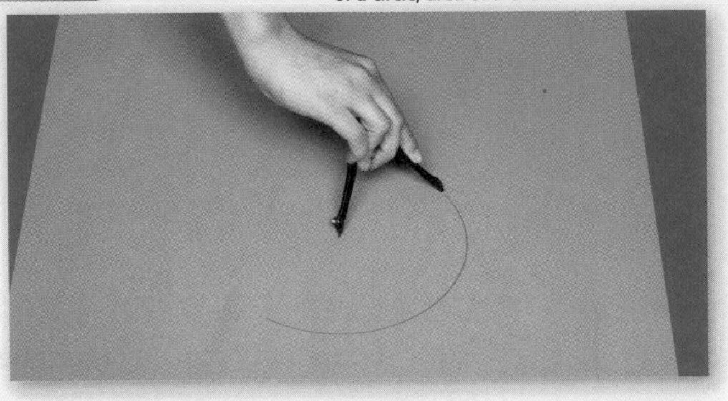

2. Use a measuring tape to measure the circle's diameter and circumference as accurately as possible.

3. Use the results from your circle to estimate π. Compare your answers with the results of the rest of the class.

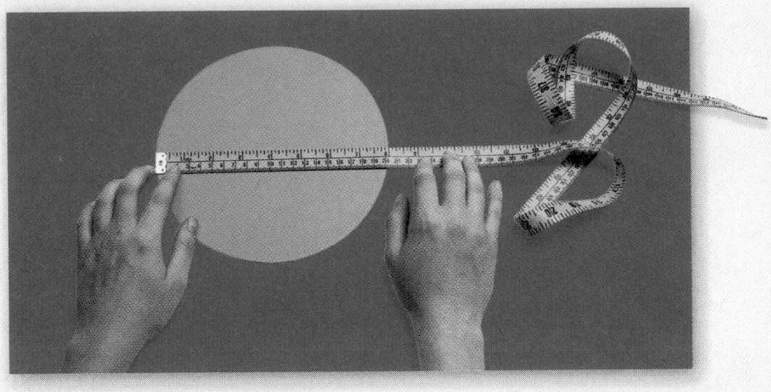

Try This

1. Do you think it is possible to draw a circle whose ratio of circumference to diameter is not π? Why or why not?
2. How does knowing the relationship between circumference, diameter, and π help you determine the formula for circumference?
3. Use a ribbon to make a π measuring tape. Mark off increments of π inches or π cm on your ribbon as accurately as possible. How could you use this π measuring tape to find the diameter of a circular object? Use your π measuring tape to measure 5 circular objects. Give the circumference and diameter of each object.

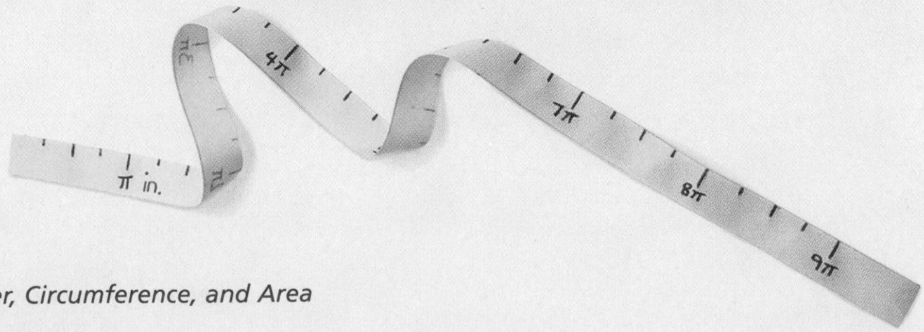

Archimedes used inscribed and circumscribed polygons to estimate the value of π. His "method of exhaustion" is considered to be an early version of calculus. In the figures below, the circumference of the circle is less than the perimeter of the larger polygon and greater than the perimeter of the smaller polygon. This fact is used to estimate π.

Activity 2

1. Construct a large square. Construct the perpendicular bisectors of two adjacent sides.

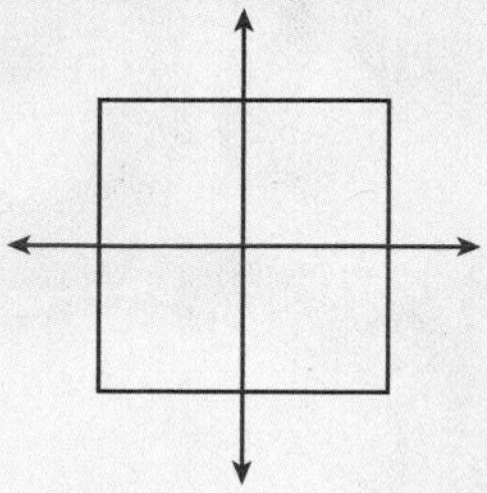

2. Use your compass to draw an inscribed circle as shown.

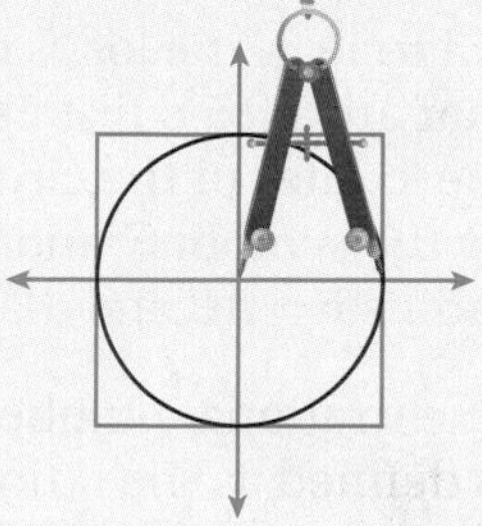

3. Connect the midpoints of the sides to form a square that is inscribed in the circle.

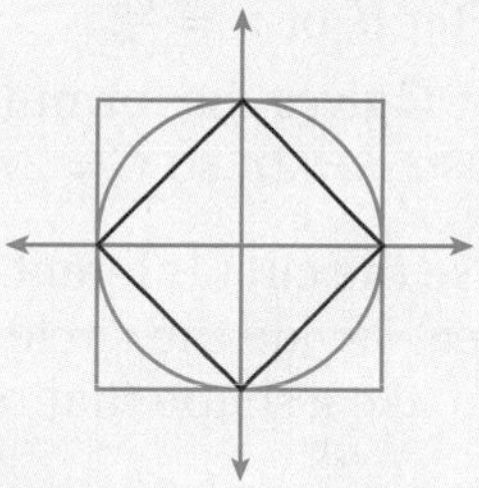

4. Let P_1 represent the perimeter of the smaller square, P_2 represent the perimeter of the larger square, and C represent the circumference of the circle. Measure the squares to find P_1 and P_2 and substitute the values into the inequality below.

$$P_1 < C < P_2$$

5. Divide each expression in the inequality by the diameter of the circle. Why does this give you an inequality in terms of π? Complete the inequality below.

$$\underline{\quad ? \quad} < \pi < \underline{\quad ? \quad}$$

Try This

4. Use the perimeters of the inscribed and circumscribed regular hexagons to write an inequality for π. Assume the diameter of each circle is 2 units.

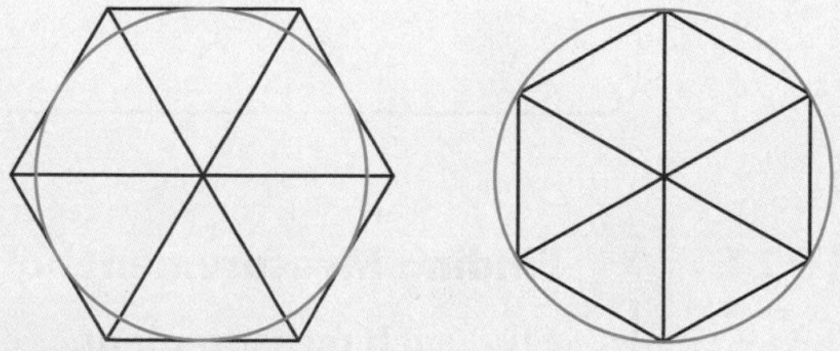

5. Compare the inequalities you found for π. What do you think would be true about your inequality if you used regular polygons with more sides? How could you use inscribed and circumscribed regular polygons to estimate π?

6. An alternate definition of π is the area of a circle with radius 1. How could you use this definition and the figures above to estimate the value of π?

COMMON CORE

10-2 Developing Formulas for Circles and Regular Polygons

CC.9-12.G.GMD.1 Give an informal argument for the formulas for the circumference of a circle, area of a circle…

Objectives

Develop and apply the formulas for the area and circumference of a circle.

Develop and apply the formula for the area of a regular polygon.

Vocabulary

circle
center of a circle
center of a regular polygon
apothem
central angle of a regular polygon

Who uses this?

Drummers use drums of different sizes to produce different notes. The pitch is related to the area of the top of the drum. (See Example 2.)

A **circle** is the locus of points in a plane that are a fixed distance from a point called the **center of the circle**. A circle is named by the symbol ⊙ and its center. ⊙A has radius $r = AB$ and diameter $d = CD$.

The irrational number π is defined as the ratio of the circumference C to the diameter d, or $\pi = \frac{C}{d}$. Solving for C gives the formula $C = \pi d$. Also $d = 2r$, so $C = 2\pi r$.

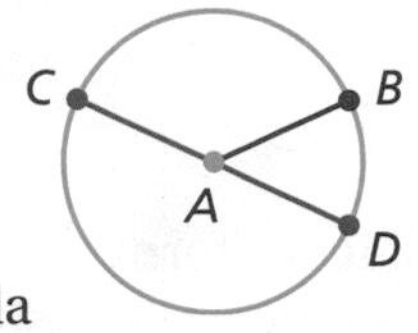

You can use the circumference of a circle to find its area. Divide the circle and rearrange the pieces to make a shape that resembles a parallelogram.

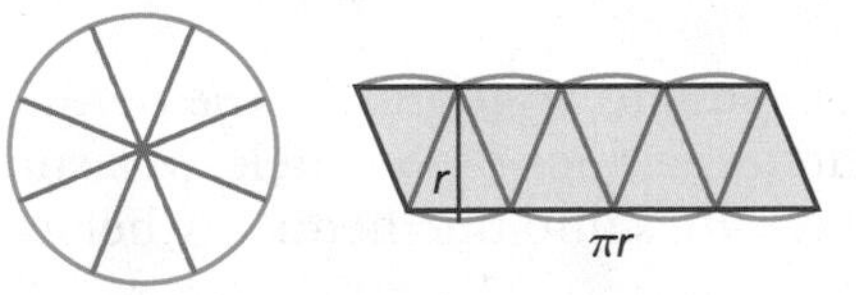

The base of the parallelogram is about half the circumference, or πr, and the height is close to the radius r. So $A \approx \pi r \cdot r = \pi r^2$.

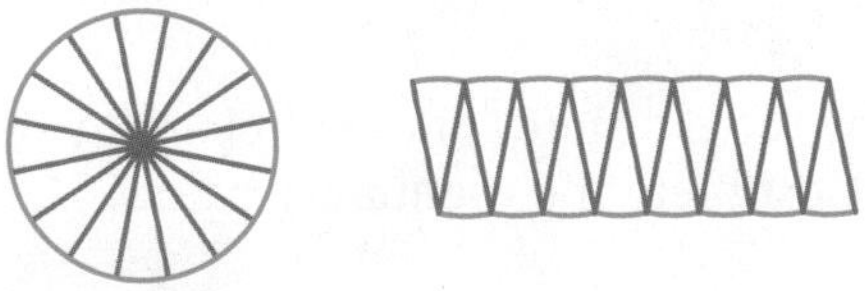

The more pieces you divide the circle into, the more accurate the estimate will be.

Know it! Note

Circumference and Area Circle

A circle with diameter d and radius r has circumference $C = \pi d$ or $C = 2\pi r$ and area $A = \pi r^2$.

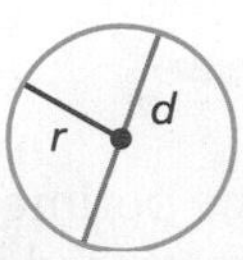

EXAMPLE 1 **Finding Measurements of Circles**

Find each measurement.

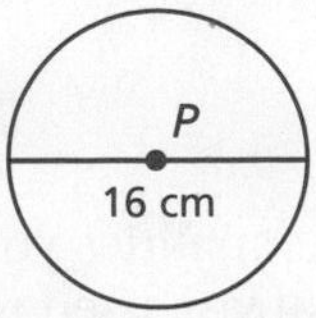

A **the area of ⊙P in terms of π**

$A = \pi r^2$	*Area of a circle*
$A = \pi(8)^2$	*Divide the diameter by 2 to find the radius, 8.*
$A = 64\pi \text{ cm}^2$	*Simplify.*

Find each measurement.

B **the radius of $\odot X$ in which $C = 24\pi$ in.**

$C = 2\pi r$ *Circumference of a circle*

$24\pi = 2\pi r$ *Substitute 24π for C.*

$r = 12$ *in.* *Divide both sides by 2π.*

C **the circumference of $\odot S$ in which $A = 9x^2\ \pi$ cm^2**

Algebra

Step 1 Use the given area to solve for r.

$A = \pi r^2$ *Area of a circle*

$9x^2\pi = \pi r^2$ *Substitute $9x^2\pi$ for A.*

$9x^2 = r^2$ *Divide both sides by π.*

$3x = r$ *Take the square root of both sides.*

Step 2 Use the value of r to find the circumference.

$C = 2\pi r$

$C = 2\pi(3x)$ *Substitute 3x for r.*

$C = 6x\pi$ cm *Simplify.*

CHECK IT OUT! **1.** Find the area of $\odot A$ in terms of π in which $C = (4x - 6)\pi$ m.

EXAMPLE 2 *Music Application*

A drum kit contains three drums with diameters of 10 in., 12 in., and 14 in. Find the area of the top of each drum. Round to the nearest tenth.

10 in. diameter	12 in. diameter	14 in. diameter
$A = \pi(5^2)$ $r = \frac{10}{2} = 5$	$A = \pi(6^2)$ $r = \frac{12}{2} = 6$	$A = \pi(7)^2$ $r = \frac{14}{2} = 7$
$\cong 78.5$ in^2	$\cong 113.1$ in^2	$\cong 153.9$ in^2

Helpful Hint

The π key gives the best possible approximation for π on your calculator. Always wait until the last step to round.

CHECK IT OUT! **2.** Use the information above to find the circumference of each drum.

The **center of a regular polygon** is equidistant from the vertices. The **apothem** is the distance from the center to a side. A **central angle of a regular polygon** has its vertex at the center, and its sides pass through consecutive vertices. Each central angle measure of a regular n-gon is $\frac{360°}{n}$.

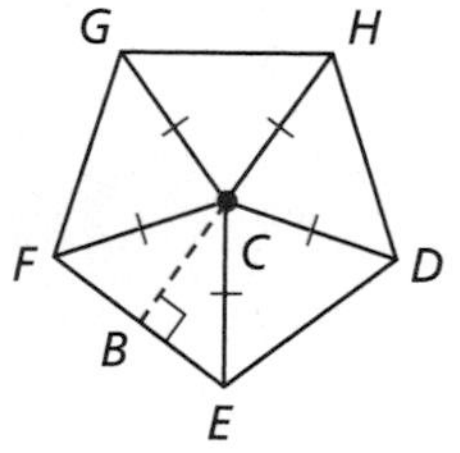

Regular pentagon *DEFGH* has center *C*, apothem *BC*, and central angle ∠*DCE*.

To find the area of a regular n-gon with side length s and apothem a, divide it into n congruent isosceles triangles.

area of each triangle: $\frac{1}{2}as$

total area of the polygon: $A = n\left(\frac{1}{2}as\right)$, or $A = \frac{1}{2}aP$ *The perimeter is $P = ns$.*

Know it! Note

Area **Regular Polygon**

The area of a regular polygon with apothem a and perimeter P is $A = \frac{1}{2}aP$.

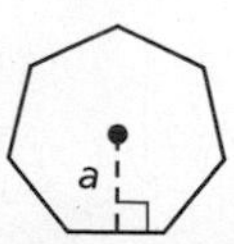

EXAMPLE 3 Finding the Area of a Regular Polygon

Find the area of each regular polygon. Round to the nearest tenth.

A **a regular hexagon with side length 6 m**

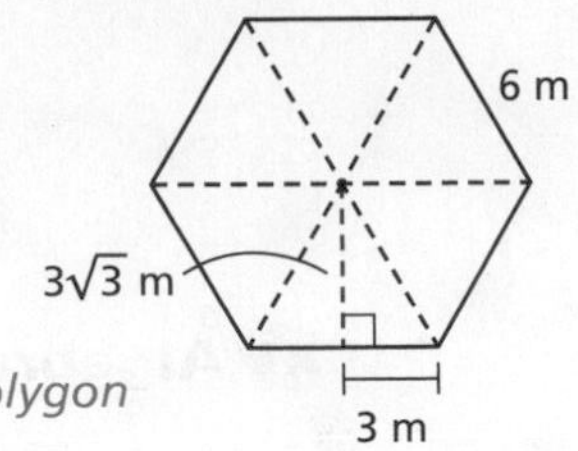

The perimeter is $6(6) = 36$ m. The hexagon can be divided into 6 equilateral triangles with side length 6 m. By the 30°-60°-90° Triangle Theorem, the apothem is $3\sqrt{3}$ m.

$A = \frac{1}{2}aP$ *Area of a regular polygon*

$A = \frac{1}{2}(3\sqrt{3})(36)$ *Substitute $3\sqrt{3}$ for a and 36 for P.*

$A = 54\sqrt{3} \cong 93.5 \text{ m}^2$ *Simplify.*

Remember!

The tangent of an angle in a right triangle is the ratio of the opposite leg length to the adjacent leg length.

B **a regular pentagon with side length 8 in.**

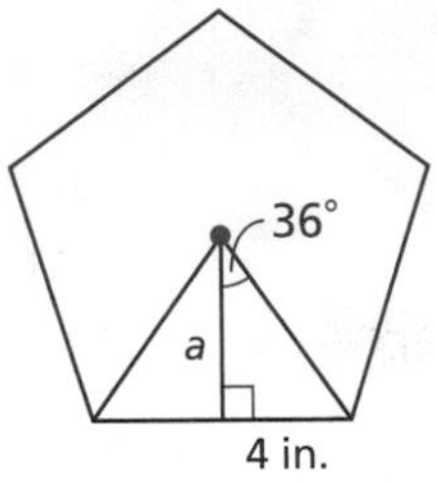

Step 1 Draw the pentagon. Draw an isosceles triangle with its vertex at the center of the pentagon. The central angle is $\frac{360°}{5} = 72°$. Draw a segment that bisects the central angle and the side of the polygon to form a right triangle.

Step 2 Use the tangent ratio to find the apothem.

$\tan 36° = \frac{4}{a}$ *The tangent of an angle is $\frac{\text{opp. leg}}{\text{adj. leg}}$.*

$a = \frac{4}{\tan 36°}$ *Solve for a.*

Step 3 Use the apothem and the given side length to find the area.

$A = \frac{1}{2}aP$ *Area of a regular polygon*

$A = \frac{1}{2}\left(\frac{4}{\tan 36°}\right)(40)$ *The perimeter is 8(5) = 40 in.*

$A \cong 110.1 \text{ in}^2$ *Simplify. Round to the nearest tenth.*

CHECK IT OUT! **3.** Find the area of a regular octagon with a side length of 4 cm.

MATHEMATICAL PRACTICES

THINK AND DISCUSS

1. Describe the relationship between the circumference of a circle and π.

2. Explain how you would find the central angle of a regular polygon with n sides.

Know it! Note

3. GET ORGANIZED Copy and complete the graphic organizer.

Regular Polygons (Side Length = 1)

Polygon	Number of Sides	Perimeter	Central Angle	Apothem	Area
Triangle					
Square					
Hexagon					

10-2 Exercises

Learn It Online
Homework Help Online
Parent Resources Online

GUIDED PRACTICE

1. **Vocabulary** Describe how to find the *apothem* of a square with side length *s*.

SEE EXAMPLE 1

Find each measurement.

2. the circumference of $\odot C$

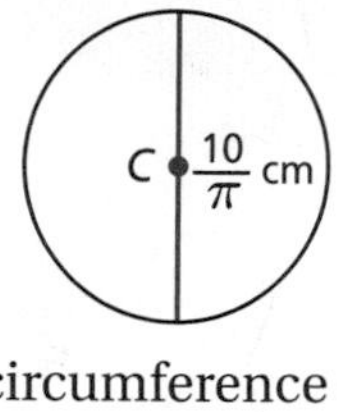

3. the area of $\odot A$ in terms of π

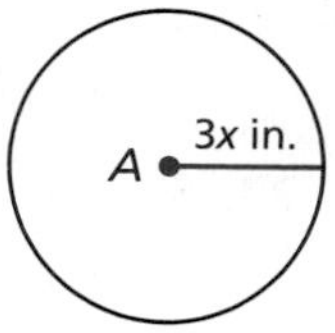

4. the circumference of $\odot P$ in which $A = 36\pi \text{ in}^2$

SEE EXAMPLE 2

5. **Food** A pizza parlor offers pizzas with diameters of 8 in., 10 in., and 12 in. Find the area of each size pizza. Round to the nearest tenth.

SEE EXAMPLE 3

Find the area of each regular polygon. Round to the nearest tenth.

6.

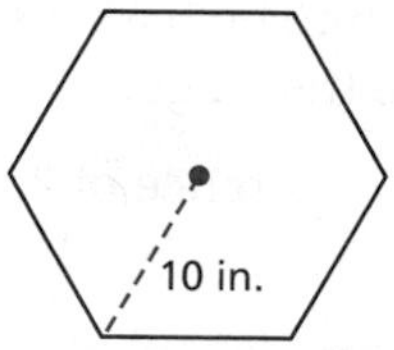

7.

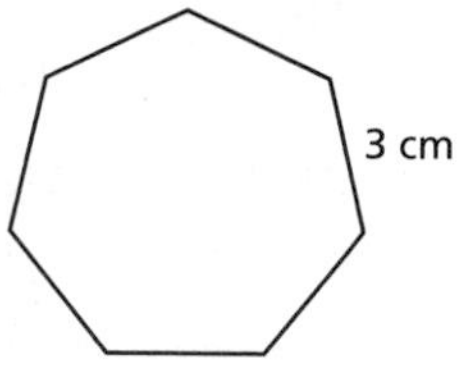

8. an equilateral triangle with an apothem of 2 ft

9. a regular dodecagon with a side length of 5 m

PRACTICE AND PROBLEM SOLVING

Independent Practice

For Exercises	See Example
10–12	1
13	2
14–17	3

Extra Practice

See Extra Practice for more Skills Practice and Applications Practice exercises.

Find each measurement. Give your answers in terms of π.

10. the area of $\odot M$

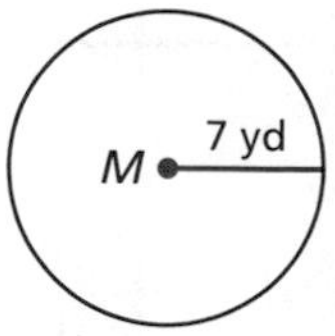

11. the circumference of $\odot Z$

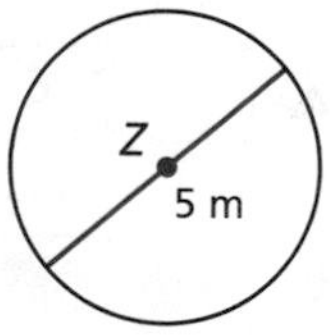

12. the diameter of $\odot G$ in which $C = 10$ ft.

13. **Sports** A horse trainer uses circular pens that are 35 ft, 50 ft, and 66 ft in diameter. Find the area of each pen. Round to the nearest tenth.

Find the area of each regular polygon. Round to the nearest tenth, if necessary.

14.

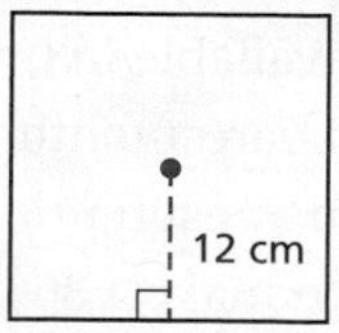

15.

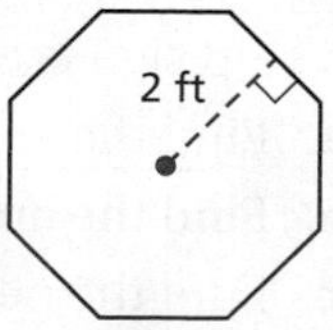

16. a regular nonagon with a perimeter of 144 in.

17. a regular pentagon with an apothem of 2 ft.

Find the central angle measure of each regular polygon. (*Hint:* To review polygon names.)

18. equilateral triangle **19.** square **20.** pentagon **21.** hexagon

22. heptagon **23.** octagon **24.** nonagon **25.** decagon

Find the area of each regular polygon. Round to the nearest tenth.

26.

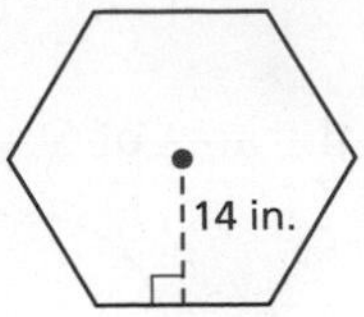

27.

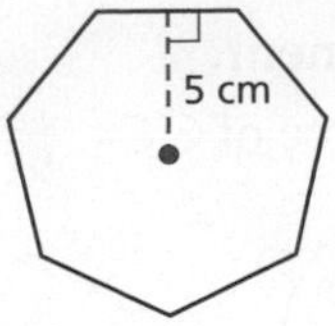

28.

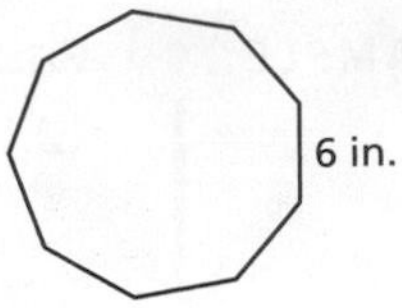

29.

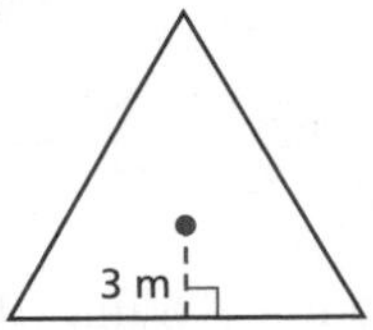

30.

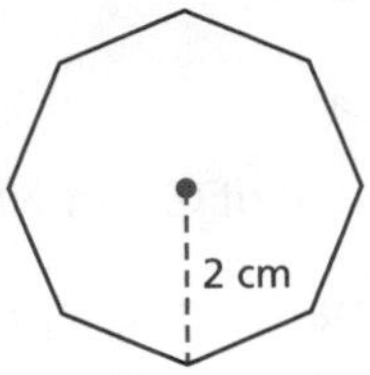

31.

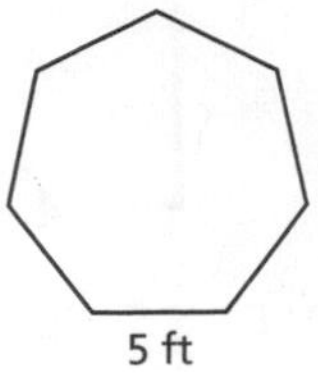

LINK

Biology

Dendroclimatologists study tree rings for evidence of changes in weather patterns over time.

32. Biology You can estimate a tree's age in years by using the formula $a = \frac{r}{w}$, where r is the tree's radius without bark and w is the average thickness of the tree's rings. The circumference of a white oak tree is 100 in. The bark is 0.5 in. thick, and the average width of a ring is 0.2 in. Estimate the tree's age.

33. ///ERROR ANALYSIS/// A circle has a circumference of 2π in. Which calculation of the area is incorrect? Explain.

A

The circumference is 2π in., so the diameter is 2 in. The area is $A = \pi(2^2) = 4\pi$ in^2.

B

The circumference is 2π in., so the radius is 1 in. The area is $A = \pi(1^2) = 2\pi$ in^2.

Find the missing measurements for each circle. Give your answers in terms of π.

	Diameter d	Radius r	Area A	Circumference C
34.	6			
35.			100	
36.		17		
37.				36π

38. Multi-Step Janet is designing a garden around a gazebo that is a regular hexagon with side length 6 ft. The garden will be a circle that extends 10 feet from the vertices of the hexagon. What is the area of the garden? Round to the nearest square foot.

MULTI-STEP TEST PREP

39. A stop sign is a regular octagon. The signs are available in two sizes: 30 in. or 36 in.

a. Find the area of a 30 in. sign. Round to the nearest tenth.

b. Find the area of a 36 in. sign. Round to the nearest tenth.

c. Find the percent increase in metal needed to make a 36 in. sign instead of a 30 in. sign.

40. **Measurement** A *trundle wheel* is used to measure distances by rolling it on the ground and counting its number of turns. If the circumference of a trundle wheel is 1 meter, what is its diameter?

41. **Critical Thinking** Which do you think would seat more people, a 4 ft by 6 ft rectangular table or a circular table with a diameter of 6 ft? How many people would you sit at each table? Explain your reasoning.

42. **Write About It** The center of each circle in the figure lies on the number line. Describe the relationship between the circumference of the largest circle and the circumferences of the four smaller circles.

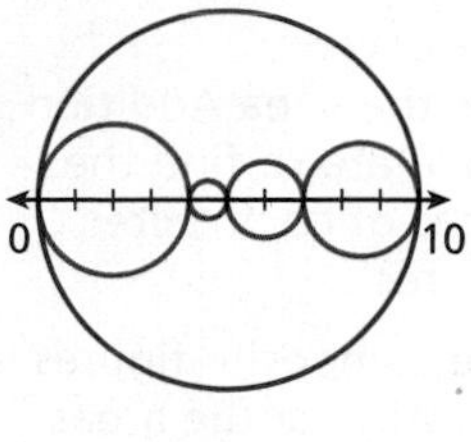

TEST PREP

43. Find the perimeter of the regular octagon to the nearest centimeter.

Ⓐ 5 Ⓑ 40 Ⓒ 20 Ⓓ 68

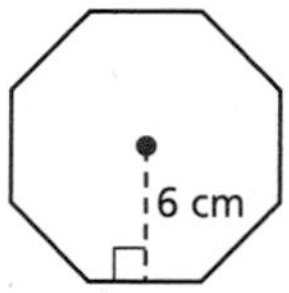

44. Which of the following ratios comparing a circle's circumference C to its diameter d gives the value of π?

Ⓕ $\frac{C}{d}$ Ⓖ $\frac{4C}{d^2}$ Ⓗ $\frac{d}{C}$ Ⓙ $\frac{d}{2C}$

45. Alisa has a circular tabletop with a 2-foot diameter. She wants to paint a pattern on the table top that includes a 2-foot-by-1-foot rectangle and 4 squares with sides 0.5 foot long. Which information makes this scenario impossible?

Ⓐ There will be no room left on the tabletop after the rectangle has been painted.

Ⓑ A 2-foot-long rectangle will not fit on the circular tabletop.

Ⓒ Squares cannot be painted on the circle.

Ⓓ There will not be enough room on the table to fit all the 0.5-foot squares.

CHALLENGE AND EXTEND

46. Two circles have the same center. The radius of the larger circle is 5 units longer than the radius of the smaller circle. Find the difference in the circumferences of the two circles.

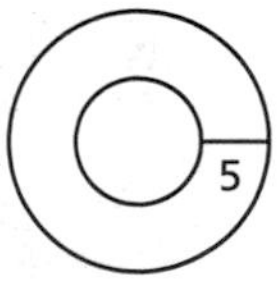

47. **Algebra** Write the formula for the area of a circle in terms of its circumference.

48. **Critical Thinking** Show that the formula for the area of a regular n-gon approaches the formula for the area of a circle as n gets very large.

COMMON CORE

10-3 Composite Figures

CC.9-12.G.MG.3 Apply geometric methods to solve design problems…* *Also* CC.9-12.G.SRT.9 (+)

Objectives

Use the Area Addition Postulate to find the areas of composite figures.

Use composite figures to estimate the areas of irregular shapes.

Vocabulary

composite figure

Who uses this?

Landscape architects must compute areas of composite figures when designing gardens. (See Example 3.)

A **composite figure** is made up of simple shapes, such as triangles, rectangles, trapezoids, and circles. To find the area of a composite figure, find the areas of the simple shapes and then use the Area Addition Postulate.

EXAMPLE 1 Finding the Areas of Composite Figures by Adding

Find the shaded area. Round to the nearest tenth, if necessary.

A

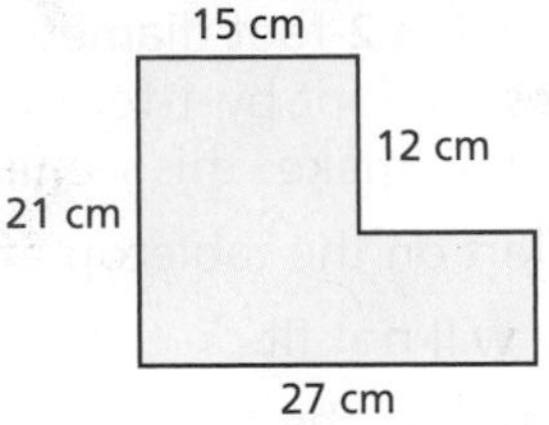

Divide the figure into rectangles.

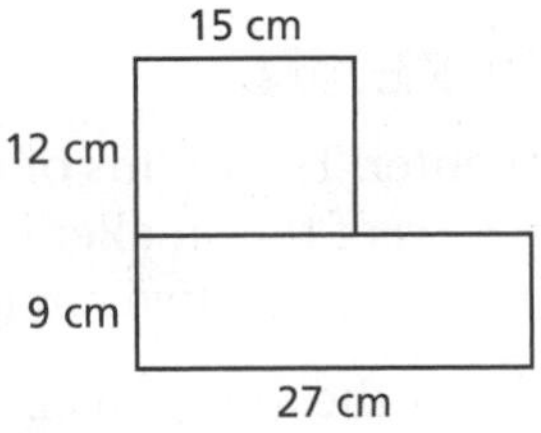

area of top rectangle:
$A = bh = 12(15) = 180 \text{ cm}^2$

area of bottom rectangle:
$A = bh = 9(27) = 243 \text{ cm}^2$

shaded area:
$180 + 243 = 423 \text{ cm}^2$

B

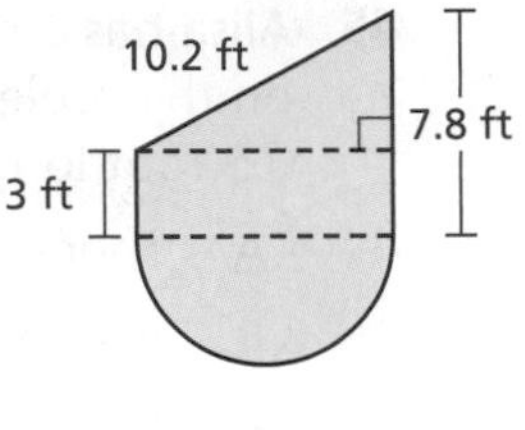

Divide the figure into parts. The base of the triangle is $\sqrt{10.2^2 - 4.8^2} = 9$ ft.

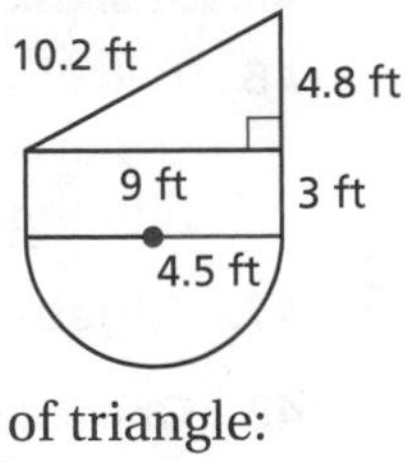

area of triangle:
$A = \frac{1}{2}bh = \frac{1}{2}(9)(4.8) = 21.6 \text{ ft}^2$

area of rectangle:
$A = bh = 9(3) = 27 \text{ ft}^2$

area of half circle:
$A = \frac{1}{2}\pi r^2 = \frac{1}{2}\pi(4.5^2) = 10.125\pi \text{ ft}^2$

shaded area:
$21.6 + 27 + 10.125\pi \approx 80.4 \text{ ft}^2$

CHECK IT OUT!

1. Find the shaded area. Round to the nearest tenth, if necessary.

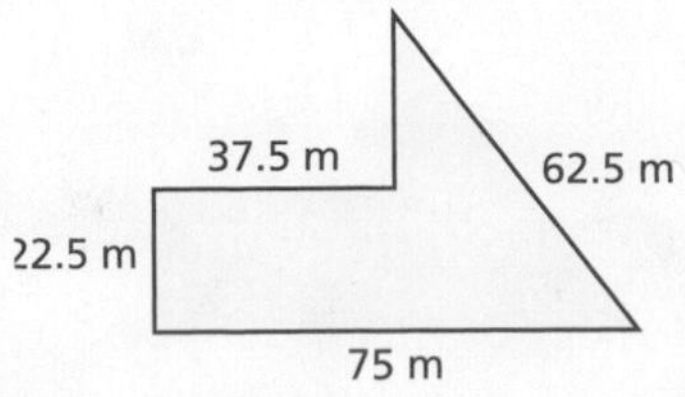

Sometimes you need to subtract to find the area of a composite figure.

EXAMPLE 2 Finding the Areas of Composite Figures by Subtracting

Find the shaded area. Round to the nearest tenth, if necessary.

A

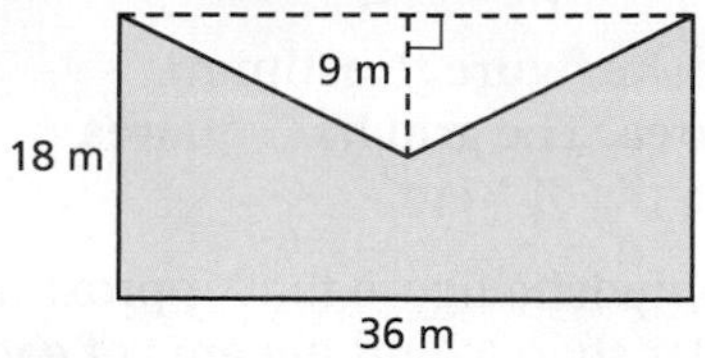

Subtract the area of the triangle from the area of the rectangle.

area of rectangle:
$A = bh = 18(36) = 648 \text{ m}^2$

area of triangle:
$A = \frac{1}{2}bh = \frac{1}{2}(36)(9) = 162 \text{ m}^2$

area of figure:
$A = 648 - 162 = 486 \text{ m}^2$

B

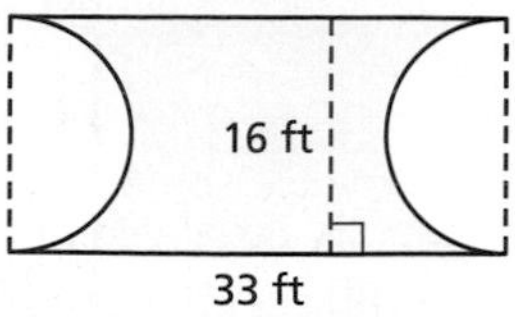

The two half circles have the same area as one circle. Subtract the area of the circle from the area of the rectangle.

area of the rectangle:
$A = bh = 33(16) = 528 \text{ ft}^2$

area of circle:
$A = \pi r^2 = \pi(8^2) = 64\pi \text{ ft}^2$

area of figure:
$A = 528 - 64\pi \approx 326.9 \text{ ft}^2$

CHECK IT OUT! 2. Find the shaded area. Round to the nearest tenth, if necessary.

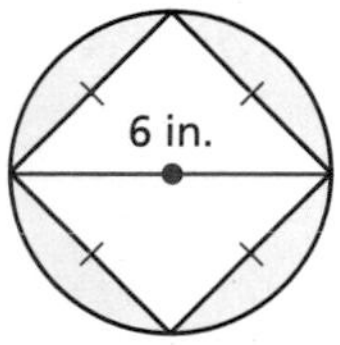

EXAMPLE 3 *Landscaping Application*

Katie is using the given plan to convert part of her lawn to a xeriscape garden. A newly planted xeriscape uses 17 gallons of water per square foot per year. How much water will the garden require in one year?

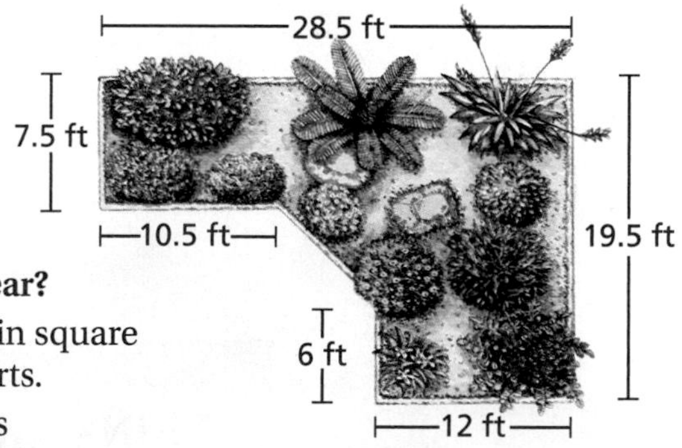

To find the area of the garden in square feet, divide the garden into parts.

The area of the top rectangle is $28.5(7.5) = 213.75 \text{ ft}^2$.

The area of the center trapezoid is $\frac{1}{2}(12 + 18)(6) = 90 \text{ ft}^2$.

The area of the bottom rectangle is $12(6) = 72 \text{ ft}^2$.

The total area of the garden is $213.75 + 90 + 72 = 375.75 \text{ ft}^2$.

The garden will use $375.75(17) = 6387.75$ gallons of water per year.

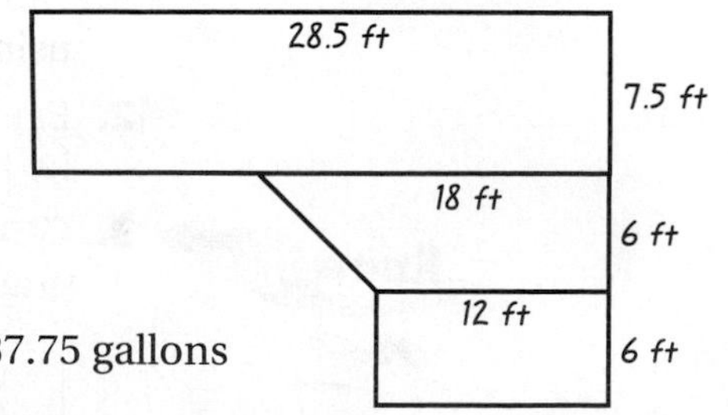

CHECK IT OUT! 3. The lawn that Katie is replacing requires 79 gallons of water per square foot per year. How much water will Katie save by planting the xeriscape garden?

To estimate the area of an irregular shape, you can sometimes use a composite figure. First, draw a composite figure that resembles the irregular shape. Then divide the composite figure into simple shapes.

EXAMPLE 4 Estimating Areas of Irregular Shapes

Use a composite figure to estimate the shaded area. The grid has squares with side lengths of 1 cm.

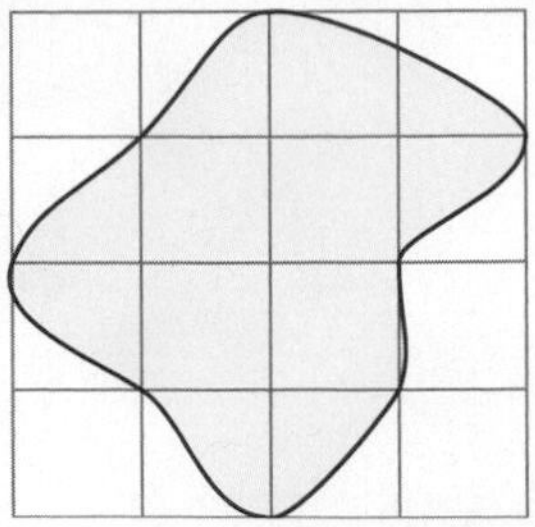

Draw a composite figure that approximates the irregular shape. Find the area of each part of the composite figure.

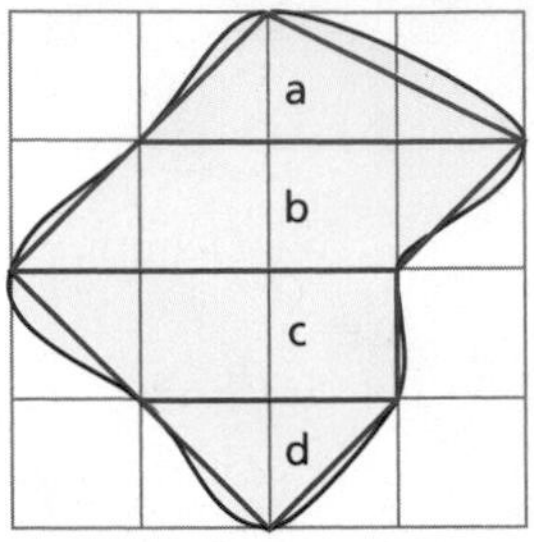

area of triangle a:

$$A = \frac{1}{2}bh = \frac{1}{2}(3)(1) = 1.5 \text{ cm}^2$$

area of parallelogram b:

$$A = bh = 3(1) = 3 \text{ cm}^2$$

area of trapezoid c:

$$A = \frac{1}{2}(3 + 2)(1) = 2.5 \text{ cm}^2$$

area of triangle d:

$$A = \frac{1}{2}(2)(1) = 1 \text{ cm}^2$$

area of composite figure:

$$1.5 + 3 + 2.5 + 1 = 8 \text{ cm}^2$$

The shaded area is about 8 cm^2.

CHECK IT OUT! 4. Use a composite figure to estimate the shaded area. The grid has squares with side lengths of 1 ft.

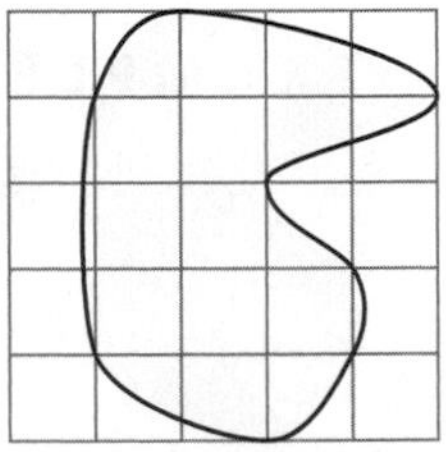

MATHEMATICAL PRACTICES

THINK AND DISCUSS

1. Describe a composite figure whose area you could find by using subtraction.
2. Explain how to find the area of an irregular shape by using a composite figure.
3. **GET ORGANIZED** Copy and complete the graphic organizer. Use the given composite figure.

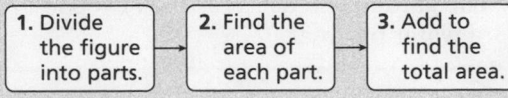

Know it! Note

1. Divide the figure into parts. → 2. Find the area of each part. → 3. Add to find the total area.

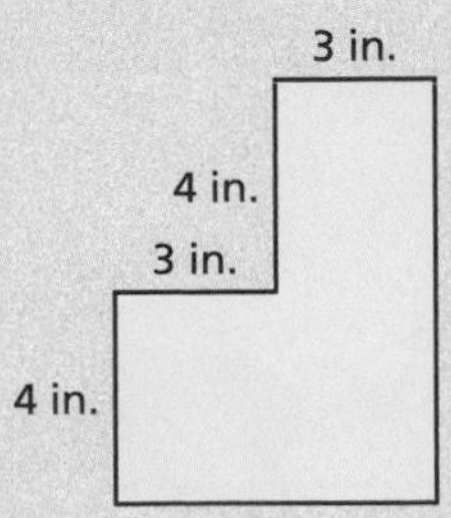

10-3 Exercises

Learn It Online
Homework Help Online
Parent Resources Online

GUIDED PRACTICE

1. **Vocabulary** Draw a *composite figure* that is made up of two rectangles.

SEE EXAMPLE 1

Multi-Step Find the shaded area. Round to the nearest tenth, if necessary.

2. 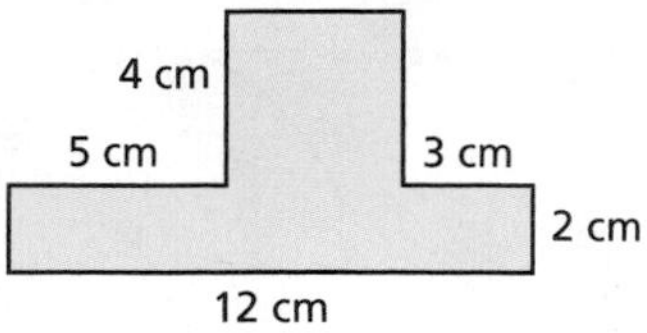

3. 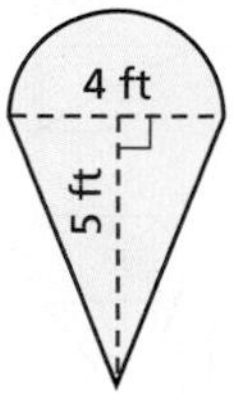

SEE EXAMPLE 2

4. 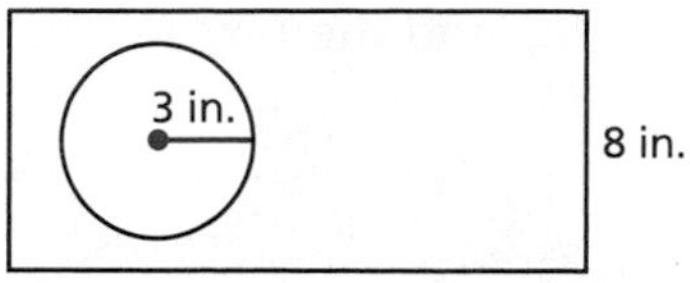

5. 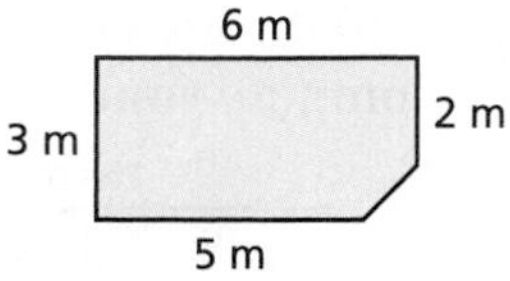

SEE EXAMPLE 3

6. **Interior Decorating** Barbara is getting carpet installed in her living room and hallway. The cost of installation is $6 per square yard. What is the total cost of installing the carpet?

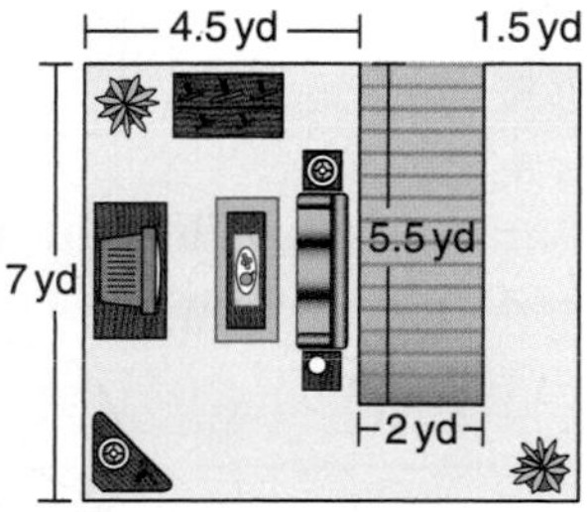

SEE EXAMPLE 4

Use a composite figure to estimate each shaded area. The grid has squares with side lengths of 1 in.

7. 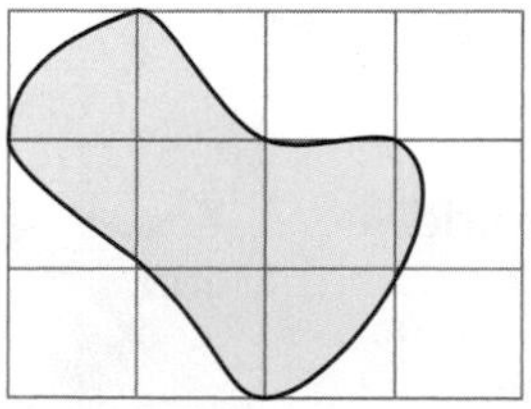

8. 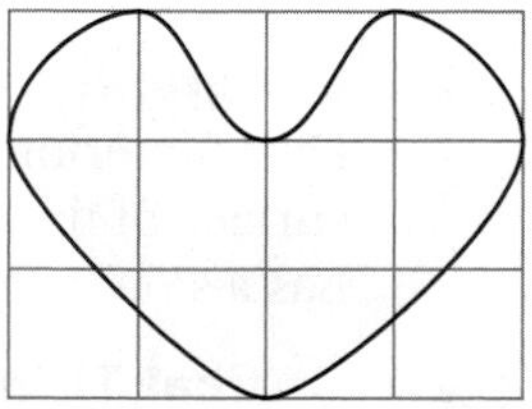

PRACTICE AND PROBLEM SOLVING

Independent Practice	
For Exercises	See Example
9–10	1
11–12	2
13	3
14–15	4

Extra Practice
See Extra Practice for more Skills Practice and Applications Practice exercises.

Multi-Step Find the shaded area. Round to the nearest tenth, if necessary.

9. 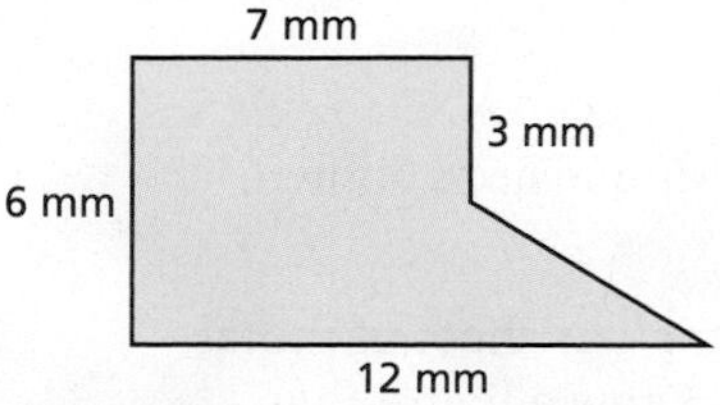

10. 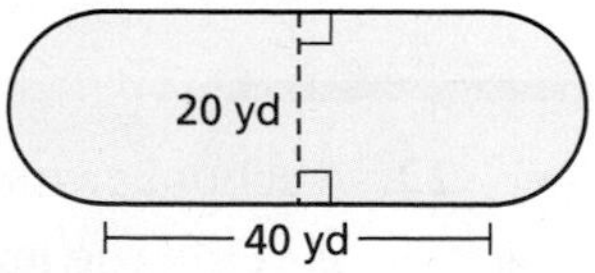

11. 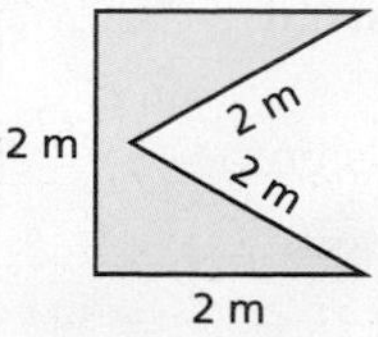

12. 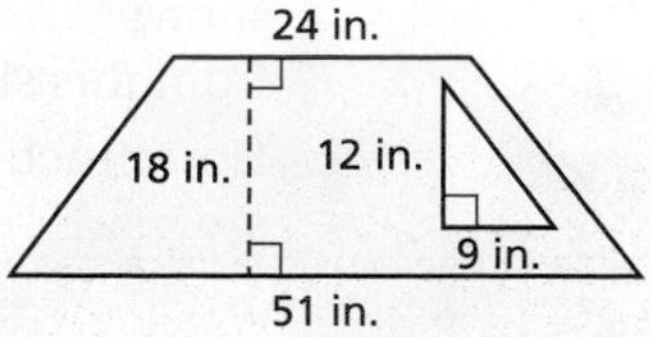

13. **Drama** Pat is painting a stage backdrop for a play. The paint he is using covers 90 square feet per quart. How many quarts of paint should Pat buy?

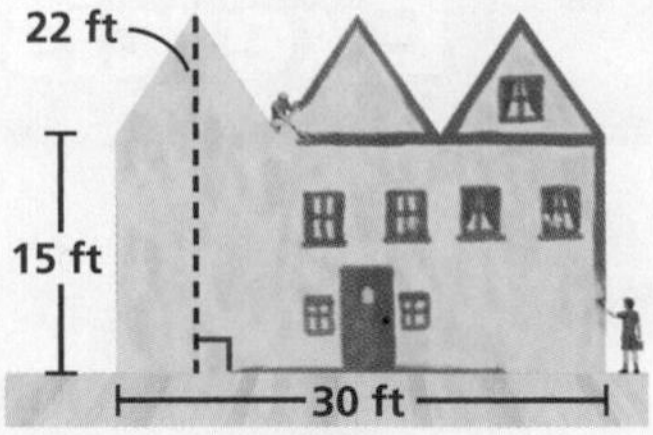

Use a composite figure to estimate each shaded area. The grid has squares with side lengths of 1 m.

14.

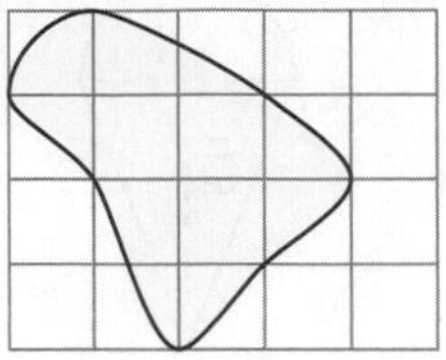

15.

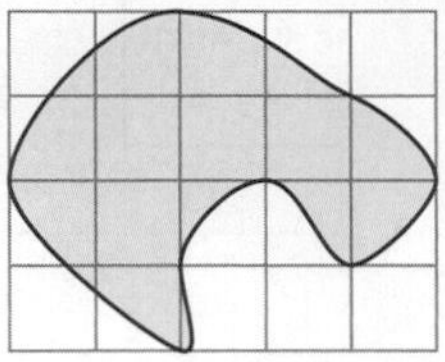

Find the area of each figure first by adding and then by subtracting. Compare your answers.

16.

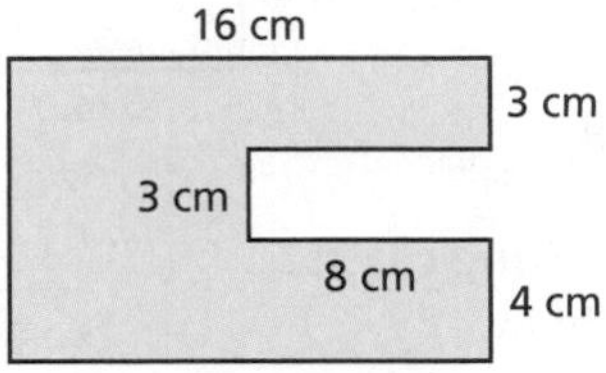

17.

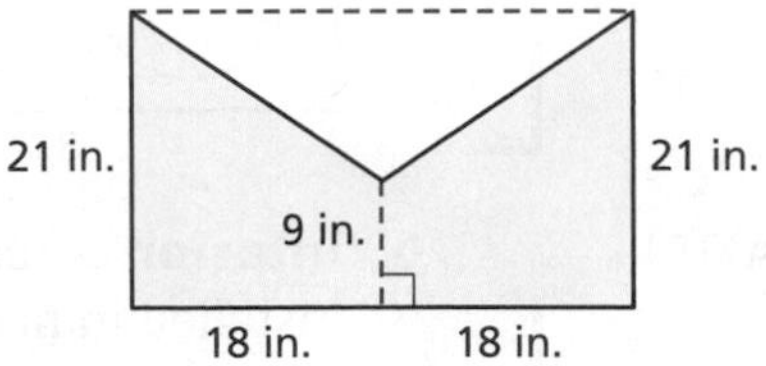

Find the area of each figure. Give your answers in terms of π.

18.

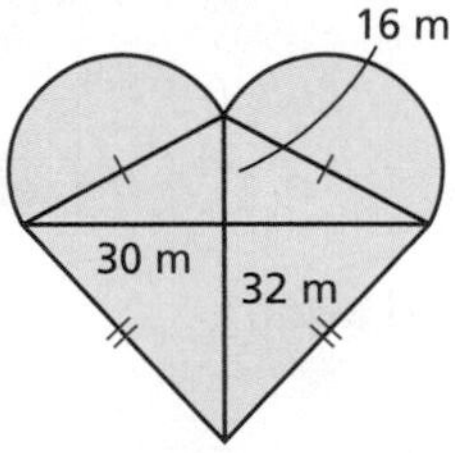

19.

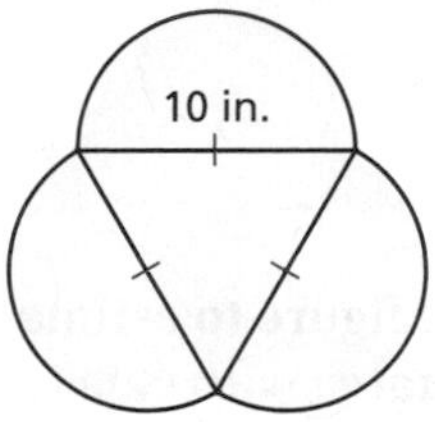

20.

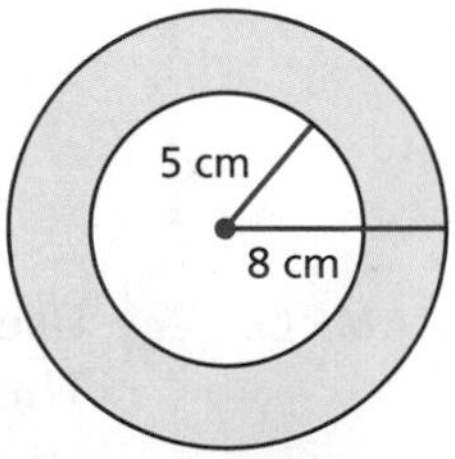

21. **Geography** Use the grid on the map of Lake Superior to estimate the area of the surface of the lake. Each square on the grid has a side length of 100 miles.

22. **Critical Thinking** A trapezoid can be divided into a rectangle and two triangles. Show that the area formula for a trapezoid gives the same result as the sum of the areas of the rectangle and triangles.

MULTI-STEP TEST PREP

23. A school crossing sign has the dimensions shown.
    a. Find the area of the sign.
    b. A manufacturer has a rectangular sheet of metal measuring 45 in. by 105 in. Draw a figure that shows how 6 school crossing signs can be cut from this sheet of metal.
    c. How much metal will be left after the six signs are made?

Multi-Step **Use a ruler and compass to draw each figure and then find the area.**

24. A rectangle with a base length of $b = 3$ cm and a height of $h = 4$ cm has a circle with a radius of $r = 1$ cm removed from the interior.

25. A square with a side length of $s = 4$ in. shares a side with a triangle with a height of $h = 5$ in. and a base length of $b = 4$ in. and shares another side with a half circle with $d = 4$ in.

26. A circle with a radius of $r = 5$ cm has a right triangle with a base of $b = 8$ cm and a height of $h = 6$ cm removed from its interior.

27. Multi-Step A lune is a crescent-shaped figure bounded by two intersecting circles. Find the shaded area in each of the first three diagrams, and then use your results to find the area of the lune. Note that AB is the diameter of the smaller circle.

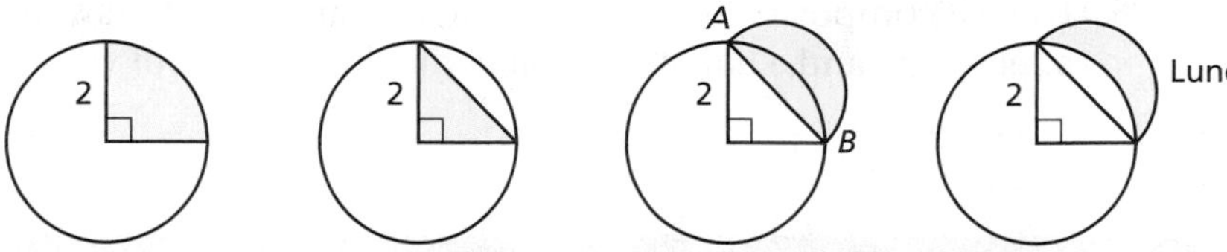

LINK

Math History

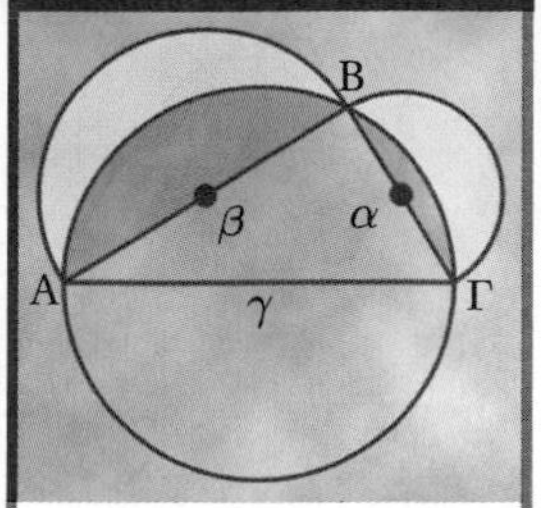

Hippocrates attempted to use lunes to solve a problem that has since been proven impossible: constructing a square with the same area as a given circle.

Estimation **Trace each irregular shape and draw a composite figure that approximates it. Measure the composite figure and use it to estimate the area of the irregular shape.**

28.

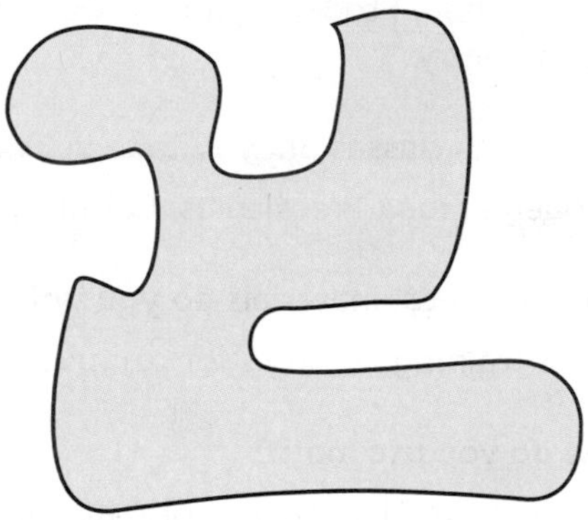

29.

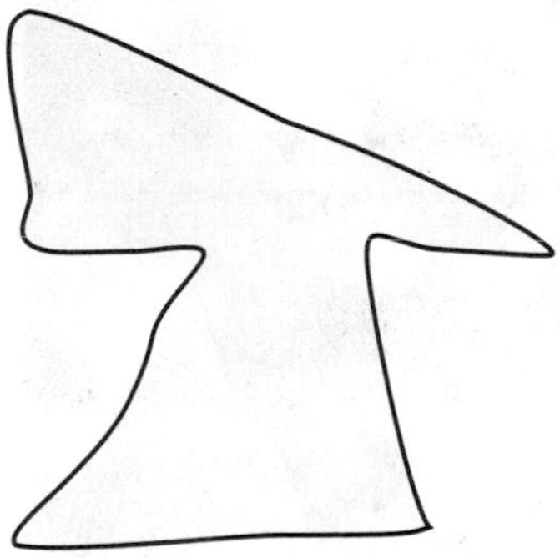

30. Write About It Explain when you would use addition to find the area of a composite figure and when you would use subtraction.

TEST PREP

31. Which equation can be used to find the area of the composite figure?

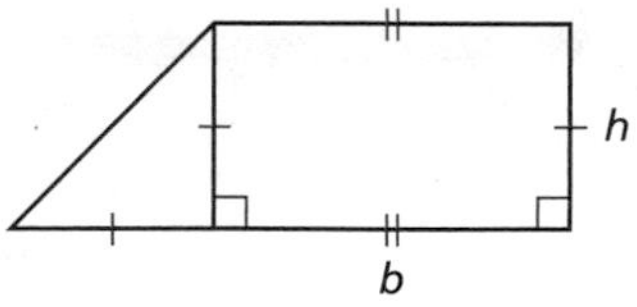

Ⓐ $A = bh + \frac{1}{2}(h)^2$

Ⓑ $A = bh + h^2$

Ⓒ $A = h + 2b + h^2$

Ⓓ $A = h + 2b + \frac{1}{2}h^2$

32. Use a ruler to measure the dimensions of the composite figure to the nearest tenth of a centimeter.

Which of the following best represents the area of the composite figure?

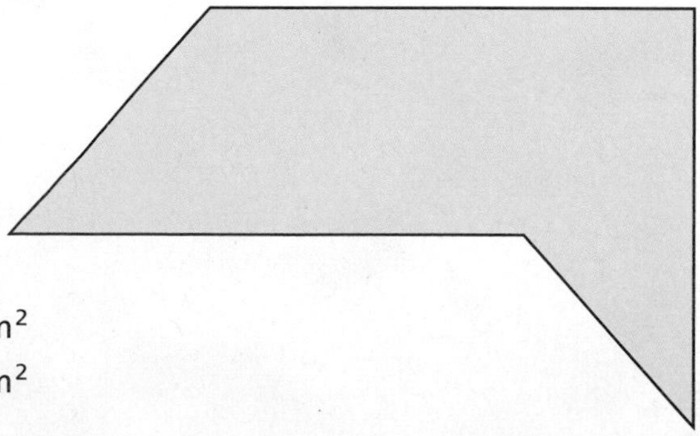

Ⓕ 4 cm^2

Ⓖ 19 cm^2

Ⓗ 22 cm^2

Ⓙ 42 cm^2

33. Find the area of the unshaded part of the rectangle.

Ⓐ 1800 m^2 Ⓒ 2925 m^2

Ⓑ 2250 m^2 Ⓓ 4725 m^2

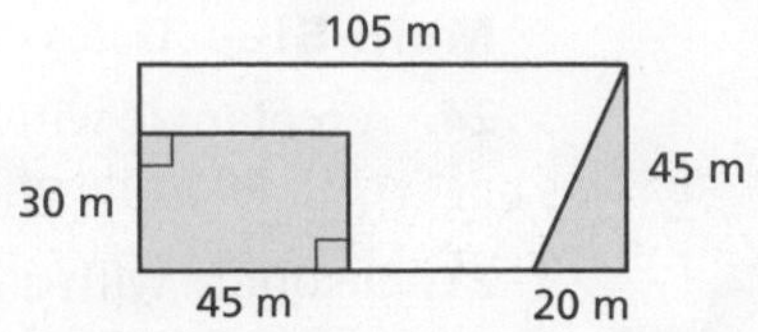

CHALLENGE AND EXTEND

34. An *annulus* is the region between two circles that have the same center. Write the formula for the area of the annulus in terms of the outer radius R and the inner radius r.

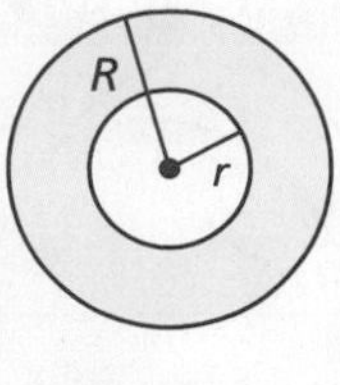

35. Draw two composite figures with the same area: one made up of two rectangles and the other made up of a rectangle and a triangle.

36. Draw a composite figure that has a total area of $10\pi \text{ cm}^2$ and is made up of a rectangle and a half circle. Label the dimensions of your figure.

Career Path

Learn It Online
Career Resources Online

Anessa Liu
Technical writer

Q: What math classes did you take in high school?

A: In high school I took Algebra 1, Geometry, Algebra 2, and Trigonometry.

Q: What math classes did you take in college?

A: In college I took Precalculus, Calculus, and Statistics.

Q: What technical materials do you write?

A: I write training manuals for computer software packages.

Q: How do you use math?

A: Some manuals I write are for math programs, so I use a lot of formulas to describe patterns and measurements.

Q: What are your future plans?

A: After I get a few more years experience writing manuals, I would like to train others who use these programs.

Connecting Geometry to

Trigonometry

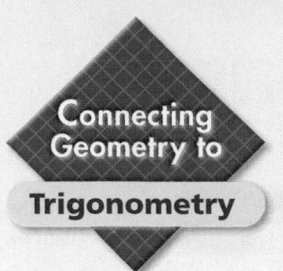

Triangle Area Formulas

You've used the formula $A = \frac{1}{2}bh$ to find the area of a triangle, and you've used trigonometric ratios to find missing lengths in right triangles. You can combine the two techniques to find the area of a triangle when you don't know the value of h.

If you are given the lengths of two sides and the included angle, you can use this information to find the area of the triangle

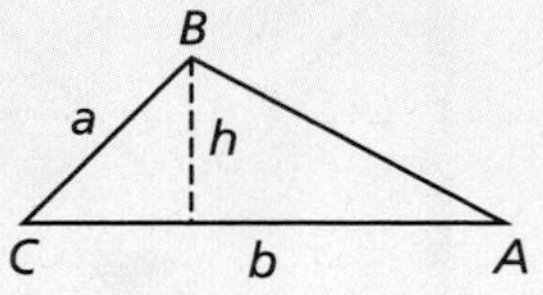

$\frac{h}{a} = \sin C$ *Write the sine of C in terms of h and a.*

$h = a \sin C$ *Multiply both sides by a to isolate h.*

$A = \frac{1}{2} ba \sin C$ *Substitute the expression for h into the area formula.*

Example

Find the area of the triangle shown.

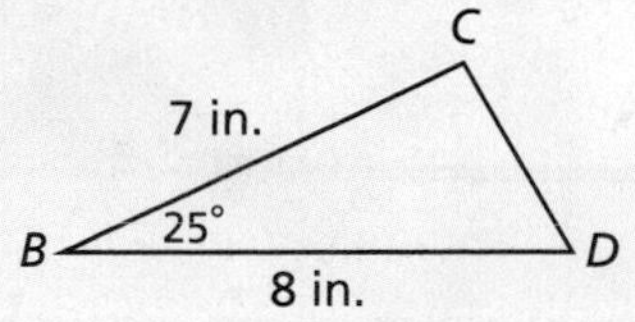

$A = \frac{1}{2} ba \sin B$

$A = \frac{1}{2}(7)(8)\sin 25°$ *Substitute the values for the side lengths and the measure of the included angle.*

$A \approx 11.8$ *Simplify.*

The area is approximately 11.8 in.^{2}.

Try This

Find the area of each triangle. Round to the nearest tenth.

1.

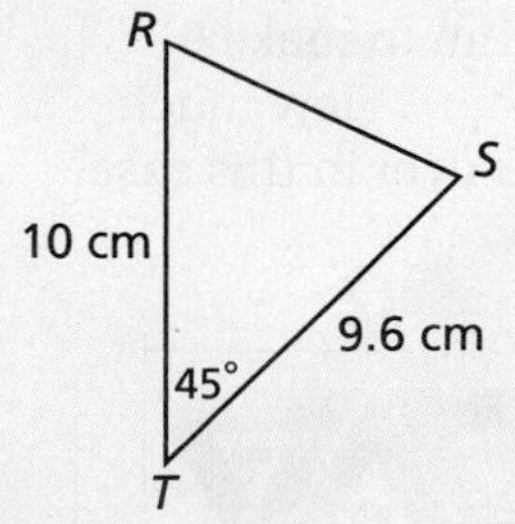

2.

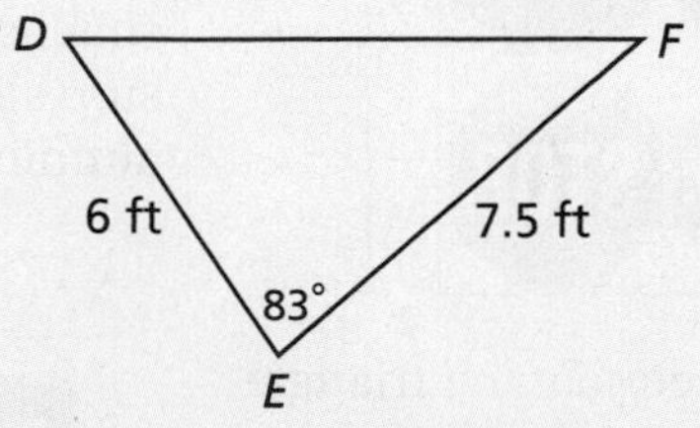

3.

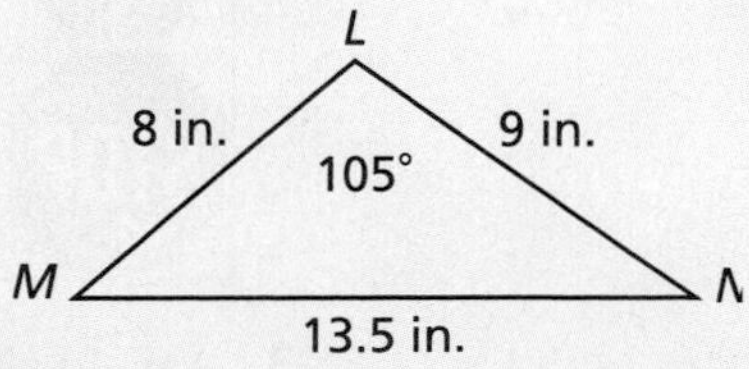

4. You can also find the area of a triangle if you only know the lengths of the sides. Heron's formula is $A = \sqrt{s(s-a)(s-b)(s-c)}$, where s is one-half of the perimeter of the triangle and a, b, and c are the side lengths of the triangle. Find s for the triangle in Exercise 3, and use Heron's formula to find the area. Round to the nearest tenth.

CHAPTER 10

MULTI-STEP TEST PREP

SECTION 10A

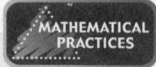

MATHEMATICAL PRACTICES **Reason abstractly and quantitatively.**

Developing Geometric Formulas

Traffic Signs Traffic signs are usually made of reflective aluminum. A manufacturer of traffic signs begins with a rectangular sheet of aluminum that measures 60 in. by 90 in.

1. A railroad crossing sign is a circle with a diameter of 30 in. The manufacturer can make 6 of these signs from the sheet of aluminum by arranging the signs as shown. How much aluminum is left over once the signs have been made?

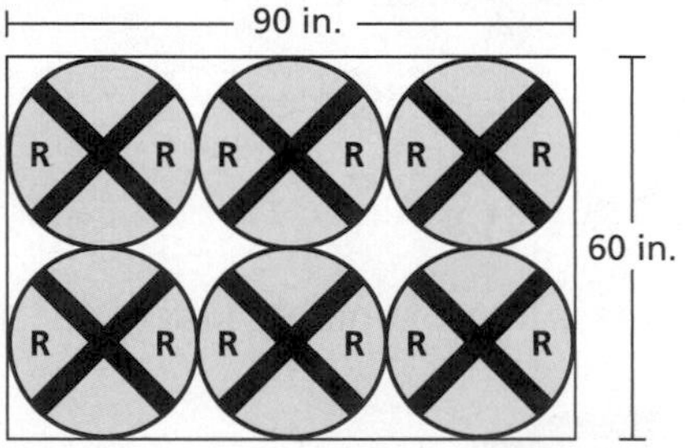

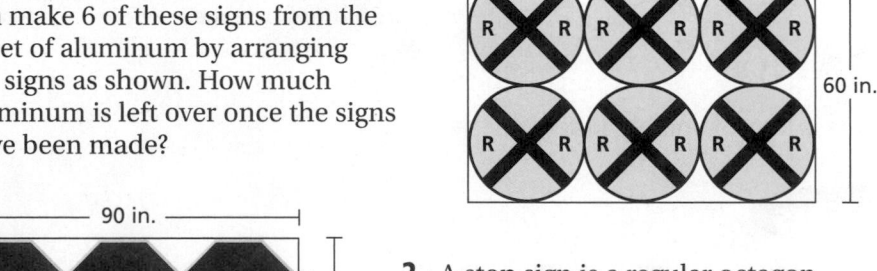

2. A stop sign is a regular octagon. The manufacturer can use the sheet of aluminum to make 6 stop signs as shown. How much aluminum is left over in this case?

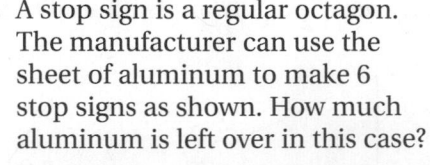

3. A yield sign is an equilateral triangle with sides 30 in. long. By arranging the triangles as shown, the manufacturer can use the sheet of aluminum to make 10 yield signs. How much aluminum is left over when yield signs are made?

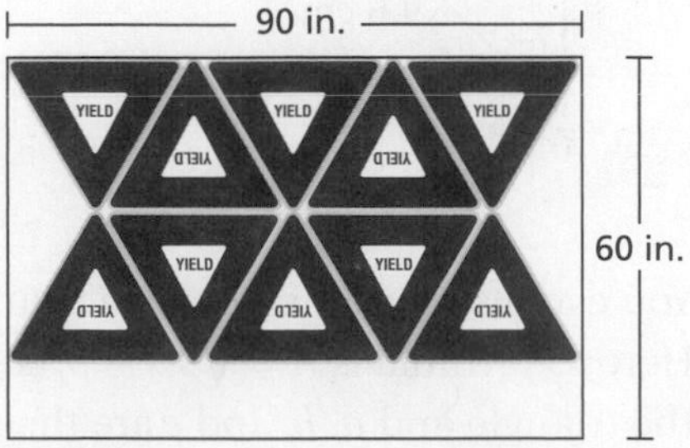

4. The making of which type of sign results in the least amount of waste?

READY TO GO ON?

Quiz for Lessons 10-1 Through 10-3

10-1 Developing Formulas for Triangles and Quadrilaterals

Find each measurement.

1. the area of the parallelogram

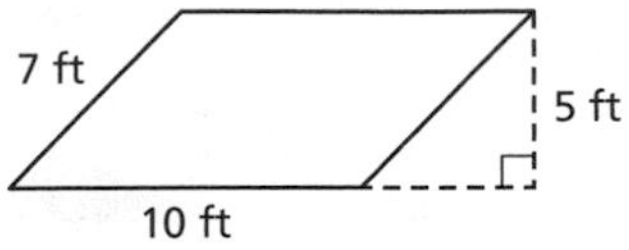

2. the base of the rectangle, in which $A = (24x^2 + 8x)$ m^2

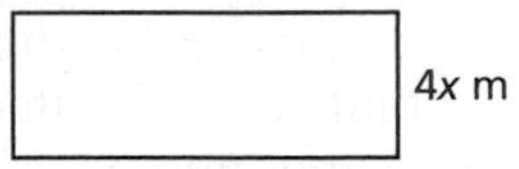

3. d_1 of the kite, in which $A = 126$ ft^2

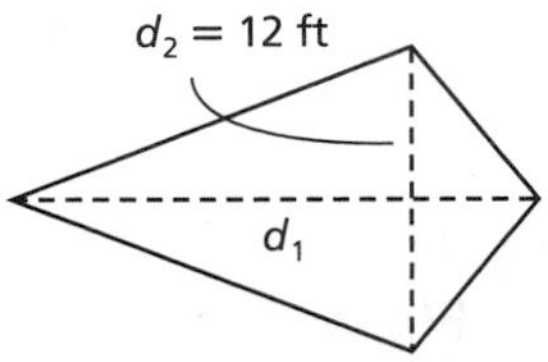

4. the area of the rhombus

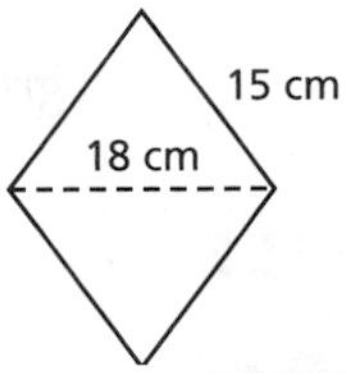

5. The tile mosaic shown is made up of 1 cm squares. Use the grid to find the perimeter and area of the green triangle, the blue trapezoid, and the yellow parallelogram.

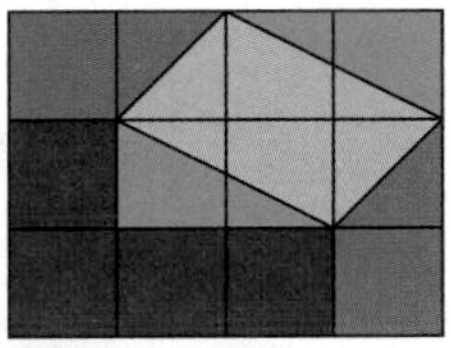

10-2 Developing Formulas for Circles and Regular Polygons

Find each measurement.

6. the circumference of $\odot R$ in terms of π

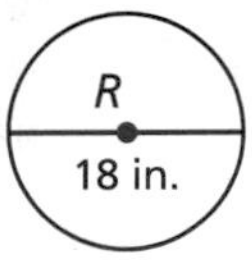

7. the area of $\odot E$ in terms of π

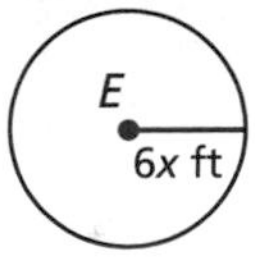

Find the area of each regular polygon. Round to the nearest tenth.

8. a regular hexagon with apothem 6 ft
9. a regular pentagon with side length 12 m

10-3 Composite Figures

Find the shaded area. Round to the nearest tenth, if necessary.

10.

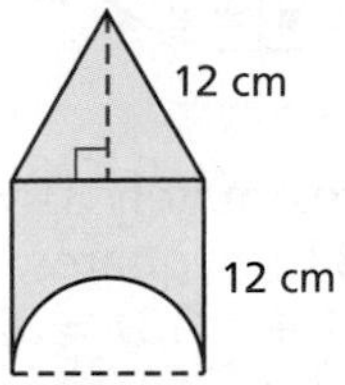

11.

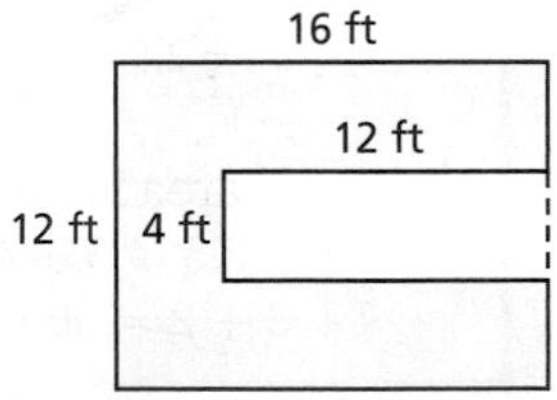

12. Shelby is planting grass in an irregularly shaped garden as shown. The grid has squares with side lengths of 1 yd. Estimate the area of the garden. Given that grass cost \$6.50 per square yard, find the cost of the grass.

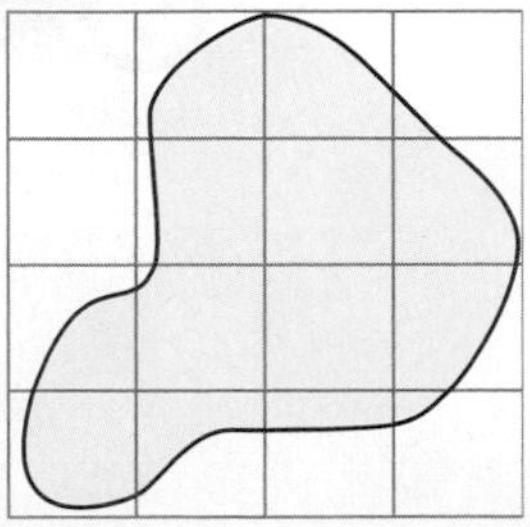

CORE

10-4 Perimeter and Area in the Coordinate Plane

CC.9-12.G.GPE.7 Use coordinates to compute perimeters…and areas…, e.g., using the distance formula.*

Objective
Find the perimeters and areas of figures in a coordinate plane.

Why learn this?
You can use figures in a coordinate plane to solve puzzles like the one at right. (See Example 4.)

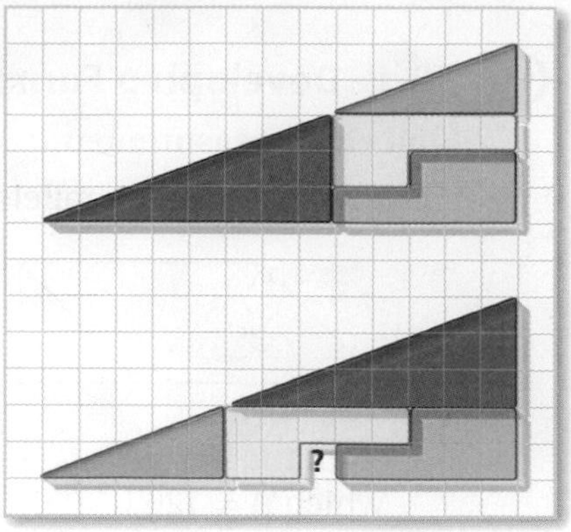

You have estimated the area of irregular shapes by drawing composite figures that approximated the irregular shapes and by using area formulas.

Another method of estimating area is to use a grid and count the squares on the grid.

EXAMPLE 1 Estimating Areas of Irregular Shapes in the Coordinate Plane

Estimate the area of the irregular shape.

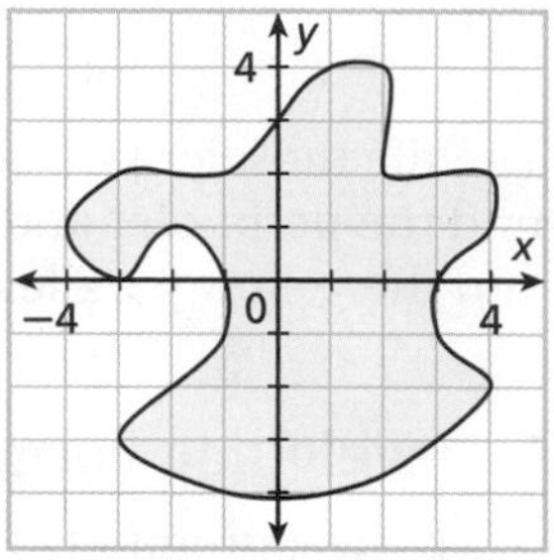

Method 1: Draw a composite figure that approximates the irregular shape and find the area of the composite figure.

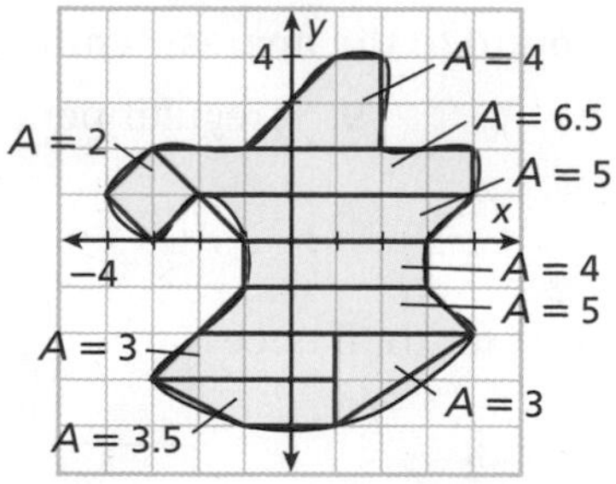

The area is approximately $4 + 6.5 + 5 + 4 + 5 + 3.5 + 3 + 3 + 2 = 36$ units^2.

Method 2: Count the number of squares inside the figure, estimating half squares. Use a ■ for a whole square and a ◢ for a half square.

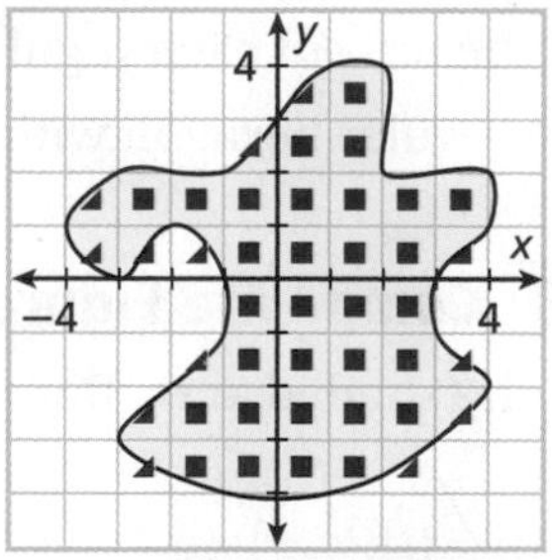

There are approximately 31 whole squares and 13 half squares, so the area is about $31 + \frac{1}{2}(13) = 37.5$ units^2.

CHECK IT OUT! **1.** Estimate the area of the irregular shape.

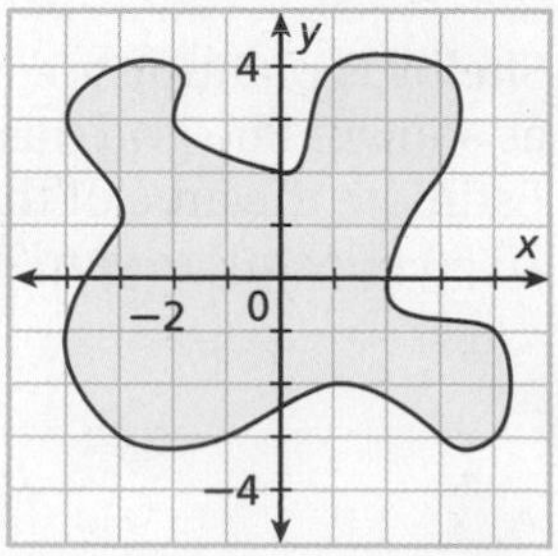

EXAMPLE 2 Finding Perimeter and Area in the Coordinate Plane

Algebra

Draw and classify the polygon with vertices $A(-4, 1)$, $B(2, 4)$, $C(4, 0)$, and $D(-2, -3)$. Find the perimeter and area of the polygon.

Step 1 Draw the polygon.

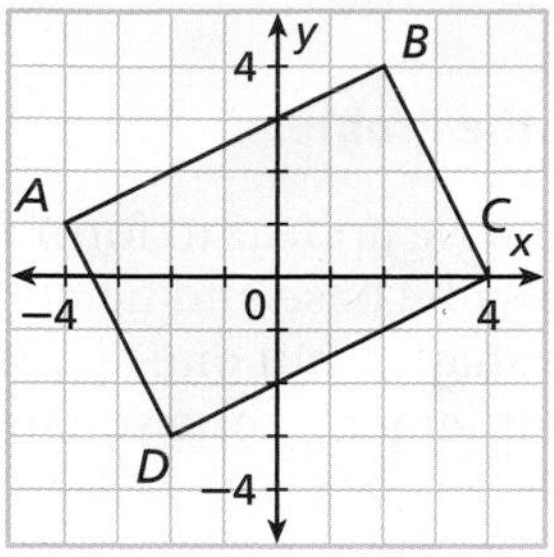

Step 2 *ABCD* appears to be a rectangle. To verify this, use slopes to show that the sides are perpendicular.

slope of $\overline{AB}$: $\frac{4-1}{2-(-4)} = \frac{3}{6} = \frac{1}{2}$

slope of $\overline{BC}$: $\frac{0-4}{4-2} = \frac{-4}{2} = -2$

slope of $\overline{CD}$: $\frac{-3-0}{-2-4} = \frac{-3}{-6} = \frac{1}{2}$

slope of $\overline{DA}$: $\frac{1-(-3)}{-4-(-2)} = \frac{4}{-2} = -2$

The consecutive sides are perpendicular, so *ABCD* is a rectangle.

Step 3 Let $\overline{CD}$ be the base and $\overline{BC}$ be the height of the rectangle. Use the Distance Formula to find each side length.

$b = CD = \sqrt{(-2-4)^2 + (-3-0)^2} = \sqrt{45} = 3\sqrt{5}$

$h = BC = \sqrt{(4-2)^2 + (0-4)^2} = \sqrt{20} = 2\sqrt{5}$

perimeter of *ABCD*: $P = 2b + 2h = 2(3\sqrt{5}) + 2(2\sqrt{5}) = 10\sqrt{5}$ units

area of *ABCD*: $A = bh = (3\sqrt{5})(2\sqrt{5}) = 30$ units^2.

> **Remember!**
>
> The distance from (x_1, y_1) to (x_2, y_2) in a coordinate plane is $d = \sqrt{(x_2 - x_1)^2 + (y_2 - y_1)^2}$, and the slope of the line containing the points is $m = \frac{y_2 - y_1}{x_2 - x_1}$.

CHECK IT OUT! 2. Draw and classify the polygon with vertices $H(-3, 4)$, $J(2, 6)$, $K(2, 1)$, and $L(-3, -1)$. Find the perimeter and area of the polygon.

For a figure in a coordinate plane that does not have an area formula, it may be easier to enclose the figure in a rectangle and subtract the areas of the parts of the rectangle that are not included in the figure.

EXAMPLE 3 Finding Areas in the Coordinate Plane by Subtracting

Find the area of the polygon with vertices $W(1, 4)$, $X(4, 2)$, $Y(2, -3)$, and $Z(-4, 0)$.

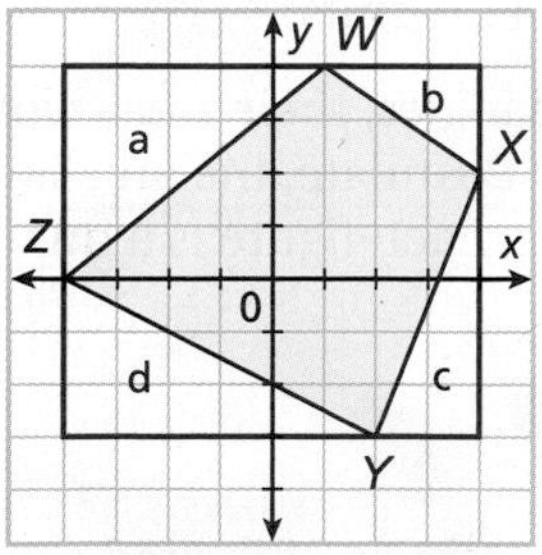

Draw the polygon and enclose it in a rectangle.

area of the rectangle: $A = bh = 8(7) = 56$ units^2

area of the triangles:

a: $A = \frac{1}{2}bh = \frac{1}{2}(5)(4) = 10$ units^2

b: $A = \frac{1}{2}bh = \frac{1}{2}(3)(2) = 3$ units^2

c: $A = \frac{1}{2}bh = \frac{1}{2}(2)(5) = 5$ units^2

d: $A = \frac{1}{2}bh = \frac{1}{2}(6)(3) = 9$ units^2

The area of the polygon is $56 - 10 - 3 - 5 - 9 = 29$ units^2.

CHECK IT OUT! 3. Find the area of the polygon with vertices $K(-2, 4)$, $L(6, -2)$, $M(4, -4)$, and $N(-6, -2)$.

EXAMPLE 4 *Problem-Solving Application*

MATHEMATICAL PRACTICES

Make sense of problems and persevere in solving them.

In the puzzle, the two figures are made up of the same pieces, but one figure appears to have a larger area. Use coordinates to show that the area does not change when the pieces are rearranged.

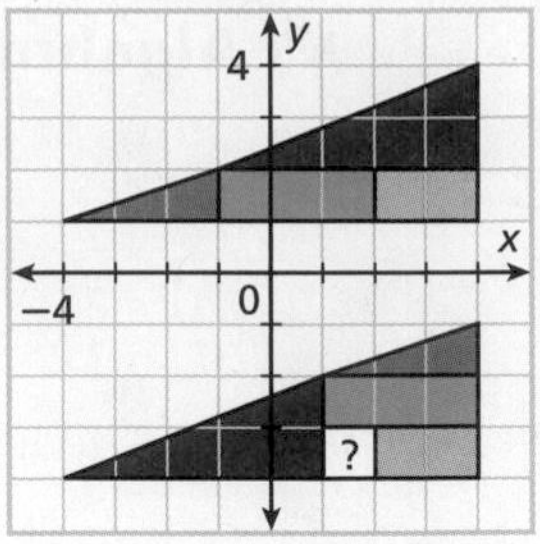

1 Understand the Problem

The parts of the puzzle appear to form two triangles with the same base and height that contain the same shapes, but one appears to have an area that is larger by one square unit.

2 Make a Plan

Find the areas of the shapes that make up each figure. If the corresponding areas are the same, then both figures have the same area by the Area Addition Postulate. To explain why the area appears to increase, consider the assumptions being made about the figure. Each figure is assumed to be a triangle with a base of 8 units and a height of 3 units. Both figures are divided into several smaller shapes.

3 Solve

Find the area of each shape.

Top figure	Bottom figure
red triangle: $A = \frac{1}{2}bh = \frac{1}{2}(5)(2) = 5 \text{ units}^2$	red triangle: $A = \frac{1}{2}bh = \frac{1}{2}(5)(2) = 5 \text{ units}^2$
blue triangle: $A = \frac{1}{2}bh = \frac{1}{2}(3)(1) = 1.5 \text{ units}^2$	blue triangle: $A = \frac{1}{2}bh = \frac{1}{2}(3)(1) = 1.5 \text{ units}^2$
green rectangle: $A = bh = (3)(1) = 3 \text{ units}^2$	green rectangle: $A = bh = (3)(1) = 3 \text{ units}^2$
yellow rectangle: $A = bh = (2)(1) = 2 \text{ units}^2$	yellow rectangle: $A = bh = (2)(1) = 2 \text{ units}^2$

The areas are the same. Both figures have an area of $5 + 1.5 + 3 + 2 = 11.5 \text{ units}^2$.

If the figures were triangles, their areas would be $A = \frac{1}{2}(8)(3) = 12 \text{ units}^2$. By the Area Addition Postulate, the area is only 11.5 units^2, so the figures must not be triangles. Each figure is a quadrilateral whose shape is very close to a triangle.

4 Look Back

The slope of the hypotenuse of the red triangle is $\frac{2}{5}$. The slope of the hypotenuse of the blue triangle is $\frac{1}{3}$. Since the slopes are unequal, the hypotenuses do not form a straight line. This means the overall shapes are not triangles.

CHECK IT OUT!

4. Create a figure and divide it into pieces so that the area of the figure appears to increase when the pieces are rearranged.

MATHEMATICAL PRACTICES

THINK AND DISCUSS

1. Describe two ways to estimate the area of an irregular shape in a coordinate plane.

2. Explain how you could use the Distance Formula to find the area of a special quadrilateral in a coordinate plane.

Know it! Note

3. **GET ORGANIZED** Copy the graph and the graphic organizer. Complete the graphic organizer by writing the steps used to find the area of the parallelogram.

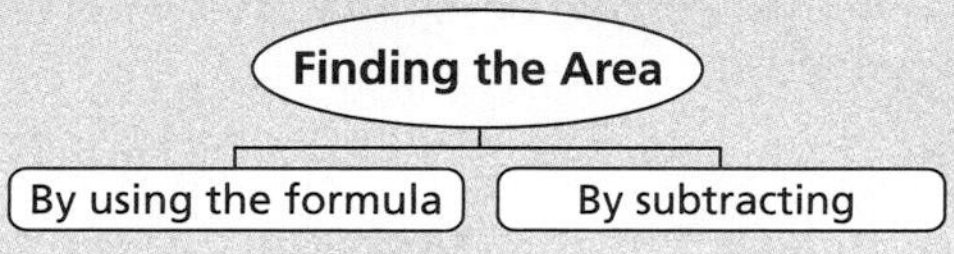

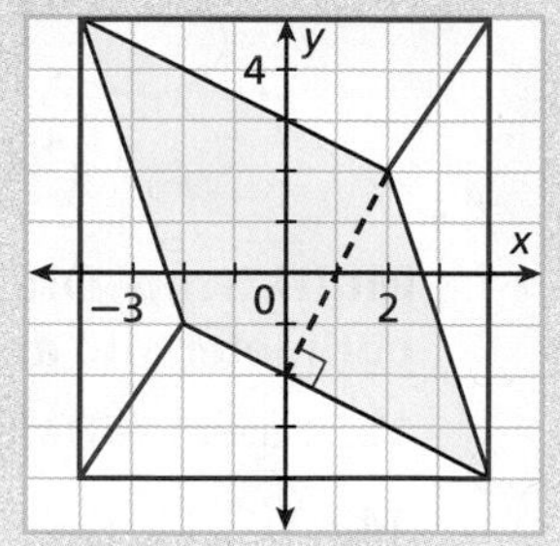

10-4 Exercises

Learn It Online
Homework Help Online
Parent Resources Online

GUIDED PRACTICE

SEE EXAMPLE 1

Estimate the area of each irregular shape.

1.

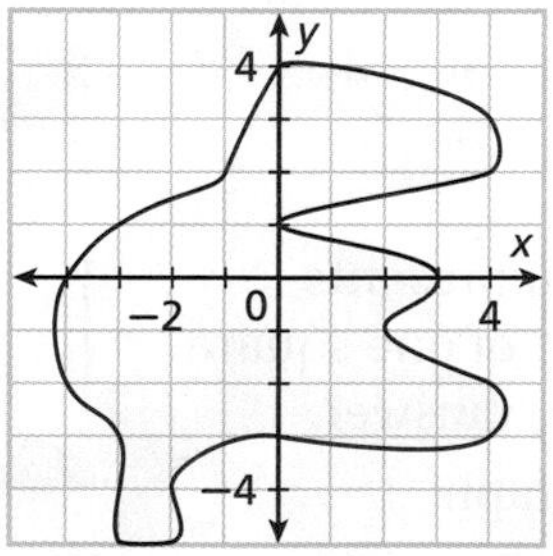

2.

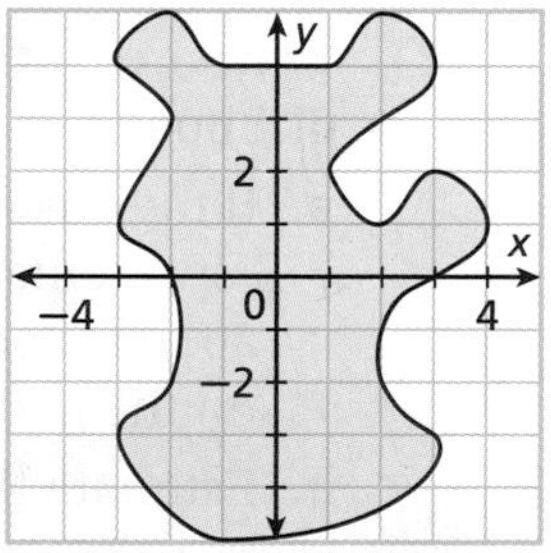

SEE EXAMPLE 2

Multi-Step Draw and classify the polygon with the given vertices. Find the perimeter and area of the polygon.

3. $V(-3, 0)$, $W(3, 0)$, $X(0, 3)$

4. $F(2, 8)$, $G(4, 4)$, $H(2, 0)$

5. $P(-2, 5)$, $Q(8, 5)$, $R(8, 1)$, $S(-2, 1)$

6. $A(-4, 2)$, $B(-2, 6)$, $C(6, 6)$, $D(8, 2)$

SEE EXAMPLE 3

Find the area of each polygon with the given vertices.

7. $S(3, 8)$, $T(8, 3)$, $U(2, 1)$

8. $L(3, 5)$, $M(6, 8)$, $N(9, 6)$, $P(5, 0)$

SEE EXAMPLE 4

9. Find the area and perimeter of each polygon shown. Use your results to draw a polygon with a perimeter of 12 units and an area of 4 units^2 and a polygon with a perimeter of 12 units and an area of 3 units^2.

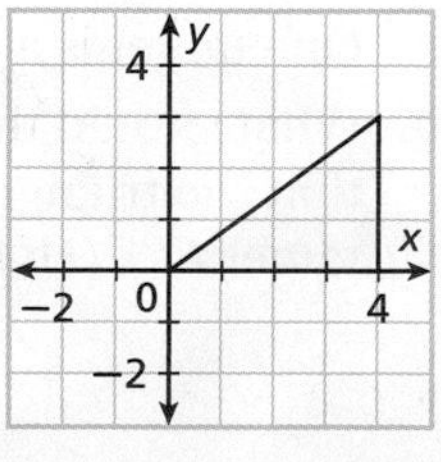

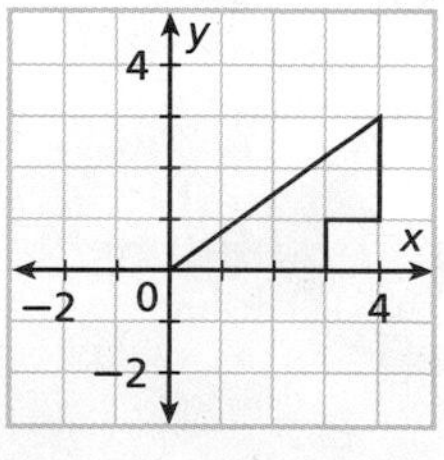

PRACTICE AND PROBLEM SOLVING

Independent Practice

For Exercises	See Example
10–11	1
12–15	2
16–17	3
18	4

Extra Practice

See Extra Practice for more Skills Practice and Applications Practice exercises.

Estimate the area of each irregular shape.

10. 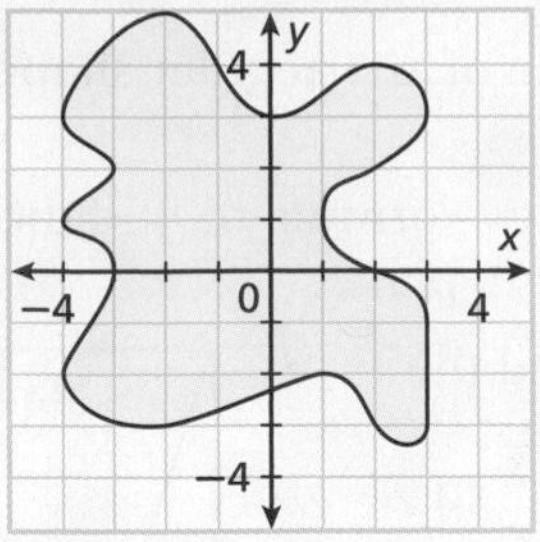

11. 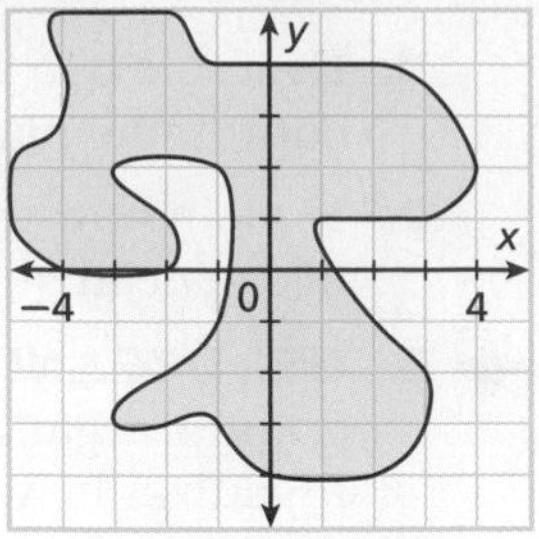

Multi-Step Draw and classify the polygon with the given vertices. Find the perimeter and area of the polygon.

12. $H(-3, -3)$, $J(-3, 3)$, $K(5, 3)$
13. $L(7, 5)$, $M(5, 0)$, $N(3, 5)$, $P(5, 10)$
14. $X(2, 1)$, $Y(5, 3)$, $Z(7, 1)$
15. $A(-3, 5)$, $B(2, 7)$, $C(2, 1)$, $D(-3, 3)$

Find the area of each polygon with the given vertices.

16. $A(9, 9)$, $B(4, -4)$, $C(-4, 1)$
17. $T(-4, 4)$, $U(5, 3)$, $V(4, -5)$, $W(-5, 1)$
18. In which two figures do the rectangles cover the same area? Explain your reasoning.

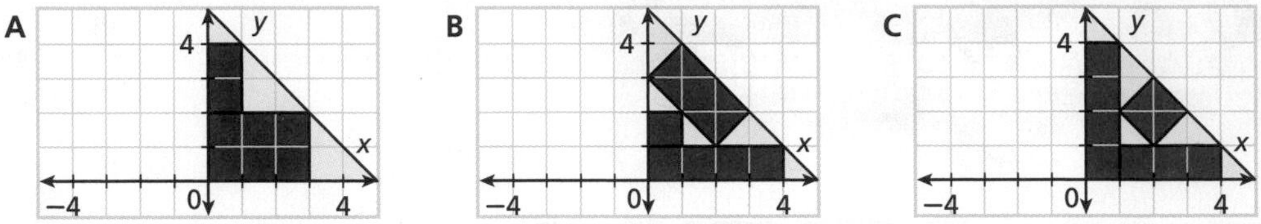

Algebra Graph each set of lines to form a triangle. Find the area and perimeter.

19. $y = 2$, $x = 5$, and $y = x$
20. $y = -5$, $x = 2$, and $y = -2x + 7$

21. **Transportation** The graph shows the speed of a boat versus time.

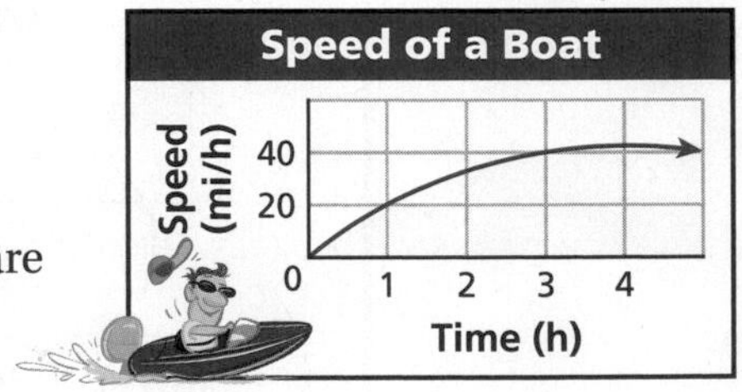

a. If the base of each square on the graph represents 1 hour and the height represents 20 miles per hour, what is the area of one square on the graph? Include units in your answer.
b. Estimate the shaded area in the graph.
c. **Critical Thinking** Use your results from part **a** to interpret the meaning of the area you found in part **b**. (*Hint:* Look at the units.)

22. **Write About It** Explain how to find the perimeter of the polygon with vertices $A(2, 3)$, $B(4, 0)$, $C(3, -2)$, $D(-1, -1)$, and $E(-2, 0)$.

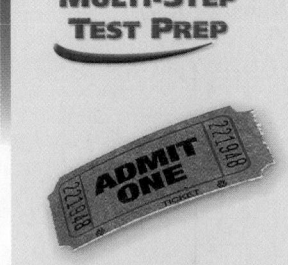

MULTI-STEP TEST PREP

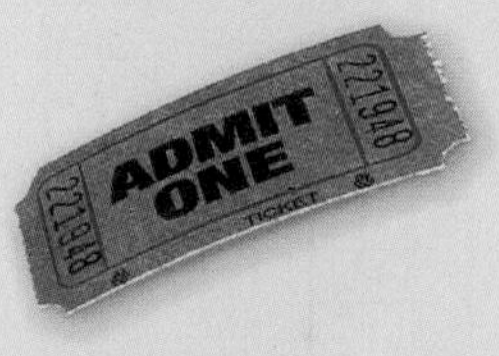

23. A carnival game uses a 10-by-10 board with three targets. Each player throws a dart at the board and wins a prize if it hits a target.

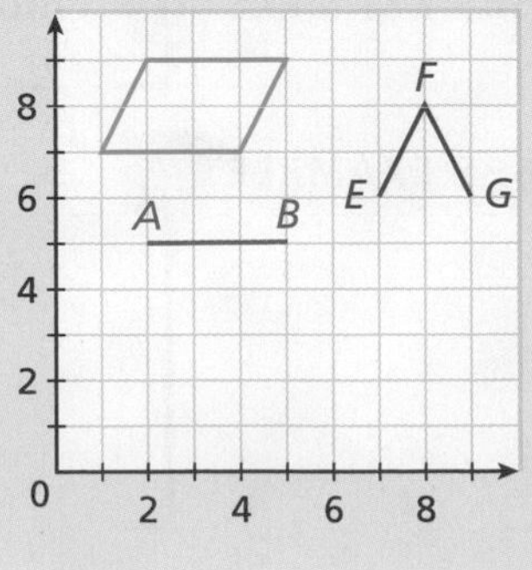

a. One target is a parallelogram as shown. Find its area.
b. What should the coordinates be for points C and H so that the triangular target $\triangle ABC$ and the kite-shaped target $EFGH$ have the same area as the parallelogram?

TEST PREP

24. A circle with center (0, 0) passes through the point (3, 4). What is the area of the circle to the nearest tenth of a square unit?

Ⓐ 15.7 Ⓑ 25.0 Ⓒ 31.4 Ⓓ 78.5

25. $\triangle ABC$ with vertices $A(1, 1)$ and $B(3, 5)$ has an area of 10 units^2. Which is NOT a possible location of the third vertex?

Ⓕ $C(-4, 1)$ Ⓖ $C(7, 3)$ Ⓗ $C(6, 1)$ Ⓙ $C(3, -3)$

26. Extended Response Mike estimated the area of the irregular figure to be 64 units^2.

a. Explain why his answer is not very accurate.

b. Explain how to use a composite figure to estimate the area.

c. Explain how to estimate the area by averaging the areas of two squares.

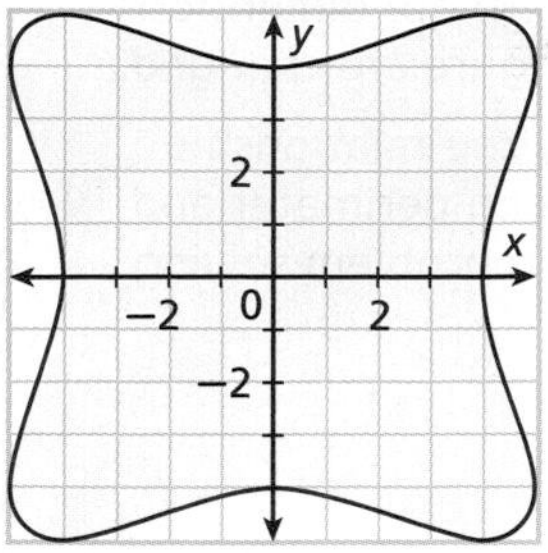

CHALLENGE AND EXTEND

Algebra Estimate the shaded area under each curve.

27. $y = 2^x$ for $0 \le x \le 3$

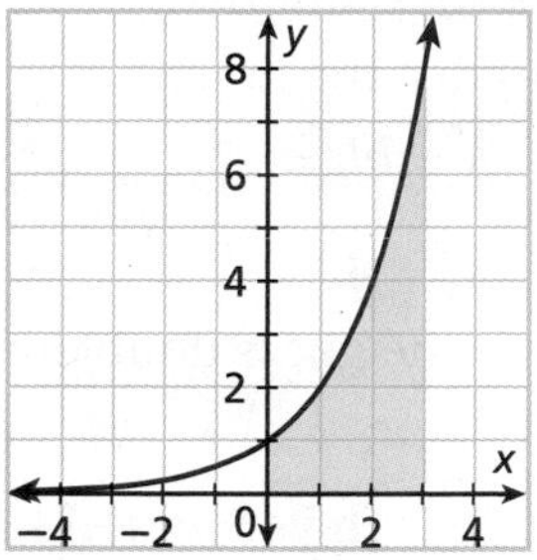

28. $y = x^2$ for $0 \le x \le 3$

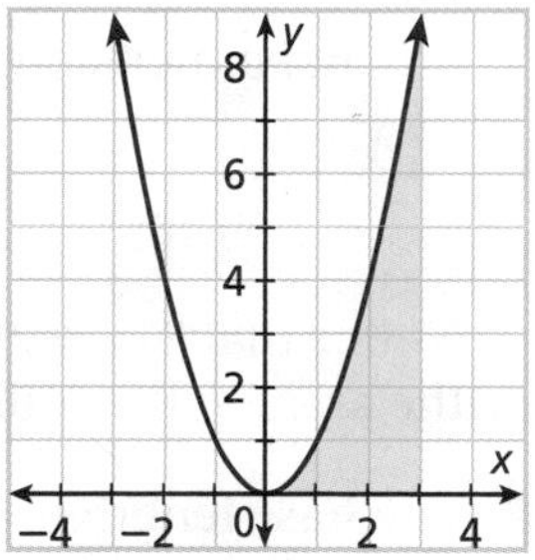

29. $y = \sqrt{x}$ for $0 \le x \le 9$

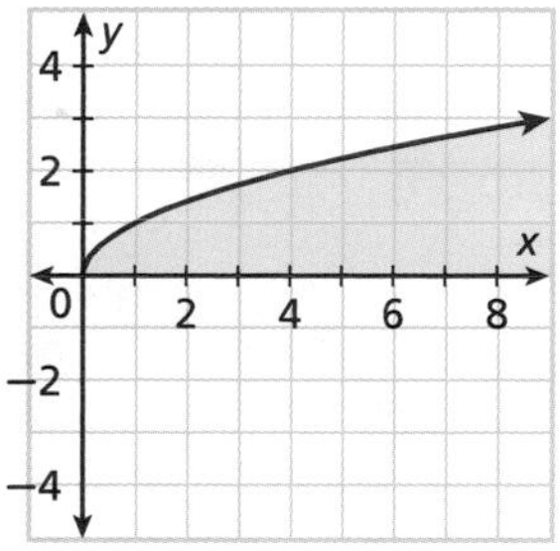

30. Estimation Use a composite figure and the Distance Formula to estimate the perimeter of the irregular shape.

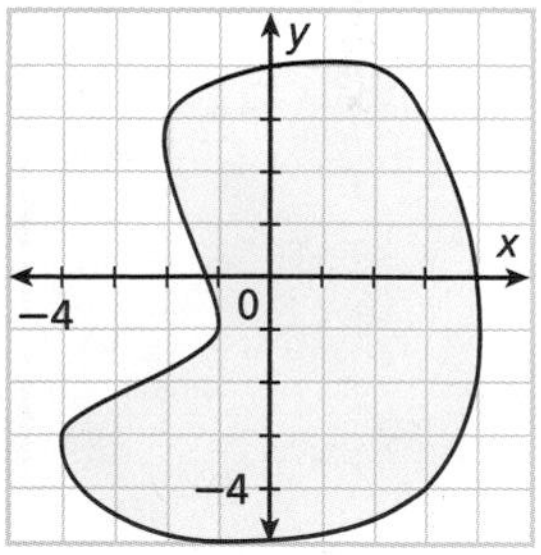

31. Graph a regular octagon on the coordinate plane with vertices on the x-and y-axes and on the lines $y = x$ and $y = -x$ so that the distance between opposite vertices is 2 units. Find the area and perimeter of the octagon.

COMMON CORE

10-5 Effects of Changing Dimensions Proportionally

CC.9-12.G.GPE.7 Use coordinates to compute perimeters…and areas…, e.g., using the distance formula.*

Objectives

Describe the effect on perimeter and area when one or more dimensions of a figure are changed.

Apply the relationship between perimeter and area in problem solving.

Why learn this?

You can analyze a graph to determine whether it is misleading or to explain why it is misleading. (See Example 4.)

In the graph, the height of each DVD is used to represent the number of DVDs shipped per year. However as the height of each DVD increases, the width also increases, which can create a misleading effect.

EXAMPLE 1 Effects of Changing One Dimension

Describe the effect of each change on the area of the given figure.

A The height of the parallelogram is doubled.

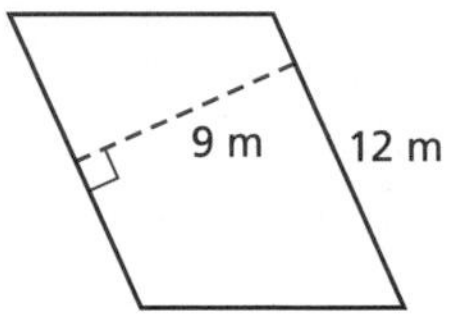

original dimensions:

$A = bh = 12(9)$

$= 108 \text{ cm}^2$

double the height:

$A = bh = 12(18)$

$= 216 \text{ cm}^2$

Notice that $216 = 2(108)$. If the height is doubled, the area is also doubled.

B The base length of the triangle with vertices $A(1, 1)$, $B(6, 1)$, and $C(3, 5)$ is multiplied by $\frac{1}{2}$.

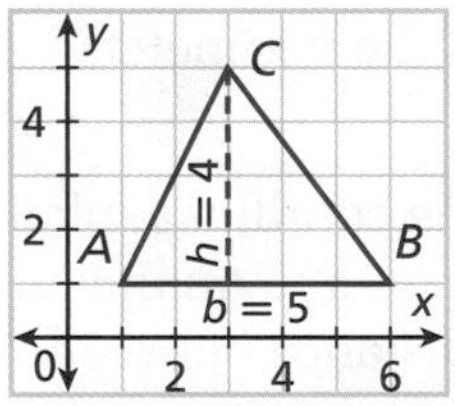

Draw the triangle in a coordinate plane and find the base and height.

original dimensions:

$A = \frac{1}{2}bh = \frac{1}{2}(5)(4) = 10 \text{ units}^2$

base multiplied by $\frac{1}{2}$:

$A = \frac{1}{2}bh = \frac{1}{2}(2.5)(4) = 5 \text{ units}^2$

Notice that $5 = \frac{1}{2}(10)$. If the base length is multiplied by $\frac{1}{2}$, the area is multiplied by $\frac{1}{2}$.

CHECK IT OUT!

1. The height of the rectangle is tripled. Describe the effect on the area.

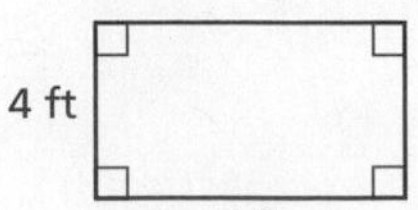

EXAMPLE 2 Effects of Changing Dimensions Proportionally

Describe the effect of each change on the perimeter or circumference and the area of the given figure.

A **The base and height of a rectangle with base 8 m and height 3 m are both multiplied by 5.**

original dimensions:

$P = 2(8) + 2(3) = 22$ m   *$P = 2b + 2h$*

$A = 83 = 24$ m^2 *$A = bh$*

dimensions multiplied by 5:

$P = 2(40) + 2(15) = 110$ m   *$5(8) = 40$; $5(3) = 15$*

$A = 40(15) = 600$ m^2

The perimeter is multiplied by 5.   *$5(22) = 110$*

The area is multiplied by 5^2, or 25.   *$25(24) = 600$*

B **The radius of $\odot A$ is multiplied by $\frac{1}{3}$.**

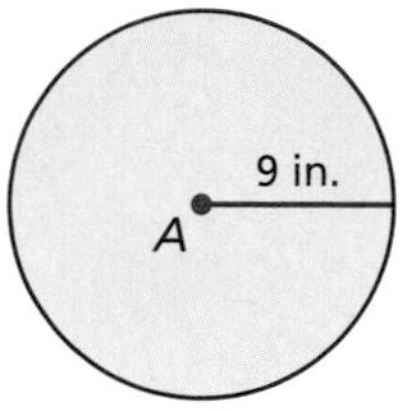

original dimensions:

$C = 2\pi(9) = 18\pi$ in.   *$C = 2\pi r$*

$A = \pi(9)^2 = 81\pi$ in^2 *$A = \pi r^2$*

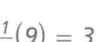

dimensions multiplied by $\frac{1}{3}$:

$C = 2\pi(3) = 6\pi$ in.   *$\frac{1}{3}(9) = 3$*

$A = \pi(3)^2 = 9\pi$ in^2

The perimeter is multiplied by $\frac{1}{3}$.   *$\frac{1}{3}(18\pi) = 6\pi$*

The area is multiplied by $\left(\frac{1}{3}\right)^2$, or $\frac{1}{9}$.   *$\frac{1}{9}(81\pi) = 9\pi$*

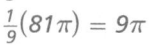

Helpful Hint

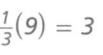

If the radius of a circle or the side length of a square is changed, the size of the entire figure changes proportionally.

CHECK IT OUT!

2. The base and height of the triangle with vertices $P(2, 5)$, $Q(2, 1)$ and $R(7, 1)$ are tripled. Describe the effect on its area and perimeter.

Know it! Note

When all the dimensions of a figure are changed proportionally, the figure will be similar to the original figure.

Effects of Changing Dimensions Proportionally		
Change in Dimensions	**Perimeter or Circumference**	**Area**
All dimensions multiplied by a	Changes by a factor of a	Changes by a factor of a^2

EXAMPLE 3 Effects of Changing Area

A **A square has side length 5 cm. If the area is tripled, what happens to the side length?**

The area of the original square is $A = s^2 = 5^2 = 25$ cm^2.

If the area is tripled, the new area is 75 cm^2.

$s^2 = 75$ *Set the new area equal to s^2.*

$s = \sqrt{75} = 5\sqrt{3}$ *Take the square root of both sides and simplify.*

Notice that $5\sqrt{3} = \sqrt{3}(5)$. The side length is multiplied by $\sqrt{3}$.

B **A circle has a radius of 6 in. If the area is doubled, what happens to the circumference?**

The original area is $A = \pi r^2 = 36\pi \text{ in}^2$, and the circumference is $C = 2\pi r = 12\pi$ in. If the area is doubled, the new area is $72\pi \text{ in}^2$.

$\pi r^2 = 72\pi$ — *Set the new area equal to πr^2.*

$r^2 = 72$ — *Divide both sides by π.*

$r^2 = \sqrt{72} = 6\sqrt{2}$ — *Take the square root of both sides and simplify.*

$C = 2\pi r = 2\pi(6\sqrt{2}) = 12\sqrt{2}\pi$ — *Substitute $6\sqrt{2}$ for r and simplify.*

Notice that $12\sqrt{2}\pi = \sqrt{2}(12\pi)$. The circumference is multiplied by $\sqrt{2}$.

CHECK IT OUT! **3.** A square has a perimeter of 36 mm. If the area is multiplied by $\frac{1}{2}$, what happens to the side length?

EXAMPLE 4 Entertainment Application

The graph shows that DVD shipments totaled about 182 million in 2000, 364 million in 2001, and 685 million in 2002. The height of each DVD is used to represent the number of DVDs shipped. Explain why the graph is misleading.

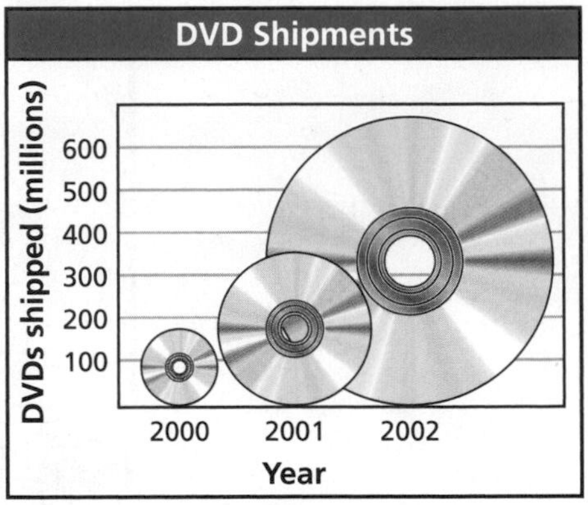

The height of the DVD representing shipments in 2002 is about 3.8 times the height of the DVD representing shipments in 2002.

This means that the area of the DVD is multiplied by about 3.8^2, or 14.4, so the area of the larger DVD is about 14.4 times the area of the smaller DVD.

The graph gives the misleading impression that the number of shipments in 2002 was more than 14 times the number in 2000, but it was actually closer to 4 times the number shipped in 2000.

CHECK IT OUT! **4.** Use the information above to create a version of the graph that is not misleading.

MATHEMATICAL PRACTICES

THINK AND DISCUSS

1. Discuss how changing both dimensions of a rectangle affects the area and perimeter.

Know it! Note **2. GET ORGANIZED** Copy and complete the graphic organizer.

If the radius of a circle is doubled …

The diameter __?__.	The circumference __?__.	The area __?__.

10-5 Exercises

Learn It Online
Homework Help Online
Parent Resources Online

GUIDED PRACTICE

SEE EXAMPLE 1

Describe the effect of each change on the area of the given figure.

1. The height of the triangle is doubled.

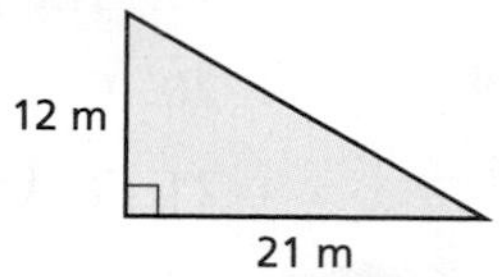

2. The height of a trapezoid with base lengths 12 cm and 18 cm and height 5 cm is multiplied by $\frac{1}{3}$.

SEE EXAMPLE 2

Describe the effect of each change on the perimeter or circumference and the area of the given figure.

3. The base and height of a triangle with base 12 in. and height 6 in. are both tripled.
4. The base and height of the rectangle are both multiplied by $\frac{1}{2}$.

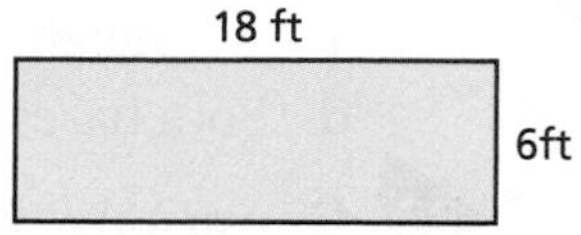

SEE EXAMPLE 3

5. A square has an area of 36 m^2. If the area is doubled, what happens to the side length?
6. A circle has a diameter of 14 ft. If the area is tripled, what happens to the circumference?

SEE EXAMPLE 4

7. **Business** A restaurant has a weekly ad in a local newspaper that is 2 inches wide and 4 inches high and costs $36.75 per week. The cost of each ad is based on its area. If the owner of the restaurant decides to double the width and height of the ad, how much will the new ad cost?

PRACTICE AND PROBLEM SOLVING

Independent Practice

For Exercises	See Example
8–9	1
10–11	2
12–13	3
14	4

Extra Practice

See Extra Practice for more Skills Practice and Applications Practice exercises.

Describe the effect of each change on the area of the given figure.

8. The height of the triangle with vertices $(1, 5)$, $(2, 3)$, and $(-1, -6)$ is multiplied by 4.
9. The base of the parallelogram is multiplied by $\frac{2}{3}$.

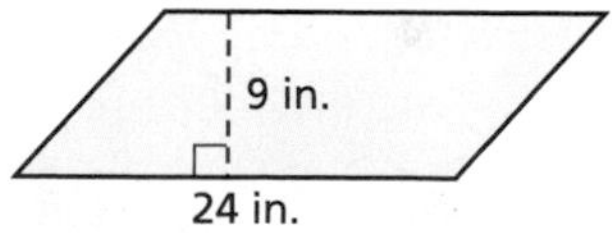

Describe the effect of each change on the perimeter or circumference and the area of the given figure.

10. The base and height of the triangle are both doubled.
11. The radius of the circle with center $(0, 0)$ that passes through $(5, 0)$ is multiplied by $\frac{3}{5}$.

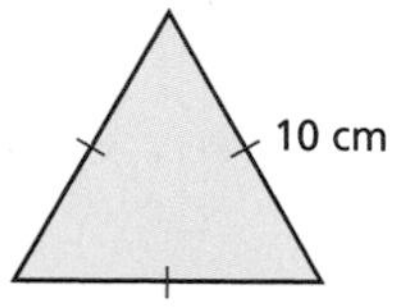

12. A circle has a circumference of 16π mm. If you multiply the area by $\frac{1}{3}$, what happens to the radius?
13. A square has vertices $(3, 2)$, $(8, 2,)$ $(8, 7)$, and $(3, 7)$. If you triple the area, what happens to the side length?
14. **Entertainment** Two televisions have rectangular screens with the same ratio of base to height. One has a 32 in. diagonal, and the other has a 36 in. diagonal.
    a. What is the ratio of the height of the larger screen to that of the smaller screen?
    b. What is the ratio of the area of the larger screen to that of the smaller screen?

Describe the effect of each change on the area of the given figure.

15. The diagonals of a rhombus are both multiplied by 8.

16. The circumference of a circle is multiplied by 2.4.

17. The base of a rectangle is multiplied by 4, and the height is multiplied by 7.

18. The apothem of a regular octagon is tripled.

19. The diagonal of a square is divided by 4.

20. One diagonal of a kite is multiplied by $\frac{1}{7}$.

21. The perimeter of an equilateral triangle is doubled.

LINK

Geography

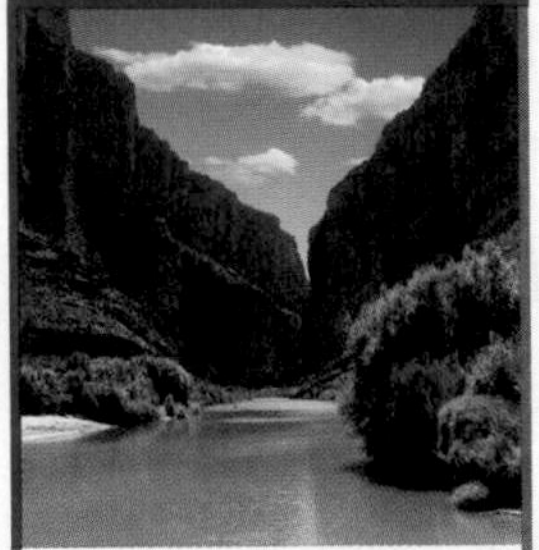

The altitude in Big Bend National Park ranges from approximately 1800 feet along the Rio Grande to 7800 feet in the Chisos Mountains.

22. Find the area of the trapezoid. Describe the effect of each change on the area.

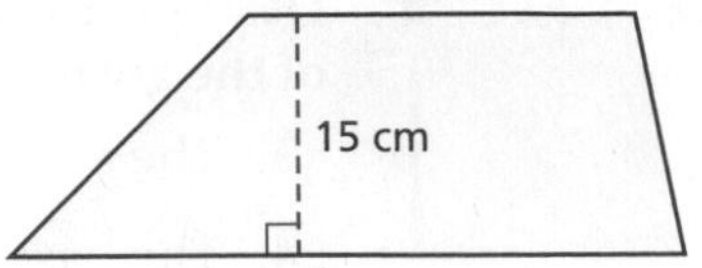

a. The length of the top base is doubled.

b. The length of both bases is doubled.

c. The height is doubled.

d. Both bases and the height are doubled.

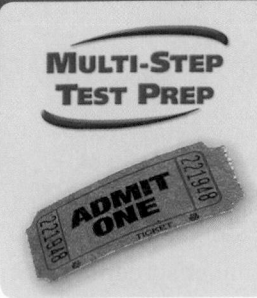

23. Geography A map has the scale 1 inch = 10 miles. On the map, the area of Big Bend National Park in Texas is about 12.5 square inches. Estimate the actual area of the park in acres. (*Hint:* 1 square mile = 640 acres)

24. Critical Thinking If you want to multiply the dimensions of a figure so that the area is 50% of the original area, what is your scale factor?

Multi-Step For each figure in the coordinate plane, describe the effect on the area that results from each change.

a. Only the x-coordinates of the vertices are multiplied by 3.

b. Only the y-coordinates of the vertices are multiplied by 3.

c. Both the x- and y-coordinates of the vertices are multiplied by 3.

25.

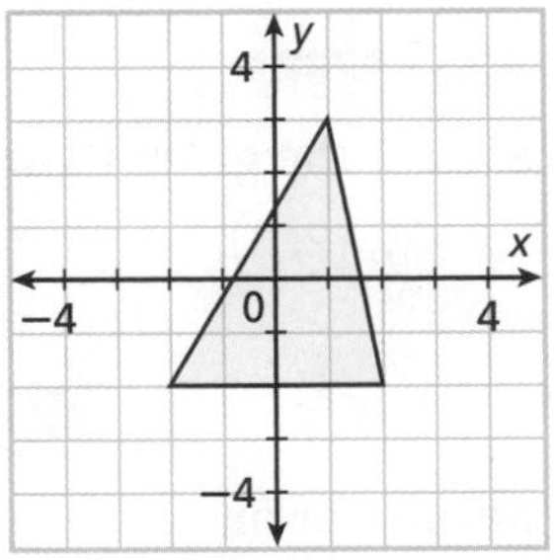

26.

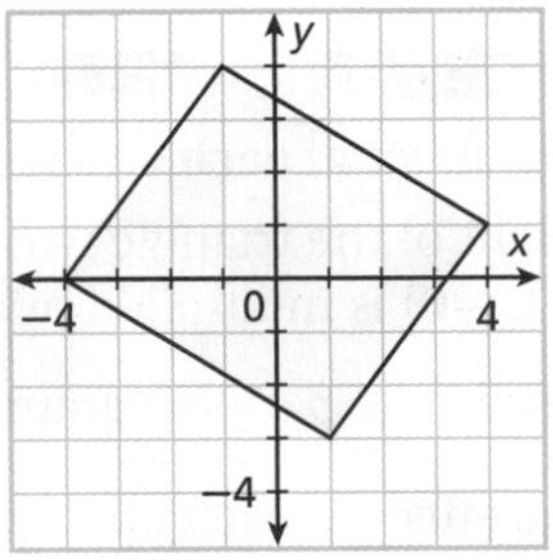

27.

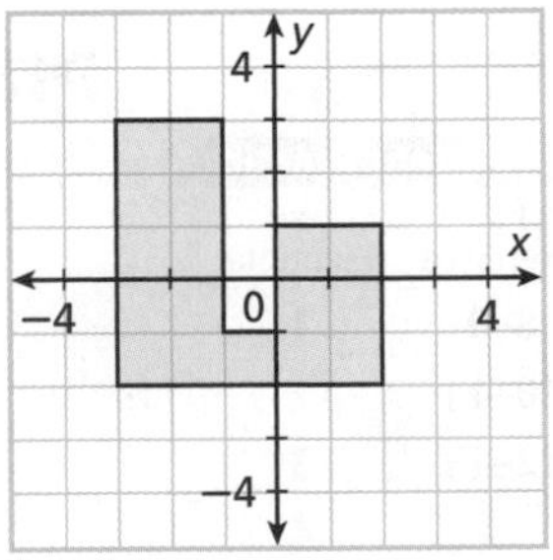

28. Write About It How could you change the dimensions of a parallelogram to increase the area by a factor of 5 if the parallelogram does not have to be similar to the original parallelogram? if the parallelogram does have to be similar to the original parallelogram?

MULTI-STEP TEST PREP

29. To win a prize at a carnival, a player must toss a beanbag onto a circular disk with a diameter of 8 in.

a. The organizer of the game wants players to win twice as often, so he changes the disk so that it has twice the area. What is the diameter of the new disk?

b. Suppose the organizer wants players to win half as often. What should be the disk's diameter in this case?

TEST PREP

30. Which of the following describes the effect on the area of a square when the side length is doubled?

- (A) The area remains constant.
- (B) The area is reduced by a factor of $\frac{1}{2}$.
- (C) The area is doubled.
- (D) The area is increased by a factor of 4.

31. If the area of a circle is increased by a factor of 4, what is the change in the diameter of the circle?

- (F) The diameter is $\frac{1}{2}$ of the original diameter.
- (G) The diameter is 2 times the original diameter.
- (H) The diameter is 4 times the original diameter.
- (J) The diameter is 16 times the original diameter.

32. Tina and Kieu built rectangular play areas for their dogs. The play area for Tina's dog is 1.5 times as long and 1.5 times as wide as the play area for Kieu's dog. If the play area for Kieu's dog is 60 square feet, how big is the play area for Tina's dog?

(A) 40 ft^2 (B) 90 ft^2 (C) 135 ft^2 (D) 240 ft^2

33. Gridded Response Suppose the dimensions of a triangle with a perimeter of 18 inches are doubled. Find the perimeter of the new triangle in inches.

CHALLENGE AND EXTEND

34. Algebra A square has a side length of $(2x + 5)$ cm . If the side length is multiplied by 5, what is the area of the new square?

35. Algebra A circle has a diameter of 6 in. If the circumference is multiplied by $(x + 3)$, what is the area of the new circle?

36. Write About It How could you change the dimensions of the composite figure to double the area if the resulting figure does not have to be similar to the original figure? if the resulting figure does have to be similar to the original figure?

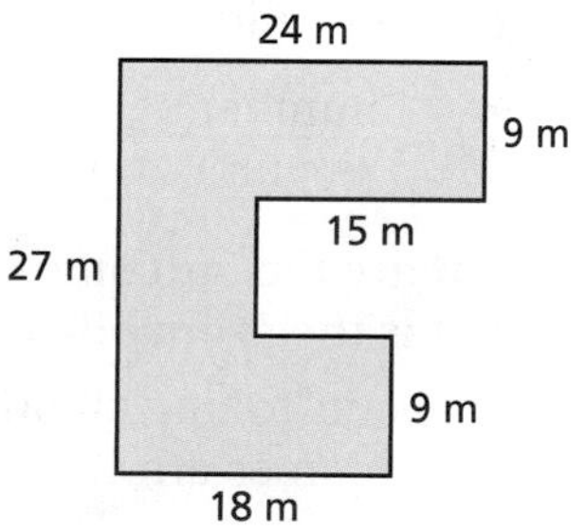

Connecting Geometry to Probability

Probability

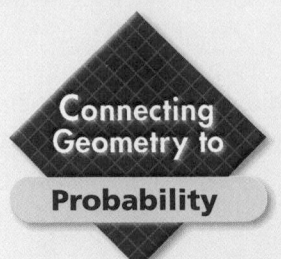

An *experiment* is an activity in which results are observed. Each result of an experiment is called an *outcome.* The *sample space* is the set of all outcomes of an experiment. An *event* is any set of outcomes.

The probability of an event is a number from 0 to 1 that tells you how likely the event is to happen. The closer the probability is to 0, the less likely the event is to happen. The closer it is to 1, the more likely the event is to happen.

An experiment is *fair* if all outcomes are equally likely. The *theoretical probability* of an event is the ratio of the number of outcomes in the event to the number of outcomes in the sample space.

$$P(E) = \frac{\text{number of outcomes in event } E}{\text{number of possible outcomes}}$$

Example 1

A fair number cube has six faces, numbered 1 through 6. An experiment consists of rolling the number cube.

A What is the sample space of the experiment?

The sample space has 6 possible outcomes.
The outcomes are 1, 2, 3, 4, 5, and 6.

B What is the probability of the event "rolling a 4"?

The event "rolling a 4" contains only 1 outcome.
The probability is

$$P(E) = \frac{\text{number of outcomes in event } E}{\text{number of possible outcomes}} = \frac{1}{6}.$$

C What are the outcomes in the event "rolling an odd number"? What is the probability of rolling an odd number?

The event "rolling an odd number" contains 3 outcomes.
The outcomes are 1, 3, and 5. The probability is

$$P(E) = \frac{\text{number of outcomes in event } E}{\text{number of possible outcomes}} = \frac{3}{6} = \frac{1}{2}.$$

If two events A and B have no outcomes in common, then the probability that A or B will happen is $P(A) + P(B)$.

The *complement of an event* is the set of outcomes that are *not* in the event. If the probability of an event is p, then the probability of the complement of the event is $1 - p$.

Example 2

The tiles shown below are placed in a bag. An experiment consists of drawing a tile at random from the bag.

A What is the sample space of the experiment?

The sample space has 9 possible outcomes. The outcomes are 1, 2, 3, 4, A, B, C, D, E, and F.

B What is the probability of choosing a 3 or a vowel?

The event "choosing a 3" contains only 1 outcome. The probability is

$$P(A) = \frac{\text{number of outcomes in event } A}{\text{number of possible outcomes}} = \frac{1}{9}.$$

The event "choosing a vowel" has 2 outcomes, A and E. The probability is

$$P(B) = \frac{\text{number of outcomes in event } B}{\text{number of possible outcomes}} = \frac{2}{9}.$$

The probability of choosing a 3 or a vowel is $\frac{1}{9} + \frac{2}{9} = \frac{3}{9} = \frac{1}{3}$.

C What is the probability of not choosing a letter?

The event "choosing a letter" contains 5 outcomes, A, B, C, D, and E. The probability is

$$P(E) = \frac{\text{number of outcomes in event } E}{\text{number of possible outcomes}} = \frac{5}{9}.$$

The event of not choosing a letter is the complement of the event of choosing a letter. The probability of not choosing a letter is $1 - \frac{5}{9} = \frac{4}{9}$.

Try This

An experiment consists of randomly choosing one of the given shapes.

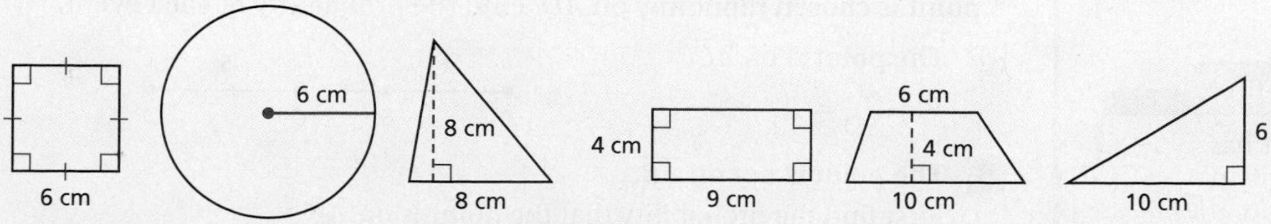

1. What is the probability of choosing a circle?
2. What is the probability of choosing a shape whose area is 36 cm^2?
3. What is the probability of choosing a quadrilateral or a triangle?
4. What is the probability of not choosing a triangle?

COMMON CORE

10-6 Geometric Probability

CC.9-12.S.CP.1 Describe events...using characteristics of the outcomes...*

Objectives
Calculate geometric probabilities.

Use geometric probability to predict results in real-world situations.

Vocabulary
geometric probability

Why learn this?

You can use geometric probability to estimate how long you may have to wait to cross a street. (See Example 2.)

Remember that in probability, the set of all possible outcomes of an experiment is called the *sample space.* Any set of outcomes is called an *event.*

If every outcome in the sample space is equally likely, the *theoretical probability* of an event is

$$P = \frac{\text{number of outcomes in the event}}{\text{number of outcomes in the sample space}}.$$

Geometric probability is used when an experiment has an infinite number of outcomes. In **geometric probability**, the probability of an event is based on a ratio of geometric measures such as length or area. The outcomes of an experiment may be points on a segment or in a plane figure. Three models for geometric probability are shown below.

Know it! Note

Geometric Probability

Model	Length	Angle Measure	Area
Example	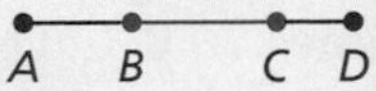		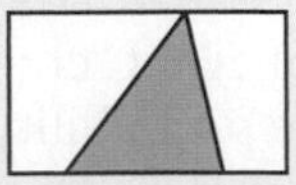
Sample space	All points on $\overline{AD}$	All points in the circle	All points in the rectangle
Event	All points on $\overline{BC}$	All points in the shaded region	All points in the triangle
Probability	$P = \frac{BC}{AD}$	$P = \frac{\text{measure of angle}}{360°}$	$P = \frac{\text{area of triangle}}{\text{area of rectangle}}$

EXAMPLE 1

Using Length to Find Geometric Probability

A point is chosen randomly on $\overline{AD}$. Find the probability of each event.

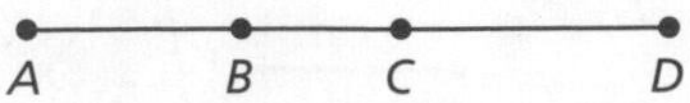

A **The point is on $\overline{AC}$.**

$P = \frac{AC}{AD} = \frac{7}{12}$

B **The point is not on $\overline{AB}$.**

First find the probability that the point is on $\overline{AB}$.

$P(\overline{AB}) = \frac{AB}{AD} = \frac{4}{12} = \frac{1}{3}$

Subtract from 1 to find the probability that the point is not on $\overline{AB}$.

$P(\text{not on } \overline{AB}) = 1 - \frac{1}{3} = \frac{2}{3}$

Remember!

If an event has a probability p of occurring, the probability of the event *not* occurring is $1 - p$.

A point is chosen randomly on $\overline{AD}$.
Find the probability of each event.

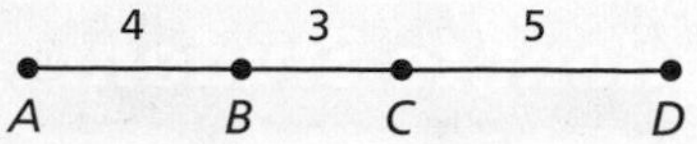

C The point is on $\overline{AB}$ or $\overline{CD}$.

$$P(\overline{AB} \text{ or } \overline{CD}) = P(\overline{AB}) + P(\overline{CD}) = \frac{4}{12} + \frac{5}{12} = \frac{9}{12} = \frac{3}{4}$$

CHECK IT OUT! 1. Use the figure above to find the probability that the point is on $\overline{BD}$.

EXAMPLE 2 Transportation Application

A stoplight has the following cycle: green for 25 seconds, yellow for 5 seconds, and red for 30 seconds.

A **What is the probability that the light will be yellow when you arrive?**

To find the probability, draw a segment to represent the number of seconds that each color light is on.

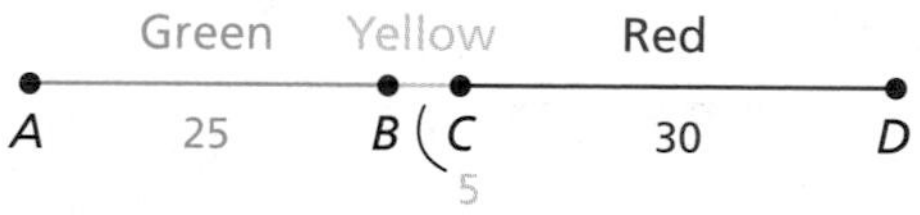

$P = \frac{5}{60} = \frac{1}{12} \approx 0.08$ *The light is yellow for 5 out of every 60 seconds.*

B **If you arrive at the light 50 times, predict about how many times you will have to stop and wait more than 10 seconds.**

In the model, the event of stopping and waiting more than 10 seconds is represented by a segment that starts at C and ends 10 units from D. The probability of stopping and waiting more than 10 seconds is $P = \frac{20}{60} = \frac{1}{3}$.

If you arrive at the light 50 times, you will probably stop and wait more than 10 seconds about $\frac{1}{3}(50) \approx 17$ times.

CHECK IT OUT! 2. Use the information above. What is the probability that the light will not be red when you arrive?

EXAMPLE 3 Using Angle Measures to Find Geometric Probability

Use the spinner to find the probability of each event.

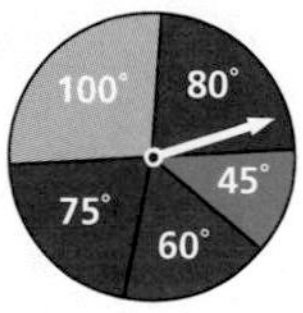

A **the pointer landing on red**

$P = \frac{80}{360} = \frac{2}{9}$ *The angle measure in the red region is 80°.*

B **the pointer landing on purple or blue**

$P = \frac{75 + 60}{360} = \frac{135}{360} = \frac{3}{8}$ *The angle measure in the purple region is 75°. The angle measure in the blue region is 60°.*

C **the pointer not landing on yellow**

$P = \frac{360 - 100}{360}$ *The angle measure in the yellow region is 100°. Substract this angle measure from 360°.*

$= \frac{260}{360} = \frac{13}{18}$

Helpful Hint

In Example 3C, you can also find the probability of the pointer landing on yellow, and subtract from 1.

CHECK IT OUT! 3. Use the spinner above to find the probability of the pointer landing on red or yellow.

Student to Student

Geometric Probability

Jeremy Denton
Memorial High School

I like to write a probability as a percent to see if my answer is reasonable.

The probability of the pointer landing on red is $\frac{80°}{360°} = \frac{2}{9} \approx 22\%$.

The angle measure is close to 90°, which is 25% of the circle, so the answer is reasonable.

EXAMPLE 4 **Using Area to Find Geometric Probability**

Find the probability that a point chosen randomly inside the rectangle is in each given shape. Round to the nearest hundredth.

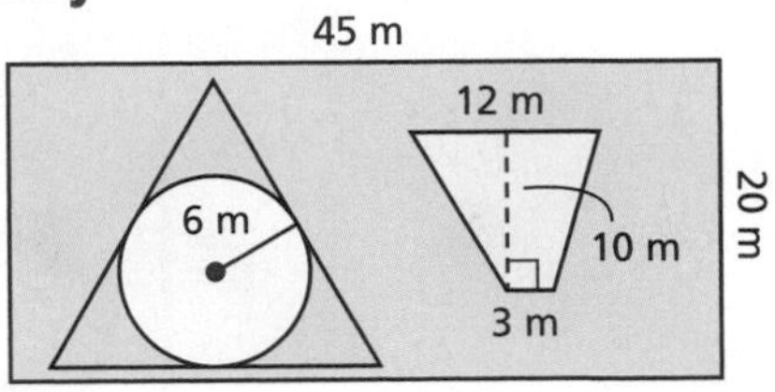

A **the equilateral triangle**

The area of the triangle is $A = \frac{1}{2}aP$

$= \frac{1}{2}(6)\left(36\sqrt{3}\right) \approx 187 \text{ m}^2.$

The area of the rectangle is $A = bh$

$= 45(20) = 900 \text{ m}^2.$

The probability is $P = \frac{187}{900} \approx 0.21.$

B **the trapezoid**

The area of the trapezoid is $A = \frac{1}{2}(b_1 + b_2)h$

$= \frac{1}{2}(3 + 12)(10) = 75 \text{ m}^2.$

The area of the rectangle is $A = bh$

$= 45(20) = 900 \text{ m}^2.$

The probability is $P = \frac{75}{900} \approx 0.08.$

C **the circle**

The area of the circle is $A = \pi r^2$

$= \pi\left(6^2\right) = 36\pi \approx 113.1 \text{ m}^2.$

The area of the rectangle is $A = bh$

$= 45(20) = 900 \text{ m}^2.$

The probability is $P = \frac{113.1}{900} \approx 0.13.$

CHECK IT OUT! **4.** Use the diagram above. Find the probability that a point chosen randomly inside the rectangle is not inside the triangle, circle, or trapezoid. Round to the nearest hundredth.

THINK AND DISCUSS

MATHEMATICAL PRACTICES

1. Explain why the ratio used in theoretical probability cannot be used to find geometric probability.
2. A spinner is one-half red and one-third blue, and the rest is yellow. How would you find the probability of the pointer landing on yellow?
3. **GET ORGANIZED** Copy and complete the graphic organizer. In each box, give an example of the geometric probability model.

Know it! Note

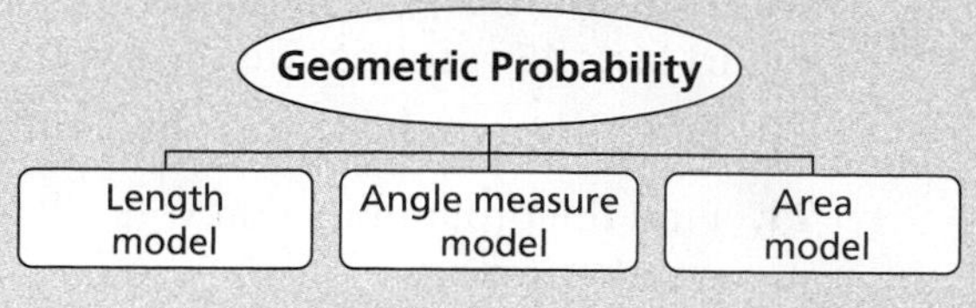

10-6 Exercises

Learn It Online
Homework Help Online
Parent Resources Online

GUIDED PRACTICE

1. **Vocabulary** Give an example of a model used to find *geometric probability.*

SEE EXAMPLE 1

A point is chosen randomly on $\overline{WZ}$. Find the probability of each event.

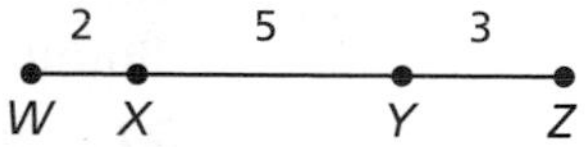

2. The point is on $\overline{XZ}$.
3. The point is not on $\overline{XY}$.
4. The point is on $\overline{WX}$ or $\overline{YZ}$.
5. The point is on $\overline{WY}$.

SEE EXAMPLE 2

Transportation A bus comes to a station once every 10 minutes and waits at the station for 1.5 minutes.

6. Find the probability that the bus will be at the station when you arrive.
7. If you go to the station 20 times, predict about how many times you will have to wait less than 3 minutes.

SEE EXAMPLE 3

Use the spinner to find the probability of each event.

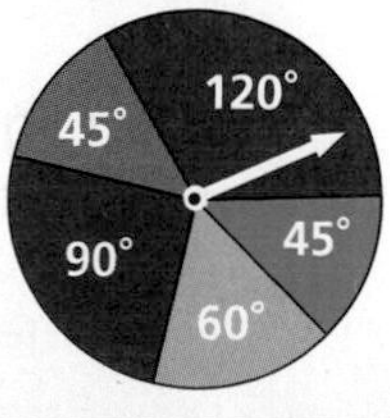

8. the pointer landing on green
9. the pointer landing on orange or blue
10. the pointer not landing on red
11. the pointer landing on yellow or blue

SEE EXAMPLE 4

Multi-Step Find the probability that a point chosen randomly inside the rectangle is in each shape. Round to the nearest hundredth.

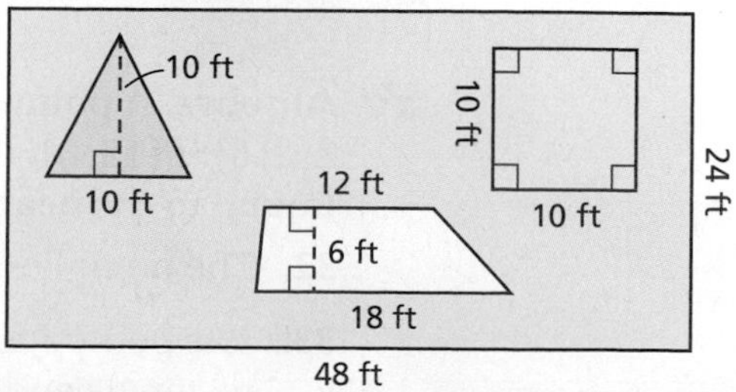

12. the triangle
13. the trapezoid
14. the square
15. the part of the rectangle that does not include the square, triangle, or trapezoid

PRACTICE AND PROBLEM SOLVING

Independent Practice

For Exercises	See Example
16–19	1
20–22	2
23–26	3
27–30	4

Extra Practice

See Extra Practice for more Skills Practice and Applications Practice exercises.

A point is chosen randomly on $\overline{HM}$. Find the probability of each event. Round to the nearest hundredth.

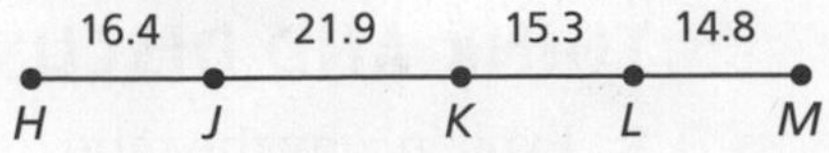

16. The point is on $\overline{JK}$.

17. The point is not on $\overline{LM}$.

18. The point is on $\overline{HJ}$ or $\overline{KL}$.

19. The point is not on $\overline{JK}$ or $\overline{LM}$.

Communications **A radio station gives a weather report every 15 minutes. Each report lasts 45 seconds. Suppose you turn on the radio at a random time.**

20. Find the probability that the weather report will be on when you turn on the radio.

21. Find the probability that you will have to wait more than 5 minutes to hear the weather report.

22. If you turn on the radio at 50 random times, predict about how many times you will have to wait less than 1 minute before the start of the next weather report.

Use the spinner to find the probability of each event.

23. the pointer landing on red

24. the pointer landing on yellow or blue

25. the pointer not landing on green

26. the pointer landing on red or green

Multi-Step **Find the probability that a point chosen randomly inside the rectangle is in each shape. Round to the nearest hundredth, if necessary.**

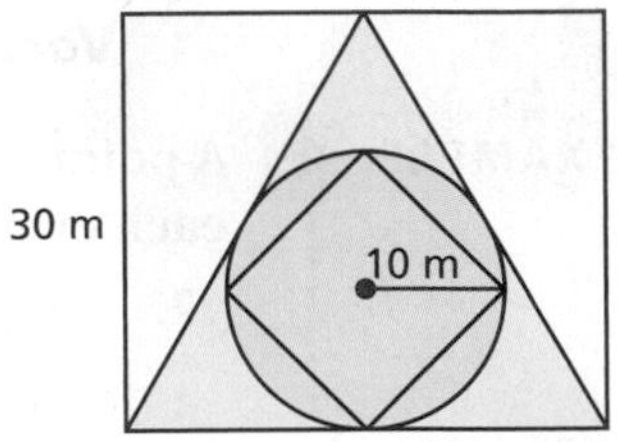

27. the equilateral triangle

28. the square

29. the part of the circle that does not include the square

30. the part of the rectangle that does not include the square, circle, or triangle

31. **ERROR ANALYSIS** In the spinner at right, the angle measure of the red region is 90°. The angle measure of the yellow region is 135°, and the angle measure of the blue region is 135°. Which value of the probability of the spinner landing on yellow is incorrect? Explain.

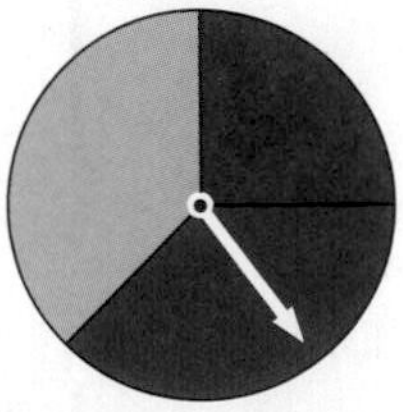

A

There are three outcomes, so the probability of the spinner landing on yellow is $\frac{1}{3}$.

B

The angle measure of the yellow sector is 135°, so the probability of the spinner landing on yellow is $\frac{135}{360} = \frac{3}{8}$.

Algebra **A point is chosen randomly inside rectangle $ABCD$ with vertices $A(2, 8)$, $B(15, 8)$, $C(15, 1)$, and $D(2, 1)$. Find the probability of each event. Round to the nearest hundredth.**

32. The point lies in $\triangle KLM$ with vertices $K(4, 3)$, $L(5, 7)$, and $M(9, 5)$.

33. The point does not lie in $\odot P$ with center $P(2, 5)$ and radius 3. (*Hint:* draw the rectangle and circle.)

Algebra **A point is chosen at random in the coordinate plane such that $-5 \le x \le 5$ and $-5 \le y \le 5$. Find the probability of each event. Round to the nearest hundredth.**

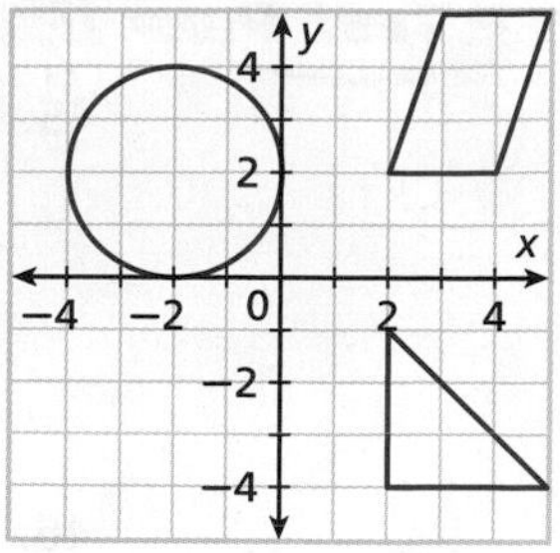

34. The point is inside the parallelogram.
35. The point is inside the circle.
36. The point is inside the triangle or the circle.
37. The point is not inside the triangle, the parallelogram, or the circle.

38. **Sports** The point value of each region of an Olympic archery target is shown in the diagram. The outer diameter of each ring is 12.2 cm greater than the inner diameter.
   a. What is the probability of hitting the center?
   b. What is the probability of hitting a blue or black ring?
   c. What is the probability of scoring higher than five points?
   d. **Write About It** In an actual event, why might the probabilities be different from those you calculated in parts **a**, **b**, and **c**?

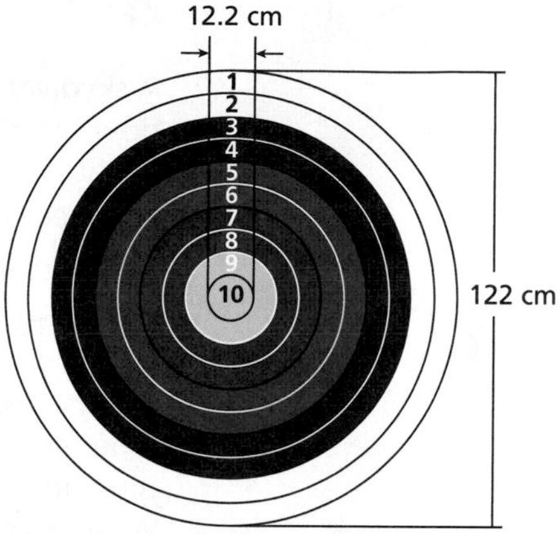

LINK

Sports

Olympic archers stand 70 m from their targets. From that distance, the target appears about the size of the head of a thumbtack held at arm's length.

Source: www.olympic.org

A point is chosen randomly in each figure. Describe an event with a probability of $\frac{1}{2}$.

39.
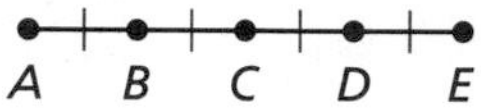

40.
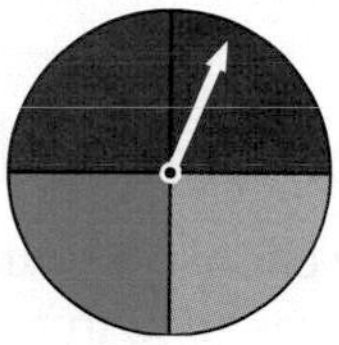

41.
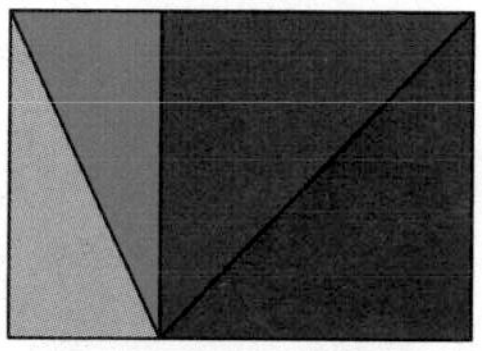

42. If a fly lands randomly on the tangram, what is the probability that it will land on each of the following pieces?
   a. the blue parallelogram
   b. the medium purple triangle
   c. the large yellow triangle
   d. **Write About It** Do the probabilities change if you arrange the tangram pieces differently? Explain.

43. **Critical Thinking** If a rectangle is divided into 8 congruent regions and 4 of them are shaded, what is the probability that you will randomly pick a point in the shaded area? Does it matter which four regions are shaded? Explain.

MULTI-STEP TEST PREP

44. A carnival game board consists of balloons that are 3 inches in diameter and are attached to a rectangular board. A player who throws a dart at the board wins a prize if the dart pops a balloon.
   a. Find the probability of winning if there are 40 balloons on the board.
   b. How many balloons must be on the board for the probability of winning to be at least 0.25?

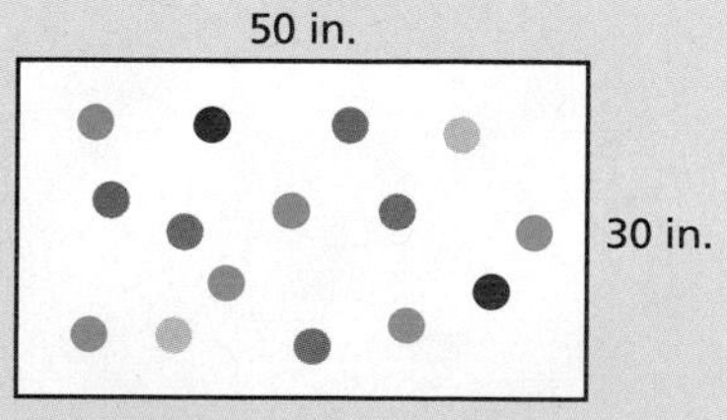

TEST PREP

45. What is the probability that a ball thrown randomly at the backboard of the basketball goal will hit the inside rectangle?

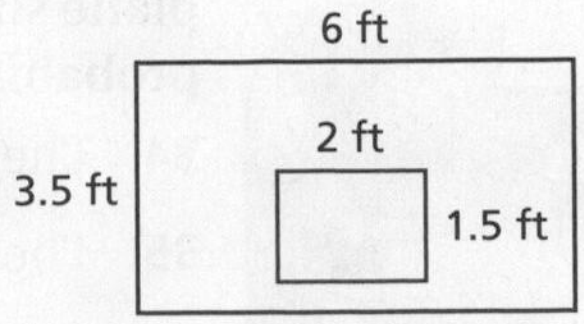

Ⓐ 0.14　　Ⓒ 0.26

Ⓑ 0.21　　Ⓓ 0.27

46. Point B is between A and C. If $AB = 18$ inches and $BC = 24$ inches, what is the probability that a point chosen at random is on $\overline{AB}$?

Ⓕ 0.18　　Ⓖ 0.43　　Ⓗ 0.57　　Ⓙ 0.75

47. A skydiver jumps from an airplane and parachutes down to the 70-by-100-meter rectangular field shown. What is the probability that he will miss all three targets?

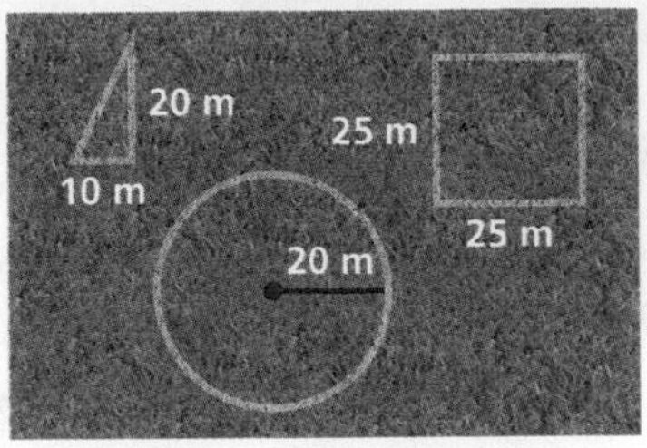

Ⓐ 0.014　　Ⓒ 0.089

Ⓑ 0.180　　Ⓓ 0.717

48. **Short Response** A spinner is divided into 12 congruent regions, colored red, blue, and green. Landing on red is twice as likely as landing on blue. Landing on blue and landing on green are equally likely.
   a. What is the probability of landing on green? Show your work or explain in words how you got your answer.
   b. How many regions of the spinner are colored green? Explain your reasoning.

CHALLENGE AND EXTEND

49. If you randomly choose a point on the grid, what is the probability that it will be in a red region?

50. You are designing a target that is a square inside an 18 ft by 24 ft rectangle. What size should the square be in order for the target to have a probability of $\frac{1}{3}$? to have a probability of $\frac{3}{4}$?

51. **Recreation** How would you design a spinner so that 1 point is earned for landing on yellow, 3 points for landing on blue and 6 points for landing on red? Explain.

10-6 Geometry LAB

Use Geometric Probability to Estimate π

Use with Geometric Probability

In this lab, you will use geometric probability to estimate π. The squares in the grid below are the same width as the diameter of a penny: 0.75 in., or 19.05 mm.

MATHEMATICAL PRACTICES **Model with mathematics.** **CC.9-12.S.CP.1** Describe events…using characteristics of the outcomes…

Activity

1 Toss a penny onto the grid 20 times. Let x represent the number of times the penny lands touching or covering an intersection of two grid lines.

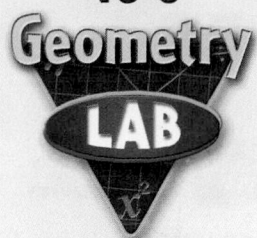

2 Estimate π using the formula $\pi \approx 4 \cdot \frac{x}{20}$.

Try This

1. How close is your result to π? Average the results of the entire class to get a more accurate estimate.
2. In order for a penny to touch or cover an intersection, the center of the penny can land anywhere in the shaded area.

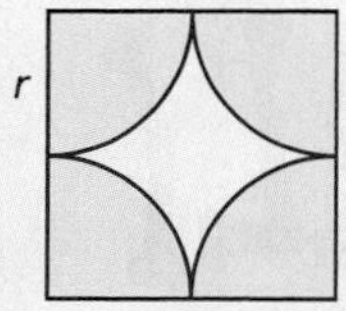

   a. Find the area of the shaded region. (*Hint:* Each corner part is one fourth of the circle. Put the four corner parts together to form a circle with radius r.)

   b. Find the area of the square.

   c. Write the expressions as a ratio and simplify to determine the probability of the center of the penny landing in the shaded area.
3. Explain why the formula in the activity can be used to estimate π.

CHAPTER 10

MULTI-STEP TEST PREP

SECTION 10B

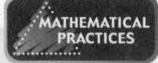

MATHEMATICAL PRACTICES **Reason abstractly and quantitatively.**

Applying Geometric Formulas

Step Right Up! A booster club organizes a carnival to raise money for sports uniforms. The carnival features several games that give visitors chances to win prizes.

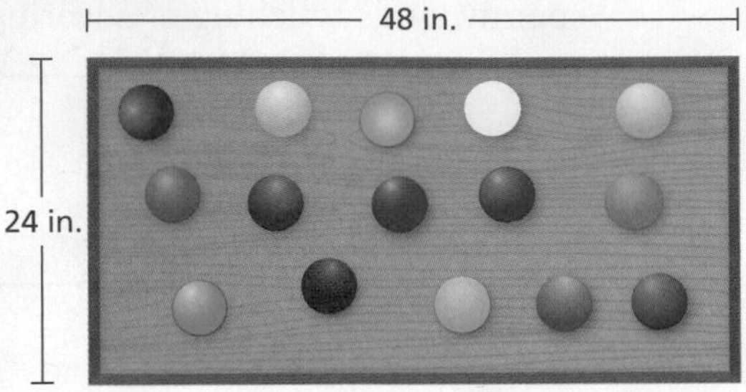

1. The balloon game consists of 15 balloons attached to a vertical rectangular board with the dimensions shown. Each balloon has a diameter of 4 in. Each player throws a dart at the board and wins a prize if the dart pops a balloon. Assuming that all darts hit the board at random, what is the probability of winning a prize?
2. The organizers decide to make the game easier, so they double the diameter of the balloons. How does this affect the probability of winning?
3. The bean toss consists of a horizontal rectangular board that is divided into a grid. The board has coordinates $(0, 0)$, $(100, 0)$, $(100, 60)$, and $(0, 60)$. A quadrilateral on the board has coordinates $A(60,0)$, $B(100, 30)$, $C(40, 60)$, and $D(0, 40)$. Each player tosses a bean onto the board and wins a prize if the bean lands inside quadrilateral $ABCD$. Find the probability of winning a prize.
4. Of the three games described in Problems 1, 2, and 3, which one gives players the best chance of winning a prize?

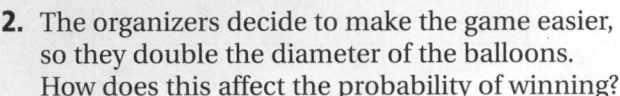

READY TO GO ON?

Quiz for Lessons 10-4 Through 10-6

10-4 Perimeter and Area in the Coordinate Plane

Draw and classify the polygon with the given vertices. Find the perimeter and area of the polygon.

1. $A(-2, 2)$, $B(2, 4)$, $C(2, -4)$, $D(-2, -2)$
2. $E(-1, 5)$, $F(3, 5)$, $G(3, -3)$, $H(-1, -3)$

Find the area of each polygon with the given vertices.

3. $J(-3, 3)$, $K(2, 2)$, $L(-1, -3)$, $M(-4, -1)$
4. $N(-3, 1)$, $P(3, 3)$, $Q(5, 1)$, $R(2, -4)$

10-5 Effects of Changing Dimensions Proportionally

Describe the effect of each change on the perimeter and area of the given figure.

5. The side length of the square is tripled.

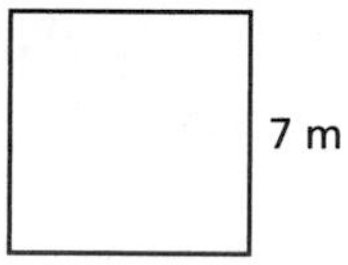

6. The diagonals of a rhombus in which $d_1 = 3$ ft and $d_2 = 9$ ft are both multiplied by $\frac{1}{3}$.
7. The base and height of the rectangle are both doubled.

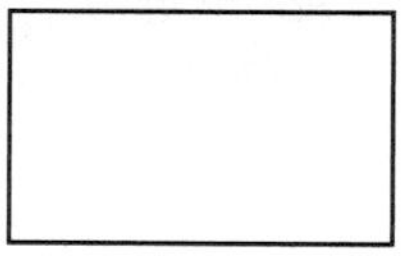

8. The base and height of a right triangle with base 15 in. and height 8 in. are multiplied by $\frac{1}{3}$.
9. A square has vertices $(-1, 2)$, $(3, 2)$, $(3, -2)$, and $(-1, -2)$. If you quadruple the area, what happens to the side length?
10. A restaurant sells pancakes in two sizes, silver dollar and regular. The silver-dollar pancakes have a 4-inch diameter and require $\frac{1}{8}$ cup of batter per pancake. The diameter of a regular pancake is 2.5 times the diameter of a silver-dollar pancake. About how much batter is required to make a regular pancake?

10-6 Geometric Probability

Use the spinner to find the probability of each event.

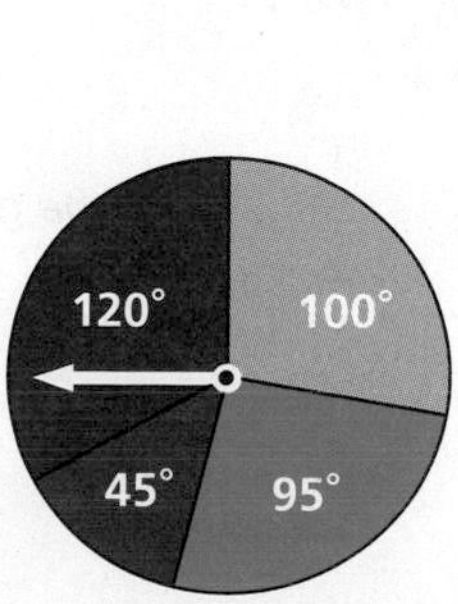

11. the pointer landing on red
12. the pointer landing on red or yellow
13. the pointer not landing on green
14. the pointer landing on yellow or blue
15. A radio station plays 12 commercials per hour. Each commercial is 1 minute long. If you turn on the radio at a random time, find the probability that a commercial will be playing.

CHAPTER 10
Study Guide: Review

Know it! Note — For a complete list of postulates, theorems, and corollaries, see p. PT2.

Vocabulary

apothem
center of a circle
center of a regular polygon
central angle of a regular polygon
circle
composite figure
geometric probability

Complete the sentences below with vocabulary words from the list above.

1. A(n) ___?___ is the length of a segment perpendicular to a side of a regular polygon.
2. The point that is equidistant from every point on a circle is the ___?___ .
3. ___?___ is based on a ratio of geometric measures.

10-1 Developing Formulas for Triangles and Quadrilaterals

EXAMPLES

Find each measurement.

- the perimeter of a square in which $A = 36\text{ in}^2$

$A = s^2 = 36\text{ in}^2$ *Use the Area Formula to find the side length.*

$S = \sqrt{36} = 6\text{ in.}$

$P = 4s = 4 \cdot 6 = 24\text{ in.}$

- the area of the triangle

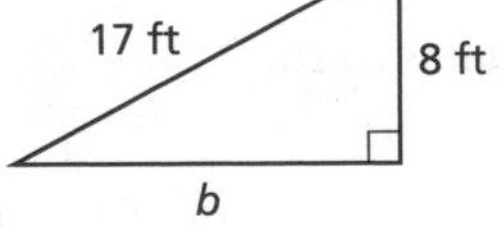

By the Pythagorean Theorem,

$8^2 + b^2 = 17^2$

$64 + b^2 = 289$

$b^2 = 225$, so $b = 15\text{ ft.}$

$A = \frac{1}{2}bh = \frac{1}{2}(15)(8) = 60\text{ ft}^2$

- the diagonal d_2 of a rhombus in which $A = 6x^3y^3\text{ m}$ and $d_1 = 4x^2y\text{ m}$

$A = \frac{1}{2}d_1d_2$

$6x^3y^3 = \frac{1}{2}(4x^2y)d_2$ *Substitute the given values.*

$d_2 = 3xy^2$ *Solve for d_2.*

EXERCISES

Find each measurement.

4. the area of a square in which $P = 36\text{ in.}$
5. the perimeter of a rectangle in which $b = 4\text{ cm}$ and $A = 28\text{ cm}^2$
6. the height of a triangle in which $A = 6x^3y\text{ in}^2$ and $b = 4xy\text{ in.}$
7. the height of the trapezoid, in which $A = 48xy\text{ ft}^2$

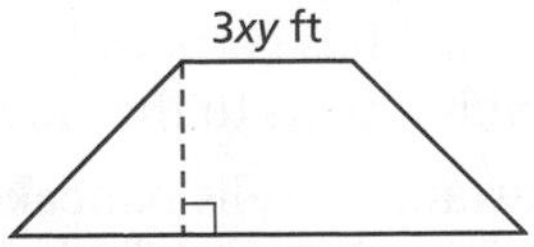

8. the area of a rhombus in which $d_1 = 21\text{ yd}$ and $d_2 = 24\text{ yd}$
9. the diagonal d_2 of the rhombus, in which $A = 630x^3y^7\text{ in}^2$

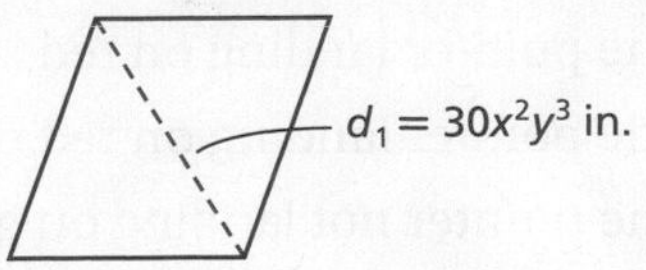

10. the area of a kite in which $d_1 = 32\text{ m}$ and $d_2 = 18\text{ m}$

10-2 Developing Formulas for Circles and Regular Polygons

EXAMPLES

Find each measurement.

- the circumference and area of $\odot B$ in terms of π

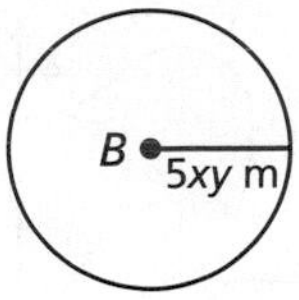

$C = 2\pi r = 2\pi(5xy)$
$= 10xy\pi$ m
$A = \pi r^2 = \pi(5xy)^2 = 25x^2y^2\pi \text{ m}^2$

- the area, to the nearest tenth, of a regular hexagon with apothem 9 yd

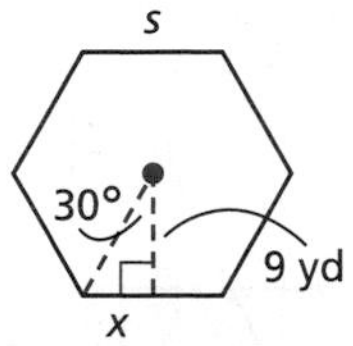

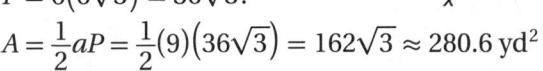

By the 30°-60°-90° Triangle Theorem, $x = \frac{9\sqrt{3}}{3} = 3\sqrt{3}$.
So $s = 2x = 6\sqrt{3}$, and
$P = 6(6\sqrt{3}) = 36\sqrt{3}$.
$A = \frac{1}{2}aP = \frac{1}{2}(9)(36\sqrt{3}) = 162\sqrt{3} \approx 280.6 \text{ yd}^2$

EXERCISES

Find each measurement. Round to the nearest tenth, if necessary.

11. the circumference of $\odot G$

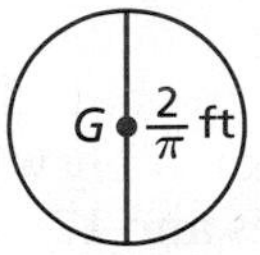

12. the area of $\odot J$ in which $C = 14\pi$ yd

13. the diameter of $\odot K$ in which $A = 64x^2\pi \text{ m}^2$

14. the area of a regular pentagon with side length 10 ft

15. the area of an equilateral triangle with side length 4 in.

16. the area of a regular octagon with side length 8 cm

17. the area of the square

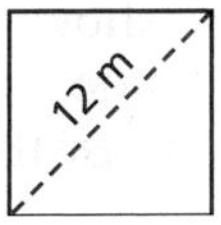

10-3 Composite Figures

EXAMPLE

- **Find the shaded area. Round to the nearest tenth, if necessary.**

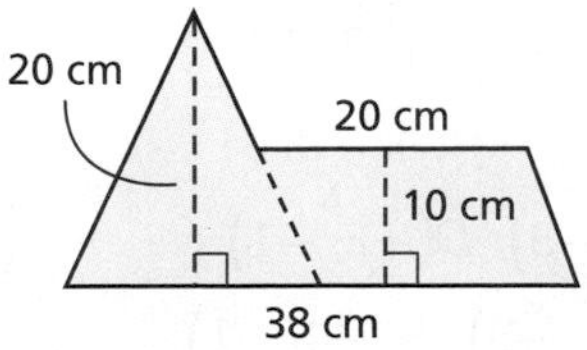

The area of the triangle is
$A = \frac{1}{2}(18)(20) = 180 \text{ cm}^2$.
The area of the parallelogram is
$A = bh = 20(10) = 200 \text{ cm}^2$.
The area of the figure is the sum of the two areas. $180 + 200 = 380 \text{ cm}^2$

EXERCISES

Find the shaded area. Round to the nearest tenth, if necessary.

18.

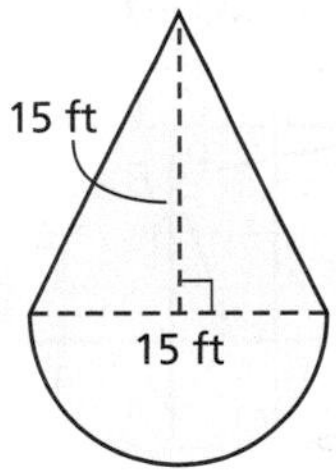

19.

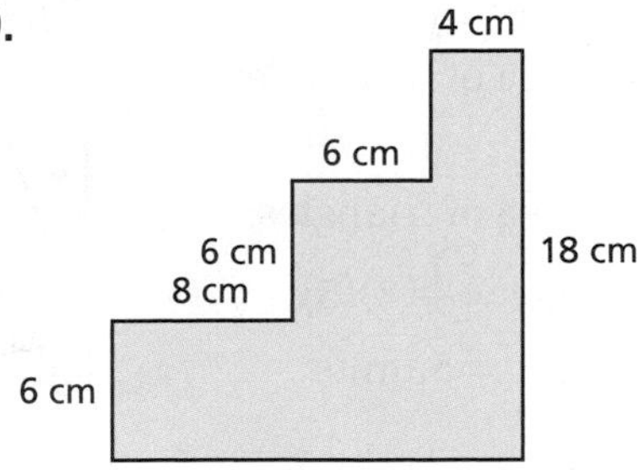

20.

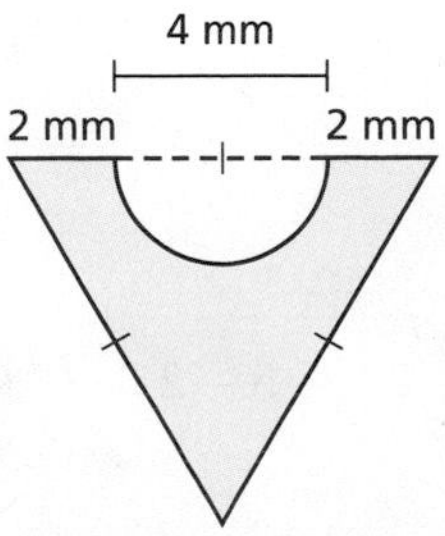

10-4 Perimeter and Area in the Coordinate Plane

EXAMPLES

■ **Estimate the area of the irregular shape.**

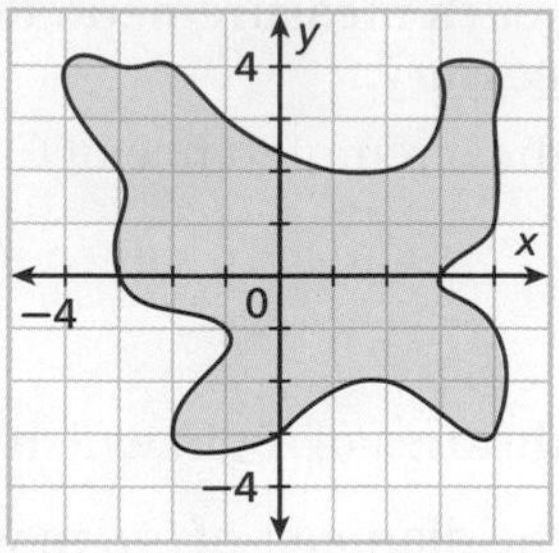

The shape has 28 approximately whole squares and 17 approximately half squares. The total area is approximately $28 + \frac{1}{2}(17) = 36.5 \text{ units}^2$.

■ **Draw and classify the polygons with vertices $R(2, 4)$, $S(3, 1)$, $T(2, -2)$, and $U(1, 1)$. Find the perimeter and area of the polygon.**

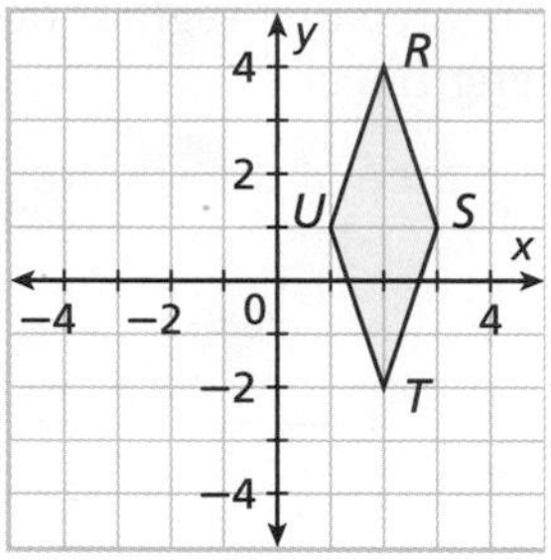

RSTU appears to be a rhombus.

Verify this by showing that the four sides are congruent. By the Distance Formula, $UR = RS = ST = TU = \sqrt{10}$ units.

The perimeter is $4\sqrt{10}$ units.

The area is $A = \frac{1}{2}d_1d_2 = \frac{1}{2}US \cdot RT = \frac{1}{2}(2 \cdot 6) = 6 \text{ units}^2$.

■ **Find the area of the polygon with vertices $A(-3, 4)$, $B(2, 3)$, $C(0, -2)$, and $D(-5, -1)$.**

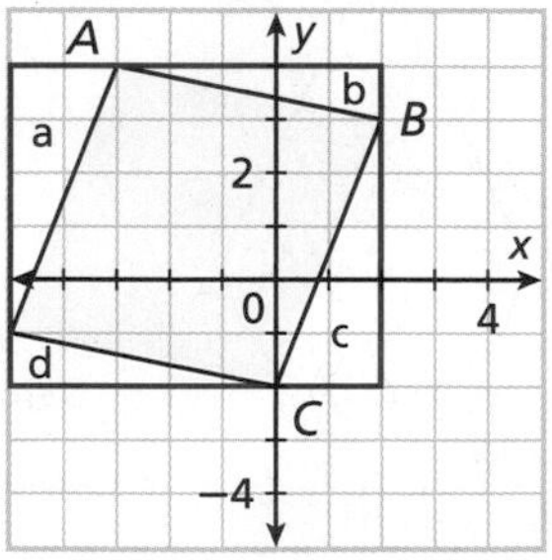

area of rectangle:

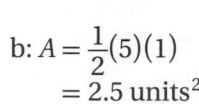

$7(6) = 42 \text{ units}^2$

area of triangles:

a: $A = \frac{1}{2}(2)(5) = 5 \text{ units}^2$

b: $A = \frac{1}{2}(5)(1) = 2.5 \text{ units}^2$

c: $A = \frac{1}{2}(2)(5) = 5 \text{ units}^2$

d: $A = \frac{1}{2}(5)(1) = 2.5 \text{ units}^2$

area of polygon: $A = 42 - 5 - 2.5 - 5 - 2.5 = 27 \text{ units}^2$

EXERCISES

Estimate the area of each irregular shape.

21.

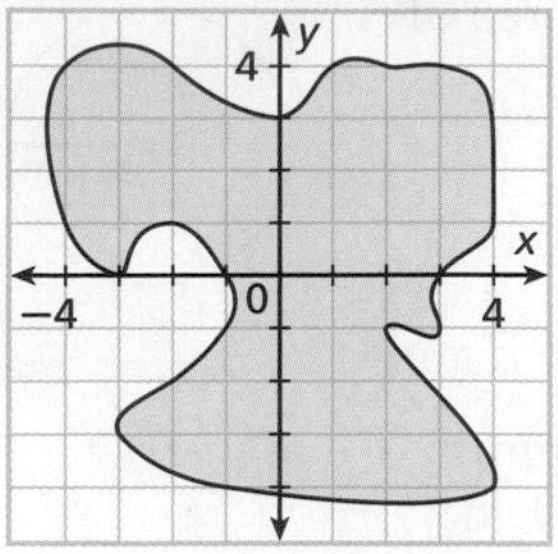

22.

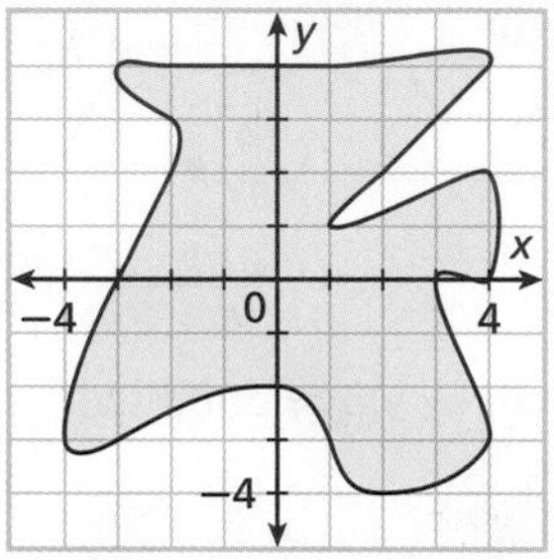

Draw and classify the polygon with the given vertices. Find the perimeter and area of the polygon.

23. $H(0, 3)$, $J(3, 0)$, $K(0, -3)$, $L(-3, 0)$

24. $M(-2, 5)$, $N(3, -2)$, $P(-2, -2)$

25. $A(-2, 3)$, $B(2, 3)$, $C(4, -1)$, $D(-4, -1)$

26. $E(-1, 3)$, $F(3, 3)$, $G(1, 0)$, $H(-3, 0)$

Find the area of the polygon with the given vertices.

27. $Q(1, 4)$, $R(4, 3)$, $S(2, -4)$, $T(-3, -2)$

28. $V(-2, 2)$, $W(4, 0)$, $X(2, -3)$, $Y(-3, 0)$

29. $A(1, 4)$, $B(2, 3)$, $C(0, -3)$, $D(-2, -1)$

30. $E(-1, 2)$, $F(2, 0)$, $G(1, -3)$, $H(-4, -1)$

10-5 Effects of Changing Dimensions Proportionally

EXAMPLE

- **The base and height of a rectangle with base 10 cm and height 15 cm are both doubled. Describe the effect on the area and perimeter of the figure.**

original: $P = 2b + 2h = 2(10) + 2(15) = 50$ cm

$A = bh = 10(15) = 150 \text{ cm}^2$

doubled: $P = 2b + 2h = 2(20) + 2(30)$
$= 100$ cm

$A = bh = 20(30) = 600 \text{ cm}^2$

The perimeter increases by a factor of 2. The area increases by a factor of 4.

EXERCISES

Describe the effect of each change on the perimeter or circumference and area of the given figure.

31. The base and height of the triangle with vertices $X(-1, 3)$, $Y(-3, -2)$, and $Z(2, -2)$ are tripled.

32. The side length of the square with vertices $P(-1, 1)$, $Q(3, 1)$, $R(3, -3)$, and $S(-1, -3)$ is doubled.

33. The radius of $\odot A$ with radius 11 m is multiplied by $\frac{1}{2}$.

34. The base and height of a triangle with base 8 ft and height 20 ft are both multiplied by 4.

10-6 Geometric Probability

EXAMPLES

A point is chosen randomly on $\overline{WZ}$. Find the probability of each event.

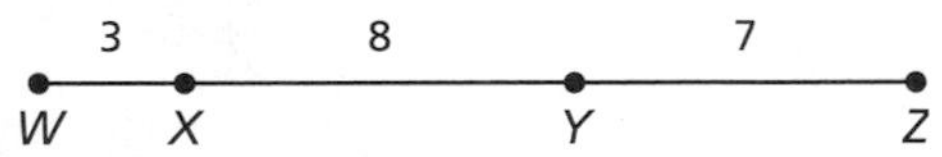

- The point is on $\overline{XZ}$.

$P(\overline{XZ}) = \frac{XZ}{WZ} = \frac{15}{18} = \frac{5}{6}$

- The point is on $\overline{WX}$ or $\overline{YZ}$.

$P(\overline{WX} \text{ or } \overline{YZ}) = P(\overline{WX}) + P(\overline{YZ}) = \frac{3}{18} + \frac{7}{18}$

$= \frac{10}{18} = \frac{5}{9}$

- **Find the probability that a point chosen randomly inside the rectangle is inside the equilateral triangle.**

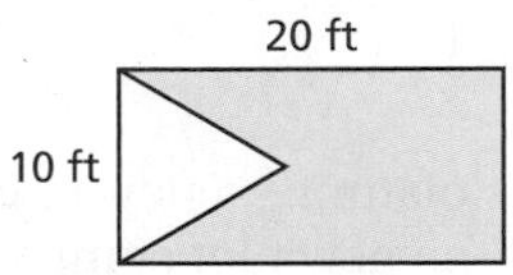

area of rectangle

$A = bh = 20(10) = 200 \text{ ft}^2$

area of triangle

$A = \frac{1}{2}aP = \frac{1}{2}\left(\frac{5\sqrt{3}}{3}\right)(30) = 25\sqrt{3} \approx 43.3 \text{ ft}^2$

$P = \frac{43.3}{200} \approx 0.22$

EXERCISES

A point is chosen randomly on $\overline{AD}$. Find the probability of each event.

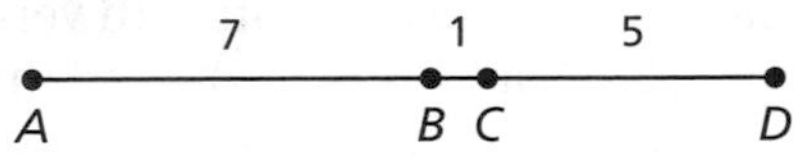

35. The point is on $\overline{AB}$.

36. The point is not on $\overline{CD}$.

37. The point is on $\overline{AB}$ or $\overline{CD}$.

38. The point is on $\overline{BC}$ or $\overline{CD}$.

Find the probability that a point chosen randomly inside the 40 m by 24 m rectangle is in each shape. Round to the nearest hundredth.

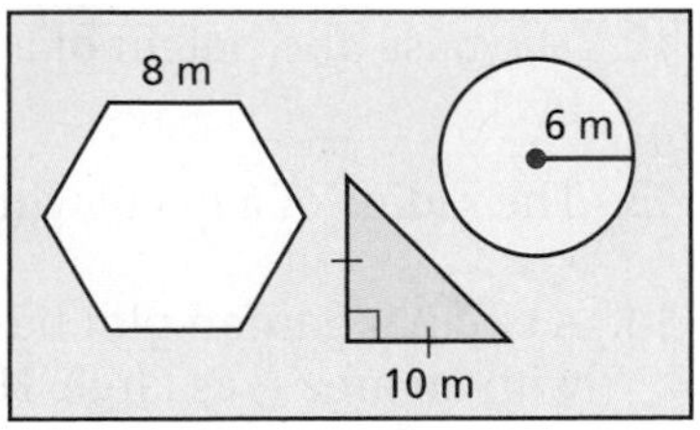

39. the regular hexagon

40. the triangle

41. the circle or the triangle

42. inside the rectangle but not inside the hexagon, triangle, or circle

CHAPTER 10

CHAPTER TEST

Find each measurement.

1. the height h of a triangle in which $A = 12x^2y$ ft^2 and $b = 3x$ ft
2. the base b_1 of a trapezoid in which $A = 161.5$ cm^2, $h = 17$ cm, and $b_2 = 13$ cm
3. the area A of a kite in which $d_1 = 25$ in. and $d_2 = 12$ in.
4. Find the circumference and area of $\odot A$ with diameter 12 in. Give your answers in terms of π.
5. Find the area of a regular hexagon with a side length of 14 m. Round to the nearest tenth.

Find the shaded area. Round to the nearest tenth, if necessary.

6.

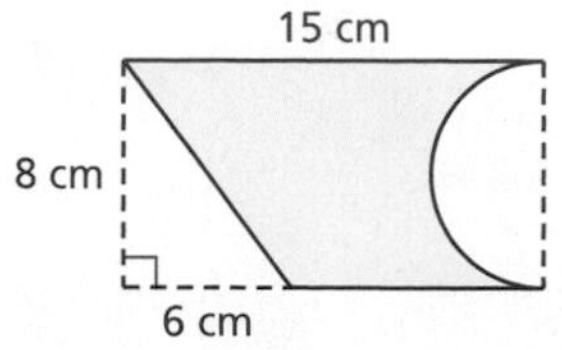

7.

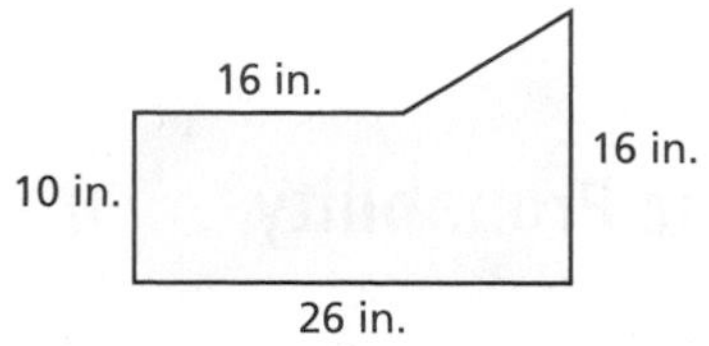

8. The diagram shows a plan for a pond. Use a composite figure to estimate the pond's area. The grid has squares with side lengths of 1 yd.

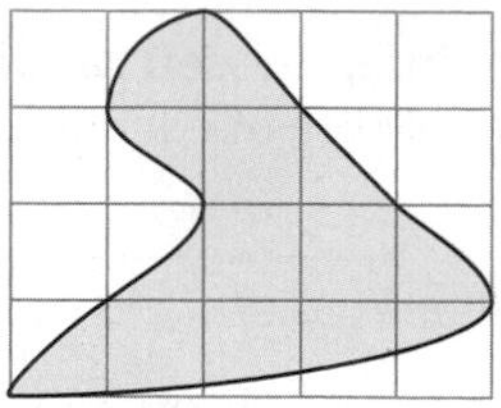

9. Draw and classify the polygon with vertices $A(1, 5)$, $B(2, 3)$, $C(-2, 1)$, and $D(-3, 3)$. Find the perimeter and area of the polygon.

Find the area of each polygon with the given vertices.

10. $E(-3, 4)$, $F(1, 1)$, $G(0, -4)$, $H(-4, 1)$
11. $J(3, 4)$, $K(4, -1)$, $L(-2, -4)$, $M(-3, 3)$

Describe the effect of each change on the perimeter or circumference and area of the given figure.

12. The base and height of a triangle with base 10 cm and height 12 cm are multiplied by 3.
13. The radius of a circle with radius 12 m is multiplied by $\frac{1}{2}$.
14. A circular garden plot has a diameter of 21 ft. Janelle is planning a new circular plot with an area $\frac{1}{9}$ as large. How will the circumference of the new plot compare to the circumference of the old plot?

A point is chosen randomly on $\overline{NS}$. Find the probability of each event.

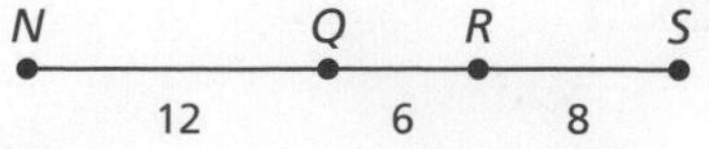

15. The point is on $\overline{NQ}$.
16. The point is not on $\overline{QR}$.
17. The point is on $\overline{NQ}$ or $\overline{RS}$.
18. A shuttle bus for a festival stops at the parking lot every 18 minutes and stays at the lot for 2 minutes. If you go to the festival at a random time, what is the probability that the shuttle bus will be at the parking lot when you arrive?

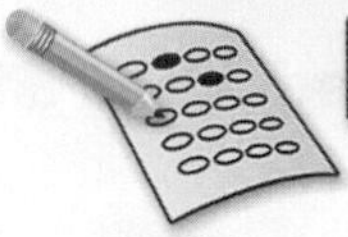

COLLEGE ENTRANCE EXAM PRACTICE

CHAPTER 10

FOCUS ON SAT STUDENT-PRODUCED RESPONSES

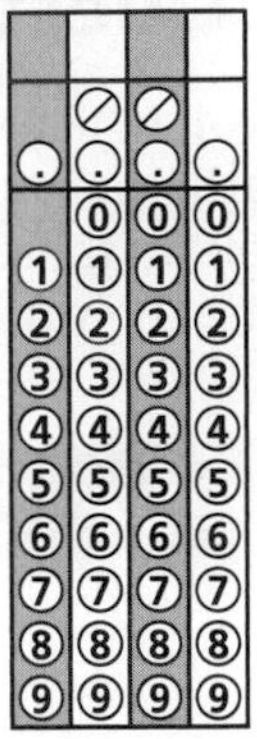

There are two types of questions in the mathematics sections of the SAT: multiple-choice questions, where you select the correct answer from five choices, and student-produced response questions, for which you enter the correct answer in a special grid.

HOT TIP! On the SAT, the student-produced response items do not have a penalty for incorrect answers. If you are uncertain of your answer and do not have time to rework the problem, you should still grid in the answer you have.

You may want to time yourself as you take this practice test. It should take you about 9 minutes to complete.

---

1. A triangle has two angles with a measure of 60° and one side with a length of 12. What is the perimeter of the triangle?

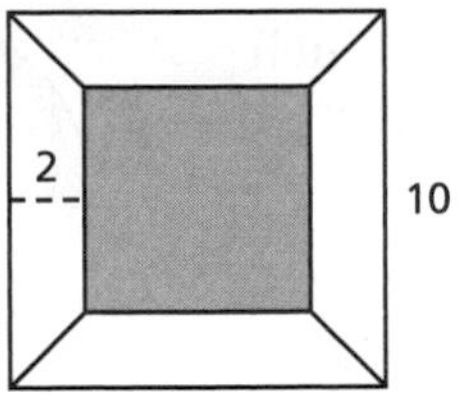

2. The figure above is composed of four congruent trapezoids arranged around a shaded square. What is the area of the shaded square?

3. If $\triangle PQR \sim \triangle STU$, $m\angle P = 22°$, $m\angle Q = 57°$, and $m\angle U = x°$, what is the value of x?

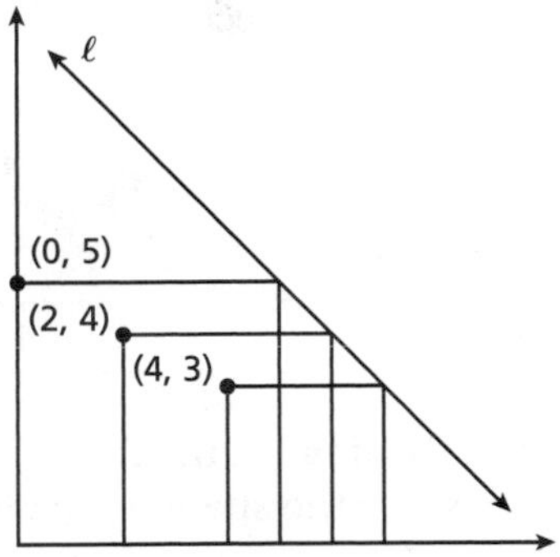

4. Three overlapping squares and the coordinates of a corner of each square are shown above. What is the y-intercept of line ℓ?

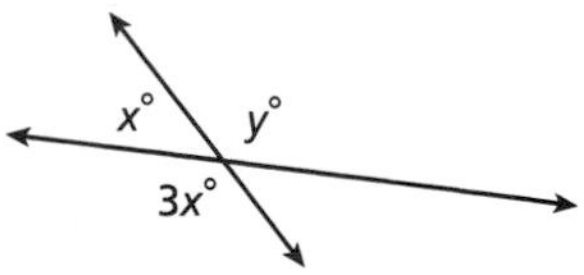

5. In the figure above, what is the value of y?

6. The three angles of a triangle have measures $12x°$, $3x°$, and $7y°$, where $7y > 60$. If x and y are integers, what is the value of x?

CHAPTER 10

TEST TACKLER

Standardized Test Strategies

Any Question Type: Use a Formula Sheet

When you take a standardized mathematics test, you may be given a formula sheet or a mathematics chart that accompanies the test. Although many common formulas are given on these sheets, you still need to know when the formulas are applicable, and what the variables in the formulas represent.

EXAMPLE 1

Mathematics Chart

Perimeter	rectangle	$P = 2\ell + 2w$ or $P = 2(\ell + w)$
Circumference	circle	$C = 2\pi r$ or $C = \pi d$
Area	rectangle	$A = \ell w$ or $A = bh$
	triangle	$A = \frac{1}{2}bh$ or $A = \frac{bh}{2}$
	trapezoid	$A = \frac{1}{2}(b_1 + b_2)h$ or $A = \frac{(b_1 + b_2)h}{2}$
	circle	$A = \pi r^2$

Multiple Choice **In the figure, a rectangle is inscribed in a circle. Which best represents the shaded area to the nearest tenth of a square meter?**

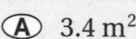

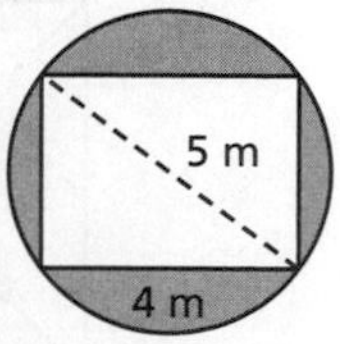

Ⓐ 3.4 m^2 Ⓒ 12.6 m^2

Ⓑ 7.6 m^2 Ⓓ 17.2 m^2

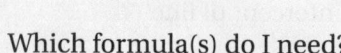

Which formula(s) do I need?

area of a circle, area of a rectangle

What do I substitute for each variable in the formulas?

To use the formula for the area of a circle, I need to know the radius. The diameter of the circle is 5 m, so the radius is 2.5 m. I should substitute 2.5 for r and 3.14 for π.

To use the formula for the area of a rectangle, I need to know its base and height. The base b is 4 m. To find the height, I can use the Pythagorean Theorem.

$$4^2 + h^2 = 5^2$$
$$16 + h^2 = 25$$
$$h^2 = 9$$
$$h = 3$$

What are the areas of the shapes?

circle: $A = \pi r^2 = \pi(2.5)^2 = 6.25\pi \text{ m}^2$

rectangle: $A = bh = 4(3) = 12 \text{ m}^2$

What do I do with the areas to find the answer?

shaded area = area of circle − area of rectangle

$= 6.25\pi - 12 \approx 7.6 \text{ m}^2$

Choice B is the correct answer.

Read each test problem and answer the questions that follow. Use the formula sheet below, if applicable.

Perimeter	
rectangle	$P = 2\ell + 2w$ or $P = 2(\ell + w)$
Circumference	
circle	$C = 2\pi r$ or $C = \pi d$
Area	
rectangle	$A = \ell w$ or $A = bh$
triangle	$A = \frac{1}{2}bh$ or $A = \frac{bh}{2}$
trapezoid	$A = \frac{1}{2}(b_1 + b_2)h$ or $A = \frac{(b_1 + b_2)h}{2}$
circle	$A = \pi r^2$
Pi	
π	$\pi \approx 3.14$ or $\pi \approx \frac{22}{7}$

Item A
The circumference of a circle is 48π meters. What is the radius in meters?

Ⓐ 6.9 meters
Ⓑ 24 meters
Ⓒ 12 meters
Ⓓ 36 meters

1. Which formula would you use to solve this problem?
2. After substituting the variables in the formula, what would you need to do to find the correct answer?

Item B
Gridded Response The area of a trapezoid is 171 square meters. The height is 9 meters, and one base length is 23 meters. What is the other base length of the trapezoid in meters?

3. What formula(s) would you use to solve this problem?
4. What would you substitute for each variable in the formula?

HOT TIP! Before you begin a test, quickly review the formulas included on your formula sheet.

Item C
Gridded Response The area of the rectangle is 48 square miles. What is the perimeter in miles?

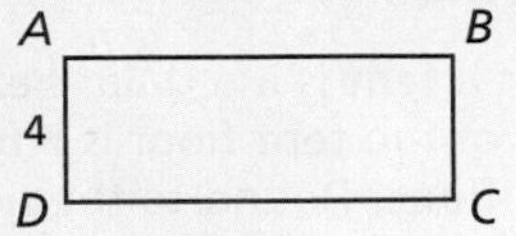

5. What formula(s) would you use to solve this problem?
6. What would you substitute for each variable in the formula?
7. After substituting the variables in the formula, what would you need to do to find the correct answer?

Item D
Short Response A point is chosen randomly inside the rectangle. Which is more likely: the point lies within the triangle, or the point does not lie inside the triangle or the trapezoid?

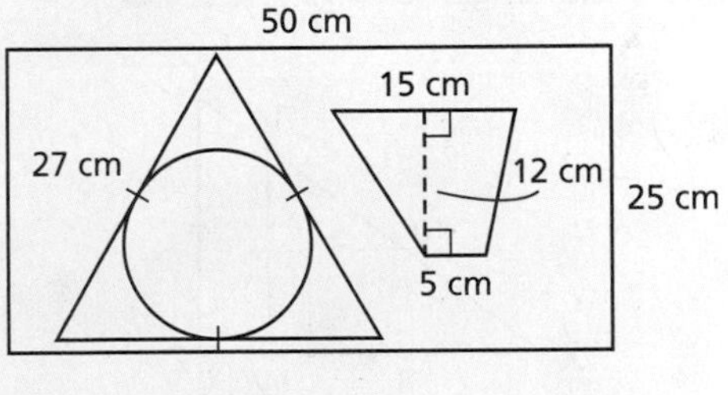

8. Which formulas would you use to solve this problem?
9. What would you substitute for each variable in the formula(s)?
10. After substituting the variables in the formula, what would you need to do to find the correct answer?

CHAPTER 10

STANDARDIZED TEST PREP

Learn It Online
State Test Practice

CUMULATIVE ASSESSMENT

Multiple Choice

1. The floor of a tent is a regular hexagon. If the side length of the tent floor is 5 feet, what is the area of the floor? Round to the nearest tenth.

Ⓐ 32.5 square feet

Ⓑ 65.0 square feet

Ⓒ 75.0 square feet

Ⓓ 129.9 square feet

2. If J is on the perpendicular bisector of $\overline{KL}$, what is the length of $\overline{KL}$?

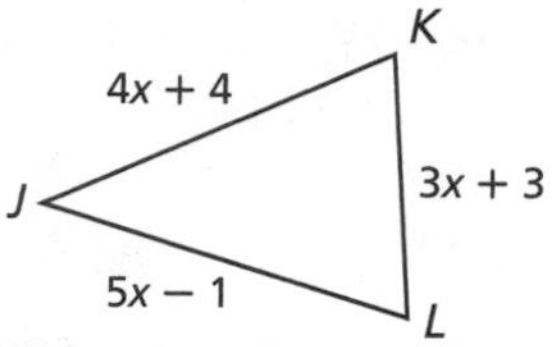

Ⓕ 12 Ⓗ 24

Ⓖ 18 Ⓙ 36

3. What is the length of $\overline{VY}$?

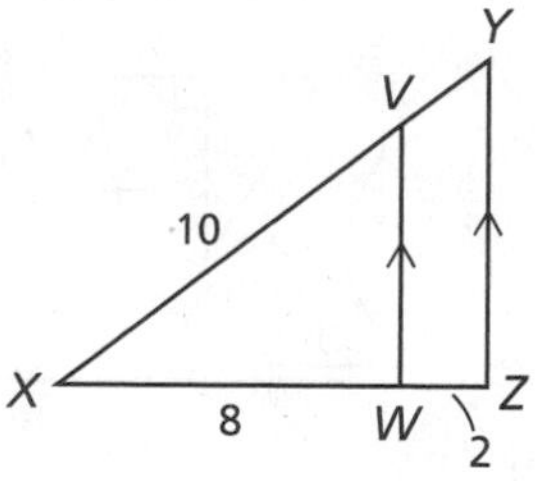

Ⓐ 1.6 Ⓒ 2.5

Ⓑ 2 Ⓓ 4

4. A sailor on a ship sights the light of a lighthouse at an angle of elevation of 15°. If the light in the lighthouse is 189 feet higher than the sailor's line of sight, what is the horizontal distance between the ship and the lighthouse? Round to the nearest foot.

Ⓕ 49 feet Ⓗ 705 feet

Ⓖ 51 feet Ⓙ 730 feet

5. If $ABCD$ is a rhombus in which $m\angle 1 = (x + 15)°$ and $m\angle 2 = (2x + 12)°$, what is the value of x?

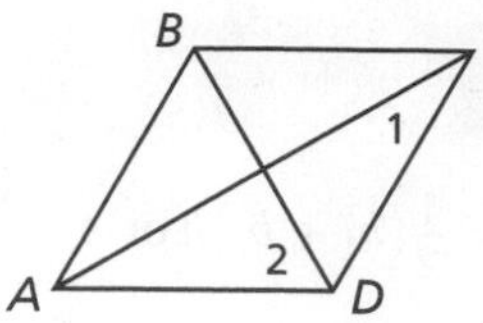

Ⓐ 3 Ⓒ 18

Ⓑ 9 Ⓓ 21

6. What is the area of the shaded portion of the rectangle?

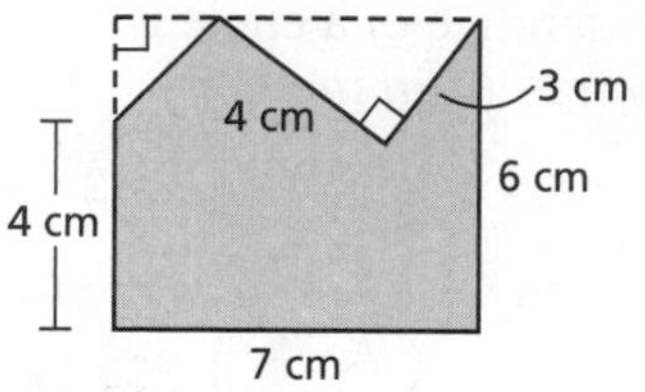

Ⓕ 34 square centimeters

Ⓖ 36 square centimeters

Ⓗ 38 square centimeters

Ⓙ 50 square centimeters

7. If $\triangle XYZ$ is isosceles and $m\angle Y > 100°$, which of the following must be true?

Ⓐ $m\angle X < 40°$ Ⓒ $\overline{XZ} \cong \overline{YZ}$

Ⓑ $m\angle X > 40°$ Ⓓ $\overline{XY} \cong \overline{XZ}$

8. The Eiffel Tower in Paris, France, is 300 meters tall. The first level of the tower has a height of 57 meters. A scale model of the Eiffel Tower in Shenzhen, China, is 108 meters tall. What is the height of the first level of the model? Round to the nearest tenth.

Ⓕ 15.8 meters Ⓗ 56.8 meters

Ⓖ 20.5 meters Ⓙ 61.6 meters

There is often more than one way to find a missing side length or angle measure in a figure. For example, you might be able to find a side length of a right triangle by using either the Pythagorean Theorem or a trigonometric ratio. Check your answer by using a different method than the one you originally used.

9. The lengths of both bases of a trapezoid are tripled. What is the effect of the change on the area of the trapezoid?

   Ⓐ The area remains the same.

   Ⓑ The area is tripled.

   Ⓒ The area increases by a factor of 6.

   Ⓓ The area increases by a factor of 9.

10. If $\angle 1$ and $\angle 2$ form a linear pair, which of the following must also be true about these angles?

    Ⓕ They are adjacent.

    Ⓖ They are complementary.

    Ⓗ They are congruent.

    Ⓙ They are vertical.

11. In $\triangle ABC$, $AB = 8$, $BC = 17$, and $AC = 2x + 1$. Which of the following is a possible value of x?

    Ⓐ 3   Ⓒ 9

    Ⓑ 4   Ⓓ 12

12. Which line is parallel to the line with the equation $y = -3x + 4$?

    Ⓕ $y - 3x = 8$

    Ⓖ $4y - 12x = 1$

    Ⓗ $3y - x = 3$

    Ⓙ $2y + 6x = 5$

Gridded Response

13. What is the radius of a circle in inches if the ratio of its area to its circumference is 2.5 square inches : 1 inch?

14. $\triangle JLM \sim \triangle RST$. If $JL = 5$, $LM = 4$, $RS = 3x - 1$, and $ST = x + 2$, what is the value of x?

15. If the two diagonals of a kite measure 16 centimeters and 10 centimeters, what is the area of the kite in square centimeters?

Short Response

16. Two gas stations on a straight highway are 8 miles apart. If a car runs out of gas at a random point between the two gas stations, what is the probability that the car will be at least 2 miles from either gas station? Draw a diagram or write and explanation to show how you determined your answer.

17. Use the figure below to find each measure. Show your work or explain in words how you found your answers. Round the angle measure to the nearest degree.

    a. m$\angle A$

    b. AC

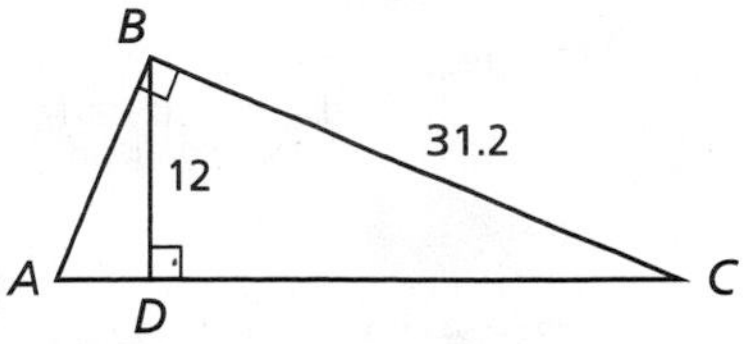

18. Given that $\overline{DE}$, $\overline{DF}$, and $\overline{EF}$ are midsegments of $\triangle ABC$, determine m$\angle C$ to the nearest degree. Show your work or explain in words how you determined your answer.

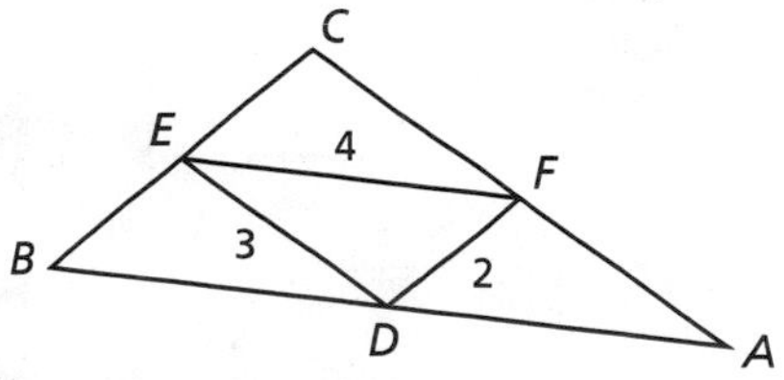

Extended Response

19. Quadrilateral $LMNP$ has vertices at $L(1, 4)$, $M(4, 4)$, $N(1, 0)$ and $P(-2, 0)$.

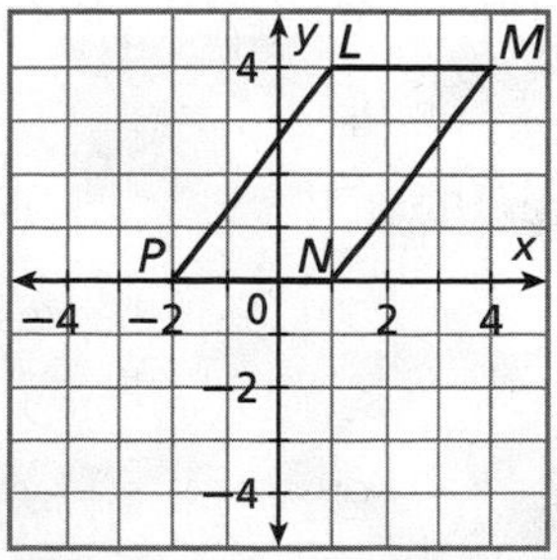

    a. Write a coordinate proof showing that $LMNP$ is a parallelogram.

    b. Draw a rectangle with the same area as figure $LMNP$. Explain how you know that the figures have the same area.

    c. Does the rectangle you drew have the same perimeter as figure $LMNP$? Explain.

CHAPTER 11

Spatial Reasoning

COMMON CORE

Chapter

- Create representations of three-dimensional figures.
- Apply formulas for volume to real-world problems.

Solid Gold!

This sculpture shows five intersecting tetrahedrons. You can use *nets* to create models of tetrahedrons and other three-dimensional figures.

Erik Dawson/Getty Images Photo Assignments/HRW Photo/ Sculpture by Dale Seymour

Learn It Online
Chapter Project Online

ARE YOU READY?

Vocabulary

Match each term on the left with a definition on the right.

1. equilateral
2. parallelogram
3. apothem
4. composite figure

A. the distance from the center of a regular polygon to a side of the polygon

B. a quadrilateral with four right angles

C. a quadrilateral with two pairs of parallel sides

D. having all sides congruent

E. a figure made up of simple shapes, such as triangles, rectangles, trapezoids, and circles

Find Area in the Coordinate Plane

Find the area of each figure with the given vertices.

5. $\triangle ABC$ with $A(0, 3)$, $B(5, 3)$, and $C(2, -1)$
6. rectangle $KLMN$ with $K(-2, 3)$, $L(-2, 7)$, $M(6, 7)$, and $N(6, 3)$
7. $\odot P$ with center $P(2, 3)$ that passes through the point $Q(-6, 3)$

Circumference and Area of Circles

Find the circumference and area of each circle. Give your answers in terms of π.

8.

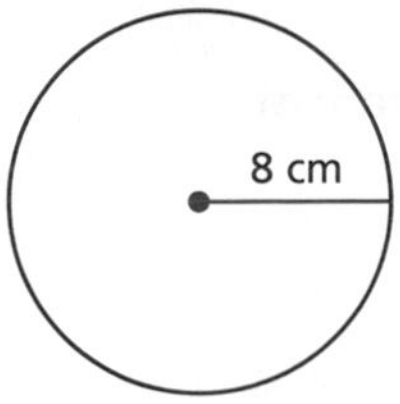

9.

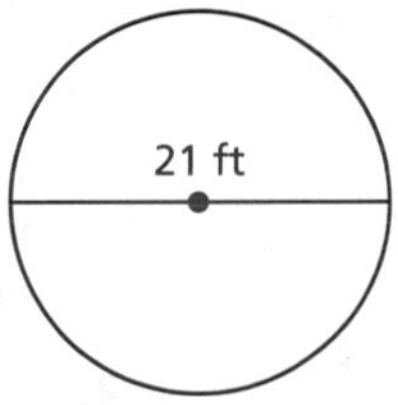

10.

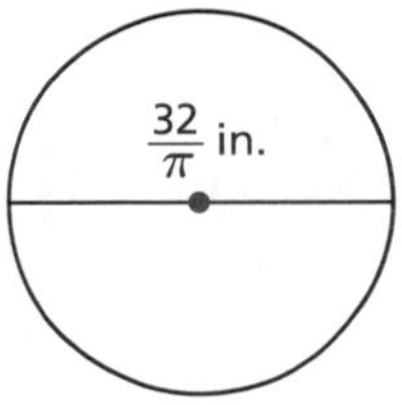

Distance and Midpoint Formulas

Find the length and midpoint of the segment with the given endpoints.

11. $A(-3, 2)$ and $B(5, 6)$
12. $C(-4, -4)$ and $D(2, -3)$
13. $E(0, 1)$ and $F(-3, 4)$
14. $G(2, -5)$ and $H(-2, -2)$

Evaluate Expressions

Evaluate each expression for the given values of the variables.

15. $\sqrt{\frac{A}{\pi}}$ for $A = 121\pi \text{ cm}^2$
16. $\frac{2A}{P}$ for $A = 128 \text{ ft}^2$ and $P = 32$ ft
17. $\sqrt{c^2 - a^2}$ for $a = 8$ m and $c = 17$ m
18. $\frac{2A}{h} - b_1$ for $A = 60 \text{ in}^2$, $b_1 = 8$ in., and $h = 6$ in.

CHAPTER 11

Study Guide: Preview

Where You've Been

Previously, you

- analyzed properties of figures in a plane.
- found the perimeters and areas of triangles, circles, polygons, and composite figures.
- studied the effects of changing dimensions of polygons proportionally.

In This Chapter

You will study

- properties of three-dimensional figures.
- the volumes of three-dimensional figures.
- the effects of changing dimensions of three-dimensional figures proportionally.

Where You're Going

You can use the skills learned in this chapter

- in all your future math classes, including Precalculus.
- to study other fields such as chemistry, physics, and architecture.
- to solve problems concerning interior design, packaging, and construction.

Key Vocabulary/Vocabulario

cone	cono
cylinder	cilindro
net	plantilla
polyhedron	poliedro
prism	prisma
pyramid	pirámide
sphere	esfera
volume	volumen

Vocabulary Connections

To become familiar with some of the vocabulary terms in the chapter, consider the following questions. You may refer to the chapter, the glossary, or a dictionary if you like.

1. The word **polyhedron** begins with the root *poly-*. List some other words that begin with *poly-*. What do all of these words have in common?
2. The word **cone** comes from the root *ko-*, which means "to sharpen." Think of sharpening a pencil. How do you think this relates to a cone?
3. The figure shown is a **net** for a cube. How do you think a net is related to a three-dimensional object?

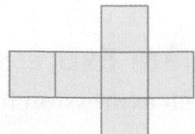

Reading and Writing Math

Writing Strategy: Draw Three-Dimensional Figures

When you encounter a three-dimensional figure such as a cylinder, cone, sphere, prism, or pyramid, it may help you to make a quick sketch so that you can visualize its shape.

Use these tips to help you draw quick sketches of three-dimensional figures.

CYLINDER

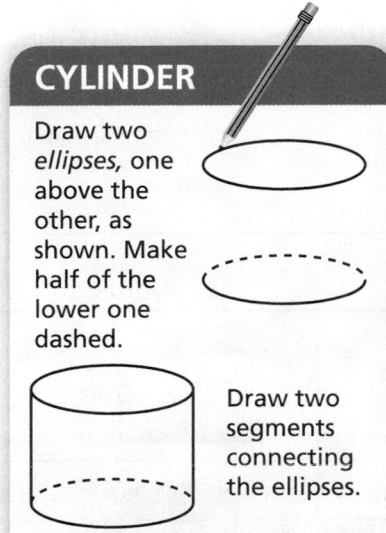

Draw two *ellipses,* one above the other, as shown. Make half of the lower one dashed.

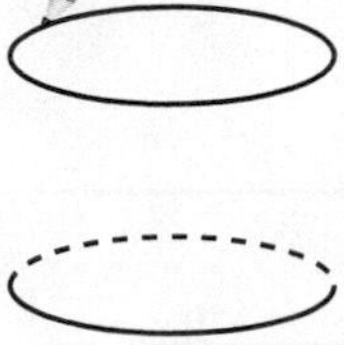

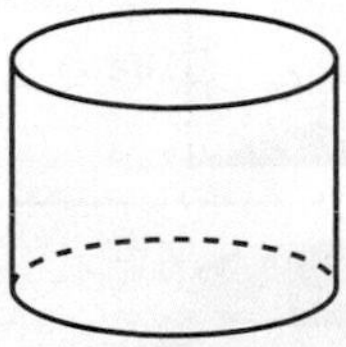

Draw two segments connecting the ellipses.

PRISM

Draw two parallelograms, one above the other. Make two sides of the lower one dashed.

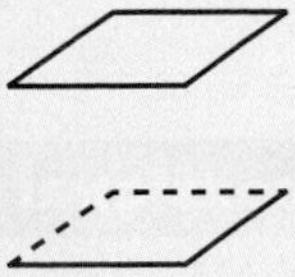

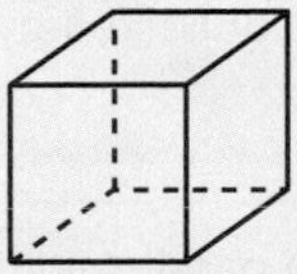

Draw segments connecting the vertices of the parallelograms. Use a dashed segment for the hidden edge.

SPHERE

Draw a circle and its center.

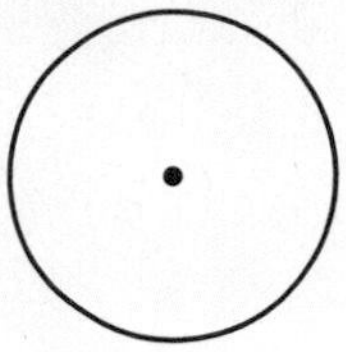

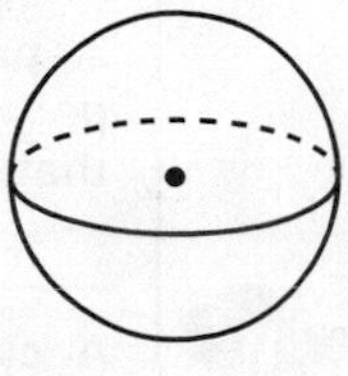

Draw an ellipse inside the circle. Make the top half of the ellipse dashed.

CONE

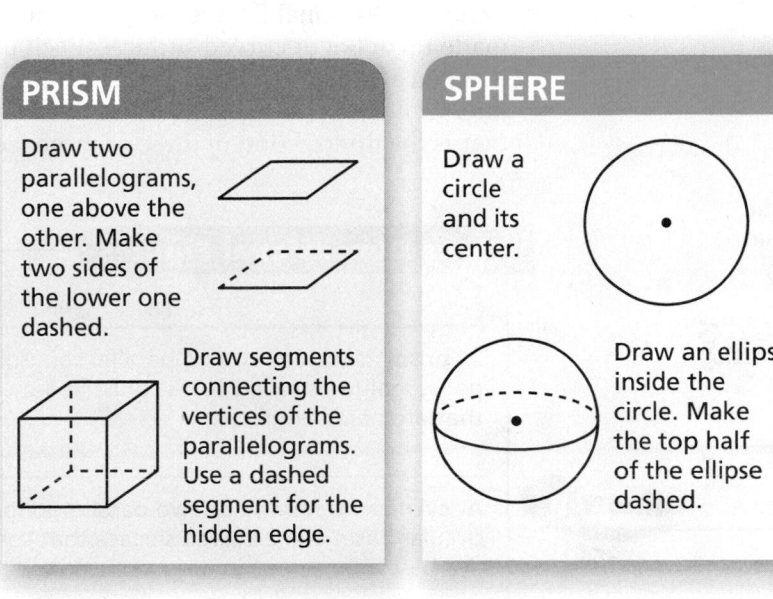

Draw an ellipse and a point above it. Make the top half of the ellipse dashed.

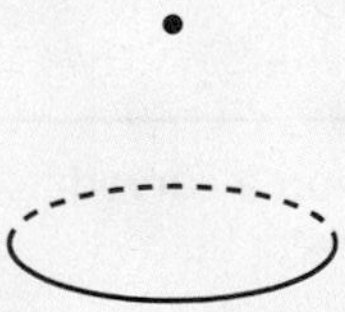

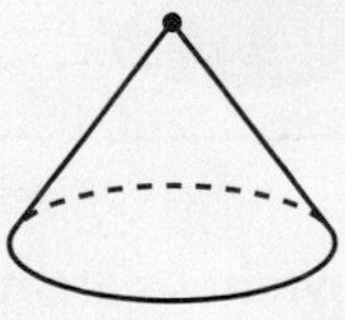

Draw two segments connecting the point to the ellipse.

PYRAMID

Draw a parallelogram and a point above it. Make two sides of the parallelogram dashed.

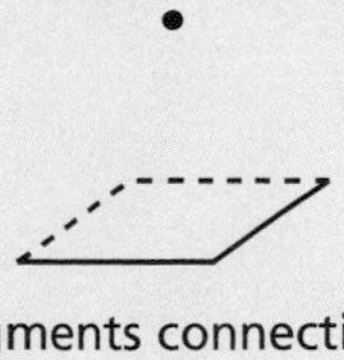

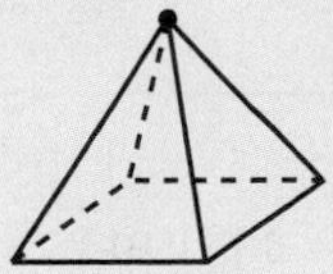

Draw segments connecting the vertices of the parallelogram to the point. Use a dashed segment for the hidden edge.

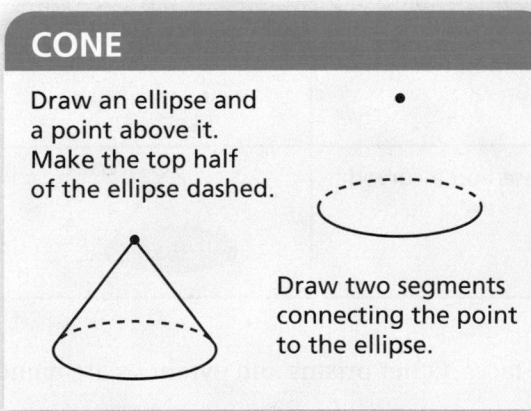

Try This

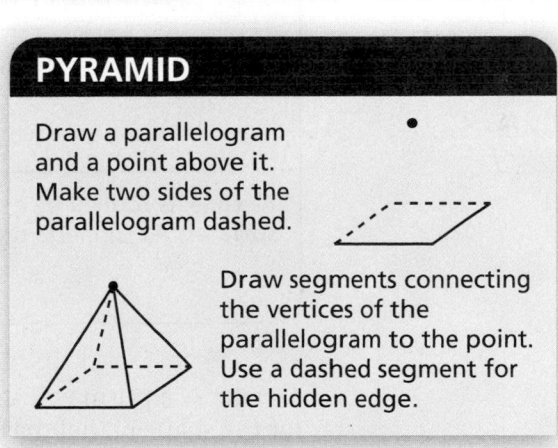

1. Explain and show how to draw a *cube*, a prism with equal length, width, and height.
2. Draw a prism, starting with two hexagons. (*Hint:* Draw the hexagons as if you were viewing them at an angle.)

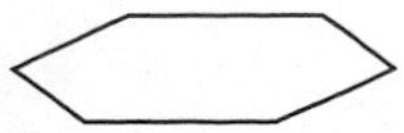

3. Draw a pyramid, starting with a triangle and a point above the triangle.

COMMON CORE

11-1 Solid Geometry

CC.9-12.G.GMD.4 Identify…cross-sections of three-dimensional objects… *Also* **CC.9-12.G.MG.3***

Objectives

Classify three-dimensional figures according to their properties.

Use nets and cross sections to analyze three-dimensional figures.

Vocabulary

face
edge
vertex
prism
cylinder
pyramid
cone
cube
net
cross section

Why learn this?

Some farmers in Japan grow cube-shaped watermelons to save space in small refrigerators. Each fruit costs about the equivalent of U.S. $80. (See Example 4.)

Three-dimensional figures, or *solids,* can be made up of flat or curved surfaces. Each flat surface is called a **face**. An **edge** is the segment that is the intersection of two faces. A **vertex** is the point that is the intersection of three or more faces.

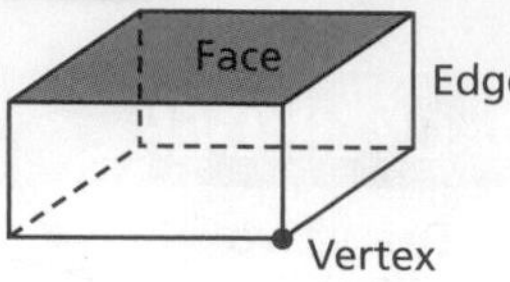

Know it! Note

Three-Dimensional Figures

TERM	EXAMPLE
A **prism** is formed by two parallel congruent polygonal faces called *bases* connected by faces that are parallelograms.	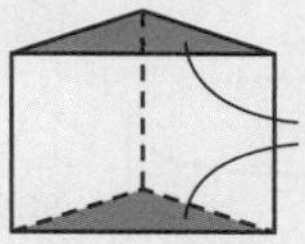
A **cylinder** is formed by two parallel congruent circular bases and a curved surface that connects the bases.	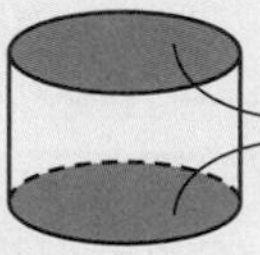
A **pyramid** is formed by a polygonal base and triangular faces that meet at a common vertex.	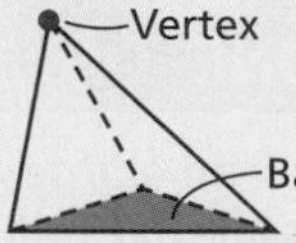
A **cone** is formed by a circular base and a curved surface that connects the base to a vertex.	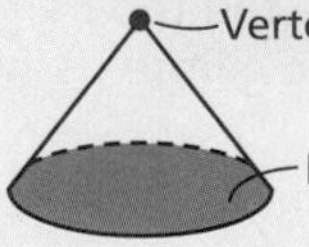

A **cube** is a prism with six square faces. Other prisms and pyramids are named for the shape of their bases.

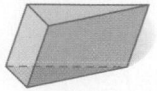

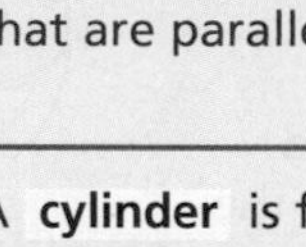
Triangular prism

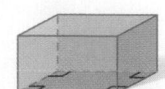

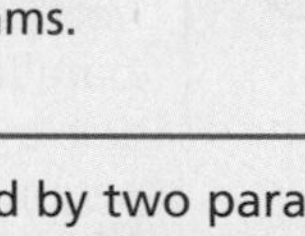
Rectangular prism

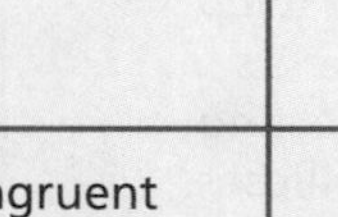
Pentagonal prism

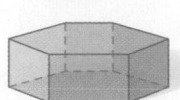

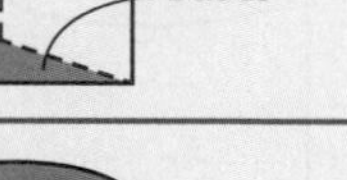
Hexagonal prism

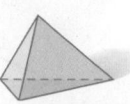

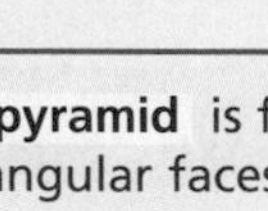
Triangular pyramid

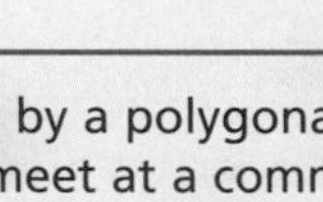
Rectangular pyramid

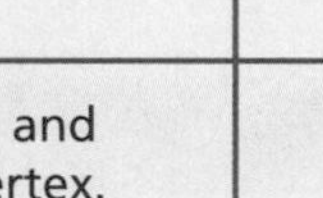
Pentagonal pyramid

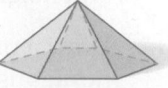

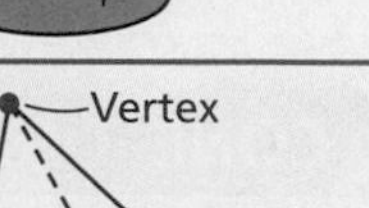
Hexagonal pyramid

EXAMPLE 1 Classifying Three-Dimensional Figures

Classify each figure. Name the vertices, edges, and bases.

A

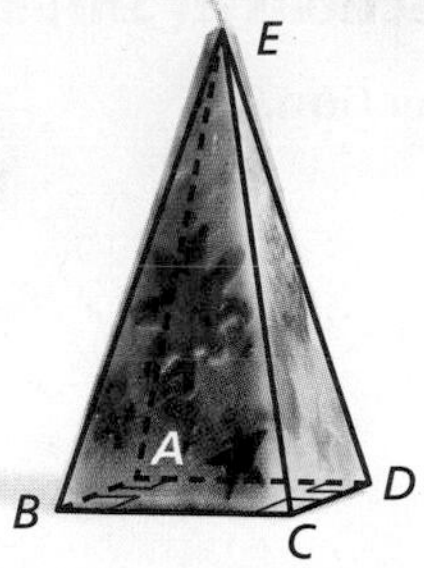

rectangular pyramid
vertices: *A, B, C, D, E*
edges: $\overline{AB}$, $\overline{BC}$, $\overline{CD}$, $\overline{AD}$, $\overline{AE}$, $\overline{BE}$, $\overline{CE}$, $\overline{DE}$
base: rectangle *ABCD*

B

cylinder
vertices: none
edges: none
bases: ⊙*P* and ⊙*Q*

CHECK IT OUT! **Classify each figure. Name the vertices, edges, and bases.**

1a.

1b.

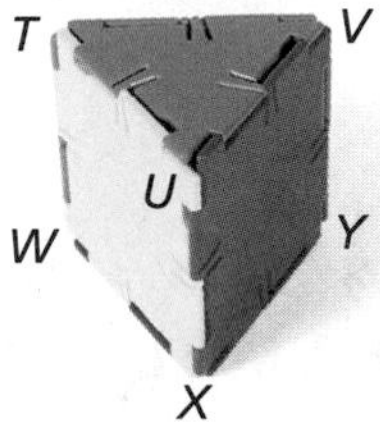

A **net** is a diagram of the surfaces of a three-dimensional figure that can be folded to form the three-dimensional figure. To identify a three-dimensional figure from a net, look at the number of faces and the shape of each face.

EXAMPLE 2 Identifying a Three-Dimensional Figure From a Net

Describe the three-dimensional figure that can be made from the given net.

A

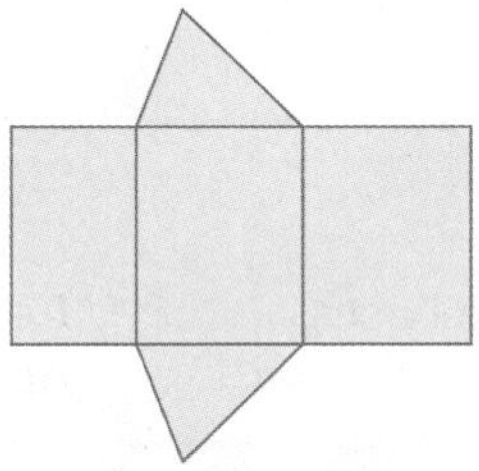

The net has two congruent triangular faces. The remaining faces are parallelograms, so the net forms a triangular prism.

B

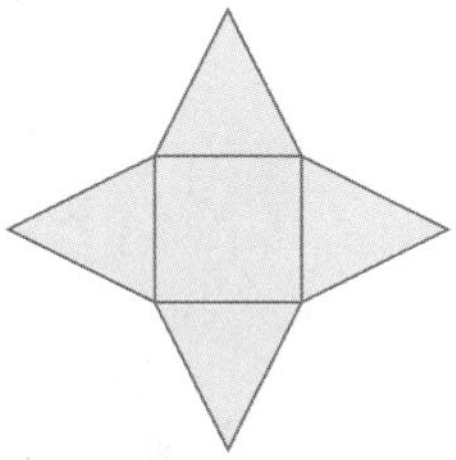

The net has one square face. The remaining faces are triangles, so the net forms a square pyramid.

CHECK IT OUT! **Describe the three-dimensional figure that can be made from the given net.**

2a.

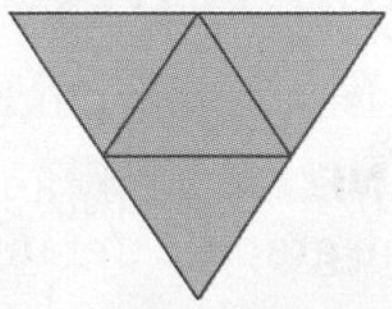

2b.

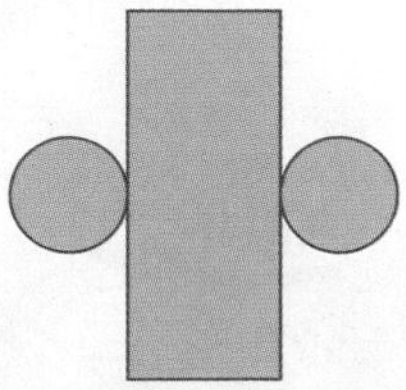

A **cross section** is the intersection of a three-dimensional figure and a plane.

EXAMPLE 3 Describing Cross Sections of Three-Dimensional Figures

Describe each cross section.

A

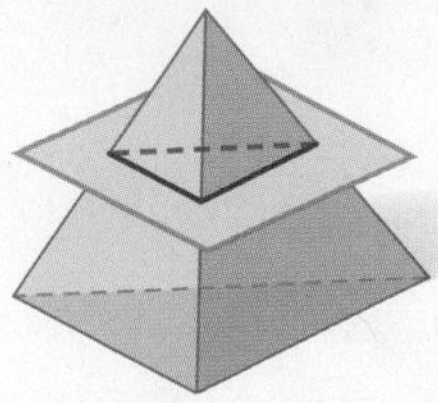

The cross section is a triangle.

B

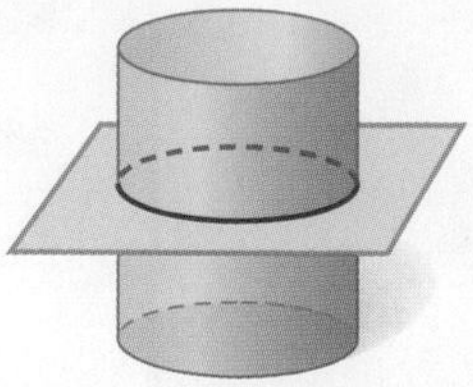

The cross section is a circle.

CHECK IT OUT! **Describe each cross section.**

3a.

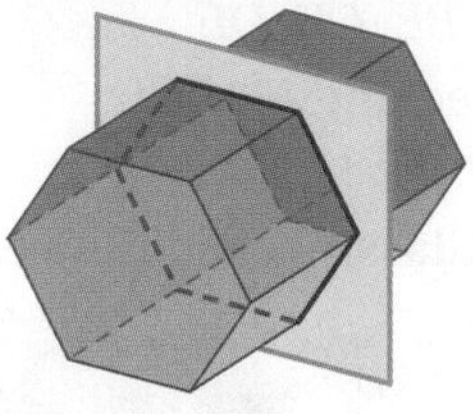

3b.

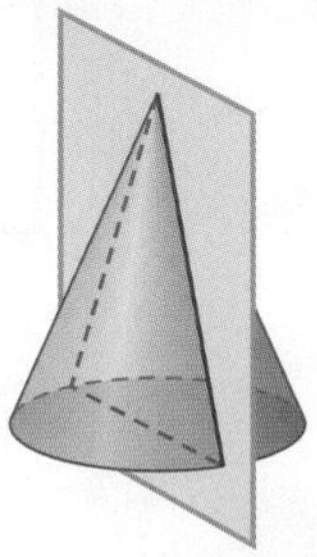

EXAMPLE 4 *Food Application*

A chef is slicing a cube-shaped watermelon for a buffet. How can the chef cut the watermelon to make a slice of each shape?

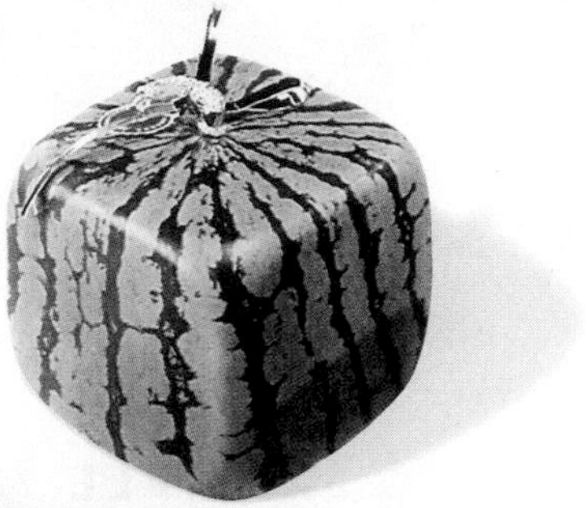

A **a square**

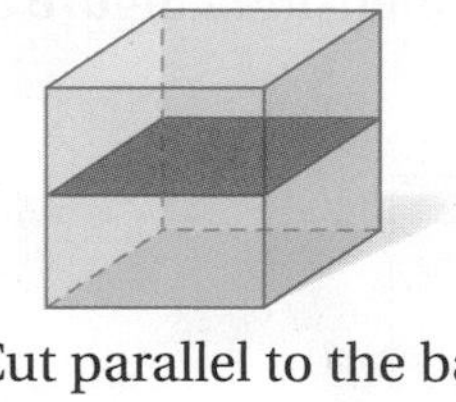

Cut parallel to the bases.

B **a hexagon**

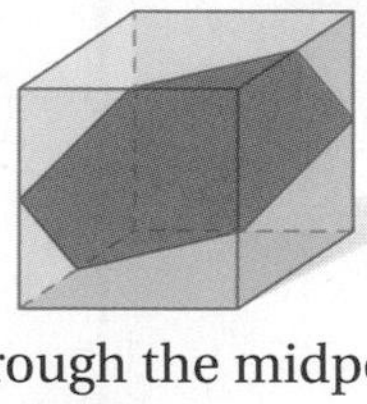

Cut through the midpoints of the edges.

CHECK IT OUT! **4.** How can a chef cut a cube-shaped watermelon to make slices with triangular faces?

MATHEMATICAL PRACTICES

THINK AND DISCUSS

1. Compare prisms and cylinders.

Know it! Note

2. GET ORGANIZED Copy and complete the graphic organizer.

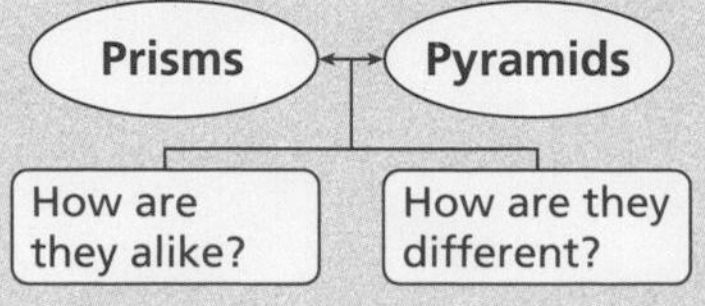
Prisms
Pyramids
How are they alike?
How are they different?

Newscom

11-1 Exercises

Learn It Online
Homework Help Online
Parent Resources Online

GUIDED PRACTICE

1. **Vocabulary** A __?__ has two circular bases. (*prism, cylinder,* or *cone*)

SEE EXAMPLE 1

Classify each figure. Name the vertices, edges, and bases.

2. 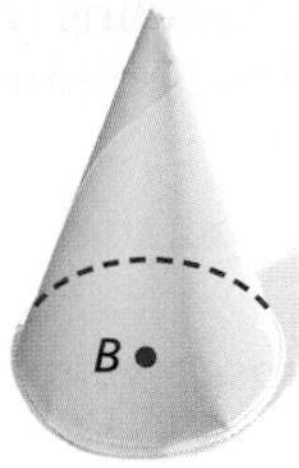

3. 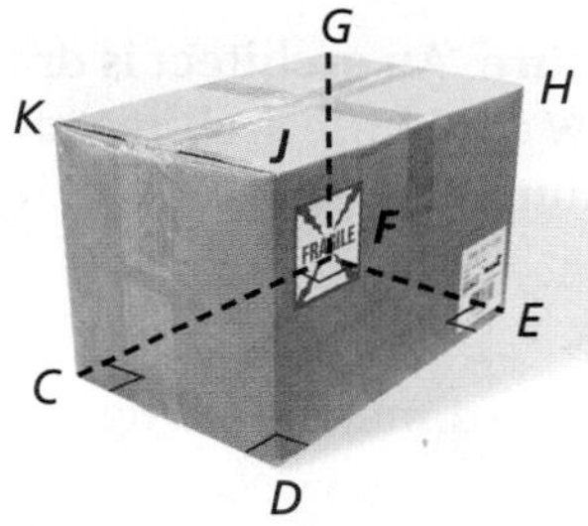

4. 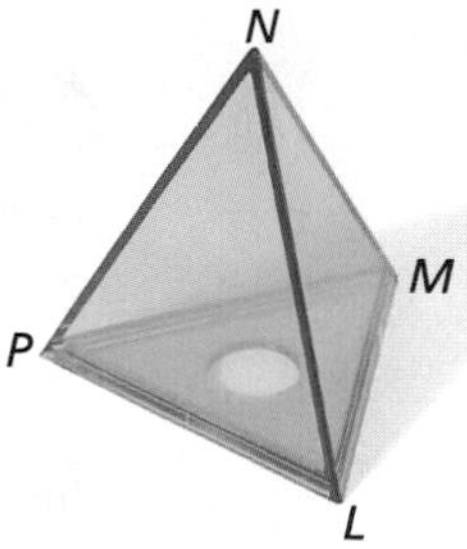

SEE EXAMPLE 2

Describe the three-dimensional figure that can be made from the given net.

5. 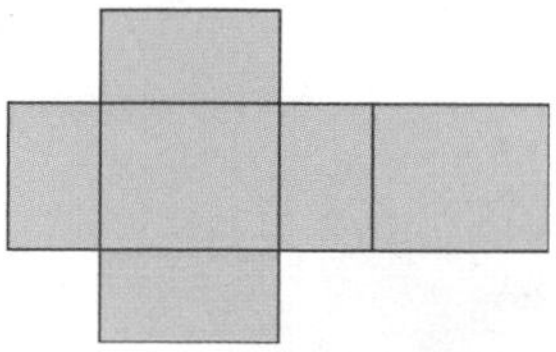

6. 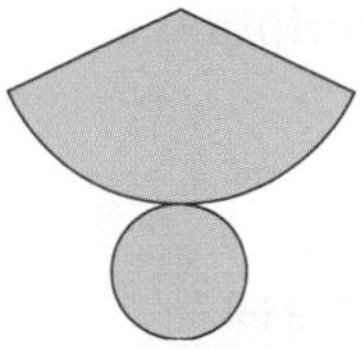

7. 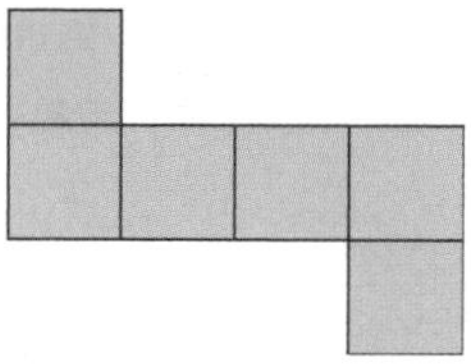

SEE EXAMPLE 3

Describe each cross section.

8. 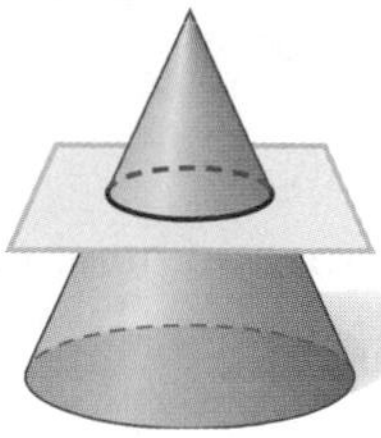

9. 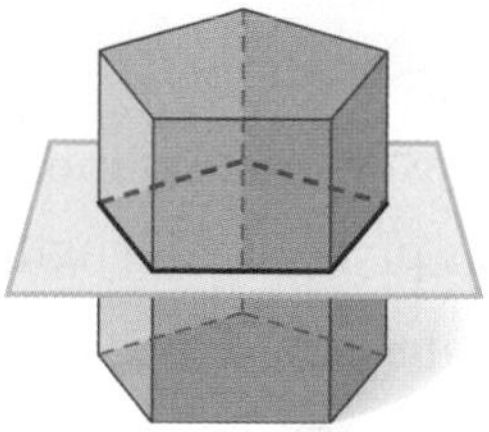

10. 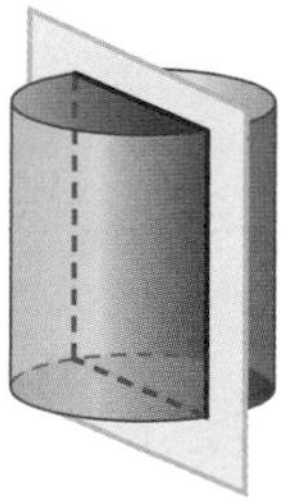

SEE EXAMPLE 4

Art **A sculptor has a cylindrical piece of clay. How can the sculptor slice the clay to make a slice of each given shape?**

11. a circle

12. a rectangle

PRACTICE AND PROBLEM SOLVING

Independent Practice

For Exercises	See Example
13–15	1
16–18	2
19–21	3
22–23	4

Extra Practice

See Extra Practice for more Skills Practice and Applications Practice exercises.

Classify each figure. Name the vertices, edges, and bases.

13. 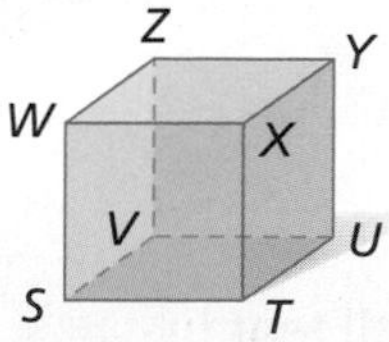

14. 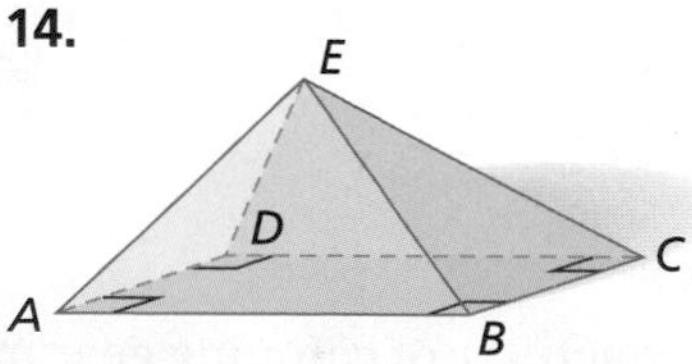

15. 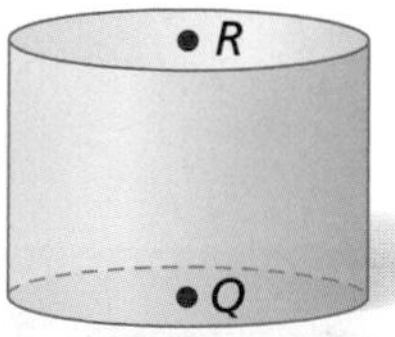

Describe the three-dimensional figure that can be made from the given net.

16. 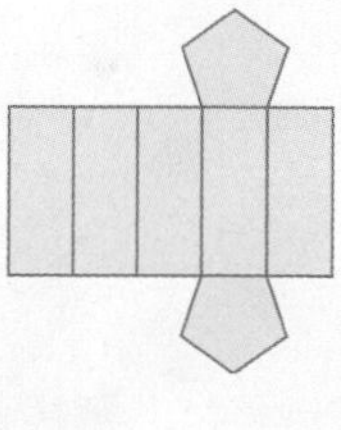

17. 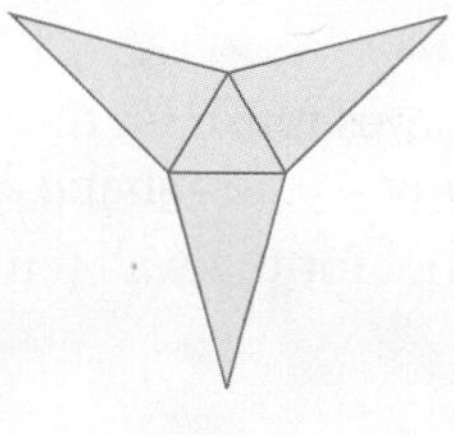

18. 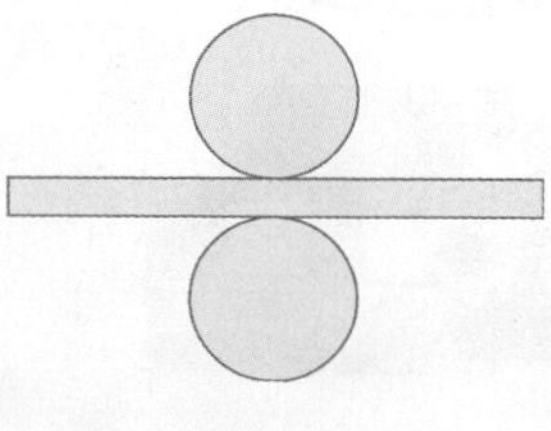

Describe each cross section.

19.

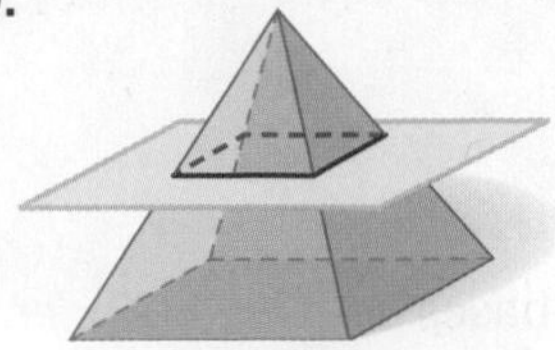

20.

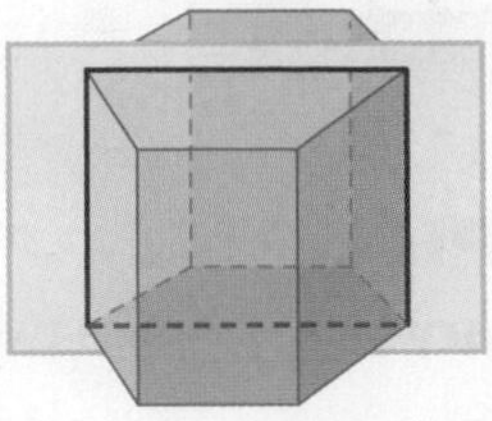

21.

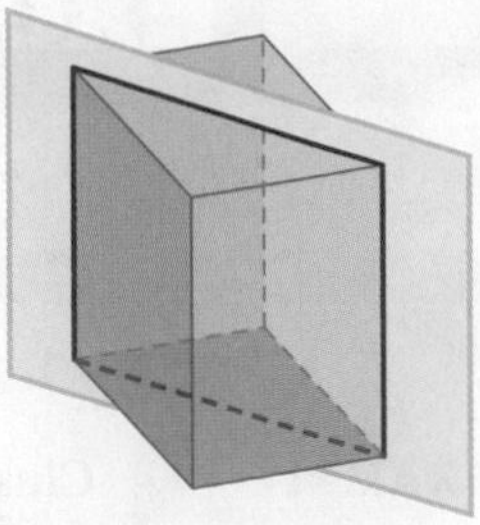

Architecture **An architect is drawing plans for a building that is a hexagonal prism. How could the architect draw a cutaway of the building that shows a cross section in the shape of each given figure?**

22. a hexagon

23. a rectangle

Name a three-dimensional figure from which a cross section in the given shape can be made.

24. square

25. rectangle

26. circle

27. hexagon

Write a verbal description of each figure.

28.

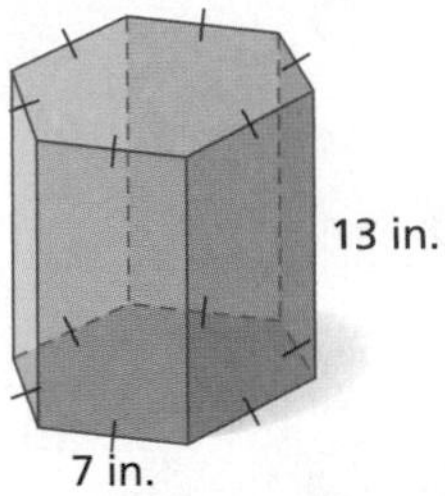

29.

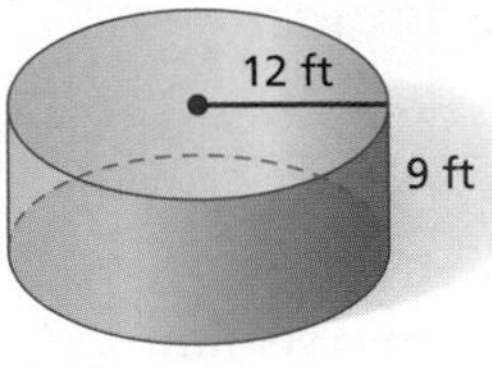

30.

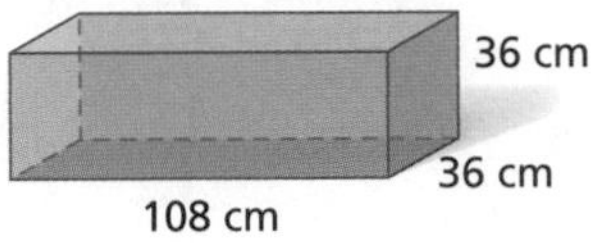

Draw and label a figure that meets each description.

31. rectangular prism with length 3 cm, width 2 cm, and height 5 cm

32. regular pentagonal prism with side length 6 in. and height 8 in.

33. cylinder with radius 4 m and height 7 m

Draw a net for each three-dimensional figure.

34.

35.

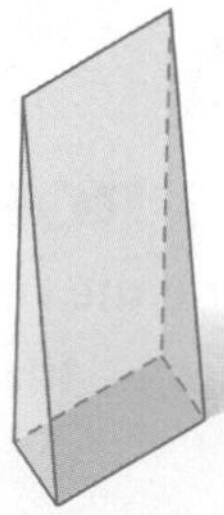

36.

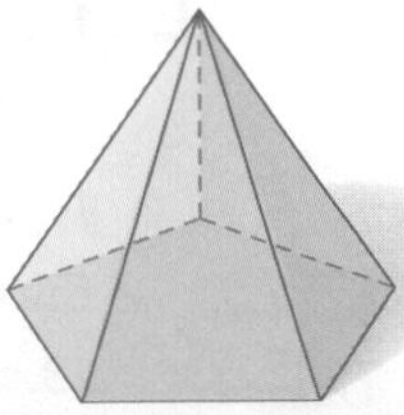

MULTI-STEP TEST PREP

37. A manufacturer of camping gear makes a wall tent in the shape shown in the diagram.

a. Classify the three-dimensional figure that the wall tent forms.

b. What shapes make up the faces of the tent? How many of each shape are there?

c. Draw a net for the wall tent.

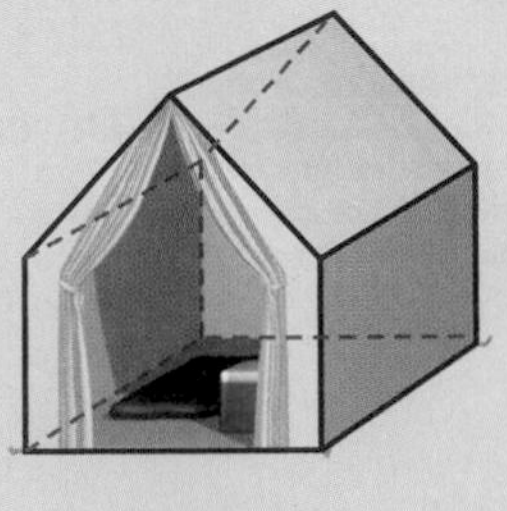

38. **ERROR ANALYSIS** A regular hexagonal prism is intersected by a plane as shown. Which cross section is incorrect? Explain.

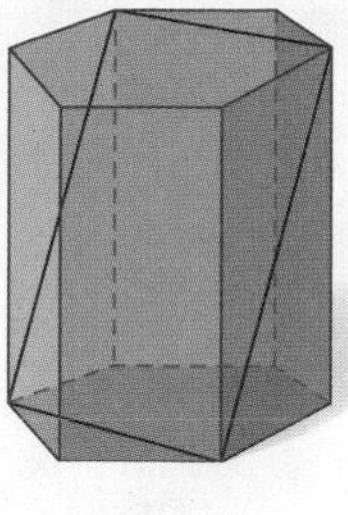

Ⓐ
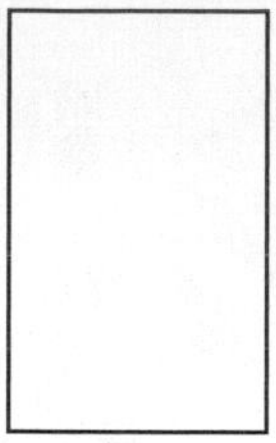

Ⓑ

39. **Critical Thinking** A three-dimensional figure has 5 faces. One face is adjacent to every other face. Four of the faces are congruent. Draw a figure that meets these conditions.

40. **Write About It** Which of the following figures is not a net for a cube? Explain.

a.
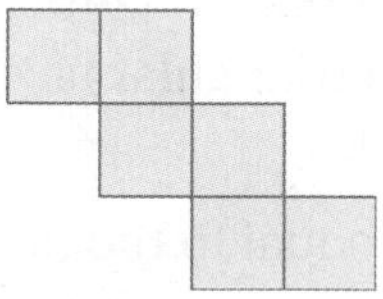

c.
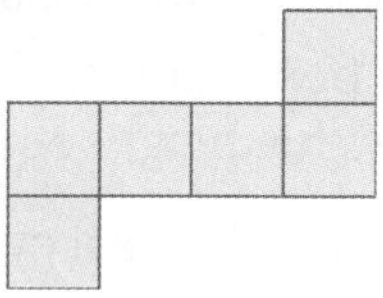

b.
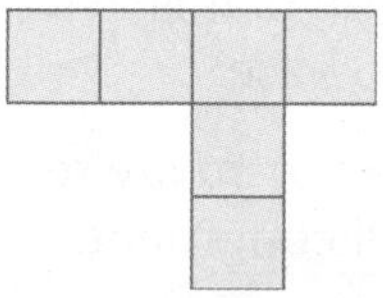

d.
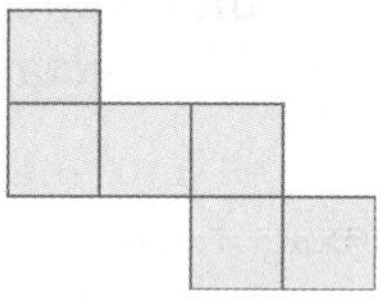

TEST PREP

41. Which three-dimensional figure does the net represent?

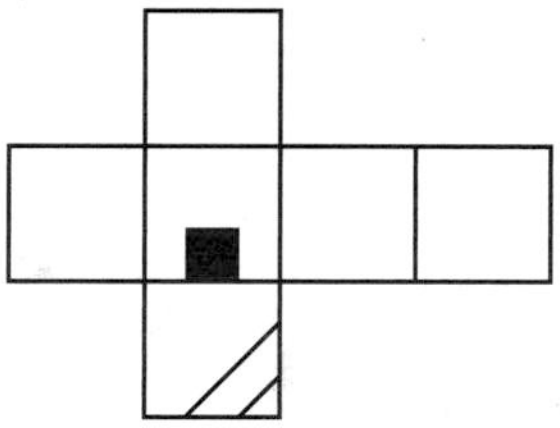

Ⓐ
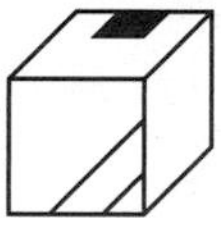

Ⓒ
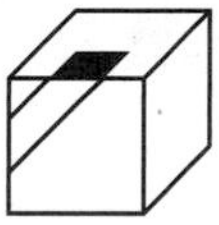

Ⓑ
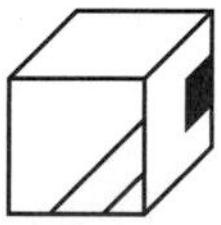

Ⓓ

42. Which shape CANNOT be a face of a hexagonal prism?

Ⓕ triangle
Ⓗ parallelogram
Ⓖ hexagon
Ⓙ rectangle

43. What shape is the cross section formed by a cone and a plane that is perpendicular to the base and that passes through the vertex of the cone?

Ⓐ circle
Ⓒ trapezoid
Ⓑ triangle
Ⓓ rectangle

44. Which shape best represents a hexagonal prism viewed from the top?

Ⓕ
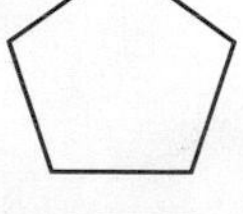

Ⓗ
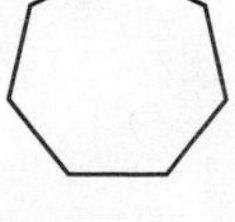

Ⓖ
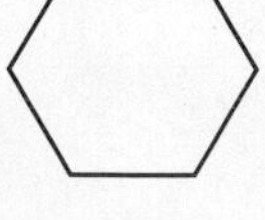

Ⓙ
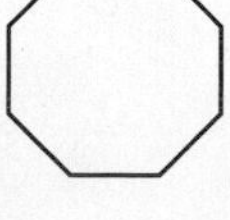

CHALLENGE AND EXTEND

A *double cone* is formed by two cones that share the same vertex. Sketch each cross section formed by a double cone and a plane.

45.

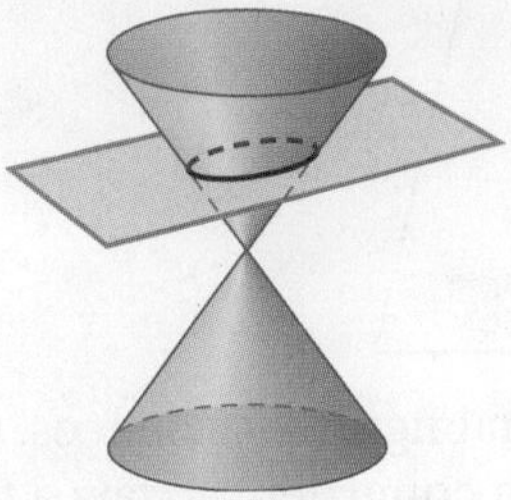

46.

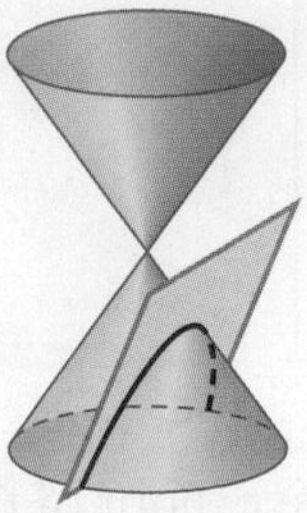

47.

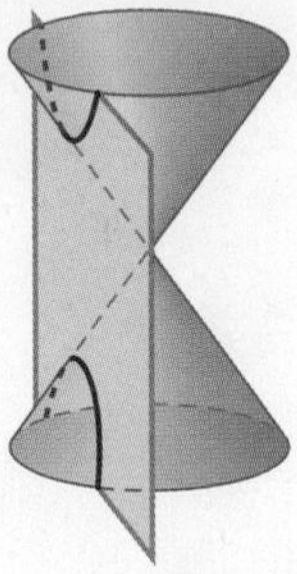

Crafts **Elena is designing patterns for gift boxes. Draw a pattern that she can use to create each box. Be sure to include tabs for gluing the sides together.**

48. a box that is a square pyramid where each triangular face is an isosceles triangle with a height equal to three times the width

49. a box that is a cylinder with the diameter equal to the height

50. a box that is a rectangular prism with a base that is twice as long as it is wide, and with a rectangular pyramid on the top base

51. A net of a prism is shown. The bases of the prism are regular hexagons, and the rectangular faces are all congruent.

a. List all pairs of parallel faces in the prism.

b. Draw a net of a prism with bases that are regular pentagons. How many pairs of parallel faces does the prism have?

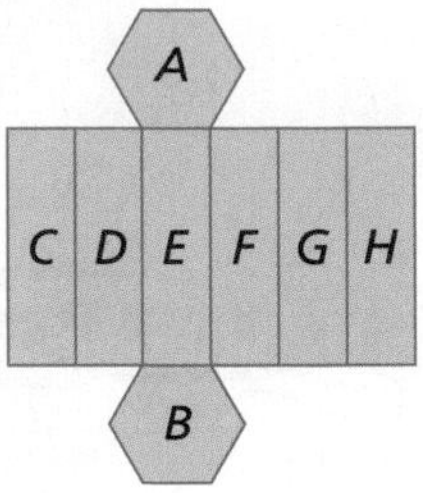

COMMON CORE

11-2 Volume of Prisms and Cylinders

CC.9-12.G.GMD.3 Use volume formulas for cylinders… * *Also* **CC.9-12.G.GMD.1, CC.9-12.G.MG.1*, CC.9-12.G.MG.2***

Objectives
Learn and apply the formula for the volume of a prism.

Learn and apply the formula for the volume of a cylinder.

Vocabulary
volume

Who uses this?

Marine biologists must ensure that aquariums are large enough to accommodate the number of fish inside them. (See Example 2.)

The **volume** of a three-dimensional figure is the number of nonoverlapping unit cubes of a given size that will exactly fill the interior.

A cube built out of 27 unit cubes has a volume of 27 cubic units.

Cavalieri's principle says that if two three-dimensional figures have the same height and have the same cross-sectional area at every level, they have the same volume.

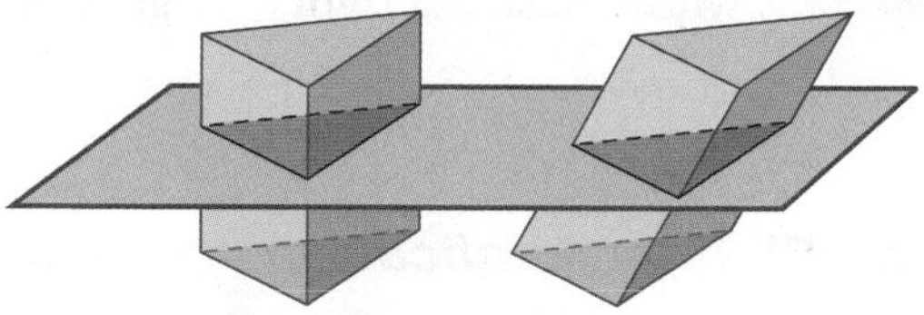

A right prism and an oblique prism with the same base and height have the same volume.

Know it! Note

Volume of a Prism

The volume of a prism with base area B and height h is $V = Bh$.

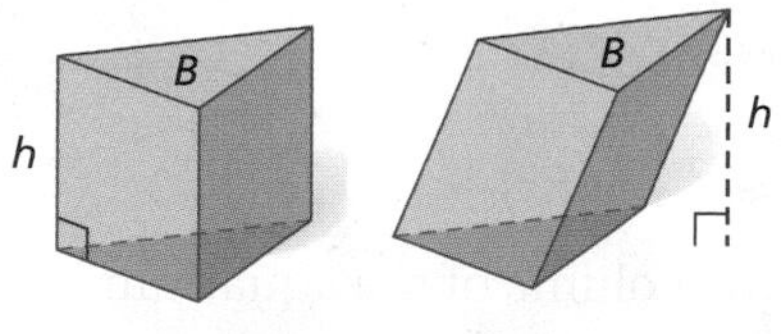

The volume of a right rectangular prism with length ℓ, width w, and height h is $V = \ell wh$.

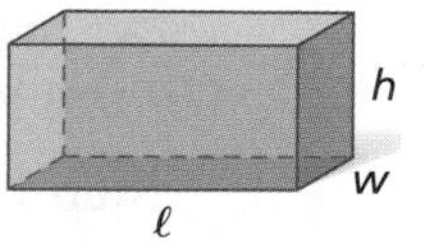

The volume of a cube with edge length s is $V = s^3$.

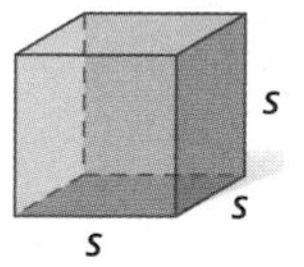

EXAMPLE 1 Finding Volumes of Prisms

Find the volume of each prism. Round to the nearest tenth, if necessary.

A

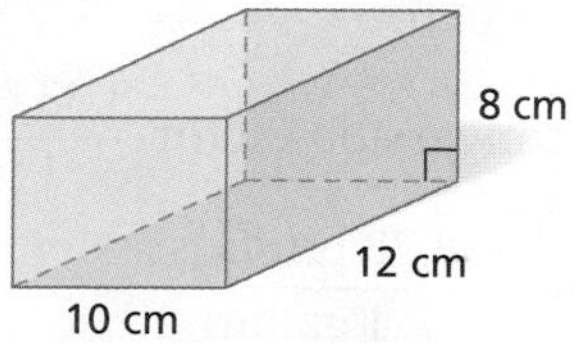

$V = \ell wh$ — *Volume of a right rectangular prism*

$= (10)(12)(8) = 960 \text{ cm}^3$ — *Substitute 10 for ℓ, 12 for w, and 8 for h.*

B **a cube with edge length 10 cm**

$V = s^3$ — *Volume of a cube*

$= 10^3 = 1000 \text{ cm}^3$ — *Substitute 10 for s.*

Find the volume of each prism. Round to the nearest tenth, if necessary.

C **a right regular pentagonal prism with base edge length 5 m and height 7 m**

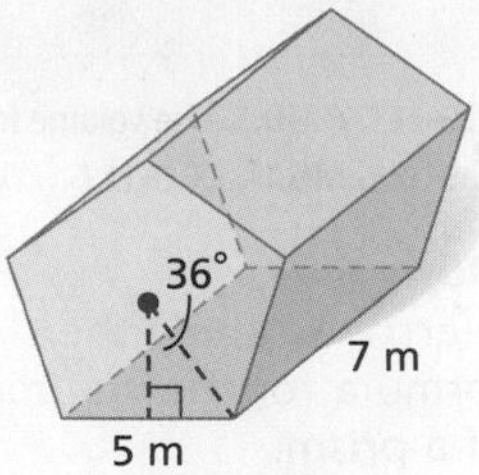

Step 1 Find the apothem a of the base. First draw a right triangle on one base as shown. The measure of the angle with its vertex at the center is $\frac{360°}{10} = 36°$.

$\tan 36° = \frac{2.5}{a}$ *The leg of the triangle is half the side length, or 2.5 m.*

$a = \frac{2.5}{\tan 36°}$ *Solve for a.*

Step 2 Use the value of a to find the base area.

$B = \frac{1}{2}aP = \frac{1}{2}\left(\frac{2.5}{\tan 36°}\right)(25) = \frac{31.25}{\tan 36°}$ *$P = 5(5) = 25$ m*

Step 3 Use the base area to find the volume.

$V = Bh = \frac{31.25}{\tan 36°} \cdot 7 \approx 301.1 \text{ m}^3$

CHECK IT OUT! **1.** Find the volume of a triangular prism with a height of 9 yd whose base is a right triangle with legs 7 yd and 5 yd long.

EXAMPLE 2 *Marine Biology Application*

The aquarium at the right is a rectangular prism. Estimate the volume of the water in the aquarium in gallons. The density of water is about 8.33 pounds per gallon. Estimate the weight of the water in pounds. (*Hint:* 1 gallon $\approx$ 0.134 ft³)

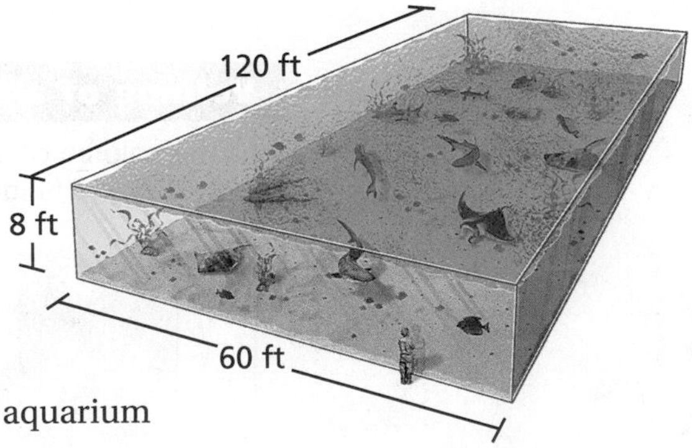

Step 1 Find the volume of the aquarium in cubic feet.

$V = \ell wh = (120)(60)(8) = 57{,}600 \text{ ft}^3$

Step 2 Use the conversion factor $\frac{1 \text{ gallon}}{0.134 \text{ ft}^3}$ to estimate the volume in gallons.

$57,600 \text{ ft}^3 \cdot \frac{1 \text{ gallon}}{0.134 \text{ ft}^3} \approx 429{,}851 \text{ gallons}$ *$\frac{1 \text{ gallon}}{0.134 \text{ ft}^3} = 1$*

Step 3 Use the conversion factor $\frac{8.33 \text{ pounds}}{1 \text{ gallon}}$ to estimate the weight of the water.

$429{,}851 \text{ gallons} \cdot \frac{8.33 \text{ pounds}}{1 \text{ gallon}} \approx 3{,}580{,}659 \text{ pounds}$ *$\frac{8.33 \text{ pounds}}{1 \text{ gallon}} = 1$*

The aquarium holds about 429,851 gallons. The water in the aquarium weighs about 3,580,659 pounds.

CHECK IT OUT! **2. What if...?** Estimate the volume in gallons and the weight of the water in the aquarium above if the height were doubled.

Cavalieri's principle also relates to cylinders. The two stacks have the same number of CDs, so they have the same volume.

Know it! Note

Volume of a Cylinder

The volume of a cylinder with base area B, radius r, and height h is $V = Bh$, or $V = \pi r^2 h$.

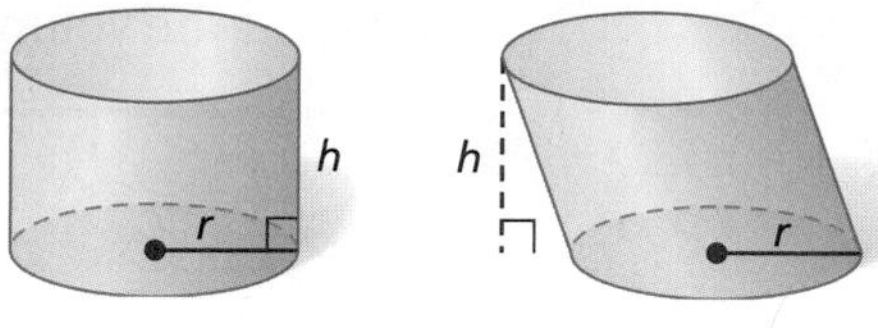

EXAMPLE 3 **Finding Volumes of Cylinders**

Find the volume of each cylinder. Give your answers both in terms of π and rounded to the nearest tenth.

A

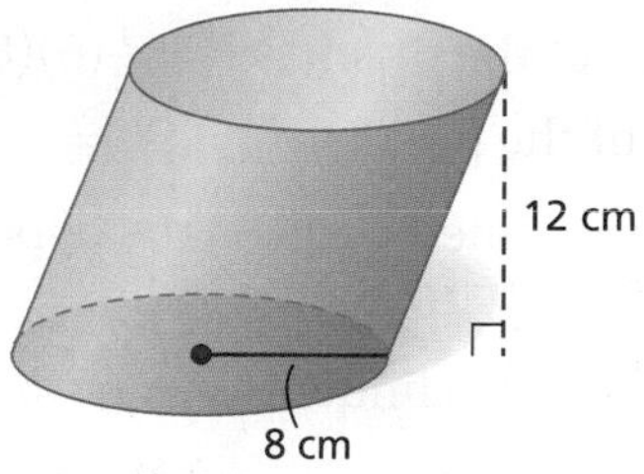

$V = \pi r^2 h$ *Volume of a cylinder*

$= \pi(8)^2(12)$ *Substitute 8 for r and 12 for h.*

$= 768\pi \text{ cm}^3 \approx 2412.7 \text{ cm}^3$

B **a cylinder with a base area of 36π in^2 and a height equal to twice the radius**

Step 1 Use the base area to find the radius.

$\pi r^2 = 36\pi$ *Substitute 36π for the base area.*

$r = 6$ *Solve for r.*

Step 2 Use the radius to find the height. The height is equal to twice the radius.

$h = 2r$

$= 2(6) = 12$ cm

Step 3 Use the radius and height to find the volume.

$V = \pi r^2 h$ *Volume of a cylinder*

$= \pi(6)^2(12) = 432\pi \text{ in}^3$ *Substitute 6 for r and 12 for h.*

$\approx 1357.2 \text{ in}^3$

CHECK IT OUT! **3.** Find the volume of a cylinder with a diameter of 16 in. and a height of 17 in. Give your answer both in terms of π and rounded to the nearest tenth.

EXAMPLE 4 Exploring Effects of Changing Dimensions

The radius and height of the cylinder are multiplied by $\frac{1}{2}$. Describe the effect on the volume.

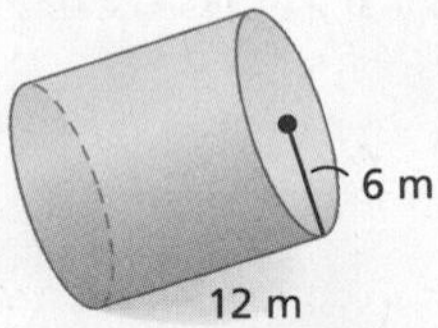

original dimensions:	radius and height multiplied by $\frac{1}{2}$:
$V = \pi r^2 h$	$V = \pi r^2 h$
$= \pi(6)^2(12)$	$= \pi(3)^2(6)$
$= 432\pi \text{ m}^3$	$= 54\pi \text{ m}^3$

Notice that $54\pi = \frac{1}{8}(432\pi)$. If the radius and height are multiplied by $\frac{1}{2}$, the volume is multiplied by $\left(\frac{1}{2}\right)^3$, or $\frac{1}{8}$.

CHECK IT OUT! **4.** The length, width, and height of the prism are doubled. Describe the effect on the volume.

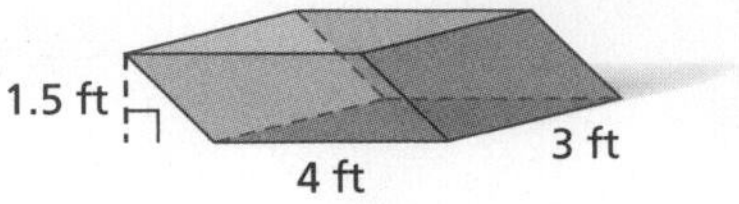

EXAMPLE 5 Finding Volumes of Composite Three-Dimensional Figures

Find the volume of the composite figure. Round to the nearest tenth.

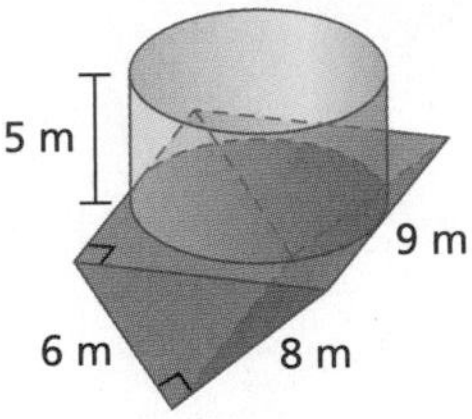

The base area of the prism is $B = \frac{1}{2}(6)(8) = 24 \text{ m}^2$.

The volume of the prism is $V = Bh = 24(9) = 216 \text{ m}^3$.

The cylinder's diameter equals the hypotenuse of the prism's base, 10 m. So the radius is 5 m.

The volume of the cylinder is $V = \pi r^2 h = \pi(5)^2(5) = 125\pi \text{ m}^3$.

The total volume of the figure is the sum of the volumes.
$V = 216 + 125\pi \approx 608.7 \text{ m}^3$

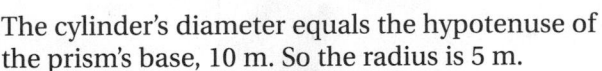

CHECK IT OUT! **5.** Find the volume of the composite figure. Round to the nearest tenth.

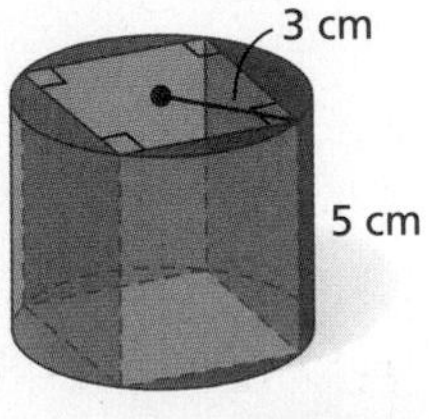

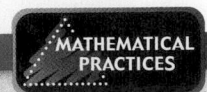

MATHEMATICAL PRACTICES

THINK AND DISCUSS

1. Compare the formula for the volume of a prism with the formula for the volume of a cylinder.

2. Explain how Cavalieri's principle relates to the formula for the volume of an oblique prism.

Know it! Note

3. GET ORGANIZED Copy and complete the graphic organizer. In each box, write the formula for the volume.

Shape	Volume
Prism	
Cube	
Cylinder	

11-2 Exercises

Learn It Online
Homework Help Online
Parent Resources Online

GUIDED PRACTICE

1. **Vocabulary** In a right cylinder, the *altitude* is ___?___ the axis. (*longer than*, *shorter than*, or *the same length as*)

SEE EXAMPLE 1

Find the volume of each prism.

2.

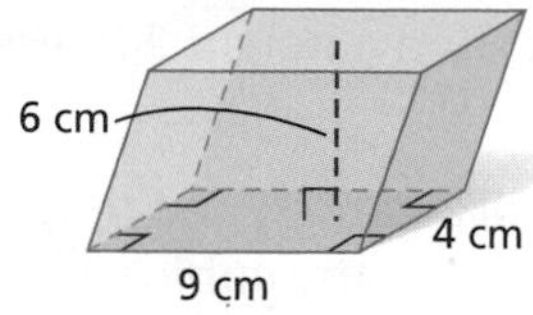

3.

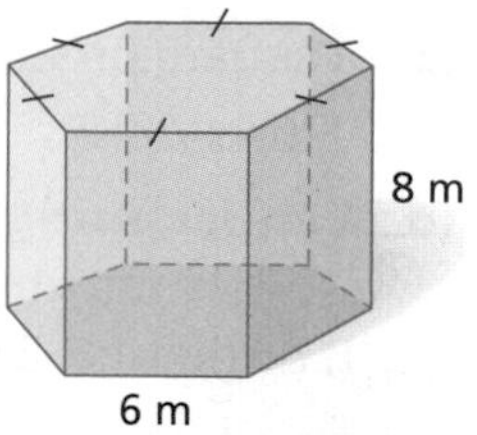

4. a cube with edge length 8 ft

SEE EXAMPLE 2

5. **Food** The world's largest ice cream cake, built in New York City on May 25, 2004, was approximately a 19 ft by 9 ft by 2 ft rectangular prism. Estimate the volume of the ice cream cake in gallons. If the density of the ice cream was 4.73 pounds per gallon, estimate the weight of the cake. (*Hint:* 1 gallon $\approx$ 0.134 cubic feet)

SEE EXAMPLE 3

Find the volume of each cylinder. Give your answers both in terms of π and rounded to the nearest tenth.

6.

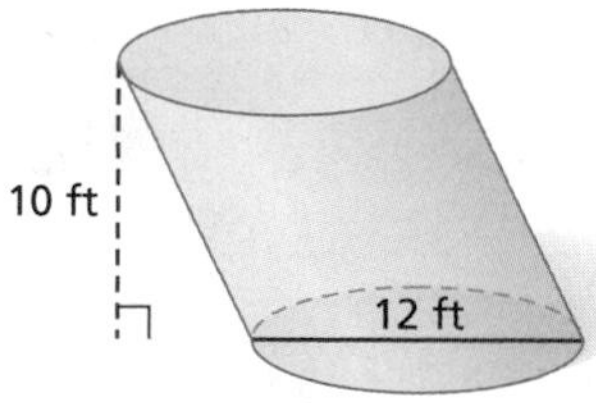

7.

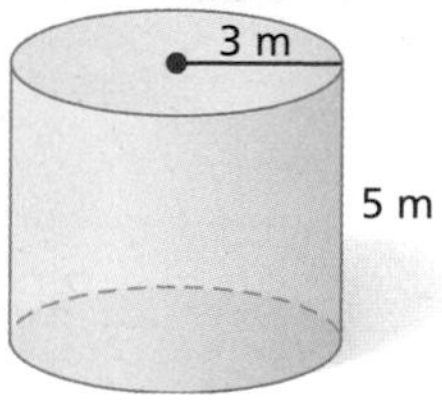

8. a cylinder with base area 25π cm^2 and height 3 cm more than the radius

SEE EXAMPLE 4

Describe the effect of each change on the volume of the given figure.

9. The dimensions are multiplied by $\frac{1}{4}$.

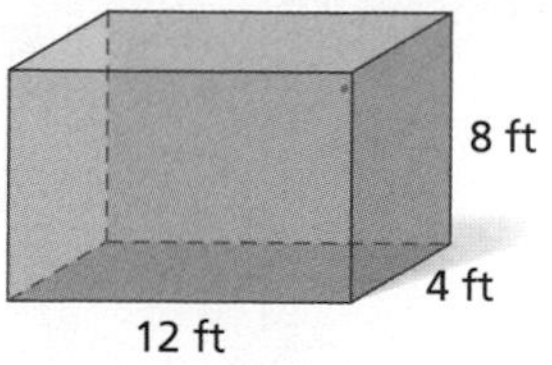

10. The dimensions are tripled.

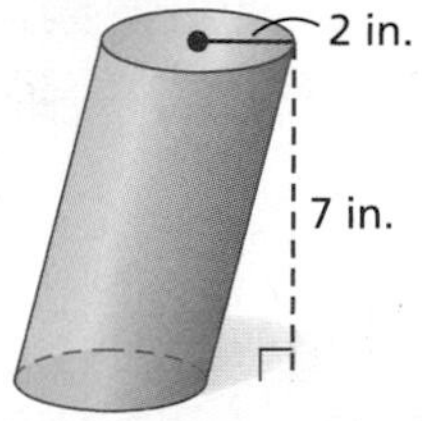

SEE EXAMPLE 5

Find the volume of each composite figure. Round to the nearest tenth.

11.

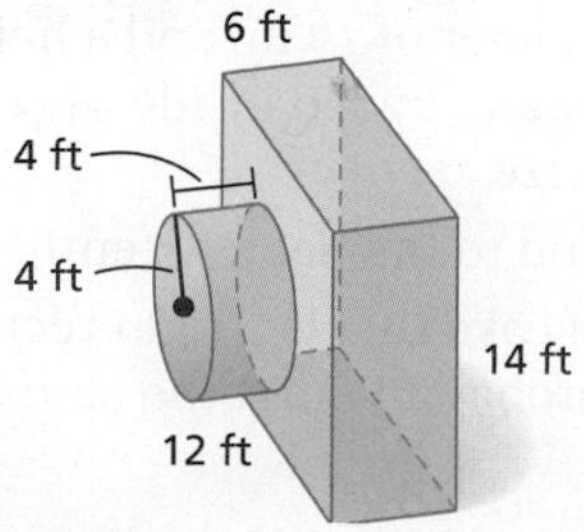

12.

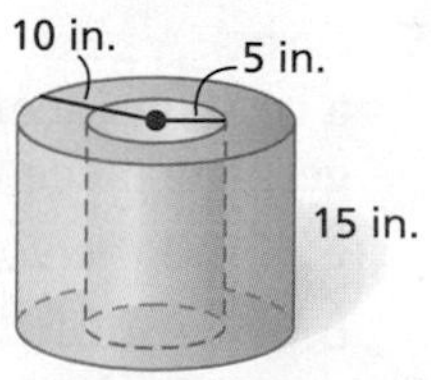

PRACTICE AND PROBLEM SOLVING

Independent Practice

For Exercises	See Example
13–15	1
16	2
17–19	3
20–21	4
22–23	5

Extra Practice

See Extra Practice for more Skills Practice and Applications Practice exercises.

Find the volume of each prism.

13.

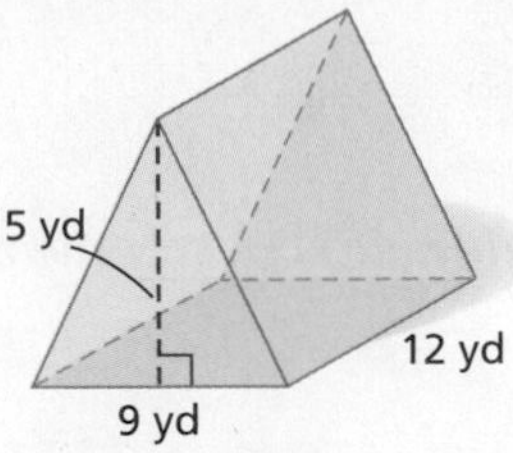

14.

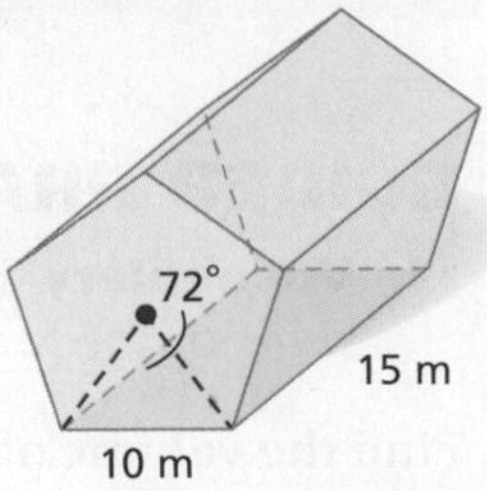

15. a square prism with a base area of 49 ft^2 and a height 2 ft less than the base edge length

16. **Landscaping** Colin is buying dirt to fill a garden bed that is a 9 ft by 16 ft rectangle. If he wants to fill it to a depth of 4 in., how many cubic yards of dirt does he need? If dirt costs \$25 per yd^3, how much will the project cost? (*Hint:* 1 yd^3 = 27 ft^3)

Find the volume of each cylinder. Give your answers both in terms of π and rounded to the nearest tenth.

17.

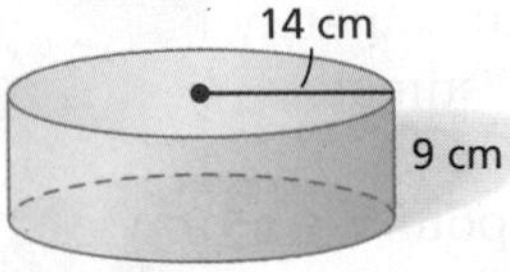

18.

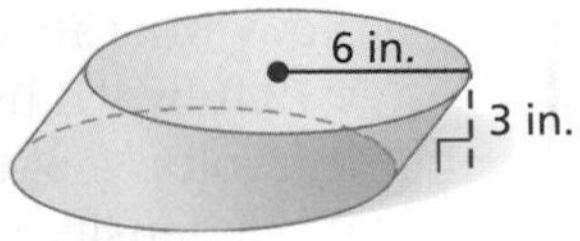

19. a cylinder with base area 24π cm^2 and height 16 cm

Describe the effect of each change on the volume of the given figure.

20. The dimensions are multiplied by 5.

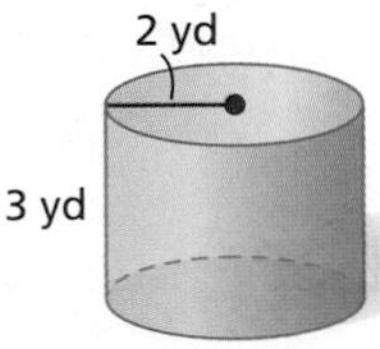

21. The dimensions are multiplied by $\frac{3}{5}$.

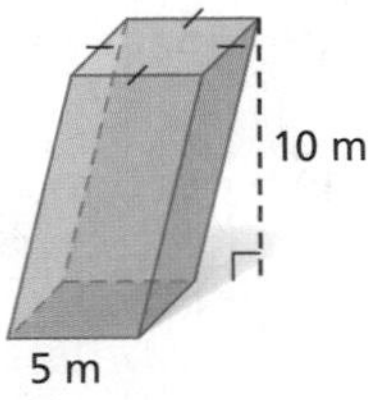

Find the volume of each composite figure.

22.

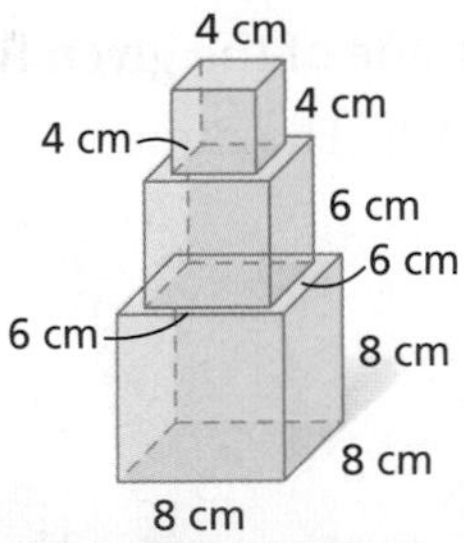

23.

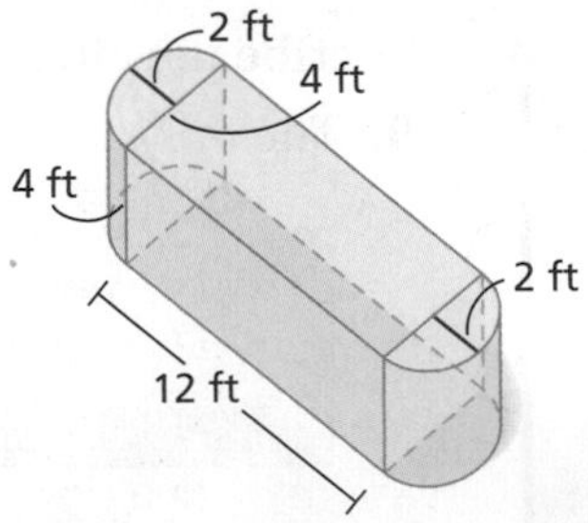

24. One cup is equal to 14.4375 in^3. If a 1 c cylindrical measuring cup has a radius of 2 in., what is its height? If the radius is 1.5 in., what is its height?

25. **Food** A cake is a cylinder with a diameter of 10 in. and a height of 3 in. For a party, a coin has been mixed into the batter and baked inside the cake. The person who gets the piece with the coin wins a prize.

a. Find the volume of the cake. Round to the nearest tenth.

b. **Probability** Keka gets a piece of cake that is a right rectangular prism with a 3 in. by 1 in. base. What is the probability that the coin is in her piece? Round to the nearest hundredth.

MULTI-STEP TEST PREP

26. A cylindrical juice container with a 3 in. diameter has a hole for a straw that is 1 in. from the side. Up to 5 in. of a straw can be inserted.
   a. Find the height h of the container to the nearest tenth.
   b. Find the volume of the container to the nearest tenth.
   c. How many ounces of juice does the container hold? (*Hint:* 1 in^3 $\approx$ 0.55 oz)

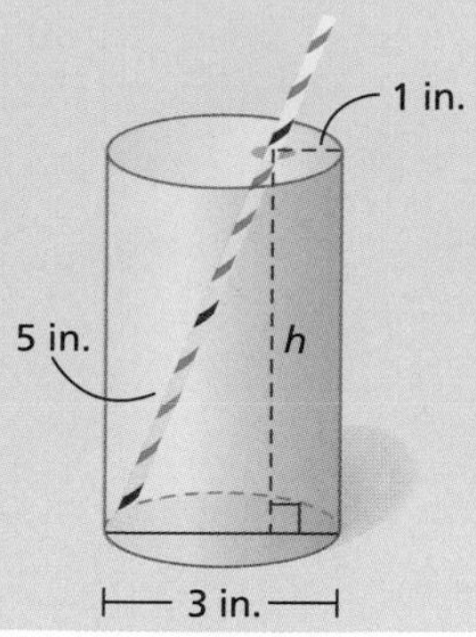

27. Find the height of a rectangular prism with length 5 ft, width 9 ft, and volume 495 ft^3.

28. Find the area of the base of a rectangular prism with volume 360 in^3 and height 9 in.

29. Find the volume of a cylinder with surface area 210π m^2 and height 8 m.

30. Find the volume of a rectangular prism with vertices $(0, 0, 0)$, $(0, 3, 0)$, $(7, 0, 0)$, $(7, 3, 0)$, $(0, 0, 6)$, $(0, 3, 6)$, $(7, 0, 6)$, and $(7, 3, 6)$.

31. You can use *displacement* to find the volume of an irregular object, such as a stone. Suppose the tank shown is filled with water to a depth of 8 in. A stone is placed in the tank so that it is completely covered, causing the water level to rise by 2 in. Find the volume of the stone.

32. **Food** A 1 in. cube of cheese is one serving. How many servings are in a 4 in. by 4 in. by $\frac{1}{4}$ in. slice?

33. **History** In 1919, a cylindrical tank containing molasses burst and flooded the city of Boston, Massachusetts. The tank had a 90 ft diameter and a height of 52 ft. How many gallons of molasses were in the tank? (*Hint:* 1 gal $\approx$ 0.134 ft^3)

34. **Meteorology** If 3 in. of rain fall on the property shown, what is the volume in cubic feet? In gallons? The density of water is 8.33 pounds per gallon. What is the weight of the rain in pounds? (*Hint:* 1 gal $\approx$ 0.134 ft^3)

35. **Critical Thinking** The dimensions of a prism with volume V and surface area S are multiplied by a scale factor of k to form a similar prism. Make a conjecture about the ratio of the surface area of the new prism to its volume. Test your conjecture using a cube with an edge length of 1 and a scale factor of 2.

36. **Write About It** How can you change the edge length of a cube so that its volume is doubled?

LINK

Math History

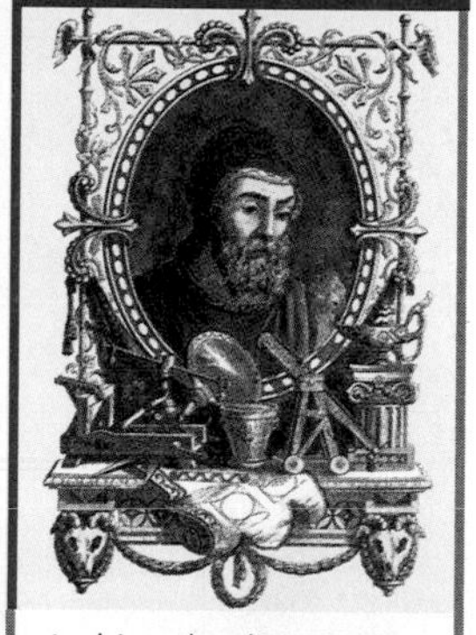

Archimedes (287–212 B.C.E.) used displacement to find the volume of a gold crown. He discovered that the goldsmith had cheated the king by substituting an equal weight of silver for part of the gold.

TEST PREP

37. Abigail has a cylindrical candle mold with the dimensions shown. If Abigail has a rectangular block of wax measuring 15 cm by 12 cm by 18 cm, about how many candles can she make after melting the block of wax?

   Ⓐ 14 Ⓑ 31 Ⓒ 35 Ⓓ 76

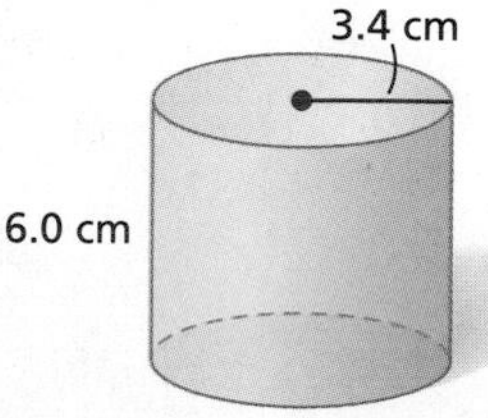

38. A 96-inch piece of wire was cut into equal segments that were then connected to form the edges of a cube. What is the volume of the cube?

Ⓕ 512 in^3 Ⓖ 576 in^3 Ⓗ 729 in^3 Ⓙ 1728 in^3

39. One juice container is a rectangular prism with a height of 9 in. and a 3 in. by 3 in. square base. Another juice container is a cylinder with a radius of 1.75 in. and a height of 9 in. Which best describes the relationship between the two containers?

Ⓐ The prism has the greater volume.
Ⓑ The cylinder has the greater volume.
Ⓒ The volumes are equivalent.
Ⓓ The volumes cannot be determined.

40. What is the volume of the three-dimensional object with the dimensions shown in the three views below?

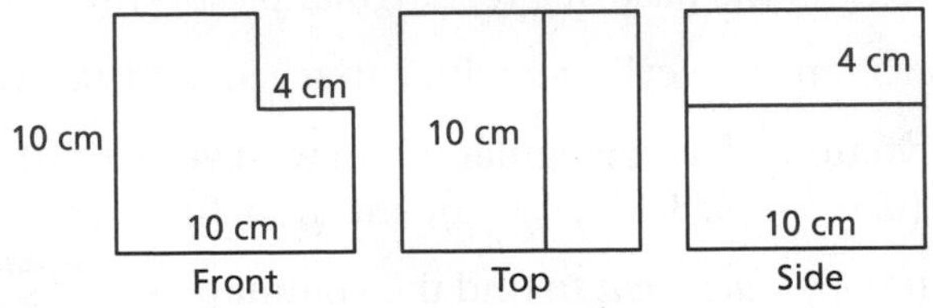

Ⓕ 160 cm^3 Ⓖ 240 cm^3 Ⓗ 840 cm^3 Ⓙ 1000 cm^3

CHALLENGE AND EXTEND

Algebra **Find the volume of each three-dimensional figure in terms of *x*.**

41.

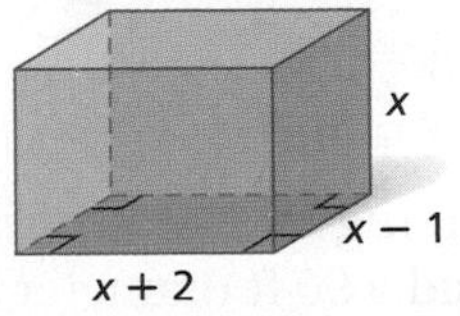

42.

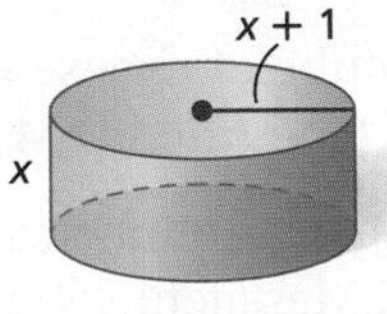

43.

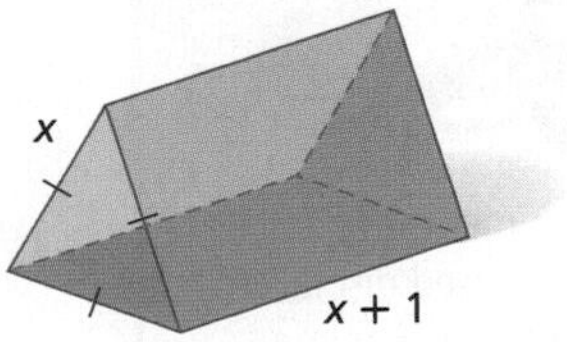

44. The volume in cubic units of a cylinder is equal to its surface area in square units. Prove that the radius and height must both be greater than 2.

COMMON CORE

11-3 Volume of Pyramids and Cones

CC.9-12.G.GMD.3 Use volume formulas for…pyramids, cones…to solve problems.*
Also **CC.9-12.G.GMD.1**

Objectives

Learn and apply the formula for the volume of a pyramid.

Learn and apply the formula for the volume of a cone.

Who uses this?

The builders of the Rainforest Pyramid in Galveston, Texas, needed to calculate the volume of the pyramid to plan the climate control system. (See Example 2.)

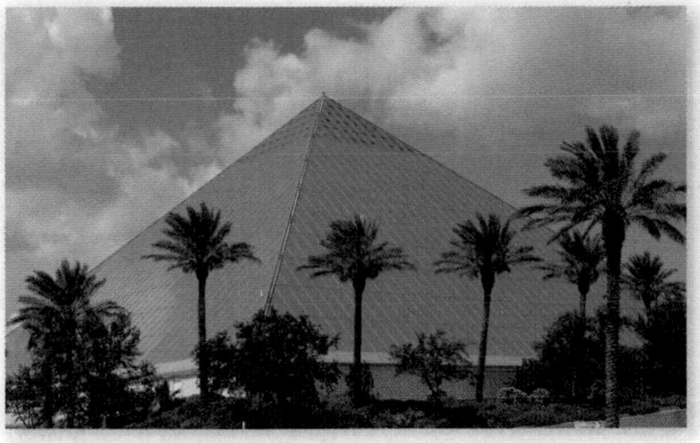

The volume of a pyramid is related to the volume of a prism with the same base and height. The relationship can be verified by dividing a cube into three congruent square pyramids, as shown.

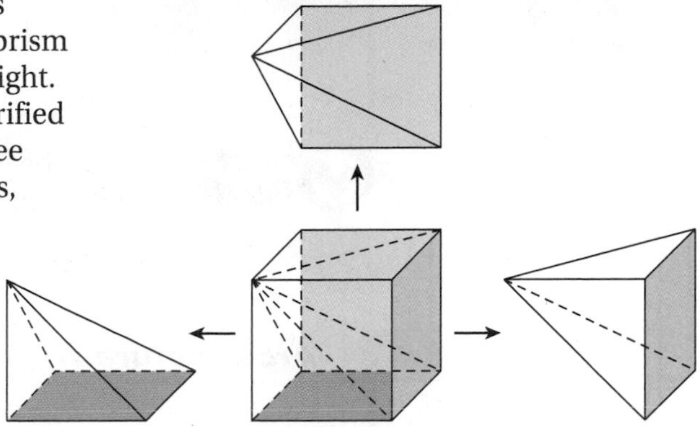

The square pyramids are congruent, so they have the same volume. The volume of each pyramid is one third the volume of the cube.

Know it! Note

Volume of a Pyramid

The volume of a pyramid with base area B and height h is $V = \frac{1}{3}Bh$.

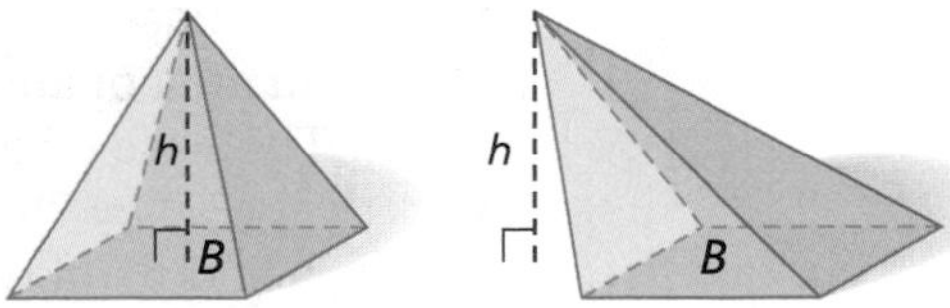

EXAMPLE 1 **Finding Volumes of Pyramids**

Find the volume of each pyramid.

A **a rectangular pyramid with length 7 ft, width 9 ft, and height 12 ft**

$$V = \frac{1}{3}Bh = \frac{1}{3}(7 \cdot 9)(12) = 252 \text{ ft}^3$$

B **the square pyramid**

The base is a square with a side length of 4 in., and the height is 6 in.

$$V = \frac{1}{3}Bh = \frac{1}{3}(4^2)(6) = 32 \text{ in}^3$$

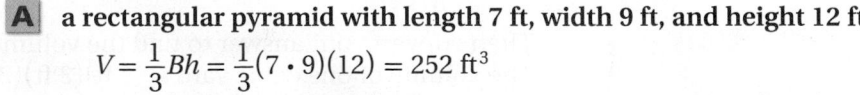

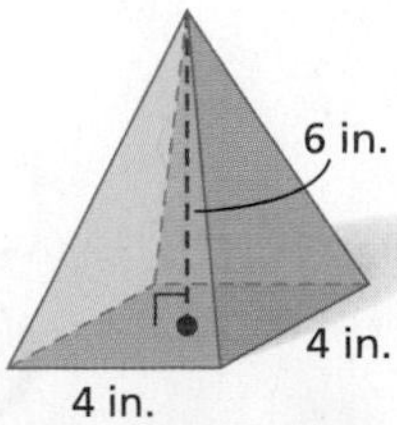

Find the volume of the pyramid.

C **the trapezoidal pyramid with base $ABCD$, where $\overline{AB} \parallel \overline{CD}$ and $\overline{AE} \perp$ plane ABC**

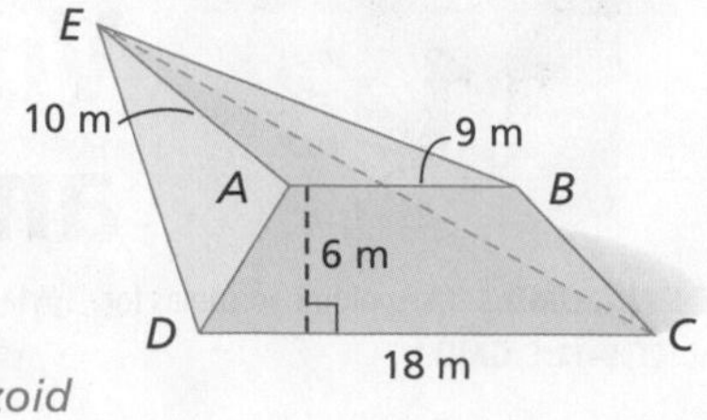

Step 1 Find the area of the base.

$B = \frac{1}{2}(b_1 + b_2)h$ — *Area of a trapezoid*

$= \frac{1}{2}(9 + 18)6$ — *Substitute 9 for b_1, 18 for b_2, and 6 for h.*

$= 81 \text{ m}^2$ — *Simplify.*

Step 2 Use the base area and the height to find the volume. Because $\overline{AE} \perp$ plane ABC, $\overline{AE}$ is the altitude, so the height is equal to AE.

$V = \frac{1}{3}Bh$ — *Volume of a pyramid*

$= \frac{1}{3}(81)(10)$ — *Substitute 81 for B and 10 for h.*

$= 270 \text{ m}^3$

CHECK IT OUT! **1.** Find the volume of a regular hexagonal pyramid with a base edge length of 2 cm and a height equal to the area of the base.

EXAMPLE 2 *Architecture Application*

The Rainforest Pyramid in Galveston, Texas, is a square pyramid with a base area of about 1 acre and a height of 10 stories. Estimate the volume in cubic yards and in cubic feet. (*Hint:* 1 acre = 4840 yd², 1 story ≈ 10 ft)

The base is a square with an area of about 4840 yd². The base edge length is $\sqrt{4840} \approx 70$ yd. The height is about $10(10) = 100$ ft, or about 33 yd.

First find the volume in cubic yards.

$V = \frac{1}{3}Bh$ — *Volume of a regular pyramid*

$= \frac{1}{3}(70^2)(33) = 53{,}900 \text{ yd}^3$ — *Substitute 70^2 for B and 33 for h.*

Then convert your answer to find the volume in cubic feet. The volume of one cubic yard is $(3 \text{ ft})(3 \text{ ft})(3 \text{ ft}) = 27 \text{ ft}^3$. Use the conversion factor $\frac{27 \text{ ft}^3}{1 \text{ yd}^3}$ to find the volume in cubic feet.

$$53{,}900 \text{ yd}^3 \cdot \frac{27 \text{ ft}^3}{1 \text{ yd}^3} \approx 1{,}455{,}300 \text{ ft}^3$$

CHECK IT OUT! **2. What if...?** What would be the volume of the Rainforest Pyramid if the height were doubled?

Know it! Note

Volume of Cones

The volume of a cone with base area B, radius r, and height h is $V = \frac{1}{3}Bh$, or $V = \frac{1}{3}\pi r^2 h$.

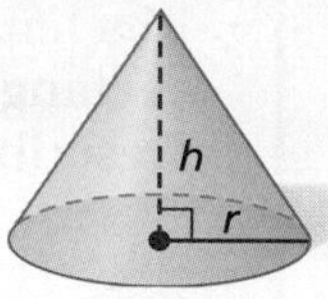

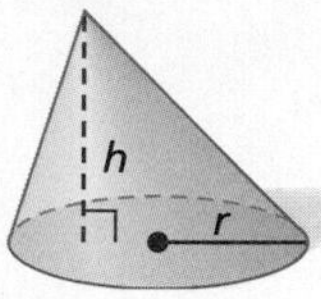

EXAMPLE 3 Finding Volumes of Cones

Find the volume of each cone. Give your answers both in terms of π and rounded to the nearest tenth.

A **a cone with radius 5 cm and height 12 cm**

$V = \frac{1}{3}\pi r^2 h$ *Volume of a cone*

$= \frac{1}{3}\pi(5)^2(12)$ *Substitute 5 for r and 12 for h.*

$= 100\pi \text{ cm}^3 \approx 314.2 \text{ cm}^3$ *Simplify.*

B **a cone with a base circumference of 21π cm and a height 3 cm less than twice the radius**

Step 1 Use the circumference to find the radius.

$2\pi r = 21\pi$ *Substitute 21π for C.*

$r = 10.5$ cm *Divide both sides by 2π.*

Step 2 Use the radius to find the height.

$2(10.5) - 3 = 18$ cm *The height is 3 cm less than twice the radius.*

Step 3 Use the radius and height to find the volume.

$V = \frac{1}{3}\pi r^2 h$ *Volume of a cone*

$= \frac{1}{3}\pi(10.5)^2(18)$ *Substitute 10.5 for r and 18 for h.*

$= 661.5\pi \text{ cm}^3 \approx 2078.2 \text{ cm}^3$ *Simplify.*

C

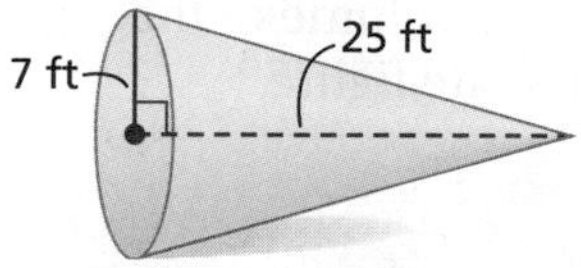

Step 1 Use the Pythagorean Theorem to find the height.

$7^2 + h^2 = 25^2$ *Pythagorean Theorem*

$h^2 = 576$ *Subtract 7^2 from both sides.*

$h = 24$ *Take the square root of both sides.*

Step 2 Use the radius and height to find the volume.

$V = \frac{1}{3}\pi r^2 h$ *Volume of a cone*

$= \frac{1}{3}\pi(7)^2(24)$ *Substitute 7 for r and 24 for h.*

$= 392\pi \text{ ft}^3 \approx 1231.5 \text{ ft}^3$ *Simplify.*

CHECK IT OUT!

3. Find the volume of the cone.

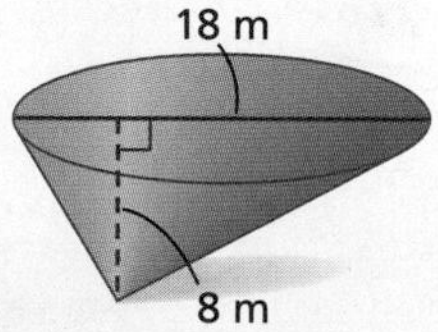

EXAMPLE 4 Exploring Effects of Changing Dimensions

The length, width, and height of the rectangular pyramid are multiplied by $\frac{1}{4}$. Describe the effect on the volume.

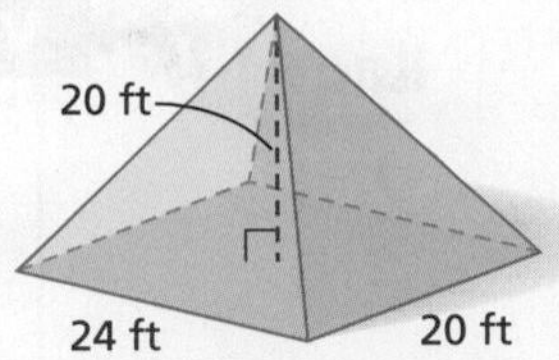

original dimensions:

$$V = \frac{1}{3}Bh$$
$$= \frac{1}{3}(24 \cdot 20)(20)$$
$$= 3200 \text{ ft}^3$$

length, width, and height multiplied by $\frac{1}{4}$:

$$V = \frac{1}{3}Bh$$
$$= \frac{1}{3}(6 \cdot 5)(5)$$
$$= 50 \text{ ft}^3$$

Notice that $50 = \frac{1}{64}(3200)$. If the length, width, and height are multiplied by $\frac{1}{4}$, the volume is multiplied by $\left(\frac{1}{4}\right)^3$, or $\frac{1}{64}$.

CHECK IT OUT! 4. The radius and height of the cone are doubled. Describe the effect on the volume.

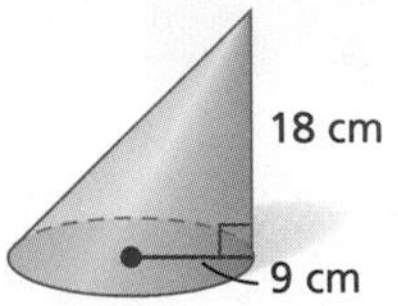

EXAMPLE 5 Finding Volumes of Composite Three-Dimensional Figures

Find the volume of the composite figure. Round to the nearest tenth.

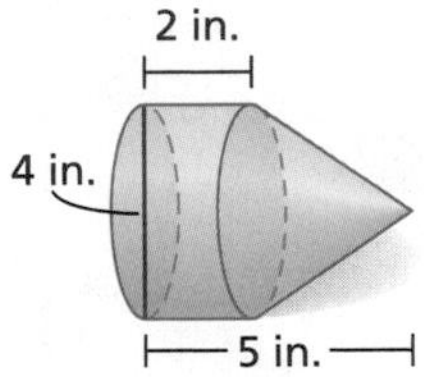

The volume of the cylinder is
$V = \pi r^2 h = \pi(2)^2(2) = 8\pi \text{ in}^3$.

The volume of the cone is
$V = \frac{1}{3}\pi r^2 h = \frac{1}{3}\pi(2)^2(3) = 4\pi \text{ in}^3$.

The volume of the composite figure is the sum of the volumes.
$V = 8\pi + 4\pi = 12\pi \text{ in}^3 \approx 37.7 \text{ in}^3$

CHECK IT OUT! 5. Find the volume of the composite figure.

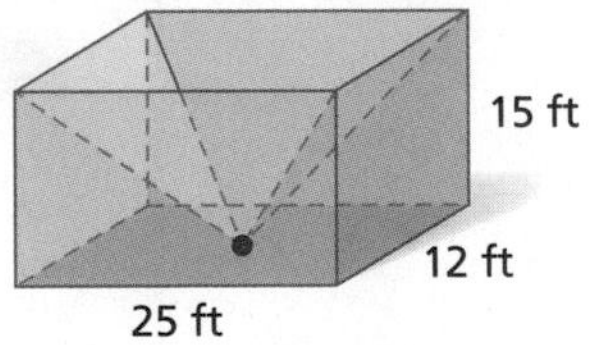

MATHEMATICAL PRACTICES

THINK AND DISCUSS

1. Explain how the volume of a pyramid is related to the volume of a prism with the same base and height.

Know it! Note

2. **GET ORGANIZED** Copy and complete the graphic organizer.

Volumes of Three-Dimensional Figures		
Formula	$V = Bh$	$V = \frac{1}{3}Bh$
Shapes		
Examples		

11-3 Exercises

Learn It Online
Homework Help Online
Parent Resources Online

GUIDED PRACTICE

1. **Vocabulary** The *altitude* of a pyramid is ___?___ to the base. (*perpendicular, parallel,* or *oblique*)

SEE EXAMPLE 1

Find the volume of each pyramid. Round to the nearest tenth, if necessary.

2. 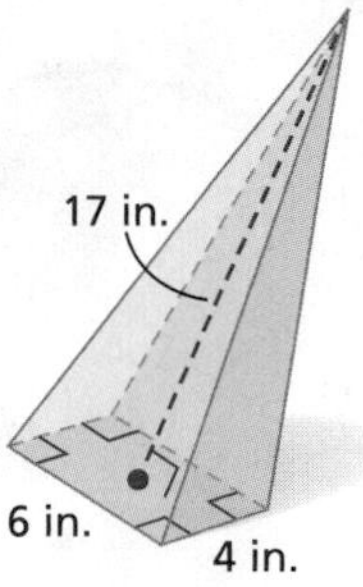

3. 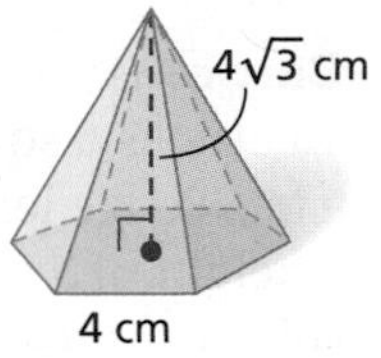

4. a hexagonal pyramid with a base area of 25 ft^2 and a height of 9 ft

SEE EXAMPLE 2

5. **Geology** A crystal is cut into the shape formed by two square pyramids joined at the base. Each pyramid has a base edge length of 5.7 mm and a height of 3 mm. What is the volume to the nearest cubic millimeter of the crystal?

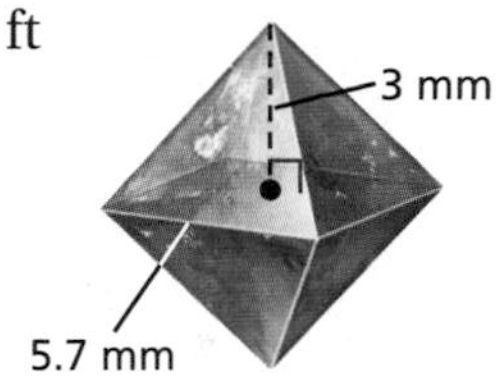

SEE EXAMPLE 3

Find the volume of each cone. Give your answers both in terms of π and rounded to the nearest tenth.

6. 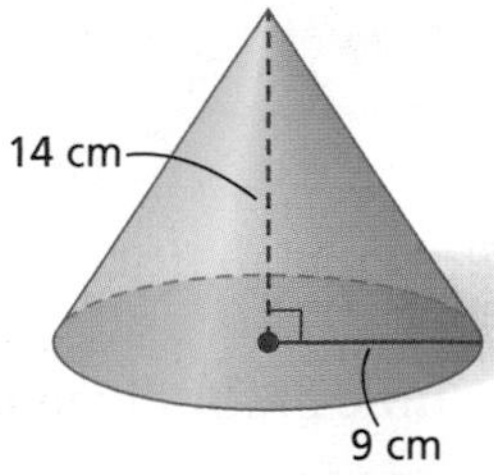

7. 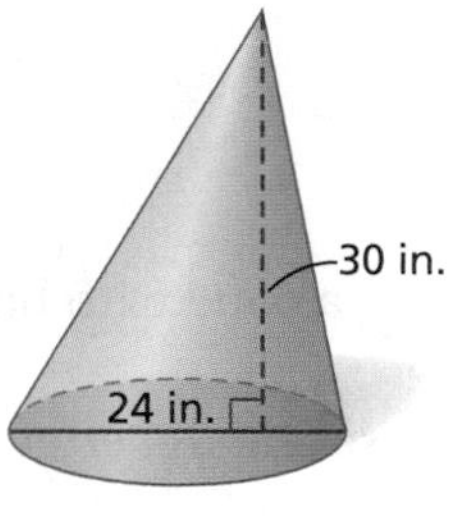

8. a cone with radius 12 m and height 20 m

SEE EXAMPLE 4

Describe the effect of each change on the volume of the given figure.

9. The dimensions are tripled.

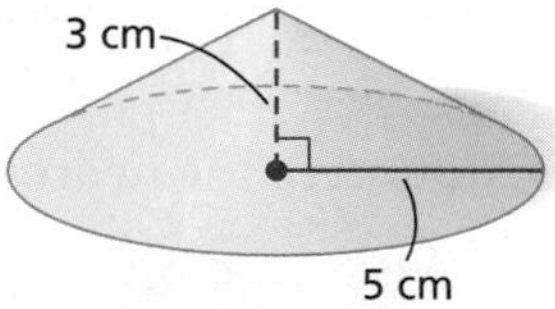

10. The dimensions are multiplied by $\frac{1}{2}$.

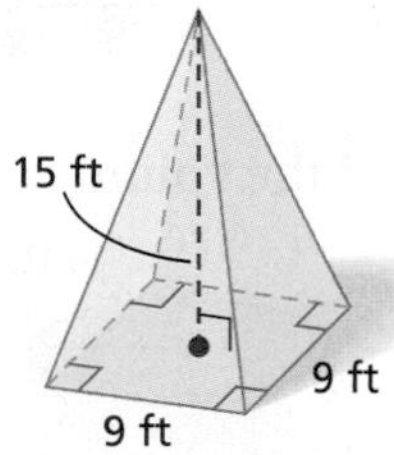

SEE EXAMPLE 5

Find the volume of each composite figure. Round to the nearest tenth, if necessary.

11. 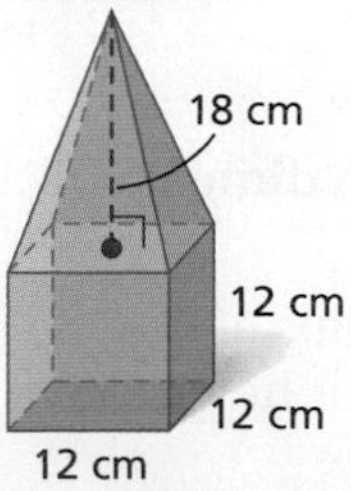

12. 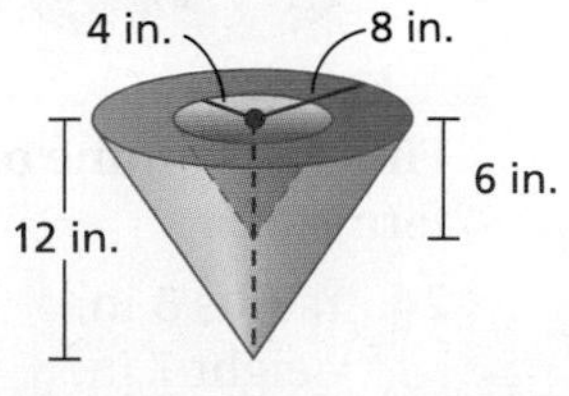

PRACTICE AND PROBLEM SOLVING

Independent Practice

For Exercises	See Example
13–15	1
16	2
17–19	3
20–21	4
22–23	5

Extra Practice

See Extra Practice for more Skills Practice and Applications Practice exercises.

Find the volume of each pyramid. Round to the nearest tenth, if necessary.

13.

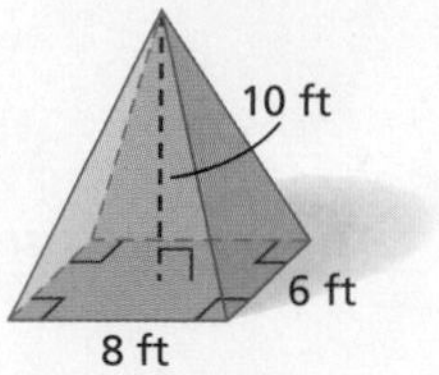

14.

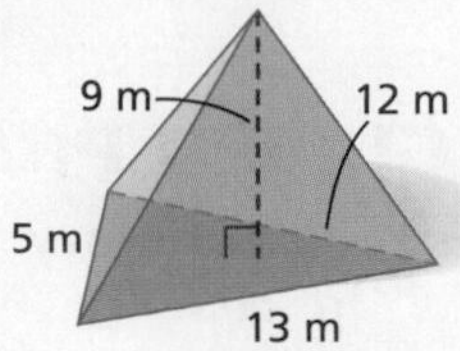

15. a regular square pyramid with base edge length 12 ft and slant height 10 ft

16. Carpentry A roof that encloses an attic is a square pyramid with a base edge length of 45 feet and a height of 5 yards. What is the volume of the attic in cubic feet? In cubic yards?

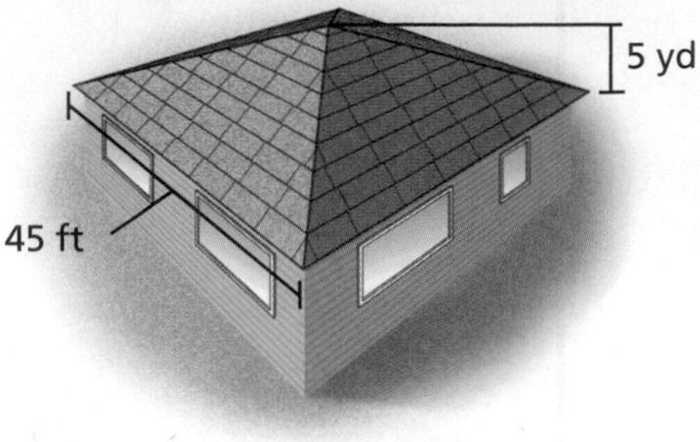

Find the volume of each cone. Give your answers both in terms of π and rounded to the nearest tenth.

17.

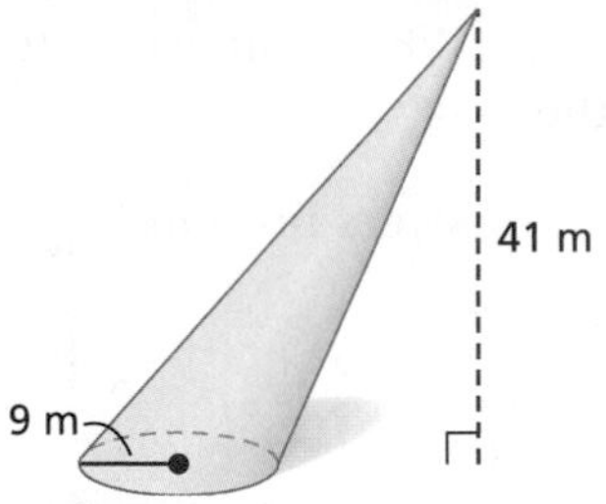

18.

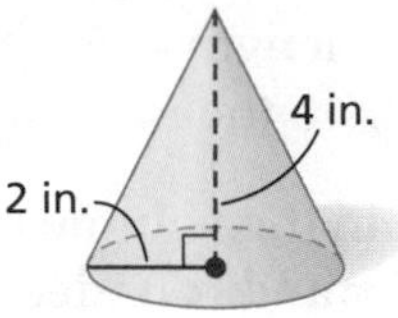

19. a cone with base area 36π ft^2 and a height equal to twice the radius

Describe the effect of each change on the volume of the given figure.

20. The dimensions are multiplied by $\frac{1}{3}$.

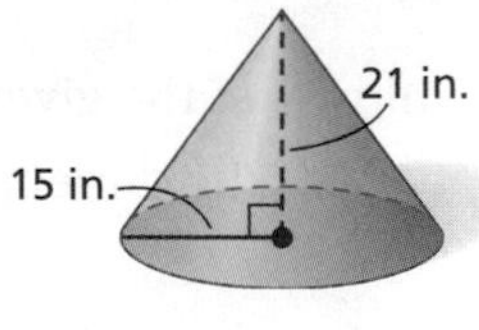

21. The dimensions are multiplied by 6.

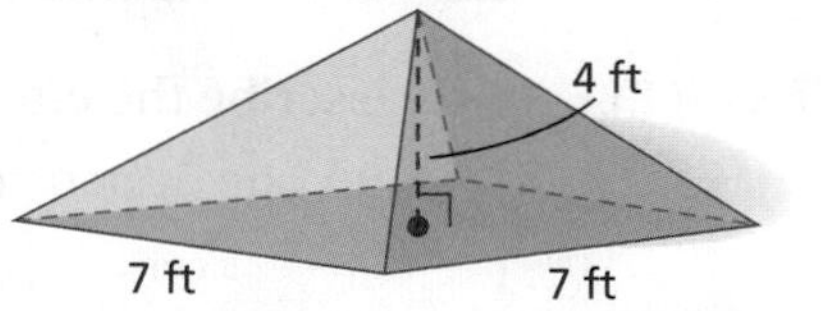

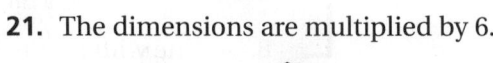

Find the volume of each composite figure. Round to the nearest tenth, if necessary.

22.

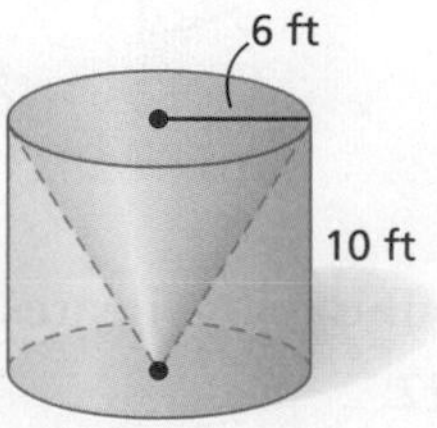

23.

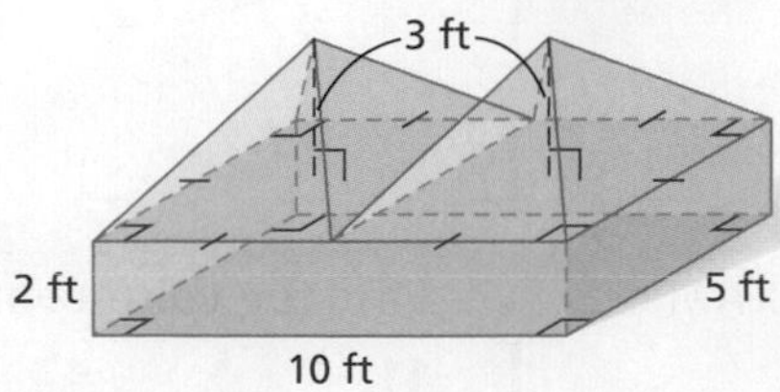

Find the volume of each right cone with the given dimensions. Give your answers in terms of π.

24. radius 3 in.
height 7 in.

25. diameter 5 m
height 2 m

26. radius 28 ft
slant height 53 ft

27. diameter 24 cm
slant height 13 cm

Find the volume of each regular pyramid with the given dimensions. Round to the nearest tenth, if necessary.

	Number of sides of base	Base edge length	Height	Volume
28.	3	10 ft	6 ft	
29.	4	15 m	18 m	
30.	5	9 in.	12 in.	
31.	6	8 cm	3 cm	

32. Find the height of a rectangular pyramid with length 3 m, width 8 m, and volume 112 m^3.

33. Find the base circumference of a cone with height 5 cm and volume 125π cm^3.

34. Find the volume of a cone with slant height 10 ft and height 8 ft.

35. Find the volume of a square pyramid with slant height 17 in. and surface area 800 in^2.

36. Find the surface area of a cone with height 20 yd and volume 1500π yd^3.

37. Find the volume of a triangular pyramid with vertices $(0, 0, 0)$, $(5, 0, 0)$, $(0, 3, 0)$, and $(0, 0, 7)$.

38. ///ERROR ANALYSIS/// Which volume is incorrect? Explain the error.

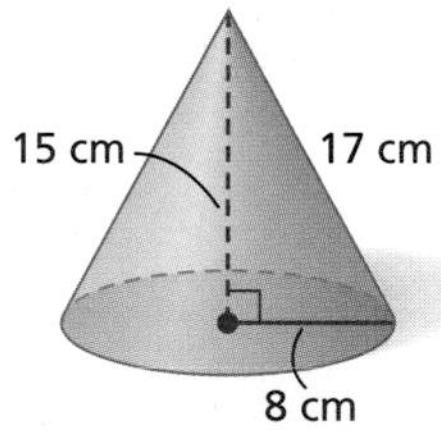

A

$V = \frac{1}{3}(8^2\pi)(17)$

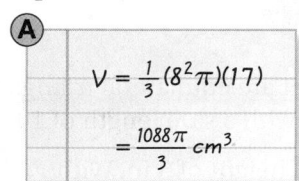

$= \frac{1088\pi}{3}$ cm^3

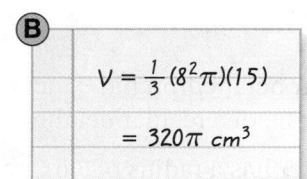

B

$V = \frac{1}{3}(8^2\pi)(15)$

$= 320\pi$ cm^3

39. Critical Thinking Write a ratio comparing the volume of the prism to the volume of the composite figure. Explain your answer.

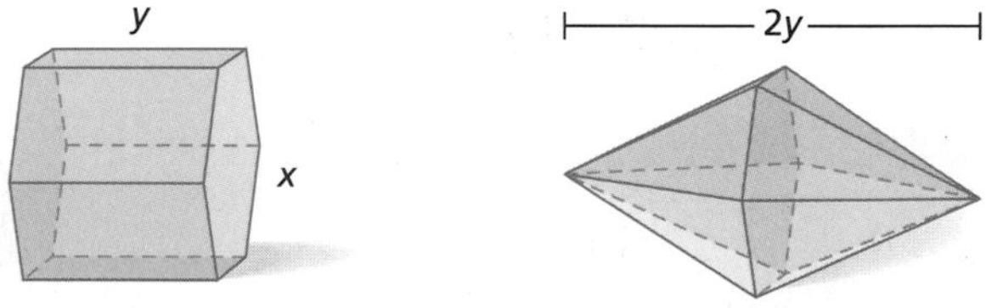

40. Write About It Explain how you would find the volume of a cone, given the radius and the surface area.

MULTI-STEP TEST PREP

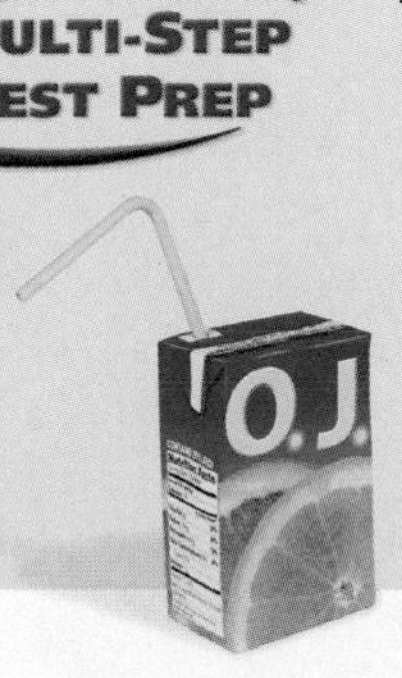

41. A juice stand sells smoothies in cone-shaped cups that are 8 in. tall. The regular size has a 4 in. diameter. The jumbo size has an 8 in. diameter.

a. Find the volume of the regular size to the nearest tenth.

b. Find the volume of the jumbo size to the nearest tenth.

c. The regular size costs \$1.25. What would be a reasonable price for the jumbo size? Explain your reasoning.

TEST PREP

42. Find the volume of the cone.

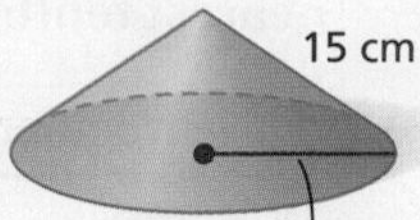

(A) 432π cm^3 (C) 1296π cm^3
(B) 720π cm^3 (D) 2160π cm^3

43. A square pyramid has a slant height of 25 m and a lateral area of 350 m^2. Which is closest to the volume?

(F) 392 m^3 (G) 1176 m^3 (H) 404 m^3 (J) 1225 m^3

44. A cone has a volume of 18π in^3. Which are possible dimensions of the cone?

(A) Diameter 1 in., height 18 in. (C) Diameter 3 in., height 6 in.
(B) Diameter 6 in., height 6 in. (D) Diameter 6 in., height 3 in.

45. **Gridded Response** Find the height in centimeters of a square pyramid with a volume of 243 cm^3 and a base edge length equal to the height.

CHALLENGE AND EXTEND

Each cone is inscribed in a regular pyramid with a base edge length of 2 ft and a height of 2 ft. Find the volume of each cone.

46.

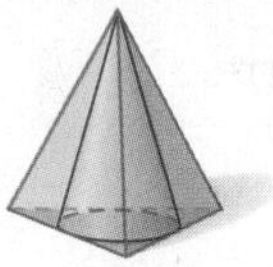

47.

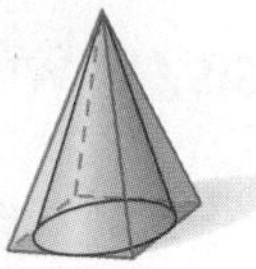

48.

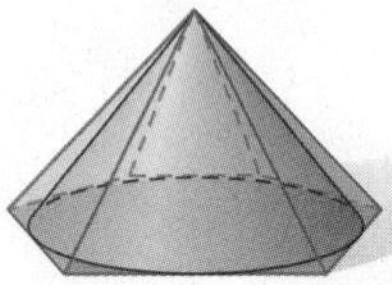

49. A regular octahedron has 8 faces that are equilateral triangles. Find the volume of a regular octahedron with a side length of 10 cm.

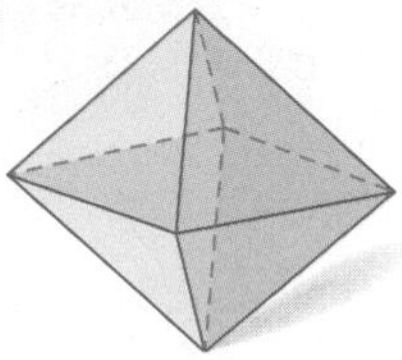

50. A cylinder has a radius of 5 in. and a height of 3 in. Without calculating the volumes, find the height of a cone with the same base and the same volume as the cylinder. Explain your reasoning.

Connecting Geometry to Algebra

Cube Roots

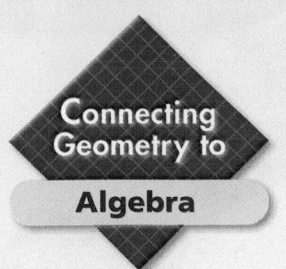

If you know the area of a square, you can find the length of a side by taking the square root of the area. How can you find the length of a side of a cube if you know the volume?

$A = 16 \text{ in}^2$ | $V = 27 \text{ in}^3$

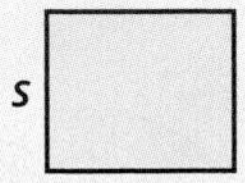

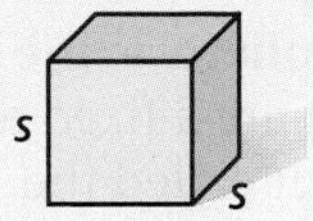

$s^2 = A$ | $s^3 = V$

$s^2 = 16$ | $s^3 = 27$

$s = \sqrt{16} = 4$ | $s = ?$

To find the side length, you need to find the *cube root* of 27. The cube root of 27 is 3 because $3^3 = 27$, so the side length of the cube above is 3 in. "The cube root of 27" can also be written as $\sqrt[3]{27}$.

Example

The volume of a cube is 64 m³. Find the side length of the cube.

$s^3 = V$

$s^3 = 64$ *Substitute 64 for V.*

$s = \sqrt[3]{64} = 4$ *$4^3 = 64$, so the cube root of 64 is 4.*

The side length of the cube is 4 m.

Try This

Given the volume, find the side length of each cube.

1. $V = 8 \text{ cm}^3$ **2.** $V = 125 \text{ ft}^3$ **3.** $V = 216 \text{ in.}^3$

4. $V = 1{,}000 \text{ yd}^3$ **5.** $V = 1 \text{ cm}^3$ **6.** $V = 0.064 \text{ m}^3$

7. Carlos wants to buy an angelfish for a pet. The pet store recommends a fish tank that holds 2,197 in³ of water. If the tank is in the shape of a cube, how long is each side?

For an integer $n > 1$, an nth root of x is a number a such that $a^n = x$. If n is also even and $x > 0$, x has both positive and negative nth roots, written as $\sqrt[n]{x}$ and $-\sqrt[n]{x}$. For example, the 4th roots of 16 are 2 and –2, because $2^4 = 16$ and $(-2)^4 = 16$. So, $\sqrt[4]{16} = 2$, and $-\sqrt[4]{16} = -2$. Simplify each expression.

8. $\sqrt[4]{81}$ **9.** $\sqrt[5]{32}$ **10.** $\sqrt[3]{729}$

11. $\sqrt[5]{243}$ **12.** $\sqrt[7]{1}$ **13.** $\sqrt[4]{0.0016}$

COMMON CORE

11-4 Spheres

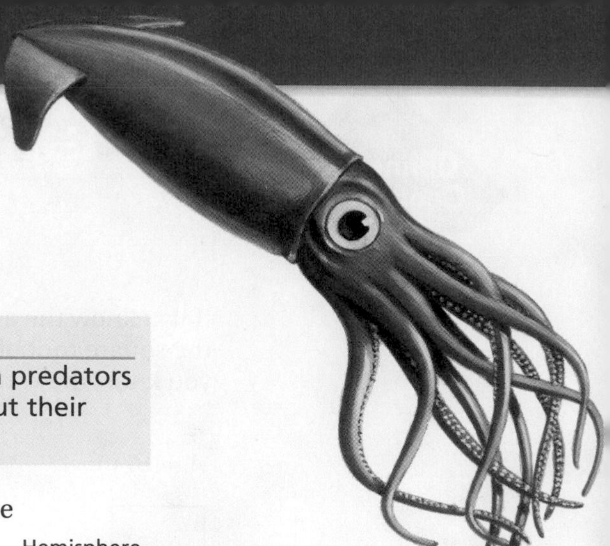

CC.9-12.G.GMD.3 Use volume formulas for...spheres to solve problems.*

Objectives

Learn and apply the formula for the volume of a sphere.

Learn and apply the formula for the surface area of a sphere.

Vocabulary

sphere
center of a sphere
radius of a sphere
hemisphere
great circle

Who uses this?

Biologists study the eyes of deep-sea predators such as the giant squid to learn about their behavior. (See Example 2.)

A **sphere** is the locus of points in space that are a fixed distance from a given point called the **center of a sphere**. A **radius of a sphere** connects the center of the sphere to any point on the sphere. A **hemisphere** is half of a sphere. A **great circle** divides a sphere into two hemispheres.

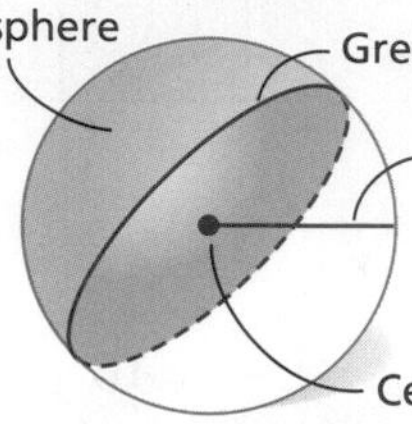

The figure shows a hemisphere and a cylinder with a cone removed from its interior. The cross sections have the same area at every level, so the volumes are equal by Cavalieri's Principle. You will prove that the cross sections have equal areas in Exercise 39.

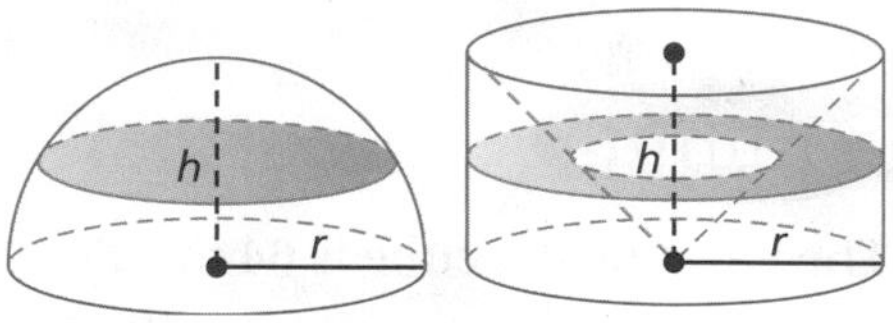

$$\begin{aligned} V(\text{hemisphere}) &= V(\text{cylinder}) - V(\text{cone}) \\ &= \pi r^2 h - \frac{1}{3}\pi r^2 h \\ &= \frac{2}{3}\pi r^2 h \\ &= \frac{2}{3}\pi r^2 (r) \\ &= \frac{2}{3}\pi r^3 \end{aligned}$$

The height of the hemisphere is equal to the radius.

The volume of a sphere with radius r is twice the volume of the hemisphere, or $V = \frac{4}{3}\pi r^3$.

Know it! Note

Volume of a Sphere

The volume of a sphere with radius r is $V = \frac{4}{3}\pi r^3$.

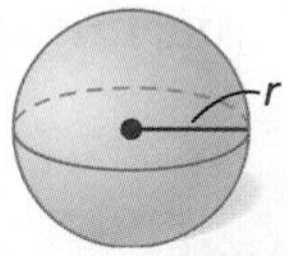

EXAMPLE 1 **Finding Volumes of Spheres**

Find each measurement. Give your answer in terms of π.

A **the volume of the sphere**

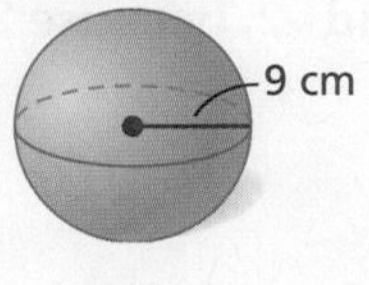

$V = \frac{4}{3}\pi r^3$

$V = \frac{4}{3}\pi (9)^3$ *Substitute 9 for r.*

$= 972\pi \text{ cm}^3$ *Simplify.*

Find each measurement. Give your answer in terms of π.

B **the diameter of a sphere with volume 972π in^3**

$972\pi = \frac{4}{3}\pi r^3$ *Substitute 972π for V.*

$729 = r^3$ *Divide both sides by $\frac{4}{3}\pi$.*

$r = 9$ *Take the cube root of both sides.*

$d = 18$ in. *$d = 2r$*

C **the volume of the hemisphere**

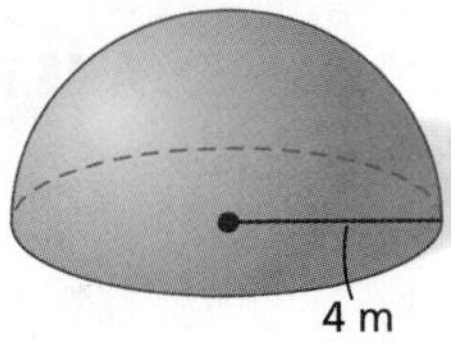

$V = \frac{2}{3}\pi r^3$ *Volume of a hemisphere*

$= \frac{2}{3}\pi(4)^3 = \frac{128\pi}{3}$ m^3 *Substitute 4 for r.*

CHECK IT OUT! 1. Find the radius of a sphere with volume 2304π ft^3.

EXAMPLE 2 *Biology Application*

Giant squid need large eyes to see their prey in low light. The eyeball of a giant squid is approximately a sphere with a diameter of 25 cm, which is bigger than a soccer ball. A human eyeball is approximately a sphere with a diameter of 2.5 cm. How many times as great is the volume of a giant squid eyeball as the volume of a human eyeball?

human eyeball:

$V = \frac{4}{3}\pi r^3$

$= \frac{4}{3}\pi(1.25)^3 \approx 8.18$ cm^3

giant squid eyeball:

$V = \frac{4}{3}\pi r^3$

$= \frac{4}{3}\pi(12.5)^3 \approx 8181.23$ cm^3

A giant squid eyeball is about 1000 times as great in volume as a human eyeball.

CHECK IT OUT! 2. A hummingbird eyeball has a diameter of approximately 0.6 cm. How many times as great is the volume of a human eyeball as the volume of a hummingbird eyeball?

In the figure, the vertex of the pyramid is at the center of the sphere. The height of the pyramid is approximately the radius *r* of the sphere. Suppose the entire sphere is filled with *n* pyramids that each have base area *B* and height *r*.

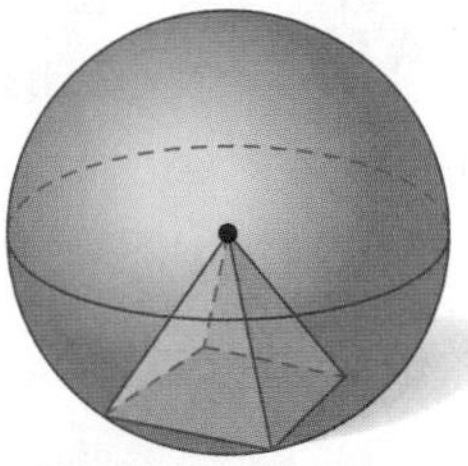

$V(\text{sphere}) \approx \frac{1}{3}Br + \frac{1}{3}Br + \ldots + \frac{1}{3}Br$ *The sphere's volume is close to the sum of the volumes of the pyramids.*

$\frac{4}{3}\pi r^3 \approx n\left(\frac{1}{3}Br\right)$

$4\pi r^2 \approx nB$ *Divide both sides by $\frac{1}{3}\pi r$.*

If the pyramids fill the sphere, the total area of the bases is approximately equal to the surface area of the sphere *S*, so $4\pi r^2 \approx S$. As the number of pyramids increases, the approximation gets closer to the actual surface area.

Know it! Note

Surface Area of a Sphere

The surface area of a sphere with radius r is $S = 4\pi r^2$.

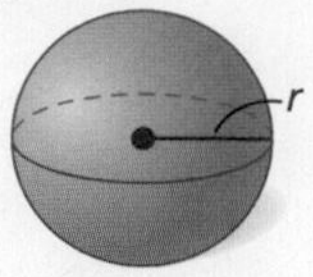

EXAMPLE 3 Finding Surface Area of Spheres

Find each measurement. Give your answers in terms of π.

A **the surface area of a sphere with diameter 10 ft**

$S = 4\pi r^2$

$S = 4\pi(5)^2 = 200\pi \text{ ft}^2$ *Substitute 5 for r.*

B **the volume of a sphere with surface area $144\pi \text{ m}^2$**

$S = 4\pi r^2$

$144\pi = 4\pi r^2$ *Substitute 144π for S.*

$6 = r$ *Solve for r.*

$V = \frac{4}{3}\pi r^3$

$= \frac{4}{3}\pi(6)^3 = 288\pi \text{ m}^3$ *Substitute 6 for r.*

The volume of the sphere is $288\pi \text{ m}^3$.

C **the surface area of a sphere with a great circle that has an area of $4\pi \text{ in}^2$**

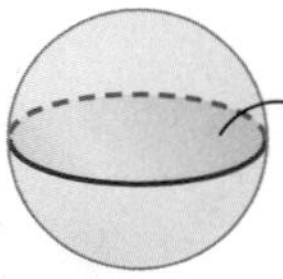

$\pi r^2 = 4\pi$ *Substitute 4π for A in the formula for the area of a circle.*

$r = 2$ *Solve for r.*

$S = 4\pi r^2$

$= 4\pi(2)^2 = 16\pi \text{ in}^2$ *Substitute 2 for r in the surface area formula.*

CHECK IT OUT! 3. Find the surface area of the sphere.

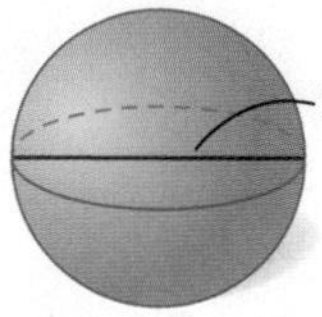

EXAMPLE 4 Exploring Effects of Changing Dimensions

The radius of the sphere is tripled. Describe the effect on the volume.

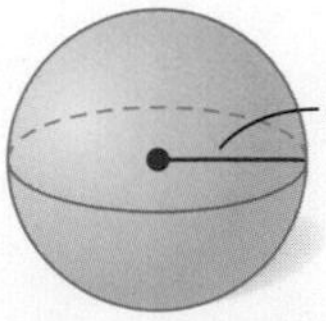

original dimensions:	radius tripled:
$V = \frac{4}{3}\pi r^3$	$V = \frac{4}{3}\pi r^3$
$= \frac{4}{3}\pi(3)^3$	$= \frac{4}{3}\pi(9)^3$
$= 36\pi \text{ m}^3$	$= 972\pi \text{ m}^3$

Notice that $972\pi = 27(36\pi)$. If the radius is tripled, the volume is multiplied by 27.

CHECK IT OUT! 4. The radius of the sphere above is divided by 3. Describe the effect on the surface area.

EXAMPLE 5 Finding Surface Areas and Volumes of Composite Figures

Find the surface area and volume of the composite figure. Give your answers in terms of π.

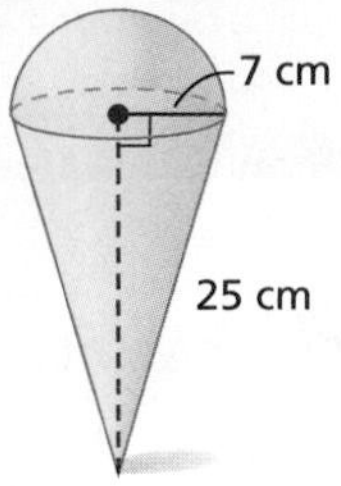

Step 1 Find the surface area of the composite figure.

The surface area of the composite figure is the sum of the surface area of the hemisphere and the lateral area of the cone.

$$S\text{ (hemisphere)} = \frac{1}{2}(4\pi r^2) = 2\pi(7)^2 = 98\pi \text{ cm}^2$$

$$L\text{ (cone)} = \pi r\ell = \pi(7)(25) = 175\pi \text{ cm}^2$$

The surface area of the composite figure is $98\pi + 175\pi = 273\pi \text{ cm}^2$.

Step 2 Find the volume of the composite figure.

First find the height of the cone.

$h = \sqrt{25^2 - 7^2}$ *Pythagorean Theorem*

$= \sqrt{576} = 24 \text{ cm}$ *Simplify.*

The volume of the composite figure is the sum of the volume of the hemisphere and the volume of the cone.

$$V\text{ (hemisphere)} = \frac{1}{2}\left(\frac{4}{3}\pi r^3\right) = \frac{2}{3}\pi(7)^3 = \frac{686\pi}{3} \text{ cm}^3$$

$$V\text{ (cone)} = \frac{1}{3}\pi r^2 h = \frac{1}{3}\pi(7)^2(24) = 392\pi \text{ cm}^3$$

The volume of the composite figure is $\frac{686\pi}{3} + 392\pi = \frac{1862\pi}{3} \text{ cm}^3$.

CHECK IT OUT! 5. Find the surface area and volume of the composite figure.

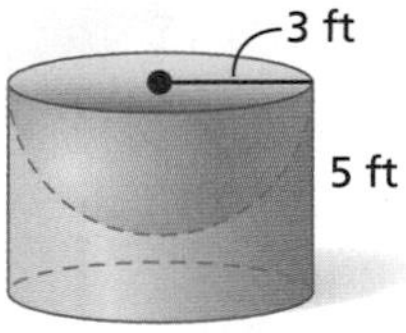

MATHEMATICAL PRACTICES

THINK AND DISCUSS

1. Explain how to find the surface area of a sphere when you know the area of a great circle.
2. Compare the volume of the sphere with the volume of the composite figure.

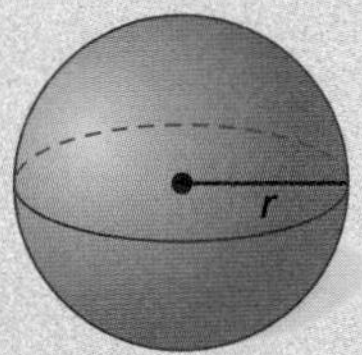

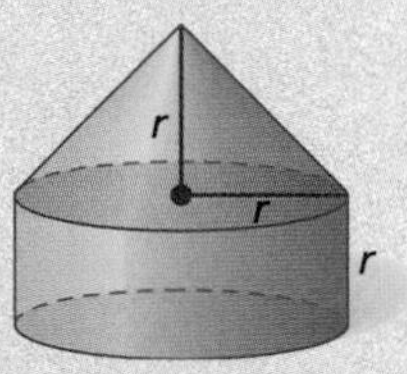

Know it! Note

3. **GET ORGANIZED** Copy and complete the graphic organizer.

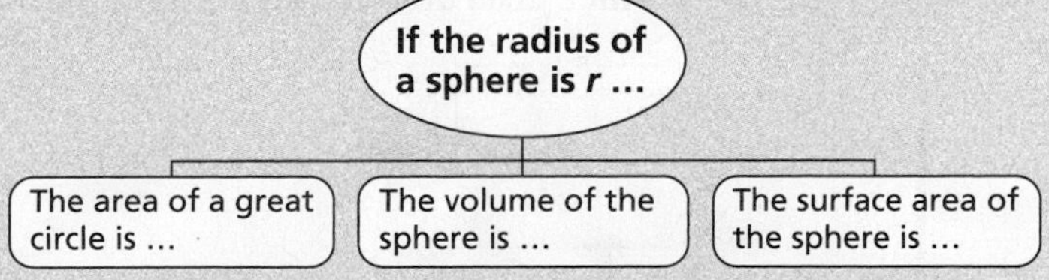

11-4 Exercises

Learn It Online
Homework Help Online
Parent Resources Online

GUIDED PRACTICE

1. **Vocabulary** Describe the endpoints of a *radius of a sphere.*

SEE EXAMPLE 1

Find each measurement. Give your answers in terms of π.

2. the volume of the hemisphere

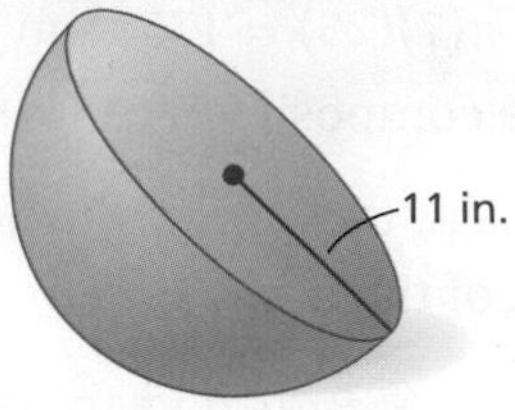

3. the volume of the sphere

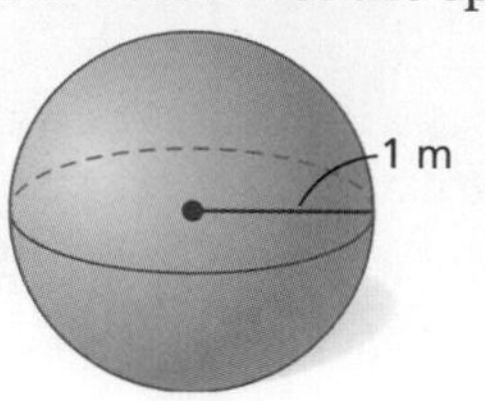

4. the radius of a sphere with volume 288π cm^3

SEE EXAMPLE 2

5. **Food** Approximately how many times as great is the volume of the grapefruit as the volume of the lime?

SEE EXAMPLE 3

Find each measurement. Give your answers in terms of π.

6. the surface area of the sphere

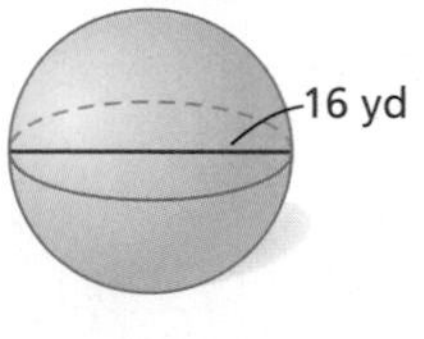

7. the surface area of the sphere

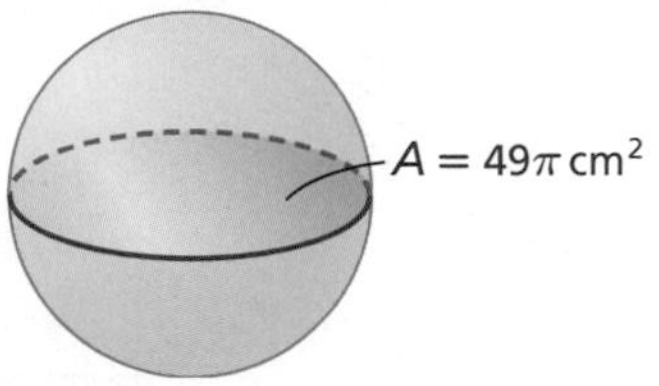

8. the volume of a sphere with surface area 6724π ft^2

SEE EXAMPLE 4

Describe the effect of each change on the given measurement of the figure.

9. surface area
   The dimensions are doubled.

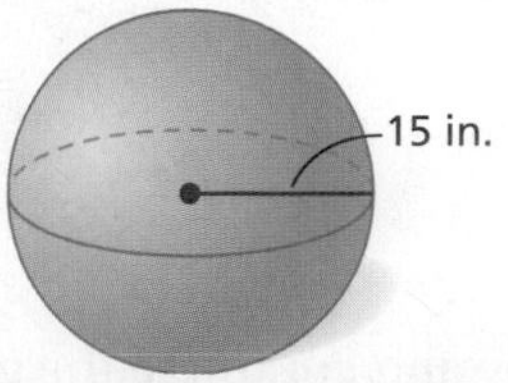

10. volume
    The dimensions are multiplied by $\frac{1}{4}$.

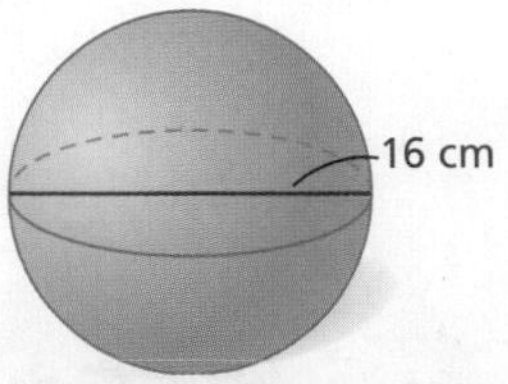

SEE EXAMPLE 5

Find the surface area and volume of each composite figure.

11.

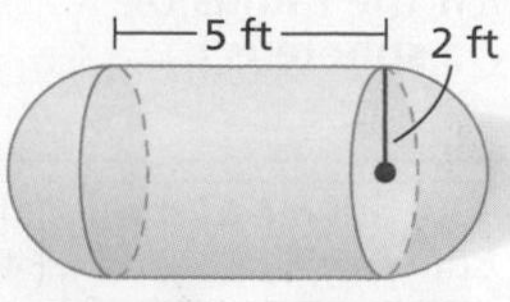

12.

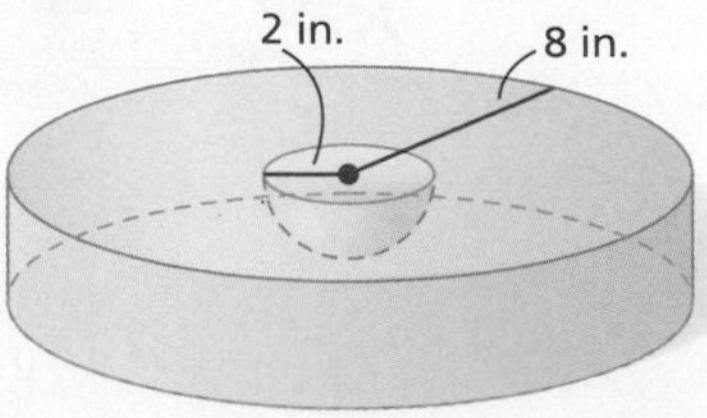

PRACTICE AND PROBLEM SOLVING

Independent Practice

For Exercises	See Example
13–15	1
16	2
17–19	3
20–21	4
22–23	5

Extra Practice

See Extra Practice for more Skills Practice and Applications Practice exercises.

Find each measurement. Give your answers in terms of π.

13. the volume of the sphere

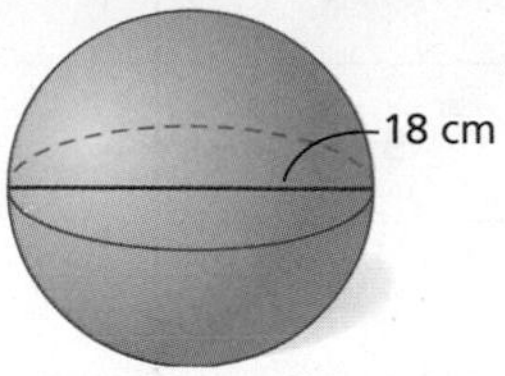

14. the volume of the hemisphere

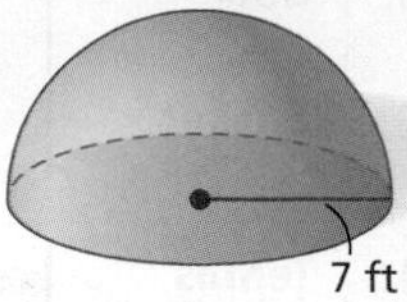

15. the diameter of a sphere with volume 7776π in^3

16. Jewelry The size of a cultured pearl is typically indicated by its diameter in mm. How many times as great is the volume of the 9 mm pearl as the volume of the 6 mm pearl?

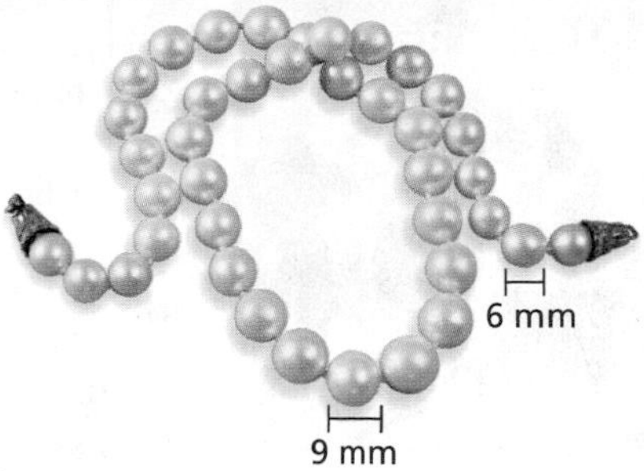

Find each measurement. Give your answers in terms of π.

17. the surface area of the sphere

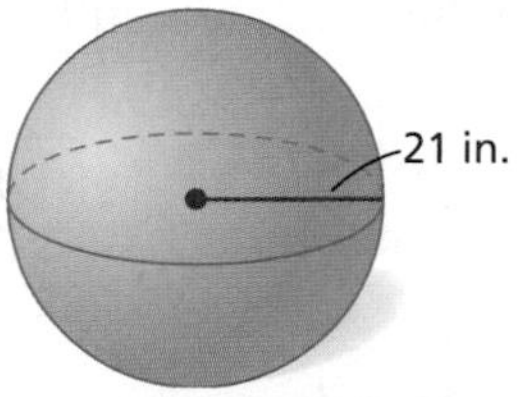

18. the surface area of the sphere

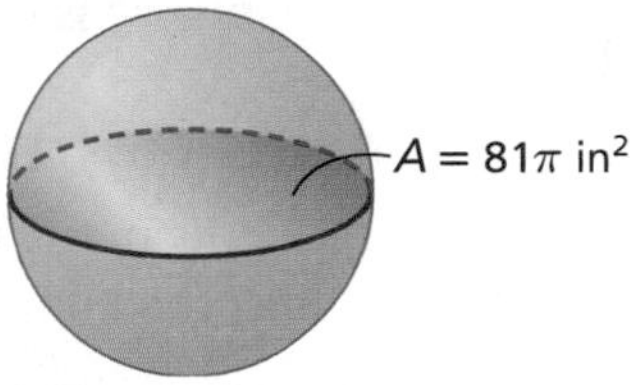

19. the volume of a sphere with surface area 625π m^2

Describe the effect of each change on the given measurement of the figure.

20. surface area
The dimensions are multiplied by $\frac{1}{5}$.

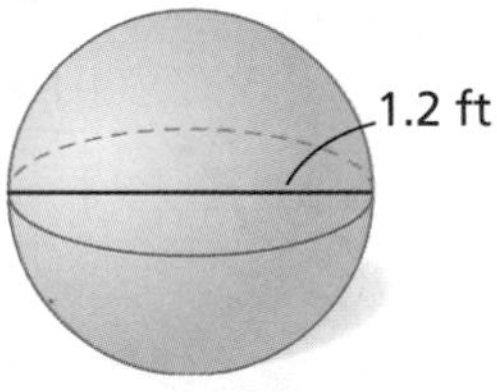

21. volume
The dimensions are multiplied by 6.

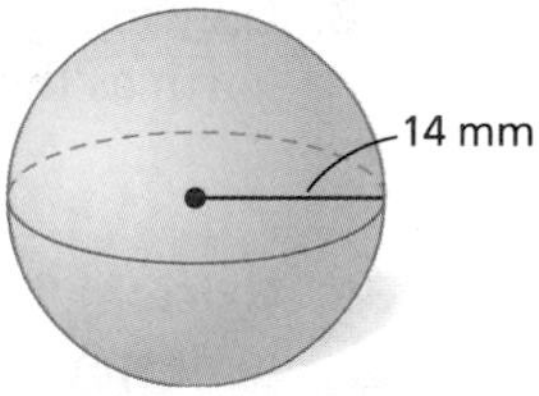

Find the surface area and volume of each composite figure.

22.

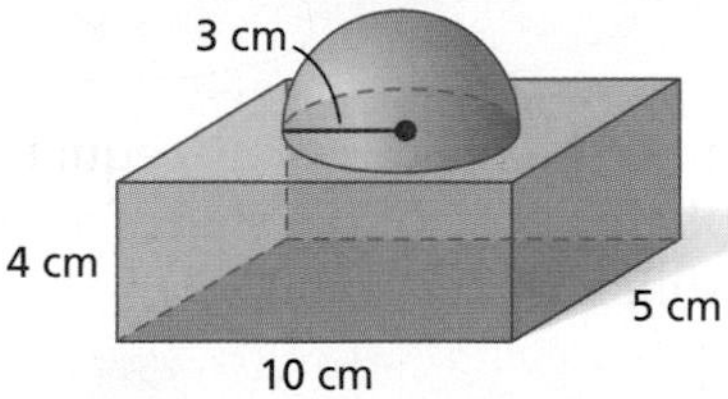

23.

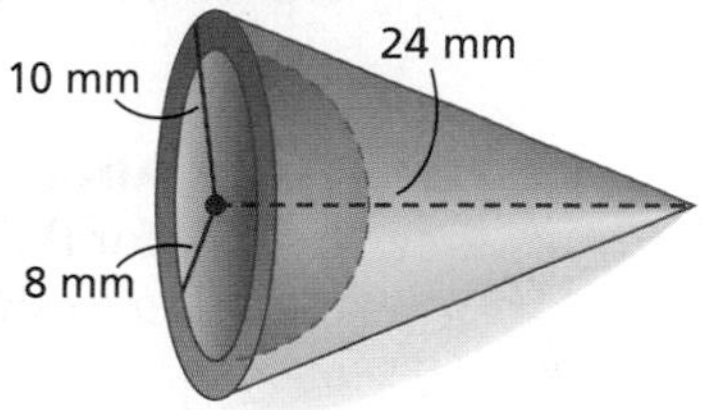

24. Find the radius of a hemisphere with a volume of 144π cm^3.

25. Find the circumference of a sphere with a surface area of 60π in^2.

26. Find the volume of a sphere with a circumference of 36π ft.

27. Find the surface area and volume of a sphere centered at $(0, 0, 0)$ that passes through the point $(2, 3, 6)$.

28. Estimation A bead is formed by drilling a cylindrical hole with a 2 mm diameter through a sphere with an 8 mm diameter. Estimate the surface area and volume of the bead.

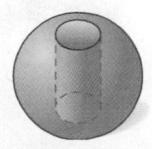

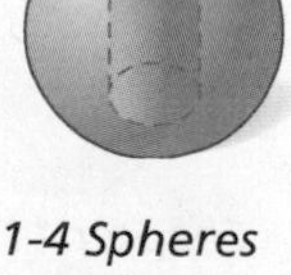

Sports Find the unknown dimensions of the ball for each sport.

	Sport	Ball	Diameter	Circumference	Surface Area	Volume
29.	Golf		1.68 in.	■	■	■
30.	Cricket		■	9 in.	■	■
31.	Tennis		2.5 in.	■	■	■
32.	Petanque		74 mm	■	■	■

LINK

Marine Biology

In 1934, the bathysphere reached a record depth of 3028 feet. The pressure on the hull was about half a ton per square inch.

33. **Marine Biology** The *bathysphere* was an early version of a submarine, invented in the 1930s. The inside diameter of the bathysphere was 54 inches, and the steel used to make the sphere was 1.5 inches thick. It had three 8-inch diameter windows. Estimate the volume of steel used to make the bathysphere.

34. **Geography** Earth's radius is approximately 4000 mi. About two-thirds of Earth's surface is covered by water. Estimate the land area on Earth.

Astronomy Use the table for Exercises 35–38.

Planet	Diameter (mi)
Mercury	3,032
Venus	7,521
Earth	7,926
Mars	4,222
Jupiter	88,846
Saturn	74,898
Uranus	31,763
Neptune	30,775

35. How many times as great is the volume of Jupiter as the volume of Earth?

36. The sum of the volumes of Venus and Mars is about equal to the volume of which planet?

37. Which is greater, the sum of the surface areas of Uranus and Neptune or the surface area of Saturn?

38. How many times as great is the surface area of Earth as the surface area of Mars?

39. **Critical Thinking** In the figure, the hemisphere and the cylinder both have radius and height r. Prove that the shaded cross sections have equal areas.

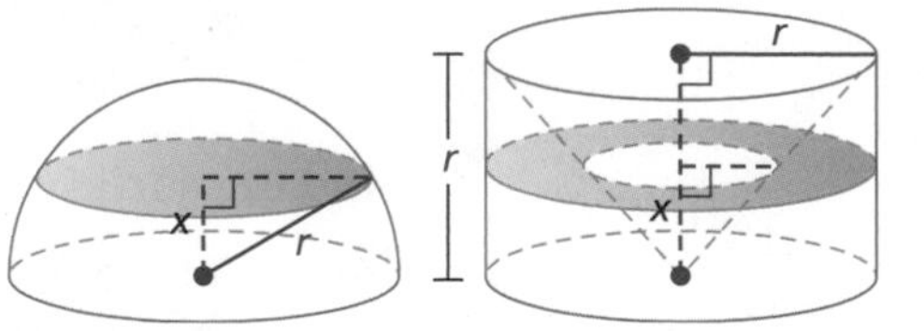

40. **Write About It** Suppose a sphere and a cube have equal surface areas. Using r for the radius of the sphere and s for the side of a cube, write an equation to show the relationship between r and s.

MULTI-STEP TEST PREP

41. A company sells orange juice in spherical containers that look like oranges. Each container has a surface area of approximately 50.3 in^2.
    a. What is the volume of the container? Round to the nearest tenth.
    b. The company decides to increase the radius of the container by 10%. What is the volume of the new container?

TEST PREP

42. A sphere with radius 8 cm is inscribed in a cube. Find the ratio of the volume of the cube to the volume of the sphere.

Ⓐ $2:\frac{1}{3}\pi$ Ⓑ $2:3\pi$ Ⓒ $1:\frac{4}{3}\pi$ Ⓓ $1:\frac{2}{3}\pi$

43. What is the surface area of a sphere with volume $10\frac{2}{3}\pi$ in^3?

Ⓕ 8π in^2 Ⓖ $10\frac{2}{3}\pi$ in^2 Ⓗ 16π in^2 Ⓙ 32π in^2

44. Which expression represents the volume of the composite figure formed by a hemisphere with radius r and a cube with side length $2r$?

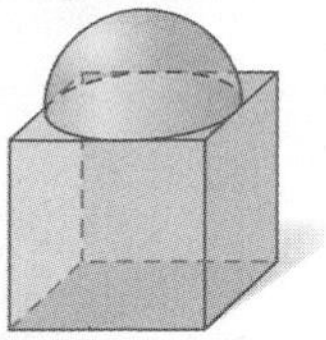

Ⓐ $r^3\left(\frac{2}{3}\pi + 8\right)$ Ⓒ $2r^2(2\pi + 12)$

Ⓑ $\frac{4}{3}\pi r^3 + 2r^3$ Ⓓ $\frac{4}{3}\pi r^3 + 8r^3$

CHALLENGE AND EXTEND

45. Food The top of a gumball machine is an 18 in. sphere. The machine holds a maximum of 3300 gumballs, which leaves about 43% of the space in the machine empty. Estimate the diameter of each gumball.

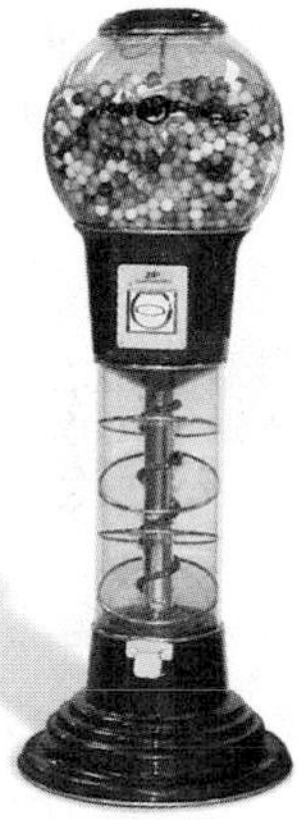

46. The surface area of a sphere can be used to determine its volume.

a. Solve the surface area formula of a sphere to get an expression for r in terms of S.

b. Substitute your result from part **a** into the volume formula to find the volume V of a sphere in terms of its surface area S.

c. Graph the relationship between volume and surface area with S on the horizontal axis and V on the vertical axis. What shape is the graph?

Use the diagram of a sphere inscribed in a cylinder for Exercises 47 and 48.

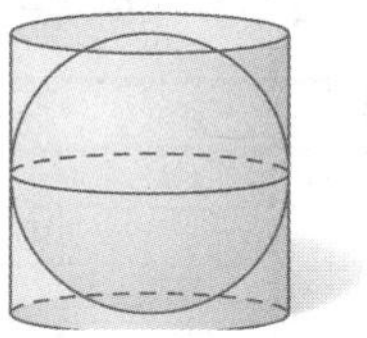

47. What is the relationship between the volume of the sphere and the volume of the cylinder?

48. What is the relationship between the surface area of the sphere and the lateral area of the cylinder?

11-4 Technology LAB

Use with Spheres

Compare Surface Areas and Volumes

In some situations you may need to find the minimum surface area for a given volume. In others you may need to find the maximum volume for a given surface area. Spreadsheet software can help you analyze these problems.

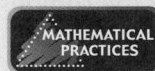

MATHEMATICAL PRACTICES **Use appropriate tools strategically.** **CC.9-12.G.GMD.3** Use volume formulas… to solve problems.*

Activity 1

1. Create a spreadsheet to compare surface areas and volumes of rectangular prisms. Create columns for length L, width W, height H, surface area SA, volume V, and ratio of surface area to volume SA/V. In the column for SA, use the formula shown.

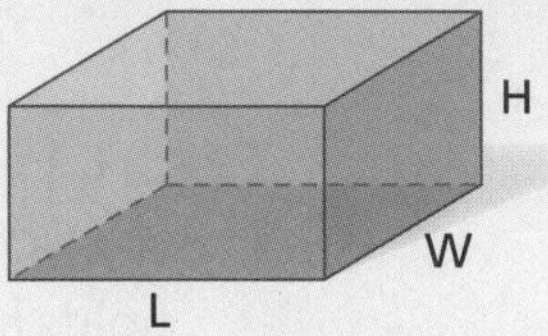

D2 | fx =2*A2*B2+2*B2*C2+2*A2*C2

	A	B	C	D	E	F
1	L	W	H	SA	V	SA/V
2				0	0	
3						
4						
5						
6						

2. Create a formula for the V column and a formula for the SA/V column.

3. Fill in the measurements L = 8, W = 2, and H = 4 for the first rectangular prism.

F2 | fx =D2/E2

	A	B	C	D	E	F
1	L	W	H	SA	V	SA/V
2	8	2	4	112	64	1.75
3						
4						
5						
6						

4. Choose several values for L, W, and H to create rectangular prisms that each have the same volume as the first one. Which has the least surface area? Sketch the prism and describe its shape in words. (Is it tall or short, skinny or wide, flat or cubical?) Make a conjecture about what type of shape has the minimum surface area for a given volume.

Try This

1. Repeat Activity 1 for cylinders. Create columns for radius R, height H, surface area SA, volume V, and ratio of surface area to volume SA/V. What shape cylinder has the minimum surface area for a given volume? (*Hint:* To use π in a formula, input "PI( )" into your spreadsheet.)

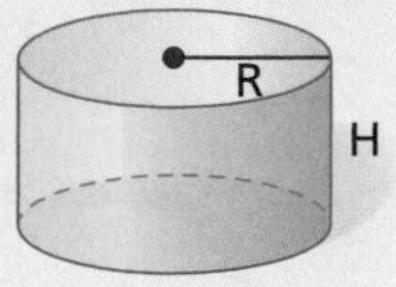

2. Investigate packages such as cereal boxes and soda cans. Do the manufacturers appear to be using shapes with the minimum surface areas for their volume? What other factors might influence a company's choice of packaging?

Activity 2

1 Create a new spreadsheet with the same column headings used in Activity 1. Fill in the measurements L = 8, W = 2, and H = 4 for the first rectangular prism. To create a new prism with the same surface area, choose new values for L and W, and use the formula shown to calculate H.

C3 ▼ fx =(112/2-A3*B3)/(A3+B3)

	A	B	C	D	E	F
1	L	W	H	SA	V	SA/V
2	8	2	4	112	64	1.75
3	6	4	3.2	112		
4						
5						
6						

2 Choose several more values for L and W, and calculate H so that SA = 112. Examine the V and SA/V columns. Which prism has the greatest volume? Sketch the prism and describe it in words. Make a conjecture about what type of shape has the maximum volume for a given surface area.

Try This

3. Repeat Activity 2 for cylinders. Create columns for radius R, height H, surface area SA, volume V, and the ratio of surface area to volume SA/V. What shape cylinder has the maximum volume for a given surface area?

4. Solve the formula $SA = 2LW + 2LH + 2WH$ for H. Use your result to explain the formula that was used to find H in Activity 2.

5. If a rectangular prism, a pyramid, a cylinder, a cone, and a sphere all had the same volume, which do you think would have the least surface area? Which would have the greatest surface area? Explain.

6. Use a spreadsheet to analyze what happens to the ratio of surface area to volume of a rectangular prism when the dimensions are doubled. Explain how you set up the spreadsheet and describe your results.

CHAPTER 11

MULTI-STEP TEST PREP

SECTION 11A

MATHEMATICAL PRACTICES **Model with mathematics.**

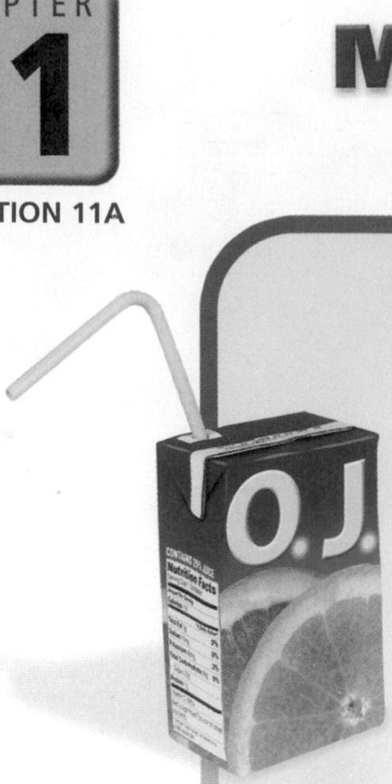

Surface Area and Volume

Juice for Fun You are in charge of designing containers for a new brand of juice. Your company wants you to compare several different container shapes. The container must be able to hold a 6-inch straw so that exactly 1 inch remains outside the container when the straw is inserted as far as possible.

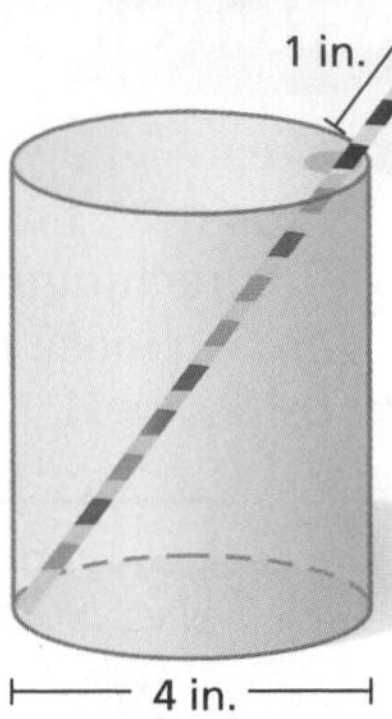

1. One possible container is a cylinder with a base diameter of 4 in., as shown. The formula for the surface area of a cylinder with radius r and height h is $S = \pi r^2 h$. Use this formula to determine how much material is needed to make this container. Round to the nearest tenth.
2. Estimate the volume of juice in ounces that the cylinder will hold. Round to the nearest tenth. (*Hint:* $1 \text{ in}^3 \approx 0.55$ oz)
3. Another option is a square prism with a 3 in. by 3 in. base, as shown. The formula for the surface area of a prism with length l, width w, and height h is $S = lwh$. Use this formula to determine how much material is needed to make this container.
4. Estimate the volume of juice in ounces that the prism will hold. (*Hint:* $1 \text{ in}^3 \approx 0.55$ oz)
5. Which container would you recommend to your company? Justify your answer.

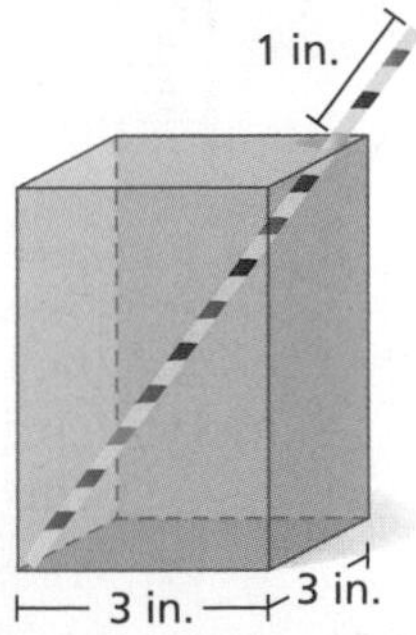

READY TO GO ON?

Quiz for Lessons 11-1 Through 11-4

11-1 Solid Geometry

Classify each figure. Name the vertices, edges, and bases.

1.

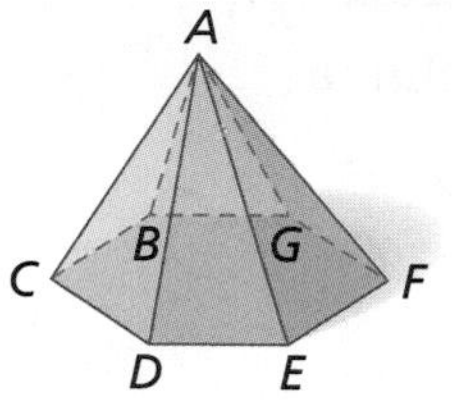

2.

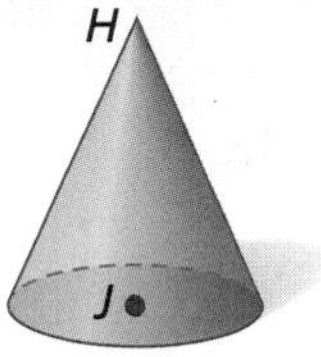

3.

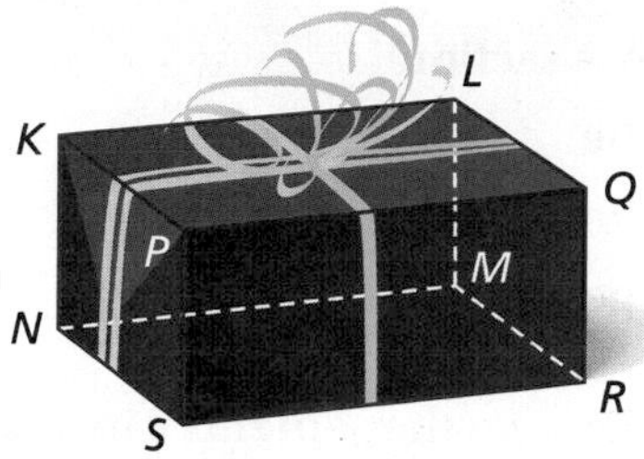

Describe the three-dimensional figure that can be made from the given net.

4.

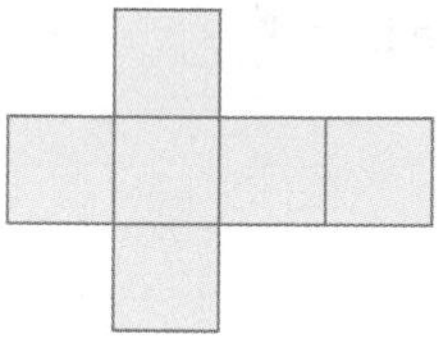

5.

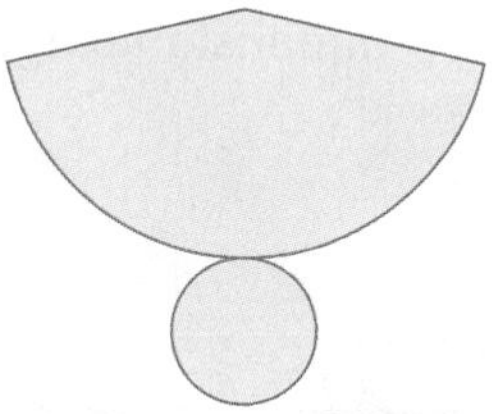

6.

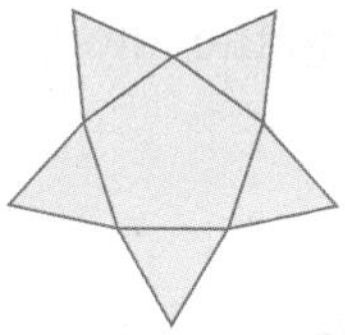

11-2 Volume of Prisms and Cylinders

Find the volume of each figure. Round to the nearest tenth, if necessary.

7. a regular hexagonal prism with base area 23 in^2 and height 9 in.
8. a cylinder with radius 8 yd and height 14 yd
9. A brick patio measures 10 ft by 12 ft by 4 in. Find the volume of the bricks. If the density of brick is 130 pounds per cubic foot, what is the weight of the patio in pounds?
10. The dimensions of a cylinder with diameter 2 ft and height 1 ft are doubled. Describe the effect on the volume.

11-3 Volume of Pyramids and Cones

Find the volume of each figure. Round to the nearest tenth, if necessary.

11.

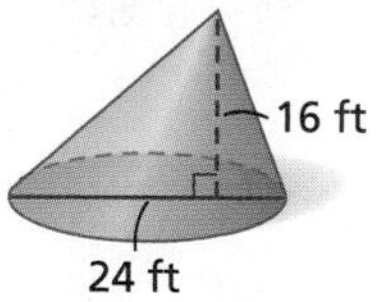

12.

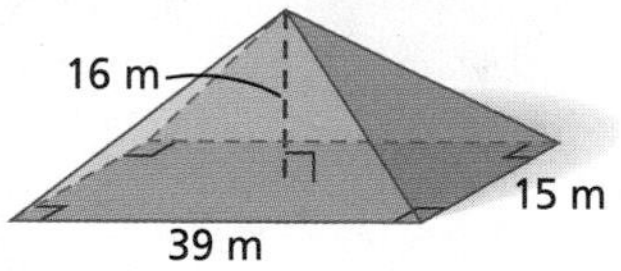

13.

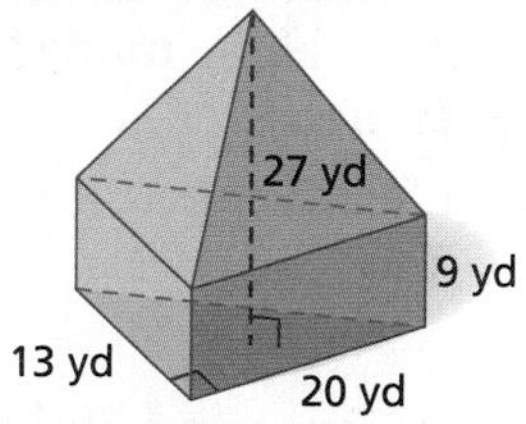

11-4 Spheres

Find the surface area and volume of each figure.

14. a sphere with diameter 20 in.
15. a hemisphere with radius 12 in.
16. A baseball has a diameter of approximately 3 in., and a softball has a diameter of approximately 5 in. About how many times as great is the volume of a softball as the volume of a baseball?

CHAPTER 11

Study Guide: Review

Know it! Note

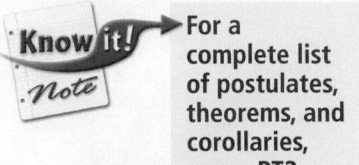

For a complete list of postulates, theorems, and corollaries, see p. PT2.

Vocabulary

center of a sphere	face	radius of a sphere
cone	great circle	sphere
cross section	hemisphere	vertex
cube	net	volume
cylinder	prism	
edge	pyramid	

Complete the sentences below with vocabulary words from the list above.

1. A(n) __?__ is a flat surface of a solid.

2. A name given to the intersection of a three-dimensional figure and a plane is __?__ .

11-1 Solid Geometry

EXAMPLES

■ **Classify the figure. Name the vertices, edges, and bases.**

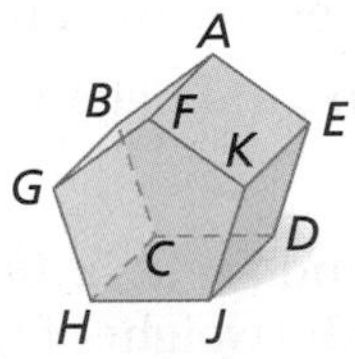

pentagonal prism

vertices: *A, B, C, D, E, F, G, H, J, K*

edges: $\overline{AB}, \overline{BC}, \overline{CD}, \overline{DE}, \overline{AE}, \overline{FG}, \overline{GH}, \overline{HJ}, \overline{JK}, \overline{KF}, \overline{AF}, \overline{EK}, \overline{DJ}, \overline{CH}, \overline{BG}$

bases: *ABCDE, FGHJK*

■ **Describe the three-dimensional figure that can be made from the given net.**

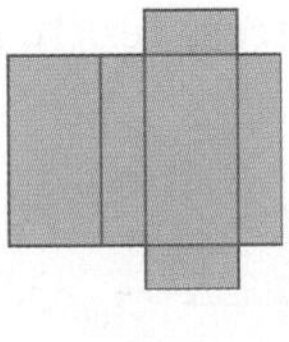

The net forms a rectangular prism.

EXERCISES

Classify each figure. Name the vertices, edges, and bases.

3.

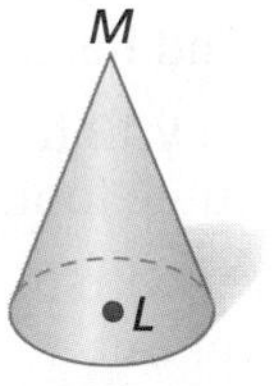

4.

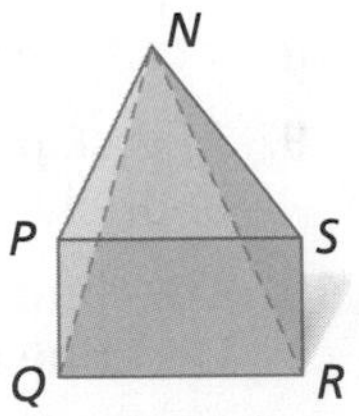

Describe the three-dimensional figure that can be made from the given net.

5.

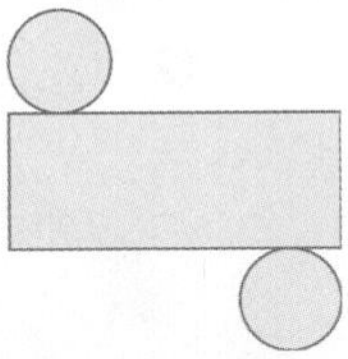

6.

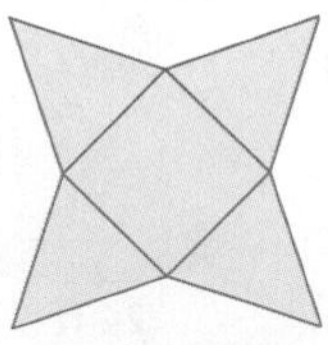

11-2 Volume of Prisms and Cylinders

EXAMPLES

■ **Find the volume of the prism.**

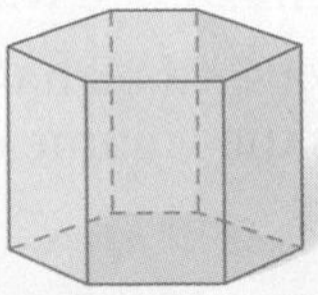

$V = Bh = \left(\frac{1}{2}aP\right)h$

$= \frac{1}{2}(4\sqrt{3})(48)(12)$

$= 1152\sqrt{3} \approx 1995.3 \text{ cm}^3$

EXERCISES

Find the volume of each prism.

7.

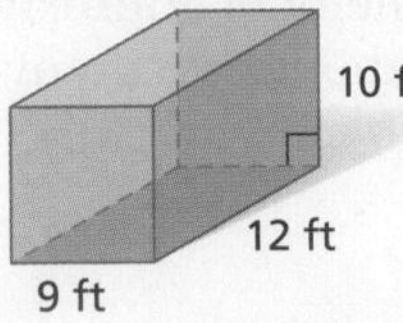

8.

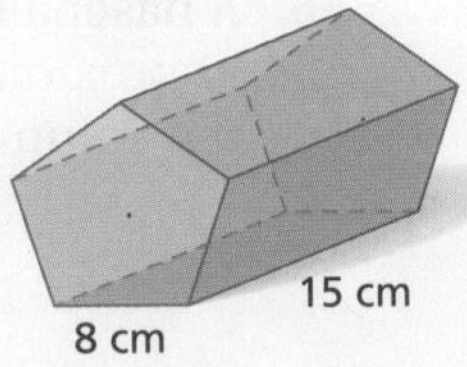

■ **Find the volume of the cylinder.**

$V = \pi r^2 h = \pi(6)^2(14)$

$= 504\pi \approx 1583.4 \text{ ft}^3$

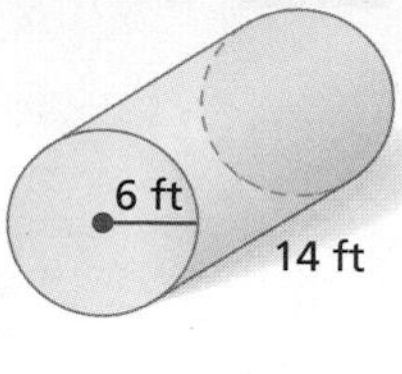

Find the volume of each cylinder.

9.

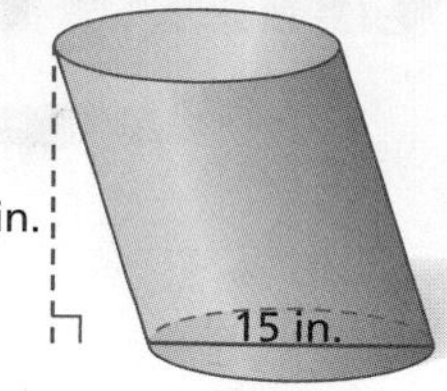

10.

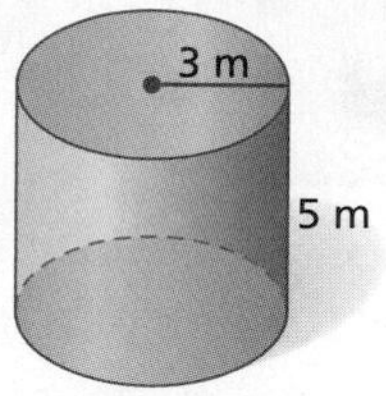

11-3 Volume of Pyramids and Cones

EXAMPLES

■ **Find the volume of the pyramid.**

$V = \frac{1}{3}Bh = \frac{1}{3}(8 \cdot 3)(14)$

$= 112 \text{ in}^3$

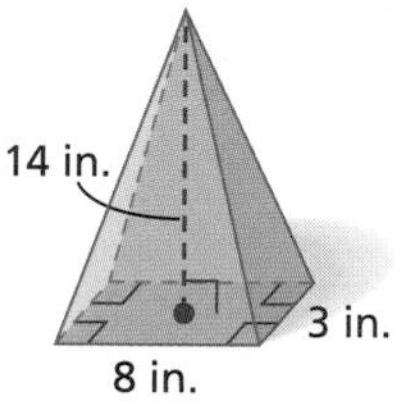

■ **Find the volume of the cone.**

$V = \frac{1}{3}\pi r^2 h = \frac{1}{3}\pi(9)^2(16)$

$= 432\pi \text{ ft}^3 \approx 1357.2 \text{ ft}^3$

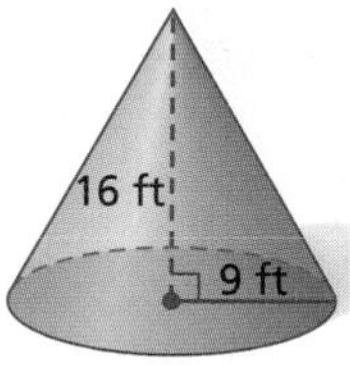

EXERCISES

Find the volume of each pyramid or cone.

11. a hexagonal pyramid with base area 42 m^2 and height 8 m

12. an equilateral triangular pyramid with base edge 3 cm and height 8 cm

13. a cone with diameter 12 cm and height 10 cm

14. a cone with base area $16\pi \text{ ft}^2$ and height 9 ft

Find the volume of each composite figure.

15.

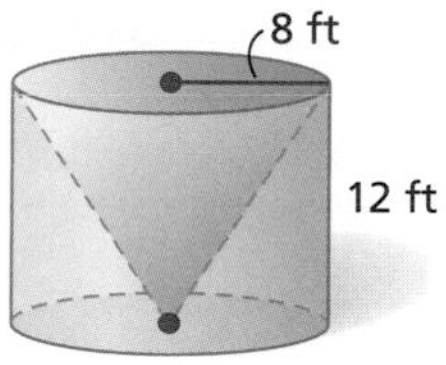

16.

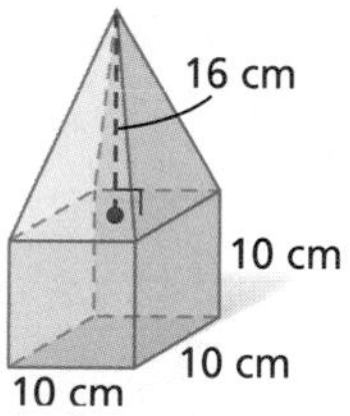

11-4 Spheres

EXAMPLE

■ **Find the volume and surface area of the sphere. Give your answers in terms of π.**

$V = \frac{4}{3}\pi r^3 = \frac{4}{3}\pi(9)^3 = 972\pi \text{ m}^2$

$S = 4\pi r^2 = 4\pi(9)^2 = 324\pi \text{ m}^2$

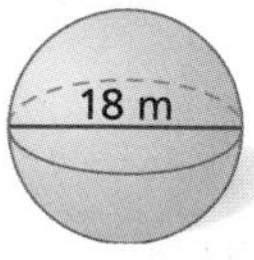

EXERCISES

Find each measurement. Give your answers in terms of π.

17. the volume of a sphere with surface area $100\pi \text{ m}^2$

18. the surface area of a sphere with volume $288\pi \text{ in}^3$

19. the diameter of a sphere with surface area $256\pi \text{ ft}^2$

Find the surface area and volume of each composite figure.

20.

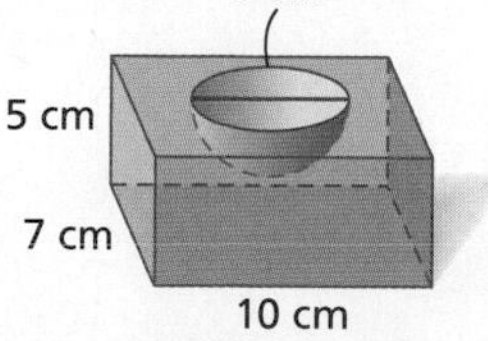

21.

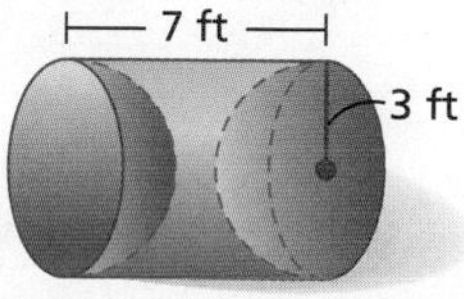

CHAPTER TEST

Use the diagram for Items 1–2.

1. Classify the figure. Name the vertices, edges, and bases.
2. Describe a cross section made by a plane parallel to the base.

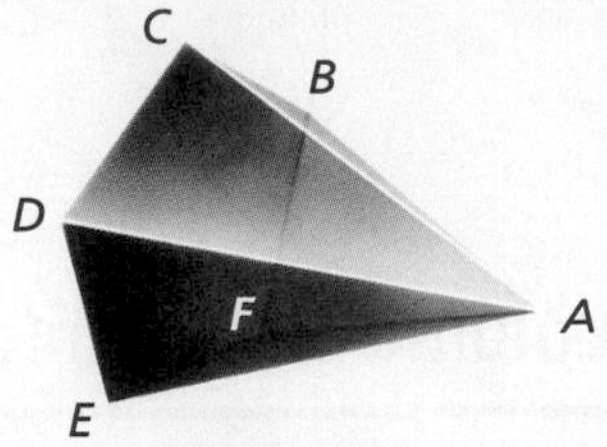

Describe each cross section.

3.

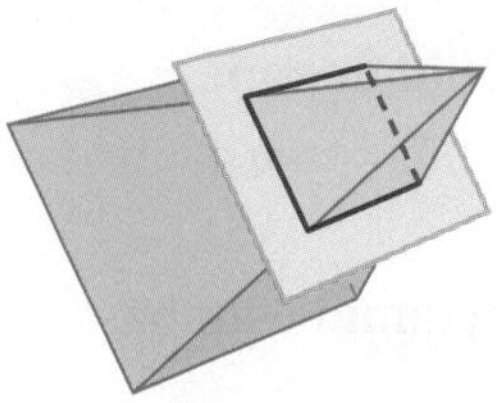

4.

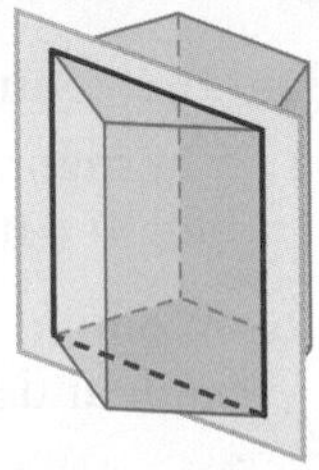

5.

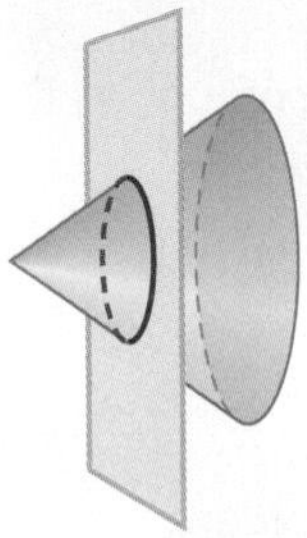

Find the volume of each figure. Round to the nearest tenth, if necessary.

6.

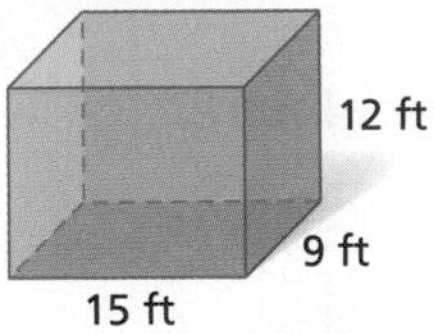

7.

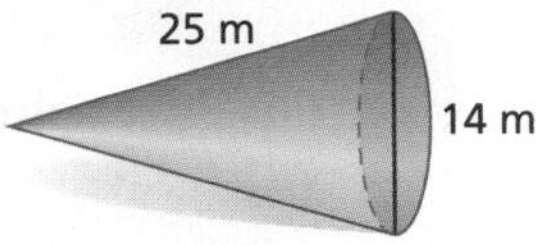

8.

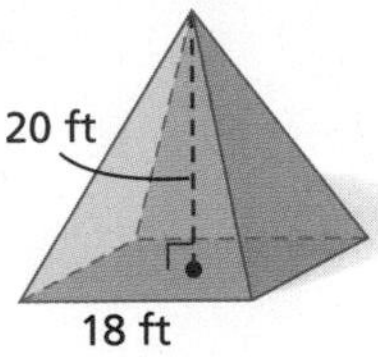

9.

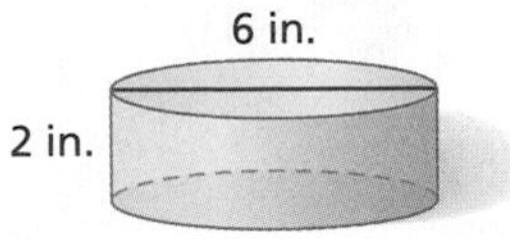

10.

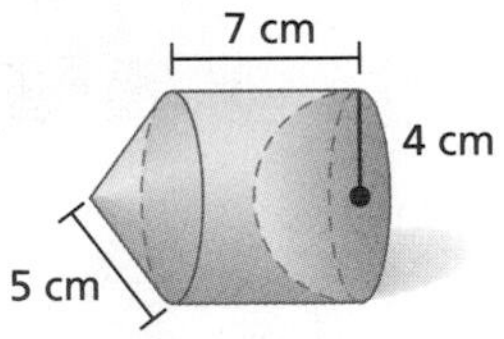

11.

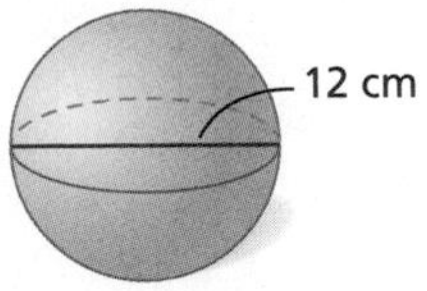

12. Earth's diameter is approximately 7930 miles. The Moon's diameter is approximately 2160 miles. About how many times as great is the volume of Earth as the volume of the Moon?

College Entrance Exam Practice

FOCUS ON SAT MATHEMATICS SUBJECT TEST

SAT Mathematics Subject Test results include scaled scores and percentiles. Your scaled score is a number from 200 to 800, calculated using a formula that varies from year to year. The percentile indicates the percentage of people who took the same test and scored lower than you did.

You may want to time yourself as you take this practice test. It should take you about 6 minutes to complete.

HOT TIP! **The questions are written so that you should not need to do any lengthy calculations. If you find yourself getting involved in a long calculation, think again about all of the information in the problem to see if you might have missed something helpful.**

1. Which three-dimensional figure has at least one cross section that is NOT a polygon?

(A) rectangular prism

(B) cube

(C) pentagonal prism

(D) cone

(E) pyramid

2. The height of a right cylinder is 4 times the radius of its base. What is the volume of the cylinder in terms of its radius *r*?

(A) $4\pi r^2$

(B) $8\pi r^2$

(C) $4\pi r^3$

(D) $8\pi r^3$

(E) $3\pi r^4$

3. What is the volume of a right cone with radius 6 ft and height 8 ft?

(A) 48π ft^3

(B) 72π ft^3

(C) 96π ft^3

(D) 288π ft^3

(E) 384π ft^3

4. If triangle *ABC* is rotated about the *x*-axis, what is the volume of the resulting cone?

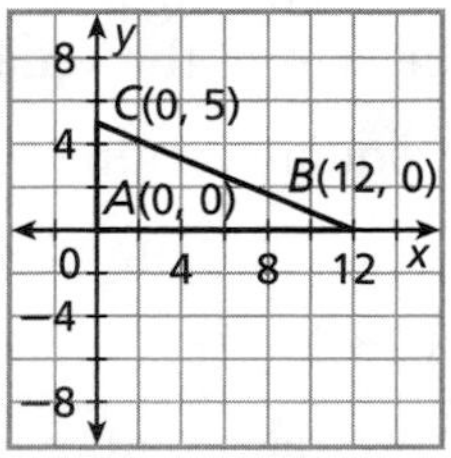

(A) 100π cubic units

(B) 144π cubic units

(C) 240π cubic units

(D) 300π cubic units

(E) 720π cubic units

5. An oxygen tank is the shape of a cylinder with a hemisphere at each end. If the radius of the tank is 5 inches and the overall length is 32 inches, what is the volume of the tank?

(A) $\frac{500}{3\pi}$ in^3

(B) $\frac{2275}{12}\pi$ in^3

(C) $\frac{1900}{3}\pi$ in^3

(D) $\frac{2150}{3}\pi$ in^3

(E) $\frac{2900}{3}\pi$ in^3

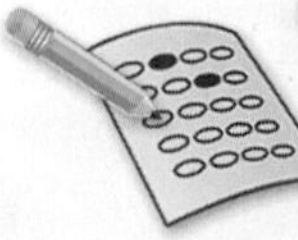

TEST TACKLER

Standardized Test Strategies

Any Question Type: Measure to Solve Problems

On some tests, you may have to measure a figure in order to answer a question. Pay close attention to the units of measure asked for in the question. Some questions ask you to measure to the nearest centimeter, and some ask you to measure to the nearest inch.

EXAMPLE 1

Multiple Choice: **The net of a square pyramid is shown below. Use a ruler to measure the dimensions of the pyramid to the nearest centimeter.**

Which of the following best represents the total surface area of the square pyramid?

Ⓐ 9 square centimeters

Ⓑ 21 square centimeters

Ⓒ 33 square centimeters

Ⓓ 36 square centimeters

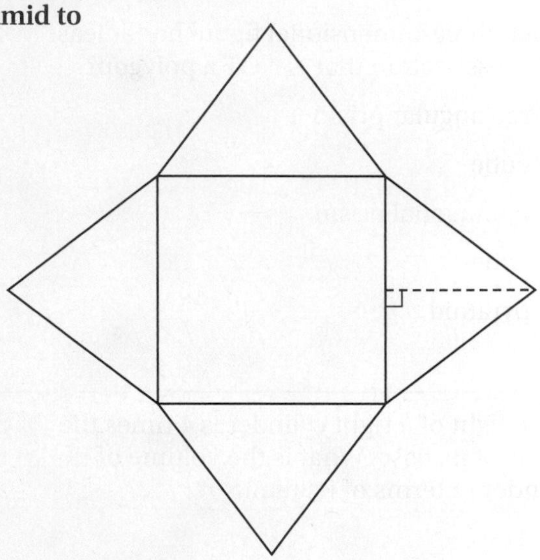

Use a centimeter ruler to measure one side of the square base. The measurement to the nearest centimeter is 3 cm. The base is a square, so all four side lengths are 3 cm.

Measure the altitude of a triangular face, which is the slant height of the pyramid. The altitude is 2 cm. Label the drawing with the measurements.

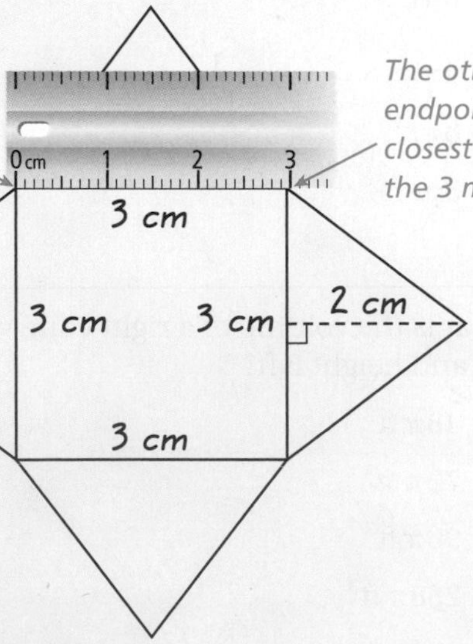

To find the total surface area of the pyramid, find the base area and the lateral area.

The base of the pyramid is a square. The base area of the pyramid is $A = s^2 = (3)^2 = 9\text{ cm}^2$.

The area of one triangular face is $A = \frac{1}{2}bh = \frac{1}{2}(3)(2) = 3\text{ cm}^2$.

The pyramid has 4 faces, so the lateral area is $4(3) = 12\text{ cm}^2$.

The total surface area is $9 + 12 = 21\text{ cm}^2$. The correct answer choice is B.

Read each test item and answer the questions that follow.

HOT TIP! Measure carefully and make sure you are using the correct units to measure the figure.

Item A

The net of a cube is shown below. Use a ruler to measure the dimensions of the cube to the nearest $\frac{1}{4}$ inch.

Which best represents the volume of the cube to the nearest cubic inch?

Ⓐ 1 cubic inch

Ⓑ 2 cubic inches

Ⓒ 5 cubic inches

Ⓓ 9 cubic inches

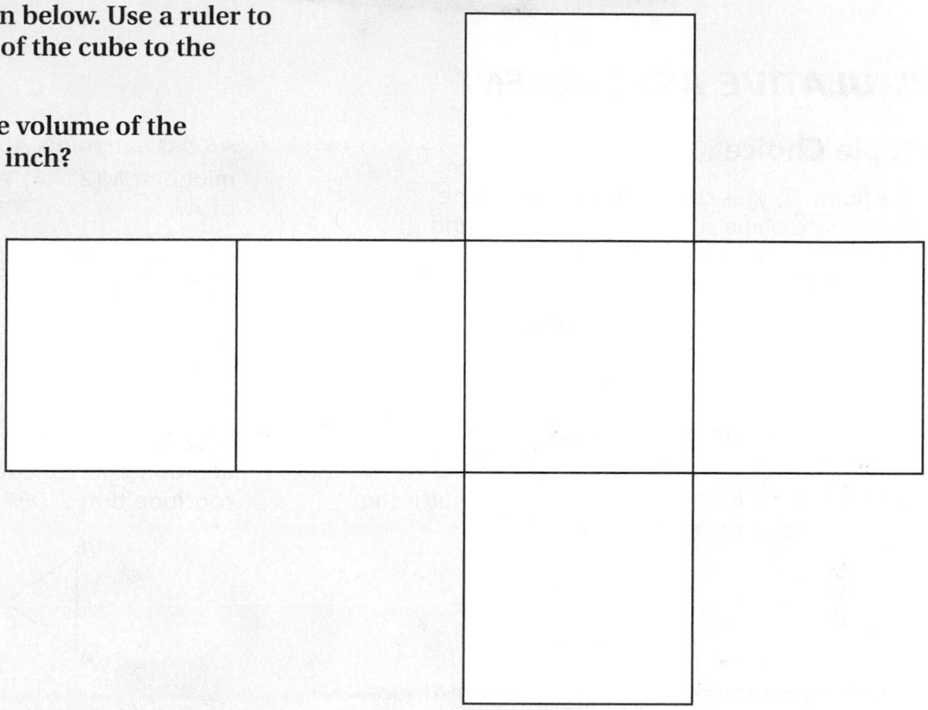

1. Measure one edge of the net for the cube. What is the length to the nearest $\frac{1}{4}$ inch?
2. How would you use the measurement to find the volume of the cube?

Item B

The net of a cylinder is shown below. Use a ruler to measure the dimensions of the cylinder to the nearest tenth of a centimeter.

Which best represents the volume of the cylinder to the nearest cubic centimeter?

Ⓕ 2 cubic centimeters

Ⓖ 6 cubic centimeters

Ⓗ 7 cubic centimeters

Ⓙ 19 cubic centimeters

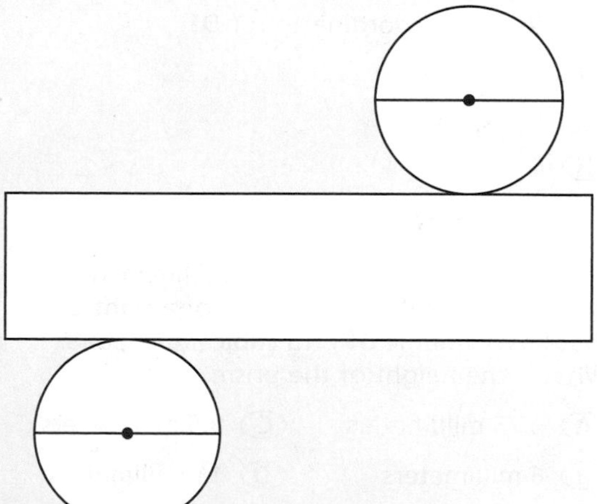

3. Which part of the net do you need to measure in order to find the height of the cylinder? Find the height of the cylinder to the nearest tenth of a centimeter.
4. What other measurement(s) do you need in order to find the volume of the cylinder? Find the measurement(s) to the nearest tenth of a centimeter.
5. How would you use the measurements to find the volume of the cylinder?

STANDARDIZED TEST PREP

Learn It Online
State Test Practice

CUMULATIVE ASSESSMENT

Multiple Choice

1. If a point (x, y) is chosen at random in the coordinate plane such that $-1 \leq x \leq 1$ and $-5 \leq y \leq 3$, what is the probability that $x \geq 0$ and $y \geq 0$?

   (A) 0.1875 (C) 0.375

   (B) 0.25 (D) 0.8125

2. $\triangle ABC \sim \triangle DEF$, and $\triangle DEF \sim \triangle GHI$. If the similarity ratio of $\triangle ABC$ to $\triangle DEF$ is $\frac{1}{2}$ and the similarity ratio of $\triangle DEF$ to $\triangle GHI$ is $\frac{3}{4}$, what is the similarity ratio of $\triangle ABC$ to $\triangle GHI$?

   (F) $\frac{1}{4}$ (H) $\frac{2}{3}$

   (G) $\frac{3}{8}$ (J) $\frac{3}{2}$

3. Which expression represents the number of faces of a prism with bases that are n-gons?

   (A) $n + 1$ (C) $2n$

   (B) $n + 2$ (D) $3n$

4. Parallelogram $ABCD$ has a diagonal $\overline{AC}$ with endpoints $A(-1, 3)$ and $C(-3, -3)$. If B has coordinates (x, y), which of the following represents the coordinates for D?

   (F) $D(-3x, -y)$

   (G) $D(-x, -y)$

   (H) $D(-x - 4, -y)$

   (J) $D(x - 2, y)$

5. Right $\triangle ABC$ with legs $AB = 9$ millimeters and $BC = 12$ millimeters is the base of a right prism that has a volume of 513 cubic millimeters. What is the height of the prism?

   (A) 4.75 millimeters (C) 9.5 millimeters

   (B) 6 millimeters (D) 11 millimeters

6. The radius of a sphere is doubled. What happens to the ratio of the volume of the sphere to the surface area of the sphere?

   (F) It remains the same.

   (G) It is doubled.

   (H) It is increased by a factor of 4.

   (J) It is increased by a factor of 8.

7. $\overline{AB}$ has endpoints $A(x, y)$ and $B(-2, 6)$ and midpoint $M(2, -6)$ What are the coordinates of A?

   (A) $A(-6, 18)$

   (B) $A(0, 0)$

   (C) $A(2, -6)$

   (D) $A(6, -18)$

8. If $\overline{DE}$ bisects $\angle CEF$, which of the following additional statements would allow you to conclude that $\triangle DEF \cong \triangle ABC$?

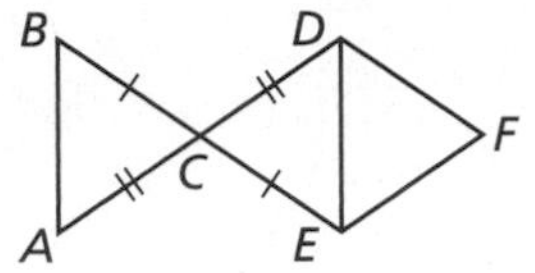

   (F) $\angle DEF \cong \angle BAC$

   (G) $\angle DEF \cong \angle CDE$

   (H) $\overline{EF} \cong \overline{CD}$

   (J) $\overline{EF} \cong \overline{EC}$

9. To the nearest tenth of a cubic centimeter, what is the volume of a right regular octagonal prism with base edge length 4 centimeters and height 7 centimeters?

   (A) 180.3 cubic centimeters

   (B) 224.0 cubic centimeters

   (C) 270.4 cubic centimeters

   (D) 540.8 cubic centimeters

10. Which of the following must be true about a conditional statement?

   (F) If the inverse is false, then the converse is false.

   (G) If the conditional is true, then the contrapositive is false.

   (H) If the conditional is true, then the converse is false.

   (J) If the hypothesis of the conditional is true, then the conditional is true.

HOT TIP! **It may be helpful to include units in your calculations of measures of geometric figures. If your answer includes the proper units, you are less likely to have made an error.**

11. A right cylinder has a height of 10 inches. The circumference of the base is 28.3 inches. To the nearest tenth of a cubic inch, what is the volume for this cylinder?

(A) 141.4 cubic inches

(B) 282.7 cubic inches

(C) 637.3 cubic inches

(D) 2544.7 cubic inches

12. The volume of the smaller sphere is 288 cubic centimeters. Find the volume of the larger sphere.

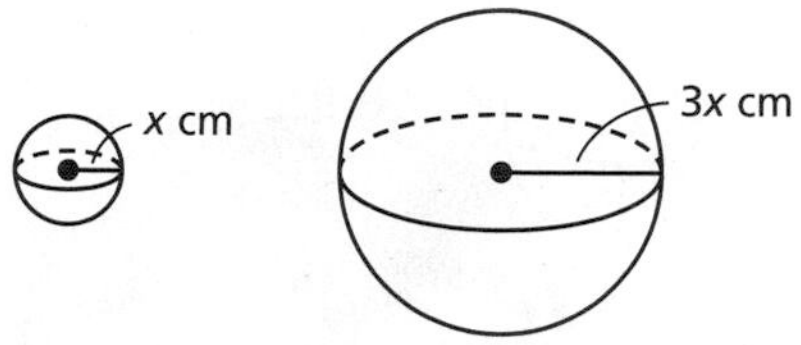

(F) 864 cubic centimeters

(G) 2,592 cubic centimeters

(H) 7,776 cubic centimeters

(J) 23,328 cubic centimeters

Gridded Response

13. $\vec{u} = \langle 3, -7 \rangle$, and $\vec{v} = \langle -6, 5 \rangle$. What is the magnitude of the resultant vector to the nearest tenth?

14. How many lines of symmetry does a regular pentagon have?

15. If Y is the circumcenter of $\triangle PQR$, what is the value of x?

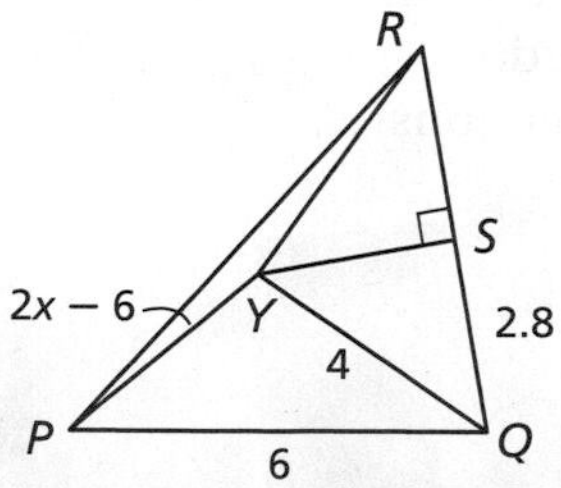

16. How many cubes with edge length 3 centimeters will fit in a box that is a rectangular prism with length 12 centimeters, width 15 centimeters, and height 24 centimeters?

Short Response

17. The area of trapezoid $GHIJ$ is 103.5 square centimeters. Find each of the following. Round answers to the nearest tenth. Show your work or explain in words how you found your answers.

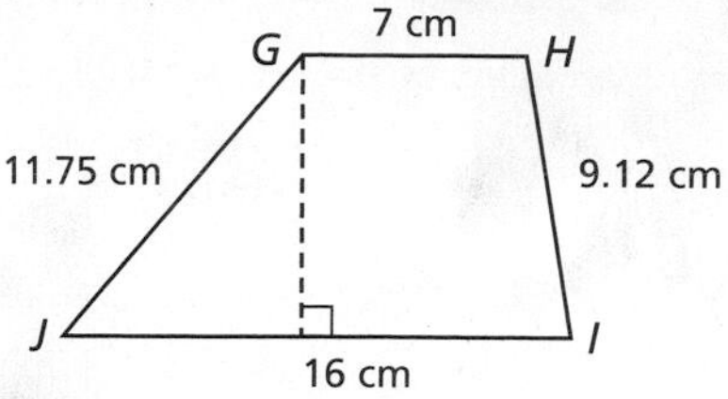

a. the height of trapezoid $GHIJ$

b. $m\angle J$

18. The figure shows the top view of a stack of cubes. The number on each cube represents the number of stacked cubes. The volume of each cube is 4 cubic inches. What is the volume of the three-dimensional figure formed by the cubes?

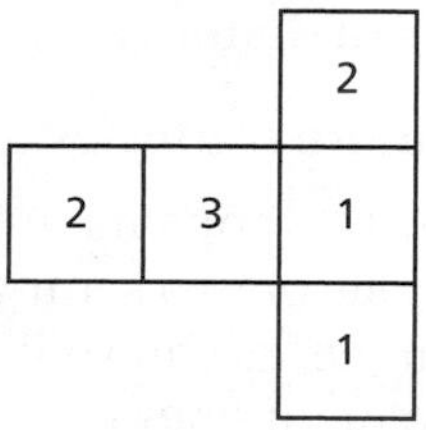

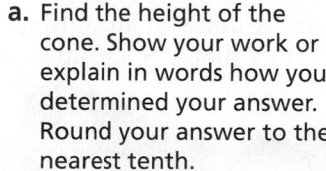

19. $\triangle ABC$ has vertices $A(1, -2)$, $B(-2, -3)$, and $C(-2, 2)$.

a. Graph $\triangle A'B'C'$, the image of $\triangle ABC$, after a dilation with a scale factor of $\frac{3}{2}$.

b. Show that $\overleftrightarrow{AB} \parallel \overleftrightarrow{A'B'}$, $\overleftrightarrow{BC} \parallel \overleftrightarrow{B'C'}$, and $\overleftrightarrow{CA} \parallel \overleftrightarrow{C'A}$. Use slope to justify your answer.

Extended Response

20. The lateral area of a right cone with radius r and slant height ℓ is $L = \pi r \ell$.

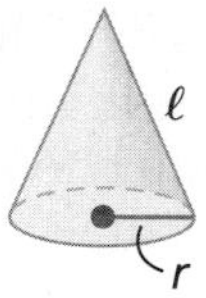

a. Find the height of the cone. Show your work or explain in words how you determined your answer. Round your answer to the nearest tenth.

b. Find the volume of this cone. Round your answer to the nearest tenth.

c. Given a right cone with a lateral area of L and a slant height of ℓ, find an equation for the volume in terms of L and ℓ. Show your work.

Real-World CONNECTIONS

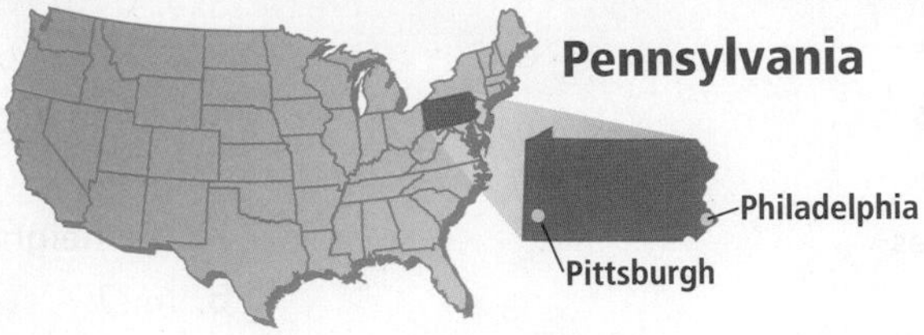

The Mellon Arena

When Pittsburgh's Mellon Arena opened in 1961, it was the world's first auditorium with a retractable roof. The arena became the home of the Penguins in 1967. In 2008, ground was broken for a new arena.

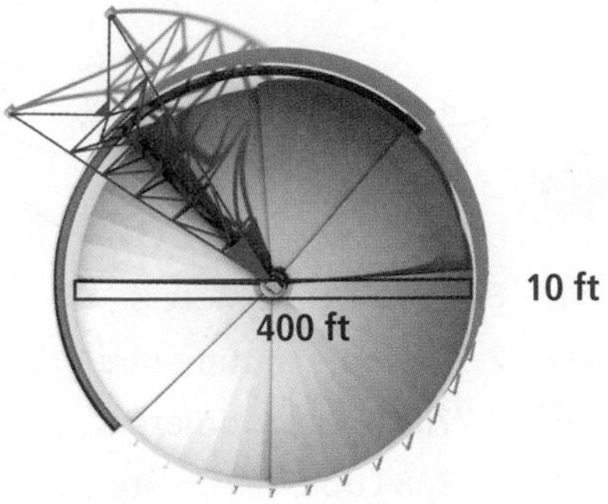

Choose one or more strategies to solve each problem.

1. The Mellon Arena appears to be a perfect circle. However it actually consists of two semi-circles that are connected by a narrow rectangle, as shown in the figure. Approximately how many acres of land does the arena cover? (*Hint:* 1 acre = 43,560 ft^2)

For 2 and 3, use the table.

2. For hockey games, the arena's standard rectangular floor is used. The ratio of the floor's length to its width is 40 : 17. What are the dimensions of the standard arena floor?

3. For special events, some of the seating can be removed to create an expanded rectangular floor. In this case, the length is 130 ft greater than the width. What are the dimensions of the expanded arena floor?

Mellon Arena Floor

	Perimeter (ft)	Area (ft^2)
Standard	570	17,000
Expanded	740	30,000

4. The arena's roof is a stainless steel dome. It consists of eight congruent wedge-shaped sections. When the roof is retracted, six of the sections rotate and come to rest under the two sections that remain fixed. Suppose you choose a seat in the arena at random. When the roof is retracted, what is the probability that you are sitting under one of the fixed sections? What is the probability that you are sitting under the open sky?

✪ The U.S. Mint

Chances are good that you have a souvenir of Philadelphia in your pocket. Since 1792, the U.S. mint has had a facility in Philadelphia, and over the years it has produced trillions of coins. In 2004 alone, the Philadelphia mint turned out approximately 3 billion pennies.

Choose one or more strategies to solve each problem. For 1–4, use the table.

1. Coins are stamped out of a rectangular metal strip that is 13 in. wide by 1,500 ft long. Given that the diameter of a quarter is just under an inch (0.955 in.), what is the minimum number of strips that would be needed to stamp out 700,000 quarters?
2. A penny contains a small amount of copper, but most of the metal in a penny is zinc. The volume of copper in a penny is about 11 mm^3. What percentage of the penny is copper?
3. Nickels are made from a metal that is a mixture of nickel and copper. About how many nickels can be made if a 1 m^3 block of this metal is melted down?
4. Rolls of 50 dimes are packaged in clear plastic sleeves. How much plastic is needed to enclose one roll of dimes?

Coin Specifications

	Diameter (mm)	Thickness (mm)
Penny	19.05	1.55
Nickel	21.21	1.95
Dime	17.91	1.35
Quarter	24.26	1.75

CHAPTER

12 Circles

COMMON CORE

Chapter Focus

- Develop and apply the properties of lines and angles that intersect circles.
- Analyze the properties of circles in the coordinate plane and use them to solve real-world problems.

Elegant Eggs!

Constructing egg shapes from curves of different radii is an ancient art form that goes back to prehistoric times.

Learn It Online
Chapter Project Online

ARE YOU READY?

Vocabulary

Match each term on the left with a definition on the right.

1. radius
2. pi
3. circle
4. circumference

A. the distance around a circle

B. the locus of points in a plane that are a fixed distance from a given point

C. a segment with one endpoint on a circle and one endpoint at the center of the circle

D. the point at the center of a circle

E. the ratio of a circle's circumference to its diameter

Tables and Charts

The table shows the number of students in each grade level at Middletown High School. Find each of the following.

5. the percentage of students who are freshman
6. the percentage of students who are juniors
7. the percentage of students who are sophomores or juniors

Year	Number of Students
Freshman	192
Sophomore	208
Junior	216
Senior	184

Circle Graphs

The circle graph shows the age distribution of residents of Mesa, Arizona, according to the 2000 census. The population of the city is 400,000.

8. How many residents are between the ages of 18 and 24?
9. How many residents are under the age of 18?
10. What percentage of the residents are over the age of 45?
11. How many residents are over the age of 45?

Residents of Mesa, AZ

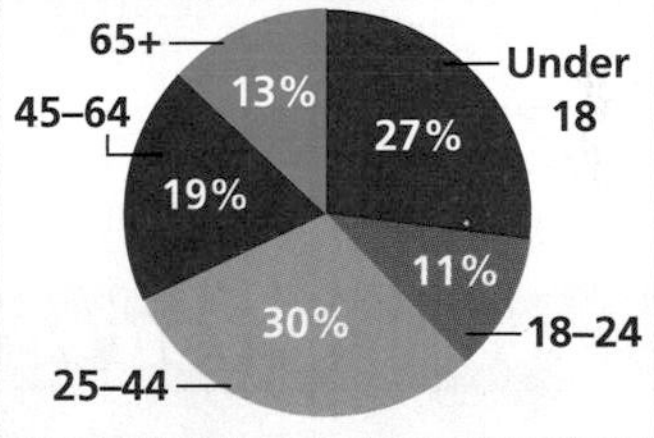

Solve Equations with Variables on Both Sides

Solve each equation.

12. $11y - 8 = 8y + 1$
13. $12x + 32 = 10 + x$
14. $z + 30 = 10z - 15$
15. $4y + 18 = 10y + 15$
16. $-2x - 16 = x + 6$
17. $-2x - 11 = -3x - 1$

Solve Quadratic Equations

Solve each equation.

18. $17 = x^2 - 32$
19. $2 + y^2 = 18$
20. $4x^2 + 12 = 7x^2$
21. $188 - 6x^2 = 38$

CHAPTER 12

Study Guide: Preview

Where You've Been

Previously, you

- used the fundamental vocabulary of circles.
- developed and applied formulas for the area and circumference of circles.
- used circles to solve problems.

In This Chapter

You will study

- solving problems involving circles.
- finding lengths, angle measures, and areas associated with circles.
- applying circle theorems to solve a wide range of problems.

Where You're Going

You can use the skills learned in this chapter

- in Algebra 2 and Precalculus.
- in other classes, such as in Biology when you explore cells, in Physics when you study the laws of motion and kinematic principles, and in Art when you create images.
- to calculate distances, interpret information in newspaper and magazine charts, and make designs.

Key Vocabulary/Vocabulario

arc	arco
arc length	longitud de arco
central angle	ángulo central
chord	cuerda
secant	secante
sector of a circle	sector de un círculo
segment of a circle	segmento de un círculo
semicircle	semicírculo
tangent of a circle	tangente de un círculo

Vocabulary Connections

To become familiar with some of the vocabulary terms in the chapter, answer the following questions. You may refer to the chapter, the glossary, or a dictionary if you like.

1. The word **semicircle** begins with the prefix *semi-*. List some other words that begin with *semi-*. What do all of these words have in common?
2. The word *central* means "located at the center." How can you use this definition to understand the term **central angle** of a circle?
3. The word **tangent** comes from the Latin word *tangere,* which means "to touch." What does this tell you about a line that is a tangent to a circle?
4. The word **secant** comes from the Latin word *secare,* which means "to cut." What does this tell you about a line that is a secant to a circle?

Reading and Writing Math

Study Strategy: Prepare for Your Final Exam

Math is a cumulative subject, so your final exam will probably cover all of the material you have learned since the beginning of the course. Preparation is essential for you to be successful on your final exam. It may help you to make a study timeline like the one below.

2 weeks before the final:

- Look at previous exams and homework to determine areas I need to focus on; rework problems that were incorrect or incomplete.
- Make a list of all formulas, postulates, and theorems I need to know for the final.
- Create a practice exam using problems from the book that are similar to problems from each exam.

1 week before the final:

- Take the practice exam and check it. For each problem I miss, find two or three similar ones and work those.
- Work with a friend in the class to quiz each other on formulas, postulates, and theorems from my list.

1 day before the final:

- Make sure I have pencils, calculator (check batteries!), ruler, compass, and protractor.

Try This

1. Create a timeline that you will use to study for your final exam.

COMMON CORE

12-1 Lines That Intersect Circles

CC.9-12.G.C.2 Identify and describe relationships among inscribed angles, radii, and chords.
Also **CC.9-12.G.C.4 (+), CC.9-12.G.CO.12**

Objectives

Identify tangents, secants, and chords.

Use properties of tangents to solve problems.

Vocabulary

interior of a circle
exterior of a circle
chord
secant
tangent of a circle
point of tangency
congruent circles
concentric circles
tangent circles
common tangent

Why learn this?

You can use circle theorems to solve problems about Earth. (See Example 3.)

This photograph was taken 216 miles above Earth. From this altitude, it is easy to see the curvature of the horizon. Facts about circles can help us understand details about Earth.

Recall that a circle is the set of all points in a plane that are equidistant from a given point, called the center of the circle. A circle with center C is called circle C, or $\odot C$.

The **interior of a circle** is the set of all points inside the circle. The **exterior of a circle** is the set of all points outside the circle.

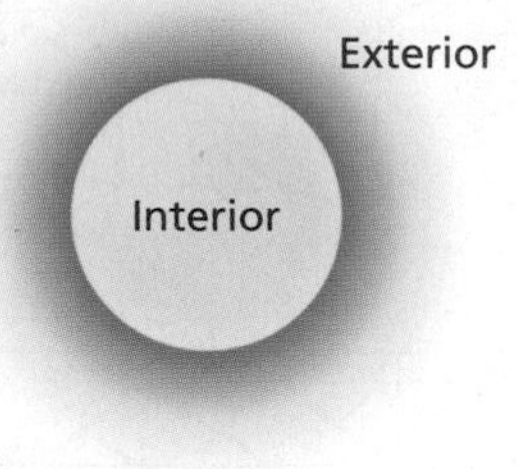

Know it! Note

Lines and Segments That Intersect Circles

TERM
A **chord** is a segment whose endpoints lie on a circle.
A **secant** is a line that intersects a circle at two points.
A **tangent** is a line in the same plane as a circle that intersects it at exactly one point.
The point where the tangent and a circle intersect is called the **point of tangency**.

DIAGRAM

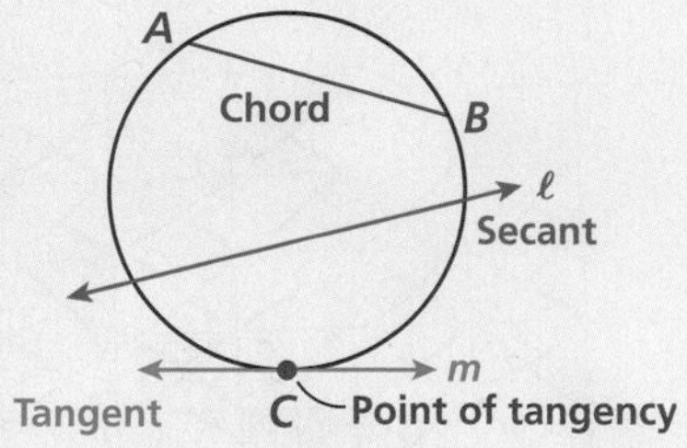

EXAMPLE 1 **Identifying Lines and Segments That Intersect Circles**

Identify each line or segment that intersects $\odot A$.

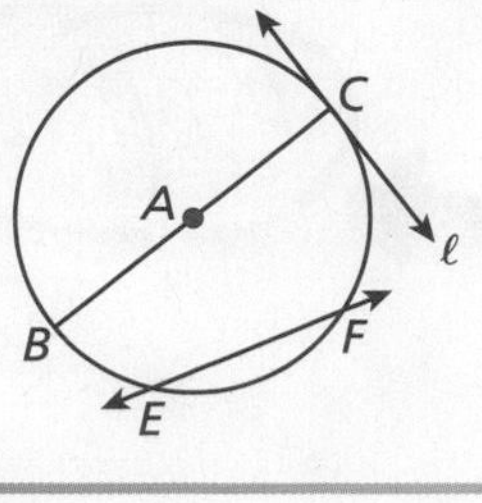

chords: $\overline{EF}$ and $\overline{BC}$

tangent: ℓ

radii: $\overline{AC}$ and $\overline{AB}$

secant: $\overleftrightarrow{EF}$

diameter: $\overline{BC}$

CHECK IT OUT! 1. Identify each line or segment that intersects $\odot P$.

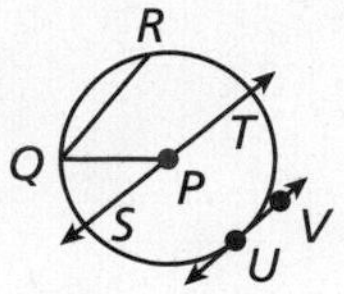

Remember that the terms *radius* and *diameter* may refer to line segments, or to the lengths of segments.

Know it! Note

Pairs of Circles

TERM	DIAGRAM
Two circles are **congruent circles** if and only if they have congruent radii.	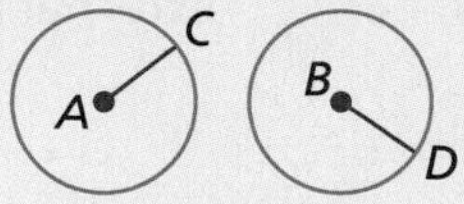 *$\odot A \cong \odot B$ if $\overline{AC} \cong \overline{BD}$.* *$\overline{AC} \cong \overline{BD}$ if $\odot A \cong \odot B$.*
Concentric circles are coplanar circles with the same center.	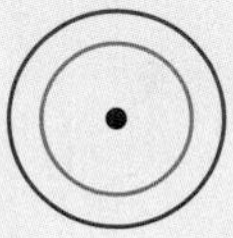
Two coplanar circles that intersect at exactly one point are called **tangent circles**.	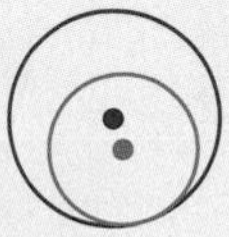 Internally tangent circles 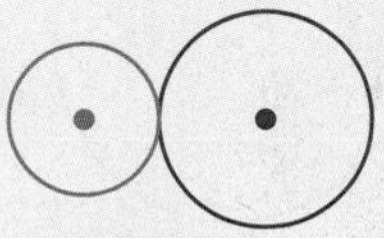 Externally tangent circles

EXAMPLE 2 Identifying Tangents of Circles

Find the length of each radius. Identify the point of tangency and write the equation of the tangent line at this point.

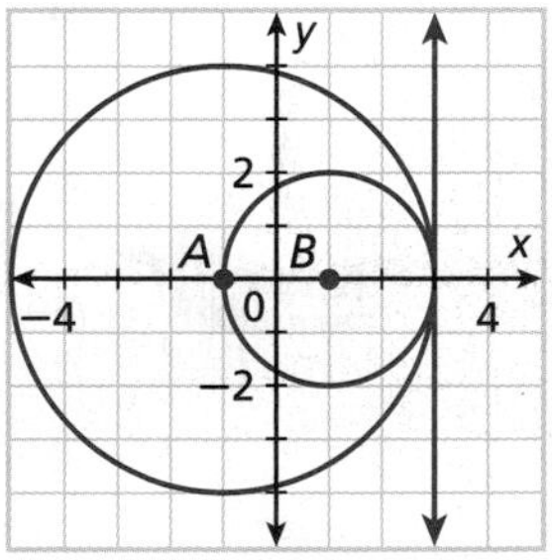

radius of $\odot A$: 4 — *Center is $(-1, 0)$. Pt. on $\odot$ is $(3, 0)$. Dist. between the 2 pts. is 4.*

radius of $\odot B$: 2 — *Center is $(1, 0)$. Pt. on $\odot$ is $(3, 0)$. Dist. between the 2 pts. is 2.*

point of tangency: $(3, 0)$ — *Pt. where the $\odot$s and tangent line intersect*

equation of tangent line: $x = 3$ — *Vert. line through $(3, 0)$*

CHECK IT OUT! 2. Find the length of each radius. Identify the point of tangency and write the equation of the tangent line at this point.

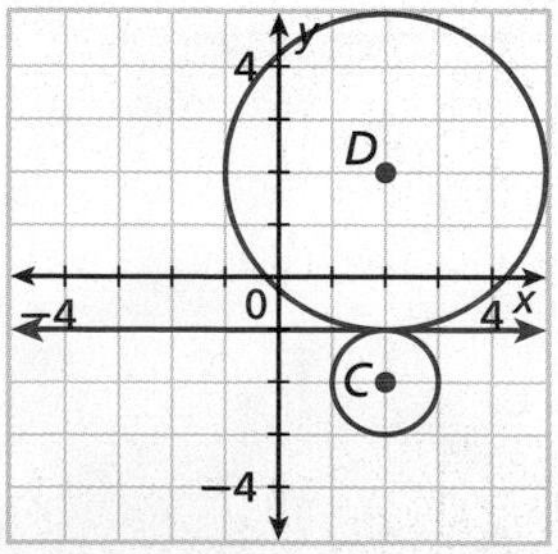

A **common tangent** is a line that is tangent to two circles.

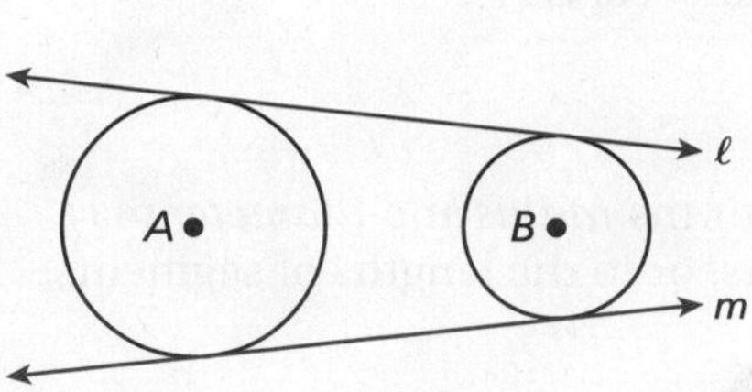

Lines ℓ and m are common external tangents to $\odot A$ and $\odot B$.

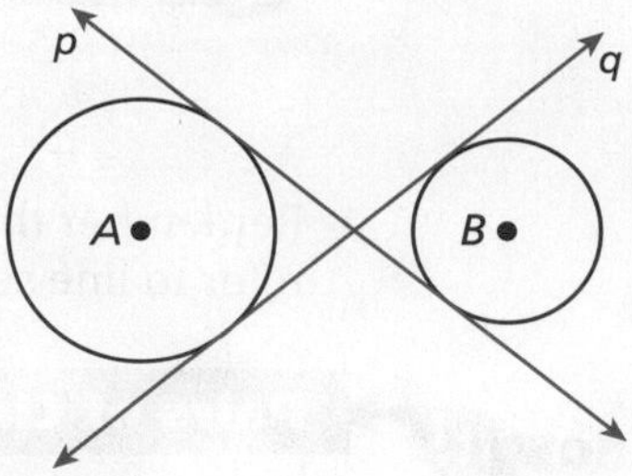

Lines p and q are common internal tangents to $\odot A$ and $\odot B$.

Construction Tangent to a Circle at a Point

1

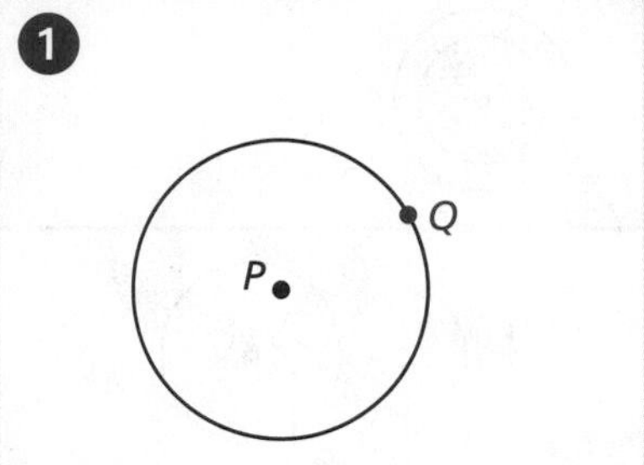

Draw $\odot P$. Locate a point on the circle and label it Q.

2

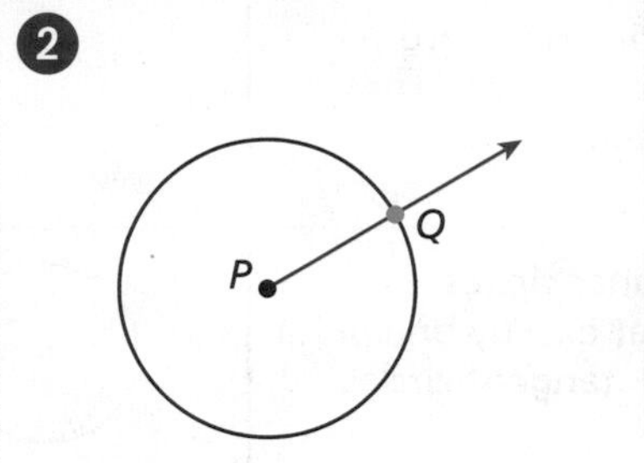

Draw $\overrightarrow{PQ}$.

3

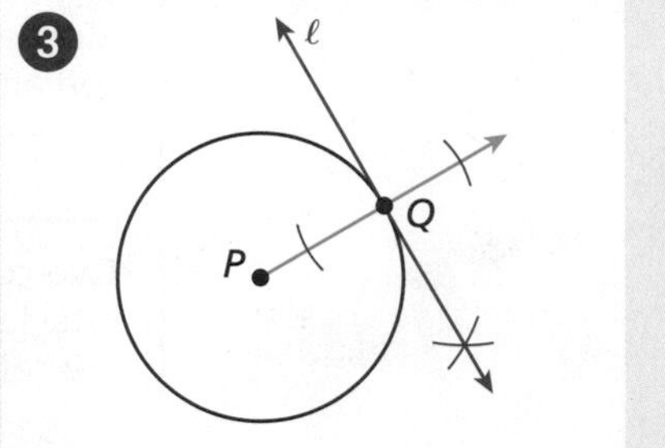

Construct the perpendicular ℓ to $\overrightarrow{PQ}$ at Q. This line is tangent to $\odot P$ at Q.

Notice that in the construction, the tangent line is perpendicular to the radius at the point of tangency. This fact is the basis for the following theorems.

Know it! Note

Reading Math

Theorem 12-1-2 is the converse of Theorem 12-1-1.

Theorems

	THEOREM	HYPOTHESIS	CONCLUSION
12-1-1	If a line is tangent to a circle, then it is perpendicular to the radius drawn to the point of tangency. (line tangent to ⊙ → line ⊥ to radius)	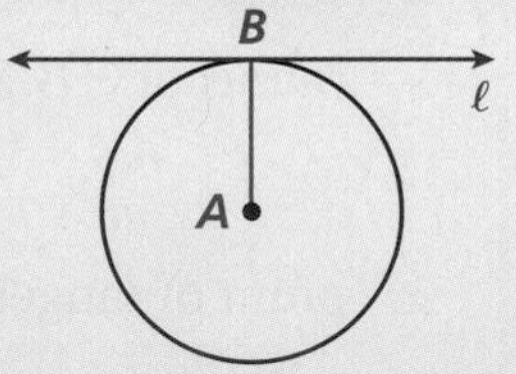 ℓ is tangent to $\odot A$	$\ell \perp \overline{AB}$
12-1-2	If a line is perpendicular to a radius of a circle at a point on the circle, then the line is tangent to the circle. (line ⊥ to radius → line tangent to ⊙)	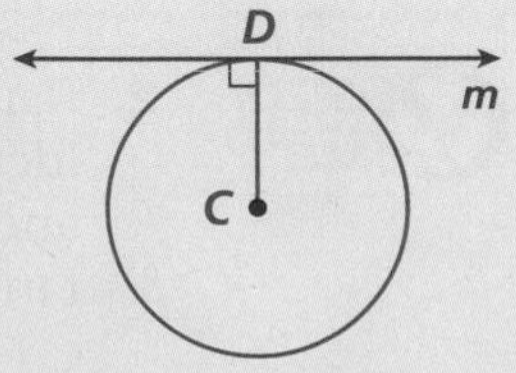 m is $\perp$ to $\overline{CD}$ at D	m is tangent to $\odot C$.

You will prove Theorems 12-1-1 and 12-1-2 in Exercises 28 and 29.

EXAMPLE 3 Problem Solving Application

x^2y Algebra

The summit of Mount Everest is approximately 29,000 ft above sea level. What is the distance from the summit to the horizon to the nearest mile?

MATHEMATICAL PRACTICES

Make sense of problems and persevere in solving them.

1 Understand the Problem

The **answer** will be the length of an imaginary segment from the summit of Mount Everest to Earth's horizon.

2 Make a Plan

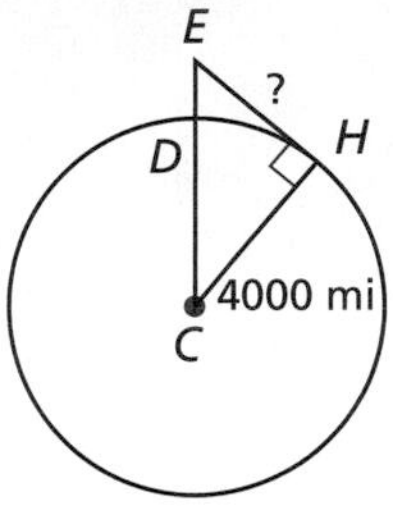

Draw a sketch. Let C be the center of Earth, E be the summit of Mount Everest, and H be a point on the horizon. You need to find the length of $\overline{EH}$, which is tangent to $\odot C$ at H. By Theorem 12-1-1, $\overline{EH} \perp \overline{CH}$. So $\triangle CHE$ is a right triangle.

Helpful Hint

5280 ft = 1 mi
Earth's radius ≈ 4000 mi

3 Solve

ED	$= \mathbf{29{,}000}$ ft	*Given*
	$= \dfrac{29{,}000}{5280} \approx 5.49$ mi	*Change ft to mi.*
EC	$= CD + ED$	*Seg. Add. Post.*
	$= \mathbf{4000} + \mathbf{5.49} = 4005.49$ mi	*Substitute 4000 for CD and 5.49 for ED.*
EC^2	$= EH^2 + CH^2$	*Pyth. Thm.*
$\mathbf{4005.49}^2$	$= EH^2 + \mathbf{4000}^2$	*Substitute the given values.*
$43{,}950.14$	$\approx EH^2$	*Subtract 4000^2 from both sides.*
210 mi	$\approx EH$	*Take the square root of both sides.*

4 Look Back

The problem asks for the distance to the nearest mile. Check if your answer is reasonable by using the Pythagorean Theorem. Is $210^2 + 4000^2 \approx 4005^2$? Yes, $16{,}044{,}100 \approx 16{,}040{,}025$.

CHECK IT OUT! 3. Kilimanjaro, the tallest mountain in Africa, is 19,340 ft tall. What is the distance from the summit of Kilimanjaro to the horizon to the nearest mile?

Know it! Note

Theorem 12-1-3

THEOREM	HYPOTHESIS	CONCLUSION
If two segments are tangent to a circle from the same external point, then the segments are congruent. (2 segs. tangent to ⊙ from same ext. pt. → segs. ≅)	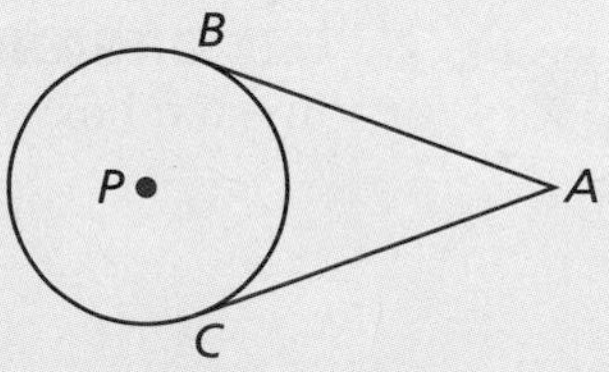 $\overline{AB}$ and $\overline{AC}$ are tangent to $\odot P$.	$\overline{AB} \cong \overline{AC}$

You will prove Theorem 12-1-3 in Exercise 30.

You can use Theorem 12-1-3 to find the length of segments drawn tangent to a circle from an exterior point.

EXAMPLE 4 Using Properties of Tangents

$\overline{DE}$ and $\overline{DF}$ are tangent to $\odot C$. Find DF.

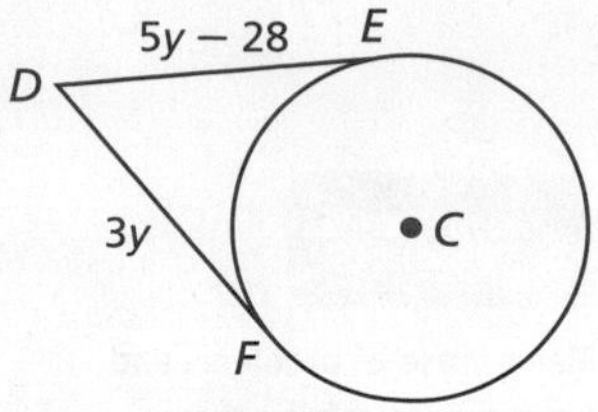

$DE = DF$	*2 segs. tangent to ⊙ from same ext. pt. → segs. ≅.*
$5y - 28 = 3y$	*Substitute 5y − 28 for DE and 3y for DF.*
$2y - 28 = 0$	*Subtract 3y from both sides.*
$2y = 28$	*Add 28 to both sides.*
$y = 14$	*Divide both sides by 2.*
$DF = 3(14)$	*Substitute 14 for y.*
$= 42$	*Simplify.*

CHECK IT OUT! **$\overline{RS}$ and $\overline{RT}$ are tangent to $\odot Q$. Find RS.**

4a.

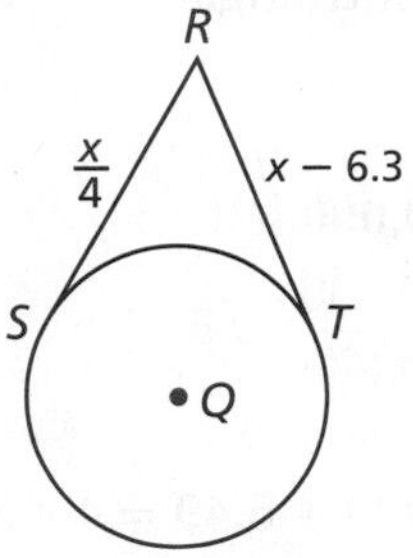

4b.

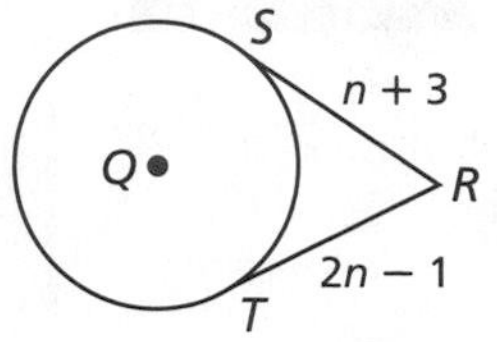

MATHEMATICAL PRACTICES

THINK AND DISCUSS

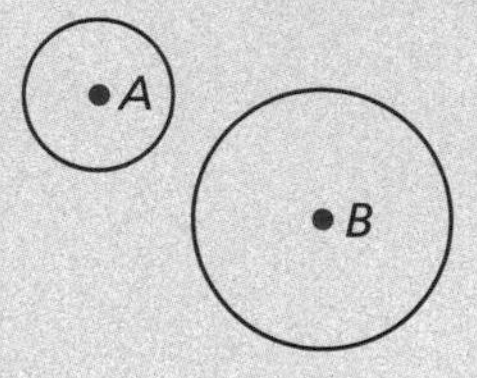

1. Consider $\odot A$ and $\odot B$. How many different lines are common tangents to both circles? Copy the circles and sketch the common external and common internal tangent lines.
2. Is it possible for a line to be tangent to two concentric circles? Explain your answer.
3. Given $\odot P$, is the center P a part of the circle? Explain your answer.
4. In the figure, $\overline{RQ}$ is tangent to $\odot P$ at Q. Explain how you can find $m\angle PRQ$.

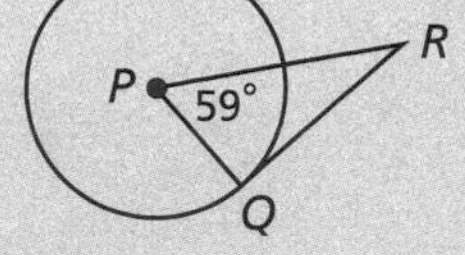

Know it! Note

5. **GET ORGANIZED** Copy and complete the graphic organizer below. In each box, write a definition and draw a sketch.

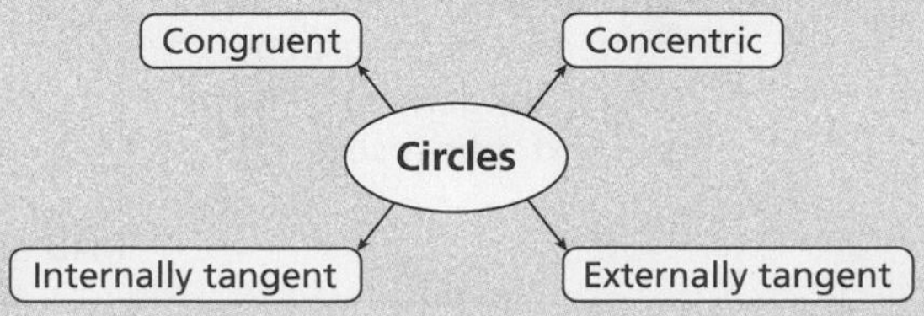

12-1 Exercises

Learn It Online
Homework Help Online
Parent Resources Online

GUIDED PRACTICE

Vocabulary **Apply the vocabulary from this lesson to answer each question.**

1. A ___?___ is a line in the plane of a circle that intersects the circle at two points. (*secant* or *tangent*)

2. Coplanar circles that have the same center are called ___?___. (*concentric* or *congruent*)

3. $\odot Q$ and $\odot R$ both have a radius of 3 cm. Therefore the circles are ___?___. (*concentric* or *congruent*)

SEE EXAMPLE 1

Identify each line or segment that intersects each circle.

4.

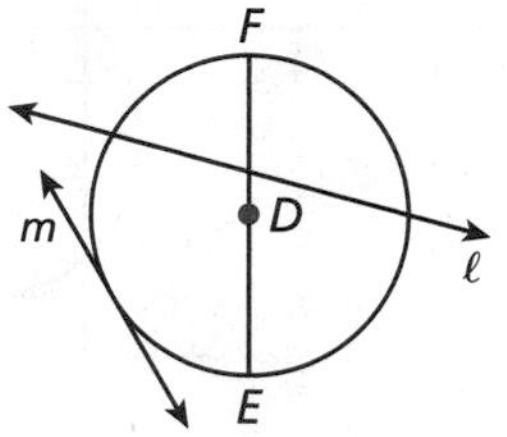

5.

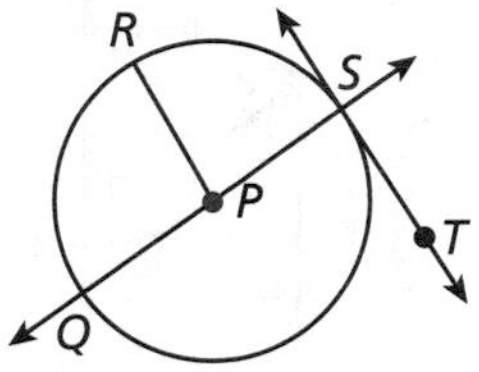

SEE EXAMPLE 2

Multi-Step **Find the length of each radius. Identify the point of tangency and write the equation of the tangent line at this point.**

6.

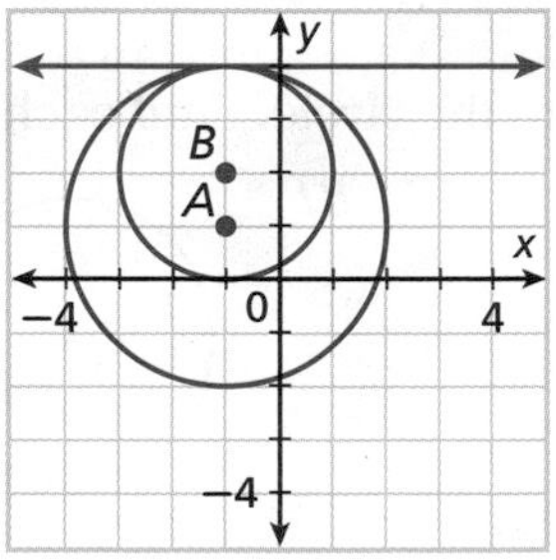

7.

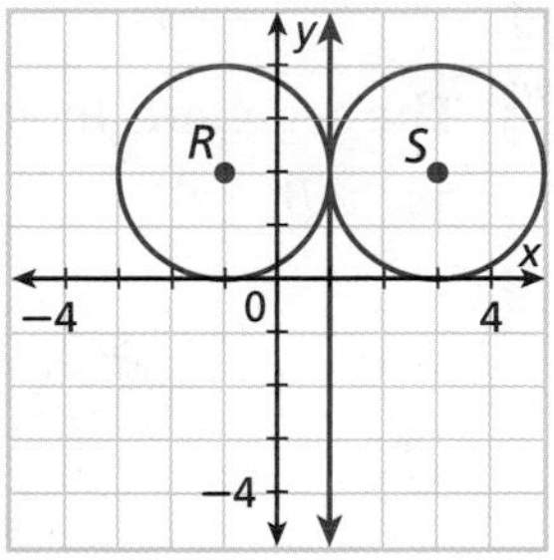

SEE EXAMPLE 3

8. **Space Exploration** The International Space Station orbits Earth at an altitude of 240 mi. What is the distance from the space station to Earth's horizon to the nearest mile?

SEE EXAMPLE 4

The segments in each figure are tangent to the circle. Find each length.

9. *JK*

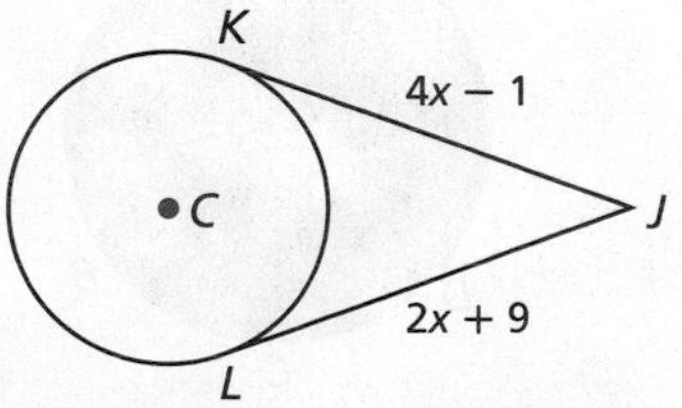

10. *ST*

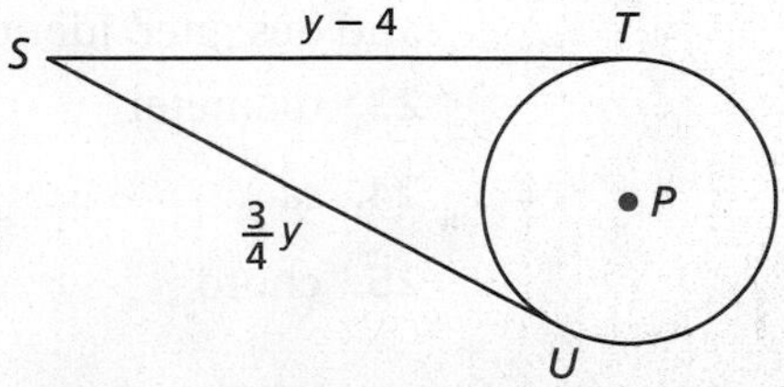

PRACTICE AND PROBLEM SOLVING

Independent Practice

For Exercises	See Example
11–12	1
13–14	2
15	3
16–17	4

Extra Practice

See Extra Practice for more Skills Practice and Applications Practice exercises.

Identify each line or segment that intersects each circle.

11.

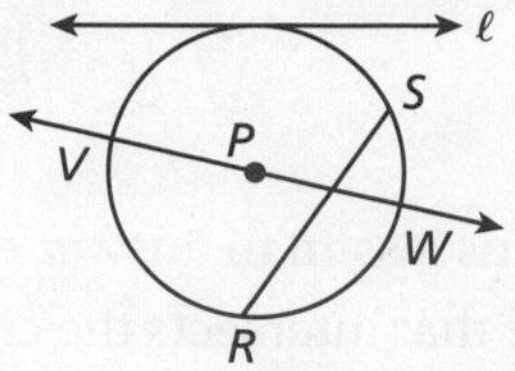

12.

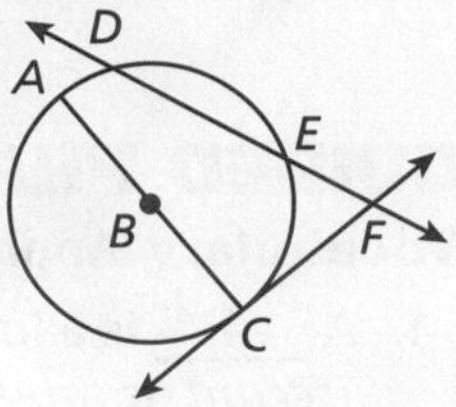

Multi-Step **Find the length of each radius. Identify the point of tangency and write the equation of the tangent line at this point.**

13.

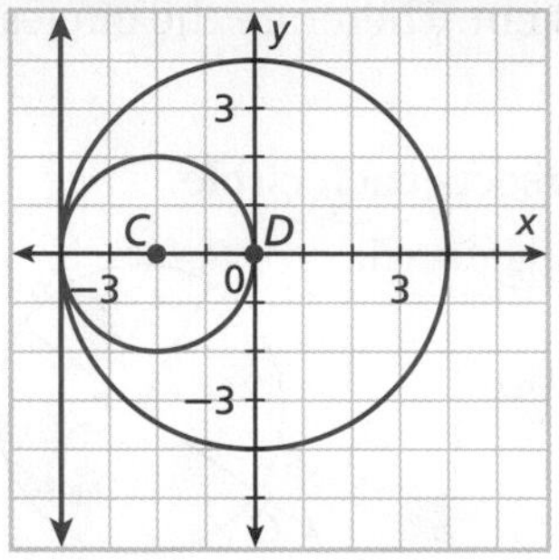

14.

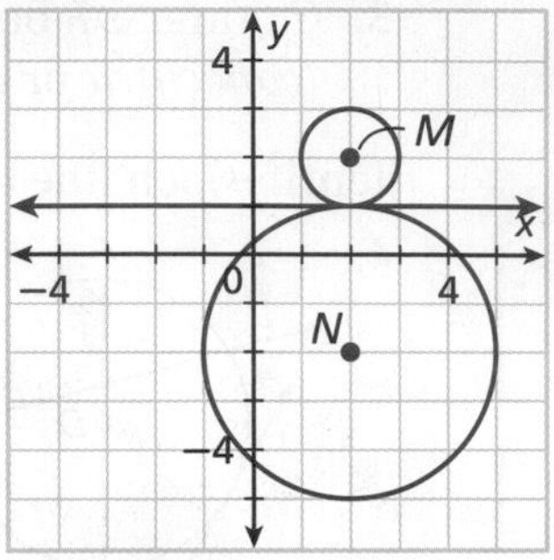

LINK

Astronomy

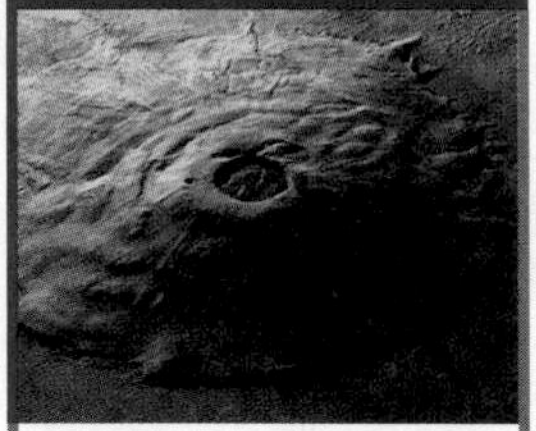

Olympus Mons, located on Mars, is the tallest known volcano in the solar system.

15. **Astronomy** Olympus Mons's peak rises 25 km above the surface of the planet Mars. The diameter of Mars is approximately 6794 km. What is the distance from the peak of Olympus Mons to the horizon to the nearest kilometer?

The segments in each figure are tangent to the circle. Find each length.

16. AB

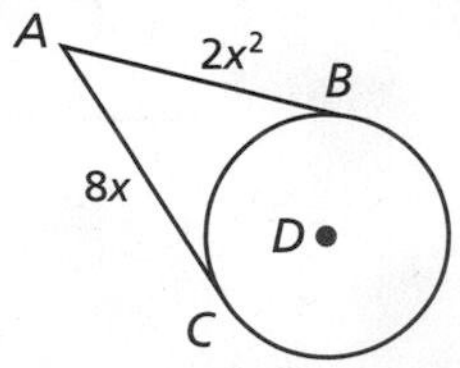

17. RT

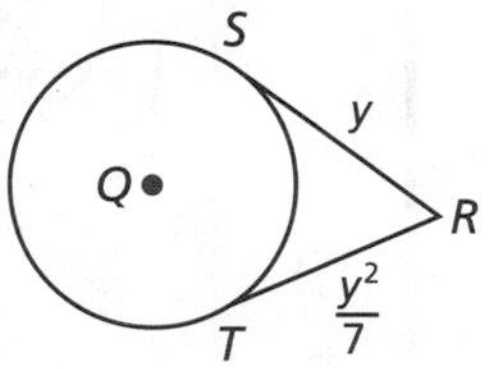

Tell whether each statement is sometimes, always, or never true.

18. Two circles with the same center are congruent.

19. A tangent to a circle intersects the circle at two points.

20. Tangent circles have the same center.

21. A tangent to a circle will form a right angle with a radius that is drawn to the point of tangency.

22. A chord of a circle is a diameter.

Graphic Design **Use the following diagram for Exercises 23–25.**

The peace symbol was designed in 1958 by Gerald Holtom, a professional artist and designer. Identify the following.

23. diameter

24. radii

25. chord

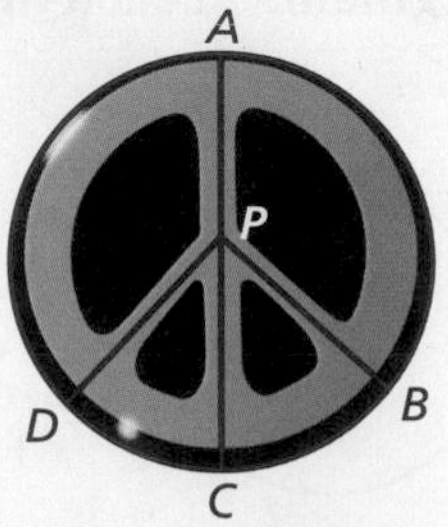

In each diagram, $\overline{PR}$ and $\overline{PS}$ are tangent to $\odot Q$. Find each angle measure.

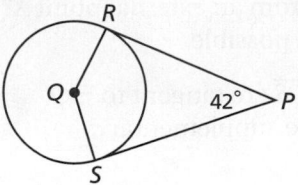

26. $m\angle Q$

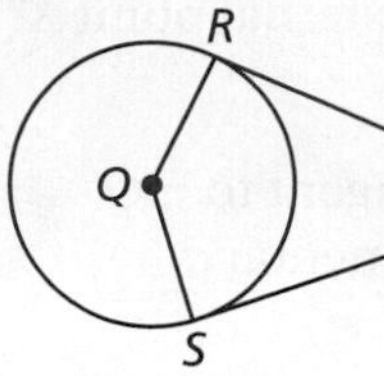

27. $m\angle P$

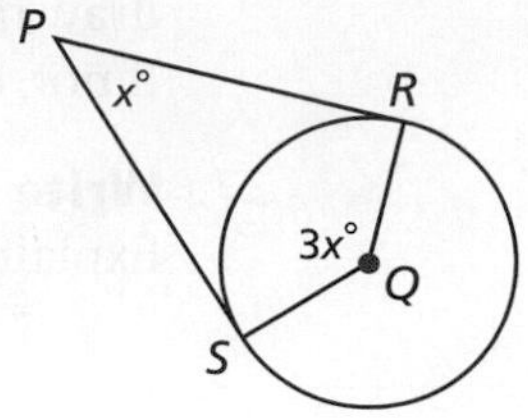

28. Complete this indirect proof of Theorem 12-1-1.
Given: ℓ is tangent to $\odot A$ at point B.
Prove: $\ell \perp \overline{AB}$

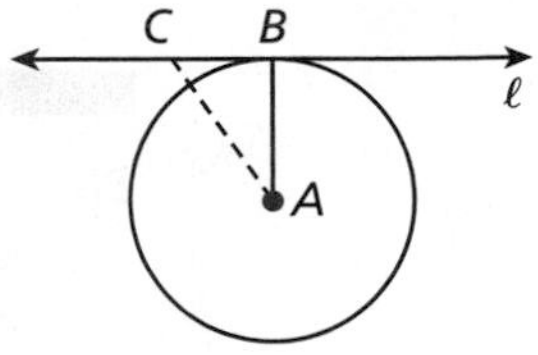

Proof: Assume that ℓ is not $\perp \overline{AB}$. Then it is possible to draw $\overline{AC}$ such that $\overline{AC} \perp \ell$. If this is true, then $\triangle ACB$ is a right triangle. $AC < AB$ because **a.** ___?___ . Since ℓ is a tangent line, it can only intersect $\odot A$ at **b.** ___?___ , and C must be in the exterior of $\odot A$. That means that $AC > AB$ since $\overline{AB}$ is a **c.** ___?___ . This contradicts the fact that $AC < AB$. Thus the assumption is false, and **d.** ___?___ .

29. Prove Theorem 12-1-2.
Given: $m \perp \overline{CD}$
Prove: m is tangent to $\odot C$.

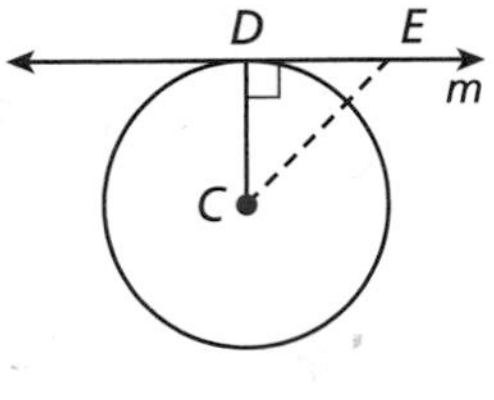

(*Hint:* Choose a point on m. Then use the Pythagorean Theorem to prove that if the point is not D, then it is not on the circle.)

30. Prove Theorem 12-1-3.
Given: $\overline{AB}$ and $\overline{AC}$ are tangent to $\odot P$.
Prove: $\overline{AB} \cong \overline{AC}$

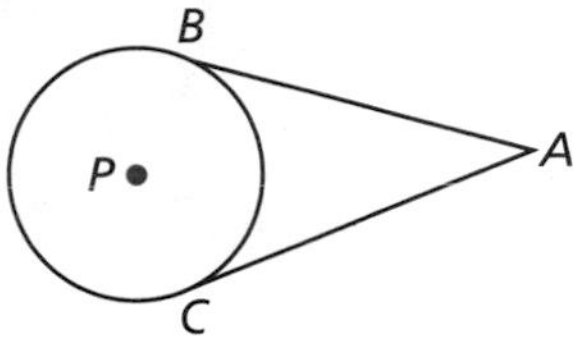

Plan: Draw auxiliary segments $\overline{PA}$, $\overline{PB}$, and $\overline{PC}$. Show that the triangles formed are congruent. Then use CPCTC.

Algebra **Assume the segments that appear to be tangent are tangent. Find each length.**

31. ST

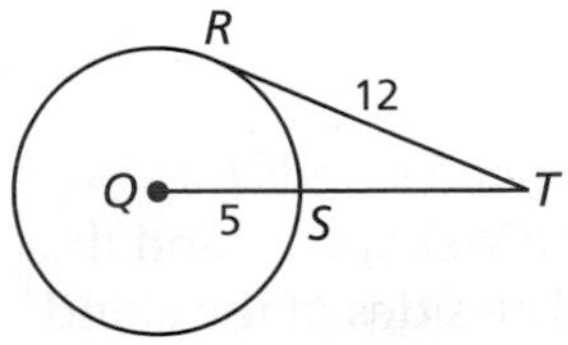

32. DE

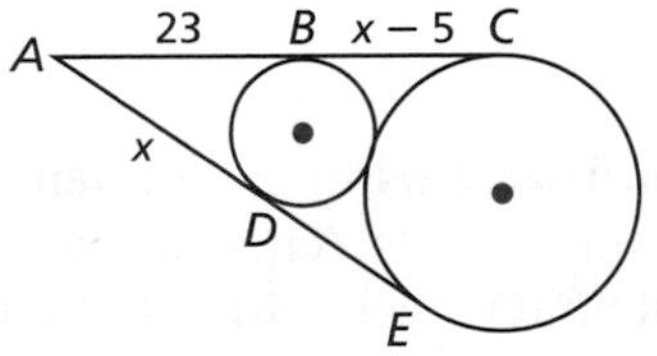

33. JL

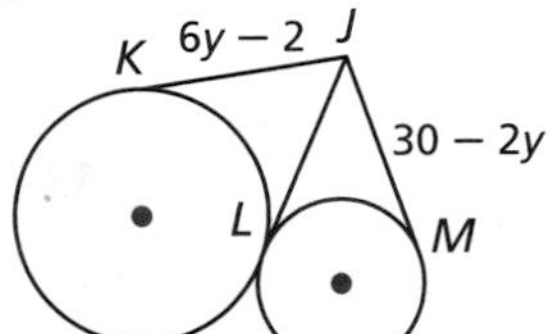

34. $\odot M$ has center $M(2, 2)$ and radius 3. $\odot N$ has center $N(-3, 2)$ and is tangent to $\odot M$. Find the coordinates of the possible points of tangency of the two circles.

MULTI-STEP TEST PREP

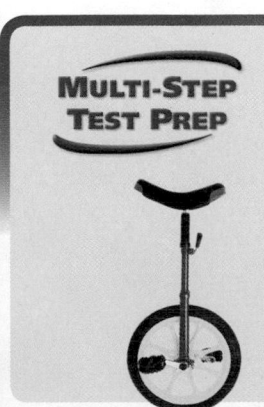

35. The diagram shows the gears of a bicycle. $AD = 5$ in., and $BC = 3$ in. CD, the length of the chain between the gears, is 17 in.

a. What type of quadrilateral is $BCDE$? Why?

b. Find BE and AE.

c. What is AB to the nearest tenth of an inch?

36. Critical Thinking Given a circle with diameter $\overline{BC}$, is it possible to draw tangents to B and C from an external point X? If so, make a sketch. If not, explain why it is not possible.

37. Write About It $\overline{PR}$ and $\overline{PS}$ are tangent to $\odot Q$. Explain why $\angle P$ and $\angle Q$ are supplementary.

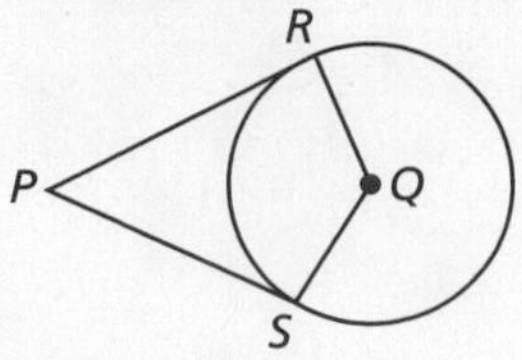

38. $\overline{AB}$ and $\overline{AC}$ are tangent to $\odot D$. Which of these is closest to AD?

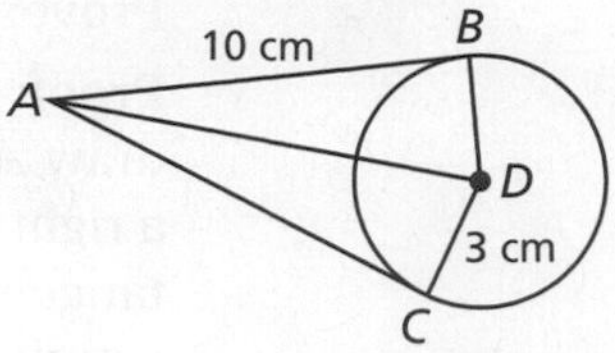

(A) 9.5 cm (C) 10.4 cm

(B) 10 cm (D) 13 cm

39. $\odot P$ has center $P(3, -2)$ and radius 2. Which of these lines is tangent to $\odot P$?

(F) $x = 0$ (G) $y = -4$ (H) $y = -2$ (J) $x = 4$

40. $\odot A$ has radius 5. $\odot B$ has radius 6. What is the ratio of the area of $\odot A$ to that of $\odot B$?

(A) $\frac{125}{216}$ (B) $\frac{25}{36}$ (C) $\frac{5}{6}$ (D) $\frac{36}{25}$

CHALLENGE AND EXTEND

41. Given: $\odot G$ with $\overline{GH} \perp \overline{JK}$
Prove: $\overline{JH} \cong \overline{KH}$

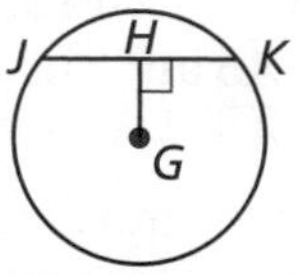

42. Multi-Step $\odot A$ has radius 5, $\odot B$ has radius 2, and $\overline{CD}$ is a common tangent. What is AB? (*Hint:* Draw a perpendicular segment from B to E, a point on $\overline{AC}$.)

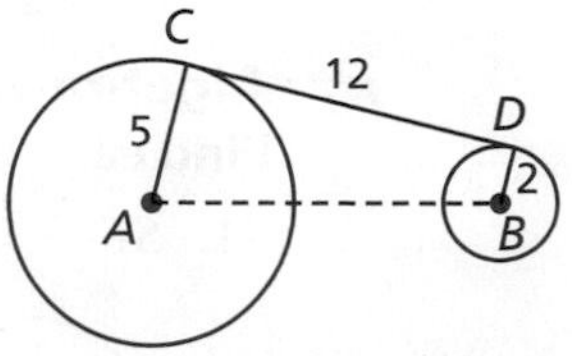

43. Manufacturing A company builds metal stands for bicycle wheels. A new design calls for a V-shaped stand that will hold wheels with a 13 in. radius. The sides of the stand form a 70° angle. To the nearest tenth of an inch, what should be the length XY of a side so that it is tangent to the wheel?

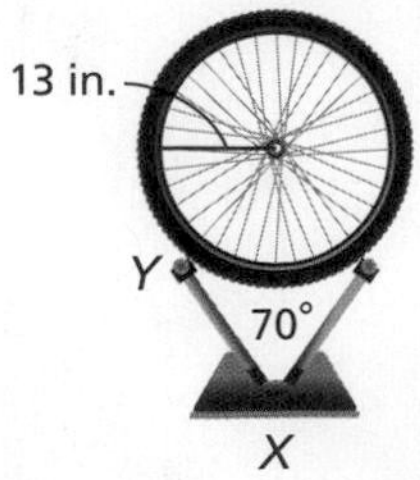

Connecting Geometry to **Data Analysis**

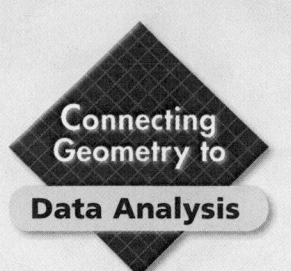

Circle Graphs

A circle graph compares data that are parts of a whole unit. When you make a circle graph, you find the measure of each *central angle*. A *central angle* is an angle whose vertex is the center of the circle.

Example

Make a circle graph to represent the following data.

Books in the Bookmobile	
Fiction	110
Nonfiction	40
Children's	300
Audio books	150

Step 1 Add all the amounts. *110 + 40 + 300 + 150 = 600*

Step 2 Write each part as a fraction of the whole.

fiction: $\frac{110}{600}$; *nonfiction:* $\frac{40}{600}$; *children's:* $\frac{300}{600}$; *audio books:* $\frac{150}{600}$

Step 3 Multiply each fraction by 360° to calculate the central angle measure.

$\frac{110}{600}(360°) = 66°$; $\frac{40}{600}(360°) = 24°$; $\frac{300}{600}(360°) = 180°$; $\frac{150}{600}(360°) = 90°$

Step 4 Make a circle graph. Then color each section of the circle to match the data.

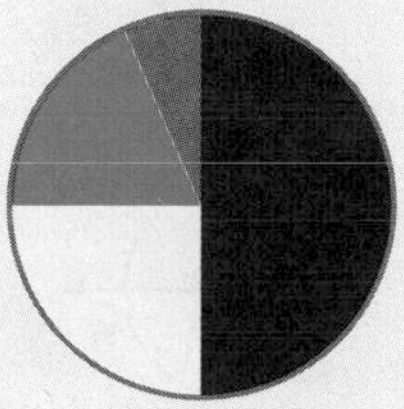

The section with a central angle of 66° is green, 24° is orange, 180° is purple, and 90° is yellow.

Try This

Choose the circle graph that best represents the data. Show each step.

A

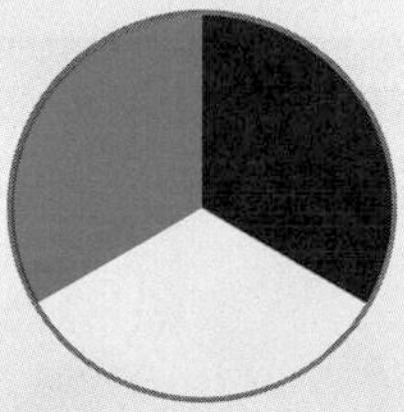

B

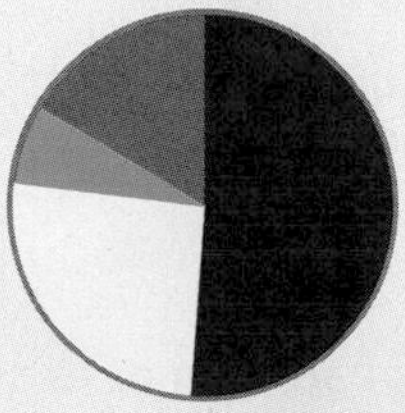

C

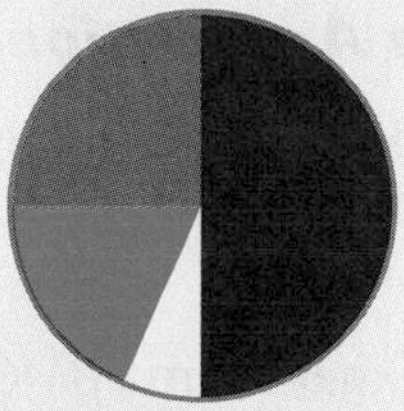

D

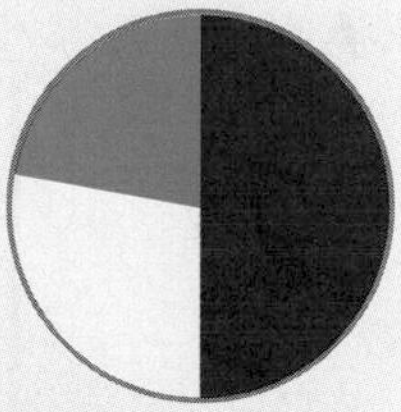

1.

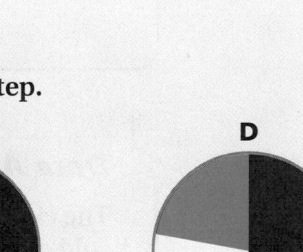

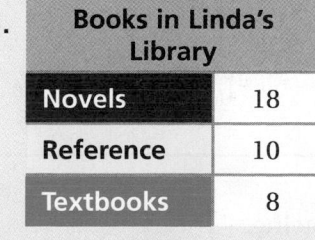

Books in Linda's Library	
Novels	18
Reference	10
Textbooks	8

2.

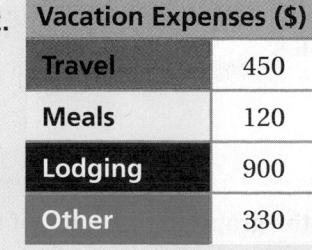

Vacation Expenses ($)	
Travel	450
Meals	120
Lodging	900
Other	330

3.

Puppy Expenses ($)	
Food	190
Health	375
Training	120
Other	50

COMMON CORE

12-2 Arcs and Chords

CC.9-12.G.C.2 Identify and describe relationships among inscribed angles, radii, and chords.
Also **CC.9-12.G.CO.12**

Objectives

Apply properties of arcs.

Apply properties of chords.

Vocabulary

central angle
arc
minor arc
major arc
semicircle
adjacent arcs
congruent arcs

Who uses this?

Market analysts use circle graphs to compare sales of different products.

A **central angle** is an angle whose vertex is the center of a circle. An **arc** is an unbroken part of a circle consisting of two points called the endpoints and all the points on the circle between them.

Know it! Note

Arcs and Their Measure

ARC	MEASURE	DIAGRAM
A **minor arc** is an arc whose points are on or in the interior of a central angle.	The measure of a minor arc is equal to the measure of its central angle. $m\overset{\frown}{AC} = m\angle ABC = x°$	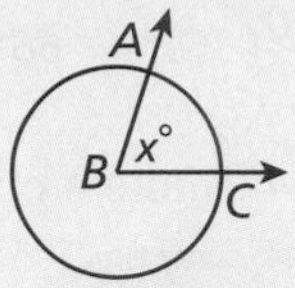
A **major arc** is an arc whose points are on or in the exterior of a central angle.	The measure of a major arc is equal to 360° minus the measure of its central angle. $m\overset{\frown}{ADC} = 360° - m\angle ABC = 360° - x°$	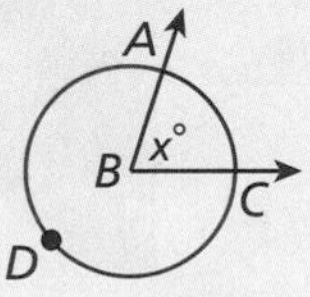
If the endpoints of an arc lie on a diameter, the arc is a **semicircle**.	The measure of a semicircle is equal to 180°. $m\overset{\frown}{EFG} = 180°$	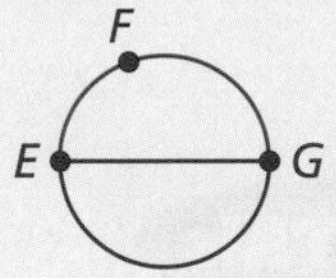

Writing Math

Minor arcs may be named by two points. Major arcs and semicircles must be named by three points.

EXAMPLE 1 ***Data Application***

The circle graph shows the types of music sold during one week at a music store. Find $m\overset{\frown}{BC}$.

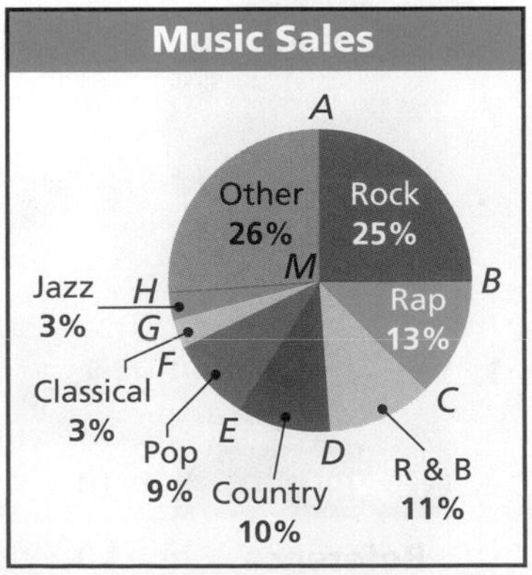

$m\overset{\frown}{BC} = m\angle BMC$ *m of arc = m of central ∠.*

$m\angle BMC = 0.13(360°)$ *Central ∠ is 13% of the ⊙.*

$= 46.8°$

CHECK IT OUT! **Use the graph to find each of the following.**

1a. $m\angle FMC$ **1b.** $m\overset{\frown}{AHB}$ **1c.** $m\angle EMD$

Adjacent arcs are arcs of the same circle that intersect at exactly one point. $\overset{\frown}{RS}$ and $\overset{\frown}{ST}$ are adjacent arcs.

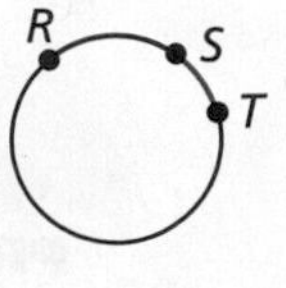

Know it! Note

Postulate 12-2-1 **Arc Addition Postulate**

The measure of an arc formed by two adjacent arcs is the sum of the measures of the two arcs.

$m\overset{\frown}{ABC} = m\overset{\frown}{AB} + m\overset{\frown}{BC}$

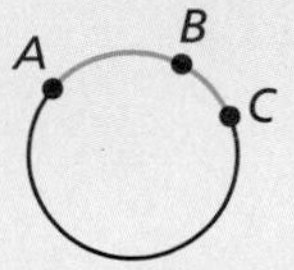

EXAMPLE 2 Using the Arc Addition Postulate

Find $m\overset{\frown}{CDE}$

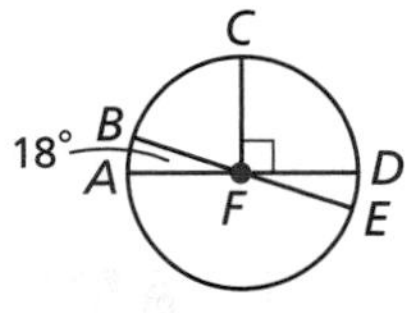

$m\overset{\frown}{CD} = 90°$	*m∠CFD = 90°*
$m\angle DFE = 18°$	*Vert. ∠s Thm.*
$m\overset{\frown}{DE} = 18°$	*m∠DFE = 18°*
$m\overset{\frown}{CE} = m\overset{\frown}{CD} + m\overset{\frown}{DE}$	*Arc Add. Post.*
$= 90° + 18° = 108°$	*Substitute and simplify.*

CHECK IT OUT! **Find each measure.**

2a. $m\overset{\frown}{JKL}$ **2b.** $m\overset{\frown}{LJN}$

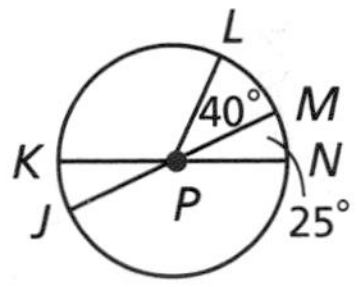

Within a circle or congruent circles, **congruent arcs** are two arcs that have the same measure. In the figure, $\overset{\frown}{ST} \cong \overset{\frown}{UV}$.

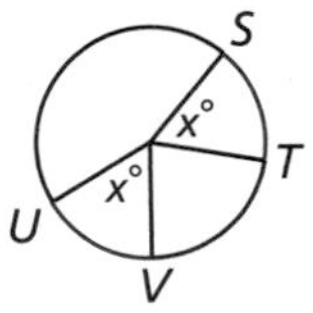

Know it! Note

Theorem 12-2-2

THEOREM	HYPOTHESIS		CONCLUSION
In a circle or congruent circles:			
(1) Congruent central angles have congruent chords.	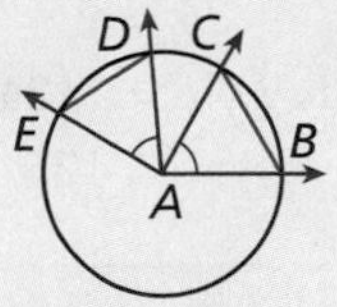	∠EAD ≅ ∠BAC	$\overline{DE} \cong \overline{BC}$
(2) Congruent chords have congruent arcs.	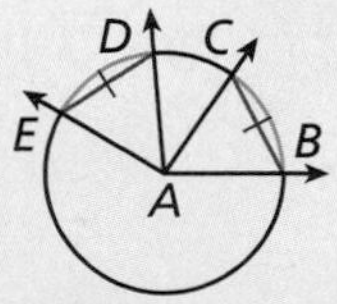	$\overline{ED} \cong \overline{BC}$	$\overset{\frown}{DE} \cong \overset{\frown}{BC}$
(3) Congruent arcs have congruent central angles.	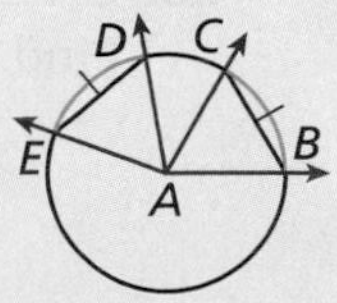	$\overset{\frown}{ED} \cong \overset{\frown}{BC}$	∠DAE ≅ ∠BAC

You will prove parts 2 and 3 of Theorem 12-2-2 in Exercises 40 and 41.

The converses of the parts of Theorem 12-2-2 are also true. For example, with part 1, congruent chords have congruent central angles.

PROOF

Theorem 12-2-2 (Part 1)

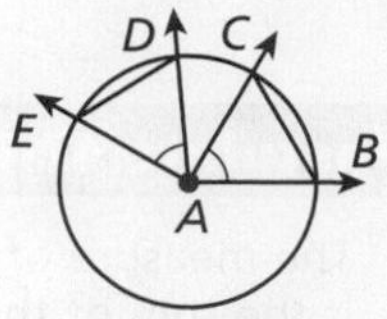

Given: $\angle BAC \cong \angle DAE$
Prove: $\overline{BC} \cong \overline{DE}$

Proof:

Statements	Reasons
1. $\angle BAC \cong \angle DAE$	1. Given
2. $\overline{AB} \cong \overline{AD}$, $\overline{AC} \cong \overline{AE}$	2. All radii of a $\odot$ are $\cong$.
3. $\triangle BAC \cong \triangle DAE$	3. SAS *Steps 2, 1*
4. $\overline{BC} \cong \overline{DE}$	4. CPCTC

EXAMPLE 3 Applying Congruent Angles, Arcs, and Chords

Find each measure.

Algebra

A $\overline{RS} \cong \overline{TU}$. Find $m\overset{\frown}{RS}$.

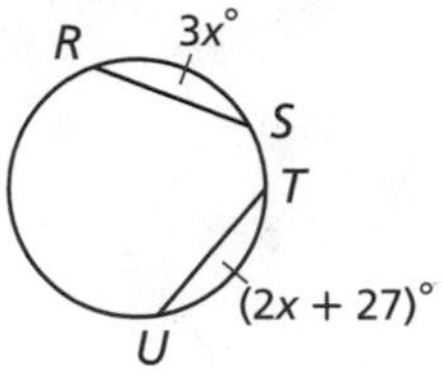

$\overset{\frown}{RS} \cong \overset{\frown}{TU}$	*$\cong$ chords have $\cong$ arcs.*
$m\overset{\frown}{RS} = m\overset{\frown}{TU}$	*Def. of $\cong$ arcs*
$3x = 2x + 27$	*Substitute the given measures.*
$x = 27$	*Subtract 2x from both sides.*
$m\overset{\frown}{RS} = 3(27)$	*Substitute 27 for x.*
$= 81°$	*Simplify.*

B $\odot B \cong \odot E$, and $\overset{\frown}{AC} \cong \overset{\frown}{DF}$. Find $m\angle DEF$.

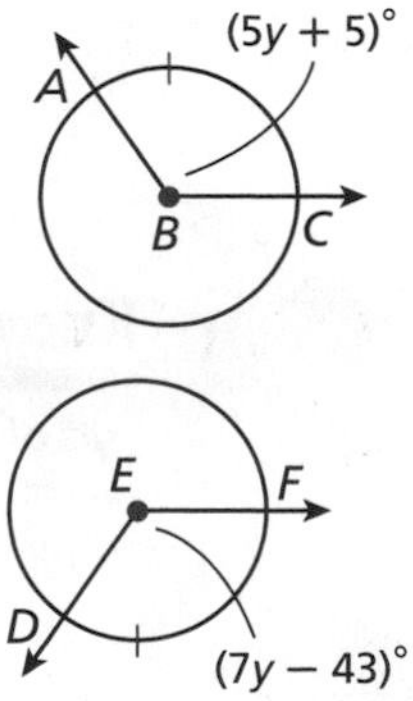

$\angle ABC \cong \angle DEF$	*$\cong$ arcs have $\cong$ central $\measuredangle$s.*
$m\angle ABC = m\angle DEF$	*Def. of $\cong$ $\measuredangle$s*
$5y + 5 = 7y - 43$	*Substitute the given measures.*
$5 = 2y - 43$	*Subtract 5y from both sides.*
$48 = 2y$	*Add 43 to both sides.*
$24 = y$	*Divide both sides by 2.*
$m\angle DEF = 7(24) - 43$	*Substitute 24 for y.*
$= 125°$	*Simplify.*

CHECK IT OUT! Find each measure.

3a. $\overrightarrow{PT}$ bisects $\angle RPS$. Find RT.

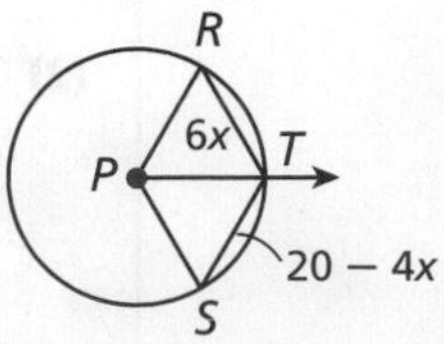

3b. $\odot A \cong \odot B$, and $\overline{CD} \cong \overline{EF}$. Find $m\overset{\frown}{CD}$.

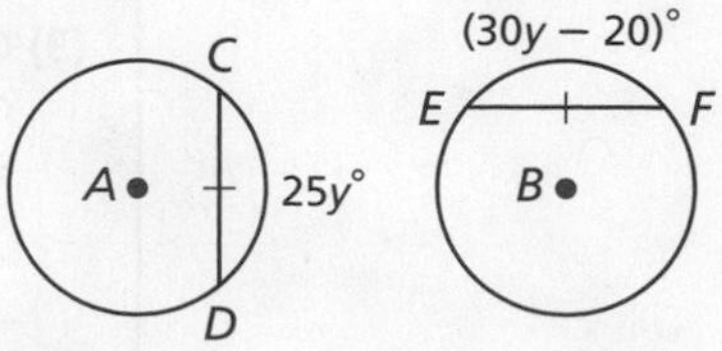

Know it! Note — Theorems

THEOREM	HYPOTHESIS	CONCLUSION
12-2-3 In a circle, if a radius (or diameter) is perpendicular to a chord, then it bisects the chord and its arc.	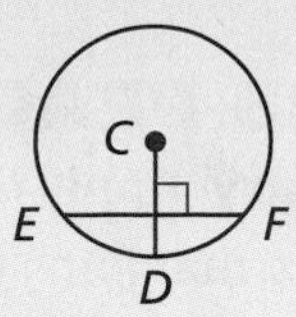 $\overline{CD} \perp \overline{EF}$	$\overline{CD}$ bisects $\overline{EF}$ and $\widehat{EF}$.
12-2-4 In a circle, the perpendicular bisector of a chord is a radius (or diameter).	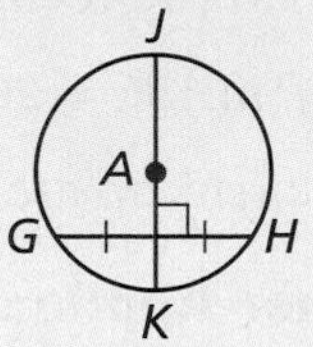 $\overline{JK}$ is $\perp$ bisector of $\overline{GH}$.	$\overline{JK}$ is a diameter of $\odot A$.

You will prove Theorems 12-2-3 and 12-2-4 in Exercises 42 and 43.

EXAMPLE 4 Using Radii and Chords

Algebra

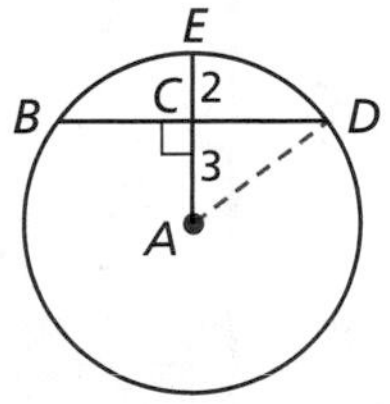

Find BD.

Step 1 Draw radius $\overline{AD}$.

$AD = 5$ — *Radii of a ⊙ are ≅.*

Step 2 Use the Pythagorean Theorem.

$CD^2 + AC^2 = AD^2$

$CD^2 + 3^2 = 5^2$ — *Substitute 3 for AC and 5 for AD.*

$CD^2 = 16$ — *Subtract 3^2 from both sides.*

$CD = 4$ — *Take the square root of both sides.*

Step 3 Find BD.

$BD = 2(4) = 8$ — *$\overline{AE} \perp \overline{BD}$, so $\overline{AE}$ bisects $\overline{BD}$.*

CHECK IT OUT! **4.** Find QR to the nearest tenth.

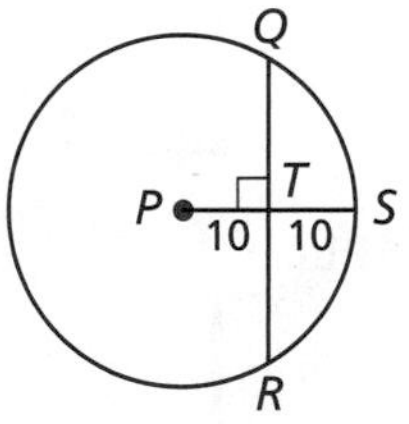

THINK AND DISCUSS

MATHEMATICAL PRACTICES

1. What is true about the measure of an arc whose central angle is obtuse?

2. Under what conditions are two arcs the same measure but not congruent?

Know it! Note

3. GET ORGANIZED Copy and complete the graphic organizer. In each box, write a definition and draw a sketch.

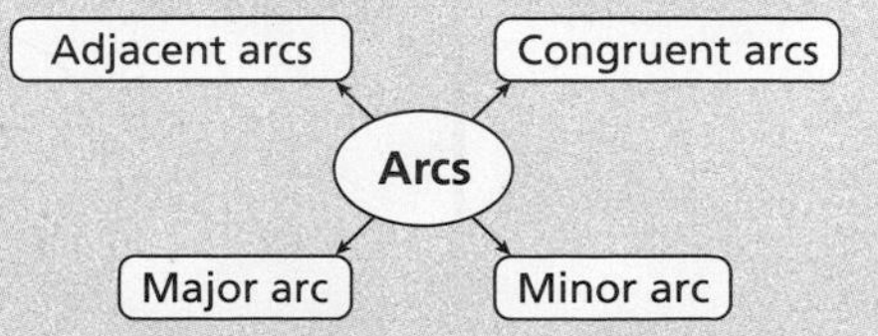

12-2 Exercises

Learn It Online
Homework Help Online
Parent Resources Online

GUIDED PRACTICE

Vocabulary **Apply the vocabulary from this lesson to answer each question.**

1. An arc that joins the endpoints of a diameter is called a ___?___ . (*semicircle* or *major arc*)
2. How do you recognize a *central angle* of a circle?
3. In $\odot P$ $m\overset{\frown}{ABC} = 205°$. Therefore $\overset{\frown}{ABC}$ is a ___?___ . (*major arc* or *minor arc*)
4. In a circle, an arc that is less than a semicircle is a ___?___ . (*major arc* or *minor arc*)

SEE EXAMPLE 1

Consumer Application **Use the following information for Exercises 5–10.**

The circle graph shows how a typical household spends money on energy. Find each of the following.

5. $m\angle PAQ$
6. $m\angle VAU$
7. $m\angle SAQ$
8. $m\overset{\frown}{UT}$
9. $m\overset{\frown}{RQ}$
10. $m\overset{\frown}{UPT}$

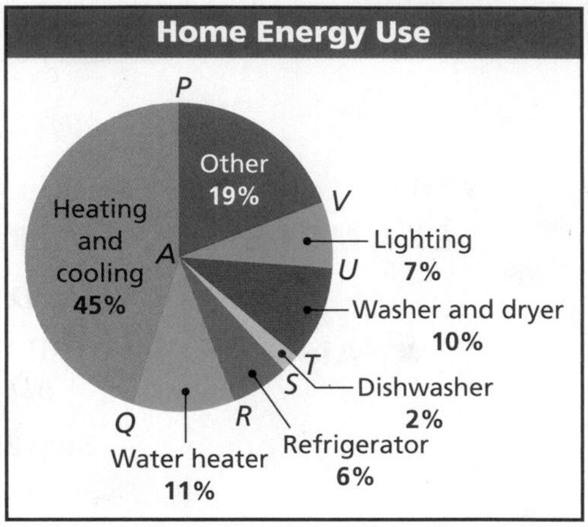

SEE EXAMPLE 2

Find each measure.

11. $m\overset{\frown}{DF}$
12. $m\overset{\frown}{DEB}$

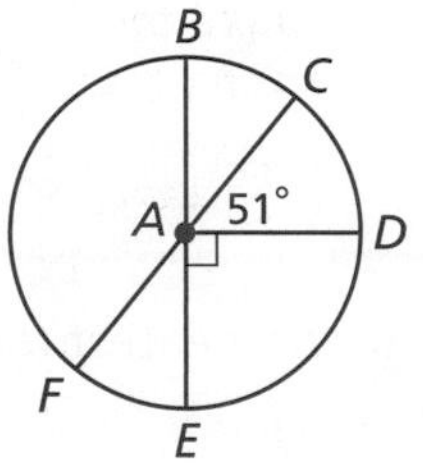

13. $m\overset{\frown}{JL}$
14. $m\overset{\frown}{HLK}$

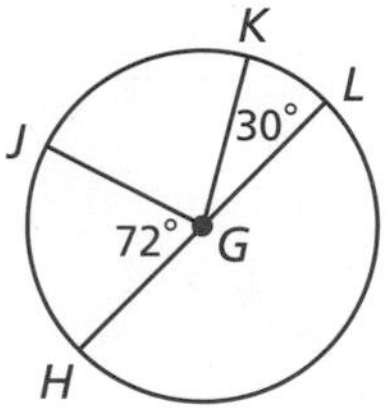

SEE EXAMPLE 3

15. $\angle QPR \cong \angle RPS$. Find QR.

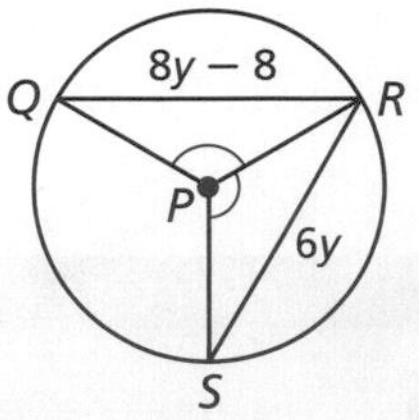

16. $\odot A \cong \odot B$, and $\overset{\frown}{CD} \cong \overset{\frown}{EF}$. Find $m\angle EBF$.

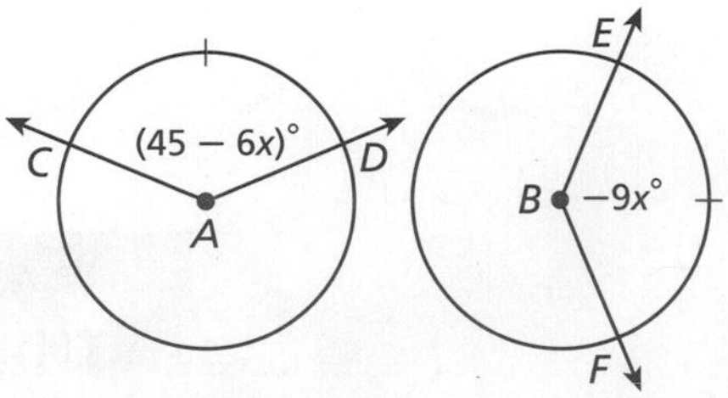

SEE EXAMPLE 4

Multi-Step **Find each length to the nearest tenth.**

17. RS

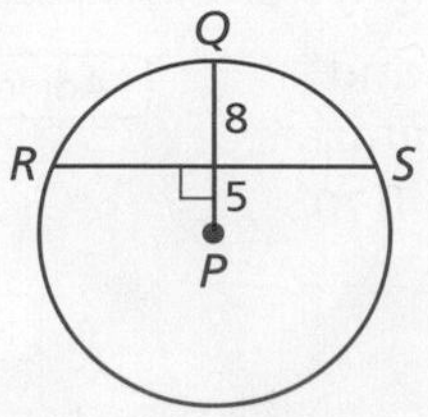

18. EF

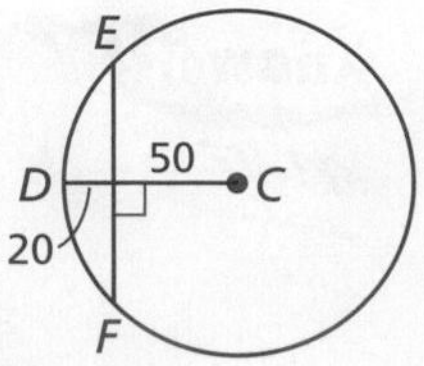

PRACTICE AND PROBLEM SOLVING

Independent Practice

For Exercises	See Example
19–24	1
25–28	2
29–30	3
31–32	4

Extra Practice

See Extra Practice for more Skills Practice and Applications Practice exercises.

Sports Use the following information for Exercises 19–24.

The key shows the number of medals won by U.S. athletes at the 2004 Olympics in Athens. Find each of the following to the nearest tenth.

Medals	
Gold	35
Silver	39
Bronze	29

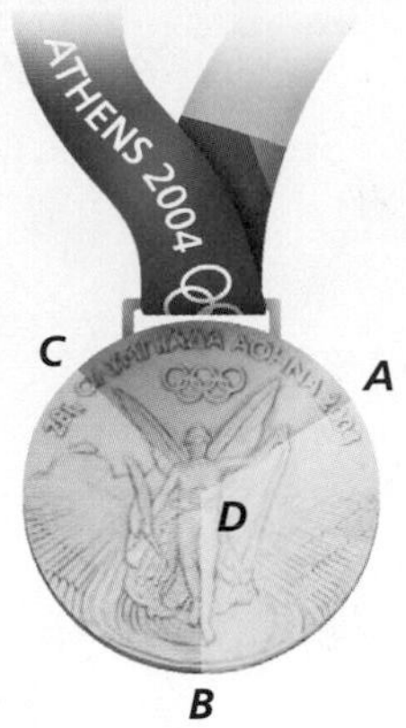

19. m∠ADB 20. m∠ADC

21. m$\widehat{AB}$ 22. m$\widehat{BC}$

23. m$\widehat{ACB}$ 24. m$\widehat{CAB}$

Find each measure.

25. m$\widehat{MP}$

26. m$\widehat{QNL}$

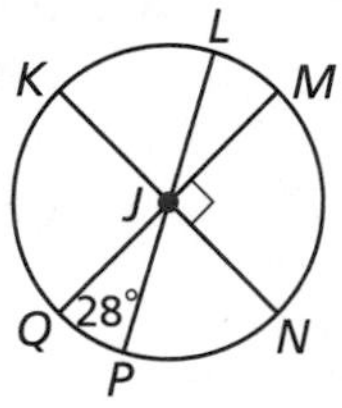

27. m$\widehat{WT}$

28. m$\widehat{WTV}$

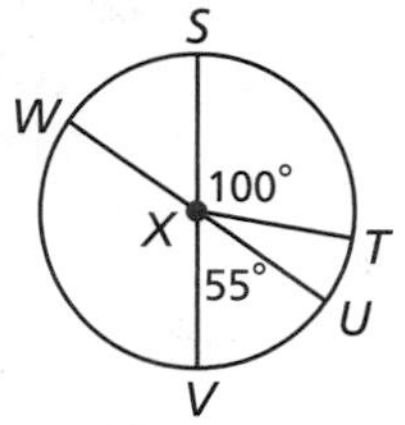

29. ⊙A ≅ ⊙B, and $\widehat{CD} \cong \widehat{EF}$. Find m∠$CAD$.

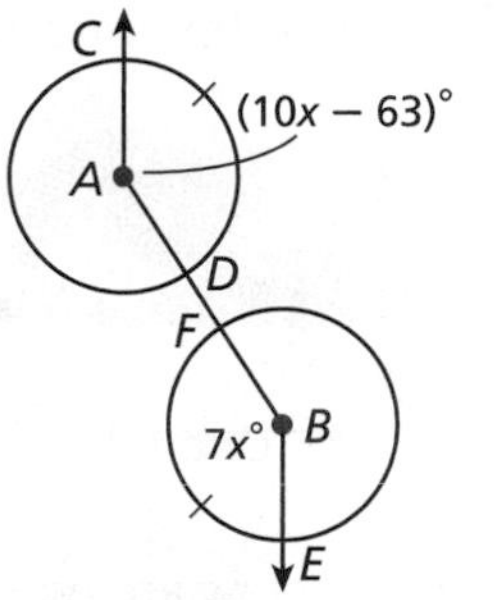

30. $\overline{JK} \cong \overline{LM}$. Find m$\widehat{JK}$.

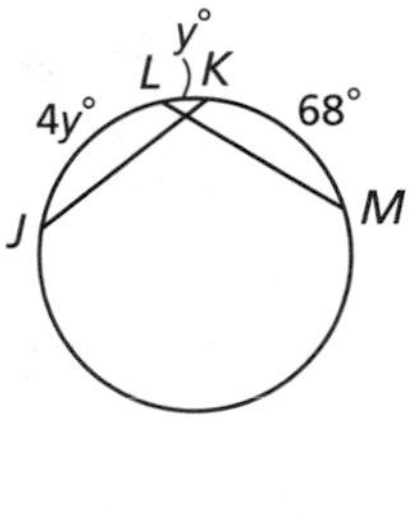

Multi-Step Find each length to the nearest tenth.

31. CD

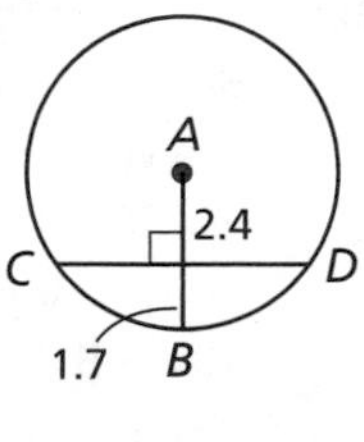

32. RS

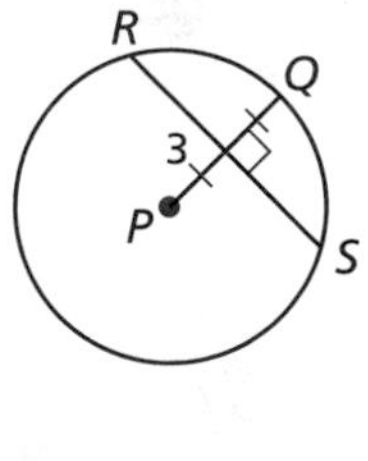

Determine whether each statement is true or false. If false, explain why.

33. The central angle of a minor arc is an acute angle.

34. Any two points on a circle determine a minor arc and a major arc.

35. In a circle, the perpendicular bisector of a chord must pass through the center of the circle.

36. **Data Collection** Use a graphing calculator, a pH probe, and a data-collection device to collect information about the pH levels of ten different liquids. Then create a circle graph with the following sectors: strong basic $(9 < \text{pH} < 14)$, weak basic $(7 < \text{pH} < 9)$, neutral $(\text{pH} = 7)$, weak acidic $(5 < \text{pH} < 7)$, and strong acidic $(0 < \text{pH} < 5)$.

37. In ⊙E, the measures of ∠AEB, ∠BEC, and ∠CED are in the ratio 3 : 4 : 5. Find m$\widehat{AB}$, m$\widehat{BC}$, and m$\widehat{CD}$.

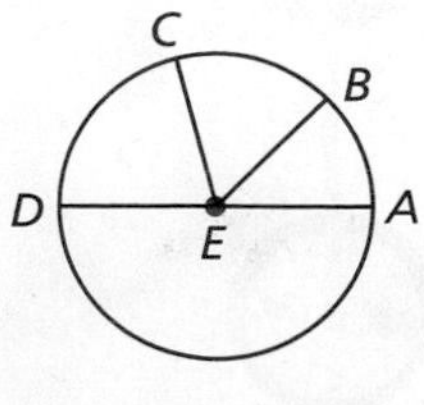

x^2y Algebra **Find the indicated measure.**

38. $m\widehat{JL}$

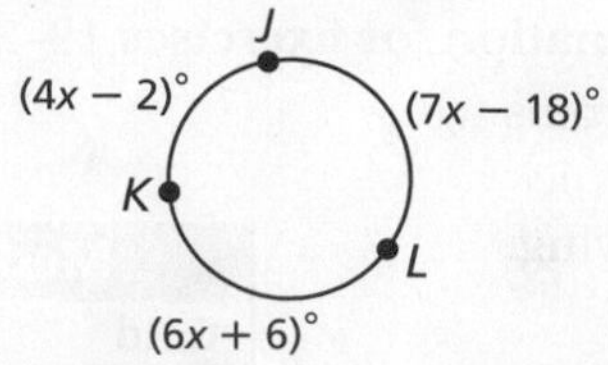

39. $m\angle SPT$

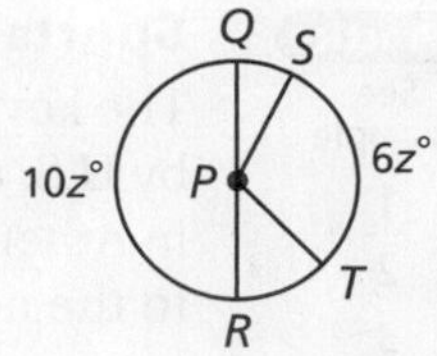

40. Prove ≅ chords have ≅ arcs.
Given: $\odot A$, $\overline{BC} \cong \overline{DE}$
Prove: $\widehat{BC} \cong \widehat{DE}$

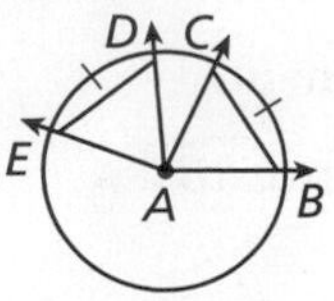

41. Prove ≅ arcs have ≅ central ∠s.
Given: $\odot A$, $\widehat{BC} \cong \widehat{DE}$
Prove: $\angle BAC \cong \angle DAE$

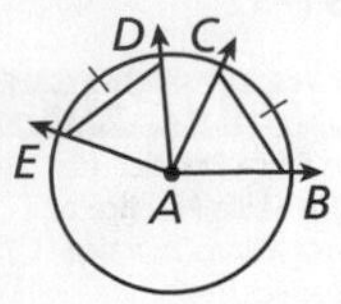

42. Prove Theorem 12-2-3.
Given: $\odot C$, $\overline{CD} \perp \overline{EF}$
Prove: $\overline{CD}$ bisects $\overline{EF}$ and $\widehat{EF}$.
(*Hint:* Draw $\overline{CE}$ and $\overline{CF}$ and use the HL Theorem.)

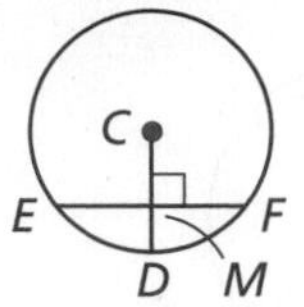

43. Prove Theorem 12-2-4.
Given: $\odot A$, $\overline{JK} \perp$ bisector of $\overline{GH}$
Prove: $\overline{JK}$ is a diameter
(*Hint:* Use the Converse of the ⊥ Bisector Theorem.)

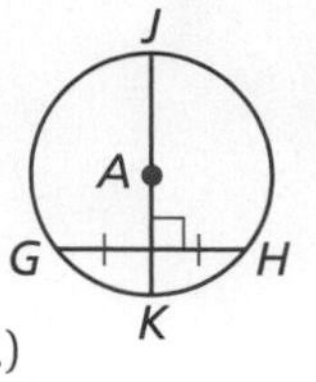

44. Critical Thinking Roberto folds a circular piece of paper as shown. When he unfolds the paper, how many different-sized central angles will be formed?

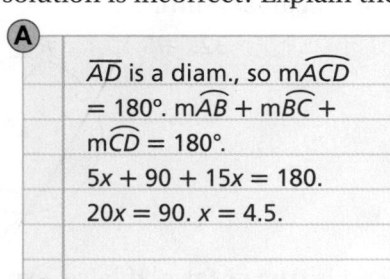

One fold　　Two folds　　Three folds

45. ///ERROR ANALYSIS/// Below are two solutions to find the value of x. Which solution is incorrect? Explain the error.

A

$\overline{AD}$ is a diam., so $m\widehat{ACD} = 180°$. $m\widehat{AB} + m\widehat{BC} + m\widehat{CD} = 180°$.
$5x + 90 + 15x = 180$.
$20x = 90$. $x = 4.5$.

B

Because they are vert. ∠s, $\angle AGF \cong \angle CGD$.
Thus $m\widehat{AF} = m\widehat{CD}$.
$16x - 5 = 15x$.
$x = 5$.

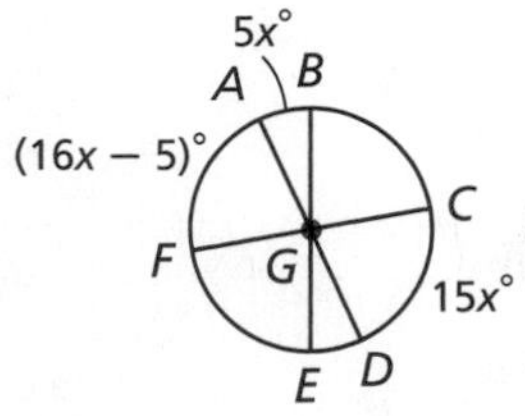

46. Write About It According to a school survey, 40% of the students take a bus to school, 35% are driven to school, 15% ride a bike, and the remainder walk. Explain how to use central angles to create a circle graph from this data.

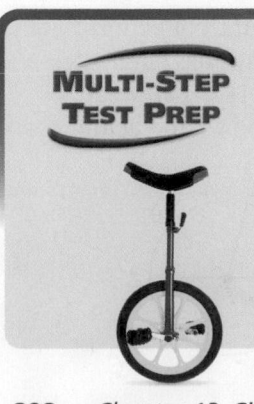

MULTI-STEP TEST PREP

47. Chantal's bike has wheels with a 27 in. diameter.

a. What are AC and AD if DB is 7 in.?

b. What is CD to the nearest tenth of an inch?

c. What is CE, the length of the top of the bike stand?

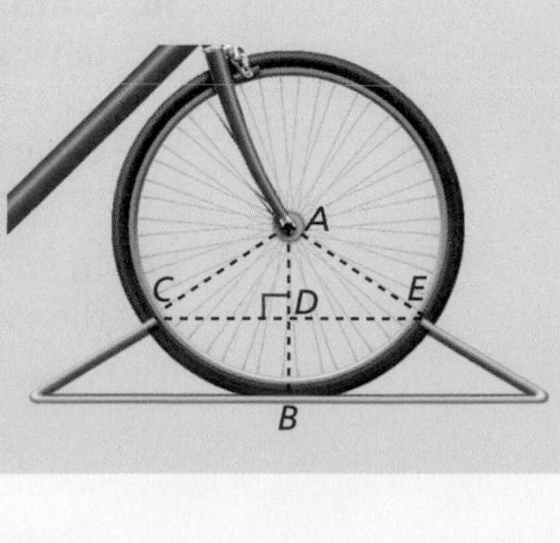

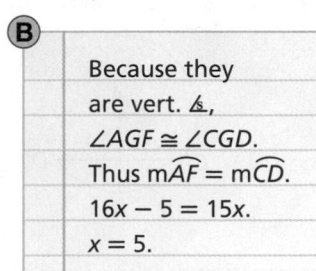

TEST PREP

48. Which of these arcs of ⊙Q has the greatest measure?

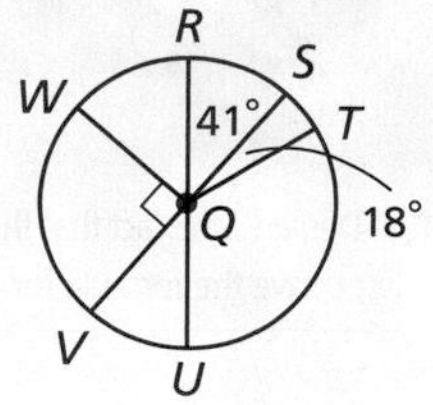

Ⓐ $\overset{\frown}{WT}$
Ⓑ $\overset{\frown}{UW}$
Ⓒ $\overset{\frown}{VR}$
Ⓓ $\overset{\frown}{TV}$

49. In ⊙A, $CD = 10$. Which of these is closest to the length of $\overline{AE}$?

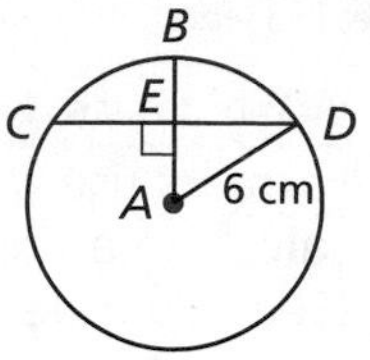

Ⓕ 3.3 cm
Ⓖ 4 cm
Ⓗ 5 cm
Ⓙ 7.8 cm

50. **Gridded Response** ⊙P has center $P(2, 1)$ and radius 3. What is the measure, in degrees, of the minor arc with endpoints $A(-1, 1)$ and $B(2, -2)$?

CHALLENGE AND EXTEND

51. In the figure, $\overline{AB} \perp \overline{CD}$. Find m$\overset{\frown}{BD}$ to the nearest tenth of a degree.

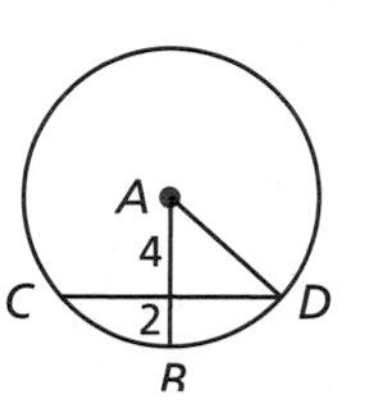

52. Two points on a circle determine two distinct arcs. How many arcs are determined by n points on a circle? (*Hint:* Make a table and look for a pattern.)

53. An angle measure other than degrees is *radian* measure. 360° converts to 2π radians, or 180° converts to π radians.
    a. Convert the following radian angle measures to degrees: $\frac{\pi}{2}, \frac{\pi}{3}, \frac{\pi}{4}$.
    b. Convert the following angle measures to radians: 135°, 270°.

Construction Circle Through Three Noncollinear Points

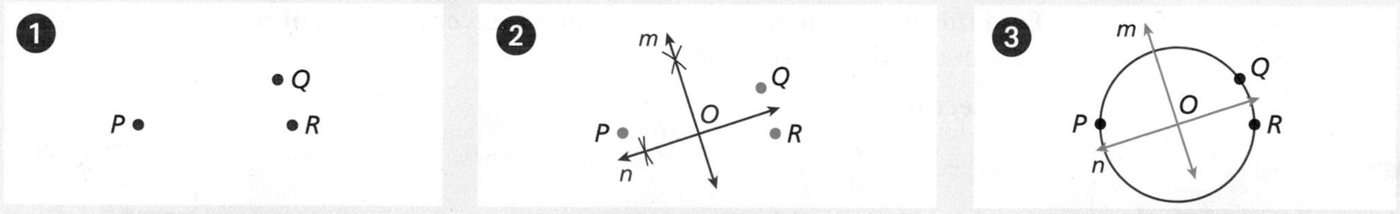

1. Draw three noncollinear points.
2. Construct m and n, the ⊥ bisectors of $\overline{PQ}$ and $\overline{QR}$. Label the intersection O.
3. Center the compass at O. Draw a circle through P.

1. Explain why ⊙O with radius $\overline{OP}$ also contains Q and R.

COMMON CORE

12-3 Sector Area and Arc Length

CC.9-12.G.C.5 Derive…the fact that the length of the arc intercepted by an angle is proportional to the radius…; derive the formula for…area of a sector.

Objectives

Find the area of sectors.

Find arc lengths.

Vocabulary

sector of a circle
segment of a circle
arc length

Who uses this?

Farmers use irrigation radii to calculate areas of sectors. (See Example 2.)

The area of a sector is a fraction of the circle containing the sector. To find the area of a sector whose central angle measures $m°$, multiply the area of the circle by $\frac{m°}{360°}$.

Know it! Note

Sector of a Circle

TERM	NAME	DIAGRAM	AREA
A **sector of a circle** is a region bounded by two radii of the circle and their intercepted arc.	sector ACB	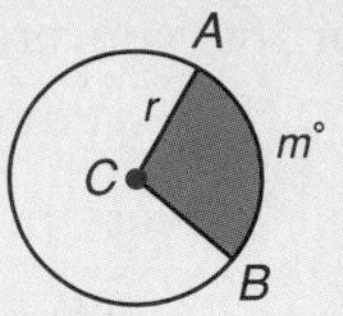	$A = \pi r^2\left(\frac{m°}{360°}\right)$

EXAMPLE 1 Finding the Area of a Sector

Find the area of each sector. Give your answer in terms of π and rounded to the nearest hundredth.

A sector MPN

$A = \pi r^2\left(\frac{m°}{360°}\right)$ *Use formula for area of a sector.*

$= \pi(3)^2\left(\frac{80°}{360°}\right)$ *Substitute 3 for r and 80 for m.*

$= 2\pi \text{ in}^2 \approx 6.28 \text{ in}^2$ *Simplify.*

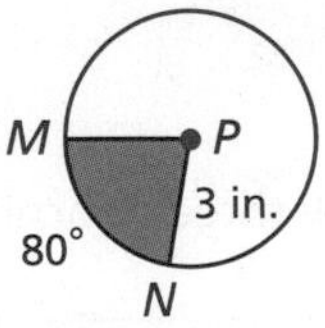

B sector EFG

$A = \pi r^2\left(\frac{m°}{360°}\right)$ *Use formula for area of a sector.*

$= \pi(6)^2\left(\frac{120°}{360°}\right)$ *Substitute 6 for r and 120 for m.*

$= 12\pi \approx 37.70 \text{ cm}^2$ *Simplify.*

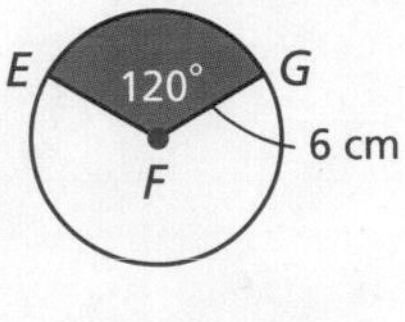

Helpful Hint

Write the degree symbol after *m* in the formula to help you remember to use degree measure not arc length.

CHECK IT OUT! **Find the area of each sector. Give your answer in terms of π and rounded to the nearest hundredth.**

1a. sector ACB

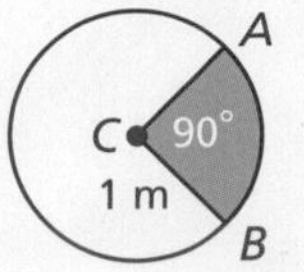

1b. sector JKL

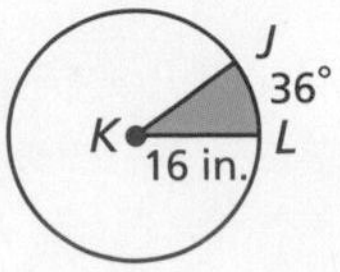

EXAMPLE 2 **Agriculture Application**

A circular plot with a 720 ft diameter is watered by a spray irrigation system. To the nearest square foot, what is the area that is watered as the sprinkler rotates through an angle of 50°?

$$A = \pi r^2\left(\frac{m°}{360°}\right)$$

$$= \pi(360)^2\left(\frac{50°}{360°}\right) \quad \textit{d = 720 ft, r = 360 ft.}$$

$$\approx 56{,}549 \text{ ft}^2 \quad \textit{Simplify.}$$

CHECK IT OUT! **2.** To the nearest square foot, what is the area watered in Example 2 as the sprinkler rotates through a semicircle?

A **segment of a circle** is a region bounded by an arc and its chord. The shaded region in the figure is a segment.

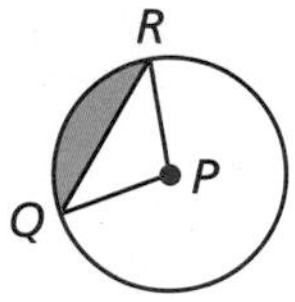

Know it! Note

Area of a Segment

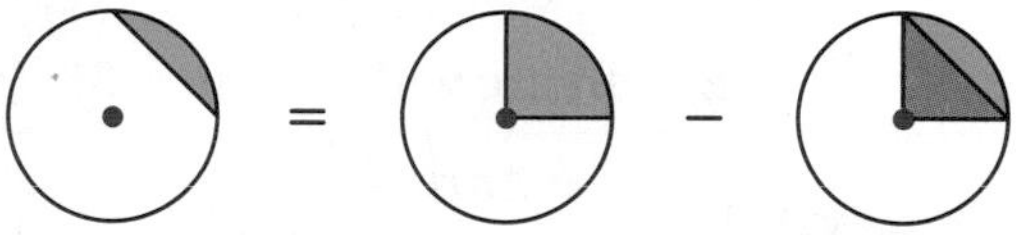

area of segment = area of sector − area of triangle

EXAMPLE 3 **Finding the Area of a Segment**

Find the area of segment *ACB* to the nearest hundredth.

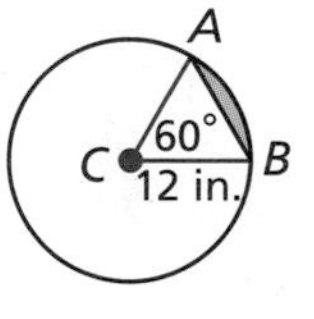

Step 1 Find the area of sector *ACB*.

$$A = \pi r^2\left(\frac{m°}{360°}\right) \quad \textit{Use formula for area of a sector.}$$

$$= \pi(12)^2\left(\frac{60°}{360°}\right) \quad \textit{Substitute 12 for r and 60 for m.}$$

$$= 24\pi \text{ in}^2$$

Step 2 Find the area of $\triangle ACB$.

Draw altitude $\overline{AD}$.

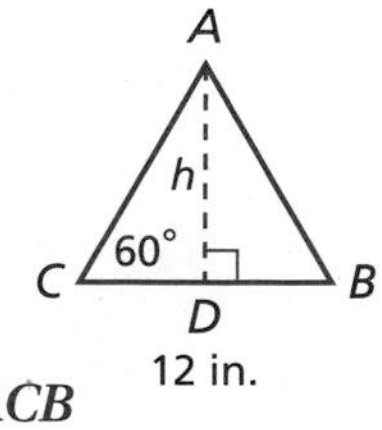

$$A = \frac{1}{2}bh = \frac{1}{2}(12)(6\sqrt{3}) \quad \textit{CD = 6 in., and h = } 6\sqrt{3} \textit{ in.}$$

$$= 36\sqrt{3} \text{ in}^2 \quad \textit{Simplify.}$$

Step 3 area of segment = **area of sector *ACB* − area of $\triangle ACB$**

$$= 24\pi - 36\sqrt{3}$$

$$\approx 13.04 \text{ in}^2$$

Remember!

In a 30°-60°-90° triangle, the length of the leg opposite the 60° angle is $\sqrt{3}$ times the length of the shorter leg.

CHECK IT OUT! **3.** Find the area of segment *RST* to the nearest hundredth.

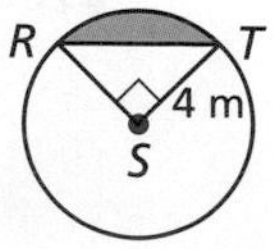

In the same way that the area of a sector is a fraction of the area of the circle, the length of an arc is a fraction of the circumference of the circle.

Know it! Note

Arc Length

TERM	DIAGRAM	LENGTH
Arc length is the distance along an arc measured in linear units.	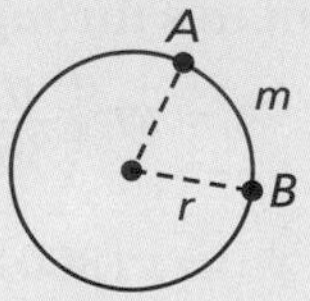	$L = 2\pi r\left(\frac{m°}{360°}\right)$

EXAMPLE 4 Finding Arc Length

Find each arc length. Give your answer in terms of π and rounded to the nearest hundredth.

A $\overset{\frown}{CD}$

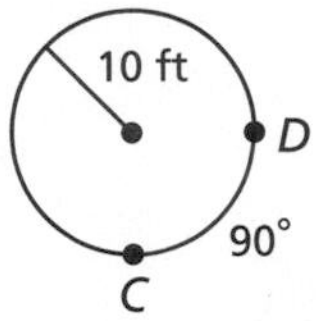

$L = 2\pi r\left(\frac{m°}{360°}\right)$ *Use formula for arc length.*

$= 2\pi(10)\left(\frac{90°}{360°}\right)$ *Substitute 10 for r and 90 for m.*

$= 5\pi \text{ ft} \approx 15.71 \text{ ft}$ *Simplify.*

B **an arc with measure 35° in a circle with radius 3 in.**

$L = 2\pi r\left(\frac{m°}{360°}\right)$ *Use formula for arc length.*

$= 2\pi(3)\left(\frac{35°}{360°}\right)$ *Substitute 3 for r and 35 for m.*

$= \frac{7}{12} \text{ in.} \approx 1.83 \text{ in.}$ *Simplify.*

CHECK IT OUT! **Find each arc length. Give your answer in terms of π and rounded to the nearest hundredth.**

4a. $\overset{\frown}{GH}$

4b. an arc with measure 135° in a circle with radius 4 cm

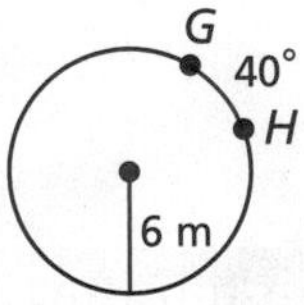

MATHEMATICAL PRACTICES

THINK AND DISCUSS

1. What is the difference between arc measure and arc length?

2. A slice of pizza is a sector of a circle. Explain what measurements you would need to make in order to calculate the area of the slice.

Know it! Note

3. GET ORGANIZED Copy and complete the graphic organizer.

	Formula	Diagram
Area of a Sector		
Area of a Segment		
Arc Length		

12-3 Exercises

Learn It Online
Homework Help Online
Parent Resources Online

GUIDED PRACTICE

1. **Vocabulary** In a circle, the region bounded by a chord and an arc is called a ___?___ . (*sector* or *segment*)

SEE EXAMPLE 1

Find the area of each sector. Give your answer in terms of π and rounded to the nearest hundredth.

2. sector PQR

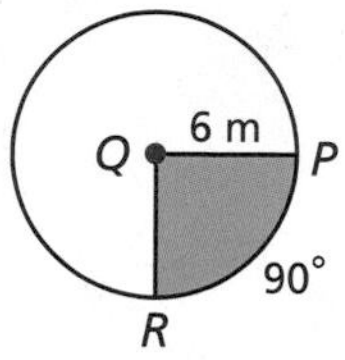

3. sector JKL

4. sector ABC

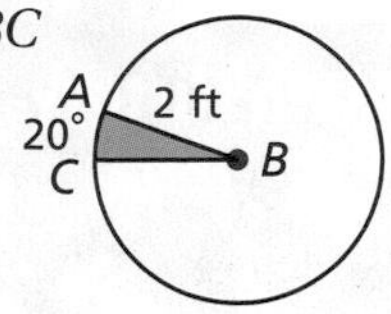

SEE EXAMPLE 2

5. **Navigation** The beam from a lighthouse is visible for a distance of 3 mi. To the nearest square mile, what is the area covered by the beam as it sweeps in an arc of 150°?

SEE EXAMPLE 3

Multi-Step **Find the area of each segment to the nearest hundredth.**

6.

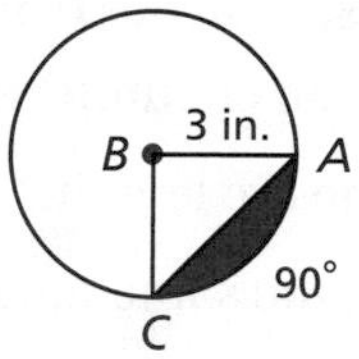

7.

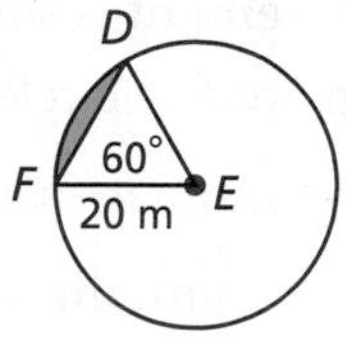

8.

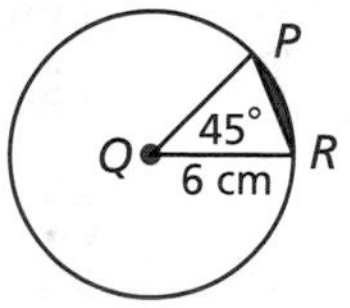

SEE EXAMPLE 4

Find each arc length. Give your answer in terms of π and rounded to the nearest hundredth.

9. $\widehat{EF}$

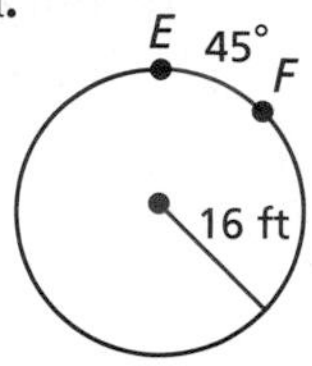

10. $\widehat{PQ}$

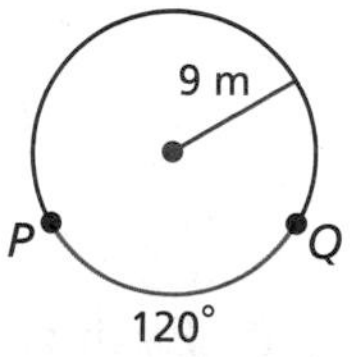

11. an arc with measure 20° in a circle with radius 6 in.

PRACTICE AND PROBLEM SOLVING

Independent Practice	
For Exercises	See Example
12–14	1
15	2
16–18	3
19–21	4

Extra Practice
See Extra Practice for more Skills Practice and Applications Practice exercises.

Find the area of each sector. Give your answer in terms of π and rounded to the nearest hundredth.

12. sector DEF

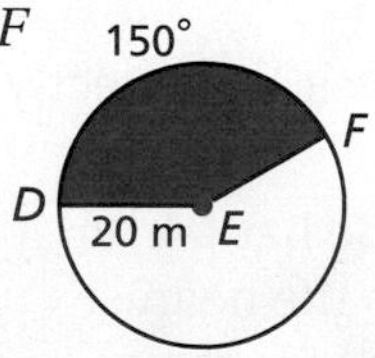

13. sector GHJ

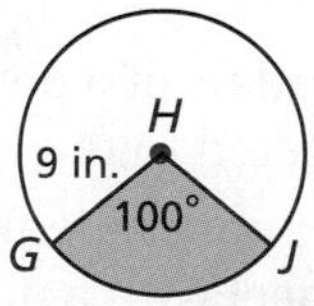

14. sector RST

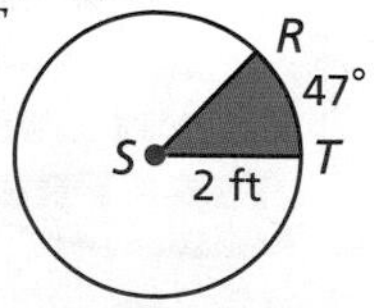

15. **Architecture** A *lunette* is a semicircular window that is sometimes placed above a doorway or above a rectangular window. To the nearest square inch, what is the area of the lunette?

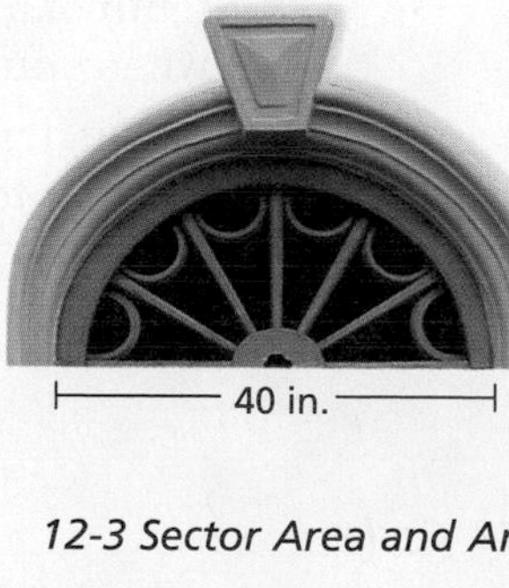

Multi-Step Find the area of each segment to the nearest hundredth.

16.

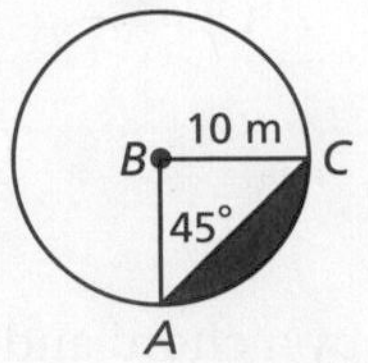

17.

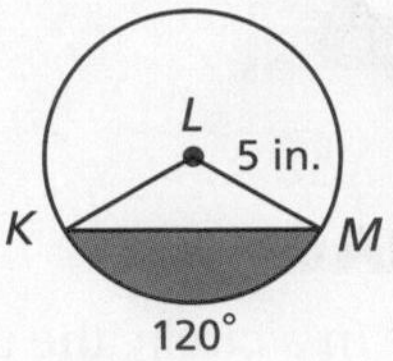

18.

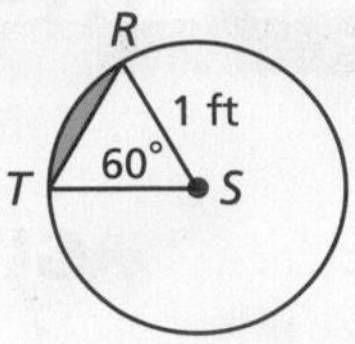

Find each arc length. Give your answer in terms of π and rounded to the nearest hundredth.

19. $\widehat{UV}$

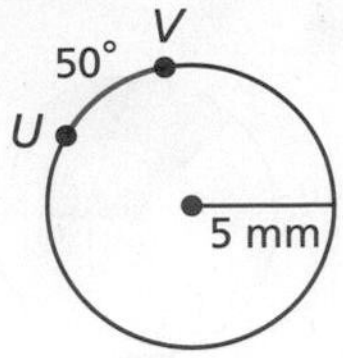

20. $\widehat{AB}$

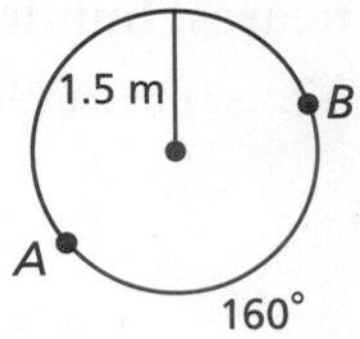

21. an arc with measure 9° in a circle with diameter 4 ft

22. Math History Greek mathematicians studied the *salinon*, a figure bounded by four semicircles. What is the perimeter of this salinon to the nearest tenth of an inch?

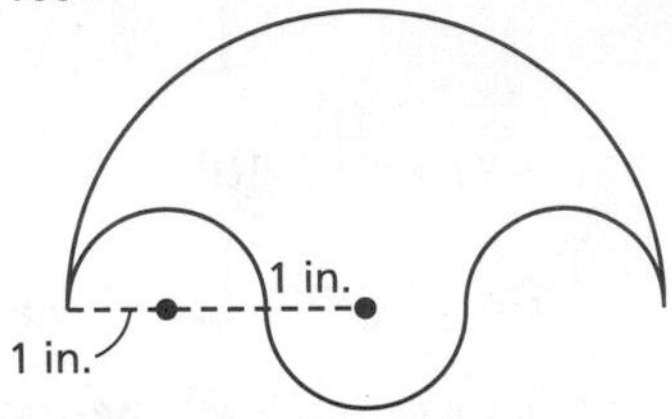

LINK

Math History

Hypatia lived 1600 years ago. She is considered one of history's most important mathematicians. She is credited with contributions to both geometry and astronomy.

Tell whether each statement is sometimes, always, or never true.

23. The length of an arc of a circle is greater than the circumference of the circle.

24. Two arcs with the same measure have the same arc length.

25. In a circle, two arcs with the same length have the same measure.

Find the radius of each circle.

26. area of sector $ABC = 9\pi$

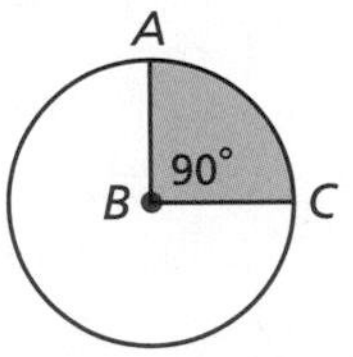

27. arc length of $\widehat{EF} = 8\pi$

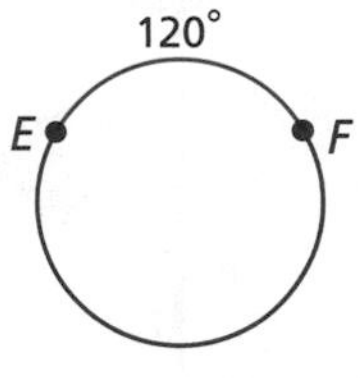

28. Estimation The fraction $\frac{22}{7}$ is an approximation for π.

a. Use this value to estimate the arc length of $\widehat{XY}$.

b. Use the π key on your calculator to find the length of $\widehat{XY}$ to 8 decimal places.

c. Was your estimate in part **a** an overestimate or an underestimate?

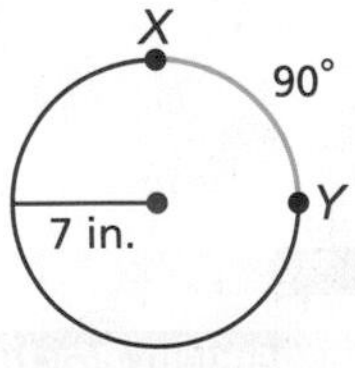

MULTI-STEP TEST PREP

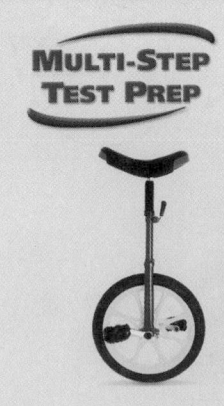

29. The pedals of a penny-farthing bicycle are directly connected to the front wheel.

a. Suppose a penny-farthing bicycle has a front wheel with a diameter of 5 ft. To the nearest tenth of a foot, how far does the bike move when you turn the pedals through an angle of 90°?

b. Through what angle should you turn the pedals in order to move forward by a distance of 4.5 ft? Round to the nearest degree.

30. **Critical Thinking** What is the length of the radius that makes the area of $\odot A = 24\ \text{in}^2$ and the area of sector $BAC = 3\ \text{in}^2$? Explain.

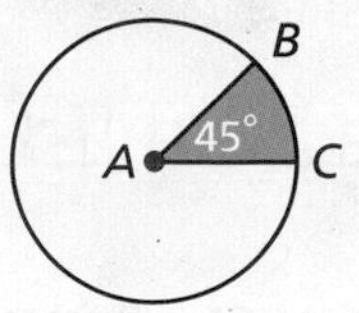

31. **Write About It** Given the length of an arc of a circle and the measure of the arc, explain how to find the radius of the circle.

TEST PREP

32. What is the area of sector AOB?

Ⓐ 4π Ⓑ 16π Ⓒ 32π Ⓓ 64π

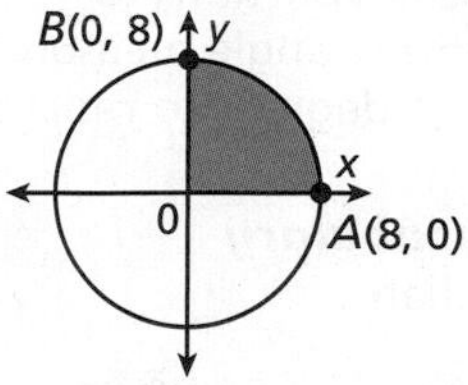

33. What is the length of $\widehat{AB}$?

Ⓕ 2π Ⓖ 4π Ⓗ 8π Ⓙ 16π

34. **Gridded Response** To the nearest hundredth, what is the area of the sector determined by an arc with measure 35° in a circle with radius 12?

CHALLENGE AND EXTEND

35. In the diagram, the larger of the two concentric circles has radius 5, and the smaller circle has radius 2. What is the area of the shaded region in terms of π?

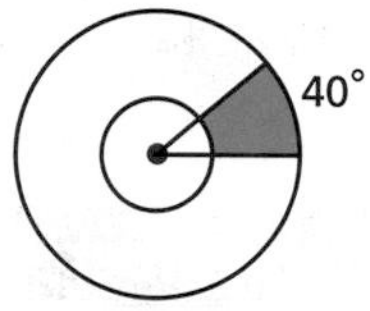

36. A wedge of cheese is a sector of a cylinder.
    a. To the nearest tenth, what is the volume of the wedge with the dimensions shown?
    b. What is the surface area of the wedge of cheese to the nearest tenth?

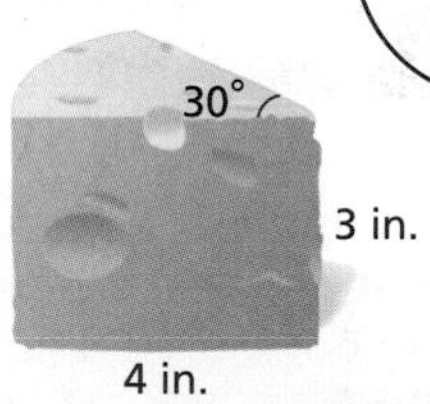

37. **Probability** The central angles of a target measure 45°. The inner circle has a radius of 1 ft, and the outer circle has a radius of 2 ft. Assuming that all arrows hit the target at random, find the following probabilities.
    a. hitting a red region
    b. hitting a blue region
    c. hitting a red or blue region

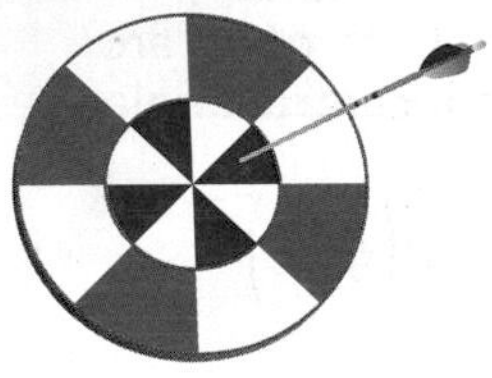

COMMON CORE

EXTENSION Measuring Angles in Radians

CC.9-12.G.C.5 ...Define the radian measure of the angle as the constant of proportionality...

Objective
Use proportions to convert angle measures from degrees to radians.

Vocabulary
radian

One unit of measurement for angles is degrees, which are based on a fraction of a circle. Another unit is called a *radian,* which is based on the relationship of the radius and arc length of a central angle in a circle.

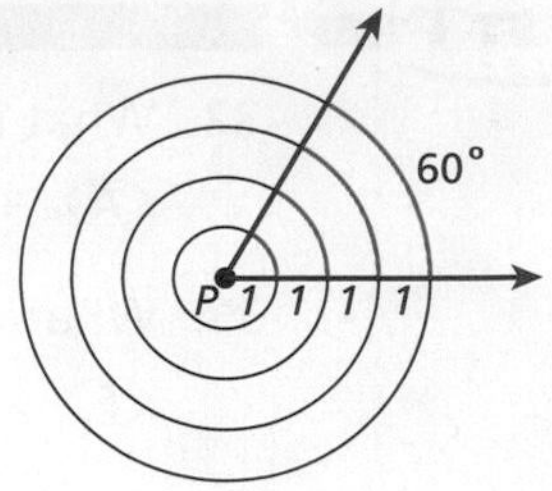

Four concentric circles are shown, with radius 1, 2, 3, and 4. The measure of each arc is 60°.

Radius	Arc Length
1	$2\pi(1)\left(\frac{60°}{360°}\right) = \frac{\pi}{3}$
2	$2\pi(2)\left(\frac{60°}{360°}\right) = \frac{2\pi}{3}$
3	$2\pi(3)\left(\frac{60°}{360°}\right) = \pi$
4	$2\pi(4)\left(\frac{60°}{360°}\right) = \frac{4\pi}{3}$

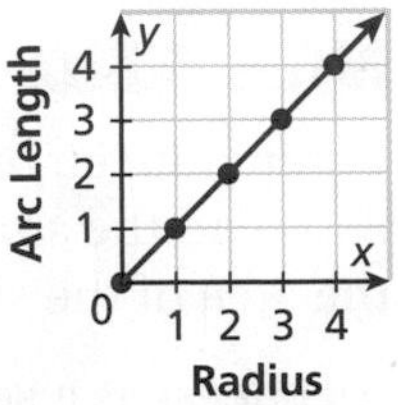

Remember!

Arc length is the distance along an arc measured in linear units. In a circle of radius r, the length of an arc with a central angle measure m is $L = 2\pi r\left(\frac{m°}{360°}\right)$.

The relationship between the radius and arc length is linear, with a slope of $2\pi\left(\frac{60°}{360°}\right) = \frac{\pi}{3}$, or about 1.05. The slope represents the ratio of the arc length to the radius. This ratio is the *radian* measure of the angle, so 60° is the same as $\frac{\pi}{3}$ radians.

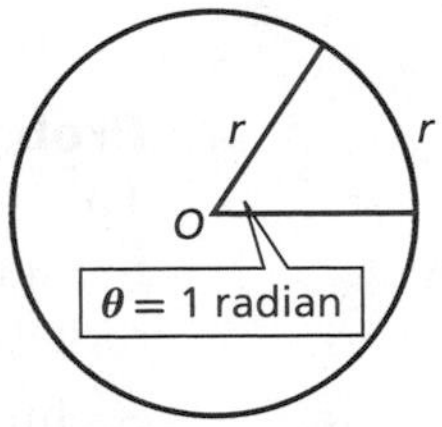

If a central angle θ in a circle of radius r intercepts an arc of length r, the measure of θ is defined as 1 **radian.** Since the circumference of a circle of radius r is $2\pi r$, an angle representing one complete rotation measures 2π radians, or 360°.

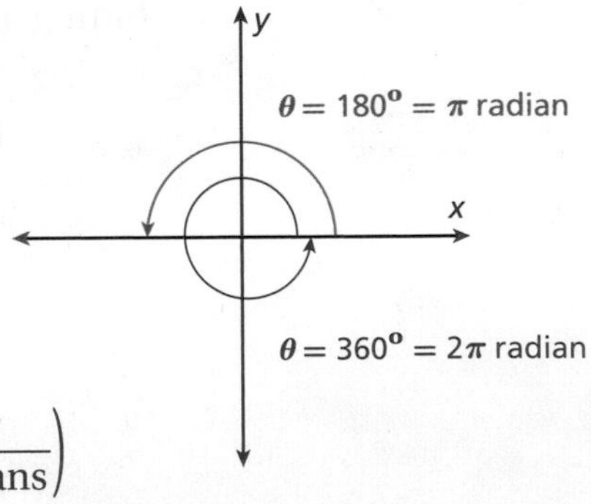

2π radians = 360° and π radians = 180°

$1° = \left(\frac{\pi \text{ radians}}{180°}\right)$ and $1 \text{ radian} = \left(\frac{180°}{\pi \text{ radians}}\right)$

Use these facts to convert between radians and degrees.

Converting Angle Measures

DEGREES TO RADIANS	RADIANS TO DEGREES
Multiply the number of degrees by	Multiply the number of radians by
$\left(\frac{\pi \text{ radians}}{180°}\right)$	$\left(\frac{180°}{\pi \text{ radians}}\right)$

EXAMPLE 1 Converting Degrees to Radians

Helpful Hint

Because the radian measure of an angle is related to arc length, the most commonly used angle measures are usually written as fractional multiples of π.

Convert each measure from degrees to radians. *Multiply by* $\left(\frac{\pi \text{ radians}}{180°}\right)$.

A 30°

$\overset{1}{\cancel{30°}}\left(\frac{\pi \text{ radians}}{\underset{6}{\cancel{180°}}}\right) = \frac{\pi}{6} \text{ radians}$

B 75°

$\overset{5}{\cancel{75°}}\left(\frac{\pi \text{ radians}}{\underset{12}{\cancel{180°}}}\right) = \frac{5\pi}{12} \text{ radians}$

CHECK IT OUT! **Convert each measure from degrees to radians.**

1a. –36° **1b.** 270°

EXAMPLE 2 Converting Radians to Degrees

Convert each measure from radians to degrees.

A $\frac{\pi}{4}$ radians

$\frac{\cancel{\pi}}{\underset{1}{\cancel{4}}} \cancel{\text{radians}}\left(\frac{\overset{45}{\cancel{180°}}}{\cancel{\pi} \cancel{\text{radians}}}\right) = 45°$

B $\frac{2\pi}{9}$ radians *Multiply by* $\left(\frac{180°}{\pi \text{ radians}}\right)$.

$\frac{2\cancel{\pi}}{\underset{1}{\cancel{9}}} \cancel{\text{radians}}\left(\frac{\overset{20}{\cancel{180°}}}{\cancel{\pi} \cancel{\text{radians}}}\right) = 40°$

CHECK IT OUT! **Convert each measure from radians to degrees.**

2a. $\frac{5\pi}{6}$ radians **2b.** $-\frac{3\pi}{4}$ radians

EXTENSION Exercises

1. **Convert each measure from degrees to radians to complete the table.**

0°	30°	45°	60°	90°	180°	270°	360°

Convert each measure from degrees to radians.

2. 215° **3.** 25° **4.** –180° **5.** 35°

6. 120° **7.** –315° **8.** 400° **9.** –60°

Convert each measure from radians to degrees.

10. $\frac{6\pi}{5}$ radians **11.** $\frac{3\pi}{5}$ radians **12.** $-\frac{\pi}{3}$ radians **13.** $\frac{5\pi}{9}$ radians

14. $\frac{\pi}{6}$ radians **15.** $\frac{2\pi}{3}$ radians **16.** $\frac{5\pi}{8}$ radians **17.** $\frac{7\pi}{2}$ radians

18. **Electronics** A DVD rotates through an angle of 20π radians in 1 second. At this speed, how many revolutions does the DVD make in 2 minutes?

19. **Clocks** Find the measure of the angle in radians formed by the minute hand on a clock at 7:35 and its position 15 minutes later.

20. **Wheels** A bicycle's wheel spins backwards, making 2 complete counterclockwise revolutions. What is the measure of the wheel's rotation angle in radians?

CHAPTER 12

MULTI-STEP TEST PREP

SECTION 12A

MATHEMATICAL PRACTICES **Reason abstractly and quantitatively.**

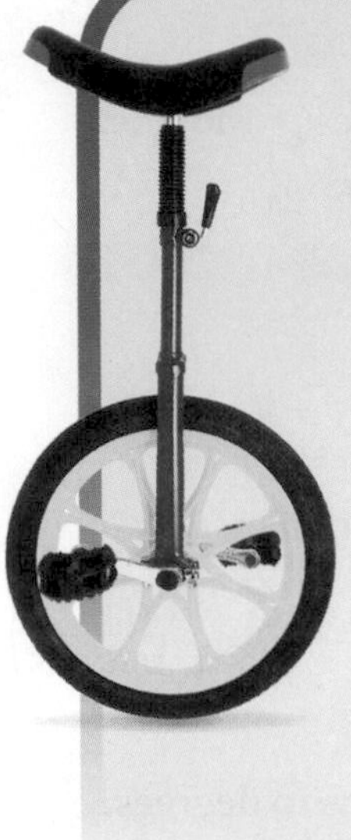

Lines and Arcs in Circles

As the Wheels Turn The bicycle was invented in the 1790s. The first models didn't even have pedals—riders moved forward by pushing their feet along the ground! Today the bicycle is a high-tech machine that can include hydraulic brakes and electronic gear changers.

1. A road race bicycle wheel is 28 inches in diameter. A manufacturer makes metal bicycle stands that are 10 in. tall. How long should a stand be to the nearest tenth in order to support a 28 in. wheel? (*Hint:* Consider the triangle formed by the radii and the top of the stand.)

2. The chain of a bicycle loops around a large gear connected to the bike's pedals and a small gear attached to the rear wheel. In the diagram, the distance AB between the centers of the gears the nearest tenth is 15 in. Find CD, the length of the chain between the two gears to the nearest tenth. (*Hint:* Draw a segment from B to $\overline{AD}$ that is parallel to $\overline{CD}$.)
3. By pedaling, you turn the large gear through an angle of 60°. How far does the chain move around the circumference of the gear to the nearest tenth?
4. As the chain moves, it turns the small gear. If you use the distance you calculated in Problem 3, through what angle does the small gear turn to the nearest degree?

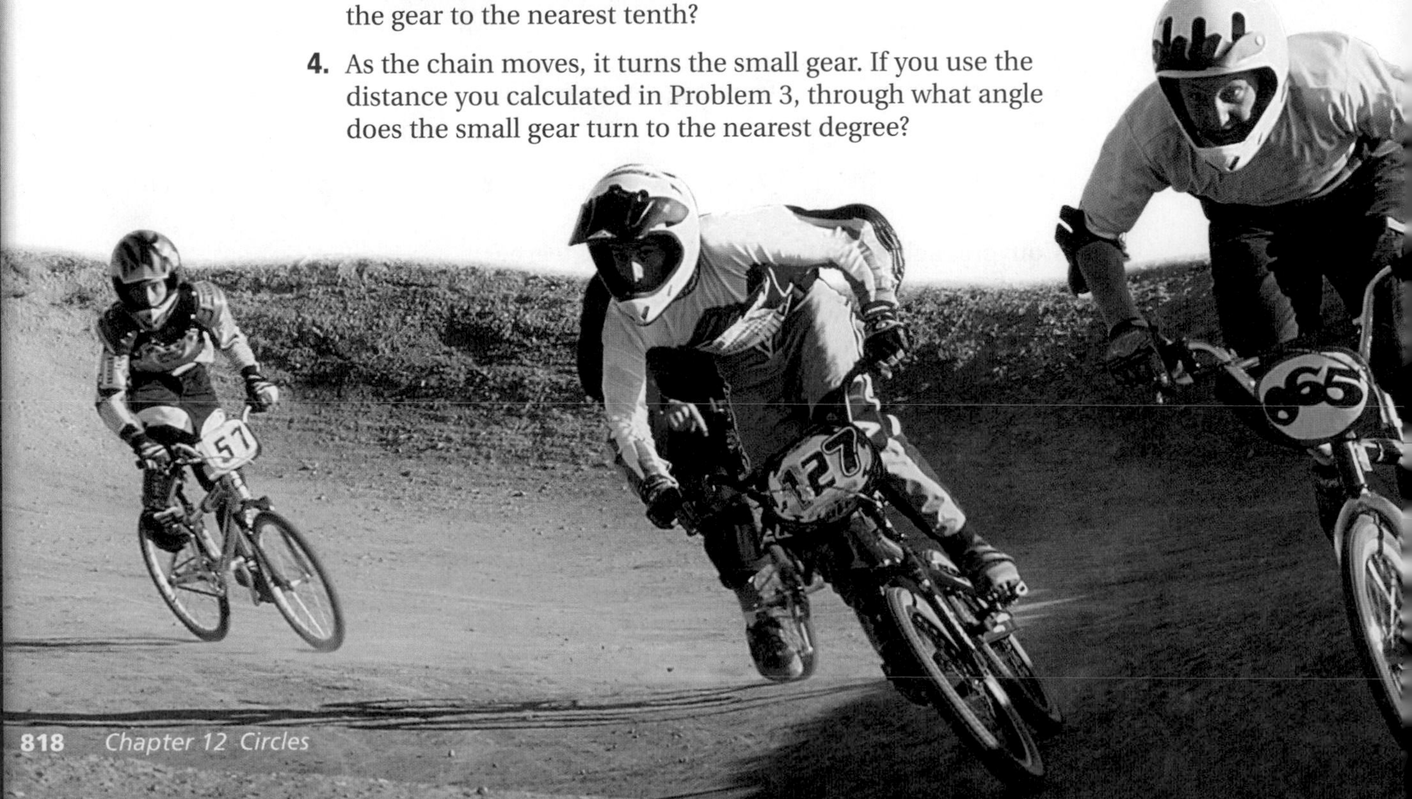

READY TO GO ON?

Quiz for Lessons 12-1 Through 12-3

12-1 Lines That Intersect Circles

Identify each line or segment that intersects each circle.

1.

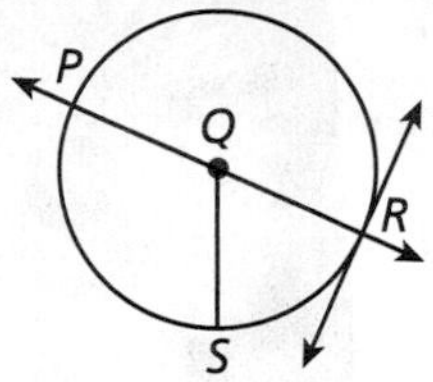

2.

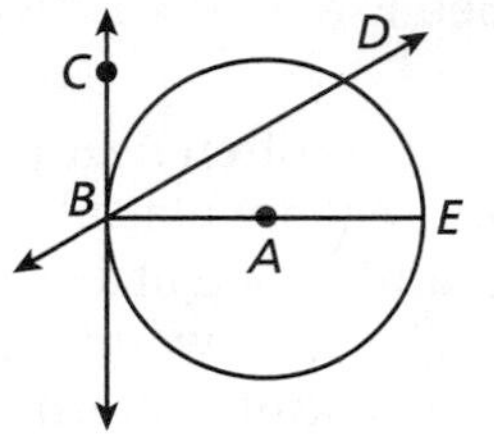

3. The tallest building in Africa is the Carlton Centre in Johannesburg, South Africa. What is the distance from the top of this 732 ft building to the horizon to the nearest mile? (*Hint:* 5280 ft = 1 mi; radius of Earth = 4000 mi)

12-2 Arcs and Chords

Find each measure.

4. $\overset{\frown}{BC}$

5. $\overset{\frown}{BED}$

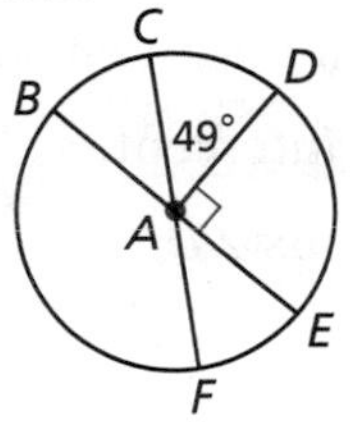

6. $\overset{\frown}{SR}$

7. $\overset{\frown}{SQU}$

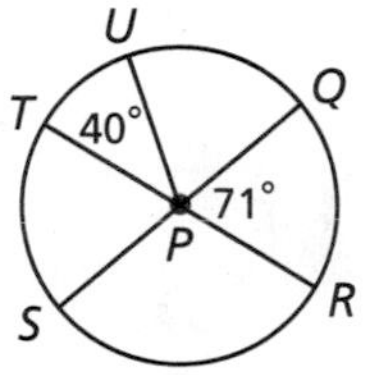

Find each length to the nearest tenth.

8. JK

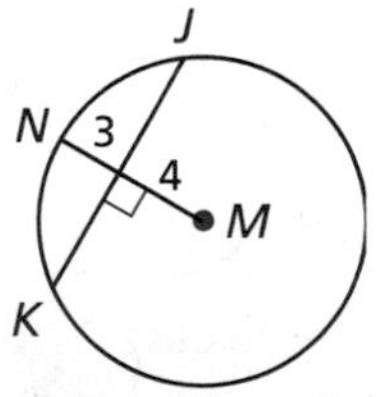

9. XY

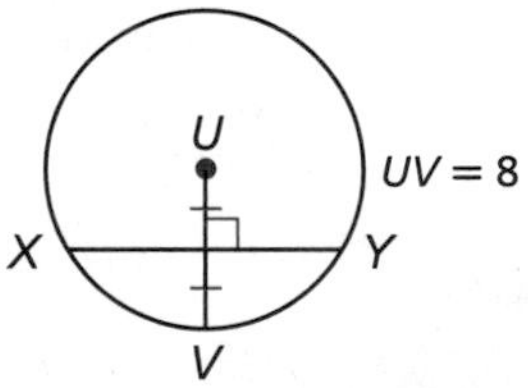

12-3 Sector Area and Arc Length

10. As part of an art project, Peter buys a circular piece of fabric and then cuts out the sector shown. What is the area of the sector to the nearest square centimeter?

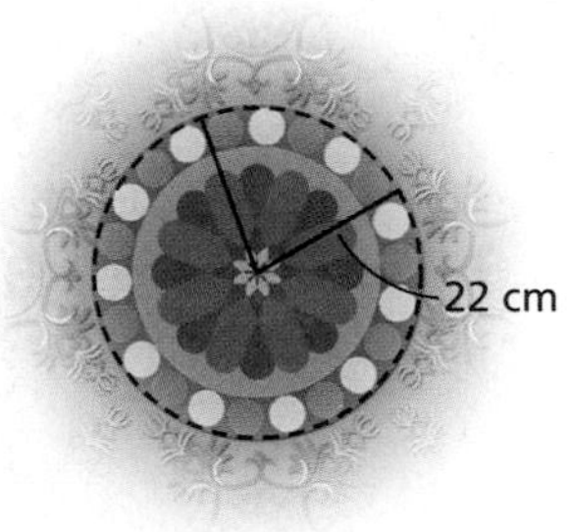

Find each arc length. Give your answer in terms of π and rounded to the nearest hundredth.

11. $\overset{\frown}{AB}$

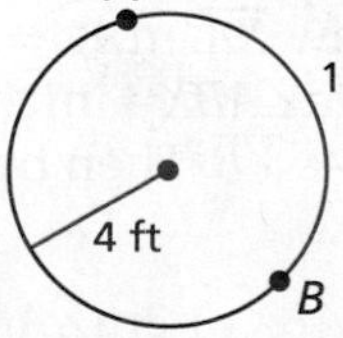

12. $\overset{\frown}{EF}$

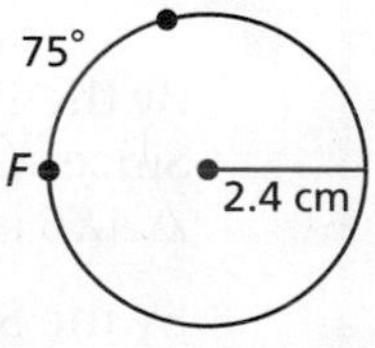

13. an arc with measure 44° in a circle with diameter 10 in.

14. a semicircle in a circle with diameter 92 m

COMMON CORE

12-4 Inscribed Angles

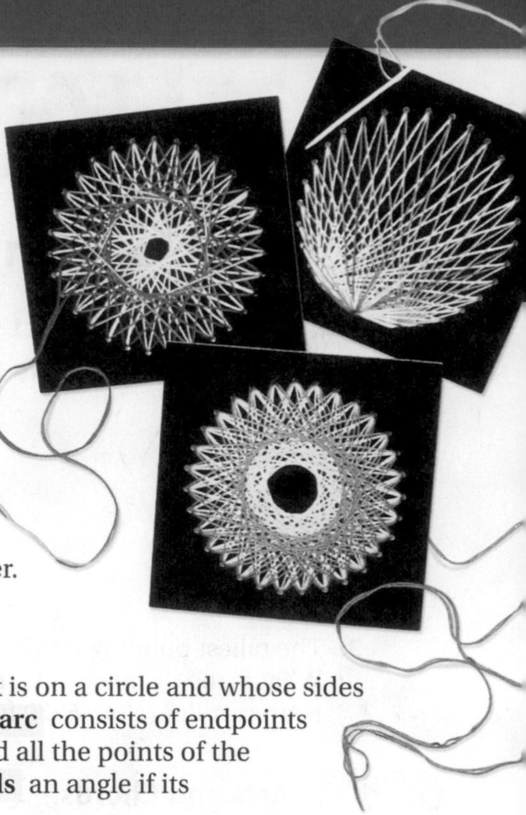

CC.9-12.G.C.2 Identify and describe relationships among inscribed angles. *Also* **CC.9-12.G.C.3, CC.9-12.G.CO.13, CC.9-12.G.CO.12**

Objectives

Find the measure of an inscribed angle.

Use inscribed angles and their properties to solve problems.

Vocabulary

inscribed angle
intercepted arc
subtend

Why learn this?

You can use inscribed angles to find measures of angles in string art. (See Example 2.)

String art often begins with pins or nails that are placed around the circumference of a circle. A long piece of string is then wound from one nail to another. The resulting pattern may include hundreds of *inscribed angles.*

An **inscribed angle** is an angle whose vertex is on a circle and whose sides contain chords of the circle. An **intercepted arc** consists of endpoints that lie on the sides of an inscribed angle and all the points of the circle between them. A chord or arc **subtends** an angle if its endpoints lie on the sides of the angle.

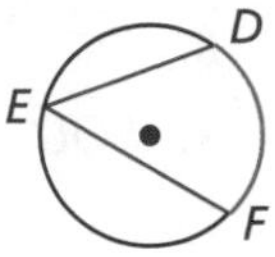

$\angle DEF$ is an **inscribed angle.**

$\overparen{DF}$ is the **intercepted arc.**

$\overparen{DF}$ subtends $\angle DEF$.

Know it! Note

Theorem 12-4-1 Inscribed Angle Theorem

The measure of an inscribed angle is half the measure of its intercepted arc.

$$m\angle ABC = \frac{1}{2}m\overparen{AC}$$

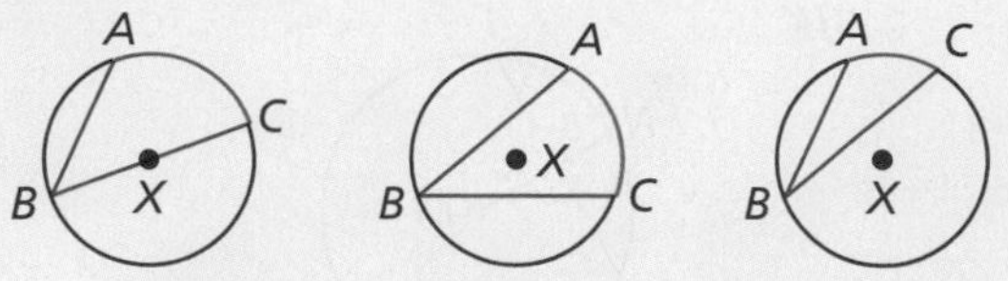

Case 1 Case 2 Case 3

You will prove Cases 2 and 3 of Theorem 12-4-1 in Exercises 30 and 31.

PROOF

Inscribed Angle Theorem

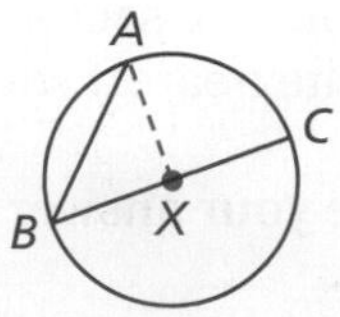

Given: $\angle ABC$ is inscribed in $\odot X$.

Prove: $m\angle ABC = \frac{1}{2}m\overparen{AC}$

Proof Case 1:

$\angle ABC$ is inscribed in $\odot X$ with X on $\overline{BC}$. Draw $\overline{XA}$. $m\overparen{AC} = m\angle AXC$.
By the Exterior Angle Theorem $m\angle AXC = m\angle ABX + m\angle BAX$.
Since $\overline{XA}$ and $\overline{XB}$ are radii of the circle, $\overline{XA} \cong \overline{XB}$. Then by definition $\triangle AXB$ is isosceles. Thus $m\angle ABX = m\angle BAX$.

By the Substitution Property, $m\overparen{AC} = 2m\angle ABX$ or $2m\angle ABC$.
Thus $\frac{1}{2}m\overparen{AC} = m\angle ABC$.

EXAMPLE 1 Finding Measures of Arcs and Inscribed Angles

Find each measure.

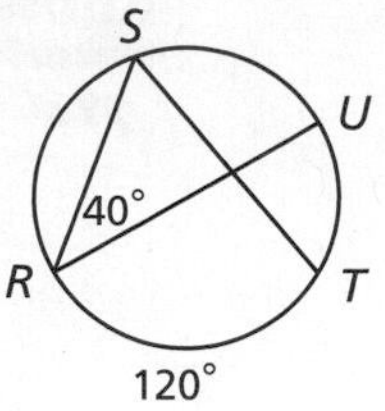

A $m\angle RST$

$m\angle RST = \frac{1}{2}m\widehat{RT}$ *Inscribed ∠ Thm.*

$= \frac{1}{2}(120°) = 60°$ *Substitute 120 for $m\widehat{RT}$.*

B $m\widehat{SU}$

$m\angle SRU = \frac{1}{2}m\widehat{SU}$ *Inscribed ∠ Thm.*

$40° = \frac{1}{2}m\widehat{SU}$ *Substitute 40 for $m\angle SRU$.*

$m\widehat{SU} = 80°$ *Mult. both sides by 2.*

CHECK IT OUT! Find each measure.

1a. $m\widehat{ADC}$

1b. $m\angle DAE$

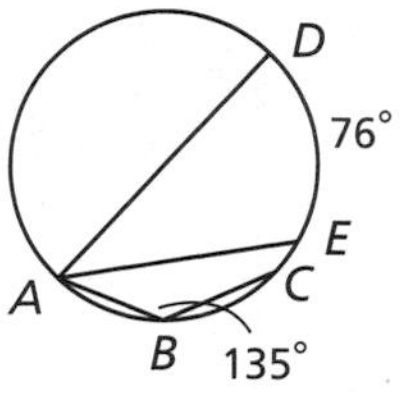

Know it! Note

Corollary 12-4-2

COROLLARY	HYPOTHESIS	CONCLUSION
If inscribed angles of a circle intercept the same arc or are subtended by the same chord or arc, then the angles are congruent.	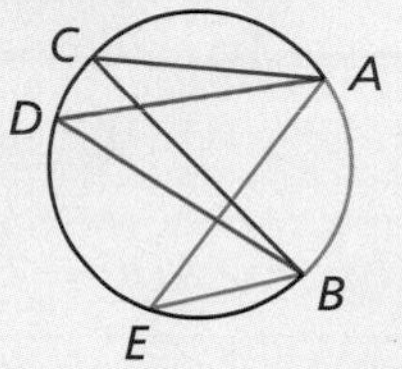 $\angle ACB$, $\angle ADB$, and $\angle AEB$ intercept $\widehat{AB}$.	$\angle ACB \cong \angle ADB \cong \angle AEB$ (and $\angle CAE \cong \angle CBE$)

You will prove Corollary 12-4-2 in Exercise 32.

EXAMPLE 2 *Hobby Application*

Find $m\angle DEC$, if $m\widehat{AD} = 86°$.

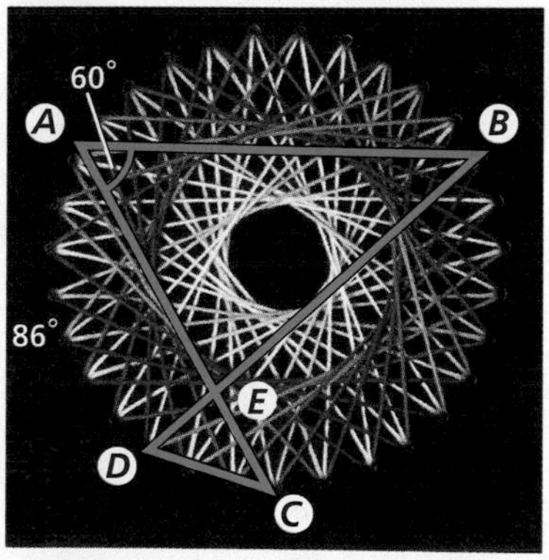

$\angle BAC \cong \angle BDC$ *∠BAC and ∠BDC intercept $\widehat{BC}$.*

$m\angle BAC = m\angle BDC$ *Def. of ≅*

$m\angle BDC = 60°$ *Substitute 60 for $m\angle BDC$.*

$m\angle ACD = \frac{1}{2}m\widehat{AD}$ *Inscribed ∠ Thm.*

$= \frac{1}{2}(86°)$ *Substitute 86 for $m\widehat{AD}$.*

$= 43°$ *Simplify.*

$m\angle DEC + 60 + 43 = 180$ *△ Sum Theorem*

$m\angle DEC = 77°$ *Simplify.*

CHECK IT OUT! **2.** Find $m\angle ABD$ and $m\widehat{BC}$ in the string art.

Know it! Note

Theorem 12-4-3

An inscribed angle subtends a semicircle if and only if the angle is a right angle.

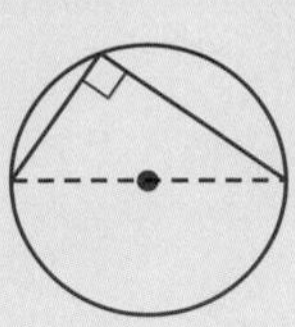

You will prove Theorem 12-4-3 in Exercise 43.

EXAMPLE 3 Finding Angle Measures in Inscribed Triangles

x^2y **Algebra**

Find each value.

A x

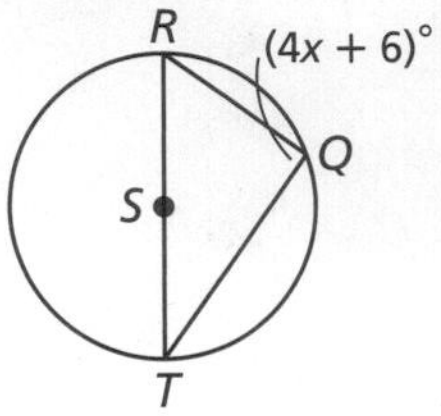

$\angle RQT$ is a right angle	*$\angle RQT$ is inscribed in a semicircle.*
$m\angle RQT = 90°$	*Def. of rt. $\angle$*
$4x + 6 = 90$	*Substitute $4x + 6$ for $m\angle RQT$.*
$4x = 84$	*Subtract 6 from both sides.*
$x = 21$	*Divide both sides by 4.*

B $m\angle ADC$

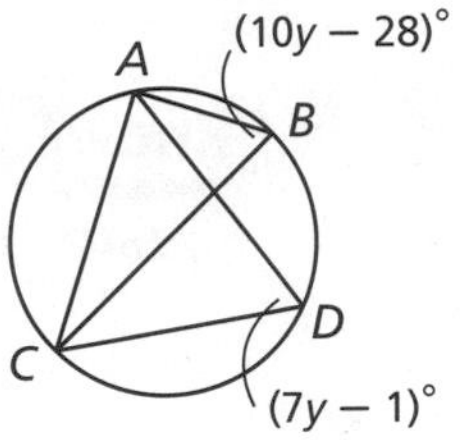

$m\angle ABC = m\angle ADC$	*$\angle ABC$ and $\angle ADC$ both intercept $\overparen{AC}$.*
$10y - 28 = 7y - 1$	*Substitute the given values.*
$3y - 28 = -1$	*Subtract 7y from both sides.*
$3y = 27$	*Add 28 to both sides.*
$y = 9$	*Divide both sides by 3.*
$m\angle ADC = 7(9) - 1 = 62°$	*Substitute 9 for y.*

CHECK IT OUT! **Find each value.**

3a. z

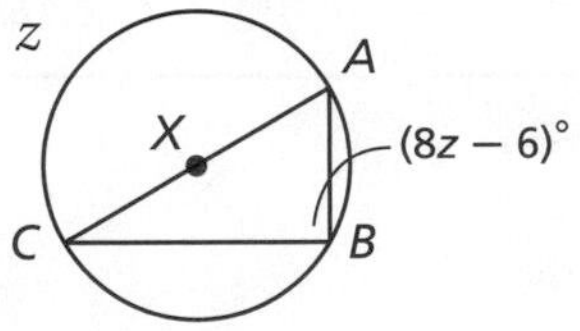

3b. $m\angle EDF$

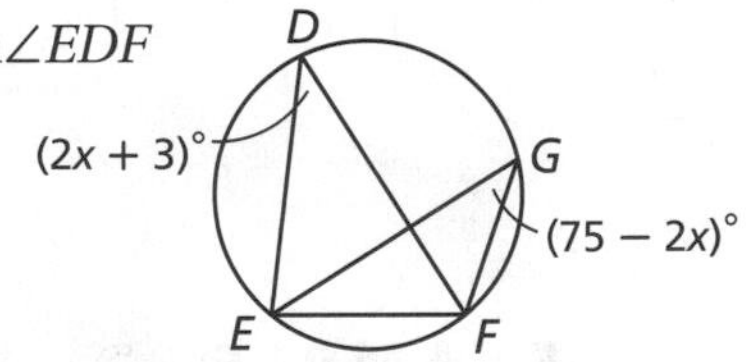

Construction Center of a Circle

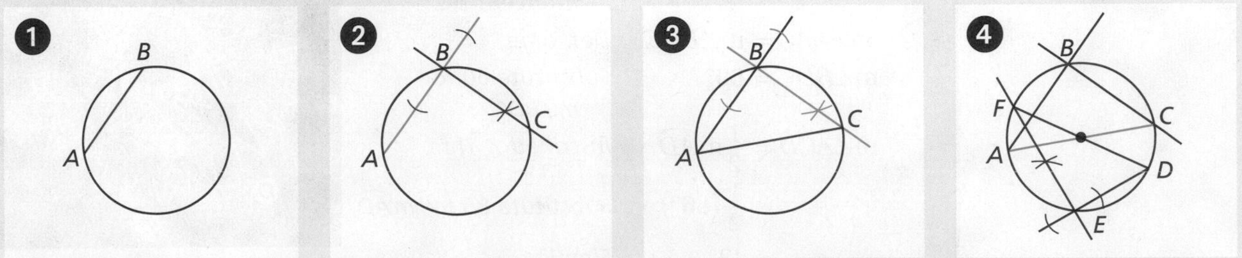

1. Draw a circle and chord $\overline{AB}$.
2. Construct a line perpendicular to $\overline{AB}$ at *B*. Where the line and the circle intersect, label the point **C**.
3. Draw chord $\overline{AC}$.
4. Repeat steps to draw chords $\overline{DE}$ and $\overline{DF}$. The intersection of $\overline{AC}$ and $\overline{DF}$ is the center of the circle.

Know it! Note

Theorem 12-4-4

THEOREM	HYPOTHESIS	CONCLUSION
If a quadrilateral is inscribed in a circle, then its opposite angles are supplementary.	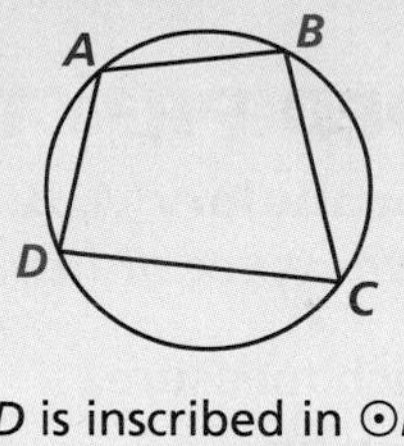 $ABCD$ is inscribed in $\odot E$.	$\angle A$ and $\angle C$ are supplementary. $\angle B$ and $\angle D$ are supplementary.

You will prove Theorem 12-4-4 in Exercise 44.

EXAMPLE 4 Finding Angle Measures in Inscribed Quadrilaterals

x^2y Algebra

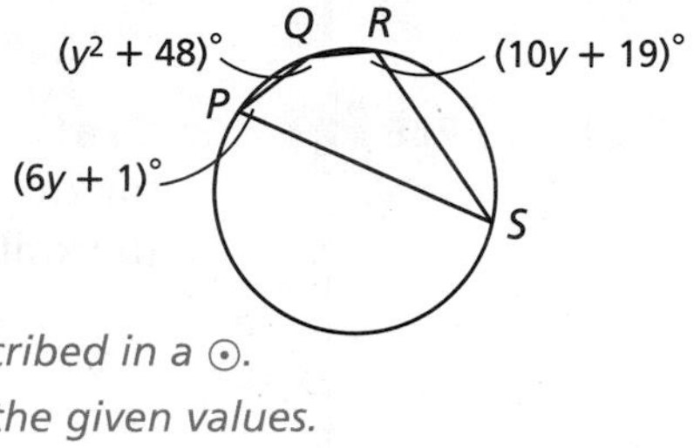

Find the angle measures of *PQRS*.

Step 1 Find the value of y.

$m\angle P + m\angle R = 180°$	*PQRS is inscribed in a ⊙.*
$6y + 1 + 10y + 19 = 180$	*Substitute the given values.*
$16y + 20 = 180$	*Simplify.*
$16y = 160$	*Subtract 20 from both sides.*
$y = 10$	*Divide both sides by 16.*

Step 2 Find the measure of each angle.

$m\angle P = 6(10) + 1 = 61°$	*Substitute 10 for y in each expression.*
$m\angle R = 10(10) + 19 = 119°$	
$m\angle Q = 10^2 + 48 = 148°$	
$m\angle Q + m\angle S = 180°$	*∠Q and ∠S are supp.*
$148° + m\angle S = 180°$	*Substitute 148 for m∠Q.*
$m\angle S = 32°$	*Subtract 148 from both sides.*

CHECK IT OUT!

4. Find the angle measures of *JKLM*.

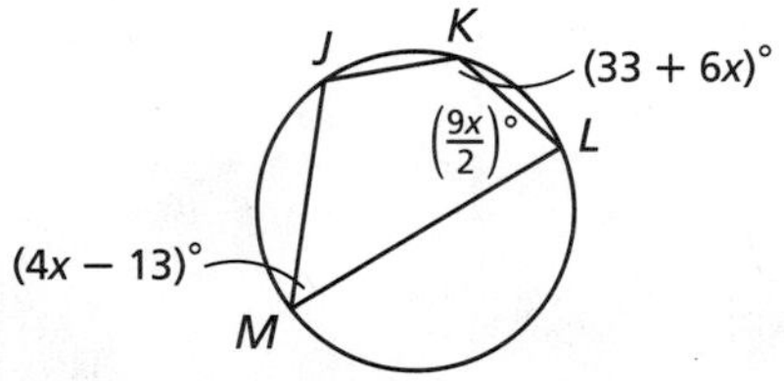

MATHEMATICAL PRACTICES

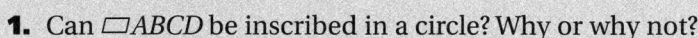

THINK AND DISCUSS

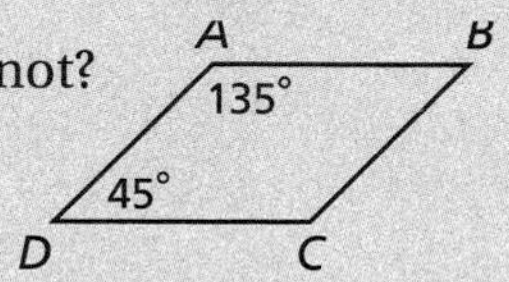

1. Can $\square ABCD$ be inscribed in a circle? Why or why not?

2. An inscribed angle intercepts an arc that is $\frac{1}{4}$ of the circle. Explain how to find the measure of the inscribed angle.

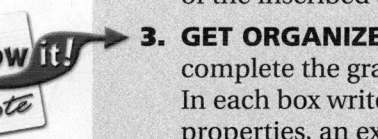

Know it! Note

3. GET ORGANIZED Copy and complete the graphic organizer. In each box write a definition, properties, an example, and a nonexample.

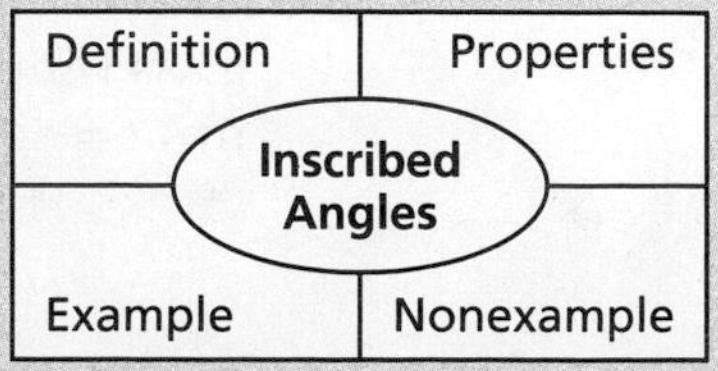

12-4 Exercises

Learn It Online
Homework Help Online
Parent Resources Online

GUIDED PRACTICE

1. **Vocabulary** *A*, *B*, and *C* lie on ⊙*P*. ∠*ABC* is an example of an ___?___ angle. (*intercepted* or *inscribed*)

SEE EXAMPLE 1

Find each measure.

2. m∠*DEF*
3. m$\overset{\frown}{EG}$

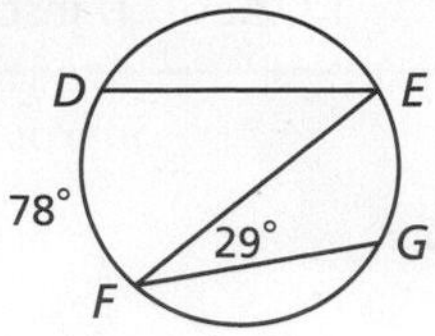

4. m$\overset{\frown}{JKL}$
5. m∠*LKM*

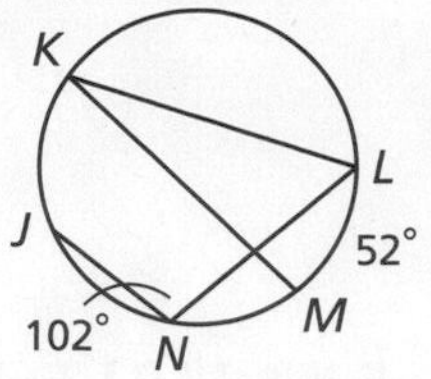

SEE EXAMPLE 2

6. **Crafts** A circular loom can be used for knitting. What is the m∠*QTR* in the knitting loom?

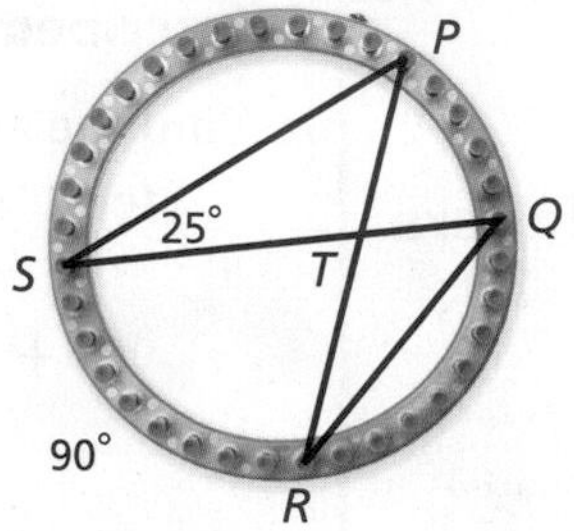

SEE EXAMPLE 3

Find each value.

7. *x*

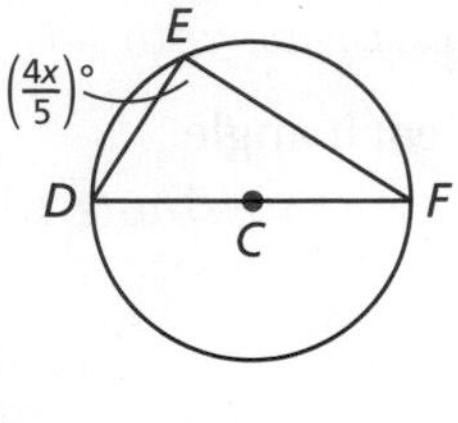

8. *y*

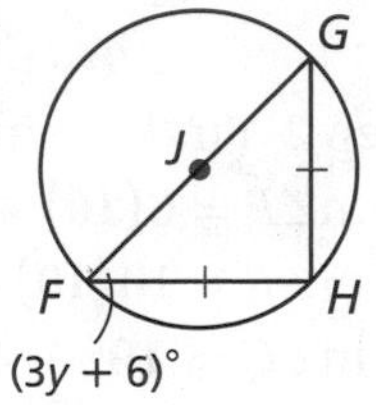

9. m∠*XYZ*

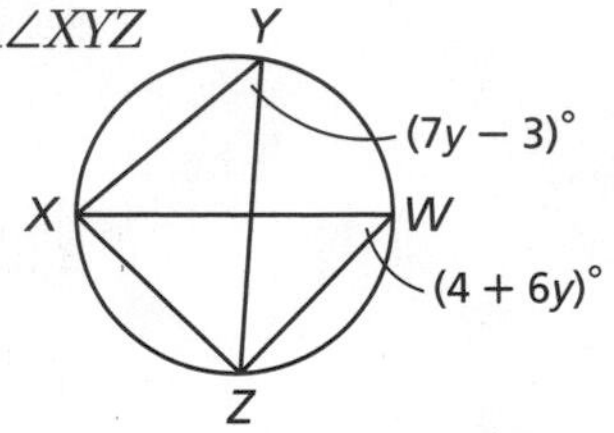

SEE EXAMPLE 4

Multi-Step **Find the angle measures of each quadrilateral.**

10. *PQRS*

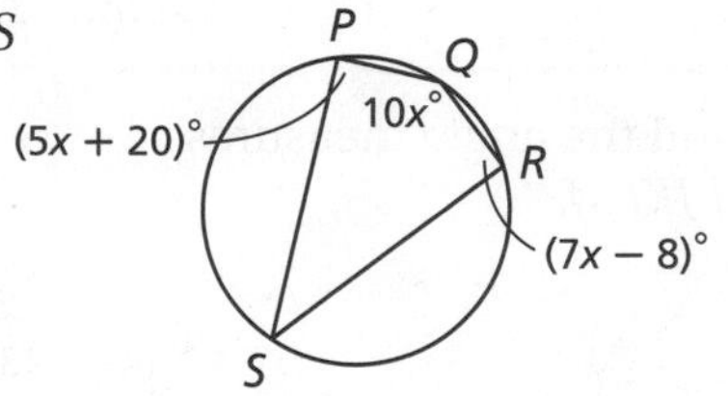

11. *ABCD*

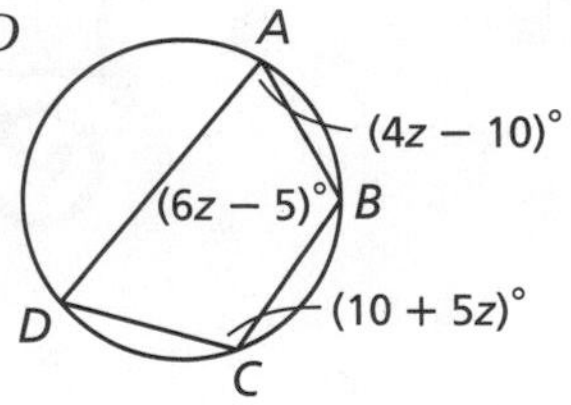

PRACTICE AND PROBLEM SOLVING

Independent Practice	
For Exercises	See Example
12–15	1
16	2
17–20	3
21–22	4

Find each measure.

12. m$\overset{\frown}{ML}$
13. m∠*KMN*

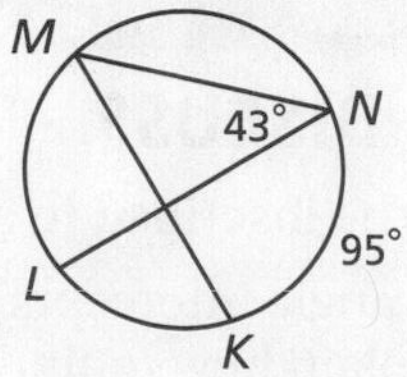

14. m$\overset{\frown}{EGH}$
15. m∠*GFH*

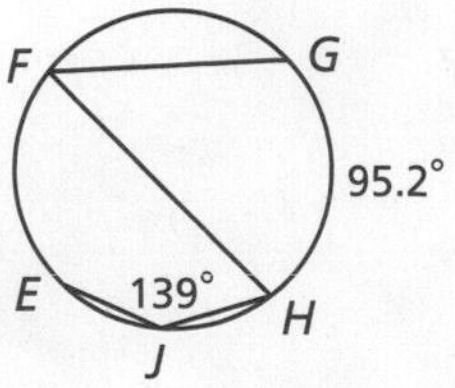

16. **Crafts** An artist created a stained glass window. If m∠*BEC* = 40° and m$\overset{\frown}{AB}$ = 44°, what is m∠*ADC*?

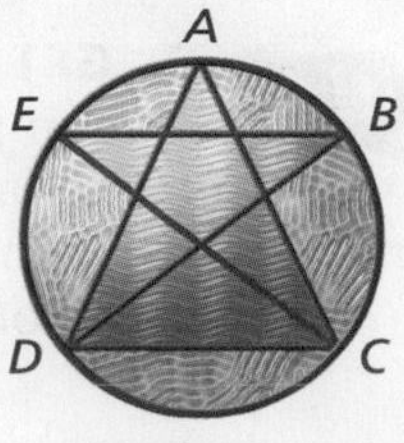

Algebra **Find each value.**

17. y

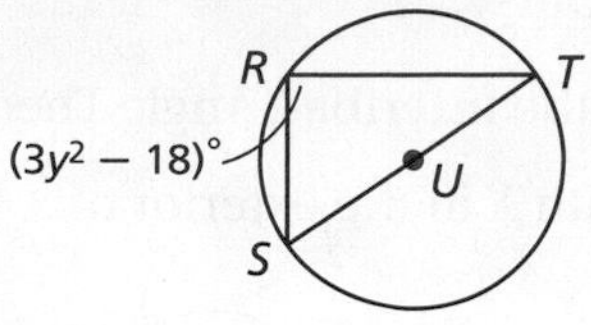

18. z

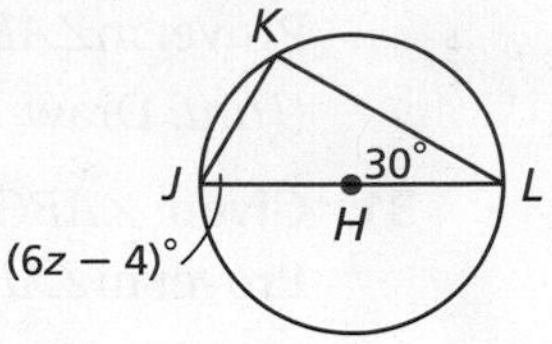

19. $m\widehat{AB}$

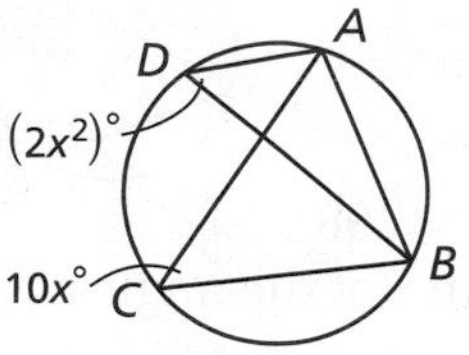

20. $m\angle MPN$

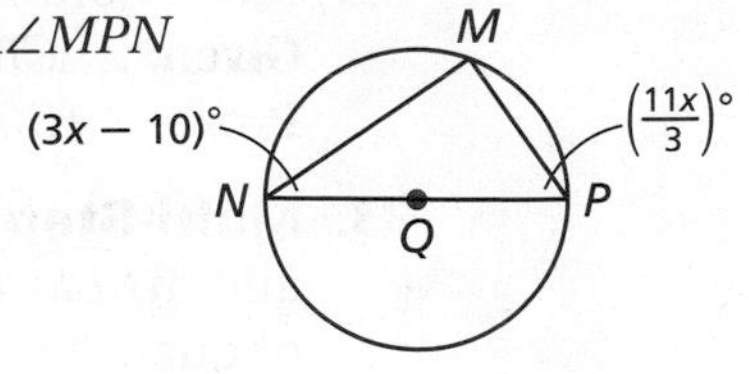

Multi-Step **Find the angle measures of each quadrilateral.**

21. $BCDE$

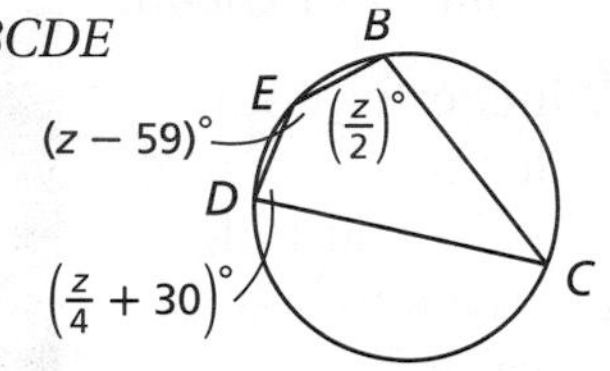

22. $TUVW$

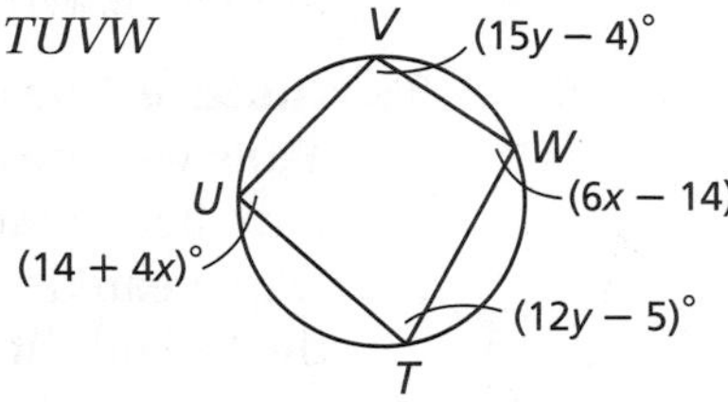

Tell whether each statement is sometimes, always, or never true.

23. Two inscribed angles that intercept the same arc of a circle are congruent.

24. When a right triangle is inscribed in a circle, one of the legs of the triangle is a diameter of the circle.

25. A trapezoid can be inscribed in a circle.

Multi-Step **Find each angle measure.**

26. $m\angle ABC$ if $m\angle ADC = 112°$

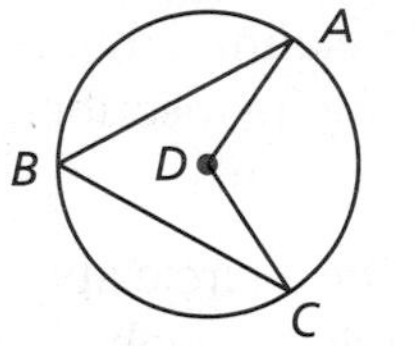

27. $m\angle PQR$ if $m\widehat{PQR} = 130°$

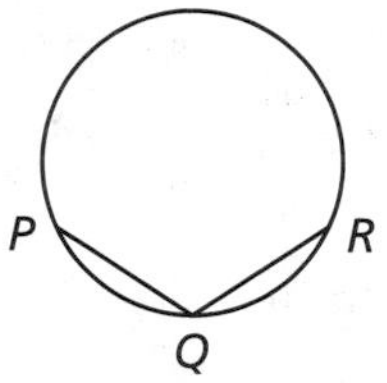

28. Prove that the measure of a central angle subtended by a chord is twice the measure of the inscribed angle subtended by the chord.
Given: In $\odot H$ $\overline{JK}$ subtends $\angle JHK$ and $\angle JLK$.
Prove: $m\angle JHK = 2m\angle JLK$

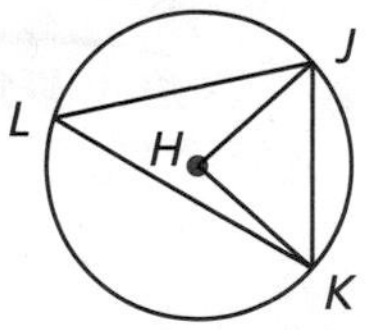

MULTI-STEP TEST PREP

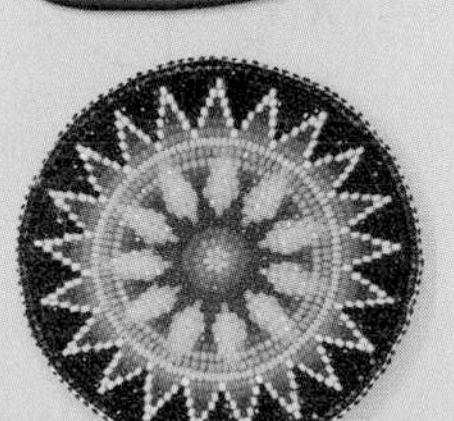

29. A Native American sand painting could be used to indicate the direction of sunrise on the winter and summer solstices. You can make this design by placing six equally spaced points around the circumference of a circle and connecting them as shown.

a. Find $m\angle BAC$.

b. Find $m\angle CDE$.

c. What type of triangle is $\triangle FBC$? Why?

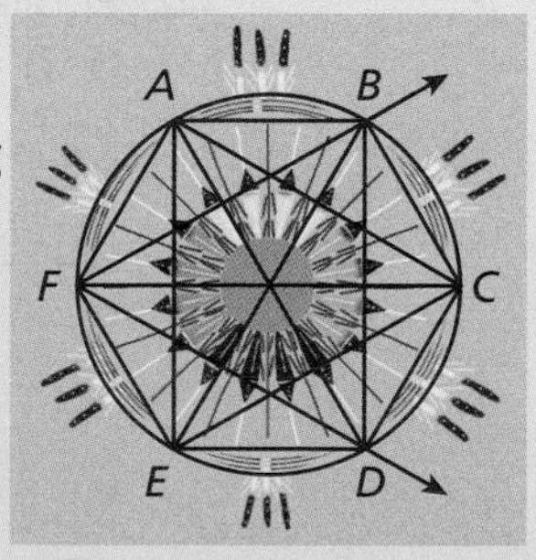

30. **Given:** $\angle ABC$ is inscribed in $\odot X$ with X in the interior of $\angle ABC$.
Prove: $m\angle ABC = \frac{1}{2} m\widehat{AC}$
(*Hint:* Draw $\overrightarrow{BX}$ and use Case 1 of the Inscribed Angle Theorem.)

31. **Given:** $\angle ABC$ is inscribed in $\odot X$ with X in the exterior of $\angle ABC$.
Prove: $m\angle ABC = \frac{1}{2} m\widehat{AC}$

32. Prove Corollary 12-4-2.
Given: $\angle ACB$ and $\angle ADB$ intercept $\widehat{AB}$.
Prove: $\angle ACB \cong \angle ADB$

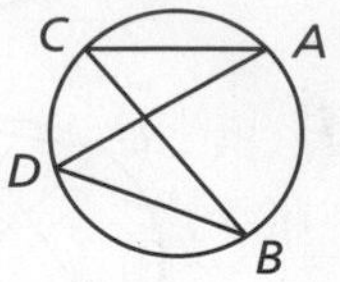

33. **Multi-Step** In the diagram, $m\widehat{JKL} = 198°$, and $m\widehat{KLM} = 216°$. Find the measures of the angles of quadrilateral $JKLM$.

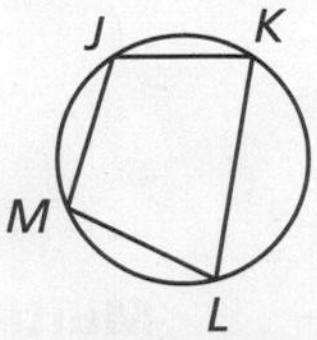

34. **Critical Thinking** A rectangle $PQRS$ is inscribed in a circle. What can you conclude about $\overline{PR}$? Explain.

35. **History** The diagram shows the Winchester Round Table with inscribed $\triangle ABC$. The table may have been made at the request of King Edward III, who created the Order of the Garter as a return to the Round Table and an order of chivalry.
   a. Explain why $\overline{BC}$ must be a diameter of the circle.
   b. Find $m\widehat{AC}$.

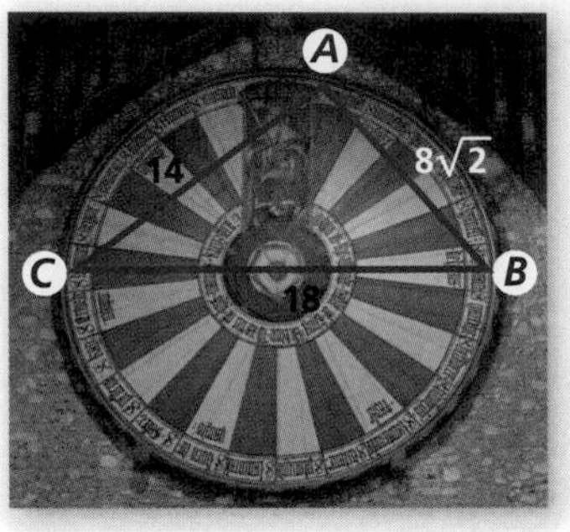

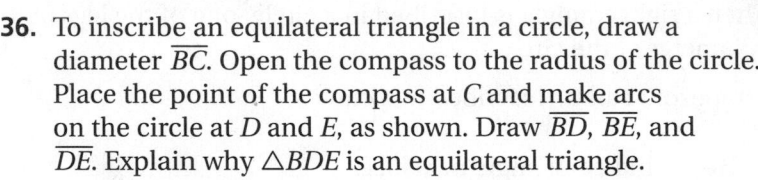

36. To inscribe an equilateral triangle in a circle, draw a diameter $\overline{BC}$. Open the compass to the radius of the circle. Place the point of the compass at C and make arcs on the circle at D and E, as shown. Draw $\overline{BD}$, $\overline{BE}$, and $\overline{DE}$. Explain why $\triangle BDE$ is an equilateral triangle.

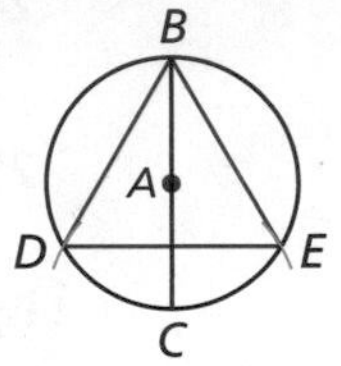

37. **Write About It** A student claimed that if a parallelogram contains a 30° angle, it cannot be inscribed in a circle. Do you agree or disagree? Explain.

38. **Construction** Circumscribe a circle about a triangle. (*Hint:* Follow the steps for the construction of a circle through three given noncollinear points.)

TEST PREP

39. What is $m\angle BAC$?

Ⓐ 38° Ⓒ 66°
Ⓑ 43° Ⓓ 81°

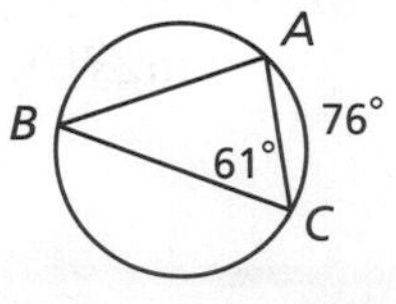

40. Equilateral $\triangle XCZ$ is inscribed in a circle. If $\overline{CY}$ bisects $\angle C$, what is $m\widehat{XY}$?

Ⓕ 15° Ⓖ 30° Ⓗ 60° Ⓙ 120°

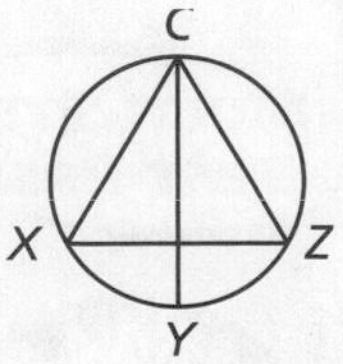

41. Quadrilateral $ABCD$ is inscribed in a circle. The ratio of $m\angle A$ to $m\angle C$ is 4:5. What is $m\angle A$?

Ⓐ 20° Ⓑ 40° Ⓒ 80° Ⓓ 100°

42. Which of these angles has the greatest measure?

Ⓕ $\angle STR$ Ⓖ $\angle QPR$ Ⓗ $\angle QSR$ Ⓙ $\angle PQS$

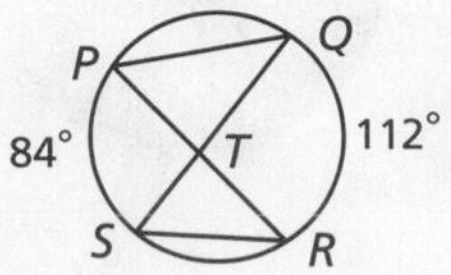

CHALLENGE AND EXTEND

43. Prove that an inscribed angle subtends a semicircle if and only if the angle is a right angle. (*Hint:* There are two parts.)

44. Prove that if a quadrilateral is inscribed in a circle, then its opposite angles are supplementary. (*Hint:* There are two parts.)

45. Find m$\overset{\frown}{PQ}$ to the nearest degree.

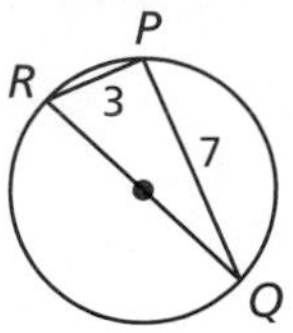

46. Find m$\angle ABD$.

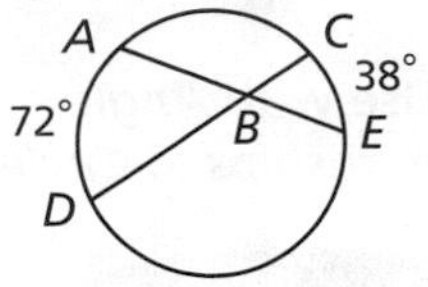

47. Construction To circumscribe an equilateral triangle about a circle, construct $\overline{AB}$ parallel to the horizontal diameter of the circle and tangent to the circle. Then use a 30°-60°-90° triangle to draw $\overline{AC}$ and $\overline{BC}$ so that they form 60° angles with $\overline{AB}$ and are tangent to the circle.

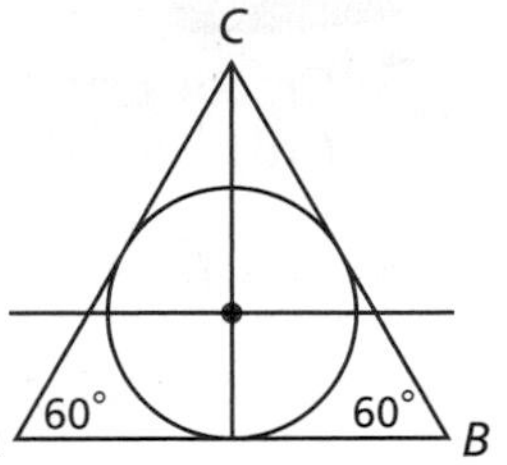

Construction Tangent to a Circle From an Exterior Point

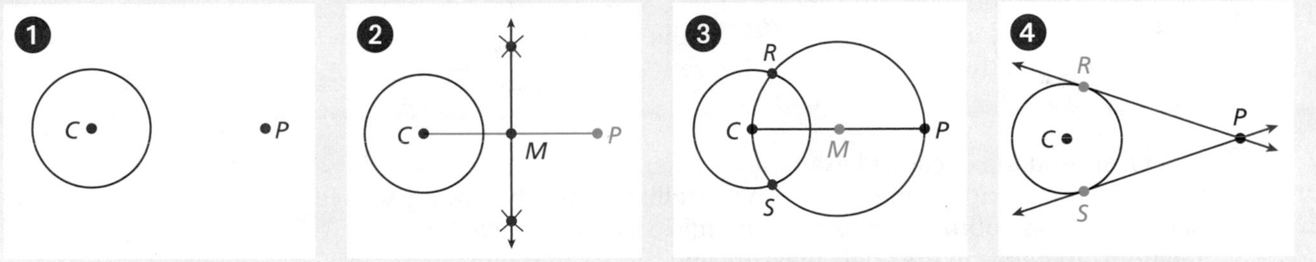

1. Draw ⊙*C* and locate ***P*** in the exterior of the circle.

2. Draw $\overline{CP}$. Construct ***M***, the midpoint of $\overline{CP}$.

3. Center the compass at *M*. Draw a circle through *C* and *P*. It will intersect ⊙*C* at ***R*** and ***S***.

4. *R* and *S* are the tangent points. Draw $\overleftrightarrow{PR}$ and $\overleftrightarrow{PS}$ tangent to ⊙*C*.

1. Can you draw $\overline{CR} \perp \overleftrightarrow{RP}$? Explain.

12-5 Technology LAB

Explore Angle Relationships in Circles

The measure of an angle inscribed in a circle is half the measure of its intercepted arc. Now you will explore other angles formed by pairs of lines that intersect circles.

Use with *Angle Relationships in Circles*

MATHEMATICAL PRACTICES **Use appropriate tools strategically.**

CC.9-12.G.C.2 Identify and describe relationships among inscribed angles, radii, and chords.

Activity 1

1. Create a circle with center A. Label the point on the circle as B. Create a radius segment from A to a new point C on the circle.

2. Construct a line through C perpendicular to radius $\overline{AC}$. Create a new point D on this line, which is tangent to circle A at C. Hide radius $\overline{AC}$.

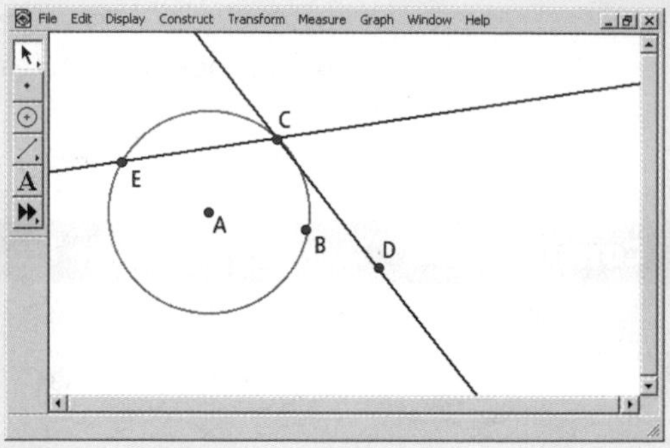

3. Create a new point E on the circle and then construct secant $\overline{CE}$.

4. Measure $\angle DCE$ and measure $\overset{\frown}{CBE}$. (*Hint:* To measure an arc in degrees, select the three points and the circle and then choose Arc Angle from the Measure menu.)

5. Drag E around the circle and examine the changes in the measures. Fill in the angle and arc measures in a chart like the one below. Try to create acute, right, and obtuse angles. Can you make a conjecture about the relationship between the angle measure and the arc measure?

m$\angle DCE$					
m$\overset{\frown}{CBE}$					
Angle Type					

Activity 2

1. Construct a new circle with two secants $\overleftrightarrow{CD}$ and $\overleftrightarrow{EF}$ that intersect *inside* the circle at G.

2. Create two new points H and I that are on the circle as shown. These will be used to measure the arcs. Hide B if desired. (It controls the circle's size.)

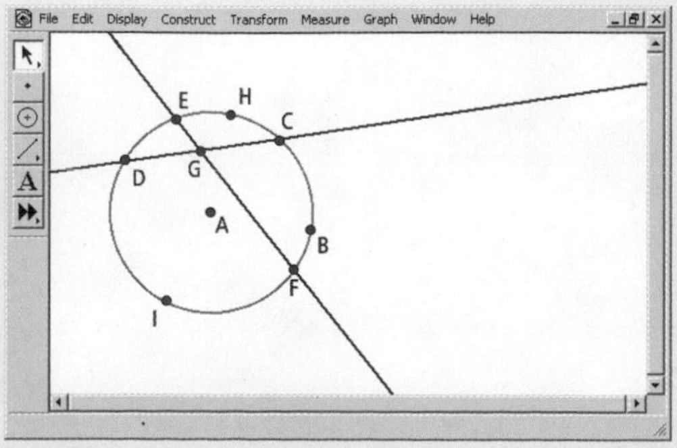

3. Measure $\angle DGF$ formed by the secant lines and measure $\overset{\frown}{CHE}$ and $\overset{\frown}{DIF}$.

4. Drag F around the circle and examine the changes in measures. Be sure to keep H between C and E and I between D and F for accurate arc measurement. Move them if needed.

5 Fill in the angle and arc measures in a chart like the one below. Try to create acute, right, and obtuse angles. Can you make a conjecture about the relationship between the angle measure and the two arc measures?

$m\angle DGF$					
$m\overset{\frown}{CHE}$					
$m\overset{\frown}{DIF}$					
Sum of Arcs					

Activity 3

1 Use the same figure from Activity 2. Drag points around the circle so that the intersection G is now *outside* the circle. Move H so it is between E and D and I is between C and F, as shown.

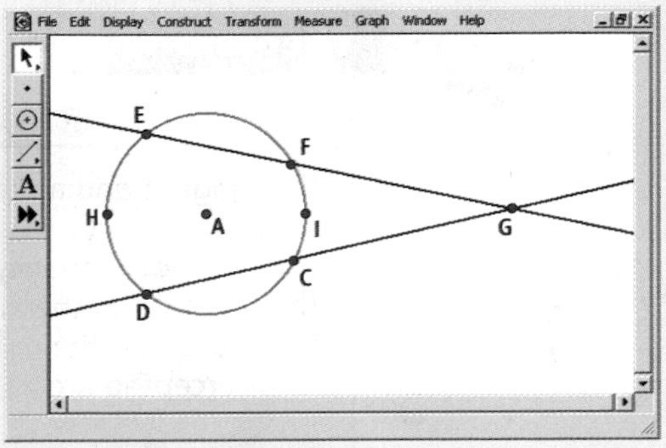

2 Measure $\angle FGC$ formed by the secant lines and measure $\overset{\frown}{CIF}$ and $\overset{\frown}{DHE}$.

3 Drag points around the circle and examine the changes in measures. Fill in the angle and arc measures in a chart like the one below. Can you make a conjecture about the relationship between the angle measure and the two arc measures?

$m\angle FGC$					
$m\overset{\frown}{CIF}$					
$m\overset{\frown}{DHE}$					
Number of Arcs					

Try This

1. How does the relationship you observed in Activity 1 compare to the relationship between an inscribed angle and its intercepted arc?
2. Why do you think the radius $\overline{AC}$ is needed in Activity 1 for the construction of the tangent line? What theorem explains this?
3. In Activity 3, try dragging points so that the secants become tangents. What conclusion can you make about the angle and arc measures?
4. Examine the conjectures and theorems about the relationships between angles and arcs in a circle. What is true of an angle with a vertex *on* the circle? What is true of an angle with a vertex *inside* the circle? What is true of an angle with a vertex *outside* the circle? Summarize your findings.
5. Does using geometry software to compare angle and arc measures constitute a formal proof of the relationship observed?

COMMON CORE

12-5 Angle Relationships in Circles

CC.9-12.G.C.2 Identify and describe relationships among inscribed angles, radii, and chords.

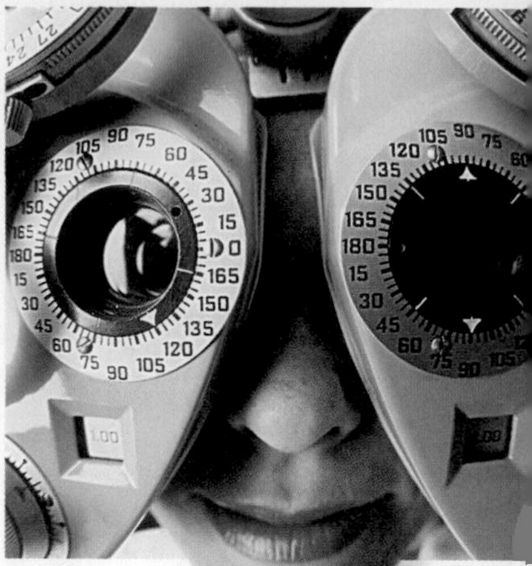

Objectives

Find the measures of angles formed by lines that intersect circles.

Use angle measures to solve problems.

Who uses this?

Circles and angles help optometrists correct vision problems. (See Example 4.)

Theorem 12-5-1 connects arc measures and the measures of tangent-secant angles with tangent-chord angles.

Know it! Note

Theorem 12-5-1

THEOREM	HYPOTHESIS	CONCLUSION
If a tangent and a secant (or chord) intersect on a circle at the point of tangency, then the measure of the angle formed is half the measure of its intercepted arc.	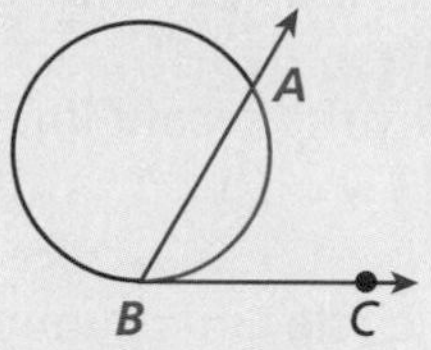 Tangent $\overrightarrow{BC}$ and secant $\overrightarrow{BA}$ intersect at B.	$m\angle ABC = \frac{1}{2}m\widehat{AB}$

You will prove Theorem 12-5-1 in Exercise 45.

EXAMPLE 1 Using Tangent-Secant and Tangent-Chord Angles

Find each measure.

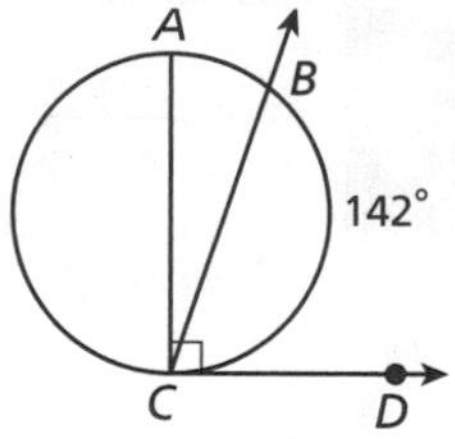

A $m\angle BCD$

$$m\angle BCD = \frac{1}{2}m\widehat{BC}$$
$$m\angle BCD = \frac{1}{2}(142°)$$
$$= 71°$$

B $m\widehat{ABC}$

$$m\angle ACD = \frac{1}{2}m\widehat{ABC}$$
$$90° = \frac{1}{2}m\widehat{ABC}$$
$$180° = m\widehat{ABC}$$

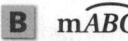

CHECK IT OUT! **Find each measure.**

1a. $m\angle STU$

1b. $m\widehat{SR}$

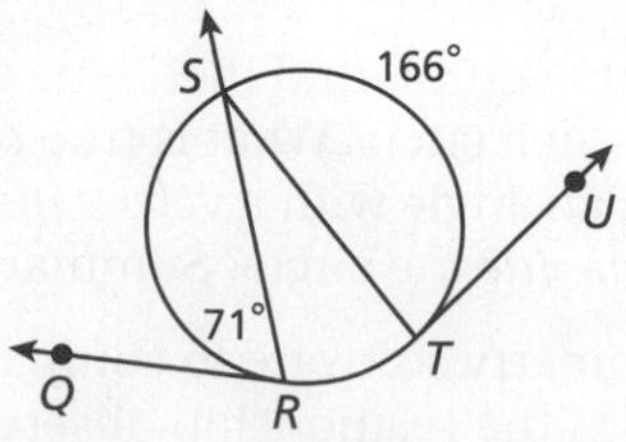

Know it! Note

Theorem 12-5-2

THEOREM	HYPOTHESIS	CONCLUSION
If two secants or chords intersect in the interior of a circle, then the measure of each angle formed is half the sum of the measures of its intercepted arcs.	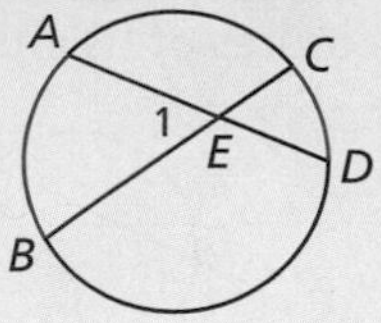 Chords $\overline{AD}$ and $\overline{BC}$ intersect at E.	$m\angle 1 = \frac{1}{2}\left(m\widehat{AB} + m\widehat{CD}\right)$

PROOF

Theorem 12-5-2

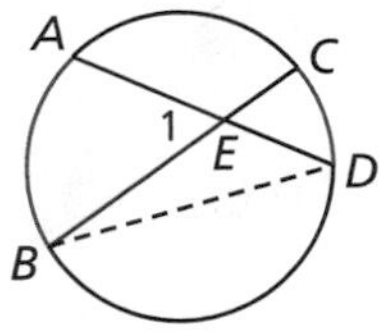

Given: $\overline{AD}$ and $\overline{BC}$ intersect at E.

Prove: $m\angle 1 = \frac{1}{2}\left(m\widehat{AB} + m\widehat{CD}\right)$

Proof:

Statements	Reasons
1. $\overline{AD}$ and $\overline{BC}$ intersect at E.	1. Given
2. Draw $\overline{BD}$.	2. Two pts. determine a line.
3. $m\angle 1 = m\angle EDB + m\angle EBD$	3. Ext. ∠ Thm.
4. $m\angle EDB = \frac{1}{2}m\widehat{AB}$, $m\angle EBD = \frac{1}{2}m\widehat{CD}$	4. Inscribed ∠ Thm.
5. $m\angle 1 = \frac{1}{2}m\widehat{AB} + \frac{1}{2}m\widehat{CD}$	5. Subst.
6. $m\angle 1 = \frac{1}{2}\left(m\widehat{AB} + m\widehat{CD}\right)$	6. Distrib. Prop.

EXAMPLE 2 Finding Angle Measures Inside a Circle

Find each angle measure.

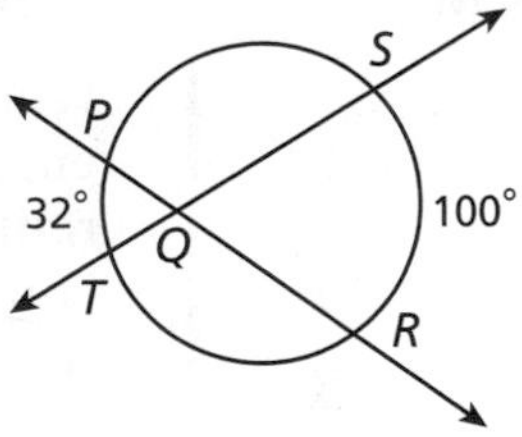

m∠SQR

$$m\angle SQR = \frac{1}{2}\left(m\widehat{PT} + m\widehat{SR}\right)$$
$$= \frac{1}{2}(32° + 100°)$$
$$= \frac{1}{2}(132°)$$
$$= 66°$$

CHECK IT OUT! **Find each angle measure.**

2a. $m\angle ABD$

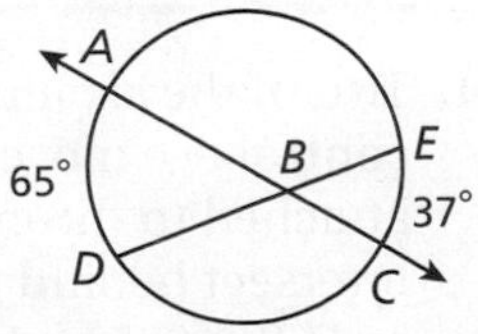

2b. $m\angle RNM$

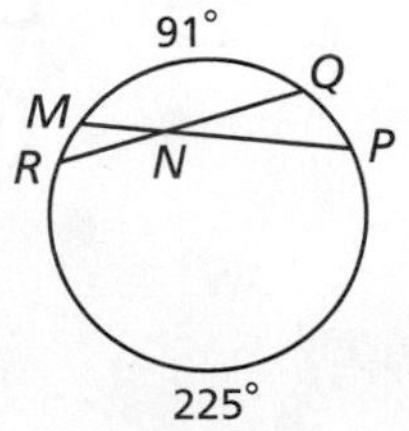

Know it! Note

Theorem 12-5-3

If a **tangent and a secant, two tangents,** or **two secants** intersect in the exterior of a circle, then the measure of the angle formed is half the difference of the measures of its intercepted arcs.

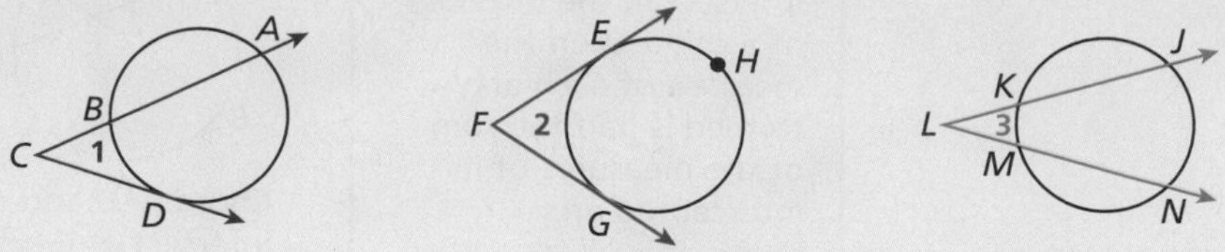

$m\angle 1 = \frac{1}{2}(m\overset{\frown}{AD} - m\overset{\frown}{BD})$ $m\angle 2 = \frac{1}{2}(m\overset{\frown}{EHG} - m\overset{\frown}{EG})$ $m\angle 3 = \frac{1}{2}(m\overset{\frown}{JN} - m\overset{\frown}{KM})$

You will prove Theorem 12-5-3 in Exercises 34–36.

EXAMPLE 3 Finding Measures Using Tangents and Secants

Find the value of x.

Helpful Hint

$\overset{\frown}{EHG}$ and $\overset{\frown}{EG}$ joined together make a whole circle. So $m\overset{\frown}{EHG} = 360° - 132° = 228°$

A

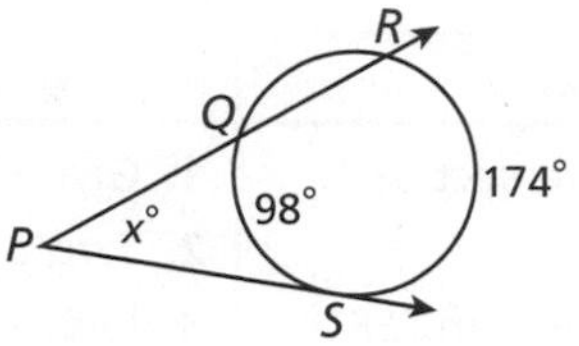

$x = \frac{1}{2}(m\overset{\frown}{RS} - m\overset{\frown}{QS})$

$= \frac{1}{2}(174° - 98°)$

$= 38°$

B

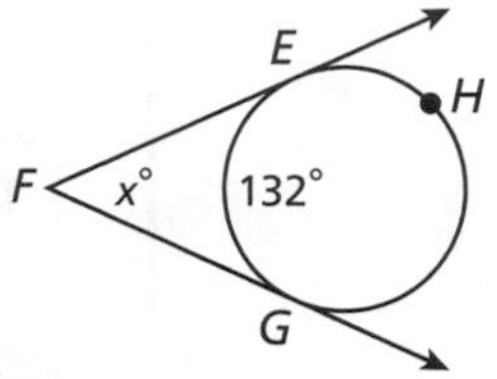

$x = \frac{1}{2}(m\overset{\frown}{EHG} - m\overset{\frown}{EG})$

$= \frac{1}{2}(228° - 132°)$

$= 48°$

CHECK IT OUT!

3. Find the value of x.

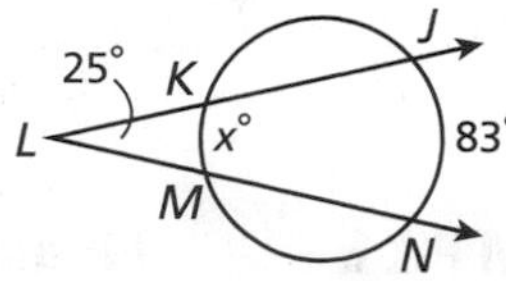

EXAMPLE 4 *Biology Application*

When a person is farsighted, light rays enter the eye and are focused behind the retina. In the eye shown, light rays converge at R. If $m\overset{\frown}{PS} = 60°$ and $m\overset{\frown}{QT} = 14°$, what is $m\angle PRS$?

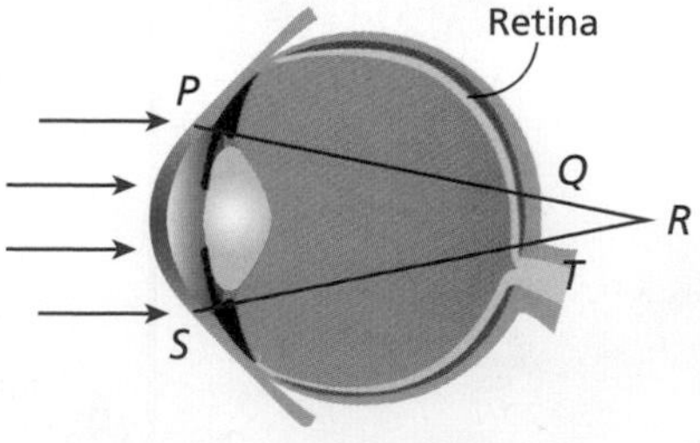

$m\angle PRS = \frac{1}{2}(m\overset{\frown}{PS} - m\overset{\frown}{QT})$

$= \frac{1}{2}(60° - 14°)$

$= \frac{1}{2}(46°) = 23°$

CHECK IT OUT!

4. Two of the six muscles that control eye movement are attached to the eyeball and intersect behind the eye. If $m\overset{\frown}{AEB} = 225°$, what is $m\angle ACB$?

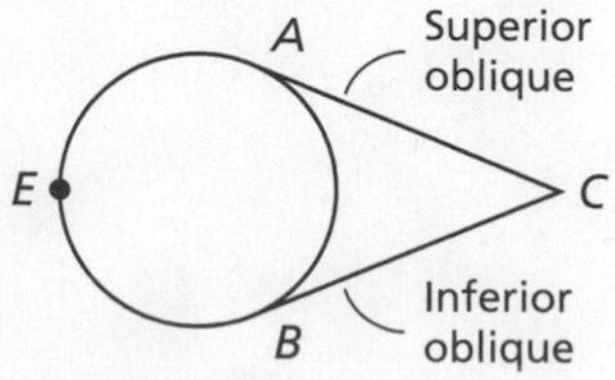

Know it! Note

Angle Relationships in Circles

VERTEX OF THE ANGLE	MEASURE OF ANGLE	DIAGRAMS	
On a circle	Half the measure of its intercepted arc	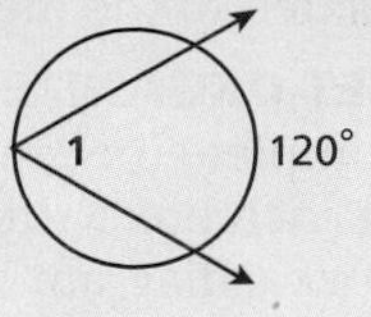 $m\angle 1 = 60°$	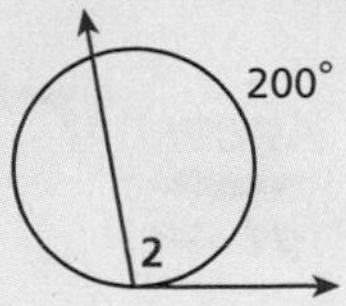 $m\angle 2 = 100°$
Inside a circle	Half the sum of the measures of its intercepted arcs	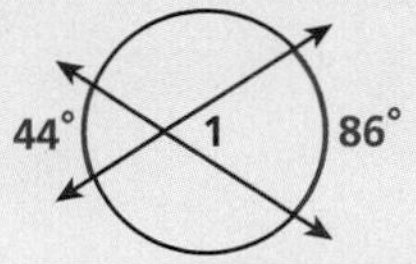	$m\angle 1 = \frac{1}{2}(44° + 86°)$ $= 65°$
Outside a circle	Half the difference of the measures of its intercepted arcs	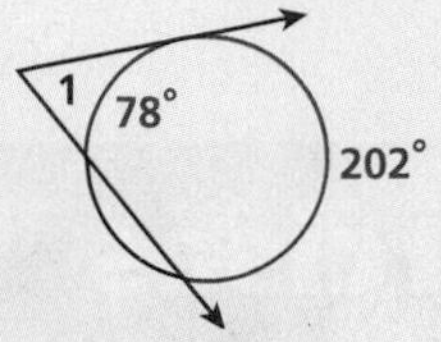 $m\angle 1 = \frac{1}{2}(202° - 78°)$ $= 62°$	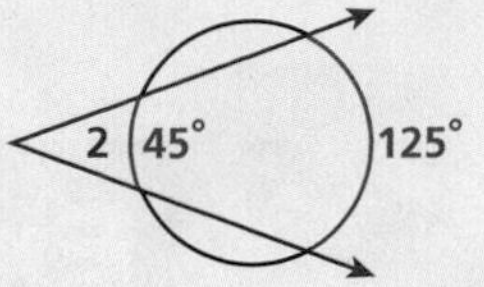 $m\angle 2 = \frac{1}{2}(125° - 45°)$ $= 40°$

EXAMPLE 5 **Finding Arc Measures**

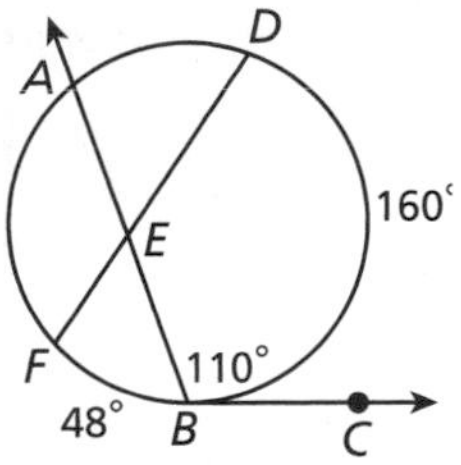

Find $m\widehat{AF}$.

Step 1 Find $m\widehat{ADB}$.

$m\angle ABC = \frac{1}{2}m\widehat{ADB}$ — *If a tangent and secant intersect on a ⊙ at the pt. of tangency, then the measure of the ∠ formed is half the measure of its intercepted arc.*

$\mathbf{110°} = \frac{1}{2}m\widehat{ADB}$ — *Substitute 110 for m∠ABC.*

$m\widehat{ADB} = 220°$ — *Mult. both sides by 2.*

Step 2 Find $m\widehat{AD}$.

$m\widehat{ADB} = m\widehat{AD} + m\widehat{DB}$ — *Arc Add. Post.*

$\mathbf{220°} = m\widehat{AD} + \mathbf{160°}$ — *Substitute.*

$m\widehat{AD} = 60°$ — *Subtract 160 from both sides.*

Step 3 Find $m\widehat{AF}$.

$m\widehat{AF} = 360° - \left(m\widehat{AD} + m\widehat{DB} + m\widehat{BF}\right)$ — *Def. of a ⊙*

$= 360° - \mathbf{(60° + 160° + 48°)}$ — *Substitute.*

$= 92°$ — *Simplify.*

CHECK IT OUT! 5. Find $m\widehat{LP}$.

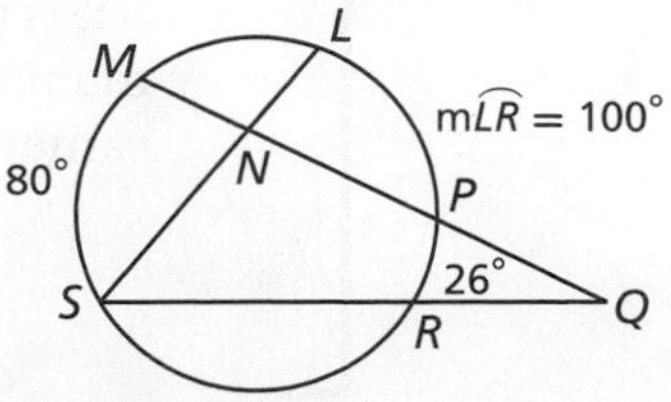

MATHEMATICAL PRACTICES

THINK AND DISCUSS

1. Explain how the measure of an angle formed by two chords of a circle is related to the measure of the angle formed by two secants.

Know it! Note

2. **GET ORGANIZED** Copy and complete the graphic organizer. In each box write a theorem and draw a diagram according to where the angle's vertex is in relationship to the circle.

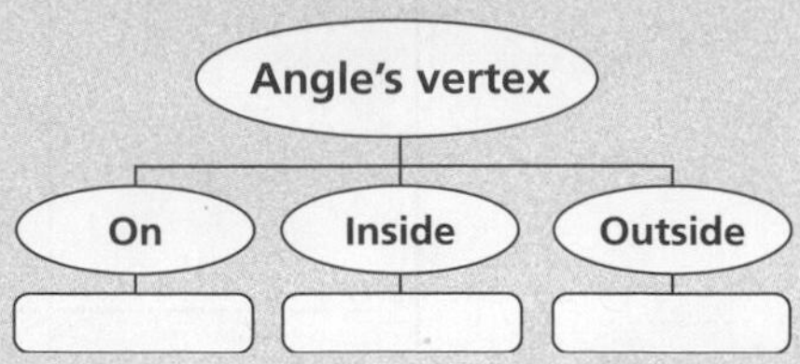

12-5 Exercises

Learn It Online
Homework Help Online
Parent Resources Online

GUIDED PRACTICE

SEE EXAMPLE 1

Find each measure.

1. m∠*DAB*
2. m$\widehat{AC}$

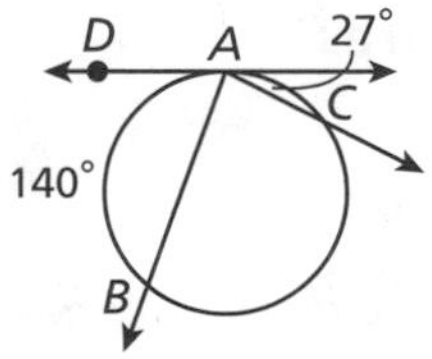

3. m$\widehat{PN}$
4. m∠*MNP*

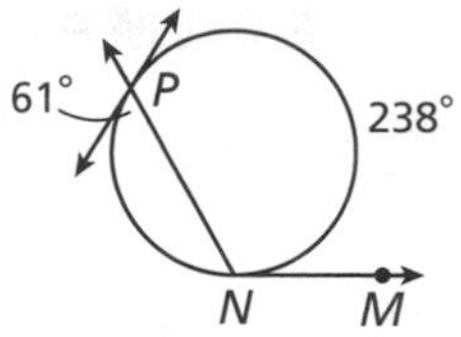

SEE EXAMPLE 2

5. m∠*STU*

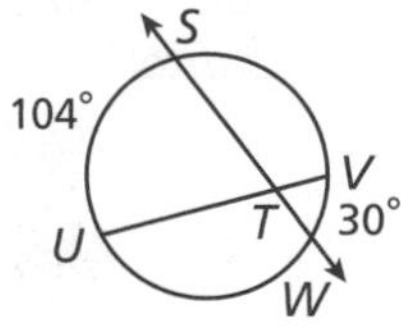

6. m∠*HFG*

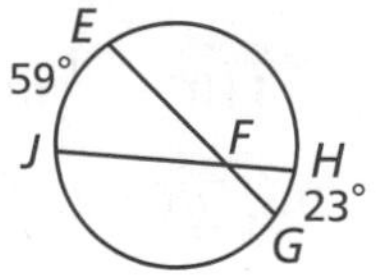

7. m∠*NPK*

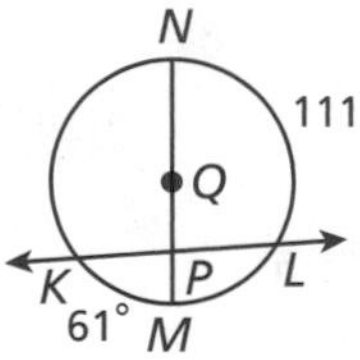

SEE EXAMPLE 3

Find the value of *x*.

8.

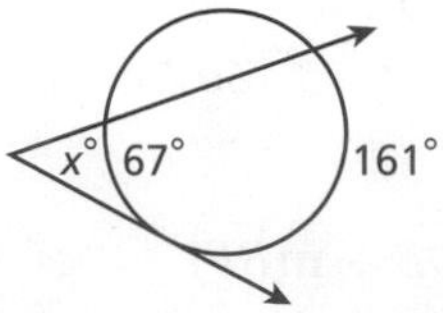

9.

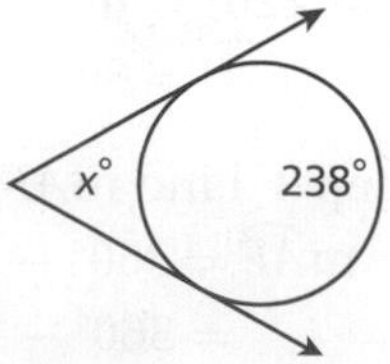

10.

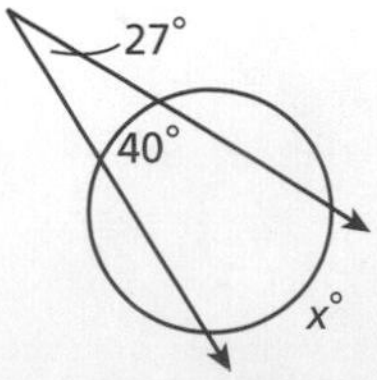

SEE EXAMPLE 4

11. **Science** A satellite orbits Mars. When it reaches *S* it is about 12,000 km above the planet. How many arc degrees of the planet are visible to a camera in the satellite?

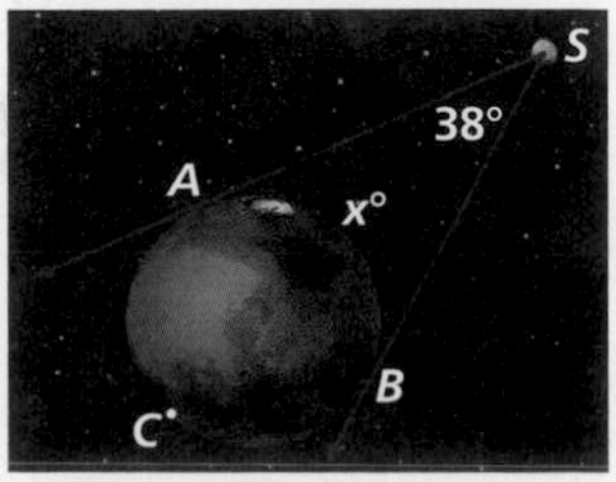

SEE EXAMPLE 5

Multi-Step Find each measure.

12. $m\widehat{DF}$

13. $m\widehat{CD}$

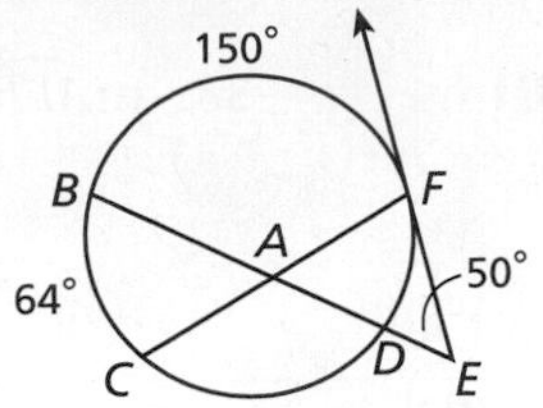

14. $m\widehat{PN}$

15. $m\widehat{KN}$

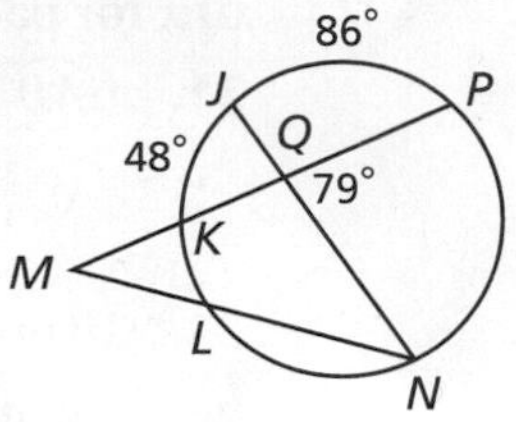

PRACTICE AND PROBLEM SOLVING

Independent Practice

For Exercises	See Example
16–19	1
20–22	2
23–25	3
26	4
27–30	5

Extra Practice

See Extra Practice for more Skills Practice and Applications Practice exercises.

Find each measure.

16. $m\angle BCD$

17. $m\angle ABC$

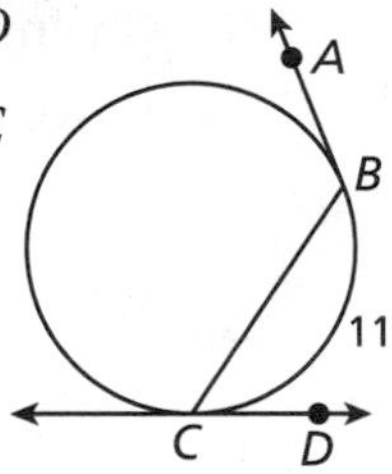

18. $m\angle XZW$

19. $m\widehat{XZV}$

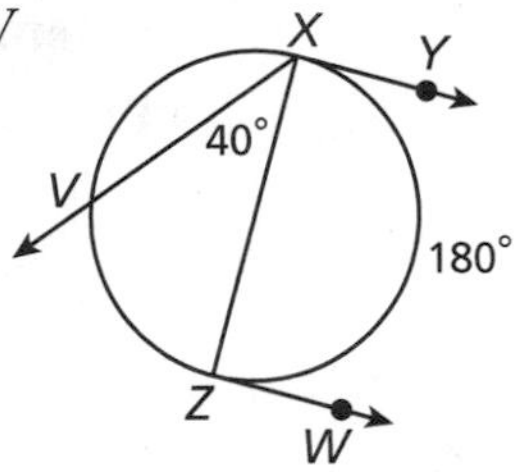

20. $m\angle QPR$

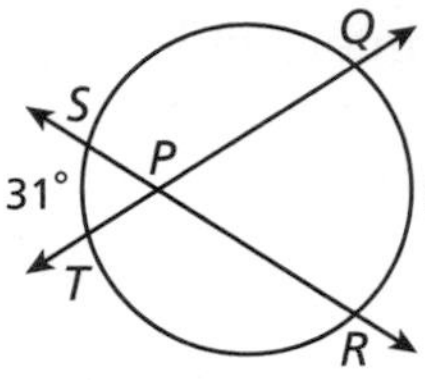

21. $m\angle ABC$

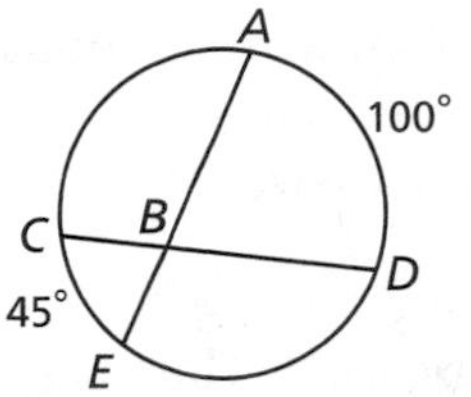

22. $m\angle MKJ$

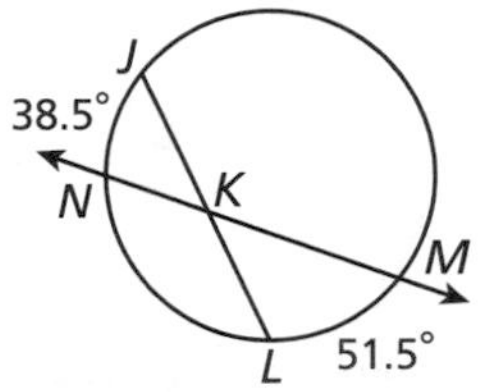

Find the value of x.

23.

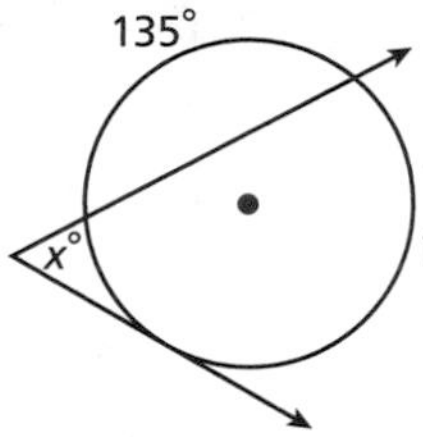

24.

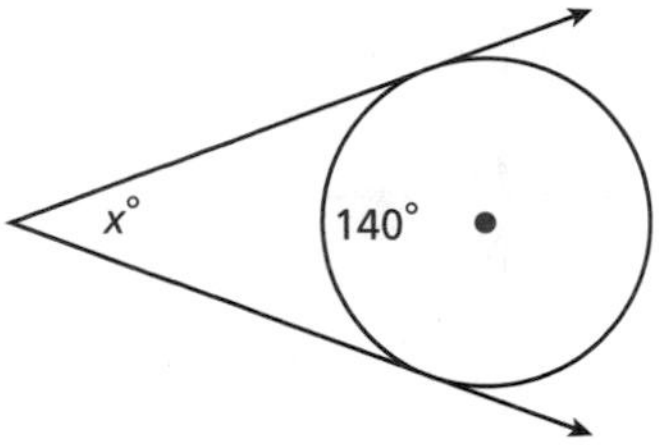

25.

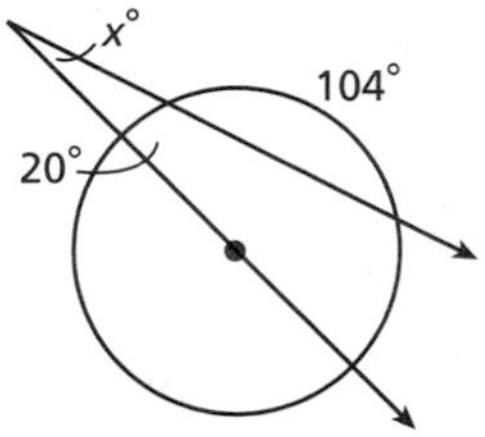

26. **Archaeology** Stonehenge is a circular arrangement of massive stones near Salisbury, England. A viewer at V observes the monument from a point where two of the stones A and B are aligned with stones at the endpoints of a diameter of the circular shape. Given that $m\widehat{AB} = 48°$, what is $m\angle AVB$?

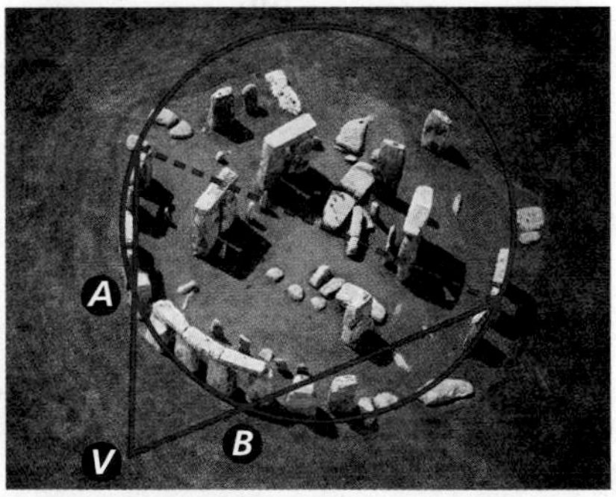

Multi-Step Find each measure.

27. $m\widehat{EG}$

28. $m\widehat{DE}$

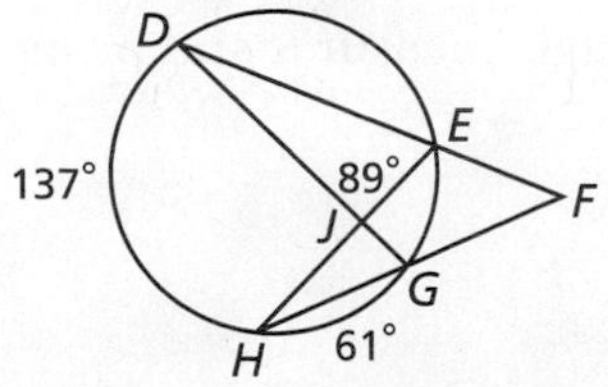

29. $m\widehat{PR}$

30. $m\widehat{LP}$

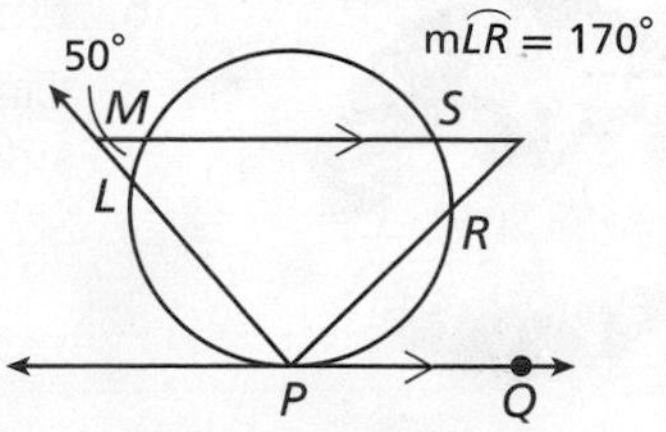

In the diagram, m∠*ABC* = *x*°. Write an expression in terms of *x* for each of the following.

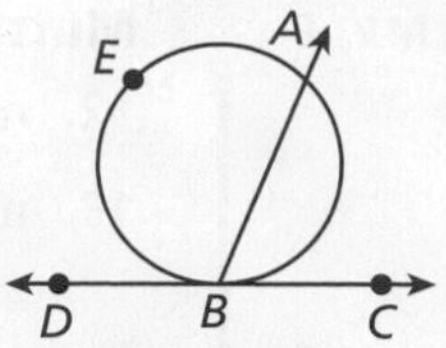

31. m$\overset{\frown}{AB}$ **32.** m∠*ABD* **33.** m$\overset{\frown}{AEB}$

34. Given: Tangent $\overrightarrow{CD}$ and secant $\overrightarrow{CA}$
Prove: $m\angle ACD = \frac{1}{2}(m\overset{\frown}{AD} - m\overset{\frown}{BD})$
Plan: Draw auxiliary line segment $\overline{BD}$. Use the Exterior Angle Theorem to show that m∠*ACD* = m∠*ABD* − m∠*BDC*. Then use the Inscribed Angle Theorem and Theorem 12-5-1.

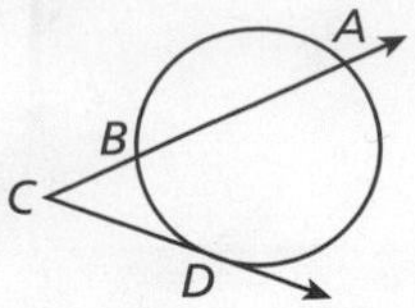

35. Given: Tangents $\overrightarrow{FE}$ and $\overrightarrow{FG}$
Prove: $m\angle EFG = \frac{1}{2}(m\overset{\frown}{EHG} - m\overset{\frown}{EG})$

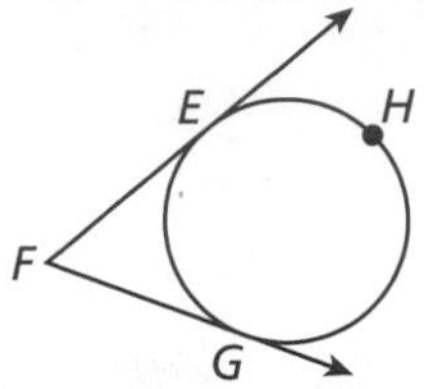

36. Given: Secants $\overline{LJ}$ and $\overline{LN}$
Prove: $m\angle JLN = \frac{1}{2}(m\overset{\frown}{JN} - m\overset{\frown}{KM})$

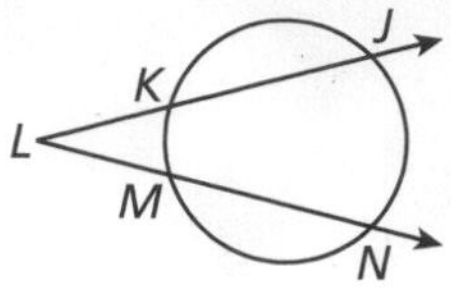

37. Critical Thinking Suppose two secants intersect in the exterior of a circle as shown. What is greater, m∠1 or m∠2? Justify your answer.

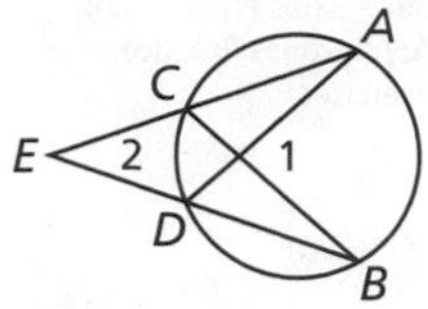

38. Write About It The diagrams show the intersection of perpendicular lines on a circle, inside a circle, and outside a circle. Explain how you can use these to help you remember how to calculate the measures of the angles formed.

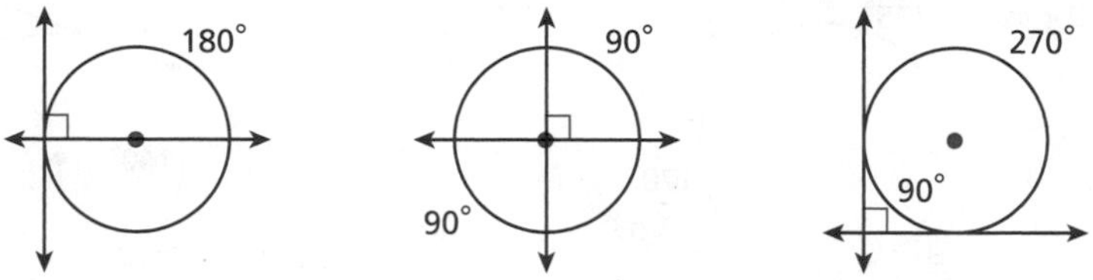

Algebra **Find the measures of the three angles of △*ABC*.**

39.

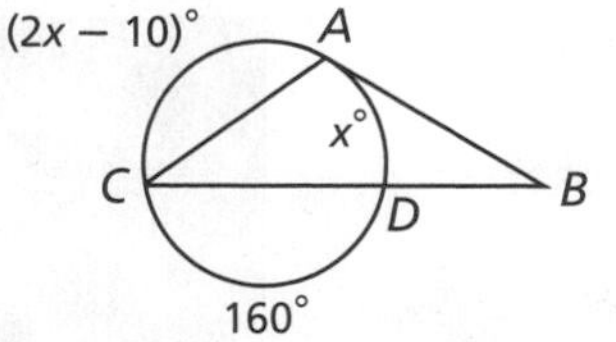

40.

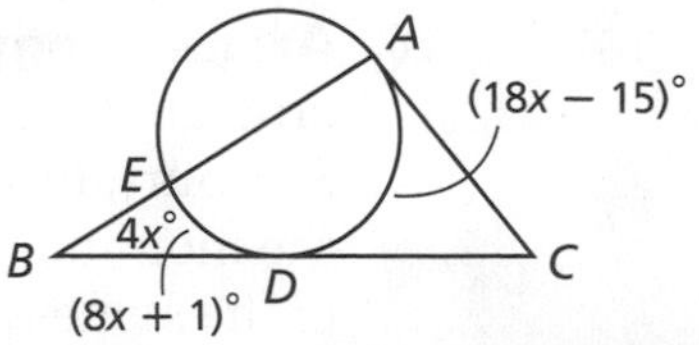

MULTI-STEP TEST PREP

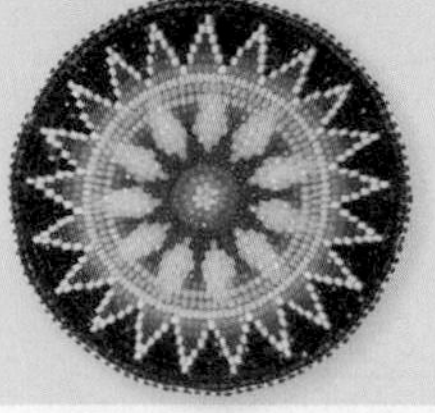

41. The design was made by placing six equally-spaced points on a circle and connecting them.

a. Find m∠*BHC*.

b. Find m∠*EGD*.

c. Classify △*EGD* by its angle measures and by its side lengths.

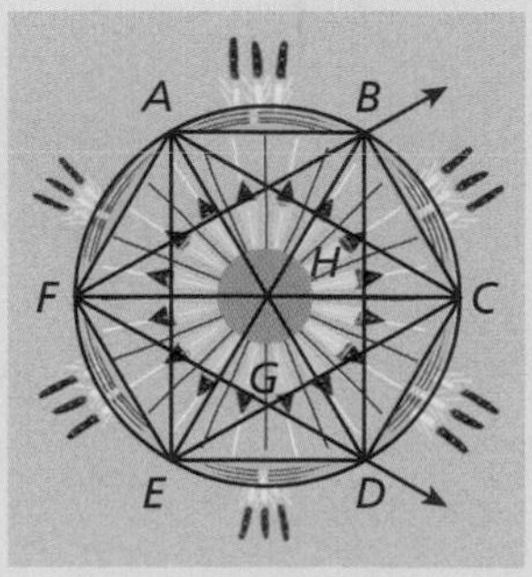

TEST PREP

42. What is $m\angle DCE$?

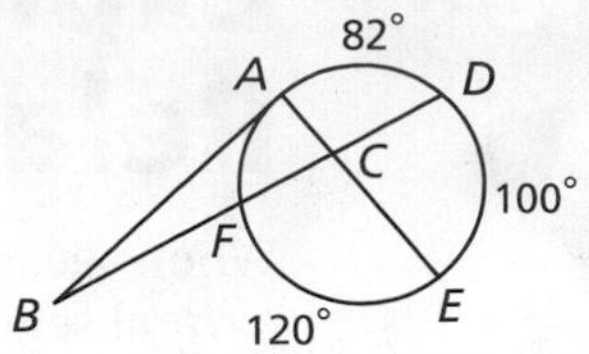

Ⓐ 19°　Ⓒ 79°

Ⓑ 21°　Ⓓ 101°

43. Which expression can be used to calculate $m\angle ABC$?

Ⓕ $\frac{1}{2}\left(m\widehat{AD} + m\widehat{AF}\right)$　Ⓗ $\frac{1}{2}\left(m\widehat{DE} - m\widehat{AF}\right)$

Ⓖ $\frac{1}{2}\left(m\widehat{DE} + m\widehat{AF}\right)$　Ⓙ $\frac{1}{2}\left(m\widehat{AD} - m\widehat{AF}\right)$

44. Gridded Response In ⊙Q, $m\widehat{MN} = 146°$ and $m\angle JLK = 45°$. Find the degree measure of $\widehat{JK}$.

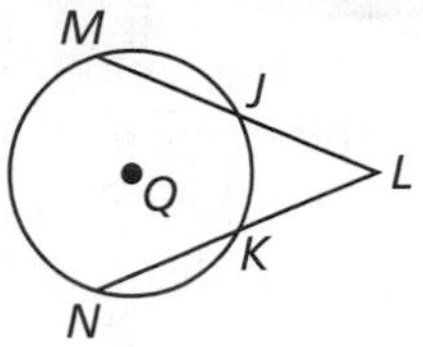

CHALLENGE AND EXTEND

45. Prove Theorem 12-5-1.
Given: Tangent $\overrightarrow{BC}$ and secant $\overrightarrow{BA}$
Prove: $m\angle ABC = \frac{1}{2}m\widehat{AB}$
(*Hint:* Consider two cases, one where $\overline{AB}$ is a diameter and one where $\overline{AB}$ is not a diameter.)

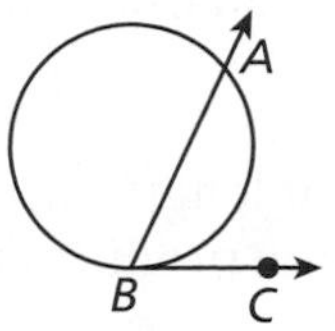

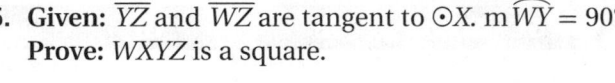

46. Given: $\overline{YZ}$ and $\overline{WZ}$ are tangent to ⊙X. $m\widehat{WY} = 90°$
Prove: $WXYZ$ is a square.

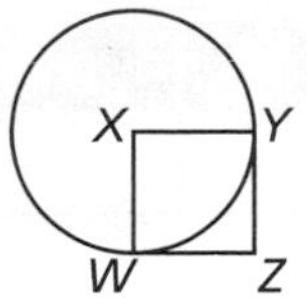

47. Find x.

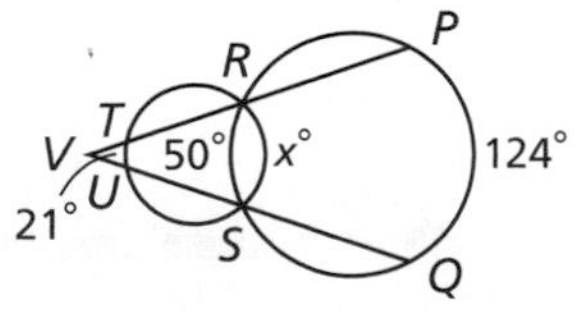

48. Find $m\widehat{GH}$.

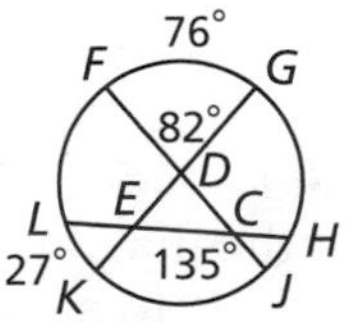

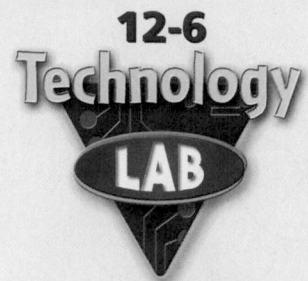

12-6 Technology LAB

Explore Segment Relationships in Circles

Use with *Segment Relationships in Circles*

When secants, chords, or tangents of circles intersect, they create several segments. You will measure these segments and investigate their relationships.

MATHEMATICAL PRACTICES **Use appropriate tools strategically.**

Learn It Online Lab Resources Online

CC.9-12.G.C.2 Identify and describe relationships among inscribed angles, radii, and chords.

Activity 1

1. Construct a circle with center *A*. Label the point on the circle as *B*. Construct two secants $\overleftrightarrow{CD}$ and $\overleftrightarrow{EF}$ that intersect *outside* the circle at *G*. Hide *B* if desired. (It controls the circle's size.)

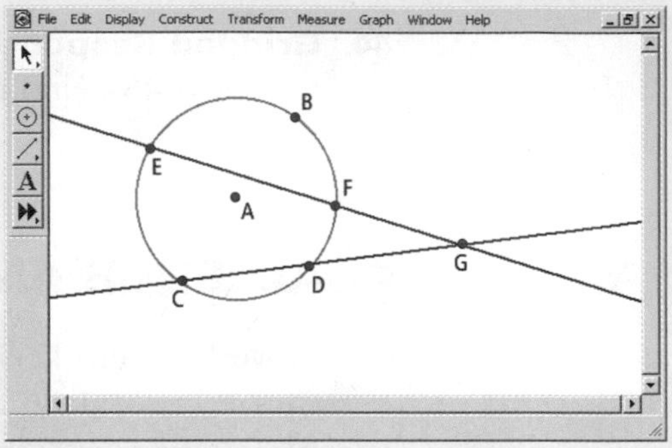

2. Measure $\overline{GC}$, $\overline{GD}$, $\overline{GE}$, and $\overline{GF}$. Drag points around the circle and examine the changes in the measurements.

3. Fill in the segment lengths in a chart like the one below. Find the products of the lengths of segments on the *same* secant. Can you make a conjecture about the relationship of the segments formed by intersecting secants of a circle?

GC	*GD*	*GC* • *GD*	*GE*	*GF*	*GE* • *GF*

Try This

1. Make a sketch of the diagram from Activity 1, and create $\overline{CF}$ and $\overline{DE}$ to create $\triangle CFG$ and $\triangle EDG$ as shown.
2. Name pairs of congruent angles in the diagram. How are $\triangle CFG$ and $\triangle EDG$ related? Explain your reasoning.
3. Write a proportion involving sides of the triangles. Cross-multiply and state the result. What do you notice?

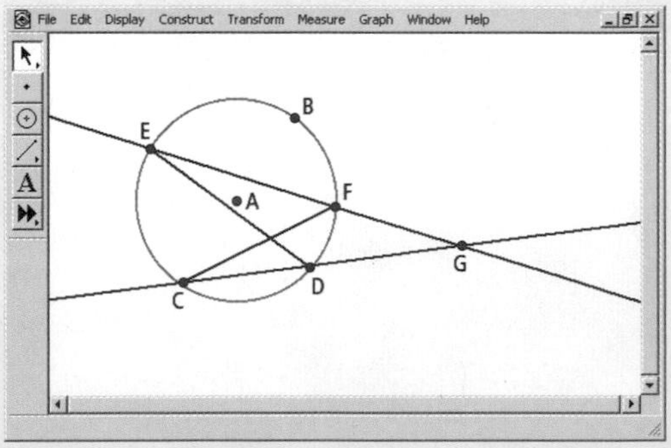

Activity 2

1. Construct a new circle with center *A*. Label the point on the circle as *B*. Create a radius segment from *A* to a new point *C* on the circle.

2. Construct a line through *C* perpendicular to radius $\overline{AC}$. Create a new point *D* on this line, which is tangent to circle *A* at *C*. Hide radius $\overline{AC}$.

3. Create a secant line through D that intersects the circle at two new points E and F, as shown.

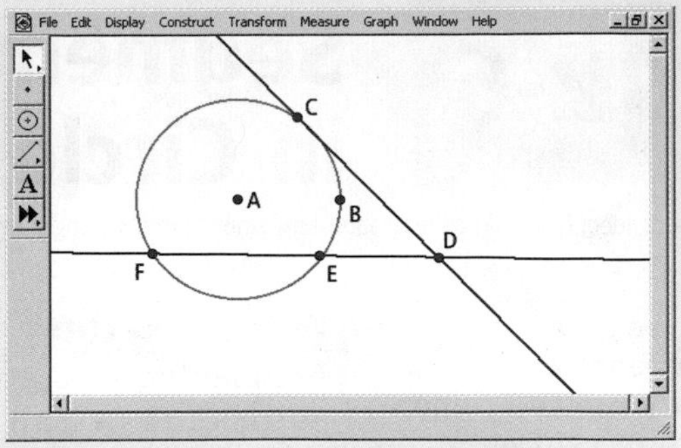

4. Measure $\overline{DC}$, $\overline{DE}$, and $\overline{DF}$. Drag points around the circle and examine the changes in the measurements. Fill in the measurements in a chart like the one below. Can you make a conjecture about the relationship between the segments of a tangent and a secant of a circle?

DE	*DF*	*DE* • *DF*	*DC*	?

Try This

4. How are the products for a tangent and a secant similar to the products for secant segments?
5. Try dragging E and F so they overlap (to make the secant segment look like a tangent segment). What do you notice about the segment lengths you measured in Activity 2? Can you state a relationship about two tangent segments from the same exterior point?
6. **Challenge** Write a formal proof of the relationship you found in Problem 2.

Activity 3

1. Construct a new circle with two chords $\overline{CD}$ and $\overline{EF}$ that intersect inside the circle at G.

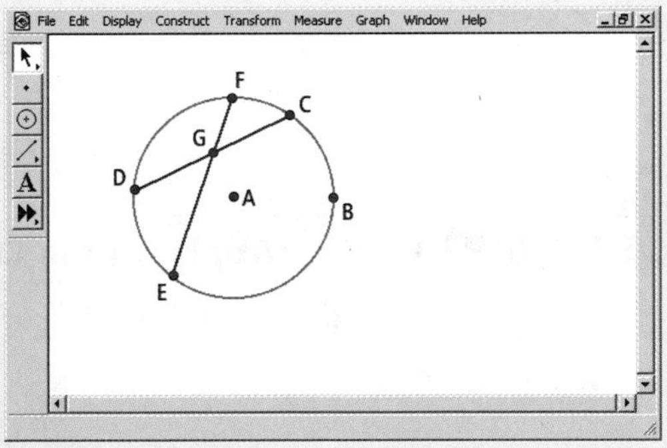

2. Measure $\overline{GC}$, $\overline{GD}$, $\overline{GE}$, and $\overline{GF}$. Drag points around the circle and examine the changes in the measurements.
3. Fill in the segment lengths in a chart like the ones used in Activities 1 and 2. Find the products of the lengths of segments on the same chord. Can you make a conjecture about the relationship of the segments formed by intersecting chords of a circle?

Try This

7. Connect the endpoints of the chords to form two triangles. Name pairs of congruent angles. How are the two triangles that are formed related? Explain your reasoning.
8. Examine the conclusions you made in all three activities about segments formed by secants, chords, and tangents in a circle. Summarize your findings.

12-6 Segment Relationships in Circles

CC.9-12.G.C.2 Identify and describe relationships among inscribed angles, radii, and chords.

Objectives

Find the lengths of segments formed by lines that intersect circles.

Use the lengths of segments in circles to solve problems.

Vocabulary

secant segment
external secant segment
tangent segment

Who uses this?

Archaeologists use facts about segments in circles to help them understand ancient objects. (See Example 2.)

In 1901, divers near the Greek island of Antikythera discovered several fragments of ancient items. Using the mathematics of circles, scientists were able to calculate the diameters of the complete disks.

The following theorem describes the relationship among the four segments that are formed when two chords intersect in the interior of a circle.

Know it! Note

Theorem 12-6-1 Chord-Chord Product Theorem

THEOREM	HYPOTHESIS	CONCLUSION
If two chords intersect in the interior of a circle, then the products of the lengths of the segments of the chords are equal.	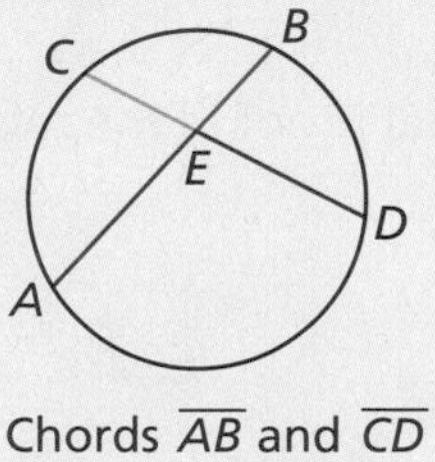 Chords $\overline{AB}$ and $\overline{CD}$ intersect at *E*.	$AE \cdot EB = CE \cdot ED$

You will prove Theorem 12-6-1 in Exercise 28.

EXAMPLE 1 Applying the Chord-Chord Product Theorem

Algebra

Find the value of *x* and the length of each chord.

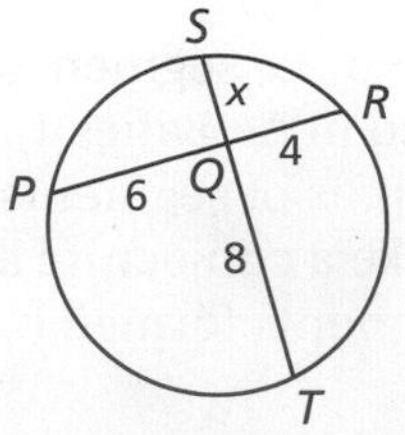

$$PQ \cdot QR = SQ \cdot QT$$
$$6(4) = x(8)$$
$$24 = 8x$$
$$3 = x$$
$$PR = 6 + 4 = 10$$
$$ST = 3 + 8 = 11$$

CHECK IT OUT!

1. Find the value of *x* and the length of each chord.

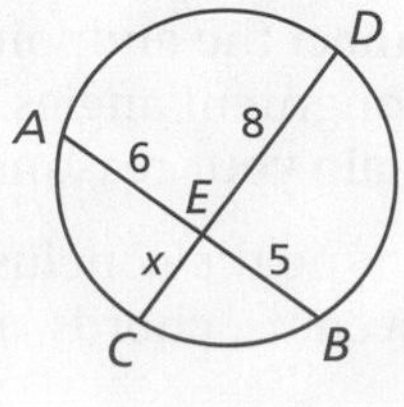

EXAMPLE 2 ***Archaeology Application***

Algebra

Archaeologists discovered a fragment of an ancient disk. To calculate its original diameter, they drew a chord $\overline{AB}$ and its perpendicular bisector $\overline{PQ}$. Find the disk's diameter.

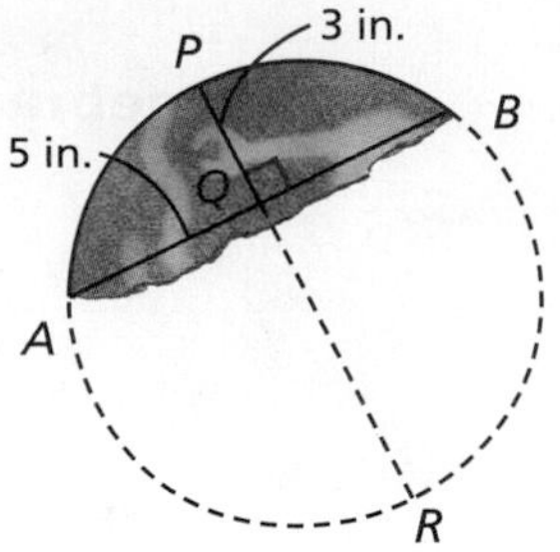

Since $\overline{PQ}$ is the perpendicular bisector of a chord, $\overline{PR}$ is a diameter of the disk.

$$AQ \cdot QB = PQ \cdot QR$$
$$5(5) = 3(QR)$$
$$25 = 3QR$$
$$8\frac{1}{3} \text{ in.} = QR$$
$$PR = 3 + 8\frac{1}{3} = 11\frac{1}{3} \text{ in.}$$

CHECK IT OUT! 2. **What if...?** Suppose the length of chord $\overline{AB}$ that the archaeologists drew was 12 in. In this case how much longer is the disk's diameter compared to the disk in Example 2?

A **secant segment** is a segment of a secant with at least one endpoint on the circle. An **external secant segment** is a secant segment that lies in the exterior of the circle with one endpoint on the circle.

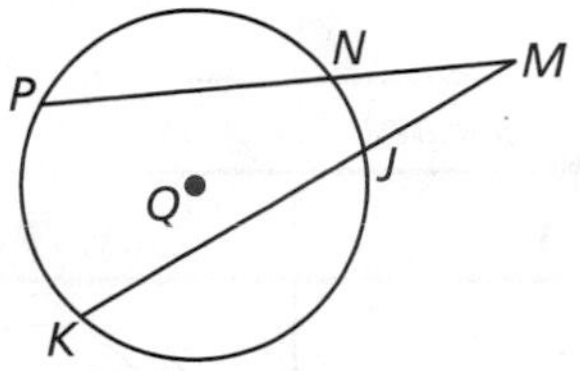

$\overline{PM}$, $\overline{NM}$, $\overline{KM}$, and $\overline{JM}$ are secant segments of $\odot Q$. $\overline{NM}$ and $\overline{JM}$ are external secant segments.

Know it! Note

Theorem 12-6-2 **Secant-Secant Product Theorem**

THEOREM	HYPOTHESIS	CONCLUSION
If two secants intersect in the exterior of a circle, then the product of the lengths of one secant segment and its external segment equals the product of the lengths of the other secant segment and its external segment. (whole • outside = whole • outside)	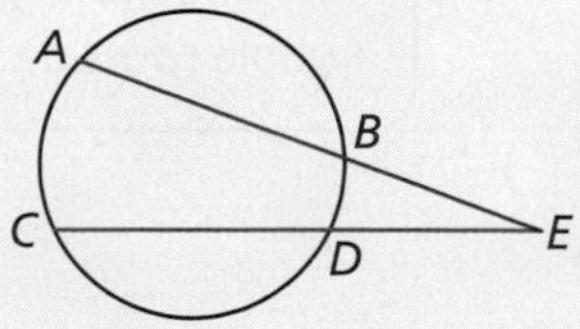 Secants $\overline{AE}$ and $\overline{CE}$ intersect at E.	$AE \cdot BE = CE \cdot DE$

PROOF **Secant-Secant Product Theorem**

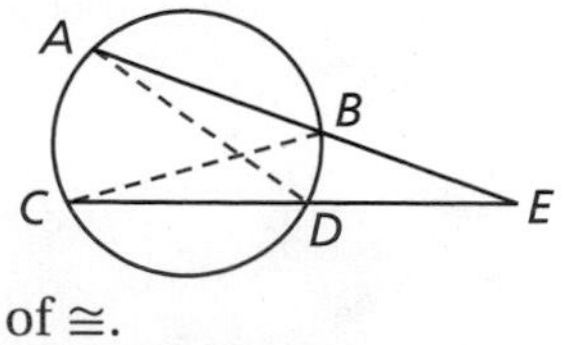

Given: Secant segments $\overline{AE}$ and $\overline{CE}$

Prove: $AE \cdot BE = CE \cdot DE$

Proof: Draw auxiliary line segments $\overline{AD}$ and $\overline{CB}$. $\angle EAD$ and $\angle ECB$ both intercept $\overset{\frown}{BD}$, so $\angle EAD \cong \angle ECB$. $\angle E \cong \angle E$ by the Reflexive Property of $\cong$. Thus $\triangle EAD \sim \triangle ECB$ by AA Similarity. Therefore corresponding sides are proportional, and $\frac{AE}{CE} = \frac{DE}{BE}$. By the Cross Products Property, $AE \cdot BE = CE \cdot DE$.

EXAMPLE 3 Applying the Secant-Secant Product Theorem

Algebra

Find the value of x and the length of each secant segment.

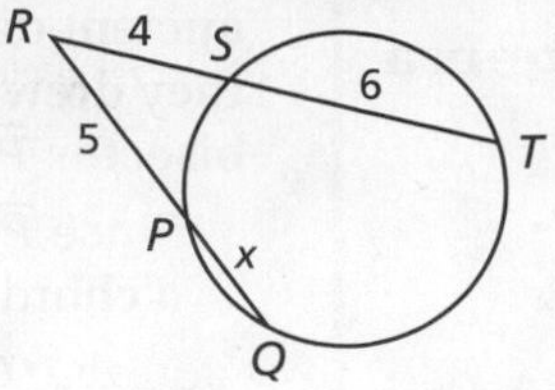

$RT \cdot RS = RQ \cdot RP$

$10(4) = (x + 5)5$

$40 = 5x + 25$

$15 = 5x$

$3 = x$

$RT = 4 + 6 = 10$

$RQ = 5 + 3 = 8$

CHECK IT OUT!

3. Find the value of z and the length of each secant segment.

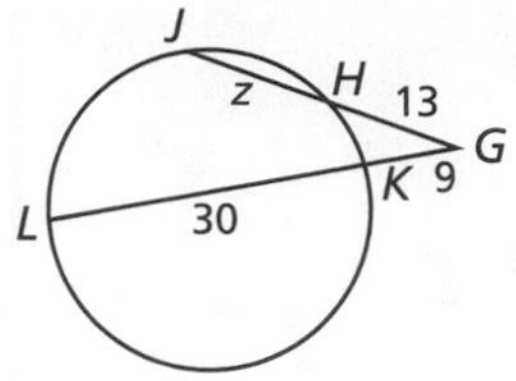

A **tangent segment** is a segment of a tangent with one endpoint on the circle. $\overline{AB}$ and $\overline{AC}$ are tangent segments.

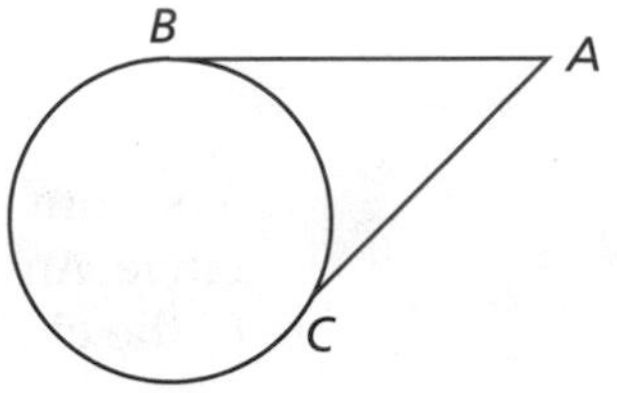

Know it! Note

Theorem 12-6-3 Secant-Tangent Product Theorem

THEOREM	HYPOTHESIS	CONCLUSION
If a secant and a tangent intersect in the exterior of a circle, then the product of the lengths of the secant segment and its external segment equals the length of the tangent segment squared. (whole $\cdot$ outside $=$ tangent^2)	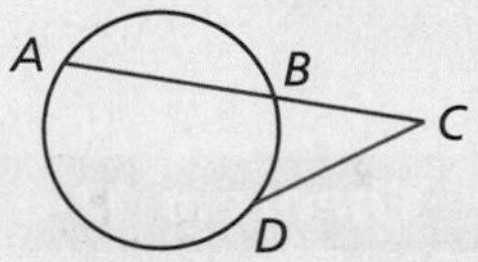 Secant $\overline{AC}$ and tangent $\overline{DC}$ intersect at C.	$AC \cdot BC = DC^2$

You will prove Theorem 12-6-3 in Exercise 29.

EXAMPLE 4 Applying the Secant-Tangent Product Theorem

Algebra

Find the value of x.

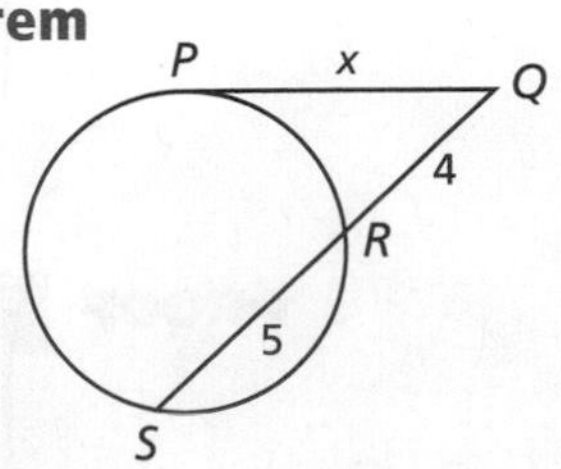

$SQ \cdot RQ = PQ^2$

$9(4) = x^2$

$36 = x^2$

$\pm 6 = x$

The value of x must be 6 since it represents a length.

CHECK IT OUT!

4. Find the value of y.

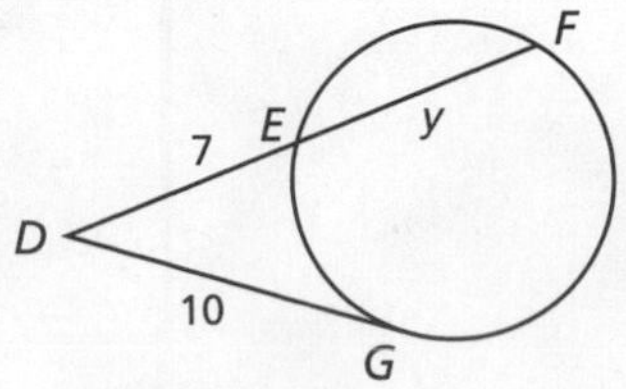

THINK AND DISCUSS

MATHEMATICAL PRACTICES

1. Does the Chord-Chord Product Theorem apply when both chords are diameters? If so, what does the theorem tell you in this case?
2. Given A in the exterior of a circle, how many different tangent segments can you draw with A as an endpoint?
3. **GET ORGANIZED** Copy and complete the graphic organizer.

Know it! Note

	Theorem	Diagram	Example
Chord–Chord			
Secant–Secant			
Secant–Tangent			

12-6 Exercises

Learn It Online
Homework Help Online
Parent Resources Online

GUIDED PRACTICE

1. **Vocabulary** $\overleftrightarrow{AB}$ intersects $\odot P$ at exactly one point. Point A is in the exterior of $\odot P$, and point B lies on $\odot P$. $\overline{AB}$ is a(n) __?__ . (*tangent segment* or *external secant segment*)

SEE EXAMPLE 1

Find the value of the variable and the length of each chord.

2. 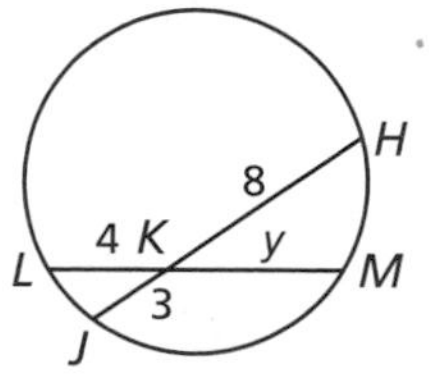

3. 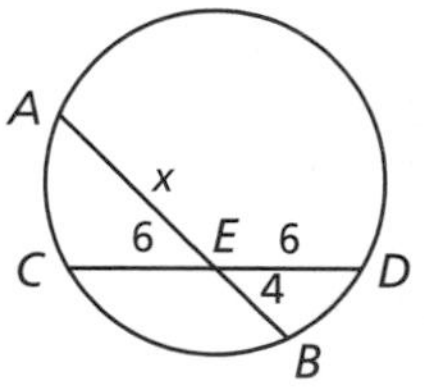

4. 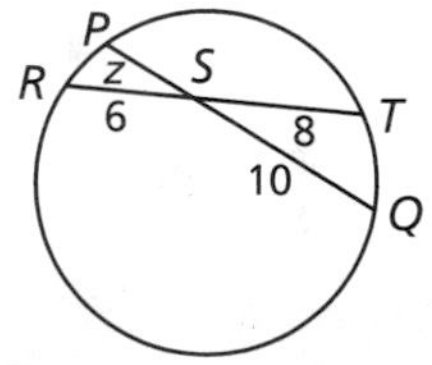

SEE EXAMPLE 2

5. **Engineering** A section of an aqueduct is based on an arc of a circle as shown. $\overline{EF}$ is the perpendicular bisector of $\overline{GH}$. $GH = 50$ ft, and $EF = 20$ ft. What is the diameter of the circle?

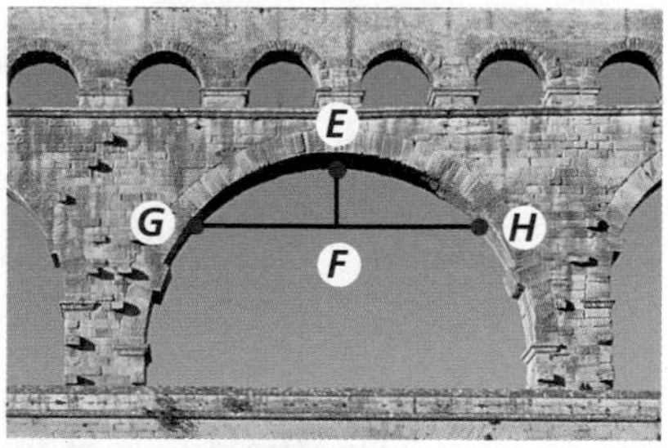

SEE EXAMPLE 3

Find the value of the variable and the length of each secant segment.

6. 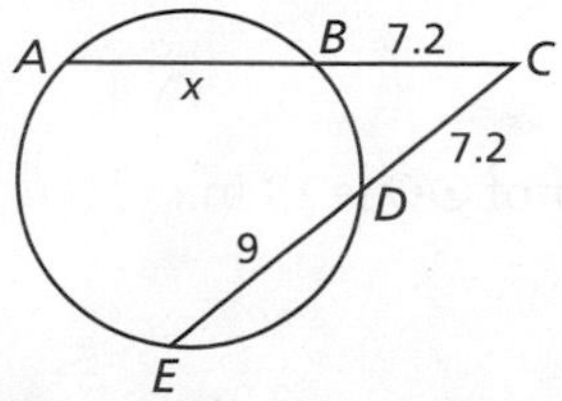

7. 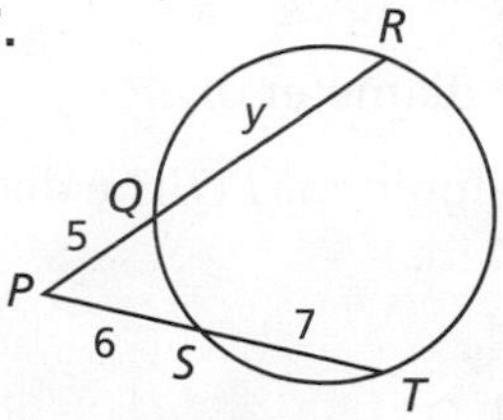

8. 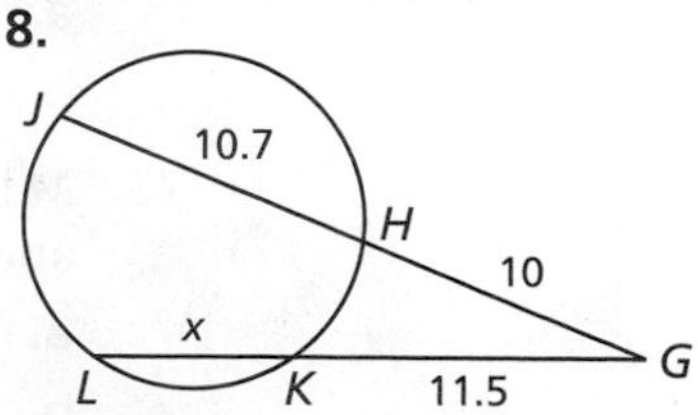

SEE EXAMPLE 4 Find the value of the variable.

9.

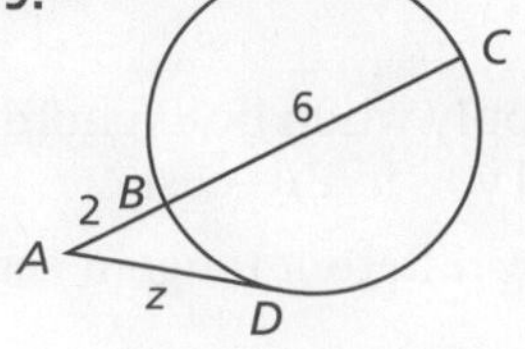

10.

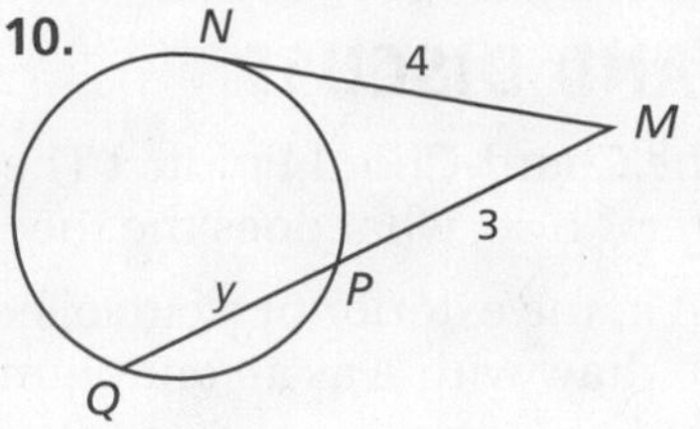

11.

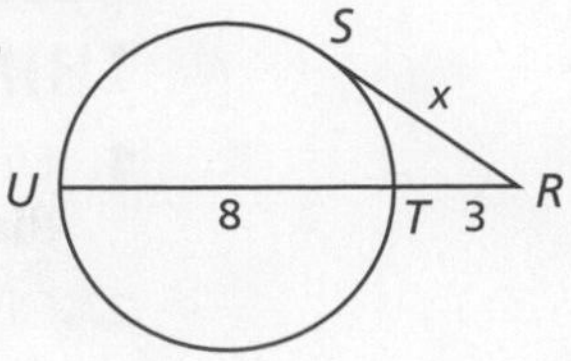

PRACTICE AND PROBLEM SOLVING

Independent Practice	
For Exercises	See Example
12–14	1
15	2
16–18	3
19–21	4

Extra Practice

See Extra Practice for more Skills Practice and Applications Practice exercises.

Find the value of the variable and the length of each chord.

12.

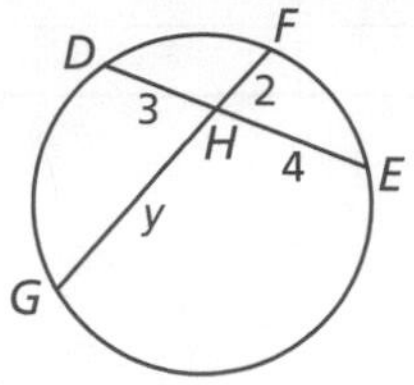

13.

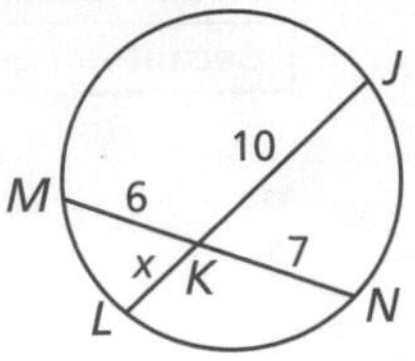

14.

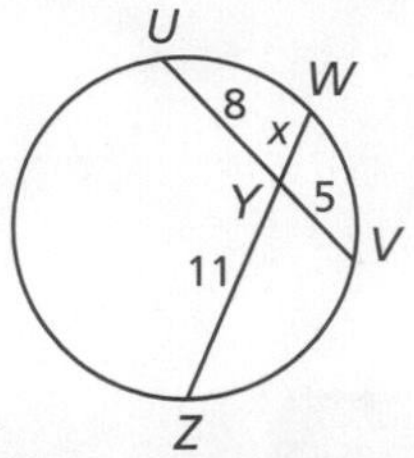

15. **Geology** Molokini is a small, crescent-shaped island $2\frac{1}{2}$ miles from the Maui coast. It is all that remains of an extinct volcano. To approximate the diameter of the mouth of the volcano, a geologist can use a diagram like the one shown. What is the approximate diameter of the volcano's mouth to the nearest foot?

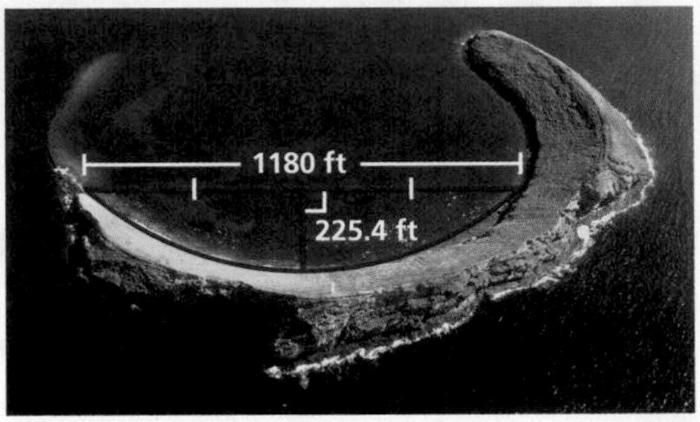

Find the value of the variable and the length of each secant segment.

16.

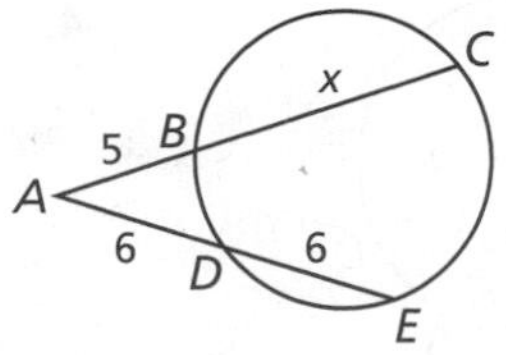

17.

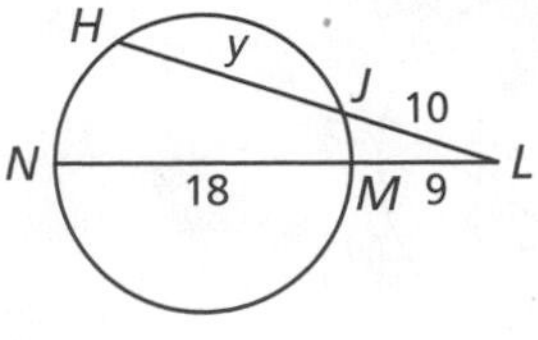

18.

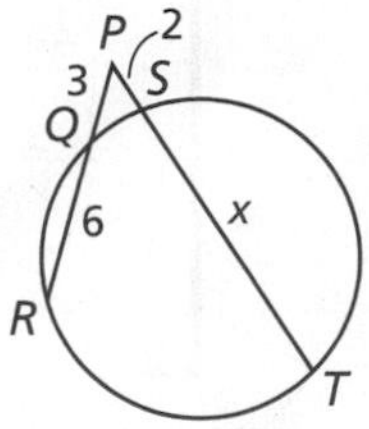

Find the value of the variable.

19.

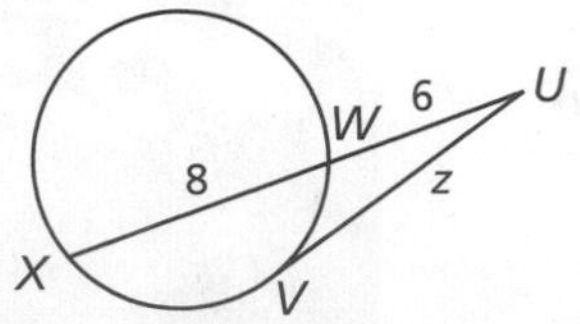

20.

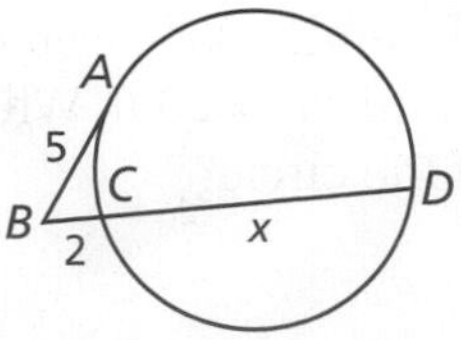

21.

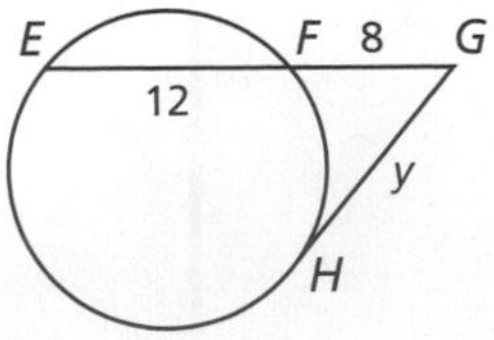

Use the diagram for Exercises 22 and 23.

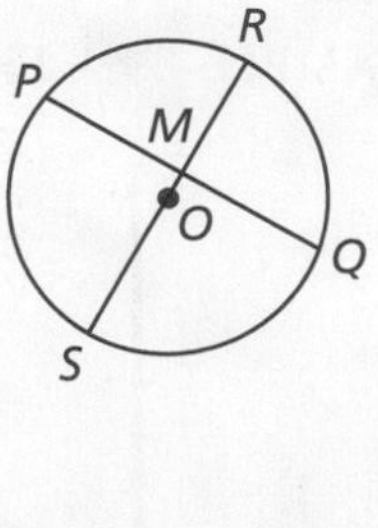

22. M is the midpoint of $\overline{PQ}$. $RM = 10$ cm, and $PQ = 24$ cm.
   a. Find MS.
   b. Find the diameter of $\odot O$.

23. M is the midpoint of $\overline{PQ}$. The diameter of $\odot O$ is 13 in., and $RM = 4$ in.
   a. Find PM.
   b. Find PQ.

LINK Meteorology

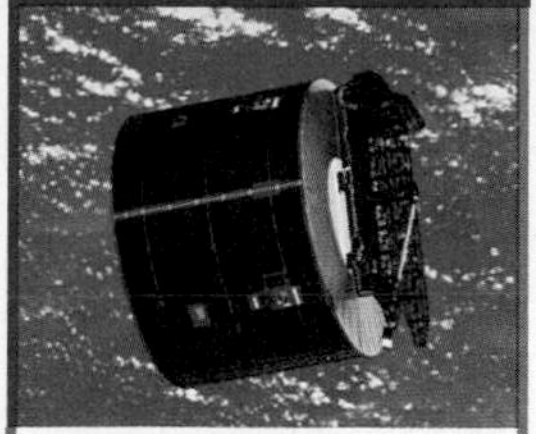

Satellites are launched to an area above the atmosphere where there is no friction. The idea is to position them so that when they fall back toward Earth, they fall at the same rate as Earth's surface falls away from them.

Multi-Step Find the value of both variables in each figure.

24.

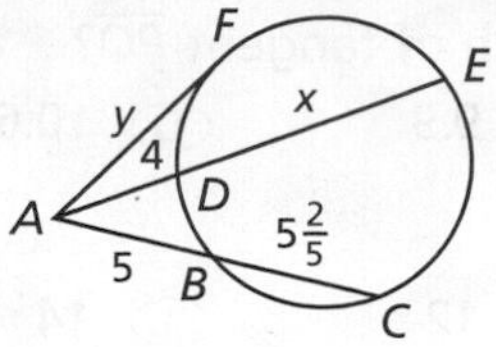

25.

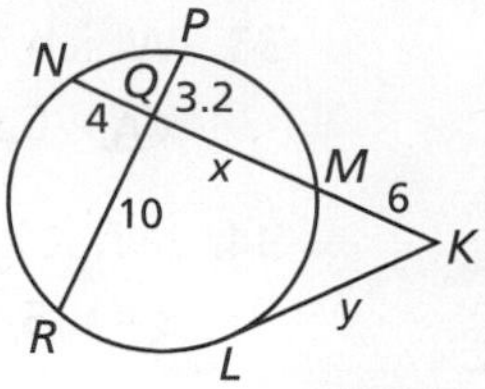

26. Meteorology A weather satellite S orbits Earth at a distance SE of 6000 mi. Given that the diameter of the earth is approximately 8000 mi, what is the distance from the satellite to P? Round to the nearest mile.

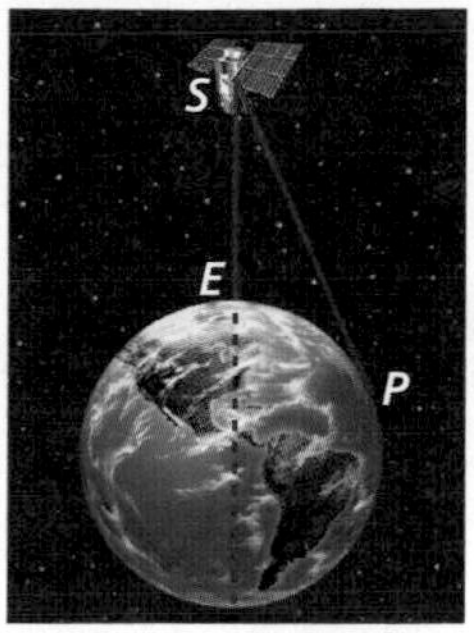

27. ERROR ANALYSIS The two solutions show how to find the value of x. Which solution is incorrect? Explain the error.

A

$AC \cdot BC = DC^2$, so
$10(4) = x^2$. $x^2 = 40$,
and $x = 2\sqrt{10}$.

B

$AB \cdot BC = DC^2$, so
$6(4) = x^2$. $x^2 = 24$,
and $x = 2\sqrt{6}$.

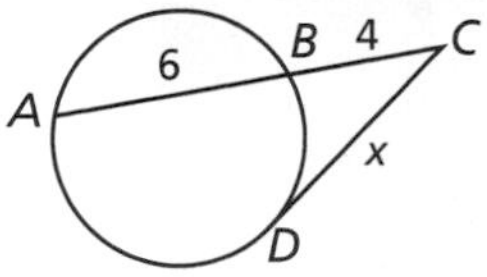

28. Prove the Chord-Chord Product Theorem.
Given: Chords $\overline{AB}$ and $\overline{CD}$ intersect at point E.
Prove: $AE \cdot EB = CE \cdot ED$
Plan: Draw auxiliary line segments $\overline{AC}$ and $\overline{BD}$. Show that $\triangle ECA \sim \triangle EBD$. Then write a proportion comparing the lengths of corresponding sides.

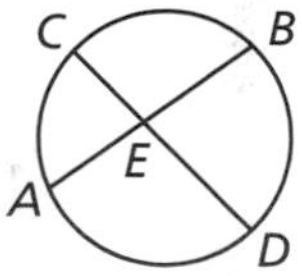

29. Prove the Secant-Tangent Product Theorem.
Given: Secant segment $\overline{AC}$, tangent segment $\overline{DC}$
Prove: $AC \cdot BC = DC^2$

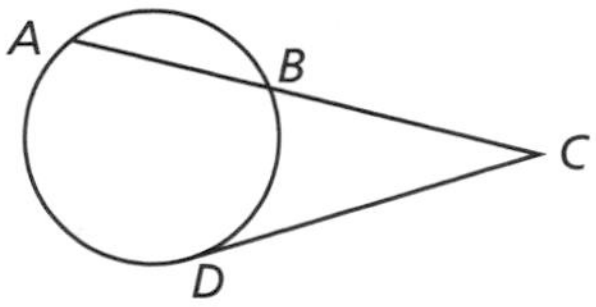

30. Critical Thinking A student drew a circle and two secant segments. By measuring with a ruler, he found $\overline{PQ} \cong \overline{PS}$. He concluded that $\overline{QR} \cong \overline{ST}$. Do you agree with the student's conclusion? Why or why not?

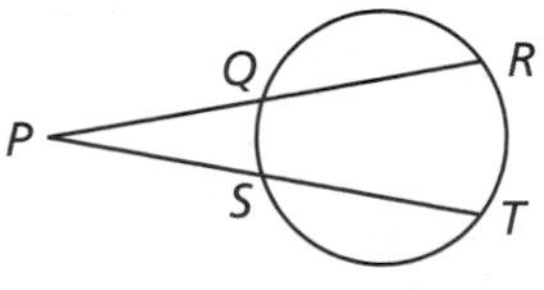

31. Write About It The radius of $\odot A$ is 4. $CD = 4$, and $\overline{CB}$ is a tangent segment. Describe two different methods you can use to find BC.

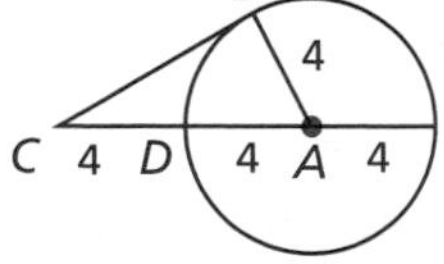

MULTI-STEP TEST PREP

32. Some Native American designs are based on eight points that are placed around the circumference of a circle. In $\odot O$, $BE = 3$ cm. $AE = 5.2$ cm, and $EC = 4$ cm.

a. Find DE to the nearest tenth.

b. What is the diameter of the circle to the nearest tenth?

c. What is the length of $\overline{OE}$ to the nearest hundredth?

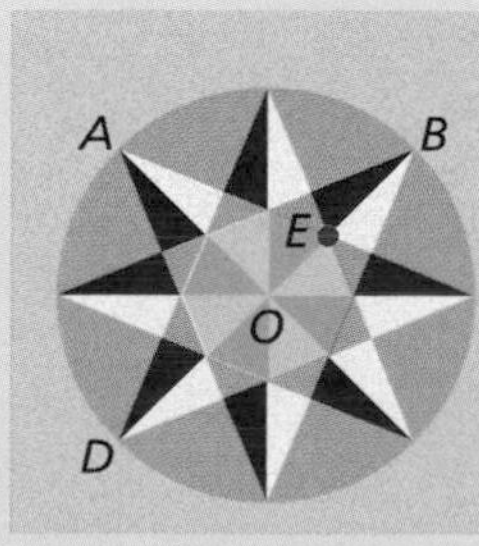

TEST PREP

33. Which of these is closest to the length of tangent $\overline{PQ}$?

Ⓐ 6.9 Ⓑ 9.2 Ⓒ 9.9 Ⓓ 10.6

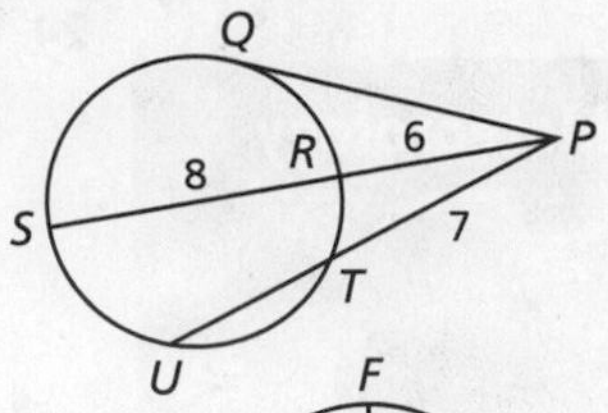

34. What is the length of $\overline{UT}$?

Ⓕ 5 Ⓖ 7 Ⓗ 12 Ⓙ 14

35. **Short Response** In ⊙A, $\overline{AB}$ is the perpendicular bisector of $\overline{CD}$. $CD = 12$, and $EB = 3$. Find the radius of ⊙A. Explain your steps.

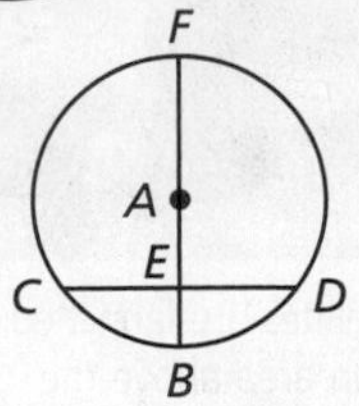

CHALLENGE AND EXTEND

36. **Algebra** $\overline{KL}$ is a tangent segment of ⊙N.
   a. Find the value of x.
   b. Classify $\triangle KLM$ by its angle measures. Explain.

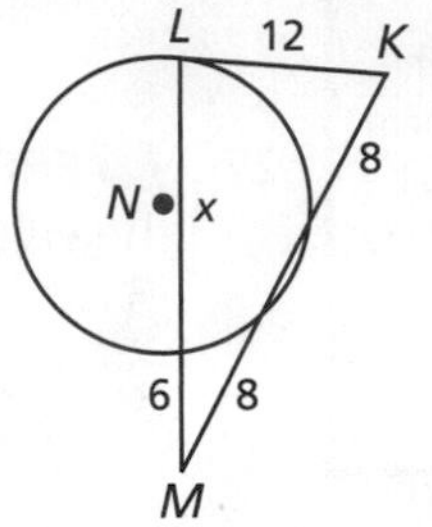

37. $\overline{PQ}$ is a tangent segment of a circle with radius 4 in. Q lies on the circle, and $PQ = 6$ in. Find the distance from P to the circle. Round to the nearest tenth of an inch.

38. The circle in the diagram has radius c. Use this diagram and the Chord-Chord Product Theorem to prove the Pythagorean Theorem.

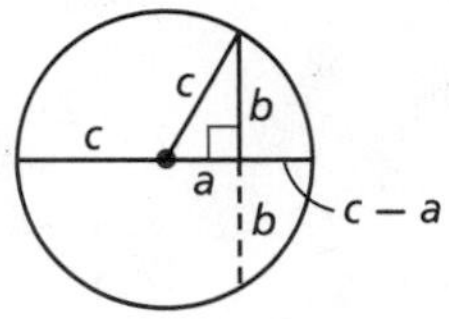

39. Find the value of y to the nearest hundredth.

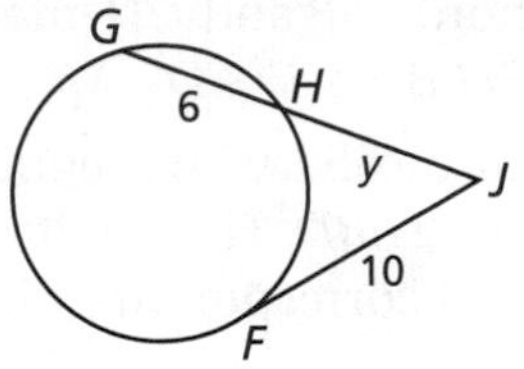

COMMON CORE

12-7 Circles in the Coordinate Plane

CC.9-12.G.GPE.1 Derive the equation of a circle…Find the center and radius of a circle given by an equation.

offthemark.com
CHANGING WEATHER PATTERNS

Objectives

Write equations and graph circles in the coordinate plane.

Use the equation and graph of a circle to solve problems.

Who uses this?

Meteorologists use circles and coordinates to plan the location of weather stations. (See Example 3.)

The equation of a circle is based on the Distance Formula and the fact that all points on a circle are equidistant from the center.

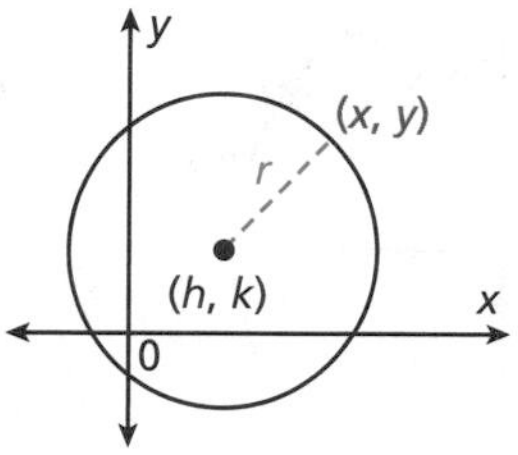

$$d = \sqrt{(x_2 - x_1)^2 + (y_2 - y_1)^2}$$ *Distance Formula*

$$r = \sqrt{(x - h)^2 + (y - k)^2}$$ *Substitute the given values.*

$$r^2 = (x - h)^2 + (y - k)^2$$ *Square both sides.*

Know it! Note

Theorem 12-7-1 Equation of a Circle

The equation of a circle with center (h, k) and radius r is $(x - h)^2 + (y - k)^2 = r^2$.

EXAMPLE 1 Writing the Equation of a Circle

Algebra

Write the equation of each circle.

A **$\odot A$ with center $A(4, -2)$ and radius 3**

$(x - h)^2 + (y - k)^2 = r^2$ *Equation of a circle*

$(x - 4)^2 + (y - (-2))^2 = 3^2$ *Substitute 4 for h, −2 for k, and 3 for r.*

$(x - 4)^2 + (y + 2)^2 = 9$ *Simplify.*

B **$\odot B$ that passes through $(-2, 6)$ and has center $B(-6, 3)$**

$r = \sqrt{(-2 - (-6))^2 + (6 - 3)^2}$ *Distance Formula*

$= \sqrt{25} = 5$ *Simplify.*

$(x - (-6))^2 + (y - 3)^2 = 5^2$ *Substitute −6 for h, 3 for k, and 5 for r.*

$(x + 6)^2 + (y - 3)^2 = 25$ *Simplify.*

CHECK IT OUT!

Write the equation of each circle.

1a. $\odot P$ with center $P(0, -3)$ and radius 8

1b. $\odot Q$ that passes through $(2, 3)$ and has center $Q(2, -1)$

If you are given the equation of a circle, you can graph the circle by making a table or by identifying its center and radius.

EXAMPLE 2 Graphing a Circle

Algebra

Graph each equation.

A $x^2 + y^2 = 25$

Step 1 Make a table of values.

Since the radius is $\sqrt{25}$, or 5, use ± 5 and the values between for x-values.

x	−5	−4	−3	0	3	4	5
y	0	±3	±4	±5	±4	±3	0

Step 2 Plot the points and connect them to form a circle.

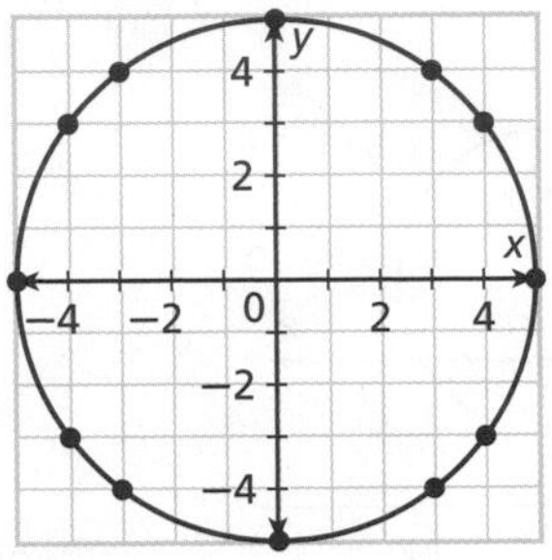

Helpful Hint

Always compare the equation to the form $(x-h)^2 + (y-k)^2 = r^2$.

B $(x+1)^2 + (y-2)^2 = 9$

The equation of the given circle can be written as $(x-(-1))^2 + (y-2)^2 = 3^2$.
So $h = -1$, $k = 2$, and $r = 3$.
The center is $(-1, 2)$, and the radius is 3.
Plot the point $(-1, 2)$. Then graph a circle having this center and radius 3.

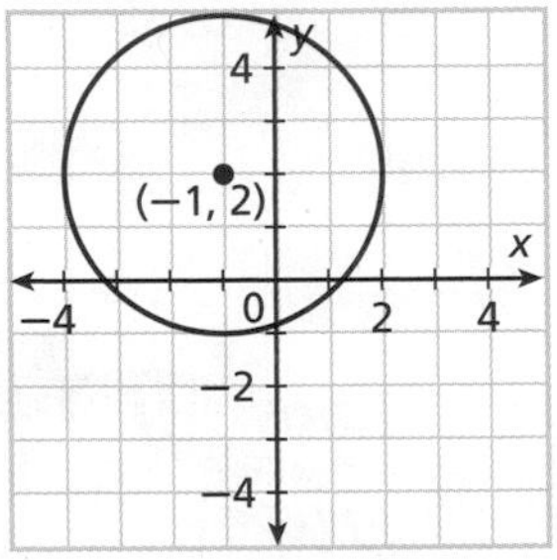

CHECK IT OUT! **Graph each equation.**

2a. $x^2 + y^2 = 9$

2b. $(x-3)^2 + (y+2)^2 = 4$

Student to Student

Graphing Circles

Christina Avila
Crockett High School

I found a way to use my calculator to graph circles. You first need to write the circle's equation in y = form.

For example, to graph $x^2 + y^2 = 16$, first solve for y.

$$y^2 = 16 - x^2$$
$$y = \pm\sqrt{16 - x^2}$$

Now enter and graph the two equations

$$y_1 = \sqrt{16 - x^2} \text{ and } y_2 = -\sqrt{16 - x^2}.$$

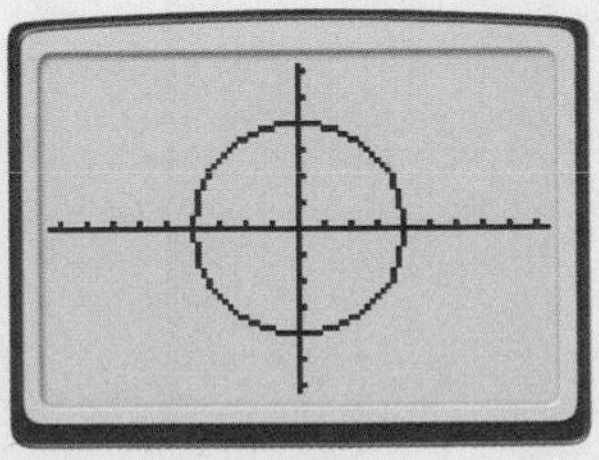

EXAMPLE 3 Meteorology Application

Meteorologists are planning the location of a new weather station to cover Osceola, Waco, and Ireland, Texas. To optimize radar coverage, the station must be equidistant from the three cities which are located on a coordinate plane at $A(2, 5)$, $B(3, -2)$, and $C(-5, -2)$.

a. What are the coordinates where the station should be built?

b. If each unit of the coordinate plane represents 8.5 miles, what is the diameter of the region covered by the radar?

Step 1 Plot the three given points.

Step 2 Connect *A*, *B*, and *C* to form a triangle.

Step 3 Find a point that is equidistant from the three points by constructing the perpendicular bisectors of two of the sides of $\triangle ABC$.

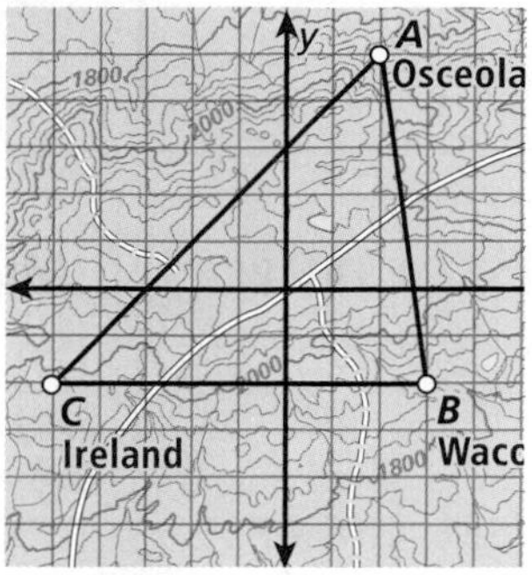

The perpendicular bisectors of the sides of $\triangle ABC$ intersect at a point that is equidistant from *A*, *B*, and *C*.

The intersection of the perpendicular bisectors is $P(-1, 1)$. *P* is the center of the circle that passes through *A*, *B*, and *C*.

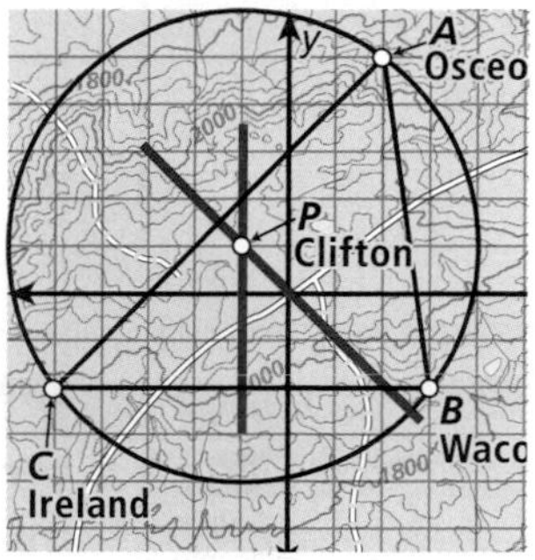

The weather station should be built at $P(-1, 1)$, Clifton, Texas.

There are approximately 10 units across the circle. So the diameter of the region covered by the radar is approximately 85 miles.

Remember!

The perpendicular bisectors of a triangle are concurrent at a point equidistant from each vertex.

CHECK IT OUT! 3. **What if...?** Suppose the coordinates of the three cities in Example 3 are $D(6, 2)$, $E(5, -5)$, and $F(-2, -4)$. What would be the location of the weather station?

MATHEMATICAL PRACTICES

THINK AND DISCUSS

1. What is the equation of a circle with radius *r* whose center is at the origin?
2. A circle has a diameter with endpoints $(1, 4)$ and $(-3, 4)$. Explain how you can find the equation of the circle.
3. Can a circle have a radius of -6? Justify your answer.
4. **GET ORGANIZED** Copy and complete the graphic organizer. First select values for a center and radius. Then use the center and radius you wrote to fill in the other circles. Write the corresponding equation and draw the corresponding graph.

Know it! Note

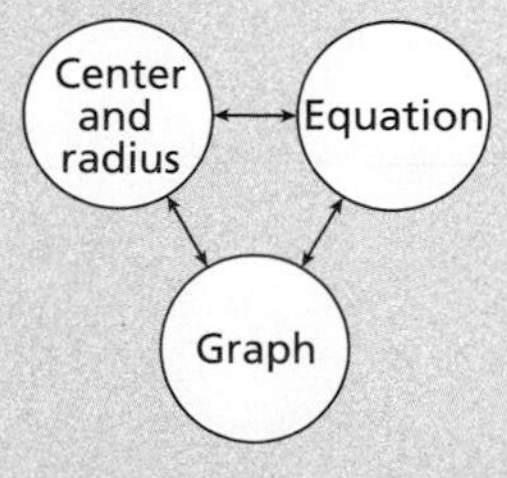

12-7 Exercises

Learn It Online
Homework Help Online
Parent Resources Online

GUIDED PRACTICE

SEE EXAMPLE 1

Write the equation of each circle.

1. $\odot A$ with center $A(3, -5)$ and radius 12
2. $\odot B$ with center $B(-4, 0)$ and radius 7
3. $\odot M$ that passes through $(2, 0)$ and that has center $M(4, 0)$
4. $\odot N$ that passes through $(2, -2)$ and that has center $N(-1, 2)$

SEE EXAMPLE 2

Multi-Step Graph each equation.

5. $(x-3)^2 + (y-3)^2 = 4$
6. $(x-1)^2 + (y+2)^2 = 9$
7. $(x+3)^2 + (y+4)^2 = 1$
8. $(x-3)^2 + (y+4)^2 = 16$

SEE EXAMPLE 3

9. **Communications** A radio antenna tower is kept perpendicular to the ground by three wires of equal length. The wires touch the ground at three points on a circle whose center is at the base of the tower. The wires touch the ground at $A(2, 6)$, $B(-2, -2)$, and $C(-5, 7)$.
   a. What are the coordinates of the base of the tower?
   b. Each unit of the coordinate plane represents 1 ft. What is the diameter of the circle?

PRACTICE AND PROBLEM SOLVING

Independent Practice

For Exercises	See Example
10–13	1
14–17	2
18	3

Extra Practice

See Extra Practice for more Skills Practice and Applications Practice exercises.

Write the equation of each circle.

10. $\odot R$ with center $R(-12, -10)$ and radius 8
11. $\odot S$ with center $S(1.5, -2.5)$ and radius $\sqrt{3}$
12. $\odot C$ that passes through $(2, 2)$ and that has center $C(1, 1)$
13. $\odot D$ that passes through $(-5, 1)$ and that has center $D(1, -2)$

Multi-Step Graph each equation.

14. $x^2 + (y-2)^2 = 9$
15. $(x+1)^2 - y^2 = 16$
16. $x^2 + y^2 = 100$
17. $x^2 + (y+2)^2 = 4$

18. **Anthropology** Hundreds of stone circles can be found along the Gambia River in western Africa. The stones are believed to be over 1000 years old. In one of the circles at Ker Batch, three stones have approximate coordinates of $A(3, 1)$, $B(4, -2)$, and $C(-6, -2)$.
    a. What are the coordinates of the center of the stone circle?
    b. Each unit of the coordinate plane represents 1 ft. What is the diameter of the stone circle?

Algebra Write the equation of each circle.

19.

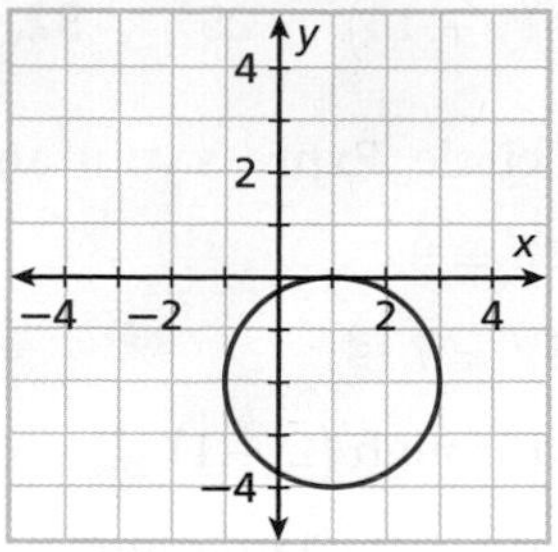

20.

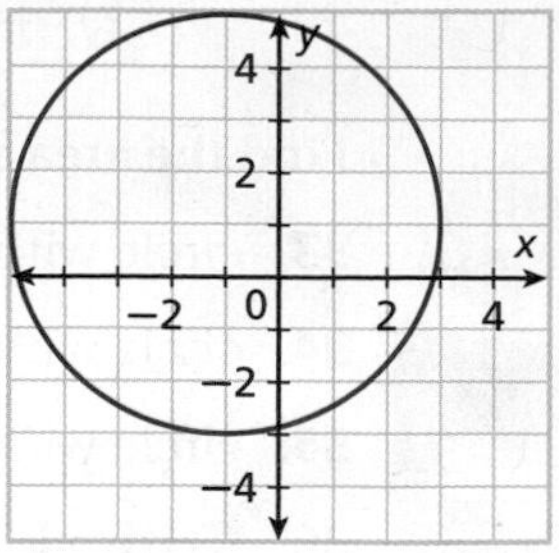

21. **Entertainment** In 2004, the world's largest carousel was located at the House on the Rock, in Spring Green, Wisconsin. Suppose that the center of the carousel is at the origin and that one of the animals on the circumference of the carousel has coordinates $(24, 32)$.
 a. If one unit of the coordinate plane equals 1 ft, what is the diameter of the carousel?
 b. As the carousel turns, the animals follow a circular path. Write the equation of this circle.

Determine whether each statement is true or false. If false, explain why.

22. The circle $x^2 + y^2 = 7$ has radius 7.
23. The circle $(x - 2)^2 + (y + 3)^2 = 9$ passes through the point $(-1, -3)$.
24. The center of the circle $(x - 6)^2 + (y + 4)^2 = 1$ lies in the second quadrant.
25. The circle $(x + 1)^2 + (y - 4)^2 = 4$ intersects the y-axis.
26. The equation of the circle centered at the origin with diameter 6 is $x^2 + y^2 = 36$.
27. **Estimation** You can use the graph of a circle to estimate its area.

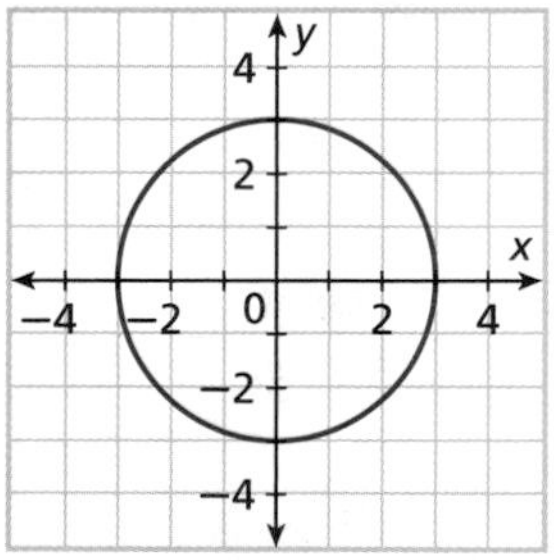

 a. Estimate the area of the circle by counting the number of squares of the coordinate plane contained in its interior. Be sure to count partial squares.
 b. Find the radius of the circle. Then use the area formula to calculate the circle's area to the nearest tenth.
 c. Was your estimate in part **a** an overestimate or an underestimate?
28. Consider the circle whose equation is $(x - 4)^2 + (y + 6)^2 = 25$. Write, in point-slope form, the equation of the line tangent to the circle at $(1, -10)$.

MULTI-STEP TEST PREP

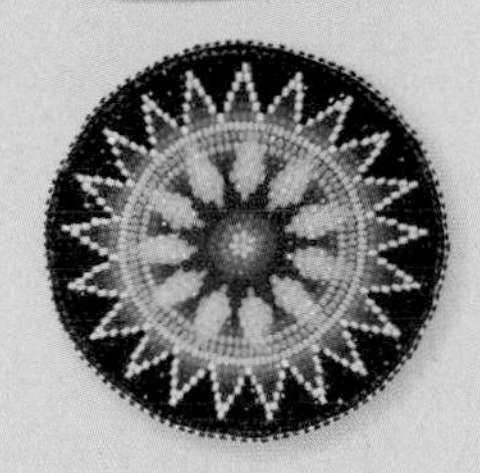

29. A *hogan* is a traditional Navajo home. An artist is using a coordinate plane to draw the symbol for a hogan. The symbol is based on eight equally spaced points placed around the circumference of a circle.

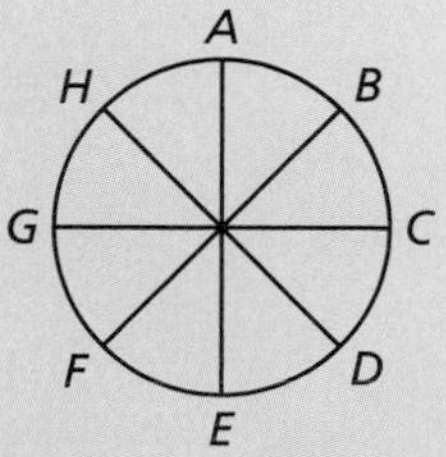

 a. She positions the symbol at $A(-3, 5)$ and $C(0, 2)$. What are the coordinates of E and G?
 b. What is the length of a diameter of the symbol?
 c. Use your answer from part **b** to write an equation of the circle.

Find the center and radius of each circle.

30. $(x-2)^2+(y+3)^2=81$ **31.** $x^2+(y+15)^2=25$ **32.** $(x+1)^2+y^2=7$

Find the area and circumference of each circle. Express your answer in terms of π.

33. circle with equation $(x+2)^2+(y-7)^2=9$

34. circle with equation $(x-8)^2+(y+5)^2=7$

35. circle with center $(-1, 3)$ that passes through $(2, -1)$

36. Critical Thinking Describe the graph of the equation $x^2+y^2=r^2$ when $r=0$.

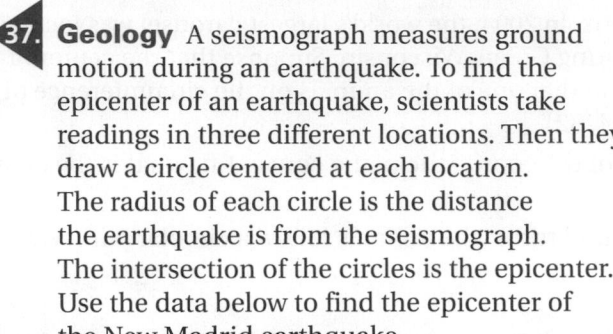

37. Geology A seismograph measures ground motion during an earthquake. To find the epicenter of an earthquake, scientists take readings in three different locations. Then they draw a circle centered at each location. The radius of each circle is the distance the earthquake is from the seismograph. The intersection of the circles is the epicenter. Use the data below to find the epicenter of the New Madrid earthquake.

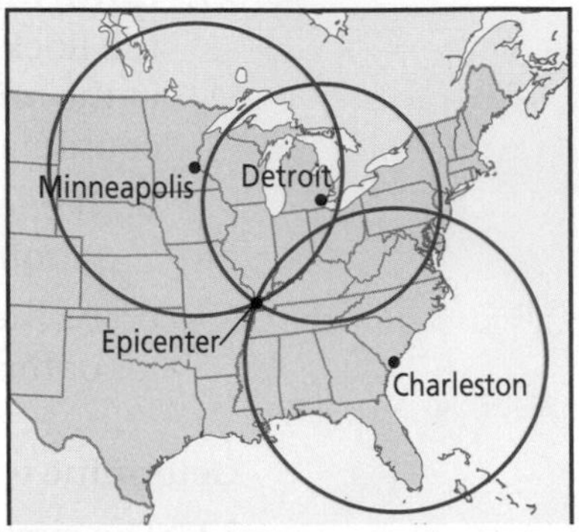

Seismograph	Location	Distance to Earthquake
A	$(-200, 200)$	300 mi
B	$(400, -100)$	600 mi
C	$(100, -500)$	500 mi

LINK

Geology

The New Madrid earthquake of 1811 was one of the largest earthquakes known in American history. Large areas sank into the earth, new lakes were formed, forests were destroyed, and the course of the Mississippi River was changed.

The Granger Collection, New York

38. For what value(s) of the constant k is the circle $x^2+(y-k)^2=25$ tangent to the x-axis?

39. $\odot A$ has a diameter with endpoints $(-3, -2)$ and $(5, -2)$. Write the equation of $\odot A$.

40. Recall that a locus is the set of points that satisfy a given condition. Draw and describe the locus of points that are 3 units from $(2, 2)$.

41. Write About It The equation of $\odot P$ is $(x-2)^2+(y-1)^2=9$. Without graphing, explain how you can determine whether the point $(3, -1)$ lies on $\odot P$, in the interior of $\odot P$, or in the exterior of $\odot P$.

TEST PREP

42. Which of these circles intersects the x-axis?

Ⓐ $(x-3)^2+(y+3)^2=4$ Ⓒ $(x+2)^2+(y+1)^2=1$

Ⓑ $(x+1)^2+(y-4)^2=9$ Ⓓ $(x+1)^2+(y+4)^2=9$

43. What is the equation of a circle with center $(-3, 5)$ that passes through the point $(1, 5)$?

Ⓕ $(x+3)^2+(y-5)^2=4$ Ⓗ $(x+3)^2+(y-5)^2=16$

Ⓖ $(x-3)^2+(y+5)^2=4$ Ⓙ $(x-3)^2+(y+5)^2=16$

44. On a map of a park, statues are located at $(4, -2)$, $(-1, 3)$, and $(-5, -5)$. A circular path connects the three statues, and the circle has a fountain at its center. Find the coordinates of the fountain.

Ⓐ $(-1, -2)$ Ⓑ $(2, 1)$ Ⓒ $(-2, 1)$ Ⓓ $(1, -2)$

CHALLENGE AND EXTEND

45. In three dimensions, the equation of a sphere is similar to that of a circle. The equation of a sphere with center (h, j, k) and radius r is $(x-h)^2 + (y-j)^2 + (z-k)^2 = r^2$.
   a. Write the equation of a sphere with center $(2, -4, 3)$ that contains the point $(1, -2, -5)$.
   b. $\overleftrightarrow{AC}$ and $\overleftrightarrow{BC}$ are tangents from the same exterior point. If $AC = 15$ m, what is BC? Explain.

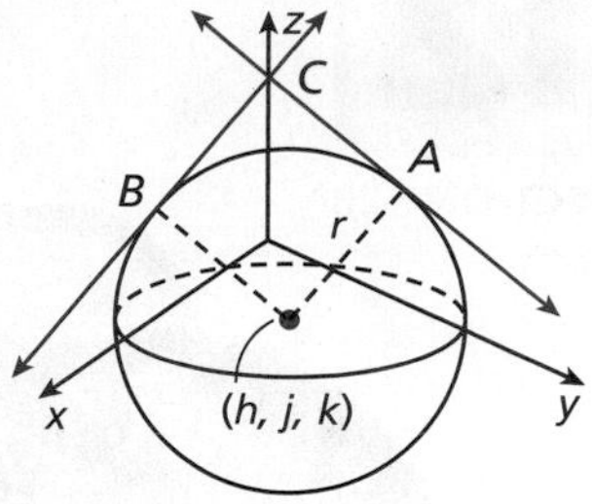

46. **Algebra** Find the point(s) of intersection of the line $x + y = 5$ and the circle $x^2 + y^2 = 25$ by solving the system of equations. Check your result by graphing the line and the circle.

47. Find the equation of the circle with center $(3, 4)$ that is tangent to the line whose equation is $y = 2x + 3$. (*Hint:* First find the point of tangency.)

Career Path

Learn It Online
Career Resources Online

Bryan Moreno
Furniture Maker

Q: What math classes did you take in high school?

A: I took Algebra 1 and Geometry. I also took Drafting and Woodworking. Those classes aren't considered math classes, but for me they were since math was used in them.

Q: What type of furniture do you make?

A: I mainly design and make household furniture, such as end tables, bedroom furniture, and entertainment centers.

Q: How do you use math?

A: Taking appropriate and precise measurements is very important. If wood is not measured correctly, the end result doesn't turn out as expected. Understanding angle measures is also important. Some of the furniture I build has 30° or 40° angles at the edges.

Q: What are your future plans?

A: Someday I would love to design all the furniture in my own home. It would be incredibly satisfying to know that all my furniture was made with quality and attention to detail.

CHAPTER 12

MULTI-STEP TEST PREP

SECTION 12B

MATHEMATICAL PRACTICES Model with mathematics.

Angles and Segments in Circles

Native American Design

The members of a Native American cultural center are painting a circle of colors on their gallery floor. They start by laying out the circle and chords shown. Before they apply their paint to the design, they measure angles and lengths to check for accuracy.

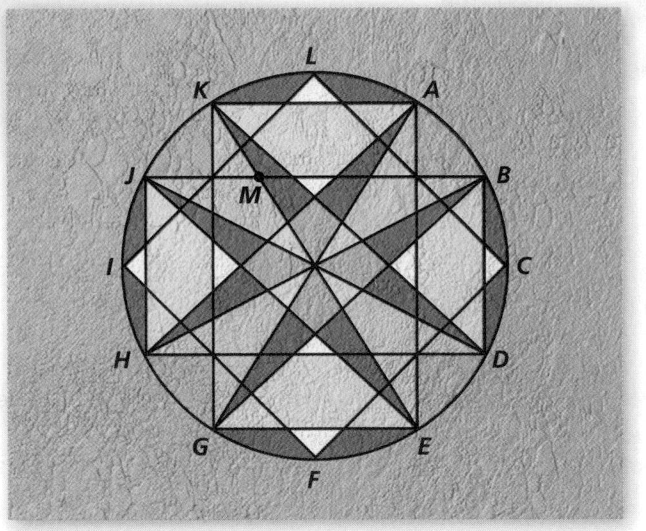

1. The circle design is based on twelve equally spaced points placed around the circumference of the circle. As the group lays out the design, what should be $m\angle AGB$?
2. What should be $m\angle KAE$? Why?
3. What should be $m\angle KMJ$? Why?
4. The diameter of the circle is 22 ft. $KM \approx 4.8$ ft, and $JM \approx 6.4$ ft. What should be the length of $\overline{MB}$?
5. The group members use a coordinate plane to help them position the design. Each square of a grid represents one square foot, and the center of the circle is at $(20, 14)$. What is the equation of the circle?
6. What are the coordinates of points L, C, F, and I?

READY TO GO ON?

CHAPTER 12

SECTION 12B

Quiz for Lessons 12-4 Through 12-7

12-4 Inscribed Angles

Find each measure.

1. $m\angle BAC$
2. $m\widehat{CD}$

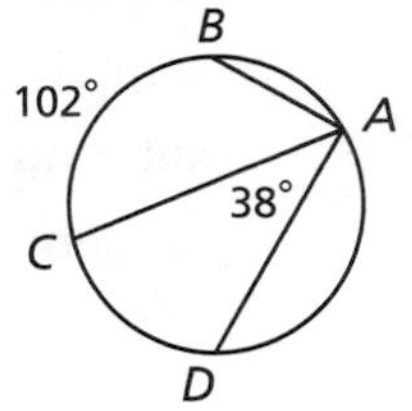

3. $m\angle FGH$
4. $m\widehat{JGF}$

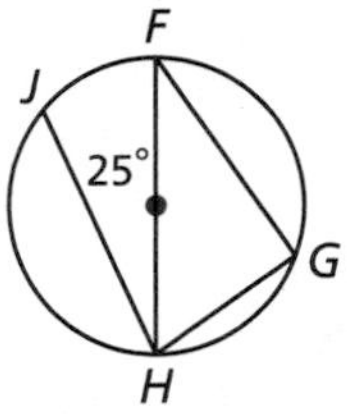

12-5 Angle Relationships in Circles

Find each measure.

5. $m\angle RST$

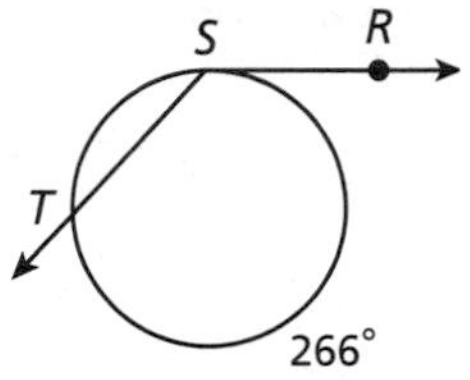

6. $m\angle AEC$

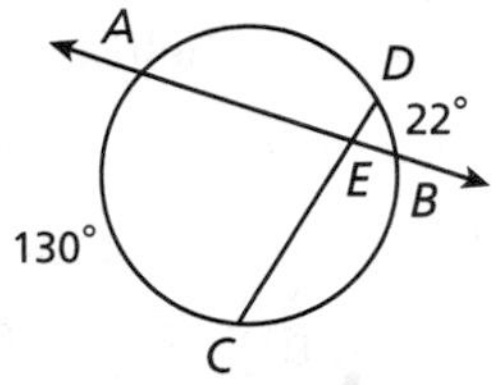

7. A manufacturing company is creating a plastic stand for DVDs. They want to make the stand with $m\widehat{MN} = 102°$. What should be the measure of $\angle MPN$?

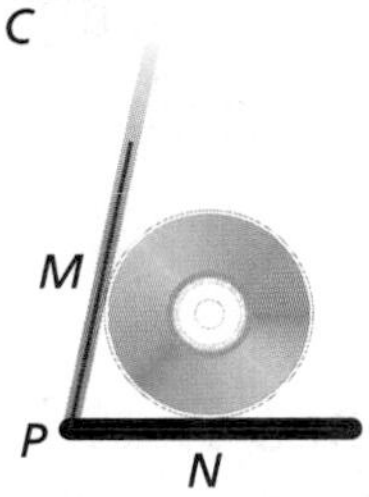

12-6 Segment Relationships in Circles

Find the value of the variable and the length of each chord or secant segment.

8.

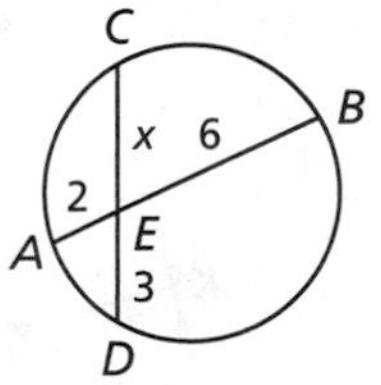

9.

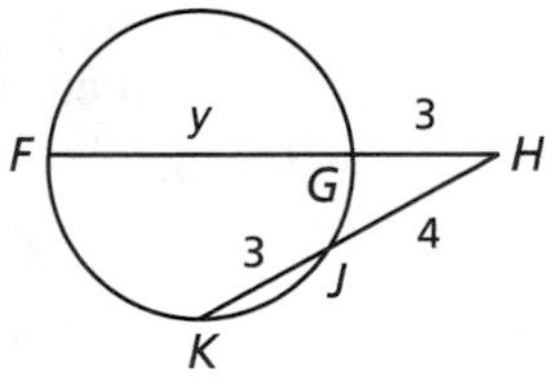

10. An archaeologist discovers a portion of a circular stone wall, shown by $\widehat{ST}$ in the figure. $ST = 12.2$ m, and $UR = 3.9$ m. What was the diameter of the original circular wall? Round to the nearest hundredth.

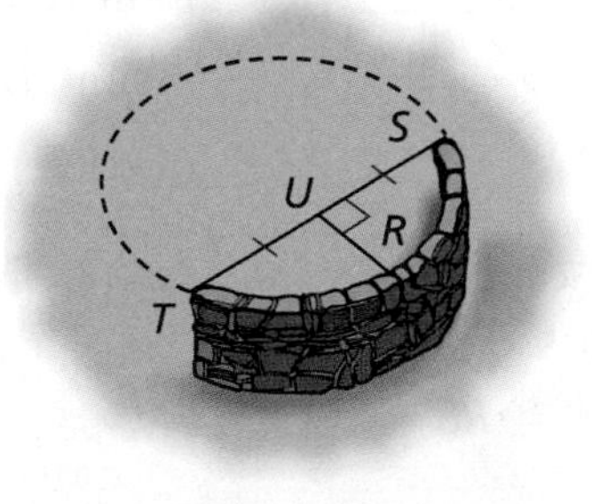

12-7 Circles in the Coordinate Plane

Write the equation of each circle.

11. $\odot A$ with center $A(-2, -3)$ and radius 3
12. $\odot B$ that passes through $(1, 1)$ and that has center $B(4, 5)$
13. A television station serves residents of three cities located at $J(5, 2)$, $K(-7, 2)$, and $L(-5, -8)$. The station wants to build a new broadcast facility that is equidistant from the three cities. What are the coordinates of the location where the facility should be built?

CHAPTER 12 Study Guide: Review

Know it! Note For a complete list of postulates, theorems, and corollaries, see p. PT2.

Vocabulary

adjacent arcs	exterior of a circle	secant segment
arc	external secant segment	sector of a circle
arc length	inscribed angle	segment of a circle
central angle	intercepted arc	semicircle
chord	interior of a circle	subtend
common tangent	major arc	tangent of a circle
concentric circles	minor arc	tangent circles
congruent arcs	point of tangency	tangent segment
congruent circles	secant	

Complete the sentences below with vocabulary words from the list above.

1. A(n) __?__ is a region bounded by an arc and a chord.

2. An angle whose vertex is at the center of a circle is called a(n) __?__ .

3. The measure of a(n) __?__ is 360° minus the measure of its central angle.

4. __?__ are coplanar circles with the same center.

12-1 Lines That Intersect Circles

EXAMPLES

■ **Identify each line or segment that intersects ⊙*A*.**

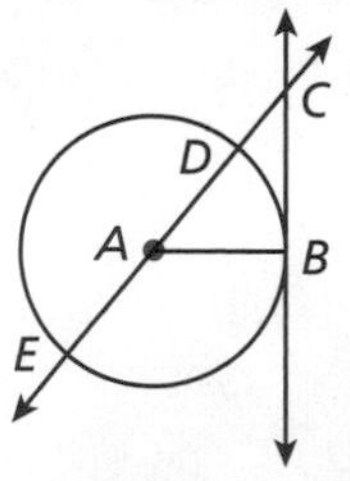

chord: $\overline{DE}$

tangent: $\overleftrightarrow{BC}$

radii: $\overline{AE}$, $\overline{AD}$, and $\overline{AB}$

secant: $\overleftrightarrow{DE}$

diameter: $\overline{DE}$

■ **$\overline{RS}$ and $\overline{RW}$ are tangent to ⊙*T*. $RS = x + 5$ and $RW = 3x - 7$. Find *RS*.**

$RS = RW$	*2 segs. tangent to ⊙ from same ext. pt. → segs. ≅.*
$x + 5 = 3x - 7$	*Substitute the given values.*
$-2x + 5 = -7$	*Subtract 3x from both sides.*
$-2x = -12$	*Subtract 5 from both sides.*
$x = 6$	*Divide both sides by −2.*
$RS = 6 + 5$	*Substitute 6 for y.*
$= 11$	*Simplify.*

EXERCISES

Identify each line or segment that intersects each circle.

5.

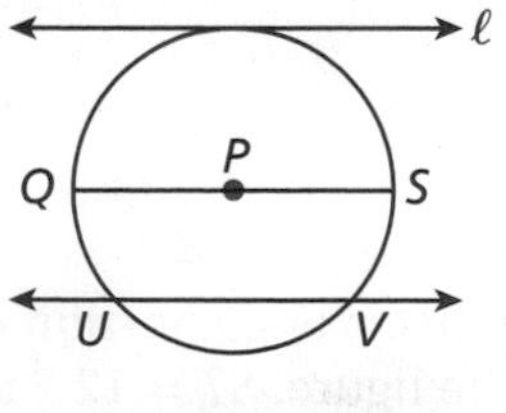

6.

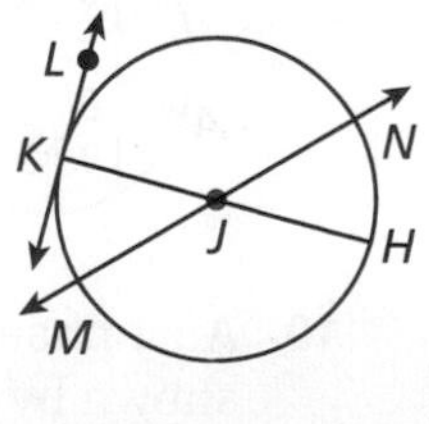

Given the measures of the following segments that are tangent to a circle, find each length.

7. $AB = 9x - 2$ and $BC = 7x + 4$. Find *AB*.

8. $EF = 5y + 32$ and $EG = 8 - y$. Find *EG*.

9. $JK = 8m - 5$ and $JL = 2m + 4$. Find *JK*.

10. $WX = 0.8x + 1.2$ and $WY = 2.4x$. Find *WY*.

12-2 Arcs and Chords

EXAMPLES

Find each measure.

- $m\overset{\frown}{BF}$

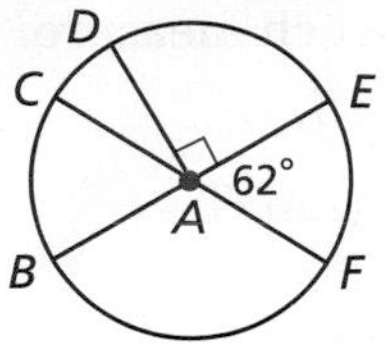

$\angle BAF$ and $\angle FAE$ are supplementary, so $m\angle BAF = 180° - 62° = 118°$. $m\overset{\frown}{BF} = m\angle BAF = 118°$

- $m\overset{\frown}{DF}$

Since $m\angle DAE = 90°$, $m\overset{\frown}{DE} = 90°$. $m\angle EAF = 62°$, so $m\overset{\frown}{EF} = 62°$. By the Arc Addition Postulate, $m\overset{\frown}{DF} = m\overset{\frown}{DE} + m\overset{\frown}{EF} = 90° + 62° = 152°$.

EXERCISES

Find each measure.

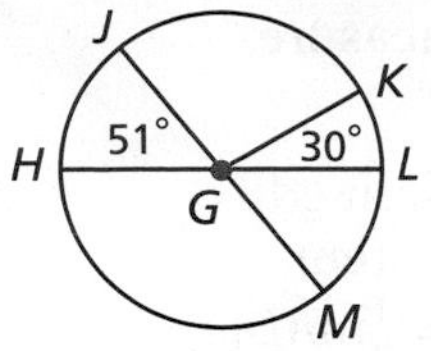

11. $m\overset{\frown}{KM}$

12. $m\overset{\frown}{HMK}$

13. $m\overset{\frown}{JK}$

14. $m\overset{\frown}{MJK}$

Find each length to the nearest tenth.

15. *ST*

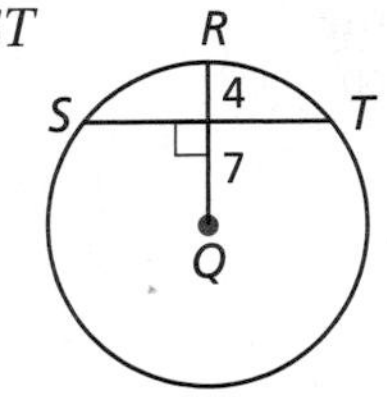

16. *CD*

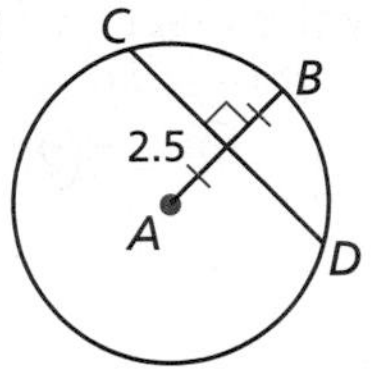

12-3 Sector Area and Arc Length

EXAMPLES

- **Find the area of sector *PQR*. Give your answer in terms of π and rounded to the nearest hundredth.**

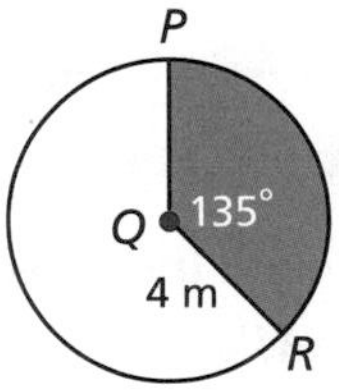

$$A = \pi r^2\left(\frac{m°}{360°}\right)$$

$$= \pi(4)^2\left(\frac{135°}{360}\right)$$

$$= 16\pi\left(\frac{3}{8}\right)$$

$$= 6\pi \text{ m}^2$$

$$\approx 18.85 \text{ m}^2$$

- **Find the length of $\overset{\frown}{AB}$. Give your answer in terms of π and rounded to the nearest hundredth.**

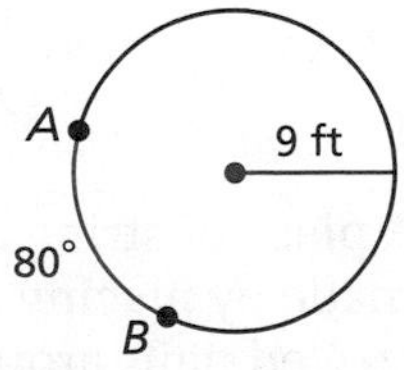

$$L = 2\pi r\left(\frac{m°}{360°}\right)$$

$$= 2\pi(9)\left(\frac{80°}{360°}\right)$$

$$= 18\pi\left(\frac{4}{9}\right)$$

$$= 8\pi \text{ ft}$$

$$\approx 25.13 \text{ ft}$$

EXERCISES

Find the area of each sector. Give your answer in terms of π and rounded to the nearest hundredth.

17. sector *DEF*

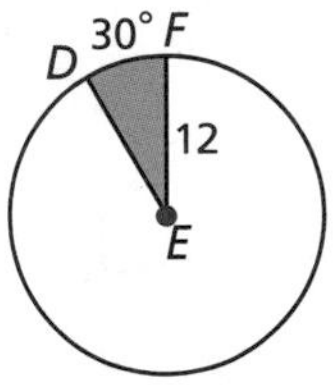

18. sector *JKL*

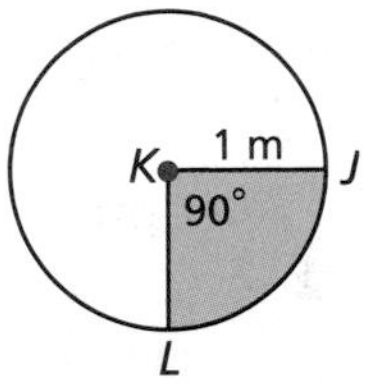

Find each arc length. Give your answer in terms of π and rounded to the nearest hundredth.

19. $\overset{\frown}{GH}$

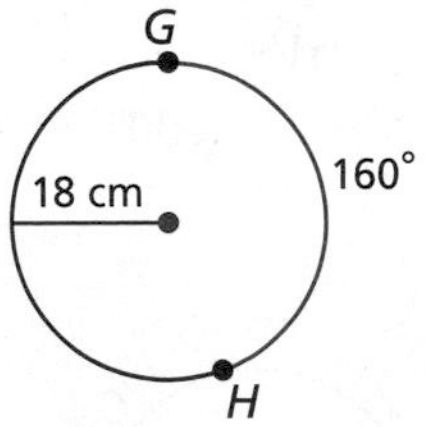

20. $\overset{\frown}{MNP}$

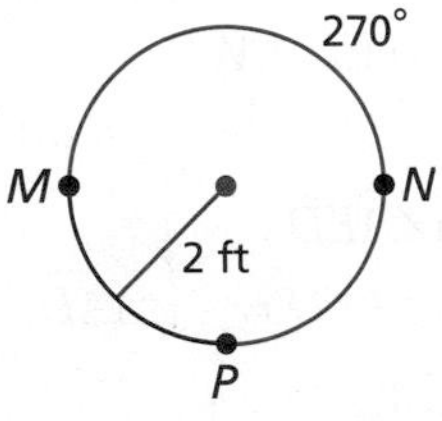

12-4 Inscribed Angles

EXAMPLES

Find each measure.

- m∠*ABD*

By the Inscribed Angle Theorem, $m\angle ABD = \frac{1}{2}m\widehat{AD}$, so $m\angle ABD = \frac{1}{2}(108°) = 54°$.

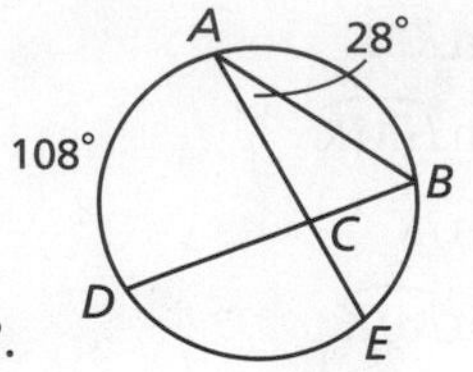

- $m\widehat{BE}$

By the Inscribed Angle Theorem, $m\angle BAE = \frac{1}{2}m\widehat{BE}$. So $28° = \frac{1}{2}m\widehat{BE}$, and $m\widehat{BE} = 2(28°) = 56°$.

EXERCISES

Find each measure.

21. $m\widehat{JL}$
22. m∠*MKL*

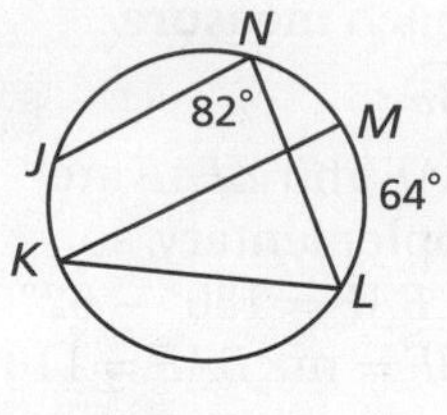

Find each value.

23. *x*

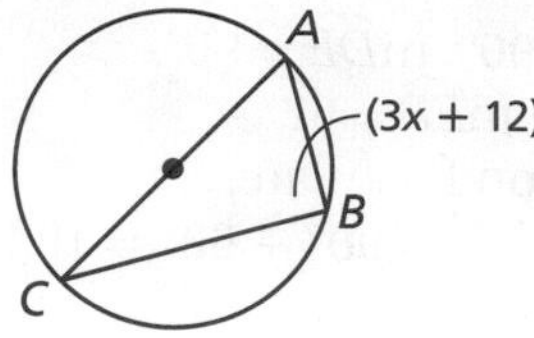

24. m∠*RSP*

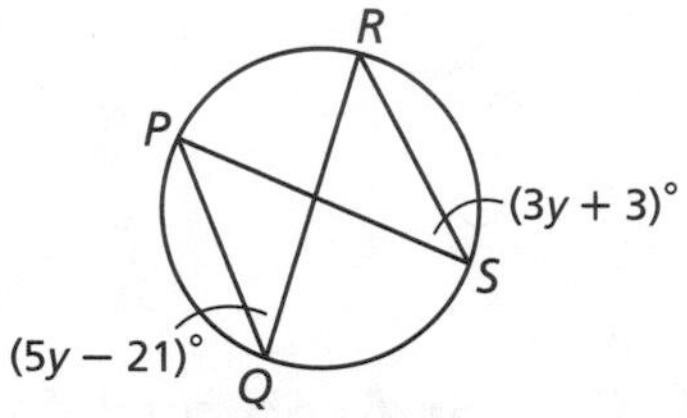

12-5 Angle Relationships in Circles

EXAMPLES

Find each measure.

- m∠*UWX*

$$m\angle UWX = \frac{1}{2}m\widehat{UW}$$
$$= \frac{1}{2}(160°)$$
$$= 80°$$

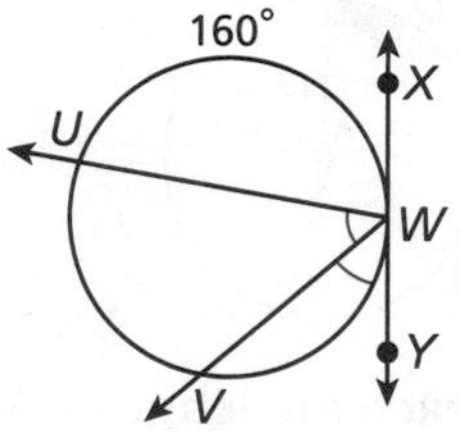

- $m\widehat{VW}$

Since m∠*UWX* = 80°, m∠*UWY* = 100° and m∠*VWY* = 50°. $m\angle VWY = \frac{1}{2}m\widehat{VW}$. So $50° = \frac{1}{2}m\widehat{VW}$, and $m\widehat{VW} = 2(50°) = 100°$.

- m∠*AED*

$$m\angle AED = \frac{1}{2}\left(m\widehat{AD} + m\widehat{BC}\right)$$
$$= \frac{1}{2}(31° + 87°)$$
$$= \frac{1}{2}(118°)$$
$$= 59°$$

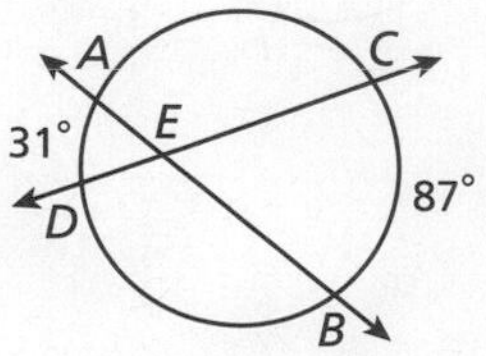

EXERCISES

Find each measure.

25. $m\widehat{MR}$
26. m∠*QMR*

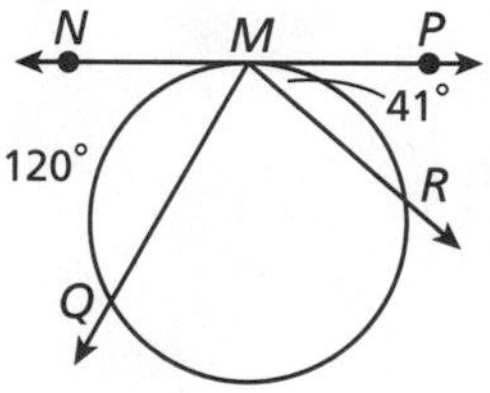

27. m∠*GKH*

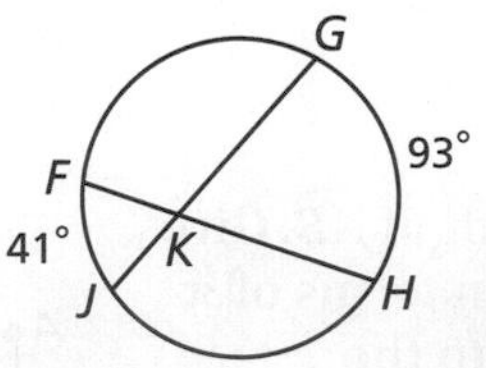

28. A piece of string art is made by placing 16 evenly spaced nails around the circumference of a circle. A piece of string is wound from *A* to *B* to *C* to *D*. What is m∠*BXC*?

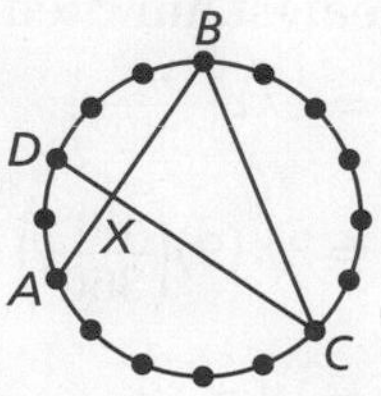

12-6 Segment Relationships in Circles

EXAMPLES

- **Find the value of x and the length of each chord.**

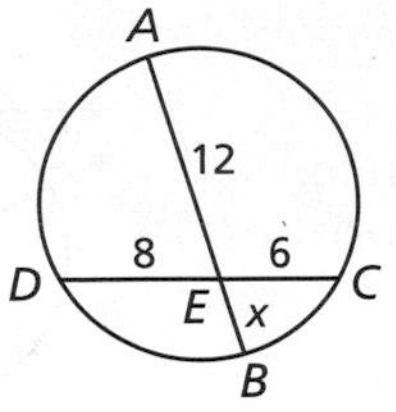

$AE \cdot EB = DE \cdot EC$

$12x = 8(6)$

$12x = 48$

$x = 4$

$AB = 12 + 4 = 16$

$DC = 8 + 6 = 14$

- **Find the value of x and the length of each secant segment.**

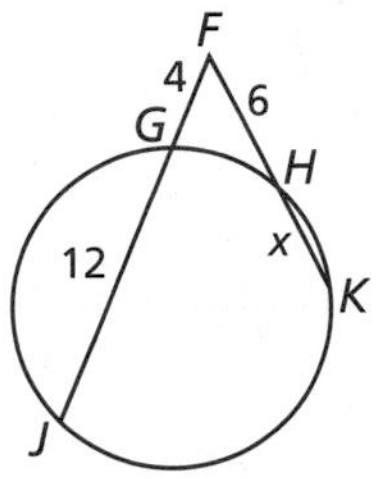

$FJ \cdot FG = FK \cdot FH$

$16(4) = (6 + x)6$

$64 = 36 + 6x$

$28 = 6x$

$x = 4\frac{2}{3}$

$FJ = 12 + 4 = 16$

$FK = 4\frac{2}{3} + 6 = 10\frac{2}{3}$

EXERCISES

Find the value of the variable and the length of each chord.

29.

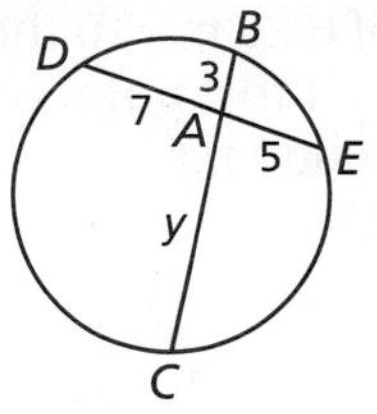

30.

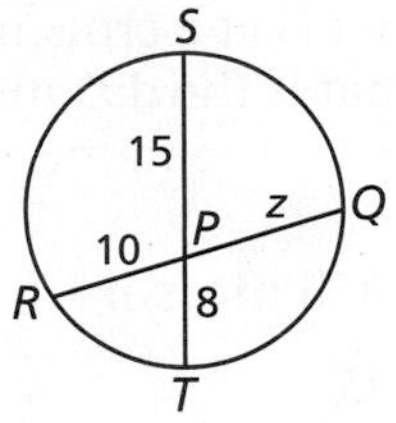

Find the value of the variable and the length of each secant segment.

31.

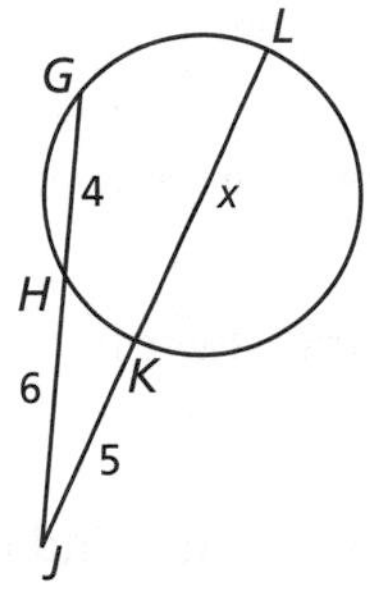

32.

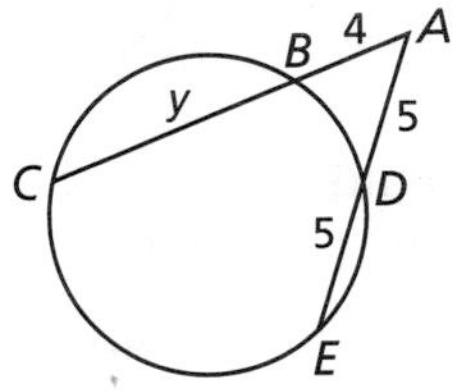

12-7 Circles in the Coordinate Plane

EXAMPLES

- **Write the equation of $\odot A$ that passes through $(-1, 1)$ and that has center $A(2, 3)$.**

The equation of a circle with center (h, k) and radius r is $(x - h)^2 + (y - k)^2 = r^2$.

$r = \sqrt{(2 - (-1))^2 + (3 - 1)^2} = \sqrt{3^2 + 2^2} = \sqrt{13}$

The equation of $\odot A$ is $(x - 2)^2 + (y - 3)^2 = 13$.

- **Graph $(x - 2)^2 + (y + 1)^2 = 4$.**

The center of the circle is $(2, -1)$, and the radius is $\sqrt{4} = 2$.

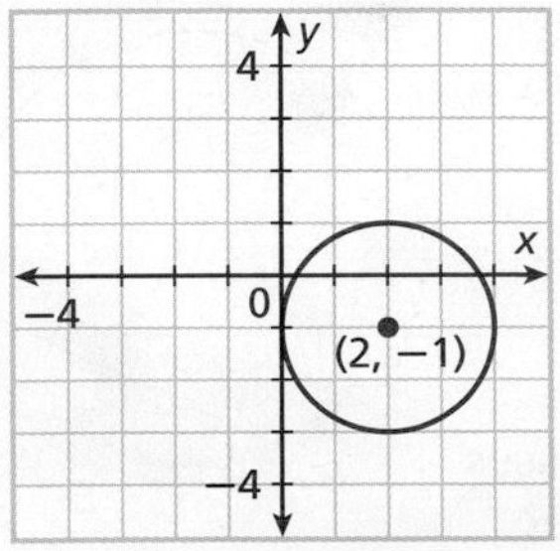

EXERCISES

Write the equation of each circle.

33. $\odot A$ with center $(-4, -3)$ and radius 3

34. $\odot B$ that passes through $(-2, -2)$ and that has center $B(-2, 0)$

35. $\odot C$

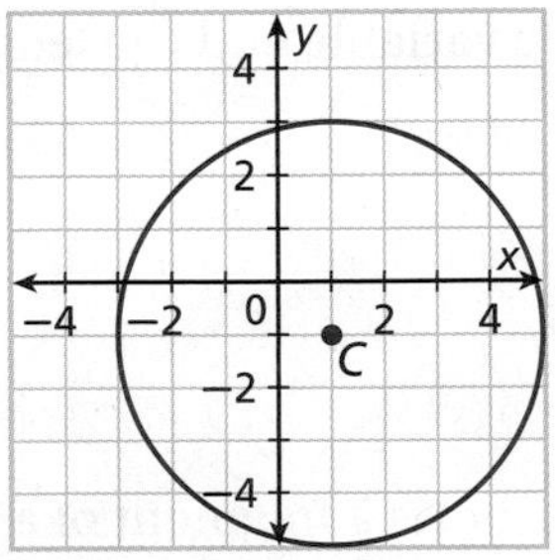

36. Graph $(x + 2)^2 + (y - 2)^2 = 1$.

CHAPTER 12 CHAPTER TEST

1. Identify each line or segment that intersects the circle.

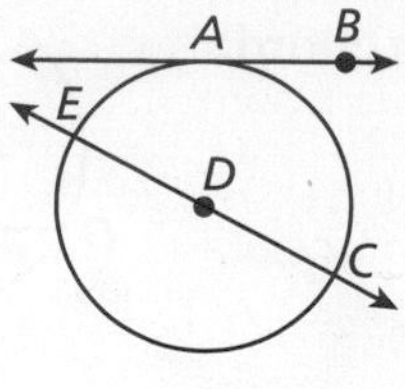

2. A jet is at a cruising altitude of 6.25 mi. To the nearest mile, what is the distance from the jet to a point on Earth's horizon? (*Hint:* The radius of Earth is 4000 mi.)

Find each measure.

3. $m\widehat{JK}$

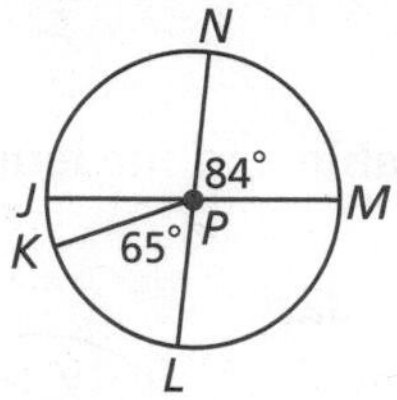

4. UV

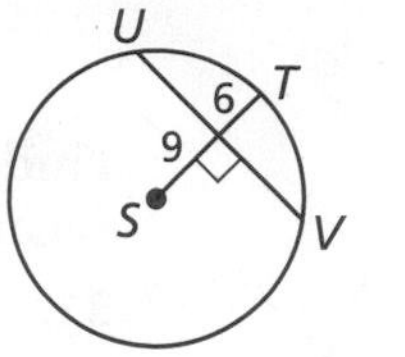

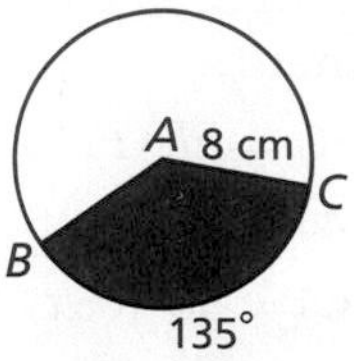

5. Find the area of the sector. Give your answer in terms of π and rounded to the nearest hundredth.

6. Find the length of $\widehat{BC}$. Give your answer in terms of π and rounded to the nearest hundredth.

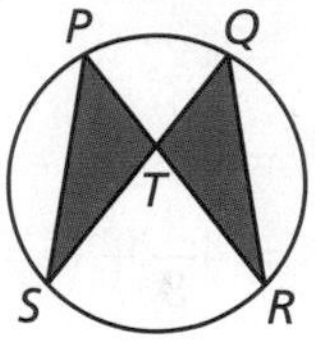

7. If $m\angle SPR = 47°$ in the diagram of a logo, find $m\widehat{SR}$.

8. A printer is making a large version of the logo for a banner. According to the specifications, $m\widehat{PQ} = 58°$. What should the measure of $\angle QTR$ be?

Find each measure.

9. $m\angle ABC$

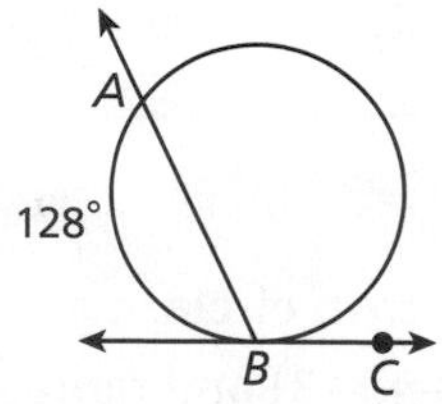

10. $m\angle NKL$

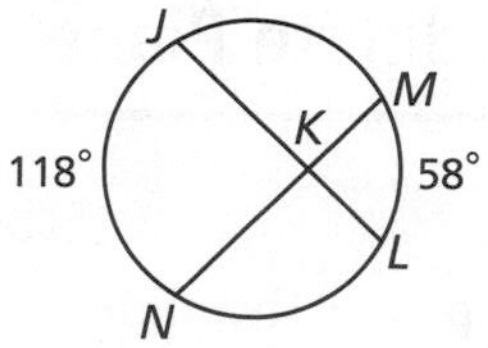

11. A surveyor S is studying the positions of four columns A, B, C, and D that lie on a circle. He finds that $m\angle CSD = 42°$ and $m\widehat{CD} = 124°$. What is $m\widehat{AB}$?

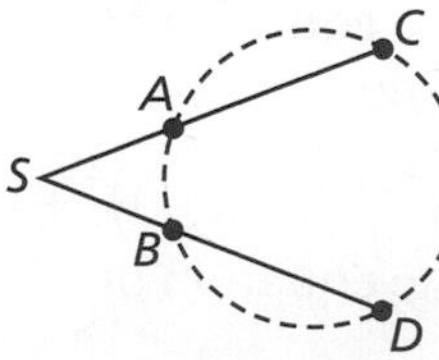

Find the value of the variable and the length of each chord or secant segment.

12.

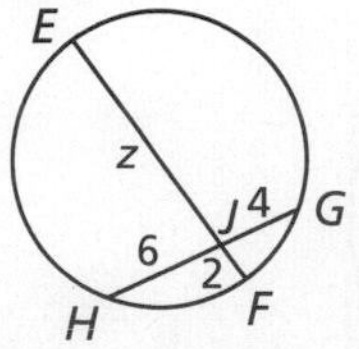

13.

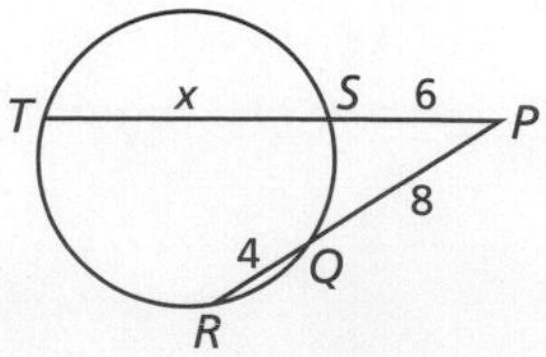

14. The illustration shows a fragment of a circular plate. $AB = 8$ in., and $CD = 2$ in. What is the diameter of the plate?

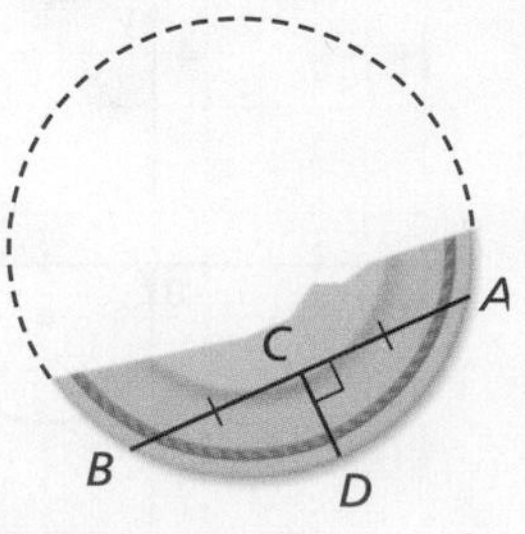

15. Write the equation of the circle that passes through $(-2, 4)$ and that has center $(1, -2)$.

16. An artist uses a coordinate plane to plan a mural. The mural will include portraits of civic leaders at $X(2, 4)$, $Y(-6, 0)$, and $Z(2, -8)$ and a circle that passes through all three portraits. What are the coordinates of the center of the circle?

College Entrance Exam Practice

FOCUS ON SAT MATHEMATICS SUBJECT TESTS

The topics covered on the SAT Mathematics Subject Tests vary only slightly each time the test is administered. You can find out the general distribution of questions across topics, then determine which areas need more of your attention when you are studying for the test.

You may want to time yourself as you take this practice test. It should take you about 6 minutes to complete.

To prepare for the SAT Mathematics Subject Tests, start reviewing course material a couple of months before your test date. Take sample tests to find the areas you might need to focus on more. Remember that you are not expected to have studied all topics on the test.

---

1. $\overline{AC}$ and $\overline{BD}$ intersect at the center of the circle shown. If $m\angle BDC = 30°$, what is the measure of minor $\widehat{AB}$?

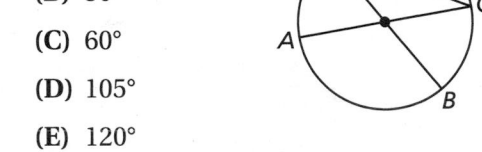

(A) 15°

(B) 30°

(C) 60°

(D) 105°

(E) 120°

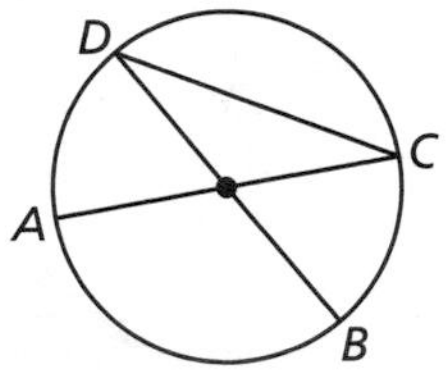

Note: Figure not drawn to scale.

---

2. Which of these is the equation of a circle that is tangent to the lines $x = 1$ and $y = 3$ and has radius 2?

(A) $(x + 1)^2 + (y - 1)^2 = 4$

(B) $(x - 1)^2 + (y + 1)^2 = 4$

(C) $x^2 + (y - 1)^2 = 4$

(D) $(x - 1)^2 + y^2 = 4$

(E) $x^2 + y^2 = 4$

---

3. If $LK = 6$, $LN = 10$, and $PK = 3$, what is PM?

(A) 7

(B) 8

(C) 9

(D) 10

(E) 11

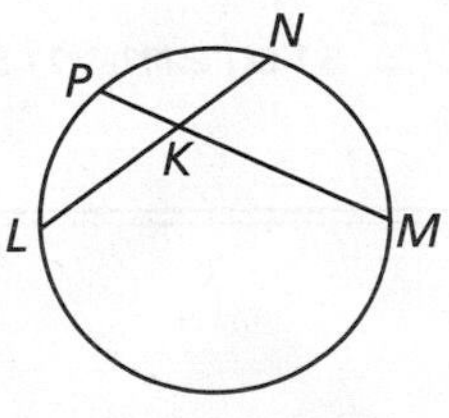

---

4. Circle D has radius 6, and $m\angle ABC = 25°$. What is the length of minor $\widehat{AC}$?

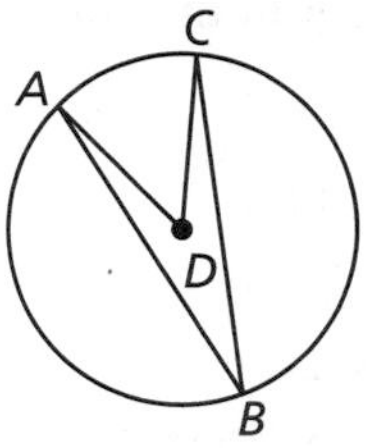

Note: Figure not drawn to scale.

(A) $\frac{5\pi}{6}$

(B) $\frac{5\pi}{4}$

(C) $\frac{5\pi}{3}$

(D) 3π

(E) 5π

---

5. A square is inscribed in a circle as shown. If the radius of the circle is 9, what is the area of the shaded region, rounded to the nearest hundredth?

(A) 11.56

(B) 23.12

(C) 57.84

(D) 104.12

(E) 156.23

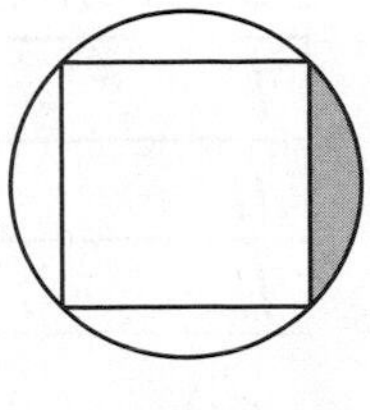

CHAPTER 12

TEST TACKLER

Standardized Test Strategies

Multiple Choice: Choose Combinations of Answers

Given a multiple-choice test item where you are asked to choose from a combination of statements, the correct response is the most complete answer choice available. A strategy to use when solving these types of test items is to compare each given statement with the question and determine if it is true or false. If you determine that more than one of the statements is correct, then you can choose the combination that contains each correct statement.

EXAMPLE 1

Given that $\ell \parallel m$ and n is a transversal, which statement(s) are correct?

I. $\angle 1 \cong \angle 3$ **II.** $\angle 2 \cong \angle 5$ **III.** $\angle 2 \cong \angle 8$

(A) I only
(B) I and II
(C) II only
(D) I and III

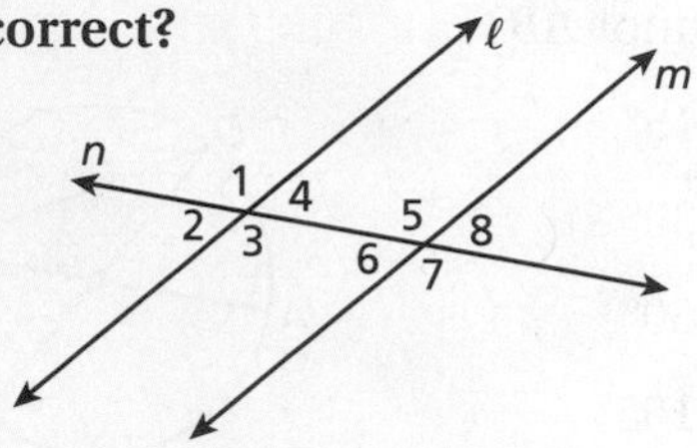

Look at each statement separately and determine if it is true or false. As you consider each statement, write true or false beside the statement.

Consider statement I: Because $\angle 1$ and $\angle 3$ are vertical angles and vertical angles are congruent, then this statement is TRUE. So the answer could be choice A, B, or D.

Consider statement II: $\angle 2 \cong \angle 4$ because they are vertical angles. $\angle 4$ and $\angle 5$ are supplementary angles because they are same-side interior angles. So $\angle 2$ and $\angle 5$ must be supplementary, not congruent. This statement is FALSE. The answer is NOT choice B or C.

Consider statement III: Because $\angle 2$ and $\angle 8$ are alternate exterior angles and alternate exterior angles are congruent, this statement is TRUE.

Since statements I and III are both true, choice D is correct.

You can also keep track of your statements in a table.

Statement	True/False
I	TRUE
II	FALSE
III	TRUE

Only I and III are TRUE statements.

HOT TIP! Make a table or write *T* or *F* beside each statement to keep track of whether it is true or false.

Read each test item and answer the questions that follow.

Item A

Which are chords of circle *W*?

I. $\overleftrightarrow{AB}$

II. $\overline{WG}$

III. $\overline{EC}$

IV. $\overline{FD}$

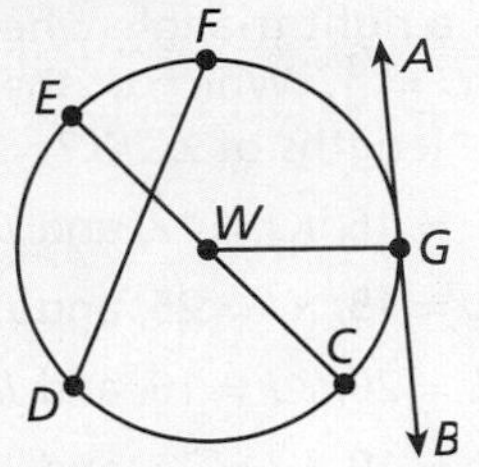

Ⓐ I only Ⓒ I and II

Ⓑ III only Ⓓ III and IV

1. What is the definition of a chord?
2. Determine if statements I, II, III, and IV are true or false. Explain your reasoning for each.
3. Kristin realized that statement III was true and selected choice B as her response. Do you agree? Why or why not?

Item B

Classify △*DEF*.

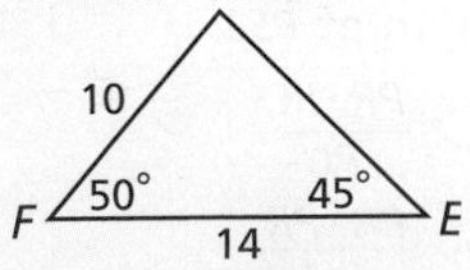

Ⓕ acute Ⓗ obtuse

Ⓖ acute scalene Ⓙ right equilateral

4. How can you use the Triangle Sum Theorem to find all of the angle measures of △*DEF*?
5. Consider the angle measures of △*DEF*. Is the triangle acute, right, or obtuse?
6. Explain how you can use your answer to Problem 5 to eliminate two answer choices.
7. Can a triangle be classified in any other way than by its angles? Explain.
8. Which choice gives the most complete response?

Item C

Which describes the arc length of $\widehat{AB}$?

I. $\frac{17}{72}(24\pi)$

II. $\frac{17\pi}{3}$

III. $\frac{17}{36}(24\pi)$

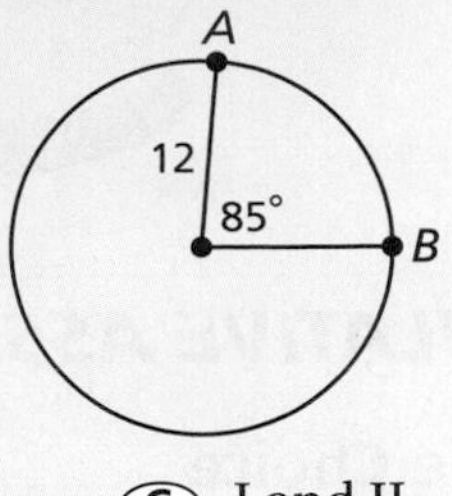

Ⓐ I only Ⓒ I and II

Ⓑ II only Ⓓ I, II, and III

9. What is the formula to find arc length?
10. Is statement I true or false? Explain.
11. Decide if statement II is true or false. Should you select the answer choice yet? Why or why not?
12. Can any answer choice be eliminated? Explain.
13. Describe how you know which combination of statements is correct.

Item D

A rectangular prism has a length of 5 m, a height of 10 m, and a width of 4 m. Describe the change if the height and width of the prism are multiplied by $\frac{1}{2}$.

I. The new volume is one fourth of the original volume.

II. The new height is 20 m, and the new width is 2 m.

III. The new surface area is less than half of the original surface area.

Ⓕ I only Ⓗ I, II, and II

Ⓖ II and III Ⓙ I and III

14. Create a table and determine if each statement is true or false.
15. Using your table, which choice is the most accurate?

CHAPTER 12

STANDARDIZED TEST PREP

Learn It Online
State Test Practice

CUMULATIVE ASSESSMENT

Multiple Choice

1. A cylinder has a volume of 24 cubic centimeters. The height of a cone with the same radius is two times the height of the cylinder. What is the volume of the cone?

(A) 8 cubic centimeters
(B) 12 cubic centimeters
(C) 16 cubic centimeters
(D) 48 cubic centimeters

2. What is the area of the polygon with vertices $A(2, 3)$, $B(12, 3)$, $C(6, 0)$, and $D(2, 0)$?

(F) 12 square units
(G) 21 square units
(H) 30 square units
(J) 42 square units

Use the diagram for Items 3–5.

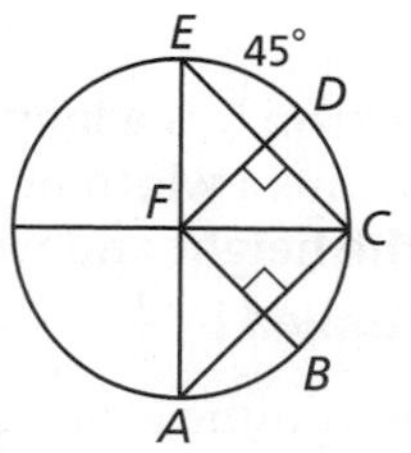

3. What is $m\widehat{BC}$?

(A) 36°
(B) 45°
(C) 54°
(D) 72°

4. If the length of $\widehat{ED}$ is 6π centimeters, what is the area of sector EFD?

(F) 20π square centimeters
(G) 72π square centimeters
(H) 120π square centimeters
(J) 240π square centimeters

5. Which of these line segments is NOT a chord of $\odot F$?

(A) $\overline{EC}$
(B) $\overline{CA}$
(C) $\overline{AF}$
(D) $\overline{AE}$

6. $\triangle JKL$ is a right triangle where $m\angle K = 90°$ and $\tan J = \frac{3}{4}$. Which of the following could be the side lengths of $\triangle JKL$?

(F) $KL = 16$, $KJ = 12$, and $JL = 20$
(G) $KL = 15$, $KJ = 25$, and $JL = 20$
(H) $KL = 20$, $KJ = 16$, and $JL = 12$
(J) $KL = 18$, $KJ = 24$, and $JL = 30$

Use the diagram for Items 7 and 8.

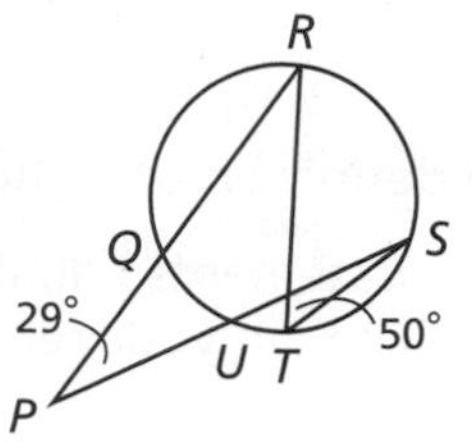

7. What is $m\widehat{QU}$?

(A) 25°
(B) 42°
(C) 58°
(D) 71°

8. Which expression can be used to calculate the length of $\overline{PS}$?

(F) $\frac{PR \cdot PQ}{PU}$
(G) $\frac{PR \cdot PR}{PU}$
(H) $\frac{PQ \cdot QR}{PU}$
(J) $\frac{PQ \cdot PR}{PS}$

9. $\triangle ABC$ has vertices $A(0, 0)$, $B(-1, 3)$, and $C(2, 4)$. If $\triangle ABC \sim \triangle DEF$ and $\triangle DEF$ has vertices $D(5, -3)$, $E(4, -2)$, and $F(3, y)$, what is the value of y?

(A) −7
(B) −5
(C) −3
(D) −1

10. What is the equation of the circle with diameter $\overline{MN}$ that has endpoints $M(-1, 1)$ and $N(3, -5)$?

(F) $(x + 1)^2 + (y - 2)^2 = 13$
(G) $(x - 1)^2 + (y + 2)^2 = 13$
(H) $(x + 1)^2 + (y - 2)^2 = 26$
(J) $(x - 1)^2 + (y + 2)^2 = 52$

HOT TIP! **Remember that an important part of writing a proof is giving a justification for each step in the proof. Justifications may include theorems, postulates, definitions, properties, or the information that is given to you.**

11. Kite $PQRS$ has diagonals $\overline{PR}$ and $\overline{QS}$ that intersect at T. Which of the following is the shortest segment from Q to $\overline{PR}$?

Ⓐ $\overline{PT}$ Ⓒ $\overline{RQ}$

Ⓑ $\overline{QP}$ Ⓓ $\overline{TQ}$

12. If the perimeter of an equilateral triangle is reduced by a factor of $\frac{1}{2}$, what is the effect on the area of the triangle?

Ⓕ The area remains constant.

Ⓖ The area is reduced by a factor of $\frac{1}{2}$.

Ⓗ The area is reduced by a factor of $\frac{1}{4}$.

Ⓙ The area is reduced by a factor of $\frac{1}{6}$.

13. The area of a right isosceles triangle is 36 m^2. What is the length of the hypotenuse of the triangle?

Ⓐ 6 meters Ⓒ 12 meters

Ⓑ $6\sqrt{2}$ meters Ⓓ $12\sqrt{2}$ meters

Gridded Response

14. The ratio of the side lengths of a triangle is 4:5:8. If the perimeter is 38.25 centimeters, what is the length in centimeters of the shortest side?

15. What is the geometric mean of 4 and 16?

16. For $\triangle HGJ$ and $\triangle LMK$ suppose that $\angle H \cong \angle L$, $HG = 4x + 5$, $KL = 9$, $HJ = 5x - 1$, and $LM = 13$. What must be the value of x to prove that $\triangle HGJ$ and $\triangle LMK$ are congruent by SAS?

17. If the length of a side of a regular hexagon is 2, what is the area of the hexagon to the nearest tenth?

18. What is the arc length of a semicircle in a circle with radius 5 millimeters? Round to the nearest hundredth.

19. What is the surface area of a sphere whose volume is 288π cubic centimeters? Round to the nearest hundredth.

20. The point $(a, -3)$ is on the circle with equation $x^2 + (y - 1)^2 = 25$ and lies in the third quadrant. What is the value of a?

Short Response

21. Use the diagram to find the value of x. Show your work or explain in words how you determined your answer.

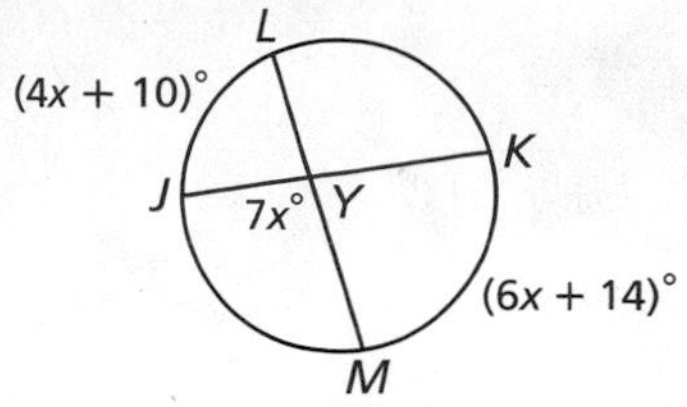

22. Paul needs to rent a storage unit. He finds one that has a length of 10 feet, a width of 5 feet, and a height of 9 feet. He finds a second storage unit that has a length of 11 feet, a width of 4 feet, and a height of 8 feet. Suppose that the first storage unit costs \$85.00 per month and that the second storage unit costs \$70.00 per month.

a. Which storage unit has a lower price per cubic foot? Show your work or explain in words how you determined your answer.

b. Paul finds a third storage unit that charges \$0.25 per cubic foot per month. What are possible dimensions of the storage unit if the charge is \$100.00 per month?

23. The equation of $\odot C$ is $x^2 + (y + 1)^2 = 25$.

a. Graph $\odot C$.

b. Write the equation of the line that is tangent to $\odot C$ at $(3, 3)$. Show your work or explain in words how you determined your answer.

24. A tangent and a secant intersect on a circle at the point of tangency and form an acute angle. Explain how you would find the range of possible measures for the intercepted arc.

Extended Response

25. Let $ABCD$ be a quadrilateral inscribed in a circle such that $\overline{AB} \parallel \overline{DC}$.

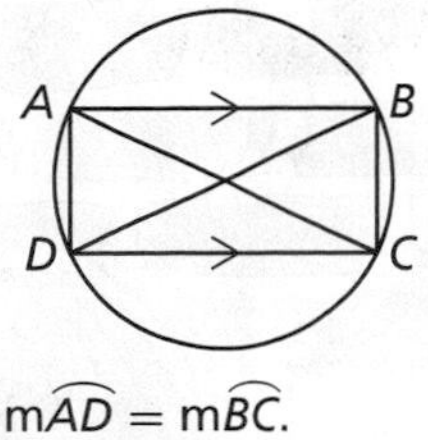

a. Prove that $m\widehat{AD} = m\widehat{BC}$.

b. Suppose $ABCD$ is a trapezoid. Show that $ABCD$ must be isosceles. Justify your answer.

c. If $ABCD$ is not a trapezoid, explain why $ABCD$ must be a rectangle.

CHAPTER

13 Probability

Chapter

- Apply concepts of probability to solve problems.
- Use tables and diagrams to find probabilities of compound events.

Wait a Second!

You can use probability and statistics to analyze *queuing,* the study of waiting in line.

Learn It Online
Chapter Project Online

ARE YOU READY?

Tree Diagrams

1. Natalie has three colors of wrapping paper (purple, blue, and yellow) and three colors of ribbon (gold, white, and red). Make a tree diagram showing all possible ways that she can wrap a present using one color of paper and one color of ribbon.

Ratios

For each circle, find the ratio of the shaded area to the entire area.

2.

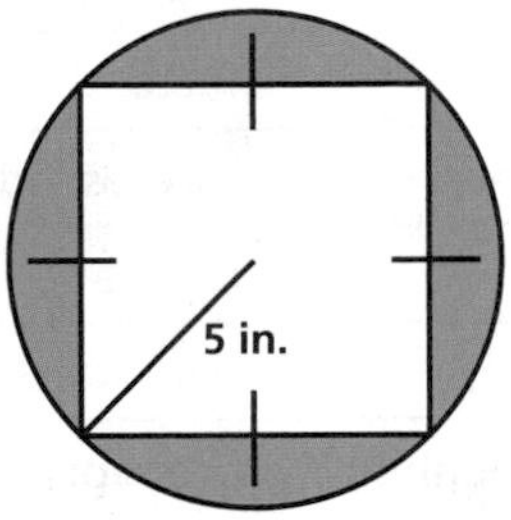

3.

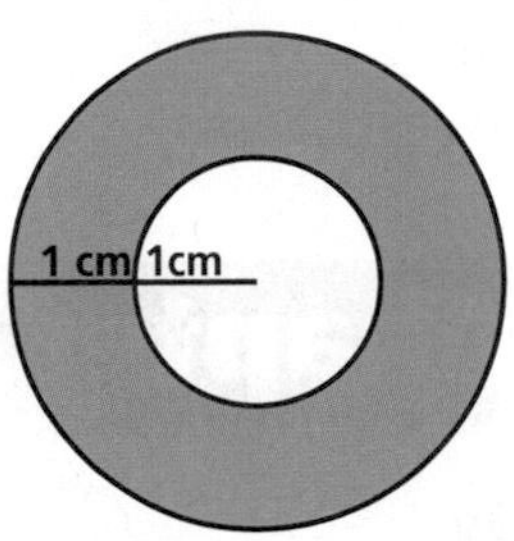

Add and Subtract Fractions

Add or subtract.

4. $1 - \frac{14}{20}$

5. $\frac{3}{8} + \frac{5}{6}$

6. $\frac{8}{15} - \frac{2}{5}$

7. $\frac{1}{12} + \frac{1}{10}$

Multiply and Divide Fractions

Multiply or divide.

8. $\frac{1}{2} \cdot \frac{3}{7}$

9. $2\frac{1}{3} \cdot \frac{1}{4}$

10. $\frac{4}{5} \div \frac{1}{2}$

11. $5\frac{1}{3} \div \frac{1}{4}$

Percent Problems

Solve.

12. What number is 7% of 150?

13. 90% of what number is 45?

14. A $24 item receives a price increase of 12%. How much was the price increased?

15. Twenty percent of the water in a large aquarium should be changed weekly. How much water should be changed each week if an aquarium holds 65 gallons of water?

CHAPTER 13

Study Guide: Preview

Where You've Been

Previously, you

- made tree diagrams to find the number of possible combinations of a group of objects.
- made lists to count and arrange objects.
- calculated measures of central tendency.

In This Chapter

You will study

- solving problems involving counting and arranging.
- finding theoretical, experimental, and binomial probabilities.
- two-way tables and conditional frequencies.

Where You're Going

You can use the skills in this chapter

- to find probabilities involved in games and events involving chance.
- to compare conditional probabilities.
- to make mathematically informed decisions.

Key Vocabulary/Vocabulario

binomial experiment	experimento binomial
combination	combinación
conditional probability	probabilidad condicional
dependent events	sucesos dependientes
experimental probability	probabilidad experimental
factorial	factorial
independent events	sucesos independientes
outcome	resultado
permutation	permutación
theoretical probability	probabilidad teórica

Vocabulary Connections

To become familiar with some of the vocabulary terms in the chapter, consider the following. You may refer to the chapter, the glossary, or a dictionary if you like.

1. A number is the product of its *factors*. What operation do you think is involved in finding a **factorial**?
2. A *theory* can be described as a sound and rational explanation. An *experiment* can be described as a procedure carried out in a controlled environment. Knowing this, how do you think **theoretical probability** differs from **experimental probability**?
3. A *conditional* is used to describe something that will be done only if another thing is done. Do you think **conditional probability** is used with **independent events** or **dependent events**? Why?
4. Each possible result of an experiment is an **outcome**. How many possible outcomes do you think a **binomial experiment** has? Why?

Reading and Writing Math

Writing Strategy: Translate Between Words and Math

It is important to correctly interpret the type of math being described by a verbal or written description. Listen/look for key words to help you translate between the words and the math.

15. In 1626, the Dutch bought Manhattan Island for $24 worth of merchandise. Suppose that, instead, $24 had been invested in an account that paid 3.5% interest **compounded** annually. Find the balance in 2008.

compounded: *Compounding indicates an exponential function.*

31. Gardeners check the pH level of soil to ensure a **pH** of 6 or 7. Soil is usually more acidic in areas where rainfall is high, whereas soil in dry areas is usually more alkaline. The pH level of a certain soil sample is 5.5. What is the difference in **hydrogen ion concentration**, or $[H^+]$, between the sample and an acceptable level?

pH

hydrogen ion concentration: *These terms indicate a logarithmic function.*

parabola: *A parabola indicates a quadratic function.*

27. You are given a **parabola** with two points that have the same *y*-value, $(-7, 11)$ and $(3, 11)$. Explain how to find the equation for the axis of symmetry of this parabola.

Try This

Identify the key word and the type of function being described.

1. Kelly invested $2000 in a savings account at a simple interest rate of 2.5%. How much money will she have in 8 months?
2. The diameter *d* in inches of a chain needed to move *p* pounds is given by the square root of 85*p*, divided by pi. How much more can be lifted with a chain 2.5 inches in diameter than by a rope 0.5 inch in diameter?
3. A technician took a blood sample from a patient and detected a toxin concentration of 0.01006 mg/cm^3. Two hours later, the technician took another sample and detected a concentration of 0.00881 mg/cm^3. Assume that the concentration varies exponentially with time. Write a function to model the data.
4. Students found that the number of mosquitoes per acre of wetland grows by about 10 to the power $\frac{1}{2}d + 2$, where *d* is the number of days since the last frost. Write and graph the function representing the number of mosquitoes on each day.

COMMON CORE

13-1 Permutations and Combinations

CC.9-12.S.CP.9 (+) Use permutations and combinations to compute probabilities…and solve problems.

Objectives

Solve problems involving the Fundamental Counting Principle.

Solve problems involving permutations and combinations.

Vocabulary

Fundamental Counting Principle
permutation
factorial
combination

Why learn this?

Permutations can be used to determine the number of ways to select and arrange artwork so as to give a new look each day. (See Example 2B.)

You have previously used tree diagrams to find the number of possible combinations of a group of objects. In this lesson, you will learn to use the **Fundamental Counting Principle**.

Know it! Note

Fundamental Counting Principle

If there are n items and m_1 ways to choose a first item, m_2 ways to choose a second item after the first item has been chosen, and so on, then there are $m_1 \cdot m_2 \cdot \ldots \cdot m_n$ ways to choose n items.

EXAMPLE 1 Using the Fundamental Counting Principle

A **For the lunch special, you can choose an entrée, a drink, and one side dish. How many meal choices are there?**

number of main dishes	times	number of beverages	times	number of sides	equals	number of choices
3	×	4	×	3	=	36

There are 36 meal choices.

B **In Utah, a license plate consists of 3 digits followed by 3 letters. The letters *I*, *O*, and *Q* are not used, and each digit or letter may be used more than once. How many different license plates are possible?**

digit		*digit*		*digit*		*letter*		*letter*		*letter*	
10	×	10	×	10	×	23	×	23	×	23	= 12,167,000

There are 12,167,000 possible license plates.

Helpful Hint

In Example 1B, there are 10 possible digits and 26 − 3 = 23 possible letters.

CHECK IT OUT!

1a. A "make-your-own-adventure" story lets you choose 6 starting points, gives 4 plot choices, and then has 5 possible endings. How many adventures are there?

1b. A password is 4 letters followed by 1 digit. Uppercase letters (A) and lowercase letters (a) may be used and are considered different. How many passwords are possible?

A **permutation** is a selection of a group of objects in which order is important.

There is one way to arrange one item A.

A second item B can be placed first or second.

A third item C can be first, second, or third for each order above.

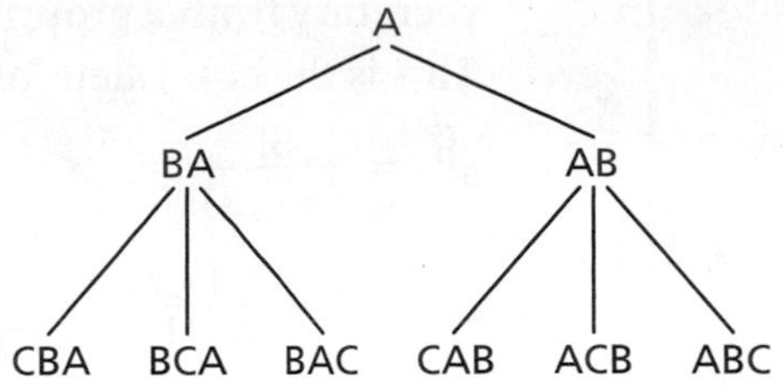

1 permutation

2 • 1 permutations

3 • 2 • 1 permutations

You can see that the number of permutations of 3 items is 3 • 2 • 1. You can extend this to permutations of n items, which is $n \cdot (n-1) \cdot (n-2) \cdot (n-3) \cdot \ldots \cdot 1$. This expression is called *n factorial*, and is written as $n!$.

Know it! Note

n Factorial

For any whole number *n*,

WORDS	NUMBERS	ALGEBRA
The **factorial** of a number is the product of the natural numbers less than or equal to the number. 0! is defined as 1.	$6! =$ $6 \cdot 5 \cdot 4 \cdot 3 \cdot 2 \cdot 1 = 720$	$n! =$ $n \cdot (n-1) \cdot (n-2) \cdot (n-3) \cdot \ldots \cdot 1$

Sometimes you may not want to order an entire set of items. Suppose that you want to select and order 3 people from a group of 7. One way to find possible permutations is to use the Fundamental Counting Principle.

First Person		Second Person		Third Person		
7 choices	•	6 choices	•	5 choices	=	210 permutations

There are 7 people. You are choosing 3 of them in order.

Another way to find the possible permutations is to use factorials. You can divide the total number of arrangements by the number of arrangements that are not used. In the example above, there are 7 total people and 4 whose arrangements do not matter.

$$\frac{\text{arrangements of 7 people}}{\text{arrangements of 4 people}} = \frac{7!}{4!} = \frac{7 \cdot 6 \cdot 5 \cdot \cancel{4} \cdot \cancel{3} \cdot \cancel{2} \cdot \cancel{1}}{\cancel{4} \cdot \cancel{3} \cdot \cancel{2} \cdot \cancel{1}} = 210$$

This can be generalized as a formula, which is useful for large numbers of items.

Know it! Note

Permutations

NUMBERS	ALGEBRA
The number of permutations of 7 items taken 3 at a time is $_7P_3 = \frac{7!}{(7-3)!} = \frac{7!}{4!}$.	The number of permutations of n items taken r at a time is $_nP_r = \frac{n!}{(n-r)!}$.

EXAMPLE 2 Finding Permutations

A **How many ways can a club select a president, a vice president, and a secretary from a group of 5 people?**

This is the equivalent of selecting and arranging 3 items from 5.

$$_5P_3 = \frac{5!}{(5-3)!} = \frac{5!}{2!} \qquad \textit{Substitute 5 for n and 3 for r in } \frac{n!}{(n-r)!}.$$

$$= \frac{5 \cdot 4 \cdot 3 \cdot \cancel{2 \cdot 1}}{\cancel{2 \cdot 1}} \qquad \textit{Divide out common factors.}$$

$$= 5 \cdot 4 \cdot 3 = 60$$

There are 60 ways to select the 3 people.

B **An art gallery has 9 fine-art photographs from an artist and will display 4 from left to right along a wall. In how many ways can the gallery select and display the 4 photographs?**

$$_9P_4 = \frac{9!}{(9-4)!} = \frac{9!}{5!} = \frac{9 \cdot 8 \cdot 7 \cdot 6 \cdot \cancel{5 \cdot 4 \cdot 3 \cdot 2 \cdot 1}}{\cancel{5 \cdot 4 \cdot 3 \cdot 2 \cdot 1}} \qquad \textit{Divide out common factors.}$$

$$= 9 \cdot 8 \cdot 7 \cdot 6$$

$$= 3024$$

There are 3024 ways that the gallery can select and display the photographs.

Helpful Hint

The number of factors left after dividing is the number of items selected. In Example 2B, there are 4 photographs and 4 factors in $9 \cdot 8 \cdot 7 \cdot 6$.

CHECK IT OUT!

2a. Awards are given out at a costume party. How many ways can "most creative," "silliest," and "best" costume be awarded to 8 contestants if no one gets more than one award?

2b. How many ways can a 2-digit number be formed by using only the digits 5–9 and by each digit being used only once?

A **combination** is a grouping of items in which order does not matter. There are generally fewer ways to select items when order does not matter. For example, there are 6 ways to order 3 items, but they are all the same combination:

6 permutations → {ABC, ACB, BAC, BCA, CAB, CBA}

1 combination → {ABC}

To find the number of combinations, the formula for permutations can be modified.

$$\textbf{number of permutations} = \frac{\textbf{ways to arrange all items}}{\textbf{ways to arrange items not selected}}$$

Because order does not matter, divide the number of permutations by the number of ways to arrange the selected items.

$$\textbf{number of combinations} = \frac{\textbf{ways to arrange all items}}{\textbf{(ways to arrange selected items)(ways to arrange items not selected)}}$$

Know it! Note

Combinations

NUMBERS	ALGEBRA
The number of combinations of 7 items taken 3 at a time is $_7C_3 = \frac{7!}{3!(7-3)!}$.	The number of combinations of n items taken r at a time is $_nC_r = \frac{n!}{r!(n-r)!}$.

When deciding whether to use permutations or combinations, first decide whether order is important. Use a permutation if order matters and a combination if order does not matter.

EXAMPLE 3 *Pet Adoption Application*

Katie is going to adopt kittens from a litter of 11. How many ways can she choose a group of 3 kittens?

Step 1 Determine whether the problem represents a permutation or combination.

The order does not matter. The group Kitty, Smoky, and Tigger is the same as Tigger, Kitty, and Smoky. It is a combination.

Step 2 Use the formula for combinations.

$$_{11}C_3 = \frac{11!}{3!(11-3)!} = \frac{11!}{3!(8!)} \quad n = 11 \text{ and } r = 3$$

$$= \frac{11 \cdot 10 \cdot 9 \cdot \cancel{8 \cdot 7 \cdot 6 \cdot 5 \cdot 4 \cdot 3 \cdot 2 \cdot 1}}{3 \cdot 2 \cdot 1(\cancel{8 \cdot 7 \cdot 6 \cdot 5 \cdot 4 \cdot 3 \cdot 2 \cdot 1})} \quad \text{Divide out common factors.}$$

$$= \frac{11 \cdot 10 \cdot 9}{3 \cdot 2 \cdot 1} = \frac{11 \cdot \cancel{10}^5 \cdot \cancel{9}^3}{{}_1\cancel{3} \cdot {}_1\cancel{2} \cdot 1} = 165$$

There are 165 ways to select a group of 3 kittens from 11.

Helpful Hint

You can find permutations and combinations by using **nPr** and **nCr**, respectively, on scientific and graphing calculators.

CHECK IT OUT! 3. The swim team has 8 swimmers. Two swimmers will be selected to swim in the first heat. How many ways can the swimmers be selected?

MATHEMATICAL PRACTICES

THINK AND DISCUSS

1. Give a situation in which order matters and one in which order does not matter.
2. Give the value of $_nC_n$, where n is any integer. Explain your answer.
3. Tell what $_3C_4$ would mean in the real world and why it is not possible.
4. **GET ORGANIZED** Copy and complete the graphic organizer.

Know it! Note

	Fundamental Counting Principle	Permutation	Combination
Formula			
Examples			

13-1 Exercises

Learn It Online
Homework Help Online
Parent Resources Online

GUIDED PRACTICE

1. **Vocabulary** When you open a rotating combination lock, order is __?__ (*important* or *not important*), so this is a __?__ (*permutation* or *combination*).

SEE EXAMPLE 1

2. Jamie purchased 3 blouses, 3 jackets, and 2 skirts. How many different outfits using a blouse, a jacket, and a skirt are possible?
3. An Internet code consists of one digit followed by one letter. The number zero and the letter *O* are excluded. How many codes are possible?

SEE EXAMPLE 2

4. Nate is on a 7-day vacation. He plans to spend one day jet skiing and one day golfing. How many ways can Nate schedule the 2 activities?
5. How many ways can you listen to 3 songs from a CD that has 12 selections?
6. Members from 6 different school organizations decorated floats for the homecoming parade. How many different ways can first, second, and third prize be awarded?

SEE EXAMPLE 3

7. A teacher wants to send 4 students to the library each day. There are 21 students in the class. How many ways can he choose 4 students to go to the library on the first day?
8. Gregory has a coupon for $1 off the purchase of 3 boxes of Munchie brand cereal. The store has 5 different varieties of Munchie brand cereal. How many ways can Gregory choose 3 boxes of cereal so that each box is a different variety?

PRACTICE AND PROBLEM SOLVING

Independent Practice

For Exercises	See Example
9–10	1
11–13	2
14	3

Extra Practice

See Extra Practice for more Skills Practice and Applications Practice exercises.

9. **Hiking** A hiker can take 4 trails to the lake and then 3 trails from the lake to the cabins. How many routes are there from the lake to the cabins?
10. The cheerleading squad is making posters. They have 3 different colors of poster board and 4 different colors of markers. How many different posters can be made by using one poster board and one marker?
11. How many ways can you choose a manager and assistant from a 9-person task force?
12. How many identification codes are possible by using 3 letters if no letter may be repeated?
13. There are 5 airplanes ready to depart. Runway A and runway D are available. How many ways can 2 planes be assigned to runways without using the same runway?
14. **Food** How many choices of 3 hamburger toppings are possible?

15. **What if...?** In the United Kingdom's National Lottery, you must correctly select a group of 6 numbers from 49. Suppose that the contest were changed to selecting 7 numbers. How many more ways would there be to select the numbers?

Evaluate.

16. $_6P_6$
17. $_5C_5$
18. $_9P_1$
19. $_6C_1$
20. $\frac{2!}{6!}$
21. $\frac{4!3!}{2!}$
22. $\frac{9!}{7!}$
23. $\frac{8! - 5!}{(8-5)!}$

Geometry Find the number of ways that each selection can be made.

24. two marked points to determine slope

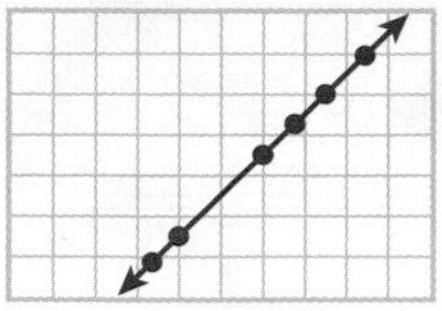

25. four points to form a quadrilateral

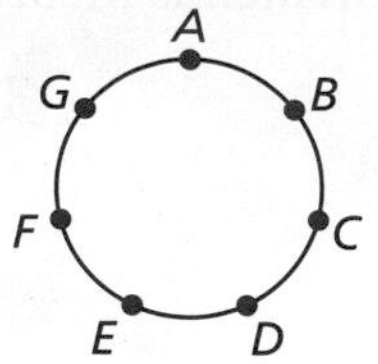

Compare. Write >, <, or =.

26. ${}_7P_3$ ■ ${}_7C_4$ 27. ${}_7P_4$ ■ ${}_7P_3$ 28. ${}_7C_3$ ■ ${}_7C_4$ 29. ${}_{10}C_{10}$ ■ ${}_{10}P_{10}$

30. Copy and complete the table. Use the table to explain why 0! is defined as 1.

$n!$	4!	3!	2!	1!
$n(n-1)!$	4(3!) = 24	■	■	■

LINK

Music

There are many change-ringing societies and groups, especially in the United Kingdom. Bell ringers work together to follow patterns and called changes to avoid repeating sequences.

31. **Critical Thinking** Why are there more unique permutations of the letters in YOUNG than in GEESE?

32. **Music** In change ringing, a *peal* is the ringing of all possible sequences of a number of bells. Suppose that 8 bells are used and it takes 0.25 second to ring each bell. How long would it take to ring a complete peal?

33. **Multi-Step** Amy, Bob, Charles, Dena, and Esther are club officers.
   a. Copy and complete the table to show the ways that a president, a vice president, and a secretary can be chosen if Amy is chosen president. (Use first initials for names.)

President	A	A	A	A	A	A	A	A	A	A	A	A
Vice President	B	B	B	C	C	C	■	■	■	■	■	■
Secretary	C	D	E	■	■	■	■	■	■	■	■	■

   b. Extend the table to show the number of ways that the three officers can be chosen if Bob is chosen president. Make a conjecture as to the number of ways that a president, a vice president, and a secretary can be chosen.
   c. Use a formula to find the number of different ways that a president, a vice president, and a secretary can be chosen. Compare your result with part **b.**
   d. How many different ways can 3 club officers be chosen to form a committee? Compare this with the answer to part **c.** Which answer is a number of permutations? Which answer is a number of combinations?

34. **Critical Thinking** Use the formulas to divide ${}_nP_r$ by ${}_nC_r$. Predict the result of dividing ${}_6P_3$ by ${}_6C_3$. Check your prediction. What meaning does the result have?

35. **Write About It** Find ${}_9C_2$ and ${}_9C_7$. Find ${}_{10}C_6$ and ${}_{10}C_4$. Explain the results.

MULTI-STEP TEST PREP

36. While playing the game of Yahtzee, Jen rolls 5 dice and gets the result shown at right.
   a. How many different ways can she arrange the dice from left to right?
   b. How many different ways can she choose 3 of the dice to reroll?

37. **ERROR ANALYSIS** Below are two solutions for "How many Internet codes can be made by using 3 digits if 0 is excluded and digits may not be repeated?" Which is incorrect? Explain the error.

A

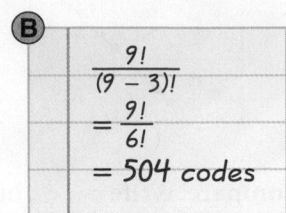

$$\frac{9!}{3!(9-3)!} = \frac{9!}{3!6!} = 84 \text{ codes}$$

B

$$\frac{9!}{(9-3)!} = \frac{9!}{6!} = 504 \text{ codes}$$

38. **Critical Thinking** Explain how to use the Fundamental Counting Principle to answer the question in Exercise 37.

TEST PREP

39. There are 14 players on the team. Which of the following expressions models the number of ways that the coach can choose 5 players to start the game?

Ⓐ $5!$ Ⓑ $\frac{14!}{5!}$ Ⓒ $\frac{14!}{9!}$ Ⓓ $\frac{14!}{5!9!}$

40. Which of the following has the same value as ${}_9C_4$?

Ⓕ ${}_9P_4$ Ⓖ ${}_4C_9$ Ⓗ ${}_9P_5$ Ⓙ ${}_9C_5$

41. **Short Response** Rene can choose 1 elective each of the 4 years that she is in high school. There are 15 electives. How many ways can Rene choose her electives?

CHALLENGE AND EXTEND

42. **Geometry** Consider a circle with two points, A and B. You can form exactly 1 segment, $\overline{AB}$. If there are 3 points, you can form 3 segments as shown in the diagram.

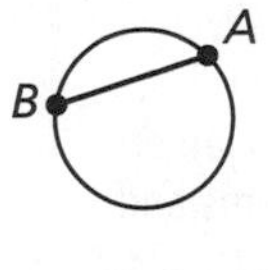

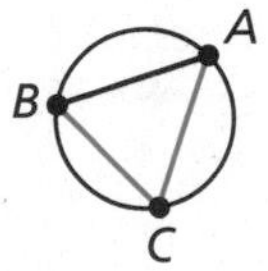

a. How many segments can be formed from 4 points, 5 points, 6 points, and n points? Write your answer for n points as a permutation or combination.

b. How many segments can be formed from 20 points?

43. **Government** How many ways can a jury of 12 and 2 alternate jurors be selected from a pool of 30 potential jurors? (*Hint:* Consider how order is both important and unimportant in selection.) Leave your answer in unexpanded notation.

Connecting Algebra to Geometry

Relative Area

In *geometric probability*, the probability of an event corresponds to ratios of the areas (or lengths or volumes) or parts of one or more figures.

In the spinners shown, the probability of landing on a color is based on relative area.

$\frac{1}{2}$ shaded $\quad$ $\frac{3}{8}$ shaded $\quad$ $\frac{1}{4}$ shaded

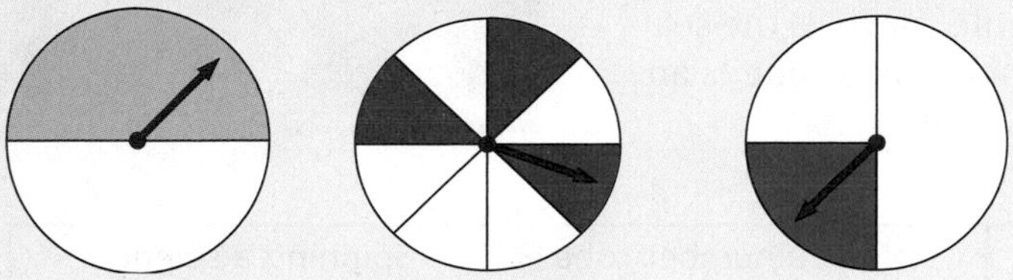

Use the area formulas at right to help you determine relative area.

Area Formulas	
Figure	**Formula**
Rectangle	$A = bh$
Square	$A = s^2$
Triangle	$A = \frac{1}{2}bh$
Trapezoid	$A = \frac{1}{2}h(b_1 + b_2)$
Circle	$A = \pi r^2$

Example

What portion of the rectangle is shaded? Write the relative area as a fraction, a decimal, and a percent.

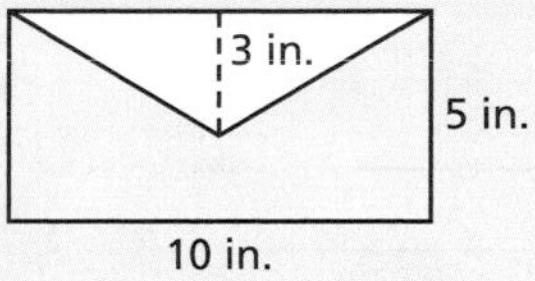

Find the ratio of the area of the shaded region to the area of the rectangle.

$A = 10(5) = 50 \text{ in}^2$ *Area of the rectangle: A = bh*

$A = \frac{1}{2}(3)(10) = 15 \text{ in}^2$ *Area of the unshaded triangle: A = $\frac{1}{2}$bh*

$$\frac{\text{area of shaded region}}{\text{area of the rectangle}} = \frac{50 - 15}{50} = \frac{35}{50} = \frac{7}{10} = 0.7, \text{ or } 70\%$$

Try This

What portion of each figure is shaded? Write the relative area as a fraction, a decimal, and a percent.

1. 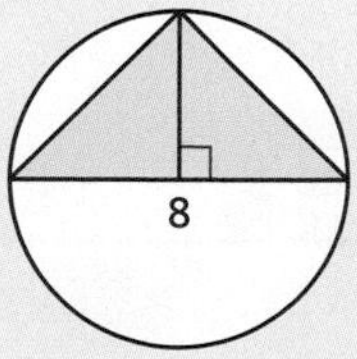

2. 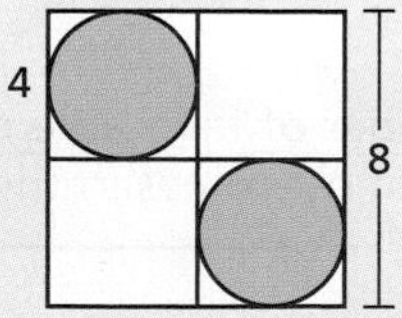

3. 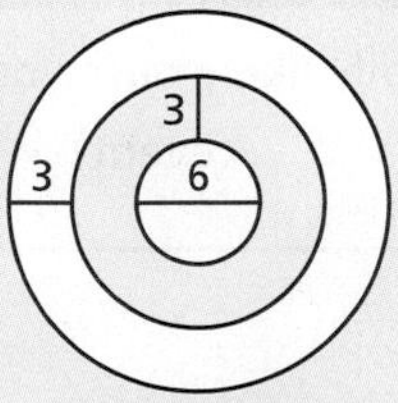

4. 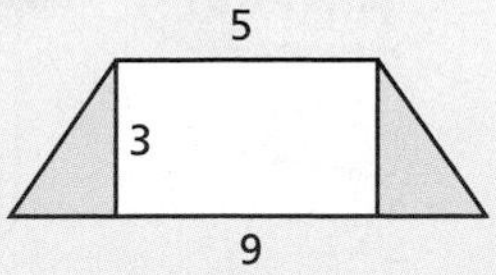

5. Write the relative area of each sector of the spinner as a fraction, decimal, and percent.

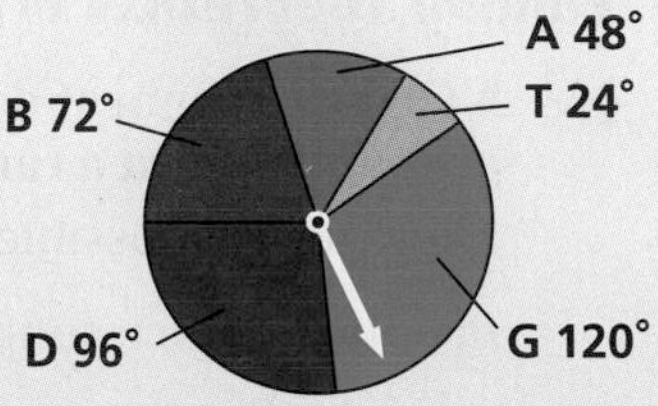

COMMON CORE

13-2 Theoretical and Experimental Probability

CC.9-12.S.MD.7 (+) Analyze decisions and strategies using probability concepts ... *Also* CC.9-12.S.CP.9 (+)

Objectives

Find the theoretical probability of an event.

Find the experimental probability of an event.

Vocabulary

probability
outcome
sample space
event
equally likely outcomes
favorable outcomes
theoretical probability
complement
geometric probability
experiment
trial
experimental probability

Why learn this?

You can use probability to find the chances of hitting or missing a target in the game Battleship. (See Example 2.)

Probability is the measure of how likely an event is to occur. Each possible result of a probability experiment or situation is an **outcome**. The **sample space** is the set of all possible outcomes. An **event** is an outcome or set of outcomes.

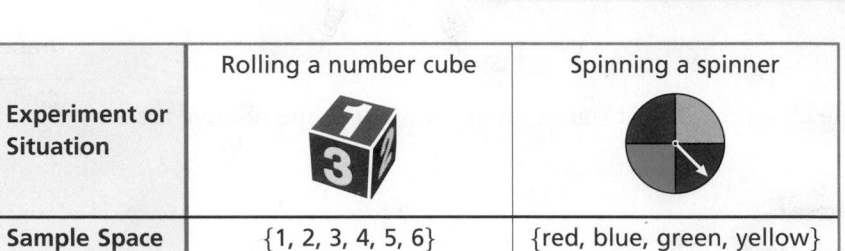

Experiment or Situation	Rolling a number cube 	Spinning a spinner 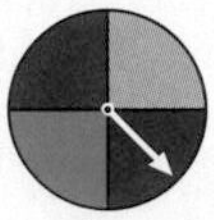
Sample Space	{1, 2, 3, 4, 5, 6}	{red, blue, green, yellow}

Probabilities are written as fractions or decimals from 0 to 1, or as percents from 0% to 100%.

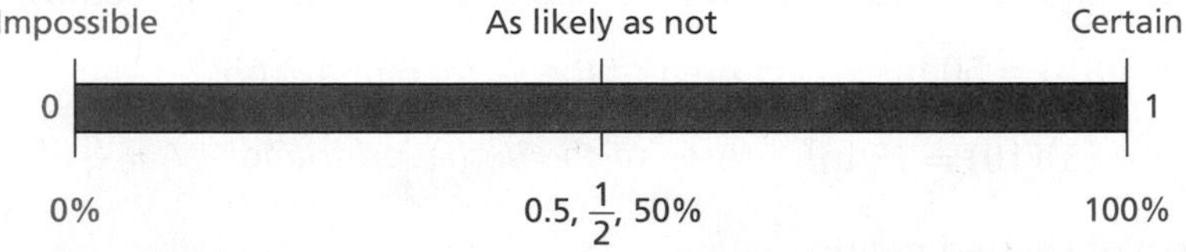

Equally likely outcomes have the same chance of occurring. When you toss a fair coin, heads and tails are equally likely outcomes. **Favorable outcomes** are outcomes in a specified event. For equally likely outcomes, the **theoretical probability** of an event is the ratio of the number of favorable outcomes to the total number of outcomes.

Know it! Note

Theoretical Probability

For equally likely outcomes,

$$P(\text{event}) = \frac{\text{number of favorable outcomes}}{\text{number of outcomes in the sample space}}.$$

EXAMPLE 1 Finding Theoretical Probability

A **A CD has 5 upbeat dance songs and 7 slow ballads. What is the probability that a randomly selected song is an upbeat dance song?**

There are 12 possible outcomes and 5 favorable outcomes.

$P(\text{upbeat dance song}) = \frac{5}{12} \approx 41.7\%$

B **A red number cube and a blue number cube are rolled. If all numbers are equally likely, what is the probability that the sum is 10?**

There are 36 possible outcomes.

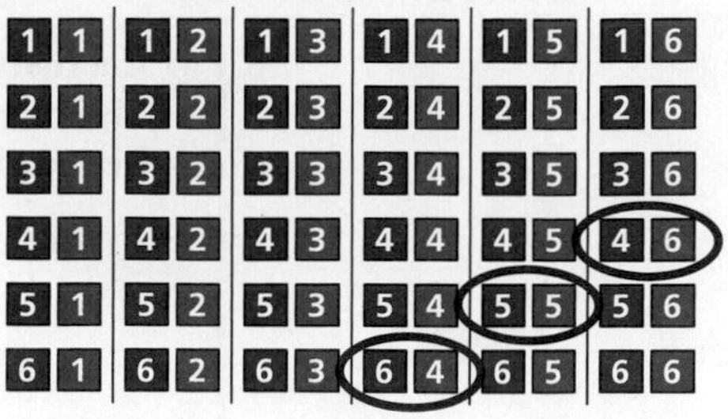

$$P(\text{sum is } 10) = \frac{\text{number of outcomes with sum of } 10}{36}$$

$$P(\text{sum is } 10) = \frac{3}{36} = \frac{1}{12}$$ *3 outcomes with a sum of 10: (4, 6) (5, 5), and (6, 4)*

CHECK IT OUT! **A red number cube and a blue number cube are rolled. If all numbers are equally likely, what is the probability of each event?**

1a. The sum is 6.

1b. The difference is 6.

1c. The red cube is greater.

The sum of all probabilities in the sample space is 1. The **complement** of an event E is the set of all outcomes in the sample space that are not in E.

Know it! Note

Complement

The probability of the complement of event E is

$$P(\text{not } E) = 1 - P(E).$$

EXAMPLE 2 *Entertainment Application*

The game Battleship is played with 5 ships on a 100-hole grid. Players try to guess the locations of their opponent's ships and sink them. At the start of the game, what is the probability that the first shot misses all targets?

$P(\text{miss}) = 1 - P(\text{hit})$ *Use the complement.*

$P(\text{miss}) = 1 - \frac{17}{100}$ *There are 17 total holes covered by game pieces.*

$= \frac{83}{100}$, or 83%

There is an 83% chance of the first shot missing all targets.

Battleship Pieces

Game Piece	Number of Holes Covered
Destroyer	2
Cruiser	3
Submarine	3
Battleship	4
Carrier	5

CHECK IT OUT! **2.** Two integers from 1 to 10 are randomly selected. The same number may be chosen twice. What is the probability that both numbers are less than 9?

EXAMPLE 3 Finding Probability with Permutations or Combinations

Each student received a 4-digit code to use the library computers, with no digit repeated. Manu received the code 7654. What was the probability that he would receive a code of consecutive numbers?

Step 1 Determine whether the code is a permutation or a combination.

Order is important, so it is a permutation.

Step 2 Find the number of outcomes in the sample space.

The sample space is the number of permutations of 4 of 10 digits.

$$_{10}P_4 = \frac{10!}{6!} = \frac{10 \cdot 9 \cdot 8 \cdot 7 \cdot \cancel{6 \cdot 5 \cdot 4 \cdot 3 \cdot 2 \cdot 1}}{\cancel{6 \cdot 5 \cdot 4 \cdot 3 \cdot 2 \cdot 1}} = 5040$$

Step 3 Find the favorable outcomes.

The favorable outcomes are the codes 0123, 1234, 2345, 3456, 4567, 5678, 6789, and the reverse of each of these numbers. There are 14 favorable outcomes.

Step 4 Find the probability.

$$P(\text{consecutive numbers}) = \frac{14}{5040} = \frac{1}{360}$$

The probability that Manu would receive a code of consecutive numbers was $\frac{1}{360}$.

CHECK IT OUT! **3.** A DJ randomly selects 2 of 8 ads to play before her show. Two of the ads are by a local retailer. What is the probability that she will play both of the retailer's ads before her show?

Geometric probability is a form of theoretical probability determined by a ratio of lengths, areas, or volumes.

EXAMPLE 4 Finding Geometric Probability

Three semicircles with diameters 2, 4, and 6 cm are arranged as shown in the figure. If a point inside the figure is chosen at random, what is the probability that the point is inside the shaded region?

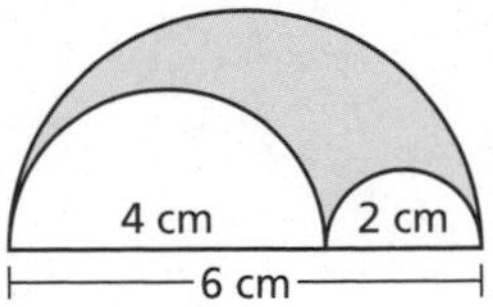

Find the ratio of the area of the shaded region to the area of the entire semicircle. The area of a semicircle is $\frac{1}{2}\pi r^2$.

First, find the area of the entire semicircle.

$$A_t = \frac{1}{2}\pi(3^2) = 4.5\pi$$ *Total area of largest semicircle*

Next, find the unshaded area.

$$A_u = \left[\frac{1}{2}\pi(2^2)\right] + \left[\frac{1}{2}\pi(1^2)\right] = 2\pi + 0.5\pi = 2.5\pi$$ *Sum of areas of the unshaded semicircles*

Subtract to find the shaded area.

$$A_s = 4.5\pi - 2.5\pi = 2\pi$$ *Area of shaded region*

$$\frac{A_s}{A_t} = \frac{2\pi}{4.5\pi} = \frac{2}{4.5} = \frac{4}{9}$$ *Ratio of shaded region to total area*

The probability that the point is in the shaded region is $\frac{4}{9}$.

CHECK IT OUT! **4.** Find the probability that a point chosen at random inside the large triangle is in the small triangle.

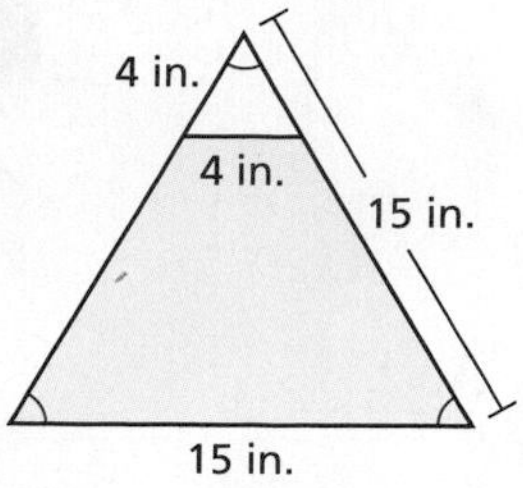

You can estimate the probability of an event by using data, or by **experiment**. For example, if a doctor states that an operation "has an 80% probability of success," 80% is an estimate of probability based on similar case histories.

Each repetition of an experiment is a **trial**. The sample space of an experiment is the set of all possible outcomes. The **experimental probability** of an event is the ratio of the number of times that the event occurs, the *frequency*, to the number of trials.

Know it! Note

Experimental Probability

$$\text{experimental probability} = \frac{\text{number of times the event occurs}}{\text{number of trials}}$$

Experimental probability is often used to estimate theoretical probability and to make predictions.

EXAMPLE 5 Finding Experimental Probability

The bar graph shows the results of 100 tosses of an oddly shaped number cube. Find each experimental probability.

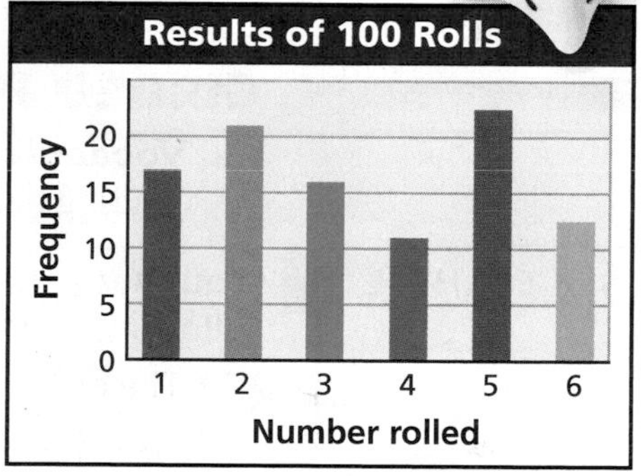

A **rolling a 3**

The outcome 3 occurred 16 times out of 100 trials.

$$P(3) = \frac{16}{100} = \frac{4}{25} = 0.16$$

Helpful Hint

Frequencies must be whole numbers, so they can be easily read from the graph in Example 5.

B **rolling a perfect square**

$$P(\text{perfect square}) = \frac{17 + 11}{100}$$

$$= \frac{28}{100} = \frac{7}{25} = 0.28$$

The numbers 1 and 4 are perfect squares. 1 occurred 17 times and 4 occurred 11 times.

C **rolling a number other than 5**

Use the complement.

$$P(5) = \frac{22}{100}$$

5 occurred 22 times out of 100 trials.

$$1 - P(5) = 1 - \frac{22}{100} = \frac{78}{100} = \frac{39}{50} = 0.78$$

CHECK IT OUT! **5.** The table shows the results of choosing one card from a deck of cards, recording the suit, and then replacing the card.

Card Suit	Hearts	Diamonds	Clubs	Spades
Number	5	9	7	5

5a. Find the experimental probability of choosing a diamond.

5b. Find the experimental probability of choosing a card that is not a club.

MATHEMATICAL PRACTICES

THINK AND DISCUSS

1. Explain whether the probability of an event can be 1.5.
2. Tell which events have the same probability when two number cubes are tossed: sum of 7, sum of 5, sum of 9, and sum of 11.
3. Compare the theoretical and experimental probabilities of getting heads when tossing a coin if Joe got heads 8 times in 20 tosses of the coin.
4. **GET ORGANIZED** Copy and complete the graphic organizer. Give an example of each probability concept.

Know it! Note

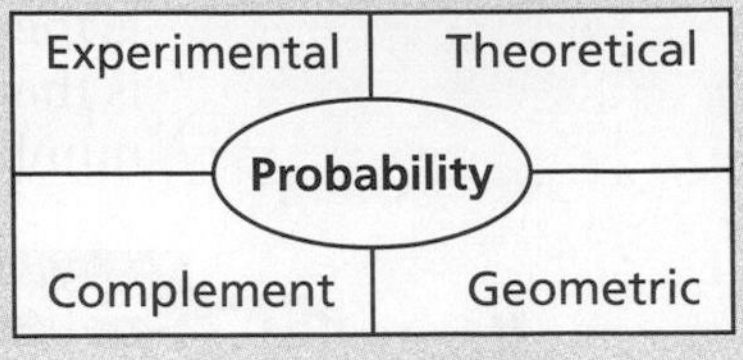

13-2 Exercises

Learn It Online
Homework Help Online
Parent Resources Online

GUIDED PRACTICE

1. **Vocabulary** A fair coin is tossed 8 times and lands heads up 3 times. The __?__ of landing heads is $\frac{1}{2}$. (*theoretical probability* or *experimental probability*)

SEE EXAMPLE 1

A quarter, a nickel, and a penny are flipped. Find the probability of each of the following.

2. The quarter shows heads.
3. The penny and nickel show heads.
4. One coin shows heads.
5. All three coins land the same way.

SEE EXAMPLE 2

6. What is the probability that a random 2-digit number (00-99) does not end in 5?
7. What is the probability that a randomly selected date in one year is not in the month of December or January?

SEE EXAMPLE 3

8. A clerk has 4 different letters that need to go in 4 different envelopes. What is the probability that all 4 letters are placed in the correct envelopes?
9. There are 12 balloons in a bag: 3 each of blue, green, red, and yellow. Three balloons are chosen at random. Find the probability that all 3 of the balloons are green.

SEE EXAMPLE 4

Use the diagram for Exercises 10 and 11. Find each probability.

10. that a point chosen at random is in the shaded area
11. that a point chosen at random is in the smallest circle

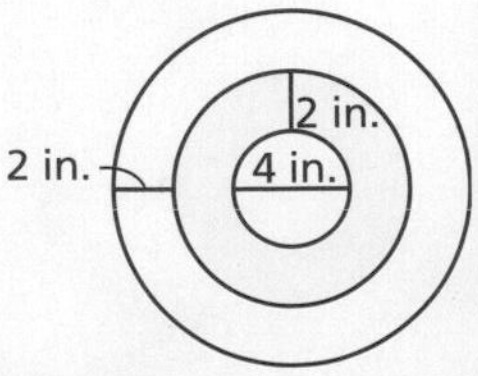

SEE EXAMPLE 5

Use the table for Exercises 12 and 13.

12. Find the experimental probability of spinning red.
13. Find the experimental probability of spinning red or blue.

Spinner Experiment

Color	Red	Green	Blue
Spins	5	8	7

PRACTICE AND PROBLEM SOLVING

Independent Practice

For Exercises	See Example
14–15	1
16	2
17–18	3
19	4
20	5

Extra Practice

See Extra Practice for more Skills Practice and Applications Practice exercises.

There are 3 green marbles, 7 red marbles, and 5 white marbles in a bag. Find the probability of each of the following.

14. The chosen marble is white.

15. The chosen marble is red or white.

16. Two integers from 1 to 8 are randomly selected. The same number can be chosen both times. What is the probability that both numbers are greater than 2?

17. Swimming The coach randomly selects 3 swimmers from a team of 8 to swim in a heat. What is the probability that she will choose the three strongest swimmers?

18. Books There are 7 books numbered 1–7 on the summer reading list. Peter randomly chooses 2 books. What is the probability that Peter chooses books numbered 1 and 2?

19. Games In the game of corntoss, players throw corn-filled bags at a hole in a wooden platform. If a bag that hits the platform can hit any location with an equal likelihood, find the probability that a tossed bag lands in the hole.

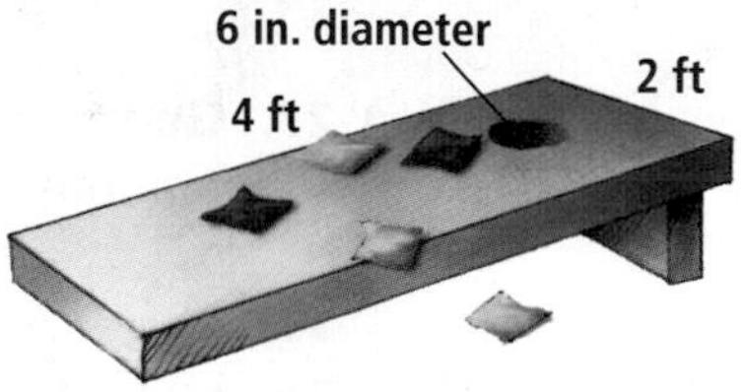

20. Cards An experiment consists of choosing one card from a standard deck and then replacing it. The experiment was done several times, and the results are: 8 hearts, 8 diamonds, 6 spades, and 6 clubs. Find the experimental probability that a card is red.

21. Critical Thinking Explain whether the experimental probability of tossing tails when a fair coin is tossed 25 times is always, sometimes, or never equal to the theoretical probability.

22. Games A radio station in Mississippi is giving away a trip to the Mississippi coast from any other state in the United States. Assuming an equally likely chance for a winner from any other state, what is the probability that the winner will be from a state that does not border Mississippi?

23. Geometry **Use the figure.**

a. A circle with radius r is inscribed in a square with side length $2r$. What is the ratio of the area of the circle to the area of the square?

b. A square board has an inscribed circle with a 15 in. radius. A small button is dropped 10,000 times on the board, landing inside the circle 7852 times. How can you use this experiment to estimate a value for π?

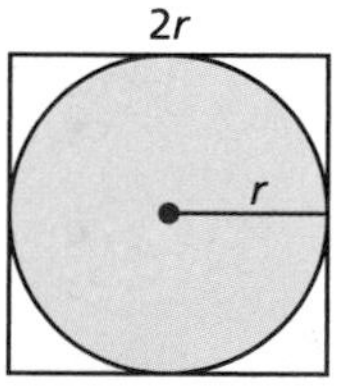

24. Games The sides of a backgammon die are marked with the numbers 2, 4, 8, 16, 32, and 64. Describe an outcome that has a probability of $\frac{2}{3}$.

25. Computer A player in a computer basketball program has a constant probability of making each free throw. Jack notes the success rate over a period of time.

a. Find the experimental probability for each set of 25 attempts as a decimal.

b. Find the experimental probability for the entire experiment.

c. What is the best estimate of the theoretical probability? Justify your answer.

Free Throw Shooting

Attempts	Free Throws Made
1–25	17
26–50	21
51–75	19
76–100	16

MULTI-STEP TEST PREP

26. While playing Yahtzee and rolling 5 dice, Mei gets the result shown at right. Mei decides to keep the three 4's and reroll the other 2 dice.

a. What is the probability that Mei will have 5 of a kind?

b. What is the probability that she will have 4 of a kind (four 4's plus something else)?

c. What is the probability that she will have exactly three 4's?

d. How are the answers to parts **a, b,** and **c** related?

27. Geometry The points along $\overline{AF}$ are evenly spaced. A point is randomly chosen. Find the probability that the point lies on $\overline{BD}$.

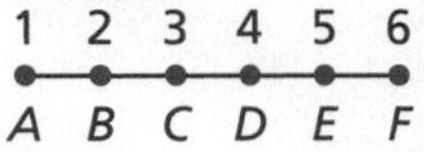

Weather **Use the graph and the following information for Exercises 28–30.**

The table shows the number of days that the maximum temperature was above 90°F in Death Valley National Park in 2002.

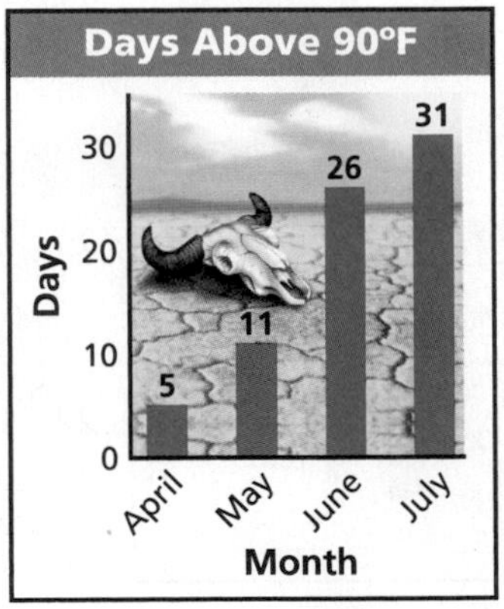

28. What is the experimental probability that the maximum temperature will be greater than 90°F on a given day in April?

29. For what month would you estimate the theoretical probability of a maximum temperature no greater than 90°F to be about 0.13? Explain.

30. May has 31 days. How would the experimental probability be affected if someone mistakenly used 30 days to calculate the experimental probability that the maximum temperature will not be greater than 90°F on a given day in May?

31. Critical Thinking Is it possible for the experimental probability of an event to be 0 if the theoretical probability is 1? Is it possible for the experimental probability of an event to be 0 if the theoretical probability is 0.99? Explain.

32 Geometry The two circles circumscribe and inscribe the square. Find the probability that a random point in the large circle is within the inner circle. (*Hint:* Use the Pythagorean Theorem.)

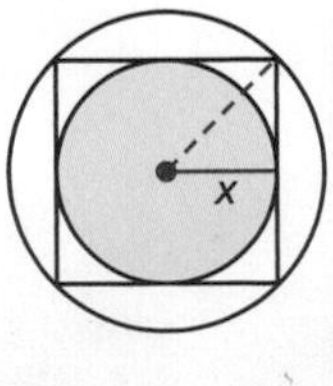

33. Critical Thinking Lexi tossed a fair coin 20 times, resulting in 12 heads and 8 tails. What is the theoretical probability that Lexi will get heads on the next toss? Explain.

34. Athletics Do male or female high school basketball players have a better chance of playing on college teams? on professional teams? Explain.

U.S. Basketball Players

	Men	Women
High School Players	549,500	456,900
College Players	4,500	4,100
College Players Drafted by Pro Leagues	44	32

Source: www.ncaa.org

35. Write About It Describe the difference between theoretical probability and experimental probability. Give an example in which they may differ.

TEST PREP

36. A fair coin is tossed 25 times, landing tails up 14 times. What is the experimental probability of heads?

Ⓐ 0.44 Ⓑ 0.50 Ⓒ 0.56 Ⓓ 0.79

37. Geometry Find the probability that a point chosen at random in the large rectangle at right will lie in the shaded area, to the nearest percent.

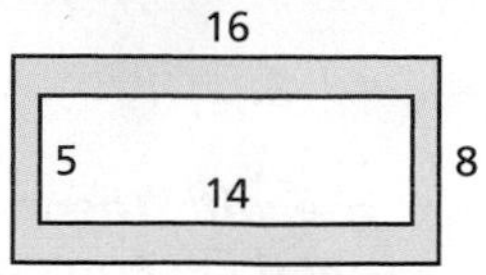

Ⓕ 18% Ⓖ 45% Ⓗ 55% Ⓙ 71%

38. How many outcomes are in the sample space when a quarter, a dime, and a nickel are tossed?

Ⓐ 3 Ⓑ 6 Ⓒ 8 Ⓓ 12

39. Two number cubes are rolled. What is the theoretical probability that the sum is 5?

Ⓕ $\frac{1}{3}$ Ⓖ $\frac{1}{6}$ Ⓗ $\frac{1}{9}$ Ⓙ $\frac{1}{12}$

40. Short Response Find the probability that a point chosen at random on the part of the number line shown will lie between points *B* and *C*.

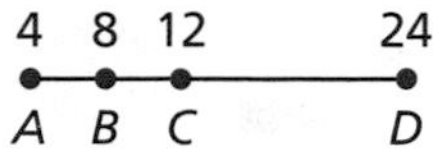

CHALLENGE AND EXTEND

41. The graph illustrates a statistical property known as the *law of large numbers*. Make a conjecture about the effect on probability as the number of trials gets very large. Give an example of how the probability might be affected for a real-world situation.

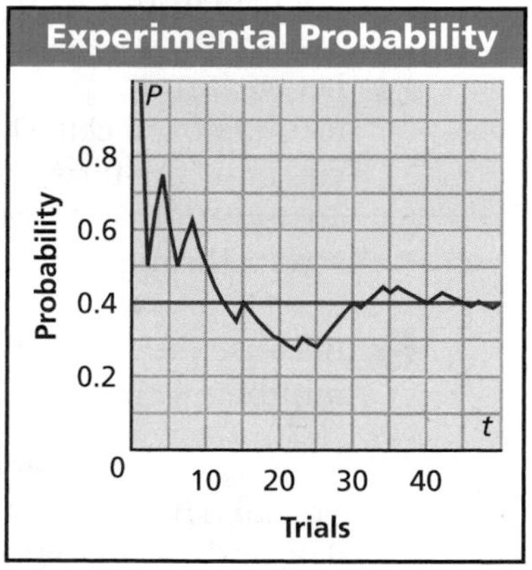

42. Four trumpet players' instruments are mixed up, and the trumpets are given to the players just before a concert. What is the probability that *no one* gets his or her trumpet back?

43. The table shows the data from a spinner experiment. Draw a reasonable spinner with 6 regions that may have been used for this experiment.

Spinner Experiment

Color	Red	Blue	Green	Yellow
Occurrences	23	44	7	26

13-2 Technology LAB

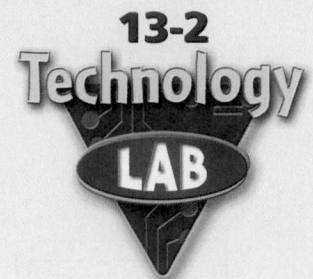

Explore Simulations

Use with Theoretical and Experimental Probability

MATHEMATICAL PRACTICES **Use appropriate tools strategically.**

CC.9-12.S.MD.7 (+) Analyze decisions and strategies using probability concepts...

A *simulation* is a model that uses random numbers to approximate experimental probability. You can use a spreadsheet to perform simulations. The **RAND( )** function generates random decimal values greater than or equal to 0 and less than 1. The **INT** function gives the greatest integer less than or equal to the input value. The functions can be used together to generate random integers as shown in the table

Random Numbers		
Formula	**Output**	**Example**
=RAND()	Decimal values $0 \le n < 1$	0.279606096
=100*RAND()	Decimal values $0 \le n < 100$	27.9606096
=INT(100*RAND())	Integers $0 \le n \le 99$	27
=INT(100*RAND())+1	Integers $1 \le n \le 100$	28

Activity

Use a simulation to find the experimental probability that a 65% free throw shooter will make at least 4 of his next 5 attempts.

1. To represent a percent, enter the formula for random integers from 1 to 100 into cell A1.

A1 fx =INT(100*RAND())+1

	A	B	C	D	E
1	38				

2. Let each row represent a trial of 5 attempts. Copy the formula from cell A1 into cells B1 through E1. Each time you copy the formula, the random values will change. To represent 10 trials, copy the formulas from row 1 into rows 2 through 10.

A1 fx =INT(100*RAND())+1

	A	B	C	D	E
1	72	98	34	74	87

3. Because the shooter makes 65% of his attempts, let the numbers 1 through 65 represent a successful attempt.

Identify the number of successful attempts in each row, or trial. There were 4 or more successes in trials 1, 3, 8, 9, and 10. So there is about a $\frac{5}{10}$, or 50%, experimental probability that the shooter will make at least 4 of his next 5 attempts.

Note that each time you run the simulation, you may get a different probability. The more trials you perform, the more reliable your estimate will be.

	A	B	C	D	E
1	✓ 25	✓ 2	✓ 62	✓ 26	✓ 38
2	✓ 30	✓ 32	66	88	✓ 9
3	✓ 27	✓ 18	✓ 9	✓ 9	93
4	98	✓ 34	✓ 10	86	99
5	87	✓ 64	✓ 4	74	✓ 36
6	✓ 5	97	69	83	✓ 51
7	✓ 39	✓ 39	80	95	97
8	✓ 32	✓ 64	✓ 51	✓ 64	✓ 46
9	✓ 52	81	✓ 39	✓ 5	✓ 36
10	✓ 48	✓ 46	✓ 45	69	✓ 21

Try This

Use a simulation to find each experimental probability.

1. An energy drink game advertises a 25% chance of winning with each bottle cap. Find the experimental probability that a 6-pack will contain at least 3 winners.
2. In a game with a 40% chance of winning, your friend challenges you to win 4 times in a row. Find the experimental probability of this happening in the next 4 games.
3. **Critical Thinking** How would you design a simulation to find the probability that a baseball player with a .285 batting average will get a hit in 5 of his next 10 at bats?

COMMON CORE

13-3 Independent and Dependent Events

CC.9-12.S.CP.3 Understand the conditional probability of *A* given *B*...and interpret independence of *A* and *B*...
Also **CC.9-12.S.CP.2, CC.9-12.S.CP.4, CC.9-12.S.CP.6, CC.9-12.S.IC.2, CC.9-12.S.ID.5, CC.9-12.S.CP.8 (+)**

Objectives

Determine whether events are independent or dependent.

Find the probability of independent and dependent events.

Vocabulary

independent events
dependent events
conditional probability

Who uses this?

Political analysts can use demographic information and probabilities to predict the results of elections. (See Example 3.)

Events are **independent events** if the occurrence of one event does not affect the probability of the other.

If a coin is tossed twice, its landing heads up on the first toss and landing heads up on the second toss are independent events. The outcome of one toss does not affect the probability of heads on the other toss. To find the probability of tossing heads twice, multiply the individual probabilities, $\frac{1}{2} \cdot \frac{1}{2}$, or $\frac{1}{4}$.

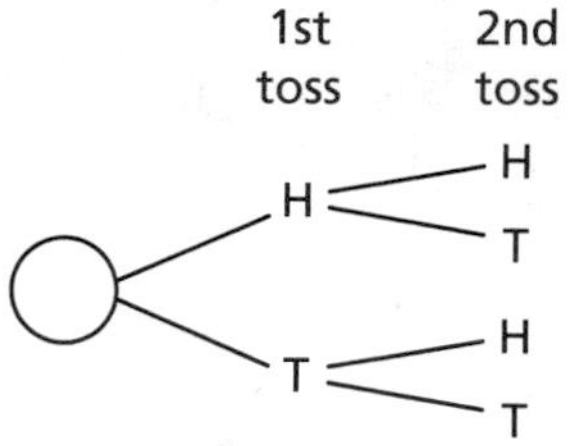

Know it! Note

Probability of Independent Events

If *A* and *B* are independent events, then $P(A \text{ and } B) = P(A) \cdot P(B)$.

EXAMPLE 1 Finding the Probability of Independent Events

Find each probability.

A spinning 4 and then 4 again on the spinner

Spinning a 4 once does not affect the probability of spinning a 4 again, so the events are independent.

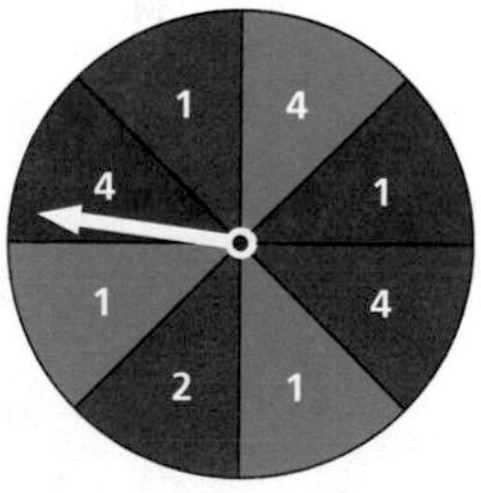

$P(4 \text{ and then } 4) = P(4) \cdot P(4)$

$\frac{3}{8} \cdot \frac{3}{8} = \frac{9}{64}$ *3 of the 8 equal sectors are labeled 4.*

B spinning red, then green, and then red on the spinner

The result of any spin does not affect the probability of any other outcome.

$P(\text{red, then green, and then red}) = P(\text{red}) \cdot P(\text{green}) \cdot P(\text{red})$

$= \frac{1}{4} \cdot \frac{3}{8} \cdot \frac{1}{4} = \frac{3}{128}$ *2 of the 8 equal sectors are red; 3 are green.*

CHECK IT OUT! **Find each probability.**

1a. rolling a 6 on one number cube and a 6 on another number cube

1b. tossing heads, then heads, and then tails when tossing a coin 3 times

Events are **dependent events** if the occurrence of one event affects the probability of the other. For example, suppose that there are 2 lemons and 1 lime in a bag. If you pull out two pieces of fruit, the probabilities change depending on the outcome of the first.

The tree diagram shows the probabilities for choosing two pieces of fruit from a bag containing 2 lemons and 1 lime.

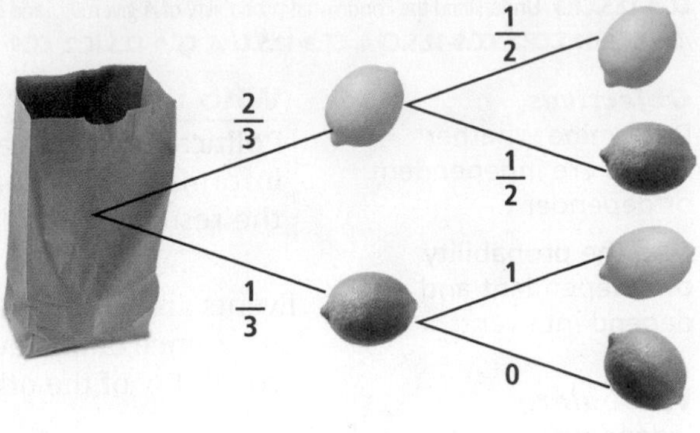

The probability of a specific event can be found by multiplying the probabilities on the branches that make up the event. For example, the probability of drawing two lemons is $\frac{2}{3} \cdot \frac{1}{2} = \frac{1}{3}$.

To find the probability of dependent events, you can use **conditional probability** $P(B \mid A)$, the probability of event B, given that event A has occurred.

Know it! Note

Probability of Dependent Events

If A and B are dependent events, then $P(A \text{ and } B) = P(A) \cdot P(B \mid A)$, where $P(B \mid A)$ is the probability of B, given that A has occurred.

EXAMPLE 2 Finding the Probability of Dependent Events

Two number cubes are rolled—one red and one blue. Explain why the events are dependent. Then find the indicated probability.

1 1	1 2	1 3	1 4	1 5	1 6
2 1	2 2	2 3	2 4	2 5	2 6
3 1	3 2	3 3	3 4	3 5	3 6
4 1	4 2	4 3	4 4	4 5	4 6
5 1	5 2	5 3	5 4	5 5	5 6
6 1	6 2	6 3	6 4	6 5	6 6

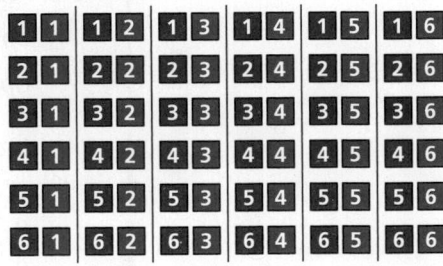

A **The red cube shows a 1, and the sum is less than 4.**

Step 1 Explain why the events are dependent.

$$P(\text{red } 1) = \frac{6}{36} = \frac{1}{6}$$ *Of 36 outcomes, 6 have a red 1.*

$$P(\text{sum} < 4 \mid \text{red } 1) = \frac{2}{6} = \frac{1}{3}$$ *Of 6 outcomes with a red 1, 2 have a sum less than 4.*

The events "the red cube shows a 1" and "the sum is less than 4" are dependent because $P(\text{sum} < 4)$ is different when it is known that a red 1 has occurred.

Step 2 Find the probability.

$$P(A \text{ and } B) = P(A) \cdot P(B \mid A)$$
$$P(\text{red 1 and sum} < 4) = P(\text{red } 1) \cdot P(\text{sum} < 4 \mid \text{red } 1)$$
$$= \frac{1}{6} \cdot \frac{2}{3} = \frac{1}{18}$$

Helpful Hint

In Example 2A, you can check to see that 2 of the 36 outcomes, or $\frac{1}{18}$, have a red 1 and a sum less than 4: $(1, 1)$ and $(1, 2)$.

Explain why the events are dependent. Then find the indicated probability.

B **The blue cube shows a multiple of 3, and the sum is 8.**

The events are dependent because $P(\text{sum is 8})$ is different when the blue cube shows a multiple of 3.

$P(\text{blue multiple of 3}) = \frac{2}{6} = \frac{1}{3}$ *Of 6 outcomes for blue, 2 have a multiple of 3.*

$P(\text{sum is 8} \mid \text{blue multiple of 3}) = \frac{2}{12} = \frac{1}{6}$ *Of 12 outcomes that have a blue multiple of 3, 2 have a sum 8.*

$P(\text{blue multiple of 3 and sum is 8}) =$

$P(\text{blue multiple of 3}) \cdot P(\text{sum is 8} \mid \text{blue multiple of 3}) = \left(\frac{1}{3}\right)\left(\frac{1}{6}\right) = \frac{1}{18}$

CHECK IT OUT! **Two number cubes are rolled—one red and one black. Explain why the events are dependent, and then find the indicated probability.**

2. The red cube shows a number greater than 4, and the sum is greater than 9.

Conditional probability often applies when data fall into categories.

EXAMPLE 3 Using a Table to Find Conditional Probability

Largest Texas Counties' Votes for President 2004 (thousands)

County	Bush	Kerry	Other
Harris	581	472	5
Dallas	345	336	4
Tarrant	349	207	3
Bexar	260	210	3
Travis	148	197	5

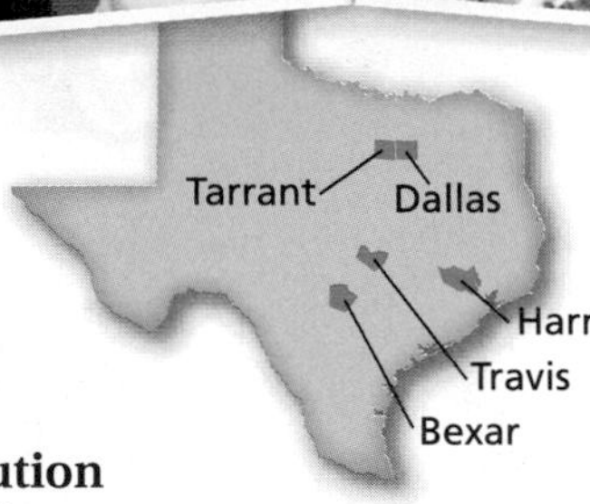

The table shows the approximate distribution of votes in Texas' five largest counties in the 2004 presidential election. Find each probability.

A **that a voter from Tarrant County voted for George Bush**

$P(\text{Bush} \mid \text{Tarrant}) = \frac{349}{559} \approx 0.624$ *Use the Tarrant row. Of 559,000 Tarrant voters, 349,000 voted for Bush.*

B **that a voter voted for John Kerry and was from Dallas County**

$P(\text{Dallas} \mid \text{Kerry}) = \frac{336}{1422}$ *Of 1,422,000 who voted for Kerry, 336,000 were from Dallas County.*

$P(\text{Kerry and Dallas} \mid \text{Kerry}) = \frac{1422}{3125} \cdot \frac{336}{1422}$ *There were 3,125,000 total voters.*

≈ 0.108

CHECK IT OUT! **Find each probability.**

3a. that a voter from Travis county voted for someone other than George Bush or John Kerry

3b. that a voter was from Harris county and voted for George Bush

In many cases involving random selection, events are independent when there is replacement and dependent when there is not replacement.

EXAMPLE 4 Determining Whether Events Are Independent or Dependent

Two cards are drawn from a deck of 52. Determine whether the events are independent or dependent. Find the probability.

> **Remember!**
> A standard card deck contains 4 suits of 13 cards each. The face cards are the jacks, queens, and kings.

A **selecting two aces when the first card is replaced**

Replacing the first card means that the occurrence of the first selection will not affect the probability of the second selection, so the events are independent.

$P(\text{ace} \mid \text{ace on first draw}) = P(\text{ace}) \cdot P(\text{ace})$

$= \frac{4}{52} \cdot \frac{4}{52} = \frac{1}{169}$ *4 of the 52 cards are aces.*

B **selecting a face card and then a 7 when the first card is not replaced**

Not replacing the first card means that there will be fewer cards to choose from, affecting the probability of the second selection, so the events are dependent.

$P(\text{face card}) \cdot P(7 \mid \text{first card was a face card})$

$= \frac{12}{52} \cdot \frac{4}{51} = \frac{4}{221}$ *There are 12 face cards, four 7's and 51 cards available for the second selection.*

CHECK IT OUT! **A bag contains 10 beads—2 black, 3 white, and 5 red. A bead is selected at random. Determine whether the events are independent or dependent. Find the indicated probability.**

4a. selecting a white bead, replacing it, and then selecting a red bead

4b. selecting a white bead, not replacing it, and then selecting a red bead

4c. selecting 3 nonred beads without replacement

MATHEMATICAL PRACTICES

THINK AND DISCUSS

1. Describe some independent events.

2. Extend the rule for the probability of independent events to more than two independent events. When might this be used?

Know it! Note

3. GET ORGANIZED Copy and complete the graphic organizer. In each box, compare independent and dependent events and their related probabilities.

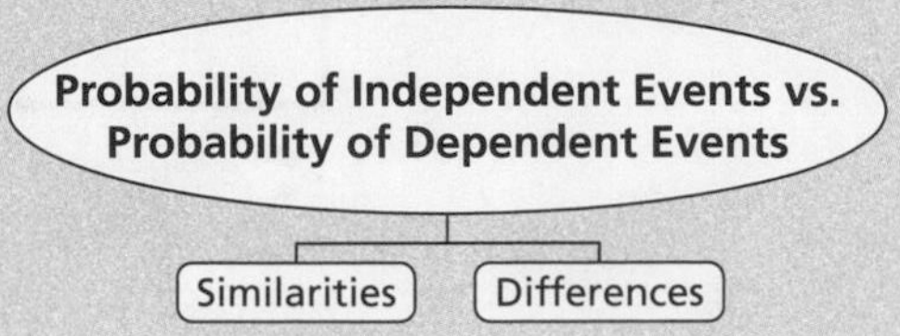

13-3 Exercises

Learn It Online
Homework Help Online
Parent Resources Online

GUIDED PRACTICE

1. **Vocabulary** Two events are __?__ if the occurrence of one event does not affect the probability of the other event. (*independent* or *dependent*)

SEE EXAMPLE 1

Find each probability.

2. rolling a 1 and then another 1 when a number cube is rolled twice
3. a coin landing heads up on every toss when it is tossed 3 times

SEE EXAMPLE 2

Two number cubes are rolled—one blue and one yellow. Explain why the events are dependent. Then find the indicated probability.

4. The blue cube shows a 4 and the product is less than 20.
5. The yellow cube shows a multiple of 3, given that the product is 6.

SEE EXAMPLE 3

The table shows the results of a quality-control study of a lightbulb factory. A lightbulb from the factory is selected at random. Find each probability.

6. that a shipped bulb is not defective
7. that a bulb is defective and shipped

Lightbulb Quality

	Shipped	Not Shipped
Defective	10	45
Not Defective	942	3

SEE EXAMPLE 4

A bag contains 20 checkers—10 red and 10 black. Determine whether the events are independent or dependent. Find the indicated probability.

8. selecting 2 black checkers when they are chosen at random with replacement
9. selecting 2 black checkers when they are chosen at random without replacement

PRACTICE AND PROBLEM SOLVING

Independent Practice

For Exercises	See Example
10–11	1
12–14	2
15–16	3
17–18	4

Extra Practice

See Extra Practice for more Skills Practice and Applications Practice exercises.

Find each probability.

10. choosing the same activity when two friends each randomly choose 1 of 4 extracurricular activities to participate in
11. rolling an even number and then rolling a 6 when a number cube is rolled twice

Two number cubes are rolled—one blue and one yellow. Explain why the events are dependent. Then find the indicated probability.

12. The yellow cube is greater than 5 and the product is greater than 24.
13. The blue cube is less than 3 and the product is 8.
14. The table shows immigration to the United States from three countries in three different years. A person is randomly selected. Find each probability.
    a. that a selected person is from Cuba, given that the person immigrated in 1990
    b. that a person came from Spain and immigrated in 2000
    c. that a selected person immigrated in 1995, given that the person was from Ghana.

Immigration to the United States

Country	1990	1995	2000
Cuba	10,645	17,937	20,831
Ghana	4,466	3,152	4,344
Spain	1,886	1,321	1,264

Employment Find each probability.

15. that a person with an advanced degree is employed

16. that a person is not a high school graduate and is not employed

Employment by Education Level, Ages 21–24		
Education Level	Employed (millions)	Not employed (millions)
Not a high school graduate	1.060	0.834
High school graduate	2.793	1.157
Some college	4.172	1.634
Bachelor's degree	1.53	0.372
Advanced degree	0.104	0.041

A bag contains number slips numbered 1 to 9. Determine whether the events are independent or dependent, and find the indicated probability.

17. selecting 2 even numbers when 2 slips are chosen without replacement

18. selecting 2 even numbers when 2 slips are chosen with replacement

Determine whether the events are independent or dependent.

19. A coin comes up heads, and a number cube rolled at the same time comes up 6.

20. A 4 is drawn from a deck of cards, set aside, and then an ace is drawn.

21. A 1 is rolled on a number cube, and then a 4 is rolled on the same number cube.

22. A dart hits the bull's-eye, and a second dart also hits the bull's eye.

LINK

Tennis

Wimbledon has been played annually since 1877 at the All England Lawn Tennis and Croquet Club.

23. **Tennis** In the 2004 Wimbledon Men's Tennis Championship final, Roger Federer defeated Andy Roddick in three sets.
   a. What was the probability that Federer won the point when his second serve was in?
   b. When Federer lost a point, what was the probability that he *double faulted*?

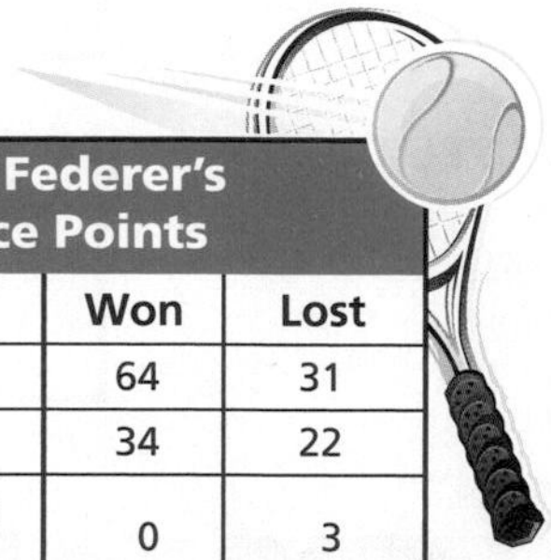

Roger Federer's Service Points		
	Won	Lost
First Serve In	64	31
Second Serve In	34	22
Second Serve Out (Double Fault)	0	3

24. **Multi-Step** At one high school, the probability that a student is absent today, given that the student was absent yesterday, is 0.12. The probability that a student is absent today, given that the student was present yesterday, is 0.05. The probability that a student was absent yesterday is 0.1. Draw a tree diagram to represent the situation. What is the probability that a randomly selected student was present yesterday and today?

MULTI-STEP TEST PREP

25. While playing Yahtzee, Jake rolls 5 dice and gets the result shown at right. The rules allow him to reroll these dice 2 times. Jake decides to try for all 5's, so he rerolls the 2 and the 3.

   a. What is the probability that Jake gets no additional 5's in either of the 2 rolls?
   b. What is the probability that he gets all 5's on his first reroll of the 2 and the 3?
   c. What is the probability that he gets all 5's on his first reroll, given that at least one of the dice is a 5?

Estimation Use the graph to estimate each probability.

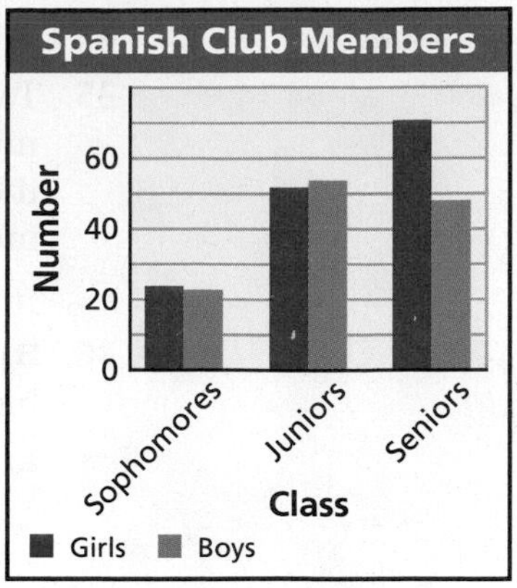

26. that a Spanish club member is a girl
27. that a senior Spanish club member is a girl
28. that a male Spanish club member is a senior
29. **Critical Thinking** A box contains 100 balloons. Eighty are yellow, and 20 are green. Fifty are marked "Happy Birthday!" and 50 are not. A balloon is randomly chosen from the box. How many yellow "Happy Birthday!" balloons must be in the box if the event "a balloon is yellow" and the event "a balloon is marked 'Happy Birthday!'" are independent?
30. **Travel** Airline information for three years is given in the table.
    a. Complete the table.
    b. What was the probability that a scheduled flight in 2004 was canceled?
    c. An on-time flight is selected randomly for study. What is the probability that it was a flight from 2005?

Scheduled Flights (thousands) January to July

	2003	2004	2005	Total
On Time	■	3197	3237	■
Delayed	598	■	877	2321
Canceled	61	68	■	■
Total	3761	■	4196	■

Source: Bureau of Transportation Statistics

31. **Write About It** The "law of averages" is a nonmathematical term that means that events eventually "average out." So, if a coin comes up heads 10 tosses in a row, there is a greater probability that it will come up tails on the eleventh toss. Explain the error in this thinking.

TEST PREP

32. What is the probability that a person's birthday falls on a Saturday next year, given that it falls on a Saturday this year?

    Ⓐ 0 Ⓑ $\frac{1}{7}$ Ⓒ $\frac{1}{2}$ Ⓓ 1

33. Which of the following has the same probability as rolling doubles on 2 number cubes 3 times in a row?

    Ⓕ A single number cube is rolled 3 times. The cube shows 5 each time.

    Ⓖ Two number cubes are rolled 3 times. Each time the sum is 6.

    Ⓗ Two number cubes are rolled 3 times. Each time the sum is greater than 2.

    Ⓙ Three number cubes are rolled twice. Each time all cubes show the same number (triples).

34. **Extended Response** Use the tree diagram.
    a. Find $P(D \mid A)$, $P(D \mid B)$, and $P(D \mid C)$.
    b. Does the tree diagram represent independent or dependent events? Explain your answer.
    c. Describe a scenario for which the tree diagram could be used to find probabilities.

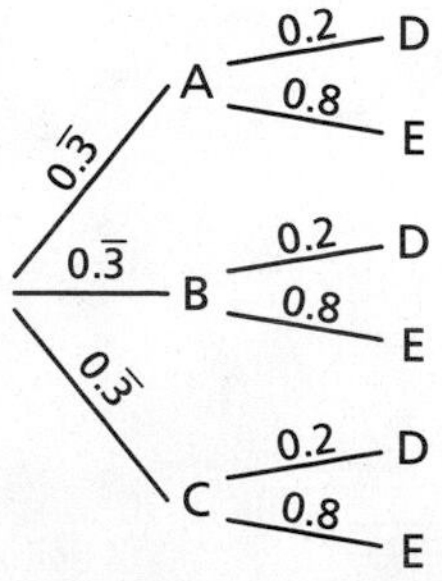

CHALLENGE AND EXTEND

35. Two number cubes are rolled in succession and the numbers that they show are added together. What is the only sum for which the probability of the sum is independent of the number shown on the first roll? Explain.

36. Birthdays People born on February 29 have a birthday once every 4 years.

a. What is the smallest group of people in which there is a greater than 50% chance that 2 people share a birthday? (Do not include February 29.)

b. What is the probability that in a group of 150 people, none are born on February 29?

c. What is the least number of people such that there is a greater than 50% chance that one of the people in the group has a birthday on February 29?

37. There are 150 people at a play. Ninety are women, and 60 are men. Half are sitting in the lower level, and half are sitting in the upper level. There are 35 women sitting in the upper level. A person is selected at random for a prize. What is the probability that the person is sitting in the lower level, given that the person is a woman? Is the event "person is sitting in the lower level" independent of the event "person is a woman"? Explain.

38. Medicine Suppose that strep throat affects 2% of the population and a test to detect it produces an accurate result 99% of the time.

a. Complete the table.

b. What is the probability that someone who tests positive actually has strep throat?

Per 10,000 People Tested

	Have strep	Do not have strep	Total
Test Positive	■	■	■
Test Negative	■	■	■
Total	■	■	10,000

Mastering the Standards

for Mathematical Practice

The topics described in the Standards for Mathematical Content will vary from year to year. However, the *way* in which you learn, study, and think about mathematics will not. The Standards for Mathematical Practice describe skills that you will use in all of your math courses.

Mathematical Practices

1. *Make sense of problems and persevere in solving them.*
2. *Reason abstractly and quantitatively.*
3. *Construct viable arguments and critique the reasoning of others.*
4. *Model with mathematics.*
5. *Use appropriate tools strategically.*
6. *Attend to precision.*
7. *Look for and make use of structure.*
8. *Look for and express regularity in repeated reasoning.*

1 Make sense of problems and persevere in solving them.

Mathematically proficient students start by explaining to themselves the meaning of a problem... They analyze givens, constraints, relationships, and goals. They make conjectures about the form... of the solution and plan a solution pathway...

In your book

Focus on Problem Solving describes a four-step plan for problem solving. The plan is introduced at the beginning of your book, and practice with the plan appears throughout the book.

Focus on Problem Solving

The Problem-Solving Plan

To be a good problem solver you need a good problem-solving plan. Using a problem-solving plan along with a problem-solving strategy helps you organize your work and correctly solve the problem. The plan used in this book is outlined below.

UNDERSTAND the Problem

- **What are you asked to find?** Make sure you understand exactly what the problem is asking. Restate the problem in your own words.
- **What information is given in the problem?** List every piece of information the problem gives you.
- **Is all the information relevant?** Sometimes problems have extra information that is not needed to solve the problem. Try to determine what is and is not needed. This helps you stay organized when you are making a plan.
- **Were you given enough information to solve the problem?** Sometimes there simply is not enough information to solve the problem. List what else you need to know to solve the problem.

Make a PLAN

- **What problem-solving strategy or strategies can you use to help you solve the problem?** Think about strategies you have used in the past to solve problems. Would any of them be helpful in solving this problem?
- **Create a step-by-step plan of how you will solve the problem.** Write out your plan in words to help you get a clearer idea of how to solve the problem mathematically.

SOLVE

- **Use your plan to solve the problem.** Translate your plan from words to math. Show each step in your solution and write your answer in a complete sentence.

LOOK BACK

- **Did you completely answer the question that was asked?** Be sure you answered the question that was asked and that your answer is complete.
- **Is your answer reasonable?** Your answer should make sense.
- **Could you have used a different strategy to solve the problem?** Solving the problem again with a different strategy is a good way to check your answer.
- **Did you learn anything that could help you solve similar problems in the future?** You may want to take notes about this kind of problem and the strategy you used to solve it.

xx *Focus On Problem Solving*

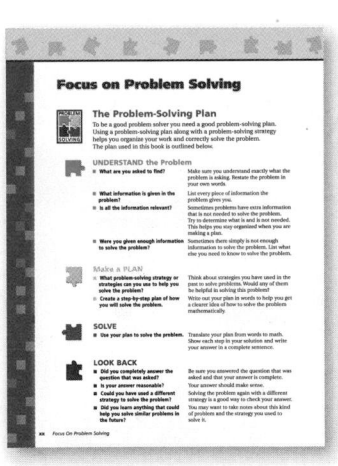

EXAMPLE 5 PROBLEM SOLVING ***Problem-Solving Application***

The cost to place an ad in a newspaper for one week is a linear function of the number of lines in the ad. The costs for 3, 5, and 10 lines are shown. Write an equation in slope-intercept form that represents the function. Then find the cost of an ad that is 18 lines long.

City Gazette

Newspaper Ad Costs

Lines	3	5	10
Cost ($)	13.50	18.50	31

1 Understand the Problem

- The **answer** will have two parts—an equation in slope-intercept form and the cost of an ad that is 18 lines long.
- The ordered pairs given in the table satisfy the equation.

2 Make a Plan

First, find the slope. Then use point-slope form to write the equation. Finally, write the equation in slope-intercept form.

3 Solve

Step 1 Choose any two ordered pairs from the table to find the slope.

$$m = \frac{y_2 - y_1}{x_2 - x_1} = \frac{18.50 - 13.50}{5 - 3} = \frac{5}{2} = 2.5 \quad \textit{Use (3, 13.50) and (5, 18.50).}$$

Step 2 Substitute the slope and any ordered pair from the table into the point-slope form.

$$y - y_1 = m(x - x_1)$$
$$y - 31 = 2.5(x - 10) \quad \textit{Use (10, 31).}$$

Step 3 Write the equation in slope-intercept form by solving for y.

$$y - 31 = 2.5(x - 10)$$
$$y - 31 = 2.5x - 25 \quad \textit{Distribute 2.5.}$$
$$y = 2.5x + 6 \quad \textit{Add 31 to both sides.}$$

Step 4 Find the cost of an ad containing 18 lines by substituting 18 for x.

$$y = 2.5x + 6$$
$$y = 2.5(18) + 6 = 51$$

The cost of an ad containing 18 lines is $51.

4 Look Back

Check the equation by substituting the ordered pairs (3, 13.50) and (5, 18.50).

$y = 2.5x + 6$	
13.50	$2.5(3) + 6$
13.5	$7.5 + 6$
13.5	13.5 ✓

$y = 2.5x + 6$	
18.50	$2.5(5) + 6$
18.5	$12.5 + 6$
18.5	18.5 ✓

Comstock/Getty Images

CHAPTER 13

MULTI-STEP TEST PREP

SECTION 13A

MATHEMATICAL PRACTICES **Reason abstractly and quantitatively.**

Experimental Probability

You can use a spinner to examine the relationship between experimental and theoretical probability. Construct a spinner like the one shown below, and use it to answer the questions.

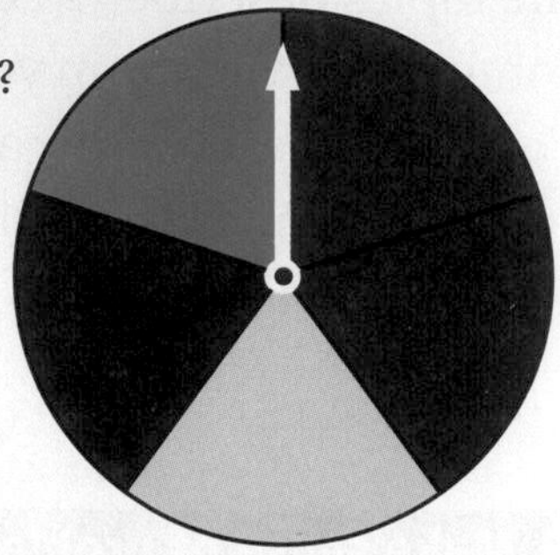

1. What is the theoretical probability of spinning yellow?
2. What is the theoretical probability of spinning red OR yellow?
3. Spin the spinner 10 times, then copy the table below and record your results.. What is the experimental probability of spinning yellow?

Spinner Experiment				
Blue	**Red**	**Yellow**	**Purple**	**Green**

4. Perform another 10 spins and record them. What is the new experimental probability of spinning yellow?
5. Share your results with the rest of the class. What is the experimental probability of the class's results as a whole?

READY TO GO ON?

Quiz for Lessons 13-1 Through 13-3

13-1 Permutations and Combinations

1. A security code consists of 5 digits (0–9), and a digit may not be used more than once. How many possible security codes are there?
2. Adric owns 8 pairs of shoes. How many ways can he choose 4 pairs of shoes to pack into his luggage?
3. A plumber received calls from 5 customers. There are 6 open slots on today's schedule. How many ways can the plumber schedule the customers?

13-2 Theoretical and Experimental Probability

4. A cooler contains 18 cans: 9 of lemonade, 3 of iced tea, and 6 of cola. Dee selects a can without looking. What is the probability that Dee selects iced tea?
5. Jordan has 9 pens in his desk; 2 are out of ink. If his mom selects 2 pens from his desk, what is the probability that both are out of ink?
6. Find the probability that a point chosen at random inside the figure shown is in the shaded area.
7. A number cube is tossed 50 times, and a 2 is rolled 12 times. Find the experimental probability of not rolling a 2.

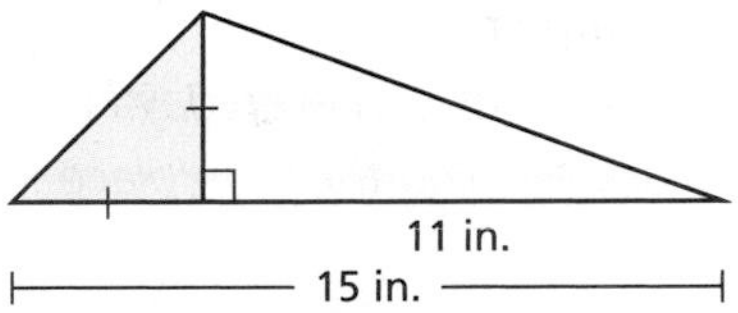

13-3 Independent and Dependent Events

8. Explain why the events "getting tails, then tails, then tails, then tails, then heads when tossing a coin 5 times" are independent, and find the probability.
9. Two number cubes are rolled—one red and one black. Explain why the events "the red cube shows a 6" and "the sum is greater than or equal to 10" are dependent, and find the probability.
10. The table shows the breakdown of math students for one school year. Find the probability that a Geometry student is in the 11th grade.
11. A bag contains 25 checkers—15 red and 10 black. Determine whether the events "a red checker is selected, not replaced, and then a black checker is selected" are independent or dependent, and find the probability.

Math Students by Grade

	Geometry	Algebra 2
9th Grade	26	0
10th Grade	68	24
11th Grade	33	94

Mastering the Standards

for Mathematical Practice

The topics described in the Standards for Mathematical Content will vary from year to year. However, the *way* in which you learn, study, and think about mathematics will not. The Standards for Mathematical Practice describe skills that you will use in all of your math courses.

Mathematical Practices

1. *Make sense of problems and persevere in solving them.*
2. *Reason abstractly and quantitatively.*
3. *Construct viable arguments and critique the reasoning of others.*
4. *Model with mathematics.*
5. *Use appropriate tools strategically.*
6. *Attend to precision.*
7. *Look for and make use of structure.*
8. *Look for and express regularity in repeated reasoning.*

4 Model with mathematics.

Mathematically proficient students can apply... mathematics... to... problems... in everyday life, society, and the workplace...

In your book

Multi-Step Test Prep and **Real-World Connections** apply mathematics to other disciplines and in real-world scenarios.

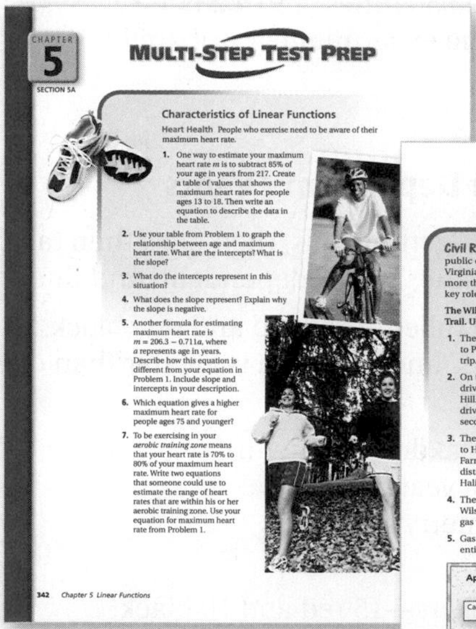

CHAPTER 5
SECTION 5A

MULTI-STEP TEST PREP

Characteristics of Linear Functions

Heart Health People who exercise need to be aware of their maximum heart rate.

1. One way to estimate your maximum heart rate m is to subtract 85% of your age in years from 217. Create a table of values that shows the maximum heart rates for people ages 13 to 18. Then write an equation to describe the data in the table.
2. Use your table from Problem 1 to graph the relationship between age and maximum heart rate. What are the intercepts? What is the slope?
3. What do the intercepts represent in this situation?
4. What does the slope represent? Explain why the slope is negative.
5. Another formula for estimating maximum heart rate is $m = 206.3 - 0.711a$, where a represents age in years. Describe how this equation is different from your equation in Problem 1. Include slope and intercepts in your description.
6. Which equation gives a higher maximum heart rate for people ages 75 and younger?
7. To be exercising in your *aerobic training zone* means that your heart rate is 70% to 80% of your maximum heart rate. Write two equations that someone could use to estimate the range of heart rates that are within his or her aerobic training zone. Use your equation for maximum heart rate from Problem 1.

342 *Chapter 5 Linear Functions*

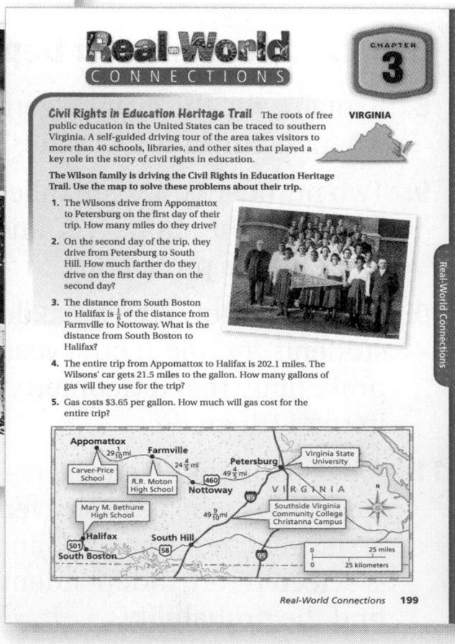

Real-World CONNECTIONS

CHAPTER 3

Civil Rights in Education Heritage Trail The roots of free public education in the United States can be traced to southern Virginia. A self-guided driving tour of the area takes visitors to more than 40 schools, libraries, and other sites that played a key role in the story of civil rights in education.

VIRGINIA

The Wilson family is driving the Civil Rights in Education Heritage Trail. Use the map to solve these problems about their trip.

1. The Wilsons drive from Appomattox to Petersburg on the first day of their trip. How many miles do they drive?
2. On the second day of the trip, they drive from Petersburg to South Hill. How much farther do they drive on the first day than on the second day?
3. The distance from South Boston to Halifax is $\frac{1}{6}$ of the distance from Farmville to Nottoway. What is the distance from South Boston to Halifax?
4. The entire trip from Appomattox to Halifax is 202.1 miles. The Wilsons' car gets 21.5 miles to the gallon. How many gallons of gas will they use for the trip?
5. Gas costs $3.65 per gallon. How much will gas cost for the entire trip?

Real-World Connections 199

Real-World Connections

COMMON CORE

13-4 Two-Way Tables

CC.9-12.S.CP.4 Construct and interpret two-way frequency tables... *Also* CC.9-12.S.CP.6, CC.9-12.S.CP.5, CC.9-12.S.MD.6 (+)

Objectives
Construct and interpret two-way frequency tables of data when two categories are associated with each object being classified.

Vocabulary
joint relative frequency
marginal relative frequency
conditional relative frequency

Who uses this?
Commuters can use two-way tables to determine the best route to work. (See Example 3.)

A *two-way table* is a useful way to organize data that can be categorized by two variables. Suppose you asked 20 children and adults whether they liked broccoli. The table shows one way to arrange the data.

	Yes	No
Children	3	8
Adults	7	2

The **joint relative frequencies** are the values in each category divided by the total number of values, shown by the shaded cells in the table. Each value is divided by 20, the total number of individuals.

The **marginal relative frequencies** are found by adding the joint relative frequencies in each row and column.

	Yes	No	Total
Children	0.15	0.4	0.55
Adults	0.35	0.1	0.45
Total	0.5	0.5	1

EXAMPLE 1 Finding Joint and Marginal Relative Frequencies

The table shows the results of a poll of 80 randomly selected high school students who were asked if they prefer math or English. Make a table of the joint and marginal relative frequencies.

	9th grade	10th grade	11th grade	12th grade
Math	10	12	11	8
English	12	11	8	8

Divide each value by the total of 80 to find the joint relative frequencies, and add each row and column to find the marginal relative frequencies.

	9th grade	10th grade	11th grade	12th grade	Total
Math	0.125	0.15	0.1375	0.1	0.5125
English	0.15	0.1375	0.1	0.1	0.4875
Total	0.275	0.2875	0.2375	0.2	1

CHECK IT OUT!

1. The table shows the number of books sold at a library sale. Make a table of the joint and marginal relative frequencies.

	Fiction	Nonfiction
Hardcover	28	52
Paperback	94	36

To find a **conditional relative frequency**, divide the joint relative frequency by the marginal relative frequency. Conditional relative frequencies can be used to find conditional probabilities.

EXAMPLE 2 Using Conditional Relative Frequency to Find Probability

A sociologist collected data on the types of pets in 100 randomly selected households, and summarized the results in a table.

		Owns a cat	
		Yes	No
Owns a dog	Yes	15	24
	No	18	43

A **Make a table of the joint and marginal relative frequencies.**

		Owns a cat		
		Yes	No	Total
Owns a dog	Yes	0.15	0.24	0.39
	No	0.18	0.43	0.61
	Total	0.33	0.67	1

Idamini/Alamy

B **If you are given that a household has a dog, what is the probability that the household also has a cat?**

Use the conditional relative frequency for the row with the condition "Owns a dog." The total for households with dogs is 0.39, or 39%. Out of these, 0.15, or 15%, also have cats. The conditional relative frequency is $\frac{0.15}{0.39} \approx 0.38$.

Given that a household has a dog, there is a probability of about 0.38 that the household also has a cat.

CHECK IT OUT! **The classes at a dance academy include ballet and tap dancing. Enrollment in these classes is shown in the table.**

		Ballet	
		Yes	No
Tap	Yes	38	52
	No	86	24

2a. Copy and complete the table of the joint relative frequencies and marginal relative frequencies.

		Ballet		
		Yes	No	Total
Tap	Yes			
	No			
	Total			1

2b. If you are given that a student is taking ballet, what is the probability that the student is not taking tap?

Notice that in Example 2, the conditional relative frequency could have been found from the original data:

$$\frac{0.15}{0.39} = \frac{15}{39} \approx 0.38$$

EXAMPLE 3 Comparing Conditional Probabilities

Tomas is trying to decide on the best possible route to drive to work. He has a choice of three possible routes. On each day, he randomly selects a route and keeps track of whether he is late. After a 40-day trial, his notes look like this.

	Late	Not Late
Route A	||||	𝍸 𝍸
Route B	|||	𝍸 ||
Route C	||||	𝍸 𝍸 ||

Use conditional probabilities to determine the best route for Tomas to take to work.

Create a table of joint and marginal relative frequencies. There are 40 data values, so divide each frequency by 40.

	Late	Not late	Total
Route A	0.1	0.25	0.35
Route B	0.075	0.175	0.25
Route C	0.1	0.3	0.4
Total	0.275	0.725	1

To find the conditional probabilities, divide the joint relative frequency of being late by the marginal relative frequency in each row.

$$P(\text{being late if driving Route A}) = \frac{0.1}{0.35} \approx 0.29$$

$$P(\text{being late if driving Route B}) = \frac{0.075}{0.25} = 0.3$$

$$P(\text{being late if driving Route C}) = \frac{0.1}{0.4} = 0.25$$

The probability of being late is least for Route C. Based on the sample, Tomas is least likely to be late if he takes Route C.

CHECK IT OUT!

3. Francine is evaluating three driving schools. She asked 50 people who attended the schools whether they passed their driving tests on the first try.

   Use conditional probabilities to determine which is the best school.

	Pass	Fail
Al's Driving	𝍸 𝍸 ||||	𝍸 |||
Drive Time	𝍸 𝍸 |	𝍸 ||
Crash Course	𝍸	𝍸

MATHEMATICAL PRACTICES

THINK AND DISCUSS

1. Describe the relationship between joint relative frequencies and marginal relative frequencies.
2. Explain how to find the conditional relative frequencies from a two-way table showing joint and marginal relative frequencies.
3. **GET ORGANIZED** Copy and complete the graphic organizer at right. In each column, explain how to find the relative frequency from a two-way table.

Know it! Note

Relative Frequencies		
Joint	Marginal	Conditional

13-4 Exercises

GUIDED PRACTICE

Vocabulary **Apply the vocabulary from this lesson to answer each question.**

1. The ___?___ relative frequencies are the sums of each row and column in a two-way table. (*joint, marginal,* or *conditional*)

2. You can compare ___?___ probabilities to evaluate the best one out of a number of options. (*joint, marginal,* or *conditional*)

SEE EXAMPLE 1

3. The table shows the results of a poll of randomly selected high school students who were asked if they prefer to hear all-school announcements in the morning or afternoon.

	Underclassmen	Upperclassmen
Morning	8	14
Afternoon	18	10

Make a table of the joint and marginal relative frequencies.

4. **Customer Service** The table shows the results of a customer satisfaction survey for a cellular service provider, by location of the customer. In the survey, customers were asked whether they would recommend a plan with the provider to a friend.

	Arlington	Towson	Parkville
Yes	40	35	41
No	18	10	6

Make a table of the joint and marginal relative frequencies. Round to the nearest hundredth where appropriate.

SEE EXAMPLE 2

5. **School** Pamela has collected data on the number of students in the sophomore class who play a sport or play a musical instrument.

		Plays a sport	
		Yes	No
Plays an instrument	Yes	47	38
	No	51	67

a. Copy and complete the table of the joint and marginal relative frequencies. Round to the nearest hundredth where appropriate.

		Play Sport		
		Yes	No	Total
Play instrument	Yes			
	No			
	Total			

b. If you are given that a student plays an instrument, what is the probability that the student also plays a sport? Round your answer to the nearest hundredth.

c. If you are given that a student plays a sport, what is the probability that the student also plays an instrument? Round your answer to the nearest hundredth.

SEE EXAMPLE 3

6. **Business** Roberto is the owner of a car dealership. He is assessing the success rates of his top three salespeople in order to offer one of them a promotion. Over two months, for each attempted sale, he records whether the salesperson made a successful sale or not. The results are shown in the chart below.

	Successful	Unsuccessful
Becky	6	6
Raul	4	5
Darrell	6	9

   a. Make a table of the joint relative frequencies and marginal relative frequencies. Round to the nearest hundredth where appropriate.
   b. Find the probability that each salesperson will make a successful sale. Round to the nearest hundredth where appropriate.
   c. Determine which salesperson has the highest success rate.

PRACTICE AND PROBLEM SOLVING

Independent Practice

For Exercises	See Example
7–8	1
9–12	2
13	3

Extra Practice

See Extra Practice for more Skills Practice and Applications Practice exercises.

7. **Fundraising** The table shows the number of T-shirts and sweatshirts sold at a fundraiser during parent visitation night at Preston High School.

	Students	Adults
T-Shirts	16	23
Sweatshirts	7	14

   Make a table of the joint relative frequencies and marginal relative frequencies.

8. **Write About It** Describe in your own words the process you use to write marginal relative frequencies for data given in a two-way table.

9. **Customer Service** The claims handlers at a car insurance company help customers with insurance issues when there has been an accident, so their customer service skills are very important.

   The claims handlers at the Trust Auto Insurance Company are divided into three teams. For one month, a customer satisfaction survey was given for each team. The results of the surveys are shown below.

	Satisfied	Dissatisfied
Team 1	20	8
Team 2	34	12
Team 3	34	10

   a. Make a table of the joint relative frequencies and marginal relative frequencies. Round to the nearest hundredth where appropriate.
   b. Find the probability that a customer will be satisfied after working with each team. Round to the nearest hundredth where appropriate.
   c. Determine which team has the highest rate of customer satisfaction.

10. **Critical Thinking** What do you notice about the value that always falls in the cell to the lower right of a two-way table when marginal relative frequencies have been written in? What does this value represent?

11. ***ERROR ANALYSIS*** One hundred adults and children were randomly selected and asked whether they spoke more than one language fluently. The data were recorded in a two-way table. Maria and Brennan each used the data to make the tables of joint relative frequencies shown below, but their results are slightly different. The difference is shaded. Can you tell by looking at the tables which of them made an error? Explain.

Maria's table

	Yes	No
Children	0.15	0.25
Adults	0.1	0.6

Brennan's table

	Yes	No
Children	0.15	0.25
Adults	0.1	0.5

12. **Estimation** A total of 107 brownies and muffins was sold at a school bake sale. The joint relative frequency representing muffins sold to seniors was 0.48. Use mental math to find approximately how many muffins were sold to seniors.

13. **Public Transit** A town planning committee is considering a new system for public transit. Residents of the town were randomly selected to answer two questions: "Do you work less than 5 miles from home?" and "Would you use the new system to get to work, if it were available?"
The results are shown below.

UpperCut Images/Getty Images

		Work less than 5 miles from home?	
		Yes	No
Use new system?	Yes	24	32
	No	44	20

a. Make a table of the joint relative frequencies and marginal relative frequencies. Round to the nearest hundredth where appropriate.

b. If residents work less than 5 miles from home, what is the probability that they would use the new system? Round to the nearest hundredth.

c. If residents are willing to use the new system, what is the probability that they don't work less than 5 miles from home? Round to the nearest hundredth.

TEST PREP

14. Students and teachers at a school were polled to see if they were in favor of extending the parking lot into part of the athletic fields. The results of the poll are shown in the two-way table.

	In Favor	Not in Favor
Students	16	23
Teachers	9	14

Which of the following statements is false?

(A) Thirty-nine students were polled in all.

(B) Fourteen teachers were polled in all.

(C) Twenty-three students are not in favor of extending the parking lot.

(D) Nine teachers are in favor of extending the parking lot.

15. A group of students were polled to find out how many were planning to major in a scientific field of study in college. The results of the poll are shown in the two-way table.

		Majoring in a science field	
		Yes	No
Class	Junior	150	210
	Senior	112	200

Which of the following statements is true?

(A) Three hundred sixty students were polled in all.

(B) A student in the senior class is more likely to be planning on a scientific major than a nonscientific major.

(C) A student planning on a scientific major is more likely to be a junior than a senior.

(D) More seniors than juniors plan to enter a scientific field of study.

16. **Gridded Response** A group of children and adults were polled about whether they watch a particular TV show. The survey results, showing the joint relative frequencies and marginal relative frequencies, are shown in the two-way table.

	Yes	No	Total
Children	0.3	0.4	0.7
Adults	0.25	x	0.3
Total	0.55	0.45	1

What is the value of x?

CHALLENGE AND EXTEND

The table shows the joint relative frequencies for data on how many children and teenagers attended a fair in one evening, and whether each bought a booklet of tickets for rides at the entrance gate.

M. Scott Brauer/Alamy

	Yes	No
Children	0.125	0.1
Teenagers	0.725	0.05

Use the table to answer questions 17–20. Round answers to the nearest hundredth where appropriate.

17. Find the marginal relative frequencies for the data.

18. Based on this data, use a percentage to express how likely it is that tomorrow evening a teenager at the fair will buy a ticket booklet at the entrance. Round your answer to the nearest whole percent, if necessary.

19. If the data represent 80 teenagers and children altogether, how many children will have bought a ticket booklet at the entrance?

20. If 12 children did not buy ticket booklets at the entrance, then how many children and teenagers altogether does the data represent?

21. A poll with the options of 'yes' and 'no' was given. If the marginal relative frequency of 'yes' is 1.0, what was the marginal relative frequency of 'no'?

	Yes	No	Total
Group 1	0.24	?	?
Group 2	0.76	?	?
Total	1.0	?	?

22. **Short Response** What is the maximum a marginal relative frequency can be, and why?

COMMON CORE

13-5 Compound Events

CC.9-12.S.CP.7 Apply the Addition Rule. . .and interpret the answer. . . *Also* CC.9-12.S.CP.9 (+), CC.9-12.S.CP.1

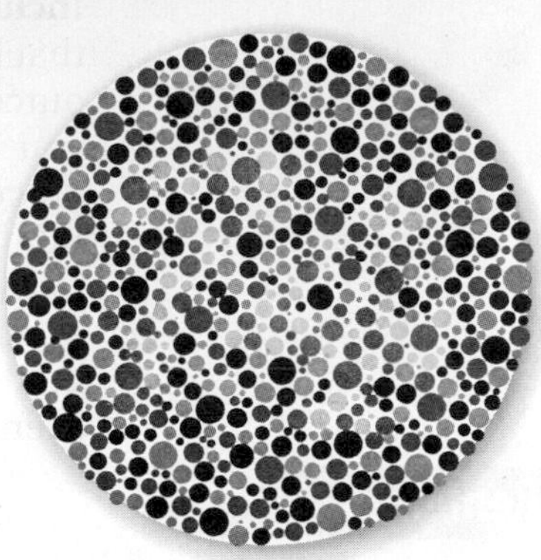

Objectives
Find the probability of mutually exclusive events.

Find the probability of inclusive events.

Vocabulary
simple event
compound event
mutually exclusive events
inclusive events

Why learn this?

You can use the probability of compound events to determine the likelihood that a person of a specific gender is color-blind. (See Example 3.)

A **simple event** is an event that describes a single outcome. A **compound event** is an event made up of two or more simple events. **Mutually exclusive events** are events that cannot both occur in the same trial of an experiment. Rolling a 1 and rolling a 2 on the same roll of a number cube are mutually exclusive events.

Mutually Exclusive Events

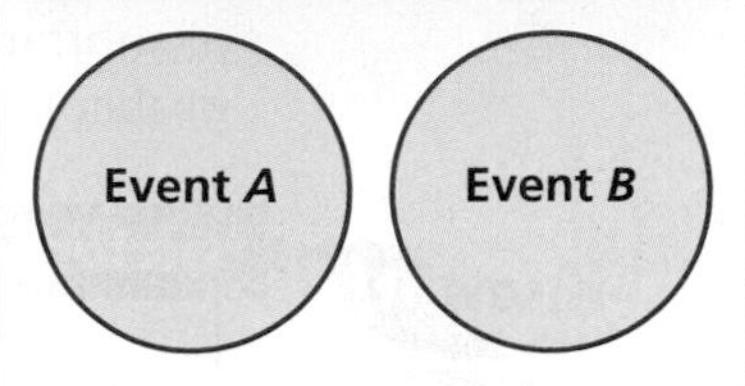

Know it! Note

Mutually Exclusive Events

WORDS	ALGEBRA	EXAMPLE
The probability of two mutually exclusive events *A or B* occurring is the sum of their individual probabilities.	For two mutually exclusive events *A* and *B*, $P(A \cup B) = P(A) + P(B)$.	When a number cube is rolled, $P(\text{less than } 3) =$ $P(1 \text{ or } 2) =$ $P(1) + P(2) = \frac{1}{6} + \frac{1}{6} = \frac{1}{3}$.

Remember!

Recall that the union symbol ∪ means "or."

EXAMPLE 1 Finding Probabilities of Mutually Exclusive Events

A drink company applies one label to each bottle cap: "free drink," "free meal," or "try again." A bottle cap has a $\frac{1}{10}$ probability of being labeled "free drink" and a $\frac{1}{25}$ probability of being labeled "free meal."

a. Explain why the events "free drink" and "free meal" are mutually exclusive.

Each bottle cap has only one label applied to it.

b. What is the probability that a bottle cap is labeled "free drink" or "free meal"?

$$P(\text{free drink} \cup \text{free meal}) = P(\text{free drink}) + P(\text{free meal})$$
$$= \frac{1}{10} + \frac{1}{25} = \frac{5}{50} + \frac{2}{50} = \frac{7}{50}$$

CHECK IT OUT!

1. Each student cast one vote for senior class president. Of the students, 25% voted for Hunt, 20% for Kline, and 55% for Vila. A student from the senior class is selected at random.

a. Explain why the events "voted for Hunt," "voted for Kline," and "voted for Vila" are mutually exclusive.

b. What is the probability that a student voted for Kline or Vila?

Inclusive events are events that have one or more outcomes in common. When you roll a number cube, the outcomes "rolling an even number" and "rolling a prime number" are not mutually exclusive. The number 2 is both prime and even, so the events are inclusive.

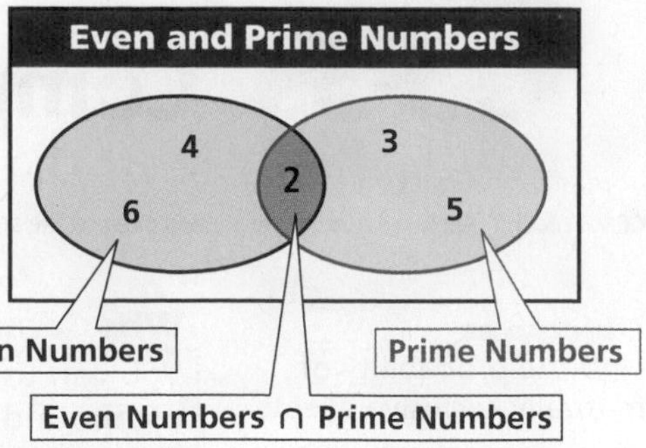

Remember!
Recall that the intersection symbol ∩ means "and."

There are 3 ways to roll an even number, $\{2, 4, 6\}$.
There are 3 ways to roll a prime number, $\{2, 3, 5\}$.

The outcome "2" is counted twice when outcomes are added $(3 + 3)$. The actual number of ways to roll an even number or a prime is $3 + 3 - 1 = 5$. The concept of subtracting the outcomes that are counted twice leads to the following probability formula.

Know it! Note

Inclusive Events

WORDS	The probability of two inclusive events *A* or *B* occurring is the sum of their individual probabilities minus the probability of *both* occurring.
ALGEBRA	For two inclusive events *A* and *B*, $P(A \cup B) = P(A) + P(B) - P(A \cap B)$.
EXAMPLE	When you roll a number cube, P(even number or prime) = $P(\text{even or prime}) = P(\text{even}) + P(\text{prime}) - P(\text{even and prime})$ $= \frac{3}{6} + \frac{3}{6} - \frac{1}{6} = \frac{5}{6}$.

EXAMPLE 2 Finding Probabilities of Inclusive Events

Find each probability on a die.

A rolling a 5 or an odd number

$$P(5 \text{ or odd}) = P(5) + P(\text{odd}) - P(5 \text{ and odd})$$

$$= \frac{1}{6} + \frac{3}{6} - \frac{1}{6} \quad \textit{5 is also an odd number.}$$

$$= \frac{1}{2}$$

B rolling at least one 4 when rolling 2 dice

$$P(4 \text{ or } 4) = P(4) + P(4) - P(4 \text{ and } 4)$$

$$= \frac{1}{6} + \frac{1}{6} - \frac{1}{36} \quad \textit{There is 1 outcome in 36 where both dice show 4.}$$

$$= \frac{11}{36}$$

CHECK IT OUT! **A card is drawn from a deck of 52. Find the probability of each.**

2a. drawing a king or a heart

2b. drawing a red card (hearts or diamonds) or a face card (jack, queen, or king)

EXAMPLE 3 Health Application

Of 3510 drivers surveyed, 1950 were male and 103 were color-blind. Only 6 of the color-blind drivers were female. What is the probability that a driver was male or was color-blind?

> **Helpful Hint**
>
> As you work through Example 3, fill in the Venn diagram with information as you find it.

Step 1 Use a Venn diagram.

Label as much information as you know. Being male and being color-blind are inclusive events.

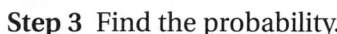

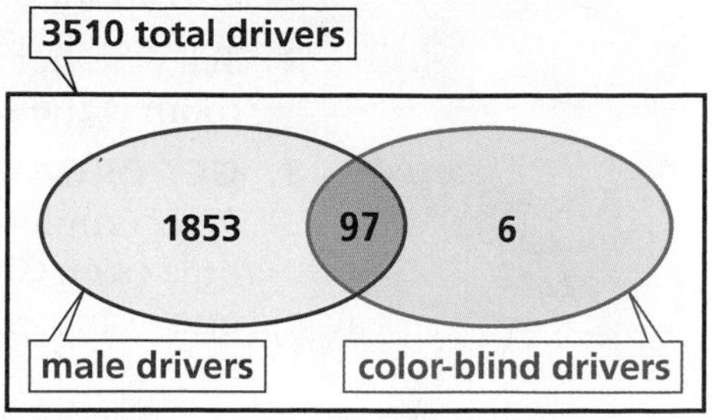

Step 2 Find the number in the overlapping region.

Subtract 6 from 103. This is the number of color-blind males, 97.

Step 3 Find the probability.

$= P(\text{male} \cup \text{color-blind}) =$

$= P(\textbf{male}) + P(\textbf{color-blind}) - P(\textbf{male} \cap \textbf{color-blind})$

$= \frac{1950}{3510} + \frac{103}{3510} - \frac{97}{3510} = \frac{1956}{3510} \approx 0.557$

The probability that a driver was male or was color-blind is about 55.7%.

CHECK IT OUT! **3.** Of 160 beauty spa customers, 96 had a hair styling and 61 had a manicure. There were 28 customers who had only a manicure. What is the probability that a customer had a hair styling or a manicure?

Recall that the complement of an event with probability p, all outcomes that are not in the event, has a probability of $1 - p$. You can use the complement to find the probability of a compound event.

EXAMPLE 4 Book Club Application

There are 5 students in a book club. Each student randomly chooses a book from a list of 10 titles. What is the probability that at least 2 students in the group choose the same book?

$P(\text{at least 2 students choose same}) = 1 - P(\text{all choose different})$ *Use the complement.*

$$P(\text{all choose different}) = \frac{\textbf{number of ways 5 students can choose different books}}{\textbf{total number of ways 5 students can choose books}}$$

$$= \frac{{}_{10}P_5}{10^5}$$

$$= \frac{10 \cdot 9 \cdot 8 \cdot 7 \cdot 6}{10 \cdot 10 \cdot 10 \cdot 10 \cdot 10} = \frac{30{,}240}{100{,}000} = 0.3024$$

$P(\text{at least 2 students choose same}) = 1 - 0.3024 = 0.6976$

The probability that at least 2 students choose the same book is 0.6976, or 69.76%.

CHECK IT OUT! **4.** In one day, 5 different customers bought earrings from the same jewelry store. The store offers 62 different styles. Find the probability that at least 2 customers bought the same style.

MATHEMATICAL PRACTICES

THINK AND DISCUSS

1. Explain why the formula for inclusive events, $P(A \cup B) = P(A) + P(B) - P(A \cap B)$, also applies to mutually exclusive events.
2. Tell whether the probability of sharing a birthday with someone else in the room is the same whether your birthday is March 13 or February 29. Explain.
3. **GET ORGANIZED** Copy and complete the graphic organizer. Give at least one example for each.

Know it! Note

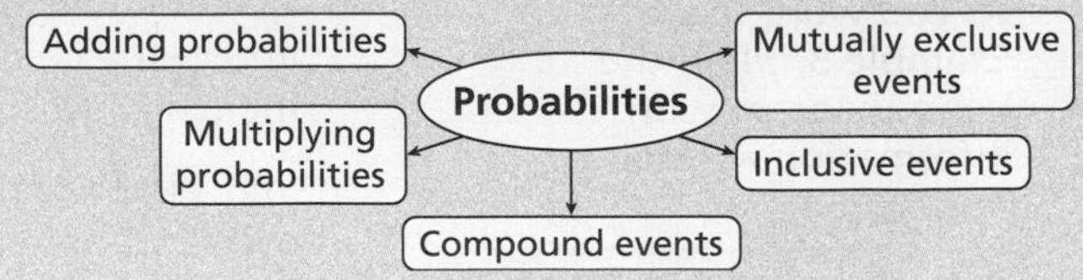

13-5 Exercises

Learn It Online
Homework Help Online
Parent Resources Online

GUIDED PRACTICE

1. **Vocabulary** A compound event where one outcome overlaps with another is made up of two __?__. (*inclusive event* or *mutually exclusive events*)

A bag contains 25 marbles: 10 black, 13 red, and 2 blue. A marble is drawn from the bag at random.

SEE EXAMPLE 1

2. Explain why the events "getting a black marble" and "getting a red marble" are mutually exclusive.
3. What is the probability of getting a red or a blue marble?
4. A car approaching an intersection has a 0.1 probability of turning left and a 0.2 probability of turning right. Explain why the events are mutually exclusive. What is the probability that the car will turn?

SEE EXAMPLE 2

Numbers 1–10 are written on cards and placed in a bag. Find each probability.

5. choosing a number greater than 5 or choosing an odd number
6. choosing an 8 or choosing a number less than 5
7. choosing at least one even number when selecting 2 cards from the bag

SEE EXAMPLE 3

Five years after 650 high school seniors graduated, 400 had a college degree and 310 were married. Half of the students with a college degree were married.

8. What is the probability that a student has a college degree or is married?
9. What is the probability that a student has a college degree or is not married?
10. What is the probability that a student does not have a college degree or is married?

SEE EXAMPLE 4

11. A vending machine offers 8 different drinks. One day, 6 employees each purchased a drink from the vending machine. Find the probability that at least 2 employees purchased the same drink.

PRACTICE AND PROBLEM SOLVING

Independent Practice

For Exercises	See Example
12–13	1
14–15	2
16–18	3
19	4

Extra Practice

See Extra Practice for more Skills Practice and Applications Practice exercises.

Jump ropes are given out during gym class. A student has a $\frac{1}{6}$ chance of getting a red jump rope and a $\frac{1}{3}$ chance of getting a green jump rope. Meg is given a jump rope.

12. Explain why the events "getting a red jump rope" and "getting a green jump rope" are mutually exclusive.

13. What is the probability that Meg gets a red or green jump rope?

The letters *A–P* are written on cards and placed in a bag. Find the probability of each outcome.

14. choosing an *E* or choosing a *G*

15. choosing an *E* or choosing a vowel

Lincoln High School has 98 teachers. Of the 42 female teachers, 8 teach math. One-seventh of all of the teachers teach math.

16. What is the probability that a teacher is a woman or teaches math?

17. What is the probability that a teacher is a man or teaches math?

18. What is the probability that a teacher is a man or does not teach math?

19. A card is drawn from a deck of 52 and recorded. Then the card is replaced, and the deck is shuffled. This process is repeated 13 times. What is the probability that at least one of the cards drawn is a heart?

LINK

Television

In 2004, about 109.6 million U.S. households had televisions. Nielsen's *rating points*, such as those for *CSI*, represent the percent of these households tuned to a show.

20. Critical Thinking Events *A* and *B* are mutually exclusive. Must the complements of events *A* and *B* be mutually exclusive? Explain by example.

21. Television According to Nielsen Media Research, on June 21, 2005, from 9 to 10 P.M., the NBA Finals Game 7 between San Antonio and Detroit had a 22 *share* (was watched by 22% of television viewers), while *CSI* had a 15 share. What is the probability that someone who was watching television during this time watched the NBA Finals or *CSI*? Do you think that this is theoretical or experimental probability? Explain.

School Arts **Use the table for Exercises 22 and 23.**

22. What would you need to know to find the probability that a U.S. public school offers music or dance classes?

23. What is the minimum probability that a U.S. public school offers visual arts or drama? What is the maximum probability?

Arts Offered by U.S. Public Schools

Class Type	Music	Visual arts	Dance	Drama and theater
Percent of Schools	94%	87%	20%	19%

24. Geometry A square dartboard contains a red square and a blue square that overlap. A dart hits a random point on the board.

a. Find $P(\text{red} \cap \text{blue})$.
b. Find $P(\text{red})$.
c. Find $P(\text{red} \cup \text{blue})$.
d. Find $P(\text{yellow})$.

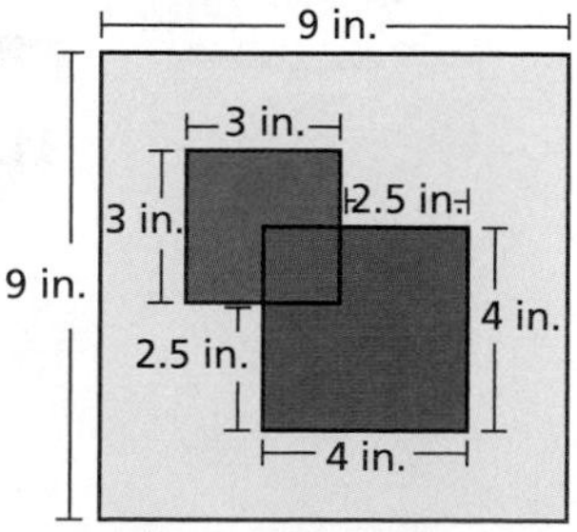

25. Genetics One study found that 8% of men and 0.5% of women are born color-blind. Of the study participants, 52% were men.

a. Which probability would you expect to be greater: that a study participant is male *and* born color-blind or that a participant is male *or* born color-blind? Explain.

b. What is the probability that a study participant is male and born color-blind? What is the probability that a study participant is male or born color-blind?

MULTI-STEP TEST PREP

26. While playing Yahtzee, Amanda rolls five dice and gets the result shown. She decides to keep the 1, 2, and 4, and reroll the 5 and 6.
    a. After rerolling the 5 and 6, what is the probability that Amanda will have a "large straight" (1-2-3-4-5) or three 4's?
    b. After rerolling the 5 and 6, what is the probability that Amanda will have a "small straight" (1-2-3-4 plus anything else) or a pair of 3's?

27. **Public Safety** In a study of canine attacks, the probability that the victim was under 18 years of age was 0.8. The probability that the attack occurred on the dog owner's property was 0.64. The probability that the victim was under 18 years of age or the attack occurred on the owner's property was 0.95. What was the probability that the victim was under 18 years of age and the attack occurred on the owner's property?

28. **Politics** A 4-person leadership committee is randomly chosen from a group of 24 candidates. Ten of the candidates are men, and 14 are women.
    a. What is the probability that the committee is all male or all female?
    b. What is the probability that the committee has at least 1 man or at least 1 woman?

29. **Multi-Step** The game Scrabble contains letter tiles that occur in different numbers. Suppose that one tile is selected.
    a. What is the probability of choosing a vowel if *Y* is not included?
    b. What is the probability of choosing a *Y*?
    c. What is the probability of choosing a vowel if *Y* is included? How does this relate to the answer to parts **a** and **b**?

Distribution of Scrabble Tiles

Tiles	Frequency
J, K, Q, X, Z	1
B, C, F, H, M, P, V, W, Y, blank	2
G	3
D, L, S, U	4
N, R, T	6
O	8
A, I	9
E	12

30. **Write About It** Demonstrate two ways to find the probability of a coin's landing heads up at least once in 2 tosses of a coin.

TEST PREP

31. For a quilt raffle, 2500 tickets numbered 0001–2500 are sold. Jamie has number 1527. The winning raffle number is read one digit at a time. The first winning number begins "One...". After the first digit is called, Jamie's chances of winning do which of the following?

    Ⓐ Go to 0
    Ⓑ Stay the same
    Ⓒ Increase from $\frac{1}{2500}$ to $\frac{1}{1527}$
    Ⓓ Increase from $\frac{1}{2500}$ to $\frac{1}{1000}$

32. A fair coin is tossed 4 times. Given that each of the first 3 tosses land tails up, what is the probability that all 4 tosses land tails up?

    Ⓕ 0.5
    Ⓖ Greater than 0.5
    Ⓗ 0.5^4
    Ⓙ Between 0.5^4 and 0.5

33. If Travis rolls a 5 on a number cube, he lands on "roll again." If Travis rolls a number greater than 3, he'll pass "start" and collect $100. What is the probability that Travis rolls again or collects $100?

Ⓐ $\frac{1}{6}$ Ⓑ $\frac{1}{5}$ Ⓒ $\frac{1}{4}$ Ⓓ $\frac{1}{2}$

34. **Short Response** What is the probability of an event or its complement? Explain.

CHALLENGE AND EXTEND

35. What is the probability that at least 2 people in a group of 10 people have the same birthday? (Assume no one in the group was born on February 29th.)

Travel For Exercises 36–38, use the Venn diagram, which shows the transportation methods used by 162 travelers. Find each probability if a traveler is selected at random.

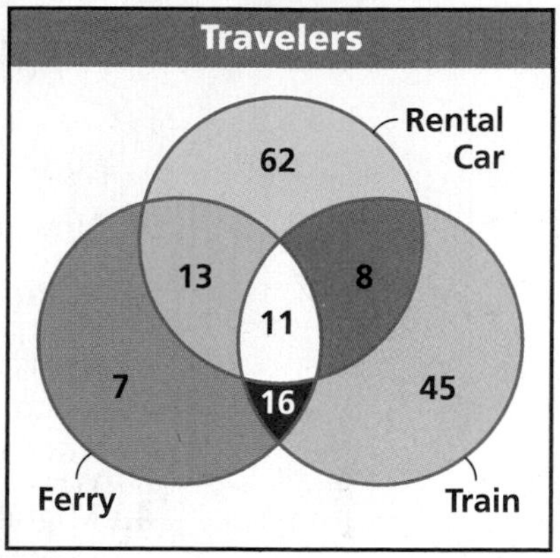

36. $P(\text{ferry or train})$

37. $P(\text{ferry or rental car})$

38. $P(\text{train and ferry, or train and rental car})$

Use the table of probabilities and the following information for Exercises 39–41. Hint: Draw a Venn diagram.

**For any three events A, B, and C, $P(A \text{ or } B \text{ or } C) =$
$P(A) + P(B) + P(C) - P(A \cap B) - P(A \cap C) - P(B \cap C) + P(A \cap B \cap C)$**

Event	$P(A)$	$P(B)$	$P(C)$	$P(A \cap B)$	$P(A \cap C)$	$P(B \cap C)$	$P(A \cap B \cap C)$
Probability	0.5	0.3	0.7	0.2	0.3	0.1	0.1

39. Find $P(B \cup C)$.

40. Find $P(A \cup B \cup C)$.

41. Find $P(B \cap (A \cup C))$.

CHAPTER 13

MULTI-STEP TEST PREP

SECTION 13B

MATHEMATICAL PRACTICES **Reason abstractly and quantitatively.**

Probability

Roll Call Yahtzee is played with 5 dice. A player rolls all 5 dice and may choose to roll any or all of the dice a second time and then a third time. At that point, the player scores points for various combinations of dice, such as 3 of a kind, 4 of a kind, or 5 of a kind.

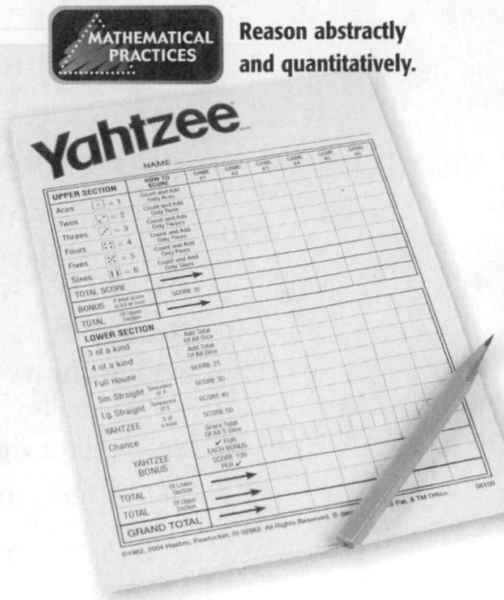

1. How many possible rolls of 5 dice are there?
2. What is the probability of rolling five 6's on the first roll of the dice?
3. What is the probability of rolling 5 of any one number on the first roll?
4. Miguel's first roll is shown at right. He decides to reroll the 6's. What is the probability that he has a 1, 2, 3, 4, and 5 after this roll?

5. What is the probability that Miguel has a 1, 2, 3, 4, and 5 after the roll, given that at least one of the dice comes up a 4?
6. What is the probability that Miguel has a 1, 2, 3, 4, and 5 or a pair of 2's after the roll in Problem 4?
7. What is the probability that Miguel has a 1, 2, 3, 4, and any other number or a pair of 4's after the roll in Problem 4?

READY TO GO ON?

CHAPTER 13

SECTION 13B

Quiz for Lessons 13-4 and 13-5

13-4 Two-Way Tables

A bookshop surveys its customers about their magazine-buying habits, summarized in the table.

1. Make a table of the joint relative frequencies and the marginal relative frequencies.
2. Given that a customer reads *Super News,* what is the probability that he or she also reads *Look Around?*
3. Given that a customer reads *Look Around,* what is the probability that he or she also reads *Super News?*

		Reads *Look Around*	
		Yes	**No**
Reads *Super News*	Yes	62	15
	No	21	136

13-5 Compound Events

Numbers 1–30 are written on cards and placed in a bag. One card is drawn. Find each probability.

4. drawing an even number or a 1
5. drawing an even number or a multiple of 7
6. Of a company's 85 employees, 60 work full time and 40 are married. Half of the full-time workers are married. What is the probability that an employee works part time or is not married?

CHAPTER 13

Study Guide: Review

Vocabulary

combination
complement
compound event
conditional probability
conditional relative frequency
dependent events
equally likely outcomes
event
experiment
experimental probability
factorial
favorable outcomes
Fundamental Counting Principle
geometric probability
inclusive events
independent events
joint relative frequency
marginal relative frequency
mutually exclusive events
outcome
permutation
probability
sample space
simple event
theoretical probability
trial

Complete the sentences below with vocabulary words from the list above.

1. If the occurrence of one event affects the probability of the other, then the events are ___?___ .
2. When arranging items, order is important when using a(n) ___?___ .
3. The ___?___ is the joint relative frequency divided by the marginal relative frequency.

13-1 Permutations and Combinations

EXAMPLES

- **If you have 8 vases to choose from, how many ways can you arrange 5 of them on a shelf?**

The order matters, so it is a permutation.

$$_8P_5 = \frac{8!}{(8-5)!} = \frac{8 \cdot 7 \cdot 6 \cdot 5 \cdot 4 \cdot \cancel{3} \cdot \cancel{2} \cdot \cancel{1}}{\cancel{3} \cdot \cancel{2} \cdot \cancel{1}}$$
$$= 8 \cdot 7 \cdot 6 \cdot 5 = 6720$$

There are 6720 ways to arrange the vases.

- **If 7 pizza toppings are available, how many ways can you choose 2 toppings?**

The order does not matter, so it is a combination.

$$_7C_2 = \frac{7!}{2!(7-2)!} = \frac{7 \cdot 6 \cdot \cancel{5} \cdot \cancel{4} \cdot \cancel{3} \cdot \cancel{2} \cdot \cancel{1}}{2 \cdot 1(\cancel{5} \cdot \cancel{4} \cdot \cancel{3} \cdot \cancel{2} \cdot \cancel{1})}$$
$$= \frac{42}{2} = 21$$

There are 21 ways to choose the toppings.

EXERCISES

4. How many different 7-digit telephone numbers can be made if the first digit cannot be 7, 8, or 9?
5. From a group of 12 volunteers, a surveyor must choose 5 to complete an advanced survey. How many groups of 5 people can be chosen?
6. In one day, a salesman plans to visit 6 out of 14 companies that are in the neighborhood. How many ways can he plan the visits?
7. How many ways can 7 people arrange themselves inside a van that has 10 seats?
8. The caterer told Kathy that she can choose 3 entrées from the 6 listed on the menu. How many groups of 3 entrées can she choose?

13-2 Theoretical and Experimental Probability

EXAMPLES

A paper clip holder has 100 paper clips: 30 are red, 20 are yellow, 25 are green, 15 are pink, and 10 are black. A paper clip is randomly chosen. Find each probability.

- The paper clip is green.

$$P(\text{green}) = \frac{\text{number of green paper clips}}{\text{total number of paper clips}}$$

$$= \frac{25}{100} = \frac{1}{4}$$

- The paper clip is not pink.

$$P(\text{not pink}) = 1 - P(\text{pink}) = 1 - \frac{15}{100} = \frac{17}{20}$$

- **Carl and Pedro each put their names in a hat for a door prize. Two names will be selected, and there are a total of 40 names in the hat. What is the probability that Carl wins the first prize and Pedro wins the second?**

The number of outcomes in the sample space is the number of ways that 2 people can be selected from 40 and then ordered.

$$P(\text{Carl, then Pedro}) = \frac{1}{{}_{40}P_2} = \frac{1}{1560}$$

- **A dart is randomly thrown at the dartboard. What is the probability that it lands in the outer ring?**

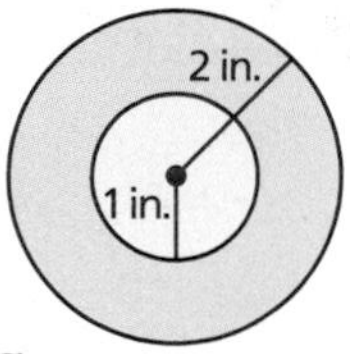

$$P(\text{outer ring}) = \frac{\text{area of outer ring}}{\text{area of dart board}}$$

$$= \frac{\text{area of large circle} - \text{area of inner circle}}{\text{area of large circle}}$$

$$= \frac{\pi(3)^2 - \pi(1)^2}{\pi(3)^2} = \frac{9\pi - 1\pi}{9\pi} = \frac{8\pi}{9\pi} = \frac{8}{9}$$

- **The table shows the results of 75 tosses of a number cube. Find the experimental probability of rolling a 4.**

1	2	3	4	5	6
10	12	16	15	9	13

$$P(4) = \frac{\text{number of times 4 occurred}}{\text{number of trials}} = \frac{15}{75}$$

$$= \frac{1}{5} = 0.2$$

EXERCISES

Two number cubes are rolled. What is the probability of each event?

9. Sum is 8.

10. Difference is 1.

11. Sum is even.

12. Product is less than 30.

13. The 10-member math team randomly selects 4 representatives to send to a meet. What is the probability that the 4 members chosen are the 4 with the lowest math grades?

14. A 5-digit code is given to all cashiers at a store to let them log onto the cash register. What is the probability that an employee receives a code with all 5 numbers the same?

15. Find the probability that a point chosen at random inside the rectangle is in the shaded area.

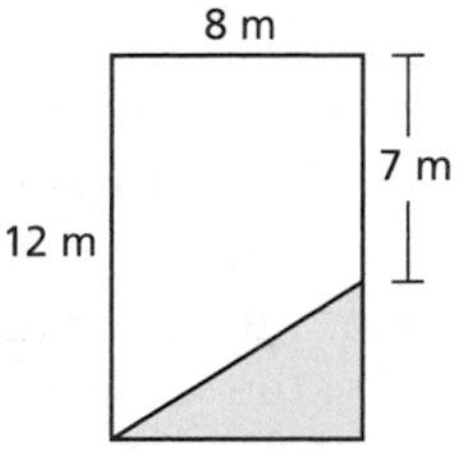

16. Find the probability that a point chosen at random inside the square is not inside the circle.

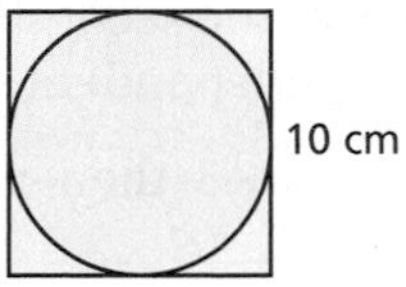

The bar graph shows the results of tossing two pennies 50 times. Find the experimental probability of each of the following.

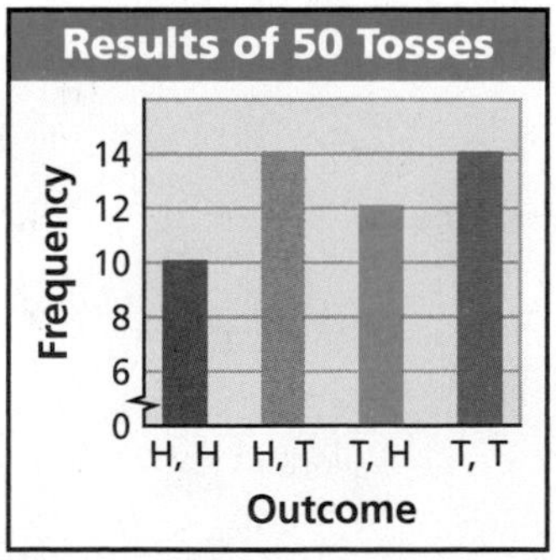

17. tossing 2 heads

18. tossing at least 1 tail

19. not tossing a head

20. tossing exactly 1 tail

Two pennies are tossed. Find the theoretical probability of each of the following.

21. tossing 2 heads

22. tossing at least 1 tail

23. not tossing a head

24. tossing exactly 1 tail

13-3 Independent and Dependent Events

EXAMPLES

A bag contains slips of papers with the following numbers: 2, 2, 3, 3, 4, 5, 6. Determine whether the events are independent or dependent, and find the indicated probability.

- You select a 3, keep the paper, and then your friend selects a 3.

  Keeping the paper with the first 3 changes the number of 3's left in the bag for your friend to choose from, so the events are dependent.

  $$P(3, \text{then } 3) = P(3) \cdot P(3 \mid 3)$$
  $$= \frac{2}{7} \cdot \frac{1}{6} = \frac{2}{42} = \frac{1}{21}$$

- You select a number greater than 3, replace the paper, and then your friend selects a number less than 3.

  Replacing the paper with the number greater than 3 means that your friend will also select from the same papers, so the occurrence of the first selection does not affect the probability of the second selection. The events are independent.

  $$P(> 3, \text{then} < 3) = P(> 3) \cdot P(< 3)$$
  $$= \frac{3}{7} \cdot \frac{2}{7} = \frac{6}{49}$$

EXERCISES

Explain why the events are independent, and find the probability.

25. rolling "doubles" 3 times in a row when rolling 2 number cubes

26. selecting a red pen and then a blue pen, when selecting 2 pens from a bag of 10 red and 15 blue pens with replacement

The table shows the age and marital status of the members of an environmental group. One person from the group is randomly selected. Find each probability.

Marital Status by Age

	18–34	35–50	51–65	66+
Married	6	20	22	4
Single	14	22	11	0

27. that the selected person is single, given that he or she is in the 35–50 age group

28. that a married person is 66 or older

29. that a person aged 18–50 is married

30. that a person in the group is single and in the 18–34 age group

13-4 Two-Way Tables

EXAMPLES

A teacher collected data on the activities the class performed last weekend and summarized the data in a table.

		Went to Park	
		Yes	No
Saw a movie	Yes	4	10
	No	5	5

- **Make a table of the joint and marginal relative frequencies.**

  Divide each value by the total of 24 to find the joint relative frequencies, and add each row and column to find the marginal relative frequencies.

		Went to Park		
		Yes	No	Total
Saw a movie	Yes	0.167	0.417	0.583
	No	0.208	0.208	0.417
	Total	0.375	0.625	1

EXERCISES

A teacher collected data on the activities the class performed on their summer break and summarized the data in a table.

		Went to Beach	
		Yes	No
Joined a sports team	Yes	10	9
	No	11	6

31. Make a table of the joint and marginal relative frequencies.

32. Given that a student went to the beach, what is the probability he or she joined a sports team?

33. Given that a student did not go to the beach, what is the probability he or she did not join a sports team?

13-5 Compound Events

EXAMPLES

Andy is using his calculator to obtain a random number from 10 to 20. Find the probability that

- Andy gets a 15 or a multiple of 2.

  10 11 12 13 14 15 16 17 18 19 20

  $\frac{1}{11} + \frac{6}{11} = \frac{7}{11}$ *The events are mutually exclusive.*

- Andy gets a multiple of 3 or a multiple of 5.

  10 11 12 13 14 15 16 17 18 19 20

  $\frac{3}{11} + \frac{3}{11} - \frac{1}{11} = \frac{5}{11}$ *The events are inclusive.*

- Andy gets all different numbers if he has the calculator randomly select 5 numbers.

  $\frac{_{11}P_5}{11^5} = \frac{11 \cdot 10 \cdot 9 \cdot 8 \cdot 7}{11 \cdot 11 \cdot 11 \cdot 11 \cdot 11} = \frac{55{,}440}{161{,}051} \approx 0.3442$

EXERCISES

A store is handing out coupons. One-third of the coupons offer a 10% discount, half offer a 15% discount, and one-sixth offer a 20% discount. A customer is handed a coupon.

34. Explain why the events "10% discount" and "15% discount" are mutually exclusive.

35. What is the probability that the coupon offers a 10% discount or a 15% discount?

A card is drawn from a deck of 52. Find the probability of each outcome.

36. drawing a red card or drawing a 5

37. drawing a club or drawing a heart

38. Of 120 males and 180 females who took an eye exam, 170 passed. One-third of the males did not pass. What is the probability that a person who took the exam passed or was male?

CHAPTER 13

CHAPTER TEST

1. A mall employee is dressing a mannequin. There are 6 pairs of shoes, 4 types of jeans, and 8 sweaters. Using 1 of each, how many ways can the mannequin be dressed?
2. How many ways can you award first, second, and third place to 8 contestants?
3. How many ways can a group of 3 students be chosen from a class of 30?
4. Four cards are randomly selected from a standard deck of 52 playing cards. What is the probability that the cards are all jacks, all queens, or all kings?
5. The table shows the results of tossing 2 coins. Find the experimental probability of tossing 2 tails.

HH	HT	TH	TT
3	6	5	6

Each letter of the alphabet is written on a card. The cards are placed into a bag. Determine whether the events are independent or dependent, and find the indicated probability.

6. The letter D is drawn, replaced in the bag, and then the letter J is drawn.
7. Three vowels are drawn without replacement.

A card is drawn from a bag containing the 9 cards shown. Find each probability.

8. selecting a C or an even number
9. selecting an odd number or a multiple of 3
10. The probability distribution for the number of absent students on any given day for a certain class is given. Find the expected number of absent students.

Number of Students Absent n	0	1	2	3	4
Probability of n Absent Students	$\frac{7}{20}$	$\frac{5}{20}$	$\frac{4}{20}$	$\frac{3}{20}$	$\frac{1}{20}$

A school is voting on a new mascot. While voting, the student body also tracked whether each person played on one of the school's sports teams. The data are presented in the table.

		Plays a sport	
		Yes	No
Mascot	Aardvark	9	75
	Fruit bat	35	56
	Plankton	51	123

11. Make a table of the joint relative frequencies and marginal relative frequencies.
12. Given that a student voted for fruit bat, what is the probability they play a sport?
13. Given that a student plays a sport, what is the probability they voted for fruit bat?
14. Given that a student plays a sport, what is the probability they did not vote for fruit bat?

COLLEGE ENTRANCE EXAM PRACTICE

CHAPTER 13

FOCUS ON SAT MATHEMATICS SUBJECT TESTS

The reference information at the beginning of a test is usually the same each time the test is given. Memorize this information so that you won't have to refer back to it during the test. When you take the test, note whether any information is different from what you expected.

You may want to time yourself as you take this practice test. It should take you about 6 minutes to complete.

HOT TIP! If you do not know how to solve a general problem, try working out a simple example or two to see if a general solution method becomes apparent. But do not spend too much time on examples. If you are still stuck after a while, move on to the next problem.

1. Two cards are drawn from a standard deck of 52 cards. What is the probability that a king and a queen are drawn?

(A) $\frac{1}{169}$

(B) $\frac{2}{169}$

(C) $\frac{8}{663}$

(D) $\frac{14}{663}$

(E) $\frac{4}{169}$

2. A poll with the options of 'yes' and 'no' was given. What is the maximum a marginal relative frequency can be for this poll, and why?

(A) The maximum is 2, because 2 is the number of options on the poll.

(B) The maximum is 0.5, because 0.5 equals one-half of the answer choices.

(C) The maximum is 1, because 1 represents 100% of the data.

(D) The maximum can't be determined from the information given.

(E) There is no maximum for the marginal relative frequencies.

3. A number cube is rolled twice. What is the probability of getting a 6 at least once?

(A) $\frac{1}{36}$

(B) $\frac{1}{6}$

(C) $\frac{11}{36}$

(D) $\frac{1}{3}$

(E) $\frac{5}{6}$

4. Your CD player can hold 6 CDs. You have 10 CDs to choose from, one of which is your favorite and is always in your player. How many ways can the player be filled if order does not matter?

(A) 126

(B) 210

(C) 720

(D) 15,120

(E) 151,200

5. Of 100 students, 37 play an instrument, 45 play sports, and 11 do both. What is the probability that a student neither plays an instrument nor plays sports?

(A) 0.145

(B) 0.18

(C) 0.29

(D) 0.40

(E) 0.82

CHAPTER 13

TEST TACKLER

Standardized Test Strategies

Multiple Choice: None of the Above or All of the Above

Given a multiple-choice test item where one of the answer choices is *none of the above* or *all of the above,* the correct response is the best, most-complete answer choice available.

To answer these types of test items, compare each answer choice with the question and determine if the answer is true or false. If you determine that more than one of the choices is true, then the correct choice is likely to be *all of the above.*

If you do not know how to solve the problem and have to guess at the answer, more often than not, *all of the above* is correct and *none of the above* is incorrect.

EXAMPLE 1

There are 8 players on the chess team. Which of the following models the number of ways that the coach can choose 2 players to start the game?

(A) ${}_8C_2$

(B) $\dfrac{8!}{2!(6!)}$

(C) 28

(D) All of the above

LOOK at each choice separately, and determine if it is true or false.

As you consider each choice, mark it "true" or "false."

Consider Choice A: *Because order does not matter, this is a combination problem. The number of combinations of 8 players, taken 2 at a time, is given by ${}_nC_r$, where $n = 8$ and $r = 2$. So, ${}_8C_2$ is a correct model of the combination.*

Choice A is *"true."* The answer could be choice A, but you need to check if choices B and C are also correct because the answer could be *all of the above.*

Consider Choice B: *The number of combinations of 8 players, taken two at a time, is given by ${}_nC_r = \frac{n!}{r!(n-r)!}$, where $n = 8$ and $r = 2$.*

$${}_nC_r = \frac{n!}{r!(n-r)!} = \frac{8!}{2!(8-2)!} = \frac{8!}{2!(6)!}$$

Choice B is also a correct model of the combination. Choice B is *"true."* The answer is likely to be choice D, *all of the above,* but you still should check to see if choice C is true.

Consider Choice C: *The number of combinations of 8 players, taken two at a time, is given by ${}_nC_r = \frac{n!}{r!(n-r)!}$, where $n = 8$ and $r = 2$.*

$${}_nC_r = \frac{n!}{r!(n-r)!} = \frac{8!}{2!(8-2)!} = \frac{8!}{2!(6)!} = 28$$

Choice C is also a correct model of the combination. Choice C is *"true."* Because choices A, B, and C are all *"true,"* the correct answer choice is choice D, *all of the above.*

HOT TIP! Be careful of problems with double negatives. Read the problem statement and each answer choice twice before selecting an answer.

Read each test item and answer the questions that follow.

Item A

Some people were polled about their support for a community garden and whether or not they had any experience growing their own food. The results of the poll are shown in the two-way table.

	Support the garden	Do not support the garden
Have grown food	7	4
Have not grown food	19	16

Which of the following statements is not true?

Ⓐ A person that supports the garden is more likely than not to have not grown food.

Ⓑ A person that hasn't grown food is more likely than not to support the garden.

Ⓒ Both statements A and B

Ⓓ None of these.

1. Read the problem statement again. If an answer choice is true, is that the correct answer? Explain.

2. Willie determined that because choice B is the reverse of choice A, choice C couldn't be correct. Do you agree? If not, what would you have done differently?

Item B

For a number cube, what is the probability of rolling a 2 or a number greater than 4?

Ⓕ 50%

Ⓖ $P(\text{rolling a 2} \cup \text{rolling 5 or 6}) = P(\text{rolling a 2}) + P(\text{rolling 5 or 6})$

Ⓗ $\frac{1}{6} + \frac{2}{6}$

Ⓙ All of the above

3. Is this event mutually exclusive or inclusive? How do you know? Determine if choice G is a true or false statement.

4. If you roll a number cube, what is the probability of rolling a 2? What is the probability of rolling a 5 or 6?

5. Simplify choice H to find its value. Is this value equivalent to any other answer choices?

6. How many answer choices are correct? What is the correct response?

Item C

Suppose that a dart lands at a random point on the circular dartboard. Find the probability that the dart lands inside only the dark gray or white region. The radius of the dartboard is 3 inches.

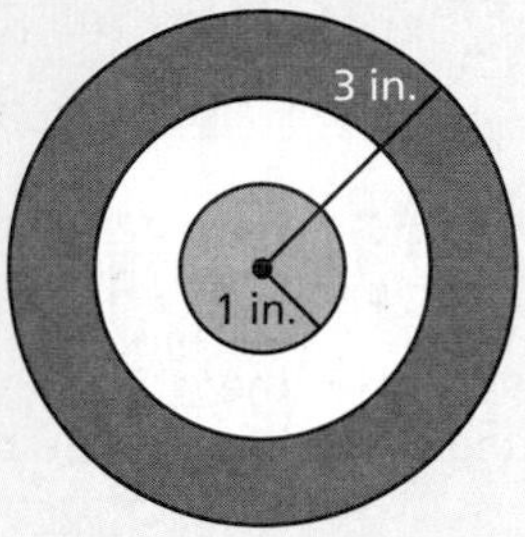

Ⓐ $\frac{1}{9}$

Ⓑ 8π

Ⓒ $\frac{8}{9}$

Ⓓ None of these

7. A student finds that both choice A and choice B are incorrect. To save time, he chooses choice D as his answer because he figures it is likely that choice C will also be incorrect. Do you think that this student made a wise decision? Explain.

8. What is the formula for the area of a circle? What is the area of this dartboard? How can you determine the area of the dark gray and white regions?

9. Find if choice A, B, or C is true, and determine the response to the test item.

Item D

Each gym member receives a 3-digit code to use for a locker combination with no digit repeated. Grace received the code 210. What was the probability that she would receive a code of consecutive numbers?

Ⓕ $1.\overline{6}\%$

Ⓖ $\frac{1}{45}$

Ⓗ $\frac{1}{{}_{10}P_3}$

Ⓙ All of the above

10. How can you determine if choice J is correct?

11. Are the values given in choices F, G, and H equivalent? What does this tell you about choice J?

CHAPTER 13

STANDARDIZED TEST PREP

Learn It Online
State Test Practice

CUMULATIVE ASSESSMENT

Multiple Choice

1. There were 8 dogs in a litter. How many ways can Mike choose 2 dogs?

Ⓐ 20,160

Ⓑ 56

Ⓒ 28

Ⓓ $\frac{1}{28}$

2. In a two-way table, the _______ are the values in each category divided by the total number of values.

Ⓕ conditional relative frequencies

Ⓖ marginal relative frequencies

Ⓗ joint relative frequencies

Ⓙ conditional probabilities

3. The table shows the number of teachers, coaches, and students at a high school of each gender. What is the probability, to the nearest hundredth, that a coach is male?

School Population and Gender

	Male	Female
Teachers	12	24
Coaches	17	9
Students	429	453

Ⓐ 0.65

Ⓑ 0.35

Ⓒ 0.04

Ⓓ 0.02

4. For $f(x) = ab^x$, if x increases by 1, the value of $f(x)$ does which of the following?

Ⓕ $f(x)$ increases by b.

Ⓖ $f(x)$ is multiplied by b.

Ⓗ $f(x)$ increases by a.

Ⓙ $f(x)$ is multiplied by a.

5. A slice of an 18-inch diameter pizza that is cut into sixths sells for \$3.25. At this rate, how much should a slice that is one eighth of a 16-inch diameter pizza sell for, to the nearest \$0.05?

Ⓐ \$1.75

Ⓑ \$1.95

Ⓒ \$2.15

Ⓓ \$2.45

6. Which graph shows a line with a slope of $-\frac{4}{3}$ that passes through $(5, 2)$?

Ⓕ
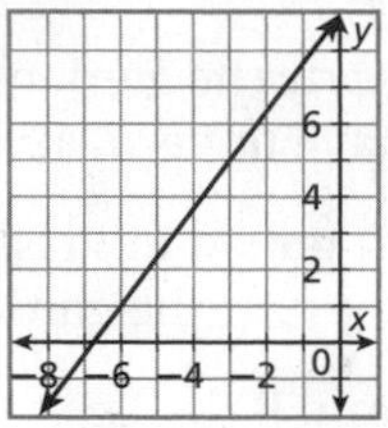

Ⓗ
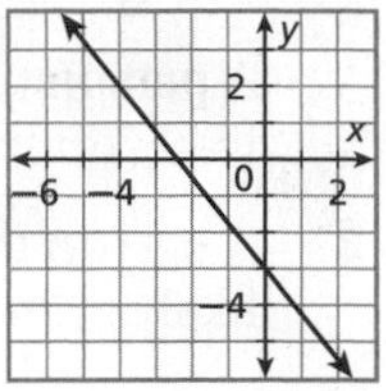

Ⓖ
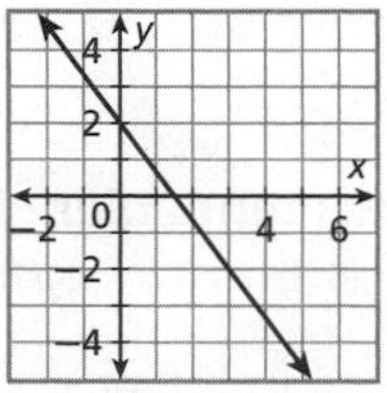

Ⓙ
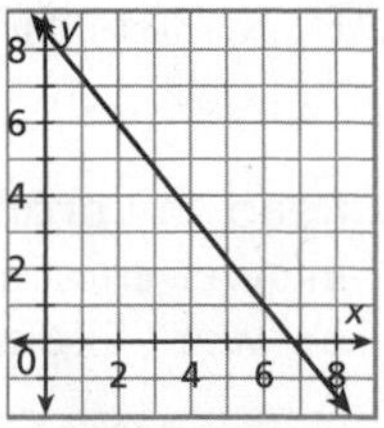

7. Which type of function is shown in the graph?

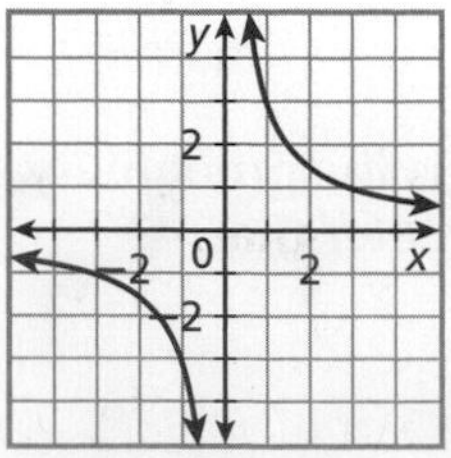

Ⓐ exponential

Ⓑ polynomial

Ⓒ radical

Ⓓ rational

8. Suppose y varies directly with x. If $y = 6$ when $x = -2$, find x when $y = -9$.

(F) -3

(G) 3

(H) 6

(J) 12

HOT TIP! **In item 9, remember that a real number with a 0 exponent is 1. You can use mental math to quickly evaluate each function and compare your result to the corresponding value in the graphed function.**

9. Which is the equation of the graph below?

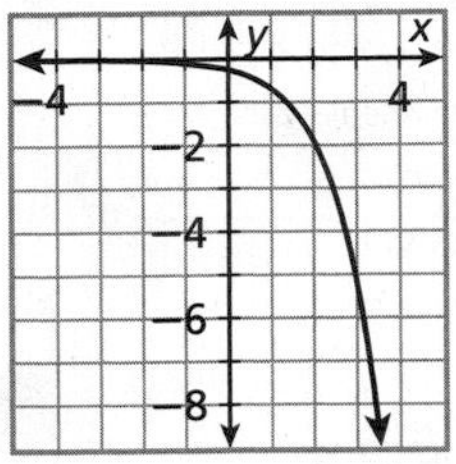

(A) $f(x) = 0.25(2.75^x)$

(B) $f(x) = -2.75(0.25^x)$

(C) $f(x) = 2.75(0.25^x)$

(D) $f(x) = -0.25(2.75^x)$

Gridded Response

10. One solution of the equation $3(x - 2) + 5 = x(x - 4) + 9$ is 2. What is the other solution?

11. Use long division to find the coefficient of the x term in the quotient.
$(2x^3 + 5x^2 + 10x + 7) \div (x + 1)$

Use the spinner for Items 12 and 13.

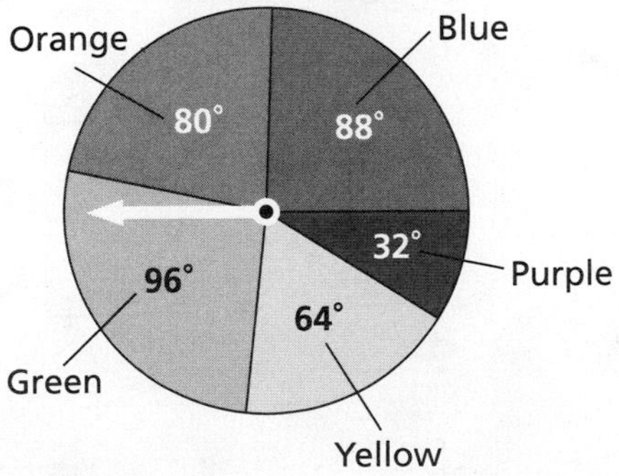

12. What is the probability of the spinner landing on the orange or purple sector, to the nearest hundredth?

13. What is the probability that the spinner will land on green in at least 2 of the next 3 spins? Write the answer to the nearest thousandth.

Short Response

14. Find the center and the radius of a circle that has a diameter with the endpoints $(-2, 8)$ and $(4, 2)$.
    a. What is the length of the diameter?
    b. The endpoints $(4, 8)$ and $(-2, y)$ are located on the circle. Find the missing value of y.

15. A test to be on a trivia show has two parts. 60% of contestants pass the first part, and 20% pass the second part.
    a. If a contestant must pass both parts of the test to be on the show, how many contestants out of a group of 50 would likely make the show? Show your work.
    b. Is it more likely that a contestant would pass both parts or fail both parts of the test? Explain.

16. The Badgers won 70% of their games this season. They won 5 of the 12 games they played during their last road trip. Before the road trip, the Badgers had won 75% of their games.
    a. How many wins and losses did the Badgers have during the season?
    b. How many wins and losses did the Badgers have before their last road trip?

Extended Response

17. Randy wants to collect 515 baseball cards. Each week Randy buys 15 baseball cards.
    a. Create a table to represent this situation where t is the amount of time in weeks and c is the number of cards that Randy still wants to buy.
    b. Write an equation to model the data in the table.
    c. Graph the equation.
    d. After how many weeks will Randy meet his goal?

Mastering the *Standards*

for Mathematical Practice

The topics described in the Standards for Mathematical Content will vary from year to year. However, the *way* in which you learn, study, and think about mathematics will not. The Standards for Mathematical Practice describe skills that you will use in all of your math courses.

Mathematical Practices

1. *Make sense of problems and persevere in solving them.*
2. *Reason abstractly and quantitatively.*
3. *Construct viable arguments and critique the reasoning of others.*
4. *Model with mathematics.*
5. *Use appropriate tools strategically.*
6. *Attend to precision.*
7. *Look for and make use of structure.*
8. *Look for and express regularity in repeated reasoning.*

5 Use appropriate tools strategically.

Mathematically proficient students consider the available tools when solving a... problem... [and] are... able to use technological tools to explore and deepen their understanding...

In your book

Algebra Labs and **Technology Labs** use concrete and technological tools to explore mathematical concepts.

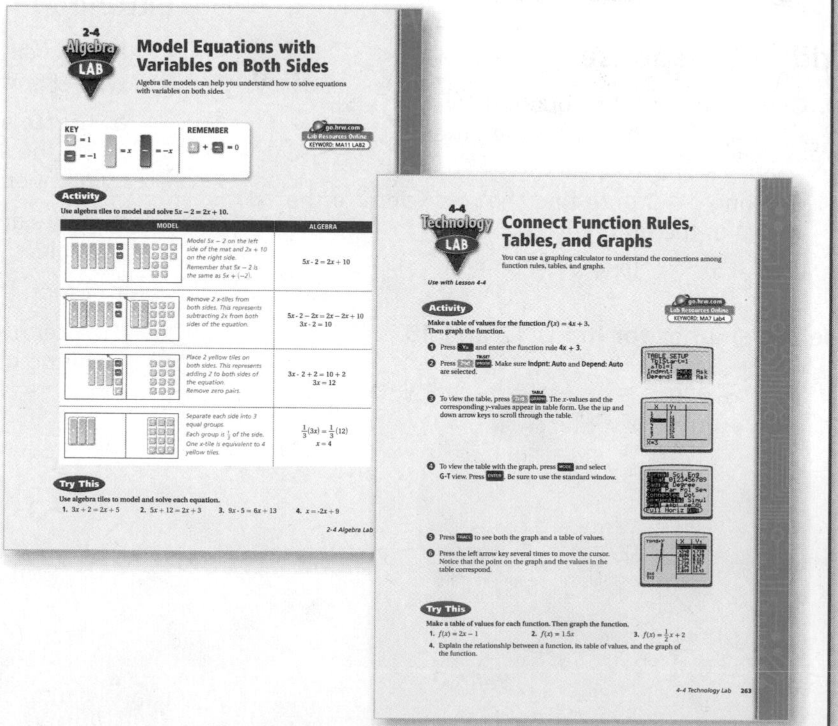
2-4 Algebra LAB

Model Equations with Variables on Both Sides

Algebra tile models can help you understand how to solve equations with variables on both sides.

Activity

Use algebra tiles to model and solve $5x - 2 = 2x + 10$.

Try This

Use algebra tiles to model and solve each equation.

1. $3x + 2 = 2x + 5$ 2. $5x + 12 = 2x + 3$ 3. $9x - 5 = 6x + 13$ 4. $x = -2x + 9$

2-4 Algebra Lab

4-4 Technology LAB

Connect Function Rules, Tables, and Graphs

You can use a graphing calculator to understand the connections among function rules, tables, and graphs.

Use with Lesson 4-4

Activity

Make a table of values for the function $f(x) = 4x + 3$. Then graph the function.

Try This

Make a table of values for each function. Then graph the function.

1. $f(x) = 2x - 1$ 2. $f(x) = 1.5x$ 3. $f(x) = \frac{1}{2}x + 2$
4. Explain the relationship between a function, its table of values, and the graph of the function.

4-4 Technology Lab 263

Student Handbook

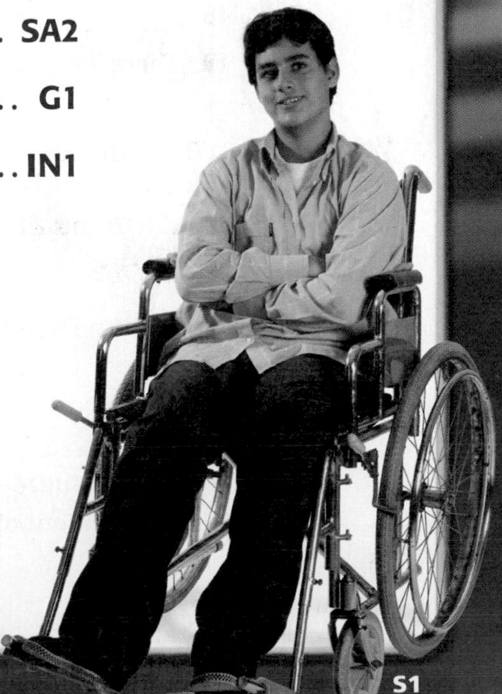

Extra Practice Chapter 1 ▪ Skills Practice

Lesson 1-1

Name each of the following.

1. two points
2. two lines
3. two planes
4. a point on $\overleftrightarrow{IH}$
5. a line that contains L and J
6. a plane that contains L, K, and H

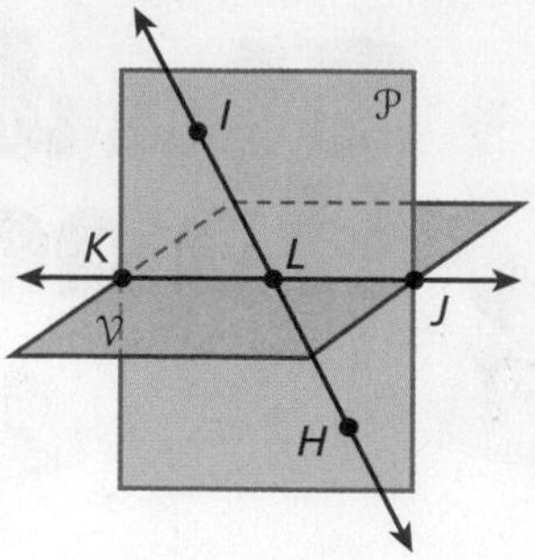

Draw and label each of the following.

7. a ray with endpoint A that passes through B
8. a line $\overleftrightarrow{PQ}$ that intersects plane $\mathcal{D}$

Lesson 1-2

Find each length.

9. MN
10. MO

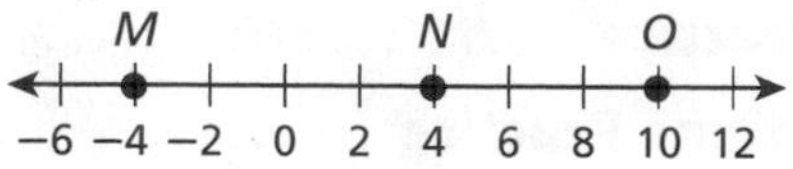

11. Segments that have the same length are ___?___ .
12. Construct a segment congruent to AB. Then construct the midpoint M.

13. M is the midpoint of $\overline{PR}$, $PM = 2x + 5$, and $MR = 4x - 7$. Solve for x and find PR.

Lesson 1-3

Z is in the interior of $\angle WXY$. Find each of the following.

14. $m\angle WXY$ if $\angle WXZ = 23°$ and $m\angle ZXY = 51°$
15. $m\angle WXZ$ if $m\angle WXY = 44°$ and $m\angle ZXY = 20°$

$\overrightarrow{EH}$ bisects $\angle DEF$. Find each of the following.

16. $m\angle DEH$ if $m\angle DEH = (10z - 2)°$ and $m\angle HEF = (6z + 10)°$
17. $m\angle DEF$ if $m\angle DEH = (9x + 3)°$ and $m\angle HEF = (5x + 11)°$
18. A ___?___ is formed by two opposite rays and measures ___?___ °.
19. There are ___?___ ° in a circle.

Lesson 1-4

Tell whether the angles are only adjacent, adjacent and form a linear pair, or not adjacent.

20. $\angle AOB$ and $\angle DOE$
21. $\angle AOE$ and $\angle DOE$
22. $\angle COE$ and $\angle EOA$
23. $\angle AOB$ and $\angle BOD$
24. Name a pair of vertical angles.

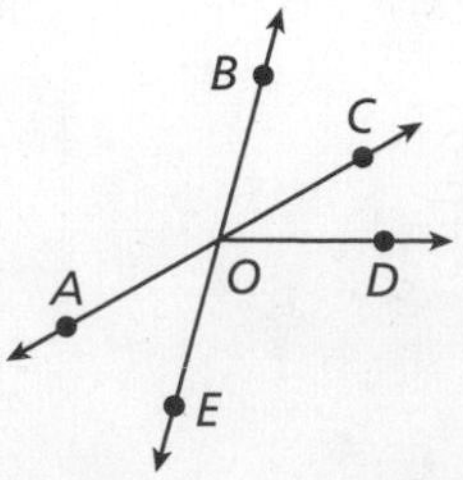

Given $m\angle A = 41.7°$ and $m\angle B = (24.2 - x)°$, find the measure of each of the following.

25. complement of $\angle A$
26. supplement of $\angle A$
27. supplement of $\angle B$

Lesson 1-5

Find the perimeter and area of each figure.

28.

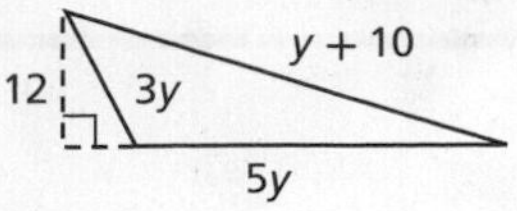

29.

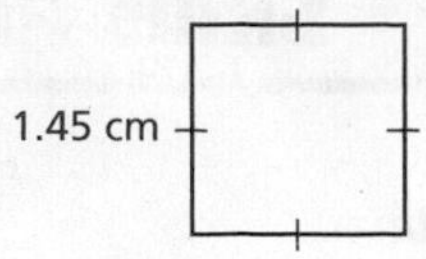

30.

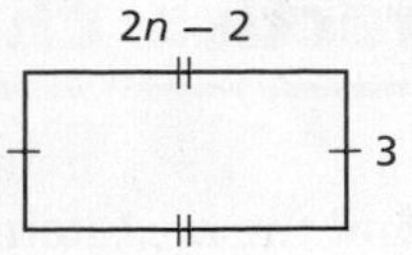

Find the circumference and area of each circle. Give your answer to the nearest hundredth.

31.

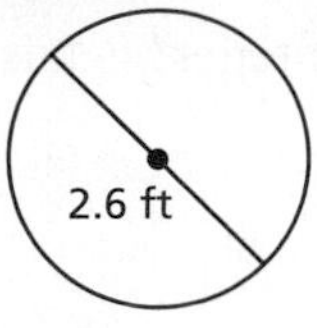

32.

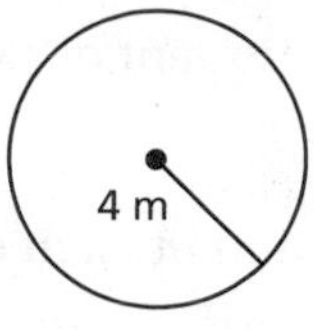

33.

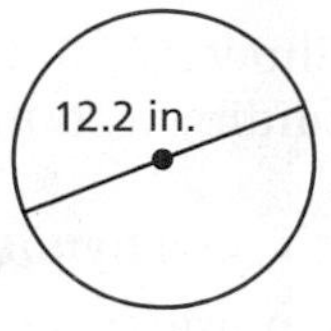

Lesson 1-6

34. The formula to find the midpoint M of $\overline{AB}$ with endpoints $A(x_1, y_1)$ and $B(x_2, y_2)$ is ___?___ .

Find the coordinates of the midpoint of each segment.

35. $\overline{WX}$ with endpoints $W(-4, 1)$ and $X(2, 9)$

36. $\overline{YZ}$ with midpoints $Y(4, 8)$ and $Z(-1, -4)$

37. M is the midpoint of $\overline{RS}$. R has coordinates $(-7, -3)$, and M has coordinates $(1, 1)$. Find the coordinates of S.

Find the length of the given segments and determine if they are congruent.

38. $\overline{VW}$ and $\overline{PQ}$

39. $\overline{RS}$ and $\overline{TU}$

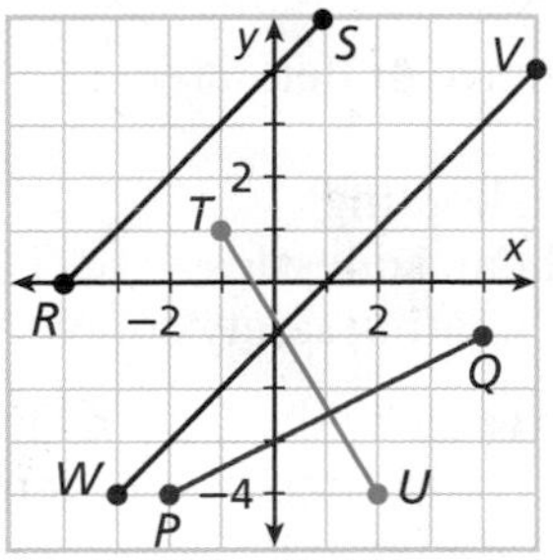

Lesson 1-7

Identify each transformation. Then use arrow notation to describe the transformation.

40.

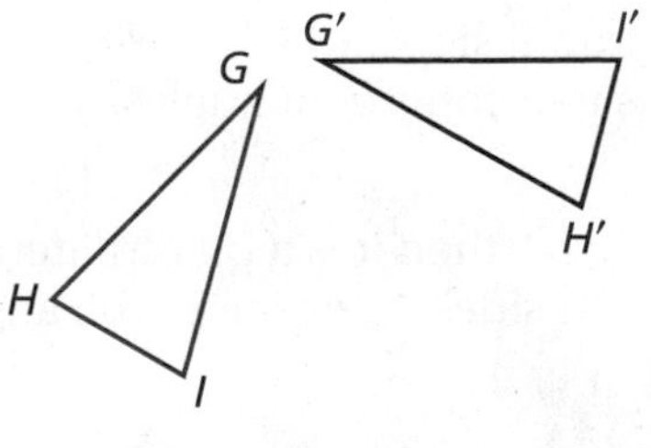

41.

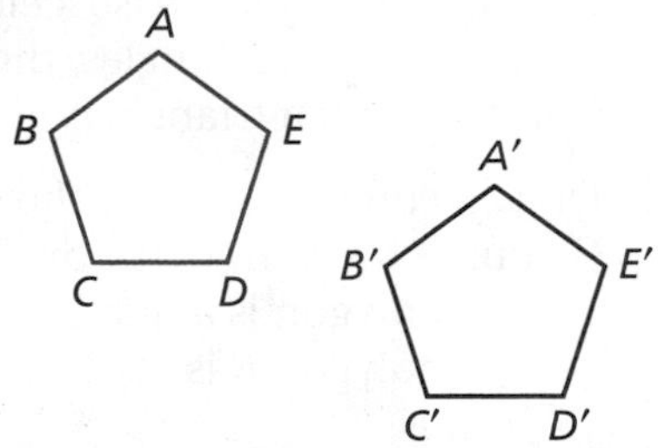

42. A figure has vertices at $(1, 1)$, $(2, 4)$, and $(5, 3)$. After a transformation, the image of the figure has vertices at $(-3, -2)$, $(-2, 1)$, and $(1, 0)$. Draw the preimage and image. Then describe the transformation.

43. A figure has vertices at $(5, 5)$, $(2, 6)$, $(1, 5)$, and $(2, 4)$. After a transformation, the image of the figure has vertices at $(5, 5)$, $(6, 8)$, $(5, 9)$, and $(4, 8)$. Draw the preimage and image. Then describe the transformation.

44. The coordinates of the vertices of quadrilateral $DEFG$ are $(3, 0)$, $(2, 3)$, $(-3, 2)$, and $(-2, -1)$. Find the coordinates for the image of rectangle $DEFG$ after the translation $(x, y) \rightarrow (x, -y)$. Draw the preimage and image. Then describe the transformation.

Lesson 2-1

Find the next item in each pattern.

1. 3, 7, 11, 15, ...
2. −3, 6, −12, 24, ...
3. Complete the conjecture "The product of two negative numbers is __?__."
4. Show that the conjecture "The quotient of two integers is an integer" is false by finding a counterexample.

Lesson 2-2

Identify the hypothesis and conclusion of each conditional.

5. A number is divisible by 10 if it ends in zero.
6. If the temperature reaches 100° F, it will rain.

Write a conditional statement from each of the following.

7. Perpendicular lines intersect to form 90° angles.
8. 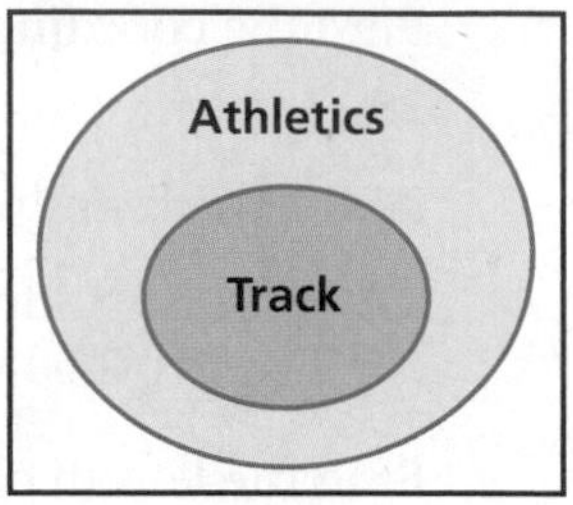

9. The sum of two supplementary angles is 180°.

Lesson 2-3

Determine if each conditional is true. If false, give a counterexample.

10. If a figure has four sides, then it is a square.
11. If $x = 3$, then $5x = 15$.
12. Does the conclusion use inductive or deductive reasoning?
To rent a boat, you must take a boating safety course. Jason rented a boat, so Jessica concludes that he has taken a boating safety course.
13. Determine if the conjecture is valid by the Law of Detachment.
Given: If a student is in tenth grade, then the student may participate in student council. Eric is a tenth-grader.
Conjecture: Eric may participate in student council.
14. Determine if the conjecture is valid by the Law of Syllogism.
Given: If a triangle is isosceles, then it has two congruent sides. If a triangle has two congruent angles, then it has two congruent sides.
Conjecture: If a triangle is isosceles, then it has two congruent angles.
15. Draw a conclusion from the given information.
Given: If the sum of the angles of a polygon is 360°, then it is a quadrilateral. If a polygon is a quadrilateral, then it has four sides. The sum of the angles of polygon R is 360°.

Lesson 2-4

16. Write the conditional statement and converse within the biconditional "A triangle is equilateral if and only if it has three congruent sides."
17. For the conditional "If a triangle is scalene, then its sides have different lengths," write the converse and a biconditional statement.
18. Determine if the biconditional "$n + 3 = -1 \leftrightarrow n = -4$" is true. If false, give a counterexample.

Write each definition as a biconditional.

19. A parallelogram is a quadrilateral with two pairs of parallel sides.
20. Congruent angles have equal measures.

Lesson 2-5

Solve each equation. Write a justification for each step.

21. $2x + 3 = 9$

22. $\frac{x+2}{5} = 3$

Write a justification for each step.

23. $AC = AB + BC$

$9x - 5 = (3x + 6) + (5x + 2)$

$9x - 5 = 8x + 8$

$x - 5 = 8$

$x = 13$

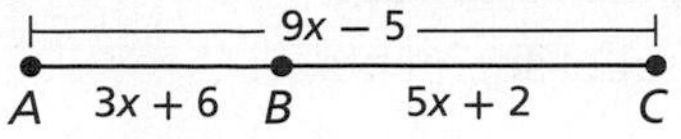

Lesson 2-6

24. Fill in the blanks to complete the two-column proof.

Given: $\angle HMK$ and $\angle JML$ are right angles.
Prove: $\angle 1 \cong \angle 3$
Proof:

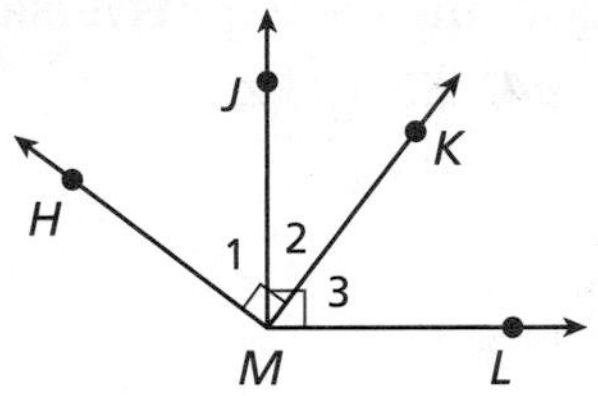

Statements	Reasons
1. a. ___?___	1. Given
2. b. ___?___ c. ___?___	2. Adjacent angles that form a right angle are complementary.
3. $\angle 1 \cong \angle 3$	3. d. ___?___

25. Use the given plan to write a two-column proof of the Transitive Property of Congruence.

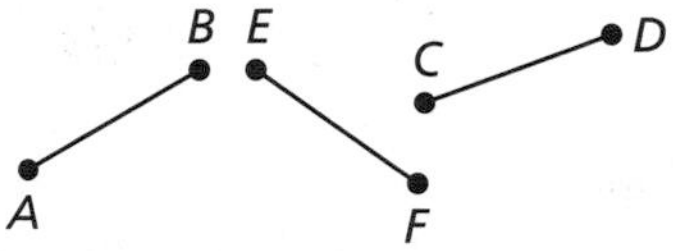

Given: $\overline{AB} \cong \overline{CD}$, $\overline{CD} \cong \overline{EF}$
Prove: $\overline{AB} \cong \overline{EF}$
Plan: Use the definition of congruent segments to write the given congruence statements as statements of equality. Then use the Transitive Property of Equality to show that $AB = EF$. So $\overline{AB} \cong \overline{EF}$ by the definition of congruent segments.

Lesson 2-7

26. Use the given two-column proof to write a flowchart proof.

Given: $\angle 2 \cong \angle 3$
Prove: $m\angle 1 = m\angle 4$
Proof:

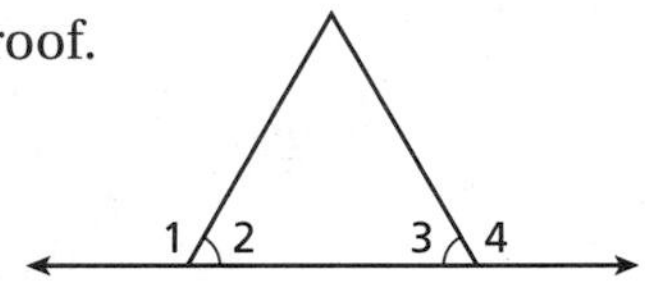

Statements	Reasons
1. $\angle 2 \cong \angle 3$	1. Given
2. $\angle 1$ and $\angle 2$ are supplementary. $\angle 3$ and $\angle 4$ are supplementary.	2. Lin. Pair Thm.
3. $\angle 1 \cong \angle 4$	3. $\cong$ Supps. Thm.
4. $m\angle 1 = m\angle 4$	4. Def. of $\cong$ ∠s

27. Use the given two-column proof to write a paragraph proof.

Given: $\angle 1 \cong \angle 3$
Prove: $\angle 4 \cong \angle 5$
Proof:

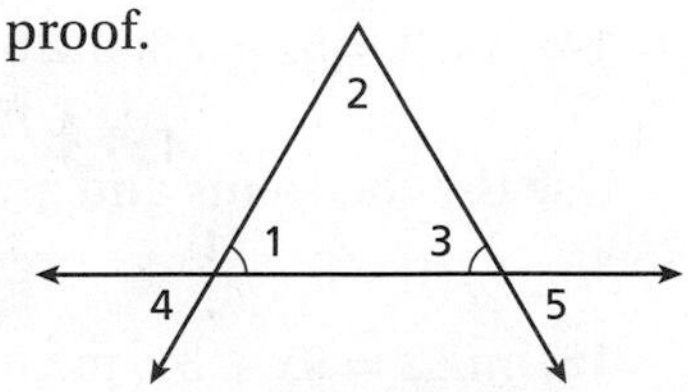

Statements	Reasons
1. $\angle 1 \cong \angle 3$	1. Given
2. $\angle 1 \cong \angle 4$, $\angle 3 \cong \angle 5$	2. Vert. ∠s Thm.
3. $\angle 1 \cong \angle 5$	3. Trans. Prop. of $\cong$
4. $\angle 4 \cong \angle 5$	4. Trans. Prop. of $\cong$

Extra Practice Chapter 3 ▪ Skills Practice

Lesson 3-1

Identify each of the following.

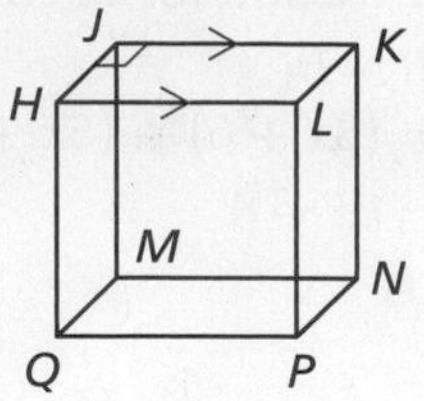

1. a pair of parallel segments
2. a pair of perpendicular segments
3. a pair of skew segments

Identify the transversal and classify each angle pair.

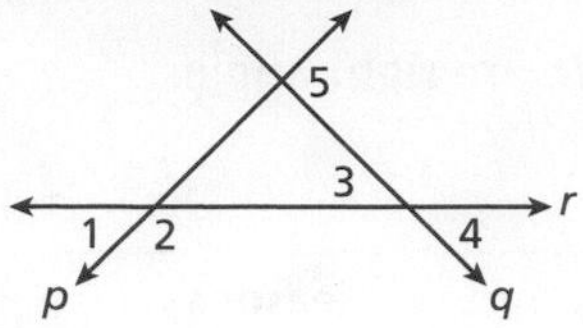

4. ∠5 and ∠3
5. ∠2 and ∠4
6. ∠5 and ∠1

Lesson 3-2

Find each angle measure.

7. m∠*XYZ*

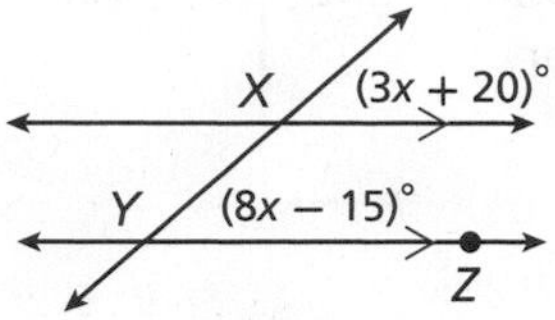

8. m∠*KJH*

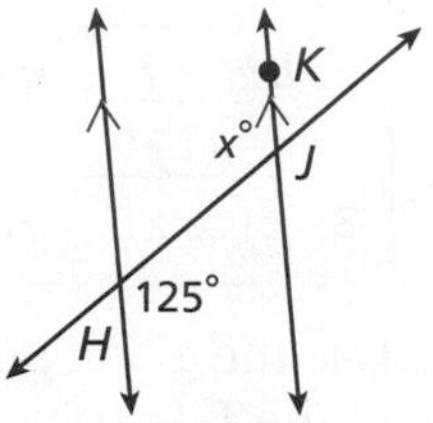

9. m∠*ABC*

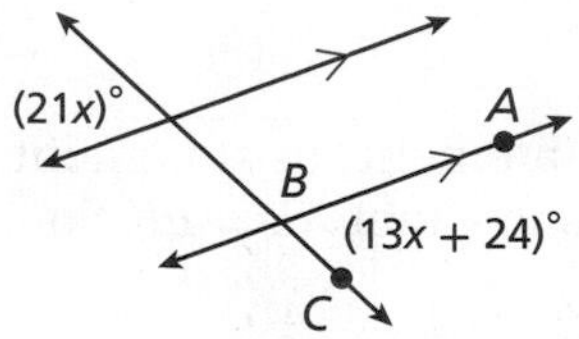

10. m∠*LMN*

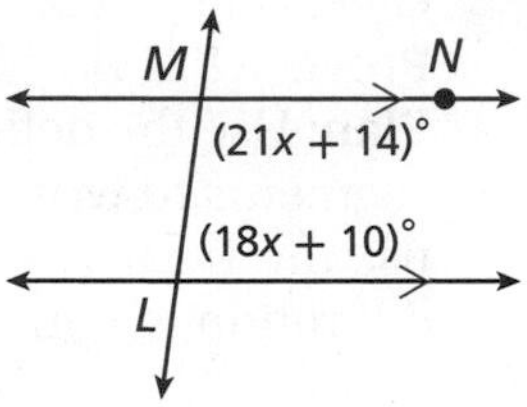

11. m∠*PQR*

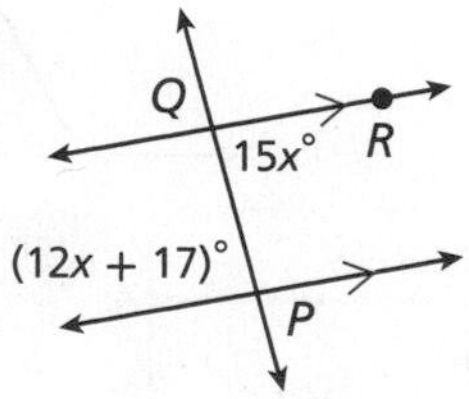

12. m∠*TUV*

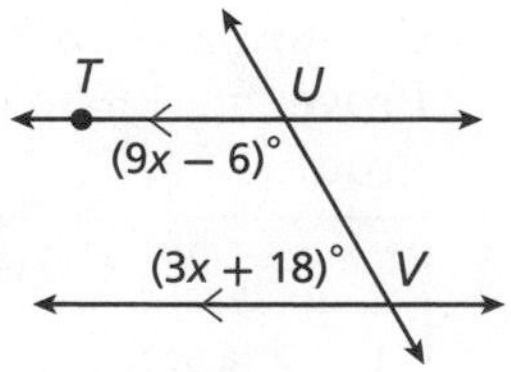

Lesson 3-3

Use the Converse of the Corresponding Angles Postulate and the given information to show that ℓ ∥ *m*.

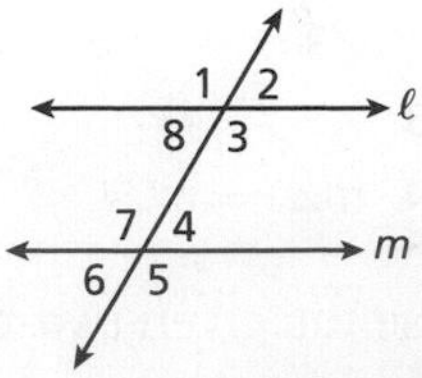

13. ∠2 ≅ ∠4
14. m∠8 = 5*x* + 36, m∠6 = 11*x* + 12, *x* = 4

Use the theorems and given information to show that *p* ∥ *q*.

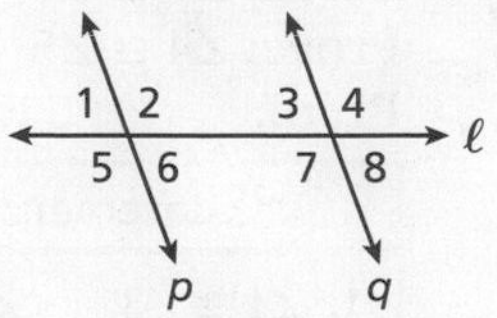

15. ∠1 ≅ ∠8
16. m∠2 = 9*x* + 31, m∠3 = 6*x* + 14, *x* = 9
17. Write a two-column proof.

Given: ∠1 and ∠5 are supplementary.
Prove: ℓ ∥ *m*

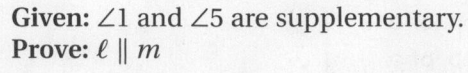

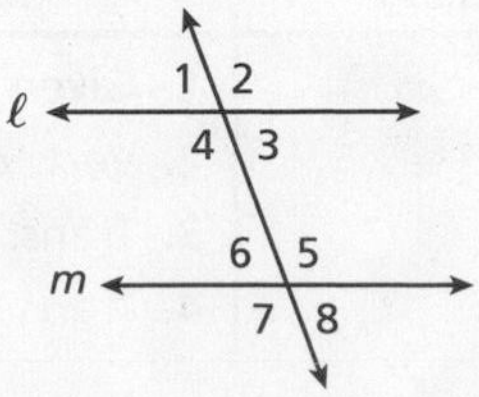

Lesson 3-4

18. Name the shortest segment from point A to $\overleftrightarrow{BE}$.

19. Write and solve an inequality for x.

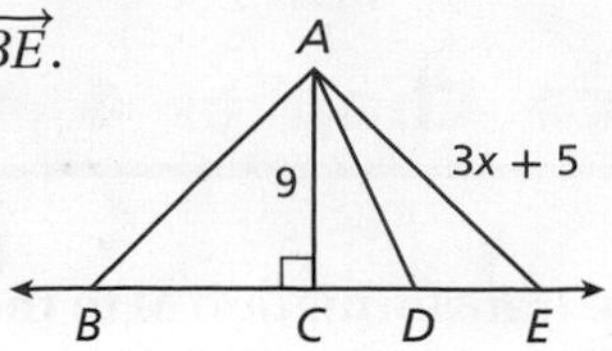

Solve for x and y in each diagram.

20.

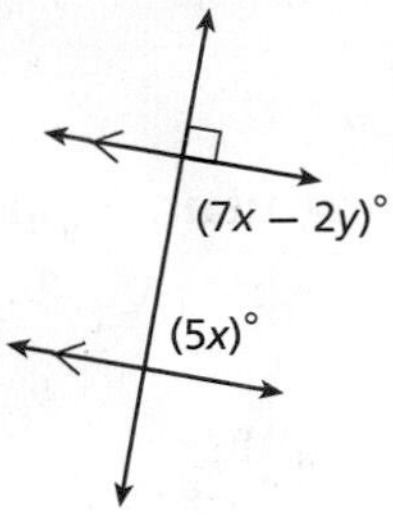

21.

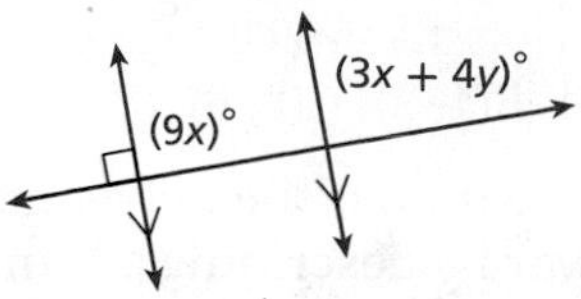

22. Write a two-column proof.

Given: $\ell \perp p$, $m \perp p$
Prove: $\ell \parallel m$

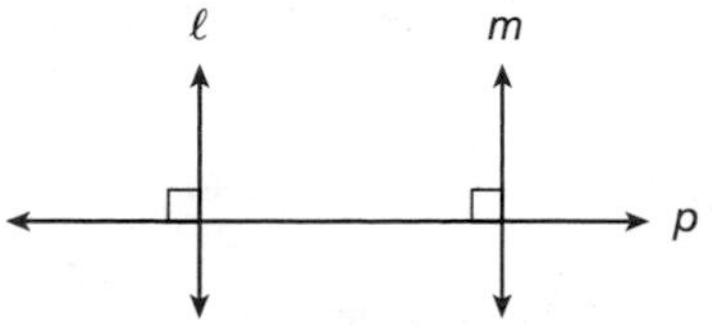

Lesson 3-5

Use the slope formula to determine the slope of each line.

23. $\overleftrightarrow{FG}$

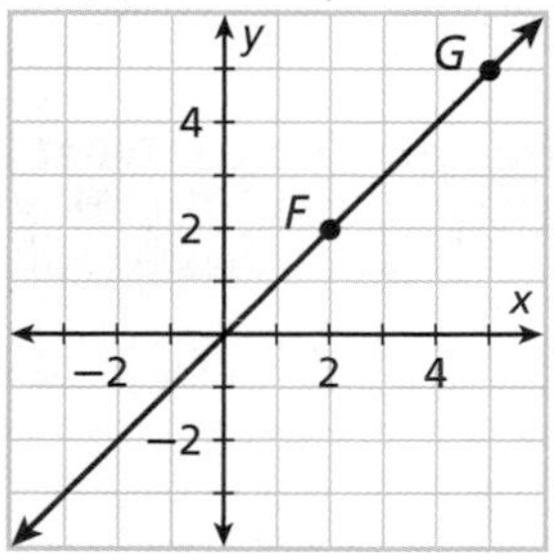

24. $\overleftrightarrow{HJ}$

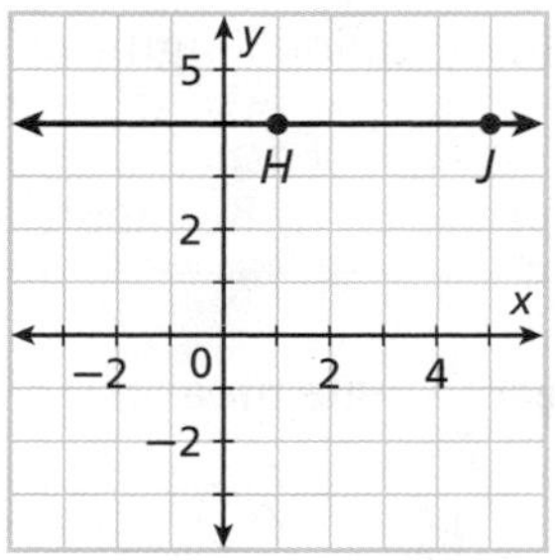

Graph each pair of lines. Use slopes to determine whether the lines are parallel, perpendicular, or neither.

25. $\overleftrightarrow{AB}$ and $\overleftrightarrow{CD}$ for $A(4, 7)$, $B(3, 2)$, $C(-3, 4)$, $D(2, 3)$

26. $\overleftrightarrow{EF}$ and $\overleftrightarrow{GH}$ for $E(-2, 4)$, $F(3, 1)$, $G(-1, -2)$, $H(4, -5)$

27. $\overleftrightarrow{JK}$ and $\overleftrightarrow{LM}$ for $J(-3, 3)$, $K(4, -2)$, $L(4, 2)$, $M(0, -4)$

Lesson 3-6

Write the equation of each line in the given form.

28. the line with slope $-\frac{2}{3}$ through $(3, -1)$ in point-slope form

29. the line through $(-2, 2)$ and $(4, -1)$ in slope-intercept form

30. the line with x-intercept -3 and y-intercept 4 in slope-intercept form

Graph each line.

31. $y = -\frac{3}{4}x + 2$

32. $y + 4 = -3(x + 2)$

33. $y = 2$

34. $x = -1$

Determine whether the lines are parallel, intersect, or coincide.

35. $y = 4x + 2$, $4x - y = 1$

36. $y = -\frac{1}{2}x + 3$, $2y + x = 6$

37. $2x + 5y = 1$, $5x + 2y = 1$

38. $2x - y = 5$, $2x - y = -5$

Extra Practice Chapter 4 ▪ Skills Practice

Lesson 4-1

Apply the transformation *M* to the polygon with the given vertices. Name the coordinates of the image points. Identify and describe the transformation.

1. $M: (x, y) \longrightarrow (-x, y)$
$A(4, 5)$, $B(1, 3)$, $C(2, 6)$

2. $M: (x, y) \longrightarrow (x - 2, y + 2)$
$P(-3, 2)$, $Q(5, 0)$, $R(4, -2)$

Determine whether the polygons with the given vertices are congruent. Support your answer by describing a transformation.

3. $X(1, -3)$, $Y(0, 2)$, $Z(-1, 4)$ and $M(3, -9)$, $N(0, 6)$, $P(-3, 12)$

Lesson 4-2

Classify each triangle by its angle measures.

4. $\triangle ABC$

5. $\triangle BCD$

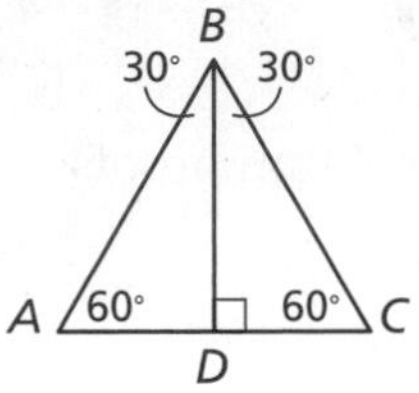

Classify each triangle by its side lengths.

6. $\triangle EFG$

7. $\triangle FGH$

8. $\triangle EFH$

9. Find the side lengths of $\triangle JKL$.

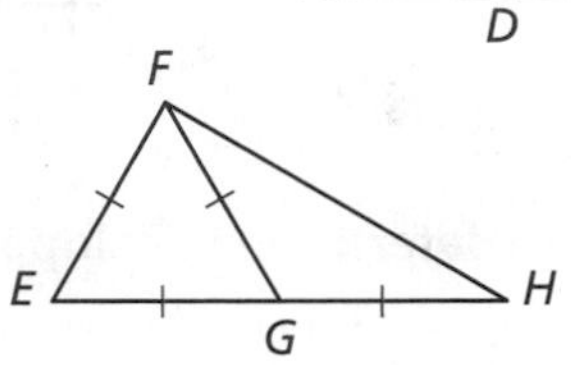

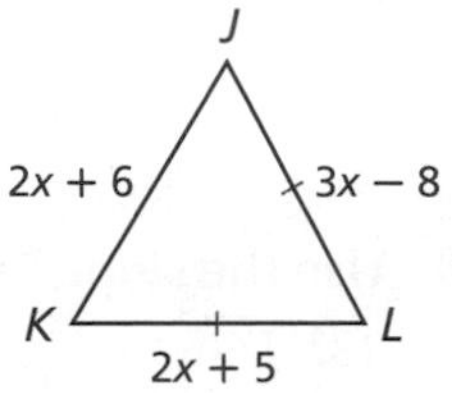

Lesson 4-3

The measure of one of the acute angles of a right triangle is given. What is the measure of the other acute angle?

10. 38°

11. 27.6°

Find each angle measure.

12. $m\angle A$

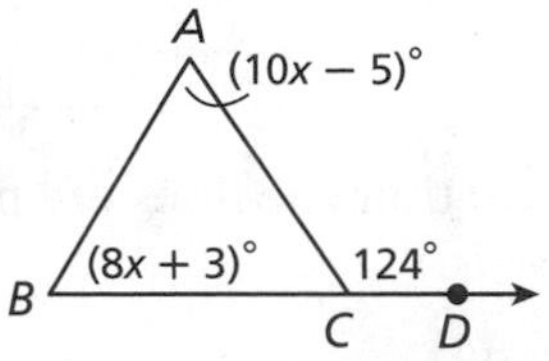

13. $m\angle J$ and $m\angle P$

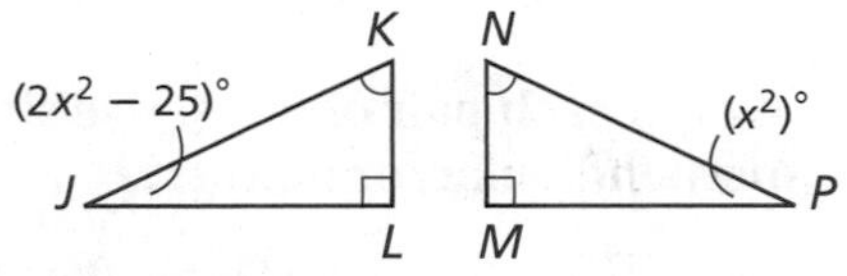

Lesson 4-4

Given: $\triangle GHI \cong \triangle JKL$. Identify the congruent corresponding parts.

14. $\overline{GH} \cong$ ___?___

15. $\overline{JL} \cong$ ___?___

16. $\angle K \cong$ ___?___

Given: $\triangle LMN \cong \triangle PQN$. Find each value.

17. x

18. $m\angle LMN$

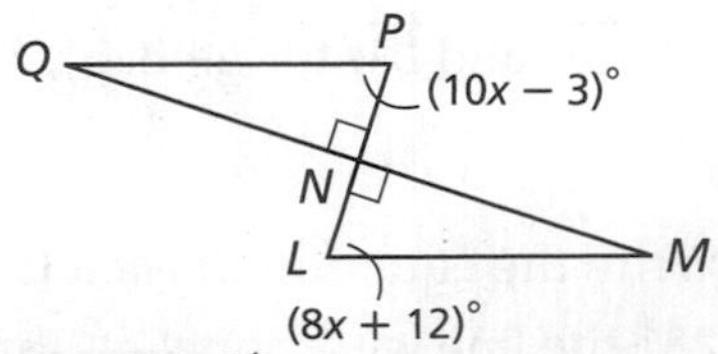

Lesson 4-5

Use SSS to explain why the triangles in each pair are congruent.

19. $\triangle QRS \cong \triangle QRT$

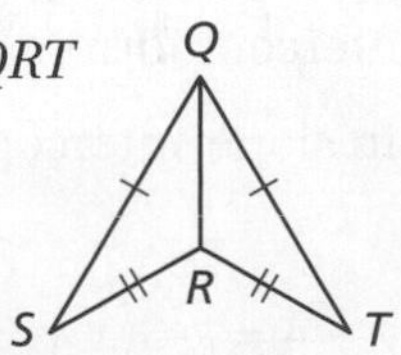

20. $\triangle UVW \cong \triangle WXU$

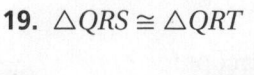

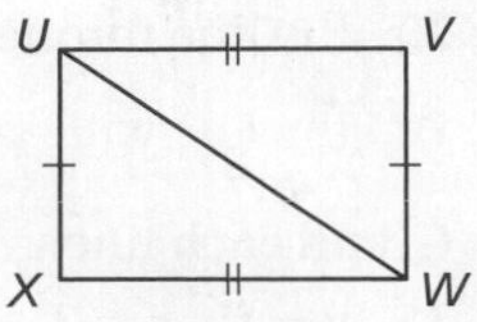

Show that the triangles are congruent for the given value of the variable.

21. $\triangle XYZ \cong \triangle ABC$, $x = 4$

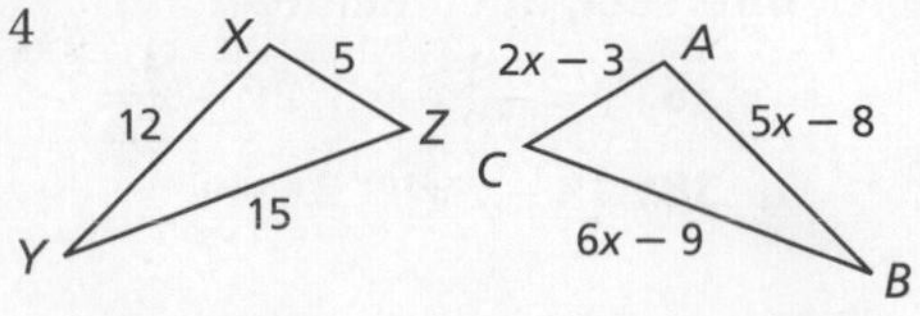

22. $\triangle DEF \cong \triangle GFE$, $y = 8$

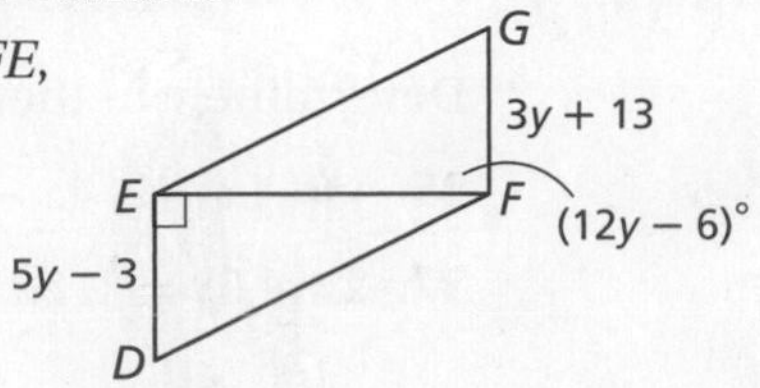

Lesson 4-6

Determine if you can use ASA to prove the triangles congruent. Explain.

23. $\triangle ACB$ and $\triangle ACD$

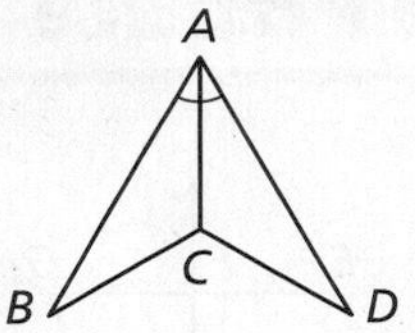

24. $\triangle EFG$ and $\triangle HGF$

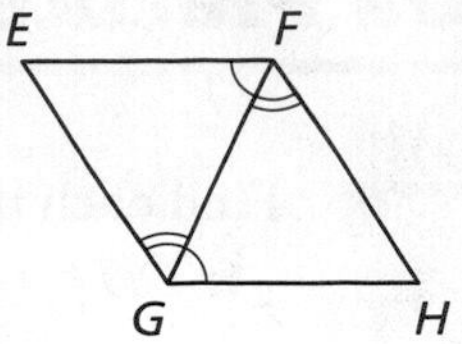

Determine if you can use the HL Congruence Theorem to prove the triangles congruent. If not, tell what else you need to know.

25. $\triangle ABC \cong \triangle EDC$

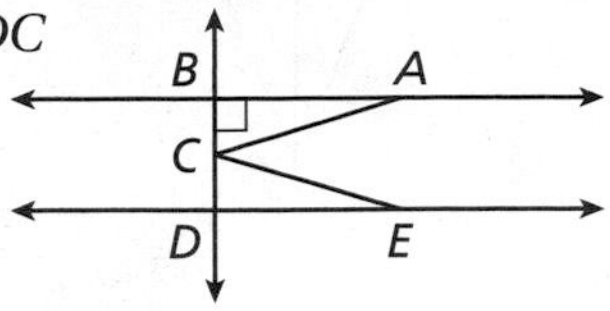

26. $\triangle FGH \cong \triangle FJH$

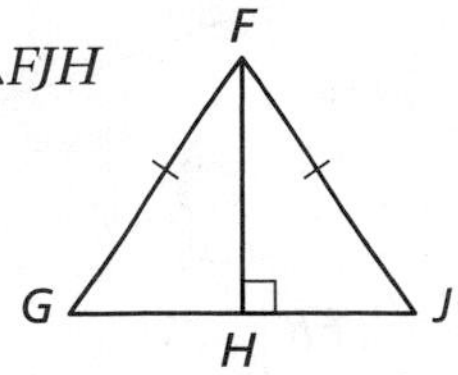

Lesson 4-7

27. **Given:** $\overline{MN} \parallel \overline{LP}$, $\angle N \cong \angle L$

Prove: $\overline{ML} \cong \overline{PN}$

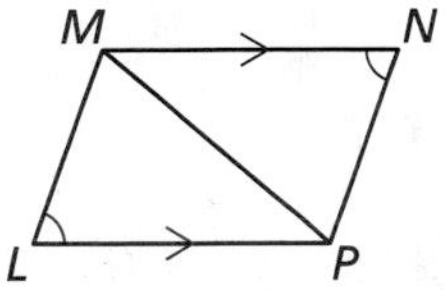

28. **Given:** $\angle 1 \cong \angle 6$, $\angle 4 \cong \angle 6$, $\angle 1 \cong \angle 3$, $\overline{AB} \cong \overline{AE}$

Prove: $\triangle ACD$ is isosceles.

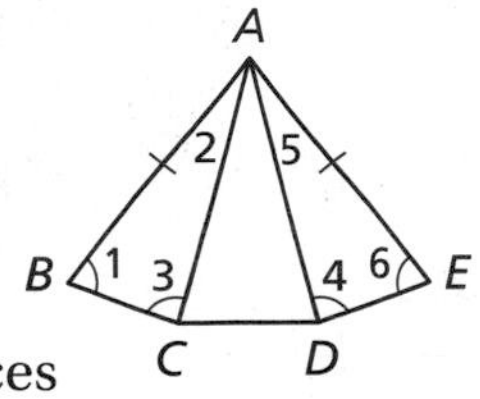

29. **Given:** $\triangle ABC$ with vertices $A(2, 4)$, $B(3, 1)$, $C(5, 2)$ and $\triangle DEF$ with vertices $D(-4, -2)$, $E(-1, -3)$, $F(-2, -5)$

Prove: $\angle BAC \cong \angle EDF$

Lesson 4-8

Position each figure in the coordinate plane.

30. a rectangle with length 7 units and width 3 units

31. a square with side length $3a$

Write a coordinate proof.

32. **Given:** Right $\triangle GHI$ has coordinates $G(0, 0)$, $H(0, 4)$, and $I(6, 0)$. J is the midpoint of $\overline{GH}$, and K is the midpoint of $\overline{GI}$.

Prove: The area of $\triangle GJK$ is $\frac{1}{4}$ the area of $\triangle GHI$.

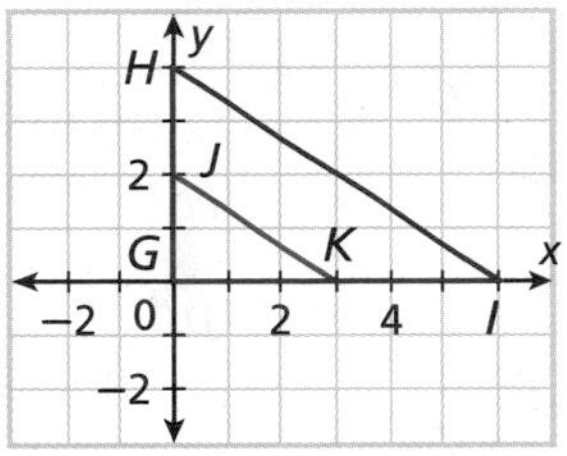

Assign coordinates to each vertex and write a coordinate proof.

33. **Given:** A is the midpoint of $\overline{XW}$ in rectangle $WXYZ$. B is the midpoint of $\overline{YZ}$.

Prove: $AB = XY$

Lesson 4-9

Find each angle measure.

34. $m\angle X$

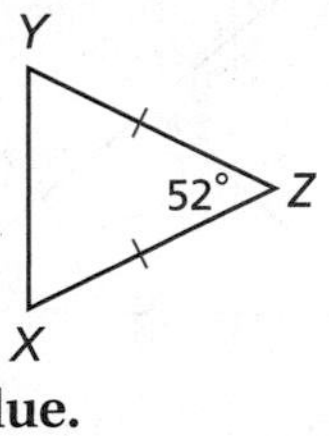

35. $m\angle A$

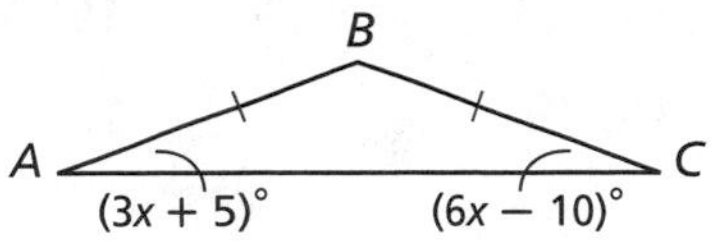

Find each value.

36. x

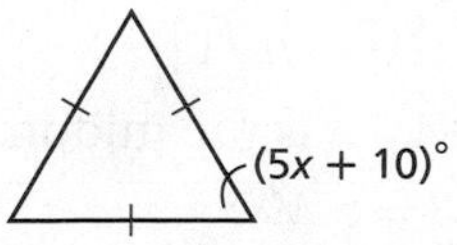

37. y

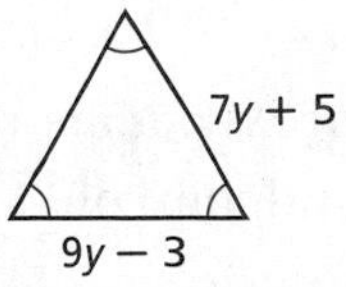

38. **Given:** $\triangle XYZ$ is isosceles. A is the midpoint of $\overline{XZ}$. $\overline{XY} \cong \overline{YZ}$

Prove: $\triangle YAZ$ is isosceles.

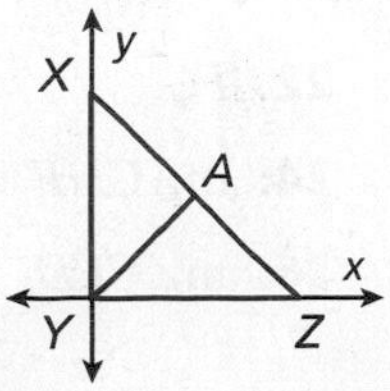

Extra Practice Chapter 5 ▪ Skills Practice

Lesson 5-1

Find each measure.

1. CD

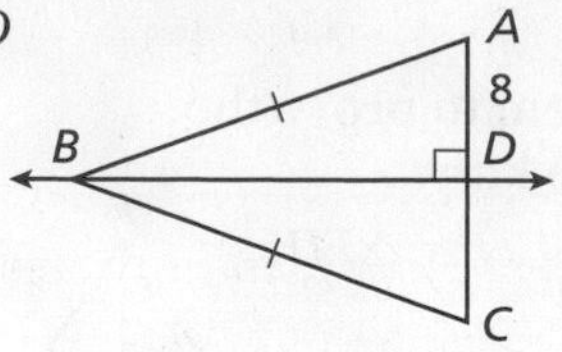

2. HG

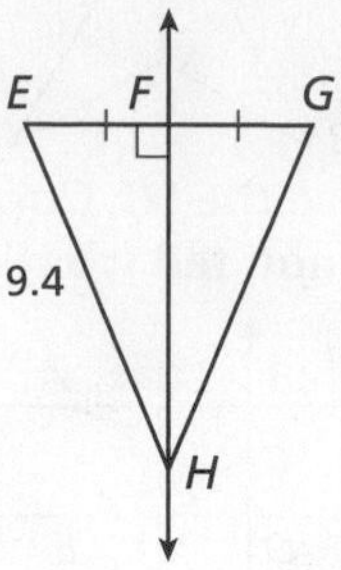

3. JM

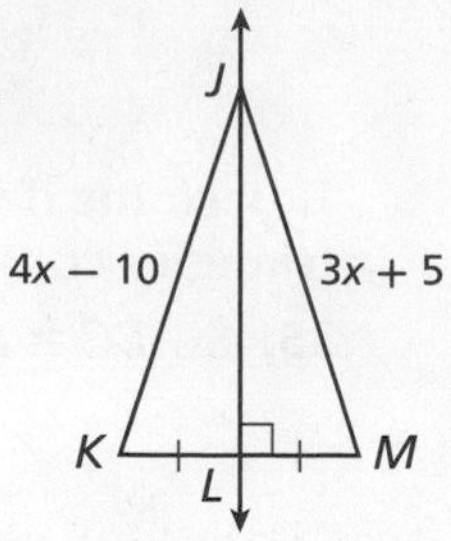

4. m∠SRT, given m∠$SRU = 126°$

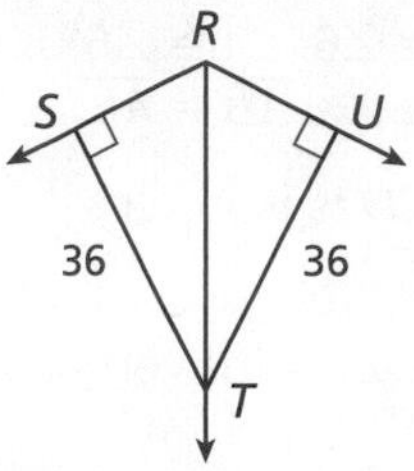

5. PQ

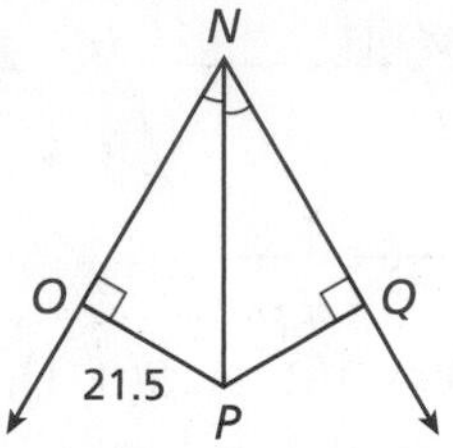

6. m∠WXV

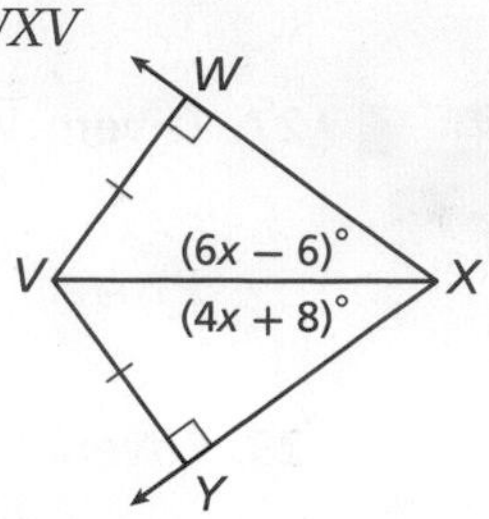

7. Write an equation in point-slope form for the perpendicular bisector of the segment with endpoints $A(1, 4)$ and $B(-5, -2)$.

Lesson 5-2

$\overline{DG}$, $\overline{EG}$, and $\overline{FG}$ are the perpendicular bisectors of △ABC. Find each length.

8. BG

9. AG

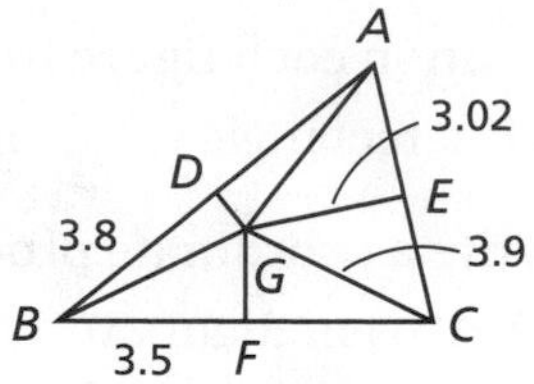

Find the circumcenter of a triangle with the given vertices.

10. $H(5, 0)$, $J(0, 3)$, $K(0, 0)$

11. $L(0, 0)$, $M(-2, 0)$, $N(0, -4)$

$\overline{QS}$ and $\overline{RS}$ are angle bisectors of △QPR. Find each measure.

12. the distance from S to $\overline{PR}$

13. m∠SQP

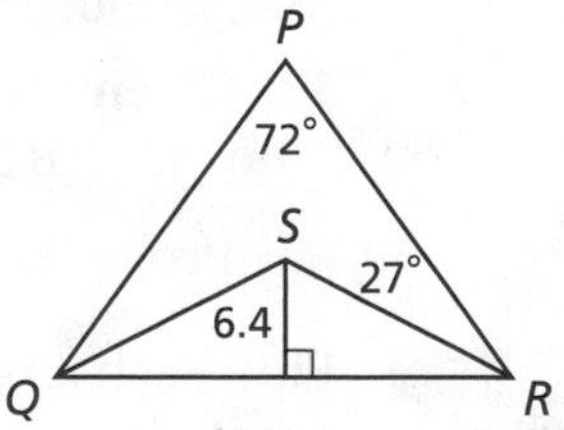

Lesson 5-3

In △DEF, $DJ = 30$, and $FM = 12$. Find each length.

14. DM

15. MJ

16. GF

17. GM

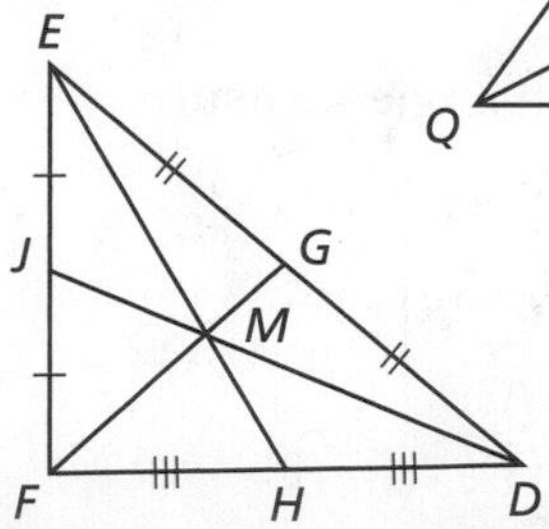

Find the orthocenter of a triangle with the given vertices.

18. $N(-2, 2)$, $P(4, 2)$, $Q(0, -2)$

19. $R(-2, 1)$, $S(2, 5)$, $T(4, 1)$

Lesson 5-4

20. The vertices of △WXY are $W(-3, 2)$, $X(5, 2)$, and $Y(1, -4)$. A is the midpoint of $\overline{WY}$, and B is the midpoint of $\overline{XY}$. Show that $\overline{AB} \parallel \overline{WX}$ and $AB = \frac{1}{2}WX$.

Find each measure.

21. DE

22. FG

23. DG

24. m∠CHF

25. m∠FHE

26. m∠CED

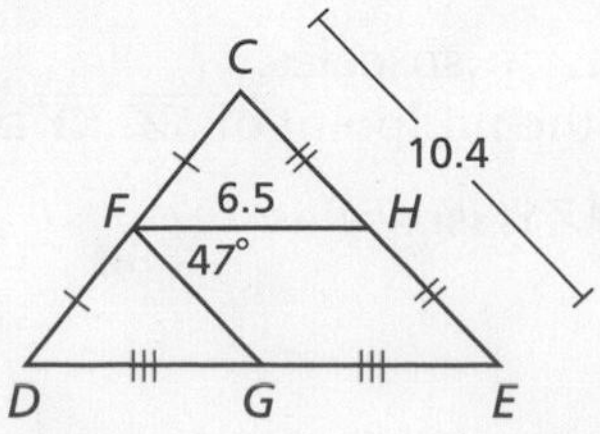

Lesson 5-5

Write an indirect proof of each statement.

27. An isosceles triangle cannot have an obtuse base angle.

28. A right triangle cannot have three congruent sides.

29. Write the angles in order from smallest to largest.

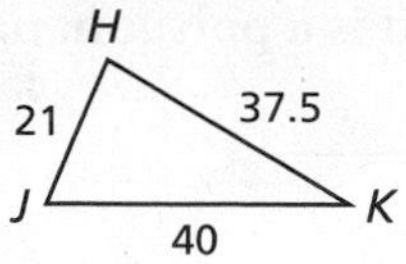

30. Write the sides in order from shortest to longest.

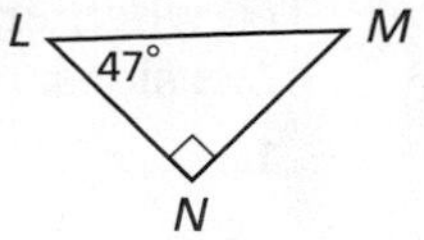

Tell whether a triangle can have sides with the given lengths. Explain.

31. 4, 7, 8

32. 7, 9, 18

33. $2x + 5$, $4x$, $3x^2$, when $x = 3$

The lengths of two sides of a triangle are given. Find the range of possible lengths for the third side.

34. 4 in., 10 in.

35. 8 ft, 8 ft

36. 6.2 cm, 12 cm

Lesson 5-6

Compare the given measures.

37. Compare *RS* and *UV*.

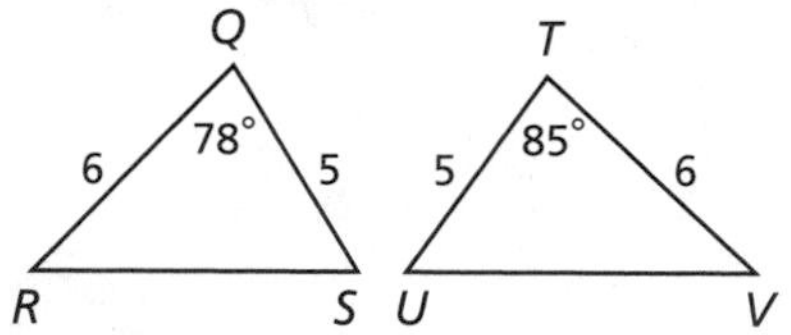

38. Compare m∠*XWY* and m∠*ZWY*.

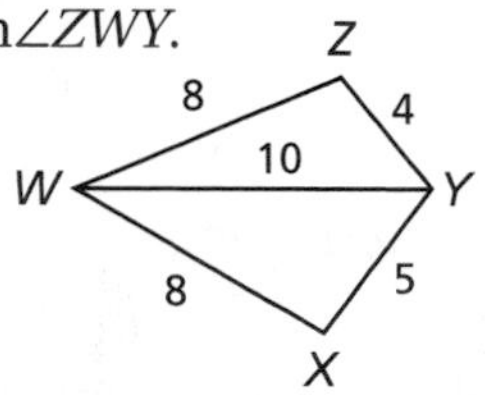

39. Find the range of values for *x*.

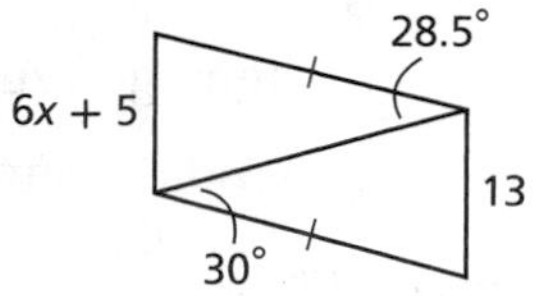

40. Write a two-column proof.

Given: m∠*X* > m∠*Y*, m∠*B* > m∠*A*

Prove: *AY* > *XB*

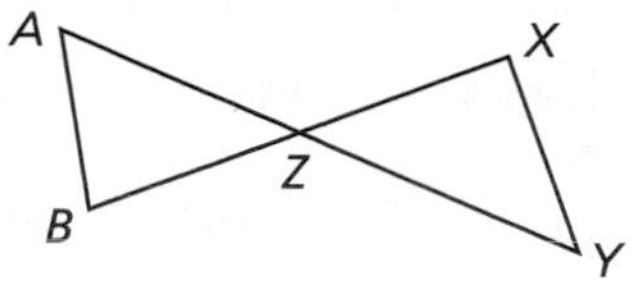

Lesson 5-7

Find the value of *x*. Give your answer in simplest radical form.

41.

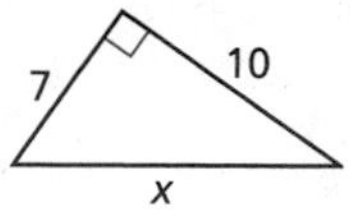

42.

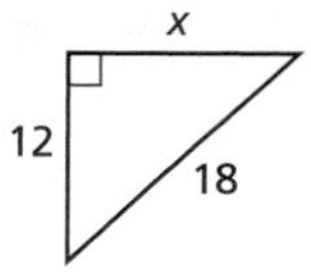

43.

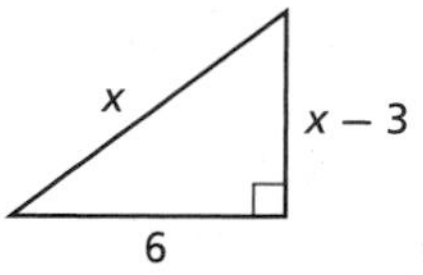

Find the missing side length. Tell if the side lengths form a Pythagorean triple. Explain.

44.

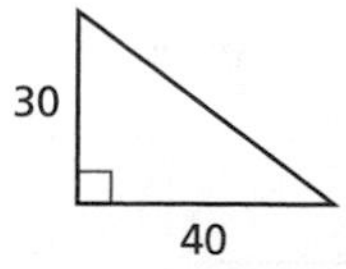

45.

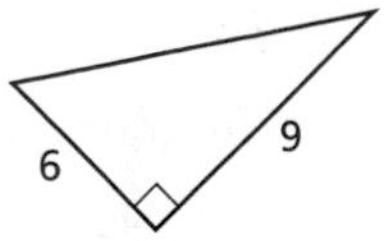

46.

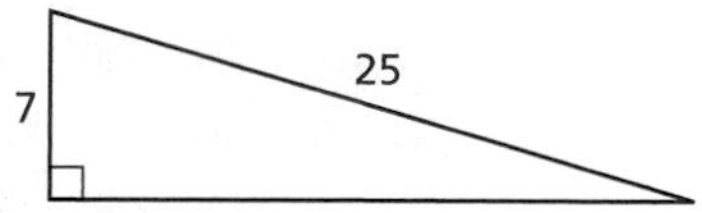

Tell if the measures can be the side lengths of a triangle. If so, classify the triangle as acute, obtuse, or right.

47. 4, 7.5, 8.5

48. 6, 10, 11

49. 9, 21, 25

Lesson 5-8

Find the value of *x*. Give your answer in simplest radical form.

50.

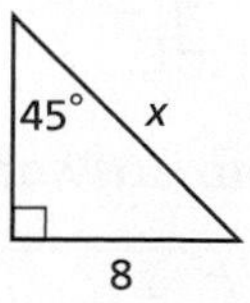

51.

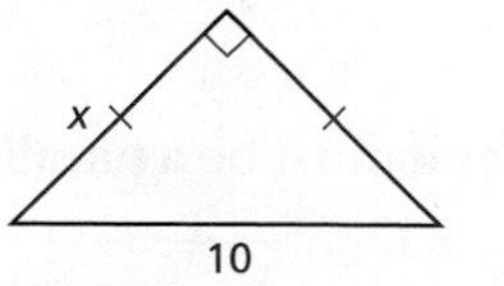

52.

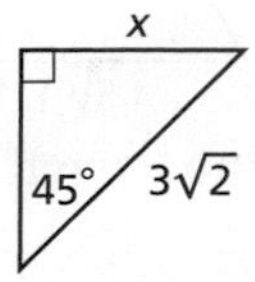

Find the values of *x* and *y*. Give your answers in simplest radical form.

53.

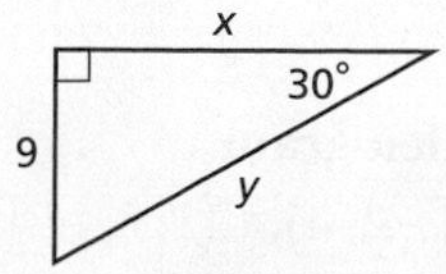

54.

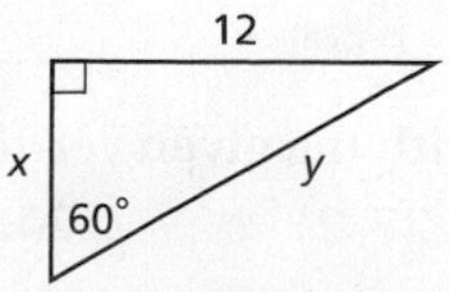

55.

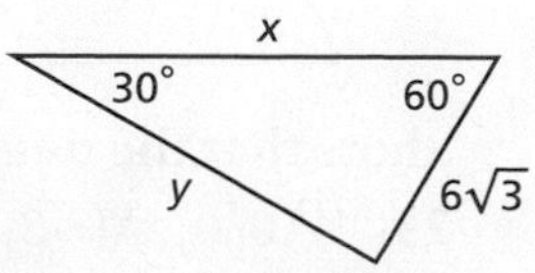

Extra Practice Chapter 6 ▪ Skills Practice

Lesson 6-1

Tell whether each figure is a polygon. If it is a polygon, name it by the number of its sides.

1. 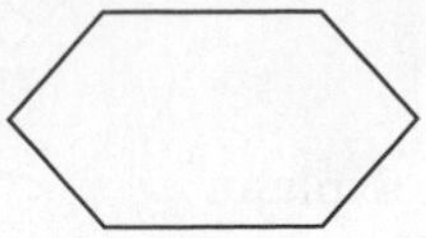

2. 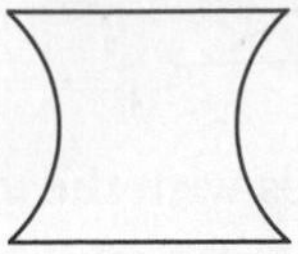

3. 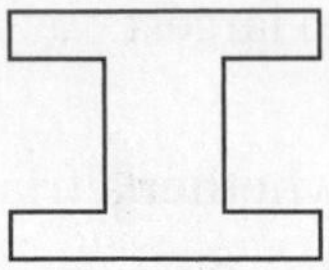

Tell whether each polygon is regular or irregular. Tell whether it is concave or convex.

4. 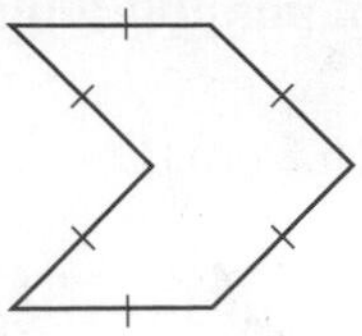

5. 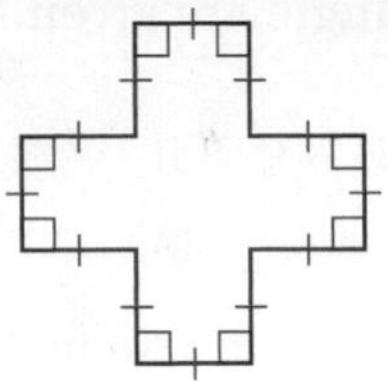

6. 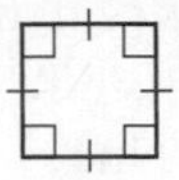

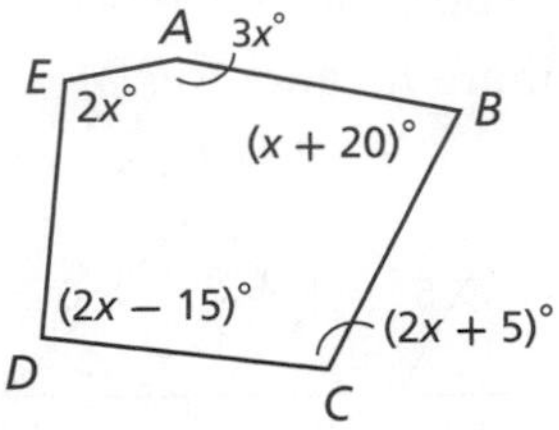

7. Find the measure of each interior angle of pentagon *ABCDE*.
8. Find the sum of the interior angle measures of a convex heptagon.
9. Find the measure of each interior angle of a regular 15-gon.
10. Find the value of x in polygon *FGHJKL*.

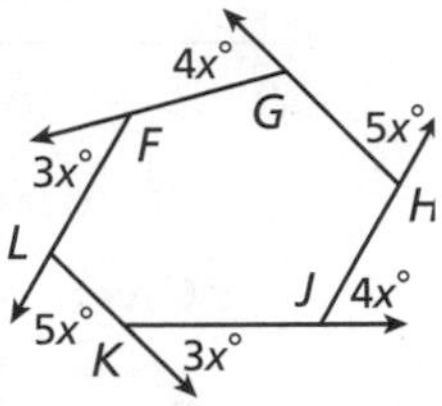

11. Find the measure of each exterior angle of a regular dodecagon.

Lesson 6-2

***MNOP* is a parallelogram. Find each measure.**

12. *MP*
13. m∠*M*
14. m∠*N*

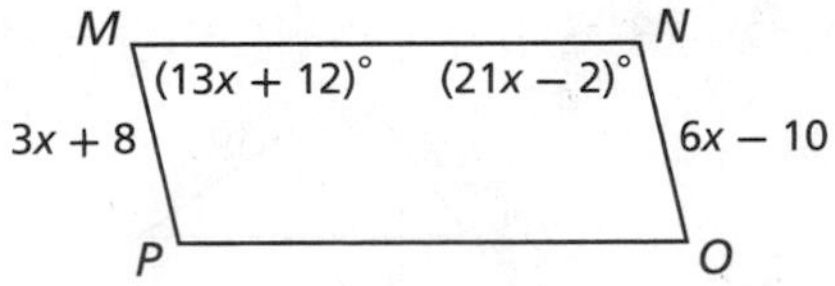

Three vertices of ▱*QRST* are given. Find the coordinates of *T*.

15. *Q*(−5, 3), *R*(3, 6), *S*(6, 4)
16. *Q*(−1, 7), *R*(3, 3), *S*(−2, 3)

Write a two-column proof.

17. **Given:** *ABFG* and *HDEG* are parallelograms.
    Prove: ∠*B* ≅ ∠*D*

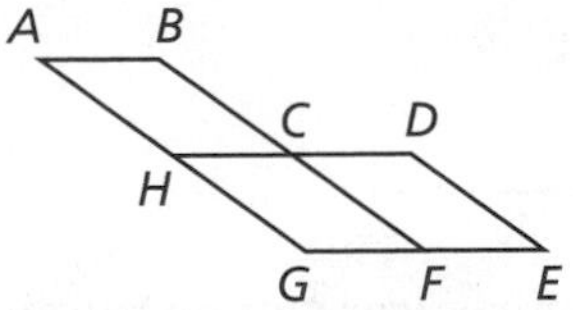

Lesson 6-3

18. Show that *RSTU* is a parallelogram for $x = 2$ and $y = 3$.

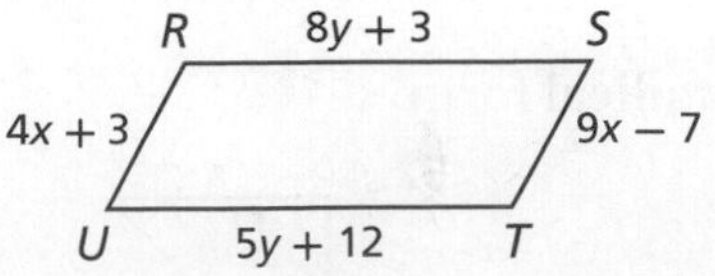

19. Show that *WXYZ* is a parallelogram for $a = 6$ and $b = 11$.

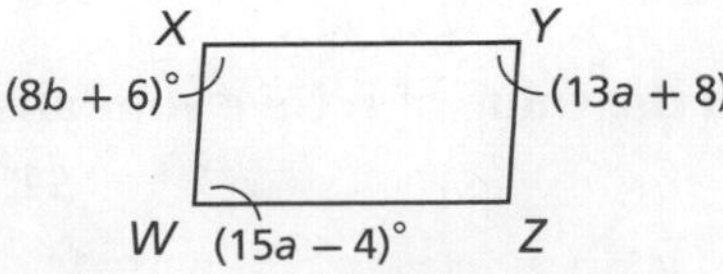

Determine if each quadrilateral must be a parallelogram. Justify your answer.

20. 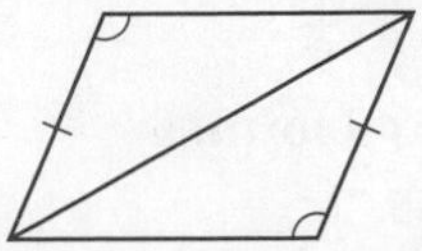

21. 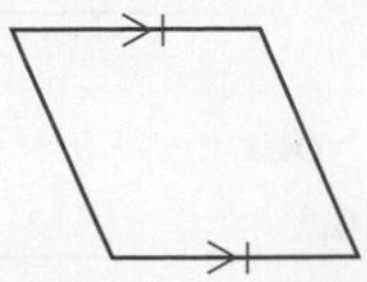

22. 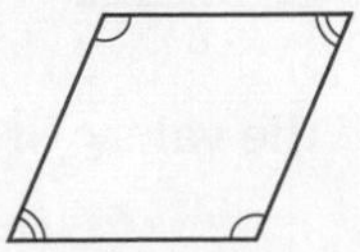

Show that the quadrilateral with the given vertices is a parallelogram.

23. *W*(0, 0), *X*(−3, 3), *Y*(5, 5), *Z*(8, 2)
24. *A*(−3, 1), *B*(−2, 4), *C*(1, 2), *D*(0, −1)

Lesson 6-4

***EFGH* is a rectangle. Find each measure.**

25. EH
26. HF

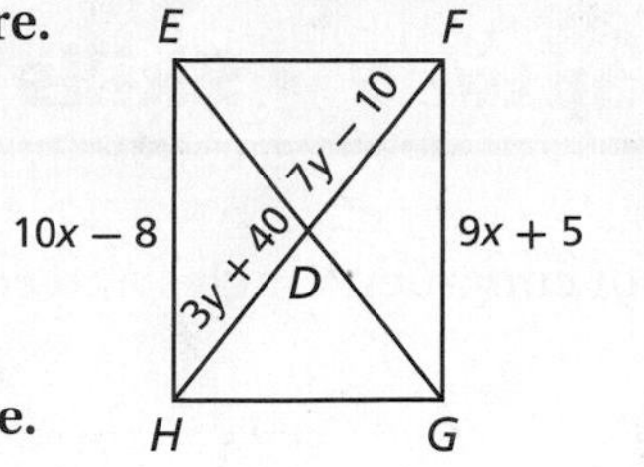

***JKLM* is a rhombus. Find each measure.**

27. JK
28. $m\angle NKL$

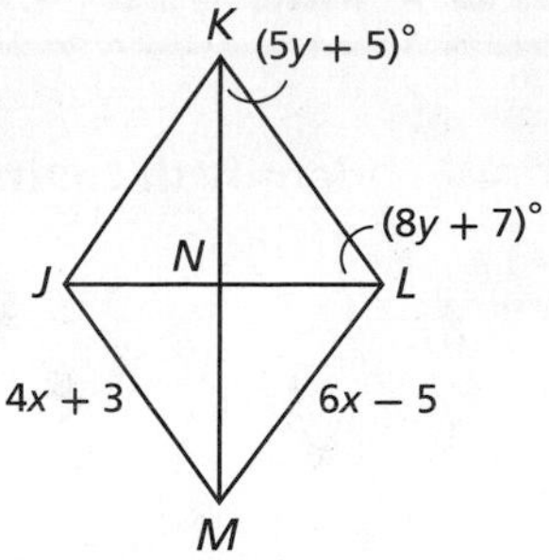

Show that the diagonals of a square with the given vertices are congruent perpendicular bisectors of each other.

29. $N(1, 4)$, $P(4, 1)$, $Q(1, -2)$, $R(-2, 1)$
30. $S(-2, 7)$, $T(2, 8)$, $U(3, 4)$, $V(-1, 3)$

31. **Given:** $WXYZ$ is a rectangle. $\overline{XB} \cong \overline{AZ}$
Prove: $\overline{WB} \cong \overline{YA}$

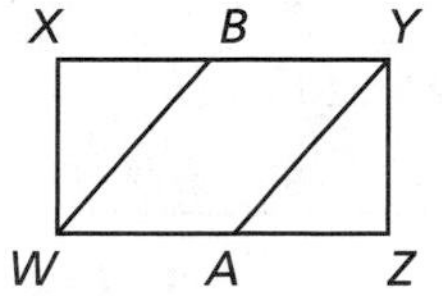

Lesson 6-5

Determine if the conclusion is valid. If not, tell what additional information is needed to make it valid.

32. Given: $\overline{XY} \parallel \overline{WZ}$, $\overline{XY} \cong \overline{WZ}$, $\overline{XZ} \perp \overline{WY}$
Conclusion: $WXYZ$ is a rhombus.

33. Given: $\overline{WX} \cong \overline{XY}$
Conclusion: $WXYZ$ is a square.

34. Given: $\overline{WX} \perp \overline{XY}$, $\overline{WX} \perp \overline{WZ}$
Conclusion: $WXYZ$ is a rectangle.

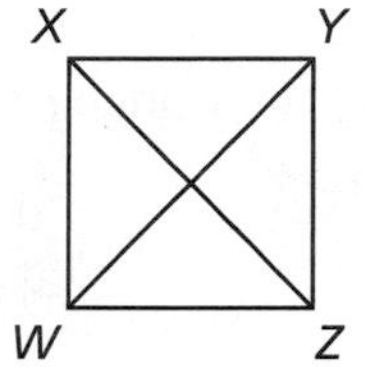

Use the diagonals to determine whether a parallelogram with the given vertices is a rectangle, rhombus, or square. Give all the names that apply.

35. $A(1, 0)$, $B(2, -4)$, $C(6, -3)$, $D(5, 1)$
36. $E(-3, -1)$, $F(-4, -4)$, $G(2, -6)$, $H(3, -3)$

Lesson 6-6

In kite *TUVW*, $m\angle XTU = 65°$, and $m\angle UVT = 32°$. Find each measure.

37. $m\angle TUX$
38. $m\angle XUV$
39. $m\angle TWX$

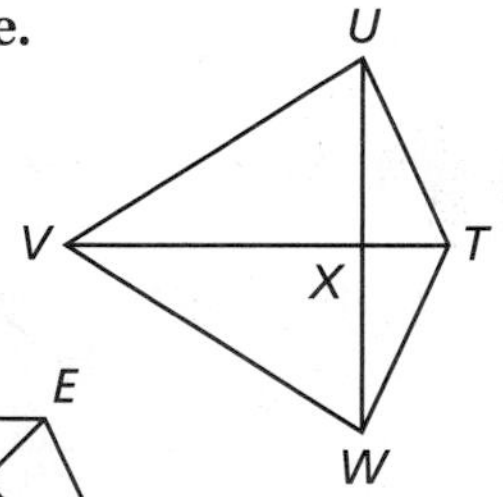

Find each measure.

40. $m\angle C$

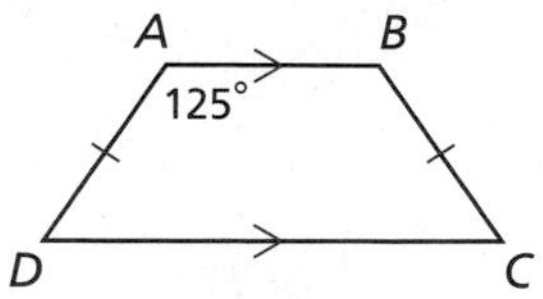

41. HJ, given that $EG = 32.8$ and $FJ = 24.3$

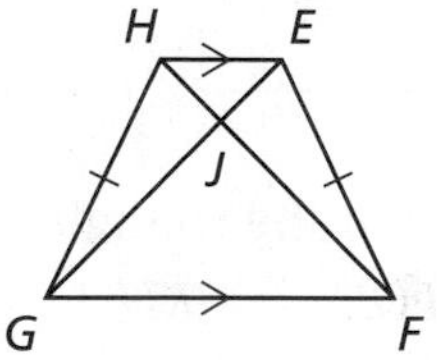

42. Find the value of x so that $JKLM$ is isosceles.

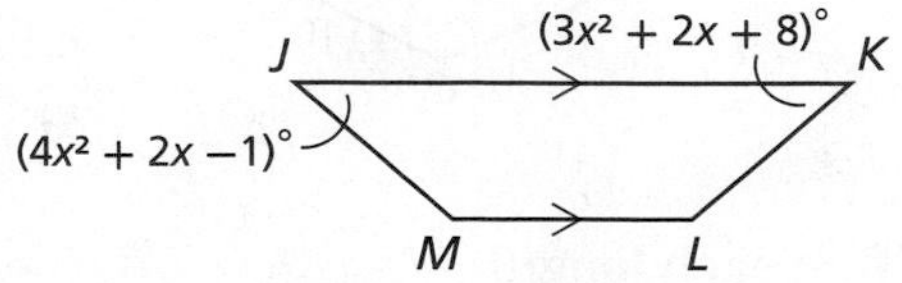

43. Given $RP = 8y - 7$ and $NQ = 10y - 12$, find the value of y so that $NPQR$ is isosceles.

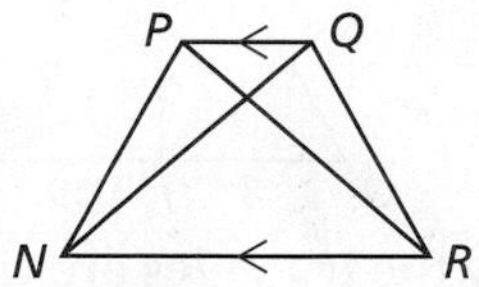

44. Find RS.

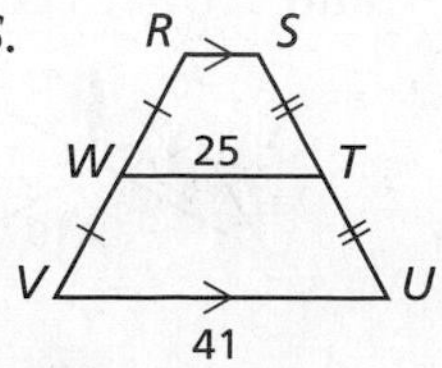

45. Find XY.

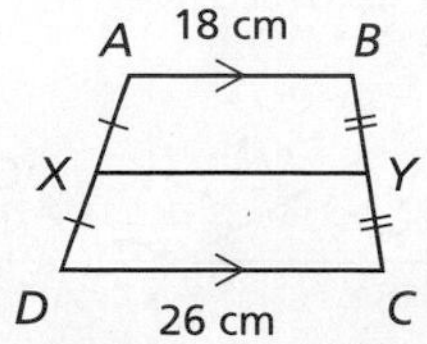

Extra Practice Chapter 7 ■ Skills Practice

Lesson 7-1

Identify the pairs of congruent angles and corresponding sides.

1.

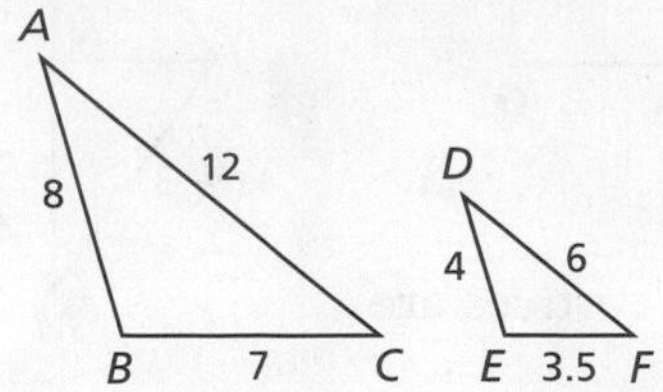

2.

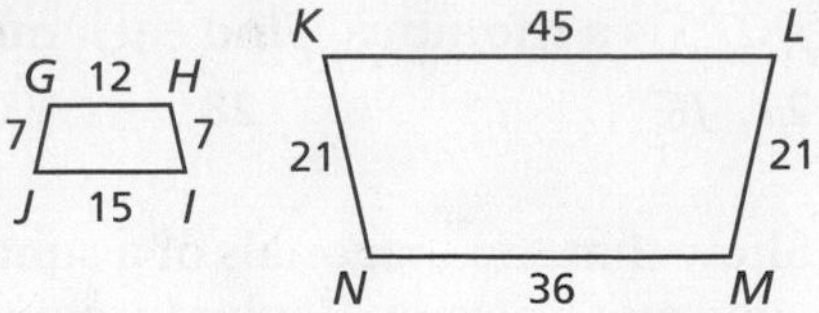

Determine whether the polygons are similar. If so, write the similarity ratio and a similarity statement.

3. rectangles *ABCD* and *EFGH*

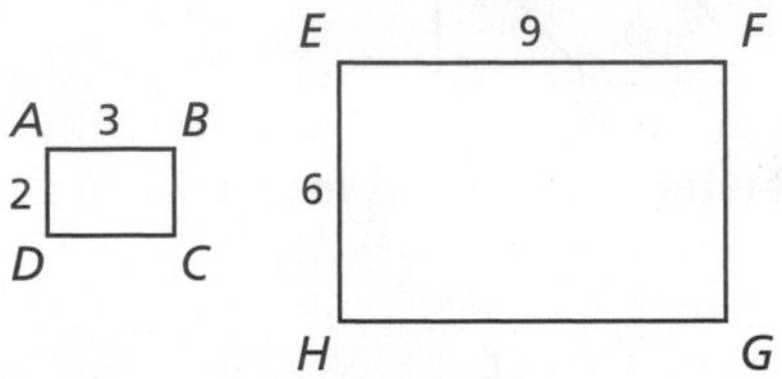

4. $\triangle JKL$ and $\triangle MNO$

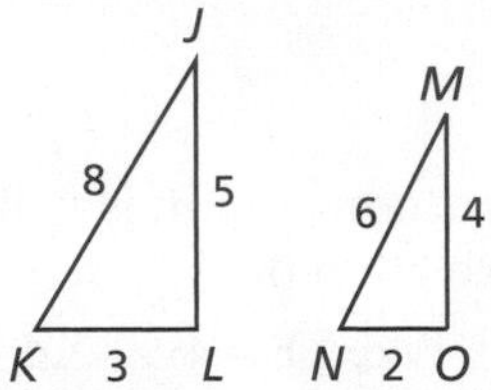

Lesson 7-2

Name the coordinates of the image points. Identify and describe the transformation.

5. $D: (x, y) \rightarrow (2x, 2y)$
$A(-2, -1)$, $B(2, 3)$, $C(0, 4)$

6. $D: (x, y) \rightarrow (1.5x, 1.5y)$
$M(-6, 2)$, $N(4, 0)$, $P(5, -8)$

7. $D: (x, y) \rightarrow (0.5x, 0.5y)$
$R(-2, 0)$, $S(10, -7)$, $T(-2, -6)$

8. $D: (x, y) \rightarrow (4x, 4y)$
$E(-0.5, 0.5)$, $F(1, -2.5)$, $G(-2, 0.75)$

Determine whether the polygons with the given vertices are similar. Support your answer by describing a transformation.

9. $E(4, 0)$, $F(-4, -12)$, $G(8, -8)$
$J(3, 0)$, $K(-3, -9)$, $L(6, -6)$

10. $P(-1, 4)$, $Q(3, 2)$, $R(1, -2)$
$X(4, 4)$, $Y(12, 0)$, $Z(8, -8)$

Lesson 7-3

Explain why the triangles are similar and write a similarity statement.

11.

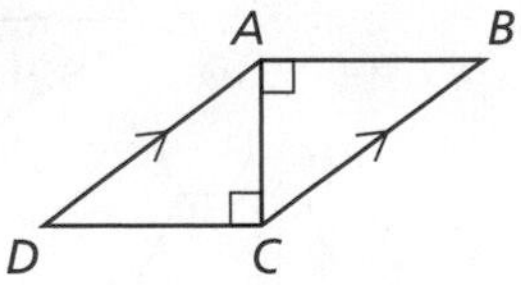

12.

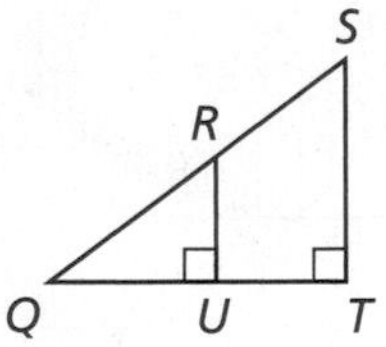

Verify that the triangles are similar.

13. $\triangle FGH \sim \triangle JKH$

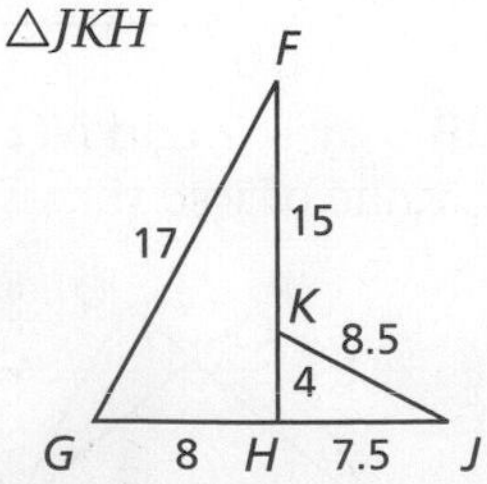

14. $\triangle ACE \sim \triangle BCD$

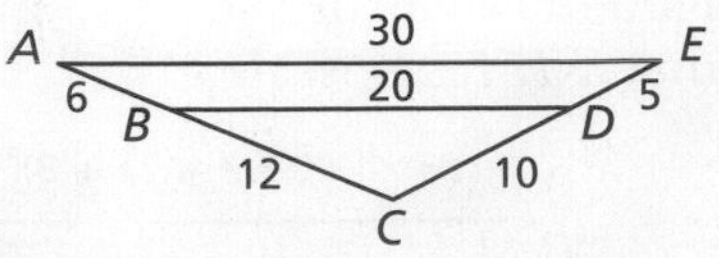

Explain why the triangles are similar and then find each length.

15. $\triangle XYZ$ and $\triangle ABC$, *BC*

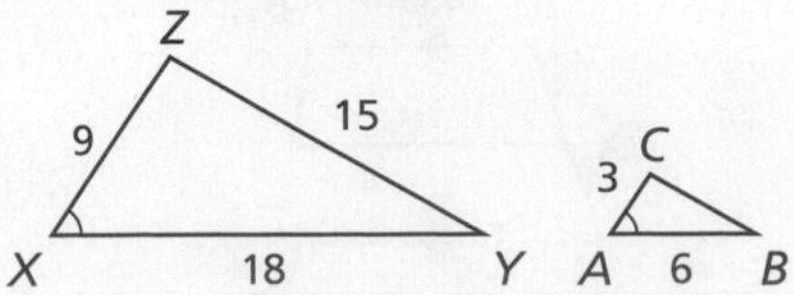

16. $\triangle RSV$ and $\triangle UST$, *TU*

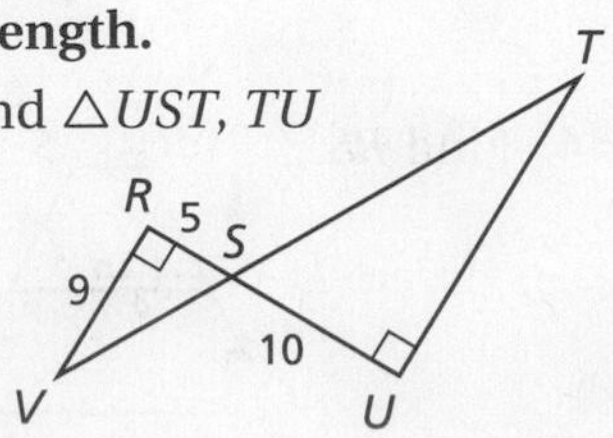

Lesson 7-4

Find the length of each segment.

17. $\overline{AE}$

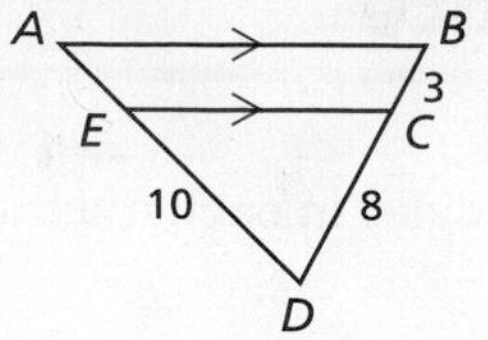

18. $\overline{KJ}$

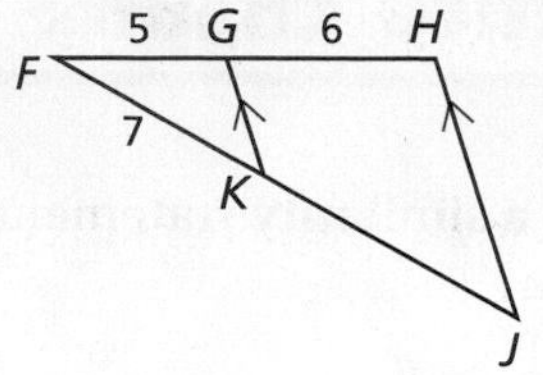

Verify that the given segments are parallel.

19. $\overline{EF}$ and $\overline{JG}$

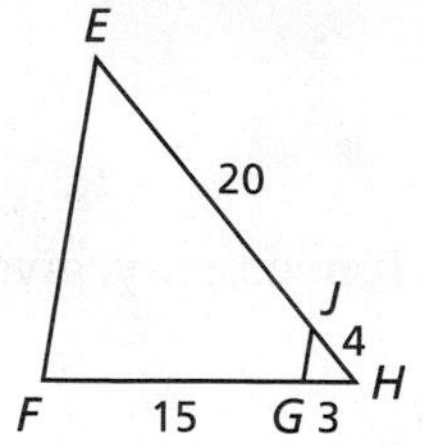

20. $\overline{LP}$ and $\overline{MN}$

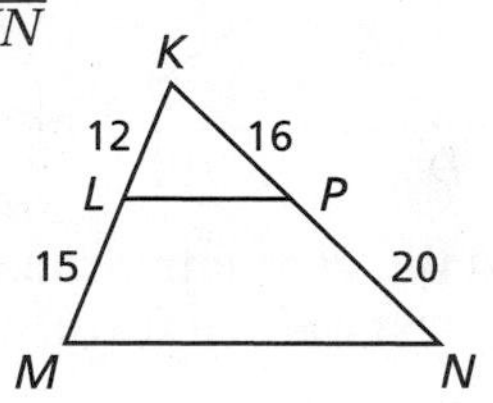

Find the length of each segment.

21. $\overline{RS}$ and $\overline{ST}$

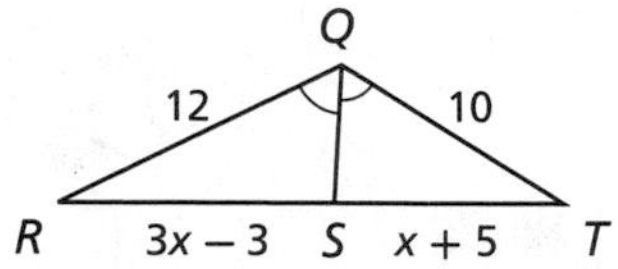

22. $\overline{XW}$ and $\overline{WZ}$

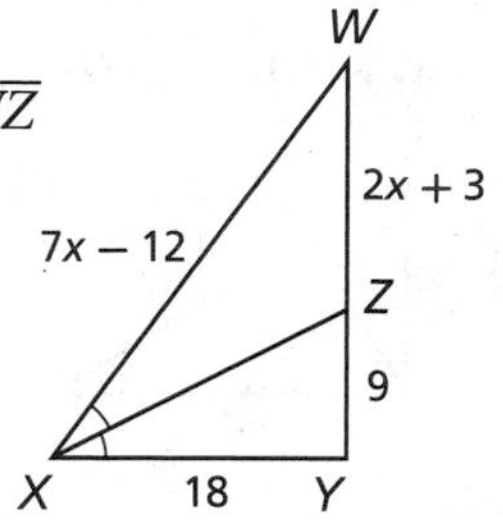

Lesson 7-5

The scale drawing of the playhouse is 1 in.: 10 ft. Find the actual lengths of the following walls.

23. $\overline{GH}$

24. $\overline{EF}$

25. $\overline{DC}$

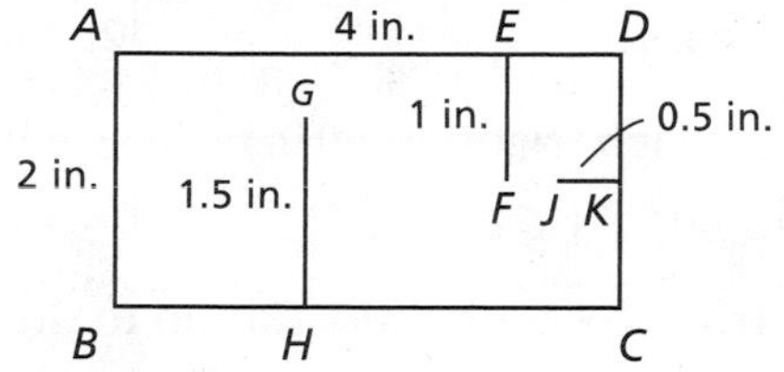

The school courtyard is 25 ft by 40 ft. Make a scale drawing of the courtyard using the following scales.

26. 1 cm: 1 ft

27. 1 cm: 5 ft

28. 1 cm: 10 ft

29. Given that $\triangle ABC \sim \triangle DEF$, find the perimeter P and area A of $\triangle DEF$.

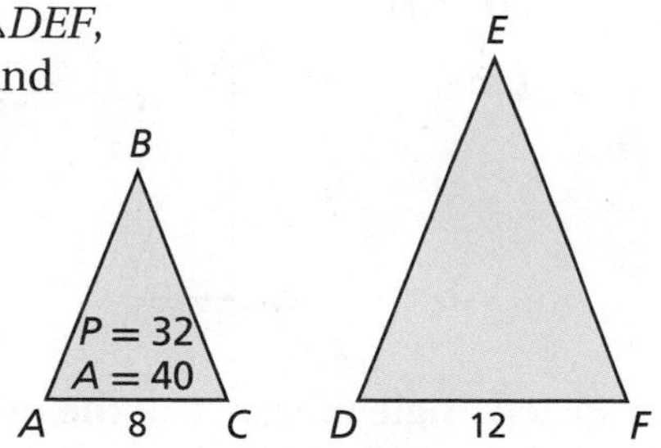

Lesson 7-6

30. Given that $\triangle RSV \sim \triangle RTU$, find the coordinates of S and the scale factor.

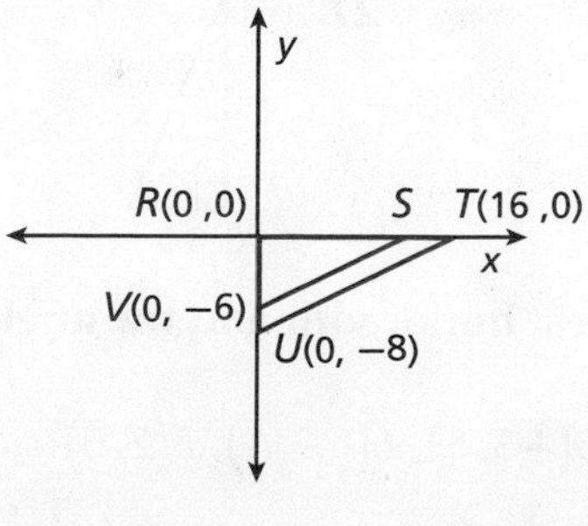

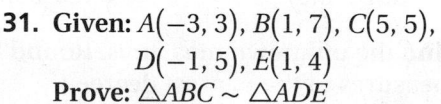

31. Given: $A(-3, 3)$, $B(1, 7)$, $C(5, 5)$, $D(-1, 5)$, $E(1, 4)$
Prove: $\triangle ABC \sim \triangle ADE$

Lesson 8-1

Write a similarity statement comparing the three triangles in each diagram.

1. 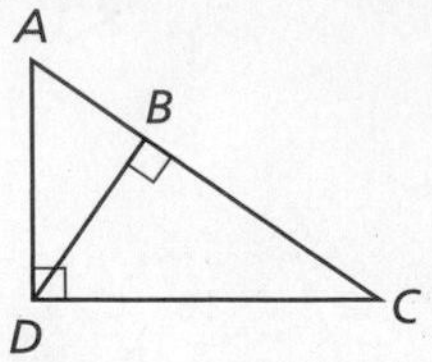

2. 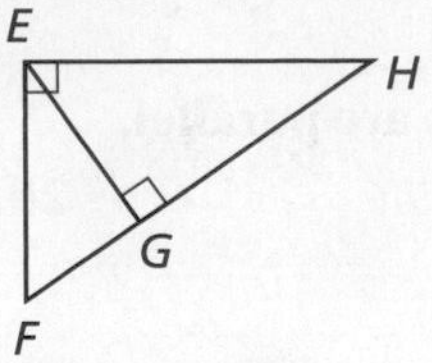

3. 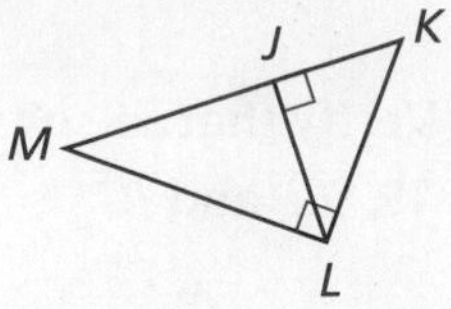

Find the geometric mean of each pair of numbers. If necessary, give the answers in simplest radical form.

4. 3 and 9

5. 4 and 7

6. $\frac{1}{2}$ and 5

Find *x*, *y*, and *z*.

7. 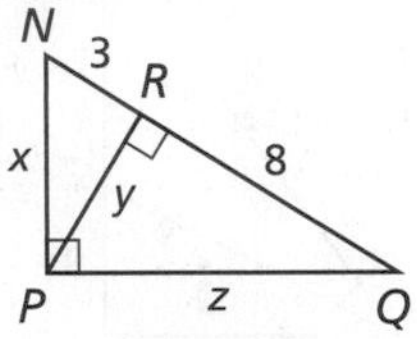

8. 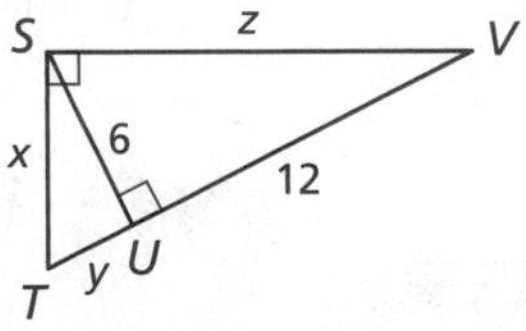

9. 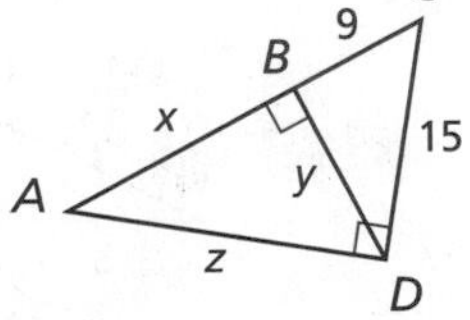

Lesson 8-2

Write each trigonometric ratio as a fraction and as a decimal rounded to the nearest hundredth.

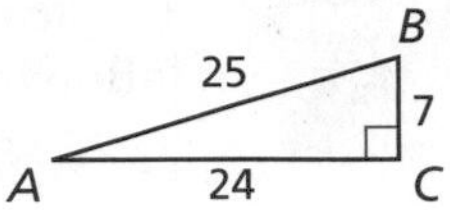

10. $\sin A$

11. $\cos A$

12. $\tan A$

Use a special right triangle to write each trigonometric ratio as a fraction.

13. $\cos 30°$

14. $\sin 45°$

15. $\tan 60°$

Use your calculator to find each trigonometric ratio. Round to the nearest hundredth.

16. $\sin 38°$

17. $\cos 47°$

18. $\tan 21°$

Find each length. Round to the nearest hundredth.

19. *DE*

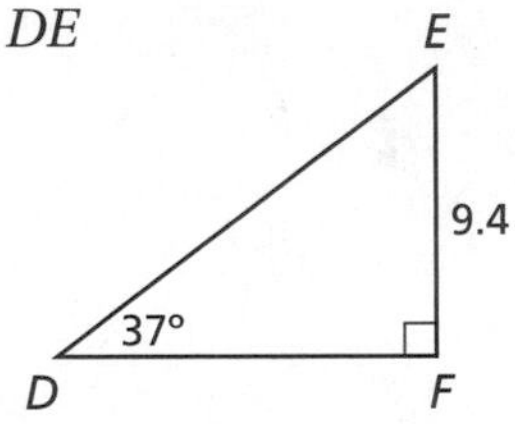

20. *GH*

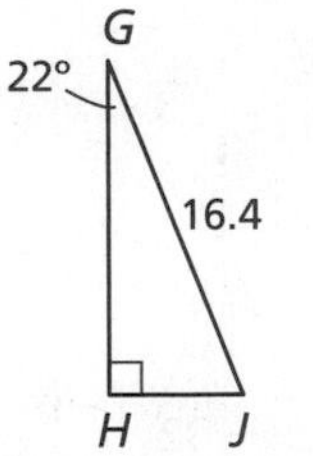

21. *KL*

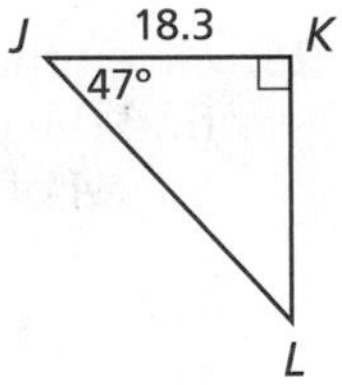

Lesson 8-3

Use your calculator to find each angle measure to the nearest degree.

22. $\tan^{-1}(3.5)$

23. $\sin^{-1}\left(\frac{1}{5}\right)$

24. $\cos^{-1}(0.05)$

Find the unknown measures. Round lengths to the nearest hundredth and angle measures to the nearest degree.

25. 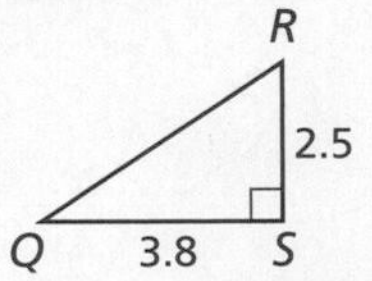

26. 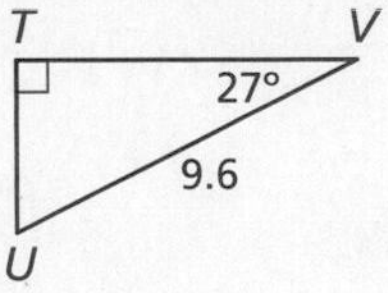

27. 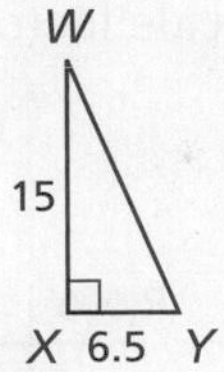

For each triangle, find the side lengths to the nearest hundredth and the angle measures to the nearest degree.

28. $A(1, 4)$, $B(1, 1)$, $C(4, 1)$

29. $D(-3, 5)$, $E(-3, 1)$, $F(2, 5)$

Lesson **8-4**

Classify each angle as an angle of elevation or angle of depression.

30. ∠1 **31.** ∠2

32. ∠3 **33.** ∠4

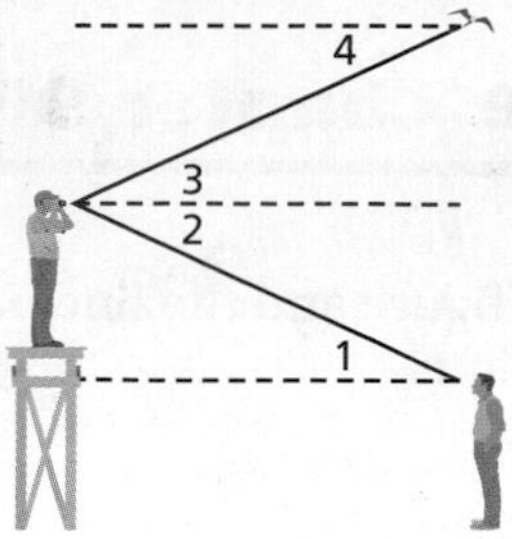

Lesson **8-5**

Use a calculator to find each trigonometric ratio. Round to the nearest hundredth.

34. cos 127° **35.** tan 131° **36.** sin 114°

37. tan 158° **38.** sin 85° **39.** cos 161°

Find each measure. Round lengths to the nearest tenth and angle measure to the nearest degree.

40. *AC*

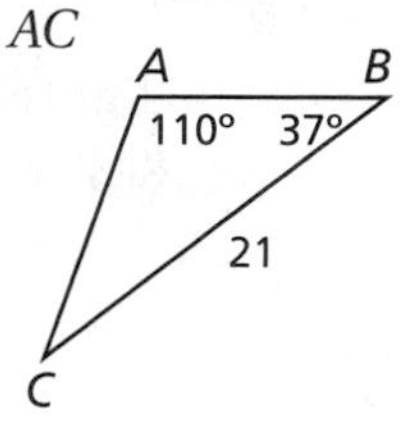

41. m∠*E*

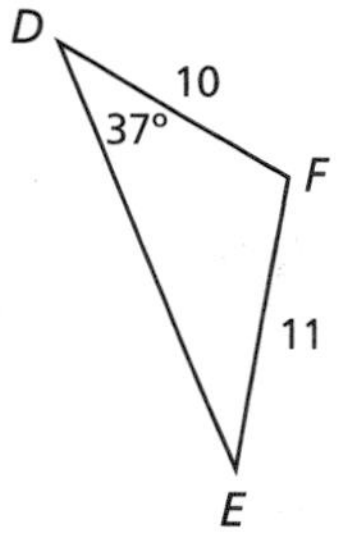

42. m∠*G*

43. m∠*T*

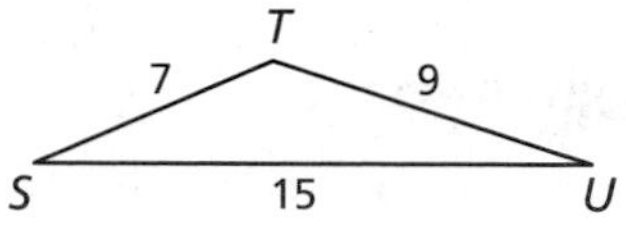

44. *VX*

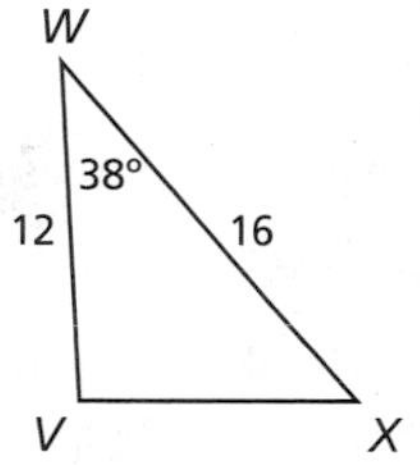

45. *BC*

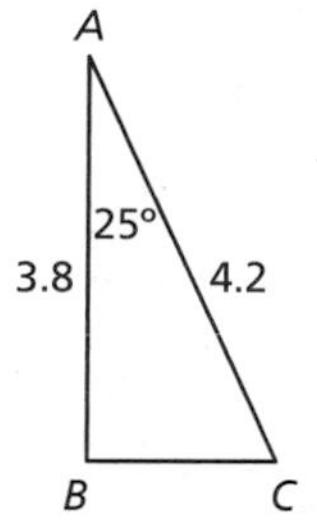

Lesson **8-6**

Write each vector in component form.

46. $\overrightarrow{AB}$ with $A(2, 3)$ and $B(5, 6)$

47. the vector with initial point $C(3, 6)$ and terminal point $D(2, 4)$

48. $\overrightarrow{EF}$

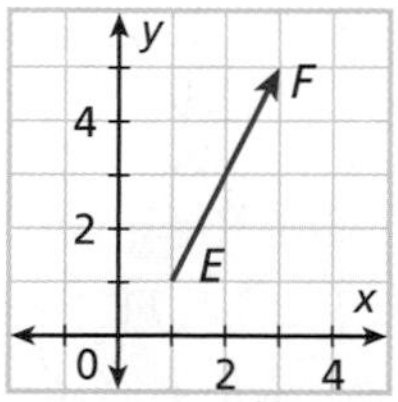

49. $\overrightarrow{GH}$

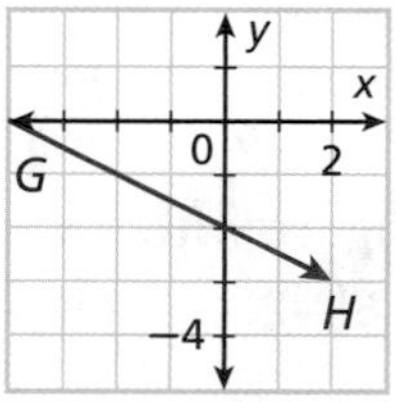

Draw each vector on a coordinate plane. Find its magnitude to the nearest tenth.

50. $\langle -3, 2\rangle$ **51.** $\langle 4, 3\rangle$ **52.** $\langle 2, -5\rangle$

Draw each vector on a coordinate plane. Find the direction of the vector to the nearest degree.

53. A wind velocity is given by the vector $\langle 3, 4\rangle$.

54. The velocity of a rocket is given by the vector $\langle 8, 1\rangle$.

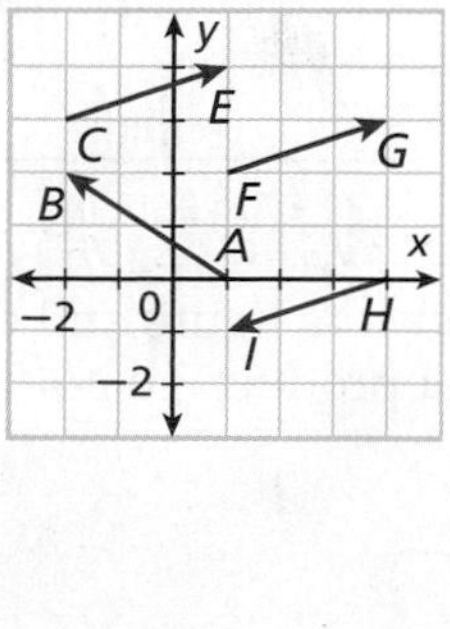

Identify each of the following in the diagram.

55. equal vectors **56.** parallel vectors

Find each vector sum.

57. $\langle 5, 0\rangle + \langle -3, 6\rangle$ **58.** $\langle -3, -1\rangle + \langle 0, -7\rangle$

59. $\langle 1, 8\rangle + \langle 2, 3\rangle$ **60.** $\langle -2, -1\rangle + \langle -7, 9\rangle$

Extra Practice Chapter 9 ▪ Skills Practice

Lesson 9-1

Copy each figure and the line of reflection. Draw the reflection of the figure across the line.

1.

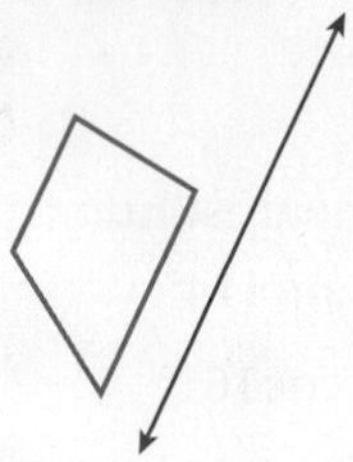

2.

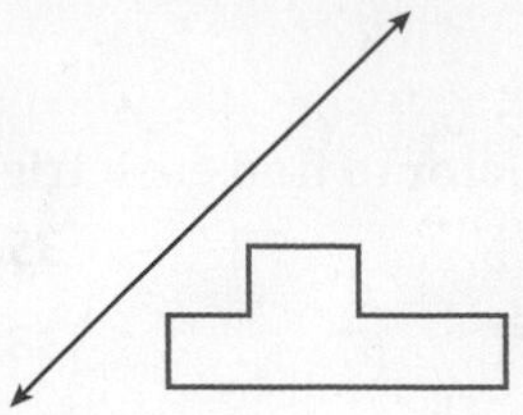

Reflect the figure with the given vertices across the given line.

3. $A(-4, 1)$, $B(2, 4)$, $C(3, -2)$; x-axis

4. $D(3, 1)$, $E(2, 4)$, $F(-2, 2)$, $G(2, -2)$; $y = x$

Lesson 9-2

Copy each figure and the translation vector. Draw the translation of the figure along the given vector.

5.

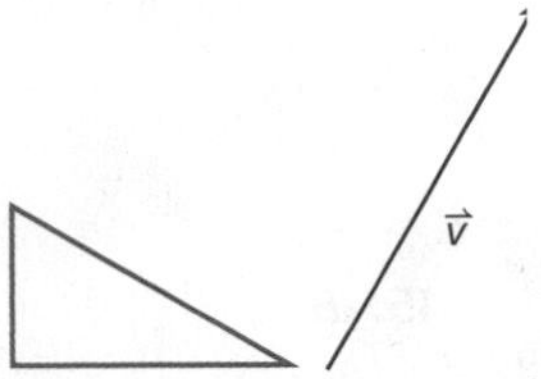

6.

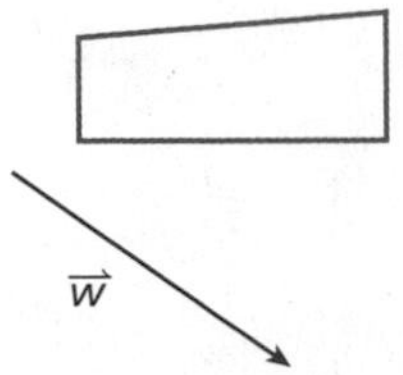

Translate the figure with the given vertices along the given vector.

7. $A(-2, 1)$, $B(4, 3)$, $C(2, -2)$; $\langle 2, 3\rangle$

8. $D(-1, 3)$, $E(2, 4)$, $F(3, 3)$, $G(3, -2)$; $\langle 2, -2\rangle$

Lesson 9-3

Copy each figure and the angle of rotation. Draw the rotation of the figure about the point P by m∠A.

9.

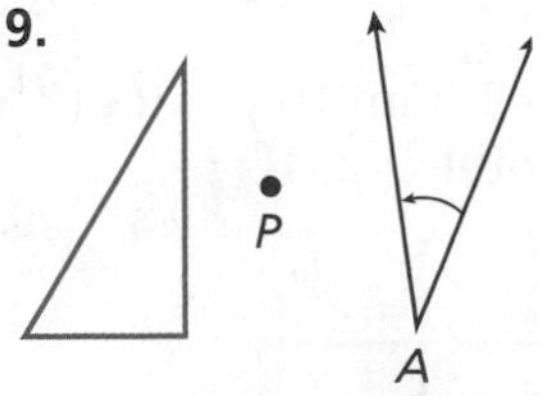

10.

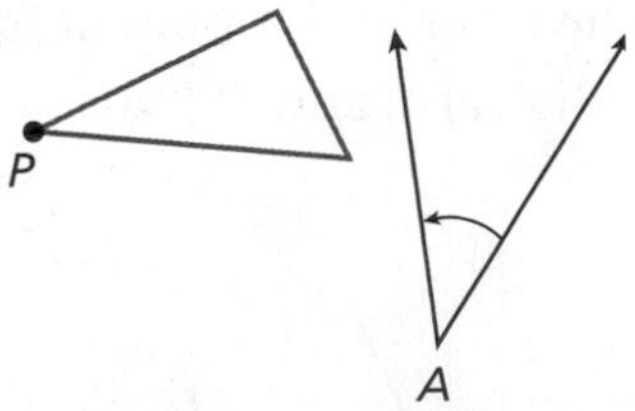

Rotate the figure with the given vertices about the origin using the given angle of rotation.

11. $A(2, 3)$, $B(-2, 1)$, $C(1, -1)$; 90°

12. $D(-2, 3)$, $E(2, 4)$, $F(3, 1)$, $G(-2, 2)$; 180°

Lesson 9-4

Draw the result of each composition of isometries.

13. Translate △ABC along $\vec{v}$ and then reflect it across line ℓ.

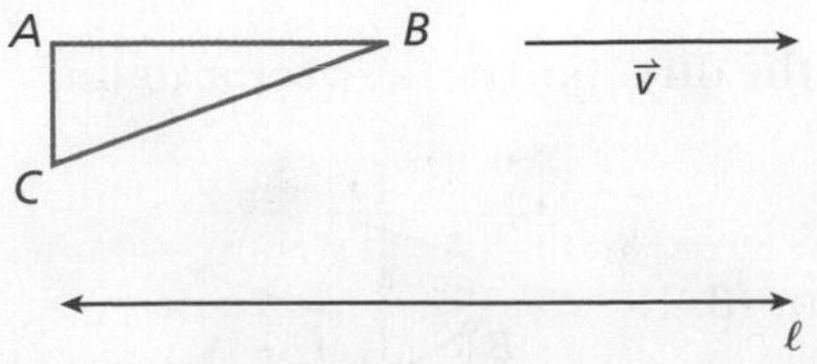

14. Reflect △DEF across line m and then translate it along $\vec{w}$.

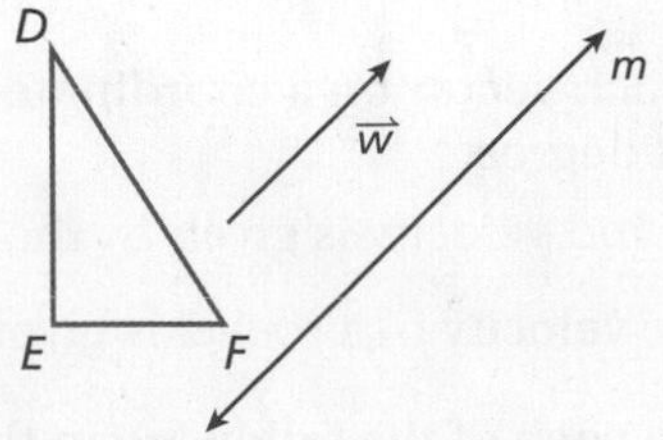

15. Copy the figure and draw two lines of reflection that produce an equivalent transformation.

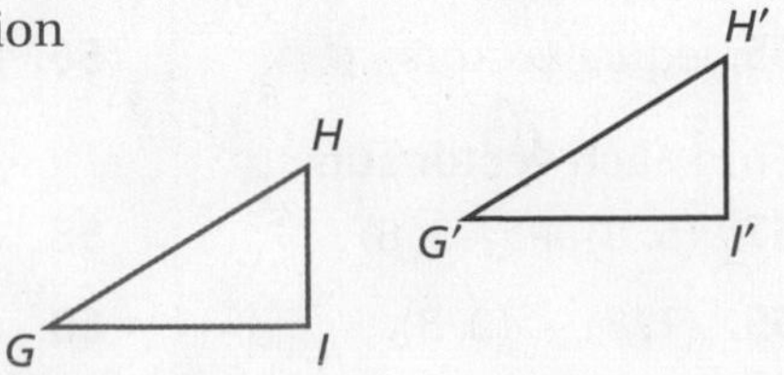

Lesson 9-5

Describe the symmetry of each figure. Copy the shape and draw all lines of symmetry. If there is rotational symmetry, give the angle and order.

16.

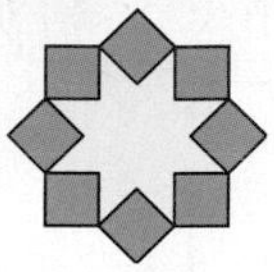

17.

18.

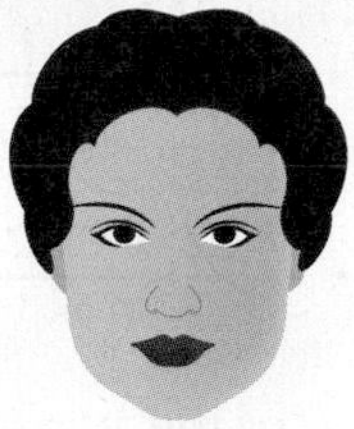

Tell whether each figure has plane symmetry, symmetry about an axis, or neither.

19.

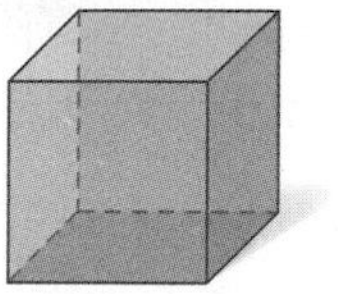

20.

21.

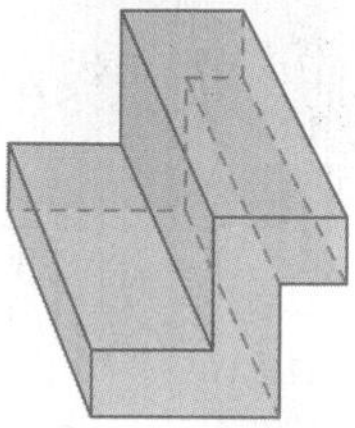

Lesson 9-6

Copy the given figure and use it to create a tessellation.

22.

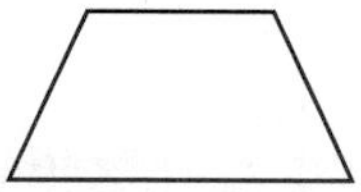

23.

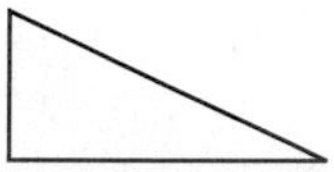

24.

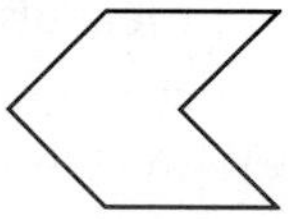

Classify each tessellation as regular, semiregular, or neither.

25.

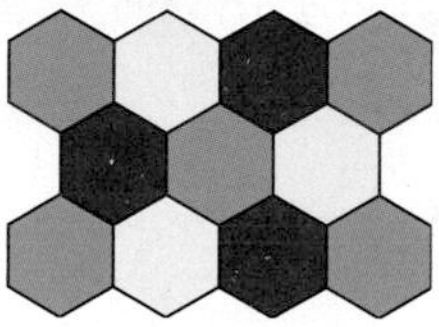

26.

27.

Lesson 9-7

Copy each figure and center of dilation *P*. Draw the image of the figure under a dilation with the given scale factor.

28. scale factor: 3

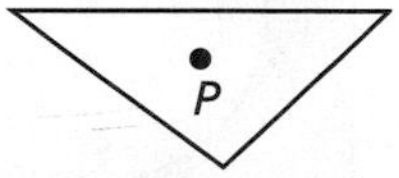

29. scale factor: $\frac{2}{3}$

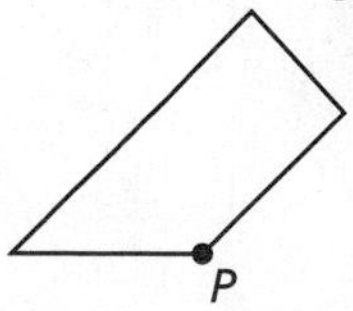

Draw the image of the figure with the given vertices under a dilation with the given scale factor centered at the origin.

30. $A(1, 3)$, $B(1, 5)$, $C(4, 3)$; scale factor 2

31. $E(-2, 2)$, $F(2, 4)$, $G(4, -2)$; scale factor $-\frac{1}{2}$

Extra Practice Chapter 10 Skills Practice

Lesson 10-1

Find each measurement.

1. the area of the parallelogram

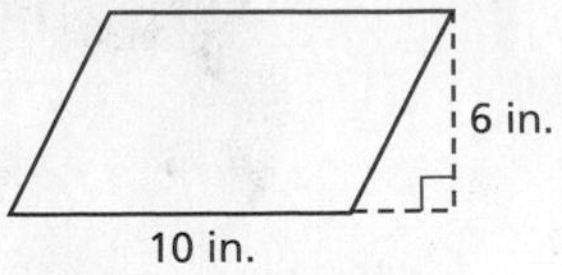

2. the perimeter of the rectangle in which $A = 15x^2$ ft^2

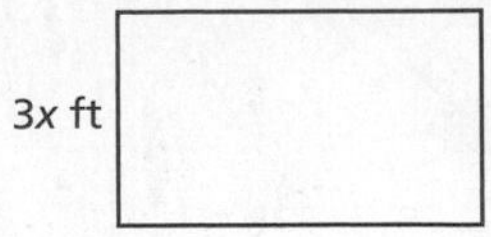

3. b_2 of the trapezoid in which $A = 35$ ft^2

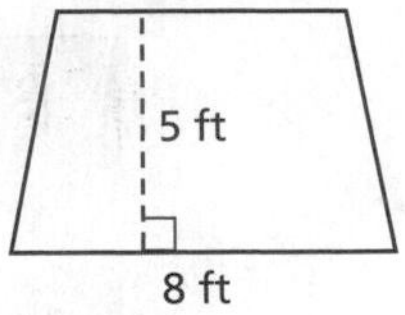

4. the area of the kite

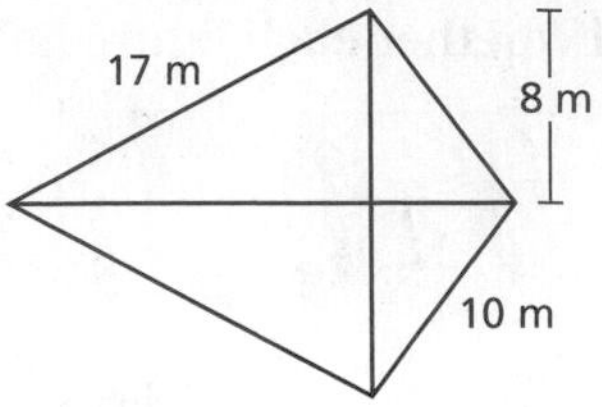

5. the base of a triangle in which $h = 9$ and $A = 135$ in^2

6. the area of a rhombus in which $d_1 = (3x + 5)$ cm and $d_2 = (7x + 4)$ cm

Lesson 10-2

Find each measurement.

7. the circumference of $\odot C$ in terms of π

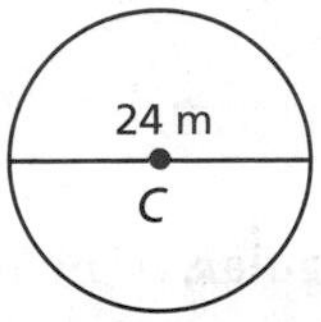

8. the area of $\odot D$ in terms of π

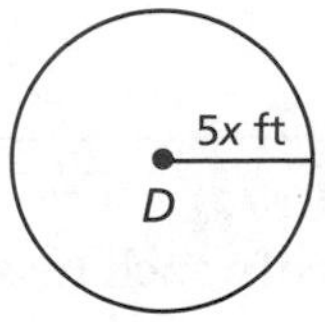

9. the circumference of $\odot F$ in which $A = 49x^2\pi$ cm^2

10. the radius of $\odot E$ in which $C = 36\pi$ in.

Find the area of each regular polygon. Round to the nearest tenth.

11. a regular hexagon with a side length of 8 in.

12. an equilateral triangle with an apothem of $\frac{5\sqrt{3}}{3}$ cm

Lesson 10-3

Find the shaded area. Round to the nearest tenth, if necessary.

13.

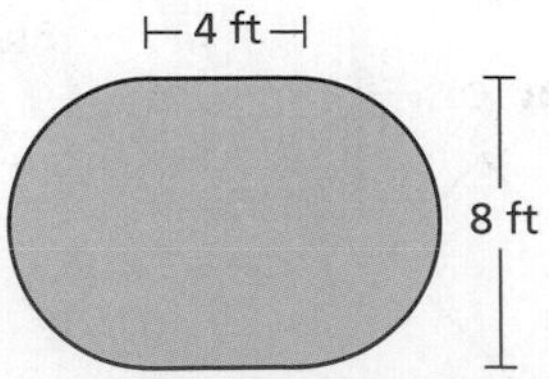

14.

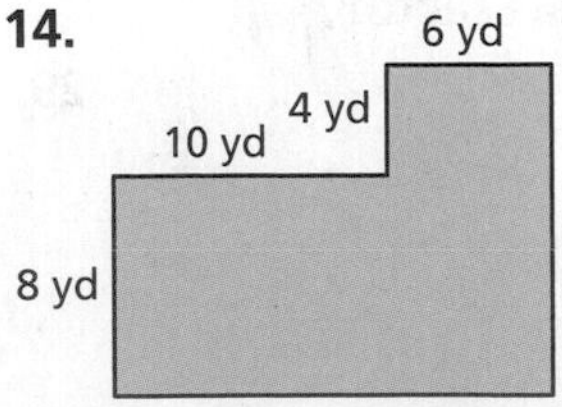

15.

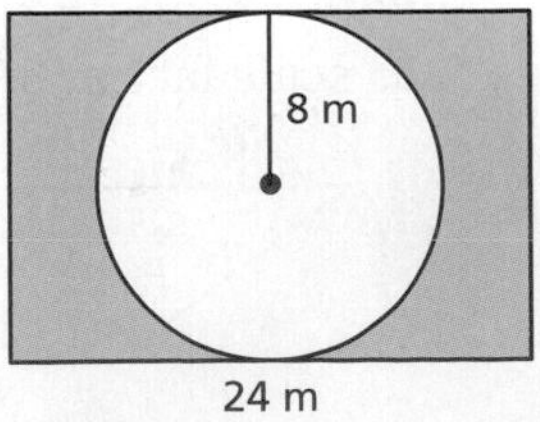

Use a composite figure to estimate each shaded area. The grid has squares with side lengths of 1 in.

16.

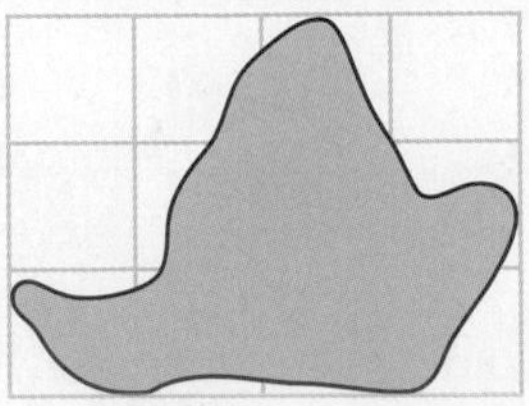

17.

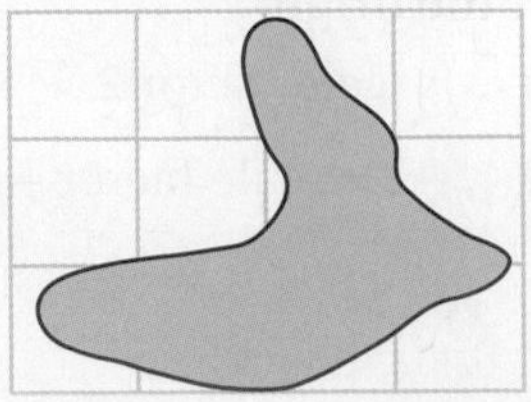

Lesson 10-4

Estimate the area of each irregular shape.

18.

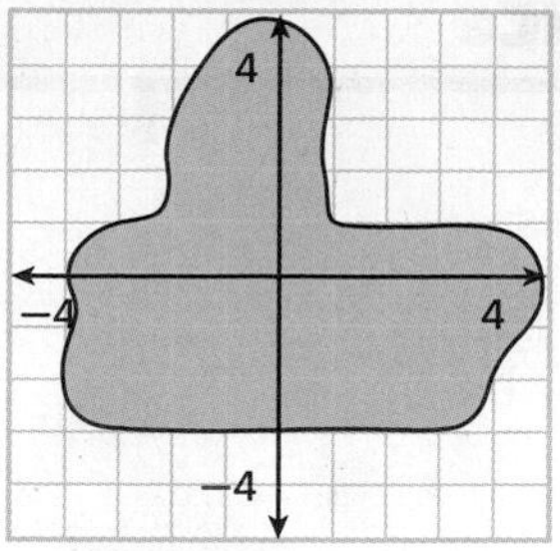

19.

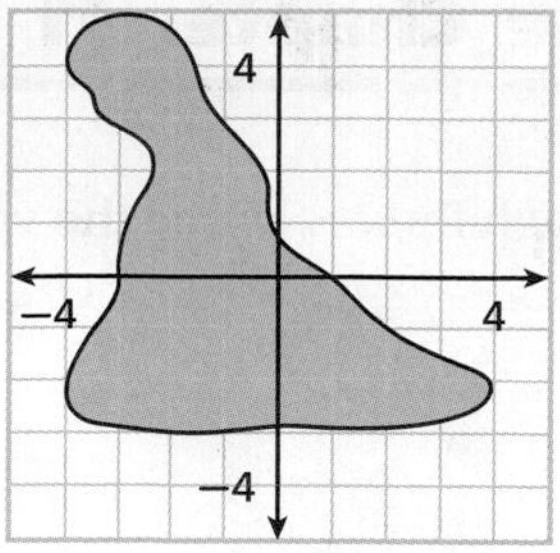

Draw and classify the polygon with the given vertices. Find the perimeter and area of the polygon.

20. $A(-2, 3)$, $B(0, 6)$, $C(6, 2)$, $D(4, -1)$

21. $E(-1, 3)$, $F(2, 3)$, $G(2, -1)$

Find the area of each polygon with the given vertices.

22. $R(-2, 3)$, $S(1, 5)$, $T(3, 1)$, $U(0, -2)$

23. $W(-4, 0)$, $X(4, 3)$, $Y(6, 1)$, $Z(2, -1)$

Lesson 10-5

Describe the effect of each change on the area of the given figure.

24. The height of the rectangle with height 10 ft and width 12 ft is multiplied by $\frac{1}{2}$.

25. The base of the parallelogram with vertices $A(-2, 3)$, $B(3, 3)$, $C(0, -1)$, $D(-5, -1)$ is doubled.

Describe the effect of each change on the perimeter or circumference and the area of the given figure.

26. The radius of $\odot E$ is multiplied by $\frac{1}{4}$.

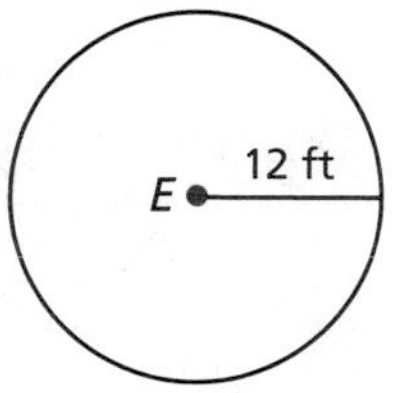

27. The base and height of a rectangle with base 6 in. and height 5 in. are multiplied by 3.

28. A square has a side length of 7 ft. If the area is tripled, what happens to the side length?

29. A circle has a diameter of 20 m. If the area is doubled, what happens to the circumference?

Lesson 10-6

A point is chosen randomly on $\overline{AD}$. Find the probability of each event.

30. The point is on $\overline{AC}$.

31. The point is on $\overline{AB}$ or $\overline{CD}$.

32. The point is not on $\overline{BC}$.

33. The point is on $\overline{BD}$.

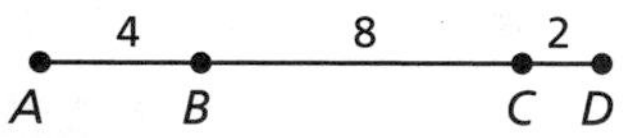

Use the spinner to find the probability of each event.

34. the pointer landing on green

35. the pointer landing on blue or red

36. the pointer not landing on orange

37. the pointer not landing on red or yellow

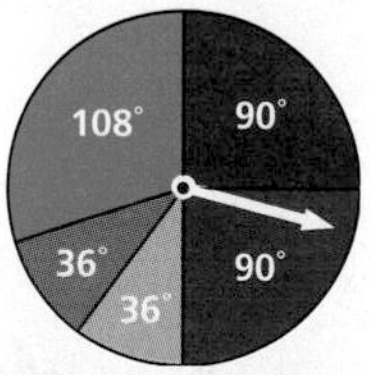

Find the probability that a point chosen randomly inside the rectangle is in each shape. Round to the nearest hundredth.

38. the equilateral triangle

39. the parallelogram

40. the circle

41. the part of the rectangle that does not include the circle, triangle, or parallelogram

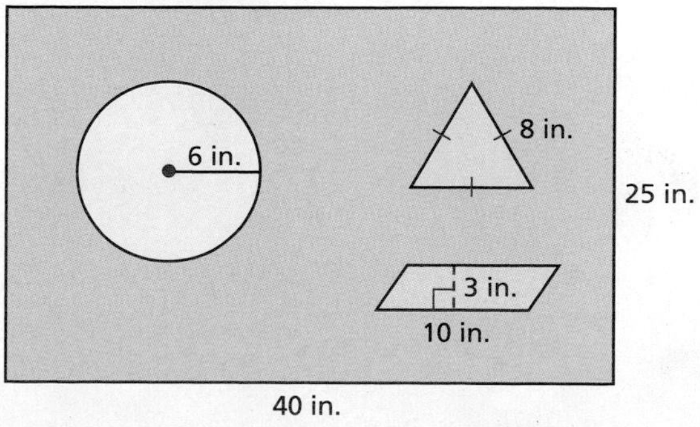

Lesson 11-1

Classify each figure. Name the vertices, edges, and bases.

1. 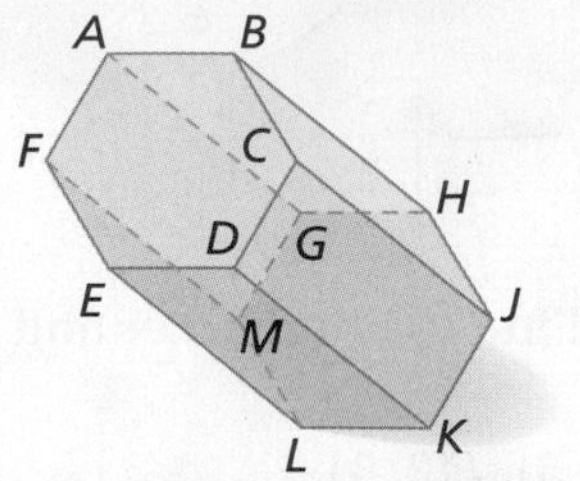

2. 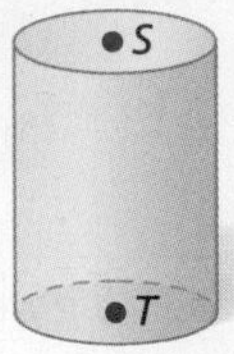

3. 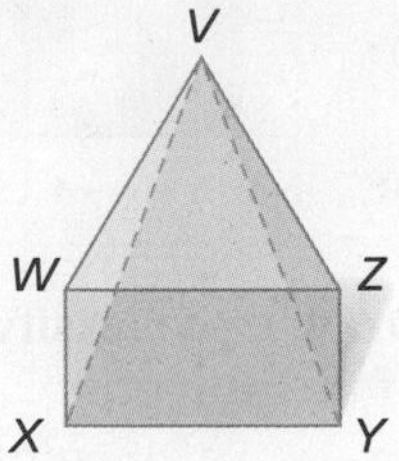

Describe the three-dimensional figure that can be made from the given net.

4. 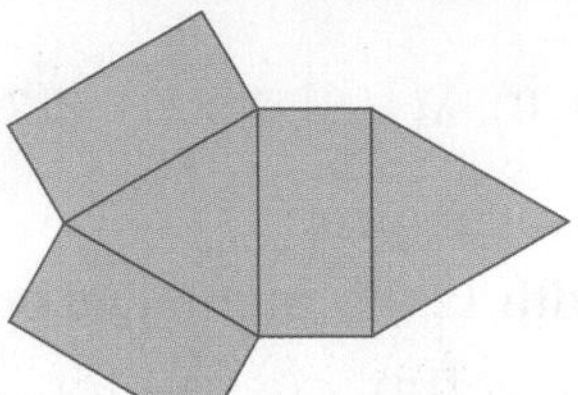

5. 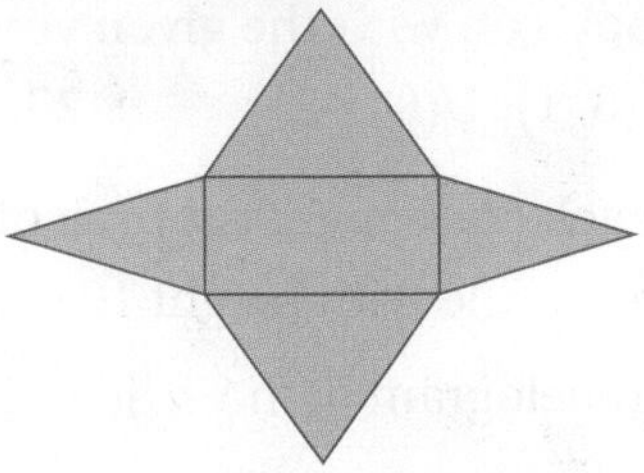

6. 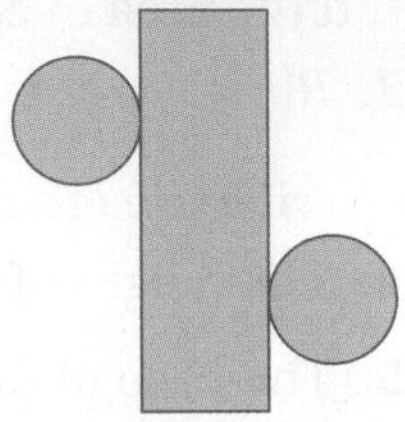

Lesson 11-2

Find the volume of each figure. Round to the nearest tenth.

7. 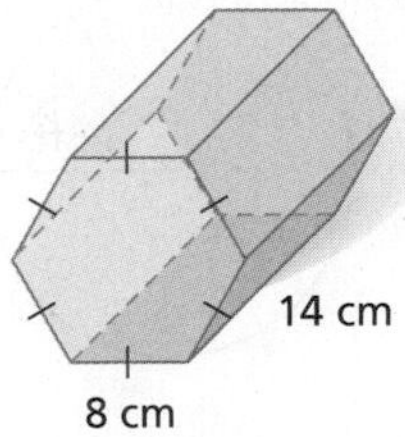

8. 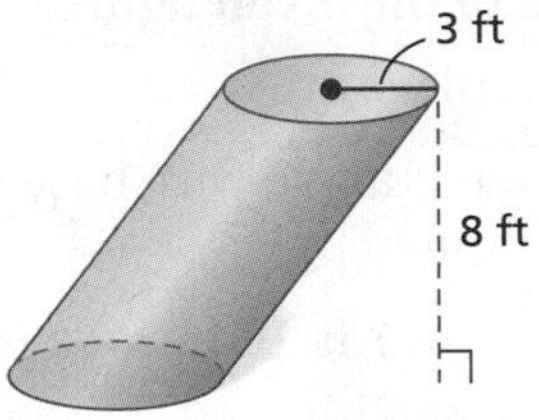

9. 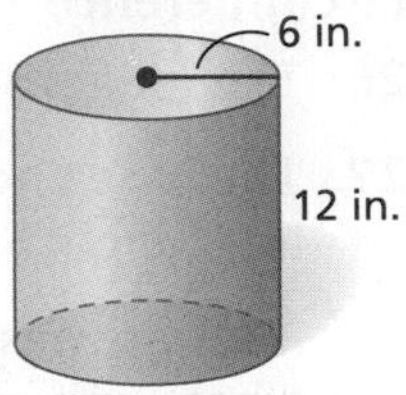

10. The dimensions of a prism with $B = 14\text{ cm}^2$ and $h = 8$ cm are doubled. Describe the effect on the volume.

11. The dimensions of a cylinder with $r = 6$ cm and $h = 4$ cm are multiplied by $\frac{2}{3}$. Describe the effect on the volume.

Lesson 11-3

Find the volume of each figure. Round to the nearest tenth.

12.

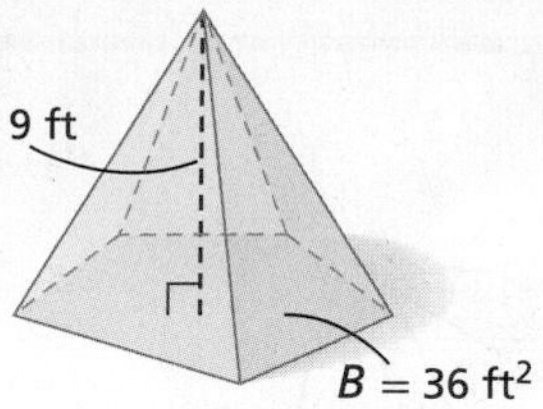

13.

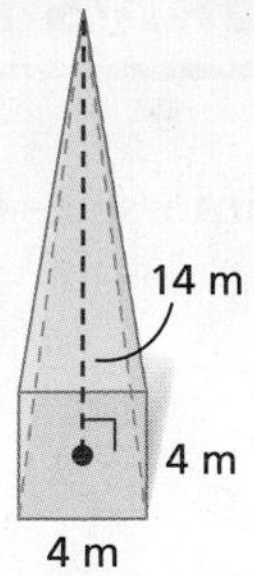

14.

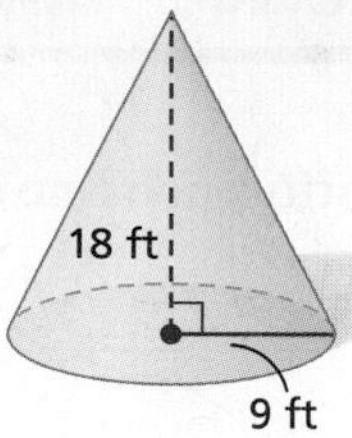

15. The dimensions of a cone with $r = 8$ cm and $\ell = 17$ cm are multiplied by $\frac{1}{2}$. Describe the effect on the volume.

16. The dimensions of a pyramid with $B = 128$ mm^2 and $h = 56$ mm are tripled. Describe the effect on the volume.

Lesson 11-4

Find the surface area and volume of each figure. Give your answers in terms of π.

17.

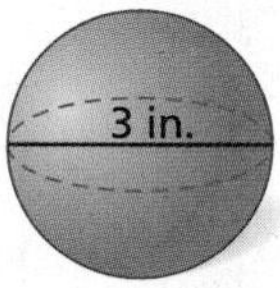

18.

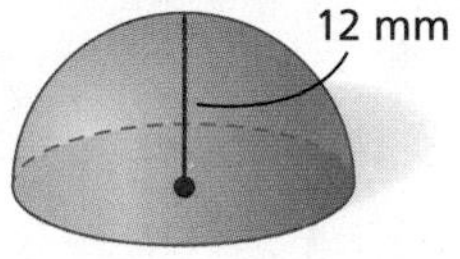

19.

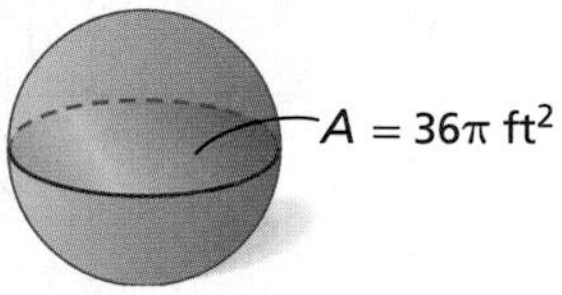

20. The radius of a sphere with $r = 24$ cm is multiplied by $\frac{1}{3}$. Describe the effect on the surface area and volume.

21. The radius of a sphere with $r = 15$ mm is multiplied by 4. Describe the effect on the surface area and volume.

Extra Practice Chapter 12 ■ Skills Practice

Lesson 12-1

Identify each line or segment that intersects each circle.

1.

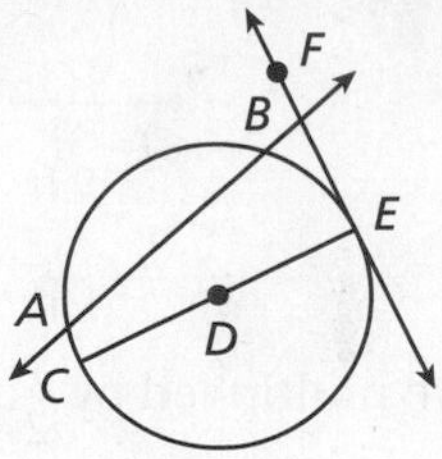

2.

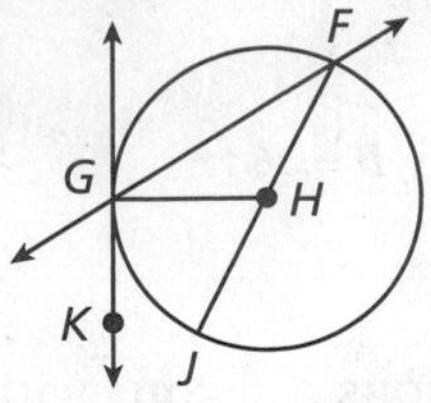

Find the length of each radius. Identify the point of tangency and write the equation of the tangent line at this point.

3.

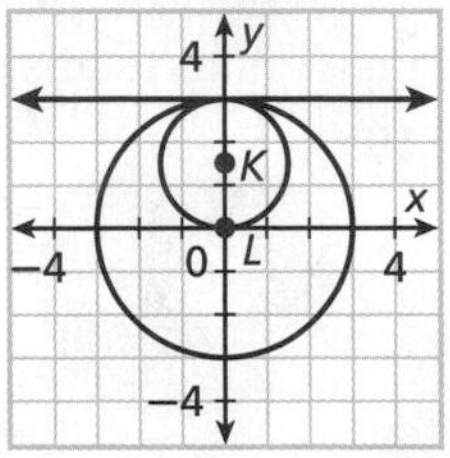

4.

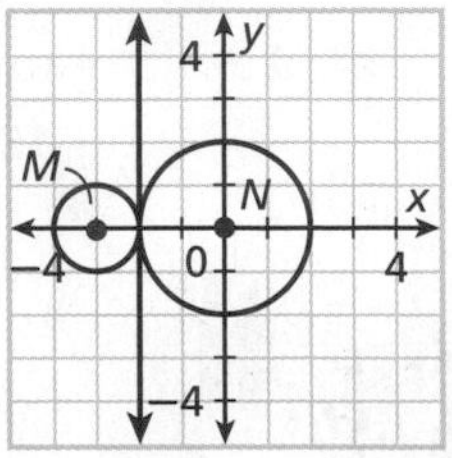

The segments in each figure are tangent to the circle. Find each length.

5. *PQ*

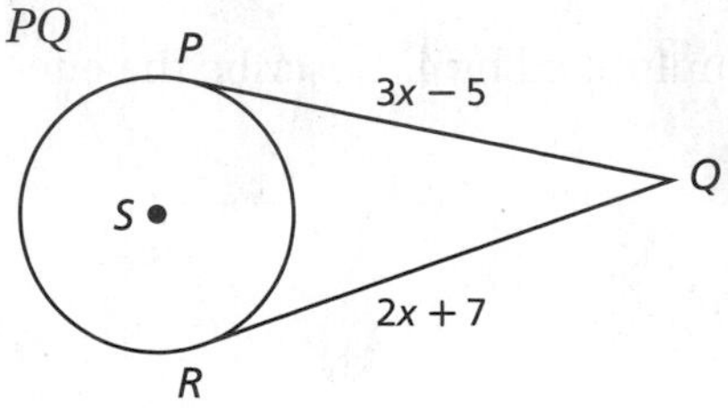

6. *WZ*

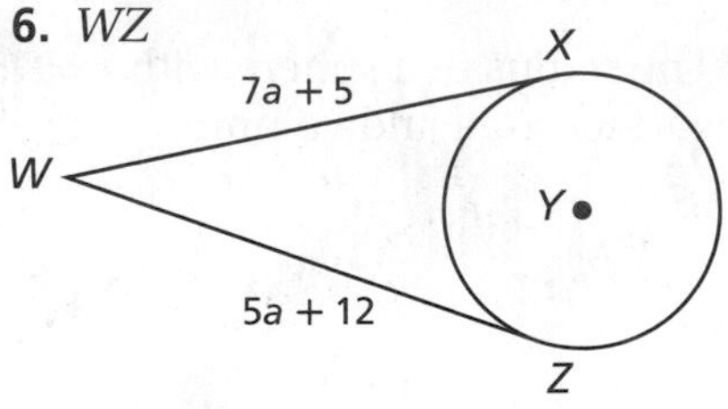

Lesson 12-2

Find each measure. Round to the nearest tenth, if necessary.

7. $m\overset{\frown}{FB}$

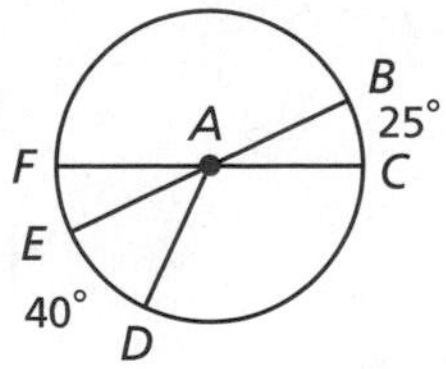

8. *PQ*

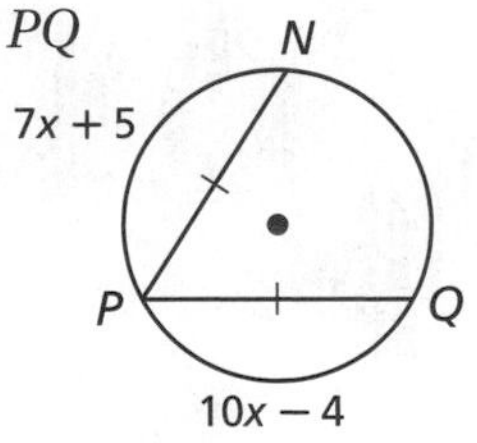

9. $\odot T \cong \odot W$. Find $m\angle VWX$.

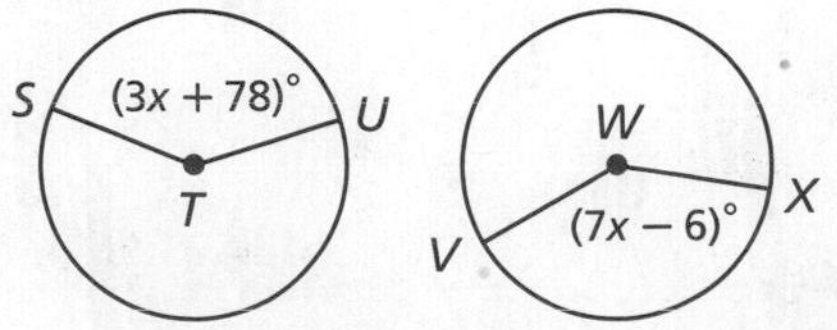

10. *BD*

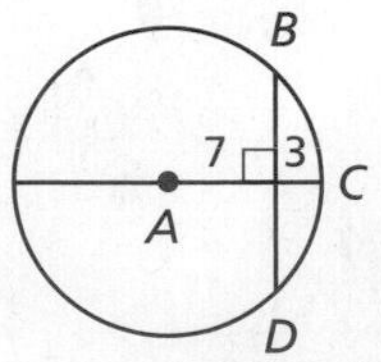

Lesson 12-3

Find the area of each sector or segment. Round to the nearest tenth.

11.

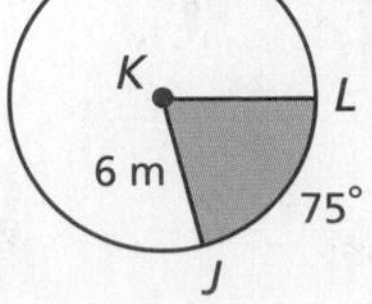

12.

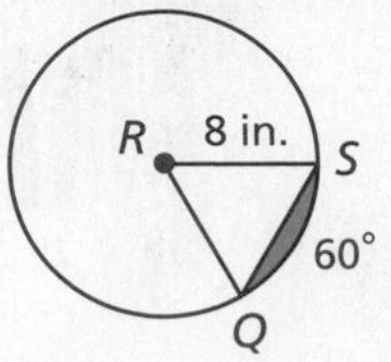

Find each arc length. Give your answers in terms of π and rounded to the nearest tenth.

13.

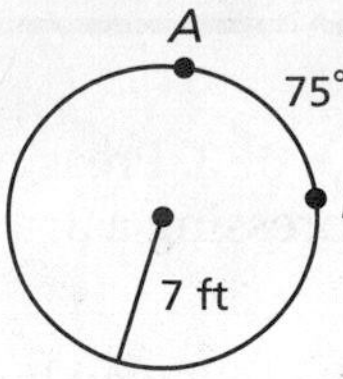

14.

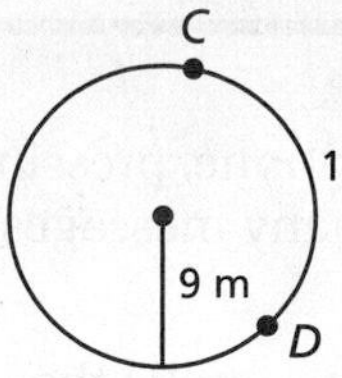

Lesson 12-4

Find each measure or value. Round to the nearest tenth, if necessary.

15. m∠ABD

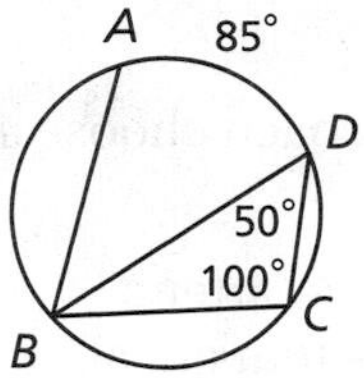

16. x

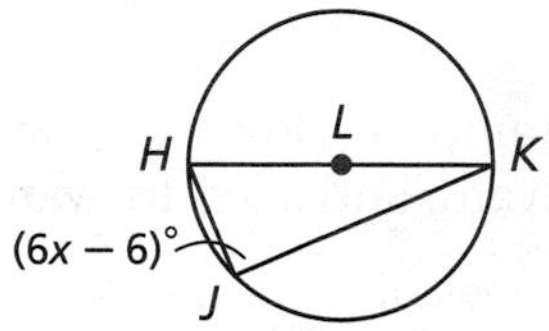

17. x

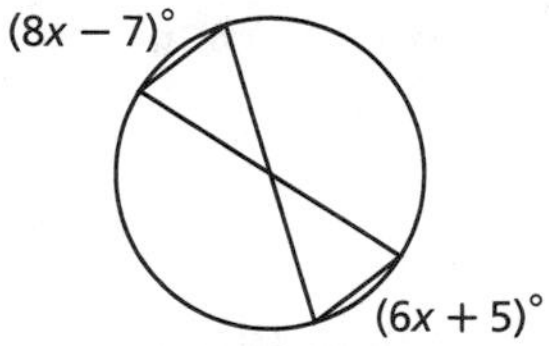

18. angle measures of $HJKL$

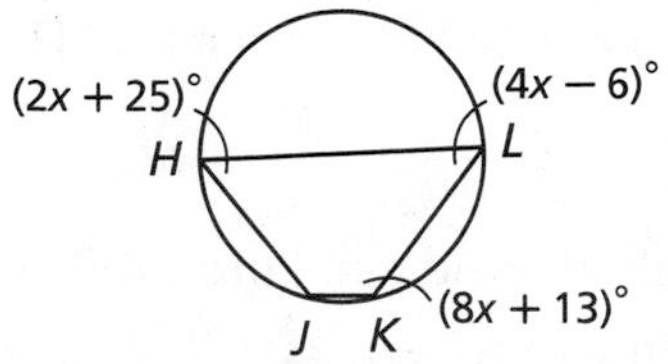

Lesson 12-5

19. m$\widehat{DF}$

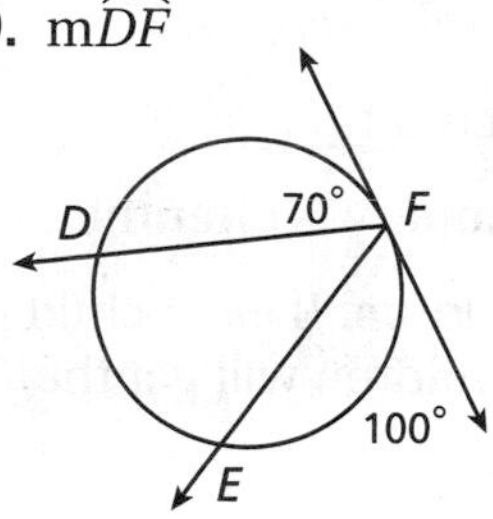

20. m∠JMK

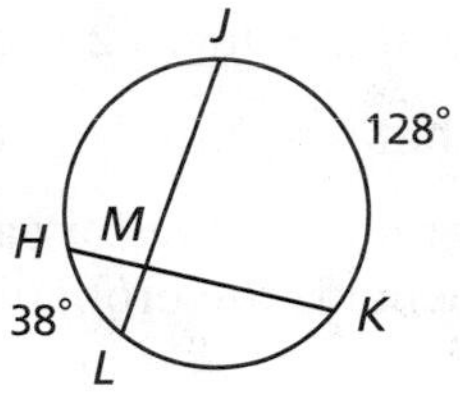

21. m∠RTQ

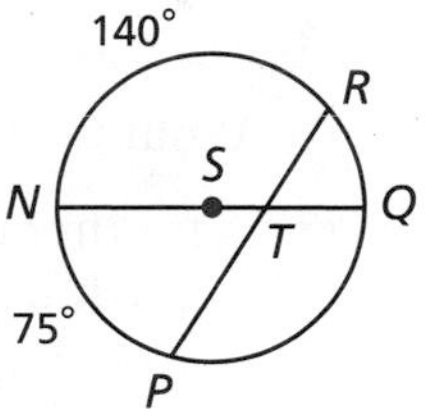

22. x

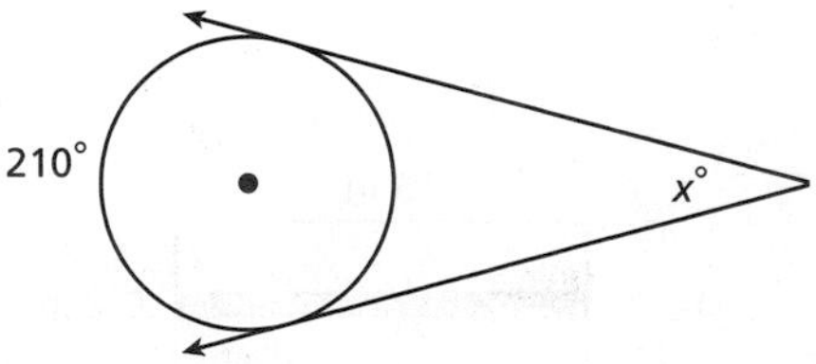

23. m∠AFE

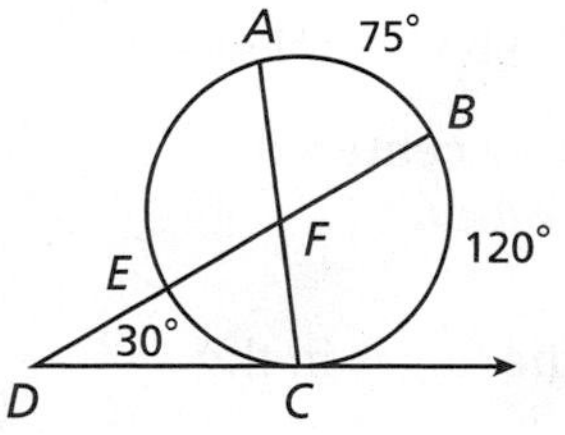

24. m$\widehat{GL}$

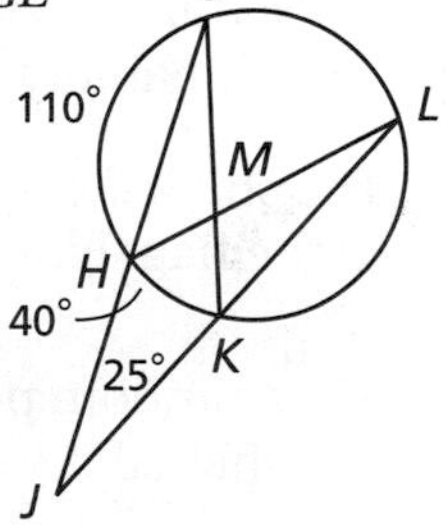

Lesson 12-6

Find the value of the variable. Round to the nearest tenth, if necessary.

25.

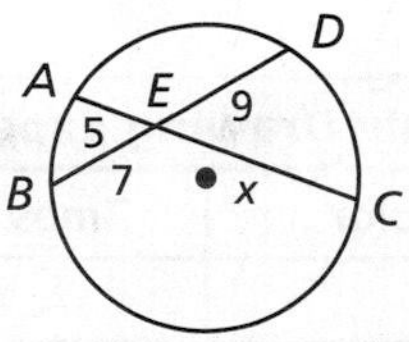

26.

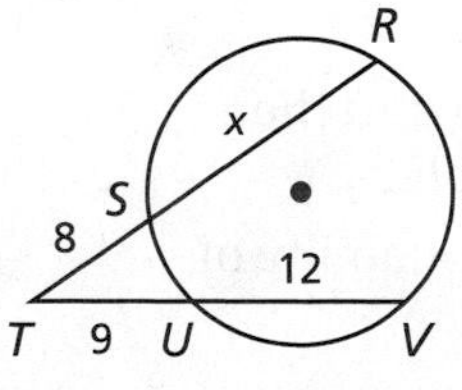

27.

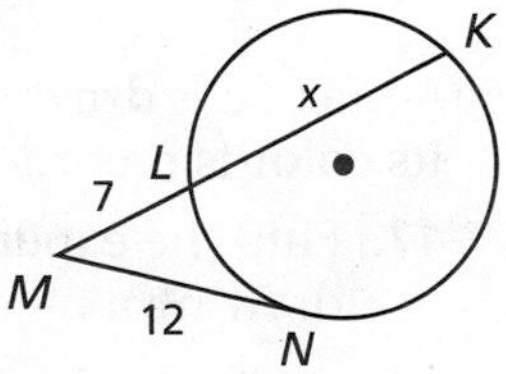

Lesson 12-7

Write the equation of each circle.

28. ⊙A with center $A(2, -3)$ and radius 6

29. ⊙B that passes through $(3, 4)$ and has center $B(-2, 1)$

Graph each equation.

30. $(x + 3)^2 + (y - 4)^2 = 1$

31. $x^2 + (y + 4)^2 = 16$

Extra Practice Chapter 13 ■ Skills Practice

Lesson 13-1

1. When text messaging on a telephone, pressing a 3 types D, E, F, or 3. Pressing a 7 types P, Q, R, S, or 7. How many messages are possible by pressing a 3, a 7, and then a 3?
2. At a company, each employee has an ID that consists of 2 digits followed by a letter. The letters Q and X are not used. How many employee IDs are possible?
3. If there are 8 finalists in a talent show, how many ways can a winner and a runner-up be chosen?
4. Jim's soccer team has 18 members. How many ways can the coach choose a right forward, a center forward, and a left forward?
5. Erin's health club offers 7 types of aerobics classes. She plans to attend 4 classes this week. How many ways can she choose 4 classes that are all different?
6. Francesca can take 4 of her 14 books on a trip. How many ways can she choose them?

Lesson 13-2

Two number cubes are rolled. Find each probability.

7. Both cubes roll the same number.
8. The sum is greater than 8.
9. The sum is 8 or less.
10. Both cubes roll even numbers.
11. What is the probability that a random 2-digit number is a multiple of 7?
12. What is the probability that a randomly selected day in January is after the 20th?
13. A mother is making different lunches for each of her 3 children. If each child grabs a lunch bag at random, what is the probability that all 3 children will get the correct bag?
14. A teacher writes MATHEMATICS on a piece of paper and then cuts out each letter and puts them all in a bag. She will draw two letters at random. What is the probability that she will select an M and an A?

The shaded region is vertically centered in the flag. Find each probability.

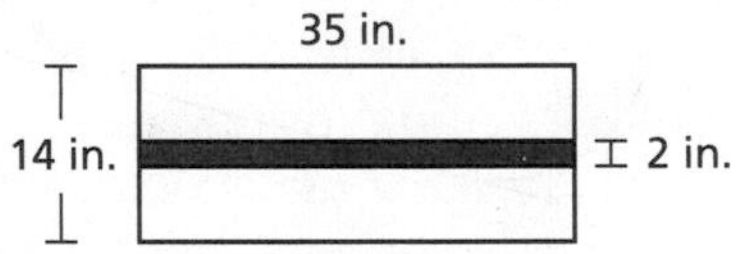

15. a random point inside the flag is in the shaded region
16. a random point inside the flag is above the shaded region

A marble is drawn from a bag and then its color is recorded in the table.

17. Find the experimental probability of drawing a blue marble.
18. Find the experimental probability of drawing a pink or a yellow marble.

Marble Drawing Experiment

Color	Times Drawn
Pink	12
Green	10
Blue	16
Yellow	12

Lesson 13-3

Find each probability.

19. rolling a number greater than or equal to 4 on a number cube twice in a row

20. drawing a face card from a deck, replacing it, and drawing a number card

21. Two number cubes are rolled—one blue and one yellow. Find the probability that the yellow cube is even, and the sum is 7. Explain why the events are dependent.

The table shows the results of a schoolwide survey on the homecoming dance. Find each probability.

Homecoming Dance Location Survey		
	Girls	Boys
Gymnasium	67	58
Cafeteria	53	37

22. A student who prefers the cafeteria is a girl.

23. A surveyed student is male and prefers the gymnasium.

A bag contains 18 beads—5 blue, 6 yellow, and 7 red. Determine whether the events are independent or dependent. Find the indicated probability.

24. selecting a yellow and then a blue bead when they are chosen with replacement

25. selecting a yellow and then a blue bead when they are chosen without replacement

Lesson 13-4

The table shows the side dish chosen with the lunch plate and the supper plate at a diner on one day.

	Salad	Fries	Broccoli	Total
Lunch	26	47	9	82
Supper	42	29	34	105
Total	68	76	43	187

26. Make a table of the joint and marginal relative frequencies. Round to the nearest hundredth where appropriate.

27. If you are given that a customer ordered a lunch plate, what is the probability that fries were chosen as the side dish?

28. If you are given that a customer ordered broccoli with the meal plate, what is the probability that it was the supper plate?

Lesson 13-5

29. A table was chosen at random in the cafeteria, and there were 2 freshmen, 5 sophomores, 7 juniors, and 2 seniors eating there. A student is chosen at random from the table. What is the probability of choosing a freshman or a senior?

The numbers 1–20 are written on cards and placed in a bag. Find each probability.

30. choosing a number less than 10 or choosing a multiple of 5

31. choosing 20 or choosing an odd number

32. In an apartment building with 50 residents, 16 residents have cats, 28 residents are students, and 9 of the students have cats. What is the probability that a resident is a student or has a cat?

33. There are 8 couples in a dance competition, and each of the 3 judges must pick the couple they believe should win. Suppose the judges picked randomly. What is the probability that at least 2 judges picked the same couple?

Athletics **Use the following information for Exercises 1–3.**

During gym class, a teacher notices the following. Decide if each resembles a point, segment, ray, or line. *(Lesson 1-1)*

1. Kyle starts running in a straight line. Suppose he does not stop running.
2. Agnes runs a quarter-mile in a straight line.
3. Jimmy stands perfectly still.

Travel **Use the following information for Exercises 4–6.**

The Perez family is driving from Austin, Texas, to Dallas, Texas. The city of Waco is the approximate midpoint between these two cities. It is 102 miles from Austin to Waco. *(Lesson 1-2)*

4. What is the total distance from Austin to Dallas?
5. The approximate midpoint from Waco to Dallas is Milford. What is the distance from Austin to Milford?
6. The Perez family averages 64 miles per hour. About how long will the entire drive take?

Probability **Use the following information for Exercises 7 and 8.**

In a carnival game, each contestant spins the wheel and wins the prize indicated by the color. *(Lesson 1-3)*

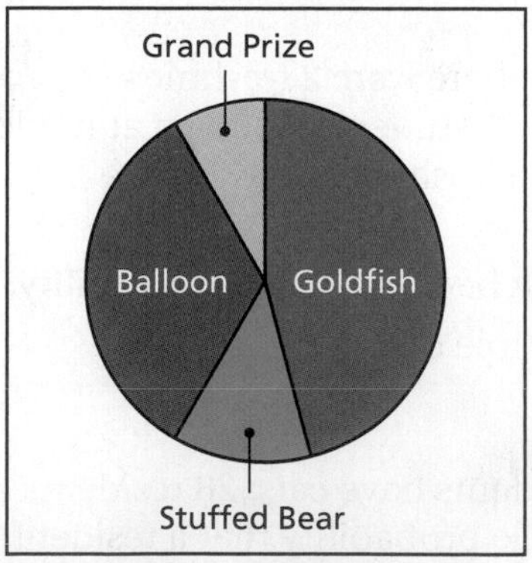

7. Using a protractor, measure each angle on the wheel.
8. Since there are 360° in a circle, the probability of the wheel landing on a given color is the number of degrees in the angle divided by 360°. Find the probability of the wheel landing on each prize. Express your answer as a fraction in lowest terms.

9. **Entomology** Because the insect is symmetrical, $\angle 1 \cong \angle 4$ and $\angle 2 \cong \angle 3$. Also, $\angle 1$ and $\angle 2$ are complementary, and $\angle 3$ and $\angle 4$ are complementary. If $m\angle 1 = 48.5°$, find $m\angle 2$, $m\angle 3$, and $m\angle 4$. *(Lesson 1-4)*

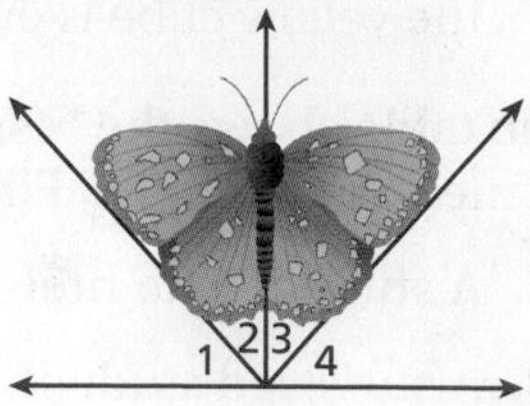

Architecture **Use the following information for Exercises 10 and 11.**

The bricks used to make a building are one-fourth as tall as they are wide, and the bricks are 2.25 inches tall. *(Lesson 1-5)*

10. What is the area of the largest face of each brick?
11. A certain exterior wall is 33 bricks long and 20 bricks tall. What is the area of the wall in square inches?
12. **Sports** A football coach has his team run sprints diagonally across a football field. If the field is 120 yards long and 160 feet wide, what is the distance they run? Write your answer to the nearest hundredth of a foot. *(Lesson 1-6)*
13. **Crafts** The picture below shows half of a stenciled design. The full design should resemble a sun. Name two transformations that can be performed on the image so that the image and its preimage form a complete picture. Be as specific as possible, referring to *L* and *P*. *(Lesson 1-7)*

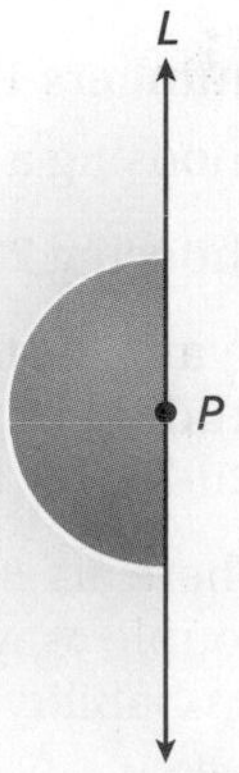

1. **Health** Mike collected the following data about the heights of twelve students in his tenth-grade class. Use the table to make a conjecture about the heights of boys and girls in the tenth grade. *(Lesson 2-1)*

Height (in.) of Tenth-Grade Students						
Boys	70	71	68	67	70	67
Girls	67	64	64	65	68	66

2. **Government** Presidential elections are held every four years. Elections for senators are held every two years. So in years not divisible by 4, only Senate seats are up for election. The table shows voter turnout for a small town during recent election years. Make a conjecture based on the data. *(Lesson 2-1)*

Voter Turnout	
Year	**Voters**
1996	12,530
1998	8,750
2000	15,210
2002	7,370
2004	14,380

3. **Biology** Write the converse, inverse, and contrapositive of the conditional statement "If an animal is a fish, then it swims in salt water." Find the truth value of each. *(Lesson 2-2)*

4. **Gardening** Write the converse, inverse, and contrapositive of the conditional statement "If a plant is watered, then it will grow." Find the truth value of each. *(Lesson 2-2)*

5. **Sports** Determine if the conjecture is valid by the Law of Detachment. *(Lesson 2-3)*
Given: If you participate in a triathlon, then you run, swim, and bike. Margie runs, swims, and bikes.
Conjecture: Margie participates in a triathlon.

6. **Health** Students are required to have certain immunizations before attending school to prevent the spread of disease. Write the conditional statement and converse within the biconditional "Students can attend public school if and only if they have the required immunizations." *(Lesson 2-4)*

7. **Weather** Hurricanes are assigned category numbers to describe the amount of flooding and wind damage they are likely to cause. Write the statement "If a hurricane has sustained winds of more than 155 miles per hour, then it is Category 5" as a biconditional statement. *(Lesson 2-4)*

8. **Athletics** The equation $c = 5w + 25$ relates the number of workouts w to the cost c of a weight training group. If Matthew plans to spend \$200 on weight training, how many workouts can he participate in? Solve the equation for w and justify each step. *(Lesson 2-5)*

9. **Nutrition** Rick has allotted himself 200 Calories for his evening snack, which consists of a glass of milk and crackers. A glass of milk has 110 Calories, and each cracker has 15 Calories. The equation $s = 110 + 15c$ relates the number of crackers c to the total number of Calories s in Rick's evening snack. How many crackers can Rick have? Solve the equation for c and justify each step. *(Lesson 2-5)*

10. **Travel** On a city map, the library, post office, and police station are collinear points in that order. The distance from the library to the post office is 2.3 miles. The distance from the post office to the police station is 5.1 miles. Which theorem can you use to conclude that the distance from the library to the police station is 7.4 miles? *(Lesson 2-6)*

11. **Recreation** Kyle is making a kite from the pattern below by cutting four triangles from different pieces of material. Write a paragraph proof to show that $m\angle 3 = 90°$. *(Lesson 2-7)*

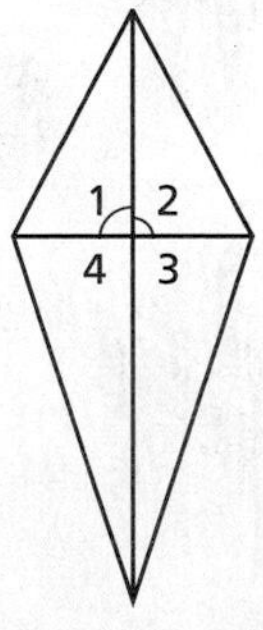

Given: $\angle 1 \cong \angle 2$
Prove: $m\angle 3 = 90°$

1. **Recreation** A scuba diver leaves a flag on the surface of the water to alert boaters of his location. Describe two parallel lines and a transversal in the flag. *(Lesson 3-1)*

2. **Carpentry** In the stairs shown, the horizontal treads and the vertical risers are all parallel. $m\angle 1 = (14x + 6)°$ and $m\angle 2 = (19x - 24)°$. Find x. *(Lesson 3-2)*

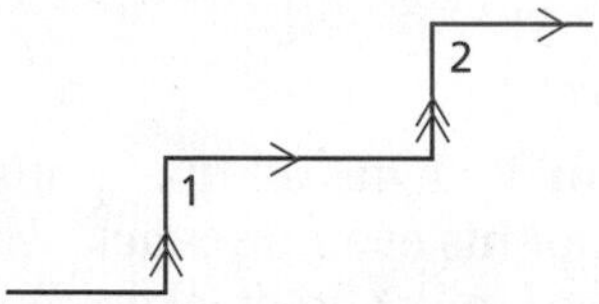

3. **Transportation** The train tracks shown cross the street lanes. The lanes of the street are parallel. Find x in the diagram. *(Lesson 3-3)*

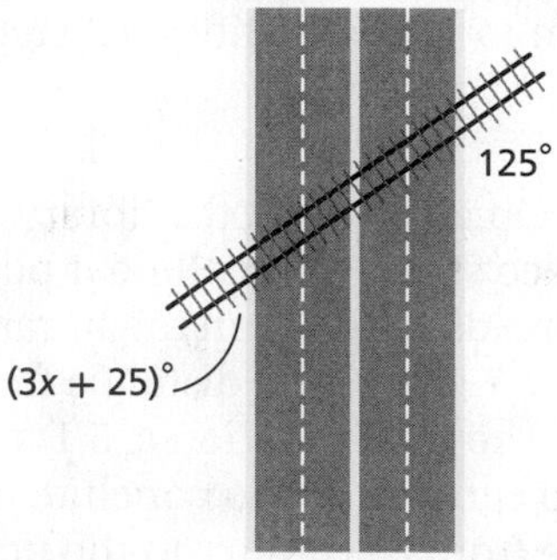

4. **Sports** At a track meet, the starting blocks are placed along a line that is a transversal to the lanes. $m\angle 1 = 12x - 8$, $m\angle 2 = 8x + 12$, and $x = 5$. Show that the lines between the lanes are parallel. *(Lesson 3-3)*

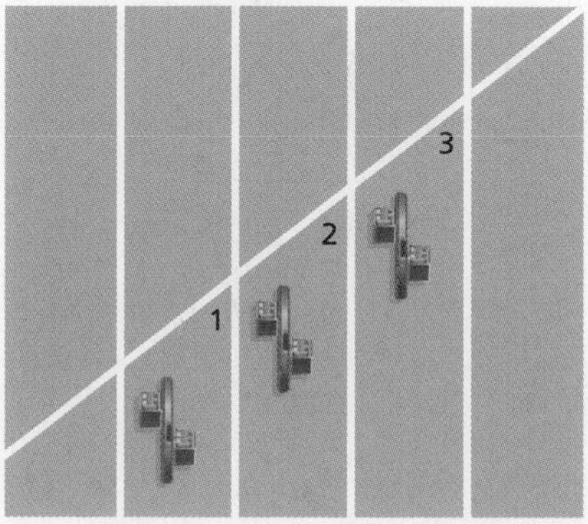

5. **Transportation** The railroad ties in the diagram are all parallel. $m\angle 1 = 19x - 5$ and $m\angle 2 = 4x + 5y$. Find x and y so that the ties are all perpendicular to the tracks. *(Lesson 3-4)*

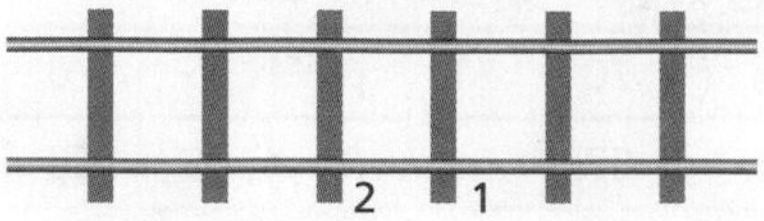

6. **Art** The sides of a picture frame are cut so that the opposite sides of the frame are parallel and the consecutive sides are perpendicular. Find the values of x and y in the diagram. *(Lesson 3-4)*

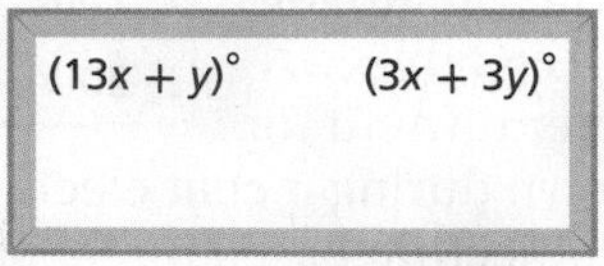

7. **Recreation** At 1:00 P.M., a boat on a river passes a point that is 3 miles from a lodge. At 5:30 P.M., the boat passes a point that is 8 miles from the lodge. Graph the line that represents the boat's distance from the lodge. Find and interpret the slope of the line. *(Lesson 3-5)*

8. **Sports** A marathon runner runs 10 miles by 3:00 P.M. and 25 miles by 4:30 P.M. Graph the line that represents her distance run. Find and interpret the slope of the line. *(Lesson 3-5)*

9. **Business** A cab company charges \$8 per ride plus \$0.25 per mile. Another cab company charges \$5 per ride plus \$0.35 per mile. For how many miles will two cab rides cost the same amount? *(Lesson 3-6)*

10. **Food** A pizza parlor is catering a school event. Pete's Pizza charges \$85 for the first 20 students and \$5 for each additional student. Polly's Pizza charges \$125 for the first 20 students and \$3 for each additional student. For how many students will the pizza parlors cost the same? *(Lesson 3-6)*

Extra Practice Chapter 4 ■ Applications Practice

1. Crafts On a coordinate plane, patterns for two pieces of stained glass have coordinates $A(4, 1)$, $B(3, 5)$, $C(1, 2)$ and $D(1, -3)$, $E(5, -2)$, $F(2, 0)$. Prove that the patterns are congruent. *(Lesson 4-1)*

2. Camping Three poles are used to create the frame for a tent. The front of the tent is an isosceles triangle with $\overline{AB} \cong \overline{BC}$. The length of the base is 1.5 times the length of the sides. The perimeter of the triangle is 21 ft. Find each side length. *(Lesson 4-2)*

3. Geography The universities in Durham, Chapel Hill, and Raleigh, North Carolina form what is known as the Research Triangle. Use the map to find the measure of the angle whose vertex is at Durham. *(Lesson 4-3)*

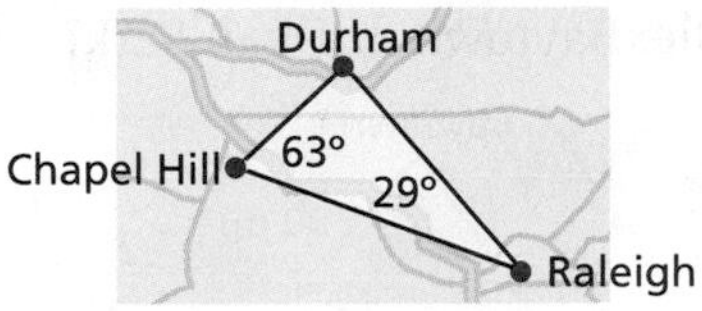

4. Business Oil derricks are used as supports for oil drilling equipment. Use the diagram to prove the following. *(Lesson 4-4)*

Given: $\overline{AB} \cong \overline{HG}$, $\overline{HB} \cong \overline{AG}$
$\angle GAB \cong \angle BHG$,
$\angle AGB \cong \angle HBG$

Prove: $\triangle AGB \cong \triangle HBG$

5. Sports A kite is made up of two pairs of congruent triangles. Use SAS to explain why $\triangle ABD \cong \triangle CBD$. *(Lesson 4-5)*

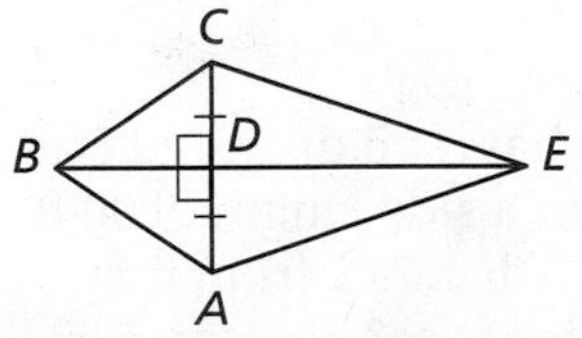

6. Recreation A student is estimating the height of a water slide. From a certain distance, the angle from where he is standing to a point on the highest part of the slide is 35°. From a distance 200 m closer, the same angle is 45°. Which postulate or theorem can be used to show that the triangle with the point at the top of the slide as one vertex, and the points where the measurements were taken as the other vertices, is uniquely determined? *(Lesson 4-6)*

7. Surveying To find the distance AB across a lake, first locate point C. Then measure the distance from C to B. Locate point D the same distance from C as B, but in the opposite direction. Then measure the distance from C to A and locate point E in a similar manner. What is the distance AB across the lake? *(Lesson 4-7)*

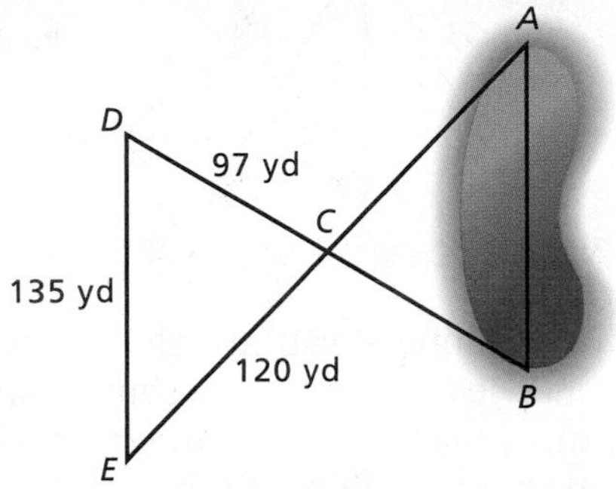

8. The first step in creating a Sierpinski triangle is to connect the midpoints of the sides of a triangle as shown. *(Lesson 4-8)*

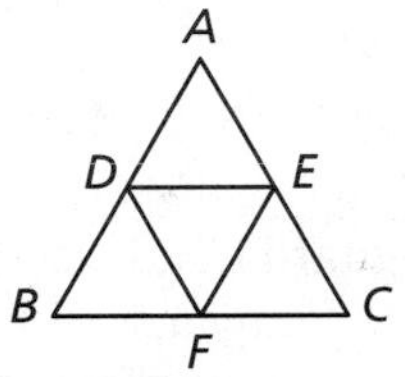

Given: Equilateral $\triangle ABC$, D is the midpoint of $\overline{AB}$, E is the midpoint of $\overline{AC}$, and F is the midpoint of $\overline{BC}$.

Prove: The area of $\triangle DEF$ is $\frac{1}{4}$ the area of $\triangle ABC$.

9. Recreation A boat is sailing parallel to the coastline along $\overleftrightarrow{XY}$. When the boat is at X, the measure of the angle from the lighthouse W to the boat is 30°. After the boat has traveled 5 miles to Y, the angle from the lighthouse to the boat is 60°. How can you find WY? *(Lesson 4-9)*

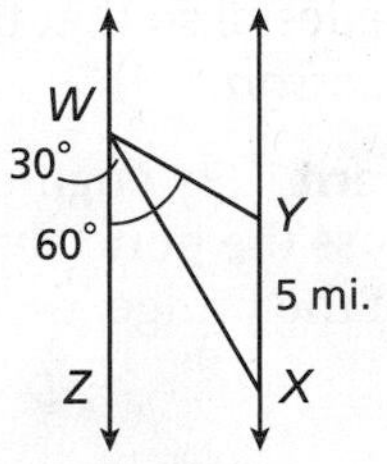

1. **Building** The guy wires $\overline{AB}$ and $\overline{CB}$ supporting a cell phone tower are congruent and are equally spaced from the base of the tower. How do these wires ensure that the cell phone tower is perpendicular to the ground? *(Lesson 5-1)*

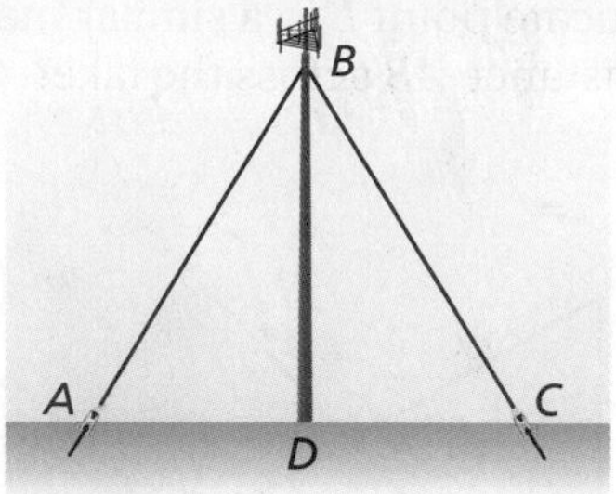

2. **Safety** City planners want to relocate their town's firehouse so that it is the same distance from the three main streets of the town. Draw a sketch to show where the firehouse should be positioned. Justify your sketch. *(Lesson 5-2)*

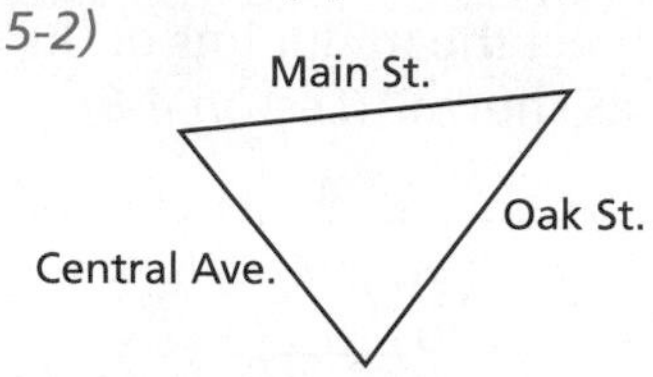

3. **Safety** A lifeguard needs to watch three areas of a water park. Draw a sketch to show where she should stand to be the same distance from all the swimmers. Justify your sketch. *(Lesson 5-2)*

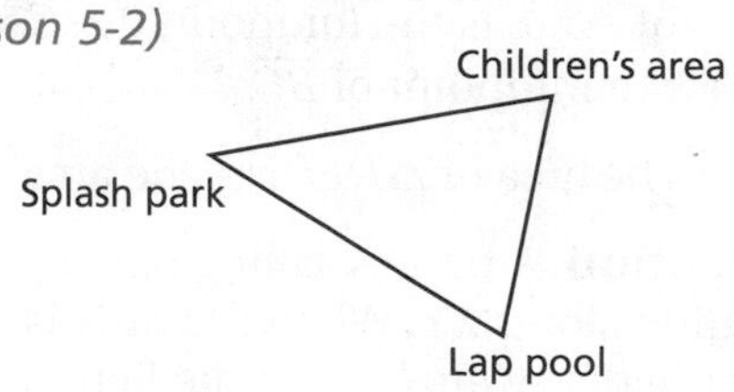

4. **Art** An artist is designing a sculpture composed of a pedestal with a triangular top. The vertices of the top are $A(-4, 2)$, $B(2, 4)$, and $C(4, -3)$. Where should the artist attach the pedestal so that the triangle is balanced? *(Lesson 5-3)*

5. **Measurement** City engineers plan to build a bridge across the pond shown. What will be the length of the bridge, GH? *(Lesson 5-4)*

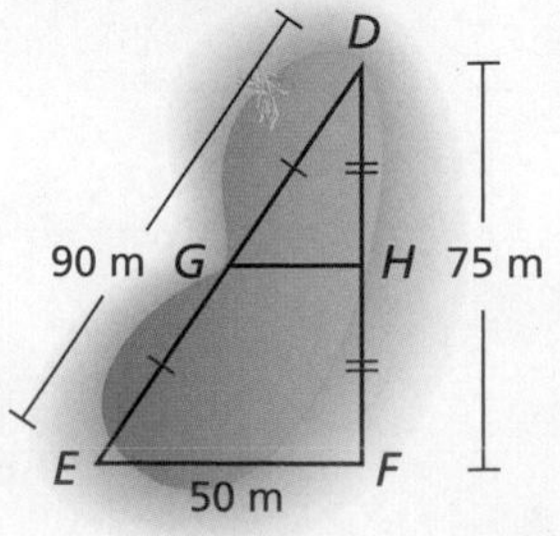

Engineering Use the following information for Exercises 6 and 7.

Playground engineers are planning a sidewalk that will connect the swings, seesaw, and slide. *(Lesson 5-5)*

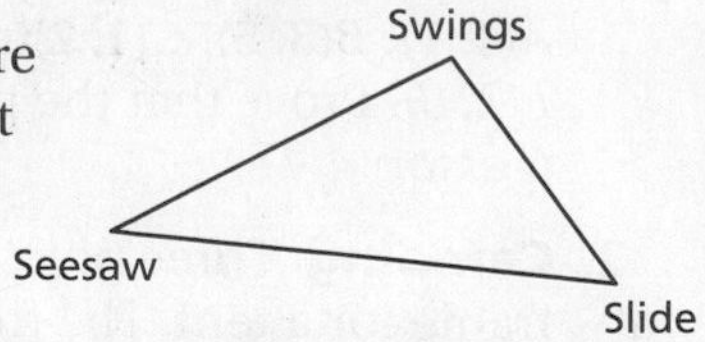

6. If the angle at the swings is the largest, which portion of the sidewalk will be the longest?

7. The distance from the swings to the slide is 37 ft. Can the lengths of the other sides be 40 ft and 50 ft? Explain.

8. **Geography** The cities of Allenville, Baytown, College City, and Dean Park are shown on the map. Baytown and Dean Park are each 30 miles from College City. Which city is closer to Allenville: Baytown or Dean Park? *(Lesson 5-6)*

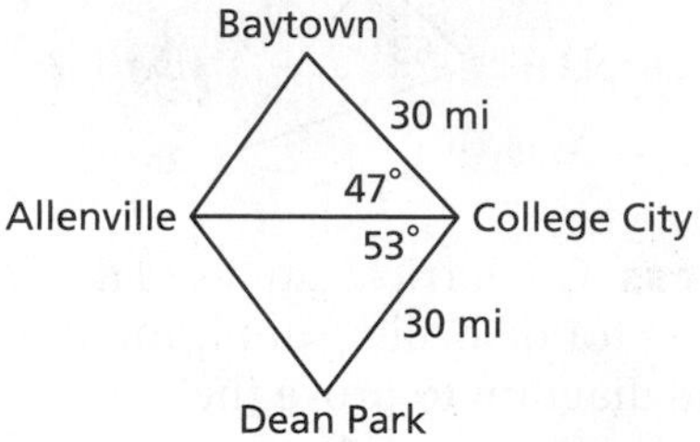

9. Mark is late for school. He usually goes around the park so he can walk along the water. Today he decides to cut through the park. About how many feet does he save by going through the park? *(Lesson 5-7)*

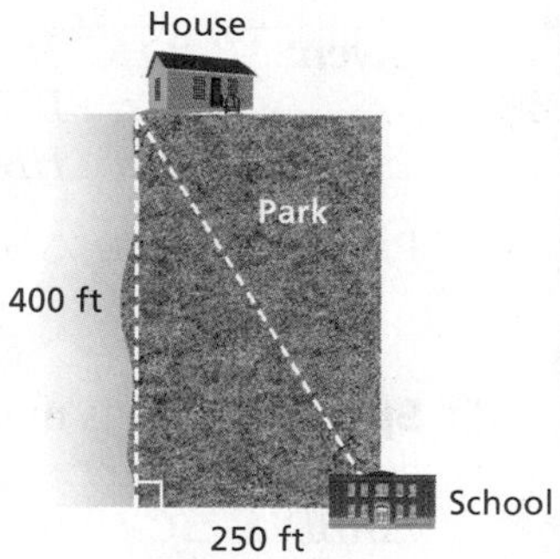

10. **Sports** A baseball diamond is a square with a side length of 90 ft. What is the distance from first base to third base? *(Lesson 5-8)*

11. **Recreation** Haley, who is 5 ft tall, is flying a kite on 100 ft of string. How high is the kite? *(Lesson 5-8)*

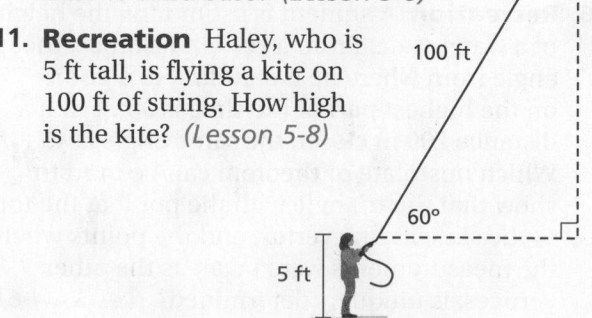

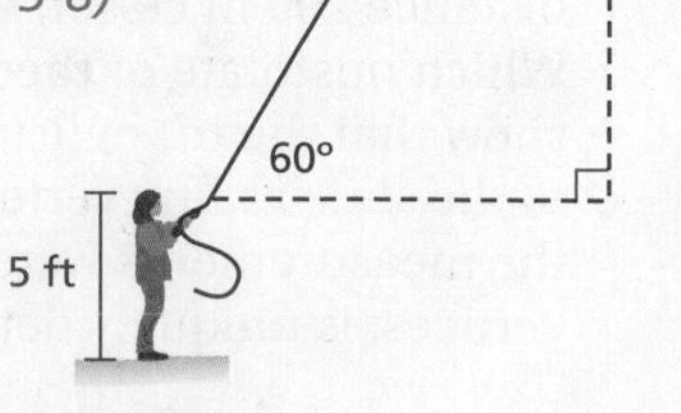

Extra Practice Chapter 6 ▪ Applications Practice

1. **Safety** A stop sign is in the shape of a regular octagon. What is the value of x? *(Lesson 6-1)*

2. **Hobbies** Nancy is planting a garden shaped like a regular pentagon. She bought metal edging to surround the garden and prevent weeds. What angle should the edging form at the vertices of the garden? *(Lesson 6-1)*

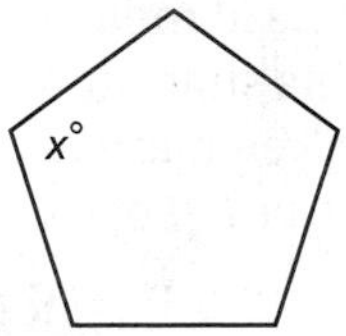

Fishing **Use the following information for Exercises 3–5.**

The hinges for the trays in a tackle box form parallelograms to ensure that the trays stay parallel to the base of the box. In ▱$ABCD$, $AB = 21$ in., $AE = 9$ in., and $m\angle BCD = 125°$. Find each measure. *(Lesson 6-2)*

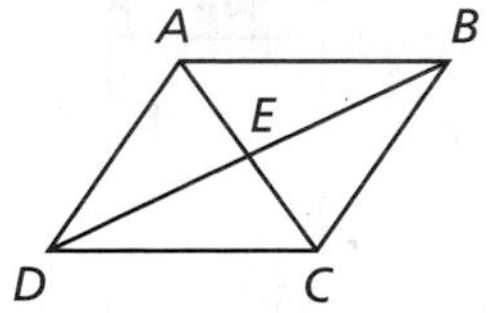

3. DC

4. EC

5. $m\angle ADC$

6. **Design** A glide rocker uses hinged parallelograms to move the chair back and forth. In ▱$ABCD$, $AB = DC$, and $AD = BC$. The sides of the parallelogram, $\overline{AD}$ and $\overline{BC}$, rotate together to move the chair. Why is $ABCD$ always a parallelogram? *(Lesson 6-3)*

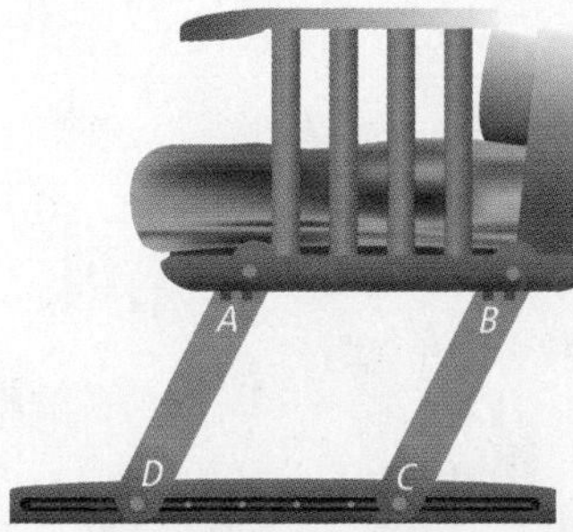

Design **Use the following information for Exercises 7–9.**

When extended, the legs of a folding table must form a rectangle so the tabletop is parallel to the ground. Given that $JK = 48$ in. and $KN = 36$ in., find each length. *(Lesson 6-4)*

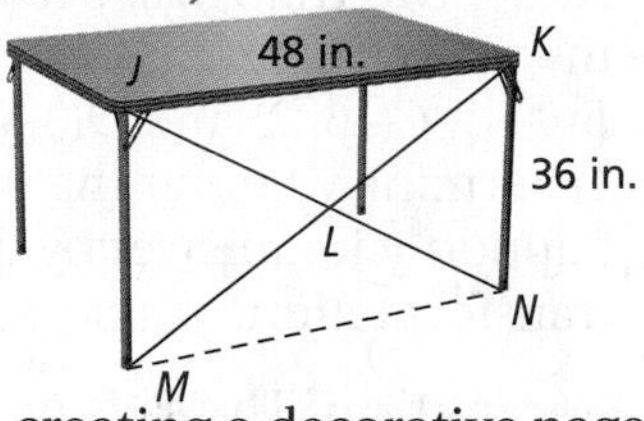

7. JM

8. JN

9. NM

10. **Hobbies** Elise is creating a decorative page for her scrapbook. She has a piece of ribbon that is 12 inches long. She wants to outline a rhombus with the ribbon. How can Elise cut the ribbon to ensure that the final shape is a rhombus? *(Lesson 6-5)*

11. **Carpentry** Luke is cutting a rectangular window frame. The dimensions of the window are to be 3 feet by 4 feet. What should the diagonal of the frame measure so that the window is rectangular? *(Lesson 6-5)*

12. **Hobbies** Addie is making a kite with diagonals of 32 inches and 18 inches. She wants to put a ribbon around the edge of the kite. She will add an 8-foot tail to the kite, made of the same ribbon. If ribbon can be purchased in packages of 3 yards, how many packages should she buy for the entire project? *(Lesson 6-6)*

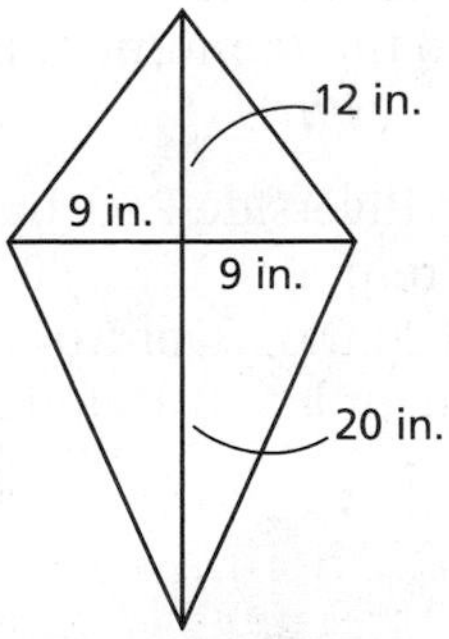

13. **Carpentry** Aaron is building a shadow box for his baseball memorabilia. The shadow box will be in the shape of a trapezoid, as shown below. The wood for the box costs \$1.59 per foot. Estimate the cost of the lumber. *(Lesson 6-6)*

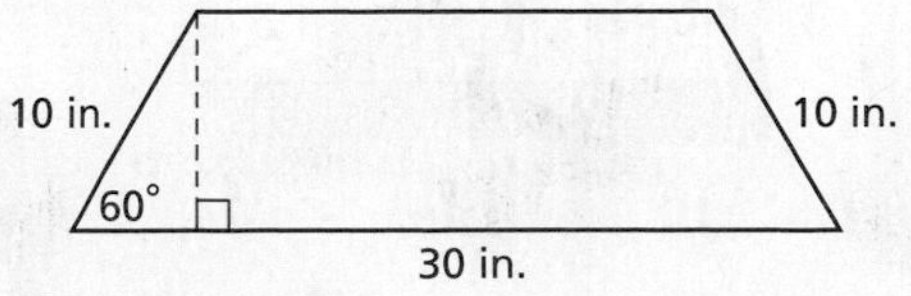

1. **Travel** A map is a scale model of a real city. The scale on the map is 1 in.:30 mi. Two cities are 165 mi apart. How far apart will the cities be on the map? *(Lesson 7-1)*

2. **Design** The logo for the Tri-City Corporation shows two triangles. On a coordinate plane, the triangles have coordinates $A(2, 0)$, $B(0, 4)$, $C(-6, 2)$ and $D(3, 0)$, $E(0, 6)$, $F(-9, 3)$. Determine whether the triangles are similar. Support your answer by describing a transformation. *(Lesson 7-2)*

3. **Recreation** The sails on the sailboat below have the given dimensions. Use similar triangles to prove $\triangle ABC \sim \triangle DEF$. *(Lesson 7-3)*

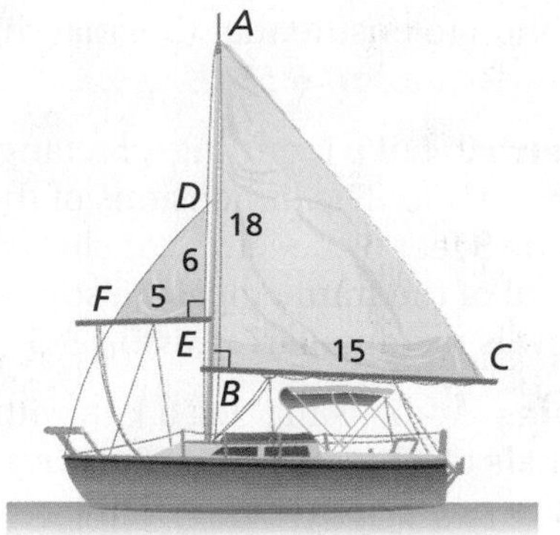

4. **Graphics** A photograph shows a smaller version of the real item. The height of the Washington Monument is approximately 555 ft. The monument in a photo is 5 in. tall. What is the scale factor of the actual monument to the monument in the photo? *(Lesson 7-3)*

5. **Geography** Riverside Park has campsites available for rent. Lot A has 50 ft of street frontage and 80 ft of river frontage. Find the river frontage for lots B, C, and D. *(Lesson 7-4)*

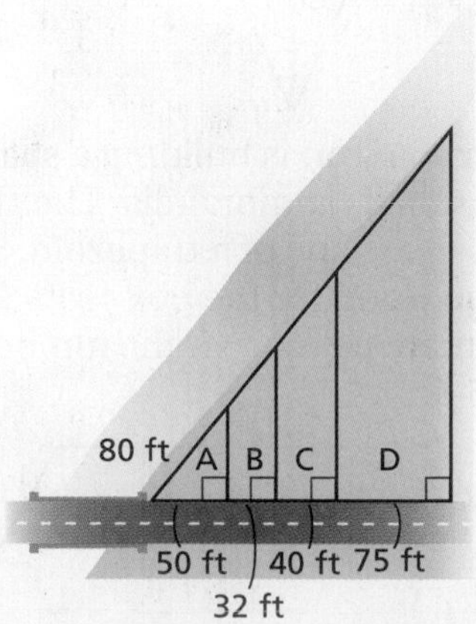

6. **Architecture** An amphitheater is being built according to the design shown. If the total footage on the right of the rows of seats is 232.5 ft, find the length of each section. *(Lesson 7-4)*

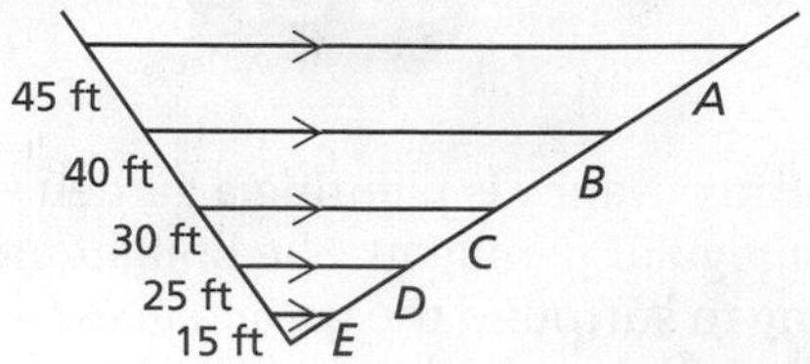

7. Jake wants to know the height of the oak tree in his front yard. He measured his height as 68 inches and his shadow as 34 inches. At the same time, the tree has a shadow of 5.5 feet. How tall is the tree? *(Lesson 7-5)*

8. **Recreation** The kiddie pool and the lap pool at Centerville Park are similar rectangles. The lap pool measures 25 ft wide by 48 ft long. The kiddie pool is 8 ft long. How wide is the kiddie pool to the nearest tenth? *(Lesson 7-5)*

9. Melissa is enlarging her 4-by-6 photo by 150%. Find the coordinates of the enlarged photo. *(Lesson 7-6)*

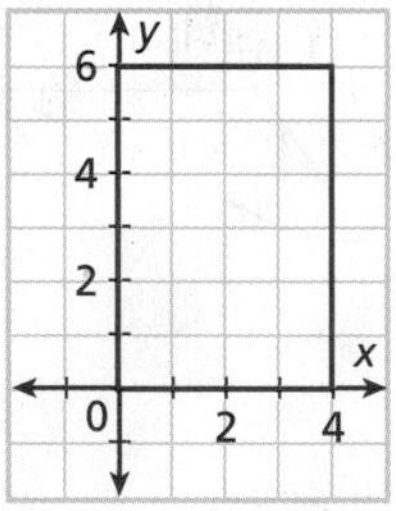

1. **Diving** To estimate the height of a diving platform, a spectator stands so that his lines of sight to the top and bottom of the platform form a right angle as shown. The spectator's eyes are 5 ft above the ground. He is standing 15 ft from the diving platform. How high is the platform? *(Lesson 8-1)*

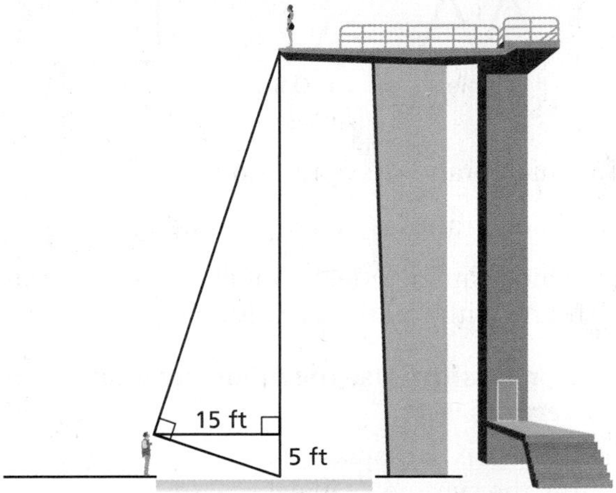

2. **Recreation** A neighborhood park has a 15-foot-long space available to install a playground slide. If the maximum height of the slide is 6 ft, what are the lengths of the slide x and ladder y that should be installed? Round to the nearest tenth of a foot. *(Lesson 8-1)*

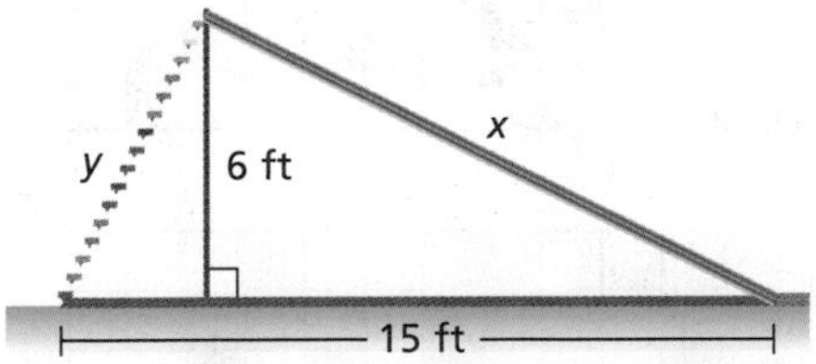

3. **Building** The escalator at the mall forms a 35° angle with the floor. The vertical distance from the bottom of the escalator to the top is 25 ft. How long is the escalator? Round to the nearest foot. *(Lesson 8-2)*

4. **Sports** A 3-foot-long skateboard ramp forms a 40° angle with the ground. How far above the ground is the end of the ramp? Round to the nearest foot. *(Lesson 8-2)*

5. **Running** A race includes a 0.25-mile hill on which runners travel from 510 ft of elevation to 570 ft of elevation. What angle does the hill form? Round to the nearest degree. *(Lesson 8-3)*

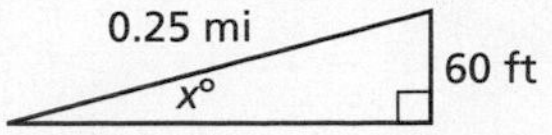

6. **Safety** A lifeguard sees a swimmer struggling in the water at an angle of depression of 15°. The stand is 10 feet tall. What is the horizontal distance from the stand to the swimmer? Round to the nearest foot. *(Lesson 8-4)*

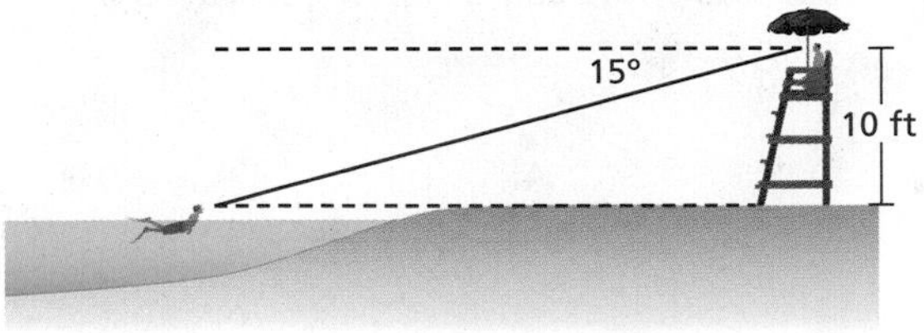

7. **Aviation** A helicopter pilot flying at an altitude of 1200 ft sees two landing pads directly in front of him. The angle of depression to the first landing pad is 40°. The angle of depression to the second pad is 28°. What is the distance between the two pads? Round to the nearest foot. *(Lesson 8-4)*

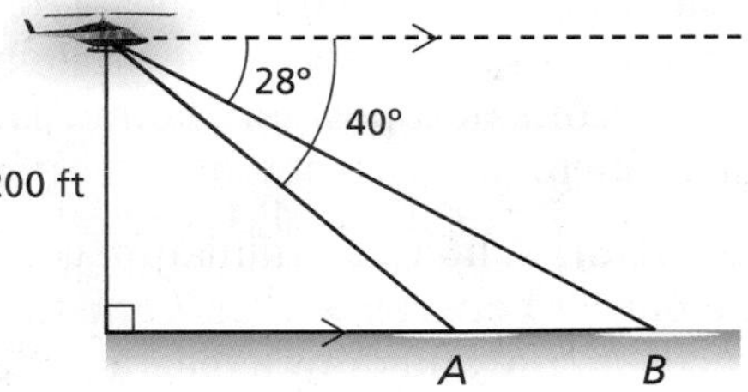

8. **Carpentry** Sean is creating a triangular frame from three wooden dowels, which are 18 in., 12 in., and 15 in. long. What are the measures of each angle of the triangle? Round to the nearest degree. *(Lesson 8-5)*

9. **Sports** To estimate the width of the sand trap on a golf course, Matthew locates three points and measures the distances shown. What is the width, XZ, of the sand trap to the nearest foot? *(Lesson 8-5)*

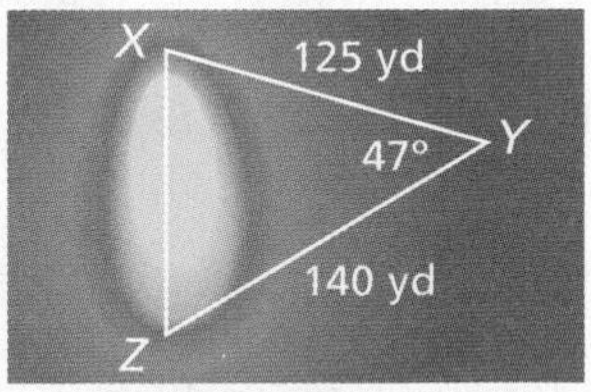

10. **Recreation** Jill swims due east across a river at 2 mi/h. The river is flowing north at 1.5 mi/h. What are Jill's actual speed and direction? Round the speed to the nearest tenth and the direction to the nearest degree. *(Lesson 8-6)*

1. **Transportation** Two towns are located on the same side of a river. Two roads are being built to meet at the same point *P* on the river. Draw a diagram that shows where *P* should be located in order to make the total length of the roads as short as possible. *(Lesson 9-1)*

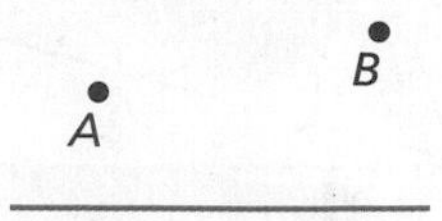

2. **Fashion** A piece of fabric used for a scarf has a repeating pattern of trapezoids. To create the pattern, translate the trapezoid with vertices $(-1, 3), (3, 3), (4, 1), (-2, 1)$ along the vector $\langle 0, -2\rangle$. Repeat to generate a pattern. What are the vertices of the third trapezoid in the pattern? *(Lesson 9-2)*

3. **Computers** A screen saver moves an icon around a screen. The icon starts at $(20, 0)$, and then it is rotated about the origin by 50°. Give the icon's next position. Round each coordinate to the nearest tenth. *(Lesson 9-3)*

4. **Recreation** A hole at a miniature golf course has a barrier between the tee *T* and the hole *H*. Copy the figure and draw a diagram that shows how to make a hole in one. *(Lesson 9-3)*

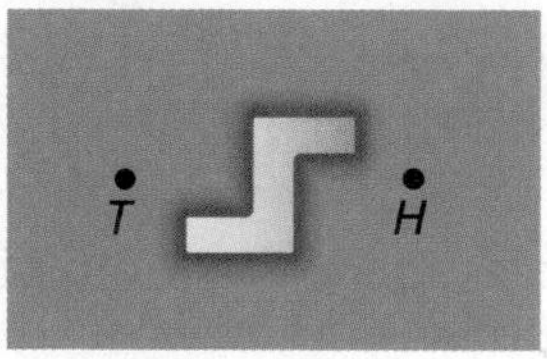

5. **Sports** A team's Web site shows a baseball moving across the screen. The ball is reflected over line ℓ and is then reflected over line *m*. Describe a single transformation that moves the ball from its starting point to its final position. *(Lesson 9-4)*

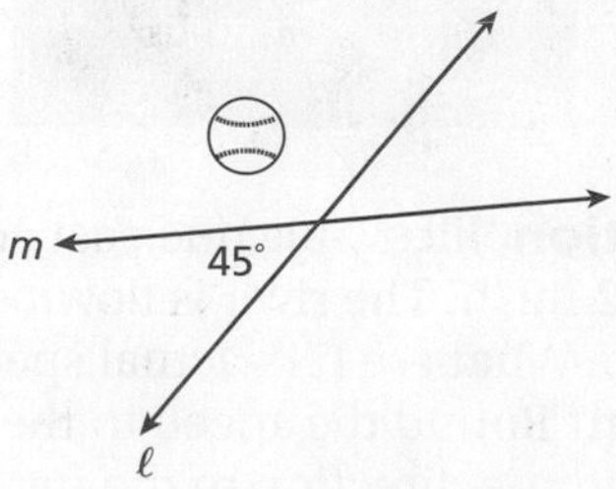

Agriculture Use the following information for Exercises 6–8.

Cattle ranchers brand their cattle to show ownership. Three different brands are shown. *(Lesson 9-5)*

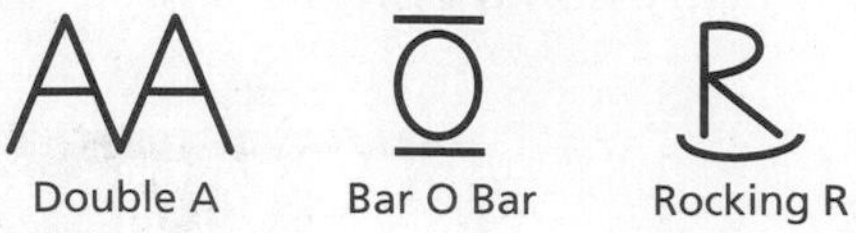

6. Which brands have rotational symmetry?
7. Which brands have line symmetry?
8. Which capital letters could be used to create a brand with rotational symmetry?

Interior Design Use the following information for Exercises 9–11.

Three kitchen backsplash tile patterns are shown. Identify the symmetry in each pattern. *(Lesson 9-6)*

9.

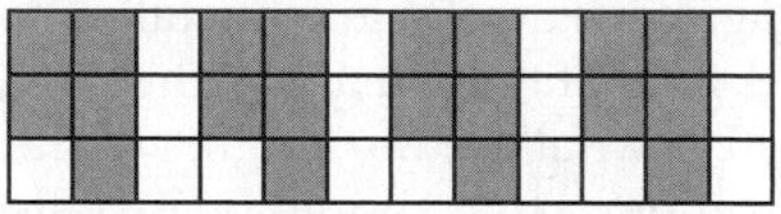

10.

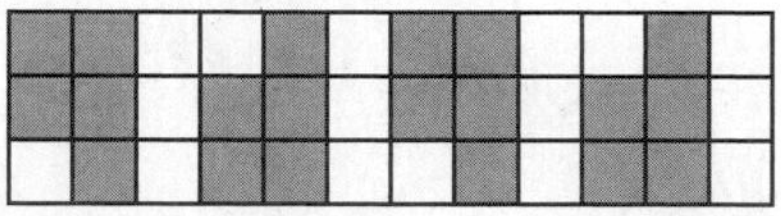

11.

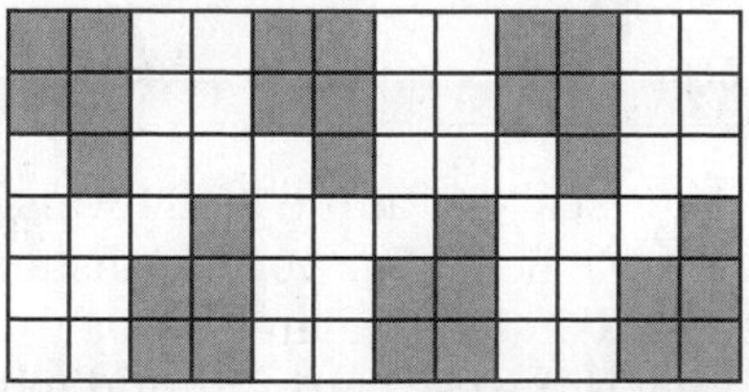

12. **Hobbies** Reid has a baseball card that is 2.5-by-3.5 inches. He wants to enlarge it to poster size using a scale factor of 8. What size poster frame should he buy? *(Lesson 9-7)*

13. **Hobbies** A 40 in. by 30 in. piece of art is being made into a 1 in. by $\frac{3}{4}$ in. postage stamp. What scale factor should be used to reduce the art? *(Lesson 9-7)*

1. **Recreation** Kathy is making a kite with diagonals of lengths 30 inches and 20 inches. How many square inches of fabric will she need? *(Lesson 10-1)*

Agriculture **Use the following information for Exercises 2 and 3. An acre is 43,560 square feet.** *(Lesson 10-1)*

2. If a one-acre piece of land is a rectangle with a base of 100 ft, what is its height?
3. If a one-acre piece of land is a square, what is the length of each side? Round to the nearest tenth.
4. The garden shown is a regular hexagon with a circular fountain at the center. What is the area of the garden? Round to the nearest square foot. *(Lesson 10-2)*

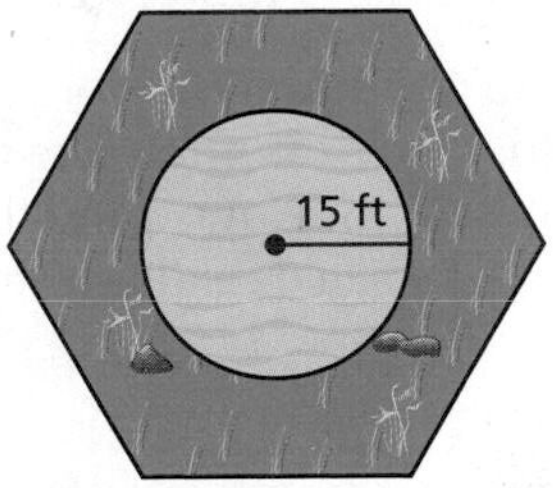

5. **Food** A bakery has cheesecake pans with three diameters: 18 cm, 22 cm, and 26 cm. Find the area of the bottom of each pan. Round to the nearest square centimeter. *(Lesson 10-2)*
6. **Recreation** A track for a toy car is a 2 ft by 2 ft square with a semicircle at each end. What is the distance around the track? Round to the nearest foot. *(Lesson 10-3)*
7. **Art** Jonas is painting the shape shown on his ceiling. If a quart of paint covers 75 square feet, will one quart be enough to paint the entire shape? Explain. *(Lesson 10-3)*

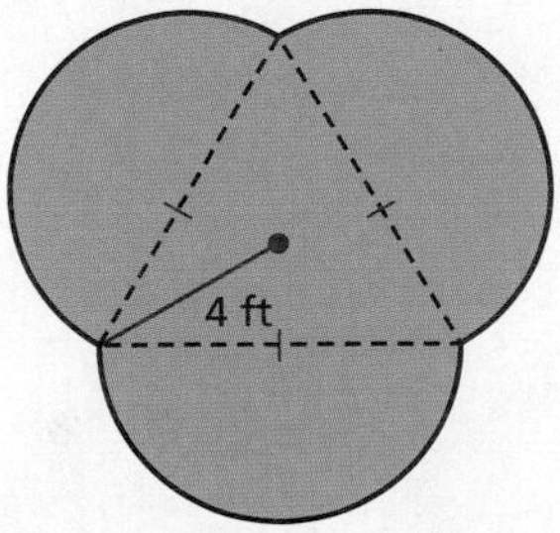

Transportation **Use the following information for Exercises 8 and 9. The graph shows the speed of a car versus time. The base of each square on the graph represents 10 minutes, and the height represents 10 miles per hour.** *(Lesson 10-4)*

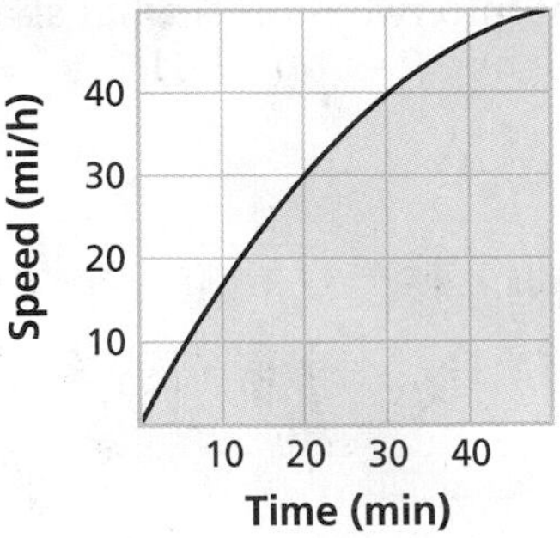

8. What is the area of one square on the graph?
9. Estimate the shaded area of the graph.
10. **Art** Rasha is cutting a mat for a poster with an area of 480 in^2. To find the dimensions of the mat, she multiplies the dimensions of the poster by 1.2. To find the dimensions of the opening, she multiplies the dimensions of the poster by 0.9. What is the area of the remaining part of the mat? *(Lesson 10-5)*
11. **Food** A restaurant sells two sizes of pizzas. The smaller pizza has a 12-inch diameter. If the area of the larger pizza is twice the area of the smaller pizza, what is the diameter of the larger pizza? Round to the nearest inch. *(Lesson 10-5)*
12. **Transportation** A commuter train stops at a station every 3 minutes and stays at the station for 20 seconds. If you arrive at the station at a random time, what is the probability that you will have to wait more than one minute for a train? Round to the nearest hundredth. *(Lesson 10-6)*
13. **Sports** A skydiver is delivering the game ball for a baseball game. Suppose he lands at a random point on the field. What is the probability that he will not land on the pitcher's mound? Round to the nearest hundredth. *(Lesson 10-6)*

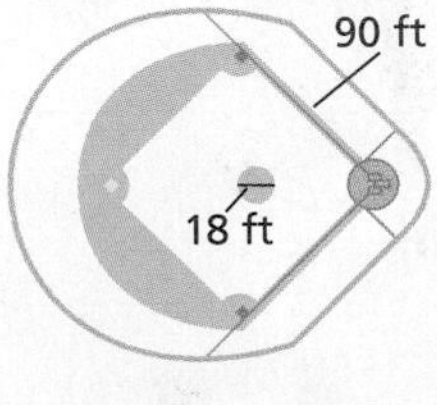

Extra Practice Chapter 11 ▪ Applications Practice

1. **Food** Cookie dough is rolled in the shape of a cylinder. How can the dough be sliced to make circular cookies? *(Lesson 11-1)*

2. **Recreation** The tent shown is in the shape of a pentagonal prism. If a wall is used to divide the tent into two rooms, what shapes could the wall be? *(Lesson 11-1)*

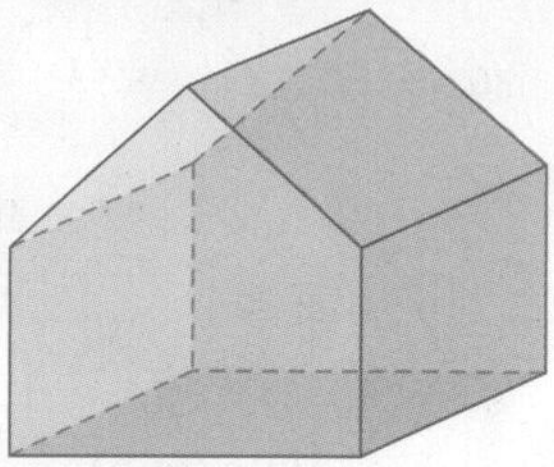

Recreation Use the following information for Exercises 3 and 4.

A cylindrical pool has a 10 ft diameter. *(Lesson 11-2)*

3. How many gallons of water are needed to fill the pool to a depth of 4 feet? Round to the nearest gallon. (*Hint:* 1 gallon $\approx$ 0.134 cubic feet.)

4. If the pool is filled to a depth of 4 feet, how much will the water weigh? Round to the nearest pound. (*Hint:* 1 gallon weighs about 8.34 pounds.)

5. **Hobbies** The greenhouse shown is in the shape of a cube with a square pyramid on top. What is the volume of the greenhouse? *(Lesson 11-3)*

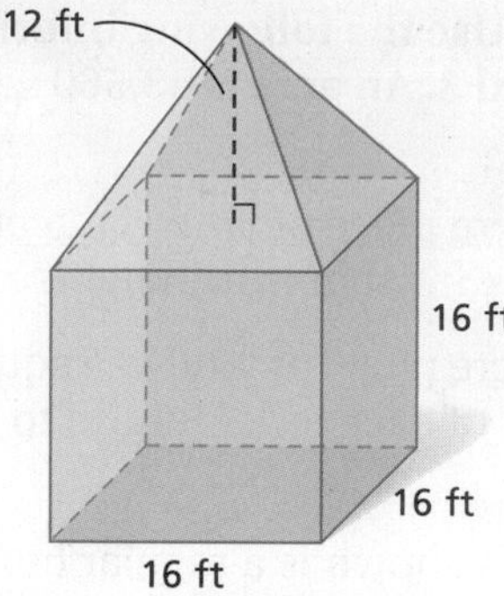

6. **Food** A snow-cone cup has a 3-inch diameter and is 4 inches tall. Another snow-cone cup has a 4-inch diameter and is 3 inches tall. Which cup will hold more? *(Lesson 11-3)*

7. **Sports** The circumference of a size 3 soccer ball is 24 in. The circumference of a size 5 soccer ball is 28 in. How many times as great is the volume of a size 5 ball as the volume of a size 3 ball? *(Lesson 11-4)*

1. **Measurement** There is a water tower near Peter's house in the shape of a cylinder. He wants to find the diameter of the tank. Peter stands 25 feet from the tower. The distance from Peter to a point of tangency on the tower is 80 feet. What is the diameter of the tank? *(Lesson 12-1)*

2. **Travel** Pikes Peak is 14,110 feet above sea level. What is the distance from the summit to the horizon, to the nearest mile? (*Hint:* Earth's radius ≈ 4000 mi) *(Lesson 12-1)*

Hobbies Use the circle graph to find each measure for Exercises 3–6 to the nearest degree.

Eric collects baseball cards. He has 85 cards from the 1970s, 95 cards from the 1980s, and 125 cards from the 1990s. *(Lesson 12-2)*

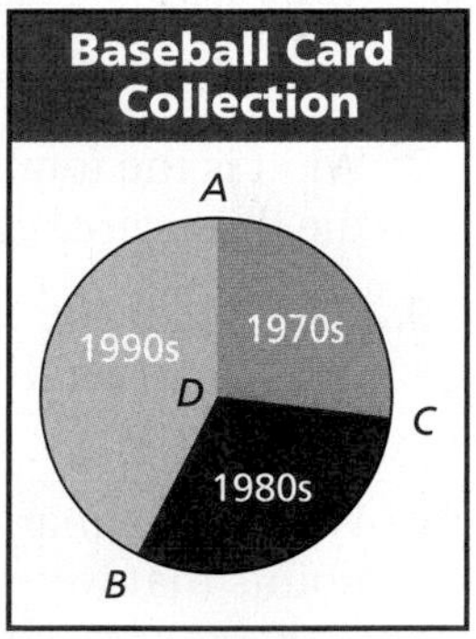

3. $\widehat{AB}$
4. $\widehat{AC}$
5. $\angle CDB$
6. $\angle ADC$

Data Use the circle graph to find each measure for Exercises 7–10 to the nearest degree.

The circle graph shows the color of cars in a parking lot at the mall. *(Lesson 12-2)*

7. $\widehat{HG}$
8. $\widehat{CD}$
9. $\angle AJH$
10. $\angle FJE$

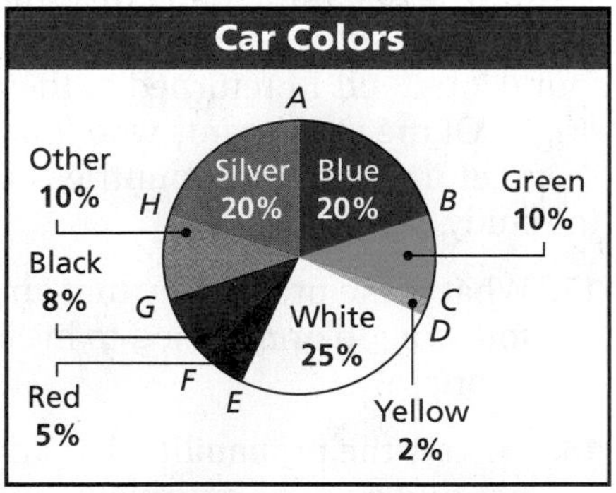

Hobbies Use the following information to find each area to the nearest tenth for Exercises 11 and 12.

A sprinkler system has three types of sprinkler heads: a quarter circle, a semicircle, and a full circle. The sprinkler will spray a distance of 15 feet from the sprinkler head. *(Lesson 12-3)*

11. What is the area of the sector that will be watered by the quarter circle sprinkler head?

12. What is the area of the sector that will be watered by the semicircle sprinkler head?

Art Use the diagram to find each value for Exercises 13–15.

The diagram represents an engraving on a stained glass window. *(Lesson 12-4)*

13. x
14. y
15. $m\widehat{FE}$

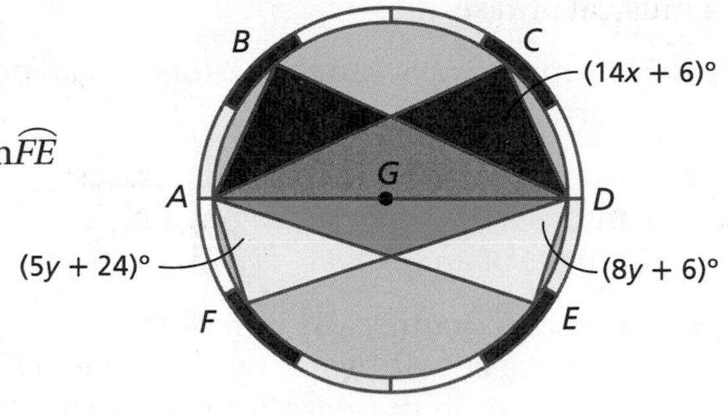

16. **Astronomy** Two satellites are orbiting Earth. Satellite A is 10,000 km above Earth, and satellite B is 13,000 km above Earth. How many arc degrees of Earth does each satellite see? *(Lesson 12-5)*

17. **Entertainment** A group of friends ate most of a pepperoni pizza. All that was left was a piece of crust. What was the diameter of the original pizza? *(Lesson 12-6)*

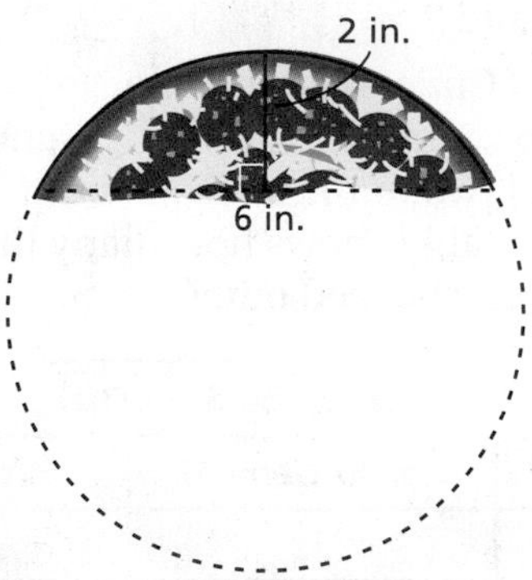

18. **Safety** Three small towns have agreed to share a new fire station. To make sure each town has equal response time, the station should be the same distance from each town. The three towns are located on a coordinate plane at (0, 0), (6, 0), and (0, 8). At which coordinates should the station be built? *(Lesson 12-7)*

Music Use the following information for Exercises 1 and 2.

Serialism is a form of music in which the composer arranges each of the 12 tones in an octave to form a musical phrase. *(Lesson 13-1)*

1. How many ways can the 12 tones of an octave be arranged?
2. How many different musical phrases could a composer create by arranging only 5 of the 12 tones of an octave?
3. **Drama** A drama class is performing the Greek tragedy *Antigone,* by Sophocles. Of the 15 students in the class, 6 will make up the chorus. How many different ways can the chorus be selected? *(Lesson 13-1)*
4. **Holidays** Of December's 31 days, the 25th and the 31st are holidays. What is the probability that a randomly chosen day in December is not a holiday? *(Lesson 13-2)*
5. **Games** If Sara's dart lands in a red equilateral triangle, she wins a prize. Each triangle has a base of 2 in. If all locations on the 12 in. diameter target are equally likely, what is the probability that Sara wins a prize? *(Lesson 13-2)*

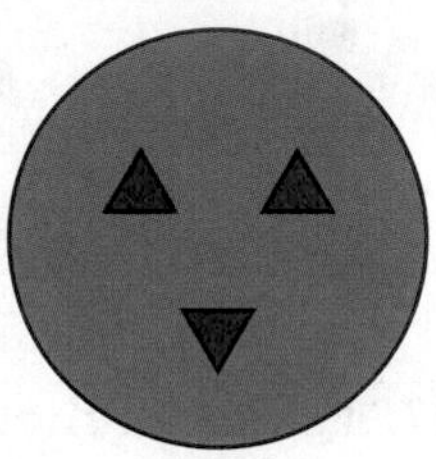

Literature Use the following information for Exercises 6 and 7.

The works of Chilean poet Pablo Neruda have been published in many languages. The school library has copies of two of his books in both English and Spanish. The table shows how many times each book has been checked out. *(Lesson 13-3)*

Books Checked Out		
	Canto General	*Extravagario*
English	23	27
Spanish	17	14

6. What is the probability that *Canto General* was checked out in Spanish?
7. What is the probability that a student who checked out a Pablo Neruda book selected *Extravagario* in English?

Basketball Use the following information for Exercises 8–11.

The table shows the numbers of points scored by the top three scorers in last week's basketball tournament that were made as 1-point shots (free throws), 2-point shots, and 3-point shots. *(Lesson 13-4)*

	1-point	2-point	3-point
Tina	11	38	21
Stella	7	24	42
Misha	17	46	6

8. What is the total number of points scored by the three girls?
9. What is the joint relative frequency that represents points scored by Misha as 2-point shots?
10. What is the marginal relative frequency of the points that were made as 3-point shots?
11. Given that a point was scored by a free throw, what it the probability that Misha scored that point?

Immigration Use the following information for Exercises 12 and 13.

A group of 100 immigrants was studied over a one-year period. During the study, 63 of the immigrants found jobs, and 14 returned to their country of origin. Of the immigrants who found jobs, 6 of them returned to their countries before the end of the study. *(Lesson 13-5)*

12. What is the probability that an immigrant found a job or returned to his or her country of origin?
13. What is the probability that an immigrant did not find a job or returned to his country of origin?

Mastering the Standards

for Mathematical Practice

The topics described in the Standards for Mathematical Content will vary from year to year. However, the *way* in which you learn, study, and think about mathematics will not. The Standards for Mathematical Practice describe skills that you will use in all of your math courses.

Mathematical Practices

1. *Make sense of problems and persevere in solving them.*
2. *Reason abstractly and quantitatively.*
3. *Construct viable arguments and critique the reasoning of others.*
4. *Model with mathematics.*
5. *Use appropriate tools strategically.*
6. *Attend to precision.*
7. *Look for and make use of structure.*
8. *Look for and express regularity in repeated reasoning.*

1 Make sense of problems and persevere in solving them.

Mathematically proficient students start by explaining to themselves the meaning of a problem... They analyze givens, constraints, relationships, and goals. They make conjectures about the form... of the solution and plan a solution pathway...

In your book

Focus on Problem Solving describes a four-step plan for problem solving. The plan is introduced at the beginning of your book, and practice with the plan appears throughout the book.

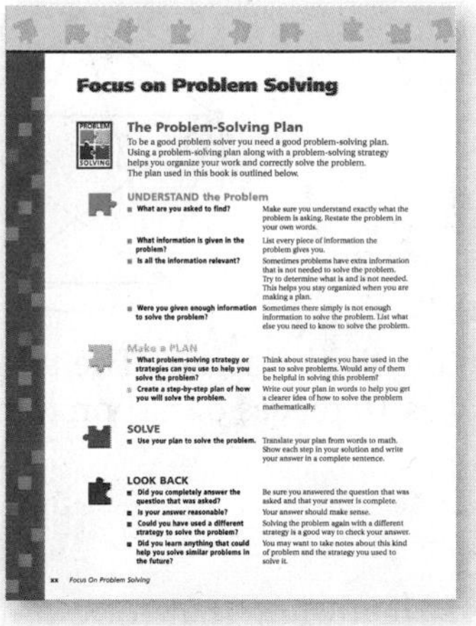

Focus on Problem Solving

The Problem-Solving Plan

To be a good problem solver you need a good problem-solving plan. Using a problem-solving plan along with a problem-solving strategy helps you organize your work and correctly solve the problem. The plan used in this book is outlined below.

UNDERSTAND the Problem

What are you asked to find?	Make sure you understand exactly what the problem is asking. Restate the problem in your own words.
What information is given in the problem?	List every piece of information the problem gives you.
Is all the information relevant?	Sometimes problems have extra information that is not needed to solve the problem. Try to determine what is and is not needed. This helps you stay organized when you are making a plan.
Were you given enough information to solve the problem?	Sometimes there simply is not enough information to solve the problem. List what else you need to know to solve the problem.

Make a PLAN

What problem-solving strategy or strategies can you use to help you solve the problem?	Think about strategies you have used in the past to solve problems. Would any of them be helpful in solving this problem?
Create a step-by-step plan of how you will solve the problem.	Write out your plan in words to help you get a clearer idea of how to solve the problem mathematically.

SOLVE

Use your plan to solve the problem.	Translate your plan from words to math. Show each step in your solution and write your answer in a complete sentence.

LOOK BACK

Did you completely answer the question that was asked?	Be sure you answered the question that was asked and that your answer is complete.
Is your answer reasonable?	Your answer should make sense.
Could you have used a different strategy to solve the problem?	Solving the problem again with a different strategy is a good way to check your answer.
Did you learn anything that could help you solve similar problems in the future?	You may want to take notes about this kind of problem and the strategy you used to solve it.

xx *Focus On Problem Solving*

EXAMPLE 5 ***Problem-Solving Application***

PROBLEM SOLVING

The cost to place an ad in a newspaper for one week is a linear function of the number of lines in the ad. The costs for 3, 5, and 10 lines are shown. Write an equation in slope-intercept form that represents the function. Then find the cost of an ad that is 18 lines long.

City Gazette

Newspaper Ad Costs

Lines	3	5	10
Cost ($)	13.50	18.50	31

1 Understand the Problem

- The **answer** will have two parts—an equation in slope-intercept form and the cost of an ad that is 18 lines long.
- The ordered pairs given in the table satisfy the equation.

2 Make a Plan

First, find the slope. Then use point-slope form to write the equation. Finally, write the equation in slope-intercept form.

3 Solve

Step 1 Choose any two ordered pairs from the table to find the slope.

$m = \frac{y_2 - y_1}{x_2 - x_1} = \frac{18.50 - 13.50}{5 - 3} = \frac{5}{2} = 2.5$ *Use (3, 13.50) and (5, 18.50).*

Step 2 Substitute the slope and any ordered pair from the table into the point-slope form.

$y - y_1 = m(x - x_1)$

$y - 31 = 2.5(x - 10)$ *Use (10, 31).*

Step 3 Write the equation in slope-intercept form by solving for y.

$y - 31 = 2.5(x - 10)$

$y - 31 = 2.5x - 25$ *Distribute 2.5.*

$y = 2.5x + 6$ *Add 31 to both sides.*

Step 4 Find the cost of an ad containing 18 lines by substituting 18 for x.

$y = 2.5x + 6$

$y = 2.5(18) + 6 = 51$

The cost of an ad containing 18 lines is $51.

4 Look Back

Check the equation by substituting the ordered pairs (3, 13.50) and (5, 18.50).

y	$= 2.5x + 6$
13.50	$2.5(3) + 6$
13.5	$7.5 + 6$
13.5	13.5 ✓

y	$= 2.5x + 6$
18.50	$2.5(5) + 6$
18.5	$12.5 + 6$
18.5	18.5 ✓

Problem-Solving Handbook

Draw a Diagram

When a problem involves objects, distances, or places, drawing a diagram can make the problem clearer. You can draw a diagram to help understand and solve the problem.

Problem-Solving Strategies

Draw a Diagram	Make a Table
Make a Model	Solve a Simpler Problem
Guess and Test	Use Logical Reasoning
Work Backward	Use a Venn Diagram
Find a Pattern	Make an Organized List

EXAMPLE

During a team-building activity, five people stand in a circle. Pieces of ribbon will be used to connect each person to each of the other four people in the circle. How many pieces of ribbon are needed to connect all five people in this way?

1 Understand the Problem

List the important information.

- There are five people standing in a circle.
- Each person should be connected to each of the other four people with a piece of ribbon.

The answer is the number of pieces of ribbon needed to connect all five people.

2 Make a Plan

Draw a diagram to represent the information in the problem.

3 Solve

Draw a circle. Add five points to the circle to represent the five people in the problem. Then draw segments to connect each point to each of the other four points.

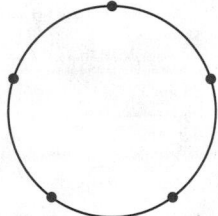

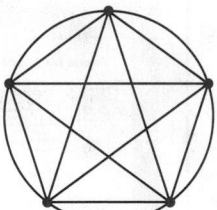

Count the number of segments in the final diagram. The total number of segments is the answer to the problem. It takes 10 pieces of ribbon to connect each person to each of the other four people.

4 Look Back

Check that the diagram is drawn correctly and that you counted the number of line segments accurately.

PRACTICE

1. A delivery truck driver travels 15 miles south to deliver his first package. He then goes 9 miles east and 6 miles north to deliver his next package. From there, the driver travels 12 miles east to make his last delivery. How far is the driver from his starting point? Round to the nearest tenth of a mile.

Make a Model

When a problem involves manipulating objects, you can use those or similar objects to make a model. This can help you to understand the problem and find the solution.

Problem-Solving Strategies

Draw a Diagram
Make a Model
Guess and Test
Work Backward
Find a Pattern
Make a Table
Solve a Simpler Problem
Use Logical Reasoning
Use a Venn Diagram
Make an Organized List

EXAMPLE

During a geometry class, Zach cuts out a parallelogram with base 12 cm and height 6 cm. Catherine cuts out a rectangle with the same base and height. Show that the two shapes have the same area.

1 Understand the Problem

List the important information.

- There are two geometric shapes, a parallelogram and a rectangle.
- The base and the height of the two shapes are the same.

To solve the problem, you need to show that the areas of the two shapes are equal.

2 Make a Plan

You can make a model of the figures by cutting them out of paper or cardboard. Then compare the areas by placing one on top of the other.

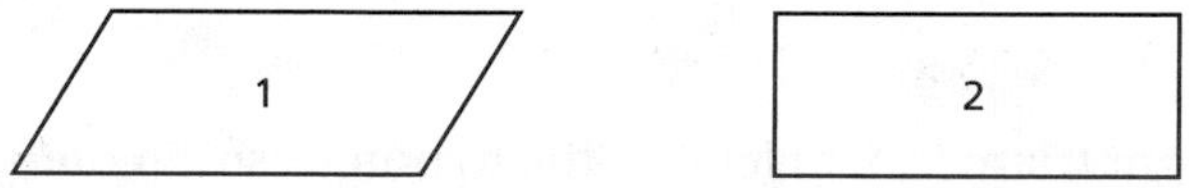

3 Solve

If the shaded area of the parallelogram is cut and moved to the opposite side, the figure becomes a rectangle.

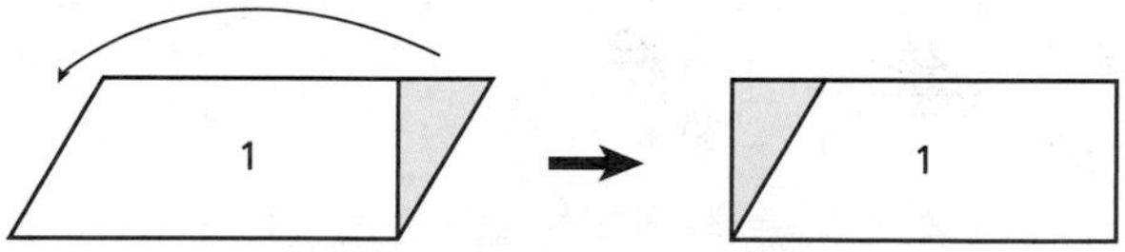

Place the two shapes on top of each other to compare the area.

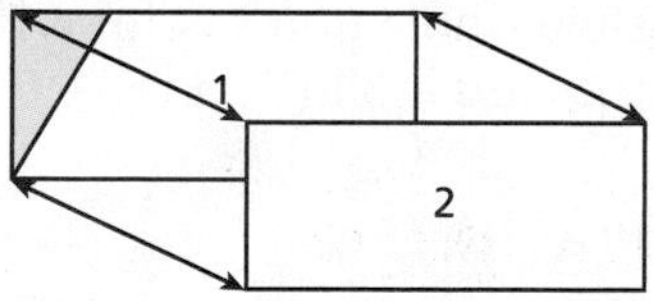

The shapes have the same base and height, so these shapes have the same area.

4 Look Back

Check that your models have the correct dimensions. Use the formulas for the area of a rectangle and a parallelogram to confirm that the shapes have the same area.

PRACTICE

1. Find the dimensions of a rectangular prism made up of 16 1-inch cubes.
2. Two triangles are formed by cutting a rectangle along its diagonal. What possible shapes can be formed by arranging these triangles?

Guess and Test

For complex problems, you can use clues to make guesses and narrow your choices for the solution. Test whether your guess solves the problem, and then continue guessing until you find the solution.

Problem-Solving Strategies

Draw a Diagram	Make a Table
Make a Model	Solve a Simpler Problem
Guess and Test	Use Logical Reasoning
Work Backward	Use a Venn Diagram
Find a Pattern	Make an Organized List

EXAMPLE

Edgar is designing a party invitation in the shape of a right triangle. If all three side measures are to be whole numbers of inches, what is the smallest possible perimeter for the birthday card?

1 Understand the Problem

List the important information.

- The invitation is to be a right triangle.
- The legs and hypotenuse must be whole numbers.

To solve the problem, you need to find the smallest possible perimeter for the right triangle.

2 Make a Plan

You can guess and test, starting with the smallest possible whole numbers.

3 Solve

Let a and b be the legs of the right triangle, and let c be the hypotenuse. So the relationship $a^2 + b^2 = c^2$ must hold. Start by using $(1, 1)$ for (a, b) and solve for c^2. Since c must be a whole number, continue to guess and test until c^2 is a perfect square.

Guess	Test
(1, 1)	$1^2 + 1^2 = 2$ ✗
(1, 2)	$1^2 + 2^2 = 5$ ✗
(1, 3)	$1^2 + 3^2 = 10$ ✗
(1, 4)	$1^2 + 4^2 = 17$ ✗
(1, 5)	$1^2 + 5^2 = 26$ ✗

Guess	Test
(2, 2)	$2^2 + 2^2 = 8$ ✗
(2, 3)	$2^2 + 3^2 = 13$ ✗
(2, 4)	$2^2 + 4^2 = 20$ ✗
(2, 5)	$2^2 + 5^2 = 29$ ✗

Guess	Test
(3, 3)	$3^2 + 3^2 = 18$ ✗
(3, 4)	$3^2 + 4^2 = 25$ ✓

Based on the tables, 5 is the smallest possible whole number for c, 3 for a, and 4 for b. So the smallest possible perimeter for the card is 3 in. + 4 in. + 5 in. = 12 in.

4 Look Back

Since $3^2 + 4^2 = 5^2$, these are reasonable dimensions for the card. The problem asks for the perimeter, which is 12 inches.

PRACTICE

1. The sum of Cary's age and his brother's age is 34. The difference between their ages is 4. How old are Cary and his brother?
2. Adult tickets for a theater performance cost \$8 and children's tickets cost \$3. A group with twice as many adults as children attends the performance and spends \$133 on tickets. How many people are in the group?

Work Backward

Some problems involve a series of events, giving you information about the last event, and then ask you to solve something related to the initial situation. You can work backward to solve these problems.

Problem-Solving Strategies

- Draw a Diagram
- Make a Model
- Guess and Test
- **Work Backward**
- Find a Pattern
- Make a Table
- Solve a Simpler Problem
- Use Logical Reasoning
- Use a Venn Diagram
- Make an Organized List

EXAMPLE

Sandy is creating a pattern made from isosceles right triangles as shown below. If the hypotenuse of the fifth triangle is 4 in., what are the dimensions of the smallest triangle?

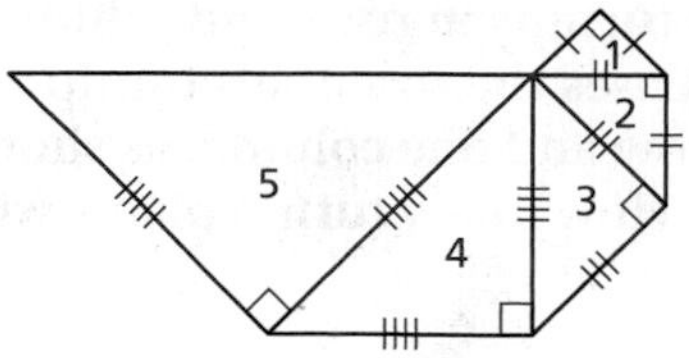

1 Understand the Problem

List the important information.

- Each triangle is an isosceles right triangle, so each triangle's legs are congruent.
- The hypotenuse of one triangle is equal to the leg length of the next triangle.
- The fifth triangle's hypotenuse is 4 in.

You must work backward to find the dimensions of the first triangle.

2 Make a Plan

Let h be the hypotenuse and s be the leg length of each triangle. Start with a hypotenuse length of 4 and work backward using the Pythagorean Theorem, which states that $h^2 = s^2 + s^2 = 2s^2$.

3 Solve

Triangle 5: $h = 4$; $s = \sqrt{8}$ — *$4^2 = 2s^2$, so $s = \sqrt{8}$*

Triangle 4: $h = \sqrt{8}$; $s = 2$ — *The hypotenuse of Triangle 4 equals the leg length of Triangle 5. $\left(\sqrt{8}\right)^2 = 2s^2$, so $s = 2$.*

Triangle 3: $h = 2$; $s = \sqrt{2}$ — *$2^2 = 2s^2$, so $s = \sqrt{2}$.*

Triangle 2: $h = \sqrt{2}$; $s = 1$ — *$\left(\sqrt{2}\right)^2 = 2s^2$, so $s = 1$.*

Triangle 1: $h = 1$; $s = \sqrt{0.5}$ — *$1^2 = 2s^2$, so $s = \sqrt{0.5}$.*

The first triangle should have a leg length of $\sqrt{0.5}$ and a hypotenuse of 1.

4 Look Back

Recreate the diagram starting with the dimensions you found for the first triangle, and confirm that the fifth triangle has a hypotenuse of 4 inches.

PRACTICE

1. In a trivia game, each question is worth twice as many points as the one before it. Chelsea answers 5 questions and earns 1550 points. How many points was her first question worth?
2. Sheryl has 4 siblings. She is 4 years younger than her sister Meagan. Meagan is twice as old as Tina. Jack is 3 years older than Tina, and Tina is 1 year older than Bryan, who is 9. How old is Sheryl?

Find a Pattern

In some problems, there is a relationship between different pieces of information. You can find a pattern to help solve these problems.

Problem-Solving Strategies

Draw a Diagram	Make a Table
Make a Model	Solve a Simpler Problem
Guess and Test	Use Logical Reasoning
Work Backward	Use a Venn Diagram
Find a Pattern	Make an Organized List

EXAMPLE

Frank plants turnips in rows and columns. Each year, he increases the size of his turnip patch by adding one row and one column, as shown in the diagram. How many turnip plants will Frank have after year 5?

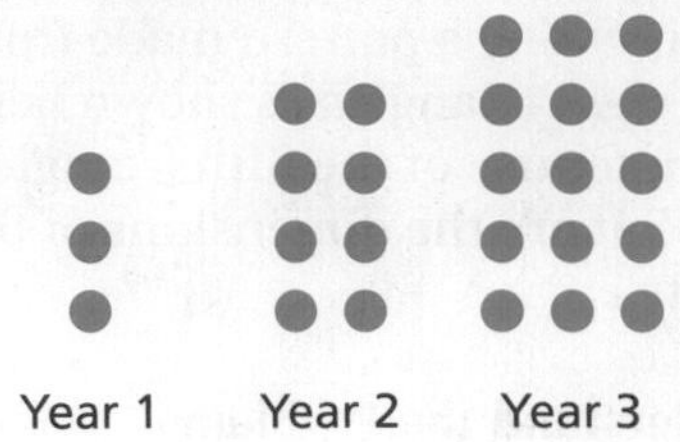

1 Understand the Problem

List the important information.

- In year 1, Frank has 3 turnip plants.
- In year 2, he has 8 turnip plants.
- In year 3, he has 15 turnip plants.

The answer will be the number of turnip plants in year 5.

2 Make a Plan

Find the pattern based on the diagram.

3 Solve

Make a table of the given information and find a pattern.

	Number of Turnip Plants	Possible Pattern
Year 1	3	$0 + 3$
Year 2	8	$3 + 5$
Year 3	15	$8 + 7$

The pattern seems to be the number of turnip plants in the previous year plus the next odd number. So in year 4, Frank will have $15 + 9 = 24$ turnip plants, and in year 5, he will have $24 + 11 = 35$ turnip plants.

4 Look Back

By thinking of the number of plants as the product of the number of rows and columns, you might notice another pattern, $n(n + 2)$, where n is the year number. Use this to confirm your answer.

Year 4: $4(4 + 2) = 24$ turnip plants

Year 5: $5(5 + 2) = 35$ turnip plants

PRACTICE

1. Use the key GDB = DAY to decode the sentence DQ DSSOH D GDB NHHSV WKH GRFWRU DZDB.

2. Describe the pattern 15, 22, 29, 36, 43, ... and find the next two numbers.

Make a Table

To solve a problem that involves a relationship between two sets of numbers, you can make a table to organize and analyze the data.

Problem-Solving Strategies

Draw a Diagram
Make a Model
Guess and Test
Work Backward
Find a Pattern
Make a Table
Solve a Simpler Problem
Use Logical Reasoning
Use a Venn Diagram
Make an Organized List

EXAMPLE

Roy's Geometry class is playing a game to practice identifying shapes. There are eight shapes in the game: an acute triangle, a right triangle, a square, a rectangle, a rhombus, a parallelogram, a kite, and an isosceles trapezoid. On Roy's turn, the teacher reads the following clues: The shape is a quadrilateral with four right angles in which all sides are not congruent. Which shape should Roy select?

1 Understand the Problem

List the important information.

- The possible shapes are an acute triangle, a right triangle, a square, a rectangle, a rhombus, a parallelogram, a kite, and an isosceles trapezoid.
- Roy's shape is a quadrilateral with four right angles.
- Roy's shape does not have four congruent sides.

The answer will be the shape that matches Roy's clues.

2 Make a Plan

Make a table and use the given information to identify Roy's shape.

3 Solve

Use the given clues to complete a table and identify Roy's shape.

Shape	Quadrilateral?	4 Right Angles?	Sides Not Congruent?
Acute triangle	N	N	N
Right triangle	N	N	N
Square	Y	Y	N
Rectangle	Y	Y	Y
Rhombus	Y	N	N
Parallelogram	Y	N	N
Kite	Y	N	Y
Isosceles trapezoid	Y	N	Y

The rectangle is the only shape that satisfies the given clues.

4 Look Back

Make sure that your answer satisfies the given clues.

PRACTICE

1. Katie gets the following clues: The shape has at least one right angle, has no parallel sides, and is not the kite. Which shape should Katie select?
2. Mary gets the following clues: The shape has no congruent sides. How many possible shapes might Mary select?

Problem-Solving Handbook

Solve a Simpler Problem

A problem with many steps or involving very large numbers can be overwhelming. Sometimes it helps to solve a simpler problem first, or to break the complex problem into multiple simpler ones.

Problem-Solving Strategies

Draw a Diagram	Make a Table
Make a Model	**Solve a Simpler Problem**
Guess and Test	Use Logical Reasoning
Work Backward	Use a Venn Diagram
Find a Pattern	Make an Organized List

EXAMPLE

Tom plans to repaint his patio, which has the measurements shown below. What is the total area that Tom needs to paint?

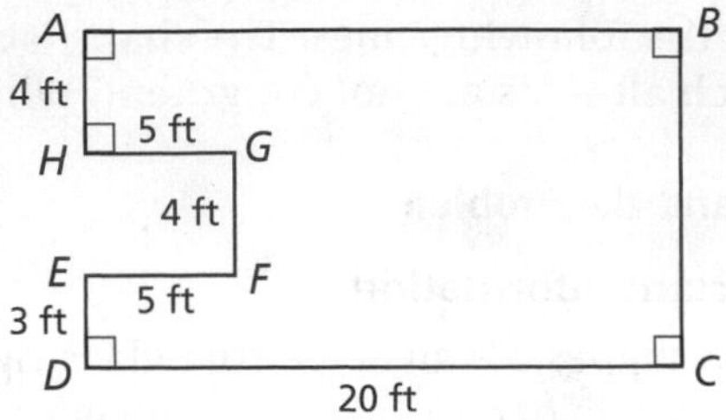

1 Understand the Problem

List the important information.

- $AH = FG = 4$ ft
- $DE = 3$ ft
- $CD = 20$ ft
- $GH = EF = 5$ ft

The answer will be the total area of the patio.

2 Make a Plan

To simplify the problem, divide the patio into basic geometric shapes and add their areas together.

3 Solve

Find the area of the patio as if it were a complete rectangle, and then subtract the area of the smaller rectangle that is not part of the patio.

Step 1: Find the area of each rectangle.

	Larger rectangle	Smaller rectangle
Length	$CD = 20$ ft	$GH = 5$ ft
Width	$AH + FG + DE = 11$ ft	$FG = 4$ ft
Area	$\ell w = (20)(11) = 220 \text{ ft}^2$	$\ell w = (5)(4) = 20 \text{ ft}^2$

Step 2: Subtract the areas to find the area of the patio.

Area of patio $= 220 - 20 = 200 \text{ ft}^2$

Tom needs to paint 200 square feet.

4 Look Back

Divide the patio into a different arrangement of smaller shapes to check your answer. For example, by dividing the patio into three rectangles stacked on top of each other, you find that $(4)(20) + (4)(15) + (3)(20) = 200 \text{ ft}^2$, which confirms the first answer.

PRACTICE

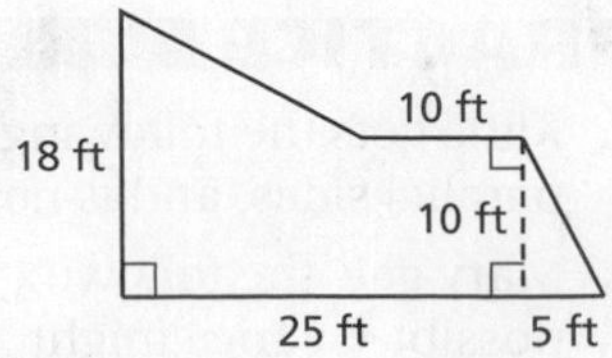

1. How much paint does Rose need to repaint her patio?
2. Rose plans to add a decorative railing around the outer edges of her patio. The railing will cover every edge except the 30-foot side of the patio that joins her house. About how many feet of railing does Rose need? Round to the nearest foot.

Use Logical Reasoning

Some problems provide clues and facts that you must use to find the solution. To use logical reasoning, identify these facts and draw conclusions from them.

Problem-Solving Strategies

Draw a Diagram	Make a Table
Make a Model	Solve a Simpler Problem
Guess and Test	**Use Logical Reasoning**
Work Backward	Use a Venn Diagram
Find a Pattern	Make an Organized List

EXAMPLE

Dawn, Chloe, and Tyra finish first through third in a cross-country race. The girls wear the numbers 7, 8, and 12. Dawn does not wear an even number. The one who wears number 8 comes in first. Chloe comes in third. Who wears which number, and in what place did each runner finish?

1 Understand the Problem

List the important information.

- Dawn wears an odd number.
- The girl who wears number 8 comes in first place.
- Chloe comes in third place.

The answer will be a list of who wears which number and each girl's finishing position.

2 Make a Plan

Start with the clues given in the problem. Use logical reasoning to determine each girl's number and finishing position.

3 Solve

Make a table. Read the clues one at a time, and mark the table appropriately.

- **Dawn wears an odd number, so she must wear number 7. No other girl can wear number 7.**
- **The girl who wears number 8 comes in first place. No other number is the first-place winner. Also, since Dawn wears number 7, she didn't come in first.**
- **Chloe comes in third. By process of elimination, Dawn must have come in second, and Tyra came in first. So Tyra wears number 8, and thus Chloe wears number 12.**

	7	8	12	1st	2nd	3rd
Dawn	✓	✗	✗	✗	✓	✗
Chloe	✗	✗	✓	✗	✗	✓
Tyra	✗	✓	✗	✓	✗	✗
1st	✗	✓	✗			
2nd	✓	✗	✗			
3rd	✗	✗	✓			

4 Look Back

Compare your answer to the facts given in the problem. Make sure none of your conclusions conflict with the given clues.

PRACTICE

1. Mike, Jack, and Ann each wear a different type of top in three different colors. The tops are a button-down shirt, a pullover, and a sweater. The colors are blue, yellow, and red. Mike wears a blue shirt, and Jack wears a button-down. The yellow top is a pullover. Who wears the sweater and who wears the red top?
2. The Warriors, Jaguars, and Cougars each have a different-colored shape on their team shirt. The colors are green, purple, and red, and the shapes are a triangle, a rectangle, and a hexagon. The Warriors' shape has the most sides, the color of the Jaguars' shape is green, and the rectangle is purple. Which team has which shape and in which color?

Problem-Solving Handbook

Use a Venn Diagram

A Venn diagram can be useful when you solve a problem involving relationships among sets or groups.

Problem-Solving Strategies

Draw a Diagram	Make a Table
Make a Model	Solve a Simpler Problem
Guess and Test	Use Logical Reasoning
Work Backward	**Use a Venn Diagram**
Find a Pattern	Make an Organized List

EXAMPLE

In a class of 15 students, ten play on at least one of the school sports teams—the basketball team or the baseball team. Five of them are on the basketball team. Three students are on both the basketball team and the baseball team. How many of the students play on the baseball team?

1 Understand the Problem

List the important information.

- 5 students play on the basketball team.
- 3 students play on both teams.

The answer is the number of students who play on the baseball team.

2 Make a Plan

Organize the information by drawing a Venn diagram.

3 Solve

Draw and label the Venn diagram.

- 3 people will be in the overlapping area.
- Since 5 people play on the basketball team, and 3 of them are also on the baseball team, only 2 people play on only the basketball team.

There are 10 student players in all, and five are already accounted for. Therefore, the remaining five play only baseball.

Adding the three students who also play basketball, a total of eight students in the class play on the baseball team.

Student Players in Class

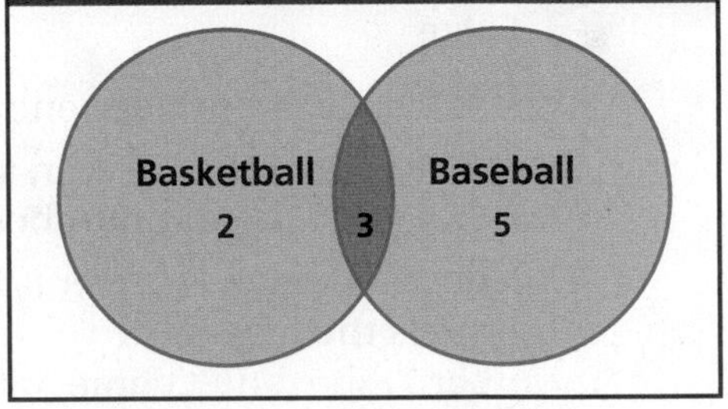

4 Look Back

Check your Venn diagram to make sure it is an accurate representation of the information given in the problem. Confirm that the numbers in each of the labeled sections add up to the total number of students in the problem.

PRACTICE

1. At Lucy's Home-Style Restaurant, four of the meals include a side salad, six include only soup as a side, and two meals come with both salad and soup as sides. If all meals come with at least one side, how many different meals are on Lucy's menu?
2. A cupboard contains 12 cups, and each cup has a lid, a handle, or both. There are seven cups with handles, and three cups with both a lid and a handle. How many cups have only a lid?

Problem-Solving Handbook

Make an Organized List

If a problem involves multiple outcomes, it may be useful to make an organized list to record the data and count the different outcomes.

Problem-Solving Strategies

Draw a Diagram	Make a Table
Make a Model	Solve a Simpler Problem
Guess and Test	Use Logical Reasoning
Work Backward	Use a Venn Diagram
Find a Pattern	**Make an Organized List**

EXAMPLE

Sally randomly selects two shapes from a bag that contains five different cut-outs: a triangle, a square, a rectangle, a pentagon, and a hexagon. The sum of the number of sides of the two shapes is eight. What combinations of shapes might Sally have selected?

1 Understand the Problem

List the important information.

- The possible shapes are a triangle, a square, a rectangle, a pentagon, and a hexagon.
- The sum of the number of sides is 9.

The answer will be the two shapes Sally selected.

2 Make a Plan

Make an organized list of the possible combinations of shapes. Then list the number of sides and the sum of the sides.

3 Solve

List the possible combinations of shapes, and find the sum of the shapes' sides.

Triangle (3)	X	X	X	X						
Square (4)	X				X	X	X			
Rectangle (4)		X			X			X	X	
Pentagon (5)			X			X		X		X
Hexagon (6)				X			X		X	X
Total number of sides	7	7	8	9	8	9	10	9	10	11

There are two combinations of shapes that have a total number of eight sides: the triangle and pentagon and the square and rectangle.

4 Look Back

Make sure all possible combinations are shown in the table. Check that the total number of sides for both combinations (triangle and pentagon, and square and rectangle) is 8.

PRACTICE

1. How many ways can you make $0.30 by using quarters, dimes, nickels, and pennies?
2. Pete's Pizza Palace has 5 choices of meat, 4 choices of vegetables, and 2 choices of cheese. You want to order a pizza with one of each. How many combinations can you order?

Postulates, Theorems, and Corollaries Chapter 1

Post. 1-1-1 Through any two points there is exactly one line.

Post. 1-1-2 Through any three noncollinear points there is exactly one plane containing them.

Post. 1-1-3 If two points lie in a plane, then the line containing those points lies in the plane.

Post. 1-1-4 If two lines intersect, then they intersect in exactly one point.

Post. 1-1-5 If two planes intersect, then they intersect in exactly one line.

Post. 1-2-1 Ruler Postulate The points on a line can be put into a one-to-one correspondence with the real numbers.

Post. 1-2-2 Segment Addition Postulate If B is between A and C, then $AB + BC = AC$.

Post. 1-3-1 Protractor Postulate Given $\overleftrightarrow{AB}$ and a point O on $\overleftrightarrow{AB}$, all rays that can be drawn from O can be put into a one-to-one correspondence with the real numbers from 0 to 180.

Post. 1-3-2 Angle Addition Postulate If S is in the interior of $\angle PQR$, then $m\angle PQS + m\angle SQR = m\angle PQR$.

Thm. 1-6-1 Pythagorean Theorem In a right triangle, the sum of the squares of the lengths of the legs is equal to the square of the length of the hypotenuse.

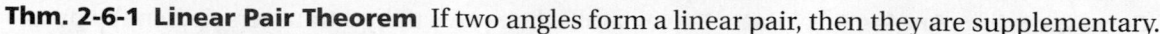

Postulates, Theorems, and Corollaries Chapter 2

Thm. 2-6-1 Linear Pair Theorem If two angles form a linear pair, then they are supplementary.

Thm. 2-6-2 Congruent Supplements Theorem If two angles are supplementary to the same angle (or to two congruent angles), then the two angles are congruent.

Thm. 2-6-3 Right Angle Congruence Theorem All right angles are congruent.

Thm. 2-6-4 Congruent Complements Theorem If two angles are complementary to the same angle (or to two congruent angles), then the two angles are congruent.

Thm. 2-7-1 Common Segments Theorem Given collinear points A, B, C, and D arranged as shown, if $\overline{AB} \cong \overline{CD}$, then $\overline{AC} \cong \overline{BD}$.

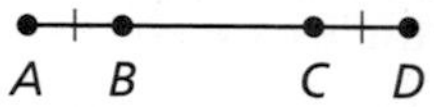

Thm. 2-7-2 Vertical Angles Theorem Vertical angles are congruent.

Thm. 2-7-3 If two congruent angles are supplementary, then each angle is a right angle.

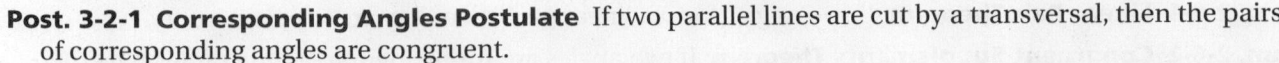

Postulates, Theorems, and Corollaries Chapter 3

Post. 3-2-1 Corresponding Angles Postulate If two parallel lines are cut by a transversal, then the pairs of corresponding angles are congruent.

Thm. 3-2-2 Alternate Interior Angles Theorem If two parallel lines are cut by a transversal, then the pairs of alternate interior angles are congruent.

Thm. 3-2-3 Alternate Exterior Angles Theorem If two parallel lines are cut by a transversal, then the two pairs of alternate exterior angles are congruent.

Thm. 3-2-4 Same-Side Interior Angles Theorem If two parallel lines are cut by a transversal, then the two pairs of same-side interior angles are supplementary.

Post. 3-3-1 Converse of the Corresponding Angles Postulate If two coplanar lines are cut by a transversal so that a pair of corresponding angles are congruent, then the two lines are parallel.

Post. 3-3-2 Parallel Postulate Through a point P not on line ℓ, there is exactly one line parallel to ℓ.

Thm. 3-3-3 Converse of the Alternate Interior Angles Theorem If two coplanar lines are cut by a transversal so that a pair of alternate interior angles are congruent, then the two lines are parallel.

Thm. 3-3-4 Converse of the Alternate Exterior Angles Theorem If two coplanar lines are cut by a transversal so that a pair of alternate exterior angles are congruent, then the two lines are parallel.

Thm. 3-3-5 Converse of the Same-Side Interior Angles Theorem If two coplanar lines are cut by a transversal so that a pair of same-side interior angles are supplementary, then the two lines are parallel.

Thm. 3-4-1 If two intersecting lines form a linear pair of congruent angles, then the lines are perpendicular.

Thm. 3-4-2 Perpendicular Transversal Theorem In a plane, if a transversal is perpendicular to one of two parallel lines, then it is perpendicular to the other line.

Thm. 3-4-3 If two coplanar lines are perpendicular to the same line, then the two lines are parallel to each other.

Thm. 3-5-1 Parallel Lines Theorem In a coordinate plane, two nonvertical lines are parallel if and only if they have the same slope. Any two vertical lines are parallel.

Thm. 3-5-2 Perpendicular Lines Theorem In a coordinate plane, two nonvertical lines are perpendicular if and only if the product of their slopes is -1. Vertical and horizontal lines are perpendicular.

Postulates, Theorems, and Corollaries Chapter 4

Thm. 4-3-1 Triangle Sum Theorem The sum of the angle measures of a triangle is 180°.

Cor. 4-3-2 The acute angles of a right triangle are complementary.

Cor. 4-3-3 The measure of each angle of an equiangular triangle is 60°.

Thm. 4-3-4 Exterior Angle Theorem The measure of an exterior angle of a triangle is equal to the sum of the measures of its remote interior angles.

Thm. 4-3-5 Third Angles Theorem If two angles of one triangle are congruent to two angles of another triangle, then the third pair of angles are congruent.

Post. 4-5-1 Side-Side-Side (SSS) Congruence Postulate If three sides of one triangle are congruent to three sides of another triangle, then the triangles are congruent.

Post. 4-5-2 Side-Angle-Side (SAS) Congruence Postulate If two sides and the included angle of one triangle are congruent to two sides and the included angle of another triangle, then the triangles are congruent.

Post. 4-6-1 Angle-Side-Angle (ASA) Congruence Postulate If two angles and the included side of one triangle are congruent to two angles and the included side of another triangle, then the triangles are congruent.

Thm. 4-6-2 Angle-Angle-Side (AAS) Congruence Theorem If two angles and a nonincluded side of one triangle are congruent to the corresponding angles and nonincluded side of another triangle, then the triangles are congruent.

Thm. 4-6-3 Hypotenuse-Leg (HL) Congruence Theorem If the hypotenuse and a leg of a right triangle are congruent to the hypotenuse and a leg of another right triangle, then the triangles are congruent.

Thm. 4-9-1 Isosceles Triangle Theorem If two sides of a triangle are congruent, then the angles opposite the sides are congruent.

Thm. 4-9-2 Converse of the Isosceles Triangle Theorem If two angles of a triangle are congruent, then the sides opposite those angles are congruent.

Cor. 4-9-3 If a triangle is equilateral, then it is equiangular.

Cor. 4-9-4 If a triangle is equiangular, then it is equilateral.

Postulates, Theorems, and Corollaries Chapter 5

Thm. 5-1-1 Perpendicular Bisector Theorem If a point is on the perpendicular bisector of a segment, then it is equidistant from the endpoints of the segment.

Thm. 5-1-2 Converse of the Perpendicular Bisector Theorem If a point is equidistant from the endpoints of a segment, then it is on the perpendicular bisector of the segment.

Thm. 5-1-3 Angle Bisector Theorem If a point is on the bisector of an angle, then it is equidistant from the sides of the angle.

Thm. 5-1-4 Converse of the Angle Bisector Theorem If a point in the interior of an angle is equidistant from the sides of the angle, then it is on the bisector of the angle.

Thm. 5-2-1 Circumcenter Theorem The circumcenter of a triangle is equidistant from the vertices of the triangle.

Thm. 5-2-2 Incenter Theorem The incenter of a triangle is equidistant from the sides of the triangle.

Thm. 5-3-1 Centroid Theorem The centroid of a triangle is located $\frac{2}{3}$ of the distance from each vertex to the midpoint of the opposite side.

Thm. 5-4-1 Triangle Midsegment Theorem A midsegment of a triangle is parallel to a side of a triangle, and its length is half the length of that side.

Thm. 5-5-1 If two sides of a triangle are not congruent, then the larger angle is opposite the longer side.

Thm. 5-5-2 If two angles of a triangle are not congruent, then the longer side is opposite the larger angle.

Thm. 5-5-3 Triangle Inequality Theorem The sum of any two side lengths of a triangle is greater than the third side length.

Thm. 5-6-1 Hinge Theorem If two sides of one triangle are congruent to two sides of another triangle and the included angles are not congruent, then the longer third side is across from the larger included angle.

Thm. 5-6-2 Converse of the Hinge Theorem If two sides of one triangle are congruent to two sides of another triangle and the third sides are not congruent, then the larger included angle is across from the longer third side.

Thm. 5-7-1 Converse of the Pythagorean Theorem If the sum of the squares of the lengths of two sides of a triangle is equal to the square of the length of the third side, then the triangle is a right triangle.

Thm. 5-7-2 Pythagorean Inequalities Theorem In $\triangle ABC$, c is the length of the longest side. If $c^2 > a^2 + b^2$, then $\triangle ABC$ is an obtuse triangle. If $c^2 < a^2 + b^2$, then $\triangle ABC$ is an acute triangle.

Thm. 5-8-1 45°-45°-90° Triangle Theorem In a 45°-45°-90° triangle, both legs are congruent, and the length of the hypotenuse is the length of a leg times $\sqrt{2}$.

Thm. 5-8-2 30°-60°-90° Triangle Theorem In a 30°-60°-90° triangle, the length of the hypotenuse is 2 times the length of the shorter leg, and the length of the longer leg is the length of the shorter leg times $\sqrt{3}$.

Postulates, Theorems, and Corollaries Chapter 6

Thm. 6-1-1 Polygon Angle Sum Theorem The sum of the interior angle measures of a convex polygon with n sides is $(n - 2)180°$.

Thm. 6-1-2 Polygon Exterior Angle Sum Theorem The sum of the exterior angle measures, one angle at each vertex, of a convex polygon is 360°.

Thm. 6-2-1 If a quadrilateral is a parallelogram, then its opposite sides are congruent.

Thm. 6-2-2 If a quadrilateral is a parallelogram, then its opposite angles are congruent.

Thm. 6-2-3 If a quadrilateral is a parallelogram, then its consecutive angles are supplementary.

Thm. 6-2-4 If a quadrilateral is a parallelogram, then its diagonals bisect each other.

Thm. 6-3-1 If one pair of opposite sides of a quadrilateral are parallel and congruent, then the quadrilateral is a parallelogram.

Thm. 6-3-2 If both pairs of opposite sides of a quadrilateral are congruent, then the quadrilateral is a parallelogram.

Thm. 6-3-3 If both pairs of opposite angles of a quadrilateral are congruent, then the quadrilateral is a parallelogram.

Thm. 6-3-4 If an angle of a quadrilateral is supplementary to both of its consecutive angles, then the quadrilateral is a parallelogram.

Thm. 6-3-5 If the diagonals of a quadrilateral bisect each other, then the quadrilateral is a parallelogram.

Thm. 6-4-1 If a quadrilateral is a rectangle, then it is a parallelogram.

Thm. 6-4-2 If a parallelogram is a rectangle, then its diagonals are congruent.

Thm. 6-4-3 If a quadrilateral is a rhombus, then it is a parallelogram.

Thm. 6-4-4 If a parallelogram is a rhombus, then its diagonals are perpendicular.

Thm. 6-4-5 If a parallelogram is a rhombus, then each diagonal bisects a pair of opposite angles.

Thm. 6-5-1 If one angle of a parallelogram is a right angle, then the parallelogram is a rectangle.

Thm. 6-5-2 If the diagonals of a parallelogram are congruent, then the parallelogram is a rectangle.

Thm. 6-5-3 If one pair of consecutive sides of a parallelogram are congruent, then the parallelogram is a rhombus.

Thm. 6-5-4 If the diagonals of a parallelogram are perpendicular, then the parallelogram is a rhombus.

Thm. 6-5-5 If one diagonal of a parallelogram bisects a pair of opposite angles, then the parallelogram is a rhombus.

Thm. 6-6-1 If a quadrilateral is a kite, then its diagonals are perpendicular.

Thm. 6-6-2 If a quadrilateral is a kite, then exactly one pair of opposite angles are congruent.

Thm. 6-6-3 If a quadrilateral is an isosceles trapezoid, then each pair of base angles are congruent.

Thm. 6-6-4 If a trapezoid has one pair of congruent base angles, then the trapezoid is isosceles.

Thm. 6-6-5 A trapezoid is isosceles if and only if its diagonals are congruent.

Thm. 6-6-6 Trapezoid Midsegment Theorem The midsegment of a trapezoid is parallel to each base, and its length is one half the sum of the lengths of the bases.

Postulates, Theorems, and Corollaries Chapter 7

Post. 7-3-1 Angle-Angle (AA) Similarity Postulate If two angles of one triangle are congruent to two angles of another triangle, then the triangles are similar.

Thm. 7-3-2 Side-Side-Side (SSS) Similarity Theorem If the three sides of one triangle are proportional to the three corresponding sides of another triangle, then the triangles are similar.

Thm. 7-3-3 Side-Angle-Side (SAS) Similarity Theorem If two sides of one triangle are proportional to two sides of another triangle and their included angles are congruent, then the triangles are similar.

Thm. 7-4-1 Triangle Proportionality Theorem If a line parallel to a side of a triangle intersects the other two sides, then it divides those sides proportionally.

Thm. 7-4-2 Converse of the Triangle Proportionality Theorem If a line divides two sides of a triangle proportionally, then it is parallel to the third side.

Cor. 7-4-3 Two-Transversal Proportionality Corollary If three or more parallel lines intersect two transversals, then they divide the transversals proportionally.

Thm. 7-4-4 Triangle Angle Bisector Theorem An angle bisector of a triangle divides the opposite side into two segments whose lengths are proportional to the lengths of the other two sides.

Thm. 7-5-1 Proportional Perimeters and Areas Theorem If the similarity ratio of two similar figures is $\frac{a}{b}$, then the ratio of their perimeters is $\frac{a}{b}$, and the ratio of their areas is $\frac{a^2}{b^2}$ or $\left(\frac{a}{b}\right)^2$.

Postulates, Theorems, and Corollaries Chapter 8

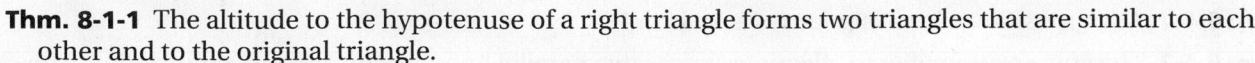

Thm. 8-1-1 The altitude to the hypotenuse of a right triangle forms two triangles that are similar to each other and to the original triangle.

Cor. 8-1-2 Geometric Means Corollary The length of the altitude to the hypotenuse of a right triangle is the geometric mean of the lengths of the two segments of the hypotenuse.

Cor. 8-1-3 Geometric Means Corollary The length of a leg of a right triangle is the geometric mean of the lengths of the hypotenuse and the segment of the hypotenuse adjacent to that leg.

Thm. 8-5-1 The Law of Sines For any $\triangle ABC$ with side lengths a, b, and c, $\frac{\sin A}{a} = \frac{\sin B}{b} = \frac{\sin C}{c}$.

Thm. 8-5-2 The Law of Cosines For any $\triangle ABC$ with sides a, b, and c, $a^2 = b^2 + c^2 - 2bc\cos A$, $b^2 = a^2 + c^2 - 2ac\cos B$, and $c^2 = a^2 + b^2 - 2ab\cos C$.

Thm. 9-4-1 A composition of two isometries is an isometry.

Thm. 9-4-2 The composition of two reflections across two parallel lines is equivalent to a translation. The translation vector is perpendicular to the lines. The length of the translation vector is twice the distance between the lines. The composition of two reflections across two intersecting lines is equivalent to a rotation. The center of rotation is the intersection of the lines. The angle of rotation is twice the measure of the angle formed by the lines.

Thm. 9-4-3 Any translation or rotation is equivalent to a composition of two reflections.

Postulates, Theorems, and Corollaries Chapter 10

Post. 10-1-1 Area Addition Postulate The area of a region is equal to the sum of the areas of its nonoverlapping parts.

Postulates, Theorems, and Corollaries Chapter 12

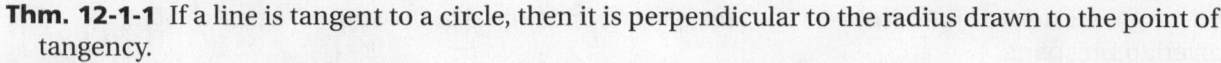

Thm. 12-1-1 If a line is tangent to a circle, then it is perpendicular to the radius drawn to the point of tangency.

Thm. 12-1-2 If a line is perpendicular to a radius of a circle at a point on the circle, then the line is tangent to the circle.

Thm. 12-1-3 If two segments are tangent to a circle from the same external point, then the segments are congruent.

Post. 12-2-1 Arc Addition Postulate The measure of an arc formed by two adjacent arcs is the sum of the measures of the two arcs.

Thm. 12-2-2 In a circle or congruent circles: (1) congruent central angles have congruent chords, (2) congruent chords have congruent arcs, and (3) congruent arcs have congruent central angles.

Thm. 12-2-3 In a circle, if a radius (or diameter) is perpendicular to a chord, then it bisects the chord and its arc.

Thm. 12-2-4 In a circle, the perpendicular bisector of a chord is a radius (or diameter).

Thm. 12-4-1 Inscribed Angle Theorem The measure of an inscribed angle is half the measure of its intercepted arc.

Cor. 12-4-2 If inscribed angles of a circle intercept the same arc or are subtended by the same chord or arc, then the angles are congruent.

Thm. 12-4-3 An inscribed angle subtends a semicircle if and only if the angle is a right angle.

Thm. 12-4-4 If a quadrilateral is inscribed in a circle, then its opposite angles are supplementary.

Thm. 12-5-1 If a tangent and a secant (or chord) intersect on a circle at the point of tangency, then the measure of the angle formed is half the measure of its intercepted arc.

Thm. 12-5-2 If two secants or chords intersect in the interior of a circle, then the measure of each angle formed is half the sum of the measures of its intercepted arcs.

Thm. 12-5-3 If a tangent and a secant, two tangents, or two secants intersect in the exterior of a circle, then the measure of the angle formed is half the difference of the measures of its intercepted arcs.

Thm. 12-6-1 Chord-Chord Product Theorem If two chords intersect in the interior of a circle, then the products of the lengths of the segments of the chords are equal.

Thm. 12-6-2 Secant-Secant Product Theorem If two secants intersect in the exterior of a circle, then the product of the lengths of one secant segment and its external segment equals the product of the lengths of the other secant segment and its external segment.

Thm. 12-6-3 Secant-Tangent Product Theorem If a secant and a tangent intersect in the exterior of a circle, then the product of the lengths of the secant segment and its external segment equals the length of the tangent segment squared.

Thm. 12-7-1 Equation of a Circle The equation of a circle with center (h, k) and radius r is $(x - h)^2 + (y - k)^2 = r^2$.

Constructions

1-1

Check It Out! 1. Possible answer: plane $\mathcal{R}$ and plane ABC
2.

3. Possible answer: plane GHF
4.
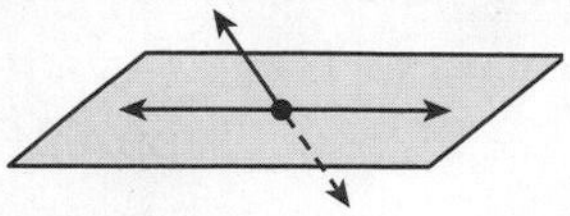

Exercises 3. A, B, C, D, E
5. Possible answer: planes ABC and $\mathcal{N}$
7.

9. Possible answer: $\overleftrightarrow{AB}$
11.
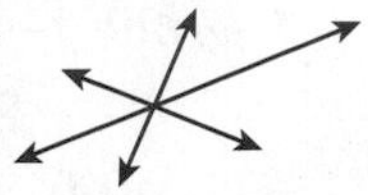
13. B, E, A **15.** Possible answer: ABC
17.
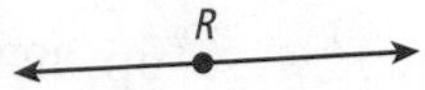

19. Possible answer: planes $\mathcal{T}$ and $\mathcal{S}$
21.

23.
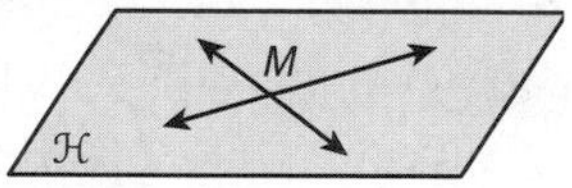

25. U **27.** U **29.** If 2 lines intersect, then they intersect in exactly 1 pt. **31.** A **33.** A **35.** Post. 1-1-3 **37.** Post. 1-1-2 **39.** C **41.** D **43.** 6 **45.** $\frac{n(n-1)}{2}$

1-2

Check It Out! 1a. $3\frac{1}{2}$ **1b.** $4\frac{1}{2}$ **3a.** $1\frac{2}{3}$ **3b.** 24 **4.** 591.25 m **5.** $RS = 4$; $ST = 4$; $RT = 8$

Exercises 1. $\overline{XM}$ and $\overline{MY}$ **3.** 3.5 **7.** 29 **9.** $x = 4$; $KL = 7$; $JL = 14$ **11.** $5\frac{11}{12}$ **15.** 5 **17.** $DE = EF = 14$; $DF = 28$ **19a.** C is the mdpt. of $\overline{AE}$. **b.** 16 **21.** 7.1 **23.** 4 **25.** S **27.** Statement A **29.** 6.5; −1.5 **31.** 3.375 **33.** 9 **37.** J **39.** H
41.
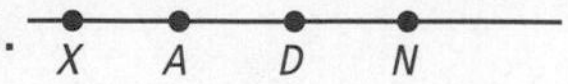

43. 14.02 m

1-3

Check It Out! 1. $\angle RTQ$, $\angle T$, $\angle STR$, $\angle 1$, $\angle 2$ **2a.** 40°; acute **2b.** 125°; obtuse **2c.** 105°; obtuse **3.** 62° **4a.** 34° **4b.** 46°

Exercises 1. $\angle A$, $\angle R$, $\angle O$ **3.** $\angle AOB$, $\angle BOA$, or $\angle 1$; $\angle BOC$, $\angle COB$, or $\angle 2$; $\angle AOC$ or $\angle COA$ **5.** 105°; obtuse **7.** 70° **9.** 28° **11.** $\angle 1$ or $\angle JMK$; $\angle 2$ or $\angle LMK$; $\angle M$ or $\angle JML$ **13.** 93°; obtuse **15.** 66.6° **17.** 20° **19.** acute **21.** acute **27.** 67.5°; 22.5° **29.** $16\frac{1}{3}$ **31.** 9 **33a.** 9 **b.** 12 **c.** $0 < x < 15.6$ **35.** $m\angle COD = 72°$; $m\angle BOC = 90°$ **37.** No; an obtuse ∠ measures greater than 90°, so it cannot be ≅ to an acute ∠ (less than 90°). **41.** D **43.** C **45.** The ⊿ are acute. An obtuse ∠ measures between 90° and 180°. Since $\frac{1}{2}$ of 180 is 90, the resulting ⊿ must measure less than 90°. **47.** 36° or 4° **49.** 8100

1-4

Check It Out! 1a. adj.; lin. pair **1b.** not adj. **1c.** not adj. **2a.** $(102 - 7x)°$ **2b.** $63\frac{1}{2}°$ **3.** 68° **4.** $m\angle 1 = m\angle 2 = 62.4°$; $m\angle 4 = 27.6°$ **5.** Possible answer: $\angle EDG$ and $\angle FDH$; $m\angle EDG \approx m\angle FDH \approx 45°$

Exercises 1. $(90 - x)°$; $(180 - x)°$ **3.** adj.; lin. pair **5.** not adj. **7.** 98.8° **9.** $(185 - 6x)°$ **11.** 69° **13.** $\angle ABE$, $\angle CBD$; $\angle ABC$, $\angle EBD$ **15.** adj.; lin. pair **17.** not adj. **19.** 33.6° **21.** $(94 - 2x)°$ **23.** $m\angle 2 = 22.3°$; $m\angle 3 = m\angle 4 = 67.7°$ **25.** $\frac{1}{3}$ **27.** 72°; 108° **29.** 61°; 29° **31.** 10°; 80° **33a.** $m\angle JAH = 64°$; $m\angle KAH = 26°$ **b.** $m\angle JAH = 131.5°$; $m\angle KAH = 48.5°$ **c.** $m\angle JAH = m\angle KAH = 7°$ **35.** F **37.** T **39.** C **41.** C **43.** 12 **45.** 30°

1-5

Check It Out! 1. $P = 14$ in.; $A = 12.25$ in^2 **2.** 65 in^2 **3.** $C \approx 88.0$ m; $A \approx 615.8$ m^2

Exercises 1. Both terms refer to the dist. around a figure. **3.** $P = 30$ mm; $A = 44$ mm^2 **5.** $P = (x + 21)$ m; $A = (2x + 6)$ m^2 **7.** $C \approx 13.2$ m; $A \approx 13.9$ m^2 **9.** $C \approx 50.3$ cm; $A \approx 201.1$ cm^2 **11.** $P = 4x + 12$; $A = x^2 + 6x$ **13.** 72 in^2 **15.** $C \approx 39.3$ ft; $A \approx 122.7$ ft^2 **17.** 82.81 yd^2 **19.** 6.1875 in^2 **21.** 17.1 cm **23.** Statement A **25.** $9y^2\pi$ **27.** For a square, the length and width are both s, so $P = 2l + 2w = 2s + 2s = 4s$ and $A = lw = s(s) = s^2$. **29.** $b = 41$ in.; $h = 38$ in. **31a.** $ac + ad + bc + bd$ **b.** $(a + 1)(c + 1)$; $ac + a + c + 1$ **c.** $(a + 1)^2$; $a^2 + 2a + 1$ **33.** 28 ft **35.** 26.46 ft^2 **37.** $25\frac{2}{3}$ yd^2 or 231 ft^2 **39.** 10 ft **41.** $\frac{14}{\pi}$ **43.** 50 **45.** Measure any side as the base. Then measure the height of the △ at a rt. ∠ to the base. **47.** B **49.** A **51.** 83.7 in^2 **53.** 5; 8; 9 **55.** width = 16 in.; length = 20 in.

1-6

Check It Out! 1. $\left(\frac{3}{2}, 0\right)$ **2.** $(4, 3)$ **3.** $EF = 5$; $GH = 5$; $\overline{EF} \cong \overline{GH}$ **4a.** 6.7 **4b.** 8.5 **5.** 60.5 ft

Exercises 1. hypotenuse **3.** $\left(1\frac{1}{2}, -4\right)$ **5.** $(0, -2)$ **7.** $\sqrt{29}$; $3\sqrt{5}$; no **9.** 15.0 **11.** 27.2 ft **13.** $\left(3\frac{1}{2}, -4\frac{1}{2}\right)$ **15.** $(8, 4)$ **17.** $2\sqrt{5}$; $\sqrt{29}$; no **19.** 8.9 **21.** 18 in. **23.** 4.47 **25.** Divide each coord. by 2. **27.** 2.5 mi **31.** 1 **33.** Let M be the mdpt. of $\overline{AC}$; $AM = MC = 5.0$ ft; $MB = MD \approx 6.4$ ft. **35.** G **37.** J **39.** ±2 **41.** $AB = \sqrt{x^2 + y^2}$

1-7

Check It Out! 1a. translation; $MNOP \to M'N'O'P'$ **1b.** rotation; $\triangle XYZ \to \triangle X'Y'Z'$ **2.** rotation; 90° **3.** $J'(-1, -5)$; $K'(1, 5)$; $L'(1, 0)$; $M'(-1, 0)$ **4.** $(x, y) \to (x - 4, y - 4)$

Exercises 1. Preimage is $\triangle XYZ$; image is $\triangle X'Y'Z'$ **3.** reflection; $\triangle ABC \to \triangle A'B'C'$ **5.** reflection across the y-axis **7.** $(x, y) \to (x + 4, y + 4)$ **9.** reflection; $WXYZ \to W'X'Y'Z'$ **11.** $A'(-1, -1)$, $B'(4, -1)$, $C(4, -4)$, $D(-1, -4)$ **13.** reflection **15.** reflection

17.

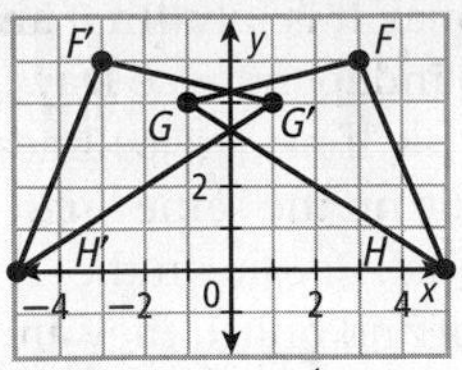

19. *B* **21.** *D* **23.** $R'(-1, -12)$; $S'(-3, -9)$; $T'(-7, -7)$

25.

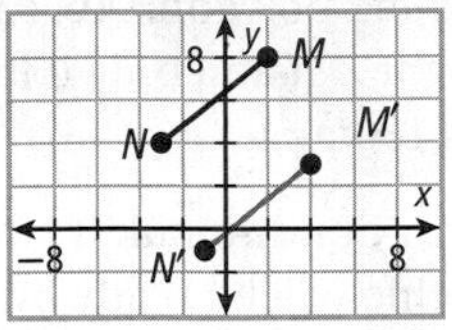

29. A **31.** A **33a.** $R''(1, 0)$; $S''(0, 3)$; $T''(4, 3)$ **b.** $(x, y) \rightarrow (x + 3, y + 2)$

35.

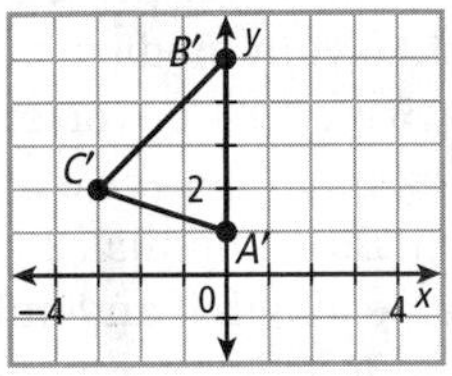

37. $(-x, y)$

Study Guide: Review

1. angle bisector **2.** complementary angles **3.** hypotenuse **4.** *A, F, E, G* or *C, G, D, B* **5.** Possible answer: $\overleftrightarrow{GC}$ **6.** Possible answer: plane *AEG*

7.

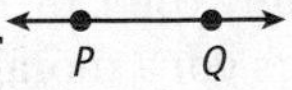

8.

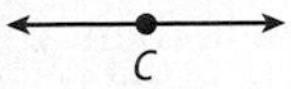

9.

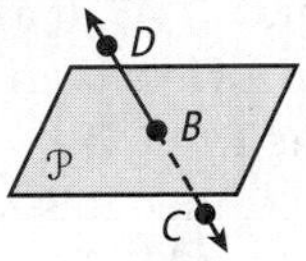

10. 3.5 **11.** 5 **12.** 7.6 **13.** 22 **14.** 13; 13; 26 **15.** 18; 18; 36 **16.** ∠*VYX*: rt.; ∠*VYZ*: obtuse; ∠*XYZ*: acute; ∠*XYW*: rt.; ∠*ZYW*: acute; ∠*VYW*: straight **17.** 59° **18.** 96° **19.** only adj. **20.** adj. and a lin. pair **21.** not adj. **22.** 15.4°; 105.4° **23.** $(94 - 2x)°$; $(184 - 2x)°$ **24.** 73° **25.** $14x - 2$; $12x^2 - 3x$ **26.** $4x + 16$; $x^2 + 8x + 16$ **27.** $x + 15$; $4x - 20$ **28.** $10x + 54$; $100x + 140$ **29.** $A \approx 1385.4\ m^2$; $C \approx 131.9$ m **30.** $A \approx 153.9\ ft^2$; $C \approx 44.0$ ft **31.** 12 m **32.** $Y(1, 3)$ **33.** $B(-9, 6)$ **34.** $A(0, 2)$ **35.** 8.5 **36.** 7.3 **37.** 8.1 **38.** 90° rotation; $DEFG \rightarrow D'E'F'G'$ **39.** translation; $PQRS \rightarrow P'Q'R'S'$ **40.** $X'(-1, 1)$; $Y'(1, 4)$; $Z'(2, 3)$

2-1

Check It Out! **1.** 0.0004 **2.** odd **3.** Female whales are longer than male whales. **4a.** Possible answer: $x = \frac{1}{2}$ **4b.** Possible answer:

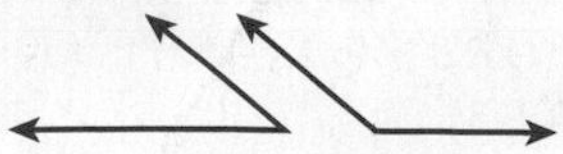

4c. Jupiter or Saturn

Exercises **3.** $\frac{4}{6}$ **5.** even **7.** The number of bacteria doubles every 20 minutes. **9.** The 3 pts. are collinear. **11.** 5 P.M. **13.**

15. $n - 1$ **17.** Possible answer: $y = -1$ **19.** $m\angle 1 = m\angle 2 = 90°$ **21.** Possible answer: each term is the previous term multiplied by $\frac{1}{2}$; $\frac{1}{16}$; $\frac{1}{32}$. **23.** $2n + 1$ **25.** F **27.** T **29.** $\frac{1}{11} = 0.\overline{09}$, $\frac{2}{11} = 0.\overline{18}$, $\frac{3}{11} = 0.\overline{27}$,...; the fraction pattern is multiples of $\frac{1}{11}$, and the decimal pattern is repeating multiples of 0.09. **31.** 34, 55, 89; each term is the sum of the 2 previous terms. **33.** odd **37.** C **39.** D **41.** 12 years **43.** $m\angle CAB = m\angle CBA$; $AC = CB$

2-2

Check It Out! **1.** Hypothesis: A number is divisible by 6. Conclusion: A number is divisible by 3. **2.** If 2 ∠s are comp., then they are acute. **3.** F; possible answer: 7 **4.** Converse: If an animal has 4 paws, then it is a cat; F. Inverse: If an animal is not a cat, then it does not have 4 paws; F. Contrapositive: If an animal does not have 4 paws, then it is not a cat; T.

Exercises **1.** converse **3.** Hypothesis: A person is at least 16 years old. Conclusion: A person can drive a car. **5.** Hypothesis: $a - b < a$. Conclusion: b is a positive number. **7.** If $0 < a < b$, then $\left(\frac{a}{b}\right)^2 < \frac{a}{b}$. **9.** T **11.** F **13.** Hypothesis: An animal is a tabby. Conclusion: An animal is a cat. **15.** Hypothesis: 8 ounces of cereal cost \$2.99. Conclusion: 16 ounces of cereal cost \$5.98. **17.** If the batter makes 3 strikes, then the batter is out. **19.** T **21.** T **25.** T **27.** F **29.** F **35.** If a person is a Texan, then the person is an American. **37a.** H: Only you can find it. C: Everything's got a moral. **b.** If only you can find it, then everything's got a moral. **43.** If a mineral has a hardness less than 5, then it is not apatite; T. **45.** If a mineral is not apatite, then it is calcite; F. **47.** If a mineral is calcite, then it has a hardness less than 5; T. **51.** H **53.** J **55.** Some students are adults. Some adults are students. **57.** 3

2-3

Check It Out! **1.** deductive reasoning **2.** valid **3.** valid **4.** Polygon P is not a quad.

Exercises **3.** deductive reasoning **5.** valid **7.** invalid **9.** deductive reasoning **11.** invalid **13.** Dakota gets better grades in Social Studies. **15.** valid **17.** valid **19.** yes; no; because the first conditional is false **23.** D **25.** 196 **27a.** If you live in San Diego, then you live in the United States. **b.** If you do not live in California, then you do not live in San Diego. If you do not live in the United States, then you do not live in California. **c.** If you do not live in the United States, then you do not live in San Diego. **d.** They are contrapositives of each other.

2-4

Check It Out! **1a.** Conditional: If an ∠ is acute, then its measure is greater than 0° and less than 90°. Converse: If an ∠'s measure is greater than 0° and less than 90°, then the ∠ is acute. **1b.** Conditional: If Cho is a member, then he has paid the \$5 dues. Converse: If Cho has paid the \$5 dues, then he is a member. **2a.** Converse: If it is Independence Day, then the date is July 4th. Biconditional: It is July 4th if and only if it is Independence Day. **2b.** Converse: If pts. are collinear, then they lie on the same line. Biconditional: Pts. lie on the same line if and only if they are collinear. **3a.** T **3b.** F; $y = 5$ **4a.** A figure is a quad. if and only if it is a 4-sided polygon. **4b.** An ∠ is a straight ∠ if and only if its measure is 180°.

Exercises **3.** Conditional: If your medicine will be ready by 5 P.M. , then you dropped your prescription off by 8 A.M. Converse: If you drop your prescription off by 8 A.M. , then your medicine will be ready by 5 P.M. **5.** Converse: If 2 segs. are ≅, then they have the same length. Biconditional: 2 segs. have the same length if and only if they are ≅. **7.** F **9.** An animal is a hummingbird if and only if it is a tiny, brightly colored bird with narrow wings, a slender bill, and a long tongue. **11.** Conditional: If a ▱ is a rect., then it has 4 rt. ∠s. Converse: If a ▱ has 4 rt. ∠s, then it is a rect. **13.** Converse: If it is the weekend, then today is Saturday or Sunday. Biconditional: Today is Saturday or Sunday if and only if it is the weekend. **15.** Converse: If a △ is a rt. △, then it contains a rt. ∠. Biconditional: A △ contains a rt. ∠ if and only if it is a rt. △. **17.** T **19.** A player is a catcher if and only if the player is positioned behind home plate and catches throws from the pitcher. **21.** yes **23.** no **25.** A square is a quad. with 4 ≅ sides and 4 rt. ∠s. **31.** no **33.** 5 **37a.** If I say it, then I mean it. If I mean it, then I say it. **39.** G **43a.** If an ∠ does not measure 105°, then the ∠ is not obtuse. **b.** If an ∠ is not obtuse, then it does not measure 105°. **c.** It is the contrapositive of the original. **d.** F; the inverse is false, and its converse is true.

2-5

Check It Out! 1. $\frac{1}{2}t = -7$ (Given); $2\left(\frac{1}{2}t\right) = 2(-7)$ (Mult. Prop. of =); $t = -14$ (Simplify.) **2.** $C = \frac{5}{9}(F - 32)$ (Given); $C = \frac{5}{9}(86 - 32)$ (Subst.); $C = \frac{5}{9}(54)$ (Simplify.); $C = 30$ (Simplify.) **3.** ∠ Add. Post.; Subst.; Simplify.; Subtr. Prop. of =; Mult. Prop. of = **4a.** Sym. Prop. of = **4b.** Reflex. Prop. of = **4c.** Trans. Prop. of = **4d.** Sym. Prop. of ≅

Exercises 3. $t - 3.2 = -8.3$ (Given); $t = -5.1$ (Add. Prop. of =) **5.** $\frac{x+3}{-2} = 8$ (Given); $x + 3 = -16$ (Mult. Prop. of =); $x = -19$ (Subtr. Prop. of =) **7.** $0 = 2(r - 3) + 4$ (Given); $0 = 2r - 6 + 4$ (Distrib. Prop.); $0 = 2r - 2$ (Simplify.); $2 = 2r$ (Add. Prop. of =); $1 = r$ (Div. Prop. of =) **9.** $C = \$5.75 + \$0.89m$ (Given); $\$11.98 = \$5.75 + \$0.89m$ (Subst.); $\$6.23 = \$0.89m$ (Subtr. Prop. of =); $m = 7$ (Div. Prop. of =) **11.** Seg. Add. Post.; Subst.; Subtr. Prop. of =; Add. Prop. of =; Div. Prop. of = **13.** Trans. Prop. of = **15.** Trans. Prop. of ≅ **17.** $1.6 = 3.2n$ (Given); $0.5 = n$ (Div. Prop. of =) **19.** $-(h + 3) = 72$ (Given); $-h - 3 = 72$ (Distrib. Prop.); $-h = 75$ (Add. Prop. of =); $h = -75$ (Mult. Prop. of =) **21.** $\frac{1}{2}(p - 16) = 13$ (Given); $\frac{1}{2}p - 8 = 13$ (Distrib. Prop.); $\frac{1}{2}p = 21$ (Add. Prop. of =); $p = 42$ (Mult. Prop. of =) **23.** ∠ Add. Post.; Subst.; Simplify.; Subtr. Prop. of =; Add. Prop. of =; Div. Prop. of = **25.** Sym. Prop. of ≅ **27.** Trans. Prop. of = **29.** $x = 16$; $2(3.1x - 0.87) = 94.36$ (Given); $6.2x - 1.74 = 94.36$ (Distrib. Prop.); $6.2x = 96.1$ (Add. Prop. of =); $x = 15.5$ (Div. Prop. of =); possible answer: the exact solution rounds to the estimate. **31.** ∠A ≅ ∠T **33.** $\frac{x+1}{2} = 3$ (Mdpt. Formula;) $x + 1 = 6$ (Mult. Prop. of =); $x = 5$ (Subtr. Prop. of =); $\frac{1+y}{2} = 5$ (Mdpt. Formula); $1 + y = 10$ (Mult. Prop. of =); $y = 9$ (Subtr. Prop. of =) **35a.** $1733.65 = 92.50 + 79.96 + 983 + 10{,}820x$ (Given); $1733.65 = 1155.46 + 10{,}820x$ (Simplify.); $578.19 = 10{,}820x$ (Subtr. Prop. of =); $0.05 \approx x$ (Div. Prop. of =) **b.** \$1.71 **37a.** $x + 15 \le 63$ (Given); $x \le 48$ (Subtr. Prop. of Inequal.) **b.** $-2x > 36$ (Given); $x < -18$ (Div. Prop. of Inequal.) **39.** B **41.** D **43.** $PR = PA + RA$ (Seg. Add. Post.); $PA = QB$, $QB = RA$ (Given); $PA = RA$ (Trans. Prop. of =); $PR = PA + PA$ (Subst.); $PA = 18$(Given); $PR = 18 + 18$ (Subst.); $PR = 36$ in. (Simplify.) **45.** $7 - 3x > 19$ (Given); $-3x > 12$ (Subtr. Prop. of Inequal.); $x < -4$ (Div. Prop. of Inequal.)

2-6

Check It Out!

1. 1. Given
2. Def. of mdpt.
3. Given
4. Trans. Prop. of ≅

2a. ∠1 and ∠2 are supp., and ∠2 and ∠3 are supp. **2b.** m∠1 + m∠2 = m∠2 + m∠3 **2c.** Subtr. Prop. of = **2d.** ∠1 ≅ ∠3

3. 1. ∠1 and ∠2 are comp. ∠2 and ∠3 are comp. (Given)
2. m∠1 + m∠2 = 90°, m∠2 + m∠3 = 90° (Def. of comp. ∠s)
3. m∠1 + m∠2 = m∠2 + m∠3 (Subst.)
4. m∠2 = m∠2 (Reflex. Prop. of =)
5. m∠1 = m∠3 (Subtr. Prop. of =)
6. ∠1 ≅ ∠3 (Def. of ≅ ∠s)

Exercises 1. statements; reasons

3. 1. Given
2. Subst.
3. Simplify.
4. Add. Prop. of =
5. Simplify.
6. Def. of supp. ∠s

5. 1. X is the mdpt. of $\overline{AY}$. Y is the mdpt. of $\overline{XB}$. (Given)
2. $\overline{AX} \cong \overline{XY}$, $\overline{XY} \cong \overline{YB}$ (Def. of mdpt.)
3. $\overline{AX} \cong \overline{YB}$ (Trans. Prop. of ≅)

7a. m∠1 + m∠2 = 180°, m∠3 + m∠4 = 180° **b.** Subst. **c.** m∠1 = m∠4 **d.** Def. of ≅ ∠s

9. 1. $\overline{BE} \cong \overline{CE}$, $\overline{DE} \cong \overline{AE}$ (Given)
2. $BE = CE$, $DE = AE$ (Def. of ≅ segs.)
3. $AE + BE = AB$, $CE + DE = CD$ (Seg. Add. Post.)
4. $DE + CE = AB$ (Subst.)
5. $AB = CD$ (Subst.)
6. $\overline{AB} \cong \overline{CD}$ (Def. of ≅ segs.)

11. 132° **13.** 59° **17.** S **19.** N **21.** $x = 16$ **25.** C **27.** D **29.** $a = 17$; 37.5°, 52.5°, and 37.5°

2-7

Check It Out!

1. 1. $RS = UV$, $ST = TU$ (Given)
2. $RS + ST = TU + UV$ (Add. Prop. of =)
3. $RS + ST = RT$, $TU + UV = TV$ (Seg. Add. Post.)
4. $RT = TV$ (Subst.)
5. $\overline{RT} \cong \overline{TV}$ (Def. of ≅ segs.)

2.

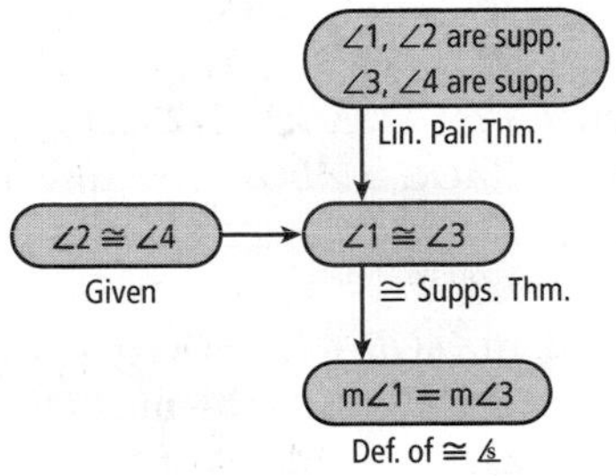

3. 1. ∠WXY is a rt. ∠. (Given)
2. m∠WXY = 90° (Def. of rt. ∠)
3. m∠2 + m∠3 = m∠WXY (∠ Add. Post.)
4. m∠2 + m∠3 = 90° (Subst.)
5. ∠1 ≅ ∠3 (Given)
6. m∠1 = m∠3 (Def. of ≅ ∠s)
7. m∠2 + m∠1 = 90° (Subst.)
8. ∠1 and ∠2 are comp. (Def. of comp. ∠s)

4. It is given that ∠1 ≅ ∠4. By the Vert. ∠s Thm., ∠1 ≅ ∠2 and ∠3 ≅ ∠4. By the Trans. Prop. of ≅, ∠2 ≅ ∠4. Similarly, ∠2 ≅ ∠3.

Exercises 1. flowchart

3. 1. ∠1 ≅ ∠2 (Given)
2. ∠1 and ∠2 are supp. (Lin. Pair Thm.)
3. ∠1 and ∠2 are rt. ∠s. (≅ ∠s supp. → rt. ∠s)

5. 1. ∠2 ≅ ∠4 (Given)
2. ∠1 ≅ ∠2 , ∠3 ≅ ∠4 (Vert. ∠s Thm.)

3. $\angle 1 \cong \angle 4$ (Trans. Prop. of $\cong$)
4. $\angle 1 \cong \angle 3$ (Trans. Prop. of $\cong$)

7. **1.** B is the mdpt. of $\overline{AC}$. (Given)
2. $\overline{AB} \cong \overline{BC}$ (Def. of mdpt.)
3. $AB = BC$ (Def. of $\cong$ segs.)
4. $AD + DB = AB$, $BE + EC = BC$ (Seg. Add. Post.)
5. $AD + DB = BE + EC$ (Subst.)
6. $AD = EC$ (Given)
7. $DB = BE$ (Subtr. Prop. of =)

9. **1.** $\angle 1 \cong \angle 4$ (Given)
2. $\angle 1 \cong \angle 2$ (Vert. $\angle$s Thm.)
3. $\angle 4 \cong \angle 2$ (Trans. Prop. of $\cong$)
4. $m\angle 4 = m\angle 2$ (Def. of $\cong$ $\angle$s)
5. $\angle 3$ and $\angle 4$ are supp. (Lin. Pair Thm.)
6. $m\angle 3 + m\angle 4 = 180°$ (Def. of supp. $\angle$s)
7. $m\angle 3 + m\angle 2 = 180°$ (Subst.)
8. $\angle 2$ and $\angle 3$ are supp. (Def. of supp. $\angle$s)

11. 13 cm; conv. of the Common Segs. Thm. **13.** 37°, Vert. $\angle$s Thm. **15.** $y = 11$ **17.** A **21.** C **23.** D

25. **1.** $\angle AOC \cong \angle BOD$ (Given)
2. $m\angle AOC = m\angle BOD$ (Def. of $\cong$ $\angle$s)
3. $m\angle AOB + m\angle BOC = m\angle AOC$, $m\angle BOC + m\angle COD = m\angle BOD$ ($\angle$ Add. Post.)
4. $m\angle AOB + m\angle BOC = m\angle BOC + m\angle COD$ (Subst.)
5. $m\angle BOC = m\angle BOC$ (Reflex. Prop. of =)
6. $m\angle AOB = m\angle COD$ (Subtr. Prop. of =)
7. $\angle AOB \cong \angle COD$ (Def. of $\cong$ $\angle$s)

27. $x = 31$ and $y = 11.5$; 86°, 94°, 86°, and 94°

Study Guide: Review

1. theorem **2.** deductive reasoning **3.** counterexample **4.** conjecture **5.** The rightmost $\triangle$ is duplicated, rotated 180°, and shifted to the right. The next 2 items are

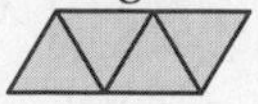

and

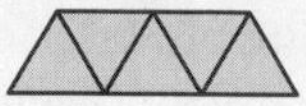

.

6. Each item is $\frac{1}{6}$ greater than the previous one. The next 2 items are $\frac{5}{6}$ and 1. **7.** The white section is halved. If the white section is a rect. but not a square, it is halved horiz. and the upper portion is colored yellow. If the white section is a square, it is halved vert. and the left portion is colored yellow. The next 2 items are

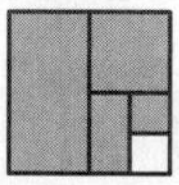

and

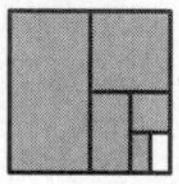

.

8. odd **9.** positive **10.** F; 0 **11.** T **12.** T **13.** F; during a leap year, there are 29 days in February. **14.** Check students' constructions. Possible answer: The 3 $\angle$ bisectors of a $\triangle$ intersect in the int. of the $\triangle$. **15.** If it is Monday, then it is a weekday. **16.** If something is a lichen, then it is a fungus. **17.** T **18.** F; possible answer: $\sqrt{2}$ and $\sqrt{2}$ **19.** Converse: If $m\angle X = 90°$, then $\angle X$ is a rt. $\angle$; T. Inverse: If $\angle X$ is not a rt. $\angle$, then $m\angle X \neq 90°$; T. Contrapositive: If $m\angle X \neq 90°$, then $\angle X$ is not a rt. $\angle$; T. **20.** Converse: If $x = 2$, then x is a whole number; T. Inverse: If x is not a whole number, then $x \neq 2$; T. Contrapositive: If $x \neq 2$, then x is not a whole number; F.
21. F **22.** T **23.** F **24.** Sara's call lasted 7 min. **25.** The cost of Paulo's long-distance call is \$2.78. **26.** No conclusion; the number and length of calls are unknown. **27.** yes

28. no; possible answer: $x = 2$
29. no; possible answer: a seg. with endpoints $(3, 7)$ and $(-5, -1)$
30. yes **31.** comp. **32.** positive
33. greater than 50 mi/h
34. $4s$ **35.** $\frac{m}{-5} + 3 = -4.5$ (Given); $\frac{m}{-5} = -7.5$ (Subtr. Prop. of =); $m = 37.5$ (Mult. Prop. of =) **36.** $-47 = 3x - 59$ (Given); $12 = 3x$ (Add. Prop. of =); $4 = x$ (Div. Prop. of =)
37. Reflex. Prop. of = **38.** Sym. Prop. of $\cong$ **39.** Trans. Prop. of = **40.** figure $ABCD$ **41.** $m\angle 5 = m\angle 2$ **42.** $\overline{CD} \cong \overline{EF}$ **43.** $I = Prt$ (Given); $4200 = P(0.06)(4)$ (Subst.); $4200 = P(0.24)$ (Simplify.); $17{,}500 = P$ (Div. Prop. of =)

44. **1.** Given
2. Def. of comp. $\angle$s
3. Given
4. Def. of $\cong$ $\angle$s
5. Subst.
6. Def. of comp. $\angle$s

45a. Given **b.** $TU = UV$
c. $SU + UV = SV$ **d.** Subst.

46. $z = 22.5$ **47.** $x = 17$

48.

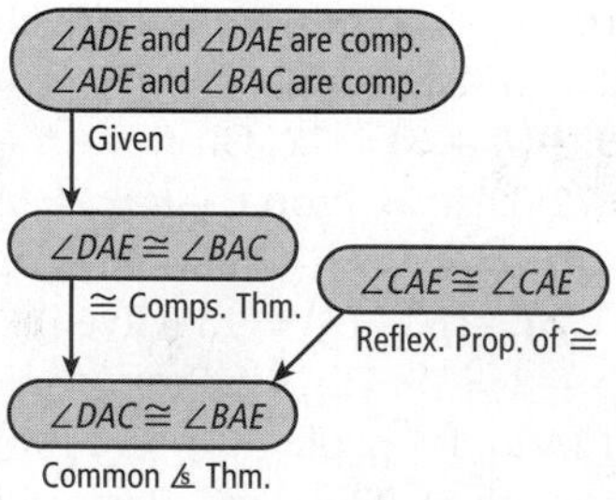

49. It is given that $\angle ADE$ and $\angle DAE$ are comp. and $\angle ADE$ and $\angle BAC$ are comp. By the $\cong$ Comps. Thm., $\angle DAE \cong \angle BAC$. By the Reflex. Prop. of $\cong$, $\angle CAE \cong \angle CAE$. By the Common $\angle$s Thm., $\angle DAC \cong \angle BAE$. **50.** $w = 45$; Vert. $\angle$s Thm. **51.** $x = 45$; $\cong$ $\angle$s supp. $\rightarrow$ rt. $\angle$s

Mastering the Standards

for Mathematical Practice

The topics described in the Standards for Mathematical Content will vary from year to year. However, the *way* in which you learn, study, and think about mathematics will not. The Standards for Mathematical Practice describe skills that you will use in all of your math courses.

Mathematical Practices

1. *Make sense of problems and persevere in solving them.*
2. *Reason abstractly and quantitatively.*
3. *Construct viable arguments and critique the reasoning of others.*
4. *Model with mathematics.*
5. *Use appropriate tools strategically.*
6. *Attend to precision.*
7. *Look for and make use of structure.*
8. *Look for and express regularity in repeated reasoning.*

4 Model with mathematics.

Mathematically proficient students can apply... mathematics... to... problems... in everyday life, society, and the workplace...

In your book

Multi-Step Test Prep and **Real-World Connections** apply mathematics to other disciplines and in real-world scenarios.

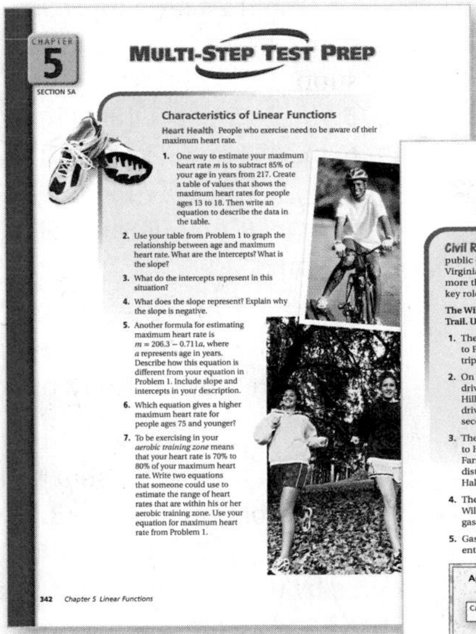

CHAPTER 5

SECTION 5A

MULTI-STEP TEST PREP

Characteristics of Linear Functions

Heart Health People who exercise need to be aware of their maximum heart rate.

1. One way to estimate your maximum heart rate m is to subtract 85% of your age in years from 217. Create a table of values that shows the maximum heart rates for people ages 13 to 18. Then write an equation to describe the data in the table.
2. Use your table from Problem 1 to graph the relationship between age and maximum heart rate. What are the intercepts? What is the slope?
3. What do the intercepts represent in this situation?
4. What does the slope represent? Explain why the slope is negative.
5. Another formula for estimating maximum heart rate is $m = 206.3 - 0.711a$, where a represents age in years. Describe how this equation is different from your equation in Problem 1. Include slope and intercepts in your description.
6. Which equation gives a higher maximum heart rate for people ages 75 and younger?
7. To be exercising in your *aerobic training zone* means that your heart rate is 70% to 80% of your maximum heart rate. Write two equations that someone could use to estimate the range of heart rates that are within his or her aerobic training zone. Use your equation for maximum heart rate from Problem 1.

342 *Chapter 5 Linear Functions*

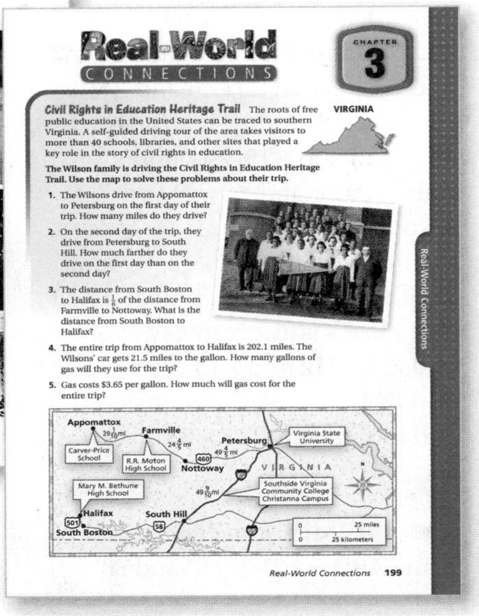

Real-World CONNECTIONS

CHAPTER 3

Civil Rights in Education Heritage Trail The roots of free public education in the United States can be traced to southern Virginia. A self-guided driving tour of the area takes visitors to more than 40 schools, libraries, and other sites that played a key role in the story of civil rights in education.

VIRGINIA

The Wilson family is driving the Civil Rights in Education Heritage Trail. Use the map to solve these problems about their trip.

1. The Wilsons drive from Appomattox to Petersburg on the first day of their trip. How many miles do they drive?
2. On the second day of the trip, they drive from Petersburg to South Hill. How much farther do they drive on the first day than on the second day?
3. The distance from South Boston to Halifax is $\frac{1}{6}$ of the distance from Farmville to Nottoway. What is the distance from South Boston to Halifax?
4. The entire trip from Appomattox to Halifax is 202.1 miles. The Wilsons' car gets 21.5 miles to the gallon. How many gallons of gas will they use for the trip?
5. Gas costs $3.65 per gallon. How much will gas cost for the entire trip?

Real-World Connections

Real-World Connections 199

PhotoDisc/Getty Images

Selected Answers ■ Chapter 3

3-1

Check It Out! **1–2.** Possible answers given. **1a.** $\overline{BF} \parallel \overline{EJ}$ **1b.** $\overline{BF}$ and $\overline{DE}$ are skew. **1c.** $\overline{BF} \perp \overline{FJ}$ **1d.** plane $FJH \parallel$ plane BCD **2a.** $\angle 1$ and $\angle 3$ **2b.** $\angle 2$ and $\angle 7$ **2c.** $\angle 1$ and $\angle 8$ **2d.** $\angle 2$ and $\angle 3$ **3.** transv. n; same-side int. $\angle$s

Exercises **1.** alternate interior angles **3–9.** Possible answers given. **3.** $\overline{AB}$ and $\overline{DH}$ are skew. **5.** plane $ABC \parallel$ plane EFG **7.** $\angle 6$ and $\angle 8$ **9.** $\angle 2$ and $\angle 3$ **11.** transv. m; alt. ext. $\angle$s **13.** transv. p, same-side int. $\angle$s **15–21.** Possible answers given. **15.** $\overline{AB}$ and $\overline{CF}$ are skew. **17.** plane $ABC \parallel$ plane DEF **19.** $\angle 1$ and $\angle 8$ **21.** $\angle 2$ and $\angle 5$ **23.** transv. q; alt. int. $\angle$s **25.** transv. p; same-side int. $\angle$s **27.** corr. $\angle$s **29.** same-side int. $\angle$s **31.** Possible answer: $\overline{CD}$ and $\overline{FG}$ **33a.** plane $MNR \parallel$ plane KLP; plane $LMQ \parallel$ plane KNP; plane $PQR \parallel$ plane KLM **b.** same-side int. $\angle$s **35–39.** Possible answers given. **35.** $\angle 5$ and $\angle 8$ **37.** $\angle 1$ and $\angle 5$ **39.** transv. n; alt. int. $\angle$s **41.** The lines are skew. **45.** G **47.** F **49.** transv. m: $\angle 1$ and $\angle 3$, $\angle 2$ and $\angle 4$, $\angle 5$ and $\angle 7$, $\angle 6$ and $\angle 8$; transv. n: $\angle 9$ and $\angle 11$, $\angle 10$ and $\angle 12$, $\angle 13$ and $\angle 15$, $\angle 14$ and $\angle 16$; transv. p: $\angle 1$ and $\angle 9$, $\angle 2$ and $\angle 10$, $\angle 5$ and $\angle 13$, $\angle 6$ and $\angle 14$; transv. q: $\angle 3$ and $\angle 11$, $\angle 4$ and $\angle 12$, $\angle 7$ and $\angle 15$, $\angle 8$ and $\angle 16$ **51.** transv. m: $\angle 1$ and $\angle 8$, $\angle 4$ and $\angle 5$; transv. n: $\angle 9$ and $\angle 16$, $\angle 12$ and $\angle 13$; transv. p: $\angle 1$ and $\angle 14$, $\angle 2$ and $\angle 13$; transv. q: $\angle 3$ and $\angle 16$, $\angle 4$ and $\angle 15$ **53.** corr. $\angle$s

3-2

Check It Out! **1.** $m\angle QRS = 62°$ **2.** $m\angle ABD = 60°$ **3.** 55° and 60°

Exercises **1.** $m\angle JKL = 127°$ **3.** $m\angle 1 = 90°$ **5.** $x = 8$; $y = 9$ **7.** $m\angle VYX = 100°$ **9.** $m\angle EFG = 102°$ **11.** $m\angle STU = 90°$ **13.** 120°; Corr. $\angle$s Post. **15.** 60°; Same-Side Int. $\angle$s Thm. **17.** 60°; Lin. Pair Thm. **19.** 120°; Vert. $\angle$s Thm. **21.** $x = 4$; Same-Side Int. $\angle$s Thm.; $m\angle 3 = 103°$; $m\angle 4 = 77°$ **23.** $x = 3$; Corr. $\angle$s Post.; $m\angle 1 = m\angle 4 = 42°$ **25a.** $\angle 1 \cong \angle 3$ **b.** Corr. $\angle$s Post. **c.** $\angle 1 \cong \angle 2$ **d.** Trans. Prop. of $\cong$ **29a.** same-side int. $\angle$s **b.** By the Same-Side Int. $\angle$s Thm., $m\angle QRT + m\angle STR = 180°$. $m\angle QRT = 25° + 90° = 115°$, so $m\angle STR = 65°$. **31.** A **35.** J **37.** $m\angle 1 = 75°$ **39.** $x = 4$; $y = 12$

3-3

Check It Out! **1a.** $\angle 1 \cong \angle 3$, so $\ell \parallel m$ by the Conv. of Corr. $\angle$s Post. **1b.** $m\angle 7 = 77°$ and $m\angle 5 = 77°$, so $\angle 7 \cong \angle 5$. $\ell \parallel m$ by the Conv. of Corr. $\angle$s Post. **2a.** $\angle 4 \cong \angle 8$, so $r \parallel s$ by the Conv. of Alt. Int. $\angle$s Thm. **2b.** $m\angle 3 = 100°$ and $m\angle 7 = 100°$, so $\angle 3 \cong \angle 7$. $r \parallel s$ by the Conv. of Alt. Int. $\angle$s Thm.

3. **1.** $\angle 1 \cong \angle 4$ (Given)
2. $m\angle 1 = m\angle 4$ (Def. $\cong$ $\angle$s)
3. $\angle 3$ and $\angle 4$ are supp. (Given)
4. $m\angle 3 + m\angle 4 = 180°$ (Def. supp. $\angle$s)
5. $m\angle 3 + m\angle 1 = 180°$ (Subst.)
6. $m\angle 2 = m\angle 3$ (Vert. $\angle$s Thm.)
7. $m\angle 2 + m\angle 1 = 180°$ (Subst.)
8. $\ell \parallel m$ (Conv. of Same-Side Int. $\angle$s Thm.)

4. $4y - 2 = 4(8) - 2 = 30°$; $3y + 6 = 3(8) + 6 = 30°$; The $\angle$s are $\cong$, so the oars are $\parallel$ by the Conv. of Corr. $\angle$s Post.

Exercises **1.** $\angle 4 \cong \angle 5$, so $p \parallel q$ by the Conv. of Corr. $\angle$s Post. **3.** $m\angle 4 = 47°$, and $m\angle 5 = 47°$, so $\angle 4 \cong \angle 5$. $p \parallel q$ by the Conv. of Corr. $\angle$s Post. **5.** $\angle 3$ and $\angle 4$ are supp., so $r \parallel s$ by the Conv. of Same-Side Int. $\angle$s Thm. **7.** $m\angle 4 = 61°$, and $m\angle 8 = 61°$, so $\angle 4 \cong \angle 8$. $r \parallel s$ by the Conv. of Alt. Int. $\angle$s Thm. **9.** $m\angle 2 = 132°$, and $m\angle 6 = 132°$, so $\angle 2 \cong \angle 6$. $r \parallel s$ by the Conv. of Alt. Ext. $\angle$s Thm. **11.** $m\angle 1 = 60°$, and $m\angle 2 = 60°$, so $\angle 1 \cong \angle 2$. By the Conv. of Alt. Int. $\angle$s Thm., the landings are $\parallel$. **13.** $m\angle 4 = 54°$, and $m\angle 8 = 54°$, so $\angle 4 \cong \angle 8$. $\ell \parallel m$ by the Conv. of Corr. $\angle$s Post. **15.** $m\angle 1 = 55°$, and $m\angle 5 = 55°$, so $\angle 1 \cong \angle 5$. $\ell \parallel m$ by the Conv. of Corr. $\angle$s Post. **17.** $\angle 2 \cong \angle 7$, so $n \parallel p$ by the Conv. of Alt. Ext. $\angle$s Thm. **19.** $m\angle 1 = 105°$, and $m\angle 8 = 105°$, so $\angle 1 \cong \angle 8$. $n \parallel p$ by the Conv. of Alt. Ext. $\angle$s Thm. **21.** $m\angle 3 = 75°$, and $m\angle 5 = 105°$. $75° + 105° = 180°$, so $\angle 3$ and $\angle 5$ are supp. $n \parallel p$ by the Conv. of Same-Side Int. $\angle$s Thm. **23.** If $x = 6$, then $m\angle 1 = 20°$ and $m\angle 2 = 20°$. So $\overline{DJ} \parallel \overline{EK}$ by the Conv. of Corr. $\angle$s Post. **25.** Conv. of Alt. Ext. $\angle$s Thm. **27.** Conv. of Corr. $\angle$s Post. **29.** Conv. of Same-Side Int. $\angle$s Thm. **31.** $m \parallel n$; Conv. of Same-Side Int. $\angle$s Thm. **33.** $m \parallel n$; Conv. of Alt. Ext. $\angle$s Thm. **35.** $\ell \parallel n$; Conv. of Same-Side Int. $\angle$s Thm. **37a.** $\angle URT$; $m\angle URT = m\angle URS + m\angle SRT$ by the $\angle$ Add. Post. It is given that $m\angle SRT = 25°$ and $m\angle URS = 90°$, so $m\angle URT = 25° + 90° = 115°$. **b.** It is given that $m\angle SUR = 65°$. From part **a**, $m\angle URT = 115°$. $65° + 115° = 180°$, so $\overleftrightarrow{SU} \parallel \overleftrightarrow{RT}$ by the Conv. of Same-Side Int. $\angle$s Thm. **39.** It is given that $\angle 1$ and $\angle 2$ are supp., so $m\angle 1 + m\angle 2 = 180°$. By the Lin. Pair Thm., $m\angle 2 + m\angle 3 = 180°$. By the Trans. Prop. of =, $m\angle 1 + m\angle 2 = m\angle 2 + m\angle 3$. By the Subtr. Prop. of =, $m\angle 1 = m\angle 3$. By the Conv. of Corr. $\angle$s Post., $\ell \parallel m$. **41.** The Reflex. Prop. is not true for $\parallel$ lines, because a line is not $\parallel$ to itself. The Sym. Prop. is true, because if $\ell \parallel m$, then ℓ and m are coplanar and do not intersect. So $m \parallel \ell$. The Trans. Prop. is not true for $\parallel$ lines, because if $\ell \parallel m$ and $m \parallel n$, then ℓ and n could be the same line. So they would not be $\parallel$. **43.** C **45.** 15 **47.** No lines can be proven $\parallel$. **49.** $q \parallel r$ by the Conv. of Alt. Int. $\angle$s Thm. **51.** $s \parallel t$ by the Conv. of Alt. Ext. $\angle$s Thm. **53.** No lines can be proven $\parallel$. **55.** By the Vert. $\angle$s Thm., $\angle 6 \cong \angle 3$, so $m\angle 6 = m\angle 3$. It is given that $m\angle 2 + m\angle 3 = 180°$. By subst., $m\angle 2 + m\angle 6 = 180°$. By the Conv. of Same-Side Int. $\angle$s Thm., $\ell \parallel m$.

3-4

Check It Out! **1a.** $\overline{AB}$ **1b.** $x < 17$
2. 1. $\angle EHF \cong \angle HFG$ (Given)
2. $\overleftrightarrow{EH} \parallel \overleftrightarrow{FG}$ (Conv. of Alt. Int. $\angle$s Thm.)
3. $\overleftrightarrow{FG} \perp \overleftrightarrow{GH}$ (Given)
4. $\overleftrightarrow{EH} \perp \overleftrightarrow{GH}$ ($\perp$ Transv. Thm.)

3. The shoreline and the path of the swimmer should both be $\perp$ to the current, so they should be $\parallel$ to each other.

Exercises **1.** $\overline{AB}$ and $\overleftrightarrow{CD}$ are $\perp$. $\overline{AC}$ and $\overline{BC}$ are $\cong$. **3.** $x > -5$ **5.** The service lines are coplanar lines that are $\perp$ to the same line (the center line), so they must be $\parallel$ to each other. **7.** $x < 11$ **9.** Both the frets are lines that are $\perp$ to the same line (the string), so the frets must be $\parallel$ to each other. **11.** $x > \frac{8}{3}$ **13.** $x = 6, y = 15$ **15.** $x = 60, y = 60$ **17.** no **19.** no **21.** yes **23a.** It is given that $\overline{QR} \perp \overline{PQ}$ and $\overline{PQ} \parallel \overline{RS}$, so $\overline{QR} \perp \overline{RS}$ by the $\perp$ Transv. Thm. It is given that $\overline{PS} \parallel \overline{QR}$. Since $\overline{QR} \perp \overline{RS}$, $\overline{PS} \perp \overline{RS}$ by the $\perp$ Transv. Thm. **b.** It is given that $\overline{PS} \parallel \overline{QR}$ and $\overline{QR} \perp \overline{PQ}$. So $\overline{PQ} \perp \overline{PS}$ by the $\perp$Transv. Thm. **25.** Possible answer: 1.6 cm **31.** C **33.** D **35a.** $n \perp p$ **b.** AB; AB; the shortest distance from a point to a line is measured along a perpendicular segment. **c.** The distance between two parallel lines is the length of a segment that is perpendicular to both lines and has one endpoint on each line.

3-5

Check It Out! **1.** $m = 2$ **2.** 390 m **3a.** $\perp$ **3b.** neither **3c.** $\parallel$

Exercises **1.** rise; run **3.** $m = -\frac{5}{9}$ **5.** $m = \frac{5}{2}$ **7.** $\parallel$ **9.** neither **11.** $m = 0$ **13.** $m = -\frac{7}{3}$ **15.** $\parallel$ **17.** $\perp$ **19.** $m = \frac{1}{10}$ **21.** $m = \frac{1}{2}$ **23.** $m < -1$ **25a.** 66 ft/s **b.** 45 mi/h **27.** F **29.** $\overleftrightarrow{JK}$ is a vert. line. **33.** Possible answer: $x = 1$, $y = -6$

3-6

Check It Out! **1a.** $y = 6$ **1b.** $y - 2 = 0$

2a.

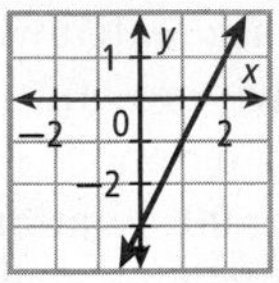

2b.

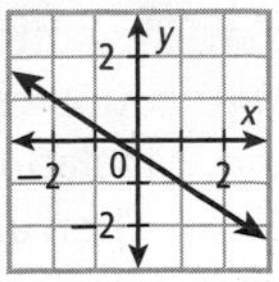

2c.

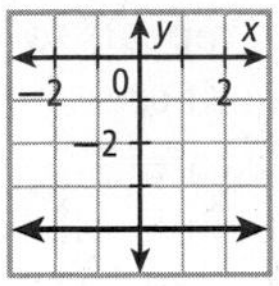

3. parallel **4.** The lines would be $\parallel$.

Exercises **1.** The slope-intercept form of an equation is solved for y. The x term is first, and the constant term is second. **3.** $y - 2 = \frac{3}{4}(x + 4)$

5.

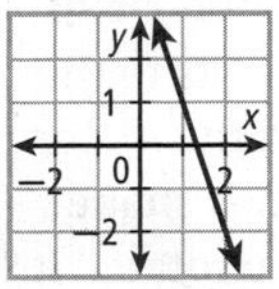

7.

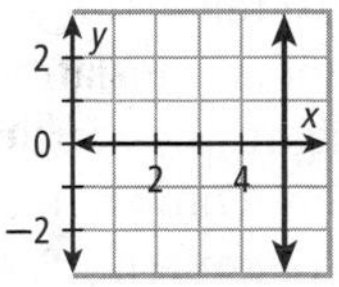

9. intersect **11.** $\parallel$ **13.** $y + 2 = 2x$ **15.** $y + 4 = \frac{2}{3}(x - 6)$

17.

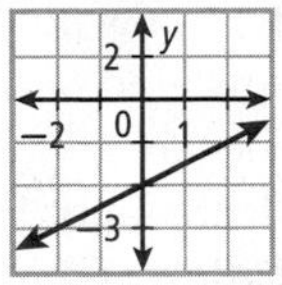

19. intersect **21.** coincide **23.** \$1000 per week **33.** no **35.** yes **37.** $\parallel$ line: $y = 3x - 3$; $\perp$ line: $y = -\frac{1}{3}x + \frac{11}{3}$ **39.** $\parallel$ line: $y = -\frac{4}{3}x + \frac{10}{3}$; $\perp$ line: $y = \frac{3}{4}x - 5$ **41.** yes; $\angle B$ **43.** no **45.** For 4 toppings, both pizzas will cost \$14. **47.** $y = -\frac{1}{2}x + \frac{17}{2}$ **49.** $y = 2x + \frac{7}{2}$ **51.** $y = 2x - 1$; $(2, 3)$; $\sqrt{5}$ units

53a–b. Distance Traveled

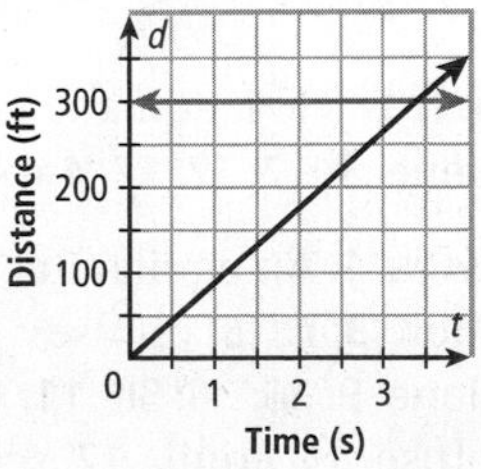

b. the time when the car has traveled 300 ft **c.** Possible answer: 3.5 s **59.** J **61.** J **63.** Possible answer: $y = -\frac{8}{15}x + 8$ **65.** no

Study Guide: Review

1. alternate interior angles **2.** skew lines **3.** transversal **4.** point-slope form **5.** rise; run **6.** Possible answer: $\overline{DE}$ and $\overline{BC}$ are skew. **7.** $\overline{AB} \parallel \overline{DE}$ **8.** $\overline{AD} \perp \overline{DE}$ **9.** plane $ABC \parallel$ plane DEF **10.** ℓ; alt. int. $\angle$s **11.** n; corr. $\angle$s **12.** ℓ; same-side int. $\angle$s **13.** m; alt. ext. $\angle$s **14.** $m\angle WYZ = 90°$ **15.** $m\angle KLM = 100°$ **16.** $m\angle DEF = 79°$ **17.** $m\angle QRS = 76°$ **18.** $\angle 4 \cong \angle 6$, so $c \parallel d$ by the Conv. of Alt. Int. $\angle$s Thm. **19.** $m\angle 1 = 107°$ and $m\angle 5 = 107°$, so $\angle 1 \cong \angle 5$. $c \parallel d$ by the Conv. of Corr. $\angle$s Post. **20.** $m\angle 6 = 66°$, $m\angle 3 = 114°$, and $66° + 114° \neq 180°$, so $\angle 6$ and $\angle 3$ are supp. $c \parallel d$ by the Conv. of Same-Side Int. $\angle$s Thm. **21.** $m\angle 1 \neq 99°$, and $m\angle 7 = 99°$, so $\angle 1 \cong \angle 7$. $c \parallel d$ by the Conv. of Alt. Ext. $\angle$s Thm. **22.** $\overline{KM}$ **23.** $x < 13$

24. 1. $\overline{AD} \parallel \overline{BC}$, $\overline{AD} \perp \overline{AB}$, $\overline{DC} \perp \overline{BC}$ (Given);
2. $\overline{AB} \perp \overline{BC}$ ($\perp$ Transv. Thm.);
3. $\overline{AB} \parallel \overline{CD}$ (2 lines $\perp$ to same line $\rightarrow$ 2 lines $\parallel$)

25. $m = -\frac{1}{7}$ **26.** $m = \frac{5}{3}$ **27.** neither **28.** $\parallel$ **29.** $\perp$ **30.** $y = -\frac{4}{9}x + \frac{11}{3}$ **31.** $y = \frac{2}{3}x - 2$ **32.** $y - 0 = 2(x - 1)$ **33.** $\parallel$ **34.** intersect **35.** coincide

Selected Answers ▪ Chapter 4

4-1

Check It Out! 1. $D'(3, 9)$, $E'(3, -6)$, $F'(9, 0)$; dilation with scale factor 3 **2.** The triangles are congruent because $\triangle ABC$ can be mapped to $\triangle PQR$ by a rotation: $(x, y) \longrightarrow (-y, x)$. **3.** The polygons are congruent because $\triangle ABC$ can be mapped to $\triangle A'B'C'$ by a translation: $(x, y) \longrightarrow (x + 5, y + 2)$; and then $\triangle A'B'C'$ can be mapped to $\triangle PQR$ by a reflection $(x, y) \longrightarrow (x, -y)$.

Exercises 1. are not **3.** $A'(2, -1)$, $B'(5, -4)$, $C'(5, -1)$; This is a reflection across the x-axis. **5.** $L'(2, -1)$, $M'(5, -4)$, $N'(5, -1)$, $O'(5, -1)$; This is a 90° rotation clockwise with a center of rotation (0, 0). **7.** The rectangles are not congruent because rectangle *ABCD* can be mapped to rectangle *WXYZ* by a dilation with scale factor $k \neq 1$. $(x, y) \longrightarrow (0.5x, 0.5y)$. **9.** The triangles are congruent because $\triangle MNO$ can be mapped to $\triangle M'N'O'$ by a reflection: $(x, y) \longrightarrow (-x, y)$. And then $\triangle M'N'O'$ can be mapped to $\triangle JKL$ by a translation: $(x, y) \longrightarrow (x, y + 2)$. **11.** Repeated horizontal reflections and horizontal translations create the wallpaper pattern. The large flower at the top is translated right and left while the stem, leaves, smaller flowers, and background design are reflected to the left and right to create an image that is congruent to the pre-image. **13.** $G'(9, -5)$, $H'(12, -1)$, $I'(12, -5)$; This is a translation 5 units right and 4 units down. **15.** $L'(-1.5, 6)$, $M'(-6, 6)$, $N'(-6, 4.5)$; This is a dilation with scale factor 1.5 and center (0, 0). **17.** $N'(0, -1)$, $O'(-1, 5)$, $P'(1, 5)$; This is a translation 1 unit left and 1 unit up. **19.** Yes, the rectangles are congruent because rectangle *JKLM* can be mapped to rectangle *ABCD* by a rotation: $(x, y) \longrightarrow (y, -x)$. **21.** Yes, the triangles are congruent because $\triangle EFG$ can be mapped to $\triangle UVW$ by a translation: $(x, y) \longrightarrow (x, y + 3)$. **23.** The triangles are congruent because $\triangle ABC$ can be mapped to $\triangle A'B'C'$ by a rotation: $(x, y) \longrightarrow (y, -x)$, and then $\triangle A'B'C'$ can be mapped to $\triangle DEF$ by a translation: $(x, y) \longrightarrow (x - 2, y)$. **25a.** The pattern was created with a 90° counterclockwise rotation and translation to the right and down. Then another 90° rotation clockwise and a translation right and down. This then repeats to fill the rectangular quilt area. **b.** The thin rectangles are congruent, as are the quilt block squares. c. The quilt would look more like a checkerboard pattern. **27.** $X'(4, 6)$, $Y'(4, -4)$, $Z'(-2, 0)$; This is a rotation 90° clockwise about (0, 0) 29. $A'(2, -5)$, $B'(4, -4)$, $C'(-1, 2)$; This is a reflection across the *x*-axis and a translation 3 units to the right. **31.** Starting in the upper left, Frank reflected his shape horizontally. Then he rotated it 90° counterclockwise and translated it to the right and up. The he reflected it vertically. This whole row he then rotated 180° and translated down. **33.** Dave is correct because the triangle was reflected, not rotated. **35.** The dilation of the figure with a scale factor of 2 will be 4 times as large as the figure with a scale factor of 0.5. A scale factor of 2 increases the figure to twice its original size. A scale factor of 0.5 decreases the figure to half its original size. **37.** D

4-2

Check It Out! 1. equiangular **2.** scalene **3.** 17; 17; 17 **4a.** 4 **4b.** 3

Exercises 1. An equilateral $\triangle$ has 3 $\cong$ sides. **3.** rt. **5.** obtuse **7.** scalene **9.** 36; 36; 36 **11.** 6 **13.** obtuse **15.** equil. **17.** scalene **19.** 8.6; 8.6 **21.** 18 ft; 18 ft; 24 ft

23.

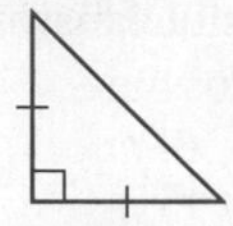

25.

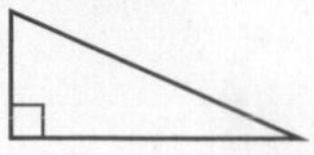

27. not possible **29.** 35 in. **31.** isosc. rt. **33a.** 173 ft; 87 ft **b.** scalene **35.** S **37.** A **41.** D **43.** D **45.** It is an isosc. $\triangle$ since 2 sides of the $\triangle$ have length *a*. It is a rt. $\triangle$ since 2 sides of the $\triangle$ lie on the coord. axes and form a rt. $\angle$. **47.** $y = -3$

4-3

Check It Out! 1. 32° **2a.** 26.3° **2b.** $(90 - x)^\circ$ **2c.** $41\frac{3}{5}^\circ$ **3.** 141° **4.** 32°; 32°

Exercises 3. auxiliary lines **5.** 36°; 80°; 64° **7.** $(90 - y)^\circ$ **9.** 28° **11.** 52°; 63° **13.** 89°; 89° **15.** 84° **17.** $(90 - 2x)^\circ$ **19.** 162° **21.** 48°; 48° **23.** 15°; 60°; 105° **29.** 36° **31.** 48° **33.** 120°; 360° **35.** 18° **37.** The ext. ∠s at the same vertex of a $\triangle$ are vert. ∠s. Since vert. ∠s are $\cong$, the 2 ext. ∠s have the same measure. **41.** C **43.** D **45.** $y = 7$ or $y = -7$ **47.** Since an ext. $\angle$ is = to a sum of 2 remote int. ∠s, it must be greater than either $\angle$. Therefore it cannot be $\cong$ to a remote int. $\angle$. **49.** 38°

4-4

Check It Out! 1. $\angle L \cong \angle E$, $\angle M \cong \angle F$, $\angle N \cong \angle G$, $\angle P \cong \angle H$, $\overline{LM} \cong \overline{EF}$, $\overline{MN} \cong \overline{FG}$, $\overline{NP} \cong \overline{GH}$, $\overline{LP} \cong \overline{EH}$ **2a.** 4 **2b.** 37°

3.
1. $\angle A \cong \angle D$ (Given)
2. $\angle BCA \cong \angle ECD$ (Vert. ∠s are $\cong$.)
3. $\angle ABC \cong \angle DEC$ (Third ∠s Thm.)
4. $\overline{AB} \cong \overline{DE}$ (Given)
5. $\overline{AD}$ bisects $\overline{BE}$, and $\overline{BE}$ bisects $\overline{AD}$. (Given)
6. $\overline{BC} \cong \overline{EC}$, $\overline{AC} \cong \overline{DC}$ (Def. of bisector)
7. $\triangle ABC \cong \triangle DEC$ (Def. of $\cong$ △s)

4.
1. $\overline{JK} \parallel \overline{ML}$ (Given)
2. $\angle KJN \cong \angle MLN$, $\angle JKN \cong \angle LMN$ (Alt. Int. ∠s Thm.)
3. $\angle JNK \cong \angle LNM$ (Vert. ∠s Thm.)
4. $\overline{JK} \cong \overline{ML}$ (Given)
5. $\overline{MK}$ bisects $\overline{JL}$, and $\overline{JL}$ bisects $\overline{MK}$. (Given)
6. $\overline{JN} \cong \overline{LN}$, $\overline{MN} \cong \overline{KN}$ (Def. of bisector)
7. $\triangle JKN \cong \triangle MLN$ (Def. of $\cong$ △s)

Exercises **1.** You find the ∠s and sides that are in the same, or matching, places in the 2 △s. **3.** $\overline{LM}$ **5.** $\angle M$ **7.** $\angle R$ **9.** $KL = 9$ **11a.** Given **b.** Alt. Int. ∠s Thm. **c.** Given **d.** Given **e.** $\overline{AE} \cong \overline{CE}$, $\overline{DE} \cong \overline{BE}$; **f.** Vert. ∠s Thm. **g.** Def. of ≅ △s **13.** $\overline{LM}$ **15.** $\angle N$ **17.** $m\angle C = 31°$ **19a.** Given **b.** Given **c.** $\angle NMP \cong \angle RMP$ **d.** $\angle NPM \cong \angle RPM$ **e.** Given **f.** $\overline{PN} \cong \overline{PR}$ **g.** Given **h.** Reflex. Prop. of ≅ **21.** $\triangle GSR \cong \triangle KPH$; $\triangle SRG \cong \triangle PHK$; $\triangle RGS \cong \triangle HKP$ **23.** $x = 30$; $AB = 50$ **25.** $x = 2$; $BC = 17$ **29.** solution A **31.** B **33.** D **35.** $x = 5.5$; yes; $UV = WV = 41.5$, and $UT = WT = 33$. $TV = TV$ by the Reflex. Prop. of =. It is given that $\angle VWT \cong \angle VUT$ and $\angle WTV \cong \angle UTV$. $\angle WVT \cong \angle UVT$ by the Third ∠s Thm. Thus $\triangle TUV \cong \triangle TWV$ by the def. of ≅ △s.

4-5

Check It Out! **1.** It is given that $\overline{AB} \cong \overline{CD}$ and $\overline{BC} \cong \overline{DA}$. By the Reflex. Prop. of ≅, $\overline{AC} \cong \overline{CA}$. So $\triangle ABC \cong \triangle CDA$ by SSS. **2.** It is given that $\overline{BA} \cong \overline{BD}$ and $\angle ABC \cong \angle DBC$. By the Reflex. Prop. of ≅, $\overline{BC} \cong \overline{BC}$. So $\triangle ABC \cong \triangle DBC$ by SAS. **3.** $DA = DC = 13$, so $\overline{DA} = \overline{DC}$ by def. of ≅. $m\angle ADB = m\angle CDB = 32°$, so $\angle ADB \cong \angle CDB$ by def. of ≅. $\overline{DB} \cong \overline{DB}$ by the Reflex. Prop. of ≅. Therefore $\triangle ADB \cong \triangle CDB$ by SAS.

4. 1. $\overline{QR} \cong \overline{QS}$ (Given)
2. $\overrightarrow{QP}$ bisects $\angle RQS$. (Given)
3. $\angle RQP \cong \angle SQP$ (Def. of bisector)
4. $\overline{QP} \cong \overline{QP}$ (Reflex. Prop. of ≅)
5. $\triangle RQP \cong \triangle SQP$ (SAS *Steps 1, 3, 4*)

Exercises **1.** $\angle T$ **3.** It is given that $\overline{MN} \cong \overline{MQ}$ and $\overline{NP} \cong \overline{QP}$. $\overline{MP} \cong \overline{MP}$ by the Reflex. Prop. of ≅. Thus $\triangle MNP \cong \triangle MQP$ by SSS. **5.** When $x = 4$, $HI = GH = 3$, and $IJ = GJ = 5$. $\overline{HJ} \cong \overline{HJ}$ by the Reflex. Prop. of ≅. Therefore $\triangle GHJ \cong \triangle IHJ$ by SSS. **7a.** Given **b.** $\angle JKL \cong \angle MLK$ **c.** Reflex. Prop. of ≅ **d.** SAS *Steps 1, 2, 3* **9.** It is given that $\overline{KJ} \cong \overline{LJ}$ and $\overline{GK} \cong \overline{GL}$. $\overline{GJ} \cong \overline{GJ}$ by the Reflex. Prop. of ≅. So $\triangle GJK \cong \triangle GJL$ by SSS. **11.** When $y = 3$, $NQ = NM = 3$, and $QP = MP = 4$. So by the def. of ≅, $\overline{NQ} \cong \overline{NM}$ and $\overline{QP} \cong \overline{MP}$. $m\angle M = m\angle Q = 90°$, so $\angle M \cong \angle Q$ by the def. of ≅. Thus $\triangle MNP \cong \triangle QNP$ by SAS. **13a.** Given **b.** $\overline{DB} \cong \overline{CB}$ **c.** $\overline{AB} \perp \overline{DC}$ **d.** Def. of ⊥ **e.** Rt. ∠ ≅ Thm. **f.** $\overline{AB} \cong \overline{AB}$ **g.** SAS *Steps 2, 5, 6* **15.** SAS **17.** neither **19.** $QS = TV = \sqrt{5}$. $SR = VU = 4$. $QR = TU = \sqrt{13}$. The △s are ≅ by SSS. **21a.** Given **b.** Def. of ≅ **c.** $m\angle WVY = m\angle ZYV$ **d.** Def. of ≅ **e.** Given **f.** $\overline{VY} \cong \overline{YV}$ **g.** SAS *Steps 6, 5, 7* **25.** Measure the lengths of the logs. If the lengths of the logs in 1 wing deflector match the lengths of the logs in the other wing deflector, the △s will be ≅ by SAS or SSS. **27.** Yes; if each side is ≅ to the corr. side of the second △, they can be in any order. **29.** G **31.** J **35.** $x = 27$; $FK = FH = 171$, so $\overline{FK} \cong \overline{FH}$ by the def of ≅. $\angle KFJ \cong \angle HFJ$ by the def. of ∠ bisector. $\overline{FJ} = \overline{FJ}$ by the Reflex. Prop. of ≅. So $\triangle FJK \cong \triangle FJH$ by SAS.

4-6

Check It Out! **1.** Yes; the △ is uniquely determined by AAS. **2.** By the Alt. Int. ∠s Thm., $\angle KLN \cong \angle MNL$. $\overline{LN} \cong \overline{LN}$ by the Reflex. Prop. of ≅. No other congruence relationships can be determined, so ASA cannot be applied.

3. Given: $\overline{JL}$ bisects $\angle KLM$, and $\angle K \cong \angle M$.
Prove: $\triangle JKL \cong \triangle JML$

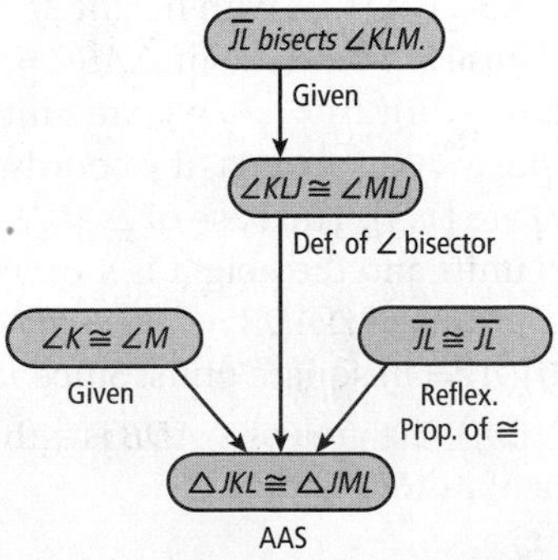

4. Yes; it is given that $\overline{AC} \cong \overline{DB}$. $\overline{CB} \cong \overline{CB}$ by the Reflex. Prop. of ≅. Since $\angle ABC$ and $\angle DCB$ are rt. ∠s, $\triangle ABC$ and $\triangle DCB$ are rt. △s, $\triangle ABC \cong \triangle DCB$ by HL.

Exercises **1.** The included side $\overline{BC}$ is enclosed between $\angle ABC$ and $\angle ACB$. **3.** Yes, the △ is determined by AAS. **5.** No; you need to know that a pair of corr. sides are ≅. **7.** Yes; it is given that $\angle D$ and $\angle B$ are rt. ∠s and $\overline{AD} \cong \overline{BC}$. $\triangle ABC$ and $\triangle CDA$ are rt. △s by def. $\overline{AC} \cong \overline{CA}$ by the Reflex. Prop. of ≅. So $\triangle ABC \cong \triangle CDA$ by HL.

9.

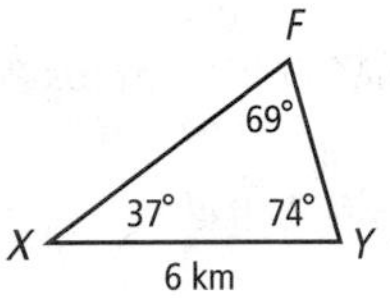

11. No; you need to know that $\angle MKJ \cong \angle MKL$. **13a.** $\angle A \cong \angle D$ **b.** Given **c.** $\angle C \cong \angle F$ **d.** AAS **15.** Yes; E is a mdpt. So by def., $\overline{BE} \cong \overline{CE}$, and $\overline{AE} \cong \overline{DE}$. $\angle A$ and $\angle D$ are ≅ by the Rt. ∠ ≅ Thm. By def. $\triangle ABE$ and $\triangle DCE$ are rt. △s. So $\triangle ABE \cong \triangle DCE$ by HL. **17.** $\triangle FEG \cong \triangle QSR$; rotation **19a.** No; there is not enough information given to use any of the congruence theorems. **b.** HL **21.** It is given that $\triangle ABC$ and $\triangle DEF$ are rt.△s. $\overline{AC} \cong \overline{DF}$, $\overline{BC} \cong \overline{EF}$, and $\angle C$ and $\angle F$ are rt. ∠s. $\angle C \cong \angle F$ by the Rt. ∠ ≅ Thm. Thus $\triangle ABC \cong \triangle DEF$ by SAS. **27.** J **29.** G **31.** Yes; the sum of the ∠ measures in each △ must be 180°, which makes it possible to solve for x and y. The value of x is 15, and the value of y is 12. Each △ has ∠s measuring 82°, 68°, and 30°. $\overline{VU} \cong \overline{VU}$ by the Reflex. Prop. of ≅. So $\triangle VSU \cong \triangle VTU$ by ASA or AAS.

4-7

Check It Out! **1.** 41 ft
2.

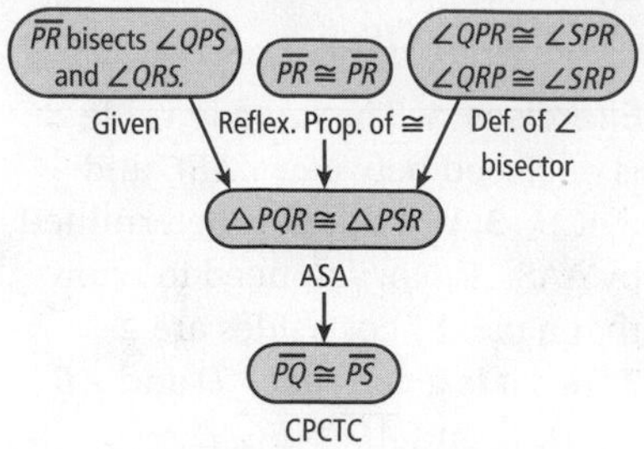

3. **1.** J is the mdpt. of $\overline{KM}$ and $\overline{NL}$. (Given)
2. $\overline{KJ} \cong \overline{MJ}$, $\overline{NJ} \cong \overline{LJ}$ (Def. of mdpt.)
3. $\angle KJL \cong \angle MJN$ (Vert. ∡ Thm.)
4. $\triangle KJL \cong \triangle MJN$ (SAS *Steps 2, 3*)
5. $\angle LKJ \cong \angle NMJ$ (CPCTC)
6. $\overline{KL} \parallel \overline{MN}$ (Conv. of Alt. Int. ∡ Thm.)
4. $RJ = JL = \sqrt{5}$, $RS = JK = \sqrt{10}$, and $ST = KL = \sqrt{17}$. So $\triangle JKL \cong \triangle RST$ by SSS. $\angle JKL \cong \angle RST$ by CPCTC.

Exercises **1.** corr. ∡ and corr. sides. **3a.** Def. of ⊥ **b.** Rt. ∠ ≅ Thm. **c.** Reflex. Prop. of ≅ **d.** Def. of mdpt. **e.** $\triangle RXS \cong \triangle RXT$ **f.** CPCTC
5. $EF = JK = 2$ and $EG = FG = JL = KL = \sqrt{10}$. So $\triangle EFG \cong \triangle JKL$ by SSS. $\angle EFG \cong \angle JKL$ by CPCTC.
7. 420 ft
9. **1.** $\overline{WX} \cong \overline{XY} \cong \overline{YZ} \cong \overline{ZW}$ (Given)
2. $\overline{ZX} \cong \overline{ZX}$ (Reflex. Prop. of ≅)
3. $\triangle WXZ \cong \triangle YZX$ (SSS)
4. $\angle W \cong \angle Y$ (CPCTC)
11. **1.** $\overline{LM}$ bisects $\angle JLK$. (Given)
2. $\angle JLM \cong \angle KLM$ (Def. of ∠ bisector)
3. $\overline{JL} \cong \overline{KL}$ (Given)
4. $\overline{LM} \cong \overline{LM}$ (Reflex. Prop. of ≅)
5. $\triangle JLM \cong \triangle KLM$ (SAS *Steps 3, 2, 4*)
6. $\overline{JM} \cong \overline{KM}$ (CPCTC)
7. M is the mdpt. of $\overline{JK}$. (Def. of mdpt.)
13. $AB = DE = \sqrt{13}$, $BC = EF = 5$, and $AC = DF = \sqrt{18} = 3\sqrt{2}$. So $\triangle ABC \cong \triangle DEF$ by SSS. $\angle BAC \cong \angle EDF$ by CPCTC.
15. **1.** E is the mdpt. of $\overline{AC}$ and $\overline{BD}$. (Given)
2. $\overline{AE} \cong \overline{CE}$; $\overline{BE} \cong \overline{DE}$ (Def. of mdpt.)
3. $\angle AEB \cong \angle CED$ (Vert. ∡ Thm.)
4. $\triangle AEB \cong \triangle CED$ (SAS *Steps 2, 3*)
5. $\angle A \cong \angle C$ (CPCTC)
6. $\overline{AB} \parallel \overline{CD}$ (Conv. of Alt. Int. ∡ Thm.)
17. 14 **25.** G **27.** G **29.** Any diag. on any face of the cube is the hyp. of a rt. △ whose legs are edges of the cube. Any 2 of these ⊿ are ≅ by SAS. Therefore any 2 diags. are ≅ by CPCTC.

4-8

Check It Out!
1. Possible answer:

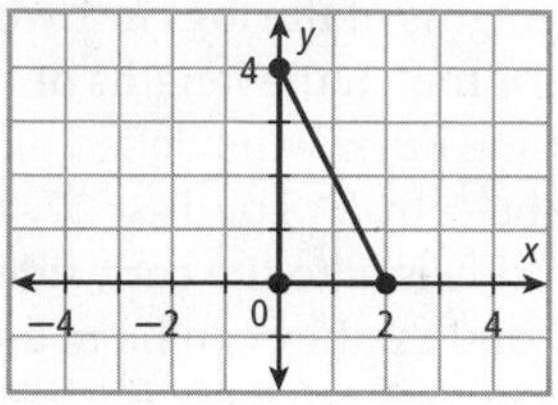

2. $\triangle ABC$ is a rt. △ with height AB and base BC. The area of $\triangle ABC$ is $\frac{1}{2}(4)(6) = 12$ square units. By the Mdpt. Formula, the coords. of D are $\left(\frac{0+4}{2}, \frac{6+0}{2}\right) = (2, 3)$. With $\overline{AB}$ as the base of $\triangle ADB$, the x-coord. of D gives the height of $\triangle ADB$. The area of $\triangle ADB = \frac{1}{2}bh = \frac{1}{2}(6)(2) = 6$ square units. Since $6 = \frac{1}{2}(12)$, the area of $\triangle ADB$ is the area of $\triangle ABC$.
3. Possible answer:

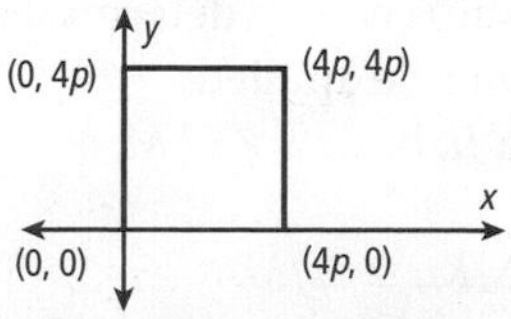

4. $\triangle ABC$ is a rt. △ with height $2j$ and base $2n$. The area of $\triangle ABC = \frac{1}{2}bh = \frac{1}{2}(2n)(2j) = 2nj$ square units. By the Mdpt. Formula, the coords. of D are (n, j). The base of $\triangle ABD$ is $2j$ units and the height is n units. So the area of $\triangle ADB = \frac{1}{2}bh = \frac{1}{2}(2j)(n) = nj$ square units. Since $nj = \frac{1}{2}(2nj)$, the area of $\triangle ADB$ is $\frac{1}{2}$ the area of $\triangle ABC$.

Exercises
7.

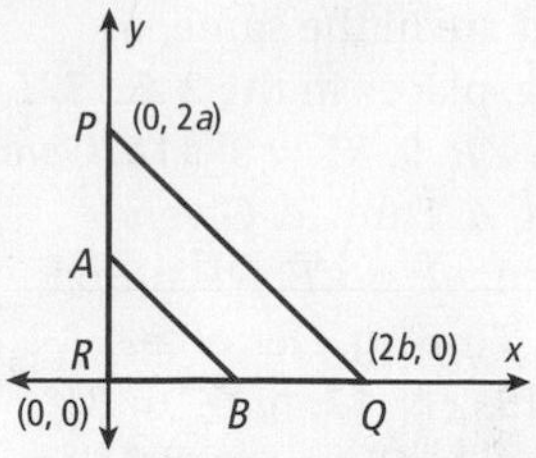

By the Mdpt. Formula, the coords. of A are $(0, a)$ and the coords. of B are $(b, 0)$. By the Dist. Formula, $PQ = \sqrt{(0 - 2b)^2 + (2a)^2} = \sqrt{(-2b)^2 + (2a)^2} = \sqrt{4b^2 + 4a^2} = 2\sqrt{b^2 + a^2}$ units. $AB = \sqrt{(0 - b)^2 + (a - 0)^2} = \sqrt{(-b)^2 + a^2} = \sqrt{b^2 + a^2}$ units. So $AB = \frac{1}{2}PQ$.
13.

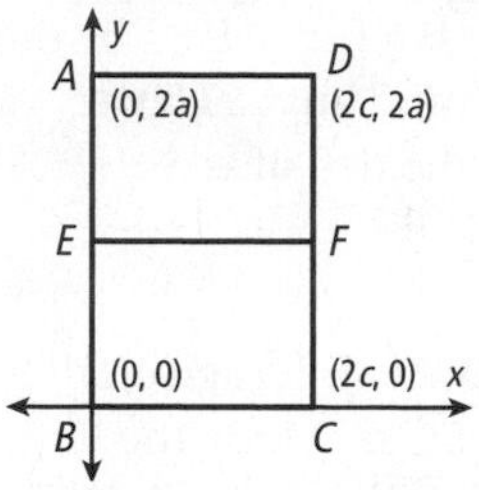

By the Mdpt. Formula, the coords. of E are $(0, a)$ and the coords. of F are $(2c, a)$. By the Dist. Formula, $AD = \sqrt{(2c - 0)^2 + (2a - 2a)^2} = \sqrt{(2c)^2} = 2c$ units. Similarly, $EF = \sqrt{(2c - 0)^2 + (a - a)^2} = \sqrt{(2c)^2} = 2c$ units. So $EF = AD$.
15a.

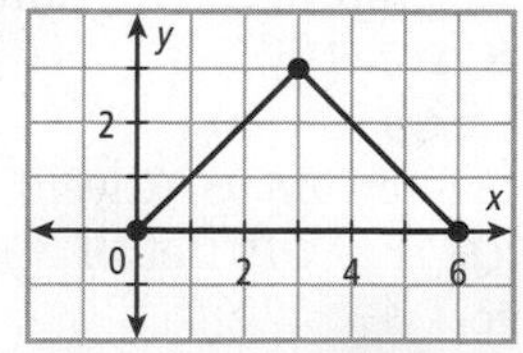

b. 8.5 mi **17.** $2s + 2t$ units; st square units **19.** $(p, 0)$ **21.** $AB \approx 128$ nautical miles; $AP = BP \approx 64$ nautical miles; so P is the mdpt. of $\overline{AB}$. **23.** By the Dist. Formula, $AB = \sqrt{(x_2 - x_1)^2 + (y_2 - y_1)^2}$ and $AM = \sqrt{\left(\frac{x_1 + x_2}{2} - x_1\right)^2 + \left(\frac{y_1 + y_2}{2} - y_1\right)^2} = \sqrt{\left(\frac{x_1 + x_2}{2} - \frac{2x_1}{2}\right)^2 + \left(\frac{y_1 + y_2}{2} - \frac{2y_1}{2}\right)^2} = \sqrt{\frac{1}{4}(x_2 - x_1)^2 + \frac{1}{4}(y_2 - y_1)^2} =$

$\frac{1}{2}\sqrt{(x_2 - x_1)^2 + (y_2 - y_1)^2}$. So $AM = \frac{1}{2}AB$. **27.** B **29.** D **31.** $(a + c, b)$

4-9

Check It Out! 1. 4.2×10^{13}; since it is 6 months between September and March, the ∠ measures will be the same between Earth and the star. By the Conv. of the Isosc. △ Thm., the ⧍ created are isosc. and the dist. is the same. **2a.** 66° **2b.** 48° **3.** 10 **4.** By the Mdpt. Formula, the coords. of X are $(-a, b)$, the coords. of Y are (a, b), and the coords. of Z are $(0, 0)$. By the Dist. Formula, $XZ = YZ = \sqrt{a^2 + b^2}$. So $\overline{XZ} \cong \overline{YZ}$ and $\triangle XYZ$ is isosc.

Exercises 1. legs: $\overline{KJ}$ and $\overline{KL}$; base: $\overline{JL}$; base ∡: $\angle J$ and $\angle L$ **3.** 118° **5.** 27° **7.** $y = 5$ **9.** 20 **11.** It is given that $\triangle ABC$ is rt. isosc., $\overline{AB} \cong \overline{BC}$, and X is the mdpt. of $\overline{AC}$. By the Mdpt. Formula, the coords. of X are(a, a). By the Dist. Formula, $AX = BX = a\sqrt{2}$. So $\triangle AXB$ is isosc. by def. of an isosc. △. **13.** 69° **15.** 130° or 172° **17.** $z = 92$ **19.** 26 **21.** It is given that $\triangle ABC$ is isosc., $\overline{AB} \cong \overline{AC}$, P is the mdpt. of $\overline{AB}$, and Q is the mdpt. of $\overline{AC}$. By the Mdpt. Formula, the coords. of P are (a, b) and the coords. of Q are $(3a, b)$. By the Dist. Formula, $PC = QB = \sqrt{9a^2 + b^2}$, so $\overline{PC} \cong \overline{QB}$ by the def of ≅ segs. **23.** S **25.** N **27a.** 38° **b.** $m\angle PQR = m\angle PRQ = 53°$ **29.** $m\angle 1 = 127°$; $m\angle 2 = 26.5°$; $m\angle 3 = 53°$ **33.** 20
39. 1. $\triangle ABC \cong \triangle CBA$ (Given)
2. $\overline{AB} \cong \overline{CB}$ (CPCTC)
3. $\triangle ABC$ is isosceles (Def. of Isosc)
43. H **47.** $(2a, 0)$, $(0, 2b)$, or any pt. on the ⊥ bisector of $\overline{AB}$

Study Guide: Review

1. isosceles triangle
2. corresponding angles
3. included side **4.** The triangles are congruent because ABC can be mapped to PQR by a rotation: $(x, y) \longrightarrow (-x, -y)$. **5.** $D'(4, 8)$, $E'(8, -12)$, and $F'(16, 0)$; dilation with scale factor 4 and center (0, 0) **6.** equiangular; equil. **7.** obtuse; scalene **8.** 60°
9. 66.5° **10.** $\overline{XZ}$ **11.** $\angle Q$ **12.** 25 **13.** 7
14. 1. $\overline{AB} \cong \overline{DE}$, $\overline{DB} \cong \overline{AE}$ (Given)
2. $\overline{DA} \cong \overline{DA}$ (Reflex. Prop. of ≅)
3. $\triangle ADB \cong \triangle DAE$ (SSS *Steps 1, 2*)
15. 1. $\overline{GJ}$ bisects $\overline{FH}$, and $\overline{FH}$ bisects $\overline{GJ}$. (Given)
2. $\overline{GK} \cong \overline{JK}$, $\overline{FK} \cong \overline{HK}$ (Def. of seg. Bisect)
3. $\angle GKF \cong \angle JKH$ (Vert. ∡ Thm.)
4. $\triangle FGK \cong \triangle HJK$ (SAS *Steps 2, 3*)
16. 1. C is the mdpt. of $\overline{AG}$. (Given)
2. $\overline{GC} \cong \overline{AC}$ (Def. of mdpt.)
3. $\overline{HA} \parallel \overline{GB}$ (Given)
4. $\angle HAC \cong \angle BGC$ (Alt. Int. ∡ Thm.)
5. $\angle HCA \cong \angle BCG$ (Vert. ∡ Thm.)
6. $\triangle HAC \cong \triangle BGC$ (ASA *Steps 4, 2, 5*)
17. 1. $\overline{WX} \perp \overline{XZ}$, $\overline{YZ} \perp \overline{ZX}$ (Given)
2. $\angle WXZ$ and $\angle YZX$ are rt. ∡. (Def. of ⊥)
3. $\triangle WZX$ and $\triangle YXZ$ are rt. ⧍. (Def. of rt. △)
4. $\overline{XZ} \cong \overline{XZ}$ (Reflex. Prop. of ≅)
5. $\overline{WZ} \cong \overline{YX}$ (Given)
6. $\triangle WZX \cong \triangle YXZ$ (HL *Steps 5, 4*)
18. 1. $\angle S$ and $\angle V$ are rt. ∡. (Given)
2. $\angle S \cong \angle V$ (Rt. ∠ ≅ Thm.)
3. $RT = UW$ (Given)
4. $\overline{RT} \cong \overline{UW}$ (Def. of ≅)
5. $m\angle T = m\angle W$ (Given)
6. $\angle T \cong \angle W$ (Def. of ≅)
7. $\triangle RST \cong \triangle UVW$ (AAS *Steps 2, 6, 4*)
19. 1. M is the mdpt. of $\overline{BD}$. (Given)
2. $\overline{MB} \cong \overline{DM}$ (Def. of mdpt.)
3. $\overline{BC} \cong \overline{DC}$ (Given)
4. $\overline{CM} \cong \overline{CM}$ (Reflex. Prop. of ≅)
5. $\triangle CBM \cong \triangle CDM$ (SSS *Steps 2, 3, 4*)
6. $\angle 1 \cong \angle 2$ (CPCTC)
20. 1. $\overline{PQ} \cong \overline{RQ}$ (Given)
2. $\overline{PS} \cong \overline{RS}$ (Given)
3. $\overline{QS} \cong \overline{QS}$ (Reflex. Prop. of ≅)
4. $\triangle PQS \cong \triangle RQS$ (SSS *Steps 1, 2, 3*)
5. $\angle PQS \cong \angle RQS$ (CPCTC)
6. $\overline{QS}$ bisects $\angle PQR$. (Def. of bisect)
21. 1. H is mdpt. of line $\overline{GJ}$, and L is mdpt. of $\overline{MK}$. (Given)
2. $GH = JH$, $ML = KL$ (Def. of mdpt.)
3. $\overline{GH} \cong \overline{JH}$, $\overline{ML} \cong \overline{KL}$ (Def. of ≅)
4. $\overline{GJ} \cong \overline{KM}$ (Given)
5. $\overline{GH} \cong \overline{KL}$ (Div. Prop. of ≅)
6. $\overline{GM} \cong \overline{KJ}$, $\angle G \cong \angle K$ (Given)
7. $\triangle GMH \cong \triangle KJL$ (SAS *Steps 5, 6*)
8. $\angle GMH \cong \angle KJL$ (CPCTC)
22. $(0, 0)$, $(r, 0)$, $(0, s)$ **23.** $(0, 0)$, $(2p, 0)$, $(2p, p)$, $(0, p)$ **24.** $(0, 0)$, $(8m, 0)$, $(8m, 8m)$, $(0, 8m)$ **25.** Use coords. $A(0, 0)$, $B(2a, 0)$, $C(2a, 2b)$, and $D(0, 2b)$. Then, by the Mdpt. Formula, $E(a, 0)$, $F(2a, b)$, $G(a, 2b)$, and $H()$. By the Dist. Formula, $EF = \sqrt{(2a - a)^2 + (b - 0)^2} = \sqrt{a^2 + b^2}$, and $GH = \sqrt{(0 - a)^2 + (b - 2b)^2} = \sqrt{a^2 + b^2}$. So $\overline{EF} \cong \overline{GH}$ by the def. of ≅. **26.** Use coords. $P(0, 2b)$, $Q(0, 0)$, and $R(2a, 0)$. Then, by the Mdpt. Formula, $M(a, b)$. By the Dist. Formula, $QM = \sqrt{(a - 0)^2 + (b - 0)^2} = \sqrt{a^2 + b^2}$, $PM = \sqrt{(a - 0)^2 + (b - 2b)^2} = \sqrt{a^2 + b^2}$, and $RM = \sqrt{(2a - a)^2 + (0 - b)^2} = \sqrt{a^2 + b^2}$. So $QM = PM = RM$. By def. M is equidistant from the vertices of $\triangle PQR$ **27.** To be a rt. △, the side lengths must have lengths such that $a^2 + b^2 = c^2$. $\sqrt{(3 - 3)^2 + (5 - 2)^2} = 3$, $\sqrt{(3 - 2)^2 + (2 - 5)^2} = \sqrt{10}$, and $\sqrt{(2 - 3)^2 + (5 - 5)^2} = 1$. Since $3^2 + 1^2 = \left(\sqrt{10^2}\right)$, or $9 + 1 = 10$, the triangle is a rt. △. **28.** $x = -5$ **29.** $RS = 13.5$ **30.** 70 units

5-1

Check It Out! **1a.** 14.6 **1b.** 10.4 **2a.** 3.05 **2b.** 126° **3.** $\overrightarrow{QS}$ bisects $\angle PQR$. **4.** $y + 1 = -\frac{2}{3}(x - 3)$

Exercises **1.** perpendicular bisector **3.** 25.9 **5.** 21.9 **7.** 38° **9.** $y - 1 = x + 2$ **11.** $y - 2 = \frac{4}{3}(x + 3)$ **13.** 26.5 **15.** 1.3 **17.** 54° **19.** $y + 3 = -\frac{1}{2}(x + 2)$ **21.** $y + 3 = \frac{5}{2}(x - 2)$ **23.** 38 **25.** 38 **27.** 24 **29.** Possible answer: $C(3, 2)$

31. **1.** $\overrightarrow{PS}$ bisects $\angle QPR$. $\overline{SQ} \perp \overrightarrow{PQ}$, $\overline{SR} \perp \overrightarrow{PR}$ (Given)
2. $\angle QPS \cong \angle RPS$ (Def. of ∠ bisector)
3. $\angle SQP$ and $\angle SRP$ are rt. ⦣. (Def. of ⊥)
4. $\angle SQP \cong \angle SRP$ (Rt. ∠ ≅ Thm.)
5. $\overline{PS} \cong \overline{PS}$ (Reflex. Prop. of ≅)
6. $\triangle PQS \cong \triangle PRS$ (AAS)
7. $\overline{SQ} \cong \overline{SR}$ (CPCTC)
8. $SQ = SR$ (Def. of ≅ segs.)

33a. $y = -\frac{3}{4}x + 2$ **b.** 2 **c.** 6.4 mi **35.** D **39.** the lines $y = x$ and $y = -x$

5-2

Check It Out! **1a.** 14.5 **1b.** 18.6 **1c.** 19.9 **2.** $(4, -4.5)$ **3a.** 19.2 **3b.** 52°

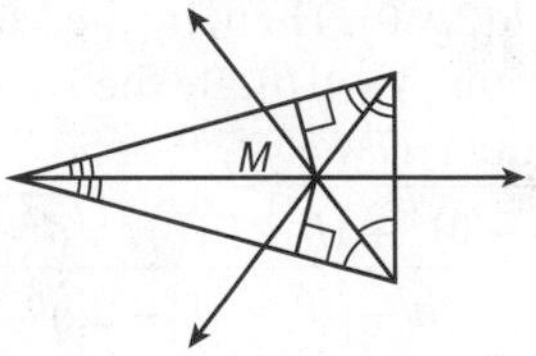

4. By the Incenter Thm., the incenter of a △ is equidistant from the sides of the △. Draw the △ formed by the streets and draw the ∠ bisectors to find the incenter, point *M*. The city should place the monument at point *M*.

Exercises **1.** They do not intersect at a single point. **3.** 5.64 **5.** 3.95 **7.** $(2, 6)$ **9.** 42.1 **11.** The largest possible ⊙ in the int. of the △ is its inscribed ⊙, and the center of the inscribed ⊙ is the incenter. Draw the △ and its ∠ bisectors. Center the ⊙ at *E*, the pt. of concurrency of the ∠ bisectors. **13.** 63.9 **15.** 63.9 **17.** $(-1.5, 9.5)$ **19.** 55° **23.** perpendicular bisector **25.** angle bisector **27.** neither **29.** S **31.** N **33.** $(4, 3)$ **35a.** ∠ Bisector Thm. **b.** the bisector of $\angle B$ **c.** $PX = PZ$ **37a.** $\left(4, -\frac{7}{6}\right)$ **b.** outside **c.** 4.2 mi **41.** F

5-3

Check It Out! **1a.** 21 **1b.** 5.4 **2.** 3; 4; possible answer: the *x*-coordinate of the centroid is the average of the *x*-coordinates of the vertices of the △, and the *y*-coordinate of the centroid is the average of the *y*-coordinates of the vertices of the △. **3.** Possible answer: An equation of the altitude to $\overline{JK}$ is $y = -\frac{1}{2}x + 3$. It is true that $4 = -\frac{1}{2}(-2) + 3$, so $(-2, 4)$ is a solution of this equation. Therefore this altitude passes through the orthocenter.

Exercises **1.** centroid **3.** 136 **5.** 156 **7.** $(4, 2)$ **9.** $(2, -3)$ **11.** $(-1, 2)$ **13.** 7.2 **15.** 5.8 **17.** $(0, -2)$ **19.** $(-2, 9)$ **21.** 12 **23.** 5 **25.** 36 units **27.** $(10, -2)$ **29.** 54 **31.** 48 **33.** Possible answer: ⊥ bisector of the base; bisector of the vertex ∠; median to the base; altitude to the base **35.** A **37.** A **41.** D **43.** D **45a.** slope of $\overline{RS} = \frac{c}{b}$; slope of $\overline{ST} = \frac{c}{b - a}$; slope of $\overline{RT} = 0$ **b.** Since $\ell \perp \overline{RS}$, slope of $\ell = -\frac{b}{c}$. Since $m \perp \overline{ST}$, slope of $m = -\frac{b - a}{c} = \frac{a - b}{c}$. Since $n \perp \overline{RT}$, *n* is a vertical line, and its slope is undefined. **c.** An equation of ℓ is $y - 0 = -\frac{b}{c}(x - a)$, or $y = -\frac{b}{c}x + \frac{ab}{c}$. An equation of *m* is $y - 0 = \frac{a - b}{c}(x - 0)$, or $y = \frac{a - b}{c}x$. An equation of *n* is $x = b$. **d.** $\left(b, \frac{ab - b^2}{c}\right)$ **e.** Since the equation of line *n* is $x = b$ and the *x*-coordinate of *P* is *b*, *P* lies on *n*. **f.** Lines ℓ, *m*, and *n* are concurrent at *P*.

5-4

Check It Out! **1.** $M(1, 1)$; $N(3, 4)$; slope of $\overline{MN} = \frac{3}{2}$; slope of $\overline{RS} = \frac{3}{2}$; since the slopes are the same, $\overline{MN} \parallel \overline{RS}$. $MN = \sqrt{13}$; $RS = \sqrt{52} = 2\sqrt{13}$; the length of $\overline{MN}$ is half the length of $\overline{RS}$. **2a.** 72 **2b.** 48.5 **2c.** 102° **3.** 775 m

Exercises **1.** midpoints **3.** 5.1 **5.** 5.6 **7.** 29° **9.** less than 5 yd **11.** 38 **13.** 19 **15.** 55° **17.** yes **19.** 17 **21.** $n = 36$ **23.** $n = 8$ **25.** $n = 4$ **27.** B **29.** Possible answer: about 18 parking spaces **31.** 11 **33.** 57° **35.** 123° **37a.** 2.25 mi **b.** 28.5 mi **39.** D **41.** D **43.** equilateral and equiangular **45.** 7 **47a.** 32; 16; 8; 4 **b.** $\frac{1}{4}$ **c.** $64\left(\frac{1}{2}\right)^n = 2^{6-n}$

5-5

Check It Out!

1. Possible answer:
Given: $\triangle RST$
Prove: $\triangle RST$ cannot have 2 rt. ⦣.
Proof: Assume that $\triangle RST$ has 2 rt. ⦣. Let $\angle R$ and $\angle S$ be the rt. ⦣. By the def. of rt. ∠, $m\angle R = 90°$ and $m\angle S = 90°$. By the △ Sum Thm., $m\angle R + m\angle S + m\angle T = 180°$. But then $90° + 90° + m\angle T = 180°$ by subst., so $m\angle T = 0°$. However, a △ cannot have an ∠ with a measure of 0°. So there is no $\triangle RST$, which contradicts the given information. This means the assumption is false, and $\triangle RST$ cannot have 2 rt. ⦣.

2a. $\angle B$, $\angle A$, $\angle C$ **2b.** $\overline{EF}$, $\overline{DF}$, $\overline{DE}$ **3a.** No; $8 + 13 = 21$, which is not greater than the third side length. **3b.** Yes; the sum of each pair of 2 lengths is greater than the third length. **3c.** Yes; when $t = 4$, the value of $t - 2$ is 2, the value of $4t$ is 16, and the value of $t^2 + 1$ is 17. The sum of each pair of 2 lengths is greater than the third length. **4.** greater than 5 in. and less than 39 in. **5.** 28 mi < *d* < 72 mi

Exercises

3. Possible answer:
Given: $\triangle PQR$ is an isosc. △ with base $\overline{PR}$.
Prove: $\triangle PQR$ cannot have a base ∠ that is a rt. ∠.
Proof: Assume that $\triangle PQR$ has a base ∠ that is a rt. ∠. Let $\angle P$ be

the rt ∠. By the Isosc. △ Thm., ∠R ≅ ∠P, so ∠R is also a rt. ∠. By the def. of rt. ∠, m∠P = 90° and m∠R = 90°. By the △ Sum Thm., m∠P + m∠Q + m∠R = 180°. By subst., 90° + m∠Q + 90° = 180°, so m∠Q = 0°. However, a △ cannot have an ∠ with a measure of 0°. So there is no △PQR, which contradicts the given information. This means the assumption is false, and therefore △PQR cannot have a base ∠ that is rt.
5. $\overline{YZ}, \overline{XZ}, \overline{XY}$ **7.** no **9.** no **11.** yes **13.** greater than 0 ft and less than 32 ft **15a.** the path from the refrigerator to the stove **b.** no **19.** $\overline{RS}, \overline{ST}, \overline{RT}$ **21.** no **23.** yes **25.** no **27.** greater than 5 km and less than 51 km **29.** greater than 1.18 m and less than 4.96 m **31.** greater than $2\frac{2}{3}$ ft and less than $10\frac{1}{3}$ ft **33.** $a > 7.5$, where a is the length of a leg. **35.** $\overline{EF}, \overline{DE}, \overline{DF}$ **37.** m∠Y < 90°, and ∠Y is an obtuse angle. **39.** $\overline{AB} \perp \overline{BC}$, and $\overline{AB} \parallel \overline{BC}$. **41.** x is a multiple of 4, and x is prime. **43.** < **45.** = **47.** > **49.** > **51.** < **53.** = **55.** ∠L, ∠K, ∠J **57.** ∠J, ∠L, ∠K **59a.** 0.4 h < t < 2 h **b.** no **61.** $1 < n < 6$ **63.** $n > 0$ **65.** $n > 0.5$ **67a.** def. of ≅ segs. **b.** Isosc. △ Thm. **c.** def. of ≅ ∠s **d.** m∠1 + m∠3 **e.** subst. **f.** m∠S **g.** Trans. Prop. of Inequal. **71.** H **73.** $\frac{3}{10}$, or 30%

5-6

Check It Out! **1a.** m∠EGF > m∠EGH **1b.** $BC > AB$ **2.** The ∠ of the swing at full speed is greater than the ∠ at low speed.
3a. **1.** C is the mdpt. of $\overline{BD}$. m∠1 = m∠2, m∠3 > m∠4 (Given)
2. $\overline{BC} \cong \overline{DC}$ (Def. of mdpt.)
3. ∠1 ≅ ∠2 (Def. of ≅ ∠s)
4. $\overline{AC} \cong \overline{EC}$ (Conv. of Isosc. △ Thm.)
5. $AB > ED$ (Hinge Thm.)
3b. **1.** ∠SRT ≅ ∠STR, $TU > RU$ (Given)
2. $\overline{ST} \cong \overline{SR}$ (Conv. of Isosc. △ Thm.)
3. $\overline{SU} \cong \overline{SU}$ (Reflex. Prop. of ≅)
4. m∠TSU > m∠RSU (Conv. of Hinge Thm.)

Exercises **1.** $AC < XZ$ **3.** $KL > KN$ **5.** $1.2 < x < 3$ **7.** the second position **9.** m∠DCA > m∠BCA **11.** $TU > SV$ **13.** $-3.5 < z < 32.5$ **15.** the second position **17.** $BC = YZ$ **19.** > **21.** = **23.** < **25.** m∠RSV < m∠TSV **27.** m∠YMX > m∠ZMX **31.** D **33.** Group A is closer to the camp.

5-7

Check It Out! **1a.** $x = 4\sqrt{5}$ **1b.** $x = 16$ **2.** 29 ft 1 in. **3a.** $2\sqrt{41}$; no; $2\sqrt{41}$ is not a whole number. **3b.** 10; yes; the 3 side lengths are nonzero whole numbers that satisfy the equation $a^2 + b^2 = c^2$. **3c.** 2.6; no; 2.4 and 2.6 are not whole numbers. **3d.** 34; yes; the 3 side lengths are nonzero whole numbers that satisfy the equation $a^2 + b^2 = c^2$. **4a.** yes; obtuse **4b.** no **4c.** yes, acute

Exercises **1.** no **3.** $x = 6\sqrt{2}$ **5.** width: 14.8 in.; height: 11.9 in. **7.** 16; yes **9.** triangle; acute **11.** triangle; right **13.** triangle; acute **15.** $x = 10$ **17.** $x = 24$ **19.** 6; no **21.** $3\sqrt{5}$; no **23.** not a triangle **25.** triangle; right **27.** triangle; acute **29.** B **31.** $x = 8 + \sqrt{13}$ **33.** $x = 4\sqrt{6}$ **35.** $x = 6\sqrt{13}$ **39.** perimeter: $16 + 4\sqrt{7}$ units; area: $12\sqrt{7}$ square units **41.** perimeter: $14 + 2\sqrt{13}$ units; area: 18 square units **43.** perimeter: 22 units; area: 26 square units **47a.** King City **b.** m∠SRM > 90° **49.** B **51a.** $PA = \sqrt{2}$; $PB = \sqrt{3}$; $PC = 2$; $PD = \sqrt{5}$; $PE = \sqrt{6}$; $PF = \sqrt{7}$ **55a.** no **b.** yes. **c.** no **d.** no

5-8

Check It Out! **1a.** $x = 20$ **1b.** $x = 8\sqrt{2}$ **2.** 43 cm **3a.** $x = 9\sqrt{3}$; $y = 27$ **3b.** $x = 5\sqrt{3}$; $y = 10$ **3c.** $x = 12$; $y = 12\sqrt{3}$ **3d.** $x = 6\sqrt{3}$; $y = 3\sqrt{3}$ **4.** 34.6 cm

Exercises **1.** $x = 14\sqrt{2}$ **3.** $x = 9$ **5.** $x = 3$; $y = 3\sqrt{3}$ **7.** $x = 21$; $y = 14\sqrt{3}$ **9.** $x = \frac{15\sqrt{2}}{2}$ **11.** $x = 18$ **13.** $x = 48$; $y = 24\sqrt{3}$ **15.** $x = \frac{2\sqrt{3}}{3}$; $y = \frac{4\sqrt{3}}{3}$ **17.** perimeter: $(12 + 12\sqrt{2})$ in.; area: 36 in^2 **19.** perimeter: $36\sqrt{2}$ m; area: 162 m^2 **21.** perimeter: $60\sqrt{3}$ yd; area: $300\sqrt{3}$ yd^2 **23.** no **25.** (10, 3) **27.** $(5, 10 - 12\sqrt{3})$ **29a.** 640 mi **b.** 453 mi **c.** 234 mi **31.** F **33.** 443.4 **35.** $x = \frac{32}{9}$

Study Guide: Review

1. equidistant **2.** midsegment **3.** incenter **4.** locus **5.** 7.4 **6.** 13.4 **7.** 5.8 **8.** 52° **9.** $y = x - 1$ **10.** $y - 6 = -0.25(x - 4)$ **11.** No; to apply the Conv. of the ∠ Bisector Thm., you need to know that $\overline{AP} \perp \overline{AB}$ and $\overline{CP} \perp \overline{CB}$. **12.** Yes; because $\overline{AP} \perp \overline{AB}$, $\overline{CP} \perp \overline{CB}$, and $\overline{AP} \cong \overline{CP}$, P is on the bisector of ∠ABC by the Conv. of the ∠ Bisector Thm. **13.** 42.2 **14.** 46 **15.** 57.6 **16.** 46 **17.** 18 **18.** 37° **19.** (4, 3) **20.** (−6, −3.5) **21.** 16.4 **22.** 8.2 **23.** 5.8 **24.** 17.4 **25.** (−6, 0) **26.** (1, 2) **27.** (7, 4) **28.** (3, 0) **29.** (3, 4) **30.** 35.1 **31.** 64.8 **32.** 32.4 **33.** 42° **34.** 138° **35.** 42° **36.** $V(-1, -1)$; $W(6, 1)$; slope of $\overline{VW} = \frac{2}{7}$; slope of $\overline{GJ} = \frac{2}{7}$; since the slopes are the same, $\overline{VW} \parallel \overline{GJ}$. $VW = \sqrt{53}$; $GJ = 2\sqrt{53}$; since $\sqrt{53} = \frac{1}{2}(2\sqrt{53})$, $VW = \frac{1}{2}GJ$. **37.** $\overline{BC}, \overline{AC}, \overline{AB}$ **38.** ∠F, ∠H, ∠G **39.** greater than 9 cm and less than 18 cm **40.** Yes; possible answer: the sum of each pair of 2 lengths is greater than the third length. **41.** No; possible answer: when $z = 5$, the value of $3z$ is 15. So the 3 lengths are 5, 5, and 15. The sum of 5 and 5 is 10, which is not greater than 15. By the △ Inequality Thm., a △ cannot have these side lengths. **43.** $PS < RS$ **44.** m∠BCA < m∠DCA **45.** $-1.4 < n < 3$ **46.** $2.75 < n < 12.5$ **47.** $x = 2\sqrt{10}$ **48.** $x = 2\sqrt{33}$

49. 6; the lengths do not form a Pythagorean triple because 4.5 and 7.5 are not whole numbers. **50.** 40; the lengths do form a Pythagorean triple because they are nonzero whole numbers that satisfy the equation $a^2 + b^2 = c^2$. **51.** triangle; obtuse **52.** not a triangle **53.** triangle; right **54.** triangle; acute **55.** $x = 26\sqrt{2}$ **56.** $x = 6\sqrt{2}$ **57.** $x = 32$ **58.** $x = 24$; $y = 24\sqrt{3}$ **59.** $x = 6\sqrt{3}$; $y = 12$ **60.** $x = \frac{14\sqrt{3}}{3}$; $y = \frac{28\sqrt{3}}{3}$ **61.** 21 ft 3 in. **62.** 15 ft 7 in.

Mastering the *Standards*

for Mathematical Practice

The topics described in the Standards for Mathematical Content will vary from year to year. However, the *way* in which you learn, study, and think about mathematics will not. The Standards for Mathematical Practice describe skills that you will use in all of your math courses.

Mathematical Practices

1. *Make sense of problems and persevere in solving them.*
2. *Reason abstractly and quantitatively.*
3. *Construct viable arguments and critique the reasoning of others.*
4. *Model with mathematics.*
5. *Use appropriate tools strategically.*
6. *Attend to precision.*
7. *Look for and make use of structure.*
8. *Look for and express regularity in repeated reasoning.*

5 Use appropriate tools strategically.

Mathematically proficient students consider the available tools when solving a... problem... [and] are... able to use technological tools to explore and deepen their understanding...

In your book

Algebra Labs and **Technology Labs** use concrete and technological tools to explore mathematical concepts.

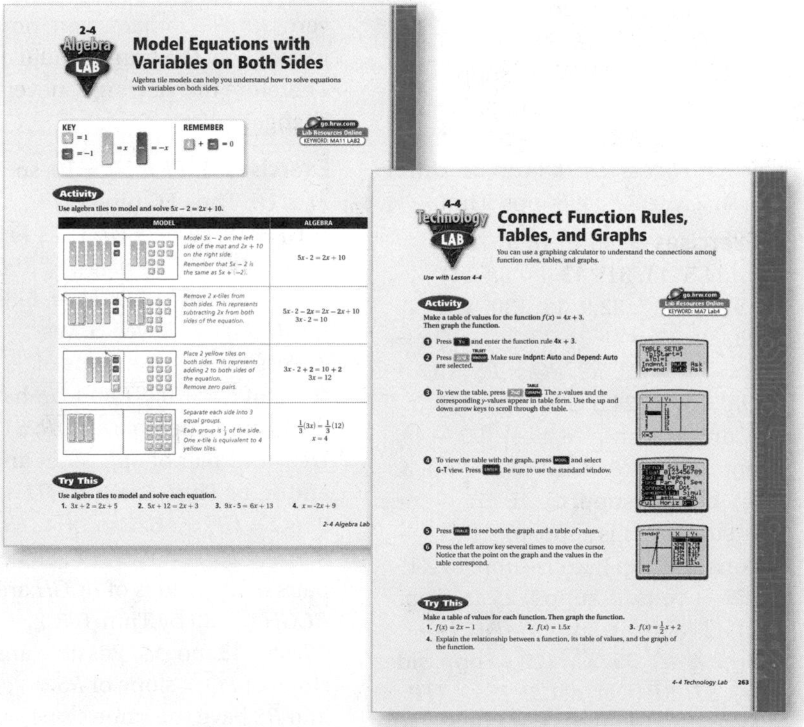
2-4 Algebra LAB

Model Equations with Variables on Both Sides

Algebra tile models can help you understand how to solve equations with variables on both sides.

KEY: = 1; = −1; = x; = $-x$ REMEMBER: + = 0

go.hrw.com Lab Resources Online KEYWORD: MA11 LAB2

Activity

Use algebra tiles to model and solve $5x - 2 = 2x + 10$.

MODEL		ALGEBRA
	Model $5x - 2$ on the left side of the mat and $2x + 10$ on the right side. Remember that $5x - 2$ is the same as $5x + (-2)$.	$5x - 2 = 2x + 10$
	Remove 2 x-tiles from both sides. This represents subtracting 2x from both sides of the equation.	$5x - 2 - 2x = 2x - 2x + 10$ $3x - 2 = 10$
	Place 2 yellow tiles on both sides. This represents adding 2 to both sides of the equation. Remove zero pairs.	$3x - 2 + 2 = 10 + 2$ $3x = 12$
	Separate each side into 3 equal groups. Each group is $\frac{1}{3}$ of the side. One x-tile is equivalent to 4 yellow tiles.	$\frac{1}{3}(3x) = \frac{1}{3}(12)$ $x = 4$

Try This

Use algebra tiles to model and solve each equation.

1. $3x + 2 = 2x + 5$ 2. $5x + 12 = 2x + 3$ 3. $9x - 5 = 6x + 13$ 4. $x = -2x + 9$

2-4 Algebra Lab

4-4 Technology LAB

Connect Function Rules, Tables, and Graphs

You can use a graphing calculator to understand the connections among function rules, tables, and graphs.

Use with Lesson 4-4

go.hrw.com Lab Resources Online KEYWORD: MA7 Lab4

Activity

Make a table of values for the function $f(x) = 4x + 3$. Then graph the function.

1. Press and enter the function rule **4x + 3**.
2. Press TBLSET. Make sure **Indpnt: Auto** and **Depend: Auto** are selected.
3. To view the table, press TABLE. The x-values and the corresponding y-values appear in table form. Use the up and down arrow keys to scroll through the table.
4. To view the table with the graph, press and select **G-T** view. Press . Be sure to use the standard window.
5. Press to see both the graph and a table of values.
6. Press the left arrow key several times to move the cursor. Notice that the point on the graph and the values in the table correspond.

Try This

Make a table of values for each function. Then graph the function.

1. $f(x) = 2x - 1$ 2. $f(x) = 1.5x$ 3. $f(x) = \frac{1}{2}x + 2$
4. Explain the relationship between a function, its table of values, and the graph of the function.

4-4 Technology Lab 263

Selected Answers ■ Chapter 6

6-1

Check It Out! **1a.** not a polygon **1b.** polygon, nonagon **1c.** not a polygon **2a.** regular, convex **2b.** irregular, concave **3a.** 2340° **3b.** 144° **4a.** 30° **4b.** $r = 15$ **5.** 45°

Exercises **3.** not a polygon **5.** not a polygon **7.** irregular, concave **9.** $m\angle A = m\angle D = 81°$; $m\angle B = 108°$; $m\angle C = m\angle E = 135°$ **11.** 3240° **13.** 72° **15.** $m\angle Q = m\angle S = 135°$ **17.** not a polygon **19.** irregular, concave **21.** irregular, convex **23.** 160° **25.** 40° **27.** 120° **29.** 61.5 **31.** 72 **33.** 10 **35.** pentagon **37.** dodecagon **39.** 3; 60° **41.** 10; 144° **43.** A **45a.** heptagon **b.** 900° **c.** 140° **53.** A **55.** D **57.** $x = 36$; $y = 36$; $z = 72$ **59.** Yes, if you allow for ∠ measures greater than 180°

6-2

Check It Out! **1a.** 28 in. **1b.** 74° **1c.** 13 in. **2a.** 12 **2b.** 18 **3.** (7,6)

4. 1. *GHJN* and *JKLM* are ▱s. (Given)
2. ∠*N* and ∠*HJN* are supp. ∠*K* and ∠*MJK* are supp. (▱ → cons. ∠s supp.)
3. ∠*HJN* ≅ ∠*MJK* (Vert. ∠s Thm.)
4. ∠*N* ≅ ∠*K* (≅ Supps. Thm.)

Exercises **3.** 36 **5.** 18 **7.** 70° **9.** 24.5 **11.** 51° **13.** (– 6, – 1) **15.** 82.9 **17.** 82.9 **19.** 130° **21.** 10 **23.** 28 **25.** (−1, 3) **27.** $PQ = QR = RS = SP = 21$ **29.** $PQ = RS = 17.5$; $QR = SP = 24.5$ **31a.** ∠3 ≅ ∠1 (Corr. ∠s Post.); ∠6 ≅ ∠1 (▱ → opp. ∠s ≅); ∠8 ≅ ∠1 (▱ → opp. ∠s ≅) **b.** ∠2 is supp. to ∠1 (▱ → cons. ∠s supp.); ∠4 is supp. to ∠1 (▱ → cons. ∠s supp.); ∠5 is supp. to ∠1 (▱ → cons. ∠s supp.); ∠7 is supp. to ∠1 (Subst.) **33.** ∠*KMP* (▱ → opp. ∠s ≅) **35.** $\overline{KM}$ (▱ → opp. sides ≅) **37.** $\overline{RP}$ (Def. of ▱) **39.** ∠*RTP* (Vert. ∠s Thm.) **41.** $x = 119$; $y = 61$; $z = 119$ **43.** $x = 24$; $y = 50$; $z = 50$ **47.** $x = 5$; $y = 8$ **49a.** no **b.** no **51.** A **53.** 26.4 **55.** (2, 4), (4, –6), (–6, –2)

6-3

Check It Out! **1.** $PQ = RS = 16.8$, so $\overline{PQ} \cong \overline{RS}$. $m\angle Q = 74°$, and $m\angle R = 106°$, so ∠*Q* and ∠*R* are supp., which means that $\overline{PQ} \parallel \overline{RS}$. So 1 pair of opp. sides of *PQRS* are ∥ and ≅. By Thm. 6-3-1, *PQRS* is a ▱. **2a.** Yes; possible answer: the diag. of the quad. forms 2 △s. 2 ∠s of 1 △ are ≅ to 2 ∠s of the other, so the third pair of ∠s are ≅ by the Third ∠s Thm. So both pairs of opp. ∠s of the quad. are ≅. By Thm. 6-3-3, the quad. is a ▱. **2b.** No; 2 pairs of cons. sides are ≅. None of the sets of conditions for a ▱ are met. **3.** Possible answer: slope of $\overline{KL}$ = slope of $\overline{MN} = -\frac{7}{2}$; slope of $\overline{LM}$ = slope of $\overline{NK} = -\frac{1}{4}$; both pairs of opp. sides have the same slope, so $\overline{KL} \parallel \overline{MN}$ and $\overline{LM} \parallel \overline{NK}$; by def., *KLMN* is a ▱. **4.** Possible answer: Since *ABRS* is a ▱, it is always true that $\overline{AB} \parallel \overline{RS}$. Since $\overline{AB}$ stays vert., $\overline{RS}$ also remains vert. no matter how the frame is adjusted. Therefore the viewing ∠ never changes.

Exercises **1.** $FJ = HJ = 10$, so $\overline{FJ} \cong \overline{HJ}$. Thus $\overline{EG}$ bisects $\overline{FH}$. $EJ = GJ = 18$, so $\overline{EJ} \cong \overline{GJ}$. Thus $\overline{FH}$ bisects $\overline{EG}$. So the diags. of *EFGH* bisect each other. By Thm. 6-3-5, *EFGH* is a ▱. **3.** yes **5.** yes **7.** Possible answer: slope of $\overline{ST}$ = slope of $\overline{UR} = 0$; $\overline{ST}$ and $\overline{UR}$ have the same slope, so $\overline{ST} \parallel \overline{UR}$; $ST = UR = 6$; 1 pair of opp. sides are ∥ and ≅; by Thm. 6-3-1, *RSTU* is a ▱. **9.** $BC = GH = 16.6$, so $\overline{BC} \cong \overline{GH}$. $CG = HB = 28$, so $\overline{CG} \cong \overline{HB}$. Since both pairs of opp. sides of *BCGH* are ≅, *BCGH* is a ▱ by Thm. 6-3-2. **11.** yes **13.** no **15.** Possible answer: slope of $\overline{PQ}$ = slope of $\overline{RS} = \frac{5}{3}$; $\overline{PQ}$ and $\overline{RS}$ have the same slope, so $\overline{PQ} \parallel \overline{RS}$; $PQ = RS = \sqrt{34}$; 1 pair of opp. sides are ∥ and ≅; by Thm. 6-3-1, *PQRS* is a ▱. **17.** no **19.** yes **21.** $a = 16.5$; $b = 23.2$ **23.** $a = 8.4$; $b = 20$ **27a.** ∠*Q* **b.** ∠*S*. **c.** $\overline{SP}$ **d.** $\overline{RS}$ **e.** ▱ **35.** B **37.** no **39.** (3, 1); (−6, −3.5)

6-4

Check It Out! **1a.** 48 in. **1b.** 61.6 in. **2a.** 42.5 **2b.** 17° **3.** $SV = TW = \sqrt{122}$, so $\overline{SV} \cong \overline{TW}$. Slope of $\overline{SV} = \frac{1}{11}$, and slope of $\overline{TW} = -11$, so $\overline{SV} \perp \overline{TW}$. The coordinates of the mdpt. of $\overline{SV}$ and $\overline{TW}$ are $\left(\frac{1}{2}, -\frac{7}{2}\right)$, so $\overline{SV}$ and $\overline{TW}$ bisect each other. So the diags. of *STVW* are ≅ ⊥ bisectors of each other.

4. Possible answer:
1. *PQTS* is a rhombus. (Given)
2. $\overline{PT}$ bisects ∠*QPS*. (Rhombus → each diag. bisects opp. ∠s)
3. ∠*QPR* ≅ ∠*SPR* (Def. of ∠ bisector)
4. $\overline{PQ} \cong \overline{PS}$ (Def. of rhombus)
5. $\overline{PR} \cong \overline{PR}$ (Reflex. Prop. of ≅)
6. △*QPR* ≅ △*SPR* (SAS)
7. $\overline{RQ} \cong \overline{RS}$ (CPCTC)

Exercises **1.** rhombus; rectangle; square **3.** 160 ft **5.** 380 ft **7.** 122°

9. Possible answer:
1. *RECT* is a rect. $\overline{RX} \cong \overline{TY}$ (Given)
2. $\overline{XY} \cong \overline{XY}$ (Reflex. Prop. of ≅)
3. $RX = TY$, $XY = XY$ (Def. of ≅ segs.)
4. $RX + XY = TY + XY$ (Add. Prop. of =)
5. $RX + XY = RY$, $TY + XY = TX$ (Seg. Add. Post.)
6. $RY = TX$ (Subst.)
7. $\overline{RY} \cong \overline{TX}$ (Def. of ≅ segs.)
8. ∠*R* and ∠*T* are rt. ∠s. (Def. of rect.)
9. ∠*R* ≅ ∠*T* (Rt. ∠ ≅ Thm.)
10. *RECT* is a ▱. (Rect. → ▱)
11. $\overline{RE} \cong \overline{TC}$ (▱ → opp. sides ≅)
12. △*REY* ≅ △*TCX* (SAS)

11. 25 **13.** $14\frac{1}{2}$ **15.** $m\angle VWX = 132°$; $m\angle WYX = 66°$

17. Possible answer:
1. *RHMB* is a rhombus. $\overline{HB}$ is a diag. of *RHMB*. (Given)
2. $\overline{MH} \cong \overline{RH}$ (Def. of rhombus)
3. $\overline{HB}$ bisects ∠*RHM*. (Rhombus → each diag. bisects opp. ∠s)

4. $\angle MHX \cong \angle RHX$ (Def. of ∠ bisector)
5. $\overline{HX} \cong \overline{HX}$ (Reflex. Prop. of ≅)
6. $\triangle MHX \cong \triangle RHX$ (SAS)
7. $\angle HMX \cong \angle HRX$ (CPCTC)

19. $m\angle 1 = 54°$; $m\angle 2 = 36°$; $m\angle 3 = 54°$; $m\angle 4 = 108°$; $m\angle 5 = 72°$ **21.** $m\angle 1 = 126°$; $m\angle 2 = 27°$; $m\angle 3 = 27°$; $m\angle 4 = 126°$; $m\angle 5 = 27°$ **23.** $m\angle 1 = 64°$; $m\angle 2 = 64°$; $m\angle 3 = 26°$; $m\angle 4 = 90°$; $m\angle 5 = 64°$ **25.** S **27.** S **29.** A **31.** S **35a.** Rect. → ▱ **b.** $\overline{HG}$ **c.** Reflex. Prop. of ≅ **d.** Def. of rect. **e.** $\angle GHE$ **f.** SAS **g.** CPCTC **41.** $28\sqrt{2}$ in. ≈ 39.60 in.; 98 in^2 **45.** D **47.** H **51.** 45

6-5

Check It Out! 1. Both pairs of opp. sides of *WXYZ* are ≅, so *WXYZ* is a ▱. The contractor can use the carpenter's square to see if 1 ∠ of *WXYZ* is a rt. ∠. If 1 ∠ is a rt. ∠, then by Thm. 6-5-1 the frame is a rect. **2.** Not valid; by Thm. 6-5-1, if 1 ∠ of a ▱ is a rt. ∠, then the ▱ is a rect. To apply this thm., you need to know that *ABCD* is a ▱. **3a.** rect., rhombus, square **3b.** rhombus

Exercises 3. valid **5.** rhombus **7.** valid **9.** square, rect., rhombus **11.** ▱, rect. **13.** ▱, rect., rhombus, square **15.** ▱, rect., rhombus, square **17.** B **19.** $\overline{PR} \cong \overline{QS}$ **21.** $(2, 6)$ **23.** $(-2, -2)$ **25.** $x = 3$ **27.** rhombus **29a.** slope of $\overline{AB}$ = slope of $\overline{CD} = -\frac{1}{3}$; slope of $\overline{AD}$ = slope of $\overline{CB} = -3$ **b.** Slope of $\overline{AC} = -1$; slope of $\overline{BD} = 1$; the slopes are negative reciprocals of each other, so $\overline{AC} \perp \overline{BD}$. **c.** *ABCD* is a rhombus, since it is a ▱ and its diags. are ⊥ (Thm. 6-5-4.) **33b.** ▱ **c.** square **39.** A **41a.** $15x = 13x + 12$; $x = 6$ **b.** yes **c.** no **d.** yes **43b.** no **c.** no

6-6

Check It Out! 1. about 191.3 in.; 3 packages **2a.** 51° **2b.** 110° **2c.** 62° **3a.** 131° **3b.** 25.4 **4.** $x = 4$ or $x = -4$ **5.** 8

Exercises 1. bases: $\overline{RS}$ and $\overline{PV}$; legs: $\overline{PR}$ and $\overline{VS}$; midsegment: $\overline{QT}$ **3.** about 20.1 in.; 3 sun catchers **5.** 63° **7.** 106° **9.** $z = 2$ or $z = -2$ **11.** 14 **13.** about 56.6 in.; about 418.3 in. **15.** 122° **17.** 62° **19.** $\pm 4\sqrt{5}$ **21.** 3.6 **23.** S **25.** N **27.** $m\angle 1 = 82°$; $m\angle 2 = 128°$ **29.** $m\angle 1 = 51°$; $m\angle 2 = 16°$ **31.** $m\angle 1 = 120°$ **33a.** $EF = FG = \sqrt{17}$, and $GH = HE = \sqrt{29}$, so $\overline{EF} \cong \overline{FG}$, and $\overline{GH} \cong \overline{HE}$. Thus *EFGH* is a kite, since it has exactly 2 pairs of ≅ cons. sides. **b.** $m\angle E = m\angle G = 126°$ **35.** 13 **37.** $m\angle PAQ = 108°$; $m\angle OAQ = 130°$; $m\angle OBP = 22°$ **41.** kite **43.** isosc. trap. **47.** B **49.** 18 **51.** $AD = 7.08$ in.; $AB = CD = 5.08$ in.; $BC = 10.16$ in.

Study Guide: Review

1. vertex of a polygon **2.** convex **3.** rhombus **4.** base of a trapezoid **5.** not a polygon **6.** polygon; △ **7.** polygon; dodecagon **8.** irregular; concave **9.** irregular; convex **10.** reg.; convex **11.** 1800° **12.** 162° **13.** 90° **14.** $m\angle A = m\angle D = 144°$; $m\angle B = m\angle E = 126°$; $m\angle C = m\angle F = 90°$ **15.** 37.5 **16.** 62.4 **17.** 37.5 **18.** 79° **19.** 101° **20.** 101° **21.** 9.5 **22.** 9.5 **23.** 54° **24.** 126° **25.** 54° **26.** 126° **27.** $T(6, -5)$
28. 1. *GHLM* is a ▱. $\angle L \cong \angle JMG$ (Given)
2. $\angle G \cong \angle L$ (▱ → opp. ∠s ≅)
3. $\angle G \cong \angle JMG$ (Trans. Prop. of ≅)
4. $\overline{GJ} \cong \overline{MJ}$ (Conv. of Isosc. △ Thm.)
5. $\triangle GJM$ is isosc. (Def. of isosc. △)

29. $m\angle A = m\angle E = 63°$; $m\angle G = 117°$; since $117° + 63° = 180°$, $\angle G$ is supp. to $\angle A$ and to $\angle E$. So 1 ∠ of *ACEG* is supp. to both of its cons. ∠s. By Thm. 6-3-4, *ACEG* is a ▱. **30.** $RS = QT = 25$, so $\overline{RS} \cong \overline{QT}$. $m\angle R = 76°$, $m\angle Q = 104°$, and $m\angle R + m\angle Q = 180°$, so $\angle R$ is supp. to $\angle Q$. Since $\angle R$ and $\angle Q$ are a pair of same-side int. ∠s, and they are supp., $\overline{RS} \parallel \overline{QT}$. So 1 pair of opp. sides of *QRST* are ∥ and ≅. By Thm. 6-3-1, *QRST* is a ▱. **31.** Yes; the diags. of the quad. bisect each other. By Thm. 6-3-5, the quad. is a ▱. **32.** No; a pair of alt. int. ∠s are ≅, so 1 pair of opp. sides are ∥. A different pair of opp. sides are ≅. None of the conditions for a ▱ are met. **33.** slope of $\overline{BD}$ = slope of $\overline{FH} = \frac{1}{5}$; slope of $\overline{BH}$ = slope of $\overline{DF} = -6$; both pairs of opp. sides have the same slope, so $\overline{BD} \parallel \overline{FH}$ and $\overline{BH} \parallel \overline{DF}$; by def., *BDFH* is a ▱. **34.** 18 **35.** 39.6 **36.** 39.6 **37.** 19.8 **38.** 25.5 **39.** 10.5 **40.** 25.5 **41.** 21 **42.** 41° **43.** 49° **44.** 82° **45.** 98° **46.** $m\angle 1 = 57°$; $m\angle 2 = 66°$; $m\angle 3 = 33°$; $m\angle 4 = 114°$; $m\angle 5 = 57°$ **47.** $m\angle 1 = 37°$; $m\angle 2 = 53°$; $m\angle 3 = 90°$; $m\angle 4 = 37°$; $m\angle 5 = 53°$ **48.** $RT = SU = 2\sqrt{10}$, so $\overline{RT} \cong \overline{SU}$. Slope of $\overline{RT} = -3$, and slope of $\overline{SU} = \frac{1}{3}$, so $\overline{RT} \perp \overline{SU}$. The coordinates of the mdpt. of $\overline{RT}$ and $\overline{SU}$ are $(-4, -3)$, so $\overline{RT}$ and $\overline{SU}$ bisect each other. So the diags. of *RSTU* are ≅ ⊥ bisectors of each other. **49.** $EG = FH = 3\sqrt{2}$, so $\overline{EG} \cong \overline{FH}$. Slope of $\overline{EG} = -1$, and slope of $\overline{FH} = 1$, so $\overline{EG} \perp \overline{FH}$. The coordinates of the mdpt. of $\overline{EG}$ and $\overline{FH}$ are $\left(\frac{7}{2}, -\frac{1}{2}\right)$, so $\overline{EG}$ and $\overline{FH}$ bisect each other. So the diags. of *EFGH* are ≅ ⊥ bisectors of each other. **50.** Not valid; by Thm. 6-5-2, if the diags. of a ▱ are ≅, then the ▱ is a rect. By Thm. 6-5-4, if the diags. of a ▱ are ⊥, then the ▱ is a rhombus. If a ▱ is both a rect. and a rhombus, then the ▱ is a square. To apply this chain of reasoning, you must first know that *EFRS* is a ▱. **51.** valid **52.** valid **53.** rhombus **54.** rect. **55.** rect., rhombus, square **56.** 64° **57.** 25° **58.** 65° **59.** 123° **60.** $m\angle R = 126°$; $m\angle S = 54°$ **61.** 51.6 **62.** 48.5 **63.** 3.5 **64.** $n = 3$ or $n = -3$ **65.** kite **66.** trap. **67.** isosc. trap.

7-1

Check It Out! 1. $\angle A \cong \angle J$; $\angle B \cong \angle G$; $\angle C \cong \angle H$; $\frac{AB}{JG} = \frac{BC}{GH} = \frac{AC}{JH} = 2$ **2.** yes; $\frac{5}{2}$; $\triangle LMJ \sim \triangle PNS$ **3.** 5 in.

Exercises 3. $\angle A \cong \angle H$; $\angle B \cong \angle J$; $\angle C \cong \angle K$; $\angle D \cong \angle L$; $\frac{AB}{HJ} = \frac{BC}{JK} = \frac{CD}{KL} = \frac{DA}{LH} = \frac{2}{3}$ **5.** yes; $\frac{2}{3}$; $\triangle RMP \sim \triangle XWU$ **7.** $\angle J \cong \angle S$; $\angle K \cong \angle T$; $\angle L \cong \angle U$; $\angle M \cong \angle V$; $\frac{JK}{ST} = \frac{KL}{TU} = \frac{LM}{UV} = \frac{MJ}{VS} = \frac{5}{6}$ **9.** yes; $\frac{7}{8}$; $\triangle RSQ \sim \triangle UZX$ **11.** 14 ft **13.** S **15.** N **17.** S **19.** 5 **23.** $\angle O$; $\angle Q$ **27.** C **29.** The ratios of the sides are not the same; $\frac{12}{3.5} = \frac{24}{7}$; $\frac{10}{2.5} = 4$; $\frac{6}{1.5} = 4$. **33a.** rect. $ABCD \sim$ rect. $BCFE$ **b.** $\frac{\ell}{1} = \frac{1}{\ell - 1}$ **c.** $\ell = \frac{1+\sqrt{5}}{2}$ **d.** $\ell \approx 1.6$

7-2

Check It Out! 1. $D'(-2, 0)$, $E'(-2, -1)$, $F'(-1, -2)$; dilation with center (0, 0) and scale factor $\frac{1}{4}$ **2.** The triangles are similar because $\triangle ABC$ can be mapped to $\triangle A'B'C'$ by a rotation: $(x, y) \longrightarrow (-y, x)$, and then $\triangle A'B'C'$ can be mapped to $\triangle PQR$ by a dilation: $(x, y) \longrightarrow (3x, 3y)$.
3. Circle A can be mapped to circle A' by a translation: $(x, y) \longrightarrow (x - 3, y - 2)$. Then circle A' can be mapped to circle B by a dilation with center $(-1, -1)$ and scale factor $\frac{1}{2}$. So, circles A and B are similar. **4.** Apply the dilation with center (0, 0) and scale factor 4: $(x, y) \longrightarrow (4x, 4y)$.

Exercises 1. similarity **3.** dilation about (0, 0) with a scale factor of 4; $A'(-4, -4)$, $B'(8, 4)$, $C'(-8, 4)$ **5.** dilation about (0, 0) with a scale factor of 2.5; $A'(5, 7.5)$, $B'(12.5, -5)$, $C'(-10, -5)$ **7.** Similar; to map $LMNO$ to $PQRS$, first dilate by a scale factor of 2: $(x, y) \longrightarrow (2x, 2y)$. Then translate 13 units up: $(x, y) \longrightarrow (x, y + 13)$. **9.** Similar; to map ABC to XYZ, first reflect: $(x, y) \longrightarrow (x, -y)$. Then dilate by a scale factor of $\frac{4}{3}$: $(x, y) \longrightarrow (\frac{4}{3}x, \frac{4}{3}y)$. The transformations could also be done in the other order. **11.** To map A to B, first translate 10 units to the left and 3 units down: $(x, y) \longrightarrow (x - 10, y - 3)$. Then dilate by a scale factor of $\frac{3}{5}$: $(x, y) \longrightarrow (\frac{3}{5}x, \frac{3}{5}y)$. **13.** Apply a dilation with center (0, 0) and scale factor 4 to the small triangle on the grid: $(x, y) \longrightarrow (4x, 4y)$. The image represents the shape of the large triangle. **15.** dilation about (0, 0) with a scale factor of 0.5; $A'(6, 3)$, $B'(0, -3)$, $C'(3, 9)$ **17.** Similar; to map ABC to XYZ, first translate 4 units to the left and 6 units up: $(x, y) \longrightarrow (x - 4, y + 6)$. Then dilate by a scale factor of $\frac{2}{3}$: $(x, y) \longrightarrow (\frac{2}{3}x, \frac{2}{3}y)$. **19.** Similar; to map $GHJK$ to $LMNO$, dilate by a scale factor of 0.5: $(x, y) \longrightarrow (0.5x, 0.5y)$; to map $LMNO$ to $GHJK$, dilate by a scale factor of 2: $(x, y) \longrightarrow (2x, 2y)$. **21.** Reggie made an error. The scale factor from ABC to $A'B'C'$ is $\frac{2}{3}$, not $\frac{3}{2}$. **23.** Place the drawing of the smaller building on a coordinate plane in a convenient position in the first quadrant. Apply the dilation with center (0, 0) and scale factor 5: $(x, y) \longrightarrow (5x, 5y)$. The image represents the larger building. **25.** A

7-3

Check It Out! 1. By the △ Sum Thm., $m\angle C = 47°$, so $\angle C \cong \angle F$. $\angle B \cong \angle E$ by the Rt. ∠ ≅ Thm. Therefore $\triangle ABC \sim \triangle DEF$ by $AA \sim$. **2.** $\angle TXU \cong \angle VXW$ by the Vert. ∠s Thm. $\frac{TX}{VX} = \frac{12}{16} = \frac{3}{4}$, and $\frac{XU}{XW} = \frac{15}{20} = \frac{3}{4}$. Therefore $\triangle TXU \sim \triangle VXW$ by SAS ~.
3. It is given that $\angle RSV \cong \angle T$. By the Reflex. Prop. of ≅, $\angle R \cong \angle R$. Therefore $\triangle RSV \sim \triangle RTU$ by AA ~. $RT = 15$.
4.1. M is the mdpt. of $\overline{JK}$, N is the mdpt. of $\overline{KL}$, and P is the mdpt. of $\overline{JL}$. (Given)
2. $MP = \frac{1}{2}KL$, $MN = \frac{1}{2}JL$, $NP = \frac{1}{2}KJ$ (△Midsegs. Thm.)
3. $\frac{MP}{KL} = \frac{MN}{JL} = \frac{NP}{KJ} = \frac{1}{2}$ (Div. Prop. of =)
4. $\triangle JKL \sim \triangle NPM$ (SSS ~ *Step 3*)
5. 5

Exercises 1. By the △ Sum Thm., $m\angle A = 47°$. So by the def. of ≅, $\angle A \cong \angle F$, and $\angle C \cong \angle H$. Therefore $\triangle ABC \sim \triangle FGH$ by AA ~. **3.** $\frac{DF}{JL} = \frac{DE}{JK} = \frac{EF}{KL} = \frac{1}{2}$, so $\triangle DEF \sim \triangle JKL$ by SSS ~. **5.** It is given that $\angle AED \cong \angle ACB$. $\angle A \cong \angle A$ by the Reflex. Prop. of ≅. Therefore $\triangle AED \sim \triangle ACB$ by AA ~. $AB = 10$
7.1. $\overline{MN} \parallel \overline{KL}$ (Given)
2. $\angle JMN \cong \angle JKL$, $\angle JNM \cong \angle JLK$ (Corr. ∠s Post.)
3. $\triangle JMN \sim \triangle JKL$ (AA ~ *Step 2*)
9. SAS or SSS ~ Thm. **11.** It is given that $\angle GLH \cong \angle K$. $\angle G \cong \angle G$ by the Reflex. Prop. of ≅. Therefore $\triangle HLG \sim \triangle JKG$ by AA ~. **13.** $\angle K \cong \angle K$ by the Reflex. Prop. of ≅. $\frac{KL}{KN} = \frac{KM}{KL} = \frac{3}{2}$. Therefore $\triangle KLM \sim \triangle KNL$ by SAS ~. **15.** It is given that $\angle ABD \cong \angle C$. $\angle A \cong \angle A$ by the Reflex. Prop. of ≅. Therefore $\triangle ABD \sim \triangle ACB$ by AA ~. $AB = 8$
17.1. $CD = 3AC$, $CE = 3BC$ (Given)
2. $\frac{CD}{AC} = 3$, $\frac{CE}{BC} = 3$ (Div. Prop. of =)
3. $\angle ACB \cong \angle DCE$ (Vert. ∠s Thm.)
4. $\triangle ABC \sim \triangle DEC$ (SAS ~ *Steps 2, 3*)
19. 1.5 ft **21.** yes; SSS ~ **23.** $x = 3$ **25a.** Pyramids A and C are ~ because the ratios of their corr. side lengths are =. **b.** $\frac{5}{4}$ **27.** 2 ft; 4 ft **31a.** The △s are ~ by AA ~ if you assume that the camera is ∥ to the hurricane (that is, $\overline{YX} \parallel \overline{AB}$). **b.** $\triangle YWZ \sim \triangle BCZ$, and $\triangle XWZ \sim \triangle ACZ$, also by AA ~. **c.** 105 mi **35.** J **37.** 30

7-4

Check It Out! 1. 7.5 **2.** $AD = 16$, and $BE = 12$, so $\frac{DC}{AD} = \frac{20}{16} = \frac{5}{4}$, and $\frac{EC}{BE} = \frac{15}{12} = \frac{5}{4}$. Since $\frac{DC}{AD} = \frac{EC}{BE}$, $\overline{DE} \parallel \overline{AB}$ by the Conv. of the △ Proportionality Thm. **3.** $LM \approx 1.5$ cm; $MN \approx 2.4$ cm **4.** $AC = 16$; $DC = 9$

Exercises 1. 30 **3.** $\frac{EC}{AC} = 1$, and $\frac{ED}{DB} = 1$. Since $\frac{EC}{AC} = \frac{ED}{DB}$, $\overline{AB} \parallel \overline{CD}$ by the Conv. of the △ Proportionality Thm. **5.** 286 ft **7.** $CD = 4$; $AD = 6$ **9.** 20 **11.** $\frac{PM}{MQ} = \frac{6.3}{2.7} = 2\frac{1}{3}$, and $\frac{PN}{NR} = \frac{7}{3} = 2\frac{1}{3}$. Since $\frac{PM}{MQ} = \frac{PN}{NR}$, $\overline{MN} \parallel \overline{QR}$ by the Conv. of the

△ Proportionality Thm.
13. $BC = 6$; $CD = 5$ **15.** CE **17.** BD
19. DF **21.** 15 in. or $26\frac{2}{3}$ in.
23.1. $\frac{AE}{EB} = \frac{AF}{FC}$ (Given)
2. $\angle A \cong \angle A$ (Reflex. Prop. of ≅)
3. $\triangle AEF \sim \triangle ABC$ (SAS ~ *Steps 1, 2*)
4. $\angle AEF \cong \angle ABC$ (Def. of ~ △)
5. $\overleftrightarrow{EF} \parallel \overline{BC}$ (Conv. of Corr. ∠s Post.)
25a. $PR = 6$; $RT = 8$; $QS = 3$; $SU = 4$
b. $\frac{PR}{RT} = \frac{QS}{SU}$, or $\frac{6}{8} = \frac{3}{4}$ **27.** 15 **33.** J

7-5

Check It Out! 1. 15 ft 7 in.
2. 900 m, or 0.9 km **3.** Check students' work. The drawing should be 3.7 in. by 3 in. **4.** $P = 14$ mm; $A = 10\frac{2}{3}$ mm^2

Exercises 1. indirect measurement
3. 12 ft **5.** 60 ft **11.** 27 cm^2
13. ≈ 57 km **19.** 864 m^2 **21.** ≈ 25 ft
23. ≈ 39 ft **25.** $\frac{4}{5}$ **27.** 0.3 ft by 1.2 ft
29. 20 in.; 12 in. **31a.** $\frac{1}{24}$ **b.** $\frac{1}{576}$
c. 24 ft^2 **33.** $\frac{1}{9}$ cm **35.** 1 cm:5 m; since each centimeter will equal 5 m, this drawing will be $\frac{1}{5}$ the size of the drawing with a scale of 1 cm:1 m. **39.** D **41.** C **43a.** 150 m
b. 1.28 cm

7-6

Check It Out! 1. The photo should have vertices $A'(0, 0)$, $B'(0, 2)$, $C'(1.5, 2)$, and $D'(1.5, 0)$.
2. $N(0, -20)$; $\frac{2}{3}$ **3.** $RS = \sqrt{2}$, $RU = 3\sqrt{2}$, $RT = \sqrt{5}$, and $RV = 3\sqrt{5}$, so $\frac{RS}{RU} = \frac{RT}{RV} = \frac{1}{3}$. $\angle R \cong \angle R$ by the Reflex. Prop. of ≅. So $\triangle RST \sim \triangle RUV$ by SAS ~. **4.** Check students' work. The image of $\triangle MNP$ has vertices $M'(-6, 3)$, $N'(6, 6)$, and $P'(-3, -3)$. $MP = \sqrt{5}$, $MN = \sqrt{17}$, and $PN = 3\sqrt{2}$. $M'P' = 3\sqrt{5}$, $M'N' = 3\sqrt{17}$, and $P'N' = 9\sqrt{2}$. $\frac{M'P'}{MP} = \frac{M'N'}{MN} = \frac{P'N'}{PN} = 3$. So $\triangle M'N'P' \sim \triangle MNP$ by SSS ~.

Exercises 1. dilation
5. $S(0, -8)$; $\frac{5}{2}$ **7.** $JK = 2\sqrt{5}$, $JM = 3\sqrt{5}$, $JL = 2\sqrt{5}$, and $JN = 3\sqrt{5}$, so $\frac{JK}{JM} = \frac{JL}{JN} = \frac{2}{3}$. $\angle J \cong \angle J$ by the Reflex. Prop. of ≅. So $\triangle JKL \sim \triangle JMN$ by SAS ~. **9.** The image of $\triangle RST$ has vertices $R'(-3, 3)$, $S'(3, 6)$, and $T'(0, -3)$. $RS = 2\sqrt{5}$, $RT = 2\sqrt{5}$, and $ST = 2\sqrt{10}$. $R'S' = 3\sqrt{5}$, $R'T' = 3\sqrt{5}$, and $S'T' = 3\sqrt{10}$. $\frac{R'S'}{RS} = \frac{R'T'}{RT} = \frac{S'T'}{ST} = \frac{3}{2}$. So $\triangle RST \sim \triangle R'S'T'$ by SSS ~. **11.** $X(-24, 0)$; $\frac{8}{3}$
13. $DE = 2\sqrt{5}$, $DG = 3\sqrt{5}$, $DF = 4\sqrt{2}$, and $DH = 6\sqrt{2}$, so $\frac{DE}{DG} = \frac{DF}{DH} = \frac{2}{3}$. $\angle D \cong \angle D$ by the Reflex. Prop. of ≅. So $\triangle DEF \sim \triangle DGH$ by SAS ~.
15. The image of $\triangle JKL$ has vertices $J'(-6, 0)$, $K'(-3, -3)$, and $L'(-9, -6)$. $JK = \sqrt{2}$, $JL = \sqrt{5}$, and $LK = \sqrt{5}$. $J'K' = 3\sqrt{2}$, $J'L' = 3\sqrt{5}$, and $L'K' = 3\sqrt{5}$. $\frac{J'K'}{JK} = \frac{J'L'}{JL} = \frac{L'K'}{LK} = 3$. So $\triangle JKL \sim \triangle J'K'L'$ by SSS ~. **17.** It is not a dilation; because it changes the shape of the figure. **21.** A
23. A **25.** 12

Study Guide: Review

1. indirect measurement **2.** dilation
3. similarity ratio **4.** scale factor
5. yes; $\frac{5}{3}$; $JKLM \sim PQRS$
6. yes; 2; $\triangle TUV \sim \triangle WXY$
7. $A'(4, 8)$, $B'(12, -4)$, $C'(-16, 0)$
8. Yes; Dilate ABC by a scale factor of 2 and reflect across the y-axis.
9.1. $JL = \frac{1}{3}JN$, $JK = \frac{1}{3}JM$ (Given)
2. $\frac{JL}{JN} = \frac{1}{3}$, $\frac{JK}{JM} = \frac{1}{3}$ (Div. Prop. of =)
3. $\frac{JL}{JN} = \frac{JK}{JM}$ (Trans. Prop. of =)
4. $\angle J \cong \angle J$ (Reflex. Prop. of ≅)
5. $\triangle JKL \sim \triangle JMN$ (SAS ~ *Steps 3, 4*)
10.1. $\overline{QR} \parallel \overline{ST}$ (Given)
2. $\angle RQP \cong \angle STP$ (Alt. Int. ∠ Thm.)
3. $\angle RPQ \cong \angle SPT$ (Vert. ∠s Thm.)
4. $\triangle PQR \sim \triangle PTS$ (AA ~ *Steps 2, 3*)
11.1. $\overline{BC} \parallel \overline{CE}$ (Given)
2. $\angle ABD \cong \angle C$ (Corr. ∠ Post.)
3. $\angle ADB \cong \angle E$ (Corr. ∠ Post.)
4. $\triangle ABD \sim \triangle ACE$ (AA ~ *Steps 2, 3*)
5. $\frac{AB}{AC} = \frac{BD}{CE}$ (Def. of ~ polygons)
6. $AB(CE) = AC(BD)$ (Cross Products Prop.)
12. 10 **13.** $3\frac{1}{3}$ **14.** $\frac{JK}{JM} = \frac{JL}{JN} = \frac{1}{2}$. Since $\frac{JK}{JM} = \frac{JL}{JN}$, $\overline{KL} \parallel \overline{MN}$ by the Conv. of the △ Proportionality Thm. **15.** $\frac{EC}{EA} = \frac{ED}{EB} = \frac{3}{7}$. Since $\frac{EC}{EA} = \frac{ED}{EB}$, $\overline{AB} \parallel \overline{CD}$ by the Conv. of the △ Proportionality Thm. **16.** $SU = 4$; $SV = 6$ **17.** 18 **18.** $4x + 8$
19. 25 ft 4 in. **20.** 3 ft **21.** By the Dist. Formula, $RS = 2\sqrt{2}$, $RU = 4\sqrt{2}$, $RT = \sqrt{10}$, and $RV = 2\sqrt{10}$. $\frac{RS}{RU} = \frac{RT}{RV} = \frac{1}{2}$. $\angle R \cong \angle R$ by the Reflex. Prop. of ≅. So $\triangle RST \sim \triangle RUV$ by SAS ~. **22.** By the Dist. Formula, $JK = \sqrt{5}$, $JM = 4\sqrt{5}$, $JL = 2$, and $JN = 8$. $\frac{JK}{JM} = \frac{JL}{JN} = \frac{1}{4}$. $\angle J \cong \angle J$ by the Reflex. Prop. of ≅. So $\triangle JKL \sim \triangle JMN$ by SAS ~. **23.** $(0, -6)$; $\frac{2}{3}$
24. The image of $\triangle KLM$ has vertices $K'(0, 9)$, $L'(0, 0)$, and $M'(12, 0)$. By the Dist. Formula, $KL = 3$, $LM = 4$, $KM = 5$, $K'L' = 9$, $L'M' = 12$, and $K'M' = 15$. $\frac{K'L'}{KL} = \frac{L'M'}{LM} = \frac{K'M'}{KM} = \frac{3}{1}$. Therefore $\triangle KLM \sim \triangle K'L'M'$ by SSS ~.

Selected Answers ▪ Chapter 8

8-1

Check It Out! **1.** $\triangle LJK \sim \triangle JMK \sim \triangle LMJ$ **2a.** 4 **2b.** $10\sqrt{3}$ **2c.** $6\sqrt{2}$ **3.** 27; $3\sqrt{10}$; $9\sqrt{10}$ **4.** 148 ft

Exercises **1.** 8 is the geometric mean of 2 and 32. **3.** $\triangle BED \sim \triangle ECD \sim \triangle BCE$ **5.** 10 **7.** 2 **9.** 20 **11.** $2\sqrt{15}$; $2\sqrt{6}$; $2\sqrt{10}$ **13.** 12; $4\sqrt{13}$; 8 **15.** $\triangle MPN \sim \triangle PQN \sim \triangle MQP$ **17.** $\triangle RSU \sim \triangle RTS \sim \triangle STU$ **19.** $3\sqrt{5}$ **21.** $2\sqrt{5}$ **23.** $\frac{3\sqrt{5}}{10}$ **25.** $20\sqrt{3}$; $10\sqrt{21}$; $20\sqrt{7}$ **27.** 1670 ft **29.** $\frac{10}{3}$, or $3\frac{1}{3}$ **31.** $x + y$ **33.** z **35.** x **37.** $4\sqrt{5}$ **39.** $\frac{\sqrt{10}}{2}$ **41.** B **43.** By Corollary 8-1-3, $a^2 = x(x + y)$, and $b^2 = y(x + y)$. So $a^2 + b^2 = x(x + y) + y(x + y)$. By the Distrib. Prop., this expression simplifies to $(x + y)(x + y) = (x + y)^2 = c^2$. So $a^2 + b^2 = c^2$. **47.** D **49.** A **51.** 7; $\sqrt{35}$; $2\sqrt{15}$ **53.** $AC \approx 15.26$ cm; $AB \approx 8.53$ cm

8-2

Check It Out! **1a.** $\frac{24}{25} = 0.96$ **1b.** $\frac{24}{7} \approx 3.43$ **1c.** $\frac{24}{25} = 0.96$ **2.** $\frac{s}{s} = 1$ **3a.** 0.19 **3b.** 0.88 **3c.** 0.87 **4a.** 21.87 m **4b.** 7.06 in. **4c.** 36.93 ft **4d.** 6.17 cm **5.** 14.34 ft

Exercises **1.** $\frac{LK}{JL}$ **3.** $\frac{4}{5} = 0.80$ **5.** $\frac{4}{5} = 0.80$ **7.** $\frac{4}{3} \approx 1.33$ **9.** $\frac{1}{2}$ **11.** $\frac{\sqrt{2}}{2}$ **13.** 0.39 **15.** 0.03 **17.** 0.16 **19.** 9.65 m **21.** 7 ft 6 in. **23.** $\frac{15}{8} \approx 1.88$ **25.** $\frac{15}{17} \approx 0.88$ **27.** $\frac{15}{17} \approx 0.88$ **29.** $\frac{1}{2}$ **31.** 1.23 **33.** 0.22 **35.** 0.82 **37.** 3.58 cm **39.** 19.67 ft **41.** 5.27 ft **43.** 6.10 m **45.** sine; cosine **47.** 60° **49.** 1.2 ft **53.** 0.6 **55.** 753 ft **59.** $\left(\frac{1}{2}\right)^2 + \left(\frac{\sqrt{3}}{2}\right)^2 = \frac{1}{4} + \frac{3}{4} = 1$ **61a.** $\sin A = \frac{a}{c}$; $\cos A = \frac{b}{c}$ **b.** $(\sin A)^2 + (\cos A)^2 = \left(\frac{a}{c}\right)^2 + \left(\frac{b}{c}\right)^2 = \frac{a^2}{c^2} + \frac{b^2}{c^2} = \frac{a^2 + b^2}{c^2} = \frac{c^2}{c^2} = 1$ **63.** 18.64 cm; 16.00 cm^2 **65.** 22.60 in.; 14.69 in^2 **69.** H **71.** $x \approx 5$; $AB \approx 20$; $BC \approx 18$; $AC \approx 27$ **75.** 1.25 **77.** 0.75

8-3

Check It Out! **1a.** $\angle 2$ **1b.** $\angle 1$ **2a.** 37° **2b.** 87° **2c.** 42° **3.** $DF \approx 16.51$; $EF \approx 8.75$; $m\angle D = 32°$ **4.** $RS = ST = 7$; $RT \approx 9.90$; $m\angle S = 90°$; $m\angle R = m\angle T = 45°$ **5.** 21°

Exercises **1.** $\angle 1$ **3.** $\angle 1$ **5.** $\angle 2$ **7.** 65° **9.** 34° **11.** 38° **13.** $RP \approx 9.42$; $m\angle P \approx 19°$; $m\angle R \approx 71°$ **15.** $YZ \approx 13.96$; $m\angle Y \approx 38°$; $m\angle Z \approx 52°$ **17.** $RS = 5$; $ST = 6$; $RT \approx 7.81$; $m\angle S = 90°$; $m\angle R \approx 50°$; $m\angle T \approx 40°$ **19.** $AB = 2$; $BC = 4$; $AC \approx 4.47$; $m\angle B = 90°$; $m\angle A \approx 63°$; $m\angle C \approx 27°$ **21.** $\angle 2$ **23.** $\angle 1$ **25.** $\angle 2$ **27.** 18° **29.** 37° **31.** 57° **33.** $JK \approx 2.88$; $LK \approx 1.40$; $m\angle L = 64°$ **35.** $QR \approx 4.90$; $m\angle P \approx 36°$; $m\angle R \approx 54°$ **37.** $MN = NP = 4$; $MP \approx 5.66$; $m\angle N = 90°$; $m\angle M = m\angle P = 45°$ **39.** 74° **41.** cos **43.** 0.93 **47a.** 5° **b.** 85° **c.** 31 ft 1 in. **49.** 23°; 67° **51.** The acute $\angle$ measure changes from about 58° to about 73°, an increase by a factor of 1.26. **53a.** $AB = 5\sqrt{2}$; $BC = 2\sqrt{10}$; $AC = \sqrt{10}$ **b.** $AC^2 + BC^2 = AB^2$, so $\triangle ABC$ is a rt. $\triangle$, and $\angle C$ is the rt. $\angle$. **c.** $m\angle A = 63°$; $m\angle B = 27°$ **55.** 35° **57.** 62° **59.** 72° **61.** 39° **65.** D **67.** A **69.** 58° **71.** 34° **73.** x

8-4

Check It Out! **1a.** angle of depression **1b.** angle of elevation **2.** 6314 ft **3.** 1717 ft **4.** 32,300 ft

Exercises **1.** elevation **3.** angle of elevation **5.** angle of elevation **7.** 18 ft **9.** 64.6 m **11.** angle of elevation **13.** angle of depression **15.** 1962 ft **17.** T **19.** F **21.** $\angle 1$ and $\angle 3$ **25a.** 424 ft **b.** 276 ft **27a.** 2080 ft **b.** 14 s **29.** J **31.** 98 m **33.** 1318 ft

8-5

Check It Out! **1a.** −0.09 **1b.** −0.03 **1c.** 0.34 **2a.** 34.9 **2b.** 29° **2c.** 26° **2d.** 17.7 **3a.** 6.5 **3b.** 30° **3c.** 7.0 **3d.** 65° **4.** 68.6 m; 54°

Exercises **1.** 0.98 **3.** −28.64 **5.** −0.68 **7.** 0.54 **9.** −0.91 **11.** 43° **13.** 44° **15.** 17.3 **17.** −0.09 **19.** −1.88 **21.** 0.99 **23.** −0.87 **25.** 0.79 **27.** 20.6 **29.** 10.4 **31.** 65° **33.** 33° **35.** 8.4 **37.** 21° **39.** 8.2 cm **41.** 50° **43.** no **45.** 63° **47.** 41.2 ft **49.** 42°; 138° **51.** Law of Sines **53.** Law of Sines **55.** $BC \approx 10.73$; $AB \approx 10.34$; $m\angle ABC \approx 50°$ **57a.** $y^2 + h^2$ **b.** b^2 **c.** $a^2 = c^2 - 2cx + x^2 + h^2$ **d.** $a^2 = c^2 + b^2 - 2cx$ **e.** $b \cos A$ **f.** Subst. **59.** A **61.** C **63.** 31°

8-6

Check It Out! **1a.** $\langle -3, -4 \rangle$ **1b.** $\langle 7, 1 \rangle$ **2.** 3.2 **3.** 23°

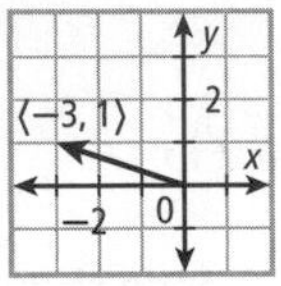

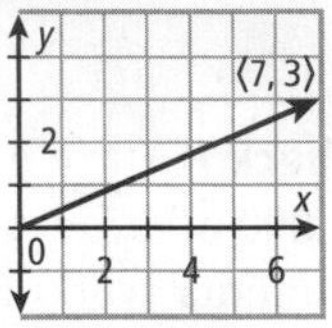

4a. $\overrightarrow{PQ} = \overrightarrow{RS}$ **4b.** $\overrightarrow{PQ} \parallel \overrightarrow{RS}$; $\overrightarrow{XY} \parallel \overrightarrow{MN}$ **5.** 4.4 mi/h; 58°, or N 32° E

Exercises **1.** equal **3.** magnitude **5.** $\langle 8, -8 \rangle$ **7.** 4.1 **9.** 5.8 **11.** 11° **13.** $\overrightarrow{CD} = \overrightarrow{EF}$ **15.** $\overrightarrow{RS} = \overrightarrow{XY}$ **17.** 4.6 mi; 20°, or N 70° E **19.** $\langle -3.5, 5.5 \rangle$ **21.** 2.0 **23.** 4.3 **25.** 36° **27.** $\overrightarrow{DE} = \overrightarrow{LM}$ **29.** $\overrightarrow{RS} = \overrightarrow{UV}$ **31.** 190.1 km/h; 54°, or N 36° E **33.** $\langle 2, 2 \rangle$ **35.** $\langle 6, 2 \rangle$ **37a.** 98° **b.** 68.9 mi/h **c.** 36° **d.** N 81° E **39.** $\langle 7.1, 1.1 \rangle$ **41.** $\langle 2.2, 5.4 \rangle$ **43a.** $\frac{1}{12}$ **b.** $\frac{1}{6}$ **45.** 4; 0° **47.** 3.6; 56° **49.** $\langle 0, 10 \rangle$, $\langle 10, 0 \rangle$; $\langle 10, 10 \rangle$; the magnitude of the resultant is $10\sqrt{2}$, and the direction of the resultant is $\tan^{-1}\left(\frac{10}{10}\right) = 45°$. **53.** $\langle 3.5, 1 \rangle$; 3.6; 16° **55.** $\langle 4, 4 \rangle$; 5.7; 45° **57a.** $\langle 1, 3 \rangle$; $\langle 2, 6 \rangle$ **b.** $\sqrt{10}$; $2\sqrt{10}$; the magnitude of $2\vec{v}$ is twice the magnitude of $\vec{v}$. **c.** 72°; 72°; the direction of $2\vec{v}$ is the same as the direction of $\vec{v}$. **d.** Multiply each component by k. **e.** $-\vec{v} = -1\vec{v} = -1\langle x, y \rangle = \langle -x, -y \rangle$ **61.** G **63.** 8.2 **65.** 180° **67.** 6.4 mi/h at a bearing of N 58° E

Study Guide: Review

1. component form **2.** equal vectors **3.** geometric mean **4.** angle of elevation **5.** trigonometric ratio **6.** $\triangle PRQ \sim \triangle RSQ \sim \triangle PSR$ **7.** 5 **8.** $\sqrt{51}$ **9.** $x = \sqrt{35}$; $y = 2\sqrt{15}$; $z = 2\sqrt{21}$ **10.** $x = 3$; $y = 3\sqrt{5}$; $z = 6\sqrt{5}$ **11.** $x = 5$; $y = \sqrt{5}$;

$z = \sqrt{30}$ **12.** 11.17 m **13.** 6.30 m **14.** 10.32 cm **15.** 1.31 cm **16.** m∠C = 68°; $AB \approx 4.82$; $AC \approx 1.95$ **17.** m∠$H \approx 53°$; m∠$G \approx 37°$; $HG \approx 5.86$ **18.** m∠$S = 40°$; $RS \approx 42.43$; $RT \approx 27.27$ **19.** m∠$Q \approx 41°$; m∠$N \approx 49°$; $QN \approx 13.11$ **20.** angle of depression **21.** angle of elevation **22.** 36 ft **23.** 458 m **24.** 22° **25.** 31.4 **26.** 20.1 **27.** 56° **28.** ⟨−7, 2⟩ **29.** ⟨1, −6⟩ **30.** ⟨−2, −5⟩

31.
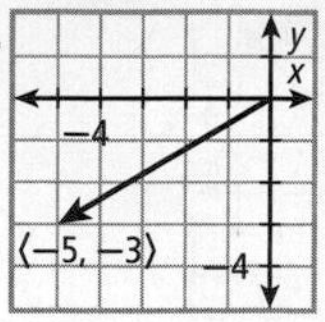

5.8

32.
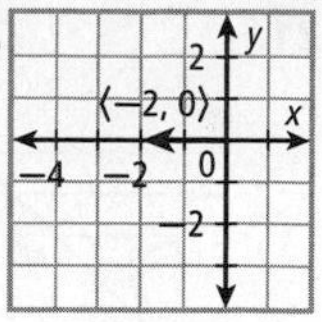

2

33.
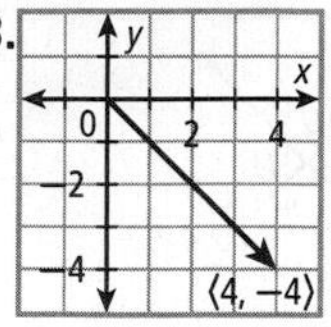

5.7

34.
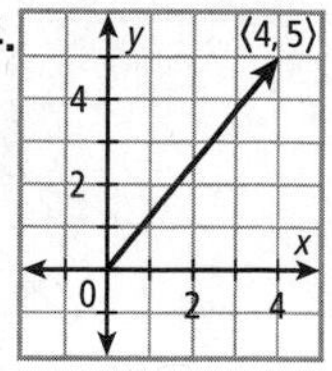

51°

35.
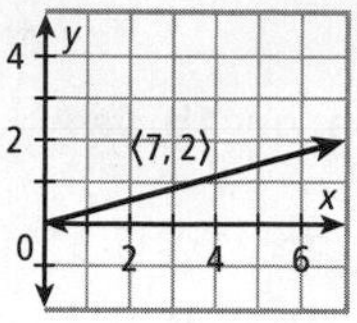

16°

36. 641.6 mi/h; 32°, or N 58° E

Selected Answers ■ Chapter 9

9-1

Check It Out! 1a. no **1b.** yes

2.

3. $\overline{AX}$ and $\overline{BX}$ would be ≅.

4.

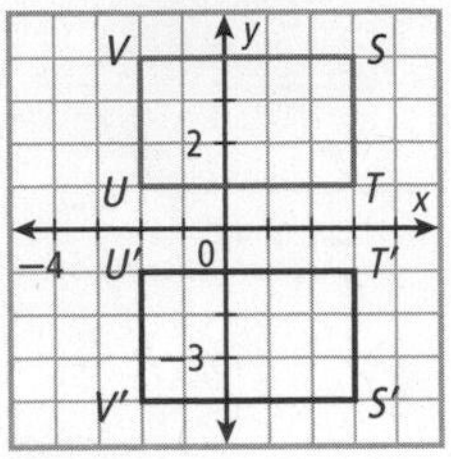

Exercises 1. They are ≅. **3.** no **5.** no

7.

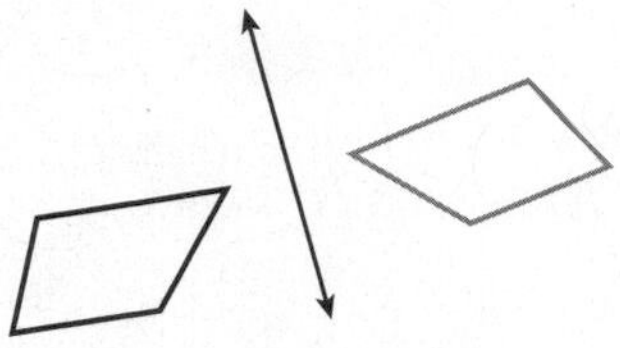

9.

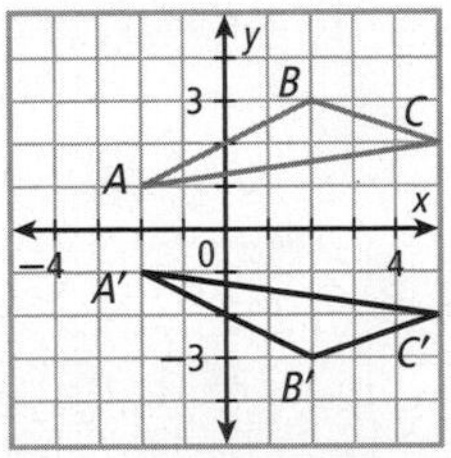

11.

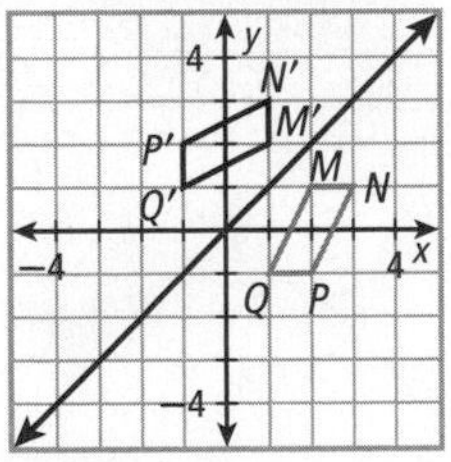

13. no **15.** yes

17.

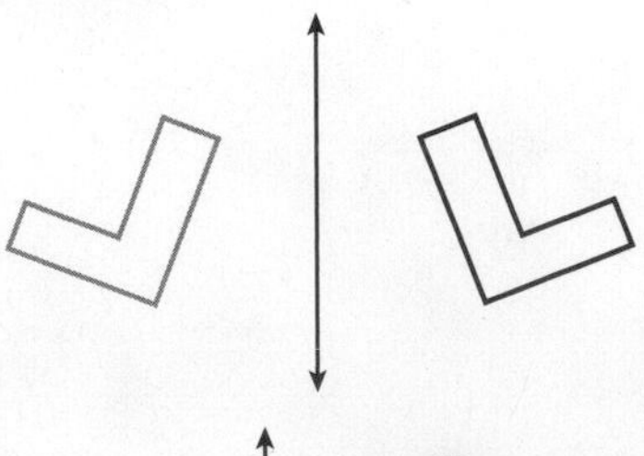

19.

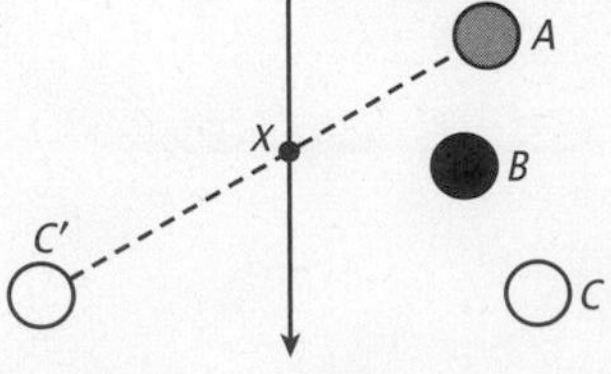

21.

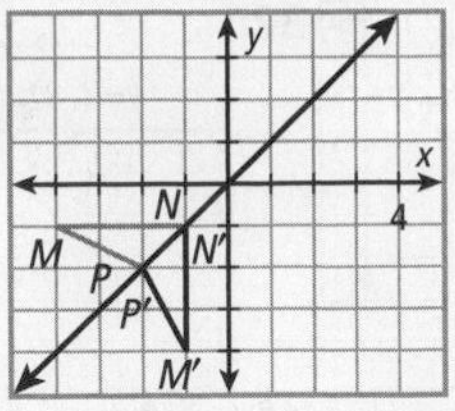

23.

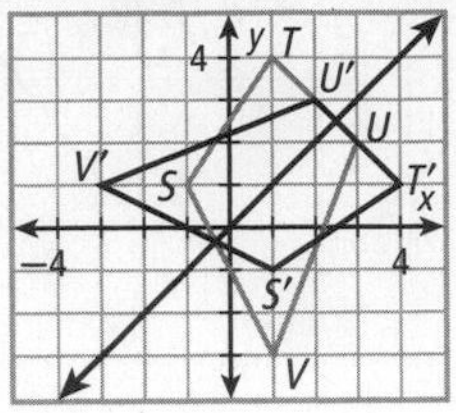

27.

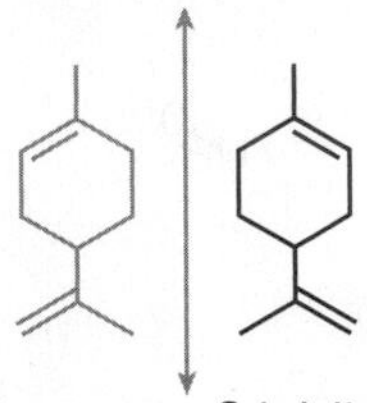

R-(+)-limonene *S*-(−)-limonene

29.

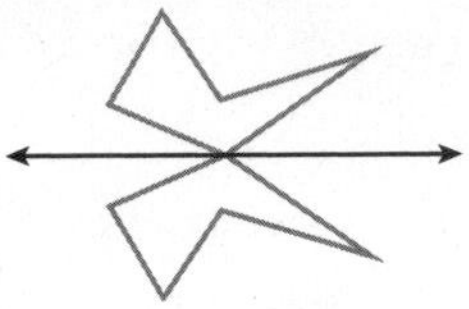

31. (5, 2) → (5, −2) **33.** (0, 12) → (0, −12) **35.** (0, −5) → (−5, 0)
37a. no **b.** (7, 4) **c.** (6, 3.5)
39. $y = x$

41.

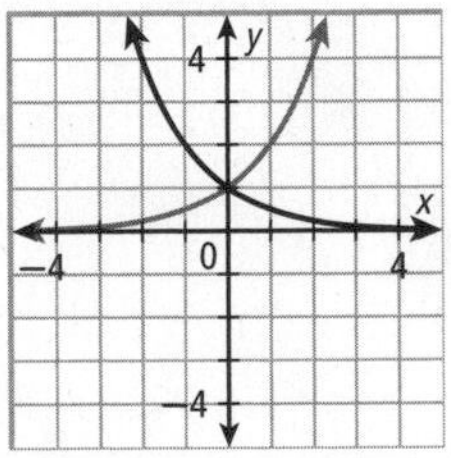

47. J **49.** (4, 4) **51.** (−1, 5)
53. Use the fact that the reflection of a seg. is ≅ to the preimage and the def. of ≅ segs. **55.** Use the fact that the reflection of a seg. is ≅ to the preimage to prove △*ABC* ≅ △*A′B′C′* by SSS.

9-2

Check It Out! 1a. Yes **1b.** no

2.

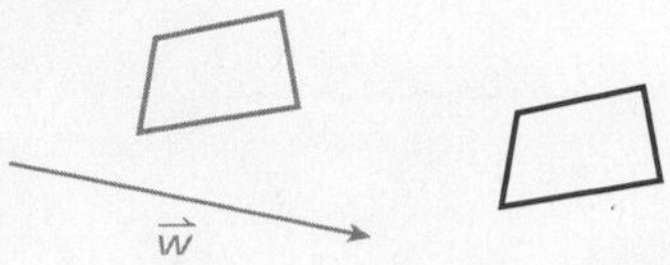

3.

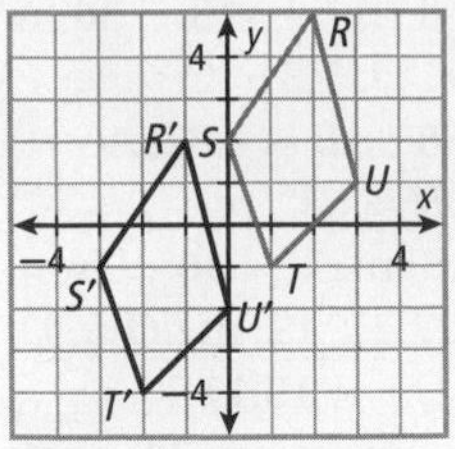

4. (16, −24)

Exercises 1. no **3.** yes

7.

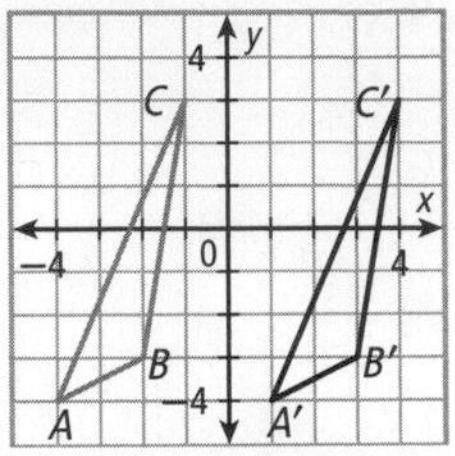

9.

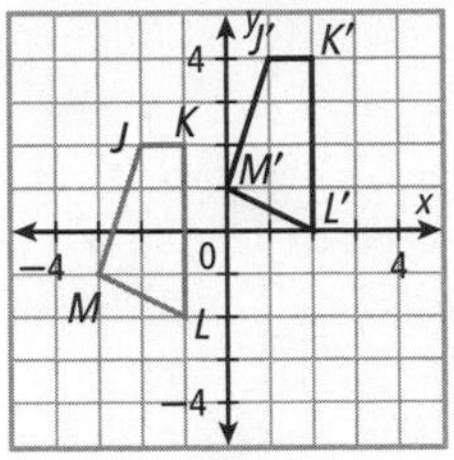

11. yes **13.** no

17.

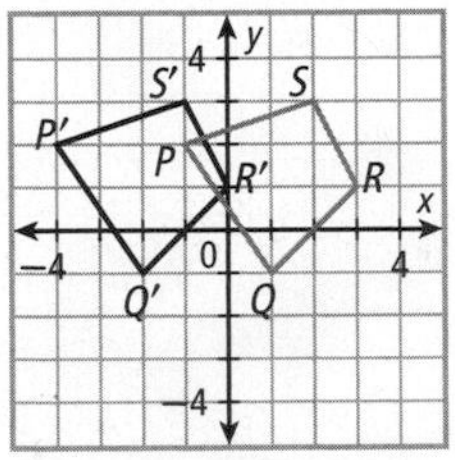

19.

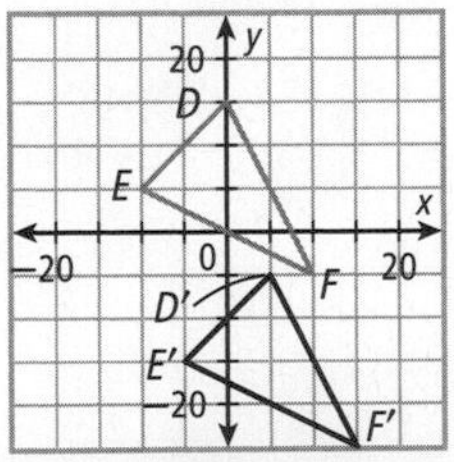

21.

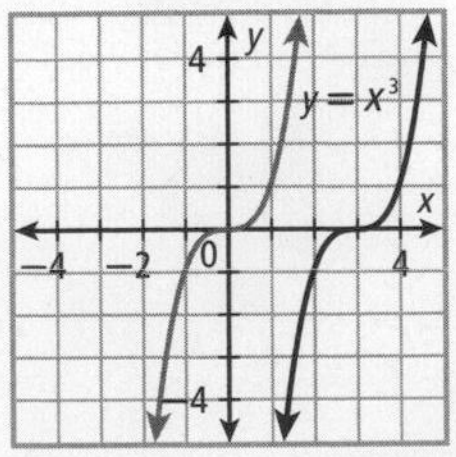

23a. $\frac{1}{4}$ **b.** $\frac{1}{2}$. **c.** 0 **27.** No; there are no fixed pts. because, by def. of a translation, every pt. must move by the same distance.
29. ⟨4, 0⟩, (−3, 2) → (1, 2)

31. ⟨−3, −2⟩, (3, −1)→ (0, −3)
33. ⟨−3, 1⟩, (3, −1) → (0, 0) **39.** A
41. C **43a.** the vector $\overrightarrow{PQ}$
b. 3.46 cm **45.** Use the fact that the translation of a seg. is ≅ to the preimage and the def. of ≅ segs.
47. Use the fact that the translation of a seg. is ≅ to the preimage to prove △*ABC* ≅ △*A'B'C'* by SSS.

9-3

Check It Out! 1a. no **1b.** yes

2.

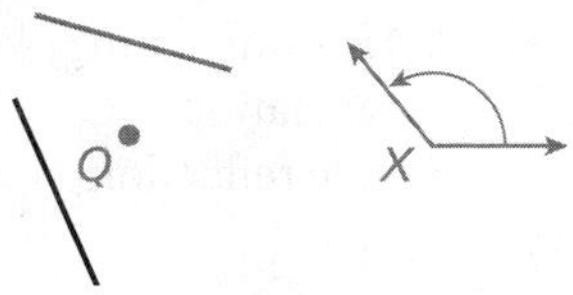

3.

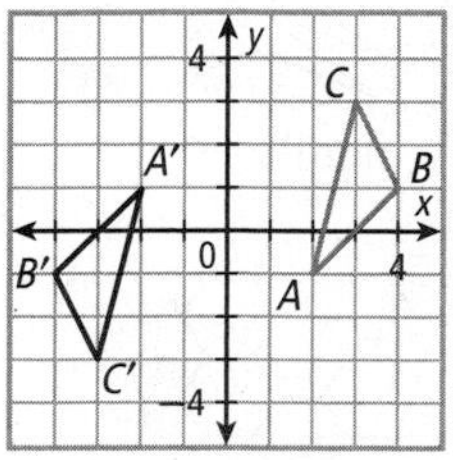

4. (20.9, 64.2)

Exercises 1. yes **3.** no

5.

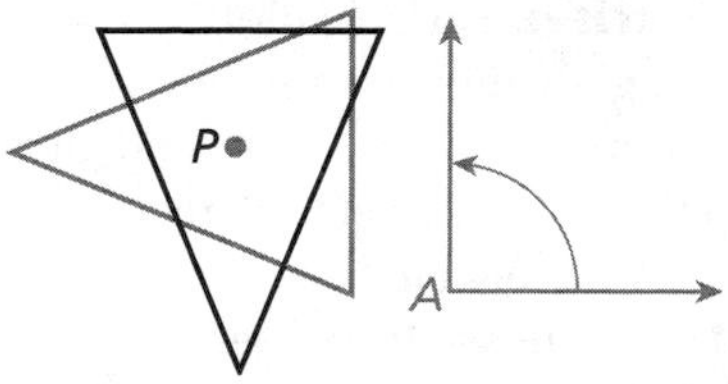

7.

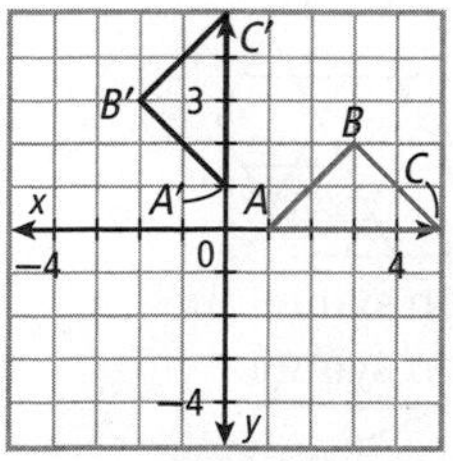

9.

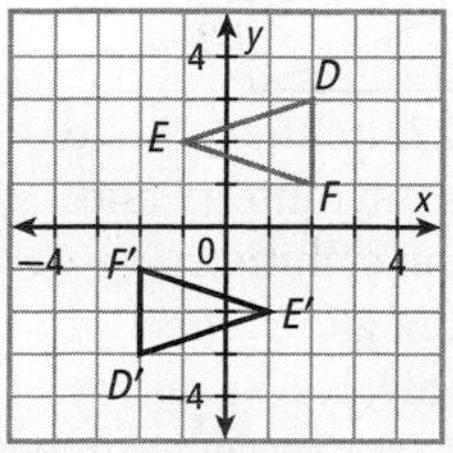

11. (8.7, 5) **13.** yes **15.** no

17.

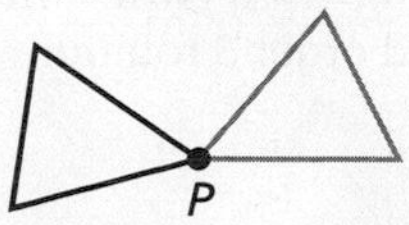

19.

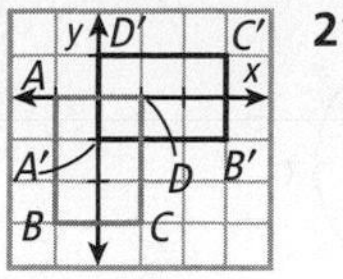

21.

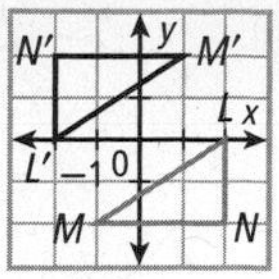

23.

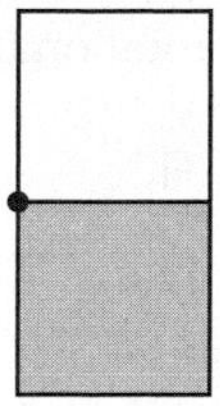

25.

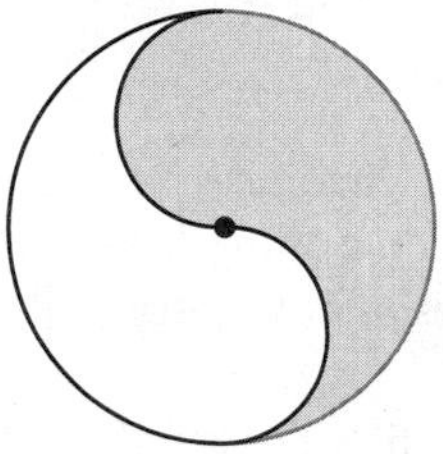

27. *T* **29.** $\overline{ST}$ **31a.** 72°
31b. (4.9, 5.9)
33.

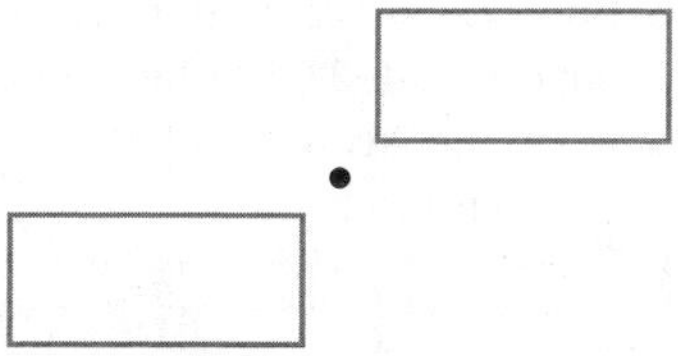

35a. 90° **35b.** 6 hours
37. No; although all pts. are rotated around the center of rotation by the same ∠, pts. that are farther from the center of rotation move a greater distance than pts. that are closer to the center of rotation.
39. *A'*(−2, 3), *B'*(−3, 0), *C'* (0, −3), D'(3, 0), E'(2, 3), **43.** H
45. 160° **47.** Use the fact that the rotation of a seg. is ≅ to the preimage and the def. of ≅ segs.
49. Use the fact that the rotation of a seg. is ≅ to the preimage to prove △*ABC* ≅ △*A'B'C'* by SSS.
51. If *A*, *B*, and *C* are collinear, then one pt. is between the other two. Case 1: If *C* is between *A* and *B*, then *AC* + *BC* = *AB*. Use the fact that the rotation of a seg. is ≅ to the preimage to prove *A'C'* + *B'C'* = *A'B'*. Then *C'* is between *A'* and *B'*, so *A'*, *B'*, and *C'* are collinear. Prove the other two cases similarly.

9-4

Check It Out!
1.

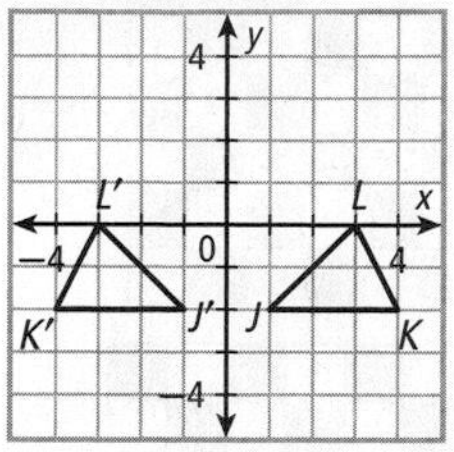

2. a translation in direction ⊥ to *n* and *p*, by distance of 6 in.
3.

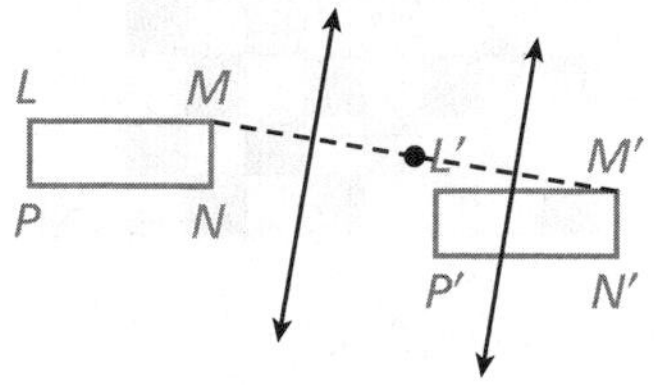

Exercises 1. Draw a figure and translate it along a vector. Then reflect the image across a line.
3.

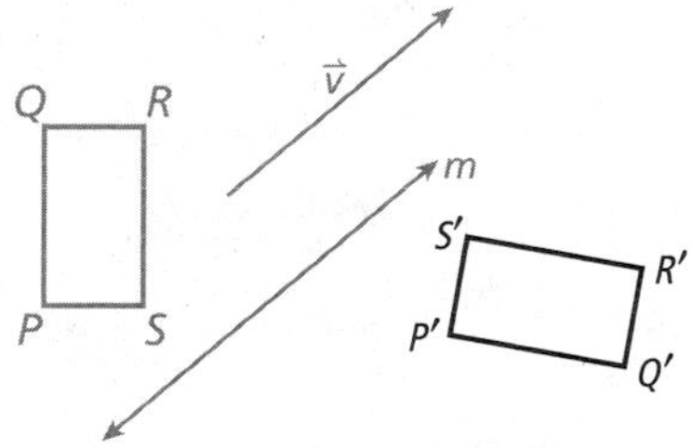

5. a rotation of 100° about the pt. of intersection of the lines
7.

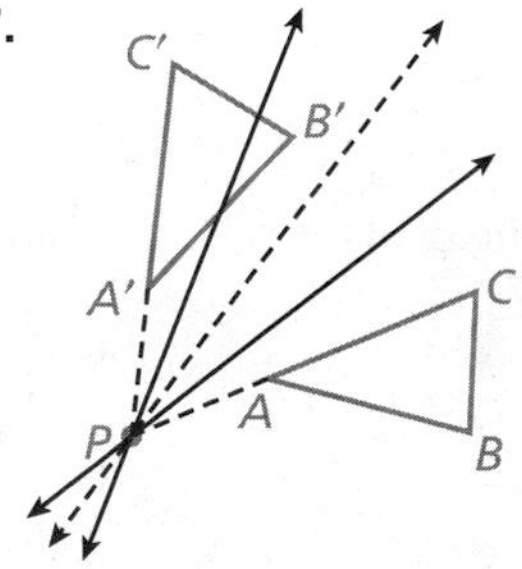

9.

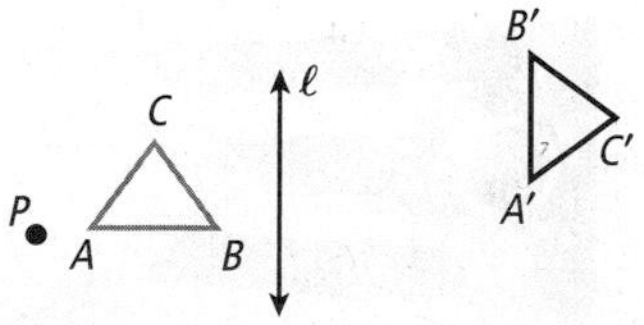

11a. The move is a horiz. or vert. translation by 2 spaces followed by a vert. or horiz. translation by 1 space.

11b.

11c.

13.

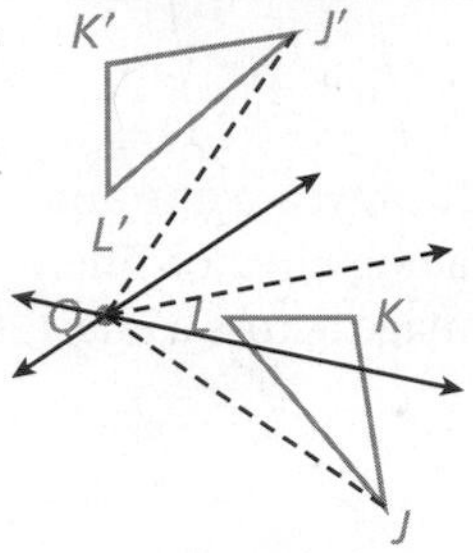

17. never **19.** always **23.** A
25. C

9-5

Check It Out!

1a. yes; 2 lines of symmetry

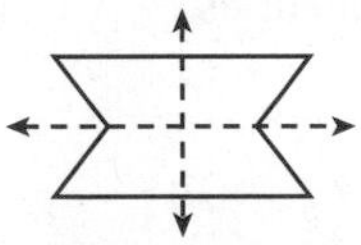

1b. yes; 1 line of symmetry

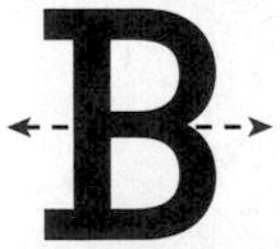

1c. yes; 1 line of symmetry

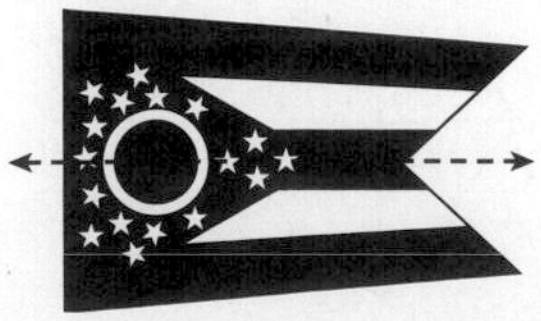

2a. yes; 120°; order: 3 **2b.** yes; 180°; order: 2° **2c.** no
3a. line symmetry and rotational symmetry; 72°; order: 5

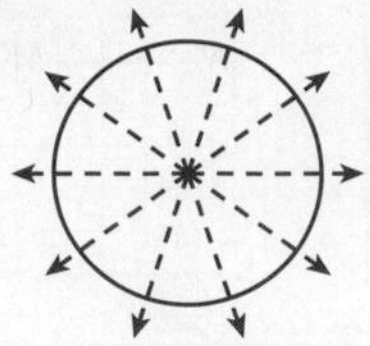

3b. line symmetry and rotational symmetry; 51.4°; order: 7
4a. both **4b.** neither

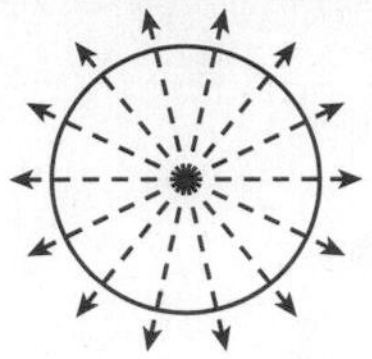

Exercises **1.** The line of symmetry is the ⊥ bisector of the base.
3. yes; 2 lines of symmetry
5. no **7.** no
9. 72°; order: 5
11. both
13. yes; 1 line of symmetry
15. no **17.** yes; 72°; order: 5
19. 90; order: 4 **21.** neither
23. isosc. **25.** scalene **27.** 0
29. line symmetry

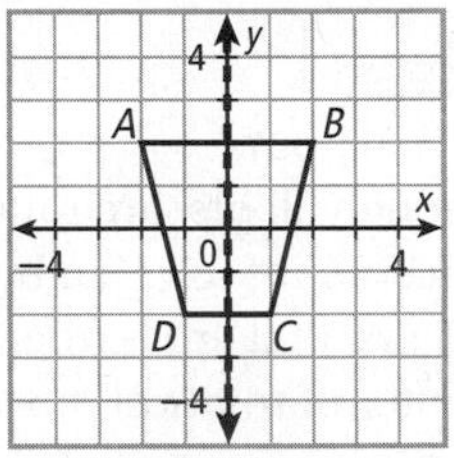

31. line symmetry

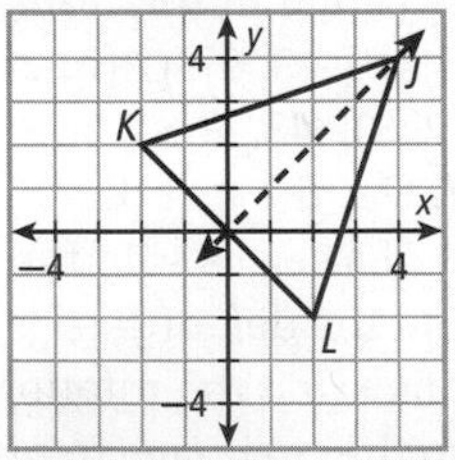

33. rotational symmetry of order 4
35. line symmetry; $x = 2$ **37a.** no **b.** yes; 180°; 2. **c.** Yes; if color is not taken into account the ∠ of rotational symmetry is 90.
39. parallelogram **41.** square
43. 15° **45.** It has rotational symmetry of order 3, with an ∠ of rotational symmetry of 120°.

47.

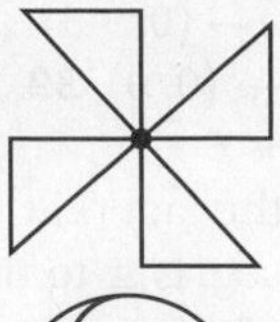

49.

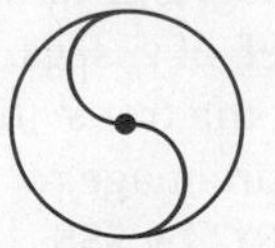

51. A **53.** C **55.** 72 **57.** $x = -4$
59. $x = 0$ **61.** 8

9-6

Check It Out! **1a.** translation symmetry **1b.** translation symmetry and glide reflection symmetry
2.

3a. regular **3b.** neither.
3c. semiregular
4a. yes

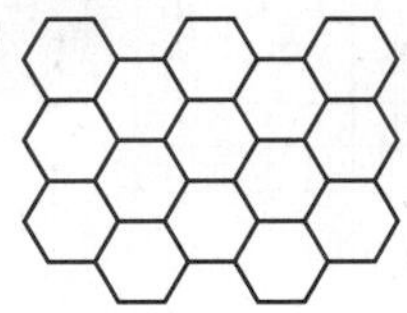

4b. no

Exercises **3.** translation symmetry and glide reflection symmetry
5. translation symmetry and glide reflection symmetry **9.** regular
11. semiregular
13. yes; possible answer

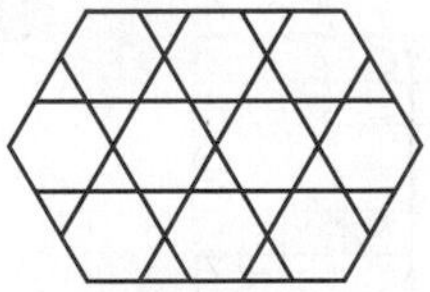

15. translation symmetry
17. translation symmetry
19.

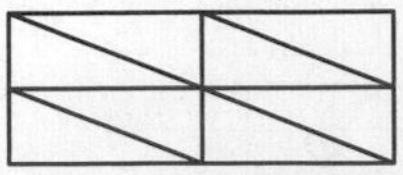

21. neither **23.** neither **25.** no
27. translation symmetry and glide reflection symmetry
29. translation, glide reflection, rotation **31.** always **33.** always
35. never **41.** The tessellation has translation symmetry, reflection symmetry, and order 3 rotation symmetry.

43. $CH_2 - CH$ (with CH_3 attached below the CH)

47. H **51.** yes

9-7

Check It Out! 1a. no **1b.** yes

2.

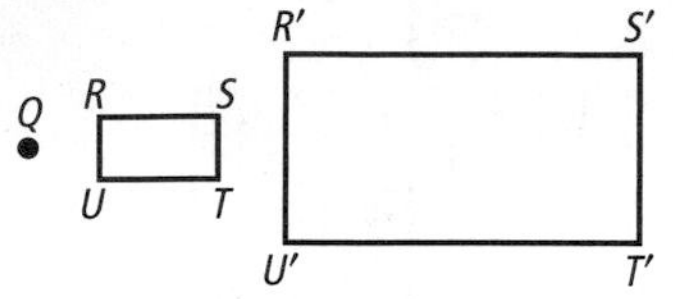

3. 1600 in^2

4.

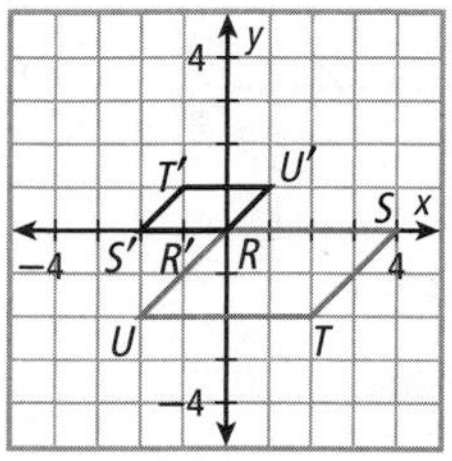

Exercises 1. The center is the origin; the scale factor is 3. **3.** yes **5.** yes

7.

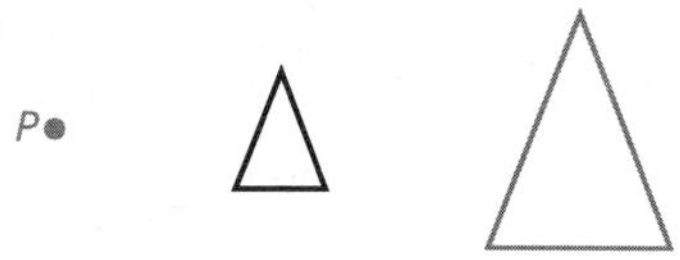

9.

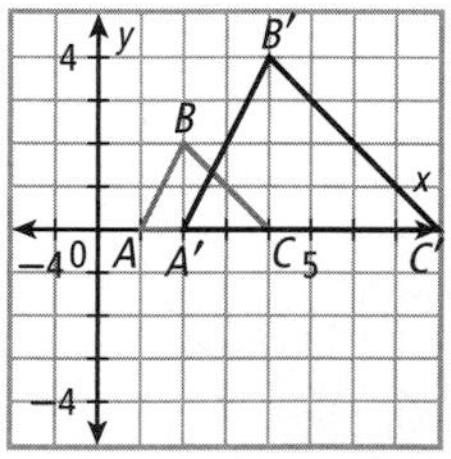

11.

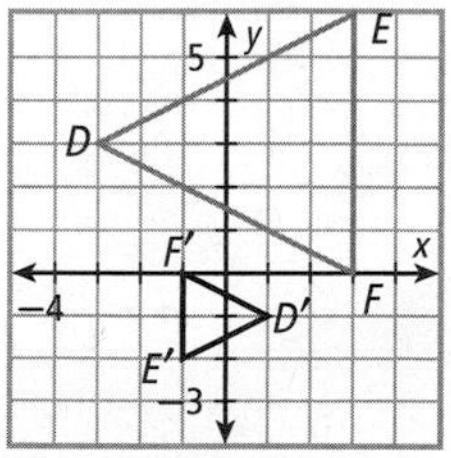

13. yes **15.** no **19.** 108

21.

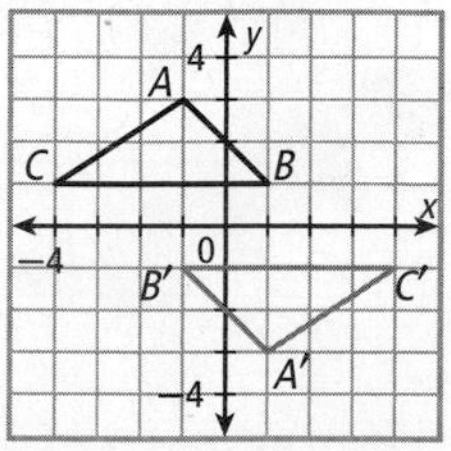

23.

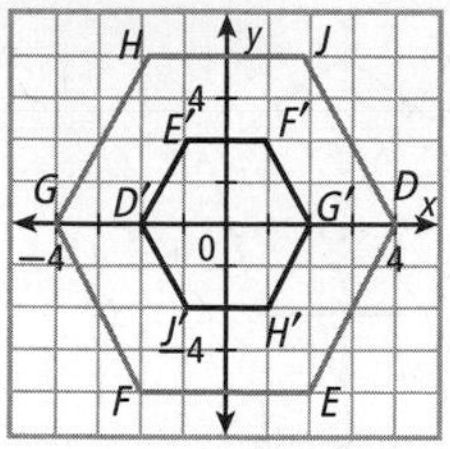

25. $ABCDE \sim MNPQR$

27.

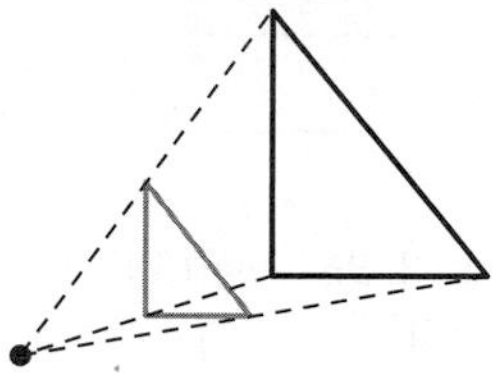

29.

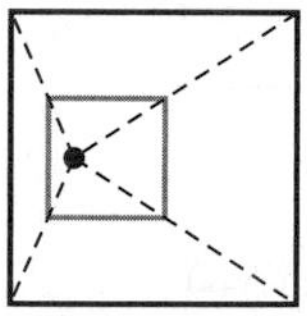

31. B **35.** -4.5×10^{-12} **37.** $k = -2$; $A'(4, -4)$, $B'(-2, -6)$ **39.** $k = 1$ and $k = -1$ **47.** H **49.** no **51.** $y = -x + 6$

Study Guide: Review

1. reg. tessellation **2.** frieze pattern **3.** isometry **4.** composition of transformations **5.** yes **6.** no **7.** no **8.** yes

9.

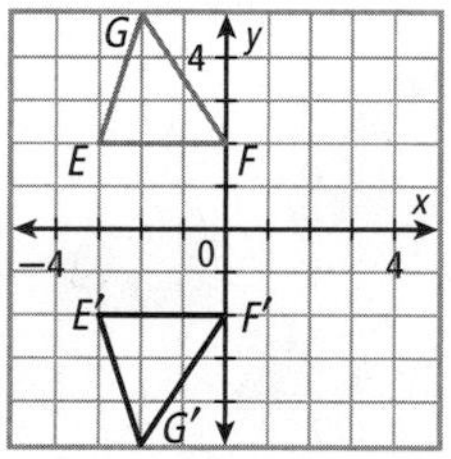

10.

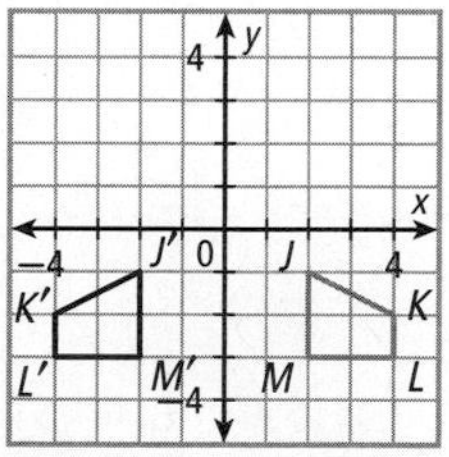

11.

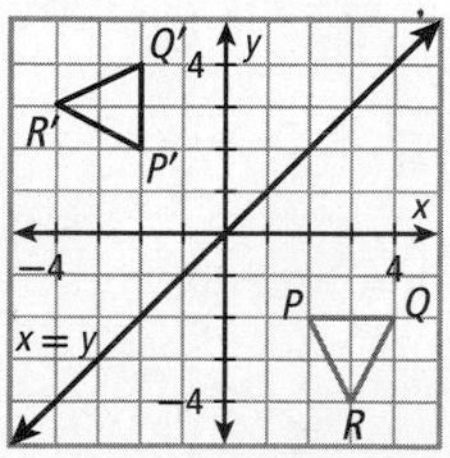

12.

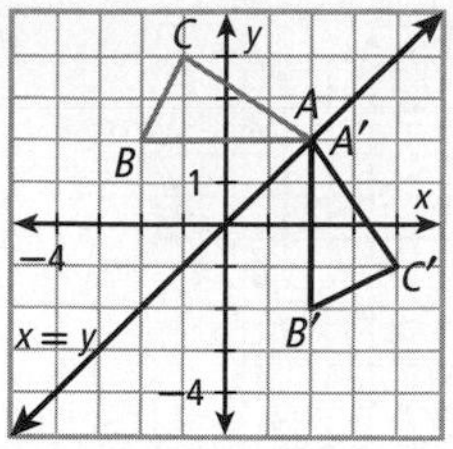

13. no **14.** yes **15.** no **16.** no

17.

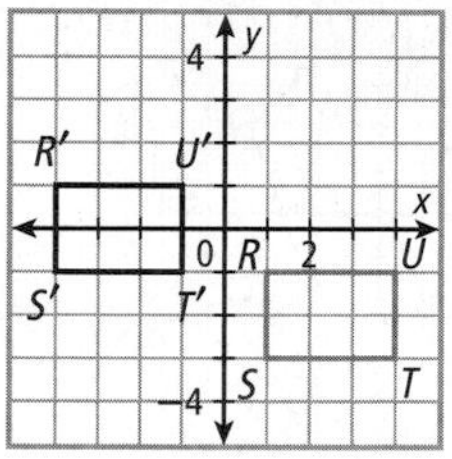

18.

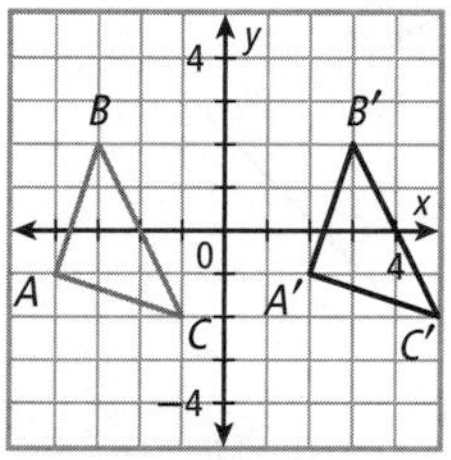

19.

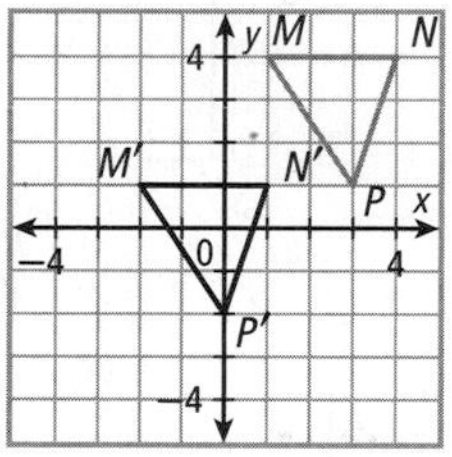

20.

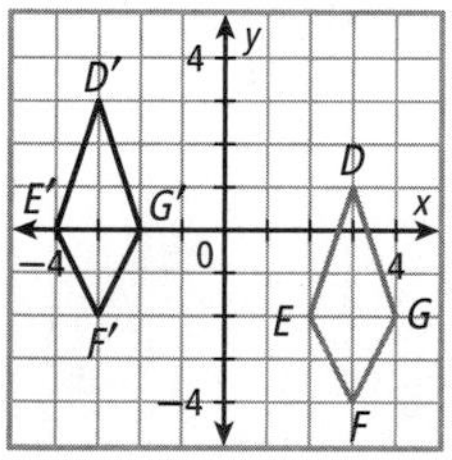

21. yes **22.** yes **23.** no **24.** no

25.

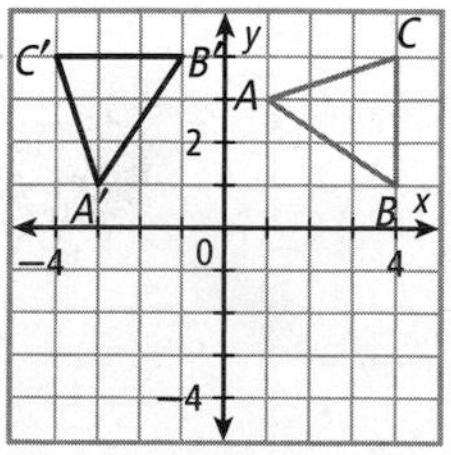

26.

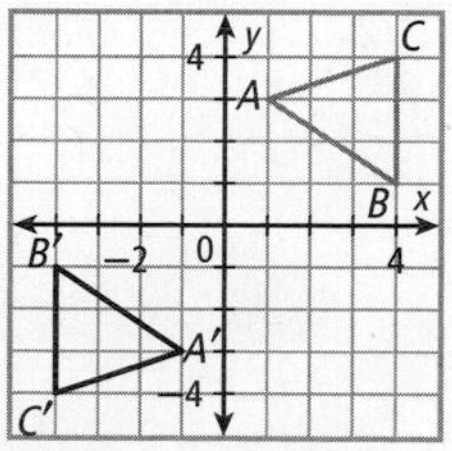

27.

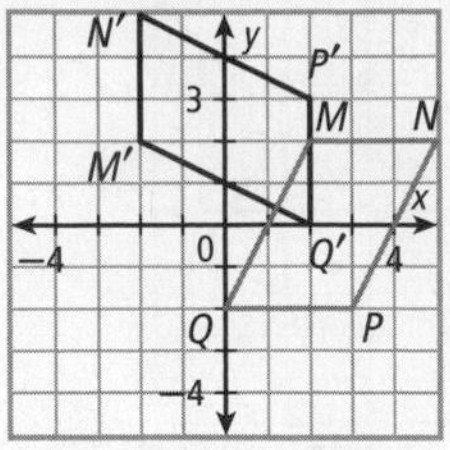

28.

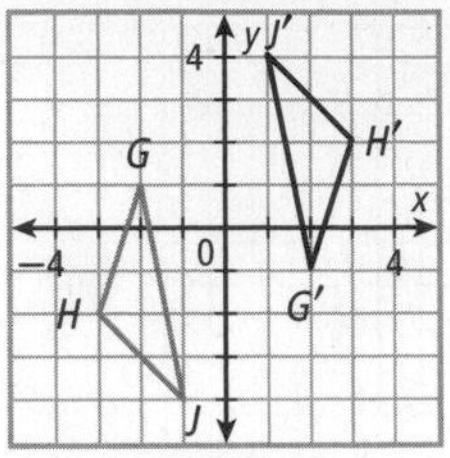

29.

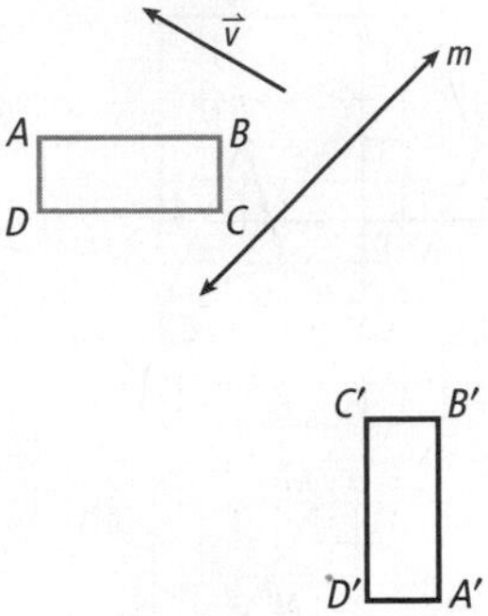

30.

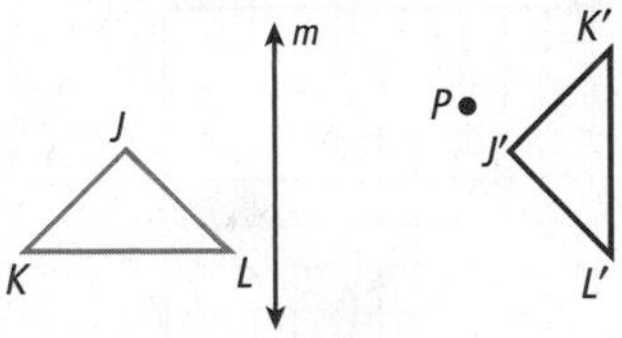

31. yes

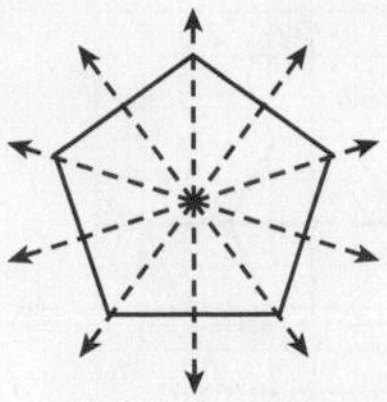

32. yes

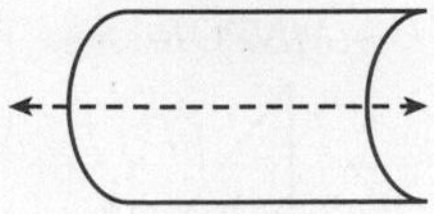

33. yes; 120°; 3 **34.** no

35. yes; 120°; 3 **36.** yes; 180°; 2

37.

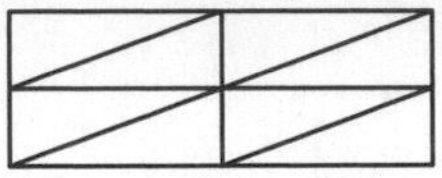

38.

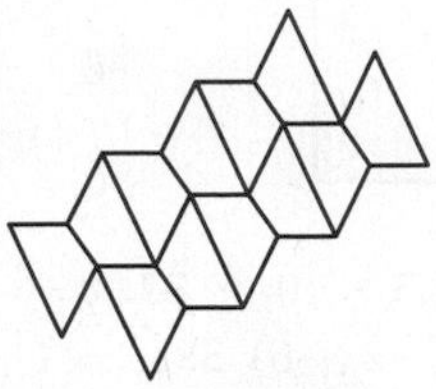

39.

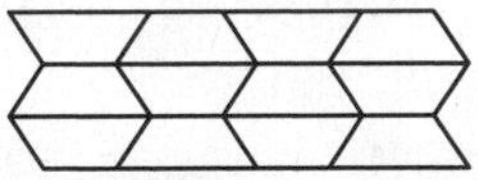

40.

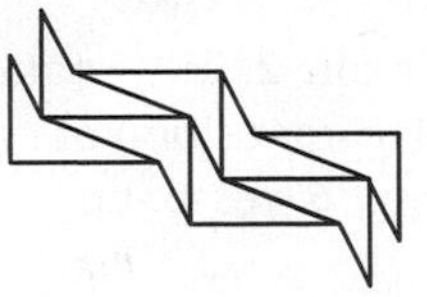

41. neither

42. semiregular **43.** yes **44.** yes

45.

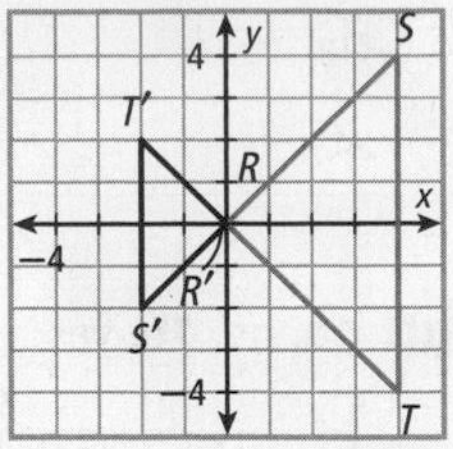

46.

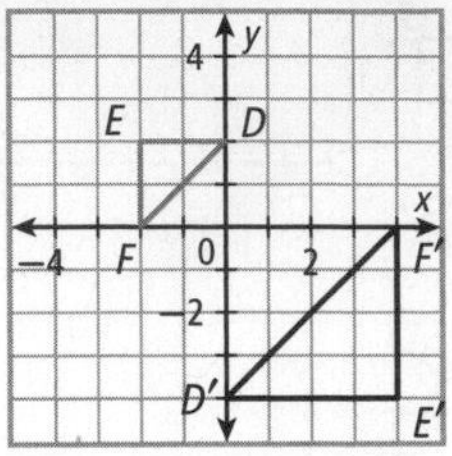

Mastering the Standards

for Mathematical Practice

The topics described in the Standards for Mathematical Content will vary from year to year. However, the *way* in which you learn, study, and think about mathematics will not. The Standards for Mathematical Practice describe skills that you will use in all of your math courses.

Mathematical Practices

1. *Make sense of problems and persevere in solving them.*
2. *Reason abstractly and quantitatively.*
3. *Construct viable arguments and critique the reasoning of others.*
4. *Model with mathematics.*
5. *Use appropriate tools strategically.*
6. *Attend to precision.*
7. *Look for and make use of structure.*
8. *Look for and express regularity in repeated reasoning.*

1 Make sense of problems and persevere in solving them.

Mathematically proficient students start by explaining to themselves the meaning of a problem... They analyze givens, constraints, relationships, and goals. They make conjectures about the form... of the solution and plan a solution pathway...

Comstock/Getty Images

In your book

Focus on Problem Solving describes a four-step plan for problem solving. The plan is introduced at the beginning of your book, and practice with the plan appears throughout the book.

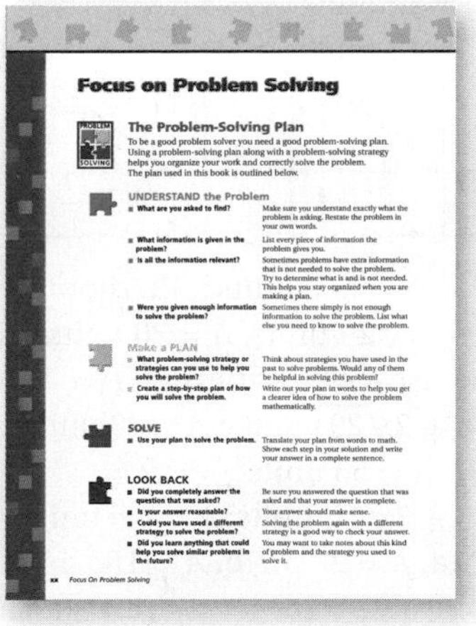

Focus on Problem Solving

The Problem-Solving Plan

To be a good problem solver you need a good problem-solving plan. Using a problem-solving plan along with a problem-solving strategy helps you organize your work and correctly solve the problem. The plan used in this book is outlined below.

UNDERSTAND the Problem

What are you asked to find?	Make sure you understand exactly what the problem is asking. Restate the problem in your own words.
What information is given in the problem?	List every piece of information the problem gives you.
Is all the information relevant?	Sometimes problems have extra information that is not needed to solve the problem. Try to determine what is and is not needed. This helps you stay organized when you are making a plan.
Were you given enough information to solve the problem?	Sometimes there simply is not enough information to solve the problem. List what else you need to know to solve the problem.

Make a PLAN

What problem-solving strategy or strategies can you use to help you solve the problem?	Think about strategies you have used in the past to solve problems. Would any of them be helpful in solving this problem?
Create a step-by-step plan of how you will solve the problem.	Write out your plan in words to help you get a clearer idea of how to solve the problem mathematically.

SOLVE

Use your plan to solve the problem.	Translate your plan from words to math. Show each step in your solution and write your answer in a complete sentence.

LOOK BACK

Did you completely answer the question that was asked?	Be sure you answered the question that was asked and that your answer is complete.
Is your answer reasonable?	Your answer should make sense.
Could you have used a different strategy to solve the problem?	Solving the problem again with a different strategy is a good way to check your answer.
Did you learn anything that could help you solve similar problems in the future?	You may want to take notes about this kind of problem and the strategy you used to solve it.

xx *Focus On Problem Solving*

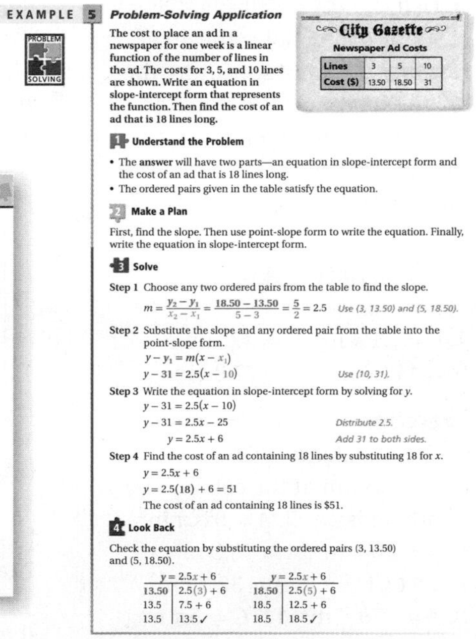

EXAMPLE 5 ***Problem-Solving Application***

PROBLEM SOLVING

The cost to place an ad in a newspaper for one week is a linear function of the number of lines in the ad. The costs for 3, 5, and 10 lines are shown. Write an equation in slope-intercept form that represents the function. Then find the cost of an ad that is 18 lines long.

City Gazette

Newspaper Ad Costs

Lines	3	5	10
Cost ($)	13.50	18.50	31

1 Understand the Problem

- The **answer** will have two parts—an equation in slope-intercept form and the cost of an ad that is 18 lines long.
- The ordered pairs given in the table satisfy the equation.

2 Make a Plan

First, find the slope. Then use point-slope form to write the equation. Finally, write the equation in slope-intercept form.

3 Solve

Step 1 Choose any two ordered pairs from the table to find the slope.

$$m = \frac{y_2 - y_1}{x_2 - x_1} = \frac{18.50 - 13.50}{5 - 3} = \frac{5}{2} = 2.5 \quad \textit{Use (3, 13.50) and (5, 18.50).}$$

Step 2 Substitute the slope and any ordered pair from the table into the point-slope form.

$y - y_1 = m(x - x_1)$

$y - 31 = 2.5(x - 10)$ *Use (10, 31).*

Step 3 Write the equation in slope-intercept form by solving for y.

$y - 31 = 2.5(x - 10)$

$y - 31 = 2.5x - 25$ *Distribute 2.5.*

$y = 2.5x + 6$ *Add 31 to both sides.*

Step 4 Find the cost of an ad containing 18 lines by substituting 18 for x.

$y = 2.5x + 6$

$y = 2.5(18) + 6 = 51$

The cost of an ad containing 18 lines is $51.

4 Look Back

Check the equation by substituting the ordered pairs (3, 13.50) and (5, 18.50).

$y = 2.5x + 6$	
13.50	2.5(3) + 6
13.5	7.5 + 6
13.5	13.5 ✓

$y = 2.5x + 6$	
18.50	2.5(5) + 6
18.5	12.5 + 6
18.5	18.5 ✓

10-1

Check It Out! 1. $b = 0.5$ yd **2.** $A = 96$ m^2 **3.** $d_2 = 8y$ m **4.** $P = \left(4 + 4\sqrt{2}\right)$ cm; $A = 4$ cm^2

Exercises 1. $A = 120$ cm^2 **3.** $P = 52$ cm **5.** $b = 13$ in. **7.** $A = 336$ in^2 **9.** $d_2 = 8xy^2$ cm **11.** $h = 1.25$ m **13.** $A = \left(21x^2 + 32x - 5\right)$ ft^2 **15.** $h = 20$ cm **17.** $A = 196\sqrt{3}$ in^2 **19.** $A = \left(12x^2 + 34x + 20\right)$ ft **21.** $A = 4.5$ in^2 **23.** $A = 30\sqrt{3}$ cm^2 **25.** $A = 300$ in^2 **27.** $A = \frac{x^2\sqrt{3}}{2}$ **29a.** $h = 31.2$ in. **b.** $A = 561.2$ in^2 **c.** 734.8 in^2 **31.** 8; 50 **33.** 9; 24 **35.** $h = 5$ cm **37.** 9 **39.** 100 **41.** $A = 108$ ft^2 **43a.** $A = \frac{1}{2}(a + b)^2$ **b.** $\frac{1}{2}ab$; $\frac{1}{2}ab$; $\frac{1}{2}c^2$ **c.** $\frac{1}{2}(a + b)^2 = \frac{1}{2}ab + \frac{1}{2}ab + \frac{1}{2}c^2$; $a^2 + b^2 = c^2$ **47a.** Possible answers: A: 4.2 cm^2; B: 3.8 cm^2; C: 4.3 cm^2 **b.** C has the greatest area. **49.** 23 cases **53.** H **55.** H **57.** $h = 4$ in. **59.** $b = (7x + 5)$ cm; $h = (6x + 3)$ cm **61a.** $A = x(12 - x)$ **b.** D: $0 < x < 12$; R: $0 < y \leq 36$ **c.** 6 ft by 6 ft **d.** Solve the area formula for y and substitute the expression into the perimeter formula. Graph, and find the minimum value.

10-2

Check It Out! 1. $A = \left(4x^2 - 12x + 9\right)\pi$ m^2 **2.** $C \approx 31.4$ in.; $C \approx 37.7$ in.; $C \approx 44.0$ in. **3.** $A \approx 77.3$ cm^2

Exercises 1. Draw a segment perpendicular to a side with one endpoint at the center. The apothem is $\frac{1}{2}s$. **3.** $A = 9x^2\pi$ in^2 **5.** $A \approx 50.3$ in^2; $A \approx 78.5$ in^2; $A \approx 113.1$ in^2 **7.** $A \approx 32.7$ cm^2 **9.** $A \approx 279.9$ m^2 **11.** $C = 5\pi$ m **13.** $A \approx 962.1$ ft^2; $A \approx 1963.5$ ft^2; $A \approx 3421.2$ ft^2 **15.** $A \approx 13.3$ ft^2 **17.** $A \approx 14.5$ ft^2 **19.** 90° **21.** 60° **23.** 45° **25.** 36° **27.** $A \approx 84.3$ cm^2 **29.** $A \approx 46.8$ m^2 **31.** $A \approx 90.8$ ft^2 **35.** $20\frac{\sqrt{\pi}}{\pi}$; $10\frac{\sqrt{\pi}}{\pi}$; $20\sqrt{\pi}$ **37.** 36; 18; 324π **39a.** $A \approx 745.6$ in^2 **b.** $A \approx 1073.6$ in^2 **c.** 44% **43.** B **45.** B **47.** $A = \frac{C^2}{4\pi}$

10-3

Check It Out! 1. $A = 1781.3$ m^2 **2.** $A \approx 10.3$ in^2 **3.** 23,296.5 gal **4.** $A \approx 12$ ft^2

Exercises 3. $A \approx 16.3$ ft^2 **5.** $A = 17.5$ m^2 **7.** $A \approx 4.5$ in^2 **9.** $A = 49.5$ mm^2 **11.** $A \approx 2.3$ m^2 **13.** 7 qt **15.** $A \approx 9$ m^2 **17.** $A = 540$ in^2 **19.** $A = \left(25\sqrt{3} + \frac{75\pi}{2}\right)$ in^2 **21.** Possible answer: 35,000 mi^2 **23a.** $A = 675$ in^2 **b.**

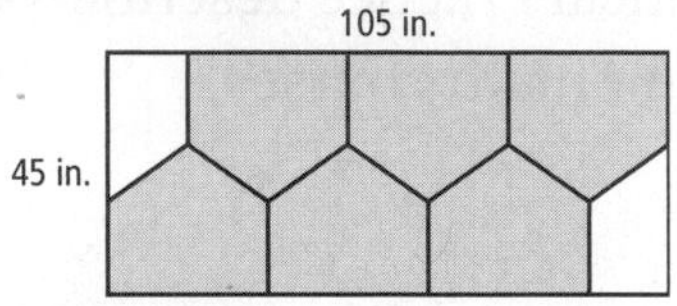

c. 675 in^2 **25.** $A = (26 + 2\pi)$ in^2 **27.** $A = 2$ **29.** Possible answer: $A \approx 10$ cm^2 **31.** A **33.** C

10-4

Check It Out! 1. $A \approx 38$ units^2 **2.** parallelogram; $P \approx 20.8$ units^2; $A = 25$ units^2 **3.** $A = 48$ units^2

Exercises 1. $A \approx 40.5$ units^2 **3.** isosceles triangle; $P = \left(6 + 6\sqrt{2}\right)$ units; $A = 9$ units^2 **5.** rectangle; $P = 28$ units; $A = 40$ units^2 **7.** $A = 20$ units^2 **9.** $A = 6$ units^2; $P = 12$ units; $A = 5$ units^2; $P = 12$ units

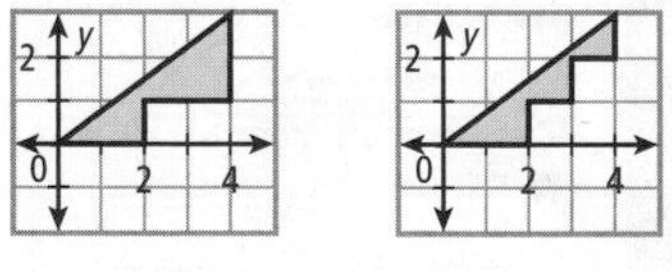

11. $A \approx 43.5$ units^2 **13.** rhombus; $P = 4\sqrt{29}$ units; $A = 20$ units^2 **15.** isosceles trapezoid; $P = \left(8 + 2\sqrt{29}\right)$ units; $A = 20$ units^2 **17.** $A = 53$ units^2 **19.** $P = \left(6 + 3\sqrt{2}\right)$ units; $A = 4.5$ units^2 **21a.** $A = 20$ mi **b.** $A \approx 150$ mi^2. The area represents the distance the boat traveled in 5 h. **23a.** $A = 6$ units^2 **b.** Possible answer: $C(2, 1)$ and $H(8, 2)$ **25.** J **27.** $A \approx 10.5$ units^2 **29.** $A \approx 17.5$ units^2 **31.** $P = 8\sqrt{2 - \sqrt{2}}$ units; $A = 2\sqrt{2}$ units^2

10-5

Check It Out! 1. The area is tripled. **2.** The perimeter is tripled, and the area is multiplied by 9. **3.** The side length is multiplied by $\frac{1}{\sqrt{2}}$. **4.** Possible answer:

DVD Shipments (millions)

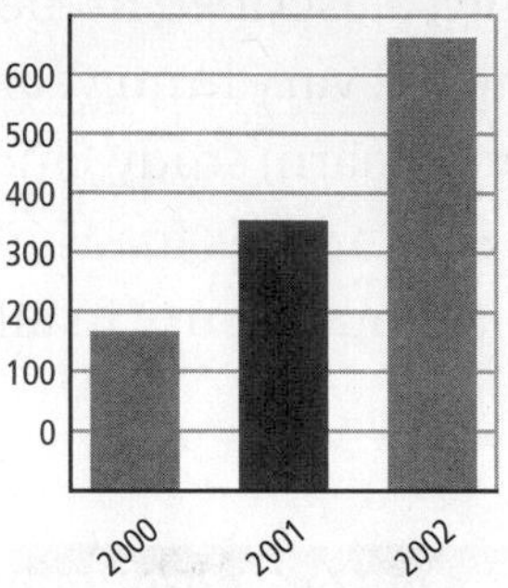

Exercises 1. The area is doubled. **3.** The perimeter is tripled. The area is multiplied by 9. **5.** The side length is multiplied by $\sqrt{2}$. **7.** $147.00 **9.** The area is multiplied by $\frac{2}{3}$. **11.** The circumference is multiplied by $\frac{3}{5}$. The area is multiplied by $\frac{9}{25}$. **13.** The side length is multiplied by $\sqrt{3}$. **15.** The area is multiplied by 64. **17.** The area is multiplied by 28. **19.** The area is divided by 16. **21.** The area is multiplied by 4. **23.** 800,000 acres **25a.** The area is multiplied by 3. **b.** The area is multiplied by 3 **c.** The area is multiplied by 9. **27a.** The area is multiplied by 3. **b.** The area is multiplied by 3. **c.** The area is multiplied by 9. **29a.** $8\sqrt{2}$ in. **b.** $4\sqrt{2}$ in. **31.** G **33.** 36 **35.** $A = \left(9\pi x^2 + 54\pi x + 81\pi\right)$ in^2

10-6

Check It Out! 1. $\frac{2}{3}$ **2.** $\frac{1}{2}$ **3.** $\frac{1}{2}$ **4.** 0.71

Exercises 3. $\frac{1}{2}$ **5.** $\frac{7}{10}$ **7.** 9 times **9.** $\frac{3}{8}$ **11.** $\frac{5}{12}$ **13.** 0.08 **15.** 0.79 **17.** 0.78 **19.** 0.46 **21.** 0.62 **23.** $\frac{1}{2}$ **25.** $\frac{3}{4}$ **27.** 0.5 **29.** 0.11 **31.** A **33.** 0.84 **35.** 0.13 **37.** 0.77 **39–41.** Possible answers given. **39.** The point lies on AC. **41.** The point lies in the blue triangle or the green triangle. **43.** $\frac{1}{2}$; it does not matter which regions are shaded because they all have the same area. **45.** A **47.** D

Study Guide: Review

1. apothem **2.** center of a circle **3.** geometric probability **4.** $A = 81\text{ in}^2$ **5.** $P = 22$ cm **6.** $h = 3x^2$ in. **7.** $h = 8$ ft **8.** $A = 252\text{ yd}^2$ **9.** $d_2 = 42xy^4$ in. **10.** $A = 288\text{ m}^2$ **11.** $C = 2$ ft **12.** $A \approx 153.9\text{ yd}^2$ **13.** $d = 16x$ m **14.** $A \approx 172.0\text{ ft}^2$ **15.** $A \approx 6.9\text{ in}^2$ **16.** $A \approx 309.0\text{ cm}^2$ **17.** $A = 72\text{ m}^2$ **18.** $A \approx 200.9\text{ ft}^2$ **19.** $A = 192\text{ cm}^2$ **20.** $A \approx 21.4\text{ mm}^2$ **21.** $A \approx 49.5\text{ units}^2$ **22.** $A \approx 44\text{ units}^2$ **23.** square; $P = 12\sqrt{2}$ units; $A = 18\text{ units}^2$ **24.** right triangle; $P = \left(12 + \sqrt{74}\right)$ units; $A = 17.5\text{ units}^2$ **25.** isosceles trapezoid; $P = \left(12 + 4\sqrt{5}\right)$ units; $A = 24\text{ units}^2$ **26.** parallelogram; $P = \left(8 + 2\sqrt{13}\right)$ units; $A = 12\text{ units}^2$ **27.** $A = 30.5\text{ units}^2$ **28.** $A = 17.5\text{ units}^2$ **29.** $A = 12\text{ units}^2$ **30.** $A = 16\text{ units}^2$ **31.** The perimeter is multiplied by 3. The area is multiplied by 9. **32.** The perimeter is doubled. The area is multiplied by 4. **33.** The circumference is multiplied by $\frac{1}{2}$. The area is multiplied by $\frac{1}{4}$. **34.** The perimeter is multiplied by 4. The area is multiplied by 16. **35.** $\frac{7}{13}$ **36.** $\frac{8}{13}$ **37.** $\frac{12}{13}$ **38.** $\frac{6}{13}$ **39.** 0.17 **40.** 0.05 **41.** 0.17 **42.** 0.66

11-1

Check It Out! 1a. cone; vertex: N; edges: none; base: $\odot M$ **1b.** triangular prism; vertices: T, U, V, W, X, Y; edges: $\overline{TU}, \overline{TV}, \overline{UV}, \overline{TW}, \overline{UX}, \overline{VY}, \overline{WX}, \overline{WY}, \overline{XY}$; bases: $\triangle TUV$, $\triangle WXY$ **2a.** triangular pyramid **2b.** cylinder **3a.** hexagon **3b.** triangle **4.** Cut through the midpoints of 3 edges that meet at 1 vertex.

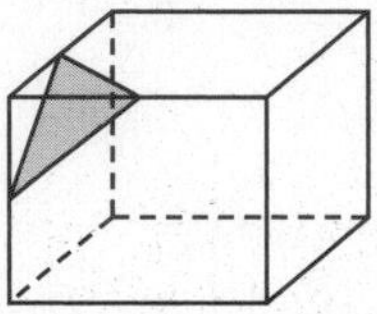

Exercises 1. cylinder **3.** rectangular prism; vertices: C, D, E, F, G, H, J, K; edges: $\overline{GH}, \overline{GK}, \overline{HJ}, \overline{JK}, \overline{GF}, \overline{HE}, \overline{JD}, \overline{KC}, \overline{FC}, \overline{CD}, \overline{DE}, \overline{EF}$; bases: $GHJK$, $CDEF$ **5.** rectangular prism **7.** cube **9.** pentagon **11.** Cut parallel to the bases. **13.** cube; vertices: S, T, U, V, W, X, Y, Z; edges: $\overline{ST}, \overline{TU}, \overline{UV}, \overline{VS}, \overline{SW}, \overline{TX}, \overline{UY}, \overline{VZ}, \overline{WX}, \overline{XY}, \overline{YZ}, \overline{ZW}$; bases: $STUV$, $WXYZ$ **15.** cylinder; vertices: none; edges: none; bases: $\odot R$, $\odot Q$ **17.** triangular pyramid **19.** square **21.** rectangle **23.** Cut perpendicular to the ground. **25.** rectangular prism **27.** hexagonal prism **29.** The figure is a cylinder whose bases each have a radius of 12 ft. The height of the cylinder is 9 ft.

31.

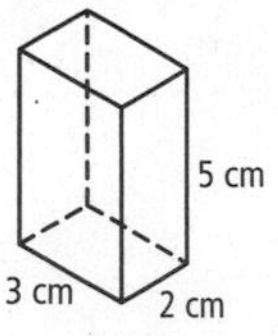

33.

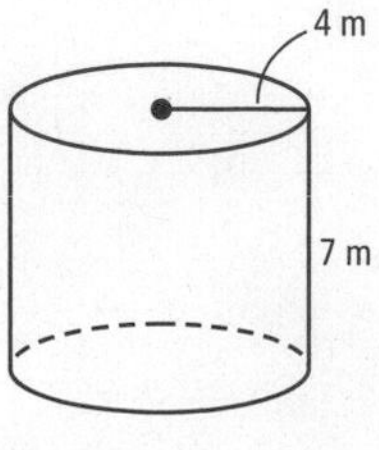

35.

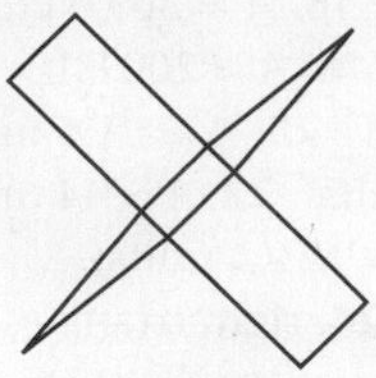

37a. pentagonal prism
b. 2 pentagons and 5 rectangles
c.

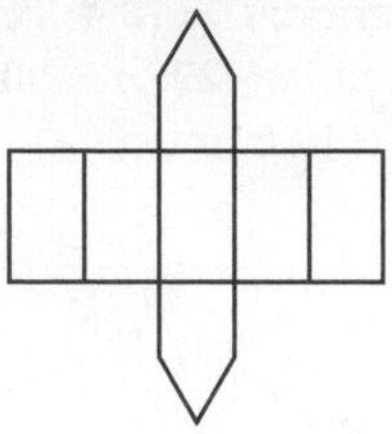

39.

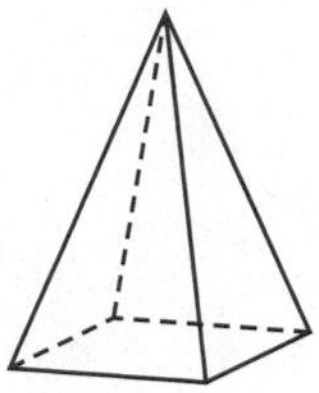

41. D **43.** B
45.

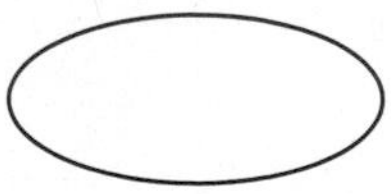

47.

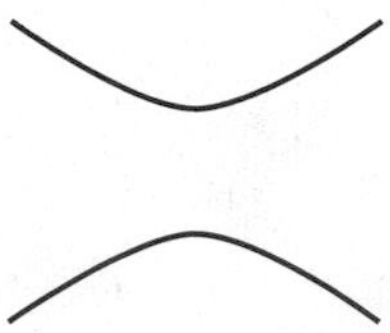

49.

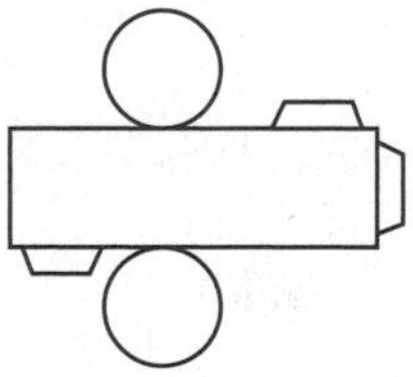

51a. A and B, C and F, D and G, E and H **b.** one

11-2

Check It Out! 1. $V = 157.5$ yd^3 **2.** 859,702 gal; 7,161,318 lb **3.** $V = 1088\pi$ in^3 ≈ 3418.1 in^3 **4.** The volume is multiplied by 8. **5.** $V \approx 51.4$ cm^3

Exercises 1. the same length as **3.** $V \approx 748.2$ m^3 **5.** 2552 gal; 12,071 lb **7.** $V = 45\pi$ m^3 ≈ 141.4 m^3 **9.** The volume is multiplied by $\frac{1}{64}$. **11.** $V \approx 1209.1$ ft^3 **13.** $V = 810$ yd^3 **15.** $V = 245$ ft^3 **17.** $V = 1764\pi$ cm^3 ≈ 5541.8 cm^3 **19.** $V = 384\pi$ cm^3 ≈ 1206.4 cm^3 **21.** The volume is multiplied by $\frac{27}{125}$. **23.** $V \approx 242.3$ ft^3 **25a.** 235.6 in^2 **25b.** 0.04 **27.** $h = 11$ ft **29.** $V = 392\pi$ m^3 **31.** 576 in^3, or $\frac{1}{3}$ ft^3 **33.** 2,468,729 gal **37.** A **39.** B **41.** $V = x^3 + x^2 - 2x$ **43.** $V = \frac{x^3\sqrt{3} + x^2\sqrt{3}}{4}$

11-3

Check It Out! 1. $V = 36$ cm^3 **2.** 107,800 yd^3 or 2,910,600 ft^3 **3.** $V = 216\pi$ m^3 ≈ 678.6 m^3 **4.** The volume is multiplied by 8. **5.** $V = 3000$ ft^3

Exercises 1. perpendicular **3.** $V = 96$ cm^3 **5.** $V \approx 65$ mm^3 **7.** $V = 1440\pi$ in^3 ≈ 4523.9 in^3 **9.** The volume is multiplied by 27. **11.** $V = 2592$ cm^3 **13.** $V = 160$ ft^3 **15.** $V = 384$ ft^3 **17.** $V = 1107\pi$ m^3 ≈ 3477.7 m^3 **19.** $V = 144\pi$ ft^3 ≈ 452.4 ft^3 **21.** The volume is multiplied by 216. **23.** $V = 150$ ft^3 **25.** $V = \frac{25\pi}{6}$ m^3 **27.** $V = 240\pi$ cm^3 **29.** 1350 m^3 **31.** 166.3 cm^3 **33.** $C = 10\pi\sqrt{3}$ cm **35.** $V = 1280$ in^3 **37.** $V = 17.5$ units^3 **39.** 3:2 **41a.** 33.5 in^3 **b.** 134.0 in^3 **c.** \$5; the large size holds 4 times as much. **43.** H **45.** 9 **47.** $V = \frac{2\pi}{3}$ ft^3 **49.** $V = \frac{1000\sqrt{2}}{3}$ cm^3

11-4

Check It Out! 1. $r = 12$ ft **2.** about 72.3 times as great **3.** $S = 2500\pi$ cm^2 **4.** The surface area is divided by 9. **5.** $S = 57\pi$ ft^2; $V = 27\pi$ ft^3

Exercises **1.** One endpoint is the center of the sphere, and the other is a point on the sphere. **3.** $V = \frac{4\pi}{3}$ m^3 **5.** about 8 times as great **7.** $S = 196\pi$ cm^2 **9.** The surface area is multiplied by 4. **11.** $S = 36\pi$ ft^2; $V = \frac{92\pi}{3}$ ft^3 **13.** $V = 972\pi$ cm^3 **15.** $d = 36$ in. **17.** $S = 1764\pi$ in^2 **19.** $V = \frac{15{,}625\pi}{6}$ m^3 **21.** The volume is multiplied by 216. **23.** $S \approx 1332.0$ mm^2; $V \approx 1440.9$ mm^3 **25.** $C = 2\pi\sqrt{15}$ in. **27.** $S = 196\pi$ units^2; $V = \frac{1372\pi}{3}$ units^3 **29.** 5.28 in.; 8.87 in^2; 2.48 in^3 **31.** 7.85 in.; 19.63 in^2; 8.18 in^3 **33.** Possible answer: 14,293 in^3 **35.** about 1408 times as great **37.** The surface area of Saturn is greater. **39.** The cross section of the hemisphere is a circle with radius $\sqrt{r^2 - x^2}$, so its area is $A = \pi(r^2 - x^2)$. The cross section of the cylinder with the cone removed has an outer radius of r and an inner radius of x, so the area is $A = \pi r^2 - \pi x^2 = \pi(r^2 - x^2)$. **41a.** 33.5 in^3 **b.** 44.6 in^3 **43.** H **45.** 1 in. **47.** The volume of the cylinder is 1.5 times the volume of the sphere.

Study Guide: Review

1. face **2.** cross section **3.** cone; vertex: M; edges: none; base: $\odot L$ **4.** rectangular pyramid; vertices: N, P, Q, R, S; edges: $\overline{NP}$, $\overline{NQ}$, $\overline{NR}$, $\overline{NS}$, $\overline{PQ}$, $\overline{QR}$, $\overline{RS}$, $\overline{SP}$; base: $PQRS$ **5.** cylinder **6.** square pyramid **7.** $V = 1080$ ft^3 **8.** $V \approx 1651.7$ cm^3 **9.** $V = 900\pi$ in^3 **10.** $V = 45\pi$ m^3 **11.** $V = 112$ m^3 **12.** $V \approx 10.4$ cm^3 **13.** $V = 120\pi$ cm^3 **14.** $V = 48\pi$ ft^3 **15.** $V = 512\pi$ ft^3 **16.** $V \approx 1533.3$ cm^3 **17.** $V = \frac{500\pi}{3}$ m^3 **18.** $S = 144\pi$ in^2 **19.** $d = 16$ ft **20.** $S \approx 338.3$ cm^2; $V \approx 293.5$ cm^3 **21.** $S \approx 245.0$ ft^2; $V \approx 84.8$ ft^3

12-1

Check It Out! 1. chords: $\overline{QR}$, $\overline{ST}$; secant: $\overleftrightarrow{ST}$; tangent: $\overleftrightarrow{UV}$; diam.: $\overline{ST}$; radii: $\overline{PQ}$, $\overline{PT}$, $\overline{PS}$ **2.** radius of ⊙C: 1; radius of ⊙D: 3; pt. of tangency: $(2, -1)$; eqn. of tangent line: $y = -1$ **3.** 171 mi **4a.** 2.1 **4b.** 7

Exercises 1. secant **3.** congruent **5.** chord: $\overline{QS}$; secant: $\overleftrightarrow{QS}$; tangent: $\overleftrightarrow{ST}$; diam.: $\overline{QS}$; radii: $\overline{PR}$, $\overline{PQ}$, $\overline{PS}$ **7.** radius of ⊙R: 2; radius of ⊙S: 2; pt. of tangency: $(1, 2)$; eqn. of tangent line: $x = 1$ **9.** 19 **11.** chords: $\overline{RS}$, $\overline{VW}$; secant: $\overleftrightarrow{VW}$; tangent: ℓ; diam.: $\overline{VW}$; radii: $\overline{PV}$, $\overline{PW}$ **13.** radius of ⊙C: 2; radius of ⊙D: 4; pt. of tangency: $(-4, 0)$; eqn. of tangent line: $x = -4$ **15.** 413 km **17.** 7 **19.** N **21.** A **23.** $\overline{AC}$ **25.** $\overline{AC}$ **27.** 45° **31.** 8 **33.** 22 **35a.** rect.; $\angle BCD$ and $\angle EDC$ are rt. ∠s because a line tangent to a ⊙ is ⊥ to a radius. It is given that $\angle DEB$ is a rt. ∠. $\angle CBE$ must also be a rt. ∠ because the sum of the ∠s of a quad. is 360°. Thus $BCDE$ has 4 rt. ∠s and is a rect. **b.** 17 in.; 2 in. **c.** 17.1 in. **39.** G **43.** 18.6 in.

12-2

Check It Out! 1a. 108° **1b.** 270° **1c.** 36° **2a.** 140° **2b.** 295° **3a.** 12 **3b.** 100° **4.** 34.6

Exercises 1. semicircle **3.** major arc **5.** 162° **7.** 61.2° **9.** 39.6° **11.** 129° **13.** 108° **15.** 24 **17.** 24.0 **19.** 122.3° **21.** 122.3° **23.** 237.7° **25.** 152° **27.** 155° **29.** 147° **31.** 6.6 **33.** F **35.** T **37.** 45°; 60°; 75° **39.** 108°

41. **1.** $\widehat{BC} \cong \widehat{DE}$ (Given)
2. $m\widehat{BC} = m\widehat{DE}$ (Def. of ≅ arcs)
3. $m\angle BAC = m\angle DAE$ (Def. of arc measures)
4. $\angle BAC \cong \angle DAE$ (Def. of ≅ ∠s)

43. **1.** $\overline{JK}$ is the ⊥ bisector of $\overline{GH}$. (Given)
2. A is equidistant from G and H. (Def. of center of ⊙)
3. A lies on the ⊥ bisector of $\overline{GH}$. (⊥ Bisector Thm.)
4. $\overline{JK}$ is a diam. of ⊙A. (Def. of diam.)

45. Solution A **47a.** 13.5 in.; 6.5 in. **b.** 11.8 in. **c.** 23.7 in. **49.** F **51.** 48.2° **53a.** 90°; 60°; 45° **b.** $\frac{3}{4}\pi$; $\frac{3}{2}\pi$

12-3

Check It Out! 1a. $\frac{\pi}{4}$ m²; 0.79 m² **1b.** 25.6π in²; 80.42 in² **2.** 203,575 ft² **3.** 4.57 m² **4a.** $\frac{4}{3}\pi$ m; 4.19 m **4b.** 3π cm; 9.42 cm

Exercises 1. seg. **3.** 24π cm²; 75.40 cm² **5.** 12 mi² **7.** 36.23 m² **9.** 4π ft; 12.57 ft **11.** $\frac{2}{3}\pi$ in; 2.09 in. **13.** $\frac{45}{2}\pi$ in²; 70.69 in² **15.** 628 in² **17.** 15.35 in² **19.** $\frac{25}{18}\pi$ mm; 4.36 mm **21.** $\frac{1}{10}\pi$ ft; 0.31 ft **23.** N **25.** A **27.** 12 **29a.** 3.9 ft **b.** 103° **33.** G **35.** $\frac{7}{3}\pi$ **37a.** $\frac{1}{8}$ **b.** $\frac{3}{8}$ **c.** $\frac{1}{2}$

12-4

Check It Out! 1a. 270° **1b.** 38° **2.** 43°; 120° **3a.** 12 **3b.** 39° **4.** 51°; 129°; 72°; 108°

Exercises 1. inscribed **3.** 58° **5.** 26° **7.** 112.5 **9.** 46° **11.** 70°; 110°; 115°; 65° **13.** 47.5° **15.** 47.6° **17.** ±6 **19.** 100° **21.** 100°; 39°, 80°; 141° **23.** A **25.** S **27.** 115° **29a.** 30° **b.** 120° **c.** Rt.; $\angle FBC$ is inscribed in a semicircle, so it must be a rt. ∠; therefore △FBC is a rt. △. **33.** 72°; 99°; 108°; 81° **35a.** $AB^2 + AC^2 = BC^2$, so by the Conv. of the Pyth. Thm., △ABC is a rt. △ with rt. ∠A. Since ∠A is an inscribed rt. ∠, it intercepts a semicircle. This means that $\overline{BC}$ is a diam. **b.** 102° **39.** D **41.** C **45.** 134°

12-5

Check It Out! 1a. 83° **1b.** 142° **2a.** 51° **2b.** 22° **3.** 33 **4.** 45° **5.** 72°

Exercises 1. 70° **3.** 122° **5.** 67° **7.** 94° **9.** 58 **11.** 142° **13.** 96° **15.** 116° **17.** 124° **19.** 260° **21.** 107.5° **23.** 57.5 **25.** 18 **27.** 45° **29.** 90° **31.** $2x°$ **33.** $(360 - 2x)°$ **39.** 115°; 30°; 35° **41a.** 60° **b.** 120° **c.** obtuse isosceles **43.** J **45.** Case 1: Assume $\overline{AB}$ is a diam. of the circle. Then $m\widehat{AB} = 180°$, and $\angle ABC$ is a rt. ∠. Thus $m\angle ABC = \frac{1}{2}m\widehat{AB}$. Case 2: Assume $\overline{AB}$ is not a diam. of the ⊙. Let X be the center of the ⊙ and draw radii $\overline{XA}$ and $\overline{XB}$. Since they are radii, $\overline{XA} \cong \overline{XB}$, so △$AXB$ is isosceles. Thus $\angle XAB \cong \angle XBA$ and $2m\angle XBA + m\angle AXB = 180$. This means that $m\angle XBA = 90 - \frac{1}{2}m\angle AXB$. By Thm. 11-1-1, $\angle XBC$ is a rt. ∠, so $m\angle XBA + m\angle ABC = 90$ or $m\angle ABC = 90 - m\angle XBA$. By subst., $m\angle ABC = 90 - \left(90 - \frac{1}{2}m\angle AXB\right)$. Simplifying gives $m\angle ABC = \frac{1}{2}m\angle AXB$. $m\angle AXB = m\widehat{AB}$ because $\angle AXB$ is a central ∠. Thus $m\angle ABC = \frac{1}{2}\widehat{AB}$. **47.** 95°

12-6

Check It Out! 1. 3.75; $AB = 11$; $CD = 11.75$ **2.** $3\frac{2}{3}$ in. **3.** $z = 14$; $JG = 27$; $LG = 39$ **4.** $7\frac{2}{7}$

Exercises 1. tangent seg. **3.** $x = 9$; $AB = 13$; $CD = 12$ **5.** $51\frac{1}{4}$ ft **7.** $y = 10.6$; $PR = 15.6$; $PT = 13$ **9.** 4 **11.** $\sqrt{33}$ **13.** $x = 4.2$; $JL = 14.2$; $MN = 13$ **15.** ≈ 1770 ft **17.** $y = 14.3$; $HL = 24.3$; $NL = 27$ **19.** $2\sqrt{21}$ **21.** $4\sqrt{10}$ **23a.** 6 in. **b.** 12 in. **25.** $x = 8$; $y = 6\sqrt{3}$ **27.** Solution B **33.** B **35.** $CE = ED = 6$ and by the Chord-Chord Product Thm., $6 \cdot 6 = 3 \cdot EF$. So $EF = 12$, $FB = 15$, and the radius AB must be 7.5. **37.** 3.2 in. **39.** 7.44

12-7

Check It Out! 1a. $x^2 + (y + 3)^2 = 64$ **1b.** $(x - 2)^2 + (y + 1)^2 = 16$

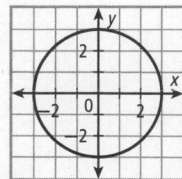

2a.

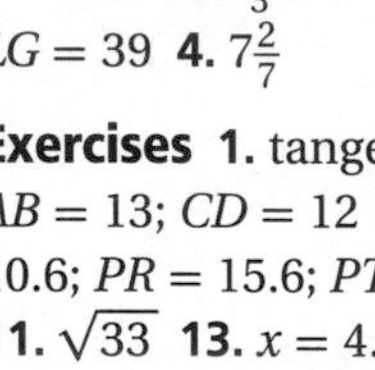

2b.

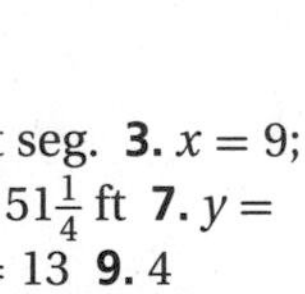

3. $(2, -1)$

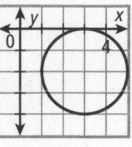

Exercises 1. $(x - 3)^2 + (y + 5)^2 = 144$ **3.** $(x - 4)^2 + y^2 = 4$

5. 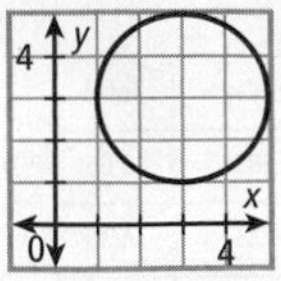

7. 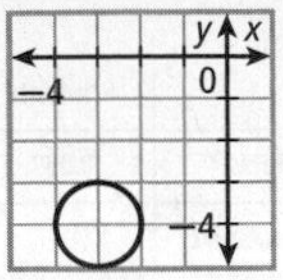

9a. $(-2, 3)$ **b.** 10 ft **11.** $(x-1.5)^2 + (y+2.5)^2 = 3$ **13.** $(x-1)^2 + (y+2)^2 = 45$

15. 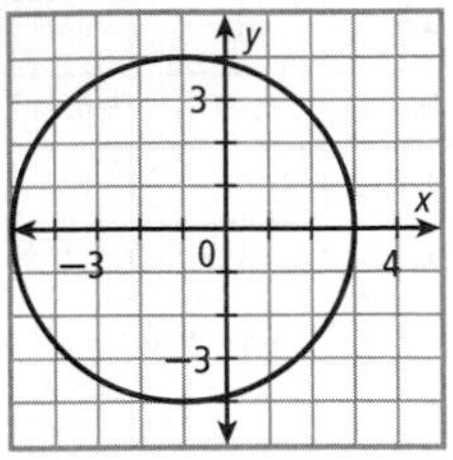

17. 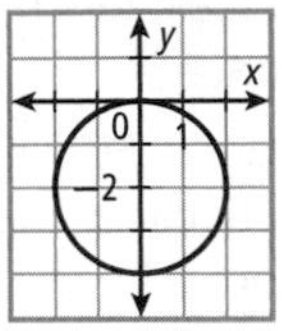

19. $(x-1)^2 + (y+2)^2 = 4$ **21a.** 80 ft **b.** $x^2 + y^2 = 1600$ **23.** T **25.** T **29a.** $E(-3, -1)$; $G(-6, 2)$ **b.** 6 **c.** $(x+3)^2 + (y-2)^2 = 9$ **31.** $(0, -15)$; 5 **33.** $A = 9\pi$; $C = 6\pi$ **35.** $A = 25\pi$; $C = 10\pi$ **37.** $(-200, -100)$ **39.** $(x-1)^2 + (y+2)^2 = 16$ **43.** H **45a.** $(x-2)^2 + (y+4)^2 + (z-3)^2 = 69$ **b.** 15; if 2 segs. are tangent to a ⊙ or sphere from the same ext. pt., then the segs. are ≅. **47.** $(x-3)^2 + (y-4)^2 = 5$

Study Guide: Review

1. segment of a circle **2.** central angle **3.** major arc **4.** concentric circles **5.** chords: $\overline{QS}$, $\overline{UV}$; tangent: ℓ; radii: $\overline{PQ}$, $\overline{PS}$; secant: $\overleftrightarrow{UV}$; diam.: $\overline{QS}$ **6.** chords: $\overline{KH}$, $\overline{MN}$; tangent: $\overleftrightarrow{KL}$; radii: $\overline{JH}$, $\overline{JK}$, $\overline{JM}$, $\overline{JN}$; secant: $\overleftrightarrow{MN}$; diams.: $\overline{MN}$, $\overline{KH}$ **7.** 25 **8.** 12 **9.** 7 **10.** 1.8 **11.** 81° **12.** 210° **13.** 99° **14.** 279° **15.** 17.0 **16.** 8.7 **17.** 12π in^2; 37.70 in^2 **18.** $\frac{\pi}{4}$ m^2; 0.79 m^2 **19.** 16π cm; 50.27 cm **20.** 3π ft; 9.42 ft **21.** 164° **22.** 32° **23.** 26 **24.** 39° **25.** 82° **26.** 79° **27.** 67° **28.** 90° **29.** $11\frac{2}{3}$; $DE = 12$; $BC = 14\frac{2}{3}$ **30.** 12; $RQ = 22$; $ST = 23$ **31.** 7; $JG = 10$; $JL = 12$ **32.** $8\frac{1}{2}$; $AC = 12\frac{1}{2}$; $AE = 10$ **33.** $(x+4)^2 + (y+3)^2 = 9$ **34.** $(x+2)^2 + y^2 = 4$ **35.** $(x-1)^2 + (y+1)^2 = 16$

36. 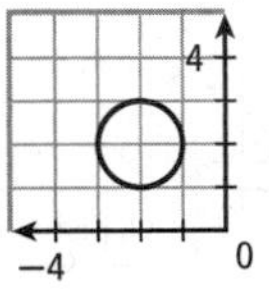

13-1

Check It Out! 1a. 120 **b.** 73,116,160 **2a.** 336 **b.** 20 **3.** 28

Exercises 1. important; permutation **3.** 225 **5.** 1320 **7.** 5985 **9.** 12 **11.** 72 **13.** 20 **15.** 71,916,768 **17.** 1 **19.** 6 **21.** 72 **23.** 6700 **25.** 35 **27.** > **29.** <

33a.

President	A	A	A	A	A	A	A	A	A	A	A	A
Vice President	B	B	B	C	C	C	D	D	D	E	E	E
Secretary	C	D	E	B	D	E	B	C	E	B	C	D

b.

President	B	B	B	B	B	B	B	B	B	B	B	B
Vice President	A	A	A	C	C	C	D	D	D	E	E	E
Secretary	C	D	E	A	D	E	A	C	E	A	C	D

60 ways

c. 60 **d.** 10; 60; 10 **37.** A **39.** D **41.** 1365 **43.** $({}_{30}C_{12})({}_{18}C_2)$

13-2

Check It Out! 1a. $\frac{5}{36}$ **b.** 0 **c.** $\frac{5}{12}$ **2.** $\frac{16}{25}$ **3.** $\frac{1}{28}$ **4.** $\frac{16}{225}$ **5a.** $\frac{9}{26}$ **b.** $\frac{19}{26}$

Exercises 1. theoretical probability **3.** $\frac{1}{4}$ **5.** $\frac{1}{4}$ **7.** $\frac{303}{365}$ **9.** $\frac{1}{220}$ **11.** $\frac{1}{9}$ **13.** $\frac{3}{5}$ **15.** $\frac{4}{5}$ **17.** $\frac{1}{56}$ **19.** $\approx\frac{1}{42}$ **21.** never **23a.** $\frac{\pi}{4}$ **25a.** 0.68; 0.84; 0.76; 0.64 **b.** 0.73 **27.** $\frac{2}{5}$ **29.** June; ≈ 0.13 **31.** no; yes **33.** $\frac{1}{2}$ **37.** G **39.** H

13-3

Check It Out! 1a. $\frac{1}{36}$ **b.** $\frac{1}{8}$ **2.** $\frac{5}{36}$ **3a.** ≈ 0.014 **b.** ≈ 0.186 **4a.** independent; $\frac{3}{20}$ **b.** dependent; $\frac{1}{6}$ **c.** dependent; $\frac{1}{12}$

Exercises 1. independent **3.** $\frac{1}{8}$ **5.** The probability that the yellow cube shows a multiple of 3 increases from $\frac{1}{3}$ if the product is 6; $\frac{1}{2}$ **7.** $\frac{1}{100}$ **9.** dependent; $\frac{9}{38}$ **11.** $\frac{1}{12}$ **13.** The probability that the product is 8 increases from $\frac{1}{18}$ if the blue cube is less than 3; $\frac{1}{36}$ **15.** ≈ 0.72 **17.** dependent; $\frac{1}{6}$ **19.** independent **21.** independent **23a.** ≈ 0.61 **b.** ≈ 0.05 **25a.** $\frac{625}{1296}$ **b.** $\frac{1}{36}$ **c.** $\frac{1}{6}$ **27.** ≈ 0.6 **29.** 40 **33.** F **35.** 7

13-4

Check It Out!

1.

	Fiction	Nonfiction	Total
Hardcover	0.133	0.248	0.381
Paperback	0.448	0.171	0.619
Total	0.581	0.419	1

2a.

Tap \ Ballet	Yes	No	Total
Yes	0.19	0.26	0.45
No	0.43	0.12	0.55
Total	0.62	0.38	1

b. 0.69 or 69%

3. Al's Driving has the best pass rate, about 64%, versus 61% for Drive Time and 50% for Crash Course.

Exercises 1. marginal

3.

	Under-classmates	Upper-classmates	Total
Morning	0.16	0.28	0.44
Afternoon	0.36	0.2	0.56
Total	0.52	0.48	1

5a.

Play instrument \ Play Sport	Yes	No	Total
Yes	0.23	0.19	0.42
No	0.25	0.33	0.58
Total	0.48	0.52	1

b. 0.55

c. 0.48

7.

	Students	Adults	Total
T-Shirts	0.267	0.383	0.65
Sweatshirts	0.117	0.233	0.35
Total	0.384	0.616	1

9a.

	Satisfied	Dissatisfied	Total
Team 1	0.17	0.07	0.24
Team 2	0.29	0.1	0.39
Team 3	0.29	0.08	0.37
Total	0.75	0.25	1

b. Team 1: 0.71; Team 2: 0.74; Team 3: 0.78

c. Team 3 has the highest rate of customer satisfaction.

11. Maria made an error; Possible answer: You can tell because the four relative frequencies have a sum of 1.1, rather than 1.

13a.

Use new system? \ Work less than 5 miles from home?	Yes	No	Total
Yes	0.2	0.27	0.47
No	0.37	0.17	0.54
Total	0.57	0.44	1

b. 0.35

c. 0.57

15. C

17.

	Yes	No	Total
Children	0.125	0.1	0.225
Teenagers	0.725	0.05	0.775
Total	0.85	0.15	1

19. 10 children

21. 0

13-5

Check It Out! 1a. Each student can vote only once. **b.** 75% **2a.** $\frac{4}{13}$ **b.** $\frac{8}{13}$ **3.** $\frac{31}{40}$ **4.** ≈ 0.1524

Exercises 1. inclusive events **3.** $\frac{3}{5}$ **5.** $\frac{4}{5}$ **7.** $\frac{7}{9}$ **9.** $\frac{54}{65}$ **11.** ≈ 0.92 **13.** $\frac{1}{2}$ **15.** $\frac{1}{4}$ **17.** $\frac{32}{49}$ **19.** $1 - 0.75^{13} \approx 0.976$ **21.** 0.37;

experimental **23.** 87%; 100% **25b.** 4.16%; 52.24% **27.** 0.49 **29a.** 0.42 **b.** 0.02 **c.** 0.44; it is the sum of the probabilities. **31.** D **33.** D **35.** ≈ 0.12 **37.** $\frac{13}{18}$ **39.** 0.9 **41.** 0.2

Study Guide: Review

1. dependent events
2. permutation
3. conditional relative frequency
4. 7,000,000 **5.** 792 **6.** 2,162,160 **7.** 604,800 **8.** 20 **9.** $\frac{5}{36}$ **10.** $\frac{5}{18}$ **11.** $\frac{1}{2}$ **12.** $\frac{11}{12}$ **13.** $\frac{1}{210}$ **14.** $\frac{1}{10{,}000}$ **15.** $\frac{5}{24}$ **16.** ≈ 0.21 **17.** $\frac{1}{5}$ **18.** $\frac{4}{5}$ **19.** $\frac{7}{25}$ **20.** $\frac{13}{25}$ **21.** $\frac{1}{4}$ **22.** $\frac{3}{4}$ **23.** $\frac{1}{4}$ **24.** $\frac{1}{2}$ **25.** $\frac{1}{216}$ **26.** $\frac{6}{25}$ **27.** $\frac{11}{21}$ **28.** $\frac{1}{13}$ **29.** $\frac{13}{31}$ **30.** $\frac{14}{99}$

31.

		Went to beach		
		Yes	No	
Joined a sports team	Yes	0.278	0.25	0.528
	No	0.306	0.167	0.472
		0.583	0.417	1

32. $\frac{10}{21} \approx 0.476$ **33.** $\frac{6}{15} = 0.4$ **34.** Each coupon offers only 1 discount. **35.** $\frac{5}{6}$ **36.** $\frac{7}{13}$ **37.** $\frac{1}{2}$ **38.** $\frac{7}{10}$

Mastering the Standards

for Mathematical Practice

The topics described in the Standards for Mathematical Content will vary from year to year. However, the *way* in which you learn, study, and think about mathematics will not. The Standards for Mathematical Practice describe skills that you will use in all of your math courses.

Mathematical Practices

1. *Make sense of problems and persevere in solving them.*
2. *Reason abstractly and quantitatively.*
3. *Construct viable arguments and critique the reasoning of others.*
4. *Model with mathematics.*
5. *Use appropriate tools strategically.*
6. *Attend to precision.*
7. *Look for and make use of structure.*
8. *Look for and express regularity in repeated reasoning.*

4 Model with mathematics.

Mathematically proficient students can apply... mathematics... to... problems... in everyday life, society, and the workplace...

In your book

Multi-Step Test Prep and **Real-World Connections** apply mathematics to other disciplines and in real-world scenarios.

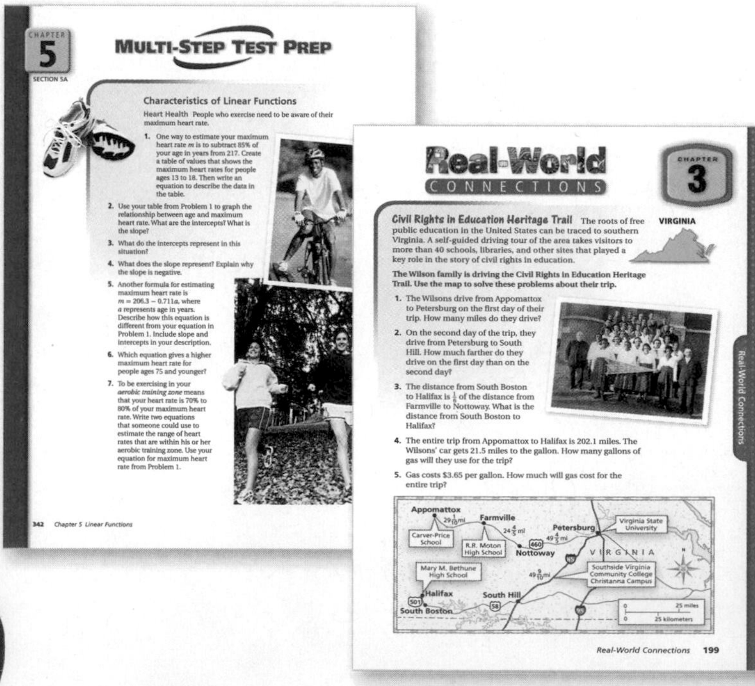

CHAPTER 5
SECTION 5A

MULTI-STEP TEST PREP

Characteristics of Linear Functions

Heart Health People who exercise need to be aware of their maximum heart rate.

1. One way to estimate your maximum heart rate *m* is to subtract 85% of your age in years from 217. Create a table of values that shows the maximum heart rates for people ages 13 to 18. Then write an equation to describe the data in the table.
2. Use your table from Problem 1 to graph the relationship between age and maximum heart rate. What are the intercepts? What is the slope?
3. What do the intercepts represent in this situation?
4. What does the slope represent? Explain why the slope is negative.
5. Another formula for estimating maximum heart rate is $m = 206.3 - 0.711a$, where a represents age in years. Describe how this equation is different from your equation in Problem 1. Include slope and intercepts in your description.
6. Which equation gives a higher maximum heart rate for people ages 75 and younger?
7. To be exercising in your *aerobic training zone* means that your heart rate is 70% to 80% of your maximum heart rate. Write two equations that someone could use to estimate the range of heart rates that are within his or her aerobic training zone. Use your equation for maximum heart rate from Problem 1.

342 Chapter 5 Linear Functions

Real-World CONNECTIONS

CHAPTER 3

Civil Rights in Education Heritage Trail The roots of free public education in the United States can be traced to southern Virginia. A self-guided driving tour of the area takes visitors to more than 40 schools, libraries, and other sites that played a key role in the story of civil rights in education.

VIRGINIA

The Wilson family is driving the Civil Rights in Education Heritage Trail. Use the map to solve these problems about their trip.

1. The Wilsons drive from Appomattox to Petersburg on the first day of their trip. How many miles do they drive?
2. On the second day of the trip, they drive from Petersburg to South Hill. How much farther do they drive on the first day than on the second day?
3. The distance from South Boston to Halifax is $\frac{1}{6}$ of the distance from Farmville to Nottoway. What is the distance from South Boston to Halifax?
4. The entire trip from Appomattox to Halifax is 202.1 miles. The Wilsons' car gets 21.5 miles to the gallon. How many gallons of gas will they use for the trip?
5. Gas costs $3.65 per gallon. How much will gas cost for the entire trip?

Real-World Connections

Real-World Connections 199

PhotoDisc/Getty Images

Glossary/Glosario

Learn It Online
Multilingual Glossary

A

ENGLISH	SPANISH	EXAMPLES
acute angle An angle that measures greater than 0° and less than 90°.	**ángulo agudo** Ángulo que mide más de 0° y menos de 90°.	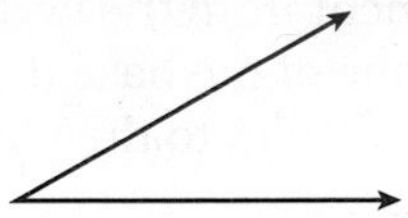
acute triangle A triangle with three acute angles.	**triángulo acutángulo** Triángulo con tres ángulos agudos.	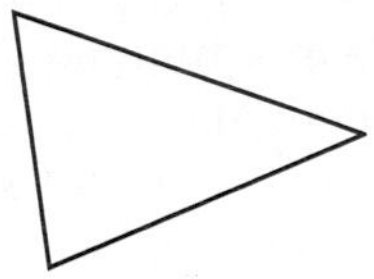
adjacent angles Two angles in the same plane with a common vertex and a common side, but no common interior points.	**ángulos adyacentes** Dos ángulos en el mismo plano que tienen un vértice y un lado común pero no comparten puntos internos.	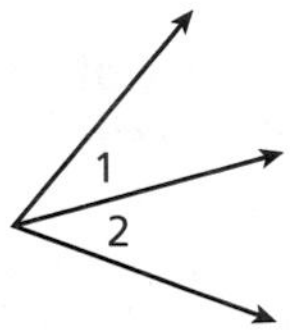 ∠1 and ∠2 are adjacent angles.
adjacent arcs Two arcs of the same circle that intersect at exactly one point.	**arcos adyacentes** Dos arcos del mismo círculo que se cruzan en un punto exacto.	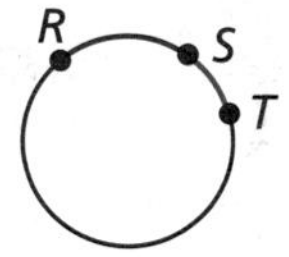 $\overset{\frown}{RS}$ and $\overset{\frown}{ST}$ are adjacent arcs.
alternate exterior angles For two lines intersected by a transversal, a pair of angles that lie on opposite sides of the transversal and outside the other two lines.	**ángulos alternos externos** Dadas dos líneas cortadas por una transversal, par de ángulos no adyacentes ubicados en los lados opuestos de la transversal y fuera de las otras dos líneas.	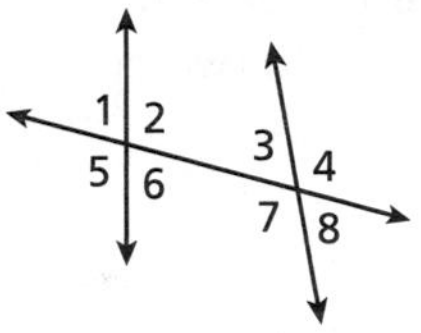 ∠4 and ∠5 are alternate exterior angles.
alternate interior angles For two lines intersected by a transversal, a pair of nonadjacent angles that lie on opposite sides of the transversal and between the other two lines.	**ángulos alternos internos** Dadas dos líneas cortadas por una transversal, par de ángulos no adyacentes ubicados en los lados opuestos de la transversal y entre las otras dos líneas.	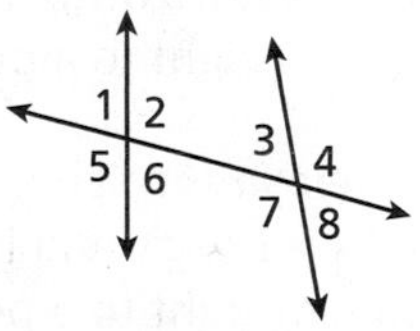 ∠3 and ∠6 are alternate interior angles.
altitude of a cone A segment from the vertex to the plane of the base that is perpendicular to the plane of the base.	**altura de un cono** Segmento que se extiende desde el vértice hasta el plano de la base y es perpendicular al plano de la base.	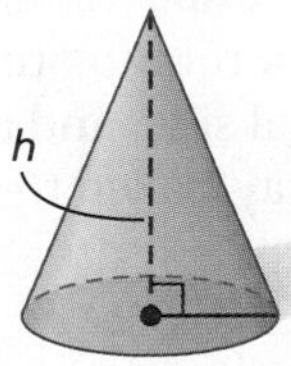
altitude of a cylinder A segment with its endpoints on the planes of the bases that is perpendicular to the planes of the bases.	**altura de un cilindro** Segmento con sus extremos en los planos de las bases que es perpendicular a los planos de las bases.	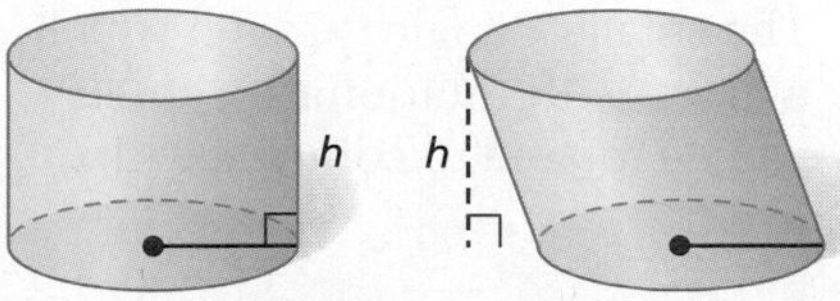

ENGLISH	SPANISH	EXAMPLES
altitude of a prism A segment with its endpoints on the planes of the bases that is perpendicular to the planes of the bases.	**altura de un prisma** Segmento con sus extremos en los planos de las bases que es perpendicular a los planos de las bases.	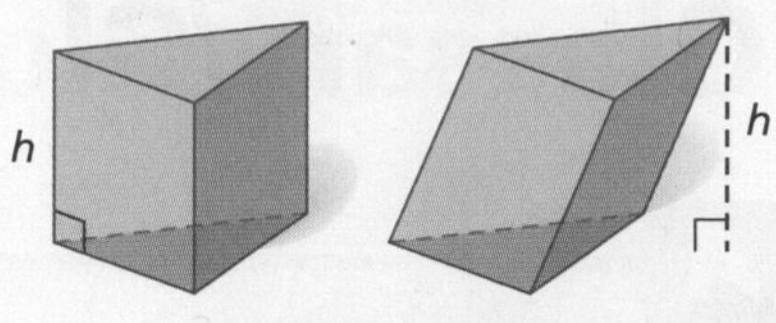
altitude of a pyramid A segment from the vertex to the plane of the base that is perpendicular to the plane of the base.	**altura de una pirámide** Segmento que se extiende desde el vértice hasta el plano de la base y es perpendicular al plano de la base.	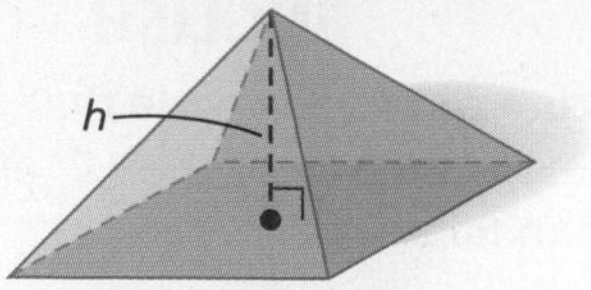
altitude of a triangle A perpendicular segment from a vertex to the line containing the opposite side.	**altura de un triángulo** Segmento perpendicular que se extiende desde un vértice hasta la línea que forma el lado opuesto.	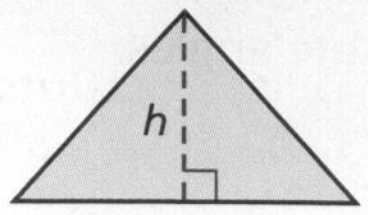
ambiguous case of the Law of Sines If two sides and a nonincluded angle of a triangle are given in order to solve the triangle using the Law of Sines, it is possible to have two different answers.	**caso ambiguo de la ley de los senos** Si se conocen dos lados y un ángulo no incluido de un triángulo y se quiere resolver el triángulo aplicando la ley de los senos, es posible obtener dos respuestas diferentes.	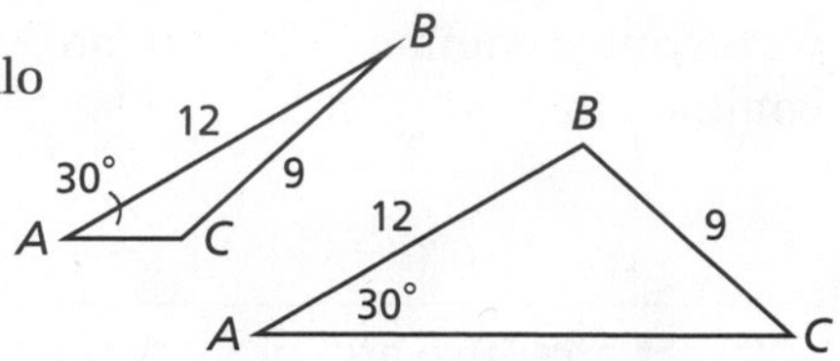
angle A figure formed by two rays with a common endpoint.	**ángulo** Figura formada por dos rayos con un extremo común.	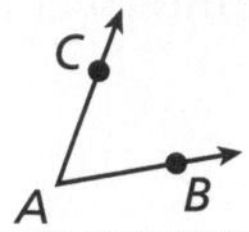
angle bisector A ray that divides an angle into two congruent angles.	**bisectriz de un ángulo** Rayo que divide un ángulo en dos ángulos congruentes.	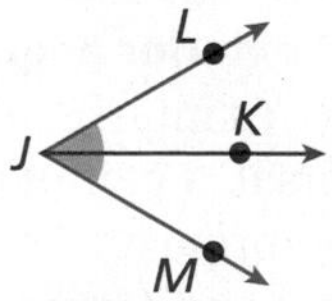 $\overrightarrow{JK}$ is an angle bisector of $\angle LJM$.
angle of depression The angle formed by a horizontal line and a line of sight to a point below.	**ángulo de depresión** Ángulo formado por una línea horizontal y una línea visual a un punto inferior.	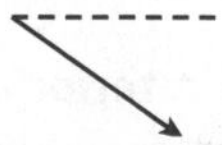
angle of elevation The angle formed by a horizontal line and a line of sight to a point above.	**ángulo de elevación** Ángulo formado por una línea horizontal y una línea visual a un punto superior.	
angle of rotation An angle formed by a rotating ray, called the terminal side, and a stationary reference ray, called the initial side.	**ángulo de rotación** Ángulo formado por un rayo rotativo, denominado lado terminal, y un rayo de referencia estático, denominado lado inicial.	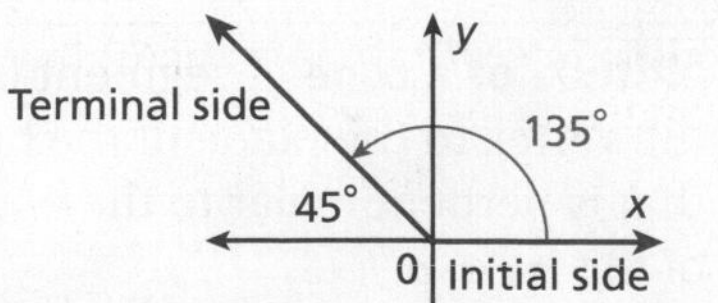 The angle of rotation is 135°.
angle of rotational symmetry The smallest angle through which a figure with rotational symmetry can be rotated to coincide with itself.	**ángulo de simetría de rotación** El ángulo más pequeño alrededor del cual se puede rotar una figura con simetría de rotación para que coincida consigo misma.	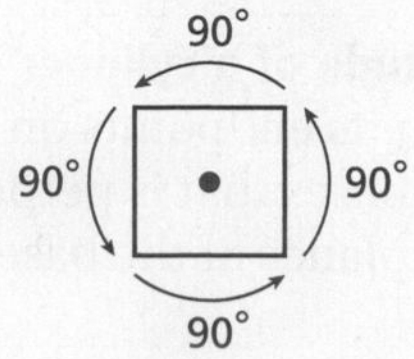

ENGLISH	SPANISH	EXAMPLES
annulus The region between two concentric circles.	**corona circular** Región comprendida entre dos círculos concéntricos.	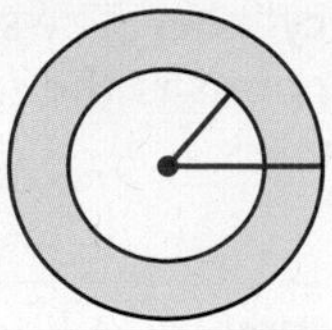
apothem The perpendicular distance from the center of a regular polygon to a side of the polygon.	**apotema** Distancia perpendicular desde el centro de un polígono regular hasta un lado del polígono.	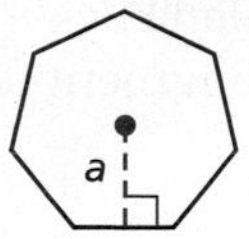
arc An unbroken part of a circle consisting of two points on the circle, called the endpoints, and all the points on the circle between them.	**arco** Parte continua de una circunferencia formada por dos puntos de la circunferencia denominados extremos y todos los puntos de la circunferencia comprendidos entre éstos.	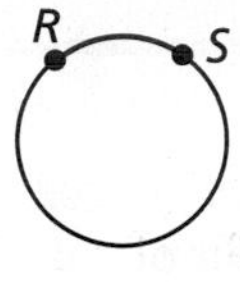
arc length The distance along an arc measured in linear units.	**longitud de arco** Distancia a lo largo de un arco medida en unidades lineales.	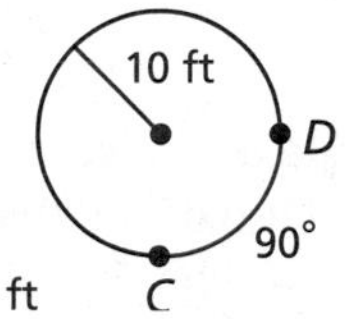 $m\widehat{CD} = 5\pi$ ft
arc marks Marks used on a figure to indicate congruent angles.	**marcas de arco** Marcas utilizadas en una figura para indicar ángulos congruentes.	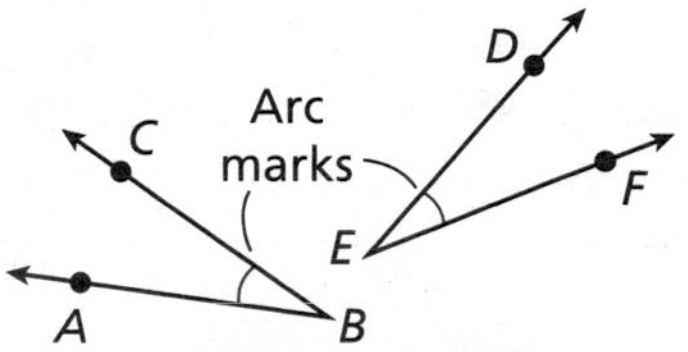
area The number of nonoverlapping unit squares of a given size that will exactly cover the interior of a plane figure.	**área** Cantidad de cuadrados unitarios de un determinado tamaño no superpuestos que cubren exactamente el interior de una figura plana.	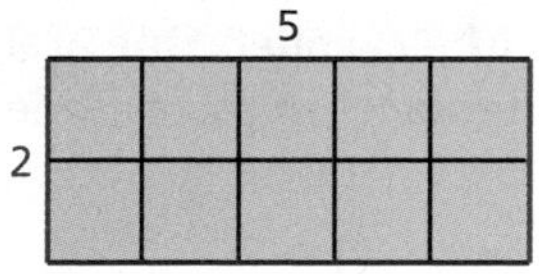 The area is 10 square units.
arrow notation A symbol used to describe a transformation.	**notación de flecha** Símbolo utilizado para describir una transformación.	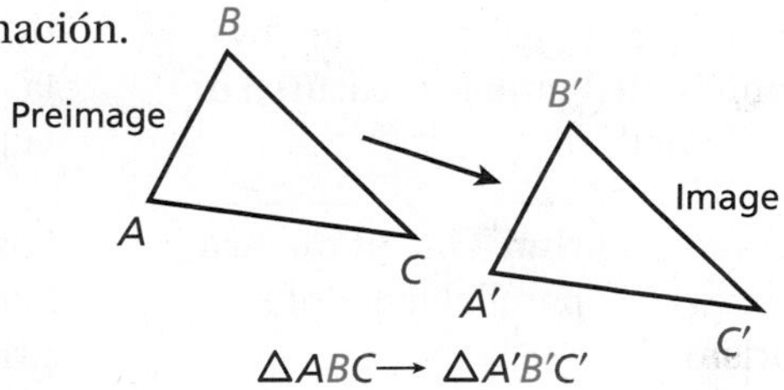 $\triangle ABC \rightarrow \triangle A'B'C'$
auxiliary line A line drawn in a figure to aid in a proof.	**línea auxiliar** Línea dibujada en una figura como ayuda en una demostración.	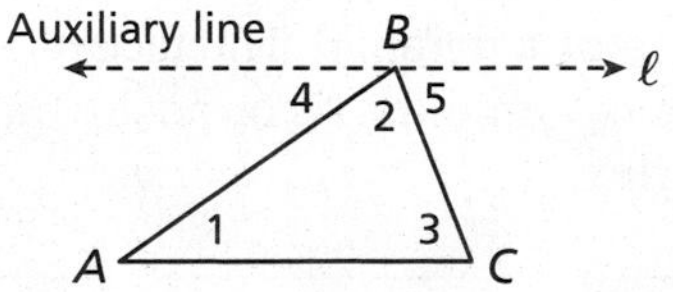
axiom *See* postulate.	**axioma** *Ver* postulado.	
axis of a cone The segment with endpoints at the vertex and the center of the base.	**eje de un cono** Segmento cuyos extremos se encuentran en el vértice y en el centro de la base.	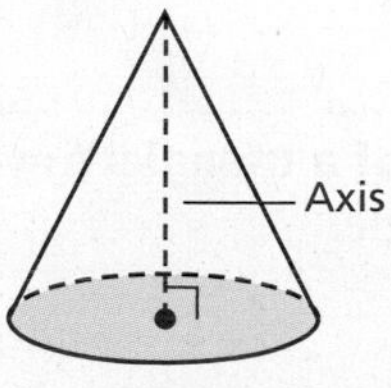

ENGLISH	SPANISH	EXAMPLES

axis of a cylinder The segment with endpoints at the centers of the two bases.

eje de un cilindro Segmentos cuyos extremos se encuentran en los centros de las dos bases.

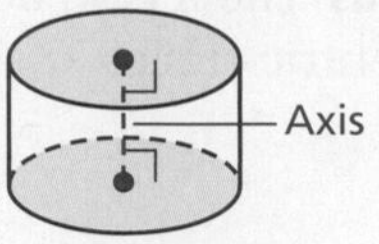

axis of symmetry A line that divides a plane figure or a graph into two congruent reflected halves.

eje de simetría Línea que divide una figura plana o una gráfica en dos mitades reflejadas congruentes.

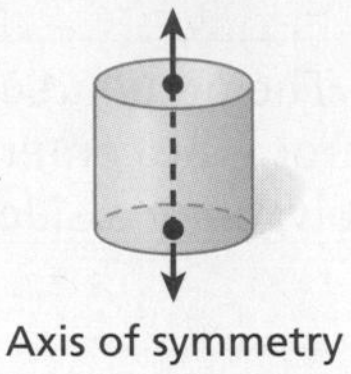

B

base angle of a trapezoid One of a pair of consecutive angles whose common side is a base of the trapezoid.

ángulo base de un trapecio Uno de los dos ángulos consecutivos cuyo lado en común es la base del trapecio.

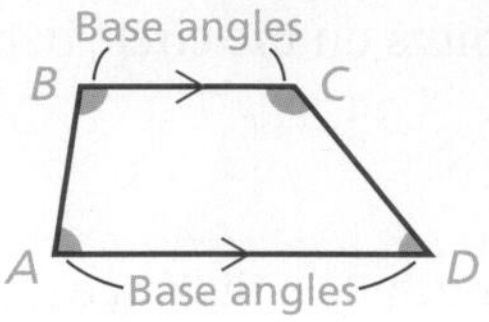

base angle of an isosceles triangle One of the two angles that have the base of the triangle as a side.

ángulo base de un triángulo isósceles Uno de los dos ángulos que tienen como lado la base del triángulo.

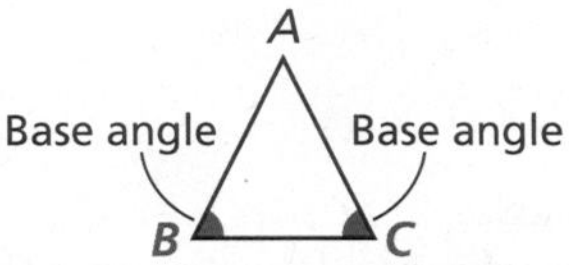

base of a cone The circular face of the cone.

base de un cono Cara circular del cono.

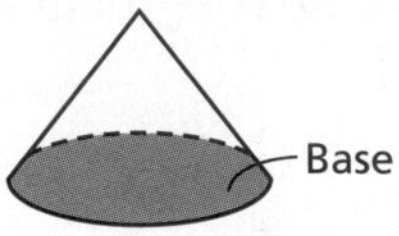

base of a cylinder One of the two circular faces of the cylinder.

base de un cilindro Una de las dos caras circulares del cilindro.

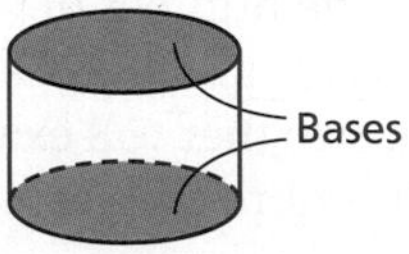

base of a geometric figure A side of a polygon; a face of a three-dimensional figure by which the figure is measured or classified.

base de una figura geométrica Lado de un polígono; cara de una figura tridimensional por la cual se mide o clasifica la figura.

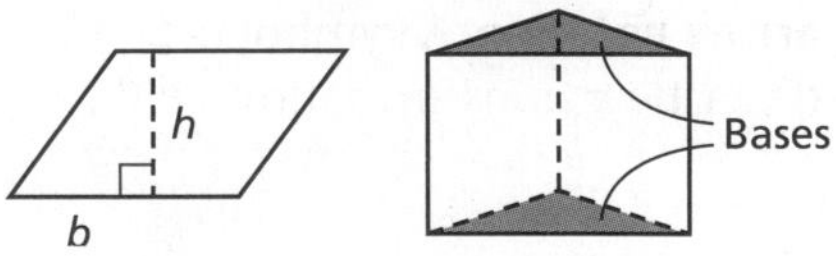

base of a prism One of the two congruent parallel faces of the prism.

base de un prisma Una de las dos caras paralelas y congruentes del prisma.

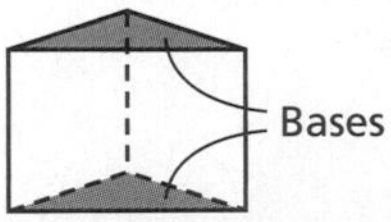

base of a pyramid The face of the pyramid that is opposite the vertex.

base de una pirámide Cara de la pirámide opuesta al vértice.

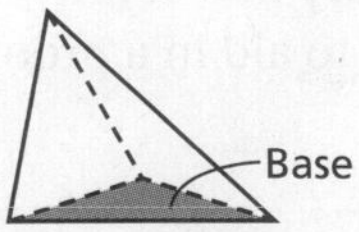

base of a trapezoid One of the two parallel sides of the trapezoid.

base de un trapecio Uno de los dos lados paralelos del trapecio.

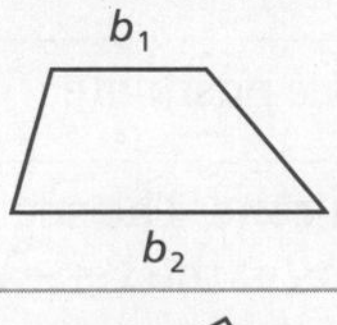

base of a triangle Any side of a triangle.

base de un triángulo Cualquier lado de un triángulo.

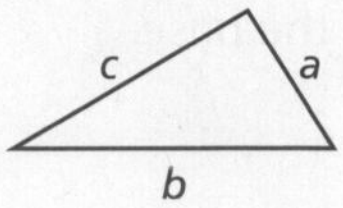

ENGLISH	SPANISH	EXAMPLES

base of an isosceles triangle The side opposite the vertex angle.

base de un triángulo isósceles Lado opuesto al ángulo del vértice.

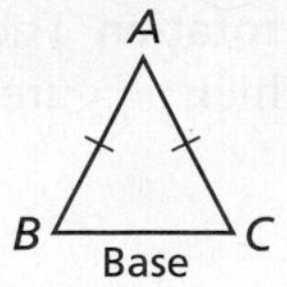

bearing Indicates direction. The number of degrees in the angle whose initial side is a line due north and whose terminal side is determined by a clockwise rotation.

rumbo Indica dirección. La cantidad de grados en el ángulo cuyo lado inicial es una línea recta en dirección norte y cuyo lado terminal se determina por una rotación en el sentido de las agujas del reloj.

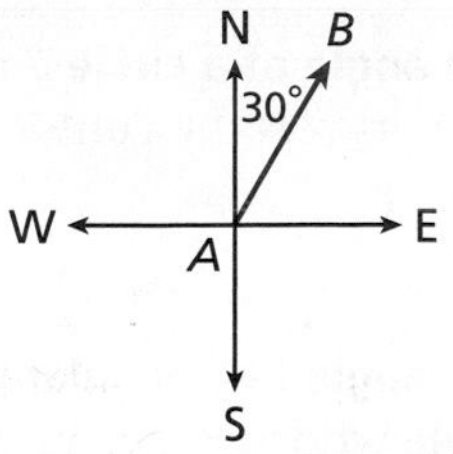

between Given three points A, B, and C, B is between A and C if and only if all three of the points lie on the same line, and $AB + BC = AC$.

entre Dados tres puntos A, B y C, B está entre A y C si y sólo si los tres puntos se encuentran en la misma línea y $AB + BC = AC$.

biconditional statement A statement that can be written in the form "p if and only if q."

enunciado bicondicional Enunciado que puede expresarse en la forma "p si y sólo si q".

A figure is a triangle if and only if it is a three-sided polygon.

bisect To divide into two congruent parts.

trazar una bisectriz Dividir en dos partes congruentes.

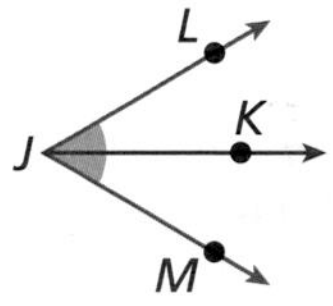

$\overrightarrow{JK}$ bisects $\angle LJM$.

C

Cartesian coordinate system *See* coordinate plane.

sistema de coordenadas cartesianas *Ver* plano cartesiano.

center of a circle The point inside a circle that is the same distance from every point on the circle.

centro de un círculo Punto dentro de un círculo que se encuentra a la misma distancia de todos los puntos del círculo.

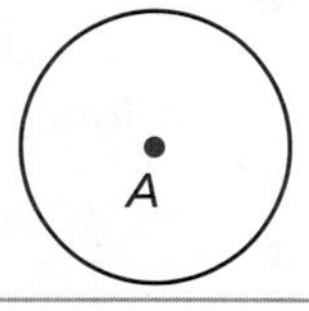

center of a regular polygon The point that is equidistant from all vertices of the regular polygon.

centro de un polígono regular Punto equidistante de todos los vértices del polígono regular.

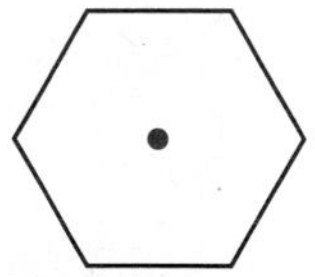

center of a sphere The point inside a sphere that is the same distance from every point on the sphere.

centro de una esfera Punto dentro de una esfera que está a la misma distancia de cualquier punto de la esfera.

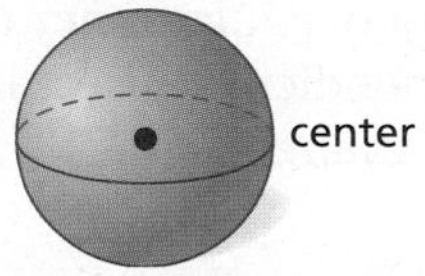

center of dilation The intersection of the lines that connect each point of the image with the corresponding point of the preimage.

centro de dilatación Intersección de las líneas que conectan cada punto de la imagen con el punto correspondiente de la imagen original.

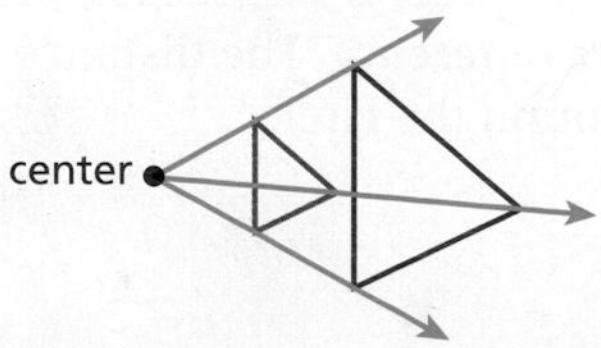

Glossary/Glosario

ENGLISH | **SPANISH** | **EXAMPLES**

center of rotation The point around which a figure is rotated.

centro de rotación Punto alrededor del cual rota una figura.

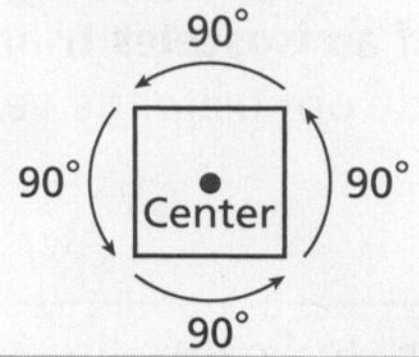

---

central angle of a circle An angle whose vertex is the center of a circle.

ángulo central de un círculo Ángulo cuyo vértice es el centro de un círculo.

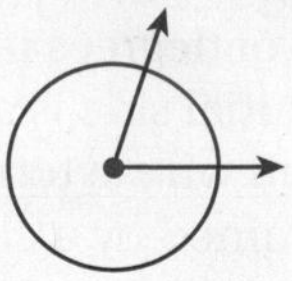

---

central angle of a regular polygon An angle whose vertex is the center of the regular polygon and whose sides pass through consecutive vertices.

ángulo central de un polígono regular Ángulo cuyo vértice es el centro del polígono regular y cuyos lados pasan por vértices consecutivos.

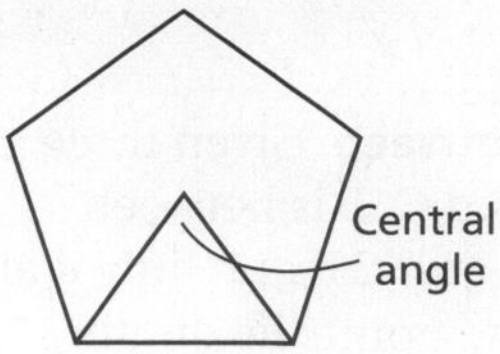

---

centroid of a triangle The point of concurrency of the three medians of a triangle. Also known as the *center of gravity*.

centroide de un triángulo Punto donde se encuentran las tres medianas de un triángulo. También conocido como *centro de gravedad.*

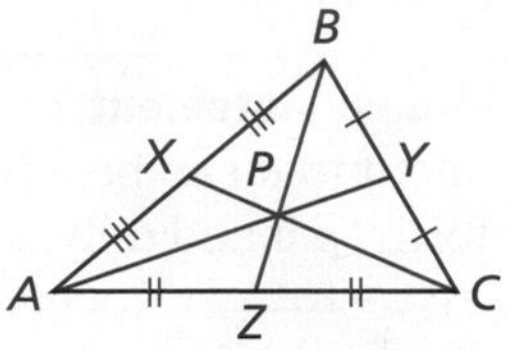

The centroid is *P*.

---

chord A segment whose endpoints lie on a circle.

cuerda Segmento cuyos extremos se encuentran en un círculo.

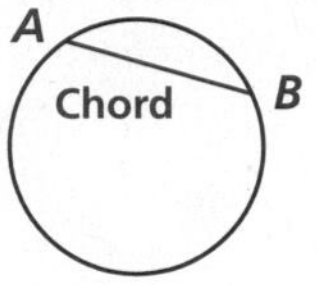

---

circle The set of points in a plane that are a fixed distance from a given point called the center of the circle.

círculo Conjunto de puntos en un plano que se encuentran a una distancia fija de un punto determinado denominado centro del círculo.

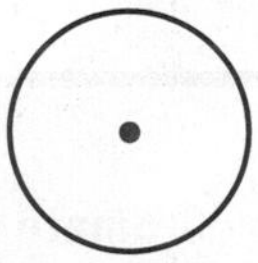

---

circle graph A way to display data by using a circle divided into non-overlapping sectors.

gráfica circular Forma de mostrar datos mediante un círculo dividido en sectores no superpuestos.

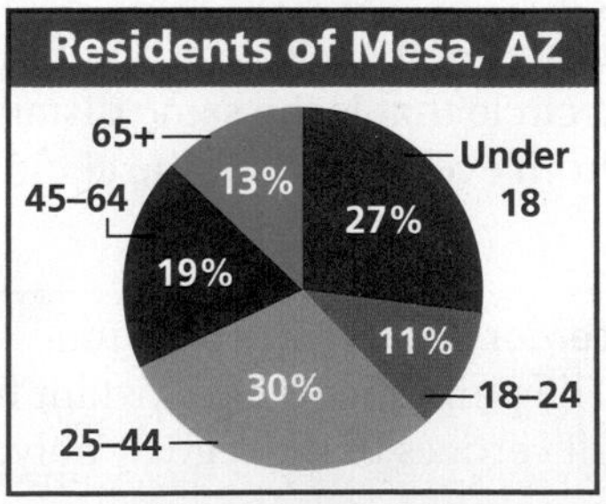

---

circumcenter of a triangle The point of concurrency of the three perpendicular bisectors of a triangle.

circuncentro de un triángulo Punto donde se cortan las tres mediatrices de un triángulo.

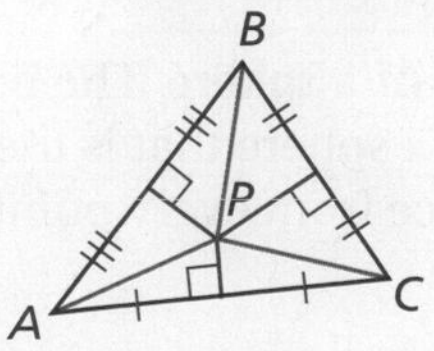

The circumcenter is *P*.

---

circumference The distance around the circle.

circunferencia Distancia alrededor del círculo.

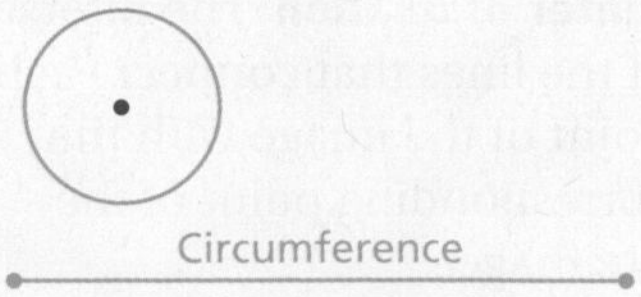

ENGLISH	SPANISH	EXAMPLES

circumscribed circle Every vertex of the polygon lies on the circle.

círculo circunscrito Todos los vértices del polígono se encuentran sobre el círculo.

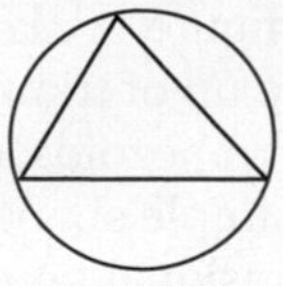

---

circumscribed polygon Each side of the polygon is tangent to the circle.

polígono circunscrito Todos los lados del polígono son tangentes al círculo.

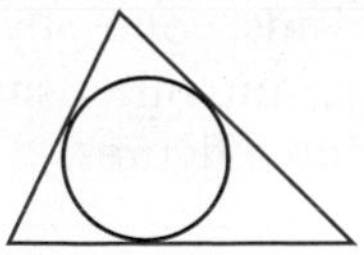

---

cofunction The trigonometric function of the complement of an angle.

cofuncion La funciona trigonométrica del complemento de un ángulo.

---

coincide To correspond exactly; to be identical.

coincidir Corresponder exactamente, ser idéntico.

---

collinear Points that lie on the same line.

colineal Puntos que se encuentran sobre la misma línea.

K, *L*, and *M* are collinear points.

---

combination A selection of a group of objects in which order is *not* important. The number of combinations of *r* objects chosen from a group of *n* objects is denoted $_{n}C_{r}$.

combinación Selección de un grupo de objetos en la cual el orden *no* es importante. El número de combinaciones de *r* objetos elegidos de un grupo de *n* objetos se expresa así: $_{n}C_{r}$.

For 4 objects *A*, *B*, *C*, and *D*, there are $_{4}C_{2} = 6$ different combinations of 2 objects: *AB, AC, AD, BC, BD, CD*.

---

common tangent A line that is tangent to two circles.

tangente común Línea que es tangente a dos círculos.

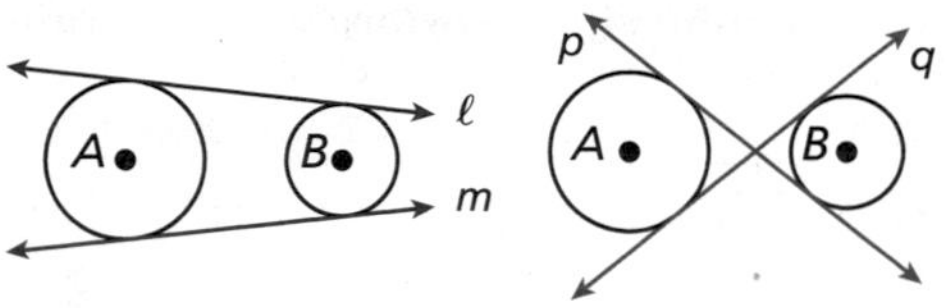

---

complement of an angle The sum of the measures of an angle and its complement is 90°.

complemento de un ángulo La suma de las medidas de un ángulo y su complemento es 90°.

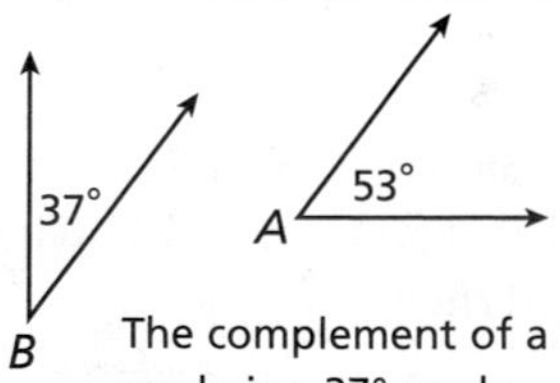

The complement of a 53° angle is a 37° angle.

---

complement of an event All outcomes in the sample space that are not in an event *E*, denoted $\overline{E}$.

complemento de un suceso Todos los resultados en el espacio muestral que no están en el suceso *E* y se expresan $\overline{E}$.

In the experiment of rolling a number cube, the complement of rolling a 3 is rolling a 1, 2, 4, 5, or 6.

---

complementary angles Two angles whose measures have a sum of 90°.

ángulos complementarios Dos ángulos cuyas medidas suman 90°.

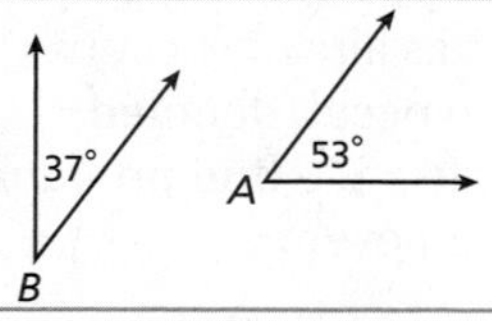

---

component form The form of a vector that lists the vertical and horizontal change from the initial point to the terminal point.

forma de componente Forma de un vector que muestra el cambio horizontal y vertical desde el punto inicial hasta el punto terminal.

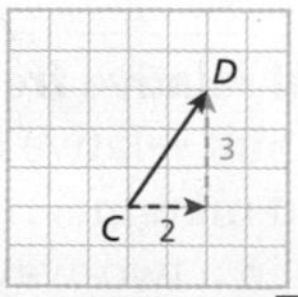

The component form of $\overrightarrow{CD}$ is $\langle 2, 3 \rangle$.

ENGLISH	SPANISH	EXAMPLES
composite figure A plane figure made up of triangles, rectangles, trapezoids, circles, and other simple shapes, or a three-dimensional figure made up of prisms, cones, pyramids, cylinders, and other simple three-dimensional figures.	**figura compuesta** Figura plana compuesta por triángulos, rectángulos, trapecios, círculos y otras figuras simples, o figura tridimensional compuesta por prismas, conos, pirámides, cilindros y otras figuras tridimensionales simples.	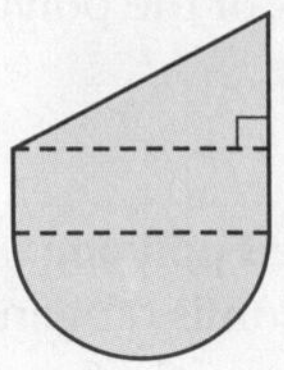
composition of transformations One transformation followed by another transformation.	**composición de transformaciones** Una transformación seguida de otra transformación.	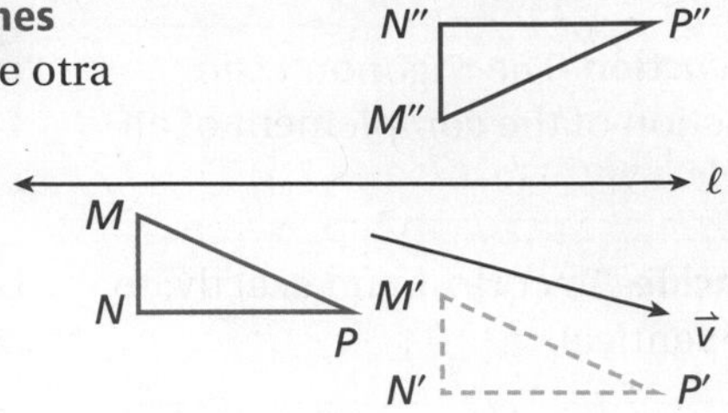
compound event An event made up of two or more simple events.	**suceso compuesto** Suceso formado por dos o más sucesos simples.	In the experiment of tossing a coin and rolling a number cube, the event of the coin landing heads and the number cube landing on 3.
compound statement Two statements that are connected by the word *and* or *or*.	**enunciado compuesto** Dos enunciados unidos por la palabra *y* u *o*.	The sky is blue and the grass is green. I will drive to school or I will take the bus.
concave polygon A polygon in which a diagonal can be drawn such that part of the diagonal contains points in the exterior of the polygon.	**polígono cóncavo** Polígono en el cual se puede trazar una diagonal tal que parte de la diagonal contiene puntos ubicados fuera del polígono.	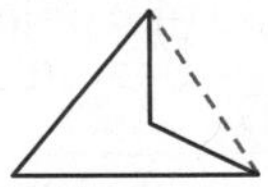 Concave quadrilateral
concentric circles Coplanar circles with the same center.	**círculos concéntricos** Círculos coplanares que comparten el mismo centro.	
conclusion The part of a conditional statement following the word *then*.	**conclusión** Parte de un enunciado condicional que sigue a la palabra *entonces*.	If $x + 1 = 5$, then $\underbrace{x = 4}_{\text{Conclusion}}$.
concurrent Three or more lines that intersect at one point.	**concurrente** Tres o más líneas que se cortan en un punto.	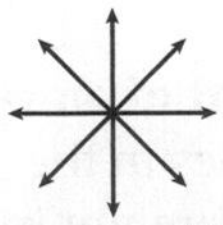
conditional probability The probability of event B, given that event A has already occurred or is certain to occur, denoted $P(B \mid A)$; used to find probability of dependent events.	**probabilidad condicional** Probabilidad del suceso B, dado que el suceso A ya ha ocurrido o es seguro que ocurrirá, expresada como $P(B \mid A)$; se utiliza para calcular la probabilidad de sucesos dependientes.	
conditional relative frequency The ratio of a joint relative frequency to a related marginal relative frequency in a two-way table.	**frecuencia relativa condicional** Razón de una frecuencia relativa conjunta a una frecuencia relativa marginal en una tabla de doble entrada.	

ENGLISH	SPANISH	EXAMPLES
conditional statement A statement that can be written in the form "if p, then q," where p is the hypothesis and q is the conclusion.	**enunciado condicional** Enunciado que se puede expresar como "si p, entonces q", donde p es la hipótesis y q es la conclusión.	If $\underbrace{x + 1 = 5}_{\text{Hypothesis}}$, then $\underbrace{x = 4}_{\text{Conclusion}}$.
cone A three-dimensional figure with a circular base and a curved lateral surface that connects the base to a point called the vertex.	**cono** Figura tridimensional con una base circular y una superficie lateral curva que conecta la base con un punto denominado vértice.	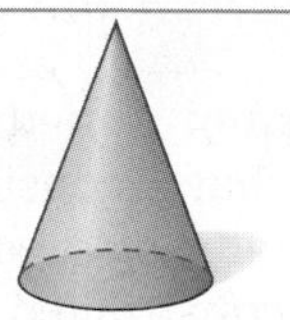
congruence statement A statement that indicates that two polygons are congruent by listing the vertices in the order of correspondence.	**enunciado de congruencia** Enunciado que indica que dos polígonos son congruentes enumerando los vértices en orden de correspondencia.	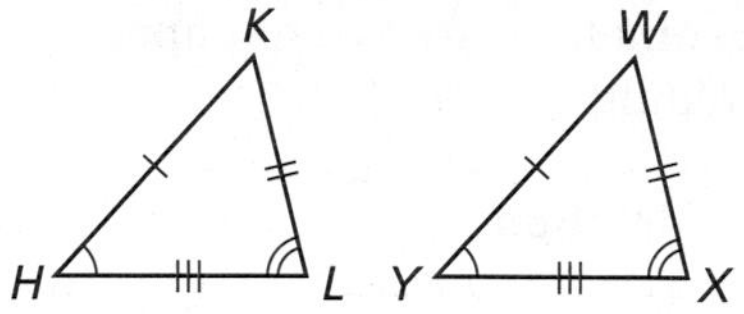 $\triangle HKL \cong \triangle YWX$
congruence transformation *See* isometry.	**transformación de congruencia** *Ver* isometría.	
congruent Having the same size and shape, denoted by ≅.	**congruente** Que tiene el mismo tamaño y la misma forma, expresado por ≅.	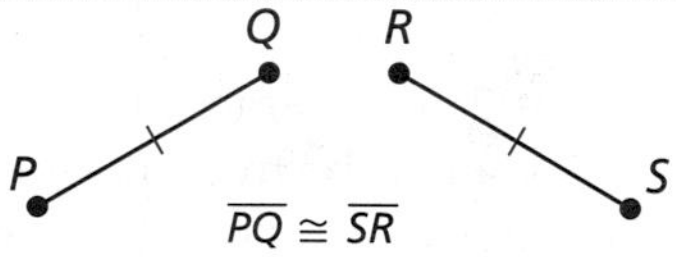 $\overline{PQ} \cong \overline{SR}$
congruent angles Angles that have the same measure.	**ángulos congruentes** Ángulos que tienen la misma medida.	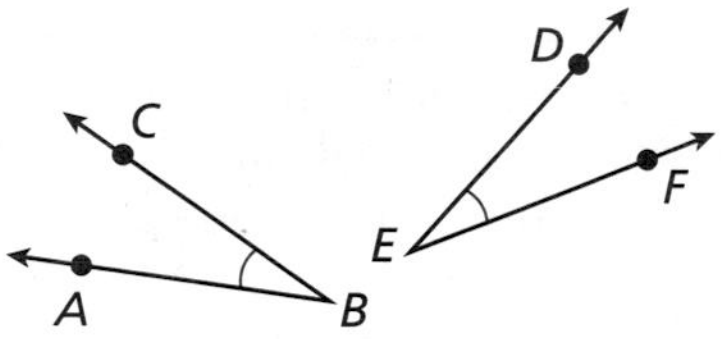 $\angle ABC \cong \angle DEF$
congruent arcs Two arcs that are in the same or congruent circles and have the same measure.	**arcos congruentes** Dos arcos que se encuentran en el mismo círculo o en círculos congruentes y que tienen la misma medida.	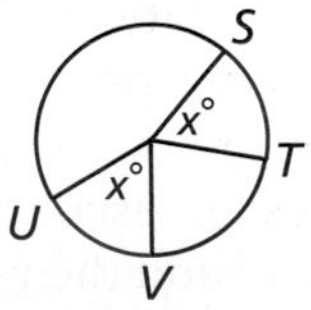
congruent circles Two circles that have congruent radii.	**círculos congruentes** Dos círculos que tienen radios congruentes.	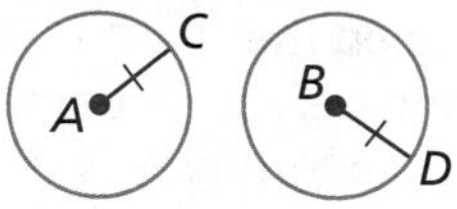
congruent polygons Two polygons whose corresponding sides and angles are congruent.	**polígonos congruentes** Dos polígonos cuyos lados y ángulos correspondientes son congruentes.	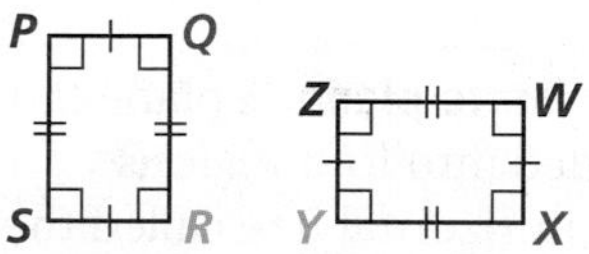
congruent segments Two segments that have the same length.	**segmentos congruentes** Dos segmentos que tienen la misma longitud.	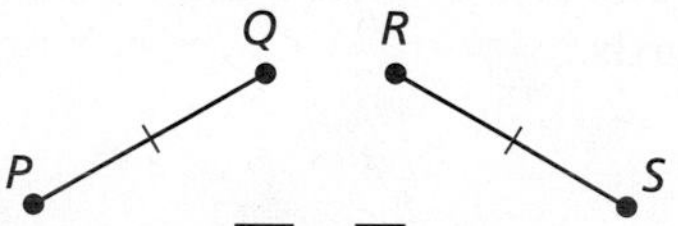 $\overline{PQ} \cong \overline{SR}$
conjecture A statement that is believed to be true.	**conjetura** Enunciado que se supone verdadero.	A sequence begins with the terms 2, 4, 6, 8, 10. A reasonable conjecture is that the next term in the sequence is 12.

ENGLISH	SPANISH	EXAMPLES
conjunction A compound statement that uses the word *and*.	**conjunción** Enunciado compuesto que contiene la palabra *y*.	3 is less than 5 AND greater than 0.
consecutive interior angles *See* same-side interior angles.	**ángulos internos consecutivos** *Ver* ángulos internos del mismo lado.	
construction A method of creating a figure that is considered to be mathematically precise. Figures may be constructed by using a compass and straightedge, geometry software, or paper folding.	**construcción** Método para crear una figura que es considerado matemáticamente preciso. Se pueden construir figuras utilizando un compás y una regla, un programa de computación de geometría o plegando papeles.	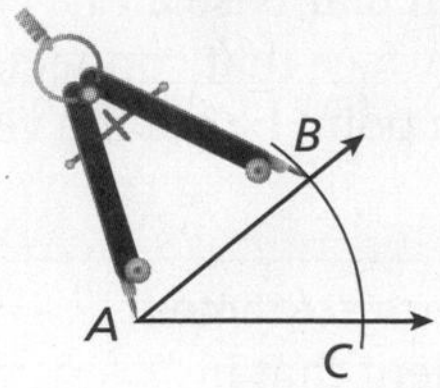
contraction *See* reduction.	**contracción** *Ver* reducción.	
contrapositive The statement formed by both exchanging and negating the hypothesis and conclusion of a conditional statement.	**contrarrecíproco** Enunciado que se forma al intercambiar y negar la hipótesis y la conclusión de un enunciado condicional.	Statement: If $n + 1 = 3$, then $n = 2$ Contrapositive: If $n \neq 2$, then $n + 1 \neq 3$
converse The statement formed by exchanging the hypothesis and conclusion of a conditional statement.	**recíproco** Enunciado que se forma intercambiando la hipótesis y la conclusión de un enunciado condicional.	Statement: If $n + 1 = 3$, then $n = 2$ Converse: If $n = 2$, then $n + 1 = 3$
convex polygon A polygon in which no diagonal contains points in the exterior of the polygon.	**polígono convexo** Polígono en el cual ninguna diagonal contiene puntos fuera del polígono.	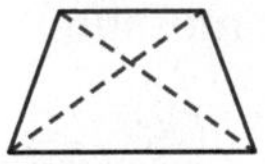 Convex quadrilateral
coordinate A number used to identify the location of a point. On a number line, one coordinate is used. On a coordinate plane, two coordinates are used, called the *x*-coordinate and the *y*-coordinate. In space, three coordinates are used, called the *x*-coordinate, the *y*-coordinate, and the *z*-coordinate.	**coordenada** Número utilizado para identificar la ubicación de un punto. En una recta numérica se utiliza una coordenada. En un plano cartesiano se utilizan dos coordenadas, denominadas coordenada *x* y coordenada *y*. En el espacio se utilizan tres coordenadas, denominadas coordenada *x*, coordenada *y* y coordenada *z*.	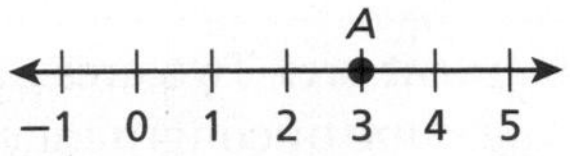The coordinate of point *A* is 3. 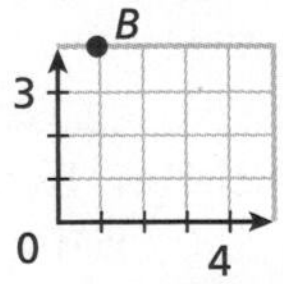The coordinates of point *B* are (1, 4).
coordinate plane A plane that is divided into four regions by a horizontal line called the *x*-axis and a vertical line called the *y*-axis.	**plano cartesiano** Plano dividido en cuatro regiones por una línea horizontal denominada eje *x* y una línea vertical denominada eje *y*.	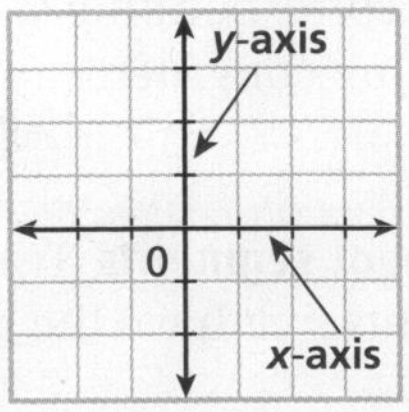
coordinate proof A style of proof that uses coordinate geometry and algebra.	**prueba de coordenadas** Tipo de demostración que utiliza geometría de coordenadas y álgebra.	

ENGLISH	SPANISH	EXAMPLES

coplanar Points that lie in the same plane.

coplanar Puntos que se encuentran en el mismo plano.

---

corollary A theorem whose proof follows directly from another theorem.

corolario Teorema cuya demostración proviene directamente de otro teorema.

---

corresponding angles of lines intersected by a transversal For two lines intersected by a transversal, a pair of angles that lie on the same side of the transversal and on the same sides of the other two lines.

ángulos correspondientes de líneas cortadas por una transversal Dadas dos líneas cortadas por una transversal, el par de ángulos ubicados en el mismo lado de la transversal y en los mismos lados de las otras dos líneas.

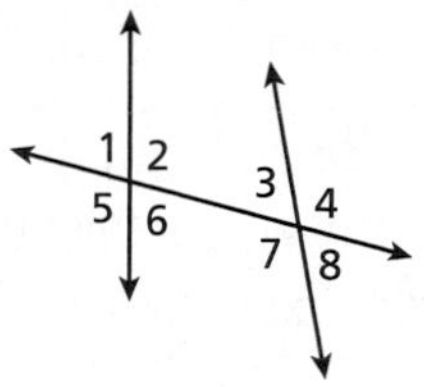

$\angle 1$ and $\angle 3$ are corresponding.

---

corresponding angles of polygons Angles in the same position in two different polygons that have the same number of angles.

ángulos correspondientes de los polígonos Ángulos que tienen la misma posición en dos polígonos diferentes que tienen el mismo número de ángulos.

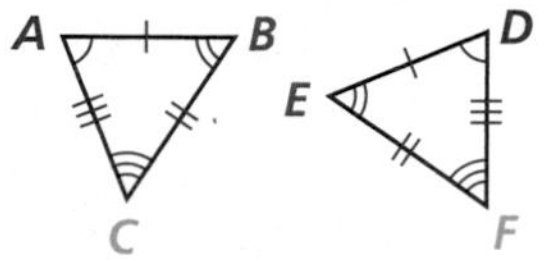

$\angle A$ and $\angle D$ are corresponding angles.

---

corresponding sides of polygons Sides in the same position in two different polygons that have the same number of sides.

lados correspondientes de los polígonos Lados que tienen la misma posición en dos polígonos diferentes que tienen el mismo número de lados.

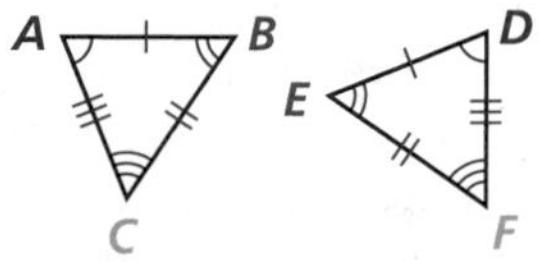

$\overline{AB}$ and $\overline{DE}$ are corresponding sides.

---

cosecant In a right triangle, the cosecant of angle A is the ratio of the length of the hypotenuse to the length of the side opposite A. It is the reciprocal of the sine function.

cosecante En un triángulo rectángulo, la cosecante del ángulo A es la razón entre la longitud de la hipotenusa y la longitud del cateto opuesto a A. Es la inversa de la función seno.

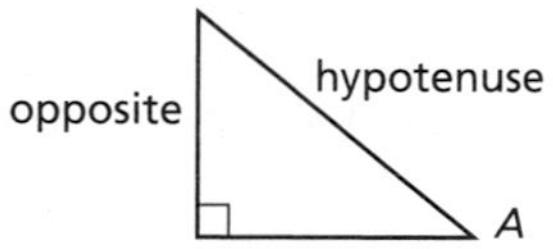

$$\csc A = \frac{\text{hypotenuse}}{\text{opposite}} = \frac{1}{\sin A}$$

---

cosine In a right triangle, the cosine of angle A is the ratio of the length of the leg adjacent to angle A to the length of the hypotenuse. It is the reciprocal of the secant function.

coseno En un triángulo rectángulo, el coseno del ángulo A es la razón entre la longitud del cateto adyacente al ángulo A y la longitud de la hipotenusa. Es la inversa de la función secante.

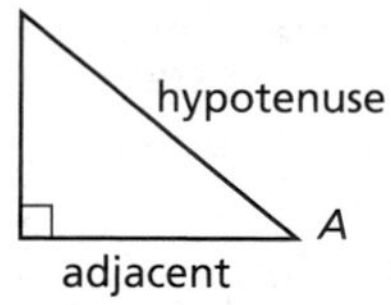

$$\cos A = \frac{\text{adjacent}}{\text{hypotenuse}} = \frac{1}{\sec A}$$

---

cotangent In a right triangle, the cotangent of angle A is the ratio of the length of the side adjacent to A to the length of the side opposite A. It is the reciprocal of the tangent function.

cotangente En un triángulo rectángulo, la cotangente del ángulo A es la razón entre la longitud del cateto adyacente a A y la longitud del cateto opuesto a A. Es la inversa de la función tangente.

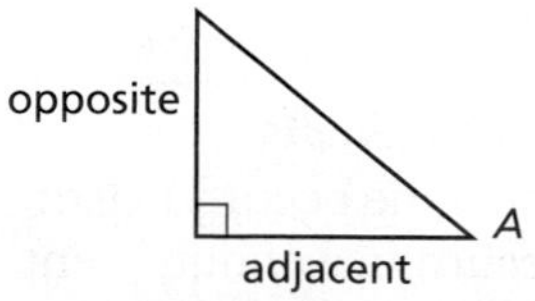

$$\cot A = \frac{\text{adjacent}}{\text{opposite}} = \frac{1}{\tan A}$$

---

counterexample An example that proves that a conjecture or statement is false.

contraejemplo Ejemplo que demuestra que una conjetura o enunciado es falso.

Glossary/Glosario

ENGLISH	SPANISH	EXAMPLES
CPCTC An abbreviation for "Corresponding Parts of Congruent Triangles are Congruent," which can be used as a justification in a proof after two triangles are proven congruent.	**PCTCC** Abreviatura que significa "Las partes correspondientes de los triángulos congruentes son congruentes", que se puede utilizar para justificar una demostración después de demostrar que dos triángulos son congruentes (CPCTC, por sus siglas en inglés).	
cross products In the statement $\frac{a}{b} = \frac{c}{d}$, bc and ad are the cross products.	**productos cruzados** En el enunciado $\frac{a}{b} = \frac{c}{d}$, bc y ad son los productos cruzados.	$\frac{1}{2} = \frac{3}{6}$ Product of means: $2 \cdot 3 = 6$ Product of extremes: $1 \cdot 6 = 6$
cross section The intersection of a three-dimensional figure and a plane.	**sección transversal** Intersección de una figura tridimensional y un plano.	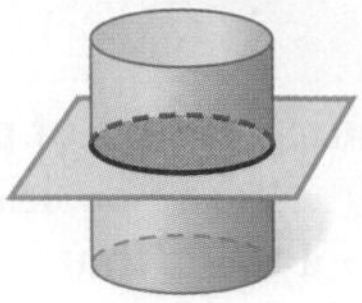
cube A prism with six square faces.	**cubo** Prisma con seis caras cuadradas.	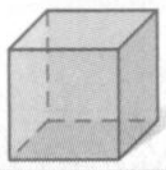
cylinder A three-dimensional figure with two parallel congruent circular bases and a curved lateral surface that connects the bases.	**cilindro** Figura tridimensional con dos bases circulares congruentes y paralelas y una superficie lateral curva que conecta las bases.	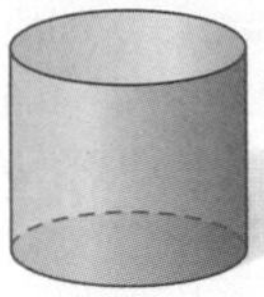

D

ENGLISH	SPANISH	EXAMPLES
decagon A ten-sided polygon.	**decágono** Polígono de diez lados.	
deductive reasoning The process of using logic to draw conclusions.	**razonamiento deductivo** Proceso en el que se utiliza la lógica para sacar conclusiones.	
definition A statement that describes a mathematical object and can be written as a true biconditional statement.	**definición** Enunciado que describe un objeto matemático y se puede expresar como un enunciado bicondicional verdadero.	
degree A unit of angle measure; one degree is $\frac{1}{360}$ of a circle.	**grado** Unidad de medida de los ángulos; un grado es $\frac{1}{360}$ de un círculo.	
dependent events Events for which the occurrence or nonoccurrence of one event affects the probability of the other event.	**sucesos dependientes** Dos sucesos son dependientes si el hecho de que uno de ellos se cumpla o no afecta la probabilidad del otro.	From a bag containing 3 red marbles and 2 blue marbles, drawing a red marble, and then drawing a blue marble without replacing the first marble.
diagonal of a polygon A segment connecting two nonconsecutive vertices of a polygon.	**diagonal de un polígono** Segmento que conecta dos vértices no consecutivos de un polígono.	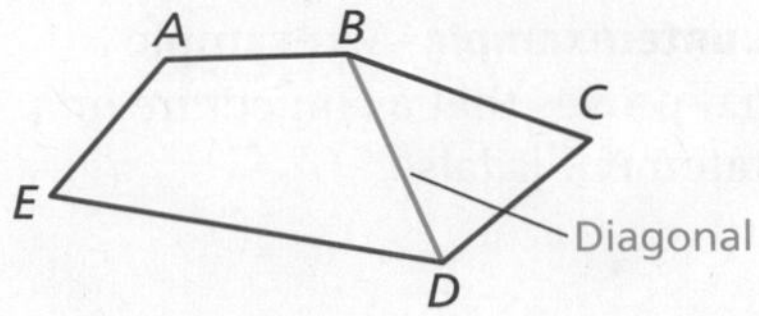

ENGLISH	SPANISH	EXAMPLES
diameter A segment that has endpoints on the circle and that passes through the center of the circle; also the length of that segment.	**diámetro** Segmento que atraviesa el centro de un círculo y cuyos extremos están sobre la circunferencia; longitud de dicho segmento.	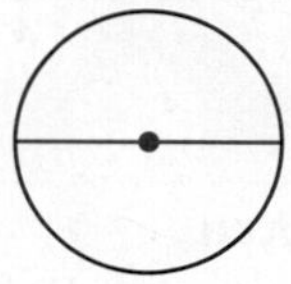
dilation A transformation in which the lines connecting every point P with its preimage P' all intersect at a point C known as the center of dilation, and $\frac{CP'}{CP}$ is the same for every point P; a transformation that changes the size of a figure but not its shape.	**dilatación** Transformación en la cual las líneas que conectan cada punto P con su imagen original P' se cruzan en un punto C conocido como centro de dilatación, y $\frac{CP'}{CP}$ es igual para cada punto P; transformación que cambia el tamaño de una figura pero no su forma.	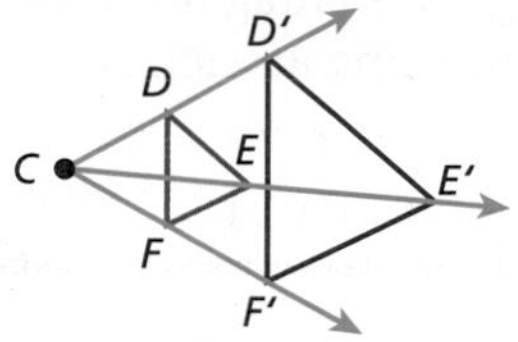
directed line segment A segment between two points A and B with a specified direction, from A to B or from B to A.	**segmento de una línea con dirección** Un segmento entro dos puntos con una dirección especificada.	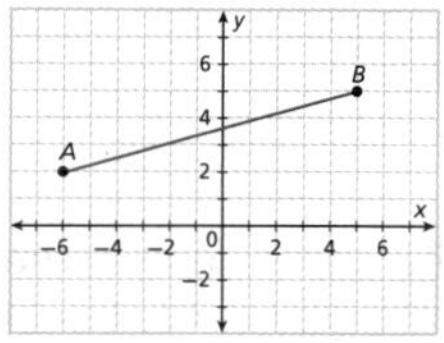
direct reasoning The process of reasoning that begins with a true hypothesis and builds a logical argument to show that a conclusion is true.	**razonamiento directo** Proceso de razonamiento que comienza con una hipótesis verdadera y elabora un argumento lógico para demostrar que una conclusión es verdadera.	
direct variation A linear relationship between two variables, x and y, that can be written in the form $y = kx$, where k is a nonzero constant.	**variación directa** Relación lineal entre dos variables, x e y, que puede expresarse en la forma $y = kx$, donde k es una constante distinta de cero.	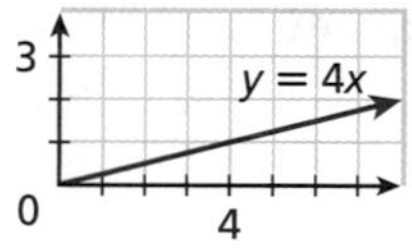
direction of a vector The orientation of a vector, which is determined by the angle the vector makes with a horizontal line.	**dirección de un vector** Orientación de un vector, determinada por el ángulo que forma el vector con una línea horizontal.	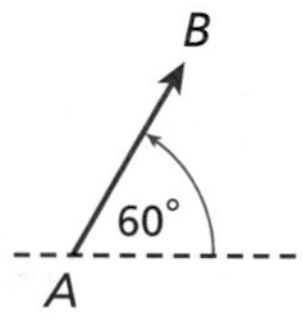
disjunction A compound statement that uses the word *or*.	**disyunción** Enunciado compuesto que contiene la palabra *o*.	John will walk to work or he will stay home.
distance between two points The absolute value of the difference of the coordinates of the points.	**distancia entre dos puntos** Valor absoluto de la diferencia entre las coordenadas de los puntos.	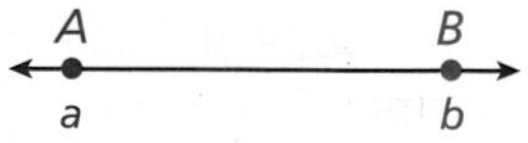 $AB = \|a - b\| = \|b - a\|$
distance from a point to a line The length of the perpendicular segment from the point to the line.	**distancia desde un punto hasta una línea** Longitud del segmento perpendicular desde el punto hasta la línea.	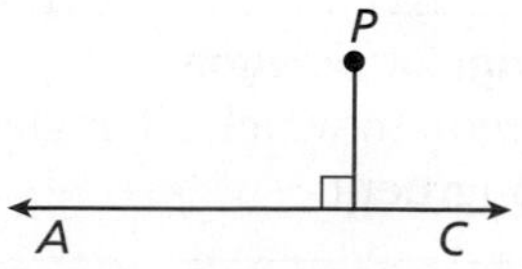 The distance from P to $\overleftrightarrow{AC}$ is 5 units.

Glossary/Glosario

ENGLISH	SPANISH	EXAMPLES
dodecagon A 12-sided polygon.	**dodecágono** Polígono de 12 lados.	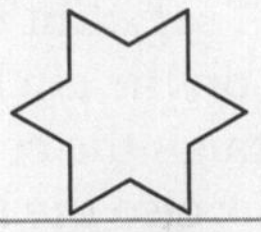
dodecahedron A polyhedron with 12 faces. The faces of a regular dodecahedron are regular pentagons, with three faces meeting at each vertex.	**dodecaedro** Poliedro con 12 caras. Las caras de un dodecaedro regular son pentágonos regulares, con tres caras que concurren en cada vértice.	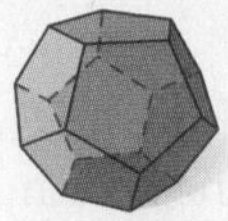

E

ENGLISH	SPANISH	EXAMPLES
edge of a graph A curve or segment that joins two vertices of the graph.	**arista de una gráfica** Curva o segmento que une dos vértices de la gráfica.	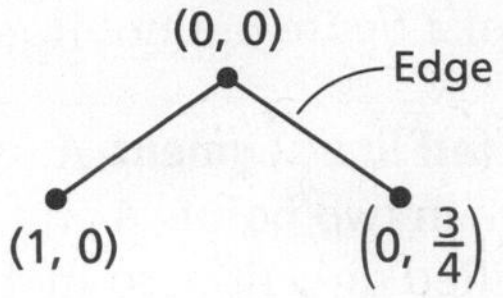
edge of a three-dimensional figure A segment that is the intersection of two faces of the figure.	**arista de una figura tridimensional** Segmento que constituye la intersección de dos caras de la figura.	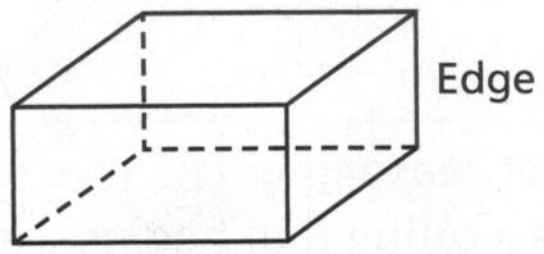
endpoint A point at an end of a segment or the starting point of a ray.	**extremo** Punto en el final de un segmento o punto de inicio de un rayo.	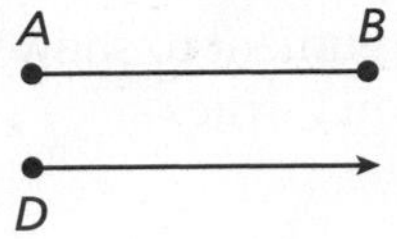
enlargement A dilation with a scale factor greater than 1. In an enlargement, the image is larger than the preimage.	**agrandamiento** Dilatación con un factor de escala mayor que 1. En un agrandamiento, la imagen es más grande que la imagen original.	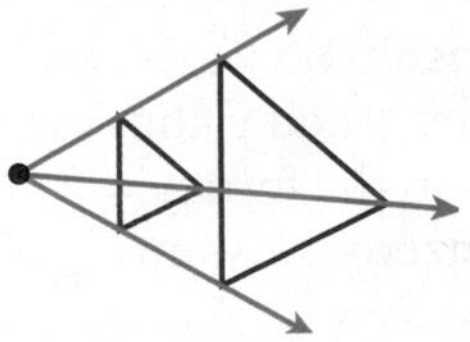
equal vectors Two vectors that have the same magnitude and the same direction.	**vectores iguales** Dos vectores de la misma magnitud y con la misma dirección.	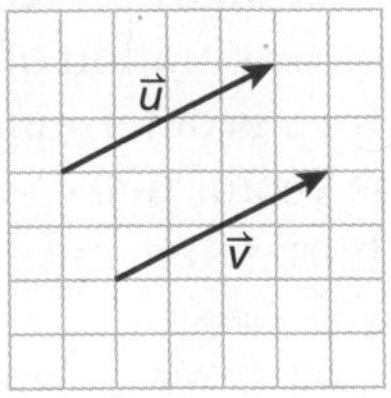 $\lvert\vec{u}\rvert = \lvert\vec{v}\rvert = 2\sqrt{5}$
equally likely outcomes Outcomes are equally likely if they have the same probability of occurring. If an experiment has n equally likely outcomes, then the probability of each outcome is $\frac{1}{n}$.	**resultados igualmente probables** Los resultados son igualmente probables si tienen la misma probabilidad de ocurrir. Si un experimento tiene n resultados igualmente probables, entonces la probabilidad de cada resultado es $\frac{1}{n}$.	If a coin is tossed, and heads and tails are equally likely, then $P(\text{heads}) = P(\text{tails}) = \frac{1}{2}$.
equiangular polygon A polygon in which all angles are congruent.	**polígono equiangular** Polígono cuyos ángulos son todos congruentes.	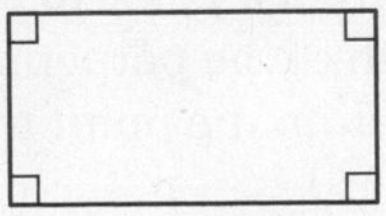
equiangular triangle A triangle with three congruent angles.	**triángulo equiangular** Triángulo con tres ángulos congruentes.	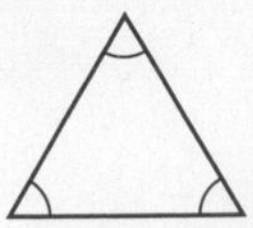

ENGLISH	SPANISH	EXAMPLES
equidistant The same distance from two or more objects.	**equidistante** Igual distancia de dos o más objetos.	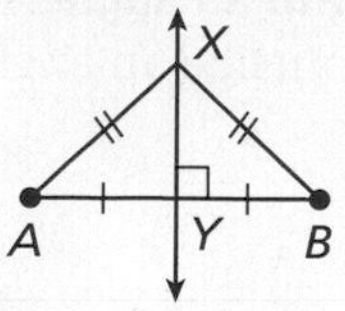 X is equidistant from A and B.
equilateral polygon A polygon in which all sides are congruent.	**polígono equilátero** Polígono cuyos lados son todos congruentes.	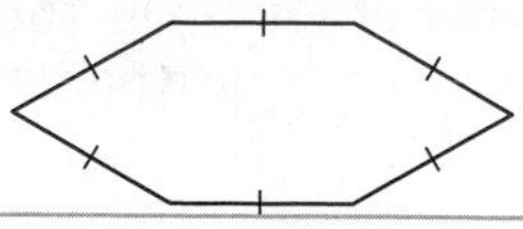
equilateral triangle A triangle with three congruent sides.	**triángulo equilátero** Triángulo con tres lados congruentes.	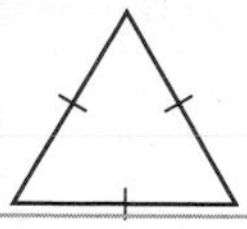
Euclidean geometry The system of geometry described by Euclid. In particular, the system of Euclidean geometry satisfies the Parallel Postulate, which states that there is exactly one line through a given point parallel to a given line.	**geometría euclidiana** Sistema geométrico desarrollado por Euclides. Específicamente, el sistema de la geometría euclidiana cumple con el postulado de las paralelas, que establece que por un punto dado se puede trazar una única línea paralela a una línea dada.	
Euler line The line containing the circumcenter (U), centroid (C), and orthocenter (O) of a triangle.	**recta de Euler** Recta que contiene el circuncentro (U), el centroide (C) y el ortocentro (O) de un triángulo.	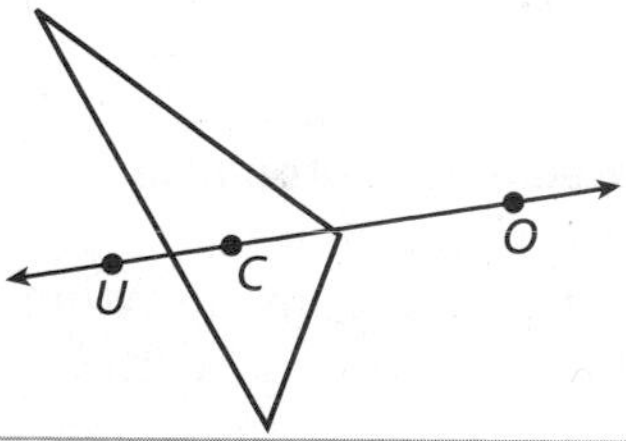
event An outcome or set of outcomes in a probability experiment.	**suceso** Resultado o conjunto de resultados en un experimento de probabilidad.	In the experiement of rolling a number cube, the event "an odd number" consists of the outcomes 1, 3, 5.
expansion *See* enlargement.	**expansión** *Ver* agrandamiento.	
experiment An operation, process, or activity in which outcomes can be used to estimate probability.	**experimento** Una operación, proceso o actividad en la que se usan los resultados para estimar una probabilidad.	Tossing a coin 10 times and noting the number of heads.
experimental probability The ratio of the number of times an event occurs to the number of trials, or times, that an activity is performed.	**probabilidad experimental** Razón entre la cantidad de veces que ocurre un suceso y la cantidad de pruebas, o veces, que se realiza una actividad.	Kendra made 6 of 10 free throws. The experimental probability that she will make her next free throw is $P(\text{free throw}) = \frac{\text{number made}}{\text{number attempted}} = \frac{6}{10}$.
exterior of a circle The set of all points outside a circle.	**exterior de un círculo** Conjunto de todos los puntos que se encuentran fuera de un círculo.	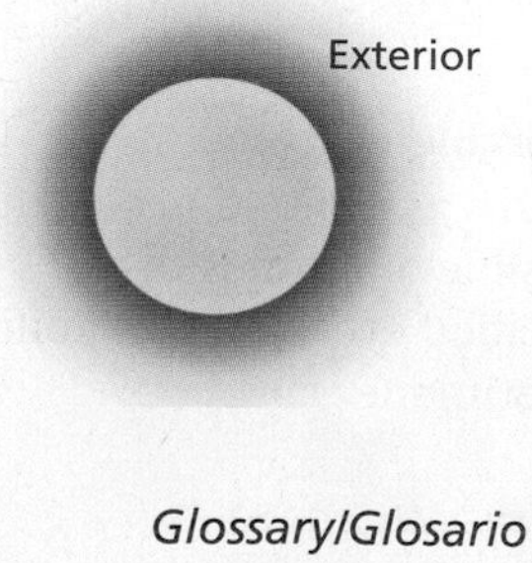

ENGLISH	SPANISH	EXAMPLES
exterior of an angle The set of all points outside an angle.	**exterior de un ángulo** Conjunto de todos los puntos que se encuentran fuera de un ángulo.	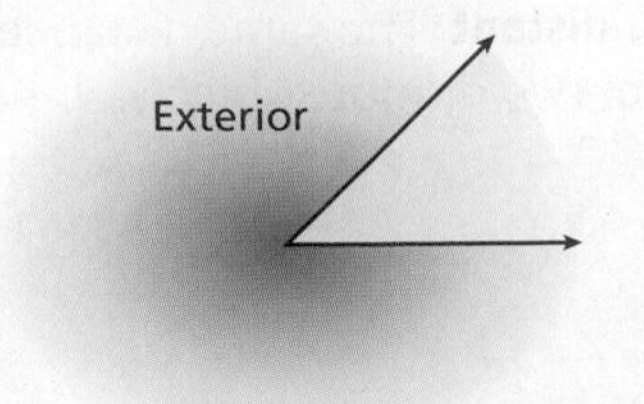
exterior of a polygon The set of all points outside a polygon.	**exterior de un polígono** Conjunto de todos los puntos que se encuentran fuera de un polígono.	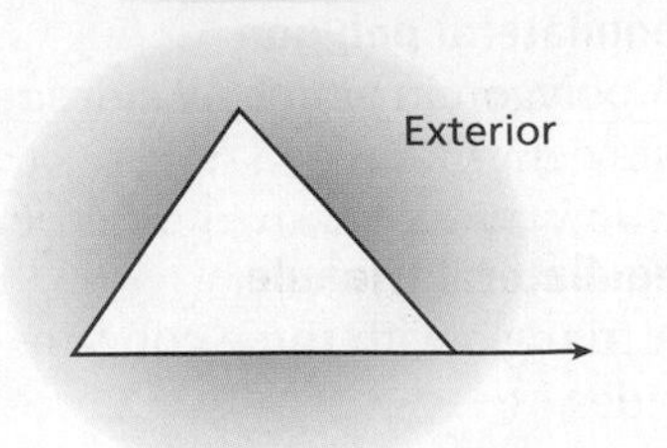
exterior angle of a polygon An angle formed by one side of a polygon and the extension of an adjacent side.	**ángulo externo de un polígono** Ángulo formado por un lado de un polígono y la prolongación del lado adyacente.	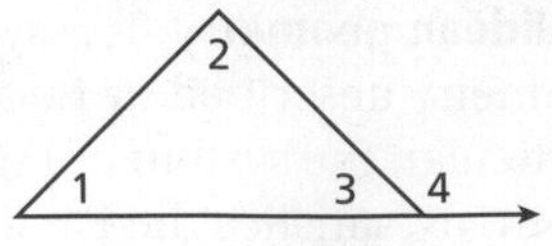 $\angle 4$ is an exterior angle.
external secant segment A segment of a secant that lies in the exterior of the circle with one endpoint on the circle.	**segmento secante externo** Segmento de una secante que se encuentra en el exterior del círculo y tiene un extremo sobre el círculo.	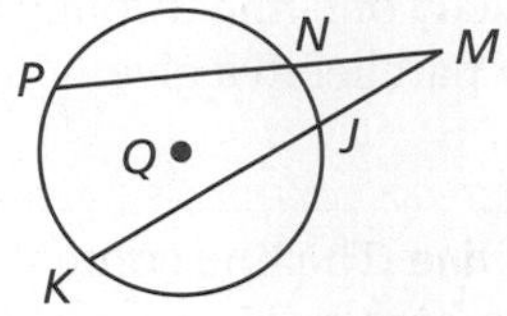 $\overline{NM}$ is an external secant segment.
extremes of a proportion In the proportion $\frac{a}{b} = \frac{c}{d}$, a and d are the extremes. If the proportion is written as $a{:}b = c{:}d$, the extremes are in the first and last positions.	**valores extremos de una proporción** En la proporción $\frac{a}{b} = \frac{c}{d}$, a y d son los valores extremos. Si la proporción se expresa como $a{:}b = c{:}d$, los extremos están en la primera y última posición.	

F

ENGLISH	SPANISH	EXAMPLES
face of a polyhedron A flat surface of the polyhedron.	**cara de un poliedro** Superficie plana de un poliedro.	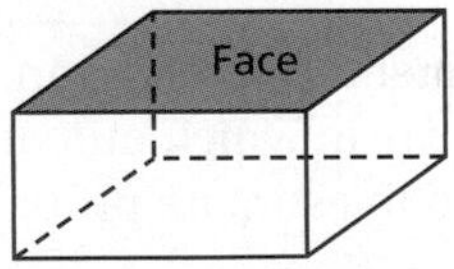
factorial If n is a positive integer, then n factorial, written $n!$, is $n \cdot (n-1) \cdot (n-2) \cdot \ldots \cdot 2 \cdot 1$. The factorial of 0 is defined to be 1.	**factorial** Si n es un entero positivo, entonces el factorial de n, expresado como $n!$, es $n \cdot (n-1) \cdot (n-2) \cdot \ldots \cdot 2 \cdot 1$. Por definición, el factorial de 0 será 1.	$7! = 7 \cdot 6 \cdot 5 \cdot 4 \cdot 3 \cdot 2 \cdot 1 = 5040$ $0! = 1$
fair When all outcomes of an experiment are equally likely.	**justo** Cuando todos los resultados de un experimento son igualmente probables.	When tossing a fair coin, heads and tails are equally likely. Each has a probability of $\frac{1}{2}$.
favorable outcome The occurrence of one of several possible outcomes of a specified event or probability experiment.	**resultado favorable** Cuando se produce uno de varios resultados posibles de un suceso específico o experimento de probabilidad.	In the experiment of rolling an odd number on a number cube, the favorable outcomes are 1, 3, and 5.

ENGLISH	SPANISH	EXAMPLES

Fibonacci sequence The infinite sequence of numbers beginning with 1, 1, … such that each term is the sum of the two previous terms.

sucesión de Fibonacci Sucesión infinita de números que comienza con 1, 1, … de forma tal que cada término es la suma de los dos términos anteriores.

1, 1, 2, 3, 5, 8, 13, 21, …

flip *See* reflection.

inversión *Ver* reflexión.

flowchart proof A style of proof that uses boxes and arrows to show the structure of the proof.

demostración con diagrama de flujo Tipo de demostración que se vale de cuadros y flechas para mostrar la estructura de la prueba.

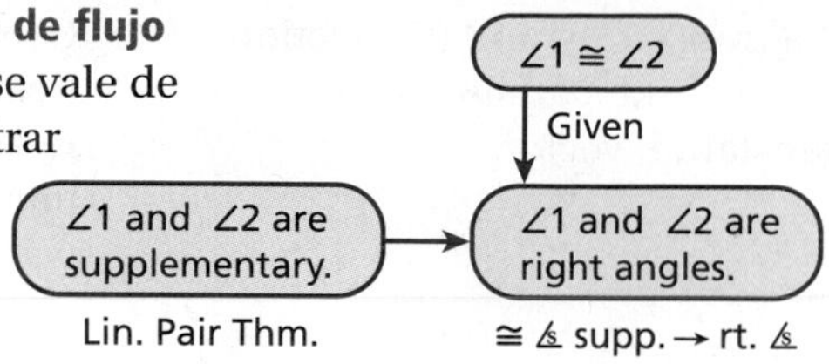

fractal A figure that is generated by iteration.

fractal Figura generada por iteración.

frieze pattern A pattern that has translation symmetry along a line.

patrón de friso Patrón con simetría de traslación a lo largo de una línea.

frustum of a cone A part of a cone with two parallel bases.

tronco de cono Parte de un cono con dos bases paralelas.

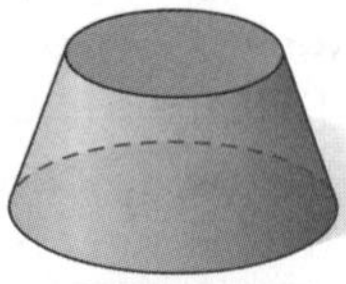

frustum of a pyramid A part of a pyramid with two parallel bases.

tronco de pirámide Parte de una pirámide con dos bases paralelas.

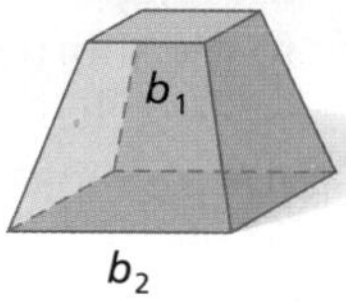

function A relation in which every input is paired with exactly one output.

función Una relación en la que cada entrada corresponde exactamente a una salida.

Function: $\{(0, 5), (1, 3), (2, 1), (3, 3)\}$

Not a Function: $\{(0, 1), (0, 3), (2, 1), (2, 3)\}$

Fundamental Counting Principle For n items, if there are m_1 ways to choose a first item, m_2 ways to choose a second item after the first item has been chosen, and so on, then there are $m_1 \cdot m_2 \cdot \ldots \cdot m_n$ ways to choose n items.

Principio fundamental de conteo Dados n elementos, si existen m_1 formas de elegir un primer elemento, m_2 formas de elegir un segundo elemento después de haber elegido el primero, y así sucesivamente, entonces existen $m_1 \cdot m_2 \cdot \ldots \cdot m_n$ formas de elegir n elementos.

If there are 4 colors of shirts, 3 colors of pants, and 2 colors of shoes, then there are $4 \cdot 3 \cdot 2 = 24$ possible outfits.

G

geometric mean For positive numbers a and b, the positive number x such that $\frac{a}{x} = \frac{x}{b}$. In a geometric sequence, a term that comes between two given nonconsecutive terms of the sequence.

media geométrica Dados los números positivos a y b, el número positivo x tal que $\frac{a}{x} = \frac{x}{b}$. En una sucesión geométrica, un término que está entre dos términos no consecutivos dados de la sucesión.

$$\frac{a}{x} = \frac{x}{b}$$
$$x^2 = ab$$
$$x = \sqrt{ab}$$

ENGLISH	SPANISH	EXAMPLES

geometric probability A form of theoretical probability determined by a ratio of geometric measures such as lengths, areas, or volumes.

probabilidad geométrica Una forma de la probabilidad teórica determinada por una razón de medidas geométricas, como longitud, área o volumen.

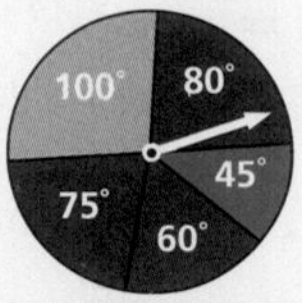

The probability of the pointer landing on red is $\frac{2}{9}$.

glide reflection A composition of a translation and a reflection across a line parallel to the translation vector.

deslizamiento con inversión Composición de una traslación y una reflexión sobre una línea paralela al vector de traslación.

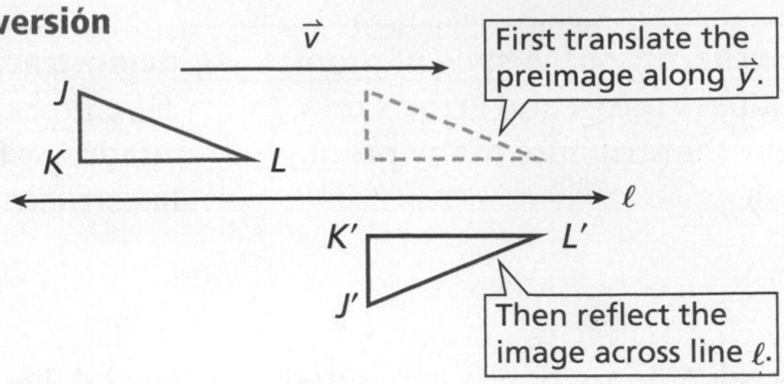

glide reflection symmetry A pattern has glide reflection symmetry if it coincides with its image after a glide reflection.

simetría de deslizamiento con inversión Un patrón tiene simetría de deslizamiento con inversión si coincide con su imagen después de un deslizamiento con inversión.

golden ratio If a segment is divided into two parts so that the ratio of the lengths of the whole segment to the longer part equals the ratio of the lengths of the longer part to the shorter part, then that ratio is called the golden ratio. The golden ratio is equal to $\frac{1+\sqrt{5}}{2} \approx 1.618$.

razón áurea Si se divide un segmento en dos partes de forma tal que la razón entre la longitud de todo el segmento y la de la parte más larga sea igual a la razón entre la longitud de la parte más larga y la de la parte más corta, entonces dicha razón se denomina razón áurea. La razón áurea es igual a $\frac{1+\sqrt{5}}{2} \approx 1.618$.

Golden ratio $= \frac{AC}{AB} = \frac{AB}{BC}$

Create segment such that

$\frac{AC}{AB} \approx 1.62$ and $\frac{AB}{BC} \approx 1.62$

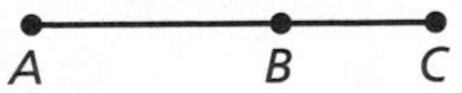

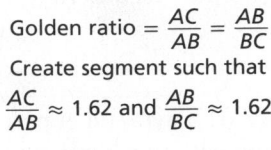

golden rectangle A rectangle in which the ratio of the lengths of the longer side to the shorter side is the golden ratio.

rectángulo áureo Rectángulo en el cual la razón entre la longitud del lado más largo y la longitud del lado más corto es la razón áurea.

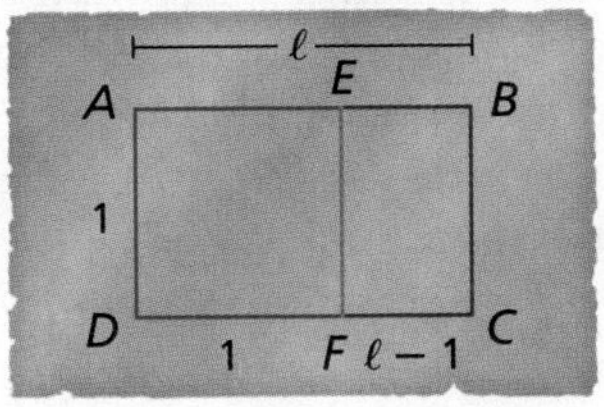

great circle A circle on a sphere that divides the sphere into two hemispheres.

círculo máximo En una esfera, círculo que divide la esfera en dos hemisferios.

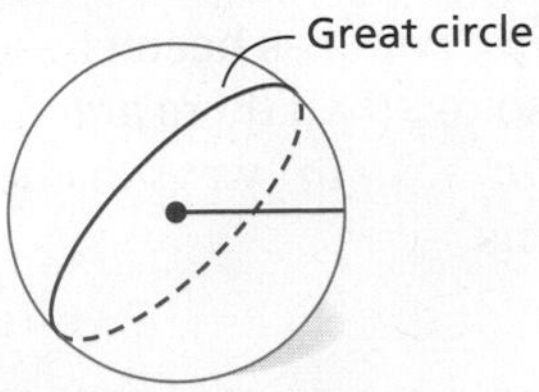

H

head-to-tail method A method of adding two vectors by placing the tail of the second vector on the head of the first vector; the sum is the vector drawn from the tail of the first vector to the head of the second vector.

método de cola a punta Método para sumar dos vectores colocando la cola del segundo vector en la punta del primer vector. La suma es el vector trazado desde la cola del primer vector hasta la punta del segundo vector.

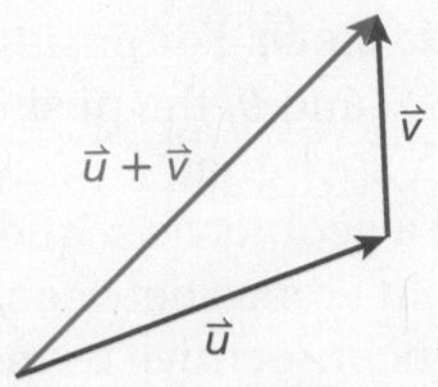

ENGLISH	SPANISH	EXAMPLES
height of a figure The length of an altitude of the figure.	**altura de una figura** Longitud de la altura de la figura.	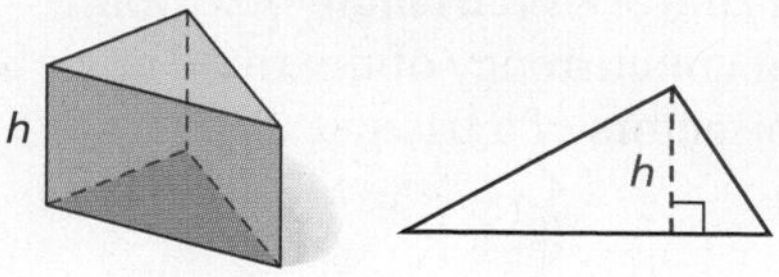
height of a triangle A segment from a vertex that forms a right angle with a line containing the base.	**altura de un triángulo** Segmento que se extiende desde el vértice y forma un ángulo recto con la línea de la base.	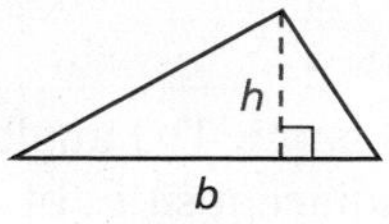
hemisphere Half of a sphere.	**hemisferio** Mitad de una esfera.	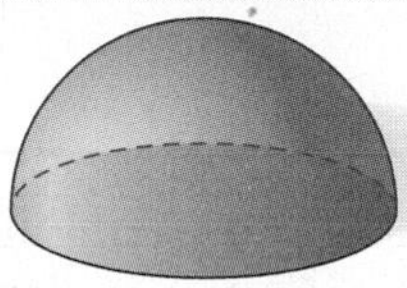
heptagon A seven-sided polygon.	**heptágono** Polígono de siete lados.	
hexagon A six-sided polygon.	**hexágono** Polígono de seis lados.	
horizon The horizontal line in a perspective drawing that contains the vanishing point(s).	**horizonte** Línea horizontal en un dibujo en perspectiva que contiene el punto de fuga o los puntos de fuga.	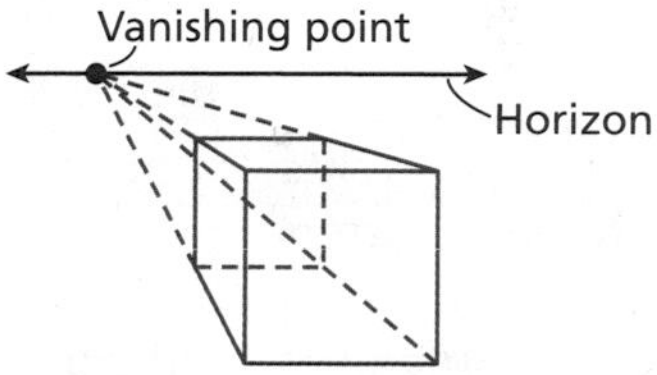
hypotenuse The side opposite the right angle in a right triangle.	**hipotenusa** Lado opuesto al ángulo recto de un triángulo rectángulo.	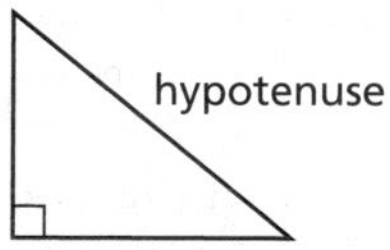
hypothesis The part of a conditional statement following the word *if*.	**hipótesis** La parte de un enunciado condicional que sigue a la palabra *si*.	If $\underbrace{x + 1 = 5}_{\text{Hypothesis}}$, then $x = 4$.

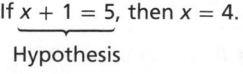

I

ENGLISH	SPANISH	EXAMPLES
icosahedron A polyhedron with 20 faces. A regular icosahedron has equilateral triangles as faces, with 5 faces meeting at each vertex.	**icosaedro** Poliedro con 20 caras. Las caras de un icosaedro regular son triángulos equiláteros y cada vértice es compartido por 5 caras.	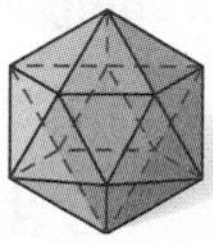
identity An equation that is true for all values of the variables.	**identidad** Ecuación verdadera para todos los valores de las variables.	$3 = 3$ $2(x - 1) = 2x - 2$
image A shape that results from a transformation of a figure known as the preimage.	**imagen** Forma resultante de la transformación de una figura conocida como imagen original.	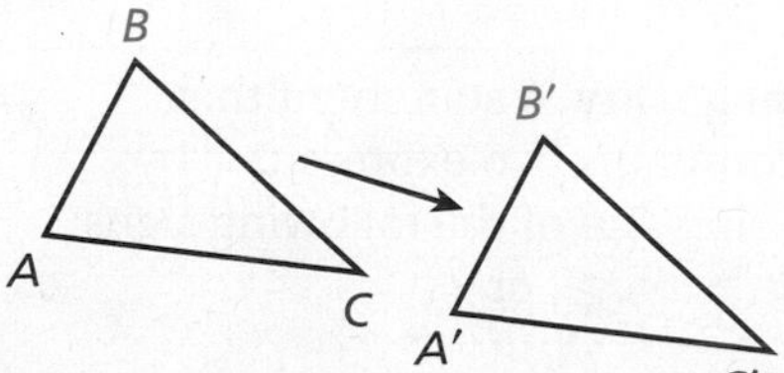

Glossary/Glosario

ENGLISH	SPANISH	EXAMPLES
incenter of a triangle The point of concurrency of the three angle bisectors of a triangle.	**incentro de un triángulo** Punto donde se encuentran las tres bisectrices de los ángulos de un triángulo.	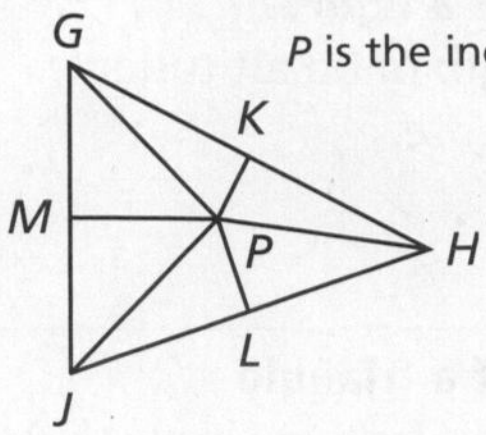 P is the incenter.
included angle The angle formed by two adjacent sides of a polygon.	**ángulo incluido** Ángulo formado por dos lados adyacentes de un polígono.	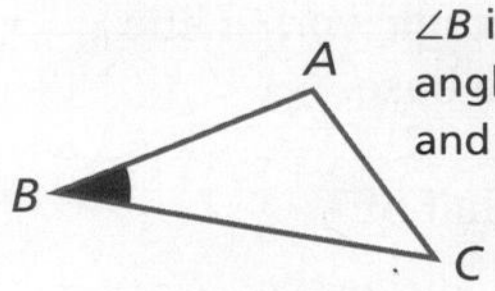 $\angle B$ is the included angle between $\overline{AB}$ and $\overline{BC}$.
included side The common side of two consecutive angles of a polygon.	**lado incluido** Lado común de dos ángulos consecutivos de un polígono.	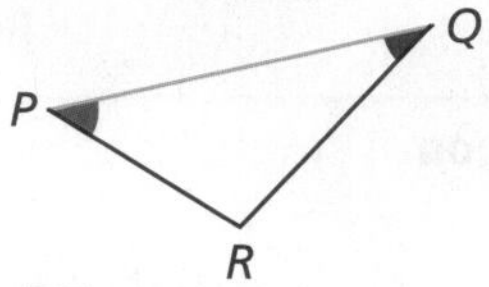 $\overline{PQ}$ is the included side between $\angle P$ and $\angle Q$.
inclusive events Events that have one or more outcomes in common.	**sucesos inclusivos** Sucesos que tienen uno o más resultados en común.	In the experiment of rolling a number cube, rolling an even number and rolling a number less than 3 are inclusive events because the outcome 2 is both even and less than 3.
independent events Events for which the occurrence or non-occurrence of one event does not affect the probability of the other event.	**sucesos independientes** Dos sucesos son independientes si el hecho de que se produzca o no uno de ellos no afecta la probabilidad del otro suceso.	From a bag containing 3 red marbles and 2 blue marbles, drawing a red marble, replacing it, and then drawing a blue marble.
indirect measurement A method of measurement that uses formulas, similar figures, and/or proportions.	**medición indirecta** Método para medir objetos mediante fórmulas, figuras semejantes y/o proporciones.	
indirect proof A proof in which the statement to be proved is assumed to be false and a contradiction is shown.	**demostración indirecta** Prueba en la que se supone que el enunciado a demostrar es falso y se muestra una contradicción.	
indirect reasoning *See* indirect proof.	**razonamiento indirecto** *Ver* demostración indirecta.	
inductive reasoning The process of reasoning that a rule or statement is true because specific cases are true.	**razonamiento inductivo** Proceso de razonamiento por el que se determina que una regla o enunciado son verdaderos porque ciertos casos específicos son verdaderos.	
inequality A statement that compares two expressions by using one of the following signs: $<, >, \leq, \geq$, or $\neq$.	**desigualdad** Enunciado que compara dos expresiones utilizando uno de los siguientes signos: $<, >, \leq, \geq$ o $\neq$.	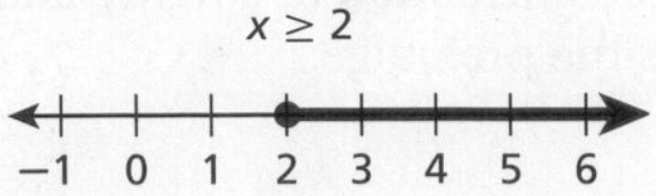

ENGLISH	SPANISH	EXAMPLES
initial point of a vector The starting point of a vector.	**punto inicial de un vector** Punto donde comienza un vector.	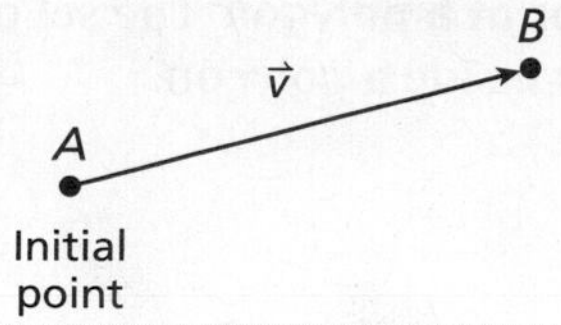
initial side The ray that lies on the positive x-axis when an angle is drawn in standard position.	**lado inicial** Rayo que se encuentra sobre el eje x positivo cuando se traza un ángulo en posición estándar.	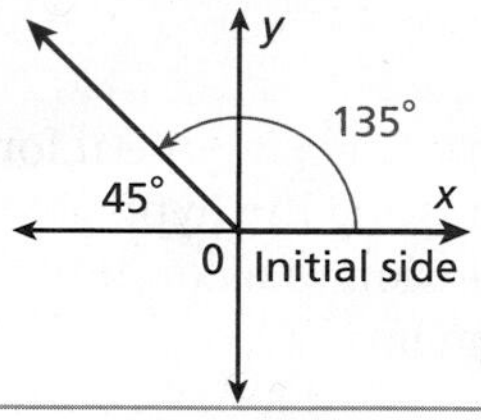
inscribed angle An angle whose vertex is on a circle and whose sides contain chords of the circle.	**ángulo inscrito** Ángulo cuyo vértice se encuentra sobre un círculo y cuyos lados contienen cuerdas del círculo.	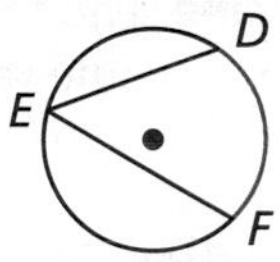
inscribed circle A circle in which each side of the polygon is tangent to the circle.	**círculo inscrito** Círculo en el que cada lado del polígono es tangente al círculo.	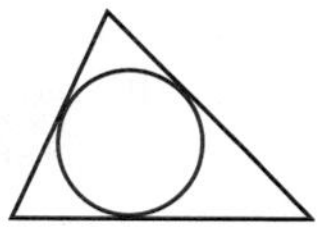
inscribed polygon A polygon in which every vertex of the polygon lies on the circle.	**polígono inscrito** Polígono cuyos vértices se encuentran sobre el círculo.	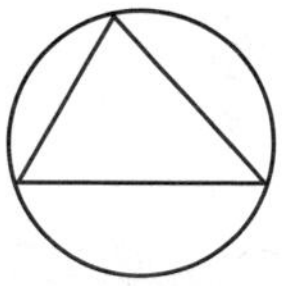
integer A member of the set of whole numbers and their opposites.	**entero** Miembro del conjunto de números cabales y sus opuestos.	$\{\ldots -3, -2, -1, 0, 1, 2, 3, \ldots\}$
intercepted arc An arc that consists of endpoints that lie on the sides of an inscribed angle and all the points of the circle between the endpoints.	**arco abarcado** Arco cuyos extremos se encuentran en los lados de un ángulo inscrito y consta de todos los puntos del círculo ubicados entre dichos extremos.	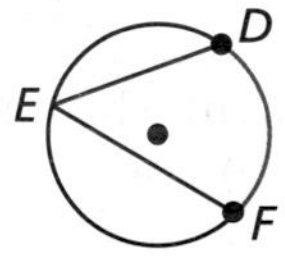 $\overset{\frown}{DF}$ is the intercepted arc.
interior angle An angle formed by two sides of a polygon with a common vertex.	**ángulo interno** Ángulo formado por dos lados de un polígono con un vértice común.	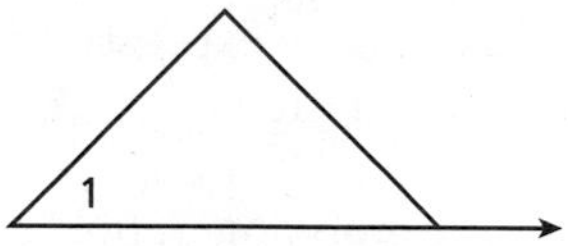 $\angle 1$ is an interior angle.
interior of a circle The set of all points inside a circle.	**interior de un círculo** Conjunto de todos los puntos que se encuentran dentro de un círculo.	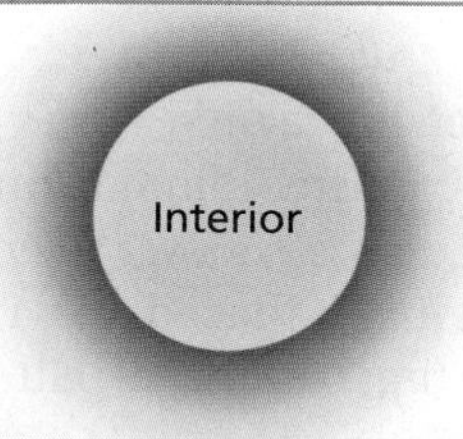
interior of an angle The set of all points between the sides of an angle.	**interior de un ángulo** Conjunto de todos los puntos entre los lados de un ángulo.	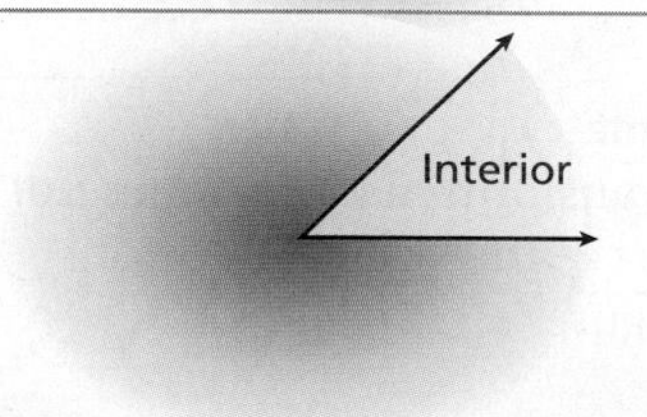

ENGLISH	SPANISH	EXAMPLES
interior of a polygon The set of all points inside a polygon.	**interior de un polígono** Conjunto de todos los puntos que se encuentran dentro de un polígono.	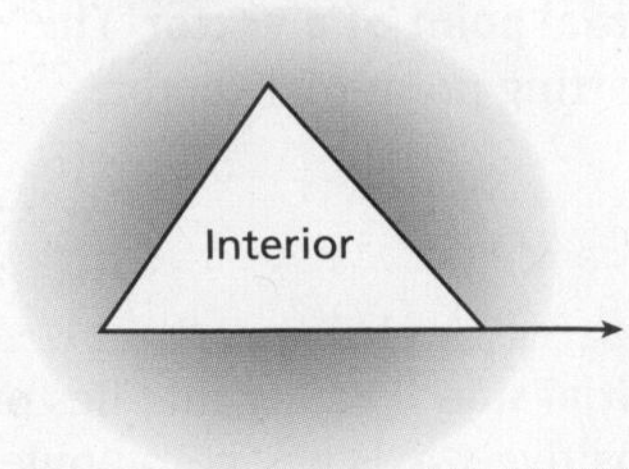
inverse The statement formed by negating the hypothesis and conclusion of a conditional statement.	**inverso** Enunciado formado al negar la hipótesis y la conclusión de un enunciado condicional.	Statement: If $n + 1 = 3$, then $n = 2$ Inverse: If $n + 1 \neq 3$, then $n \neq 2$
inverse cosine The measure of an angle whose cosine ratio is known.	**coseno inverso** Medida de un ángulo cuya razón coseno es conocida.	If $\cos A = x$, then $\cos^{-1}x = m\angle A$.
inverse function The function that results from exchanging the input and output values of a one-to-one function. The inverse of $f(x)$ is denoted $f^{-1}(x)$.	**función inversa** Función que resulta de intercambiar los valores de entrada y salida de una función uno a uno. La función inversa de $f(x)$ se indica $f^{-1}(x)$.	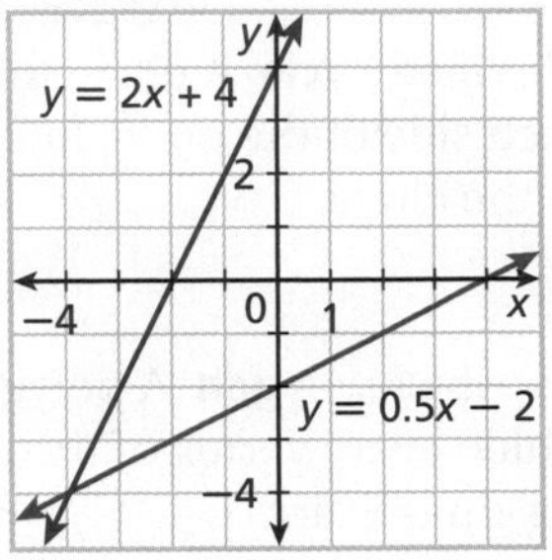 The function $y = \frac{1}{2}x - 2$ is the inverse of the function $y = 2x + 4$.
inverse sine The measure of an angle whose sine ratio is known.	**seno inverso** Medida de un ángulo cuya razón seno es conocida.	If $\sin A = x$, then $\sin^{-1}x = m\angle A$.
inverse tangent The measure of an angle whose tangent ratio is known.	**tangente inversa** Medida de un ángulo cuya razón tangente es conocida.	If $\tan A = x$, then $\tan^{-1}x = m\angle A$.
irrational number A real number that cannot be expressed as the ratio of two integers.	**número irracional** Número real que no se puede expresar como una razón de dos enteros.	$\sqrt{2}, \pi, e$
irregular polygon A polygon that is not regular.	**polígono irregular** Polígono que no es regular.	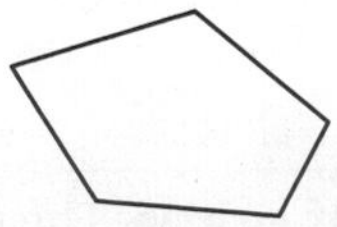
isometric drawing A way of drawing three-dimensional figures using *isometric dot paper*, which has equally spaced dots in a repeating triangular pattern.	**dibujo isométrico** Forma de dibujar figuras tridimensionales utilizando *papel punteado isométrico*, que tiene puntos espaciados uniformemente en un patrón triangular que se repite.	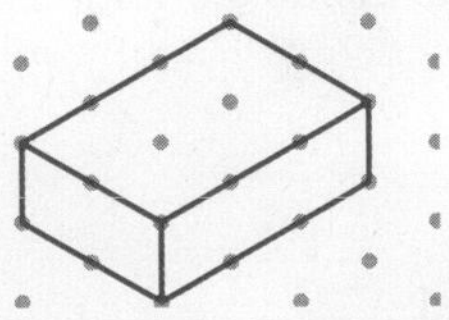
isometry A transformation that does not change the size or shape of a figure.	**isometría** Transformación que no cambia el tamaño ni la forma de una figura.	Reflections, translations, and rotations are all examples of isometries.

ENGLISH	SPANISH	EXAMPLES

isosceles trapezoid A trapezoid in which the legs are congruent.

trapecio isósceles Trapecio cuyos lados no paralelos son congruentes.

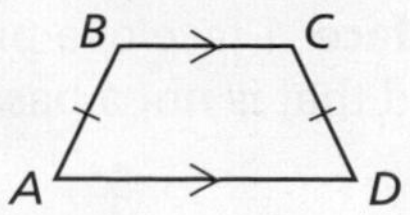

isosceles triangle A triangle with at least two congruent sides.

triángulo isósceles Triángulo que tiene al menos dos lados congruentes.

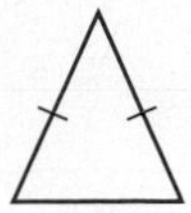

iteration The repetitive application of the same rule.

iteración Aplicación repetitiva de la misma regla.

J

joint relative frequency The ratio of the frequency in a particular category divided by the total number of data values.

frecuencia relativa conjunta La razón de la frecuencia en una determinada categoría dividida entre el número total de valores.

K

kite A quadrilateral with exactly two pairs of congruent consecutive sides.

cometa o papalote Cuadrilátero con exactamente dos pares de lados congruentes consecutivos.

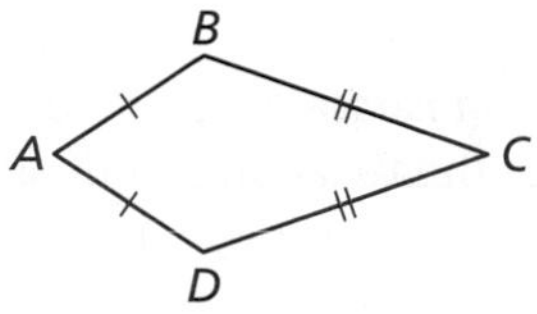

Kite *ABCD*

Koch snowflake A fractal formed from a triangle by replacing the middle third of each segment with two segments that form a 60° angle.

copo de nieve de Koch Fractal formado a partir de un triángulo sustituyendo el tercio central de cada segmento por dos segmentos que forman un ángulo de 60°.

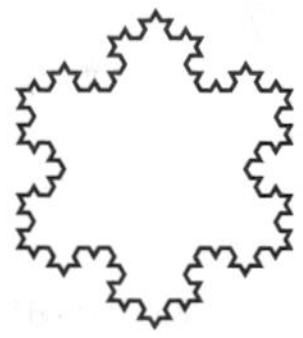

L

lateral area The sum of the areas of the lateral faces of a prism or pyramid, or the area of the lateral surface of a cylinder or cone.

área lateral Suma de las áreas de las caras laterales de un prisma o pirámide, o área de la superficie lateral de un cilindro o cono.

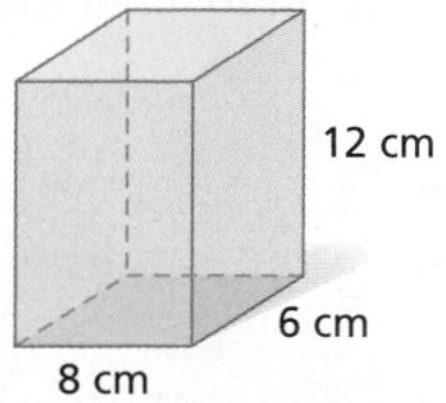

Lateral area $= 4(6)(12) = 288 \text{ cm}^2$

lateral edge An edge of a prism or pyramid that is not an edge of a base.

arista lateral Arista de un prisma o pirámide que no es la arista de una base.

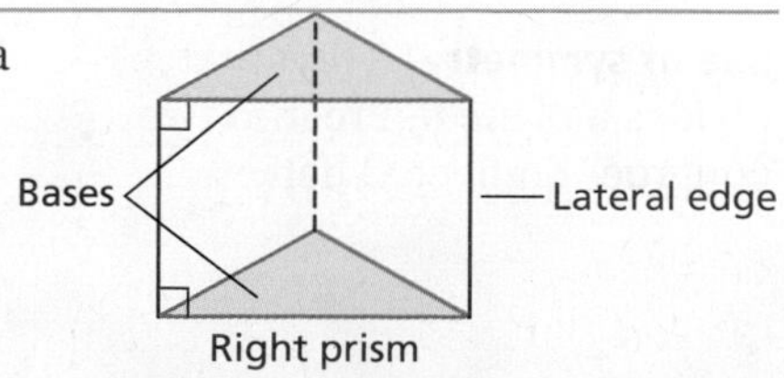

ENGLISH	SPANISH	EXAMPLES
lateral face A face of a prism or a pyramid that is not a base.	**cara lateral** Cara de un prisma o pirámide que no es la base.	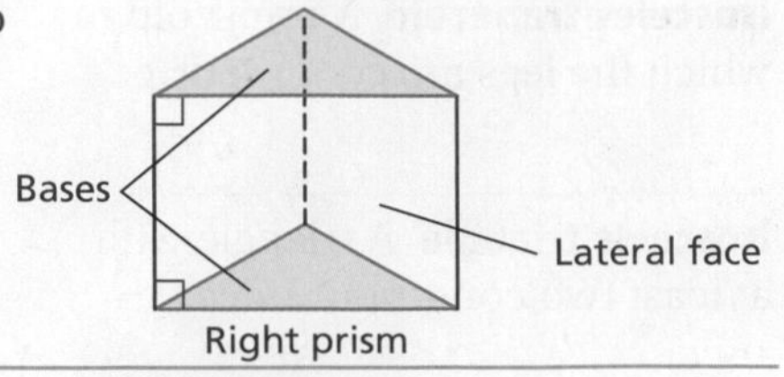
lateral surface The curved surface of a cylinder or cone.	**superficie lateral** Superficie curva de un cilindro o cono.	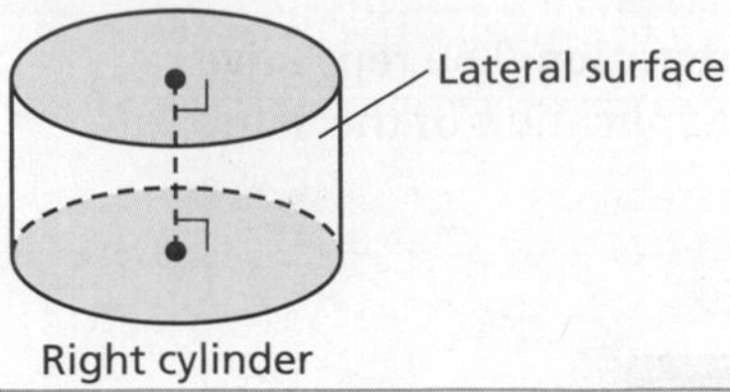
leg of a right triangle One of the two sides of the right triangle that form the right angle.	**cateto de un triángulo rectángulo** Uno de los dos lados de un triángulo rectángulo que forman el ángulo recto.	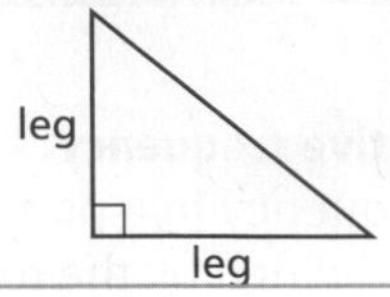
leg of a trapezoid One of the two nonparallel sides of the trapezoid.	**cateto de un trapecio** Uno de los dos lados no paralelos del trapecio.	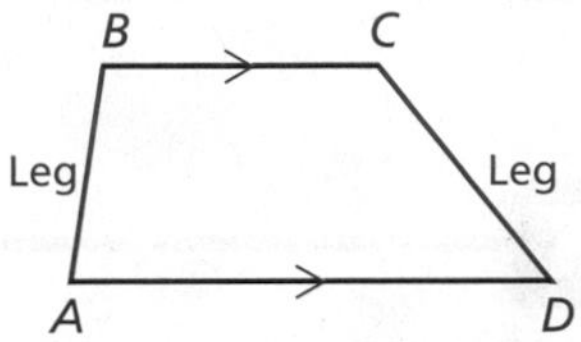
leg of an isosceles triangle One of the two congruent sides of the isosceles triangle.	**cateto de un triángulo isósceles** Uno de los dos lados congruentes del triángulo isósceles.	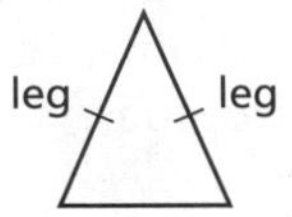
length The distance between the two endpoints of a segment.	**longitud** Distancia entre los dos extremos de un segmento.	 $AB = \|a - b\| = \|b - a\|$
line An undefined term in geometry, a line is a straight path that has no thickness and extends forever.	**línea** Término indefinido en geometría; una línea es un trazo recto que no tiene grosor y se extiende infinitamente.	
line of best fit The line that comes closest to all of the points in a data set.	**línea de mejor ajuste** Línea que más se acerca a todos los puntos de un conjunto de datos.	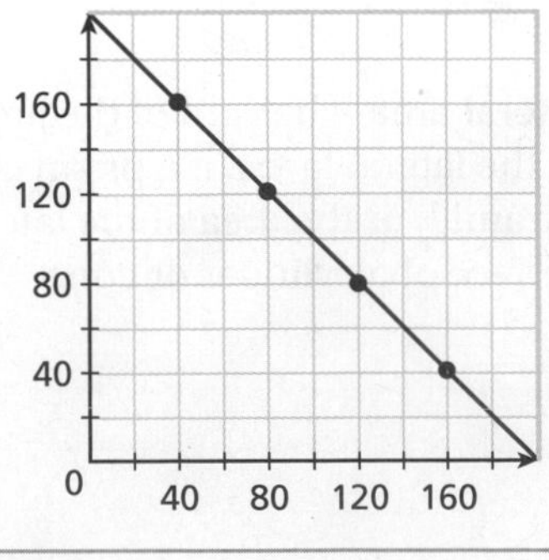
line of symmetry A line that divides a plane figure into two congruent reflected halves.	**eje de simetría** Línea que divide una figura plana en dos mitades reflejas congruentes.	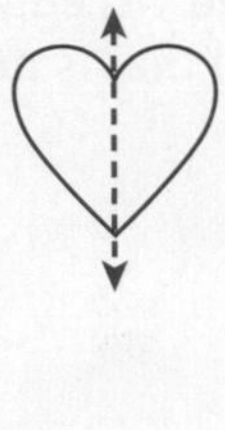

ENGLISH	SPANISH	EXAMPLES

line symmetry A figure that can be reflected across a line so that the image coincides with the preimage.

simetría axial Figura que puede reflejarse sobre una línea de forma tal que la imagen coincida con la imagen original.

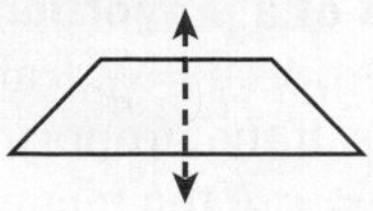

---

linear pair A pair of adjacent angles whose noncommon sides are opposite rays.

par lineal Par de ángulos adyacentes cuyos lados no comunes son rayos opuestos.

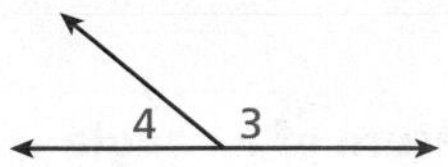

$\angle 3$ and $\angle 4$ form a linear pair.

---

literal equation An equation that contains two or more variables.

ecuación literal Ecuación que contiene dos o más variables.

$d = rt$ $\quad A = \frac{1}{2}h(b_1 + b_2)$

---

locus A set of points that satisfies a given condition.

lugar geométrico Conjunto de puntos que cumple con una condición determinada.

---

logically equivalent statements Statements that have the same truth value.

enunciados lógicamente equivalentes Enunciados que tienen el mismo valor de verdad.

M

magnitude The length of a vector, written $|\overrightarrow{AB}|$ or $|\vec{v}|$.

magnitud Longitud de un vector, que se expresa $|\overrightarrow{AB}|$ o $|\vec{v}|$.

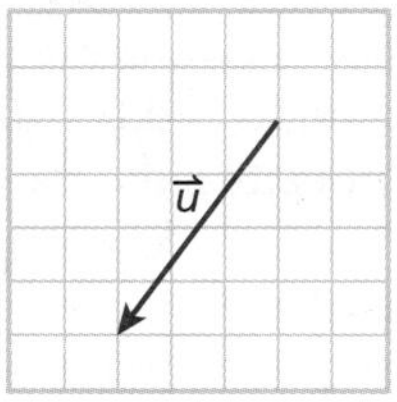

$|\vec{u}| = 5$

---

major arc An arc of a circle whose points are on or in the exterior of a central angle.

arco mayor Arco de un círculo cuyos puntos están sobre un ángulo central o en su exterior.

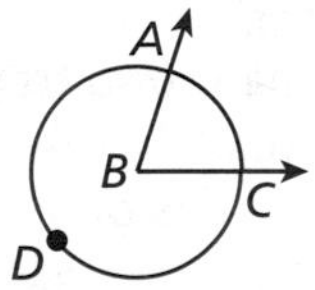

$\overset{\frown}{ADC}$ is a major arc of the circle.

---

mapping An operation that matches each element of a set with another element, its image, in the same set.

correspondencia Operación que establece una correlación entre cada elemento de un conjunto con otro elemento, su imagen, en el mismo conjunto.

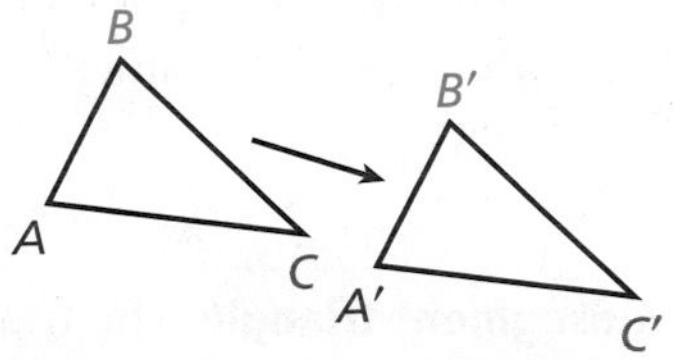

---

marginal relative frequency The sum of the joint relative frequencies in a row or column of a two-way table.

frecuencia relativa marginal La suma de las frecuencias relativas conjuntas en una fila o columna de una tabla de doble entrada.

---

matrix A rectangular array of numbers.

matriz Arreglo rectangular de números.

$$\begin{bmatrix} 1 & 0 & 3 \\ -2 & 2 & -5 \\ 7 & -6 & 3 \end{bmatrix}$$

ENGLISH	SPANISH	EXAMPLES

means of a proportion In the proportion $\frac{a}{b} = \frac{c}{d}$, b and c are the means. If the proportion is written as $a:b = c:d$, the means are in the two middle positions.

valores medios de una proporción En la proporción $\frac{a}{b} = \frac{c}{d}$, b y c son los valores medios. Si la proporción se expresa como $a:b = c:d$, los valores medios están en las dos posiciones del medio.

measure of an angle Angles are measured in degrees. A degree is $\frac{1}{360}$ of a complete circle.

medida de un ángulo Los ángulos se miden en grados. Un grado es $\frac{1}{360}$ de un círculo completo.

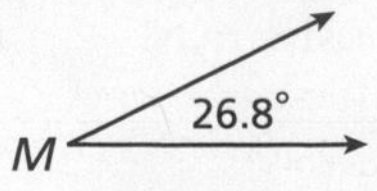

$m\angle M = 26.8°$

measure of a major arc The difference of 360° and the measure of the associated minor arc.

medida de un arco mayor Diferencia entre 360° y la medida del arco menor asociado.

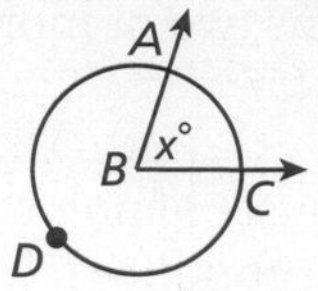

$m\widehat{ADC} = 360° - x°$

measure of a minor arc The measure of its central angle.

medida de un arco menor Medida de su ángulo central.

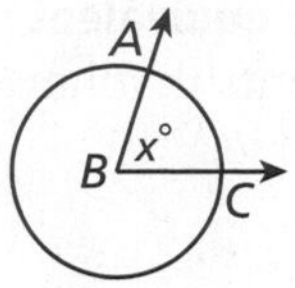

$m\widehat{AC} = x°$

median of a triangle A segment whose endpoints are a vertex of the triangle and the midpoint of the opposite side.

mediana de un triángulo Segmento cuyos extremos son un vértice del triángulo y el punto medio del lado opuesto.

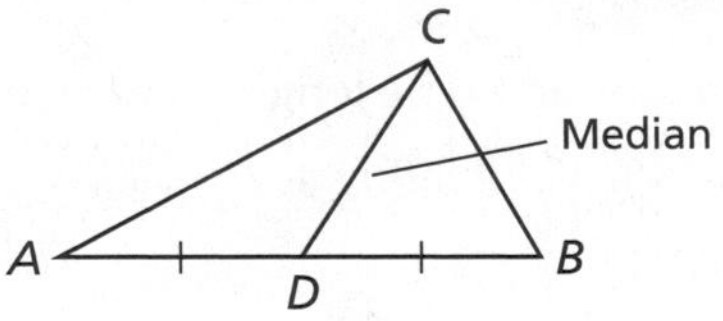

midpoint The point that divides a segment into two congruent segments.

punto medio Punto que divide un segmento en dos segmentos congruentes.

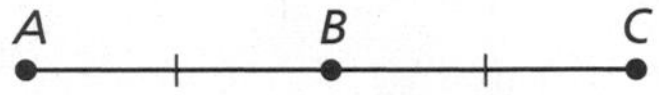

B is the midpoint of $\overline{AC}$.

midsegment of a trapezoid The segment whose endpoints are the midpoints of the legs of the trapezoid.

segmento medio de un trapecio Segmento cuyos extremos son los puntos medios de los catetos del trapecio.

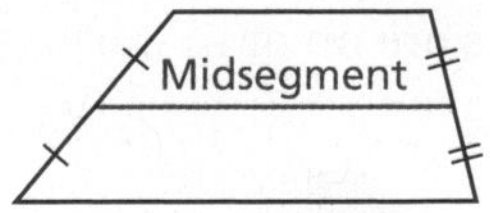

midsegment of a triangle A segment that joins the midpoints of two sides of the triangle.

segmento medio de un triángulo Segmento que une los puntos medios de dos lados del triángulo.

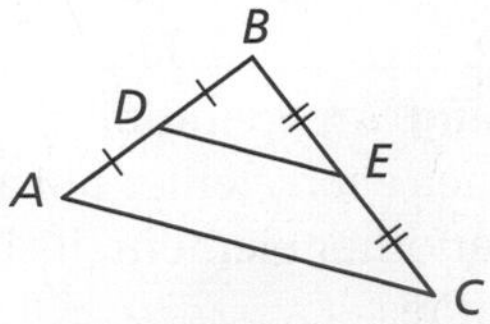

midsegment triangle The triangle formed by the three midsegments of a triangle.

triángulo de segmentos medios Triángulo formado por los tres segmentos medios de un triángulo.

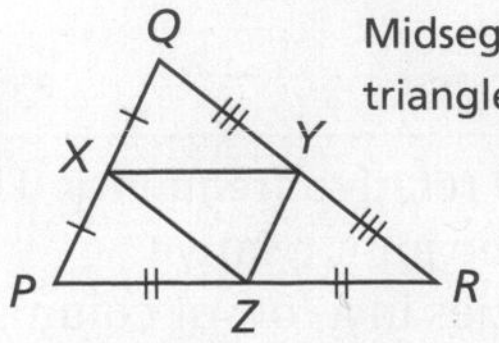

Midsegment triangle: $\triangle XYZ$

minor arc An arc of a circle whose points are on or in the interior of a central angle.

arco menor Arco de un círculo cuyos puntos están sobre un ángulo central o en su interior.

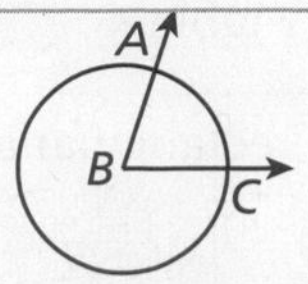

$\widehat{AC}$ is a minor arc of the circle.

ENGLISH	SPANISH	EXAMPLES
mutually exclusive events Two events are mutually exclusive if they cannot both occur in the same trial of an experiment.	**sucesos mutuamente excluyentes** Dos sucesos son mutuamente excluyentes si ambos no pueden ocurrir en la misma prueba de un experimento.	In the experiment of rolling a number cube, rolling a 3 and rolling an even number are mutually exclusive events.

N

ENGLISH	SPANISH	EXAMPLES
natural number A counting number.	**número natural** Número que sirve para contar.	1, 2, 3, 4, 5, 6, ...
negation The negation of statement p is "not p," written as $\sim p$.	**negación** La negación de un enunciado p es "no p", que se escribe p.	
negation of a vector The vector obtained by negating each component of a given vector.	**negación de un vector** Vector que se obtiene por la negación de cada componente de un vector dado.	The negation of $\langle 3, -2\rangle$ is $\langle -3, 2\rangle$.
net A diagram of the faces of a three-dimensional figure arranged in such a way that the diagram can be folded to form the three-dimensional figure.	**plantilla** Diagrama de las caras de una figura tridimensional que se puede plegar para formar la figura tridimensional.	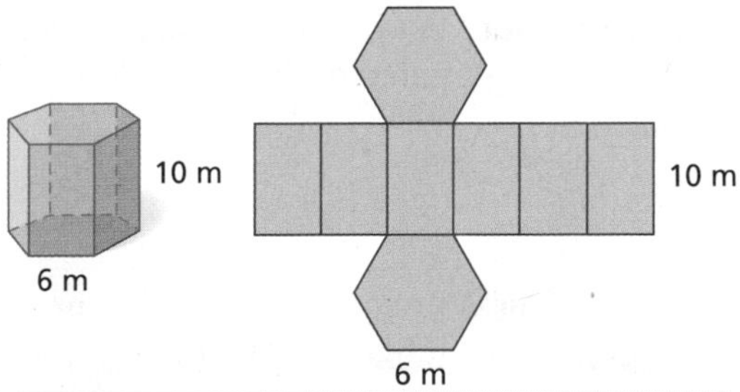
network A diagram of vertices and edges.	**red** Diagrama de vértices y aristas.	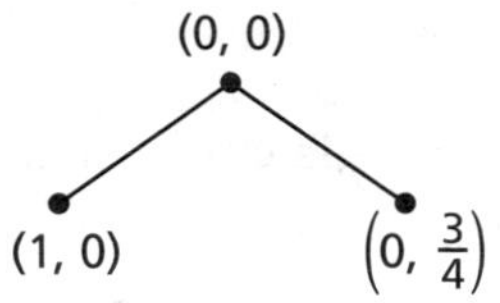
***n*-gon** An n-sided polygon.	***n*-ágono** Polígono de n lados.	
nonagon A nine-sided polygon.	**nonágono** Polígono de nueve lados.	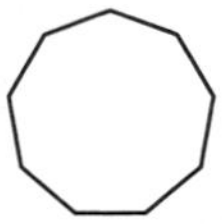
noncollinear Points that do not lie on the same line.	**no colineal** Puntos que no se encuentran sobre la misma línea.	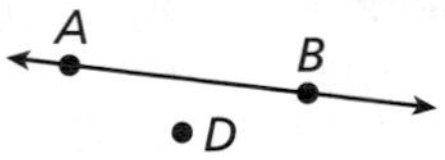 Points A, B, and D are not collinear.
non-Euclidean geometry A system of geometry in which the Parallel Postulate, which states that there is exactly one line through a given point parallel to a given line, does not hold.	**geometría no euclidiana** Sistema de geometría en el cual no se cumple el postulado de las paralelas, que establece que por un punto dado se puede trazar una única línea paralela a una línea dada.	In spherical geometry, there are no parallel lines. The sum of the angles in a triangle is always greater than 180°.

Glossary/Glosario

ENGLISH | **SPANISH** | **EXAMPLES**

noncoplanar Points that do not lie on the same plane.

no coplanar Puntos que no se encuentran en el mismo plano.

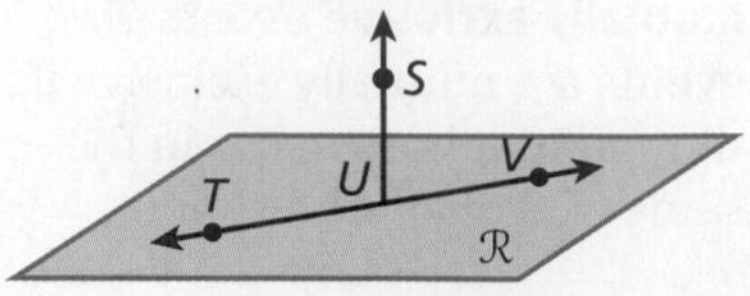

T, U, V, and *S* are not coplanar.

---

numerator The top number of a fraction, which tells how many parts of a whole are being considered.

numerador El número superior de una fracción, que indica la cantidad de partes de un entero que se consideran.

The numerator of $\frac{3}{7}$ is 3.

O

oblique cone A cone whose axis is not perpendicular to the base.

cono oblicuo Cono cuyo eje no es perpendicular a la base.

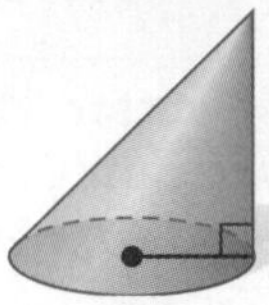

---

oblique cylinder A cylinder whose axis is not perpendicular to the bases.

cilindro oblicuo Cilindro cuyo eje no es perpendicular a las bases.

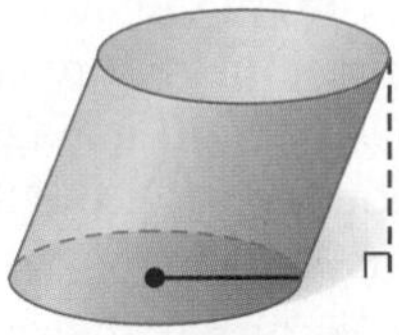

---

oblique prism A prism that has at least one nonrectangular lateral face.

prisma oblicuo Prisma que tiene por lo menos una cara lateral no rectangular.

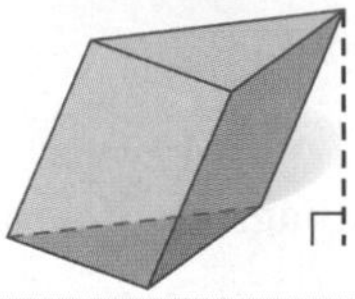

---

obtuse angle An angle that measures greater than 90° and less than 180°.

ángulo obtuso Ángulo que mide más de 90° y menos de 180°.

---

obtuse triangle A triangle with one obtuse angle.

triángulo obtusángulo Triángulo con un ángulo obtuso.

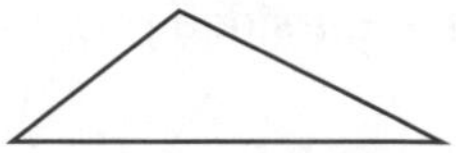

---

octagon An eight-sided polygon.

octágono Polígono de ocho lados.

---

octahedron A polyhedron with eight faces.

octaedro Poliedro con ocho caras.

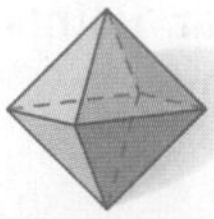

---

one-point perspective A perspective drawing with one vanishing point.

perspectiva de un punto Dibujo en perspectiva con un punto de fuga.

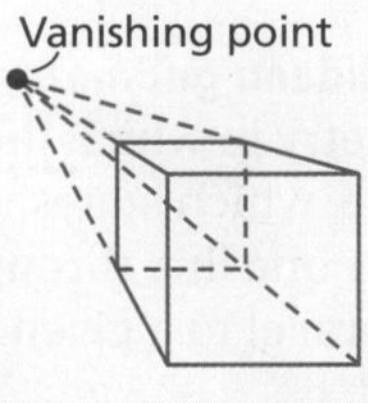

---

opposite rays Two rays that have a common endpoint and form a line.

rayos opuestos Dos rayos que tienen un extremo común y forman una línea.

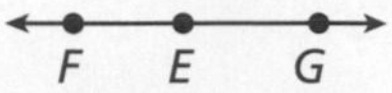

$\overrightarrow{EF}$ and $\overrightarrow{EG}$ are opposite rays.

ENGLISH	SPANISH	EXAMPLES
opposite reciprocal The opposite of the reciprocal of a number. The opposite reciprocal of a is $-\frac{1}{a}$.	**recíproco opuesto** Opuesto del recíproco de un número. El recíproco opuesto de a es $-\frac{1}{a}$.	The opposite reciprocal of $\frac{2}{3}$ is $\frac{-3}{2}$
order of rotational symmetry The number of times a figure with rotational symmetry coincides with itself as it rotates 360°.	**orden de simetría de rotación** Cantidad de veces que una figura con simetría de rotación coincide consigo misma cuando rota 360°.	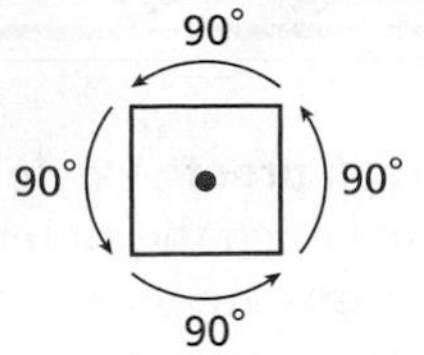 Order of rotational symmetry: 4
ordered pair A pair of numbers (x, y) that can be used to locate a point on a coordinate plane. The first number x indicates the distance to the left or right of the origin, and the second number y indicates the distance above or below the origin.	**par ordenado** Par de números (x, y) que se pueden utilizar para ubicar un punto en un plano cartesiano. El primer número indica la distancia a la izquierda o derecha del origen y el segundo número indica la distancia hacia arriba o hacia abajo del origen.	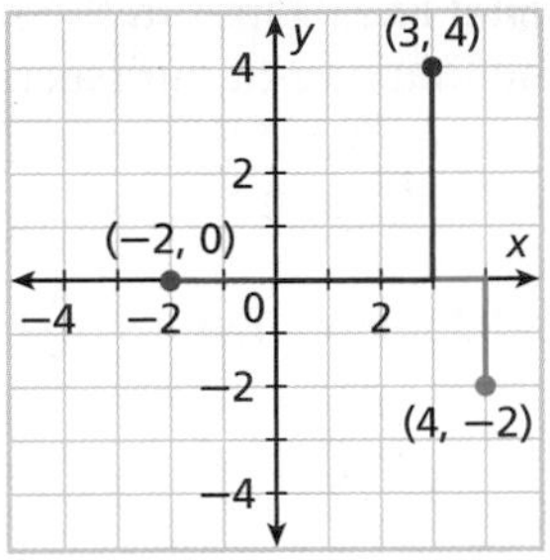
ordered triple A set of three numbers that can be used to locate a point (x, y, z) in a three-dimensional coordinate system.	**tripleta ordenada** Conjunto de tres números que se pueden utilizar para ubicar un punto (x, y, z) en un sistema de coordenadas tridimensional.	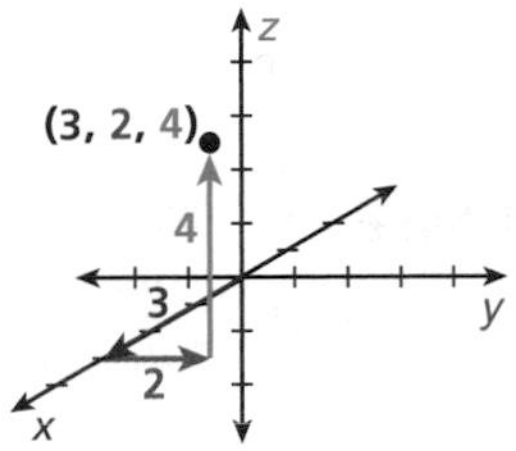
origin The intersection of the x- and y-axes in a coordinate plane. The coordinates of the origin are $(0, 0)$.	**origen** Intersección de los ejes x e y en un plano cartesiano. Las coordenadas de origen son $(0, 0)$.	
orthocenter of a triangle The point of concurrency of the three altitudes of a triangle.	**ortocentro de un triángulo** Punto de intersección de las tres alturas de un triángulo.	P is the orthocenter. 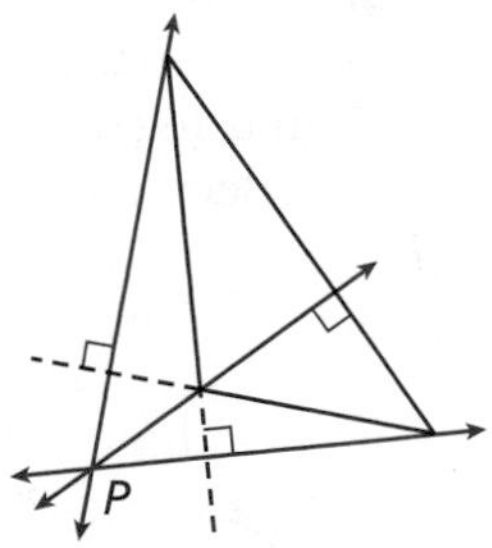
orthographic drawing A drawing that shows a three-dimensional object in which the line of sight for each view is perpendicular to the plane of the picture.	**dibujo ortográfico** Dibujo que muestra un objeto tridimensional en el que la línea visual para cada vista es perpendicular al plano de la imagen.	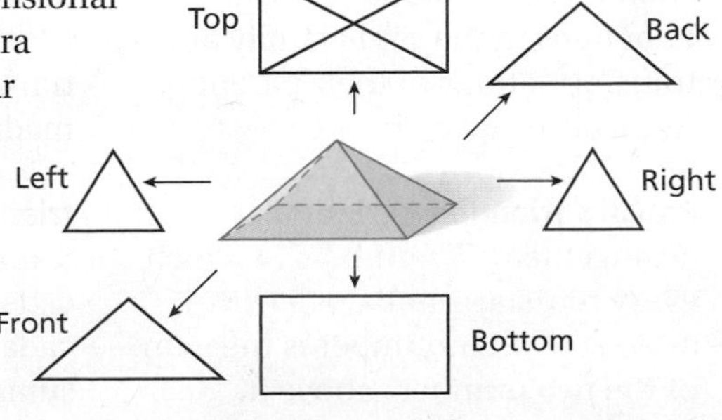

ENGLISH	SPANISH	EXAMPLES
outcome A possible result of a probability experiment.	**resultado** Resultado posible de un experimento de probabilidad.	In the experiment of rolling a number cube, the possible outcomes are 1, 2, 3, 4, 5, and 6.

P

paragraph proof A style of proof in which the statements and reasons are presented in paragraph form.

demostración con párrafos Tipo de demostración en la cual los enunciados y las razones se presentan en forma de párrafo.

parallel lines Lines in the same plane that do not intersect.

líneas paralelas Líneas rectas en el mismo plano que no se cruzan.

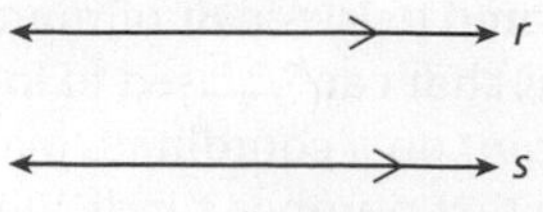

$r \parallel s$

parallel planes Planes that do not intersect.

planos paralelos Planos que no se cruzan.

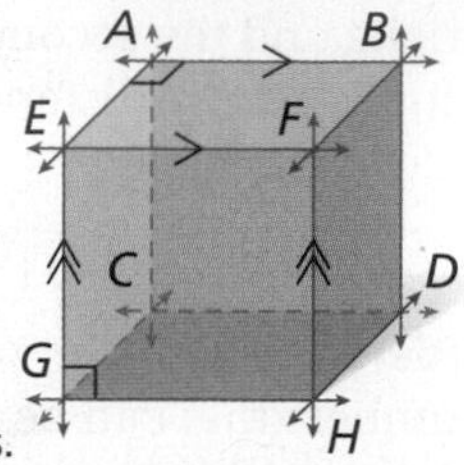

Plane *AEF* and plane *CGH* are parallel planes.

parallel vectors Vectors with the same or opposite direction.

vectores paralelos Vectores con dirección igual u opuesta.

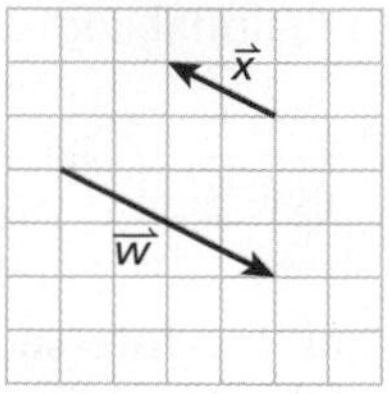

$|\vec{w}| = 2\sqrt{5}$
$|\vec{x}| = \sqrt{5}$

parallelogram A quadrilateral with two pairs of parallel sides.

paralelogramo Cuadrilátero con dos pares de lados paralelos.

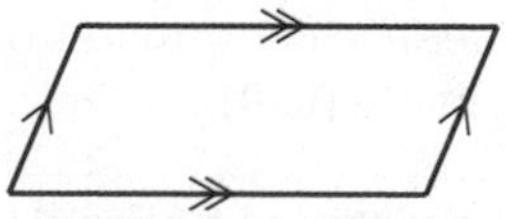

parallelogram method A method of adding two vectors by drawing a parallelogram using the vectors as two of the consecutive sides; the sum is a vector along the diagonal of the parallelogram.

método del paralelogramo Método mediante el cual se suman dos vectores dibujando un paralelogramo, utilizando los vectores como dos de los lados consecutivos; el resultado de la suma es un vector a lo largo de la diagonal del paralelogramo.

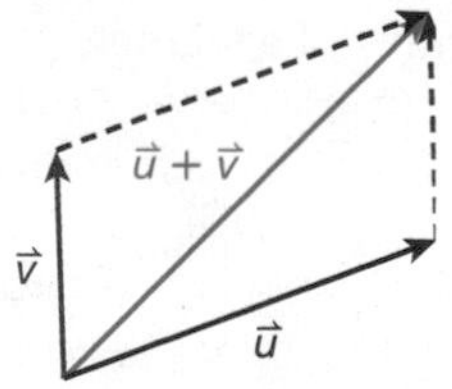

parent function The simplest function with the defining characteristics of the family. Functions in the same family are transformations of their parent function.

función madre La función más básica que tiene las características distintivas de una familia. Las funciones de la misma familia son transformaciones de su función madre.

$f(x) = x^2$ is the parent function for $g(x) = x^2 + 4$ and $h(x) = 5(x + 2)^2 - 3$.

Pascal's triangle A triangular arrangement of numbers in which every row starts and ends with 1 and each other number is the sum of the two numbers above it.

triángulo de Pascal Arreglo triangular de números en el cual cada fila comienza y termina con 1 y cada uno de los otros números es la suma de los dos números que están encima de él.

1
1 1
1 2 1
1 3 3 1
1 4 6 4 1

ENGLISH	SPANISH	EXAMPLES
pentagon A five-sided polygon.	**pentágono** Polígono de cinco lados.	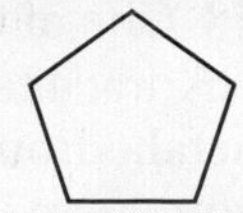
perimeter The sum of the side lengths of a closed plane figure.	**perímetro** Suma de las longitudes de los lados de una figura plana cerrada.	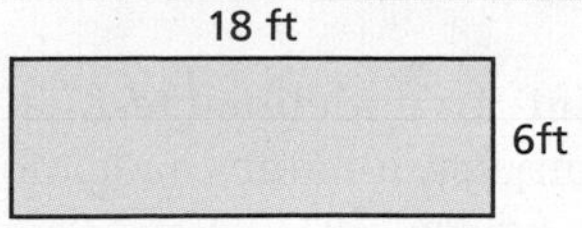 Perimeter = 18 + 6 + 18 + 6 = 48 ft
permutation An arrangement of a group of objects in which order is important. The number of permutations of *r* objects from a group of *n* objects is denoted ${}_nP_r$.	**permutación** Arreglo de un grupo de objetos en el cual el orden es importante. El número de permutaciones de *r* objetos de un grupo de *n* objetos se expresa ${}_nP_r$.	For 4 objects *A, B, C,* and *D,* there are ${}_4P_2 = 12$ different permutations of 2 objects: *AB, AC, AD, BC, BD, CD, BA, CA, DA, CB, DB,* and *DC.*
perpendicular Intersecting to form 90° angles, denoted by $\perp$.	**perpendicular** Que se cruza para formar ángulos de 90°, expresado por $\perp$.	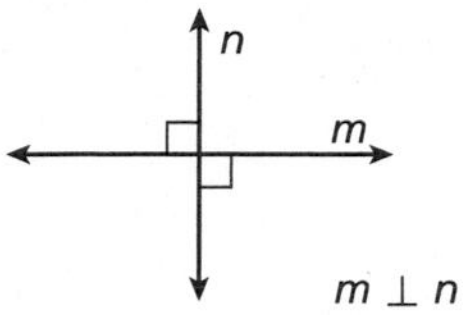 $m \perp n$
perpendicular bisector of a segment A line perpendicular to a segment at the segment's midpoint.	**mediatriz de un segmento** Línea perpendicular a un segmento en el punto medio del segmento.	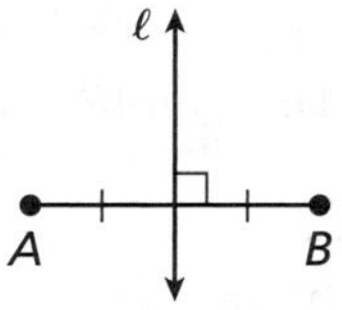 ℓ is the perpendicular bisector of $\overline{AB}$.
perpendicular lines Lines that intersect at 90° angles.	**líneas perpendiculares** Líneas que se cruzan en ángulos de 90°.	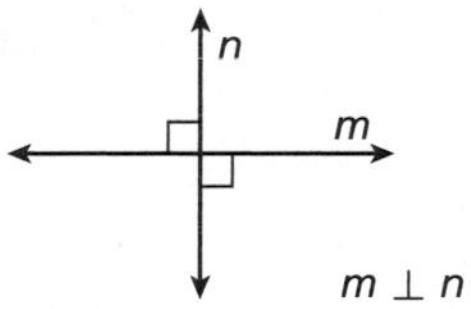 $m \perp n$
perspective drawing A drawing in which nonvertical parallel lines meet at a point called a *vanishing point.* Perspective drawings can have one or two vanishing points.	**dibujo en perspectiva** Dibujo en el cual las líneas paralelas no verticales se encuentran en un punto denominado *punto de fuga.* Los dibujos en perspectiva pueden tener uno o dos puntos de fuga.	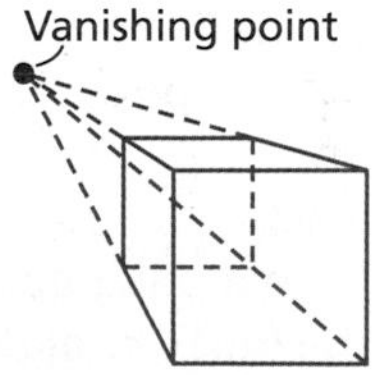
pi The ratio of the circumference of a circle to its diameter, denoted by the Greek letter π (pi). The value of π is irrational, often approximated by 3.14 or $\frac{22}{7}$.	**pi** Razón entre la circunferencia de un círculo y su diámetro, expresado por la letra griega π (pi). El valor de π es irracional y por lo general se aproxima a 3.14 ó $\frac{22}{7}$.	If a circle has a diameter of 5 inches and a circumference of *C* inches, then $\frac{C}{5} = \pi$, or $C = 5\pi$ inches, or about 15.7 inches.
plane An undefined term in geometry, it is a flat surface that has no thickness and extends forever.	**plano** Término indefinido en geometría; un plano es una superficie plana que no tiene grosor y se extiende infinitamente.	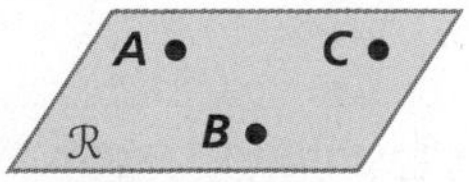 plane *R* or plane *ABC*
plane symmetry A three-dimensional figure that can be divided into two congruent reflected halves by a plane has plane symmetry.	**simetría de plano** Una figura tridimensional que se puede dividir en dos mitades congruentes reflejadas por un plano tiene simetría de plano.	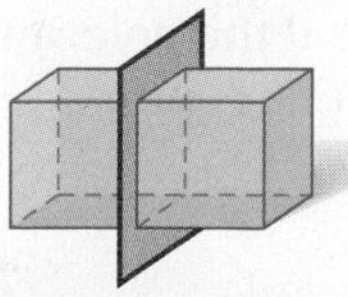 Plane symmetry

Glossary/Glosario

ENGLISH	SPANISH	EXAMPLES
Platonic solid One of the five regular polyhedra: a tetrahedron, a cube, an octahedron, a dodecahedron, or an icosahedron.	**sólido platónico** Uno de los cinco poliedros regulares: tetraedro, cubo, octaedro, dodecaedro o icosaedro.	
point An undefined term in geometry, it names a location and has no size.	**punto** Término indefinido de la geometría que denomina una ubicación y no tiene tamaño.	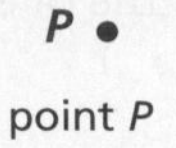
point matrix A matrix that represents the coordinates of the vertices of a polygon. The first row of the matrix consists of the x-coordinates of the points, and the second row consists of the y-coordinates.	**matriz de puntos** Matriz que representa las coordenadas de los vértices de un polígono. La primera fila de la matriz contiene las coordenadas x de los puntos y la segunda fila contiene las coordenadas y.	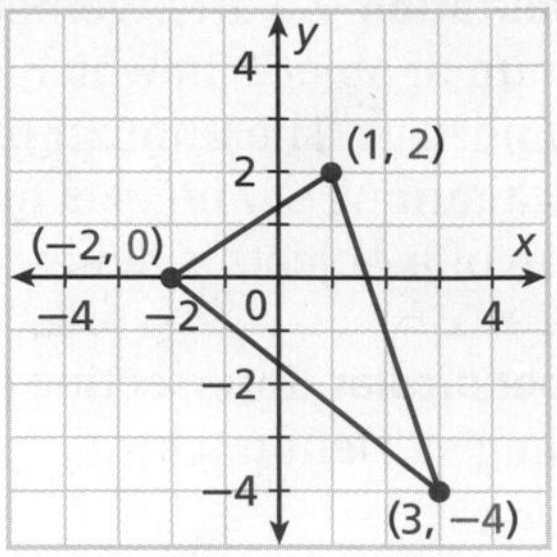 $\begin{bmatrix} 1 & -2 & 3 \\ 2 & 0 & -4 \end{bmatrix}$
point of concurrency A point where three or more lines coincide.	**punto de concurrencia** Punto donde se cruzan tres o más líneas.	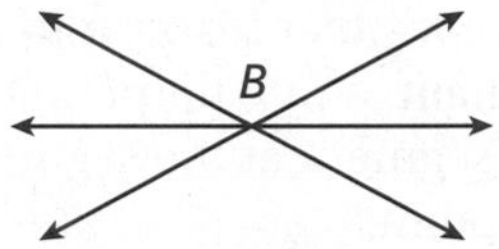
point of tangency The point of intersection of a circle or sphere with a tangent line or plane.	**punto de tangencia** Punto de intersección de un círculo o esfera con una línea o plano tangente.	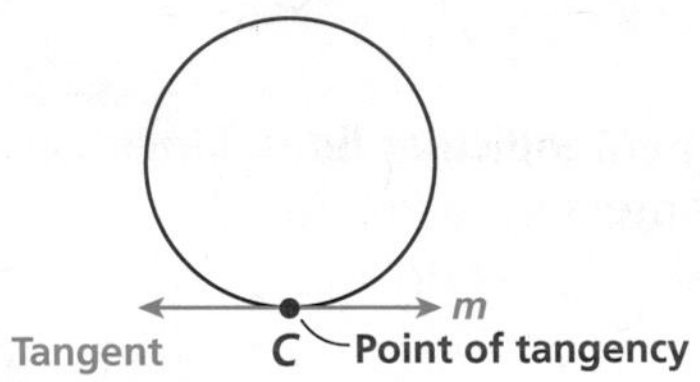
point-slope form $y - y_1 = m(x - x_1)$, where m is the slope and (x_1, y_1) is a point on the line.	**forma de punto y pendiente** $(y - y_1) = m(x - x_1)$, donde m es la pendiente y (x_1, y_1) es un punto en la línea.	
polar axis In a polar coordinate system, the horizontal ray with the pole as its endpoint that lies along the positive x-axis.	**eje polar** En un sistema de coordenadas polares, el rayo horizontal, cuyo extremo es el polo, que se encuentra a lo largo del eje x positivo.	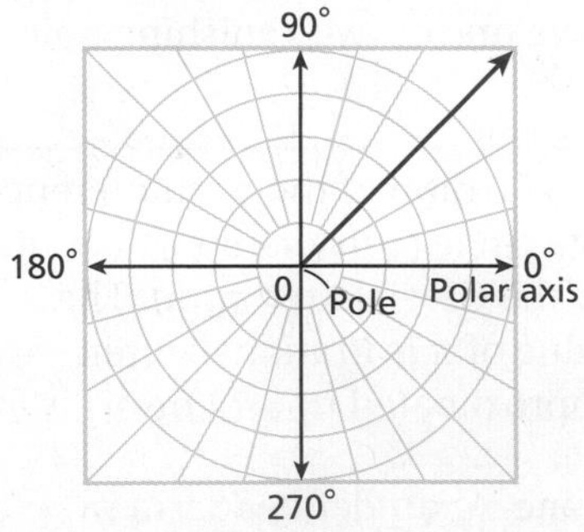
polar coordinate system A system in which a point in a plane is located by its distance r from a point called the pole, and by the measure of a central angle θ.	**sistema de coordenadas polares** Sistema en el cual un punto en un plano se ubica por su distancia r de un punto denominado polo y por la medida de un ángulo central θ.	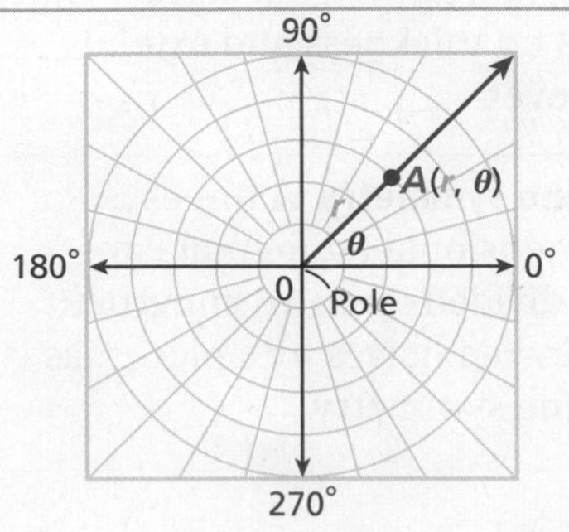

ENGLISH	SPANISH	EXAMPLES

pole The point from which distances are measured in a polar coordinate system.

polo Punto desde el que se miden las distancias en un sistema de coordenadas polares.

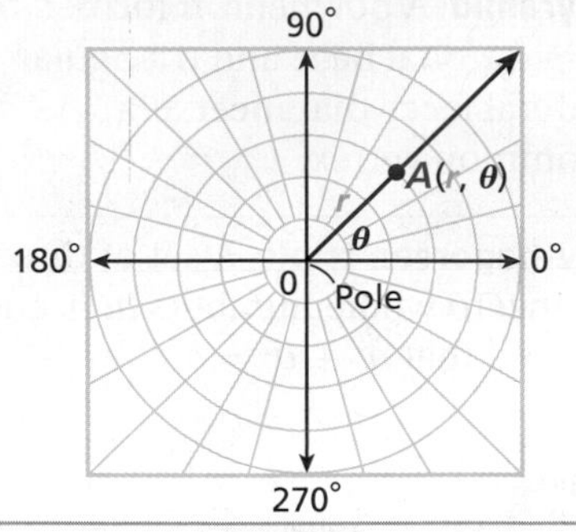

---

polygon A closed plane figure formed by three or more segments such that each segment intersects exactly two other segments only at their endpoints and no two segments with a common endpoint are collinear.

polígono Figura plana cerrada formada por tres o más segmentos tal que cada segmento se cruza únicamente con otros dos segmentos sólo en sus extremos y ningún segmento con un extremo común a otro es colineal con éste.

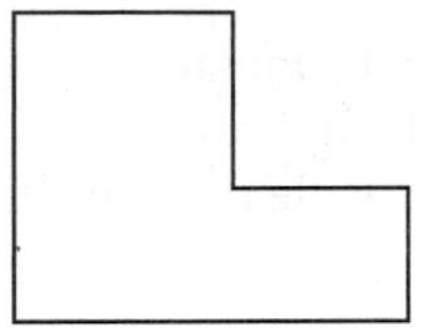

---

polyhedron A closed three-dimensional figure formed by four or more polygons that intersect only at their edges.

poliedro Figura tridimensional cerrada formada por cuatro o más polígonos que se cruzan sólo en sus aristas.

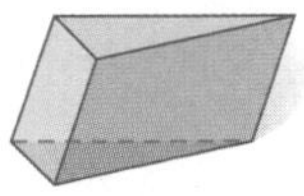

---

postulate A statement that is accepted as true without proof. Also called an *axiom*.

postulado Enunciado que se acepta como verdadero sin demostración. También denominado *axioma*.

---

preimage The original figure in a transformation.

imagen original Figura original en una transformación.

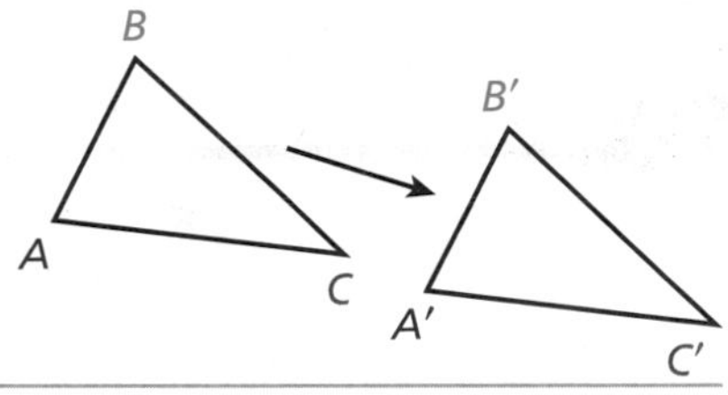

---

primes Symbols used to label the image in a transformation.

apóstrofos Símbolos utilizados para identificar la imagen en una transformación.

A′B′C′

---

prism A polyhedron formed by two parallel congruent polygonal bases connected by lateral faces that are parallelograms.

prisma Poliedro formado por dos bases poligonales congruentes y paralelas conectadas por caras laterales que son paralelogramos.

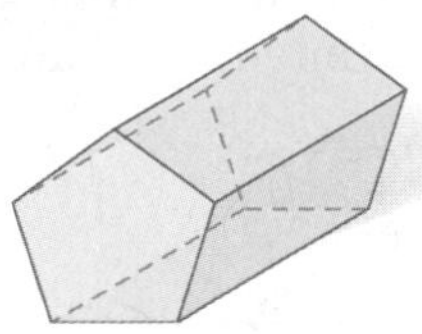

---

probability A number from 0 to 1 (or 0% to 100%) that is the measure of how likely an event is to occur.

probabilidad Número entre 0 y 1 (o entre 0% y 100%) que describe cuán probable es que ocurra un suceso.

A bag contains 3 red marbles and 4 blue marbles. The probability of randomly choosing a red marble is $\frac{3}{7}$.

---

proof An argument that uses logic to show that a conclusion is true.

demostración Argumento que se vale de la lógica para probar que una conclusión es verdadera.

---

proof by contradiction *See* indirect proof.

demostración por contradicción *Ver* demostración indirecta.

ENGLISH	SPANISH	EXAMPLES
pyramid A polyhedron formed by a polygonal base and triangular lateral faces that meet at a common vertex.	**pirámide** Poliedro formado por una base poligonal y caras laterales triangulares que se encuentran en un vértice común.	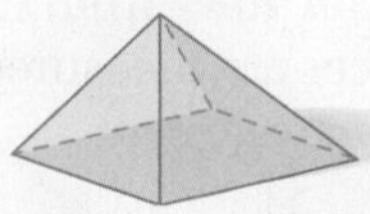
Pythagorean triple A set of three nonzero whole numbers a, b, and c such that $a^2 + b^2 = c^2$.	**Tripleta de Pitágoras** Conjunto de tres números cabales distintos de cero a, b y c tal que $a^2 + b^2 = c^2$.	$\{3, 4, 5\}$ $3^2 + 4^2 = 5^2$

Q

quadrant One of the four regions into which the x- and y-axes divide the coordinate plane.	**cuadrante** Una de las cuatro regiones en las que los ejes x e y dividen el plano cartesiano.	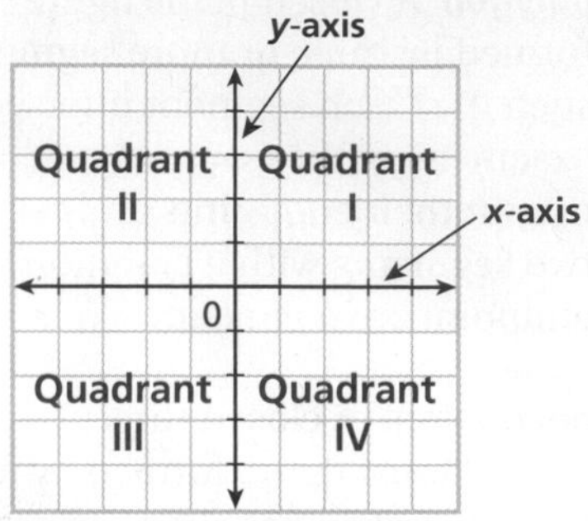
quadrilateral A four-sided polygon.	**cuadrilátero** Polígono de cuatro lados.	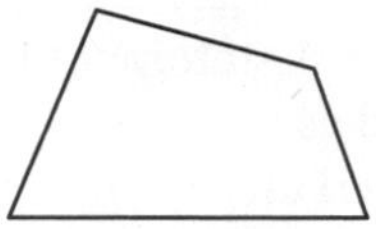

R

radial symmetry *See* rotational symmetry.	**simetría radial** *Ver* simetría de rotación.	
radian A unit of angle measure based on arc length. In a circle of radius r, if a central angle has a measure of 1 radian, then the length of the intercepted arc is r units. 2π radians = 360° 1 radian ≈ 57°	**radián** Unidad de medida de un ángulo basada en la longitud del arco. En un círculo de radio r, si un ángulo central mide 1 radián, entonces la longitud del arco abarcado es r unidades. 2π radians = 360° 1 radian ≈ 57°	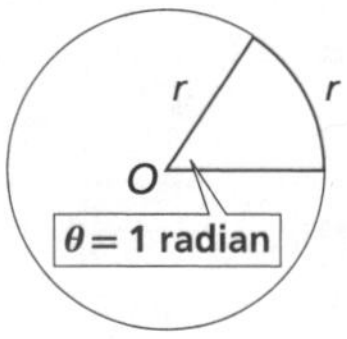
radical symbol The symbol $\sqrt{}$ used to denote a root. The symbol is used alone to indicate a square root or with an index, $\sqrt[n]{}$, to indicate the nth root.	**símbolo de radical** Símbolo $\sqrt{}$ que se utiliza para expresar una raíz. Puede utilizarse solo para indicar una raíz cuadrada, o con un índice, $\sqrt[n]{}$, para indicar la enésima raíz.	$\sqrt{36} = 6$ $\sqrt[3]{27} = 3$
radicand The expression under a radical sign.	**radicando** Número o expresión debajo del signo de radical.	Expression: $\sqrt{x + 3}$ Radicand: $x + 3$

ENGLISH	SPANISH	EXAMPLES
radius of a circle A segment whose endpoints are the center of a circle and a point on the circle; the distance from the center of a circle to any point on the circle.	**radio de un círculo** Segmento cuyos extremos son el centro y un punto de la circunferencia; distancia desde el centro de un círculo hasta cualquier punto de la circunferencia.	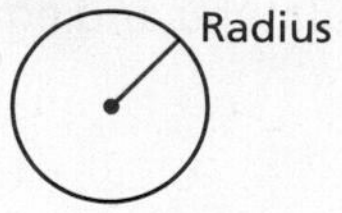
radius of a sphere A segment whose endpoints are the center of a sphere and any point on the sphere; the distance from the center of a sphere to any point on the sphere.	**radio de una esfera** Segmento cuyos extremos son el centro de una esfera y cualquier punto sobre la esfera; distancia desde el centro de una esfera hasta cualquier punto sobre la esfera.	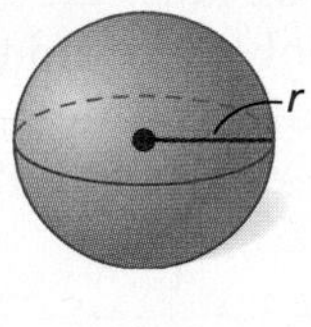
rate of change A ratio that compares the amount of change in a dependent variable to the amount of change in an independent variable.	**tasa de cambio** Razón que compara la cantidad de cambio de la variable dependiente con la cantidad de cambio de la variable independiente.	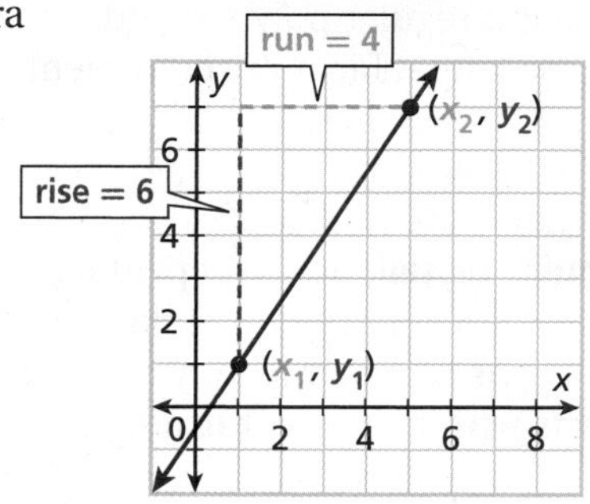 Rate of change $= \frac{\text{change in } y}{\text{change in } x} = \frac{6}{4} = \frac{3}{2}$
rational number A number that can be written in the form $\frac{a}{b}$, where a and b are integers and $b \neq 0$.	**número racional** Número que se puede expresar como $\frac{a}{b}$, donde a y b son números enteros y $b \neq 0$.	3, 1.75, $0.\overline{3}$, $-\frac{2}{3}$, 0
ray A part of a line that starts at an endpoint and extends forever in one direction.	**rayo** Parte de una línea que comienza en un extremo y se extiende infinitamente en una dirección.	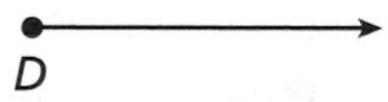
rectangle A quadrilateral with four right angles.	**rectángulo** Cuadrilátero con cuatro ángulos rectos.	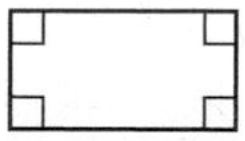
reduction A dilation with a scale factor greater than 0 but less than 1. In a reduction, the image is smaller than the preimage.	**reducción** Dilatación con un factor de escala mayor que 0 pero menor que 1. En una reducción, la imagen es más pequeña que la imagen original.	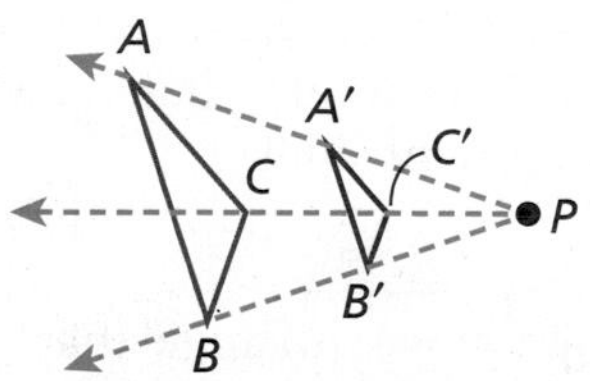
reflection A transformation across a line, called the line of reflection, such that the line of reflection is the perpendicular bisector of each segment joining each point and its image.	**reflexión** Transformación sobre una línea, denominada la línea de reflexión. La línea de reflexión es la mediatriz de cada segmento que une un punto con su imagen.	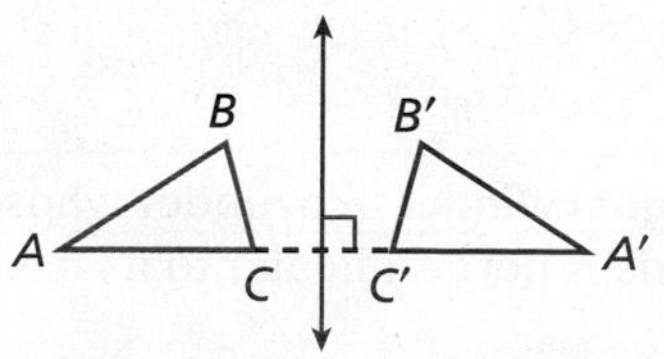
reflection symmetry *See* line symmetry.	**simetría de reflexión** *Ver* simetría axial.	

Glossary/Glosario

ENGLISH	SPANISH	EXAMPLES
regular polygon A polygon that is both equilateral and equiangular.	**polígono regular** Polígono equilátero de ángulos iguales.	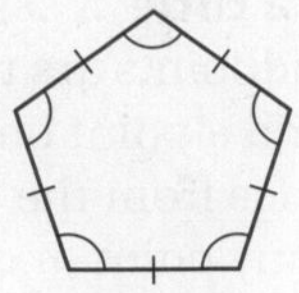
regular polyhedron A polyhedron in which all faces are congruent regular polygons and the same number of faces meet at each vertex. *See also* Platonic solid.	**poliedro regular** Poliedro cuyas caras son todas polígonos regulares congruentes y en el que el mismo número de caras se encuentran en cada vértice. *Ver también* sólido platónico.	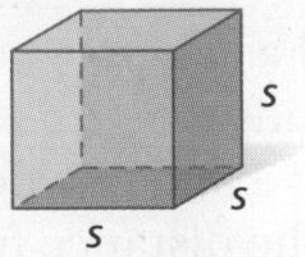
regular pyramid A pyramid whose base is a regular polygon and whose lateral faces are congruent isosceles triangles.	**pirámide regular** Pirámide cuya base es un polígono regular y cuyas caras laterales son triángulos isósceles congruentes.	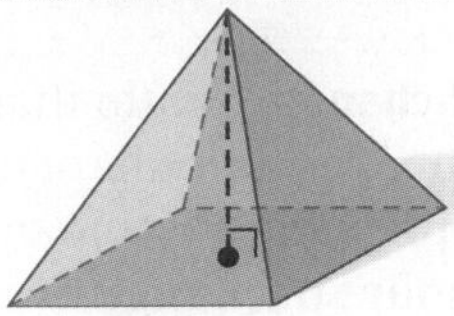
regular tessellation A repeating pattern of congruent regular polygons that completely covers a plane with no gaps or overlaps.	**teselado regular** Patrón que se repite formado por polígonos regulares congruentes que cubren completamente un plano sin dejar espacios y sin superponerse.	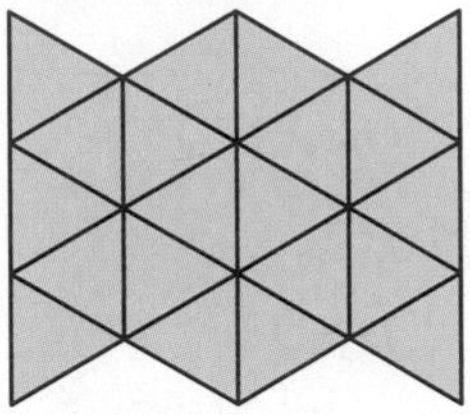
relation A set of ordered pairs.	**relación** Conjunto de pares ordenados.	{(0, 5), (0, 4), (2, 3), (4, 0)}
remote interior angle An interior angle of a polygon that is not adjacent to the exterior angle.	**ángulo interno remoto** Ángulo interno de un polígono que no es adyacente al ángulo externo.	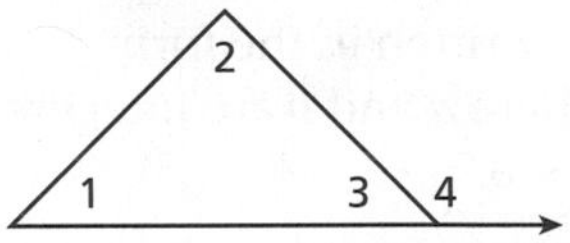 The remote interior angles of ∠4 are ∠1 and ∠2
resultant vector The vector that represents the sum of two given vectors.	**vector resultante** Vector que representa la suma de dos vectores dados.	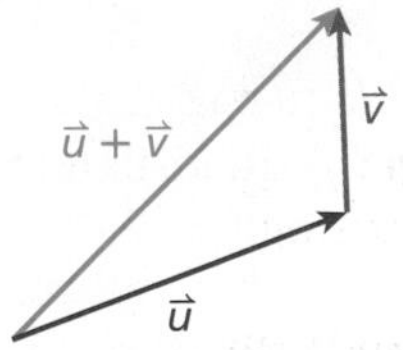
rhombus A quadrilateral with four congruent sides.	**rombo** Cuadrilátero con cuatro lados congruentes.	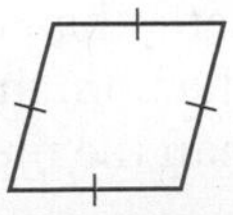
right angle An angle that measures 90°.	**ángulo recto** Ángulo que mide 90°.	
right cylinder A cylinder whose axis is perpendicular to its bases.	**cilindro recto** Cilindro cuyo eje es perpendicular a sus bases.	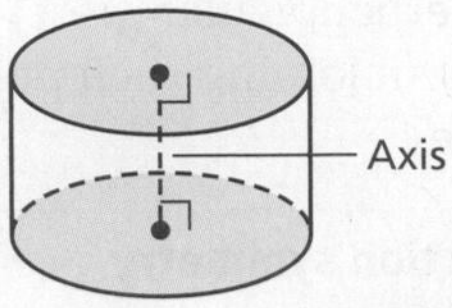

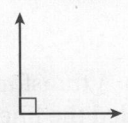

Glossary/Glosario

ENGLISH	SPANISH	EXAMPLES
right prism A prism whose lateral faces are all rectangles.	**prisma recto** Prisma cuyas caras laterales son todas rectángulos.	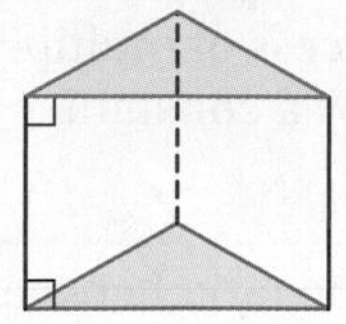
right triangle A triangle with one right angle.	**triángulo rectángulo** Triángulo con un ángulo recto.	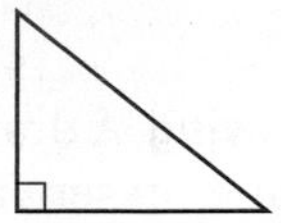
rigid motion *See* isometry.	**movimiento rígido** *Ver* isometría.	
rigid transformation A transformation that does not change the size or shape of a figure.	**transformación rígida** Transformación que no cambia el tamaño o la forma de una figura.	
rise The difference in the y-values of two points on a line.	**distancia vertical** Diferencia entre los valores de y de dos puntos de una línea.	For the points $(3, -1)$ and $(6, 5)$, the rise is $5 - (-1) = 6$.
rotation A transformation about a point P, also known as the center of rotation, such that each point and its image are the same distance from P. All of the angles with vertex P formed by a point and its image are congruent.	**rotación** Transformación sobre un punto P, también conocido como el centro de rotación, tal que cada punto y su imagen estén a la misma distancia de P. Todos los ángulos con vértice P formados por un punto y su imagen son congruentes.	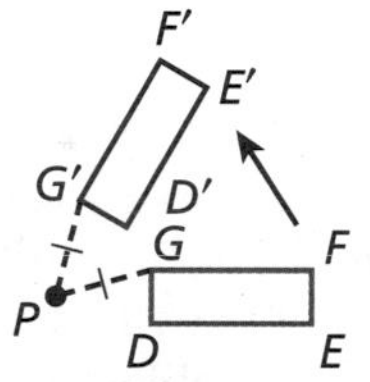
rotational symmetry A figure that can be rotated about a point by an angle less than 360° so that the image coincides with the preimage has rotational symmetry.	**simetría de rotación** Una figura que puede rotarse alrededor de un punto en un ángulo menor de 360° de forma tal que la imagen coincide con la imagen original tiene simetría de rotación.	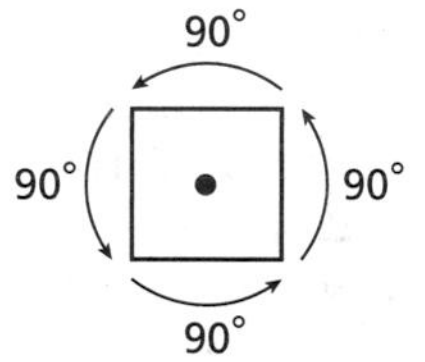 Order of rotational symmetry: 4
run The difference in the x-values of two points on a line.	**distancia horizontal** Diferencia entre los valores de x de dos puntos de una línea.	For the points $(3, -1)$ and $(6, 5)$, the run is $6 - 3 = 3$.

S

ENGLISH	SPANISH	EXAMPLES
same-side interior angles For two lines intersected by a transversal, a pair of angles that lie on the same side of the transversal and between the two lines.	**ángulos internos del mismo lado** Dadas dos líneas cortadas por una transversal, el par de ángulos ubicados en el mismo lado de la transversal y entre las dos líneas.	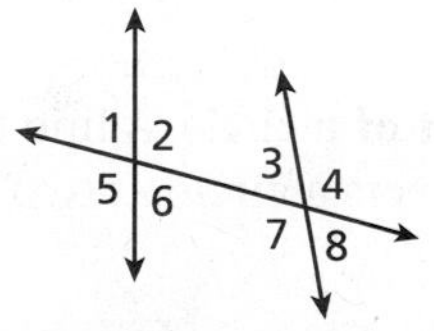 $\angle 2$ and $\angle 3$ are same-side interior angles.
sample space The set of all possible outcomes of a probability experiment.	**espacio muestral** Conjunto de todos los resultados posibles de un experimento de probabilidad.	in the experiment of rolling a number cube, the sample space is {1, 2, 3, 4, 5, 6}.

ENGLISH	SPANISH	EXAMPLES
scalar multiplication of a vector The process of multiplying a vector by a constant.	**multiplicación escalar de un vector** Proceso por el cual se multiplica un vector por una constante.	$3\langle -8, 1\rangle = \langle -24, 3\rangle$
scale The ratio between two corresponding measurements.	**escala** Razón entre dos medidas correspondientes.	1 cm : 5 mi
scale drawing A drawing that uses a scale to represent an object as smaller or larger than the actual object.	**dibujo a escala** Dibujo que utiliza una escala para representar un objeto como más pequeño o más grande que el objeto original.	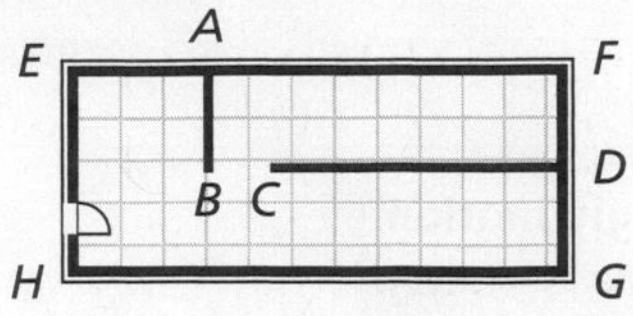 A blueprint is an example of a scale drawing.
scale factor The multiplier used on each dimension to change one figure into a similar figure.	**factor de escala** El multiplicador utilizado en cada dimensión para transformar una figura en una figura semejante.	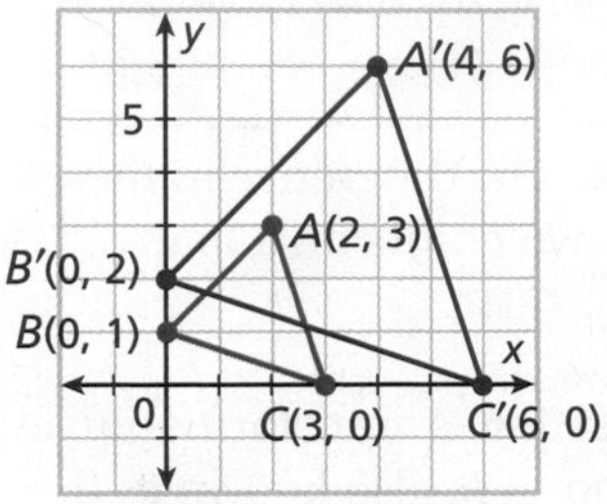 Scale factor: 2
scale model A three-dimensional model that uses a scale to represent an object as smaller or larger than the actual object.	**modelo a escala** Modelo tridimensional que utiliza una escala para representar un objeto como más pequeño o más grande que el objeto real.	
scalene triangle A triangle with no congruent sides.	**triángulo escaleno** Triángulo sin lados congruentes.	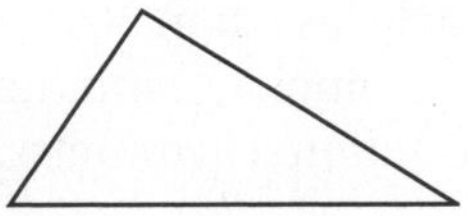
scatter plot A graph with points plotted to show a possible relationship between two sets of data.	**diagrama de dispersión** Gráfica con puntos que se usa para demostrar una relación posible entre dos conjuntos de datos.	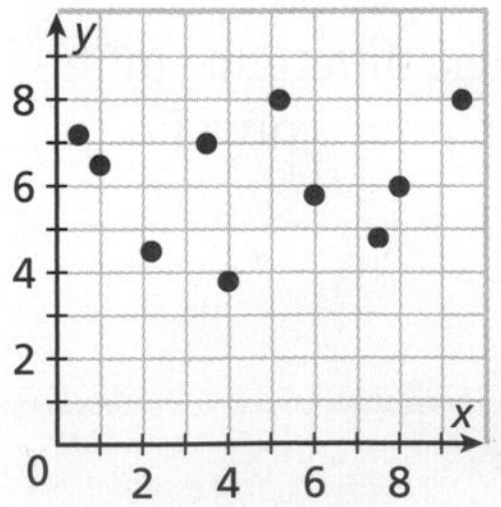
secant of a circle A line that intersects a circle at two points.	**secante de un círculo** Línea que corta un círculo en dos puntos.	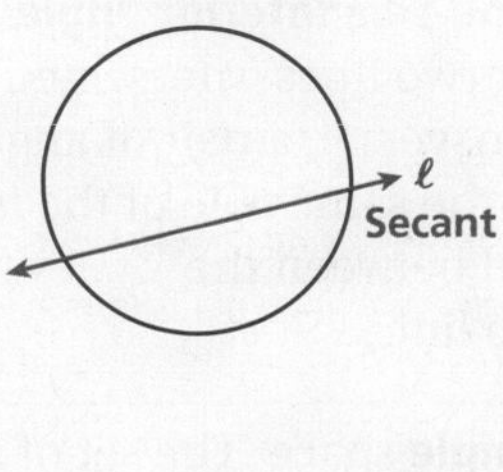

ENGLISH	SPANISH	EXAMPLES

secant of an angle In a right triangle, the ratio of the length of the hypotenuse to the length of the side adjacent to angle *A*. It is the reciprocal of the cosine function.

secante de un ángulo En un triángulo rectángulo, la razón entre la longitud de la hipotenusa y la longitud del cateto adyacente al ángulo *A*. Es la inversa de la función coseno.

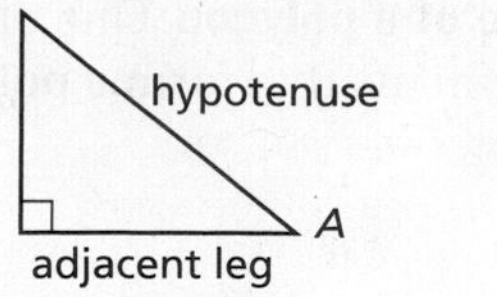

$$\sec A = \frac{\text{hypotenuse}}{\text{adjacent}} = \frac{1}{\cos A}$$

secant segment A segment of a secant with at least one endpoint on the circle.

segmento secante Segmento de una secante que tiene al menos un extremo sobre el círculo.

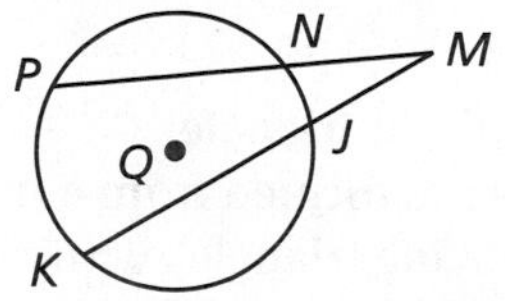

$\overline{NM}$ is an external secant segment.
$\overline{JK}$ is an internal secant segment.

sector of a circle A region inside a circle bounded by two radii of the circle and their intercepted arc.

sector de un círculo Región dentro de un círculo delimitado por dos radios del círculo y por su arco abarcado.

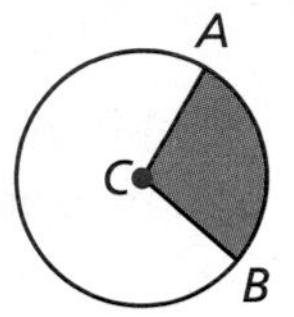

segment bisector A line, ray, or segment that divides a segment into two congruent segments.

bisectriz de un segmento Línea, rayo o segmento que divide un segmento en dos segmentos congruentes.

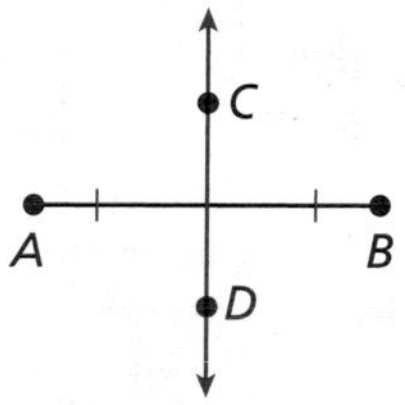

segment of a circle A region inside a circle bounded by a chord and an arc.

segmento de un círculo Región dentro de un círculo delimitada por una cuerda y un arco.

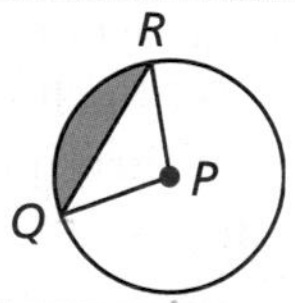

segment of a line A part of a line consisting of two endpoints and all points between them.

segmento de una línea Parte de una línea que consiste en dos extremos y todos los puntos entre éstos.

self-similar A figure that can be divided into parts, each of which is similar to the entire figure.

autosemejante Figura que se puede dividir en partes, cada una de las cuales es semejante a la figura entera.

semicircle An arc of a circle whose endpoints lie on a diameter.

semicírculo Arco de un círculo cuyos extremos se encuentran sobre un diámetro.

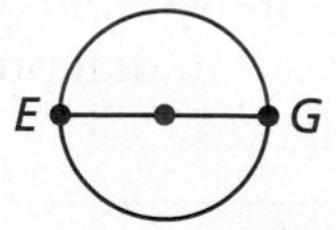

semiregular tessellation A repeating pattern formed by two or more regular polygons in which the same number of each polygon occur in the same order at every vertex and completely cover a plane with no gaps or overlaps.

teselado semirregular Patrón formado por dos o más polígonos regulares en el que el mismo número de cada polígono se presenta en el mismo orden en cada vértice y cubren un plano completamente sin dejar espacios vacíos ni superponerse.

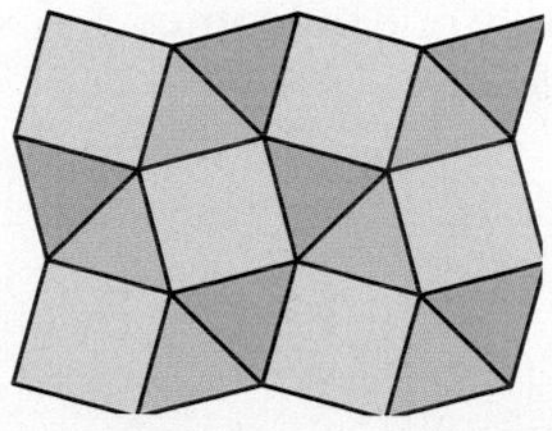

Glossary/Glosario

ENGLISH	SPANISH	EXAMPLES

side of a polygon One of the segments that form a polygon.

lado de un polígono Uno de los segmentos que forman un polígono.

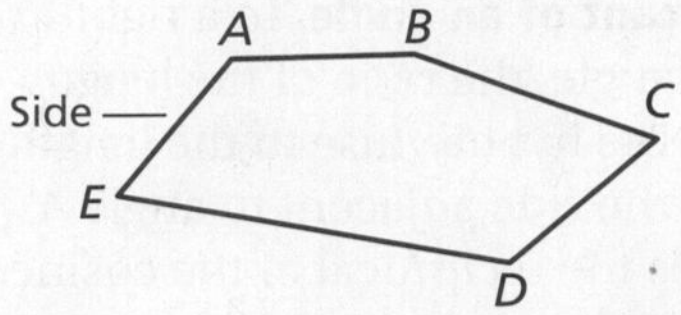

---

side of an angle One of the two rays that form an angle.

lado de un ángulo Uno de los dos rayos que forman un ángulo.

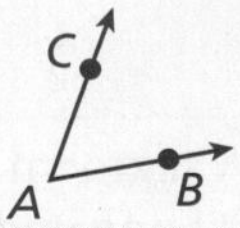

$\overrightarrow{AC}$ and $\overrightarrow{AB}$ are sides of $\angle CAB$.

Sierpinski triangle A fractal formed from a triangle by removing triangles with vertices at the midpoints of the sides of each remaining triangle.

triángulo de Sierpinski Fractal formado a partir de un triángulo al cual se le recortan triángulos cuyos vértices se encuentran en los puntos medios de los lados de cada triángulo restante.

---

similar Two figures are similar if they have the same shape but not necessarily the same size.

semejantes Dos figuras con la misma forma pero no necesariamente del mismo tamaño.

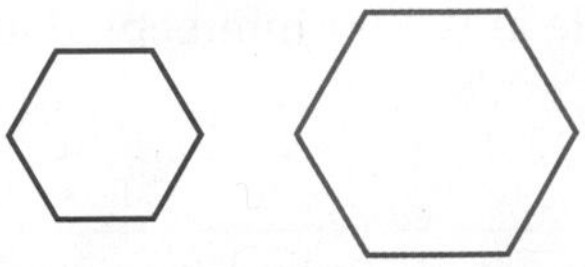

---

similar polygons Two polygons whose corresponding angles are congruent and whose corresponding side lengths are proportional.

polígonos semejantes Dos polígonos cuyos ángulos correspondientes son congruentes y cuyos lados correspondientes tienen longitudes proporcionales.

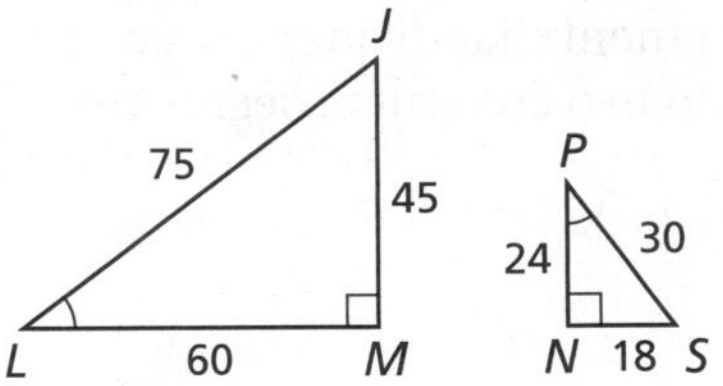

---

similarity ratio The ratio of two corresponding linear measurements in a pair of similar figures.

razón de semejanza Razón de dos medidas lineales correspondientes en un par de figuras semejantes.

Similarity ratio: $\frac{3.5}{2.1} = \frac{5}{3}$

---

similarity statement A statement that indicates that two polygons are similar by listing the vertices in the order of correspondence.

enunciado de semejanza Enunciado que indica que dos polígonos son semejantes enumerando los vértices en orden de correspondencia.

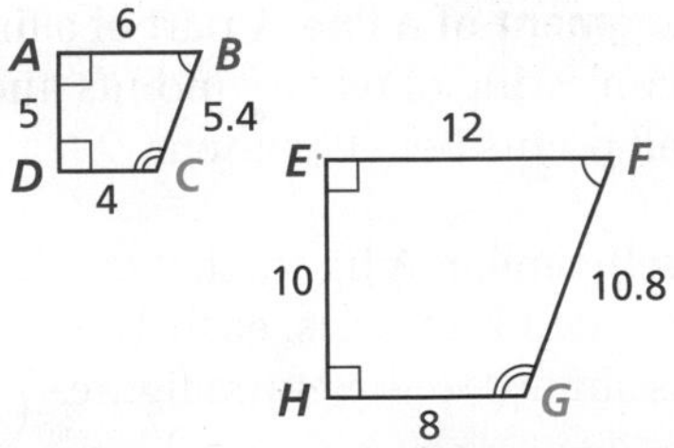

quadrilateral *ABCD* ~ quadrilateral *EFGH*

---

similarity transformation A transformation that produces similar figures.

transformación de semejanza Una transformación que resulta en figuras semejantes.

Dilations are similarity transformations.

---

simple event An event consisting of only one outcome.

suceso simple Suceso que contiene sólo un resultado.

In the experiment of rolling a number cube, the event consisting of the outcome 3 is a simple event.

ENGLISH	SPANISH	EXAMPLES

sine In a right triangle, the ratio of the length of the leg opposite $\angle A$ to the length of the hypotenuse.

seno En un triángulo rectángulo, razón entre la longitud del cateto opuesto a $\angle A$ y la longitud de la hipotenusa.

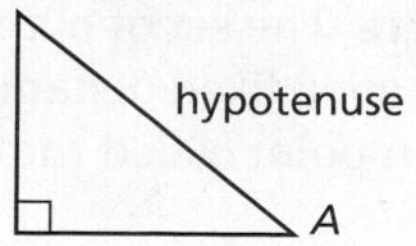

$\sin A = \dfrac{\text{opposite}}{\text{hypotenuse}}$

---

skew lines Lines that are not coplanar.

líneas oblicuas Líneas que no son coplanares.

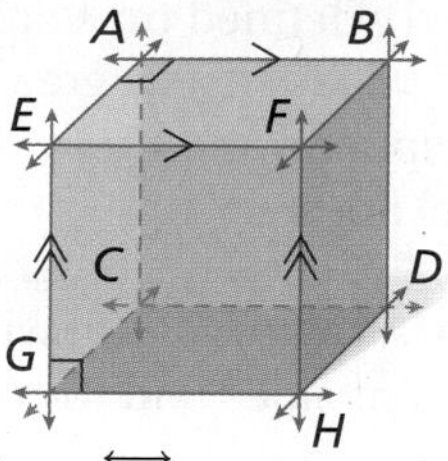

$\overleftrightarrow{AE}$ and $\overleftrightarrow{CD}$ are skew lines.

---

slide *See* translation.

deslizamiento *Ver* traslación.

---

slope A measure of the steepness of a line. If (x_1, y_1) and (x_2, y_2) are any two points on the line, the slope of the line, known as m, is represented by the equation $m = \frac{y_2 - y_1}{x_2 - x_1}$.

pendiente Medida de la inclinación de una línea. Dados dos puntos (x_1, y_1) y (x_2, y_2) en una línea, la pendiente de la línea, denominada m, se representa con la ecuación $m = \frac{y_2 - y_1}{x_2 - x_1}$.

---

slope-intercept form The slope-intercept form of a linear equation is $y = mx + b$, where m is the slope and b is the y-intercept.

forma de pendiente-intersección La forma de pendiente-intersección de una ecuación lineal es $y = mx + b$, donde m es la pendiente y b es la intersección con el eje y.

---

solid A three-dimensional figure.

cuerpo geométrico Figura tridimensional.

$y = -2x + 4$
The slope is -2.
The y-intercept is 4.

---

solving a triangle Using given measures to find unknown angle measures or side lengths of a triangle.

resolución de un triángulo Utilizar medidas dadas para hallar las medidas desconocidas de los ángulos o las longitudes de los lados de un triángulo.

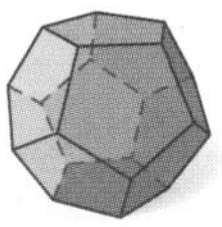

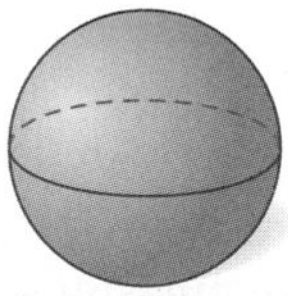

---

space The set of all points in three dimensions.

espacio Conjunto de todos los puntos en tres dimensiones.

---

special parallelogram A rectangle, rhombus, or square.

paralelogramo especial Un rectángulo, rombo o cuadrado.

---

special quadrilateral A parallelogram, rectangle, rhombus, square, kite, or trapezoid.

cuadrilátero especial Un paralelogramo, rectángulo, rombo, cuadrado, cometa o trapecio.

---

special right triangle A 45°-45°-90° triangle or a 30°-60°-90° triangle.

triángulo rectángulo especial Triángulo de 45°-45°-90° o triángulo de 30°-60°-90°.

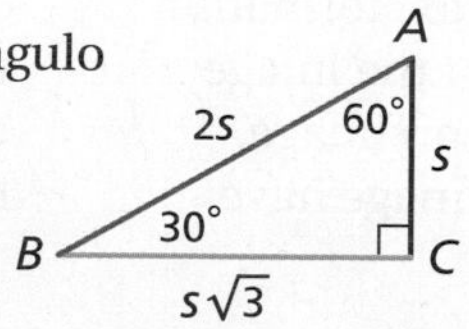

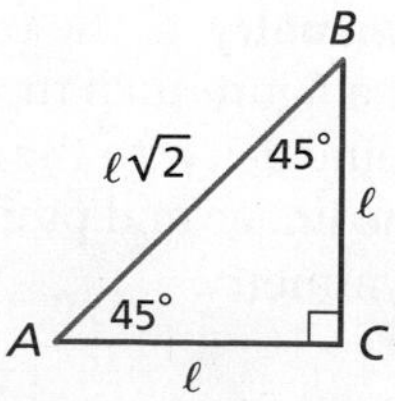

ENGLISH | **SPANISH** | **EXAMPLES**

sphere The set of points in space that are a fixed distance from a given point called the center of the sphere.

esfera Conjunto de puntos en el espacio que se encuentran a una distancia fija de un punto determinado denominado centro de la esfera.

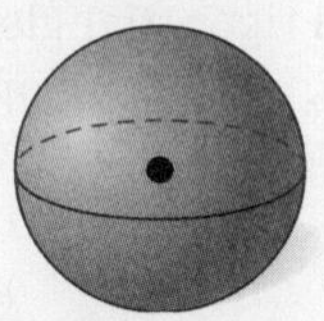

---

spherical geometry A system of geometry defined on a sphere. A line is defined as a great circle of the sphere, and there are no parallel lines.

geometría esférica Sistema de geometría definido sobre una esfera. Una línea se define como un gran círculo de la esfera y no existen líneas paralelas.

---

square A quadrilateral with four congruent sides and four right angles.

cuadrado Cuadrilátero con cuatro lados congruentes y cuatro ángulos rectos.

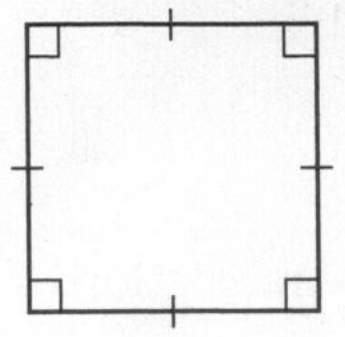

---

standard position An angle in standard position has its vertex at the origin and its initial side on the positive x-axis.

posición estándar Ángulo cuyo vértice se encuentra en el origen y cuyo lado inicial se encuentra sobre el eje x positivo.

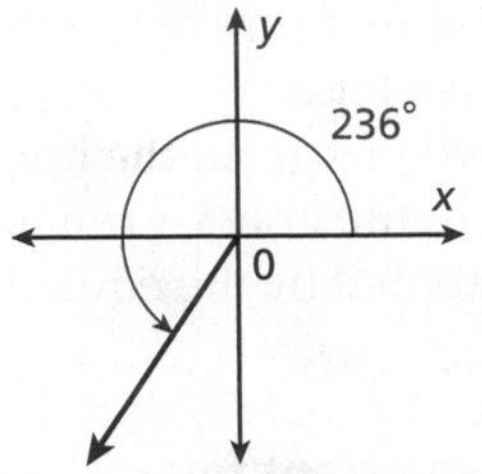

---

straight angle A 180° angle.

ángulo llano Ángulo que mide 180°.

subtend A segment or arc subtends an angle if the endpoints of the segment or arc lie on the sides of the angle.

subtender Un segmento o arco subtiende un ángulo si los extremos del segmento o arco se encuentran sobre los lados del ángulo.

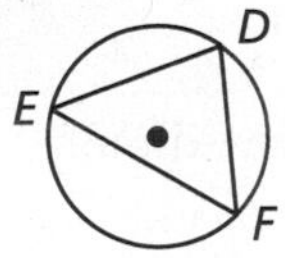

If D and F are the endpoints of an arc or chord, and E is a point not on $\overline{DF}$, then $\overset{\frown}{DF}$ or $\overline{DF}$ is said to subtend $\angle DEF$.

---

supplementary angles Two angles whose measures have a sum of 180°.

ángulos suplementarios Dos ángulos cuyas medidas suman 180°.

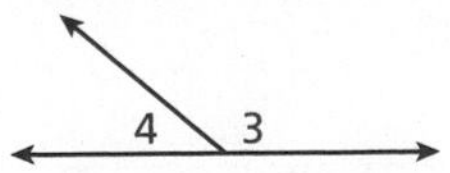

$\angle 3$ and $\angle 4$ are supplementary angles.

---

surface area The total area of all faces and curved surfaces of a three-dimensional figure.

área total Área total de todas las caras y superficies curvas de una figura tridimensional.

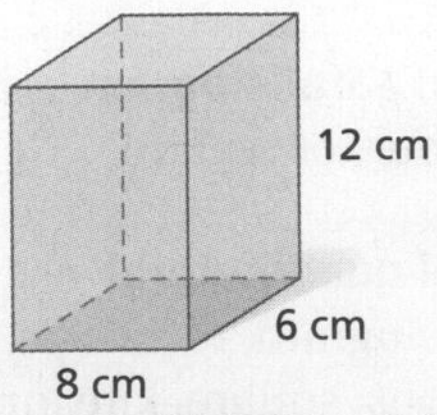

Surface area $= 2(8)(12) + 2(8)(6) + 2(12)(6) = 432 \text{ cm}^2$

---

symmetry In the transformation of a figure such that the image coincides with the preimage, the image and preimage have symmetry.

simetría En la transformación de una figura tal que la imagen coincide con la imagen original, la imagen y la imagen original tienen simetría.

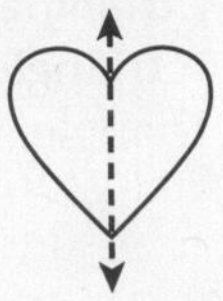

ENGLISH | **SPANISH** | **EXAMPLES**

symmetry about an axis In the transformation of a figure such that there is a line about which a three-dimensional figure can be rotated by an angle greater than 0° and less than 360° so that the image coincides with the preimage, the image and preimage have symmetry about an axis.

simetría axial En la transformación de una figura tal que existe una línea sobre la cual se puede rotar una figura tridimensional a un ángulo mayor que 0° y menor que 360° de forma que la imagen coincida con la imagen original, la imagen y la imagen original tienen simetría axial.

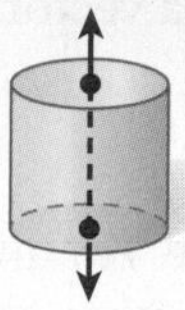

system of equations A set of two or more equations that have two or more variables.

sistema de ecuaciones Conjunto de dos o más ecuaciones que contienen dos o más variables.

$$2x + 3y = -1$$
$$3x - 3y = 4$$

T

tangent circles Two coplanar circles that intersect at exactly one point. If one circle is contained inside the other, they are *internally tangent*. If not, they are *externally tangent*.

círculos tangentes Dos círculos coplanares que se cruzan únicamente en un punto. Si un círculo contiene a otro, son *tangentes internamente*. De lo contrario, son *tangentes externamente*.

tangent of an angle In a right triangle, the ratio of the length of the leg opposite $\angle A$ to the length of the leg adjacent to $\angle A$.

tangente de un ángulo En un triángulo rectángulo, razón entre la longitud del cateto opuesto a $\angle A$ y la longitud del cateto adyacente a $\angle A$.

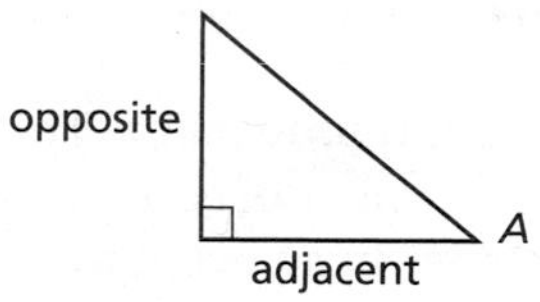

$$\tan A = \frac{\text{opposite}}{\text{adjacent}}$$

tangent segment A segment of a tangent with one endpoint on the circle.

segmento tangente Segmento de una tangente con un extremo en el círculo.

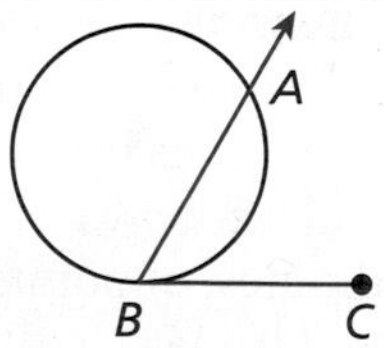

$\overline{BC}$ is a tangent segment.

tangent of a circle A line that is in the same plane as a circle and intersects the circle at exactly one point.

tangente de un círculo Línea que se encuentra en el mismo plano que un círculo y lo cruza únicamente en un punto.

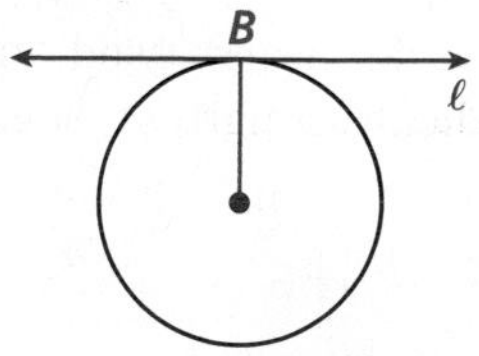

tangent of a sphere A line that intersects the sphere at exactly one point.

tangente de una esfera Línea que toca la esfera únicamente en un punto.

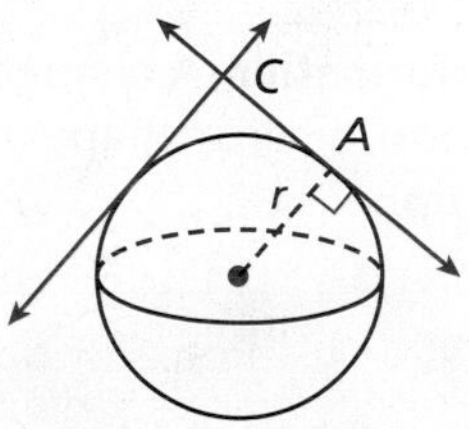

ENGLISH	SPANISH	EXAMPLES
terminal point of a vector The endpoint of a vector.	**punto terminal de un vector** Extremo de un vector.	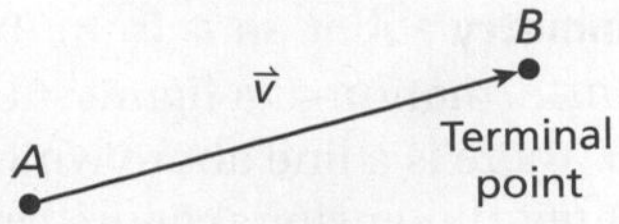
terminal side For an angle in standard position, the ray that is rotated relative to the positive x-axis.	**lado terminal** Para un ángulo en posición estándar, el rayo que se rota en relación con el eje x positivo.	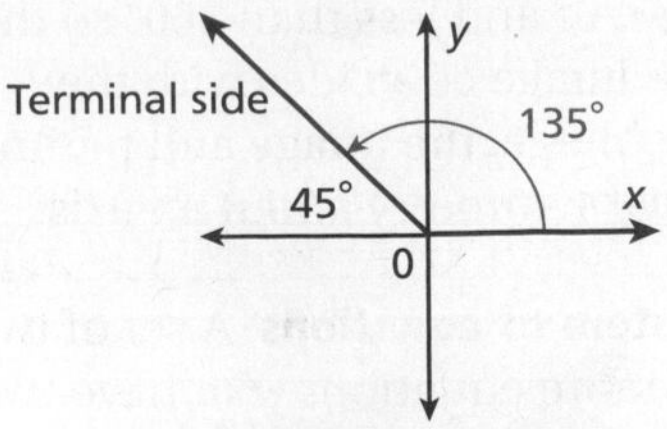
tessellation A repeating pattern of plane figures that completely covers a plane with no gaps or overlaps.	**teselado** Patrón que se repite formado por figuras planas que cubren completamente un plano sin dejar espacios libres y sin superponerse.	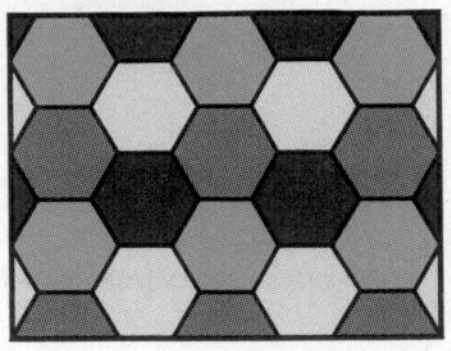
tetrahedron A polyhedron with four faces. A regular tetrahedron has equilateral triangles as faces, with three faces meeting at each vertex.	**tetraedro** Poliedro con cuatro caras. Las caras de un tetraedro regular son triángulos equiláteros y cada vértice es compartido por tres caras.	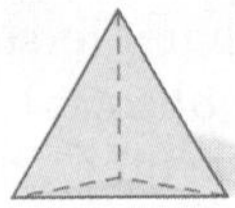
theorem A statement that has been proven.	**teorema** Enunciado que ha sido demostrado.	
theoretical probability The ratio of the number of equally likely outcomes in an event to the total number of possible outcomes.	**probabilidad teórica** Razón entre el número de resultados igualmente probables de un suceso y el número total de resultados posibles.	In the experiment of rolling a number cube, the theoretical probability of rolling an odd number is $\frac{3}{6} = \frac{1}{2}$.
three-dimensional coordinate system A space that is divided into eight regions by an x-axis, a y-axis, and a z-axis. The locations, or coordinates, of points are given by ordered triples.	**sistema de coordenadas tridimensional** Espacio dividido en ocho regiones por un eje x, un eje y un eje z. Las ubicaciones, o coordenadas, de los puntos son dadas por tripletas ordenadas.	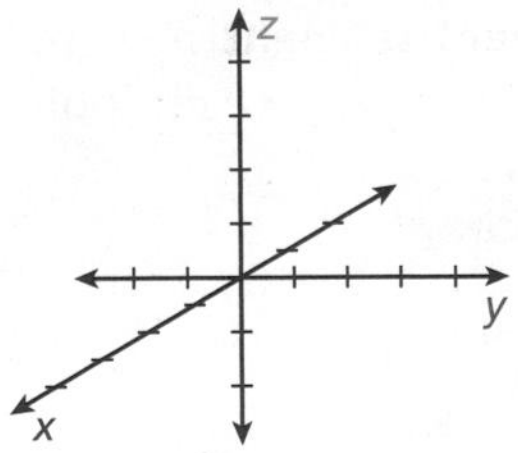
tick marks Marks used on a figure to indicate congruent segments.	**marcas "|"** Marcas utilizadas en una figura para indicar segmentos congruentes.	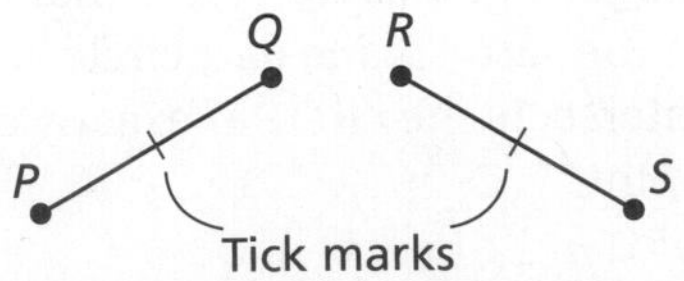
tiling *See* tessellation.	**teselación** *Ver* teselado	
transformation A change in the position, size, or shape of a figure or graph.	**transformación** Cambio en la posición, tamaño o forma de una figura o gráfica.	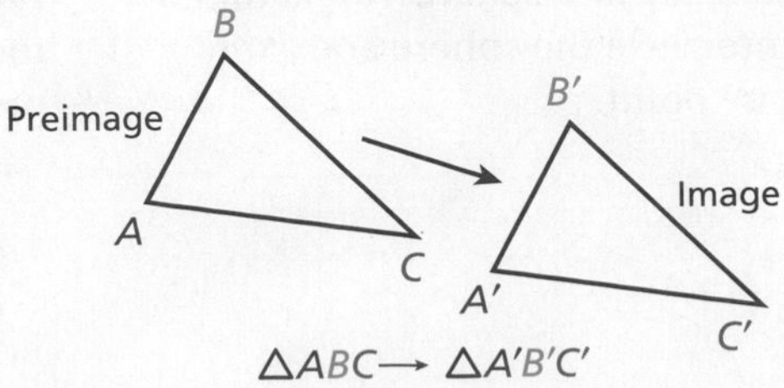

Glossary/Glosario

ENGLISH	SPANISH	EXAMPLES

translation A transformation that shifts or slides every point of a figure or graph the same distance in the same direction.

traslación Transformación en la que todos los puntos de una figura o gráfica se mueven la misma distancia en la misma dirección.

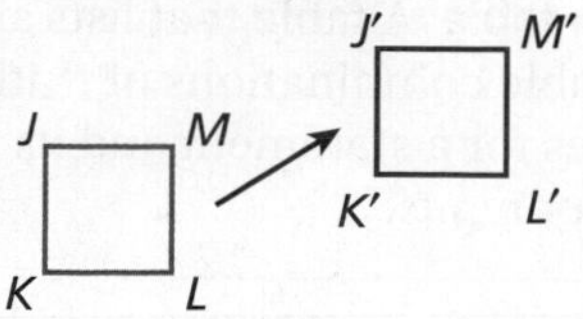

translation symmetry A figure has translation symmetry if it can be translated along a vector so that the image coincides with the preimage.

simetría de traslación Una figura tiene simetría de traslación si se puede trasladar a lo largo de un vector de forma tal que la imagen coincida con la imagen original.

transversal A line that intersects two coplanar lines at two different points.

transversal Línea que corta dos líneas coplanares en dos puntos diferentes.

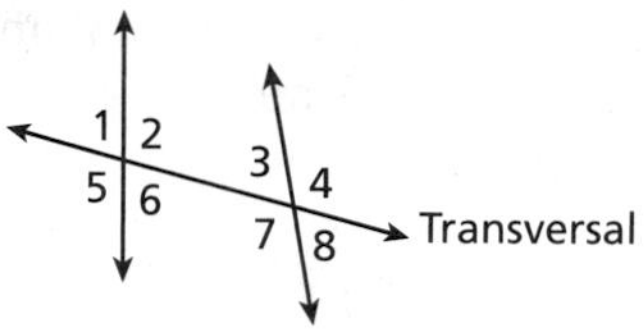

trapezoid A quadrilateral with exactly one pair of parallel sides.

trapecio Cuadrilátero con sólo un par de lados paralelos.

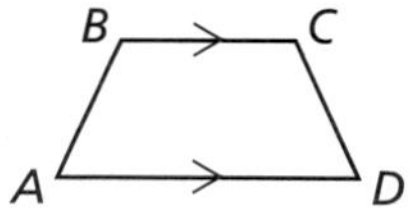

trial In probability, a single repetition or observation of an experiment.

prueba En probabilidad, una sola repetición u observación de un experimento.

In the experiment of rolling a number cube, each roll is one trial.

triangle A three-sided polygon.

triángulo Polígono de tres lados.

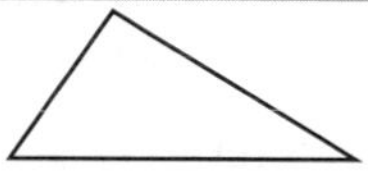

triangle rigidity A property of triangles that states that if the side lengths of a triangle are fixed, the triangle can have only one shape.

rigidez del triángulo Propiedad de los triángulos que establece que, si las longitudes de los lados de un triángulo son fijas, el triángulo puede tener sólo una forma.

triangulation The method for finding the distance between two points by using them as vertices of a triangle in which one side has a known, or measurable, length.

triangulación Método para calcular la distancia entre dos puntos utilizándolos como vértices de un triángulo en el cual un lado tiene una longitud conocida o medible.

trigonometric ratio A ratio of two sides of a right triangle.

razón trigonométrica Razón entre dos lados de un triángulo rectángulo.

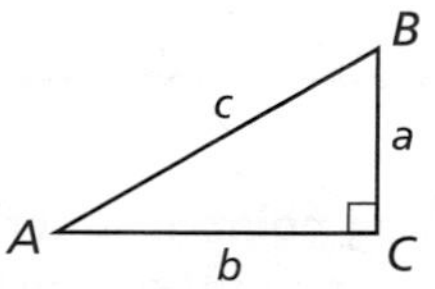

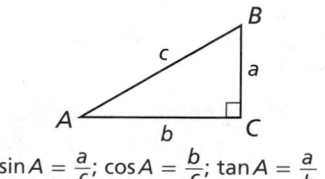

$\sin A = \frac{a}{c}$; $\cos A = \frac{b}{c}$; $\tan A = \frac{a}{b}$

trigonometry The study of the measurement of triangles and of trigonometric functions and their applications.

trigonometría Estudio de la medición de los triángulos y de las funciones trigonométricas y sus aplicaciones.

trisect To divide into three equal parts.

trisecar Dividir en tres partes iguales.

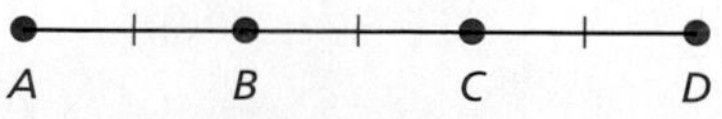

$\overline{AD}$ is trisected.

ENGLISH	SPANISH	EXAMPLES
truth table A table that lists all possible combinations of truth values for a statement and its components.	**tabla de verdad** Tabla en la que se enumeran todas las combinaciones posibles de valores de verdad para un enunciado y sus componentes.	
truth value A statement can have a truth value of true (T) or false (F).	**valor de verdad** Un enunciado puede tener un valor de verdad verdadero (V) o falso (F).	
turn *See* rotation.	**giro** *Ver* rotación.	
two-column proof A style of proof in which the statements are written in the left-hand column and the reasons are written in the right-hand column.	**demostración a dos columnas** Estilo de demostración en la que los enunciados se escriben en la columna de la izquierda y las razones en la columna de la derecha.	
two-point perspective A perspective drawing with two vanishing points.	**perspectiva de dos puntos** Dibujo en perspectiva con dos puntos de fuga.	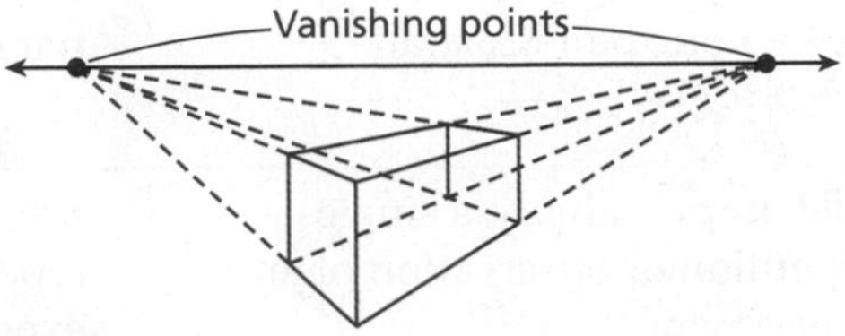

U

undefined term A basic figure that is not defined in terms of other figures. The undefined terms in geometry are point, line, and plane.	**término indefinido** Figura básica que no está definida en función de otras figuras. Los términos indefinidos en geometría son el punto, la línea y el plano.	
unit circle A circle with a radius of 1, centered at the origin.	**círculo unitario** Círculo con un radio de 1, centrado en el origen.	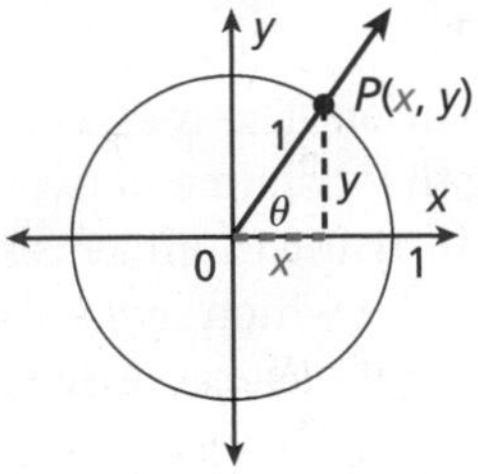Unit circle

V

vanishing point In a perspective drawing, a point on the horizon where parallel lines appear to meet.	**punto de fuga** En un dibujo en perspectiva, punto en el horizonte donde todas las líneas paralelas parecen encontrarse.	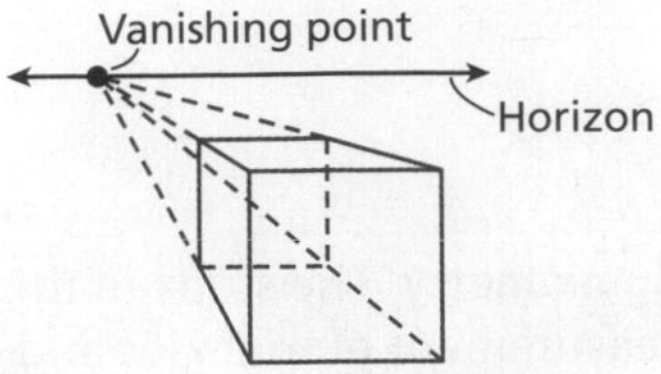
vector A quantity that has both magnitude and direction.	**vector** Cantidad que tiene magnitud y dirección.	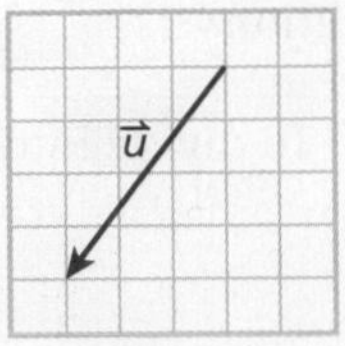

ENGLISH | **SPANISH** | **EXAMPLES**

Venn diagram A diagram used to show relationships between sets.

diagrama de Venn Diagrama utilizado para mostrar la relación entre conjuntos.

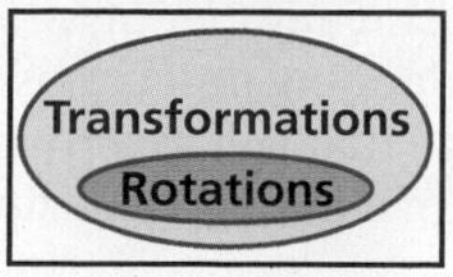

---

vertex angle of an isosceles triangle The angle formed by the legs of an isosceles triangle.

ángulo del vértice de un triángulo isósceles Ángulo formado por los catetos de un triángulo isósceles.

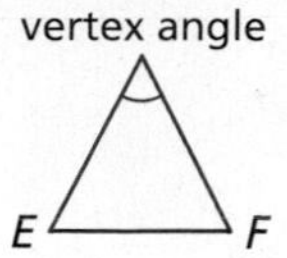

---

vertex of a cone The point opposite the base of the cone.

vértice de un cono Punto opuesto a la base del cono.

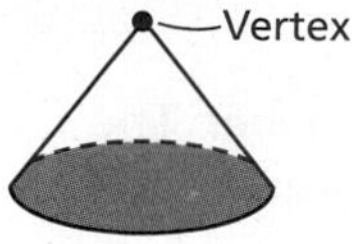

---

vertex of a graph A point on a graph.

vértice de una gráfica Punto en una gráfica.

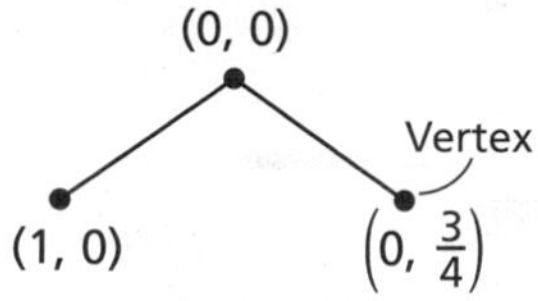

---

vertex of a polygon The intersection of two sides of the polygon.

vértice de un polígono La intersección de dos lados del polígono.

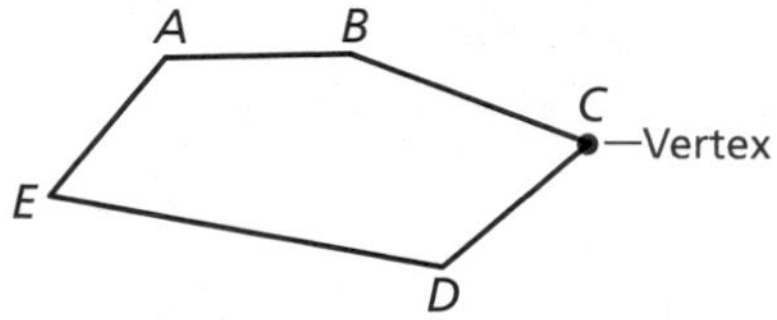

A, *B*, *C*, *D*, and *E* are vertices of the polygon.

---

vertex of a pyramid The point opposite the base of the pyramid.

vértice de una pirámide Punto opuesto a la base de la pirámide.

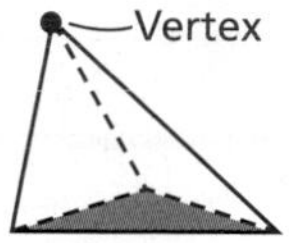

---

vertex of a three-dimensional figure The point that is the intersection of three or more faces of the figure.

vértice de una figura tridimensional Punto que representa la intersección de tres o más caras de la figura.

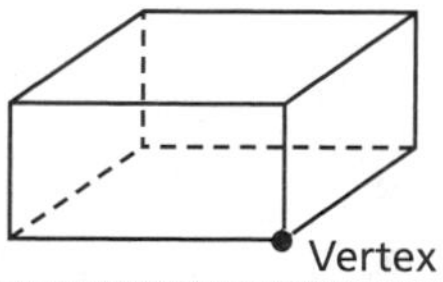

---

vertex of a triangle The intersection of two sides of the triangle.

vértice de un triángulo Intersección de dos lados del triángulo.

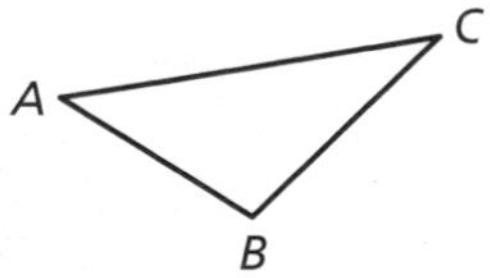

A, *B*, and *C* are vertices of $\triangle ABC$.

---

vertex of an angle The common endpoint of the sides of the angle.

vértice de un ángulo Extremo común de los lados del ángulo.

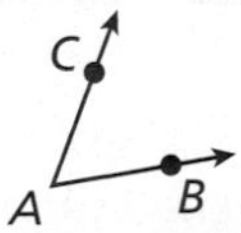

A is the vertex of $\angle CAB$.

---

vertical angles The nonadjacent angles formed by two intersecting lines.

ángulos opuestos por el vértice Ángulos no adyacentes formados por dos rectas que se cruzan.

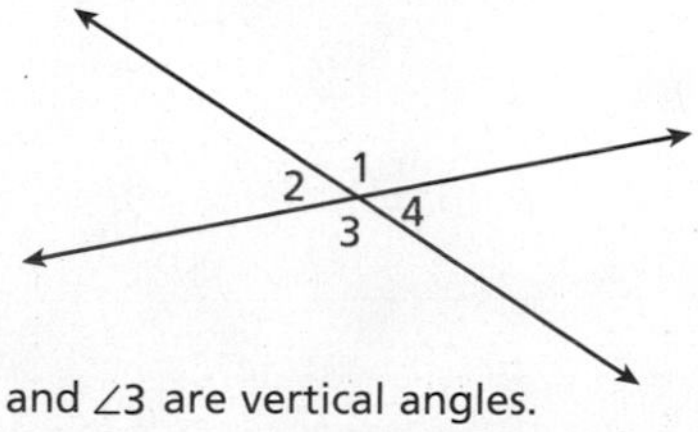

$\angle 1$ and $\angle 3$ are vertical angles.
$\angle 2$ and $\angle 4$ are vertical angles.

ENGLISH	SPANISH	EXAMPLES
volume The number of nonoverlapping unit cubes of a given size that will exactly fill the interior of a three-dimensional figure.	**volumen** Cantidad de cubos unitarios no superpuestos de un determinado tamaño que llenan exactamente el interior de una figura tridimensional.	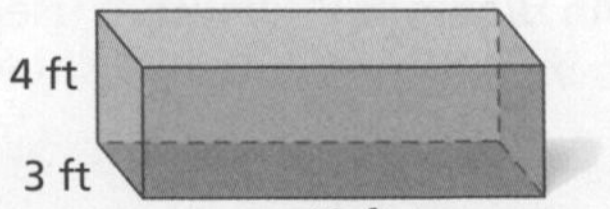 Volume = (3)(4)(12) = 144 ft^3

W

whole number The set of natural numbers and zero.	**número cabal** Conjunto de los números naturales y cero.	{0, 1, 2, 3, 4, 5, ...}

X

***x*-axis** The horizontal axis in a coordinate plane.	**eje *x*** Eje horizontal en un plano cartesiano.	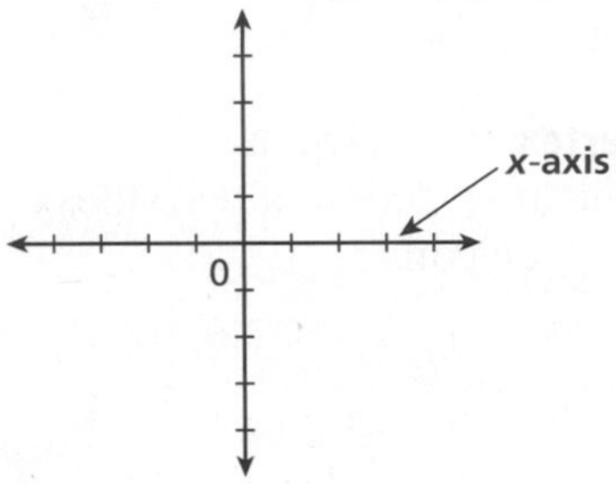

Y

***y*-axis** The vertical axis in a coordinate plane.	**eje *y*** Eje vertical en un plano cartesiano.	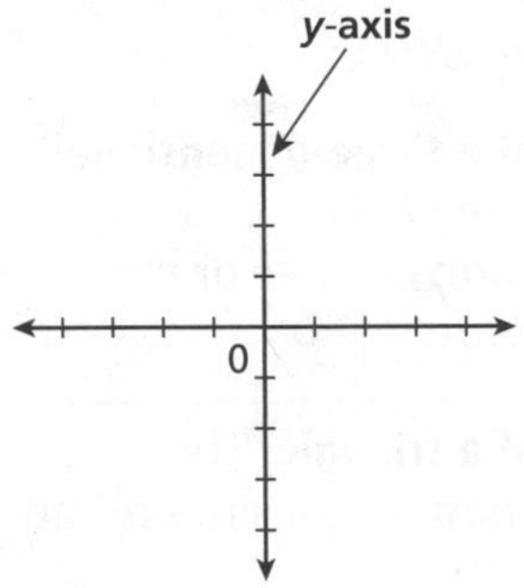

Z

***z*-axis** The third axis in a three-dimensional coordinate system.	**eje *z*** Tercer eje en un sistema de coordenadas tridimensional.	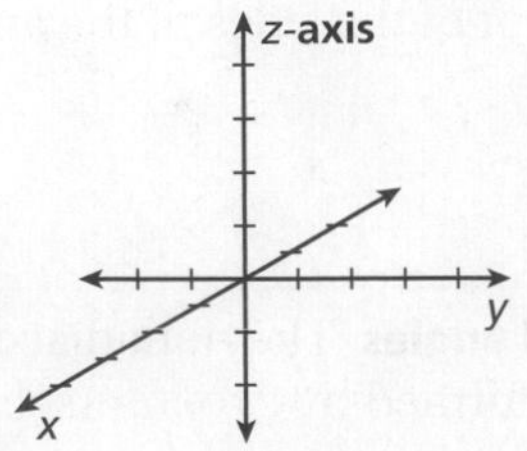

Index

A

Index

B

C

Index

Index

D

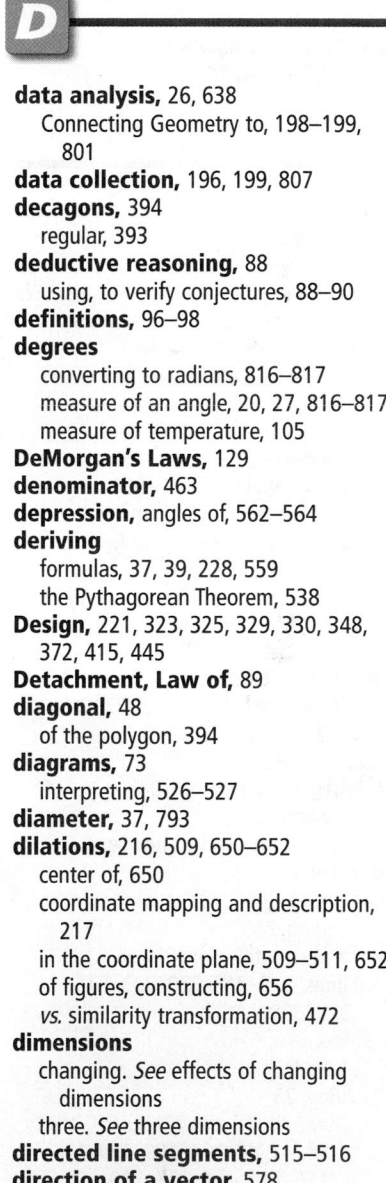

Index

E

F

J

K

L

M

Index

Q

R

S

T

U

V

W

X

Y

Z

Index